"Knowledge is of two kinds. We know a subject ourselves, or we know where we can find information on it."

—Samuel Johnson

This directory is published by:

New Riders Publishing
201 West 103rd Street
Indianapolis, IN 46290 USA

CIP data available upon request

Warning and Disclaimer

This book is designed to provide information about the Internet. Every effort has been made to make this book as complete and as accurate as possible, but no warranty or fitness is implied. The information is provided on an "as is" basis. The author(s) and New Riders Publishing shall have neither liability nor responsibility to any person or entity with respect to any loss or damages arising from the information contained in this book or from the use of the disks or programs that may accompany it.

Publisher	*Don Fowley*
Publishing Manager	*Emmett Dulaney*
Marketing Manager	*Mary Foote*
Managing Editor	*Carla Hall*

Software Specialist
Steve Flatt

Development Editors
Amy Bezek
John Sleeva

Acquisitions Editors
Pete Bitar
Jeff Durham

Copy Editors
Ami Frank
Charles Gose
Stacia Mellinger
Greg Pearson
Cliff Shubs
Molly Warnes

Associate Marketing Manager
Tamara Apple

Acquisitions Coordinator
Stephanie Layton

Publisher's Assistant
Rosemary Graham

Cover Designer
Karen Ruggles

Book Designer
Ann Jones

Production Manager
Kelly Dobbs

Production Team Supervisor
Laurie Casey

Production Team
Heather Butler
Daniel Caparo
Kim Cofer
Cindy Fields
Tricia Flodder
Daniela Raderstorf
Beth Rago
Erich J. Richter
Christy Wagner
Megan Wade

Indexers
Chris Cleveland
Brad Herriman
Erika Millen
Tina Trettin

Trademark Acknowledgments

Acknowledgments

A special tip of the hat goes to Amy Bezek and John Sleeva for their extraordinary work on this book. New Riders' would also like to thank the following contributing editors who worked so feverishly to help author this book:

Daniel Bryan
Julian Cates
Jeff Chandler
Jay Hinkleman
Kristina Horn
Damon Jordan
David Rizley
Suzanne Snyder
Rebecca Tapley

New Riders would also like to thank the following sources that provided information for this book:

The Larousse Desk Reference. New York: Larousse Kingfisher Chambers Inc., 1995.

The New York Public Library Desk Reference, Second Edition. New York: Prentice Hall General Reference, 1993.

Running Press Cyclopedia. Philadelphia: Running Press Book Publishers, 1995.

And finally, New Riders thanks the following Web pages that provided listservs and ftp sites, respectively:

tile.net (http://tile.net)
Monster FTP Sites List (http://hoohoo.ncsa.uiuc.edu/ftp)

Contents at a Glance

Introduction, 1

1 Introducing the World Wide Web, 3

2 Introducing the Internet, 9

3 Internet E-Mail and Usenet Newsgroups, 21

4 What You Need to Link to the Web, 31

5 Examining WWW Browsers, 41

Directory of Listings

Animals, 57

Art, 71

Books & Authors, 97

Business, 121

Children, 149

Computer Games, 159

Computers, 177

Education, 291

Employment, 321

Entertainment, 335

Environment, 361

Family Issues, 379

Food & Drink, 393

Government & Politics, 413

Health & Fitness, 427

History, 455

Hobbies & Crafts, 477

Home Improvement, 505

Humanities, 517

Internet Resources, 553

Law, 585

Media, 599

Movies, 623

Music, 647

Paranormal Phenomena, 685

Reference, 701

Religion & Philosophy, 723

Science & Engineering, 749

Sexuality, 795

Shopping, 805

Society & Culture, 823

Sports, 839

Television, 867

Transportation, 893

Travel, 901

Weddings, 923

A Colleges & Universities, 931

B FTP Sites, 967

Index, 1011

TABLE OF CONTENTS

Introduction   **1**

Features and Uses of the World Wide Web   **1**
- Business 1
- Education 1
- Travel 2

About This Directory   **2**

Further Reading   **2**

New Riders Publishing   **2**

Chapter 1
Introducing the World Wide Web   **3**

Exploring the Web's Foundation   **3**
- Looking at Hypermedia 3
- How the Web Started 4
- Mosaic—A Dawn of a New Era 5

Looking at the Web Today   **6**
- The Growth of the Web 7
- Business and the Web 7
- Looking Toward the Web's Future 8

Chapter 2
Introducing the Internet   **9**

Defining the Internet   **9**
- Looking at TCP/IP 10

Connecting to the Internet   **10**
- Making IP Connections 11

Defining the Internet/Web Relationship   **11**
- Web Browsers 11
- Hypermedia Documents 14
- Web Servers and the HyperText Transfer
  Protocol (HTTP) 15
- Uniform Resource Locators (URLs) 15
- Putting It All Together 17

Using the Internet Properly   **17**
- Learning the Basics 17
- Understanding Netiquette 18
- Dousing the Flames 18
- Signatures 18
- Don't Be a Cyberstalker 19

**Understanding Frequently Asked
Questions (FAQs)**   **19**

Chapter 3
Internet E-Mail and Usenet Newsgroups   **21**

Introducing E-Mail   **21**

Working with E-Mail   **22**
- E-Mail Problems: Privacy 22
- E-Mail Problems: Addressing 22
- E-Mail Addressing Theory 23
- Mailing Lists 24

Using E-Mail Basics   **24**
- Using Netscape E-Mail Manager 24
- Troubleshooting Sending Mail 25

Selecting an E-Mail Interface   **26**

Working with Usenet Newsgroups   **28**

Getting a News Interface   **28**

Chapter 4
What You Need to Link to the Web   **31**

Finding the Right Hardware   **31**
- Picking Out Your Modem 32
- Examining ISDN Connections 33
- Choosing CPU System Speed 33
- Choosing Graphics Hardware 34
- Selecting Audio Hardware 34

Examining Web Software Requirements   **34**
- Finding Internet Providers 35

Chapter 5
Examining WWW Browsers   **41**

Examining Browser Types   **41**

Features to Look for in a Browser   **42**
- HTML 3.2 Support 43
- Netscape Extensions 43
- Netscape Plug-Ins 44
- VRML 44
- Java and JavaScript 44
- ActiveX 45

Installing Your Browser   **46**
- Customizing Your Browser 46
- Navigation Advice 46
- Examining Browser Viewing Capabilities 47

Text Wars   **47**
    Graphics Wars 49
    Supporting Other Internet/Usenet Tools 49
    Working Quickly 49

Examining a Selection of Browsers   **50**
    Netscape Navigator 2.0 50
    Netscape Navigator Gold 2.0 51
    NCSA Mosaic 2.1.1 51
    Microsoft Internet Explorer 3.0 51
    Spyglass Enhanced Mosaic 52
    AIR Mosaic 53
    Cello 53
    Lynx 54
    NetCruiser 54
    SlipKnot 54

Animals   **57**

Animal Parks   **57**
    National Zoological Park Home Page 57
    Neopolis Zoo 57
    San Diego Wild Animal Park 57
    Sea World/Busch Gardens 57
    Singapore Zoological Gardens 57
    Terry Polk's Zoological E-mail Directory 57
    Zoo 57
    ZooNet 57

Birds   **57**
    Audubon 57
    Birds, United States National Park Service (NPS)
        (Information Center for the Environment) 57
    Caring for Your New Bird 57
    The Eagle Page from Rocky
        Mountain High 58
    The Fabulous Kakapo
        (Strigops Habroptilus) 58
    Michael's Photo Gallery 58
    The Pet Bird Page 58
    UAS Home Page 58
    United States Fish and Wildlife
        Service Home Page 58
    Virtual Birding in Tokyo 58

Cats   **58**
    Cat Fanciers' Home Page 58
    Cat House (EFBC/FCC) Home Page 58

    Cats On the Internet 58
    Happy Household Pet Cat Club 58
    Index of /multimed/pics/feline 58
    JESSICATS Home Page 59
    LAL Cat Archive 59
    Savage Studios Homepage 59
    The Traditional Cat Association Home Page 59
    The Zoe Foundation 59

Dogs   **59**
    Akbash Dog Home Page 59
    Bernese Mountain Dog Home Page 59
    Border Collies 59
    Borzoi Info Online 59
    Canine Activity Calendar 59
    Canine Vaccination Schedule 59
    Caucasian Ovcharka Info 59
    Choosing a Dog Breed 60
    Dog Breeding 60
    Dog-Play 60
    Dog Term Glossary 60
    Greyhound Starting Gate 60
    Pomeranian Dog Home Page 60
    Portuguese Water Dog Index 60
    The Pug Dog Home Page 60
    Rhodesian Ridgebacks 60
    Rottweiler Home Page 60
    Schipperke Page 60
    Tibetan Mastiff Home Page 61
    The Visual Rhodesian Ridgeback 61
    Westies Home Page 61

Dolphins   **61**
    The Dolphin Alliance 61
    Dolphin Information Server—Home Page 61
    The Dolphin Page 61
    The Wild Dolphin Project 61

Ferrets   **61**
    Electronic Zoo/NetVet—Ferret Page 61
    Ferret Central 61
    Ferret World! 61

General Information   **62**
    Amphibian and Reptile Collection 62
    Animal Rights Resource Site 62
    Animals 62
    The Bunny Thymes 62

Donald Firsching's Chicken Page 62
Endangered Species 62
Exotic Pets 62
Getting a Pet 62
The House Rabbit Society Home Page 63
How to Put Your Pet on the Web 63
Index of /animal_gifs/ 63
Inter-species Telepathic Communication 63
Nature Subject Page 63
Pet Care Corner 63
Pet Grief Support 63
PetBunny Home Page 63
The Remembrance Page 63

Horses 63
EquiLinQ 63
The Horse Zone 63
The Horseman's Advisor 64
WWW Library—Livestock Section 64

Whales 64
Canada Whale Watching 64
Welcome to the Tirpitz Whaling Web Page 64
Whale Adoption Project Home Page 64
The Whale Information Network 64
Whale Songs 64
The Whale Watching Web 64

Wildlife 64
Adam's Fox Box 64
Antarctica and Its Environment 64
The Bear Den 65
Cochrane Wildlife Reserve 65
Deer Net 65
Eastern Slope Grizzly 65
Frontier Technologies' Lion Gallery 65
GORP—Nature & Wildlife 65
Hyenas 65
Introduced Wild Animals in Australia 65
Kaehler's Mill Farm 65
Kids' Action: Rainforest Animals 66
Lion Pictures of the Month 66
LlamaWeb 66
Manatees 66
OSU's Breeds of Livestock 66
The Polar Regions 66
Turtle Trax—A Marine Turtle Page 66
Wolf Resource Page 66

The Wolf Studies Project 66
The Wolf's Den: Home Page of Wolf McSherry 66
Wombats, Marsupials, and Other Animals 66
The Wonderful Skunk and Opossum Page 66
The World Wide Raccoon Web 66

Newsgroups 67

Listservs 68
ANMGT-L—Animal Management Discussion Forum 68
ANSCI-L—Animal Science Students 68
AQUARIUM—Fish and Aquaria 68
AZARC-L—Association of Zoos and Aquariums Research Coordinators 68
CANINE-L—Discussion Forum for Dog Fanciers 68
CAT-CHAT 68
CONSGIS—Biological Conservation and GIS 68
DAIRY-L—Dairy Discussion List 68
EMBRIO—Basic Embryology for Medical Students 68
EQUINE-L—Discussion Forum for Horse Fanciers 68
FELINE-L—Discussion Forum for Cat Fanciers 68
FERRET—The Domestic Ferret Electronic Mailing List (FML) 68
GERBILS—Gerbil Discussion List 68
GISAB-L—Gibbs Sampling in Animal Breeding 69
GROOMERS-L—Pet Groomers Helping Each Other 69
KSUPET-L—KSU Pet Health News 69
MAMMAL-L—Mammalian Biology 69
MARMAM—Marine Mammals Research and Conservation Discussion 69
MATBI-L—Marine All Taxa Biological Inventories 69
PETBUNNY—Forum for Folks with Companion Rabbits 69
POODLE-L—All Poodle Discussion Group 69
PROTECTION-DOGS-L—Protection Dogs Discussion List 69
URBWLF-L—Urban Wildlife Working Group: Ecology, Education, Planning 69
WDAMAGE—Wildlife Damage Management 69
WLREHAB—Wildlife Rehab List 69
ZOOGNUS—News from the National Zoological Park, Washington, DC 69
ZOOGRAD—Department of Zoology Grad Students 70

Art 71

Art History 71

The Age of Enlightenment 71
ArtServe 71
The Ashmolean Museum of Art and Archaeology 71
Israel Museum—Jerusalem 71
The Risk Map of Cultural Heritage in Italy 71

Art Resources 71

ADG Graphix Home Page 71
Advanced Cultural Technologies 71
African Art 71
Akteo Watch Boutique 71
Allen Toney's Home Page 71
Amsterdam Valley 71
ANIMA 72
Arizona Museum for Youth 72
Art Crimes Index 72
Art Links on the World Wide Web 72
Art To Live with Original Prints 72
Art.Online 72
Art? 72
Artix 72
ArtMap 72
ArtScape 72
ArtScene 73
ArtSource 73
Artworld (ArtMap) Online Links and Listings 73
AS220 73
Ballinakill Studios 73
Brookhouse Studio 73
Business Volunteers for the Arts—Houston 73
The Butler Institute of American Art 73
BYU Performing Arts Management 73
Capacity Index 73
CBC Radio Trial 73
Center for Research in Computing and
    the Arts (CRCA) 73
CERN MusiClub 73
The Chrysler Museum 74
Cloud Gallery 74
Colorburst Studios Online Catalog 74
Danclink 74
Daniel Vogel 74
Daum On-line 74
Dia Center for the Arts 74
DigiPen Applied Computer Graphics School 74
Enterzone 74

Eric Boutilier-Brown 74
eSCENE 1995 74
The Eye Produce CD ROM Home Page 74
Flaming Jewels 74
Flapping 74
FrameMakers 75
The Framers Corner 75
Free Art Website (Laurie McCanna's Home Page) 75
Frida Kahlo Art Pages 75
Front Home 75
gallery.html (Edison Gallery) 75
Gen Art 75
The Getty Art History Information Program 75
The Graphix Exchange 75
The Great Books of Western Civilization 75
Hal's Virtual Furniture Gallery 75
Harmony Music List 75
The Heard Museum 76
Hollywood Archaeology 76
The iGallery 76
INM Home Page 76
International Sculpture Center's
    On-line Resource 76
Jayhawk 76
Jordan, Robert 76
Kaleidospace Home Page 76
Krannert Art Museum 76
Krypton Neon—The Internet's Neon Shop 76
Le Ministère de la Culture Direction
    des Musées de France 76
Lewis Carroll Home Page 77
Lysator Computer Society 77
Metaverse 77
Michael C. Carlos Museum, Emory University 77
Mill Valley Film Festival 77
Millennium Productions 77
Motorcycle Collectible Art Gallery 77
The Multimedia Cultural Information Service 77
Musée des Arts et Métiers's World Wide Web
    (Museum of Art and Craft) 77
Museum Web from Art-ROM 77
Museums in the Netherlands 77
National Museum of American Art 77
The National Museum of the American Indian—
    George Gustav Heye Center 77
Noel Ford Cartoonist/Illustrator/Author 77
OBD—Organization of Black Designers 77
On-Line Books 78
Online Source Register (Services) 78

Optical Illusions 78
Patrick Gallagher, Celtic Art 78
A Purgatory of Semiotics 78
Rare Treasures 78
rEX's wORLd 78
Rittners School of Floral Design 78
Shakespeare 78
Synergy Music and Art Workshop 78
Syracuse University Computer Graphics
   for the Visual Arts 78
Tele-Garden 78
The Tokugawa Art Museum 78
U'Mista Cultural Centre 79
University Art Museum and Pacific Film Archive 79
University Art Museum Art Exhibitions 79
Vancouver Arts Index 79
VCU Arts Home Page 79
A Very Usable Film and Cinema Directory 79
VFS Multimedia 79
VI&P Animation Art Resources 79
WebArtWed 79
Welcome to VIPER 79
The West Australian Virtual Arts Community 79
What I Believe by J.G. Ballard 79
Wonders of the World 80
The WORD Online 80

Electronic Arts   80
@art gallery 80
Alternative Virtual Biennial 80
Atelier Nord 80
Auricular Home Page 80
Christine Thea Partridge* Gallery 80
Cyberbabe 80
Duncan Hopkins Web Site 80
Electronic Art Gallery 80
Graficas Art and Design 80
Hillustration 81
Hiway Technologies Graphics Portfolio 81
HypArt 81
Joe Walker's Page 81
Lectro-Art 81
Lightside Art Gallery 81
Martin Action Art 81
Media West Editions 81
Museum Web 81
NCSA Digital Gallery CD-ROM 81
Netwash 81

Pix Gallery 81
the place 82
Rainbow of Chaos 82
REIFF II Museum 82
Robert Derr's Virtual Gallery 82
Sample the Dog Design 82
Spanky Welcome (The Spanky Fractal Database) 82
Tom Reed/Photographer 82
Vancouver Cyberspace Association 82
The WebWeavers 82

Fine Arts   82
911 Gallery Home Page 82
Abulafia Gallery 82
The Akron Art Museum 82
The Allen Memorial Art Museum 82
Andy Warhol Museum 83
Anti-Art Productions 83
Art by Belinda Di Leo 83
Art by Tim Pascoe 83
The Art Kelderie 83
The Art of Barbara Weigel 83
Art on the Net 83
Art Planet 83
Arthole 83
The Arthur Ross Gallery Home Page 83
The ArtMetal Project 83
ArtStudio 83
Asian Arts 83
AusArts 84
Bruce Museum 84
Burton Levitsky 84
Center on Contemporary Art 84
The Centre for Contemporary Art in Warsaw 84
Connie Tunick's Paintings in Watermedia 84
Crosswire Images 84
Crucible Chicago 84
Daddazio—The Bronze Necktie 84
DaliWeb The Official Salvador Dali Museum
   Web Site 84
Dallas Museum of Art Online 84
The Digital Cathedral 84
Digital Giraffe 85
Donajski's Digital Gallery 85
The Douglas Albert Gallery State College, PA 85
Duane Hilton High Sierra Fine Art 85
Eagle Aerie Gallery 85
Edoardo Villa 85

The Electric Gallery 85
The Electronic Chronicles 85
Exhibition of Paintings by Stanley Pettigrew 85
FineArt Forum Gallery 85
Galeria MexPlaza 85
Heirloom Art 85
Herbert R. Mears, Contemporary American Artist 85
The Identity Box Collective 85
ImageMaker Gifts for Dog Lovers 85
International Masters Group 86
The International Museum of Art 86
Kaufman, Karin 86
Khazana 86
Kjell Ringi Art Exhibition 86
Koh-Varilla Guild 86
La Trobe University Art Museum 86
Liros Gallery 86
Los Angeles County Museum of Art 86
*The Meridian Gallery Contemporary Art,
   in the Heart of San Francisco* 86
Michael Rubin 86
The Minneapolis Institute of Arts 86
*MIT Center for Educational Computing
   Initiatives Virtual Museum* 86
Musée National D'Histoire Et D'Art 87
Na-Te-So Workshop 87
Nico Roos 87
Ohio State University at Newark 87
*Okanagan University College, Department
   of Fine Arts* 87
Parallax Gallery 87
Pavilion of Polyhedreality 87
Pearl St. Online Gallery 87
Project Gutenberg 87
*RACE Research into Artifacts, Center
   for Engineering* 87
The Roger Whitney Gallery of Artists 87
Santa Fe Fine Art 87
Sculptor/Stone Carver 87
Sculpture Tour 88
Sierra Wave Art Gallery 88
Sonoma State University Alumni Art Exhibition 88
Stained Glass by Steve 88
The Surrealism Server 88
*Surrey Institute of Art and Design's
   World Wide Web Server* 88
Susan Aaron-Taylor Profile of an Artist 88
Techno-Impressionist Art 88
Tel Aviv Museum of Art 88

Treasures of the Louvre 88
Tucson Museum of Art and Historic Block 88
University of Wyoming Art Museum 88
The Watercolors of Sherry Zuker 88
WebMuseum 89
Welcome to the aRt_sLab @ UCSD 89
Whitney Museum Information 89
The Will James Art Company 89
Windshadow 89

Performing Arts   **89**
Alaskan Dance Theater 89
Arthur Hall and Black Dance in America 89
As-Sayf Oriental Dance Home Page 89
AXIS Dance Troupe 89
B.A.W.P. Spoken Word Audio Recordings 89
Booth Milton Sculptor 89
Dancescape 89
Henry's Dance Hotlist 90
International Folk Dancers Of Ottawa Home Page 90
Internet Dance Resources 90
Marjan 90
*Ohio State University, Department of
   Dance Home Page* 90
PDX TheatreSports 90
Talk about Dance 90
Tango Dance Notation Argentina Argentine 90

Photography   **90**
3-D Stuff 90
50th Bristol International Salon of Photography 90
(Art)n Galleries 90
The Attic Window (by Diane Fenster) 90
Black and White Gallery 90
The Cemetery 90
Cincinnati Parks' Butterfly Show 91
Citizen Kane Gallery 91
Crayon Design & Communications 91
*Cypress College Photography
   Department (First Stop)* 91
*Detroit Publishing Company
   Photographic Collection* 91
Digital Photography Exhibit 91
digital wave photography gallery 91
Edgerton Center's Online Photo Gallery 91
Florida Wildflower Showcase 91
FocalPoint f/8 91
Fotogruppe der Studiobühne und Filmwerkstatt 91
Frolic 91

GallerySight 92
Hiroshima and Nagasaki Gallery Exhibition 92
imago 92
Michael's Photo Gallery 92
Michigan Photo Contest 92
Misa 92
Molecular Expressions (Microscapes) 92
Mythago 92
Nature Gallery 92
New Mexico 92
The New York Public Library
   Photography Collection 92
Non Facturé 92
Oxford Photographs 92
The Photo Archive 92
Photo Perspectives 93
The Photographers Gallery 93
PhotoLink Gallery 93
Picture Projects 93
Portfolio of Architechtural Photographs 93
Postcards from Bahia 93
PPSA Photo Gallery 93
Prairie Dog Artworks 93
Probus Photos 93
Remembering Nagasaki 93
Rogers Virtual Gallery (Beauty #2) 94
Ruby's Gallery 94
Russian Reminiscence 94
Sam's Shoebox 94
A Shot in the Dark 94
SITO 94
SolarColor Photography by Michael Fastoso 94
Stereoscopic Imaging by Ray 3D 94
United in Anger 94
The Unofficial Cincinnati Butterfly Show 94
Vintage Postcards 94
The Zone I Gallery 94

Newsgroups 95

Listservs 95

AAT-L—Art & Architecture Thesaurus
   Discussion List 95
ARLIS-L—Art Libraries Society Discussion List 95
ART193—Fine Arts Computing Group 95
ARTCRIT—Art Criticism Discussion Forum 95
ARTIST-L—Student Artist Discussions 95
ARTLIST—Discuss Issues Relevant to
   Contemporary Art 95
ARTNEWS—UA Fine Arts News Releases 95
ARTNINE—Discusses Especially the Contemporary
   Art in the Nineties 96
BOOK_ARTS-L—The Book Arts: Binding,
   Typography, Collecting 96
CAAH—Consortium Of Art And Architectural
   Historians 96
CLASSICAL—Moderated Classical Music List 96
CLASSM-L—Classical Music List 96
CLAYART—Ceramic Arts Discussion List 96
COLLAB-L—Theatre and Musical Artists,
   Composers, etc. 96
DESIGN-L—Basic and Applied Design
   (Art and Architecture) 96
LARCH-L—Landscape Architecture
   Electronic Forum 96
MUSEUM-L—Museum Discussion List 96
PERFORM—Medieval Performing Arts 96
RLGART-L—RLG Art and Architecture 96
SAH-L—Society of Architectural Historians 96
UAARTED—Art Education Issues 96

Books & Authors 97

Authors 97

Douglas Adams 97
Louisa May Alcott: Flower Fables 97
V.C. Andrews 97
http://www.csh.rit.edu/~cwalker/vcandrews/ 97
Piers Anthony 97
Isaac Asimov 97
Margaret Atwood Information Site 97
Nicholson Baker 97
Clive Barker 97
Donald Barthelme 97
Richard Bausch 97
Greg Bear 97
Aphra Behn Page 98
Edward Bellamy 98
Jorge Luis Borges—The Garden of Forking Paths 98
Ray Bradbury 98
Richard Brautigan 98
David Brin 98
Charlotte Brontë 98
The Brontë Sisters 98
Rita Brown 98
Charles Bukowski 98
Edgar Rice Burroughs 98
William S. Burroughs 99

Albert Camus 99
Truman Capote 99
Jim Carroll 99
Lewis Carroll: An Overview 99
Raymond Carver 99
Willa Cather 99
Miguel de Cervantes 99
The Kate Chopin Project 99
Agatha Christie 99
Tom Clancy 99
Arthur C. Clarke Chapter of "The Silicon Jungle" 100
Douglas Coupland—Snapshots 100
Stephen Crane 100
Michael Crichton 100
Cyber-Seuss 100
Roald Dahl 100
Le Marquis de Sade 100
Fyodor Dostoevsky 100
Dr. Seuss 100
Marguerite Duras 100
Umberto Eco 100
William Faulkner 101
F. Scott Fitzgerald 101
Ian Fleming 101
Johann Wolfgang von Goethe 101
John Grisham 101
Thomas Hardy 101
Nathaniel Hawthorne 101
Ernest Hemingway (The Papa Page) 101
L. Ron Hubbard 101
Zora Neale Hurston 101
Robert Jordan 102
James Joyce (Work in Progress) 102
Jonathan Kellerman 102
Jack Kerouac 102
Stephen King 102
Stephen King 102
Barbara Kingsolver 102
Dean Koontz 102
Katherine Kurtz 102
Louis L'Amour 102
Ring Lardner (Lardnermania) 102
Ursula K. Le Guin 102
C.S. Lewis and the Inklings 102
C.S. Lewis (Into the Wardrobe) 103
The Libyrinth 103
H. P. Lovecraft 103
Anne McCaffrey 103

Cormac McCarthy 103
Herman Melville 103
Henry Miller (18, villa seurat) 103
Yukio Mishima Archive 103
N. Scott Momaday 103
Vladmir Nabokov (Zembla) 103
Anaïs Nin 103
Joyce Carol Oates (Celestial Timepiece) 104
Edgar Allen Poe 104
Marcel Proust (Proust Said That) 104
Ayn Rand 104
Anne Rice 104
Tom Robbins (The AFTRLife) 104
Philip Roth 104
Antoine de Saint-Exupery 104
J.D. Salinger (The Bananafish Home Page) 104
George Sand 104
Mary Shelley 105
Gertrude Stein 105
John Steinbeck 105
Amy Tan 105
Mark Twain (Ever the Twain Shall Meet) 105
Jules Verne 105
Gore Vidal 105
William T. Vollmann 105
Alice Walker 105
Eudora Welty 105
Oscar Wilde (The Wild Wilde Web) 105
Thomas Wolfe 106
Virginia Woolf 106
Roger Zelazny 106

Electronic Literature　　　　　　　　　　106

The Adventures of Tom Sawyer 106
Alice's Adventures in Wonderland 106
American Literary Classics 106
Baker Street Connection 106
Bob Book Online 106
The Citadell of Riva 106
The Commonplace Book 106
The Electronic Labyrinth 106
The Electronic Library 106
Great Books of Western Civilization 107
Gutter Press 107
The Hunting of the Snark: an Agony in Eight Fits 107
HyperLiterature/HyperTheory 107
Literary Works: Mark Twain 107
Little Women-DataText 107

The Lost World (Randomhouse) 107
Mark Twain: Huckleberry Finn 107
The Martian Chronicles Study Guide 107
Online Books FAQ 107
TeleRead 107
Tree Fiction on the World Wide Web 108
The Wonderful Wizard of Oz 108
Zuzu's Petals Literary Resource 108

Journals and E-Zines   108
@Ezine 108
Alternative-X 108
American Planet Galactic News 108
Anagram 108
Canboulay, The Caribbean Literature Quarterly 108
The Cream City Review 108
CrossConnect 108
De Proverbio 108
Dimension² 108
Early Modern Literary Studies 109
Exemplaria 109
Harvard Gay and Lesbian Review 109
The Milton Quarterly 109
NorthWords 109
Plaintext 109
Qui Parle 109
Renditions 109
Romanticism On the Net 109
Sapphic Ink 109
Science Fiction Weekly 109
Transculture 110
Wespennest 110

Online Book Resources   110
alt.books.reviews 110
alt.books.technical 110
Amazon.com 110
Banned Books On-line 110
Book Banning, Burning, and Censorship 110
Bookbinding, a tutorial 110
BookWorld 110
Conservation OnLine 110
A Hundred Highlights from the Koninklijke Bibliotheek 110
Hungry Mind Review Discussion 111
Index 111
L'Art Medical Antiquarian Books 111
Macmillan Publishing USA (The Information SuperLibrary) 111

Notable Children's Books 111
The Preservation Educators' Exchange 111
ReadersNdex 111
rec.arts.books 111
The Romance Pages 111
A Sherlockian Holmepage 111
The Tolkien Society 111
Ultimate Romance Novel Website 111
Vintage Books Reading Group Guides 112
Willy Wonka Lyrics 112

Online Bookstores   112
Antiquarian Booksellers' Association of America 112
Association of American University Presses (AAUP) Online Catalog/Bookstore 112
Astrology et al Bookstore 112
Bantam Doubleday Dell—BDD Online 112
Bonder Bookstore, Inc. 112
Book Hunter 112
BookLink 112
BookSite 112
Bookstore at Houghton Mifflin 112
Christian Book Connection 113
A Clean Well-Lighted Place for Books 113
Cody's Books 113
Comics at Bendigo Books 113
David Morrison Books 113
Deep Politics Bookstore 113
Fast Books 113
Gareth Stevens Publishing 113
Gary Holmes Books 113
It's a Mystery 113
Joseph-Beth Booksellers 113
JourneyWare Media 113
Loganberry Books 114
Login Brothers Book Company 114
Mage Publishing 114
Mare's Nest Publishing 114
Midnight Special Bookstore 114
Moe's Books 114
Navrang, Inc. 114
New World Books 114
Norwegian Bookshop 114
The Old Bookroom 114
Pacific Book Auction Galleries 114
Pantera Publishing 114
Pas de chance 114
Polonia Bookstore 115

Revolution Books 115
Science Express, Inc. 115
Secret Staircase Bookshop 115
Shen's Books and Supplies 115
SPITE! Books 115
Stone Bridge Press 115
Svoboda's Books Online—State College, PA 115
Time-Life Explorer 115
UNARIUS Academy of Science 115
Zanadu Comics 115

Newsgroups   **116**

Listservs   **117**
AIDSBKRV—AIDS Book Review Journal 117
AMLIT2-L—Discussion of American
    Literature from 1880-Present 117
ARBOOKS—Discussion of Books by Anne Rice 117
BOOKTALK—Childrens Literature and
    Classroom Use 118
COMP-REV—Book Review Forum: Rhetoric
    & Composition 118
CTHEORY—CTHEORY Is an International,
    Electronic Review of Books 118
DESIRELIT-LIST—Desire & Literature List 118
DOROTHYL—Mystery Literature
    E-Conference 118
ENG1162—Book Discussion Questions 118
ENG212—ENG212-BUSINESS WRITING 118
ENG213—ENG213-TECHNICAL WRITING 118
FEM-BIBLIO—Discussion of Books Relating
    to Women and/or Spirituality 118
FICTION—Fiction Writing Workshop 118
HORROR—Horror in Film and Literature 118
JPL-L—Electronic Publishing Mailing List 118
NEWBOOKS—New Books in Communication 118
RW-L—Romance Writer's Discussion List 118
TAA-L—Textbook Authors Association 118
TECHWR-L—Technical Writers List; For
    All Technical Communication Issues 119
TOW—The Online World Book Info 119
WFILES—Archive Files for the WRITERS List 119
WRITERS—WRITERS 119
WRITERS-CLUB—Information, Motivation, and
    Inspiration for Every Writer 119
WRITING—Writing Workshop Discussion List 119

Business   **121**

Banking   **121**
The Credit Union Home Page 121
Infogroup S.p.A. 121
The World Bank Home Page 121
World Currency Converter 121

Business Process Reengineering   **121**
The Benchmarking Exchange 121
Leverage Technologists Home Page 121
Navatar—Organizational Renewal and Business
    Reengineering 121
The Phoenix Business Renewal Site 121

Business-Related Careers   **121**
The Business Job Finder 121
Chancellor and Chancellor, Inc. 121
Dick Williams and Associates 121
DXI Corporation 122
IOMA Information Services for Professionals 122

Consumer Issues   **122**
ClearStar Security Network 122
Consumer Fraud Alert Network 122
The Consumer Law Page 122
Criminal Enforcement Bulletin 122
Diamond Resources 122
Get Organized 122

Corporate Home Pages   **122**
3M Innovation Network 122
AT&T Home Page 122
FedEx Home Page 122
GE Home Page 123
Goodyear Tire and Rubber Company 123
JCPenney Home Page 123
McDonnell Douglas Aerospace 123
MCI Home Page 123
Shell Oil Company 123
SONY Online 123
Tandy Corporation 123
UPS Home Page 123
Walgreen Co. 123

International Business   **123**
Adnet 123
African Sky Video 123

Agora Language Marketplace 124
Asian Business Daily 124
Ask Us For 124
Australasian World Publishing Systems 124
Australian Pacific Advertising 124
Australian Stock Market Web Page 124
Austrian Worldport Austrian Business Connection 124
Batey Ads Singapore 124
Canada Net Pages 124
Canadian Business InfoWorld 124
Catalogue Production Management Services 124
Cyber Planet Korea 125
The Econsult Group WWW Page 125
Extra Trade, Inc. 125
How to Do Business in Mexico 125
ICC Communications Centre 125
INFOCENTRO 125
Ingvar's Home Page 125
The London Mall Magazine and HQ 125
Mega-Directory of US/Canada International
    Exports—U.S. Trade Center Directory 125
Microswiss-Centre North-South 125
Mobile Phones for UK Users 125
Moscow Libertarium 125
The NAFTA Watch 125
OCEANOR—Oceanographic Company
    of Norway 126
Octagon Technology Group, Inc. 126
Pristine Communications 126
Rainforest Health Project 126
Selling Your Products Abroad 126
The South African Futures Exchange 126
TN-1 NAFTA Home Page 126
U.S. Council for International Business 126
Valore International 126
Virtual Business Plaza 126
VR Cargo International Home Page 126
Welcome to the European Market 126
Welcome to Molson Canadian 127

Investments & Financial Planning   127
Accel Partners 127
Allegiance Financial Advisors 127
American Stock Exchange—The Smarter
    Place to Be 127
The American Stock Report, Inc. 127
A.S.K. Financial Digest 127
Chicago Mercantile Exchange 127
CyberFund 127

FFP Securities 127
Fin-Atlantic Securities, Inc. 127
How to Become a Real-Time Commodity Futures
    Trader—From Home 127
InterQuote 127
The Mutual Fund Home Page 128
Nesbitt Burns, Inc. 128
Olsen & Associates 128
Pawws Financial Network 128
Perception Global Market Predictions 128
The Philadelphia Stock Exchange 128
Precision Investment Services, Inc. 128
Quote.Com 128
Security APL Quote Server 128
SGA Goldstar Research 128
The Siegel Group, Inc. 128
Silicon Investor 129
Stockdeck Online 129
StockMaster at MIT 129
A Trader's Financial Resource Guide 129
Wall Street Net 129
Wall Street Online 129
Woodbridge and Associates 129

Miscellaneous Business Sites   129
Acer America Career Opportunities 129
AdMorInk 129
American Computer Resources, Inc. 129
Aquatic Network 129
Automation Specialists 130
Broadway Video, Inc. 130
Bubble Technology Industries, Inc. 130
The Business Incorporating, Guide 130
Bytewise Consulting, Inc. 130
Chastain Research Group, Inc. 130
Copyright Clearance Center Online 130
Duoforce Enterprises, Inc. 130
Evolving Technologies Corporation 130
EXPOguide Home Page 130
Farg's Cost Accounting Home Page 130
FiberNet Communications 130
Global Business Network 130
Global Trade Center 131
Habia Cable AB 131
HADCO Corporation 131
Harris Digital Telephone Systems 131
HSiN Semiconductor Pte Ltd. 131
Ideal Point Home Page 131
Inland Answering Service 131

International Typeface Corporation 131
Internet Bankruptcy Library 131
ISO Easy 131
Jones, Hall, Hill, and White 131
KAB Konsult AB 132
Khem Products, Inc. 132
Kingston Telecommunication Laboratories 132
LEXIS-NEXIS Communication Center 132
Manufacturing Resources 132
McDonnell Information Systems 132
MicroBiz 132
MTAC Home Page 132
N-Vision Systems 132
Nijenrode Business Webserver 132
North American Power Brokers 132
ODIN Oil Network 133
Opportunity Network 133
Paracel, Inc. 133
Perceptics Corporation 133
Peters-de Laet, Inc. 133
Porter Novelli 133
Process Technologies Incorporated 133
Regional Economic Models, Inc. 133
Research Dynamics 133
The Resource Group 133
Rodex Technologies for the
   Manufacturing Industry 133
Rogers Communications, Inc. 133
SABRE Decision Technologies 133
Scope Systems—Worldwide Industrial Electronics
   Repair and Services 134
Screenwriters Online 134
Seals on Wheels 134
The Service Bureau, LLC 134
Seven Technologies 134
Shape Memory Applications, Inc. 134
STAT-USA 134
Submarine Cables of the World 134
The TechExpo on WWW 134
Tele-Communications, Inc. (TCI) 134
TeleService Resources, Inc. 134
Time Machine 134
Vaughn Communications, Inc. 134
Video Publishing House 135
Virtual Design Center 135
Waters Corporation 135
Welcome to MLMBBS 135

Windy Hills Professional Laboratories 135
World of Commercial Ballooning 135

Patent Information   135

Patent Portal Internet PatentResources 135
SBH Patent Marketing Group 135
Shadow Patent Office 135
U.S. Patent and Trademark Office General
   Information Concerning Patents 135

Real Estate   135

The ADLIST Real Estate Database 135
The Advant Home 136
ALWAYS OPEN!—HouseLink US Real Estate Guide 136
bestagents.com 136
Eastern Mortgage Services, Inc. 136
Electronic Resource Services Property Finder 136
Exquisite Homes and Properties 136
Fidelity Union Mortgage 136
First Pacific Financial 136
FractalNet Real Estate Server 136
Home Builder's Utopia 136
Home Improvement Loans 136
HomeOwners Finance Center 136
How I Made 1 Million Dollars In Real Estate
   With No Money Down 136
Insiders Track Capital Funding Aid 137
Internet Real Estate Listings 137
Internet Real Estate Network 137
J.C. Mortgage 137
Levien-Rich Associates, Inc. 137
The LOAN STORE 137
The Mortgage Calculator 137
The Mortgage Manager 137
The Mortgage Manager Version 5.00 137
National Homes Online 137
National InterAd Real Estate Page 137
The Real Estate Junction 137
The Real Estate Pages 137
Real Estate Recruiting/Careers Education 138
Real Estate Registry 138
Real Estate Shop 138
Real Estate Web 138
Security First Funding 138
Timbergreen Custom Homes 138
Who's Who in Luxury Real Estate 138
WRENet—World Real Estate Network 138

Sales, Marketing, & Advertising   138

Advertising, Boelter & Lincoln 138
AfterHours Communications Corp. 138
Allen & Associates, Ltd. 138
American Demographics/Marketing Tools 138
Another Color, Inc. 139
Austin Knight's KnightNet 139
B.A.A.S. Boating Advertising, Advice, and Service 139
Biggs Gilmore Communications 139
BMP DDB Needham 139
Business-to-Business Marketing Exchange 139
Carter Waxman 139
CEO Access Across the Street or Around the World ... 139
Chiat/Day, Inc. 139
Cohn & Wells 139
Cortex Marketing Resources 139
curious pictures 139
Electronic Product Catalog Systems 140
Farago Advertising 140
Forest Green Media 140
Galaxy Communications, Inc. 140
GBH Handsfree Communication 140
Goswick Advertising 140
HERMES, Consumer and Corporate Surveys 140
Ingalls, Quinn & Johnson 140
Institute for the Study of Business Markets 140
Kern Media Associates 140
Liggett Stashower 140
Marcus Advertising 140
Market Place Media 141
Marketing to Consumers 141
McMonigle & Spooner 141
Michael J. Motto Advertising 141
Mintz & Hoke Advertising and Public Relations 141
Mousetracks—NSNS Marketing Resources 141
O'KEEFE WORLD 141
Reckless Design Limited 141
Richards Group 141
Sales Plus 141
Sharrow Advertising and Marketing Information
    Resource Center 141
Sidea 142
TAL Marketing Services, Inc. 142
TEAMS Marketing and Sales
    Assessment Software 142
Tech Image, Ltd. 142
Tom Davis+Company 142
Wahlstrom & Company 142

Wall Street Journal 142
Web Digest for Marketers 142
WebReach Internet Advertising & Marketing 142
Weightman Group 142
Western Direct's Home Page 142
Wimsey Information Services 142
Winkler McManus 142
Young & Roehr, Inc. 143

Small & Home-Based Businesses   143

Bucknell University Small Business
    Development Center 143
Cobweb 143
Creative Edge 143
The Entrepreneur Network 143
FranNet 143
Inc. Business Resources Library 143
On-Line Marketing 143
SBA Service Corps of Retired Executives 143
Simple Solutions 143
Small and Home-Based Business Links 143
Xerox Small Office 144

Taxes   144

Citizens for an Alternative Tax System 144
L.A. Professionals Online 144
TaxSites—Income Tax Information in Internet 144
United States Tax Code Online 144

Newsgroups   144

Listservs   146

ALSBNEWS—Academy of Legal Studies in
    Business (ALSB) News 146
AOL-EZONE—"Your Business Newsletter" -
    America Online's Weekly Small Bus+ 146
BETS-L—Business Ethics Teaching Society 147
BIZNEWS—News Service Business
    News Releases 147
BSN-D—Business Sources on the Net -
    Distribution List 147
BTECH94—Business Technology 147
BUSHEA—Health-Related Information for
    Business and Industry 147
BUSLAW-L—Business Law List 147
BUSLIB-L—Business Libraries Discussion List 147
BUSREC—Business Recovery 147
CORP-L—Corporate Accountability List 147
EHCOLUMN—Economic History Columns 147

INBUSINESS— Internet In Business
Discussion List 147
KSINDX-L—KS Index of Leading
Econ. Indicators 147
LABOR-L—Forum on Labor in the
Global Economy 147
MBA-L—BA Discussion List 147
NASIRN-L—North American Service
Industries Research Network List 148
NDSRB-L—Students for Responsible Business 148
PCBR-L—Pacific Business Researchers
Forum (PCBR-L) 148
ROUNDTABLE—International Business
Roundtable 148
TOES97—The Other Economic Summit
USA 1997 148

Children   149

4Kids Treehouse 149
1996 Olympic Games Side 149
AHA! Kids Network 149
Awesome Site for All Ages 149
BigKid Network 149
Child Prodigies 149
Children Page 149
Children's Pages at WombatNet 149
Children's Stories, Poems and Pictures 149
Childrens Internet Site, Upstate SC 149
Colgate Kid's World 149
Cyberhaunts for Kids 149
Cynthia and Winston's Kids' Page 149
Flitter Adventure Land 150
Free Kids Page 150
FreeZone 150
FutureScan 150
Girl Talk 150
Global Show-n-Tell Museum Wings 150
Horse Country 150
I Spy 150
Info Guide—For Kids Only 150
Interesting Places for Kids 150
Internet for Kids 150
Jackson's Page for Five Year Olds 151
Katie's Workshop 151
Kay's Kid's Collection 151
KID List 151
Kid's Web 151
Kid's Window 151

Kid's Zone 151
Kidland 151
kidlinks 151
Kids Club 151
Kids Hits 151
Kids on Campus 151
Kids on the Web 151
Kids World 2000 152
The Kids' Place 152
Kids' WB 152
Kids' Web 152
KidsCom Home Page 152
KidsHealth.org 152
KidsNet 152
KidStuff 152
KidWeb 152
Knowledge Adventure 152
LEGO Group 152
Link-4-Kids 152
Maddy Mayhem's Kid's Stuff! 152
MBG Network 153
MCA Home Entertainment Playroom 153
Munchkin Lady 153
NFL Kids 153
Nicky's Kid Links 153
Nucleus Kids' Page 153
Oasis * Here and There * Kids Corner 153
Palos Verdes Kid's Corner 153
Pasadena Kid's Pages 153
Patricia's Kids' Links 153
Planet Blortland 153
Platypus Family Playroom 153
Playroom 154
Rachel's Kids Page 154
REACH Summer Science Camp 154
Reference Links 154
Route 6-16 154
The Sugar Bush 154
Terrific Web Sites 154
Tessa's Cool Links for Kids 154
thekids.com 154
Tristan and Tiffany's Daily Cool Stuff for Kids 154
Uncle Bob's Kids' Page 154
Visa Olympics of the Imagination 154
Web.Kids 155
World Surfari 155
World Wide Kids, Welcome Aboard! 155

Xplore Kids 155
Yahooligans 155
Youth Central Community 155
Youth Connection 155

Newsgroups — 155

Listservs — 156

ABUSE-L—Professional Forum for
Child Abuse Issues 156
ADDKIDS—ADDKids- The List for Children
with Attention Deficit Disorder 156
BEHAVIOR—Behavioral and Emotional
Disorders in Children 156
CAPHARM—CAPharm/Child-Pharm 156
CARINGKD—Caringkids Discussion 156
CHILDRI—Discussion UN Convention on
the Rights of the Child 156
CPPARENT—CPPARENT Discussion for Parents
of Children with Cerebral Pal+ 156
CSHCN-L—Children with Special Health
Care Needs 156
DADVOCAT—DADVOCAT—Dads of Children
with Disabilities or Special Health+ 156
DEAFKIDS—DeafKids List for Deaf Children 156
ECENET-L—Early Childhood Education/
Young Children (0–8) 156
ECEOL-L—Early Childhood Education On-Line
Mailing List 157
ECPOLICY-L—Policy Issues Related to
Young Children 157
KIDCAFE—KIDLINK List: Youth Dialog—
Age 10–15 Only 157
KIDLIT-L—Children and Youth Literature List 157
KIDNEWS—KIDLINK List: For Newsletter
Distribution 157
KIDPEDIA—Child-Authored Encyclopedia 157
KIDZMAIL—KIDZMAIL: Kids Exploring Issues
And Interests Electronically 157
NOVNET—National Operational Volunteers
For Girl Scouts, USA 157
QUAKER-K—Discussion List for Young Quakers
Ages 5 to 12 157
SAC-L—School Aged Child Care Issues
and Concerns 157
SCOUTS-L—Youth Groups Discussion List 157
SICKKIDS—Kids Talking to Kids 157
WYCOOL-L—Way Cool Software Reviews by
Children, Teachers, and Parents 157

YANX-DEP—YANX-DEP Child and Adolescent
Anxiety and Depression Forum 158
YAWRITE—The Children and Young Adult
Writing List 158
YNGLRNGP—Young Learners Group 158

Computer Games — 159

3D Action Games — 159

The 3D Gaming Scene 159
The All-Time Best DOOM Levels 159
CyberMage 159
Dark Forces Editors and Utilities 159
Djinni's Hexen-Editing Page 159
DOOM and DOOM II Secrets 159
Duke Nukem 3D Resource Page 159
GameNet 159
id software 159
Mech Warrior 2 and Clan of the Ghost Bear Page 159
Quake 159
The Tenth Planet 160
Terminator Future Shock 160

3D Strategy Games — 160

Crusader No Remorse 160
Diablo 160
Ishi Press 160
Justin's Command and Conquer Web Page 160
Player's Lists 160
Raptor's Warcraft and Warcraft II Page 160
Welcome To Dave's Warcraft 2 page 160

Adventure Games — 161

Activision Zork Nemesis 161
Daggerfall 161
Dungeon Keeper 161
The Myst Hint Guide 161
Prepare to Get Maxxed AutoDesk 3D Studio 161
Return to Krondor 161
Review of Phantasmagoria 161
Welcome to the Shrine of Zork 161

Companies — 161

7th Level 161
Aristoplay, Ltd. 161
Bethesda Software Current Projects 161
Capstone Software 162
Cosmic JamStain 162

Epic Megagames 162
InterPlay Productions 162
LucasArts Entertainment Company Presents 162
Microprose Software 162
Pop Rocket, Inc. 162
Shadow Island Games 162
Sierra On-Line 162
Sony Electronic Publishing 162
Virgin Zesty Bytes 163
Virtual Entertainment 163

Flight Simulators   **163**
Air Havoc Controller for Windows 163
Battlecruiser 3000AD Unofficial FAQ
   and Home Page 163
Embry-Riddle Flight Simulation Links 163
First Eurofighter Air Wing 163
Flight Unlimited 163
Military Simulations Back to Baghdad 163
Military Simulations, Inc. 163
TekMate Home of the Skunks 163
Terran Confederate Underground 164
Thrustmaster Home Page 164
U.S. Navy Fighters: The Unofficial Home Page 164
The USENET Guide to Falcon 3 164
Warbirds Internet Multi-Player Flight
   Simulation 164
Welcome to CRC and the Air Warrior Community 164
Werewolf vs. Commanche 164

Game Developer Sites   **164**
3D Engine List 164
Commercial 3D Graphic Game Engines 164
Digital Dialect 164
EVPA 165
G.A.C. Computer Services 165
Gray Design Associates 165
IBM OS/2 Games Home Page 165
Jeff Lander's Home Page 165
Pie in the Sky Software 165

Hardware   **165**
CH Products 165
Creative Zone 165
Diamond Multimedia 165
Forte Vfx1 165
head on by Eiger Labs 165
Mag zine 166
Virtual I/O 166
Welcome to the SpaceTec IMC WebKeep 166

Horror Games   **166**
Computer Games Rating Guide 166
Fade to Black 166
Gabriel Knight Help and Hints Home Page 166
Into the Void 166
Psychic Detective 166
Shivers 166
Trilobyte Software 166

Humorous Games   **167**
Cannon Fodder II 167
Earthworm Jim II 167
Gearheads 167
Information about Lemmings 3D the Demo 167
Orion Burger 167
You Don't Know Jack 167

Life Simulators   **167**
The Civilization Page 167
Jerry Moore's Sim Stuff Web Page 167
Maxis, Inc. Home Page 167

Magazines   **167**
Coming Soon! Magazine 167
Computer Gaming World 168
Electronic Gaming Monthly 168
Game Guide 168
Game Informer 168
hyper@ctive 168
NEXT Generation Magazine 168
Nuke InterNETWORK 168
PC Gamer Online 168

MUDs: Multiple User Dungeons   **168**
The Angel's Roleplaying Bookmarks 168
Arcadia MUD 168
Kingdoms 168
Mortal Realms 169
The MUD List 169
The MUD/MUSH/MOO Catalog of Catalogs 169
OuterSpace 169
The Realm 169
Welcome to the World Wide Web Dungeon 169

Shareware/Freeware Games   **169**

Directories   **169**
Gamer's Inn 169
Games Domain 169
Happy Puppy's PC Hit 100 Game Downloads 169
Intel Software Showcase 169

Moonlite Software 170
shareware.com 170
Welcome to the New Guru Online 170

Sports-Related Games   **170**
Computer Baseball and Basketball Games 170
Trophy Bass 170
The Unofficial Need for Speed Page 170
VR Soccer 170
Welcome to My NBA Live 96 Page 170
Whiplash 170
X-Car 170

War Simulations   **170**
Avalon Hill Games of Strategy 170
The E-Hawk Cadre 171
Enemy Lock On 171
The Goat Locker 171
Great War Series Aces of the Deep 171
HPS Simulations 171
Multiplayer Games and Simulations 171
The Silent Service Wargaming Club 171
The Tanker's Homepage 171
The War Page 171

Newsgroups   **172**

Listservs   **173**
*A3R— A Discussion List for the Games
  ADVANCED THIRD REICH and RISING SUN* 173
*ADND-L—Advanced Dungeons and Dragons
  Discussion List* 174
*ALTEREGO-L—Alter Ego Games
  Discussion List* 174
ARIA-L—Last Unicorn's Aria Game List 174
CHESS-L—The Chess Discussion List 174
CONSIM-L—Conflict Simulation Games 174
*GAMEHENDGE—Gamehendge MUSH
  Users Mailing List* 174
GAMES-L—Computer Games List 174
GMAST-L—Gamemasters Interest Group 174
*GSPE-NL—Discussion List in the Field
  of Gaming, Simulation* 174
*ISAGA-L—Int'l Simulation and Gaming
  Association Forum* 174
*MIDGARD-L—Midgard PBM Game
  Discussion List* 174
*MUD-L—Multi-User Dungeons and Other
  Simulated Real-Time Environments* 174
*MYTHUS-L—Mythus Fantasy Roleplaying
  Game List* 174

*PC-GAMES-NEW—Shareware.com
  PC-Games-New List* 174
*PC-GAMES-TOP—Shareware.com
  Pc-Games-Top List* 175
QMS-L— QM Studio Games List 175
UD-L—Ultimate Dungeon List 175

Computers   177

Computer Companies   **177**
Alps Electric USA 177
Altera 177
Amdahl Open Enterprise Systems 177
American Digital Network 177
Apache Digital Corporation 177
Apple Computer Home Page 177
AST Support Information 177
*AT&T Global Information Solutions
  WWW Homepage!* 177
Belhaven Group 177
Bell Microproducts, Inc. 177
Beyond 2000 Systems 177
CGI Systems, Inc. 178
Citac Corporation 178
Client Systems, Inc. 178
Comdisco, Inc. 178
CommTech Systems, Inc. 178
Compaq Online 178
Computer House/ISMAX 178
CTE Computer Training Center 178
Cunningham & Cunningham, Inc. 178
Darwin Micro Systems 178
Data Exchange Corporation 178
Data-Doc Electronics, Inc. 178
Database Excelleration Systems 179
Dataserv Middle East & Africa Ltd 179
DataWave Technologies 179
DayStar Digital 179
DDB Needham Interactive Communications 179
Dell Computer 179
Digital PC 179
Distinct Corporation 179
Downtown Digital 179
DPI 179
DVC Company 179
Eltec International 180
EMD 180
eSoft, Inc. 180
Explorer Communication 180

Fujitsu Systems Business of America Home Page 180
Global Computing, Inc. 180
Great Computer 180
Hewlett Packard 180
IBM Client/Server Computing 180
IBM Person to Person Conferencing 180
Meiko Computers 180
Micropolis Corporation 181
News—Planet Xerox Products 181
Nightware Energy Saving Switch for
   Laser Printers 181
Parsytec Computer GmbH 181
Perfection Services, Inc. 181
Performance Engineering Corporation 181
Persoft 181
Point & Click Software, Inc. 181
PRC 181
Quality HiTec Services 181
Quantum Research Corporation 181
Schofield Computer Organization 181
Sea Change Corporation 182
SEIKO EPSON 182
SITE Computer Services, Inc. 182
Speech Systems, Inc. 182
Sprague Magnetics 182
SRA International, Inc. 182
Storage Computer Corp. Presents 182
Storage Systems Solutions 182
Sun Microsystems 182
Sybex 182
Sylvest Management Systems 182
Synapse Communications, Inc. 183
Synergetic Resource Corporation 183
Systems Solutions 183
TechWorks 183
Tecnation Digital World 183
Texas Micro Home Page 183
TradeNet International, Inc. 183
Turbosales 183
Twenty Twenty 183
Unicomp, Inc. 183
UniPress Worldwide 183
VA Research, Inc. 184
Validity Corporation 184
Vive Synergies, Inc. 184
Voice Recognition Systems 184
Willow Peripherals 184

Wordlink, Inc. 184
XPRO Systems 184

Computer Science   184

Argonne National Laboratory: Mathematics
   and Computer Science Division 184
Computer Oriented Abbreviations
   and Acronyms 184
Cornell Theory Center 184
Cray Research 184
CS-100 The History of Computing 185
Historic Computer Images 185
IEEE Communications Society Technical
   Committee on Gigabit Networking 185
Intelligent Systems Integration Program 185
The Innovation Network 185
List of the World's Most Powerful
   Computing Sites 185
MetaCenter Computational Science Highlights 185
MIT Artificial Intelligence Laboratory 185
NASA High Performance Computing and
   Communications 185
North Carolina Supercomputing
   Center Homepage 185
PARC Xerox Palo Alto Research Center 185
Smithsonian Computer History 186
Software Tools for Logistics Problem Solving 186
Spectral Research Technologies 186
Welcome to The Computer Museum 186

Consultants   186

123 Consulting 186
ActionCall Help Desk Service 186
AHK & Associates 186
AIT 186
Amadeus Consulting 186
Apple Support 186
Bennett Products—Computer Sales/Networking/
   Consulting/Internet 186
Cambridge Technology Partners 187
Cascade Consulting 187
CCI Consulting 187
Clara Vista Corporation 187
Commonwealth Data Systems, Inc. 187
Communicopia Environmental Research and
   Communications 187
CompAdept Corporation 187
Comport Consulting Corporation 187
Compusult Limited 187

Computer Power Group 187
Computerized Data Management 188
ComputerPeople/Dci 188
CooperSoft 188
CoreLAN Communications, Inc. 188
CP Systems 188
CSI.NET, Inc. 188
Daedalus Design Group 188
Dokken Consulting, Inc. 188
Dowdell Business Services 188
Durango Computer Classroom 188
Eccosys, Ltd. 188
EPMOD Consultants, Inc. 188
ESDX 189
The FIEN Group 189
Fly-By-Day Consulting 189
Folio Corporation 189
For-to-Win 189
Full Spectrum Communications 189
Galaxy Systems, Inc. 189
Garbee and Garbee 189
Genoa Technology 189
Georg Heeg 189
GlobalNET 189
Godin London Incorporated 190
GroupWise Information 190
GulfNet Technologies 190
Guru Technologies, Inc. 190
Halo Network Management 190
HD Industries 190
Hartford Computer Group 190
Hieroglyphics 190
hot-n-GUI 190
HTA Link 190
Ian Freed Consulting, Inc. 190
IC Group, Inc. 190
Inacom Corp. 191
Index 191
Information Builders, Inc 191
Ingres Consultant 191
Integrated Systems Solutions Corporation 191
InterComp Internet, Unix, and
    World Wide Web Services 191
IPC Technologies, Inc. on the World Wide Web 191
J P Mclaughlin & Associates, Inc. 191
Jackson-Reed, Inc. 191
Jewell, Chris 191
JimWare, Inc. 191

JM Consulting and Cheap Advice 191
Keystone Technology 191
Kitchen Wisdom Publishing 192
Kratzer Computer Consultants 192
Lavallée & Associates 192
Lodestone Research, L.L.C. 192
MacMedic 192
MBS Industries, Inc. 192
MC2 Cyberspace Research 192
MediaGlobe 192
MetaCase Consulting 192
Mike Salitter Consultant Services 192
The Millennium Solution 192
Minerva Technology 192
MultiMedia Enterprises 192
MVS Training, Inc. 193
Mystech Enterprises 193
Netplan ApS. Consultants in
    Telecommunications 193
Pangea Visions 193
Phoenix Systems Internet Publishing 193
PLATINUM Solutions 193
PRC Inc. Home Page 193
ProSoft Consulting 193
Relational Information Systems, Inc. 193
SAIC Los Altos Home Page 193
Software Dynamics Consulting 193
Specs™ Manufacturing Instructions 194
Spire Technologies 194
Sterling Information Group 194
STS 194
Technology Futures, Inc. 194
TeKnowlogy Education Centers 194
Telecommunications Technology Corp. 194
The Whole Shebang 194
Winsor Computing 194
Word Master, Inc. 194
Xephon 194

Desktop Publishing   **194**
Adobe PageMaker 194
DTP Internet Jumplist 195
ECS Custom Personalized Scalable
    Truetype Fonts 195
A First Guide to PostScript 195
Free Software from Adobe 195
Freedom System Integrators, Inc. 195
i am Iomega 195

Imagine Adobe 195
INFOSEARCH PrintNet 195
MacroMedia Fontographer 195
New World Graphics and Publishing 195
Newspaper Production Using PageMaker 5 ... 195
Quark, Inc. 196
Serif, Inc. 196
So Cal Graphics 196
A Tomato Foundry Technical
   Writing and Design 196
The Xpresso Bar 196
What's New at Quark, Inc.'s Web Site 196

Graphics   196

Adobe Illustrator What's New 196
AnimaTek, Inc. 196
Anton's Freehand Page 196
Artifice, Inc. 196
AspenGrafix 196
Astrobyte 197
Autodesk Home Page 197
Blue Sky Research 197
Cadkey Corp. 197
CadSoft Computer GmbH 197
Caema Ltd. 197
CGD.Graphix 197
CHRIS DICKMAN'S CorelNet 197
Cimio CADCAM Conversion Software 197
Click 3x 197
ComCom Systems, Inc 197
Computer Chrome Presentation Graphics 198
Computer Graphics Systems Development
   Corporation (CGSD) 198
Corel's FTP Site 198
Creative Eye 198
Creative Services 198
CyberTec Commercial Art, Inc. 198
Cytopia Software Incorporated 198
DAIR Computer Systems Logo Design 198
Data Image Systems 198
DesignSphere Online 198
Digio Media 199
Edifika 199
EDS Unigraphics Division 199
Electronic Design Automation Companies 199
Evans & Sutherland Computer Corporation ... 199
Fractal Design Corporation 199

The Graphics Gallery 199
Hamrick Software 199
ICE 199
IDEAL Scanners & Systems 199
InfoImaging Technologies Home Page 199
Intergraph Corp 200
Kai's Power Tips and Tricks for Adobe Photoshop 200
Lightscape Technologies, Inc. 200
Limit X 200
Live Picture, Inc. 200
Lockheed Martin REAL 3D® 200
MacroMedia Freehand Page 200
Management Graphics, Inc. USA 200
Marine Graphics, Inc. 200
MaxVision Online 200
Mentor Graphics Corporation 200
Number Nine Visual Technologies 201
Optix The Internet Document
   Management System 201
Pacific Animated Imaging 201
Parallel Performance Group 201
Parametric Technology Corporation 201
Pathtrace Systems 201
Pattern Corporation 201
Paul Mace Software 201
Performing Graphics Company 201
PhotoModeler 201
Photoshop Folder FTP Site 201
Play Incorporated 201
Precision Graphics of Texas 202
Quadrat Communications 202
Renaissance Technologies 202
Render-Cam Images 202
Scientific Visualization Sites 202
Silicon Surf 202
Software Publishing Corporation Home Page 202
Stephens Design 202
Subia 202
team smartyPANTS! 202
tela computer consulting + design 202
Triffet Design Group 203
Ventana's Photoshop f/x Online Companion 203
Virtus Corporation 203
Visual CADD Home Page 203
WebFlow Communications Group 203
Zycad Corporation 203

Hardware   **203**

1st Solutions, Inc. 203
ACCESS Computer Hardware 203
American Power Conversion 203
ATI Technologies Online 203
Autotime Corp. 203
Bandwidth Brokers International (BBI) 203
BizWeb Category Computer Hardware 204
Black Box Corporation 204
Boca Research 204
BusLogic, Inc. 204
BVM 204
Central Data 204
Colorgraphic Communications Corporation 204
Commax Technologies, Inc. 204
Computer Companies and Vendor
   WWW Home Pages 204
Computer Hardware Page 204
DTK Computers, Inc. 204
Hauppauge Computer 205
Hewlett Packard Products 205
ICS 205
The Image 205
Image Manipulation Systems 205
IMT Systems 205
Information Data Products Corp. 205
Intel Information for Developers 205
Intergraph Corporation 205
Maxtor Current Product Information 205
Memory USA 205
Micro House International 205
MIPS Product Information 205
Power Computing Corporation 206
Praegitzer Industries Web Server 206
PSI Ltd. 206
Rockwell Collins Printed Circuits 206
Samsung Group 206
SCEPTRE 206
Tadpole Technology 206
TechnoGraphy & Storage Computer in Japan 206
Thinking Machines Corporation 206
TouchWindow 206
TTi Technologies, Inc. 206
ViewSonic Corporation 207

Languages   **207**

Amzi! Prolog + Logic Server 207
Benaroya 207
C Programming v.2.6 207

CONSULTIX, the Unix Training Experts 207
Free Compilers and Interpreters 207
hav.Software 207
Hyperparallel Technologies 207
Index of /1/perlinfo/scripts 207
LEARN C/C++ TODAY
   (A list of resources/tutorials) 207
Management Information Technologies, Inc. 208
OC Systems AdaMania Page 208
Rigal Language Home Page 208
Software Translation Tools 208
The C++ Virtual Library 208
Tutorials Need Help with C/C++
   and Other Languages? 208
Unofficial FutureBASIC Web Page 208
Welcome to the WWW Home of COBOL 208

Magazines   **208**

BYTE Magazine 208
Communications Week Interactive 208
Computer Shopper Online 208
Computer Sun Times 208
HotWired 209
Ice-9 Publications 209
MacUser/MacWeek Special on Apple's Future 209
PC-TRANS 209
Pure Power 209
Scientific Computing and Automation Magazine 209
The List of Free Computer-Related Publications 209
Virtual Computer Library Journals 209
ZDNet 209

Mobile Computing   **209**

Adaptec AIRport™ Family 209
Apex PCMCIA Modems 209
BarCode1—A Web of Information
   about Bar Code 209
Cellular Works 209
Columbia University Mobile
   Computing Laboratory 210
DataLink by Timex 210
Introduction to ARDIS 210
It's a Wireless World 210
Mobile and Wireless Computing 210
Mobile Office Magazine 210
Mobile Planet 210
MobileWare Corporation 210
NDS Distributing 210
Psion Incorporated 210

Road Warrior Outpost Solutions for the
Mobile Professional 210
Special Topics in Engineering 210
The World of Newton 211

Multimedia 211

Atomic Vision, Inc. 211
Auricle Control Systems 211
Avalanche Systems, Inc. 211
AVM Summit 211
CA Natalie Associates 211
CD Learn: Personalized Training For Your Favorite
Application Packages 211
CD Warehouse 211
CD Works 211
CD-ROM Online 211
Chick Enterprises Ltd. 212
Cinax Designs Inc. 212
Constant Synthesis Project 212
Crystal River Engineering 212
Darim Vision Co. 212
DayStar Digital, Inc. 212
Demo and Tutorial Builders from MIKSoft, Inc. 212
Digital Creators 212
Digital Movie News 212
Due North 213
EDGE Interactive Media, Inc. 213
Edit & Copy Communications 213
EMA Multimedia, Inc. 213
Entertainment Through Technology Association 213
HJF Digital Media 213
IBM 3D Interaction Accelerator 213
IDM 213
Incite 213
Jack 213
Loviel Computer Corporation 213
MakeMPEG—the Home Page 214
Magnum Resources 214
Media Solutions International 214
Metatec Corporation 214
MidiMan's Official Web Site 214
Mimesis Technology 214
Multimedia Archives 214
Murray MultiMedia 214
Music Screeners 214
Net-One System's Personalized CDs 214
North Communications 214
NuReality 214
Pangaea Creative Media 214

Photodex Corporation 215
Pinnacle Post 215
QuickMedia 215
QuickMedia—Living Album 215
Ramworks 215
Scala Computer Television AS (Norway) 215
Sealworks, Inc. 215
SimPhonics, Inc. 215
Software Tools for Artists 215
Sound & Vision Media 215
Sprite Interactive 215
StarMan Group, Multimedia Productions 216
Station Graphics, Inc. 216
ThreeToad Multimedia 216
Two Guys Named Hank 216
Virtual Artists 216
Visionary Designs 216
vivid studios 216
Welcome to macromedia.com 216
Worlds Inc. 216
X Communications Multimedia 216
Xpand, Inc. 217
XSI MeDIA 217
Zfx, Inc. 217

Networking 217

AppWare Developers Association 217
Alcatel Data Networks 217
Banyan Systems, Inc 217
Capella Networking 217
CrossComm Corporation 217
CygnaCom Solutions, Inc. 217
Designed Information Systems Corporation 218
Digital Network Product Business 218
Emulex Network Systems 218
Engage Communication 218
Enterprise Network Solutions 218
Florida Atlantic University 218
HDS Network Systems 218
HELIOS Software 218
Integrated Communications 218
Intel Smart Network Devices 218
Internet Database Consultants 218
Interphase 219
InterWorking Labs 219
John Mayes & Associates 219
K-Net Ltd 219
KarlBridge 219

Kinesix 219
Klever Computers 219
LAN Solutions 219
Lancom Technologies 219
Maxperts, Inc. 219
MSI Communications 219
Myricom, Inc. 219
Net Guru Technologies, Inc. 219
NETiS Technology, Inc. 219
NetMagic, Inc. 220
Network Communication Computers and Arrays 220
Networks Incorporated 220
NeuroSolutions, Inc. 220
Newbridge Networks Corporation 220
Nortel Northern Telecom 220
Novell, Inc. 220
NTG International 220
NTT Data Communications Systems 220
Onion Peel Software 220
Ornetix Network Computing 221
PC DOCS, Inc. 221
Plaintree Systems 221
Retix Web 221
Rnet 221
Sietec Document Management and Archives 221
SoftLinx, Inc. 221
StonyBrook Software 221
Strategic Networks Consulting, Inc. 221
Structured Network Systems 221
System Resources Corporation 221
TENET Computer Group, Inc. 222
VISIT Computer Telephony Integration 222
Word Master, Inc. 222
XLNT Designs, Inc. 222
Yost Serial Device Wiring Standard 222

Online Sales   **222**

BreakThrough Technologies 222
Campus Network Solutions 222
CJC Graphic Design, Inc. 222
Computer Direct 222
Computer Express 222
Computer Literacy Bookshops, Inc. 222
Computer Marketplace, Inc. 223
Computer Price Cruncher 223
Computer Recycler 223
Computer Warehouse 223
Comstar 223

Continental Resources Computer Division 223
Cyberian Outpost 223
CyberStar 223
DAKCO PC Products Division, Inc. 223
Datalink Direct 223
Datamini Systems 223
Digital Dimensions 223
Direct Connections 223
Domanski-Irvine Book Company 224
Egghead Software 224
EMJ Data Systems Limited 224
Essential Data, Inc. 224
EZ Systems 224
F. F. Tronixs 224
Global Computing, Inc. 224
Global Union Square Internet Shopping Mall 224
Grey-Tech Computer, Inc. 224
Hamilton Rentals Place 224
HNR Computers 224
Icon Technologies, Inc. 225
IPC Technologies, Inc. 225
L & H Computers 225
Laser Express 225
Laser Products and Services Group 225
Laser Renewal 225
LinkStor 225
LMB Microcomputers 225
Logic Approach 225
Lotus Selects Catalog 225
Mac Talk, Inc's WWW Page 225
MacZone Internet Superstore 225
Mantissa Computer Systems 225
Micro-Rent Corporation 226
Micro/Station at UIC 226
Microtrader 226
MicroWarehouse, Inc. 226
National Parts Depot 226
NCA Computer Products 226
Networks Plus Computers 226
New England Computer Supply 226
New Technology Computers 226
New Wave Computers 226
Newman Group Computer Services 226
North American Digital 227
PC Heidens 227
Phoenix Software Solutions, Inc. 227
Powercom and One Com 227
Printer Works 227

The Q Group 227
S.P.C. Microcomputer 227
SBI Computer Distribution 227
SNC International 227
Spectrum Trading 227
Sunshine Computers 228
Team America 228
TENET Computer Group, Inc. 228
Total Systems, Inc. (TSI) Home Page 228
United Computer Exchange Corp. (UCE) 228
Used Computers, Etc 228
Welcome to the Computer Shop 228
Z-Law Software, Inc. 228

Online Services   228

The Allegro Group 228
Alta Vista digital.com 228
Amris, Ltd. 228
APCiNet 229
AT&T Business Network 229
Axess Communications 229
BrainLINK International 229
Brazilnet BBS 229
CDM Distributors 229
CNI Communications Network
   International GmbH 229
Cogent Software, Inc. 229
CommNet Data Systems 229
Community ConneXion 229
CompuHelp Online 230
ConnectUSA 230
CrossLink Internet Access 230
Cyber Technologies International 230
CyberDiner Internet Cafe Systems 230
Damar Group 230
Dataworld 230
DirectNet 230
The Dream Machine 230
E-Doc 230
e.m.a.N.a.t.e. 230
The Emporium 231
ENVISIONET, Inc. 231
Epublish 231
Excite 231
Flamingo Communications Inc. 231
Florida Online 231
Global One 231

Green Bay Online! 231
GroMedia 231
Hot City Networking 231
I. Net Solutions, Inc. 231
Icanet 232
Indiana University's UCS Knowledge Base 232
Intercom 232
Internet Home Users Group (IHUG) 232
Interstate FiberNet 232
Intertex 232
Jay Barker's Online Connection 232
JUMBO! Shareware Archive 232
Merisel's Sun Division 232
OAK Software Repository 232
pixel Generation, Inc. 232
Planet Communications 232
PObox EMail Service 233
Qpage.Com 233
Quay Information 233
Quick.Net 233
r.u.there? 233
SenseMedia Online 233
SoftInfo Software Information Center 233
Sojourn Systems 233
SPAN Information Technology, Inc. 233
Southwest Web 233
Stat Tech 233
SuperLink.NET 233
System Optimization Information 234
ThoughtPort Authority, Inc. 234
Tiger Mountain Productions 234
Total Connectivity Providers 234
TRG, Inc. 234
U-NET 234
Vector Internet Services 234
Virtual Communications 234
Web Professionals, Inc. 234
Web Weavers Publishing 234
WebPub Communications 234
WebSpace 234
The Well Connected Mac 235
Whitey's Web Works & Internet Services 235
WonderNet Digital Communications, Inc. 235
World Information Network 235
WWW. WIN.COM 235
XXL 235

Operating Systems **235**

Apple Software Updates (ftp.info.apple.com) 235

ARDI Executor 235

Current Operating Systems Projects and
OS-Related Research 235

Florida Tech HELP DESK 235

Openstep for Windows 235

OS/2 versus Windows 95Battle for
Operating System Domination 236

OS/2 Warp Product Family Home Page 236

PC-DOS 7 236

Que's Complete List of Windows 95 Products 236

Slackware Professional Linux 236

Randy's Windows 95 Resource Center 236

This Week's Popular Unix Downloads 236

Xiaomu Niu's Internet Application Collection
for Windows 236

Personal Computers **236**

Acer Computer 236

Acorn Computer Group 236

Cult of Macintosh 236

Dell Computer Home Page 237

Elek-Tek 237

GW2K.COM 237

IBM Personal Computers Home Page 237

IBM Personal Computers in the U.S. Aptiva 237

Micron 237

NEC Home Page 237

Northstar 237

Packard Bell 237

Swan Technologies 237

Security **238**

American Power Conversion 238

Atlantic Systems Group 238

Anonymity and Privacy on the Internet 238

ByteBox Computer Enclosures 238

Community Connextion 238

Computer Security Day 238

Cryptography and PGP Page 238

Exide Electronics 238

Index of Privacy Resources 238

Internet Firewalls Frequently Asked Questions 238

McAfee VirusScan for Windows 238

National Computer Security Association 239

Network Systems Corporation 239

NH&A 239

NIST Computer Security Resource Clearinghouse 239

Raptor Systems, Inc. 239

S&S International PLC-Dr. Solomon's Online 239

Secure Computing Corporation 239

Security Engineering Services, Inc. 239

UN*X Net for Computer Security
in Law Enforcement 239

VeriSign, Inc. 239

ViaCrypt 240

The World Wide Web Security FAQ 240

ZD Net Trailblazer Security 240

Software **240**

20/20 Software 240

4GL Computing, Ltd. 240

Ablaze Business Systems, Inc. 240

Absoft Corporation 240

Abstract Technologies 240

ACC Corp., Inc. 240

Accsys Corporation 240

Achieve Technology 240

ACI Company 240

Advanced Computing Systems Company 241

Advanced Paradigms, Inc. 241

Advanced Quick Circuits, L.P. 241

Agorics, Inc. 241

Aladdin Knowledge Systems, Ltd. 241

Aliah, Inc. 241

Alpha Microsystems Services Operation 241

Analytical Software Packages, Inc. 241

ANGOSS Software ntl. 241

Applix, Inc. 242

AquaNet 242

Arcada Software 242

Archive Comparison Test (A.C.T.) 242

ARGUS 242

Ashlar, Inc. 242

Aslan Computing, Inc. 242

ATI Technologies 242

Atlantic Information Systems, Inc. 243

The Attachmate Internet Products Group 243

Austin Software Foundry 243

Automata Design, Inc. (ADI) 243

Axis Communications AB 243

B & E Technology Group 243

Bentley Systems 243

Bernstein & Associates, Inc. 243

BGS Systems 243

Bismarck Group	243
Bluestone, Inc.	243
Blyth Software	243
BMC Software, Inc.	244
Brickell Research, Inc.	244
Brightware Corporation	244
Broadcast Management Plus	244
Bryant Software	244
Business Systems of America, Inc.	244
Caldera, Inc.	244
Cambridge Computer Corp.	244
Camellia Software Corporation	244
Candle Corporation	244
Caravelle Networks Corporation	244
CastCAE	245
Catron Custom Software	245
CE Software	245
CEO Software	245
CharterHouse Software Corporation	245
Chemical Safety	245
Chicago-Soft, Ltd	245
CIAO Software Solutions, Inc.	245
Clarion for Windows Icetips	245
Classic Variety AIPS	245
Clayton Wallis	246
clySmic Software	246
Coconut Info	246
Cogent Computing Software	246
Collabra Software, Inc.	246
Columbia Data Products, Inc.	246
Computers and Learning A/S	246
Computervision Corp.	246
Compuware Corporation	246
Connectivity Custom Controls	246
Core Systems	246
Cornelius Concepts	247
Cort Directions, Inc.	247
CPI Electronic Publishing	247
CPsoft Consulting	247
Crescent Division	247
CrossWind Technologies, Inc.	247
Custom Innovative Solutions (CIS)	247
CVS Bubbles	247
CyberMedia	247
CyberMedia, Inc. WWW Home Page	247
Cyclic Software	248
Cygnus Support Information Gallery	248
Databyte	248
Data Logic	248
DataViz	248
David Whitt & Associates, Inc.	248
Delphi Information Systems	248
Delphic Medical Systems	248
DGA	248
Diamond International Systems Ltd.	248
Dragon's Eye Software	248
DS Diagonal Systems	249
Dubl-Click Software	249
Dun & Bradstreet Software	249
Élan Computer Group	249
Electric Gypsy Software & Consulting	249
Electronic Book Technologies	249
Electronic Learning Systems, Inc.	249
emotion, Inc.	249
Engineering Graphical Solutions	249
EnviroAccount Software	249
Environmental Systems Research Institute	249
Eòlas Technologies Incorporated	250
ERDAS	250
ExperTelligence	250
FCR Software	250
Fineware Systems	250
Focus GbR Software	250
Fundamental Software	250
Futuristic Software & Computing Group	250
Gamma Productions, Inc.	250
Gemini Systems Software, Inc.	250
GeneCraft	250
Generator	251
GIS/Solutions, Inc.	251
Golden Diamonds	251
GrafTek Inc.	251
Gryphon Software Corporation	251
Harlequin	251
Hearne Scientific Software	251
Helios Software	251
HMS Software	251
Honeysuckle Computing	251
Hummingbird Software	251
I-Kinetics, Inc.	251
iambic Software	252
Illustra Information Technologies, Inc.	252
ImageFX	252
Imageware	252
Imagix	252
Imaja Home Page	252

IMB Managing for Profit	252
Immortal Software Productions	252
InContext Systems	252
Inference	252
INFORIUM, The Information Atrium Inc.	252
Information Builders, Inc.	253
The Information Systems Manager, Inc.	253
Insight Designs, Inc.	253
Insignia Solutions	253
Integrated Research	253
Interactive Software Engineering	253
InterMind	253
International Knowledge Systems	253
International Software Systems, Inc.	253
Interpretive Software	253
ISPW	253
J-MAC System Inc.	254
Jandel Scientific Software	254
JOBSCOPE Manufacturing Management System	254
Kinfonetics Technology	254
Knowledge Engineering Pty Ltd.	254
LandWare	254
Law Enforcement/Police Software	254
Legal Computer Solutions	254
Lex Systems	254
Lexitech, Inc.	254
LifeGuide	254
Lighthouse Software, Inc.	254
Lilly Software Associates, Inc.	255
LMSoft	255
Look Software Systems, Inc.	255
Mabry Software	255
Macola Software from Osiris	255
MacNeal-Schwendler Corporation	255
Magna Computer Corp.	255
Maui Software	255
Mayflower Software	255
MCAE Inc.	255
Medlin Accounting Shareware	255
MentorPlus Software, Inc.	255
Merlin Software	255
The Message Board System	256
MetaWare Incorporated	256
Micro-Frame Technologies, Inc.	256
MicroExcel Software	256
Microstar Software Ltd.	256
Microsystems Software, Inc.	256
Milestone Technologies, Inc. (MTI)	256
MKS Source Integrity Product	256
MLL Software and Computers	256
Modular Software Corporation	256
The Molloy Group, Inc.	257
NeoLogic Systems	257
new stuff inc.	257
Notes Solution Software	257
The Numerical Algorithms Group Ltd	257
Pacific Numerix Corporation	257
PaperFree Systems	257
Peninsula Advisors, Inc.	257
Personal Library Software, Inc.	257
Pierian Spring Educational Software	257
Pinnacle Software	258
The Plant Software, Inc.	258
Praxis International	258
Prime Time Freeware	258
Process Analysts, Inc.	258
Prode	258
ProSoft International, Inc.	258
Qbik Software	258
Quality Software Management	258
Quadrillion Data Analysis Software for Semiconductor Manufacturers	258
Quality America Incorporated	258
Quality Software Management	258
Quest Software, Inc.	259
RABA Technologies, Inc.	259
Robert McNeel & Associates	259
S.S.I.T.E. Windows 3.x Utilities	259
Safetynet, Inc. AntiVirus and Security	259
Sage Solutions, Inc.	259
Sanctuary Woods Multimedia	259
Scandinavian Softline Technology	259
Second Nature Software, Inc.	259
Sequent Computer Systems, Inc.	259
Shana Corporation	259
Shock Software	260
SiliconSoft	260
Simucad	260
Sirius Software	260
Skylonda Group	260
Smithmicro	260
SoftPlan Systems	260
SoftSell Business Systems, Inc.	260
Software Consulting Services	260
Software Tailors	260

Solid Oak Software, Inc. 260

SouthWare Innovations, Inc. 261

SPARTA, Inc. 261

Specialized Business Solutions 261

SpeedSim, Inc. 261

SST, Inc. 261

Stonehand Inc. 261

StrandWare Home Page 261

Strawberry Tree, Inc. 261

Subtle Software 261

Sunbelt Software 261

Sunvalley Software 261

Superlative Software Solutions 261

SurfWatch Software 261

SW International Systems Pte Ltd 262

SymCon Software 262

Synapse Communications, Inc. 262

Syntax 262

Systemcorp 262

Systems Alliance, Inc. 262

TEC Solutions 262

TECHCO 262

Technetix Unix/Internet Tools 262

Thermal Solutions 262

Thinque Systems Corporation 262

Thomson Software Products 262

Thunderstone Software 262

Tibco 263

Time Crafter (shareware) 263

TimeLess Technologies Schedule Wizard Software 263

Tosoft Children's Educational and
    Quit Smoking Page 263

The Total Point of Sale Solution 263

Tower Concepts, Inc. 263

Traffic Software 263

Trax Softworks, Inc. 263

Tumbleweed Software Corp. 263

Ubi Soft 263

UNIBOL 263

Uniplex 263

Uptime Computer Solutions, Inc. 263

Van Dyke Technologies 264

Vantageware 264

Veritas Software 264

VersaFax 264

Viewpoint Software Solutions 264

Visigenic 264

Vision XXI 264

VYSOR Integration, Inc. 264

Wall Street Software 264

Welcome to Computer Associates 264

Welcome to HPI on the World Wide Web 265

Welcome to Microsoft 265

Wind River Systems 265

Wingra Technologies 265

Wingra Technologies 265

Zinc Software, Inc. 265

Telecommunications 265

Applied Signal Technology 265

Archtek Telecom Corp. 265

Commercial Speech Recognition 265

Cromack Industries, Inc. 265

EMJ Data Systems 265

FAQ: How can I use the Internet as a telephone? 266

Genesys LLC Home Page—Premier Telephony
    Products for Windows 266

Internet Phone Download a Free Copy 266

ISDN Infocentre 266

M&S Hourdakis SA 266

MedConnect 266

MediaLogic, ADL Inc. 266

MediaSoft Telecom 266

Metricon Welcome 266

Motorola Information Systems Group 266

Multi-Tech Systems, Inc. 266

National Telecommunications And Information
    Administration 267

Nokia 267

Practinet Practical Perhipherals Home Page 267

Research Program on Communications Policy 267

Source, Inc. 267

Stylus Innovation, Inc. 267

Symplex Communications 267

Tascomm Engineering 267

Telecommunications News and Journals 267

Terminate Home Page, the Final Terminal 267

Universal Group Of Companies 268

Videoconferencing Systems, Inc. 268

The World Wide Web Virtual Library of
    Communications and Telecommunications 268

Welcome to the Fibersphere 268

Welcome to Sprint Stop 268

User Groups 268

Autodesk North American User Groups 268

GUIDE International—An IBM User Group 268

Hull Community Artworks 268
IEEE Computer Society—Purdue
   Student Chapter 268
InfoWest Windows 95 Software Archive 268
International Computer Association Home Page 268
Newsletters on the Web 268
The Ottawa Microsoft Users Group (TOMUG) 269
Portland PC Users Group 269
SGI User Groups 269
Sun User Group Java SIG 269
Tampa Bay Linux GNU Technical Society 269
Victoria Macintosh Users Group 269

Newsgroups   **270**

Listservs   **281**

AAASCS—AAAS Computer Systems 281
ACL-L—ACL Software Users List 281
ACORN-L—ACORN Computers Discussion List 281
ACSOFT-L—Academic Software
   Development 281
AECP-L—Apple Education Consultants Program 281
AIBIBL—ACADEMIC INITIATIVE IBM,
   PROJECT "LIBRARY SYSTEMS," AIBIBL 281
AMIGAHAR—AMIGAGHAR
   COMP.SYS.AMIGA.HARDWARE redist. 281
APPLE-PL 281
APPLE2-L—Apple II List 281
APPLE3-L—Apple III Discussion Group 281
APPLENOOZ—AppleNooz Newsletter 281
ASSEMBLER-LIST—IBM Mainframe
   Assembler List 282
ASSEMBLER-LIST—IBM 370 Assembly
   Programming Discussion List 282
ASSMPC—"Assembly for the IBM-PC" 282
BAYSGI-L—Bay Area Silicon Graphics
   Users Group 282
BESTCOM—Hardware You Would Like Others
   to Know About 282
BESTOS—Operating Systems You Would Like
   Others to Try 282
BESTSOFT—Software You'd Like Others
   to Know About 282
BIOPI-L—Secondary Biology Teacher
   Enhancement PI 282
BLIND-L—Computer Use by and for the Blind 282
BMDP-L—BMDP(R)Statistical Software
   Discussion List 282
CADAM-L—Computer Aided Design and
   Manufacturing (CADAM) Interest Group 282

CADAPP-L—CAD Applications Discussion List 282
CADLIST—CAD General Discussion Group 282
CAEDS-L—Computer Aided Engineering Design
   (CAEDS) Interest Group 282
CARR-L—Computer-assisted Reporting
   & Research 282
CECS-L—MU Computer Engineering and
   Computer Science 283
CG-CHAR—Computer Graphics Character
   Animation 283
CGE—Computer Graphics Education Newsletter 283
CNEDUC-L—Computer Networking
   Education Discussion List 283
COCO—Tandy Color Computer List 283
COMM-L—Communications/Modems/BBSs
   Discussion List 283
CRYPTOAPI—Microsoft Cryptographic API 283
CRYPTYCH-L—Cryptych Magazine
   Discussion List 283
CUMREC-L—Administrative Computer Use 283
CYBERIA-L—Law & Policy of Computer
   Communications 283
CYBERVPM—Online Networking for Volunteer
   Program Managers 283
DELTA-L—DELTA Software Discussion List 283
DEOS-R—Distance Education Online Research 283
DERR-L—Distance Education Research
   Roundtable 283
DIRECT-L—Macromedia Director for
   Macintosh and Windows 283
DTPBID—Electronic & Desktop Publishing
   Tenders 284
EMULPC—Emulation SW & HW on the
   IBM-PC 284
ETHCSE-L—Ethical Issues in Software
   Engineering 284
GRAPH-L—Mathematical aspects of Computer
   Graphics, Caos, Fractal 284
GRAPH-L—Yale University Graphics Users 284
GRAPHICS—Graphic Design discussion 284
HP-48—HP-48 Hand Held System 284
HP-USERS-L—A forum for Hewlett Packard
   workstation owners/administrators 284
HP3000-L—HP-3000 Systems Discussion 284
HPMINI-L—Hewlett-Packard 9000 Series Mini
   Computer Discussion 284
IBM-HESC—IBM Higher Education
   Consortium 284
IBM-MAIN—IBM Mainframe Discussion List 284
IBM-NETS—IBM Networking 284

IBMDCE-L—Discussion of IBM DCE Products, Platforms & Usage 284

IBMSND-L—MSDOS Sound Card Forum and Discussion List 284

IBMTCP-L—IBM TCP/IP List 284

IEEETCPC—IEEE Technical Committee on Personal Communications 285

IMAMEDIA—Compatibility of Multimedia Applications 285

INFINI-D—Macintosh Infini-D Discussion 285

INFO-IBMPC—IBMPC-L 285

INFO-IBMPC—INFO-IBMPC Digest 285

INFO-IBMPC—INFO-IBMPC Digest 285

INFO-IBMPC—INFO-IBMPC Digest 285

IO-MUG—I/O MUG - Internet ONLY Macintosh User's Group 285

IOMUG-L—ILLINET Online Music Users Group 285

JCMST-L—Journal Of Computers In Mathematics And Science Teaching 285

JPL-L—Electronic Publishing Mailing List 285

JPSOFT—JP Software products (4DOS/4OS2 et al) 285

ANMAN-L—MS Windows NT Server and Relatives Discussion List 285

LANSRV-L—IBM LAN Server 285

LINUX-ATALK—Appletalk on Linux 285

MAC-FORUM-NEWS—News of the Macintosh Computing Forums on America Online 285

MAC-HELP-NEWSLETTER—News of the Macintosh Help Forum on America Online 286

MACAPPLI—Usage Tips about Macintosh Applications 286

MACHRDWR—Macintosh Hardware an d Related Perpherials 286

MACINTOSH-TOP—Shareware.com macintosh-top list 286

MACLAB—Mac Hardware for Physiologists 286

MACMULTI—Macintosh Multimedia Discussion List 286

MACNET-L—Macintosh Networking Issues 286

MACPCI-L—Macintosh PCI Discussion List 286

MACPPC-L—Macintosh Power PC List (MACPPC-L) 286

MACPROG—Macintosh Programming Discussion List 286

MAC_ED-L—AOL Mac Education & Technology Forum Newsletter 286

MAX—Discussion of Interactive Music/Multimedia Standard Environments 286

MCMANNOUNCE—AOL Mac Comms and Networking Forum Announcements 286

MIBSRV-L—IBM Antiviral Update List 286

MODEMS-L—MODEMS-L Mailing List 286

MS-WINDOWS95-NEW—Shareware.com ms-windows95-new list 286

MS-WINDOWS95-TOP—Shareware.com MS-WINDOWS95-TOP list 287

MSMAIL-L—Microsoft Mail Discussion List 287

MSSQL-L—Microsoft SQL Server Discussion List 287

MSVC—This is a Discussion List for Microsoft Visual C++ Programmers 287

MUSE-L—MUSE Software Discussion List 287

MYTHUS-L—Mythus Fantasy Roleplaying Game List 287

NET-L—STUDENT'S INTERNET/EARN DISCUSSION LIST 287

NET-ND—Notre Dame Campus Networking News 287

NETMONTH—NetMonth Magazine 287

NETV-L—IBM's NETView Discussion List 287

NEWTON-L—Discussion of Apple Newton Family of Equipment 287

NEXTSTEP—NeXTSTEP 3.x & NeXTSTEP 486 for Intel 287

NOVAE—NOVAE GROUP Teachers Networking for the Future 287

NV-L—Discussion of IBM NetView and POLYCENTER Manager on NetView et alia 287

OHIOMM—Ohio Multimedia Development 287

ORCS-L—Operations Research/Computer Science Interface 288

OS2-L—IBM OS/2 Unedited Discussion List 288

OS2PRO-L—IBM OS/2 Unedited Programmers Forum 288

PACS-L—Public-Access Computer Systems Forum 288

PAGEMAKR—PageMaker for Desktop Publishers 288

PCBUILD—Building and Repairing PC Computers - Hardware Only 288

PCSUPT-L—Forum for the Discussion of PC User Support Issues 288

PCTECH-L—MS-DOS Compatibles Support Group 288

POWER-L—POWER-L IBM RS/6000 POWER Family 288

POWER-PC—IBM Power PC Discussion 288

POWERH-L—Discussion List for the PowerHouse Software 288

QPS-USERS—Discussion Among Users of the Quark Publishing System 288

QUARKXPR—The Quark Express List 288
SOFTREVU—Small Computing Systems
   Software Issues Discussion List 288
SP1-L—IBM SP1 Discussion 288
STPP—Science, Technology, and Society
   Discussion and Networking Group 288
SUPERIBM—Super Computing Issues Forum 289
TAA-L—Textbook Authors Association 289
TIDBITS—A Newsletter for Mac Users 289
TIP—List Of Theoretical Computer Science, Tip 289
TOW—The Online World Book Info 289
TYPO-L—TYPO-L Discussion of Type and
   Typographic Design 289
VBDATA-L—Discussion for Microsoft Visual
   Basic Data Access 289
VBSCRIPT—Visual Basic Scripting Edition 289
VFORT-L—VS-Fortran Discussion List 289
VISBAS-L—Visual Basic List 289
VPIEJ-L—Electronic Journal Publishing List 289
WAVEFR-L—WaveFront Software 289
WAYCOOL-L—Way Cool Software Reviews
   by Children, Teachers, and Parents 289
WEBPOST—Microsoft WebPost API 289
WFW-L—Microsoft Windows for Workgroups 289
WIN95-L—Windows 95 Give-And-Take List 289
WINDOWS—MICROSOFT WINDOWS (R),
   NT (R) AND 95 (R) 290
WINHLP-L—Windows Help Compiler (WINHELP)
   Discussion List 290
WPWIN-L—WordPerfect For Windows
   Discussion List 290
WVRK12-L—Ruralnet Forum on Computer
   Networking in Education 290
XLFORT-L—XL FORTRAN Compilers
   Disscussion List 290

Education   291

Education Resources   291

A.Word.A.Day Home Page 291
Academy One 291
Adult Education 291
AIMS Education Foundation 291
The Amistad Research Center 291
Apple Higher Education: The Apple Virtual Campus .. 291
The AskERIC Virtual Library 291
Biology(Science) 291
CALI: The Center for Computer-Assisted Legal
   Instruction 291
Cartoon Laws of Physics 291
Center for Talented Youth (CTY) of the Johns
   Hopkins University 291
Childaware 291
CIC, Center for Library Initiatives 292
The Comer School Development Program 292
Computer as Learning Partner 292
Cornell Theory Center Math and
   Science Gateway 292
Department of Clothing, Design, and Technology,
   MMU 292
The Digital Frog 292
Education Virtual Library—Primary School 292
EDUCOM—Home Page 292
The Egyptian Gallery 292
Federal and State-Run Servers 292
The Geometry Forum 292
Heritage Map Museum 292
Hillside Elementary School 293
ICDL 293
Interactive Multimedia Education Resources 293
The Internet Educational Resources Guide 293
IPL Building Directory 293
ISN KidNews 293
Knox Junior High Home Page 293
Little Toy Store on the Net 293
Magic Learning Systems 293
The Mark Twain Library 293
Math and Science Gateway (Cornell Theory Center) ... 293
MATHMOL—K–12 Mathematics and Molecules 293
The Media Literacy On-line Project Home Page 294
MediaPro 294
Medical/Clinical/Occupational Toxicology
   Resource Home Page 294
MEOL 294
Mount St. Helens 294
MU CoE Links to Education Resources 294
NASA Education Sites 294
Network Nuggets 294
The New York Open Center 294
The Nine Planets 294
The OSPI Math, Science, and
   Technology Server 294
Parenting Skills on Video 295
Persimmon Software for Children 295
Peterson's Education Center 295
Placer County Office of Education 295
Private School Resource 295
Project LEAP (Learn Earn and Prosper) 295
Project Libellus 295

Scholarly Electronic Forums Web Page 295
Schoolhouse Videos and CDs (CD-ROMs) 295
SciEd: Science and Mathematics
    Education Resources 295
Second Nature 295
SERESC 295
Small is Beautiful 295
Street Cents Online 296
The Tecla Home Page from Birkbeck
    College London 296
TENET 296
TESL-EJ Master Page 296
Theodore Tugboat 296
TIESnet 296
UEWeb 296
The United States EducationDepartment/OERI 296
Videodiscovery 296
VOTEC Home Page 296
The Washington Center for Internships &
    Academic Seminars 296
Web 66 297
Web66: K-12 Schools Registry 297
Welcome to MegaMath 297
Welcome to the United States Civil
    War Center 297
Whales: A Thematic Web Unit 297
Window-To-Russia Home Page 297
Winston Churchill High School Web Server 297
WisDPI—The Wisconsin Department of
    Public Instruction 297
Women in Higher Education 297
The World Lecture Hall 297
The World of Benjamin Franklin 297
The World of the Vikings Home Page 298

Financial Aid 298

Financial Aid Information Page 298
Money for College 298

Home Schooling 298

Homeschooling Resources 298
Jon's Home-School Resource Page 298

International Education 298

Friends and Partners 298
Hello India! 298
The Human-Languages Page 298
I*EARN 298
IMD International Institute for
    Management Development 299

Le Coin des Francophones et Autres Grenouilles 299
Live from Antarctica 299
World Kids Press Home Page 299

K–12 Education 299

About the NDLC 299
Alpine Valley School—Home Page 299
ArtsEdge Network 299
Book Nook 299
Brooke High WWW Server 299
Busy Teachers WebSite K–12 299
Cold Spring Harbor Fish Hatchery and Aquarium 299
Columbia Public Schools Home Page 300
Council of the Great City Schools Online 300
The Cyberspace Middle School 300
FYI, RFC #1578-Schools, and Internet 300
Galileo 300
HotList of K–12 Internet School Sites 300
K–12 Education 300
K–12 Technology 300
NCSA Education Program 300
NYSERNet 300
Turner Adventure Learning 300
Welcome K–12 300

Online Teaching & Learning 300

Canadian Institute of Applied Learning, Inc. 300
Canadian Kids' Page 301
Classroom Connect 301
The Community Learning Network 301
Cornell Computer Science Graphics Course 301
Distance Ed 301
Distance Education Clearinghouse 301
Distance Education Resources 301
Distance Learning Directory 301
Distance Learning Resources 301
Educational Online Sources 301
election.html 301
The Electronic Prehistoric Shark Museum 301
Exploratorium Home Page 301
Garfield Co. Public Library System 302
GCRIO On-line Student Activities 302
Genetic Engineering Taught Through
    Telecommunications 302
HotList: Virtual Exhibits 302
Impact! Online Home Page 302
The Interactive Frog Dissection:
    An On-line Tutorial 302

Intercultural E-Mail Classroom Connections 302
JASON Project 302
Landegg Academy Online 302
Math Education Resources 302
MathMagic Internet 302
Online Reference Works 302
The Open University 302
Reed Interactive's Global Classroom 303
The Study in the USA Online Directory 303
The Technology and Distance Education Branch 303
Total Recall 303
Traveler's Japanese with Voice 303
Virtual Frog Dissection Kit 303
Welcome to TEAMSnet 303
The World-Wide Web Virtual Library 303

Organizations 303
Arrow Publishing 303
Banned Books On-line 303
Ethical, Legal, and Social Issues in Science 303
Faculty of Asian Studies, Australian National
    University 304
Florida Institute of Technology—School of
    Aeronautics 304
Global Ecology Study Abroad/IHP 304
Grolier Interactive 304
GROW—Opportunity Wales 304
Harry Singer Foundation 304
International Federation of Library Associations
    and Institutions (IFLA) 304
Junior Achievement Purpose/Facts 304
Macroscale Land Surface Hydrology
    Modeling at the UW 304
Natural Resources Defence Council (NRDC) 304
Northwest Service Academy Page 304
The Smithsonian Institution Home Page 305
TERC 305
United States Naval Sea Cadet Corps 305
Welcome to the Council of the Great City
    Schools Online 305

Research 305
Alabama Supercomputer Authority 305
Brunel University Artificial
    Intelligence Area 305
The Centre for Alternative
    Transportation Fuels 305
CEPS/NASM Smithsonian Institution 305
Concepts in Science through Molecular
    Modeling 305

DreamLink 305
The Environmental Education Network 306
ILTweb: LiveText: Index 306
Image Analytics Corporation 306
IUB Libraries: Research Collections and
    Services Department 306
John and Janice's Research Page 306
Middlebrook's Structured Analog Design 306
Monterey Academy of Oceanographic Science 306
Norm's Home Page 306
Research at BYU Integrated
    Microelectronics Lab 306
Waterford Institute 306

Standards & Testing 306
Environmental Training Group Inc's
    ENVIROPAGE 306
Guidelines for Educational Uses of Networks 306
North Central Regional Educational Laboratory 307
Technology for All Americans Project 307

Student Resources 307
CASAA Student Leadership Resource Centre 307
Children's Literature Web Guide 307
Classroom at the Internet Schoolhouse 307
College Prep Page 307
CyberKids Home 307
English as a Second Language 307
Exchange—Learning.English Language Culture 307
FredNet MOO 307
The Homework Page 308
Inkspot 308
Jefferson-Scranton Community Schools 308
Kids Web A World Wide Web Digital Library for
    Schoolkids 308
Kids' Space 308
North American Historical Re-Enactor Web Site
    (West Site) 308
Private Schools Online 308
Sylvan Learning Centers 308
Voices of Youth Home Page 308
Welcome to the DeweyWeb 308
Welcome to Virtual FlyLab 308
Writing at MU 308

Teacher Resources 308
Ainsworth Keyboard Training Systems 308
Ameritech Education Resources 309
Carrie's Sites for Educators 309
Cisco Educational Archives and Resources Catalog 309

Dole 5-A-Day Home Page 309
DPI InfoWeb 309
Ed Web Home Page 309
Education 309
Education (Social Sciences) 309
Education Sites 309
eduMall 309
ELTI Charlotte's English Aids 309
Explorer Home Page 309
GENII Home Page 309
Gifted and Talented (TAG) Resources Home Page 310
Heinemann World 310
InfoList Home Page 310
InforMNs 310
inQuiry Almanack, March 1995 310
Integrating Technology Schools Home Page at
    University of New Mexico 310
Judi Harris' Network-Based
    Educational Activity Collection 310
Kidding Around 310
Lesson Plans and Activities 310
Mining the Internet Columns 310
NASA Spacelink—An Electronic
    Information System for Educators 310
National Science Foundation World Wide
    Web Server 310
National Teachers Enhancement Network 310
Newton's Apple Educational Materials! 311
The North Dakota ICICLE Project 311
The Old School House Studio 311
School and Community Networking Resources 311
The Tech Classics Archive 311
The Virtual English Language Center 311

Newsgroups   **312**

Listservs   **313**
AACSB—Business School Accredidation 313
AEPDCC—Adult Basic and Literacy Education
    Professional Development Discussion 313
AERA—American Educational Research
    Association List (AERA) 313
AJCUFAID—AJCU Financial Aid Directors 313
CALIBK12—California K-12 Librarians 313
CCE—Council of Counselor Educators 314
CELVR001—CEL's Virtual Classroom 001 314
COENEWS—College of Education
    Employee Discussion 314
CRITTHINKT-L—Teaching Critical Thinking 314

CSTEP—Academic and Scholarship Information
    for Students 314
DEOS-L—The Distance Education Online
    Symposium 314
DEOSNEWS—The Distance Education Online
    Symposium 314
DR-ED—Medical Education Research and
    Development 314
DSSHE-L—Disabled Student Services in Higher
    Education 314
EAIE-L—A Discussion List for International
    Educators in Europe and be+ 314
ECENET-L—Early Childhood Education/Young
    Children (0-8) 314
ECEOL-L—Early Childhood Education
    On-Line mailing list 314
ED220—Issues in Distance Education 314
EDINTL-L—Education School International
    Committee 314
EDLIB-L—Academic Education Librarians 315
EE246—EE246-TCHG MATH ELEMENTARY
    SCHOOL 315
FAMSTECH—Financial Aid Systems - Technical
    Discussion List 315
FINAID-L—ADMINISTRATION of USA
    Financial Aid Offices 315
FLTEACH—Foreign Language Teaching Forum 315
GC-L—Global Classroom: International Students
    E-mail Debate 315
GLB-HLT—Global Forum on Medical Education
    and Practice 315
GRAPH-TI—Discussion of TI Graphing Calculators
    in Education 315
HEALTH-L—International Discussion on Health
    Research 315
HMEDRSCH—Home Education Research
    Discussion List 315
IMSE-L—Institute for Math and
    Science Education 315
IRSU-L—International Relations Student
    Union List 315
ISSSAB-L—International Student and Scholar
    Services Advisory Board List 316
I_STUD—Members of the Student Chapter of the
    Institute for Op. Research 316
K-12GEOGED—ND K-12 Geography
    Educators 316
K12ADMIN—K-12 Educators Interested in
    Educational Administration 316
K12SMALL—A Forum for Education in Small or
    Rural Schools 316

KINDED—Discussion Group for Course Education in Kindergarten 316

LRN-ED—Provide Support and Information to K12 Teachers 316

MAC_ED-L—AOL Mac Education & Technology Forum Newsletter 316

MIDDLE-L—Middle level education/early adolescence (10-14) 316

MIFINAID—Federal Education Loan Program 316

MSIRE-L—RI Math & Science Resource Discussion List 316

MULTC-ED—Multicultural Education Discussion 316

MUSIC-ED—MUSIC-ED Music Education 316

MWERA-H—Midwest Education Research Assn - H 317

NAFSA8-L—NAFSA: AIEE (Association of International Educators) 317

NETINTRO—Workshops For Grades K-12: Applications of the Internet 317

NETSRCH—Workshops For Grades K-12: Internet Searching for Educators 317

NEXUS-L—Nexus-L Research and Studies 317

NYSFA-L—NYS Student Financial Aid List 317

OISNEWS—News For IU International Students and Scholars 317

ONLINEED—Faculties of Education Online Education Forum 317

QUALRSED—Qualitative Research in Education 317

RPE-L—Restructuring Public Education Discussion List 317

SA—Student Association Information and Discussion 317

SERVICE—Student Service Leaders 317

SNURSE-L—An International Nursing Student List 318

SSMP-L—Student Success Mentoring Program 318

STCOAL—Student Coalition of Disabled Students 318

SUNYTRC—SUNY Teaching Resource Centers List 318

SUPERK12—High Performance Internet & Computer Apps in K-12 Schools 318

T321-L—Teaching Science in Elementary Schools 318

TAG-L—Talented and Gifted Education 318

TAMHA—Teaching American History 318

TARPS—Teachers as Research Partners 318

TEACH-L 318

TEACH-RI—News and Information for K-12 Teachers in Rhode Island 318

TEACHART—NMAA Art Curriculum Teacher Conference 318

TERSG-L—NRC: Teacher Education Research Study Group 318

TOW—The Online World Book Info 318

UBITA-L—International Teaching Assistants 319

VIRTCOL1—Virtual College Course 1 319

VIRTED—SJU Virtual Education List 319

VT-HSNET—VT K-12 School Network 319

WIOLE-L—Writing Intensive Online Learning Environments 319

WOMYNWIT—Women Professors of Adult Education 319

Employment — 321

Careers — 321

The Airbase 321

The Airline Employment Assistance Corps 321

Attorney Jobs 321

BackStreet Studios 321

Bolack Total Travel Academy 321

Career Atlas for the Road 321

Career Crafting 321

Career Management International 321

Career Resource Homepage 321

CareerWEB 321

CyberMania! 321

Federal Law Enforcement Careers Employment Guide 321

Getting Past Go 322

High Technology Careers 322

Hot Jobs 322

How To Find a Creative Job in The Real World 322

Library Job Hunting 322

MECA (MBA Employment Connection Association) 322

NetConnections 322

Occupational Resources 322

Ronaldi's MBA Job Finder 322

Westech Career Expo 322

Employment Services — 322

4Work 322

Access Careers & Jobs Resources 323

America's Employers 323

Amerisoft 323

Atlantic Management Resources 323

The Best Jobs in the USA Today 323
Butterfass, Pepe & MacCallan, Inc. 323
CACEE WorkWeb 323
Caldwell Partners On-line Directory 323
CareerMart 323
CareerSite 323
Cromwell Partners Interactive 323
The D.L. Weaver Difference 324
E-Span 324
Employment Search International, Inc. 324
Employment Search Productions 324
Freelance Online 324
Groupweb 324
InPursuit's Employment Network 324
The JobExchange 324
Michael Latas & Associates, Inc. 324
Michigan Association of Personnel Services 324
The Monster Board 324
National Association of Colleges and Employers 324
National Consulting Network 325
National Internship Directory 325
ProMatch '96 325
Recruiters OnLine Network 325
whatNOW? 325

Human Resources   **325**
Achievement Corporation 325
The Analysis Group 325
Benefit Associates 325
CareerLab 325
Edwards and Associates 325
Fortune Personnel Consultants 326
Human Resource News and Issues 326
Pemberton and Associates 326
Total Human Resources 326

Job Fairs   **326**
Career Expo 326
CyberFair 326
Job Fair Home Page 326
SENET Career Expo Home Page 326
The Virtual Job Fair 326
Which Job Fair Is Right for You? 326

Résumé Services   **326**
Career Résumés 326
Employnet, Inc. 326
The Extreme Résumé Drop 327

Graphiti Printing & Graphics' Online
    Résumé Service 327
Job-Link 327
unisoft.net 327

Training Services   **327**
ACME Training, Inc. 327
Advanced Training Professionals 327
American Management Association 327
The Ankarlo Training Group Home Page 327
CaBiT Development 327
Career Connection 327
ClearWord Communications and Training 327
Conceptual Systems, Inc. 328
Damar Group 328
The Image Maker 328
InfoDesign Group 328
The Jacks Institute 328
The McKinley Group, Inc. 328
National Center for Tooling & Precision
    Components (NCTPC) 328
Peritas Online 328
Practical Management, Inc. 328
RootLearning, Inc. 328
Scaffold Training Institute 328
Stressmaster 329
Success Express Journal 329
TLC Seminars 329
Training Express 329
Vital Learning Corporation 329

Newsgroups   **330**

Listservs   **332**
ALIENS-L—Taxation/Witholding/Reporting
    Requirements for Payments to Aliens 332
BLIND-JOBS-L—Employment Issues Concerning
    Blind People 332
CAREER-L—SUNY-wide Career
    Development Organization List 332
ECOLOG-L—Ecological Society of America:
    Grants, Jobs, News 332
FEDJOBS—Federal Job Bulletin Board 332
ICEN-L—ICEN-L International Career and
    Employment Network (NAFSA) 333
JOB-LIST—Job Offers from EARN
    Institute members 333
JOB-TECH—Technology and Employment
    Conference 333

JOBANALYSIS[—Jobanalysis Discussion List 333
JOBPLACE—JobPlace (Self Directed Job Search
   Techniques and Job Placement) 333
JOBVAC-L—OSU Job Vacancy Listings 333
LABNEWS—News of Labor Unions & Workplace
   Organizing 333
LIBJOBS—Library and Information Science
   Jobs mailing List 333
MBACAREER-L—Career Counsellors for
   MBA Students 333
MOONLIGHT-L— 333
SLAJOB—Special Libraries Association
   Employment Opportunities 333
STC—School to Careers- the Purpose of
   Public Education 333
STUDEMP—Issues Related to Student
   Employment 333
SUMMJOBS—Summer Job Information List
   from Career Services 334
SWJOBS—AD&A Software Jobs Weekly 334
TESLJB-L—Jobs and Employment Issues
   (TESL-L sublist) 334

Entertainment 335

Acting 335

Casting on the Web 335
CastingOnline 335
Hollywood Actors Network 335
Raymond Interactive Theatre, Ltd. 335
VCV Stunts—Stuntmen on the Net 335
The Virtual Headbook 335

Comics & Animation 335

The 3-D Zone 335
Alternative Comics—A WWW Guide 335
Austin Anime-Niacs Association 335
Calvin and Hobbes on the World Wide Web 335
Comics 'n Stuff 335
Gen13 Animation's Next GEN 336
Jonah Weiland's Comic Book Resources 336
Marvel Comics 336
Museum of Fine Arts, 3D Animation 336
Planet Millennium 336
Sirius Entertainment 336
Spider Man Figure Archive 336

Games & Online Toys 336

A Simple Rhyming Dictionary 336
Alexander Jean-Claude Bottema's Home Page 336
Bluedog Can Count 336
Boggle 336
Build Your Own Critter 336
Carlo's Coloring Book 337
Chris' Collection of Drinking Misc. 337
Complaint Letter Generator 337
Cool Lego Site of the Week 337
Crejaculabryrinth 337
The Crystal Ball 337
The Cyrano Server 337
The Daily 100 337
The Destruction Derby Games 337
Dogz 337
Duck Hunt—Find the Fowl 337
Ferret Frenzy 337
The First Simpson Dating Game on the Web 337
The Fruit Game 338
Fun with Grapes 338
Funny Bunny Trail 338
Guess the Dictator and/or Television
   Sit-Com Character 338
Handy Spanish Phrase 338
Heretical Rhyme Generator 338
Home Appliance Shooting 338
How Bored Are You 338
Husband Lover Spy 338
IBM—the Electric Origami Shop 338
ID Archives—Doom 338
The Insult Page 338
Interactive Model Railroad 339
Ipizza 339
Joe's Amazing Relationship Problem Solver 339
Kooks Museum 339
Kurt Cobain's Talking Eight Ball 339
Lee's Useless Superhero Generator 339
Lemonade Stand 339
Lite Board 339
Lloyd's Coke Machine 339
Looney Tunes Karaoke 339
Makin Bacon 339
Manic Maze 340
Mark's Apology Note Generator 340
Mindgames 340
Oeno Phile's Mood Detector 340
Optical Illusions—A Collection 340
PhoNETic 340
Piercing Mildred 340
Pig Latin Converter 340

Play Chess on the Net 340
Random Topic Generator 340
Riddle du Jour 340
Rock Mall's Trivia Challenge 340
Rock, Paper, Scissors 340
Salon Betty's Interactive Paper Doll 341
Send an Electronic Postcard 341
Similarities Engine II 341
Star Trek: The Next Generation—
   The Daily Test 341
The Tele-Garden 341
Test Borkifier 341
Tic-Tac-Toe 341
The Tick's Dart Games 341
The Ultimate Oracle—Pray Before the
   Head of Bob 341
The Vain Game 341
Virtual Bubble Wrap 341
Virtual Media 342
Virtual Mr. Spud Head 342
Web-a-Sketch 342
WebBattleship 342
Webcube 342
Welcome to Faces 342
Welcome to Find-the-Spam 342
Welcome To the Connect Four Homepage 342
Welcome to the Web Wumpus 342
Wizards of the Coast, Inc. 342
WWW Anagram Generator 342
The WWW Fortune Cookie Machine 342
WWW Interactive Crossword 342

Humor   **343**
Air Guitar 343
The Amazing Pecking Chicken 343
Big Green Button 343
The Bottom 95% of the WWW 343
Center for the Easily Amused 343
Cruel Site of the Day 343
Crunch 343
Cursing in Swedish 343
The Daily Double Awards 343
The Daily Muse 343
Dave's Web of Lies 343
David Hasselhoff is the AntiChrist 343
The Dog Ate My Homework—1,001 Excuses
   for Home, Work, and Play 343

A Duck's Memoirs 344
Evil Little Brother's Excuse Generator 344
Exploding Heads 344
Georgetown Gonzo 344
The Great Barbie Naming Contest 344
Heather Has Two Mommies 344
Internet Advertising Hall of Shame 344
Internet Squeegee Guy 344
It's the French Fries 344
Jadie's Warped Mind 344
Jim's All New, Fresher Smelling Home Page ...344
LaughWeb 344
Lip Balm Anonymous 345
The Lunacy Catapult 345
Make James Earl Jones Speak 345
The Miraculous Winking Jesus 345
Mirky's Worst of the Web 345
The Oracle of Bacon at Virginia 345
Oracle Service Humor Archive 345
PElvis 345
Penny's Skulls of Fate 345
Personalized Shakespearean Insult Service 345
Planet Wallywood One Liner Comedy Diner 345
Punch Rush Limbaugh Page 345
Random Elizabethan Curse Generator 345
Random Jokes about Yo Mama 346
The Rock and Roll Hall of Shame 346
Rodney Dangerfield Home Page 346
The Scamizdat Memorial 346
Solid Space 346
Spam Haiku Archive 346
Spatula City 346
TEI's Random Joke Server 346
The Textual Abuse Page 346
Thinking Bob's Image of the Day 346
Top Ten Ways to Tell if You Have a
   Sucky Home Page 346
Twisted Tunes Home Page 346
Webcrawler—Deep Thought of the Day 347
White Trash Homepage—Phrantic's Trailerpark 347
World Headquarters for Burrito and
   Burrito-Related Information 347
WWW Fights 347

Miscellaneous   **347**
101 Hollywood Blvd. 347
Campfire Tales 347
Cyber City '96 347

Glenfiddich—Weird and Wonderful Websites 347
Hell's Buddhas 347
The Magic 8 Bra 347
Marvin the Martian 347
Mr. Showbiz 348
Net Frog 348
The Sneeze Page 348
Southern California Real Time Traffic Report 348
Supermarket Tabloid Headlines 348
Virtual Flowers 348
The Virtual Keyboard 348
Welcome to the Adventures of Spacedog 348

Radio — 348

94.7 NRK—The New Rock Revolution 348
440 Satisfaction 348
*AudioNet—The Broadcast Network on
   the Internet* 348
Blue Planet 348
Cinemedia Radio 349
The FCC 349
The Howard Stern Show Sounds Page 349
The Internet Karaoke Store 349
Media Watchdog 349
The Museum of Television and Radio 349
Radio on the Internet 349
*Radio Online—Radio's Starting Point
   on the Net* 349
Sounds of Silence 349

Sound — 349

8-Track Heaven 349
CES News 350
Lucasfilm's THX Home Page 350
RealAudio Audio on Demand for the Internet 350
Secrets of Home Theater and High Fidelity 350
See Hollywood and Vine 350
Sound Site 350
Welcome to Dolby Laboratories 350
Xing Technology's StreamWorks 350

Theater — 350

The Complete Works of William Shakespeare 350
Larry Stark's Theater Mirror 351
London Theatre Guide—On Line 351
New York's Capital District Theater Page 351
New York City Theater 351
Red Herring Productions 351
The SITCOM Home Page 351

TenEyck Design Studio 351
Triad Productions Presents 351

Virtual Worlds — 352

Desiderata—The Reststop 352
Electric Saloon 352
The Enterprise City Home Page 352
Mariam's Cyberspace Park 352
The Social Cafe 352
The Tin Cup Coffee House 352
Virtual Vegas 352
World of Paths Headquarters 352

Newsgroups — 353

Listservs — 357

ANIME-L—rec.arts.anime Newsgroup 357
*ASUENTER—ASU Entertainment Press Release
   Distribution List* 357
*DQMW-L—Dr. Quinn Medicine Woman
   TV Show* 357
*ENTERTAINMENT-NEWS—Entertainment
   Channel Newsletter* 357
*ER-L—ER-L Discussions on ER
   (Crichton's TV Series)* 357
FILMUS-L—Film Music Discussion List 357
FKFIC-L—Forever Knight TV Show Stories 357
*FKSPOILR—Forever Knight TV Show -
   Spoiler Topic List* 357
FORKNI-L—Forever Knight TV Show 357
FRIENDS—The NBC Comedy Friends 357
*GIGGLES—House of Laughter; Jokes, Stories,
   and Anecdotes* 357
GOODIES-L—Discussion List for the Goodies 357
GS-L—Game Shows Discussion List 357
HIGHLA-L—Highlander Movies and TV Series 358
HLFIC-L—Highlander TV Show Stories 358
HORROR—Horror in Film and Literature 358
HUMOR—Good Clean Funny Stuff 358
HUMOR—UGA Humor List 358
*HUMORSCOPE—A Humorous Horoscope
   by Ron Lunde* 358
*LAZARUS-L—The Lazarus Man'
   Discussion List* 358
*LAW-AND-ORDER—Discussion of the
   TV Series* 358
*LOISCLA—The Lois & Clark: The New
   Adventures of Superman Discussion List* 358
MERELEWIS—Life & Works of C.S. Lewis 358
*MISC-HUMOR-L—Miscellaneous Humor
   Mailing List* 358

MOPO-L—Movie Poster Discussion 358

PARTNERS—Discussion of the FOX
   sitcom Partners 358

RRA-L—Romance Readers Anonymous 358

SCREEN-L—Film and TV Studies
   Discussion List 359

STCMD-L—Internet Star Trek Command Council 359

STHL-L—The Star Trek Humour League 359

THEATRE-SOUND—Discussion List for
   People Working in Sound for Live Theatre 359

TWAIN-L—Mark Twain Forum 359

Environment   361

Companies   361

Amway 361

BASF Ecology 361

Chrysler Corporation—Recycling & Conservation 361

Department of the Navy Environmental Programs 361

Disaster's Edge Environmental
   Education Center 361

DuPont: Safety, Health, and the
   Environment 361

Ford Environmental Report 361

Goldman Prize Winners 361

Conservation   361

Alaska Safari Club Home Page 361

American Association of Zoo Keepers 361

Arbor Day 361

Atlantic Salmon Federation 362

The Butterfly Website: Conservation and Ecology 362

Conservation Breeding Specialist Group 362

Conservation International 362

The Coral Reef Alliance 362

Endangered Plants: Images 362

Endangered Species 362

GreenLife Society—North America 362

International Palm Society 362

John Muir Exhibit 363

League of Conservation Voters 363

Maine Solar House 363

The Marine Fish Conservation Network 363

Mr. Solar Home Page 363

National Audubon Society 363

Sempervirens Fund 363

Surfrider Foundation USA 363

USDA—Natural Resources Conservation Service 363

Disasters   364

The Most Contaminated Spot on the Planet 364

Oil Spill Public Information Center 364

The Sea Empress Oil Spill 364

Ecology   364

Cliff Ecology Research Group 364

Earth Watch 364

Ecologia 364

Ecological Monitoring and Assessment Network 364

Ecology Action Centre 364

Envirolink 364

Envirolink Freenet 365

International Center for Tropical Ecology 365

Missouri Botanical Garden 365

PlanetKeepers 365

Questions About Biodiversity 365

Sci.environment 365

Talk.environment 365

Education   365

Arizona EarthVision 365

Ask An Earth Scientist 365

Community Environmental Action Web 365

Connecting With Nature 365

The Earth System Science Community
   Home Page 366

EE Link 366

Environmental Information Center 366

FICUS 366

The GLOBE Program 366

GREENGUIDE—How to Trim Your
   Office Waste 366

Handbook for a Better Future 366

Institute for Earth Education 366

Okefenokee Joe's Natural Education Center 366

Plastic Bag Information Clearinghouse 366

Texas Environmental Center 367

World Transformation 367

Pollution   367

The Air That Kills Us 367

Breath Taking 367

Burning Issues/Clean Air Revival 367

Ecocide in the U.S.S.R. 367

The Economics of Industrial Pollution
   Home Page 367

EPIC Home Page 367

Friends of the Earth Local Groups 367

Georgia Pollution Prevention
Assistance Division 367
Geothermal Energy 368
How To Survive Without a Car 368
Impact of Lead-Contaminated Soil on
Public Health 368
National Pollution Prevention Center
for Higher Education 368
Natural History Book Service 368
Pollution 368

Preservation 368

The Air & Waste Management Association 368
Arctic National Wildlife Refuge 368
Australian Environment Online 368
Earthwise Travels 369
Environmental Defense Fund 369
Fragile Legacy 369
Green Cross International 369
Greenpeace USA 369
Headwaters Forest 369
International Greens 369
U.S. Environmental Protection Agency 369
Welcome to Sherwood 369
Whale and Dolphin Conservation Society 369
The Whale Museum's Orca Adoption Program 370

Products & Services 370

Anatomy 370
Black-Gold Oil Conditioning Systems 370
Buy Green 370
Earth Folk Catalog 370
Earth Shirts 370
Eco-Heads 370
Eco-Motion 370
Eco Store 370
The Electronic Lobbyist for Renewable Energy 370
Environmental Software Resources 370
Environmentally Sound Products 371
Geotechnical & Geo-environmental
Software Directory 371
Green Bean 371
GreenDesign 371
Greenway 371
Hemp Baby 371
Hugg-A-Planet 371
Jade Mountain 371

Mother Nature's General Store 371
Real Goods 371
Smokeless Cooking Products 372
The Video Project 372
ZAP Power Systems 372

Publications 372

The Atlantic Monthly Election
Connection: Environment 372
Conscious Choice 372
CNN—Environment News Main Page 372
Duke Environment Magazine 372
The Dying Sea 372
E Online 372
Earth First! Journal 372
The Earth Times Home Page 372
EcoLink 373
Electronic Green Journal 373
Environmental Ethics Journal 373
Environmental News Network 373
Forty Tips to Go Green 373
Grassroots Youth Magazine 373
GreenBeat! 373
GREENLines 373
Greenpeace Magazines & Newsletters 373
Natural Areas Journal 373
The Online Better World Magazine 374
Our Environment—Online 374
People & the Planet 374
Rachel's Environment & Health Weekly 374
Ranger Rick 374
Science & The Environment 374
SCOPE Newsletter 374
Senior Network News 374
Suncoast Wildlife/Ecology 374
Viva La Tortuga! 374
The WWW Virtual Library—Environment 374

Recycling 374

Cleaning Up C.E. Cole 374
Commonly Recycled Materials 375
The Consumer Recycling Guide: Index to
Local Recycling Centers 375
GreenDisk 375
GREENGUIDE—Reduce/Reuse/Recycle 375
National Oil Recycler's Association 375
The Recycle Link 375
Recycle Locally 375
Recycler's World 375

Newsgroups   **376**

Listservs   **376**
ACTIV-L—Activists Mailing List 376
AERE-L—Association of Environmental and
   Resource Economists 376
AQUIFER—Pollution and Groundwater Recharge 376
CERES-L—Collaborative Environments for
   Conserving Earth Resources 376
CONSLINK—CONSLINK - The Conservation
   Network 376
CUSEN-L—Canadian Unified Student
   Environmental Network 376
ECDM—Environmentally Conscious Design
   & Mfg List 376
ECOLOGIC—EcoLogic Mailing List 376
ENTREE-L—Environmental Training in
   Engineering Education 377
ENVINF-L—List for Environmental
   Information 377
ENVIRON—Miami University
   Environmental Information 377
ENVST-L—Environmental Studies
   Discussion List 377
GREENGRP—Inst. for the Environment 377
COASTNET—Coastal Management
   Conference 377
CUSN-L—Canadian Unified Student
   Environmental Network 377
GROUNDWATER—GROUNDWATER 377
H-ASEH—American Society for
   Environmental History 377
ISEA-L—International Students for Environmental
   Action 377
ONE-L—Organization and the Natural
   Environment 377
PS085—PS085-GLOBAL ECOLOGY 377
QEN-L—Queen's Environmental Network 377
SEAUGA—Students for Environmental
   Awareness 378

Family Issues   **379**

Adoption: Growing Families   **379**
Adoption Advocates: Adoption Policy
   Resource Center 379
Adoption Benefits: Employers as Partners
   in Family Building 379
Adoption Resources on the Internet 379

Adoption—Where Do I Start? 379
AdoptioNetwork 379
Adoptions 379
The Adoptions Connections Project:
   Women's Journeys 379
AIS Exchange List 1996—Community Resources 379
The Alliance For Children 380
Christian World Adoption 380
Domestic Infant Adoption Advice 380
Faces of Adoption—America's
   Waiting Children 380
Family Law Center—Adoption 380
Growing Families Inc. 380
Having Your Child Adopted 380
Help the Children 380
Holt International Children's Services 380
Independent Adoption Center
   Home Page 380
National Adoption Organizations 380
Precious in HIS Sight—Adoption
   Information on the Internet 380
Roots and Wings Adoption Magazine 381
The Texas Adoption Resource Exchange 381
Voices of Adoption 381

Adoption: Searching for a Birthfamily   **381**
Adoptee & Genealogy Page from
   Carrie's Crazy Quilt! 381
Adoptees and Birthparents 381
Adoption on the Usenet 381
BirthQuest 381
Jeff Hartung's Adoptees Resources Home Page 381
Treasure Maps 381

Divorce & Custody   **382**
10 Questions About Child Custody 382
CCADE Web 382
C.H.I.L.D: Children Hurt in Legal Decisions 382
Child Custody: Building Agreements that Work 382
Child Custody in the USA 382
Child Support Home Page 382
Children's Rights Counsel Home Page 382
CourtTV Divorce 382
Custody and Access 382
Divorce 382
Divorce Care Home Page 382
Divorce Helpline Home Page 383
Divorce Helpline: The Legal Divorce
   vs. The Real Divorce 383

Divorce Law Home Page 383
Divorce Online 383
The Divorce Page: Child Support and Custody 383
The Divorce Page: Parenting and Children 383
Divorce Roadmap: Help Around
   the Legal System 383
Family Law Advisor Home Page 383
Family Law Advisor Message Board 383
Family Law Links 383
Kids' Turn 383
Law Offices of Keith M. Carter:
   Child Custody and Visitation 384
Legal dot Net 384
Nolo's Fast Facts: Custody and Visitation 384

**Domestic Violence, Child Abuse, &
   Missing Children**   **384**
Amber Hagerman's Missing
   Children Home Page 384
America's Lost Children Television Network 384
Blain Nelson's Abuse Pages 384
Child Abuse Prevention Network 384
Child Abuse: Statistics, Research,
   and Resources 385
Child CyberSEARCH: English Home Page 385
Child Quest International 385
Child Search: National Missing
   Children's Center 385
Child Sexual Abuse 385
Child Sexual Abuse 385
Child Sexual Abuse or Exploitation:
   What to Do 385
Children's House Home Page 385
Children's Safety Network Home Page 385
CyberPages International Inc:
   Missing Children 385
Domestic Violence Page 386
Family Law Center—Child Abuse and Neglect 386
How to Identify Child Abuse 386
The Institute for the Prevention of
   Child Abuse 386
Kathy's Resources on Parenting, Domestic Violence,
   Abuse, Trauma, and Disassociation 386
Kevin Collins Foundation for Missing Children 386
The KEYEYE Making Kids Safe Page 386
KidsPeace: The National Center for
   Kids in Crisis 386
Mental Health Net: Responding
   to Sexual Child Abuse 386

Minnesota Higher Education Center Against
   Violence & Abuse 386
National Center for Missing
   and Exploited Children 387
National Center on Child Abuse and Neglect 387
OUDPS: Kids Safety on the Internet 387
PeaceDove 387
Safe-T-Child Online 387
SAVE: Survivors and Victims Empowered 387
Survivor Organizations and Agencies 387

Parenting   **387**
365 TV-Free Activities 387
All About Kids Online 387
D.O.S.A. Parenting Home Page 387
Empowering People Home Page 387
family.com 388
Family Planet Home Page 388
Family Resiliency 388
KidsHealth.org 388
The Mommy Times 388
Moms-at-Home Page 388
Nashville Parent 388
National Child Care Information Center
   Home Page 388
Our Kids 388
Parent Soup 388
Parent's Place.Com 389
Parenting New Mexico 389
ParentingMatters 389
Parents and Children Together Online 389
Positive Parenting Home Page 389
Twins Magazine Home Page 389
The Wonderwise Parent Home Page 389

Newsgroups   **390**

Listservs   **390**
ABLETECH-L—For parents, teachers, and
   others concerned with disabilities 390
ABUSE-L—Professional Forum for
   Child Abuse Issues 390
ABUSE-PARTNERS-L—Support for Partners
   of Abuse Survivors 390
ADOPTEES—List Adoptees/Adoptees
   Mailing List 390
BLINDFAM—SJU List for Families of the Blind 390
CARINGPARENTS—How Do Kids Cope
   with Illness? 390

CEL-KIDS—Celiac/Coeliac Wheat/
Gluten-Free Children List 390

CO-OCCURRING-DISORDERS—Discuss
Co-occurring Mental Health & Substance Abuse
Disorders 391

CPPARENT—Discussion for Parents of Children
with Cerebral Palsy 391

DADVOCAT—Dads of Children with
Disabilities or Special Health+ 391

FAM-MATH—Family Math 391

FAMCOMM—Marital/Family & Relational
Communication 391

FAMILY-L—Academic Family Medicine
Discussion 391

FATHERS—US Department of HHS: Fatherhood
and Social Service Programs 391

FREE-L—Fathers' Rights and
Equality Exchange 391

GERINET—Geriatric Health Care
Discussion Group 391

HEALING—Healing: Survivors of
Intimate Abuse 391

MFTC-L—MFTC-L Marriage and Family Therapy
Counseling Discussion 391

MOMSONLINE—Moms Online Main
Mailing List 391

NFWNET-L—Nebraska Family
Wellness Network 391

OPEN-ADOPTION—Open Adoption List
(formerly BRTHPRNT) 391

PARENTING-L—Discussion of Parenting 391

PARENTS—Announcements, Information and
Discussion Related to Parenting 392

PSNEWS—Parent Soup Newsletter 392

REGAYN—Drug Abuse Prevention 392

S-YOUTH—Stolen Youth Mental Health,
Abuse Problems of Youth 392

SP-SUBSTANCE-ABUSE-LIST—Substance
Abuse Information 392

TCS—Taking Children Seriously: Non-coercive
Parenting/Education 392

UIUCPARENT-L—U of I Parents
Advocacy Group 392

VIOLEN-L—Violence Discussion Forum 392

WITCHHNT—Is There a Child Sex Abuse
Witchhunt? 392

WS238-L—Women, Work, and Family in the
20th Century 392

Food & Drink 393

Beverages 393

Acats Internet Bar Pages 393
Beamish & Crawford Brewery 393
Brew Hawaii Magazine 393
Bud On-Line 393
Cafe MAM 393
Capulin Coffee 393
Cat's Meow 3: Internet Beer Recipe Database 393
Celebration Vineyards 393
Coca-Cola 393
Cocktail.Com 393
Cyber Grape and Grain 393
Edinburgh Malt Whisky Tour 394
Eric's Simple Fermented Beverages 394
Grapevine 394
Heineken 394
Internet Wine Rack 394
Jack Daniel's 394
Jolt Cola 394
Mother City Espresso 394
Moxie Collector's Page 394
Napa Valley Virtual Visit 394
Newcastle Brown Home Page 394
Over the Coffee 394
Perrier 395
Real Beer Page 395
Redhook Brewery 395
Rosswog Farm Distillery 395
S.P.S. Beer Stuff 395
SmartWine Online 395
Snapple 395
Stoli Central 395
Virtual Pub 395
Virtual Vineyards 396
Wines on the Internet 396
World Wide Web Winemaking Home Page 396
zima.com 396

Companies 396

Anytime Snacks 396
Aunt Ida's Southern Kitchen 396
Ben & Jerry's 396
Buckeye Beans & Herbs, Inc. 396
CalWine Gourmet Food Shop 396

Campbell Soup Company 396
Caroline Gold Cheese 396
ChefsOnline 396
Chile Today Hot Tamale 397
Constant Creation 397
Dean & Deluca 397
Fax Foods 397
Frito-Lay Main Menu 397
Hacienda Flores Salsa 397
The Highland Trail Company 397
Hot Hot Hot 397
J.R. Wood, Inc. 397
Krema Nut Company 397
Linsey Foods 397
Lotsa Hotsa Salsas, Hot Sauces and More 397
Myer's Gourmet Popcorn 398
Neu Coffee 398
North Fork Exchange 398
Olympia Bakery and Catering 398
Ore-Ida Foods, Inc. 398
Oregon Cupboard 398
PizzaHut 398
Pop 'n Stuff, Inc. 398
Queen's Kitchen & Pantry 398
Saguaro Food Products 398
Scubber's 398
A Taste of Texas 398
Taste of Texas Market 398
Truly Special Gourmet Foods 399
The Virtual Gourmet 399
Watkins Recipes 399

Confectionaries   **399**
Ann Hemyng Candy, Inc.'s
  Chocolate FACTORY 399
Candy 399
ChocolateTown U.S.A. 399
Food Works by Swiss Connection 399
Godiva Online 399
I Need My Chocolate! 399

Culinary Education/Nutrition   **399**
Department of Food Science & Nutrition 399
Dole 5 a Day 399
Electronic Gourmet Guide (eGG) 399
Professor Geoff Skurray's Food &
  Nutrition Information 400

Food A-Z   **400**
B's Cucumber Page 400
Bagel Page 400
BBQ—A Southern Cultural Icon 400
Bovril Shrine 400
Bread 400
Breakfast Cereal Hall of Fame 400
Broccoli Central 400
Buffalo Chicken Wing Home Page 400
Burrito Page 400
Caviar & Caviar, Ltd. 400
Cheeseburger in Paradise 400
CheeseNet 95 401
Chicken Wing Central 401
Cranberry Home Page 401
Dan's Doner Kebab Registry 401
Dinner Co-op 401
Food Resource 401
FoodPlex 401
Official French Fries Page 401
Garlic Page 401
Hot Roast Beef Sandwiches 401
Idaho Potato Expo 401
The Italian Food Market 401
Mmmm... Toast 401
National Pork Producer's Council 402
Pasta Home Page 402
Pickle Preservation Society 402
Potato Miscellany 402
Ranch Worship Page 402
The Raspberry Web Page 402
Rhubarb Compendium 402
Rolling Your Own Sushi 402
Snax.Com 402
Spam Page 402
Strawberry Facts Page 402
Thai Fruits 402
Wild Mushrooms 402

Recipes   **403**
Callahan's Cookbook 403
Cape Breton Pictorial Cookbook 403
Chicken Wing Central 403
Chil E-Heads 403
Chili! 403
Cooking Recipes of the Institute
  of Nuclear Chemistry 403

Creole and Cajun Recipe Page 403
A Culinary World Tour 403
Directory of /pub/rec.food.recipes 403
Directory of /pub/Vegetarian/Recipes/FatFree 403
Epicurious 403
FATFREE Vegetarian Mailing List Archive 403
Filipino Cuisine 404
Friends and Partners Kitchen 404
FYNet's Collection of Malaysian Recipes 404
Hawaii's Favorite Recipes 404
Hawaiian Electric Kitchen 404
Janet Starosta's Recipes 404
Ketchum Kitchen 404
Kitchens of Gordon Bleu 404
Kosher Express 404
La Comeda Mexicana 404
La Pagina dela Salsa Mole 404
Mama's Cookbook 404
Medieval/Renaissance Food Home Page 404
My Favorite Recipes 405
New England Lobster 405
Nomius Eye—Sasa Recipes 405
Notte's Cookbook 405
Pedro's Kitchen 405
Prapapun's Hobby Kitchen 405
Recipe Archive Index 405
RecipeNet 405
Recipes for Traditional Food in Slovenia 405
Recipes from Kathy 405
Restaurant Le Cordon Bleu 405
Ridiculously Easy Recipes 405
Stuart's Chinese Recipes 405
Turkish Cuisine 405
USENET Cookbook 405
Virtual Health 406
Virtual Kitchen 406
VNO: Food—Cooking and Recipes 406
YACB: Yet Another CookBook 406

Restaurants **406**
Boston Restaurant Guide 406
Chrone's Virtual Diner 406
Diner's Grapevine 406
Dining Out on the Web 406
MenuNet FoodFinder 406
Paolo's 406

Sally's Place 406
Virginia Diner 407
World-Wide Sushi Restaurant Reference 407

Vegetarian & Natural Foods **407**
Algy's Herb Page 407
BabyfishNet's Vegan Recipes 407
Earthrise Spirulina home page 407
Gardenburger 407
Herbs & Spices 407
Index to Gluten-Free and Wheat-free Diets pages 407
Mycelium 407
Native American Foods 407
Noah's Ark 407
Oils of Aloha 407
Tamilian Cuisine 407
U.S. Soyfoods Directory 408
Vegetarian Pages 408
Veggies Unite! 408
Whole Foods Market 408
World Guide To Vegetarianism 408

Newsgroups **409**

Listservs **411**
2020_VIS—WKKF Food-Systems-Professions-
  Education-Initiative in Texas 411
ADD-L—Forum for Discussion of Concerns
  of Drinking and Driving 411
DAIRYNET—Professionals Advising The Dairy
  Foods Industry 411
DF225-L—VA. Seafood Faculty 411
DS225-L—VA. Seafood Support 411
EAT-DIS—Eating Disorders List 411
EAT-L—Foodlore/Recipe Exchange 411
FOODTALK—Read it... Do it: Food,
  Nutrition, Food Safety 411
FOODWINE—Discussion List for
  Food and Wine 411
FSPETAMU—WKKF Food-Systems-Professions-
  Education-Initiative in Texas 411
IPFANR-L—"Intl Program for Food, Agri, and
  Natural Resources" 411
SLA-FAN—Special Libraries Association—
  Food Agriculture and Nutrition 412
VCE-FNNEWS—Virginia Cooperative Extension
  Food Nutrition News 412

Government & Politics — 413

Agencies & Offices — 413

BosniaLINK 413
Census Bureau 413
CIAWEB: Central Intelligence Agency Website 413
DefenseLINK 413
Federal Election Commission 413
Federal Information Exchange 413
The Federal Justice Center 413
The Federal Web Locator 413
FedWorld Information Network 413
The House of Representatives WWW Service 413
The Japan Technology Program 413
The Library of Congress Home Page 414
Minority Business Development Agency 414
The National Endowment for the Arts 414
The Office of Management and Budget 414
Social Security On Line 414
Thomas: The U. S. Congress 414
U. S. Department of Agriculture 414
U. S. Department of Commerce: Stat-USA 414
U.S. Department of Education 414
U.S. Department of Energy 414
U.S. Department of Health and Human Services 415
U.S. Department of Housing
    and Urban Development 415
U.S Department of Justice 415
U.S. Department of Labor 415
U.S. Department of the Interior 415
U.S. Department of Transportation 415
U.S. Patent and Trademark Office 415
U. S. Postal Service 415
U.S. Travel and Tourism Administration 415
The United States Senate WWW Server 415
The White House Home Page 415

Campaigns — 416

All Things Political 416
The Almanac of American Politics 416
American Political Network 416
American Voter '96 416
The C-SPAN Networks Site 416
Campaign and Elections Online 416
CBS News: Campaign '96 416
CNN/Time: All Politics 416
Decision '96 416

ElectionLine 416
ElectNet 416
The Gallup Organization:
    1996 Presidential Elections 416
GoverNet 417
KidsNet: Election '96 417
The League of Women Voters' Election '96 417
Majority '96 417
Mother Jones Magazine's
    On the Campaign Trail 417
NetVote '96 417
The Political Participation Project 417
PoliticsUSA 417
Project Vote Smart 417

Foreign Policy — 417

DOSFAN: Department of State
    Foreign Affairs Network 417
The Electronic Embassy 417
The Embassy Page 418
NATO: The North Atlantic Treaty
    Organization 418
The United Nations 418

Miscellaneous Politicals — 418

Hardball '96 418
Political Americana Online 418
Primary Colors 418
President '96 418
The Right Company 418

Political Consulting — 418

Greer, Margolis, Mitchell, Burns & Associates 418
Grossfeld/Severin, Inc. 418
Praxis Online Campaigns 418
Silicon Media, Inc. 418

Political Parties — 419

College Democrats of America 419
College Republican National
    Committee Home Page 419
The Democratic Caucus 419
Democratic National Committee 419
Independence/Reform Party 419
Libertarian Party Headquarters 419
Republican National Committee 419
Republicans Abroad International 419
Young Democrats of America 419
Young Republican National
    Federation Home Page 419

Newsgroups   **420**

Listservs   **423**
ACTVST-L—Political Activist List 423
AERA-L—Division L: Educational
    Policy and Politics 423
APGOVPOL—Advance Placement
    Government and Politics 423
CENASIA—Former Soviet Republic - Central Asia
    Political Discussion List 423
CROSSFIRE—Sophists Political Science Society
    Discussion List 423
CRP—McGill Students for the Renewal of the
    Political Process List 423
GEOPOL—Discussion List for Political
    Geography 423
GILS-L—DHHS Government Information
    Locator Service 423
GOVDOC-L—Discussion of Government
    Document Issues 423
GOVERN-L—Governance Committee Listserv 423
GOVERNANCE-RIN-LIST—Governance Project -
    Regional Information Network 423
GOVMANAG—Management and Leadership in
    Government 423
GOVPUB—Local and State Government Info on the
    Internet 424
GOVREL-L—Discussion of AACRAO
    Government Relations Topics 424
GRC-L—AALL Government Relations
    Committee 424
GSPMTALK—Graduate School of Political
    Management Discussion List 424
H-POL—H-Net Political History
    Discussion List 424
IRL-POL—Discussion of Irish Politics 424
KENTUCKY—KY Civic and Political
    Discussion 424
LGA-L—Local Government
    Administration List 424
LPSSBI-L—Information Management Issues
    Related to Law, Political Science 424
MOPOLY-L—Discussion of Missouri
    Political Issues 424
PCM100—Political Communication
    Discussion Group 424
PEA—Political Economy of Agriculture 424
POLCOMM—Study of Political
    Communication 425
POLI-PSY—Political Science-
    Psychology/Psychiatry 425

POLITICS—Forum for the Discussion of Politics 425
POLS-L—Political Science Major Forum 425
POSCIM—POlitical SCIences Mailinglist 425
PSALUM—Political Science Alumni 425
PSGRAD—Political Science Graduate Students 425
PSRT-L—Political Science Research and
    Teaching List 425
REPUB-L—Discussion of Republican Politics 425
SA_TALK—South African Social and
    Political Issues Forum 425
SGANET—Student Government Global
    Mail Network 425
STAFFGOV—Staff Governance in
    Higher Education 425
STATEPOL—Politics in the American States 426

Health & Fitness   427

Addiction & Recovery   427

Cenikor Foundation, Inc. 427
Drinkwise 427
Habit Smart 427
Lenair Technique, Inc. 427
Prevline: Prevention Online 427
Recovery Home Page 427
Sex and Love Addiction Recovery Home Page 427
U.S. Recovery, Addiction, and Abuse Resources 427

Alternative Medicine   427

Actual Natural Source 427
Acupuncture Home Page 427
Alexandra Health Center 427
The Alternative Medicine Home Page from Falk
    Library of the Health Sciences, University
    of Pittsburgh 427
Conscious Choice 427
HANS—The Health Action Network Society 428
Health and Longevity 428
Herbal Hall 428
Natural Health and Nutrition Shop 428
Nature's Medicine 428
People's Place 428
Welcome to Acupuncture 428
WorldWide Wellness 428

Companies   428

Alliance Health Products 428
Cell Tech Super Blue Green Algae 428
Code Four Medical 428
D&M Sales 428

Designs for Health 428
Doody Publishing Health Science Book Reviews 429
Dragon Herbarium 429
E-Zee Vision Prescription Eyeglasses 429
Green Page—Natural Health/Nutrition 429
My Life International 429
Pharmavite Corporation 429
Springboard Health and Nutrition Products 429
Swan Medical, Inc. 429
Tapestry Books—Adoption/Infertility Book Catalog 429

Death & Dying   **429**
A Place to Honor Grief 429
Bereavement Research Network 429
DeathNET 429
Euthanasia World Directory 429
International Association for
   Near-Death Studies 429
Internet Cremation Society 429
Natural Death Centre 430
Sociology of Death and Dying 430
Summum Mummification 430

Dentistry   **430**
Dental Ethics 430
Dental Implant Home Page 430
Dental Information Home Page 430
Dental Related Internet Resources 430
DENTal TRAUMA Server 430
Frequently Asked Questions 430
Mercury Page 430
Oral Health Country Profiles 430
Scholarly Opportunities in Dentistry 430
So, You Want to be a Dentist? 430

Dieting & Weight Loss   **430**
AromaTrim Weight Loss System 430
Body/Mind Restoration Retreats 1996 430
CyberDiet 431
Fat Person's Home Page 431
FITE—Fat is the Enemy 431
Hacker's Diet 431
Health Vision 431
International No Diet Day 431
Largesse: The Network for Size Esteem 431
The Magic of Believing 431
Magic of Believing 431
Medical Sciences Bulletin 431
Michael D. Myers, MD Inc./Myers
   Information Services 431

Modern Methods—Fat Burning Specialists 431
Nutri/System Online 431
Tell-Me-Y, Inc. 431
TOPS—Take Off Pounds Sensibly 431
Weight Watchers 432

Disabilities   **432**
Ability OnLine Support Network 432
Access Ability Travel 432
Archimedes Project 432
Blind Childrens Center, Inc. Home Page 432
CHATBACK Trust 432
Deaf World Web 432
Disability Net 432
Mankato State University Department of
   Communication Disorders 432
National Sports Center for the Disabled 432
Sibling Support Project 432

Diseases & Conditions   **432**
AIDS Bytes 432
AIDS Information for Young People 432
AIDS Walk Los Angeles 432
Alzheimer Disease Web Site 433
American Diabetes Association 433
American Heart Association National Center 433
American Lyme Disease Foundation 433
Arthritis—Doctor's Guide to the Internet 433
Bad Breath Research 433
Breast Cancer Information 433
Cardiovascular Institute of the South 433
Caring for People With Huntington's Disease 433
CDC National AIDS Clearinghouse 433
Down Syndrome WWW Page 433
Endometriosis 433
Eye Diseases and Conditions 433
Gastroenterology Consultants 434
Heart Mind Body Institute 434
Herpes: The Hidden Disease 434
HYPHECAN Fingertip Cap 434
Introduction to Skin Cancer 434
Introduction to Vision Correcting Procedures
   by Med-Source, Inc. 434
Jeffrey Modell Foundation 434
Kaiser Family Foundation 434
Malaria Weekly 434
Medicine On Line 434
The Merck Manual 434
Muscular Dystrophy Association 434

National Osteoporosis Foundation 435
Parkinson's Web 435
Pediatric Rheumatology Home Page 435
Prostate Cancer InfoLink 435
Rehabilitation Learning Center 435
Roxane Pain Institute 435
Scoliosis 435
The Skin (Diseases) Page 435
Sudden Infant Death Syndrome (SIDS)
    Information Home Page 435
Vision Impairments: A Guide for the Perplexed 435
World of Multiple Sclerosis 435

Emergency Services **435**
Avalanche Dogs! 435
EMBBS: Emergency Medicine and Primary Care
    Home Page 436
Emergency 436
Emergency Preparedness Information eXchange 436
Global Emergency Medicine Archives 436
Mountain Rescue Association 436
National Collegiate EMS Foundation Home Page 436
Team Dispatch 436
UBC (University of British Columbia) MultiCentre
    Research Network 436
UTHSCSA Trauma Home Page 436

Fitness **436**
Aerobics! 436
Alexander Technique 436
Balance: Fitness on the Net 436
The Blonz Guide to Nutrition, Food Science,
    and Health 436
CyberNutrition Online Dole 5 A Day 437
Dole 5 A Day 437
Food & Nutrition Information Center 437
Food Pyramid 437
Hiking and Walking Home Page 437
IFIC Foundation 437
International Yoga School 437
Krispin Komments 437
Mirkin Report 437
MSU Athletic Training 437
Netlife Health Products 437
NutriGenie 438
The Nutrition Expert 438
The Nutrition Pages 438
Nutritive Value of Foods 438

Online Digital Fitness Solutions 438
Peak Performance 438
Professor Geoff Skurray's Food & Nutrition
    Information 438
Sci.Med.Nutrition 438
Yoga Paths: An Overview of Different Schools
    and Traditions 438

General Health **438**
General Complementary Medicine 438
Good Health Web 438
Health Resource 438
HealthCom, Inc. 438
Healthtouch 438
International Health News 439
Linda Sy Skin Care 439
MEDMarket Virtual Industrial Park 439
Minority Health Network 439
Narhex 439
Natracare, LLC 439
Navigator's Health and Nutrition Page 439
SkinCare Program 439
Word on Health 439
World Health Network 439

Geriatrics & Aging **439**
Aging Research Centre 439
Creative Learning Stroke Support Web Site 439
Geropsychology 439
Guide to Retirement Living Online 439
Home Modification: A NARIC Resource Guide 439
Institute for Brain Aging and Dementia 440
Portals Aging 440
SeniorSites 440
Social Security Online 440

Health Administration **440**
American College of Healthcare Executives 440
Aspen Publishers, Inc. 440
BONES: The Biomedically Oriented Navigator of
    Electronic Services 440
Healthcare Financial Management Association 440
Healthcare Information and
    Management Systems Society 440
Innervation Technology Corp. 440
National Association of Health
    Authorities and Trusts 440
Society for Medical Decision Making 440

Health Care   440

Center for Rural Health and
Social Service Developers 440
Chiropractic Page 441
Colorado HealthNet 441
Indigent Patient Services 441
Internal Capsule 441
Internet Medical Products Guide 441
Marijuana as a Medicine 441
Marquette University Program in
Physical Therapy 441
MDB Information Network 441
MedSearch America 441
Patti Peeples' Guide to Health Economics, Medical,
and, Pharmacy Resources on the Net 441
Physical Therapy WWW Page 441
SPA in Italy 441

Health Insurance   441

AFLAC 441
Employers Health Insurance 441
FHP Health Care 442
Inscon: Insurance Consultants, Inc. 442
Insurance for Students, Inc. 442
Insurance Research Network 442
Managed Health Care 442
Rusty Chambers Insurance Agent—Life,
DI, Disability, Health 442
Value-Care 442
Worldwide Med 442

Institutes   442

Arkansas Children's Hospital 442
Catholic Health Association of Wisconsin 442
Charities USA 442
Hair Loss Handbook and Support Group Network 442
Interactive Media Lab 442
International Cancer Alliance 442
Missouri Institute of Mental Health 442
New England Medical Center 443
Radiation Effects Research Foundation 443
OSHA: Occupational Safety and
Health Administration 443

Medical History   443

Michigan Digital Historical Initiative in
the Health Sciences 443
Scientific and Medicinal Antiques 443

Medicine   443

Cyberspace Hospital 443
Department of Neurosurgery at
New York University 443
Department of Otorhinolaryngology at
Baylor College of Medicine 443
Experimental Organ Preservation 443
Harvard Biological Labratories'
Biosciences-Medicine 443
Interactive Patient 443
Medical Education Page 443
MedLink International 444
Medscrip Windows Prescription
Writer for Physicians 444
Northwestern University Department
of Radiology 444
Osteopathic Source 444
PLink—The Plastic Surgery Link 444
Telemedicine Information Exchange—TIE 444
Three-Dimensional Medical Reconstruction 444
Virtual Environments and Real-time Deformations
for Surgery Simulation 444

Men's Health   444

Chronic Prostatitis 444
Circumcision Issues 444
Geddings Osbon, Sr. Foundation
Impotence Resource Center 444
Male Factor Infertility 444
Male Fertility 444
Men's Health 444
Men's Health Issues 445
Successfully Treating Impotence 445
Testicular Cancer: Survival High with
Early Detection 445
Urologic and Male Genital Diseases 445

Mental Health   445

Acclaim Professional Counseling 445
Center for Anxiety and Stress Treatment 445
Cybernetic Stress Control 445
Cyber-Psych 445
Institute of Psychiatry 445
National Alliance for the Mentally Ill Home Page 445
National Coalition of Arts Therapies
Associations 445
Noodles's Panic-Anxiety Page 445
Psychiatry and Psychotherapy 445

Psyrix Help-Net and High Performance Consultants 446
Recreational Therapy Home Page 446
Shyness Home Page 446

Nursing   **446**
ADN/RN Concepts 446
HomeCareNurse Web Page 446
Idea Nurse 446
International Network for Interfaith Health Practices 446
MacNursing 446
Nursing Lists 446
Telephone Triage and Nurse Consultation 446
WholeNurse 446

Nutrition   **446**
Arizona Health Sciences Library 446
Austin Reference Guide for Vitamins 446
Center for Food Safety and Applied Nutrition 446
Dietetics Online 447
Fast Food Finder 447
Macrobiotics Online 447
Magnesium Deficiency, Heart Attack, and Drinking Water 447
MN-NET Home Page 447
Nutrition Pages 447
Organic Gardening 447

Pharmacology   **447**
Controlled Substances: Uses and Effects 447
Fischer Pharmaceuticals Laboratories 447
Hedonistic Imperative 447
Pharmaceutical Information Network 447
Pharmacokinetics, Pharmacodynamics, and Biopharmaceutics Home Page 447
PhRMA Home Page 448
PPS OnLine 448
RxList: The Internet Drug Index 448

Travel Resources   **448**
AEE Wilderness Safety and Emergency Care 448
Comprehensive Healthcare for International and Wilderness Travelers 448
Executive Registry 448
HealthNet 448
Healthy Flying 448
International Traveler's Clinic 448
Moon Publications 448

Outdoor Action Guide to High Altitude Acclimatization and Illness 448
Travel First Aid Kit 448
Traveler's Diarrhea 448
Traveler's Medical and Immunization Service 448
World Wide Drugs 449

Women's Health   **449**
Atlanta Reproductive Health Centre 449
Avon's Breast Cancer Awareness Crusade 449
Breast Cancer Information 449
Bright Innovations 449
Emergency Contraception 449
Endometriosis 449
Health and Science 449
Health Articles by Patricia Older 449
Labor of Love 449
OB/GYN Toolbox 449
S.P.O.T.: The Tampon Health Web Site 449
Women of the World 449
WomenCare 449
WomenSpace 449

Workplace Health & Safety   **450**
American Industrial Hygiene Association 450
Computer Related Repetitive Strain Injury 450
CTD News Online 450
Eastern Analytical Services 450
EMF-Link 450
Health and Computers 450
Howger Services, Inc. 450
NewsPage 450
OSHA-DATA 450
Rocky Mountain Center for Occupational and Environmental Health 450
Typing Injury FAQ 450

Newsgroups   **451**

Listservs   **453**
C+HEALTH—The Health Effects of Computer Use 453
CANCHID—Canadian Network on Health in International Development 453
FIT-L—Exercise/Diet/Wellness Talk List 453
GERINET—Geriatric Health Care Discussion Group 454
HEALTH-L—International Discussion on Health Research 454

H-INFOED—Education for Health Info &
   Library Wk 454
INHEALTH—International Health
   Communication 454
L-CHDH—Culture, Human Development,
   and Health 454
NHSC—National Health Service Corps 454
SCOHRP—Study Committee on Health-Related
   Programs Discussion List 454
SPHHS—School of Public Health & Health Services
   Discussion Group 454
TLTHS—Teaching and Learning Technologies
   for the Health Sciences 454

History   455

American History   455

African-American History 455
American and British History Resources 455
American Civil War Home Page 455
American Civilization Internet Resources 455
American History 455
American Memory 455
The American Revolution and the Struggle
   for Independence 455
American Studies Web 455
Anti-Imperialism in the United States,
   1898–1935 455
Indiana Historical Society 455
Isis: Our Story 455
Life Histories—American Memory Project 456
Oregon—World War II Farming 456
United States—History 456

Ancient History   456

ABZU 456
Akkadian Language (Babylonian and Assyrian
   Cuneiform Texts) 456
Alexandria, Egypt 456
Ancient City of Athens 456
Archaeological Survey in the
   Eastern Desert of Egypt 456
Assyria On-line 456
Didaskalia: Home Page 457
Diotima: Women & Gender in the
   Ancient World 457
Exploring Ancient World Cultures 457
Kelsey Museum Educational
   and Outreach Program 457

Oriental Institute 457
Perseus Project Home Page 457
Peter Konin's Ancient Rome Page 457
Pompeii 457
Pompeii Forum 457

Archaeology   457

ArchNet: Main Menu 457
Classics and Mediterranean Archaeology
   Home Page 457
Fossil Hominids 457
GIS and Remote Sensing for Archaeology:
   Burgundy, France 458
Gopher and WWW Servers 458
The Institute of Egyptian Art and Archaeology 458
Leptiminus Archaeological Project 458
NEH Archaeology Projects Online 458
Newstead Project 458
The Ohio State University Excavations at
   Isthmia 458
Online Archaeology-An Electronic Journal
   of Archaeological Theory 458
Oriental Institute Archaeology 458
OWAN 458

European History   458

Armenian Research Center Home Page 458
Berlin Wall Falls Project 458
European History 458
Europe/Russia/Eastern Europe 458
Germany—Database of German Nobility 459
The Historical Text Archive 459
History Pages 459
Hungarian Images and Historical Background 459
Irish History on the Web 459
Irish Potato Famine 459
REESWeb: Russian and East European Studies 459
Russian Information 459
Soviet Archives: Entrance Room 459
The Victorian Web 459

Historical Figures   459

Abraham Lincoln Online 459
Educational Sources for George Washington 459
Empires Beyond the Great Wall: The Heritage
   of Genghis Khan 460
Fair Play 460
JFK Resources Online 460
Leonardo da Vinci Museum 460

Spectrum Biography Library 460
Thomas Jefferson 460
Thomas Paine 460
Twisted Freaks of History 460
The United States Presidents: Welcome Page 460

Medieval Studies 460
Articles on Medieval/Renaissance Subjects 460
Avalon: Arthurian Heaven 460
Byzantium: The Byzantine Studies Page 460
Labyrinth WWW Home Page 460
Vikings Home Page 461
WWW Medieval Resources 461

Military History 461
Cold War Hot Links 461
Cybrary of the Holocaust 461
D-Day 461
George Rarey's Journals of the 379th
   Fighter Squadron 461
Gulf War Photo Gallery 461
Korean War Project 461
Military History 461
Operation Desert Storm Debriefing Book 461
Remembering Nagasaki 461
Salvation of Bulgarian Jews during WW II 461
Salzburg 1945–1955: Introduction 461
Vietnam Veterans Home Page 462
The War from a Parlor: Stereoscopic Images of the
   Philippine-American War and Soldiers'
   Letters Home 462
Worlds of Late Antiquity 462
World War I (1914-1918) 462
World War II on the Web 462

Miscellaneous Historical Sites 462
ADFA History: History on the Internet 462
Arctic Circle 462
Ari's Today Page 462
BUBL Information Service Web Server 462
Castles on the Web 462
Gangsters! 462
The Heritage Post Interactive 463
The Historical Text Archive 463
History Computerization Project 463
The History of Costume by Braun 463
Index of /expo/ 463
Intentional Communities 463
James B. Ross' Home Page 463
Lords of the Earth: Maya/Aztec/Inca Exchange 463

The Maritime History Virtual Archives 463
Mary Rose Virtual Maritime Museum 463
Maya 463
The Maya Astronomy Page 463
Media History, Studies, and Education 463
Mithraism 464
Musei 464
The Museum Professional 464
Mutiny on the HMS Bounty 464
The National Inventors Hall of Fame 464
Native American Cultural Resources
   on the Internet 464
Papyrology Home Page 464
Paris Museums 464
Pirates 464
Romarch List Home Page 464
Shikhin 464
Shore Line Trolley Museum 465
UNESCO World Heritage List 465
Voice of the Shuttle Home Page 465

Science & Technology 465
The Art of Renaissance Science 465
History of Astronomy 465
History of Science, Technology and Medicine 465
History of Space Exploration 465
Institute for Human Sciences—Vienna 465
NASA Astronautics History 465

Newsgroups 466

Listservs 467
AERA-F—Division F: Educational History
   and Historiography 467
AEROSP-L—Aeronautics & Aerospace
   History 467
AMERCATH—A Discussion List On The
   History Of American Catholics 467
ANCIEN-L—History of the Ancient
   Mediterranean 467
ASHR-L—American Society for the History
   of Rhetoric 467
ASTR-L—Theatre History Discussion List -
   Amer. Soc. for Theatre Research 467
ASTRO-L—History of Astronomy in Canada 467
ATHG—Alcohol and Temperance
   History Group 467
AZTLAN—Pre-Columbian History 467
CAAH—Consortium Of Art And
   Architectural Historians 467

CHA-97—Canadian Historical
Association 1997 467

CHEIRON—Society for the History of the
Social and Behavioral Sciences 467

COMHIST—History of Human
Communication 468

COMM-ORG—H-Net/H-Urban Seminar on
History of Community Organizing 468

EARLYSCIENCE-L—History of Science Society -
Early Science Interest Group 468

EH-TEST—Economic History Testing 468

EHCOLUMN—Economic History Columns 468

ELIAS-I—Figurational Studies in Social Science,
History and Psychology 468

ESPORA-L—History of the Iberian Peninsula 468

ETHNOHIS—General Ethnology and History
Discussion List 468

GAHIST-L—Georgia History Discussion List 468

GHOSTLETTERS—Conversations as Fictional
or Historical Characters! 468

H-AFRICA—H-NET List for African History 468

H-ALBION—H-Net British and Irish
History List 468

H-ALBION—H-NET British and Irish
History List 468

H-AMREL—H-Net American Religious
History Discussion Group 469

H-ANTIS—History of Antisemitism List 469

H-ASEH—American Society for
Environmental History (H-NET List) 469

H-ASIA—H-Net list for Asian History
and Culture 469

H-CANADA—H-Net List for
Canadian History 469

H-CIVWAR—H-Net US Civil War History
Discussion List 469

H-DEMOG—H-Net Historical
Demography List 469

H-DIPLO—H-Net Diplomatic History List 469

H-DIPLO—H-Net Diplomatic History list 469

H-ETHNIC—H-NET List on Ethnic History 469

H-ETHNIC—H-Net Ethnic History
Discussion List 469

H-FRANCE—H-Net History of France List 470

H-FRANCE—H-NET French History
Discussion Group 470

H-GERMAN—H-NET List on German History 470

H-GRAD—H-Net History Graduate Students
Discussion List 470

H-IDEAS—H-NET Intellectual History List 470

H-ITALY—Italian History List from H-NET 470

H-JAPAN—H-NET/KIAPS List for
Japanese History 470

H-LABOR—H-Net Labor History
Discussion List 470

H-LATAM—H-Net Latin-American
History List 470

H-LAW—H-Net and ASLH Legal History
Discussion list 470

H-LAW—H-Net and ASLH Legal History
Discussion list 470

H-LOCAL—H-Net DISCUSSION LIST
FOR LOCAL AND STATE HISTORY 470

H-MAC—H-NET List for the History and
Macintosh Society 470

H-RHETOR—H-Net History of Rhetoric
Discussion List 471

H-RHETOR—H-NET HISTORY OF
RHETORIC DISCUSSION LIST 471

H-RURAL—An H-Net List for Discussion
of Rural & Agricultural History 471

H-RUSSIA—H-Net Russian History list 471

H-RUSSIA—H-Net Russian History List 471

H-SHEAR—H-NET List for History of the
Early American Republic 471

H-SKAND—H-Net List on Scandinavian
History & Culture 471

H-SOUTH—H-Net Southern History
Discussion List 471

H-TEACH—H-Net List for Teaching College
History and Related Fields 471

H-TEACH—H-Net List for Teaching History
and Related Fields 471

H-URBAN—H-Net Urban History
Discussion List 471

H-WAR—H-Net Military History
Discussion List 471

H-WEST—H-Net Western History List 471

H-WEST—H-Net Western History List 472

H-WOMEN—H-NET List for
Women's History 472

H-WORLD—H-NET List for World History 472

HASTRO-L—History of Astronomy
Discussion Group 472

HIS—History and Computing
Discussion Group 472

HISLAW-L—History of Law
(Feudal, Common, Canon) 472

HIST-L—History - Peer Distribution List 472

HISTARCH—Historical Archaeology 472

HISTNEWS—Historians' Newsletter 472
HISTORY 472
HISTORY—History - Peer Distribution List 472
HISTOWNR—Discussion List for Owners
  of History-Related Lists 472
HN-ASK-L—History Network Forum 472
HN-ORG-L—The History Network 472
HOLOCAUS—H-Net History of the
  Holocaust List 473
HOPOS-L—A Forum for Discussion of the
  History of the Philosophy of Sci+ 473
HPSST-L—History and Philosophy of Science
  and Science Teaching 473
HTECH-L—History of Technology Discussion 473
ISLAM-L—History of Islam 473
JSH—Journal of Southern History 473
MAPHIST—Map History Discussion List 473
MEDART-L—Medieval Art History 473
MEDIEV-L—Medieval History 473
MENA-H—History of the Mideast
  and North Africa 473
MIL20C-L—20th Century Military History
  for Amateur Historians 473
MILHST-L—Military History 473
MISSIONS—Missions History Discussion Group
  (MISSIONS) 473
MONON—Monon Railroad Historical &
  Technical Society discussion Group 473
NAHIA-L—North American Historians
  of Islamic Art 474
NFDANCE—Newfoundland Traditional/Historical
  Dance List 474
OHA-L—Oral History Association
  Discussion List 474
PHILOFHI—PHILosophy OF HIstory and
  Theoretical History 474
PRINTS-L—Devoted to the Study of Historical
  & Contemporary Prints 474
PUBLHIST—Public History Discussion List 474
RENAIS-L—Early Modern History -
  Renaissance 474
SAH-L—Society of Architectural
  Historians 474
SISTER-L—History & Contemporary Concerns
  of Catholic Women Religious 474
SLAVERY—The History of Slavery, the Slave Trade,
  Abolition and Emancipation 474
SPORTHIST—ISPHES - Sport History
  Scholars List 474

TAMHA—Teaching American History 474
TARIKH-L—Iran History Forum
  (TARIKH-L) 474
WHIRL—Women's History in Rhetoric
  and Language 474
WHR-L—Women's History in Rhetoric 475
WISHFORD—Crafts, Recreation, Historical
  Methods List 475
WOMHIST—Women's History Discussion 475
WORLD-L—Forum on Non-Eurocentric
  World History 475

Hobbies & Crafts — 477

Amateur Radio — 477

100 Years of Radio 477
The Amateur Radio Elmers Resource
  Directory 477
Amateur Radio Resources 477
The American Radio Relay League's
  World Wide Web Service 477
Ham Radio Outlet 477
Ham University Home Page 477
List of Mail Order Electronics Companies 477
The Packet Radio Home Page 477
Personal Database Applications 477
WWW Ham Radio Servers List 477

Antiques & Collectibles — 477

A–Z Antique & Collectible Directory 477
About the Lighthouse Depot 477
Alien Antiques 478
Auntie Q's Antiques & Collectibles 478
BJS Enterprises Collectibles and
  Crafts Mini Mall 478
Bob's Rock Shop 478
Campus Collectibles 478
The Canadian Online Bottle Collecting Network 478
Cape Cod Teddy Bear 478
Casecrafters 478
Cellophane Square 478
CG Publishing, Inc. Home Page 478
Classifieds–Collectibles–Selling 478
Collectibles by R&T 478
Collectibles by R&T Musical Merry-Go-Rounds 479
Collector Online 479
Collectors COIN UNIVERSE 479
The Collectors' Index 479

Cottage Catalogs 479
Cybercinema Links 479
Dolls By Christine 479
Dr. Wax 479
Dream-Land Dollies!!! 479
East Coast Cards and Collectibles 479
Funtiques Antiques Home Page 479
Glass Insulators 479
Global Art Marketing 479
Haynet on the Web 479
Henry Gitner Philatelists, Inc. 480
Hershey's Collectibles 480
Ilene & Wayne Productions: Collectibles 480
Incredible Collectibles Home Page 480
The Internet Auction List 480
Internet Classifieds: 1500–1599
    Collectibles Index 480
Island Imports, Ltd. 480
Jan-Ken-Po—The Trading Card Game for
    Kids of All Ages 480
Just Matchbox!! 480
Kaila's Country Collectibles 480
KBC Antiques and Collectibles Sites List 480
Kringle Kottage Collectibles 480
Medals of America 481
Moments On-Line 481
MOODY'S Sports Autographs and
    Memorabilia 481
Numismatists Online 481
Perfect Image Sportscards and
    Memorabilia 481
Portal Disney FANtasEARS-
    Mouse-Sell-aneous Forum 481
Railroad Scripophily 481
Rick's GAMEROOM Collectibles 481
Roger's Collector's Marketplace 481
Rusty Zipper—Vintage Clothing
    on the Web 481
Santa Fe Southwest Artists Marketspace 481
Santa Fe Traditions, Inc. 481
Sea Creations 482
Sports, Collectibles, and Money 482
SportsCards, Etc. 482
Sun Tile 482
Web Mill Business District—Bears By The Sea 482
Web Mill Business District—Teddy Bear Directory 482
Whispers in Time 482

World Wide Collectors Digest—
    Your Collectibles Outlet 482
World Wide Mall:™ Arts, Crafts, & Antiques 482
World Wide Mall:™ Collectibles, Dolls, & More 482

Astronomy 482

Astronomy and Astrophysics 482
The Galaxy Page 483
NASA 483
National Space Science Data Center (NSSDC) 483
Novagraphics Space Art Gallery 483
Raben Software & Graphics 483
Radio-Sky Publishing 483
Skywatcher's Diary 483
The Society of Amateur Radio
    Astronomers (SARA) 483
Students for the Exploration and
    Development of Space (SEDS) 483

Birding 484

The Academy of Natural Sciences 484
The Backyard Birdfeeder 484
The Bird Guide, Inc. 484
Birding in Southeast Arizona 484
Birding on the Web 484
Birding on the Web 484
Fugleskue Birdwatch Birdbase 484
Hotspot for Birds 484
NPFauna and NPFlora 484
Ontario Birdwatching Home Page 484
Wild Bird Marketplace 484

Ceramics & Pottery 485

Archie Bray Foundation for the Ceramic Arts 485
Carl Baker Stoneware and Raku Pottery 485
CDI Ceramic Devices, Inc. 485
CEEN, The Crafts Equipment
    Exchange Newsletter 485
Centre for Technical Ceramics, CTK 485
Ceramic Industry 485
Ceramic Solutions 485
Ceramics and Artifacts Restoration 485
Dynamic Ceramic 485
The Forum On-Line Antiques Mall for Potter,
    Porcelain and Ceramics 485
Keith Ceramic Materials LTD 485
Mesa Verde Pottery 486
Orton's Firing Tips 486

The Potter's Page 486
Pottery 486
Scientific Report, Chapter 2: Ceramics and
  Ceramic Composites 486
Virtual Ceramics Exhibit 486
WWW Virtual Library: TechnicalCeramics 486

Coins 486

American Gold Coins 486
The American Numismatic Association 486
Ancient and Medieval Coins 486
Buying Gold Silver Jewelry Coins 486
Coin Universe 487
Coins 487
The Department of the Treasury of
  the United States 487
E Pluribus Unum 487
History of Money from Ancient Times
  to the Present Day 487
Superior Stamp and Coin 487

Furniture Refinishing & Repair 487

BUILD.COM: The Building and Home
  Improvement Products Network 487
Furniture and Refinishing 487
Furniture Medic® 487
The Furniture Repair and Refinishing Wizard 487
Hartmann House Antiques 488
LIBERON/Star Finishing Supplies 488
North American Refinisher'sAssociation 488
Technical Guidelines, Finishing
  Schedules & Product Information 488

Gardening 488

AgriGator 488
The Garden Gate 488
Gardening 488
The Gardening Archive 488
The Gardens at Thunder Ridge 488
The Germinator 488
Howard Garrett's Basic OrganicProgram 488
Joe and Mindy's WebGarden 489
The Virtual Garden 489

Jewelry Making & Metalworking 489

Ancient Circles 489
Associate Jeweler's Tradeshop 489
Design in Metal 489
Hansen Designs—Fine Art Jewelry and Gems 489
Keith Farley/Metalsmith 489

Main Lobby for Jewelry Making 489
The Making of JEEP COLLINS Jewelry 489
Metalwork Using the Sand-Matrix
  Design Process 489

Models 489

Aero-Pac 489
Books/Videos 490
C & M Train Depot 490
DP Industries Home Page 490
Florida's Largest Train Store 490
Logic Rail Technologies 490
Mini Automania 490
Model Railroad.Com 490
Monroe Astronomical Rocket Society 490
Nautical Research and Shipmodeling Links 490
Palatine Hobby's Railroad Page 490
Pmcg's Vicious Model Boat Page 490
Polyterrain Water Soluble Scenery Materials 491
Rocket Works 491
Roecks Railroad Concepts 491
The RR Depot 491
Rutger Friberg's World of Model
  Railroad Electronics 491
S. Shiota's Model Rocket Page 491
A Scale Model Collection 491
Scale Modeling 491
South Bay Model Shipwrights 491
TraiNutz 491

Movie Memorabilia 491

Big Reel 491
CinaMedia 491
Collecting 492
CyberCinema 492
Hollywood Toy and Poster Company 492
Movie Collector's World 492
Movie Poster Warehouse 492
Sources for Still Photographs, Posters and
  Other Film Memorabilia 492
World Collectible Center 492

Origami 492

The Electric Origami Shop 492
An Introduction to Origami and
  The Peace of Paper 492
Jasper's Origami Menagerie 492
Joseph Wu's Origami Page 492
Marbleized Paper 493

Origami Books in Local Libraries 493
Origami Tips 493
Origami USA Main Menu 493
The Pavilion of Polyhedreality 493
Schoolhouse Videos and CDs 493
The Word Chains 493

Photography 493

@rtweb Art Gallery 493
1002situations 493
ABC of Bird Photography 493
Alan Dorow Gallery 493
Alder Yarrow's Photography 493
Allen Rose 494
Anderson Galleries 494
Ansel Adams—Fiat Lux 494
Atlanta Photography Group 494
Atlanta Photojournalism Seminar 494
Australian Outback Gallery Photography 494
Barry Anderson Photography 494
California Museum of Photography 494
Chiossone Studio, NYC 494
The Discovery Catalogue 494
Figure 1: The Visual Sector 494
Hans de Kort Photography 494
*Home Page of Photographer, Sculptor
    David C. Franson* 494
Hot Pictures: Russian Photography 494
Impact Studio 495
Jay Stoegbauer Photography 495
The Jazz Photography of Ray Avery 495
Kodak 495
Michigan Press Photographers 495
Mythago 495
*Northwest College Photographic
    Communications* 495
Online PhotoWeb 495
The Photography Spot 495
The Photography Yellow Pages 495
The Photojournalist's Coffee House 495
PhotoServe 496
Professional Photography Portfolios 496
Ron Lowry's Home Page 496
Sacred Faces, Sacred Spaces 496
*Scott Freeman's Underwater
    Photography Page* 496
*Specializing in Natural Light and
    Nature Images* 496

Travels with Samantha 496
Virtual Gallery (Korea) 496
Virtual Portfolio (London) 496
The Web Nebulae 496

Rocks, Gems, & Minerals 496

Arris International Corporation 496
Crystals and Minerals 496
Gems 496
Hunterian Museum of Rocks and Minerals 497
Mineralogical Meanderings 497
Rockhounds Information Page 497
Web Dexter 497

Stamps 497

Bjorn Much's Stamps Page 497
ELA Auctions, Inc. 497
Th Iceladic Stamp's Page 497
Joseph Luft's Philatelic Resources on the Web 497
New Zealand First Day Covers 497
The Philatelic Trading Post 497
Revenue and Telegraph Stamps 498
Stamp Collecting Basics 498
Stamps, Covers, and Anything Philatelic 498
U.S. 1995 Stamp Program 498
Ukrainian Stamps 498

Textiles 498

Amish Quilts 498
A Brief History of Quilting 498
Computers and Quilting 498
*Counted Cross Stitch, Needlework, and
    Stitchery Page* 498
Creative Quilting 498
*International Web Exchange:
    Quilting Exchange* 499
Misc Quilting Information 499
The Quilting Page 499
The True PA Dutch Country Souvenir 499
World Wide Quilting Page 499

Woodworking 499

Arbortech 499
Carleton Woodworking 499
Chris Melhorn's Woodworking Gallery 499
The Oak Factory Bulletin Board 499
Prairie Woodworking 499
Quality Woodwork and Supply, Inc. 499
W5: Woodworking on the World Wide Web 500

WoodLink 500
Woods of the World 500
WoodWeb 500
Woodworking in Western Montana 500

Newsgroups   **501**

Listservs   **503**
AANDC—Arts and Crafts Era Collectors list 503
ASTRONOMY—This is a Discussion List for
   Amateur and Professional Astronomy 503
ATCA—Antique Telephone Collectors 503
BIRDCHAT—National Birding Hotline
   Cooperative (Chat Line) 503
BIRDCNTR—National Birding Hotline
   Cooperative (Central) 503
BIRDEAST—National Birding Hotline
   Cooperative (East) 503
BIRD_RBA—National Birding Hotline
   Cooperative Business List 503
BIRDTECH-L—The Companion
   Bird Forum 503
BIRDWEST—National Birding Hotline
   Cooperative (West) 504
CLAYART—Ceramic Arts Discussion List 504
CLOTEX-L—Extension Textile and
   Clothing List 504
FUNASTR—Interesting New Discoveries
   in Astronomy 504
GARDENS—Gardens & Gardening 504
OGL—Organic Gardening Discussion List 504
PHOTOASSIST—The Photographer's
   Assistant Mail List 504
PHOTOPRO—The Professional
   Photographers Mail List 504
PHOTOTECH—The Photographers
   Technical Mail List 504
SEW-OLD—Sew-Old Antique Sewing Machine
   Collectors List 504
SQFT—Square Foot Gardening 504
SSUG-L—ShopSmith Woodworking Users
   Group List 504
STAMPS—The Stamps List 504
WOODWORK—Woodworking Discussions 504

Home Improvement   **505**

Architecture   **505**
Architecture & Design 505
Art for Architecture 505

HBA Architecture and Interior Design 505
International Architecture and Design
   Home Page 505
MBT Architecture 505
Open Building Architecture
   For Residential Construction 505
V.C.net 505

Automation   **505**
CBI Systems, Inc. 505
DHSL: Data Home Systems Limited 505
Home Automation Association 505
Home Automation Association (HAA) 505
Home Automator 506
The Home Team 506
HomeTheater Com 506
Intelligent Home Technologies, Inc. 506
JDS Technologies 506
Media Dimensions 506
ProSpec 506
The Spectacular Powerhouse Page 506
Vantage 506

Construction & Woodworking   **506**
The Construction Zone 506
Cyberwood Express 506
The Dulux Paint Assistant 507
THE HOME IMPROVEMENT
   and CONSTRUCTION CONNECTION 507
Home Improvement Home Page 507
Home Improvement Net 507
HomeSource 507
Jonathan Press Woodworking and
   Home Improvement Books and Plans 507
New Home Builders 507
New Home Interactive Cyber
   Home Building Site 507
Pete's Dry Dock 507
Professional Woodgraining Kits 507
Quality Woodwork & Supply, Inc. 507
Remodeler Online 507
The Sound Home Resource Web Home Page 507
The Woodworking Catalog 507

Education   **508**
DO IT YOURSELF HQ 508
Home Improvement 508
Home Improvement How-to Videos 508
Hometime 508

Lamb Home Videos U-DO IT YOURSELF 508
Materials Engineering and Research Laboratory 508

Flooring   508
Advanced Flooring, Inc. 508
Anderson Hardwood Floors 508
Carpets.com 508
Carpet One 508
Country Oak Flooring 509
Dalton Carpet Outlets 509
Floor Coverings International 509
Sculptured Carpet Selections 509
TrustMark 509

Furniture   509
Amboan & Badinia Furniture of Spain 509
Bayviewer Chair Company 509
Blue Canyon Woodworks 509
Crazy Creek Products 509
The Family Room Store 509
Furniture First Aid 509
Furniture, Furniture, Furniture 509
Furniture On Line 509
Leisure Home Center 509
The Online Furniture Refinisher 510
The Sturdy Artistics Catalogue Pages 510
Welcome to the Furniture Fair! 510

General Home Improvement   510
Builders Graphics 510
Home Ideas 510
Home Line Talk Radio 510
Home Repair Hotline 510
Lowe's Home Improvement Warehouse 510
National Consumer Alert Hotline 510
On The House with The Carey Brothers 510
This Old House 511
United Consumers Club 511
Voyager Plus Home Improvement Specialists 511

Inspection   511
Accu-Spect Home Inspection Institute 511
Advanced Home Inspection 511
American Society of Home Inspection 511
AmeriSpec Home Inspection Service 511
Home Inspection Resources 511
Home Spec Inspection Services, Inc. 511
HomeSpec 101 511

Professional Home Inspections, Inc. 511
Wedgwood Service Group, Inc. 512

Interior Decorating   512
Cascade Blinds 512
Colton, Inc. 512
Cuvs Factory Outlet Store 512
Decorating Dimensions, Inc. 512
Decorating Online 512
Dion's Secrets of Home Decorating guide 512
Home Decorator 512
Mainely Shades 512
National Decorating Products Association 512
Roc On Drywall Paint & Wallpaper 512
Southwest Decor 512
Sudberry House new Location! 513
Suzanne Seely's "Make it Beautiful" Decorating
    Newsletter 513
Symbol-Talk 513

Landscaping   513
Centre for Landscape Research 513
Jeff Chorba Landscape Design 513
LandNET—American Society
    of Landscape Architects 513
Landscape Architecture Virtual Library 513
Pennsylvania Horticultural Society 513
University of Delaware Botanic Gardens 513

Plumbing   513
Best Mfg. Co. 513
Faucet Outlet Online 513
GROHE 514
Pipe Trades Association 514
theplumber.com 514

Newsgroups   515

Listservs   515
ARCITRON—Architronic: The Electronic
    Journal of Architecture 515
DESIGN-L—Basic and Applied Design
    (Art and Architecture) 515
LARCH-L—Landscape Architecture
    Electronic Forum 515
PLUMBERS-L—Plumbers Discussion List 515
TREETM-L—Sustainable Landscapes,
    Woody etc. Plants 516

Humanities — 517

Anthropology — 517

ANTHAP—The Applied Anthropology Computer Network ... 517
Anthropoetics: The Electronic Journal of Generative Anthropology ... 517
Anthropology of East Europe Review (AEER) ... 517
Anthropology Resources on the Internet ... 517
The Ascent of Mind: Ice Age Climates and the Evolution of Intelligence ... 517
The Castles of Wales ... 517
Center for Anthropology Communications Home Page ... 517
Center for Visual Anthropology (CVA) ... 517
Centre for Social Anthropology and Computing (CSAC) Ethnographics Gallery ... 517
Exploring Ancient World Cultures ... 518
Fourth World Documentation Project ... 518
Gnostic Institute of Anthropology—London U.K. ... 518
The Gorilla Home Page ... 518
Grottos of the American Midwest ... 518
Hopi Basketry Presentation ... 518
Journal of World Anthropology ... 518
Maxwell Museum of Anthropology ... 518
Maya Adventure ... 518
MayaQuest '96 Home Page ... 518
Museum of Anthropology— University of Michigan ... 518
Native American Net Server ... 519
NativeWeb ... 519
Nicole's AnthroPage ... 519
Origins Of Mankind Home Page ... 519
Primate Info Net (PIN) ... 519
Seeker1's CyberAnthropology Home Page ... 519
Sisseton Wahpeton Sioux Tribe ... 519
The Society for the Anthropology of Europe (SAE) Web Site ... 519
Society for Economic Anthropology ... 519
UCSB Anthropology Web Site ... 520
University of Chicago Press Anthropology and Archaeology Catalog ... 520
University of Manitoba Anthropology Department ... 520
The UVa AnthroNet ... 520
World Scripture: A comparative anthology of sacred texts ... 520

Archaeology — 520

The Aerial Archaeology Newsletter ... 520
The Ancient City of Athens ... 520
Anasazi Archaeology ... 520
Annual Egyptological Bibliography (AEB) ... 520
Archaeological Fieldwork Opportunities ... 520
Archaeological Resource Guide for Europe ... 521
Archaeology at Mt. Vernon Plantation ... 521
Archaeology Magazine ... 521
ArchNet: WWW Virtual Library— Archaeology ... 521
Biblical Archaeologist ... 521
British Archaeology ... 521
Classics and Mediterranean Archaeology Home Page ... 521
COMBINED CAESAREA EXPEDITIONS— Underwater Excavations of Sebastos: King Herod's Harbor ... 521
The Council for Independent Archaeology ... 521
Dino Russ's Lair ... 521
Dinosaur Provincial Park ... 521
Duke Papyrus Archive ... 522
Encyclopedia Smithsonian: Archaeology ... 522
FAQ—Career in Archaeology in the U.S. ... 522
Field Museum Online ... 522
GIS and Remote Sensing for Archaeology: Burgundy, France ... 522
The Indiana Jones WWW Page ... 522
Institute of Nautical Archaeology (INA) ... 522
Internet Archaeology ... 522
National Park Service: Links to the Past— Archaeology ... 522
Native American History and Archaeology Resources on the Internet ... 522
The Oriental Institute—University of Chicago ... 523
Pan-American Institute of Maritime Archaeology (PIMA) ... 523
Papers from the Institute of Archaeology (UCL) ... 523
Prehistory Press ... 523
RADIOCARBON WWW Server ... 523
Reeder's Egypt Page ... 523
ROMARCH—Roman Art and Archaeology ... 523
Royal Commission on the Ancient and Historical Monuments of Scotland (RCAHMS) ... 523
Royal Tyrrell Museum Web Site ... 523
SAAweb—Society for American Archaeology ... 524
The Skull Page ... 524
South Dakota Archaeology ... 524
SouthWestern Archaeology ... 524
Stone Pages ... 524
T.W. Rutledge ... 524
U.C. Berkeley Museum of Paleontology ... 524
UK Archaeology on the Internet ... 524

General Humanities   524

Center for Electronic Texts
  in the Humanities 524
Center for the Humanities 524
Computing in the Humanities
  Users Group (CHUG) 524
H-Net—Humanities OnLine 525
Humanities and Social Sciences—
  University of Chicago LibInfo 525
Humanities HUB 525
Humanities National Database Search 525
The Humanities Report 525
Institute for Human Sciences—Vienna 525
National Endowment for
  the Humanities (NEH) 525
National Humanities Institute Home Page 525
The Stanford Electronic Humanities Review 526
Research Institute for the Humanities (RIH) 526
Voice of the Shuttle: Web Page for
  Humanities Research 526
WWW Virtual Library—Humanities 526

Geography   526

AGI GIS Dictionary 526
Area Accurate Map / The Peters Projection 526
The Association of American Geographers 526
The Association of Chinese Professionals
  in Geographic Information Systems 526
Canadian WWW Central Index/Liste centrale
  des serveurs WWW canadiens 526
Cartography—Indiana State University 526
ChartWrite's Data-on-the-Map 526
E-scapes: Electronic Resources for the Study
  of Ancient Landscapes 527
Federal Geographic Data Committee (FGDC) 527
Geographic Institutes around the World 527
Geographic Nameserver 527
GEOGRAPHY USA: A Virtual Textbook 527
The Global Positioning System (GPS) 527
Heritage Map Museum 527
The History of Cartography Project 527
How far is it? 527
Institute of Arctic and Alpine Research 527
Interactive Geographical Index 527
International Map Trade Association (IMTA) 527
The Laboratory for Remote Sensing and
  Geographic Information Systems (LRSGIS) 528
Making Maps Easy to Read 528
Mapmaker, Mapmaker, Make Me a Map 528

MAPublisher 528
NAISMap WWW-GIS Home Page 528
National Center for Geographic Information
  and Analysis (NCGIA) 528
The Natural Area Coding System 528
Oregon Geographic Alliance (OGA) 528
Project GeoSim 528
RETKI GPS Land Navigation Software 528
The RYHINER-Project at the University Library
  of Berne 528
Spatial Odyssey: GIS Literature Database 529
TIGER Mapping Service 529
TOPO!™ Interactive Maps 529
U.S. Geological Survey (USGS) National Mapping
  Information World Wide Web Server 529
Xerox PARC Map Viewer 529

Languages/Linguistics   529

The American Dialect Society (ADS) 529
American Sign Language Linguistic
  Research Project 529
The Association for Computational Linguistics 529
Australian National Dictionary Centre 530
CELEX Dutch Centre for Lexical Information 530
Center for Applied Linguistics (CAL) 530
Center for Machine Translation 530
Center for Spoken Language Understanding 530
The Chomskybot 530
Colibri Home Page 530
English as a Second Language Home Page 530
ETHNOLOGUE: Languages of the World 530
EUROLANG Optimizer 530
FoLLI, the European Association for Logic,
  Language, and Information 530
Haskins Laboratories 531
The Human-Languages Page 531
Journal of Child Language 531
Journal of Pidgin and Creole Languages 531
The Klingon Language Institute 531
Kualono: 'Olelo Hawai'i 531
Lexeme-Morpheme Base Morphology (LMBM) 531
The Lingua Project 531
The LINGUIST Network 531
Linguistic Fun 531
Loglan 532
The Mayan Epigraphic Database Project 532
Mayan Hieroglyphic Syllabary 532
Model Languages 532
Multilingual PC Directory 532

Natural Language Computing Home Page 532
Old English Pages 532
Russian Manual Alphabet 532
Semiotics for Beginners 532
TsaLaGi (English/Cherokee Dictionary) 532
*UCREL—University Centre for Computer Corpus
   Research on Language* 533
*University of Chicago Press Cognitive Science and
   Linguistics Catalog* 533
The Web Journal of Modern Language Linguistics 533
Word Manager 533
WordSmith Tools 533
The Yuen Ren Society 533

Psychology   533

Ages & Stages 533
Altered States of Consciousness 533
*The American Academy of Child & Adolescent
   Psychiatry Homepage (AACAP)* 533
American Psychoanalytic Association 533
*American Psychological Association—
   PsychNET* 533
American Psychological Society (APS) 534
*The Arc, a national organization on
   mental retardation* 534
Attention Deficit Disorder WWW Archive 534
*C.G. Jung, Analytical Psychology,
   and Culture* 534
The C.G. Jung Institute of Los Angeles 534
Canadian Psychological Association 534
Cyber-Psych 534
Depression FAQ 534
DreamLink 534
The ERIC Digests 534
Evolution's Voyage 535
*The Institute of Psychology, Russian
   Academy of Sciences (IP RAS)* 535
*International Association for Cross-Cultural
   Psychology (IACCP)* 535
Internet Mental Health 535
*Institute for the Psychological Study
   of the Arts (IPSA)* 535
The Journal of Mind and Behavior (JMB) 535
The Keirsey Temperament Sorter 535
*KidsPeace®, The National Center
   for Kids in Crisis* 535
The Mental Edge—Sport Psychology 535
Mental Relativity 535
Mind Tools 535

National Institute of Mental Health (NIMH) 536
Online Psychological Services 536
Personality Test 536
PREP—Psychology Preprint Server 536
The Primal Psychotherapy Page 536
Professional Psychology 536
Psychology of Religion Page 536
Psychguide 536
Psychiatry & Psychotherapy 536
Psychiatry On-Line 536
Psychological Type Profiles 536
Psychology of Invention 536
*Psychology Self-Help Resources
   on the Internet* 537
Psychology Software Tools, Inc. 537
Rorschach Inkblot Test 537
School Psychology Resourses Online 537
Sigmund Freud 537
The Society for Computers in Psychology 537
Subintellect's Personality Test 537
Teaching Clinical Psychology 537
Tools for Practical Self Development 537
The Whole Brain Atlas 537

Sociology   537

American Civilization Homepage 537
American Sociological Association (ASA) 538
Association for Humanist Sociology 538
The Canadian Journal of Sociology (CJS) 538
Center for Rural Studies (CRS) 538
Center for the Study of Online Communities 538
Centre for Media Sociology (CeMeSo) 538
*Centre for Social Theory and
   Technology (CSTT)* 538
*Consortium for International Earth Science
   Information Network (CIESIN)* 538
CTHEORY 539
*The Economic and Social Research Council
   Data Archive* 539
Electronic Journal of Sociology© 539
*European Research Centre on Migration and
   Ethnic Relations (ERCOMER)* 539
European Sociological Association (ESA) 539
Filmakers Library 539
The Future of Children 539
*GALLERY OF SOCIAL STRUCTURES:
   Network Visualization* 539
The Human Rights Web Home Page 539
The Institute for Propaganda Analysis 539

International Network for Social
Network Analysis (INSNA) 540

International Sociological Association (ISA) 540

Journal of Criminal Justice and
Popular Culture 540

The Journal of Latin American Perspectives 540

Journal of World-Systems Research 540

National Criminal Justice Reference
Service (NCJRS) 540

Population Index 540

Population Reference Bureau (PRB) 540

Population Studies Center—
University of Michigan 540

Society for Applied Sociology 540

Sociological Research Online 540

Sociology Gopher Resources 541

The SocioWeb 541

SOCNET 541

United Nations Scholars' Workstation at
Yale University 541

United Nations Population Information Network
(POPIN) 541

University of Chicago Press Sociology Catalog 541

U.S. Agency for International Development 541

U.S. Civil Rights Code 541

World Neighbors 541

Worldwide Demography Resources 541

Women's Studies   **542**

American Association of University Women
(AAUW) 542

The Center for the American Woman and
Politics (CAWP) 542

Center for Women's Global Leadership
(CWGL) 542

Centre for Women's Studies
in Education (CWSE) 542

A Celebration of Women Writers 542

Colleen's Feminism Home Page 542

CRLP: Women of the World 542

Cybergrrl Webstation 542

Diotima: Women & Gender in the
Ancient World 542

Encyclopedia of Women's History 542

Electronic Access to Research on Women:
A Short Guide, 2nd Edition 543

Expect the Best from a Girl 543

Feminism and Women's Resources 543

Feminist Bookstores 543

Feminist Majority Online 543

Feminist Science Fiction, Fantasy, & Utopia 543

Feminist Studies in Aotearoa
Electronic Journal (FMST) 543

FEMINIST.COM 543

Gender Equity in Sports 543

Global Fund for Women 543

Guerrilla Girls 543

Her Own Words® 544

InforM Women's Studies Database 544

Internet Resources for Women's Legal and
Public Policy Information 544

Isis 544

Library Resources for Women's Studies 544

Lifetime Online 544

Linkages FOURTH WORLD CONFERENCE
ON WOMEN site 544

The Legal Rights of Women 544

The National Organization for Women (NOW) 544

Resources for Feminist Research/Documentation
sur la recherche féministe (RFR/DRF) 544

Spinsters Ink 545

The United Nations and the Status of Women 545

VOWworld: Voices of Women 545

WIDNET (Women In Development NETwork) 545

The Women & Politics Home Page 545

Women Leaders Online (WLO) 545

Women's Books Online 545

Women's History Month 545

The Women's Studies Reference Roadmap 545

Women's Wire 545

WomensNet@igc 546

WomenSpace 546

The World's Women On-Line! 546

Yale Journal of Law and Feminism 546

Newsgroups   **547**

Listservs   **548**

ABSLST-L—Association of Black
Sociologists 548

AGGRESS—Aggression-Psychology 548

ALT—The Association for Linguistic Typology 548

ANIMUS—Philosophy in the Third Millenium 548

ANTHRO-L—General Anthropology
Bulletin Board 548

APASD-L—APA Research Psychology Network 548

ARCH-L—Archaeology List 548

ARCHCOMP-L—Computational
Archaeology 548

ARCO—Arco/Art & Literature, Psychology
and Communication 548

ASAONET—Oceanic Anthropology
Discussion Group 548

ASASCAN—Computers and Sociology 548

ASPSYCH—Applied Social Psychology
Discussion Group 548

ASSESS-P—Psychological Assessment-
Psychometrics Discussion 549

C-PSYCH—Cross-Cultural Psychology
Discussion List 549

CAPSYCH—CAPsych Child-Psych 549

CLINICAL-PSYCHOLOGISTS—
Clinical Psychologists 549

COMPSYCH—Community Psychology Listserv 549

COUNPSY—Counseling Psychology
Practice and Science 549

E-SAE—Society for Anthropology of Europe
Editorial Board List 549

FORENPSY—Forenpsy Forensic Psychology 549

FUNKNET—Discussion of Issues in
Functional Linguistics 549

GEOGED—Geography Education List 549

H-SAE—An H-Net List for the Society for
Anthropology of Europe 549

IAPSY-L—Interamerican Psychologists List
(SIPNET) 549

IFPE—Psychoanalysis and Education 549

IOOB-L—Industrial Psychology 549

IOPSYCH—Industrial/Organizational Psychology
Discussion Group 550

JWA—The Journal of World Anthropology 550

LEFTGEOG—Socialist/Radical Geography 550

LINGUIST—The LINGUIST Discussion List 550

LITHICS-L—The Archaeological Lithic
Analysis Discussion List 550

MATHSOC—Mathematical Sociology
Discussion Group 550

PAN-L—Physical Anthropology News List 550

PHILOS-L—Paleoanthropological & Biological
Basis of Ethics & Aesthetics 550

PSA-ED—Psychoanalysis and Education
Discussion Network 550

PSI-L—Parapsychology Discussion Forum 550

PSY-LANG—Language and
Psychopathology Discussion 550

PSYART—Institute for Psychological Study
of the Arts 550

PSYADMIN—Psych-Admin Psychiatry
Administration 550

PSYCH-CI—List Name PSYCH-CI -
Current Issues in Psychology and Psychiatry 551

PSYCH-DD—Developmental Disabilities 551

PSYCHL—PSYCHL Psychiatry 551

PSYCHAT—PsyUSA Network -
Collegial Chat 551

PSYCHNEWS—PsychNews International 551

PSYCHOAN—Psychoanalysis 551

PSYCHOLOGICAL-TYPE—Psychological-Type
Discussion List 551

PSYMEA-L—Developmental Psychology 551

PSYSTS-L—Psychology Statistics Discussion 551

RADANTH-L—Radical Anthropologists List 551

RES-GARD—Research & Educational Gardens—
Urban & Socio-Horticulture 551

RURSOC-L—Rural Sociology Discussion List 551

SANALST—Study of North American
Anthropology Discussion 551

SLLING-L—Sign Language Linguistics List 552

SOCTALK—Sociology Discussion List 552

SPIRAMED—Spiramed Spiritual Implications
for Medicine and Psychology 552

SPORTPSY—Exercise and Sports Psychology 552

SPORTSOC—Sociological Aspects of Sports
Discussion 552

SUB-ARCH—Underwater Archaeology
Discussion List 552

SWIP-L—Society for Women in Philosophy
Information and Discussion List 552

TRANSCULTURAL-PSYCHOLOGY 552

WMST-L—Women's Studies List 552

WISE-L—European Women's Studies 552

WSCC-L—Women's Studies Curriculum
Committee 552

WSCD—Women's Studies Collection
Development List 552

URBGEOG—Urban Geography 552

Internet Resources — 553

Access Providers — 553

Charm Net Personal IP Page 553

CyberSight 553

EFF's (Extended) Guide to the Internet 553

Enterprise Internet Services 553

Fountainhead Internet Systems 553

Fusion Advertising and Communications 553

GeoCities 553

GHG Corp 553

GTLug ISP Index 553
How To Select an Internet Service Provider 553
I-2000 553
Icanect 553
ICNet: The Original Internet Provider for the
   Eastern Shore 553
Imagine.com 554
Industrial Peer-to-Peer 554
InReach 554
Inspiration Software 554
InstaNet (Instant Internet Corp.) 554
Infonet 554
Internet Access Phoenix Arizona 554
Internet Application Services, Inc. 554
Internet Channel 554
Internet Delaware 554
Internet Direct 554
Internet Express, Inc. 554
Internet Front 554
Intergate 554
Internet Interface Systems 554
Internet Light and Power 555
Internet MainStreet 555
Internet North 555
Internet On-Ramp, Inc. 555
Internet Services Montana 555
InterServe Communications 555
IntrepidNet 555
ISDN Internet Access 555
LavaNet, Inc. 555
LI.Net 555
Linkage Online 555
Magnetic Page 555
MapleNet Technologies, Inc. 555
Medius Communications, Inc. 555
Michigan Internet Cooperative Association 556
Micron Internet Services 556
MJC Inc. Computer Services 556
Minnesota MicroNet 556
Minnesota Regional Network (MRNet) 556
MonadNet 556
Mojoski Net Tools 556
Moran Communications Group 556
Mountain Internet 556
Nantucket.Net 556
National Knowledge Networks, Inc. 556
NetAccess Worldwide List 556
NetAxis 556

NETCOM Online Communications Services, Inc. 556
NetDepot 557
NETHEAD 557
NetPoint Communications, Inc. 557
NetPress Communications 557
NetReach 557
Netropolis 557
Netside Network 557
NETWave Internet Access Provider 557
Northwest Link 557
Novagate 557
Valiquet Lamothe, Inc. 557

Browsers & Interfaces   557

About Web/Genera 557
Cyberspace Connection 557
Easy Mosaic and Introductory Web Surfing 558
Global Network Navigator Home Page 558
Hill Holliday Advertising 558
Internet Group/Internet Business Center 558

Chats, Messaging, & Conferences   558

Internet Conference Calendar 558
Internet Relay Chat Games 558
IRC Galley 558
IRC Poker Channels Home Page 558
MeGALiTH's Sensational Visual IRC
   Beta Home Page 558
Quarterdeck Global Chat 558
TeamWARE AB 558
World Wide Web Consortium 558
Worlds Chat 558

Cyberspace Issues   559

BBN on the World Wide Web 559
Blacklist of Internet Advertisers 559
c | net: the computer network 559
Censorship and the Internet 559
Cybertown 559
EFFweb—The Electronic Frontier Foundation 559
Executive Guide to Marketing on the New Internet 559
Hermes Project 559
Information Economy 559
Internet Companion 559
Internet Society 559
Mapping the Internet 559
Netscape: J.P. Morgan's Equities Research 560
NetWatchers Legal Cyberzine 560
SurfWatch Home Page 560
What's New in Japan 560

Educational & Tutorial Listings **560**

Beginner's Guide to Effective E-mail 560
Center for the Application of
   Information Technology 560
FutureNet 560
Gestalt Systems, Inc. 560
Global Institute for Interactive Multimedia 560
Glossary of Internet Terms 560
Hideki's Home Page: How To Use
   Japanese on Internet 560
How To Search a WAIS Database 560
ICC Seminar Series 560
INFO Online 560
INFOMINE 561
Information Management Group 561
Information Resources 561
Inter-Links 561
Internet Learning Center 561
Internet Web Text 561
Introduction to the Internet II 561
Kids on Campus (Cornell Theory Center) 561
Learning Edge Corp. 561
Library Solutions Institute and Press 561
Magnett Internet Gateway 561
Management Concepts, Inc. 561
MicroMedium, Inc. 561
Multimedia Help Page 562
Net Guru Technologies, Inc. 562
Net: User Guidelines and Netiquette, by
   Arlene Rinaldi 562
Netscape Tutorial 562
Online World Resources Handbook 562
Patrick Crispen's Internet Roadmap 562
Setting Up Shop on the Internet 562
Surfin' the Net 562
Teach Yourself the Internet Support Page 562
UK Index Beginner's Guide: the Net 562
Web Weavers: Tools for Aspiring Web Authors 562
Winsock Connections 562
Writing the Information Superhighway 563
Youth Quake 563
Zen and the Art of the Internet 563

Guides, Tours, & Cool Site Resources **563**

Best of the Net 563
George Coates Performance Works 563
GO! Online Communications 563
Greene Communications Design, Inc. 563
Hajjar/Kaufman New Media Lab 563

Cool Site of the Day 563
Exploring the Internet 563
Glass Wings 564
GNN Select Top 50 564
GNN Tour 564
Guided Web Tours 564
Handy Guide 564
High-Tech Investor 564
Hit The Beach! 564
Hybrid Communications 564
InfoMedia 564
Internet ProLink SA/AG 564
Internet Resources 564
Internet Tour 564
Meta-list of What's New Pages 564
Mirsky's Worst of the Web 564
Net Trek Cafe 565
nicejob Media 565
NickNet 565
Overall Knowledge Company, Inc. 565
Point Survey and Escort 565
Thousand Points of Sites 565
ThreadTreader's WWW Contests Guide 565
Today Page 565
UnderWorld Links 565
Unusual or Deep Site of the Day 565
Virtual Town City Limits 565
WEBula 565

HTML & Other Languages **565**

Bare Bones Guide to HTML 565
Beginner's Guide to HTML 566
Cerebral Systems Development—
   Home of Webber™ 566
ColorEditor for Windows 566
David B. Martin's VRML Page 566
HTML Info Page 566
Introduction to HTML: Table of Contents 566
Personal Home Page of Bob Hunter 566
Primer for Creating Web Resources 566
tkHTML Editor Information 566
Web Letter, a Guide to HTML/Web Publishing 566
Web Resources 566

Resources **566**

Aether Madness 566
All-Internet Shopping Directory 566
Ansible's Web Page Design Services 567
Argus/Univeristy of Michigan Clearinghouse 567

Aspen Systems Corp. 567
Association of Internet Users 567
Association of University Technology Managers 567
Autopilot 567
Autorama 567
Babbs's Bookmarks 567
Banana Report Easy Visual Basic Tips 567
Canada Net Pages 567
Canadian Internet Handbook/Advantage
  Home Page 567
Categorical Catapult 567
Cnet—Canada 567
Commercial Services on the Net 568
Common Internet File Formats 568
Connect, Inc.—Audio Innovations 568
CRAYON—CReAte Your Own Newspaper 568
CSUSM Windows World 568
E-Minder Free Reminder-By-E-mail Service 568
Economics of Networks Internet Site 568
EINet Galaxy 568
FLFSoft, Inc. Home Page 568
FutureMedia Services 568
FutureTel, Inc. 568
Glistening Trail Records 568
Global Village Stock Footage 569
G.T.A. Business Solutions 569
Harter Image Archives 569
Hippermedia 569
HFSI 569
Hirt & Carter Owlnet 569
Home Run Pictures 569
Information Age, Inc. 569
InfoScan 569
Innovative Computer Associates, Inc. 569
Instruction Set, Inc. 569
InteliSys Technologica, Inc. 569
Interactive Data Systems, Inc. 570
Interactive Voice Applications 570
International Industrial Intelligence 570
Internet Business Solutions 570
Internet Info Store Directory 570
Internet Resources Newsletter 570
Internet Servers for the Mac OS 570
Internet World 570
Internet Systems, Inc. 570
iWORLD 570
INTRANET Technologies, Inc. 570
Island Services Network 570

Knighted Computers 570
Knossopolis 571
Life on the Internet 571
List of WWW Archie Services 571
Logical Operations 571
LookUp! 571
Lopez Communications 571
Marketing Masters 571
MindSphere Design for Communication 571
Miramar Productions 571
Media Connection of New York—Links Page 571
Monster FTP Sites List 571
Network Hardware Suppliers List 571
Newton Online 571
Norcov Research 571
Novia Internetworking 571
Omega West 572
Presence—An Information Design Studio 572
Q-D Software Development 572
RealAudio Home Page 572
Sibylla: The WWW Software Development Kit 572
SpectraFAX Corp. Home Page 572
Strategis 572
SWITCH—Swiss Academic and Research Network 572
Timothy W. Amey Resource Links 572
Virtual Tourist 572
Washington Web 572
Web Week 572
Welcome to Netscape 572
Windows95 InterNetworking Headquarters 573
WorldTel Global Marketing Network 573

Searchers & Databases   **573**

Business Directions International 573
InterNIC Directory of Directories 573
Four11 White Page Directory 573
Business Researcher's Interests 573
College and University Home Pages 573
COMMA Hotlist Database 573
Database Demos 573
Explorer 573
High Performance Cartridges 573
Index 573
Index of Australian Indexes 573
InfoCafé 574
International Business Resources on the WWW 574
Internet Pearls Index 574
Internet Sleuth 574

Joel's Hierarchical Subject Index 574
Lycos Home Page: Hunting WWW Information 574
Media Logic's Index of Economic and Financial
   Resources 574
MediaTel's Newsline 574
Micro Service & Training 574
Montana Communications Network (MCN) 574
Mother-of-all BBS 574
NET Compass 574
New Riders' Official World Wide Web
   Yellow Pages 574
New User's Directory 575
NlightN: Finding What You Want To Know Now 575
Nothin' But Net 575
Planet Earth Home Page 575
Publicize Your Home Page 575
Recondite Reference Desk 575
Search, Find—Internet Resource Locators 575
Searching the Web 575
shareware.com 575
Starting Point 575
Starting Points for Internet 575
URL-Minder: Your Own Personal Web Robot 575
Virtual Libraries 575
VSL Front Desk at the OAK Repository 575
WAIS Access Through the Web 576
WebAnts Home Page 576
Yahoo! 576

Statistics & History   **576**
Economic FAQs about the Internet 576
Internet Business Center 576
Rampages 576
World Wide Web: Origins and Beyond 576

Web Publishing   **576**
5 Top Internet Marketing Successes of 1994 576
Artzilla Surf Constructions 576
Building Web Servers 576
Business of the Internet 576
Carter & Associates WEB Studios 576
Copyright Website 576
Dunn & Edwards Services 577
Dynamic Diagrams Home Page 577
Four Lakes Colorgraphics, Inc. 577
Free Range Media, Inc. 577

FRS Associates Training and Education Division 577
Garry's Web Services 577
Gates, Jeff 577
Headquarters.Com Internet 577
Hijinx 577
Home Space Builder 577
Hourglass Internet Services 577
HudsoNet 577
Hyper Design Technologies 577
Iconomics 578
Image Alchemy Digital Imaging 578
Image Compression for Publishing Online 578
Image House Digital Photography Studio 578
imedia 578
Infowerks Creative Web Services 578
Integra Software Corp. 578
Inter//Web Development 578
INTERCAT 578
Interglobal Mutltimedia 578
International Business Center 578
Internet Advertising Solutions 578
Internet Business Connection 578
Internet Pilots 578
Making Money on Internet 579
Manhattan MultiMedia, Inc. 579
MediaBox Communications 579
Metrotel Multi-Media Ltd 579
MFD Consult 579
MGL Systems 579
Moshofsky/Plant Creative Services 579
MultiMedia Dimensions—New Horizons
   in Sight and Sound 579
NetCasters, Inc. 579
NetWorXs of California 579
new3, Inc. 579
Program One Online Service 579
RAMWORKS 579
Stannet WWW Designing and
   Publishing Company 580
Vannevar New Media 580
Web Developer 580
Web Publishing Australia 580
WebDesigns 580
Winfield Design Group 580
WorldWide Information and Netcasting Services 580
World Wide exPRess 580

Newsgroups 581

Listservs 582
AOL-MONITOR—AOL Internet Systems
Root-Mail List 582
BEYON—User Services Internet in the
Colleges Working List 582
BONSAI—Internet Bonsai Club 582
CLICK4HP—Health Promotion on the Internet
(Discussion) 582
EDRES-DB—Educational Resources on
the Internet - Database 582
GNN-MONITOR—GNN Internet Systems
Root-Mail List 582
IAP—Small Internet Access Providers 583
IBASICS—Internet Basics: An Online Tutorial 583
IDA—Internet Developers Association
Announcement Mailing List 583
IE-HTML—Internet Explorer—HTML 583
IMARCOM—The Internet Marketing
Communications Mailing List 583
INBUSINESS—Internet In Business
Discussion List 583
INET-L—OCC Internet Committee 583
INETUSE—Internet Use Discussion List 583
INTERCAT—OCLC Internet Cataloging project 583
IO-MUG—Internet ONLY Macintosh
User's Group 583
ISP-ADMIN-LIST—Internet Service
Provider Admin Resource Mailing List 583
IUFOG-L—Administrative Discussions of the
Internet UFO Group Project 583
IUS-L—Internet Ultra Society 583
MMATRIX—Internet Medical Resource
Development 583
NANOSNET—Neuro-Ophthalmology
Internet Mail Group 584
NETEX—The Internet Experience 584
NETHELP—TJL Internet User Help 584
PACESIG—Special Internet Group 584
PRIE-L—Packet Radio Internet Extension List 584
SHAMANS—Shamans Impact of the Internet
on Religion 584
STCMD-L—Internet Star Trek Command
Council 584
TOURBUS—The Internet TourBus - A Virtual
Tour of Cyberspace 584
WEB-INT—Internet Integration Team 584

WEBLIST—Internet Workshop Discussion Group 584
WWWIIG-L—UA World Wide Web Internet
Interest Group Discussion 584

Law 585

Criminal Law 585
Cecil Greek's Criminal Justice Page 585
COPNet & Police Resource List 585
Criminal Law Links 585
Guide to Internet Resources in Criminal Law and
Criminal Justice 585
Justice Information Center (NCJRS) 585
Partnerships Against Violence Network (PAVNET) 585
Scott Carpenter's TOP Page 585
U.S. Criminal Law 585

Cyber Law 585
CyberLaw™ World Wide 585
CyberSpace Law Center 585
E-Law 3.0 585
ICLU—Your Rights in Cyberspace 586
Information Highway Advisory Counsel (IHAC)
of Canada 586
The Information Law Web 586
Internet, the Law, and Related Topics 586
OwlLex Law Links—The CyberSpace Law Links 586
Netwatchers Cyberzine 586

Environmental Law 586
CCE - CCA - CEC (Commission for Enviromental
Cooperation) 586
Environmental Law Alliance Worldwide 586
Environmental Law Around the World 587
Environmental Law Resources 587
Environmental Law World Wide Web Site 587
U.S. Environmental Protection Agency 587
United Nations Environment Programme 587
The WWW Virtual Library: Law:
International & Environmental Law 587

Family Law 587
Divorce Helpline Home Page 587
Divorce Law Home Page 587
The Divorce Page 587
Family Law 588
Family Law Advisor Home Page 588
Fathers' Rights and Equality Exchange 588

Legal dot Net—Family Law, and Overview 588
Same-Sex Marriage Home Page 588

International Law 588
American Journal of International Law 588
Foreign and International Law Page 588
The International Law Page 588
International Trade Law—ITL 588
The Internet Immigration Law Center 588
JurWeb 588
*United Nations Crime and Justice Information
    Network* 589

Law Schools 589
FindLaw: Law Schools of Canada 589
FindLaw: US News Top 25 Law Schools 589
ILRG: Brennan's Law School Rankings 589
Law School Admission Council Online 589
Law School and the LSAT 589
Law School Dot Com 589
Law School Quotes 589
The Law Student Web 589
The Princeton Review: Law School and the LSAT 589
Yale Law School Homepage 589

Legal Organizations 590
ACLU Freedom Network 590
American Bar Association 590
American Immigration Lawyers Association 590
The Better Business Bureau 590
International Association of Constitutional Law 590
NYSDA Public Defense Backup Center Home Page 590
The Sovereign Patriot Group 590

Legal Publications 591
The American Indian Law Review 591
American Journal of Criminal Law 591
European Law Journal 591
Federal Communications Law Journal 591
Global Legal Studies Journal 591
Human Rights Brief 591
Journal of Information, Law, and Technology 591
Journal of International Law and Practice 591
The Journal of Online Law 591
Law Journal Extra! 592
Law Library Journal 592
legal.online 592

Legal Resources 592
ALSO! Main Page 592
Counsel Connect Web 592

CourtTV Home Page 592
Hieros Gamos 592
Law.Net 592
LawMall 592
LawMarks...The Legal Resource Database 592
The 'Lectric Law Library 593
Legal Information Institute 593
P-LAW Legal Resources Locator 593
Web Journal of Current Legal Issues 593

Miscellaneous Law Sites 593
The Constitution of the United States of America 593
LAW EMPLOYMENT CENTER 593
LawTalk 593
Lawyer Jokes 593
Legalitees T-Shirts Home Page 593
Murphy's Law 593
*THE SEAMLESS WEBsite...lawyer law
    firm expert* 594

Newsgroups 595

Listservs 595
*ADA-LAW—Americans with Disabilities
    Act Law* 595
*ALSBFEM—Academy of Legal Studies in
    Business (ALSB) Feminist* 596
*ALSBNEWS—Academy of Legal Studies in
    Business (ALSB) News* 596
*ALSBTALK—Academy of Legal Studies in
    Business (ALSB) Talk* 596
BUSLAW-L—Business Law List 596
*CALL-L—Canadian Association of Law
    Libraries List* 596
*CYBERIA-L—Law & Policy of Computer
    Communications* 596
EDLAW—Law and Education 596
*FEMJUR—Discussions and Information
    About Feminist Legal Issues* 596
*INTLAW-L—Internet and Computer Law
    Association* 596
*LAT-LAW—Latin American Legal
    Discussion Group* 596
*LAWCOM-L—Commission on
    Communication and Law Discussion List* 596
LAWSCH-L—Law School Discussion List 596
*LEGALTEN—Topical Evaluation Network
    Legal List* 596
*LGUILD-L—The National Lawyers Guild
    Electronic Mailing List* 597

LRW—Legal Research and Writing
Adjuncts' Discussion Group 597
LSE—Legal Studies Education 597
MAALL—Mid-America Association of
Law Libraries 597
MALSLC—Mid-America Law School Library
Consortium Resource Sharing 597
MINLAW-L—Law School Experiences
of Minorities 597
MPLA—Minority Pre-Law Association 597
NCLSMTG—National Conference of Lawyers
and Scientists 597
PSYCOP—PsyUSA Network - Psychologists
in Law Enforcement 597
PSYLAW-L—Psychology and Law,
International Discussion 597
SPORTLAW 597
TECHLAW—"Journal of Technology
Law & Policy" 597
WRIFELL—Legal Research and Writing
Fellows Discussion Group 598
YLOPEARL—Asian Pacific American Law
Professors Discussion Group 598

Media   599

Magazines   599

Access ET 599
Acoustic Musician Magazine 599
Adventure Online Gaming 599
Adventurous Traveler Bookstore 599
Advertising Age 599
AE Magazine 599
American Country Collectibles 599
American Wine 599
Aquanaut 599
Architronic Home Page 599
Asia, Inc. Online 599
Astronomer Magazine 599
basilisk 599
Boardwatch Magazine 600
Car Collector Home Page 600
Chicago Moving Image Scene 600
Column that Nobody Reads 600
Condé Nast Traveler 600
Cyber Cyclist 600
cyberSPOKESMAN 600
Cyberwest Magazine 600
Dirty Linen 600
Discover Magazine 600
Editor & Publisher 600
Electronic Green Journal 600
Electronic Newsstand 600
Esquireb2b 600
Family World Home Page 600
Felix Culpa Home Page 601
FH: Canada Travel Home Page 601
Fix—Funkier Than Blown Vinyl 601
Folk Roots Home Page 601
Fortran Journal 601
FutureNet:.net—Index 601
Galaxy Entertainment 601
Gigaplex 601
Glass Wings: Sensual Celebrations 601
Good Medicine Magazine 601
Grass Roots Magazine 601
Great Lakes Skier Magazine 601
High Country News Home Page 601
Interactive Age Home Page 601
Internet Writer Resource Guide 602
InterText: The Online Fiction Magazine 602
JEST Home Page 602
KLON'S JazzAvenue Jazz Information Service 602
Knowledge Industry Publications, Inc. 602
LIFE Photo Home Page 602
Living Poets, EJournal Home Page 602
Logical Alternative—Front Door 602
MacNet Journal 602
Macworld Online Web Server 602
Mercury Center Home Page 602
Millennium Whole Earth Catalog 602
MMWIRE WEB 602
Mobilia Magazine 602
MoJo Wire 603
Motorcycle Online 603
Muse Magazine 603
NCS Career Magazine 603
Net Traveler 603
Oceanography—The Magazine 603
Online Access Web Edition 603
Online Educator 603
Outside Online 603
Pan Asian Publications Home Page 603
Penthouse on the Internet 603
Perspective 603

Playboy Home Page 603
PM Zone 603
Popular Science Magazine 603
Positive Planet 604
PowerPC News 604
Redundantly, Online 604
Rippin' Good Yarn 604
Scripps Howard Home Page 604
Sea Frontiers 604
Serif: The Magazine of Type & Typography 604
South Carolina Point 604
Tharunka Home 604
Travel Weekly 604
TravelASSIST Magazine 604
Typofile Magazine—Home 604
Unix News 604
UT Science Bytes 604
Videomaker's Camcorder & Desktop Video Site 605
Virtual Pathways 605
Walls & Ceilings Magazine 605
Wave~Length Paddling Network 605
Web Week Home Page 605
Welcome to Carbon 14 605
Welcome to Computer Shopper 605
Welcome To HotWired! 605
Welcome to Infobahn Magazine 605
Welcome to Pathfinder 605
Welcome to ZD Net 605
Where the Buffalo Roam 605

News 605

American Reporter 605
Associated Press 605
FCC Welcome Page 606
infoMCI 606
International Pages 606
Internet Disaster Information Center 606
libraries.americas 606
NewsLink Menu 606
NJ Online Weather 606
NOS TeleTekst 606
Omnivore 606
RadioSpace Home Page 606
RealAudio: ABC News 606
South African Broadcasting Corporation
   Welcome Page 606
Time Daily News Summary 606
USIA International Broadcasting 606

Newspapers 606

Campus Newspapers on the Internet 606
The Capital 607
City Paper 607
Financial Times Group 607
Gazeta Wyborcza 607
Hastings Tribune Internet Edition 607
Indianapolis Star and News 607
Jerusalem Post 607
Kamloops Daily News—Online 607
Knoxville News Sentinel 607
Maui News 607
Money & Investing Update—Welcome 607
Newspaper / Diario LA NACION—
   San Jose, Costa Rica 607
Newsshare Corporation 607
Personal Technology Home Page 607
Private Eye 607
Providence Business News 608
Southam, Inc. 608
The St. Petersburg Times 608
Stanford Daily Home Page 608
Sydney Morning Herald 608
Tech 608
Telluride Times-Journal 608
Times Higher Education Supplement 608
Vocal Point 608
Wall Street Journal Link 608
Welcome to USA TODAY 608

Publishing 608

Academic Press 608
Addison Wesley Longman 608
Albion Books 608
Alldata 608
Association of American University Presses 609
Astrology et al Bookstore 609
Atomic Books "Literary Finds for Mutated Minds" 609
Audiobook Source 609
Baltzer Science Publishers 609
BDD: Home Page 609
Beach Holme Publishing 609
Bioenergetics Press 609
Blackwell Science 609
Blue Heron Publishing 609
Book Stacks—Home Page 609
Bookish 609
BookWire—The First Place To Look
   for Book Information 609

BookZone 610
Borders Books and Music 610
BradyGAMES Home Page 610
BRP Publications, Inc. 610
Cambridge University Press 610
Carswell Publishing 610
Catalogue Index 610
CatchWord Ltd 610
ChemTech Publishing 610
Christian Warehouse 610
Cocoon 610
Cold Spring Harbor Laboratory Press 610
Colorado Independent Publisher's Association 610
Commercial Publications 611
Conari Press 611
Coteau Books 611
Creative Virtue Press 611
Doody Publishing, Inc. 611
Drama Book Publishers 611
Dream Garden Press 611
East View Publications, Inc. Home Page 611
Editorial Experts, Inc. (EEI) 611
Elsevier Science—Home Page 611
HarperCollins Publishers Home Page 611
Harvard Advocate Home Page 611
Hayden Books 611
HMSO 611
Hodder & Stoughton 612
Houghton Mifflin Company 612
IDG Books 612
index.html 612
Information SuperLibrary 612
INFOSEARCH—PrintNet 612
Internet Book Fair: Publishers Index 612
Internet Road Map to Books 612
IPL Books 612
iWORLD Home Page 612
Jacobs Publishing, Ltd. 612
Karoma Publishers 612
Keski-Uusimaa 612
Kluwer Academic Publishers 612
Koinonia House 613
Kraken Press, Titles 613
Little, Brown & Company 613
Manic D Press 613
McGraw Hill 613
M.E. Sharpe 613
MIT Press 613

Monterey Press 613
Multimedia Newsstand home 613
Natural History Book Service—Home Page 613
New Riders Publishing 613
Nomad Press 613
Norwegian Bookshop Home Page 613
O'Reilly Home Page 613
Online Islamic Bookstore—Home Page 614
Oxford University Press 614
Para Publishing 614
Peachpit Press 614
Penguin USA 614
PennWell Publishing Company 614
pgrmli.txt 614
Prentice Hall Home Page 614
Press Association 614
Publisher's Catalogues Home Page 614
Putnam Berkley Online 614
QUE Publishing Home Page 614
Random House 614
Reed Interactive 615
Resolution Business Press 615
Saint Mary's Press 615
Sams Publishing 615
Sapphire Press UNCAT 615
Shogakukan Home Page 615
Small Media and Large 615
Software Net Product Menu 615
Springer-Verlag 615
Straight Line Medium, Inc. 615
Strangelove Internet Enterprises 615
Thomsom Publishing 615
Time-Life Explorer 615
Times Mirror Higher Education Group 615
TOR SF and Fantasy 616
W. W. Norton & Company, Inc. 616
Warner Aspect 616
Web Art Publishing 616
Wellsweep Press 616
West Publishing 616
Wiley 616
WWW VL Electronic Journals List: Publishers 616

Radio   **616**

Amateur Radio Books and Open
Repeater Database 616
Brent Albert's Radioland 616
Chris Smolinski's Radio Page 616
Deutche Welle Radio & TV—English Home Page 616

Javiation 617
Monitor Radio 617
NPR Online 617
Old Time Radio (OTR) WWW Page 617
Radio Centro 617
Radio HK 617
Radio JAPAN 617
Radio Prague 617
RadioWorld Europe 617
RealTime 617
Rob Mayfield 617
RTHK on the Internet Home Page 617
Thistle and Shamrock Stations List at the
   Ceolas Archive 617
Welcome to BBC Radio 617

Newsgroups   **618**

Listservs   **620**
ADEC-STC—ADEC Satellite
   Telecommunications Coordinators 620
AHECTA-L—Assoc. of Higher Education
   Cable Television Administrators 620
ALAORPC—ALAO Research and Publication
   Committee 620
CAN-MEDIA—Canadian Student Media
   Mailing List 621
CURRENT—Campus Newspaper Discussion List 621
DUBNET—A Forum for Public Radio Folks
   to Swap Dubs 621
FANZINE—Discussion of Fanzines, Small Press
   and Self Publishing 621
IBSRAD-L—College/Community Radio
   Association 621
L-MEDIA—Media Discussion Group 621
MAGAZINE 621
MEDIA-L—Media in Education 621
NETV-L—IBM's NETView Discussion List 621
NV-L—Discussion of IBM NetView and
   POLYCENTER Manager on NetView 621
P-ONS—Traffic Departments of Public
   Television Stations 621
PRFORUM—Public Radio Discussion Group 621
PTV-DCOM—Public Television Station
   Development & Communications Departments 621
PUBRADIO—Public Radio Discussion Group 622
SCREEN-L—Film and TV Studies Discussion List 622
SNPA—Southern Newspaper Publishers
   Association 622
TELECOM—Telecommunications List 622
WISP-L—Women in Scholarly Publishing
   Discussion List 622

Movies   **623**

Action/Adventure   **623**

Alien 623
Apollo 13 623
Braveheart 623
Congo the Movie 623
Crimson Tide: Danger Runs Deep 623
Dr. NO 623
The Hunt for Red October 623
In the Name of the Father 623
The Indiana Jones WWW Page 623
James Bond 007 623
The Killer 623
Killing Zoe 624
Last of the Mohicans 624
Nathan's Apocalypse Now Page 624
The Professional 624
Terminator/Terminator 2: Judgment Day FAQ List 624
Tombstone 624

Actors & Actresses   **624**

Clint Eastwood The World Wide Web Page 625
KeanuNet 625
The Marilyn Pages 625
Welcome to Brandoland 625

Children's   **625**

The Adventures of Pinocchio 625
All Dogs Go To Heaven 2 625
Ariel Forever 625
Babe 625
Beauty and the Beast 626
Casper Audio/Video Library 626
The Dark Crystal 626
The Dove Foundation's Home Page 626
Hunchback of Notre Dame 626
It Takes Two 626
James and the Giant Peach 626
Lion King 626
Mighty Morphin Power Rangers Megadventure 626
Miracle on 34th Street 627
Muppet Movie Links 627
Pocahontas 627

Toy Story 627
Willy Wonka and the Chocolate Factory 627

Classics 627

Casablanca 627
Citizen Kane 627
Gone With the Wind 627
The Jazz Singer (1927) 627
Metropolis 627
The Wizard of Oz 628

Comedies 628

Airplane!—The Movie 628
Brazil 628
Caddyshack Movie Sound Archive 628
Cher Horowitz's Home Page 628
A Christmas Story 628
Clerks 628
Ferris Bueller's Day Off 628
Four Rooms 628
Ghostbusters 628
The Goon Docks 628
Groundhog Day 628
The Jerk 628
Joe Versus the Volcano 628
Kids in the Hall Brain Candy 629
Loser 629
National Lampoon's Animal House 629
October Films Presents, Nadja 629
The Princess Bride 629
Reality Bites 629
Rosencrantz and Guildenstern Are Dead 629
The Saxonian Blues Brothers Page 629
Shaft 629
Shallow Grave 629
Smoke 629
Super Fly 629
Tank Girl 630
Three O'Clock High 630
Too Wong Foo, Thanks for Everything!
    Julie Newmar 630
The Unofficial Addams Family Movie Home Page 630

Companies 630

Buena Vista MoviePlex 630
Elstree—remember me? 630
Fine Line 630
Fox Film 630
The Lion's Den 630

MCA/Universal 630
Media House Films 630
Miramar Productions 630
Miramax Cafe 631
Movies.Com 631
New Line Cinema 631
October Films 631
Paramount Pictures Online Studio 631
Polygram Filmed Entertainment 631
Sony Pictures Entertainment Page 631
Walt Disney 631
Warner Bros. Online 631

Cult 631

Bloodlust 631
The Buckaroo Banzai Jump-Station 631
A Clockwork Orange 632
The Cult Shop 632
Dr. Strangelove Or: How I Learned to Stop
    Worrying and Love the Bomb 632
Heathers 632
Mystery Science Theater 3000: The Movie 632
Ray Wolfe's Online Guide to Eraserhead 632
Rocky Horror Picture Show 632
Spinal Tap 632
The Unofficial Monty Python Home Page 632

Drama 632

Barton Fink 632
Basketball Diaries 632
The Crow 633
Dead Man Walking 633
Forrest Gump 633
The Godfather Trilogy 633
Goodfellas 633
Hackers 633
Heat 633
Il Postino (The Postman) 633
Jane Eyre 633
Leaving Las Vegas 633
Martin Scorsese 634
Mean Streets 634
Othello 634
Photographic Gallery of the Film Trilogy
    of Krzysztof Kieslowski, Three Colors 634
Powder 634
Pulp Fiction Apothecarys Page 634
Quiz Show 634
Reservoir Dogs 634

Scarface 634
Showgirls 634
A Taxi Driver Page 634
True Romance 634
(Unofficial) Hoop Dreams 634

Festivals 635
Cannes Film Festival Official Web Site 635
Chicago Underground Film Festival 635
Cinema Festivals 635
The Film Festivals Server 635
Low Res film and video festival 635
Sundance Film Festival 635

Film & Production Resources 635
The Character Shop 635
CinemaSpace 635
Dolby Laboratories 635
DTS Theatrical 635
Film Resources 636
The Independent Film and Video Makers
   Internet Resource Guide 636
Knight Productions, Inc. 636
LucasArts 636
Makin' Waves Studio 636
Mass F/X 636
New York Film and Animation Co. Ltd. 636
Production Magic 636
Rhythm & Hues Studios 636
Shades of Light Studios 636
THX 636
Virtual Studio Ltd, London 636
WAVE—Wognum Art's Virtual Exchange 636
Welcome to EPSONE.COM 637

Horror 637
The Cabinet of Dr. Casey 637
David Cronenberg Home Page 637
Halloween 637
The Hannibal Lecter Home Page 637
Jaws 637
Lord of Illusions 637
A Nightmare on the Web 637
The Return of the Texas Chainsaw Massacre 637
The Shining 637

Miscellaneous 637
The Academy of Motion Picture Arts and Sciences 638
American Cinema Page 639
Best Video 639

Bright Lights Film Journal 639
Cinema Sites 639
Cinemania Online 639
Critics Roost 639
Early Motion Pictures 1897–1916 639
Films in the Works 639
The Internet Movie Database 639
Movie Reviews.com 639
The Movies Cliché List 639
The Movie Sounds Page 640
Movie Target 640
MovieLink 777-FILM Online 640
Movienet 640
MovieWEB 640
MPEG Movie Archive 640
Mr. Showbiz 640
San Francisco Chronicle Film Review 640
Showtimes Home Page 640
Star Seeker Movie Page 640
United Film Distributors 640
Widescreen Links 640

Mystery 641
Clue 641
Fargo 641
The Hitchcock Page 641
Seven 641
Usual Suspects 641
Vertigo 641

Products 641
CyberCinema 641
The Entertainment Connection 641
HSS Wholesale Home Page 641
Movie Madness Merchandise 641
The Movie Poster Page 641
The Ultimate Resource for Vintage Posters 642

Science Fiction/Fantasy 642
2001: A Space Odyssey 642
2019: Off-World (Blade Runner Page) 642
Back to the Future 642
Bob's Godzilla Shrine 642
Dune 642
Flash Gordon 642
Harp on Batman Forever 642
Mithral Web 642
Nuke Home Page 642
Phantasm 642

Star Trek: WWW 643
The Star Wars Collectors Home Page 643
Star Wars Home Page at UPENN 643
The Tron Home Page 643
Until the End of the World 643
War Games Fan Page 643
Waterworld 643

Newsgroups   **644**

Listservs   **645**
CINEMA-L—Discussions on All Forms
   of Cinema 645
Film Music Discussion List 645
FRAMEWORKS—Experimental Film
   Discussion List 645
H-FILM—H-NET List for Scholarly Studies
   and Uses of Media 645
Movie Poster Discussion 645
SCREEN-L—Film and TV Studies
   Discussion List 646

Music   647

Alternative   **647**
Be Happy or Die! 647
The Cure 647
D'CuCKOO 647
Depeche Mode Home Page 647
Ectophiles' Guide to Good Music 647
fourtuoh 647
The High Lonesome 647
Hyperreal 647
Index 647
Kraftwerk infobahn 647
MEGO 647
Lou Reed's Web Home 647
Pet Shop Boys Virtually 648
R.E.M. Home Page 648
Talking Heads 648
They Might Be Giants: Home-away-from-
   Home Page 648
Tom Waits Digest 648
Turmoil's Seattle Music Web 648
Wood and Wire 648

Awards   **648**
Academy Awards, for Music, 1960s and 1970s 648
Grammy Awards on the Internet 648

Bluegrass   **648**
Bluegrass Unlimited Reviews 648
Central Texas Bluegrass Association 648
Doc Hamilton's Bluegrass Home Page 648
Doc Watson 648
Old Time Music Bulletin Board 648
Welcome to Planet Bluegrass! 649

Charts   **649**
Air Top 20 Chart 649
Alternative World 649
Black Music Department Top R&B Album
   and Singles Chart 649
Casey's Top 40 649
CD Album Top 100 of All Time 649
DJ Dom A's Top Twenty Club Charts 649
DJ Special Blend's Top 10 649
HitsWorld 649
Hype! One Hit Wonder Compilation 649
Rick Dee's Weekly Top 40 649

Christian   **650**
"Almost" Definitive Contemporary Christian
   Music Hot 650
Christian Music Online 650
Michael W. Smith 650
Susan Ashton 650

Classical   **650**
Allegro 650
American Music Center 650
Aspen Music Festival 650
BalletWeb 650
Boston Chamber Ensemble 650
Building a Library: A Collector's Guide 650
Cecilia Bartoli FanWeb (Unofficial) 650
Chamber Music Conferences 651
Chicago Concert Search 651
Classical MIDI Archives 651
Classical Music Home Page 651
Classical Music on the Web 651
Cleveland Concert Search 651
Current Opera Website 651
CyberDance: Ballet on the Web 651
DCI: Drum Corps International 651
Electronic Early Music 651
FAQ: rec.music.classical 651
FutureNet: Classic CD 651

Galliard String Quartet 652
Gilbert and Sullivan Archive 652
Gregorian Chant Home Page 652
Indiana University School of Music 652
Indianapolis Symphony Orchestra 652
Katia and Marielle Labeque Home Page 652
La Ma de Guido 652
Le Nozze di Figaro 652
Maestronet 652
Music Hall 652
Music under Soviet Rule 653
New York Philharmonic 653
Opera Schedule Server 653
opera-l_home_page 653
Opera Stories and Background 653
Performing Arts Sites 653
Renaissance Consort 653
SCA Music and Dance Home Page 653
T. M. McComb: Music Home Page 653
Unknown Composers Page 653
Worldwide Internet Music Resources 653

Commercial Music Resources   **654**
Ace Ticket Service—Concert Tickets 654
Akers Mic 654
Andrak Music 654
HMV Toronto Superstore 654
Hot Platters 654
Jazz Music Stores around the World 654
Rounder Records 654
Transatlantic Management 654
Virtual Radio 654
WholeARTS Directory of Musical Entertainment 654

Country   **654**
Basket Full of Country 654
History of Country Music 654
Obvious Gossip Home Page 654
planet garth 655
Reba McENTIRE 655

Databases   **655**
AMG Online Music 655
Digital Tradition Folk Song Database 655
Discographies (and More) 655
Friedman/Fairfax Publishers 655
GEMM: Global Electronic Music Marketplace 655
Hype! Music 655

Mammoth Music Meta-List @ VIBE 655
Monsterbit Media 655
Random '80s Lyrics 655
Random Band Name 655
Rockmine Archives 655
Similarities Engine 656
Ultimate Band List 656
Worldwide Internet Music Resources 656

Education   **656**
Brent Hugh's Music Instruction
   Software Page 656
MIDI Home Page 656
Neil Hume DJ Page 656

Ethnic Music   **656**
Abayudaya Jews in Uganda: Music 656
Afro-Caribbean Music 656
Afropop Worldwide 656
Ain't Whistlin' Dixie 656
Ari Davidow's Klezmer Page 657
Australian Music World Wide Web Site 657
Bali & Beyond Home Page 657
Batish Institute of Indian Music and Fine Arts 657
Celtic Music Index Page 657
Ceolas Celtic Music Archive 657
Chinese Music Page 657
Clannad WWW Home Page 657
Classical Music Home Page: N.S. Sundar 657
Cuban Music 657
Flamenco Home Page 658
Hindi Movie Songs 658
Home Page of MT&C Music Club 658
Indian Classical Music 658
Indian Music: Recordings and Instruments 658
Indonesian Music 658
Irish Folk Songs 658
Larry Aronson Home Page 658
MIZIK 658
Music from Africa and the African Diaspora 658
Northern Journey: Canadian Folk Music Website 658
Rashid Sales Co. 658
Richard Robinson's Tunebook 659
Roots/World Music FAQ 659
RootsWorld: Music on the Net 659
Russian Music 659
Samba in Sweden 659
Sami's Urdu/Hindi Film Music Page 659

Shona Music 659
Some Peruvian Music 659
Tara: The World of Jewish Music 659
Temple Records 659
TuneWeb 659
Turkish Music Home Page 659
WOMEX '96 659
World Music/Boston 660

Events 660
29th Montreux Jazz Festival Official Site 660
ABSOLUTELY WORTHLESS Calendar
   of New England Folk Concerts 660
Creation 96 660
Lollapalooza Information (Unofficial) 660
MBNA College Quartet Contest 660
Musi-Cal Performer Index 660
National Folk Festival 660
Rob Kenney Presents: Kerrville Folk Festival 660
Ron Smith Oldies Calendar 660
Strawberry Music Festivals 660
UFOJOE Presents: Information
   about Canadian Folk Festivals 660

Folk 660
Fasola Home Page 660
Folk Music Home Page 661
Folk on the Radio 661
Folk Stuff 661
FolkBook 661
Mary Chapin Carpenter 661
Southern Folklife Collection 661
Unofficial John Prine Page 661

Karaoke 661
Karaoke 661
Karaoke Home Page 661

Instruments 661
Accumulated Accordian Annotations 661
Autoharp Page 661
Banjo Tablature Archive 662
Bodhran Page 662
Bottom Line Archive 662
CONCERTINA! 662
Digeridoo Page 662
DREAMTIME, The Didjeridu W3 Server 662
Drums and Percussion Page 662
GUITAR.NET 662

Harmonica World 662
Harp Page 662
Historical Harp Society Page 662
Horn Players' FAQ 662
IDRS WWW 662
Lark in the Morning 663
Mandolin Pages 663
Musicmaker's Kits, Inc. 663
Official Hammered Dulcimer Page 663
Phillip Mann's Banjo Tab Collection and Bluegrass
   Information Site 663
Piano Page 663
Violette Instruments 663
Wayne's Lute Page 663
Will Clifton, Double Basses
   and Some Other Things 663

Jazz 663
Alabama Jazz Hall of Fame 663
Arizona Jazz, Rhythm and Blues Festival 663
Electric Gallery 663
Hard Bop Cafe™ 664
Jazz Central Station 664
Jazz Improvisation 664
Jazz in France 664
Jazz Net 664
Jazz Roots 664
Pacific Blues & Jazz 664
Tom Morgan's Web Site for Jazz and Blues 664
Traditional Jazz (Dixieland) 664
Virtual Jazz Fest! 664
William Ransom Hogan Archive
   of New Orleans Jazz 664
WNUR-FM JazzWeb 664

Lyrics 665
Jessica Ross and Her Amazing Mondegreen Circus 665
Lyrics Page 665
Twisted Tunes 665

Magazines 665
Addicted To Noise 665
Cybergrass—The Internet Bluegrass Magazine 665
Electric Magic—The Led Zeppelin Chronicle 665
ICE On-Line 665
Northern Journey: Canadian Folk Music Website 665
OffBeat Magazine 665
Stirrings Folk Mag 665
Synthesis: Electronic Dance Music Page 666

Musicals 666

Les Miserables Home Page 666

On Broadway WWW Information Page 666

The Really Useful Company Presents
Sir Andrew Lloyd Webber 666

Rec.Arts.Theatre.Musicals 666

New Age 666

Björk's—Web Sense 666

Enya—Unofficial World Wide Web Home Page 666

Malahat Mountain Music 666

Vangelis—The Man and The Music 666

Organizations & Clubs 666

American Music Center 666

BMG 666

Club ZigZag 667

Muscle Music, Inc. 667

National Music Foundation 667

Wolverine Antique Music Society 667

Pop 667

ABBAnatic 667

Amy Grant Site in College Park, MD 667

and through the wire 667

Beastie Boys 667

The Boy George Home Page 668

Bryan Adams Home Page 668

Clash 668

Caribbean Soul: The Jimmy Buffett
Parrot(t)head Page 668

Chicago O(+> Nation 668

Counting Crows 668

Disgraceland 668

ELP—Emerson, Lake & Palmer 668

Elvis Costello Home Page 668

Enigma 668

EXCESS OF INXS, AN 668

Finally Found a Page: A Web Site
Dedicated to Huey Lewis and the News 668

Frankie Goes to Hollywood Fan Pages 668

Future Love Paradise: The Seal WWW Site 668

Gaia: Olivia Newton-John Home Page 668

Gloria Estefan/MSM 669

Lloyd Robbins' Moody Blues Page 669

Madonna Home Page 669

Men Without Hats: The (Unofficial) Home Page 669

Mike Markowski's Beatles Page 669

Nicks Fix 669

Original Mariah Carey Home Page 669

Original Unofficial Elvis Home Page 669

Pete Lambie's Bruce Springsteen Page 669

Planet Janet 669

ROSS 669

Roxette: Home Page 669

Sarah McLachlan Homepage 670

Simon and Garfunkel Home Page 670

Simple Minds—Good News From the Web 670

Sinead O'Connor Home Page 670

Sting—The Soul Pages 670

22nd Row 670

Tori Amos 670

VH1 Music First 670

Welcome to HIStory! 670

Zar's Paula Abdul 670

R&B 670

Biscuit Time on Blues Web 670

Blue Highway 670

Bluenote 671

BluesNet 671

DC Blues Home Page 671

House of Blues 671

Live Blues and Blues Radio, Steamin' Stan Ruffo 671

Record Labels 671

About Time Music Company 671

Acorn Music 671

Alternet Sonic Realities 671

American Gramaphone Records 671

American Recordings Home Page 671

Angel Thorne Music 671

Asphodel Records 672

Atlantic Records Home Page 672

Axiom/Laswell Web Site 672

Badcat Records 672

Bedazzled 672

Black Rock Coalition 672

Bogus Records 672

Boy's Life Records 672

Caroline Records 672

Castle von Buhler Records 672

Catasonic Records 672

Caulfield Records 672

Changing Tones Records 672

China Records 673

Curb Records 673

East Side Digital Records 673
Geffen Records 673
Go Kart Records 673
Grand Royal 673
Hi-Bias Records Inc. 673
ID&T Records 673
Indochina 673
Landphil Records' Online Information Dump 673
Lunch Records 673
Magic Island 674
Manifest Records 674
Marathon Records 674
Metal Blade Records 674
Monkeyland Records 674
Moonshine Music 674
Mute Liberation Technologies 674
Nettwerk 674
Oh Boy Records 674
PolyGram Records, Inc. 674
Pop Gun Records 674
Propulsion Records 674
Rage Records 674
RCA Victor 674
Red Phraug Modern Medium 674
Reservoir Records 675
Restless Records 675
Rhino Records Home Page 675
Rockadillo Records 675
Sesha Press Records 675
Silver Girl Records 675
Sin-Drome Records 675
Slumberland Records 675
Squealer Music 675
Supernova Records 675
Surfdog Records 675
TeenBeat Records 675
Verb Audio 675
Village Pulse 676
Wa Nui Records 676
Warner Bros. Records 676
Windham Hill Records 676

Recording   **676**
Marketing Music on the Web 676
Moneymaking Music Resources 676
Patrick's Musicians' Page 676
Planet StarChild 676

Rock   **676**
Aerosmith 676
The David Bowie File 676
The Death of Rock 'n' Roll 676
The Grateful Dead 676
Green Day 677
Hanspeter Niederstrasser's Def Leppard Page 677
Hyper Idol II 677
Iron Maiden Page 677
Jane's Addiction and Porno for Pyros 677
Jethro Tull Music Archive 677
Kinks Web Sites 677
KISS OTAKU 677
L.A. Rock & Roll Road Map 677
Led Zeppelin Home Page 677
Mazzy Star Home Page 677
Meat Puppets Home Page 677
Merger 677
Metallica 677
MÖTLEY CRÜE 678
nine inch nails: the unofficial home page 678
Phish.Net 678
Pink Floyd Home Page 678
Queen 678
RADISH—Hot Original Rock! 678
Rock and Roll Hall of Shame 678
Rolling Stones Web Site 678
*Room Full of Mirrors: The Official
   Jimi Hendrix Web Site* 678
Stranglehold—The Ted Nugent Page 678
Welcome to the Jungle 678

Newsgroups   **679**

Listservs   **681**
*ACTMUS-L—Asian Contemporary Music
   Discussion Group* 681
ALLMUSIC—Discussions on All Forms of Music 681
BGRASS-L—Bluegrass Music Discussion 681
*BLUE-EYED-POP—Bjork/Sugarcubes/Icelandic
   Music Mailing List* 681
BLUES-L—Blues Music List 682
BOSTON-M—Boston Music Scene 682
*C-OPERA—Contemporary Opera and
   Music Theatre* 682
CLASSICAL—Moderated Classical Music List 682
CLASSM-L—Classical Music List 682
*COLLAB-L—Theatre and Musical Artists,
   Composers, etc.* 682

EMUSIC-L—Electronic Music Discussion List 682
FILMUS-L—Film Music Discussion List 682
FOLKBIZ—Folk Musician Issues 682
IRTRAD-L—Irish Traditional Music List 682
LAMC-L—Academic Discussion of
    Latin American Music 682
ROCKLIST—Academic Discussion of
    Popular Music 682
STABWEST-L—The College Rock Music
    Interest Group 682
SYNTH-L—Electronic Music "Gearhead" List 683
WMUSIC-L—Center for the Study of
    World Musics 683

Paranormal Phenomena 685

Alchemy 685

Alchemy, Taoism, God & all that Stuff 685
The Alchemy Virtual Library 685
Philosophers of Nature 685
Philosopher's Stone/Elixir of Life 685

Astrology 685

Asian Astrology 685
The Astrological Association of Great Britain 685
Astrology Alive! 685
Astrology Online Magazine 685
Astrology: A Theological Science 685
Astrology—The Ultimate Original Science 685
The Cosmic Palette 686
The Harmony of Heaven 686
How and Why Astrology Works 686
Kramer—Fishing guide to the Stars 686
The Metalog Yellow Pages 686
The Nine Planets 686
Oracle's Astrology Chart 686
The Skeptics Dictionary—Astrology 686
The Underground Astrologer 686
Welcome to Daka's Buddhist Astrology 686
Zodiacal Zephyr 687

Ghost Stories 687

Arcadia 687
Are Ghosts For Real? 687
Asylem 687
A Directory of Haunted Dining and
    Lodging in the U.S. 687
The Earthlight Productions Haunted Page 687
Ghost Hunters Gallery 687
Ghost Lore 687
The Ghost Watcher 687
Ghosts 687
Ghosts—The Charles J. Adams Home Page 687
Ghosts of New Mexico 687
Haunted Toys R Us 688
Hauntings Today 688
The Legend of Sleepy Hollow 688
The Ooga Booga Page 688
Paranormal Belief Survey 688
A Philippine Ghost Story 688
Schloss Reichenstein 688
The Virtual Library—Angel Encounters 688
The WWW Virtual Library—Ghost
    Stories and Folklore 688

Numerology 688

Animals and Karma 688
Astro-numerology 688
Entropic Fine Art Inc. 688
How Does the Kalabalarian Philosophy Differ
    from Numerology? 689
Numerology 689
Numerology 689
Numerology by Cheryl Lee Terry 689
Numerology—I've Got Your Number 689
Numerology, The Science of Vibration 689
Numerology—What do the Numbers Mean? 689
Prime—Advanced Numerology Profiler 689
Six Hundred and Sixty Six But not 666 689
The Skeptics Dictionary—Numerology 689
Sun Angel 689
The Wonderful World of Numerology 689

Occult 689

The Alternative Spiritualities Club Home Page 689
Angelnet 690
Aunt Agatha's Occult Emporium 690
The Land of Oz 690
Necronomi.com—The Familiar Spirit BBS 690
The Nine Houses of Gaia 690
Occult Gateway 690
Occult Page 690
Occultism—The Shawn Knight Page 690
Paganlink 690
Pentagram—the Internet's Pagan and
    Occult Superstore 690
Servants of the Light—School of Occult Science 690

The Shroud of Turin 690
Urdco's Mystic Visions 690
You lack Slack, Jack—The Church of the Subgenius 691

Reincarnation 691
22 Topics on Past Lives 691
Electronic Newsletter—Reincarnation 691
Human Understood Reincarnation 691
Joe's Reincarnation Link 691
Karma and Reincarnation—Yoga 691
Past Lives and Reincarnation 691
Reincarnation 691
Reincarnation 101 691
Reincarnation & Karma 691
Reincarnation Case History 691
Reincarnation—Have We Lived Before? 692
Reincarnation—Is Reincarnation a Christian Concept? 692
Reincarnation and the Theory of Tri-chart 692
Synthetic Reincarnation 692
The True Reincarnation of Panchen Rinpoche 692
What is Reincarnation? 692

Tarot 692
Innerspace Station 692
Introduction To Tarot Magic 692
Learning the Tarot—An Online Course 692
Lord of Illusions—Clive Barker's Tarot Cards 692
Michael's Tarot Pages 692
Michele's Tarot Page 692
The Original WWW Tarot Site 693
The Tarot Cards 693
Tarot Cards—Maelstrom 693
Tarot Inspiration 693
Tarot—Tools and Rites of Transformation 693
Tarot Web 693
Tarot Weekly 693
Vibrations—The Layman's Answer to Tarot Cards! 693

UFOs 693
8-Tracks and UFOs 693
Alien Bob's Command Post 693
Alien Information 693
Area 51 694
Aufora—The Alberta UFO Research Association 694
BUFORA—British UFO Research Association 694
The Conspiracy Pages 694
Flying Saucer Review 694

Internet UFO Group—Government 694
Jody's "ET Phone-Home!" Page 694
PBS' Nova Solves UFO and Alien Abduction Phenomena! 694
Roswell UFO Crash Page 694
Smitty's UFO Page 694
Stan Friedman's UFO Page 694
UFO Books—The Serious Literature 694
UFO Sightings by Astronauts 695
Unidentified Flying Objects 695
The X-Files 695

Voodoo 695
African Religion Syncretism 695
The Electric Gallery-Voodoo Flags 695
A New Look at Juju 695
A Primer on Voodoo 695
The Role of the Patient's Religion in Healthcare Setting 695
Voodoo 695
Voodoo-Angelique Kidjo 695
Voodoo and Cemeteries 696
Voodoo Culture in the US Bibliography 696
Voodoo: From Medicine to Zombies 696
Voodoo Information Pages 696
Voodoo Museum 696
Voodoo Products and Information 696
The Voodoo Queen 696
VoodooTour—A Cultural Trip to Benin 696

Witchcraft 696
About Witchcraft 696
Bewitched 696
The Hazelnut 696
The Killing of Witches-A Chronicle of the Burning Times 697
Rosegate—The Council of Elders 697
Satanism and the History of Wicca 697
Strand by Strand 697
What about Witches 697
Witchcraft 697
Witchcraft 697
Witchcraft 697
Witchcraft in Salem 697
Witchcraft: Some Answers for the Curious 697
Witchcraft (Wicca) 697
Witches League for Public Awareness 697
Witch's Brew—For All of Mother's Children 698

Newsgroups   **699**

Listservs   **699**
IUFOG-L—Administrative Discussions of
the Internet UFO Group Project 699
UFO-L—FORUM FOR UFOLOGY 699

Reference   **701**

Calendars   **701**
The Calendar 701
CalendarLand 701
Calendars and Their History 701
Chinese Astrology Calendar 701
Compact Calendar 701
Conversion Between Chinese and
Gregorian Calendar 701
Ecclesiastical Calendar 701
Gregorian-Hijri Dates Converter 701
The Hebrew Date for Today 701
Heichal Shlomo Interactive Calendar 701
Home Page for Calendar Reform 701
J World 701
Leap Years 702
Literary Hyper Calendar 702
Olivian Calendar 702
One-World Global Calendar 702
Ron Smith Oldies Calendar 702
Steffen Thorsen's Calendar Page 702

Census   **702**
1990 U.S. Census Lookup 702
TIGER Mapping Service 702
U.S. Gazetteer 702

Dictionaries & Thesauri   **702**
ARTFL Project: ROGET'S Thesaurus Search Form 702
The Climbing Dictionary 702
Dictionary of Cell Biology 703
The Free On-Line Dictionary of Computing 703
Hacker's Jargon 703
Hypertext Webster Interface 703
LC Thesaurus for Graphic Material: Topical Terms
for Subject Access 703
STING software engineering glossary 703
The WorldWideWeb Acronym
and Abbreviation Server 703

English Language   **703**
The 11 Rules of Grammar 703
The American Dialect Society 704
BritSpeak: English as a Second
Language for Americans 704
The Collective Nouns 704
Cool Word of the Day 704
The Electronic Beowulf 704
The Electronic Text Center
at the University of Virginia 704
ENGL 310: History of the English Language 704
The Etymology of First Names 704
Grammar and Style Notes 704
The Logical World of Etymology 705
Old English Pages 705
The On-line Books Page 705
A.Word.A.Day 705
Word for Word 705
The Word Page 705
WordNet 705
The WWW Anagram Generator 705

Etiquette   **705**
Dance Floor Etiquette 705
Toilet Training: An Online Guide
to Urinal Etiquette 705
USENET Etiquette 705

Flags   **705**
Betsy Ross Homepage 705
The Flag of the United States of America 706
The Flag-Burning Page 706
Flags of the 19th and 20th Century 706
National Flag Foundation 706
Save Old Glory From Flames Home Page 706

Genealogy   **706**
Cool Site of the Month for Genealogists 706
The Genealogy Home Page 706
The Genealogy Page 706
Genealogy Resources on the Internet 706
Genealogy Resources on the Internet 706
Roots Surname List Name Finder 706
Treasure Maps: The "How-To" Genealogy Site 706

Holidays   **707**
Happy Birthday, America! 707
Christmas around the World 707
Chinese New Year 707

Easter in Cyberspace: A Christian Perspective 707
Kwanzaa Information Center 707
Passover on the Net 707
World Wide Holidays and Events 708
The Yom Tov Page 708

Libraries   **708**
AcqWeb 708
American Society of Indexers home page 708
Building Digital Libraries on the Web 708
Celebrate Libraries 708
Christian Classics Ethereal Library 708
Internet Public Library 708
Internet Resources for Cataloging 708
Librarians' professional resources 709
Library Job Hunting 709
The Library of Congress 709
Library Resource List 709
National Archives and Records Administration 709
OCLC Online Computer Library Center, Inc. 709
A Plethora of Web Sites: The Librarian's Meta-List 709
School Libraries on the Web: A Directory 709
Smithsonian Institution Libraries 709
Understanding Call Numbers 710
WWW Library Directory 710

Maps   **710**
Color Landform Atlas of the United States 710
Country Maps from W3 Servers in Europe 710
International Map Trade Association 710
Mapmaker, Mapmaker, Make Me a Map 710
MapQuest 710
National Atlas Information Service (of Canada) 710
The Perry-Castañeda Library Map Collection 710
Rare Map Collection at the Hargrett Library 710
National Atlas of Canada on SchoolNet 710
VIBE's World Map 711

Measurements   **711**
Conversion Factor Table 711
Engineering, Scientific Unit Converter 711
Measurements Converter 711

Miscellaneous Reference   **711**
The Better Business Bureau 711
Bow Brummell: Where Cyberians Learn the
    Manly Art of Tying a Bow Tie 711
Central Notice 711

Clocks and Time 711
The Consumer Information Center 711
The DataStar Information Retrieval Service 711
Disaster Information Network 711
Find-A-Grave 712
Gray Ghost: The Links You Use Everyday 712
Internet Nonprofit Center 712
Jumble & Crossword Solver 712
Morse Code and the Phonetic Alphabets 712
Morse Code Translator 712
MRX - Morse Receive and Transmit Training 712
My Virtual Reference Desk 712
The Nobel Foundation 712
The Nobel Prize Internet Archive 712
The Obituary Page 712
The Official Wicked Hair-Dyeing Page 712
On-Line Reference Works 713
The Reporter's Internet Survival Guide 713
Research-It! 713
The Scout Report 713
Standard Industrial Classifications (SIC) Index 713
"Ten Codes" 713
THOR+: The Virtual Reference Desk 713
Tipping 713
Today's Fun Fact 713
The WWW Virtual Library 713
UTLink: Resources by Subject 714
The World Fact Book 1995 714
World Population 714
World Population Figures 714

Patents   **714**
European Patent Office 714
National Association of Patent Practitioners 714
Source Translation & Optimization (STO)
    Internet Patent Search System 714
U.S. Patent and Trademark Office 714
Wacky Patent of the Month 714

Phone Numbers   **714**
555-1212.com Area Code Look-Up 714
Airline Toll-Free Numbers and Websites 714
American Computer Resources, Inc. 715
The AmeriCom Long Distance AREA DECODER 715
AT&T Internet Toll Free 800 Directory 715
BigBook 715
BigYellow 715

Central Source Yellow Pages 715
The Internet 800 Directory 715
Mutual Fund Company Directory 715
National Telephone & Communications (NTC)
  Tele-Locator 715
PC Phone List 716
Period.Com Airlines! 716
PhoNETic 716
Switchboard 716
Telephone Directories on the Web 716
What does your phone number spell? 716
World Telecom Directories 716
World Yellow Pages Network (wyp.net) 716
Yellow Pages Online, Inc. 716
YellowNet 716

Postal Information   716

Geographic Nameserver 716
National Address and ZIP+4 Browser 716
United States Postal Service 717
The Zipper 717

Quotations   717

Advertising Quotes 717
Ash's Choice Quotations 717
Bartlett's Familiar Quotations 717
The "Best of" Edward Gibbon's Decline and
  Fall of the Roman Empire 717
Bon Mots from the Supermodels 717
Conventional Wisdom: Selected Quotations
  Illustrating the Illusions of Popular History 717
The Curmudgeon Quotelist 717
Dave's Searchable Quote Database 717
Don's Doctor Who Interesting Quote Archive 718
Frank Lloyd Wright Quotes 718
Labor Quotes Page 718
The Official Internet Quayle Quote List 718
Outriders of Reality Reference Manual &
  Travel Guide 718
Quotations 718
Quotations About Libraries and Librarians 718
Quotations of William Blake 718
Quotes, Quotes, and More Quotes 718
Welcome to the Introspect Library 718
Zappa Quote of the Day 718

Newsgroups   719

Listservs   720

3MPLUS-LIST—3 Million Library Volumes 720
GEDCOM-L—Genealogical Data
  Communications Specs 720
GEN-MEDIEVAL—Medieval Genealogy
  Discussion List 720
GENCMP-L—Genealogy Computing
  Discussion List 720
GENMSC-L—General Genealogical Discussions 720
GO4LIB-L—Library Gopher List 720
IACRL—Illinois Association of College & Research
  Libraries 720
JEWGEN—Jewish Genealogy Discussion Group 720
LIBFAP—Purdue Libraries 720
LIBREF-L—Discussion of Library
  Reference Issues 721
LINES-L—LifeLines Genealogical System 721
ROOTS-L—ROOTS-L Genealogy List 721
TFTD-L—Thought for the Day 721
TJLDESK—TJL Reference Desk 721
TJLREF-L—Thomas Jefferson Library
  Reference List 721

Religion & Philosophy   723

Atheism   723

Atheist Manifesto 723
International Atheistic Secular
  Humanist Conspiracy [Canada Division] 723
The Secular Web 723

Bible Study & Christian Research   723

Bible Gateway 723
ECOLE Institute 723
Holy Bible—King James Version 723
Logos Research Systems 723
New Media Communications 723
Our Daily Bread 723
RTS's Totally Righteous Home Page for
  Paul the Apostle 723
Scrolls from the Dead Sea 723
University of St. Michael's College,
  Faculty of Theology 724

Buddhism   **724**

Access to Insight 724
Buddhist Scripture Information Retrieval 724
DEFA Home Page 724
International Meditation Centres
  (in the Tradition of Sayagyi U Ba Khin) 724
International Research Institute
  for Zen Buddhism 724
Journal of Buddhist Ethics 724
New Kadampa Tradition 724
Nichiren Shoshu Buddhism 724
Shin Buddhism Network 725
Shin Buddhist Resource Center 725
Tiger Team Buddhist Information
  Network 725
Zen Garden 725
Zen Mountain Monastery 725
Zen@SunSITE 725

Christian Denominations   **725**

American Baptist Churches Mission Center Online 725
Anglicans Online 725
Association of Vineyard Churches 725
Baptist Faith and Message 725
Canada Toronto East Mission 725
Catholic Online 726
East 7th Street Baptist Ministry—Graffiti 726
Evangelical Lutheran Church
  in America Home Page 726
Famous Unitarian Universalists 726
Harvest Online 726
Lutheran Church-Missouri Synod Home Page 726
Orthodox Christian Page 726
Orthodox Ministry ACCESS 726
Presbyterian Church USA 726
Religious Society of Friends WWW site 726
SBC "Maverick" Home Page 726
SDANet 727
United Church of Christ 727
United Pentecostal Church International 727

Christian Media   **727**

Baker Book House 727
Christian Articles Archive 727
Christian Book Connection 727
Christian Classics Ethereal Library 727

Christian Computing Magazine 727
Christian Cyberspace Companion 727
Christian Poetry 727
Electronic Book of Common Prayer 727
Gospel Films, Inc. 727
GROKNet—Comedyatre and Resources 727
ICMC Home Page 728
Jesus Film Project 728
Minister's Reference Center 728
National Religious Broadcasters 728
Saint Mary's Press 728
Serious Developments—Christian
  Software Catalog 728
This Week in Bible Prophecy 728
Tien Dao Christian Media 728
Wire 728

Christian Ministries & Organizations   **728**

Christian Recovery Connection 728
Computerized AIDS Ministries 728
Family Research Council 729
Greater Grace World Outreach 729
InterVarsity Christian Fellowship 729
Jesus Army 729
Jesus Fellowship Home Page 729
Life and Faith Network 729
Lutheran Marriage Encounter 729
Monastery of Christ in the Desert 729
National Association of Evangelicals 729
Promise Keepers Unofficial Home Page 729
Renewal Ministries: De Colores and Ultreya 729
St. Louis Life News 730
Tough Guys 730
Web Chapel—Prayer Request 730

Christian Philosophy   **730**

Answers in Action Home Page 730
APOLOGIA—To Offer a Reason 730
In the Footsteps of the Lord 730
Project Wittenberg 730

Christian Resources   **730**

Brother Mark's Christian Material 730
Christian Connections 730
Christian Resource Network 730
GOSHEN Internet Christian Resource Directory 730
Not Just Bibles 730

Creation/Evolution   731

Answers About Evolution 731
Center for Scientific Creation 731
Creation Science Home Page 731
Creationism Connection 731
Evolution vs. Creation Science 731
Talk.Origins Archive 731

Cults   731

A-Z of Cults 731
AFF Cultic Studies 731
Cults 731
Cults 'R Us 731
Destructive Cults 731
.ex-cult Archive 731
Jehovah's Christian Witnesses 732
Jehovah's Witnesses 732
Loki Cult Web Page 732
Ms. Guidance on Strange Cults 732
Sacrespace 732
Waco Never Again 732

Hinduism   732

Bhagavad Gita 732
Global Hindu Electronic Network 732
Hinduism 732
Hinduism Today Home Page 732
Kundalini Research Foundation, Ltd. 732
Spirituality, Yoga, and Hinduism 732

Islam   733

CyberMuslim Information Collective 733
Ibrahim Shafi's Page in Islam 733
Islam 733
Islam's Home Page 733
Islamic Society of Wichita 733
Online Islamic Bookstore 733
Salaam Ailaikum 733
WAMY IslamNet (World Assembly
   of Muslim Youth) 733

Jainism   733

Jain Studies 733
Jain World Wide Web Page 733

Judaism & Messianic Judaism   734

A–Z of Jewish & Israel-Related Resources 734
Aish Ha Torah Discovery 734
Chabad Lubavitch in Cyberspace 734
Jerusalem One WWW Network 734

Jewish Federation/Jewish Exponent 734
Jewish on the WELL 734
Jewish Theological Seminary 734
Jewishnet 734
Jews for Jesus Home Page 734
Judaism and Jewish Resources 734
Menorah Ministries 734
Messianic Jewish Alliance of America 734
National Jewish Committee on Scouting 735
Shamash 735
Shtetl, Yiddish Language and Culture Home Page 735
Society Hill Synagogue of Philadelphia 735
World ORT Union 735
Yaohushua, the Genuine Messiah 735

Miscellaneous Religion   735

Baha'i Resources on the Internet 735
The Bastard Son of the Lord 735
The Church of the SubGenius BRAIN TOOLKIT
   AND SURREALITY REBOOT 735
CyberINDIA: India at your Fingertips 735
Free Daism 735
Friends of Osho 736
Haqqani Foundation Home Page 736
Hare Krishna Home Page 736
Israelite Handbook 736
Logictarian Christian Home Page 736
McChurch 736
Pagan Pages 736
Pathways to Metaphysics 736
Stanford University Zoroastrian Group 736
Taoism Information Page 736
Taoist Resource Center 737
Theosophical Society 737
Universal Life Church 737
Urantia Book 737
Yoga Paths, An Overview Of Different
   Schools and Traditions 737

Mysticism   737

Al Azif: The Manuscript Liber Logaeth 737
Aleister Crowley 737
The Egyptian Book of the Dead 737
The Golden Dawn FAQ 737
The Kabballah Connection 737
Mysticism in World Religions 737
Shawn's Rituals Collection 737
Tarot Reading 737
Wayfarer's Rest 738

Philosophy													738
    American Philosophical Association 738
    ANALYSIS Home Page 738
    Arisbe: A Home for Charles S. Peirce Studies 738
    Augustine 738
    Australasian Philosophy Network: Home Page 738
    BEARS in Moral and Political Philosophy 738
    Cybernetics and Systems Theory 738
    Electronic Journal of Analytic Philosophy 738
    Environmental Ethics 738
    International Philosophical Preprint Exchange 738
    Mechanosphere 738
    Nietzsche Page at USC 738
    Philosophy and Religion 739
    Philosophy in Cyberspace—Home Page 739
    Philosophy Resources 739
    PSYCHE: an interdisciplinary journal
      of research and consciousness 739
    Tech Classics Archive 739
    University of Chicago Philosophy Project 739
    White Mountain Education—A Source
      for the Ageless Wisdom 739

Sikhism													739
    Fort: Panth Khalsa 739
    Sikhism: Religion of the Sikh People 739

Scientology													739
    Alt.religion.scientology 739
    The Church of Scientology vs. The Net 739
    Dianetics Home Page 739
    Johnny Get Your Modem—Scientology's
      War with the Internet 740
    L. Ron Hubbard Home Page 740
    Scientology Home Page 740

Newsgroups													741

Listservs													743
    ACE-NET-L—Association of Christian Economists 743
    ALPHA-CHURCH—A Place for Christians
      Who Share 1st Century Church Beliefs 743
    AMERCATH—AMERCATH - A Discussion
      List on the History of American Catholicism 743
    ANIMUS—Philosophy in the Third Millenium 743
    APACIC-L—American Philosophical Association 744
    ARCANA—ARCANA Discussion List for
      the Study of the Occult 744
    ARIL-L—"Association for Religion and
      Intellectual Life" 744

    AYN-RAND—Moderated Discussion
      of Objectivist Philosophy 744
    AYN-REVU—Moderated Discussion
      of Objectivist Philosophy 744
    AYN-TECH—Moderated Discussion
      of Objectivist Philosophy — Technical 744
    BETMIDRASH—Information from the Seminary
      of Judaic Studies, Jerusalem 744
    BUDDHA-L—Buddhist Academic
      Discussion Forum 744
    BUSSOC—Business and Society Course,
      Philosophy Dept. 744
    CAGS-L—Christian Anthropology Grad Students 744
    CCC_VT—Campus Crusade for Christ
      Mailing List 744
    CHPSSTU—Committee On The History
      And Philosophy Of Science At UMCP 744
    CHRISTIANITY-ONLINE—Christianity Online
      Connection Newsletter 744
    CJ-L—Discussion of Beliefs and Practices
      of Conservative Judaism 745
    COMETHIC—Ethical Issues and Computer
      Science Course Philosophy Dept. 745
    CONCHR-L—Conservative Christian
      Discussion List 745
    COVR—Colloquium on Violence and Religion 745
    CYBERMIND—Philosophy and Psychology
      of Cyberspace 745
    DIG-NEWS—LesBiGay Catholic News 745
    DIGNITY—LesBiGay Catholic List 745
    EDPHIL2-L—Philosophy of Education,
      Open Access 745
    EJAP—The Electronic Journal
      of Analytic Philosophy 745
    FEMREL-L—Open Discussion of Women,
      Religion, and Feminist Theology 745
    HINDU-D—Hindu Digest 745
    HOPOS-L—A Forum for Discussion of
      the History of the Philosophy of Science 745
    IMBAS—The IMBAS List for Celtic Pagans 746
    ISL-SCI—Issues on Islam and Science 746
    ISLAM—Islam Discussion List 746
    ISLAM-L—History of Islam 746
    IVCF-L—InterVarsity Christian Fellowship List 746
    JEWGEN—Jewish Genealogy Discussion Group 746
    LDS-PHIL—LDS Philosophy List 746
    MSA-L—Muslim Student Association List 746
    MUSLIMS—The Islamic Information &
      News Network 746

NEWLIFE—Helping the New Christian
  on Their Walk with God 746
PHILCOMM—Philosophy of Communication 746
PHILOS-L—Paleoanthropological & Biological
  Basis of Ethics & Aesthetics 746
PHTECH-L—Philosophy and Technology 746
POMO—Discussions in Post-Modern Jewish
  Philosophy and Theology 747
RELNET—Religious Internet 747
RENEW-L—Catholic Reform and Renewal 747
SHAMANS—Shamans Impact of the Internet
  on Religion 747
SSREL-L—Scientific Study of Religion 747
SWIP-L—Society for Women in Philosophy
  Information and Discussion List 747
VINCENT—Vincent Vincentian Philosophy
  and Practice 747
VISIONS—Christian Visions Discussion List 747
WMSPRT-L—Women's Spirituality and
  Feminist-Oriented Religions 747

Science & Engineering — 749

Agriculture — 749

Ag-Links 749
Agriculture Online 749
AgriGator Commercial Agriculture Sites 749
Agrinet 749
Center for Soybean Tissue and Genetic Engineering ... 749
Economic Research Service 749
Farmland Information Library 749
GrainsGenes 749
High Plains Journal—The Farmer-Rancher Paper 749
John Deere—Agricultural Equipment 749
NewCrop 749
Pest & Crop Management Production Newsletter 749
Rationale 749
USDA 749
The Voice of Agriculture 750

Astronomy — 750

Air Force Maui Optical Station (AMOS) 750
American Astronomical Society 750
Art of Renaissance Science: Galileo and Perspective 750
Astro!Info 750
Astronomical Data Center 750
Astronomical Museum in Bologna 750
Astronomical Resources on the Internet 751
Astronomy HyperText Book 751
Astronomy-Related Web Sites 751
AstroWeb Astronomy/Astrophysics on the Internet 751
Aztec Books 751
Brief Tour of Our Universe! 751
Caltech Space Society 751
CCD Images of Galaxies 751
Center for Advanced Space Studies (CASS)
  Home Page 751
Compton Observatory Science Support Center 751
CyberSky 751
Discovery Program Home Page 751
HEASARC Video Archive 751
Henrietta Leavitt Flat Screen Space Theater 751
High Energy Astrophysics Science Archive
  Research Center 752
Humans in Space 752
Information Leaflets 752
Institute for Space Astrophysics C.N.R. 752
International Astronomical Union 752
International Occultation Timing
  Association (I.O.T.A.) Home Page 752
The Long Duration Exposure Facility 752
Mount Wilson Observatory 752
NASA Astrophysics Data System Home
  Page—Classic System 752
NASA-JSC Digital Image Collection 752
NASA World Wide Web Information Services 752
NCSA Relativity Group 752
Planetary Society Home Page 752
Purdue SEDS (Students for the Exploration
  and Development of Space) 752
SEDS Internet Space Warehouse 753
Sensors and Instrument Technology Planetary
  Tour Guide 753
Sky Online Home Page 753
Solar System Live 753
Southern Cross Astronomical Society 753
Space Explorer's Guide 753
Space Settlement 753
StarBits—Acronyms, Abbreviations, and More 753
StarWorlds—Astronomy
  and Related Organizations 753
STELAR Project Demos 753
Usenet FAQs Space 753
Views of the Solar System 753
Web Nebulae 753

WebStars Astrophysics in Cyberspace 753
Welcome to Loch Ness Productions 754
Welcome to Project CLEA 754
Welcome to SkyView 754
Welcome to the Planets 754
World Wide Web Home Page of the
    Canadian Astronomy Data Centre (CADC) 754
Wormhole Interactive 754

Aviation   **754**
Air Affair 754
Airship: The Home Page
    for Lighter-Than-Air Craft 754
Aviation Enthusiast Corner 754
Aviation Image Archives 754
Basics of Space Flight Learners' Workbook 754
Canard's Aviator's Page 754
Federal Aviation Regulations 754
First General Aviation WWW Server 754
NASA Dryden Flight Research Center 755
NASA Information Services via World Wide Web 755
NASA Television on CU-SeeMe 755
On Board STS-70 755

Biology   **755**
Anatomy Images 755
Anderson's Timesaving Comparative Guide 755
Auditory Perception 755
BiochemWeb 755
Biodiversity and Biological Collections Web Server 755
BioForce Labs 755
BIOS Scientific Publishers 755
BioSupplyNet 755
CSU BIOWEB 756
The Gene Expression Information Resource Project 756
The Genome Database 756
Horizon Scientific Press: Molecular Biology Books 756
Journals, Conferences, and Current
    Awareness Services (Biosciences) 756
LLNL Biology and Biotechnology
    Research Program 756
Mendelweb 756
Microworlds Exploring the Structure
    of Materials 756
National Center for Biotechnology Information 756
NRC Biotechnology Research Institute 756
Tools for Molecular Biology, Genetics,
    and Microbiology 756

Tree of Life 757
Virus Databases Online 757
Welcome to Virtual FlyLab 757
The World Wide Web Virtual Library,
    Evolution (Biosciences) 757

Botany   **757**
Balogh Scientific Books 757
Botanical Gardens 757
Botany 757
Brief Overview of the National Herbarium 757
Connecticut Botanical Society 757
Geobotanical Institue 757
Internet Directory for Botany 757
National Institute of Agricultural Botany 757
Nature Described: Learning to Look at the World 757
University of Wisconsin-Madison
    Botanical Garden 758

Chemistry   **758**
The American Chemical Society 758
The Armchair Scientist 758
Atmospheric Chemistry 758
Brain Page 758
ChemCAI: Instructional Software for Chemistry 758
Chemical Demonstrations—Table of Contents 758
Chemistry Hypermedia Project 758
Chemistry Teacher Resources 758
Composite Materials Research
    Group—University of Mississippi 758
CTI Centre for Chemistry Software Catalogue 758
Dalton Chemical Laboratories, Inc. 758
George Goble (GHG) Extended Home Page 759
Introduction to Alchemy 759
Los Alamos National Laboratory of
    Energetic Materials 759
Mendeleev Communications 759
Periodic Table of the Elements 759
SoftShell Online 759
Software Reviews from the CTI Centre
    for Chemistry 759
STM Image Gallery 759
Understanding Our Planet Through Chemistry 759
WWW Chemistry Sites at Academic Institutions 759

Cognitive Science   **760**
Esoteric Psychology 760
Frequently Asked Questions about Parapsychology 760
Internet Resources for Cognitive Science 760

Interpsych 760
MIT Artificial Intelligence Laboratory 760
Neurosciences on the Internet 760
North West Artificial Intelligence
   Applications Group 760
Psych Central—Dr. John Grohol's
   Mental Health Page 760
Scholarly Psychology Resources on the Web 760
The Social Worker Networker 760

Computer Science   760

Brussels Free University (ULB)
   Computer Science Department: Bookmarks 760
Computer Vision and Image Processing Group 760
Computing Center, Academy of Sciences, Russia 761
Cornell Theory Center 761
Electronic Desktop Project Home Page 761
Electronic Visualization Lab 761
European Software Institute (ESI) 761
Los Alamos Group XTM Home Page 761
Projects in Scientific Computing 761
San Diego Supercomputer Center 761
UCSD Optoelectronic Computing Group 761

Earth Science   761

Earth Sciences and Resources Institute 761
EOS Buchantiquariat Benz 761
Hanford Site 762
Idaho National Engineering Laboratory 762
National Center for Atmospheric Research 762
Online Earth Science Journals 762
Rain Forest Action Network Home Page 762
Science and Public Policy Program 762
Science and Technology Corporation (STC) 762
Science Applications International Corp. (SAIC) 762
Supplements to Atmospheric &
   Oceanic Publications 762
Technadyne Engineering Consultants 762
VolcanoWorld 762

Ecology   762

Abbey's Web 762
The Access Fund 763
Earth Viewer 763
EcoLink 763
Ecology and Human Rights Information 763
The Ecology Channel 763
Ecovote Online 763

Greenpeace 763
Natural Resources Conservation
   Service—U.S. Dept. of Agriculture 763
Rainforest Workshop Home Page 763
Ralph Maughan's Wolf Report 763
Sierra Club 763
U.I.A. Freshwater Ecology
   (The Chironomid Home Page) 764
U.S. Fish and Wildlife Service 764
Welcome to Coastal America's Home Page 764
World Forum for Acoustic Ecology 764

Energy   764

Alternative Energy Engineering 764
The American Nuclear Society 764
Bioenergy 764
Brookhaven National Laboratory 764
Clustron Science Corporation 764
CREST'S Guide to Alternative Energy 764
Ed's News Page 764
Energy Science and Technology Software Center 764
Home Power Magazine 764
Investigating Wind Energy 765
Nova Structure 765

Engineering   765

All Electrical Engineering Academic
   Programs (Almost) 765
American Institute of Chemical Engineers 765
Chemical Engineering URLs Directory 765
Crazy about Constraints! 765
D Banks—Microengineering/MEMS 765
Fraunhofer Institute for Materials
   Physics and Surface Engineering 765
Institution of Electrical Engineers Home Page 765
Meetings Information 765
Micromath's Home Page 765
National Society Of Black Engineers at SDSU 766
NU Student Chapter ASCE 766
Reliability Analysis Center (RAC) Home Page 766
Software Engineering Archives 766
Statistical Reports on United States Science
   and Engineering 766
UAB Thermal and Fluids Engineering Group 766
UCF ASET 766
Unofficial Chemical Engineering Home Page 766
Virginia Geotechnical Services 766

Welcome to Internet Directory
of Biotechnology Resources 766
World Wide Web Virtual Library: Aerospace 766
WWW Archive for Electric Power
Engineering Education 766

Environmental Science   766

BCRI On-Line 766
Earth and Environmental Science 767
EMF-Link 767
Environmental Chemical Corporation 767
Florida Center for Environmental
Studies' Home Page 767
Giovanni Guglielmo's Research Page
on Salt Tectonics 767
Greenspan Technology 767
IFIAS 767
Infrastructure Technology Institute (ITI) 767
National Soil Erosion Research Laboratory 767
United Nations Environment
Programme (UNEP), Geneva 767
WWW Virtual Library—Environment 768

Geography   768

Althausen's WWW Wonderland 768
Chesapeake Bay Program 768
Clinch River Restoration Program 768
Color Landform Atlas of the United States 768
Geographic Nameserver 768
Geography—A Diverse Discipline 768
Internet Resources for Geographers 769
Michael Braun's Home Page 769
TIGER Mapping Service 769
United States Gazetteer 769
Xerox PARC Map Viewer 769

Geology   769

Centre for Earth and Ocean
Research—University of Victoria 769
Civil Engineer's Calendar 769
CNC Relief Maps 769
Data Catalog 769
Data Zoo 769
Earthquake Info from the U.S.G.S. 769
Nevada Bureau of Mines and Geology 769
New Mexico Bureau of Mines and
Mineral Resources 769

Niel's Timelines and Scales of Measurement List 770
Smithsonian Gem and Mineral Collection 770
United States Department of the Interior/Geological
Survey/Pacific Marine Geology 770
United States Geological Survey:
Earth and Environmental Science 770

Mathematics   770

AMATH, Inc. 770
Beauty of Chaos 770
Ben Cheng's Home Page 770
Calculus & Mathematica Home Page 770
Chaos at Maryland 770
Chaos Network Sign-In 770
Chartwell-Bratt 770
Common Weights and Measures 770
Computational Logic, Inc. 770
CPLEX Optimization, Inc. Home Page 771
CSC Mathematical Topics 771
CSC Mathematical Topics: Visualizations 771
Data Modeling Web Site 771
Dave's Math Links 771
Design-By-Example 771
Dynamical Systems and Technology Project 771
e-Math Home Page 771
Eisenhower National Clearinghouse DCL 771
Electronic Textbook: Integrated Course in
Chemistry, Mathematics, and Physics 771
Fractal Gallery 771
Fractal Image Compression 772
Fractal Microscope 772
Fractals Calendar Home Page 772
Fractals Frequently Asked Questions and Answers 772
Future Graph, Inc. Home Page 772
GAMS: Guide to Available Mathematical Software 772
Guide to Math Resources 772
History of Mathematics 772
IMA WWW Server 772
IMSA Home Page 772
Intercall 772
Internet Center for Mathematics Problems 772
Logal Software Home Page 772
Math Teaching Assistant 772
Mathematica World 773
Mathematics Archives WWW Server 773
Mathlab 773

MathSearch—Search a Collection
of Mathematical Web Material 773
MathSoft Home Page 773
MathSolutions, Inc. Home Page 773
MathSource Home Page 773
MathType Home Page 773
MathWorks Home Page 773
More Fractal Pictures 773
Netlib Repository at UTK/ORNL 773
Numerical Algorithms Group Ltd. 773
Online Image Archiver 773
Precision Large-Scale Dimensional
Metrology/Measurement 773
Principia Consulting Home Page 774
Quantum Books Home Page 774
Steven M. Christensen and Associates, Inc. 774
TMP at Imperial College London 774
Transmath—A CBL Mathematics Tutor 774
Union Mathematica Argentina 774
Video Vita 774
Waterloo Fractal Compression Page 774
World-Wide Web Virtual Library: Mathematics 774

Meteorology 774

AgriWeather 774
Alden Electronics 774
Atlantic Tropical Weather Center 775
Automated Weather Source—Nationwide
School Weather Network 775
Current Weather Maps/Movies 775
Defense Meteorological Satellite Program 775
Earth Watch Communications, Inc. 775
Intellicast 775
Interactive Marine Observations 775
Interactive Weather Browser 775
International Weather Watchers
Official Home Page 775
NASA Weather Archive 775
National Center for Atmospheric Research 775
National Hurricane Center
Tropical Prediction Center 775
National Severe Storms Laboratory 775
National Weather Service 776
Seismological Laboratory 776
Space Science and Engineering Center (SSEC)
Real-Time Data 776
Storm Chaser Home Page 776
Warren Faidley's Storm Chasing Home Page 776
Weather and Climate Images 776

Weather and Global Monitoring 776
Weather Channel 776
Weather Net 776
Weather Page 776

Miscellaneous Science Sites 776

American Electronics Association 776
The Aphrodisiac Home Page 776
California Academy of Sciences 776
CMU Artificial Intelligence Repository 777
Consciousness Research Laboratory 777
Exploratorium 777
Explorer Home Page 777
Fun with Grapes—A Case Study 777
Great Canadian Scientists 777
ISB Working Group on Footwear Biomechanics 777
National Chipcard Forum 777
National Museum of Natural History 777
National Science Foundation 777
Nondestructive Testing Information Analysis
Center Home Page 777
Nye Labs 777
Olivetti Research Laboratory 777
On Being a Scientist: Responsible
Conduct in Research 778
Point Source Ltd. 778
Sargent Welch Scientific Company 778
Science Television 778
Society for Scientific Exploration 778
SRI's Optical Technology Group 778
Superplasticity 778
Systems Realization Laboratory 778
Technology Review Magazine 778
Vibrant Technology, Inc. 778
Virtually Hawaii 778
Web Station—New Media Science 778
Westinghouse Science and Technology Center 778
X-Ray and Gamma-Ray Coefficients 778
Yale NMR Research Group 779

Oceanography 779

ASLO Home Page 779
Coral Health and Monitoring Home Page 779
CSIRO Division of Oceanography 779
El Nino Theme Page 779
GLOBEC Information 779
List of Oceanography Resources 779
National Marine Fisheries Service 779
NEMO—Oceanographic Data Server 779

NOAA Coastal & Estuarine
  Oceanography Branch 779
NOAA Home Page 780
NOAA Paleoclimatology Program 780
Ocean Planet Home Page 780
Oceanography Links: Oceanography
  on the World Wide Web 780
Oceanography Society 780
Parallel Ocean Program (POP) Simulation ... 780
Pathfinder Cafe 780
Safari Splash 780
Satellite Oceanography Laboratory 780
Scripps Institution of Oceanography Library ... 780
Sea Surface Temperature Satellite Images ... 780
SeaWiFS Project Home Page 781
SelectSite Ocean Technology 781
TAMU Oceanography Welcome Page 781
Topex/Poseidon—The Ocean
  Topography Experiment 781
United States JGOFS Home Page 781
United States WOCE Home Page 781
Welcome to OCEANIC 781
Woods Hole Oceanographic Institution (WHOI) ... 781
Word about the International
  Oceanographic Foundation 781
World Wide Web Virtual Library: Oceanography ... 781

Paleontology　　781
Columbus Rock and Mineral Society 781
Dino Russ's Laur 781
Dinosauria On-Line 781
Palaeolithic Painted Cave at Vallon-Pont-d'Arc ... 782
Exposure Excursions 782
Gulf Of St. Lawrence Microfossil Catalogue ... 782
Museum of Paleontology 782
Raymond M. Alf Museum 782
UC Berkeley's Museum of Paleontology 782
University of California Museum of Paleontology:
  Bringing Life's Past and People Together ... 782

Physics　　782
Accelerator Physics at SLAC 782
American Institute of Physics 782
American Physical Society 782
ASM International Home Page 783
CERN European Laboratory for Particle Physics ... 783
CMB Astrophysics Research Program 783
Fermilab—Discovering the Nature of Nature ... 783
HyperSpace at UBC 783

Interactive Physics Problem Set 783
Jean-Marie Vaneskahian's Physics Home Page ... 783
Lawrence Livermore National Laboratory ... 783
Laws List 783
Listing of Physics Resources
  on the World Wide Web 783
Livermore Labs Atmospheric Research 783
Nanotechnology 783
Nanoworld Home Page 783
NIH Guide to Molecular Modeling 784
Nuclear Physics 784
Physics and Space Technology Directorate ... 784
Physics around the World 784
Physics Demonstrations at UC Berkeley 784
Physics News 784
Physics Problems 784
Physics Servers and Services around the World ... 784
Physics Unbound 784
Physics World Electronic News 784
Quantum Magazine Home Page 784
Virtual Science Class 784
WARP Home 784
Welcome to the Institute of Physics 784
Welcome to the Laboratory for Terrestrial Physics ... 785
World Wide Web Virtual Library: Physics ... 785

Zoology　　785
Absearch 785
AlpacaNet 785
Cornell Ornithology Collection 785
Electronic Zoo 785
Insect Behavior Group 785
NetVet Veterinary Resources 785
NetVet Veterinary Resources and the Electronic Zoo ... 785
Virtual Emu 785
Zoology Department 785
Zoological Record 785

Newsgroups　　786

Listservs　　789
AAASEST—Perspectives on Ethical Issues
  in Science and Technology 789
ANSCI-L—Animal Science Students 789
ASEE-L—American Society of Engineering
  Education Students 789
ASUSCI—ASU Science and Research Press Release
  Distribution List 790
AWISNEOC—Association of Women In
  Science — N. E. Ohio Chapter 790

BIOM-SCI—Events Concerning the Biomedical Sciences Graduate Program 790
CECS-L—MU Computer Engineering and Computer Science 790
CHEME-L—Chemical Engineering List 790
COUNPSY—Counseling Psychology Practice and Science 790
DISTLABS—Teaching Science Labs Via Distance 790
EARLYSCIENCE-L—History of Science Society - Early Science Interest Group 790
EMFLDS-L—Electromagnetics in Medicine, Science & Comunications 790
ENG263-L—Popular Literature of Contemporary Science 790
ESIPLIST—Elementary Science Integration Project 790
FAMLYSCI—Family Science Network 790
GEOED-L—Geology and Earth Science Education Discussion Forum 790
GEONET-L—GEONET-L Geoscience Librarians & Information Specialists 790
H-NEXA—H-NEXA: the Science-Humanities Convergence Forum 791
HEC-L—Higher Education Consortium for Mathematics and Science 791
HUMSCI—Human Sciences Program 791
IMSE-L—Institute for Math and Science Education 791
ISL-SCI—Issues on Islam and Science 791
KSUSCI-L—KSU Science News 791
KYCCS—Center for Computational Sciences 791
MAES-L—Society of Mexican American Engineers and Scientists 791
MEDDCHEM—Macromolecular Engineering, Drug Design and Chemistry 791
MEDSCI-L—Medieval Science Discussion List 791
MSIRE-L—RI Math & Science Resource Discussion List 791
MST—Math, Science and Technology Mentors 791
NCLSMTG—National Conference of Lawyers and Scientists 791
NCPRSE-L—Reform Discussion List for Science Education 792
NEURL—Neuroscience Strategic Planning 792
NSBELINE—NSBE National Society of Black Engineers 792
NYSESM-L—Earth Science Mentors List 792
ORNITH-L—The Scientific Discussion of Ornithology 792

QMSTE-L—Mathematics, Science, and Technology Education Group 792
SCI-CULT—Science-as-Culture 792
SCIALL-L—NIH Science Alliance 792
SCIFRAUD—Discussion of Fraud in Science 792
SCINEWS—News Service Science News releases 792
SMART—Science/Math Teacher Training List 792
SSREL-L—Scientific Study of Religion 792
STPPNEWS—Science, Technology, and Public Policy News Group 792
SUSIG—Teaching in the Mathematical Sciences with Spreadsheets 793
SWE-L—Society of Women Engineers 793
TSS-LIST—Transportation Science Section List 793
WISENET—Women In Science and Engineering NETwork 793
WVUSTW-L—Scientific and Technical Writing Group 793

Sexuality   795

Abuse   795

Breaking the Cycle 795
Child Sexual Abuse 795
Images of Children, Crime, and Violence 795
National Coalition Against Sexual Assault 795
No More Victims 795
Stop It Now 795
Survivors Network of Those Abused by Priests 795

Dating Services   795

Christian Singles 795
Christian Single Online 795
Jewish Singles Connection 795
Match.Com—"We met on the net" 795
Ulti-Mate Dating Service 795
Webpersonals.com 795

Erotic E-Zines, Publications, and Other Resources   796

The Aphrodisiac Home Page 796
The Bio Keeper Archives 796
Body Politic 796
The Church of Tantra 796
Dark Nites 796
eaRoS 796
EroticaTender 796
The Erotic Pen 796
Libido Magazine 796

Penthouse Online 796
Red Hot Amsterdam 796
The Stories of Mary Anne Mohanraj 797
The Loving Center: Your Source for Information
    on Tantric Loving 797
Yellow Silk 797

Erotiproducts   **797**
Classic Lady 797
Cyber-Sex-Toys 797
EVN Mail Order Factory Outlet 797
Exxxtasy Adult Television 797
Plainwrapped Chocolates 797
Playware Limited 797
Sensuous You 797
Sin 797
TriRSex 797

Rocky Road Resources   **798**
The Chamber of Goddess Dianna Vesta 798
The Different Loving Page 798
Sex and Food 798
Stasya's Main Zoo Page 798

Safer Sex Resources   **798**
Condoms Express/Condom Club
    International 798
Contraceptive Research and
    Development Program 798
Information about Contraception
    and Reproductive Health 798
The Safer Sex Page 798

Same Sex Resources   **798**
Blair 798
Dyke TV 798
The Gay & Lesbian Bar Guide 798
The Gay & Lesbian National Hotline 799
Grassroots Queers 799
The Isle of Lesbos 799
The Lesbian Herstory Project 799
OutNOW Live 799
The Pines Guesthouse 799

Sexual Health Resources   **799**
American Social Health Association 799
Herpes Zone 799
International Planned Parenthood Federation 799
SHAPE: Sexual Health Advocate Peer Education 800

Sexual Purity Tests   **800**
The 100-Point Purity Test
    for Non-Virgins 800
The 100-Point Bondage/Dominance
    Sadism/Masochism Purity Test 800

Newsgroups   **801**

Listservs
AMANSEEKINGAWOMAN—Ads For Men
    Seeking Women 802
ANAHITA—Women and Gender in the
    Ancient World 802
AUGLBC-L—TAU: Gay, Lesbian and
    Bisexual Community 802
AWOMANSEEKINGAMAN—Ads
    For Women Seeking Men 802
GENDER—Study of Communication and Gender 802
GENDERCB—Gender Marketing and Consumer
    Behavior Discussion List 802
GENDEREQ—RI Gender Equity Discussion &
    Information List 803
GLMGLBCN—Great Lakes/Midwest Gay, Lesbian,
    Bisexual College Network 803
LEADER—Gender and Leadership Case Studies
    Discussion Group 803
MINERVA—Discussion of Women and the
    Military and Women in War 803
NGLB-L—List for NASPA Network on Gay,
    Lesbian, and Bisexual Concerns 803
NGO-CONF—Global Women's Issues Discussed
    in World Women's Conferences 803
RSVPP—RSVPP List for Research in Sex, Violence,
    and Pregnancy Prevention 803
SEX-L—For General Discussion of Sexual Issues 803
SEXTALK—For Intellectual Discussion
    on Issues Related to Sexuality 803
STOPRAPE—Sexual Assault Activist List 803
STWTTF-L—Gender Issues in Science Fiction 803
WITCHHNT—Is There a Child
    Sex Abuse Witchhunt? 803
WOMEN-IN-MINISTRY—Women in Ministry 803

Shopping   **805**

Apparel   **805**
2(x)ist Underwear 805
America's Tall Catalog 805
Bonté Casuals 805

Camalgori: A Representative Collection
of Fashion Made in Italy 805
Discreet Boutique 805
Express Online 805
Genius T-Shirts 805
Graphiti 805
Hot Couture Clothing Company 805
Lebow Bros. Clothing for Men and Boys 805
Main Sequence Astronomical Apparel 805
Menswear Unlimited 805
Planet Greek 805
Rainbow Rags 805
Salonwear 806
Soft Wear by ColorTech 806

Automobiles **806**
AutoPages of Internet 806
CAR-LINK 806
Hot Rods World Wide 806
The Ultimate New Auto Club in Canada 806

Flowers **806**
1-800-FLOWERS 806
1-800-Roses 806
Absolutely Fresh Flowers 806
Buning the Florist 806
Fleurs d'Eté 806
Flora Designs 806
Flower Stop 806
FTD Internet 807
Royer's Flowers 807
Teleflora—at the Spectra.Net Mall 807
Total Flower Exports 807

Gifts **807**
à la Gift Basket Headquarters 807
Christmas Shop 807
Crafter's Showcase 807
Erre Esse Gifts 807
Giftnet 807
Parkleigh World-Wide 807
The Private Source 807

Health & Beauty **807**
American Supply International 807
The Beauty Department at CyberShop 807
Body Doubles Skin Care 807
Certified European Image Consultant 808
Health-Max Your Maximum Health Connection 808

J. Crow Company—Herbs, Spices, Oils, Incense 808
Le Parfum 808
Maui Amenities 808
Nature's Wealth 808

Home & Office **808**
Atlas Pen and Pencil Corporation 808
Cyberian Outpost 808
The Electronics Department at CyberShop 808
Haworth Furniture for What's Next 808
In Home Shopping 808
Leonardo Collection Co. 808
Marshall on the Internet 809
Shopping Planet 809
Southern Reprographics 809
STI Internet Toner Depot 809
Valentine & Company 809
WoodWrite Wood Pens 809

Internet & Multimedia Services **809**
After Hours Media Duplication Service 809
Allegro New Media 809
AzTech Interactive 809
Connect Homepage 809
Punch & Brodie Productions 809

Jewelry **809**
Abundant Discoveries 809
The Amber Lady 809
Gem Search International 810
J & M Coin, Stamp, and Jewellery Ltd. 810
The Jewelers of Las Vegas 810
Milne Jewelry Company 810
NetDiamonds, Inc. 810
Rhinestone Jewelry Word Pins 810
Silver Jewellery 810

Miscellaneous Shopping Sites **810**
A&H Internet Shopping Service 810
Ada's Store 810
AmericaNet.Com—Free Classified Advertising 810
The Americas 810
AMOC (A Matter of Clay) 810
Ancient World 810
Another Victim of Santa Fe Style 811
Antiques World 811
Aquarium World Market 811
Art of the States 811
Blue Green Algae Enzymes 811

Builders Graphics 811
Business and Safety Cartoons by Goff 811
California Crafts Marketplace 811
Cartoon Heaven 811
Castle Attic 811
Catalog Live 811
Charleston: A Magical History Tour 811
Coherent Communications Systems Corporation 811
CouponNet 812
CraftBase 812
Dakota Engraving, Etc. 812
Delblau Company 812
Discovering Success with Gary Viterise, Ph.D. 812
Distant Caravans 812
dotSpiegel 812
eShop Inc. 812
Essex Wood Products 812
Eureka! The Web Junction 812
Facet Collector's Showcase 812
Fanco International Corp. 812
Feathered Friends 812
For Sale By Owner Magazine 813
Fox Color and Light Home Page 813
The Front Page 813
Gilltro-Electronics, Inc. 813
Global Innovations 813
Good Stuff Cheap 813
The Hahn Company 813
Handcrafts Unlimited 813
Hawaiian Express Unlimited 813
Ideal Engraving Co., Inc. 813
InfoWell 813
Internet Auction List 813
Internet Green Marketplace 813
J.R. Antiques and China Registry 813
John Charles Antiques 814
Jordan Manufacturing Company, Inc. 814
Keller's Appaloosas 814
KRAMER Handgun Leather 814
Laid Back Designs 814
LifeTime Filters 814
Lucia's Little Houses 814
Made in America 814
Magazine Warehouse 814
Maude Asbury 814
Maverick Communications 814
Musicmaker's Kits, Inc. 814

Neuromedical Supplies, Inc. 814
Next to Nothing 814
Newbury Comics, Interactive 815
Northwest Neon 815
Paramount Custom Cabinetry 815
Perspective Visuals, Inc. 815
Pet Supplies On-line 815
PolyEster Records and Books 815
Posters from Your Photos and Computer Files 815
The Quiltery 815
Rip-Tie 815
Roctronics Lighting 815
Rubber Stamp Queen 815
SCHWA Online 815
Scintilla Alternative Lighting, Gifts,
    and Accessories 815
SeaVision USA 815
Shopping2000 816
Stealth Technologies 816
Sumeria Product List 816
Surplus United States Government Sales 816
Tampa Machinery Auction, Inc. 816
Tickets and Travel, Inc. 816
Tough Traveler Gear 816
Traders' Connection 816
Uncommon Connections 816
Winona 816
Woman Made Catalog Showroom 816
The World Shopping & Information Network 816

Security & Surveillance Equipment   817
Alarm Systems 817
The Codex 817
Electronic Countermeasures, Inc. 817
Special Electronic Security Products Ltd. 817
Spy Supply Online 817
STANCOM, Inc. 817

Software   817
Confluent, Inc. 817
Diskovery Educational Systems 817
KeyStone Learning Systems Corporation 817
Layer Eight Systems, Inc. 817
Lighten, Inc. 817
Lumina Decision Systems, Inc. 817
MECC 817
NeuroSolutions: The Neural Network Simulation
    Environment 818

ObjectSpace, Inc. 818
Ovation Software Testing, Inc. 818
Second Chair Corporation 818
Sunquest Information Systems, Inc. 818
Virtual AdVentures 818

Sporting Goods 818
The Amazing Baseball Card Auction 818
New England Ski and Scuba 818
Online Sports 818
S & S Enterprises 818
Score It 818
Steve's Multi-Sport Catalog 818
SunFun Collection 818
Sunglasses.Com 818
The Sunglasses, Shavers, and More Home Page 819

Toys 819
Baby Joy Toys 819
MotoMini—Quality Motorcycle Collectibles 819
PGT Toys 819
Stratton's Collector Toy Network 819
The Virtual Toy Store 819
The World of Breyer Model Horses 819

Virtual Malls 819
American Shopping Mall 819
BizCafe Mall 819
Branch Mall 819
CityMart Shopping Mall 819
The Cyber-Shopping Network 819
Flea Market @FUW 819
IndustryNET Industry's Online Mall 820
Internet Shopping Galleria 820
Internet Shopping Network 820
Leonardo Park 820
Meetings Industry Mall 820
Microplay Video Game Stores 820
Roblyn's Shopping Mall 820
Shopper's Utopia 820
Spectra.Net Mall 820
Star-Byte Shopping Mall 820
The UK Shopping City 820
WebMart Virtual Mall And Web
    Development Services 820
The Web Plaza—Online Marketplace 820
Xplore Shopping 820

Newsgroups 821

Listservs 822
ACCIBD—American Council
    on Consumer Interests 822
BIG-E-DEALS—Discounts, Deals, and
    Bargains for Consumers by E-mail 822
GENDERCB—Gender Marketing and Consumer
    Behavior Discussion List 822

Society & Culture 823

Alternative Living 823
AERO—The Alternative Education
    Resource Organization 823
Alternative Living 823
Cohousing Network 823
Eco-Village Information Service 823
Fellowship for Intentional Community 823
The Intentional Family Connection 823
Vision of Sanctuary 823

Censorship 823
24 Hours of Democracy 823
Bonfire of Liberties: Censorship
    of the Humanities 823
Citizens Internet Empowerment Coalition 823
The Indecency Page 823
Index on Censorship 823
Know Your Enemies 824
Project Censored 824
Project 2000: The Cyberporn Debate 824
Sex, Censorship, and the Internet 824

Civil Rights 824
American Civil Liberties Union 824
Amnesty International Online 824
Center for Democracy and Technology 824
Cornucopia of Disability Information
    Gopher Server 824
Euthanasia World Directory 824
Fear—Forfeiture Endangers American Rights 824
Global Vision—The Other Network...
    Rights & Wrongs 825
Human Rights Web 825
The Martin Luther King Jr. Directory 825
Votelink...the Voice of the Net 825

Crime 825
Crime-Free America 825
Crime Prevention Initiatives 825
Emergency Net 825
Fugitive Watch 825
Justice Net 825
National Victim Center 825
Parents of Murdered Children 826
Prison Legal News 826
Rape Victim Advocates 826
Rate Your Risk 826
Serial Killers 826
Shattered Love Broken Lives 826
United Nations Crime and Justice
    Information Network 826
United States Department of Justice 826

Cross-Cultural Resources 826
Diversity and Pluralism 826
The ERaM Programme 826
Interracial Voice 826
ITI's Multi-Cultural Network 826
Minority Affairs Forum 827
Museum of Tolerance 827
National Civil Rights Museum 827
The National Multicultural Institute 827
The Web of Culture 827

Senior Citizens 827
AARP 827
The Adopt a Grandparent Program 827
Caregiver Network, Inc. 827
Elderhostel 827
Grand Times 827
Seniors-Site 827
SWT Age Page 828

Social Issues 828
American Firearms Association 828
Drug Use is Life Abuse/Project: No Gangs ... 828
EZ Connect 828
Gunfree 828
Institute for Global Communications 828
just 828
The Knowledge Source 828
NARAL 828
National Right to Life 828
Planned Parenthood Federation of America ... 828
Soapbox Issues 828

Soundprint Historical and Social Issues 829
Urban Legends Archive 829
U.S. Pro-Life Directory 829
Today in Perspective 829
Vote Smart Web 829

Social Services 829
American Red Cross 829
The Carter Center 829
Contact Center Network 829
HandsNet 829
National Civic League 829
The National Coalition for the Homeless 830
River of Hope 830
An Unofficial Guide to Rotary 830
VISTA Web 830
Who Cares 830

Veterans' Affairs 830
The American Legion 830
Baudo's Vet Links 830
Department of Veterans Affairs 830
Military Family Institute 830
Veterans Archive 830
Vietnam Veterans Home Page 830

Newsgroups 831

Listservs 836
AAASHRAN—AAAS Human Rights
    Action Network 836
AASNET-L—African American Student Network 836
AFAM-L—African-American Research 836
AFAMHED—African-Americans
    in Higher Education 836
AFAMLIT—African American Literature
    Discussion Forum 836
AFRICA-L—Pan-Africa Discussion List 836
BIRG—Black Issues Research Group 836
BLKCRIM—Black Criminologists
    Discussion List 836
CJMOVIES—Journal of Criminal Justice
    and Popular Culture 836
CJUST-L—CJUST-L: Criminal Justice
    Discussion List 836
FREE-L—Fathers' Rights and Equality Exchange 837
H-AFRLITCINE—H-NET List for African
    Literature and Cinema 837
HRS-L—Systematic Studies of Human Rights 837
NCS-L—National Crime Survey Discussion 837

*NSBELINE—NSBE National Society
   of Black Engineers* 837
*SA_TALK—South African Social and
   Political Issues Forum* 837
*VPAD-L—Veterans Program
   Administrators Discussion List/VPAD-L* 837
*Y-RIGHTS—Y-Rights: Kid/Teen Rights
   Discussion Group* 837

Sports　　　　839

Auto Racing　　　839
candelaMotorsport 839
GALE FORCE F1 839
The IndyCar Enthusiast 839
Matt's Solar Car Page 839
*Motorsports Media Service
   International Home Page* 839
The Racer Archive 839
Specialty Car Page 839

Baseball　　　839
Baseball Hall of Fame 840
ESPNet SportsZone: Major League Baseball 840
Fastball 840
Instant Baseball 840
Japanese Professional Baseball 840
John Skilton's Baseball Links 840
Little League Baseball 840
Major League Baseball 840
Nando Baseball Server 840
New York Yankees Home Plate 841
World Youth Baseball 841

Basketball　　　841
College Basketball Page 841
Michael Jordan's Home Page 841
Nando Basketball Server 841
On Hoops 841
Scottie Pippen's Home Court 842
Ultimate Basketball Home Page 842
*Unofficial Australian National
   Basketball League (NBL) Page* 842

Boating & Sailing　　　842
Adventure Schools, Inc. 842
Boatnet 842
Common Sense Design's Home Page 842
The Flying Scot Page 842

Internet Sea Kayaking 842
Offshore Powerboat Racing 842
*Perception, Inc.'s Kayaking
   Home Page—20 Years of Fun* 842
RC—Sailing Infocenter 842
SailWeb 842
United States Power Squadrons Web Page 842
White Water Rafting 843
WWW Sailing Index 843

Cycling　　　843
Cyber Cylcery 843
CycLinks 843
Emory Bicycle Manufacturing Company 843
Fat Tire Wire 843
MuDsLuTs 843
Spring City Cycles 843
VeloNet 843
The Velonews 843
VeloZine 843
WOMBATS on the Web 843
The WWW Bicycle Lane 843

Extreme Sports　　　844
Edge Magazine 844
Hang Gliding Page 844
Hang Gliding WWW Server 844
ISF World Snowboarding Rankings 844
The Maui Windsurfing Report 844
New England Windsurfing Journal 844
Parachute Industry Association 844
Sailboard Vacations 844
SkyDance SkyDiving 844
Skydive Archive 844
Windsight Windsurfing Wind Reports 844

Fantasy Leagues　　　845
Conway's Sports Research 845
Cosmic Baseball Association 845
CyberSoccer 845
Fantasy Baseball 845
Fantasy Baseball Home Page 845
Fantasy Insights 845
Football Stats Analyzer Shareware 845
The Grandstand 845
Highlight Fantasy—The Draft Kit 845
Midwest Express Fantasy Game Co. 845
NFL POOL 845

Onondaga/Oswego Fantasy Football Page 845
Small World 846
WinAmerica! Fantasy Football 846

Fishing · 846
Anglers Online 846
Flyfishing Antventures 846
J.P.'s Fishing Page 846
King of the Hill Fly Fishing Co. 846
Nautical Net 846
Nor'east Saltwater Magazine 846
Sportfishing Industry Newsletter 846
Virtual Flyshop 846
World of Fishing 847

Football · 847
AllSports.Com Football Hotlist 847
College Football WWW Site 847
College Sports Internet Channel 847
Nando Football Server 847
NFL Executive Accessories 848
Team NFL 848
Traveller Information Service 848
Two-Minute Warning 848
USA Football Center Online 848

Golf · 848
The 19th Hole 848
Alberta 848
Fore Play Golf Home Page 848
The Golf Circuit 848
Golf Courses of British Columbia 848
The Golf Depot 848
Golf Magazine 848
Golf Web 849
NBC Golf Tour 849
Official PGA Championship Web Site 849
Princeton Golf Archives 849
Ryder Cup Home Page 849

Hiking · 849
Above the Clouds 849
Backcountry Home Page 849
Orienteering and Rogaining Home Page 849
Volksmarch and Walking Index 849

Hockey · 849
Hockey Hall of Fame 850
National Hockey League Players' Association 850

NHL OPEN NET 850
NHL Schedule 850
NHL Wreckroom 850

Horse Sports · 850
Horse Country 850
Thoroughbred Horse Racing and Breeding 850
Three Chimneys Farm Home Page 850
The Washington Handicapper 851

Martial Arts · 851
Aikido Information 851
CyberDojo 851
The Danzan-Ryu Jujutsu Homepage 851
Judo Information Site 851
The Martial Arts As I've Learned Them 851
Piedmont Budokan (Judo and JuJitsu) 851
The T'ai Chi Connection 851

Miscellaneous Sports Sites · 851
American Poolplayers Association 851
The Art of Fencing 851
AWESOME Sports Site of the Week 851
Ballistic Batteries 851
British Society of Sports History 852
Canada's Sports Hall of Fame 852
College Athletics WWW Pages 852
College Lacrosse USA 852
David B. Martin's Water Polo Page 852
ESPNET Sports Zone 852
Frisbee Freestyle 852
The Gym Forum 852
Internet Athlete 852
Irish Sports Report 852
La Tauromaquia: The Art of Bullfighting 852
Mart's In-Line Stating Page 852
Nando.Net Sports Server 852
PBA Tour 853
Physique Techniques Fitness Consultants 853
Planet Reebok 853
Quick Stats Service 853
Rowing 853
The Sporting Life 853
Sports Illustrated 853
Sports Network 853
Sports Source 853
Sports Souvenirs & Memorabilia 853
Sports Videos 853

SportsArena 854
Sportsworld 854
Sprague Mat Club 854
Stadiums and Arenas 854
Sumo Infomation Page 854
Tenpin World 854
The Ultimate Internet Sports Guide 854
The Ultimate Sports Page 854
United States Air-Table-Hockey
   Association (USAA) 854
US Fencing Association Online 854
USA Today Sports 854
the virtual greensward 854
Wide Web of Sports 855
World Squash Federation 855

Motorcycle Racing 855
AFMWeb 855
Speedway Home Page 855

Olympics 855
Guide to the 1996 Olympic Games 855
The XVIII Olympic Winter Games 855

Outdoors 855
Arkatents USA—High Quality
   Camping Accessories 855
Great Outdoor Recreation Pages (GORP) 855
Outside Online 855
Roller Warehouse News 855
Sk8er's Home Page 855
The Upper Midwest Traveler
   and Adventure Guide 855

Rugby 856
International Rugby League Home Page 856
WWW Rugby Information Service 856

Running 856
Running Page 856
Sportsworld 856

Scuba Diving 856
Aquanaut 856
Diving Server 856
Mad Dog Expeditions 856
Maui Scuba Page—Ed Robinson's
   Diving Adventures 856
NAUI (National Association
   of Underwater Instructors) 856

Scuba Central 856
Scuba Net 856

Skiing 857
CRN—Colorado Resort Net 857
The FALL LINE Home Page 857
Jump 857
Northern Vermont X-Country, Backcountry,
   and Telemark Skiing 857
Pedersen's Ski and Sport 857
Powder Hound Ski Report 857
The SnowPage 857
Wasatch Powderbird Guides 857
World Skiing 857

Soccer 857
ESPNet SportZone Soccer 857
International Soccer 857
Soccer Cybertour 857
SoccerNet 858
SoccerNews Online 858
TSI Soccer 858
U.S. Soccer Web Pages 858

Surfing & Waterskiing 858
Bodysurfing 858
Drop In 858
FreeSurf 858
Surf Lingo 858
Water Skier's Web 858
Welcome to the Lip 858
Windsurfer.com 858

Swimming 858
Home Page for United States Swimming, Inc. 858
Web Swim 859

Tennis 859
ATP Tour Home Page 859
Tennis Country 859
United States Tennis Association/
   Mid-Atlantic Section 859
World Wide Web Tennis Server 859

Volleyball 859
USA Volleyball Home Page 859
Volleyball WorldWide 859

Winter Sports 859
Figure Skater's Web Page 859
Snow Page 859

Speed Skating 859
The Winter Sports Page 859

Newsgroups 860

Listservs 866
AUTORACE—A Discussion of Auto Racing 866
B10WB-L—Big 10 Women's Basketball 866
CBR—Honda CBR motorcycles 866
HRACING—Horse Racing Discussion 866
MUFC—Manchester United Football Club (Soccer) ... 866
NYMETS-L—New York Mets Baseball Talk 866
PHILS—Phillies Discussion List 866
RANGERS—Discussion of Texas Rangers
  Major League Baseball Team 866
SOCCER-L—Soccer Boosters List 866
SOCREF-L—Discussion of Topics
  for Soccer Referees 866
SPORTS-CARDS—Buy/Sell/Trade and
  Discussion of Sports Cards 866
STATLG-L—Baseball (and Lesser Sports)
  Discussion List 866
UTAHJAZZFANS—Discussion of Utah
  Jazz Basketball 866
VB-CLUB—Club Volleyball Discussion List 866

Television 867

Children 867
2 Stupid Dogs 867
The Adventures of Pete and Pete 867
The alt.tv.tiny-toon FAQ 867
Animaniacs 867
Bananas in Pajamas 867
Batfink 867
Batman: The Animated Series 867
Beakman's World Home Page 867
Captain Caveman 868
Captain Planet 868
Cartoon World 868
Cartoons of the '80s Home Page 868
Children's Television Workshop 868
Clarissa Explains It All 868
Count Duckula Page 868
Craig's Comic & Cartoon Page 868
Danger Mouse 868
Davey and Goliath 868
Deron's Muppet Page 868
Dinosaucers 868
Dungeons and Dragons 869

Earthworm Jim 869
The Flintstones Unofficial Home Page 869
Fraggle Rock 869
Freakazoid! 869
Frostbite Falls 869
G.I. Joe—A Real American Hero 869
Goosebumps 869
Gumby on the Web 869
The Jetsons 869
Keeper's Cartoon Files 870
Kids.Cool 870
Mighty Morphin Power Documents 870
Mister Rogers' Neighborhood 870
Muppets Home Page 870
Phil's Faboo Animaniacs Web Page 870
Pigs in CyberSpaaaaaaaaaaace... 870
Pinky and the Brain 870
The ReBoot Home Page 870
The School House Rock Page 870
The Secret World of Alex Mack
  Unofficial Home Page 870
Some of the 100 or Some Odd Smurfs 870
The Superfriends Archive 870
The Sylvester and Tweety Mysteries 871
Taz-Mania Page 871
Teen Court TV 871
That's Warner Bros.! 871
Thomas the Tank Engine 871
Thunderbirds 871
The Tick Page 871
The Unofficial Sid and Marty Krofft Home Page 871
Welcome to Casper's Whipstaff Manor 871
You Can't Do That On Television 871

Comedies & Sitcoms 871
Absolutely Fabulous 871
The ALF Page by Kyle 872
The Alice TV-Show Home Page 872
All in the Family 872
alt.tv.brisco-county 872
America's Favorite Radio Station 872
The Andy Griffith Show Home Page 872
Beavis and Butthead 872
Better Dead Than SMEG 872
Bewitched Home Page 872
Blossom 873
The Bob Newhart Unofficial Homepage 873
Bosom Buddies Home Page 873

Boston Common 873
Boy Meets World 873
Café Nervosa 873
California Dreams 873
The Carol Burnett Show Episode Guide 873
Caroline in the City 873
Cheers Home Page 873
Clueless 874
C'mon, Get Happy! 874
The Comedy Store Fan Club Home Page 874
Common Law 874
The Critic 874
Dinosaurs 874
Dr. Katz 874
Dream On 874
Duckman! 874
Eerie, Indiana 874
Encyclopedia Brady 874
The Facts of Life Unofficial Home Page 874
Family Ties 874
Fawlty Towers Episode Guide 875
The Fresh Prince of Bel-Air 875
Friends 875
Full House 875
Get a Life Program Guide 875
The Get Smart Home Page 875
Gilligan's Island 875
The Golden Girls 875
Grace Under Fire 875
Growing Pains 875
The Hangin' with Mr. Cooper Home Page 875
Herman's Head 875
Hogan's Heroes 876
Home of Home Improvement Cyberfans 876
The Honeymooners Picture Depot 876
Hudson Street Home Page 876
The Indispensable I Dream of Jeannie Page 876
The John Larroquette Show 876
Kids In the Hall by Jeff 876
The Larry Sanders Show 876
Mad About You 876
The Mad TV Home Page 876
Mama's Family 876
Maniac Mansion 877
Married…With Children Home Page 877
MASH Archives 877
Mel Loves I Love Lucy 877

Mook's the Simpsons Page 877
Moon Over Parma 877
Moonlighting, on the Web 877
Murphy Brown 877
My So-Called Life 877
The Nanny Unofficial Home Page 877
The Ned and Stacey Home Page 877
The New Web Site of Love Mystery
    Science Theatre 3000 877
The NewsRadio Station 878
The Official Unofficial Seinfeld Page 878
Parker Lewis Can't Lose 878
The Red Green Show 878
The R.M.P.S.S. 878
Roseanne 878
Saturday Night Archives 878
Saved By The Bell 878
The Simpsons Source 878
The Single Guy ("How about something
    simple, like…") 878
Sledge Hammer! Arsenal 878
Spin City 878
The State's Virtual Whatever… 878
Sup's Blackadder Page 878
Third Page from the Official 879
Townies 879
TV Nation 879
Welcome Back, Kotter 879
Whose Line Is It Anyway? 879
Wings 879
The Wonder Years 879

Dramas — 879

Chicago Hope Home Page 879
Dangerous Minds 879
Dead At 21 879
The Dr. Quinn, Medicine Woman
    Official Web Site 879
ER 880
The Little House on the Prairie
    Unofficial Home Page 880
The Moose's Guide to Northern Exposure 880
My So-Called Life 880
NYPD Blue Home Page 880
Party of Five 880
The Perry Mason Pages 880
The Real World 880
The thirtysomething Episode Guide 880

The Twin Peaks Lodge 880
The Unofficial Picket Fences
    Home Page 881

Educational   881
Bill Nye the Science Guy's Nye Labs Online 881
Biography 881
Building America—Eye On Business 881
Collecting Across America 881
CTN 881
The Doctor Is In 881
Great Canadian Parks 881
The Joy of Painting with Bob Ross 881
Newton's Apple 881
No Dogs or Philosophers Allowed 881
Where in the World Is Carmen Sandiego? 882

News   882
The C-Span Networks 882
CNN Newsroom 882

Science Fiction & Fantasy   882
Babylon 5 file Area 882
Battlestar Galactica 882
Broadsword 882
Dark Shadows 882
The Dominion Sci-fi Channe 882
The Extraterrestrial Biological Entity (EBE) Page 882
Forever Knight 882
Hyperlight Enterprises 882
Lurker's Guide to Babylon 5 883
Planet X 883
Sliders 883
Songs of the Blue Bird 883
Starship Portfolio 883
Starship Store 883
Tales from the Crypt 883
Terminal X 883
Trader 800 Trekker 883
Trek Reviews Archive 884

Soap Operas   884
All My Children 884
The Another World Fan Club Official Home Page 884
As the World Turns 884
The Bold and the Beautiful 884
Days of Our Lives Page 884
General Hospital 884
Guiding Light 884

One Life To Live: The History Page 884
Soap Opera Pen Pal Page 884
The Young and the Restless 884

Talk Shows   884
alt.fan.howard-stern 884
alt.tv.talkshows.daytime 884
alt.tv.talkshows.late 885
Andy Richter: King of the Couch 885
David Letterman 885
The Ed Sullivan Show 885
FAQ—alt.tv.talkshows.late 885
The George and Alana Show Home Page 885
Hereeeeeeeeee's Conan 885
The Late Late Show with Tom Snyder 885
Later with Greg Kinnear 885
Lauren Hutton 885
The Oprah Winfrey Show 885
The Politically Incorrect Unofficial Home Page 886
The Richard Bey Show 886
The Ricki Lake Show Home Page 886
Rolonda 886
The Rosie O'Donnell Show 886
Sony Pictures Before They Were Stars 886
Tempestt 886
The Tonight Show with Jay Leno 886
The Unofficial Talk Soup Web Page 886

Television Resources   886
All TVs Center 886
Columbia Music Video Resources 887
Comedy Central 887
NBC 887
PBS Online 887
Tooncers Web Page Fantasmic 887
TV5 887
The Ultimate TV List 887
Vanderbilt Television News Archive 887
Welcome to the BBC 887

Newsgroups   888

Listservs   891
DQMW-L—Dr. Quinn Medicine
    Woman TV Show 891
FORKNI-L—Forever Knight TV show 891
HIGHLA-L—Highlander movies and TV series 891
LAW-AND-ORDER—Discussion of the TV Series 891
MASTVF-L—Martial Arts in Television and films 891
PTV-SERV—Public Television Station Service 892

SCREEN-L—Film and TV Studies
Discussion List 892
SO-CALLED—Discussion of the TV series
"My So-Called Life" 892

Transportation   893

Alternative Fuel Vehicles   893
Citicar: My Electric Vehicle 893
Electric Vehicle Association of the Americas 893
Formula Lightning 893

Buyer's Guides   893
AutoPlus 893
Car and Driver Buyer's Guide 1996 893
Car Tips 893
CARveat Emptor 893
Edmund's Automobiles Buying Guides 893
The Internet CarGuide 893
New Car Comparison Guide 893
Tallweb—Cars 894
Used Car Buying Guide 894

Clubs   894
CHVA 894
Hudson-Essex-Terraplane Club, Inc. 894
Rolls-Royce Owners' Club 894

Driving   894
Art of Driving 894
Natural Born Drivers 894
Teen New Drivers' Home Page 894

Four Wheel Drives   895
4WD: Four Wheel Drive and All Wheel Drive 895
America's 4¥4 4U Video Magazine 895
Dakar Official Site 895
My Jeep Adventures 895
Off-Road.com 895
Warn Adventure Morocco '96 895

Makes & Models   895
AC Cobra Page 895
Alfa Romeo GTA 895
Aston Martin 895
DeLorean Home Page 895
Javelin AMX Home Page 895
Paul Murtagh's Lamborghini Web Site 896
Waletail's Porsche and 959 Home Page 896

Motorcycles   896
Longriders Internet Bikers' Club House 896
Motorcycle Tips and Techniques 896
WetLeather Home Page 896

Museums   896
Auto Museum at Wells 896
Cole Land Transportation Museum 896
Henry Ford Museum & Greenfield
Village On-Line 896
Vette Americana On-Line 896

Organizations   896
American Truck Historical Society 896
Mid-America Old Time Auto Association 897

Trains   897
Amtrak 897
Burlington Northern Santa Fe Corporation 897
Grand Canyon Railway 897

Trucks   897
European Trucks 897
Sport Trucks 897
Truck Safety Page 897
Trucking Times 897

Vintage Automobiles   898
Boulder Bob's Roadster Page 898
Car Junkie 898
Classic Car Gallery 898
Classic Car Pictures Archive 898
Classic Showcase 898
Coys of Kensington 898
Hillsborough Concours d'Elegance 898
Schiemer's Page 898
Tangerine Dream Vintage Car Locator Service 898
Wambo! 898
XK's Unlimited 898

Newsgroups   899

Listservs   899
AEROSP-L—Aeronautics & Aerospace History 899
AIRCRAFT—The Aircraft Discussion List 899
AUTORECY—Automobile Recycling 899
CCEVS—Carolinas Consortium for
Electrical Vehicles 900
CETM-L—Canadian Executive
Transportation Management 900

CYCLNG-L—UGA Cycling Club Discussion List 900
EV—Electric Vehicle Discussion List 900
EM_TRANS—Emerging Methods in
   Transportation 900
HYDROGEN—Hydrogen as an Alternative Fuel 900
NTEAA-L—North Texas Electric Auto Association ... 900
NUMAP—Nuclear Utility Materials
   and Procurement 900
RBIKE—Road Bicycling 900

Travel   901

Adventure Travel   901
Adventure Travel 901
Adventure Travel for Women 901
Alaska—Mt. McKinley 901
Alpine Guides Alaska 901
Arctic Adventours, Inc. 901
Big Island Air 901
Eagle Canyon Airlines 901
EarthWise Journeys 901
Helinet Helicopter Tours 901
Mayuc—Ecological Tourism 901
New Brunswick, Canada Outdoor Adventures 901
Resort Sports Network 901
Safari Helicopters 902
Sierra Mountain Guides 902
Touring Exchange 902
TravelBase 902
Wildwest Travel, Inc. 902

Airlines   902
Above It All 902
Aer Lingus 902
Aeroflot 902
Air Canada 902
Air Charter Guide 902
Air Travel Card Control Tower 902
Air UK 902
Airlines of the Web 902
American Airlines 902
Ansett Australia 903
Canadian Airlines Intl. 903
Cathay Pacific 903
Comair 903
Eagle Canyon Airlines 903
Emirates Airline Page 903
Finnair 903
Frontier Airlines 903

International Airport Codes 903
Japan Airlines 903
Lauda Air 903
Lufthansa Timetable Info 904
Mexicana Airlines 904
Mount Cook Airlines 904
New England Airlines 904
Quantas Airlines 904
Scenic Airlines 904
Virgin Atlantic Airlines 904

Automobile Travel   904
ASIRT-Association for International Road Travel 904
Bumper Stickers 904
National Auto League 904
Rental Agencies 904
Route 66 904
Scenic Byways and Other Recreational Drives 904
Traveling in the USA 904

Books & Publications   905
Adventurous Traveler Bookstore 905
Travel Publications 905
Traveler's Book Club 905
Travels with Samantha 905
World of Maps 905

Cruise Ships   905
Accent's Cruise Connection 905
Adventure Cruising in the North Atlantic 905
Cruise Review Library 905
Cruise Shoppes America, Ltd. 905
Cruises, Inc. 905
Freighter World Cruises 905
Norwegian Cruise Line 905
Royal Caribbean Cruise Line 906
Travel Discounts Cruise Index 906

International Travel   906
Air Brokers International World Travel
   Specialist 906
Alchemy of Africa 906
Ansett Australia 906
Antigua & Barbuda 906
Australia Travel Directory 906
Automated Travel Center 906
Brochure Flow 906
The Civilized Explorer 907
Costa Travel Online 907
Council Travel 907

Country Maps of Europe 907
Cyprus 907
Czech Info Center 907
Dublin Pub Review 907
Endeavour Travel 907
European and British Rail Passes 907
Eurostar Internet 907
Far & Away Travel Services 907
FranceEscape 907
Freesun News 908
Going to Belgium 908
Great Australian Travel Co. 908
Hong Kong Online Guide 908
Indonesia 908
InteleTravel International 908
International Travel Agency (ITA) 908
The Internet Guide to Hostels 908
Intra Travel 908
Jerusalem Mosaic 908
Jordan 908
Lanka Internet Services 908
Lonely Planet Travel Centre 908
Middle World 908
The Monaco Home Page 909
Salzburg, Austria 909
Sinbad Travel 909
TGV French High Speed Train 909
Tour Canada without Leaving Your Desk 909
Tourist Office of Spain Homepage 909
Travel Home 909
Travel to Finland 909
United Kingdom Pages 909
Vancouver, British Columbia 909
Victoria, British Columbia 909
Welcome to Future Net—Queensland, Australia 909

Island Travel   910
America's Caribbean Paradise 910
Bahamas Online 910
CaribWeb 910
Charlotte's Caribbean Connection 910
Holman Travel 910
Maui Interactive 910
NetWeb Bermuda Home Page 910

Lodging   910
American Youth Hostels 910
Bed & Breakfast Inns Online 910

California Travel and Parks Association 910
Campground Directory 910
Choice Hotels 910
Homeless Shelters in the United States 910
Hostelling International 911
International Bed And Breakfast Guide 911
Nude 2000 911
Professional Association of Innkeepers
   International 911
Travel Web 911
United Hostels of Europe 911
World Wide Lodging Guide 911

Train Travel   911
Burlington Northern—Sante Fe 911
Canadian National 911
European Rail System 911
Liberty's Amtrak Page 911
Union Pacific Railroad Excursion Information 911
VI Rail-Canada's Passenger Train Network 911
Welcome to Amtrak's Station on the WWW 912

Travel Databases   912
America's Best 912
City Net 912
GNN Travel Center 912
The Inn Traveler—International Bed & Breakfast
   and Country Inn Guide 912
The North American Virtual Tourist 912
rec.travel.library 912
Round-The-World Travel Guide 912
TII—Tourism Info Internet 912
Travel & Entertainment Network
   (TEN-IO) Home Page 912
Travel Information 912
Travel Online 912
The Travel Page 913
Travel Web Search Page 913
TravelSearch 913
TravelSource 913
Virtual Tourist II 913
The Webfoot's Travel Guides 913
WL The World Library From Scescape 913
The Yankee Traveler 913

Travel Tips   913
Air Traveler's Handbook 913
Currency Exchange Rates 913
The Electronic Embassy 913

ELVIS+, Co. 914
Foreign Language for Travelers 914
GNN/Koblas Money Converter 914
Information about Duty Free/Tax Free Shopping 914
Interactive Travel Guide 914
International Traveler's Clinic 914
Railroad Timetables 914
Travel Discounts 914
Travel Web Sites 914
United States State Department Travel Warnings
    and Consular Info Sheets 914
Web Travel Review 914

U.S. Travel 914

Access New Hampshire 914
ACUMUG—Arkansas Index
    of Internet Resources 915
Alabama 915
Alaska Information Cache 915
Allons! Acadiana 915
America's Land of Enchantment 915
AMI News—Recreation and Travel 915
The Arizona Guide 915
Atlanta Web Guide 915
Boston Area Map of WWW Resources 915
California Do Your Own Thing 915
Cambridge, Massachusetts 915
Chicago Information System 916
CLEVE.NET A Guided Tour of the North Coast 916
Clickable Connecticut Area Map 916
Front Desk 916
Gold Canyon Multimedia 916
Grand Rapids, Michigan 916
Greensboro Online 916
HobokenX 916
Idaho Home Page 916
Index 916
Index 916
Indiana Virtual Tourist 916
Information Access Websites 916
Iowa Virtual Tourist 917
Kentucky Network Services 917
Las Vegas 917
Los Angeles Traffic Report 917
Maine WWW Resources 917
Minneapolis 917
Missouri WWW Resources 917
Nashville Scene 917

Nebraska Travel and Tourism 917
The Oklahoma Image Map 917
Oregon Online 917
Palo Alto, California 917
Peaks—An Online Magazine About Montana 917
RING. Online Michigan's Electronic Magazine 918
Santa Barbara County 918
South Carolina Supernet—LocalNet 918
South Dakota World Wide Web Site 918
Staunton, Virginia 918
St. Louis, Missouri 918
Texas, Austin 918
U/Seattle 918
USA CityLink 918
Utah! Travel and Adventure Online 918
The Vail Valley Home Page 918
Vermont/New Hampshire WWW Resources 918
VISIT Virginia 919
The Washington DC City Pages 919
Washington State Online Travel Information 919
Web Texas 919
Weekend Getaways 919
Welcome to the Ohio Web 919
The West Virginia Web 919

Newsgroups 920

Listservs 920

AGING-L—University of Connecticut's
    Traveler's Center on Aging 920
SCUBA-SE—SouthEast US Scuba Diving
    Travel list 920
TRAVABLE—Travel for the Disabled 921
TRAVEL-L—Travel-L Discussion of
    Travel Experiences 921
TRAVELUK-L—Travel in the United
    Kingdom 921

Weddings 923

Announcements, Invitations, & Registries 923

Bridal Gallery 923
Bridal Net: Online Bridal Registry 923
Club Wed Press 923
Historical Wedding Invitations 923
Personal Wedding Pages on the Net 923
The Wedding Center 923

Gifts — 923

Groom's Gift Collection 923
Peachtree Circle Inc. 923
Sophisticated Chocolates 923
Wedding Decorations and Gifts 923
Wedding Marketplace 923
The Wedding Registries Directory 923

Miscellaneous Wedding Sites — 924

The Alt.Wedding Home Page 924
The American Humanist Association 924
Automatic Wedding Speech Writer 924
The Bride and Groom's World Wedding Fair 924
The Bride's Page 924
Celebration Vineyards 924
Collected Domestic Partners Information 924
Elegant Bride 924
I Do 924
Rialto Archive: Period and SCA Weddings 924
Same-Sex Marriage Home Page 924
soc.couples.wedding WWW Page 924
A Way Cool Wedding Every Week 925
Wedding Bell Blueprint 925
Wedding Bells 925
Wedding Circle Home Page 925
The Wedding Source 925
The Wedding Spot 925
Weddings Online, The Internet's
   Wedding Information Resource 925

Wedding & Honeymoon Locations — 925

Caribmoon 925
Island Weddings, SuperClubs 925
Wedding Gardens 925
A Wedding Made in Paradise 925
Weddings, with Makana 926

Wedding Gowns & Accessories — 926

Ans Bolk Personal Design Bridal Couture 926
The Bridal Veil Home Page 926
The Dessy Creations Home Page 926
Hora Bridal Accessories 926
Imagi-Nations 926
NetDiamonds, Inc. 926
Sposabella Bridal—La Sposa Veil 926
Watters and Watters 926
The Wedding Band Center 926

Wedding Planning — 926

Bridal Expo Online 926
Coconut Coast Weddings and Honeymoons 926
Emily Post's Complete Guide to Weddings 927
Leslie's Guide to Wedding Planning 927
Melanet Online African Wedding Guide 927
My Wedding Companion 927
Ninga Software Corporation:
   "The Wedding Planner" 927
Northwest Wedding Network 927
A Pagan Wedding 927
Simply Software: "Bridesmaids for Windows" 927
The TouchSoft: "I Do Ultimate Wedding Planner" 927
Wedding Web Home Page 927
Wedding Wise 927
Weddings by IPS 928
WedNet —The Wedding Network 928

Newsgroups — 929

Listservs — 929

1YEAR2GO—Planning and Information
   for Upcoming Weddings 929
COUPLES-L—Aspects of Concern
   in Heterosexual Relationships 929
FAMCOMM—Marital/Family & Relational
   Communication 929
FAMLYSCI—To Enhance Communication
   among Family Scientists 929
MFTC-L—Marriage and Family Therapy
   Counseling Discussion 929
PHOTOWED—The Wedding Photographers
   Mailing List 929
WME-L—Worldwide Marriage
   Encounter Discussion 929

Appendix A
Colleges & Universities — 931

Appendix B
FTP Sites — 967

Index — 1011

Introduction

The Internet is a collection of interconnected computer networks from around the world that provides a wealth of information on nearly any topic you can imagine. The World Wide Web, often simply called the Web, is a subsystem of the Internet. The Web has become the definitive "hot spot" for Internet users primarily because it enables anyone to graphically and visually "advertise" themselves or a specific cause, and have this representation 24 hours a day. Many individuals do not have the need to create their own Web page, as this type of representation is called, but they do want to have access to and be able to view the Web sites of others. Whatever your situation, you will be utterly amazed by the tremendous variety and amount of information that is available on the World Wide Web and captured in this book.

Features and Uses of the World Wide Web

The Web can link together information from anywhere in the world and make it available to anyone. A grade-school student can jump from Dun & Bradstreet's financial information to a pictorial tour of Croatia's capital, Zagreb, to the state of the Internet in southern Africa, without ever leaving his desk.

There's far more to the Web than just information. You can learn static facts from any encyclopedia. The information stored in the Web is constantly updated. With the Web, you'll always have the freshest information at your fingertips.

The Web also dynamically links information into a seamless whole. You may start your information hunt next door and finally track down your quarry somewhere in Singapore. From where you sit, however, the distance between the two online data sources makes no difference. The Web enables you to move around the world as easily as to the local library—with a click of a mouse.

Although the Web has existed for a relatively short time, it is already being used in numerous areas by both public and private institutions. Businesses have discovered how beneficial advertising and performing transactions on the Web can be. Educational institutions also are making more information available on the Web, and students are discovering that they can get increasingly more research done by searching Web pages rather than library books. You can make travel plans, buy houses, read about your favorite hobby, and make new friends via the Web.

Business

Individual companies have set up advertisements on the Web. Before long, it will be almost unprofitable for any major company—especially one that deals in new technologies—to exist without its own site to show advertisements and product information. Buyers, moreover, are rapidly finding out that it is far easier to take a look at a new product by going to a business's Web page than by physically going to the store to look for a product or searching advertisements in the newspaper. In addition to finding advertisements on the Web, consumers can do their shopping on the Web as well.

Do you want to actually purchase an item that you've been viewing? Step into a shopping mall! These malls allow users to place orders for items that can then be shipped to their homes or businesses. Holiday shopping couldn't be easier! No longer will you have to stand in lines at stores or wait on hold for the attendant at the mail-order company to take your order. Instead, you can find the item you want and enter your credit card information to have it shipped right away.

Users can order almost anything from the Web: chocolate, books, games, clothing, music, or anything else they might desire. This directory contains listings for numerous stores and shopping centers.

Education

Many educational resources already are available through the Web. Libraries are adding their catalogs and universities are posting information about degree programs. You can find research documents containing information about almost any subject. Before long, travelling to a library to find this information will become a nearly obsolete venture. Instead, students will be able to find information they need without leaving their desks.

The possibilities for education on the Web are amazing. Many college and university classes presently create Web pages for semester class projects. Research papers on many different topics are also available. Even elementary school students are using the Web to access information and pass along news to other students. Exchange students can communicate with their classmates-to-be long before they actually arrive at their new school. It won't be long before students will be able to take language classes that are actually taught in the country where the language is spoken.

Many elementary and secondary schools have created and are maintaining Web pages. Students and teachers work together to decide what information should be included on the site, and to prepare it for publication. By doing this, not only do they make more information available to the community, but students gain useful knowledge of new technologies and their use.

Travel

Planning a vacation? There are many sites on the Web that can help you solidify your travel plans, or give you ideas of places you might want to visit. These sites offer information about tours and hotel accommodations, as well as car rentals, airfare, and other forms of transportation. Cruise lines have Web pages that outline various types of cruise packages and describe destinations. Many cities sponsor Web pages as well, where you can learn about restaurants, sightseeing and shopping opportunities, and local points of interest.

About This Directory

This directory lists more than 9,000 selected World Wide Web sites. Each listing presents the site's title and URL, as well as a brief description of the site.

The sites have been placed in categories, such as Children, Health, Music, Religion, and Travel, and are then presented alphabetically in subcategories. Because New Riders Publishing wanted to present as many sites as possible in this directory, maximum effort has been made to avoid site duplication from category to category, even if the site's contents qualifies it for more than one category (for example, a site about church music could conceivably fall under either the Music or Religion category). For the widest range of listings under a given subject, therefore, please check our comprehensive index that lists Web site titles under an extensive number of subject headings.

Further Reading

There are many books and articles about the World Wide Web; moreover, any relatively recent book about the Internet will contain some material on the subject of the Web. Here are some possible sources for further information:

Inside the World Wide Web, Second Edition, New Riders Publishing.

Riding the Internet Highway, Intenetworks Edition, New Riders Publishing.

New Riders' Official World Wide Web Yellow Pages, 1997 Edition, New Riders Publishing.

New Riders Publishing

The staff of New Riders is committed to bringing you the very best in computer reference material. Each New Riders book is the result of months of work by authors and staff who research and refine the information contained within its covers.

As part of this commitment to you, the reader, New Riders invites your input. Please let us know if you enjoy this book, if you have trouble with the information and examples presented, or if you have a suggestion for the next edition.

Please note, though: New Riders staff cannot serve as a technical resource for the World Wide Web or for questions about software- or hardware-related problems. Moreover, the World Wide Web is a dynamic environment that changes daily. Because changes will inevitably have taken place between the time of this book's compilation and its publication date, New Riders welcomes and solicits your feedback regarding inaccuracies or possible improvements and additions for subsequent editions. We, therefore, invite you to fill out the form provided for this purpose in the back of this book.

If you have a question or comment about any New Riders book, there are several ways to contact us. We will respond to as many readers as we can. Your name, address, or phone number will never become part of a mailing list or be used for any purpose other than to help us continue to bring you the best books possible. You can write us at the following address:

New Riders
Attn: Publisher
201 W. 103rd Street
Indianapolis, IN 46290

If you prefer, you can fax New Riders at (317) 581-4670.

You can send e-mail to New Riders at the following Internet address:

edulaney@newriders.mcp.com

Or you may visit the New Riders Web site at the following location:

http://www.mcp.com/newriders

NRP is an imprint of Macmillan Computer Publishing. To obtain a catalog or information, or to purchase any Macmillan Computer Publishing book, call (800) 428-5331.

Thank you for selecting this directory!

Chapter 1
Introducing the World Wide Web

Before there was the World Wide Web, before there was an Internet, there was the dream of Xanadu. In Xanadu, all of human knowledge, all documents, images, sounds, and videos would be instantly accessible to anyone who had a computer, anywhere, anytime.

Xanadu was the dream of Ted Nelson, a computer visionary. He foresaw a world where all information could be linked together in a worldwide web of hypertext and hypermedia. In short, he saw a world where the constant Babel of incompatible data formats and protocols would be replaced by a universal library of information. It would be a world transformed; one that would have as little in common with our world as ours does with the one before Gutenberg invented the printing press.

This chapter introduces you to the World Wide Web and focuses on the following points:

- Hypermedia and hypertext

- The evolution of the Web

- World Wide Web browsers

- Business on the Web

- The growth of the Web

Exploring the Web's Foundation

Xanadu was the dream. Today we have a reality: the World Wide Web (WWW). It's not the reality envisioned by Ted Nelson—his Xanadu project soldiers under the guidance of Serious Cybernetics in Melbourne, Australia. But, although the Web might not be quite what Nelson envisioned, it attempts the same grand unification theory of information. It will change the world as perhaps no other invention has, save the printing press and the computer.

Those are strong words, but consider this: The Web can link together information from anywhere in the world and make it available to anyone. A grade-school student can jump from Dun & Bradstreet's financial information to a virtual tour of Croatia's capital, Zagreb (see fig. 1.1), to the state of the Internet in southern Africa, without ever leaving his desk.

Figure 1.1

Without leaving your office, you have a world of information at your fingertips.

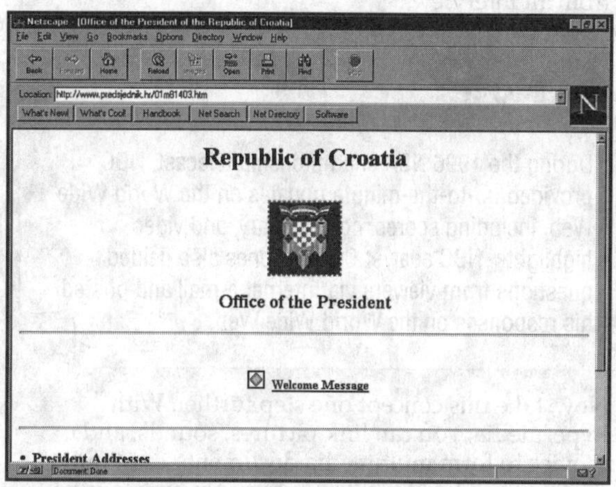

There's far more to the Web than just information. You can learn static facts from any encyclopedia. The information stored on the Web is constantly updated. With the Web, you'll always have the freshest information, as well as a seemingly endless archive of reference material.

The Web also dynamically links information into a seamless whole. You may start your information hunt next door and finally track down your quarry somewhere in Singapore. From where you sit, however, there's no difference between the two online data sources. The Web enables you to move around the world as easily as to the local library—with a click of a mouse.

The Web manages this feat by employing the twin concepts of *hypertext* and *hypermedia*. Both concepts date back to Ted Nelson.

Looking at Hypermedia

In hypertext, related information is linked together. Instead of being forced to move linearly from page 1 to page 2 and so on, a hypertext document lets you leap from word to word using links.

In a hypertext encyclopedia, for example, you could be reading about Michael Jordan and find a reference to the Chicago Bulls winning the NBA championship in 1996, and that makes you wonder which team won the championship the year before. In an ordinary book, you're stuck; you must either go to the index or continue reading through the book searching for the information you seek. In hypertext, however, a simple click on the phrase "NBA championship" can take you to the next occurrence of the phrase or to a fuller description of the NBA championship's history. With the addition of multimedia items in Web pages now, you might even get a video clip of a game or an audio clip taken from an interview.

> **Note:**
>
> During the 1996 NBA championship telecast, NBC provided up-to-the-minute updates on the World Wide Web, including scores, commentary, and video highlights. NBC analyst Charlie Jones also fielded questions from viewers via Internet e-mail and posted his responses on the World Wide Web.

Now, take this concept one step further. With hypermedia, you can link pictures, sounds, and movies to form multimedia documents—not only words are linked together, but images and sounds are bound together as well.

Hypermedia tries to make computers work the way people think; that is, jumping around rather than always moving straight forward or backward. It is not perfect, of course. Hyperdocument links might lead you far astray from the destination you have in mind. Still, hypermedia can be a great help in chasing down elusive information.

How the Web Started

In short, the Web is a part of the Internet, which is a worldwide network of computers and computer databases. In concept, the Web is a client/server database management system that uses a common information retrieval architecture (this is how your Web browser software accesses the information on the Web). There's nothing particularly special about this because advanced database designs have been doing it for years.

> **Note:**
>
> A browser is a program that enables you to access the World Wide Web. If you like the information superhighway analogy, you can think of a browser as your car that lets you drive from one Web site to another.

Tim Berners-Lee, a British computer programmer, did something different from that which had gone before. He combined hypermedia with the Internet's vast information resources. Before the Web, you could do an untold number of interesting things on the Internet, but none of them easily.

In 1989, Berners-Lee was working at the European Particle Physics Laboratory (CERN) in Geneva, Switzerland. Berners-Lee faced the eternal problem of getting people the information they needed to work together effectively on many projects in real time.

Berners-Lee's solution uses hypertext technology to form a web of documents. Unlike books or many databases, there is no hierarchical structure to his information web. Instead, there are many possible connections between documents without a beginning or an end. All the messy details of how this information is linked is hidden by a character-based hypertext interface. With the Web, a physicist can jump from an article on particle theory in a local machine to a glossary of nuclear physics terms on a system ten thousand miles away. She can do so with less trouble than a reader has paging through a book's glossary for the same information.

Web documents must be written in a special format that enables the hypertext links to work. This format is HyperText Markup Language (HTML). HTML is a subset of Standard Generalized Markup Language (SGML). SGML is an International Standards Organization (ISO) standard for defining formatting in text documents. Although SGML is meant for desktop publishing, Berners-Lee and his companions seized upon its hyperlink capacity to form the basis of the first Web documents.

To access the first early strands of the Web, you had to use a line-based Web browser, an interface that was so simple that it couldn't even use a full-screen character interface. Rather, it was limited to a single line of information. To get to the interface, you had to use an Internet tool called Telnet to connect either of the first two Web servers: info.cern.ch or nxo01.cern.ch. This first version, which you ran with the login www, had only two commands: start a search and follow a link.

That link capability might not sound like much, but it really is. With the introduction of the Web, users had the ability to seek information without worrying about where it was or how to unlock it. Much of the data with which the Web dealt was not in hypertext format, so the hypertext advantage was not clear, and the Web often came across as simply another Internet data-hunting tool with a more consistent interface.

The result was that the Web grew very slowly. If you were to ask Internet information jockeys what was hot in Internet information retrieval four years ago, chances are that most of them would have mentioned Wide Area Information Servers (WAIS). What changed the Web from being an interesting, but neglected, part of the Internet to being the hottest news ever to hit the Net was Mosaic.

Mosaic—A Dawn of a New Era

No one set out with a plan to build an interface (a browser) that would free the power of the Web. Instead, Mosaic (see fig. 1.2) began as a project by Marc Andreessen, an undergraduate student at the University of Illinois at Urbana-Champaign (UIUC). In 1993, Andreessen faced the same problems at his part-time job at the National Center for Super-computing Applications (NCSA) that Berners-Lee had dealt with at CERN: many people working on many projects at once who needed to share information. Specifically, Andreessen was working on tools for scientific visualization.

Figure 1.2

The latest version of Mosaic.

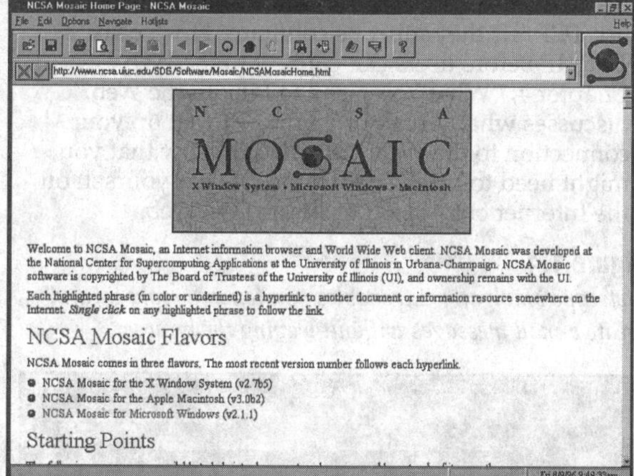

In the course of working toward that goal, Andreessen began to build Mosaic. At first, he didn't even know of the Web's existence. Not being one to reinvent the wheel, he searched for existing solutions and found the Web. After he discovered the Web's potential, he began turning Mosaic into a Web browser. In April 1993, the first version, Mosaic 1.0 for the X Window System, appeared. The program took off like wildfire, and the Web's popularity exploded with it.

Because of Mosaic's popularity (due in large part because it was freeware for anyone to download and use), the NCSA developed Microsoft Windows and Apple Macintosh versions of the browser. These programs were released in the early autumn of

1993—just in time for Mosaic to ride the wave of Internet interest to the beaches of broad popular acceptance.

Because the NCSA's resources were designed to provide supercomputer resources to researchers rather than help Microsoft Windows users navigate the difficulties of setting up Mosaic, the NCSA gave several companies, such as Spry, Mosaic Communications, and Quarterdeck, the right to develop Mosaic commercially.

This proved only a short-term solution because the NCSA found itself in a commercial world that it was ill-suited to deal with. Finally, in August 1994, the NCSA gave Spyglass Incorporated the right to commercially develop and license Mosaic. There continues to be a freeware version of Mosaic, however, which includes some Spyglass improvements.

Although the Spyglass decision washed NCSA's hands of the difficulties of commercializing Mosaic, it also muddied the Mosaic marketplace. With numerous "Mosaics" moving into the marketplace, telling one version from another became confusing. Today, there are several companies developing Mosaic from its older versions, while others use Spyglass' Enhanced Mosaic as their base.

In 1994, Mark Andreessen left NCSA to help form a new company—Netscape Communications—and produce a revolutionary Web browser named Netscape Navigator. Within weeks (perhaps even days!) of Navigator's initial release in beta format, Navigator became the most popular browser on the market. Navigator 2.0 (see fig. 1.3), released in January 1996, is still the number one selling browser, and Netscape Communications' is one of the busiest sites on the World Wide Web.

Figure 1.3

Netscape Navigator 2.0 is the top-selling Web browser.

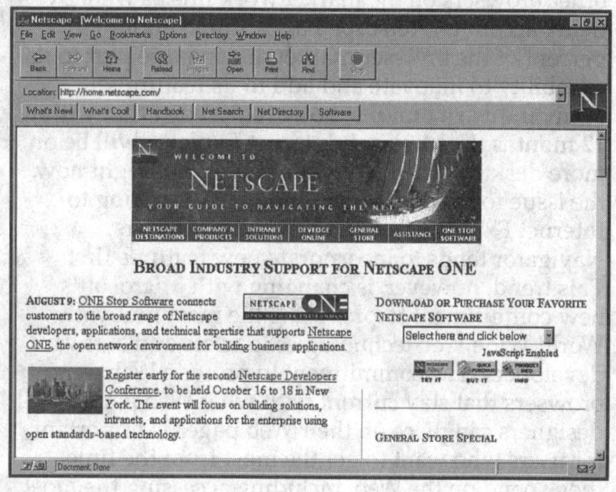

Note:

As an interesting sidebar to Web history, Netscape Communications' first choice for a company name was Mosaic Communications. NCSA pressured the new company to change its name, which it did—to Netscape Communications. A term you might encounter as you surf the Web is Mozilla. Mozilla is a Netscape term used to stand for "Mosaic Killer," showing the company's real feelings about NCSA and its Mosaic product.

Looking at the Web Today

If you are presently deciding between Web browsers, your choice likely depends upon your operating system's needs, plus the performance and features you desire. Although today you can pretty much get data from any Web server by using any graphical Web browser, in the future, that won't be the case as the Web itself grows more fragmented. Many Web sites offer extended features that require you to use specific Web browsers. Some of the extended features you might encounter include sites that have applications created by a new programming language called Java and virtual reality pages that have been created with the Virtual Reality Modeling Language (VRML). You might also encounter Web pages that include ActiveX, JavaScript, and Visual Basic Script applications. With older versions of browsers (including Netscape 1.2), you cannot access these features.

As of this writing, two browsers have emerged as the leaders of the pack: Netscape Navigator and the Internet Explorer from Microsoft. For simple Web navigation, both browsers work fine. In fact, most other browsers on the market work fine as well. By many accounts, Netscape has captured about 70 percent of the browser market due in large part to its capability to innovate and add to its feature set. Many industry pundits, however, predict that within 12 months the Microsoft Internet Explorer will be on more desktops than Netscape Navigator. Right now, the issue for many users thinking of migrating to Internet Explorer is that, of the two browsers, Navigator tends to incorporate new features first. This trend, however, is changing with Microsoft's new commitment to providing the most innovative World Wide Web technologies to users and software developers. The commitment to provide Web browsers that stay current with what Web page designers can place on their Web pages is important for users who want to get the most from the time they spend on the Web, including accessing the most up-to-date resources available.

Another problem with browsers, but one that is likely to disappear soon, is that most Web browsers are not universal front ends to all Internet services. Although any Web client can use Gopher, most of them can't read newsgroup messages, or read and write e-mail. Developers are working, however, to make Web browsers that enable you to do anything your heart desires on the Internet. Netscape Navigator 2.0, for instance, enables you to access ftp, Gopher, news, and mail services within the browser. The Netscape e-mail window is shown in figure 1.4.

Although Web browsers are all very easy to use, and they are becoming easier to install and configure, attaching to the Web can still be a headache. Depending on the operating system you use, you might spend a few hours configuring your software and hardware to work together to get you connected properly. If you use Windows 95, you have a better chance of configuring the software without too much hassle than you would if you use Windows 3.1.

The primary hurdle to cross when establishing a Web connection is setting up TCP/IP support on your computer. TCP/IP, or Transmission Control Protocol/Internet Protocol, is a network protocol that enables all the computers on the Internet to talk to one another. It is the language of the Internet. Because most computers in the world today do not use TCP/IP, they must be configured to "speak" TCP/IP before users can connect to the Web. Chapter 4, "What You Need to Link to the Web," discusses what you need and how to set up your connection to the Web. You should know that you might need to bring in some help to get yourself on the Internet before you try to surf the Web.

Figure 1.4

Netscape Navigator 2.0 enables you to read, reply to, and create e-mail messages without leaving the browser.

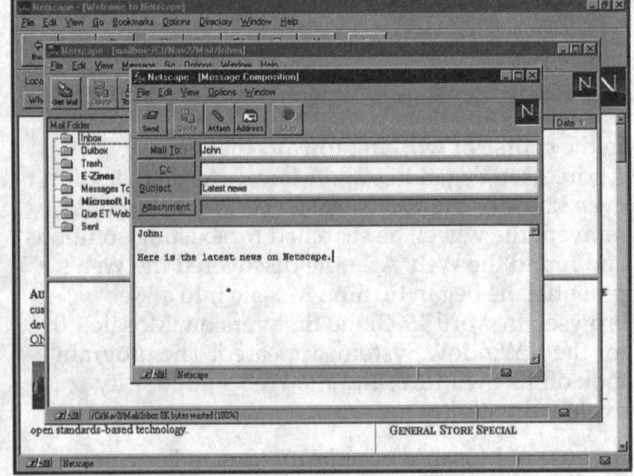

The Growth of the Web

The Web is continuing to expand at a remarkable rate. You can't watch a prime-time television show without seeing an advertisement that includes a Web site address for more information. In fact, many television shows and stations have their own presence on the World Wide Web. On the Internet, you can read messages posted on Usenet newsgroups devoted to Web servers (such as comp.infosystems.www.providers) to see that a new Web server pops up on the Web every day.

Note:

A *Web site* is an Internet system that holds a Web server. A *Web server* is the software on a site that enables Web browsers to access Web documents sitting on the Web site.

Newsgroups are services on the Internet that enable users to communicate using an electronic bulletin board system.

This surge in Web servers springs from several factors. A large part can be attributed to the fact that Web servers are relatively easy to set up and are becoming less expensive to implement in businesses and organizations. Also, as more and better HTML editors and text converters have emerged, which enable users to create Web documents to place on Web servers, new Web servers will flood the Internet. Equally important is that Web servers enable businesses to enter the Internet.

Business and the Web

In the past, because of the Internet's long-standing acceptable use policies, it was impossible for commercial traffic to use the Net. This changed in 1991 with the beginning of the Commercial Internet Exchange (CIX).

The CIX was created by the Internet service providers behind AlterNet, CERFnet, and PSInet, whose goal was to create a system by which commercial traffic could flow freely through the Internet. The effort was a success because now businesses can use the Internet to share information from one office to another. A company based in Pasadena, California, for instance, can use the Internet to access their accounting records in Bangor, Maine. At the same time, however, CIX inadvertently created the expectation that other Internet services also could be used for commercial purposes, such as selling goods or services.

Note:

These early efforts were feeble at best. At their worst, companies engaged in mass e-mail mailings and using Usenet newsgroups for advertising. This is analogous to receiving dozens of pieces of junk mail in your regular mail—but you have to pay the postage! Many users became irritated when they received unsolicited e-mail from companies they were not interested in hearing from. In response to this, users turned around and sent messages (in many cases thousands of messages) back to the original sender, flooding the company's Internet server.

The Web, however, offered new ways for companies to venture into the Internet. Here, companies can project an attractive appearance while simultaneously selling their services or goods through a Web server hyperlink. For example, if the traditional Sears & Roebuck mail-order catalog existed on the Web, it would have text and illustrations just like its paper counterpart. Unlike mere paper and ink, Web catalogs let users find out more about a product than they could ever learn from an ordinary catalog, then enable them to post orders instantly. And that's the least you can do with Web interactions and catalogs. Silicon Graphics' catalogs (see fig. 1.5), for example, let you try their high-end systems from across the Web when you access their catalog.

Figure 1.5

Businesses, such as Silicon Graphics, use the Web to offer more than simple product information for customers interested in their products.

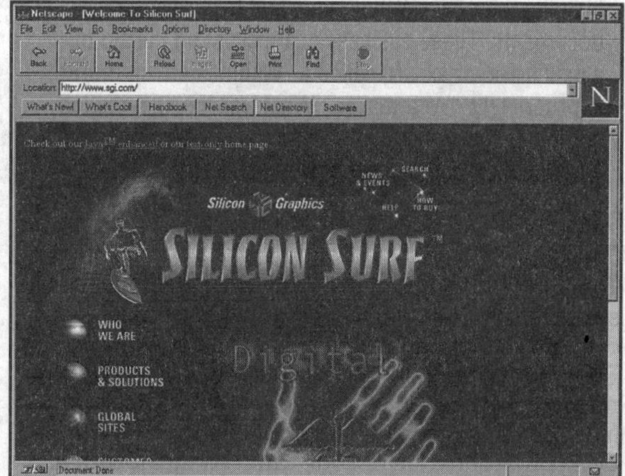

Other companies, particularly computer companies, can offer technical support services over the Web. Federal Express, for instance, enables you to track your packages using its Web site (see fig. 1.6). The

Web lends itself to this use because users can easily find their way to the solutions for their problems thanks to the hypertext format.

Figure 1.6

If your package is not there when you need it, track it down on Federal Express' Web site at http://www.fedex.com.

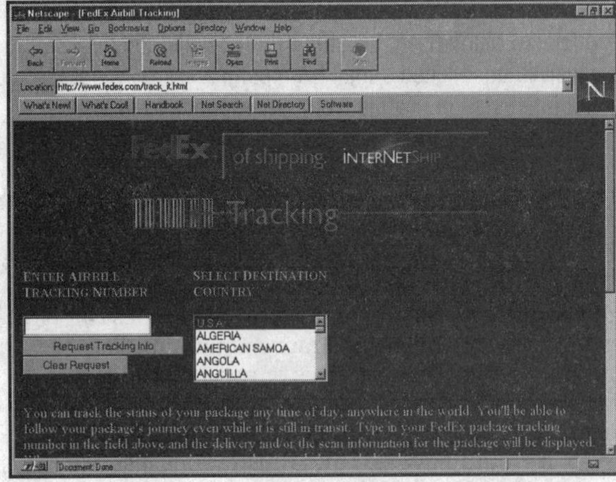

Other businesses are using the Web as a publishing venture. Their magazines and newspapers exist only as electronic text and graphics. Though this format might not appeal to all readers, it does offer a way for both old and new publications to gain a world-wide online presence without substantial capital investment.

Note:

Some companies are venturing onto the Internet by building their own Web servers and hypermedia documents. These businesses are enlisting the aid of a new breed of expert, called a "Webmaster" or, more appropriately, "Webweaver." Whatever the title, the job combines the work of network administrator, technical writer, editor, computer programmer, and desktop publisher.

To make commerce on the Web work, the Web needs secure encryption standards so that a user in Tulsa can send her credit card number to a company in San Francisco without worrying someone will steal the number. *Secure encryption* is a method of encrypting a document so only those computers that have the decryption software or code can read the document. To do this, Web businesses are building encryption schemes into their Web servers to make sure that anyone intercepting credit or debit card numbers will only pick up garbage.

All solutions come with their own set of problems. One such problem is that encryption schemes are not compatible with one another. This could mean that even if you have a secure Web browser, you might not be able to buy things from every secure Web site.

Looking Toward the Web's Future

In the next few years, you'll see many Web developments. The Web browser of the year 2000 will be as easy to install as a simple word processor is today; in fact, it will be part of the operating system in the next version of Windows, now called Windows 97 (code named Nashville). Future programs will combine all Internet services into a single, easy-to-use graphical user interface (GUI) that will be both keyboard-, mouse-, and voice-activated.

What won't change, however, is that the Web will still be difficult for some kinds of information retrieval. Although there are current efforts to standardize and catalog Web data, there is no consensus on how this should be done. Even if rules on how to catalog the Web's data existed, it seems questionable that these could be in place on the majority of Web servers. The Web will always be somewhat confusing. That is why a catalog of Web sites like the New Riders' Official World Wide Web Yellow Pages is valuable to help you manage and find resources on the Web.

Overall, you'll also see faster performance from software and the Internet itself. In particular, integrated services digital networks (ISDNs), will increase the throughput speed of modem users from a top of 28,800 bps to 64,000 bps.

There will also be some incompatibility problems between browsers and Web servers. Netscape Communications has added some extensions to HTML. Documents written in this new variant of HTML might not be displayed properly by some browsers.

A more serious problem is that as the language of the Web, HTML, matures and evolves, and as new technologies emerge to create Web resources, users stuck with older Web browsers will be limited to the type of information and resources they can access. Many Web sites now require Netscape Navigator 3.0 and/or the Microsoft Internet Explorer 3.0 to view their site in the most optimal way.

The Web's potential is as unlimited as human communications. The next chapter takes a closer look at the system behind the Web—the Internet.

CHAPTER 2

INTRODUCING THE INTERNET

The Internet is the biggest network the world has ever seen. A network is a term that describes two or more computers that are hooked together by a physical device, such as cable, or a wireless device, such as infrared or satellite wavelengths. Tens of millions of people use it every day, but few truly understand how it works. This chapter gives you a basic understanding of what the Internet is and how the World Wide Web relates to it.

Specifically, the chapter covers the following:

- What the Internet is

- Connecting to the Internet

- Understanding how the Web relates to the Internet

- Understanding Netiquette

- Understanding frequently asked questions (FAQs)

Defining the Internet

If you're slightly confused about what the Internet is, you're in good company. There's no neat answer. A definition that most experts can live with is that it's a Transmission Control Protocol/Internet Protocol (TCP/IP)-bound network of networks and their common, accessible resources. In short, it is a series of computers connected together that speak the same networking language (TCP/IP).

The Internet was born from many fathers, but ARPAnet, a U.S. Defense agency, and hence the Internet, sprang from the Cold War. The new network was meant to be one that would keep working even if parts were destroyed in a nuclear war. Data would be lost, but communications would continue.

In the late 1960s, the U.S. Department of Defense's Advanced Research Projects Agency (ARPA) set about developing a network that tied together geographically distant computers using a technology of sharing data lines called packet-switching. In short, packet-switching lets data be divided into small chunks and sent across data lines (such as telephone lines) to another computer or to several computers. When the chunks of data arrive at the other end, they are assembled again in the original form.

From this original Internet (called the DARPAnet at the time) came other services such as e-mail, file transfer protocol (ftp), and Gopher. Eventually, the World Wide Web was added as well.

One service, Usenet newsgroups, though often confused with the Internet, is actually only one of its supersets. Usenet really isn't a network at all, but a distribution system whose messages consist of e-mail and publicly available messages bundled by topic (known as newsgroups).

Beyond even the Internet and Usenet is what Internet expert John Quartermain calls the Matrix. The Matrix is the sum of all networks that can communicate with each other. Every bulletin board system with Internet mail capacity and all important online services, such as America Online, CompuServe, and the Microsoft Network, are all part of the Matrix. In short, the Matrix is the superset of all networks that can communicate with each other—including the Internet.

Note:

The Internet is big and getting bigger every day. Although much of this growth springs from new Internet machines coming online, the major commercial online services are also merging with the Internet. America Online, CompuServe, and the Microsoft Network have added direct connections to the Internet by providing TCP/IP support to the Internet. This means that consumers can purchase an account with one of these services to get Internet and Web access, as well as access the propriety information on the commercial service.

Who controls the Internet? Although there's no grand committee of scientists or a federal agency in charge of the Internet, there are organizations that guide the Internet. These groups, such as the Internet Society (ISOC), Internet Engineering Task Force (IETF), and the Internet Architecture Board (IAB), try to direct, design, and approve changes in the Internet. These groups lead the worldwide Internet community by consensus rather than by any dicta or legal authority.

When someone wants to make a change to the Internet they submit a proposal to the IETF in the form of a Request for Proposal (usually referred to as RFCs). RFC documents, which automatically expire after six months, are essentially working notes, and not hard and fast standards. You can find all of the submitted RFCs by visiting the IETF Web site at `http://www.ietf.org`.

The Internet is no one's property. It's an open network that welcomes anyone who can connect with it and obey the rules of the road. You might think of the Internet as being the property of your

Internet provider or your Internet software company; it's not. Although the Internet isn't free, one way or the other, access is always paid for. No company or government has any claim over its totality. Parts, to be sure, are controlled by companies such as IBM or consortiums such as the Commercial Internet Exchange (CIX, pronounced *kicks*), but even the largest group holds only a part of the whole Internet picture.

Looking at TCP/IP

In the early '70s, work progressed on a network protocol that could handle interconnecting heterogeneous networks. The resulting protocol was Transmission Control Protocol/Internet Protocol (TCP/IP). TCP/IP's great strength is that it easily enables computers of different architectures and operating systems to communicate with each other.

For the Internet to make any sense of where a message or file should go, an addressing scheme is needed. On the Internet, each Internet host (or server) has a domain name. A domain name consists of labels separated by periods, such as in the following example:

`vna.digex.net.`

Computers don't understand the English language, as shown in the preceding domain name. What the Internet hosts use as addresses are IP addresses, which are integers separated by periods. In the preceding example, vna.digex.net's IP address is 164.109.213.7. Web addresses, such as www.disney.com, are actually IP addresses using the domain name addressing scheme. As you can see, it's much easier to remember domain names instead of a string of seemingly arbitrary numbers.

When you connect to the Internet, you must have a unique IP address that identifies you. You receive this IP address from your network administrator if you connect to the Internet using a local area network (such as at work) or an Internet Service Provider (ISP), which is usually the case if you connect to the Internet using a modem.

Note:

In many cases when you dial into the Internet through an ISP, you are assigned a dynamic IP address. Dynamic IP addresses are not permanently assigned to you but are assigned from a pool of IP addresses when you log into the ISP.

Normally, no one has to worry about IP addresses because the distributed name and address directory program, the Domain Name System (DNS), takes care of translating from domain names to IP addresses. This is a significant TCP/IP advantage. Sometimes, however, your DNS server will either be down or its address list will be incorrect. In that case, you might need to use the actual IP address to access the service or Web site.

Another TCP/IP advantage is that it's not bound in any way to a physical medium. Whether it's wireless, token-ring, ordinary phone lines, or smoke signals, if you can transmit data through it, you can use TCP/IP on it. This interoperability is an important issue because of the diversity of computer systems and operating systems around the World connected to the Internet. If a system in Paris, France offers an online tour of Le Louvre Museum on a Sun Sparc Station (a type of computer that runs Unix), for example, you can view the site via the Web even if you are sitting in Chicago, IL running a Windows 95 computer. TCP/IP makes this connectivity possible.

Connecting to the Internet

There are three different end-user Internet connection levels, all of which spring from Internet Points of Presence (POP). An Internet Point of Presence is simply a place with modems, routers, and terminal servers that enables outside users to call in and connect to the Internet. The types of connections that are available as follows:

- Unix-to-Unix Copy Protocol (UUCP)

- Shell

- IP

Note:

If you're interested in what happens when you call a POP, read this. If not, skip to the section "Making IP Connections." When you call a POP, you first connect with a modem. Your signal is then relayed to a server, which translates your call into TCP/IP data. The server then sends your transformed data to the local Internet host computer. In return, the server translates the Internet's computer responses into signals that your modem understands. The host computer, in turn, uses special networking hardware called routers to connect with the rest of the Internet. From where you sit, this process is completely invisible.

The only type of connection you should use to connect to the World Wide Web is IP. Although the other two connections enable you to connect to the Internet, and, in the case of the shell connection to the Web, you can't get all the features of the Web using these two connections. For this reason, only the IP connection is discussed here.

Making IP Connections

There are two ways to make an IP connection to the Internet when you dial into an ISP using a modem—SLIP and PPP. The method used is determined by the service you dial into. The oldest method is SLIP, Serial Line Internet Protocol, and is generally associated with older Unix systems. SLIP connections can still be made using Windows or Macintosh computers, but the installation process is usually difficult.

SLIP, although still popular, is slowly being over-hauled by Point-to-Point Protocol (PPP). One advantage that PPP has over SLIP is that it can automatically assign IP addresses, making it easier for the general populace (such as you and me) to establish an Internet connection. PPP can also encapsulate other network layer protocols, such as Novell NetWare's IPX, instead of just IP. The latter makes PPP useful for hooking into non-TCP/IP networks that are connected to the Internet by a router.

With either SLIP or PPP, your machine becomes an actual part of the Internet. To make use of the connection to the Internet and to access the Web, you also need TCP/IP programs, such as Telnet, ftp, or Web browsers (such as Netscape Navigator), installed on your computer.

Note:

There are several advantages to accessing the Internet through an IP connection. For instance, you can run multiple programs at once. In one Telnet window, you can be chatting with someone using Internet Relay Chat (IRC), transferring a file using an ftp utility, while at the same time surfing the Web using a Web browser.

Defining the Internet/Web Relationship

"So how does the Web fit into all this?" you ask. Very easily, actually. From a structural point of view, the Web is made up of four parts, as follows:

- Browser

- Hypermedia Documents

- HyperText Transfer Protocol (HTTP)

- Uniform Research Locator (URL)

Before we go into specifics, here are the basics. Like the Internet, the Web isn't under anyone's control. It is simply an open set of standards that work because everyone who uses it agrees to play by its rules.

The World Wide Web Consortium (W3C) guides the Web. The goal of the W3C is to develop the Web into a global information infrastructure capable of supporting commercial as well as research activities. In particular, the W3C intends to make sure that the Web doesn't fragment into incompatible sub-webs. There are other groups that shepherd the Web. Perhaps the most important of them is the same Internet Engineering Task Force (IETF) that establishes technical guidelines for the Internet.

The reason for this close relationship between the Internet and the Web is quite simple: The Web can't exist without the Internet. The Web runs on the Internet like cars over bridges.

Web Browsers

A browser is the client in the Web's client-server model. A client program is one that you interact with. The server, which you don't touch, supplies information to the client as it relays your requests to it. In short, a browser is your gateway to the Web. Everything that you see on the Web passes through the lens of your browser.

A browser can display only files that it understands. Most files you'll run into will be hypermedia files written in the HyperText Markup Language (HTML), and any Web browser will be able to read them. Figure 2.1 shows you a raw HTML file; figure 2.2 shows you this same file in a Web browser.

Figure 2.1

HTML files enable users to view documents on the Web.

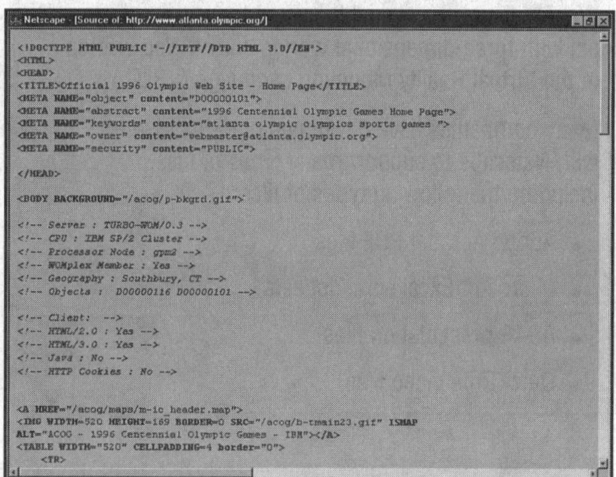

```
<!DOCTYPE HTML PUBLIC "-//IETF//DTD HTML 3.0//EN">
<HTML>
<HEAD>
<TITLE>Official 1996 Olympic Web Site - Home Page</TITLE>
<META NAME="object" content="D00000101">
<META NAME="abstract" content="1996 Centennial Olympic Games Home Page">
<META NAME="keywords" content="atlanta olympic olympics sports games ">
<META NAME="owner" content="webmaster@atlanta.olympic.org">
<META NAME="security" content="PUBLIC">

</HEAD>

<BODY BACKGROUND="/acog/p-bkgrd.gif">

<!-- Server : TURBO-WOM/0.3 -->
<!-- CPU : IBM SP/2 Cluster -->
<!-- Processor Node : gpm2 -->
<!-- WOMplex Member : Yes -->
<!-- Geography : Southbury, CT -->
<!-- Objects :  D00000116 D00000101 -->

<!-- Client:  -->
<!-- HTML/2.0 : Yes -->
<!-- HTML/3.0 : Yes -->
<!-- Java : No -->
<!-- HTTP Cookies : No -->


<A HREF="/acog/maps/m-ic_header.map">
<IMG WIDTH=520 HEIGHT=169 BORDER=0 SRC="/acog/b-tmain23.gif" ISMAP
ALT="ACOG - 1996 Centennial Olympic Games - IBM"></A>
<TABLE WIDTH="520" CELLPADDING=4 border="0">
    <TR>
```

Figure 2.2

The HTML file in figure 2.1 displayed in a Web browser.

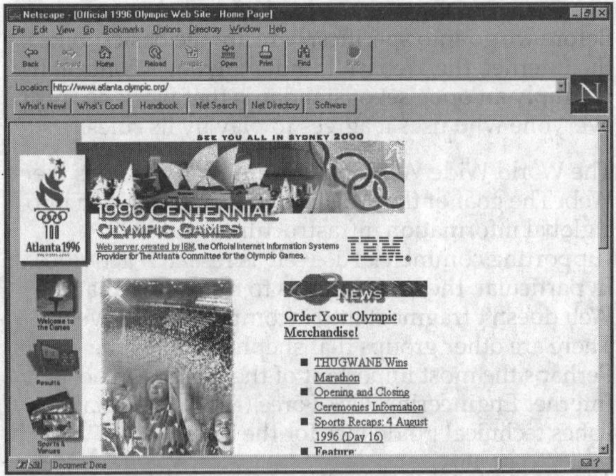

There will be some files that your browser may not understand. For example, most of the images and illustrations that you'll find on the Web will either be in Graphics Interchange Format (GIF) or Joint Photographics Experts Group (JPEG). Some files, such as other graphics files or files created in standard word processors (such as Microsoft Word), require the browser to use another program, called a viewer or helper application, to display these files. As time goes by and browsers mature, browsers will start incorporating viewers. Some viewers are available on the Internet and can be downloaded using your Web browser.

Note:

With the release of Netscape Navigator 2.0, another type of viewer application is supported—plug-ins. Plugs-in are applications that you install to work with Netscape to view and work with files that Netscape cannot handle directly. One such plug-in is WebFX. WebFX displays and enables users to view and interact with three-dimensional worlds on the Web written in the Virtual Reality Modeling Language (VRML).

Many companies have developed plug-ins to work with Netscape to support many types of files, including the following types of files:

- Adobe Acrobat PDF files
- Microsoft Excel spreadsheets
- ASAP presentation files
- QuickTime video files

Web browsers try to deal with the file type problem by using Multipurpose Internet Mail Extensions (MIME). MIME began as extensions to the Internet's Simple Mail Transport Protocol (SMTP) (see table 2.1 for a sampling of MIME types), enabling mail messages to carry binary data such as programs, sounds, and pictures (instead of just plain text like e-mail messages). Since then, it's become a de facto standard for identifying file types on the Web.

Table 2.1
MIME Types

MIME Types/MIME SubTypes	Extensions
application/mac-binhex40	hqx
application/msword	doc
application/pdf	pdf
application/postscript	ai, eps, ps
application/rtf	rtf
application/zip	zip
audio/basic	au, snd
audio/x-aiff	aif aiff aifc
audio/x-wav	wav
image/gif	gif
image/jpeg	jpeg, jpg, jpe
image/tiff	tiff tif
image/x-portable-bitmap	pbm
image/x-portable-pixmap	ppm
image/x-xbitmap	xbm
image/x-xpixmap	xpm
text/html	html
text/plain	asc, txt
video/mpeg	mpeg, mpg, mpe
video/quicktime	qt, mov, moo
video/x-msvideo	avi

Your browser's configuration settings has an area in which you define MIME types and helper applications to enable your browser to recognize and activate a helper application when you encounter a certain file type. Figures 2.3 and 2.4 show the configuration dialog boxes for two different Web browsers. Check your browser's documentation for the exact way you need to get your browser to work in cooperation with a helper application.

Figure 2.3

In Mosaic 2.0, you use the Viewers tab on the NCSA Mosaic for Windows Preference dialog box to set helper applications.

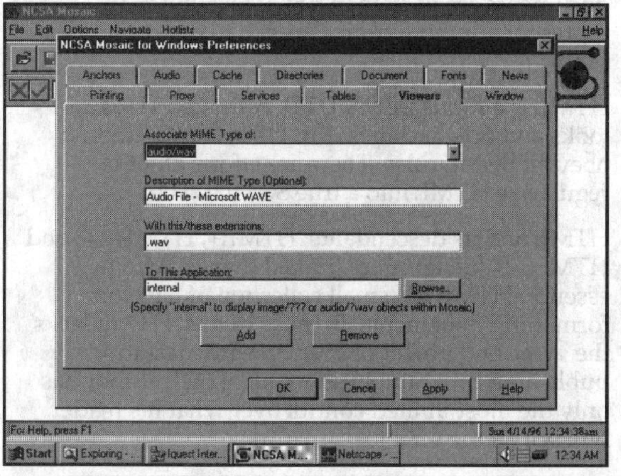

Figure 2.4

In Netscape Navigator 2.0, you use the Helpers tab in the Preferences dialog box to set helper applications.

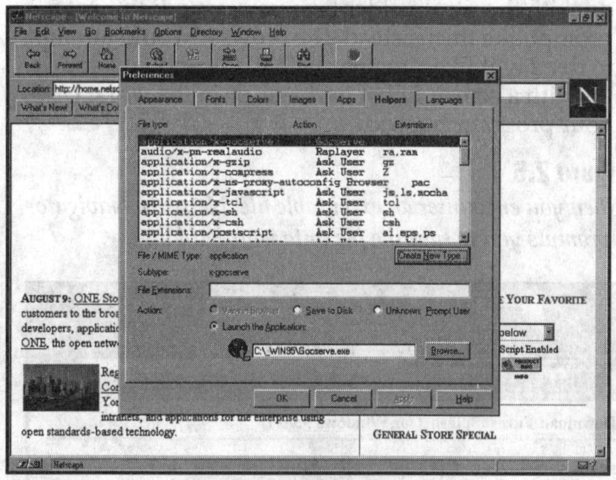

Some of the most popular viewers for the file types that you're likely to encounter are listed in table 2.2.

Table 2.2
MIME Types and Viewer Programs

Type/Subtypes	Mac Viewers	Windows Viewers
application/msword	MS-Word	MS-Word
application/pdf	Acrobat	Acrobat
application/postscript	Not Needed	GhostScript
application/rtf	MS-Word	MS-Word
application/wordperfect	WordPerfect	WordPerfect
application/zip	StuffIt	PKzip
audio/basic	Sound Machine	WPlany
audio/x-aiff	Sound Machine	WPlany
audio/x-wav (wav)	Sound Machine	WPlany
image/gif	JPEGView	LView
image/jpeg	JPEGView	LView
text/html	Netscape, Mosaic	Netscape, Mosaic
text/plain text	Netscape, Mosaic	Netscape, Mosaic
video/mpeg	Sparkle	MPEGPlay
video/quicktime	Simple Player	QuickTime Video Player
video/x-msvideo	N/A	Video for Windows

What happens when your browser can't determine the file type? The browser will display a screen like the one shown in figure 2.5. This screen prompts you to make a decision about what the browser should do with the file. In older browsers, you didn't get a prompt like this; instead, the browser would attempt to display it like a regular HTML file and you ended up with a screen full of garbage, or in the worst cases your program crashed.

Figure 2.5

When you encounter an executable file, Netscape Navigator 2 prompts you to save the file onto your hard disk.

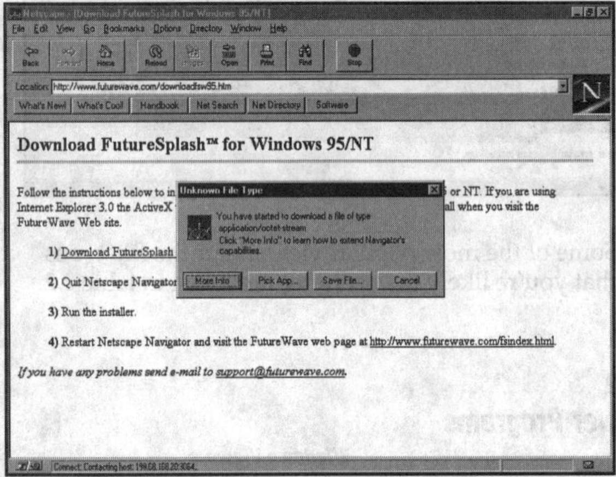

Note:

With Microsoft Internet Explorer 3.0, you can set it up to automatically execute programs you download from the World Wide Web or Internet. Although this is a quick way to launch programs, you should probably first download the file to your hard drive and then run a virus-checking program to determine if the program you just downloaded is safe from damaging viruses. After you check the program and it is safe, you then can execute it from your hard drive.

Hypermedia Documents

If it weren't for hypermedia documents, we wouldn't have a Web to play on. The vast majority of Web documents are written in HTML. HTML, as you'll see, isn't without its problems for online publishers, so some authors are looking toward other hypermedia authoring languages or systems. The most important of these is Adobe's Acrobat and its Portable Document Format (PDF).

Before we discuss conflicting standards, let's take a closer look at HTML and PDF. HTML comes from

Standard General Makeup Language (SGML), ISO 8879h. SGML is a set of rules for creating document grammars—the rules on how a document should be formatted. The specification for the SGML rules is a Document Type Definition (DTD). In SGML, documents are written in ASCII text, but may represent anything from a speech to dance choreography.

HTML is a rogue SGML DTD. Although HTML looks and acts like an SGML DTD, HTML doesn't obey all SGML rules. There are efforts afoot to regularize HTML into a true SGML DTD.

HTML and its descendants, HTML+, HTML 2.0, and HTML 3.0, are far more limited than SGML. In essence, HTML is a small collection of tags for formatting documents. Because of this, HTML lacks the grace and power of even an early desktop publishing program. In short, an HTML author has only the most limited control over what his reader will see on the screen.

Note:

The latest version of HTML is HTML 3.2. The World Wide Web Consortium (W3C), headed by Tim Berners-Lee and made up of representatives of several leading Internet developers (including Netscape, Microsoft, IBM, and Macromedia), agreed to release HTML 3.2 in mid-1996 as a benchmark for later revisions to the HTML specifications. Up to this point, many developers have created their own HTML tags to work only with their Web browser, splintering the HTML language and making it difficult for Web page authors and developers to know which HTML tags are approved by the W3C. The W3C has agreed to include HTML tags developed and published prior to December 31, 1995 in HTML 3.2. Tags and extensions to HTML, such as style sheets and page layout specifications, developed after this date will be added to later HTML versions that are adopted as supplemental documents to the HTML specifications. You can read more about HTML by looking at the Internet Resources section in the directory part of this book.

So why do we use HTML? It's really very simple. HTML is an open standard. Anyone can use it without paying a penny for it. Although HTML editors, such as Microsoft FrontPage 1.1, SoftQuad's HoTMetaL Pro, Netscape's Navigator Gold 2.0, and Brooklyn Software's HTML Assistant Pro, make writing HTML documents easier, you can write in HTML with any ASCII editor. One such ASCII editor is Notepad, which is distributed with Windows 3.1 and Windows 95.

Browsers and servers can both be configured to use HTML documents with assurance that any server or browser that comes their way will be able to use their documents. Another important point here is that these documents can be read on any platform. Whether you're using a Macintosh, a PC, or an X-terminal, you can read HTML documents.

Note:

In response to author and publisher problems with HTML, Adobe is suggesting that their Acrobat 2.0 portable document format editor is the solution. Although Acrobat offers writers and publishers much greater control over the look of their documents, and it's far more powerful for organizing documents and making them searchable, its problems are the reverse of HTML's. Adobe is making free PDF readers available, and the application programming interface (API) is an open standard, but you still need Acrobat to create PDF documents.

Another problem with Acrobat files is their size. A PDF document carries along its own collection of fonts which means that the PDF files are bigger and take longer to transport across the Internet, a real issue for users connected via slow-speed modems.

Web Servers and the HyperText Transfer Protocol (HTTP)

As you've read, the Internet and WWW comprises many computers connected in a large, worldwide network. Not all of these computers on the Internet offer Web content. Some offer content and files in other formats. On the other hand, many computers do offer Web content, and new Web servers appear weekly. For a computer to provide Web content, it must have the HyperText Transfer Protocol installed on it.

HyperText Transfer Protocol (HTTP) is a simple data transfer protocol that binds the Web together. Essentially, the protocol consists of a set of messages and replies for both servers and browsers. In HTTP, documents, files, menus, and graphics are all treated as objects. HTTP relies on the Universal Resource Identifier (URI), enclosed in the Universal Resource Locator (URL), to identify files.

HTTP runs on Web servers, not on the computer that has the Web browser. A Web server is software that, upon receiving a browser request, sends the requested document back to the browser. The server doesn't worry about what the document looks like or how a menu is presented to the client—that's the browser's job. If for some reason it can't send the

file—maybe the machine that document is on is down for repairs or upgrades—the server sends a simple error message letting the user on the other end know that the server is not responding.

Another issue that Web servers have to support is some type of security mechanism. Until recently, servers have had no way of encrypting information or authenticating users. Secure servers work by encoding sensitive information. The exact method varies from system to system, but the idea is always the same. Your private information is encrypted so only the receiver can read it.

This issue of security might not seem very important for most users and most sites to date. However, if you conduct any form of business over the Web, this is vital. Likewise, if you purchase anything over the Web, you want to be sure your transaction is secure.

One form of doing business on the Internet is a credit card transaction. Commercial sites must have a way of making sure that a customer's credit card number is secure and not accessible to others. Such sites must also make certain that any valuable information they send out can't be read by Internet eavesdroppers or anyone not authorized to receive the information. Business-class Web servers, such as Netscape Communications' Secure Commerce Server and Microsoft Internet Information Server 2.0, can handle these concerns. Freeware servers, however, do not have these capacities. Unfortunately, for businesses and consumers, freeware servers make up the majority of the Web today.

Note:

Why are freeware servers so popular if they lack security? Because they are free. Freeware applications, such as Web servers, are products in the public domain that anyone can freely download and use. Although the price is right, usually freeware products have limitations or lack of advanced features you might find in expensive commercial products.

Uniform Resource Locators (URLs)

Uniform Resource Locators are the addresses of Web resources. Usually, an URL (pronounced *earl*) leads to a Web document or file, but that's not always the case. An URL can point you to a single record in a database, the front-end of an Internet program such as Gopher, or the results of a query you made using another program. URLs give you more information about your destination than just ordinary file names. Not to remind you of Freshman English, but figure 2.7 demonstrates how to diagram the URL found in figure 2.6.

The first section (http:) tells you the type of resource you're connecting to. In this case, it's an HTTP resource. Other common resource types are the following:

- ftp:
- gopher:
- news:
- mailto:

Figure 2.6

A typical Web page with its URL.

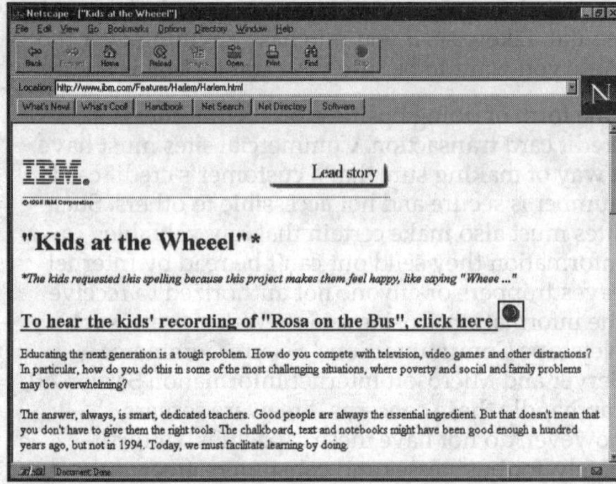

Figure 2.7

Here, the URL in figure 2.6 is diagrammed.

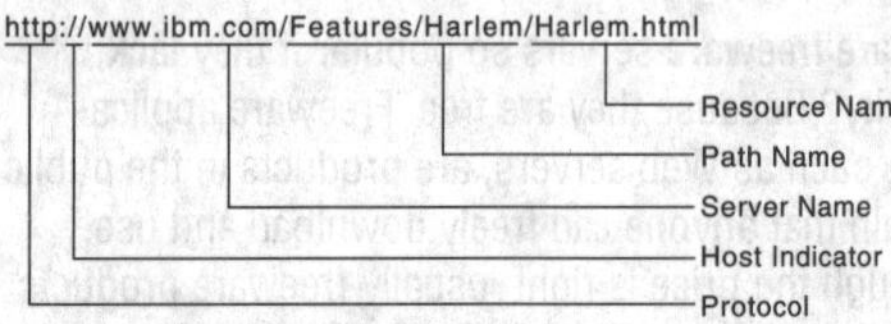

The double slashes (//) in the URL address indicate that you're requesting information from a Web server. If you are accessing a file on your local machine, you would use triple slashes (///).

Next, you have the Internet domain name and address of the Web server (www.ibm.com). When you have a complete address such as this, it's called a fully qualified domain name. The letters at the end of the address, depending on the naming style used by the site, either tell you something about who owns the server or where the server is located.

In the U.S., most, but not all, sites use organizational type designators. Some sites do use geographical identifiers, in which case they usually correspond to the site's home state. A few sites mix organizational and geographical domain names. The most well-known organizational identifiers are shown in table 2.3.

Table 2.3

Designator	Meaning
com	Commercial Site
edu	Educational Site
int	International Site
mil	Military Site
net	Internet Site #
org	Organization Site *

These are sites that are meant primarily to enable people to connect with the Internet.

* Sites that are run by an organization like the Electronic Freedom Foundation use this designator.

Almost all non-U.S. sites use two-letter country identifiers after the organization identifier (this is the .com in the preceding example). For example, ".uk" is the United Kingdom, ".ja" is Japan, and so on. (This example is a site located in the U.S. and was accessed in the U.S., so no country identifier is needed.)

In some countries, notably the U.K., the order in the domain name fields are reversed from typical U.S. practice. That is, instead of the following:

www.thisplace.somwhere.uk

the address in the U.K. would read:

www.uk.somewhere.thisplace

Both styles are equally valid.

Continuing with the example URL, the /Features/ Harlem/ part is the path to the destination file. Windows and DOS users in particular should note two things about this path structure:

- On the Web, like almost all of the Unix-based Internet, directories use forward slashes instead of back-slashes for directory names.

- Both upper- and lowercase letters are used and are significant, which means that "a.txt" is not the same as "A.txt".

At the end of the URL is the actual resource or resource name. In this example, it is a file Harlem.html. The file extension (.html) tells you that the file is an HTML document. Systems that cannot handle file names with extensions longer than three letters, such as MS-DOS or Windows 3.1, use three letters instead. For example, a Windows 3.1 server would list the same file with an extension of .htm.

Windows 95 and Windows NT, on the other hand, can support long file names. On these servers you can have files ending in .html.

Putting It All Together

When you put all the components together, the address works in the following manner. The whole network is held together by links. Your browser scampers over the strands of TCP/IP with an HTTP request to an URL. At the other end of the URL sits an HTTP server that sends the requested information back, using HTTP.

If you start with your browser and take it step by step, the first thing you will see is the loading of your default home page. This home page is the document that's been set for you to visit whenever you start the browser. A home page can be stored on your local machine or on a remote Web site.

Next, it takes your home page's URL and tries to find the IP address for its Internet site. A browser, like almost all client-server Internet applications, does this by checking with its known DNS. If it can't find the DNS, the program returns an error message. Now, armed with the IP address of the destination site, your browser sends out an HTTP request.

If all goes well, this request is received by the server's HTTP program. Normally, HTTP programs run as *daemons*—programs that are always running in the background and are constantly checking to see if they need to perform their job. After the HTTP daemon receives your request, it relays it to the appropriate service.

When your request is an HTML document, the HTTP daemon fetches the document and sends it to you using HTTP. If it's some other resource that HTTP can access directly, it still follows this routine.

Note:

HTTP works differently, however, when you call upon other Internet services such as ftp or Gopher. In these cases, HTTP acts as your go-between. For instance, when you transfer a file with ftp, the HTTP server logs you in with a login id of anonymous and uses your Internet address as a password.

This might all sound terribly complicated, but you really don't need to be concerned. When all you want to do is use the Web, you never see the layers of complexity underlying your browser. This, after all, is the idea of the Web—to make information access easy. What you do need to be concerned with,

however, is how you use the tools that the browser puts at your disposal. This is discussed in the next section.

Using the Internet Properly

The Tragedy of the Commons is a historical concept that explains the economic collapse of medieval English villages. Because everyone in a village tended to overuse and abuse the land held in common (which is where the "commons" got its name), the village commons were ruined for everyone. What does that have to do with the Internet and the Web? Everything.

Like the commons, Internet resources are not infinite. As more and more users crowd into the Internet, the "free" resources of the Internet—from ftp sites to WWW servers—are pushed to work harder and harder. In the immediate future, it will become more difficult to get a quick response from many Web resources. Worse still, you might not be able to use some Internet resources at all because they are too busy.

In this situation, you should be patient. Many of these resources are maintained by volunteers or workers for whom your desire to access a file comes way behind the needs of the group that owns the server. Getting pushy will only help bring about the day when some resources are closed to the general population. Eventually, the Internet's resources will catch up with demand, but the key word is eventually. The biggest improvement for the Internet will be the expansion of high-speed backbones. As more of these come online, the Net's overall speed will rise to meet demand. In the meantime, practice patience.

Tip

Don't take out your frustrations on your ISP's help desk staff. Most slowdown and blockage problems have nothing to do with your ISP.

Learning the Basics

Almost all Internet sites that carry resources do not supply these resources as their primary job. This situation is changing, however. Many Web sites are being set up expressly for the purpose of supplying Web services to users, not to supply the Web with information. For better or worse, most of these new sites are commercial sites, and you will more than likely experience difficulties if you call on them during normal business hours. Accessing resources will almost certainly be slower, and you're likely to find tighter restrictions on the use of the resource. Nights and weekends are the best times for Internet surfing. According to many studies conducted, the bulk of Internet traffic is between the hours of 11:00 am and 1:00 pm, when most people are on their lunch time.

Tip

A good reason for noting a resource site's location is that the closer you are to a resource, the more likely you are to have a connection take only a few jumps. The fewer links between you and another Internet computer, the better your chance of getting a clean, fast connection.

Is your session running slowly? You might want to turn off the inline images feature, using whatever method is appropriate to your browser. You won't get the pretty pictures, but you will get the text much faster.

To avoid the busy, popular sites, look around for mirror sites, which contain the exact same information as their primary sites. Once found, mirror sites are great for saving time and energy. If a site is an international link, it may be slower than a domestic connection. The Internet is global, but think local whenever possible.

Understanding Netiquette

What is Netiquette? Netiquette is *online etiquette*. In its most essential form, it can be summed up as the Golden Rule: Do unto others as you would have them do unto you.

Netiquette begins with respecting your fellow users. Far too many people seem to think that just because they're online, they've been given license to be rude. Wrong! Insults sting just as hard when written on cathode ray tubes as they do in person. In fact, words often sting even harder in e-mail and newsgroup messages than they do face-to-face. What's written in cold letters of electron fire cannot be softened by a light-hearted tone. On the Internet, no one can see you smile. What you think is funny or light-hearted might be taken in deadly earnest. Think twice and write once—you'll be far happier for it.

Dousing the Flames

Online arguments can get quite heated, but there's never any call to resort to insults. Unlike real life, where sometimes you can't walk away from an argument, on the Internet, you can always walk away.

When online arguments occur in newsgroups and they don't die down, the message threads, or discussions, in which they occur are called *flames*. When things get really out of hand and arguments are breaking out in all discussions, you have a *flame fest*—something you never want to get involved with.

If you find yourself involved in a flame, try to get out of it. Most of the time, you can't win online arguments—you can only pour more fuel on the fire. Unless your idea of a good time is spending every day arguing, the best way to treat a flame is to "just say no." In other words, you could just refuse to respond to the argumentative message, or you could send one last message saying, "I have my view, you have your view, we don't agree; I'm not going to post to you on the newsgroup or the mailing list about this issue anymore." That's it.

If you can't stand hearing from someone again, check to see if your browser's newsreader has an automatic kill function, which is a setting that automatically deletes someone's message based on their Internet address, subject matter, or what have you. That way, you never have to read another word from whoever is annoying you.

Signatures

There are other points of netiquette that are important. First, when you're sending e-mail or Usenet newsgroup postings, you should attach what's called a signature to your message. This should be your name, your e-mail address, and perhaps a few words about yourself. What it shouldn't be is long. Resist the temptation to insert long quotes or ASCII art in each and every one of your e-mail addresses. An ideal signature is no more then three lines long. If you want to tell the world more about yourself, you can always set up a personal home page on the Web and include its URL in your signature.

Another no-no is sending a newsgroup message out asking if anyone knows where so-and-so is. Those millions of newsgroup readers don't know where so-and-so is and couldn't care less. Because almost all browsers have built-in links to Internet white pages services, there's no need to pester other news readers with your request.

Before posting anything to a newsgroup, you need to ask yourself what would be appropriate for the group and of interest to its members. The only way to know if what you have to say is important is, very simply, to read the newsgroup. Once you have a feel for its subject, then you can start writing. Before posting to any newsgroup, look for its frequently asked question (FAQ) file. More on FAQs in an upcoming section.

There are several other related issues. When you reply to a message, don't copy the entire—or even most of—the message in your response. Nothing is more annoying than reading screen after screen of quoted text to see "And I agree" at the end.

You should also resist the temptation to post messages to more than one newsgroup—lest ye be flamed. Find the one newsgroup that's appropriate for your message and send it to that group alone. In the same vein, make sure that your subject line is specific and concise.

Another thing to consider is where your article is going to go. Most of the main newsgroups are distributed throughout the world. If you want to sell your computer, it's not a good idea to post it somewhere where there really aren't any potential buyers. Someone in Zambia should not have to consider whether a thousand bucks is too much for your Apple IIc when it's unrealistic for them to buy it at all. (It's about a 100 times too much, by the way.)

The trick here is to use the distribution feature. When the news system prompts you for a distribution, don't press Enter. When you hit Enter, the system usually defaults to "world," and that's not where you want your ad to go. Instead, after checking with your POP's help feature, type a more appropriate distribution. For instance, many sites have a distribution of just the state that the system is in so that your ad would only go out to people nearby.

Warning

By the way, don't think of actually advertising for a commercial business over Usenet newsgroups. It's highly frowned upon.

Don't Be a Cyberstalker

Many online women, or users with feminine names, get tons of unwelcome attention. All too often, they're constantly bombarded with lewd mail messages or online chat requests from jerks who know nothing about them save they might be female. Okay, guys, in two words: Stop it! Acting like an idiot doesn't get you anywhere in the world, and it doesn't get you anywhere on the Internet either. Yes, you can meet people and make friends on the Internet—even your spouse-to-be—but you don't do it by pounding on every available door. You certainly don't do it by trying to smash through someone's virtual window. No one likes a cyberstalker.

When you were sixteen, did you expect to be able to climb into a car and drive it away into the rush hour crush? No, you probably didn't. You might have understood how the wheel turned, how to push down the gas pedal, and how to slam on the brakes, but you hadn't yet learned the finer, more important details of driving.

Learning how to drive on the Internet highway can be a lot like your first time in a car. You might know the commands to cruise around the Web and how to mail a message to a newsgroup, but that does not mean you're an expert. To answer both basic and advanced questions, users throughout the Internet turn to FAQ files.

FAQs are exactly that: collections of questions and, more importantly, answers. Some FAQs cover the nut-and-bolt details of getting Internet tools to work. Others are about making the best possible use of Internet resources, explaining a newsgroup's theme, or how to behave in certain areas of the Internet. FAQs can tell you everything from what the "T" in James T. Kirk stands for (Tiberius), to how to find a Web server for AmigaOS.

FAQs are invaluable for learning how to be a responsible Internet driver. Whether you're using a new resource or beginning to read a new Usenet newsgroup, one of the first things you should do is look for its FAQ.

You can find FAQs in many places. Most FAQs began in Usenet newsgroups, and that's where the vast majority of them can still be found. In newsgroups, FAQs are published on irregular schedules. Some are published as often as every week, others are updated perhaps as seldom as once a year.

Two moderated newsgroups, alt.answers and news.answers, consist entirely of FAQs and other regularly published information of interest to the entire Net community. Even if you're not interested in newsgroups, you should, at the very least, sign up for news.answers. If you're new to the Internet, you should also sign up for news.newsusers.questions and news.announce.newsusers. Here, you can find all the vital FAQs. The FAQs you can't live without are shown in the following list:

- A Primer On How To Work With The Usenet Community

- Answers To Frequently Asked Questions About The Usenet

- Emily Postnews Answers Your Questions About Netiquette

- Hints On Writing Style For Usenet
- FAQ: How To Find People's E-Mail Addresses
- FAQ: International E-Mail Accessibility
- How to Find The Right Place to Post
- Introduction to News Announcements
- Introduction To the *.Answers Newsgroups
- Internet Services Frequently Asked Questions and Answers
- Rules for Posting To Usenet
- What is Usenet?
- World Wide Web Frequently Asked Questions

All of the above, save the last, can be found in the news.answers, news.newusers.questions, and news.announce.newusers newsgroups. The World Wide Web FAQ is found in the comp.infosystems.www.users and comp.infosystems.www.providers newsgroups. If you don't have newsgroup access, don't despair. You can go to the following URL for a HTML front-end to the FAQ.

```
http://www.cis.ohio-state.edu/hypertext/faq/usenet/
FAQ-List.html
```

CHAPTER 3
INTERNET E-MAIL AND USENET NEWSGROUPS

Electronic mail (called e-mail) is the tool you can use to send electronic correspondence to another user. Usenet newsgroups are electronic bulletin boards where you can leave or read messages pertaining to selected topics of interest.

Technically, these tools differ from the Internet and Web tools in that they don't require an Internet protocol connection to the Net. They are, however, a vital resource and service for all Internet and Web surfers. Practically speaking, e-mail and the newsgroups are the communication tools that bind the users of the Usenet and the Internet together.

In this chapter, you will read about the following:

- E-mail
- E-mail addressing
- Usenet newsgroups
- Picking a newsreader

Introducing E-Mail

Even with the World Wide Web growing daily, the application that makes the Internet world go around is e-mail. By many accounts, over 70 percent of the traffic on the Internet is e-mail. E-mail enables someone in Aberdeen, Maryland to communicate quickly (and cheaply) with someone in Aberdeen, Scotland. E-mail has transformed the way corporations and small businesses conduct work and distribute information. E-mail has also found many users new friends they didn't know they had.

One of the basic complaints of many Web browser users has been the lack of fully functioning support for e-mail in the browser itself. Unfortunately, e-mail support is where Web browsers have traditionally been the weakest. Until the release of Netscape Navigator 2.0, no browsers offered a decent e-mail front-end, much less a good one. With Netscape 2.0, you get a great Web browser and a good e-mail utility (see fig. 3.1). For most users, however, the best strategy is to have both a strong Web browser to navigate the Web and a powerful, but separate e-mail application to read, sort, store, and send e-mail messages.

Figure 3.1

The Netscape 2.0 e-mail window.

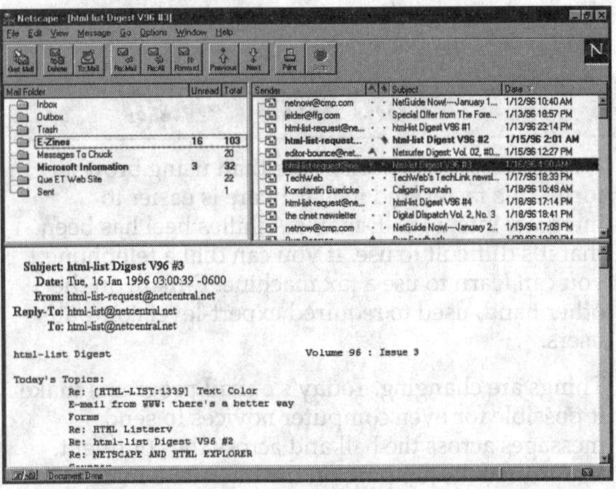

The closest that Web browsers come to e-mail is the use of forms found on many Web sites. Forms are HTML documents that can send fill-in-the-blank messages back to the Web server. Although you could use these HTML documents to build a true e-mail system, it would be rather cumbersome.

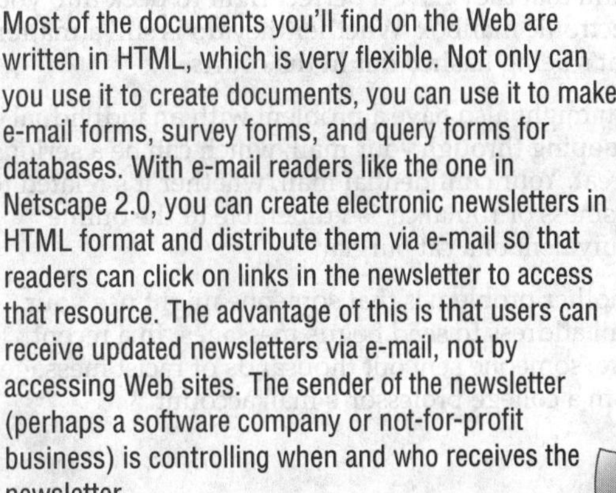

Note:

Most of the documents you'll find on the Web are written in HTML, which is very flexible. Not only can you use it to create documents, you can use it to make e-mail forms, survey forms, and query forms for databases. With e-mail readers like the one in Netscape 2.0, you can create electronic newsletters in HTML format and distribute them via e-mail so that readers can click on links in the newsletter to access that resource. The advantage of this is that users can receive updated newsletters via e-mail, not by accessing Web sites. The sender of the newsletter (perhaps a software company or not-for-profit business) is controlling when and who receives the newsletter.

Forms are usually used for feedback to Web site administrators and for commercial purposes. Forms, for example, might ask you for your opinion on the Web server you're visiting or for your credit-card number when you want to buy something.

There are many things you need to know about Internet e-mail, however, that have nothing to do with the interface. No matter the look and feel of a program, there are many things about Internet mail that are true regardless of your application.

Working with E-Mail

E-mail has always been better than using browser forms. It's faster, and its hardware is easier to integrate into a PC. E-mail's Achilles heel has been that it's difficult to use. If you can dial a telephone, you can learn to use a fax machine. E-mail, on the other hand, used to required expert-level computer users.

Things are changing. Today's e-mail programs make it possible for even computer novices to send messages across the hall and across the continent. Unfortunately, jumping on the Internet e-mail bandwagon still isn't easy. E-mail interfaces are far more friendly than they once were, but difficulties still abound. The following sections examine some of these concerns.

E-Mail Problems: Privacy

First, e-mail is not the U.S. Postal Service. Large gray areas exist in the law when it comes to privacy rights and e-mail. If you're using your company's or school's Internet system, the system owners may claim that they have a perfect right to peek into your electronic mailbox. Whether they do is still a matter that's being hashed out in the courts.

You might also have a problem with an individual snooping through your mail, which can be a serious threat. Your confidential mail, whether it's related to business or romance, is vulnerable to the online equivalent of a cat burglar.

Another problem is that someone might use your mail address to send bogus messages. In a recent case, someone sent out thousands of racist messages from a college professor's mail account.

Tip

Sounds unlikely doesn't it? Maybe not. Consider that one rude electronic note to your boss, a colleague, or a client, by someone else's hand—but in your name—

could prove disastrous. At the very least, turn off your Internet connection when you're not around.

To combat online peeping Toms, you must employ some security basics. First, security starts with people. An old cracker joke, that's painfully true, is that the easiest way to break into a system is to make friends with someone in the office. (And in case you are not aware of the difference, *crackers* are hackers with criminal intent. Hackers hack for the heck of it.)

If you want to make sure that your secrets don't walk, you can start by making sure that your password isn't easy to guess, changing it on a regular basis, and not telling anyone what it is. Equally important, don't write it down on paper or in your desk. Too many people do this, and every snoop knows it.

Another way to safeguard your privacy is to use an encryption program with your e-mail. By far the most popular of these on the Internet is Philip Zimmerman's Pretty Good Privacy (PGP). PGP encrypts your mail so that nobody but the intended recipient can read it.

You can also use PGP to sign your public messages with a unique digital signature. You use this option when you want to make it absolutely clear that you are the author of a particular message. If you want to know more about PGP, look for the FAQ in the alt.security.pgp, alt.answers, or news.answers newsgroup.

E-Mail Problems: Addressing

Most people find e-mail addressing to be their biggest headache. For all of e-mail's virtues, getting mail from one system to another can be monstrously difficult.

Much of this problem isn't that e-mail addressing is really that difficult. It's just that with dozens of different e-mail systems out there, it can be tricky determining which method is right for getting the mail from one specific system to another. Sending messages from user to user on the Internet, for instance, is pretty straightforward. On the other hand, sending a message from the friendly confines of the Internet to someone on America Online or CompuServe can be more complex.

The crux of this difficulty is that the "who, how, and what" of e-mail addressing is hard to come by. Most systems hide this vital information away in so-called help files. In essence, addressing really isn't the problem; it's finding the address in the first place. Later in this chapter, you'll deal with this problem. For now, background information on mail addressing might help you get a feel for the issue.

E-Mail Addressing Theory

No man may be an island, but e-mail systems certainly can be. Sitting alone in splendid isolation, an e-mail system can make it mindlessly simple to send a message to another on the same system. At the same time, it can be practically impossible to send messages to someone on another system.

The current concern with sending e-mail from one system to another, however, is with addressing. A typical Internet e-mail address consists of two parts: a mailbox name and a domain name. This address can be represented in many formats. For example, were I to send you a message from the Internet, my address might read:

```
rtidrow@iquest.net (Rob Tidrow)
```

or

```
Rob Tidrow <rtidrow@iquest.net>
```

Whichever way you type it, the important part is the section containing the *at* (@) sign. The name listing is purely an optional convenience so you'll know who's sitting behind an often cryptic address. The following address syntax, for example, works well:

```
rtidrow@iquest.net
```

The information to the left of the at sign is the mailbox address. On many mail systems, this usually is a version of your name, or, in this example, my first initial and last name.

> **Note:**
>
> Some mailbox names contain percentage signs (%) or periods, which usually means that the mailbox name is a forwarding address. When you send a note to a forwarding address, the address is expanded to its full size by the receiving machine. This is frequently the solution used within an internal network. The following address, for example, sends a message to my Lotus Notes mail account, which is connected to the Internet by the mail.zd.ziff.com gateway system.
>
> ```
> sjvn.Notes@mail.zd.ziff.com
> ```

There are fundamental problems with full names, however. Not only are some mail systems unable to deal with very long names, but some systems can't handle mixed cases in addresses. A message sent to the hypothetical mailbox, Heidi_Patton@testcase.bit net, for instance, would generate a "nasty-gram" from the system mailer daemon (an automatic mailer program) because it couldn't figure out, or, as it is said in the business, *resolve*, the address.

> **Note:**
>
> In an address, *mixed case* is simply the use of upper- and lowercase letters in an address element, such as user name.

Another concern with mixed-case addresses is that they are usually treated precisely. If you sent a message to rtidrow@iquest.net, I would get it; if you sent one to Rtidrow@iquest.net, however, I would never see it because Rtidrow is not the same thing as rtidrow to most mailers. To prevent confusion, most users go with e-mail names, or *handles*, in all lowercase letters. You would be wise to adopt the same convention.

On the right side of the address is the domain address (iquest.net in this case). At the extreme right, you'll find the top-level domain. Other elements in this section of the address are referred to as sub-domains. These work just like the Internet site addresses you looked at in the last chapter.

Domain addresses normally resemble the U.S. Postal Service system of addressing. The more specific address elements come first and the more general ones come last. There are thousands of .com sites (commercial sites), for instance. The next subdomain, as you move closer to the at sign, tells you more specifically where the user's e-mail account can be found. Table 3.1 shows how postal addresses are similar to Internet e-mail addresses:

Table 3.1
RFC822 Addressing

Postal Address	E-Mail
Rob Tidrow	rtidrow@
123 Some Street	well
New York, New York 21202	iquest or sf.ca
USA	net

> **Tip**
>
> There are two exceptions to address ordering. In the United Kingdom and New Zealand, some mailers read the address in reverse. These systems expect to see something like the following:
>
> ```
> example@uk.cambridge.csdept
> ```
>
> Fortunately, most modern mailers can handle either address form.

You'll notice that there can be more than one subdomain, which can represent geographic entities, as you can see from the Well address with San Francisco, California in table 3.1. A subdomain can also represent a particular computer in a network or a department inside a larger business or organization. For example, an address may read as follows:

```
sjvn@vna.digex.net
```

In this case, vna is a single computer within the larger digex organization. This is an especially popular addressing scheme in university communities where addresses such as test@history.mit.edu are common.

Mailing Lists

You might occasionally bump into mailbox names with dashes (-) in them. These are almost always mailing list addresses.

A mailing list is simply a single mail address that corresponds to a list of other e-mail addresses. Thus, when you send a message to a mailing list, the message is automatically forwarded to all the people on the list. Mailing lists are used for everything from keeping college friends in touch with one another, to students of heraldry, to serious discussions of the C++ computer language.

If a list's subject matter sounds interesting to you, you can usually ask to be added to the list by sending a message to the following address:

```
listname-request@domain_name.system_type
```

Note that the word "request" is critical. If you send a message to the list itself, which is what would happen if the address didn't include "request," everyone on the list would get your message. Soon thereafter, you would get mail from many people on the list telling you not to bother them with your requests.

For instance, if you want to join the mailing list devoted to Traveler, a science-fiction role playing game, you'd send a message to the following address:

```
traveler-request@engrg.uwo.ca
```

Other lists use programs to manage their lists. These lists will have mailbox names such as listserv, majordomo, listproc, and mail-serv. Each of these uses a slightly different method to place you on a mailing list. To find out how to join a list, send a message to the list management program consisting simply of the word "help."

Once you're on a list, you'll automatically get all mail sent to the list, including any mail you send. Some systems also enable you to set up your own lists. Check with your Internet provider to see if it's possible. Small lists are easy to maintain and can be invaluable for keeping people with common interests in contact.

The one common name with a hyphen that is not a list is MAILER-DAEMON. Whenever you get a message from MAILER-DAEMON or a similar name, it's almost always an error message from the mail-handling program, or, as they're known in the trade, a *mailer*.

Using E-Mail Basics

There are too many Internet e-mail interfaces to go into much detail on how to use them. Nevertheless, here are the basics for using the Netscape e-mail manager in Netscape Navigator 2.0. Check your manual or your Internet provider's help desk for more information.

Using Netscape E-Mail Manager

You can start the Netscape e-mail manager by using the Netscape Mail option in the Window menu in Netscape. When you do this, a new window displays that is the e-mail manager. (If you have not configured your e-mail preferences first, you'll need to configure them now using the Mail and News Preferences option in the Options menu.) The e-mail window looks like the one in figure 3.2.

Figure 3.2

The Netscape e-mail manager window has three panes to help you manage and read your e-mail messages.

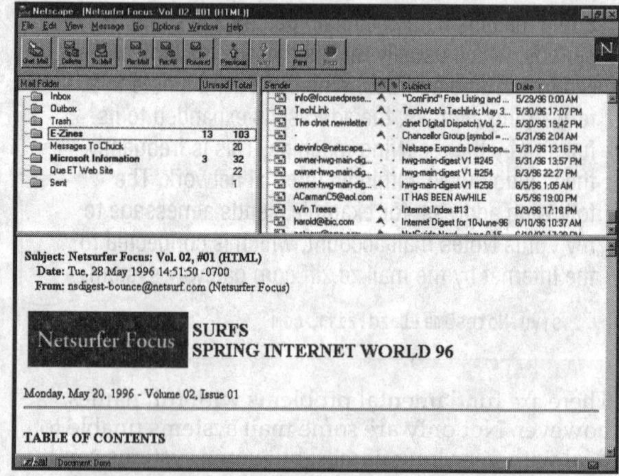

Notice how the window is broken into three panes. These panes are described in the following list:

- **Mail folders pane.** The top left pane includes the names of the folders in which your mail is stored. By default, two folders are included: Inbox and Trash. The Inbox folder holds messages you've received. The Trash folder holds messages you've deleted. When you create and send a new message, a new folder, Sent, is created automatically. You can further add to this list of folders by adding your own as you need to organize your messages.

- **Message headers pane.** The top right pane contains a list of the messages you have in the selected folder. Usually this list will display the messages in the Inbox folder to see which messages you've received so far. Messages in boldface indicate those you have not read yet. To read a message, click on its name in the message headers pane and you'll see the message in the bottom pane.

- **Message text pane.** The lower pane shows the text of the message you're reading.

Tip

The panes in the e-mail window can be resized by moving the thick bar separating each window with your mouse. You may need to do this if you can't read information in one of the panes. Usually, the top left pane (mail folders pane) does not need to be very large.

An element of the e-mail window that you'll want to get used to using is the toolbar. By moving your mouse over a button and holding it steady for a second or two, a *tooltip* displays, telling you the name of the button. At the same time, in the status bar at the bottom of the screen, you'll get a longer description of the tool's use. The primary toolbar button you'll use is the New message button and the Reply button. These buttons enable you to create a new e-mail message and reply to a message that you've selected.

To create a new message, select the New message toolbar button or select File, New message. The message composition window displays (see fig. 3.3). From here, you can click on the Mail To: button and select users to whom you want to send the message. You can do the same for Cc: (carbon copied) recipients by using the Cc: button. In the Subject line, enter a title for the message.

In the message text area at the bottom of the screen, enter your message. As a form of courtesy, you should not use ALL UPPERCASE lettering unless you want to mimic SHOUTING. All-uppercase messages are difficult to read, and seasoned e-mail readers will assume you are yelling at them and will be annoyed.

Figure 3.3

You create new messages in the message composition window in the Netscape e-mail manager.

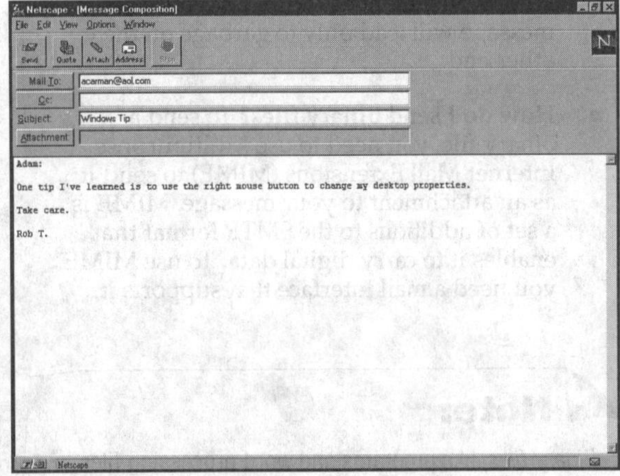

After your message is created, you can send it by clicking on the Send button or selecting File, Send Now. If you are online when you create the message, Netscape sends the message over the Internet to the recipient (unless you requested Netscape to spool your messages first). If you are not online, Netscape will display your dial-up software window letting you know you need to connect and log into the Internet before your message can be sent.

Tip

To read more about using the Netscape e-mail manager, click on the Help window and select Handbook. If you are online, you will connect automatically to Netscape Communications' Web site and can select from a variety of help topics. If you do not use Netscape for your e-mail package, consult that individual's help system or look for information in books or online.

Troubleshooting Sending Mail

When sending mail, there are several problems that often trip up users. If you avoid these common mistakes, you'll be on your way to using intersystem e-mail successfully.

- **Why did my e-mail come out like gibberish?** The first thing to remember is to send only ASCII text. Word processing files might look like ASCII to you, but they're loaded with formatting codes, which means they'll be turned into gibberish if you send them as is. If you need to send a document, first save it into an ASCII format.

You can send binary files, such as graphics, programs, and spreadsheets, over Internet mail, but you can't send them as ordinary mail. That's why trying to send a Word-Perfect document as the text of your message will lead only to garbage on the other end.

- **How do I send binary files?** To send a binary file, you need to use Multipurpose Internet Mail Extensions (MIME) to send it as an attachment to your message. MIME is a set of additions to the SMTP format that enables it to carry digital data. To use MIME, you need a mail interface that supports it.

Note:

Binary files, like programs and word processing files, can't be sent through ordinary e-mail. There are two ways around this: Multipurpose Internet Mail Extension (MIME) and uuencode. Both translate binary files into formats that can be sent through mail. MIME is easy to use, but it can only be used if you have a MIME-capable mail program and can't be used to transfer binary files at all to address outside the Internet proper.

Uuencode, in contrast, is difficult to use, but can be used with most mail programs and, if your receiver has the right software, can send binary messages to users on Usenet systems. For more information, check your software documentation.

- **What's a good program for use with binary files?** Your best move for a mail front-end/editor combination might be QualComm's PC Eudora or Macintosh Eudora, which come in freeware and commercial versions at the following address:

  ```
  ftp://ftp.qualcomm.com/
  ```

- **Is there a good way to find others' e-mail addresses?** Of course, before you can send someone a message, you need to know their address. How do you find out what someone's address is? Truly, the best way is simply to ask them or to have them send you a message to your address. Although there is a network White Pages (see fig. 3.4), it's an address book for systems and network connections, not users.

There are several white pages systems available on the Internet. Many Web browsers, including Mosaic and Netscape, have built-in addresses for some of the more popular white pages services. Unfortunately, none of these come close to having complete listings of Internet addresses. Nevertheless, something is still better than nothing. They also are not updated often, so they can be out of date.

Figure 3.4
Internet white pages can be useful, such as this one from Four 11, but they don't have complete listings, and their records are quickly outdated.

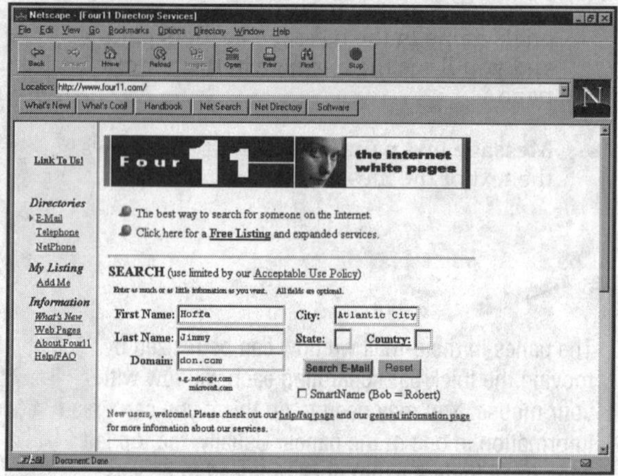

After you've gotten the hang of Net addresses, they're easy to use. You can also use Internet mail to send mail to users on other networks or online services. For the address format for several popular online services, see table 3.2.

Table 3.2
Online Service Address Formats

Service Name	Address Format
America Online	user_name@aol.com
CompuServe*	user_number@compuserve.com
Delphi	user_name@delphi.com
Microsoft Network	user_name@msn.com
Prodigy	user_number@prodigy.com

* To send mail to CompuServe users, use a period instead of a comma in the user number.

Selecting an E-Mail Interface

What do you do if your Web browser does not include an e-mail utility, or if you don't prefer the one the browser has? You get a stand-alone e-mail program, of course.

There are several things you should look for in a mail program.

- **First, it should be capable of using aliases**. No one wants to type ladeda@somewhere.or.the.other.com every time they want to send a message. An alias is a feature that enables you to type a one-word nickname for a user's full e-mail address. A good mail program also has an address book so you can keep all your aliases and addresses in one place. The best mail program also lets you store more than one name to an alias so you can easily send mail to a group of business associates or friends—that is, you can give a mailing list an alias.

- **Another important feature is the capability to place your mail in various folders.** If you're on a mailing list or two, it won't take long for your mail to get too unwieldy for a single virtual mailbox.

- **Be binary-file capable.** Your mail program should also be capable of sending binary attachments with MIME. E-mail is a great way of getting vital documents to people far away. Eudora Light enables you to attach and receive binary files with ease.

- **Your e-mail should keep working in the background.** If you're like the author, you'll want a mail program that can run in the background and gather your mail automatically on a timed schedule. This way, you always get your mail within minutes of its arrival without having to strike a single key to get it.

- **Get a mail sorter.** A good mail program is capable of letting you sort your mail in a variety of ways. Some people like their mail sorted by date order in last-in, first-out order, while others prefer their mail to be listed alphabetically by address.

- **Get a mail filter.** The best mail programs filter your mail for you. Say that you don't want to read any more junk mail from an annoying correspondent. An excellent mail reader can set up a "twit" filter that will automatically dump these messages into the bit-bucket. An absolutely top-of-the-line mail program could also be set to sort your mail. You could, for example, set your mail program to place mail from your boss in a business folder while putting notes from your significant other in a romance folder.

- **E-mail bells and whistles.** There are other bits of chrome you might want for your mail program. One popular option is to have the mail program attach your signature to your messages. Although you're looking for a mail program, you might want to use QualComm's Eudora (see fig. 3.5). This freeware program doesn't do everything, but it comes pretty darn close. Versions of Eudora exist for both the Macintosh and Windows systems.

Figure 3.5

Eudora might be freeware, but it includes several advanced features such as mail folders, signature files, and binary transfer capacity.

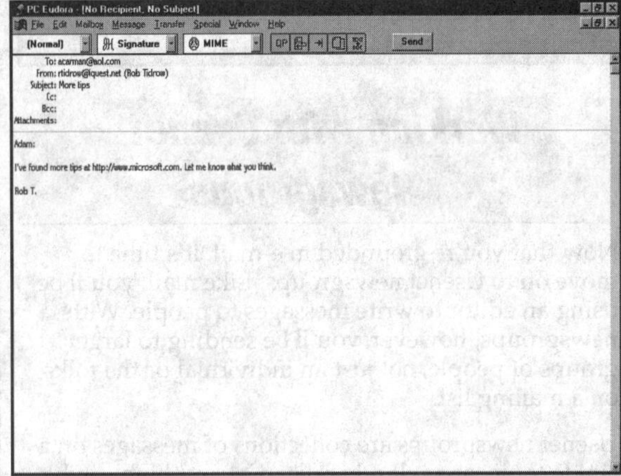

Another e-mail program you might try is Microsoft Internet Mail (see fig. 3.6). This program is a stand-alone program that Microsoft lets you download and use for free. Internet Mail features an easy-to-use interface with customizable folders to store messages, an address book to add frequently used e-mail addresses, and a message composition window that lets you add a signature file and attached files to your outgoing messages. You can download Internet Mail from http://www.microsoft.com.

Figure 3.6

Microsoft's Internet Mail program is easy to use and is free.

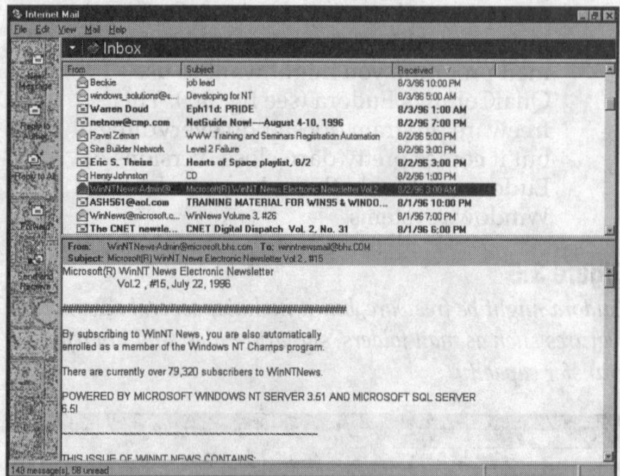

Working with Usenet Newsgroups

Now that you're grounded in e-mail, it's time to move on to Usenet newsgroups. Like mail, you'll be using an editor to write messages to people. With newsgroups, however, you'll be sending to large groups of people, not just an individual or the folks on a mailing list.

Usenet newsgroups are collections of messages on a single topic, or as closely related as anything can be in the formalized anarchy known as the Internet. For instance, whether you're a fan of the Irish singer Enya, Windows 95, or (like me) both, there's a newsgroup for you.

Note:

Usenet groups, along with parts of the Internet e-mail system, define the Usenet. Any system that gives users access to newsgroups is part of the Usenet. Any particular system, however, will not carry all Usenet newsgroups. The defining point is not how many—it's whether the system lets you access Usenet news at all.

With thousands of topics, tens of thousands of networked computers, and hundreds of thousands of readers, it doesn't take much to turn Usenet reading into drudgery rather than a joy. There's invaluable information hidden away in Net news; the problem is finding it.

Besides pure volume, Usenet newsgroups have other problems that make them difficult to read. The most common of these are flaming and spamming. *Flaming* occurs when people start arguing online, and the argument goes from disagreement to insults. These online battles can go on forever. The best solution to a flame war is to walk away.

Spamming is when someone sends the same message to numerous newsgroups. It is barely tolerable when the same message is sent to related newsgroups, but it's totally unacceptable when the same message, or a slight variation, is sent to unrelated groups. In two words: Don't spam. Send your message only to the most appropriate newsgroup.

Tip

Don't fall prey to the temptation of subscribing to interesting but nonessential newsgroups. You could spend your entire life reading and writing to newsgroups if you subscribe to too many.

Getting a News Interface

Similar to the way some Web browsers include e-mail utilities, some also include newsreaders. Most Web browsers let you access newsgroups or view the Web browser window, but you cannot respond to or post new messages to the newsgroup. You can simply read them. Mosaic 2.1, for instance, includes the news reader shown in figure 3.7. You can read, reply to, and create new messages using this utility.

Figure 3.7

The latest version of Mosaic includes a strong newsreader feature.

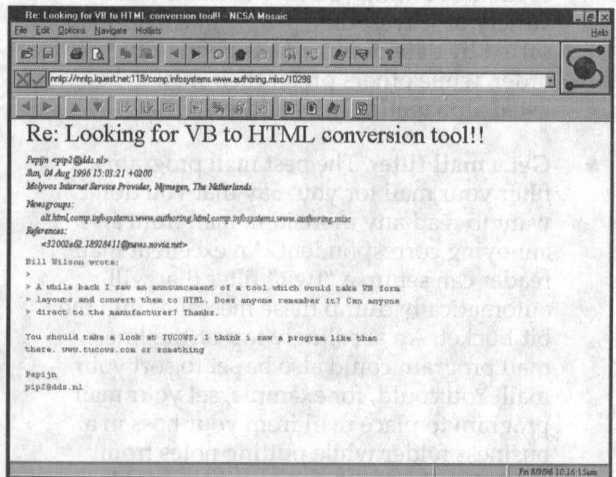

Even with Web browsers that include more powerful newsreaders, you might want to acquire a separate newsreader that does a better job of handling newsgroups. When you go shopping for a news interface, there are several features you should look for. First, the interface must be capable of threading messages. In threading, messages are presented to you in conversational order. For example, if you read a conversation between John and Liz about the Web, you would see their responses one after another as their "conversation" continues.

Some news programs only display messages in chronological order, which is something entirely different. In this arrangement, you see the messages only in the order that they were written. This means you would find it much harder to read Web discussions because dozens of other messages might be interposed between the messages you want to read.

The chronological order method is used by most Web browsers with any news-reading capabilities. As you can see in figure 3.8, one Web browser, Netscape, can handle threaded news discussions.

Figure 3.8

Netscape 2.0 includes a great newsreader.

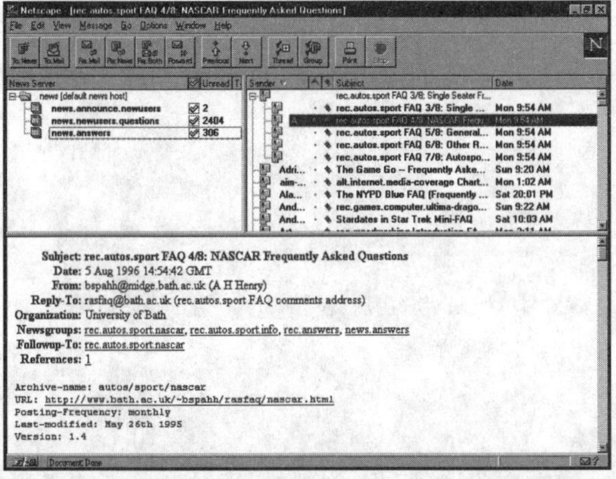

Tip

Similar to its Internet Mail program, Microsoft recently released a newsreader program called Internet News. Internet News includes an interface similar to Internet Mail, with two main panes. One pane includes message headers, and the other includes the body of the subject. Internet News enables you to view newsgroup articles, compose new articles, respond to articles, and subscribe to newsgroups. One nice feature of Internet News is its Options dialog box (select News, Options), which enables you to configure Internet News and customize it to your specifications. You can, for instance, have Internet News spell-check your articles before posting them and specify how often the news server is checked to see if any new articles have been posted to newsgroups to which you are subscribed. You can download Internet News from http://www.microsoft.com for free.

Newsgroup articles, for example, often have what's called a header. In the *header*, you'll find useful information, such as the subject of the message, and some not-so-useful information, such as the number of lines in the message.

Some newsreaders, such as NetManage's AIRNews, let you organize your newsgroups into newsgroup sections. That way, you can have your set of newsgroups for fun, when you have the time for them, and another set for business, which you always turn your attention to.

Tip

A great feature of the newsreader in Netscape 2.0 is its capability to handle binary files. If a message includes an attachment, such as a graphics file, you can view the image in the newsreader window without saving the file to your hard disk and unencoding the file first.

If you want a more sophisticated newsreader, you might want to get a newsreader program such as Fortes Free Agent. The key to enjoying newsgroups is managing the incredible flood of information that roars through them.

CHAPTER 4

WHAT YOU NEED TO LINK TO THE WEB

Someday soon, hooking into the Internet—and from there the Web—will be easy. Today is not that day.

Today, the newest versions of all operating systems include Internet connectivity and a Web browser. Unix has always had it, OS/2 Warp has it, and Windows 95 recently included it. Even with operating systems coming bundled with Web browsers, you still must have the right mix of hardware and software to explore the Web. This chapter describes the specific hardware and software you need to hook onto the Web.

Specifically, this chapter focuses on the following points:

- Putting together your Web computer

- Establishing a SLIP or PPP connection to the Internet

- Examining viewer software

Finding the Right Hardware

Most modern PCs are capable of running the software you need for the Web. For acceptable performance, you need (at the *very* least) the features listed in table 4.1. You can get by with less powerful equipment, but performance will be marginal at best.

Table 4.1
Bare Minimum Hardware Requirements

Hardware	PC	Macintosh
Processor	80386SX	68030
Speed	25 MHz	25 MHz
RAM	4 MB	5 MB
Disk space	8 MB	8 MB
Graphics	VGA	Color
Modem	9,600 bps	9,600 bps

If you're content to use only character-based applications, you can get along by using almost any computer that can talk to a modem and a character-based WWW browser, such as Lynx. Most users demand more, however. Table 4.2 lists what you

need for better than rock-bottom performance in running the software you need for the Web. Finally, if you have the cash, consider getting the Web dream machine outlined in table 4.3.

Table 4.2
Acceptable Hardware Requirements

Hardware	PC	Macintosh
Processor	80486SX	68030
Speed	25 MHz	40 MHz
RAM	8 MB	8 MB
Disk space	8 MB	8 MB
Graphics	Super-VGA	8-bit, 256-color
Modem (or)	28,800 bps	28,800 bps
Network card	Ethernet	Ethernet

Table 4.3
Optimal Hardware Requirements

Hardware	PC	Macintosh
Processor	Pentium 100	PowerPC-601
Speed	33/66 MHz	40 MHz
RAM	16 MB	16 MB
Disk space	8 MB	8 MB
Graphics	Super-VGA	8-bit, 256-color
Modem	28,800 bps/ISDN	28,800 bps/ISDN

Interestingly enough, except for the modem requirements, there's nothing top-of-the-line about any of these requirements. To run a Web browser, you really don't need a fast Pentium or PowerPC chip. Compared to the demands of most modern programs, Web browsers require very little in the way of resources.

The most critical part of any system you use to explore the Web is your Internet connection. Whether you're using a modem or a network connection, the speed of your Internet connection, more than any other, determines how quickly your Web browser runs.

Note:

Because this book assumes you will be attaching to the Internet using a dial-up connection, the hardware and software needed to attach via a local area network (LAN) is not covered. If you are in a company or organization that has Internet access through a LAN and a fast connection, consider yourself lucky. You won't have to read this chapter, and the speed you experience on the Web will be very satisfying.

Picking Out Your Modem

To get on the Web, unless you have a network connection, you need a high-speed modem with both data compression and error correction. Don't bother trying to hitchhike on the Net with less than a 14,400 bits per second (bps), V.32bis/V.42bis-compliant modem. A V.34 modem, with its 28,800 bps, is better still. Table 4.4 shows a list of the modem standards.

Tip

You can connect with slower modems, but you should avoid using a modem without V.42 error correction and V.42bis data compression. Because Serial Line Internet Protocol (SLIP) doesn't include any error correction, the least bit of line noise can knock your network connection for a loop. You need data compression because SLIP has a *high latency* (SLIP takes its own sweet time transferring information). Anything that improves SLIP throughput, which is where data compression comes in, is a good idea.

Table 4.4
Modem Standards

Designation	Definition
V.22	1,200 bps modem speed
V.22bis	2,400 bps modem speed
V.29	9,600 bps fax speed
V.32	9,600 bps modem speed
V.32bis	14,400 bps modem speed
V.32ter	19,200 bps modem speed/Not CCITT
V.34/V.Fast	28,800 bps modem speed
V.FC	28,800 bps modem speed/Not CCITT
V.42	Error correction
V.42bis	Data compression

Before you shop for a modem, check with your Internet provider to see what kind of modems they use. Although most modems work with most other modems, the odds are you'll get more consistent connections (and troubleshooting is easier) if you and the provider have the same brand.

Furthermore, a rocket-fast 28,800 bps modem won't do you a bit of good if your service supports only speeds up to 14,400 bps. Even if you decide not to get a twin of your provider's modem, the company can advise you which modems to avoid. Remember, not all modems are created equal.

Note:

Not all telephone lines are created equal, either. Normal analog telephone lines were never meant to handle high-speed data transfers. Your connection may rarely get up to its theoretical top speed. Go ahead and have your telephone company check your line, but don't be surprised if your speed doesn't improve, even on a "repaired" line.

Note:

The most important modem standards are made by the Consultative Committee for International Telephony and Telegraphy (CCITT). This international standards group sets the V-series of standards. Unlike some standards, the CCITT rules are recognized and obeyed by almost every modem and fax manufacturer in the world.

Other standards are de facto rather than de jure standards. Microcom's Microcom Networking Protocols (MNP) are the best known of these standards. Although no standard-setting organization stands behind MNP, almost all modem and communication vendors recognize the MNP standards.

A couple of modem terms that might puzzle you are *bits per second* and *baud*. Most of the confusion surrounding these terms arises because, at low speeds, bps and baud have the same value. For instance, a 300-bps modem transmits data at the exact same rate as a 300-baud modem. *Baud* measures the line-switching speed of a communications line. Thus, a 600-baud modem can transmit or receive, in one second, 600 frequency or voltage changes on a line. *Bps*, on the other hand, measures how many bits of data can be sent or received (per second) on a line.

Another point to consider is the difference between simplex, half-duplex, and full-duplex devices. *Simplex* devices can only transmit or receive data in a single session. V.17 fax-modems are an example of this kind of modem. With a *half-duplex* device, or when you operate a modem in *half-duplex* mode, data can be transmitted and received—but only one or the other at any given time. You probably have guessed already that *full-duplex* modems are capable of simultaneously transmitting and receiving data.

Examining ISDN Connections

Even better than any modem is an Integrated Services Digital Network (ISDN) connection. This telecommunications standard lays the groundwork for local digital telephone connections capable of transmitting voice, video, and data at a rate of up to 64 kilobits per second (Kbps). You also can combine the voice and data connections to achieve speeds of up to 128 Kbps.

Note:

There are ISDN adapters for both PCs and Macintoshes. Many well-known modem companies, such as Hayes, Intel, and ZyXEL, make ISDN adapters.

Also, if you are using Windows 95, you can obtain a file that upgrades Windows 95 to work with ISDN connections automatically. You can find this file on the Microsoft Web site at `http://www.microsoft.com`.

Although ISDN connections offer a lot in terms of speed, one major drawback right now is that ISDN services can be very difficult to acquire and configure. Many large metropolitan areas, such as New York and San Francisco, are just now starting to get ISDN services.

Tip

Because the telephone companies continue to drag their feet in making ISDN widely available, don't hold your breath if your area doesn't have it. On the other hand, it doesn't hurt to check. You might already have ISDN in your area. Remember, however, that even if you can get ISDN, you'll gain no speed advantage at all unless your Internet Service Provider (ISP) also has ISDN lines. If this is the case, you might need to look into changing ISPs if another one is available in your area. Also expect to pay a premium price for ISDN Internet services.

With the passage of the telecommunications bill in February 1996, many cable television providers are looking into providing Internet connectivity to homes and businesses. Some test sites have already been set up to test this technology. If it works out—which seems likely—you soon may be able to use cable TV lines to hook into the Internet at high speeds of 10 Mbps, or even faster. One Long Island cable television company is experimenting with 16 Mbps speeds, which is fast enough for television-like video streams.

Choosing CPU System Speed

Believe it or not, system CPU speed is probably the least important factor in putting together a Web-capable system. That's because your overall speed is dictated by the entire system's slowest component, which, on the Web, is almost certainly going to be your modem or the network itself.

But don't dig out your 4.77 MHz IBM PC from the attic. You do need some system speed to be happy with your Web connection. The recommendation is to go no slower than a 25 MHz processor on any PC.

And you don't have to worry about floating point units (FPU), also known as math co-processors. No Internet-related programs use these chips.

Note:

An exception to the preceding statement is when you encounter Web sites that include applications created using new programming languages, such as Java and ActiveX Java. Java is a language that enables developers to create applications that are not platform- or operating system-specific. The developers then can post these programs on the Web for users to interact with while online. Depending on the type of program (Java programs included in Web sites are called Java *applets*) and size of it, you might want to go with a fast processor for your base system. It's hard to go wrong with a Pentium processor that is at least 75 MHz.

ActiveX, formerly called Object Linking and Embedding (OLE), is a technology by Microsoft designed to distribute applications, audio, video, animations, and interactivity to the World Wide Web. ActiveX is designed to work with the Microsoft Internet Explorer 3.0 Web browser and other Microsoft applications to extend the Web from a passive client/server distribution medium to a more interactive environment. Like Java, however, ActiveX requires more system resources than a standard Web-surfing computer.

Also, CPU speed is important in translating graphics and PostScript files into viewable formats. If you think that you're going to be dealing extensively with these file types, go ahead and get a faster processor.

On the Macintosh side of the house, you needn't dither over PowerPC computers versus the older 680x0 systems. A fast 680x0 works as well as a slow PowerPC for most practical Web-wandering purposes.

CPU speed is less important than the total amount of memory. Given a choice between a faster processor and more memory, go with the RAM. With a large amount of memory, you can cache more Web pages on your local system, which means that you'll need to access the Web site less frequently. As a result, your system will be much more responsive when you need to move back to a document you were looking at earlier.

A fast hard drive is important, but not vital for decent Web browser performance. Any modern drive with an access speed of 28 milliseconds or less should serve you well.

Another component you don't need to be too concerned about is the drive interface. Whether you're using *small computer system interface* (SCSI), *integrated drive electronics* (IDE), *extended IDE* (EIDE), or an older technology doesn't matter a fig to Web browsers.

Choosing Graphics Hardware

Graphics is another area in which speed is nice but not critical. The critical factors you should look at in a graphics card are the following:

- Its graphics processor
- Its onboard memory
- Its interface to the motherboard

A graphics processor, such as ATI's Mach128, essentially speeds up your graphics in two ways. First, it takes the work of displaying graphics away from your main processor. Second, the graphics processor's chips specialize in speeding up the graphic routines that all programs use to display their images.

One thing you don't need is a card that specializes in rendering 24-bit color images—most Web images are rendered in 8-bit color.

You can still get by with only 1 MB of video memory because most color images on the Web have only 256 colors and 640×480 pixel resolution. As time goes on, this situation will change—to images with up to 16.7 million colors and 1024×768 resolution. This change isn't going to happen quickly, however, because even the Internet backbone networks simply don't have the bandwidth to tolerate the sending back and forth of huge, true-color images. If you want to look toward the future, get video cards with 2 MB of RAM.

Tip

As the Web matures and more sites are adding high-color graphics and video to their documents, the strain on your graphics hardware is going to increase. The types of graphics files that need the fastest and highest color support are three-dimensional graphics and virtual reality files. To take advantage of these types of files, invest in a high-performance graphics card and monitor, including support for 24-bit color.

For the most part, however, a standard monitor with good color is all you need if you are a typical Web surfer. Monitors that you purchase with a PC at your local computer store work fine. The bottom line with monitors is that you should try them out before you buy them. If you don't like the way they look in the store, you won't like them any better when you take them home.

Selecting Audio Hardware

Audio requirements are perhaps the easiest for Web users to meet. Macintosh users already have all the sound equipment they need to deal with Web audio files. PC users must get Sound Blaster-compatible sound cards. (That's a cinch because almost all PC audio cards are Sound Blaster-compatible.) You also need a set of speakers or headphones to hook to the sound card.

Examining Web Software Requirements

Your software is as important as your hardware. Unless everything works together as a team, you can't connect with the Web. If you already have the hardware necessary to get on the Internet, table 4.5 lists and summarizes the software and configuration information you need to make a connection to the Internet. Because most readers who need help getting an Internet connection are dialing up using a modem, this chapter assumes that. If you have an Internet connection from work through your local area network, you might need to ask your system administrator or manager for directions on setting up a connection to the Internet.

Table 4.5
What You Need to Get On the Internet

Item	Description
Internet Service Provider (ISP)	Similar to your telephone company that provides you phone service, an ISP provides you with access to the Internet. Each time you connect to the Internet, you first dial your ISP using your modem, enter a username and password, and the ISP then gives you access to the Internet. Many times the ISP is referred to as an "on ramp" to the Internet. When you establish an account with an ISP, you are provided with some information you use to configure your computer to access your ISP.
TCP/IP support	TCP/IP is a computer language (called a *network protocol*) that enables computers to communicate with one another. All computers that connect to the Internet and World Wide Web must use TCP/IP, including your personal computer. Windows 95 and Windows NT 4.0 include built-in support for TCP/IP, as does the Macintosh. If you have Windows 3.11, you need to obtain TCP/IP software, sometimes called a *protocol stack*. One such stack is called Trumpet Winsock. You are shown in the section called "Setting Up Windows 95 for the Internet" how to configure Windows 95 for the Internet.
Connection software	After you configure your TCP/IP software, you need connection software to dial up and connect to your ISP. This software is sometimes called *dialer software*. Windows 95's Dial-Up Networking feature enables you to dial up an ISP to access the Internet. Trumpet Winsock includes its own dialer, if you use Winsock to connect Windows 3.11 to the Internet.
Internet and Web software	Besides the TCP/IP software and dialer, the Internet and Web software is the most important piece you need for successful Web navigation. Chapter 5, "Examining WWW Browsers," describes the most popular Web browsers available, as well as what features to look for in a Web browser. In Chapter 3, "Internet E-Mail and Usenet Newsgroups," you are introduced to e-mail and newsgroup software you can use on the Internet. Other Internet software you might want to obtain includes ftp, Gopher, and Telnet software. Internet software suites, such as Spry's Internet in a Box, Microsoft's Internet Starter Kit, and Quarterdeck's InternetSuite 2, provide you with all the software you need to use the Internet and World Wide Web.

Finding Internet Providers

As recently as four years ago, if your school, office, or military installation couldn't get you a connection, you were out of luck. Those days are long gone. Today, you can pick from your phone company, your cable TV company, a local or national Internet provider, or an online service such as CompuServe. All these providers are called Internet Access Providers or Internet Services Providers (ISPs).

Before you can do anything on the Web, you have to find a connection. In particular, what you're looking for is an Internet provider that enables you to hook up with an IP connection. Many businesses are set up to provide users access to the Internet and World Wide Web. A few of these companies you are probably already familiar with, such as AT&T, MCI, CompuServe, and America Online. Other companies, however, you might not have heard of yet, such as BBN Planet, PSINet, and UUNET Technologies.

What to Look for in an ISP

The key to finding an Internet provider is to first determine your needs and wants for accessing the Internet. Some of the reasons you might want to connect to the Internet are given in the following list:

- Your business or career requires you to work online, including using e-mail, transferring files, and using Web resources.

- You are interested in connecting to the Internet for recreational purposes, perhaps to replace your television viewing time with Web surfing.

- You want to get your children acclimated to working online and accessing the large repositories of information and data available on the Internet and Web.

- You want to set up a business online and offer services and products using the Web as a marketing tool.

Unless you use an ISP in your local phone service area, one of the first things you need to ask a potential ISP is whether they have a 1-800 number. If they do not, you'll need to factor in the expense of local distance tolls, in addition to the basic monthly surcharge for the service. This is one hidden cost that many users in rural areas do not realize until they receive their first month's phone bill after they attach to the Internet. They are amazed at how much time they actually spend online, racking up long distance charges without knowing it.

Some other options you should look for in an ISP include the following:

- **24-hour, 7-day a week customer service.** Many users do not turn on their computer to "surf" until late in the evening when the kids fall asleep or on weekends (instead of mowing the lawn). Make sure that your ISP has someone on staff you can call at strange hours.

- **User documentation.** Ask for software documentation or user manuals for the services and utilities the ISP offers.

- **Online technical support.** Along with a phone number that you can call, make sure the ISP has an e-mail address you can send questions to.

- **Training.** Ask the ISP if they offer training on how to use the Internet efficiently and productively. You can waste a lot of time and money if you don't know where to look and how to look for resources you need.

- **Home page areas.** Many ISPs are letting customers set up a personal Web page online for other users to access. Ask if this service is available with your ISP.

Tip

If you are looking to put your business on the Web, the following are some additional services you might want to look for in an ISP:

- Managed security services and security analysis

- ISDN support for remote access

- 24-hour, 7-day customer service for security and access questions

- Web page creation and maintenance services

Where to Find ISPs

After you understand your needs, you can look at the different payment schemes that providers offer and go about locating providers in your area. People in suburban and urban areas have the advantage over their country cousins. If you're in or near a city, you can find an Internet provider by looking in the business section of your local newspaper. If that doesn't work, ask around your circle of friends or business associates.

Another source of information is computer and technical magazines. Many Internet providers advertise nationally. In particular, look for copies of *BoardWatch*, *Internet World*, and *NetGuide*, all of which are reputable magazines that offer extensive coverage of the Internet and other online services.

You should also call your local phone company or your long-distance provider to inquire about Web access. MCI's InternetMCI package, for instance, enables customers to access the Web with Netscape Communications' Netscape browser.

Tip

It's not easy to tell which Internet service is good and which isn't. Word of mouth usually concentrates on support, or the lack thereof. The problem with this is that almost all Internet providers these days are on the verge of being swamped. A system with good service today might have bad service tomorrow because of increased business. If a service seems to consistently have a bad reputation, then stay away; otherwise, give them the benefit of the doubt.

Table 4.6 is a comprehensive list of National ISPs. Because rates change about every month (fortunately they are tending to go down instead of rising), you should contact several of these ISPs for more information about the services they offer and their monthly rates. Lately, the going rate for most national ISPs, including AT&T Worldnet, is $19.95 per month for unlimited hours. Some other services have rates of around $6.95 per month and you get 5 hours of "free" access time per month. Additional charges are added for each hour over the first 5 hours (usually around $2.00/hour).

Table 4.6
National ISPs

Company Name	Contact Information
Ans CO+RE Systems, Inc	Elmsord, N.Y. (800) 456-8267 http://www.ans.net
AT&T Worldnet	Bridgewater, N.J. (800) 967-5363 http://www.att.com/worldnet
BBN Planet	Cambridge, MA (800) 472-4565 http://www.bbn.com
CerfNet, Inc.	San Diego, CA (800) 876-4103 http://www.cerf.net
CompuServe, Inc	Columbus, OH (800) 524-3388 http://www.compuserve.com
Global Enterprise Services, Inc.	Princeton, N.J. (609) 897-7300 http://www.ges.com

Company Name	Contact Information
IBM Internet Connection	Armonk, N.Y. (800) 888-4103 http://www.ibm.com/globalnetwork
MCI Telecommunication, Inc.	Washington, D.C. (800) 550-0927 http:// www.internetmci.com
Netcom On-Line Communications Services, Inc.	San Jose, CA (800) 353-6600 http://www.netcom.com
PSINet, Inc	Herndon, VA (800) 827-7482 http://www.psi.net
Sprint	Kansas City, KA (800) 225-5408 http://www.sprintbiz.com
Spry/CompuServe Internet	Bellevue, WA (800) 777-9638 http://www.spry.com
UUNET Technologies, Inc.	Fairfax, VA (800) 488-6384 http://www.uu.net

Although all of the services listed in the table offer full Internet and Web access, some services—such as CompuServe and Netcom—use their own interfaces to enable you to explore the Web. With these services you might have a choice to stick with the proprietary interface or use the Web browser of your choice. Sometimes, however, some services do not support other Web browsers. Although this lack of support restricts your choice to their front-end program, it also means you get better technical support from these services because the technical support staff does not need to become experts on half-a-dozen different TCP/IP programs and as many more Web interfaces.

The real advantage of these interfaces over their competitors is their ease of setup. Because these interfaces have built-in defaults about where to find things such as the DNS and the gateway system, you don't need to get your hands dirty with these details. You usually follow a set of setup screens when signing up for the service.

What Your ISP Assigns You

As mentioned in table 4.5, when you sign up with an ISP, you will be given some information you need to configure your computer to access the Internet. When you are given this information, be sure to write it down and store it in a safe place. Even after you configure your computer and everything is working fine, you might have to reconfigure your software if something goes wrong at a later date.

The following list describes each of the items your ISP will give you. In some cases, you might be given more information or less. If you think you are missing something, be sure to ask your ISP.

- **Phone number.** Your ISP has a dial-up number you use for your modem to dial into the ISP. You do not use the regular telephone number that you used to call the ISP to set up your account.

- **Login name or username.** This is a unique name you are assigned that lets you login in to the ISP. Usually, login names are eight characters long (they can be shorter or longer) and are derived from your name, such as your first initial and last name. Pat Buckman, for instance, may be pbuckman.

- **Internet e-mail address.** E-mail addresses are used for you to send and receive e-mail once you are connected to the Internet. Usually, the e-mail address is your username and domain name of the ISP. It is made up of three parts, the username, *at* symbol (@) and the domain name, such as pbuckman@isp.com. The trick to using and sharing your e-mail address is to use it exactly as you are given it. You cannot, for instance, hyphenate it or change it without first requesting to do so from your ISP.

- **Password.** When you log into your ISP, you are required to enter a login name and password to confirm that you are authorized to access the Internet from the ISP you are dialing. If either or both your password or login name does not match the ISP's list of users, you will not be able to connect to your ISP. Make sure you keep your password secret from other users.

- **IP address.** This is your Internet IP address that your ISP gives you. IPs are analogous to street addresses but are made up of numbers only. IP addresses are four-part numbers separated by periods, such as 170.203.93.5. IP addresses must be entered exactly as your ISP gives it to you. In many cases, however, you will not be given an IP address to enter on your computer if your ISP assigns one to you each time you log into the Internet. These types of IP addresses are called dynamic IP addresses and enable the ISP to re-use IP addresses when some members are not attached to the Internet. Be sure to ask your ISP if you should have an IP address or not.

- **Domain name.** A domain name is the name assigned to your ISP, such as compuserve.com, iquest.net, or microsoft.com.

- **Host name.** This is your computer's name on the Internet. Although you might want to assign this yourself, your ISP must do this because it is only effective when you are connected to the ISP. Usually, the host name is simply your username, sometimes with an additional character such as 1 added to it.

- **DNS Server.** Like the IP address, the DNS server is a four-part number separated by periods that is assigned to your ISP.

- **News and e-mail server names.** These are the names of the ISP's usenet news and e-mail servers. An e-mail server name may be something like pop.uunet.com. A news server name may be nntp.uunet.com. Be sure to copy these down exactly as your ISP gives them to you. If you don't, you will not be able to access your e-mail or subscribe to usenet newsgroups.

Note:

While you have your ISP on the phone, ask them if they provide you with Internet and Web software and with installation software to help you get connected. Some ISPs have their own software utilities that come preconfigured to make it easier for you to get online.

Setting Up Windows 95 for the Internet

Once you set up an account with an ISP and have all the necessary software, hardware, and information, you need to configure your system to access the Internet. If your ISP sends you software to help you configure your computer, use it. Otherwise, follow these steps for setting up Windows 95 for Internet capabilities. You'll need to have your Windows 95 Setup disks or CD-ROM handy while working through these steps.

Note:

This section assumes that you are using Windows 95 to connect to the Web. If you are using another operating system, such as Windows 3.11 or the Macintosh, you should consult the documentation for that operating system to see how to set up TCP/IP support. If you have a Macintosh, you can use the built-in MacTCP software.

1. Click on the Start button and select Programs, Accessories, Internet Tools, Internet Setup Wizard. This launches the Internet Setup Wizard (see fig. 4.1).

Figure 4.1
The Internet Setup Wizard.

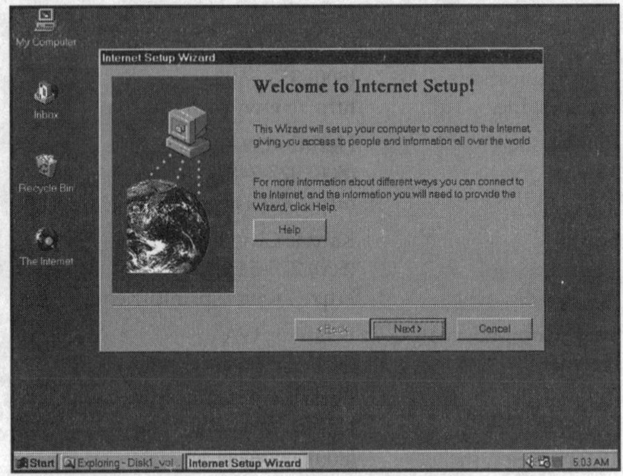

2. Click the Next button, to show the next wizard screen. This screen informs that you need to set up a modem to connect to the Internet.

3. Click the Next button to display the Install New Modem screen. Windows 95 can automatically detect your modem if it is connected to your computer and turned on. If you do not know how to install a modem, see the documentation that comes with your modem. If you do not want Windows 95 to look for your modem, click the Don't detect my modem; I will select if from a list option. If you let Windows 95 locate your modem, you might have to wait several minutes before Windows continues. The following steps assume that you manually locate your modem.

4. Click the Next button to display the Install New Modem screen with a list of modems and manufacturer names (see fig. 4.2). Scroll down the Manufacturer list and click on the name of your modem manufacturer. In the Models list, select the modem model. Click Next.

5. Select a port to attach your modem to.

6. Click the Next button to display the Location Information screen. Here you fill out the country and area code you are calling from, and any numbers you need to dial to get an outside line (such as 5 or 9).

7. Click the Next button and then the Finish button. Windows 95 completes the modem installation.

Figure 4.2

Select your modem from the Manufacturers and Models list.

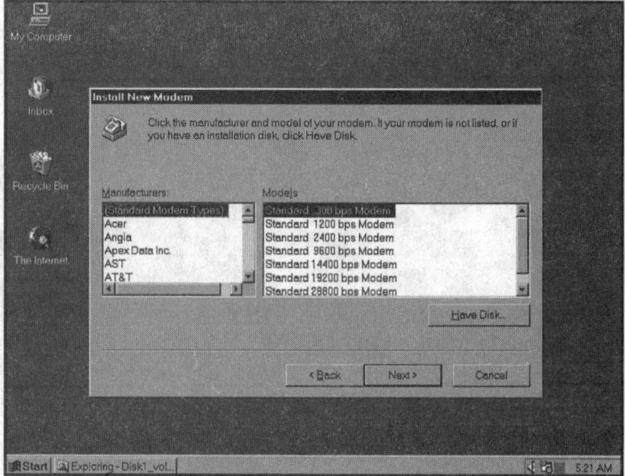

8. The Internet Setup Wizard next displays the How to Connect screen. Here you let Windows 95 know if you are using the Microsoft Network (MSN) or another company as you ISP. Select the appropriate choice. These steps assume you are using an ISP other than MSN.

9. Click the Next button. On the Internet Mail screen select whether you want to use Microsoft Exchange as your e-mail application or if you have another e-mail package you want to use. These steps assume the latter.

10. Click the Next button. The Installing Files screen displays. Click Next. If you are prompted for the Windows 95 Setup disks or CD-ROM, be sure to insert the correct one that the wizard asks for.

11. In the Service Provider Information screen, enter the name of your ISP.

12. Click the Next button. In the Phone Number screen, fill in phone number for the ISP.

13. Click the Next button. In the User Name and Password screen, fill in the login or username for your account, as well as the password. When you enter the password, you only see asterisks to help keep your password private.

14. Click the Next button, to display the IP Address screen (see fig. 4.3). If your ISP gave you an IP address, click the Always use the following option and enter the IP Address and Subnet Mask fields. Otherwise, keep the top option selected.

Figure 4.3

Most ISPs use dynamic IP addresses, so you do not have to fill out the IP Address screen.

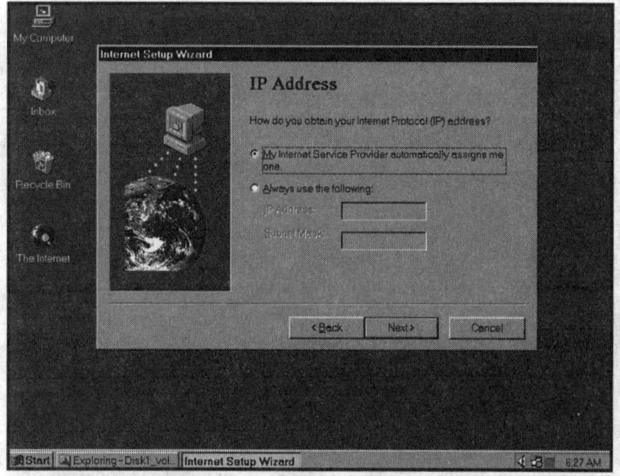

15. Click the Next button to display the DNS Server Address screen. Here you must enter the DNS (Domain Name Service) server your ISP gave you. If the ISP gave you an alternate DNS server, fill in that name as well. You must fill in at least the DNS Server field.

16. Click the Next button to display the Finished Setup screen. Click the Finish button to complete the installation.

17. Click Yes to restart Windows 95.

After Windows 95 restarts, you are ready to set up the Dial-Up Networking feature so you can dial up your ISP and connect to the Internet. Use the following steps to do this.

Note:

In some cases, Windows 95 automatically creates a dial-up networking icon during the Internet Setup Wizard steps. If this is the case, all you need to do at this point is to double-click on the My Computer icon, open the Dial-UP Networking folder, and double-click the new icon. It will be labeled the name you gave it during Step 11 in the preceding steps. Fill in your password and then click the Connect button to connect to the Internet.

1. Double-click on the My Computer icon on the Windows 95 desktop and double-click on the Dial-Up Networking folder.

2. Double-click on the Make New Connection icon to launch the Make New Connection wizard (see fig. 4.4).

Figure 4.4

The Make New Connection wizard helps you set up dial-up networking for your ISP.

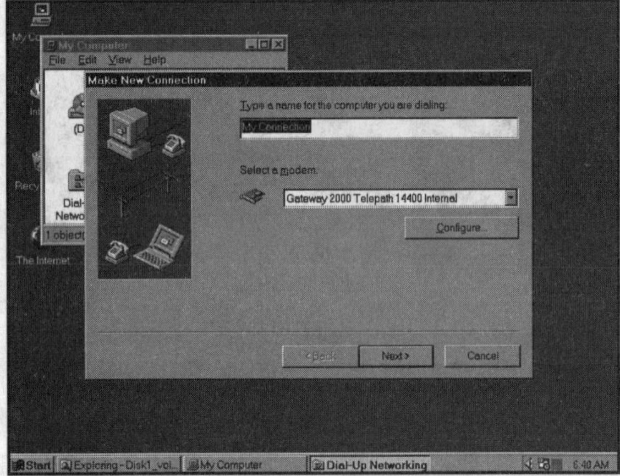

3. Enter a name for the connection, such as **Internet Connection**.

4. Click the Next button. On the next screen, enter the phone number of your ISP.

5. Click the Next button and then the Finish button. The new connection icon appears in the Dial-Up Networking folder.

6. Double-click on the new connection icon and fill in your user name and password in the Connect To dialog box.

7. Click the Connect button to dial your ISP and to connect to the Internet.

You now are on the Internet. Chapter 5, "Examining WWW Browsers," shows you how to use a Web browser to navigate on the Web.

EXAMINING WWW BROWSERS

Once upon a time, you had one good choice for a Web browser: NCSA Mosaic. Things have changed. Today, everyone and her uncle has a Web browser they want to sell you.

By far, the leader of the pack, both in market penetration and feature set, is Netscape Navigator. With its recent release of two new browsers— Navigator 2.0 and Navigator Gold 2.0—Netscape remains at the top of the charts. Snapping at Netscape's tail, however, is Microsoft's Internet Explorer 2.0. Although Microsoft has a long way to go to overtake Netscape's 70–90 percent market share, that does not mean it cannot happen within the next 12–18 months.

For users, this stiff competition means that browser technology will continue to mature quickly and the prices will be reasonable. In fact, Microsoft gives away their Web browser. Many users have two or three browsers installed on their system and are always looking for a new one to download and try.

For those of you just starting out, examine this chapter and decide on at least one browser to use. This chapter won't simply tell you to do this or that. Although it shows you specific browsers, those browsers change so quickly there's little point in making precise recommendations. What the chapter does do is tell you what features to look for in your Web browser.

This chapter looks at the following:

- Available browser types

- Features to look for in a browser

- A selection of browsers

Examining Browser Types

Four basic types of browsers are available. The first type requires a TCP/IP connection. Another type— America Online, Pipeline, and Prodigy are ex- amples—work only when used with a particular online service. (Although at the time of this writing AOL agreed to use the Microsoft Internet Explorer as their primary Web browser, the transition to the new browser had not taken effect at press time.) The tried-and-true character-based interfaces—such as Lynx and WWW—offer a third type. The final browser type—for example, SlipKnot—gives you a graphical interface while working with an ordinary shell account connection.

Before shopping for any Web browser, take a look at what's already on your computer. If you purchased a

computer in the last year that came with Windows 95 pre-installed, you probably got a copy of Internet Explorer on your system (see fig. 5.1). When you first start Windows 95 you'll see an icon called The Internet that you can click on to set up Internet support in Windows 95. After you set up your system for the Internet, you can then use Internet Explorer to navigate the Web. If you are an IBM OS/ 2 Warp 3.0 user, the BonusPak includes utilities that enable you to access the Internet.

Figure 5.1

Windows 95 and Internet Explorer 3.0 provides a quick and easy way to connect to and start navigating the Web.

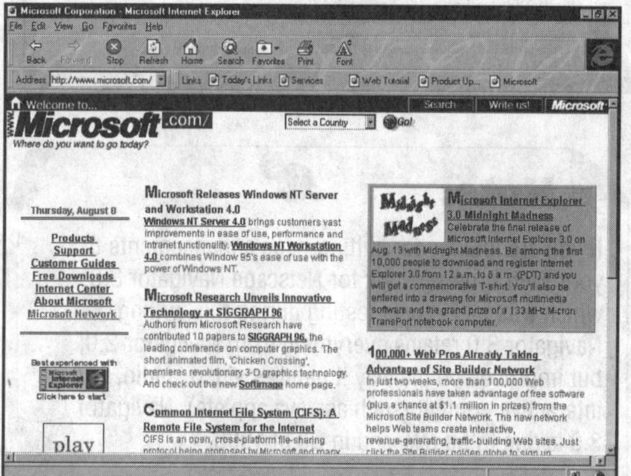

> **Note:**
>
> Just because your system comes with a Web browser, don't be afraid to look for another browser if the one you have doesn't meet your needs. With a multitude of choices, there's no reason to stick with a browser you don't like. With my current Windows 95 setup, I have five browsers installed: Netscape Navigator 2.0 and 3.0, Netscape Navigator Gold 2.0, Microsoft Internet Explorer 3.0, and NCSA Mosaic 2.01. Depending on the type of resource I'm accessing, I may switch browsers to the one that handles the resource the best.

NCSA Mosaic was at one time the most popular Web browser. It became the spark application that ignited the Web explosion. Thanks to its blazing success, the browser field expanded quickly. NCSA Mosaic has long since ceased to be the hottest browser around. That honor now belongs to Netscape (see fig. 5.2).

Figure 5.2

Netscape Navigator 2.0 still is the best-selling Web browser, regardless of the efforts of Microsoft and others to usurp its leadership.

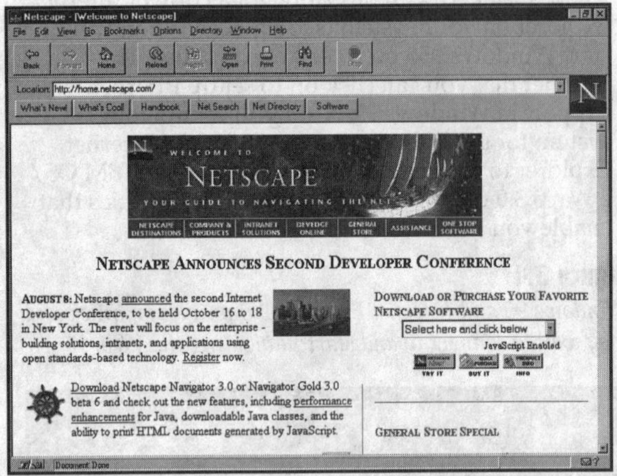

You can get a browser in a number of different ways. In addition to having one bundled with your operating system, you might find that your new computer already has the front end to either an Internet provider—such as NetCom—or an online service—such as CompuServe or America Online—that includes a Web browser.

Many browsers, such as Cello, NCSA Mosaic, and Explorer 2.0, are given away free on the Internet or online services. Netscape Navigator, however, is not free, but you can download a copy from the Netscape Web site and register the copy online for $49. You also can purchase a copy of the browser at many retail shops for around $29.99 to $39.99.

Tip

If you are an educational institute or government agency, you can download and use Netscape free of charge. You still need to go through the registration process, but you must indicate at which school or agency you work.

Note:

If you are looking for cutting-edge enhancements to your Web browser, look for Netscape Navigator 3.0, which was still in beta testing during this writing. Navigator 3.0 retains everything from Navigator 2.0, but improves on the way it handles video, audio, and interactive content (such as Java applets). Navigator 3.0 is due to be released in Q3 of 1996.

Another way to try Netscape Navigator before you buy is to become an active member of Netscape's beta program. A beta program is one in which a software company provides users copies of new applications while in testing. By accessing the Netscape home page at `http://home.netscape.com` you can learn more about which applications are in beta.

Other browsers also can be purchased at many software or retail outlets, such as Netscape Navigator 2.0, CompuServe/SPRY's AIR Mosaic, and QuarterDeck's Internetsuite. Still others, such as NetCom's NetCruiser, are shareware (that is, you can try it for free, but to continue using the browser, you must, or should, pay for it) that you can find online.

Features to Look for in a Browser

So how do you find the browser that's right for you? The first thing you should look for is a browser that works with your computer system. Web browsers are available for major operating systems, including those in the following list:

- Windows 95

- Windows NT 3.51 and 4.0

- Windows 3.1 and Windows for Workgroups

- Macintosh

- Unix and XWindow

- OS/2 Warp

- CP/M (shell accounts only)

Tip

Even if you don't have the world's most powerful system with the fastest Internet connection, you still can use the Web. The most bare-bones system—say an old KayPro CP/M computer with a 300 bps modem—can use the Web with a shell account and a character-based browser. It might not be as much fun as Netscape running on an ISDN line at 128 Kbps and a 133 Mhz Pentium system, but it can be done.

The following list describes the ideal Web browser:

- Is easy to install

- Is easy to customize

- Enables you to navigate the Web easily

- Enables you to view most common Web document types

- Supports secure transactions

- Supports other Internet/Usenet tools

- Works quickly

In addition to this list, if you are interested in accessing Web sites that offer the latest in multimedia, three-dimensional worlds, and application development, you'll need to make sure the browser supports the following technologies:

- HTML 3.2 support

- Netscape extensions, including frames support

- Netscape Plug-Ins

- VRML (Virtual Reality Modeling Language)

- Java and JavaScript programming languages

- ActiveX support

Each of these is covered separately.

HTML 3.2 Support

The heart of the Web is the content that resides on it. Most of this content is created using the Hypertext Markup Language (HTML). Originally, Web browsers had to support only one version of HTML, HTML 1.0. Through the years, different companies, organizations, and individuals have proposed new features to be added to the HTML language. This meant that Web browser developers had to reengineer their browsers to work with these new features.

An example of this change occurred when the second major version of the HTML standard was approved. With HTML 2.0, Web page designers (the people who create Web pages using HTML) had more control over how the Web page looked. HTML 2.0 features included headings, paragraphs, lists, inline images, and forms. If you've had any opportunity to see the Web or work on it, you know that these features are used in almost all Web pages now, including images.

Because the Web doesn't stop and wait for anyone, including those who are driving it, a new HTML standard has emerged over the past several months. Originally, this standard was earmarked as HTML+, but has since been called HTML 3.0.

With HTML 3.2, which was recently adopted, Web designers can do the following:

- Insert tables on the page (see fig. 5.3)

- Center and right-align text on the page

- Align text and images

- Include mathematical equations in pages

If your browser does not support HTML 3.2, you might experience problems viewing some sites on the Web. Usually, if a site is optimized for HTML 3.2, you'll see a warning that the site is best viewed by Netscape Navigator 2.0. This is because Netscape 2.0 is one of the few browsers currently supporting HTML 3.2. If you don't want to use Netscape 2.0 as your browser, you can also use Internet Explorer 3.0 to view many of the HTML 3.2 features. Many of the Netscape extensions discussed in the following section have been included in the HTML 3.2 specifications.

Figure 5.3

Tables add a lot of organization to a Web page.

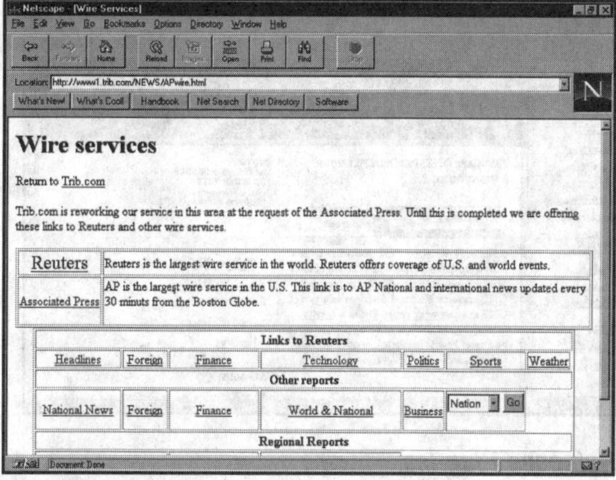

Netscape Extensions

Along with HTML 3.2 features, Netscape supports a set of HTML codes (usually called HTML tags) known as Netscape Extensions. Netscape Extensions were (and currently are) developed so that Web designers could avoid some of the problems and limitations inherent within HTML.

One of these limitations is that HTML dictates how a Web page will look on a browser. HTML only hints or suggests how the page should look. Unlike this page in this book, which was printed with an exact page layout specification, the way a Web page looks is ultimately controlled by the way the viewer's Web browser happens to display it. So, if in this book the type size for chapter titles is set to 48 points, that is the way the printer will print it, and each book will have chapter titles the same point size, regardless of who reads it. HTML doesn't give you that kind of control over the page.

Although you still cannot dictate the size of a type-face, you can give it a relative size (such as larger or smaller than another font), and you can give it a specific color (such as red or maroon). The major problem with these Extensions is that with browsers that do not support Netscape Extensions, such as Mosaic, Web pages using Extensions may look weird.

Another type of Netscape feature is the introduction of frames to Web pages. Frames allow Web designers to divide the Web browser window into different "panes" or frames. Within each frame, a different type of information can be displayed, such as what is shown in figure 5.4. If a Web browser does not support frames, only one page will display instead of the other pages of information.

Figure 5.4

Frames enable Web designers to deliver their content in new ways.

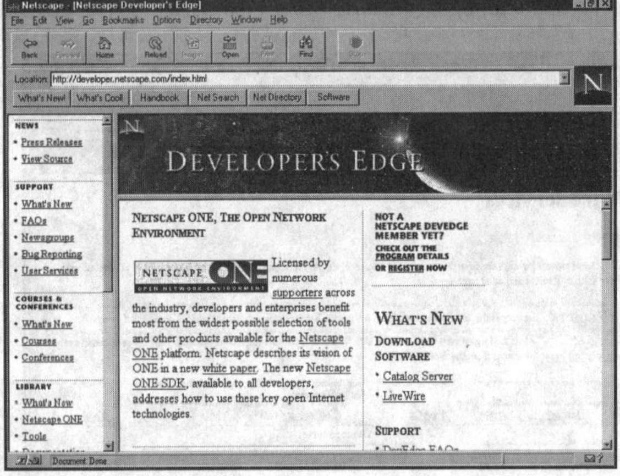

Netscape Plug-Ins

One of the most aggravating problems with Web browsers is their inability to handle diverse file types. In the past, if it wasn't an HTML document or an image file you were accessing, you had to use a helper application. In fact, only GIF and XBM (a Unix file format) graphics could be displayed inside a Web page for the longest time. Now, you can view JPG/JPEG as well. The problem with this is that not everyone works in HTML, and as you've just seen, HTML is limited in its page display capabilities.

To combat the problem of unrecognized file types and to limit the number of applications a browser has to call to as helper applications, Netscape developed support for plug-ins. Plug-ins are applications created by third-party developers that work "inside" Netscape Navigator 2.0 to display various file types, such as Macromedia Director files, Excel worksheets, and ASAP presentations.

VRML

We live in a three-dimensional world. Why don't we interact with our computers in a three-dimensional environment? Well, we just may start doing that in the near future using a programming language called VRML (you can pronounce it ver'muhl if you want to be hip).

VRML is described by one of its co-developers, Mark Pesce, as follows:

> VRML is a new computer language that provides a framework for space and virtual environments on the Internet—essentially, it turns the Internet into a great big space, in the same way that the Web turned the Internet into a great big document.

> —from *VRML Flying Through The Web*, Mark Pesce, New Riders 1996.

What this means is that you will be able to interact with documents, files, databases, and other users in a three-dimensional space. A document can be represented by a 3D picture of a document, not a piece of text with a link associated with it.

Java and JavaScript

Another feature you should look for in a browser is support for Java and JavaScript. Java is a new programming language from Sun Microsystems that enables program developers to write one set of code and then have that code be used on any operating system (this is called cross-platform support). With traditional programming languages, programmers must write a separate set of code for each operating system they want to support. This is why, when you acquire a piece of software (such as a Web browser or word processor), you must make sure the software was written for your particular operating system.

Java promises a day when a program will run on your computer regardless of the operating system or version of operating system you have. The first wave of this is now being seen on the Web. One of the reasons Java is so exciting for online users and developers is that, much like the way HTML works cross-platform, Java applets can be placed inside a Web page and any user can execute the program as long at they have the right browser. (Java applets are programs written in the Java language and inserted inside Web documents.) The first Windows 95 and Macintosh browser to support Java is Netscape Navigator 2.0. Microsoft Internet Explorer 3.0 also supports Java. And, if you are a Unix user, you can use Sun's HotJava Web browser.

JavaScript, which is loosely related to Java, is a scripting language from Netscape that uses some of the same principles of Java. One of the key differences between JavaScript and Java is the former is less complicated and may be easier for most users to learn to use. (Java is similar to programming in C++, which is a programming language used to develop many applications on the market today, and requires an extensive knowledge of programming and skills.) Like Java, Web pages can include JavaScript programs that run when you visit that page. Some JavaScript programs are activated automatically when you download that page; others are run by on-screen buttons or controls.

Tip

No one really knows yet the security ramifications of including Java applets and JavaScript programs in Web documents. Because most computer viruses reside in computer programs, it would be very easy for someone to hide a virus inside a Java applet or JavaScript program. Then, when you run that program on your computer, your computer would be infected with the virus.

Because of this potential, Netscape includes an option in its Security Preferences dialog box that enables you to shut off Java and JavaScript support (see fig. 5.5).

Figure 5.5

You can use the Security options in Netscape Navigator 2.0 to shut off Java or JavaScript support.

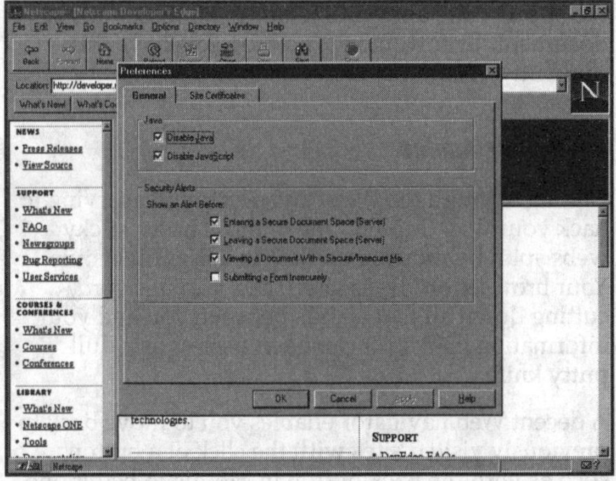

ActiveX

With Internet Explorer 3.0, Microsoft is introducing its new ActiveX technologies. *ActiveX* is a development environment for software developers and Web designers to create dynamic Web pages. What this

means is that instead of static Web pages you can view online, Web pages will have animation, virtual reality, video, and other types of content available online. ActiveX used to be called Object Linking and Embedding (OLE), which many Windows users have become familiar with since its release in Windows 3.1.

ActiveX lets Web page authors create applications to embed in HTML pages that the visitor can immediately interact with. Instead of relying on the user to have a browser or utility available to run the application, an ActiveX application can run on any computer that is running an ActiveX-compliant Web browser (such as Internet Explorer 3.0). Another feature of ActiveX that makes it attractive to Web page designers is that if the user who is visiting the site does not have the ActiveX feature installed on their machine yet, the Web page author can have the ActiveX application prompt the user if he or she wants to install the components now. If so, the ActiveX code is designed to find the latest components on the World Wide Web and download them to the user's computer.

Although ActiveX is not a predominate technology on the Web today, in the next 12 months you can expect to see a growing number of sites that feature ActiveX applications. This is due in large part to Microsoft's heavy-handed marketing campaign for ActiveX, as well as the relative ease of programming ActiveX applications using popular programming tools like Visual Basic and Visual C++. This is in large contrast to Java, which is difficult to understand and has a steeper learning curve than ActiveX.

To find out more information on ActiveX, see the Microsoft Site Builder Network Web site at `http://www.microsoft.com/workshop` (see fig. 5.6).

Figure 5.6

Microsoft's Site Builder Network Web site contains ActiveX content, as well as other Web site authoring information.

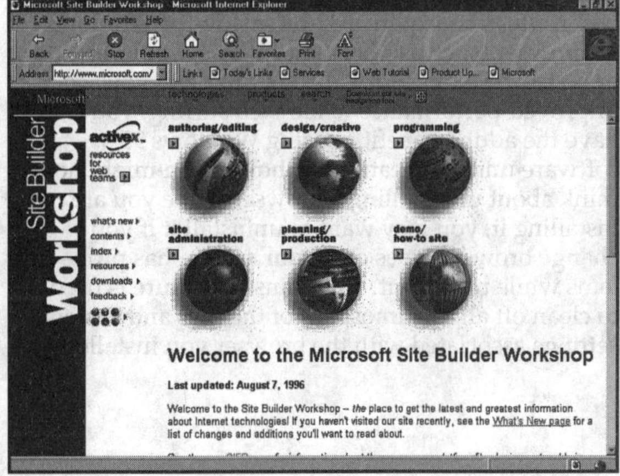

Installing Your Browser

As previous chapters indicate, setting up an Internet connection can be a bear of a job. If you go with a stand-alone TCP/IP browser, such as NCSA Mosaic or Netscape, you have to wrestle that bear.

If you're not eager for hand-to-paw combat with the network, your best move is to use an online service's Web service, such as CompuServe. If you are a Windows user, for example, you can use CompuServe's latest membership startup disk to install Internet support by following the Setup instructions on-screen. When you are through and have specified to include Internet support through CompuServe, you'll have a copy of CompuServe's Winsock (which is TCP/IP software) on your system. You then can dial up CompuServe and start navigating the Web using the built-in Spry Mosaic browser. As an alternative to Spry Mosaic, CompuServe now lets you select Netscape Navigator 2.0 as your main Web browser.

Some Microsoft Windows browsers require that Windows be upgraded with Win32s. Win32s, now up to version 1.25, is a Windows enhancement that enables Windows 3.1 and Windows for Workgroups to run some non-NT or Windows 95-specific 32-bit Windows programs.

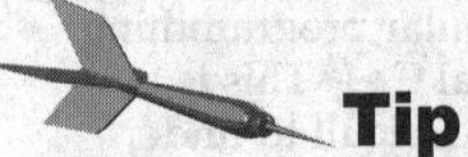

Tip

Sometimes Win32s is bundled with your browser. More often, however, you have to hunt it down from ftp sites. You can always find the most recent copy of the file at the following site:

```
http://www.ncsa.uiuc.edu/SDG/Software/WinMosaic/
win32s.htm
```

If you are a Windows 95 user, you can use the Internet Setup Wizard to set up Internet support on your computer (see Chapter 4). Once set up, your best route is to acquire a 32-bit, made-for-Windows 95 browser (such as Microsoft Internet Explorer 3.0 or Netscape Navigator 2.0). Not only will you see improved performance while Web surfing, you also have the added benefit of using Windows 95's software uninstall feature. Although you might not think about uninstalling a browser while you are installing it, you may want to uninstall it if you change browser types or if your system has problems while running it. The uninstall feature is used to clean off all (or almost all) of the files and system settings associated with the browser you installed.

Customizing Your Browser

You might think that customizing a Web browser isn't that important—it is. Customizing a browser isn't just a matter of making it look pretty; it's a matter of configuring the browser so that it works successfully with the Web.

Although most of the Web is written in HTML and most of its graphics are in JPEG and GIF formats, many documents and images are in other formats. To handle these foreign formats, either your browser must be able to work directly with these formats or you must be able to customize your browser so that you can use helper applications to view the foreign formats.

Ideally, your browser would not need helper applications, but with everything from Notes databases to Word for Windows documents appearing on the Web, that's just a pipe dream. The next best thing is to have a browser that makes it easy to associate helper applications to deal with new file formats, and, in the case of Netscape Navigator 2.0, lets you use plug-in applications to extend the power of the browser.

The character-based interface browsers normally fare the worst when it comes to helper applications. Not only are they incapable of dealing with graphics, but they cannot cope with such non-HTML text files as those in the PostScript or Portable Document Format (PDF) page description formats.

Most of the current wave of browsers—Netscape Navigator 2.0, Microsoft Internet Explorer 3.0, and NCSA Mosaic 2.0—enable you to to configure the software (including helper applications) by using menu options. The ultimate browser would suggest the appropriate applications for the foreign format document. Unfortunately, no browsers have this capability yet.

Navigation Advice

Getting through the Web can be as tough as trying to hack your way through one of those nasty, sticky webs spun by monster spiders in a B-grade movie. Your browser can be as sharp as a vorpal sword, cutting down all that stands between you and your information goal, or it can be as useless as a dull putty knife.

A decent Web navigator enables you to move back to previously visited sites with the click of a button, such as with the Back button in Mosaic. A better one enables you to decide exactly how far you want to backtrack along your route, rather than forcing you to laboriously walk back step-by-step. One such navigation tool for this is the History list in Netscape Navigator 2.0 (see fig. 5.7). The History list shows the last 15 Web sites you visited during the current session. This way you can immediately return to a site you liked but can't remember how you got there in the first place.

Figure 5.7

Netscape Navigator's History list helps you remember the most recently visited sites during your current Web session.

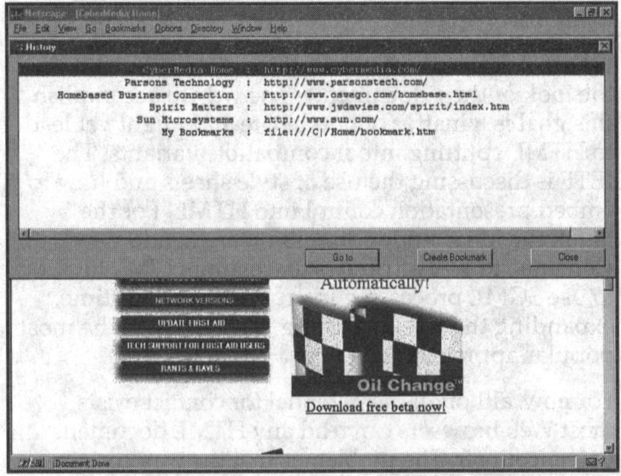

The best Web navigator enables you to keep a permanent record of favorite destinations. This feature is usually called bookmarking and is invaluable if you spend any serious amount of time on the Web. You can keep bookmarks of favorite sites much like you bookmark a page in a book you're reading or referencing.

> ### Note:
>
> Microsoft uses the terms shortcuts and favorites instead of bookmarks. *Shortcuts* is the same term they use for establishing aliases to files or programs on your desktop in Windows 95. By using this term for Internet bookmarks as well, Microsoft is blurring the lines between the files and resources on your personal computer and those that are online.

Although such Web mapping is a common feature, Web browsers have a way to go to perfect that feature. Many browsers don't enable you to organize your bookmarks any special way. Netscape Navigator 2.0, on the other hand, includes a much improved bookmarking system that enables you to set up your bookmark list the way you want. You can, for example, create and name folders into which you can place your bookmarks. You also can instruct Netscape to show only a specific folder on your bookmark list, further helping you navigate to only those sites of most interest to you. Finally, Netscape also includes a feature that lets you dictate into

which folder new bookmarks should be placed when you are browsing and want to quickly save that site in your bookmarks list. Most other browsers don't include this feature.

> ### Note:
>
> Another nice addition to this feature would be the capability to make notes on each site, for when you're trying to remember exactly what it was that fascinated you about a particular site a month ago. Both Mosaic 2.0 and Netscape Navigator 2.0 include ways to add descriptions to your bookmarks or add annotations about the site.

Examining Browser Viewing Capabilities

Previously, this chapter touched on the problem of viewing foreign file formats. As the Web grows, more formats are being used to make Web documents. Consequently, sometimes even to view a page you need a browser that's up to the task.

A browser must be able to read HTML 1.0 and GIF89a—the basics. Those used to be the only capabilities it needed. Today, a browser should also be able to handle HTML 3.2 documents and Adobe Acrobat PDF file format for text. Graphically speaking, your browser should be literate in GIF89a, GIF24, and JPG/JPEG. These are the most common types of graphic file types you'll encounter on the Web.

The well-equipped Web explorer also has helper applications to handle QuickTime, Microsoft Video for Windows, and MPEG movies, and Microsoft Word for Windows and PostScript documents. For the foreseeable future, these extras are strictly optional.

Why does your browser need the capability to handle so many different formats? The answer lies in the next two sections, which briefly examine the world of text and graphics standards on the Web.

Text Wars

At one time, all text on Web pages was in HTML. Time moved on, and with it went the unity of a single hypermedia language. Today, several HTML variants and other document formats are used in Web pages.

This shift signals a change in the Web from a friendly place, where any Web browser can be used with virtually any document, to a hostile world, where not all browsers work with all Web documents.

This has always been something of a problem for Web browsers—it's the reason for viewers. In the future, this problem will only get worse. Pure HTML is no longer the only language of the land, and more file formats are being used to carry the basic textual information of the Web. Let's take a look at the players in the Web language wars.

Before HTML, there was Standard Generalized Markup Language (SGML). SGML is an International Standards Organization (ISO) page description standard (ISO 8879). SGML itself does not describe how to format a document. Rather, it provides a set of rules, or grammar, to create Document Type Definitions (DTDs). A DTD specifies how to identify structural items, such as keywords, end notes, and words in italics by specifying tags and their meanings for a class of documents. HTML is a variation from the SGML theme and can be thought of as a DTD for hypermedia documents.

> ## Note:
>
> Until recently, pure SGML was regarded as too complex for Web documents. Now, some Web designers are exploring the use of SGML on the Web. The SGML community is also lobbying for HTML to move closer to SGML orthodoxy. They claim SGML offers readers far more sophisticated textual resources—such as the capability to bounce more easily from text to footnote to bibliography and back again— than does HTML.

The *Text Encoding Initiative* (TEI), for example, an SGML DTD for the humanities, enables authors to combine different editions of a text into a single hypertext document. You can have both the manuscript and its final published form in one document, for instance, and easily go back and forth between the two versions.

> ## Note:
>
> SGML most likely will fade into a document format hidden behind an HTML mask. Electronic Book Technologies' DynaWeb points the way to this future. DynaWeb is a Unix Web server that automatically translates SGML documents into HTML for Web browsers. Some SGML documents will prove too complex for timely automatic translations. For these, manual translations into HTML will be their way onto the Web. Fortunately, this tedious job will be semi-automated with the use of tools like Avalanche Development Company's SGML Hammer, an SGML-to-HTML translator.

In the meantime, the mainstream of Web document designers are moving from HTML 2.0 to HTML 3.0. The first version of HTML, HTML 0.9, though still used with some documents, is now considered antique. HTML 1.0 and 2.0 remain the most popular Web document formats. Fortunately, those with hours invested in legacy documents do not need to update these items. Most Web browsers can read these documents.

HTML 3.2 gives authors additional ways to control the look of their documents. The way to accomplish this goal is a matter of hot debate and might yet lead to HTML splitting into incompatible variants. The IETF is discussing the use of style sheets and how to embed presentation control into HTML. For the latter, the ideas under discussion are to add new elements, to add attributes to existing HTML tags, or to use SGML processing instructions. At this time, expanding the role of existing HTML tags is the most popular approach.

For now, although the potential for conflict exists, most Web browsers can read any HTML document you encounter. The problem is that the way certain items display, if at all, is determined by the HTML standard used and the browser you're using. Although there may come a time when HTML will not be the only accepted Web language, many companies have attempted to introduce proprietary languages to the Web and have not received a warm welcome. The main problem with proprietary Web pages is that you must have a specific browser to view the page, which limits the number of visitors to a site.

> ## Note:
>
> Some Web designers, desiring absolute control over document presentation, are starting to use Adobe Acrobat's PDF. PDF enables authors to send documents with PostScript-like quality to the original but without PostScript's size and compatibility penalties. Today, with Netscape embracing PDF as a supported format, there is some interest in using PDF as an HTML replacement. For now, though, PDF is more commonly used as a viewer file type. The Internal Revenue Service (IRS), for example, uses HTML for their Web pages, but IRS forms are kept in PDF.

So what do these projected changes mean for you? They mean that the Web is going to be divided into incompatible sections. If there is popular support for standard HTML and open systems, you will still be able to roam over most of the Web freely. If not, then expect an end to the days when you could explore the Web without restriction. Your only response will be to stay informed and update your Web browser often.

Graphics Wars

You might not believe it, especially if you're new to the Web, but once there was no question concerning Web graphics. The Web's inline graphics were GIF. Today, GIF is no longer the guaranteed inline graphics format of choice because Unisys, the patent owner on the Lempel-Ziv-Welch (LZW) data compression algorithm, began demanding licensing fees for programs using LZW (which GIF uses). CompuServe, GIF's owner, then started charging fees for programs using GIF.

These charges don't affect Web designers or users directly. You can use and view GIFs in your pages to your heart's content without payment. The changes do affect vendors that make programs that create, edit, or (and this is the important one) view GIFs—browsers.

When news of the licensing fee first came out, the graphics and online services programming communities blew up at the very notion. For years, the GIF format, though copyrighted by CompuServe, had been the free, de facto graphics standard of not only CompuServe and the Web, but for most of the online world. Graphics designers and programmers started to feel as if someone had changed the rules on them in mid-stream. They began to look for alternatives to GIF.

Browser programmers responded to GIF licensing fees by adding JPG support to their browsers. Despite this early support, JPG hasn't become the dominant inline image format, and it probably won't make further inroads. JPG isn't as flexible as GIF for design purposes. JPG is a fine format for an image to end up in (if you don't mind the loss of some resolution). It's also very hard to edit.

The immediate result of all this has been to slow down Unisys' requests for licensing fees. CompuServe, faced with outraged developers, decided to dump LZW from GIF and come up with a new GIF. This new format, GIF24, promises to be the "free, clear, and open format" for all developers that GIF was meant to be.

Over the past few years, graphics developers have been working on other alternatives to GIF. The Portable Network Graphics (PNG, pronounced ping) format offers the most popular alternative. PNG designers hope PNG will replace GIF for inline images. PNG produces smaller graphic files than GIF. It also includes 24-bit TrueColor support, and is free of all LZW licensing problems. For the down and dirty details, examine PNG's source code at the following site:

```
ftp://ftp.uu.net:/graphics/png.
```

What does the preceding information mean for Web designers? First, although PNG has a great deal of freeware and shareware author support, the big-name graphics developers haven't put their support behind it. Aldus Photoshop, for example, has no plans right now for PNG input and output mechanisms. Consequently, some considerable time is going to pass before many top-quality PNG images become available.

More importantly (for our purposes), the Web browser developers currently are sitting on the sidelines. Will PNG get their support? Will the designers continue to support GIF? Right now, Web browser developers are supporting GIF and JPG primarily, and looking at ways to offer support for other file formats with the better helper application support and plug-in technology.

Supporting Other Internet/Usenet Tools

All Web browsers are capable of supporting some other Internet tools. You can, for example, access ftp and Gopher servers from a browser. In addition, Web browsers are adding other jobs as they move from being strictly Web browsers to all-in-one Internet front ends.

Some users who like to pick just the right application for the job don't care whether their browser can do anything other than roam the Web. Other users like the convenience of a one-stop Internet front end. If you prefer to use your Web browser to replace all the Internet tools, the minimal additional tools you should expect are Usenet newsgroups and e-mail. Not all Web browsers have full e-mail support, but many enable you to send messages out. With Netscape Navigator 2.0, you have a fully integrated e-mail and newsgroup applications that work very well with the Web browser. Netscape Navigator 2.0 also enables you to replace its e-mail package with Microsoft Exchange if you use Windows 95.

Having Usenet newsgroup support isn't enough in itself. You want your newsgroup reader to support easy newsgroup selection, message threading, and sophisticated message-reply options. With anything less, you get more annoyance than enjoyment from Usenet news. For now, the browser that makes Usenet news the most fun is Netscape.

Moving one level up, you probably want a browser that supports Telnet and its mainframe cousin, Telnet-3270. Many Web browsers do not include Telnet support directly, but do enable you to assign a separate Telnet application to work with your Web browser. This way, when you encounter a Telnet site, the associated Telnet application automatically starts.

Working Quickly

More than anything else, your browser's speed depends on the speed of your Internet connection.

Having that said, your browser can make it seem as if you are moving much faster on the Web than you actually are.

Netscape Navigator 2.0 offers this bit of magic. Netscape—and now other browsers—displays the text of a Web site first, and then takes its time bringing up the graphics. It doesn't sound like much, but the overall effect makes Netscape "seem" much quicker when you are online. Rather than waiting for a 20-KB GIF to appear in its entirety, you can decide early whether you want to stick around for the whole image based on the already displayed words from a page.

Another trick in working performance wonders involves displaying information as soon as it arrives. Some browsers do this poorly, showing information in screen-blurring displays as it is received. These displays leave you rubbing your eyes and wondering whether or not you made the right decision in trading in your TV set for a Pentium and a Web hookup. The speed secret here is for the browser to smoothly show information as it appears.

Note:

Netscape Navigator 2.0 also supports a new JPG file type called progressive JPG/JPEG. Progressive JPG files display faster than other files because they display in "chunks" as the Web page is downloaded. When a page has a progressive JPG file, you'll see the image display gradually, kind of like a fade-in in a movie, and then after all the text of the Web page has displayed, the image will finish.

The final touch, completing the illusion of speed, enables you to stop an incoming page so that you can move on to something else. There's nothing quite as frustrating as waiting for a page to appear so you can get on with another job. Many programs, like Netscape, now enable you to hit the Esc key or click on the Stop button to discontinue the download of the current page. You then can return to a previous page, click on any links that are showing on the current page, or type in the URL for another page.

Examining a Selection of Browsers

Now that you have the basics, you're ready to take a look at browsers. Remember as you go through this section that browsers are changing on an almost weekly basis and that new ones are coming out at an even faster clip. Regard this information, therefore, as more of a general guide than specific recommendations.

Netscape Navigator 2.0

Netscape Navigator 2.0 (Mac, Unix, Windows 3.x, Windows 95) is, without question, the leading Web browser today. It's faster than the other browsers, loaded with features, and available in versions for more operating systems than any other browser. There's little to dislike and a great deal to love about Netscape.

Netscape comes in two versions. The first can be obtained from the Web at `http://home.netscape.com`. If you're in school, or you're working for a non-profit group, you can use this edition for free. Otherwise, you can order a copy of Netscape by sending e-mail to the following address:

`sales@netscape.com`

Netscape is one program that lacks scarcely any features. It comes ready to work with secure servers that use the SSL protocol. Netscape also supports e-mail and has an easy-to-use and powerful Usenet newsreader. Although it has no other Internet applications, Netscape makes it easy to link up with pre-existing Internet programs, such as Telnet clients. Netscape is also easy to install and configure.

Note:

For more features of Netscape Navigator 2.0, see the earlier section "Features to Look For in Browsers."

One small but delightful feature is Netscape's status bar at the bottom of the display. From this bar you can determine exactly what the browser is doing at any given moment, such as the percentage of the current Web page and its graphics that have downloaded to your computer. Although this information might not be terribly useful, it does help keep the impatient user at bay, showing that something is indeed happening and gives you an idea of how much time is left to complete the current download.

Where Netscape really kills the competition is speed. Netscape displays graphics faster than anyone else in the business. The browser uses great caching to boost your speed when you need to look back a page. The program also enables you to display and interact with text and links—before the complete graphics display arrives.

Netscape's navigation aids are also of championship quality. The History utility, for example, enables you to create a permanent bookmark for a site long after you've left it behind.

The program is also popular with many vendors. Netscape has struck deals with CompuServe, General Electric, and several other companies to be their official browser of choice.

Netscape Navigator Gold 2.0

Netscape Navigator Gold 2.0 is a recently released Web browser that includes all the features of Netscape Navigator 2.0. What differentiates Gold from Netscape 2.0 is its HTML editing window. With Gold, you can create, edit, and publish your own Web pages.

Although there are several HTML editors available, such as HTML Assistant Pro from Brooklyn North Software, Gold is the first to incorporate an editing tool with the Web browser. Gold also features an editing interface that displays your Web page as it will be viewed in the Web browser. Other HTML editors only show raw HTML code, requiring you to view the HTML document in a Web browser before you know what the page will look like. With Gold, you can reduce the guesswork of creating and editing Web pages.

If you are interested in Netscape Gold, you can get more information about it at `http://home.netscape.com`. The price of Gold has not been determined yet, but will probably be around $80.

NCSA Mosaic 2.1.1

NCSA Mosaic (Mac, Unix, Windows), the grandfather of all graphics browsers, might be getting a little long in the tooth, but it's still a good program (see fig. 5.8).

Figure 5.8

The newest version of NCSA Mosaic isn't quite as powerful as the top browsers, but it doesn't suffer by comparison either.

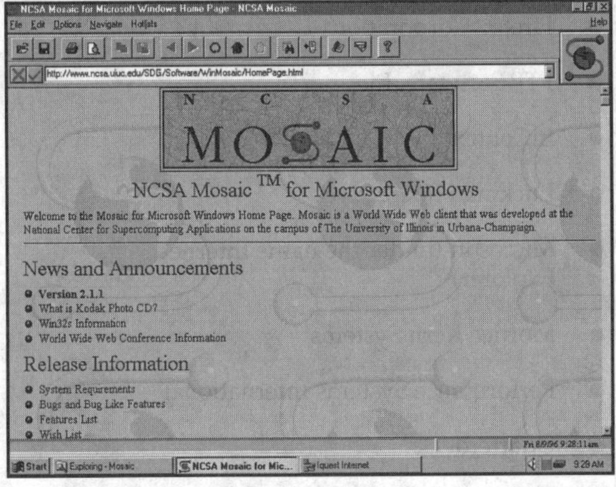

Mosaic helps you navigate the Web in several ways. You can make annotations on pages you've visited. These comments then appear at the bottom of a page the next time you visit it. The program also enables you to create a hotlist of URLs, as well as cascaded menus of URLs using the Hotlist Manager.

Mosaic is also in the forefront of supporting the newest HTML standards. Mosaic supports many of the HTML 3.0 features. However, you might encounter some problems when a page includes some of the Netscape extensions that Mosaic doesn't support yet.

The newest Mosaic also includes a top-notch customization tool. Those who have wept over the pain of adjusting Mosaic by tweaking the INI file will jump for joy over this development. User preferences are set using the Mosaic Options dialog box, which includes several different tabs of choices you can set.

The new, improved Mosaic also comes with outgoing e-mail and newsgroup support. Although the program is no Netscape, these features do set it above less sophisticated browsers.

At this time, Mosaic does not support a security protocol. Once the protocol competition is settled—which shouldn't be long—Mosaic will likely support the winning protocol.

Some other browsers might have more features or better speed, but NCSA Mosaic is solid, has great HTML support, and best of all, is free. You can check out your copy at the following URL:

`http://www.ncsa.uiuc.edu/SDG/Software/Mosaic/`

Microsoft Internet Explorer 3.0

A browser you're going to hear a lot about (if you haven't already) is the Microsoft Internet Explorer (see fig. 5.10).

Although Internet Explorer lacks some of the features of Netscape Navigator 2.0, including a full-feature newsreader and e-mail utility (although Windows 95 users might want to use Microsoft Exchange as their e-mail program), Internet Explorer has an advantage over Netscape; every computer sold with Windows 95 on it includes a copy of Internet Explorer.

Figure 5.9

The Microsoft Internet Explorer 3.0 browser promises some new features that will help it gain market share.

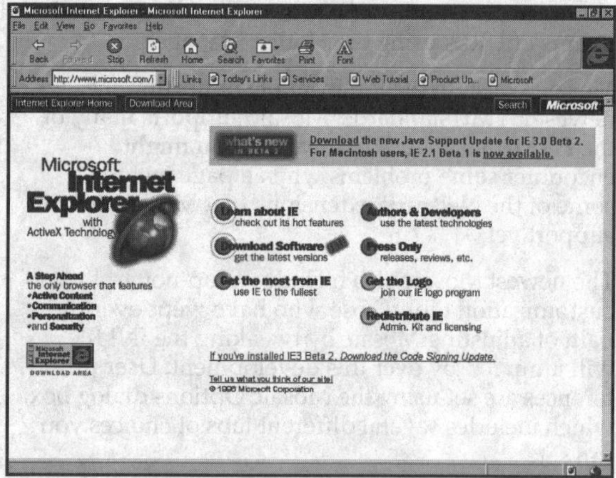

Note:

Although Internet Explorer 3.0 does not have built-in e-mail or newsreaders, you can download Internet Mail and Internet News from Microsoft for free. These applications are discussed in Chapter 3, "Internet E-Mail and Usenet Newsgroups."

Besides coming pre-installed on Windows 95, you can also download it from the Microsoft Web site at `http://www.microsoft.com` and use it for free. Recently, Microsoft and America Online agreed to make Internet Explorer the standard, built-in Web browser for AOL's members (which tops 5 million customers). What this means is when you purchase a new computer with Windows 95 preinstalled on it, an icon for AOL appears on the desktop that you can double-click to sign up for an AOL membership.

Some of the new features of Internet Explorer 3.0 include the following:

- **Resizable toolbar.** Provides Quick Links to World Wide Web pages. You can slide the toolbar to hide the Quick Links buttons, or slide them out to let you see buttons called Today's Links, Services, Web Tutorial, Product Update, and Microsoft.

- **Internet rating system.** Use the Internet rating system to block certain sites inappropriate for children.

- **ActiveX support.** Internet Explorer 3.0 is the first Web browser to support ActiveX documents and applications. You can, for instance, view Microsoft Word documents in

your Web browser instead of launching a separate application to read the documents.

- **Separate file download window.** Instead of waiting for a file to download before surfing to another site, with Internet Explorer 3.0, you can start a download session in a separate window and then continue your surfing.

- **Visual Basic Script support.** Visual Basic Script is a programming language similar to Visual Basic for Applications available in several Microsoft Office applications. With VBScript, Web authors can create dynamic and enhanced Web pages.

- **Security.** Internet Explorer 3.0 includes the latest online security features to make it safer than ever to send credit card information over the Internet for online commerce.

Spyglass Enhanced Mosaic

Spyglass won the right to take NCSA Mosaic and turn it into a commercial product. The company's first attempts at Enhanced Mosaic (Mac, Unix, Windows) have added functions to Mosaic, such as form and printing support, but the program still feels more like NCSA Mosaic with the edges smoothed off rather than a new product.

Spyglass normally sells Enhanced Mosaic to other companies, who then modify it and bundle it with their own TCP/IP offerings. The following is a list of businesses currently marketing Enhanced Mosaic under their own name:

- AT&T Global Information Solutions

- Corel Corporation

- Digital Equipment Corporation

- Firefox Corporation

- FTP Software, Inc.

- InContext

- Luckman Interactive

- Microsoft (under the name Internet Explorer)

- Mortice Kern Systems

- Performance Systems International

- Quarterdeck

- SPRY

If you're running a browser from any of the companies just listed, you're working with Enhanced Mosaic. Some, like SPRY, have heavily modified the program; others have done little with the base program.

No matter the version, Enhanced Mosaic always supports SHTTP. You shouldn't have any security worries in the commercial Web of tomorrow.

Generally, Enhanced Mosaic installs easily. The Windows version requires Win32s support. Customization was troublesome in early versions of Enhanced Mosaic. At times, in the Windows version, you even had the dubious pleasure of manually editing the INI file.

Unlike with the other programs, your first stop when visiting the Web with Enhanced Mosaic is not a predetermined Web site. Instead, you're presented with a home page located on your home PC. From here, a variety of useful Web sites are presented for your Web running selection. This simple trick makes Enhanced Mosaic the fastest browser at the starting gun. Once you're on the Web, Enhanced Mosaic slows down to typical browser speeds.

One feature Enhanced Mosaic can boast that few others can is its support for multiple browser sessions. You can connect to multiple hosts and switch between windows. It's a nice feature, but don't think about using it unless you have a 28,800 bps or faster connection.

Like Netscape, Enhanced Mosaic enables you to abort out of a troublesome or slow Web connection by hitting the Esc key. You might think that you won't use this feature often, but once you've been on the Web for awhile, you'll appreciate the ability to walk away from a downloading attempt.

On the less satisfactory side, Enhanced Mosaic lacks some navigation tools, and it doesn't inform you of the status of ongoing downloads. When you get impatient, wondering whether or not a GIF is ever going to show up on your screen, this drawback is no small matter.

Enhanced Mosaic is being further enhanced every day. Furthermore, each seller adds its own twists to the program and to the program's add-ons. Coming up with a simple judgment, therefore, is quite difficult. All in all, Enhanced Mosaic is a good, but not spectacular, Web browser. To find out more about Enhanced Mosaic, visit its Web site at the following URL:

```
http://spyglass.www.com
```

You also can contact them at 708-505-1010; fax, 708-505-4944; or e-mail, `info@spyglass.com`.

AIR Mosaic

SPRY's AIR Mosaic represents the first commercial Web browser. (SPRY is a division of CompuServe.) Though it can be slow, especially when displaying large GIFs, AIR Mosaic features a Spyglass-based interface that is easy to use and to configure (as far as IP-based browsers go).

For a trial run, download a test version of the program, using ftp, from the following URL address:

```
ftp://ftp.spry.com/demo/AirMosaicDemo/
```

The commercial version is available in several packages, including SPRY's Internet in a Box, AIR Series, and Mosaic in a Box. It is also the default Web browser for CompuServe users who want Web access.

One of AIR Mosaic's strongest points is its ease of installation. Unlike other Windows TCP/IP browsers, you don't need to add Win32s support.

Another AIR Mosaic plus is that you can file documents into folders, which can be added to the menu bar. You can create up to 15 hotlist folders. Each of these folders can handle approximately 200 URLs. Each of these features combine to make mapping your way through the Web much simpler.

One feature unique to AIR Mosaic is its Kiosk mode. In Kiosk mode, you see the Web page without the visual obstruction of a menu. Although this mode works well when you want to get the fullest look at a homepage, it does have its limitations. In Kiosk mode, you cannot use any of the program's navigation tools; you are limited to navigating by hyperlinks.

Overall, AIR Mosaic is a good, though somewhat slow, Windows browser. For more information, contact SPRY at 800-777-9638, ext. 26; 206-447-0300; fax, 206-447-9008; e-mail, `info26@spry.com`.

Cello

Many browsers tend to look alike, mainly because they're all chips off the Mosaic block. Netscape and AIR Mosaic, for example, both have original Mosaic designers behind them. Cello (Windows) is carved from its own rock.

Different doesn't mean bad. Cello, an IP-based browser developed by programmers at Cornell Law School's Legal Information Institute, works more quickly than other freeware browsers. It is available over the Internet, using ftp, from the following URL:

```
ftp://ftp.law.cornell.edu/pub/LII/Cello/cello.zip
```

In addition to its speed, Cello includes several other Internet tools. You can use Cello to read Usenet news, send (but not retrieve) e-mail, and perform

WAIS searches. Cello also bundles a Telnet and a 3270 terminal emulator in its bag of goodies.

Cello does have its imperfections. The program doesn't render graphics well. Many HTML pages appear crude in Cello. Another more annoying trait is that when you resize a Window, you must reload the document before you can view it properly. Further, Cello does not support any Web security protocols.

These points are bad enough, but far more damaging to Cello's future as a Web browser is that it is no longer being updated. As the Web grows more complicated, Cello is quickly becoming an antique program. Still, if you want a freeware, all-in-one Web browser and interface, Cello has its strengths.

Lynx

If you don't care for graphics and just want your information straight from the Web, then Lynx—the premier character-based Web browser—is for you. Because Lynx runs on VT100 terminals (or in a Telnet session), you can only see or hear multimedia items by downloading them.

Lynx is not limited ASCII text. The newest version, 2.2, supports Curses, a Unix text-based windowing system. Curses makes seeing links much easier than with other text-based interfaces.

Another plus, if you're using a dial-up shell account, is that you can download a file—with Zmodem or the like—to your local PC while your Unix system is still receiving a file from an ftp server or you're wandering the Web. It's as close to on-screen multitasking as you're going to get with a VT100-bound shell session.

The program also has the twin virtues of being cheap and free of installation. Most shell accounts already have access to a Lynx client, in which case all you have to do is type in lynx and you're on your way to the Web.

Further, Lynx comes with a feature that not all fancy graphical browsers have: an integrated Usenet news-reader. Some features, of course, such as support for a security protocol or non-HTML text files like PDF, are beyond Lynx. If that's fine by you, then Lynx's meat-and-potatoes approach to the Web might be exactly what you need. If your Internet site doesn't have a copy of Lynx, you can download one from the following:

ftp2.cc.ukans.edu

NetCruiser

NetCom On-Line Communication Services' NetCruiser is the graphical front end to NetCom's Internet access service. NetCruiser comes with a full array of Internet and Usenet tools. Unfortunately, only a few of them work quite right. The Web browser, for example, has some problems and crashes quite a bit.

On the plus side, NetCruiser is one Internet application that is easy to install. It's not quite "plug-and-play" yet, but it's close.

Like any proprietary interface, of course, you're stuck with the tools that NetCom offers. With NetCruiser, for example, you won't be able to use the Eudora mail reader. The flip side is that you do get to use a single, integrated front end.

On the minus side, NetCruiser doesn't offer sophisti-cated Web navigation tools. Further, the program does not inherently support much more than the HTML and GIF formats. NetCom is, however, constantly working on NetCruiser. In fact, Net-Cruiser is probably the most rapidly updated Web browser available.

A beginner will probably be happy with NetCruiser, but a more experienced user might get frustrated with its restrictions. Still, the software is free, and at $19.95 for a month of service, you're not going to go broke from giving NetCruiser a try. You can arrange to take the browser out for a drive around the virtual block by calling NetCom at 800-501-8649, 408-983-5970; fax, 408-241-9145; or sending e-mail to info@netcom.com.

SlipKnot

Do you want the Web's graphics without the headaches of TCP/IP connectivity? Then you are a candidate for SlipKnot. SlipKnot is a shareware program that works with any Internet provider shell account that also provides either the Lynx or WWW browser.

SlipKnot works by using Lynx or WWW for basic connectivity, and then translating their input into a graphical Web display. Unfortunately, SlipKnot skims on some basics. You cannot, for example, resize windows. Still, though the program's a little slow, it does give you the basics of graphical Web browsing.

SlipKnot comes with the basic set of browser tools. Don't look for anything fancy here, like a news-reader, but for walking around the Web, SlipKnot serves quite well. Because SlipKnot also comes with a terminal mode, you can always get directly to

Usenet and Internet host-based character applications, like the trn. newsreader and the elm mail front end.

As you might expect, SlipKnot comes with only minimal support for Web text and graphic formats. Further, the program does not come with any security support. By its very nature, such support would be difficult to implement.

Installation is not terribly easy. It is, however, much easier to install than any of the IP applications. You can give it a try yourself by using ftp to get it from the following URL:

```
ftp://ftp.netcom.com/pub/pbrooks/slipknot
```

ANIMALS

Animal Parks

National Zoological Park Home Page

http://www.si.edu/organiza/museums/zoo/homepage/nzphome.htm

Web site of the National Zoo. Includes a user questionnaire, news, and information, as well as a photo library. Also includes links to the Smithsonian Institution. Includes downloadable files that contain press coverage of the zoo. Coffee drinkers, take note: the site contains an interesting legend about Lewak coffee.

Neopolis Zoo

http://www.neosoft.com/neopolis/zoo/default.html

Meet Dupree the iguana at this animal-filled Web site. The page opens with a picture of a panda couple and offers links to other animal photos and sites on the Web.

San Diego Wild Animal Park

http://www.infopost.com/sandiego/points/sdzoo.html

Lets you make an online visit to the San Diego Wild Animal Park, a park that features animals in their natural habitats—without fences or cages. Offers a montage of the animals that live in the park.

Sea World/Busch Gardens

http://www.bev.net/education/SeaWorld/homepage.html

Contains an animal information database maintained by the Sea World Busch/Gardens theme parks. Includes "Ask Shamu," a column that features animal-related questions. Also includes images on numerous zoo species and information on zoological park careers.

Singapore Zoological Gardens

http://www.ncb.gov.sg/sog/att/abal/zoo.html

Features information on the Singapore Zoo's orang-utans and tigers and offers a short video clip of the zoo animals.

Terry Polk's Zoological E-mail Directory

http://www.wcmc.org.uk/infoserv/zoodir.html

Archives e-mail addresses of professionals in the zoological fields, which also helps locate particular aquariums or zoos.

Zoo

http://sensemedia.net/sprawl/38047

Provides an online tour of a zoo. Uses an image map to guide you from exhibit to exhibit.

ZooNet

http://www.mindspring.com/~zoonet/

Attempts to provide information about every zoo in the world. Includes the ZooLinks page, which offers jumps to hundreds of zoos and zoo-related information. Offers the ZooNet Image Archives, which features numerous jumps to online zoos and animal pictures.

Birds

Audubon

http://www.audubon.org/audubon/

This site, the home page of the National Audubon Society, provides information on the conservation issues and programs the Society is currently working on. Those campaigns currently target the marine ecosystems of the world and bird sanctuaries that protect wildlife habitats. Learn about the Audubon's action agenda for the 104th Congress. You can also get travel, education, and membership information.

Birds, United States National Park Service (NPS) (Information Center for the Environment)

http://ice.ucdavis.edu/US_National_Park_Service/NPS_birds.html

Provides a searchable index of birds in the United States National Park system. Includes information about NPFlora and NPFauna, national PC-based databases of vertebrate and vascular plant occurrences in the US.

Caring for Your New Bird

http://www.ddc.com/~kjohnson/birdcare.htm

This 23-page book includes information on local pet stores, mail order supply catalogs, veterinarians, and bird clubs. Includes info on choosing breeders and choosing a bird, the first few days, handling your new bird, household safety, nutrition, diseases and injuries, and more. This page was chosen as a Hot Site by Starting Point, a WWW database searching tool.

The Eagle Page from Rocky Mountain High

`http://www.sky.net/~emily/eagle.html`

Pays homage to birds of prey and provides a resource list of other related sites. A diverse site that provides info (or points you in the right direction) about the U.S. Bald Eagle Protection Act, information on adopting an eagle, and poems and song lyrics about eagles.

The Fabulous Kakapo (Strigops Habroptilus)

`http://www.resort.com/~ruhue/kakapo.html`

Focuses on the Kakapo bird, a rare nocturnal, flightless parrot that is native to New Zealand. Once prevalent throughout the area, the Kakapo population is slowly diminishing. There are only about 56 Kakapo left. This site details how New Zealanders are working to help the population recover.

Michael's Photo Gallery

`http://www.netaxs.com/~mhmyers/image.html#birdtel`

Caters to the virtual birdwatcher and contains a plethora of photos, including Cardinals, Blue Jays, Sparrow, Robins, and Finches. Offers a straightforward presentation and includes links to other sites as well as other nature photos.

The Pet Bird Page

`http://aloha.net/~granty/`

With facts about everything from the Maroon Bellied Conure to the African Gray Parrot, this site serves as a guide to pet birding. Includes FAQs and newsgroup connections in addition to specific information on most of the major breeds of commonly domesticated birds.

UAS Home Page

`http://www.upatsix.com/upatsix/`

Introduces aviary practices. Provides software on aviculture and birding.

United States Fish and Wildlife Service Home Page

`http://www.fws.gov/`

Offers information on numerous species (both endangered and non-endangered), including migratory habits and habitats.

Virtual Birding in Tokyo

`http://www.st.rim.or.jp/~koike/`

Provides exquisite pictures of wild and domestic birds in Tokyo, Japan.

Cats

Cat Fanciers' Home Page

`http://www.fanciers.com/`

Provides cat-related information. Offers numerous FAQs on different cat breeds, feline health, and care issues. Offers links to show schedules, cat organizations, FTP and Gopher sites, as well as links to commercial sites, picture sites, and cat owners' home pages.

Cat House (EFBC/FCC) Home Page

`http://www.cathouse-fcc.org/`

Contains pictures and some audio clips straight from the cat's mouth. The Cat House (a.k.a. the Feline Conservation Center) is a desert zoo that contains a variety of wild cat species. More than 50 cats, representing 13 species, live at the compound. Includes photos of recent births.

Cats On the Internet

`http://http2.sils.umich.edu/~dtorres/cats/cats.html`

This photo-filled site primarily features links to other people's World Wide Web pages about their cats. The page includes five browsing categories, as well as a link to the author's own personal Web page for her cat Maggie. Listen to a "hello" from the nation's first cat, Socks.

Happy Household Pet Cat Club

`http://www.best.com/~slewis/HHPCC`

The Happy Household Pet Cat Club (HHPCC), a 28-year-old international organization, is geared toward cat owners who want to exhibit their feline companions in cat shows. HHPCC's Web site offers access to a bi-monthly newsletter, membership information, and info on how you can get the most out of showing your household cat in shows.

Index of /multimed/pics/feline

`http://sunsite.sut.ac.jp/multimed/pics/feline/`

Lets visitors view and/or download images of lions, tigers, cougars, cheetahs, and other large cats.

JESSICATS Home Page

http://steps.atsi.edu/tca/term.html

Features many photos of Siamese cats. The site includes a link to the Traditional Cat Association Home Page.

LAL Cat Archive

http://lal.cs.byu.edu/cats/cats.html

Offers pictures of cats—many cat pictures in .GIF format, many of them quite large. Also contains links to more cat pictures as well as other cat-related sites. Lets you send your cat's picture for display.

Savage Studios Homepage

http://www.awod.com/gallery/wgd/savage/

Features information on cats of all shapes and sizes. Offers links to big cat organizations and the Zoe Foundation, which is dedicated to helping endangered, large cats survive.

The Traditional Cat Association Home Page

http://www.covesoft.com/tca/

The Traditional Cat Association (TCA) is a non-profit organization dedicated to preserving the health, longevity, and physical characteristics of cats. The group's objectives include establishing a registry for Traditional cat breeds, and bringing back and maintaining the "old style" look of each breed. This site includes links to cat breeders, a newsletter, photos, membership information, and more.

The Zoe Foundation

http://www.awod.com/gallery/probono/zoe/index.html

The Zoe Foundation is dedicated to helping endangered large cats avoid extinction. Funds are raised through product sales, licensing, and donations. The special focus of the foundation is on the Indochinese tiger, panthera tigris corbetti. View photos of some big cats, get info about foundation products, and learn how you can join the preservation effort.

Dogs

Akbash Dog Home Page

http://www.upei.ca/akbash/akbash.htm

The Akbash Dog is a livestock-protection dog found in rural Turkey. This site lets you view pictures of Akbash dogs, read their history and breed description, and learn about Ashkash Dogs International and its rescue program.

Bernese Mountain Dog Home Page

http://www.prairienet.org/~mkleiman/berner.html

Focuses on the Bernese Mountain dog. Includes photos, links to mailing lists, FAQs, information about getting a Bernese puppy, and links to owner sites.

Border Collies

http://mendel.berkeley.edu/dogs/bcs.html

Picture-filled site that provides special information on border collie e-mail lists and an FTP site dedicated to border collie information. Includes information for those individuals thinking about getting a border collie, as well as an online training manual.

Borzoi Info Online

http://www.clark.net/pub/bdalzell/borzoiinfo.html

Provides information on the Borzoi breed. The Borzoi is a large hunting dog of Russia. Includes pictures and a link to the Borzoi Geneology Database. Also offers articles and links to additional general dog-related information.

Canine Activity Calendar

http://www.acmepet.com/canine/civic/k9_act.html

Provides a one-stop-shopping list of canine shows scheduled throughout North America.

Canine Vaccination Schedule

http://www.acmepet.com/canine/k9vacsch.html

If you're a pet owner, you know how difficult it can be to keep up with your pet's inoculation schedule. However, there is an easier way: visit this site, which contains a schedule for canine vaccinations from age 6 weeks on up to 18 months. The site also provides descriptions on how each vaccine is administered and describes the illness the vaccine treats.

Caucasian Ovcharka Info

http://pasture.ecn.purdue.edu/~laird/Dogs/Ovcharka/

Focuses on the Caucasian Mountain dog, a flock guardian that has served as a livestock guard, a home guardian, and a fighting dog. Includes special information on the national club for this breed, and contact information for the Caucasian Mountain Dog Club of America, Inc.

Choosing a Dog Breed

http://www.acpub.duke.edu/~hendrix/choosing.html

Offers guidance and suggestions to those who are thinking about getting a dog. Includes answers to a list of frequently asked questions. Includes a list of reading resources, including books and links to other sites.

Dog Breeding

http://www.clark.net/pub/bdalzell/21stcent.html

Covers how to properly care for and raise a dog. Includes tips. Discusses aspects of several different breeds. Includes the electronic version of the *Merck Veterinary Manual* and information about CompuPed, a pedigree management program.

Dog-Play

http://www.dog-play.com/

Gives pet owners something different to think about—animal-assisted therapy. The author of this site details the experience of using dogs to help reach out to the elderly and confined individuals. The site includes links to organizations involved in animal-assisted therapy, books and publications on therapy dogs, and links to other dog-related sites.

Dog Term Glossary

http://pasture.ecn.purdue.edu/~laird/Dogs/glossary.html

Presents terminology both common and uncommon to the canine field. Provides many links to additional sites, as well as pointers to other parts of the glossary. Also contains contact information for Humane Societies and the American Kennel Club.

Greyhound Starting Gate

http://pasture.ecn.purdue.edu/~laird/Dogs/Greyhound/

Did you know you can play a greyhound's ribs like an air guitar? Well, not really—but at this site, you

can learn the other "Top 10" reasons you should adopt a greyhound. This site focuses on finding homes for retired racing greyhounds. It provides background information on the greyhound and its history in the United States.

Pomeranian Dog Home Page

http://www.u-net.com/~galley/

Provides information on the Pomeranian. Includes links to pictures, history, and breed standards, as well as information on other links related to the Pomeranian.

Portuguese Water Dog Index

http://pasture.ecn.purdue.edu/~laird/Dogs/PWD/index.html

Offers information on the Portugese Water Dog, also referred to as the Fisherman's Dog. Offers links to other related sites, including the Pacific NW Portugese Water Dog Club site, which incorporates HTML 3.0 background imaging techniques.

The Pug Dog Home Page

http://www.camme.ac.be/~cammess/www-pug/home.html

This thorough site presents the Pug dog, a member of the Toy group. Find out why this dog is a great choice for potential pet owners who live in a dwelling with no outdoor yard or dog run. The site also provides a guestbook to record comments for passers-by.

Rhodesian Ridgebacks

http://warthog.cns.udel.edu/richard/RhoRidge/rrfaq.html

Offers information on e-mail lists of owners of the Ridgeback dog (sometimes called the African Lion Hound), a native of South Africa. Presents a list of frequently asked questions for potential owners of Ridgebacks.

Rottweiler Home Page

http://www.in.net/~katl/rottpage/rottie.html

Thinking of getting a Rottweiler? Check out this site, which contains listings of Rottweilers across the country that need a home. This site also contains smaller images designed to identify links that provide more information.

Schipperke Page

http://www.eskimo.com/~baubo/schip.html

Includes information and pictures on the Scipperke breed of dog (pronounced "schipperkey"). Features a list of additional sites that offer information on canines, including medical projects and veterinary studies.

Tibetan Mastiff Home Page

http://www.idyllmtn.com/tm/

Focuses on the Tibetan Mastiff breed of dog. Includes Tibetian Mastiff-related links to clubs, pictures, purchasing, and information on relevent health matters.

The Visual Rhodesian Ridgeback

http://wintermute.sr.unh.edu/ridgeback/ridgeback.html

Focuses on the Rhodesian breed. Contains some links to adorable pictures of the young ridgeback and the owners that love them. Provides additional links to other canine sites.

Westies Home Page

http://www.stpt.usf.edu/~greek/westies.html

Displays pictures of small terriers and doggie cartoon images. Also provides information to other terrier-oriented sites.

Dolphins

The Dolphin Alliance

http://envirolink.org/arrs/ahimsa/tda/

The Dolphin Alliance is a citizen's action group established in 1992 that works to preserve dolphin and whale rights and the protection of their environment. The Alliance has several goals, including working to stop all capture of whales and dolphins within U.S. waters. The group hopes to do this through public education and legislative reform.

Dolphin Information Server— Home Page

http://elpc54136.lboro.ac.uk/

Serves as a simple resource for pictures and information on dolphins, killer whales, and other marine mammals. Includes information about Keiko (the whale in the motion picture *Free Willy*).

The Dolphin Page

http://mingus.loni.ucla.edu:1028/FURMANSKI/dolphin2.html

Provides information on the dolphin, including protection issues, research, sound, and graphics.

The Wild Dolphin Project

http://wwwa.com/dolphin/project.htm

The Wild Dolphin Project was started in 1985 to study the history and communication systems of Atlantic spotted dolphins in the Bahamas. The project focuses on understanding dolphin behavior, interactions, and communication. This colorful Web site offers information about the project and includes photos, background information on dolphins, and information on how you can join an expedition.

Ferrets

Electronic Zoo/NetVet—Ferret Page

http://netvet.wustl.edu/ferrets.htm

Ferret lovers, come together! This site contains a listing of links to other sites and other helpful info for ferret owners, including a link to the American Ferret Association, Inc., the California Domestic Ferret Association, and Ferret Lover's Clubs throughout the country.

Ferret Central

http://www.optics.rochester.edu:8080/users/pgreene/central.html

This site includes FAQs, veterinary information, and a photo gallery of ferrets. Includes links to a mailing list of ferret owners and links to related sites.

Ferret World!

http://www.csc.peachnet.edu/~rpoore/Ferrets/

Did you know there are approximately five to seven million pet ferrets in the United States? That fact and more can be found at this Web page, which offers lots of ferret-related info on topics such as: "Care and Keeping of Domestic Ferrets," "Going on Trips with Your Ferret," and "What Is Your Ferret Eating?" View ferret pictures in the Photo Gallery.

General Information

Amphibian and Reptile Collection

http://www.mip.berkeley.edu/mvz/mvzherpe.html

Describes the MVZ reptilian/amphibian collection, which includes more than 200,000 specimens from around the world. Includes a few pictures. Also contains a link to information about their animal tissue collection, which can be used for DNA research.

Animal Rights Resource Site

http://envirolink.org/arrs/index.html

The Animal Rights Resource Site, sponsored by the Envirolink Network, provides information for those involved in the support of animal rights. An icon-based menu takes you to FAQs, journals, the latest news, and extra resources. Includes information about the annual International Animal Rights Symposium in Washington, DC. Information on vegetarianism and veganism also is available at this site.

Animals

http://rs306.ccs.bbk.ac.uk/flora/animals.htm#inverts

Contains an abundance of information about all kinds of mammals, birds, amphibians, reptiles, and butterflies. Offers many links to other animal specific sites.

The Bunny Thymes

http://hiddencharms.com/inscape/thyme_in.html

The Bunny Thymes is a bi-monthly newsletter that contains articles by veterinarians, book reviews, vegetarian recipes, children's pages, and information on rabbit care. Visitors to this site can subscribe to the newsletter online.

Hey Ma, What's for Dinner?

Having chicken tonight? As you pour on the barbeque sauce, consider the following about our delicious friend. Check out Donald Firsching's Chicken Page for more juicy morsels.

- The domestication of the chicken (Gallus domesticus) is believed to have taken place about 3000 B.C. in India.

- Most of the breeds we know today are the result of a widespread enthusiasm for poultry breeding in America and England in the nineteenth century.

- Today there are over seven billion chickens in the world.

- Each year nearly 300 million chickens are raised for egg production in the United States alone. They produce about 65 billion eggs annually.

- More than three billion fryers or broilers (the chicken most commonly found in food stores) are grown each year in large commercial flocks.

Donald Firsching's Chicken Page

http://ccwf.cc.utexas.edu/~ifza664/index.html

Did you know that the average American eats 20 chickens a year? That's according to Firsching Enterprises, the sponsor of this site. This page includes other "cool chicken facts" and "great chicken connections" (links to other sites/info). Contains links to information on the history of chickens, the poultry industry, and how to raise and care for chickens. Also offers hen and rooster .WAV sound files.

Endangered Species

http://www.nceet.snre.umich.edu/EndSpp/Endangered.html

Provides information on endangered species. Contains a large list of extinct species and clickable image maps that identify at-risk species by region.

Exotic Pets

http://dca.net:80/exoticpets/

Online exotic pet shop. Specializes in birds, reptiles, frogs, ferrets, iguanas, snakes, hedgehogs, chinchillas, emus, fish, turtles, chameleons, sugar gliders, wolf dogs, rabbits, and more. Lets you place classified ads for buying or selling (for a fee). Also includes an Online Exotic Pet Breeder Directory.

Getting a Pet

http://www.tezcat.com/~ermiller/getapet.html

This sight will come in handy for those who are thinking of getting a dog or cat and need advice on where/how to get started. The site offers information on choosing a breed, descriptions of different types of animal shelters, advice on why you should avoid pet stores, and the truth about puppy mills. Includes links to related sites.

The House Rabbit Society Home Page

http://www.psg.lcs.mit.edu/~carl/paige/HRS-home.html

The House Rabbit Society is a non-profit organization that works to rescue abandoned rabbits and find permanent homes for them. The Society also educates the public and assists humane societies. This Web site offers information about rabbits that are available for adoption, plus pictures and bios. It also offers links to Web sites of HRS local chapters, and provides general information about rabbits as house pets.

How to Put Your Pet on the Web

http://www.dynamo.net/dynamo/pets/howto.html

So you want to show the whole world that great photo you took of Tabby or Buttons, but you don't have your own Web site. No problem—Pet Pages will post your pet's photo on the World Wide Web for you. It's easy and free. Just follow the instructions and soon your friendly feline friend or favorite pooch can be seen online by other pet enthusiasts.

Index of /animal_gifs/

http://aazk.ind.net/animal_gifs/

Contains an archive of stock photos of animals. Indexes animals by species.

Inter-species Telepathic Communication

http://www.asyst.net/animal/telepath.htm

Do you believe humans can communicate telepathically with pets? If so, you're not alone. This site describes one dog owner's experiences in communicating telepathically with her dog, and includes submissions by other pet owners who detail similar communications with their animals. This page also refers you to reading material on the subject, videos, and workshops around the country on inter-species communication.

Nature Subject Page

http://secondnature.com/nature.htm

This photo- and graphics-laden site features photographic artwork of animals in their natural habitat. It also includes screen savers of nature shots that users can download—for a small fee. Includes photos of other nature venues, and links to other sites about nature and travel.

Pet Care Corner

http://www.familyinternet.com/pet/pet-vet.htm

Authored by Lowell Ackermann, a board-certified veterinary dermatologist and author of 34 books on animal health, this site provides answers to owner's questions about their pets' health.

Pet Grief Support

http://ourworld.compuserve.com/homepages/edwilliams/

For pet owners who are grieving over the death of a pet or an ill pet, this site offers support and encouragement. One highlight is the Monday Evening Candle Ceremony, a weekly event in which people across the country (who have lost a pet) light candles in memory of their departed companions. The site also includes the Rainbow Bridge story, which provides an answer to the question: "Where do our pets go when they die?" (You might want to keep a tissue handy for this one.)

PetBunny Home Page

http://www.mit.edu:8001/people/klund/bunny/bunny.html

PetBunny, which includes a mailing list for rabbit owners, is an open forum for people who are interested in discussing rabbits. The discussion includes such topics as diet, behavior, and medical problems. The site includes a few links to specific rabbit home pages.

The Remembrance Page

http://www.primenet.com/~meggie/bridge.htm

This site, which offers an outlet for grieving pet owners, includes poems, tributes, and photos from owners who want to share memories of animals. Visitors can also access links to pages that contain tributes to specific dogs, cats, and birds.

Horses

EquiLinQ

http://www.wsmith.com/equilinq/

Provides sales information about horses and horse-related gear. Includes links to the red bluff bull and gelding sale.

The Horse Zone

http://www.thinktek.com/horses.htm

If you're looking for a horse to buy, or need a saddle or other riding gear, the Horse Zone might be what you're looking for. This site contains that information and more. Home of the Equestrian Resource Center, this page contains a listing of classified ads, a discussion group, and a photo gallery of horses.

The Horseman's Advisor

http://www.spyder.net/horseadvice/

This Web site serves as a clearinghouse for articles and products on horse-related topics. Includes a discussion forum, classifieds, and links to other sites.

WWW Library—Livestock Section

http://www.ansi.okstate.edu/library/equine.html

This strictly basics Web site provides a listing of horse resources, including information on breeds and selection, horse publications, publications on diseases, disorders, and parasites of the horse, and general information such as behavior and training, buying a horse, care and horse shoeing, nutrition and feeding, and more.

Whales

Canada Whale Watching

http://www.csi.nb.ca/tourism/page1.html

Provides information about the lesser-known whale species in the Canadian seas. Also includes information about whale-watching tours in New Brunswick on the Bay of Fundy, where more than 20 types of whales have been sighted.

Welcome to the Tirpitz Whaling Web Page

http://tirpitz.ibg.uit.no/wwww/ss.html

Focuses on whales and the whaling industry. Provides links to the latest news, FAQs, organizations, Internet whale information, and literature on whaling.

Whale Adoption Project Home Page

http://www.Webcom.com/~iwcwww/whale_adoption/waphome.html

Learn how you can adopt a humpback whale for yourself or as a gift for a friend. View photos of humpback whales and learn how the whaling industry is threatening the survival of this species. Features "Whalewatch," a newsletter of the Whale Adoption Project.

The Whale Information Network

http://www.macmedia.com.au/whales/

The Whale Information Network (WIN) works to assist the research, understanding, and conservation of some 25 species of whales and dolphins. The site includes photos, whale-watching guidelines, whale facts, and background info on whales throughout history.

Whale Songs

http://kingfish.ssp.nmfs.gov/songs.html

Presents the sounds of whales. Includes a small archive of audio files.

The Whale Watching Web

http://www.physics.helsinki.fi/whale/

Serves as the whale-watchers network on the Internet. Offers pictures, information about whales, information about countries around which whales are active.

Wildlife

Adam's Fox Box

http://tavi.acomp.usf.edu/foxbox/

This colorful, graphics-filled, and award-winning site gives you the scoop on everything you ever needed to know about the fox. Points you to articles, books, stories, songs, and poems, photos, and more. Great site for kids and adults alike.

Antarctica and Its Environment

http://icair.iac.org.nz/reports/nz/visitor.html

Examines the ecosystems and wildlife, including fish, seals, whales, penguins, and sea birds, on the Antarctic continent. Includes descriptions about how wildlife has adapted to the extreme cold of Antarctica, such as fish that have been able to adapt to temperatures blow the freezing point of their body fluids.

The Bear Den

`http://www2.portage.net/~dmiddlet/bears/index.html`

This site, which contains a wealth of information and photos about bears, provides up-to-date information about initiatives to protect endangered grizzlies. Describes the evolution of bears and details the different species, including Brown, Polar, and Panda bears. Includes a link to The Cub Den, a new Web site for children that contains bear info geared to young readers. A sound file lets you hear a bear roar.

Cochrane Wildlife Reserve

`http://www.cuug.ab.ca:8001/~scholefp/swiftfox.html`

Focuses on reintroducing the swift fox species back into the wild. Stylish, colorful, and contains good reading. Includes links to other sites, such as the International Wildlife Coalition and the African Wild Dog Conservation Fund.

Deer Net

`http://cervid.forsci.ualberta.ca/deernet/deernet.html`

Focuses on the impact of humans on Canadian wildlife and their habitats. Provides interesting facts on the grizzly and livestock diversification. Provides some species information including the white tail deer, which can be found in every state in the Continental U.S.

Eastern Slope Grizzly

`http://www.rr.ualberta.ca/~lmorgant/grizzly.html`

Concerned about human land use and grizzly bear mortality, environmental groups and other agencies formed the Eastern Slopes Grizzly Bear Steering Committee in 1994. This group works to identify and implement research that will predict the effects of development on grizzly bears. This site describes the Committee's activities and also includes photos of grizzlies.

Frontier Technologies' Lion Gallery

`http://www.frontiertech.com/gall.htm`

Did you know the lion's tail is the only one in the cat family with a tassel at the tip? Learn about this and more lion facts at this colorful and photo-filled site. The award-winning Web page boasts several contributors' submissions—in the form of photos, factoids, stories, and other items about lions. Take a moment to hear a lion roar.

GORP—Nature & Wildlife

`http://www.gorp.com/gorp/activity/wildlife.htm`

Provides information about almost any conceivable animal-related topic—from bird watching to protection/preservation societies, including the U.S. National Parks, U.S. National Forests, U.S. National Monuments, and U.S. Fish and Wildlife Service.

Hyenas

`http://www.csulb.edu/~persepha/hyena.html`

Focuses on the much maligned and misunderstood spotted hyena, a carnivore that roams the deserts of Africa. Includes lots of photos. This award-winning site garnered the "Point Survey Top Five Percent of the Web."

Introduced Wild Animals in Australia

`http://kaos.erin.gov.au/life/end_vuln/Threats/wildanim.html`

Provides detailed information on Australian wildlife evolution. Takes an intriguing look at the impact of animals, such as the cane toad, English starling, rabbit, and fox, that were introduced into the Australian ecosystem—and subsequently altered the habitat of the wildlife already there.

Kaehler's Mill Farm

`http://www.execpc.com/~slc/k-m.html`

Contains information about Galloway cattle and Targhee sheep. Describes a farming technique called Management Intensive Grazing. Interesting site for those curious about cattle and sheep farming.

Coffee

`http://www.nwwp.com/volcano/sendme.htm`

The Volcano Coffee Company harvests it's coffee beans from the volcanic regions of the south sea islands. Request a sample of the Kona Roast, Mo'a Mana Blend, or the monthly special.

Kids' Action: Rainforest Animals

http://www.ran.org/ran/kids_action/animals.html#pagetop

This site gives a kid's-eye view of the animals from the tropical rainforest, one of the oldest ecosystems of the world. Explains why more species live in the rainforest than any other area of the world. Answers other frequently asked questions.

Lion Pictures of the Month

http://www.frontiertech.com/gall.htm

Exhibits a monthly gallery of fine feline photography. Contains not only lots of photos, but also links to other sites and the "Lion Factiod of the Month." Lets you download a .WAV file of a lion raoring. Winner of the "Magellan 3 Star Site" award.

LlamaWeb

http://www.webcom.com/~degraham/

This site focuses on llamas, the South American camelid. Contains pictures of llamas, the lineage of specific llamas, and all about llama shows, products, literature, and llama associations. The site has been voted among the top five percent of Web sites by Point Communications, and also received a four-star rating by Magellan.

Manatees

http://www.bev.net/education/SeaWorld/manatee/manatees.html

Provides information on the habits, habitat, diet, and just about anything else you would want to know about the manatee. Sponsored by Sea World Education Department, this site also contains links to Sea World of Florida, Texas, California, and Ohio.

OSU's Breeds of Livestock

http://www.ansi.okstate.edu/breeds/

Showcases a comprehensive list of the various breeds of livestock, including cattle, goats, horses, sheep, and swine. Sponsored by the Department of Animal Science, Oklahoma State University, this site also provides background information and terminology on animal breeds.

The Polar Regions

http://www.stud.unit.no:80/~sveinw/arctic/wild.html

Offers links to arctic wildlife and resources, including wolves, foxes, polar bears, and Antarctic life.

Turtle Trax—A Marine Turtle Page

http://www.io.org/~bunrab/

Provides information on marine turtles, which are larger and more interesting than the ones from the store. Also points out that marine turtles are endangered and explains the issue, including how you can help.

Wolf Resource Page

http://www.greywolf.com/wolf.html

Lists wolf resources and provides special reports on wolf-related news throughout the country.

The Wolf Studies Project

http://www.wolf.org/

Includes a chance to listen to the howl of the wolf, pictures of wolves, and links to newsgroups that cover wolves.

The Wolf's Den: Home Page of Wolf McSherry

http://www.widomaker.com/~wolf/

This site provides information on wolves and wolf recovery, as well as Native American info, amateur radio, and more. Provides updates on brutality incidents against wolves. Includes wolf photos and graphics.

Wombats, Marsupials, and Other Animals

http://www.batnet.com/wombat/animals.html

Serves as a resource site for marsupials as well as other kinds of existing and extinct species in the animal kingdom.

The Wonderful Skunk and Opossum Page

http://elvis.neep.wisc.edu/~firmiss/mephitis-didelphis.html

Do you know the difference between a possum and an opossum? Find out about that and other interesting facts at this Web site. Contains drawings and newsgroup information, skunk and possum trivia, stories, photos, further reading, and a little historical perspective about these two critters.

The World Wide Raccoon Web

http://deja-vu.oldiron.cornell.edu/~sjm1/raccoons/

Features pictures and stories about raccoons, raccoon wildlife management, and links to a raccoon lovers' mailing list.

Newsgroups

alt.animals

alt.animals.badgers

alt.animals.bears

alt.animals.dolphins

alt.animals.felines

alt.animals.foxes

alt.animals.raccoons

alt.aquaria

alt.chinchilla

alt.fan.lemurs

alt.pets.ferrets

alt.pets.hamsters

alt.pets.rabbits

alt.skunks

alt.support.grief.pet-loss

alt.wolves

alt.wolves.hybrid

rec.animals.wildlife

rec.aquaria

rec.aquaria.freshwater.goldfish

rec.aquaria.freshwater.misc

rec.aquaria.freshwater.plants

rec.aquaria.marine.misc

rec.aquaria.marine.reefs

rec.aquaria.marketplace

rec.aquaria.misc

rec.aquaria.tech

rec.equestrian

rec.hunting.dogs

rec.pets

rec.pets.birds

rec.pets.cats

rec.pets.dogs

rec.pets.dogs.activities

rec.pets.dogs.behavior

rec.pets.dogs.breeds

rec.pets.dogs.health

rec.pets.dogs.info

rec.pets.dogs.misc

rec.pets.dogs.rescue

rec.pets.herp

Listservs

ANMGT-L—Animal Management Discussion Forum

University of Nebraska Computing Services Network, Lincoln, NE

You can join this group by sending the message "sub ANMGT-L your name" to `listserv@unlvm.unl.edu`

ANSCI-L—Animal Science Students

You can join this group by sending the message "sub ANSCI-L your name" to `listserv@listserv.okstate.edu`

AQUARIUM—Fish and Aquaria

You can join this group by sending the message "sub AQUARIUM your name" to `listserv%emuvm1.bitnet@listserv.net`

AZARC-L—Association of Zoos and Aquariums Research Coordinators

Kansas State University; Manhattan, KS

You can join this group by sending the message "sub AZARC-L your name" to `listserv@ksuvm.ksu.edu`

CANINE-L—Discussion Forum for Dog Fanciers

Pennsylvania State University

You can join this group by sending the message "sub CANINE-L your name" to `listserv@psuvm.psu.edu`

CAT-CHAT

You can join this group by sending the message "sub CAT-CHAT your name" to `listserv@lsv.uky.edu`

CONSGIS—Biological Conservation and GIS

You can join this group by sending the message "sub CONSGIS your name" to `listserv%uriacc.bitnet@listserv.net`

DAIRY-L—Dairy Discussion List

University of Maryland CSC, College Park, MD 20742-2411

You can join this group by sending the message "sub DAIRY-L your name" to `listserv%umdd.bitnet@listserv.net`

EMBRIO—Basic Embryology for Medical Students

Temple University, Philadelphia, PA 19122

You can join this group by sending the message "sub EMBRIO your name" to `listserv@vm.temple.edu`

EQUINE-L—Discussion Forum for Horse Fanciers

Pennsylvania State University

You can join this group by sending the message "sub EQUINE-L your name" to `listserv@psuvm.psu.edu`

FELINE-L—Discussion Forum for Cat Fanciers

Pennsylvania State University

You can join this group by sending the message "sub FELINE-L your name" to `listserv@psuvm.psu.edu`

FERRET—The Domestic Ferret Electronic Mailing List (FML)

City University of New York/University Computing Center

You can join this group by sending the message "sub FERRET your name" to `listserv@cunyvm.cuny.edu`

GERBILS—Gerbil Discussion List

Rice University Information Systems, Houston, Texas

You can join this group by sending the message
"sub GERBILS your name" to
`listserv@ricevm1.rice.edu`

GISAB-L—Gibbs Sampling in Animal Breeding

University of Nebraska Computing Services Network, Lincoln, NE

You can join this group by sending the message
"sub GISAB-L your name" to `listserv@unlvm.unl.edu`

GROOMERS-L—Pet Groomers Helping Each Other

You can join this group by sending the message
"sub GROOMERS-L your name" to
`listserv@home.ease.lsoft.com`

KSUPET-L—KSU Pet Health News

Kansas State University; Manhattan, KS

You can join this group by sending the message
"sub KSUPET-L your name" to
`listserv@ksuvm.ksu.edu`

MAMMAL-L—Mammalian Biology

Smithsonian Institution, Washington, DC 20560

You can join this group by sending the message
"sub MAMMAL-L your name" to
`listserv@sivm.si.edu`

MARMAM—Marine Mammals Research and Conservation Discussion

University of Victoria, Victoria, BC

You can join this group by sending the message
"sub MARMAM your name" to
`listserv@uvvm.uvic.ca`

MATBI-L—Marine All Taxa Biological Inventories

Smithsonian Institution, Washington, DC

You can join this group by sending the message
"sub MATBI-L your name" to `listserv@sivm.si.edu`

PETBUNNY—Forum for Folks with Companion Rabbits

You can join this group by sending the message
"sub PETBUNNY your name" to
`listserv@lsv.uky.edu`

POODLE-L—All Poodle Discussion Group

eWorld, Apple Online Services, Cupertino, CA, USA

You can join this group by sending the message
"sub POODLE-L your name" to
`listserv@mail.eworld.com`

PROTECTION-DOGS-L—Protection Dogs Discussion List

eWorld, Apple Online Services, Cupertino, CA, USA

You can join this group by sending the message
"sub PROTECTION-DOGS-L your name" to
`listserv@mail.eworld.com`

URBWLF-L—Urban Wildlife Working Group: Ecology, Education, Planning

You can join this group by sending the message
"sub URBWLF-L your name" to
`listserv%uriacc.bitnet@listserv.net`

WDAMAGE—Wildlife Damage Management

You can join this group by sending the message
"sub WDAMAGE your name" to
`listserv@listserv.nodak.edu`

WLREHAB—Wildlife Rehab List

You can join this group by sending the message
"sub WLREHAB your name" to
`listserv@listserv.nodak.edu`

ZOOGNUS—News from the National Zoological Park, Washington, DC

Smithsonian Institution, Washington, DC 20560

You can join this group by sending the message
"sub ZOOGNUS your name" to
`listserv@sivm.si.edu`

ZOOGRAD—Department of Zoology Grad Students

Arizona State University, Tempe, AZ

You can join this group by sending the message "sub ZOOGRAD your name" to
listserv@asuvm.inre.asu.edu

ART

Art History

The Age of Enlightenment

http://dmf.culture.fr/files/imaginary_exhibition.html

For students of art history, this site highlights the paintings of France's national museums concerning the Age of Enlightenment. Presents the information from an historical and artistic perspective.

ArtServe

http://rubens.anu.edu.au/

Australian National University server. Offers a variety of image collections and small presentations dealing with art history. Includes more than 10,200 images, which include 2,800 prints ranging from the 15th to the 19th century, over 8,500 images of architecture and architectural sculpture from the Mediterranean and beyond, and a small selection of Islamic monuments.

The Ashmolean Museum of Art and Archaeology

http://www.ashmol.ox.ac.uk/

One of the four museums of the University of Oxford, founded in 1683, which is regarded as Britain's oldest public museum. Contains the University's archaeological and art historical collections. This museum includes both temporary and permanent exhibitions.

Israel Museum—Jerusalem

http://www.imj.org.il

Emphasizes the material culture (past, present, and future) of the land of Israel and the Jewish people. The Israel Museum (founded in 1965) fosters public education and strives to preserve, study, and display the collections.

The Risk Map of Cultural Heritage in Italy

http://www.uni.net/aec

A project promoted by Italian Istituto Centrale per il Restauro on preventative restoration and programmed maintenance.

Art Resources

ADG Graphix Home Page

http://www.earthlink.net/~anthony/index.html

Offers links to African American sites on the Web, as well as other sites, including the design and graphics arts community.

Advanced Cultural Technologies

http://www.ACTinc.bc.ca/

Provides a multimedia catalog of participating Canadian museums and gallerys. Site utilizes sound bytes, text, digitized photographs, and narration. Also provides a newsletter and a "Virtual Museum" project.

African Art

http://www.lib.virginia.edu/dic/exhib/93.ray.aa/African.html

The University of Virginia's Bayly Art Museum presents an exhibit of African art, including an overview of African aesthetics, pictures and descriptions of masks, headdresses, statuettes, and other artifacts.

Akteo Watch Boutique

http://www.tiac.net/users/uwc

Affords opportunity to view and/or purchase AKTEO watches designed by J. C. Mareschal.

Allen Toney's Home Page

http://marshall.edu/~jtoney/

Displays the art work of Allen Toney, the 1st place winner of the 1995 Fractal Designs "Painter" International Computer Art Contest. His work "weds liquid, sensual, neoclassical forms with mystical, mathematical, and surreal sensibilities."

Amsterdam Valley

http://valley.interact.nl/av/int/home.html

Contains an eclectic mix of off-beat publications, forums for musicians, and high-tech businesses. Amsterdam Valley provides a wide range of activities, from touring a virtual art gallery known for its mood enhancing paintings and artistic sounds to sampling Dutch culture by viewing the online windmill collection.

ANIMA

http://www.anima.wis.net//ANIMAhome.html

ANIMA is the Arts Network for Integrated Media Applications, a global cultural information source for the media arts. Links an array of categories: art work, spectrum, atlas, nexus, techne, persona, and connections.

Arizona Museum for Youth

http://www.primenet.com/art-rom/museumweb/azmusyou/azmusyou.html

Displays exhibits with intent of introducing children to the fine arts world to generate interest in non-virtual visits to the museum.

Art Crimes Index

http://www.gatech.edu/desoto/graf/Index.Art_Crimes.html

Displays graffiti art from around the world, providing explanations and examples of "art crime." Also provides links to other art-related sites.

Art Links on the World Wide Web

http://amanda.physics.wisc.edu/outside.html

Contains links to most of the major and minor galleries on the Web featuring new and innovative art, music, video, photography, and 3D renderings. You can contact other artists; view paintings, sketches, and renderings in virtual art galleries; check out current events in the art field; or submit your own art-related Web site for others to view.

Art To Live with Original Prints

http://www.arttolivewith.com/

Includes original prints by internationally recognized artists such as Appel, Chamberlain, Hamaguchi, Tooker, Wesselmann, and more, and offers the opportunity to purchase art.

Art.Online

http://bighorn.terra.net/artonline/

Highlights African American, Native American, wildlife, nautical, and rock art. Enables you to view and purchase limited edition art.

Art?

http://www.directnet.com/Crash/Art/index.html

Contains a nontraditional perspective on art that claims art's death. Art? maintains that since art's death, "we find ourselves free of two dead weights." This means that everyone is now an artist, and art's audience has "regained its innocence."

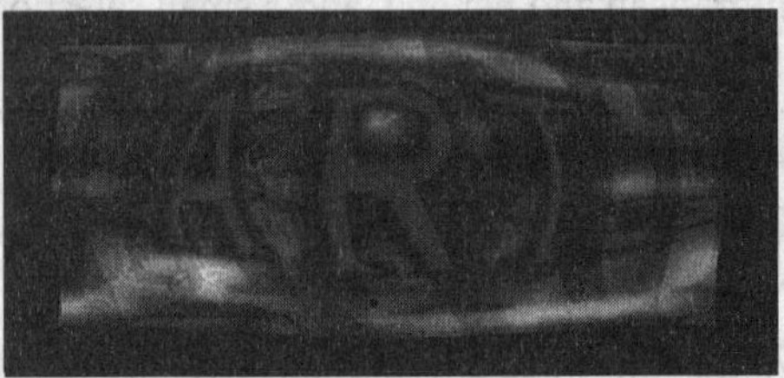

Artix

http://www.artix.com/biz/artix/

Artix is a Web site home for many New York City galleries and artists. Provides links to individual gallery home pages and an alphabetical listing of all their artists represented.

ArtMap

http://www.anima.wis.net//ARTWORLDonline.html

Contains links to the visual arts and galleries, mass media and pop culture, literary arts and online libraries, animation, film and video, performance in the audio arts of music and sound, and architecture, environmental planning, and urban design.

ArtScape

http://www.artscape.com/

Provides a means for artists to display their work, share their philosophies and inspirations, demonstrate techniques, and network with other artists and art enthusiasts who share their interests. Offers artists' samples and networking opportunities, and plans to include a searchable index, QuickTime movies demonstrating technique, information on professional organizations, and art show schedules.

ArtScene

http://artscenecal.com/

Guide to art galleries and museums in Southern California. This site includes schedules, area maps, articles, an image bank, a calendar of openings and special events, and a user's forum.

ArtSource

http://www.uky.edu/Artsource/artsourcehome.html

Points you to a variety of electronic art galleries, online exhibits, research materials, and art-related periodicals. This site includes links to resources on the net, as well as original materials submitted by art and architechture scholars. They state, however, that this site is "intended to be selective rather than comprehensive."

Artworld (ArtMap) Online Links and Listings

http://www.anima.wis.net//ARTWORLDonline.html#VISUALARTS

Indexes a wealth of actual images, as well as artists, magazines, events, and so forth, and overviews current art (including literature) in Canada.

AS220

http://www.ids.net/~as220/home.html

AS220 is an artist-owned complex that manages two galleries, a performance space, a cafe, 11 artist studios, and 12 residential studios in Rhode Island.

Ballinakill Studios

http://gellersen.valpo.edu/~jgordon/art.html

Advertises art courses offered at Ballinakill Studios in Ireland. This site also houses a repository of information concerning education in Ireland.

Brookhouse Studio

http://www.ni.net/brookhouse.com/

Offers more than 300 images that reflect Brookhouse Studio's services, which include commercial photography and graphics, 3D models, stock images, and fine art.

Business Volunteers for the Arts— Houston

http://www.fine-art.com/org/bva.html

Provides business expertise through volunteers to non-profit arts and cultural organizations.

The Butler Institute of American Art

http://www.cisnet.com/butler/

Displays information regarding the Butler Institute of American Art, in Youngstown, Ohio. Includes links to other museums.

BYU Performing Arts Management

http://visitor.byu.edu/pam/homepage.html

Includes links that enable you to order tickets to all performances of all Brigham Young University's performing arts and a schedule of national and international places at which BYU groups perform.

Capacity Index

http://www.wimsey.com/Capacity/

Canadian magazine that seeks to expand the boundaries of art and culture (current and back issues available online).

CBC Radio Trial

http://www.radio.cbc.ca/

Offers Canadian Broadcasting Corporation radio products, including a complete listing of available program transcripts, aired broadcasts, and digital radio program samples.

Center for Research in Computing and the Arts (CRCA)

http://crca-www.ucsd.edu/

Deals with applying computing technology to a wide array of artistic endeavors, including music, visual arts, theatre, literature, and media. Also contains a listing of concerts, seminars, and art-related workshops, as well as links to other sites.

CERN MusiClub

http://www.cern.ch/CERN/Clubs/Music/musiclub.html

Includes press releases, sounds, and pics from CERN bands. The CERN MusiClub is divided into two sections, classical and rock/jazz.

The Chrysler Museum

http://www.whro.org/cl/cmhh/

Provides information about the museum, including photographs, addresses, and some specifics about the house in which the museum is contained.

Cloud Gallery

http://www.commerce.digital.com/palo-alto/CloudGallery/home.html

Contains downloadable fine art photographs of sky backgrounds. Includes tips on angels and ways to watch clouds and offers the means to order more sky images.

Colorburst Studios Online Catalog

http://www.teleport.com/~paulec/catalog.html

Offers a catalog of Niobium jewelry, handcrafted by Paul Crabtree and Tess Yevka, for which you can place orders online.

Danclink

http://www.cts.com/~danclink/

Point of departure for dance enthusiasts who want more than just Internet connections. Includes not only complete video instructions on how to dance, but also provides a "dating service" (helps you find a dance partner), video dating services such as online chatting with other members, as well as membership in an adult movie club.

Daniel Vogel

http://www.eciad.bc.ca/~dvogel/personal.html

Displays Daniel Vogel's home page and a series of pages that further display his work. Includes art and graphics accompanied by explanatory text and an eclectic set of links.

Daum On-line

http://www.daum.co.kr

Concentrates only on artistic areas such as photography, cinema, cartoon, and fashion. Provides links to several subsites and several mirror sites for Korean users.

Dia Center for the Arts

http://www.diacenter.org/

Shows exhibitions and the Dia Center for the Arts' permanent collection, and provides links to many other art-related sites.

DigiPen Applied Computer Graphics School

http://www.digipen.com/High/DPHP.htm

One page in a series of pages regarding classes and background of Vancouver's DigiPen Applied Computer Graphics School—the page on which the students can display their work.

Enterzone

http://enterzone.berkeley.edu/enterzone.html

Online magazine designed for people who like to read a little bit about everything; an eclectic mix of various forms of art, short stories, and news media. Previous editions available.

Eric Boutilier-Brown

http://www.isisnet.com/empire/ebb/

Showcases black-and-white fine art photography, predominantly of the nude and of archaeological ruins.

eSCENE 1995

http://www.etext.org/Zines/eScene

Furnishes yearly anthology of short fiction published online (available in ASCII, PDF, and PostScript formats).

The Eye Produce CD ROM Home Page

http://www.earthlink.net/~rogue/cd.html

Hosts hundreds of royalty free pictures and photographs, mostly backgrounds and textures.

Flaming Jewels

http://www.prairienet.org/~jjewels/jewel.html

An online exhibition of writings by jewel (Julieann M. Brown-Micklo). Poetry, prose, and letters are included here.

Flapping

http://www.slip.net/~atombee

Presents illustrated allegorical sci-fi spoof of Chervil Orbane's saga, including his moment of clarity, the big ideas, the good guys, the bad guys, the gratuitous sex, the great epiphany, the happy ending, and the ipso and the facto, as it were, of fin-de-siècle metaphysical thought.

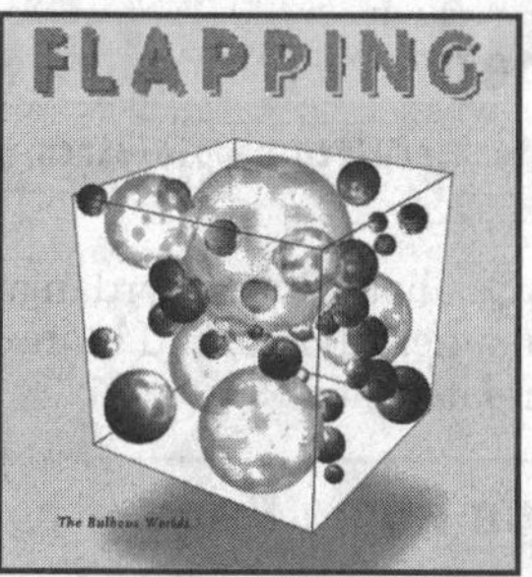

FrameMakers

http://www.prairienet.org/arts/framing/homepage.html

FrameMakers began as a framing shop and has now expanded to selling prints over the Internet. Provides links to artists, prints, copyright and ordering info, as well as their newsletter, books, featured prints, and other art-related pages.

The Framers Corner

http://www.traveller.com/mall/hsv/framer

Specializes in limited edition prints by Terry Redlin, Daniel Moore, John Seery-Lester, Alan Hunt, and many others.

Free Art Website (Laurie McCanna's Home Page)

http://www.mccannas.com/

Lets you view the art work of Laurie McCanna, a freelance illustrator and WWW graphics designer, as well as download icons, textures, and Photoshop tips.

Frida Kahlo Art Pages

http://www.cascade.net/kahlo.html

Showcases the work of Frido Kahlo, provides facts about her life, and points to a bibliography for further reading.

Front Home

http://www.anima.wis.net//SHELF/FrontTOC.html

Electronic newsletter for a cultural center in Vancouver, Canada. Offers gallery and performance space, as well as a simple meeting place for local artists. Includes pages to the magazine, the place, the artists, and their work.

gallery.html (Edison Gallery)

http://www.wimsey.com/~panic/gallery.html

Elaborates on the gallery's background, upcoming exhibits, and images of previous artists.

Gen Art

http://www.emedia.net/genart/

Displays the work of young artists and provides exhibitions, online catalog, and links to other art-related sites.

The Getty Art History Information Program

http://www.ahip.getty.edu/ahip/Text_home.html

Disseminates research and information about artistic and cultural heritage. Provides text and graphics versions of pages.

The Graphix Exchange

http://www.rust.net/TGX_WWW_pgs/TGX.html

Growing resource directory of freelance talent from around the world. Furnishes a database of artists (to whom you can send e-mail directly from this site) and links to many artists' personal home pages.

The Great Books of Western Civilization

http://www.ilinks.net/~lnoles/grtbks.html

Provides access to the great literary works of the western world. This site is based on the Great Books Program, started at Mercer University in the Early '80s.

Hal's Virtual Furniture Gallery

http://www.xensei.com/users/hipjr

Presents handcrafted pieces ranging from grandfather clocks to Belizian deck chairs.

Harmony Music List

http://orpheus.ucsd.edu/mbreen/harmony.html

Indexes nearly 1,000 music-related links and contains a built-in search engine for finding sources in the Harmony list, including major headings such as Artists, Classical, Cultures, Discographies, Instruments and Equipment, Jazz, Music Labels, Magazines, Radio stations, Studios, and more.

The Heard Museum

http://hanksville.phast.umass.edu/defs/independent/
Heard/Heard.html

Promotes appreciation and respect for native people and their cultural heritage and emphasizes the traditional cultures of the Greater Southwest and the evolving Native American Fine Art Movement. Over the years the Heard Museum (established in 1929) has grown and today boasts a collection of more than 30,000 works of art and artifacts; 45,000 pieces of archival materials including significant papers, books, and photographs; and a membership of nearly 5,000.

Hollywood Archaeology

http://www.echonyc.com/~hwdarch

Contains five separate subsections, one of which traces the life and career of wrestler and movie heavy, Mike Mazurki (text by conceptual artist Lowell Darling, design by Jim Newman). Includes 40 examples of film found in the streets of Hollywood by Darling in the early '70s.

The iGallery

http://www.igallery.com

Presents a collection of eclectic art work from around the world, including beaded and metal jewelry, iron furniture, decorated masks, and much more.

INM Home Page

http://www.inm.de/

The Institute for New Media, a research site and forum for art, science, and technology in new media. Includes four levels of cooperative projects in the fields of audio, video, 3D-graphics, and interactive media.

International Sculpture Center's On-line Resource

http://www.dgsys.com/~sculpt/

Nonprofit organization devoted to issues related to contemporary sculpture. Publishes *Sculpture and Maquette* magazine, holds technical workshops and conferences, brokers sculpture shows, and administrates Sculpture Source, a database for contemporary sculpture.

Jayhawk

http://www.klab.caltech.edu/~flowers/jayhawk/

Presents the Jayhawk series, a cyberpunk fantasy by Mary K. Kuhner, serialized in 144 parts and stored in the order in which the author posted them on the Web (except for the story background, an explanatory piece posted partway through the story to help bring new readers up to date).

Jordan, Robert

http://www.cc.gatech.edu/ftp/people/viren/www/jordan/
jordan.html

Focuses on FAQs about Robert Jordan and presents readings on dreamers, lyrics, and humor. Also offers links to other related sites.

Kaleidospace Home Page

http://kspace.com

Offers a mix of art and publications: you can select where you want to go from a color wheel, relax in the Reading Room, chat with artists online in the Kaleidospeak forum, see what's new in the Art Studio, or check out the new tunes in the Music Kiosk, to name a few of your many options. Also allows you to place online orders for work by Kspace artists.

Krannert Art Museum

http://www.art.uiuc.edu/kam/

Provides information about the University of Illinois' Krannert Art Museum. Includes exhibition schedules, a guide to the permanent collection, special events at the museum, a virtual tour, and shopping at the museum shop.

Krypton Neon—The Internet's Neon Shop

http://www.neonshop.com

Offers neon signs, neon art, neon special effects, and more. Demonstrates the art of making neon. Includes neon FAQs and more.

Le Ministère de la Culture Direction des Musées de France

http://dmf.culture.fr/

Displays exhibit, titled "The Age of Enlightenment in the Paintings of France's National Museums," offered by the French Ministry of Culture. Offers complete French version in addition to the English site.

Lewis Carroll Home Page

http://www.students.uiuc.edu/~jbirenba/carroll.html

Highlights listings of Carroll's publications online, *Alice in Wonderland* graphics, and links to other related sites, including a *Jabberwocky* translation page.

Lysator Computer Society

http://www.lysator.liu.se

Maintains a collection of books, artworks, and literature resources divided into three broad subject areas: The Science Fiction/Fantasy Archive (contains reviews, bibliographies, news lists, electronic magazines, and art work), Anime and Manga (a collection of Japanese comics and animations), and Project Runeberg (publishes electronic texts in Scandinavian).

Metaverse

http://metaverse.com/index.html

Offers much in the way of art and entertainment. A true multimedia Web site.

Michael C. Carlos Museum, Emory University

http://www.cc.emory.edu/CARLOS/carlos.html

Offers a virtual tour of the museum with downloadable video files.

Mill Valley Film Festival

http://www.well.com/mvff

Offers the 17th Annual Mill Valley Film Festival, a line-up of American and international films, tributes, and a three-day videofest and interactive exhibition.

Millennium Productions

http://www.arts-online.com/

Hosts the home pages of many visual artists, performing artists, and writers.

Motorcycle Collectible Art Gallery

http://www.rwga.com/motor2.htm

Displays a montage lithograph of the history of Harley-Davidson for collectors and provides

information on how they can (for a price) paint your portrait into this picture.

The Multimedia Cultural Information Service

http://www.wimsey.com/anima/ARTWORLDhome.html

Provides an online art gallery and links to other related Web sites on visual arts, design, video, literature, and performance.

Musée des Arts et Métiers's World Wide Web (Museum of Art and Craft)

http://web.cnam.fr/museum/

Offers many collections, displays, and unique graphics. Currently, most of this site is in French, with no English translation available.

Museum Web from Art-ROM

http://www.primenet.com/art-rom/museumweb/

Directory to museum and gallery sites on the World Wide Web.

Museums in the Netherlands

http://www.xxlink.nl/nbt/museums/

Provides links to information about museums in the Netherlands. Supports many languages. Text only.

National Museum of American Art

http://www.nmaa.si.edu/

Presents information and exhibitions for the National Museum of American Art.

The National Museum of the American Indian—George Gustav Heye Center

http://www.interport.net/~logomanc/heye.html

Displays information about The National Museum of the American Indian. Provides links to other Native American cultural sites.

Noel Ford Cartoonist/Illustrator/Author

http://193.118.187.101/help/extra/people/noel-ford-cart

Features general information about Noel Ford, a UK cartoonist and author.

OBD—Organization of Black Designers

http://www.core77.com/OBD

A nonprofit professional association. Addresses the unique needs of African American design professionals.

On-Line Books

http://cs.indiana.edu/metastuff/bookfaq.html

Offers an index of Internet servers that offer electronic reading materials. Contains archive sites for books and electronic text as well as a list of known books freely available on the Web. Also gives information on related Usenet groups.

Online Source Register (Services)

http://www.interstat.net/serv.html

Includes Internet advertising, telecommunications, e-mail setups, job lead reports, contracting services, and more.

Optical Illusions

http://www.lainet.com/~ausbourn

Contains a collection of some famous optical illusions.

Patrick Gallagher, Celtic Art

http://www.planet.net/celtart

Provides lists of exhibitons, where to learn the art form, bibliographies, examples and samples, and a news page.

A Purgatory of Semiotics

http://www.sonoma.edu/Exhibits/Semiotics

Contains a selection of poems by Michael Mollo of Wine County, California, as well as author information, a searchable table of contents for the poems and other exhibits.

Rare Treasures

http://www.ip.net/rt

Presents a gallery of fine porcelains to art collectors, museums, and fine arts establishments.

rEX's wORLd

http://www.cea.edu/rex

Presents pieces of original art work from rEX and friends.

Rittners School of Floral Design

http://www.tiac.net/users/stevrt/index.html

Provides workshop courses in floral designing. Also includes information about floral design, with other information about courses offered at the school.

Shakespeare

http://the-tech.mit.edu/Shakespeare/works.html

Contains the complete works of William Shakespeare. Offers a chronological and categorical listing of plays, Bartlett's familiar Shakespearean quotations, and a section of frequently asked questions.

Synergy Music and Art Workshop

http://www.eirenet.net/cork/synergy/

Promotes music, art, and entertainment.

Syracuse University Computer Graphics for the Visual Arts

http://ziris.syr.edu/curriculum/mainmenu2.html

Provides information on Syracuse University and links to students' pages.

Tele-Garden

http://www.usc.edu/dept/garden/

Enables you to control a robot arm to plant and tend a real garden. Provides color images of the garden and detailed logs record the growth of the plants and the social interactions between gardeners.

The Tokugawa Art Museum

http://cjn.meitetsu.co.jp/tokugawa/index.html

Highlights the Tokugawa Art Museum, the third oldest privately endowed museum in Japan. Uses a map of the museum to give a virtual tour.

U'Mista Cultural Centre

http://www.swifty.com/umista/

Provides online site for the U'Mista Cultural Center. The center presents artwork and cultural exhibits of the Kwagu' people. Includes artwork, center background, and a catalog from the gift shop.

University Art Museum and Pacific Film Archive

http://www.uampfa.berkeley.edu

Contains current exhibitions of film and art from an exciting museum/cinematheque.

University Art Museum Art Exhibitions

http://www.uampfa.berkeley.edu/exhibits.html

Provides links to the UCB University Art Museum exhibitions. Provides links to artist's work.

Vancouver Arts Index

http://giant.mindlink.net/sloth/art/

Serves as directory for the arts in Vancouver, Canada. Includes community, university, and private performances and galleries, as well as a virtual gallery. Contains built-in room for expansion, artists' home pages, upcoming events, and so on.

VCU Arts Home Page

http://128.172.172.6/.SOTASERVER/sota.html

Provides comprehensive information about The School of the Arts at Virginia Commonwealth University (VCU).

A Very Usable Film and Cinema Directory

http://www.movies.net

Contains the best of the best, all the usual, as well as unique features, such as production information and a list of local theatre showtimes called "Now Playing."

VFS Multimedia

http://www.multimedia.edu/

Provides information about the Vancouver Film School's Multimedia Productions department. Contains gallery of digital images. Offers links that integrate other information about the school.

VI&P Animation Art Resources

http://www.earthlink.net/~sworth/

Provides information of interest to collectors of original animation drawings and cels. Includes topics on care and restoration, authentication, appraising, and more.

WebArtWed

http://www.aec2000.it:80/waw/

Acts as a bulletin board for Italian happenings about art, cultural heritage, research projects, new books, and more.

Welcome to VIPER

http://www.viper.ch/viper

Dedicated to the most advanced aesthetic strategies in the audiovisual sphere—a challenge to map the gray area between technological innovation and poetic imagination. Acts both as a public forum for critical discussion and a meeting place for artists, critics, and the public.

The West Australian Virtual Arts Community

http://www.arts.uwa.edu.au/MegsWWW/intro.html

Presents material from various artists and arts companies in West Australia, as well as visual and audio galleries, an arts funding game, pages from the southern hemisphere's premiere cyber-nightclub, a magazine, game reviews—high and low art and culture.

What I Believe by J.G. Ballard

http://www.cnw.com/~miki/index.html

Offers a link-enhanced list of quotations from the work of English science-fiction writer J.G. Ballard.

Wonders of the World

http://www.eznet.com/wow/ww_intro.html

Wonders of the World is a small shop in an Old Flour Mill located in Spokane, Washington, a purveyor of the ancient and the mysterious, the beautiful and the exotic, the rare and extraterrestrial. Collectors of museum quality art, artifacts, and adornments.

The WORD Online

http://rampages.onramp.net/~voorhees/

Acts as a monthly guide to the arts and literature in Dallas, Texas. Includes listings of events, articles on art-related subjects, book reviews, interviews with artists, and information about the literary and art communities. Accepts unsolicited submissions of articles about art or literature and pays with byline credit and copies. Also accepts submissions of art work for inclusion and for cover art and pays in copies and byline credit.

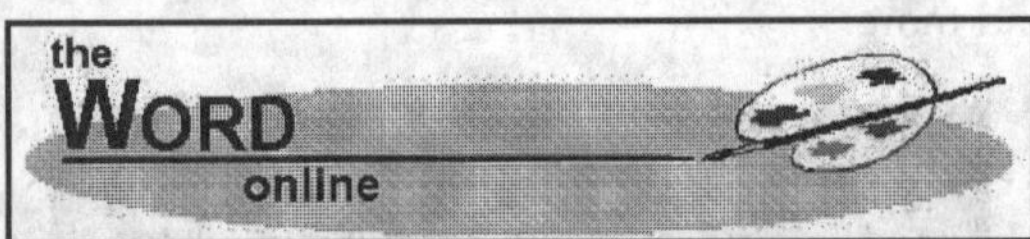

Electronic Arts

@art gallery

http://gertrude.art.uiuc.edu/@art/gallery.html

Features new exhibitions and archives past exhibitions. Provides links to talented and mature contemporary artists. UIUC faculty members curate the exhibitions.

Alternative Virtual Biennial

http://www.interport.net/avb/

Presents an alternative view of art, providing comprehensive explanations of the art and artists.

Atelier Nord

http://www.oslonett.no/home/atelier/index.html

Oslo, Norway site that displays the work of artists in residence at Atelier Nord, including projects on the Internet, multimedia, electronic images, computer animation, video, sound, performance, and printmaking.

Auricular Home Page

http://128.218.7.140/Auricular.html

Explores sights, sounds, and beyond and includes collections of computer-generated art, experimental music catalogs, and many links to the alternative and (they say) amazing. Also offers to design Web sites for you.

Christine Thea Partridge* Gallery

http://www.wimsey.com/~thea/gallery.html

Contains one artist's gallery of her work. Worth visiting particularly if you're an artist exploring the possibility of doing art direction and Web page development commercially.

Cyberbabe

http://www.yes.net/cyberbabe/

A virtual magazine devoted to women electronic artists, featuring visual art as well as essays.

Duncan Hopkins Web Site

http://www.eden.com/~dhopkins/

Specializes in multimedia and information graphic design, from interactive multimedia to Web site development, as well as animation, 3D modeling, and illustration.

Electronic Art Gallery

http://www.pixelpushers.wis.net//Texindex.html

Offers many thumbnails of the Pixel Pushers, for viewing and for sale.

Graficas Art and Design

http://iquest.com/~tbuzbee/

A site designed to electronically present the art and design work of artists. Links are provided to their clients' work and to an experimental page where they are attempting to develop résumés with image mapping techniques.

Art

Hillustration

http://www.hillustration.com/~mhill/

Samples traditional and digital illustration, along with examples of Web page design and interface design.

Hiway Technologies Graphics Portfolio

http://www.hway.com/sp/

Provides a collection of images created by Hiway Technologies' graphics and logo design department, as well as Web services and Internet consulting.

HypArt

http://rzsun01.rrz.uni-hamburg.de/cgi-bin/HypArt.sh

Stands for Hyper-Art, the artistical equivalent to hypertext. Features many pictures created based on the idea that several people create a single picture.

Joe Walker's Page

http://www.oz.net/~jwalk/

Provides a rotating display of Joe Walker's personal art and page design services, as well as links to other pages he has created.

Lectro-Art

http://www.artnet.org/iamfree/IAMFREE/html/elecart.html

Dave Parmley is an electronic art wizard who resides in Monte Sereno, California. Parmley was inspired by eastern philisophical concepts in design as well as his own hand. These elements culminate in his piece, "Seeing Is Not Believing," available for downloading.

Lightside Art Gallery

http://www.lightside.net/ArtGallery/ArtGallery.html

This small gallery includes both art created by computers and those created on other media (such as paintings on canvas).

Martin Action Art

http://www.bluemarble.net/~bcs/cauldron/catalog.html

"Edge, raw, computer-mediated art with an out-there text component." Electronic art for sale. Many are signed and numbered limited editions.

Media West Editions

http://www.wimsey.com/Pixel_Pushers

Features works of original digital art created wholly on computers and works from the Pixel Pushers Exhibition of Original Digital Art.

Museum Web

http://www.primenet.com/links/graphics.html

Enables you to explore some of the world's most famous art galleries on the Web today, in addition to eclectic sites such as The Shiki Internet Haiku Salon, Shremagraphs, 3D Kinetic Art, and Thant's Animation Index.

NCSA Digital Gallery CD-ROM

http://www.ncsa.uiuc.edu/SDG/DigitalGallery/DG_readme.html

Offers a wide range of NCSA Scientific Software for the Macintosh, IBM PC, SGI, Sun, and X Window servers, along with approximately 250 MB of images and animation sequences produced by researchers around the world. You also can view scientific animations in the Science Theater in the upper level of the gallery.

Netwash

http://www.umn.edu/nlhome/g023/filmsoc/chris/netwash.html

Exhibits a series of images made of pictures and text collected on the Infobahn during the current week—the trash and treasures you can find along the side of the information superhighway, dressed up like art.

Pix Gallery

http://www.nynex.co.uk/nynex/pix/index.html

Includes information on the British Computer Arts Association and Art Technology.

Healthy Choice Software

http://www.healthychoice.com/FreeStuff/html/FreeStuff.htm

Are you trying to eat better and exercise more? Healthy Choice supports a program that might help. Visit their site to download a free demo of Life Form, a program that helps you track your diet, exercise, and medical condition.

the place

`http://gertrude.art.uiuc.edu/ludgate/the/place.html`

Evolving repository of art work created specifically for distribution on the Web. Includes many graphics, very little text.

Rainbow of Chaos

`http://www.indy.net/~gemini/`

Serves as an environment in which computer-oriented artists who use primarily the Amiga personal computer can display their artistic accomplishments. Offers pieces of art and displays the graphics capabilities of the Amiga.

REIFF II Museum

`http://www.informatik.rwth-aachen.de/Reiff2/`

An electronic art museum available in both the German and English language. Exhibits digitized images and fast frame art.

Robert Derr's Virtual Gallery

`http://www.neosoft.com/~kcderr/rcd.html`

Presents the black-and-white and digital imagery of Robert Derr.

Sample the Dog Design

`http://www.teleport.com/~sample/`

Slaves to digital imaging, layout, graphical concept, and video.

Spanky Welcome (The Spanky Fractal Database)

`http://spanky.triumf.ca/`

Serves the mildly curious with simple fractal images and challenges the avidly interested with links to in-depth discussions and projects in nonlinearality.

Tom Reed/Photographer

`http://www.his.com/~reedpix`

Tom Reed focuses on image creation analog and digital, location and studio tailored toward advertising, corporate, and editorial use. Specializes in making the familiar strange and the strange familiar, photographing people and technology at the point where they meet.

Vancouver Cyberspace Association

`http://www.anima.wis.net//VCA.html`

Provides information about the Vancouver Cyberspace Association, an association of arts organizations interested in promoting the visual, performing, and literary arts on the Internet. Offers links to related magazines, events, and so forth.

The WebWeavers

`http://www.anima.wis.net//WebWeavers.html`

A networked group of artists and computer professionals dedicated to promoting and developing multimedia applications on the Internet. Provides information about and links to the people generating and operating on self-proclaimed "synarchist principles."

Fine Arts

911 Gallery Home Page

`http://www.iquest.net/911/iq_911.html`

A frequently updated virtual gallery of largely American artists. You can purchase art shown here off-line by contacting the artists or galleries.

Abulafia Gallery

`http://www.cgrg.ohio-state.edu/~mlewis/Gallery/gallery.html`

Highlights the work of artists who work in any medium, including computers. Offers choice for large or small monitor viewing. *Hint:* Choose the small option for faster results. Includes a VRML section—you can obtain the best results if you have the WebSpace viewer and an SGI computer, although a PC and a VRML viewer do work, the results are just of low resolution and without textures.

The Akron Art Museum

`http://www.winc.com/~aam/`

Showcases artists of our time and the recent past and offers links to modern art for visitors of all ages. Provides links to other museums around the world as well.

The Allen Memorial Art Museum

`http://www.oberlin.edu/wwwmap/allen_art.html`

Displays art objects, including paintings, ivories, and bronzes received. It also includes schedules and contacts at the museum. The Allen Memorial Art Museum is a museum on the campus of Oberlin College.

Andy Warhol Museum

http://www.warhol.org/warhol

Features extensive permanent collections of art and archives by Warhol, and regularly presents temporary exhibitions that may include the work of other artists. As well as electronic representations of the two-dimensional art, there is a virtual tour, films, and a link to the museum's stores.

Anti-Art Productions

http://www.nauticom.net/www/dada/index.html

Claims to be an independent artistic endeavor whose purported goal is "to expose the truth which lies underneath the complacent mediocre facade of the contemporary human condition."

Art by Belinda Di Leo

http://gort.ucsd.edu/mw/bdl.html

Appalachian artist Belinda Di Leo demonstrates the relationships between culture, religion, and death in her art. The paintings depict these interrelationships with a sense of place, character, and spiritual conviction, all of which are reinforced by a repetition of visual imagery.

Art by Tim Pascoe

http://www.hub.co.uk/intercafe/tpascoe/Pascoe.cArt1.HTML

Tim Pascoe presents an online exhibition of his sculptures, some of which are accompanied by essays.

The Art Kelderie

http://www.xs4all.nl/~mad/kelderie/kelderie.htm

Shows the work of Theo Kelderman over the last 20 years in different media: acrylic, air-brush, and oil paintings, as well as some black-and-white photos from his early years.

The Art of Barbara Weigel

http://198.66.88.2/blw/blwhome.html

Presents the art of Barbara Weigel, a New Orleans artist who specializes in a brightly colored, hard-edged style that has evolved into dramatic figures and portraits on canvas and wood cutouts.

Art on the Net

http://www.art.net

Serves as site to which artists can come to curate their own studios and gallery rooms, share their works, and help each other learn how to use the Web. Includes links to art-related topics other than visual art and to other art-related sites.

Art Planet

http://www.artplanet.com/

Comprehensive online art directory that features an artist search database. Provides links to sites designed and created by Art Planet. Also features the Art Cellar Exchange service.

Arthole

http://www.mcs.net/~wallach/arthole.html

Contains a plentitude of art and photography for display. This site also includes several movies in QuickTime format, as well as sponsored exhibitions.

The Arthur Ross Gallery Home Page

http://www.upenn.edu/ARG/index.html

An exhibition gallery of the University of Pennsylvania, featuring fine art shows from around the world. This page is well-maintained, and offers links to schedules, events, archives, and visitor information.

The ArtMetal Project

http://wuarchive.wustl.edu/edu/arts/metal/ArtMetal.html

Picked one of the Top 5% from Point Communications, Inc., this site is written and designed by a not-for-profit group of metalsmiths and includes special stories, movies, graphics, and sound files about metalwork.

ArtStudio

http://www.vt.com/artstudio/

Offers fishermen and art lovers a unique Game Fish series, including the rainbow trout, cutbow trout, yellowbelly sunfish, and the bluegill, in signed, frame-ready prints. Offers a full-color preview of the series, by Texas artist Norm Browne, as well as an opportunity to order the set or individual prints.

Asian Arts

http://www.webart.com/asianart/index.html

Online Asian art gallery that contains exhibitions, galleries, and articles (includes Buddhism-influenced art).

AusArts

http://online.anu.edu.au/ITA/AusArts/

Maintained by Australian National University. Contains links to the Institute of the Arts library server, Canberra University, and the electronic library. Offers avenue to information about the arts and higher education in Australia.

Bruce Museum

http://www.primenet.com/art-rom/museumweb/brucemus/brucemus.html

Displays images from exhibits at the Bruce Museum, which is a teaching museum of the arts and earth sciences. Includes crafts and natural history galleries.

Burton Levitsky

http://www.cruzio.com/~scva/blevitsky.html

Features highly detailed oil paintings of California, Ireland, and fantasy landscapes.

Center on Contemporary Art

http://www.subpop.com/coca

Contains Seattle's Center on Contemporary Art's virtual gallery. Also includes membership information, schedule, directions, and more.

The Centre for Contemporary Art in Warsaw

http://www.nask.org.pl/Others/CSW/

Features Polish artists and art from the collection at The Centre for Contemporary Art in Warsaw.

Connie Tunick's Paintings in Watermedia

http://www.centcon.com./~atun

Contains a virtual gallery of watercolor and watermedia paintings. Exhibits images of original floral and abstract paintings.

Crosswire Images

http://cuiwww.unige.ch/Chloe/OtisCrosswire/index.html

Presents a collection of art (an experiment in collaborative art that features starter, manipulated, and finished images, called CROSSWIRE) produced by the organizational efforts of OTIS, an electronic art gallery.

Crucible Chicago

http://www.mcs.net/~poleary/crucible/crucible.html

Contains images of the work of four Chicago artists, primarily sculpture, but also furniture and lighting design.

Daddazio—The Bronze Necktie

http://www.gems.com/showcase/daddazio/

Features sculptures modeled in plaster or wax and subsequently cast in bronze for eternity, and you can purchase the sculptures you want online.

DaliWeb The Official Salvador Dali Museum Web Site

http://www.highwayone.com/dali/daliweb.html

Presents interactive look at the Salvador Dali Museum in St. Petersburg, Florida. Includes museum history, some of Dali's greatest works, and information on how friends of the museum help it and this site continue to grow and develop.

Dallas Museum of Art Online

http://www.unt.edu/dfw/dma/www/dma.htm

Provides information and images from the museum. Contains approximately 200 digital images of art works owned by the Dallas Museum of Art.

The Digital Cathedral

http://marshall.edu/~stock1/index.html

Features "an ever-more-detailed cybernetic-artistic exploration of reality." Also features related Mac links.

Digital Giraffe

http://redshift.com/~cwhit

Online studio/gallery of electronic painting and fun. Exhibition changes every month, as does the art-smart quiz (sassy questions on art subjects designed to challenge your mind and provoke a grin).

Donajski's Digital Gallery

http://www.atm.com.pl/COM/Art-Gallery/Art-Gallery.html

Presents a variety of digital arts, including exhibits, projects, studio work, and a section for new art featured on this site.

The Douglas Albert Gallery State College, PA

http://www.epicom.com/arts/albert/index.htm

Features a variety of works by today's prominent artists. Offers the opportunity to purchase pieces from both local and international artists.

Duane Hilton High Sierra Fine Art

http://www.dnai.com/~antares/hilton/hilton.html

Offers a selection of original miniature oil paintings and limited edition prints of Eastern Sierra landscapes and wildlife.

Eagle Aerie Gallery

http://www.advantage.com/EAG/EAG.html

Features the art of Roy Henry Vickers. Offers a catalogue and the means to make online purchases.

Edoardo Villa

http://www.fine-art.com/artist/villa.html

Presents the art of Edoardo Villa, the South African artist.

The Electric Gallery

http://www.egallery.com/

Offers virtual tours and displays of modern art. This site gives the opportunity to purchase works, as well as the ability to find many different styles from modern artists.

The Electronic Chronicles

http://www.awa.com/artnetweb/projects/ahneed/first.html

Fictional site that contains a story about a futuristic archaeological dig that finds archaic 20th century electronic documents, and speculates on what the future will think of us.

Exhibition of Paintings by Stanley Pettigrew

http://www.internet-eireann.ie/pettigrew/petpla5.htm

Makes the oil paintings of Irish landscape painter, Stanley Pettigrew, available for viewing and for sale.

FineArt Forum Gallery

http://www.msstate.edu/Fineart_Online/gallery.html

Offers electronic art gallery for works by contemporary artists. Requires JPEG viewer for some files.

Galeria MexPlaza

http://mexplaza.udg.mx/Ingles/Galeria

Promotes Mexican artists and their work throughout the world.

Heirloom Art

http://www.desiderata.com/Art/Artists/Heirloom/

Old Master and Impressionist oil reproductions supplied to galleries, collectors, designers, and hotel groups. Brochure are available, as are links to art and artists.

Herbert R. Mears, Contemporary American Artist

http://www.wwma.com/mears/

Offers the chance to view Texan artist Herbert R. Mears' romantic paintings reminiscent of Bonnard, Ensor, and Matisse.

The Identity Box Collective

http://www.mcs.net/~ibc/home/ibc.htm

Showcases the artistic creation of Sam Jennings, including paintings and images from the past three years of his painting career.

ImageMaker Gifts for Dog Lovers

http://fender.onramp.net:80/imagemaker/

Makes available artist Monique Akar's pen and ink drawings of approximately 150 dogs for imprinting on a variety of quilts, umbrellas, photo albums, or aprons, or simply transferring to nearly anything.

International Masters Group

http://www.fine-art.com/gallery/masters.html

Wholesale fine art distributor. Specializes in limited edition lithographs.

The International Museum of Art

http://www.nettap.com/~iart/

Preserves and promotes rice straw art, an ancient Indian art form. Displays pieces and offers them for sale.

Kaufman, Karin

http://www.execpc.com/~skaufman/karin.html

Presents a virtual art gallery of Karin's colored pencil drawings, which she calls "illustrated dreams."

Khazana

http://www.winternet.com/~khazana/index.html

Fine and folk art from India and Nepal purchased directly from the artisans themselves. Provides links to the gallery, which includes painting, music, castings, and apparel. Ordering information included.

Kjell Ringi Art Exhibition

http://www.wca95.org/ringi/

Displays Kjell Ringi's paintings, sketches, graphics, and posters.

Koh-Varilla Guild

http://www.mcs.com/~kvg/

Consists of classical realist artists who specialize in portrait and monumental sculpture, limited editions of bronze and terra cotta sculptures, still life oil paintings, and fine drawings. Accepts commissions. Offers classes in figurative and portrait sculpture.

La Trobe University Art Museum

http://www.latrobe.edu.au/Glenn/Museum/ArtMuseumHome.html

Offers an online view of exhibitions taking place at the La Trobe University Art Museum. Doesn't link to other art-related sources.

Liros Gallery

http://media1.hypernet.com/liros.html

Specializes in the sale of fine paintings, Russian icons, and prints. Offers many 19th and 20th century Russian icons, as well as American and European paintings, prints, and maps. Also offers details on how to contact Liros Gallery regarding the purchase or sale of fine art.

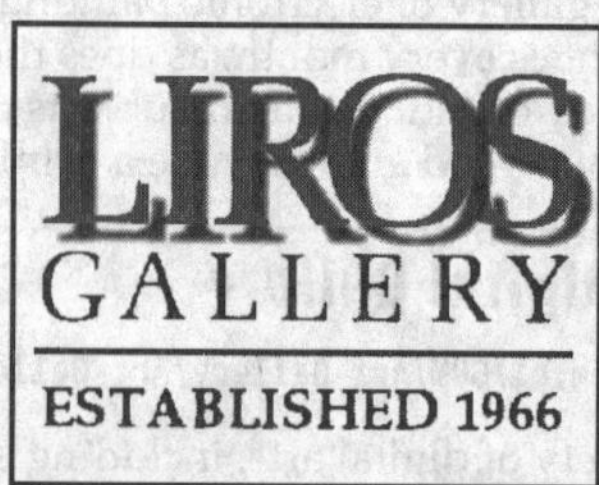

Los Angeles County Museum of Art

http://www.lacma.org/

Displays the exhibits in the Los Angeles County Museum of Art. You can watch a QuickTime movie, sift through online catalogs, pick out favorite categories in the exhibition schedule, or visit the museum shop. Also offers links to other online art museums.

The Meridian Gallery Contemporary Art, in the Heart of San Francisco

http://www.homenet.com/meridian/

Presents contemporary art from throughout the Americas, in the heart of San Francisco's gallery district, including exhibitions, visual, literary, and performing artists.

Michael Rubin

http://www.fine-art.com/artist/rubin.html

Presents the art of Michael Rubin, which he claims represents the next aesthetic stage in pure abstraction.

The Minneapolis Institute of Arts

http://www.mtn.org/MIA/

Provides information on The Minneapolis Institute of Arts, including exhibitions, galleries, events, and shopping. Doesn't link to other art-related sites.

MIT Center for Educational Computing Initiatives Virtual Museum

http://abelard.mit.edu/cgi-bin/museum-entrance/

Allows you to search the available database for pictures of interest and view Harold E. Edgerton's high-speed photography, including a variety of photographs from which to select; for example, apples split by bullets, Vortex motion pictures, and birds and balloons in flight.

Musée National D'Histoire Et D'Art

http://www.men.lu/~fumanti/LuxMusee.html

Invites you to take tour of Luxembourg's National Museum of Art and History and provides many links to other art-related resources on the Web.

Na-Te-So Workshop

http://www.qadas.com/nateso

Exhibits original handcrafted Southwestern art works in wood, silver, and paintings created by artists of the Na-Te-So Workshop, which is located in Indian Hills, Colorado.

Nico Roos

http://www.fine-art.com/artist/roos.html

Includes 16 one-man exhibitions and a retrospective exhibition at the Pretoria Art Museum in 1993, the work of Nico Roos, abstract landscape painter and professor of Fine Art at Pretoria University.

Ohio State University at Newark

http://www.cgrg.ohio-state.edu:80/mkruse/osu.html

Exhibits the Art Gallery, established at Ohio State University at Newark in 1968. Enables you to download a movie (MPEG) of the gallery's interior as well as tour the gallery in German and Spanish.

Okanagan University College, Department of Fine Arts

http://oksw01.okanagan.bc.ca/fiar/home.html

Describes programs, resources, and so forth avaliable at the Department of Fine Arts, and provides useful general information and links to related sites.

Parallax Gallery

http://www.colossus.net/rwsa/parallax_gallery.html

Includes a collection of art objects, fine art, jewelry, mineral specimens, sculpture, blown glass, and espresso.

Pavilion of Polyhedreality

http://www.li.net/~george/pavilion.html

Polyhedreality—an almost magical transformation of the banal (in this case, paper clips) into multi-sided, symmetrical, structures.

Pearl St. Online Gallery

http://antics.com/pearl.html

Exhibits computer-colored images of the southwestern United States, Colorado Wildflowers by Steven P. Cone, three images from within the Hoh River rain forest, and images from Colorado.

Project Gutenberg

http://jg.cso.uiuc.edu/PG/welcome.html

Contains complete texts for more than 100 works of literature, ranging from Light Literature (for example, *Alice in Wonderland, Through the Looking Glass, Peter Pan, Aesop's Fables,* and so on) to Heavy Literature (for example, the Bible or other religious documents, Shakespeare, *Moby Dick, Paradise Lost,* and so forth) to References (for example, *Roget's Thesaurus,* almanacs, a set of encyclopedias, dictionaries, and so on).

RACE Research into Artifacts, Center for Engineering

http://brains.race.u-tokyo.ac.jp/RACE.html

Offers images that depict art, technology, and their relationship to the surrounding environment, as well as links to several of the university professors to find out their views and contributions to this and other projects.

The Roger Whitney Gallery of Artists

http://www.rwga.com/index.html

Displays a selected variety of Roger Whitney's works, as well as works by "some of his famous friends." You can purchase art as well as view it.

Santa Fe Fine Art

http://www.sffa.com

Features the work of photographers, painters, sculptors, and printmakers from the southwestern United States.

Sculptor/Stone Carver

http://www.mcs.com/~sculptor/home.html

Contains a variety of sculptures, including gargoyles and grotesques, custom fireplaces, signage and entry panels, and public sculptures.

Sculpture Tour

http://loki.ur.utk.edu/sculpture/sculpt.html

Presents over 200 pieces of sculpture on the Knoxville campus of the University of Tennessee as well as links to the other exhibitions.

Sierra Wave Art Gallery

http://www.dnai.com/~antares/wave/wave.html

Showcases the work of photographers, painters, sculpters, writers, and other artists who live in the Eastern Sierra region of California and Nevada.

Sonoma State University Alumni Art Exhibition

http://www.sonoma.edu/exhibits/alumni/

Contains the art work of 16 former students of Sonoma State University.

Stained Glass by Steve

http://www.craftweb.com/org/steve/steve.shtml

Features stained glass windows and fused glass visual images. Offers opportunity to get in touch with the artist.

The Surrealism Server

http://pharmdec.wustl.edu/juju/surr/surrealism.html

Attempts to simultaneously explain surrealism and entertain. Covers surrealism from all angles. Offers links to other surrealistic pages.

Surrey Institute of Art and Design's World Wide Web Server

http://www.surrart.ac.uk/

Offers, among other draws, links to pages related to graphic design.

Susan Aaron-Taylor Profile of an Artist

http://www.cris.com/~greenlak/sat/satmain.shtml

Profiles Susan Aaron-Taylor, who has had exhibitions at the Detroit Institute of Arts and teaches at the Center for Creative Studies.

Techno-Impressionist Art

http://www.interport.net/~tkarp

Features the work of the techno-impressionist artists. Provides information on the origins of techno-impressionism, quotes from the artists, a history of 21st Century art, fables, and more.

Tel Aviv Museum of Art

http://www.macom.co.il/ta-museum/index.html

Displays the best of Israel's art and sculpture from the 1920s to the contemporary work of today's established and newly discovered Israeli artists. Contains the Museum's graphics collection of more than 20,000 prints and drawings.

Treasures of the Louvre

http://www.paris.org/Musees/Louvre/Treasures/

Offers a selection of the art treasures you can see in the real museum in Paris.

Tucson Museum of Art and Historic Block

http://www.primenet.com/art-rom/museumweb/tucartm/tucartm.html

Provides information about the museum and displays images of exhibits and the permanent collection of Roberto Marquez.

University of Wyoming Art Museum

http://www.primenet.com/art-rom/museumweb/uwyartm/uwyartm.html

Displays examples from the collections and exhibits of the museum.

The Watercolors of Sherry Zuker

http://www.halcyon.com/hzuker/colors/sazpage.htm

Presents Northwest artist Sherry Zuker's bright, bold watercolors and watercolor collages.

WebMuseum

http://sunsite.unc.edu/wm/

Exhibits art collections and exhibits primarily from a very famous Paris museum. Provides access to many network points for faster display. Includes downloadable classical music files (AU format). Also provides links to other art-related sites.

Welcome to the aRt_sLab @ UCSD

http://jupiter.ucsd.edu/~webmngr/

Displays examples of student work at UCSD (and maintained by UCSD art students). Provides links to many interesting displays of art.

Whitney Museum Information

http://www.uky.edu/Artsource/whitneyhome.html

Represents the Whitney Museum of American Art in New York, and portrays a listing of exhibitions (dating from 1931 to 1997), as well as of events and performances. Describes all pieces of art in great detail, but doesn't display them. Also features traveling exhibits.

The Will James Art Company

http://www.imt.net/~murphy/mainhomepage01.HTML

Owns all copyrights to Will James art and books, and provides much information about Will James and his work. Reproduces art from the originals and sells a wide variety of high-quality prints. Offers limited edition prints of oils and pencil sketches for sale, as well as the art and books of Will James.

Windshadow

http://www.wimsey.com/~bobg/index.html

Displays images of Canadian Michael Duncan's Windshadow series prints for sale.

Performing Arts

Alaskan Dance Theater

http://www.alaska.net/~ethan/adt.html

Covers primarily ballet, but offers a variety of links both to other dance sites and Alaska. Mostly text.

Arthur Hall and Black Dance in America

http://www.columbia.edu/~jw157/arthur.hall.html

Covers Arthur Hall's life and impact on African American dance and cultural development in America and offers links to broader pages regarding Hall's Yoruba culture of Nigeria.

As-Sayf Oriental Dance Home Page

http://www.ivo.se/as-sayf/englishindex.html

Dance group that offers traditional Middle Eastern and North African performances (such as belly dancing).

AXIS Dance Troupe

http://picasso.ucsf.edu/~schmitz/axis.html

Provides information regarding the particular dance troupe (which includes wheelchair-bound dancers), their awards, background, upcoming shows, and provides links to more information on this troupe and others like it.

B.A.W.P. Spoken Word Audio Recordings

http://www.cs.brown.edu:80/fun/bawp/

Contains downloadable spoken word performances (ranging in theme from computers to love) made in movie-quality sound. Features several artists at a time and updates selections monthly.

Booth Milton Sculptor

http://www.alchemedia.net/boothmilton/index.html

Contains thumbnails of the sculptor Booth Milton's metal and wood creations (strictly a virtual gallery—no pricing information—but you can contact the artist).

Dancescape

http://wchat.on.ca/dance/pages/dscape.htm

Offers comprehensive coverage of the world of competitive ballroom dancing and dance sport. Includes a wide range of information, ranging from upcoming competitions to national personals.

Art

Henry's Dance Hotlist

http://zeus.ncsa.uiuc.edu:8080/~hneeman/
dance_hotlist.html#tango

Provides a list of Internet pages, events, supplies, magazines, and more, all related to dance.

International Folk Dancers Of Ottawa Home Page

http://lucas.incen.doc.ca/ifdo.html

Ottawa-based nonprofit participatory recreational dance group. Provides links to local and other dance events.

Internet Dance Resources

http://www.nando.net/events/dance/dsource.html

A directory of dance resources available through World Wide Web. Links to dance pages already separated by type. Also includes newsgroup and link access.

Marjan

http://www.cybernetics.net/users/jwkjr/marjhome.htm

Marjan is a belly dancer in Dallas, TX. Site includes her photo, but more importantly, links to other pages on belly dancing.

Ohio State University, Department of Dance Home Page

http://www.dance.ohio-state.edu

Distributes original material related to dance. Provides information on dance history, dance and technology, and musicians in dance.

PDX TheatreSports

http://www.spiretech.com/~richie/pdxts.html

Offers improvisational comedy with a competitive twist, in which teams of improvisors compete in improvisational games scored by a panel of judges or the audience. Includes plenty of information about TheatreSports, as well as links to other groups and improv pages.

Talk about Dance

http://www.nando.net/events/dance/dance.html

Represents the American Dance Festival (ADF), which has sponsored several hundred dance works. Features columns, profiles, and dance reviews originally published in the *Raleigh News & Observer*. Contains the ADF dance schedule and upcoming events, as well as links to other dance sites.

Tango Dance Notation Argentina Argentine

http://litwww.epfl.ch/~shawn/tango/

Provides all the information you might ever want to obtain (and maybe more) concerning dancing the Tango, including where to do it, as well as plenty of interrelated (and unrelated) links.

Photography

3-D Stuff

http://www.fishnet.net/~3dstereo

Both of your eyes will enjoy this site. Here you'll see one of the Web's greatest collection of odd and exciting stereo images and information.

50th Bristol International Salon of Photography

http://www.avonibp.co.uk/bps/salon/advert.htm

An invitation to submit slides for consideration for inclusion in one of the world's leading international photographic exhibitions.

(Art)ⁿ Galleries

http://www.artn.nwu.edu/Galleries/

Gallerie: virtualPhotography is produced by the (Art)ⁿLaboratory located at Northwestern University. This particular gallery was "arranged & hung" by Janine Fron. Welcome to the world of virtual photography.

The Attic Window (by Diane Fenster)

http://www.art.net/Studios/Visual/Fenster/ritofab_Home/
fenster.html

An aptly named artist and project, this site is part essay, part poem, part art show, and part gallery. It is also an award winner.

Black and White Gallery

http://world.std.com/~sjh/

A gallery showing changing photographic exhibits. The current exhibit at the time of this writing is one by Franco Forleo of South Africa.

The Cemetery

http://loki.stockton.edu/~whitew/cemetery/cemetery.html

Photographs from an ongoing image/text project, describing the historically Black communities of southern New Jersey.

Cincinnati Parks' Butterfly Show

`http://www.cinci.com/recreation/special/butterfly/index.html`

A nice page constructed by the same man who constructed the official Cincinnati Butterfly Show— Alan Fraser. There are some nice pictures of butterflies and children enjoying the beauty of nature.

Citizen Kane Gallery

`http://rohan.sdsu.edu/faculty/rosebud/homepage`

Based at a server at San Diego State University, the Citizen Kane Gallery features a black-and-white exhibit and two "photography book" exhibits called Pictures of You I and II.

Crayon Design & Communications

`http://www.infobahnos.com/~crayon/`

A design company with some photographs of sample designs. If you are interested in design, advertising, or photography, this site might be for you.

Cypress College Photography Department (First Stop)

`http://www.newart.com/cypress/`

Touted as a "progressive and comprehensive" photography department, their offer to the World Wide Web is a great place for students and teachers to display their work.

Detroit Publishing Company Photographic Collection

`http://lcweb2.loc.gov/detroit/dethome.html`

Part of the Library of Congress, the photos from the Detroit Publishing Company (1820–1920) are an avenue to turn of the century America. There is a search engine that is helpful, as well as a way to order photographic reproductions of some of the prints.

Digital Photography Exhibit

`http://www.bradley.edu/exhibit95/`

Although the URL implies a year in photos, there are actually three years here. Based at Bradley University, this page is a very well-designed site that anyone who enjoys photography will like.

digital wave photography gallery

`http://www.digitalwave.org/cgibin/var/exhibit/index.html`

Broken up into smaller pages that are bandwidth-friendly, this site gives photographers a chance to display their very interesting work; from photo essays to digital galleries, you'll find it here.

Edgerton Center's Online Photo Gallery

`http://the-tech.mit.edu/Gallery/gallery.html`

Present at MIT's photography site are a featured artist and collaborative work between the Edgerton Center at MIT and *The Tech*, MIT's student newspaper. Portfolios and digitally enhanced photography are what you'd expect from the MIT community.

Florida Wildflower Showcase

`http://www-wane.scri.fsu.edu/~mikems/`

Full of beautiful pictures of Florida's wildflowers, there is also a great deal of information about flowers at this site. This site has won awards for its excellent collection of photographs.

FocalPoint f/8

`http://www.f8.com/`

FocalPoint f/8 is an experimental design and production group that presents democratic photojournalism and uses the Web as its digital conduit. Many different photojournalists are involved with the project, and it features different exhibitions all the time.

Fotogruppe der Studiobühne und Filmwerkstatt

`http://www.uni-koeln.de/zentral/studio/foto/index_e.html`

An interactive gallery, this site, (obviously) located in Germany, is written in English, has photos in both galleries and archives, and invites submissions from people around the world.

Frolic

`http://www.ddb.com/olegv/trippage.shtml`

A travelogue and photo essay by a student at the University of Minnesota, this page is a pleasure to view for both the photographs and the layout.

GallerySight

http://www.webcom.com/~zume/GallerySight/welcome.html

There are photo essays by various photographers here, and new shows go up all the time. One of the nicest aspects of this site is the photographers' comments that accompany their respective essays.

Hiroshima and Nagasaki Gallery Exhibition

http://www.oneworld.org/gallery/index.html

The Hiroshima and Nagasaki exhibition is somber but needs to be seen. Whatever a person's politics, to forget such tragedy would be inhuman.

imago

http://www.users.interport.net/~edb/

imago is a site that is well-formatted, well-constructed, full of great photographs, and even has an agenda—how human perception of certain images are coupled. All these great photographs and something to think about, too.

Michael's Photo Gallery

http://www.netaxs.com/~mhmyers/image.html

A strangely grouped collection of photographs are available at this site. From birds, to the moon, to city pictures, Michael's Photo Gallery has some interesting images to view.

Michigan Photo Contest

http://www.ring.com/contest2.htm

Open to all! For photographs and images of Michigan People, Places and Closeups. Prizes from Applebee's Grill & Bar, Marsh Ridge Resort, and PDG.

Misa

http://www.users.interport.net/~misa/

Based in New York, this exhibit features what many might perceive as strange and usual aspects of living in Manhattan. New images are added here every week.

Molecular Expressions (Microscapes)

http://micro.magnet.fsu.edu/

Photographs from beneath the microscope, this site has some beautiful images that look frighteningly like fractals. One wouldn't think that such beauty could come from such strange places as amino acids, cocktails, or cholesterol.

Mythago

http://www.lavondyss.com/gallery/mythago.html

This gallery of photography has a permanent collection and an exhibit that changes biweekly. They also sell prints, posters, and coffee-table books.

Nature Gallery

http://www.cohsoft.com.au/nature/gallery/

The Nature Gallery presents photographs of animals—winged and footed—from around the world. You are invited to search by region on a clickable image map.

New Mexico

http://www-swiss.ai.mit.edu/philg/new-mexico/album.html

A very bizarre photo essay that describes the housing situation in New Mexico. In fact, you might think that the author of this site is bluffing.

The New York Public Library Photography Collection

http://www.nypl.org/research/chss/spe/art/photo/photo.html

Filled with links and information, the photography collection located at the New York Public Library contains 200,000 original photos from an international base of photographers.

Non Facturé

http://www.univ-paris8.fr/~alex/

Two French photographers are going from Paris to Moscow to capture the European landscape and what one of the photographers calls "Eastern Faces." It should be interesting.

Oxford Photographs

http://www.comlab.ox.ac.uk/archive/ox/photos.html

There are photographs of Oxford, a virtual tour, links, and collections and archives located here.

The Photo Archive

http://orion.pet.cam.ac.uk/photo.htm

This archive located at Orion in the United Kingdom contains over 50 images. The photos here are freely available for personal use, but if you want to use any of them commercially, you must contact the photographer.

Photo Perspectives

`http://www.i3tele.com/photo_perspectives_museum/faces/perspectives.home.html`

The Photo Perspectives gallery is designed to be an interactive museum, to allow direct access to publications and museum-quality exhibitions via the World Wide Web. The photos presented are for an examination of contemporary society and culture.

The Photographers Gallery

`http://www.sfn.saskatoon.sk.ca/arts/tpg/index.html`

The home page of a gallery located in Saskatoon, Saskatchewan, the Photographers Gallery has an online gallery available for perusal. The gallery is composed of a cooperative of photographers interested in learning to express themselves artistically through the medium of photography.

PhotoLink Gallery

`http://www.netins.net/showcase/fotolink/`

The PhotoLink Gallery features 3D graphics and scenery as the interface between you and the photos. This site really tries to make you feel at home— as though you were in a gallery, rather—but is graphically-intense, so be ready for large download times.

Picture Projects

`http://www.itp.tsoa.nyu.edu/~student/picture_projects/`

Picture Projects is a page dedicated to documentary photography. As is often its nature, these photographs can be quite disturbing and aren't for the weak of heart.

Portfolio of Architechtural Photographs

`http://rampages.onramp.net/~blitz/lreens/ap.html`

This site, complete with a mirror site in Italy (appropriately), is set up as a photography magazine with volumes and series numbers. The exhibit at the time of this writing was an essay called "The Silence of Ruins."

Postcards from Bahia

`http://www.brazilonline.com/lita/`

An exhibit divided into three sections for convenience, this site has city, landscape, and portrait photos from the Bahia region. Photographer Lita Cerqueira gives a glimpse into life and the world.

PPSA Photo Gallery

`http://www.ppsa.com/Graphics/photo.html`

There are photographs and travelogues of friends known, scenery captured, and recent road trips taken by the author. There are also links to stories, travel sites, and pieces of art.

Prairie Dog Artworks

`http://www.awinc.com/Cybermall/shops/dunn/`

The home page of Prairie Dog Artworks features the photography of dogs, people, interactions, and life. These photos can be purchased in the form of postcards, posters, and art prints.

Probus Photos

`http://www.users.mis.net/~jgleas/index.html`

An award-winning site, this gallery is bandwidth-heavy but worth seeing. There is a Java applet as you enter, as well as links to the gallery, an exhibit schedule, an introduction, and more. Make sure you have a Netscape-compatible browser, though, if you really want to enjoy this site.

Remembering Nagasaki

`http://www.exploratorium.edu/nagasaki/`

Commentary, photography, first-hand accounts, and commemorations are present at this dark but attractive site. Inspired by an invitation from the Exploratorium to the denizens of the Internet to post their opinions and ideas of the bombing of Hiroshima and Nagasaki, this site blossomed into a presentation-style result of a public forum.

Campbell's Recipes

`http://www.campbellsoups.com/recipes/holiday/`

Can't decide what to fix for dinner? Campbell Soup Company offers online recipes in a variety of categories including courses, low fat, main ingredients, and Campbell's brands and products.

Rogers Virtual Gallery (Beauty #2)

http://www.rogers.com/Beauty2/

When you get here, you stand outside the gallery doors. There is a directional key at the bottom of the page, as well as instructions on how to use it. Browse the gallery by walking the halls and clicking on pictures of the art for a closer look.

Ruby's Gallery

http://www.ivn.com/Gallery/index.html

There are pictures here featured by IVN New Media and Global Bytes. The pictures here change every few weeks and are in a variety of formats so you can download them to use as you see fit.

Russian Reminiscence

http://www.wfu.edu/~david/russia/

An amateur photographer who went to Russia offers this online photo gallery. Obviously all based in Russia, there are pictures of people and places for your perusal.

Sam's Shoebox

http://www.mcs.net/~florio/photos.htm

This page has an interesting take on information exchange and art. There are small galleries of personal portraits, city scapes, and other scenic shots. A great page to just look around in.

A Shot in the Dark

http://www.sys.uea.ac.uk/Recreation/Sport/reading/shotin/shot.html

Some interesting sports photography is included at A Shot in the Dark. Mostly a photo essay reporting on the Reading Football (Soccer) Club, there is some introductory text and photos of both atheletes and fans.

SITO

http://www.sito.org/

After a *Romeo and Juliet* style fight about the former name of this site with the Otis School of Art and Design, the name has been turned upside-down but still stands for "Operative Term Is Stimulate." It is an archive and art-collaborative that is interesting to peruse—if not just plain big.

SolarColor Photography by Michael Fastoso

http://pacificnet.net/~fastoso/start.html

The SolarColor Portfolio is often updated, so new pictures are available about once a month. All of the photographs are silver gelatin prints whose effects are achieved by several different types of chemical baths.

Stereoscopic Imaging by Ray 3D

http://www.ray3d.com/

Ray Hannisian's home page features an interesting photographic phenomenon—3D photography on the Internet. There are two different techniques to see these photos in 3D, and neither of them require special software or equipment. It was voted a USA Today Hotsite and with good reason.

United in Anger

http://www.panix.com/~boyfren/

There are photographs from the United in Anger project shown at this site. The UIA is a photo-documentary of AIDS activists from around the globe and wants to present an honest look at those whose lives have been affected by this tragic disease.

The Unofficial Cincinnati Butterfly Show

http://w3.one.net/~a_fraser/butterfly/index.html

A lovely sort-of companion to the official Cincinnati Parks' Butterfly show, there are photographs of children, butterflies, and nature present here.

Vintage Postcards

http://www.paris.org/Expos/Vintage/

An exposition located at the Paris Pages' server, this site contains photo-reproductions of postcards from Paris in the earlier part of the 20th century. Browse through several peoples' collections to see gargoyles, parks, and old buildings in Paris.

The Zone I Gallery

http://www.gate.net/~eak3/

The Zone I Gallery is a showcase for African-American photography. It has been noticed by Magellan and the Microsoft Network as a formidible presence on the Internet.

Newsgroups

alt.architecture

alt.architecture.alternative

alt.art.colleges

alt.art.marketplace

alt.arts.nomad

alt.art.scene

alt.art.virtual-beret

alt.artcom

alt.arts.ballet

alt.binaries.pictures.fine-art.misc

alt.binaries.pictures

alt.censorship

alt.postmodern

alt.surrealism

fj.rec.fine-arts

rec.arts.dance

rec.arts.fine

rec.arts.sf.marketplace

rec.arts.misc

rec.folk-dancing

rec.photo

Listservs

AAT-L—Art & Architecture Thesaurus Discussion List

University of Illinois at Chicago, Chicago, IL

You can join this group by sending the message " sub AAT-L your name" to listserv@listserv.uic.edu

ARLIS-L—Art Libraries Society Discussion List

You can join this group by sending the message " sub ARLIS-L your name" to listserv@lsv.uky.edu

ART193—Fine Arts Computing Group

The George Washington University Computer Center, Washington, DC

You can join this group by sending the message " sub ART193 your name" to listserv@gwuvm.gwu.edu

ARTCRIT—Art Criticism Discussion Forum

You can join this group by sending the message " sub ARTCRIT your name" to listserv@yorku.ca

ARTIST-L—Student Artist Discussions

University of Arkansas Main Campus - Fayetteville

You can join this group by sending the message "sub ARTIST-L your name" to listserv@uafsysb.uark.edu

ARTLIST—Discuss Issues Relevant to Contemporary Art

University of Arizona, Tucson, AZ

You can join this group by sending the message "sub ARTLIST your name" to listserv@listserv.arizona.edu

ARTNEWS—UA Fine Arts News Releases

University of Arizona, Tucson, AZ

You can join this group by sending the message "sub ARTNEWS your name" to `listserv@listserv.arizona.edu`

ARTNINE—Discusses Especially the Contemporary Art in the Nineties

You can join this group by sending the message "sub ARTNINE your name" to `listserv@urzinfo.urz.uni-heidelberg.de`

BOOK_ARTS-L—The Book Arts: Binding, Typography, Collecting

Syracuse University

You can join this group by sending the message "sub BOOK_ARTS-L your name" to `listserv@listserv.syr.edu`

CAAH—Consortium Of Art And Architectural Historians

Princeton University, Princeton, NJ

You can join this group by sending the message "sub CAAH your name" to `listserv@pucc.princeton.edu`

CLASSICAL—Moderated Classical Music List

You can join this group by sending the message "sub CLASSICAL your name" to `listserv@home.ease.lsoft.com`

CLASSM-L—Classical Music List

Brown University, Providence, RI

You can join this group by sending the message "sub CLASSM-L your name" to `listserv@brownvm.brown.edu`

CLAYART—Ceramic Arts Discussion List

You can join this group by sending the message "sub CLAYART your name" to `listserv@lsv.uky.edu`

COLLAB-L—Theatre and Musical Artists, Composers, etc.

Pennsylvania State University

You can join this group by sending the message "sub COLLAB-L your name" to `listserv@psuvm.psu.edu`

DESIGN-L—Basic and Applied Design (Art and Architecture)

Pennsylvania State University

You can join this group by sending the message "sub DESIGN-L your name" to `listserv@psuvm.psu.edu`

LARCH-L—Landscape Architecture Electronic Forum

Syracuse University

You can join this group by sending the message "sub LARCH-L your name" to `listserv@listserv.syr.edu`

MUSEUM-L—Museum Discussion List

University of New Mexico, Albuquerque, NM

You can join this group by sending the message "sub MUSEUM-L your name" to `listserv@unmvma.unm.edu`

PERFORM—Medieval Performing Arts

University Computing Services, Indiana University

You can join this group by sending the message "sub PERFORM your name" to `listserv@iubvm.ucs.indiana.edu`

RLGART-L—RLG Art and Architecture

Yale University Computer Center, New Haven, CT

You can join this group by sending the message "sub RLGART-L your name" to `listserv@yalevm.cis.yale.edu`

SAH-L—Society of Architectural Historians

Smithsonian Institution, Washington, DC

You can join this group by sending the message "sub SAH-L your name" to `listserv@sivm.si.edu`

UAARTED—Art Education Issues

University of Arizona, Tucson, AZ

You can join this group by sending the message "sub UAARTED your name" to `listserv@listserv.arizona.edu`

BOOKS & AUTHORS

Authors

Douglas Adams

http://www.umd.umich.edu/~nhughes/dna/

Several links to FAQs, lists of works by Adams that are available online, and membership information for the semi-official fan club, ZZ9 Plural Z Alpha. There's even a search engine, in case you want to find out exactly where in Adams' works the Babel fish is first mentioned. The site is maintained by the maintainer of the alt.fan.douglas-adams FAQ.

Louisa May Alcott: Flower Fables

http://www.inform.umd.edu:8080/EdRes/Topic/ WomensStudies/ReadingRoom/Fiction/FlowerFables

Flower Fables is a site that contains the entirety of a book of fables originally published in 1854. Readers and scholars alike might find useful and informative information contained here.

V.C. Andrews

http://www.csh.rit.edu/~cwalker/vcandrews/

Another book list, with descriptions of most of the books. Also has a family tree of the Foxworth family from the *Flowers in the Attic* series.

Piers Anthony

http://malkuth.sephiroth.org/~corwin/authors/panthony/ index.html

Contains a short biography and a complete list of Piers Anthony's books (including some short descriptions).

Isaac Asimov

http://www.clark.net/pub/edseiler/WWW/ asimov_home_page.html

A wonderful site for Asimov fans! Comprehensive booklists, stores and publishers that sell them, transcripts of reviews and interviews, and even sound files of Asimov himself.

Margaret Atwood Information Site

http://www.io.org/~toadaly/

This is the official Margaret Atwood site, open mainly to students and scholars of her work. There are several sections, including bibliographical information, essays on writing and other subjects, as well as a link to ameliorate the search for more information on the writer of novels such as *The Handmaid's Tale* and *Cat's Eye*.

Nicholson Baker

http://www.cts.com/browse/jwalk/nbaker/

The Nicholson Baker Fan Page is a page filled with facts about the books and the life of Nicholson Baker. There are links to reviews and comments, and perhaps most enjoyably, the first sentence of each novel is present in its description.

Clive Barker

http://www.barkerverse.com/.

The official Clive Barker Web site lists books, films, and comics, and details about book tours and special video releases. Includes discussion forums and transcripts of IRC interviews with Barker.

Donald Barthelme

http://weber.u.washington.edu/~daspaz/barthelme.html

Largely a collection of stories, this site is an already well-defined work-in-progress. Present here are stories, excerpts, and essays either by or about Donald Barthelme.

Richard Bausch

http://web.gmu.edu/departments/writing/bausch.html

An instructor at George Mason University, writer Richard Bausch is widely published and acclaimed. His works have been featured in such periodicals as *The Atlantic*, *Harper's*, *The New Yorker*, and *Esquire*.

Greg Bear

http://www.kaiaghok.com/gregbear/gregbear.htm

Biography, bibliography, and some original work by Bear himself, exclusive to the Web ("for the time being"). Also contains bitmaps of some of Bear's paintings.

Aphra Behn Page

http://ourworld.compuserve.com/homepages/r_nestvold/

This site is dedicated to the first professional woman writer in the English language. A prolific playwright (second only to John Dryden in the Restoration), Aphra Behn is known largely for her prose. This site has links to information about Aphra Behn and other women writers.

Edward Bellamy

http://oak.cats.ohiou.edu/~aw148888/bellamy.html

Edward Bellamy is the 19th century writer of *Looking Backward*. This site, evolved from the Center for Utopian Studies, has links to essays and excerpts by Bellamy, as well as links to related sites.

Jorge Luis Borges—The Garden of Forking Paths

http://www.microserve.net/~thequail/libyrinth/borges.html

Perhaps one of the best-formatted literature pages on the Web, the Garden of Forking Paths (*El Jardín de Senderos que se Bifurcan*) is home to the Magical Realist Jorge Luis Borges. Not only good-looking, this site is also quite complete. Certainly worth the time.

Ray Bradbury

http://freenet3.scri.fsu.edu:81/users/brig/bradbury.html

A biography and a list of books, films, and TV works by Ray Bradbury.

Richard Brautigan

http://www.cnct.com/home/jen/rich.html

One of the only sites dedicated to this British Black Satirist, this page has a library and a "Trader's Corner." Configured for Netscape-compatible browsers.

David Brin

Contains an FAQ, bibliographies, excerpts, and links to some original online fiction.

Charlotte Brontë

http://www.stg.brown.edu/projects/hypertext/landow/victorian/cbronte/bronteov3.html

Dedicated to the Victorian author of *Jane Eyre*, this site also boasts links to literary and artistic relations, as well as a cultural context section.

The Brontë Sisters

http://www.sbbs.se/hp/cfalk/bronteng.htm

Both biographical information and essays concerning their novels are present at this site. Also, links to each individual sister—Emily, Charlotte, and Anne—are available.

Rita Brown

http://mchip00.med.nyu.edu/lit-med/lit-med-db/webdocs/webauthors/brown283-au-.html

This page concerns Rita Mae Brown, lesbianism, and medicine in the humanities. This page has links to these and other issues.

Charles Bukowski

http://realbeer.com/buk/

Strange that a drunk, self-described "dirty old man" would have such a nice home on the Web. There is a biography, a newsletter, an art section, and letters to the author.

Edgar Rice Burroughs

http://www.tarzan.com/

Probably as close as a person can come to an "official" Edgar Rice Burroughs page, this site has an autobiographical sketch, essays, and other information about the writer of the Tarzan series (and other fantasies).

William S. Burroughs

http://www.hyperreal.com/wsb/

Whenever a person begins to study William S. Burroughs, there are usually words of warning or at least a *caveat lector*. This site keeps with that tradition but gives great insight into the life of the writer of books such as *Naked Lunch* and *Junky*.

Albert Camus

http://www.wolfenet.com/~willej/indexa.htm

Although this page is probably too heavily formatted, the information presented is at least interesting. There are several essays about Camus, a biography, and photographs of the Algerian/French Absurdist.

Truman Capote

http://www.sgi.net/marbles/zeno/capote.html

Mainly dedicated to the new-journalistic novel *In Cold Blood*, this site also has biographical information and other points of interest about Truman Capote.

Jim Carroll

http://ernie.bgsu.edu/~ccarter/carroll.htm

Jim Carroll's home on the Web seems to want to dispel anything known by the public about the author of *The Basketball Diaries*. Indeed, Carroll is a multipracticed artist in music, letters, and spoken-word performance; however, this site claims him the messiah of the nouveau Renaissance.

Lewis Carroll: An Overview

http://www.stg.brown.edu/projects/hypertext/landow/
victorian/carroll/carrollov.html

Lewis Carroll (née Charles Dodgson) was not only the writer of the famous *Alice in Wonderland* stories, he also was a mathematician and scientist. This site houses information about Carroll as a whole person—his literary tactics, religion and philosophy, and his work in a political and social context.

Raymond Carver

http://world.std.com/~ptc/

This site has biographical information and essays about Raymond Carver. His stories have become very popular in the recent past, perhaps because of Robert Altman's film *Short Cuts*; however, Carver died of cancer in 1988. This page is the only one of its kind.

Willa Cather

http://icg.harvard.edu/~cather/

A well-formatted site available from the Harvard Web server, this page has information about Cather, her work, and scholarly conferences in her honor. Her very astute picture of America in the early 20th century should be impetus enough for a reader to look at the information included at this site.

Miguel de Cervantes

http://csdl.tamu.edu/cervantes/

A project of the Cervantes International Bibliography Online and the Anuario Bibliográfico Cervantino, this site is dedicated to solve the "problem of currency, thoroughness, and accessibility which now hampers research on Cervantes." There is a record of the books, articles, dissertations, reviews, and other points of interest included here to this end.

The Kate Chopin Project

http://www.lacollege.edu/chopin/chopin.html

The Kate Chopin Project Web site concentrates not only on biography and bibliographical information, but also the stories and writings of Kate Chopin. Very well-formatted for graphical browsers, the project utilizes the World Wide Web's hypertext platform for footnoting the stories.

Agatha Christie

http://www.nd.edu/~rwoodbur/christie/christie.htm

Provides a chronogical listing of most of Christie's works, grouped optionally by featured detective. The maintainer of the page promises that all the books and plays listed will eventually have complete descriptions (including whodunnit, for the impatient!).

Tom Clancy

http://malkuth.sephiroth.org/~corwin/authors/tclancy/
index.html

This site has some biographical information and also some information concerning Tom Clancy's novels. It is heavily formatted for Netscape-compatible browsers, but it is very well done.

Arthur C. Clarke Chapter of "The Silicon Jungle"

http://www.clark.net/pub/rothman/jungle.htm

Relates one person's experiences communicating with Clarke via telecommunications satellite in 1985, before the Internet was known outside of military and research institutions.

Douglas Coupland—Snapshots

http://boris.qub.uk/tony/coupland

Of interest to many people concerning their everyday lives with computers and technology, this site features writer Douglas Coupland (author of the satire *Microserfs*), interviews, and bibliographical and biographical information.

Stephen Crane

http://www.en.utexas.edu/~mmaynard/Crane/crane.html

This page was written by several students at the University of Texas at Austin for a project in their English class; however, this doesn't diminish its relevance to the study of Stephen Crane. It is quite complete and has biography, bibliography, and excerpts from Crane's work—both audio and text.

Michael Crichton

http://http.tamu.edu:8000/~cmc0112/crichton.html

The writer of such novels as *Jurassic Park*, *The Eaters of the Dead*, and *Congo*, and all-around American media entrepreneur Michael Crichton finds a welcome home at this page. There are many good links to information about his life, books, and other entertainment efforts.

Cyber-Seuss

http://www.afn.org/~afn15301/drseuss.html

A good Dr. Seuss page, with all kinds of links, including information on the "Great Grinch Debate."

Roald Dahl

http://www.nd.edu/~khoward1/Roald.html

This good-humored home page is a place that Roald Dahl would have been proud of. His biography and bibliography shows Dahl's life in a good light, and also makes apparent the breadth of his *oeuvre*. His adult writing and his (perhaps more famous) children's writing is exemplified here.

Le Marquis de Sade

http://www.tsrcom.com/users/sodoku/sade.htm

Tastefully written, this site contains much information about the infamous French noble from the 18th century. There are quotes, excerpts, and a chronology available here.

Fyodor Dostoevsky

http://grove.ufl.edu/~flask/Dostoevsky.html

This page, though dark, is styled very nicely. A great resource for people searching information concerning the (arguably) first existentialist novelist, this page contains facts and text to further study of this 19th century novelist.

Dr. Seuss

http://www2.interconnect.net/drseuss/home.html

Great images, book listings, pieces of interviews and commentaries, and a copy of Seuss' death announcement. Includes a copy of the humor piece, "What if Dr. Seuss Were a Technical Writer?"

Marguerite Duras

http://www.uta.fi/~trkisa/duras/duras.html

Marguerite Duras died in the spring of 1996 in her Paris apartment. Since that time, her fans have taken time to construct very complete archives of her work and tributes to her life. This page is the most complete of those, including essays and *ses oeuvres* in three languages.

Umberto Eco

http://www4.ncsu.edu/eos/users/m/mcmesser/www/eco.html

A computer-friendly semiotician, Umberto Eco's work has been hailed by philosophers, scholars, and readers all over the world. This site provides a good overview of the work of this important Italian writer.

William Faulkner

http://www.mcsr.olemiss.edu/~egjbp/faulkner/

The site to visit for any sort of information about William Faulkner. John B. Padgett, currently a Ph.D. student at the University of Mississippi (located at Oxford, whence Faulkner hailed), maintains this completists' page with more information on Faulkner than anyone could want.

F. Scott Fitzgerald

http://www.csd.scarolina.edu/fitzgerald/index.html

Based at the University of South Carolina, this site dedicated to F. Scott Fitzgerald is in celebration of the centennial of his birth. The mission statement of the page states that "this site celebrates his writings, his life, and his relationships with other writers of the 20th century." True to this, you'll find biography, writings, and beautiful photos of the famous author from the Roaring '20s.

Ian Fleming

http://www.mcs.net/~klast/www/fleming.html

You might think that the Ian Fleming Web page might as well be called "Oh, yeah, and for the guy who actually created James Bond," however, this page is chock-full of history, biography, and news clips relating to the British author. Of course, you'll find plenty of 007, too.

Johann Wolfgang von Goethe

http://www.cris.com/~Huntress/goethe.shtml

A brief biography and some different links to matters concerning Goethe are present at this site. Also, if your equipment can support it, there are some nice multimedia aspects here.

John Grisham

http://www.bdd.com/athwk/bddathwk.cgi?w=06-19-95

This site created by the publisher of Grisham's books has information on the author, pictures, and features the ability to e-mail John Grisham, if you so desire.

Thomas Hardy

http://pages.ripco.com:8080/~mws/hardy.html

A large site about the author, it includes what you might expect—biography, e-texts, pictures—as well as some very entertaining sound bites of excerpts of works by Hardy and Monty Python's take on him.

Nathaniel Hawthorne

http://www.tiac.net/users/eldred/nh/hawthorne.html

"Dedicated to enhancing our understanding and appreciation of Hawthorne's writings and life," this site has complete e-texts of his novels and stories. There are readings, pictures, and information about this American author of the 19th century.

Ernest Hemingway (The Papa Page)

http://www.ee.mcgill.ca/~nverever/hem/cover.html

Probably the definitive Hemingway site, The Papa Page brings pictures, bibliographies, and biography of Ernest Hemingway to the World Wide Web. There are good references here to print resources that can be obtained at any bookstore or library.

L. Ron Hubbard

http://www.lronhubbard.org/

A wonderful site to visit for its accessibility, layout, and information on L. Ron Hubbard. It offers a profile of Hubbard, his poetry, songs and music, philosophy, and (of course) his books. There's also a link to the Church of Scientology. Includes audio clips of some of his lectures and writings.

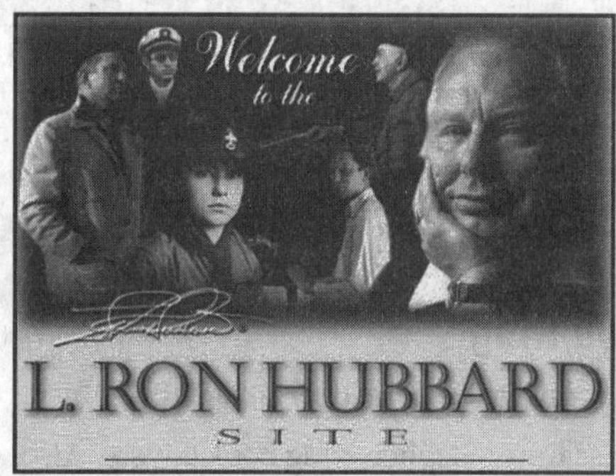

Zora Neale Hurston

http://pages.prodigy.com/zora/

A site dedicated to the writer of the famous novel *Their Eyes Were Watching God*. There are links, many photographs, and links to other Hurston and literature sites.

Robert Jordan

`http://www.cc.gatech.edu/ftp/people/viren/www/jordan/jordan.html`

A whimsical FAQ to Robert Jordan's work, with humor, language guides, and more.

James Joyce (Work in Progress)

`http://www.2street.com/joyce/`

There are many joys to this site—pictures of the author, his family, and those people mentioned in his work; important songs and readings by Joyce himself; links to articles and Internet groups who study Joyce; and maps of the places mentioned in his work. Give yourself some time, though—this site is worth it.

Jonathan Kellerman

`http://malkuth.sephiroth.org/~corwin/authors/jkellerman/index.html`

Contains a brief biography and book list of Jonathan Kellerman, as well as some books with descriptions culled from the dust jackets.

Jack Kerouac

`http://www-hsc.usc.edu/~gallaher/k_speaks/kerouacspeaks.html`

Many recordings of Jack Kerouac reading from his prose. (Sometimes he sings, too.)

Stephen King

`http://wwwcsif.cs.ucdavis.edu/~pace/king.html`

Full of many interesting links that one might not imagine Stephen King would relate himself with. In other words, you will find photos, FAQs, and biographies about King here, but you will also find a guess at his mailing address and a copy of some liner notes King wrote for Michael McDermott's new album.

Stephen King

`http://www.netropolis.net/slayer/sking.htm`

Lots of scans of Stephen King book covers. Also includes a complete list of his movies, novels and collections, some with descriptions and additional graphics.

Barbara Kingsolver

`http://www.csc.eku.edu/honors/kingsolver/`

Pictures of her book covers, essays by students, and a biography compose this site dedicated to the writer of *Pigs in Heaven*.

Dean Koontz

`http://www.hway.com/zebster/koontz/`

FAQ, bibliography, reviews, interviews, readers' polls, and an index page of links—all with a very attractive interface.

Katherine Kurtz

`http://arrogant.itc.icl.ie/KatherineKurtz.html`

Contains listings of Katherine Kurtz's works and a short biography, as well as a Deryni FAQ.

Louis L'Amour

`http://www.accessnow.com/ll/welcome.html`

A self-proclaimed "celebration of American History and the Wild West," this site gives more than just information about L'Amour and his prolific amount of novels—it approaches all things from the American West. The author of this site has written it in such a way that is very inviting, and he has included reviews, pictures, and (kindly) a list of updates made on the page.

Ring Lardner (Lardnermania)

`http://ourworld.compuserve.com/homepages/Topping/`

The Lardnermania page includes links, a chronology, and a selected bibliography of secondary sources. This site is a great starting point for students and researchers of Ring Lardner.

Ursula K. Le Guin

`http://www.uic.edu/~lauramd/sf/leguin.html`

A biography, contact and agent information, lists of awards won by LeGuin, and a complete bibliography, arranged both chronologically and by type of work (poetry, novel, etc.)

C.S. Lewis and the Inklings

`http://ernie.bgsu.edu/~edwards/lewis.html`

A site devoted not only to Lewis, but to the Inklings—the group of English and Irish writers that spawned

Lewis, J.R.R. Tolkein, and others. Contains a list of available audio- and videotapes of Lewis, as well as an Inklings Photogallery with a map of Narnia.

C.S. Lewis (Into the Wardrobe)

http://www.cache.net/~john/cslewis/index.html

Into the Wardrobe has many tidbits and large chunks of useful information for the scholar, reader, and fan of C.S. Lewis. One of the best parts of this site is its completist attitude toward studying Lewis and his work—it even includes a Useful Contacts page.

The Libyrinth

http://www.microserve.net/~thequail/libyrinth/index.html

A very large and intricate Web unto itself, the Libyrinth features information and links about 20th century authors and their influence on (and by) Magical Realism or Post Modernism. Several authors are included here, and several more are in the midst of being added.

H. P. Lovecraft

http://www.primenet.com/~dloucks/hplpage.html

Biography, chronological list of tales, a Lovecraft FAQ, information regarding the "Necronomicon," and a photo-tour of New England locations related to Lovecraft's work.

Anne McCaffrey

http://arrogant.itc.icl.ie/AnneMcCaffrey.html

Contains links to bibliographies, a list of awards, and sample chapters from Anne McCaffrey's latest books. There's also a link to DragonWeb and a list of fan clubs.

Cormac McCarthy

http://pages.prodigy.com/cormac/index.htm

The Cormac McCarthy home page is a good place to start for someone interested both in the writing of Cormac McCarthy and the literature of the American Southwest. Often compared to William Faulkner, McCarthy has recently become very popular among certain literary circles. Perhaps with the proliferation of novels such as *All The Pretty Horses*, reading will again become an American pastime.

Herman Melville

http://www.melville.org/

Alright, so maybe you didn't like reading *Moby Dick* in high school; that doesn't mean that it wasn't worthwhile, though, right? Melville is actually a pretty approachable author, not to mention his

importance to the American tradition. Try him again here—you'll find a comprehensive amount of information about the author of arguably "the great American novel."

Henry Miller (18, villa seurat)

http://astro.ocis.temple.edu/~bwalsh/miller/miller.htm

At 18, villa seurat, you'll find artwork, a bibliography, a chronology, and criticism concerning the once owner of a speakeasy in New York and otherwise infamous author of the early 20th century.

Yukio Mishima Archive

http://www.injapan.net/members/tokyojon/cjourn.htm

This site is dedicated to the Japanese writer of the famous short story "Patriotism." Currently present is a brief biography (of sorts) and a picture gallery.

N. Scott Momaday

http://users.mwci.net/~lapoz/Momaday.html

A very ambitious Web page, this page promises to provide links to information "about every article and book written by or about N. Scott Momaday." Already present (as of this writing) are biographical and bibliographical information and reviews of Momaday's work.

Vladmir Nabokov (Zembla)

http://www.libraries.psu.edu/iasweb/nabokov/nsintro.htm

A formidable presence on the World Wide Web in terms of layout, content, and conciseness, Zembla offers a great amount and breadth of information concerning Vladmir Nabokov.

Anaïs Nin

http://www.informatik.uni-leipzig.de/privat2/beckmann/
public_html/nin.html

This home page includes links to resources concerning Anaïs Nin's work, a bibliography, and a biography. Perhaps best known for her diaries, Nin was also a prose writer, a fact that the writer of this page doesn't forget to cover.

Joyce Carol Oates (Celestial Timepiece)

`http://storm.usfca.edu/~southerr/jco.html`

Heavily Netscape formatted, Celestial Timepiece gives a full view of Oates' work. This site features a well-laid out table of contents that covers her life and gives access to resources for research on Oates and her work.

Edgar Allen Poe

`http://www.cs.umu.se/~dpcnn/eapoe/ea_poe.html`

Author of "The Raven," Edgar Allen Poe is also famous for his short stories that were meant to "expand the human soul." This Web site is very popular, and deservedly so—it features biography, links to e-text, and a chat room.

Marcel Proust (Proust Said That)

`http://www.yahoo.com/Arts/Humanities/Literature/Genres/Literary_Fiction/Authors/Proust__Marcel__1871_1922_/`

This site calls itself "the highly unofficial organ of the totally unofficial, utterly unacademic Marcel Proust Support Group of San Francisco," but it is probably the best Proust source on the Web yet. There is an interesting hyperlinked biography, as well as some other tidbits, including recipes and articles only slightly relating to Proust.

Ayn Rand

`http://www.aynrand.org/`

Dedicated to Rand's novels and philosophy, there are many links to biographies, bibliographies, mission statements, and objectivism. The philosophy of reason and egoism lives here.

Anne Rice

`http://www.personal.psu.edu/users/l/m/lms5/aboutar.html`

A very large site in honor of the horror writer from New Orleans. Anne Rice's books have become very popular in the last few years, and this site is testimony to that. There are pictures, biographies, bibliographies, sounds, and even information about Rice's house in New Orleans.

Tom Robbins (The AFTRLife)

`http://www.rain.org/~da5e/tom_robbins.html`

A self-described Tom Robbins playground, the AFTRLife is a fun place to look around and learn about Tom Robbins' work. It is Java enhanced and well formatted. A good place to spend a few minutes if you are looking for the author of *Still Life With Woodpecker*.

Philip Roth

`http://omni.cc.purdue.edu/~royald/roth.htm`

A straightforward page concerning Philip Roth's work as a novelist and critic. There are biographies, bibliographies, interviews, and articles present here.

Antoine de Saint-Exupery

`http://www.sas.upenn.edu/~smfriedm/exupery/`

Perhaps known mostly for his book *The Little Prince*, Antoine de Saint-Exupery was also an adult novelist and pilot. At this site, there are links to quotes, a bibliography, and e-texts available in several languages.

J.D. Salinger (The Bananafish Home Page)

`http://slf.gweep.net/~sfoskett/jds/index.html`

Salinger's wish for privacy and ownership have kept some of the best sites down, leaving sites only the ability to provide biography and bibliography. If anyone has any recent pictures of Salinger, this guy would probably appreciate them.

George Sand

`http://www.eden.com/~gebbie/gsand/gs_home.html`

George Sand, French writer of the 19th century, finds a very well-constructed Web home here. There are biography, bibliography, and chronology pages present, and perhaps most impressive is the gallery of pictures of Sand.

Mary Shelley

http://www.netaxs.com/~kwbridge/maryshel.html

This site houses information about Mary Shelley, Percy Shelly, the Romantics, and, of course, her popular novel *Frankenstein*. Newly updated, there is a gothic air to this site, including a musical background.

Gertrude Stein

http://www.magibox.net/~stein/

The most "official" Gertrude Stein page, this site features a reproduction of the wallpaper Stein and Alice B. Toklas bought for their Paris apartment. Of course, too, there are some pictures and quotes from the author.

John Steinbeck

http://www.sjsu.edu/depts/steinbec/srchome.html

The San Jose State University is home to the Steinbeck Research Center, and this is its home on the Web. There are chronologies, biographical information, bibliographies, and an interesting link called Steinbeck Country with pictures and other tidbits.

Amy Tan

http://www.alchemyweb.com/~alchemy/amytan/

Amy Tan On The Web gives excerpts, sound bites, interviews, links, and pictures of this influential contemporary American author. Her work has been widely translated and deserves the recognition that it has attained.

Mark Twain (Ever the Twain Shall Meet)

http://www.lm.com/~joseph/mtwain.html

This site seems to know its stuff. It has links to e-text versions of several of Twain's novels—both downloadable and in HTML—and other very interesting links to Twain around the Web.

Jules Verne

http://avery.med.virginia.edu/~mtp0f/flips/jules.html

A well-maintained, chatty site dedicated to the author of *20,000 Leagues Under the Sea* and *Around the World in 80 Days* (among others), this page is easily navigated and has good links to biography, reviews, pictures, and the like.

Gore Vidal

http://www.randomhouse.com/atr/fall95/vidal.html

A very interesting man, Gore Vidal has led his life behind the typewriter and in the public eye. His acid accuracies concerning contemporary America are astounding and are presented here in this interview.

William T. Vollmann

http://FTPhome1.gte.net/csweet/vollmann.htm

Quickly becoming very popular, William T. Vollmann is a writer who very clearly could have died many pages ago—his work is voluminous and his exploits are infamous. This site pays homage to the man who has spent months above the Arctic Circle while doing research on a novel. There is an hour-long interview in RealAudio format here, if you have the time.

Alice Walker

http://www.alchemyweb.com/~alchemy/alicew/

Essays, articles, criticism, poetry, short stories, excerpts—you name it, you'll find it here. Also, this site is well formatted and is filled with links to this contemporary American writer.

Eudora Welty

http://www.lacollege.edu/depart/ejl/south/welty.html

Eudora Welty is often compared to William Faulkner in both theme and time frame. This site houses her publication history, some essays, criticism, and bibliographies concerning Welty and her work.

Oscar Wilde (The Wild Wilde Web)

http://www.clients.anomtec.com/oscarwilde/

The Wild Wilde Web has beautiful pictures, a nice biography, and a comprehensive bibliography for you to peruse if you are looking for the controversial playwright from the turn of the century. There is also an interesting page filled with quotes about Wilde.

Thomas Wolfe

`http://www.cms.uncwil.edu/~connelly/wolfe.html`

Thomas Wolfe was a reader's writer. Legend has it that before he seriously wrote any novels, he read the entire library at the University of North Carolina at Chapel Hill. At this site, you won't find that much text, but you will find a bountiful amount of information about the writer of *Look Homeward Angel*.

Virginia Woolf

`http://www.aianet.or.jp/~orlando/VWW/`

The Virginia Woolf Web has quotes, e-texts, and information about the Bloomsbury group with which Woolf is associated. This page is consistently updated, and contains information about Woolf that is found nowhere else on the Web.

Roger Zelazny

`http://intele.net/~ferenczy/rogerz.html`

Detailing the work that Roger Zelazny had in progress at his death in 1995.

Electronic Literature

The Adventures of Tom Sawyer

`http://www.cs.cmu.edu/Web/People/rgs/sawyr-table.html`

The complete text, from the Project Gutenberg edition, linkable by chapter.

Alice's Adventures in Wonderland

`http://www.cstone.net/library/alice/alice-w.html`

The complete text, linkable by chapter, with colorized versions of the John Tenniel illustrations.

American Literary Classics

`http://www.mindport.net/~arezis/`

A great site to visit if you want to catch up on reading you know you should be doing, but don't

have much time to dedicate to it. This site gives a chapter a day of a classic American novel. (For instance, *Moby Dick* was featured at the time of this writing.) In addition to the chapter, the rest of the novel is present if you'd like to read it in its entirety, and links to the author of the featured book and some other interesting links are also available.

Baker Street Connection

`http://www.citsoft.com/holmes.html`

Contains the texts of the Sherlock Holmes novels and short stories. Also includes scans of illustrations from Holmes books, and a canon word search feature.

Bob Book Online

`http://www.gigaplex.com/books/bob/index.htm`

Are you an okay guy? Well, here is a book that is a celebration of the ultimate okay guy. The Bob Book deals with the who, what, why, and how issues of Bobness. Includes complete explanations with pictures and text from famous Bobs from Dylan to Barker.

The Citadell of Riva

`http://linnea.asogy.stockholm.se/~mp95askm/David_Eddings/`

Provides a biography of writer David Eddings, scans of artwork, and links to other pages. Also contains some excerpts from some of Eddings' works.

The Commonplace Book

`http://sunsite.unc.edu/ibic/Commonplace-Book.html`

Traditionally, a "commonplace book" is a place to put notable passages people find in their reading to memorialize those ideas. This page is an electronic version of one of those books made by a variety of readers.

The Electronic Labyrinth

`http://www.ualberta.ca/~ckeep/elab.html`

Home to hypertext in literature, there are links to articles, e-texts, and other resources concerning hypertext in the area of writing. Essays by important authors are also present and link to other related articles.

The Electronic Library

`http://www.books.com/scripts/lib.exe`

This virtual library is available for the free dissemination of e-texts by thousands of different authors. There is a nice search engine that is available to find anything present in the "stacks."

Great Books of Western Civilization

`http://www.ilinks.net/~lnoles/grtbks.html`

A self-study sort of course that should give the reader a well-rounded liberal education. The interesting twist on this, though, is that the books in the course are online (for the most part—some would infringe on copyrights).

Gutter Press

`http://www.io.org/~gutter/`

Provides radical literature and fiction to the reader of new or dangerous fiction. Provides links to other small presses, quarterly publications, and new and existing titles and authors.

The Hunting of the Snark: an Agony in Eight Fits

`http://etext.lib.virginia.edu/cgibin/ browse-mixed?id=CarSnar&tag=public&images=images/modeng&data=/lv1/Archive/eng-parsed`

The complete text of Lewis Carroll's poem, including his preface, and scanned images of many of the original illustrations.

HyperLiterature/HyperTheory

`http://ebbs.english.vt.edu/hthl/HyperLit_Home.html`

HyperLiterature/HyperTheory has an annotated bibliography, some readings, and some works by students who are studying this exciting new field.

Literary Works: Mark Twain

`http://www.literature.org/Works/Mark-Twain/`

Contains the complete text of *Huck Finn* and *Connecticut Yankee*, with more to come.

Little Women-DataText

`http://www.datatext.co.uk/library/alcott/littlew/chapters.htm`

The complete text of the book, linkable by chapter.

The Lost World (Randomhouse)

`http://www.randomhouse.com/site/lostworld`

A page maintained by the publisher, devoted to the *Jurassic Park* sequel. Contains ordering info, excerpts. Also contains links to other sites' articles on such subjects as dinosaurs, electric/hybrid vehicles, and chaos theory.

Mark Twain: Huckleberry Finn

`http://etext.lib.virginia.edu/twain/huckfinn.html`

Browse the complete text, chapter by chapter if you like, and look at the first edition illustrations. Includes early reviews and "the obscene sales prospectus illustration."

The Martian Chronicles Study Guide

`http://www.wsu.edu:8080/~brians/science_fiction/martian_chronicles.html`

Maintained by Washington State University, this is a useful page for those wishing to study and critique Bradbury's writing style.

Online Books FAQ

`http://www.cs.indiana.edu/metastuff/bookfaq.html`

A Frequently Asked Question list concerning the availability of online works, with links to archives and other directories, and information about public domain laws.

TeleRead

`http://www.clark.net/pub/rothman/telhome.html`

A project to bring books and reading to everyone. It includes articles, links, and papers written by scholars in support of electronic publishing.

Education Supplies

`http://co-nect.bbn.com/WWW/Opportunities/free_stuff.html`

Become the coolest teacher in school with these free supplies. This site provides addresses, phone numbers, and descriptions of products available including CD-ROMs that tackle today's environmental issues, assistive technology for parents and teachers of children with special needs, posters, and science experiments.

Tree Fiction on the World Wide Web

`http://www.cl.cam.ac.uk/users/gdr11/tree-fiction.html`

Gareth Rees' paper concerning hypertext and the World Wide Web presents differing ideas about the use of hypertext in today's literature. He even offers that certain games are a form of hypertext; in fact, he maintains that these are the most interactive type.

The Wonderful Wizard of Oz

`http://www.literature.org/Works/L-Frank-Baum/wizard/`

The complete text of the book, linkable by chapter.

Zuzu's Petals Literary Resource

`http://www.hway.net/zuzu/homelink.htm`

Filled with links, Zuzu's Petals is the place to start looking for any online resource to literature and the arts. There are also links to related issues, such as censorship, artists, movie lovers, and Web designers.

Journals and E-Zines

@Ezine

`http://www.vitter.com/ezine/@ezine.htm`

Essays, commentary, short fiction, poetry, visual arts, and cultural interest grace the pages of this well-designed e-zine. There are also links to many of the artists' home pages and galleries.

Alternative-X

`http://marketplace.com/alt.x/althome.html`

A pleasingly interesting site, Alternative-X gives a forum for new writers, hypertext aficionados, and even ancient Greeks. There are texts of many different genres, but all are grouped logically into subsections of the e-zine.

American Planet Galactic News

`http://www.americanplanet.com/`

A quirky e-zine that is reportedly updated weekly, this zine features poetry, links, current events, public affairs, and pictures that might be of interest to young adults.

Anagram

`http://www.jhu.edu/~anagram/`

This is a literary journal based at The Johns Hopkins University and dedicated to Asian-Americans. Although most of the contributors are students at Johns Hopkins, there are also writers from other venues presented.

Canboulay, The Caribbean Literature Quarterly

`http://www.talkin-drum.com/canboulay/bitss.html`

A journal dedicated to creative works and critical studies centered around Caribbean literature. Of course, writers from around the world are presented here, too.

The Cream City Review

`http://www.uwm.edu/People/noj/tccr/about.htm`

Based at the University of Wisconsin at Milwaukee, this is the literary journal of their English department. The name comes from the town's nickname, "The City of Cream-Colored Bricks."

CrossConnect

`http://tech1.dccs.upenn.edu/~xconnect/`

CrossConnect is a triannual electronic journal examining and presenting contemporary art. It is based at the University of Pennsylvania in Philadelphia. This page is very well-formatted and popular. The current issue is at the forefront, but back issues are available, too.

De Proverbio

`http://ftp.utas.edu.au/docs/flonta/`

This is an electronic journal of international proverb studies. Several issues are available to be accessed and read, and there are other links available to reach the editors and editorial board of the periodical.

Dimension^2

`http://members.aol.com/germanlit/dimension2.html`

This is a journal of contemporary German-language literature. It is available in both the original German as well as in English. Also present at this site is original artwork by a contemporary German artist.

Early Modern Literary Studies

http://unixg.ubc.ca:7001/0/e-sources/emls/emlshome.html

Dedicated to the English language, literature, and literary culture from the 16th and 17th century, this journal is very interactive, featuring the capability to respond to its published papers in a Reader's Forum.

Exemplaria

http://www.clas.ufl.edu/english/exemplaria/

A journal of theory in medieval and Renaissance studies, Exemplaria is based at the University of Florida. Read articles concerning literature and culture from the formative Middle Ages.

Harvard Gay and Lesbian Review

http://www.hglc.org/hglc/review.htm

Considered the premier journal for gay and lesbian studies, the *Harvard Gay and Lesbian Review* is now online. There are indexes, articles, and excerpts from big-named scholars in the area of sexuality, such as Camille Paglia and Edmund White.

The Milton Quarterly

http://voyager.cns.ohiou.edu/~somalley/milton.html

A journal related to John Milton and his work. There are abstracts and excerpts from the journal, as well as various other information about John Milton and his work.

NorthWords

http://www.catalyst-highlands.co.uk/nortword.htm

Produced in the Scottish Highlands, NorthWords is a journal that focuses on the literature of "the North." Their definition of "North" is particularly interesting, though, and doesn't hold any sort of provincial boundary. Not only is creative work featured here, interviews and book reviews also are present.

Plaintext

http://www.plaintext.com/

Plaintext is (amazingly) a self-described "literary daily." Its aim is to present reviews, essays, stories, and articles each day—often in hypertext format. Readers can also submit to this online e-zine by e-mail.

Qui Parle

http://garnet.berkeley.edu:4045/

The home page for the journal of the liberal arts. This periodical covers a wide range of topics, interdisciplinary and otherwise.

Renditions

http://www.cuhk.edu.hk/renditions/

Renditions is a magazine dedicated to Chinese literature and language. At this site, you'll find such interesting topics as Chinese poetry, essays, and story excerpts. You also can order books by Renditions Publishing.

Romanticism On the Net

http://users.ox.ac.uk/~scat0385/

A great site about Romanticism in general, this online journal presents many articles, links, and the ability to publish online—that is, if you have something to say about Romanticism.

Sapphic Ink

http://www.lesbian.org/sapphic-ink/

A lesbian literary journal that features fiction, poetry, book reviews, and a hotlist. Also available is the ability to read about and get in contact with the contributors and editors of the magazine.

Science Fiction Weekly

http://www.scifi.com/sfw/

An electronic SF magazine. Covers books, movies, TV, games, artwork, and merchandise, and even some interviews.

Transculture

http://www.ilstu.edu/depts/forlangs/tculture.htm

A journal of interpretations and applications of cultural studies in language. Mostly abstracts from the printed journal, this site invites you to read more about the impact of multicultural studies.

Wespennest

http://www.ping.at/wespennest/wespennest.html

A literary magazine in both English and German. This site has links to literature sites, journals, and specimen articles in the PDF (Acrobat) format. There are also archives, offers, and a form to order this journal in print.

Online Book Resources

alt.books.reviews

news://alt.books.reviews

This newsgroup gives reviews of books, but there is not much discussion here. If you're interested in a book and want just a little more information about it before you buy it, then you might want to look here first.

alt.books.technical

news://alt.books.technical

Provides information about technical books, mostly centering on computer books. This newsgroup also attracts the sale and resale of books about technical topics.

Amazon.com

http://www.amazon.com/

Touted as the "Earth's Biggest Bookstore," Amazon.com maintains and sells over one million titles. With a well-developed search engine, you can search by just about anything you know about a book or author—even if it is just one word.

Banned Books On-line

http://www.cs.cmu.edu/Web/People/spok/banned-books.html

Banned Books On-line celebrates the freedom to read. There are links to e-texts on the Web featuring authors who have at one time been banned in America and elsewhere. Also present is some censorship history of the books featured on the page.

Book Banning, Burning, and Censorship

http://www.banned.books.com/

A multimedia experience concerning banned books, censorship, and its impact on the world. There are quotes, pictures, audio files, and the use of client-side pull to present its case—make sure you are using a Netscape-compatible browser to experience this site to its fullest.

Bookbinding, a tutorial

http://www.cs.uiowa.edu/~jones/book/

An instruction guide to repairing books that might be falling apart, this site has been carefully researched and represents the work of a true bibliophile.

BookWorld

http://www.bookworld.com/

A very useful reference site for anyone who buys books or wants to publish a book of their own. This site has samples of hundreds of titles under a myriad of subjects. It also provides information about publishing and marketing a book over the Internet, and it includes links to many publishers and related services.

Conservation OnLine

http://palimpsest.stanford.edu/

A guide to preserving books, articles, pictures, and other media for professionals and amateurs alike. This site is dedicated to the preservation of information of many media.

A Hundred Highlights from the Koninklijke Bibliotheek

http://www.konbib.nl/100hoogte/hh-en.html

This large, Dutch library has a searchable index of resources. There are also many pictures present that were either created specifically for the library or are archived at the library. This library mainly houses older books, so this presentation is to bring them to the public in a way that makes them less vulnerable to battery and the caustic effects of being in the open.

Hungry Mind Review Discussion

`http://www.bookwire.com/HMR.discussion`

A place to discuss titles, subjects, genres, or just about anything concerning reading. There are archives of discussions from the past. Feel free to join any of the many discussions.

Index

`http://www.bookwire.com/links/other_booksellers/other_booksellers.html`

If you're looking for a particular type of book, click on the links and the list of booksellers will appear. Provides links to computer, gay and lesbian, science fiction, children's, travel booksellers, and many, many more. Also gives a link to other bookseller sites.

L'Art Medical Antiquarian Books

`http://www.xs4all.nl/~artmed/`

The history of medicine, antique books, and a place to register in a "wish-list" for certain titles. There are links to a mailing list and the Netherlands Antiquarian Bookseller's Network.

Macmillan Publishing USA (The Information SuperLibrary)

`http://www.mcp.com/`

The Information SuperLibrary is chock-full of interesting and useful information about computer-related titles, including a link to the online version of the book, *New Riders' Official World Wide Web Yellow Pages*.

Notable Children's Books

`http://www.ala.org/alaorg/alsc/notbooks.html`

This site sponsored by the Association for Library Service to Children is filled with suggested reading for children and is organized to separate younger, middle, and older children's books. There are also suggested readings for children of all ages.

The Preservation Educators' Exchange

`http://www.well.com/user/bronxbob/presed-x/presed-x.html`

A site to exchange information that might be valuable to anyone who wishes to learn more about archiving or preserving books and library science. There are announcements of upcoming events, items of interest, and even syllabi of library science classes at different universities.

ReadersNdex

`http://www.readersndex.com/`

This is a great site if you love books. Provides links to authors, publishers, book stores, discussion panels, and a reading room of articles and book samples. Includes personalized subscription services that provide information based upon interests.

rec.arts.books

`news://rec.arts.books`

This newsgroup is a generic discussion of anything relating to books or writing. There are many postings here, so you are certain to find something that interests you.

The Romance Pages

`http://www.ivdev.com/booksource/romance/index.html`

Maintained by Integrated Visions, this site lists many contemporary romance authors and their newest works (including some excerpts and scans of book covers).

A Sherlockian Holmepage

`http://watserv1.uwaterloo.ca/~credmond/sh.html`

Contains many links to electronic Holmes and Conan Doyle resources.

A Sherlockian Holmepage

The Tolkien Society

`http://info.ox.ac.uk/~tolksoc/ts.html`

Home page for a British charity organization aimed at promoting the works of J.R.R. Tolkien.

Ultimate Romance Novel Website

`http://www.icgnet.com/romancebooks/`

Enables you to offer your opinions on romance novels you've read. Take a look at their gallery of cover art, and read up on publishers, writers, illustrators, and cover models.

Vintage Books Reading Group Guides

http://www.randomhouse.com/knopf/read/

A novel idea about the reading group (and perhaps a very good way to promote books, too), the Vintage Books Reading Group Guides are like the discussion questions that you might find at the end of a story in a high school anthology (only for adults). There is more here, though—there is author biography, pictures of the books and authors, and a selected further reading list. If you are in charge of a reading group and can't think of a good place to start discussion, try this site first.

Willy Wonka Lyrics

http://www.stcloud.msus.edu/~hazelc01/wonka/lyrics.html

The lyrics to each song from the movie, including the songs of the Oompa Loompas.

Online Bookstores

Antiquarian Booksellers' Association of America

http://www.abaa-booknet.com

Specializes in rare and antiquarian books, maps, and prints. Provides a search service by specialty and location, catalogs and links to other services for over 140 booksellers, current information on book fairs nationwide, links to online public access catalogs at libraries worldwide, and articles of interest to book sellers and book collectors from the ABAA Newsletter.

Association of American University Presses (AAUP) Online Catalog/ Bookstore

http://aaup.pupress.princeton.edu/

Online bookstore that is a made up of member university presses. Open for business but still under construction, the AAUP introduction states that it expects to have more than 100,000 titles from almost 100 imprints. Provides links to individual university presses. Includes the ability to search for an entire association or by individual university imprint.

Astrology et al Bookstore

http://www.wolfe.net/~astroetl/index.html

Features online catalog of astrology, occult, pagan, UFO, metaphysical, and other related titles. Includes

listing of out-of-print and hard to find books that they have in stock.

Bantam Doubleday Dell—BDD Online

http://www.bdd.com

Catalogs, forums, puzzles, and interviews with the authors of new books. Check out their author of the week. Science fiction fans should check out the Spectra SF Forum.

Bonder Bookstore, Inc.

http://www.bonder.com

Provides online sales site for the Montreal, Quebec based bookstore. Includes order form for purchasing any book in print over the Web.

Book Hunter

http://www.i1.net/~bhunter/

Provides a book-finding service specializing in, but not limited to, technical books. Includes price quote service, search, and order forms. Also includes company profile and account establishment information.

BookLink

http://www.intac.com/~booklink

Specializes in distributing ESL (English as a Second Language) and multicultural books. Also sells children's books and any British book in print.

BookSite

http://www.booksite.com/

An online bookstore that provides search tools for a two-million-book database, new release information, and ordering information. Includes testimonials from satisfied customers.

Bookstore at Houghton Mifflin

http://www.hmco.com/trade/

Provides online sales for one of the largest printing houses in the world. The store is broken down into six sections with book listings, book excerpts, news, and discussion groups. Also included are links and resources for related information and research.

Christian Book Connection

http://www.xmission.com/~seer/Christian-Book/index.html

Online Christian bookstore. Features a catalog of nearly 30,000 items including books, Bibles, Bible software, CDs, and cassettes. Also presents the monthly Christian best-sellers lists of books and music.

A Clean Well-Lighted Place for Books

http://www.well.com/www/jwscott

Why fight traffic, weather, and crowds when you can go to the local bookstore in your own home? This site provides sales and reviews for thousands of titles in many different categories. Also provides many links to other related topics and fields.

Cody's Books

http://www.parentsplace.com/shopping/codys/index.cgi

Provides online sales and home site for Cody's Books. Offers a catalog of over 80,000 titles organized by category. Includes Cody's Books staff suggestions and recommendations. Also includes ordering and contact information.

Comics at Bendigo Books

http://www.prodata.com.au/~benbooks

Specializes in comics, role-playing games, books, and graphic novels. Offers list of best sellers and weekly new releases. Lets you subscribe to comics direct from the Web.

David Morrison Books

http://www.teleport.com/~morrison/

Provides catalog and online sales for David Morrison Books, which specializes in titles on art, architecture, decorative arts, and photography. Includes book descriptions and information.

Deep Politics Bookstore

http://www.copi.com/deepbook.htm

Provides home site and sales for political texts and books. Includes book and author background, as well as ordering information.

Fast Books

http://www.moreinfo.com.au/fastbooks/

Provides online book sales specializing in self-publishers. Includes company catalog, self-publishing information, previews, and ordering information.

Gareth Stevens Publishing

http://market.net/literary/gsinc/index.html

Provides online catalog of Gareth Stevens series books, descriptions of titles, prices, and ordering information. Books are indexed by category (nature, science, social studies, biography, picture books, reference, and bibliotherapy).

Gary Holmes Books

http://www.gmi.edu/~gholmes/Welcome.html

Gary Holmes' site acts as a book buyer and seller. Will sell books or look for specific titles for you. Large collection of juvenile literature like the Hardy Boys books. Also provides links to lists of movie and TV show locations on the Web.

It's a Mystery

http://www.mysterybooks.com/

If you're looking for collectibles or just browsing for a new hard-cover mystery book, this is the site for you. Also join the book club and check out the fun and mysterious links.

Joseph-Beth Booksellers

http://www.mis.net/jbeth/jbmain.html

A listing of Joseph-Beth Bookstores in the Ohio and Kentucky area. Click on the store nearest you for news, events, and information.

JourneyWare Media

http://www.journeyware.com/

Software products and books for lifelong learning, family relationships, and responsible living. Browse the online catalog or place an order.

Loganberry Books

http://www.logan.com/loganberry/

Offering book-of-the-month clubs specializing in
women's, children's, arts, and out of print books.
Choose the club that is right for you.

Login Brothers Book Company

http://www.lb.com/

A book company specializing in books and videos
for the health professional. Search for medical,
nursing, or health-related profession titles. Also
carries a limited selection of legal texts including
Blonds Legal Notes and the Blackletter series.

Mage Publishing

http://gpg.com/mage/

Persian literature and culture, English language
publisher. Order from their catalog or even from
books out of print.

Mare's Nest Publishing

http://www.poptel.org.uk/password/marenest.html

Publisher of Nordic poetry and fiction in the United
Kingdom, some new, some in translation dating back
over 1,000 years. Links to their catalog, stock list, and
the Password home page.

Midnight Special Bookstore

http://msbooks.com/msbooks/

A social and cultural, independent bookstore
featuring political, social science, history, and related
books, weekly events, video and Web connections.
Provides access to other independent bookstores and
asks you to bypass the chains and support the
independent booksellers.

Moe's Books

http://sunsite.unc.edu/ibic/Moeshome.html

Contains more than 500,000 titles in stock at a discount. Includes rare children's books, hard-to-find
import titles, new books, remainder books, and used
books. Also offers free searches if you can't find the
book you want.

Navrang, Inc.

http://catalog.com/navrang/

Comics, books, or magazines published in or about
India or by Indian authors. Links to ordering
information as well as other interesting links on or
about India.

New World Books

http://branch.com/books/books.html

You can order any book in print by mail and save up
to 30%, as long as you know the author/title.
Provides links to book news, university presses,
book summaries, and more.

Norwegian Bookshop

http://www.oslonett.no/home/paul/nw.html

If you're interested in buying Norwegian books or
products, check our this site. They offer study
material, books about Norway, children's books, and
other information.

The Old Bookroom

http://www.ozemail.com.au/~oldbook/

A secondhand and antiquarian bookshop specializing in books, prints, and maps on Asia, Africa, and
the Middle East.

Pacific Book Auction Galleries

http://www.nbn.com/pba/

Provides home site for Pacific Book Auction Galleries, which deals in rare and old books. Includes
current catalog, upcoming auctions, absentee
bidding information, prices paid, and the Pacific
Currents newsletter.

Pantera Publishing

http://www.iquest.net/~kingman/book.html

Provides information and online sales for the book
Tall Weeds and Big Dogs by John Kingman. This
book is a career and job-survival handbook.
Includes testimonials and reviews of the work.

Pas de chance

http://www.interlog.com/~ian/

Produces and provides small print-run, obscure
writings and poetry. Includes company catalog,

artwork, and ordering information. Pas de chance is definitely not your usual publishing house.

Polonia Bookstore

http://www.wtinet.com/wti/polonia.htm

Provides sales of books for Polish-Americans. Includes catalog of books in English with Polish themes and books, magazines, and newspapers in Polish. Also includes book previews, links to Polish sites, and ordering information.

Revolution Books

http://virtumall.com/RevBooks/

Provides online catalog and sales for Revolution Books. Specializes in history, politics, and culture texts. Includes books, magazines, T-shirts, and periodicals.

Science Express, Inc.

http://www.sci-exp.com/

Provides online sales of a large catalog of computer books. The catalog covers nearly all of topics from a range of publishers. Includes searchable index, book descriptions, and reviews. Also includes online ordering information.

Secret Staircase Bookshop

http://www.secretstaircasebooks.com/

Provides online sales for the Secret Staircase Bookshop. Specializes in children's books and adult mysteries. Includes a listing of autographed books in stock, reviews, catalogs, a store calendar, and ordering information. Also provides links to reading and other related sites.

Shen's Books and Supplies

http://www.shens.com/

Provides online catalog sales of children's books from Asia, South America, Europe, and Australia. Offers titles in English and other languages. Includes indexed catalog and company recommendations. Also includes company history, new release information, and monthly themes.

SPITE! Books

http://www.ukshops.co.uk:8000/spite/

Home to self-published work of all persuasions. Features comics and zines. Includes links to other related sites.

Stone Bridge Press

http://www.stonebridge.com/~sbp/

Provides online catalog and sales for Stone Bridge Press books, software, and videos. Specializes in books and products about Japan. Includes complete catalog, excerpts, cover artwork, reviews, and author profiles.

Svoboda's Books Online—State College, PA

http://www.epicom.com/svobodas

Specializes in academic and technical titles, but offers access to anything in American Books-in-Print. Lets you place book orders from your computer.

Time-Life Explorer

http://www.timelife.com

Lets you explore the many products Time-Life offers in books, music, and videos.

UNARIUS Academy of Science

http://www.cts.com/~unarius/

Provides information and online sales for the UNARIUS line of psychology and consciousness books. Includes background of Unarius and listing of workshops available.

Zanadu Comics

http://www.aa.net/~zanadu

Specializes in alternative and mainstream comics, graphic novels, and more. Features reviews by staff and customers, promotions, a trivia contest, and a virtual catalog.

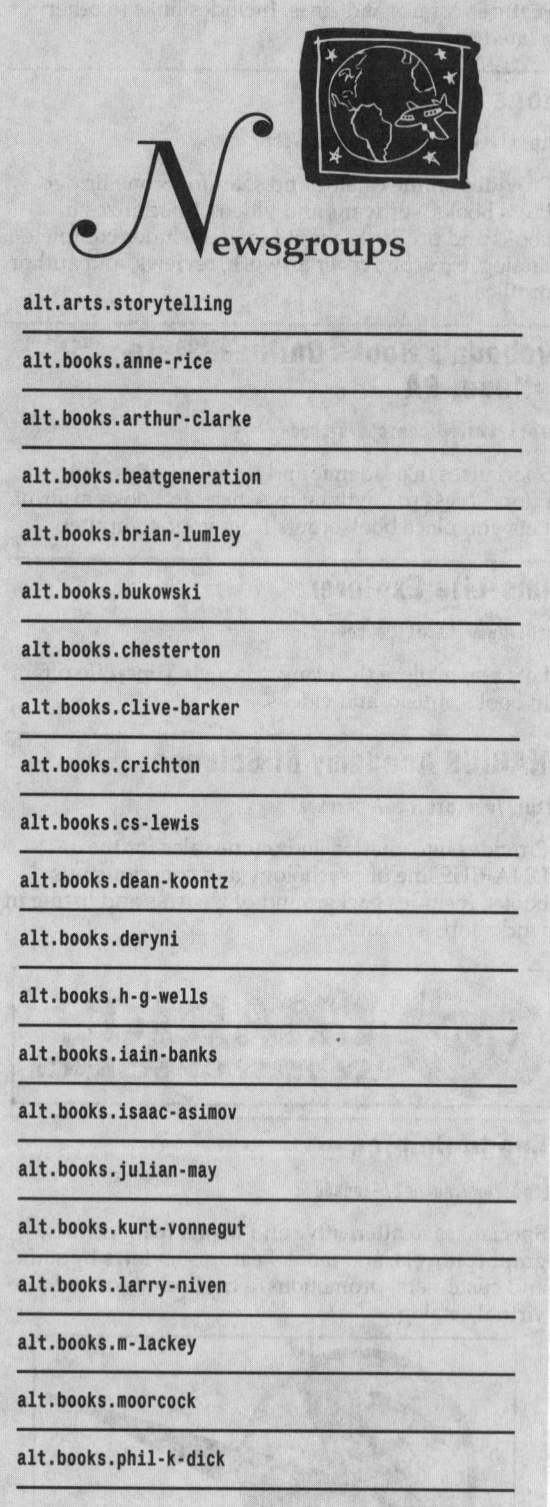

Newsgroups

alt.arts.storytelling

alt.books.anne-rice

alt.books.arthur-clarke

alt.books.beatgeneration

alt.books.brian-lumley

alt.books.bukowski

alt.books.chesterton

alt.books.clive-barker

alt.books.crichton

alt.books.cs-lewis

alt.books.dean-koontz

alt.books.deryni

alt.books.h-g-wells

alt.books.iain-banks

alt.books.isaac-asimov

alt.books.julian-may

alt.books.kurt-vonnegut

alt.books.larry-niven

alt.books.m-lackey

alt.books.moorcock

alt.books.phil-k-dick

alt.books.pratchett

alt.books.raymond-feist

alt.books.reviews

alt.books.robert-rankin

alt.books.sf.melanie-rawn

alt.books.stephen-king

alt.books.technical

alt.books.terry-brooks

alt.books.toffler

alt.books.tom-clancy

alt.comp.shareware.authors

alt.fan.authors.stephen-king

alt.fan.douglas-adams

alt.fan.eddings

alt.fan.harlan-ellison

alt.fan.heinlein

alt.fan.pern

alt.fan.piers-anthony

alt.fan.pooh

alt.fan.pratchett

alt.fan.tolkien

alt.fan.tom-clancy

alt.fan.tom-robbins

alt.fantasy.conan

alt.jokes.limericks

alt.legend.king-arthur

alt.sex.stories

alt.sex.stories.d

alt.startrek.creative.erotica

asu.books.exchange

aus.books

aus.org.acs.books

biz.books.technical

clari.living.books

humanities.lit.authors.shakespeare

misc.books.technical

misc.writing.screenplays

pnet.books.review

pnet.books.rlstine

pnet.books.talk

rec.arts.books

rec.arts.books.childrens

rec.arts.books.hist-fiction

rec.arts.books.marketplace

rec.arts.books.reviews

rec.arts.books.tolkien

rec.arts.erotica

rec.arts.mystery

rec.arts.sf.written

rec.arts.sf.written.robert-jordan

rec.arts.startrek.current

rec.arts.startrek.reviews

relcom.fido.su.books

sdnet.books

slac.rec.books

soc.libraries.talk

tnn.books

tnn.books.magazine

tnn.books.new

ucb.market.books

ucd.swap.books

uiuc.misc.bookcoop

uk.media.books.sf

Listservs

AIDSBKRV—AIDS Book Review Journal

University of Illinois at Chicago, Chicago, IL

You can join this group by sending the message "sub AIDSBKRV your name" to listserv@uicvm.uic.edu

AMLIT2-L—Discussion of American Literature from 1880-Present

Texas A&M University Computing Services Center

You can join this group by sending the message "sub AMLIT2-L your name" to listserv@tamvm1.tamu.edu

ARBOOKS—Discussion of Books by Anne Rice

Pennsylvania State University

You can join this group by sending the message "sub ARBOOKS your name" to `listserv@psuvm.psu.edu`

BOOKTALK—Childrens Literature and Classroom Use

NE Regional Data Center, Univ. of Florida campus, Gainesville, FL

You can join this group by sending the message "sub BOOKTALK your name" to `listserv@nervm.nerdc.ufl.edu`

COMP-REV—Book Review Forum: Rhetoric & Composition

Computing Services Center, University at Albany, Albany, NY

You can join this group by sending the message "sub COMP-REV your name" to `listserv@cnsibm.albany.edu`

CTHEORY—CTHEORY Is an International, Electronic Review of Books

You can join this group by sending the message "sub CTHEORY your name" to `listserv@vm1.mcgill.ca`

DESIRELIT-LIST—Desire & Literature List

State University of New York at Buffalo

You can join this group by sending the message "sub DESIRELIT-LIST your name" to `listserv@listserv.acsu.buffalo.edu`

DOROTHYL—Mystery Literature E-Conference

You can join this group by sending the message "sub DOROTHYL your name" to `listserv@listserv.kent.edu`

ENG1162—Book Discussion Questions

The George Washington University Computer Center, Washington, DC

You can join this group by sending the message "sub ENG1162 your name" to `listserv@gwuvm.gwu.edu`

ENG212—ENG212-BUSINESS WRITING

University of Missouri-St. Louis

You can join this group by sending the message "sub ENG212 your name" to `listserv@umslvma.umsl.edu`

ENG213—ENG213-TECHNICAL WRITING

University of Missouri-St. Louis

You can join this group by sending the message "sub ENG213 your name" to `listserv@umslvma.umsl.edu`

FEM-BIBLIO—Discussion of Books Relating to Women and/or Spirituality

America Online, Inc. (1-800-827-6364 in USA/ Canada)

You can join this group by sending the message "sub FEM-BIBLIO your name" to `listserv@listserv.aol.com`

FICTION—Fiction Writing Workshop

Pennsylvania State University

You can join this group by sending the message "sub FICTION your name" to `listserv@psuvm.psu.edu`

HORROR—Horror in Film and Literature

University Computing Services, Indiana University

You can join this group by sending the message "sub HORROR your name" to `listserv@iubvm.ucs.indiana.edu`

JPL-L—Electronic Publishing Mailing List

Clark Internet Services Inc, 10600 Route 108, Ellicott City, MD

You can join this group by sending the message "sub JPL-L your name" to `listserv@listserv.clark.net`

NEWBOOKS—New Books in Communication

Rensselaer Polytechnic Institute, Troy, NY

You can join this group by sending the message "sub NEWBOOKS your name" to `listserv@vm.its.rpi.edu`

RW-L—Romance Writer's Discussion List

St. John's University, Jamaica, NY

You can join this group by sending the message "sub RW-L your name" to `listserv@sjuvm.stjohns.edu`

TAA-L—Textbook Authors Association

The University of Georgia, Athens, GA

You can join this group by sending the message "sub TAA-L your name" to `listserv@uga.cc.uga.edu`

TECHWR-L—Technical Writers List; For All Technical Communication Issues

You can join this group by sending the message "sub TECHWR-L your name" to listserv@listserv.okstate.edu

TOW—The Online World Book Info

You can join this group by sending the message "sub TOW your name" to listserv@listserv.nodak.edu

WFILES—Archive Files for the WRITERS List

Massachusetts Institute of Technology, Cambridge, MA

You can join this group by sending the message "sub WFILES your name" to listserv@mitvma.mit.edu

WRITERS—WRITERS

Massachusetts Institute of Technology, Cambridge, MA

You can join this group by sending the message "sub WRITERS your name" to listserv@mitvma.mit.edu

WRITERS-CLUB—Information, Motivation, and Inspiration for Every Writer

America Online, Inc. (1-800-827-6364 in USA/Canada)

You can join this group by sending the message "sub WRITERS-CLUB your name" to listserv@listserv.aol.com

WRITING—Writing Workshop Discussion List

Pennsylvania State University

You can join this group by sending the message "sub WRITING your name" to listserv@psuvm.psu.edu

BUSINESS

Banking

The Credit Union Home Page

http://www.cu.org/

Serves as a gathering place for credit unions on the Internet, featuring information on credit unions ranging from joining a credit union to running one. Includes information on the philosophy of credit unions, consumer information, and services available.

Infogroup S.p.A.

http://www.infogroup.it/UK/home_uk.htm

Based in Florence, Italy, Infogroup offers software for the banking industry. Quality information systems are their main focus. Access to descriptions and services is offered.

The World Bank Home Page

http://www.worldbank.org/

Provides information about the World Bank, including current events, press releases, bank news, publications, research studies, and country- and project-related information.

World Currency Converter

http://www.dna.lth.se/cgi-bin/kurt/rates

Lets you choose a currency of the world, and then choose another currency to compare against it, which gives you the exchange rate. Rates are provided by the Federal Reserve Bank of New York and are updated daily.

Business Process Reengineering

The Benchmarking Exchange

http://www.benchnet.com

Information and communication system dedicated to benchmarking, reengineering, process improvement, and quality improvement.

Leverage Technologists Home Page

http://stout.levtech.com/home.html

Specializes in software reverse engineering and reengineering tools, training, and consulting services. Offers off-the-shelf tools and in-house training and products in various computer languages.

Navatar—Organizational Renewal and Business Reengineering

http://www.navatar.ca/

Offers up-to-date information on BPR and change management. Offers links to other sites covering business process reengineering, business process redesign, IT, public service reengineering projects, treasury board IQE, and related subjects. Also lists upcoming BPR seminars and courses.

The Phoenix Business Renewal Site

http://www.phoenix.ca:80/bpr/

Provides information related to business process reengineering, total quality management, and process modeling. Offers enterprise modeling software.

Business-Related Careers

The Business Job Finder

http://www.cob.ohio-state.edu/dept/fin/osujobs.htm

Designed to help recent college graduates get started on careers in the business world. Focuses on job searches in areas of accounting, finance, and management. Contains information about job descriptions, salaries, future outlook, and leading employers. Offers many links to organizations.

Chancellor and Chancellor, Inc.

http://www.chancellor.com

A brokerage firm offering comprehensive placement services for computer technology professionals. Specializes in services for contractors, contract employees, and full-time software professionals. Contains resources for contractors and links to related sites.

Dick Williams and Associates

http://www.netrep.com/home/dwa

Specializes in high technology recruiting. Looks for company clients and individual candidates for executive/manager positions in the following fields:

sales and marketing, key account, product, design engineers, field and customer service, technical, and process and application engineers.

DXI Corporation

`http://isotropic.com/dxicorp/dxihome.html`

Provides contract services to the information processing industry. Lists positions available for contractors. Also includes a newsletter and a list of reasons for hiring contractors.

IOMA Information Services for Professionals

`http://starbase.ingress.com/ioma/`

Institute of Management and Administration. Offers trial subscriptions to business newsletters that include career-enhancing information for professionals. Provides a directory of business-related resources by topic, including finance and investment, human resources, information systems, sales and marketing, and small businesses.

Consumer Issues

ClearStar Security Network

`http://www.clearstar.com/`

Serves as a listing service of locksmiths, alarm installers, safe technicians, and other security professionals who belong to security associations.

Consumer Fraud Alert Network

`http://www.world-wide.com/homebiz/fraud.htm`

Provides information about the latest scams that professional con men and scam artists are using to rob you of your money. Offers advice about how you can protect yourself from being ripped off and who you can contact for help.

The Consumer Law Page

`http://seamless.com/alexanderlaw/txt/intro.html`

Provides information related to consumer law. Offers articles on topics such as insurance fraud and product liability, brochures on topics such as automobiles, funerals, and banking, and useful links to other resources related to consumer law.

Criminal Enforcement Bulletin

`http://www.haledorr.com/criminal_news.html`

Provides information for owners and managers considering internal investigation into possible criminal activities by employees.

Diamond Resources

`http://www.teleport.com/~raylc/master/diamonds.html`

Offers resources that include a guide for understanding more about diamonds, gemological information with images, appraisal information, and a diamond price guide. Also offers an Ask the Gemologist section in which you can e-mail questions to a certified gemologist.

Get Organized

`http://www.get-organized.com`

A personal organizational consultant provides tips for small and large businesses and individuals regarding managing time, resources, and paper. The goals are to reduce stress, eliminate chaos, and simplify your life. Tips are updated monthly.

Corporate Home Pages

3M Innovation Network

`http://www.mmm.com`

Provides information about 60,000 innovative 3M products for the home, business, and industry. Also offers information on market centers, worldwide operations, and company news.

AT&T Home Page

`http://www.att.com/`

Includes information about AT&T products and services, activities, news, employment opportunities, and investment information.

FedEx Home Page

`http://www.fedex.com/`

Features free package tracking with the identification number. Also contains information related to available services, free downloadable software, and delivery options.

GE Home Page

`http://www.ge.com/index.htm`

Includes information about GE products and services, company news and events, current stock quotes, and research, development, investment, and employment opportunities.

Goodyear Tire and Rubber Company

`http://www.goodyear.com/`

Provides information about specifications and preferences regarding tires. Gives advice on the purchase and care of tires. Includes a catalog of Goodyear tires. Also gives contact information to the nearest Goodyear store, including hours and services offered.

JCPenney Home Page

`http://www.jcpenney.com/`

Provides information on investor relations, gift registry, and online shopping. Includes a store locator and a customer survey.

McDonnell Douglas Aerospace

`http://pat.mdc.com/MDA_Houston.html`

Includes some corporate information, as well as information on robotics and 3D animated human mannequins. Uses the 3D human modeling system to analyze human body fit and function within a geometric structure.

MCI Home Page

`http://www.mci.com`

Takes you on a virtual tour of MCI. Offers links to Internet MCI, Gramercy Press, MCI Developers Lab, and the Small Business Center. Describes available products and services, and offers online customer service.

Shell Oil Company

`http://www.shellus.com`

Provides information about Shell's activities, products, and research.

SONY Online

`http://www.music.sony.com/`

Contains information about Sony products and services. Includes categories of music, movies, games, electronics, television, theaters, radio, and merchandise.

Tandy Corporation

`http://www.tandy.com/`

Encompasses Radio Shack, Computer City, and Incredible Universe. Provides history of Tandy and information on future activities, press releases, and investments.

UPS Home Page

`http://www.ups.com/`

Contains service information, software, UPS news, and contact information. Also contains a section on package tracking.

Walgreen Co.

`http://www.walgreens.com`

Includes Walgreen's corporate information, career opportunities, company history, store locations, and links to other pharmacy-related sites.

International Business

Adnet

`http://www.adnet.ie/Adnet/`

Provides an interactive resources directory of Ireland. Site has links to various Irish businesses and chambers of commerce. A good place to start when inquiring about business in Ireland.

African Sky Video

`http://www.active.co.za/~askvideo/`

Pictoral travel directory of tourism facilities in Botswana, Namibia, Zimbabwe, and South Africa.

Agora Language Marketplace

http://www.agoralang.com:2410

Provides a place for vendors and consumers of language-related publications, materials, and services to congregate. Offers an online newsletter also available by subscription. Permits people to post their queries directly to the pages that relate to their request, including publications, study abroad, language services, and workshops. Also contains extensive resources for foreign language professionals.

Asian Business Daily

http://infomanage.com/~icr/abd/

Contains real-time information on financial, political, and economic matters in Pacific Rim countries. Useful for trade, stocks, industry trends, and company decisions, or simply as an educational site. Contains daily sections, with stories sorted by country.

Ask Us For

http://www.webcom.com/~wrsl/askusfor.html

Offers monthly newsletters by e-mail about the international business sector in Bermuda. Also contains reports on other related issues.

Australasian World Publishing Systems

http://www.wps.com.au/

Provides and publishes World Wide Web services for Australia and the Asian Basin. Features an Australian travel page, business page, and real estate page. These pages cover many subsections and have links to many businesses and services throughout Australia. Also features listings of Australasian World Publishing Systems mulitmedia services and prices. For the travel and business pages alone, this is a valuable resource to utilize.

Australian Pacific Advertising

http://www.nt.com.au/apa/

Provides Internet advertising and marketing for Australia and the Pacific rim. Site is still under construction, so many of the links are not yet established. Features information and links on real estate, services, and general features in Australia.

Australian Stock Market Web Page

http://www.wp.com/paritech

Includes information on Australian stock exchange data vendors, Australian companies and brokers on the Net, and Australian and overseas data for purchase.

Austrian Worldport Austrian Business Connection

http://www.worldport.co.at/worldport/

Serves as database of commerce. Contains about 3,000 business home pages from all over the world, including major business sites in Austria, international trade, technology, industry, manufacturing services, tourism, culture, and entertainment. (In English and German.)

Batey Ads Singapore

http://bateyads.com.sg/

Provides advertising services throughout Asia and Australia. Includes extensive company history and policies along with listings of resources and clients. Also provides creative showcase of work done.

Canada Net Pages

http://www.visions.com

Comprehensive resource of Canadian business and finance data, including a white pages, a business directory, and information on Canadian products and services, stocks and bonds, tourism, and real estate.

Canadian Business InfoWorld

http://csclub.uwaterloo.ca/u/nckwan/index.html

Provides Canadian business-related information. Includes Canadian business directory, business resource database, stock market links, business school links, and job-related information.

Catalogue Production Management Services

http://www.webcom.com/~thames/cpms/welcome.html

Helps United States direct mail companies into Europe. Provides information about direct marketing in Europe, including sources for the most competitive print and paper prices.

Cyber Planet Korea

`http://www.cpk.co.kr/`

Contains information on Korean culture, travel, entertainment, a virtual jazz conference, and Netscafe. Information on kids, religion, education, health, news, and TV and radio. (In English and Korean.)

The Econsult Group WWW Page

`http://www.egroup.com/home.html`

International management and business consultants that specialize in information technology, economic consulting, business and market research, executive mentoring, and property development management. Provides offices in Australia, Malaysia, Papua New Guinea, Singapore, and Thailand.

Extra Trade, Inc.

`http://www.interport.net/~extra`

Supplier of U.S.-made beer and canned fruits and vegetables from Greece and Bulgaria to Europe, Asia, and South America. Lists details about inventory available for sale.

How to Do Business in Mexico

`http://daisy.uwaterloo.ca/~alopez-o/busfaq.html`

Provides general information about Mexican business practices, including business hours, dress codes, negotiations, the wage structure, social practices, and sources of help and information.

ICC Communications Centre

`http://www1.usa1.com/~ibnet/iccomhp.html`

Paris-based company linking the international community with the World Business Organization, its commissions, committees, and events. Provides links to publications, press releases, speeches and articles, chambers of commerce, and more.

INFOCENTRO

`http://www.infotec.conacyt.mx/info_i.shtml`

Provides information about Mexico, including commercial, culture, travel, education, science and technology, and state governments. Includes a search engine that lets you search Hispanic written documents on the Internet, as well as specialized directories. (Also in Spanish.)

Ingvar's Home Page

`http://www.ingvar.is`

Icelandic firm that provides information on engineering and consulting, import and export, and aqua- and mariculture. (Also in German and Icelandic.)

The London Mall Magazine and HQ

`http://www.londonmall.co.uk/_edit.htm`

A combination magazine, shopping center, showcase, and information source. Offers articles and information on topics ranging from politics to weather to beer.

Mega-Directory of US/Canada International Exports—U.S. Trade Center Directory

`http://www.grasmick.com/ustrade.htm`

Contains directory of professionals who can assist Canadians exporting to and doing business with the United States. Offers categorized listing. Also includes information on Canadian companies sending employees to the U.S. and U.S. companies hiring Canadians.

Microswiss-Centre North-South

`http://www.htl-bw.ch/~mswiss/welcome2.html`

Swiss government program that promotes microelectronics applications for small and medium enterprises. Offers courses, trainings, and workshops. (Also in German.)

Mobile Phones for UK Users

`http://www.demon.co.uk/mobiles`

Provides information on mobile phones, including specifications, special features, prices, and networks available in the United Kingdom.

Moscow Libertarium

`http://feast.fe.msk.ru/libertarium/`

Features information and articles on liberal movement, thinking, and studies. (In Russian and English.)

The NAFTA Watch

`http://www.aescon.com/naftam/index.htm`

Contains a weekly newsletter focusing on business opportunities in Mexico and other related topics.

OCEANOR—Oceanographic Company of Norway

http://www.oceanor.no

Specializes in the marine environment. The company has developed marine environmental and performance monitoring and forecasting systems through a combination of expertise in meteorology, oceanography, biology, ocean engineering, and instrumentation. Markets these systems worldwide.

Octagon Technology Group, Inc.

http://www.otginc.com

Provides worldwide business and financial services that allow companies to compete in the international marketplace. Provides multilingual and multi-jurisdictional sales, marketing, and distribution services.

Pristine Communications

http://www.pristine.com.tw/

Provides a wide range of communications services for companies looking to business in Asia. Offers translation, interpretation, media, and WWW services for Asia. Concentrates focus on South Korea, China, and Japan. Includes services offered and contact information.

Rainforest Health Project

http://www.mps.org/rhp

Nonprofit international relief organization recognized in the United States and Peru. Sells art and artifacts created by the indigenous peoples of the Peruvian rain forests and reinvests the proceeds into RHP to help fund the organization, which sends teams of volunteers to the Peruvian jungle to help local villagers with sanitation and nutrition and to provide medical and dental care.

Selling Your Products Abroad

http://www.kcilink.com:80/brc/marketing/v2n10.html

Contains general information for product export, market opportunities, and market research. Also provides information on locating foreign markets and financing.

The South African Futures Exchange

http://www.safex.co.za/

Offers information about the financial and agricultural derivatives market in South Africa, as well as downloadable statistics and prices.

TN-1 NAFTA Home Page

http://www.grasmick.com/nafta.htm

The TN-1 permit is a U.S. immigration permit only for Canadians. The law office of Joseph C. Grasmick provides information relating to applying for immigration and work permits.

U.S. Council for International Business

http://www.uscib.org/

Describes the functions and purpose of the U.S. Council for International Business. Provides a section on ATA Carnet, the merchandising passport for doing business in foreign countries. Provides links to information concerning exporting.

Valore International

http://www.florin.com/valore/

An electronic journal covering issues in international trade and development. Provides articles and related links.

Virtual Business Plaza

http://zocalo.net/cz/

Presents the Czech and Slovak market, companies, classified ads, and other information. (In English and Czech.)

VR Cargo International Home Page

http://www.kolumbus.fi/cargo/

Provides information about Finnish railways as a transportation link between the West and East. Includes links to Russian and railroad Web sites, statistics about Finland, maps, and a traffic survey.

Welcome to the European Market

http://www.sme.com/lukas.consulting

Specializes in European strategy, marketing, and sales, to help non-Europeans enter the European market successfully. Provides expertise in computer and communications systems, products, services, and contents. Emphasizes multimedia. Reaches from

Scandinavia to Sicily, from Portugal to the Urals, but focuses on Paris, France and Munich, Germany.

Welcome to Molson Canadian

http://www.molson.com/canadian/

Focuses on Canada: culture, events, travel in Canada, and hockey. Also offers e-mail, bulletin boards, and a well-developed chat facility.

Investments & Financial Planning

Accel Partners

http://www.accel.com

Invests in entrepreneurial companies of selected technology-driven markets. Provides links for company background, investment strategy, and resources for entrepreneurs.

Allegiance Financial Advisors

http://www.ibp.com/pit/allegiance/

Specializes in individualized asset management for individuals, businesses, retirement plans, and trusts.

American Stock Exchange—The Smarter Place to Be

http://www.amex.com/

Provides all kinds of financially related information, including market information, market news, listed companies, options and derivatives, and an information exchange section. Claims to be the first U.S. stock market on the Web.

The American Stock Report, Inc.

http://www.awod.com/gallery/business/asr/

Newsletter targeted at the busy individual who wants to build equity by purchasing stock in American companies. Provides a review of selected growth stocks rated favorably by established and widely read American financial publications.

A.S.K. Financial Digest

http://www.cloud9.net/~dkirchen/ask

Monthly newsletter that helps investors trade stocks, bonds, and mutual funds for intermediate financial cycles.

Chicago Mercantile Exchange

http://www.cme.com/

Contains financial-related information. Provides information related to products and prices, educational resources, and CME member firms. Includes a CME news center, general information about CME, and links to other financial resources.

CyberFund

http://www.cyberfund.com

The CyberFund Investment Account program is a managed investment advisory service of Hammer Capital Management, Inc. It is designed to participate in the growth of the computer, telecommunications, and advancing technology industries. It invests only in publicly traded companies listed on the major U.S. and foreign stock exchanges.

FFP Securities

http://awebs.com/33487/ThomasEMurray

Provides services in the following areas: estate planning, trust planning and preparation, pensions, mutual funds, annuity products, and fixed income products.

Fin-Atlantic Securities, Inc.

http://www.gate.net/~stocks

Investment banking and securities brokerage firm. Offers stocks, bonds, options, mutual funds, new issues, and other securities. Offers Internet users one free no-commission trade.

How to Become a Real-Time Commodity Futures Trader—From Home

http://www.crocker.com/~futures

Presents a trading guide recommended by *Futures Magazine*. Covers details from initial home setup to advanced strategies.

InterQuote

http://www.interquote.com

Provides a collection of affordable Internet-based financial information services, including real-time, delayed, and end-of-day information on stocks, options, indices, mutual funds, and futures from most United States and Canadian exchanges.

The Mutual Fund Home Page

http://www.brill.com/features.html

Features articles on what's happening in the mutual fund industry, including topics such as "Investing for Retirement" and "The Best Choices in Variable Annuities."

Nesbitt Burns, Inc.

http://204.138.60.75/nesbitt.html

Serves the needs of individuals, corporations, and institutions from a network of Canadian and international offices. Provides investment and related information. If the information you need is not available, you can leave a message, and they will send it to you.

Olsen & Associates

http://www.olsen.ch/

Provides economic research in the field of financial markets. Specializes in the forecasting and historical analysis of foreign exchange rates. Also provides trading models and a currency ranking analysis.

Pawws Financial Network

http://pawws.com

Provides information for investors. Allows quick access to the vast amounts of information necessary for successfully managing a securities portfolio. Seamlessly integrates services for portfolio accounting, securities and market research, and online trading.

Perception Global Market Predictions

http://www.manawatu.gen.nz/pages/business/perception

A Neural Network technically oriented financial market prediction service for global markets. Includes futures, options, and indices.

The Philadelphia Stock Exchange

http://www.libertynet.org/~phlx/

The oldest stock exchange in the nation and the first on the Net (although they are not the only ones to claim this honor). Includes a history of the exchange, information on sectors index options, currency

options, equity options, and links to other financial sites. Also includes a QuickTime VR scene of the Philadelphia Stock Exchange options floor.

Precision Investment Services, Inc.

http://powertrader.com

Presents PowerTrader, a fully integrated, real-time stock quotation, technical analysis and portfolio management suite of software products. PowerTrader software reads the data you receive from your data service and displays the delayed or real-time quote information on your monitor. Enables you to collect data and analyze up to 32,000 instruments in any market: equities, options, futures, indices, bonds, money markets, and mutual funds.

Quote.Com

http://www.quote.com

Provides financial market data to the Internet community, including current quotes on stocks, options, commodity futures, mutual funds, and bonds. Also provides business news, market analysis and commentary, fundamental data, and company profiles.

Security APL Quote Server

http://www.secapl.com/cgi-bin/qs

Provides online trading, real-time quotes, information on portfolio accounting, financial calculators, news, and research.

SGA Goldstar Research

http://www.sgagoldstar.com/sga/

Presents a daily financial newsletter that offers the opinions and recommendations of successful stock market experts. Contains information on stocks, bonds, options, futures, securities, gold, the NYSE, and American and NASDAQ stock exchanges, as well as Dow Jones, over the counter, and Canadian stocks.

The Siegel Group, Inc.

http://www.fredsiegel.com

Specializes in providing financial news analysis and consulting to the broadcast media, primarily to local radio and television affiliates of the national networks. Includes links to several sites that provide commentary about activity in the financial markets.

Silicon Investor

`http://www.techstocks.com/`

Consists of five innovative areas for technology investors: Company Profiles, Groups, Chart Generator, StockTalk, and Spotlight. These areas let you participate in discussion forums, create individual charts and comparison charts, view company profiles, and get quotes and other financial information.

Stockdeck Online

`http://www.stockdeck.com/`

Features corporate profiles on more than 600 publicly traded companies. Lets you request additional information such as financial reports or news releases online, as well as 15-minute delayed stock quotes.

StockMaster at MIT

`http://www.ai.mit.edu/stocks.html`

Provides recent stock market information, including current prices and the previous day's closing prices, one-year graphics of stock movements, and ticker symbols. Also contains links related to finance. Categories include daily stock charts, bimonthly mutual fund charts, and top stocks.

A Trader's Financial Resource Guide

`http://www.libertynet.org/~beausang/`

Serves as a financial resource guide to sites dealing with stocks, currencies, exchanges, banks, brokers, mortgages, futures, newspapers, sports pages, research, and search utilities.

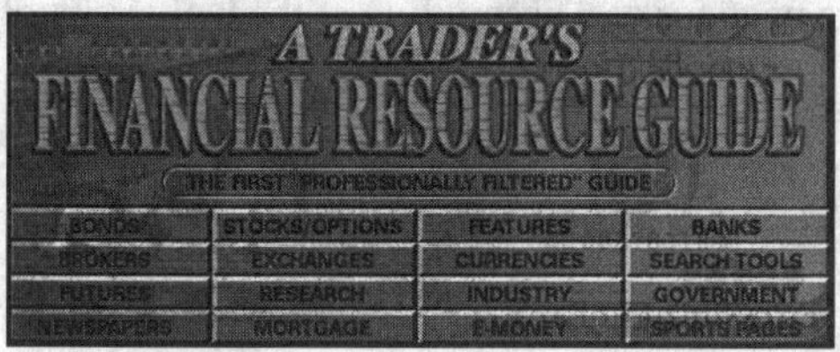

Wall Street Net

`http://www.netresource.com/wsn/home.html`

Provides the latest news in the world of corporate debt and equity financing for issuers and investment bankers. Also contains archival data on transactions over the past 12 months.

Wall Street Online

`http://www.wso.com/wso/`

Presents a collection of daily investment advisory services, including Prostock, Instant Advisor, IPO Outlook, and The Pristine Day Trader.

Woodbridge and Associates

`http://www.calypso.com/woodbridge/`

Offers information on increasing the profitability of your investments through investing in emerging growth companies.

Miscellaneous Business Sites

Acer America Career Opportunities

`http://www.acer.com/aac/about/jobs.htm`

Provides online career oportunities in numerous fields within the corporation, including customer service, engineering, manufacturing, marketing, sales, and Web teams. Also includes capability to apply over the Web for all fields.

AdMorInk

`http://www.focusoc.com/admorink/`

AdMorInk is a small publisher of booklets on various subjects. Site provides information, catalogs, and samples of many of their assorted titles. Subject matter varies from do-it-yourself booklets to travel and art titles.

American Computer Resources, Inc.

`http://www.the-acr.com/`

Provides wholesale sale of IBM, Compaq, Packard Bell, and other computer companies' products. Includes product listings, technical support, company history, and import/export library. Also provides services such as study Web and an international calling code directory.

Aquatic Network

`http://www.brainiac.com/aquanet`

Serves as an information server for the aquatic world. Includes information on aquaculture, conservation, fisheries, marine science and oceanography, maritime heritage, ocean engineering, and seafood.

Automation Specialists

http://www.cyberport.com/mall/autospec/

Provides sales of application design engineering and automation solution products. Also provides sales of transducers, generators, solar panels, and batteries. Includes a description of the technical features of products that are offered.

Broadway Video, Inc.

http://www.broadwayvideo.com/

Provides home site for Broadway Video, Broadway Comics, and the Broadway Interactive Group. Includes BV forum and chat rooms. Also includes previews of upcoming titles and listings of comic retailers nationwide.

Bubble Technology Industries, Inc.

http://intranet.on.ca/~bubble/

Produces radiation protection products and services. Includes company and product profiles with photographs. Text background is currently under construction.

The Business Incorporating, Guide

http://www.corporate.com/

Contains details on how to form your own corporation in any state. Also provides information on the advantages of incorporating, types of corporations, Internet resources, and incorporating software.

Bytewise Consulting, Inc.

http://www.ticllc.net/~ccasey/bytewise/bw_welc.htm

Specializes in assisting legal, medical, accounting, architectural, and other professional firms, as well as small and home-based businesses, in incorporating new technologies into their business operations. Services include identifying technology needs, analyzing hardware and software options, coordinating the introduction of the new technology, and training personnel.

Chastain Research Group, Inc.

http://www.best.com/~chastain

Serves as a consulting firm dedicated to meeting the requirements of biotechnology/pharmaceutical companies and professionals.

Copyright Clearance Center Online

http://www.openmarket.com/copyright/

Nonprofit organization providing copyright licensing, clearance, and usage services. Contains catalogs for searching for material.

Duoforce Enterprises, Inc.

http://www.netwave.net/duoforce/

Provides consulting, skills training, and seminar services on networking, office communications, and public relations. Includes listing of services and products offered. Also includes contact information and a communications skills test.

Evolving Technologies Corporation

http://www.evolvingtech.com/

A value-added reseller, developer, and consulting firm. Creates analytic tools for the financial industry, complex electronic documents for regulatory compliance in the pharmaceutical industry, and departmental and enterprise network design and installation.

EXPOguide Home Page

http://www.expoguide.com/

Offers details about trade shows, conferences, exhibitions, and links to related associations and resources.

Farg's Cost Accounting Home Page

http://darkwing.uoregon.edu:80/~nfargher/

Home page for cost accounting at the University of Oregon. Includes class notes and references to related articles and accounting resources.

FiberNet Communications

http://www.allware.com/fibernet/ldrates.html

Provides long distance carrier services and reselling products. Includes service listings and product catalog, as well as contact information.

Global Business Network

http://www.gbn.org/

A membership organization specializing in scenario thinking and collaborative learning about the future. Brings together members from business, science, the arts, and academia to explore uncertainties and to reframe executives' mental models and increase the organization's perceptive powers.

Global Trade Center

http://www.tradezone.com/tz/

Provides resources and information for people interested in world trade and mail order. Provides links to trade resources and sites around the world, trade news, business opportunities, and much more.

Habia Cable AB

http://www.habia.se/

A German company with offices in Europe offering cable to meet any industrial or business requirement. Provides links and descriptions of products and ordering information.

HADCO Corporation

http://www.hadco.com:8080/

For those in the electronics industry, offers printed circuit board technological excellence. Links to services, volume manufacturing, and tech centers.

Harris Digital Telephone Systems

http://www.dts.harris.com/

Provides telecommunications platforms and software, switching systems, wireless communications products, etc., for public telephone networks and private switching environments. Provides links to product info, training and employment opportunities, what's new, contact information, etc.

HSiN Semiconductor Pte Ltd.

http://www.singnet.com.sg/~hx1008/

A semiconductor and electronics component distributor stocking mainly SGS Thomson and Philips Components. Links to what's new, their mission, profile, other Web links, and ordering information.

Ideal Point Home Page

http://www.ipoint.com

A research and development company focusing on technologies that enhance interaction, communication, and learning.

Inland Answering Service

http://www.citivu.com/usa/ias/index.html

A personal, professional, nationwide telephone answering service. Will take orders, send messages to your voice mail or pager, schedule appointments, or broadcast faxes. Check out their long list of services for your business.

International Typeface Corporation

http://www.esselte.com/itc/

This corporation has designed and licensed typeface designs for numerous companies. Links to license, sales, and marketing info, press releases, stuff to download, and more.

Internet Bankruptcy Library

http://bankrupt.com

Provides worldwide troubled-company resources for the bankruptcy and insolvency professional, including discussion groups, a worldwide directory of professionals, and notices of conferences.

ISO Easy

http://www.exit109.com/~leebee/

Provides assistance in understanding and implementing the ISO 9000 model for quality assurance. Contains a FAQ list and links to other sites on quality assurance standards and other ISO 9000 resources.

Jones, Hall, Hill, and White

http://www.jhhw.com

A professional law corporation practicing exclusively in the area of municipal finance as bond counsel, underwriter's counsel, special tax counsel, and rebate compliance counsel. Includes links to other public finance resources as well.

St. Ives Rebate and Beauty Tips

http://www.StIves.com/contents.html

If you're not sure what hairstyle is right for you or what skin care products you should try, visit the St. Ives site. Find tips on how to improve your hair and skin health. Also get a rebate on a St. Ives product.

KAB Konsult AB

http://www.dataphone.se/~kab/indexe.html

A publishing, consulting, and reselling IT-company located in Europe. Several company links available.

Khem Products, Inc.

http://www.khem.com/khem/home.html

A chemical inventory, waste, and MSDS database. Releases Khem modules, which track and report hazardous and nonhazardous chemicals, and provide an affordable building block approach to chemical inventory management and EPA regulatory compliance, as well as addressing the community right to know laws in the areas of EPCRA, RCRA, SARA, and CERCLA.

Kingston Telecommunication Laboratories

http://www.ktl.co.uk/ktl/

European company specializing in testing and consulting services related to telecommunications equipment. Testing services include analog, CRA, safety, digital, and EMC.

LEXIS-NEXIS Communication Center

http://www.lexis-nexis.com/

An online legal, news, and business information retrieval, storage, and management service. Describes the services and products available worldwide.

Manufacturing Resources

http://www.warwick.ac.uk/~esrjf/manufact.html

Subject guide and directory containing links to resources relevant to the manufacturing community. Topics include manufacturing strategy and management, manufacturing engineering and technology, product introduction and disposal, funding and grants, and educational and professional organizations.

McDonnell Information Systems

http://www.mdis.com/

Provides software, hardware, management, training, consulting, maintenance services, computer solutions, and development tools for your company. Links to a variety of sales groups.

MicroBiz

http://www.carroll.com/microbiz/

MicroBiz offers their computerized business control system for a variety of businesses. Check out their Auto Repair Shop Controller, Video Store Controller, Dry Cleaner Controller, their remote computing and accounting software, hardware, and other varieties of services and product support.

MTAC Home Page

http://oracle.mtac.pitt.edu/WWW/MTAC.html

Mid-Atlantic Technology Applications Center. One of six regional technology transfer centers funded by NASA. Promotes use of NASA technologies in the private sector to help U.S. firms improve their competitiveness.

N-Vision Systems

http://www.iquest.net/kiosk/index.html

Specializes in kiosk manufacturing and implementation. Also acts as a full-service multimedia consulting company serving government, industry, and institutions.

Nijenrode Business Webserver

http://www.nijenrode.nl/resources/bus/

Webserver at the Netherlands Business School. Provides resources relevant to students, faculty, and researchers at business schools. Offers links to information about careers, business news, other business schools, and other business-related directories.

North American Power Brokers

http://nyx10.cs.du.edu:8001/~jrozyck

An energy purchasing consultant that promises to lower energy rates for consumers. Provides information about the U.S. utility industry and the benefits that NAPB can provide for consumers.

ODIN Oil Network

http://www.oil.net

Presents an Internet network designed for companies and individuals involved in the international oil industry. Enables people involved with exploration and drilling, production, seismic, and personnel to get in touch with each other and with the service and supply companies they need to access.

Opportunity Network

http://www.oppnet.com/ern

Promotes opportunities in all communications media: by mail, through a highly targeted database, through the Internet on the Web, by telephone networking, and by attending major regional trade and consumer expositions.

Paracel, Inc.

http://www.paracel.com

Develops leading-edge information filtering and categorizing technologies for the Internet, enterprise, bioinformatic, and government industries.

Perceptics Corporation

http://www.usit.net/info

Develops, designs, manufactures, integrates, and supports specialized information systems for applications in document management and imaging systems.

Peters-de Laet, Inc.

http://www.pdel.com/

Distibutes electronic, electrical, and fastener products including connectors, sockets, fasteners, and much more. Includes catalog, new product, and company information.

Porter Novelli

http://www.porternovelli.com/

Provides public relations services specializing in new media applications. Includes client listings, services offered, and the CyberLifestyle online services demographic information. Includes links to many related sites and contact information.

Process Technologies Incorporated

http://www.execpc.com/~pti

Manufactures glass phototooling on a small scale. Produces chromium and iron-oxide photo tools for the microelectronics industries.

Regional Economic Models, Inc.

http://www.crocker.com/~remi/

Constructs models that forecast the economic and demographic effects that policy initiatives or external events might cause in a local economy. Provides information about the company and lists upcoming seminars.

Research Dynamics

http://www.txdirect.net/resdyn/

Provides home site for Research Dynamics. Includes corporate structure, job listings, and contact information.

The Resource Group

http://www.in.net/resource/index.html

Assists organizations and individuals in working toward personal and professional growth and development through using the tools of the information age. The group has three divisions: Technical Resources, The Resource Group Bookstore, and The Resource Group Consulting.

Rodex Technologies for the Manufacturing Industry

http://www.magi.com/~rodex/

Supplies manufacturing technologies such as equipment, software systems, and engineering expertise from Canada to manufacturers worldwide.

Rogers Communications, Inc.

http://www.rogers.com/

Provides home site for Rogers Communications, Inc., a large Canadian telecommunications, media, and cable television corporation. Includes corporate profile and detailed information about Rogers' services and products. Also includes facilities tour, job openings, cable channel lineups, and contact information for all divisions.

SABRE Decision Technologies

http://www.sdt.com/SDT

Provides business solutions and consulting services to the travel and transportation industry and related fields. Has recently expanded to include clients in other fields, including food services, insurance, retailers, and manufacturers.

Scope Systems—Worldwide Industrial Electronics Repair and Services

http://www.charm.net/~scope

Specializes in the repair and remanufacture of industrial electronic circuit boards and assemblies. Includes analog, digital, power supplies, A/C and D/C drives, video monitors, and process control systems.

Screenwriters Online

http://screenwriter.com/insider/news.html

Offers trade secrets, advice, and insider information from professional screenwriters. Publishes "The Screenwriter's Insider Report," a subscription-based industry newsletter that features insider interviews with screenwriters, studio heads, and agents.

Seals on Wheels

http://www.acoates.com/seals

Provides mobile notary, small claims, and finger-printing services in the San Francisco Bay area. Office visits available.

The Service Bureau, LLC

http://www.xmission.com/~rexm/tsb.html

Provides credit reporting services and Credit Manager software for businesses. Includes company profile and services and products offered. Also includes contact and pricing information.

Seven Technologies

http://www.sevent.dk

A Danish software company working toward professional solutions for professional computer users. Provides process visualization, automation tools, graphical user interfaces, supervision systems, transaction systems, security management systems, and information about how to get in touch with the company.

Shape Memory Applications, Inc.

http://www.sma-inc.com/

Supplies and uses NiTi shape memory and superelastic alloys. Provides information on products and services offered, as well as technical and industry news.

STAT-USA

http://www.stat-usa.gov/

Provides daily economic news, statistical releases, export and trade databases and information, and domestic economic databases and information.

Submarine Cables of the World

http://www.teleport.com/~simoriah/scow/sub.htm

Provides information about underwater cable protection. Includes committee background, resources guide, and very detailed information about underwater cables.

The TechExpo on WWW

http://www.techexpo.com/

Provides information about high technology companies in the areas of engineering and life sciences. Includes information on their products and services, societies, universities, magazines, and newsletters.

Tele-Communications, Inc. (TCI)

http://www.tcinc.com/

Provides home site for TCI telecommunications. Includes links to many sites and contact information.

TeleService Resources, Inc.

http://www.amrcorp.com:80/amr_mgmt/teleserv/teleserv.htm

Provides online reservation services for the travel and hotel industry. Includes listing of services offered, company partners, company profile, and contact information.

Time Machine

http://webmart.org/timelaps/

Produces special effects for the motion picture, television, and advertising industries. Includes many different examples of effects created for many famous companies. Provides background information on how effects are created.

Vaughn Communications, Inc.

http://www.primenet.com/~vaughn/

Provides video tape duplication services, digital production training, along with film and video production. Includes links to Vaughn's different divisions, a company profile, and a services-offered listing. Provides contact information for each company area.

Video Publishing House

http://www.vphi.com/cgi-bin/choose.pl

Produces and provides sales of The Signature Line of training videos. Includes lengthy company catalog, program information, company profile, philosophy, and ordering information.

Virtual Design Center

http://www.vdc.com/

Presents a corporate communication and marketing system for furniture design and marketing. Contains information about the office furniture industry and about buying and selling used office furniture.

Waters Corporation

http://www.waters.com/

Analytic instrument and chromatography chemistries manufacturer, specializing in High Performance Liquid Chromatography (HPLC) technology. Provides information about the company, its products, and related technologies.

Welcome to MLMBBS

http://www.mlmbbs.com

Serves as a common meeting ground for MLMers/ entrepreneurs around the world. Includes training articles, special reports, mailing lists, newsletters, online classifieds, and recommendations.

Windy Hills Professional Laboratories

http://perry.gulfnet.com/advertisers/drug_testing/ drug1.htm

Provides drug-testing services. Includes company background and ordering information. Results can be received through e-mail as well as traditional means.

World of Commercial Ballooning

http://www.aero.com/ballooning/commercial/main.htm

Provides information and details about commerical ballooning and its advertising uses. Provides ample information about the technical, media, and marketing angles for using a hot air balloon.

Patent Information

Patent Portal Internet Patent Resources

http://www.law.vill.edu/~rgruner/patport.htm

Serves as an entry point for patent-related information. Identifies resources, organizes and indexes links to resources, and presents new material on patent issues that are currently shaping patent law. Also allows patent searches and searches of patent attorneys and agents.

SBH Patent Marketing Group

http://www.inlink.com/~sbh/index.html

Specializes in licensing and selling existing U.S. patents. Recognizes that many inventors have achieved greater success in creating patents than in selling or licensing them. Acts as an agent for individual inventors, corporations, and institutions in marketing United States patents.

Shadow Patent Office

http://www.spo.eds.com/patent.html

Provides information about United States patents, including a searchable database of the full text of the U.S. Patent and Trademark Office patents issued from January 1, 1972 to the present. Updated weekly.

U.S. Patent and Trademark Office General Information Concerning Patents

http://www.uspto.gov/web/patinfo/toc.html

Provides general information about application for and granting of patents in nontechnical language. Intended for inventors, students, and prospective applicants for patents.

Real Estate

The ADLIST Real Estate Database

http://www.adlist.com/re/

Offers opportunities to add your real estate link to the database, search for real estate. Advertise your real estate.

The Advant Home

http://www.sccsi.com/Advant/homes.html

Designs custom homes. Presents sample designs and information.

ALWAYS OPEN!—HouseLink US Real Estate Guide

http://www.wirelink.com/houselink/index.html

HouseLink lets you view and list real estate nation-wide. Realtors and brokers can submit their existing sites for a free listing. Can also provide all your Web advertising needs.

bestagents.com

http://www.bestagents.com/

Provides information for home buyers and sellers. Serves as a network of exclusive real estate agents who become your personal advisors, consultants, and negotiators.

Eastern Mortgage Services, Inc.

http://www.eastmortg.com/

First mortgage and home equity lender specializing in poor credit loan programs, low-rate mortgages, refinance, debt consolidation and home improve-ment loans. 24-hour pre-approval.

Electronic Resource Services Property Finder

http://www.erspros.com/propfind.html

Provides listings of real estate professionals, land or housing for sale, and commercial properties for sale or lease across the U.S.

Exquisite Homes and Properties

http://www.exquisite.com/index.html

Provides a real estate listing service for homes and properties in the U.S., Europe, and the Caribbean. Also includes information on mortgages, title services, lending institutions, realtors, remodeling, and landscaping.

Fidelity Union Mortgage

http://www.dirs.com/mortgage/fidelity/

Home loans and mortgages for every purpose: home improvements, purchases, construction, refinancing, equity loans, and more. Strives for fast, professional service.

First Pacific Financial

http://www.firstpacificfinancial.com

First Pacific Financial is a full-service mortgage broker for any residential real estate loan.

FractalNet Real Estate Server

http://www.fractals.com/realestate.html

Offers listings for residential real estate on the Internet and advertising to real estate agents and home owners interested in selling real estate.

Home Builder's Utopia

http://www.dfw.net/~custmbld/utopia.html

Serves as a guide to links to professional homebuilders on the Internet. Also lists building associations and products and services.

Home Improvement Loans

http://realinfo.com/homeimprovement

Funding from Home Improvement Loans can help you add a new room, kitchen, or expand your house.

HomeOwners Finance Center

http://www.homeowners.com/homeowners/index.html

Provides the latest interest rates, rate analysis, market trends, featured loan programs, histories of adjustable rate indices, a mortgage dictionary, a mortgage calculator, and online forms for purchas-ing and refinancing. Lets you join a mailing list for updates on the latest news in mortgage rates.

How I Made 1 Million Dollars In Real Estate With No Money Down

http://www.pwrnet.com/freepage/1million/

Offers strategies for building quick cash and wealth in the '90s. Real estate investor answers questions. Learn how to earn $5,000 to $10,000 in 30–60 days.

Insiders Track Capital Funding Aid

http://www.pennet.net/commercial/itcfa/

Provides an inside view of the capital funding process to start-up or expansion companies. Insiders Track Capital Funding Aid can verify, recommend, or negotiate a capital funding process.

Internet Real Estate Listings

http://www.map.com/irel

An Internet real estate listing service for anyone wishing to buy or sell real estate.

Internet Real Estate Network

http://www.iren.com/

Free Web pages for real estate properties, professionals, and organizations. Fully searchable database. HTML/CGI authoring and other custom services are also available. Provides answers to frequently asked questions and links to other related sites.

J.C. Mortgage

http://www.crossnet.com/jcmortgage

J.C. Mortgage offers home improvement loans and loans designed to consolidate debt. Also converts excess credit card interest into tax deductible mortgage interest.

Levien-Rich Associates, Inc.

http://www.brainlink.com/~levien

Consultants to the real estate and construction industries. Offers objective evaluation and monitoring of real estate construction projects.

The LOAN STORE

http://www.neosoft.com/~infowell/loans/loanfinal.html

Offers Commercial Pro Money Mortgage Loans. No credit check, no application fee, and no employment verification are necessary. All loans are based on the equity in the real estate.

The Mortgage Calculator

http://ibc.wustl.edu/mort.html

Calculates mortgage payments when you input details about the mortgage. Includes a conversion factor for Canadian users. Contains links to other search calculation pages on the Web.

The Mortgage Manager

http://www.fairfield.com/mindtrek/index.html

Provides step-by-step instructions on how to save money on the interest on your mortgage and cut your payment time in half. Provides information about managing your mortgage and principal prepayment.

The Mortgage Manager Version 5.00

http://web.idirect.com/~klg

Offers an advanced mortgage and loan amortization program for professionals, used by banks, lawyers, accountants, insurance companies, real estate agents, and mortgage brokers. Includes an order form.

National Homes Online

http://nationalhomes.com

Site where buyers and sellers can place the real estate they have for sale. Also has a personal classifieds section where you can put items, such as a lamp or a table, up for sale.

National InterAd Real Estate Page

http://www.nia.com/homes

Offers illustrated listings for real estate, including houses, condominiums, and land. Includes information on real estate agents and services, as well as home buyers' tips.

The Real Estate Junction

http://www.valleynet.com/~webcity/

Provides real estate listings by category, including residential, farm and ranch, commercial and investment properties, and recreation/resort/retirement properties.

The Real Estate Pages

http://www.newmarkets.com/real_estate.htm

Real estate listings from all 50 states and around the world.

Real Estate Recruiting/Careers Education

http://www.realestateeducation.com

Web site with information on real estate careers, recruiting real estate agents, and real estate education on the West Coast.

Real Estate Registry

http://www.rereg.com/

A complete online site that assists in listing property, both commercial and residential.

Real Estate Shop

http://www.bsoftware.com/reshop.htm

Contains homes, real estate want ads, realtor advertisements, and a unique real estate catalog. Brings together real estate buyers, sellers, and agents. Find the dream house to buy by using Real Estate ON LINE. Sellers can also put their property listings on the ON LINE section. Also helps you locate excellent real estate agents in an area near you.

Real Estate Web

http://www.infi.net/REWeb/

Lets you browse all listings of property for sale in coastal Virginia, based on price, type of property, and number of bedrooms. Also lets you view agent profiles or add your own property for sale.

Security First Funding

http://www.dirs.com/mortgage/sfft1

They are FHA approved and offer loan programs for home improvement, purchase, or refinancing. FHA Title 1 loans up to $25,000 with no equity or appraisal.

Timbergreen Custom Homes

http://www.dfw.net/~custmbld/timbergreen.html

Provides information about Timbergreen Custom Homes, which has been designing and building high-end custom homes in and around Dallas, Texas since 1983. Contains information about the company and present homes available. Also contains photographs, floor plans, and elevations of various projects built by Timbergreen Custom Homes.

Who's Who in Luxury Real Estate

http://www.luxury-realestate.com/jbl/

An international network of independent real estate brokers. Specializes in the finest properties in the world. Includes more than 350 brokers representing 47 states and 22 foreign countries. Offers properties online and provides listing information.

WRENet—World Real Estate Network

http://www.wren.com

A public real estate search service that includes all types of property (residential, commercial, industrial commercial investment, ranch, and land) all over the world. Also includes a list of FAQs.

Sales, Marketing, & Advertising

Advertising, Boelter & Lincoln

http://www.advbl.com/

Provides Web site advertising and marketing along with traditional advertising. Site provides complete company history, capabilities (technical and otherwise), data of the firm's effectiveness, and a list of Web sites Boelter & Lincoln created. Also provided is a group of affiliations and customers.

AfterHours Communications Corp.

http://www.primenet.com/~ahours/

Provides complete advertising services including online marketing and advertising. Includes Web site design and construction. Also provides a list of customers and their sites, "Top 10 Ways to Tell If You Have a Sucky Home Page," and "Top 10 Tips to Better Web Sites."

Allen & Associates, Ltd.

http://www.radix.net/~eallen/

Provides company background, portfolio, and gallery for marketing communications graphics arts studio. Includes Web site nexus of sites created by Allen & Associates.

American Demographics/Marketing Tools

http://www.marketingtools.com/

Provides *American Demographics*, a Dow Jones publication, online, which covers consumer trends and demographics from a business perspective. Also presents *Marketing Tools* magazine, which covers information-based marketing, including database marketing, research, advertising, and media.

Another Color, Inc.

`http://www.csgi.com/AC/`

Contains information and background of services offered by this graphics designs firm based in Washington, D.C. Provides extensive list of clients with portfolios of work in marketing promotion, package design, corporate identity, Web site creation, and other related work.

Austin Knight's KnightNet

`http://www.ak.com/`

Provides U.S. home site for worldwide advertising agency. Includes company history, profile, listings of service, international location sites, portfolio of work done, and awards received.

B.A.A.S. Boating Advertising, Advice, and Service

`http://www.dataplace.nl/baas`

Specializes in advertising for the marine market, represents yachting magazines, b-to-b and consumer magazines, and Webvertising.

Biggs Gilmore Communications

`http://www.Biggs-Gilmore.com/icecream/`

Provides home site for Michigan-based advertising and communications firm. Includes company background and walks the user through the steps Biggs Gilmore uses with a client. Also includes portfolio of work done and listing of contracts. The artwork at this site is very eye-catching and well done.

BMP DDB Needham

`http://www.bmp.co.uk/bmp/home.htm`

Provides information and background of services offered by this international advertising firm. Includes examples of work in media and interactive marketing, with listings of clients who utilize BMP DDB Needham. Also includes register of effective advertising awards.

Business-to-Business Marketing Exchange

`http://www.btob.wfu.edu/b2b.html`

Contains access information related to the American Marketing Association, international marketing associations, job listings, and marketing bulletin boards and Internet resources.

Carter Waxman

`http://www.carwax.com`

Provides home site for the Carter Waxman advertising agency based in the Silicon Valley. Includes company background and portfolio of work. The most interesting part of the site is a weird, lurid, and yes, fictional soap opera called *The Valley of the Chips*. This self-described "continuing saga of lust and intrigue in an era of technology" is rather funny, if not just strange. You will see nothing comparable in any other business site.

CEO Access Across the Street or Around the World

`http://www.ceo-access.com/index.html`

Organizes resources, information, and relationships needed for businesses to grow. Offers advertising and marketing service for a fee. Includes links to newspaper, journalism, and electronic-related sites.

Chiat/Day, Inc.

`http://www.chiatday.com/factory/`

Provides home site for Chiat/Day, Inc. and TBWA advertising firms that have recently merged. Includes merger reasoning and preview of services to come to this site.

Cohn & Wells

`http://www.cohn-wells.com/`

Provides marketing, advertising, and communications services across many types of media. Provides company profile, philosophy, services, and capibilities. Includes links to clients' Internet pages.

Cortex Marketing Resources

`http://www.netweb.com/cortex/content/mktg/`

Provides high-end consulting and Internet software. Compiles marketing resources. Concentrates on listing agencies, suppliers, publications, and so on that are not presently on the Internet.

curious pictures

`http://found.cs.nyu.edu/curious/`

Provides full-service graphics production for TV commericals, computer graphics, and interactive media. Based in New York City, curious pictures has worked on many recognizable on-air spots and commercials. Site includes company profile along with full services-offered listings. Also includes internship information, career opportunities, and an online guided tour of the offices.

Electronic Product Catalog Systems

`http://www.intbc.com/ibc2/csad.html`

Produces custom business electronic media for sales automation and market expansion, and develops modern marketing tools for businesses. Offers an electronic product demonstrator catalog.

Farago Advertising

`http://www.farago.com`

Provides home site for Farago Advertising, which provides full-service advertising for traditional media and new media alike. Includes services offered, client listings, and an "ask the 8-ball" section to answer questions. Also includes contact information.

Forest Green Media

`http://fgreen.com/fgm/`

Company that provides interactive marketing for the Web and multimedia. Specializes in unique, high-tech graphics. Provides links to current projects, clients, demos, as well as net stocks, what's new, and Internet search engines.

Galaxy Communications, Inc.

`http://www2.portal.ca/~galaxy/`

Galaxy provides audio-visual equipment for businesses, education, and churches. Provides pictures of products, links to descriptions and pricing, and monthly specials.

GBH Handsfree Communication

`http://nia.com/headsets/`

GBH provides hands-free communications equipment such as headsets, teleconferencing, telecommuting, and videoconferencing products for the ergonomically correct office. Links are provided to their products with descriptions and pictures. Links to ordering info also are provided.

Goswick Advertising

`http://www.goswick.com/`

An advertising firm capable of creating broadcast and print advertising, multimedia services on the Internet, and commercial online service marketing. Includes links to past and current projects, the agency, and the advertising team.

HERMES, Consumer and Corporate Surveys

`http://www.umich.edu/~sgupta/hermes/`

Provides free access to results from the project's research on commercial uses of the Web. Currently offers results from four user surveys, based on more than 30,000 responses. Also enables companies who use the Web to communicate with their customers or suppliers to register to become corporate panel members (also free).

Ingalls, Quinn & Johnson

`http://www.iqj.com/`

Advertising, PR, and multimedia solutions for your business, especially clients in TV, radio, and print. Provides links to numerous arms of their agency, as well as employment opportunities.

Institute for the Study of Business Markets

`http://www.smeal.psu.edu/isbm/`

Contains current information related to ISBM activities, including seminars, research projects, publications, and membership in the organization.

Kern Media Associates

`http://www.maine.com/kern/`

Radio, TV, and cable ad agency located in Gloucester, Maine. Links to free newsletters and services, clients, services, and more.

Liggett Stashower

`http://www.liggett.com/`

A marketing communications company based in Cleveland, Ohio. Their clients range from local charities to international organizations. Includes links to services, marketing, consulting, creative services, and more.

Marcus Advertising

`http://www.marcusad.com/marcus/`

A long-time full-service advertising agency specializing in creative services, print and broadcast production, PR, multimedia, Web publishing, and much more. Provides access to their clients and their current projects.

Market Place Media

http://www.marketmedia.com/

A marketing company to help you target your product with the right media to the right audience—students, seniors, military, or minorities. Expert in direct marketing, posters, radio, specialized newspapers and magazines, promotions, and more.

Marketing to Consumers

http://metro.turnpike.net/metro/tuvok/guide.html

Provides an outline of the stages of marketing management concepts, based on notes from class lectures.

McMonigle & Spooner

http://www.primenet.com/~mands/index.html

An advertising, design, and marketing firm specializing in a variety of services, including corporate development, design, media planning, TV and radio production, audio/video, and promotion.

Michael J. Motto Advertising

http://www.gti.net/motto/

If you have advertising or marketing needs on or off the Internet, Michael J. Motto Advertising will handle your questions by phone or stop in for a visit (the first visit's on them). They can help your company maximize your profit potential using the Internet.

Mintz & Hoke Advertising and Public Relations

http://www.mintz-hoke.com/

An advertising agency that will go directly to your target audience to find out how to design your campaign.

Mousetracks—NSNS Marketing Resources

http://nsns.com/MouseTracks/

Offers links to and commentary on marketing activities and resources available on the Net for educational and professional use.

O'KEEFE WORLD

http://www.okeefe.com

The home of O'Keefe Marketing, a full-service ad agency integrating Web site development with traditional marketing.

Reckless Design Limited

http://www.arlington.com/~reckless/reckless.html

Provides print and new media advertising services. Includes sample artwork, client listings, and contact information.

Richards Group

http://www.x-ads.com/

Provides advertising services specializing in Internet, animation, and graphics creation. Includes clients' ads, art portfolio, and company philosophies.

Sales Plus

http://www.salesplus.com/

Contains information related to sales and marketing. Contains prospecting, video and audio tapes, books and software, trade shows, and consulting information related to sales and marketing.

Sharrow Advertising and Marketing Information Resource Center

http://www.dnai.com/~sharrow/register.html

Hosts marketing topics, including a mail-order catalog, advertising opportunities, and lists of advertising and marketing resources on the Web.

Freebies for Kids

http://www.icv.net/cgi-bin/free.cgi?pag

Free stuff isn't just for adults. Kids can write to one of the companies on this page or call an 800 number for newsletters designed for kids, educational videos, and more.

Sidea

`http://www.sidea.com/`

Provides homesite for Sidea (Service, Information, Demonstrations, Evalutations, Assistance), a retail marketing company. Sidea produces demonstration booths and set-ups so customers can experience products in the store. Includes services, products, and contact information.

TAL Marketing Services, Inc.

`http://moose.erie.net/~talerie`

Offers extensive experience in print, media, multi-media, audio/video, interactive, broadcast, direct mail, and outdoor marketing.

TEAMS Marketing and Sales Assessment Software

`http://mtg-teams.com`

Offers TEAMS (Total Evaluation and Analysis of Marketing and Sales), a sales and marketing assessment software program designed to evaluate and improve your company's marketing and sales activities. Includes samples of the TEAMS question-naire and report and an electronic order form.

Tech Image, Ltd.

`http://www.techimage.com/techimage`

Provides public relations and marketing communi-cation support services to high-technology compa-nies. Combines traditional public relations capabilities with emerging online communication tools. Also offers international PR services.

Tom Davis+Company

`http://www.tdavisco.com/home.html`

Provides a wide range of artwork and design work for companies. Includes online portfolio and examples of work done for clients. Also includes company profile, philosophies, and contact informa-tion.

Wahlstrom & Company

`http://www.wahlstrom.com/`

Provides yellow page advertising consulting and services. Publishes the Wahlstrom Reports newsletter about directory advertising and new electronic media. Includes clients' listings and contact information.

Wall Street Journal

`http://www.adnet.wsj.com/`

Online guide for advertising on the Net, Web sites, and general Internet directory. Lets you search the directory by category and alphabetically. Also includes lists of companies advertising in the *Wall Street Journal* related to catalog shopping, travel planning, mutual funds, education, corporate annual reports, and an annual subscription guide.

Web Digest for Marketers

`http://www.advert.com/wdfm/wdfm.html`

Offers links to other marketing-related sites. Also offers advertising- and catalog-related information.

WebReach Internet Advertising & Marketing

`http://www.io.com/~webreach/`

Provides services to build and maintain WWW home pages to advertise your business or organization on the Internet.

Weightman Group

`http://www.weightman.com/`

Provides advertising and public relation services in both old and new media. Includes company profile, resources, philosophy, portfolio, and contact information.

Western Direct's Home Page

`http://www.westerndirect.com`

Provides support for telemarketing, Internet services, and other direct marketing campaigns.

Wimsey Information Services

`http://www.wimsey.com`

Wimsey is home of Canada's largest commercial Web site. Provides links to business pages, services, magazines, help and references, and advertising info.

Winkler McManus

`http://www.winklermcmanus.com/`

Provides home site for Winkler McManus Advertis-ing. Includes portfolio, company philosophy, profile, news, and contact information.

Young & Roehr, Inc.

http://www.teleport.com/~davidwh/

Provides full advertising services from direct mail to new media. Provides handling of Web site creation, public relations, and strategic planning. Includes services offered, client listings, artwork samples, and links to sites created.

Small & Home-Based Businesses

Bucknell University Small Business Development Center

http://www.bucknell.edu/~sbdc

Provides business and engineering assistance for small businesses on a variety of topics, including starting a new business, accounting, personnel, marketing and sales, inventory, and computer systems.

Cobweb

http://www.netresource.com/cobweb/intro.html

Offers a catalog of products offered by small business enterprises. Sells items produced by small companies from around the world at no cost to the company. Encourages such companies to contact them.

Creative Edge

http://www.halcyon.com/midnight/

Serves as a resource center for growing companies. Provides information on advertising, promotions, sponsorships, and funding opportunities.

The Entrepreneur Network

http://bizserve.com/ten/

Nonprofit corporation focused on helping Midwestern inventors and entrepreneurs with information and connections. Provides information on business opportunities, new products wanted, private and public sector resources, and details about membership organizations.

FranNet

http://www.frannet.com

Provides basic information to help you select the right franchise. Also includes a listing by category of a large number of franchise opportunities and franchise home pages that provide more detailed information on franchise opportunities.

Inc. Business Resources Library

http://nmq.com:80/emgbiznc/cntprovs/products/incbiz/

A division of *Inc.* magazine. Provides entrepreneurs with information about starting and managing a growing business. Categories include business startup, planning, time management, managing people, and customer service. Provides resources via books, videotapes, and computer software.

On-Line Marketing

http://www.shore.net/olm/

Provides affordable advertising opportunities for the tourism and hospitality industry, small businesses, and individuals. Six-line ads cost $15 per month. Also contains ads for vacation properties and holiday rentals.

SBA Service Corps of Retired Executives

http://www.sbaonline.sba.gov/business_management/score.html

A volunteer program sponsored by the U.S. Small Business Administration. Matches volunteers with small businesses that need expert management and technical advice.

Simple Solutions

http://fbsolutions.com/prieto/simple1.htm

A home-based consulting business providing advice and services related to upgrading your computer system, desktop publishing, designing a Web page, and choosing an Internet access server.

Small and Home-Based Business Links

http://www.ro.com/small_business/homebased.html

Offers small and home-based business links, including reference, franchises, marketing, newsgroups, services, and opportunities for home-based businesses.

Xerox Small Office

http://www.xerox.com/soho.html

Provides information for small offices, including small business resources, customer support, software, recycling programs, descriptions of Xerox products and services for the small office, and lists of retailers where Xerox products are sold.

Taxes

Citizens for an Alternative Tax System

http://www.intac.com/~gbaren/cats.html

Houses the national public interest group for an alternative tax system and tax reform. Talks mainly about the group's manifesto and related information.

L.A. Professionals Online

http://www.primenet.com/~laig/proserve

Provides generic information from attorneys, certified public accountants, and medical professionals. Offers a bulletin section that contains information about tax issues, including an analysis of IRS guidelines for independent contractors and employee status.

TaxSites—Income Tax Information in Internet

http://www.best.com/~ftmexpat/html/taxsites.html

Provides income tax-related information. Also contains links to several related sites, including tax forms, FAQs, U.S. and state tax laws, and tax software.

United States Tax Code Online

http://www.fourmilab.ch/ustax/ustax.html

Provides interactive access to the complete text of United States Internal Revenue Code.

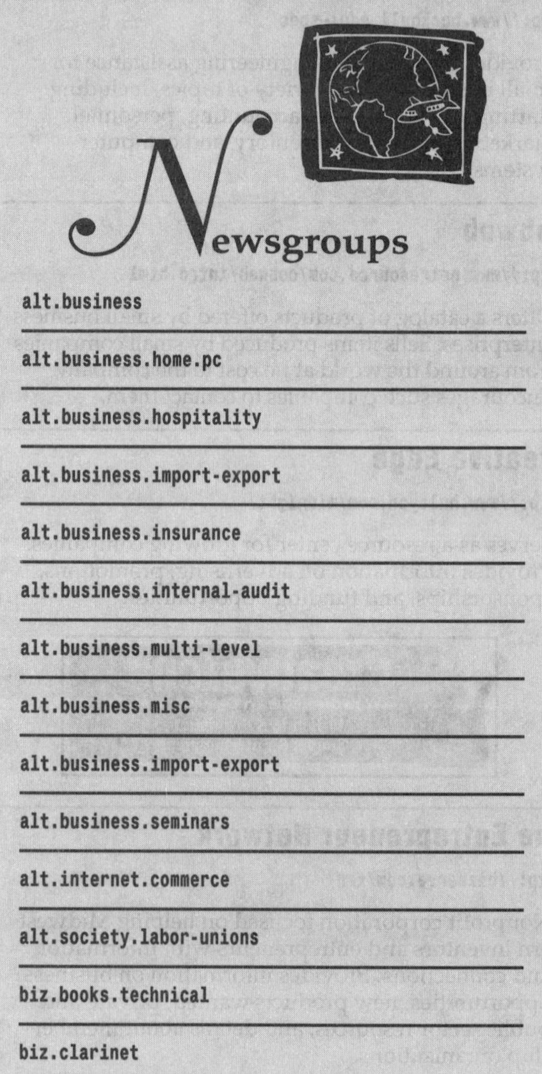

Newsgroups

alt.business

alt.business.home.pc

alt.business.hospitality

alt.business.import-export

alt.business.insurance

alt.business.internal-audit

alt.business.multi-level

alt.business.misc

alt.business.import-export

alt.business.seminars

alt.internet.commerce

alt.society.labor-unions

biz.books.technical

biz.clarinet

biz.clarinet.sample

biz.comp.accounting

biz.comp.mcs

biz.comp.telebit

biz.config

biz.control

biz.digex.announce

biz.digital.announce

biz.digital.articles

biz.general

biz.jobs.offered

biz.marketplace.computers.discussion

biz.marketplace.computers.mac

biz.marketplace.computers.other

biz.marketplace.computers.pc-clone

biz.marketplace.computers.workstation

biz.marketplace.discussion

biz.marketplace.international

biz.marketplace.international.discussion

biz.marketplace.non-computer

biz.marketplace.services.computers

biz.marketplace.services.discussion

biz.marketplace.services.non-computer

biz.next.newprod

biz.oreilly.announce

biz.pagesat

biz.pagesat.weather

biz.stolen

biz.tadpole.sparcbook

biz.test

biz.univel.misc

biz.zeos.announce

biz.zeos.general

clari.biz.briefs

clari.biz.earnings

clari.biz.economy

clari.biz.economy.world

clari.biz.features

clari.biz.finance

clari.biz.industry.agriculture

clari.biz.industry.automotive

clari.biz.industry.aviation

clari.biz.industry.banking

clari.biz.industry.broadcasting

clari.biz.industry.construction

clari.biz.industry.dry_goods

clari.biz.industry.energy

clari.biz.industry.food

clari.biz.industry.health

clari.biz.industry.insurance

clari.biz.industry.manufacturing

clari.biz.industry.mining

```
clari.biz.industry.print_media
```

```
clari.biz.industry.real_estate
```

```
clari.biz.industry.retail
```

```
clari.biz.industry.services
```

```
clari.biz.industry.tourism
```

```
clari.biz.industry.transportation
```

```
clari.biz.market.commodities
```

```
clari.biz.market.misc
```

```
clari.biz.market.news
```

```
clari.biz.market.report
```

```
clari.biz.market.report.asia
```

```
clari.biz.market.report.europe
```

```
clari.biz.market.report.top
```

```
clari.biz.market.report.usa
```

```
clari.biz.market.report.usa.nyse
```

```
clari.biz.mergers
```

```
clari.biz.misc
```

```
clari.biz.review
```

```
clari.biz.top
```

```
clari.biz.urgent
```

```
clari.biz.world_trade
```

```
clari.news.labor
```

```
clari.news.labor.layoff
```

```
clari.news.labor.strike
```

```
cu.business.general
```

```
cu.business.general.distance
```

```
cu.business.grad.mba
```

```
cu.business.grad.ms
```

```
cu.business.grad.phd
```

```
cu.business.ugrad
```

```
misc.consumers.frugal-living
```

```
misc.entrepreneurs
```

```
misc.invest.funds
```

```
misc.invest.real-estate
```

```
misc.invest.stocks
```

```
misc.invest.technical
```

```
misc.taxes
```

```
misc.taxes Archive
```

```
misc.taxes.moderated
```

Listservs

ALSBNEWS—Academy of Legal Studies in Business (ALSB) News

Miami University, Oxford, OH

You can join this group by sending the message "sub ALSBNEWS your name" to listserv@miamiu.muohio.edu

AOL-EZONE—"Your Business Newsletter" - America Online's Weekly Small Bus+

America Online, Inc. (1-800-827-6364 in USA/ Canada)

You can join this group by sending the message "sub AOL-EZONE your name" to listserv@listserv.aol.com

BETS-L—Business Ethics Teaching Society

University of Illinois at Chicago, Chicago, IL

You can join this group by sending the message "sub BETS-L your name" to `listserv@uicvm.uic.edu`

BIZNEWS—News Service Business News Releases

Purdue University, West Lafayette, IN

You can join this group by sending the message "sub BIZNEWS your name" to `listserv@vm.cc.purdue.edu`

BSN-D—Business Sources on the Net - Distribution List

You can join this group by sending the message "sub BSN-D your name" to `listserv@listserv.kent.edu`

BTECH94—Business Technology

University of Missouri-St. Louis

You can join this group by sending the message "sub BTECH94 your name" to `listserv@umslvma.umsl.edu`

BUSHEA—Health-Related Information for Business and Industry

Southern Illinois University at Carbondale, Carbondale, IL

You can join this group by sending the message "sub BUSHEA your name" to `listserv%siucvmb.bitnet@listserv.net`

BUSLAW-L—Business Law List

Humber College, Toronto, ON

You can join this group by sending the message "sub BUSLAW-L your name" to `listserv@admin.humberc.on.ca`

BUSLIB-L—Business Libraries Discussion List

Boise State University, Boise, ID

You can join this group by sending the message "sub BUSLIB-L your name" to `listserv@idbsu.idbsu.edu`

BUSREC—Business Recovery

Wayne State University, Detroit, MI

You can join this group by sending the message "sub BUSREC your name" to `listserv@cms.cc.wayne.edu`

CORP-L—Corporate Accountability List

The American University, Washington, DC

You can join this group by sending the message "sub CORP-L your name" to `listserv@american.edu`

EHCOLUMN—Economic History Columns

Miami University, Oxford, OH

You can join this group by sending the message "sub EHCOLUMN your name" to `listserv@miamiu.muohio.edu`

INBUSINESS— Internet In Business Discussion List

America Online, Inc. (1-800-827-6364 in USA/Canada)

You can join this group by sending the message "sub INBUSINESS your name" to `listserv@listserv.aol.com`

KSINDX-L—KS Index of Leading Econ. Indicators

Kansas State University, Manhattan, KS

You can join this group by sending the message "sub KSINDX-L your name" to `listserv@ksuvm.ksu.edu`

LABOR-L—Forum on Labor in the Global Economy

You can join this group by sending the message "sub LABOR-L your name" to `listserv@yorku.ca`

MBA-L—BA Discussion List

University of Missouri-St. Louis

You can join this group by sending the message "sub MBA-L your name" to `listserv@umslvma.umsl.edu`

NASIRN-L—North American Service Industries Research Network List

America Online, Inc. (1-800-827-6364 in USA/Canada)

You can join this group by sending the message "sub NASIRN-L your name" to
`listserv@listserv.aol.com`

NDSRB-L—Students for Responsible Business

University of Notre Dame, Notre Dame, IN

You can join this group by sending the message "sub NDSRB-L your name" to
`listserv@vma.cc.nd.edu`

PCBR-L—Pacific Business Researchers Forum (PCBR-L)

You can join this group by sending the message "sub PCBR-L your name" to
`listserv%uhccvm.bitnet@listserv.net`

ROUNDTABLE—International Business Roundtable

You can join this group by sending the message "sub ROUNDTABLE your name" to
`listserv@home.ease.lsoft.com`

TOES97—The Other Economic Summit USA 1997

Syracuse University

You can join this group by sending the message "sub TOES97 your name" to
`listserv@listserv.syr.edu`

4Kids Treehouse

`http://www.4kids.com/~4kids/~4kids/`

Contains sections devoted to entertainment, a playroom, projects, reading, science, and social studies. Site is both entertaining and educational with interactive games and readings.

1996 Olympic Games Side

`http://www.atlanta.olympic.org/acog/fun/d-index.html`

Contains Olympic trivia for children, news, event schedule, and general Olympic history and entertaining information. Also features Izzy, an animated host, and his friends and family to guide you through the site.

AHA! Kids Network

`http://www.aha-kids.com/`

Created by Al Hyslop, the producer of *Captain Kangaroo*, *Sesame Street*, and *3-2-1 Contact*, this site is an interactive playground for kids of all ages. Contains cute graphics, video, and songs. Features an entertaining section for children 2–5, mysteries for ages 6–12, science for ages 5–12, and a section for teenagers.

Awesome Site for All Ages

`http://www.marlo.com/`

Present witty ClickToons, cartoons for all ages, illustrated children's stories online, and children's jokes. Also allows for the making of customized greeting cards online. Does offer areas for 15–95 year olds.

BigKid Network

`http://www.ecst.csuchico.edu/~bigkid/bigkidnetwork.html`

Entertaining site containing sections about museums, science, sports, zoos, aquariums, cities and countries, and amusement parks. Also has a fun and games section.

Child Prodigies

`http://www.pic.net/~jari/cprodigy.html`

A publication designed to help motivate children to write. Features children's submitted writings up to age 16.

Children Page

`http://www.pd.astro.it/local-cgi-bin/kids.cgi/forms/`

Web site for children containing many links to other children's Web sites around the world.

Children's Pages at WombatNet

`http://www.batnet.com/wombat/children.html`

Contains links to Web sites for children about animals, dinosaurs, high schools, libraries, hobbies, magazines, museums, news, space, toys, and travel.

Children's Stories, Poems and Pictures

`http://www.comlab.ox.ac.uk/oucl/users/jonathan.bowen/children.html`

Contains stories, pictures, sound, and poems. Also features many links to other children's sites.

Childrens Internet Site, Upstate SC

`http://www.cris.com/~Tjpsys/community/child/child.htm`

For kids, by kids, about kids. Lets kids submit Web art and lets them speak up on the Internet about whatever topics they find important to them. Contains art by kids and other kids' home pages.

Colgate Kid's World

`http://www.colgate.com/Kids-world/index.html`

Site contains information about cavity prevention, games, stories, a coloring book, interesting information, and pictures from around the world.

Cyberhaunts for Kids

`http://www.freenet.hamilton.on.ca/~aa937/Profile.html`

Site contains links for children of all ages to visit. Features itemized link categories on space, sound, literature, general children's pages, sports, communications, art, computer, science fun, music, misc., animals, and games. Great location to start when browsing the Internet.

Cynthia and Winston's Kids' Page

`http://www.webcom.com/~cynspot/kids.html`

Features stories by and for children. Also contains many science and reading links appropriate for children to use in learning more about their world.

Flitter Adventure Land

http://www.connecti.com/~flitter/

Web site where children can play and enjoy themselves at. Contains stories, games, and mazes. Site is both fun and educational and a good place to start young children exploring on the Internet.

Free Kids Page

http://walden.mo.net/~jennings/index.html

Children's Web site devoted to the entertaining and education of young children. Contains comics, puzzles, educational software, science information and experiments, an education section, and an area for preschoolers. Also contains links to other children's Web sites.

FreeZone

http://freezone.com

Web site devoted to children. Contains games, educational areas, comics, e-pal areas, chat areas, and a home page creator for children ages 9–15.

FutureScan

http://www.futurescan.com/

Site developed for young adults (ages 11–18) to provide helpful information in their career decisions. Featuring actual career stories, FutureScan attempts to help teens in choosing an appealing career to pursue. Though set up for teens, this Web site welcomes anyone who may be curious or interested in a different career.

Girl Talk

http://www.pleiades-net.com/voices/girl/girl.html

Web site where teenage girls can get together and discuss topics relevant to their lives. Features topics on friends, computers, school, pen pals, sexuality, siblings, relationships, and parents. Site is an alternative place where adolescent girls can discuss teen-related issues with others in similar situations.

Global Show-n-Tell Museum Wings

http://www.manymedia.com/show-n-tell/

Site allows for children to submit their accomplishments or projects to "show and tell" about them. Promotes pride and self esteem within children while developing communication skills. Also includes links to other children-related sites.

Horse Country

http://www.pathology.washington.edu/Horse/

Web site for young people interested in horses. Contains information and links to various horse associations, equestrian news and events, the Junior Riders Mailing List, Horse Owners Club For Kids, and the Junior Riders International Pen Pal List. Entertaining site for riders of all ages and skill levels.

I Spy

http://www.lexmark.com/data/spy/spy.html

Online children's game that helps to develop pattern recognition and cognitive skills. Contains several different games that help with geology, mathematics, and general enterainment.

Info Guide—For Kids Only

http://www.wchat.on.ca/info/kid.htm

Web site containing numerous links around the world devoted solely to children. These sites vary from educational to entertaining.

Interesting Places for Kids

http://www.crc.ricoh.com/people/steve/kids.html

Selected as a "4-Star" site by the McKinley Group, this site contains many entertaining and educational topics for children. Contains sections on getting around the Internet, art and literature, music, museums, science and math, toys and games, movies, and arts and crafts. Also features a collection of art, writing, and other interesting things submitted by children.

Internet for Kids

http://www.sybex.com/i4kids/

Produced by educational consultants, this is the companion site to the book *Internet for Kids*. Contains

Gophers, activities, mailing lists, and other information to assist children in their search on the Internet.

Jackson's Page for Five Year Olds

`http://www.islandnet.com/~bedford/jackson.html`

Site developed for preschool children. Contains activities and games to help with cognitive and recognition skills. Features fun pictures and coloring books along with some adventures of another five year old.

Katie's Workshop

`http://www.primenet.com/~hightek/katie/katie.htm`

Site developed by a five year old containing links to other children's sites. Also features sections on Barbie, Power Rangers, and paper dolls.

Kay's Kid's Collection

`http://fox.nstn.ca/~tmonk/kayskids/kay.html`

Contains a story book, picture page, and a funny page. Has links to sites devoted to crafts, Disney, games, girl guides and Brownies, family and friend pages, pictures, science and history, television, and other fun children's sites.

KID List

`http://www.clark.net/pub/journalism/kid.html`

Over 100 links to children's sites that are not religious, commercial, or political.

Kid's Web

`http://www.npac.syr.edu/textbook/kidsweb/`

A World Wide Web Digital Library for school children. Contains information in the categories of art, science, social studies, miscellaneous, and other digital libraries. Within each heading, features several specific subcategories to ease searching.

Kid's Window

`http://jw.stanford.edu/KIDS/kids_home.html`

A Web site in English developed to educate children about Japan and its culture. Contains pictures, a dictionary, and stories.

Kid's Zone

`http://www.spokane.net/kidzone/`

Educational Web site containing areas for children, parents, and teachers. Contains games and stories to help children learn fundamental skills.

Kidland

`http://www.kidland.com/`

Kids can leap with Webbie, an animated frog, from site to site. Contains an index of kids' sites, activities, books, cartoons, educational information, games, and other topics related to children.

kidlinks

`http://www.carroll.com/ridgewood_elem/kidlinks.htm`

Site created by an elementary school in New Jersey. Features numerous links to entertaining and educational sites appropriate for children. Gives good descriptions of individual sites to assist in searching.

Kids Club

`http://www.olworld.com/kidsclub/`

Site for children containing online chat, games, stories, and links to other children's sites.

Kids Hits

`http://www.nchcpl.lib.in.us/Library/LibraryInfo/KidzHitz.html`

Contains a large alphabetical listing of sites designed especially for children. Also provides a good description of each site.

Kids on Campus

`http://www.tc.cornell.edu/Kids.on.Campus/WWWDemo/`

Site developed for children. Contains sections about planets and space, dinosaur and science museum exhibits, disasters (earthquakes, volcanoes, tornadoes) weather, butterfly pictures, and many other exciting areas for children to explore and learn.

Kids on the Web

`http://www.zen.org/~brendan/kids.html`

Contains valuable information for children and their parents to read before youngsters cruise the Web. Also features links to educational sites, games, and children's books.

Kids World 2000

http://www.ecst.csuchico.edu/~bigkid/kidsworldindex.html

Contains hundreds of children's links around the world for children to explore. Primarily educational and entertaining, these are divided into museums, science, sports, fun and games, zoos and aquariums, cities and countries, amusement parks, and government and politics. Also features other interesting sites and a mystery site of the week.

The Kids' Place

http://www.islandnet.com/~bedford/kids.html

Children's Web site containing a pen pal section, interactive area, children's home pages, online adventures, puzzles and games, fish and marine animal section, and space and astronomy area. Site is a fun and safe place for children of all ages to explore and learn.

Kids' WB

http://www.pathfinder.com/KidsWB/home.html

Web site of the Warner Brother's. This site contains information about many of the most popular cartoons produced by Warner Brother's. Also features sound and video clips, character descriptions and voice biographies.

Kids' Web

http://www.primenet.com/~sburr/index.html

Site developed for children. Contains stories and activities, links organized by topic, software recommendations, children's art gallery, and access to *ComputED Gazette* (a quarterly newsletter devoted to computer education).

KidsCom Home Page

http://www.kids.com/

A children's Web site for ages 4–15. Presents versions in English, French, Spanish, and Dutch. Entertaining site that contains projects, games, jokes, and resources.

KidsHealth.org

http://kidshealth.org/

Site contains interactive articles about children's healthcare, medicine, surgery, and parenting. There are fun games, Kids Vote health polls, and Nemours media guide.

KidsNet

http://www.PonyShow.com/KidsNet/website.htm

Site developed for children to learn computer skills. This is accomplished through games, activities, and stories. Also features areas on software, art, books, puzzles, travel, and cooking.

KidStuff

http://members.aol.com/vergi/webdetective/kidstuff.html

Contains links to children's sites. Features lengthy descriptions about each site and its offerings.

KidWeb

http://www.teleport.com/~rhubarbs/kidweb/kidweb.shtml

Contains hundreds of links to sites appropriate for children of all ages. Also features kid's home pages, a survey, and areas divided for different age groups.

Knowledge Adventure

http://www.adventure.com/

A safe and exciting 3D world for kids. It features educational games, a monthly scavenger hunt with prizes, a complete reference library, and more!

LEGO Group

http://www.LEGO.com/

The official LEGO universe: products, services, Legoland, company history, and recent press releases.

Link-4-Kids

http://www.bltg.com/link4kid.html

Site contains many children's links and descriptions to assist the young surfer. Also features areas for parents that addresses Web safety and offers links to the top Internet security software.

Maddy Mayhem's Kid's Stuff!

http://wchat.on.ca/merlene/kid.htm

Lots of fun kid's links. A safe Web site for children. Links to penpal connections, fun sites, and more.

MBG Network

http://MBGnet.mobot.org/MBGnet/

Educational site that has areas for children, schools, and parents. Features pictures and videos of and about the environment. Also offers activities online and projects that can be done at home.

MCA Home Entertainment Playroom

http://www.mca.com/home/playroom/

A safe, fun, and creative place for children of all ages to come and enjoy themselves. Features stories and games that will excite and amuse children.

Munchkin Lady

http://www.uncg.edu/~jmarnese/index.html

Contains adventures, cartoons, and coloring books. Also features links to many popular children's sites.

NFL Kids

http://nflhome.com/kids/kids.html

Site geared for children that contains NFL profiles, statistics, news, and trivia. Also contains a searchable database, index, calendar, and shop.

Nicky's Kid Links

http://www.geocities.com/SiliconValley/2565/

This is a place suitable for kids of all ages. Contains different educational material and links to children's sites including NASA and online magazines.

Nucleus Kids' Page

http://www.nucleus.com/kids.html

Contains many links to sites for children. Site provides subcategories of education, reading material, places to visit, things to do, movies for kids, TV on the Net, music, toys, kid's work on the Web, penpals, a variety of links for fun and education, products, and links for parents.

Oasis * Here and There * Kids Corner

http://www.ot.com/kids/

Web site for children that contains entertaining games, a picture puzzle, an art gallery, an interactive story, and links to other children's sites.

Palos Verdes Kid's Corner

http://wwwsmart.com/~shui/PV/Kids.html

Site developed for kids by kids. Allows for submission of ideas, art, drawings, jokes, and stories.

Permits online viewing of submissions from other children.

Pasadena Kid's Pages

http://www.e-znet.com/kids/

Contains a daily calendar of events for children for the Pasadena, California and surrounding suburbs.

Patricia's Kids' Links

http://www.ghgcorp.com/wrholland/kidlinks.html

Contains links to many sites appropriate for children.

Planet Blortland

http://blortland.netserv.com/

Visit the Planet Blortland, an underwater adventure for children. While there, children can take a guided tour, solve a mystery, win prizes, and meet an e-pal!

Platypus Family Playroom

http://www.orst.edu/~dickt/playroom/playroom.html

A Web site for children that offers both English and Spanish versions. Contains self-reading short stories, singing songs in harmony, interactive activities, a maze of the week, map quizzes, and different family activities.

Magazine

http://www.toro.com/HotStuff/FreeStuff.shtml

Get a free one year subscription to Toro Horsepower Magazine—filled with valuable product information and yard care tips.

Playroom

http://openweb.vassar.edu/students/dohernandez/
kids'corner/Playroom.html

Site for kids of all ages. Contains links to sites about animals, education, games, homepages, literature, toys, and visual graphics.

Rachel's Kids Page

http://exo.com/~jess/

Home page of Rachel, a four year old, that contains children software and links that will entertain any preschooler.

REACH Summer Science Camp

http://www.ee.mcgill.ca/~reach/

Site contains exciting science projects and experiments for children grades 4–9 and teachers. Also features links to other science Web sites designed for children.

Reference Links

http://www.lws.com/kidsweb/links.htm

Site designed and run by children that contains reference links about general history, news, weather, and children's sites. Also features a children's picture gallery.

Route 6-16

http://www.microsys.com/616/

An entertaining and educational site developed for kids ages 6–16, parents, and teachers. Contains a playground with areas devoted to games and toys, art, music and books, movies and TV, outdoors and sports, oceans and space, animals, vacation and travel, and puzzles and hobbies. Site also features over 2,000 links.

The Sugar Bush

http://intranet.ca/~dlemire/sb_kids.html

Site where children can enjoy themselves and make friends. Offers stories, crafts, projects, and fun and educational adventures. Also contains a treasure hunt and links to other children's sites.

Terrific Web Sites

http://www.westnet.com/~rickd/Kids.html

Site developed by The Eastchester Middle School provides both educational and entertaining links for middle school students. Featuring two main

categories, academic studies and fun sites for kids, several subcategories, and multiple directories within each subcategory makes it easy to locate particular interests quickly.

Tessa's Cool Links for Kids

http://www.islandnet.com/~bedford/tessa.html

Web site created for pre-teens contains links to movies, coloring books, pictures, and software. Features both educational and amusing sites that will entertain your children.

thekids.com

http://www.thekids.com/kids/

Site features extensively illustrated stories, rhymes, fables, folk and fairy tales from around the world, plus discussion groups, games, contests, and information for parents. Also contains to their favorite educational sites.

Tristan and Tiffany's Daily Cool Stuff for Kids

http://www.polar7.com/tnt/

Created by children for children, this site features links to many entertaining sites.

Uncle Bob's Kids' Page

http://gagme.wwa.com/~boba/kids.html

Created for students K–12, this site features many links to "children safe" Web sites including news, world events, games, puzzles, trivia, and more.

Visa Olympics of the Imagination

http://www.enw.com/visakids/

Art contest challenging children worldwide ages 11–13 to draw or paint their own Olympic sport of the future. Includes instructions to teachers, and previous winning pictures.

Web.Kids

http://www.hoofbeats.com/

Science fiction site for children. Contains stories, graphics, story ideas, and adventures.

World Surfari

http://www.supersurf.com/

Monthly virtual tour of a different country. Features information on the people, society, history, and other interesting facts of the particular country.

World Wide Kids, Welcome Aboard!

http://pages.prodigy.com/USFY50A/ldever_c.html

Site features links to books, games, and other fun stuff for kids on the Web. Also contains some original stories.

Xplore Kids

http://www.xplore.com/xplore500/medium/kids.html

Web site designed for children to help them learn about animals, find a penpal, publish art and stories, work on projects for school, or play games and have fun.

Yahooligans

http://www.yahooligans.com/

Web site search engine for children containing sections devoted to history, the arts, politics, computers and games, entertainment, sports and recreation, daily news events, weather, and comics. Also features a school section that contains programs and homework answers.

Youth Central Community

http://www.youthcentral.apple.com/

Site designed for kids by kids. Features news, a poster contest, poems, stories, shareware, entertainment, pictures, sports, and much more.

Youth Connection

http://www.ingenius.com/product/cyberhd/youth/youth.htm

A youth-oriented forum that includes sections on art, money, games, and more. Also contains many links designed for children.

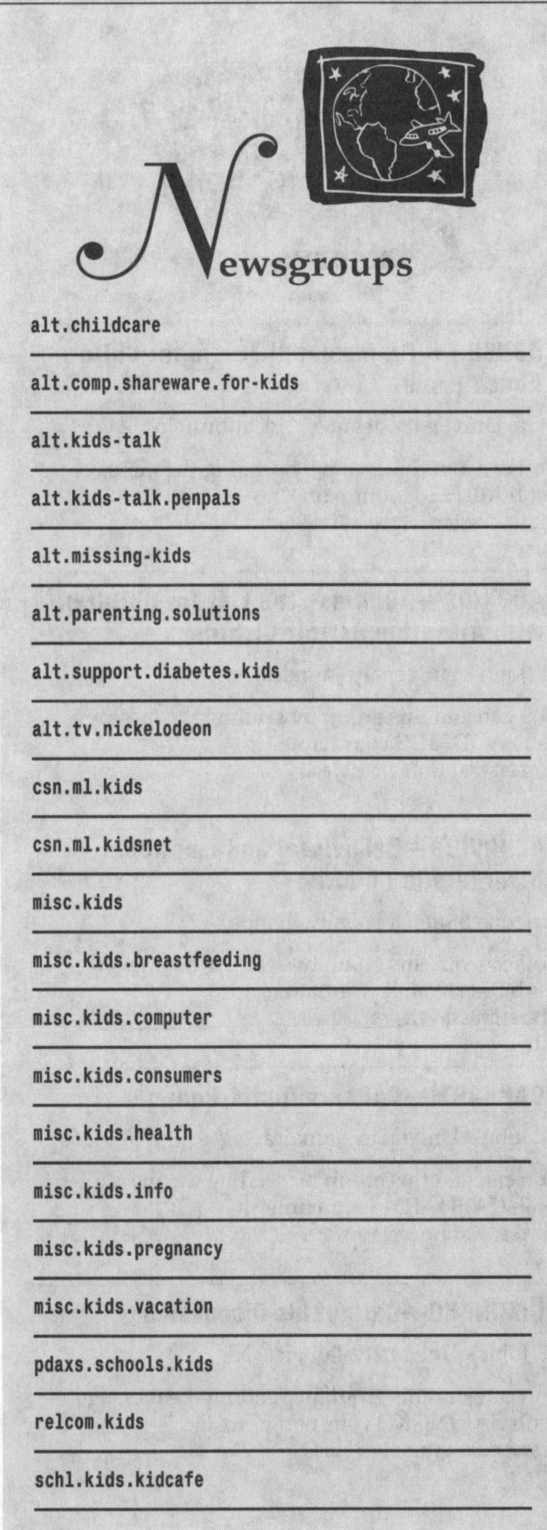

Newsgroups

alt.childcare

alt.comp.shareware.for-kids

alt.kids-talk

alt.kids-talk.penpals

alt.missing-kids

alt.parenting.solutions

alt.support.diabetes.kids

alt.tv.nickelodeon

csn.ml.kids

csn.ml.kidsnet

misc.kids

misc.kids.breastfeeding

misc.kids.computer

misc.kids.consumers

misc.kids.health

misc.kids.info

misc.kids.pregnancy

misc.kids.vacation

pdaxs.schools.kids

relcom.kids

schl.kids.kidcafe

Listservs

ABUSE-L—Professional Forum for Child Abuse Issues

State University of New York at Buffalo

You can join this group by sending the message "sub ABUSE-L your name" to
`listserv@ubvm.cc.buffalo.edu`

ADDKIDS—ADDKids- The List for Children with Attention Deficit Disorder

St. John's University, Jamaica, NY

You can join this group by sending the message "sub ADDKIDS your name" to
`listserv@sjuvm.stjohns.edu`

BEHAVIOR—Behavioral and Emotional Disorders in Children

Arizona State University, Tempe, AZ

You can join this group by sending the message "sub BEHAVIOR your name" to
`listserv@asuvm.inre.asu.edu`

CAPHARM—CAPharm/Child-Pharm

St. John's University, Jamaica, NY

You can join this group by sending the message "sub CAPHARM your name" to
`listserv@sjuvm.stjohns.edu`

CARINGKD—Caringkids Discussion

St. John's University, Jamaica, NY

You can join this group by sending the message "sub CARINGKD your name" to
`listserv@sjuvm.stjohns.edu`

CHILDRI-—Discussion UN Convention on the Rights of the Child

University Center of Information services (UCI), Nijmegen, The Netherlands

You can join this group by sending the message "sub CHILDRI- your name" to
`listserv@nic.surfnet.nl`

CPPARENT—CPPARENT Discussion for Parents of Children with Cerebral Pal+

St. John's University, Jamaica, NY

You can join this group by sending the message "sub CPPARENT your name" to
`listserv@sjuvm.stjohns.edu`

CSHCN-L—Children with Special Health Care Needs

NE Regional Data Center, Univ. of Florida campus, Gainesville, FL

You can join this group by sending the message "sub CSHCN-L your name" to
`listserv@nervm.nerdc.ufl.edu`

DADVOCAT—DADVOCAT—Dads of Children with Disabilities or Special Health+

You can join this group by sending the message "sub DADVOCAT your name" to
`listserv@lsv.uky.edu`

DEAFKIDS—DeafKids List for Deaf Children

St. John's University, Jamaica, NY

You can join this group by sending the message "sub DEAFKIDS your name" to
`listserv@sjuvm.stjohns.edu`

ECENET-L—Early Childhood Education/ Young Children (0–8)

University of Illinois, Urbana, IL

You can join this group by sending the message "sub ECENET-L your name" to
`listserv@postoffice.cso.uiuc.edu`

ECEOL-L—Early Childhood Education On-Line Mailing List

University of Maine System, Orono, ME

You can join this group by sending the message "sub ECEOL-L your name" to
`listserv@maine.maine.edu`

ECPOLICY-L—Policy Issues Related to Young Children

University of Illinois, Urbana, IL

You can join this group by sending the message "sub ECPOLICY-L your name" to
`listserv@postoffice.cso.uiuc.edu`

KIDCAFE—KIDLINK List: Youth Dialog—Age 10–15 Only

You can join this group by sending the message "sub KIDCAFE your name" to
`listserv@listserv.nodak.edu`

KIDLIT-L—Children and Youth Literature List

State University of New York at Binghamton

You can join this group by sending the message "sub KIDLIT-L your name" to
`listserv@bingvmb.cc.binghamton.edu`

KIDNEWS—KIDLINK List: For Newsletter Distribution

You can join this group by sending the message "sub KIDNEWS your name" to
`listserv@listserv.nodak.edu`

KIDPEDIA—Child-Authored Encyclopedia

St.John's University, Jamaica, NY

You can join this group by sending the message "sub KIDPEDIA your name" to
`listserv@sjuvm.stjohns.edu`

KIDZMAIL—KIDZMAIL: Kids Exploring Issues And Interests Electronically

Arizona State University, Tempe, AZ

You can join this group by sending the message "sub KIDZMAIL your name" to
`listserv@asuvm.inre.asu.edu`

NOVNET—National Operational Volunteers For Girl Scouts, USA

University Computing Services, Indiana University

You can join this group by sending the message "sub NOVNET your name" to
`listserv@iubvm.ucs.indiana.edu`

QUAKER-K—Discussion List for Young Quakers Ages 5 to 12

University of Illinois, Urbana, IL

You can join this group by sending the message "sub QUAKER-K your name" to
`listserv@postoffice.cso.uiuc.edu`

SAC-L—School Aged Child Care Issues and Concerns

University of Illinois, Urbana, IL

You can join this group by sending the message "sub SAC-L your name" to
`listserv@postoffice.cso.uiuc.edu`

SCOUTS-L—Youth Groups Discussion List

Texas Christian University, Fort Worth, TX

You can join this group by sending the message "sub SCOUTS-L your name" to
`listserv@tcubvm.is.tcu.edu`

SICKKIDS—Kids Talking to Kids

St.John's University, Jamaica, NY

You can join this group by sending the message "sub SICKKIDS your name" to
`listserv@sjuvm.stjohns.edu`

WYCOOL-L—Way Cool Software Reviews by Children, Teachers, and Parents

The University of Connecticut, Storrs, CT

You can join this group by sending the message "sub WYCOOL-L your name" to
`listserv@uconnvm.uconn.edu`

YANX-DEP—YANX-DEP Child and Adolescent Anxiety and Depression Forum

St.John's University, Jamaica, NY

You can join this group by sending the message "sub YANX-DEP your name" to
listserv@sjuvm.stjohns.edu

YAWRITE—The Children and Young Adult Writing List

Pennsylvania State University

You can join this group by sending the message "sub YAWRITE your name" to
listserv@psuvm.psu.edu

YNGLRNGP—Young Learners Group

Texas A&M University Computing Services Center

You can join this group by sending the message "sub YNGLRNGP your name" to
listserv@tamvm1.tamu.edu

Children

COMPUTER GAMES

3D Action Games

The 3D Gaming Scene

http://www.pol.umu.se/html/ac/mainpage.htm

Describes in detail every 3D action game available, beginning with the original—Wolfenstein 3D. Download working demos and shareware versions from this page, or just read a helpful description of each game. Includes a screen shot from each game, the type of 3D engine used in the game, and provides cheat FAQs and walkthroughs.

The All-Time Best DOOM Levels

http://doomgate.cs.buffalo.edu/~williams/

The best DOOM and DOOM II add-on levels are now available in one place. You no longer have to hunt far and wide for add-on DOOM levels, only to find that they stink. This page provides dozens of the best levels available. Most of these levels include new monsters; new textures, lighting, and sound; and even new weapons. Get ready to die!

CyberMage

http://www.ea.com/origin/english/prod-info/pc-cd/
current-titles/cybermage/index.html

Download screen shots of the shareware version of Origin's CyberMage, meet the designer, or check out the steep system requirements of this highly acclaimed futuristic sorcery game.

Dark Forces Editors and Utilities

http://www2.best.com/~dalton/DarkForces/utils.html

Provides level and monster editors, math coprocessor patches, graphics file converters, and screen savers for LucasArts' Dark Forces 3D action game.

Djinni's Hexen-Editing Page

http://www.geocities.com/Hollywood/2298/

A well-organized site for fans of Hexen, one of the best-selling 3D action games ever. This sword and sorcery follow up to Heretic can now be customized using a number of different utilities. This site provides the best MAP editors, Lump tools (for adding your own graphics), and notebuilders available. Also included are FAQs, technical specs, sound lists, and parts inventories.

DOOM and DOOM II Secrets

http://www.cen.uiuc.edu/~mb9530/secrets.html

A complete description of every secret area in every version of DOOM, Ultimate DOOM, DOOM II, and Heretic. Click on one of the listed games to see a text description, or choose to see a map of each level.

Duke Nukem 3D Resource Page

http://www.3drealms.com/duke3d.html

Contains every conceivable piece of information on Duke Nukem 3D, the hottest action shoot 'em up since Doom II. This site provides a comprehensive FAQ (which you are encouraged to read before sending e-mail to 3D Realms), a list of bug fixes in the latest software update, and fixes for problems with different CPUs. Also included in this site is a list of every ftp site containing Duke Nukem's shareware and updates and links to every available Duke Nukem and 3D Realms Web site.
NOTE: Access this site first because the other Duke Nukem sites are always busy, which means snail's pace access times.

GameNet

http://www.gamenet.com/

A Mac gamer subscriber service. Provides 24-hour access to BBS and server (for play) devoted to Mac games such as Marathon, Power Poker, and Chuck Yeager's Air Combat. Subscribers can order games at discount prices.

id software

http://www.idsoftware.com/

Home page of the creators of DOOM, DOOM II, and the long awaited Quake. The success of id software's games is so great that accessing this site is almost impossible. Check out similar sites first to see if the softare updates, levels, or patches you need are available.

Mech Warrior 2 and Clan of the Ghost Bear Page

http://www.lookup.com/Homepages/69636/Mech/
mech_text.html

Complete resource for the 3D battle simulator MechWarrior II, from Activision. This site includes detailed information on the best way to fight different Mechs and all the cheat codes for Mechwarrior II and the expansion pack. In addition, an invaluable list of utilities includes Mech editing software, patches for version 1.1 and Windows 95, information on running the game from the hard drive, and custom .AVIs.

Quake

http://www.texas.net/~wise/quake.htm

A comprehensive site for id software's long awaited sequel to DOOM II. Quake is a true 3D MUD that uses FTP/IP and runs on a server. Access this site to find a lengthy description of the game's new technology, proposed features, and design history. This site also includes a number of documents listing console commands, technical specs for level editor programmers, and release notes from id. Find out what makes Quake so different from DOOM and the DOOM engine.

The Tenth Planet

`http://www.bethsoft.com/cgi-bin/10thplanet.cgi?Lite`

Bethesda's team-up with Centropolis Entertainment, the producers of Independence Day and Stargate, promises to be a breakthrough in 3D science fiction action games. Find out about the storyline for The Tenth Planet, the game's development (it isn't finished yet), and download screen shots and sounds from the game.

Terminator Future Shock

`http://www.bethsoft.com/cgi-bin/futureshock.cgi?Lite`

What's the third installment of the Terminator series like? Download an awesome demo (19 MB!), check out screen shots of the game, view movies of the intro, or upgrade the commercial version. This site has a little something for every Terminator gaming fan.

3D Strategy Games

Crusader No Remorse

`http://www.ea.com/origin/english/prod-info/pc-cd/current-titles/crusader/index.html`

Meet the designer of this 3D action shooter from Origin with an interface similar to Command and Conquer. Download a video demo (.AVI or .MOV), or check out the sound clips. Click on Product Demos to access Origin's game demo software.

Diablo

`http://www.blizzard.com/diablo.htm`

What's all the fuss about the most anticipated RPG game of 1996? Check out the awesome graphics of this game, read the storyline, and see if your system can handle Blizzard's RPG juggernaut.

Ishi Press

`http://www.portal.com/~rww/pub_ishi.html`

Complete information, including software, for the ancient Japanese game of GO. Links to tutorials, books, software, game sets, and so on.

Justin's Command and Conquer Web Page

`http://www.cam.org/~jlee06/cc.html`

A detailed site dedicated to Command and Conquer, voted by many as the best PC game of 1995. This site is filled with tips for beating your opponents, getting out of messes, and multiplayer tactics. Invaluable is the files section, which includes the latest patches and a new level editor, CCEDIT. Includes links to other interesting sites dedicated to Command & Conquer.

Player's Lists

`http://www.zorda.com/playlst/`

Join a players list for Hexen, DOOM I/II, CivNET, Command and Conquer, and Warcraft II. Simply choose the game, click on Add Yourself to the <game> List, then fill out the form. A great resource for 3D game strategists.

Raptor's Warcraft and Warcraft II Page

`http://www.accent.net/jsdurand/war.htm`

Page provides links to Warcraft II leagues, downloadable demos of Warcraft (I and II), screen shots, the Warcraft newsgroup, the Kali patch for playing over the Internet, and a PUD area, where you can download battlefields made by other Warcraft fanatics.

Welcome To Dave's Warcraft 2 page

`http://www.teleport.com/~conrad/war2/war2.shtml`

A good fan page for Blizzard's Warcraft II: Tides of Darkness strategy game. Includes reviews of the game, cheats, screen shots of the game, strategy guides, software add-ons, newsgroups, and links to related pages.

Adventure Games

Activision Zork Nemesis

http://www.activision.com/zorknem/zorkhome.html

Activision's Zork page introduces the latest chapter in the Zork saga. The page describes the game, discusses its connection with the Zork legacy, provides screen shots of each of the puzzles and more.

Daggerfall

http://www.bethsoft.com/cgi-bin/daggerfall.cgi?Lite

The latest 3D adventure game is the sequel to Bethesda Software's The Elder Scrolls: Arena. This site describes the game in detail, provides a downloadable demo, includes hundreds of screen shots, and even MIDI files from the game.

Dungeon Keeper

http://www.bullfrog.co.uk/games/dungeon/index.html

Read about Bullfrog software's first role-playing adventure game—Dungeon Keeper. This page includes a description of the game (you are in control of monsters that must guard a treasure) and images.

The Myst Hint Guide

http://www.astro.washington.edu/ingram/myst/index.html

Clues to solving those vexing puzzle problems in Myst are now available. This site, one of the top five percent visited on the Web, provides hints organized by world. There is no walkthrough at this URL, but the hints should help you solve traps when you're completely stumped. If you ever wondered why such a mentally torturous game was ever created, FAQs near the end of the page will answer your questions.

Prepare to Get Maxxed AutoDesk 3D Studio

http://server1.autodesk.com/prod/mm/3d.htm

Ever wonder what game designers use to create the beautiful virtual worlds seen in such classics as Myst and Buried in Time 2? 3D Studio is one of the most popular 3D packages for digital artists in the gaming world and is also used in television, movies, and even the courtroom. Check out the demos link to download .MPEG movies and stills of works created with this amazing 3D animation package.

Return to Krondor

http://www.7thlevel.com/sevlinfo/pressrel/krondor.htm

The sequel to the successful Betrayal at Krondor is under wraps, but this press release might give you some clues to how it will play. Stay tuned at this site for more info on this anticipated sequel.

Review of Phantasmagoria

http://www.ozemail.com.au/~larme/phantas.html

Detailed Web site for Sierra On-Line's mysterious, beautiful, and controversial adventure game Phantasmagoria. This site includes all the hints, cheats, and walkthrough information you'll need if you get really stumped. More interesting, however, is a detailed account on why this game has been banned in Australia! If you haven't played the game yet, this site will certainly pique your interest.

Welcome to the Shrine of Zork

http://www.bf.rmit.edu.au/~s9205250/Zork_Shrine.html

All things Zork, from the very beginning, when Zork was a text-only adventure. FAQs, complete solution guides to every game, interviews with Zork creators, game maps, and a guest sign-in book complement this site.

Companies

7th Level

http://www.7thlevel.com/

These guys have been busy, and it shows. Read about the latest gaming project, check out their Free Demos section, visit the Company Store, or try out their Chat feature, where you can communicate with other gaming fiends.

Aristoplay, Ltd.

http://intergalactic.com/aris.htm

Provides company information and a catalog for this maker of educational computer games. Also provides Aristokids, a free newsletter that offers games and fun facts.

Bethesda Software Current Projects

http://www.bethsoft.com/cgi-bin/upcoming.cgi

This unusual home page for one of the best-known gaming companies provides a number of links to other pages at the bottom of the home page. Descriptions of current projects appear before the links. Click on the current project of interest to learn more about each game, to see screen shots, and to download playable demos.

Capstone Software

http://www.intracorp.com/capstone.html

Provides home site for Capstone Software, producers of Witchaven II, Chronomaster, William Shatner's Tek War, and the original Witchaven video games. Includes downloadable demos and screen shots. Also includes ordering information and technical support.

Cosmic JamStain

http://uptown.turnpike.net/~Makari/CJS/

Producers of "Attack of the Schmoog" video game and the upcoming "The Fall." Includes game background, producer's history, and suggestions page.

Epic Megagames

http://www.epicgames.com/

See some examples of why Epic's motto is "Only for Pentium. Only for Windows 95." This site provides information on Epic's latest releases and tantalizing upcoming products. Download demos of their latest 2D and 3D shoot 'em ups, contact Epic employees, or read the latest news on their collaboration with other game companies.

InterPlay Productions

http://www.interplay.com/website/default.html

Hot site from the creators of Descent II, Virtual Pool, and Stonekeep. Download new Interplay demos, read about their game ports to Sony PlayStation and Sega Saturn, see what's brewing with their Hollywood connections, or check out the company store. This colorful site also includes The MUD List, a lengthy list of MUDs on the Net.

LucasArts Entertainment Company Presents

http://www.lucasarts.com/menu.html

If you've got a few minutes, enter this page's URL, then go grab a cold one. Although the graphics are a little ambitious for a 28.8 connection, the page provides unique, useful links not found at other sites. Check out LucasArts' *Entertainer* magazine, shop the company store, or download demos from their library of games. The Recruitment Center is for all those who dreamed of working in the gaming business.

Microprose Software

http://www.microprose.com/mpshp.html

Creators of the award-winning Civilization and X-Com strategy games. This humorous site includes info on future projects, Cool Stuff—Microprose products—and technical help.

Pop Rocket, Inc.

http://www.poprocket.com/

Provides home site for Pop Rocket games, producers of Total Distortion. Includes game background, links to the Shockwave Game Arena, Rocket Shop, press releases, and interviews with the game designers. Also includes online contests, merchandise, and ordering information.

Shadow Island Games

http://www.pbm.com/

Play by electronic mail (PBEM) Olympia and Arena at this site. Provides game background, dice server services, and information about PBEM games.

Sierra On-Line

http://www.sierra.com/

This opening page and the Guest page for Sierra On-Line is small compared to the Welcome page you can access if you join their "club." Click on Join to sign up for Sierra's club; click on Members if you are already a member. If you can find their Demos link, you will have hit paydirt. This site is updated daily.

Sony Electronic Publishing

http://www.sepc.sony.com/SEPC/index.html

Do you want to get the latest information on Sony PlayStation and Psygnosis games and products? This site provides upcoming game information, technical specifications, and previews.

Virgin Zesty Bytes

http://www.virgin.com/

Virgin Interactive's home page provides a number of snack treats for the gaming addict. Dip into the Tasty Samples to read about Virgin's current product line and to download several working demos. The publisher of the immensely popular 11th Hour sequel to 7th Guest, provides links and information for this salty brain stumper.

Virtual Entertainment

http://www.cts.com/~vrman/

Provides information about VR Slingshot interactive virtual sport games. Includes detailed descriptions, pictures, and ordering information. Provides online test version of VR Slingshot.

Flight Simulators

Air Havoc Controller for Windows

http://com.primenet.com/rainbow/

Instead of simulating flying the plane, this time you simulate being an air traffic controller. Air Havoc utilizes 3D graphics at 640×480 resolution along with 28 different aircraft. Site provides sample images and video clips of the game.

Battlecruiser 3000AD Unofficial FAQ and Home Page

http://lookup.com/homepages/55306/battle.html

Find out the status of Take 2's Battlecruiser 3000AD. Read the gossip on its delays and beta pirates, download the demo, check out screen shots and the latest FAQ, and read e-mail from the game's principal developer.

Embry-Riddle Flight Simulation Links

http://macwww.db.erau.edu/www_virtual_lib/aviation/flightsim.html

Can you think of a better place to access flight simulator links than from the largest flying school in the country? This page includes dozens of links to the best Web sites on flying games and flight simulators.

First Eurofighter Air Wing

http://www.ef2000.com/

For pilots of the flight simulator Eurofighter 2000, published by Ocean Software. Visit with other pilots

in the Officer's Club, find that cheat code you've heard about in the Pilot Forum, download the latest patch and FAQ file, or ask for technical help in the Maintenance Hanger. A thorough site for Eurofighter fans.

Flight Unlimited

http://www.lglass.com/flight.html

Considered by many to be the most realistic flight simulator to date, the home page for this amazing program provides screen shots and descriptions of different planes and courses in the game. Really only an introduction to Flight Unlimited.

Military Simulations Back to Baghdad

http://www.military-sim.com/

Can Falcon Gold be eclipsed? Find out if Back to Baghdad's F-16 is more accurate. This page describes the game's development, provides a contest for registered users, and includes links to companies that helped develop the game, including SPOT satellite imagery, Thrustmaster, CH, and Digital Workshop.

Military Simulations, Inc.

http://www.military-sim.com/

Professional-type flight simulators for your personal computer. Check out their newest title, "Back to Baghdad—The Ultimate Desert Storm Simulation." Other products and ordering information also provided.

TekMate Home of the Skunks

http://rampages.onramp.net/~tekmate/

The makers of Virtual Skunks, plane add-on software to Microsoft Flight Simulator and Flight Sim's Aircraft Factory includes free downloadable airplanes, a gallery of aircraft, and a "plane locator." If you're interested in flying your favorite WWII bomber, Thompson Trophy classic, '90s jet airliner, or anything else, chances are good you'll find it in one of TekMate's 23 plane collections.

Terran Confederate Underground

http://cray-ymp.acm.stuorg.vt.edu/~bryantpe/underground/

Covers the Wing Commander series of games by Origin. Download patches, mission profiles, ship and weapon editors, and many other files for tweaking Wing Commander I-IV. Read the story for each game, learn about the characters and view every ship, and search the index for information on other elements of this series.

Thrustmaster Home Page

http://www.thrustmaster.com/

The manufacturer of the most advanced flight controls available provides help setting up controllers in Windows 95, patches and updates, technical support, FAQs about Thrustmaster products, developer support, and the latest news.

U.S. Navy Fighters: The Unofficial Home Page

http://wwwedu.cs.utwente.nl/~kamps/usnf.html

This highly detailed fan page for Electronic Arts' U.S. Navy Fighters provides secret key codes and cheats for the game, lengthy help and information on the Ukraine 1997 Campaign and Marine Fighters add-ons, information on EA's ATF flight simulator, and files that let you fly any plane. This page also contains a number of custom missions.

The USENET Guide to Falcon 3

http://cactus.org/~knutson/UGF3/UGF3.book.html

Incredibly detailed listing of Usenet threads about Spectrum Holobyte's famous Falcon 3.0 flight simulator. This well-organized site has ten sections, including Trivia, Setup, Tips and Strategy, and Quirks and Bugs. These categories are broken down into hundreds of subcategories. If you can't find it here, you dreamt it!

Warbirds Internet Multi-Player Flight Simulation

http://www.icigames.com/

Download the Warbirds software, then sign up to fly against other Internet gaming fanatics. This site provides a FAQ to answer all your questions (a must

read), the demo for downloading, and rates for playing on the Warbirds Internet network. Exciting!

Welcome to CRC and the Air Warrior Community

http://www.cris.com/~Flitesim/index.shtml

The place to link up with other Air Warrior pilots who want to fly with or against each other using the CRC network. Download Kesmai's multiplayer game—Air Warrior—find out about Upcoming Scenarios (simulated WWII battles), read how to subscribe to CRC, or check out links to Military, Aviation, Gaming, and WWII sites.

Werewolf vs. Commanche

http://www.novalogic.com/wvsc.html

Novalogic's head-to-head helicopter action game/ flight simulator is described in detail at this site. If you're looking for a complex deathmatch with an opponent in helicopters, this game is it.

Game Developer Sites

3D Engine List

http://www.cs.tu-berlin.de/%7Eki/engines.html

Check out the Special Categories sidebar on this page; it includes dozens of demos, shareware engines, and even a full working engine for developing your own 3D action game. This nicely organized site includes tons of 3D gaming information.

Commercial 3D Graphic Game Engines

http://www.cs.tu-berlin.de/~ki/game_eng.html#dnukem

Provides simple, informative information on the type of 3D game "engine" used by 3D games, such as DOOM, Hexen, and Duke Nukem. Simple page is helpful if you need specific info on the capabilities of each game.

Digital Dialect

http://www.primenet.com/~mcase/

Develops 3D game engines and 3D games for Sega, Sony PlayStation, and the PC. Read about Digital

Dialect's latest 3D game engine, CANCUN, which boasts sloping walls, correct perspective at all angles (even looking up and down), six degrees of camera movement, dynamic lighting, and 3D monsters.

EVPA

http://market.net/gaming/ev/index.html

Provides home site for EVPA, an association that concentrates on game play-testing and demonstrations. Includes membership information, provisions, and contact information.

G.A.C. Computer Services

http://rampages.onramp.net/~campbel/

Develops games for BBSs, PCs, and Web servers. Provides catalogs and demos of products, which you can download and pay for via credit card. Game modules include Lucky Star Casino Ship, InterLORD, and the Realm of Vanadia.

Gray Design Associates

http://delta.com/gda.com/gda.htm

Provides educational (typing tutors) and entertainment programs for teachers, parents, and game enthusiasts to download or purchase. Specializes in 3D action-adventure games and jigsaw puzzle games. Provides links to game demos, pricing, and ordering info.

IBM OS/2 Games Home Page

http://www.austin.ibm.com/os2games

IBM home page for OS/2 game developers and game enthusiasts. Includes product announcements, demos, press releases, a developer's corner, and gaming tips.

Jeff Lander's Home Page

http://www.lainet.com/~jeffl/

Showcases the Dagger 3D engine, which is being used to develop a new game called Varuna's Forces for Sega, Sony PlayStation, PC, and other platforms. Examine the technical specs on this engine and several utilities included with it, such as the Havoc renderer and Height Mapping Terrain System.

Pie in the Sky Software

http://www.catalog.com/psky/

Provides sales of Pie's 3D GCS (Games Creation System) software. Includes detailed product back-ground, links to games created with GCS, downloadable demos, and ordering information.

CH Products

http://www.chproducts.com/

If you're a die-hard flight simulator fanatic, check out the F-16 Series link on the Gaming Gear page. CH's F-16 Fighterstick, Pro Peddles, and Pro Throttle will turn heads (watch your six!). This page also lets you leave messages for the company, download CH drivers and other free software, and get technical specs on all CH "sticks."

Creative Zone

http://www.creaf.com/zonemenu.html

Creative Technologies' Web site provides three publications: Music Pub, Entertainment Arcade, and Business Center. Check out these publications to see the latest in gaming and sound technology. The Creative Zone also includes links to a directory of every Web page they have, information on anything you'd ever want to know about their Sound-, Modem-, and VideoBlaster products, and an online newsstand. This is a huge Web site.

Diamond Multimedia

http://www.diamondmm.com/

Click on Entertainment and Visual Systems to read about Diamond's newest 3D graphics accelerators and video cards. Read about their next trade show, employment opporunities, and product specs.

Forte Vfx1

http://www.fortevr.com

VR headsets are hot these days, and Forte's Web site shows why the Vfx1 is one of the hottest. Download the newest drivers for their headset, play with beta drivers for Windows 95, see how you can use this headset with VRML, and find out which games are compatible with this device.

head on by Eiger Labs

http://www.eigerlabs.com/headon.htm

Read about Eiger's modem, which lets you talk to your opponent while you play modem games against each other. Find retailers, locate opponents with their directory, and see if your favorite game is compatible.

Mag zine

`http://www.maginnovision.com/`

Tired of your 14" monitor you bought with that AT back in 1990? Check out Mag's DX17T monitor or choose the perfect monitor using their Select-A-Screen decision maker. This site also lets you contact tech support, learn more about monitors using their Glossary of Monitor Terms, and e-mail Mag employees.

Virtual I/O

`http://www.vio.com/`

See what free stuff is available for the Virtual I/O glasses, locate retailers, see which games are compatible, talk to developers, and read company info. Currently these glasses are the leader in VR headset sales.

Welcome to the SpaceTec IMC WebKeep

`http://www.spacetec.com/Hard%20Disk/WEB_SITE/Spacetec.html#imc`

Home page for the Spaceball Avenger, a 3D six-axis game controller that is a hit among 3D action gamers. Read about the Avenger and SpaceTec's other products, check to see if your favorite game is compatible, get tech support and FAQs, or click on Cool Quotes to see what other game players have to say.

Horror Games

Computer Games Rating Guide

`http://www.ozemail.com.au/~larme/phguide.html`

Read what it takes to get an RC, MA, M, or G rating on a computer game. This measuring system is similar to the National Motion Picture Rating Association's movie ratings. This page also discusses the possible reasons why Phantasmagoria was banned in several countries.

Fade to Black

`http://www.atw.fullfeed.com/~jkrutke/f2b.htm`

A violent, nerve-wracking 3D game with villians and monsters that resembles the older, less sophisticated Alone in the Dark. This page provides hints, lets you

download the demo, displays screen shots taken from the game, and provides technical information.

Gabriel Knight Help and Hints Home Page

`http://www.westga.edu/~jgibson/gk2/`

Reviews the original Gabriel Knight game and the sequel—The Beast Within. Download patches for the original Sins of the Fathers, sign the Guestbook, and download the complete walkthrough. This site also provides e-mail help. If you get stuck, send an e-mail to the Webmaster of this page. Very helpful!

Into the Void

`http://www.playmatestoys.com/pages/pie/itv.htm`

Will you survive against alien races bent on your destruction? Read about this space simulation that takes place largely in the nebulous void of empty space. This page provides a detailed synopsis of the game and screen shots.

Psychic Detective

`http://www.ea.com/eastudios/psychic/psychic.html`

What's so frightening about this Electronic Arts game? Check out the screen shots on this page to see the types of characters you'll be dealing with to solve this murder mystery. This site also provides a downloadable film of the intro (it's 10 MB!).

Shivers

`http://www.iinet.net.au/~quandary/issue5/shiv.html`

Provides a lengthy review of Sierra's spooky horror game for teenagers.

Trilobyte Software

`http://www.tbyte.com/digs/door.htm`

This graphically intense (read: slow) site for the company that created 7th Guest and 11th Hour includes a number of "rooms" to explore (access | the Map page). Check out the Gallery, Theater, and Music Room for neat images, movies, and sound. The Table of Contents link has e-mail addresses for every employee of Trilobyte.

Humorous Games

Cannon Fodder II

`http://happypuppy.com/games/link/canfod2.htm`

Download a working demo of one of the silliest "strategy" games made. The only instructions that come with this game are "Kill all enemies." Black humor at its finest in the gaming world.

Earthworm Jim II

`http://www.playmatestoys.com/pages/pie/ewjpc.htm`

Download the demo to this hilarious weirdfest with Earthworm Jim and his sidekick Snott. This page includes .WAVs of Jim's infamous expressions, screen shots from the game, and the storyline. Fun!

Gearheads

`http://spider.media.philips.com/media/games/cat_rom/`
`games/gearheads/gh_main.html`

Find out how violent wind-up toys can be in this crazy 3D strategy game. This page describes the game and includes screen shots, a downloadable demo, and Gearheads merchandise.

Information about Lemmings 3D the Demo

`http://www.cs.umu.se/~mnlchm/l3demo.html`

This fan page provides links for downloading Pygnosis' latest Lemmings adventure—Lemmings 3D. You can also download the cheat codes and the walkthrough or contact other Lemmings nuts at the Lemmings newsgroup.

Orion Burger

`http://www.sanctuary.com/cgi-bin/htimage/conf/`
`EntProducts.conf?64,291`

See screen shots of Sanctuary Woods' latest children's game, read the press release, or order it on the spot. At press time, the only way to get a demo of this was to buy the *PC Gamer Magazine's* CD-ROM.

You Don't Know Jack

`http://www.berksys.com/www/products/ydkj.html`

The hottest game on the party circuit has a Web page with info on question packs, a free demo, system

requirements, and press releases. If you think one of the answers is in error, you can e-mail the Webmaster. If you do, be funny!

Life Simulators

The Civilization Page

`http://www.lilback.com/civilization/`

A detailed Netscape 2 Web page for the Microprose simulation Civilization. This Web site discusses in detail the purpose of the computer game and Avalon Hill's original board game. You can also download FAQs, files from sections for the Mac, Amiga, and PC, and get information on CivNet and Civilization II, the sequel to this popular game.

Jerry Moore's Sim Stuff Web Page

`http://www.vcnet.com/jmoore/simstuff.htm`

Download cheat programs written in Visual Basic for SimCity 2000, Simlife, SimAnt, and other Maxis simulators. A description for each program is provided. This page also includes different winning cities created by Jerry Moore and other SimCity addicts.

Maxis, Inc. Home Page

`http://www.maxis.com/index.html`

If this page doesn't look right and you become a little concerned, you probably need to be playing more games. This detailed Web site for the largest computer "simulation" gaming company includes a company store, tips and hints, the latest Maxis news, and game demo downloads.

Magazines

Coming Soon! Magazine

`http://www.megatoon.com/~t15/index.html`

This Web e-zine provides dozens of reviews for all the gaming platforms, monthly articles about gaming hardware compatibility, and sneak preview articles for games that haven't been released. Other gaming industry news appears at the bottom of the page.

Computer Games

Computer Gaming World

http://www.zdnet.com/gaming/

This popular gaming magazine provides tons of reviews of the latest games, an online archive of back issues, a library of patches and demo files, and the latest Features stories and cover articles. The What's New link also provides daily industry news. The only way to get to this page was through the Ziff-Davis home page.

Electronic Gaming Monthly

http://www.nuke.com/egm/egm.htm

This busy site has everything imaginable for gaming fanatics. Like the magazine, this site is organized into topics. Read the latest feature articles, check out reviews on games EGM considers hot, and see who in the gaming world is in the spotlight in the Interview section.

Game Guide

http://techweb.cmp.com/ng/gameguide/gameguid.htm

Find out about interactive games on the Web, see what Game Guide considers the best.

Game Informer

http://www.winternet.com/~gionline/

You can subscribe to the real "paper lovers" edition of this video gaming mag (the kind you get by snail mail), or just peruse the links on this page. Check out the Back Issues link for select articles found in the magazine. The Secret Access: Codes of the Week choice is a must see if you think you've done everything possible on that PlayStation game you wore out.

hyper@ctive

http://hyperactive.com/games/index2.html

E-zine out of Australia that provides previews of new games, reviews, a download area, a cheats section, and the vault, a collection of reviews of "older" games (it seems anything over 6 months).

NEXT Generation Magazine

http://www.next-generation.com/

A busy site filled with live chat, the latest reviews of games for every PC, Mac, and video gaming

platform, and a number of downloadable videos of gaming in progress. Their well-organized archives let you search by platform; hundreds of reviews and news flashes are available. This site is updated daily.

Nuke InterNETWORK

http://www.nuke.com/

Check out the great interface of this online magazine and magazine publisher that strives to use the hottest technology available. Sendai, the parent company of such popular gaming magazines as *Electronic Gaming Monthly*, *Computer Games Magazine*, and *Cinescape*, provides a number of unique features at this Web site. Their Chat forums on gaming let you communicate in real time with anyone else. Register for their monthly contest.

PC Gamer Online

http://www.pcgamer.com/

Check the contents of the latest issue of *PC Gamer*, contact *PC Gamer* staff, or read about their new CD that comes with the magazine. The Demos area lists a number of game demos you can download that aren't on the monthly CD-ROM.

MUDs: Multiple User Dungeons

The Angel's Roleplaying Bookmarks

http://www.io.com/~lange/mudlists/mudlists.html

A lengthy list of dozens of MUDs, MUSHes, and MOOs organized by science fiction, horror, fantasy, superheroes, and more.

Arcadia MUD

http://www.arcadia.net/

Find out if you would like to join this detailed MUD by reading the FAQ and history of Arcadia. See a list of all the characters, contact the game administrators and Web page designers, and check out 3D maps of the Arcadia world.

Kingdoms

http://www.dd.chalmers.se/~kingdoms/Kingdoms.html

A straightforward page that describes this medieval-esque fantasy MUD. Connect to Telnet by clicking on A Telnet Connection to Kingdoms, see who's currently playing, or read the Kingdom's documentation for Wizards (the FAQ).

Mortal Realms

`http://192.216.48.20/`

If you have Windows, download the MrTerm Terminal Package so that you can play this extensive MUD with a simple command interface. Experienced players can also download utilities to add areas to this world.

The MUD List

`http://www.interplay.com/mudlist/mud/list.aph`

The most complete MUD list on the Web, with over 600 MUDs listed. The list is alphabetical and includes the MUD name, address, IP number, and port. Updated quarterly.

The MUD/MUSH/MOO Catalog of Catalogs

`http://www.educ.kent.edu/mu/catofcat.html`

This simple site provides links to the largest MUD and other Internet game lists in the country.

OuterSpace

`http://mud.stack.urc.tue.nl/`

Check out a new MUD out of the Netherlands. This site provides info on the MUD's setting, FAQs on joining as a Wizard and signing up to play, information on usable domains, and a connection for beginning the game.

The Realm

`http://www.realmserver.com/`

Sierra On-line's graphical MUD promises to be the future in Internet MUD gaming. Create a 3D character and enter him or her into the fantasy world. You can also chat and solve puzzles using this service.

Welcome to the World Wide Web Dungeon

`http://www.cling.gu.se/~cl0polau/3wd/3wd.htm`

This isn't really a MUD, but is an interesting 3D dungeon you navigate through on the Web. Eventually all MUDs might look like this. The interface provides six arrows; click on the direction you want to go, wait a few seconds, and you're closer to your goal.

Shareware/Freeware Game Directories

Gamer's Inn

`http://www.gamersinn.org/`

Click on the Levels link to access Deathmatch levels for DOOM, DOOM II, Descent, and Heretic. The Files link takes you to an easy to use page with Arcade, Adventure, and Simulation games for the Mac and PC. Click on GPB to see a list of gamers who want to play deathmatches over the Internet. A well-organized site.

Games Domain

`http://www.gamesdomain.co.uk/`

The oldest gaming resource on the Web now has sites in the U.K., U.S., and Russia. You can search for a particular game using the search engine at the top of the page. This page also provides the latest news on additions to the Domain and information on *GD Magazine*.

Happy Puppy's PC Hit 100 Game Downloads

`http://happypuppy.com/games/link/index.html`

Your one-stop HQ for demos/crippleware/shareware of the 100 hottest games on the market. Scroll through the candy aisle and click on your game of interest. Stop by the Boneyard for downloads of slideshows and demos of older games. This well-designed site should be bookmarked if you're addicted to gaming.

Intel Software Showcase

`http://pentium.intel.com/procs/homepc/software/index.htm#ent`

Intel's shareware/freeware page contains entertainment, productivity, and educational software that "...take advantage of the powerful multimedia capabilities of today's fastest PCs." Although the game section is limited, the demos included mostly contain 3D graphics and full motion video.

Moonlite Software

http://www.synapse.net/~moonlite/welcome.htm

Shareware computer games to download, such as Clyde's Revenge, Taking Care of Business, Crazy Eights, and more, with complete downloading instructions.

shareware.com

http://www.cnet.com/Resources/Software/

Part of the excellent c/net electronic magazine, this well-designed site provides over 100,000 programs for downloading. To see the latest and greatest shareware, demos, and freeware for PCs and Macs, try to find the c/net selections choice. This Web site is considered by many to be the shareware and freeware resource.

Welcome to the New Guru Online

http://www.anime.net/~go/

Site devoted to rating video games, game machines, and magazines. After you register, you can vote on a number of different topics. Although this is purely for video games and has no downloads to speak of, the Vote and Sponsored Pages links may give you ideas about your next game purchase.

Sports-Related Games

Computer Baseball and Basketball Games

http://www.imsworld.com/somgames/

Home page for Strat-O-Matic's PC-based baseball and basketball simulations. This page describes how each game incorporates statistical game management features, the auto play and schedule packages, and other features. Click on the basketball, baseball, or other games icons to download a working demo of each Strat-O-Matic game.

Trophy Bass

http://www.sierra.com/games/tb/

Check out screen shots of Sierra's fishing simulation or download the 6 MB demo. This site also describes the game and its nine different lakes.

The Unofficial Need for Speed Page

http://www.atw.fullfeed.com/~bix/nfs.htm

This fan page for the road racing simulator by Electronic Arts includes secret cheat codes and hints, technical information on the cars, reviews and e-mail, and the downloadable demo. You can submit your

best lap times, download a Track Editor, and contact other fans on the Need for Speed mailing list.

VR Soccer

http://www.vrsports.com/website/products/soccer.html

A 360° field of vision and 20-player network capability make this one of the hottest sports titles available. Download a demo or check out screen shots from the game.

Welcome to My NBA Live 96 Page

http://www.msilink.com/~solso/nbalive96.html#Hardware

An excellent site if you're researching EA's latest NBA PC game. This site includes personal e-mail and reviews from dozens of NBA Live fanatics. Sounds from the game, troubleshooting, patches, player editors, and more make this site more valuable than EA's own NBA Live 96 site.

Whiplash

http://www.interplay.com/website/sales/whiplash.html

Interplay's road race spectacle lets you duke it out with 15 other racers on a crazy, twisting racetrack. Download the demo (5.3 MB!), check out screen shots of the game, and see if your machine can handle it.

X-Car

http://www.bethsoft.com/cgi-bin/xcar.cgi?Lite

Bethesda software's hot racing simulation may help cure that lead foot you've had since Night Rider stopped airing. Compare this game's advanced features to other racing simulations and download screen shots of the game or the upcoming demo.

War Simulations

Avalon Hill Games of Strategy

http://members.aol.com/ahgames/games_page.html

Check out the latest War simulations from Avalon Hill, the father of war games. This page provides descriptions on all of Avalon's current line up. Click on Coming Soon to read about Avalon's soon-to-be-released simulations.

The E-Hawk Cadre

http://www.olcommerce.com/cadre/index.html

Need information on military history, or current declassified projects at the Defense Department? This site divides Military history and information into three categories: click on Mil-Cat to access Defense Department information; De re militari chronicles military history before the 20th century; and Mil-Hist, a military history library. Incredibly detailed site for the war game fanatic.

Enemy Lock On

http://www.elo.com/elomag/

Online gaming magazine devoted to combat simulators. Download previous issues of Enemy Lock On!, read the latest rumors, download artwork, or check out their detailed Links page.

The Goat Locker

http://www.mbnet.mb.ca/~moreau/harpoon.html

Web site for the Harpoon and Harpoon II submarine simulation. Information on Harpoon Usenet groups, mailing lists, and Department of Defense Web sites are included. You can also download a number of Harpoon (I and II) scenarios created by fans of the game.

Great War Series Aces of the Deep

http://www.mindspring.com/~jphooper/index.htm

A great page for Command: Aces of the Deep, the WWII Submarine simulator from Sierra/Dynamix. A detailed review of the game and an in-depth discussion on how to play are available. This page also provides information on Fast Attack, another sub simulator by Dynamix.

HPS Simulations

http://www.cris.com/~sturmer/

Index page for games offered, such as Tigers on the Prowl, Point of Attack, Panthers in the Shadows. Anything for the military game enthusiast, such as the military history calendar.

Multiplayer Games and Simulations

http://www.teleport.com/~caustic/

Provides information on every multiplayer game available. Find out about Internet gaming, online games, commercial and BBS game servers, gaming groups, and network game help. Click on a game of interest in the Games and Resources section to access Web pages and FAQs. Consider adding this to your bookmarks.

The Silent Service Wargaming Club

http://mypage.direct.ca/s/smithd/index.html

Detailed wargaming page devoted to Allied General, Panzer General, and Steel Panthers. After you join, take part in games in progress to see if you can make it to the ladder (hall of fame).

The Tanker's Homepage

http://www.rapidramp.com/tanker/

An excellent resource for the war strategy gaming fanatic. This incredibly detailed site provides information on computer games and board games. Topics are organized as Gaming, Military History, Movie Reviews, Online Discussions, Free Software, and What's New. The Gaming section is divided in Ground Warfare, Aerial Warfare, and Naval Warfare. The reviews of these games are thorough and helpful.

The War Page

http://www.cs.usm.maine.edu/~burns/war.html

This thorough site lists every known computer war game in the Computer Wargames section. This site also has information on military history, political theory, weapons, and military science. A valuable site if you're looking for a particular war game.

Crafts

http://www.ppi-free.com/freestf2.htm

If you like to sew, press flowers, make candles, or design earrings, visit this site for a list of addresses and 800 numbers to receive free supply samples.

Newsgroups

alt.binaries.games

alt.binaries.games.discussion

alt.games

alt.games.air-warrior

alt.games.apogee

alt.games.civnet

alt.games.command-n-conq

alt.games.command.and.conquer

alt.games.dark-forces

alt.games.descent

alt.games.doom

alt.games.doom.announce

alt.games.doom.ii

alt.games.doom.newplayers

alt.games.down-economy

alt.games.duke3d

alt.games.dune-ii.virgin-games

alt.games.dust

alt.games.final-fantasy

alt.games.final-fantasy.rpg

alt.games.frp.dnd-util

alt.games.frp.live-action

alt.games.frp.nurpg

alt.games.frp.tekumel

alt.games.gb

alt.games.heretic

alt.games.illuminati

alt.games.ki

alt.games.killer-instinct

alt.games.lynx

alt.games.marathon

alt.games.mechwarrior2

alt.games.mk

alt.games.mk.mk3

alt.games.mornington.crescent

alt.games.mornington.cresent

alt.games.mtrek

alt.games.netrek.paradise

alt.games.omega

alt.games.quake

alt.games.rpg.spacequest

alt.games.rpg.ufa

alt.games.sf2

alt.games.test2

alt.games.tiddlywinks

alt.games.torg

alt.games.tradewars

alt.games.ultima.dragons

alt.games.upcoming-3d

alt.games.vampire.the.masquerade

alt.games.vga-planets

alt.games.vga-planets.binaries

alt.games.video.alien-trilogy

alt.games.video.classic

alt.games.video.coming-soon

alt.games.video.import.japanese

alt.games.video.sony-playstation

alt.games.video.sony-playstation.faqs

alt.games.warcraft

alt.games.wc3

alt.games.whitewolf

alt.games.whitewolf.rage

alt.games.wing-commander

alt.games.worms

alt.games.wrestling

alt.games.xband

alt.games.xpilot

alt.games.xtrek

comp.graphics

comp.graphics.animation

comp.sys.ibm.pc.games

comp.sys.ibm.pc.games.action

comp.sys.ibm.pc.games.adventure

comp.sys.ibm.pc.games.announce

comp.sys.ibm.pc.games.flight-sim

comp.sys.ibm.pc.games.marketplace

comp.sys.ibm.pc.games.misc

comp.sys.ibm.pc.games.rpg

comp.sys.ibm.pc.games.sports

comp.sys.ibm.pc.games.strategic

rec.games.computer

rec.games.computer.doom.announce

rec.games.computer.doom.editing

rec.games.computer.doom.fascists

rec.games.computer.doom.help

rec.games.computer.doom.misc

rec.games.computer.doom.playing

rec.games.computer.quake.announce

rec.games.computer.quake.editing

rec.games.computer.quake.misc

rec.games.computer.xpilot

Listservs

A3R—A Discussion List for the Games ADVANCED THIRD REICH and RISING SUN

You can join this group by sending the message "sub A3R your name" to listserv@sjuvm.stjohns.edu

ADND-L—Advanced Dungeons and Dragons Discussion List

You can join this group by sending the message "sub ADND-L your name" to
`listserv@utarlvm1.uta.edu`

ALTEREGO-L—Alter Ego Games Discussion List

Wizards of the Coast, Inc.

You can join this group by sending the message "sub ALTEREGO-L your name" to
`listserv@oracle.wizards.com`

ARIA-L—Last Unicorn's Aria Game List

Brown University, Providence, RI

You can join this group by sending the message "sub ARIA-L your name" to
`listserv@brownvm.brown.edu`

CHESS-L—The Chess Discussion List

You can join this group by sending the message "sub CHESS-L your name" to
`listserv@nic.surfnet.nl`

CONSIM-L—Conflict Simulation Games

You can join this group by sending the message "sub CONSIM-L your name" to
`listserv@listserv.uni-c.dk`

GAMEHENDGE—Gamehendge MUSH Users Mailing List

NetSpace Project, Brown University, Providence, RI

You can join this group by sending the message "sub GAMEHENDGE your name" to
`listserv@netspace.org`

GAMES-L—Computer Games List

Brown University, Providence, RI

You can join this group by sending the message "sub GAMES-L your name" to
`listserv@brownvm.brown.edu`

GMAST-L—Gamemasters Interest Group

University of Tennessee at Chattanooga

You can join this group by sending the message "sub GMAST-L your name" to
`listserv@utcvm.utc.edu`

GSPE-NL—Discussion List in the Field of Gaming, Simulation

University Center of Information

You can join this group by sending the message "sub GSPE-NL your name" to
`listserv@nic.surfnet.nl`

ISAGA-L—Int'l Simulation and Gaming Association Forum

You can join this group by sending the message "sub ISAGA-L your name" to
`listserv%uhccvm.bitnet@listserv.net`

MIDGARD-L—Midgard PBM Game Discussion List

You can join this group by sending the message "sub MIDGARD-L your name" to
`listserv@home.ease.lsoft.com`

MUD-L—Multi-User Dungeons and Other Simulated Real-Time Environments

You can join this group by sending the message "sub MUD-L your name" to
`listserv@vm3090.ege.edu.tr`

MYTHUS-L—Mythus Fantasy Roleplaying Game List

Brown University, Providence, RI

You can join this group by sending the message "sub MYTHUS-L your name" to
`listserv@brownvm.brown.edu`

PC-GAMES-NEW—Shareware.com PC-Games-New List

You can join this group by sending the message "sub PC-GAMES-NEW your name" to
`listserv@dispatch.cnet.com`

PC-GAMES-TOP—Shareware.com Pc-Games-Top List

You can join this group by sending the message "sub PC-GAMES-TOP your name" to `listserv@dispatch.cnet.com`

QMS-L— QM Studio Games List

You can join this group by sending the message "sub QMS-L your name" to `listserv@brownvm.brown.edu`

UD-L—Ultimate Dungeon List

You can join this group by sending the message "sub UD-L your name" to `listserv%uriacc.bitnet@listserv.net`

COMPUTERS

Alps Electric USA

http://www.alpsusa.com/

Provides product information, technical support, and drivers for manufacturers of computer peripherals equipment. Includes full product line and background along with purchasing information. Also provides contact to Alps components division.

Altera

http://www.altera.com/

Provides company background, training information, product listings, employment opportunities, sales information, and distributors list for this manufacturer of progammable logic devices and computer-aided logic development tools. Sight also includes an electronic access contact sight for technical support and general product information.

Amdahl Open Enterprise Systems

http://www.amdahl.com/doc/products/oes.html

Provides A+ Performance Engineered systems, networks, applications, and services. Includes product information, service listings, press release index, and technical information.

American Digital Network

http://www.adnc.com/

Provides USR 28.8 v.34 digital modems, full digital IDSN, Web services, and Web site design. Includes full product information, technical support, service listings, software, and sales contacts.

Apache Digital Corporation

http://www.apache.com/

Provides information on ALPHA-based, NeXTSTEP, Linux/BSD Unix, Windows NT, SPARC-based, and other custom design systems that they sell. Also provides online custom design form, company background, policies, and detailed additional product information.

Apple Computer Home Page

http://www.apple.com/

Provides information on Apple's latest products and also supplies software updates. Although the rumor mills are flying about this company's fate, Apple's Web site obviously is full of information on new products and software enhancements. Check out this site for the latest on Apple technology.

AST Support Information

http://www.ast.com/support.htm

AST introduces their new "direct line" to technical support. This well-organized site provides quick access to bios upgrades, patches, technical support, e-mail, and file indexes.

AT&T Global Information Solutions WWW Homepage!

http://www.attgis.com/

Home page for NCR, the new name of AT&T Global Information Solutions. AT&T's split into three divisions and freed NCR from their identity crisis under AT&T's moniker. Find out about their new direction, current and future computer products, and download a detailed RealAudio message from the CEO, Lars Nyberg.

Belhaven Group

http://www.owt.com/belhaven/

Home site for Belhaven Group companies that produce computer hardware, system sales, and provide Internet services. Provides links to group companies such as Belhaven Instrumentation and Control, Belhaven Applied Technologies, Belhaven Systems, and One World Communications.

Bell Microproducts, Inc.

http://www.bellmicro.com/

Distributes many various computer products including superconductors, storage subsystems, digital optical equipment, and various software packages. Provides technical support, product information, company profile, and services listings.

Beyond 2000 Systems

http://www.beyond2000.com/

Supplies and sells computer systems, network products, and services. Provides product background, corporate profile, and online career opportunities with Beyond 2000. Includes information about WebCentral services.

CGI Systems, Inc.

http://www.cgisystems.com/

CGI is an IBM company that designs and delivers custom produced hardware, software, and applications packages created to serve client needs and structures. Specializes in Lotus Notes sales automation and the creation of networks, groupware, and work applications. Provides lengthy company background with detailed listings of services and products offered.

Citac Corporation

http://www.wta.com/citac/

Produces hardware and software that translates from English to Chinese. Includes information about CITAC computerized language tutor products. Provides demonstration of system by offering a translation of one page of text.

Client Systems, Inc.

http://www.clientsys.com/

Distributes and provides support for Hewlett-Packard and Oracle hardware, software, services, and other miscellaneous products. Includes lengthy company profile, Oracle news, HP updates, and hardware and software products listings. Also provides contact numbers and e-mail addresses for all of North America.

Comdisco, Inc.

http://www.comdisco.com/

Designs, produces, and provides disaster recovery software, systems integration services, and risk consultations. Products include CLASS, and ComPAS disaster recovery products. Includes complete listing of services offered that range from disaster recovery consulting to computer leasing.

CommTech Systems, Inc.

http://www.ctsystems.com/commtech/

Develops and produces computer hardware and software for both PCs and larger scale business operations. Includes information about Rescue data recovery software, Trouble-Shooter diagnostic programs, and other monitoring products. Provides free software and ordering information.

Compaq Online

http://www.compaq.com/

Access Compaq's Web services for corporate information, worldwide service center directories, technical support, and press releases on Compaq's newest Web servers and pricing.

Computer House/ISMAX

http://emanate.com/ismax/

Provides international importing and exporting of computer hardware, software, and other products. Specializes in doing business in Korea for government and corporate clients. Includes product listing of hardware and systems carried by Computer House.

CTE Computer Training Center

http://www.ctetrain.com/cte/

Specializes in computer training in Microsoft and Macintosh computing. Includes full schedule of classes and training courses offered. Also includes information about on-site training.

Cunningham & Cunningham, Inc.

http://www.c2.com/

Specializes in computer training and custom programming. Includes company profile, contact information, and philosophies utilized in services. Includes links to Web pages created by Cunningham & Cunningham.

Darwin Micro Systems

http://www.deltanet.com/users/darwin/

Produces file servers, mulitimedia systems, and workstations both for networks and stand-alone situations. Includes online price quotes and contact information.

Data Exchange Corporation

http://www.dex.com/

Provides a wide range of technical repair services for everything from hard drives to printers. Also provides technical support services, spare parts, and a wide array of other services. Includes services offered, contact information, job opportunities, and data exchange.

Data-Doc Electronics, Inc.

http://www.datadoc.com/

Supplies sales for connection products such as interface cables, adapters, and printer share equipment. Includes detailed product catalog with technical specifications and contact information.

Database Excelleration Systems

http://www.desdbx.com/

Produces DES Database Excellerator products that improve speed and performance through their solid state design. These products are compatable with Sybase, Oracle, or RBDMS networking systems. Includes services offered, product background, and specifications. Also includes contact information.

Dataserv Middle East & Africa Ltd

http://www.wp.com/dataserv/home.html

Supplier of second hand IBM mini- and main-frame equipment to countries in the Middle East and Africa.

DataWave Technologies

http://usa.net/datawave/

Researches, develops, and produces custom designed software and hardware for the scientific and medical fields. Includes technologies packages for data acquistion and data analysis for diciplines such as neuroscience, pshychology, biology, neurology, and many more. Includes application types and contact information.

DayStar Digital

http://www.daystar.com/

This manufacturer of high-performance multiprocessor upgrades for Macs provides a simple, graphical Web site for registering products, downloading updates and related Mac software, or learning more about Daystar's product line. Also learn about their new Genesis system of Mac-compatible systems.

DDB Needham Interactive Communications

http://www.ddbniac.com/

Develops and produces applications for data management, telecommunications, interactive media, and multimedia. Includes Internet design, communications, video conferencing, digital library,

and many other products. Includes work samples, art gallery, and contact information.

Dell Computer

http://www.us.dell.com/us/

Introductory page for Dell's U.S. Web site. From here you can choose among Dell's systems for education, businesses of different sizes, home, government, and personal use. The Web presence of this company is so large that their pages try to lead you to the products you want to see. This site also includes choices for technical support and online ordering.

Digital PC

http://www.pc.digital.com/

Aside from Digital's typical Web services, such as technical support, current product information, and International center addresses, is their own search engine—Alta Vista. Add this to your list of favorites in case your current search engines disappoint.

Distinct Corporation

http://www.distinct.com/

Designs and produces connectivity products and services. Distinct's line includes TCP/IP Developers Kits (SDK), TCP/IP Applications, and other related applications and hardware. This site includes product specifications, technical support, ordering information, and listings of international resellers.

Downtown Digital

http://www.dtd.com/home/

Provides a wide range of services in interactive technology. Includes Internet access, CD-ROM creation, custom software design, animation, and video services. Also includes contact information. The best part of this site is a link to "Gigabox!", an online games service provided by Downtown Digital. Gigabox includes trivia games, top ten lists, and contests. It's a neat site.

DPI

http://www.digprod.com/

Produces NETPrint and JETXPrint network print servers along with other printing and peripheral products. Includes product specifications, technical support, company profile, and news. Also includes purchasing information and a resellers list.

DVC Company

http://www.edt.com/dvc/dvc.html

Designs and produces "DigitEyes" family of digital and analog video cameras and other related products. Includes lengthy product technical background and company profile. Provides ordering and contact information.

Eltec International

http://www.eltec.de/Ehomeint.html

Produces controllers, network, communications, and image processing products including CPUs, I/O, and software. Includes product information, company references, and contact information.

EMD

http://www.mps.org/emd

Find out more about the mysterious company that designs, prototypes, manufactures, and tests services for printed circuit board assemblies.

eSoft, Inc.

http://www.esoft.com/

Produces Internet connectivity products specializing in access provisioning. Provides information about the Internet Protocol Adapter (IPAD) access products. Includes product specifications, corporate profile, technical support, and contact information.

Explorer Communication

http://www.explorercomm.com/

Produces computer peripherals such as modems and communication driver cards. Includes technical specifications, ordering information, customer support, and reference glossary.

Fujitsu Systems Business of America Home Page

http://www.fujitsu.com:80/FSBA/

Provides online Help, CAD, and desktop conferencing products. This site also explains the corporate structure of Fujitsu Japan, a $30 billion per year company.

Global Computing, Inc.

http://www.planet-hawaii.com/global/

Provides low price computer hardware, software, and networking products. Provides links to their electronic catalog, pricing and ordering, warranties, company information as well as other cool sites such as computer manufacturers and information and general sites on the subjects of art, government, Internet, and so forth.

Great Computer

http://www.a2z.com/a2z/cr00001a.html

Buy computers over the Internet. Provides computer upgrades, network installation, and new systems. Provides links to descriptions, pricing, ordering information, and a link to the computer dealer page.

Hewlett Packard

http://www.hp.com/

The leader in desktop hardware and network servers provides a multi-lingual Web site that is much more international than most other computer manufacturers. Jump from this site to learn about HP's Latin American division, their newest systems in other countries, and technical information on HP printers.

IBM Client/Server Computing

http://www.csc.ibm.com

Business and technical information for planning and disseminating distributed multi-vendor application solutions. Provides links to the home page, problem solving, demos, and Lotus Notes software.

IBM Person to Person Conferencing

http://www.hursley.ibm.com/p2p/P2P.html

Offers desktop conferencing products to businesses and organizations. Provides links to Person-to-Person info, ordering info, a search engine, an introduction to desktop publishing, and testimonials from Person-to-Person clients.

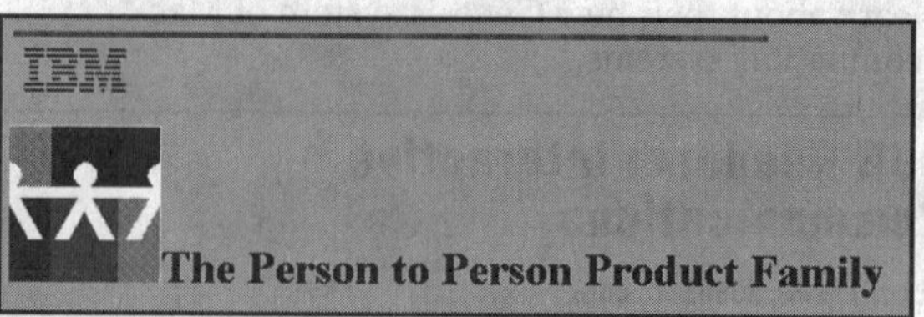

Meiko Computers

http://www.meiko.com/

Manufacturers of Massively Parallel Computing (MPP) systems and developers of software for these systems. This site provides technical information on Meiko products, announcements, and reviews. Find out how MPP systems are beginning to replace Massive Mainframes by clicking on News, Reviews, and Announcements.

Micropolis Corporation

http://www.micropolis.com

Produces high-capacity, high-performance storage products, including AV-optimized hard disk drives, RAID subsystems and controllers, and video-on-demand systems. This basic Web site includes the standard product information, tech support, recent news, and company profile information.

News—Planet Xerox Products

http://www.xerox.com/

What's new at Xerox? Check out the Research link to the Palo Alto Research Center and find out about Xerox's latest projects.

Nightware Energy Saving Switch for Laser Printers

http://www.nightware.com

Describes their energy-saving Nightware product for computer printers.

Parsytec Computer GmbH

http://www.parsytec.de/

Designs and produces cognitive automation, communication, recognition, and industrial recognition products. Specializes in products that process handwritten documents, surface inspection, quality control, and other repetitive work. Includes product technical specifications, example applications, and contact information.

Perfection Services, Inc.

http://ivory.lm.com/~psi

Produces systems engineering products and services for the data processing industry. Includes company profile, philosophy, and contact information. Also includes company references with links to clients.

Performance Engineering Corporation

http://www.p-e-c.com/

Produces and provides systems engineering products and services. Specializes in system appraisal and custom design. Includes services offered,

company resources, clients listings, and contact information. Provides company organization, news, and employment opportunities.

Persoft

http://www.persoft.com

Produces SmarTerm PC connectivity products, and Intersect wireless ethernet and token-ring network bridges. Includes company profile, product specifications, trade show attendance dates, technical support, and press releases. Also provides new product information.

Point & Click Software, Inc.

http://www.point-and-click.com/pcsi/

Produces custom developed software and networking. Also provides WWW services, graphics creation, scripting, and consulting. Includes company profile, resources, listing of services and products offered. Also includes clients with links to sites created.

PRC

http://www.prc.com/

Provides home site for PRC, a large government and corporate computer contractor and service provider. Designs and manufactures many products in many technologies. Produces custom designed software, image solutions, systems integration, and large network design services. Includes services offered, markets covered, products utilized, and contact information based upon client needs.

Quality HiTec Services

http://www.qhs.com/

Provides a wide array of network, Internet, server, and security products and services.

Quantum Research Corporation

http://www.qrc.com/

Provides computer technology and information database solutions for science agencies through the development of data collection and analysis support systems. Includes listing of clients and projects. Provides services offered and technologies utilized.

Schofield Computer Organization

http://fox.nstn.ca/~rschofie/index.html

Provides database programming, Web site creation, and computer consulting services. Creates software products and custom designed applications. Includes products and services offered.

Sea Change Corporation

http://www.seawest.seachange.com/

Produces networking, Firewall, security, system, and software products. Offers consulting, training, and development services. Includes detailed product background and service philosophies. Provides corporate profile, press releases, trade show attendance dates, links to related sites, and technical support services.

SEIKO EPSON

http://www.epson.co.jp/

Provides world-wide home site for Seiko Epson, which produces a diverse line of products spanning the technical world. Includes vast information about all of Seiko Epson's divisions, products, and companies. Includes a corporate profile and contact information.

SITE Computer Services, Inc.

http://www.ansa.com/~site/home.html

Provides business computer design, set-up, and management services. Includes services offered, technologies utilized, links to related sites, and contact information. Also includes online network evaluation and price quotes.

Speech Systems, Inc.

http://www.speechsys.com/

Designs and produces high-technology speech recognition and text conversion computer products. Includes information about The Phonetic Engine speech to text converter and the SpeechNet client/server software family. Provides complete product line and technical specifications. Also includes press releases and white papers.

Sprague Magnetics

http://www.earthlink.net/~sprague-magnetics/

Provides many repair services for computer hardware and audio equipment. Includes repair of hard drives, optical equipment, DAT tape machines, and

many more. Site includes technical support, services offered, and contact information.

SRA International, Inc.

http://www.sra.com/

Specializes in communications solutions and consulting for the health care industry, media, and legal fields. Provides system design, custom software, network management, and much more. Includes a search index of services provided and products offered.

Storage Computer Corp. Presents

http://www.storage.com/

Manufacturer and installer of fault-tolerant storage solutions for use in client/server, online transaction processing (OLTP), large database, multimedia, and imaging applications. This Web site has so many news items, product and language links, and platform and contact links that you're not sure where to click.

Storage Systems Solutions

http://www.ell.com/

Provides custom storage system creation, client/server propriertary server, and Web site development services and products. Includes product features, services offered, and contact information.

Sun Microsystems

http://www.sun.com/

The home page from the creators of the new Java Web language is a must see for Web fanatics. Click on their Search icon to access Java information quickly, or to find info on specific topics. The monthly e-zine SunWorld Online provides a wealth of information about Web servers, diagnostic software, and recent Net information.

Sybex

http://www.sybex.com/

Produces a large catalog of tutorial, reference, handbook, and network products. Includes software, books, and manuals. Provides online catalog, contact, and ordering information.

Sylvest Management Systems

http://www.sylvest.com/

Provides a wide range of products and services for companies networking, connectivity, and system problems. Includes comapany profile, technical partnership, product background, and services offered. Also includes client listings and contact information.

Synapse Communications, Inc.

http://www.synapse.com/

Produces WinTwin and WinAPPC connectivity products. Includes technical specifications, company history, and contact information.

Synergetic Resource Corporation

http://www.synernet-indy.com/src/

Provides a wide range of services and products including hardware consulting and support, Web site design, corporate Internet access services, and much more. Includes client listings, company profile, and contact information.

Systems Solutions

http://www.syspac.com/

Designs and produces business solutions software, hardware, and applications. Provides custom system design and consulting services. Includes listing of services and products developed. Also includes detailed company profile and contact information.

TechWorks

http://www.techwrks.com/

Produces add-on performance products for PCs, workstations, and laser printers. Includes information about add-on memory, acceleration devices, and other products. Includes reseller listings, technical support, and contact and ordering information.

Tecnation Digital World

http://www.tecnation.com/

Develops a wide range of technologies and products. Includes information about the AMX Pagemaker, BitBOPPER audio and visual effects products, and the Artwalker project (an online art gallery). Provides a detailed company background and profile.

Texas Micro Home Page

http://www.texmicro.com

Manufacturer of rack mount, mobile, and benchtop PCs for use in industrial applications. See what it takes to make a PC virtually bulletproof, read about their latest systems, or order a free catalog. You can also contact customer service and technical support.

TradeNet International, Inc.

http://goldray.com/used_computers/index.sht

Used PC exporter and broker. Check their inventory or find out more about Annapolis, MD—their hometown.

Turbosales

http://www.turbosales.com/~turbos/info/index.html

Provides Web site design and marketing services along with Turbosales custom software packages. Services offered include site development, advertising, and page management. Includes information about Turbosales specialized software.

Twenty Twenty

http://netsurf.net/2020/

Produces communications solutions for companies using a wide range of technologies, systems, and services. Includes company philosophies and communications background. Also includes contact information.

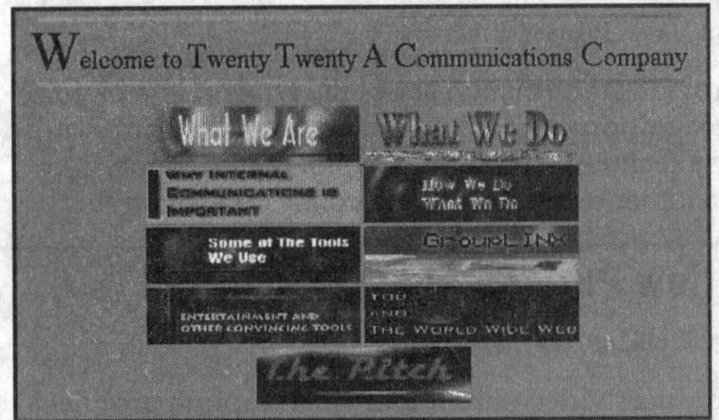

Unicomp, Inc.

http://www.fortran.com/fortran/unicomp.html

Provides a wide range of Fortran services. Includes testing, training, and other services especially for Fortran 90. Also supplies information about The Fortran Journal.

UniPress Worldwide

http://www.unipress.com/w3/

Produces UniPress software for Web publishing and site maintenence. Also provides WWW site services including page development, training, and consultation. Includes detailed listing of services and products offered along with technical and client references.

VA Research, Inc.

`http://www.varesearch.com/`

Produces PC components and other products for Linux configuration needs. Includes information about the VA Linux System catalog, ordering details, and links to Linux sites on the Web.

Validity Corporation

`http://www.primenet.com/~valcorp/`

Provides custom system, network, and software design and engineering services. Also provides consulting, training, and systems testing services. Includes information about Department of Defense systems Validity supports. Also includes client links and contact information.

Vive Synergies, Inc.

`http://www.vive.com/`

Produces automated call back and call routing devices and systems. Includes informaton about the AutoConnect and AutoRoute lines. Provides product details, reviews, downloadable overview, and contact information.

Voice Recognition Systems

`http://www.iglou.com/vrsky/`

Provides information about the Dragon line of voice recognition systems. Includes system and application technical specifics, downloadable demos, customer testimonials, and contact information.

Willow Peripherals

`http://willow.com/peripherals/`

Produces video output and video capture products. Includes information about the VGA-CTV graphics controller and the VGA-TV video output graphics card. Includes company profile, links to resource sites, and contact information.

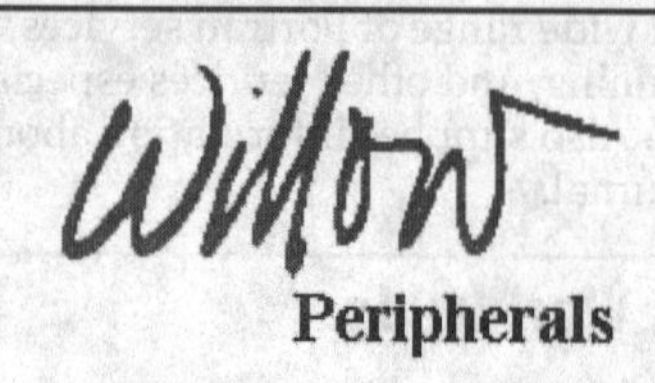

Wordlink, Inc.

`http://www.wordlink.com/`

Provides custom business information software solutions, application, and network integration services. Also provides Web site design and training services. Includes company profile, detailed service background, and contact information.

XPRO Systems

`http://www.conres.com/xtop.htm`

PC clone manufacturer for business environments. Find out about their rack mount, notebook, and desktop Pentium systems.

Computer Science

Argonne National Laboratory: Mathematics and Computer Science Division

`http://www.mcs.anl.gov/`

Scaleable parallel computing, high-performance I-WAY networks, and High-Performance Computing and Music research are currently under way at this federally funded institute. Another fascinating research project is the CAVE, a ten-foot cube that provides a stereo optical, real time, virtual environment. Check out how this works!

Computer Oriented Abbreviations and Acronyms

`http://www.access.digex.net/~ikind/babel95b.html`

A lengthy glossary of computer-oriented abbreviations and acronyms, updated three times a year (January, May, and September). This page takes a while to load because of its length, but its thoroughness is worth a bookmark or a printout.

Cornell Theory Center

`http://www.tc.cornell.edu`

One of four supercomputing centers funded by the National Science Foundation. This center experiments with powerful parallel processing structures in a number of disciplines, including aerospace engineering, economics, epidemology, physics, and visualization.

Cray Research

`http://www.cray.com/`

If you think your desktop Pentium is powerful, check out Cray's latest desktop systems, some of which are wireless.

CS-100 The History of Computing

http://calypso.cs.uregina.ca/Lecture/

A detailed discussion of the history of computing presented in a slide show format. Find out about Charles Babbage's infamous "Difference Engine," Blaise Pascal's revolutionary "Pascaline," ENIAC, and the Altair computer. A thorough and well-designed trip through computing history.

Historic Computer Images

http://ftp.arl.mil/ftp/historic-computers/

Download large GIF photos of famous, early computers, such as the ENIAC, EDVAC, ORDVAC—a fascinating Web site.

IEEE Communications Society Technical Committee on Gigabit Networking

http://info.gte.com/ieee-tcgn

Lists upcoming Gigabit Workshops and IEEE white papers and reports on gigabit computing. Includes links to other gigabit networking projects, researchers, and sites.

Intelligent Systems Integration Program

http://www.augusta.co.uk/isip

Joint initiative by the Department of Trade and Industry (DTI) and the Engineering and Physical Sciences Research Council (EPSRC) to encourage the use of intelligent systems in UK business. This site describes the technology transfer clubs, special interest groups, demonstration projects, and latest news of the ISIP program, which strives to incorporate these pattern-recognition agents in standard software development toolkits.

The Innovation Network

http://innovate.si.edu/

Founders of the Computerworld Smithsonian Awards, which have honored individuals who creatively used information technology (also known as IT) to improve humanity. Check out the Applications of Technology Information link and the Interviews link to find out how recent winners of this award used IT in their projects.

List of the World's Most Powerful Computing Sites

http://www.mordor,com/gunter/

This spartan site provides links to the fastest computers on the planet. Be sure to check out the Supercomputer Pictures link to see what Intel Paragon, Cray, and Fujitsu supercomputers look like.

MetaCenter Computational Science Highlights

http://www.tc.cornell.edu/Research/MetaScience/

Provides information in the form of text, images, sound, and animations on more than 10,000 National Science Foundation research projects. All the sites listed on this Web page have used NSF facilities to conduct research. Download computer animations of Comet Shoemaker-Levy impacting Jupiter, theoretical 3D models of action inside the sun, and many more fascinating images.

MIT Artificial Intelligence Laboratory

http://www.ai.mit.edu/index.html

The MIT AI lab's research ranges from learning and vision and robotics to development of new computers. Check out the Our Research link to read about projects in Machine Vision, Robotic Touch, Virtual and Enhanced Reality, and SodaBot software agents.

NASA High Performance Computing and Communications

http://cesdis.gsfc.nasa.gov/hpccm/factsheets.html

This program works with American businesses and universities to accelerate the development of high-performance computing technologies for use in future NASA Earth and space missions. Find out what a teraflop is (a trillion floating point operations per second), and the size of a petabyte, which is equivalent to 2,300 years of digitized video!

North Carolina Supercomputing Center Homepage

http://www.ncsc.org/

Find out how NCSC promotes the use of supercomputing at North Carolina schools. Read about their new Cray "flyer" computer, and find out more about research being conducted with their equipment.

PARC Xerox Palo Alto Research Center

http://www.parc.xerox.com/

Find out more about the 25th anniversary of the computing center that invented laser printers, graphical user interfaces, ethernet technology, and Object Oriented Programming languages. Check out personal pages of PARC researchers and employees and find out about current projects, such as nano-technology and machine vision. A prerequisite for any true technophile is to download the map to PARC's campus.

Smithsonian Computer History

http://www.si.edu/perspect/comphist/computer.htm

Take an online tour of this recent Smithsonian exhibit, which includes the original ENIAC computer, WWII German ENIGMA encryption devices, and high definition TV. Download a slide show of the exhibit, and read what famous scientists, such as Robert Ballard and Seymour Cray, have to say about the age of information.

Software Tools for Logistics Problem Solving

http://primal.iems.nwu.edu/~levi/tools.html

Group of researchers and students who develop software for supply chain/logistics/vehicle routing applications using geographic information systems (GIS). If you like puzzles or demo software and you're running Netscape 2.0 in Windows 95 or Unix, click on the Software Demonstration button for an example of their software. Cool maps!

Spectral Research Technologies

http://www.tenn.com/srt/srt.html

Provides research and produces SPECTRA6 quantitative analysis systems. SPECTRA6 is utilized in data analysis of radiation from stellar sources and related thermodynamic properties. Includes contact information.

Welcome to The Computer Museum

http://www.net.org/

The largest computer museum in the U.S., based in Boston, Massachusetts, continually updates and expands this Web address with information on new exhibits, museum clubs for adults and kids, upcoming events, and behind the scenes of their most popular exhibits.

Consultants

123 Consulting

http://www.webplaza.com/pages/Computers/123Consulting/123Consulting.html

Offers consulting, application conversions, and training services. This site includes Windows NT Server Setup and training in Seattle, Washington and Windows 95 Setup and Training in San Jose, Califor-

nia and Seattle. Site also provides numerous links to many search engines on the Net.

ActionCall Help Desk Service

http://www.actioncall.com

Provides a calling card that you can use 24 hours a day-seven days a week to call for computer help. Page provides different packages, including the Action Call Gold Card.

AHK & Associates

http://www.value.net/ahk/html/

Provides a complete list of services, products, and support to be used with ISDN products. Site includes a full equipment catalog, consulting services, Internet accessing with ISDN, and Web site of interest to ISDN subscribers.

AIT

http://access.digex.net/~solson/

Provides consulting on Oracle CASE (Versions 5.0 and 5.1), Oracle DBA (Versions 6 and 7), troubleshooting, and project management. Also provides Web site development and interactive database creation.

Amadeus Consulting

http://www.wolfgang.com/

Develops 32-bit, object-oriented applications. Amadeus also designs internets and firewalls. Provides listings of software, Web services, company background, their clients, development information, and listings of public Internet introductions.

Apple Support

http://www.support.info.apple.com/

If your Mac is sick, go to the source for a quick solution to any Mac problem. Technical support provides a number of ways to get help, including FAQs, e-mail access, and a troubleshooting index.

Bennett Products—Computer Sales/Networking/Consulting/Internet

http://www.bennettpro.com

Provides computer sales, consulting, networking, and Internet access and support. Their ftp site provides a small collection of the best shareware and freeware available.

Cambridge Technology Partners

`http://www.ctp.com/`

Installs, implements, and integrates business computing systems. Specializes in working on fast and tight time frames. Includes company profile, lengthy service listings, and representative work with clients. Also provides consulting and investment information.

Cascade Consulting

`http://www.omix.com/sites/cascade/home.html`

Provides software project consulting and evaluating with a set of goals listed in the site. Includes company background and services provided.

CCI Consulting

`http://cciworld.com/ccieng.html`

Provides Internet consulting and services including animation, Web site design, and bulletin board setup. Includes company background and services offered by CCI Consulting.

Clara Vista Corporation

`http://www.fiesta.com/CVista/`

Consults, creates, and supports businesses in the creation and maintence of World Wide Web pages and a home site. Provides ample company background with full listings of services offered. Includes links to sites created by Clara Vista.

Commonwealth Data Systems, Inc.

`http://www.mnsinc.com/bradshaw/cds_inc1.html`

Provides consultation specializing in customized software development in various system languages including DELPHI, C++, Pascal, and many more. Services include development and integration for Windows, LAN, and TurnKey systems. Includes example work done for OSHA.

Communicopia Environmental Research and Communications

`http://communicopia.bc.ca/`

Provides Internet and media consulting services to environmental and natural resource based companies and government agencies. Services include Web page, communications, system, and database design and development.

CompAdept Corporation

`http://www.compadept.com/`

Personal computer and network consulting company.

Comport Consulting Corporation

`http://www.comport.com/`

Provides consulting, technical support, and sales for Digital Equipment products. Also provides software applications in warehousing distribution. Includes company profile and product specifications with current news on each.

Compusult Limited

`http://www.compusult.nf.ca/`

Provides computer consulting services and custom computer products for the the scientific and technical areas for businesses and government agencies. Includes listing of services offered and specialized software systems. Also includes information about Applications for Rural Communites (ARC) and Compusult Integrated Data Access Systems (CIDAS) specialized software.

Computer Power Group

`http://www.cpsg.com.au/cpg/welcome.html`

Provides computer systems consulting and training for Australia and the Asian Basin. Includes full service listings, group profile, press releases, and contact information. Also includes stock reports and investment information.

Fellowship Programs

`http://www.nas.edu/fo/index.html`

The Fellowship Office of the National Research Council offers guidelines and application materials for predoctoral, dissertation, and postdoctoral fellowships.

Computerized Data Management

`http://www1.minn.net/~cdm`

Offers training and support for the home user and small business owner in the St. Paul and Minneapolis areas.

ComputerPeople/Dci

`http://www.computerppl.com/`

Provides consulting for custom designed software and systems. Includes company profile and listing of services offered. Includes contact information and career opportunities listings with Dci.

CooperSoft

`http://www.getnet.com/~joeco/`

Specializes in custom software applications, Web site design, and network creation. Includes links to pages CooperSoft created and search engines. Provides contact information.

CoreLAN Communications, Inc.

`http://www.corelan.com/`

Provides consultation services and products specializing in network communications, database systems, and Internet access integration. Includes client and technological partners links. Also includes full service listings and corporate profile.

CP Systems

`http://204.249.266.117;80/cps/`

Provides consulting and development of custom software packages and applications. Includes services offered listings and contact information. Also includes examples of WWW sites that CP systems consulted with and helped design.

CSI.NET, Inc.

`http://www.csi.net/`

Provides and produces network and Internet consulting along with custom designed applications and software. Includes consultation information on firewalls, ISDN services, Internet access, connectivity issues, and specialized applications creation. Also includes company profile and contact information.

Daedalus Design Group

`http://www.ime.net/~ddg/`

Provides consulting and services dealing with Internet development, mulitmedia design, and graphics. Includes service listings, company portfolio, and contact information. Interesting note is "Top 10 Web Design DOs and DON'Ts" that is quite informative.

Dokken Consulting, Inc.

`http://imt.net/~dokken/`

Provides consulting software development, relational database creation, and Internet relations. Specializes in object oriented software, graphical user intefaces, and databases. Includes listing of services offered, technologies utilized, and clients. Also includes company profile and contact information.

Dowdell Business Services

`http://www.dowdell.com`

Consultant for Windows NT/Novell real-time database interfaces. Check out the link to the atomic clock in Boulder, Colorado.

Durango Computer Classroom

`http://animas.frontier.net/~mkatz/`

Provides computer consulting and training services. Specializes in software design and group applications training. Includes courses listings, company news, and hiring opportunities.

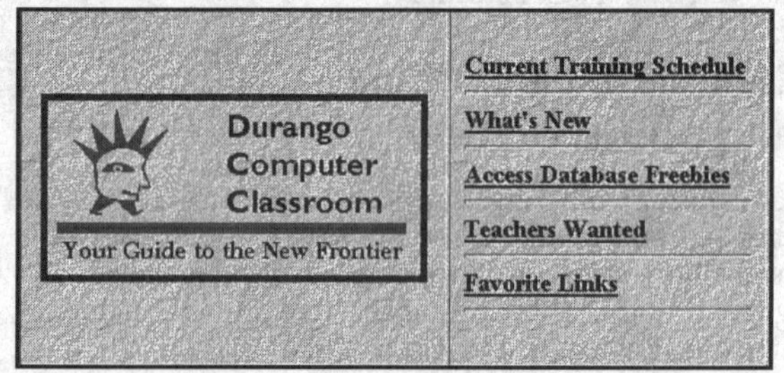

Eccosys, Ltd.

`http://www.eccosys.com/ECCOSYS/es.html`

Provides and produces Internet consulting, custom Internet software development, and systems integration services. Includes service listings, current projects, and contact information. Also includes career opportunities.

EPMOD Consultants, Inc.

`http://www.ibp.com/pit/epmod/`

Provides business consulting using "the EPMOD Concept" a methodology for improvement of information system and resource management. Includes contact information.

ESDX

`http://www.esdx.org/esdhome.html`

Provides a home site for ESDX, a nonprofit management information technology association for companies specializing in health, enviromental, and safety. Includes association news, abstracts, members, and cases featured. Also includes links to member companies and a search index.

The FIEN Group

`http://www.fiengroup.com/`

Provides consulting on a wide range of computer system needs. Consulting services include client/server application development, WWW publishing, Folio Views Infobase Technology uses, and much more. Provides technical partner listings, links to sites created, and contact information.

Fly-By-Day Consulting

`http://www.mindspring.com/~cavu`

Provides software consulting services in C and Unix, specializing in communications and porting. Also offers many aviation links, including current weather observations and forecasts.

Folio Corporation

`http://www.folio.com/`

Provides for the professional user links to download Folio's award winning Web retriever, access to their computer products buyer's guide, educational services, intranet seminars, and an application for their beta test program.

For-to-Win

`http://weber.ucsd.edu/~rtrippi/for2win2.htm`

Company to rewrite and convert your DOS/Fortran programs to make them compatible with Win 3.1/Win95. Provides link to download a financial engineering demo written in Fortran 90 and converted to Win 3.1 or Win95. Consultants possess over 20 years of experience.

Full Spectrum Communications

`http://www.fsc.com/fsc/`

Provides professional consulting and educational services in networking. Can fine tune an existing network or design from the ground up. Provides links to complete profiles of consulting and educational services and well as information on their more popular classes: internetworking on the Internet and design optimization of networks.

Galaxy Systems, Inc.

`http://www.interport.net/galaxy/`

An employment site for computer consultants. Provides links and descriptions to consulting positions, some permanent, as well as the Galaxy Office and staff. Send your resume.

Garbee and Garbee

`http://www.gag.com/`

This is the personal home page of Bdale and Karen Garbee who do pro bono consulting particularly for Amateur Radio and Amateur Satellite Services. Provides links to their current undertakings.

Genoa Technology

`http://www.gentech.com`

Genoa Technology will design and develop test solutions for manufacturers of computer printers and facsimile devices to assure interoperability. Links are provided to testing services, products, training classes, publications, and so forth.

Georg Heeg

`http://www.heeg.de/english/Welcome.html (English page)`

Distributes products and services in object-oriented methodologies. Links to new products such as VisualWave as well as object databases, development environments, services, and training courses offered. Employment opportunities also listed.

GlobalNET

`http://www.globalus.com/global3.html`

An Internet consultant who can recommend the best connection for your business, the best access provider and arrange for a server to fit your needs. Will design your Web site and get your business up and running on the Internet.

Godin London Incorporated

http://www.godin.com/godin/

Providing computer applications for your company's information management needs. Provides business management for a variety of companies including travel agents, bookstores, and restaurants. Check out their current software applications.

GroupWise Information

htt://www.dws.net/groupwise.html

Will get your company up and running with e-mail with MailWise and GroupWise—the hassle-free, secure way to send business e-mail. Provides links to other consulting services, descriptions and downloading/ordering info for products, and other interesting links to sofware and computer user groups.

GulfNet Technologies

http://199.44.46.2/

A small business in Perry, Florida offering several computer-related services to businesses and individuals such as Accounting Systems, Internet Access, Desktop Computer Systems, and Networks.

Guru Technologies, Inc.

http://www.gurutech.com/

Develop hardware and software solutions for semiconductor, networking, and graphics systems companies. Provide tech support and productivity enhancement. Provides links to clients, courses, professional associations, and company information.

Halo Network Management

http://www.commerce.com/halonet/

Will install a new network or upgrade your existing one. Primarily in the New York and New Jersey area. Will develop the best system for your needs. Provides links to Halo Test Center, Training, Novell, and Artisoft information, as well as contact information.

HD Industries

http://www.Infoservice.com/HDIndustries/

Consulting firm based in Sacramento, California for the Macintosh user, database solutions written in 4th Dimension or Panorama. Current consulting projects include sports teams off the coast of Africa and recreation districts in California.

Hartford Computer Group

http://www.awa.com/hartford/

Sells, services, and leases a full line of computers, peripherals, and equipment from manufacturers such as Apple, IBM, Compaq, NEC, AST, and Texas Instruments. Offers free technical support, fast delivery, warranties, and more.

Hieroglyphics

http://www.webcom.com/~hiero/welcome.html

Web Consultants offering Internet/Intranet, Graphic Design, Multimedia, Catalog and Newsletter design, and much more for your business. Provides links to clients' pages, services, pricing, Java, plug-ins, animation, and other groovy sites.

hot-n-GUI

http://www.hotngui.com/

A large application cross-platform developer. Links to their consulting services, add ons (commerical and freeware), and other useful pages.

HTA Link

http://www.swcp.com/htalink/

Network consulting firm that provides on-site network design, installation, and servicing.

Ian Freed Consulting, Inc.

http://www.ifc.com/

Telecommunications and computer consulting for your business or organization. Provides links to company profile, projects, clients, lab, and employment opportunitites.

IC Group, Inc.

http://pobox.com/icg/fromyahoo.html

Basic and extended WWW services, e-mail, and technical and future oriented consulting for your business or organization. Provides links to clients, projects, and other information.

Inacom Corp.

http://www.inacom.com/

Helping your business utilize the full capacity of information technology. Inacom offers your company desktop management, LAN design, training, consulting, and much more. Provides access to company profile, tech links, and what Inacom can do for you.

Index

http://www.telematrix.com/

The International Telecom Center is for anyone, business or individual, who would like to advertise their goods and services on the Internet. Browse the store or check out their advertising and consulting services.

Information Builders, Inc

http://www.ibi.com

Home page for this large, multinational computer consulting firm and software developer for client/server environments. Uses FOCUS EDA/SQL, and LEVEL5 in their work.

Ingres Consultant

http://www.cris.com/~Sb/cv.html

Personal résumé of Shaun Bliss who lists himself as a database consultant specializing in application and design in the client-server Internet environment. Will design Web pages or administer your Web site. Includes a long list of skills.

Integrated Systems Solutions Corporation

http://www.issc.ibm.com/

An IBM subsidiary that helps its business customers manage their information technology more efficiently or develop new services. Links to services, publications, and career and contact information.

InterComp Internet, Unix, and World Wide Web Services

http://www.panix.com/~tab/intercomp/

A custom programming, training, and consulting firm for your business. Links to services, company background, and experience.

IPC Technologies, Inc. on the World Wide Web

http://www.iptechinc.com/

Consulting firm for client/server networks that is based in Richmond, Virginia. Take advantage of their link to a list of computer companies on the Web, or check out their job listings.

J P Mclaughlin & Associates, Inc.

http://www.jpmac.com/JPMA_Frame.html

A firm to manage your information technologies. Personal solutions to help your company become more productive. Provides planning and information management, security and anti-virus systems, and technology integration and design using a variety of tools.

Jackson-Reed, Inc.

http://www.halcyon.com/prreed/jackreed.html

Educational and consulting services to support the computing environment. On site courses offered. Some client/server products offered are Microsoft/SQL server, Oracle, Java, Unix, and more.

Jewell, Chris

http://www.wco.com/~jewellcj/

The personal home page of Chris Jewell with a link to Jewell Consulting, which provides software solutions for businesses. Uses object-oriented technology and familiar with AS/400 systems.

JimWare, Inc.

http://www.prairienet.org/~jdpierce/homepage.html

Tool and utilities for OS/400 and VM used by system professionals. Links to JimWare, product catalog and ordering, other interesting links, and search engines.

JM Consulting and Cheap Advice

http://pages.prodigy.com/IL/jomoor/

A brief home page with a link to the consulting page and information about "what JM Consulting knows." Will, answer your PC questions or questions about Chicago restaurants!

Keystone Technology

http://www.keytech.com/

Oklahoma City company providing Internet access, Web services, and any computer related solutions your business requires. Mac, Intel, LAN, WAN, networking, telephony, and many more solutions.

Kitchen Wisdom Publishing

http://www.wiskit.com/

Kitchen Wisdom, a one-time publisher of cookbooks, now offers software development and consulting based on their own problems with desktop publishing. Provides consulting for Unix, Internet connections, and will run a free custom network diagnosis on your system.

Kratzer Computer Consultants

http://www.greatbasin.net/~kratzer/kratz.htm

Provides links to get help with minor and even disaster-level problems you may have with your home or business computer system.

Lavallée & Associates

http://www.io.org/~lcl/lassoc.html

Company specializing in Web and Internet applications, business re-engineering, systems analysis, project management, and more. Contact them for your consulting needs.

Lodestone Research, L.L.C.

http://www.aescon.com/lodeston/index.htm

Qualitative and quantitative research skills for the high tech industry, helping to develop usable hardware and software products. Look through their survey and market research, client references, and more.

MacMedic

http://www.pacificrim.net/~macmedic/

Networking solutions, hardware and software troubleshooting, hardware repair, telecommunications, training, and phone support for the Mac user.

MBS Industries, Inc.

http://www.mbsii.com/mbs/

For your internet presence needs, training, consulting, software, and Web page development.

MC2 Cyberspace Research

http://www.mc2-csr.com/

A virtual marketing and consulting firm for all your company's Internet needs. Links to their services, customers, upcoming events, other links of interest, and more.

MediaGlobe

http://www.mediaglobe.com/

Company providing businesses the assistance needed to connect to and exploit the Internet. Check out their FTP Archive, product info and catalog, and services.

MetaCase Consulting

http://www.jsp.fi/metacase/

A software company specializing in system integration and modelling and object-oriented graphics. Their software features MedaEdit Personal, MetaEdit+, and MetaEdit+ Method Workbench. Access to product descriptions, press releases, ordering info, and more.

Mike Salitter Consultant Services

http://knet.flemingc.on.ca/~msalitte/mscs.html

Network consulting and troubleshooting for many environments including Windows, Novell Netware, Windows for Workgroups, Unix, and others, plus many platforms and languages.

The Millennium Solution

http://www.prairienet.org/~dwcollin/millen.html

Sells the Millennium Solution package, which is a checklist of tasks IS managers can perform to avoid the year 2000 crisis, when computers based on two digit year systems will reset. Read about the potential cost of this imminent problem.

Minerva Technology

http://www.minerva.ca/

Client/server consulting firm with links to services, jobs, awards and news, company, and contact information.

MultiMedia Enterprises

http://www.world-wide.com/multimedia/

Personal Web page of Mike Jenkins, consultant. He will develop a Web presence for businesses or individuals. Check out his résumé.

MVS Training, Inc.

http://www.pittsburgh.net/MVS/

A training provider for individuals who work with mainframe computers, midrange, and PC computers. Will also deliver basic writing and speaking skill training. Check out their long list of training offerings and client testimonials.

Mystech Enterprises

http://www.primenet.com/~valenti/index.html

A company providing client/server solutions as well as custom photography (because of the owner's hobby). Links to current consulting projects and software solutions—and recent photographs from Yosemite Park.

Netplan ApS. Consultants in Telecommunications

http://www.netplan.dk/netplan/enetp1.htm

Danish telecommunications and computing consulting firm with an English language Web page. This site provides a few links that describe Netplan's services. Descriptions are nicely done although a few translation mistakes occur. Can you find them?

Pangea Visions

http://www.fortnet.org/~pangea/index.html

Provides Web site consulting, advertising, home site design, and database creation. Includes services offered, company profile, resourses utilized, and links to Web sites created. Also includes WWW use statistics and facts.

Phoenix Systems Internet Publishing

http://www.biddeford.com/phoenix/

Provides a wide array of Internet services including consulting, publishing, Web site creation, Internet research, and systems installation. Includes client listings, technical archive, and services offered.

PLATINUM Solutions

http://www.platsol.com/

A company dedicated to creating "Customer Based Solutions" via education, consulting, task insourcing services, and integration. Their core services include information and systems management, applications solutions, and education services.

PRC Inc. Home Page

http://www.prc.com/

Unusually plain home page for a huge government contractor that provides computer system integration, software development, facilities management, and energy-related engineering services. Find out about PRC's corporate culture and strategy, and learn more about recent work.

ProSoft Consulting

http://www.c2.org/~prosoft/index.shtml#Consulting

New York City area computer consultants specializing in Web page design, remote technical support, and network setup consultants.

Relational Information Systems, Inc.

http://wl.iglou.com/ris/

Provides consulting and custom software development services. Specializes in Unix-based, database management systems. Includes information about CA-INGRES and CA-UNICENTER products. Also includes contact information.

SAIC Los Altos Home Page

http://www.saic.com/

Employee owned research and development company based in San Diego that specializes in energy, environment, information technology, health care, telecommunications, and transportation. Click on an industry of interest (telecommunications, for example) to read about SAIC services or to learn more about recent client work.

Software Dynamics Consulting

http://www.sdcnet.com/

Provides Oracle and Microsoft consultation services. Specializes in software, project management, and methods development. Includes links to Midwest Oracle Users Group Papers and contact information.

Specs™ Manufacturing Instructions

http://www.sonic.net/~richw/zip.html

Provides consulting services and products for companies utilizing MS-DOS and especially Paradox based systems. Includes information about custom database set-up and advantages. Also includes technical specifications and background of work done.

Spire Technologies

http://www.spiretech.com/

Provides a wide range of consulting and other services. Includes Web site design, AutoCAD design, Internet provisions, and connectivity solutions. Includes products and services offered listings along with links to client sites.

Sterling Information Group

http://www.sterinfo.com

Software and management consultants, and custom software developers based in Austin, Texas. This simple site discusses Sterling services.

STS

http://www.alaska.net/~lafferty/sts.html

Provides home site for STS (Scientific Technical Services), which provides system consultation and custom programming services. Includes company profile and contact information.

Technology Futures, Inc.

http://www.tfi.com/

Provides corporate computer consulting and reporting services. Includes listing of clients, reports made, seminars offered, and publications created. Provides contact information.

TeKnowlogy Education Centers

http://www.teknowlogy.com/

Provides training, education, and testing services on many different computer systems, languages, and applications. Includes course dates, classes offered, and services provided. Also includes business partners, company profile, and contact information.

Telecommunications Technology Corp.

http://www.teltechinc.com/

Provides computer system consulting services and products to the banking, transportation, and manufacturing industries. Includes information about systems development, database management, and custom software applications design. Provides listing of clients served and contact information.

The Whole Shebang

http://www.shebang.com/

Provides database, a WWW site, integration consulting, and services. Includes client and services offered listings. Also includes information about WWW development software used in formatting, writing, and production.

Winsor Computing

http://www1.usa1.com/~dwinsor

Provides consulting and programming services for custom software, CD-ROM, multimedia, and graphic design production. Specializes in the use of C++, Pascal, and BASIC. Includes company profile, related links, and contact information.

Word Master, Inc.

http://www.interaccess.com/wmi/wm/

Provides consulting and custom systems design services. Specializes in OMNIS consulting and custom applications development. Also includes Web page design services.

Xephon

http://www.xephon.co.uk/

Provides consultation, information, and products about IBM compatible enterprise systems. Includes listings of Xephon publications, services, and information about IBEX mainframes. Also includes contact information and links to other enterprise system sites.

Desktop Publishing

Adobe PageMaker

http://w1000.mv.us.adobe.com/Apps/PageMaker/

Learn about PageMaker's latest enhancements, and download sample PDF and technical notes. The FTP link from this site lets you access new filters and clip art for use in PageMaker documents.

DTP Internet Jumplist

http://www.cs.purdue.edu/homes/gwp/dtp/dtp.html

Well-organized and popular with graphic designers and page layout specialists, this site may be the easiest way to find that freeware texture or public domain photo you heard was on the Net. The Topic Search List included on this page is organized by category; click on QuarkXPress, for example, to access hot links to mailing lists, Usenet groups, Web sites, and ftp sites. A well-designed site that is a must-see for desktop publishers.

ECS Custom Personalized Scalable Truetype Fonts

http://www.ahoynet.com/business/imart/ecs_home.html

Convert your signature or a company logo into scalable TrueType fonts using ECS font technology. Download samples for Windows 3.1 and newer versions.

A First Guide to PostScript

http://www.cs.indiana.edu/docproject/programming/
postscript/postscript.html

An excellent site for desktop publishers and programmers who want to learn more about the PostScript language. If you have been using PostScript for years and still aren't sure how it works, or if you want to learn more about the language, check out this site. Includes topics on graphics, transformations in PostScript, and more. Check out the Funky Stuff link for info on modifying the printout of a document.

Free Software from Adobe

http://w1000.mv.us.adobe.com/Software.html

A treasure trove of patches, updates, plug-ins, drivers, and printer software for Adobe software products. Check out this site for the latest updates to Photoshop, Acrobat, Premiere and other products. This site is invaluable for graphic designers and typographers.

Freedom System Integrators, Inc.

http://southwind.net/fsi/

Provides products, brochures, and tools for desktop publishers and newspaper publishing. Provides links to other desktop publishing pages and college newspapers. Also provides a key word search engine.

i am Iomega

http://www.iomega.com/

Fun site from the manufacturer of the ZipDisk, a removable diskette that is popular with graphic designers and page layout staff. Although your only choices are Cool Products, Tech Stuff, and New Stuff, you can still find out about Iomega's products, access tech support, and read all the news that's fit to print.

Imagine Adobe

http://www.adobe.com/

Download a free copy of Adobe Acrobat or check to see if a patch or update is available for Photoshop or any other Adobe product. The Customer Spotlights page includes articles detailing how Adobe products are used by various companies—a great way to get ideas for your next project.

INFOSEARCH PrintNet

http://www.xmission.com/~insearch/printnet.html

A vast repository of links and information for graphic designers, computer users, and advertising agencies. If you cannot find exactly what you need in their categorical index of hundreds of hardware and software links, use the built in Lycos WebCrawler search engine.

MacroMedia Fontographer

http://www.macromedia.com/Tools/Fontographer/

The leading font program for the Mac and PC includes a Web site featuring product updates and free downloadable PostScript and TrueType fonts created by Fontographer designers. This site also includes the usual product support links and new features information.

New World Graphics and Publishing

http://www.nwgraphics.com/

Sit back and pop a cold one while this image-heavy page crawls across the Web. Puts small businesses on the WWW in Spanish and English. Find out how much this service costs, and what other clients have signed up.

Newspaper Production Using PageMaker 5

http://www.cs.purdue.edu/homes/gwp/dtp/topic_sw.html

This page from the Worsley Press includes articles important to newspaper publishers, such as half black/half white headings, using grids, and eliminating ugly quotes. Each newsletter sent out to Worsley's customers is included at this site.

Quark, Inc.

http://www.quark.com/

Creates desktop publishing, graphics, and multimedia software applications tools. Includes information about the QuarkImmedia graphics viewer, QuarkXpress publishing software, and other applications. Includes technical specifications, links to related sites, product reviews, and contact information.

Serif, Inc.

http://www.serif.com/

Produces desktop publishing and graphics software and products. Includes a company profile and infomation about PagesPlus, ArtPacks, and DesignerPage software. Provides product features, reviews, and technical specifications.

So Cal Graphics

http://turnpike.net/emporium/S/socal/index.html

Provides desktop publishing services and products. Includes services such as design, production, scanning, and product lists. Also includes links to other graphic sites and contact information.

A Tomato Foundry Technical Writing and Design

http://www.iquest.net/tomato

This technical writing, document design, and page layout firm provides a colorful home page with free, downloadable textures, images, and unique fonts created at the foundry. If you grew up in the eighties, check out the Rotten Tomato link for a laugh; graphic designers can get ideas from the Early Girl Gallery.

The Xpresso Bar

http://www.halcyon.com/bobgale/xpresso.html

A fun and helpful site packed with Quark Xtensions, FAQs, and Quark-to-HTML converters. Check out the Easter Eggs link to learn about hidden Quark features and funny additions, such as the deleting Martian. The Interaction section is invaluable if you want to get an expert's opinion on a Quark problem you may be having.

What's New at Quark, Inc.'s Web Site

http://www.quark.com/

A straightforward company page featuring a helpful search engine for finding that elusive Xtension, a file library FTP link, a discussion group list, and even a phone directory for Quark's employees.

Adobe Illustrator What's New

http://w1000.mv.adobe.com/Apps/Illustrator/

An easy-to-use site that stresses updates to Adobe Illustrator for Macs and PCs. The Adding On link lists all the products Adobe supplies that enhance Illustrator artwork. The At Work link is invaluable if you use Illustrator for your work; it provides examples of Illustrator use by other professionals.

AnimaTek, Inc.

http://www.animatek.com/

Developers of 3D technologies, virtual environments, and artifical inhabitants. Provides information about 3DS BonesPro IPAS, AnimaTek's World Builder landscape editor, and other products. Also provides lists of development services and technologies for sale.

Anton's Freehand Page

http://www.euro.net/ecompany/afpindex.html

One of the best stops for everything Freehand. Besides the standard links to Usenet groups and mailing lists, this page includes links to Freehand demos and updates, bugs and problems FAQs, information on enhancing Freehand, and FAQs for fixing printing problems.

Artifice, Inc.

http://artifice.com/foyer.html

Creates tools, software, and media for enviroment designers. Provides company background, extensive product information, great buildings showcase, technical support, and press release library. Includes great detail about DesignWorkshop technical background and features.

AspenGrafix

http://www.AspenGrafix.com/

Develops Web site logos and custom company logos. Provides online portfolio with examples of work done for clients.

Astrobyte

http://www.astrobyte.com/

Producers of BeyondPress software that enables conversions from Xpress to HTML. Provides product overviews, reviews, links to sites using Astrobyte software, downloadable evaluation tools, and information on Japanese versions of their software. Includes links to reference and learning of HTML.

Autodesk Home Page

http://www.autodesk.com/

Information on AutoCAD, 3D Studio, and Animator—three of the most popular professional software packages in the world—can be found at this site. Also available are links to Autodesk job listings, user groups, and the latest products. This site is well-organized and downloads quickly.

Blue Sky Research

http://www.bluesky.com/

Produces Textures, LaTeX, TeX, and font software. Also produces technical manuals that go with their products. Provides technical support, company news, upgrade information, and relevant links such as CTAN, the "Comprehensive TeX Archive Network."

Cadkey Corp.

http://www.cadkey.com/

Produces CAD products including systems, hardware, and software. Includes lengthy product descriptions, company history, technical support, press releases, features in trade magazines, and online order forms. The product and company backgrounds are extensive and informative.

CadSoft Computer GmbH

http://www.CadSoft.DE/

Provides information about CadSoft's EAGLE software, which allows you to design printed circuit boards. Provides the usual technical support and online product descriptions, but also includes an exhaustive world-wide list of distributors, and a link for downloading updates, new drivers, and a free, fully functional demo version of EAGLE.

Caema Ltd.

http://www.sci.fi/~tsuomine/caema.htm

Produces MecDesign software applications for MicroDesign, MicroStation, and PowerDraft systems for use in the mechanical design and engingeering fields. Provides online demonstrations, product descriptions, technical support, developmental business partners, and tutorials.

CGD.Graphix

http://www.cgd.graphix.co.at/cgd/

Designs and produces graphics for multimedia productions, Web page creation, animation, and CD-ROM conceptions. Also provides training for mulitmedia applications. Includes lengthy list of work done and links to clients sites created.

CHRIS DICKMAN'S CorelNet

http://www.corelnet.com/

An online independent resource site for Corel users who need to find service bureaus or special Corel files, learn tips, or talk with authors. The site encourages you to visit the discussion groups first, which are organized by topic. CorelNet also sponsors live discussion events using Global Stage software.

Cimio CADCAM Conversion Software

http://www.cimio.co.uk/

Cimio's ConvertX CADCAM data exchange software enables you to freely exchange CADCAM data among AutoCAD (DWG and DXF rev 10-13), CADDS3, CADDS4X, CADDS5, CATIA V3, I/EMS, IDEAS drafting, Medusa (rev 5, 6, 7, 12), and Microstation environments.

Click 3x

http://www.click3x.com

Produces and provides full service computer graphics services including animation and interactive production. Includes studio equipment and staff listings. Also provides computer graphics created for many commercials and companies.

ComCom Systems, Inc

http://www.intbc.com/comcom/

Produces ELA Office and ELA Office Batch, Windows based OCR, and image database software. Office Batch eliminates the need to type and file forms; you simply scan in the forms and Office Batch reads them. ELA View and ELA Network are advanced document imaging systems that can handle tens of thousands of documents per day.

Tattoo

http://www.texnews.com/cowboys/reagan/tattoo.html

Make Mom proud with this free temporary tattoo. Just fill out the form and it's yours.

Computer Chrome Presentation Graphics

http://www.compchrome.com/

Provides and sells computer graphic services and products. Includes listings of the products and services offered with contact information.

Computer Graphics Systems Development Corporation (CGSD)

http://www.cgsd.com

Produces simulation and virtual reality products. Also produces a computer graphics industry newsletter Real Time. Provides consulting and specialized software design. Includes information about systems integrations research, visual stimulation real time systems, and other software products.

Corel's FTP Site

ftp://ftp.corel.ca/pub

An ftp site that includes every free patch, update, and enhancement for every version of CorelDraw. Also included are updates for using Kodak PhotoCD in CorelDraw and special filters.

Creative Eye

http://bensonassoc.com/bensonassoc/pct/pctres.html

Provides Web publishing and site design specializing in getting small to medium sized business on the World Wide Web. Includes listing of services offered, client listings, and portfolio of sites created. Also includes contact information.

Creative Services

http://sec.dgsys.com/creative.html

Provides Web site design, graphic design, and server set up. Includes listing of services offered with a questionnaire to provide pricing. Includes portfolio of work accomplished with links to sites created.

CyberTec Commercial Art, Inc.

http://www.wln.com/~grafx/index.html

Provides full service computer and traditional graphics services. Includes Web site creation, brochures, t-shirts, and layout and design. Also includes company logo creation, four-color process separations, and camera ready artwork. Site provides full service listings, samples of work done, and contact information.

Cytopia Software Incorporated

http://www.cytopia.com/

Designs and produces graphics software and applications. Includes information about SocketSet, PhotoLab, and Image Xpress ScanPrepPro products. Includes technical specifications, downloadable samples, technical support, and an art portfolio. Also includes press releases and contact information.

DAIR Computer Systems Logo Design

http://www.vpm.com/dair/daircs.htm

Produces commercial logo designs, 3D graphics, and other related computer design work. Includes online portfolio and examples. Also includes graphic secrets, company awards, 3D links, and contact information.

Data Image Systems

http://bigweb.com/mall/don/index.html

Provides sales on graphics equipment and software. Includes product specifications and contact information. Also includes links to other graphics-related sites.

DesignSphere Online

http://www.dsphere.net/

Provides industry news and information on a number of topics that tie with computer graphics, multimedia design, lithography, and other visual forms. Includes links to online zines, career opportunities, graphics businesses, portfolios, and numerous tips.

Digio Media

`http://www.digio.com/`

Provides home site for Digio Media, a full service graphics firm based in Seattle, Washington. Includes links to clients and staff credentials. Also includes a performance lab with examples of work done.

Edifika

`http://ournet.clever.net/edifika/hp.html`

Produces graphics software, applications, and products that are used in architecture, Web design, and computer animation. Specializes in the use of OTVR virtual reality technologies from Apple. Includes services offered, work examples, and contact information.

EDS Unigraphics Division

`http://www.ug.eds.com/`

Produces the Unigraphics CAD/CAM/CAE System family of applications and products. Also provides a wide array of consulting and services with the creation of automation systems, training, and custom system design. Includes technical information, clients' success stories, and products under development news.

Electronic Design Automation Companies

`http://www.edac.org/`

Provides home site and information for the Electronic Design Automation industry. Includes publications directory, services, and listings with links to all member companies. Also includes resources information, job listings, and contacts.

Evans & Sutherland Computer Corporation

`http://www.es.com/`

Designs and produces real-time 3D graphics systems for simulation and virtual reality needs. Includes company product catalog, technical specifications, and examples of real-time movies along with other graphics. Provides contact information and links to related sites.

Fractal Design Corporation

`http://www.fractal.com/`

Download working demos of the award winning Fractal Design Painter or Dabbler—an easy to use Paint program—or learn more about new Fractal products, such as Poser. A must see is the Art Gallery, a collection of amazing artwork created with Fractal products.

The Graphics Gallery

`http://www.infi.net/~gallery/`

Experienced designers, artists, and technicians will take your business file or document and convert it to another format, create slides, develop advertising media—anything that can be done! Provides links to services, prices, new media, technical info, and so on.

Hamrick Software

`http://www.primenet.com/~hamrick/`

Check out VuePrint image viewer for Windows to print or download Internet images. Links to more product info, tech support, and "fun things to do."

ICE

`http://www.iced.com/`

High performance graphics—the Desktop RealTime Engine series— for GFLOPS throughput used by movie directors to engineers. Access to links about product information, application and development, and technical information.

IDEAL Scanners & Systems

`http://www.ideal.com/`

An imaging data management company for your business needs. Provides links to product information, training, AutoDesk software, CAD information, publications, and conferences.

InfoImaging Technologies Home Page

`http://www.infoimaging.com`

Makers of 3D Fax, considered by John Dvorak to be one of the most amazing software products of 1994. Download a free working demo of this unusual product, which enables you to send password-protected digital files from your PC's fax modem to any other fax-modem-equipped PC. Find out how this amazing product works by accessing the 3D Fax Product Information area.

Intergraph Corp

http://www.ingr.com/usa/index.html

Find out about Intergraph, a Huntsville, Alabama company, that makes high-end 3D drafting and design workstations and software. Learn more about their new TDZ multiple-Pentium Pro systems, which use Windows NT and the OpenGL standard for 3D graphics. To see what Intergraph systems are capable of, search for Golden Mouse in their search engine. Amazing!

Kai's Power Tips and Tricks for Adobe Photoshop

http://the-tech.mit.edu/kpt.html

The best jumping off point for Kai's Power Tool users. This site includes links to online galleries, tips and tricks for Kai's users, and newsletters full of Photoshop tips. The Background Gallery is a must-see for Web page designers.

Lightscape Technologies, Inc.

http://www.lightscape.com/

The Lightscape Visualization System is the "most powerful visualization application on the market today." View images, models, and see the possibilities for your graphics needs.

Limit X

http://dino.ccm.itesm.mx/AM3/pageengl.html

This is a page of graphics (jpg and gif files), specifically of VR-041 renders of a robot. If you have the capability, the legs actually move.

Live Picture, Inc.

http://www.livepicture.com/

For the high-end professional market, imaging software and technologies for designers, production specialists, photo labs, and photographers. Check out their new software, live picture network, other cool links, and more.

Lockheed Martin REAL 3D®

http://www.mmc.com/real3d/real3d.html

REAL 3D† commercial graphics and other real time graphics engines and simulations for your Internet

needs. Access to product descriptions, press releases, ordering information, trade shows, and more.

MacroMedia Freehand Page

http://www.macromedia.com/Tools/Freehand/index.html

Home page for the main competitor to Abode Illustrator. Check out the Macromedia's Gallery to see what Freehand designers have created with this powerful program.

Management Graphics, Inc. USA

http://www.mgi.com/

If you're in the digital color graphics industry, this site will provide quality printing and imaging solutions for you. Offers a complete line of film recorders and support as well as news, announcements, and links to other sites.

Marine Graphics, Inc.

http://nwlink.com/graphics/

"Virtual Relettering" for your boat. They will take the picture you send, scan it, and create a full size vinyl graphic that you can preview on the Internet in only a few days to see what it will look like on your boat. If you're in the Seattle area, they'll install it too. If you're not, they provide complete installation instructions.

MaxVision Online

http://www.maxvision.com/

CAD experts specializing in modeling, visualization, and CAD graphics on MaxVision Symbion Workstations. MaxVision will provide the support you need for your workstation, or do the work for you.

Mentor Graphics Corporation

http://www.mentorg.com/

Integrated system design products and services, including hardware and software design, education, and training. Check out their many benefits for your business.

Number Nine Visual Technologies

`http://www.nine.com/`

Graphic display solutions for personal computers, for the novice to the experienced user. Links to customer support, product information, and specifications.

Optix The Internet Document Management System

`http://www.blueridge.com`

Web site for Blueridge Technologies' Optix document management system. This page describes Optix features, such as COLD (Computer Output to Laser Disk) and OCR (Optical Character Recognition); permits you to access technical support, and includes links to imaging-related sites.

Pacific Animated Imaging

`http://www.pai-west.com`

Designs custom animated software products for clients. Check out their Custom Projects page and download MPEG or FLC videos of prior 3D animation work for clients.

Parallel Performance Group

`http://www.ppgsoft.com/ppgsoft/loox.html`

Produces the LOOXS interactive graphics development system and applications. Includes product features, advantages, and system requirements.

Parametric Technology Corporation

`http://www.ptc.com/`

Produces support software for the Pro/ENGINEER mechanical design system. Includes company profile, product specifications, consulting services offered, and investment background. Also includes resellers listings and contact information.

Pathtrace Systems

`http://mfginfo.com/cadcam/edgecam/pathtrace.htm`

Produces CAD/CAM-based manufacturing design software, applications, and products. Includes information about EdgeCam, EdgeMilling, and other related products. Provides technical specifications and contact information.

Pattern Corporation

`http://www.panix.com/pattern/`

Provides a wide range of multimedia design services. Includes examples of works done, resources utilized, and contact information. Also includes links to many related sites.

Paul Mace Software

`http://www.pmace.com/`

Designs and produces Expo (GRASP) animation graphics systems along with other related products. Includes technical support, pricing, downloadable demos, online Expo demonstration, and contact information.

Performing Graphics Company

`http://www.pgc.com/`

Provides home site for Performing Graphics which specializes in real-time meetings pages and performance graphics. Meetings pages are sites set up for teleconferencing with graphics exchanged for companies. Includes articles about the utilization of graphics and icons. Also includes service listings including Web site design, and telefacilitation training.

PhotoModeler

`http://www.photomodeler.com/`

Find out about this bizarre software, which converts objects in photograph into 3D objects on the computer. Visit their VRML pages (you need a VRML viewer to do this), read FAQs about the capabilities of this software, download demos, and link to other related pages. A fascinating site for photographers and artists.

Photoshop Folder FTP Site

`ftp://ftp.asi.com/pub/photoshop`

A small but valuable site for Photoshop and Kai's users who want to try out freeware and shareware filters and other Photoshop add-ons.

Play Incorporated

`http://www.play.com/`

Designs and produces the Snappy Video Snapshot digital image producer. The Snappy can take any image from a camcorder, VCR, or a TV and make a digital still for a PC. Includes detailed technical specifications and features. Provides downloadable demo software. Also includes company profile and upcoming product information.

Precision Graphics of Texas

`http://mfginfo.com/service/precision/precision.htm`

Provides graphics design and production in new and old media. Includes services and products offered by Precision Graphics. Also includes a search engine of professional graphic resources.

Quadrat Communications

`http://www.interlog.com/~quadrat/`

Provides graphic design and other publication services. Includes service listings, artwork portfolio, and contact information for this small Toronto, Ontario firm.

Renaissance Technologies

`http://www.rentech.com/`

Provides graphics services and products. Services include Web site creation, custom graphics production, and access service. Also includes sales of Sitescapes graphic templates for WWW publishing and Rainbow color selection applications.

Render-Cam Images

`http://www.crl.com/~rci/rci.htm`

Supplies graphics and 3D production services, including computer animation, morphing, modeling, and 3D layout. Includes company portfolio and links to WWW sites created. Provides services offered listing and contact information.

Scientific Visualization Sites

`http://www.nas.nasa.gov/RNR/Visualization/annotatedURLs.html`

Collection of links to every known scientific visualization site on the Web. Each Web page from related universities that have such projects is described and compared to other Web sites. Very helpful for scientists interested in modeling their experiments.

Silicon Surf

`http://www.sgi.com/`

Besides the usual complement of product specs, customer support, and reseller directories, this Web site includes Silicon's unique Extreme Tech, Serious Fun, and Surf Zone links. Check out the Serious Fun link to download freeware, join SGI's Surf Zone club (a 3D Web navigator), and SGI's Image gallery.

Software Publishing Corporation Home Page

`http://www.spco.com`

Developers of Harvard Graphics and the new ASAP WordPower program, which lets you create presentation quality graphics from text files. Check out the ASAP Webshow Gallery for downloads of presentations created with SPC products.

Stephens Design

`http://www.opendoor.com/StephensDesign/`

Provides graphic design and production services for advertising, Web publishing, and more. Includes example graphics created, portfolio of artwork, and company profile.

Subia

`http://www.subia.com/subia/`

Provides a wide array of graphics and related design services. Includes detail color scanning, Web site creation, graphic design production, and digital proof services. Includes services background and contact information.

team smartyPANTS!

`http://www.eden.com/~smarty/`

Provides a wide range of graphics and Web publishing services. Includes 3D artwork creation, Web site design, writing HTML, and much more. Offers links to sites created, example artwork, and contact information.

tela computer consulting + design

`http://www.tela.bc.ca/tela/`

Provides graphic design services along with Web site creation, and electronic logo conversion. Includes service particulars and clients served. Also includes sample artwork and links to sites created. Site provides Web starting point with links to many different pages.

Triffet Design Group

http://www.primenet.com/~martman/TDG.html

Creates Web sites and provides graphic design services. Includes client list and contact information.

Ventana's Photoshop f/x Online Companion

http://www.vmedia.com/data/vvc/onlcomp/phshpfx/index.html

Submit your artwork to the Photoshop f/x Gallery and win a free book. This site also includes links to Internet clip art, a mountain of shareware and freeware for the Mac and Windows platforms, and an archive of mailing list messages related to Photoshop.

Virtus Corporation

http://www.virtus.com/

Produces desktop 3D graphics and virtual reality software. Includes information about the 3D Website Builder, WalkThroughPro, and other graphics tools. Provides company history, product background, and contact information.

Visual CADD Home Page

http://www.numera.com

Numera Software is the creator of Visual CADD, a Windows CAD package. Try their free, 30-day trial version of this CADD package, access their developers network, and read the latest news about Numera products.

WebFlow Communications Group

http://fox.nstn.ca/~webflow/

Provides graphic design, Web site creation, digital imaging, and other services. Includes clients listing, example work, and company contacts.

Zycad Corporation

http://www.zycad.com/

Produces computer design software and tools for engineering, prototyping, and simulations applications. Includes information about the Paradym XP Simulation Accelerator and other products. Provides company profile, press releases, financial information, office locations, and contacts.

Hardware

1st Solutions, Inc.

http://www.firstsol.com/

Provides sales for 50 Series Hardware in the United States and Canada. Also provides licensed hardware and software, consulting for Prime users, and the offering of a self developed multi-host RAID7 that can run simultaneously on Prime or other CPU platforms.

ACCESS Computer Hardware

http://www.electriciti.com/~access/

Provides sales, set-up, service, support, and consulting for small to medium sized technology companies that are moving into international markets or looking to expand export business. Also provides information on the use of Sparc Clone Workstations, hard drives, and other products.

American Power Conversion

http://www.apcc.com/products.htm

Click on one of APC's Uninterruptible Power Supply products to read about its features and capabilities. You can also view a picture of each product, download demo software, and leave questions for their marketing department.

ATI Technologies Online

http://www.atitech.ca/

The colorful home page for this successful manufacturer of video accelerator boards and multimedia products provides links to Public Relations, and provides information for investors and developers. The Products section discusses in depth ATI video products. Click on Current Drivers to download the latest ATI drivers.

Autotime Corp.

http://www.teleport.com/~autotime/

Producers of memory converters, HYPERcable printer cables, and LASERBuddy printer forms. This site is currently under construction, but will eventually feature technical support. Includes product features and pricing.

Bandwidth Brokers International (BBI)

http://www.bbi.com/

Provides exchange for buying and selling of digital circuits. Includes listing of products on hand and services information. Also provides CyberBell Online Trading database.

BizWeb Category Computer Hardware

http://www.bizweb.com/keylists/computer.hardware.html

This long list of computer hardware-related Web sites has hundreds of links to such companies as DEC, Cray, Creative Labs, Epson, and GammaLink. If you can't find the company you're looking for here, it doesn't exist! A thorough site.

Black Box Corporation

http://www.blackbox.com/

Provides online catalog for Black Box, which produces and sells data communications and digital connectivity products. Includes a searchable catalog, technical support services, online reference guide, and product background information. Also provides ability to receive hard copy version of catalog through the mail.

Boca Research

http://www.bocasearch.com

Produces a wide assortment of internal and multi-media modems along with other products from video graphic to PC card adapters. Site provides a well organized introduction to Boca Research, both the company and their products.

BusLogic, Inc.

http://www.buslogic.com/

Supplies Small Computer Systems Interface (SCSI) products for use in PCs and networks. Includes information about the Flash Point Family Ultra SCSI, and MultiMaster Ultra SCSI families of host adapters. Provides technical support, a company profile, and purchasing information along with a list of links to related sites.

BVM

http://www.bvmltd.co.uk/welcome/

Develops and manufactures VMEbus boards, controllers, disc modules, and other related hardware along with software supports. Provides detailed product background, press releases, and news clippings about BVM and their products.

Central Data

http://www.cd.com/

Produces SCSI and ethernet connectivity and host interface products such as serial port controllers, modem, and terminal servers. Includes product

benefits and pricing information along with listings of support services. The site also provides technical support and a customer feedback column.

Colorgraphic Communications Corporation

http://www.colorgfx.com/

Produces multi-screen video adapters for Windows and Microstation products. Enables to run different applications on separate monitors from one PC. Includes product specifications and technical support. Also provides ordering information.

Commax Technologies, Inc.

http://www.commax.com/

Produces computer hardware specializing in Pentium Processor CD-ROM notebooks. Includes company news, technical support, and contact information. Provides links to mobile technology sites on the Web.

Computer Companies and Vendor WWW Home Pages

http://acd.ucar.edu/www.pages.html

Nicely organized site lists computer hardware manufacturers on the Web. Other categories and links on this page include Computer Software, Vendors, and Supplies. Worth a visit!

Computer Hardware Page

http://infotique.lm.com/cgi-bin/phpl.cgi?comphard.html

MegaMall site for computer hardware new and used. Many different brands and types offered. Provides an A-to-Z search index and ordering information.

DTK Computers, Inc.

http://www.gan.net/dtk/

Produces Novell authorized microcomputer products and services. Includes product reviews, service, ordering, and contact information. Provides background for the GAN family of workstations.

Hauppauge Computer

http://www.hauppauge.com/hcw/index.htm

Provides digital video boards for PCs. Provides links to product listings, product specs, image files, software, service and support info, and special offer and ordering info.

Hewlett Packard Products

http://www.hp.com:80/ahp/Products.html

One of the most successful computer hardware manufacturers in the U.S. provides a number of links on their Products page. Find out more about HP's computer equipment, including laptops, palmtops, printers, desktop and tower computers, servers, monitors, and more. This site also provides links to HP's Medical, Chemical, and test measurement equipment.

ICS

http://www.relay.net/~gcw/memory.html

Simm memory/CPU distributor for home or office. Motherboard and multimedia upgrades, Web consulting. Provides links to product info, prices, and upgrade kits.

The Image

http://www.lainet.com/image/

An Internet monitor repair center for monitors used for CAD workstations, graphics design, and medical imaging. Provides pricing and order information. Also offers monitors for sale.

Image Manipulation Systems

http://www.imageman.com/

Offers video output (I/O, JPEG CODEC) cards and teleconferencing cards for company needs. Provides information on software support, sites of interest, and product inquiries.

IMT Systems

http://mfginfo.com/comp/imtsystems/imt.htm

You specify what you want—will build a computer system to fit your needs. Novell certified tecnhicians on staff. Access to hardware descriptions, order and

pricing information. Also use their search engine for other computer manufacturers and suppliers.

Information Data Products Corp.

http://www.planet.net/idpc/

Wide area networking products including new and refurbished hardware. Links to products, specials, hardware, and other resources of interest.

Intel Information for Developers

http://www.intel.com/design/

The king of computer hardware provides an easy-to-use "quick navigator" for developers interested in a specific Intel CPU or technology. This page also provides important news, links to Intel's online magazine, and specific language information for programmers.

Intergraph Corporation

http://www.ingr.com/

Hardware and software for the technical desktop. Software for engineering, publishing, mapping/geographical systems. Links to products and services, user groups, news, and related search engines.

Maxtor Current Product Information

http://www.maxtor.com/products.html

Read about Maxtor's 2.5" and larger hard disk drives, which range in size from 837 MB to 2 GB. This page provides links for their notebook and desktop products, FAQs, and retail sales outlets.

Memory USA

http://www.mu.com/

If you're looking to upgrade your memory on your home or business computers, Memory USA will buy, sell, or trade memory for competitive prices.

Micro House International

http://www.microhouse.com/

Service and support for the PC hardware including hard drive and modem tech support guides. Find out more about their products and services as well as browse links to "hot deals" and other sites of interest.

MIPS Product Information

http://www.mips.com/Mips_Chip_Rm.html

Provides information on MIPS' RISC-based Unix computers. Read about MIPS' powerful computers that use the MIPS RISC chip. The technical spec pages aren't very graphical, but the humorous Egyptian theme on this page is good for a chuckle.

Power Computing Corporation

http://www.powercc.com/

Produces the 225mHz PowerTower Pro desktop system, the fastest desktop currently being made. Includes PowerTower technical specifics, magazine reviews, technical support, reference matierials, and ordering information. Also includes company profile.

Praegitzer Industries Web Server

http://www.pii.com/

Designs and manufactures printed circuit boards. Includes company profile, services offered, technnologies utilized, and corporate philosophy. Provides investor information, trade show appearance dates, job openings, and future technology previews.

PSI Ltd.

http://204.131.249.1:80/psi/

Produces interface boards and data retrieval products. Includes product background and benefits along with listings of popular boards. Provides ordering information.

Rockwell Collins Printed Circuits

http://www.rockwell.com/rockwell/bus_units/cca/cpc/

Produces multi-layer circuit boards for the telecommunications, military, microwave, and other industrial technology needs. Includes company profile, services offered, price quote form, and contact information.

Samsung Group

http://www.samsung.co.kr/news/news.html

How is Samsung involved in electronics? The question should be, "What aren't they involved in?" Find out about Samsung's 1 GB RAM chips, their latest semiconductor plants, camera operations, and computer CD-ROM drives. The company also makes chemicals, the world's largest ships, and even office buildings!

SCEPTRE

http://www.gus.com/emp/sceptre/sceptre.html

Produces 486 notebook computers, and 17" and 15" color monitors. Includes technical specifications, features, and contact information.

Tadpole Technology

http://www.tadpole.com/

Produces the SPARCbook family of portable notebook computers and the Alphabook 1 software development notebook. Includes product specifications, technical support, resellers listings, and contact information.

TechnoGraphy & Storage Computer in Japan

http://www.storage.com/japan.html

Produces enterprise-wide storage systems. Includes product technical information, customers listings, and contact information.

Thinking Machines Corporation

http://www.think.com/

The company that introduced parallel computing to the world now is also a software developer. Find out more about their CM-5x parallel computer products, including the massive CM-500, which can have up to 4,096 separate super-SPARC processors!

TouchWindow

http://www.touchwindow.com/

Provides information and features on the TouchWindow monitors. TouchWindow monitors are screen interaction enabled. Includes detailed product background and ordering information.

TTi Technologies, Inc.

http://www.hypermart.com/tti/default.htm

Provides online sales and service of a large catalog of computer hardware. Includes distribution of BIOS upgrates and sales of motherboards, hard drives, and computer systems. Includes detailed catalog and ordering information.

ViewSonic Corporation

http://www.viewsonic.com/

Produces a large line of color monitors. Includes product features, company profile, reviews, technical support, and resellers listings.

Languages

Amzi! Prolog + Logic Server

http://www.amzi.com/

Produces Amzi! Prolog + Logic Server, a software add-on you embed in C++ and other programming languages to create logic-based intelligent agents and intelligent components, which are used in software that relies on artificial intelligence. Amzi!'s products assist programmers who need to create software that configures, schedules, diagnoses, advises, recognizes, lays out, plans, understands, or teaches. Downloadable demos and tutorials are provided to show how this Prolog-based programming language works.

Benaroya

http://www.portal.com/~sedit/rexxgrph.html

Producers of the REXX programming language that integrates system commands into composites. Provides background and uses for the REXX language, including work references and reviews. Includes listings of company products and services.

C Programming v.2.6

http://www.cit.ac.nz/smac/cprogram/default.htm

Download FAQs and online books about C programming. This site also provides many C utilities and compilers.

CONSULTIX, the Unix Training Experts

http://www.halcyon.com/yumpy/

Provides Unix training and other advanced language training for Fortune 500 companies and the Federal Government. This site lists upcoming classes, their structure, and how they fit into certification programs. CONSULTIX teaches the following languages: C, AWK, Bourne shell, and Korn shell languages, Unix System administration, Unix security, and Linux (the Unix look-alike system).

Free Compilers and Interpreters

http://cuiwww.unige.ch/cgi-bin/freecomp

Enter the name of the free (public-domain) compiler, compiler generator, interpreter, or assembler you need and the search engine will find it. You can also search by category.

hav.Software

http://www.neosoft.com/~hav/default.html

Provides two C++ Neural Net libraries for C++ developers in PC-DOS, Windows, NT, and Unix—IBM, HP, SUN, SGI. Also provides contract and custom software development and project management services to business, scientific, and research interests.

Hyperparallel Technologies

http://www.ppgsoft.com/ppgsoft/hc_main.html

HyperC is a programming language used to program parallel computers from Hyperparallel Technologies. Provides links to features and characteristics, technical information, and programming examples.

Index of /1/perlinfo/scripts

http://www.metronet.com/1/perlinfo/scripts/

An amazingly spartan page with a number of downloadable scripts written in Perl. There's no home page button or anything else except PERL scripts. This site is only for the serious PERL tinkerer.

LEARN C/C++ TODAY (A list of resources/tutorials)

http://www.cis.ohio-state.edu/hypertext/faq/usenet/
C-faq/learn-c-cpp-today/faq.html

A detailed page for C++ beginners. Includes reviews of dozens of C++ books, TXT, and FAQ files; recommends C++ packages for a number of platforms, and discusses the best way to start learning this important language. Although the site is rarely updated, the information is still relevant and valuable.

Poster

http://www.mergent.com/poster.html

For all of you archers out there (come on, we know you're there), check out the free poster you can get from Mergent.

Management Information Technologies, Inc.

http://www.vyp.com/miti/miti.html

Offers you the ability to access any information written in any language or file format without having the original application or even knowing the subject matter or language used. Links to contact information as well as the Management Information Technologies home page.

OC Systems AdaMania Page

http://ocsystems.com/

Develops the Powerada compiler for the Power PC.

Rigal Language Home Page

http://www.ida.liu.se/labs/pelab/members/vaden/rigal.html

Learn about the Rigal language, which uses atoms, lists, and labeled trees for data structures. Download published papers, see code examples, and read FAQs from the University of Latvia's ftp site.

Software Translation Tools

http://www.netusa.net/~mpsinc

Develops software translators, converters, and provides translation services in a number of languages. This company also makes fertility forecasting software for hospitals. Download demonstration programs of these conversion and migration tools.

The C++ Virtual Library

http://info.desy.de/user/projects/C++.html

A great resource for C++ beginners and intermediate users. This site includes information on upcoming conferences, free C++ software and reviews of commercial packages, and a number of tutorials for the beginner.

Tutorials Need Help with C/C++ and Other Languages?

http://www.andrews.edu/~maier/tutor.html

An online library that provides a number of FAQs and entire books online that you can download to teach yourself C++, ANSI C, Unix, HTML, vi, and e-mail. All the documents at this site are public domain or freeware. An excellent site for novice programmers in any of these languages.

Unofficial FutureBASIC Web Page

http://www.ids.net/~paumic/FutureBasic/Index.html

FutureBASIC is a powerful BASIC programming language for the Macintosh. This site includes source code, utilities and demos, chat groups, and articles on this easy-to-use language.

Welcome to the WWW Home of COBOL

http://www.cobol.org/

An organization of hardware manufacturers and COBOL software developers that provides information about COBOL developments. Read about the Great COBOL Debate that took place at DB Expo in December 1995 to see into the future of COBOL.

Magazines

BYTE Magazine

http://www.byte.com/

Contains a five year, searchable archive of *BYTE magazine*. Enter a search term and Presto! Articles that include this word appear in an easy-to-retrieve format. You can download files and shareware mentioned in *BYTE* articles, and download *BYTE*'s benchmark tests. A valuable site worth a bookmark in your browser software.

Communications Week Interactive

http://techweb.cmp.com/techweb/cw/current/

A colorful site with news for corporate network managers. This publication provides testing, reviews, industry news, and funny tidbits on the world of networking and information management.

Computer Shopper Online

http://www.zdnet.com/cshopper/

Check out the top stories for the latest edition of *Computer Shopper*, considered to be the monthly computer "bible" for computer buyers. Articles on the absolute latest in computer technology can be found in the CyberCentral area.

Computer Sun Times

http://www.rmii.com/cstimes/

Online computer publication that features hardware and software reviews.

HotWired

http://www.hotwired.com/

The slickest mag in the industry has a Web page with articles on the arts, politics, and technology. Before you can access much of anything, however, you have to join (free of charge). If you decide to sign up and are looking for something to do, check out the Arts and Renaissance articles first.

Ice-9 Publications

http://info.pitt.edu/~depst8/

A must-see for the information unconscious. The background completely obscures the text on this page. Fun!

MacUser/MacWeek Special on Apple's Future

http://www.zdnet.com/macuser/applefuture/

Interested in the latest on Apple's future? Visit this site for recent information on Apple and all the rumors.

PC-TRANS

http://kuhub.cc.ukans.edu/~pctrans/

Provides home site for *PC-TRANS*, a trade magaine for PC users in the transportation industry. Site provides technical support, discussion forum, and bulletin board. Includes contact information for the group and the magazine.

Pure Power

http://www.magicnet.net/purepower

Pure Power magazine's Web page provides author contact, Powerbuilder tips, back issues, user group links, and new developments in the Powerbuilder community. You can also download the first issue free.

Scientific Computing and Automation Magazine

http://gordonpub.loyola.edu/

A colorful Web site for a magazine devoted to computer analysis software for scientists and engineers. Read articles from the latest issue, link to related sites and sites of software developers, such as IBM and National Instruments, or access chemical databases.

The List of Free Computer-Related Publications

http://www.soci.niu.edu/~huguelet/TLOFCRP/

If you've ever been buried by catalogs arriving right before Christmas, you'll appreciate this site. Jim

Huguelet provides an alphabetical list of addresses and phone numbers for magazines he receives free, yet never asked for. Several publishers that discovered this list requested to be removed; they are listed here, too.

Virtual Computer Library Journals

http://www.utexas.edu/computer/vcl/journals.html

Lists a number of Web sites for e-zines and magazines about computers.

ZDNet

http://www.zdnet.com/home/filters/maina.html

Home page for Ziff Davis, the publisher of *PC Magazine*, *Computer Shopper*, *MacUser* and *MacWeek*, *Computer Gaming World*, *PC Computing*, and many others. Like other online magazines, access to the really good stuff requires registering. If you decide to join, Ziff Davis creates a Personal Profile page you can use to customize the types of articles you want to see.

Mobile Computing

Adaptec AIRport™ Family

http://www.adaptec.com/sales/980222-031.html

Read about Adaptec's infrared peripherals that let you transfer data from your PC to laptop without wires. Page describes setup, capabilities, different kits, and technical information.

Apex PCMCIA Modems

http://warrior.com/apex/index.html

Manufactures high-quality PCMCIA modems, ethernet adapters, and Fax/modem/ethernet cards for notebook computers. Their Mobile Plus Data/Fax modem is a 28.8, cellular-ready PCMCIA modem for mobile data communication.

BarCode1—A Web of Information about Bar Code

http://www.adams1.com/pub/russadam/barcode1.html

Online publication about bar code and other automatic identification technologies. Includes extensive, original information and a collection of bar code shareware.

Cellular Works

http://virtumall.com/Cell/

Provides new, hard to find, and discontinued cellular accessories, such as pagers and Motorola MicroTAC and Classic phone accessories. Download a catalog or shop online; this site is part of the VirtuMall shopping service.

Columbia University Mobile Computing Laboratory

http://www.mcl.cs.columbia.edu/mobile.html

This site explains Columbia's MCL goals, which are to create small, wireless, mobile computers that are capable of being networked all the time, anywhere on the planet. This site lists the people involved, current research projects and their status reports, and source code files for downloading. The site also links to other mobile computing efforts at leading universities.

DataLink by Timex

http://www.xmission.com/~turq/Timex_DataLink

Informative page from Milne Jewelry Company about the amazing DataLink Watch by Timex, which provides wireless PC-to-watch communication.

Introduction to ARDIS

http://www.ardis.com/ardis_hp/website2.htm

Find out about the next step in mobile computing: wireless, two-way communication using the ARDIS Network. This network is already available in over 400 metropolitan areas in the U.S., Puerto Rico, and the Virgin Islands. Be sure to check out the Coverage Maps link, which lets you zoom in on any ARDIS coverage area. Neat graphics!

It's a Wireless World

http://www.cyberramp.net/~wireless/

Web page for the wireless computing nut. The menu provides dozens of topics on wireless news, upcoming tradeshows, publications, and scientific information, just to name a few. If you're interested in this technology, this site is a must-see.

Mobile and Wireless Computing

http://snapple.cs.washington.edu:600/mobile/mobile_www.html

A well-stocked page of links to every known Web site related to mobile computing. A description of each link is provided, and the links are divided into categories, such as conferences, journals, research projects, wireless providers, and organizations.

Mobile Office Magazine

http://www.mobileoffice.com/mobile.html

A straightforward site that provides news on mobile computing issues, information about companies involved in the mobile industry, and a feedback forum. The special Webcrawler search link is perfect for finding mobile computing-related info on the Web.

Mobile Planet

http://www.mplanet.com/

The source for laptops, handheld computers, portable accessories, wireless, paging, pen-based computers, and any other mobile computing need for your home or office.

MobileWare Corporation

http://www.mobileware.com/

Software and applications to help you access resources from anywhere. Check out their wireless services and new software.

NDS Distributing

http://www.ndsdistributing.com/

Distributor of a full line of mobile office products from a variety of brand name companies. Click on the company logos to view the products and services available for your office.

Psion Incorporated

http://www.psioninc.com/

Home page for the manufacturers of the Psion Series 3a, a handheld computer made in the UK that makes an appearance in Steven Segal's turbo action flic, *Executive Decision*. The Psion software archives contain free Psion software. Click on buttons to access third-party Psion peripheral companies, e-mail tech support, or join their developers group.

Road Warrior Outpost Solutions for the Mobile Professional

http://warrior.com/

Afraid your notebook computer's hard drive will fill up on your next sales trip? Upgrade it or anything else in your computer at Road Warrior's upgrade center. This site also provides GPS and printer information and an online monthly e-zine.

Special Topics in Engineering

http://www.contrib.andrew.cmu.edu/usr/sums/wearable.html#top

Read about the future of mobile computing on this page, a special course given at Carnegie Mellon University. This page starts by presenting a survey of current products and technologies, then provides a number of links and information about research on speech synthesis, wearable computers, remote control devices, and wireless communication.

The World of Newton

`http://newton.info.apple.com/newton/newton.html`

A well-designed site for Apple's Newton PDA. Access technical support, download Newton development toolkits and sample code, or read about Newton software and hardware updates.

Multimedia

Atomic Vision, Inc.

`http://www.atomicvision.com/`

Produces and develops digital media products. Includes client listings, case studies, company processes, and purchasing information. The visuals of this site are very well done. Includes writings about the digital medium covering all pertinent subjects from the technical to the philosophical aspects of the new media. This is a business site that is not only selling the product, but raising questions about the technology and its direction.

Auricle Control Systems

`http://www.webcom.com/~auricle/`

Home site for the Oscar winning Auricle multimedia music composition tools. Professional composers and movie fans alike would find this site interesting. Provides product information, technical background, and pricing. Also provides information about how music for films is made, the art of film music, examples of where technology was used, and photo gallery of composers at work.

Avalanche Systems, Inc.

`http://www.avsi.com/`

Produces interactive media products. Includes list of services offered and links to clients sites on the web.

AVM Summit

`http://www.well.com/www/manatee/summit.html`

The "semi-official" source for information on AVM PC audio technical products. Includes product background, availability, support numbers, and troubleshooting tips.

CA Natalie Associates

`http://www.cana.com/cana/`

Provides Web and Internet services ranging from site creation to database programming. Concentration of services are based in Web marketing, publishing, and WWW server work. Site includes company profile, work done with clients, service listings, and pricing. Also provides listings of job opportunities with CA Natalie Associates.

CD Learn: Personalized Training For Your Favorite Application Packages

`http://www.netaxs.com/~irp/cdlearn/cdlearn.html`

Offers CD-ROMs that provide interactive, CD-ROM lessons and reference guides for popular applications such as Microsoft Word, WordPerfect, Excel, and Windows 95.

CD Warehouse

`http://www.ecn.com/cd_warehouse`

Provides more than 3,000 CD-ROM titles at low warehouse prices. Check out the new weekly specials or download an online catalog.

CD Works

`http://www.tiac.net/users/cdworks/`

Produces and replicates CD-ROMs along with handling sales of CD recording hardware and software. Includes formats and guidelines for data and label artwork for submission. Provides company background, services provided and links to other pertinent CD-ROM sites.

CD-ROM Online

`http://www.li.net/~nsi/cdrom.html`

A free, online e-zine that reviews PC-based CD-ROM products every month. Download back issues, check out the top 20 best-selling CD-ROM titles, or suggest titles you'd like to see reviewed.

Chick Enterprises Ltd.

http://www.infomatch.com/~chick/chick.htm

Provides and produces a wide range of computer based multimedia services and World Wide Web home page creation duties. Includes company background and full listings of services offered. On a humerous note, this site also provides links to various chicken sites.

Cinax Designs Inc.

http://www.cinax.com/

Creates and Develops iFilm interactive film software products. Includes iFilmStudio digital editing software and iMotion seamless playback servers. These technologies are for use by filmmakers, game builders, and in the creation of interactive software. Includes iFilm samples, technology explanations, product background, client and portfolio listings. Provides "The Bench," an interactive movie. An interesting site for someone interested in multimedia technologies and their applications.

Constant Synthesis Project

http://www.sanctuary.com/haven/consynpro/

Provides site for a small network of San Francisco area artists who work in CD-ROM, internet, and computer graphics technologies. Includes artist listings, gallery sampling of work, and collective projects. There is some nice artwork here done in the new media.

Crystal River Engineering

http://www.cre.com/cre

Creator of AudioReality, a 3D sound technology for entertainment, multimedia, virtual reality, and professional audio. Download free demos of Audio-Reality software and sample 3D spatial sounds, which can be played on any stereo system.

Darim Vision Co.

http://www.darvision.com/

Designs and produces a wide array of multimedia hardware and software products for the individual to companies. Includes information about MPEGator, MARS, DVMPEG, and TeleGenesis products with full product specifications. Also includes technical support, downloadable software, and contact information.

DayStar Digital, Inc.

http://www.daystar.com/

Produces Genesis MP workstations, software, and applications that are used in media publishing such as 3D graphics and animation. Includes performance papers, technical specifications, full product catalog, and technical support. Provides company store, history, and resellers index.

Demo and Tutorial Builders from MIKSoft, Inc.

http://www.cnj.digex.net/~mik/

Produces StDemo and ShowBasic Development Kit, two script-based Windows Demo players. This site explains the program's advantages over Windows Recorder and lets you download a copy of StDemo Player—a demo builder. Also includes an opportunity to watch a unique demo presentation of ShowBasic—a demo/tutorial/CBT/presentation development kit for Windows. If this is it what you need, order by e-mail or on the phone.

Digital Creators

http://www.digitalcreators.com/dc/

Specializes in multimedia, Web site page development, and computer graphics creation. Services offered include training, animation, CD-ROM, and home page creation. Includes links to sites created, graphics portfolio, CD-ROMs developed, and contact information.

Digital Movie News

http://spider.lloyd.com/~dmnews/

Interested in the latest issue of the e-zine Digital Movie News? This site's Table of Contents link includes exclusive articles on hundreds of topics, including software reviews, interviews with movie makers, and conference information. The home page includes a number of FAQs for those interested in starting their own digital moviemaking enterprise.

Due North

http://www.icw.com/duenorth/duenorth.html

Creates multimedia educational products for accelerated learning. Includes foreign language, personal change, and PhotoReading products. Provides contact and ordering information.

EDGE Interactive Media, Inc.

http://www.edgegames.com/

Produces and provides interactive games, 3D multimedia systems, EDGE PCs, *EDGE* magazine, and various Web services. Includes job opportunities, product and service information.

Edit & Copy Communications

http://www.smartpages.com/editcopy/

Provides wide array of multimedia and graphics services for use in Web page design, graphics creation, and video tape and CD-ROM production. Includes Internet and production services offered. Also includes technology demonstrations, clients listings, and information about electronic publishing. Provides contact information and company profile.

EMA Multimedia, Inc.

http://www.emamulti.com/

Provides a wide array of services including logo creation, packaging, interactive media, Web site design, and other mulitmedia productions. Includes examples of work, links to sites created, and contact information.

Entertainment Through Technology Association

http://www.ibmpcug.co.uk/~ettc/

Provides home site for ETTA, an association of entertainment and technology companies. The goal of the organization is to merge together new technologies and entertainment. Includes links to member organizations and a shared information database. Also includes membership and contact information.

HJF Digital Media

http://www.aloha.com/~redmond/

Provides digital media, graphics, and sound production to businesses and individuals. Provides links to animation, 3D, audio and video CD-ROM production, desktop publishing, Web page services and promotional screen savers.

IBM 3D Interaction Accelerator

http://www.research.ibm.com/3dix

Workstation-based interactive 3D software that enables real-time visualization and inspection of large and complex mechanical and architectural CAD models. Web site outlines latest features of this accelerator and provides examples of how this product is being used by customers. A must-see is the Pictures and Animations link, which provides large images you can download of 3D environments. Be sure to check out the Frauen Kirche project by IBM of Germany.

IDM

http://www.jaring.my/at-asia/idm/id_hpage.html

Interactive Digital Media campaign for businesses and companies. Provides links to past projects, services, and contact information.

Incite

http://www.incite.com/

High bandwidth multimedia communications at peak performance. Check out Desktop Multimedia or Conversational Media ™ for your performance needs. Links to support, marketing, contact info, and much more.

Jack

http://www.cis.upenn.edu/~hms/jack.html

Jack is a human modeling and simulation system developed at the University of Pennsylvania. Provides a 3D interactive environment for a variety of applications. Links to news, information, demos, and more.

Loviel Computer Corporation

http://www.loviel.com/

Manufacturer of external SCSI storage devices, specializes in digital video, multimedia, and video conferencing, and offers services such as media integration, computer peripherals, value added services, set-up, tech support, training, and more.

MakeMPEG—the Home Page

`http://www.fl.com.au/mpeg/`

This page is a detailed FAQ providing information on MakeMPEG software for 3D Studio. This page hasn't been updated since July 1995, so whether the information is still accurate is questionable.

Magnum Resources

`http://www.magnum.com/index.html`

Offers WWW and multimedia products and services. Includes Web site creation for companies that include retail features. Includes client listings, artwork gallery, and contact information.

Media Solutions International

`http://www.msi-usa.com/`

A software development company for multimedia applications located in Atlanta, Georgia.

Metatec Corporation

`http://www.metatec.com/`

A company offering network support, software development, and optical disc manufacturing and distribution for your publishing needs. Find out more about the company's bio, events, press releases, clients, and more.

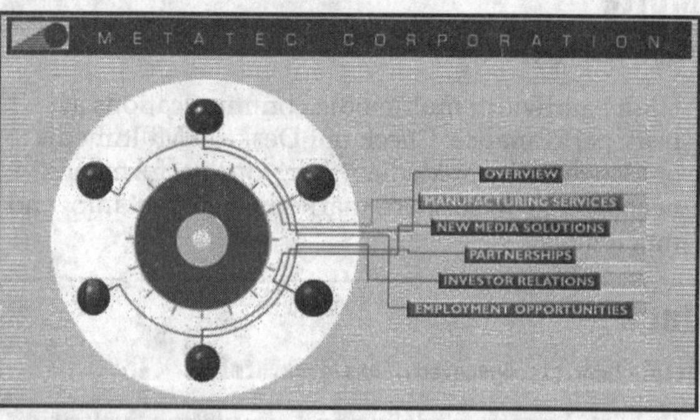

MidiMan's Official Web Site

`http://www.midifarm.com/midiman/`

If you're into musical production via computer, then check out this site. Lots of product and ordering information, troubleshooting ideas, and new ideas to try. Check out their newsgroup or FTP site, too.

Mimesis Technology

`http://rampages.onramp.net/~mimesis/`

Affordable digital video services and development for your media needs. Will encode or produce video CDs for an hourly rate.

Multimedia Archives

`http://sunsite.nus.sg/ftpmultimedia.html`

A treasure trove of sounds, images, and MPEG animations for adding to your multimedia presentations. The multimedia exhibit links are a must-see, although you can't use their images in your work.

Murray MultiMedia

`http://www.murraymedia.com/murray/`

Creative interactive and print media including advertising, packaging, exhibits and displays, photographs, announcements, and more. Links to demos, media, info, and jobs.

Music Screeners

`http://www.sony.com/Music/Screeners`

Download a free trial of Sony Music Video's Screeners, which are editable music video screen savers.

Net-One System's Personalized CDs

`http://www.primenet.com/~net-one`

Small outfit that makes personalized CD-ROMs of music or data. This site is still under construction.

North Communications

`http://www.infonorth.com/`

Interactive multimedia technology developer among North American, European, and Australian offices. Powerful solutions to government, businesses, and individuals.

NuReality

`http://www.nureality.com/`

Incredible 3D products for your home theatre, computer, or game system. Links to demos, stores, reviews, and other cool sites.

Pangaea Creative Media

`http://www.magi.com/~brett/pangaea.html`

Provides multimedia services including Web site construction, The Cyberlink multimedia newsletter, Web publishing, and graphic design. Includes contact information and links to related sites.

Develops multimedia technology products and software. Specializes in applications that enable multimedia presentations to work similar to television. Produces the Human Touch graphical user interface and Scala Interactive Television (ITV) software. Includes product features, corporate profile, technical support, and contact information.

Photodex Corporation

http://www.photodex.com/

Produces CompuPic (CPIC) graphics software and media library CD-ROMs. Includes product background and contact information. Provides links to online multimedia forums.

Pinnacle Post

http://www.halcyon.com/pinnacle/welcome.html

Provides home site for Pinnacle Post, a multimedia graphics production company. Includes services offered, pricing, company news, and contact information.

QuickMedia

http://www.quickmedia.com

Produces Living Album multimedia software that enables photo prints, audio, and video storage on floppy disks and CDs. Includes product technical specifications, reviews, and ordering information.

QuickMedia—Living Album

http://www.quickmedia.com

Download a free version of Living Album lite, software that lets you assemble multimedia albums and copy them to disks, CD-ROMs, and the WWW. Visit the Gallery to see how artists and computer gurus are using Living Album, and read the latest news about this product.

Ramworks

http://www.ramworks.com/ramworks/

Provides home site for Ramworks, a multimedia graphics and publishing production studio. Includes information about Shockwave graphics software, client listings, services offered, and contact information.

Scala Computer Television AS (Norway)

http://www.scala.com/Welcome.html

Sealworks, Inc.

http://www.libertynet.org/~swi/

Sealworks is a multimedia and Internet consulting and product company. Includes services, products, and resources utilized. Provides seminar dates, training services, and client listings.

SimPhonics, Inc.

http://www.simphonics.com/

Produces high-technology digital audio systems for simulation devices. Includes information about the FX-3000 hardware and software family used in many government and corporate flight simulators. Provides company profile, history, and contact information.

Software Tools for Artists

http://webcom.com/~stfa/

Provides sales and information about Algorithmic, DNA, and MIDI music software. Includes lengthy background information about music software, catalog of software available, and links to many related music software sites. For the technology explanations and links alone, this is a worthy site to check out for those interested in computers and music.

Sound & Vision Media

http://www.svmedia.com/svmedia/

Provides a wide range of multimedia services and products. Includes Web site development, multimedia database design, and graphics creation. Site includes links to sites created, artwork examples, and information about The Presence Engine online catalog creation software.

Sprite Interactive

http://www.cityscape.co.uk/users/di50/

Offers multimedia production and related software development. Services include Web site design, graphics creation, 3D modeling, and many more. Develops custom Photoshop, QuarkXPress, HTML, and others. Includes company background, portfolio, and contact information.

StarMan Group, Multimedia Productions

http://www.primenet.com/~star-man

Provides a wide range of multimedia services and products. Specializes in Java database development software and business site creation.

Station Graphics, Inc.

http://www.pic.net/~station/

Produces the VideoShow family of multimedia presentation products. Includes company profile and information about the VideoShow HQ Multimedia System. Provides technical specifications and contact information.

ThreeToad Multimedia

http://threetoad.com/

Develops custom multimedia software, WWW sites, computer based graphic design, and other services. Includes company profile, artwork portfolio, WWW browser comparison, and contact information.

Two Guys Named Hank

http://www.twohanks.com

Provides multimedia services including Web site design, computer animation, 3D modeling, and video production. Includes company background, and examples of work done.

Virtual Artists

http://www.va.com.au/va/

Provides a wide range of multimedia services including Web site creation, 3D graphics, computer animation, and other interactive media productions. Includes detailed company and personal background along with examples of work done.

Visionary Designs

http://www.visdesigns.com/

Provides a wide array of multimedia services and products. Includes computer animation, 3D graphics, CD-ROM creation, Web site design, and other multimedia services. Site includes company history, staff background, work examples, product listings, and contact information.

vivid studios

http://www.vivid.com/

Provides Web site construction, CD-ROM production, specialized interface creation, and other multimedia production services. Includes company profile, sites created, current projects, and links to many different sites.

Welcome to macromedia.com

http://www.macromedia.com/index.html

Headquarters for the producer of such hot multimedia authoring packages as Freehand, Director, Fontographer, and Authorware. Choose Lo Bandwidth at this opening screen if you are using anything slower than a 28.8 modem.

Worlds Inc.

http://www.worlds.net/

Produces Worlds Chat multi-user 3D environment and the Alpha World virtual place. Includes detailed company history, background, philosophies, and product information. Provides technical specifics, downloadable demos, resellers listings, and contact information. This is a very detailed business site that goes into the concepts surrounding virtual reality technologies. If interested in this subject, this site is highly recommended.

X Communications Multimedia

http://www.webcom.com/~xcomm/

Provides multimedia services such as Web page design. Includes links pages to created by X Communications, the magic "8-ball," and linky links. From this site you can access quite a few music and entertainment pages.

Xpand, Inc.

http://www.xpand.com/

Produces and provides multimedia and virtual reality technology products and services. Includes information about the Xpand family of products and other multimedia creation tools. Also includes service listings such as Web creation, Internet consulting, and training. Site provides art portfolio, links to sites created, downloadable demos, company profile, pricing models, and contact information.

XSI MeDIA

http://www.xsimedia.com/

Provides multimedia services including computer animation, Web design, CD-ROM, print, film and video production. Includes listing of services offered, technologies utilized, company resources, and contact information.

Zfx, Inc.

http://www.tricon.net/Comm/zfx/zfxhome2.html

Provides various multimedia services including computer animation and Web site creation. Includes designers notebook, links to sites created, animation portfolio, and contact information.

Networking

AppWare Developers Association

http://www.digitalprairie.com/adeva/

Non-profit organization that educates developers and the public about Novell's AppWare. The Libraries link provides an easy to use visual map of ADevA's ftp site; simply click on a particular folder to see the files you can download. These include FAQs, information about known bugs, newsgroup newsletters, mailing lists, and patches.

Alcatel Data Networks

http://www.adn.alcatel.com/

Provides company profile, news releases, product information, and hot topics list for high performance data systems company. Gives full background on Avanza switching architectures, and Alcatel platforms. Also provides information, enrolling procedures, and course listings for their Ashburn training facilities.

Banyan Systems, Inc

http://www.banyan.com/

Develops enterprise network software products that allow organizations to integrate diverse computing resources into unified, global networks. Banyan produces TCP/IP products, Unix/SMTP networking products, the StreetTalk™ naming service, and the popular VINES™ network operating system.

Capella Networking

http://plaza.xor.com/capella/

Produces and supplies a wide range of products and services for network and internetwork needs. Capella offers LAN/WAN access, DOS and Unix interoperability, and more for internetworking demands. Includes links to companies whose products they utilize.

CrossComm Corporation

http://www.crosscomm.com/

Develops and produces network, Internet, and communications products for everything from LANs to workstations. Specializes in ATM technologies and services. Includes information about ClearPath and the XL families of products for use with networks and internets. Provides technical specifications and applications of CrossComm products. Also includes pricing and ordering information.

CygnaCom Solutions, Inc.

http://www.cygnacom.com/

Produces and provides products and services for service engineering, network creation, server applications, and data security. Includes company philosophies and service listings. Provides company background and profile along with contact information.

Software

http://www.desktopPublishing.com/

Get free software from Alien Skin Software or Monotype Typography.

Computers

Designed Information Systems Corporation

http://www.aurora.net/disc.html

Specializes in design and implementation of LANs, WANs, and multi-platform networks. Provides Novell service center and products. Includes listings of manufacturer relationships and contact information.

Digital Network Product Business

http://www.networks.digital.com/

Researching the purchase of a new server for your business? This site from Digital Equipment Corporation includes extensive technical specifications on Digital's newest server products through the Network Products Guide link. An Application Stories link provides examples of Digital servers currently used in the business environment, and a Seminars, Training, and Events link lets you know when Digital will be demonstrating their products in your town.

Emulex Network Systems

http://www.emulex.com/

Designs and produces hardware and software for network access, communications, and time management. Products specialize in the managing of data between computers and peripheral equipment. Includes detailed product listings, upgrade programs, technical support, and company profile.

Engage Communication

http://www.engage.com/engage/

Produces routers and other products for networking PCs, Macintoshes, and Unix networks. Includes product specifications, technical support, and contact information.

Enterprise Network Solutions

http://www.lanology.com/

Produces a wide array of products for network servers from workstation connectivity to peripheral management and more. Includes product database with technical specifications and support. Provides service listings, contact information, technical partners, and links to related sites.

Florida Atlantic University

http://www.fau.edu/academic/cont-ed/cneip.htm

Florida Atlantic University offers a one month CNE immersion program through its certified Novell Education Center. This page explains the core courses you will take toward CNE certification taught by veteran CNI Frank Moore, the registration process, lodging, costs, and benefits of the program.

HDS Network Systems

http://www.hds.com

HDS Network Systems manufactures and sells multimedia X Window stations, and creates software for these systems in a multivendor open-system environment. HDS X terminals offer analog and digital video, IP Multicasting, and live TV/cable displays.

HELIOS Software

http://www.helios.de

Developers of color management and client/server software, including Helios EtherShare, PCShare, EtherShare OPI, and Helios ColorSync 2 Xtension.

Integrated Communications

http://www.intcom.net/

This cool site provides information about integrated network solutions such as LAN and WAN for your business. Will work with an existing network or develop a new one. Links to WAN and LAN info, support, and company info.

Intel Smart Network Devices

http://www.intel.com/comm-net/index.html

A site with links to Intel products and information for your business. Networking, video conferencing, and Internet are some of the options.

Internet Database Consultants

http://www.clark.net/infouser/endidc.htm

Will custom design Internet and intranet applications. Also provides links to the demos of A-Xorion, their easy-to-use Internet application server.

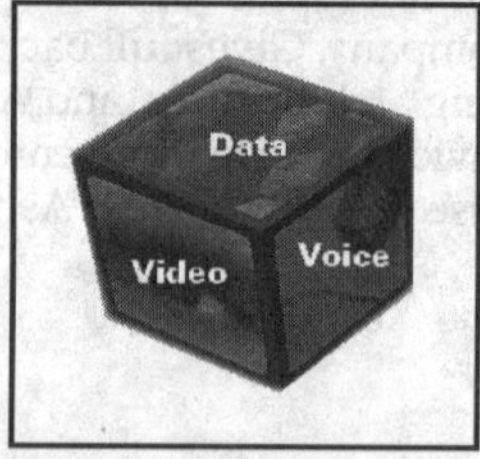

Interphase

http://www.iphase.com/

Products for mass storage and high speed networks. Links to products, support, news, and employment opportunities.

InterWorking Labs

http://www.iwl.com/

Offers Test Suite software products that test SNMP network hardware, such as routers, printers, hubs, servers, and UPSs. Find out about their products, download a free SNMP test suite demo, and contact IWL staff.

John Mayes & Associates

http://www.jma.com/

Firewall and network address translation products for your organization. Links to private link information, press releases, contact info, customer support, technical info, and more.

K-Net Ltd

http://www.k-net.co.uk/

Manufacturer and distributor of Fore Systems ATM switches, adapters, and routers. Our products include a stackable ATM ethernet bridge and stackable ATM video codec. Links to products, support, and employment information.

KarlBridge

http://www.karlnet.com/

Bridges and routers to solve your network security problems. Pictures and links to products and information, applications, pricing.

Kinesix

http://www.kinesix.com/

Manufacturer of Sammi, which allows you to integrate network applications without writing any network or graphical user interface code. Several links to learn more about Sammi, including current users, tech support, employment opportunities, and more.

Klever Computers

http://www.klever.com/

LAN product manufacturer based in California. Links to product info, tech support, what's new, and their FTP site from product and software demos and more.

LAN Solutions

http://www.aimnet.com/~yungi/lansol.html

Based in the San Francisco bay area, the leading Novell network integrator. Check out the long list of services provided by their CNEs.

Lancom Technologies

http://www.inforamp.net/~lancom/

Lancom Technologies provides all the courseware you need to become CNA or CNE certified. Provide this courseware for your students or yourself at reduced costs.

Maxperts, Inc.

http://www.maxperts.com/

Client/server solutions for SGI platforms and Mac. Create a WAN or get your business up and running on the Internet.

MSI Communications

http://www.msic.com/

Data, voice, and video integration solutions including WAN, LAN, consulting, network engineering and design, management, and maintenance.

Myricom, Inc.

http://www.myri.com/

An inexpensive, high-speed network provider based in sunny California. Myrinet is their LAN based on Mosaic technology and they offer a variety of products, performance info, client info, and more related to Myrinet.

Net Guru Technologies, Inc.

http://www.internet-is.com/netguru/index.html

Explains the different classes offered by Net Guru in such topics as Internet firewalls, TCP/IP, and Unix. Learn more about the instructors, student comments, or register immediately online!

NETiS Technology, Inc.

http://www.netistech.com/

A manufacturer and service provider for all your individual, business, and institutional computer needs. Check out their corporate profile, services and support, product info and press releases, promotionals, and more.

NetMagic, Inc.

http://www.aristosoft.com/ifact/inet.htm?who=unknown

High performance Web servers for Windows 95 and Windows NT, featuring Commerce Builder and Communications Builder. Links to sites that use Commerce Builder, downloading and purchasing information, product information, support and technical info.

Network Communication Computers and Arrays

http://tribeca.ios.com/~ideal/index.html

IDEAL computers, servers for LANs and WANs. Lots of product specs and information provided for your organization.

Networks Incorporated

http://205.138.166.1/networks/

Computer and consulting services for your network installation or troubleshooting. Links to product service and information, the benefits of networks, and more information.

NeuroSolutions, Inc.

http://www.nd.com/

A neural network simulation environment that supports any neural models. Check out their product and simulation demos, press releases, screen shots, and more.

Newbridge Networks Corporation

http://www.newbridge.com/

Design, manufacture, sale, and support of multime-dia networking solutions for corporations. Links to their products, features, user groups, investors, and more.

Nortel Northern Telecom

http://www.nortel.com/home/home.html

Nortel offers secure networks to ensure privacy. Check out their networking solutions and their training programs to benefit your organization.

Novell, Inc.

http://www.novell.com

The persistent leader in networking software provides information on new products, technical support questions, online manuals, and different networking solutions for business and government. Choose the smart country page for your location to see a neat map of all the countries in your continent. You will end up with information about Novell training courses, conferences, and other events in your city.

NTG International

http://www.ntg-campus.com/ntg/

The Network Technology group can help you with a small or large project, providing you with network technology solutions and training. Check out their list of products and services, including upcoming conferences.

NTT Data Communications Systems

http://www.unisql.com/

The UniSQL server will manage object-relational data better than relational systems, used by leading engineering, telecommunications, health care, manufacturing, and defense groups. Find out about their many products and services.

Onion Peel Software

http://www.ops.com/

Application developer for HP's OpenView Network Management platform. Download a demo program describing Onion Peel products, including RoboMap for HP Openview, and ROVE for HP OpenView.

Ornetix Network Computing

http://www.ornetix.spacenet.de/index.html

Maker of CDVision, a server-based CD-ROM manager that can accommodate up to 392 SCSI CD-ROM drives and multiple users. Download a 30-day full-user version, or practice your German by reading the Deutsch version of this page.

PC DOCS, Inc.

http://www.pcdocs.com

Produces PC-DOCS open document management systems for enterprise networks. Includes product background, press releases, case studies, and sales information. Also includes trade show appearance dates, job openings with PC DOCS, and technical partners listings.

Plaintree Systems

http://www.plaintree.com

Produces the WaveSwitch family of network connectivity products along with other Ethernet switches, converters, and software. Includes product specifications, technical support, and ordering information.

Retix Web

http://www.retix.com/

Creates internetworking products, applications, and tools. Includes information about the SWITCHStak 500 Ethernet switch, ROUTERXchange 7000 network router, NETXchange400 Ethernet bridges, and the RETIXVision network software. Provides technical specifications, press releases, and contact information.

Rnet

http://www.edb.com/rnet/index.html

Provides background and contact information for Rnet real-time message distributor systems. Includes product features and a listing of customers using Rnet.

Sietec Document Management and Archives

http://www.sietec.de/arc/arc.en

Produces LAN/WAN networking products and services for workstation and workgroup communication. Includes information about OfficeWorld

products and Sietec consultant services. Provides links to Siemens Nixdorf and contact information.

SoftLinx, Inc.

http://www.softlinx.com

Makes Replix Network Fax Software for enterprise-wide networks. This simple site provides traditional services, such as product and price info, technical support, reseller database, and support information.

StonyBrook Software

http://www.sbrook.com/

Produces RouterManager and WANServices software for network management and communication. Includes press releases, technical support, upgrades, and online demo software. Also includes career opportunities and contact information.

Strategic Networks Consulting, Inc.

http://www.snci.com/

Provides network design, management, and evaluation consulting services. Includes online essays and articles dealing with computer networking problems and solutions. Also includes job opportunities and contact information.

Structured Network Systems

http://www.structured.net/

Provides a wide array of networking services and products. Includes services offered, product listings, and contact information.

System Resources Corporation

http://www.srcorp.com/

Provides many different services and network system solutions for corporate, government, and defense clients. Includes company profile, philosophies, and services offered. Also includes client listings and contact information.

TENET Computer Group, Inc.

http://www.tenet.com

A Canadian Novell Netware network reseller and installer. Practice your French on their French version of this page, peruse their links to network-related publications, or find out about their product line.

VISIT Computer Telephony Integration

http://www.nortel.com/english/visit/

Provides a wide range of telecommunication services and products. Includes information about wireless, enterprise, and broadband networking products. Also includes company profile, solutions index, and contact information.

Word Master, Inc.

http://www.interaccess.com/wmi/wm/

Software developer of relational database managers for client/server environments.

XLNT Designs, Inc.

http://www.xlnt.com/

Designs and produces QuikStack family of LAN switches. Includes detailed company profile and product line technical specifications. Also includes technical support, online product registration, and technical partners.

Yost Serial Device Wiring Standard

http://www-scf.usc.edu/~khendric/info/yost.html

Describes the Yost serial device wiring standard. Find out why this standard is superior to null modem cables and the many different types of connections that are possible with this standard.

Online Sales

BreakThrough Technologies

http://www.programmer.com/

Provides online catalog and contact information for BreakThrough Technologies. Includes consulting services background, product specifications, and specials.

Campus Network Solutions

http://www.halcyon.com/routers/campus/

Provides a vast online catalog of various computer connectivity products for use with PCs to network size systems with all points in between. Campus Network Solutions is a large distributor of PairGain Technologies Inc. Includes product specifications, technical support, equipment reviews, and pricing comparisons.

CJC Graphic Design, Inc.

http://www.panix.com/~charl/

Provides listings of graphics-based and other software that CJC Graphic Design sells. Includes product background and contact information.

Computer Direct

http://www.worldgate.com/compdirect/

Provides sales and support of hardware, software, and other peripheral products. Specializes in Atari and Macintosh products. Includes product information, demonstration software, and Atari links.

Computer Express

http://cexpress.com:2700

Online computer superstore. Check out their Clearance section to see if that old computer game you could never find is still available. Provides a customer service link to help you out if you can't find a specific computer-related product.

Computer Literacy Bookshops, Inc.

http://www.clbooks.com/

Sells computer books. Click on Browse Our Full Database and search for a specific author or topic to find all the books in print. A free book search and e-mail ordering are available.

Computer Marketplace, Inc.

http://www.mkpl.com/

Provides sales and support for a wide range of computer systems including workstations, network systems, and other peripheral goods. Includes details catalog with product specifics and ordering information for the world.

Computer Price Cruncher

http://www.killerapp.com/

Provides sales and background on a myriad of computer products from hardware to peripherals. Includes a search index with pricing and technical specifications. Also provides a directory of computer resources that outlines many computer products.

Computer Recycler

http://www.coolsville.com/recycler/

Provides sales on new and pre-owned PCs and Macs. Includes products listing and pricing. Also provides Web Treks links to many different sites computer based and otherwise.

Computer Warehouse

http://usashopping.com/cgi-win/cw/cwnet.exe

Provides online sales for a wide array of computer products from power protection to network connectivity and all points between. Includes a shopping search index and ordering information.

Comstar

http://www.comstarinc.com/

Provides sales on new and used networking products including WAN, LAN, and 3270 equipment. Includes contact information, current sales, and product specifics.

Continental Resources Computer Division

http://www.conres.com/ctop.htm

Sells integrated systems and networks, PC hardware and peripherals, and provides rentals and service on new and used equipment.

Cyberian Outpost

http://www.cybout.com/

Provides sales on a wide range of computer products from PCs to games and all between. Includes browsing and search ability indexes.

CyberStar

http://www.vistech.net/users/cstar/

Deals in used and refurbished communications and networking equipment. Product lines include everything for LAN and WAN networking systems. Also includes modems, ISDN, transceivers and many more items. Includes sales, buying prices, and ordering information.

DAKCO PC Products Division, Inc.

http://dakco.lm.com/

Provides sales of PC components and accessories for individuals and resellers alike. Includes product information, technical support, and contact information. Specializes in custom built PCs with DAKCO's STEELBLUE Economy Services.

Datalink Direct

http://www.datalinkrdy.com/

Provides sales, pricing, and consultation for data communications products and equipment. Datalink carries a wide array of products from many companies. Includes catalog with product description, online price quote service, and contact information.

Datamini Systems

http://www.net1.net/comm/datamini.html

Wholesale distributes Pentium systems and other various products ranging from modems to monitors. Includes products available and prices. Also includes contact information.

Digital Dimensions

http://www.unicomp.net/lantz/

Retailer of computer memory. Provides quotes concerning memory and RAM pricing.

Direct Connections

http://www.owplaza.com/dc/dcindex.html

Supplies hard drives, DAT drives, optical drives, monitors, CD-ROMs, scanners, and raid systems.

Find out if CD-ROM recorders are finally under $1,000. Get free magazine subscriptions with the purchase of $500 or more from Direct Connections.

Domanski-Irvine Book Company

http://www.u-net.com/~dibookco/

Publishers of books specializing in database architecture. Find out about their self-published *A Practical Guide to Writing and Publishing Your Own Books.... and Marketing on the Internet.*

Egghead Software

http://www.egghead.com/

Provides online computer store that offers nearly anything for the home computer user or businesses. Includes product search field, category search index, and ordering information. Also provides local store and contact information.

EMJ Data Systems Limited

http://www.emj.ca/

Provides home site and information for EMJ, an international distributor of computer hardware, software, and peripherals. Includes information broken down into offices in Canada, the United States, Brazil, and Hungary. These sites includes company background, technical support, product information, catalog, and ordering information.

Essential Data, Inc.

http://netmar.com/mall/shops/edi/

Provides sales of computer peripherals and related products. Includes company catalog, ordering information, downloadable software, and links to product manufacturers.

EZ Systems

http://register.com/drives/

Provides sales and repair of tape and optical drive systems. Includes products offered, service listings and contact information.

F. F. Tronixs

http://www.fftron.com/fftron/

Distributes and sells surge protection equipment and communications products. Includes product catalog that provides technical specifications and ordering information. Also includes a detailed company profile.

Global Computing, Inc.

http://www.planet-hawaii.com/global/

Offers computer hardware, software, and networking items from Hawaii.

Global Union Square Internet Shopping Mall

http://www.gus.com/gus-home.html

A "shopping mall" divided into 16 categories. Categories include travel, computer products, gifts and flowers, clothing, health, real estate, and more. An unusual site.

Grey-Tech Computer, Inc.

http://www.inforamp.net/~greytech/

Buy computers and computer products over the Internet. Provides links to inventory, descriptions, prices. Put together the system you want for your home or office.

Hamilton Rentals Place

http://www.hamilton.co.uk/

Mid-range computer system reseller and largest computer system rental in the UK. Provides links to digital and HP products, refurbished products, software and PC offers, purchase and rental pricing information. For the small business owner.

HNR Computers

http://www.hnr.com/

A wholesale distributor of microcomputer products to South Africa. Provides links to reseller's guides, online ordering, specials, computer publications, other vendors, product descriptions, and support.

Icon Technologies, Inc.

http://www.icontech.com/

Computer engineering firm for businesses, individuals, and organizations in the Northeastern Pennsylvania area. Allows you to customize the computer system you need for the lowest price.

IPC Technologies, Inc.

http://www.ipctechinc.com/

Buy your computer hardware and software from the Austin Direct catalog. Low prices on computers. Access to product information, pricing, and ordering.

L & H Computers

http://www.citivu.com/rc/lnh/index.html

Design the computer system you want for your home or business. Click on the price range and go from there.

Laser Express

http://emporium.turnpike.net/D/dcservice/wg/krantin.htm

A laser printer toner cartridge re-manufacturer based in Pennsylvania. Pricing and order information provided. Other cartridge services available also.

Laser Products and Services Group

http://www.infoanalytic.com/laser/

Laser printer, fax, and copier supplies at low costs for your home or business. New and re-manufactured products available. On site laser printer repair also available.

Laser Renewal

http://www.infi.net/~elspence/

Based in Roanoke, Virginia, toner cartridge re-manufacturing, computer supplies, and laser printer equipment company for your home or office.

LinkStor

http://www.linkstor.com/

Will find that hard to locate mass storage or networking item for you corporation. Check out their

large product line, networking equipment, adapters, CD-ROMs, and more.

LMB Microcomputers

http://www.lmb.iquest.net/

A computer reseller offering products, desktop support, development, educational, and technical support. Access to any of their products, departments, and employment opportunities.

Logic Approach

http://www.eden.com/~logic/

A growing site specializing in buying, selling, and advertising new, used, and hard to find computer hardware equipment. Check out their catalog, products, sales, and more.

Lotus Selects Catalog

http://nyweb.com/lotus/

One-stop shopping for Lotus upgrades and enhancements, software suites, books, and video products.

Mac Talk, Inc's WWW Page

http://www.primenet.com/~mactalk/

Macintosh reseller providing a digital catalog of Mac products. Choose Cool Links if you'd like to give your eyes a workout.

MacZone Internet Superstore

http://www.maczone.com/maczone?mzstart@255202dmql

Carries a complete line of Macintosh hardware, software, and peripherals. If you are a customer of MacZone, access their customer service for quick help to nagging problems. This site also features links to PCZone, a catalog retailer of PC hardware and software. This site also offers overnight delivery, secure online ordering, and the chance to win free computer products.

Mantissa Computer Systems

http://www.epix.net/~lance/mcsi.html

A computer reseller and solution provider in Bethlehem, Pennsylvania. Check out this site if you're wondering how neon lite blue text looks on a Web page.

Micro-Rent Corporation

http://www.deltanet.com/micro-rent/

Rent, rent to own, or purchase computer equipment from this California-based company. Equipment is guaranteed and also comes with technical support.

Micro/Station at UIC

http://www.MicroStation.uic.edu/

This is the page for the campus computer store at the University of Illinois at Chicago. Purchase computer software and hardware directly from MicroStation. UIC faculty, staff, and students are eligible for manufacturers' discounts.

Microtrader

http://www.microtrader.mb.ca/index.html

A computer reseller based in Winnipeg, Canada. If you need a part for a "dinosaur," check here first. Or if you want to purchase an "off lease" or reconditioned computer at a reasonable rate, you can do that too. Some even come with warranties. Also carries a full range of new computers and upgrades.

MicroWarehouse, Inc.

http://www.warehouse.com/

Browse the MacWarhourse or MicroWarehouse catalogs, or search all available catalogs for computer equipment. Links to information on educational and government sales, security, shareware and product/software demos, and more. Order by 11 p.m. for overnight delivery.

National Parts Depot

http://www.megasoft.com/npd/

If you need parts for your computer, this is the site to check out first. Offering parts for a long list of computer manufacturers, you can download their catalog and place orders for overnight delivery.

NCA Computer Products

http://www.mediacity.com/NCA/

Memory storage devices and video displays and cards for sale at low prices. Provides support and service for the products sold and gives discounts to its business customers and their employees. Check out their catalog and ordering info.

Networks Plus Computers

http://www.sierra.net/ntwkplus/

Computer consulting, repair, upgrading, and training in the Lake Tahoe area. Also a full service computer store for purchase or rent. Check out their monthly specials.

New England Computer Supply

http://emanate.com/necs/

Brand name computer products, supplies, ergonomic aids, peripherals, and more for the workplace. Browse their database, and if they don't stock something you want, they will get it.

New Technology Computers

http://www.indirect.com/www/newtech/

A computer hardware recycling center that will buy, sell, or trade your used computers. They also offer a full line of new computers for sale.

New Wave Computers

http://www.neosoft.com/~synergy/

Upgrades, repairs, and builds custom PC clones, and sells new and used system parts. If you live in Texas, check out the Free Flea Market and the Hot Prices on Parts list; these prices may be the lowest you'll find.

Newman Group Computer Services

http://www.dpi.com/Newman/catalog.htm

Online sales of computers, computer products, memory, new and used equipment. If you know what you want, they can get it for you.

North American Digital

http://biz.rtd.com/nad/index.html

International software and hardware supplier, Novell reseller, IBM, Compaq, and HP computer system retailer. Check out their Designer Series Software ©.

PC Heidens

http://www.teleport.com/~pcheiden/

Provides sales on a wide array of computer hardware, software, peripherals, and products. Includes indexed catalog with updated prices and ordering information.

Phoenix Software Solutions, Inc.

http://www.tcpxray.com/tcpxray/

Provides sales and service for X Server and networking connectivity products. Includes online catalog, technical support, pricing, and sales.

Powercom and One Com

http://www.powercom.com/

Provides sales, support, and distribution of networking, connectivity, voice and data integration products. Includes product index with technical specifics. Also includes ordering and contact information.

Printer Works

http://www.printerworks.com/index.html

Provides online catalog and sales for Printer Works. Specializes in computer printers, parts, service, and peripherals. Includes an indexed catalog with technical specifications. Also includes reference links by manufacturer and model for parts acquisition.

The Q Group

http://www.dfw.net/~tqg/

Provides sales and technical support of personal computing hardware. Includes online catalog, prices, and ordering information.

S.P.C. Microcomputer

http://www.primenet.com/~spc/

Provides sales, service, and support of Novell Netware, custom software development, computer upgrades, and Web site design. Includes listing of services offered and contact information.

SBI Computer Distribution

http://www.the-wire.com/SBI/

Provides sales and distribution of a wide array of computer products including hardware, software, applications, and peripherals. Includes upgrades, processors, notebooks, power supplies, and many more in SBI's online catalog. Also includes ordering information.

SNC International

http://www.sncint.com/sncint/home.html

Provides online catalog sales of computer peripheral products. Includes product specifications, contact and ordering information.

Spectrum Trading

http://www.spectrum-t.com/

Provides online catalog sales and upgrades of Spectrum PC and Kingston Technology products. Includes detailed catalog, technical support, and secure ordering.

Reminders via E-Mail

http://www.netmind.com/e-minder/e-minder.html

If you have forgotten a birthday or special event lately, sign up for free e-mail reminders. The *e-minder* will send you a message reminding you of your important event.

Sunshine Computers

`http://www.sunshinec.com/`

Computer hardware mail order company. Provides links to different types of hardware for sale.

Team America

`http://www.vir.com/JAM/team.html`

Buys and sells used computer equipment. Includes online catalog of products for sale and buying prices for equipment. Provides online ordering information.

TENET Computer Group, Inc.

`http://www.tenet.com/`

Provides sales, support, and service of a wide catalog of products. Also provides Internet services and computer publications. Includes online product and service index.

Total Systems, Inc. (TSI) Home Page

`http://www.lynqs.com/TSI/`

Authorized reseller of SGI, Novell, DEC, IBM, and other companies' systems. TSI also manufactures custom business PCs. Find out their monthly specials, search their 30,000-item catalog, configure your own 486 or Pentium system, or check out links to the company's favorite sites.

United Computer Exchange Corp. (UCE)

`http://www.uce.com/`

Offers online buyer and seller services. Includes exchange services and sales. Provides online catalog, exchange rules, press releases, and online index of used computer prices.

Used Computers, Etc

`http://www.xmission.com/~gastown/goldpages/used1.htm`

Provides sales of used computers and software. Also provides repair services. Includes online prices and contact information. Also includes links to many Baltimore, Annapolis, and Washington DC sites.

Welcome to the Computer Shop

`http://www.preferred.com/shop/index.html`

If you need anything computer, this site may have it. Click on one of 62 different categories to see if they carry what you need.

Z-Law Software, Inc.

`http://mmink.com/mmink/dossiers/zlaw/zlaw.html`

Provides sales of a wide range of real estate-related software, hardware, and peripherals. Includes a search indexed online catalog with technical specifications of each product. Also includes secure online ordering and contact information.

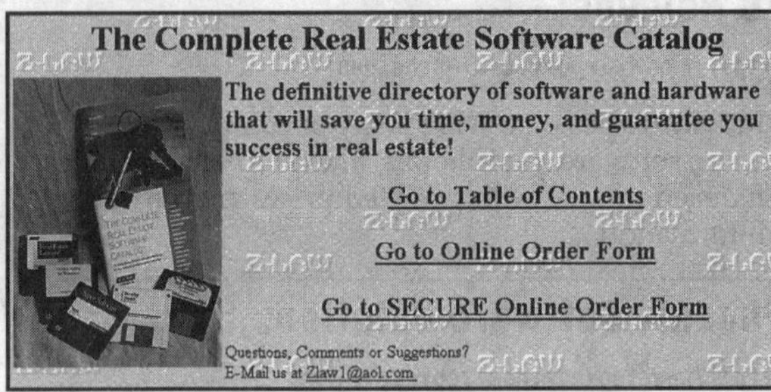

Online Services

The Allegro Group

`http://www.allegro.net/`

Provides Internet connectivity to organizations with GroupWise Internet access, Web hosting services, training and consulting. Also provides demonstrations, clients listings, technical support, site technical background, and a question answering forum.

Alta Vista digital.com

`http://www.altavista.digital.com/cgi-bin/`
`query?pg=about&what=web`

Currently, the most powerful search engine available. Digital Equipment's Alta Vista search engine contains text from more than 22 million Web pages. To narrow your search, make sure you read the Simple Query and Advanced Query information, or you'll wind up with more information than you could ever handle.

Amris, Ltd.

`http://www.iijnet.or.jp/amris/elead_pp/ad_ele_e.html`

Specializes in translation and creation of Web sites in Japanese. Includes samples of sites created. Provides list of Amris. Ltd. other services.

APCiNet

`http://www.apci.net/`

A well organized internetwork with links to many great sites under many subjects. Features MultiPlayer Game Server software and Internet access. Includes subscription information for the interested.

AT&T Business Network

`http://www.att.com/bnet/`

A recent arrival to the online access world is AT&T's Interchange Online Network. This new service requires special software, although the Web pages are visible in any browser. You can download the software at this site, sign up for a free trial membership, then take advantage of such powerful business services as CNN, Dow Jones, the Thomas Register, and TRW databases.

Axess Communications

`http://www.axess.com/`

Provides wide range of Internet services for both corporations and individuals. Includes subject links to hundreds of sites under a myriad of subjects. Also provides list and links of corporate clients, user home pages, and Internet background information.

BrainLINK International

`http://www.brainlink.com/`

Provides Internet access and various services for business and individuals alike. Based out of New York City, BrainLINK offers Web site creation and Internet support services. Features business and special interest sites that are based on BrainLINK along with many other links on various subjects.

Brazilnet BBS

`http://www.brazilnet.net/index.html`

Provides Internet access, consultation, and Web site creation for both individuals and companies. Services include Firewall and proxy set up, training, software development, and many others. Includes many links on various subjects that are from all around the world.

CDM Distributors

`http://www.iquest.net/cdm/index.html`

Distributes and sells computer hardware. Includes everything from motherboards to modems and more. Includes special rates for resellers and online ordering information.

CNI Communications Network International GmbH

`http://www.cni.net/`

Designs and produces custom made communications networks for various companies in industry, utilities, and finance. Includes information about ComVAN family of network products. Provides technical specifications, company profile, and listings of services offered.

Cogent Software, Inc.

`http://www.cogsoft.com/`

Provides an array of online services with sales of related hardware and software. Services include World Wide Web marketing, dial up, and high bandwidth connections. Also provides Internet tutorials, technical support, and company profile. Contains links to customers pages.

CommNet Data Systems

`http://www.comm.net/`

Provides a wide range of Internet and World Wide Web services. Includes dedicated and dial access services to companies, Web site creation, and technical support. Site includes Internet starting points, hot sites, an art gallery, and "The Psychic Dancehall" music site.

Community ConneXion

`http://www.c2.org/`

Provides Internet access and provider services specializing in security and privacy for their customers. Includes sign-up information, company policies, prices, and starting point for the Internet.

CompuHelp Online

`http://www.connix.com/~shpilber/`

Produces and provides Web site design and related consulting services. Includes detailed profile of design services with pricing information. Also includes starting points and hot links to a myriad of sites.

ConnectUSA

`http://www.connectusa.com/`

Provides Internet and Web services to individuals and companies alike. Includes site construction, Internet access, WWW Servers, FTP Servers, and pricing information. Also includes essays about Internet benefits for companies.

CrossLink Internet Access

`http://www.crosslink.net/`

Provides Internet accessibility for individuals and businesses with a wide array of services. Includes dedicated access and dial-in access provisions. Site includes services pricing and contact information.

Cyber Technologies International

`http://shrine.cyber.ad.jp/`

Provides an online site for the exchange of ideas and information as virtual creations can exist. Contains home pages from all over the world and anonymous FTP archives.

CyberDiner Internet Cafe Systems

`http://www.cyberplace.com/cyberdiner.html`

Provides services and products that allow any restaurant or bar to become online cyber cafes. Includes advantages, background information, product specifications, and links to cyber cafés around the world. Also provide Internet access and Web services for companies wishing to become "cyber."

Damar Group

`http://www.dgl.com/`

Provides computer training and Internet access for LANs. Includes course listings, technical support, DGL Search Engine, and product catalog. Provides contact and ordering information.

Dataworld

`http://www.datawld.com/`

Provides Internet access, service and products for individuals and companies. Includes Web site creation, dedicated access accounts, notebook computers, and Pentium computer sales. Also includes full product and services index that includes pricing.

DirectNet

`http://www.directnet.com/`

Provides miscellaneous Web services including server, Web site, frame relay , 14.4 and 28.8 connections. Includes links to search engines and a bevy of other sites.

The Dream Machine

`http://www.dreamagic.com/`

Provides computer consulting, WWW marketing, Internet starting point and network services. Includes links to many different business and leisure sites.

E-Doc

`http://www.edoc.com/`

Provides services and products in the electronic publishing arena. Includes information about Virtual Journal, a WWW publishing system. Also includes technical specifications, services offered, and contact information.

e.m.a.N.a.t.e.

`http://emanate.com/`

Provides a wide range of business services on the WWW. Includes business site creation, marketing, and advertising. Also includes links to many sites created by emaNate and contact information.

The Emporium

`http://www.vrsystem.com/`

Provides online links to businesses, entertainment, and educational sites. Includes links to VR Systems & Consulting designers of The Emporium.

ENVISIONET, Inc.

`http://www.envisionet.net`

Provides Internet related services, products, and consulting. Services include access for individuals as well as businesses with a wide array of types of connections. Also provides Web site creation, server connections, and software configuration. Includes service listings and contact information.

Epublish

`http://www.fullfeed.com/epub/index.html`

Provides a wide range of Internet publishing services including page creation, document, and multimedia formatting. Includes service listings and contact information.

Excite

`http://www.atext.com/`

Provides home for the Excite Navigation Services and search engine. Includes company background, press releases, and magazine articles about Excite. Site also provides City.Net, a comprehensive set of links to community sites all over the world.

Flamingo Communications Inc.

`http://www.fcom.com/`

Flamingo Communications is an Internet provider for California's South Bay area and its Web page includes local sports, weather, and television listings. However, it also provides the basic user with links to Web browsers and libraries, "cool sights," public service pages, national weather, and sports.

Florida Online

`http://digital.net/`

Florida Online provides a service to help computer hobbyists develop their own home pages. Several examples are given, from the Florida Online Internet surf team's individual home pages to business pages and family pages.

Global One

`http://www.globalone.net/`

Provides online service for your business. Will design Web pages, provide Web space, dial up numbers. Also offers Internet training courses. Links to business message boards, hot sites, and search engines.

Green Bay Online!

`http://www.dct.com/`

A Public and commercial service based in Green Bay, Wisconsin. Provides links to search engines, software archives, businesses and info, pages of their clients, as well as local news and weather.

GroMedia

`http://www.iea.com/~mikevm/`

This is an index link from the Computech Page. Computech is an online service provider for the inland northwest. Provides links to newsgroups, public service pages, Web classes, and clients' Web pages.

Hot City Networking

`http://www.hotcity.com/`

Directory of home pages indexed by Hot City Networking. Provides links to BBS, users, and other Web news.

I. Net Solutions, Inc.

`http://www.mke.com/`

Offers Internet services to individuals and businesses in Milwaukee and southeastern Wisconsin. Provides links to real estate and automobile info, tourism, community and services.

Icanet

http://www.compass.net/

Provides full range of Internet services. Includes providing access for individuals and businesses. Site has links to many different search engines and other pages.

Indiana University's UCS Knowledge Base

http://sckb.ucssc.indiana.edu/kb/

A database of more than 4,000 questions and answers about computers and computing. Simply enter a search term and press Submit Query; related questions and answers will appear on a follow-up page. Very simple to use.

Intercom

http://www.intercom.es/ingles/

Telecommunications services for businesses and individuals based in Spain. Offers online service, game connections, software.

Internet Home Users Group (IHUG)

http://ihug.co.nz/

An Internet user group in New Zealand. Access to home pages, software and support, charges, membership info, news and other services.

Interstate FiberNet

http://www.mindspring.com/~itchold/itc/ifn/ifn.html

Telecommunications transport services at low costs for your business located in the Southern United States. Links to and information about services offered.

Intertex

http://www.algonet.se/~intertex/

A Sweden-based communications product developer and manufacturer. Links to many products, ordering info, news and press releases, contact info, and more.

Jay Barker's Online Connection

http://www.accessone.com/~shwaap/onlinec/index.html

An excellent site that compares each of the major online information providers and national Internet service providers (ISPs). Price, software features, access speeds, exact costs per hour, and subscription packages are compared and presented in a simple list. This is a must see site if you are considering a national ISP or online service, such as AOL or CompuServe.

JUMBO! Shareware Archive

http://www.jumbo.com

The perfect site for the miserly Web surfer. Jumbo! offers thousands of freeware and shareware programs in such categories as business, games, personal, programming, utilities, and graphics. Searching for your favorite shareware title is easy. Click on the category and find it alphabetically. New programs are added every day.

Merisel's Sun Division

http://www.merisel.com/

A Fortune 500 company and wholesale distributor of computer software and hardware products, based in California. Access to their products, placing an order, and how to become a customer of Merisel.

OAK Software Repository

http://www.acs.oakland.edu/oak/oak.html

A well-organized Web page that offers links to a number of software archives and repositories on a number of different subjects. Lets you search the directory by subject area.

pixel Generation, Inc.

http://www.pixgen.com/

Provides Web consultation, access, and page design. Includes listing of services offered, company philosophy, and contact information.

Planet Communications

http://www.tc.net/planet/

Provides Internet services including Web site creation, consulting, marketing, and access connectivity. Includes services offered, client listings, and company profile.

PObox EMail Service

http://www.pobox.org.sg/

Tired of your e-mail address constantly changing? PObox provides an electronic mail forwarding service. Includes service features and online ordering.

Qpage.Com

http://www.Qpage.com/

Provides self page creation on the WWW with Qpage services. Includes background info about Qpage and Qpage Deluxe. Also includes ordering and contact information.

Quay Information

http://www.quay.co.uk/

Provides WWW services such as Web site creation, Internet training, and consulting. Includes online portfolio of graphics work, links to sites created, and listing of services offered. Also includes links to related sites and contact information.

Quick.Net

http://www.cloverleaf.com/

Provides Internet access for business and individuals along with a long list of related services and products. Includes consultation and design of Web sites and home pages. Also includes price listings of services and products.

r.u.there?

http://www.personalnet.com/

Provides real-time online conversation services over the Internet. Includes company profile, services offered, software background, and ordering information. Also provides technical partners listings.

SenseMedia Online

http://sensemedia.net/

Provides Internet access services, Web site creation, and links to almost anywhere in the virtual world. Includes company background and links to local servers from Malaysia to Hawaii to Oregon and beyond.

SoftInfo Software Information Center

http://www.icp.com/softinfo/homepg_3.html

Search for a particular software program, company, service related to information technology using this popular search engine. Perform a full name, company, product name, alphabetical list, or categorical search using their simple interface.

Sojourn Systems

http://www.sojourn.com/

Provides internet management and access services for businesses and individuals. Includes listing of services offered and pricing information. Also includes links to many sites, company news, and newsgroup information.

SPAN Information Technology, Inc.

http://www.spanit.com/

Provides Internet access services for Canada. Includes links to many different Canadian sites. A great place to start if looking into information about business, travel, government, and culture up north.

Southwest Web

http://www.southwestweb.com/

Provides online access and Web site design services. Includes links to sites created and services offered. Also includes contact information and a glossary of Internet terminology.

Stat Tech

http://www.stattech.com.au/

Produces the E-Publish line of electronic Internet publishing products. Includes company profile, product background, downloadable demos, and links to other related electronic publishing sites.

SuperLink.NET

http://www.superlink.net/

Provides a wide range of Web services including Web site creation, access, and virtual mall services. Includes technical services, links to sites created, and contact information.

Computers

System Optimization Information

http://www.dfw.net/~sdw/index.html

A popular, helpful site that provides a number of FAQs, reviews, and lists of computer performance-related information. Find out which manufacturer has the fastest motherboard, or choose a particular category, such as chipsets, to read about ways to improve their speed.

ThoughtPort Authority, Inc.

http://www.thoughtport.com/

Provides WWW access services and Web site design for businesses and individuals. Includes links to many different sites and search engines.

Tiger Mountain Productions

http://www.halcyon.com/mkinder/Tiger.html

Provides Web and multimedia services including Web site design, CD-ROM production, and a wide range of training courses. Includes listing of services offered, company resources, and contact information.

Total Connectivity Providers

http://www.tcp.co.uk/

Provides Internet access solutions and related services and support. Includes Web site creation and maintenance along with Internet training services. Site provides clients listing, company news, and contact information.

TRG, Inc.

http://www.trglink.com

Web site for USAGroup's TRG open forum, which presents major issues impacting higher education. This Web site includes a feedback forum, links to universities that are expanding students' access to information technology, and studies of students' knowledge of computers.

U-NET

http://www.u-net.com/

Provides a showcase and links to many different commercial sites. Includes search index and a subject browser.

Vector Internet Services

http://www.visi.com/

Provides Internet access services and Web site creation for businesses, organizations, and individuals. Includes services offered, pricing, and contact information. Also includes links to many sites and search engines.

Virtual Communications

http://www.slip.net/~wieneke/

Specializes in Web site creation and support services. Includes listing of services offered, links to sites created, example artwork, and customer testimonials.

Web Professionals, Inc.

http://www.professionals.com/

Provides Web site services including page design, Internet access, publishing, and more. Includes service specifics, pricing, links to sites created, Web news, and contact information.

Web Weavers Publishing

http://www.keytech.com/~weavers/index.shtml

Provides Web site pagination and publishing services. Includes service details, pricing, and samples of work completed.

WebPub Communications

http://www.io.com/~webpub/

Provides a wide range of Web publishing services including Web site design, artwork creation, graphics manipulation, and more. Includes links to clients sites, company resources, and contact information.

WebSpace

http://www.wwwcom.com/

Provides Web consulting, server, design, and marketing services. Includes Web page creation, management, and publicity advertising. Site includes work examples, pricing, and contact information.

The Well Connected Mac

http://www.macfaq.com/

Online guide to everything Macintosh, including FAQ lists, vendor contacts, software, Web sites, mailing lists, upcoming events, reviews of Mac-related books, periodicals, and more.

Whitey's Web Works & Internet Services

http://www.rmii.com/~whitey/

Provides Web publishing services, Internet consulting, marketing, training, and research services. Includes featured listings of services offered, pricing, links to sites created, and contact information.

WonderNet Digital Communications, Inc.

http://www.wondernet.com/

Provides Internet marketing services including company Web access, site development, and advertising services. Includes client listings, company profile, philosophies, and contact information.

World Information Network

http://www.winnet.net/

Provides Internet access services for businesses and individuals. Includes indexed links and search engine access. Also provides Web site development and maintenance services.

WWW. WIN.COM

http://www.win95.com

Touts itself as the one stop necessary for all your Windows file needs. Search for Windows 95 and Windows NT files and home pages.

XXL

http://www.xxl.com/

Provides a wide range of Internet services including access, site creation, maintenance, and consultation. Includes services offered, pricing, links to sites created, and contact information. Also includes links to many sites under a table of contents.

Operating Systems

Apple Software Updates (ftp.info.apple.com)

http://cgi.info.apple.com/cgi-bin/lister-pl?Apple.Support.Area/Apple.Software.Updates/US

FTP site containing all the updates for Apple software products. If you need to update your version of Apple System 7, or need a patch for a Windows printer driver, look here first.

ARDI Executor

http://www.ardi.com

Download a working demo of Executor, a 100% native software Macintosh emulator for DOS, Linux, and NEXTSTEP. Enter a specific Mac program, such as Illustrator 5.5 in the Online Documentation link search engine to find out if it has been tested on Executor.

Current Operating Systems Projects and OS-Related Research

http://www.cs.arizona.edu/people/bridges/oses.html

An incredibly detailed compendium of every known OS research project worldwide. If you're interested in the future of computer operating systems, check out the Full Alphabetical List of OS Projects, which describes dozens of OS research projects currently underway at universities and companies such as Sony, Sandia, Bell Labs, and Sun.

Florida Tech HELP DESK

http://sci-ed.fit.edu/arcshelpdesk.html

Provides FAQs, online books, articles, and reviews about Unix for those who are new to the language. An excellent resource for the budding Unix guru and future Web master.

Openstep for Windows

http://www.next.com/OpenStep/Welcome.html

The OPENSTEP development language from NEXT provides businesses with an object-oriented environment for creating custom client/server applications on any platform. This site explains NEXT's advanced environment, their product line, and lists authorized sales centers. Click on About NEXT to see screen shots of each of their products in use.

OS/2 versus Windows 95 Battle for Operating System Domination

http://www.brainiac.com/brian/oswin.html

Provides a detailed comparison of these two operating systems. This page discusses the crash protection features of OS/2 and Win95, multitasking characteristics, and each product's interface. A good place to start when comparing modern GUIs.

OS/2 Warp Product Family Home Page

http://www.austin.ibm.com/pspinfo/os2.html

Information for newcomers to the Warp operating system and support for existing users. This page has dozens of links to e-zines, technical support, Usenet groups, and developers conferences. Newcomers should click on the billboard on this page to download a free working demo of the Warp operating system.

PC-DOS 7

http://www.austin.ibm.com/pspinfo/supplemt.html

Are 16-bit operating systems still available? You bet! IBM's recent update to PC-DOS includes built in Stacker compression, memory optimized commands, built in REXX programming language, and more. This page describes at length version 7's endless number of features.

Que's Complete List of Windows 95 Products

http://www.mcp.com/que/win95/complete.html

Lists every upcoming book on Windows 95 and Win95 software. If you don't see a title here you may eventually need, you're probably a Microsoft programmer! All the book titles are organized by category, such as Excel 95, Winword 95, and PowerPoint 95.

Slackware Professional Linux

http://www.morse.net/spro.html

Comprehensive discussion of the Slackware version of Linux, currently considered the most complete and easiest to use version of this public domain Unix environment. The Slackware Linux package is only $25.00 and comes on 4 CD-ROMs with a 500-page user manual. Added features include a complete X Window environment, multimedia extensions, full TCP/IP networking, and a number of useful applications.

Randy's Windows 95 Resource Center

http://www.cris.com/~randybrg/utils.html

The software includes a helpful review of the program, a link to its author, and the date it was uploaded to the site. A helpful page for the Win95 user.

This Week's Popular Unix Downloads

http://www.shareware.com/top/UNIX-table.html

Lists in order the 30 most popular Unix programs downloaded from shareware.com's Web site. To download your own copy of any of these programs, simply click on a file name. This list usually includes the best freeware/shareware Unix software available.

Xiaomu Niu's Internet Application Collection for Windows

http://sage.cc.purdue.edu/%7Exniu/winsock/

Well-designed site provides hundreds of the most recommended Win 3.1 and Win95 Internet programs. Simply find the type of software you're looking for and click on the program Xiaomu recommends. This site is broken up into a Win 3.1 and Win95 section and further divided into the different types of communication on the Internet (FTP, Telnet, IRC, WWW, and so on).

Personal Computers

Acer Computer

http://www.acer.com/aac/index.htm

Enter a monthly drawing for a free computer and check out Acer's newest product lines, such as the Aspire. The Windows 95 Information link provides a search feature to help you find information on specific Windows 95 topics—a very helpful feature for Acer owners.

Acorn Computer Group

http://www.acorn.co.uk/

Contains information about Acorn Computer Products. Includes links to Acorn Education, which provides a special program for schools.

Cult of Macintosh

http://www.utu.fi/~jsirkia/mac/index.html

A beautifully designed site that provides Mac worshippers with every imaginable convenience. This Netscape 2 enhanced page offers links to games, newsgroups, software search engines and archives, Power Mac FAQs, MUGs, Powerbook help, a Propaganda page for Mac skeptics, and the top 20 Mac Web pages in existence.

Dell Computer Home Page

http://www.dell.com/

The home page for this billion dollar PC manufacturer requires that you choose from one of 24 countries! The next screen provides choices based on your type of business, such as education, government, home office, or a large or small corporation. After a few more screens, you can examine Dell's latest servers, portables, and desktop computers.

Elek-Tek

http://www.elektek.com

Humorous Web site for this computer retailer. Take a survey, check out their online catalog, enter a few contests, and read the latest technology news. Their catalog features more than 8,000 products.

GW2K.COM

http://www.gateway2000.com/

Even if you don't have a Gateway, this site is so well-designed and visually interesting that it is worth a hit. Click on some great graphics to access and join the Gateway club and the kids club. Be sure to visit the Cow Zone, a strange, enjoyable page with contests and cow trivia.

IBM Personal Computers Home Page

http://www.pc.ibm.com/

Home page for IBM U.S. personal computers. Click on Aptiva, Servers, ThinkPad, Desktop, Monitors, or Options to access the type of hardware desired. Click on Options to access the support section and use searchable database to find patches, software updates, and popular utilities in IBM libraries.

IBM Personal Computers in the U.S. Aptiva

http://www.pc.ibm.com/aptiva/index.html

A colorful page describing the special features of the Aptiva line of PCs. This site also includes links to a searchable database of over 5,000 files and a helpful support library of questions and answers.

Micron

http://www.micron.com/

A simple home page for an extremely successful computer company. Find out about Micron's other products, such as SRAM, DRAM, PCBs, radio frequency ID, and field emission display (FED) products used in camcorders. Click on Micron Electronics to access their Web site for Micron computers.

NEC Home Page

http://www.nec.com/

Besides the common technical support, product info, and news releases, the Research and Development link, Trade Show info, and Career Opportunities may satisfy that insatiable information thirst.

Northstar

http://www.northstar-mn.com/

Computer repair for many manufacturer's laptops, monitors, printers, PCs, and more. Links to pricing and rate information.

Packard Bell

http://www.packardbell.com/index.html

Besides the support, product catalogs, and company news, Packard Bell's unique Home PC User Survey provides important information on trends in home PC use. This link includes charts and articles revealing who is using home PCs (a surprising number of older adults) and how their use is changing with the addition of new technologies.

Swan Technologies

http://www.tisco.com/swan/

PC clone mail order manufacturer. If you're looking for a new system, try out Swan's unique Confi-O-Matic. Choose the features and hardware you want for your PC, and out pops a price on such a system.

Newsgroup Filtering Service

http://sift.stanford.edu/

SIFT (Stanford Information Filtering Tool) is a free service that can help you search through different newsgroups. SIFT can filter your search according to author, organization, conversational thread, or newsgroup/e-mail list.

Security

American Power Conversion

http://www.apcc.com/

American Power Conversion is a builder of power surge protection devices. Site provides company background along with a guided tour about power and its ability to damage computers from PCs to networks. Includes a thorough list of customer references, business partners, technical support, and an online "Determine your Risk" quiz.

Atlantic Systems Group

http://www.ASG.unb.ca/

Designs, consults, and programs security systems including featured TurnStyle Firewall system. Provides ample information and reviews about TurnStyle. Includes trade show attendance listings, product information, dealer and distributor listings.

Anonymity and Privacy on the Internet

http://www.stack.urc.tue.nl/~galactus/remailers/

Informative site discusses how you can protect your privacy and security on the Internet using remailers, encryption software, file wipe utilities, and pass phrases. Download all the software you'll need to keep your computer secure.

ByteBox Computer Enclosures

http://www.bytebox.com/bytebox/

Produces and markets ByteBox protective enclosures for computers and other technical equipment. Includes technical specifications and purchasing information.

Community Connextion

http://www.c2.org/

Internet privacy page lets you send anonymous e-mail directly from this Web site—no e-mail software necessary. Click on the anonymity link to sign up for an anonymous e-mail account.

Computer Security Day

http://www.acm.usl.edu/Home/CSD/

Created by the Association for Computing Machinery, Security Day is intended to remind computer users of the need to see if their computers or data are at risk. This page explains the origins and purpose of Security Day and provides addresses to important figures in public office.

Cryptography and PGP Page

http://rschp2.anu.edu.au:8080/crypt.html

This site includes a detailed discussion of PGP that introduces cryptography to newcomers (the cryptography FAQ goes into more detail). Also included is the actual program for the DOS, MAC, Unix, and OS/2 environments.

Exide Electronics

http://www.exide.com/exide/

Designs and produces a wide array of power surge protection products. Includes background of products including technical specifications and applications. Provides company profile, ordering information, and technical support.

Index of Privacy Resources

http://www.hotwired.com/Lib/Privacy/

Excellent site for computer users interested in protecting themselves from Net weasels and Big Brother. This Wired magazine archive of government documents, legislation, articles on wiretapping and cryptography, and Internet groups provides useful news about security and the right to privacy.

Internet Firewalls Frequently Asked Questions

http://www.v-one.com/pubs/fw-faq/faq.htm

One of the hottest security topics these days is setting up a shield or "firewall" Web server that separates the Internet from a company's network. This site provides more information than you can probably handle in one sitting, including diagrams of Firewall topologies.

McAfee VirusScan for Windows

http://www.mcafee.com/

Maker's of the best-selling VirusScan software for Windows 95. Check out McAfee's other products, sign the Guest Book, download 30-day evaluation copies of all their software, or read the latest press releases.

National Computer Security Association

http://www.ncsa.com/

The Main Menu for this organization lists conferences, online seminars, and books about computer security; hot links are available for Internet firewalls, virus information, and late-breaking alerts. The Cool Stuff section provides free directories and tutorials created by NCSA; the Hot Links section lists hundreds of important Web sites concerned with security.

Network Systems Corporation

http://www.network.com/

Network security and Firewall systems to protect your valuable information. Check out their disaster recovery plan and information. Links to products and professional services, customer information, and frequently asked questions.

NH&A

http://www.nha.com/

An independent provider of network management, anti-virus, and security software. Check out the many products and companies they represent, including McAfee, TBAV, and others. Downloading information provided.

NIST Computer Security Resource Clearinghouse

http://www.first.org/welcome.html

This site contains information on dozens of security related topics, such as viruses, risks, privacy, conferences, public keys, and trust. The page includes information on security publications, patches, training material, software tools, and alerts.

Raptor Systems, Inc.

http://www.raptor.com/

Develops network security software for use in government and business applications. Includes company profile, product specifications, and articles about their EAGLE Firewall family of products. Includes technical partners listings, network security library, and contact information.

S&S International PLC-Dr. Solomon's Online

http://www.sands.com

Provides online information about computer viruses and security issues. Also provides background of the Dr. Solomon line of computer security and auditing devices including the Anti-Virus Toolkit and Audit. Includes links to other virus related sites and contact information.

Secure Computing Corporation

http://www.sctc.com/

Specializes in security and authentication products for network servers. Includes information about the LOCKout family of identification products. Also includes information about WebTrack security applications and more. Includes technical specifics and product features. Provides investment, technical partner, and contact information.

Security Engineering Services, Inc.

http://www.blackmagic.com/ses/ses.html

Provides a wide range of consulting and systems security information and services. Includes information about the COMSEC system, INFOSEC papers, and TEMPEST program management.

UN*X Net for Computer Security in Law Enforcement

http://fox.nstn.ca/~cooke/

Unix security resource with information on PGP, security IDs, anti-virus, and disaster recovery planning. Site also discusses U.N.C.L.E. staff and services.

VeriSign, Inc.

http://www.verisign.com/

Produces digital authentication products and services. Includes information about the Digital ID Center, which provides validity services of identification cards. Also includes facts about the Certificate familiy of identification products.

ViaCrypt

http://www.viacrypt.com/

Produces encrypting tools and software. Includes product facts, technical support, pricing, and ordering information. Includes press releases and reviews of ViaCrypt products.

The World Wide Web Security FAQ

http://www-genome.wi.mit.edu/WWW/faqs/www-security-faq

An invaluable resource for webmasters and employees setting up Web servers. This 120K(!) FAQ includes solutions for protecting documents, creating secure PERL scripts, creative, effective, fair user logs, security concerns with JAVA, and reviews of different operating environments.

ZD Net Trailblazer Security

http://www.zdnet.com/zdi/tblazer/secur.html#network

Information HQ for security and privacy. This site describes on-going projects at universities, recommended security-related Web sites, hacker sites, virus info, security FAQs, online magazines, and more.

Software

20/20 Software

http://www.twenty.com/~twenty/

Develops and markets PC-Install, an installation program for developers and consumers. Also produces PC-Loan, a graphical analysis tool for analyzing mortgages, car loans, and other types of money borrowing.

4GL Computing, Ltd.

http://www.demon.co.uk/4gl/

Provides Silicon Grafics Workstations, software sales, support, and services for the United Kingdom. Site also provides a full product guide.

Ablaze Business Systems, Inc.

http://www.radix.net/~ablaze

Provides information, sales, and support in association management software. Also provides Internet services ranging from page creation to Internet training to Java development.

Absoft Corporation

http://www.absoft.com/

Provides information, sales, technical support for FORTRAN 77, Fortran 90, and C/C+ software. Also provides download product information, Absoft Fortran Newsletter, and "Fred's Link O' The Week."

Abstract Technologies

http://www.abstract.co.nz/

Manufactures peripherals for IBM RISC System/8000 workstations. Site provides information about products, support, and technologies used. This includes downloadable software, product guides, and links to IBM technical tips and techniques.

ACC Corp., Inc.

http://www.acc-corp.com/

Site provides information and background about Red Hat Software, which is a leader Linux technology. Provides vast information about Linux, complete catalog of products, press releases, and applications information.

Accsys Corporation

http://info.acm.org/~rkaplan/homepage.html

Provides information about custom designed software, little language design, and Newton Products. Includes information about AMIGO, a software application English/Spanish dictionary and reference translation system for Newton Software.

Achieve Technology

http://www.mv.com/biz/achieve-tech/

Develops software for companies and organizations to comply with state and federal regulations. Includes training, regulation management, SARA Title III Compliance, and hazard communication software. Also provides complete and detailed history of company and their products.

ACI Company

http://www.caciasl.com/

Creates modeling and simulation software for the use in system and network design. Produces COMNET III, SIMPROCESS, MODSIM III, and SIMSCRIPT II.5 simulation tools and language. Provides information and background on these and other products. Includes company profile and listings of trade shows that CACI will be in attendance.

Advanced Computing Systems Company

http://acsc.com

Produces Personal Data Cache, Network Removable Media Librarian, and a number of Unix device drivers. Personal Data Cache manages file storage on client machines in a distributed environment.

Advanced Paradigms, Inc.

http://www.paradigms.com/

Provides software development, training, systems consulting, and engineering for federal agencies and other companies. A.P.I. is a certified Microsoft trainer, and has a highly certified staff of engineers and developers. Also provides a list of contracts, partners, and affiliates.

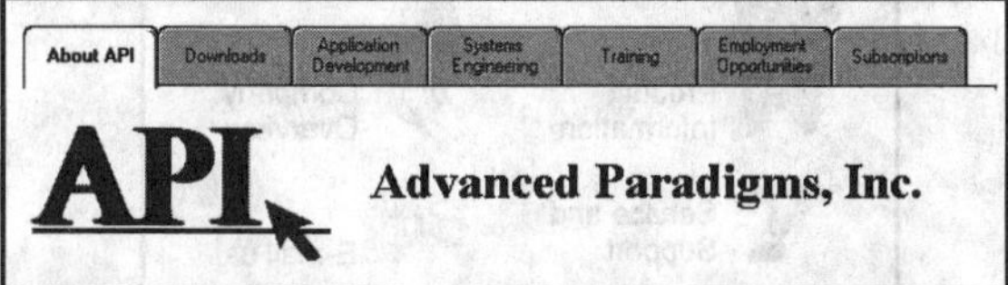

Advanced Quick Circuits, L.P.

http://www.iu.net/aqc/

Provides products and services specializing in quick-turn, high layer count, multilayer, dense packaging, advanced technology. Site also provides a general price quote service online, PCB problems survey, technical updates, and employment opportunities at Advanced Quick Circuits.

Agorics, Inc.

http://www.agorics.com/~agorics/

Provides design and production of custom software packages. Includes a full history of the company, technology background, customer listings, technical library, and a list of hot links to related technical papers and economic sites.

Aladdin Knowledge Systems, Ltd.

http://www.hasp.com/

Provides information and history on Aladdin Knowledge Systems and their products. Includes corporate and investors forum, Next Generation smartcard development information, FAST team merger background. Also provides links to HASP protections systems and HOPE programming enviroments.

Aliah, Inc.

http://www.aliah.com/

Provides background, software demos, methodologies, training, and support information for AliahTHINK. Includes features such as computer-based training, AliahSTRATEGY evaluations, and free software.

Alpha Microsystems Services Operation

http://www.alphamicro.com/

Provides company background, product information, services listings, technical support, AlphaCONNECT news, and AlphaSEARCH for more specific questions. Also provides Alpha stock information and employment opportunities.

Analytical Software Packages, Inc.

http://www.emi.net/~asp

Provides services and software in Web page creation, OS/2 software, and Windows software development. Includes links to World Wide Web pages that Analytical Software created.

ANGOSS Software ntl.

http://www.angoss.com

Produces Angoss SmartWare, an application development tool that also can be set up for system management and as a cross-platform application suite. Their KnowledgeSEEKER product analyzes databases and creates decision trees of relationships it finds in the database. This information can help in company planning. Another product—Argoss Voice—lets you create applications that respond to voice commands.

Applix, Inc.

http://www.applix.com/

Developers of Anyware software that utilizes Java technology. Provides company background, product information, technical support, alliances, demos, and overview of Anyware's abilities. The graphic design and artwork of this site is very well done.

AquaNet

http://www.finite-tech.com/fti/aquanet.html

Designs, develops, and manufactures software for the use in pressurized pipe networks. Provides information on platform support and pricing.

Arcada Software

http://www.arcada.com/

Develops tools and applications in data management for storage, management, and information access. Provides extensive product information. Also provides company background, trade show appearance dates, and information for doing business with Arcada.

Archive Comparison Test (A.C.T.)

http://www.mi.net/act/act.html

A monthly report that compares 45 different compression programs (archivers) for speed and compression sizes. If you work with graphics and often have to archive or transfer them, click on the bitmap graphic test to see where your archiver stands. WinZIP, for example, is one of the slowest and most average compression utilities.

ARGUS

http://www.argusmap.com

Home page for ARGUS net mapping technologies. Provides detailed information, and downloadable Argus Map Viewer to be used with their Virtual World. Also provides links to data partners in

software development. Available for downloading is a map of the United States that has over 3 gigabytes of geographic and demographic data.

Ashlar, Inc.

http://www.ashlar.com

Produces computer-aided design software for drafting and design companies. Features background and technical information about Vellum 3D CAD software packages. Includes technical support, service, company history, lengthy product information, and customer satisfaction notices.

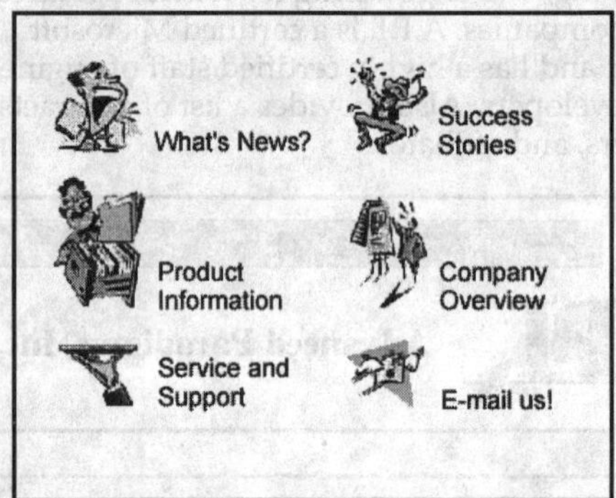

Aslan Computing, Inc.

http://www.aslaninc.com/

Produces problem solving and custom designed developmental support software for Microsoft systems. Also produces database building and Web site creation packages. Site provides company background, problem solving listings, product information, clients list with links, and technical development partners list with links.

ATI Technologies

http://www.atitech.ca/

Produces multimedia applications software, graphics accelerators, and other related products. Provides feature and specifications for all ATI products. Also provides driver information, press releases, and developer relations information.

Atlantic Information Systems, Inc.

http://www.learning.com/AIS/AISHome

Develops database software for use in nonprofit organizations. Provides online technical support, product background, software update section, and services listing.

The Attachmate Internet Products Group

http://www.twg.com/

Produces the EMISSARY line of desktop Internet software and products. Includes company profile, product technical specifics, and contact information.

Austin Software Foundry

http://www.foundry.com/

Software development company that creates applications for client/server architectures using an object-oriented development approach. Uses Powerbuilder, Lotus Notes, and proprietary software to develop corporate solutions.

Automata Design, Inc. (ADI)

http://www.adiva.com/

Produces Pro Circuit Builder software for the printed circuit fabrication industry. Provides sales, support, and product information.

Axis Communications AB

http://www.axis.se/

Develops and produces CD-ROM servers and print servers. Provides product information, distribution network, company profile, and technical support services. Includes Axis t-shirt online contest.

B & E Technology Group

http://www.ibetechgrp.com/

Develops and produces Visual Basic and Windows software. Includes reviews of their products. Site is under construction and should be more developed over time.

Bentley Systems

http://www.bentley.com/

Produces MicroStation and other engineering use software. Includes Mechanical Engineering, GeoEngineering, and Building/Plant Engineering lines of products. Provides extensive product information, technical support, listing of services, and the Bentley Gallery of images created with their software. Also provides links to Bentley Europe, Mid-World, and Africa online.

Bernstein & Associates, Inc.

http://www.b-and-a.com/

Provides software, training, and consulting. Includes work with VAX, ALPHA, Unix, and Windows NT. Also includes lists and links of Berstein & Associates' clients.

BGS Systems

http://www.bgs.com/

Develops BEST/1 Performance software and systems. Provides product information, sample graphics, technical support, and company news. Also provides contact addresses for BGS Systems world wide, including e-mail links.

Bismarck Group

http://www.bismarck.com/

Produces customized software and integration packages. Provides downloadable software samples, and links to client sites. Also includes hiring information.

Bluestone, Inc.

http://www.bluestone.com/

Produces developmental software packages and tools for use with Java, Motif, and Windows. Bluestone provides training, technical services, and consulting. Site includes corporate profile, services background, and product information.

Blyth Software

http://www.blyth.com/index.html

Produces OMNIS products for developmental client and server applications. Site provides downloadable software, product information, technical support, consulting, and training services.

BMC Software, Inc.

`http://www.bmc.com/`

A worldwide developer and vendor of software for the automation of applications and data on different types of computers in host-based and open systems environments. This site includes the latest news on applications and application suites BMC uses with clients, a calendar of free seminars in specific cities, and includes forums for questions and answers with BMC Software's research and development staff.

Brickell Research, Inc.

`http://www.shadow.net/~roland/soap.html`

Designs and produces custom software, tools and systems that are used in the medical field for information storage and billing. Also produces document imaging technology systems. Provides product and service information along with hot links to other medical sites.

Brightware Corporation

`http://www.brightware.com/`

Supplies technology products and software application consulting. Produces ART*Enterprise client/server retrieval software tools for systems building. Provides product background, service listings, and work done for clients.

Broadcast Management Plus

`http://www.bmp.com/`

Produces PC software for the media advertising industry. Provides product information, development forum, technical support, and features a media sales job opportunities list.

Bryant Software

`http://www.bryant.com/`

Produces Internet software and consulting. Company is undergoing changes and site is in flux. Includes e-mail addresses for technical support and service information.

Business Systems of America, Inc.

`http://www.webcom.com/~bsa/`

Provides sales and support for accounting software and systems. Includes company background, current news, product information, downloadable demonstration software, technical support, and free public software.

Caldera, Inc.

`http://www.caldera.com/`

Creates and markets network support software and workstations based upon Linux operating systems. Provides company profile, product specifications, technical support, online network documentation, development resources, and a link to Linux online reference. Also provides dealer and reseller information for the world.

Cambridge Computer Corp.

`http://cam.com/~cam`

Produces connectivity products for Windows and communications software for Macintosh. Includes vxConnect and vxServer for Microsoft Windows computers and mxConnect and mxServer for Apple Macintosh computers. Provides product specifications and contact e-mail addresses.

Camellia Software Corporation

`http://www.halcyon.com/camellia/`

Produces Batch Job Server, a batch job management program for Windows NT. Download a free working version of the program, access technical support, or order the full version of the program.

Candle Corporation

`http://www.candle.com/`

Develops and produces software applications including the Candle Command Center for Distributed Systems. This system can be configured to be used with Unix, Oracle and Sybase, Windows NT, NetView for AIX, and NetWare. This nicely organized site provides ample product information, company history, and customer support. Also includes job listings with Candle Corporation.

Caravelle Networks Corporation

`http://www.caravelle.com/`

Develops and produces monitoring software that works with hardware systems and applications of networks, intranets, and the Internet. Caravelle's WATCHER family of products and services are toolkits that monitor and report systems online availability, speed, and performance. Provides company background, product specifics, and technical support. Includes downloadable demonstration software.

CastCAE

http://www.castech.fi/

Produces CastCAE software for use in engineering applications such as tool and die, moldings, and other casting creation. Includes details about CastCAE 2.0's new features. Provides information about CastCHECK structural analysis design software for the metals industry.

Catron Custom Software

http://www.tiac.net/users/cgb/catron/

Specializes in custom designed software for business or home use. Also provides data conversions. Includes e-mail and telephone contacts.

CE Software

http://www.cesoft.com/

Producers of QuicKeys, WebArranger, and other software for use with Macintosh and Microsoft computers. CE Software centers around use with e-mail and Web service applications. Includes company background, product information, press releases, and technical support services. Includes links to different areas within the company from sales to employment opportunities.

CEO Software

http://www.the-wire.com/usr/ceo/

Develops financial planning corporate software. Also offers financial software consulting. Site provides information about products such as CEO*Plan, CEO*PlanPlus, CEO*Risk, and CEO*Demographics software. Also provides company history and product reviews.

CharterHouse Software Corporation

http://www.earthlink.net/~charterhouse/

Provides information and ordering information on Levinson Lyon Power Accounting software. This site

is rather sparse and does not go into depth about the software and its specifications.

Chemical Safety

http://www.portal.com/~austin/chemsafe/index.html

Produces Enviromental Management Systems (EMS) software for environmental, health, and safety management. Provides product information and area applications. Includes downloadable demonstration software. Also includes regulatory updates of changing federal, state, and local laws.

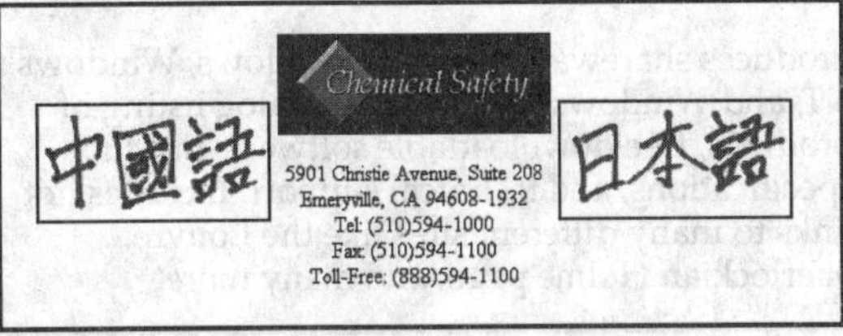

Chicago-Soft, Ltd

http://www.quickref.com

Developers of mainframe software, such as MVS/Quick-Ref and MVS/Quick-Ref for Windows, which enable you to access online message descriptions and programming information on VMS systems.

CIAO Software Solutions, Inc.

http://www1.usa1.com/~jurgen/

Provides information and background on CIAO Software Solutions that specializes in World Wide Web home page and site creation and maintenance. Includes a step by step process of how a home page and a Web site are created. Also includes contact E-mail address.

Clarion for Windows Icetips

http://www.io.com/~hanover/cw.html

Provides information and background on Clarion developmental software for the use with Windows. Includes upcoming product news, links to related sites, and career opportunities with Clarion.

Classic Variety AIPS

http://info.cv.nrao.edu/aips/aips-home.html

Develops and produces AIPS (Astronomical Image Processing System) software packages for tasks used in the gathering and processing of astronomical data. Specializes in software for radio astronomy. Includes software specifications, samples of image processing, and links to other astronomy sites. Provides ordering information.

Clayton Wallis

http://www.claytonwallis.com/index.html

Produces software, applications, and other tools like CompExec for use in finance, human resource, and consultant offices and firms. Includes editions for the desktop and office. Provides product background, company profile, downloadable software, and a guide to human resource-related Web sites.

clySmic Software

http://www.albany.net/~rsmith/

Produces shareware for DOS, Windows, Windows NT, and Windows 95. Includes catalog listing of products, free downloadable software, product specifications, and technical support. Includes hot links to many different sites like the Louvre, Sherlockian Holme page, and many more.

Coconut Info

http://www.dublclick.com/coconutinfo

Develops and offers software, training, and technical support for business and education under many systems, especially Macintosh. Includes company profile, product catalog, and listing of services offered. Also includes a hot link listing of sites ranging from Hawaiian weather forecast to pictures on Mars.

Cogent Computing Software

http://www.rt66.com/sjburke/

Provides software designed for public and educational institutions. Budget Director manages grants & contracts; C-Quest creates exams, quizzes, and questionnaires; and CC-Track manages tasks.

Collabra Software, Inc.

http://www.collabra.com/

Designs and produces "groupware" packages for companies for use in desktops and networks. Includes articles and press releases about Collabra and groupware systems. Provides product information, pricing, downloadable demos and evaluation software.

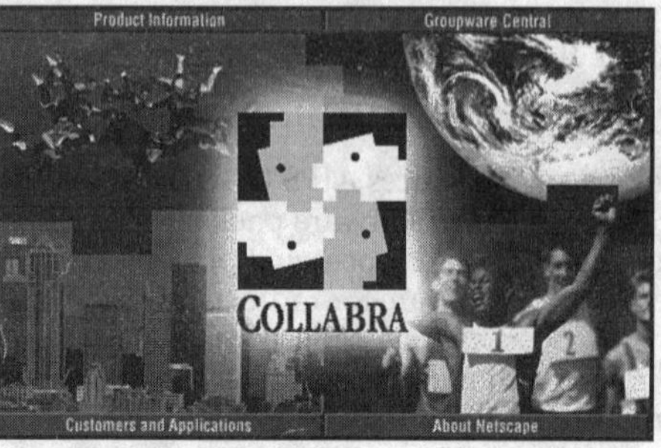

Columbia Data Products, Inc.

http://www.cdpi.com/

Produces SnapBack network software for disaster recovery and live backup. Includes background and technical specifications on the SnapBack family of products. Provides company profile and contact information world wide.

Computers and Learning A/S

http://www.oslonett.no/html/adv/Candle/candle.html

Develops and produces CANDLE software development platform products. Includes listing of products and services available. Provides extensive background and technical specifications for the Candle Authoring System and its related software products. Includes downloadable shareware and software demos.

Computervision Corp.

http://www.cv.com/

Produces and offers desktop and network product development including PDM products for data management and CAD/CAM software for automated design companies. Includes detailed product information and services offered listings. Provides Computervision stock and investor information.

Compuware Corporation

http://www.compuware.com/

Produces UNIFACE applications development software along with products for custom designed products. Includes company profile and in depth overview of products and services provided. Also includes Compuware news and upcoming trade shows.

Connectivity Custom Controls

http://www.toupin.com/~etoupin/ccc.html

Provides information about Plug-n-Play connectivity software products. Includes brief synopsis of Connectivity Custom Control Pack for network communications capabilities. Also provides contact information.

Core Systems

http://www.win.net/~core/

Produces Internet-Connect networking software packages for accessibility to the Internet. Includes product specifications, downloadable demonstration software, and contact information.

Cornelius Concepts

http://www.teleport.com/~concepts/

Develops and produces software applications using Delphi Rapid Application Development (RAD) environment for Windows. Includes company profile, clients listings, and personal background of Cornelius Concepts key officers.

Cort Directions, Inc.

http://www.empnet.com/cort/

Specializes in payroll and human resources software for client/server (Windows) and the HP3000.

CPI Electronic Publishing

http://www.citation.com/

Produces environmental, health, and safety compliance software. Includes information about the Regulatory Compliance CD-ROM that includes registration with the Federal Environmental and Safety Authority (FESA). Provides links to other related sites.

CPsoft Consulting

http://www.azstarnet.com/~cpsoft/index.html

Produces Easy Time Payroll software for automated payroll systems. Includes product information, download sample software, and ordering information. Also provides links to Game Cheats, IU Music Resources, and Grendel's Archive sites.

Crescent Division

http://www.progress.com/crescent/

Designs and produces the PROGRESS line of software, applications, and products for professional IS organizations that are system databased in Oracle, Sybase, SQL Server, ODBC, and DB2/400. Includes product and service background technical information. Provides technical support, press releases, and ordering information.

CrossWind Technologies, Inc.

http://www.crosswind.com/

Produces the SYNCHRONIZE cross-platform task scheduling management software family of products. Includes lengthy product background and technical information. Also includes downloadable sample software, company news, and ordering information.

Custom Innovative Solutions (CIS)

http://www.cisc.com/

Develops and produces custom designed software and applications packages. Provides a large company profile and product information background. Includes downloadable software and company philosophies. This includes the "Loser User Awards," a strange yet enlightening group of quotes and e-mail, dealing with copyright infringement and company ethics.

CVS Bubbles

http://www.loria.fr/~molli/cvs-index.html

Produces CVS simultaneous file configuration software family. Includes tutorials, product specifications, trade publication articles, and contact information. Also includes links to FTP and WWW sites to related CVS products.

CyberMedia

http://www.cybermedia.com/

Produces AutoFix family software and other products for computer self maintenance and reference. Includes information about Oil Change for Windows 95 and First Aid 95 software. Provides technical specifications, product information, and ordering contacts.

CyberMedia, Inc. WWW Home Page

http://www.internet-is.com/cybermedia/index.html

Manufactures First Aid for Windows 95 and PC911 for DOS, software troubleshooting programs for PCs with software conflicts and other problems. First Aid fixes Windows configuration problems automatically. PC911 keeps track of DOS configuration files.

Cyclic Software

http://www.cyclic.com/

Specializes in software support applications for CVS, including porting new platforms and custom enhancements. Includes product specifications, free software, and company profile.

Cygnus Support Information Gallery

http://www.cygnus.com/

Provides commercial support and maintenance for free software. Includes working with G++, GDB, PRMS, and GAS. Site includes many different types of downloadable "Groupware," technical support, and manuals. Also includes company profile and contact information.

Databyte

http://www.databyte.com/home.html

Developer of Flexx, accounting software for client/server environments. Check out the JavaMania choice to download pre-built Java applets from Databyte.

Data Logic

http://www.datlog.co.uk/

Produces health care industry custom-made software, computer products for telephone connections, and security equipment for firewalls and internets. Includes product profile and corporate background. Also includes contact information.

DataViz

http://199.186.148.129/

Develops and produces file translation, conversion, and connectivity software applications for interaction between Macintosh and PCs. Includes information about MacLinkPlus, MacOpener, Conversions Plus, and other translation products. Provides technical specifications, resellers information, distributors contacts, company profile, and news.

David Whitt & Associates, Inc.

http://www.gate.net/~pdwhitt/

Develops, produces, and installs portable data terminals and software products. Specializes in real-time warehouse and inventory management software. Includes client list of installations and contact information.

Delphi Information Systems

http://www.delphinfo.com/~delphi/

Produces automation systems software and applications for the insurance and brokerage fields. Includes information about the VISTA family of products and a Delphi corporate profile. Provides contact information.

Delphic Medical Systems

http://www.delphic.co.nz/

Designs and produces medical laboratory computer applications and products. Provides company profile, technical specifications, and support. Includes links to other New Zealand companies and sites.

DGA

http://www.dga.co.uk/

Designs and produces connectivity software, applications, and products. Specializes in gateways that link Lotus Notes and cc:Mail to IBM SNADS and NJE mail systems. Produces the Gateway family of products. Includes company profile, technical specifications, and links to other related sites.

Diamond International Systems Ltd.

http://www.hk.net/~drummond/diammain.html

Produces accounting software including customized applications and packages for transport companies and other firms. Includes account structuring, special functions, and reporting background information on Diamond's products. Also includes contact information.

Dragon's Eye Software

http://dragonseye.vservers.com/

Produces K-Free software that monitors free memory, disk space, and system resources. Includes product background and ordering information.

DS Diagonal Systems

http://www.diagonal.com/

Develops and produces productivity software that monitors links in application design. Includes information about WAVE-Link, CAT-Link, and Best Bench series of products that are used in program development productivity. Includes technical specification, company profile, and contact information.

Dubl-Click Software

http://www.dublclick.com

Makes products for the Macintosh, Windows, and Newton computer. Download demos of their Calculator Construction Kit, Calx for Newton advanced calculator.

Dun & Bradstreet Software

http://www.dbsoftware.com/

Produces client/server software including the SmartStream family of applications and products. Includes company profile, news, product background, services offered, business and technological partners. Provides technical support, contact information, and training services.

Élan Computer Group

http://www.elan.com/

Produces Elan License Manager and other license management systems and products. Includes product specifications, technical support, licensing issues information, and evaluation software. Provides company profile and contact information.

Electric Gypsy Software & Consulting

http://www.tyrell.net/~elecgpsy/

Provides consulting and development of custom software for Unix, Windows, or DOS. Includes service listings and contact information.

Electronic Book Technologies

http://www.ebt.com/

Produces DynaBase Web Management systems, publishing products and services. Provides publishing content production services for the WWW and CD-ROM creation. Includes technical specifications, service listings, technical support, press releases, and product reviews.

Electronic Learning Systems, Inc.

http://www.vector.net/~elstech/

Produces Mac Manager and ChatNet software for Macintosh computer products. Includes technical specifications, downloadable demos, and contact information.

emotion, Inc.

http://www.emotion.com/emotion/

Produces the Creative Partner family of software for Macintosh and Microsoft computers that enable distribution of data for collaborative work across networks and beyond. Includes product specifications, company profile, technical support, and contact information.

Engineering Graphical Solutions

http://www.egsx.com/

Designs and produces Graphical User Interfaces (GUI) and development software for Unix-based computers utilizing the X Window System. Includes lengthy company profile and product technical specifications. Provides related links and contact information.

EnviroAccount Software

http://wheel.dcn.davis.ca.us/go/earthaware/

Produces environmental awareness and education software. EarthAware is an environmental literacy educational tool for use in schools and the home. Includes product background and ordering information.

Environmental Systems Research Institute

http://www.esri.com/

Produces GIS geographic information system technologies and desktop mapping software. Includes full product information along with reviews and press releases. Includes technical support, career opportunities, technical partners, and ordering information.

Eòlas Technologies Incorporated

`http://www.eolas.com/`

Produces FastApp Internet software and other application tools for intranet development, management, security, and tracking. Includes company profile and product technical specifications. Provides downloadable demonstration software, Web search index, and contact information.

ERDAS

`http://www.erdas.com/`

Produces ImagingGIS software and products. Includes product specifications, customer testimonials, company profile, ordering information, and upcoming trade show appearances. Provides technical support, upgrade information, and new product news.

ExperTelligence

`http://www.expertelligence.com/`

Designs and produces an extensive line of development tools, systems, and software applications. Includes information about Action! interface development tools and specialized applications for needs as diverse as air tanker refueling and aircraft seat layout. Includes product specifications, company profile, and contact information.

FCR Software

`http://www.fcr.com/homepage.html`

Develops portable network LAN and WAN software for OEM systems products. Includes product catalog, technical support, dealers listings, and company profile. Also includes job opportunities information.

Fineware Systems

`http://www.fineware.com`

Makers of the distinguished shareware products, Peeper, 1st Alert, Space Hound, and File Ferret. Read about these products, download them, and see if they'll help your work.

Focus GbR Software

`http://www.liii.com/~louiev/focusgbr.html`

Graphic Recall and Graphic Recall.pro are visual databases used by the graphic artist, video artist, and animator working on an Amiga computer. Links are provided to download demo software with the capability to play "mini movies."

Fundamental Software

`http://www.funsoft.com/funsoft.html`

Company describes itself as "the only System/370 Plug Compatible Mainframe manufacturer able to put the mainframe in a laptop." Provides links to various OPEN/370 models and configurations.

Futuristic Software & Computing Group

`http://www.entrepreneurs.net/futuregroup/`

Computer software company offering Visual Basic and C programming, multimedia services, Web page design, as well as links to free software sites, shopping and points of interest on the Web, and much more.

Gamma Productions, Inc.

`http://www.gammapro.com/`

"Supplier of Unicode based Internet enabled ActiveX" technology for windows and Unix users. Links to ordering info, press releases, and other interesting sites.

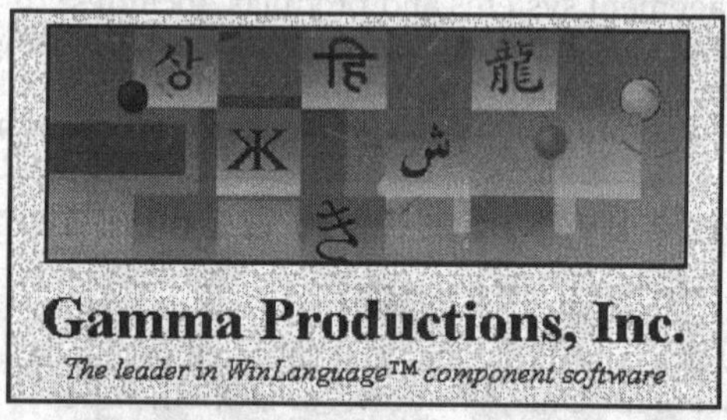

Gemini Systems Software, Inc.

`http://www.geminisystems.com/`

Gemini Systems provides software for POS/Inventory Control/Accounting for the building materials industry. Provides links to the software, ordering info, testimonials, company info, and press releases of their most recent products.

GeneCraft

`http://www.genecraft.com/vectdir/`

GeneCraft manufactures the Vector Detector, gene cloning software for Macintosh users. Provides links to information explaining intelligent cloning software, advanced features, ordering/downloading info, pricing info (academic discounts), and company info.

Generator

http://www.iea.com/~stevem/brochure.html

Generator is designed to be used with Microsoft Excel on IBM compatibles. It is a computer program designed to solve any mathematical problem you can define on an excel spreadsheet. Provides definitive links to genetic algorithms, what Generator can do, demos to download, and performance and application information.

GIS/Solutions, Inc.

http://www.gisedm.com/gisedm/gisedm.html

Offers industry standard software to environmental professionals who manage chemistry, geology, and hydrology information on PC compatibles. Provides 3D visualization capability. Links to sales representative.

Golden Diamonds

http://haven.ios.com/~cbsa/

Computer software for the retail, wholesale, and manufacturing industries. Links to software descriptions, product information, and ordering information. Also provides information about advertising your business on the Internet.

GrafTek Inc.

http://www.labelview.com/graftek/

GrafTek developed LabelView for Windows/DOS. It is a bar-code label design package for businesses and is easy to use. Provides links to a demo copy as well as to their other releases, most recently one that includes drivers for thermal transfer pictures.

Gryphon Software Corporation

http://www.gryphonsw.com/

This five star site provides software for two distinct groups: video professionals and graphic designers, and software for children. They are most known for their MORPH software. Provides links to other software products, pricing and ordering info, demos, beta info, and other Web sites of interest.

Harlequin

http://www.harlequin.com

Provides symbolic processing, electronic publishing, and custom applications. Programs in C, C++, Dylan, Lisp, ML, PostScript, and Prolog.

Hearne Scientific Software

http://www.hearne.com.au/

Mathematical, statistical, and graphing and forecasting software distributor in Australia and New Zealand. Provides links to products, catalogs, product samples, and ordering and pricing info.

Helios Software

http://www.helios.de/

A software company based in Germany, provides client/server solutions for Macintosh, PCs, and Unix/Risk based systems. Also provides color management solutions. Complete software descriptions and information provided.

HMS Software

http://www.wst.com/hms

Project management software and services, training and consulting, for your project management needs.

Honeysuckle Computing

http://pages.prodigy.com/GA/honeysoft/honeysoft.html

Multimedia and windows software development for the home or business. Provides links to shareware products for your home business such as Santa, Valentine, and Easter letters software, and software to start and organize your home day care business.

Hummingbird Software

http://www.primenet.com/~awong/legaudit.html

Provides software to streamline the legal auditing process. Fee $aver ™ will save your firm time and money. If you have a big job, Hummingbird will process it for you. Links to software, ordering and pricing information.

I-Kinetics, Inc.

http://www.i-kinetics.com/

CORBA component software for Enterprise Information Systems for businesses and organizations. Several new links to company info, products and services, press releases, seminars and training, and more.

iambic Software

`http://www.iambic.com/iambic/`

Company that designs, manufactures, and markets software applications for the personal digital assistant market. Provides links to the company, products, ordering, employment, support, other links, and news.

Illustra Information Technologies, Inc.

`http://www.illustra.com/`

Object-relational database management system to help businesses manage any kind of information. Provides links to company profile, products and services, demos, customer solutions, and virtual tours.

ImageFX

`http://www.imagefx.com`

Multimedia and imaging components for any sort of Web publishing. Provides demos, product and announcement links. FXTools version 4.0 for special effects publishing on CD-ROMs, presentations, ads, demo is available. Product and technical information provided for other software as well.

Imageware

`http://www.iware.com/`

Business software for point processing, reverse engineering, and rapid prototyping used by hundreds of companies. Provides links to product info, support info, current customers.

Imagix

`http://www.teleport.com/~imagix`

Offers program understanding tools for software developers working with legacy or complex software. Download a trial copy of Imagix 4D, get pricing info, customer support, other products and Web sites of interest.

Imaja Home Page

`http://www.imaja.com/imaja/`

Offers animation, multimedia, educational, and music software for the Mac user. Provides access to software demos and samples, artwork, calendars, other info of interest.

IMB Managing for Profit

`http://www.imb.com`

Home page for the developer of PEOPLE-PLANNER, labor management software, which projects business and labor requirements and creates optimum employee schedules. The Resource Center button helps you determine the best type of labor management software to use; Customers Say describes in detail how existing customers take advantage of People Planner software.

Immortal Software Productions

`http://www.synapse.net/~immortal/`

Specializes in music software production. Access to information on the production group and members, products, contact information, and downloading purchasing information.

InContext Systems

`http://www.incontext.ca/`

SGML and Web software for your business. Provides links to customer support, demos to download, business info, new products, tech info, and much more.

Inference

`http://www.inference.com/`

A cool site for information management software for your business or organization. Watch their upcoming events scroll across the bottom of your screen. Access to products, services, support, customers, and more.

INFORIUM, The Information Atrium Inc.

`http://www.e-commerce.com/inforium.htm`

Information management software that uses SGML and SQL relational database technology, solving your open information exchange needs. LivePAGE will manage graphics, text, and multimedia in a relational database. Links to company info, products, services, contacts.

Information Builders, Inc.

`http://www.ibi.com/`

Independent software solution vendor for any level of business that needs products and services for business analysis, reporting, data warehousing, and more. Provides links to products, tech support, user group, bookstore, consulting and training, press releases and announcements, and demo software to download.

The Information Systems Manager, Inc.

`http://www.infosysman.com/`

Creates multiplatform application tools for software and system development. Includes information about PowerFlex architecture and services offered by ISM. Provides corporate profile, product features, and contact information.

Insight Designs, Inc.

`http://www.phoenix.net/~insight/`

Provides software in order for your company to make the transition to filing your financial documents electronically, using the electronic data gathering and analysis system of the U.S. Securities and Exchange Commission. Links to software and database information, and other useful sites of interest.

Insignia Solutions

`http://www.insignia.com/`

Software allowing your business to use Windows applications on many different platforms. Information links for Mac and PC users. Links to products, catalog, tech support, press releases, and more.

Integrated Research

`http://www.zdepth.com/integ/`

A developer of software for digital media integration on Silicon Graphics workstations. Links to products

such as video production software, FAQs, integrated video info, support services, press releases, and more.

Interactive Software Engineering

`http://www.eiffel.com/`

Provider of Eiffel, the method and language to revolutionize software by reusing software components. Links to many Eiffel related topics, training sessions, subscription info, downloading info, and much more.

InterMind

`http://www.intermind.com/`

A new software manufacturing company for individuals and organizations who need to manage many communications tasks simultaneously. More information about this company will be available later in 1996.

International Knowledge Systems

`http://iks.com/`

Internet software development and consulting company experienced in JAVA applications.

International Software Systems, Inc.

`http://www.issi.com/issi/issi-home_page.html`

If your organization or business is looking for an integrated, graphical adaptable software package with services for process improvement, check out the ProSLCSE ™ products. Links to products and services, employee home pages, and other interesting links.

Interpretive Software

`http://www.execpc.com/~isi/`

Business education software for computer-based simulations. Links to simulations, products descriptions and ordering, newsletter, and more.

ISPW

`http://www.ispw.com/`

ISPW ™—Integrated Software Processing Workframe—will help increase the productivity of your application development and maintenance staff. Access to a technical overview, base system and options, benefits, FAQs, and more.

J-MAC System Inc.

`http://www.j-mac.co.jp/`

Based in Sapporo, Japan, a software company for the medical industry. Software to file, analyze, and transfer images. Links to company, software, staff pages, and more.

Jandel Scientific Software

`http://www.jandel.com`

Originally a microcomputer software tools developer for scientists, now an analytics and graphics software developer for scientists and engineers. Links to products and support, applications solutions, what's new, and much more.

JOBSCOPE Manufacturing Management System

`http://web.sunbelt.net/~jobscope`

Manufacturing management software for your contract-driven company. Special services if you are an aircraft repair and overhaul facility. Links to product information, services, employment opportunities, and more.

Kinfonetics Technology

`http://www.io.org/~cyourth/`

A software company based in Canada that specializes in customizing your applications for workflow automation. Links to products and information, some not requiring royalties, other interest areas, and contact information.

Knowledge Engineering Pty Ltd.

`http://www.ke.com.au/`

Company in Australia that develops database software, specializing in structured and textual data

high speed retrieval. Links to products, clients, demos, courses, and more.

LandWare

`http://www.landware.com/`

Software solutions for the Mac, PDA, or Windows users who are existing Landware customers. Browse through their list of new products and press releases.

Law Enforcement/Police Software

`http://www.augusta.net/alert1.htm`

Windows-based records management system for law enforcement agencies. Links to demos, features, tech support, and employment opportunities for law enforcement officers.

Legal Computer Solutions

`http://www.lcsweb.com/`

Software, management, and training applications for law offices. Links to research sites, the news room, and more.

Lex Systems

`http://www.link.ca/~lex/`

LEXIFILE is library automation software for PCs and can run on a LAN. Download a sample program or get more information and links.

Lexitech, Inc.

`http://www.lexitech.com/`

Software to bridge standard kiosk operation and the Internet. Download a sample, read customer testimonials, get up to date news, and more.

LifeGuide

`http://www.compuoffice.com/lg.html`

Canadian-based life insurance software system for comparisons, surveys, quotes, and information necessary to agents, brokers, and financial planners. Download the demo or order the software.

Lighthouse Software, Inc.

`http://www.lighth.com/~lighth/`

Business productivity tools and software development on many operating systems and in many computer languages. Links to their products and support services.

Lilly Software Associates, Inc.

http://mfginfo.com/cadcam/visual/visual.htm

VISUAL Manufacturing is integrated manufacturing software developed by Dick Lilly for one to one thousand users. Explore the specifications and benefits this software can offer you or your company.

LMSoft

http://www.lmsoft.ca/

HyperPage multimedia software integrates animation, video, sound, images, and hypertexts easily for use on the Web. Order a free demo CD or download other cool stuff.

Look Software Systems, Inc.

http://look.com/

Anti-virus software for your home or office. Links to products, support, and performance information.

Mabry Software

http://www.halcyon.com/mabry/

A computer software company based in Seattle, Washington. Products include MIDI Pack (to create and manipulate data from Visual Basic), an Internet Pack with new controls, and IniCon OCX, and Wave OCX. Check out their site and download sample software.

Macola Software from Osiris

http://www.osiris.com/osiris/products/macola/index.html

Develops accounting software for DOS, Unix, and Windows. Download a Powerpoint presentation of their latest Windows Macola package.

MacNeal-Schwendler Corporation

http://www.macsch.com/

For those in the field of computer aided engineering, software designed for finite element analysis and modeling. Links to products and support, technology, their featured "model of the month," and more.

Magna Computer Corp.

http://magna.magna.net/

Computer software for the resort industry, timeshare resort hardware and software, consulting, support, and opportunities. Provides a long list of resort clients.

Maui Software

http://hookomo.aloha.net/~mauisw

Creator of TimeTracker software for the Macintosh. All programs are shareware and are free to download. TimeTracker, an easy-to-use application for recording time tasks on the Macintosh, is also supported at this site. Check out the latest updates to TimeTracker and find out about TimeSlice, a more powerful time-tracking product.

Mayflower Software

http://www.maysoft.com/

Basic computer solutions software, disaster recovery, and specialty products for Lotus ™ Notes.

MCAE Inc.

http://www.ppgsoft.com/ppgsoft/inertia.html

Desktop software for design engineers, cutting your design and production time incredibly. Software will interface with your system's hardware, for complete integration and multitasking.

Medlin Accounting Shareware

http://community.net/~medlinsw/

Accounting shareware for Windows or DOS, including payroll, accounts payable/receivable, and general ledger. Click on the links to download.

MentorPlus Software, Inc.

http://www.webcom.com/~criteria/mentorp/

MentorPlus specialized in navigational software for pilots. Links to their products, news, and job information.

Merlin Software

http://www.deltanet.com/merlin/

Merlin Software features Proposal Wizard, a proposal generation software for systems integrators. Check out their Pro and Lyte versions, Mac and Windows updates, Beta testing, tech support, computers for sale, and other links.

The Message Board System

http://www.netins.net/showcase/message/tmb.html

Provides information about The Message Board System of programs and applications that provide conference attendance message and registration capabilities. Includes product features, customers served, and contact information.

MetaWare Incorporated

http://www.metaware.com/

If you are a professional programmer, check out MetaWare's software development kits with components such as assembler, compiler, debugger, and others. Links to technology descriptions, customers, tech support, and more.

Micro-Frame Technologies, Inc.

http://www.microframe.com

The largest manufacturer of software for managing government contract costs and schedule reports in the U.S.. Find out about training seminars, new updates to Micro Frame Program Manager and other products, access technical support, and learn about new developments at this successful software company.

MicroExcel Software

http://www.microexcel.com/mxsoft/mxweb.htm

Perfect Recall software allows you to store anything you find on the Internet and then load it into any other software package you prefer to use. Or load the images into another browser off-line.

Microstar Software Ltd.

http://www.microstar.com/

Computer Aided Document Engineering along with document design and authoring make Microstar the provider of end-to-end document management solutions for your corporation. Check out what they can do for your company, as well as download their free software.

Microsystems Software, Inc.

http://www.microsys.com

Developers of security and accessibility software, such as CyberPatrol, which protects kids from adult material on the Net, and CyberSentry, a program that monitors employees' use of the Internet. Download time-restricted working demos, read company publications and press releases, or read about their support of free speech. Their Route 6-16 link connects you to a list of Web sites that are safe for kids and suitable for family interests.

Milestone Technologies, Inc. (MTI)

http://spadion.com/mti/

Data broadcasting applications software and consulting, including SATX ™ file transfer software. Can be used to transfer data over any broadcasting network including cable television, Direct Broadcast Satellites, FM subcarriers, and others.

MKS Source Integrity Product

http://www.mks.com/useful/

Software configuration management for client/server and Web development for your organization. Their Integrity Products help to manage teams across remote locations. Check out their demo software, sales, training opportunities, and more.

MLL Software and Computers

http://www.ppgsoft.com/ppgsoft/wz_main.html

Check out their breakthrough WIZDOM-Pro that will change object-oriented technology to an effective development environment. Links to concepts, features, development facilities, product info, site licenses, and more.

Modular Software Corporation

http://www.primenet.com/~modsoft/

This company offers a variety of software packages including PicLan Networking software and FULL-VIEW for windowing. Check out their full line of products and support.

The Molloy Group, Inc.

http://www.planet.net/molloy

Developers of Cognitive Processor software for technical support departments. Find out what cognitive processing is and how it is used in this software.

NeoLogic Systems

http://www.neologic.com/~neologic/

Object oriented applications for software developers. Download NeoLogic software or find out more about their products, support, success stories, information, and jobs.

new stuff inc.

http://www.newstuff.com/

Manufacturer of fashion software including B. Famous on Stage for the fashion or costume designer. Check out their product demonstration or order your own copy.

Notes Solution Software

http://www.dct.com/NOTES/

A registered Lotus ™ Partner and Adobe Acrobat ™ developer offering consulting, custom notes application and development, desktop publishing solutions, and more.

The Numerical Algorithms Group Ltd

http://www.nag.co.uk:70/

Develops and produces scientific and technical software for mathematical problem solutions. Includes online catalog and a detailed background of the NAG group. Also provides white pagers, reviews, and contact information.

Pacific Numerix Corporation

http://www.crl.com/~pacnum/pnc.html

Develops electronic design validation tools and related software applications. Includes technical specifications, demonstration slide show, and contact information.

PaperFree Systems

http://paperfree.com/edi/index.htm

Developers of Electronic Data Exchange (EDI) technologies and applications. Includes background data about EDI developments and benefits. Also includes contact information for product catalog and ordering.

Peninsula Advisors, Inc.

http://www.best.com/~iris/

Creates IRIS (Integrated Real Estate Information Systems) management software for portfolio tracking, contract, and client services. Includes product specifications and services offered by Peninsula. Provides company profile, contact information, and links to real estate related sites.

Personal Library Software, Inc.

http://www.pls.com/

Produces information retrieval software that has graphical interfaces as well as textual. Includes detailed technical background and features on PL Web, PL Sync, and other Personal Library Software products. Provides downloadable demos, technical partners information, career opportunities, and clients using PL Web.

Pierian Spring Educational Software

http://www.pierian.com/

Creates educational software for schools and individuals. Includes product profile, company background, and links to many educational sites. Provides a media gallery, and online ordering information.

Downloadable Calendars

http://www.intellinet.com/CoolTools/CalendarMaker/

Hit this site if you want a calendar generated for you. Download it, print it, fry it up, grill it, etc.

Pinnacle Software

`http://WWW.CAM.ORG/~pinnacl/`

Produces custom designed software and consulting services along with a series of Pinnacle developed applications. Includes services and products offered with detailed specifications. Provides free demos, shareware, and links to many other sites.

The Plant Software, Inc.

`http://www.theplant.com/`

Produces E-Glue annotation utility for Windows based systems. Includes product features and contact information.

Praxis International

`http://www.praxisint.com/`

Provides software and consulting for database, data replication, and data warehouse applications. Page includes information on their data replication, training classes, and professional services.

Prime Time Freeware

`http://www.cfcl.com/ptf/`

Publishes mixed-media CD-ROMs, books, and provides collections of free software. Includes company catalog, ordering, and contact information.

Process Analysts, Inc.

`http://www.pai-colo.com/pai/`

Produces custom designed automation and management software and applications. Specializes in process integration, environmental monitoring, and data acquisition systems. Includes technical support, job opportunities, and contact information.

Prode

`http://www.prode.milano.it/prode.html`

Produces software for the chemical industry and scientific chemistry research. Includes information about the Prode Calculator graphical interface database tool. Provides company background, products catalog, and contact information. Also provides links to related sites.

ProSoft International, Inc.

`http://www.webcom.com/~prosoft/`

Provides information and demos of FileView developers utility software and applications. Includes technical specification, technical support, pricing, and ordering information.

Qbik Software

`http://nz.com/NZ/Commerce/creative-cgi/special/qbik/qbik.htm`

Produces developmental software for OaSIS Internet Services and creates other specialized Internet software applications. Includes information about Mail Monitor and WinGate software. Provides contact information.

Quality Software Management

`http://www.utopia.com/companies/qsm/home.html`

Provides custom software design, process improvement, and language creation consulting, services, and products. Includes in depth company philosophy, services, and background.

Quadrillion Data Analysis Software for Semiconductor Manufacturers

`http://www.quadrillion.com/`

Developer of Q-Yield, analysis software for semiconductor engineers, provides technical product information, information on obtaining free working demos, training information, and links to other semiconductor sites.

Quality America Incorporated

`http://www.theriver.com/qa-inc/`

Produces analysis, planning, and training software specializing customization for client needs. Includes product and service background with articles about Quality America's business and development philosophies. Provides information about training services, foreign distribution, and contacts worldwide.

Quality Software Management

`http://www.utopia.com/companies/qsm/home.html`

Provides custom software design, process improvement, and language creation consulting, services, and products. Includes in depth company philosophy, services, and background.

Quest Software, Inc.

`http://quests.com/`

Produces the Netbase Suite, VistaPlus, and many other families of output and database management software tools. Includes product technical specifications and features along with performance reviews. Provides company profile, technical support, services offered, and contact information.

RABA Technologies, Inc.

`http://www.raba.com/`

Develops and produces Unix-based custom software, applications, and systems. Also provides systems integration and consulting services. Includes technical references, product specifications, and services offered listings.

Robert McNeel & Associates

`http://www.mcneel.com/`

Provides home site for Robert McNeel & Associates developers of Rhino modeling software and other development and rendering products. Includes technical specifications and features, technical support, and training information.

S.S.I.T.E. Windows 3.x Utilities

`http://home.ptd.net/~dkt/util/utility.htm`

A nicely designed page that provides the best Windows shareware compression utilities and other utilities. Read about each product, then download it if you like what you see.

Safetynet, Inc. AntiVirus and Security

`http://www.safe.net/safety/`

Develops computer security, virus protection, inventory, and distribution software. This Web site lets you access product information and press releases, download software, and ask for technical support. Employment and Reseller Opportunities.

Sage Solutions, Inc.

`http://www.sagesoln.com/`

Develops custom designed software applications and products. Includes client list, company philosophy, and contact information. Provides detailed accounting of company resources and allocations.

Sanctuary Woods Multimedia

`http://www.sanctuary.com/`

Designs and produces interactive educational software for schools and individuals. Includes information about Major League Math software. Provides company background, link to education sites, and contact information.

Scandinavian Softline Technology

`http://www.softline.fi/`

Produces the SST Server, Open Edicom, and GMS SMS families of communications software. Includes technical specifications, company background, and online product updates.

Second Nature Software, Inc.

`http://www.secondnature.com/`

Develops and produces custom screen saver packages. Includes downloadable samples, licensing information, and available packages. Provides many artwork examples and dealers information.

Sequent Computer Systems, Inc.

`http://www.sequent.com/public/index.html`

Creates client/server platforms, software, and systems for a wide range of companies. Includes information about Sequent SMP systems, company philosophies, resources, and clients. Includes detailed company and product background.

Shana Corporation

`http://www.shana.com`

Develops forms processing software for Macs. Download the free full version of Informed Designer, forms layout software, or see if Shana's extensive library of updates, patches, demos, and crippleware has something you could use. Back at the home page, read how current customers are using Shana software in their work.

Shock Software

http://www.shock.co.uk/

Offers a wide array of services and products specializing in Web services, database development, and third party technical support on many popular systems and applications. Services include Java script creation, ShockWave development, graphic design, search engine set-up, data analysis, and conversion utilities. Includes service specifications and contact information.

SiliconSoft

http://he.tdl.com/~silicons/

Produces a wide line of PC software applications and products. Includes information about DacqEditor for DOS and services offered by SiliconSoft. Provides links to the Silicon Valley and tech services.

Simucad

http://www.simucad.com/

Produces SILOS III Simulation Environment logic EDA software. Includes company profile, product background, demo software, press releases, and contact information.

Sirius Software

http://www.siriusacct.com/sirius/

Produces business accounting software and develops custom accounting systems. Includes information about Sirius GT Accounting products and development services offered. Includes links to related sites and contact information.

Skylonda Group

http://www.skylonda.com/skyhome.html

Produces environmental, health, and safety software and products for companies. Includes consulting information, custom systems development, and product background. Provides client listings, technical partners, and contact information.

Smithmicro

http://www.smithmicro.com/

Produces communications and connectivity products. Includes information about AudioVision video phone software, HotFax for Windows, and HotDisk products. Includes technical specifications, online ordering, and contact information.

SoftPlan Systems

http://www.softplan.com/websoft

Produces architectural design software and products. Includes information about SoftPlan products and training services along with online demo software. Provides company background and ordering information.

SoftSell Business Systems, Inc.

http://www.softsell.com/

Designs and produces the VersaTest and Relate testing, simulation, and support software and products. Includes technical specifications, client listings, and contact information.

Software Consulting Services

http://nscs.fast.net/

Provides consulting and software products for newspapers and other periodicals. Includes information about Layout-8000 products. Also includes company profile, customer, and contact information.

Software Tailors

http://www.traveller.com/~rew/tailors.html

Provides custom software development, Web site creation, and Internet training. Includes listings of services offered, products utilized, company philosophies, and contact information.

Solid Oak Software, Inc.

http://www.solidoak.com/

Produces Internet software systems like CyberSitter adult material filters, Re:PLY e-mail applications, Re:PUBLIC client Internet software, and other products. Includes technical specifications, company news, technical support, and online ordering.

SouthWare Innovations, Inc.

http://www.excelco.com/swinfo.html

Produces the Excellence Series of business software and other office products. Includes information about inventory and management software products. Provides technical specifications, features, and ordering information.

SPARTA, Inc.

http://www.huntsville.sparta.com/

Provides software development, corporate management, systems engineering, and other technology services. Includes listing of services offered, technologies utilizes, SPARTA resources, clients, and contact information.

Specialized Business Solutions

http://www.some.com/sbs/

Produces Keystroke point of sale software and products. Includes product specifications and features along with downloadable demonstration software. Provides dealers and contact information.

SpeedSim, Inc.

http://www.speedsim.com/speedsim/

Provides a home site and information about Cycle-Based Simulation software that validates logic designs. Includes information about the SpeedSim line of simulation software. Also includes information about support products for Windows NT and Linux operating systems. Provides detailed company profile and contact information.

SST, Inc.

http://www.webcom.com/~sstinc/

Provides information about SST Inc. (Systems, Software, and Technology). Produces Winsock debugging tools and the TraceStock family of products. Includes technical specs, ordering and contact information.

Stonehand Inc.

http://www.stonehand.com/

Develops and licenses software text formatting tools and products. Includes information about the Stonehand Composition Toolbox formatting library. Provides technical reference and contact information.

StrandWare Home Page

http://www.primenet.com/~strandw/

Provides bar code design and printing software for the personal computer. Includes a corporate profile, product fact sheet, and industry newsletter, Automatic I.D. News. If you're lost, click on the Where is Eau Claire, Wisconsin link to see a nice map and learn about this exciting little city.

Strawberry Tree, Inc.

http://www.strawberrytree.com/

Provides data acquisition and analysis software applications solutions and products. Includes company history and facts about WorkBench products. Includes ordering information and distributors for the United States and international customers.

Subtle Software

http://world.std.com/~subtle/index.html

Produces the Subtleware product line for use with Windows sytsems. Products are used for database creation. Includes product specifics and contact information.

Sunbelt Software

http://www.ntsoftdist.com/ntsoftdist

Provides Windows NT utilities, such as event log, fault tolerance, virus protection, and batch job programs. Order online or link to other Windows NT sites.

Sunvalley Software

http://www.kwanza.com/~embleton/service.html

Produces QuickTime VR interactive media software and Custom Kiosks applications. Includes technical specifications and discussions on virtual reality. Provides ordering information.

Superlative Software Solutions

http://www.cat.syr.edu/3Si/

Provides custom software development and training services. Specializes in Java client/server applications and C++ operation services. Includes training service listings, company profile, and contact information.

SurfWatch Software

http://www.surfwatch.com/

Provides information about Spyglass Inc.'s SurfWatch adult material filter software. SurfWatch helps to filter out adult oriented and explicit Web sites for families and organizations. Includes product specifics and contact information.

SW International Systems Pte Ltd

http://www.swi.com.sg/

Develops client/server, research, and development software for the health industry. Includes company profile, products offered, and contact information.

SymCon Software

http://www.interlog.com/~symcon/

Produces software for accounting needs, desktop publishing, and Web design. Also provides custom software development and programming. Includes services offered and contact information.

Synapse Communications, Inc.

http://www.synapse.com

Develops Windows software for connecting to IBM AS/400 computer system. Find out about their software products, access tech support, read the latest news, and read about new products.

Syntax

http://www.syntax.com/

Produces the TotalNET line of network operating and systems integration software. Includes TotalNET features and technical specifications, Internet access services, training schedule, and contact information.

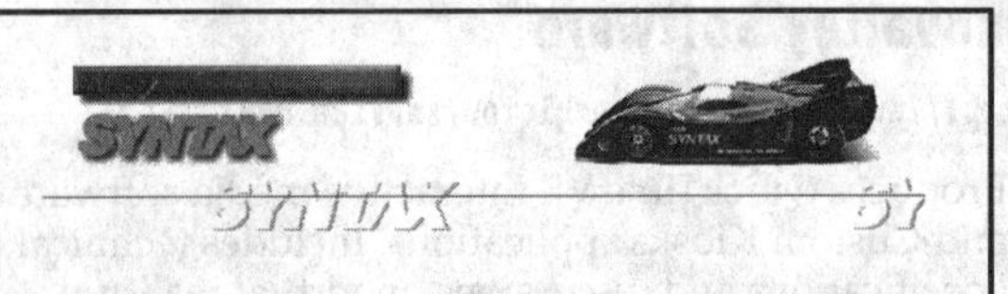

Systemcorp

http://www.systemcorp.com/index.html

Produces ready-made data and document management software on CD-ROMs. Includes information about the TrackFlow 9000 task management software. Provides product specifications and contact information.

Systems Alliance, Inc.

http://www.access.digex.net/~golshan/alliance.html

Provides custom software development and consultation services. Includes technical partners information, company resources, and contact services.

TEC Solutions

http://www.tecs.com/tecs

Produces the TECS WebServer line of software and products. Includes company profile, product technical specifics, and contact information.

TECHCO

http://www.primenet.com/~techco/

Provides network engineering, systems integration, custom software design, and database development services. Includes list of services and consultation available.

Technetix Unix/Internet Tools

http://teknetix.com/UNIX.html

Produces e-mail interoffice message software. Includes product specifics and ordering information.

Thermal Solutions

http://www.sauna.com/tsi/

Produces Sauna thermal design and electronic equipment modeling software. Includes product features, online technical support, pricing, and demo information.

Thinque Systems Corporation

http://www.thinque.com/isis/

Develops and produces software for the mobile communications and retail sales industries. Includes information about the ThinqNet Mail Gateway, Instant Wireless, Sales Traq, and other software products. Provides technical specifications, press releases, and contact information.

Thomson Software Products

http://www.thomsoft.com

Developer of application development and information management software. Read about their Nomad, Ada, and TeleUse language products, contact technical support, or examine their Site Index to find exactly the information you need.

Thunderstone Software

http://www.thunderstone.com/

Produces business software and applications for data management solutions. Includes information about the Metamorph and Texis families of software. Provides company profile, product background, job openings, and contact information.

Tibco

`http://www.tss.com/`

Produces the Information Bus family of software and Marketsheet financial applications. Includes product features, technical partners listing, corporate profile, and contact information.

Time Crafter (shareware)

`http://www.goldinc.com/Tour/LongBeach/Businesses/ASR/TimeCrafter.html`

Home page for this inexpensive shareware timing diagram documentation tool, which is used by engineers and programmers to document the way a circuit operates. Download the latest shareware release, contact the author, or download FAQs on how to use this product.

TimeLess Technologies Schedule Wizard Software

`http://www.timelesstech.com/`

Makers of Schedule Wizard Sports Scheduling Software, easy to use software for creating round robin schedules for any type of sport. Download a demo of this product, a trial version, or check out links to other sports-related Web pages.

Tosoft Children's Educational and Quit Smoking Page

`http://www.teleport.com/.~tosoft/`

Download free demo copies of their Dinosaur database for kids, Memory game, and Quit Smoking scheduler.

The Total Point of Sale Solution

`http://www.netaxs.com/people/bsc/index.html`

Produces Birds-of-Prey retail sales software and applications. Includes point-of-sale details, downloadable demonstration software, company profile, and technical partners information.

Tower Concepts, Inc.

`http://www.tower.com/`

Produces Razor integrated problem tracking and management software system. Includes online technical manual and contact information.

Traffic Software

`http://www.traffic.is/`

Produces ObjectFAX software and other business application products. Includes product features, technical support, sales and contact information.

Trax Softworks, Inc.

`http://www.webcom.com/~traxsoft/`

Produces TeamTalk group information sharing applications and Cypress authoring tools. Includes product specifications, company profile, and contact information.

Tumbleweed Software Corp.

`http://www.twcorp.com/`

Developers of Novell Envoy, a document viewer, Tumbleweed Publishing Essentials, and other electronic document viewing products. Download the Envoy plug-in for Netscape or other Tumbleweed products, talk to the webmaster, or read the latest news on Tumbleweed products.

Ubi Soft

`http://www.ubisoft.com/`

Provides the world-wide home site for Ubi Soft, developer of educational and entertainment software and applications products. Includes product background, technical support, trade show appearance dates, and contact information.

UNIBOL

`http://www.unibol.com/`

Produces the Unibol 36 and Unibol 400 native environments for open systems families of products. Includes technical specifications, product support, and contact information.

Uniplex

`http://www.uniplex.co.uk/`

Produces business applications and software for use with the Open Enterprise Workgroup environment. Includes information about onGo workgroup software products and the Uniplex line. Provides technical specifications, world-wide resellers listings, and contact information.

Uptime Computer Solutions, Inc.

`http://www.uptime1.com/`

Produces Lotus Notes workgroup software and other database applications. Includes product specifics, company philosophy, Web publishing services, and clients listings.

Van Dyke Technologies

http://www.vandyke.com/vandyke/

Produces the CRT windsock terminal that supports telnet and roglin protocol. Includes technical specifications, online product registration, and contact information.

Vantageware

http://www.vantageware.com/

Produces MasterMove warehousing and distributions software. Includes product features, technical support, and ordering information.

Veritas Software

http://www.veritas.com/

Produces storage maintenence and management products. Also produces FirstWatch high availability management software. Includes company profile, technical white papers, and contact information.

VersaFax

http://www.cosi.com/

Provides product features, technical support, and contact information about VersaFax software. VersaFax is a fax command line interface broadcasting and transmission tool.

Viewpoint Software Solutions

http://www3.servtech.com/viewpoint/

Produces LabVIEW and VisualBasic systems integrations software and tools. Provides custom software development services. Includes product features, service listings, links to related sites, and contact information.

Visigenic

http://odbc.visigenic.com/

Produces database and distributed object connectivity software. Includes information about the VisiODBC sereics and the Visibroker for Java and C++. Includes company profile, product features, technical partners listings, and ordering information.

Vision XXI

http://www.hic.net/hicpersonal/d/vxxi2.html

Specializes in the creation of software and applications for use in credit union automated loan systems. Includes information about the Inhouse system and LoanLink automated system. Provides detailed product background and contact information.

VYSOR Integration, Inc.

http://www.synapse.net/~vysor/welcome.htm

Develops Windows software developer and image systems integrator. Includes information about the V-Image Remote System and PiXCL Tools interpreted languge products. Includes online FAQ files, technical support, and ordering information.

Wall Street Software

http://www.fastlane.net/homepages/wallst/wallst.html

Produces PC investment monitoring, ordering, and management software. Includes information about Stock Watch 2000 and other investment applications and products. Provides ordering and contact information.

Welcome to Computer Associates

http://www.cai.com/

CA's Web site lets you leave messages for CA consumer relations, examine CA products, read press releases, and even check on the company's financial situation. Their Search This Site function simplifies searches for a specific topic or product.

Welcome to HPI on the World Wide Web

http://www.instalit.com/

Develops installer programs for several computer platforms. Visual Release for Windows lets you develop a sophisticated installation (setup) program. Download a working demo, read about HPI's installers for other platforms, or send e-mail for technical help.

Welcome to Microsoft

http://www.microsoft.com/

Select a specific software package using Microsoft's Select a Product field, or select one of 16 countries to see a Web page in your language. The home page for the king of software includes daily news releases, free downloads of their Explorer Web browser, directories of Microsoft partners and resellers, and lists of upcoming events.

Wind River Systems

http://www.wrs.com/

Produces embedded development software and tools. Includes detailed information about the Tornado line of products. Site provides white papers, product reviews, company profile, and ordering information.

Wingra Technologies

http://www.wingra.com/

Produces Missive messaging software systems and Jnet connectivity products. Includes product technical specifications, company news, and links to related sites.

Wingra Technologies

http://www.wingra.com/

Produces Missive messaging software systems and Jnet connectivity products. Includes product technical specifications, company news, and links to related sites.

Zinc Software, Inc.

http://www.zinc.com/

Produces C++ libraries and utilities for applications creation. Includes company background, technical partners, product technical specifications, and contact information.

Applied Signal Technology

http://www.appsig.com/

Home site for design, development, and manufacturer of signal processing equipment for telecommunications signals. Provides company background, product information, and press release file. Includes Applied Signal Techology job opportunities and college recruitment information.

Archtek Telecom Corp.

http://www.archtek.com.tw/

Manufactures SmartLink telecommunications products. Provides company profile, technical partners, support information, and a very comprehensive product line classified by telecommunication needs.

Commercial Speech Recognition

http://www.tiac.net/users/rwilcox/speech.html

This organized site provides hundreds of links to Web pages on Usenet groups, FAQs, ftp sites, mailing lists, research labs, recognition engines, telephony, and text-to-speech vendors. A valuable resource for businesses interested in this technology.

Cromack Industries, Inc.

http://www.cromack.com/

Produces Data Communications Equipment and Systems for both network and wireless markets. Includes product specifications, online data sheets, press releases, and contact information. Also includes technical updates and upcoming products release information.

EMJ Data Systems

http://www.emj.ca

Distributes of Apple, CAD, Unix, networking and telephonyr products, and peripherals in Canada, the U.S., Brazil, and Hungary.

FAQ: How can I use the Internet as a telephone?

`http://www.northcoast.com/~savetz/voice-faq.html`

Detailed discussion of how Internet phones work, their strengths and weaknesses, things you can do with them, and answers to many other questions. This FAQ also lists many of the Iphones now available. Worth a download if you're interested in this technology.

Genesys LLC Home Page—Premier Telephony Products for Windows

`http://www.teleport.com/~genesys/index.shtml`

Manufacturer of telephony products, such as CallerEGO DX, a graphical call management system for Windows, and RACom, a remote agent communicator for the ROLM CBX. A list of modem manufacturers, a press kit, and descriptions of their products are available at this site.

Internet Phone Download a Free Copy

`http://www.vocaltec.com/homep.htm`

Download a working demo of the latest copy of Internet Phone—the "phone" that lets you talk to other Internet users. Besides being one of the top 5 percent most-visited sites on the Web, this software is so hot that hundreds of phone servers have sprouted up on the Internet to handle the "calls."

ISDN Infocentre

`http://www.isdn.ocn.com/`

Heard about ISDN but still not sure what it is? Click on the Start Here button to learn about ISDN in plain English. This site's detailed links compare ISDN providers, provide technical help for hooking up ISDN, and review ISDN hardware. An excellent site for the ISDN curious.

M&S Hourdakis SA

`http://www.stepc.gr/~sweetie/hourd.html`

Information technology company located in Greece, serving Europe. Originally a manufacturer of circuit boards, the company has expanded to offer a variety of electronics needs including functionally tested through hole and SMD boards.

MedConnect

`http://netmar.com/medconnect/`

Physician to Patient voice messaging service to provide medical results quickly and securely to your patients by phone.

MediaLogic, ADL Inc.

`http://www.adlinc.com/adlinfo/`

An "Intelligent Data Warehouse" and developer of the first SSA-Capable Tape Library. Check out their long list of products, what's new, press releases and product overviews, ordering information, and more.

MediaSoft Telecom

`http://www.mediasoft.ca/`

Software for interactive communication systems. Check out their consulting services and product line for your organization.

Metricon Welcome

`http://www.metricom.com/`

Home page for a leader in two-way wireless data communication using cellular modems and the Internet. This site discusses Ricochet, their wireless Internet packet radio service, Metricon's cellular modems, UtiliNet, and Metricon's corporate structure. Their coverage maps show where the Ricochet service is available.

Motorola Information Systems Group

`http://www.motorola.com/MIMS/ISG/`

Communications products for the business or the home, including modems, terminal adaptors, access devices, routers, and other networking devices.

Multi-Tech Systems, Inc.

`http://www.multitech.com/`

Computer communications and networking products, in particular, modems and multiplexers, to international markets. Links to technical and purchasing info, as well as product and contact information.

National Telecommunications And Information Administration

`http://www.doc.gov/resources/csd/csntia.html`

Text page describes the President's advisory committee on telecommunications policy and regulation. Provides addresses of contacts in Washington who are part of this group.

Nokia

`http://www.nokia.com/`

International telecommunications group located in Finland, providing mobile computing products, home and multimedia products, and networking solutions.

Practinet Practical Perhipherals Home Page

`http://www.practinet.com/`

Need to upgrade the flash bios in your modem? Are you researching modems before you buy one? Practical Peripherals manufactures some of the fastest and most affordable modems for Macs and PCs. This site is for current modem owners and those who need more information on Practical Peripherals products.

Research Program on Communications Policy

`http://far.mit.edu/Pubs/index.html`

Home page for MIT's research forum on communications. This page lists a number of MIT-related research papers, reports, and articles on future communications-related technology, such as HDTV, high-resolution imaging, Internet broadcasting, electronic media, and many other topics.

Source, Inc.

`http://www.unicomp.net/sourcetele/`

Produces and provides sales of telecommunications hardware, software, applications, and other products. Includes an online catalog, services offered listing, technical support, and technical discussions forum. Also includes training and repair services.

Stylus Innovation, Inc.

`http://www.stylus.com/stylus`

Sells Windows-based tools for building computer telephony and voice processing applications, such as interactive voice response, fax-on-demand, and voice mail. If you're interested in the world of telephony, download one of several interactive tutorials free, or click on How to Get Started with Computer Telephony.

Symplex Communications

`http://www.iea.com/~symplex/`

Produces DirectRoute WAN/ISDN routers and other frame relay line applications. Includes product technical specifications, support, company profile, and contact information.

Tascomm Engineering

`http://www.tascomm.fi/`

Specializes in software telecommunications products. Includes information about the WATER line of router products and DTS family of integration applications. Includes Tascomm profile, product specifications, and contact information.

Telecommunications News and Journals

`http://www.sf.co.kr/t.telecom/news.html`

Simple interface provides links to popular telecom magazines such as Communications Week, infoHIGHWAY, and Pen-based Computing.

Terminate Home Page, the Final Terminal

`http://www.gpl.net/terminate/`

Developers of Terminate, advanced DOS communication software for terminal and Internet communication, provides a visually interesting page. Download a working demo of the program, check out some Terminate-related pages in Europe and the U.S., or link to some interesting FidoNet pages.

Subway Navigator

`http://metro.jussieu.fr:10001/bin/cities/english`

You're in Helsinki. You have to ride the subway. How's the best way to get from point A to point B? Check out this site to find out. The subway navigator enables you to find the best subway routes in cities around the world.

Universal Group Of Companies

http://www.universalgroup.co.uk/

Provides systems consulting and products for the telecommunications industry. Includes products offered, services provided, and contact information.

Videoconferencing Systems, Inc.

http://www.vsin.com/

Produces the Omega family of video conferencing tools and products. Includes company profile, product capabilities, press releases, and ordering information.

The World Wide Web Virtual Library of Communications and Telecommunications

http://www.analysys.co.uk/vlib/reseller.htm

An excellent resource listing all the U.K. long distance operators. Click on a company name to access its Web page.

Welcome to the Fibersphere

http://homepage.seas.upenn.edu/~gaj1/fiber.html

An exerpt from *Telecosm*, a new book by George Gilder. This lengthy excerpt, which appeared in Forbes ASAP (12/02/92) describes how companies want their telephone carriers to provide them with "dark," fiber-optic, cable-dumb, leased lines for their smart computer systems.

Welcome to Sprint Stop

http://www.sprint.com/home/sprintstop.html

A fun site with more than just the usual company pitch. Check out the Cyber Diner for real-time chats, Hollywood and political news (same thing, right?), and netiquette. Internet Ahead provides a Freeware area, emoticon directory (goofy!), and links to a number of search engines.

User Groups

Autodesk North American User Groups

http://www.autodesk.com/user_grp/noamusgp.htm

Provides a map of North America and the Caribbean for locating a specific user group. Click on the country of choice, then click on the state or province; a list of names and addresses of every user group will appear.

GUIDE International—An IBM User Group

http://www.guide.org/

IBM user group with a mission to define the future of Information Technology (IT). This site's main purpose is to list upcoming conference information and describe this non-profit group's mission in more detail. A number of publications are also available that you can order via fax.

Hull Community Artworks

http://uptown.turnpike.net/I/Image/INDEX.HTML

Workshop located in Hull, England that specializes in short courses and open access workshops on multimedia authoring, Web page design, digital imaging, nonlinear digital editing, and 3D graphics and animation.

IEEE Computer Society—Purdue Student Chapter

http://purcell.ecn.purdue.edu/~ieeecs

Provides information on membership, student interest groups, administration, and short courses on Perl, HTML, and Java.

InfoWest Windows 95 Software Archive

http://www.netex.net/w95

Go directly to the Windows 95 software archive or choose the HyperNews Discussion Forums link to speak with other Win95 gurus. A definite must-see is the Rumors link with a number of threads discussing all kinds of crazy stuff.

International Computer Association Home Page

http://www.gol.com/ica/index.html

A Tokyo-based computer group founded 26 years ago that serves as a forum for information and technology in Japan. Provides information about the organization in English, along with a phone number (in Japan) you can use to obtain the most recent copy of their newsletter.

Newsletters on the Web

http://www.melbpc.org.au/others/newslet.htm

Lists dozens of e-zines on the WWW from computer user groups and computer clubs around the world.

The Ottawa Microsoft Users Group (TOMUG)

http://www.icons.net/tomug/

User group provides information on Special Interest Groups (SIGs), back issues of the TOMUG Signals newsletter, a schedule of events, and membership info. Download the latest Windows 95 patch to fix minor bugs.

Portland PC Users Group

http://odin.cc.pdx.edu/~psu01435/index.html

A busy site with more information than most groups provide. Join online, read about recent presentations, send email to the sysop of a SIG, or check out this group's PC training schedule.

SGI User Groups

http://www.cc.gatech.edu/services/sgiusers.html

Lists every Silicon Graphics user group worldwide, including Israel, Australia, and Europe. This list is broken down by state and city for the U.S.; a few listed sites have links to their home page.

Sun User Group Java SIG

http://www.sug.org/java-sig.html

Created to meet the needs of the Sun User Group's interest in Java. This site describes the Java SIG and how to join, has a selection for the Cool Java Applet of the week, and provides an archive of Java applets for members only.

Tampa Bay Linux GNU Technical Society

http://www.intnet.net/tblgnuts/

Nicely designed page for Tampa Linux users that provides information on events, the latest Linux news and files, archives of Linux goodies, and a list of programming projects currently underway.

Victoria Macintosh Users Group

http://www.islandnet.com/~vmug

Macintosh Users Group for Victoria, Canada. A number of links to interesting Mac Web sites, information on how to join, and information on this group's goals are provided.

Computers

Newsgroups

adass.archiving

alc.archive

alc.tools.misc

alt.2600

alt.2600.crackz

alt.2600.hackerz

alt.2600.warez

alt.amiga.slip

alt.bbs

alt.bbs.adsalt.bbs Computer

alt.bbs.iniquity

alt.bbs.internet

alt.bbs.lists

alt.bbs.lists.d

alt.bbs.wildcat

alt.binaries.multimedia

alt.binaries.multimedia.d

alt.binaries.multimedia.erotica

alt.binaries.multimedia.utilities

alt.binaries.pictures.fine-art.graphics

alt.binaries.warez.ibm-pc

alt.binaries.warez.ibm-pc.old

alt.binaries.warez.mac

alt.binaries.warez.snes

alt.cd-rom

alt.cd-rom.reviews

alt.chinese.text

alt.cobol

alt.comp.hardware.homedesigned

alt.comp.shareware

alt.computer.consultants

alt.computer.consultants.ads

alt.computer.consultants.moderated

alt.dcom.telecom

alt.folklore.computers

alt.geo-software

alt.japanese.text

alt.lang.basic

alt.multimedia.director

alt.multimedia.toolbook

alt.org.team-os2

alt.os.linux

alt.os.linux.caldera

alt.os.windows95.crash.crash.crash

alt.philosophy.debate

alt.security

alt.security.keydist

alt.security.pgp

alt.security.ripem

alt.sex.cd-rom

alt.sys.amiga.blitz

alt.sys.icl

alt.uu.comp.os.linux.questions

alt.video.dvd

alt.warez.ibm-pc

alt.warez.ibm-pc.old

alt.windows.cde

alt.www.hotjava

aus.archives

aus.aswec

aus.computers.linux

aus.stats.s

av.qnet

ba.market.computers

belwue.sw

bionet.software

bionet.software.acedb

bionet.software.gcg

bionet.software.sources

bionet.software.srs

bionet.software.staden

bionet.software.www

bionet.software.x-plor

bit.listserv.banyan-1

bit.listserv.cdromlan

bit.listserv.dectei-1

bit.listserv.os2-1

bit.software.international

biz.marketplace.computers.mac

biz.marketplace.computers.other

biz.marketplace.computers.pc-clone

biz.marketplace.computers.workstation

bln.comp.pub

bln.net.news

bnr.software-eng

calstate.gina.support

can.schoolnet.comp.jr

can.schoolnet.comp.sr

cern.asis

chile.soft-1

clari.tw.computers.pc.hardware

clari.tw.computers.pc.hardware.releases

clari.tw.computers.networking

clari.tw.computers.networking.releases

clari.tw.computers.pc.software

clari.tw.computers.pc.software.releases

clari.tw.computers.unix

clari.tw.new_media

clari.tw.new_media.releases

clari.tw.telecom.misc

Computers

clari.tw.telecom.releases

comp.ai.doc-analysis.ocr

comp.arch.bus.vmebus

comp.arch.storage

comp.bbs.majorbbs

comp.bbs.misc

comp.bbs.waffle

comp.bbs.tbbs

comp.binaries.os2

comp.cad.autocad

comp.cad.i-deas

comp.cad.microstation

comp.databases

comp.databases.gupta

comp.databases.informix

comp.databases.object

comp.databases.theory

comp.databases.xbase.fox

comp.dcom.fax

comp.dcom.lans.misc

comp.dcom.modems

comp.dcom.sys.wellfleet

comp.dcom.telecom

comp.edu.languages.natural

comp.graphics

comp.graphics.algorithms

comp.graphics.animation

comp.graphics.apps.alias

comp.graphics.apps.wavefront

comp.graphics.misc

comp.graphics.packages.3dstudio

comp.graphics.rendering.raytracing

comp.groupware

comp.groupware.lotus-notes.apps

comp.infosystems.www.servers.ms-windows

comp.lang.basic.misc

comp.lang.basic.visual.3rdparty

comp.lang.basic.visual.announce

comp.lang.basic.visual.database

comp.lang.basic.visual.misc

comp.lang.c++

comp.lang.c++.leda

comp.lang.c++.moderated

comp.lang.cobol

comp.lang.java

comp.lang.javascript

comp.lang.misc

comp.lang.pascal.delphi.components

comp.lang.pascal.delphi.databases

comp.lang.pascal.delphi.misc

comp.lang.perl

comp.lang.perl.announce

comp.lang.perl.misc

comp.lang.perl.tk

comp.laser-printers

comp.mail.eudora.mac

comp.mail.eudora.ms-windows

comp.mail.list-admin.software

comp.mail.multi-media

comp.multimedia

comp.networks.noctools.wanted

comp.org.user-groups.apcug

comp.org.user-groups.management

comp.org.user-groups.meetings

comp.org.user-groups.misc

comp.org.user-groups.newsletters

comp.os.cpm.amethyst

comp.os.geos

comp.os.geos.binaries

comp.os.linux.advocacy

comp.os.linux.announce

comp.os.linux.answers

comp.os.linux.development.apps

comp.os.linux.development.system

comp.os.linux.hardware

comp.os.linux.m68k

comp.os.linux.misc

comp.os.linux.networking

comp.os.linux.setup

comp.os.linux.x

comp.os.ms-windows.advocacy

comp.os.ms-windows.announce

comp.os.ms-windows.apps

comp.os.ms-windows.apps.misc

comp.os.ms-windows.apps.utilities

comp.os.ms-windows.misc

comp.os.ms-windows.networking.misc

comp.os.ms-windows.networking.ras

comp.os.ms-windows.networking.tcp-ip

comp.os.ms-windows.networking.win95

comp.os.ms-windows.nt.admin.misc

comp.os.ms-windows.nt.advocacy

comp.os.ms-windows.nt.announce.

comp.os.ms-windows.nt.misc

comp.os.ms-windows.nt.pre-release

comp.os.ms-windows.nt.setup.hardware

comp.os.ms-windows.nt.setup.misc

omp.os.ms-windows.nt.software.compatibility

comp.os.ms-windows.nt.software.services

comp.os.ms-windows.programmer

comp.os.ms-windows.programmer.misc

comp.os.ms-windows.programmer.tools

comp.os.ms-windows.programmer.vxd

comp.os.ms-windows.programmer.win32

```
comp.os.ms-windows.setup
comp.os.ms-windows.win95.misc
comp.os.ms-windows.win95.setup
comp.os.msdos.4dos
comp.os.msdos.apps
comp.os.msdos.djgpp
comp.os.msdos.misc
comp.os.msdos.programmer
comp.os.os2.advocacy
comp.os.os2.announce
comp.os.os2.apps
comp.os.os2.beta
comp.os.os2.bugs
comp.os.os2.comm
comp.os.os2.games
comp.os.os2.mail-news
comp.os.os2.misc
comp.os.os2.multimedia
comp.os.os2.networking.misc
comp.os.os2.networking.tcp-ip
comp.os.os2.networking.www
comp.os.os2.programmer.misc
comp.os.os2.programmer.porting
comp.os.os2.programmer.tools
comp.os.os2.setup.misc
comp.os.os2.setup.storage
comp.os.os2.setup.video
comp.os.plan9
comp.os.research
comp.parallel
comp.protocols.appletalk
comp.protocols.ibm
comp.protocols.kermit.misc
comp.protocols.tcp-ip
comp.protocols.tcp-ip.domains
comp.protocols.tcp-ip.ibmpc
comp.publish.cdrom.hardware
comp.publish.cdrom.multimedia
comp.publish.cdrom.software
comp.security.announce
comp.security.firewalls
comp.security.misc
comp.security.unix
comp.software-eng
comp.software.config-mgmt
comp.software.international
comp.software.licensing
comp.software.testing
comp.software.testing
comp.sources.games
comp.sources.games.bugs
comp.sources.mac
```

comp.sources.misc

comp.sources.sun

comp.sources.testers

comp.sources.wanted

comp.sources.x

comp.std.c++

comp.sw.components

comp.sys.acorn.networking

comp.sys.amiga.advocacy

comp.sys.amiga.announce

comp.sys.amiga.applications

comp.sys.amiga.audio

comp.sys.amiga.cd32

comp.sys.amiga.datacomm

comp.sys.amiga.emulations

comp.sys.amiga.games

comp.sys.amiga.graphics

comp.sys.amiga.hardware

comp.sys.amiga.introduction

comp.sys.amiga.marketplace

comp.sys.amiga.misc

comp.sys.amiga.multimedia

comp.sys.amiga.networking

comp.sys.amiga.programmer

comp.sys.amiga.software

comp.sys.amiga.tech

comp.sys.amiga.uucp

comp.sys.amstrad.8bit

comp.sys.apple2.usergroups

comp.sys.atari.announce

comp.sys.atari.st.tech

comp.sys.convex

comp.sys.handhelds

comp.sys.hp.apps

comp.sys.ibm.pc.hardware

comp.sys.ibm.pc.hardware.cd-rom

comp.sys.ibm.pc.hardware.chips

comp.sys.ibm.pc.hardware.comm

comp.sys.ibm.pc.hardware.misc

comp.sys.ibm.pc.hardware.networking

comp.sys.ibm.pc.hardware.storage

comp.sys.ibm.pc.hardware.systems

comp.sys.ibm.pc.hardware.video

comp.sys.ibm.pc.misc

comp.sys.ibm.pc.soundcard

comp.sys.ibm.pc.soundcard.advocacy

comp.sys.ibm.pc.soundcard.games

comp.sys.ibm.pc.soundcard.misc

comp.sys.ibm.pc.soundcard.music

comp.sys.ibm.pc.soundcard.tech

comp.sys.intergraph

comp.sys.mac.advocacyb

```
comp.sys.mac.announce
comp.sys.mac.apps
comp.sys.mac.comm
comp.sys.mac.databases
comp.sys.mac.digest
comp.sys.mac.graphics
comp.sys.mac.hardware
comp.sys.mac.hypercard
comp.sys.mac.misc
comp.sys.mac.oop.macapp3
comp.sys.mac.oop.misc
comp.sys.mac.oop.tcl
comp.sys.mac.portables
comp.sys.mac.programmer
comp.sys.mac.programmer.codewarrior
comp.sys.mac.programmer.help
comp.sys.mac.programmer.info
comp.sys.mac.programmer.misc
comp.sys.mac.programmer.tools
comp.sys.mac.scitech
comp.sys.mac.system
comp.sys.mac.wanted
comp.sys.newton.programmer
comp.sys.next.hardware
comp.sys.next.marketplace
comp.sys.next.software

comp.sys.newton.announce
comp.sys.newton.misc
comp.sys.newton.programmer
comp.sys.palmtops
comp.sys.pen
comp.sys.psion
comp.sys.sgi.hardware
comp.sys.sun.apps
comp.text.desktop
comp.text.frame
comp.text.interleaf
comp.theory
comp.unix.admin
comp.unix.advocacy
comp.unix.amiga
comp.unix.bsd.misc
comp.unix.cray
comp.unix.misc
comp.unix.osf.misc
comp.unix.osf.osf1
comp.unix.programmer
comp.unix.questions
comp.unix.shell
comp.unix.unixware
comp.unix.unixware.announce
comp.unix.unixware.misc
```

comp.unix.user-friendly

comp.unix.wizards

comp.virus

comp.windows.garnet

comp.windows.interviews

comp.windows.suit

comp.windows.ui-builders.teleuse

comp.windows.ui-builders.uimx

comp.windows.x

comp.windows.x.announce

comp.windows.x.apps

comp.windows.x.i386unix

comp.windows.x.intrinsics

comp.windows.x.motif

comp.windows.x.pex

ctdl.lang.c++

cu.cs.systems+software

cz.comp.amiga

de.admin.news.software

de.alt.bbs.waffle

de.alt.comm.mgetty

de.comm.infosystems.www.servers

de.comm.internet.software

de.comm.isdn Digitale

de.comm.software.crosspoint

de.comm.software.pmail

de.comm.software.ums

de.comp.dtp

de.comp.gnu

demon.ip.winsock.dics

dungeon.announce.os2-archive

dungeon.announce.windows-archive

eug.bbs.excelsior

fido.ger.basic

fido.ger.dtp

fido.ger.hardware

fido.ger.informatik

fido.ger.maximus

fido.ger.storage

fido.ger.transputer

fido7.c_cpp

fido7.cbcs

fido7.crypt

fido7.dtp

fido7.dtp.fonts

fido7.fax

fido7.fido-anywhere

fido7.finsoft

fido7.graphics

fido7.hardw

fido7.hardw.cdrom

fido7.hardw.chainik

```
fido7.hardw.check

fido7.hardw.hsmodem

fido7.hardw.other

fido7.hardw.pc.media

fido7.hardw.pc.motherboard

fido7.hardw.pc.peripheral

fido7.hardw.pc.video

fido7.hardw.pc_sound

fido7.hardw.phones

fido7.hardw.schemes

fido7.hardw.support.arvid

fido7.hardw.uuencode

fido7.mo.softexcg

fido7.mo.softexcg.arvid

fido7.mo.softmarket

fido7.multimedia

fido7.os2

fido7.os2.comm

fido7.os2.drv

fido7.os2.faq.d

fido7.os2.marginal

fido7.os2.prog

fido7.os2.src

fido7.os2.wanted

fido7.security

fido7.softad
```

```
fido7.spb.softw

fido7.telecom

fido7.windows.nt

fido7.windows.nt.prog

fido7.windows.wanted

fj.comp.image

fj.comp.theory

fj.fleamarket.comp

fj.lang.c++

fj.lang.cobol

fj.lang.java

fj.lang.misc

fj.os.bsd.misc

fj.os.misc

fj.os.os2

fj.os.windows-nt

fj.sys.ibmpc

francom.multimedia

gnu.g++.announce

gnu.g++.bug

gnu.g++.help

han.comp.misc

han.comp.security

hannet.ml.firewalls

hannet.ml.mac.anf

hepnet.lang.c++
```

ieee.tcos

iijnet.multimedia

iijnet.os

iijnet.sys.ibm-pc

it.comp.sicurezza.varie

ka.markt.computer

kw.networks

maus.hardware

maus.os.os2.prog

maus.sys.atari.desktop

memphis.networking

misc.education.multimedia

misc.forsale.computers.mac-specific.software

misc.forsale.computers.modems

misc.forsale.computers.net-hardware

misc.forsale.computers.other.software

misc.forsale.computers.pc-specific.software

mit.eecs.discuss

mn.net

muc.lists.firewalls

nersc.c++

nj.market.computers

okinawa.os.misc

or.ojgse.cis641

pdaxs.ads.computers

pdaxs.ads.printing

pdx.telecom

pnet.comp.mac

pnet.comp.pc

rain.firewalls

relcom.commerce.computers

relcom.comp.lang.basic

relcom.comp.os.cmp

relcom.comp.os.os2

relcom.comp.os.os2.comm

relcom.comp.os.os2.drv

relcom.comp.os.os2.faq.d

relcom.comp.os.os2.marginal

relcom.comp.os.os2.prog

relcom.comp.os.os2.src

relcom.comp.os.os2.wanted

relcom.comp.os.windows.nt

relcom.comp.security

relcom.fido.su.c-c++

relcom.fido.su.hardw

sanet.tech

sci.crypt.research

sdsu.c++

slac.lang.c++

t-netz.linux

talk.politics.crypto

thenet.support.linux for Linux

thenet.support.windowsnt

t-netz.cd-rom

tn.linux

tnn.internet.firewall

tnn.internet.mobile

tnn.multimedia

tnn.multimedia.cdrom

tnn.multimedia.cdrom

tnn.os

tnn.os.linux

tnn.os.os2

tnn.os.research

tnn.os.windows-nt

tnn.software

tnn.sys.ibm-pc

tor.forsale.computers

triangle.graphics

triangle.java

tw.bbs.comp.hardware

tw.bbs.comp.hardware.cdrom

tw.bbs.comp.lang.java

tw.bbs.comp.language

tw.bbs.comp.linux

tw.bbs.comp.mswindows.nt

tw.bbs.comp.multimedia

tw.bbs.comp.security

tw.bbs.comp.software

ucb.org.callug

ucb.os.linux

ucb.os.os2

uiuc.campusnet

uiuc.org.acm.sigops

uiuc.org.acm.sigsoft

uiuc.org.os2ug

uiuc.sw.linux

ukr.comp.hardware

ukr.comp.software

umich.linux

umn.cs.windows.x

umn.local-lists.linux-activists

umn.net-lists.linux-activists

utexas.comp.windows-nt

uw.cgl

uw.cgl.software

uw.cgl.system

uw.icr.hardware

uw.x-hints

uwo.comp.security

vmsnet.networks.misc

windows.nt.software.compatibility

windows.programmer.controls

windows.programmer.graphics

```
windows.programmer.memory
```

```
windows.programmer.nt.kernel-mode
```

```
windows.programmer.tools.mfc MFC-based
```

```
windows.programmer.tools.misc
```

```
windows.programmer.tools.owl
```

```
windows.programmer.winhelp
```

```
z-netz.alt.linux
```

```
z-netz.rechner.cd-rom
```

```
za.net.misc
```

Listservs

AAASCS—AAAS Computer Systems

The George Washington University Computer Center, Washington, DC

You can join this group by sending the message "sub AAASCS your name" to listserv@gwuvm.gwu.edu

ACL-L—ACL Software Users List

You can join this group by sending the message "sub ACL-L your name" to listserv@etsuadmn.etsu.edu

ACORN-L—ACORN Computers Discussion List

Ege University Bornova, Izmir, Turkey

You can join this group by sending the message "sub ACORN-L your name" to listserv@vm3090.ege.edu.tr

ACSOFT-L—Academic Software Development

You can join this group by sending the message "sub ACSOFT-L your name" to listserv@wuvmd.wustl.edu

AECP-L—Apple Education Consultants Program

You can join this group by sending the message "sub AECP-L your name" to listserv@listserv.unb.ca

AIBIBL—ACADEMIC INITIATIVE IBM, PROJECT "LIBRARY SYSTEMS," AIBIBL

You can join this group by sending the message "sub AIBIBL your name" to listserv@plearn.edu.pl

AMIGAHAR—AMIGAGHAR COMP.SYS.AMIGA.HARDWARE redist.

You can join this group by sending the message "sub AMIGAHAR your name" to listserv@vm.gmd.de

APPLE-PL

You can join this group by sending the message "sub APPLE-PL your name" to listserv@plearn.edu.pl

APPLE2-L—Apple II List

You can join this group by sending the message "sub APPLE2-L your name" to listserv@brownvm.brown.edu

APPLE3-L—Apple III Discussion Group

You can join this group by sending the message "sub APPLE3-L your name" to listserv@wvnvm.wvnet.edu

APPLENOOZ—AppleNooz Newsletter

eWorld, Apple Online Services, Cupertino, CA

You can join this group by sending the message "sub APPLENOOZ your name" to listserv@mail.eworld.com

ASSEMBLER-LIST—IBM Mainframe Assembler List

You can join this group by sending the message "sub ASSEMBLER-LIST your name" to `listserv@uga.cc.uga.edu`

ASSEMBLER-LIST—IBM 370 Assembly Programming Discussion List

You can join this group by sending the message "sub ASSEMBLER-LIST your name" to `listserv@vm.gmd.de`

ASSMPC—"Assembly for the IBM-PC"

You can join this group by sending the message "sub ASSMPC your name" to `listserv@usachvm1.bitnet`

BAYSGI-L—Bay Area Silicon Graphics Users Group

You can join this group by sending the message "sub BAYSGI-L your name" to `listserv@sjsuvm1.sjsu.edu`

BESTCOM—Hardware You Would Like Others to Know About

You can join this group by sending the message "sub BESTCOM your name" to `listserv@vm3090.ege.edu.tr`

BESTOS—Operating Systems You Would Like Others to Try

You can join this group by sending the message "sub BESTOS your name" to `listserv@vm3090.ege.edu.tr`

BESTSOFT—Software You'd Like Others to Know About

You can join this group by sending the message "sub BESTSOFT your name" to `listserv@vm3090.ege.edu.tr`

BIOPI-L—Secondary Biology Teacher Enhancement PI

Kansas State University, Manhattan, KS

You can join this group by sending the message "sub BIOPI-L your name" to `listserv@ksuvm.ksu.edu`

BLIND-L—Computer Use by and for the Blind

You can join this group by sending the message "sub BLIND-L your name" to `listserv@uafsysb.uark.edu`

BMDP-L—BMDP(R)Statistical Software Discussion List

You can join this group by sending the message "sub BMDP-L your name" to `listserv@vm1.mcgill.ca`

CADAM-L—Computer Aided Design and Manufacturing (CADAM) Interest Group

You can join this group by sending the message "sub CADAM-L your name" to `listserv@listserv.syr.edu`

CADAPP-L—CAD Applications Discussion List

You can join this group by sending the message "sub CADAPP-L your name" to `listserv@ubvm.cc.buffalo.edu`

CADLIST—CAD General Discussion Group

You can join this group by sending the message "sub CADLIST your name" to `listserv@listserv.syr.edu`

CAEDS-L—Computer Aided Engineering Design (CAEDS) Interest Group

You can join this group by sending the message "sub CAEDS-L your name" to `listserv@listserv.syr.edu`

CARR-L—Computer-assisted Reporting & Research

You can join this group by sending the message "sub CARR-L your name" to `listserv@ulkyvm.louisville.edu`

CECS-L—MU Computer Engineering and Computer Science

You can join this group by sending the message "sub CECS-L your name" to `listserv@mizzou1.missouri.edu`

CG-CHAR—Computer Graphics Character Animation

You can join this group by sending the message "sub CG-CHAR your name" to `listserv@morgan.ucs.mun.ca`

CGE—Computer Graphics Education Newsletter

You can join this group by sending the message "sub CGE your name" to `listserv@vm.marist.edu`

CNEDUC-L—Computer Networking Education Discussion List

You can join this group by sending the message "sub CNEDUC-L your name" to `listserv@tamvm1.tamu.edu`

COCO—Tandy Color Computer List

You can join this group by sending the message "sub COCO your name" to `listserv@pucc.princeton.edu`

COMM-L—Communications/Modems/BBSs Discussion List

You can join this group by sending the message "sub COMM-L your name" to `listserv@sakaau03.bitnet`

CRYPTOAPI—Microsoft Cryptographic API

You can join this group by sending the message "sub CRYPTOAPI your name" to `listserv@listserv.msn.com`

CRYPTYCH-L—Cryptych Magazine Discussion List

You can join this group by sending the message "sub CRYPTYCH-L your name" to `listserv@oracle.wizards.com`

CUMREC-L—Administrative Computer Use

You can join this group by sending the message "sub CUMREC-L your name" to `listserv@listserv.nodak.edu`

CYBERIA-L—Law & Policy of Computer Communications

You can join this group by sending the message "sub CYBERIA-L your name" to `listserv@listserv.aol.com`

CYBERVPM—Online Networking for Volunteer Program Managers

You can join this group by sending the message "sub CYBERVPM your name" to `listserv@listserv.aol.com`

DELTA-L—DELTA Software Discussion List

You can join this group by sending the message "sub DELTA-L your name" to `listserv@nic.surfnet.nl`

DEOS-R—Distance Education Online Research

Central Michigan University, Mt. Pleasant, MI

You can join this group by sending the message "sub DEOS-R your name" to `listserv@cmuvm.csv.cmich.edu`

DERR-L—Distance Education Research Roundtable

Central Michigan University, Mt. Pleasant, MI

You can join this group by sending the message "sub DERR-L your name" to `listserv@cmuvm.csv.cmich.edu`

DIRECT-L—Macromedia Director for Macintosh and Windows

You can join this group by sending the message "sub DIRECT-L your name" to `listserv@uafsysb.uark.edu`

DTPBID—Electronic & Desktop Publishing Tenders

You can join this group by sending the message "sub DTPBID your name" to `listserv@listserv.unb.ca`

EMULPC—Emulation SW & HW on the IBM-PC

You can join this group by sending the message "sub EMULPC your name" to `listserv@usachvm1.bitnet`

ETHCSE-L—Ethical Issues in Software Engineering

You can join this group by sending the message "sub ETHCSE-L your name" to `listserv@utkvm1.utk.edu`

GRAPH-L—Mathematical aspects of Computer Graphics, Caos, Fractal

You can join this group by sending the message "sub GRAPH-L your name" to `listserv@brufpb.bitnet`

GRAPH-L—Yale University Graphics Users

You can join this group by sending the message "sub GRAPH-L your name" to `listserv@yalevm.cis.yale.edu`

GRAPHICS—Graphic Design discussion

You can join this group by sending the message "sub GRAPHICS your name" to `listserv@ulkyvm.louisville.edu`

HP-48—HP-48 Hand Held System

You can join this group by sending the message "sub HP-48 your name" to `listserv@listserv.nodak.edu`

HP-USERS-L—A forum for Hewlett Packard workstation owners/administrators

You can join this group by sending the message "sub HP-USERS-L your name" to `listserv@postoffice.cso.uiuc.edu`

HP3000-L—HP-3000 Systems Discussion

You can join this group by sending the message "sub HP3000-L your name" to `listserv@utcvm.utc.edu`

HPMINI-L—Hewlett-Packard 9000 Series MiniComputer Discussion

University of Arkansas Main Campus - Fayetteville

You can join this group by sending the message "sub HPMINI-L your name" to `listserv@uafsysb.uark.edu`

IBM-HESC—IBM Higher Education Consortium

You can join this group by sending the message "sub IBM-HESC your name" to `listserv@freya.cc.pdx.edu`

IBM-MAIN—IBM Mainframe Discussion List

You can join this group by sending the message "sub IBM-MAIN your name" to `listserv@ua1vm.ua.edu`

IBM-NETS—IBM Networking

You can join this group by sending the message "sub IBM-NETS your name" to `listserv@uga.cc.uga.edu`

IBMDCE-L—Discussion of IBM DCE Products, Platforms & Usage

You can join this group by sending the message "sub IBMDCE-L your name" to `listserv@ucsbvm.ucsb.edu`

IBMSND-L—MSDOS Sound Card Forum and Discussion List

You can join this group by sending the message "sub IBMSND-L your name" to `listserv@brownvm.brown.edu`

IBMTCP-L—IBM TCP/IP List

You can join this group by sending the message "sub IBMTCP-L your name" to `listserv@vm.marist.edu`

IEEETCPC—IEEE Technical Committee on Personal Communications

You can join this group by sending the message "sub IEEETCPC your name" to
`listserv@ccvm.sunysb.edu`

IMAMEDIA—Compatibility of Multimedia Applications

You can join this group by sending the message "sub IMAMEDIA your name" to
`listserv@umdd.bitnet`

INFINI-D—Macintosh Infini-D Discussion

You can join this group by sending the message "sub INFINI-D your name" to
`listserv@uafsysb.uark.edu`

INFO-IBMPC—IBMPC-L

You can join this group by sending the message "sub INFO-IBMPC your name" to
`listserv@nic.surfnet.nl`

INFO-IBMPC—INFO-IBMPC Digest

You can join this group by sending the message "sub INFO-IBMPC your name" to
`listserv@tamvm1.tamu.edu`

INFO-IBMPC—INFO-IBMPC Digest

You can join this group by sending the message "sub INFO-IBMPC your name" to
`listserv@ubvm.cc.buffalo.edu`

INFO-IBMPC—INFO-IBMPC Digest

You can join this group by sending the message "sub INFO-IBMPC your name" to
`listserv@uga.cc.uga.edu`

IO-MUG—I/O MUG - Internet ONLY Macintosh User's Group

You can join this group by sending the message "sub IO-MUG your name" to
`listserv@utarlvm1.bitnet`

IOMUG-L—ILLINET Online Music Users Group

You can join this group by sending the message "sub IOMUG-L your name" to
`listserv@postoffice.cso.uiuc.edu`

JCMST-L—Journal Of Computers In Mathematics And Science Teaching

You can join this group by sending the message "sub JCMST-L your name" to
`listserv@vm.cc.purdue.edu`

JPL-L—Electronic Publishing Mailing List

You can join this group by sending the message "sub JPL-L your name" to
`listserv@listserv.clark.net`

JPSOFT—JP Software products (4DOS/40S2 et al)

You can join this group by sending the message "sub JPSOFT your name" to
`listserv@irishvma.bitnet`

ANMAN-L—MS Windows NT Server and Relatives Discussion List

You can join this group by sending the message "sub ANMAN-L your name" to
`listserv@list.nih.gov`

LANSRV-L—IBM LAN Server

You can join this group by sending the message "sub LANSRV-L your name" to
`listserv@vm.marist.edu`

LINUX-ATALK—Appletalk on Linux

You can join this group by sending the message "sub LINUX-ATALK your name" to
`listserv@netspace.org`

MAC-FORUM-NEWS—News of the Macintosh Computing Forums on America Online

You can join this group by sending the message "sub MAC-FORUM-NEWS your name" to
`listserv@listserv.aol.com`

Computers

MAC-HELP-NEWSLETTER—News of the Macintosh Help Forum on America Online

You can join this group by sending the message "sub MAC-HELP-NEWSLETTER your name" to `listserv@listserv.aol.com`

MACAPPLI—Usage Tips about Macintosh Applications

You can join this group by sending the message "sub MACAPPLI your name" to `listserv@listserv.dartmouth.edu`

MACHRDWR—Macintosh Hardware and Related Perpherials

You can join this group by sending the message "sub MACHRDWR your name" to `listserv@listserv.dartmouth.edu`

MACINTOSH-TOP—Shareware.com macintosh-top list

You can join this group by sending the message "sub MACINTOSH-TOP your name" to `listserv@dispatch.cnet.com`

MACLAB—Mac Hardware for Physiologists

You can join this group by sending the message "sub MACLAB your name" to `listserv@listserv.hea.ie`

MACMULTI—Macintosh Multimedia Discussion List

You can join this group by sending the message "sub MACMULTI your name" to `listserv@fccj.bitnet`

MACNET-L—Macintosh Networking Issues

You can join this group by sending the message "sub MACNET-L your name" to `listserv@yalevm.cis.yale.edu`

MACPCI-L—Macintosh PCI Discussion List

You can join this group by sending the message "sub MACPCI-L your name" to `listserv@mitvma.mit.edu`

MACPPC-L—Macintosh Power PC List (MACPPC-L)

You can join this group by sending the message "sub MACPPC-L your name" to `listserv@yalevm.cis.yale.edu`

MACPROG—Macintosh Programming Discussion List

You can join this group by sending the message "sub MACPROG your name" to `listserv@wuvmd.wustl.edu`

MAC_ED-L—AOL Mac Education & Technology Forum Newsletter

You can join this group by sending the message "sub MAC_ED-L your name" to `listserv@listserv.aol.com`

MAX—Discussion of Interactive Music/Multimedia Standard Environments

You can join this group by sending the message "sub MAX your name" to `listserv@vm1.mcgill.ca`

MCMANNOUNCE—AOL Mac Comms and Networking Forum Announcements

You can join this group by sending the message "sub MCMANNOUNCE your name" to `listserv@listserv.aol.com`

MIBSRV-L—IBM Antiviral Update List

You can join this group by sending the message "sub MIBSRV-L your name" to `listserv@ua1vm.ua.edu`

MODEMS-L—MODEMS-L Mailing List

You can join this group by sending the message "sub MODEMS-L your name" to `listserv@vm.its.rpi.edu`

MS-WINDOWS95-NEW—Shareware.com ms-windows95-new list

You can join this group by sending the message "sub MS-WINDOWS95-NEW your name" to `listserv@dispatch.cnet.com`

MS-WINDOWS95-TOP—Shareware.com MS-WINDOWS95-TOP list

You can join this group by sending the message "sub MS-WINDOWS95-TOP your name" to `listserv@dispatch.cnet.com`

MSMAIL-L—Microsoft Mail Discussion List

You can join this group by sending the message "sub MSMAIL-L your name" to `listserv@yalevm.cis.yale.edu`

MSSQL-L—Microsoft SQL Server Discussion List

You can join this group by sending the message "sub MSSQL-L your name" to `listserv@dukefsb.bitnet`

MSVC—This is a Discussion List for Microsoft Visual C++ Programmers

You can join this group by sending the message "sub MSVC your name" to `listserv@lime.ease.lsoft.com`

MUSE-L—MUSE Software Discussion List

You can join this group by sending the message "sub MUSE-L your name" to `listserv@cmsa.berkeley.edu`

MYTHUS-L—Mythus Fantasy Roleplaying Game List

Brown University, Providence, RI

You can join this group by sending the message "sub MYTHUS-L your name" to `listserv@brownvm.brown.edu`

NET-L—STUDENT'S INTERNET/EARN DISCUSSION LIST

You can join this group by sending the message "sub NET-L your name" to `listserv@man.torun.pl`

NET-ND—Notre Dame Campus Networking News

You can join this group by sending the message "sub NET-ND your name" to `listserv@vma.cc.nd.edu`

NETMONTH—NetMonth Magazine

You can join this group by sending the message "sub NETMONTH your name" to `listserv@vm.marist.edu`

NETV-L—IBM's NETView Discussion List

You can join this group by sending the message "sub NETV-L your name" to `listserv@vm.marist.edu`

NEWTON-L—Discussion of Apple Newton Family of Equipment

You can join this group by sending the message "sub NEWTON-L your name" to `listserv@listserv.dartmouth.edu`

NEXTSTEP—NeXTSTEP 3.x & NeXTSTEP 486 for Intel

University of Notre Dame, Notre Dame, IN

You can join this group by sending the message "sub NEXTSTEP your name" to `listserv@vma.cc.nd.edu`

NOVAE—NOVAE GROUP Teachers Networking for the Future

You can join this group by sending the message "sub NOVAE your name" to `listserv@idbsu.idbsu.edu`

NV-L—Discussion of IBM NetView and POLYCENTER Manager on NetView et alia

You can join this group by sending the message "sub NV-L your name" to `listserv@ucsbvm.ucsb.edu`

OHIOMM—Ohio Multimedia Development

You can join this group by sending the message "sub OHIOMM your name" to `listserv@miamiu.muohio.edu`

ORCS-L—Operations Research/Computer Science Interface

You can join this group by sending the message "sub ORCS-L your name" to listserv@listserv.okstate.edu

OS2-L—IBM OS/2 Unedited Discussion List

You can join this group by sending the message "sub OS2-L your name" to listserv@nic.surfnet.nl

OS2PRO-L—IBM OS/2 Unedited Programmers Forum

You can join this group by sending the message "sub OS2PRO-L your name" to listserv@nic.surfnet.nl

PACS-L—Public-Access Computer Systems Forum

You can join this group by sending the message "sub PACS-L your name" to listserv@uhupvm1.uh.edu

PAGEMAKR—PageMaker for Desktop Publishers

You can join this group by sending the message "sub PAGEMAKR your name" to listserv@listserv.iupui.edu

PCBUILD—Building and Repairing PC Computers - Hardware Only

You can join this group by sending the message "sub PCBUILD your name" to listserv@idbsu.idbsu.edu

PCSUPT-L—Forum for the Discussion of PC User Support Issues

You can join this group by sending the message "sub PCSUPT-L your name" to listserv@yalevm.cis.yale.edu

PCTECH-L—MS-DOS Compatibles Support Group

You can join this group by sending the message "sub PCTECH-L your name" to listserv@vm3090.ege.edu.tr

POWER-L—POWER-L IBM RS/6000 POWER Family

You can join this group by sending the message "sub POWER-L your name" to listserv@listserv.nodak.edu

POWER-PC—IBM Power PC Discussion

You can join this group by sending the message "sub POWER-PC your name" to listserv@uga.cc.uga.edu

POWERH-L—Discussion List for the PowerHouse Software

You can join this group by sending the message "sub POWERH-L your name" to listserv@listserv.unb.ca

QPS-USERS—Discussion Among Users of the Quark Publishing System

You can join this group by sending the message "sub QPS-USERS your name" to listserv@listserv.aol.com

QUARKXPR—The Quark Express List

You can join this group by sending the message "sub QUARKXPR your name" to listserv@iubvm.ucs.indiana.edu

SOFTREVU—Small Computing Systems Software Issues Discussion List

You can join this group by sending the message "sub SOFTREVU your name" to listserv@listserv.aol.com

SP1-L—IBM SP1 Discussion

You can join this group by sending the message "sub SP1-L your name" to listserv@uga.cc.uga.edu

STPP—Science, Technology, and Society Discussion and Networking Group

You can join this group by sending the message "sub STPP your name" to listserv@gwuvm.gwu.edu

SUPERIBM—Super Computing Issues Forum

You can join this group by sending the message "sub SUPERIBM your name" to
`listserv@lsv.uky.edu`

TAA-L—Textbook Authors Association

The University of Georgia, Athens, GA

You can join this group by sending the message "sub TAA-L your name" to `listserv@uga.cc.uga.edu`

TIDBITS—A Newsletter for Mac Users

You can join this group by sending the message "sub TIDBITS your name" to
`listserv@ricevm1.rice.edu`

TIP—List Of Theoretical Computer Science, Tip

You can join this group by sending the message "sub TIP your name" to `listserv@plearn.edu.pl`

TOW—The Online World Book Info

You can join this group by sending the message "sub TYPO-L your name" to
`listserv@listserv.nodak.edu`

TYPO-L—TYPO-L Discussion of Type and Typographic Design

You can join this group by sending the message "sub BLIND-L your name" to
`listserv@listserv.hea.ie`

VBDATA-L—Discussion for Microsoft Visual Basic Data Access

You can join this group by sending the message "sub VBDATA-L your name" to
`listserv@peach.ease.lsoft.com`

VBSCRIPT—Visual Basic Scripting Edition

You can join this group by sending the message "sub VBSCRIPT your name" to
`listserv@listserv.msn.com`

VFORT-L—VS-Fortran Discussion List

You can join this group by sending the message "sub VFORT-L your name" to
`listserv@listserv.rediris.es`

VISBAS-L—Visual Basic List

You can join this group by sending the message "sub VISBAS-L your name" to
`listserv@peach.ease.lsoft.com`

VPIEJ-L—Electronic Journal Publishing List

You can join this group by sending the message "sub VPIEJ-L your name" to
`listserv@vtvm1.cc.vt.edu`

WAVEFR-L—WaveFront Software

You can join this group by sending the message "sub WAVEFR-L your name" to
`listserv@psuvm.psu.edu`

WAYCOOL-L—Way Cool Software Reviews by Children, Teachers, and Parents

You can join this group by sending the message "sub WAYCOOL-L your name" to
`listserv@uconnvm.uconn.edu`

WEBPOST—Microsoft WebPost API

You can join this group by sending the message "subWEBPOST your name" to
`listserv@listserv.msn.com`

WFW-L—Microsoft Windows for Workgroups

You can join this group by sending the message "sub WFW-L your name" to `listserv@umdd.bitnet`

WIN95-L—Windows 95 Give-And-Take List

You can join this group by sending the message "sub WIN95-L your name"
`tolistserv@peach.ease.lsoft.com`

WINDOWS—MICROSOFT WINDOWS (R), NT (R) AND 95 (R)

You can join this group by sending the message "sub WINDOWS your name" to listserv@vm1.mcgill.ca

WINHLP-L—Windows Help Compiler (WINHELP) Discussion List

You can join this group by sending the message "sub WINHLP-L your name" to listserv@admin.humberc.on.ca

WPWIN-L—WordPerfect For Windows Discussion List

You can join this group by sending the message "sub WPWIN-L your name" to listserv@listserv.acsu.buffalo.edu

WVRK12-L—Ruralnet Forum on Computer Networking in Education

You can join this group by sending the message "sub WVRK12-L your name" to listserv@wvnvm.wvnet.edu

XLFORT-L—XL FORTRAN Compilers Disscussion List

You can join this group by sending the message "sub XLFORT-L your name" to listserv@uga.cc.uga.edu

EDUCATION

Education Resources

A.Word.A.Day Home Page

http://lrdc5.lrdc.pitt.edu/awad/home.html

Provides information about the listserv AWAD, which sends a new vocabulary word a day to your e-mail address. Also offers links to other word-related Internet resources.

Academy One

http://www.nptn.org:80/cyber.serv/AOneP/

Provides resources for students, parents, and K–12 educators and administrators. Sponsors Internet projects throughout the year, including a Mousetrap-Powered Vehicle Competition, the TeleOlympics, and the Math Olympics. Also offers a curriculum database and an index of other online projects.

Adult Education

http://galaxy.einet.net/galaxy/Social-Sciences/
Education/Adult-Education.html

Offers links to several resources on adult education. Enables the combination of distance education, adult education, and the Internet to deliver instruction. Invites contributions to the collection of resources.

AIMS Education Foundation

http://204.161.33.100/AIMS.html

Presents the world of hands-on science and math investigations for K–9 students. Integrates the study of mathematics and science in a meaningful manner, which prompts students to quickly realize the value of mathematics and learn to "work like scientists."

The Amistad Research Center

http://www.arc.tulane.edu/

Archives African-American history and culture. Also contains information about many other minority groups. Offers links to the center's manuscript collection, several art collections, traveling history exhibits, and library.

Apple Higher Education: The Apple Virtual Campus

http://www.info.apple.com/hed/

Showcases Apple's vision of the campus of the future, while strengthening the technologies of today. Lists learning technologies such as distance learning, talks about collaboration and information access, and the mobile student. Also contains a link to Highway 1, a nonprofit organization formed to support innovative use of new technologies in the legislative environment and democratic process. A Quicktime virtual tour of the University of Southern California is also included.

The AskERIC Virtual Library

http://ericir.syr.edu

Contains select resources for both education and general use. Includes lesson plans, ERIC digests, information guides and publications, reference tools, government information, and educational listserv archives.

Biology(Science)

http://galaxy.einet.net/galaxy/Science/Biology.html

Offers links to all things scientific that might be of use to teach K–12 or university teachers and students. Categorizes sections by subset of biology, most recent additions, software, and collections, to name a few.

CALI: The Center for Computer-Assisted Legal Instruction

http://cali.org/

Nonprofit consortium of more than 155 United States law schools. Supports the production, distribution, and use of computer-based instructional materials.

Cartoon Laws of Physics

http://abacus.bates.edu/~jburke/open1/physics.html

Adds humor to the standard laws of physics. Illustrates each law using cartoon characters.

Center for Talented Youth (CTY) of the Johns Hopkins University

http://www.jhu.edu:80/~gifted/

Serves the gifted population with special programs, job opportunities, and other resources. Provides details about all the CTY programs, and also offers links to other resources.

Childaware

http://www.inetcom.net/test/index.html

Offers positive interaction with other parents of preschoolers. Includes a manual and resources for preschoolers to help check readiness for first grade.

CIC, Center for Library Initiatives

`http://www.cic.net/cic/cli.html`

Provides information for librarians, educators, and institutions, particularly those within the CIC (Big Ten universities, plus the University of Chicago).

The Comer School Development Program

`http://info.med.yale.edu/comer`

Provides information about the School Development Program, a national school reform project directed by James P. Comer, M.D., the renowned child psychiatrist at the Yale Child Study Center.

Computer as Learning Partner

`http://www.clp.berkeley.edu/CLP.html`

Gives information on integrating computer use to improve middle school science instruction. Provides curriculum guides, software links, and project information.

Cornell Theory Center Math and Science Gateway

`http://www.tc.cornell.edu:80/Edu/MathSciGateway/`

Provides links to resources in mathematics and science for educators and students in grades 9–12. Divides the resources into standard subject areas and includes links to online field trips and museums. Also offers journal and research articles.

Department of Clothing, Design, and Technology, MMU

`http://www.doc.mmu.ac.uk/hol/cdt.html`

Details courses, staff, students, and the work done in this department. Contains examples of designs produced by students and staff and also details some of the conferences and shows scheduled.

The Digital Frog

`http://www.sentex.net/~dfi`

Focuses on producing high-quality educational software. Features The Digital Frog CD-ROM. Describes DFI and contains a full-featured Web version of The Digital Frog.

Education Virtual Library—Primary School

`http://www.csu.edu.au/education/primary.html`

Alphabetically catalogs several interesting K–12 curriculum resources from around the world. Helps you research trends in education and creates multicultural or foreign language units. Also highlights links to a Web site created in Russian using the Cyrillic alphabet.

EDUCOM—Home Page

`http://educom.edu:80/`

Offers searchable archives of EDUCOM Review, archives of the listserv EDUPAGE, and other online documents. Supports EDUCOM's focus on educational technology in higher education. Also offers links to several other telecom/educational technology-related site and programs.

The Egyptian Gallery

`http://www.mordor.com/hany/egypt/egypt.html`

Provides information on the modern state, such as the national anthem, pictures of modern cities, and sound clips. Also presents pictures and text about ancient Egypt.

Federal and State-Run Servers

`http://edweb.cnidr.org:90/gophwww.gov.html`

Lists all current federally- and state-run Gopher and Web servers with an educational focus. Lists a link to each site along with a brief description of the site.

The Geometry Forum

`http://forum.swarthmore.edu/`

Focuses on geometry and math education. Offers links to resources such as the Coalition of Essential Schools, a Web-based lesson on vectors, a geometry listserv, and more. Also offers a section on projects for students, such as "Ask Dr. Math."

Heritage Map Museum

`http://www.carto.com`

Displays hundreds of original 15th to 19th century antique maps. Focuses on displaying and selling original works of the masters of cartography. Offers the works of Schedel, Munster, Ortelius, Mercator, Blaeu, Hondius, and many others.

Hillside Elementary School

http://hillside.coled.umn.edu/

Contains activities and projects. Lets students make their own home pages and have e-mail addresses, and use the Internet for research.

ICDL

http://acs-info.open.ac.uk/info/other/ICDL/ICDL-Facts.html

Offers links to a free Telnet database, a quarterly publication about distance learning, and the ICDL Gopher server.

Interactive Multimedia Education Resources

http://www.ems.psu.edu/Earth2/E2Top.html

Contains images and other multimedia files related to earth science. Offers an online tutorial to learn how to use the resources.

The Internet Educational Resources Guide

http://www.aber.ac.uk/~magwww/index_ht1.html

Offers a searchable collection of educational links, but offers more than just links to school subject areas. Also reviews online magazines and books about the Internet, and has information about Gophers, FTP sites, Telnet databases, and listservs.

IPL Building Directory

http://ipl.sils.umich.edu:80/bldg.dir/

Consists of four main divisions: reference, youth services, services for librarians and information professionals, and the education division. Contains resources, interactive exhibits, and discussion areas.

ISN KidNews

http://www.umassd.edu/SpecialPrograms/ISN/KidNews.html

News service for students and teachers around the world. Lets you use stories from the services as long as you credit the author, and lets you submit stories. Encourages comments about news gathering, teaching, and computer-related issues in the Discussion sections for students and teachers.

Knox Junior High Home Page

http://www.geopages.com/CapitolHill/1444

Provides important links for research and training students and teachers to use the vast resources of the Internet.

Little Toy Store on the Net

http://www.suba.com/~chicago/lts.html

Specializes in fun and educational toys for children. Offers a list of resources for educators, parents, and kids on the net.

Magic Learning Systems

http://www.xmission.com/~stageone/mls.html

Develops and markets educational and self-improvement software and shareware, combining the latest technologies with time-tested educational methods for the individual, the classroom, and the home.

The Mark Twain Library

http://hydor.colorado.edu/twain/

Provides electronic texts of Mark Twain's works. Offers several works. Also lists other pages with Mark Twain resources.

Math and Science Gateway (Cornell Theory Center)

http://www.tc.cornell.edu/Edu/MathSciGateway/

Provides a wide range of educational services to the national community. Provides links to resources in mathematics and science for educators and students in grades 9–12.

MATHMOL—K–12 Mathematics and Molecules

http://www.nyu.edu/pages/mathmol/

Provides students, teachers, and the general public information about the rapidly growing field of molecular modeling. Also provides K–12 students with basic concepts in mathematics and their connection to molecular modeling. Contains supporting materials for this project, such as a hypermedia textbook, a library of 3D molecular models, and online challenges for students.

The Media Literacy On-line Project Home Page

`http://interact.uoregon.edu/MediaLit/HomePage`

Provides information and resources to educators, producers, students, parents, and others interested in the influence of electronic media on children, youth, and adults. Contains a database on media literacy, as well as links to Internet resources related to the topic.

MediaPro

`http://www.widdl.com/MediaPro/`

Features the Magic Carpet series of interactive learning software (in English or Mandarin Chinese). Provides ordering information and information on a 30-day free trial basis.

Medical/Clinical/Occupational Toxicology Resource Home Page

`http://www.pitt.edu/~martint/welcome.htm`

Provides information for practioners, educators, and researchers in medical, clinical, and occupational toxicology. Also provides poison information.

MEOL

`http://meol.mass.edu:70/0/home`

Serves as a cooperative gateway to all of Massachusetts' educational agencies and organizations. Offers easily accessible FAQs, listings of current online projects, and job postings.

Mount St. Helens

`http://volcano.und.nodak.edu/vwdocs/msh/msh.html`

Provides image maps of more than 1,490 still images of the mountain before, during, and after the eruption. Provides information about the people, Mount St. Helens and other volcanoes, other Mount St. Helens resources, plants and animals, and curriculum.

MU CoE Links to Education Resources

`http://tiger.coe.missouri.edu/Resource.html`

Offers many links on education and resources. Includes an entire section devoted to mathematics, science, and technology.

NASA Education Sites

`http://quest.arc.nasa.gov/OER/`

Offers a collection of servers specifically geared for teachers, students, and administrators. Offers a selection of math and science education resources, connectivity to numerous education servers, journals, and grant and project participation information.

Network Nuggets

`http://www.etc.bc.ca/~tcoop/index.html`

Shares information about educationally relevant Internet resources. Provides list members with a message each day during the school year to help them find resources on the Internet. Offers an organized main index, and the listserv is one way to keep up with the Internet one day at a time.

The New York Open Center

`http://www.panix.com/~openctr`

Nonprofit center for holistic learning and culture in New York City. Offers nearly 1,000 courses annually on topics of alternative health and bodywork disciplines, depth psychologies, sociocultural issues, spiritual and meditative teachings, and multicultural arts. Includes program information and a preview of the center's journal.

The Nine Planets

`http://seds.lpl.arizona.edu/nineplanets/nineplanets/nineplanets.html#to`

Presents a multimedia essay about the solar system, using text, pictures, sounds, and an occasional movie. Briefly describes each of the planets and major moons in the solar system, and illustrates them using pictures from NASA spacecraft.

The OSPI Math, Science, and Technology Server

`http://www.ospi.wednet.edu/`

Contains a collection of online math and science resources, as well as information on WEdNet. Also offers links to public and private online schools and Washington state colleges and universities.

Parenting Skills on Video

`http://www.novia.net/~video`

Contains parenting enhancement skills that you can use throughout your impressionable child's life. Presents guidelines for raising happy, healthy children.

Persimmon Software for Children

`http://www.dnai.com/persimmon`

Chooses a different monthly aspect of the arts and humanities to create an interactive, multimedia presentation that engages children and promotes creative learning.

Peterson's Education Center

`http://www.petersons.com:8080/`

Seeks to catalog all United States K–12 schools, colleges, and universities, both public and private, as well as community and technical colleges. Also plans to offer transcript services and scholarship information.

Placer County Office of Education

`http://placercoe.k12.ca.us`

Lists California K–12 and community colleges, as well as several links for teachers, students, and administrators.

Private School Resource

`http://www.brigadoon.com/psrnet/`

Presents a collection of many resources for private, independent, and religiously affiliated schools. Includes separate sections for organizations, school home pages, private school resources guides, and vendor information.

Project LEAP (Learn Earn and Prosper)

`http://www.olemiss.edu/depts/project_leap`

Provides basic skills, GED, job skills, and life-coping skills to a wide range of programs including literacy programs, family literacy, and workplace literacy.

Project Libellus

`http://osman.classics.washington.edu/libellus/libellus.html`

Contains free classic Greek and Latin electronic texts. Offers pointers to other classic texts found at other archives, organized by institution or archive.

Scholarly Electronic Forums Web Page

`http://www.oise.on.ca/~arojo/forums.html`

Offers contextualized information on scholarly electronic discussion groups. Provides information for potential and present users and listowners. Serves as a resource for electronic communication scholars, practitioners, and students.

Schoolhouse Videos and CDs (CD-ROMs)

`http://www.nando.net/ads/gift/school.htm`

Offers hundreds of topics and thousands of videos and CD-ROMs, from algebra to gardening to music.

SciEd: Science and Mathematics Education Resources

`http://www-hpcc.astro.washington.edu/scied/science.html`

Offers an organized math and science virtual bookshelf. Offers pointers to online scientific and mathematical reference works and charts, as well as links to the usual science and math subject areas. Also includes information on ethics in science and software and equipment suppliers.

Second Nature

`http://www.2nature.org`

Nonprofit environmental organization that helps institutions of learning, such as colleges and universities, produce graduates who will become environmental leaders. Provides information about Second Nature's unique educational philosophy.

SERESC

`http://reg.seresc.k12.nh.us/`

Contains links to a short list of very useful educational Internet resources. Also offers information on grants, government agencies, and museums.

Small is Beautiful

`http://www.nas.nasa.gov/NAS/Education/nanotech/nanotech.html`

Lists resources on nanotechnology. Includes DNA nanotechnology, molecular manufacturing, and computational nanotechnolgy.

Street Cents Online

http://www.screen.com/streetcents.html

Tied to the Canadian television show *Street Cents*, which teaches young people how to be informed consumers. Covers all of the highlights of the week's program, and also offers a kids club and discussion list.

The Tecla Home Page from Birkbeck College London

http://www.bbk.ac.uk/Departments/Spanish/TeclaHome.html

Text magazine written for learners and teachers of Spanish, produced weekly during the school year. Provides text in Spanish, with vocabulary listed below the text.

TENET

http://gopher.tenet.edu

Serves as a Web site and Gopher for state educators and general use. Includes state educational news, policies, and reform information. Also offers college planning, field trip plans, and connectivity to educational Gophers around the world.

TESL-EJ Master Page

http://violet.berkeley.edu/~cwp/TESL-EJ/index.html

Online journal. Covers teaching English as a second language from many perspectives.

Theodore Tugboat

http://www.cochran.com/

Based on a Canadian TV show, *Theodore Tugboat*, and designed for young children. Lets kids send a postcard to a friend, download a coloring book page, and help write an interactive story. Also offers a parent/teacher area.

TIESnet

http://tiesnet.ties.k12.mn.usandgopher://
tiesnet.ties.k12.mn.us

Technology and Information Educational Services of Minnesota, the older sister of InforMNs. Includes access to numerous ongoing school projects, as well as lesson plans, research information, and connectivity to InforMNs.

UEWeb

http://eric-web.tc.columbia.edu/

Provides information on and for urban students, their families, and the educators who serve them. Includes manuals, brief articles, annotated bibliographies, reviews publications, and conference announcements in urban education, among other features.

The United States Education Department/OERI

http://gopher.ed.gov

Offers an information server that acts as a reference desk for all things educational. Includes educational software, Goals 2000 information, as well as primary, secondary, and vocational information.

Videodiscovery

http://www.videodiscovery.com/vdyweb

Provides information about interactive CD-ROM and laserdisc multimedia for science and math education, plus cool science facts, a guide to Internet education resources, educational technology primers, and more.

VOTEC Home Page

http://www.ed.uiuc.edu/COE/VOTEC/home.html

Provides information about vocational/technical education. Includes information on workplace literacy, tech prep, thinking skills, and training.

The Washington Center for Internships & Academic Seminars

http://www.fga.com/twc

Propones the idea that the key to student success is active involvement in the educational process. Provides internships and academic seminar programs to college students that challenge them personally and professionally. Students apply academic theory through practical experience, discover their professional strengths and weaknesses, question chosen career paths, interact with students from across the country, and develop a broad sense of civic and professional responsibility.

Web 66

`http://web66.coled.umn.edu`

Seeks to be a catalyst that integrates the Internet into K–12 school curricula. Facilitates the introduction of Internet technology into K–12 schools by helping them set up servers, design home pages, and find other online schools.

Web66: K-12 Schools Registry

`http://hillside.coled.umn.edu/others.html`

Consists of a clickable map of the United States, Canada, and Mexico, and each click takes you to a different region's online schools. Provides the same information in a text format. Also offers school listings by country. Helps find keypals or partners for an online project.

Welcome to MegaMath

`http://www.c3.lanl.gov/mega-math/welcome.html`

Aims to bring unusual and important mathematical ideas to elementary school classrooms so that young people and their teachers can think about them together. Provides an online workbook with activities for teachers and students, as well as lesson plans and curriculum guides.

Welcome to the United States Civil War Center

`http://www.cwc.lsu.edu/`

Serves as a clearinghouse for all Civil War materials. Offers links to many Civil War exhibits, continuously updated. Seeks to be objective and look and the causes, events, and aftermath from every viewpoint possible.

Whales: A Thematic Web Unit

`http://curry.edschool.Virginia.EDU/~kpj5e/Whales/Contents.HTML`

Focuses on K–5 kids. Contains images, activities, and project ideas.

Window-To-Russia Home Page

`http://www.kiae.su/www/wtr/`

Offers resources in both Russian and English, as well as links that tell you how to install a Netscape-readable Cyrillic font. Offers online art exhibits, an interactive Russian-English dictionary, basic country information, and more.

Winston Churchil High School Web Server

`http://lancelot.chs.lane.edu/`

Hosts various WWW documents written by Churchill High School students or about Churchill High School.

WisDPI—The Wisconsin Department of Public Instruction

`http://badger.state.wi.us:70/0h/agencies/dpi/www/dpi_home.html`

Includes resources about education and libraries. Contains a variety of K–12 projects, lesson plans, and educational links.

Women in Higher Education

`http://www.itis.com/wihe`

Presents Women in Higher Education, a monthly newsletter for women university administrators, faculty, and staff. Includes news and articles and current job listings.

The World Lecture Hall

`http://www.utexas.edu/world/lecture/`

Offers links to faculty world-wide who use the Web to deliver class materials. Includes syllabi, assignments, lecture notes, exams, multimedia textbooks, and resource materials on almost any subject.

The World of Benjamin Franklin

`http://sln.fi.edu/franklin/rotten.html`

Provides multimedia information about Ben Franklin using pictures, documents, and movies. Covers his family, inventions, diplomacy, philosophy, and leadership. Provides a bibliography for further study of Franklin, his accomplishments, and the time period.

Document Covers

`http://www.cover-rite.com/sample.htm`

Avoid tacky coffee stains on your business report or research paper with Cover-Rite document covers. Visit this site to learn how to receive a free sample.

The World of the Vikings Home Page

http://www.demon.co.uk/history/vikings/vikhome.html

Provides information about the World of the Vikings CD-ROM and research project. The CD-ROM includes two separate resources—the Research Database, created for academic researchers, libraries and schools, and Evidence Boxes, which collect together the best resources from the main archive for younger children. Also offers links to other Internet Viking resources.

Financial Aid

What's Your Major?

The following are the five oldest universities in the United States. Thinking of applying? Check out the sites in this section for information on how to save a buck or two.

- Harvard—founded in 1636

- Yale—founded in 1701

- University of Pensylvania—founded in 1740

- Moravian College—founded in 1742

- Princeton—founded in 1746

Financial Aid Information Page

http://www.cs.cmu.edu/afs/cs.cmu.edu/user/mkant/Public/
FinAid/finaid.html

Offers a collection of financial aid information on the Internet. Includes links to all online scholarship and fellowship databases and information about grants and loans, as well as links to university financial aid Web and Gopher servers and a link to the online version of Octameron Associates' book, *Don't Miss Out: The Ambitious Student's Guide to Financial Aid*.

Money for College

http://emporium.turnpike.net/D/dcservice/wg/lenn4.htm

Offers assistance in finding money for higher education. Loans, grants, and scholarships are available if you know where to find them, and they do.

Home Schooling

Homeschooling Resources

http://www.eskimo.com/~billb/home.html

Contains home schooling resources, divided into home schooling Web sites, relevant educational directories, and ERIC information guides.

Jon's Home-School Resource Page

http://www.midnight beach.com/hs

Provides information about home schooling. Offers links to other Web pages, online curriculum guides, listservs, newsgroups, and so on.

International Education

Friends and Partners

http://solar.rtd.utk.edu/friends/home.html

Promotes understanding between Americans and Russians. Provides information on almost every aspect of life in the two cultures, and also links to learning and using the Cyrillic alphabet. Offers a related listserv that you can join or access.

Hello India!

http://www.helloindia.com

Serves the Indian community. Contains information about Indian food, music, culture, entertainment, events, and the online version of India Today.

The Human-Languages Page

http://www.willamette.edu/~tjones/Language-Page.html

Focuses on bringing together information about the languages of the world. The language resources listed here come from all around the world, and range from dictionaries to language tutorials to spoken samples of languages. Offers the page in several languages. Provides Quick-Jump links for easy navigation, and should soon be searchable.

I*EARN

http://www.igc.apc.org/iearn/

I*EARN is the International Education and Resource Network, composed of teachers and young people working together in different parts of the world via a global telecommunications network. The purpose of I*EARN is to enable participants to undertake projects designed to make a meaningful difference in

the health and welfare of the planet and its people.
Contains information from all the international
projects, as well as entry points for the I*EARN
member newsgroups.

IMD International Institute for Management Development

http://www.imd.ch/

Offers a solid reputation for pioneering the development of executive education, bringing a truly
international perspective to management development in cooperation with some of the most successful companies around the world.

Le Coin des Francophones et Autres Grenouilles

http://www.cnam.fr/fr/

Offers links to almost all other French-related sites.
Includes pointers to popular tourist attractions,
learning and using the language, and more.

Live from Antarctica

http://quest.arc.nasa.gov/livefrom/livefrom.html

Connects students and teachers to Antarctica.
Includes field journals of scientists, teachers guides,
Q & A forums, links to resource materials, and so on.

World Kids Press Home Page

http://www.webpub.com/worldkids/

Offers audiotape and coloring book packages
designed to introduce the concept of foreign
languages to children from preschool level to age 8
or 9 through fun with music, read-alongs, and
coloring.

K–12 Education

About the NDLC

http://www.occ.uky.edu/NDLC/NDLCexplain.html

Serves as a free resource for K–12, higher education,
and adult education, distance learning. Offers a free
Telnet database. Explains how to use the database,
who to call for help, and NCLD's mission.

Alpine Valley School—Home Page

http://www.well.com/user/artbrock/avs/

A K–12 independent day school located in Denver at
which the students completely design their own
education and participate in governing the school.
Provides detailed information about the school's
philosophy, mission, enrollment process, and
generally presents a very bright picture of the school.

ArtsEdge Network

http://artsedge.kennedy-center.org/artsedge.html

Focuses on using technology to increase access to
arts resources and increase arts education in the K–
12 school environment. Features an online newsletter, an information gallery, curriculum guides, and
links to other arts-related online information.

Book Nook

http://i-site.on.ca/Isite/Education/Bk_report/

Presents book reports by kids on kids' literature.
Links reports worldwide into one central point of
reference.

Brooke High WWW Server

http://168.216.219.18

Provides information about Brooke High School,
located in the northern panhandle of West Virginia,
40 miles southeast of Pittsburgh. Includes its
newspaper, *Babbling Brooke*, which gives information
about the school system and surrounding
coummunities, and information on how to install a
Web server and slip servers. Offers thousands of
educational and shareware files for ftp/Gopher
transfer.

Busy Teachers WebSite K–12

http://www.gatech.edu/lcc/idt/Students/Cole/Proj/K-12/TOC.html

K–12 Internet resource for teachers. Organized by
subject area with annotated links to sites that lead
directly to source materials.

Cold Spring Harbor Fish Hatchery and Aquarium

http://www.okc.com/fish

Offers a wide variety of hands-on educational
programs for K–12 students. Presents indoor and
outdoor displays. Provides trout and other fish to
lakes and streams throught the region.

Columbia Public Schools Home Page

http://www.ims.columbia.k12.mo.us

Serves 15,000 K–12 students. Features student and staff work and technical information for other schools.

Council of the Great City Schools Online

http://www.cgcs.org

Nonprofit organization that represents the nation's largest public school systems. Links to local chapter pages.

The Cyberspace Middle School

http://www.scri.fsu.edu/~dennisl/CMS.html

Contains links to science fairs, *Midlink Magazine* (for kids by kids), and Virtual Bus Stops (links to online middle schools). Also offers many helpful links for students, such as an online Periodic Table, how to read a map, and so on.

FYI, RFC #1578-Schools, and Internet

http://chs.cusd.claremont.edu/www/people/rmuir/rfc1578.html

Provides an Internet FAQ on the Internet and K–12 schools. Offers a clickable table of contents for browsing and contains useful information for anyone considering putting the Internet into a K–12 environment.

Galileo

http://www-hpcc.astro.washington.edu/scied/galileo.html

Offers a downloadable collection of science lesson plans for K–12 science teachers for classroom use.

HotList of K–12 Internet School Sites

http://www.sendit.nodak.edu/k12

Contains links to all United States K–12 schools with Internet access, divided by state, and lists the level of access each school currently has (Gopher, Web, e-mail only, and so on).

K–12 Education

http://galaxy.einet.net/galaxy/Social-Sciences/Education/K12-Education.html

Offers many K–12 links, searchable and subdivided into primary and secondary education, and also into document type.

K–12 Technology

http://www.cvu.cssd.k12.vt.us/K12TECH/K12TECH.HTM

Describes what is called "Simple School Internet Protocol"—that is, a way to get schools online.

NCSA Education Program

http://www.ncsa.uiuc.edu/Edu/

Seeks to bridge the gap between scientific research and education and make the tools for computation available in the classroom (K–12). Offers jumps for teachers looking for resource materials.

NYSERNet

http://nysernet.org

Offers a wide variety of K–12 tools. Includes class projects, teaching tools, discussion groups, career guidance, reference information, and school reform plans.

Turner Adventure Learning

http://cee.indiana.edu/turner/tal.html

Contains information about Turner Adventure Learning, electronic field trips for K–12. Contains text documents, graphics, and Web links related to each field trip.

Welcome K–12

http://www.gatech.edu/lcc/idt/Students/Cole/Proj/K-12/K12wel.html

Focuses on teachers learning to use the Internet while online, as well as those who have very limited access time. Arranged alphabetically by subject area with two different tables of content—one with subheadings and pictures for those who want to browse and the other with just plain text links to resources. Addresses the real problem of teachers and time.

Online Teaching & Learning

Canadian Institute of Applied Learning, Inc.

http://www.inforamp.net/~canial/index.html

Offers courses in hardware and software training. Carries courses to train students to become certified Novell Engineers and Administrators (CNE and CNA certification). Also offers courses on PC repair and service.

Education

Canadian Kids' Page

`http://www.onramp.ca/~lowens/107kids.htm`

Serves as a starting place for parents and children exploring the Web together.

Classroom Connect

`http://www.classroom.net`

Online magazine for K–12 educators using the Internet in the classroom. Both in print and online, Classroom Connect has become a source of pointers and features related to using the Internet in formal education for more than 8,000 monthly readers.

The Community Learning Network

`http://cln.etc.bc.ca`

Provides information pertinent to United States education as well. Includes distance learning resource information, connections to other educational and Canadian government Gophers and CLN software.

Cornell Computer Science Graphics Course

`http://www.tc.cornell.edu:80/Visualization/Education/cs418/`

Plans to develop an online service for the students to review lab procedures and results, as well as present lecture material and project animations for all to view.

Distance Ed

`http://www.cudenver.edu/~mryder/itc_data/distance.html`

Offers several links to good distance education resources, especially for colleges and universities. Serves as a good starting point for researching distance learning examples and practices.

Distance Education Clearinghouse

`http://www.uwex.edu/disted/home.html`

Gathers information on teleconferencing technologies, instructional design, programs and courses, and other distance learning resources.

Distance Education Resources

`http://tenb.mta.ca/disted.html`

Offers links to international distance learning resources for community and higher education.

Distance Learning Directory

`http://199.125.205.20/WebPages/dll/DIST-LRN/dld.htm`

Provides a listing of Web sites, Gopher sites, listservs, and newsgroups associated with distance education.

Distance Learning Resources

`http://www.crl.com/~gorgon/distance.html`

Offers a list of links (all resources for distance education) that have Internet support of distance learning included in the definition. Also describes each link.

Educational Online Sources

`http://netspace.students.brown.edu/eos/main_image.html`

Plans to become a central "welcoming" and jump station for educators on the Internet. Contains links to educational conferences, policy and reform archives, and subject guides to online resources.

election.html

`http://buckman.pps.k12.or.us/election/election.html`

Presents the Toon Town Election Page, an example of an online interactive project. Students from about 50 classes sent in their votes on which cartoon should be "Mayor of ToonTown," and one class posted the results on the Web. They used e-mail ballots and accepted write-in candidates.

The Electronic Prehistoric Shark Museum

`http://turnpike.net/emporium/C/celestial/epsm.htm`

Features fossil shark teeth (photos and descriptions) from the prehistoric Great White to the jaws of a modern-day shark. Also offers links to other paleontological sites and posts additional shark sightings on the Internet.

Exploratorium Home Page

`http://www.exploratorium.edu/`

Features, among other exhibits, "Diving in to the Gene Pool," "Remembering Nagasaki," "Ask Us A Question," and a digital library. Also offers The Learning Studio, a collection of science resources for parents, teachers, and kids.

Garfield Co. Public Library System

http://www.colosys.net/garfield.html

Provides access to online books, magazines, and reference tools. Includes searchable library catalogs.

GCRIO On-line Student Activities

http://www.gcrio.org/eduStd.html

Offers a collection of links to online science-oriented interactive projects that students can participate in. Also offers subject guides to resources and grant information.

Genetic Engineering Taught Through Telecommunications

http://kadets.d20.co.edu:80/~lundberg/index.html

Genetic Engineering (plant tissue culture/ recombinant DNA) is taught to 36 other schools in the state of Colorado using the Internet.

HotList: Virtual Exhibits

http://sln.fi.edu/tfi/jump.html

Offers links to many online interactive exhibits, where you control the action on the other end, such as a robot or telescope. Also offers links to online exhibits, such as the Amazon jungle or the Louvre.

Impact! Online Home Page

http://www.ed.uiuc.edu/Impact/impact_homepage.html

Consists of hypertext documents in English, with links giving pronunciation, part of speech, and meaning.

The Interactive Frog Dissection: An On-line Tutorial

http://curry.edschool.Virginia.edu:80/~insttech/frog/

Uses photographs and QuickTime movies to illustrate step-by-step the dissection of a frog. Provides tests along the way to help the student judge mastery of the content.

Intercultural E-Mail Classroom Connections

http://www.stolaf.edu/network/iecc/

Provides listings of teachers and classes needing keypals for cross-cultural exchanges and partners for online projects at the K–12 and the college level. Also offers links to listservs and other collections of keypal requests and online projects.

JASON Project

http://seawifs.gsfc.nasa.gov/scripts/JASON.html

Collaborative learning experience for students around the world. Each year, a two-week scientific expedition is mounted in a remote part of the world and broadcast in real-time, using state-of-the-art technology, to a network of educational, research, and cultural institutions in the United States, Canada, Bermuda, and the United Kingdom. Lets participating students at the interactive downlink sites "go live" (using telepresence) to the expedition, operate the scientific equipment being used, and talk directly with the scientists at the expedition site.

Landegg Academy Online

http://www.landegg.org/landegg/

Serves as a learning environment in which people from all parts of the world can gather to search for new answers to the needs of contemporary society.

Math Education Resources

http://www.teleport.com/~vincer/math.html

Offers links to many good online math sites. Lists lesson plans, curriculum guides, and interactive links such as the Gallery of Interactive Geometry. Also offers listings of math-related newsgroups.

MathMagic Internet

http://forum.swarthmore.edu/mathmagic/

Seeks to involve teachers and students in problem solving. Pairs up registered teams from all over the world to discuss and find ways to solve the challenges posted in each of four categories: K–3, 4–6, 7–9, and 10–12.

Online Reference Works

http://www.cs.cmu.edu/Web/references.html

Lists several different online reference sources, such as a hypertext Webster's dictionary, a thesaurus, and an acronym dictionary. Also offers several foreign language dictionaries, and computing dictionaries.

The Open University

http://www.open.ac.uk/

The British institution that pioneered distance education as a way to broaden educational opportunities across the country. Offers a comprehensive program that serves as a model for other programs. Also offers links to other online resources.

Reed Interactive's Global Classroom

http://www.reedbooks.com.au/index.html

Offers online projects centering around specific themes, and encourages international participation. Also offers an international keypal search and find center and access to education-related newsgroups.

The Study in the USA Online Directory

http://www.studyusa.com/

Serves as a resource for international students seeking to study at a quality American university, college, or English language institute. Lets you browse informative articles and program descriptions, and use the online request information forms to e-mail the school in which you're interested for more information.

The Technology and Distance Education Branch

http://www.etc.bc.ca/etc.html

Focuses on the development of a community learning network. Also offers links to other good distance education sites and guidebooks.

Total Recall

http://www.demon.co.uk/sharpsw/total.html

Presents an amazing online training course that teaches you how to dramatically improve your memory powers—improve exam grades, learn foreign vocabulary, and more.

Traveler's Japanese with Voice

http://www.ntt.jp/japan/japanese/

Uses the Internet to teach basic language skills. Divides modules by subject. Plays an audio clip that provides proper pronunciation of any word you click. Also provides historical and cultural information.

Virtual Frog Dissection Kit

http://george.lbl.gov/ITG.hm.pg.docs/dissect/info.html

Provides a learning tool instead of dissecting a real frog. The program uses 3D and MRI images that you can manipulate to see the various parts of the body. Includes online tests.

Welcome to TEAMSnet

http://teams.lacoe.edu/

Offers information on both distance education and Internet in the classroom. Lists online projects, links to resources, and professional development information. Also offers a page on preservice teacher preparation.

The World-Wide Web Virtual Library

http://www.w3.org/hypertext/DataSources/bySubject/Overview.html

Cross-references everything from aboriginal studies to zoos. Details the links by alphabetical order, by era, and by region. Offers clickable maps of the world and specific information about many countries. Also offers a list of other online resources.

Organizations

Arrow Publishing

http://www2.interpath.net:80/spadion/arrow/

Lists videos, software, and publications designed to increase literacy. Produces literacy-oriented educational materials. Also offers an order form that you can print out and fill in to receive more information or materials.

Banned Books On-line

http://www.cs.cmu.edu/Web/People/spok/banned-books.html

Discusses literary censorship and offers links to each work mentioned that is available in electronic format. Also offers a Most Frequently Challenged Books of the 1990s page, as well as links to other sites dealing with censorship.

Ethical, Legal, and Social Issues in Science

http://www.lbl.gov/Education/ELSI/ELSI.html

Tackles tough issues that face scientists every day. Discusses basic versus applied research, breast cancer and genetic screening, and more.

Faculty of Asian Studies, Australian National University

http://online.anu.edu.au/asianstudies/

Provides Asian Studies teaching-and-learning resources, pointers to a vast wealth of Asian Studies research material, information about the programs of the Faculty of Asian Studies at the Australian National University, pointers to information about the University, Australia, and studying in Australia.

Florida Institute of Technology— School of Aeronautics

http://www.fit.edu/soa

Offers five accredited degree programs in aviation management, aeronautical science, and aviation computer science. Offers FAA-approved flight training.

Global Ecology Study Abroad/IHP

http://world.std.com/~ihp/ihp.html

Study global ecology and travel around the world to England, India, Philippines, New Zealand, Mexico. Earn college credit, live with families, small group, international faculty. Offers courses in anthropology, biology, ecology, and economic development. Provides an online catalog, slide file, and application.

Grolier Interactive

http://www.grolier.com

Presents Grolier Interactive, the international CD-ROM multimedia reference and entertainment publisher of the Grolier Multimedia Encyclopedia, Encyclopedia Americana, Guinness Multimedia Disc of Records, Science Fiction encyclopedia, World Cup Soccer, and Modern Art.

GROW—Opportunity Wales

http://194.72.34.100/grow/

Nonprofit organization that administers a variety of placement schemes and internships (some United Kingdom government-sponsored) for graduates and undergraduate students seeking experience of working for UK-based small- and medium-sized enterprises.

Harry Singer Foundation

http://www.redshift.com/~singerf

The Harry Singer Foundation was created to get people, especially high school and college students, more actively interested in public policy. Provides free information such as books and pamphlets, as well as points of contact for further interest.

International Federation of Library Associations and Institutions (IFLA)

http://www.nlc-bnc.ca/ifla/home.html

Provides librarians around the world with a forum for exchanging ideas, promoting international cooperation, research and development in all fields of library activity. Presents members and interested individuals an evolving range of electronic information resources and services through the use of Internet technologies.

Junior Achievement Purpose/Facts

http://www.baynet.com/junior/intro.html

Provides information about Junior Achievement, such as the purpose, mission, goals, and national contact information. Also lists answers to commonly asked questions and tells why you should volunteer to help this worthwhile organization.

Macroscale Land Surface Hydrology Modeling at the UW

http://atlas.ce.washington.edu/~lettenma/mlshm.html

Applies the VIC-2L model, a soil-vegetation-atmospere transfer scheme (SVATS), for macroscale hydrologic simulations of the water and energy balance.

Natural Resources Defence Council (NRDC)

http://www.nrdc.org/nrdc

Nonprofit environmental organization with 170,000 members nationwide and a staff of scientists, lawyers, and environmental experts. Features the latest news from the Hill, plus information everyone should have on the state of our air, water, land, and health. NRDC's mission is to protect the world's natural resources and improve the quality of the human environment.

Northwest Service Academy Page

http://www.teleport.com/~nwsa

Addresses unmet environmental and community needs. Also contains an application.

The Smithsonian Institution Home Page

`http://www.si.edu/`

Features links to What's New (exhibits), Perspectives, Activities, and Resources, which all provide information on a variety of subjects.

TERC

`http://hub.terc.edu:70/hub/owner/TERC`

Researches, develops, and disseminates innovative programs in science, mathematics, and technology for educators, schools, and other learning environments. Contains information for educators interested in trying new ideas in learning environments.

United States Naval Sea Cadet Corps

`http://www.tucson.com/nscc`

Provides a year-round Naval youth education program for young men and women ages 11–18 years old. Learn new skills and gain confidence while aboard Naval ships or air stations.

Welcome to the Council of the Great City Schools Online

`http://www.cgcs.org/`

Nonprofit organization that represents the United States's largest school systems. Offers "legislative alerts," information on instruction, curriculum, and standards, as well as other information necessary to the functioning of large urban school systems. Also provides hypertext versions of the council newsletters, council reports, and conference highlights.

Research

Alabama Supercomputer Authority

`http://sgisrvr.asc.edu/index.html`

Provides state-of-the-art technology in supercomputing and networking to educational institutions, government agencies, and private industry.

Brunel University Artificial Intelligence Area

`http://http1.brunel.ac.uk:8080/depts/AI/`

Features information on artificial intelligence, including artificial life and genetic algorithms. Also contains many links to other AI sites.

The Centre for Alternative Transportation Fuels

`http://www.bcr.bc.ca/catf\default.htm`

The Centre for Alternative Transportation Fuels is operated by BC Research Inc. (BCRI) in Vancouver, B.C., Canada. Maintains a database of technical papers to support the technical and business community in this rapidly moving technological area.

CEPS/NASM Smithsonian Institution

`http://ceps.nasm.edu:2020/homepage.html`

Serves as a jumping-off point for exploring planetary and other astronomical data from the Center for Planetary Studies, Regional Planetary Image Facility, and the National Air and Space Museum. Offers links that provide information useful for classes such as activities, images, and calendars of events.

Concepts in Science through Molecular Modeling

`http://www.nyu.edu/pages/mathmol/modules/modules.html`

Contains many activities for use in the classroom. Includes a section for teachers and for students.

DreamLink

`http://www.iag.net:80/~hutchib/.dream/`

Contains current information and resources on dream translation techniques and different theoretical orientations regarding dreams. Provides a journal to post dreams and receive feedback. Features an archive and guest dreamer.

Hair Care Samples

`http://www.salon.net/gifts/giftssamples.html`

Matrix, Rusk, Paul Mitchell, and more. Request free samples and gift incentives of your favorite salon products.

The Environmental Education Network

http://www.envirolink.org/enviroed/

Serves as a jumping-off point for using the Internet to research the environmental issues. Offers categorized links to resources for teachers, resources for students, and also for higher education.

ILTweb: LiveText: Index

http://daemon.ilt.columbia.edu/k12/livetext/

The LiveText project is based on the belief that the educational applications enabled by networked multimedia technologies will provide the opportunity for educational reform. Provides supporting curricula, lesson plans, and instructional design resources.

Image Analytics Corporation

http://www.imsworld.com/image

Provides cost effective hardware and software systems for microscopic and macroscopic image analysis. A full system performs morphometric cell analysis (length, area, velocity, and shape), currently used for AIDS, neuroimmunology, and biological research. Includes ftp Demo file. Offers basic software and frame grabber board. Also offers color analysis.

IUB Libraries: Research Collections and Services Department

http://www.indiana.edu/~librcsd/

Serves the humanities and social sciences. Builds the printed and electronic collections, instructs classes and individuals, and offers general and specialized reference and research assistance to the students, faculty, and staff of Indiana University.

John and Janice's Research Page

http://k12.cnidr.org/janice_k12/states/states.html

Provides continually updated education-and-the-Internet and other telecom-related statistics. Provides numbers to convince anyone not sure that the Internet really is useful in a learning environment. Lists information in a summary document, and also by state.

Middlebrook's Structured Analog Design

http://www.ardem.com/middlebrook/

Offers techniques to help improve design quality and save design time in the analog world.

Monterey Academy of Oceanographic Science

http://205.155.54.2/maos/home.html

Student-driven pages from a school-within-a-school on the campus of Monterey High School, along California's central coast.

Norm's Home Page

http://www.together.com/home/norm

Explores the use of high-tech construction materials like epoxy methacrylate. Provides educational information on waterproofing, concrete repair, and restoration.

Research at BYU Integrated Microelectronics Lab

http://www.ee.byu.edu/ee/iml/research/research.html

Innovative research takes place in the BYU Integrated Microelectronics Lab, including MEMS, IC processing techniques, MCMs, and TCAD.

Waterford Institute

http://www.xmission.com/~waterfrd/index.html

Provides the latest in educational research and products for the home and school.

Standards & Testing

Environmental Training Group Inc's ENVIROPAGE

http://www.etg-inc.com

Provides United States environmental and occupational safety and health regulations. Emphasizes on training. Contains updates on agency interpretations and regulations.

Guidelines for Educational Uses of Networks

http://www.ed.uiuc.edu/Guidelines/guidelines.html

Offers a collection of several different works related to setting up and managing an educational network, mostly philosophical and focused on educational outcomes.

North Central Regional Educational Laboratory

http://cedar.cic.net/ncrel/

Nonprofit organization devoted to researching and implementing the best practices in public schools so that all students achieve standards of educational excellence. Contains an online newsletter, educational resources you can order, and other useful resources. Provides standards information.

Technology for All Americans Project

http://scholar.lib.vt.edu/TAA/TAA.html

Seeks to create a forum for developing national standards for K–12 technology education. Contains press releases, consensus building workshops, and a newsletter.

Student Resources

CASAA Student Leadership Resource Centre

http://www.sentex.net/~casaa

Focuses on providing fresh student leadership materials, ideas, and support for the student activity advisor.

Children's Literature Web Guide

http://www.ucalgary.ca/~dkbrown/index.html

Catalogs Internet resources related to books for children and young adults. Lists recommended books, recent awards, new authors, resources for parents, teachers, and story tellers, movies based on children's books, and much more. Provides information on how to get your children or class involved in online publication, so the whole world can enjoy their creativity.

Classroom at the Internet Schoolhouse

http://www.packet.net:80/schoolhouse/inside.html

Offers a collection of educational and interactive resources. Includes Internet projects, art, civics, interactive games, and science.

College Prep Page

http://www.tpoint.net/~jewels/college.html

Presents a collection of resources for planning your education. Provides information on financial aid, admissions, career planning, and more.

CyberKids Home

http://www.woodwind.com:80/cyberkids/

CyberKids was created as a place for kids to learn and have fun. Offers a free online magazine that contains stories and artwork created by kids, as well as online puzzles, games, and more. Also provides keypals from around the globe in CyberKids Interactive.

English as a Second Language

http://www.ed.uiuc.edu/edpsy-387/rongchang-li/esl/

Brings together resources for teaching ES/FL, such as matching audio to text to help comprehension. Also offers links to the Word a Day vocabulary building e-mail service, and idiom of the Week.

Exchange—Learning.English Language Culture

http://www.deil.lang.uiuc.edu.exchange/

Serves primarily ES/FL students, but also works for multicultural lessons or thematic units. Consists of contributions from international students, such as "Did you know?" about little cultural differences. Also serves as a place to publish your writing (for ES/FL students).

FredNet MOO

http://www.fred.net/cindy/frednet.html

Lets you attend Lincoln's assassination, visit a biochemical laboratory, examine ancient artifacts at the Iceman Museum, and more. Provides a tutorial for new MOOers. Also contains a handy MOO command index for reference.

The Homework Page

http://www.tpoint.net/~jewels/homework.html

A general subject guide page. Categorizes links by subject matter and by age group.

Inkspot

http://www.interlog.com/~ohi/inkspots/young.html

Offers a collection of useful resources for young writers, and anyone teaching young writers. Includes references to workshops, online style guides, publications accepting submissions, and contests.

Jefferson-Scranton Community Schools

http://molebio.iastate.edu/js/homepage.html

Provides high school students the opportunity to explore the Internet through the Web.

Kids Web A World Wide Web Digital Library for Schoolkids

http://www.infomall.org/kidsweb/

Provides a collection of multimedia and other resources useful in education. Caution: The fun and humor link leads to a general Internet humor archive, an area that might not be entirely appropriate for children.

Kids' Space

http://www.interport.net/~sachi

Kids Space has been planned for children to enhance basic computer skills through their real participation and use of the Internet. Provides tools for creation of student's own Web pages.

North American Historical Re-Enactor Web Site (West Site)

http://www.webcom.com/~custer/

Contains a register of societies and clubs dedicated to re-creating historical events for preservation of artifacts and experiencing other periods of history.

Private Schools Online

http://www.thinkthink.com/schools/

Provides students information about private preparatory schools directly from the institution. Offers listings from several private schools.

Sylvan Learning Centers

http://www.magicnet.net/cge/sylvan/

Offers supplemental education to every type of student. Provides information on their services and locations.

Voices of Youth Home Page

http://www.unicef.org/voy/

Contains messages from the World Summit for Social Development. Pertains to topics discussed at the Summit, and although the server doesn't currently accept new messages, you can browse and search old messages by topic.

Welcome to the DeweyWeb

http://ics.soe.umich.edu/

Provides information to students and attempts to provide them a chance to contribute their own observations, findings, and reflections.

Welcome to Virtual FlyLab

http://vflylab.calstatela.edu/edesktop/VirtApps/VflyLab/IntroVflyLab.html

Lets you play the role of a scientist investigating genetic inheritance: manipulate the matings of different fruit flies and see the genetic results of the matings.

Writing at MU

http://www.missouri.edu/~wleric/writery.html

Online discussion site for writers. Offers four direct links to information exchange with other writers. Includes other links to assorted Internet sites, mostly related to writing, as well. Note: A few might not be appropriate for children.

Teacher Resources

Ainsworth Keyboard Training Systems

http://www.qwerty.com

Keyboard training for teachers, executives, writers, etc. Includes demo of Ainsworth Keyboard Trainer, as well as special warm-up exercises to improve efficiency and end writer's block.

Ameritech Education Resources

`http://www.aads.net:1081/education/`

Features the Schoolhouse, which contains a Recreation Area (information on hands-on projects and hobbies), a Teacher's Lounge (lesson plans and curriculum guides), and a Student Activities Center (online activities and projects). Also features the Internet InfoCenter.

Carrie's Sites for Educators

`http://www.mtjeff.com/~bodenst/page5.html`

Provides a table of contents to make browsing easy. Offers a collection of resources, from humanities to math to science to software.

Cisco Educational Archives and Resources Catalog

`http://sunsite.unc.edu/cisco/edu-arch.html`

Provides information to help educators and schools connect to the Internet. Provides technical information (because Cisco produces networking hardware), but also offers examples of school networking projects. Also offers the Virtual Schoolhouse.

Dole 5-A-Day Home Page

`http://www.dole5aday.com`

Offers educational nutrition information and delivers it in a clever and fun way: 36 fruit and vegetable characters host the site and make eating five fruits and vegetables a day fun for everyone. Provides nine areas: 5 A Day Program, CD-ROM, Nutrition Center, Fan Mail, Fun Stuff, 5 A Day at School, Newsroom, and Dole.

DPI InfoWeb

`http://www.dpi.state.nc.us`

Provides access to ERIC, employment opportunities, and the state standardized curriculum. Also offers an online telephone directory for the DPI, and a nice teacher and administrator resource page. Features an outline that shows exactly what information links off which page.

Ed Web Home Page

`http://edweb.cnidr.org:90/`

Centers on resources showing technology and its role in school reform. Lets you hunt down online educational resources around the world, learn about trends in education policy and information infrastructure development, and examine success stories of computers in the classroom.

Education

`http://www.lib.umich.edu/chouse/tree/edu.html`

Provides a listing of Internet resources, and rates the linked sites to help Internet users plow through the vast amount of information.

Education (Social Sciences)

`http://aw.com/educatio.html`

Provides a listing of Internet educational resources, organized by topic and type of resource.

Education Sites

`http://www.fn.net/education.html`

Serves as a subject-oriented guide to Internet resources. Categories include art, health, online museums and libraries, math, science, social sciences, and other resources. Offers art and health links.

eduMall

`http://edumall.com/`

Offers education products. Includes mall locations: Mall Central for mall events, freebies, and latest information; the Learning Center; Bookstore; Administrator's Connection; Campus Shops; Stadium; and Kiosk.

ELTI Charlotte's English Aids

`http://www.coe.uncc.edu/~brmattin/adds.html`

Lists several sample letters for different situations, intended to be models for ES/FL students or others learning written English.

Explorer Home Page

`http://server2.greatlakes.k12.mi.us/`

Acts as a curriculum resource. Contains a searchable database of lesson plans and curriculum guides aimed at math and science. Also categorizes lists of Web classroom resources.

GENII Home Page

`http://139.132.40/GENII/GENIIHP.html`

Teaches teachers how to utilize the resources of the Internet so that they can incorporate the technology into their lesson plans. Lists the mission, virtual faculty, and other relevant data for this project.

Education

Gifted and Talented (TAG) Resources Home Page

http://www.eskimo.com:80/~user/kids.html

Describes many resources for talented and gifted children, their parents, and educators. Overviews giftedness, and lists mailing lists, schools with TAG programs, summer programs, and publications to name a few. Also offers a keypal contact page.

Heinemann World

http://www.heinemann.co.uk

Offers news on educational books, events and technology, guides to relevant sites of use for class and coursework, and sample material to download.

InfoList Home Page

http://www.electriciti.com:80/~rlakin/

Helps teachers begin using the Internet as an educational tool. Contains back issues of the InfoList Digest, to which you also can subscribe free via e-mail.

InforMNs

http://informns.k12.mn.us

Includes teacher discussions, lesson plans, and a collection of Gopher lists.

inQuiry Almanack, March 1995

http://sln.fi.edu/qanda/qanda3.html

Monthly magazine for educators interested in using the Internet to support inquiry-based learning in the classroom. Offers Internet "hunts," online puzzles, and experiments. Focuses on science education.

Integrating Technology Schools Home Page at University of New Mexico

http://www.unm.edu/~jeffryes/its.html

Helps teachers both in the field and preservice learn how to integrate technology into the classroom. Offers online project ideas, subject guides, and how-to's for the Internet.

Judi Harris' Network-Based Educational Activity Collection

http://www.ed.uiuc.edu/Activity-Structures/

Offers a collection of 236 network-based educational activities, collected by Judi Harris.

Kidding Around

http://alexia.lis.uiuc.edu/~watts/kiddin.html

Offers links to the Internet designed for middle-school-age students. Features current affairs, celebrity information, movie and music reviews, and educational links.

Lesson Plans and Activities

http://www.c3.lanl.gov/~cjhamil/solarsystem/education/index.html

Provides information for educators trying to incorporate astronomy into their curriculum.

Mining the Internet Columns

http://www.ed.uiuc.edu/Mining/Overview.html

Presents articles (in HTML) written by Judi Harris for "The Computing Teacher," including tips and information on using computers, telecommunications, and the Internet in the classroom.

NASA Spacelink—An Electronic Information System for Educators

http://spacelink.msfc.nasa.gov/

Contains NASA's public online library of lesson plans, satellite and shuttle images, and more. Also offers information on space careers, interdisciplinary units, and software.

National Science Foundation World Wide Web Server

http://stis.nsf.gov

Provides information for educators and administrators. Contains information on NSF education projects, grants, and publications.

National Teachers Enhancement Network

http://www.montana.edu/~wwwxs/index.html

Offers graduate-credit science and mathematics courses to teachers nationally. Lets teachers participate in the telecomputing courses from convenient home or work locations by using dial-up modem connections or Internet access. Provides teachers with high-quality graduate science courses taught by university scientists, engineers, and mathematicians.

Newton's Apple Educational Materials!

http://ericir.syr.edu/index.html

Contains 26 lessons from the 12th season of the television show, Newton's Apple. Topics range from brain mapping to bread chemistry to the Hubble telescope to printing money to a raptor hospital: includes activities, questions, and further investigation suggestions.

The North Dakota ICICLE Project

http://calvin.cc.ndsu.nodak.edu/wayne/icicle.html

Offers a library of reviewed K–12 curriculum and instructional materials (lesson plans, pictures, subject matter, and so on) available on the Internet, indexed according to subject area.

The Old School House Studio

http://www.pikeperry.co.uk/ppp/pd/courses.htm

Offers inspirational personal development workshops. Also offers the one-year, part-time dramatherapy certificate course, which commences every September and spans six weekends, as well as a summer school (validated by Worcester College).

School and Community Networking Resources

http://www.nas.nasa.gov/HPCC/K12/EDRC21.html

Contains several pointers to good technical guides to getting your school online. The links reference FAQs, lists of Internet providers, and technology plans from other online schools.

The Tech Classics Archive

http://the-tech.mit.edu/Classics/

An archive of 184 works by 17 classical authors (in translation). Provides texts in HTML format and as raw text files. Segments each work into the different books, sections, parts, and so on, whenever possible.

The Virtual English Language Center

http://www.comenius.com/index.html

Provides information for ES/FL teachers and students. Includes such resources as interactive exercises and text/audio playback. Also features "Idiom of the Week," a keypal registry, and a recommended software listing. Also offers links to related Internet sites.

Baby Food Newsletter

http://www.earthsbest.com/famtimes.html

Earth's Best produces baby food made with certified organic ingredients. Find out more by subscribing to their newsletter, which contains feature articles by doctors and answers to parent questions.

Newsgroups

alt.education.alternative

alt.education.bangkok

alt.education.bangkok.cmc

alt.education.bangkok.databases

alt.education.bangkok.planning

alt.education.bangkok.research

alt.education.bangkok.student

alt.education.bangkok.theory

alt.education.disabled

alt.education.distance

alt.education.email-project

alt.education.higher.stu-affairs

alt.education.home-school.christian

alt.education.ib

alt.education.ib.tok

alt.education.research

alt.education.student.government

alt.education.university.vision2020

aus.education.bio-newtech

bit.listserv.slart-l

clari.news.education

clari.news.education.higher

comp.edu

comp.edu.composition

comp.edu.languages.natural

comp.lang.logo

k12.chat.elementary

k12.chat.junior

k12.chat.senior

k12.chat.teacher

k12.ed.art

k12.ed.business

k12.ed.comp.literacy

k12.ed.health-pe

k12.library

k12.ed.comp.literacy

k12.ed.life-skills

k12.ed.math

k12.ed.music

k12.ed.science

k12.ed.soc-studies

k12.ed.special

k12.ed.tag

k12.ed.tech

k12.lang.art

k12.lang.deutsch-eng

k12.lang.esp-eng

k12.lang.francais

k12.lang.russian

k12.sys.projects

misc.education

misc.education.adult

misc.education.home-school.christian

misc.education.home.school.misc

misc.education.language.english

misc.education.medical

misc.education.multimedia

misc.education.science

news:alt.education.alternative

news:alt.education.distance

news:alt.education.email-project

news:alt.education.research

news:alt.literacy.adult

news:alt.usage.english

news:misc.education

news:uk.education.16plus

rec.arts.books.childrens

sci.edu

sci.cognitive

sci.med.pharmacy

sci.op-research

sci.stat.edu

soc.college.teaching-a sst

uk.education.misc

uk.education.teachers

Listservs

AACSB—Business School Accredidation

University of Missouri-St. Louis

You can join this group by sending the message "sub AACSB your name" to listserv@umslvma.umsl.edu

AEPDCC—Adult Basic and Literacy Education Professional Development Discussion

Texas A&M University Computing Services Center

You can join this group by sending the message "sub AEPDCC your name" to listserv@tamvm1.tamu.edu

AERA—American Educational Research Association List (AERA)

Arizona State University, Tempe, AZ

You can join this group by sending the message "sub AERA your name" to listserv@asuvm.inre.asu.edu

AJCUFAID—AJCU Financial Aid Directors

You can join this group by sending the message "sub AJCUFAID your name" to listserv@listserv.georgetown.edu

CALIBK12—California K-12 Librarians

San Jose State University, San Jose, CA

You can join this group by sending the message "sub CALIBK12 your name" to listserv@sjsuvm1.sjsu.edu

CCE—Council of Counselor Educators

University of Central Florida

You can join this group by sending the message "sub CCE your name" to `listserv@ucf1vm.cc.ucf.edu`

CELVR001—CEL's Virtual Classroom 001

Central Michigan University, Mt. Pleasant, MI

You can join this group by sending the message "sub CELVR001 your name" to `listserv@cmuvm.csv.cmich.edu`

COENEWS—College of Education Employee Discussion

University of South Florida, Tampa, FL

You can join this group by sending the message "sub COENEWS your name" to `listserv@cfrvm.cfr.usf.edu`

CRITTHINKT-L—Teaching Critical Thinking

University of Illinois, Urbana, IL

You can join this group by sending the message "sub CRITTHINKT-L your name" to `listserv@postoffice.cso.uiuc.edu`

CSTEP—Academic and Scholarship Information for Students

Syracuse University

You can join this group by sending the message "sub CSTEP your name" to `listserv@listserv.syr.edu`

DEOS-L—The Distance Education Online Symposium

Pennsylvania State University

You can join this group by sending the message "sub DEOS-L your name" to `listserv@psuvm.psu.edu`

DEOSNEWS—The Distance Education Online Symposium

Pennsylvania State University

You can join this group by sending the message "sub DEOSNEWS your name" to `listserv@psuvm.psu.edu`

DR-ED—Medical Education Research and Development

Michigan State University, East Lansing, MI

You can join this group by sending the message "sub DR-ED your name" to `listserv@msu.edu`

DSSHE-L—Disabled Student Services in Higher Education

State University of New York at Buffalo

You can join this group by sending the message "sub DSSHE-L your name" to `listserv@ubvm.cc.buffalo.edu`

EAIE-L—A Discussion List for International Educators in Europe and be+

University Center of Information services (UCI), Nijmegen, The Netherlands

You can join this group by sending the message "sub EAIE-L your name" to `listserv@nic.surfnet.nl`

ECENET-L—Early Childhood Education/ Young Children (0-8)

University of Illinois, Urbana, IL

You can join this group by sending the message "sub ECENET-L your name" to `listserv@postoffice.cso.uiuc.edu`

ECEOL-L—Early Childhood Education On-Line mailing list

University of Maine System, Orono, ME

You can join this group by sending the message "sub ECEOL-L your name" to `listserv@maine.maine.edu`

ED220—Issues in Distance Education

The George Washington University Computer Center, Washington, DC

You can join this group by sending the message "sub ED220 your name" to `listserv@gwuvm.gwu.edu`

EDINTL-L—Education School International Committee

Purdue University, West Lafayette, IN

You can join this group by sending the message
"sub EDINTL-L your name" to
`listserv@vm.cc.purdue.edu`

EDLIB-L—Academic Education Librarians

Wayne State University, Detroit, MI

You can join this group by sending the message
"sub EDLIB-L your name" to
`listserv@cms.cc.wayne.edu`

EE246—EE246-TCHG MATH ELEMENTARY SCHOOL

University of Missouri-St. Louis

You can join this group by sending the message
"sub EE246 your name" to `listserv@umslvma.umsl.edu`

FAMSTECH—Financial Aid Systems - Technical Discussion List

Arizona State University, Tempe, AZ

You can join this group by sending the message
"sub FAMSTECH your name" to
`listserv@asuvm.inre.asu.edu`

FINAID-L—ADMINISTRATION of USA Financial Aid Offices

Pennsylvania State University

You can join this group by sending the message
"sub FINAID-L your name" to
`listserv@psuvm.psu.edu`

FLTEACH—Foreign Language Teaching Forum

State University of New York at Buffalo

You can join this group by sending the message
"sub FLTEACH your name" to
`listserv@ubvm.cc.buffalo.edu`

GC-L—Global Classroom: International Students E-mail Debate

You can join this group by sending the message
"sub GC-L your name" to
`listserv%uriacc.bitnet@listserv.net`

GLB-HLT—Global Forum on Medical Education and Practice

University of Illinois at Chicago, Chicago, IL

You can join this group by sending the message
"sub GLB-HLT your name" to
`listserv@listserv.uic.edu`

GRAPH-TI—Discussion of TI Graphing Calculators in Education

L-Soft International, Inc.

You can join this group by sending the message
"sub GRAPH-TI your name" to
`listserv@peach.ease.lsoft.com`

HEALTH-L—International Discussion on Health Research

University College Dublin, Ireland

You can join this group by sending the message
"sub HEALTH-L your name" to
`listserv@irlearn.ucd.ie`

HMEDRSCH—Home Education Research Discussion List

East Texas State University, Commerce, TX

You can join this group by sending the message
"sub HMEDRSCH your name" to
`listserv@etsuadmn.etsu.edu`

IMSE-L—Institute for Math and Science Education

University of Illinois at Chicago, Chicago, IL

You can join this group by sending the message
"sub IMSE-L your name" to
`listserv@listserv.uic.edu`

IRSU-L—International Relations Student Union List

Yale University Computer Center, New Haven, CT

You can join this group by sending the message
"sub IRSU-L your name" to
`listserv@yalevm.cis.yale.edu`

ISSSAB-L—International Student and Scholar Services Advisory Board List

State University of New York at Buffalo

You can join this group by sending the message "sub ISSSAB-L your name" to
`listserv@ubvm.cc.buffalo.edu`

I_STUD—Members of the Student Chapter of the Institute for Op. Research

University of Missouri-St. Louis

You can join this group by sending the message "sub I_STUD your name" to
`listserv@umslvma.umsl.edu`

K-12GEOGED—ND K-12 Geography Educators

You can join this group by sending the message "sub K-12GEOGED your name" to
`listserv@listserv.nodak.edu`

K12ADMIN—K-12 Educators Interested in Educational Administration

Syracuse University

You can join this group by sending the message "sub K12ADMIN your name" to
`listserv@listserv.syr.edu`

K12SMALL—A Forum for Education in Small or Rural Schools

University of Arkansas Main Campus - Fayetteville

You can join this group by sending the message "sub K12SMALL your name" to
`listserv@uafsysb.uark.edu`

KINDED—Discussion Group for Course Education in Kindergarten

You can join this group by sending the message "sub KINDEDU your name" to
`listserv@listserv.kent.edu`

LRN-ED—Provide Support and Information to K12 Teachers

Syracuse University

You can join this group by sending the message "sub LRN-ED your name" to
`listserv@listserv.syr.edu`

MAC_ED-L—AOL Mac Education & Technology Forum Newsletter

America Online, Inc. (1-800-827-6364 in USA/Canada)

You can join this group by sending the message "sub MAC_ED-L your name" to
`listserv@listserv.aol.com`

MIDDLE-L—Middle level education/early adolescence (10-14)

University of Illinois, Urbana, IL

You can join this group by sending the message "sub MIDDLE-L your name" to
`listserv@postoffice.cso.uiuc.edu`

MIFINAID—Federal Education Loan Program

Michigan State University, East Lansing, MI

You can join this group by sending the message "sub MIFINAID your name" to `listserv@msu.edu`

MSIRE-L—RI Math & Science Resource Discussion List

You can join this group by sending the message "sub MSIRE-L your name" to
`listserv%uriacc.bitnet@listserv.net`

MULTC-ED—Multicultural Education Discussion

University of Maryland CSC, College Park, MD

You can join this group by sending the message "sub MULTC-ED your name" to
`listserv%umdd.bitnet@listserv.net`

MUSIC-ED—MUSIC-ED Music Education

University of Minnesota, St. Paul Computing Services, St. Paul, MN

You can join this group by sending the message "sub MUSIC-ED your name" to `listserv@vm1.spcs.umn.edu`

MWERA-H—Midwest Education Research Assn - H

The University of Akron, Akron, OH

You can join this group by sending the message "sub MWERA-H your name" to `listserv@vm1.cc.uakron.edu`

NAFSA8-L—NAFSA: AIEE (Association of International Educators)

Temple University, Philadelphia, PA

You can join this group by sending the message "sub NAFSA8-L your name" to `listserv@vm.temple.edu`

NETINTRO—Workshops For Grades K-12: Applications of the Internet

University Computing Services, Indiana University

You can join this group by sending the message "sub NETINTRO your name" to `listserv@iubvm.ucs.indiana.edu`

NETSRCH—Workshops For Grades K-12: Internet Searching for Educators

University Computing Services, Indiana University

You can join this group by sending the message "sub NETSRCH your name" to `listserv@iubvm.ucs.indiana.edu`

NEXUS-L—Nexus-L Research and Studies

FUNET (CSC / Finnish University and research NETwork), Espoo, Finland

You can join this group by sending the message "sub NEXUS-L your name" to `listserv@fiport.funet.fi`

NYSFA-L—NYS Student Financial Aid List

State University of New York - Central Administration, Albany, New York

You can join this group by sending the message "sub NYSFA-L your name" to `listserv%snycenvm.bitnet@listserv.net`

OISNEWS—News For IU International Students and Scholars

University Computing Services, Indiana University

You can join this group by sending the message "sub OISNEWS your name" to `listserv@iubvm.ucs.indiana.edu`

ONLINEED—Faculties of Education Online Education Forum

Queen's University Computing Services

You can join this group by sending the message "sub ONLINEED your name" to `listserv@qucdn.queensu.ca`

QUALRSED—Qualitative Research in Education

University of New Mexico, Albuquerque, NM

You can join this group by sending the message "sub QUALRSED your name" to `listserv@unmvma.unm.edu`

RPE-L—Restructuring Public Education Discussion List

You can join this group by sending the message "sub RPE-L your name" to `listserv%uhccvm.bitnet@listserv.net`

SA—Student Association Information and Discussion

Rice University Information Systems, Houston, TX

You can join this group by sending the message "sub SA your name" to `listserv@ricevm1.rice.edu`

SERVICE—Student Service Leaders

University of Notre Dame, Notre Dame, IN

You can join this group by sending the message "sub SERVICE your name" to `listserv@vma.cc.nd.edu`

SNURSE-L—An International Nursing Student List

State University of New York at Buffalo

You can join this group by sending the message "sub SNURSE-L your name" to `listserv@ubvm.cc.buffalo.edu`

SSMP-L—Student Success Mentoring Program

Rensselaer Polytechnic Institute, Troy, NY

You can join this group by sending the message "sub SSMP-L your name" to `listserv@vm.its.rpi.edu`

STCOAL—Student Coalition of Disabled Students

You can join this group by sending the message "sub STCOAL your name" to `listserv@listserv.iupui.edu`

SUNYTRC—SUNY Teaching Resource Centers List

State University of New York at Buffalo

You can join this group by sending the message "sub SUNYTRC your name" to `listserv@ubvm.cc.buffalo.edu`

SUPERK12—High Performance Internet & Computer Apps in K-12 Schools

Syracuse University

You can join this group by sending the message "sub SUPERK12 your name" to `listserv@listserv.syr.edu`

T321-L—Teaching Science in Elementary Schools

University of Missouri-Columbia, Columbia, MO

You can join this group by sending the message "sub T321-L your name" to `listserv@mizzou1.missouri.edu`

TAG-L—Talented and Gifted Education

You can join this group by sending the message "sub TAG-L your name" to `listserv@listserv.nodak.edu`

TAMHA—Teaching American History

Wayne State University, Detroit, MI

You can join this group by sending the message "sub TAMHA your name" to `listserv@cms.cc.wayne.edu`

TARPS—Teachers as Research Partners

Texas A&M University Computing Services Center

You can join this group by sending the message "sub TARPS your name" to `listserv@tamvm1.tamu.edu`

TEACH-L

Purdue University, West Lafayette, IN

You can join this group by sending the message "sub TEACH-L your name" to `listserv@vm.cc.purdue.edu`

TEACH-RI—News and Information for K-12 Teachers in Rhode Island

You can join this group by sending the message "sub TEACH-RI your name" to `listserv%uriacc.bitnet@listserv.net`

TEACHART—NMAA Art Curriculum Teacher Conference

Smithsonian Institution, Washington, DC

You can join this group by sending the message "sub TEACHART your name" to `listserv@sivm.si.edu`

TERSG-L—NRC: Teacher Education Research Study Group

State University of New York at Buffalo

You can join this group by sending the message "sub TERSG-L your name" to `listserv@ubvm.cc.buffalo.edu`

TOW—The Online World Book Info

You can join this group by sending the message "sub TOW your name" to `listserv@listserv.nodak.edu`

UBITA-L—International Teaching Assistants

State University of New York at Buffalo

You can join this group by sending the message "sub UBITA-L your name" to `listserv@ubvm.cc.buffalo.edu`

VIRTCOL1—Virtual College Course 1

St. John's University, Jamaica, NY

You can join this group by sending the message "sub VIRTCOL1 your name" to `listserv@sjuvm.stjohns.edu`

VIRTED—SJU Virtual Education List

St. John's University, Jamaica, NY

You can join this group by sending the message "sub VIRTED your name" to `listserv@sjuvm.stjohns.edu`

VT-HSNET—VT K-12 School Network

Virginia Tech

You can join this group by sending the message "sub VT-HSNET your name" to `listserv@vtvm1.cc.vt.edu`

WIOLE-L—Writing Intensive Online Learning Environments

University of Missouri-Columbia, Columbia, MO

You can join this group by sending the message "sub WIOLE-L your name" to `listserv@mizzou1.missouri.edu`

WOMYNWIT—Women Professors of Adult Education

Texas A&M University Computing Services Center

You can join this group by sending the message "sub WOMYNWIT your name" to `listserv@tamvm1.tamu.edu`

EMPLOYMENT

The Airbase

http://www.airforce.com/

Filled with information about joining the U.S. Air Force, this is where you need to go if you want even more information about becoming an Airman or Airwoman.

The Airline Employment Assistance Corps

http://www2.csn.net/AEAC/

Often visited, the AEAC helps people find jobs in the airline field.

Attorney Jobs

http://www.attorneyjobs.com/

The Attorney Jobs Web site is filled with links to Federal Reports, nationwide attorney placement, career counseling, and selected job vacancies. This site is obviously useful for students of law and practicing lawyers.

BackStreet Studios

http://www.cybercom.net/~bstreet/

This site is dedicated to helping graphics artists and designers find employment in their chosen field. It provides links to different résumés and samples of creative talent, as well as employers who are seeking artists.

Bolack Total Travel Academy

http://www.bolack.com/school.htm

This site has information for people who are already in travel or who are considering a career in travel. There are links to seminars, class schedules, and other important aspects of discovering success in the travel business.

Career Atlas for the Road

http://isdn.net/nis/

FAQs, résumés, and other answers for the career-minded professional. You can even e-mail career questions to this site's professional staff.

Career Crafting

http://www.well.com/user/careerc/

This site is home to a type of reconsideration therapy. Find out how to quit the job you always hated, get the job you always wanted, and how not to fear bills and other obstacles.

Career Management International

http://www.cmi-lmi.com/

Specializing in human resources, there are many links here useful for business-oriented career professionals.

Career Resource Homepage

http://www.rpi.edu/dept/cdc/homepage.html

This site is filled mainly with links. You can look at career services at universities, an Internet Job Surfer, professional societies, and more.

CareerWEB

http://www.cweb.com/

CareerWEB is an extensive search tool useful for just about anyone seeking information about a professional career. There are listings, a résumé pool, and all other sorts of information.

CyberMania!

http://www.vni.net/~murtaza/chem395/

CyberMania! is designed to provide chemists and biochemists links to employment opportunities. Whether you are a chemist, a biotechnician, or in medicine, you can find all the links you need at this site.

Federal Law Enforcement Careers Employment Guide

http://www.gnatnet.net/~fcfjobs/

You can order a booklet at this site that lists law enforcement careers in the federal government.

Getting Past Go

http://lattanze.loyola.edu/MonGen/home.html

Getting Past Go is a resource for new and recent college graduates. There is plenty of documentation here that will help you find exactly what you are looking for.

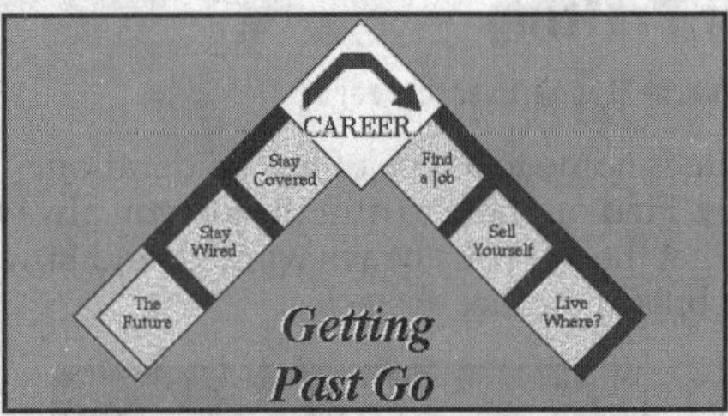

High Technology Careers

http://www.hightechcareers.com/

Career management and development, technology trends, and future outlooks are what you'll find available at this site. You can submit your résumé to this site, and they'll post it for you.

Hot Jobs

http://www.career.com/PUB/hotjob.html

A simple listing of jobs that are available from mostly electronics companies.

How To Find a Creative Job in The Real World

http://www.ici.net/cust_pages/dawn1/dawn1.html

This site is essentially a "CyberEd" course in looking for artistic jobs. You can read stories and check resources here as well.

Library Job Hunting

http://tigger.cc.uic.edu/~aerobin/libjob.html

If you are looking to find hands-on experience and are in Library Science, this is the place to look. This page was written by a person who collected information in a search for a job for himself.

MECA (MBA Employment Connection Association)

http://www.webcom.com/~meca/

An Internet firm that helps connect highly skilled and talented MBA professionals with businesses. Whether you are a recruiter or a professional, you'll find links that will help you here.

NetConnections

http://www.christworks.net/

A career networking organization, NetConnection groups different resources by region. You can also peruse the NASS Membership Directory, the PARW Membership Directory, or other links at this site.

Occupational Resources

http://orion.adnc.com/~occupational/

This site is filled with links to find employers, employment, education, or jobs. They call themselves the Opportunity On-Ramp. Check out this site for plenty of links.

Ronaldi's MBA Job Finder

http://www.wvu.edu/~colbe/person/students/resumes/marcus.htm

This page is provided by West Virginia University in order to provide a clearinghouse of career related information for MBA students. Whether you are seeking a job with a worldwide employer, in a particular city, or by a particular type of company, you'll find what you need at this address.

Westech Career Expo

http://www.vjf.com/pub/westech/

At this site, you can put your résumé in a database or check out job fairs that are close to your hometown—they even include maps. You can also peruse other resources, such as career magazines and other resources.

Employment Services

4Work

http://4work.com

Use a keyword search to find a job, volunteer opportunities, internships, or student jobs. You can search individual or all states in the U.S.

Access Careers & Jobs Resources

`http://www.hawk.igs.net/jobresources/`

A site prepared for career-minded individuals who wish to access useful links to a variety of different utilities that may help them find a job. For example, links to a personality profile, a research mechanism, and a résumé bulletin board are at this site.

America's Employers

`http://www.americasemployers.com/`

There are résumé banks, company databases, job search FAQs and other links that might help you find a job available at this site.

Amerisoft

`http://www.apk.net/amerisoft/`

If you are from the U.S. and wish to be an executive abroad, or if you are an executive in another country who wishes to work in the U.S., check out this site. Mostly specializing in data processing and automation consulting, this firm has much information for bright and eager candidates at this Web site.

Atlantic Management Resources

`http://users.aol.com/amrecruit/amr.htm`

A list of current positions, special openings, interviewing tips, and other information is available at this site.

The Best Jobs in the USA Today

`http://www.bestjobsusa.com/index.html-ssi`

For both potential employees and employers, this site hosts many links to aid in employment. There is a Best Jobs Database, a Recruiter's Boardroom, and other important links to assist in your search.

Butterfass, Pepe & MacCallan, Inc.

`http://www.bpmi.com/`

With links to the executive search process, principals, specialization, and other areas of functional exper-

tise, this site promises to give information for managers, consultants, and executives.

CACEE WorkWeb

`http://www.cacee.com/`

Brought to you by the Canadian Association of Career Educators and Employers, this organization wishes to help students and graduates find meaningful employment. You can check out links to career educators, employers, and other people who may be helpful in finding a job.

Caldwell Partners On-line Directory

`http://www.caldwellpartners.com/`

An executive search formed in 1970, this firm's clients are businesses and public organizations that wish to fill positions within their respective assemblages. Check this site for professional resources, contacts, and a directory.

CareerMart

`http://www.careermart.com/`

An extensive career search based on the familiar job fair that you might find at the local university or armory. Search by region, state, or just about in any other fashion.

CareerSite

`http://www.careersite.com/va/`

Filled with many companies, this site is truly a smart way to find or fill a job. By filling out forms, you can give your desires of where and what jobs you want.

Cromwell Partners Interactive

`http://www.cromwell-partners.com/`

Cromwell Partners Interactive is a company that wishes to help place people into executive positions. If you are qualified, please check out this well-developed site for more information.

The D.L. Weaver Difference

http://www.dlweaver.com/

In such disparate industries as health care to finance, this company is in the business of placing professionals. They look for people who have the experience, personality, and style to fill a professional position.

E-Span

http://www.espan.com/

The first place to look if you are considering using the Web as an employment search tool is E-Span. The site provides a ResumePro Database that you can submit your résumé to for employers to peruse, or you can try either the CareerPro MasterFile Database or the CareerPro Database to search for new job listings.

Employment Search International, Inc.

http://www.poweramp.net/~esi/

If you are looking for employment opportunities, this may be the site you have been seeking. Here, you'll find links and information concerning meaningful employment through technologically advanced media.

Employment Search Productions

http://www.employvideo.com/

If you wish to find another job, are unemployed, or simply feel that you are underpaid, you should look at this site. There are links to video self-teaching programs, tips, and other useful links located at this site.

Freelance Online

http://haven.ios.com/~freelans/

If you are a freelancer—writer, editor, salesperson, or just about anything else—you may consider making this your start page. It includes links to contract jobs, forums, and other information needed by freelance employees.

Groupweb

http://groupweb.com/opening/jobs.htm

A Web site dedicated to employers and job seekers. Employers can post job openings, while seekers can submit résumés.

InPursuit's Employment Network

http://www.inpursuit.com/e-network/

Built from the success of Shawn's Internet Résumé Center, InPursuit has built an entire employment network. Consisting of many career-related services and products, this network allows "the job seeker and the employer to come together."

The JobExchange

http://www.jobexchange.com/

Featuring membership opportunities for job search and recruiting, this site also boasts a candidate database to help search for qualified individuals to fill positions.

Michael Latas & Associates, Inc.

http://www.latas.com/

A full-service executive search and professional recruiting firm, Michael Latas & Associates has an ideology of divide and conquer; they have divisions that work exclusively in different areas of expertise. Check out this site to request information or read more about this firm's ideology and impressive record.

Michigan Association of Personnel Services

http://www.michjobs.com/

The Michigan Association of Personnel Services was founded in 1945 with the objective of providing personnel services to clients within Michigan and the United States. This site has links to Officers and Directors, member firms, and geographical location of employment opportunities.

The Monster Board

http://www2.monster.com:80/

This site is called the Monster Board for a reason. It is filled with plenty of links associated with jobs, careers, and companies.

National Association of Colleges and Employers

http://www.jobweb.org/about-us.htm

A "bridge between higher education and the world of work," the National Association of Colleges and

Employers is an association that brings two often disparate worlds together. Of course, many people attend college with the idea of landing a job that will make them a fortune, but it seems that only the lucky few actually do—this site may assist in that endeavor.

National Consulting Network

http://rampages.onramp.net/~ncn/

This network consists of the nation's top search professionals to assist in your job search. Whatever industry you are involved in, this firm claims that they are qualified to help you find the best job. Employers and job seekers alike—check out their center for available candidates and open positions.

National Internship Directory

http://www.tripod.com/work/internships/

Purporting that one of the best ways to get what you want from a career is to try it out in college. It has a nice résumé builder, too, that will give you clues on how to construct an efficient résumé.

ProMatch '96

http://www.promatch.org/

Simply a page filled with links, it can help with program outlines, a résumé profile, and an industry council. You also have the chance to join this organization, so check out the link called Membership Requirements if this group meets your career needs.

Recruiters OnLine Network

http://www.ipa.com/

As a worldwide online association and resource to help discover meaningful employment, this site has many links to help you find a job. RON is a large association of individuals and firms linked together in the online community as a virtual association of employment professionals. Check out the different links that give listings, résumés, and associates for the latest information in your job search.

whatNOW?

http://www.halcyon.com/whatnow/

Techiniques to land the job that you want are located at this site. There are links to tips, topics, career

resource centers, and experts that you can look at, or if you'd rather, you can purchase the video that promises to "turn interviews into job offers."

Achievement Corporation

http://www.acorp.co.uk/

Bringing a range of Human Resources and Internet communications services to you from the Web. Check out links to different services that might help you find a job.

The Analysis Group

http://www.nichecom.com/~analysis/

Founded in 1988, the Analysis Group offers candidate development services, including full search and recruitment and training in all aspects of recruiting and sourcing.

Benefit Associates

http://www.benefitassociates.com/

Benefit Associates is a recruiting company that specializes in the placement of human resources and employee benefit personnel. There are links to different specializations, as well as jobs and candidates available.

CareerLab

http://www.careerlab.com/

This site is very user-friendly. There are links to an online bookstore, a quick tour, a testing and assessment area, and information about the company.

Edwards and Associates

http://www.worldleader.com/eaa/

Need a part-time manager for your small business? Then this site might have what you are looking for. Browse around corporate magazines, FAQs, or get in contact with this firm.

Fortune Personnel Consultants

http://www.conterra.com/fortune/

This page is geared toward finding qualified candidates for staffing the needs of your company. At this site, you'll find positions in manufacturing and legal positions, as well as information about how to contact this leading placement firm.

Human Resource News and Issues

http://www.newspage.com/NEWSPAGE/cgi-bin/walk.cgi/
NEWSPAGE/info/d11/d3/

This page is simply filled with links about today's human resource issues.

Pemberton and Associates

http://www.biddeford.com/pemberton/

A "comprehensive human resource solution," this site is filled with information about this company's services. Whether you need compensation and benefit administration, recruitment services, or training and development programs, this company can help.

Total Human Resources

http://www.totalhr.com/thr/

If you are looking for fair policies for your company that are current and uphold today's federal and state laws, this site is for you. Total Human Resources is a consulting firm with comprehensive help.

Job Fairs

Career Expo

http://www.eos.net/careerex/

If you are looking to become involved in a job fair, this company is the place to check out. They have been organizing fairs for about 15 years, bringing together engineering, information systems, computer science, and many other professionals with leading U.S. and Canadian companies.

CyberFair

http://www.career.com/cyberfair.html

A new twist on the conventional job fair, this site features a place for employers and job seekers to send for information about potential employment.

Job Fair Home Page

http://www.iupui.edu/it/jobfair/

Select from two different fairs, the Indiana Collegiate Job Fair or the Multicultural Job Fair. Check out employer lists, or contact the coordinator of the fair.

SENET Career Expo Home Page

http://www.senetcareer.com/

A source employment network, SENET Career Expo wishes to provide job placement through career expos, diversity and minority job fairs, effective résumé writing skills, and other career programs. There are many links at this site to peruse.

The Virtual Job Fair

http://www.vjf.com/

The Virtual Job Fair is exactly what it says it is. There is a library here, links to searches and expos, a résumé center, and high tech careers. Formatted for both graphical browsers and text-only browsers, you can look at a table of contents or use an image map of the fair to navigate the site.

Which Job Fair Is Right for You?

http://www.psijobfair.com/a-fair.html

This site consists of a list of different types of job fairs. Each description is relatively short, and has links to locations, times, and dates.

Résumé Services

Career Résumés

http://branch.com/cr/cr.html

With the idea that a résumé should be a marketing tool instead of a simple history, Career Résumés has opportunities for both job seekers and corporations.

Employnet, Inc.

http://employnet-inc.ksi.com/

Recruiters can register with Employnet online to search a database filled with résumés of potential employees. Job seekers and employers alike should peruse this Web site for help in the job search.

The Extreme Résumé Drop

`http://www.mainquad.com/quad/careerfair/resDrop/index.html`

This site is very well formatted, filled with companies, and accessible. All you have to do is fill out your résumé, then choose the companies to whom you'd like to send it. Very easy and a great idea!

Graphiti Printing & Graphics' Online Résumé Service

`http://www.nmia.com/~graphiti/rsmeform.html`

This site enables the potential employee to fill out a résumé by filling in forms, or by downloading an Adobe PDF file that can be e-mailed back to the company.

Job-Link

`http://www.job-link.com/`

This site offers you the opportunity to fill out a member form to be added to their site.

unisoft.net

`http://www.unisoft.net/`

Bandwidth heavy, but very nice-looking, unisoft.net offers a program called CVexe. In an attempt to help make your résumé more attractive to potential employers, CVexe wants to help present your résumé in a unique and accessible way.

Training Services

ACME Training, Inc.

`http://www.gus.com/acme/`

A supplier of custom training for corporate clients, ACME training also specializes in Adobe Acrobat (PDF) documents for many uses. Their home page will direct you through several pages, including a company philosophy, a list of projects, and examples of their work.

Advanced Training Professionals

`http://www.trainingpros.com/`

Providing training services at below-industry standard, Advanced Training Professionals is dedicated to delivering world-class training to all forms of industries. Whether you are in business, education, or just want to learn, ATP promises they can help.

American Management Association

`http://www.tregistry.com/ttr/ama.htm`

The AMA provides the business community with a complete management resource. This page gives you information about membership and what it takes to get in contact with this group.

The Ankarlo Training Group Home Page

`http://www.ankarlo.com/`

This home page is filled with information about how to advance in today's competitive business environment. It stresses creativity and leadership to attain those goals, and gives advice on how to seek them.

CaBiT Development

`http://rampages.onramp.net/~cabit/`

CaBiT Development stands for Computer Based Training Development & Delivery Tools. It consists of a suite of several Windows-based programs that run on PCs used in client/server network environments. This site is where you can find information about obtaining this service.

Career Connection

`http://www.sna.com/musicbiz/`

On the job training for qualified individuals of audio recording can be found from the company that owns this site. You'll find information about how to contact this firm, as well as other information about what they do.

ClearWord Communications and Training

`http://www.tgx.com/clearword/`

Clear Modern English for international business and industry is stressed here. Obviously, language is important on both sides—native speakers need to avoid colloquialisms and other turns of phrase that are allusive to non-natives.

Conceptual Systems, Inc.

http://www.concepsys.com/

Creative solutions to complex problems can be found by seeking the help of CSI. Their Web page has links to people, products, CSI news, and clients.

Damar Group

http://www.dgl.com/cspromo.html

This site presents two different packages and a new approach to training. Both courses are designed to give you training on the Internet.

The Image Maker

http://www.intranet.on.ca/~jwaisvisz/

A training company based in the U.S. and Canada, the Image Maker has skills seminars offered in English and French. This page has many links that describe the information here.

InfoDesign Group

http://www.infodsn.com/

This company offers complete documentation, technical support, and training design and development services. This site has such links as Helping Business into the Future and What InfoDesign Can Do for Your Company.

The Jacks Institute

http://www.jackstax.com/

A trainer of tax industry professionals, the Jacks Institute's Web site has links to tax courses and books, tax tips, and a guest book.

The McKinley Group, Inc.

http://www.itg.com.inter.net/mckinley/

This home page for the McKinley Group provides information about their developmental workshops made to meet a company's specific needs. It also includes links related to this company's service.

National Center for Tooling & Precision Components (NCTPC)

http://www.utoledo.edu/www/nctpc/

This Web site for the nonprofit organization formed to provide programs in training, education, technical and business assistance, and research and development to "improve the competitive positions of U.S. tooling and manufacturing companies."

Peritas Online

http://www.peritas.com/

A very well-formatted page, there is an online training promotion available at this site. You can also check out the KnowledgePool consortium—the World's largest commercial training education group.

Practical Management, Inc.

http://www.tregistry.com/ttr/practmgt.htm

Management and instructor development are what you'll find at Practical Management's home page. There is much information here, as well as links to some courses.

RootLearning, Inc.

http://rootlearning.com/

They call themselves pioneers in the emerging technology of Learnegy. Filled with Macromedia documents, this page claims that everyone "from the CEO to the shop floor operator" must "understand and respond to the vital economic, competitive, productivity, and customer (quality and value) issues that will shape the organization's future."

Scaffold Training Institute

http://www.scaffold-training.com/

Training programs, services and pricing, instructor qualifications, and more are available from this site that concerns construction safety.

Stressmaster

http://www.tregistry.com/ttr/smaster.htm

The self-proclaimed "Leader in Stressmastery Training and Products," this site is very businesslike in approach—simple, dignified. Read lists of different types of programs or follow links to programs offered by the company.

Success Express Journal

http://www.success.ie/

The Success Express Journal's online home is host to a weekly magazine. Check out the Tips from the Top, Book Reviews, and more at this site.

TLC Seminars

http://www.tlcsem.com/

A training seminar based in choice. There are links to several different types of training sessions, including Presentation Skill Training, Instructor Training, and Custom Training Development.

Training Express

http://www.trainx.com/

Not only nice looking, the Training Express Web site is filled with information about their systems, how to order them, and an online catalog of training materials. There is also a page filled with links concerning training.

Vital Learning Corporation

http://www.vital-learning.com/

The Vital Learning Corporation is an online training academy that offers state-of-the-art tools developed for computer-based training. At this site, you can request more information, read about products, and join a mailing list.

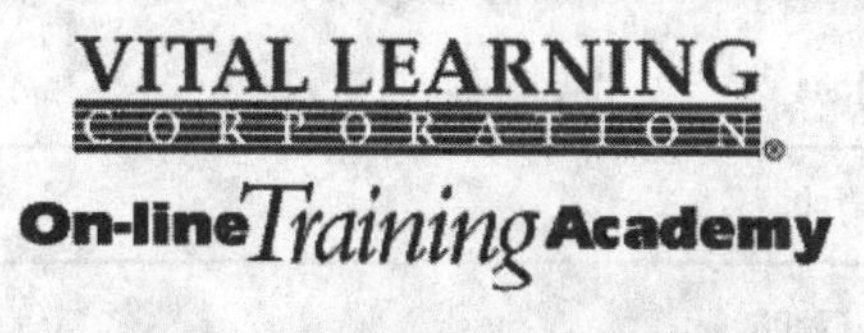

Tektronix Information

http://www.tek.com/Color_Printers/free/free.html

Get free stuff from Tektronix including print samples, downloadable template files, and a booklet on color printers, color printing technology, and how to purchase a color printer. Also register to win free prizes.

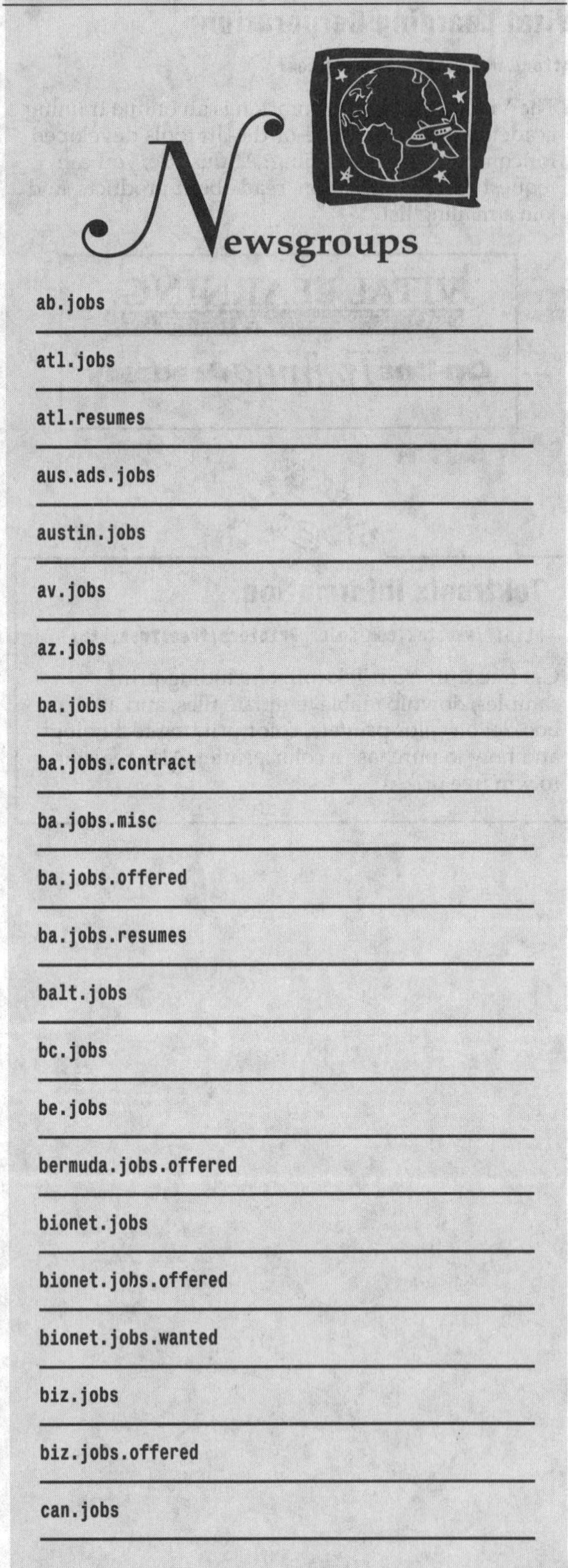

Newsgroups

ab.jobs

atl.jobs

atl.resumes

aus.ads.jobs

austin.jobs

av.jobs

az.jobs

ba.jobs

ba.jobs.contract

ba.jobs.misc

ba.jobs.offered

ba.jobs.resumes

balt.jobs

bc.jobs

be.jobs

bermuda.jobs.offered

bionet.jobs

bionet.jobs.offered

bionet.jobs.wanted

biz.jobs

biz.jobs.offered

can.jobs

chi.jobs

cmh.jobs

comp.jobs

cuug.jobs

dc.jobs

dfw.jobs

dod.jobs

fl.jobs

han.misc.jobs

hepnet.jobs

houston.jobs

houston.jobs.offered

houston.jobs.wanted

hsv.jobs

ie.jobs

iijnet.jobs

il.jobs.misc

il.jobs.offered

in.jobs

ithaca.jobs

kc.jobs

kw.jobs

la.jobs

li.jobs

lou.lft.jobs

man.jobs.offered

md.jobs

me.jobs.

memphis.employment

mi.jobs

milw.jobs

misc.jobs.contract

misc.jobs.fields.chemistry

misc.jobs.offered

misc.jobs.offered.entry

misc.jobs.resumes

misc.jobs.wanted

mn.jobs

nb.jobs

nc.jobs

ne.jobs

ne.jobs.contract

nebr.jobs

niagara.jobs

nj.jobs

nm.jobs

nv.jobs

nyc.jobs.contract

nyc.jobs.misc

nyc.jobs.offered

nyc.jobs.wanted

oh.jobs

ont.jobs

osu.jobs

ott.jobs

pa.jobs.offered

pa.jobs.wanted

pdaxs.jobs

pdaxs.jobs.clerical

pdaxs.jobs.computers

pdaxs.jobs.construction

pdaxs.jobs.delivery

pdaxs.jobs.domestic

pdaxs.jobs.engineering

pdaxs.jobs.management

pdaxs.jobs.misc

pdaxs.jobs.resumes

pdaxs.jobs.retail

pdaxs.jobs.sales

pdaxs.jobs.secretary

pdaxs.jobs.temporary

pdaxs.jobs.wanted

pgh.jobs.offered

pgh.jobs.wanted

phl.jobs.offered

phl.jobs.wanted

qc.jobs

sac.jobs

sat.jobs

scot.jobs

sdnet.jobs.offered

sdnet.jobs.services

sdnet.jobs.wanted

seattle.jobs.offered

seattle.jobs.wanted

sk.jobs.offered

slac.jobs

slo.jobs

stl.jobs

swnet.jobs

tnn.jobs

tor.jobs

triangle.jobs

tx.jobs

uark.jobs

ucb.jobs

ucd.jobs

us.jobs.contract

us.jobs.offered

us.jobs.resumes

ut.jobs

utcs.jobs

va.jobs

vegas.jobs

wyo.jobs

za.ads.jobs

Listservs

ALIENS-L—Taxation/Witholding/Reporting Requirements for Payments to Aliens

You can join this group by sending the message
"sub ALIENS-L your name" to
listserv@utkvm1.utk.edu

BLIND-JOBS-L—Employment Issues Concerning Blind People

You can join this group by sending the message
"sub BLIND-JOBS-L your name" to
listserv@sjuvm.stjohns.edu

CAREER-L—SUNY-wide Career Development Organization List

You can join this group by sending the message
"sub CAREER-L your name" to
listserv@bingvmb.cc.binghamton.edu

ECOLOG-L—Ecological Society of America: Grants, Jobs, News

University of Maryland CSC, College Park, MD

You can join this group by sending the message
"sub ECOLOG-L your name" to
Listserv%umdd.bitnet@listserv.net

FEDJOBS—Federal Job Bulletin Board

Dartmouth College, Hanover, NH

You can join this group by sending the message
"sub FEDJOBS your name" to
Listserv@listserv.dartmouth.edu

ICEN-L—ICEN-L International Career and Employment Network (NAFSA)

University Computing Services, Indiana University

You can join this group by sending the message "sub ICEN-L your name" to Listserv@iubvm.ucs.indiana.edu

JOB-LIST—Job Offers from EARN Institute members

You can join this group by sending the message "sub JOB-LIST your name" to listserv@gumncc.terena.nl

JOB-TECH—Technology and Employment Conference

University of Illinois at Chicago, Chicago, IL

You can join this group by sending the message "sub JOB-TECH your name" to listserv@uicvm.uic.edu

JOBANALYSIS[—Jobanalysis Discussion List

Virginia Tech

You can join this group by sending the message "sub JOBANALYSIS your name" to listserv@listserv.vt.edu

JOBPLACE—JobPlace (Self Directed Job Search Techniques and Job Placement)

National Association of Colleges and Employers, Bethlehem, PA

You can join this group by sending the message "sub JOBPLACE your name" to listserv@news.jobweb.org

JOBVAC-L—OSU Job Vacancy Listings

You can join this group by sending the message "sub JOBVAC-L your name" to listserv@listserv.okstate.edu

LABNEWS—News of Labor Unions & Workplace Organizing

You can join this group by sending the message "sub LABNEWS your name" to listserv@ucbcmsa.bitnet

LIBJOBS—Library and Information Science Jobs mailing List

National Library of Canada, Ottawa, Ontario, Canada

You can join this group by sending the message "sub LIBJOBS your name" to listserv@infoserv.nlc-bnc.ca

MBACAREER-L—Career Counsellors for MBA Students

You can join this group by sending the message "sub MBACAREER-L your name" to LISTSERV@PDOMAIN.UWINDSOR.CA

MOONLIGHT-L—

You can join this group by sending the message "sub moonlight-l your name" to listserv@netcom.com

SLAJOB—Special Libraries Association Employment Opportunities

University Computing Services, Indiana University

You can join this group by sending the message "sub SLAJOB your name" to listserv@iubvm.ucs.indiana.edu

STC—School to Careers- the Purpose of Public Education

You can join this group by sending the message "sub STC your name" to listserv@listserv.syr.edu

STUDEMP—Issues Related to Student Employment

University of Arizona, Tucson, AZ

You can join this group by sending the message "sub STUDEMP your name" to listserv@listserv.arizona.edu

SUMMJOBS—Summer Job Information List from Career Services

You can join this group by sending the message "sub SUMMJOBS your name" to
`listserv@ricevm1.rice.edu`

SWJOBS—AD&A Software Jobs Weekly

L-Soft International, Inc.

You can join this group by sending the message "sub SWJOBS your name" to
`listserv@peach.ease.lsoft.com`

TESLJB-L—Jobs and Employment Issues (TESL-L sublist)

You can join this group by sending the message "sub TESLJB-L your name" to
`listserv@cunyvm.cuny.edu`

ENTTERTAINMENT

Acting

Casting on the Web

http://www.actors.it/defe.htm

Search for models, actors, and new faces by indicating the type of person you need. This service for casting directors and show organizers includes a detailed form for narrowing your search. Includes complete information on models and talent.

CastingOnline

http://hookomo.aloha.net/~wrap/

A one-stop cybercasting site for the performing arts industry. Click on the continent of your choice or read about the latest casting projects nationwide. Includes casting info for actors, musicians, voice-overs, and multimedia projects.

Hollywood Actors Network

http://www.hollywoodnetwork.com/hn/acting/index.html

Lists advertisers who can help you break into Hollywood and articles on people in the business. This site includes a number of directories you can join or examine detailing information on acting, broadcasting, and screenwriting. Provides links to everything imaginable regarding Hollywood and the entertainment industry.

Raymond Interactive Theatre, Ltd.

http://www.rit.com/

This is truly a unique site, a home for the Raymond Interactive Theatre. Based on the same technologies as popular computer games, this interactive theater enables you to interact online with the production. Includes information about becoming a RIT ticketholder. If computer game shoot-'em-ups have become stale, then this may be the entertainment option you have been waiting for.

VCV Stunts—Stuntmen on the Net

http://www.procom.com/~daves/vcvstunt.html

Offers professional stunt actors for live action, motion pictures, and video.

The Virtual Headbook

http://www.xmission.com/~wintrnx/virtual.html

Provides a collection of actors' resumés and head shots that casting directors, agents, and directors can search for free. Actors can join online, get tax help, or sign with a California agent. Sound and video clips of actors at work are also available.

Comics & Animation

The 3-D Zone

http://www.leonardo.net/3dzone/

Publishes comic books in 3D, including work by Steve Ditko, Bill Ward, and others. Read about the latest publications, or pull out your 3D glasses and click on 3-D Fun.

Alternative Comics—A WWW Guide

http://bronze.ucs.indiana.edu/~mfragass/
altncom.html#anim

Includes links to e-zines, animation resources, and dozens of art galleries. A good jumping-off point for animation fans interested in WWW and mailing list fanzines.

Austin Anime-Niacs Association

http://www.io.com/~count/anime.html

Japanese animation and comics fan club from Austin, Texas, provides info on upcoming conventions and Anime links. Read "What are Manga and Anime" for a lengthy description of this art form.

Calvin and Hobbes on the World Wide Web

http://eos.kub.nl:2080/calvin_hobbes/

If you like the comic strip, you'll be in heaven when you click on Gallery and scroll down to an exhaustive list of Calvin information. Peruse the book list, and then examine the latest *Calvin and Hobbes* picture books. This site also includes icons and desktop patterns, a popularity poll, a random picture generator, links to newsgroups, and interviews with the creator, Bill Watterson. Although this site is unofficial, it is incredibly thorough.

Comics 'n Stuff

http://www.phlab.missouri.edu/~c617145/comix.html

This award-winning site contains hundreds of Web sites that include actual comics you can read.

You can also access a Web chat room, perform a comics query search, or download FAQs about comics and the Web.

Gen13 Animation's Next GEN

http://www.unf.edu/students2/jbacan/gen_13_4.html

Read about the direct-to-video movie adaptation of Scott Campbell's successful *Gen13* comic series. This page discusses the movie and includes stills from the animation and links to other *Gen13* sites.

Jonah Weiland's Comic Book Resources

http://envisionww.com/jonahw/comics/comiclinks.html

Nice site that includes special sections with hundreds of links regarding Marvel, DC, Dark Horse, miscellaneous, independent, and self-published comics. One of the few Web pages that can be considered a decent proxy for Marvel's absence on the Web.

Marvel Comics

http://garnet.berkeley.edu/~net-dq/project.html

This informative fan page is about as close as you'll get to a Marvel Comics corporate page. For whatever reason, Marvel does not yet have a Web site, but this page tentatively makes up for the loss with a Marvel history, the industry top 100 comics, and links to DC Comics.

Museum of Fine Arts, 3D Animation

http://www.smfa.edu/students/ploc/3DANHOME.html

Check out stills of 3D animation created by students at this prestigious arts school and museum.

Planet Millennium

http://www.planet-millennium.com/

A graphically rich page focusing on ways to build up your self-esteem. Click anywhere on the large planet to begin your journey toward resolving a conflict. This site also provides information on Planet Millennium comic books devoted to self-esteem.

Sirius Entertainment

http://www.insv.com/sirius

This comic book publisher lets you examine its titles, which include *Dawn*, *Animal Mystic*, *Poison Elves*, *Akiko*, and more. Be sure to visit the Sirius Gallery for hot .JPEG files of its art.

Spider Man Figure Archive

http://pegasus.acs.ttu.edu/~wvjgg/spidey/sphead.html

Serious action figure collectors will enjoy this summary of the Spider Man figure that appeared on toy shelves in 1994. Includes pictures and detailed explanations of every character in the *Spider Man* series and links to other Spidey sites.

Games & Online Toys

A Simple Rhyming Dictionary

http://bobo.link.cs.cmu.edu/cgi-bin/dougb/rhyme.cgi

This page offers a simple online rhyming dictionary that provides a list of words that rhyme with any entered word. Also provides homonyms, as long as the entered word is in the dictionary.

Alexander Jean-Claude Bottema's Home Page

http://www.csd.uu.se/~alexb/

Although this guy has a serious bias toward Microsoft, he has one ingenious home page. The site features online Java versions of Pacman and Asteroids. Also contains Alex's research interests.

Bluedog Can Count

http://kao.ini.cmu.edu:5550/bdf.html

A toy for your mathematical enjoyment. Bluedog will bark out the answer to any simple math problem you can input. But be careful about imaginary numbers.

Boggle

http://www.cs.mu.oz.au/~dnich/bgl_intro.html

One of the original word games is now online. Choose the number of rounds, time constriction, dimension of the board, and maximum word length.

Build Your Own Critter

http://www.cgrg.ohio-state.edu/~nvishnev/Onfire/Webs/BuildUrOwn/buildani.html

You, too, can play with biotechnology on the WWW—although it isn't exactly Jurassic Park. Site features an online "Critter" construction game.

Carlo's Coloring Book

http://www.ravenna.com/coloring/

Choose one of seven images to color from Carlo's page. Coloring book consists of templates pasted on a limited version of Paintbrush.

Chris' Collection of Drinking Misc.

http://www.rain.org/~uring/tvdrink/tv.htm

A page for the entertainment of college students or other procrastinator types. Site features a large number of network shows turned into drinking games. Click on the show, and a set of rules are shown.

Complaint Letter Generator

http://www-csag.cs.uiuc.edu/individual/pakin/complaint

Generate your own personalized complaint letter by entering a few details and facts. Just sit back and enjoy the complaint generated in as many paragraphs as you like.

Cool Lego Site of the Week

http://www.fibblesnork.com/lego/cool/

Check out this site to see the amazing things they are doing with Legos these days, not just the lunar lander you had as a kid. Also features links to other Lego pages.

Crejaculabryrinth

http://www.xs4all.nl/~kessels/Puzzel04.html

Learn how to make a straight angled line, if you dare. This site is another fun logic game that will have you bouncing off your bedroom walls.

The Crystal Ball

http://www.react.com/bin/nph-form.cgi?type=crystal

This site provides a gruesome vision of your future. You must enter a friend's name, your name, your favorite food, and an animal sound. Then, like magic, your fortune is told.

The Cyrano Server

http://www.nando.net/toys/cyrano.html

This site was created for the shy and unimaginative person in love. Cyrano will write your love letters for you and mail them electronically. Cyrano will also perform that nasty breakup, if necessary, so you won't have to go through the anguish.

The Daily 100

http://www.80s.com/Entertainment/Movies/Daily100/

A fantastic site featuring 80's movie trivia. They provide the clip, you provide the actor, movie, and year it debuted. Site keeps track of players; that is, it's a contest.

The Destruction Derby Games

http://www.psygnosis.com/secure/derby/

An online destruction derby is found at this site. Click on an image of an older automobile. Then watch the destruction via blunt instruments.

Dogz

http://www.dogz.com/

Download a digital dog for free from the site. You can choose a Mac or PC dog or cat. He'll even fetch a bone on your screen.

Duck Hunt—Find the Fowl

http://aurora.york.ac.uk/ducks.html

The people from York University bring us an online duck hunt. In the spirit of the "Where's Waldo®" game, find the duck in these pictures. Also contains some fun links.

Ferret Frenzy

http://www.delphi.co.uk/delphi/interactive/ferrets/intro.html

With good reason, this is the only online Ferret racing game. Choose your ferret, place a bet, and watch the race.

The First Simpson Dating Game on the Web

http://www.accent.net/ams/robert/date2.htm

The only game on the Web based on the TV animated series *The Simpsons*. Answer a few questions and receive your ultimate dream date in the cartoon land of Springfield.

The Fruit Game

http://www.2020tech.com/fruit/index.html

Offers the challenging "fruit game." Players remove fruit from the screen; the last player to remove fruit loses. Try this mathematical adventure.

Fun with Grapes

http://www.sci.tamucc.edu/~pmichaud/grape/

A theatrical and scientific study is performed here concerning the effect on grapes exposed to high levels of microwave radiation. Amusing results and discussions describe the experiment as well as the page in general.

Funny Bunny Trail

http://banzai.neosoft.com/citylink/easter/default.html

Hunt for Easter eggs on the WWW by surfing sites. Game is based on the USA Citylink Project. If you are really good, you could win some money. Check out this site for more information.

Guess the Dictator and/or Television Sit-Com Character

http://sp1.berkeley.edu/dict.html

Those wacky Berkeley kids brought us another way to kill time. This game is based on the premise that you are your favorite dictator or television sitcom star. The site will ask you yes/no questions and tell you which dictator/star you are. It's amazing.

Handy Spanish Phrase

http://www.umr.edu/~tommy/span1.html

Need a handy Spanish phrase to interject into a conversation? Look no further. The handy Spanish phrase generator is here to supply you with phrases such as "Su prima es en fuego," which means "Your cousin is on fire."

Heretical Rhyme Generator

http://zenith.berkeley.edu/seidel/Po/

Generates a rhyme for every line entered by the browser. Don't be surprised if you are slightly appalled by the assault on the aesthetic.

Home Appliance Shooting

http://www.csn.net/~dcbenton/has.html

Take out your aggressions here on those troublesome home appliances. Features the destruction of a gas grill and a television set.

Home Appliance Shooting

How Bored Are You

http://www.kfu.com/~nsayer/bored/

Features a game called "How Bored Are You." Game involves following the rules and doing absolutely nothing while the page counts the seconds.

Husband Lover Spy

http://www.hollywoodnetwork.com:80/hn/games/hls/opcenter.html

A strange online sleuth game of searching for Friedrich Ludwig Stammberger. The kick is that Friedrich really did disappear. Clues, tips, and geopolitical data are provided. Can you help?

IBM—the Electric Origami Shop

http://www.ibm.com/Stretch/EOS/

The Electric Origami Shop features kaleidoscopes shots, fractals, high tech art, and some very tough puzzles for the mathematically inclined. Also features an interesting site traveler that one could explore for days.

ID Archives—Doom

http://www.idsoftware.com/archive.html

You can download a wealth of *Doom* levels and scenarios from this Web site. *Heretic and Shadow of the Serpent Riders* and *Quake* are also available here.

The Insult Page

http://www.io.com/~rasto/ins.cgi

Provides a random insult to the unsuspecting browser. Also contains a very nice search engine index if you are tired of doing the same old searches.

Interactive Model Railroad

`http://rr-vs.informatik.uni-ulm.de/RR/RR.html`

An online model railroad that you can operate from your Web browser, brought to you from the University of Ulm. Site also contains other railroad-related links.

Ipizza

`http://www.internetuniv.com/pizza/ipizza.htm`

Thank a friend or coworker for his or her time. Send an online pizza. It's free and ever so tasty. User required to pick the toppings and provide an e-mail address.

Joe's Amazing Relationship Problem Solver

`http://studsys.mscs.mu.edu/~carpent1/probsolv/rltprob0.html`

This amazing page will solve all your relationship problems, maybe. You must answer several yes/no questions to have your problem solved for you. It is also recommended you read the disclaimer.

Kooks Museum

`http://www.teleport.com/~dkossy/`

The title describes it all. Take a course in crackpot-ology or kookology. Also features the "Hall of Hate" and "Library of Questionable Scholarship."

Kurt Cobain's Talking Eight Ball

`http://www.webcom.com/xcomm/cobain/`

In true bad taste, this page provides a bit of wisdom from the former grunge icon Kurt Cobain. Site requires the appropriate plug-in software.

Lee's Useless Superhero Generator

`http://fly.hiwaay.net/~lkseitz/comics/herogen/herogen.cgi`

Are you looking for a superhero that role-playing games just can't give you? Look here for your own personalized superhero. Type in a few guidelines, and he or she is yours to play with.

Lemonade Stand

`http://www.feist.com/~jmayans/lemonade/lemonade.cgi`

Provides an online version of the popular computer game. You operate a lemonade stand in an attempt to make as much money as possible and retire to the Hall of Fame. It is not as easy as it sounds, either.

Lite Board

`http://asylum.cid.com/lb/lb.html`

A masterpiece of a Web page. Site features an interactive online version of the classic game of lights, Lite Brite. Choose from seven different colors to create a work of art.

Lloyd's Coke Machine

`http://www.ugcs.caltech.edu/~walterfb/coke/coke.html`

Look here for an interactive Coke machine located at Caltech. You can send an LED message to a real Coke machine. Check out the schematics for a description of some amazing work. Cheers to the Caltech Coke machine guys.

Looney Tunes Karaoke

`http://www.kids.warnerbros.com/karaoke/cmp/list.htm`

Here are your favorite *Looney Tunes* songs sung on your very own PC. Application requires Real Audio software plug-in. Choose from nine songs to sing along with your PC.

Makin Bacon

`http://www.mindspring.com/~mab/kevin/kevin.html`

Kevin Bacon, star of the silver screen, is now the focus of all deranged movie fans due to this jewel of a game. Site provides proof that the world revolves around Kevin Bacon. Also provides a submission form to the game master if you get stumped.

Manic Maze

http://www.worldvillage.com/maze.htm

Interactive online maze featuring prizes and other fun stuff. Check out some other fantastic links while you're at it.

Mark's Apology Note Generator

http://net.indra.com/~karma/formletter.html

Let Mark help you deal with life with his apology generator. Look here for a fill-in-the-blank ad-lib apology note that will be electronically mailed.

Mindgames

http://weber.u.washington.edu/~jlks/mindgame.html

Stump your friends with these amazing feats of psychological wizardry. Choose from five mind games and four puzzles. Site also features links to Behavior Online.

Oeno Phile's Mood Detector

http://www.chrysalis.org/oeno/testmood.htm

If you didn't get enough of these in the '70s, or if you weren't around in the '70s, this site is for you. This online mood ring site may tell you what you do not want to hear.

Optical Illusions—A Collection

http://lainet3.lainet.com/~ausbourn/

Very nicely done optical images can be viewed at this site. Explanations of the illusion and descriptions of what to expect are given as well. Very nice images.

PhoNETic

http://www.soc.qc.edu/phonetic/

If you lack creativity, this site will tell you what word your phone number will spell based on the corresponding letters on a telephone keypad. User can set parameters for 3 to 10 numbers or even go from words to numbers.

Piercing Mildred

http://streams.com/pierce/

Creativity is not lacking at this site. Choose from three characters and apply tattoos, piercing, and scars as your heart desires. Site requires quite of bit of instruction. You'll have to read it.

Pig Latin Converter

http://voyager.cns.ohiou.edu/~jrantane/menu/pig.html

Converts Web pages from English into Pig Latin by simply entering the URL address. A language rarely seen in print, Pig Latin is very difficult for the untrained eye to read, but try it if you have the spare time.

Play Chess on the Net

http://www.outland.com/OutlandChess.html

Play the ancient game in a real-time online form. Site features optional game clocks, chat boxes, and UCSF Player Ratings.

Random Topic Generator

http://www.compassnet.com/~rdeneefe/topicgen.htm

This site was created to fill in those embarrassing conversation pauses by providing you with a random topic to quickly interject. Site also comes with random electric jazz music.

Riddle du Jour

http://www.new3.com/riddle/

An online sphinx will ask the riddle. Can you solve it? Hone your wits, for there are prizes at stake. Site also contains a Labryinth and "Mondo Trivia."

Rock Mall's Trivia Challenge

http://www.rockmall.com/arcade.htm

Sharpen your wits, trivia junkies, for here is your site. Cruise through this site if you know everything about nothing important. Some questions here will stump all challengers.

Rock, Paper, Scissors

http://www.shadow.net/~proub/rps.html

The famous game that entertained you as a child and left you with bruised arms when you lost is back and online. Site also features a "cheat" option for those who can't take losing. Also contains a comments and doomsday philosophy page.

Salon Betty's Interactive Paper Doll

`http://www.imusic.com/Paperdoll/`

Provides an image of Betty, who can be dressed in one of four "grunge" outfits. Music is also available to download from this site.

Send an Electronic Postcard

`http://linux.hartford.edu/~azmizar/postcard/`

Choose from a variety of postcards from a selection of locations. Type in a message and send your friend a postcard.

Similarities Engine II

`http://www.ari.net/se/`

Enter your favorite artist, and the similarities engine will tell you other bands you might like. An amazing database of music talent characterizes this page.

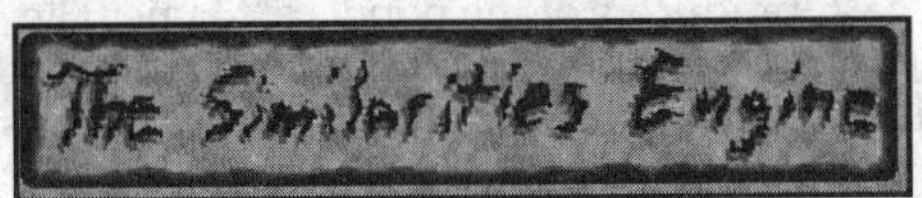

Star Trek: The Next Generation—The Daily Test

`http://www.sci.kun.nl/thalia/funpage/startrek/`

Features an online challenge for the *Star Trek* fan. You must match a picture from a specific episode with the episode title. Good luck. Engage.

The Tele-Garden

`http://www.usc.edu/dept/garden/`

Conceptual genius defines this site, a tele-robotic installation that enables WWW users to view and interact with a remote garden filled with real live plants. By using an industrial robot arm, you can watch the progress as the plants grow. You need a valid e-mail address and a caring hand.

Test Borkifier

`http://astro.queensu.ca/~dursi/borker.html`

Enables you to take any English phrase and transform it into "Swedish chef" mumblings. An amazing feat to mystify your friends with your new form of speech.

Tic-Tac-Toe

`http://http.bsd.uchicago.edu/~e-pikat/TicTacToe/ttt.html`

If you didn't get enough of this game as a child, or if you have too much free time, try this site. We all know how the game will finish. But try it nonetheless.

The Tick's Dart Games

`http://www.islandnet.com/~cwalker/sites.html`

Help the Tick destroy some forms of evil present in today's society—like Garfield. You can choose one of several media icons or political figures to throw darts at.

The Ultimate Oracle—Pray Before the Head of Bob

`http://www.resort.com/~banshee/Misc/8ball/index.html`

The online version of the legendary Magic Eight Ball. Ask Bob any question and you are sure to get a response. You can even ask in four different languages.

The Vain Game

`http://www.xs4all.nl/~kessels/Puzzel.html`

Try this site if you need a good intellectual humbling. The game is challenging and entertaining and will, of course, suck your time from you.

Virtual Bubble Wrap

`http://www.mackerel.com/bubble.html`

The packaging material you loved to destroy as a child is now available online. Look here for the virtual version. You must have the appropriate plug-in software.

Hockey Equipment Buyer's Guide

`http://www.barint.on.ca/mostly/cdrom.html`

Download the Mostly Hockey Barrie Equipment Buyer's Guide. The guide contains over 150 items and many full-color images.

Virtual Media

http://www.iaw.on.ca/~virtualm/

Home site for the video clip and sound byte of the week. Includes site background and information.

Virtual Mr. Spud Head

http://www.westnet.com/~crywalt/pothead/pothead.html

The game you lost all the pieces to as a child is back. Mr. Potato Head is here, under an online, non-copyrighted form. You are able to place eyes, nose, teeth, mouth, whatever, onto the Potato. A new twist is also available—change the vegetable if you like.

Web-a-Sketch

http://www.digitalstuff.com/web-a-sketch/

In the true spirit of the immortal Etch-a-Sketch comes Web-a-Sketch. The lines are a great deal harder to draw, but let's face it—you got the time. If your picture is good enough, it might make drawing of the week.

WebBattleship

http://info.gte.com/gtel/fun/battle/battle.html

The online version of the classic game, except you cannot choose where you want to place your battleships. Always entertaining, and the computer is pretty formidable.

Webcube

http://info.gte.com/cgi-bin/cube/cube?RESET

The game you hated as a child, but that caught on as a cultural phenomena. The only catch is that you can't take this one apart in order to win.

Welcome to Faces

http://www.web-usa.com/faces/

This site enables you to create police sketches of famous celebrities by combining heads, eyes, and mouths of different individuals.

Welcome to Find-the-Spam

http://sp1.berkeley.edu/findthespam.html

One of the many Spam worshipping pages on the Web. The game here is Find-the-Spam. It is not as simple as one would think, either.

Welcome To the Connect Four Homepage

http://csugrad.cs.vt.edu/~jhines/ConnectFour.html

The game you loved as a child is back. An online interactive version of Connect Four is available from this site. Opponent is the computer.

Welcome to the Web Wumpus

http://www.bu.edu/Games/wumpus.html

Look here for an online version of the game "Hunt the Wumpus." Your goal is to hunt the wumpus and shoot it before it gets you. Site includes game instructions.

Wizards of the Coast, Inc.

http://www.wizards.com/

Provides home site and information for Wizards of the Coast, producers of the popular "Magic: The Gathering" card came. Includes information about Magic and other games produced by the Wizards. Also includes company background and news.

WWW Anagram Generator

http://csugrad.cs.vt.edu/~eburke/anagrams.html

Take any of your favorite words or phrases and generate quite a few anagrams of it. Also contains news and upcoming features of the anagram generator.

The WWW Fortune Cookie Machine

http://www.mind.net/sage/fortune/

Receive a piece of distilled silicon wisdom from this page, without a bland cookie. You can also submit a fortune, if you think you have the karma it takes.

WWW Interactive Crossword

http://www.phillynews.com/crossword/

An online crossword puzzle brought to you by the Philadelphia newspapers. Choose from a slew of previous newspaper puzzles put online to play. You can even choose an "easy" mode.

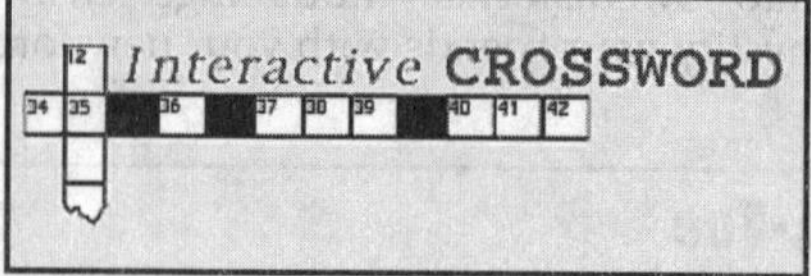

Humor

Air Guitar

http://www.digitalrag.com/mirror/air/air.html

Tired of watching your friends play air guitar at the Steve Miller concert, and wishing you had the talent? Well, take an online lesson here. Also contains 100 links to other entertaining sites.

The Amazing Pecking Chicken

http://www.vanderbilt.edu/~dotedu/staff/cluck/

A site of extreme silliness is found here. Investigate this site for images of a disco chicken, a pecking chicken, and the history of the pecking chicken home page.

Big Green Button

http://www.geocities.com/Hollywood/5945/press01.html

Creative genius spawned this site. Captivating and equally silly and useless. But you'll keep coming back to it. Site features a large green button to push.

The Bottom 95% of the WWW

http://www.dartmouth.edu/~jaundice/bottom95/

Tired of all the "Top 5 percent of the Web" icons? Here is the pirate site professing the remaining 95 percent. Look here for a great many links to sites not listed by Point's survey.

Center for the Easily Amused

http://www.islandnet.com/~cwalker/

A phenomenal site at which to waste copious amounts of time browsing. Site contains links organized by category to make up one the best lists of odd humor on the WWW.

Cruel Site of the Day

http://www.cruel.com/

This site offers a cynical look at the Web by providing sites that are the most perturbing and cruel, as well as entertaining. Also a great starting point for the obscure on the Web.

Crunch

http://www.ice.net/~crunch/

A perverse look at our nation's favorite breakfast cereals. Look here to find a list of cereal toys inside every imaginable cereal type.

Cursing in Swedish

http://www.bart.nl/~sante/enginvek.html

Learn how to swear in Swedish. Page claims that the Swedish language is remarkably limited when it comes to cursing and using four-letter words. So let this page help you take out your aggressions.

The Daily Double Awards

http://weber.u.washington.edu/~jgurney/dd/

This site, updated daily, recognizes the most impressive and least impressive site of the week. The site author is correct in his choice of lame sites—they are most intolerable.

The Daily Muse

http://www.cais.net/aschnedr//muse1.htm

Tired of the daily news as reported by the well-groomed authoritative media? Look here for a cynical twist to the news, heavily seasoned with political humor.

Dave's Web of Lies

http://www.cs.man.ac.uk/~hancockd/lies.htm

Completely useless information is contained here. Unless you need a random falsehood to use in any searchable situation, don't come here. But in a time of need, this site may be your salvation.

David Hasselhoff is the AntiChrist

http://www.indirect.com/www/warren/baywatch.html

This Web site author proposes one of the scariest possible theories in show business. Decide for yourself whether you subscribe to this eerie possibility about our favorite star of *Baywatch*.

The Dog Ate My Homework—1,001 Excuses for Home, Work, and Play

http://users.aol.com/rkoul/dogindex.htm

Contains 1,001 novel excuses for general use in all parts of your life. Excuses are organized into groups based on work, home, politicians, and so on.

A Duck's Memoirs

`http://www.wam.umd.edu/~twoflowr/photos.htm`

A duck's life portrayed in black and white still photos constructed for the people in those late-night silly moods. A nice parody of Forrest Gump—investigate it.

Evil Little Brother's Excuse Generator

`http://www.dtd.com/excuse/`

Just like when you were growing up, your evil little brother is here to give you an excuse. Site requires a few bits of information to generate your perfect excuse for any situation.

Exploding Heads

`http://www.king.net/gilmore/head/`

See your favorite Republican or Microsoft icon blow up in front of your eyes. Page features five famous figures exploding.

Georgetown Gonzo

`http://sunsite.unc.edu/martin/gonzo.html`

A Georgetown underground journalist put together this little gem in the true spirit of "Gonzo Journalism." Biting satire and a willingness to throw any essay on the page make this enjoyable.

The Great Barbie Naming Contest

`http://www.sff.net/people/pitman/barbie.htm`

Details the overthrow of girls by the tool of slavery known as Barbie. Rather than destroy these cultural icons, this page serves to provide Mattel with more creative ideas to sell Barbie by giving them a new name.

Heather Has Two Mommies

`http://www.swiss.ai.mit.edu/zoo/heather-has-two-mommies.html`

A parody of the popular children's book *Heather Has Two Mommies*. Page contains hardened views of modern gender issues, as well as scathing remarks which might incite quite a few misgivings. So investigate at your own risk.

Internet Advertising Hall of Shame

`http://www.privnet.com/adshame.html`

The people who just can't seem to relax about the WWW wound up here. Don't let this happen to your company. Page features an index of sites whose gross exploitation of this form of communication seemed to appall its author.

Internet Squeegee Guy

`http://www.website1.com/squeegee`

This page will wash the inside of your monitor for you when you pull up to a stoplight on the information dirt road. You can choose to give him some change or look the other way.

It's the French Fries

`http://www.select-ware.com/fries/`

They're hot and they're tasty. They are also the staple of the American diet. So look here for everything you never wanted to know about the skinny deep-fried potatoes.

Jadie's Warped Mind

`http://www.geocities.com/Hollywood/3128/`

Acts as the catharsis for Jadie's warped mind. Page features random thoughts and tidbits of humor. You can read one after another paragraph of humorous random thoughts.

Jim's All New, Fresher Smelling Home Page

`http://www.cruzio.com/~jimg/index.html`

A page characterized by a dry, skewed sense of humor that the over-educated will enjoy thoroughly. A site worthy of several minutes of uninterrupted surfing. Nicely done introductory pictures as well.

LaughWeb

`http://world.std.com/~joeshmoe/laughweb/lweb_ns.html`

LaughWeb provides a small bit of humor to your e-mail account to brighten your morning. Subscription is free, and you can add jokes and anecdotes if you want.

Lip Balm Anonymous

`http://members.aol.com/LipBalmA/index.html`

This site promotes the casting out of all lip balms based on lip balm's psychologically addictive tendencies. Contains the history of lip balm and "The Industry of Addiction."

The Lunacy Catapult

`http://www.epix.net/~wayne26/`

A site constructed for pure silliness and amusement. Contains the "Goofy Picture Show" and the "Play a Day Center." Also several links to more craziness.

Make James Earl Jones Speak

`http://www.tiac.net/users/nolan/jej/`

The most dashing authoritative baritone in show business is here to talk for you. Page enables users to input sentences that Mr. Jones will speak. User must have sound capabilities, though.

The Miraculous Winking Jesus

`http://www.fastlane.net/~sandman/jesus/`

A mild spoof of the religious miracles observed around the world. The Winking Jesus page provides a detailed sketch of Jesus that periodically winks. Users can submit their observations if desired.

Mirky's Worst of the Web

`http://mirsky.com/wow/`

Some hilariously funny and equally atrocious sites dot this home page. Look here for sites that would be better off deleted but are fairly entertaining.

The Oracle of Bacon at Virginia

`http://www.cs.virginia.edu/~bct7m/bacon.html`

Another site professing the power of Kevin Bacon. Check here for your favorite actors' "bacon number," or how many movies they are away from Kevin Bacon.

Oracle Service Humor Archive

`http://www.synapse.net/~oracle/Contents/HumorArch.html`

Assembled from e-mail forwardings, this humor archive is immense. Categories include political humor, daily life, computer humor, and of course, *Star Trek*.

PElvis

`http://www.princeton.edu/~pelvis/`

The King lives in the mind and jeans of the Princeton students who created this page. Provides a cynical look at drugs and alcohol. Contains numerous Elvis links and a not-so-serious look at the man behind the gold suit.

Penny's Skulls of Fate

`http://www.dtd.com/skulls/`
`sklskl01.cgi?skull=siss1&ind=846281688`

If you need to know the meaning of life, phrase the question in a yes or no format and ask the skulls of fate at this site. Also contains links to "Dr. Fellowbug's Laboratory of Fun & Horror."

Personalized Shakespearean Insult Service

`http://kite.preferred.com/insults/insult.cgi`

Get insulted by Bill Shakespeare himself. Insults such as "Vanessa said 'thou art a swag-bellied puny skainsmate!'" are found within.

Planet Wallywood One Liner Comedy Diner

`http://www.halcyon.com/gwally/cgi-pvt/welcome.pl`

Contains a large database of comedians, including biographies on most of them. Site organized into "Comedians," "Television," and "Fun Web Sites" categories.

Punch Rush Limbaugh Page

`http://www.indirect.com/www/beetle87/rush/index.html`

That's right, punch everyone's favorite politically untrained conservative radio personality. He looks even better when you give him a black eye.

Random Elizabethan Curse Generator

`http://www.tower.org/disease/insult.html`

Simply click on the Curse button to be randomly cursed in the glorious Elizabethan style. Site contains lots of random links to "computer geek" things.

Random Jokes about Yo Mama

http://www.bus.miami.edu/~ldouglas/yomama/yomama.html

This site is for those fans of the immortal "your mother" jokes. Luckily, the site is organized into categories such as "So Big/Fat...", or "So Nasty, Greasy, Hairy, Stank..." to organize your mother into nice digestible bits.

The Rock and Roll Hall of Shame

http://pathfinder.com/@@q2StgAcAbwY4*3GW/people/hall/

Is your music collection littered with bad drum solos and big hair? If so, you will love this site. Even the classic artists are assaulted here for any slip-ups. Features a lengthy list of intolerable groups and song lyrics.

Rodney Dangerfield Home Page

http://www.rodney.com/

The original bad boy of humor is back with a home page. Site contains joke of the day and the "no respect" contest. You can also download sound files and a telephone answering machine in Rodney's voice.

The Scamizdat Memorial

http://www.well.com/user/jerod23/clam.html

The site provides a scathing and humorous look at the Church of Scientology through many different perspectives. A vast amount of the articles at this site are taken from e-mail messages gathered together to leave a lasting impression of the religion.

Solid Space

http://redwood.northcoast.com/~shojo/Solid.html

Another randomly funny page featuring Fabio, Pez, and Mr. T versus a very large tree. Contains a great link to an online "view master."

Spam Haiku Archive

http://www.naic.edu/~jcho/spam/sha.html

Learn how to construct poetry in the rigorous haiku and Spam format. Over 4,600 "Spamkus," most of which are not as funny as they are curiously silly.

Spatula City

http://www.wam.umd.edu/~twoflowr/spatula.html

You'll find more than just egg scrapers here. Site contains a wealth of information organized into groups of "The Silly Zone," "Checkout List," "Black List," and "Kitchen and Candy." Check out the staring contest link.

TEI's Random Joke Server

http://www.totalweb.com/ent/jokehome.html

Choose from a large list of categories the type of joke you want. Categories include "Light Bulb Jokes," "Couples," "Blondes," and so on.

The Textual Abuse Page

http://www.shamus.com/abusepage.html

Another insult page for the overbearing browser. Customize your insult based on intelligence, gender, or political affiliation.

Thinking Bob's Image of the Day

http://adsint.bc.ca/thinkbob/

This site provides a very strange look into the mind of Thinking Bob. Contains many links to many random sites that would constitute wasting time.

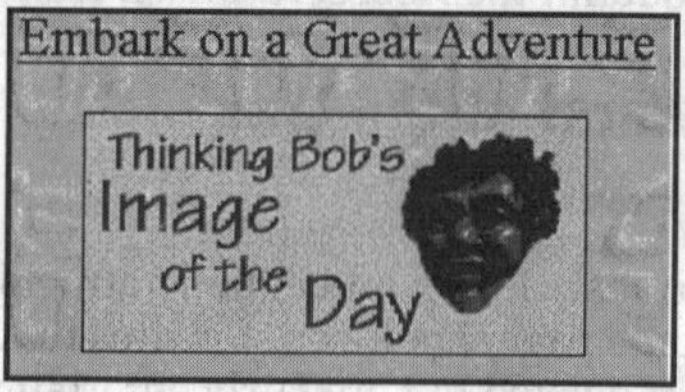

Top Ten Ways to Tell if You Have a Sucky Home Page

http://www.glover.com/sucky.html

Does your home page just not make the cut? Look here for clues hinting at a bad home page, as well as links on how to get on track. Also contains other general WWW advice.

Twisted Tunes Home Page

http://www.twistedtunes.com/

This site is a must for the loyal "Weird Al" Yankovic fan. Features parodies of rock 'n' roll songs, updated weekly. Site requires RealAudio software for performance, which is available for download from this site.

Webcrawler—Deep Thought of the Day

`http://www.webcrawler.com/select/humor.11.html`

The humor series spawned by *Saturday Night Live* stakes its one claim on the Web. Check here for a new daily Deep Thought by Jack Handy.

White Trash Homepage—Phrantic's Trailerpark

`http://www.webserve.com/phrantic/tribune.htm`

Enjoy the working-class humor of this page written by white collar individuals. This online trailer park community may amuse you if you find the right link. Link to the "Phrantic's Public Housing Project," which is leading the fight for squatting rights in cyberspace.

World Headquarters for Burrito and Burrito-Related Information

`http://www.infobahn.com/pages/rito.html`

Contains humorous and insightful information on the food that ties many of our colons together. Page also contains excerpts from Steinbecks's *Tortilla Flat* and other landmark texts in burritology, not to mention more burrito links than you ever wanted.

WWW Fights

`http://www.cheme.cornell.edu/~slevine/`

Grudge matches against media personalities are featured here. Whether you want to read about "Joe Camel fights Spud Mackenzie" or "The Sweat Hogs versus WKRP," the suspense is gripping.

Miscellaneous

101 Hollywood Blvd.

`http://home.navisoft.com/brewpubclub/101.htm`

A creative site featuring the faces of many famous people intertwined into a gripping plot lightly speckled with beer. Don't miss Hugh Grant's mug shot.

Campfire Tales

`http://www.netlink.co.uk/users/avid-eye/jackanory/`

Read one of four frightening fables of intrigue from this site. Also contains a very nice cowboy image on the home page.

Cyber City '96

`http://ccity.iwe96.infoweb.or.jp/e/index_e.html`

An online "3D city" where you can communicate with people around the world. Be careful not to get lost in the Japanese advertisements.

Glenfiddich—Weird and Wonderful Websites

`http://www.glenfiddich.co.uk/home.html`

If the fine single malt Scotch does not get you interested in this Web site, its weird and wonderful Web site of the week will tickle your fancy. Site also features a contest.

Hell's Buddhas

`http://www.hellsbuddhas.com/`

This site serves as the contact point for an ongoing five-month motorcycle road trip through the country of India. In charge is Asokananda, the lead singer of a German punk rock band. Follow them through their journey to spiritual destinations.

The Magic 8 Bra

`http://www.cyborganic.com/people/carla/Rumpus/Toychest/8bra/`

Believe in a higher cup size and your fortune will flow. Just follow the directions and receive this questionable wisdom. Site also provides some strange links worth trying.

Marvin the Martian

`http://www.frii.com/~engserv/marvin.htm`

The country's favorite little green man is back from the pages of Looney Tunes. Look here for some nicely done GIF images of Marvin, his dog, Bugs Bunny, and Duck Dodgers.

Mr. Showbiz

http://www.mrshowbiz.com/

A site that dives into the depths of Hollywood, bringing you "News," "Features," "Star Bios," and a large archive. Learn just about anything you want about any actor you can think of.

Net Frog

http://curry.edschool.Virginia.EDU/go/frog/home.html

This interactive frog dissection was designed for high school students, but it is fun for all—that is, assuming you were not emotionally scarred enough the first time you did this.

The Sneeze Page

http://www.claritin.com/Sneeze/Sneeze.html

Whether it is entertainment or not, who knows? Check out these ten downloadable sneezes. Ranging from a nasal sneeze to an allergy sneeze.

Southern California Real Time Traffic Report

http://www.scubed.com/caltrans/transnet.html

Look here if you are really in need for some random entertainment or if you are travelling in Southern California. Site features online traffic reports, including accidents.

Supermarket Tabloid Headlines

http://www.planetary.net/cgi-bin/
spew.pl?number=5&headline=enquirer&newtitle=Super
market+Tabloid+Headlines

Generates up to 10 National Enquirer Headlines at a time. Site also contains a link that will generate five fictitious grunge band names at a time, all of which are presumably in the formation stage in Seattle.

Virtual Flowers

http://www.virtualflowers.com/

Send a free online bouquet of flowers from this site to your sweetheart or significant other. Browse around the site for other floral shop items.

The Virtual Keyboard

http://www.xmission.com/~mgm/misc/keyboard.html

The name says it all. Yes, a virtual keyboard that is so slow, it takes five minutes to play *Mary Had a Little Lamb*. The page author also adds some useful suggestions to possible applications for the WWW virtual keyboard.

Welcome to the Adventures of Spacedog

http://www.spacedog.org/

The contact site for all your Spacedog needs, including fan club information, fun links, and movies. Site also contains links to other fun links checked out by "webmom."

Radio

94.7 NRK—The New Rock Revolution

http://ww2.AudioNet.com/pub/knrk/knrk.htm

Jack into this live alternative station out of Oregon. If the radio stations in your town suck, no problem; with RealAudio 2.0 and a 28.8 modem, you can now bypass that noise pollution and listen to tunes you would never hear in your town.

440 Satisfaction

http://www.aloha.net/~hijohn/

Focuses on the deejays, news people, and unsung radio people from earlier days in radio. Check out the "Reel Top 40 Radio Depository" to hear sound checks and news from some of the biggest DJs of the '60s and '70s. A real blast!

AudioNet—The Broadcast Network on the Internet

http://www.audionet.com/

With the RealAudio 2.0 player, you can listen to AudioNet's radio shows, which include sports, talk radio, and specialty programming. Includes live broadcasting from more than 50 college stations, dozens of talk shows from around the country, and news.

Blue Planet

http://www.demon.co.uk/blueplanet/index.html

Online guide to the club scene in the United Kingdom. Click on an area, such as The Midlands, to see a list of all the clubs. Includes addresses, telephone numbers, and live music calendars for each club. Covers England, Wales, and Scotland.

Cinemedia Radio

http://www.afionline.org/CINEMEDIA/CineMedia.radio.html

Provides links to hundreds of radio stations worldwide that have a Web presence. Also includes hundreds of links to radio-related sites for celebrities, shows, directories, controversy, and more. If you're into radio, visit this site first.

The FCC

http://www.fcc.gov/

Read up on the FCC's Telecom Act of 1996, which will save you from everything evil and sadistic on the Internet and infringe on your First Amendment rights just a little bit more. Here's where it all begins.

The Howard Stern Show Sounds Page

http://www2.liglobal.com/stern/

Listen to excerpts from the Howard Stern radio or TV show. Includes sound clips from Stern, his sidekick Robin Quivers, Stuttering John, and others. Also includes sounds about the OJ trial, guests and celebrities on the show, and the usual parade of puppets.

The Internet Karaoke Store

http://www.primenet.com/~karaoke/index.html

One-stop shopping for karaoke laserdiscs and CDs. Includes links to karaoke manufacturers and related Web sites.

Media Watchdog

http://theory.lcs.mit.edu/~mernst/media/

This collection of online media watchdog groups includes time-sensitive information, censorship resources, media criticism articles, and dozens of newsletters devoted to the monitoring and analysis of biased media.

The Museum of Television and Radio

http://www.mtr.org/

Take a virtual tour of the museums in New York and Los Angeles. Includes information on their gallery shows, daily screenings of radio and television specials, and an exhibit calendar. Provides visiting hours and directions to museums in Los Angeles and New York.

Radio on the Internet

http://www.town.hall.org/radio/index.html

This online radio service has been "broadcasting" since early 1993 and includes hundreds of hours of material that you can download. Includes information on technology, art, public affairs, and a list of radio stations that are experimenting with Internet audio.

Radio Online—Radio's Starting Point on the Net

http://www.radio-online.com/talent.htm

Click on a radio host to see his or her Web page. Includes dozens of deejays. If you're a deejay for a major station, you can submit your URL for review.

Sounds of Silence

http://www.silence.net

This home page for a Nashville ISP includes music charts and reviews, the Blue Power Radio Show, *Cash Box* magazine, and the home page for Gibson Guitars.

Sound

8-Track Heaven

http://www.bway.net/~abbot/8track/

Rediscover everything you wanted to forget about the breakthrough 8-track recording technology. Part of the quarterly publication *8-Track Mind* and an extension of alt.collecting.8-track-tapes, this Web page includes a FAQ about the technology, a detailed history, and collector notes. If you grew up on cassettes, feel fortunate and download the sound clip of an 8-track changing programs. Also includes Windows wallpaper and icons, the "8 Noble Truths," and the enquiring 8-Track and UFOs connection. A hilarious site!

CES News

http://www.eia.org/CEMA/cesnews/ontext11.htm

One of the largest trade shows in the U.S., the Consumer Electronics Show now has an audio/home theater show in Florida every May. Check out the lists of audio exhibitors, learn more about the CES digital fair, and read about other new shows in North America. Download images from recent shows.

Lucasfilm's THX Home Page

http://www.lum.com:80/thx/

The current leader in audio reproduction for movie and home theaters includes information on the THX sound system, THX-approved equipment, technical specs, and THX laserdiscs at this site.

RealAudio Audio on Demand for the Internet

http://www.prognet.com/

Download the latest release of the RealAudio player and be part of live Internet audio. This site provides information on the RealAudio player from Progressive Networks, and also its server and encoder products. You can access several Web sites with a significant amount of RealAudio files, including PBS, ABC, NPR, and the Live Events site.

Secrets of Home Theater and High Fidelity

http://www.sdinfo.com/

Click on an object in the home theater room to learn more about that component. This site also includes movie and music reviews for the home theater nut, a "What's New" section that describes the latest gizmos, and a search engine and index to articles. A great place to explore home theater.

See Hollywood and Vine

http://www.hollywoodandvine.com/

This hip site from Capitol Records includes hundreds of sound clips from each of its artists. Choose artists from the list, click on Search, and download one of their songs or visit their Web site. Be sure to visit the Hollywood and Vine tourist trap, a collection of attractions with more audio and video than you could ever ask for. Have fun!

Sound Site

http://www.soundsite.com/

Provides helpful information on audio and video recording technologies. Help and information includes a troubleshooting guide, history of audio and video, and a section on home theater and setting the time on your VCR. Also includes audio/video industry news, manufacturers lists, and information on new technologies.

Welcome to Dolby Laboratories

http://www.dolby.com/

If you've ever been confused as to what Dolby actually does, check out the Dolby Technologies hyperlink. Read about Dolby Digital, the latest theater sound; download the Dolby Digital trailer you've seen at theaters; review helpful hints for home theater setup; and see what's on the horizon with theater sound.

Xing Technology's StreamWorks

http://204.62.160.251/

Download StreamWorks to play sound files on the Internet. This audio player for Windows, Macintosh, and Unix lets you listen to live audio. After you download the player, click on one of the radio station sites to listen to live radio, or choose other links to download songs and speeches. Neat stuff!

Theater

The Complete Works of William Shakespeare

http://the-tech.mit.edu/Shakespeare/works.html

In addition to providing the complete text of every Shakespeare play and poem, this site includes a discussion area, chronological and alphabetical lists of the plays, Bartlett's familiar Shakespeare quotations, and a funeral elegy by the old man himself. An unbelievable site!

Larry Stark's Theater Mirror

http://northshore.shore.net/~greenrm/

Lengthy reviews of new plays in Boston are only part of this rich Web resource. Page includes a calendar of shows, upcoming plays, the casting call board, and notes on recent productions.

London Theatre Guide—On Line

http://www.londontheatre.co.uk/online/

Use this handy page to find info on West End shows, the Royal National Theatre, and other London theaters. Includes addresses, seating arrangements, reviews of current shows, ballet and opera listings, and a monthly e-mail update service.

New York's Capital District Theater Page

http://www.albany.net/~danorton/theatre/

Lists all the plays currently running in Albany, New York. This page also includes audition information, class and workshop information, and active theater company shedules. The "Other Related Web Sites" and "Theater-related Newsgroup" sections provide dozens of links and Usenet addresses.

New York City Theater

http://www.mediabridge.com/nyc/entertainment/theater/

Provides brief descriptions of plays currently in production on and off Broadway. Addresses and phone numbers are also included.

Red Herring Productions

http://www.bayne.com/wolfBayne/mystery/

Web site for this interactive theater production company. Find out about its mysteries, westerns, and melodramas that get the audience involved.

The SITCOM Home Page

http://www.ccp.uchicago.edu/grad/Dan_Goldstein/sitcom.html

Information on the SITCOM program of improvised half-hour "shows," which mimic rehearsed and planned TV comedy. Provides a blend of structuralist literary criticism and artificial intelligence—a live show that converts audience suggestions into full-length, improvised TV sitcoms that unfold live on stage.

TenEyck Design Studio

http://www.inch.com/~kteneyck/

Web page for a set design company in New York City. Be sure to enter the door to learn more about its designs for plays such as *The Tempest* and *La Traviata*. The Observatory includes information on all the productions for which TenEyck has designed sets.

Triad Productions Presents

http://www.wizard.com/~patrick/triad.html

Produces live role-playing plays in which you are part of the cast. Read more about these plays and how they work at this site.

Lipton Recipes

http://www.lipton.com/new.html

Lipton provides free online recipes, special offers, and order forms for publications about nutrition and health, tea, and food preparation.

Virtual Worlds

Desiderata—The Reststop

`http://www.dfw.net/~custmbld/desid.html`

A "rest stop" on the information highway. This site features an annotated version of *Desiderata*, the guide for life.

Electric Saloon

`http://www.st.rim.or.jp:80/~liliko/e-saloon.html`

A fun 3D "saloon" that serves a few drinks and has plenty of characters. Check out the Quicktime movie of the saloon, click on a character to talk to, then see what Web links he or she recommends. Slightly weird, slightly innocent, but still interesting.

The Enterprise City Home Page

`http://www.thebook.com/enterprise/city.htm`

Take a taxi, ride the monorail, or walk through Enterprise city, a fictitious town with all types of characters and stories. This town comprises a collection of characters, stories, and essays by Dominic R. Villari.

Mariam's Cyberspace Park

`http://www.skypoint.com/members/mariam`

Nine "parks" await your visit. Take a ride on the roller coaster at EuroDisney, or visit the theme park at the Mall of America. There is also a Psychology park, a Poetry park, a Religion park, and a Sports park. A great way to organize and display links to other pages.

The Social Cafe

`http://www.social.com/social/index.html`

Become a member (it's free) or just visit and talk with others. This site, by social.com, includes a "Sports and Social Clubs" area, a message area where you can discuss different topics, the "Woman's Page," and the latest news on the social scene. The "Fun" link includes comics, sports info, and games on the Internet.

The Tin Cup Coffee House

`http://www.tincup.com/`

Check out Web sites around the Twin Cities (Minneapolis and St. Paul, Minnesota), read the Coffee House Review of all the coffee houses in the area, or listen to great RealAudio files.

Virtual Vegas

`http://www.virtualvegas.com`

Believe it or not, you can now travel to Las Vegas on your PC. This site provides a virtual trip to Las Vegas. Includes casinos (just for fun of course), the Lizard Lounge, and much more. Also provides links to sites in the "real" Las Vegas. Virtual Vegas is a cool site.

World of Paths Headquarters

`http://www.aloha.com/~william/vpdest1.html`

The fantasy world detailed on this page and in an electronic book called *At Dream's End* is described on this page. Take a visual tour of this world, check out screen shots of the map of this world, or click on Expanded Sneak Preview to read excerpts from the book.

Newsgroups

alt.acting

alt.animation.spumco

alt.animation.warner-bros

alt.ascii-art.animation

alt.binaries.multimedia.d

alt.binaries.pictures.anime

alt.cartoon.reboot

alt.comedy.firesgn-thtre

alt.comedy.improvisation

alt.comedy.standup

alt.comics.2000ad

alt.comics.alan-moore

alt.comics.alternative

alt.comics.batman

alt.comics.classic

alt.comics.dilbert

alt.comics.elfquest

alt.comics.fan-fiction

alt.comics.image

alt.comics.lnh

alt.comics.peanuts

alt.comics.superman

alt.fan.actors

alt.fan.actors.dead

alt.fan.british-actors

alt.fan.cfny

alt.fan.dave_barry

alt.fan.don-imus

alt.fan.don-n-mike

alt.fan.fi.glover

alt.fan.howard-stern

alt.fan.kroq

alt.fan.mark-brian

alt.fan.sailor-moon

alt.games

alt.geek

alt.home-theater.misc

alt.humor.best-of-usenet

alt.humor.best-of-usenet.d

alt.humor.bluesman

alt.humor.puns

alt.internet.talk-radio

alt.misc.forteana

alt.neo-tech

alt.radio.college

alt.radio.digital

alt.radio.networks.cbc

alt.radio.networks.npr

alt.radio.online-tonight

alt.radio.paul-harvey

alt.radio.pirate

alt.radio.scanner

alt.radio.scanner.uk

alt.radio.talk

alt.radio.uk

alt.radio.uk.talk-radio

alt.radio.whadya-know

alt.radio.wpkn

alt.revenge

alt.rush-limbaugh

alt.sport.paintball

alt.sports.radio

alt.sports.radio.ferrall

alt.stagecraft

alt.tasteless.jokes

alt.testing.testing.

alt.toys.gi-joe

ba.broadcast

bit.listserv.radio-l

chi.media

chile.comics

clari.living.comics.bizarro

clari.living.comics.cafe_angst

clari.living.comics.doonesbury

clari.living.comics.forbetter

clari.living.comics.foxtrot

clari.living.comics.ozone_patrol

dc.media

fido7.humor.filtered

fiod7.su.humor

fj.jokes

fj.rec.animation

fj.rec.comics

han.rec.humor

kw.theatre

misc.news.east-europe.rferl

nebr.humor

niagara.arts

no.alt.radio-tv.irma-1000

no.radio-tv

pdaxs.arts.radio

phl.media

phl.theatre

pnet.rec.humor

pnet.rec.radio.amateur.announce

pnet.rec.radio.amateur.talk

rec.antiques.radio+phono

rec.arts.animation

rec.arts.anime

rec.arts.anime.fandom

```
rec.arts.anime.info

rec.arts.anime.marketplace

rec.arts.anime.misc

rec.arts.anime.models

rec.arts.anime.music

rec.arts.comics.alternative

rec.arts.comics.creative

rec.arts.comics.dc.lsh

rec.arts.comics.dc.universe

rec.arts.comics.dc.vertigo

rec.arts.comics.elfquest

rec.arts.comics.info

rec.arts.comics.marketplace

rec.arts.comics.marvel.universe

rec.arts.comics.marvel.xbooks

rec.arts.comics.misc

rec.arts.comics.other-media

rec.arts.comics.strips

rec.arts.disney.animation

rec.arts.theatre

rec.arts.theatre.misc

rec.arts.theatre.musicals

rec.arts.theatre.plays

rec.arts.theatre.stagecraft

rec.gambling

rec.gambling.misc

rec.gambling.other-games

rec.games.backgammon

rec.games.board

rec.games.board.marketplace - Tr

rec.games.bridge

rec.games.chess

rec.games.chess.analysis

rec.games.chess.computer

rec.games.chess.misc

rec.games.chess.play-by-email

rec.games.chess.politics

rec.games.chinese-chess

rec.games.design

rec.games.go

rec.games.misc

rec.games.pinball

rec.games.trading-cards.jyhad

rec.games.trading-cards.startrek

rec.games.video.arcade

rec.games.video.arcade.collecting

rec.games.video.classic

rec.games.video.marketplace

rec.games.video.misc

rec.humor

rec.humor.d

rec.humor.funny
```

rec.models.rc.air

rec.models.rc.land

rec.models.rc.misc

rec.models.rc.water

rec.puzzles

rec.puzzles.crosswords

rec.radio.amateur.antenna

rec.radio.amateur.digital.misc

rec.radio.amateur.equipment

rec.radio.amateur.homebrew

rec.radio.amateur.misc

rec.radio.amateur.policy

rec.radio.amateur.space

rec.radio.broadcasting

rec.radio.cb

rec.radio.info

rec.radio.noncomm

rec.radio.scanner

rec.radio.shortwave

rec.radio.swap.

rec.sport.paintball

relcom.comp.animation

relcom.humor

relcom.humor.lus

relcom.radio

relcom.radio.diagrams

relcom.radio.ham

sanet.radio.packet

sbay.hams

sci.med.radiology

slac.rec.ham_radio

su.org.ham-radio

talk.bizarre

talk.bizarre.nice

tamu.kanm.radio

tnn.internet.itr

tnn.radio.amateur

tnn.radio.life

triangle.radio

tw.bbs.rec.radio

tw.bbs.talk.joke

uiuc.org.anime

uiuc.org.synton

uk.media.radio.archers

uk.media.radio.bbc-r4

uk.radio.amateur

uwarwick.societies.amateur-radio

z-netz.freizeit.video

Listservs

ANIME-L—rec.arts.anime Newsgroup

Virginia Tech

You can join this group by sending the message "sub ANIME-L your name" to `listserv@vtvm1.cc.vt.edu`

ASUENTER—ASU Entertainment Press Release Distribution List

You can join this group by sending the message "sub ASUENTER your name" to `listserv@asuvm.inre.asu.edu`

DQMW-L—Dr. Quinn Medicine Woman TV Show

You can join this group by sending the message "sub DQMW-L your name" to `listserv%emuvm1.bitnet@listserv.net`

ENTERTAINMENT-NEWS—Entertainment Channel Newsletter

You can join this group by sending the message "sub ENTERTAINMENT-NEWS your name" to `listserv@listserv.aol.com`

ER-L—ER-L Discussions on ER (Crichton's TV Series)

Pennsylvania State University

You can join this group by sending the message "sub ER-L your name" to `listserv@psuvm.psu.edu`

FILMUS-L—Film Music Discussion List

University Computing Services, Indiana University

You can join this group by sending the message "sub FILMUS-L your name" to `listserv@iubvm.ucs.indiana.edu`

FKFIC-L—Forever Knight TV Show Stories

Pennsylvania State University

You can join this group by sending the message "sub FKFIC-L your name" to `listserv@psuvm.psu.edu`

FKSPOILR—Forever Knight TV Show - Spoiler Topic List

Pennsylvania State University

You can join this group by sending the message "sub FKSPOILR your name" to `listserv@psuvm.psu.edu`

FORKNI-L—Forever Knight TV Show

Pennsylvania State University

You can join this group by sending the message "sub FORKNI-L your name" to `listserv@psuvm.psu.edu`

FRIENDS—The NBC Comedy Friends

Dartmouth College, Hanover, NH

You can join this group by sending the message "sub FRIENDS your name" to `listserv@listserv.dartmouth.edu`

GIGGLES—House of Laughter; Jokes, Stories, and Anecdotes

You can join this group by sending the message "sub GIGGLES your name" to `listserv@listserv.vt.edu`

GOODIES-L—Discussion List for the Goodies

America Online, Inc. (1-800-827-6364 in USA/Canada)

You can join this group by sending the message "sub GOODIES-L your name" to `listserv@listserv.aol.com`

GS-L—Game Shows Discussion List

Ege University Bornova, Izmir, Turkey

You can join this group by sending the message "sub GS-L your name" to `listserv@vm3090.ege.edu.tr`

HIGHLA-L—Highlander Movies and TV Series

Pennsylvania State University

You can join this group by sending the message "sub HIGHLA-L your name" to listserv@psuvm.psu.edu

HLFIC-L—Highlander TV Show Stories

Pennsylvania State University

You can join this group by sending the message "sub HLFIC-L your name" to listserv@psuvm.psu.edu

HORROR—Horror in Film and Literature

University Computing Services, Indiana University

You can join this group by sending the message "sub HORROR your name" to listserv@iubvm.ucs.indiana.edu

HUMOR—Good Clean Funny Stuff

You can join this group by sending the message "sub HUMOR your name" to listserv@listserv.dartmouth.edu

HUMOR—UGA Humor List

You can join this group by sending the message "sub HUMOR your name" to listserv@uga.cc.uga.edu

HUMORSCOPE—A Humorous Horoscope by Ron Lunde

You can join this group by sending the message "sub HUMORSCOPE your name" to listserv@listserv.aol.com

LAZARUS-L—The Lazarus Man' Discussion List

You can join this group by sending e-mail to maiser@mirkwood.ucc.uconn.edu, in the body of the message, type SUBSCRIBE LAZARUS-L.

LAW-AND-ORDER—Discussion of the TV Series

America Online, Inc. (1-800-827-6364 in USA/Canada)

You can join this group by sending the message "sub LAW-AND-ORDER your name" to listserv@listserv.aol.com

LOISCLA—The Lois & Clark: The New Adventures of Superman Discussion List

You can join this group by sending the message "sub LOISCLA your name" to listserv@vm3090.ege.edu.tr

MERELEWIS—Life & Works of C.S. Lewis

You can join this group by sending the message "sub MERELEWIS your name" to listserv@listserv.aol.com

MISC-HUMOR-L—Miscellaneous Humor Mailing List

You can join this group by sending the message "sub MISC-HUMOR-L your name" to listserv@listserv.aol.com

MOPO-L—Movie Poster Discussion

The American University, Washington, DC

You can join this group by sending the message "sub MOPO-L your name" to listserv@american.edu

PARTNERS—Discussion of the FOX sitcom Partners

You can join this group by sending the message "sub PARTNERS your name" to listserv@listserv.dartmouth.edu

RRA-L—Romance Readers Anonymous

You can join this group by sending the message "sub RRA-L your name" to listserv@listserv.kent.edu

SCREEN-L—Film and TV Studies Discussion List

You can join this group by sending the message "sub SCREEN-L your name" to

`listserv@ua1vm.ua.edu`

STCMD-L—Internet Star Trek Command Council

University of Arkansas Main Campus - Fayetteville

You can join this group by sending the message "sub STCMD-L your name" to

`listserv@uafsysb.uark.edu`

STHL-L—The Star Trek Humour League

University Center of Information services (UCI), Nijmegen, The Netherlands

You can join this group by sending the message "sub STHL-L your name" to `listserv@nic.surfnet.nl`

THEATRE-SOUND—Discussion List for People Working in Sound for Live Theatre

You can join this group by sending the message "sub THEATRE-SOUND your name" to

`listserv@listserv.aol.com`

TWAIN-L—Mark Twain Forum

You can join this group by sending the message "sub TWAIN-L your name" to `listserv@yorku.ca`

ENVIRONMENT

Companies

Amway

http://www.amway.com/amway/partners/environ/

Documents Amway's environmental efforts, including the on-complex recycling center, participation in cleanup programs, Amway's environmental sponsorships, and their environmental awards.

BASF Ecology

http://www.basf.com/eco/

BASF is a very large international company well-known for its manufacture of chemicals, plastics, nylon fibers, magnetic media, and more. They are committed to pollution prevention, ecology, and environmental care. This page contains much information about BASF's dedication to environmental preservation.

Chrysler Corporation—Recycling & Conservation

http://www.chryslercorp.com/environment/recycling.html

Chrysler's environmental page which documents their push to minimize waste. Recycling projects and conservation procedures are documented. Also available are full size images of Chrysler's print ads on environmental goals, conservation, and recycling.

Department of the Navy Environmental Programs

http://enviro.navy.mil/

This site documents the U.S. Navy's environmental programs, including conservation, compliance, cleanup, pollution prevention, technology, and environmental planning.

Disaster's Edge Environmental Education Center

http://www2.third-wave.com/cccd/disaster.html

This company offers environmental training workshops targeted at specific groups. Children, high school students, and adults alike can benefit from an environmental training session with these guys. They also do custom workshops.

DuPont: Safety, Health, and the Environment

http://www.dupont.com/corp/gbl-company/she/index.html

DuPont's dedication to the environment is clearly demonstrated at their Web site. You can read their commitment, view their Environmental Audit, and review their official report to the EPA at this site.

Ford Environmental Report

http://www.ford.com/corporate-info/environment/ERintro.html

This site is the environmental report from Ford Motor Company. Alternatives to gas-powered vehicles, automotive recycling, and "How to Drive Green" are among the topics explored.

Goldman Prize Winners

http://www.goldmanprize.org/goldman/

In 1996, the Goldman Environmental Foundation of San Francisco awarded a total of $450,000 to six environmental heroes from around the world. This page tells the story of each of these heroes, from whom every environmentalist can draw inspiration.

Conservation

Alaska Safari Club Home Page

http://www.interax.com/~huntfishalaska/Hunting/asc/Akshome.shtml

Safari Club International is a group of conservationist hunters. They believe that the best method of preservation is controlled hunting to keep habitat and herds balanced. Interestingly, a list of animals that have become un-endangered thanks to selective hunting is included.

American Association of Zoo Keepers

http://adams.ind.net/

This nonprofit organization, made up of professional zoo keepers, is dedicated to animal care and conservation. Browse this site to learn how you can help save the endangered Eurasian Lynx population. While you're at it, try your hand at "Bowling for Rhinos."

Arbor Day

http://www.arborday.com/

Learn how you can help the environment by planting a tree in your community. Learn about the many Arbor Day programs for supplying trees to communities and educating the population about the importance of trees.

Atlantic Salmon Federation

http://www.flyfishing.com/asf/

As if the salmon of North America didn't have enough trouble having to swim upstream, now they have the possibility of extinction to contend with. The ASF's goal is to find solutions to all issues that could possibly affect the salmon's survival.

The Butterfly Website: Conservation and Ecology

http://mgfx.com/butterfly/ecology/index.htm

Provides articles calling for the conservation of butterflies. Also has articles describing the Montes Azules Biosphere Preserve which includes butterfly ranching among its many projects.

Conservation Breeding Specialist Group

http://www.cbsg.org/index.html

A conservation group who's mission is "to assist conservation of threatened animal and plant species through scientific management of small populations in wild habitats, with linkage to captive populations where needed." Check out their site to learn more about their programs and publications, read the current issue of their newsletter, or find out how you can assist.

Conservation International

http://www.conservation.org/

Learn all about the company that works in rainforests, coastal and coral reef systems, dry forests, deserts, and wastelands in over twenty-two countries. Also, find out what you can do to assist actor Harrison Ford, Intel Chairman/CEO Gordon Moore, and the rest of CI in their ongoing fight to conserve our environment.

The Coral Reef Alliance

http://www.coral.org/

This site is the diving-in point for an alliance made up of snorkelers, divers, and others who realize the value of our coral reefs and are working to preserve them. The alliance sponsors a number of conservation projects which you can sign up for online.

Endangered Plants: Images

http://www.nceet.snre.umich.edu/EndSpp/ESimages/ESplants.html

When one thinks of endangered species, one typically thinks solely of animals. Several species of plants, however, are threatened and endangered as well. They are shown here along with information regarding their status and location.

Endangered Species

http://www.nceet.snre.umich.edu/EndSpp/Endangered.html

View recent additions to the endangered species list, as well as the entire list sorted by group or region. View a list of extinct animals. This site also contains many images of creatures on the list.

GreenLife Society—North America

http://nceet.snre.umich.edu/greenlife/index.html

The goal of the GLSNA is to conribute to the protection and conservation of endangered flora and fauna. They feel that every species has a right to exist regardless of whatever resource value they hold for man. The organization was founded in 1983 and is staffed primarily by volunteers.

GreenLife Society - North America (GLSNA)

International Palm Society

http://www.palms.org/

The IPS is a group consisting of almost 3,000 members in over 80 countries dedicated to study, culture, and preservation of palm trees around the world. Their Web site gives general information about the society, membership information, and offers access to several palm-oriented publications.

John Muir Exhibit

http://www.sierraclub.org/john_muir_exhibit/

Learn about the great naturalist, conservationalist, and founder of the Sierra Club. The site includes pictures, a time line of Muir's life, his writings, and more. Learn how to celebrate "John Muir Day."

League of Conservation Voters

http://www.lcv.org/

The League believes that the best way to achieve environmental results is through successful environmental legislation. Their goal is to elect members to congress who truly care about the environment. They provide a scorecard, which lets the public know how the House and Senate rate in environmental voting, in addition to providing a means to contact representatives to let them know that we care and are watching them.

Maine Solar House

http://solstice.crest.org/renewables/wlord/index.html

A great way to conserve energy (thereby reducing strain on the environment) is by using sustainable forms of energy. This site is an example of the practical use of solar energy in a home. It includes house plans and information about solar heat and energy.

The Marine Fish Conservation Network

http://www.netspace.org/MFCN/

Due to decades of overfishing, our nation's marine life is severely depleted, and fisheries are going bankrupt. Learn how you can be part of the solution to this marine crisis.

Mr. Solar Home Page

http://www.netins.net/showcase/solarcatalog/

"Mr. Solar" is a man in Utah who along with his wife has been living on solar energy for over eighteen years. His goal is to help everyone become as self sufficient as he and his wife have been. His site includes the "Ask Mr. Solar" column, over 100 articles on alternative energy, and how tos on setting up your own solar electric system.

National Audubon Society

http://www.audubon.org/audubon/

Get background information on the Society, its namesake John James Audubon, and his natural art.

Find your local chapter and get membership information. You can even join online.

Sempervirens Fund

http://reality.sgi.com/employees/ctb/sempervirens/

A nonprofit land conservancy (the oldest in California), the fund works to protect redwood forests from threats such as population growth and logging. Learn how you can help keep these magnificent trees available for public enjoyment.

Surfrider Foundation USA

http://www.sdsc.edu/SDSC/Partners/Surfrider/

This grassroots eco-surf organization is dedicated to the preservation of biological diversity on our coasts. They emphasize low-impact "surfaris" and environmental education among surfers and others to maintain a synergy between man and beach.

USDA—Natural Resources Conservation Service

http://www.ncg.nrcs.usda.gov/Welcome.html

The NRCS helps private landowners to develop conservation systems suited to their land. They also work with rural and urban communities alike to reduce erosion, conserve water, and solve other resource problems.

Posters

http://spso.gsfc.nasa.gov:80/eos_posters/order_form.html

Seven posters are available from the Earth Observing Systems Science site. Word of advice—tell them you're affiliated with a school.

Disasters

The Most Contaminated Spot on the Planet

http://www.clarityconnect.com/webpages/grunberg/chel.htm

Dedicated to the victims of radiation in the area of Chelyabinsk, Russia, this site provides information about the various calamities that have befallen the area. Learn why the area was closed to foreigners for over 45 years.

Chelyabinsk: The Most Contaminated Spot on the Planet

In the late 1940's, about 80 kilometers north of the city of Chelyabinsk, an atomic weapons complex called "Mayak" was built. Its existence has only recently been acknowledged by Russian officials, though, in fact, the complex, bordered to the west by the Ural Mountains, and to the north by Siberia, was the goal of Gary Powers's surveillance flight in May of 1960.

For forty-five years, the Chelyabinsk province of Russia was closed to all foreigners. Only in January of 1992 did President Boris Yeltsin sign a decree changing that. As a result, western scientists who studied the region, declared Chelyabinsk to be the most polluted spot on earth.

Plutonium and Tritium for Soviet nuclear weapons are produced at three closely guarded locations, each of which includes a "closed" city for workers. These cities do not appear on maps, and until recently, travel to and from them was all but prohibited. Even now, foreign visitors have been allowed to see only two of the sites. Each of the sites has an official

Oil Spill Public Information Center

http://www.alaska.net/~ospic/

In March of 1989, the *Exxon Valdez* spilled 11 million gallons of oil into Prince William Sound. This site is a wealth of information concerning this major ecological disaster, including maps, photos, and information about the effects of the spill on wildlife.

The Sea Empress Oil Spill

http://www.a40infobahn.com/pembroke/oilspill/empress.htm

Pembrokeshire Coast National Park, Britain's only Coastal National Park was the site of a great ecological disaster when The *Sea Empress* ran aground carrying a full cargo of light crude oil. Read the information compiled from various groups involved in the cleanup process.

Ecology

Cliff Ecology Research Group

http://www.uoguelph.ca/CBS/Botany/index.htm

A group of ecologists dedicated to the study of . . . cliffs! Learn about ancient cedars on cliffs, effects of human trampling, and cryptoendolithic organisms.

Earth Watch

http://www.earthwatch.org/

A nonprofit membership organization that sponsors scientific field research projects. Their mission is "to improve human understanding of the planet, the diversity of its inhabitants, and the processes that affect the quality of life on Earth."

Ecologia

http://ecologia.nier.org/ecologia/

ECOlogists Linked for Organizing Grassroots Initiatives and Action is a group that "replaces cold war competition with environmental cooperation." Headquartered in the U.S., this group's mission is to provide assistance to environmental groups in the Former Soviet Union and Eastern Europe.

Ecological Monitoring and Assessment Network

http://www.cciw.ca/eman-temp/intro.html

EMAN is a network where ecologists from around the globe can share research, experiments, and ideas. Here ecologists can discuss emerging issues and trends and also develop options for future ecological policies.

Ecology Action Centre

http://www.cfn.cs.dal.ca/Environment/EAC/EAC-Home.html

The EAC has been protecting the environment since 1972. Their site contains several environmental FAQs, including definitions for the ever-growing list of enviromental acronyms. The Information Centre also contains access to their library, policy papers, and their quarterly magazine "Between the Issues."

Envirolink

http://envirolink.org

Envirolink provides a comprehensive amount of up-to-date environmental resources. Fellow environmentalists can communicate here via live video-conferencing and chat rooms as well as access an environmental library and real-time environmental data.

Envirolink Freenet

`telnet://envirolink.org`

Obtain a free account on the Envirolink network. Access the Internet Green Marketplace, Worldwide Environmental Bulletin Boards, and online Enviroservices, such as EnviroChat. By signing on with the freenet, you also get an e-mail account.

International Center for Tropical Ecology

`http://ecology.umsl.edu/`

Combining the expertise of ecologists and systematists from both the University of Missouri-St. Louis and the Missouri Botanical Garden, the ICTE promotes research and education in biodiversity, conservation, and the sustainable use of tropical ecosystems.

Missouri Botanical Garden

`http://www.mobot.org/`

The MBG's Web site contains beautiful photographs of some of the many rare plants grown at their greenhouse. Information is also available from the research division in the field of biodiversity. A collection of online books is also accessible.

PlanetKeepers

`http://galaxy.tradewave.com/editors/wayne-pendley/plankeep.html`

An environmental site that feautures readings, inspirational quotes, a list of upcoming events, and a list of things that you can do today to help keep our Earth beautiful and healthy.

Questions About Biodiversity

`http://www.ns.ec.gc.ca/biodiversity/whtbiod.html`

Answers basic enivironmental questions from "What is biodiversity?" to "How can I help protect biodiversity?"

Sci.environment

`news:sci.environment`

An unmoderated Usenet newsgroup aimed at environmental scientists and activists. Topics of discussion include ozone depletion, overpopulation, pesticides, nuclear energy, sustainable agriculture, and much, much more.

Talk.environment

`news:talk.environment`

An unmoderated Usenet newsgroup whose focus is the environment and environmental issues. This group is posted by environmentalists and anti-environmentalists alike, to make for a lively discussion.

Education

Arizona EarthVision

`http://earthvision.asu.edu/`

Utilizing communications methods such as CU-SeeMe video conferencing and audio transmissions, this site provides high school students with an infusion of environmental education. An e-mail discussion list is also available. Many guest speakers have their speeches broadcast from here.

Ask An Earth Scientist

`http://www.soest.hawaii.edu/GG/ASK/askanerd.html`

The Department of Geology and Geophysics at the University of Hawaii generously provides this question answering service. If you have a question about geochemistry, the environment, pollution, or other earth-related subjects, the faculty will do their best to provide you with an answer.

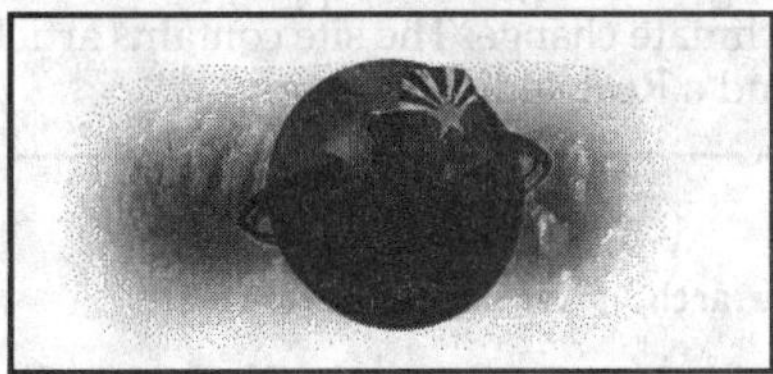

Community Environmental Action Web

`http://www.commpages.com/globe/`

The main focus of this site is ACTION! This site will help you fight ignorance and evaluate choices, the first two steps toward taking action. It also posts experiences of those who have taken action in order for all likeminded individuals to share and benefit from, as well as offer advice.

Connecting With Nature

`http://www.pacificrim.net/~nature/`

The University of Global Education presents Project Natureconnect, a project which has as its goal the reconnection of humans with nature. Take advantage of PNC's books, e-mail courses, workshops, and mailing list to help gain back personal and global sanity.

The Earth System Science Community Home Page

http://www.circles.org/

When learning Earth Science, students need resources that are not always readily available in the classroom. Enter the ESSC. Their goal is to provide students and teachers with advanced scientific resources via the WWW which will enable them to quickly and easily begin learning about the Earth system.

EE Link

http://nceet.snre.umich.edu/

Focuses on spreading information and ideas that help educators and students to explore the environment together. Contains classroom resources and activities, educational contacts, reference material, and more.

Environmental Information Center

http://www.eic.org/

The EIC serves as a "war room" for public environmental education in the areas of protecting America's endangered species and ecosystems, protecting drinking water supplies, and reacting to global climate change. The site contains articles, links, and a RealAudio program.

FICUS

http://www.arch.usf.edu/ficus/default.htm

The Florida Internet Center for Understanding Sustainability seeks to provide a forum for the exchange of information about Florida's ecosystem, biodiversity, water, and exotic species.

The GLOBE Program

http://www.globe.gov/

Global Learning and Observations to Benefit the Environment is a group of students, teachers, and scientists who work together to learn more about our Earth. GLOBE students, with the help of their teachers, gather scientific data at their schools and pass it along to other students via the Internet. Scientists analyze the data and share their findings. The result is a better understanding of the Earth system.

GREENGUIDE—How to Trim Your Office Waste

http://esp.pnl.gov:2080/esp/greenguide/appa.html

This page contains practical guidelines for making your office a more efficient, waste-free organization. You'll learn how electronic publishing, use of recycled materials, and efficient purchasing can reduce waste. (And you might even save some money to boot!)

Handbook for a Better Future

http://www.mit.edu:8001/people/howes/environ.html

Developed as a guide to show what individuals can do to make the future better. Divided into two parts, "Situation" and "Solutions," the handbook contains articles by top scientists and authors. Also included is a suggested reading list for background environmental education.

Institute for Earth Education

http://slnet.com/cip/iee/default.htm

Dedicated to creating educational experiences that instill good feelings for the natural world, lessen our impact on our planet, and develop personal relationships with the earth and its systems. Many educational products are available, including books, pamphlets, and more.

Okefenokee Joe's Natural Education Center

http://www.gravity783.com/joe1.html

Visit Joe's "Critter Center" and learn about the residents of the Okefenokee swamp, a 700 square mile area that is one of the last remaining places where natural balance exists. Also visit the "Natural Garden" to learn more about Okefenokee's plant life.

Plastic Bag Information Clearinghouse

http://www.plasticbag.com/

This site provides information that will prepare you for the next time you hear "Paper or plastic?" In addition, an environmental IQ test, free lesson plans available for teachers, and a section just for kids is available.

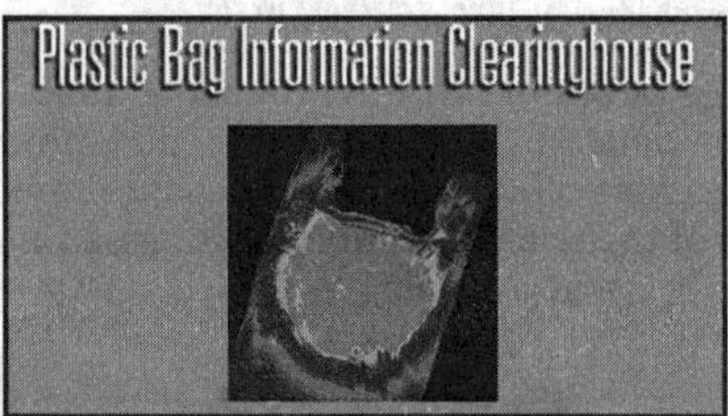

Texas Environmental Center

http://www.tec.org/

Access to environmental resources concerning water quality resources, documentaries, the Texas Environmental Almanac, GreenBeat!, and other environmental Internet resources.

World Transformation

http://newciv.org/worldtrans/

Is a page dedicated to helping people change their lifestyle in an attempt to become more harmonious with the Earth. Includes sections such as Positive Vibrations, New Civilization, Spiritual Evolution, and more.

Pollution

The Air That Kills Us

http://www.ottawa.net/~pugglers/air5.htm

This page was written by Scott Lewko, a 15-year-old Canadian who is aware of the dangers of air pollution. Scott documents what the major sources of air pollution are and offers solutions so we can all breath a little bit easier.

Breath Taking

http://www.nrdc.org/trbreath/tableGu.html

Did you know that an estimated 64,000 people will die this year as a direct result of air pollution? This site documents the number of mortalities per state, with some interesting figures detailing pollutant concentration in 239 metropolitan areas.

Burning Issues/Clean Air Revival

http://www.webcom.com/~bi/

Learn about the hazards of wood burning. This site should be of particular interest to anyone who owns and uses a fireplace. Learn the contents of wood smoke and the effects of just one person burning wood.

Ecocide in the U.S.S.R.

http://westy.jtwn.k12.pa.us/~mjr/ecocide.html

Chernobyl was only one of many economic travesties in the former Soviet Union. This site contains information about the environmental horrors at Chernobyl, Chelyabinsk, Petropavlovsk, and more. Interestingly, this site shows how the USSR brought about its own demise by disregarding its environmental obligations.

The Economics of Industrial Pollution Home Page

http://www.worldbank.org/html/prdei/ipps/home.html

In an effort to cut down on industrial pollution on a global scale, PRDEI has conducted several studies on the effectiveness of regulatory policies. Find out which polices work, which don't, and why. This site also houses an industrial pollution FAQ.

EPIC Home Page

http://146.138.5.107/EPIC.htm

This page is the Department of Energy's Pollution Prevention Information Clearinghouse. The site was developed as a medium for the exchange of pollution prevention information between various levels of government, academic institutions, and the general public.

Friends of the Earth Local Groups

http://www.foe.co.uk/lcd/index.html

Friends of the Earth is a network of environmental activists consisting of over 250 local groups in England, Wales, and Northern Ireland. To find the local group nearest to you, check out their Web page.

Georgia Pollution Prevention Assistance Division

http://www.state.ga.us/Departments/DNR/P2AD/

This site, maintained by the Georgia Department of Natural Resources, provides access to issues of its newsletter, From The Source, and also has a staff of online engineers and scientists available to answer pollution questions submitted by users.

Geothermal Energy

http://solstice.crest.org/renewables/geothermal/grc/index.html

As we all become more environmentally aware, we search for ways to eliminate pollution. One way suggested to reduce air pollution is by utilizing renewable heat energy from deep in the earth. Browse this page to learn all you ever wanted to know about geothermal energy.

How To Survive Without a Car

http://radawana.cg.tuwien.ac.at/~martinpi/nocar.html

You've seen it in foreign countries—streets filled with bicycles and not a car in sight. Some people feel that living without a car is a great way to cut down on air pollution. This is a practical guide on how to successfully manage without an auto in the U.S.

Impact of Lead-Contaminated Soil on Public Health

http://atsdr1.atsdr.cdc.gov:8080/cxlead.html

Lead pollution is a very serious danger to public health, and can lead to anything from increased hypertension to death. Learn what you can do to protect yourself in this very thorough paper published by the U.S. Department of Health and Human Services.

National Pollution Prevention Center for Higher Education

http://www.snre.umich.edu/nppc/

The NPPC's goal is to educate students about pollution prevention. To this end, they develop educational materials that can be used by university faculty to increase their students' prevention awareness. They also offer internships, professional training, and conferences.

Natural History Book Service

http://www.nhbs.co.uk/

This book ordering service is designed to take care of all the environmental book needs of individuals and organizations alike. They have over 25,000 titles online, including books, CD-ROMs, and other materials. Everything can be ordered via e-mail for convenience.

Pollution

http://www.mb.doe.ca/ENGLISH/POLLUTION/

This page published by Environment Canada gives pollution data and research information, promotes strategies for pollution prevention, and provides the full text of many anti-pollution acts passed in Canada. It is also available in French.

Preservation

The Air & Waste Management Association

http://www.awma.org/

The AWMA's purpose is "to enhance environmental knowledge and provide quality information on which to base environmental decisions." At their home site, one can find information on becoming a member and a calendar of events that includes annual meetings and workshops. Potential environmental scholars can find a list of schools that offer advanced degrees in Environmental Science here.

Arctic National Wildlife Refuge

http://www.igc.apc.org/refuge/

Dedicated to keeping the ANWR from becoming an oilfield wasteland. Learn about the refuge, alternatives to development in the area, and, most importantly, what you can do to help keep "America's Serengeti" from becoming just another oilfield.

Australian Environment Online

http://www.erin.gof.au/

These pages contain information on air, land, and water conservation. You can find out here what you can personally do to learn more about our environment, help preserve endangered species, and save energy. This site also provides an extensive library service, allowing you to access the Environment Librarians Network and many key environmental publications.

Natural Food Samples

http://villagenet.com/vnf

Obtain free samples of national brand nutritional supplements, as well as information on how to order at the "absolute lowest prices."

Earthwise Travels

http://www.teleport.com/~earthwyz/

Provides resources for travelers who want to be socially responsible. Explains why socially responsible travel is important, and what can be done to reverse the effects of negative tourism trends.

Environmental Defense Fund

http://www.edf.org

The group that formed in 1967 to fight the use of DDT is still going and is over 300,000 strong. They need your help in addressing what they feel are the nine most critical environmental issues of the '90s. Check out their site to find out what those are and what you can do.

Fragile Legacy

http://www.npsc.nbs.gov/resource/distr/others/sdrare/
sdrare.htm

The endangered, threatened, and rare animals of South Dakota. The site contains pictures, maps, and descriptions of these endangered birds, fish, insects, reptiles, and mammals. Information is also provided for what you should do if you happen to see one of the animals on this list.

Green Cross International

http://greencross.unige.ch/greencross/gcimain.html

Initiated at the 1992 Rio Summit and headed by Mikhail Gorbachev, the organization works to achieve a sustainable balance between development and environment. Learn about the group's current projects and find out where your national chapter is.

Greenpeace USA

http://www.greenpeace.org/~usa/

As Chief Seattle said in 1854, "The Earth does not belong to us; we belong to the Earth...We did not weave the web of life; we are merely a strand in it. Whatever we do to the web, we do to ourselves." Here you can find out what Greenpeace is all about and get yourself involved in saving our planet.

Headwaters Forest

http://www.igc.apc.org/headwaters/

Headwaters forest is the last unprotected ancient redwood forest on Earth and is about to be cut down by loggers. Get background information on the forest and learn what you can do to help prevent its demise. Includes a list of influential people you can write to for help.

International Greens

http://www.dru.nl/maatschappij/politiek/groenen/
intlhome.htm

Read about the developments of green political parties worldwide from 1994–1996, and what the agendas are for the remainder of 1996–1998. Also gives overviews of all green political parties worldwide, sorted by continent.

U.S. Environmental Protection Agency

http://www.epa.gov/

At the EPA home page, you can access documents such as official EPA press releases, the EPA Journal and more. All EPA programs are documented online, from "Acid Rain" to "Wetlands." Through this page you can send your comments directly to the EPA, as well as apply for employment with them.

Welcome to Sherwood

http://www.sherwoodinitiative.co.uk/

Sherwood Forest, once the great woodland hideout of the famed Robin Hood, is becoming a wasteland. Learn about the Sherwood Initiative and what it's doing to preserve this famous wood.

Whale and Dolphin Conservation Society

http://www.glen.co.uk/wdcs

The WDCS "campaigns against those countries and people who continue to kill whales and dolphins for profit." At their home page you can find information about how to protect whales and dolphins from foes such as commercial whalers and tuna fishermen.

The Whale Museum's Orca Adoption Program

http://www.pacificrim.net/~bydesign/adopt.html

What better way to "save the whales" than by adopting one? By adopting Ralph, Saratoga, Missy, Princess Angeline, Deadhead, Raven, or any of the number of orcas that swim the waters of Puget Sound and southern British Columbia, you'll be supporting orca research and education.

Products & Services

Anatomy

http://www.aveda.com/products/anatomy/anatomy.html

Anatomy is a company that produces clothing with minimal environmental impact. In their production, they utilize recycled materials, botanical dyes, plant material as fabric, and don't use any hazardous processing. In addition to being environmentally safe, their clothing line is surprisingly trendy.

Black-Gold Oil Conditioning Systems

http://www.ozarksonline.com/blackgold/

Black-Gold Enterprises offers companies a means to reclaim their wasted oil, thus cutting down on waste. Oil reclaimation saves the company money and saves our environment from unnecessary pollution.

Buy Green

http://www.buygreen.com/

This site is an excellent resource for learning to buy more "green" items. It maintains a list of companies that have developed guidelines and standards for green products, and a list of green products.

Earth Folk Catalog

http://www.gravity783.com/jpro.html

Here you can purchase products from naturalist artists such as Doug Elliot, James Billie, and Okefenokee Joe. Products include videos, cassettes, T-shirts, and more.

Earth Shirts

http://www.mind.net/darnell/

Earth Shirts is a cottage company from the woods of Southern Oregon that offers ecosafe T-shirts, biodegradable cleanup cloths, coffee mugs, and an incredible meat-free burger mix.

Eco-Heads

http://www.eco-heads.com/

Lovers of baseball caps and the environment rejoice! Eco-Heads provides a complete line of caps produced entirely from organic cotton and wool. Caps are also available with environmental logos from organizations such as Greenpeace and The Wilderness Society.

Eco-Motion

http://www.halcyon.com/slough/ecomotion

A company that specializes in electric automobiles. The site explains the advantages of owning and operating an electric car, the costs involved, and its practicality. This site also provides many links to "anyone who has anything to do with electric cars."

Eco Store

http://www.pcw100.com/ecostore.htm

Eco Store offers paper products made from 100 percent post-consumer recycled materials and soy-based ink products. Products include letterheads, envelopes, greeting cards, and even a papermaking kit to help turn your junk mail into something useful.

The Electronic Lobbyist for Renewable Energy

http://www.pic.net/~stevie2/pages/cemail.html

At this site you can find out who your congressperson is, check their voting record on renewable energy, and lobby them by sending e-mail in support of wind, biomass, solar, and hydroelectric energy.

Environmental Software Resources

http://www.envirosw.com/software.html

The Environmental Software Resource Guide is a maintained database containing information for over 2,200 environmental software products from over 600 software vendors. Information is provided concerning the programs' major functions and what environmental media they deal with.

Environmentally Sound Products

http://virtumall.com/ESP/ESPmain.html

Here you can purchase all sorts of environmentally safe products such as natural cleaning products, homemade soap, recycled paper products, books, bags, and the must-have for all the environmentally conscious—bumper stickers.

Geotechnical & Geo-environmental Software Directory

http://www.ibmpcug.co.uk/~bedrock/gsd/

Provided as a free resource for all geotechnical and geo-environmental engineers, this directory catalogues over 600 pieces of software dealing mainly with Soil Mechanics, Rock Mechanics, and Geotechnical Engineering. Listings are free for all software suppliers.

Green Bean

http://yourinfo.com/green/bean.html

A source for environment friendly products such as biodegradable toothbrushes, "save the earth" lunch bags, homemade soaps and shampoos, flannel diapers, and more.

GreenDesign

http://www.envirolink.org/greenmarket/greendesign/

A Web page design company that specializes in pages for socially and environmentally responsible organizations. Services include Web site design, photo scanning, Web site promotion, Web hosting, and CGI scripting.

Greenway

http://pages.prodigy.com/CA/palm/behpage1.html

Take the "How Green are You?" test, and then increase your score by using Greenway's environmentally sound products. Greenway offers products for home and personal care, as well as tips to help you get your home clean without the use of toxic chemicals.

Hemp Baby

http://www.transport.com:80/~hempbaby/catalogue.html

Hemp Baby provides a full line of baby clothing, both for Spring/Summer and Fall/Winter. There is a twist, however—their entire line of clothing is made entirely from hemp! Products include baseball caps, overalls, and winter jackets.

Hugg-A-Planet

http://www.dreamn.com/hugg-a-planet.html

Selected as one of the top ten environmentally friendly products in the country, Hugg-A-Planet is a cotton pillowball that looks like the planet earth. It is available with or without political boundaries and in sizes up to two feet. As the Hugg-A-Planet folks say, "It's hard to hurt something you've hugged."

Jade Mountain

http://www.indra.com/jade-mtn/contents.html

Jade Mountain is an environment-friendly company that dates back to 1972. Their 112-page catalog contains over 4,000 products including energy efficient lighting, air purification devices, plans for electric transportation, cotton shower curtains, and much, much more.

Mother Nature's General Store

http://www.mothernature.com/

A supplier of environmentally sound products, the General Store has items for sale in the areas of appliances, diet products, bath and dental supplies, groceries, herbs, pet supplies, vitamins, books, and more.

Real Goods

http://www.realgoods.com

Real Goods provides tools to promote a sustainable living environment, emphasizing independent living and energy self-sufficiency. Those interested in solar powered housing, electric automobiles, and renewable energy will find this site particularly appealing.

Smokeless Cooking Products

http://www.ecomall.com/class/bbq.htm

Those aware of the harmful by-products of charcoal and wood burning will cherish being able to cook using only the power of the sun. With these smokeless grills, not only will you be sparing our environment, you'll also never burn your hot dogs again.

The Video Project

http://www.videoproject.org/videoproject/

An abundance of videos about the environment. Videos are available concerning all aspects of the environment, from endangered species to sustainable development, water, and wildlife.

ZAP Power Systems

http://www.sonic.net/zap/

Zero Air Pollution (ZAP) Power Systems promotes the use of electric vehicles as a cleaner means of transportation. Their line is a collection of electric powered bicycles for use by young and old alike. They also sell a patented power system that can be installed on an existing bicycle.

Publications

The Atlantic Monthly Election Connection: Environment

http://www.theatlantic.com/atlantic/election/connection/environ/environ.htm

This environmental page of *The Atlantic Monthly*, a publication "Devoted to Politics, Society, the Arts, and Culture since 1857" contains many well written articles about our environment.

Conscious Choice

http://www.consciouschoice.com/

The *Journal of Ecology & Natural Living*. This bimonthly publication of the American Midwest focuses on environmental issues and natural alternatives in health care, food, and nutrition. Regular departments include News of the Earth, Legislative Action, The Holistic M.D., Eco Surf, and Veggie Links, as well as book and movie reviews.

CNN—Environment News Main Page

http://www.cnn.com/EARTH/index.html

In addition to being a news superchannel on cable television, CNN also maintains a large WWW presence. Tune in to their environment page to keep abreast of the latest breaking environmental news as it happens.

Duke Environment Magazine

http://www.env.duke.edu/Duke-Env/magazine.html

Published twice yearly by Duke University, this magazine contains articles devoted to valuing nature, ecology, wetlands, recycling, and more.

The Dying Sea

http://www3.nando.net/sacbee/dyingsea/

The Sea of Cortez, one of the great natural wonders of the world, is being destroyed. This is a touching series that gives pertinent information about the destruction with photos.

E Online

http://www.emagazine.com/

E/The Environmental Magazine also has an online version which provides valuable environmental insights. Those who are interested in leading a "green" life will enjoy the articles that E provides. Also available is Ask E, where one can submit environmental questions to be answered by the knowledgeable staff of E.

Earth First! Journal

http://www.envirolink.org/orgs/ef/

Are you a radical ecologist? Do you believe in "monkeywrenching" and "ecotage?" If so, you'll likely enjoy this collection of journals that are intentionally provocative, controversial, and fun. Incidentally, the *Earth First! Journal* is published eight times a year, once on each Pagan holiday.

The Earth Times Home Page

http://www.igc.apc.org/earthtimes/

Earth Times is an environmental newspaper published twice a month. Bill Clinton, Al Gore, Jimmy Carter, George Bush, and many other world leaders have been known to grace the opinion pages here.

You can find out how to subscribe to the print edition, or browse recent issues online.

EcoLink

http://www.envirolink.org/EcoLink/new.html

The current issue of this journal hosted by the Envirolink Network is dedicated to articles about nonindiginous species. Previous issues of the journal devote their pages to Tropical Rainforests and Landscape Ecology. Also available is a photo page which contains all of the photos from all articles of the current issue collected on one page.

Electronic Green Journal

http://drseuss.lib.uidaho.edu:70/docs/egj.html

The *Journal* is an electronic publication with new issues being made available on an irregular basis by the University of Idaho Library. Currently five issues are available, each with a wealth of articles and reviews on the subjects of assessment, conservation, development, disposal, education, hazards, pollution, resources, technology, and treatment.

Environmental Ethics Journal

http://www.cep.unt.edu/enethics.html

This site plays home to a vast collection of articles that concentrate on the philosophical side of environmental issues. Through this site you can access *The Whole Earth Review*, *Green Earth Observer*, and *The Bear Essential*.

Environmental News Network

http://www.enn.com/

The ENN see themselves as "your one stop on the Internet for timely news and information on the environment." This may well be true. Featured here are listings of companies who offer environmental products and services, a calendar of upcoming events and workshops, an environmental newsletter, and much, much more.

Forty Tips to Go Green

http://www.ncb.gov.sg/jkj/env/greentips.html

On Earth Day 1992, this flyer was distributed by the Jalan Hijau, which means "Go Green" in Malay. It consists of 40 very valuable tips to living a more eco-conscious life at home, while shopping, on the road, and at work.

Grassroots Youth Magazine

http://www.envirolink.org/greenmarket/grassroots/youth/index.html

Selected articles from *Grassroots Youth Magazine*, a publication dedicated to providing kids with environmental information. The articles are written by kids and are intended to be read by kids.

GreenBeat!

http://www.tec.org/greenbeat/index.html

An Internet magazine published monthly by the Texas Environmental Center. Issues are available back to November 1995 and are devoted to Drought, Air Quality, Earth Day, Pathways to Involvement, Wastewater, Bioregionalism, Green Building, and Water Quality respectively.

GREENLines

http://www.defenders.org/gline-h.html

GREENLines is a one-page environmental newssheet published each and every day. This site is perfect for those who want a quick update on relevant environmental happenings but don't have a lot of time to read in-depth articles.

Greenpeace Magazines & Newsletters

http://www.alternatives.com/envgmags.htm

A collection of Greenpeace publications—including *Greenpeace Magazine*, *Greenpeace Action*, *Greenlink*, *Greenpeace Examiner*, and *Greenpeace Business*.

Natural Areas Journal

http://www.vmedia.com/naj/

The *Journal*, published by the Natural Areas Association, is a communication medium for those involved in preservation, protection, and management of natural areas. Naturalists can find articles which focus on natural parks and preserves, rare and endangered species, and land preservation, as well as book reviews and a calendar of forthcoming conferences and workshops.

The Online Better World Magazine

http://www.betterworld.com/index.htm

An electronic magazine that offers feature articles on living a "greener" life. The magazine also features editorials, opinions, book reviews, and interactive discussions.

Our Environment—Online

http://maui.net/~jstark/ournvmag.html

This issue, number four, deals primarily with energy facts, technology, and conservation. The first three issues are also available, entitled "The Alarming Language of Pollution," "How Hot Is It?" and "Where Have All the Flowers Gone?"

People & the Planet

http://www.oneworld.org/patp/index.html

Provides a means to subscribe to the print version of the magazine or just browse the articles online. Articles have various environmental content. Videos are also available.

Rachel's Environment & Health Weekly

gopher://ftp.std.com:70/11/FTP/world/periodicals/rachel

An extensive collection of articles on the subjects of pesticides, sustainable development, global warming, waste management, and much more.

Ranger Rick

http://www.nwf.org/nwf/lib/rr/index.html

Remember *Ranger Rick*? This children's magazine now has several of its articles published on the net, not to mention an index of topics that goes all the way back to 1968!

Science & The Environment

http://www.cais.net/publish/voyage.htm

This bimonthly magazine contains chapters on Biodiversity & Wildlife, Health, Population, & Agriculture, Marine Ecology, Clean Water, Alternative Energy & Fuels, Climate Change & Atmospheric Studies, Waste Management & Recycling, and Clean Air.

SCOPE Newsletter

http://www.asi.fr/scope/

The Newsletter, published by the Scientific Committee on Phosphates in Europe is devoted to information concerning phosphates, detergents, sewage treatment, and the environment. The Newsletter contains objective articles containing scientific information on the effects of detergents, phosphate and non-phosphate, on the environment.

Senior Network News

http://www.comet.net/easi/netnews.html

Published by the Environmental Alliance for Senior Involvement, this newsletter is directed towards senior citizens who want to leave their grandchildren with a healthy Earth. It provides information on environmental issues, model programs, and success stories.

Suncoast Wildlife/Ecology

http://www.flsun.com/wild_eco.htm

A collection of articles dealing with a variety of "critters" in Florida's Suncoast, such as dolphins, jewfish, and sea turtles. Also discussed are coral reefs, native plants, and anything else relevant to the Suncoast environment.

Viva La Tortuga!

http://www.earthisland.org/ei/strp/strpindx.html

Viva La Tortuga! is the newsletter of the Sea Turtle Restoration Project of Earth Island Institute. Inside you can find information on sea turtle activism, including where to buy turtle-safe shrimp.

The WWW Virtual Library—Environment

http://ecosys.drdr.virginia.edu/Environment.html

A directory of many environmental articles based on the subjects of Biodiversity & Ecology, Earth Sciences, Energy, Environmental Law, Forestry, Landscape Architecture, Oceanography, and Sustainable Development.

Recycling

Cleaning Up C.E. Cole

http://www.enter.net/~tquire/cole.html

The kids of Mr. Yelles and Mr. Kondisko's classes at C.E. Cole intermediate school are concerned about their environment. They started several recycling projects, including this recycling Web page that documents their efforts.

Commonly Recycled Materials

`http://www.best.com/~dillon/recycle/guides/common.html`

Consider this Web page to be Recycling 101. It explains everything you might not have previously understood about recycling, including those cryptic looking recycling markers. The work here is an effort to make recycling a natural part of everyone's everyday life.

The Consumer Recycling Guide: Index to Local Recycling Centers

`http://www.best.com/~dillon/recycle/local/index.html`

So you want to become environmentally conscious and start recycling, but you don't know where to do it? Not a problem once you access this index to find a local recycling center near you. The list is always growing and has listings for all 50 states, as well as select international sites.

GreenDisk

`http://imagelinc.com/greendisk/`

GreenDisk helps reduce the landfill problem by taking obsolete software and recycling it into usable blank floppy diskettes. This process saves tons of plastic from taking up valuable landfill space and provides end users with inexpensive, high-quality diskettes.

GREENGUIDE—Reduce/Reuse/Recycle

`http://esp.pnl.gov:2080/esp/greenguide/appe.html`

The table on this page provides valuable information on how to reduce our consumption, reuse frequently discarded items, and recycle materials that can be reprocessed. It also contains special handling instructions for materials from batteries to wood pallets.

National Oil Recycler's Association

`http://www.webcom.com/~infoserv/customer/nora/welcome.html`

NORA's purpose is to get everyone to properly recycle their used oil, oil filters, antifreeze, and the like. Find out what NORA membership can do for your company.

The Recycle Link

`http://www.recycle.org/`

This page, brought to you by Cyber Recycle, Inc., will both help you find a recycling program in your area and teach you what exactly can or cannot be recycled. You can also find information on manufacturers who utilize recyclables and the products they make.

Recycle Locally

`http://www.umr.edu/~ems/recycle.html`

Did you ever wonder what happens to the materials you recycle once they're out of your hands? The city of Rolla documents its recycling program and tells its citizens exactly where their recycled goods are headed.

Recycler's World

`http://www.sentex.net/recycle/`

The mother of all recycling sites! You will find pages for every possible recyclable material, from automotive parts to wood and plastics. It even has a section for organic and food waste recycling.

Ribbon Shredder

`http://www.versanet.net/giftbox/gb.html`

This freebie is yours when you fill out the Gift Box Corporation guest book. What more can you ask for?

Newsgroups

alt.earth.crisis

alt.earth.system.science

alt.org.earth-first

alt.politics.greens

alt.politics.scorched-earth

alt.save.the.earth

ca.environment

earth.general

own.greenpeace.press

sci.bio.conservation

sci.environment

talk.environment

uk.environment

Listservs

ACTIV-L—Activists Mailing List

University of Missouri-Columbia, Columbia, MO

You can join this group by sending the message "sub ACTIV-L your name" to listserv@mizzou1.missouri.edu

AERE-L—Association of Environmental and Resource Economists

You can join this group by sending the message "sub AERE-L your name" to listserv@lsv.uky.edu

AQUIFER—Pollution and Groundwater Recharge

Tecnopolis CSATA Novus Ortus - Valenzano (BA), Italy

You can join this group by sending the message "sub AQUIFER your name" to listserv%ibacsata.bitnet@listserv.net

CERES-L—Collaborative Environments for Conserving Earth Resources

West Virginia Network for Educational Telecomputing

You can join this group by sending the message "sub CERES-L your name" to listserv@wvnvm.wvnet.edu

CONSLINK—CONSLINK - The Conservation Network

Smithsonian Institution, Washington, DC

You can join this group by sending the message "sub CONSLINK your name" to listserv@sivm.si.edu

CUSEN-L—Canadian Unified Student Environmental Network

Queen's University Computing Services

You can join this group by sending the message "sub CUSEN-L your name" to listserv@qucdn.queensu.ca

ECDM—Environmentally Conscious Design & Mfg List

University of Windsor

You can join this group by sending the message "sub ECDM your name" to listserv@pdomain.uwindsor.ca

ECOLOGIC—EcoLogic Mailing List

Rensselaer Polytechnic Institute, Troy, NY

You can join this group by sending the message "sub ECOLOGIC your name" to `listserv@vm.its.rpi.edu`

ENTREE-L—Environmental Training in Engineering Education

University Center of Information services (UCI), Nijmegen, The Netherlands

You can join this group by sending the message "sub ENTREE-L your name" to `listserv@nic.surfnet.nl`

ENVINF-L—List for Environmental Information

University Center of Information services (UCI), Nijmegen, The Netherlands

You can join this group by sending the message "sub ENVINF-L your name" to `listserv@nic.surfnet.nl`

ENVIRON—Miami University Environmental Information

Miami University, Oxford, OH

You can join this group by sending the message "sub ENVIRON your name" to `listserv@miamiu.muohio.edu`

ENVST-L—Environmental Studies Discussion List

Brown University, Providence, RI

You can join this group by sending the message "sub ENVST-L your name" to `listserv@brownvm.brown.edu`

GREENGRP—Inst. for the Environment

The George Washington University Computer Center, Washington DC

You can join this group by sending the message "sub GREENGRP your name" to `listserv@gwuvm.gwu.edu`

COASTNET—Coastal Management Conference

You can get info on this group by sending the message "info coastnet your name" to `listserv@uriacc.uri.edu`

CUSN-L—Canadian Unified Student Environmental Network

You can get info on this group by sending the message "info Cusn-l your name" to `listserv@qucdn.queensu.ca`

GROUNDWATER—GROUNDWATER

To subscribe to GROUNDWATER send e-mail to: `majordomo@ias.champlain.edu` In the body of the e-mail type the command: subscribe GROUNDWATER

H-ASEH—American Society for Environmental History

You can join this group by sending the message "sub H-ASEH your name" to `listserv@h-net.msu.edu`

ISEA-L—International Students for Environmental Action

University Center of Information services (UCI), Nijmegen, The Netherlands

You can join this group by sending the message "sub ISEA-L your name" to `listserv@nic.surfnet.nl`

ONE-L—Organization and the Natural Environment

Clarkson University Schuler Resouces Center

You can join this group by sending the message "sub ONE-L your name" to `listserv@clvm.clarkson.edu`

PS085—PS085-GLOBAL ECOLOGY

University of Missouri-St. Louis

You can join this group by sending the message "sub PS085 your name" to `listserv@umslvma.umsl.edu`

QEN-L—Queen's Environmental Network

Queen's University Computing Services

You can join this group by sending the message "sub QEN-L your name" to
`listserv@qucdn.queensu.ca`

SEAUGA—Students for Environmental Awareness

The University of Georgia, Athens, GA

You can join this group by sending the message "sub SEAUGA your name" to
`listserv@uga.cc.uga.edu`

Adoption: Growing Families

Adoption Resources

In addition to the Web sites listed in this section, you can also contact the following organizations for information about adoption:

Adoptive Families of America
333 Highway 100 W
Minneapolis, MN 55422
612-535-4829

National Adoption Information Clearinghouse
1400 Eye Street, NW
Washington, DC 20005
202-842-1919

Orphan Voyage
2141 Road 2300
Cedaredge, CO 81413
303-856-3937

Yesterday's Children
P.O. Box 1554
Evanston, IL 60204
312-545-6900

Adoption Advocates: Adoption Policy Resource Center

`http://www.fpsol.com/adoption/advocates.html`

Provides federal and state legislative news and analysis (including statutes and court decisions), adoption assistance (subsidy) information resources, legal resources, and advocacy resources.

Adoption Benefits: Employers as Partners in Family Building

`http://www.adopting.org/employer.html`

Provides information about company-sponsored adoption benefit plans, including who is eligible for benefits, how company-sponsored benefit plans actually work, covered expenses and when they are paid, the types of adoption the benefit plans cover, adoption leave of absence from the workplace, a list of companies that offer adoption benefits, as well as other adoption assistance programs. If you are considering adopting a child, this is a great place to go for information regarding company-sponsored benefits.

Adoption Resources on the Internet

`http://www.hal.com/users/karen/adoption.html`

Provides numerous links to other sites regarding adoption, including topics such as books and magazines for adults and children, photolistings of children available for adoption (including international adoption), newsgroups, and mailing lists.

Adoption—Where Do I Start?

`http://www.infi.net/adopt/iii1st.html`

Offers information about the process of adoption, including the type of children available for adoption, who is eligible, steps for agency adoption and independent adoption, guide books, and a list of national adoption organizations.

AdoptioNetwork

`http://www.infi.net/adopt/`

Provides information that encompasses the broad scope of adoption, including lists of agencies and photolistings, legal resources, information about international adoptions, FAQs for children about adoption, a walk-through of the adoption home study process, and much more.

Adoptions

`http://ourworld.compuserve.com/homepages/The_Open_Door/homepage.htm`

Site geared toward birthmothers who choose adoption for their unborn child. The Open Door Adoption Agency is a Christian, non-profit organization that provides temporary living and counseling in the placement of a child for adoption. This site also provides information about Eastern European, Chinese, and Latin adoptions.

The Adoptions Connections Project: Women's Journeys

`http://www.sover.net/~adopt/index.html`

Site geared toward women that offers stories of adoptees, birthmothers, and adoptive mothers, provides conference and workshop information, and a free monthly online publication called *The Adoption Connections Newsletter*. Great support site for women touched by adoption.

AIS Exchange List 1996—Community Resources

`http://www.halcyon.com/adoption/04.html`

Offers a list with descriptions of adoption agencies and organizations within the United States. The descriptions include address and phone number information, fees, membership information (when applicable).

The Alliance For Children

`http://www.adoption.com/alliance/`

Provides information about the Ecuador Adoption Program, the Romania Adoption Program, and the China Adoption Program provided by this agency. Also includes a list of criteria for which adoptive parents must qualify.

Christian World Adoption

`http://www.cwa.org/cwa.html`

Site of a nonprofit international child placement agency. In conjunction with local service agencies, place children from other countries, such as Russia, Paraguay, Brazil, and Mexico, in families throughout the United States.

Domestic Infant Adoption Advice

`http://www.openadoption.org/bbetzen/`

Written by Bill Betzen, this site concentrates on providing information about "open adoptions," including information to anyone considering the placement of an infant (including a checklist to use when searching for an agency), recommendations for anyone considering the adoption of an infant, and infant adoption cost questions and issues.

Faces of Adoption—America's Waiting Children

`http://www.adopt.org/adopt/`

Comprehensive site that provides 143 pages of photolistings of children available for adoption, categorized by age and sex. Also includes information on legislation, the adoption process, lists of adoption agencies and organizations, conferences and seminars, and other material pertinent to all aspects of adoption. This is a must visit!

Family Law Center—Adoption

`http://www.courttv.com/legalhelp/family/1084.html`

Part of CourtTV, this site provides a straightforward explanation of the adoption process, private and agency adoptions, out-of-state and foreign adoptions, and choosing adoption for your child.

Growing Families Inc.

`http://www.thesphere.com/~gfi/gfi2.html`

Site of adoption licensed agency and counseling services. Provides comprehensive material about the adoption process, types of adoption, procedures, international and domestic adoption, counseling, and fees.

Having Your Child Adopted

`http://www.webcom.com/~nfediac/BPPageT1.html`

Site for birthparents and adoptive parents. Provides a list of basic rights of birthmothers, information about open adoption, personal stories, and letters from adoptive parents waiting to adopt.

Help the Children

`http://www.adopting.org/htc.html`

Site of a private, not-for-profit, adoptive-parent-led corporation, specializing in the preparation and support of families and single persons wishing to adopt from the United States and several countries around the world. Includes licensing information, fee structure, and general information about international adoption and policies. This site also has a comprehensive photolisting of children available for adoption that includes health and development information, the circumstances under which children came into custody, and recommendations for placement.

Holt International Children's Services

`http://www.thesphere.com/~holtbear/index.html`

Provides services to reunite children with birth families, or places them with adoptive families in the country of their birth or another country.

Independent Adoption Center Home Page

`http://www.webcom.com/~nfediac/welcome.html`

Provides information and support for birthparents and adoptive parents, information and resources for professionals in the adoption field, and links to other Web sites that provide information about adoption.

National Adoption Organizations

`http://www.infi.net/adopt/nao.html`

Lists branches of the federal government concerned with adoption, national organizations concerned with adoption, and other groups with specialized interest in adoption, such as advocacy, education, and financial support. Also includes links for international, national, and regional adoption exchanges, and photo listings.

Precious in HIS Sight—Adoption Information on the Internet

`http://www.adoption.com/others.html`

Provides photolistings of children from the former Soviet Union and China. The site of Association of

American Nonprofit Adoption Agencies, Inc. is an Arkansas corporation that does not place children for adoption, but rather contracts with licensed agencies to coordinate adoptions from the former Soviet Union and in some cases China. Although the individual listings do not provide as much health and development information as other sites, you can request video tapes and further information from AANAA, Inc. This site also provides a list of adoption agencies associated with AANAA, Inc. You can find other information related to adoption, such as a list of books, country-specific adoption and general adoption information, and resources for special-need children.

Roots and Wings Adoption Magazine

http://www.webcom.com/~webweave/rw.html

Quarterly magazine that contains articles that cover the broad scope of adoption. Included are personal stories, specialized columns, and advice for adoptees, adoptive parents, and birthparents.

The Texas Adoption Resource Exchange

http://www.dhs.state.tx.us./tdprs/adoption/tare.html

This site is a first in that it is the first state to put its waiting-child photolisting on the Internet. Provides pictures and descriptions of children in custody of the state who are available for adoption. The listings also include information about the children, such as age, personality traits, needs, and whether the child is physically, emotionally, mentally, or developmentally challenged.

Voices of Adoption

http://www.best.com/~savage/adoption.html

Adoptee's and birthparent's stories, adoption issues, and search stories are a few of the offerings of this site. Also includes reader responses and links to other adoption sites.

Voices of Adoption

Adoption: Searching for a Birthfamily

Adoptee & Genealogy Page from Carrie's Crazy Quilt!

http://www.mtjeff.com/~bodenst/page3.html

Offers a wealth of information regarding searching for a birthparent or relinquished child, from infor-mation you will need to get started on your search (and how that info will help) to links to other adoption/search sites. If you are searching, you will appreciate the numerous links provided.

Adoptees and Birthparents

http://www.instantech.com/users/martin/adoptees.htm

Kathy Martin offers search assistance at no charge (donations suggested however). This page clearly states the type of help you can expect from Kathy when searching for an adoptee or birthparent.

Adoption on the Usenet

http://www.webcom.com/kmc/adoption/faqs.html

This comprehensive site contains tons of important information for those searching for birthparents, children, or siblings. You can find booklists (with reviews), legislative information, newsgroups (alt.adoption), FAQs regarding the alt.adoption newsgroup, and a list of support groups, broken down by country and state. This site also contains links to must-read information if you are considering the use of a searcher in your quest.

BirthQuest

http://www.access.digex.net

Offers an online international searchable database dedicated to searching adoptees, birth parents, adoptive parents, and siblings. Enables you to register in the database as well as search for others in the database. To register for the database, you must provide your e-mail address.

Jeff Hartung's Adoptees Resources Home Page

http://psy.ucsd.edu/~jhartung/adoptees.html

Provides up-to-date information about adoption-related events and legislation, lists of books related to searching for children and birthparents, other links, newsletters, and newsgroups. This is a must-visit for anyone searching.

Treasure Maps

http://www.firstct.com/fv/tmapmenu.html

Great site with many tools for searching and tracking your family history. Useful in searching for birthfamily. This site contains helpful tools such as suggestions for "getting past the stone wall," a tutorial on the U.S. Federal Census, research outlines, and collections of compiled and original family records.

Divorce & Custody

10 Questions About Child Custody

http://kpix.com/xtra/keane/QA-01Feb-162305-L.html

Informative page by KPIX Legal Analyst, Peter Keane. The 10 questions are those that are frequently asked by parents when trying to determine custody issues. The 10 questions cover topics such as the definition of custody, mediation and arbitration, the best interest of the child, and modification of current custody agreements.

CCADE Web

http://forensic.nova.edu/

Site where professionals interested in child custody and dependency evaluation can meet and discuss topics of mutual interest. Provides online and other custody and dependency resources (legal, psychological, general, and professional), mailing lists for those involved in custody evaluations, conference announcements, and the capability to search this site for specific information.

C.H.I.L.D: Children Hurt in Legal Decisions

http://www.cei.net/~canichol/child.html

Site of a non-profit organization that is dedicated to monitoring courts and decisions so that the best interest of the child is the primary concern of decision makers. Offers case scenarios, e-mail, objectives, and general information regarding "the best interest of the child."

Child Custody: Building Agreements that Work

http://gnn.com/gnn/bus/nolo/cust/

Great page and links for working through custody issues. Offers suggestions, plans, and strategies for working in the best interest of the child. Topics include taking stock of your situation, negotiating visitation and financing, mediation and arbitration, nontraditional families, state and federal laws affecting child custody, and worksheets.

Child Custody in the USA

http://www.islandnet.com/~wwlia/us-cus.htm

Incredible site with a wealth of information about the issue of child custody in the United States. Some topics included are types of custody arrangements and how those decisions are made, influences on decision-making, the child's wishes, mediation, and modifiability of custody and access orders.

Child Support Home Page

http://www.acf.dhhs.gov/ACFPrograms/CSE/index.html

Provides helpful information about the child support system, including basic child support program facts, newsletters and announcements, recent policy documents, and opportunity to offer feedback. Be sure to visit the External Information link for information about child support guidelines specific to your state.

Children's Rights Counsel Home Page

http://www.vix.com/crc/aboutcrc.htm

Site of Children's Rights Council (CRC), a national, non-profit, tax exempt, IRS 501(3) children's rights organization based in Washington, D.C.. Provides information about children's rights, legislation regarding children's rights, and data on the state and national levels.

CourtTV Divorce

http://www.courttv.com/legalhelp/survival/divorce/index.html

Offers straightforward information about the divorce process (including common grounds for divorce and no-fault divorce), child custody and visitation, child support and how to file for it, and suggestions to consider when choosing an attorney. The information presented at this site is clear and easy to understand. Excellent starting point for anyone fact-gathering.

Custody and Access

http://129.128.19.117/docs/custody.html

Site geared toward Canadian law regarding child visitation and access. List of FAQs and answers that address topics such as court orders, modification of agreements, custodial interference, and child support. Difficult to read because of the format and colors, but provides useful information.

Divorce

http://www.maricopa.gov/supcrt/ssc/sscinfo/divorce/divorce.html

Ongoing site that provides court information to the public. The information available is general but in easy-to-understand language and covers legal terminology used in divorce, child custody and child support issues, court papers, and property and debt.

Divorce Care Home Page

http://www.divorcecare.com/

Site of the Divorce Care support group. Provides a list of Divorce Care support groups in your area, resources for self help, information on children and divorce, financial survival, and more.

Divorce Helpline Home Page

http://www.divorcehelp.com/

Provides a "Short Divorce Course" that contains valuable information and outlines the process of divorce. Offers articles that relate to divorce, a self-help resource directory, and worksheets that help you get organized and focused when preparing for separation or divorce. Also provides links to other helpful sites.

Divorce Helpline: The Legal Divorce vs. The Real Divorce

http://206.214.38.18/SC/C11Real.html

Part of Divorce Helpline, this site provides a clear but gentle explanation about the differences between "legal" and the emotional, spiritual, and practical divorce.

Divorce Law Home Page

http://www.agate.net/~corbeau/lyons.html#toc

Great site that contains links to family law in a state-by-state format, information about child custody and support, women's resources, men's resources, newsgroups and mailing lists, articles on family law and divorce, and more.

Divorce Online

http://www.divorce-online.com/

An electronic resource for people involved in, or facing the prospect of, divorce. Offers free articles and information on divorce-related topics and contains a Professional Referral section to help locate professional assistance near you. Also contains a FAQs section that applies to divorce.

The Divorce Page: Child Support and Custody

http://www.primenet.com/~dean/csp_cust.html

Great site that contains news on child support issues, ways to remain involved with your kids when

divorcing your partner, and links to child support laws in a state-by-state format.

The Divorce Page: Parenting and Children

http://www.primenet.com/~dean/parent.html

Site that provides links to sites related to children and divorce, single parenting, support groups for kids of divorce, and a list of other available resources regarding children and divorce.

Divorce Roadmap: Help Around the Legal System

http://www.divorcehelp.com/../SC/C12Map.html

Walks you through the complicated route of the law and divorce. Includes definitions for those great legalese terms, diagrams of the divorce process, and tips on how to get what you want from divorce. This is a great place for straightforward information. Be sure to click on the "beat the system" link for more valuable info.

Family Law Advisor Home Page

http://www.divorcenet.com/welcome.html

Contains FAQs to the most common questions pertaining to divorce and family law, an online newsletter and index, a state-by-state resource center, an interactive bulletin board, international and national laws pertaining to child abduction along with a link to the U.S. State Department, and more. Also contains helpful information regarding child custody and child support.

Family Law Advisor Message Board

http://www.divorcenet.com/messages/msgs.html

Bulletin board on which you can post questions and answers pertaining to family law. Updated daily. Good place for support and sharing experiences as well as sharing knowledge.

Family Law Links

http://www.value.net/~markwelch/famlaw.htm

Comprehensive list of links to other sites that cover family law, divorce, child custody and support issues, self-help for those experiencing separation or divorce, long-distance parenting, and more. Great site to visit when you're not sure what to search for in the family law arena.

Kids' Turn

http://members.aol.com/kidsturn/

Good site for kids and parents going through separation or divorce. Geared toward the child's best interest, this site, offers suggestions for guiding kids through the "divorce zone," workshop information, list of suggested readings, and links to other organizations.

Law Offices of Keith M. Carter: Child Custody and Visitation

http://sdguide.com/law/child.html

Excellent description and explanation of the issues of child custody and visitation in a question/answer format. The questions are realistic and the answers are well thought out. If you have children and are considering separation or divorce, this is a good place to get general information.

Legal dot Net

http://www.legal.net/

Offers information about divorce and separation (somewhat specific to the state of California), data about child support, and family law news. Also provides columns and articles related to divorce, a directory of legal services, and an attorney registry.

Nolo's Fast Facts: Custody and Visitation

http://bin.gnn.com/gnn/bus/nolo/nffchild.html

Excellent page by the Editors of Nolo Press that addresses frequent questions asked about custody and visitation. Areas covered are court issues regarding custody and visitation, physical versus legal custody, custodial interference, child support, mediation, and modification of custody agreements. A great resource.

Domestic Violence, Child Abuse, & Missing Children

Child Abuse Resources

In addition to the Web sites in this section, you can also contact the following organizations for information about child abuse:

American Association for Protecting Children
c/o American Humane Association
9725 East Hampton Avenue
Denver, CO 80231
800-227-5242

Clearinghouse on Child Abuse and Neglect Information

Department of Health and Human Services
P.O. Box 1182
Washington, DC 20013
202-251-5157

National Committee for Prevention of Child Abuse
332 South Michigan Avenue
Chicago, Il 60064
312-663-3520

National Network of Youth Advisory Boards
P.O. Box 402036
Ocean View Bridge
Miami Beach, FL 33140
305-532-2607

Parents Anonymous
6733 South Sepulveda
Los Angeles, CA 90046
213-410-9732

Amber Hagerman's Missing Children Home Page

http://www.sliceoflife.com/Official/Missing/amber.html

Dedicated to the memory of Amber Hagerman, this site provides information about runaway prevention, parental child stealing prevention, child neglect, child protection agencies, emotional abuse, abduction prevention and awareness, and links to missing children Web sites.

America's Lost Children Television Network

http://alctv.com/

Site of a non-profit corporation based in Missouri whose purpose is to provide the general public with information about America's lost children via television stations and cable companies on a full time basis. Site provides satellite broadcast info, a section on helping law enforcement, and forms that enable you to list a missing child.

Blain Nelson's Abuse Pages

http://marie.az.com/%7Eblainn/dv/index.html

Great site that provides personal experience with abuse (the giving and receiving end), questions to help you determine whether you are an abuser or have been abused, information about the "cycle of abuse," and links to other sites that pertain to this subject.

Child Abuse Prevention Network

http://child.cornell.edu/

This site is dedicated to enhancing Internet resources

for the prevention of child abuse and neglect. Offers a list of state-level programs on the prevention of child abuse, electronic newsletter that keeps you up-to-date on the developments of this site, and links to other helpful sites.

Child Abuse: Statistics, Research, and Resources

http://www.jimhopper.com/abstats.html#caut

Site offers wealth of information, including statistics, methodological issues, sexual abuse of girls, sexual abuse of boys, substantiated cases, issue of memory, and additional resources.

Child CyberSEARCH: English Home Page

http://www.childcybersearch.org/ccscengl.htm

Canadian site that provides a database of missing children, a list of Canada's missing children agencies, a library that contains helpful tips, pamphlets, special interest articles about missing children, child-care, and parenting. Mostly geared toward Canadians, but some information is universal.

Child Quest International

http://www.childquest.org/

Site dedicated to the recovery of missing, abused, and exploited children. Offers safety tips to keep your kids safe, lists of other resources that can answer questions you may have, and links to other important sites dedicated to the safety of children.

Child Search: National Missing Children's Center

http://rampages.onramp.net/~child/

Provides support services for those whose children are missing, such as crisis counseling, search assistance, photo distribution assistance. Also provides photo-listings of missing children, child ID kits, and safety tips for parents.

Missing Children Photos

Child Sexual Abuse

http://www.commnet.edu/QVCTC/student/LindaCain/sexabuse.html#horror

Supportive site that provides personal stories as well as legal info and statistics on child abuse, bibliographic reference of films, videos, documentaries and presentations, list of journals and articles that pertain to child abuse, and directories listing agencies for services related to child sexual abuse. This is a great site that has tons of great information to offer.

Child Sexual Abuse

http://www.cs.utk.edu/~bartley/sacc/childAbuse.html

Not a lot of bells and whistles at this sight, but really good, must-know information about child sexual abuse. Offers sections on symptoms, feelings the child (and the parent) may have, protecting kids, and listening to children.

Child Sexual Abuse or Exploitation: What to Do

http://www.discribe.ca/childfind/victim.hte

Page that provides instructions for family and school if a child indicates that he or she has been abused. Offers dos and don'ts and specific steps to take in the event that something like this should take place. Geared toward a loving approach to children.

Children's House Home Page

http://childhouse.uio.no/

Site that is an interactive resource center—a meeting place for the exchange of information that serves the well being of children. Offers workshops and training, information resources on the well being of children, information about early childhood, and a spot about children's rights.

Children's Safety Network Home Page

http://www.edc.org/HHD/csn/

Contains publications and resources produced by CSN and other EDC injury prevention projects that include full-text in HTML format that can be viewed, downloaded, and printed directly from this site.

CyberPages International Inc: Missing Children

http://www.cyberpages.com/MISSING.HTM

Provides a list of missing children. This page is free of charge and enables you to add to the list. Also provides a list of other sites on the Intenet that provide a similar service.

Domestic Violence Page

http://www.iquest.net/~gtemp/famvi.htm

Site devoted to fighting all forms of family violence. Great info here, such as facts about domestic violence, readers stories, suggestions for where to get help, suggested reading list, and links to other sites that pertain to domestic violence.

Family Law Center—Child Abuse and Neglect

http://www.courttv.com/legalhelp/family/1086.html

Part of courtTV, this site provides information in a straightforward fashion about child abuse and neglect, what to do if you suspect abuse, child representation in abuse situations, and more. Good place to start when investigating this topic.

How to Identify Child Abuse

http://www.hdmdigital.com/vpucf/identify.html

Detailed descriptions of symptoms to look for in a child that is being abused (emotionally, physically, sexually) and description of symptoms displayed by abusers. Difficult to read because of the nature, but imperative information to have if you suspect child abuse.

The Institute for the Prevention of Child Abuse

http://www.interlog.com/~ipca/ipca.html

Canadian site of a child abuse education and information center. Provides information, such as handbooks for recreational leaders, conference, and publications, to professionals, community agencies, and the public.

Kathy's Resources on Parenting, Domestic Violence, Abuse, Trauma, and Disassociation

http://www.mcs.net/~kathyw/home.html

Offers tons of information about the different aspects of violence, including information for parents; data and info on trauma and disassociation, abuse, rape, and domestic violence; and a Net ratings guide.

Kevin Collins Foundation for Missing Children

http://www.northcoast.com/kevin_collins/collins.html

Site of volunteer organization that is dedicated to providing immediate response and experienced guidance for the families of stranger abducted children. Also provides an online directory of missing children, literature about stranger abductions, and links to other sites pertaining to missing children.

The KEYEYE Making Kids Safe Page

http://www.keyeye.com/

Site dedicated to teaching personal safety to children. Offers videotapes that help teach your child how to recognize ploys of abductors, safety tips for parents and children, and links to other safety pages.

KidsPeace: The National Center for Kids in Crisis

http://good.freedom.net/kidspeace/

Loaded with graphics (be prepared to wait), this site provides data from the Salk Research Center, a quiz parenting quiz, and parenting tips that include child abuse prevention, parenting standards, information about kids in crisis and how to help, and how to talk with your preteen.

Mental Health Net: Responding to Sexual Child Abuse

http://www.cmhcsys.com/factsfam/rspdabus.htm

Site that contains suggestions for adults who suspect child abuse or are approached by a child indicating that he or she has been abused. Suggestions are specific to your reaction to the child and what you should do after the discussion with the child.

Minnesota Higher Education Center Against Violence & Abuse

http://www.umn.edu/mincava/newstuff.htm

Site of an electronic clearinghouse via the World Wide Web for issues that pertain to domestic violence. Offers information about domestic violence in the forms of research papers and book suggestions, support for professionals, school safety info, list of treatment guidelines, gallery of children's art, poetry and prose by survivors, and links to help resources and other sites.

National Center for Missing and Exploited Children

http://www.missingkids.org/

Site of a private, non-profit organization working in cooperation with the U.S. Department of Justice dedicated to the search for missing children and pursuit of child protection. Offers training for those involved in child protection and recovery, search assistance to those looking for missing children, and provides publications and resources pertinent to the safety of children. Also provides access to a missing children database.

National Center on Child Abuse and Neglect

http://www.acf.dhhs.gov/ACFPrograms/NCCAN/index.html

Provides facts about the Child Abuse and Neglect program, statistics on child abuse and neglect, a national clearinghouse on child abuse and neglect information, and access to the National Data Archive on Child Abuse And Neglect.

OUDPS: Kids Safety on the Internet

http://www.uoknor.edu/oupd/kidsafe/start.htm

Provides an array of topics on which you would want to educate your child, such as Internet safety, drugs and alcohol, home safety, stranger danger, and so on. This is a site that you can share with your children!

PeaceDove

http://www.wam.umd.edu/~dove/pd2.html

Provides links to missing children sites. The other sites aren't necessarily huge, but the info contained at those sites are equally as important.

Safe-T-Child Online

http://yellodyno.safe-t-child.com/

Site that is an electronic resource for the prevention of lost, missing, abducted, or abused children. Offers tips and suggestions for educating your kids about abuse and strangers in a non-fearful, entertainment-driven way (including books and songs), online newsletters, information about corporate sponsorships, and I.D. card kits.

SAVE: Survivors and Victims Empowered

http://www.goshen.net/SAVE/

Dedicated to stopping the physical, emotional, and sexual assault on children. Provides a Child Protection Guide, a list of speakers on child abuse, and access to a Survivors & Victims Resource Database that contains over 350 resources in the U.S. and Canada.

Survivor Organizations and Agencies

http://www.csbsju.edu/isti/03txt.html

Provides list of organizations and agencies in the United States for victims and survivors of child abuse and includes addresses, phone numbers, and fax numbers.

Parenting

365 TV-Free Activities

http://family.starwave.com/funstuff/activity/tvtoc.html

Great site that really does offer numerous suggestions of things to do with your kids that do NOT involve the television. Activities are listed by category, such as Arts and Crafts, Indoor/Outdoor Play, Tire 'em Out (one of my favorites!), and Older Kids Play, just to name a few. Excellent place to visit!

365 TV-FREE ACTIVITIES
YOU CAN DO WITH YOUR CHILD

All About Kids Online

http://www2.aak.com/aak/

Way cool site that is about families and parenting. Features great articles about hot topics, such as choosing prenatal care, education in the United States, Attention Deficit Disorder, and so on. Also offers a "virtual community," calendar of family events, and a parent's forum.

D.O.S.A. Parenting Home Page

http://www.mbnet.mb.ca/~ahawkins/

Site that provides all kinds of information for parents, such as tips for taming your child (great perspective!), and links to recommended sites for parents.

Empowering People Home Page

http://www.twinsmagazine.com/

Site contains a lot of good info for interacting with others, but the section for parents and teachers is great! Offers tips and articles from avoiding barriers between parents and children to changing behavior with positive discipline.

family.com

http://www.family.com/

Super cool site that offers information on the following topics: activities, computing, education, travel, entertainment, and finance sections are just for starters. These sections are then broken down into sections of the United States. This site makes topics easy to find and provides great articles and information. This is a must-visit!

Family Planet Home Page

http://family.starwave.com/

Web magazine for families with kids 12 and under. Provides family news, expert advice for FAQs, Web site reviews, movie reviews, community opportunities with other parents, and the capability to send and receive responses to what's offered at this site. Good stuff here!

Family Resiliency

http://www.glue.umd.edu/~fraz/

Provides tools and suggestions for ways to enrich and fortify the family's ability to cultivate strengths to positively meet the challenges of life. Some of the topics covered in this site are educating parents, child care, public policy, and communities. Also provides links to other parenting sites.

KidsHealth.org

http://kidshealth.org/

Provides info about the health of kids, ranging from child behavior and development, to nutrition, general health, surgery, and immunizations. Offers a section for children that contains health FAQs for kids, games, and more. Also contains many tips and fun facts to know and tell. Lots of good info at this site!

The Mommy Times

http://www.mommytimes.com/

Site written and maintained by moms for moms (dedicated to preserving the sanity of all moms). Offers support network on the Web for moms, articles about motherhood, suggestions for all types of working mothers (those inside and outside of the home), and opportunities to share your experience with others. Great site for new moms, providing you can find the time!

Moms-at-Home Page

http://iquest.com/~jsm/moms/

Way cool site that is geared toward parents that forego outside employment and stay at home with kids, although not exclusive for stay-at-home parents. Offers an e-mail pen pal page for kids, at-home moms and dads, and grandparents; parenting tips and resources that include Internet access and family health and safety; books and magazine lists; online medical help; links to other parenting sites; and more! This site has just about everything you could ask for in a parenting/family site—and what it doesn't have, you will find a link! Great site.

Nashville Parent

http://www.nashvilleparent.com/

Great online, monthly magazine that has feature articles (April's issue included "Educating Your Children About HIV and AIDS" and "Preparing Kids for the Dentist," just to name a couple), a section that addresses parenting matters, and other links for parents and kids. Be patient, however; the graphics are great, but seem to take forever to load.

National Child Care Information Center Home Page

http://ericps.ed.uiuc.edu/nccic/nccichome.html

Offers information about child care and federal programs for child care, tips for looking for and finding child care, a list of organizations serving child care and related professions, and links to other child care-related sites on the Net.

Our Kids

http://wonder.mit.edu/ok/

Web site dedicated to parents who raise kids with special needs. Provides a reading list for kids, nutrition information, as well as links to other parenting resources. Provides links and support for specific challenges, such as ADD, Chromosome X, and Down Syndrome, and access to national databases, such as GCRC Rare Disorder Network Database and NORD (National Organization for Rare Diseases).

Parent Soup

http://www.parentsoup.com/cgi-bin/genobject/pmp000

Offers a wealth of information about raising kids of all ages. Some features include the "Chill Out" room, which offers suggestions to parents for relaxation, explaining money and chores (and that connection) to children, Internet access for kids, as well as bulletin boards to talk with other parents.

Parent's Place.Com

`http://www.parentsplace.com/`

Home-based site that offers info on midwifery, nutrition, education for your kids, adolescent and teen info, and single parenting. Also has daily and weekly features, such as violence in the family and sibling rivalry. Also offers online shopping where merchandise is geared towards the parenting market. Cool site!

Parenting New Mexico

`http://www.whc.net/dsrelp/pnm/index.html`

Good site that offers articles and online resources. Also provides calendar of events, but unless you actually live in New Mexico, the calendar probably won't be of much use. The articles, however, address daily issues that parents face, such as home video reviews, info on Montessori, and children facing death and dying. Also has online resources to other sites.

ParentingMatters

`http://lifematters.com/parentn.html`

Great site that features a parent support interactive forum, articles on respectful parenting, four goals of misbehavior, handling kid's aggression, bridging the generation gap, and more! This site even contains a grandparenting column!

Parents and Children Together Online

`http://www.indiana.edu/~eric_rec/fl/pcto/menu.html`

An online magazine for parents and children whose focus is family literacy. Offers opportunities for you and your children to write and share family stories; features articles geared toward grades preschool through 3, 4 through 6, and older; and book reviews. Also offers interactive story telling—very cool! This is a great site for family interaction!

Positive Parenting Home Page

`http://www.fishnet.net/~pparents/`

Features parenting tips, such as "9 things to do instead of spanking," "How to handle sibling rivalry," and "Saying, I love you." Also provides articles on parenting and online resources for parents and professionals.

Twins Magazine Home Page

`http://www.twinsmagazine.com/`

Site that offers information on twin pregnancy, childhood, and adulthood. Features monthly articles and back articles about issues that parents and twins face.

The Wonderwise Parent Home Page

`http://www.ksu.edu/wwparent/wondhome.htm`

Site interested in teaching parent/child interaction. Features articles on responsive discipline (how do I, as a parent, react?), an encyclopedia of parenting, and humor pages that offer anecdotes and quips.

Newsgroups

alt.adoption

alt.adoption.agency

alt.child-support

alt.missing-kids

alt.parenting.solutions

alt.parenting.spanking

alt.parenting.twins-triplets

alt.support.divorce

alt.support.single-parents

alt.support.step-parents

clari.news.childrn+family

fj.life.children

soc.culture.jewish.parenting

soc.support.depression.family

Listservs

ABLETECH-L—For parents, teachers, and others concerned with disabilities

You can join this group by sending the message "sub ABLETECH-L your name" to
listserv@listserv.okstate.edu

ABUSE-L—Professional Forum for Child Abuse Issues

State University of New York at Buffalo

You can join this group by sending the message "sub ABUSE-L your name" to
listserv@ubvm.cc.buffalo.edu

ABUSE-PARTNERS-L—Support for Partners of Abuse Survivors

You can join this group by sending the message "sub ABUSE-PARTNERS-L your name" to
listserv@sjuvm.stjohns.edu

ADOPTEES—List Adoptees/Adoptees Mailing List

St. John's University, Jamaica, NY

You can join this group by sending the message "sub ADOPTEES your name" to
listserv@sjuvm.stjohns.edu

BLINDFAM—SJU List for Families of the Blind

St. John's University, Jamaica, NY

You can join this group by sending the message "sub BLINDFAM your name" to
listserv@sjuvm.stjohns.edu

CARINGPARENTS—How Do Kids Cope with Illness?

You can join this group by sending the message "sub CARINGPARENTS your name" to
listserv@sjuvm.stjohns.edu

CEL-KIDS—Celiac/Coeliac Wheat/ Gluten-Free Children List

St. John's University, Jamaica, NY

You can join this group by sending the message "sub CEL-KIDS your name" to
listserv@sjuvm.stjohns.edu

CO-OCCURRING-DISORDERS—Discuss Co-occurring Mental Health & Substance Abuse Disorders

You can join this group by sending the message "sub CO-OCCURRING-DISORDERS your name" to `listserv@listserv.aol.com`

CPPARENT—Discussion for Parents of Children with Cerebral Palsy

St. John's University, Jamaica, NY

You can join this group by sending the message "sub CPPARENT your name" to `listserv@sjuvm.stjohns.edu`

DADVOCAT—Dads of Children with Disabilities or Special Health+

You can join this group by sending the message "sub DADVOCAT your name" to `listserv@lsv.uky.edu`

FAM-MATH—Family Math

You can join this group by sending the message "sub FAM-MATH your name" to `listserv@uicvm.uic.edu`

FAMCOMM—Marital/Family & Relational Communication

Rensselaer Polytechnic Institute, Troy, NY

You can join this group by sending the message "sub FAMCOMM your name" to `listserv@vm.its.rpi.edu`

FAMILY-L—Academic Family Medicine Discussion

You can join this group by sending the message "sub FAMILY-L your name" to `listserv@lsv.uky.edu`

FATHERS—US Department of HHS: Fatherhood and Social Service Programs

You can join this group by sending the message "sub FATHERS your name" to `listserv@ulist.nih.gov`

FREE-L—Fathers' Rights and Equality Exchange

You can join this group by sending the message "sub FREE-L your name" to `listserv@listserv.iupui.edu`

GERINET—Geriatric Health Care Discussion Group

You can join this group by sending the message "sub GERINET your name" to `listserv@ubvm.cc.buffalo.edu`

HEALING—Healing: Survivors of Intimate Abuse

You can join this group by sending the message "sub HEALING your name" to `listserv@sjuvm.stjohns.edu`

MFTC-L—MFTC-L Marriage and Family Therapy Counseling Discussion

You can join this group by sending the message "sub MFTC-L your name" to `listserv@sjuvm.stjohns.edu`

MOMSONLINE—Moms Online Main Mailing List

You can join this group by sending the message "sub MOMSONLINE your name" to `listserv@listserv.aol.com`

NFWNET-L—Nebraska Family Wellness Network

You can join this group by sending the message "sub NFWNET-L your name" to `listserv@unlvm.unl.edu`

OPEN-ADOPTION—Open Adoption List (formerly BRTHPRNT)

You can join this group by sending the message "sub OPEN-ADOPTION your name" to `listserv@home.ease.lsoft.com`

PARENTING-L—Discussion of Parenting

University of Illinois, Urbana, IL

You can join this group by sending the message "sub PARENTING-L your name" to `listserv@postoffice.cso.uiuc.edu`

PARENTS—Announcements, Information and Discussion Related to Parenting

You can join this group by sending the message "sub PARENTS your name" to `listserv%uriacc.bitnet@listserv.net`

PSNEWS—Parent Soup Newsletter

You can join this group by sending the message "sub PSNEWS your name" to `listserv@listserv.aol.com`

REGAYN—Drug Abuse Prevention

You can join this group by sending the message "sub REGAYN your name" to `listserv@lsv.uky.edu`

S-YOUTH—Stolen Youth Mental Health, Abuse Problems of Youth

You can join this group by sending the message "sub S-YOUTH your name" to `listserv@sjuvm.stjohns.edu`

SP-SUBSTANCE-ABUSE-LIST—Substance Abuse Information

You can join this group by sending the message "sub SP-SUBSTANCE-ABUSE-LIST your name" to `listserv@listserv.acsu.buffalo.edu`

TCS—Taking Children Seriously: Non-coercive Parenting/Education

You can join this group by sending the message "sub TCS your name" to `listserv@listserv.aol.com`

UIUCPARENT-L—U of I Parents Advocacy Group

University of Illinois, Urbana, IL

You can join this group by sending the message "sub UIUCPARENT-L your name" to `listserv@postoffice.cso.uiuc.edu`

VIOLEN-L—Violence Discussion Forum

University of Sao Paulo, Sao Paulo, SP

You can join this group by sending the message "sub VIOLEN-L your name" to `listserv%bruspvm.bitnet@listserv.net`

WITCHHNT—Is There a Child Sex Abuse Witchhunt?

You can join this group by sending the message "sub WITCHHNT your name" to `listserv@mitvma.mit.edu`

WS238-L—Women, Work, and Family in the 20th Century

State University of New York at Buffalo

You can join this group by sending the message "sub WS238-L your name" to `listserv@ubvm.cc.buffalo.edu`

Beverages

Acats Internet Bar Pages

http://www.epact.se/acats/

Consider this site your online bartender. Contains an exhaustive index of mixed drink recipes available in a searchable database by drink name or type of liquor. Learn the tools of the trade and check out postings for employment opportunities. Visit Jim's Saloon for some humorous barkeep stories.

Beamish & Crawford Brewery

http://www.aardvark.ie/beamish/

Brewing Beamish Genuine Irish Stout in Cork for more than 200 years. Contains a movie file about the brewery.

Brew Hawaii Magazine

http://aloha-mall.com/brew/

Discusses beer, wine, whiskey, sake, brewing, and cigars in Hawaii, the Pacific, and Asia. Features a guide to beer etiquette.

Bud On-Line

http://www.budweiser.com/

A colorful, innovative site from Budweiser, the King of Beers. Features information on the history of beer and how Budweiser is improving the quality of beer. Order Budweiser paraphernalia, check out the latest Budweiser sponsored/endorsed events and download the Budweiser screen saver.

Cafe MAM

http://mmink.cts.com/mmink/dossiers/cafemam.html

An environmentally conscious and socially responsible Mayan cooperative with a wide variety of fine coffee roasts and blends and other Cafe MAM paraphernalia available for online ordering.

Capulin Coffee

http://emall.com/ashcreek/

Offers a traditionally dried 100% natural jungle coffee grown on Mexico's Pacific coast. Proceeds from the sale of Capulin benefit a conservation project, which grows and harvests these beans.

Cat's Meow 3: Internet Beer Recipe Database

http://alpha.rollanet.org/cm3/recs/

The quintessential site for home brewers and micro-breweries alike. Hundreds of recipes ranging from traditional lagers to herb and spiced beers. Recipes dating from the 1500s to the present day are classified and well-organized in an exhaustive index. The site also contains detailed information for the first-time brewer, as well as links for beer recipe formulating software for most operating systems and platforms. If you consider yourself a beer aficionado, be sure to bookmark this site—you'll be returning frequently.

Celebration Vineyards

http://www.deltanet.com/intersphere/cv

Offers custom-labeled champagne and sparkling cider table favors for weddings and other special occasions.

Coca-Cola

http://www.coca-cola.com

Provides information about the most renowned soft drink company. Buy, sell, and trade Coca-Cola paraphernalia online. Check out Coca-Cola–sponsored sporting events. See how Coca-Cola is doing in the business world before you decide to buy some stock in soft drinks.

Cocktail.Com

http://www.cocktail.com/

Another cyberbar beautifully presented. Test your drink knowledge with a quick quiz, brush up on some cocktail alchemy, see what drinks are in season, jump to other mixology sites, and stimulate your brain with Dr. Pseudocryptogram's list of literary interests.

Cyber Grape and Grain

http://www.ari.net/webworks/finewine

Houses The Wine Specialist, an international mail-order and retail Washington, D.C., supplier of fine wines, malt whiskeys, and other premium liquors. Contains a monthly newsletter, wine and malt liquor-related links, and special offers. Lets you order premium liquors directly from the site.

Edinburgh Malt Whisky Tour

http://www.dcs.ed.ac.uk/home/jhb/whisky/

The definitive guide to malt whisky. Provides information about the history and manufacturing of malt whisky in Scotland. Contains an image map to Scotland's malt distilleries. Also categorizes and rates various whisky brands and distilleries.

Eric's Simple Fermented Beverages

http://www.mcp.com/people/ericg/ferment.html

Contains detailed information about making ciders, meads, and fruit wines out of ingredients from the grocery store.

Grapevine

http://www.terra.net/grapevine

An Internet e-zine that provides reviews and information on international wines and vineyards.

Heineken

http://www.Heineken.nl/

Provides history of the Heineken brewery and offers a virtual tour. Send customized e-mail postcards and participate in Heineken's online game to win prizes. As a service, Heineken provides a running clock displayed in all time zones—worth a bookmark just for this fact.

Internet Wine Rack

http://www.shelby.com/pub/wine/

Offers a wide variety in both selection and price of wine, beer, and other alcoholic beverages. Suggestions are offered for the connoisseur, as well as the adventurous amateur. Order by mail or telephone.

Jack Daniel's

http://www.infi.net/jackdaniels/index.html

Take a virtual tour of Lynchburg, Tennessee or the Jack Daniel's distillery itself, and enjoy its 125-year-old heritage. Pour yourself a drink (via sound files) while you download the Jack Daniel's screen saver. Sample recipes incorporating this fine whiskey as one of the ingredients. According to search engine surveys, this site is worth a visit.

Jolt Cola

http://www.joltcola.com/

Arguably one of the best sites on the Web now. With the advantage of having a computer-oriented core audience, Jolt presents a Java-powered site featuring information on the beverage of choice of hackers and college students. Test your vital signs on the Jolt-o-meter. See the impact Jolt has had on the entertainment industry. Get a glimpse of Jolt culture. A good site for pure entertainment value.

Mother City Espresso

http://www.seas.upenn.edu/~cpage/mothercity.html

Provides a guide to the culture of Seattle coffee houses with reviews of the best and worst bean roasters and coffee house environments. Contains addresses and telephone numbers to order from with a 20% discount.

Moxie Collector's Page

http://www.xensei.com/users/iraseski/

Learn all there is to know about the first soft drink, which was endorsed by Ted Williams and remains a staple in most New England refrigerators. The only commercial product to become synonymous with a personal attribute, Moxie even played a role in history. Download rare movie footage of an alien drinking Moxie.

Napa Valley Virtual Visit

http://www.freerun.com/cgi-bin/home.o

Explore various Napa Valley wineries or purchase wines and wine management software. This site provides sightseeing, dining, and catering ideas, as well as current events. If you're looking to make a "real" visit, check out the information on accommodations. Also contains links to other Valley sites.

Newcastle Brown Home Page

http://www.communicata.co.uk/broonale/

Provides information about "The One and Only" Nut Brown Ale developed in 1927 at Newcastle Breweries on the Tyne. Offers a brewery tour, heritage of the product, and a downloadable screen saver.

Over the Coffee

http://www.cappuccino.com/

Lets you express your personal opinions about a good cup of joe, read the opinions of your fellow coffee lovers, or access other coffee-related sites on the Internet. You know, coffee talk! No big whoop.

Perrier

http://www.perrier.com/

Nature's original beverage refresher in bottled form. Perrier's site provites information about the company and offers a restaurant guide to New York, Los Angeles, Chicago, Washington, D.C., and New Orleans. View Perrier's past, present, and future advertising artwork. Enter the bottle art contest or order some Perrier apparel and paraphernalia.

Real Beer Page

http://realbeer.com/rbp/rbp.html

The quintessential site for beer enthusiasts provides a microbrewery tour, tips about brewing, brewspapers and brew magazines, drinking games, and fellow beer drinkers' audio submissions on the Burp Me page.

Redhook Brewery

http://www.redhook.com/

Provides information on the Washington state-based microbrewery that has begun to make its existence known nation-wide for its diversity and excellence. Take a virtual tour of the brewery. Evaluate the stock value of this up-and-coming brewery.

Rosswog Farm Distillery

http://medianet.nbnet.nb.ca/medianet/atlantic/rosswog/rosswog.htm

Provides information on the traditional schnapps, as well as the blueberry and maple liqueurs, made by the Rosswogs. Also offers some schnapps recipes.

S.P.S. Beer Stuff

http://www.beerstuff.com/index.htm

A visually impressive site presenting an online catalog of homebrewing equipment and supplies. The catalog includes over 100 varieties of malt extracts from around the world. Also includes some brewing recipes from visitors. *The* site for homebrewers.

SmartWine Online

http://smartwine.com/

Claiming to be the largest wine-related site on the Web, SmartWine Online provides links to a variety of sites devoted to wine. Peruse some wine tasting notes before you imbibe, select the best wine to complement your meal, glean some health facts about wine, and find out all about the wine industry, all with the click of your mouse.

Snapple

http://www.snapple.com/

Made from the best stuff on earth, Snapple's site offers information on its current and future flavored beverages—Vote for your favorite! Enter the Snapple-a-day sweepstakes and win free Snapple products.

Stoli Central

http://www.stoli.com/

Stolichnaya, synonymous with vodka, provides a well-designed site for those seeking information about premium liquor of the world via Carillon importers. Visit England for gin, Mexico for tequila, and, of course, Russia for vodka. Download Stoli's artistic ads. Online ordering is available for self-indulgement or generosity to a friend.

Virtual Pub

http://lager.geo.brown.edu:8080/virtual-pub/

An award-winning Web site where beer aficionados exchange information on their favorite brews. Also contains an eclectic collection of information on beer with a healthy representation of links to other beer-related sites.

National Computer Security Association

http://www.ncsa.com/

Download "The Catalog"—a free guide to published material on firewalls and other aspects of Internet security.

Virtual Vineyards

http://www.virtualvin.com/vvdata/620506318/main.html

Your one-stop wine shop provides online shopping for regional California wines by varietals, wineries, and vineyards. Also provides a section that pairs food with the appropriate wine accompaniment. Be sure to check out What's New at Virtual Vineyards.

Wines on the Internet

http://www.wines.com/

A provocative resource for wine-related topics. Provides links to online wineries and vineyards, features a "virtual" tasting room, online wine shopping, and other notes of interest for the connoisseur and novice wine drinker alike. Also details upcoming events for wine enthusiasts.

World Wide Web Winemaking Home Page

http://www.uidaho.edu/~stevep/wine/winehome.html

Provides recipes and information on making your own wine. Also provides links to suppliers, other recipe pages, downloadable software to make your own wine labels, and other wine-related sites.

zima.com

http://www.zima.com/

Contains most of what there is to know about Zima Clearmalt. Most impressive is the collection of bar/restaurant reviews categorized geographically—a useful tool when out and about.

Companies

Anytime Snacks

http://www.thehost.com/anytimesnacks/

A snack delivery service, perfect as a gift or for yourself. Anytime Snacks delivers an assortment of individually wrapped cookies and name brand candies via UPS within 7–10 days of your order and can include a personalized greeting.

Aunt Ida's Southern Kitchen

http://www.net-link.net/auntidas/

A collection of delicious treats, including gourmet homemade cookies, cinnamon rolls, flavored pecans, pies, cakes, and special gifts. All of these items can be ordered by fax or directly over the Internet.

Ben & Jerry's

http://www.benjerry.com/

Visit the globally conscious ice cream company that reinvented the way we think about ice cream. Find out what flavors you're missing out on from the complete Flavor List. Find out what flavors you're missing in the Flavor Graveyard. Also, learn about the history of the company and the directions it's taking. Stock prices available online soon. Be sure to check out Ben & Jerry's new line of sorbets.

Buckeye Beans & Herbs, Inc.

http://www.buckeyeranch.com/

Black Bean Bart and the Pinto Kid team up to bring you a collection of the finest beans, spices, and pasta around. Dry ingredients are sent straight to your home, where you add ingredients of your own to come up with a flavorful masterpiece.

CalWine Gourmet Food Shop

http://www.calwine.com/foodshop.html

At CalWine, you can choose from the very best the Napa Valley has to offer. Browse wines by winery or variety, peruse gourmet selections such as chocolate wine sauces and grape seed oil, and then order by fax or toll-free number.

Campbell Soup Company

http://www.campbellsoups.com/Welcome1.html

Find out what makes soup "mmm, mmm" good. Plan a menu, or search Campbell's impressive recipe database for some new eating experiences. Evaluate Campbell's stock worth for investment considerations, and learn about the Campbell family of companies.

Caroline Gold Cheese

http://www.frontiercomm.net/~fkostlev/gold.html

Caroline, Wisconsin is home to Caroline Kountry Gold Cheese, Mehlberg's Maple Syrup, Jim's Blue Ribbon Sausage, and Vern's Cheese Spreads. Order any combination to create a custom gift basket, or choose from a variety of predesigned baskets.

ChefsOnline

http://www.i1.com/chefs/

Provides a selection of gourmet "dinners for four," which are frozen and delivered to your door. You can then prepare them in minutes with a conventional oven, microwave, or just a pot of boiling water and a good pair of scissors.

Chile Today Hot Tamale

http://eMall.com/chile/

Offers Chile, Hot Sauce, and Salsa and Chip of the Month Clubs, as well as dried chiles and exotic sauces from around the world. Also provides a list of spicy recipes to try on your own.

Constant Creation

http://fox.nstn.ca/~ccgc/

An online ordering company specializing in condiments. Dress up ordinary dishes and desserts with the truly unique and flavorful condiments, sauces, and glazes Constant Creation has to offer. From raspberry ketchup to the award-winning Maple Cream Coulis.

Dean & Deluca

http://www.ishops.com/dd/

Here you can order a variety of kitchen and gourmet products from this New York landmark. Products include copper and stainless steel kitchenware, caviar, jams, coffees & teas, and gifts.

Fax Foods

http://www.faxfoods.com/

They won't satisfy the rumbling in your stomach, but these food replicas from Fax Foods just might do wonders for your advertising, and they'll never go bad on you. Try some today and "beef up" your food displays.

Frito-Lay Main Menu

http://www.fritolay.com/

The junk food aficionado's guide to Frito-Lay products complete with recipes (Fritos Fixin's). Contains downloadable wallpapers of icon Chester Cheetah.

Hacienda Flores Salsa

http://shop-utopia.com/flores_salsa/flores.html

A company specializing in gourmet salsa. Provides a secure online form to order your salsa.

The Highland Trail Company

http://www.highlandtrail.co.uk/highlandtrail/

Offers online shopping of Scottish products, including smoked salmon, smoked venison, malt whiskey, and gifts.

Hot Hot Hot

http://www.hothothot.com/

If you take a liking to food seasoned with hot sauce named Nuclear Hell or Ring of Fire, Hot Hot Hot is the online hot sauce source for you. Over 100 varieties of sauces from around the globe can be searched by various criteria, including heat level, origin, ingredients, or name. Also contains articles from Chile Pepper Magazine.

J.R. Wood, Inc.

http://www.jrwood.com/

A company that deals in fruits, vegetables, purees, juices, and concentrates, as well as specialty items such as baby food. Information can be requested directly from the company, and corporate contacts are provided online.

Krema Nut Company

http://teraform.com/~schapman/krema/

Established in 1898, the Krema Nut Company offers the old fashioned peanut butter that gave the company its reputation, as well as an overwhelming variety nuts and nut butter gift packages available through their online catalog. If you like nuts, this is definitely the place for you.

Linsey Foods

http://www.linsey.com/

Find out about Linsey's collection of make-your-own-salad kits and dessert solutions, which are available at your local grocery. The site also includes recipes for desserts and salads that can be used in conjunction with their kits.

Lotsa Hotsa Salsas, Hot Sauces and More

http://www.lotsa-hotsa.com/

Gourmet hot sauces, salsas, recipes, and more from Chardonnay Artichoke salsa to Hellfire and Damnation Hot Sauce. Color photos, descriptions, and an online order entry. Also contains links to some of the most popular food-related sites on the Web.

Myer's Gourmet Popcorn

http://www.aus.xanadu.com/GlassWings/arcade/myers/mgp.html

A gift ordering service for the popcorn lover in your life (even if it's yourself). Select from flavors like Cajun, Tutti Frutti, or plain old buttered popcorn. Your gift can be packaged in one of the many decorative tins offered.

Neu Coffee

http://www.iea.com/~neucof

Provides gourmet Arabica coffee and espresso from the world's most renowned coffee producing countries. Also offers a wide variety of specialty foods. Includes bulk order discounts, wholesale, retail, espresso, and office accounts.

North Fork Exchange

http://www.ncia.com/~rbalam/

A smoke house and specialty foods store, they carry a full line of meat and jerky products. Meat products are limited to Washington state, but specialty items can be shipped anywhere. They also sell equipment and supplies for home smokers.

Olympia Bakery and Catering

http://www2.olympiabakery.com/Olympia/

A family owned bakery and deli since 1924. They offer a full line of cakes including wedding cakes, sculpted cakes, and even X-rated cakes. Located in Tampa, FL, they also do catering for events such as weddings.

Ore-Ida Foods, Inc.

http://www.oreida.com/

At Ore-Ida's Web site you can read about their product line, which includes a variety of potato products. Recipes are provided online as well as some interesting facts, like how many tater tots you'd have to place end-to-end to circle the Earth.

Oregon Cupboard

http://amsquare.com/cupboard/index.html

A variety of specialty foods from the artisans of Oregon. Some of the foods featured include jams, pie fillings, honeys, smoked salmon, and coffee syrups. There is also a complimentary recipe exchange maintained at this site.

PizzaHut

http://www.pizzahut.com

Order pizza with your favorite toppings from Pizza Hut's online order form. Consider this an alternative method of faxing in your order.

Pop 'n Stuff, Inc.

http://www.imall.com/stores/popnstuff/

Many flavorful products can be found here, including a number of flavored popcorns, Jelly Belly jelly beans, nuts, pretzels, gift baskets and more. Shipping is available and items can be ordered by phone, mail, or fax.

Queen's Kitchen & Pantry

http://www.pantry.com

Internet retail shopping of unusual and exotic foods and related products and services. Contains links to several commercial food sites.

Saguaro Food Products

http://pavilions.com/Saguaro.htm

A chip lover's delight! Products include chips of all sorts: potato, corn, blue corn, and more. Salsas are also on the menu with a full selection available to be shipped anywhere in the continental U.S.

Scubber's

http://www.scubbers.com/

Scubber's provides high-quality Buffalo wings, sandwiches, and finger foods to their in-store customers, but if you're not lucky enough to live close to them, you can still have their products shipped to you via UPS. Shippable products include baskets, bags of wings, and bottles of sauce.

A Taste of Texas

http://www.dallas.net/~atastetx/

A source for authentic Texas sauces and gifts. You can order online from their collection of sauces, which include an award-winning fat free three-bean salsa. Recipes are provided with every order.

Taste of Texas Market

http://www.cycorp.com/shopping.cgi/tasteoftexas/index.html

A great site for jalapeno lovers and misplaced Texans. A variety of pepper products are available including jalapeno jelly, jalapeno mustard, and Senor Jalapeno's Hot Flash for the more adventurous types.

Truly Special Gourmet Foods

http://www.netline.net/~kathy/special/special.html

Offers a wide variety of specialty foods and condiments and provides an unparalleled opportunity to enjoy the American Dream.

The Virtual Gourmet

http://www.foood.com/

Meets all your specialty food needs. Sink your teeth into fine cheeses, drinks, baked goods, meat, and snacks, as well as linen and utensils to eat them with. Provides info about all kinds of great wine.

Watkins Recipes

http://www.polaris.net:80/user-www/mande/index.html

Provides a well-rounded collection of recipes featuring Watkins spices. Offers links to Watkins order forms and other product-related services.

Confectionaries

Ann Hemyng Candy, Inc.'s Chocolate FACTORY

http://mmink.cts.com/mmink/dossiers/choco.html

Provides a wide selection of nut, cream, fresh fruit, and gift assortment options. Contains a wide variety of personalized chocolates that can be ordered from a secure online order form.

Candy

http://www.cs.cmu.edu/~mjw/recipes/candy/index.html

Provides a small index of candy recipes.

ChocolateTown U.S.A.

http://www.microserve.net/~hershey/welcome.html

Hershey's own tempting Web site, replete with information, recipes, online shopping, and stock reports on the Great American Chocolate Factory.

Food Works by Swiss Connection

http://www.leswiss.com/

Learn about Swiss chocolates and coffee, baking couvertures, gourmet pastry shells, and dessert concepts using products engineered for today's everyday gourmet. The products are offered by some of the best names in the dessert biz.

Godiva Online

http://www.godiva.com/

Presents the online catalog of the world famous Belgian chocolatier. Also contains Godiva chocolate's own batch of death-by-chocolate recipes ranging from simple brownies to Chocolate Espresso Fudge Cake . For entertainment, Godiva offers their own story version of the "Taster's Choice" couple.

I Need My Chocolate!

http://www.qrc.com/~sholubek/choco/start.htm

This is *the* Internet resource for chocolate lovers! Contains several databases of chocolate dessert recipes, links to just about every chocolate-related site on the Internet, and views and experiences by other chocolate lovers.

Culinary Education/Nutrition

Department of Food Science & Nutrition

http://www.fsci.umn.edu/

Provides information on the programs and courses offered by the University of Minnesota. Offers nutritionists tools that calculate your energy needs and analyze the nutritive value of food items.

Dole 5 a Day

http://www.dole5aday.com/

A graphics-rich site devoted to the health and nutrition benefits of fruits and vegetables. A fantastic educational tool for teachers.

Electronic Gourmet Guide (eGG)

http://www.2way.com/food/egg/index.html

A monthly Internet e-zine devoted to food and cooking. Complete with culinary trivia and articles. Also contains links to any food-related Web site you could possibly want.

Professor Geoff Skurray's Food & Nutrition Information

http://hotel.hawkesbury.uws.edu.au/~geoffs/

An informative site providing such information as: adult recommended daily allowances of nutrients, dietary guidelines, athletic dietary concerns, and links to other nutritional sites. A viable bookmark for health-conscious Web surfers.

Food A-Z

B's Cucumber Page

http://www.lpl.arizona.edu/~bcohen/cucumbers/info.html

For those interested in cucumbers and their various uses, this page provides recipes and information about commercial and greenhouse growing of cucumbers. Also included are 20 reasons why cucumbers are at least as good as men.

Bagel Page

http://jaka.ece.uiuc.edu/~scott/bagels/

Recipes and other information about bagels. Also contains links to other bagel-related sites.

BBQ—A Southern Cultural Icon

http://darwin.clas.virginia.edu/~ld9d/bbq.html

A graduate project with an introduction and history of Southern barbecue, a description of the differences between barbecuing regions, and an archive of barbecue menus and recipes. Well written and fully documented with photos and diagrams.

Bovril Shrine

http://medianet.nbnet.nb.ca/medianet/curioso/bovril/bovril.HTM

Dedicated to Bovril, which is essentially liquid beef. Contains anecdotal accounts of experiences with Bovril, information about the health benefits of Bovril, and related information.

Bread

http://www.cs.cmu.edu/~mjw/recipes/bread/bread.html

Provides an index of bread recipes.

Breakfast Cereal Hall of Fame

http://198.3.117.222/

A good deal of information about breakfast cereal. There is a featured "cerealebrity" about which you can view more information. There are also articles on the price of cereal, cereal art, and more.

Broccoli Central

http://ucsu.colorado.edu/~banasn/Home.html

Everything you could possibly want to know about the green vegetable and quite a few things that you didn't. That is, of course, unless you were looking for information on how to cook and eat it, which is nowhere to be found on this page.

Buffalo Chicken Wing Home Page

http://www.moran.com/htmld/bcw/

A page that takes Buffalo wings very seriously. Learn why Buffalo claims them, where they originated, and who makes the best wings. Vote for your favorite wing restaurant, and collect or submit Buffalo wing recipes.

Burrito Page

http://www.infobahn.com/pages/rito.html

A humorous look at a staple Mexican food item. Practices burritology—learn about yourself through the burrito toppings you choose. Contains links to other sites about burritos that enable you to learn about, order, and deconstruct the mystery of the burrito.

Caviar & Caviar, Ltd.

http://virtumall.com/Caviar/home.html

Discover all there is to know about gourmet fish eggs—how to serve them, store them, prepare them, and enjoy them. Also learn about the different varieties of caviar.

Cheeseburger in Paradise

http://www.fdu.com/fdu/cburger.htm

A listing of the best places to find a cheeseburger of world-class caliber. No matter if you're in Chicago or Cairo, there's always a good cheeseburger somewhere.

Posters

http://spso.gsfc.nasa.gov:80/eos_posters/order_form.html

Seven posters are available from the Earth Observing Systems Science site. Word of advice—tell them you're affiliated with a school.

CheeseNet 95

http://www.wgx.com/cheesenet/

The graphics-rich cheese bible of the Web—how to make it, its history, the different variations, a picture gallery, cheese literature, and cheese language. Features a cheese-making demonstration.

Chicken Wing Central

http://ucsu.colorado.edu/~alums/wings.html

Heaven for Buffalo Wing lovers. Recipes for all types of wings from the well-known hot-wings to some lesser known fringe recipes like Thai peanut butter wings. Also links to a wings newsletter.

Cranberry Home Page

http://www.scs.carleton.ca/~palepu/cranberry.html

Contains much information about cranberries: cranberry products, cranberries and the urinary tract, cranberry beer, and even some recipes for making things with cranberries.

Dan's Doner Kebab Registry

http://student.uq.edu.au/~cs315886/Dan/kebab.html

Doner Kebabs, also known as gyros, are considered by some to be the food of the gods. Dan certainly is taken with them and offers reviews of kebab shops from around the world, kebab recipes, and links to other kebab pages.

Dinner Co-op

http://gs216.sp.cs.cmu.edu/dinnercoop/home-page.html

This site offers more than your run-of-the mill food-related site. Over 1,500 links to sites concentrating on recipes, culinary education, restaurant reviews, and online food stores. Well-organized and useful—definitely worth a bookmark!

Food Resource

http://www.orst.edu/food-resource/food.html

A comprehensive index of food-related sites. Choose from a plethora of links to recipe sites, restaurant databases, colorful images of food, sites on culinary education, and anything else even remotely connected with food.

FoodPlex

http://www.gigaplex.com/wow/food/index.htm

Possibly the most entertaining food-related site on the Web, the FoodPlex contains humorous information about food, as well as other trivia such as the distribution of animals in a box of animal crackers. There are also sections on taste-testing dog biscuits, where to find the best ice cream in America, and a guide to enjoying TV dinners. Don't pass this site by!

Official French Fries Page

http://www.select-ware.com/fries/

Fun-filled information about the world's most popular side dish. Besides the normal uses for french fries (eating), find out the legal specifications of french fries, how to make them, learn about their history, and find out about alternative condiments and applications of the world's greatest snack food.

Garlic Page

http://www.broadcast.com/garlic/

Provides information on how to grow garlic, how to prepare garlic, garlic recipes, the different varieties of garlic, and what makes the variations of garlic special. Also explains how you can use garlic to improve your health.

Hot Roast Beef Sandwiches

http://members.aol.com/donwdowney/
HotRoastBeefSandwiches.html

Searches America for the perfect roadside hot roast beef sandwich. Restaurants are critiqued by their roast beef's forkiness, as well as by their choice of bread and side items.

Idaho Potato Expo

http://www.sisna.com/Idaho_Potato_Expo/

Take a virtual tour of the Expo, which is located in the "Potato Capital of the World," Blackfoot, Idaho. Also check out potato recipes and gift items from Idaho.

The Italian Food Market

http://www.italianfood.com/

It's enough to make you want to lick your screen. Everything from ciabatta to tagliatelli to soppresata. Get out the credit card because it's going to be hard not to place an order.

Mmmm... Toast

http://198.83.6.18/studspac/STUDENTS/PGRIFF/toast.htm

Questions about toast? Check out the FAQAT (Frequently Asked Questions About Toast) and find out everything you wanted to know but were afraid to ask. Remember: "Toast... It's good."

National Pork Producer's Council

http://www.nppc.org/

Find out all there is to know about "the other white meat," including industry facts, health statistics, pig facts, and the quintessential pork recipe of the day.

Pasta Home Page

http://www.ilovepasta.org/

Answers to frequently asked questions about pasta, information about the National Pasta Association and their brands, pasta nutritional information, information about various pasta shapes and which sauces to use them with, and several pasta recipes.

Pickle Preservation Society

http://www.ithaca.edu/orgs/pickle/pickle1/pickleweb.html

The place for pickle lovers of all sorts to come together and discuss their gherkins. Find out all sorts of pickle tidbits, including recipes. Also find out about starting your own chapter of the society.

Potato Miscellany

http://www.infi.net/~cksmith/famine/Miscellany.html

Links to a variety of pages that all deal with the potato. Read about new potatoes in Ireland, a better potato, potatoes as dust containment and paint removers, and more.

Ranch Worship Page

http://www.math.grin.edu/~boley/ranch/

Dedicated to enlightening the world about the many values of ranch dressing (sometimes also known as "House"). There is a list of ranch's top 10 uses, and a form for submitting your favorite to be added to the list.

The Raspberry Web Page

http://www.xnet.com/~mego/will/berry.htm

Intended to be the most comprehensive site on raspberries, this page provides raspberry recipes, general raspberry info, raspberry art & photos, and a variety of raspberry links.

Rhubarb Compendium

http://www.clark.net/pub/dan/rhubarb/rhubarb.html

The history and description of rhubarb, how to grow, harvest, store, and use rhubarb, tons of rhubarb recipes, and a rhubarb photo gallery.

Rolling Your Own Sushi

http://www.rain.org/~hutch/sushi.html

Learn the Japanese fine art of preparing raw fish as an edible delicacy. Acquire the basic skills with terminology, equipment, and food supplies, or extend your own knowledge with the several different styles presented with graphics and text.

Snax.Com

http://www.snax.com/

A site catering to those who like crunchy snack foods. Sample the audio files and see if you can guess the snack associated with the crunch. Try your hand at some new chip dips, no matter what your eating habits are. Enter the Snax.Com contest and win a T-shirt. If you have time to be a couch potato, you have time to visit this site.

Spam Page

http://www.rsi.com/spam/

More than you ever wanted to know about Spam, the amazing meat product from Hormel. Includes the Spam story, Spam recipes, brewing with Spam, and Spam haiku.

Strawberry Facts Page

http://vanbc.wimsey.com/~jmott/sbfacts/

An award-winning site containing recipes and everything you ever wanted to know about "the perfect berry."

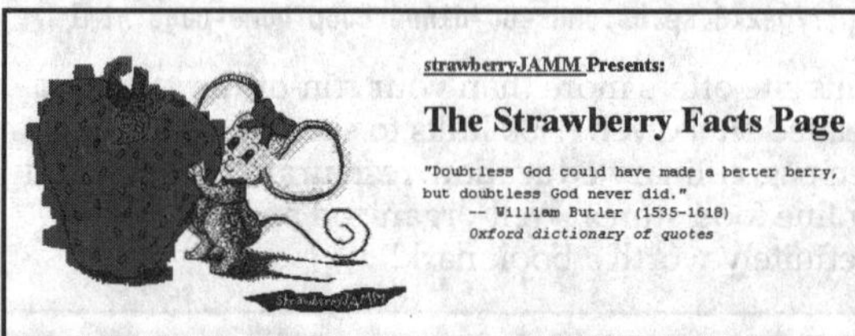

Thai Fruits

http://www.su.ac.th/thailand/fruits/fruits.html

An overview of the many fruits indigenous to Thailand. Learn about mangoes, jackfruit, rambutan, and perhaps the most coveted fruit of all, the durian.

Wild Mushrooms

http://www.ijs.si/slo/country/food/gobe/

Provides information on how to pick, prepare, cook, and eat your own wild mushrooms without making a fatal error. Contains a list of good, and bad and ugly (poisonous) mushrooms, as well as a glossary, and several recipes.

Recipes

Callahan's Cookbook

http://www.ruhr-uni-bochum.de/callahans/cookbook.html

An eclectic collection of recipes contributed by readers of the alt.callahans newsgroup.

Cape Breton Pictorial Cookbook

http://gnn.com/wic/wics/cook.17.html

Contains a compilation of recipes from the various cultures that have settled on Cape Breton Island in Nova Scotia. Displays many graphics, using them to present both the foods and the land.

Chicken Wing Central

http://ucsu.colorado.edu/~alums/wings.html

If you're looking for a different way to prepare chicken wings, look no further. This site features numerous different recipes for traditional Buffalo wings, as well as some more unusual flavors such as Sweet Maple wings and Goat Cheese wings. Ensure your immortality in the Valhalla of wings by submitting your own original recipes.

Chil E-Heads

http://neptune.netimages.com/~chile/

Chile pepper culture: recipes, restaurants, botany, festivals, and trivia.

Chili!

http://www.tpoint.net/Users/wallen/chili.html

Offers different tried-and-true chili recipes, each one with a unique twist. From Texas chili to Cincinnati chili, you're sure to find a chili recipe to suit your taste or constitution.

Cooking Recipes of the Institute of Nuclear Chemistry

http://quasar.physik.unibas.ch/~tommy/nanni/recipes.html

Contains easy-to-make and inexpensive recipes collected by German chemists and physicists. Recipes are available in both English and German. Includes a metric conversion chart.

Creole and Cajun Recipe Page

http://www.webcom.com/~gumbo/recipe-page.html

"New Orleans food is as delicious as the less criminal forms of sin." (Mark Twain, 1884). A comprehensive guide with recipes that distinguishes the fine art of New Orleans Cajun and Creole cuisine. Also contains links to several online cookbooks and food-related sites.

A Culinary World Tour

http://www.webcom.com:80/~gumbo/world-food.html

Provides a nice representation of international recipes ranging from African Bobotie, a curried bread custard with lamb, to Kloi Buad Chi, a dessert from Thailand.

Directory of /pub/rec.food.recipes

ftp://ftp.neosoft.com/pub/rec.food.recipes/

A gargantuan collection of recipes provided by the rec.food.recipes newsgroup. If you are looking for the definitive online recipe source, go no further.

Directory of /pub/Vegetarian/Recipes/ FatFree

ftp://ftp.geod.emr.ca/pub/Vegetarian/Recipes/FatFree/

An extremely large archive of lowfat/vegetarian recipes ranging from bread machine recipes to savory vegetarian stews. These recipes were collected from the FATFREE mailing list.

Epicurious

http://www.epicurious.com/epicurious/home.html

This online magazine offers more than just recipes, although a searchable database of recipes from *Gourmet* and *Bon Appetit* is nothing to sneeze at. Learn the etiquette of playing with your food, explore the delights of drinking while eating, and plan a daily menu straight from the source of good eating.

FATFREE Vegetarian Mailing List Archive

http://www.fatfree.com/

Contains 2,391 fat-free and lowfat vegetarian recipes that can be accessed from a searchable archive. Also contains links to other lowfat/vegetarian oriented Internet resources.

Filipino Cuisine

`http://pubweb.acns.nwu.edu/~flip/food.html`

Provides information on Filipino restaurants, cookbooks, recipes, and substitutions for hard-to-find ingredients. Also contains links to other Filipino cooking-related sites.

Friends and Partners Kitchen

`http://solar.rtd.utk.edu/friends/life/cookbooks/master.html`

Offers American, Russian, and International cuisine recipes. Also supports an international chef chat room for culinary tips and treasures. Contains links to other online cookbooks.

FYNet's Collection of Malaysian Recipes

`http://ucsee.eecs.berkeley.edu/~soh/recipe.html`

Looking to try something a little different? Try this site which contains links to four Internet recipe sources of Malaysian cuisine.

Hawaii's Favorite Recipes

`http://hisurf.aloha.com/Recipes.html`

Aunty Leilani posts new recipes each week for those who like the flavor of the islands.

Hawaiian Electric Kitchen

`http://www.hei.com/heco/ekitchen/ekitchen.html`

A Web site based on the TV show by the same name. Features Hawaiian dishes ranging from Pineapple-Macadamia Nut Bread to Jellyfish salad. Also contains a link to their Gopher site that contains recipe archives from 1994 and 1995.

Janet Starosta's Recipes

`http://metro.turnpike.net/J/jrs/janet.html`

An impressive personal collection of recipes organized in the typical cookbook fashion.

Ketchum Kitchen

`http://www.recipe.com/`

Considering themselves pioneers in cooking, the people of Ketchum Public Relations Worldwide in San Francisco prove themselves worthy with two online cookbooks (time consuming and time cutting), seasonal cooking tips, featured celebrity chefs, and a Dear Sandy column devoted to culinary topics.

Kitchens of Gordon Bleu

`http://www.aus.xanadu.com/GlassWings/food.html`

An impressive collection of recipes with a slant towards vegetarianism. Nonetheless, get ready to toss out your paperbound cookbooks. Make sure to check out the Chocolate Biscuits of Doom recipe from the Desserts and Other Atrocities page.

Kosher Express

`http://www.marketnet.com/mktnet/kosher/recipes.html`

A generous collection of Kosher recipes for Passover. Also contains links to Usenet Kosher recipe archives.

La Comeda Mexicana

`http://mexico.udg.mx/Cocina/menu.html`

Read about the history of Mexican food, and try out recipes for both traditional and interesting dishes from south of the border. This site is available in both English and Spanish.

La Pagina dela Salsa Mole

`http://www.slip.net/~bobnemo/mole.html`

Mole is a spicy chili-chocolate sauce used in traditional Mexican cooking. This site contains a fairly complete listing of recipes, a geographical listing of where to locate hard-to-find ingredients, and interesting facts on the history of Mole, as well as a list of links to other food-related sites.

Mama's Cookbook

`http://www.eat.com/cookbook/index.html`

A graphics-rich collection of Italian-style recipes using Ragu products. Contains a pasta and cooking glossary for those just starting out.

Medieval/Renaissance Food Home Page

`http://fermi.clas.virginia.edu/~gl8f/food.html`

Offers references and recipes for anyone who wants to make a medieval feast or sample medieval cooking just for themselves. Includes references for European and Islamic dishes.

My Favorite Recipes

`http://www.ece.ucdavis.edu/~darsie/recipes.html`

A personal collection of vegetarian recipes presented in simulated easy-to-follow, bulleted recipe cards.

New England Lobster

`http://www.nelobster.com/`

Offers fresh lobster, guaranteed overnight delivery. Provides online ordering through a secure server. Be sure to check out the extensive indexed collection of seafood recipes.

Nomius Eye—Sasa Recipes

`http://www.nomius.com/~sasa/sasarec.htm`

A personal collection of recipes from Slovakia. A metric to U.S. measurement conversion table is provided.

Notte's Cookbook

`http://www.niagara.com/~mnotte/cookbook.html`

A well-designed online personal cookbook of international recipes. Definitely worth a bookmark and some printouts.

Pedro's Kitchen

`http://superior.carleton.ca/~pwigfull/pedro.html`

A collection of authentic Brazilian recipes from a self-proclaimed Renaissance man.

Prapapun's Hobby Kitchen

`http://www.gezi.com:80/gzworld/recipe.html`

Traditional Thai recipes with a little cooking humor mixed in. Try your hand as a chef in the guest kitchen where you submit recipes via e-mail.

Recipe Archive Index

`http://www.cs.cmu.edu/~mjw/recipes/`

A master recipe archive collected by Amy Gale ranging from crockpot recipes to ethnic dishes.

RecipeNet

`http://www.indi.net/welcome.html`

A stylish commercial online cookbook offering service and recipes for the culinary inclined for a small fee. Includes some sample recipes with colorful pictures.

Recipes for Traditional Food in Slovenia

`http://www.ijs.si/slo/country/food/recipes/`

An award-winning site providing recipes for traditional Slovenian dishes as well as some information concerning wine making and a guide to "virtual" Slovenia.

Recipes from Kathy

`http://cyspacemalls.com/cook/recipe.html`

Recipes from the "Executive Pastry Chef" of the AA Restaurant in Santa Fe, New Mexico. Be sure to check out Kathy's Recipe Club containing an incrementally increasing collection of submitted recipes that you can add to.

Restaurant Le Cordon Bleu

`http://sunsite.unc.edu/expo/restaurant/restaurant.html`

A graphics-rich site from the renowned French cooking school. Offers recipes for seven full menus— one for each day of the week.

Ridiculously Easy Recipes

`http://www.sar.usf.edu/~zazuetaa/recipe.html`

A collection of easy-to-make recipes put together by college students for college students or anyone looking for the easy way out of preparing a meal.

Stuart's Chinese Recipes

`http://www-hons-cs.dcs.st-andrews.ac.uk/~sab/Chinese_Recipes.html`

An impressive collection of Chinese food recipes gathered from submissions by visitors of the site. Visitors are encouraged to add their Chinese culinary wisdom to the present collection.

Turkish Cuisine

`http://www.metu.edu.tr:80/~melih/recipes.html`

Authentic recipes from Turkey. Cooking difficulties range from amateur to expert.

USENET Cookbook

`http://www.astro.cf.ac.uk/misc/recipe/`

Online archive of recipes collected from various newsgroups. Recipes can be found from a searchable index or scanning the alphabetical listing. Measurements available in metric and non-metric formats.

Virtual Health

http://health.net/Virtual/

The site of the Virtual Health store provides healthy and delicious-looking recipes listed with nutritional information. Also offers gift baskets to purchase.

Virtual Kitchen

http://pathfinder.com/@@StnnhPJVIwMAQEir/twep/kitchen/index.html

Provides recipes and cooking tips from award-winning Master Chef Marcel Desaulniers. Also contains information about wine and wine-making, as well as reviews for a collection of recommended cookbooks with some sample recipes.

VNO: Food—Cooking and Recipes

http://yatcom.com/neworl/food/recipes/bytype.html

Offers New Orleans-style cooking including the traditional gumbo, jambalaya, and red beans and rice recipes.

YACB: Yet Another CookBook

http://www.csrd.uiuc.edu/koufaty/yacb/

A large collection of traditional Venezuelan recipes available in English and Spanish. Some non-Venezuelan recipes are thrown in at the end for good measure.

Restaurants

Boston Restaurant Guide

http://www.hubnet.com/

Provides reviews of recommended restaurants in Boston. Lets you search for your favorite restaurant by name alphabetically, as well as by type of cuisine or location. Includes a list of recently added or closed restaurants. Lets you submit your own reviews.

Chrone's Virtual Diner

http://www.neb.com/noren/diner/Chrones.html

Learn all about the American entrepreneurial institution of diners. Get a hold of a menu of a diner in your area, or glance at some reviews listed state-by-state. Learn to distinguish a "real" diner from a hash-slinging restaurant posing as a diner.

Diner's Grapevine

http://www.dinersgrapevine.com/

The ultimate site for those who like to eat out. Enter specifics of geographic location, price range, ambiance, entertainment, type of cuisine, and special features of the restaurant you're interested in and Grapevine will offer you a variety of selections. A truly invaluable tool for the adventurous diner.

Dining Out on the Web

http://www.ird.net/diningout.html

A comprehensive site that links you to hundreds of restaurant sites and search engines organized by geographical location. Helps you narrow your search to find the restaurant you're looking for. An amazing feat in Web usefulness!

MenuNet FoodFinder

http://www.foodfinder.com

A restaurant directory structured geographically and by type of food that displays menus and advertising for U.S., Canadian, and European restaurants. The success of this site is largely based upon visitor input. Here's your chance to play restaurant critic!

Paolo's

http://www.acoates.com/paolos

Do you know the way to San Jose? If you do, make sure you visit Paolo's for award-winning regional Italian cuisine. Features a seasonal menu and wine list.

Sally's Place

http://www.bpe.com/

Actually, this site covers a lot more than just restaurants. Food and travel usually come hand in hand and this site blends the two nicely. Sample some ethnically diverse recipes, search for a restaurant on your travels, or find out about your favorite beverages.

Virginia Diner

http://www.infi.net/vadiner/index.html

Provides information about the Diner's history, an online catalog of gifts, some Southern peanut recipes, and other information about peanuts.

World-Wide Sushi Restaurant Reference

http://wwwipd.ira.uka.de/~maraist/Sushi/sushi-rests-top.html

A comprehensive searchable guide to the sushi restaurants of the world. Reviews organized by country, state, and city. Learn basic sushi terminology so you'll know what you're eating before you eat it. Collect some sushi recipes and learn basic sushi etiquette. Also provides links to other sushi-related sites.

Vegetarian & Natural Foods

Algy's Herb Page

http://www.pair.com/algy

A Netscape-enhanced site devoted to herbs. Provides information about obtaining seeds, how to use herbs ornamentally, enhance your cooking with herbs, and find online herb catalogs.

BabyfishNet's Vegan Recipes

http://www.umich.edu/~babyfish/recipes.html

This small but growing page has vegan recipes for breads, appetizers, soups, and entrees. Be sure to read the introduction section for a brief explanation of veganism and "freeganism."

Earthrise Spirulina home page

http://www2.earthrise.com/spirulina/

Offers a natural food product catalog of spirulina blue green algae, green superfoods, and nutriceuticals. Also offers a spirulina scientific reference library. Explains how spirulina is ecologically grown at Earthrise Farms in California.

Gardenburger

http://www.gardenburger.com/

An environmentally conscious company that offers a healthier, meatless alternative to the traditional hamburger. The site provides recipes, product information, and a searchable database to help you find Garden-burgers, Gardendogs, and Gardensausage in your local restaurants and food stores.

Herbs & Spices

http://www.teleport.com/~ron1/herbs/herbs.html

For the naturalist in all of us, this site provides a graphics-rich index of herbs and spices with recipes and information about growing, storing, and cooking with your own bit of mother nature.

Index to Gluten-Free and Wheat-free Diets pages

http://www.wwwebguides.com/nutrition/diets/glutenfree/

A vital guide for those requiring gluten-free or wheat-free diets. Also contains information and links to sites dealing with the Celiac condition.

Mycelium

http://www.igc.apc.org/mushroom/welco.html

Everything you ever wanted to know about mushrooms but were afraid to ask. Provides recipes, mushroom anatomy, tips on mushroom gathering, and links to other sites about this deliciously edible fungus.

Native American Foods

http://www.ortel.org/Foster_Foods.html

Order a variety of traditional Native American food products, including naturally grown wild rice, nuts, syrups, berries and more.

Noah's Ark

http://www.rain.org/~sals/my.html

A site devoted to the science of organic farming and living. The cherimoya, fruit of the Incas, and reputed to be one of the finest fruits on God's green earth is spotlighted. Provides links to other sites centered on the organic movement.

Oils of Aloha

http://alohamall.aloha.com/~Oils

The Hawaiian source for Kukui and Macadamia nut oils.

Tamilian Cuisine

http://www.cba.uh.edu/~bala/tamilnadu/food.html

Collection of Tamil recipes and links to Tamil/vegetarian newsgroups.

U.S. Soyfoods Directory

http://www.in.net/soy/index.html

Provides information about soy-based food products, including health facts, recipes, links to other soy-related sites, and a searchable database to help you locate soyfoods in your area. This site is a must for people considering soy as an alternative to meat.

Vegetarian Pages

http://www.veg.org/veg/

An award-winning site that is the definitive guide to Internet resources for vegetarians and vegans. If you're curious to see what's online and devoted to vegetarianism, you'll most likely find it here.

Veggies Unite!

http://www.honors.indiana.edu/~veggie/recipes.cgi

A well-designed site for committed and non-commited vegetarians, replete with a searchable recipes archive, nutritional information, a guide to vegetarian-minded events, and links to other vegetarian sites.

Whole Foods Market

http://www.wholefoods.com/wf.html

A national food chain of more than 40 natural food supermarkets in 10 states. Provides information on organically grown foods and gives you an opportunity to try out recipes. All household and personal care items have been proven safe through nonanimal testing methods. Also offers links to agricultural, vegetarian, homeopathic, and humanitarian sites.

World Guide To Vegetarianism

http://catless.ncl.ac.uk/veg/Guide/

An international targeted site providing lists and links of vegetarian organizations, publications, cooking schools, and travel agencies devoted to vegetarians. The most useful aspect of the site is a searchable database, by city, of restaurants that cater to vegans and vegetarians.

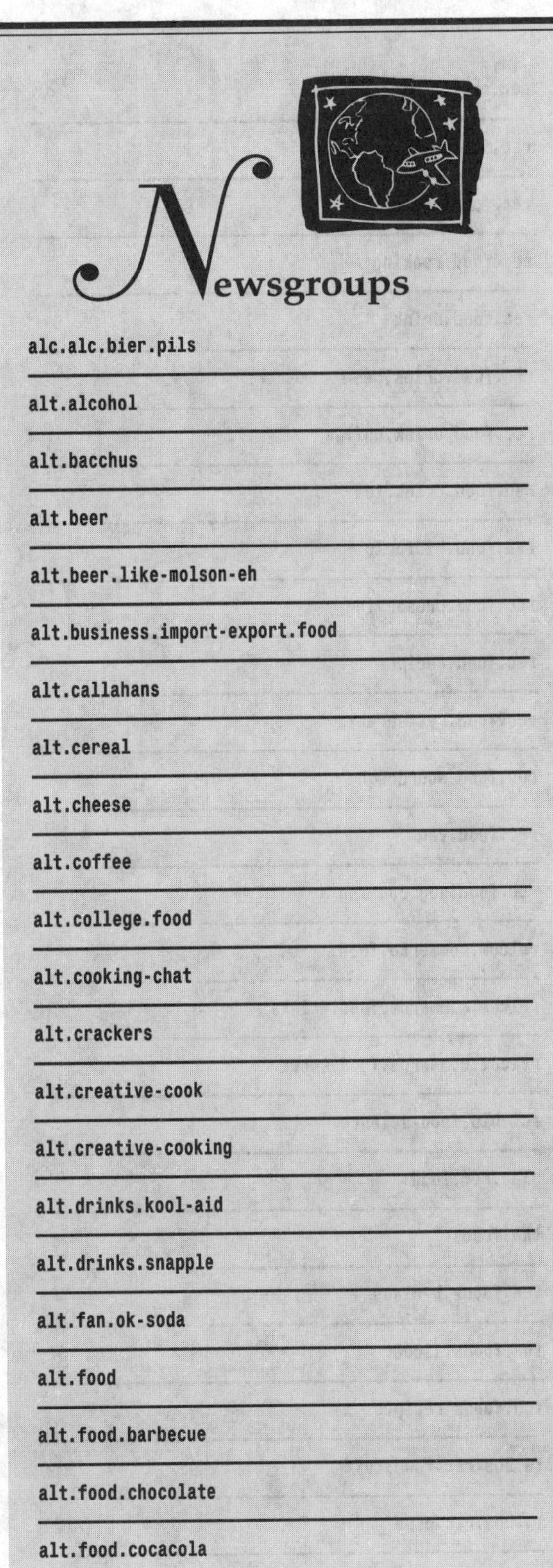

Newsgroups

alc.alc.bier.pils

alt.alcohol

alt.bacchus

alt.beer

alt.beer.like-molson-eh

alt.business.import-export.food

alt.callahans

alt.cereal

alt.cheese

alt.coffee

alt.college.food

alt.cooking-chat

alt.crackers

alt.creative-cook

alt.creative-cooking

alt.drinks.kool-aid

alt.drinks.snapple

alt.fan.ok-soda

alt.food

alt.food.barbecue

alt.food.chocolate

alt.food.cocacola

alt.food.coffee

alt.food.dennys

alt.food.fast-food

alt.food.fat-free

alt.food.grits

alt.food.ice-cream

alt.food.low-fat

alt.food.mcdonalds

alt.food.pancakes

alt.food.peeps

alt.food.pez

alt.food.professionals

alt.food.red-lobster

alt.food.sushi

alt.food.taco-bell

alt.food.waffle-house

alt.food.wine

alt.gourmand

alt.hangover

alt.kegs

alt.malta

alt.org.food-not-bombs

alt.pub.dragons-inn

alt.recipes.hawaii

alt.recovery.compulsive-eat

alt.restaurants

alt.support.food-allergies

alt.tv.networks.tvfood

alt.zima

aus.foodtech

austin.food

ba.food

clari.biz.industry.food

clari.biz.industry.food.cbd

clari.biz.industry.food.releases

clari.biz.industry.food.retail.releases

clari.biz.industry.household.cbd

fido7.mo.beer

fido7.ru.beer

fj.rec.drink.liquor

fj.rec.food

fj.rec.wine

chan.rec.food

iijnet.food

kanto.rec.food

maus.bigfood

ne.food

neworleans.info

niagara.wine

nyc.food

pnet.community.diner

rec.crafts.brewing

rec.crafts.winemaking

rec.food.baking

rec.food.chocolate

rec.food.cooking

rec.food.drink

rec.food.drink.beer

rec.food.drink.coffee

rec.food.drink.tea

rec.food.historic

rec.food.preserving

rec.food.recipes

rec.food.restaurants

rec.food.sourdough

rec.food.veg

rec.food.veg.cooking

relcom.commerce.food

relcom.commerce.food.drinks

relcom.commerce.food.sweet

sci.bio.food-science

slac.rec.food

tnn.foods

tnn.foods.b-class

tnn.foods.liquor

tnn.foods.recipes

tw.bbs.rec.foodstuff

tw.bbs.rec.wine

Listservs

2020_VIS—WKKF Food-Systems-Professions-Education-Initiative in Texas

Texas A&M University Computing Services Center

You can join this group by sending the message "sub 2020_VIS your name" to
listserv@tamvm1.tamu.edu

ADD-L—Forum for Discussion of Concerns of Drinking and Driving

Humber College, Toronto, Ontario, Canada

You can join this group by sending the message "sub ADD-L your name" to
listserv@admin.humberc.on.ca

DAIRYNET—Professionals Advising The Dairy Foods Industry

University of Maryland CSC, College Park, MD

You can join this group by sending the message "sub DAIRYNET your name" to
listserv%umdd.bitnet@listserv.net

DF225-L—VA. Seafood Faculty

Virginia Tech

You can join this group by sending the message "sub DF225-L your name" to
listserv@listserv.vt.edu

DS225-L—VA. Seafood Support

Virginia Tech

You can join this group by sending the message "sub DS225-L your name" to
listserv@listserv.vt.edu

EAT-DIS—Eating Disorders List

St. John's University, Jamaica, NY

You can join this group by sending the message "sub EAT-DIS your name" to
listserv@sjuvm.stjohns.edu

EAT-L—Foodlore/Recipe Exchange

Virginia Tech

You can join this group by sending the message "sub EAT-L your name" to listserv@listserv.vt.edu

FOODTALK—Read it... Do it: Food, Nutrition, Food Safety

University of Nebraska Computing Services Network, Lincoln, NE

You can join this group by sending the message "sub FOODTALK your name" to
listserv@unlvm.unl.edu

FOODWINE—Discussion List for Food and Wine

Central Michigan University, Mt. Pleasant, MI

You can join this group by sending the message "sub FOODWINE your name" to
listserv@cmuvm.csv.cmich.edu

FSPETAMU—WKKF Food-Systems-Professions-Education-Initiative in Texas

Texas A&M University Computing Services Center

You can join this group by sending the message "sub FSPETAMU your name" to
listserv@tamvm1.tamu.edu

IPFANR-L—"Intl Program for Food, Agri, and Natural Resources"

NE Regional Data Center, Univ. of Florida campus, Gainesville, FL

You can join this group by sending the message "sub IPFANR-L your name" to
listserv@nervm.nerdc.ufl.edu

SLA-FAN—Special Libraries Association—Food Agriculture and Nutrition

You can join this group by sending the message "sub SLA-FAN your name" to listserv@lsv.uky.edu

VCE-FNNEWS—Virginia Cooperative Extension Food Nutrition News

Virginia Tech

You can join this group by sending the message "sub VCE-FNNEWS your name" to listserv@listserv.vt.edu

Agencies & Offices

BosniaLINK

`http://www.dtic.dla.mil/bosnia/`

This is the Department of Defense's link to information on the military's operations in the former Yugoslavia. You can access maps, charts, transcripts of operation briefings and even NATO command e-mail addresses.

Census Bureau

`http://www.census.gov/`

This has to be one of the most expansive sites in the Net. You can get data maps of every county and major city in the nation. There is so much data available through this site that you just have to go there. If you need population information, they've got it.

CIAWEB: Central Intelligence Agency Website

`http://www.odci.gov/cia`

For an organization that has an image of being secretive, this is a pretty large information site. You can take a virtual tour of CIA headquarters, order publications, and even send e-mail to the director. But don't expect to find top secret documents.

DefenseLINK

`http://www.dtic.mil/defenselink/`

This is the Department of Defense's main link to the Office of the Secretary, the Joint Chiefs, the Army, Navy, Marine Corps, Air Force, Coast Guard, Reserves, and the worldwide defense theatres of command. A great starting place for U.S. defense research.

Federal Election Commission

`http://www.fec.gov/`

Find out the laws and rules regulating compaign finance and contributions. You can also download the national mail-in voter registration form.

Federal Information Exchange

`http://web.fie.com/`

The FIE is the interface between the federal government and America's institutions of higher learning. An excellent research platform for linking up with various university computer systems. There's a good link here called MOLIS that links the nation's minority colleges.

The Federal Justice Center

`http://www.fjc.gov/`

Here you can get information on the entire federal court system including the Supreme Court. One unique feature is the telephone directory with office and fax numbers for every section of the center including the directors office. You can also order from an extensive catalog of FJC publications.

The Federal Web Locator

`http://www.law.vill.edu/Fed-Agency/fedwebloc.html#doj`

Posted by the Villanova Center for Information Law and Policy, this site is a large list of links to federal agencies, especially the Department of Justice. No direct information here, but the links will take you just about anywhere you want to go in the federal government's Web.

FedWorld Information Network

`http://www.fedworld.gov/`

FedWorld links to every federal government Web site there is. It is pretty easy to get around in and has some of the most valuable links listed on the main page, including listings of all federal job openings and a way to download all tax forms.

The House of Representatives WWW Service

`http://www.house.gov`

Students needing information on the legislative process for school could not find a better source. All the committees, legislation, and of course, the congressional members are accessible here. You can search alphabetically by name or by state. However, only postal or "snail-mail" addresses are provided. You can get to the House e-mail Gopher, but it looks like an antique.

The Japan Technology Program

`http://www.doc.gov/aptp/what.html`

The JTP assists U.S. industry and researchers to access and utilize Japanese technology. The site allows you to access publications, find joint cooperative activities with Japanese private and government agencies, and apply for a fellowship program.

The Library of Congress Home Page

http://lcweb.loc.gov/

This site has links to all the Congressional sites and other government sites. The National Digital Library, Library Reading Rooms, and access to copyright laws and information make this a pretty useful site allowing researchers to access library services.

Minority Business Development Agency

http://www.doc.gov/resources/MBDA_info.html

The MBDA is under the Department of Commerce and provides information and services to promote the growth of women and minority owned businesses. This is a good link for the minority entrepreneur.

The National Endowment for the Arts

http://arts.endow.gov/

Listings of upcoming NEA events and the 56 state and jurisdictional arts agencies across the country.

The Office of Management and Budget

http://www.whitehouse.gov/WH/EOP/omb

The OMB is the department of the executive branch that handles budgeting so you can get copies of the *Federal Register* and the budget reports. If you are looking for a federal job, there's a listing of all the OMB job openings and how to apply.

Social Security On Line

http://www.ssa.gov/SSA_Home.html

All SSA questions can be answered here. There is a special feedback section for e-mailing complaints and problems regarding program benefits. There is a great deal of statistical data available, and there are explanations of benefits and programs available in Spanish.

Thomas: The U. S. Congress

http://thomas.loc.gov/

Named after Thomas Jefferson, this site allows researchers to analyze legislation in the making and the voting records of those bills. It's a good use of the Library of Congress' resources. Easy to get around in and you can download the Constitution.

U. S. Department of Agriculture

http://www.usda.gov/

You might be surprised by some of the offices under the auspices of the USDA, including the Forestry Service and the Departmant of Natural Resources. The USDA even runs its own Graduate School to which you can link.

U. S. Department of Commerce: Stat-USA

http://www.stat-usa.gov/

The DOC calls it "the world's largest source of trade, business and economic information." It's a great place for research with statistical data on the foreign and domestic economy and a daily economic report. You can also order commerce publications.

U.S. Department of Education

http://www.ed.gov/

Find out about grants, contracts, and any of the Secretary's initiatives like Goals 2000; School-to-Work; Direct Loans; Safe, Disciplined, and Drug-free Schools; and the Individuals with Disabilities Education Act (IDEA).

U.S. Department of Energy

http://www.doe.gov/

The most exciting part of the DOE site is the Electronic Exchange, which has lots of software to download and computer hardware designs.

Pain Reliever

http://www.iminet.com/tpi/sample.html

Get a free sample of RHEMU—analgesic lotion with Emu oil. Perfect for temporary relief from sore feet, back pain, muscle strain, joint pain, or just about anything else that ails you.

U.S. Department of Health and Human Services

http://www.os.dhhs.gov/

This site has access to information on all HHS programs including the National Institute of Health, the Food and Drug Administration, and the Administration on Aging. One important note: the Social Security Administration became a separate agency on March 31, 1995.

U.S. Department of Housing and Urban Development

http://www.hud.gov/

Community planning agencies can use this site to download information and access fair housing laws. The section called *Doing Business with HUD* is valuable to those business people seeking an avenue into government contracts.

U.S Department of Justice

http://www.usdoj.gov/

Attorney General Janet Reno's Justice Department is accessible here. View press releases and link up with the Federal Bureau of Investigation, the Drug Enforcement Administration, or any of the other Justice divisions.

U.S. Department of Labor

http://www.dol.gov/

The DOL has information here on labor law and trends. There is information here on grants and government labor contracts and, if you are looking for a job, search *America's Job Bank*.

U.S. Department of the Interior

http://info.er.usgs.gov/doi/doi.html

Under the auspices of the DOI are such agencies as the Bureau of Indian Affairs, the Bureau of Land Management, the National Park Service, the U.S. Fish and Wildlife Service and the U.S. Geological Survey. You can search here for employment and volunteer opportunities as well.

U.S. Department of Transportation

http://www.dot.gov/

Check out the latest from the Federal Aviation Administration, the Federal Highway Administration, the Federal Railroad Administration, the National Highway Traffic Safety Administration and more.

U.S. Patent and Trademark Office

http://www.uspto.gov/

Here's where you can go to order the proper papers and materials to get legal protection for your intellectual property. It's also a good place to search for previosly patented devices that may be of use to you or your business.

U. S. Postal Service

http://www.usps.gov

The Postal Service has built a site you can use. Here you can find your ZIP code by street or get tips on how to make business mailings more efficient and effective. Of course, you can also see and order the latest stamps.

U.S. Travel and Tourism Administration

http://www.doc.gov/resources/USTTA_info.html

The USTTA site can put you in touch with marketing offices all over the world.

The United States Senate WWW Server

http://www.senate.gov/

This is a lot like the House of Representative's server legislatively, but it offers more. The "gallery" link allows surfers to peruse the Senate art gallery and see photos of all the senators. Even more impressive is the virtual tour of the halls of congress.

The White House Home Page

http://www2.whitehouse.gov/WH/Welcome.html

This site takes a while to load if you have a slower modem, but it's worth it. Besides looking great, it's full of resources. It's an excellent historical site and provides access to all the most recent White House press briefings. You can even send e-mail to the President, Vice President, and First Lady. Major go-getters can look into the White House fellowships.

Campaigns

All Things Political

http://www.federal.com/Political.html

A collection of political newsgroups and speeches. Not very interactive, but it provides some information that's hard to find elsewhere.

The Almanac of American Politics

http://politicsusa.com/PoliticsUSA/resources/almanac/

An interactive version of Michael Barone's and Grant Ujifusa's definitive study of the nation's political districts and figures. George Will calls the Almanac "the Bible of American Politics." Searchable by states, districts, and committees.

American Political Network

http://www.apn.com

This is a hub of several sites, including The Hotline, Greenwire, The American Healthline, and The Abortion Report. You need to subscribe, however, in order to access it.

American Voter '96

http://voter96.cqalert.com/cq_home.htm

This is a great looking site put up by *Congressional Quarterly* magazine. All the links are well-marked. The news is updated daily and, to the political surfer, the CQ Hotlist is a great source for candidates' and elected officials' home pages. CQMall allows surfers to order from an extensive catalog of merchandise.

The C-SPAN Networks Site

http://www.c-span.org

Just as dry, yet informative and up-to-date as C-SPAN. Complete listings of programming on C-SPAN 1 and 2. You can download RealAudio files and scan C-SPAN's Hotlinks and check out where the C-SPAN School Bus is this week. C-SPAN in the Classroom is a great link for teachers and students.

Campaign and Elections Online

http://www.camelect.com/

The Web site of the *Campaign and Elections* magazine is a good introduction to the political campaign business. Listings of events and seminars and even a trivia contest make this an interesting site. The marketplace links are also of interest to those who like political memorabilia.

CBS News: Campaign '96

http://www.cbsnews.com/campaign96/home/

This site is very CBS. From the graphics to the regular reports like "Eye on the Issues," this site evokes the CBS Evening News. Good coverage of the issues, the personalities, and the polls. A good place for the political novise is the link Elections 101. A good introduction to the electoral system.

CNN/Time: All Politics

http://allpolitics.com

If you're a fan of the CNN show *Inside Politics*, you'll love this site. It's updated daily with news from Washington, the states and the campaigns. There's even a link to the interactive election game called President '96. A must for the political junkie.

Decision '96

http://www.decision96.msn.com/

NBC News and the Microsoft Network have their political site. The Calendar tracks the candidates and the major political events of the year. Vox Box is a chat room/newsgroup for posting opinions.

ElectionLine

http://www.electionline.com/

ElectionLine is the product of *ABC News*, *The Washington Post,* and *Newsweek Magazine.* However, most of the content is provided by *roll call magazine.* Similarly structured to PoliticsUSA site, and so it should be no surprise that the two sites have announced plans to merge in the future. Still, while you're waiting, it has some good articles that you can't get anywhere else on the Net, especially the *Money Talks* column about campaign contributions.

ElectNet

http://www.e1.com/GOV/gov.html

This election site specializes in Gubernatorial and Congressional races. Organized well with a clickable map, but the information is never totally up-to-date.

The Gallup Organization: 1996 Presidential Elections

http://www.gallup.com/1996.html

The people who practically invented the political public opinion poll have brought you an Internet site that lets you study all the political trends for the entire election season.

GoverNet

`http://www.governet.com/`

Here you can order your legislators' voting records e-mailed directly to you. Download campaign management software.

KidsNet: Election '96

`http://www.dayton.com/kidsnet/election.html`

This is a great place to start explaining the election system to kids. It's all here for them: the Electoral College, Who Can Vote, the Two Party System, and even a mock election.

The League of Women Voters' Election '96

`http://www.electriciti.com/~lwvus/elect.html`

The League is trying to "Power the Vote." Promotes voter registration and campaign finance reform.

Majority '96

`http://www.cais.com/majority96/`

The Majority '96 site supports the national grass-roots effort promoting Democratic challengers and open-seat candidates in Senate and House races. You can find out about the candidates, get on the mailing list, or join the "CyberActivists Network."

Mother Jones Magazine's On the Campaign Trail

`http://www.mojones.com/election_96/hunt.html`

MoJo's got a pretty informative site here. It's definitely to the left, but the reporting is solid, and it's easy to get where you want to go.

NetVote '96

`http://netvote96.mci.com`

The graphics on this site are impressive. Besides running surveys and other events, you can register to vote through NetVote '96.

The Political Participation Project

`http://www.ai.mit.edu/projects/ppp/groups.html`

The PPP Web site is a listing of grassroots groups and ways to contact them, including e-mail.

PoliticsUSA

`http://politicsusa.com`

PoliticsUSA has access to poll results and polls you can participate. The news reporting here is spiced up with regular columns from pollster William Schneider and reporters Jack Germond and Jules Witcover. Links to advocate groups and campaigns are also valuable. Soon to merger with ABC's ElectionLine.

Project Vote Smart

`http://www.vote-smart.org`

Complete listings of programming on C-SPAN 1 and 2. You can download RealAudio files and scan C-SPAN's Hotlinks and check out where the C-SPAN School Bus.

Foreign Policy

DOSFAN: Department of State Foreign Affairs Network

`http://dosfan.lib.uic.edu/index.html`

If you plan a trip overseas, you might want to check the travel advisories put out by the U.S. Department of State first. This is a great site for research into U.S. foreign policy, with special sections on China, Bosnia, and Cuba. Of course, you can also look for overseas jobs.

The Electronic Embassy

`http://www.embassy.org/`

Links to the staffs and resources of the Washington D.C. embassy community. Contacts in business and industry, education, the press, and government.

The Embassy Page

http://www.embpage.org/

The Embassy Page is a connection to most of the U.S.-based embassies and consulates. Part of GlobeScope Internet Services.

NATO: The North Atlantic Treaty Organization

http://www.nato.int/

If you want to know what the international organization that beat communism in Europe has planned for an encore, plug this one in. It's a pretty informative site and one of the better looking governmental sites.

The United Nations

http://www.un.org/

If you have the information resources of all the nations on earth, then you can put up a pretty good Web site. Hence, the U.N. Web site is a pretty good one. Students and teachers can use this site to its utmost.

Miscellaneous Politicals

Hardball '96

http://www.liddygame.com

This is ex-Nixon associate and ex-con G. Gordon Liddy's online site for selling his low-tech political board game.

Political Americana Online

http://www.persimmon.com/PolAmericana/

Political Americana is a place to shop for the latest buttons, bumperstickers, T-shirts, mugs, posters, rare political books, and signed presidential documents. Divided into the GOP Shoppe, The Democratic Store, The Great Seal Shop, and soon The White House Store.

Primary Colors

http://www.randomhouse.com/site/election96/primarycolors/

For as long as Random House keeps hyping this book, this site will be pretty cool. It gives background on all the characters and excerpts from the book.

President '96

http://www.pres96.com

This is an ongoing, interactive game where you run your own candidate for president. The weekly news that affects the race mirrors the real news to a certain extent.

The Right Company

http://www.bnt.com/jester/rightco/

Did you ever wonder where you could find a Republican mouse pad? Just pull up the Right Company home page for all kinds of right-wing merchandise.

Political Consulting

Greer, Margolis, Mitchell, Burns & Associates

http://www.gmmb.com/gmmb3.html

A liberal issue-based political consulting firm.

Grossfeld/Severin, Inc.

http://www.g-s.com/

Campaign and election consulting for progressive candidates and issues.

Praxis Online Campaigns

http://www.nextpolitics.com/praxis/

A consulting firm that directs its campaigns using up-to-date information technology and focusing on progressive political candidates.

Silicon Media, Inc.

http://www.smedia.com/

Internet-oriented political consulting for Republican campaigns and associations.

Natural Food Samples

http://villagenet.com/vnf

Obtain free samples of national brand nutritional supplements, as well as information on how to order at the "absolute lowest prices."

Political Parties

College Democrats of America

http://www.democrats.org/college_democrats/

The College Democrat site explains the mission, history, and issues of this branch of the party. Membership is available at this site.

College Republican National Committee Home Page

http: www.crnc.org

Alphabetical listing of College Republican chapters throughout the country.

The Democratic Caucus

http://www.house.gov/demcaucus/welcome.html

This is where the policies of the Democratic Congressional Membership can be accessed. Good research stuff for students.

Democratic National Committee

http://www.democrats.org/

Here you can find out everything the Democrats are doing. You can find out about their events, sign up for their electronic newsletter and even join the party.

Independence/Reform Party

http://www.emf.net/~cr/reform-party.html

Ross Perot has started a national political party and if you want to help, just scroll down to your state and find out what you can do to help. There are lots of transcripts from Perot speeches to be downloaded.

Libertarian Party Headquarters

http://www.lp.org/lp/

This site isn't very graphic-heavy, but it is dense with Libertarian issues and positions. Those positions are also very Internet-oriented. As with all the political party sites, you can join too.

Republican National Committee

http://www.rnc.org/

The RNC has a pretty interesting home page. It looks like a small town main street, and the icons are the storefront windows. You can link with candidates and get their e-mail addresses and, of course, join the party.

Republicans Abroad International

http://www.cyberserv.com/rai/

This site allows cyber-Republicans who live outside the U.S. to stay in touch and active in the GOP.

Young Democrats of America

http://www.democrats.org/young_democrats/

This site offers a map of the U.S. that you can click on to find the contact information and upcoming YD events for your area.

Young Republican National Federation Home Page

http://ourworld.compuserve.com/homepages/yrnf/

A listing of upcoming events and links to Young Republican chapters throughout the country.

Newsgroups

alabama.politics

alt.conspiracy.area51

alt.current-events.clinton.whitewater

alt.government.abuse

alt.hemp.politics

alt.india.progressive

alt.mindcontrol

alt.motherjones

alt.pissed.federal.employees

alt.politics.black.helicopters

alt.politics.british

alt.politics.bush

alt.politics.clinton

alt.politics.correct

alt.politics.corruption.mena

alt.politics.datahighway

alt.politics.democrats.d

alt.politics.ec

alt.politics.economics

alt.politics.elections

alt.politics.equality

alt.politics.europe.misc

alt.politics.greens

alt.politics.homosexuality

alt.politics.immigration

alt.politics.korea

alt.politics.larouche

alt.politics.libertarian

alt.politics.media

alt.politics.nationalism.black

alt.politics.nationalism.white

alt.politics.org.batf

alt.politics.org.cia

alt.politics.org.fbi

alt.politics.org.misc

alt.politics.org.nsa

alt.politics.org.un

alt.politics.org.yps

alt.politics.perot

alt.politics.radical-left

alt.politics.reform

alt.politics.scorched-earth

alt.politics.sex

alt.politics.socialism.mao

alt.politics.socialism.trotsky

alt.politics.usa.congress

alt.politics.usa.constitution

alt.politics.usa.misc

alt.politics.usa.newt-gingrich

alt.politics.usa.republican

alt.politics.white-power

alt.politics.youth

alt.president.clinton

alt.privacy

alt.religion.sexuality

alt.society.anarchy

alt.society.conservatism

aus.politics

austin.politics

az.politics

ba.politics

bermuda.politics

bit.listserv.politics

brasil.politica

ca.govt-bulletins

ca.politics

can.politics

chi.politics

chsv.politics

clari.local.california.sfbay.gov

clari.news.corruption

clari.news.issues.censorship

clari.news.usa.law.supreme

clari.usa.gov

clari.usa.gov.general

clari.usa.gov.politics

clari.usa.gov.state+local

clari.usa.politics

clari.usa.politics.personalities

clari.world.gov.politics

co.politics

co.politics.amend2.discuss

co.politics.amend2.info

csoc.politics

dc.politics

dfw.politics

eug.local.connectivity.politics

eunet.politics

fido7.pol politics

fj.soc.politics

fl.politics

git.politics

hawaii.politics

houston.politics

ia.gov.house

ia.gov.senate

info.firearms.politics

me.politics

mex.politica

misc.immigration.usa

mn.politics

ne.politics

nebr.gov

nj.politics

ny.politics

nyc.politics

nz.politics

or.politics

pa.ne.politics

pa.politics

pnet.local.politics

pnet.local.politics.talk

pnet.talk.politics

qc.politique

realtynet.government

rec.games.chess.politics.

relcom.politics

ri.politics

sanet.talk.politics,

scot.politics

seattle.politics

slo.politics

soc.culture.burma

soc.culture.colombia

soc.culture.cuba

soc.culture.estonia

soc.culture.jewish

soc.culture.kenya

soc.culture.palestine

soc.culture.polish

soc.culture.south-africa

soc.politics.arms-d Arms

talk.politics.animals

talk.politics.china

talk.politics.crypto

talk.politics.crypto

talk.politics.drugs

talk.politics.european-union

talk.politics.guns

talk.politics.libertarian

talk.politics.medicine

talk.politics.mideast

talk.politics.misc

talk.politics.soviet

talk.politics.theory

talk.politics.tibet

tnn.forum.asia-economy-p

tnn.interv.official

uk.gov.local

Listservs

ACTVST-L—Political Activist List

The American University, Washington, DC

You can join this group by sending the message "sub ACTVST-L your name" to listserv@american.edu

AERA-L—Division L: Educational Policy and Politics

Arizona State University, Tempe, AZ

You can join this group by sending the message "sub AERA-L your name" to listserv@asuvm.inre.asu.edu

APGOVPOL—Advance Placement Government and Politics

Arizona State University, Tempe, AZ

You can join this group by sending the message "sub APGOVPOL your name" to listserv@asuvm.inre.asu.edu

CENASIA—Former Soviet Republic - Central Asia Political Discussion List

You can join this group by sending the message "sub CENASIA your name" to listserv@vm1.mcgill.ca

CROSSFIRE—Sophists Political Science Society Discussion List

Southern Illinois University at Carbondale, Carbondale, IL

You can join this group by sending the message "sub CROSFIRE your name" to listserv%siucvmb.bitnet@listserv.net

CRP—McGill Students for the Renewal of the Political Process List

You can join this group by sending the message "sub CRP your name" to listserv@vm1.mcgill.ca

GEOPOL—Discussion List for Political Geography

You can join this group by sending the message "sub GEOPOL your name" to listserv@lsv.uky.edu

GILS-L—DHHS Government Information Locator Service

You can join this group by sending the message "sub GILS-L your name" to listserv@list.nih.gov

GOVDOC-L—Discussion of Government Document Issues

Pennsylvania State University

You can join this group by sending the message "sub GOVDOC-L your name" to listserv@psuvm.psu.edu

GOVERN-L—Governance Committee Listserv

Yale University Computer Center, New Haven, CT

You can join this group by sending the message "sub GOVERN-L your name" to listserv@yalevm.cis.yale.edu

GOVERNANCE-RIN-LIST—Governance Project - Regional Information Network

State University of New York at Buffalo

You can join this group by sending the message "sub GOVERNANCE-RIN-LIST your name" to listserv@listserv.acsu.buffalo.edu

GOVMANAG—Management and Leadership in Government

You can join this group by sending the message "sub GOVMANAG your name" to listserv@list.nih.gov

GOVPUB—Local and State Government Info on the Internet

You can join this group by sending the message "sub GOVPUB your name" to `listserv@listserv.nodak.edu`

GOVREL-L—Discussion of AACRAO Government Relations Topics

Arizona State University, Tempe, AZ

You can join this group by sending the message "sub GOVREL-L your name" to `listserv@asuvm.inre.asu.edu`

GRC-L—AALL Government Relations Committee

State University of New York at Buffalo

You can join this group by sending the message "sub GRC-L your name" to `listserv@ubvm.cc.buffalo.edu`

GSPMTALK—Graduate School of Political Management Discussion List

The George Washington University Computer Center, Washington DC

You can join this group by sending the message "sub GSPMTALK your name" to `listserv@gwuvm.gwu.edu`

H-POL—H-Net Political History Discussion List

Kansas State University, Manhattan, KS

You can join this group by sending the message "sub H-POL your name" to `listserv@ksuvm.ksu.edu`

H-POL—H-Net Political History Discussion List

University of Illinois at Chicago, Chicago, IL

You can join this group by sending the message "sub H-POL your name" to `listserv@uicvm.uic.edu`

IRL-POL—Discussion of Irish Politics

You can join this group by sending the message "sub IRL-POL your name" to `listserv@listserv.hea.ie`

KENTUCKY—KY Civic and Political Discussion

You can join this group by sending the message "sub KENTUCKY your name" to `listserv@lsv.uky.edu`

LGA-L—Local Government Administration List

University of Regina, Regina, Saskatchewan

You can join this group by sending the message "sub LGA-L your name" to `listserv@max.cc.uregina.ca`

LPSSBI-L—Information Management Issues Related to Law, Political Science

You can join this group by sending the message "sub LPSSBI-L your name" to `listserv@listserv.kent.edu`

MOPOLY-L—Discussion of Missouri Political Issues

University of Missouri-Columbia, Columbia, MO

You can join this group by sending the message "sub MOPOLY-L your name" to `listserv@mizzou1.missouri.edu`

PCM100—Political Communication Discussion Group

The George Washington University Computer Center, Washington, DC

You can join this group by sending the message "sub PCM100 your name" to `listserv@gwuvm.gwu.edu`

PEA—Political Economy of Agriculture

Katholieke Universiteit Leuven (KUL), Leuven, Belgium

You can join this group by sending the message "sub PEA your name" to `listserv@cc1.kuleuven.ac.be`

POLCOMM—Study of Political Communication

Rensselaer Polytechnic Institute, Troy, NY

You can join this group by sending the message "sub POLCOMM your name" to
`listserv@vm.its.rpi.edu`

POLI-PSY—Political Science-Psychology/Psychiatry

St. John's University, Jamaica, NY

You can join this group by sending the message "sub POLI-PSY your name" to
`listserv@sjuvm.stjohns.edu`

POLITICS—Forum for the Discussion of Politics

Villanova University, Villanova, PA

You can join this group by sending the message "sub POLITICS your name" to
`listserv%villvm.bitnet@listserv.net`

POLS-L—Political Science Major Forum

University of Missouri-Columbia, Columbia, MO

You can join this group by sending the message "sub POLS-L your name" to
`listserv@mizzou1.missouri.edu`

POSCIM—POlitical SCIences Mailinglist

GMD Sankt Augustin, Germany

You can join this group by sending the message "sub POSCIM your name" to `listserv@vm.gmd.de`

PSALUM—Political Science Alumni

University of Missouri-St. Louis

You can join this group by sending the message "sub PSALUM your name" to
`listserv@umslvma.umsl.edu`

PSGRAD—Political Science Graduate Students

University of Missouri-St. Louis

You can join this group by sending the message "sub PSGRAD your name" to
`listserv@umslvma.umsl.edu`

PSRT-L—Political Science Research and Teaching List

University of Missouri-Columbia, Columbia, MO

You can join this group by sending the message "sub PSRT-L your name" to
`listserv@mizzou1.missouri.edu`

REPUB-L—Discussion of Republican Politics

Marist College

You can join this group by sending the message "sub REPUB-L your name" to
`listserv@vm.marist.edu`

SA_TALK—South African Social and Political Issues Forum

Temple University, Philadelphia, PA

You can join this group by sending the message "sub SA_TALK your name" to
`listserv@vm.temple.edu`

SGANET—Student Government Global Mail Network

Virginia Tech

You can join this group by sending the message "sub SGANET your name" to
`listserv@listserv.vt.edu`

STAFFGOV—Staff Governance in Higher Education

You can join this group by sending the message "sub STAFFGOV your name" to
`listserv@listserv.nodak.edu`

STATEPOL—Politics in the American States

West Virginia Network for Educational Telecomputing

You can join this group by sending the message "sub STATEPOL your name" to listserv@wvnvm.wvnet.edu

HEALTH & FITNESS

Addiction & Recovery

Cenikor Foundation, Inc.

http://www.neosoft.com/~cenikor

A nonprofit organization with a focus on assisting people in developing skills they need to live a lifestyle free from substance abuse. Provides free residential, treatment, education, and prevention services to people over the age of 18.

Drinkwise

http://www.med.umich.edu/drinkwise/

An educational program that helps people reduce alcohol consumption. Includes a self-evaluation form and phone number to contact Drinkwise for more information.

Habit Smart

http://www.cts.com:80/~habtsmrt/

Provides information about addictive behavior: theories of habit strengths, persistence, and change. Also offers tips for managing problematic behavior.

Lenair Technique, Inc.

http://internet.village.com/business/Lenair/

A non–12-step approach toward removing the physical and psychological desire for addictive behaviors.

Prevline: Prevention Online

http://www.health.org/

Provides information for those people battling substance abuse, or who know someone battling substance abuse. Contains press releases, publications, forums, and calendars of upcoming events.

Recovery Home Page

http://www.shore.net/~tcfraser/recovery.htm

Table of contents includes Alcoholics Anonymous information, other 12-step recovery programs, events, treatment centers, commercial recovery sources, and mailing lists.

Sex and Love Addiction Recovery Home Page

http://www.wam.umd.edu/~lihn/sexlove/

Covers the building blocks and other forms of sex addiction, love addiction, dysfunctional families, and steps to recovery.

U.S. Recovery, Addiction, and Abuse Resources

http://www.contact.org/usrecov.htm

Includes organizations, guidelines and directories, and periodicals covering subjects such as rape, domestic violence, Overeaters Anonymous, and Parents of Murdered Children.

Alternative Medicine

Actual Natural Source

http://floralsnw.ark.com/health.html

Focuses on the uses of bee pollen extract for different ailments of the body.

Acupuncture Home Page

http://www.demon.co.uk/acupuncture/index.html

Provides information about acupuncture, including conditions treated, training, research, practitioners, and other resources.

Alexandra Health Center

http://www.aescon.com/alexandra/index.htm

Provides knowledge about natural medicine and homeopathy. Also provides concise descriptions on the medicine for sale.

The Alternative Medicine Home Page from Falk Library of the Health Sciences, University of Pittsburgh

http://www.pitt.edu/~cbw/altm.html

Serves as a jumpstation for sources of information on unconventional, unorthodox, unproven, or alternative, complementary, innovative, and integrative therapies.

Conscious Choice

http://www.consciouschoice.com/

Online bimonthly Midwestern magazine that reports on environmental issues and natural alternatives in health care, food, and nutrition.

HANS—The Health Action Network Society

http://www.hans.org/

Involves current issues such as acupuncture, chiropractice, disease, fluoride, food, government, pesticides, vitamins, and water. Offers films, books, and videos for sale.

Health and Longevity

http://www.sims.net/organizations/naturopath/naturopath.html

Includes information on naturopathy, herbology, nutrition, and homeopathy. Derives information from its monthly newsletter.

Herbal Hall

http://www.crl.com/~robbee/herbal.html

Focuses on all things herbal. Includes a list of resources, books, schools, and herbalists. Also features pictures and text.

Natural Health and Nutrition Shop

http://www.pixi.com/~gedwards/health/welcome.html

Provides information about nutritional supplements. Includes antioxidant protection, skin treatments, weight loss, and athletic performance.

Nature's Medicine

http://www.halcyon.com/jerryga/welcome.html

Provides natural alternatives to Western medicine. Specializes in targeted nutritionals for better health. Offers more than 200 products.

People's Place

http://peopleplace.com

Provides information and resource listings for health, personal growth, alternative medicines and therapies, healthy eating, fitness, yoga and meditation, books, vegetarianism, macrobiotics, and ayurveda. Also lists resorts, retreats, and related workshops and events.

Welcome to Acupuncture

http://www.acupuncture.com/

Contains information on acupuncture, Oriental and Chinese medicine, herbology, Qi Gong (a.k.a. Chi Kung, Chi Gong, and Qi Kung), a practitioner referral list, and a list of accredited schools for Chinese medicine. Also provides state laws regarding acupuncture.

WorldWide Wellness

http://www.doubleclickd.com/wwwellness.html

Provides a database of alternative and wholistic health information and resources. Lists events and expos going on in the Maryland area.

Companies

Alliance Health Products

http://www.websrus.com/websrus/alliance/

Offers a complete line of health food products to improve your fitness and diet, including vitamins, herbal health care products, and a natural weight loss program.

Cell Tech Super Blue Green Algae

http://www.gate.net/~clever/home.html

Provides information about Cell Tech Super Blue Green Algae, which helps strengthen the body's immune system.

Code Four Medical

http://web.idirect.com/~cfm

A public health and safety company that provides training, consulting, and supplies.

D&M Sales

http://www.srv.net/~dia/vitamins/opening.html

Provides company catalog and ordering information for Vitamin Power products. Includes ordering information and D&M Sales satisfaction guarantees.

Designs for Health

http://branch.com/vitamin/vitamin.html

Provides catalog information about DFH Discount Supplements. Includes a contact e-mail address and phone numbers.

Doody Publishing Health Science Book Reviews

http://www.doody.com/

Targets people interested in newly published health sciences books—professionals, students, librarians, bookstore staff, and publishers of health sciences literature. Offers access to a book reviews database that consists of bibliographic and descriptive information on 5,000 titles with original reviews of 3,000 of them (by paid subscription), but offers a free one-day trial.

Dragon Herbarium

http://www.teleport.com/~seahorse/dragon/

An online herbal store. Offers many herbs, spices, essential oils, tinctures, potions, lotions, and more. Features an online catalog and price list.

E-Zee Vision Prescription Eyeglasses

http://www.eyeglass.com

Offers prescription eyeglasses, factory-direct. Features high-resolution color images and sound.

Green Page—Natural Health/Nutrition

http://www.nmia.com/~sethguy/herbgreen.html

Discusses high-tech natural nutrition and weight management methods.

My Life International

http://www.cashflow.com/mylife

Markets organically sourced health products, including BioGen Plus.

Pharmavite Corporation

http://www.vitamin.com/

Offers information on vitamins and nutritional supplements.

Springboard Health and Nutrition Products

http://www.springbeech.com/springboard

Offers health and nutrition products.

Swan Medical, Inc.

http://www.vnet.net/swanmed/

Provides information about the latest in minimally invasive surgical equipment and instrumentation.

Also distributes CooperSurgical and EuroMed in North Carolina and South Carolina.

Tapestry Books—Adoption/Infertility Book Catalog

http://www.webcom.com/~tapestry

Serves as a source for adoption and infertility books and information. Offers the *Adoption Book Catalog*, which contains more than 275 books on adoption, infertility, and parenting challenges.

Death & Dying

A Place to Honor Grief

http://www2.dgsys.com:80/~tgolden//honor.html#

Allows men and women a place to write about lost loved ones as part of their grief and healing.

Bereavement Research Network

http://bereavement.org/

Includes the Men's Grief Resource and information on support, resources, conferences and workshops, and e-mail courses.

DeathNET

http://www.rights.org/~deathnet/

Offers pages related to the legal, moral, medical, historical, and cultural aspects of human mortality.

Euthanasia World Directory

http://www.efn.org/~ergo/

Includes pages on the Euthanasia Research and Guidance Organization; the World Federation of Right to Die Societies; and acts, laws, and news about euthanasia.

International Association for Near-Death Studies

http://www.iands.org/iands/

For those with an interest in near-death experiences, those who have had near-death experiences, and those who research the phenomena.

Internet Cremation Society

http://www.cremation.org/

Contains links to cremation providers and societies, scattering options, and U.S. and Canadian society participants.

Natural Death Centre

http://newciv.org/worldtrans/naturaldeath.html

A nonprofit project established to support dying people both in their home life and their careers, and to help them arrange funerals. Includes lists of publications and articles.

Sociology of Death and Dying

http://www.trinity.edu/~mkearl/death.html

Contains pages dealing with how people die, death across cultures and time, death and religion, moral debates, and personal impacts of death.

Summum Mummification

http://www.summum.org/mum.htm

Offers ideas on modern mummification, philosophical examination of mummification, and pet memorials.

Dentistry

Dental Ethics

http://ourworld.compuserve.com/homepages/SEYMOUR_YALE/

Seeks to "address the future of American dentistry" through a discussion of modern dental ethics.

Dental Implant Home Page

http://www.dental-implants.com/

Provides information on placing and restoring dental implants. Includes seminars, articles, study groups, and patient treatment overviews.

Dental Information Home Page

http://128.146.79.87/

Provides links on topics such as dentures, bleaching, erosion, bridges, and temporomandibular disorders.

Dental Related Internet Resources

http://www.nyu.edu/Dental/intres.html

New York University College of Dentistry provides connections to other dental education sites, office supplies, government-related information, and insurance.

DENTal TRAUMA Server

http://www.unige.ch/smd/orthotr.html

Dedicated to the dissemination of basic and therapeutic knowledge of dentofacial trauma.

Frequently Asked Questions

http://www.dentistinfo.com/topics/faq.htm

A FAQ sheet with in-depth information on such subjects as root canal therapy, crowns, and gum disease.

Mercury Page

http://vest.gu.se/~bosse/MercuryPage.html

At this site you will find text, links, and abstracts related to mercury and amalgam as environmental and health issues, and the facts, prejudices, thoughts, and ideas that may be contained in them.

Oral Health Country Profiles

http://www.whocollab.odont.lu.se./index.html

Presents information on dental diseases and oral health services for countries around the world.

Scholarly Opportunities in Dentistry

http://weber.u.washington.edu/~dentistry/scholops.htm

Includes information on grants, scholarships and fellowships, calls for papers, and symposia and seminars.

So, You Want to be a Dentist?

http://www.vvm.com/~bond/home.html

For those considering dentistry as a career. Covers different types of dentists, how to care for teeth, and how to become a dentist.

Dieting & Weight Loss

AromaTrim Weight Loss System

http://www.m5proc.com/aromatrim/home.htm

A weight loss system that provides a scientifically formulated fragrance that will help you control hunger and snacking. The plan comes with a video and claims that you can lose up to 15 pounds in 7 days.

Body/Mind Restoration Retreats 1996

http://users.aol.com/bodymindr/

A two-week program designed to detoxify, nourish, and assist the body and mind to reach optimum health. Includes dates and tuition information.

CyberDiet

http://www.cyberdiet.com/

Contains pages on food facts, menus and meal plans, recipes, and exercise.

Fat Person's Home Page

http://www.io.com/~joeobrin/fat/html

Contains text of a National Institute of Health study concluding that an effective method for weight loss and control does not exist. Also covers other "size acceptance" resources.

FITE—Fat is the Enemy

http://www.bright.net/~fite/

A support and advocacy group being formed for overweight Americans. Excess dietary fat is one of America's leading killers, and this group feels that something needs to be done to stop it.

Hacker's Diet

http://www.fourmilab.ch/hackdiet/www/hackdiet.html

An online book to help everyone find the diet plan that's right for them.

Health Vision

http://www1.mhv.net/~donn/diet.html

Offers links to FAQs on different exercises, diet and food myths, and a "powerful but spooky technique" to help start the diet journey.

International No Diet Day

http://www.fatso.com/fatgirl/largesse/indd/

An informational page about the holiday. Designed to warn people about the dangers of obsessive and compulsive dieting. INDD aims to make people feel good about themselves no matter what size they are.

Largesse: The Network for Size Esteem

http://www.fatso.com/fatgirl/largesse

A feminist resource center and clearinghouse for non-diet and size rights communities worldwide.

The Magic of Believing

http://www.swlink.net/~colonel/morris2.html

A nonprofit group of individuals dedicated to supporting those who are overweight. Membership is free and includes a forum for sharing strategies and methodologies for weight loss, as well as giving and getting emotional support.

Magic of Believing

http://www.geocities.com/Athens/1953/

Provides information on joining Magic of Believing, a support group that discusses diets, obesity, medical advances, fitness, and nutrition.

Medical Sciences Bulletin

http://pharminfo.com/pubs/msb/seroton.html

Reprint of an article on serotonin and eating disorders.

Michael D. Myers, MD Inc./Myers Information Services

http://www.weight.com/

Written by a physician, this page contains overviews of eating disorders, treatments and current topics related to obesity, and obesity-related medical conditions.

Modern Methods—Fat Burning Specialists

http://fatloss.com/dd.htm

Provides background information on metabolism and how your body burns fat. After you are given the background information, you are granted the opportunity to purchase the diet plan claimed to be the "most effective fat burning diet ever."

Nutri/System Online

http://www.nutrisystem.com/

At Nutri/System's Web site, you can read about the features and benefits of joining, read testimonies from clients who have had success with Nutri/System, find out where the centers are located, and sign up for free stuff.

Tell-Me-Y, Inc.

http://www.cnct.com/~tellmey/

Provides the phone number for The Solution Hotline, a charge-per-minute connection to discussions of topics including hypnotherapy and food addiction.

TOPS—Take Off Pounds Sensibly

http://www3.ns.sympatico.ca/stoner/tops.html

An unofficial TOPS page created by one of its members. Included is information on how and why to join TOPS, nifty ideas for TOPS programs, information on TOPS retreats, and more.

Weight Watchers

http://www.weight-watchers.com/

The online page of the popular weight loss program. Gives information about Weight Watchers and its many plans. Also includes an interactive portion where users can read and post success stories, challenges and solutions, exercise, and recipes.

Disabilities

Ability OnLine Support Network

http://www.ablelink.org/

An electronic bulletin that connects young people with disabilities or chronic illness to disabled and non-disabled peers and mentors.

Access Ability Travel

http://www.disabled-travel.com/

Specializes in vacations that meet the special needs of travelers with disabilities.

Archimedes Project

http://kanpai.stanford.edu/arch/arch.html

Seeks to promote equal access to information for individuals with disabilities by influencing the early design stages of tomorrow's computer-based technology.

Blind Childrens Center, Inc. Home Page

http://www.primenet.com/bcc/

Nonprofit organization. Provides resources and assistance to visually impaired children and their families. Offers information on an educational preschool program, family services, the current newsletter, and a calendar of upcoming events. Also lists links to other related sites.

CHATBACK Trust

http://www.tcns.co.uk/chatback/

Serves as a place where children who have disabilities can organize their own dialogue. Functions primarily as an e-mail exchange through a related listserv. Provides information about this service.

Deaf World Web

http://deafworldweb.org/deafworld/

Lists some information in German and French, as well as English, and is fairly international in scope.

Provides information on deaf studies, deaf culture, useful services, and more.

Disability Net

http://www.globalnet.co.uk/~pmatthews/DisabilityNet/

A non-political service for people with disabilities run *by* people with disabilities.

Mankato State University Department of Communication Disorders

http://www.mankato.msus.edu/dept/comdis/kuster2/welcome.html

Covers topics including child language disorders, dysphagia, fluency disorders, stuttering, and hearing disabilities.

National Sports Center for the Disabled

http://www.nscd.org/nscd/

Discusses its role as the largest and most successful outdoor recreation program for those with disabilities. Includes both winter and summer activities.

Sibling Support Project

http://www.chmc.org/departmt/sibsupp/

Dedicated to the interests of brothers and sisters of people with special health and developmental needs. Offers support groups, workshops, and newsletters.

Diseases & Conditions

AIDS Bytes

http://www.clients.anomtec.com/AidsBytes/

A project to demystify the terms associated with AIDS and increase the public's knowledge of the disease. Words are clearly defined and even pronounced if you are capable of playing WAV files.

AIDS Information for Young People

http://www.oneworld.org/avert/young.htm

Provides timely information for teens, including what AIDS is, what causes it, and how one might become infected.

AIDS Walk Los Angeles

http://www.bonsai.com/LAAIDS/

Register for the AIDS Walk.

Alzheimer Disease Web Site

http://med-www.bu.edu/Alzheimer/home.html

Serves as a reference site for clinicians, investigators, and caregivers interested in Alzheimer's disease and other related dementias.

American Diabetes Association

http://www.diabetes.org/

Take a simple test and determine your risk for diabetes. Then find the diabetes center that is closest to you. Learn about living with diabetes and what you can do to help out the association and those who suffer from diabetes.

American Heart Association National Center

http://www.amhrt.org/

The American association that fights heart disease and stroke. They maintain an extensive heart and stroke guide that contains over 300 articles from the association on various subjects such as aspirin, cigarette smoking, and exercise.

American Lyme Disease Foundation

http://www.w2.com/docs2/d5/lyme.html

Information about Lyme Disease, including how to spot early symptoms and general precautions for avoiding ticks, thus avoiding the disease altogether.

Arthritis—Doctor's Guide to the Internet

http://www.pslgroup.com/ARTHRITIS.HTM

Medical news and alerts about arthritis. Includes an overview of arthritis and a study of rheumatoid arthritis. Provides links to discussion groups and newsgroups and other sites that have arthritis-related information.

Bad Breath Research

http://www.tau.ac.il/~melros/Welcome.html

Interesting reading on the subject of halitosis. The questions and answers, articles, and online publications should be of interest to anyone who suffers from oral malodor or has a spouse that does.

Breast Cancer Information

http://nysernet.org/bcic/

Presents many things women should know about breast cancer, including how to detect breast cancer, toll-free numbers for information hotlines, questions and answers about cancer, and much more.

Cardiovascular Institute of the South

http://www.cardio.com/

Center for the advanced diagnosis and treatment of heart and circulatory disease. Offers a wide range of reports covering the full spectrum of prevention, diagnosis, and nonsurgical and surgical treatment of circulatory problems.

Caring for People With Huntington's Disease

http://www.kumc.edu/hospital/huntingtons/

Although not intended to be an authoritative work, this page provides valuable information about Huntington's disease. The helpful tips at this page include communication strategies, help for eating and swallowing, and more. Also provides links to other HD sources.

CDC National AIDS Clearinghouse

http://www.cdcnac.org/

A searchable database of AIDS/HIV information, including information from the XI International Conference on AIDS and the Presidential Advisory Council on HIV/AIDS Progress Report. Also includes a gallery of AIDS-awareness posters.

Down Syndrome WWW Page

http://www.nas.com/downsyn/

Information on Down Syndrome, including articles, health care guidelines, a worldwide list of organizations, and education resources. The site also features a "brag book" containing photos of a number of children with the syndrome.

Endometriosis

http://www.ivf.com/endohtml.html

A variety of information on the puzzling disease. The site includes a lengthy FAQ, case studies, and a number of articles on the subject. A photo gallery is also included.

Eye Diseases and Conditions

http://www.eyenet.org/public/faqs/faqs.html

The American Academy of Ophthalmology has developed a collection of FAQs answering questions about a variety of eye diseases. Here you can find information about cataracts, glaucoma, amblyopia, and more.

Gastroenterology Consultants

http://www.gastro.com/

Drs. Peter Gardner and Stuart Waldstreicher provide an informational page about gastroenterology and liver disease, as well as their own practice treating such disorders. Links are provided to descriptions of symptoms, videos of intestinal surgery, facts and stats on digestive disease, and more patient information.

Heart Mind Body Institute

http://www.power.net/hbm/hbm1.html

Explains new approaches in the prevention and reversal of coronary heart disease without open heart surgery. Seeks to help you free yourself from any kind of heart disease using this new approach.

Herpes: The Hidden Disease

http://www.azstarnet.com/~joanna/herpes.htm

Information on the sexually transmitted disease herpes. Provides a variety of links to sites with detailed information and addresses for herpes resource centers.

HYPHECAN Fingertip Cap

http://www.eskimo.com/~vanming/hpc_intro.html

A doctor-developed fingertip cap for fingertip injuries. Recommended by medical professionals. Links to usage information, free samples, and business opportunities for distributions.

Introduction to Skin Cancer

http://www.maui.net/~southsky/introto.html

Intended as a general introduction to skin cancer, this page provides basic information such as determining what causes skin cancer, what it is, what your personal risks are, and how to reduce those risks.

Introduction to Vision Correcting Procedures by Med-Source, Inc.

http://www.ozarksol.com/medsource/

Informs the public about vision-correcting procedures, including radial keratotomy (RK) for nearsightedness, astigmatic keratotomy (AK) for astigmatism, automated lamellar keratoplasty (ALK) for farsightedness, and the soon-to-be FDA-approved photorefractive keratectomy (PRK) for nearsightedness.

Jeffrey Modell Foundation

http://www.mssm.edu/peds/modell/home-pag.html

Dedicated to Primary Immune Deficiency, an inherited defect in the immune system.

Kaiser Family Foundation

http://www.kff.org/kff/

An independent health care philanthropy dealing with health and development in South Africa, HIV policy, health policy, and reproductive health. Foundation is located in California, and its site provides many links to AIDS-related topics.

Malaria Weekly

http://www.newsfile.com/1m.htm

The world's only newsweekly dedicated entirely to this tropical disease. Contains all the cutting-edge information available about this leading cause of death by infectious agent. Headlines and glimpses of the stories are available for free, but to get the full articles, you must subscribe. Sample issues are available.

Medicine On Line

http://meds.com

Serves as a commercial online medical information service. Provides health care professionals and consumers a convenient place to obtain medical information. Serves as a gateway to access other health information services on the Internet. Currently focuses on cancer information.

The Merck Manual

http://www.merck.com/!!rGBNN2da4rGBNN2da4/pubs/mmanual/html/sectoc.htm

A definitive source of information about disease. Topics covered range from infectious diseases to nutritional and metabolic disorders to neurologic and psychiatric disorders. The manual has an extensive list of tables and figures and is very technical in nature.

Muscular Dystrophy Association

http://www.mdausa.org/

Learn all about the MDA and what it does to help combat neuromuscular diseases. Also learn about what you can do to help besides just watching the Jerry Lewis telethon.

National Osteoporosis Foundation

`http://www.nof.org/`

The NOF seeks to reduce the incidences of osteoporosis by making the public more informed about it. Its site provides background information on the disease, information about who's at risk, and prevention and treatment ideas.

Parkinson's Web

`http://neuro-chief-e.mgh.harvard.edu/parkinsonsweb/Main/PDmain.html`

Serves as a resource directory, pointing you to sources of information on Parkinson's disease.

Pediatric Rheumatology Home Page

`http://www.wp.com/pedsrheum`

Provides information for children and young adults who have arthritis and other rheumatic diseases of childhood, their families, and the physicians who care for them.

Prostate Cancer InfoLink

`http://www.comed.com/Prostate/`

Includes pages on screening for prostate cancer, understanding diagnosis and treatments, and where to find support groups.

Rehabilitation Learning Center

`http://weber.u.washington.edu/~rlc/`

Seeks to create a computer-based multimedia rehabilitation environment designed to educate and train individuals with acute or chronic spinal cord injuries so they can successfully leave the in-patient rehabilitation environment and function in society. Provides information about their plans and progress.

Roxane Pain Institute

`http://www.Roxane.com`

Offers cancer and AIDS pain management services. Serves as a resource for pain sufferers and clinicians. Offers educational materials, including newsletters, clinical articles, presentation slides on cancer pain management, and a schedule of upcoming pain management seminars.

Scoliosis

`http://www.rad.washington.edu/Books/Approach/Scoliosis.html`

An article on the skeletal disease, written by Dr. Michael L. Richardson, MD. The article shows the various classifications of scoliosis and provides illustrations to further demonstrate the effects of the disease.

The Skin (Diseases) Page

`http://www.pinch.com/skin/`

The home to archives of various skin disease-related Usenet newsgroups. Also provides descriptions of the various skin diseases and links to other skin-related sites.

Sudden Infant Death Syndrome (SIDS) Information Home Page

`http://q.continuum.net/~sidsnet/`

Provides information about Sudden Infant Death Syndrome. "This page will grow and evolve as we progress up the learning curve together. Your patience, understanding, and contributions to this page will make it grow into a true network of people and information dedicated to stopping SIDS, the number one killer of infants between the ages of one month and one year." —Chuck Mihalko, President, SIDS Network.

Vision Impairments: A Guide for the Perplexed

`http://www.wimsey.com/~jlyon/index.html`

Provides contact information about agencies, consumer groups, Internet resources, and vendors of adaptive technology for persons with vision impairments. Covers international resources and those local to British Columbia and Western Canada. Also carries discussions that cover the experience of vision impairment.

World of Multiple Sclerosis

`http://www.ifmss.org.uk/`

FAQs, publications, research, products, services, forums, book reviews, a glossary of terms, and other information of interest to anyone involved in any way with multiple sclerosis.

Emergency Services

Avalanche Dogs!

`http://weber.u.washington.edu/~danc/avalanche.html`

Discusses training dogs for search and rescue missions.

EMBBS: Emergency Medicine and Primary Care Home Page

http://www.njnet.com/~embbs/

Provides educational resources and job opportunities for emergency and primary care physicians and health care providers.

Emergency

http://www.catt.citri.edu.au/emergency/

Hopes to provide an insight into emergency services around the world through action photos, a virtual emergency, a training room, and a notice board.

Emergency Preparedness Information eXchange

http://hoshi.cic.sfu.ca/epix/

Promotes the exchange of ideas about the prevention of, preparation for, and recovery from natural and sociotechnological disasters.

Global Emergency Medicine Archives

http://gema.library.ucsf.edu:8081/

Online journal featuring articles, online discussion forums, and keyword searches of the GEMA text archives.

Mountain Rescue Association

http://www.mra.org/

A volunteer organization that provides mountain safety education and volunteers for search and rescue operations.

National Collegiate EMS Foundation Home Page

http://www.ncemsf.org/

Clearinghouse of information for campus Emergency Medical System groups. Also maintains two e-mail discussion lists and information on conferences.

Team Dispatch

http://www.sitegroup.com/teamdisp/

Program designed to bring more awareness to EMS, Fire and Rescue, and police and sheriff department dispatchers.

UBC (University of British Columbia) MultiCentre Research Network

http://www.interchg.ubc.ca/emerg_vh/ubc_multicentre.html

Emergency medicine research consortium made up of the emergency medicine research divisions of three teaching hospitals, Royal Columbian Hospital, St Paul's Hospital, and Vancouver Hospital. Outlines information about the network's current and recent research activities. Also outlines recent publications, abstracts, presentations, and text book chapters. Functions as a bulletin board-type service, whereby members can post intra-network messages using a password-controlled link. Also offers links to a faculty-wide e-mail directory.

UTHSCSA Trauma Home Page

http://rmstewart.uthscsa.edu/

Focuses on issues of injury, injury prevention, and surgical critical care. Contains trauma-evaluation forms, a trauma and critical care e-mail directory, and trauma patient presentations.

Fitness

Aerobics!

http://grove.ufl.edu/~evilgreg/aerobics.html

Contains a FAQ sheet, a library of aerobics patterns, and a calendar of fitness events.

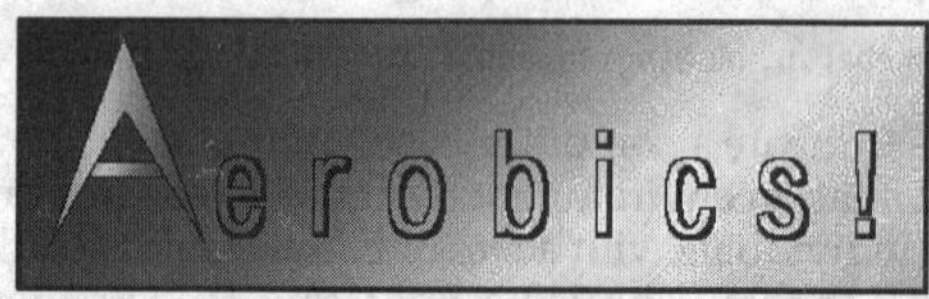

Alexander Technique

http://www.alextech.com/

Developed to improve balance and posture and help alleviate back pain.

Balance: Fitness on the Net

http://hyperlink.com:80/balance

Online magazine covering sports nutrition and therapy and the International Register of Personal Trainers, as well as general fitness and exercise.

The Blonz Guide to Nutrition, Food Science, and Health

http://www.blonz.com/blonz/index.html

Authored by Ed Blonz, Ph.D., this site is designed to help you discern the valuable nutrition sites on the

Web from those that are mere cyberjunk. The page provides many links to the sites that are considered the best and is also available in a version that contains frames and Java.

CyberNutrition Online Dole 5 A Day

http://www.dole5aday.com/

An excellent source for kids and parents alike to find out the values of eating fruits and vegetables on a daily basis. Remember, "Five a day is the magic rule—more is OK, less is uncool!"

Dole 5 A Day

http://chd.syr.edu/chd/CyberNutrition2.html

Sponsored by the Syracuse College for Human Development, this page enables you to send in nutritional questions that are answered and then presented in archive form for the benefit of all. Ask about anything from riboflavin deficiencies to the healthful qualities of beer and pizza.

Food & Nutrition Information Center

http://www.nalusda.gov/fnic/

Provides information about healthy eating, dietary guidelines, food labeling, and other nutritional information. Contains links to many "nutritional" sites.

Food Pyramid

http://www.ganesa.com/food/index.html

Getting good nutrition is easy if you follow the food pyramid guide. This page is a graphical representation of the pyramid, with each food group depicted being a link to a short discussion about its nutritional qualities.

Hiking and Walking Home Page

http://www.teleport.com/~walking/hiking.html

Offers hiking and walking resources, organizations, philosophy, and updates on gear.

IFIC Foundation

http://ificinfo.health.org/

The home page of the International Food Information Council. Provides information for health professionals, educators, parents, and consumers. Includes FAQs and other publications.

International Yoga School

http://www.webzone1.co.uk/www/simon/iys/

Offers diploma courses in professional stress management, yoga teaching, diet and nutrition, aromatherapy, massage, and reflexology.

Krispin Komments

http://www.krispin.com/

Contains two very informative articles, the Potassium Chronicles, and Protein Basics. Includes information on getting enough of each of these in your daily diet, complete with recipes.

Mirkin Report

http://www.wdn.com/mirkin/

Breakthroughs in health, fitness, nutrition, and sexuality. Includes discussions of scientific discoveries and information about Dr. Mirkin's radio programs and books.

MSU Athletic Training

http://vax1.mankato.msus.edu/~k061252/MSUATC.html

Provides information for people interested in the athletic training profession. Provides information about Mankato State University and a curriculum program and information concerning it. Also offers a number of other athletic training or related links, such as program information, alumni information, history, an athletic training listserver discussion directory, and staff.

Netlife Health Products

http://www.interlog.com/~noahs/

The best health supplements, herbs, green foods, high-end vitamins, and beauty-related products at the lowest prices. Browse the catalog, place an order, or link to other health-related sites.

Free Classified Ads Placement

http://www.recycler.com/

Running low on the dough? Place a classified ad on the Web or in a paper ad for free. Who knows, maybe someone really will want to buy that lime green sofa.

NutriGenie

`http://pages.prodigy.com/CA/nutrigenie/`

A nutrition software publisher, including titles for weight loss, disease and nutrition, high blood pressure, heart disease, special diets, sports, allergies, and much more. Also includes other health-related sites and information for downloading.

The Nutrition Expert

`http://www.alaska.net/~tne/`

A group of registered dietitians whose goal is to provide timely nutritional information to the Internet community. Here you can find information on weight loss, including several dieting FAQs, sports nutrition, health food, and eating disorders.

The Nutrition Pages

`http://deja-vu.oldiron.cornell.edu/~jabbo/`

Contains a "Current Topics" section where articles can be read and submitted, and a "Just the FAQs" section that answers questions about nutrition. Check this page out and find out why a healthful diet is "funkier than chitlins with gravy and grits...."

Nutritive Value of Foods

`http://www.fsci.umn.edu/fscnprivate/handbook8.htp`

At this site you can look up data on any of the 1,170 standard foods, a service provided by the U.S. Department of Agriculture. Entering a food's name will get you a complete list of its fats, proteins, vitamins, and more.

Online Digital Fitness Solutions

`http://www.lmg.com/odfs/menu.htm`

Discusses various types of heart rate monitors and how they can improve performance.

Peak Performance

`http://www.siteworks.co.uk/pperf/conts.htm`

A scientific newsletter devoted to improving stamina, strength, and fitness.

Professor Geoff Skurray's Food & Nutrition Information

`http://www.hawkesbury.uws.edu.au/~geoffs/`

A wealth of nutritional information, including information on reducing fat and improving athletic performance through proper nutrition; and dietary guidelines for adults, adolescents, and children.

Sci.Med.Nutrition

`news:sci.med.nutrition`

A Usenet newsgroup for those trying to improve their health through proper nutrition. This includes formulating a balanced diet and the use of vitamin and nutrient supplements.

Yoga Paths: An Overview of Different Schools and Traditions

`http://zeta.cs.adfa.oz.au/Spirit/Yoga/Overview.html`

Lists 23 types of yoga and offers links to more information about the forms.

General Health

General Complementary Medicine

`http://www.forthrt.com/~chronicl/archiv.htm#5`

Offers links to other health and medicinal home pages.

Good Health Web

`http://www.social.com/health/index.html`

Provides daily health news (and an archive); a library of health articles; discussions; and lists of FAQs, newsgroups, and mailing lists.

Health Resource

`http://www.coolware.com/health/joel/health.html`

Provides information about health, stress, sexuality, and many other health problems that people can encounter.

HealthCom, Inc.

`http://www.gdesystems.com/IIS/ORIGHTML/healthcom.html`

Site for patient-focused health care support systems for providers of health care. Links to patient-charting systems and other health care pages of interest.

Healthtouch

`http://www.healthtouch.com/`

Provides updates on health, diseases, wellness and illness, a resource directory guide to organizations and government agencies, access to pharmacies in your community, and a drug search program that enables you to find information about prescription and over-the-counter drugs.

International Health News

http://www.perspective.com/health/index.html

Presents a monthly electronic newsletter and discussion group for people who want to gain a better understanding of news and research on the relationship between health, nutrition, and lifestyle.

Linda Sy Skin Care

http://www.fractals.com/sy/html/sy_intro.html

Skin-care products for sensitive skin, developed by dermatologists. Browse the products and place your order directly from your computer.

MEDMarket Virtual Industrial Park

http://www.frontier.net/MEDMarket/

The medical industry's Internet headquarters. Includes links to featured services, announcements, and MEDMarket tenants.

Minority Health Network

http://www.pitt.edu/~ejb4/min/

Lists minority health resources by minority group, subject, and disease. Also includes lists of upcoming events and publications.

Narhex

http://www.odyssey.com.au/uspecies/narhex/welcome.html

A company offering skin-care products, lotions, alpha hydroxy, and more. Check out its special offers. Also provides a link to HIV research information.

Natracare, LLC

http://www.indra.com/natracare/

The only natural, unbleached feminine hygiene products available to reduce health risks. Check out Natracare's full line of products, references, and women's health-related links on the Internet.

Navigator's Health and Nutrition Page

http://www.nav.com/home/hnpage.html

Includes jumps to a wide range of health and medicine sources from around the country. Serves as a starting point for any health-related search.

SkinCare Program

http://shani.co.il/~skincare/

Provides information and products that deal with psoriasis and other skin ailments. Includes an online catalog, medical updates, and contact information.

Word on Health

http://www.webcom.com/~revista/

Focuses on a few topics, such as vitamins and medicine. Changes every three months.

World Health Network

http://www.worldhealth.net/

Dedicated to health, vitality, and longevity. Contains information on anti-aging, nutrition and exercise, and traditional and alternative health care.

Geriatrics & Aging

Aging Research Centre

http://www.hookup.net/mall/aging/agesit59.html

Provides information to those interested in learning about the aging process. Includes books, theories, newsgroups, conferences, and laboratories.

Creative Learning Stroke Support Web Site

http://www.tpoint.net/creative/

Focuses on a software system designed to help stroke and trauma victims recover language abilities.

Geropsychology

http://www.premier.net/~gero/geropsyc.html

Includes a listing of gerontology, senior information, dementia, Parkinson's Disease, stroke, assessment, and psychology resources.

Guide to Retirement Living Online

http://dataprompt.com/neteng/retire_liv.html

Provides retirement options, including nursing care, independent living facilities, and home health care, as well as links to legal, financial, and moving services.

Home Modification: A NARIC Resource Guide

http://www.cais.net/naric//hm.html

Provides information on making housing more accessible, including publications, organizations, and identification of products.

Institute for Brain Aging and Dementia

http://www.alz.uci.edu/

Discusses the institute's research into discovering the fundamental mechanisms behind dysfunction, and then applying those findings to prevent and reverse dementia.

Portals Aging

http://www.portals.pdx.edu/~isidore/aging.html

Provides links to resources for people to find information on the aging process. Covers discussion groups, databases, library cataloges, and aging-related home pages.

SeniorSites

http://www.seniorsites.com/

Provides a national listing of nonprofit senior housing, health care, and service organizations.

Social Security Online

http://www.ssa.gov/

Provided by the Social Security Administration, this site includes agency and benefit information, a guide for employers, international information, legislation, and research and statistics.

Health Administration

American College of Healthcare Executives

http://www.ache.org/

A professional membership society for health care executives. Offers publications, policy statements, and educational programs.

Aspen Publishers, Inc.

http://www.aspenpub.com/

Lists products and articles on adminitration, health care, and law and business.

BONES: The Biomedically Oriented Navigator of Electronic Services

http://bones.med.ohio-state.edu

Provides faculty, staff, and students in the health sciences with a starting point for Internet exploration.

Healthcare Financial Management Association

http://www.hfma.org/

A membership organization for financial management professionals. Provides a common ground for the exchange of ideas related to hospital finance.

Healthcare Information and Management Systems Society

http://www.himss.org/

A not-for-profit organization dedicated to promoting a better understanding of health care information and management systems.

Innervation Technology Corp.

http://www.innervation.com/inner/

Consulting and support services for those in the health care industry. Links to the company overview, products and services available on the Web, and other sites of interest to the medical community.

National Association of Health Authorities and Trusts

http://www.nahat.net/

Brings together NHS health authorities, Scottish health boards, and Northern Ireland health and social services boards to exchange information on support services, conferences, research, and publications.

Society for Medical Decision Making

http://www.nemc.org/SMDM

Focuses on promoting rational and systematic approaches to decisions about health policy and the clinical care of patients. Includes decision analysis, applications of quantitative methods in clinical settings and medical research, studies of human cognition and the psychology of clinical reasoning, medical ethics, medical informatics and decision making, artificial intelligence, evaluation of medical practices, and cost-effectiveness or cost-benefit assessments.

Health Care

Center for Rural Health and Social Service Developers

http://www.siu.edu/~crhssd/

Seeks to bring together university resources and health care agencies to address health concerns. The center conducts research and training, tests new models of health care delivery, and develops policy recommendations to improve the health of the rural populations.

Chiropractic Page

http://www.mbnet.mb.ca/~jwiens/chiro.html

Primarily serves as a pointer to health-related subjects, focusing on information for chiropractors, students, other health care practitioners, and interested laypersons. Offers many sites and links.

Colorado HealthNet

http://bcn.boulder.co.us/health/chn/index.html

Provides information on chronic illnesses, complementary therapies, health care plans, and information on state and federal agencies.

Indigent Patient Services

http://www.bayanet.com/Customers/indigent/index.html

Helps indigent patients receive medication necessary for health and well-being.

Internal Capsule

http://www.voicenet.com/1/voicenet/homepages/levinson/index.html

Provides resources and information on physical therapy, including music-related injuries and a PT student page.

Internet Medical Products Guide

http://www.medicom.com/medicom/home.html

Provides a database of medical product sales and technical information for health care providers.

Marijuana as a Medicine

http://www.calyx.com/~olsen/MEDICAL/medical.html

Continues the controversy of using marijuana to relieve medical ailments.

Marquette University Program in Physical Therapy

http://www.mu.edu/dept/pt

Includes information about the Master's in Physical Therapy Program at Marquette University and about the profession of physical therapy itself. Offers many links to other physical therapy and health-related topics.

MDB Information Network

http://mdbinfonet.com

Provides objective information for health care decision-makers. Helps health care providers reduce risk, contain costs, and increase efficiencies by providing reliable data, strategic analysis, and counsel. Delivers services through three divisions: MDB Technology Services, MDB Information Services, and MDB Financial Network.

MedSearch America

http://www.medsearch.com

Online job postings and résumés for the health care field.

Patti Peeples' Guide to Health Economics, Medical, and Pharmacy Resources on the Net

http://www.exit109.com/~zaweb/pjp/

Lists national and international links to biotech firms, medical libraries, journals, employment opportunities, and health databases.

Physical Therapy WWW Page

http://www.mindspring.com/~wbrock/pt.html

Provides general information about physical therapy. Includes physical therapy today, research, treatment, typical work settings, specialization, and credentials.

SPA in Italy

http://www.travel.it/ter/

Promotes the belief that the hot springs in Italy can bring relief from every type of problem, from allergies to metabolism to stress.

Health Insurance

AFLAC

http://www.aflac.com/

Provides guaranteed renewable supplemental health insurance.

Employers Health Insurance

http://www.employershealth.com/

Focuses on helping small businesses provide benefits.

FHP Health Care

http://www.fhp.com

Targets anyone who wants to assess his or her own health or learn more about HMOs.

Inscon: Insurance Consultants, Inc.

http://inscon.com/

Writes and administers insurance programs for colleges nationwide and K–12 institutions in a 10 state region.

Insurance for Students, Inc.

http://www.ins-for-students.com/

Includes policies for colleges and universities, international programs, nursery and daycare, athletics, and camps.

Insurance Research Network

http://mmink.cts.com/mmink/dossiers/irn.html

Offers a free health insurance quote.

Managed Health Care

http://ourworld.compuserve.com/homepages/MANDR/

Home page for a consulting firm that offers assistance in Medicaid consulting, HMO products and mergers, self-insured health plans, and insurance company consulting.

Rusty Chambers Insurance Agent— Life, DI, Disability, Health

http://www.intellinet.com/~rusty

Includes a brief list of insurance products and services. Also offers quotes for any type of insurance.

Value-Care

http://www.packplus.com/~protech/integra.html

Supplemental insurance to cover dental, vision, hearing, and prescription drug needs.

Worldwide Med

http://www.silo.com/services/wwmed/medsrc.htm

Independent insurance brokers offering temporary medical plans.

Institutes

Arkansas Children's Hospital

http://www.ach.uams.edu/

Private, nonprofit institution. Offers children comprehensive medical care from birth to age 21, from every county in Arkansas and from many nearby states, regardless of a family's ability to pay.

Catholic Health Association of Wisconsin

http://www.execpc.com/~chaw

Nonprofit state association that serves more than 100 Catholic health care facilities in Wisconsin. Provides information about the association's purpose, educational programming, newsletters, and ethical information.

Charities USA

http://www.charitiesusa.com/charitiesusa/fedmain/mraamain.html

Includes links to many medical research groups and foundations. Offers a toll-free number for those with donations to help fight disease.

Hair Loss Handbook and Support Group Network

http://www.hairnow.com/

Targets the countless number of men and women who want to learn more about hair loss.

Interactive Media Lab

http://griffith.dartmouth.edu/iml/iml.html

Part of the Dartmouth Medical School. Specializes in using computers, media, and communications technologies for medical simulations.

International Cancer Alliance

http://www2.ari.net/icare/

ICA is a nonprofit organization ensuring that high-quality, focused, patient-centered cancer information is available to patients and physicians. Includes information on programs and background and a sign-up site for more information.

Missouri Institute of Mental Health

http://www.missouri.edu/~mimhmj

Highlights the research, education, and multimedia efforts with which the Missouri Institute of Mental Health currently is involved.

New England Medical Center

http://www.nemc.org

Provides information about the tradition and history of the prestigious New England Medical Center. Offers comprehensive inpatient and outpatient care for adults and children.

Radiation Effects Research Foundation

http://www.rerf.or.jp/

Dedicated to studying the effects of the atomic bombings of Hiroshima and Nagasaki during World War II.

OSHA: Occupational Safety and Health Administration

http://www.osha.gov/

From the U.S. Department of Labor. Establishes and enforces protective standards and offers technical assistance to protect the American workforce.

Medical History

Michigan Digital Historical Initiative in the Health Sciences

http://http2.sils.umich.edu/HCHS/

Contains archival, manuscript, and museum materials; images of documents, photographs, graphic art and artifacts; exhibits and galleries on special topics; educational products; and online assistance.

Scientific and Medicinal Antiques

http://www.duke.edu/~tj/sci.ant.html

Includes information on electrical and magnetic items, calculating, surveying, surgical instruments, bloodletting, pharmaceuticals and medical chests, electrotherapy devices, and more.

Medicine

Cyberspace Hospital

http://ch.nus.sg

Provides one-stop access to medical Web servers around the world. Organizes the links into medical specialty departments by using a virtual hospital setting.

Department of Neurosurgery at New York University

http://mcns10.med.nyu.edu/

Serves as a resource center on a broad range of neurosurgical issues for patients, families, and health care professionals. Also describes the surgical specialties and research of the staff of the Department of Neurosurgery at the New York University Medical Center.

Department of Otorhinolaryngology at Baylor College of Medicine

http://www.bcm.tmc.edu/oto/page.html

Provides information from the Department of Otorhinolaryngology, including faculty and resident directory, residency and fellowship information, audiology program information, grand rounds archives, subscription information for the OTOHNS-Online Otolaryngology discussion group, and links to other otolaryngology resources.

Experimental Organ Preservation

http://sapphire.surgery.wisc.edu/

Focuses on organ preservation and transplantation. Also discusses UW Solution, an organ preservation solution.

Harvard Biological Labratories' Biosciences-Medicine

http://www.ohsu.edu/cliniweb/wwwvl/

Provides information about what many colleges offer in their health/medicine field, as well as search units to find key topics about health questions, such as pharmacy, epidemiology, and even veterinary medicine.

Interactive Patient

http://medicus.marshall.edu/medicus.htm

Presents a program that enables you to simulate an actual patient encounter, intended as a teaching tool for physicians, residents, and medical students.

Medical Education Page

http://www.scomm.net/~greg/med-ed

Targets pre-med and medical students. Lists medical schools in the U. S., offers links to medical reference materials and ftp sites, provides lists of specialists, and more.

MedLink International

http://www.medlink.com

Links physicians with practice opportunities around the world. Assists physicians seeking employment opportunities, as well as medical organizations recruiting qualified doctors.

Medscrip Windows Prescription Writer for Physicians

http://www.rust.net/~skindell/medscrip.html

Offers a Windows prescription writer program for physicians, written by physicians for physicians. Reduces the workload and decreases the probability of errors.

Northwestern University Department of Radiology

http://pubweb.acns.nwu.edu/~dbk675/nwu_radiology.html

Offers links to current radiological information and case presentations, as well as a description of services provided, staff, residency, and fellowship programs.

Osteopathic Source

http://avicom.net/thesource/index.html

Targets osteopathic medical students, osteopathic physicians, the allopathic medical community, and people considering medicine as a career.

PLink—The Plastic Surgery Link

http://www.IAEhv.nl/users/ivheij/plink.html

Offers a collection of plastic surgery–related links. Targets physicians and interested lay readers. Includes hospital Web pages, journals, books, and general information.

Telemedicine Information Exchange—TIE

http://tie.telemed.org/

A nonprofit research organization. Provides the Telemedicine Information Exchange (TIE), a database of information on telemedicine.

Three-Dimensional Medical Reconstruction

http://www.ge.com/crd/ivl/three_dim_medical.html

Provides 3D MPEG format movies of the human body, brain, skull, colon, heart, torso, and heart arteries.

Virtual Environments and Real-time Deformations for Surgery Simulation

http://www.cc.gatech.edu/gvu/visualization/surgsim/

Focuses on simulating the perceived environment that a surgeon encounters during endoscopic surgery. Offers a large downloadable MPEG movie.

Men's Health

Chronic Prostatitis

http://www.parsec.it/summit/po.htm

Offers sections on classification, diagnostic approaches, treatments, and anatomy and physiology. The author offers some of his own insights into different treatment methods.

Circumcision Issues

http://www.eskimo.com/%7egburlin/circ.html

Covers facts, information and resource pages, and negative aspects of circumcision and foreskin restoration. Includes a small section on female circumcision.

Geddings Osbon, Sr. Foundation Impotence Resource Center

http://impotence.org/

A nonprofit organization dedicated to improving the quality of life by promoting a better understanding of sensitive medical disorders. Offers causes, treatments, facts, and a woman's perspective.

Male Factor Infertility

http://www.ivf.com/male.html

Covers impotence, nutrition as related to male infertility, artificial insemination, transrectal ultrasound, and treatment of varicocele.

Male Fertility

http://www.dash.com/netro/nwx/tmr/tmr0595/fertility0595.html

Provides tips on enhancing fertility and ensuring a healthier baby.

Men's Health

http://h-devil-www.mc.duke.edu/h-devil/men/men.htm

Offers information on urinary tract infections, testicular self-exams, premature ejaculation, and erectile dysfunction.

Men's Health Issues

http://medic.med.uth.tmc.edu/ptnt/00000391.htm

Shows links to information on fitness for a healthy heart, fat and cholesterol, and prostate cancer screening.

Successfully Treating Impotence

http://www2.impotent.com/caverject/

Covers myths, facts, and prescription drugs, and provides a quiz, a free information kit, and the names of doctors in your area who specialize in treating impotence.

Testicular Cancer: Survival High with Early Detection

http://www.fda.gov/fdac/features/196_test.html

Encourages self-exams, includes a "how to," and explains the three stages of cancer and treatment, including side effects.

Urologic and Male Genital Diseases

http://www.mic.ki.se/Diseases/c12.html

An extensive list of potential problems in male health and where to find more information.

Mental Health

Acclaim Professional Counseling

http://www.mindspring.com/~brydaguy/acclaim.html

Offers links to short self-help articles on marriage, better sex, recovery from depression, and other happy thoughts.

Center for Anxiety and Stress Treatment

http://www.cts.com/~health/

Provides resources and services for the treatment of anxiety and stress-related mental ailments. Includes an online sale of books and audio tapes. Also provides links to treatment centers, workshops, and counseling services.

Cybernetic Stress Control

http://wchat.on.ca/romberg/

Provides background and information for Dr. Romberg Programs. Includes contact information.

Cyber-Psych

http://www.charm.net/~pandora/psych/index.html

Offers psychological information and relevant links for mental health information and resources.

Institute of Psychiatry

http://www.iop.bpmf.ac.uk/

Post-graduate school at the University of London, recognized by the World Health Organization as a collaborating center for research and training in mental health. Seeks to promote excellence in the research, development, and teaching of psychiatry and its allied subjects, and to apply and disseminate knowledge through the development of treatment for the relief of suffering. Contains information and research on mental health, psychiatry, and neuroscience.

National Alliance for the Mentally Ill Home Page

http://www.cais.com/vikings/nami/index.html

Focuses on improving the lives of people who have severe mental illness and the lives of their families.

National Coalition of Arts Therapies Associations

http://membrane.com/ncata/

Provides information on six creative arts therapies—art, dance/movement, drama, music, psych, and poetry—that use creative processes to facilitate change in therapeutic, rehabilitative, community, and educational settings.

Noodles's Panic-Anxiety Page

http://frank.mtsu.edu/~sward/anxiety/abw.html

Targets the 5–15 percent of the population expected to suffer from an anxiety-related disorder during their lives. Includes theories, support, stories, and pharmacological data.

Psychiatry and Psychotherapy

http://www-leland.stanford.edu/~corelli/

Offers links to mental health information and resources. Provides information on psychiatric diagnosis, personality disorders, and other areas of psychological interest. Offers links to information on psychotherapy and psychopharmacology. Includes a personal reading list in areas of psychiatry, psychotherapy, and Jungian psychology.

Psyrix Help-Net and High Performance Consultants

http://www.ottawa.net/~helpnet

Connects you with highly trained and experienced professionals in clinical and performance psychology. Offers you advice from experienced psychotherapists from a variety of specialties, including the fields of drugs and alcohol, sex and relationships, sleep, anxiety and depression, child and family counseling, medication, and general psychology.

Recreational Therapy Home Page

http://152.30.11.86/hpr/students/Jeffmansfield/rt.html

Uses activities such as sports, games, dance, and field trips to maintain the physical, emotional, and mental well-being of patients.

Shyness Home Page

http://www.shyness.com/

Helps those with social phobias to overcome "maladaptive thoughts and beliefs" and achieve personal and professional goals through learning new behaviors.

Nursing

ADN/RN Concepts

http://www.azstarnet.com/~jlichty/rn.htm

Forum for current issues, education, health reform, and other nursing topics. Also offers current hot topics and links to other sites.

HomeCareNurse Web Page

http://junior.apk.net/~nurse

Dedicated to providing information to home care nurses. Includes a forms library and "a day in the life of a home care nurse."

Idea Nurse

http://www.silcom.com/~peter/nurse.html

Maintained by a nurse, this page provides links to other sites to promote continuing education for nurses.

International Network for Interfaith Health Practices

http://www.interaccess.com/ihpnet/

An electronic forum for resources-sharing among persons of all religious faiths and backgrounds regarding the relationship between spirituality and health.

MacNursing

http://www.community.net/~sylvan/MacNursing.html

Offers shareware and freeware, résumés, and hospital unit information systems.

Nursing Lists

http://www.callamer.com/itc/nurse/nrslist.html

Offers links to electronic mailing lists on topics of interest to nurses. Includes lists for opthalmic nurses, intravenous therapy, graduate nursing discussions, and international nursing.

Telephone Triage and Nurse Consultation

http://ally.ios.com/~webster/index.html

Offers sites of interest to telephone triage nurses, including health administration, medical, and marketing resources.

WholeNurse

http://www.wholenurse.com/

Provides information to nurses, patients, and medical personnel of all types in an effort to keep up with the growing amount of information posted online.

Nutrition

Arizona Health Sciences Library

http://www.medlib.arizona.edu/educ/nutrition.htm

Provides links to sites related to health, including exercise, nutrition, dietetics sources, foods and recipes, and diseases and health.

Austin Reference Guide for Vitamins

http://www.realtime.net/anr/vitamins.html

Contains information on the B vitamins; vitamins C, D, and E; biotin; folic acid; and niacin. Also contains links to reference guides for nutrients, minerals, herbs, and amino acids.

Center for Food Safety and Applied Nutrition

http://vm.cfsan.fda.gov/list.html

FDA site describing cosmetics, food additives and pesticides, labeling, press releases, and women's health. Also includes a seafood hotline.

Dietetics Online

http://www.dietetics.com/

Home page for the World-Wide Network of Nutrition and Dietetic Professionals. Includes a marketplace and a link to the Dietetics Online archives.

Fast Food Finder

http://www.olen.com/food/

Searchable database for information on nutrition and fast-food restaurants.

Macrobiotics Online

http://www.macrobiotics.org/

Nutrition based on Yin/Yang diet selection and preparation. Includes lifestyle suggestions, classes, recovery stories, recipes, and a FAQ sheet.

Magnesium Deficiency, Heart Attack, and Drinking Water

http://www.execpc.com/~magnesum/

Provides information on the magnesium deficiency problem and how it relates to the beverage industry.

MN-NET Home Page

http://www.idrc.ca/mi/mnnet.htm

Provides information on micronutrient malnutrition. Includes discussion of vitamin and mineral deficiencies, current events, and prevalance and control program status.

Nutrition Pages

http://deja-vu.oldiron.cornell.edu/~jabbo/index.html

Contains articles discussing current topics such as dairy products, vegetarianism, saturated fat, poisonous plants, and food safety.

Organic Gardening

http://www.av.qnet.com/~supak/org.htm

Devoted to organic farming, this page shares information on the cost of chemicals, instructions for building a 3-bin vermicomposter, and recipes using organically grown food items.

Pharmacology

Controlled Substances: Uses and Effects

http://www.wellesley.edu/Personnel/AdminHandbook/drugchart.html

DEA-provided basic lists of narcotics, depressants, stimulants, hallucinogens, and cannabis. Outlines medical uses, physical/psychological dependence, tolerance, duration, and methods of administration.

Fischer Pharmaceuticals Laboratories

http://www.dr-fischer.com

Researches, develops, and manufactures dermatology preperations, skin-care lines, sunscreen protection, and eye and cosmetic products.

Hedonistic Imperative

http://www.pavilion.co.uk/david-pearce/hedonist.htm

Believes that within the next 1,000 years, genetic engineering and chemical psychopharmacology will eradicate the biological substrates of suffering.

Pharmaceutical Information Network

http://pharminfo.com/

Discusses publications, conferences, job listings, and software developments related to pharmaceutical care.

Pharmacokinetics, Pharmacodynamics, and Biopharmaceutics Home Page

http://griffin.vcu.edu/~gkrishna/PK/pk.html

Provides definitions, suggested readings, and news and job opportunities for these three disciplines.

Digital Photographs

http://magnet.mwci.net/mall/free/offer/

Send a 35mm or 5×7 photograph to have it digitized. Add it to your Web site or send it to your friends.

PhRMA Home Page

http://www.phrma.org

Provides an overview of PhRMA, which represents more than 100 U. S. pharmaceutical research companies. Also provides answers to frequently asked questions about pharmaceuticals, the latest news, a health guide series, and an interactive stroke survey.

PPS OnLine

http://www2.pps.ca/pps.html

Online pharmaceutical product ordering and information service. Targets health care professionals. Presents the PPS Online Pharma-Response_System, a pharmaceutical information system developed for consumers.

RxList: The Internet Drug Index

http://www.rxlist.com/

Lets you type in the names of specific drugs, and then returns information regarding generic names, brand names, and categories of classification.

Travel Resources

AEE Wilderness Safety and Emergency Care

http://www.princeton.edu/~rcurtis/wildsafe.html

Covers workshops and conferences and lists first aid resources for planning a wilderness trip.

Comprehensive Healthcare for International and Wilderness Travelers

http://www-leland.stanford.edu/~naked/stms.html

The Travel Medicine Service at Stanford University Hospital provides pretravel health care and counseling on health issues. Site includes a control panel, government agency reference sites, and related links to other health care sites.

Executive Registry

http://www.med.cornell.edu/nyhexr/exr5.html

A network of medical centers designed to assist executive travelers. A consulting service and an emergency evacuation service.

HealthNet

http://www.idsc.gov.eg/health/index.htm

Of interest to those planning trips to Egypt. Lists medical centers, physicians, and other health care providers.

Healthy Flying

http://www.maui.net/diana/

Tips for airplane travel. Covers jet lag, fear of flying, airline food, time zones, and blocked ears.

International Traveler's Clinic

http://www.intmed.mcw.edu/ITC/Health.html

Includes tips on traveling while pregnant and packing a travel medicine kit; lists environmental hazards, such as altitude and motion sickness and auto accidents; and gives an overview of different diseases and vaccinations.

Moon Publications

http://www.moon.com/

Publishes travel guides for North America, Mexico, Central America and the Caribbean, Asia, and the Pacific Islands. Includes a special section on "Staying Healthy in Asia, Africa, and Latin America," which covers what to do before leaving, preventing and treating illness while overseas, and what to do after returning home.

Outdoor Action Guide to High Altitude Acclimatization and Illness

http://www.princeton.edu/~rcurtis/altitude.html

Discusses symptoms, what causes high altitude illnesses, and how to prevent them. Also covers the different types of illnesses.

Travel First Aid Kit

http://regina.ism.ca/trakker/Medical/TravMedK.htm

Explains items to pack in case of an emergency, including antinausea treatment, antiseptics, Calamine lotion, insect repellent, water purification tablets, dental items, and more.

Traveler's Diarrhea

http://regina.ism.ca/trakker/Medical/TravDiar.htm

Discusses this acute illness that most often occurs in regions where sanitation is a problem. Covers prevention, treatment of symptoms, antibiotics, and the Giardia parasite.

Traveler's Medical and Immunization Service

http://www.tmis.com/

Offers an individualized preventative medical program based on your travel itinerary, medical history, physical condition, and exposure risk.

World Wide Drugs

http://community.net/~neils/new.html

Lists medical and pharmaceutical hospitals and sites.

Women's Health

Atlanta Reproductive Health Centre

http://www.mindspring.com/~mperloe/index.html

Provides information in areas of women's health, including infertility, endometriosis, contraception, sexually transmitted diseases, menopause, stress management, and PMS. Also provides information about the doctor's purpose and credentials regarding opinions within the Web site.

Avon's Breast Cancer Awareness Crusade

http://www.pmedia.com/Avon/avon.html

Provides information about breast cancer and breast health. Includes a list of more than 250 breast cancer support groups across the country.

Breast Cancer Information

http://nysernet.org/bcic/

Provides information for breast cancer patients and their families.

Bright Innovations

http://www.earthlink.net/~bright/

Provides tutorials and explanations of techniques regarding cervical cancer screening.

Emergency Contraception

http://opr.princeton.edu/ec/ec.html

Provides information about prescription emergency contraception such as ECPs, minipills, and the copper-T.

Endometriosis

http://www.iuf.com/endohtml.html

Discusses the immune system, environmental factors, and irritable bowel syndrome, including theories, diagnosis, and treatment.

Health and Science

http://www.polaris.net/~health/

Offers a specialty health food store and a guide to understanding and controlling PMS, fertility, menopause, and osteoporosis.

Health Articles by Patricia Older

http://pages.prodigy.com/HYEW27A/womart.htm

Articles include information on acupuncture, exercise, walking, and "dancing away the menopause blues."

Labor of Love

http://www.ultimate.org/MIDWIFE/

Contains international listings of midwives, childbirth educators, and lactation consultants, along with information on pregnancy, childbirth, breastfeeding, and parenting.

OB/GYN Toolbox

http://www.cpmc.columbia.edu/homepages/morrowj/tools/tools.html

An educational resource for the medical community. Contains a body surface area calculator, endometriosis scoring, a gestational age calculator, and an OB ultrasound analyzer.

S.P.O.T.: The Tampon Health Web Site

http://critpath.org/~tracy/spot.html

Women dedicated to informing other women through "articles and information about the hazards of synthetic tampon use and resources for healthy alternatives."

Women of the World

http://www.echonyc.com/~jmkm/wotw/

Federal laws and policies affecting reproductive rights.

WomenCare

http://www.womencare.com/

For women over 40. Discusses hot flashes, breast exams, PAP tests, and other resources.

WomenSpace

http://www.womenspace.com/

Targets young women and girls. Offers promos and free stuff. Sponsored by The Women's Pharmacy, which enables women to shop at home for pharmacy products.

Workplace Health & Safety

American Industrial Hygiene Association

http://www.aiha.org/

"Dedicated to the anticipation, recognition, evaluation, and control of environmental factors arising in or from the workplace that may result in injury, illness, impairment, or affect the well-being of workers and members of the community." Includes links to public relations, continuing education, and government affairs pages.

Computer Related Repetitive Strain Injury

http://engr-www.unl.edu/ee/eeshop/rsi.html

Contains an introduction to RSI, symptoms, prevention, and sites to learn more about the problem.

CTD News Online

http://ctdnews.com/

Covers repetitive motion injuries. Includes information on massage therapy on the job, tips for safe lifting, carpal tunnel syndrome, and back issues of the *CTDNews* magazine.

Eastern Analytical Services

http://www.EASInc.com/

An independent environmental and industrial hygiene laboratory established to provide analytical services for such containments as radon gas, formaldehyde, hydrocarbons, volatile organic compounds, PCBs, pesticides, and metals.

EMF-Link

http://infoventures.com/

Provides information on biological and health effects of electric and magnetic fields from sources such as power lines, electrical wiring, appliances, medical equipment, communciations facilities, cellular phones, and computers.

Health and Computers

http://wwwpenninfo.upenn.edu:1962/tiserve.mit.edu/9000/25204.html

A short list of links to articles about the relationship between health and computers. The links include eye problems, tendonitis, and the hazards of typing.

Howger Services, Inc.

http://www.ns.net/users/howger/index.html

Provides information on drugs in the workplace, including articles on the pros and cons of drug testing, federal drug and alcohol testing regulations, and employee-assistance programs.

NewsPage

http://www.newspage.com/NEWSPAGE/cgi-bin/walk.cgi/NEWSPAGE/info/d14/d1/d7/

Provides a daily update of workplace safety in the news. Lists brief summaries of articles; entire text is available for a small fee.

OSHA-DATA

http://www.oshadata.com/

Private corporation offering safety inspection records of companies inspected by the U.S. Department of Labor Occupational Safety and Health Administration. OSHA-DATA will help determine which companies have a better commitment to the workplace environment.

Rocky Mountain Center for Occupational and Environmental Health

http://rocky.utah.edu/

An institute dedicated to the assessment and prevention of occupation- and envrionment-related diseases. Includes information on ergonomics and safety, occupational health nursing, industrial hygiene, and continuing education.

Typing Injury FAQ

http://www.cs.princeton.edu/~dwallach/tifaq/

Provides general information about typing injuries, a list of items to replace or update a keyboard, alternative pointing devices, software monitoring tools, and new furniture.

Sunscreen

http://solargear.com/solargear/freestuf.html

Take a step toward keeping your skin healthy by ordering a $1 off coupon for sunscreen, which will come in handy if you win the trip to Tahiti.

Newsgroups

alt.backrubs

alt.building.health-safety

alt.drugs.caffeine

alt.drugs.usenet

alt.folklore.herbs

alt.forsale.nutrition

alt.health.ayurveda

alt.health.cfids-action

alt.health.oxygen-therapy

alt.med.cfs

alt.med.ems

alt.med.fibromyalgia

alt.med.veterinary

alt.meditation

alt.meditation.transcendental

alt.personals.herpes

alt.recovery.aa

alt.recovery.na

alt.society.mental-health

alt.support.anxiety-panic

alt.support.arthritis

alt.support.asthma

alt.support.ataxia

alt.support.attn-deficit

alt.support.cancer

alt.support.cancer.prostate

alt.support.cerebral-palsy

alt.support.crohns-colitis

alt.support.diabetes.kids

alt.support.diet

alt.support.diet.rx

alt.support.dystonia

alt.support.eating-disord

alt.support.endometriosis

alt.support.epilepsy

alt.support.glaucoma

alt.support.hemophilia

alt.support.herpes

alt.support.inter-cystitis

alt.support.kidney-failure

alt.support.learning-disab

alt.support.menopause

alt.support.mult-sclerosis

alt.support.ocd

alt.support.personality

alt.support.post-polio

alt.support.schizophrenia

alt.support.skin-diseases

alt.support.skin-diseases.psoriasis

alt.support.sleep-disorder

alt.support.spina-bifida

alt.support.stop-smoking

alt.support.stuttering

alt.support.thyroid

alt.support.tinnitus

alt.support.tourette

bionet.biology.vectors

bionet.immunology

bit.listserv.c+health

bit.listserv.humage-l

bit.listserv.mednews

bit.listserv.snurse-l

clari.biz.industry.health

clari.biz.industry.health.care

clari.biz.industry.health.care.releases

clari.biz.industry.health.cbd

clari.biz.industry.health.pharma

clari.biz.industry.health.pharma.releases

clari.news.aging

clari.news.alcohol

clari.news.minorities

clari.tw.health

clari.tw.health.aids

clari.tw.health.misc

misc.education.medical

misc.emerg-services

misc.fitness

misc.fitness.misc

misc.fitness.aerobic

misc.fitness.weights

misc.health

misc.health.aids

misc.health.alternative

misc.health.arthritis

misc.health.diabetes

misc.health.infertility

misc.health.injuries.rsi.misc

misc.health.injuries.rsi.moderated

misc.health.therapy.occupational

misc.kids.health

own.health.aromatherapy

own.health.bach_flowers

own.health.herbs

own.health.homoeopathy

own.health.misc

own.health.reiki

pdaxs.schools.fitness

pdaxs.services.fitness

pnet.health.braininjury

pnet.health.drug-alcohol

pnet.health.talk

sci.bio.phytopathology

sci.med

alt.med.allergy

sci.med.cardiology

sci.med.dentistry

sci.med.diseases.als

sci.med.diseases.cancer

sci.med.diseases.hepatitis

sci.med.diseases.lyme

sci.med.diseases.hepatitis

sci.med.diseases.lyme

sci.med.immunology

sci.med.informatics

sci.med.laboratory

sci.med.midwifery

sci.med.nursing

sci.med.nutrition

sci.med.occupational

sci.med.orthopedics

sci.med.pathology

sci.med.pharmacy

sci.med.prostate.cancer

sci.med.psychobiology

sci.med.radiology

sci.med.telemedicine

sci.med.transcription

soc.support.fat-acceptance

soc.retirement

su.org.hpp-aerobics

talk.politics.medicine

thelinq.student.health

tnn.living.health

tw.bbs.sci.medicine

Listservs

C+HEALTH—The Health Effects of Computer Use

America Online, Inc. (1-800-827-6364 in USA/ Canada)

You can join this group by sending the message "sub C+HEALTH your name" to listserv@listserv.aol.com

CANCHID—Canadian Network on Health in International Development

You can join this group by sending the message "sub CANCHID your name" to listserv@yorku.ca

FIT-L—Exercise/Diet/Wellness Talk List

East Texas State University, Commerce, TX

You can join this group by sending the message "sub FIT-L your name" to listserv@etsuadmn.etsu.edu

GERINET—Geriatric Health Care Discussion Group

State University of New York at Buffalo

You can join this group by sending the message "sub GERINET your name" to
listserv@ubvm.cc.buffalo.edu

HEALTH-L—International Discussion on Health Research

You can join this group by sending the message "sub HEALTH-L your name" to
listserv@listserv.hea.ie

H-INFOED—Education for Health Info & Library Wk

You can join this group by sending the message "sub H-INFOED your name" to
listserv@listserv.iupui.edu

INHEALTH—International Health Communication

Rensselaer Polytechnic Institute, Troy, NY

You can join this group by sending the message "sub INHEALTH your name" to
listserv@vm.its.rpi.edu

L-CHDH—Culture, Human Development, and Health

Pennsylvania State University

You can join this group by sending the message "sub L-CHDH your name" to listserv@psuvm.psu.edu

NHSC—National Health Service Corps

You can join this group by sending the message "sub NHSC your name" to listserv@lsv.uky.edu

SCOHRP—Study Committee on Health-Related Programs Discussion List

You can join this group by sending the message "sub SCOHRP your name" to
listserv@listserv.kent.edu

SPHHS—School of Public Health & Health Services Discussion Group

The George Washington University Computer Center, Washington, DC

You can join this group by sending the message "sub SPHHS your name" to listserv@gwuvm.gwu.edu

TLTHS—Teaching and Learning Technologies for the Health Sciences

West Virginia Network for Educational Telecomputing

You can join this group by sending the message "sub TLTHS your name" to listserv@wvnvm.wvnet.edu

American History

African-American History

http://www.msstate.edu/Archives/History/USA/Afro-Amer/afro.html

A page devoted to the history of African Americans, with text and documents relating to Buffalo soldiers, the history of slavery in the United States, African American scientists, writers, musicians, and much more. Links to related sites.

American and British History Resources

http://info.rutgers.edu/rulib/artshum/amhist.html

Provides a large archive of links to material concerning American and British history. Offers maps, online books and essays by such people as Francis Bacon, Samuel Johnson, John Locke, William Penn, Thomas Paine, Benjamin Franklin, and Thomas Jefferson.

American Civil War Home Page

http://funnelweb.utcc.utk.edu/~hoemann/cwarhp.html

A gateway to numerous civil-war related sites, including timelines, letters, graphic images, specific battles and much more. A must for Civil War enthusiasts.

American Civilization Internet Resources

http://www.georgetown.edu/departments/amer_studies/internet.html

An immense compilation of links concerning American studies, from revolutionary war topics to current history.

American History

http://www.academic.marist.edu/history/hisamer.htm

A massive series of links to all major periods of American history, each with additional links. A wonderful starting point for related searches.

American Memory

http://lcweb2.loc.gov/amhome.html

Contains collections of American culture and history, mostly derived from Library of Congress special collections. Photographic panoramas, sound files, movies, photos, and documents can be found in abundance.

The American Revolution and the Struggle for Independence

http://grid.let.rug.nl/~welling/usa/revolution.html

Presents American history, from the colonial period until World War I. Contains many images and accompanying historical descriptions. Has links to a large number of historical sources.

American Studies Web

http://www.library.yale.edu/internet/americanstudies.html

Provides links to every known topic concerning American studies (seriously, this is quite possible). Includes literature, art, history, ethnicity, religion, and so on.

Anti-Imperialism in the United States, 1898–1935

http://web.syr.edu/~fjzwick/

Focuses on presenting information and literature about the anti-imperialist movement in the United States, including several documents penned by Mark Twain. Focuses on the period 1898–1935 and provides numerous links to texts by people and organizations active at that time in the movement. Provides backgrounds for different pieces.

Indiana Historical Society

http://www..ihs1830.org/ihs.html

Nonprofit membership organization. Collects, preserves, and promotes the history of Indiana. Features information on the Society's collections, exhibitions, publications, and numerous other activities.

Isis: Our Story

http://www.netdiva.com/ourstory.html

A net page devoted to African American women and their achievements. Intersting and little-known facts, documents, and images. Links to related sites.

Life Histories—American Memory Project

http://lcweb2.loc.gov/wpaintro/wpahome.html

Presents a collection of life histories sponsored by the Manuscript Division of the Library of Congress and written for the United States Works Progress Administration's Federal Writer's Project between 1936 and 1940. Includes 2,900 documents that represent the work of more than 300 writers from 24 states. Lets you access these documents by various search means, including by region or state.

Oregon—World War II Farming

http://arcweb.sos.state.or.us/osuhomepage.html

Exhibits "Fighters on the Farm Front: Oregon's Emergency Farm Labor Service, 1943—1947," which includes more than 60 images and printed documents.

United States—History

gopher://wiretap.spies.com/11/Gov/US-History

Contains texts of historically significant United States documents, including the Declaration of Independence, Emancipation Proclamation, Monroe Doctrine, W.W.II surrenders of Germany and Japan, Tonkin Gulf Resolution, and more.

Ancient History

Seven Wonders of the Ancient World

The following are the seven wonders of the ancient world. To learn more about ancient history, visit the sites in this section.

- Artemision at Ephesus
- Colossus of Rhodes
- Hanging Gardens of Babylon
- Mausoleum at Halocarnassus
- Olympian Zeus
- Pyramids of Egypt
- Tower of Pharos

ABZU

http://www-oi.uchicago.edu/OI/DEPT/RA/ABZU/ABZU.HTML

Provides information concerning the ancient Near East including information and pictures about specific sites, museum exhibits, journals, and so forth. Provides a number of resources to ancient Egypt and Mesopotamia, including architectural information and texts.

Akkadian Language (Babylonian and Assyrian Cuneiform Texts)

http://www.sron.ruu.nl/~jheise/akkadian/index.html

Contains an introduction to the culture and history of ancient Mesopotamia, including documents in cuneiform and transliterations. Discusses grammar of Akkadian and Semitic languages and contains links to many related sites.

Alexandria, Egypt

http://pharos.bu.edu/Egypt/Alexandria

Provides information about the ancient Egyptian city of Alexandria. Includes history, maps, and visitor information.

Ancient City of Athens

http://www.indiana.edu/~kglowack/Athens/Athens.html

Includes many images of the historical sites of Athens, Greece, as well as insights into Greek history. Offers links to other sites concerning Greek history and architecture.

Archaeological Survey in the Eastern Desert of Egypt

http://rome.classics.lsa.umich.edu/projects/coptos/desert.html

A thorough archaeological study of the ancient site of Coptos, providing information about the transdesert trade routes between the Nile Valley and the Red Sea which linked early Mediterranean civilizations with those of the Indian Ocean between 300 B.C. and A.D. 400.

Assyria On-line

http://www.cs.toronto.edu/~jatou

A comprehensive resource to all subjects related to ancient Assyria, including the law code of Hammurabi, the Epic of Gilgamesh, Assyro-Babylonian mythology, and links to related sites.

Didaskalia: Home Page

http://www.warwick.ac.uk./didaskalia/

Provides information about ancient dance, drama, and music. Also provides access to Didaskalia itself (a journal on the Greek and Roman theater) and other related Internet sites.

Diotima: Women & Gender in the Ancient World

http://www.uky.edu/ArtsSciences/Classics/gender.html

A resource specifically designed for historical information concerning women in the ancient Mediterranean. Features documents, discussions, images, and links.

Exploring Ancient World Cultures

http://cedar.evansville.edu/~wcweb/wc101

Not only does this site provide detailed information on eight ancient cultures, it also provides links to other fascinating (and highly specialized) historical Web sites, including the International Museum of the Horse.

Kelsey Museum Educational and Outreach Program

http://classics.lsa.umich.edu/~Kelseydb/

Exhibits a variety of objects from the ancient meccas of culture, from Greece to Rome to Egypt. Also provides coverage of the Karanis excavations in Egypt and maps of the ancient world.

Oriental Institute

http://www-oi.uchicago.edu

Provides information about the University of Chicago's Oriental Institute museum and philology projects. Includes information and visual images on ancient Near East regions, through ABZU, an immense database of links. Also includes a new bibliographic reference, "Women in the Ancient Near East."

Perseus Project Home Page

http://medusa.perseus.tufts.edu/

Presents an interactive multimedia database on ancient Greece. Includes ancient texts and information about sites and artifacts. Includes a searchable database for finding coins, vases, and more.

Peter Konin's Ancient Rome Page

http://www.detour.com/~pkonin

The ultimate Web site for information about the Roman Empire. Features images, documents, maps, and countless links. Covers topics ranging from history and architecture to Roman cooking.

Pompeii

http://www.tulane.edu/pompeii/text/pompeii.html

Features interesting topics from Pompeii, including the famed mosaic of the Battle of Issus (between Alexander the Great and Darius) and pictures of the House of Faun, one of the largest and most elegant homes of Pompeii.

Pompeii Forum

http://jefferson.village.virginia.edu/pompeii/page-1.html

Includes maps and pictures of the unfortunate (but well-preserved) Roman city of Pompeii. Also serves as a forum for discussions about Pompeii and Roman architecture in general.

Archaeology

ArchNet: Main Menu

http://spirit.lib.uconn.edu/archnet/archnet.html

Provides links to and information regarding archaeology on the Internet. Includes the following subject areas: archeometry, ceramics, educational materials, ethnohistory, ethnoarchaeology, geo-archaeology, and a fabulous list of links to museum Web pages.

Classics and Mediterranean Archaeology Home Page

http://rome.classics.lsa.umich.edu/welcome.html

Focuses on Mediterranean and classical archaeology, but also provides access to all sorts of archaeological links, including articles, journals, projects, exhibits, images, related academics, museums, geographic information, other Internet resources, and more. An excellent resource.

Fossil Hominids

http://rumba.lcs.edu:8080/faas/fossil-hominids.html

Short summaries of the different species and subspecies of early man, including a timeline.

GIS and Remote Sensing for Archaeology: Burgundy, France

http://deathstar.rutgers.edu/projects/france/france.html

Sums up most of the major modern technological techniques for excavating and sensing underground.

Gopher and WWW Servers

http://www.icomos.org/irg-servers.html

Describes what you can find on Web servers dedicated to archaelogy. Offers links to historical societies, archaeology sites, museums, architectural preservation sites, Gophers, FAQs, and servers.

The Institute of Egyptian Art and Archaeology

http://www.memst.edu/egypt/main.html

Presents exhibits online that include mummies and other artifacts. Offers the chance to see the relics of old or take a Web tour of Egypt.

Leptiminus Archaeological Project

http://rome.classics.lsa.umich.edu/projects/lepti/lepti.html

Represents a cooperative effort between the University of Michigan and the Institute National du Patrimoine of Tunisia. Provides information about the fieldwork conducted from 1990–1993, as well as images of the site.

NEH Archaeology Projects Online

http://www.neh.fed.us/documents/rkpubs.html

Presents currently ongoing projects including histories and images of archaeology projects sponsored by the National Endowment for the Humanities. Includes images in the reports.

Newstead Project

http://www.brad.ac.uk/acad/archsci/field_proj/newstead/newstead.html

Focuses on the archeological exploration of settlements surrouding a Roman fort, called Trimontium, in southern Scotland.

The Ohio State University Excavations at Isthmia

http://www.acs.ohio-state.edu/history/isthmia/isthmia.html

Covers the excavations at The Sanctuary of Poseidon at Isthmia (Greece). Examines the work and describes several points of interest in the area.

Online Archaeology-An Electronic Journal of Archaeological Theory

http://avebury.arch.soton.ac.uk/Journal/journal.html

Electronic journal. Focuses on "promoting rapid dissemination of speculative ideas about archaeology." Covers various thoughts about archaeology.

Oriental Institute Archaeology

http://www-oi.uchicago.edu/OI/PROJ/OI_Archaeology.html

Covers many ongoing excavations and other archaeological projects by the Oriental Institute at the University of Chicago. Offers links to many different projects.

OWAN

http://www.wesleyan.edu/classics/OWAN.html

The *Old World Archaeology Newsletter (OWAN)* covers the conferences, research, and publications concerning archaeology. Includes editorials and announcements.

European History

Armenian Research Center Home Page

http://www.umd.umich.edu:80/dept/armenian/

Provides Armenian culture and history, as well as information on the Armenian genocide. Offers a link to the Society for Armenian Studies.

Berlin Wall Falls Project

http://192.253.114.31/Berlin/Introduction/Berlin.html

Presents the collaborative Web project, the "Berlin Wall Falls: Perspectives from 5 Years Down the Road." Involves students and researchers around the globe.

European History

http://www.academic.marist.edu/history/hiseuro.htm

An immense collection of links to sites devoted to different aspects (and periods) of European history. Some sites have graphics. Many sites relating to more modern eras have sound files.

Europe/Russia/Eastern Europe

http://execpc.com/~dboals/europe.html

An enormous series of links to sites connected to European history, from ancient days to modern times. A great starting place for more specific searches.

Germany—Database of German Nobility

http://faui80.informatik.uni-erlangen.de/html/

Targets historians and geneologians. Focuses on the family tree of Charlemagne, but also features a database of biographies and portraits of German nobility.

The Historical Text Archive

http://www.msstate.edu/Archives/History

Award-winning site that contains links to East and West European history topics. Historical information, images, and documents relating to many countries, including Estonia, Iceland, France, the Netherlands, and more.

History Pages

http://ux1.cso.uiuc.edu/~kundert/josh/../history/history.html

Focuses on Celtic history. Plans to add pages on Saxon and Frankish history. Provides information on the Celts, including maps and links to other Celtic sites.

Hungarian Images and Historical Background

http://www.msstate.edu/Archives/History/hungary/hungary.html

Richly detailed summaries of the salient points of Hungarian history. Features images of coats of arms, crown jewels, maps, and more.

Irish History on the Web

http://wwwvms.utexas.edu/~jdana/

A vast number of links relating to Irish history. Features information on many historical and contemporary topics, including a "This week in Irish History" page.

Irish Potato Famine

http://www1.cc.emory.edu/FAMINE

Images and contemporary reports and interviews about the Irish Potato famine (1845-1851) and related Web sites.

REESWeb: Russian and East European Studies

http://www.pitt.edu/~cjp/rees.html

A massive collection of links to historic and contemporary information about Russia and Eastern Europe.

Anything from maps of the former Soviet Union to the home page of Bucharest can be found here.

Russian Information

http://www.valley.net/~transnat/russsubj.html

A good starting point for Russian history on the Web. Features a chronology of Russian history, an illustrated history of Russia and the USSR, links to Mikhael Gorbachev's home page, and more.

Soviet Archives: Entrance Room

http://sunsite.unc.edu/expo/soviet.exhibit/entrance.html

Provides the Library of Congress Soviet Exhibit, divided into two categories: The Internal Workings of the Soviet System and The Soviet Union and the United States.

The Victorian Web

http://www.stg.brown.edu/projects/hypertext/landow/victorian/victov.html

An expansive collection of information on 19th century British culture, with documents, links, and images.

Historical Figures

Abraham Lincoln Online

http://www.netins.net/showcase/creative/lincoln.html

Documents, images, speeches and links to other sites relating to Abraham Lincoln. A great source of information about the great emancipator.

Educational Sources for George Washington

http://www.mountvernon.org/image/george.html

Many documents on the first American President, George Washington. Discusses his life history, myths about George Washington, anecdotes, and excerpts from his journal.

Potomac Mills

http://www.potomac-mills.com/shop/coupon.html

Get a free gift from one of the world's largest outlet malls.

Empires Beyond the Great Wall: The Heritage of Genghis Khan

`http://vvv.com/khan`

A virtual exhibit of the great Khan's artifacts, period clothing and armor, pottery, documents, and a biography of Genghis Khan.

Fair Play

`http://rmii.com/~jkelin/fp.html`

Online magazine. Focuses on giving Lee Harvey Oswald a fair shake. Presents articles concerning various views on the JFK assassination.

JFK Resources Online

`http://www.cybercom.net/~jimas/cheryl/jfk.html`

A page devoted to JFK. Includes his inaugural address, memories of those who knew him, selected quotes, samples of his humor, photos, and sound bites. Also covers information about President Kennedy's assasination. Has many links to other pages, mostly devoted to the assasination controversy.

Leonardo da Vinci Museum

`http://cellini.leonardo.net/museum/gallery.html`

Sketches, paintings, drawings and information about the life and times of this Renaissance genius. Offers additional links.

Spectrum Biography Library

`http://www.autobaun.com/~kbshaw/Biographies/BioLibrary.html`

Short but information-packed biographies of famous and interesting people, including Scott Joplin, Amelia Earhart, Wyatt Earp, Julius Caesar, and more. The list is still growing.

Thomas Jefferson

`http://grid.let.rug.nl/~welling/usa/jefferson.html`

Graphics, a biography, documents, and related links about the sage of Monticello, the third president of the United States and primary author of the Declaration of Independence, Thomas Jefferson.

Thomas Paine

`http://freethought.tamu.edu/freethought/thomas_paine/`

A complete source of documents written by that free-thinking American revolutionary, Thomas Paine.

Twisted Freaks of History

`http://www.tiac.net/users/jclark/index.html`

A page devoted to the famously weird and their weird ideas. Well-written and entertaining, with graphics and loads of information. The featured freak changes every six to eight weeks.

The United States Presidents: Welcome Page

`http://utkvx1.utk.edu/~razz2/uspres1.html`

Covers some of the highlights of each president's administration, including representative quotes. Also describes some of the problems with which each president struggled during his tenure, shows an image of each president, and briefly analyzes each administration.

Medieval Studies

Articles on Medieval/Renaissance Subjects

`http://www.honors.indiana.edu/~atrium/script/articles.html`

A page devoted to articles concerning the Renaissance. A storehouse of Renaissance-related articles. Part of a Web site that also contains period texts and manuscripts. Links to other sites, maps, and images.

Avalon: Arthurian Heaven

`http://Reality.sgi.com/employees/chris_manchester/guide.html`

The place to be if you're interested in both the historical and mythical King Arthur. Many links to other sites, including one that features the Monty Python "Holy Grail" script.

Byzantium: The Byzantine Studies Page

`http://www.bway.net/~halsall/byzantium.html`

A gateway to the numerous (and constantly growing) sites dedicated to the history, culture, and art of the Eastern Roman Empire. While western Europe struggled through the dark ages, civilization was alive and well in Byzantium.

Labyrinth WWW Home Page

`http://www.georgetown.edu/labyrinth/labyrinth-home.html`

Provides complete information about medieval studies on the Web. Also provides search capabilities.

Vikings Home Page

http://control.chalmers.se/vikings/viking.html

Provides topics on Viking cults, the Vikings of Russia, and Vikings of today. Also features a Swedish-Viking-English dictionary and offers links to other Viking-related Web servers.

WWW Medieval Resources

http://ebbs.english.vt.edu/medieval/medieval.ebbs.html

Offers links to different resources relating to medieval times.

Military History

Cold War Hot Links

http://www.stmartin.edu/~dprice/cold.war.html

Films, images, documents and links concerning the cold war, including formerly classified documents, information on McCarthy, period speeches, and much more.

Cybrary of the Holocaust

http://www2.best.com/~mddunn/cybrary/

Provides information on the Holocaust. Offers details on the rise of Nazism in Germany and its subsequent effects on the Jews. Includes pictures, eyewitness descriptions of concentration camps, and historical perspectives.

D-Day

http://192.253.114.31/D-Day/Table_of_contents.html

Provides Army and Navy news reels, past issues of the *Stars & Stripes* newspaper, famous speeches from the National Archives, and a collection of maps and battle plans from the Center for Military History.

George Rarey's Journals of the 379th Fighter Squadron

http://www.nbn.com/home/rareybird/index.html

Provides the journal of a young cartoonist who was drafted into the Army Air Corps in World War II. Documents his various drawings throughout the war. Provides images and accompanying text.

Gulf War Photo Gallery

http://users.aol.com/andyhosk/gulf-war.html

Presents a Gulf War photo gallery, compiled by Ronald A. Hoskinson. Displays images taken primarily from the personal collection of Norman Jarvis. Offers a few links to other Gulf War sites.

Korean War Project

http://www.onramp.net/~hbarker/index1.htm

Photos, maps, casualty lists and historical documents, all related to the Korean War. Numerous links to related sites.

Military History

http://www.cfcsc.dnd.ca/links/milhist/

A good access of links through many of the world's most famous (infamous?) wars. Find links to the Hundred Year's War, the French Revolution, or even the Persian Gulf War. If you're looking for military history, this is the place to start.

Operation Desert Storm Debriefing Book

http://www.nd.edu/~aleyden/contents.html

Provides information concerning military and political aspects of the Gulf War. Includes backgrounds on politicians, descriptions of military hardware, statistics, and links to other Gulf War sites.

Remembering Nagasaki

http://www.exploratorium.edu/nagasaki/

Observes the 50th anniversary of the dropping of atomic bombs on Hiroshima and Nagasaki. Includes photographs taken by Yosuki Yamahata of Nagasaki the day after, which create a backdrop for discussion and reflection on issues concerning the atomic age. Lets you share your views and read those of others.

Salvation of Bulgarian Jews during WW II

http://ASUdesign.eas.asu.edu/places/Bulgaria/Jewish/

Provides an archive of material regarding the rescue of Bulgarian Jews during World War II. Offers links to various documents and other sites pertaining to the Holocaust and related Jewish topics. Also provides a short bibliography.

Salzburg 1945–1955: Introduction

http://www.image.co.at/image/salzburg/

Presents Austrians and American G.I.'s sharing remembrances of the "Era of Occupation" of Salzburg, Austria, subsequent to the defeat of Nazi Germany in 1945. Includes links to images and text interviews.

Vietnam Veterans Home Page

http://www.vietvet.org/

Focuses on Vietnam veterans from both sides of the conflict. Provides a forum for exchange of information, stories, poems, songs, art, pictures, and experiences.

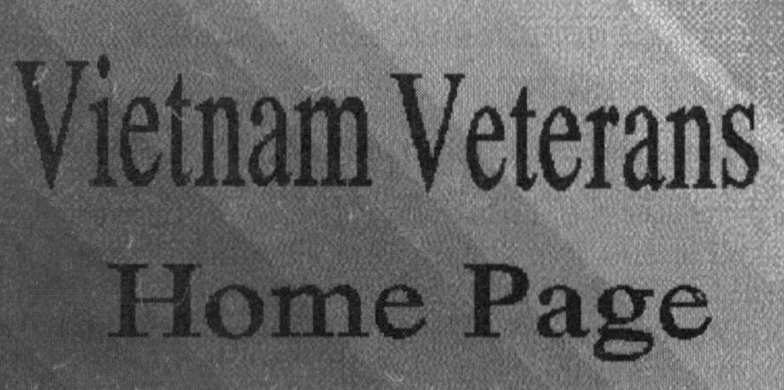

The War from a Parlor: Stereoscopic Images of the Philippine-American War and Soldiers' Letters Home

http://www.maxwell.syr.edu/unofficial/fjzwick/centennial/stereo

Juxtaposes the visual (stereoscopic images) with excerpts from letters written by United States soldiers during the Philippine-American War.

Worlds of Late Antiquity

http://ccat.sas.upenn.edu/jod/wola.html

A home page devoted to Late Roman and early medieval information. No images, but many interesting documents.

World War I (1914-1918)

http://www.cfcsc.dnd.ca/links/milhist/wwi.html

A page dedicated to World War I, featuring links to many Great War subjects: propaganda, aerial combat, trench warfare, the Versailles treaty, lost poets, and more.

World War II on the Web

http://www.bunt.com/~mconrad/

A long list of links to sites concerning the second world war, including art, photos, documents, information for memorabilia collectors, access to films, and much more.

Miscellaneous Historical Sites

ADFA History: History on the Internet

http://www.adfa.oz.au/HISTORY/links.html

A gargantuan series of links to historical sites, with photos, documents and multimedia resources on virtually any historical subject.

Arctic Circle

http://www.lib.uconn.edu/ArcticCircle/

Maps, information, and images of the circumpolar north, including history, culture, and current events. Strap on your snow shoes and take a look. Links to other pages.

Ari's Today Page

http://www.uta.fi/~blarku/today.html

A great source of information for what happened today in history. Features birthdays of famous people, historical information and important calendar days for the Jewish and Muslim faiths as well as important US oriented dates.

BUBL Information Service Web Server

http://www.bubl.bath.ac.uk/BUBL/History.html

Offers links to various history sites on the Net. Includes many topics other than history. Contains links to Russian, Vietnam War, United States, French and Indian War, Viking, medieval, and Civil War historical sites.

Castles on the Web

http://fox.nstn.ca/~tmonk/castle/castle.html

Provides a collection of sites that offer information about and pictures of castles from around the world.

Gangsters!

http://www.well.com/user/mod79

If you want information on gangsters, start here. Offers history, images, biographies of criminals and crime fighters, a bibliography of organized crime in print and on film, and links to related sites.

The Heritage Post Interactive

http://heritage.excite.sfu.ca/hpost.html

Tidbits of Canadian history and information about current Canada. Features documents and images.

The Historical Text Archive

http://www.msstate.edu/Archives/History/index.html

Archives historical texts from various countries and periods. Includes a large collection from the United States. Offers many links to other historical resources.

History Computerization Project

http://www.directnet.com/history/

Provides a database for libraries, historians, museums, libraries and more, dedicated to the exchange of historical information. Includes access to many other directories of interest.

The History of Costume by Braun

http://www.siue.edu/COSTUMES/history.html

An online version of an old German book that features fashion through the ages, from Egypt to Russian folk dress of the late nineteenth century. Excellent graphics.

Index of /expo/

http://sunsite.unc.edu/expo

Provides an index to exhibits that include the Library of Congress's "Scrolls of the Dead Sea," "The 'Palace' of Diocletian at Split," and exhibits of paleontology, the Soviet Union, the Vatican, and more. Offers a list of terms relating to Middle Eastern and classical terms. Includes downloadable .JPEG and .GIF files.

Intentional Communities

http://www.well.com/user/cmty/index.html

Seeks to be an inclusive title for information on ecovillages, cohousing, residential land trusts, communes, student co-ops, urban housing cooperatives, and other related projects.

James B. Ross' Home Page

http://134.129.87.200/jrhome.htm

Serves as a starting point for exploring history sites on the Internet. Offers an incredible amount of links.

Lords of the Earth: Maya/Aztec/Inca Exchange

http://www.realtime.net/maya

History, geography and art relating to the indigenous inhabitants of the Americas in the days before Columbus.

The Maritime History Virtual Archives

http://pc-78-120.udac.se:8001/WWW/Nautica/Nautica.html

Includes an archive on maritime history, organized under topics such as ships, shipbuilding, rigging, health of seamen, and seamanship. Also includes images of various vessels and links to other maritime sites. Provides versions in Swedish and English.

Mary Rose Virtual Maritime Museum

http://www.synergy.net/homeport.html

Offers a fascinating look at a recovered Tudor-period warship that sank in 1545. Provides links to other sites featuring ships of old.

Maya

http://www.realtime.net/maya/

Includes history, geography, geology, astronomy, archaeology, anthropology, and art forms related to the Americas before Christopher Columbus's discovery. Includes information on the Maya, Aztec, and American Indians.

The Maya Astronomy Page

http://www.astro.uva.nl/michielb/maya/astro.html

Focuses on Mayan civilization. Presents the Mayan creation story. Provides information about Mayan astronomy, mathematics, and their calendar. Offers links to other Mayan sites.

Media History, Studies, and Education

http://omnibus-eye.rtvf.nwu.edu/links/studies.html

A large number of links to history as recorded by film and other media. Many interesting sites, from the Documentary Educational Resources to the National Public Broadcasting Archives, scholarly works on Chinese Cinema, the D-Day News Reels Archive, and more.

Mithraism

http://www.lglobal.com/~hermes3/mithras.htm

Presents a look at Mithraism, a religion of the pre-Christian Roman Empire, for those interested in the roots of Western religion.

Musei

http://www.christusrex.org/www1/vaticano/0-Musei.html

Provides around 600 images of holdings of the Vatican museums. Also offers links to hundreds of images of the Sistine Chapel and the Raphael Stanze. Includes writings of John Paul II, access to News from the Holy SEE, and more.

The Museum Professional

http://www.sirius.com/~robinson/musprof

Serves as a starting point for accessing online resources in the museum field. Includes links to museum Web site lists, virtual museums, and specialization resources. Has a new forum for people in the museum field to share information.

Mutiny on the HMS Bounty

http://wavefront.wavefront.com/~pjlareau/bounty.html

Images, information and links about what is probably the most famous mutiny of all.

The National Inventors Hall of Fame

http://www.invent.org

Biographies, images, and inventions of famous inventors. Additional information on virtual exhibits and information on BFGoodrich's Collegiate Inventor's Program. An interesting stop.

Native American Cultural Resources on the Internet

http://hanksville.phast.umass.edu/misc/NAculture.html

A massive series of links to Native American sites. A good source of related history, documents, and current information.

Papyrology Home Page

http://www-personal.umich.edu/~jmucci/papyrology

Provides access to papyrology collections world-wide, literature from and concerning the collections, and images of papyri including fragments from the *Book of the Dead*.

Paris Museums

http://www.paris.org/Musees/

Contains images and information for more than 20 museums in Paris, including the Louvre, Centre Pompidou, L'Orangerie, Auguste Rodin, and la Cité des Sciences et de l'Industrie.

Pirates

http://tigger.cc.uic.edu/~toby-g/pirates.html

The page for swashbucklers and rogues, featuring facts, myths, and legends about piracy, the history of piracy, famous people, places and images connected to pirates.

Romarch List Home Page

http://www.umich.edu/~pfoss/ROMARCH.html

Provides a "crossroads for Web resources on the art and archaeology of Italy and the Roman provinces, from ca. 1000 B.C. to A.D. 600." Offers many links to sites that contain images of Roman art and architecture.

Shikhin

http://www.colby.edu/rel/Shikhin.html

A site dedicated to helping find and identify the lost city of Shikhin in Israel. Presents the story of Shikhin, known for its pottery in its day, with text, pictures, and maps.

Miscellaneous Freebies

http://www.winternet.com/~julie/fbthiswk.html

Visit this site to find weekly special offers, contests, and 800 numbers for discounts on some of your favorite products—everything from envelopes to cool beverages.

Shore Line Trolley Museum

http://www.panix.com/~christos/TrolleyPage.html

Exhibits the Shore Line Trolley museum of East Haven, CT. Provides information about museum operations, including hours and directions, as well as a tour of some streetcars in Shore Line's collection.

UNESCO World Heritage List

http://www.cco.caltech.edu/~salmon/world.heritage.html

Links to images and information on world renowned historical places like the Acropolis of Athens, India's Taj Mahal, Hadrian's Wall in England, and much more.

Voice of the Shuttle Home Page

http://humanitas.ucsb.edu/

A Web page devoted to the study of humanities, offering many links to humanities topics: archaeology, anthropology, architecture, art, general humanities, history, linguistics, literature, minority studies, philosophy, religous studies, women's studies, and more.

Science & Technology

The Art of Renaissance Science

http://www.setn.org/pubs/index.html

Photos, sound, animation, and documents tell the history of astronomy, anatomy, architecture, and art of the Renaissance, as narrated by Professor Joseph Dauben.

History of Astronomy

http://aibn55.astro.uni-bonn.de:8000/~pbrosche/
astoria.html

Focuses on the history of astronomy and in general, on science. Contains links to biographies of important people, images from observatories around the world and other archives, museums, and astronomy exhibits on the Net.

History of Science, Technology and Medicine

http://www.asap.unimelb.edu.au/hstm/hstm_ove.htm

A large database of historical information relating to science, technology, and medicine, with search features, biographies, graphics, links to museums and more.

History of Space Exploration

http://bang.lanl.gov/solarsys/

Provides information on the history of space exploration. Includes images of spacecraft and planets.

Institute for Human Sciences—Vienna

http://www.ping.at/iwm/iwmhome.htm

Provides information on an independent, interdisciplinary institute for advanced study that offers in-residence fellowships for scholars in the humanities, and that operates a number of long-term policy projects in the nations of the former Eastern bloc. Encourages both senior and junior scholars with similar research interests to explore this site.

NASA Astronautics History

http://www.hq.nasa.gov/office/pao/History/
astronautics.html

Provides key historical documents about NASA space flight, human space flight, planetary probes, lunar probes, and more.

History

Newsgroups

alt.conspiracy.jfk

alt.culture.cajun

alt.culture.us.1980s

alt.fan.ernst-zundel

alt.genealogy

alt.history.living

alt.history.ocean-liners.titanic

alt.history.what-if

alt.war.civil.usa

alt.war.vietnam

bit.listserv.history

can.schoolnet.history

clari.living.history

clari.living.history.today

fido7.fido-history

k12.ed.soc-studies

rec.food.historic

school.subjects.humanities

sci.classics

soc.culture.assyrian

soc.culture.berber

soc.culture.french

soc.culture.german

soc.culture.indian.karnataka

soc.culture.jewish.holocaust

soc.culture.kuwait

soc.culture.tamil

soc.culture.welsh

soc.genealogy.african

soc.genealogy.computing

soc.genealogy.german

soc.genealogy.hispanic

soc.genealogy.methods

soc.genealogy.methods

soc.history

soc.history.living

soc.history.medieval

soc.history.moderated

soc.history.science

soc.history.war.misc

soc.history.war.us-civil-war

soc.history.war.us-revolution

soc.history.war.vietnam

soc.history.war.world-war-ii

soc.history.what-if

soc.roots

Listservs

AERA-F—Division F: Educational History and Historiography

Arizona State University, Tempe, AZ

You can join this group by sending the message "sub AERA-F your name" to `listserv@asuvm.inre.asu.edu`

AEROSP-L—Aeronautics & Aerospace History

Smithsonian Institution, Washington, DC

You can join this group by sending the message "sub AEROSP-L your name" to `listserv@sivm.si.edu`

AMERCATH—A Discussion List On The History Of American Catholics

You can join this group by sending the message "sub AMERCATH your name" to `listserv@lsv.uky.edu`

ANCIEN-L—History of the Ancient Mediterranean

You can join this group by sending the message "sub ANCIEN-L your name" to `listserv@ulkyvm.louisville.edu`

ASHR-L—American Society for the History of Rhetoric

Pennsylvania State University

You can join this group by sending the message "sub ASHR-L your name" to `listserv@psuvm.psu.edu`

ASTR-L—Theatre History Discussion List - Amer. Soc. for Theatre Research

University of Illinois, Urbana, IL

You can join this group by sending the message "sub ASTR-L your name" to `listserv@postoffice.cso.uiuc.edu`

ASTRO-L—History of Astronomy in Canada

Memorial University of Newfoundland, St. John's, Newfoundland, Canada

You can join this group by sending the message "sub ASTRO-L your name" to `listserv@morgan.ucs.mun.ca`

ATHG—Alcohol and Temperance History Group

Miami University, Oxford, OH

You can join this group by sending the message "sub ATHG your name" to `listserv@miamiu.muohio.edu`

AZTLAN—Pre-Columbian History

You can join this group by sending the message "sub AZTLAN your name" to `listserv@ulkyvm.louisville.edu`

CAAH—Consortium Of Art And Architectural Historians

Princeton University, Princeton, NJ

You can join this group by sending the message "sub CAAH your name" to `listserv@pucc.princeton.edu`

CHA-97—Canadian Historical Association 1997

Memorial University of Newfoundland, St. John's, Newfoundland, Canada

You can join this group by sending the message "sub CHA-97 your name" to `listserv@morgan.ucs.mun.ca`

CHEIRON—Society for the History of the Social and Behavioral Sciences

You can join this group by sending the message "sub CHEIRON your name" to `listserv@yorku.ca`

COMHIST—History of Human Communication

Rensselaer Polytechnic Institute, Troy, NY

You can join this group by sending the message "sub COMHIST your name" to
`listserv@vm.its.rpi.edu`

COMM-ORG—H-Net/H-Urban Seminar on History of Community Organizing

University of Illinois at Chicago, Chicago, IL

You can join this group by sending the message "sub COMM-ORG your name" to
`listserv@uicvm.uic.edu`

EARLYSCIENCE-L—History of Science Society - Early Science Interest Group

Virginia Tech

You can join this group by sending the message "sub EARLYSCIENCE-L your name" to
`listserv@listserv.vt.edu`

EH-TEST—Economic History Testing

Miami University, Oxford Ohio

You can join this group by sending the message "sub EH-TEST your name" to
`listserv@miamiu.muohio.edu`

EHCOLUMN—Economic History Columns

Miami University, Oxford Ohio

You can join this group by sending the message "sub EHCOLUMN your name" to
`listserv@miamiu.muohio.edu`

ELIAS-I—Figurational Studies in Social Science, History and Psychology

University Center of Information services (UCI), Nijmegen, The Netherlands

You can join this group by sending the message "sub ELIAS-I your name" to `listserv@nic.surfnet.nl`

ESPORA-L—History of the Iberian Peninsula

University of Kansas, Lawrence, KS

You can join this group by sending the message "sub ESPORA-L your name" to
`listserv@ukanvm.cc.ukans.edu`

ETHNOHIS—General Ethnology and History Discussion List

University Center of Information services (UCI), Nijmegen, The Netherlands

You can join this group by sending the message "sub ETHNOHIS your name" to
`listserv@nic.surfnet.nl`

GAHIST-L—Georgia History Discussion List

The University of Georgia, Athens, GA

You can join this group by sending the message "sub GAHIST-L your name" to
`listserv@uga.cc.uga.edu`

GHOSTLETTERS—Conversations as Fictional or Historical Characters!

America Online, Inc. (1-800-827-6364 in USA/Canada)

You can join this group by sending the message "sub GHOSTLETTERS your name" to
`listserv@listserv.aol.com`

H-AFRICA—H-NET List for African History

Michigan State University, East Lansing, MI, 48824-1042

You can join this group by sending the message "sub H-AFRICA your name" to `listserv@msu.edu`

H-ALBION—H-Net British and Irish History List

Michigan State University, East Lansing, MI

You can join this group by sending the message "sub H-ALBION your name" to `listserv@msu.edu`

H-ALBION—H-NET British and Irish History List

University of Illinois at Chicago, Chicago, IL

You can join this group by sending the message "sub H-ALBION your name" to
`listserv@uicvm.uic.edu`

H-AMREL—H-Net American Religious History Discussion Group

You can join this group by sending the message "sub H-AMREL your name" to
`listserv@h-net.msu.edu`

H-ANTIS—History of Antisemitism List

University of Illinois at Chicago, Chicago, IL

You can join this group by sending the message "sub H-ANTIS your name" to
`listserv@uicvm.uic.edu`

H-ASEH—American Society for Environmental History (H-NET List)

You can join this group by sending the message "sub H-ASEH your name" to `listserv@h-net.msu.edu`

H-ASIA—H-Net list for Asian History and Culture

You can join this group by sending the message "sub H-ASIA your name" to `listserv@h-net.msu.edu`

H-CANADA—H-Net List for Canadian History

Michigan State University, East Lansing, MI

You can join this group by sending the message "sub H-CANADA your name" to `listserv@msu.edu`

H-CIVWAR—H-Net US Civil War History Discussion List

Michigan State University, East Lansing, MI

You can join this group by sending the message "sub H-CIVWAR your name" to `listserv@msu.edu`

H-CIVWAR—H-Net US Civil War History Discussion List

University of Illinois at Chicago, Chicago, IL

You can join this group by sending the message "sub H-CIVWAR your name" to
`listserv@uicvm.uic.edu`

H-DEMOG—H-Net Historical Demography List

Michigan State University, East Lansing, MI

You can join this group by sending the message "sub H-DEMOG your name" to `listserv@msu.edu`

H-DEMOG—H-Net Historical Demography List

University of Illinois at Chicago, Chicago, IL

You can join this group by sending the message "sub H-DEMOG your name" to
`listserv@uicvm.uic.edu`

H-DIPLO—H-Net Diplomatic History List

Michigan State University, East Lansing, MI

You can join this group by sending the message "sub H-DIPLO your name" to `listserv@msu.edu`

H-DIPLO—H-Net Diplomatic History list

University of Illinois at Chicago, Chicago, IL

You can join this group by sending the message "sub H-DIPLO your name" to
`listserv@uicvm.uic.edu`

H-ETHNIC—H-NET List on Ethnic History

Michigan State University, East Lansing, MI

You can join this group by sending the message "sub H-ETHNIC your name" to `listserv@msu.edu`

H-ETHNIC—H-Net Ethnic History Discussion List

University of Illinois at Chicago, Chicago, IL

You can join this group by sending the message "sub H-ETHNIC your name" to
`listserv@uicvm.uic.edu`

History

H-FRANCE—H-Net History of France List

University of Illinois at Chicago, Chicago, IL

You can join this group by sending the message "sub H-FRANCE your name" to `listserv@uicvm.uic.edu`

H-FRANCE—H-NET French History Discussion Group

Purdue University, West Lafayette, IN

You can join this group by sending the message "sub H-FRANCE your name" to `listserv@vm.cc.purdue.edu`

H-GERMAN—H-NET List on German History

You can join this group by sending the message "sub H-GERMAN your name" to `listserv@h-net.msu.edu`

H-GRAD—H-Net History Graduate Students Discussion List

University of Illinois at Chicago, Chicago, IL

You can join this group by sending the message "sub H-GRAD your name" to `listserv@uicvm.uic.edu`

H-IDEAS—H-NET Intellectual History List

University of Illinois at Chicago, Chicago, IL

You can join this group by sending the message "sub H-IDEAS your name" to `listserv@uicvm.uic.edu`

H-ITALY—Italian History List from H-NET

University of Illinois at Chicago, Chicago, IL

You can join this group by sending the message "sub H-ITALY your name" to `listserv@uicvm.uic.edu`

H-JAPAN—H-NET/KIAPS List for Japanese History

You can join this group by sending the message "sub H-JAPAN your name" to `listserv@h-net.msu.edu`

H-LABOR—H-Net Labor History Discussion List

Michigan State University, East Lansing, MI

You can join this group by sending the message "sub H-LABOR your name" to `listserv@msu.edu`

H-LABOR—H-Net Labor History Discussion List

University of Illinois at Chicago, Chicago, IL

You can join this group by sending the message "sub H-LABOR your name" to `listserv@uicvm.uic.edu`

H-LATAM—H-Net Latin-American History List

You can join this group by sending the message "sub H-LATAM your name" to `listserv@h-net.msu.edu`

H-LAW—H-Net and ASLH Legal History Discussion list

Michigan State University, East Lansing, MI

You can join this group by sending the message "sub H-LAW your name" to `listserv@msu.edu`

H-LAW—H-Net and ASLH Legal History Discussion list

University of Illinois at Chicago, Chicago, IL

You can join this group by sending the message "sub H-LAW your name" to `listserv@uicvm.uic.edu`

H-LOCAL—H-Net DISCUSSION LIST FOR LOCAL AND STATE HISTORY

Michigan State University, East Lansing, MI

You can join this group by sending the message "sub H-LOCAL your name" to `listserv@msu.edu`

H-MAC—H-NET List for the History and Macintosh Society

Michigan State University, East Lansing, MI

You can join this group by sending the message "sub H-MAC your name" to `listserv@msu.edu`

H-RHETOR—H-Net History of Rhetoric Discussion List

Michigan State University, East Lansing, MI

You can join this group by sending the message "sub H-RHETOR your name" to listserv@msu.edu

H-RHETOR—H-NET HISTORY OF RHETORIC DISCUSSION LIST

University of Illinois at Chicago, Chicago, IL

You can join this group by sending the message "sub H-RHETOR your name" to listserv@uicvm.uic.edu

H-RURAL—An H-Net List for Discussion of Rural & Agricultural History

Michigan State University, East Lansing, MI

You can join this group by sending the message "sub H-RURAL your name" to listserv@msu.edu

H-RURAL—An H-NET List for Discussion of Rural & Agricultural History

University of Illinois at Chicago, Chicago, IL

You can join this group by sending the message "sub H-RURAL your name" to listserv@uicvm.uic.edu

H-RUSSIA—H-Net Russian History list

Michigan State University, East Lansing, MI

You can join this group by sending the message "sub H-RUSSIA your name" to listserv@msu.edu

H-RUSSIA—H-Net Russian History List

University of Illinois at Chicago, Chicago, IL

You can join this group by sending the message "sub H-RUSSIA your name" to listserv@uicvm.uic.edu

H-SHEAR—H-NET List for History of the Early American Republic

Kansas State University; Manhattan, KS

You can join this group by sending the message "sub H-SHEAR your name" to listserv@ksuvm.ksu.edu

H-SKAND—H-Net List on Scandinavian History & Culture

You can join this group by sending the message "sub H-SKAND your name" to listserv@h-net.msu.edu

H-SOUTH—H-Net Southern History Discussion List

Michigan State University, East Lansing, MI

You can join this group by sending the message "sub H-SOUTH your name" to listserv@msu.edu

H-TEACH—H-Net List for Teaching College History and Related Fields

Michigan State University, East Lansing, MI

You can join this group by sending the message "sub H-TEACH your name" to listserv@msu.edu

H-TEACH—H-Net List for Teaching History and Related Fields

University of Illinois at Chicago, Chicago, IL

You can join this group by sending the message "sub H-TEACH your name" to listserv@uicvm.uic.edu

H-URBAN—H-Net Urban History Discussion List

University of Illinois at Chicago, Chicago, IL

You can join this group by sending the message "sub H-URBAN your name" to listserv@uicvm.uic.edu

H-WAR—H-Net Military History Discussion List

Kansas State University, Manhattan, KS

You can join this group by sending the message "sub H-WAR your name" to listserv@ksuvm.ksu.edu

H-WEST—H-Net Western History List

Michigan State University, East Lansing, MI

You can join this group by sending the message "sub H-WEST your name" to listserv@msu.edu

H-WEST—H-Net Western History List

University of Illinois at Chicago, Chicago, IL

You can join this group by sending the message "sub H-WEST your name" to `listserv@uicvm.uic.edu`

H-WOMEN—H-NET List for Women's History

You can join this group by sending the message "sub H-WOMEN your name" to `listserv@h-net.msu.edu`

H-WORLD—H-NET List for World History

Michigan State University, East Lansing, MI

You can join this group by sending the message "sub H-WORLD your name" to `listserv@msu.edu`

HASTRO-L—History of Astronomy Discussion Group

West Virginia Network for Educational Telecomputing

You can join this group by sending the message "sub HASTRO-L your name" to `listserv@wvnvm.wvnet.edu`

HIS—History and Computing Discussion Group

West Virginia Network for Educational Telecomputing

You can join this group by sending the message "sub HIS your name" to `listserv@wvnvm.wvnet.edu`

HISLAW-L—History of Law (Feudal, Common, Canon)

You can join this group by sending the message "sub HISLAW-L your name" to `listserv@ulkyvm.louisville.edu`

HIST-L—History - Peer Distribution List

University of Kansas, Lawrence, Kansas

You can join this group by sending the message "sub HIST-L your name" to `listserv@ukanvm.cc.ukans.edu`

HISTARCH—Historical Archaeology

Arizona State University, Tempe, AZ

You can join this group by sending the message "sub HISTARCH your name" to `listserv@asuvm.inre.asu.edu`

HISTNEWS—Historians' Newsletter

University of Kansas, Lawrence, Kansas

You can join this group by sending the message "sub HISTNEWS your name" to `listserv@ukanvm.cc.ukans.edu`

HISTORY

University College Dublin, Ireland

You can join this group by sending the message "sub HISTORY your name" to `listserv@irlearn.ucd.ie`

HISTORY—History - Peer Distribution List

University of Kansas, Lawrence, Kansas

You can join this group by sending the message "sub HISTORY your name" to `listserv@ukanvm.cc.ukans.edu`

HISTOWNR—Discussion List for Owners of History-Related Lists

State University of New York at Buffalo

You can join this group by sending the message "sub HISTOWNR your name" to `listserv@ubvm.cc.buffalo.edu`

HN-ASK-L—History Network Forum

University of Kansas, Lawrence, Kansas

You can join this group by sending the message "sub HN-ASK-L your name" to `listserv@ukanvm.cc.ukans.edu`

HN-ORG-L—The History Network

University of Kansas, Lawrence, Kansas

You can join this group by sending the message "sub HN-ORG-L your name" to `listserv@ukanvm.cc.ukans.edu`

HOLOCAUS—H-Net History of the Holocaust List

University of Illinois at Chicago, Chicago, IL

You can join this group by sending the message "sub HOLOCAUS your name" to
`listserv@uicvm.uic.edu`

HOPOS-L—A Forum for Discussion of the History of the Philosophy of Sci+

You can join this group by sending the message "sub HOPOS-L your name" to `listserv@lsv.uky.edu`

HPSST-L—History and Philosophy of Science and Science Teaching

Queen's University Computing Services

You can join this group by sending the message "sub HPSST-L your name" to
`listserv@qucdn.queensu.ca`

HTECH-L—History of Technology Discussion

Smithsonian Institution, Washington, DC

You can join this group by sending the message "sub HTECH-L your name" to `listserv@sivm.si.edu`

ISLAM-L—History of Islam

You can join this group by sending the message "sub ISLAM-L your name" to
`listserv@ulkyvm.louisville.edu`

JSH—Journal of Southern History

Rice University Information Systems, Houston, TX

You can join this group by sending the message "sub JSH your name" to `listserv@ricevm1.rice.edu`

MAPHIST—Map History Discussion List

Harvard University, Office for Information Technology, Cambridge, MA

You can join this group by sending the message "sub MAPHIST your name" to
`listserv%harvarda.bitnet@listserv.net`

MEDART-L—Medieval Art History

You can join this group by sending the message "sub MEDART-L your name" to
`listserv@listserv.utoronto.ca`

MEDIEV-L—Medieval History

University of Kansas, Lawrence, Kansas

You can join this group by sending the message "sub MEDIEV-L your name" to
`listserv@ukanvm.cc.ukans.edu`

MENA-H—History of the Mideast and North Africa

You can join this group by sending the message "sub MENA-H your name" to
`listserv@ulkyvm.louisville.edu`

MIL20C-L—20th Century Military History for Amateur Historians

Memorial University of Newfoundland, St. John's, Newfoundland, Canada

You can join this group by sending the message "sub MIL20C-L your name" to
`listserv@morgan.ucs.mun.ca`

MILHST-L—Military History

University of Kansas, Lawrence, KS

You can join this group by sending the message "sub MILHST-L your name" to
`listserv@ukanvm.cc.ukans.edu`

MISSIONS—Missions History Discussion Group (MISSIONS)

Yale University Computer Center, New Haven, CT

You can join this group by sending the message "sub MISSIONS your name" to
`listserv@yalevm.cis.yale.edu`

MONON—Monon Railroad Historical & Technical Society discussion Group

University Computing Services, Indiana University

You can join this group by sending the message "sub MONON your name" to
`listserv@iubvm.ucs.indiana.edu`

NAHIA-L—North American Historians of Islamic Art

Michigan State University, East Lansing, MI

You can join this group by sending the message "sub NAHIA-L your name" to `listserv@msu.edu`

NFDANCE—Newfoundland Traditional/Historical Dance List

Memorial University of Newfoundland, St. John's, Newfoundland, Canada

You can join this group by sending the message "sub NFDANCE your name" to `listserv@morgan.ucs.mun.ca`

OHA-L—Oral History Association Discussion List

You can join this group by sending the message "sub OHA-L your name" to `listserv@lsv.uky.edu`

PHILOFHI—PHILosophy OF HIstory and Theoretical History

You can join this group by sending the message "sub PHILOFHI your name" to `listserv@yorku.ca`

PRINTS-L—Devoted to the Study of Historical & Contemporary Prints

University of Kansas, Lawrence, KS

You can join this group by sending the message "sub PRINTS-L your name" to `listserv@ukanvm.cc.ukans.edu`

PUBLHIST—Public History Discussion List

You can join this group by sending the message "sub PUBLHIST your name" to `listserv@listserv.iupui.edu`

RENAIS-L—Early Modern History - Renaissance

You can join this group by sending the message "sub RENAIS-L your name" to `listserv@ulkyvm.louisville.edu`

SAH-L—Society of Architectural Historians

Smithsonian Institution, Washington, DC

You can join this group by sending the message "sub SAH-L your name" to `listserv@sivm.si.edu`

SISTER-L—History & Contemporary Concerns of Catholic Women Religious

Syracuse University

You can join this group by sending the message "sub SISTER-L your name" to `listserv@listserv.syr.edu`

SLAVERY—The History of Slavery, the Slave Trade, Abolition and Emancipation

You can join this group by sending the message "sub SLAVERY your name" to `listserv@listserv.uh.edu`

SPORTHIST—ISPHES - Sport History Scholars List

University of Windsor

You can join this group by sending the message "sub SPORTHIST your name" to `listserv@pdomain.uwindsor.ca`

TAMHA—Teaching American History

Wayne State University, Detroit, MI

You can join this group by sending the message "sub TAMHA your name" to `listserv@cms.cc.wayne.edu`

TARIKH-L—Iran History Forum (TARIKH-L)

Yale University Computer Center; New Haven, CT

You can join this group by sending the message "sub TARIKH-L your name" to `listserv@yalevm.cis.yale.edu`

WHIRL—Women's History in Rhetoric and Language

Pennsylvania State University

You can join this group by sending the message "sub WHIRL your name" to `listserv@psuvm.psu.edu`

WHR-L—Women's History in Rhetoric

Pennsylvania State University

You can join this group by sending the message "sub WHR-L your name" to `listserv@psuvm.psu.edu`

WISHFORD—Crafts, Recreation, Historical Methods List

You can join this group by sending the message "sub WISHFORD your name" to `listserv@uriacc.uri.edu`

WOMHIST—Women's History Discussion

Temple University, Philadelphia, PA

You can join this group by sending the message "sub WOMHIST your name" to `listserv@vm.temple.edu`

WORLD-L—Forum on Non-Eurocentric World History

State University of New York at Buffalo

You can join this group by sending the message "sub WORLD-L your name" to `listserv@ubvm.cc.buffalo.edu`

Hobbies & Crafts

Amateur Radio

100 Years of Radio

http://www.alpcom.it/hamradio/

Includes the history of ham radio, from Marconi's invention of the wireless communication in 1895 to present day projects such as the Radio Gateway Project.

The Amateur Radio Elmers Resource Directory

http://www.gonix.com/pschleck/elmers/index.html

Includes an extensive list of technical people in the field of amateur radio. The "Elmers List" has been serving the amateur radio community since 1991.

Amateur Radio Resources

http://crompton.nadc.navy.mil/amateur.html

Includes over 40 amateur radio links to other sites on the Internet, and several amateur radio files for downloading.

The American Radio Relay League's World Wide Web Service

http://www.arrl.org/

The American Radio Relay League is one of the largest amateur radio groups in the world. It specializes in providing a national resource for the public. By joining this league members obtain product reviews of the latest radios and accessories, information about upcoming conventions, and the Hamfest Calendar.

Ham Radio Outlet

http://www.hamradio.com/

Ham Radio Outlet is the world's largest supplier of amateur radio equipment. Their selection of stores spans from California to Virginia.

Ham University Home Page

http://www.oz.net/mica/hamu.html

Ham University provides quizzes for testing yourself or developing mock exams. There is a library of hypertext files for the novice user and the more technical user. Ham University provides you with three different ways to learn Morse code and enables you to link to various other ham radio sites.

List of Mail Order Electronics Companies

http://www.funhouse.com/jfw/RF_PARTS.txt

A listing of companies selling electronic components in small quantities. This sites lists distributors and sellers of new components, surplus electronics, specialty components such as crystals and toroidal cores, kits such as ham radio and random electronic kits, and publications for not only electronics, but for low-power amateur radio enthusiasts.

The Packet Radio Home Page

http://www.tapr.org/tapr/html/pkthome.html

The Packet Radio Home Page includes a virtual library and various home pages of digital communications, Packet Radio ftp archives, Packet-oriented newsgroups, and related topics.

Personal Database Applications

http://www.mindspring.com/~pda/

Provides software and accessories for ham radio. The PDA includes numerous links to related amateur radio sites.

WWW Ham Radio Servers List

http://www.alpcom.it/hamradio/w3hr.html

A complete listing of WWW ham radio servers. Sites include various technical pages, information about packet radio and networking, satellites, various ham resources, ham associations and clubs, and SWL & Ute listeners.

Antiques & Collectibles

A–Z Antique & Collectible Directory

http://www.eskimo.com/~pither/Web_Directory/

An index of antique and collectible sites on the Web. Categories include advertising, art, entertainment, military memorabilia, racing, toys, and much more. Descriptions of the sites are also presented.

About the Lighthouse Depot

http://www.biddeford.com/lhdigest/catalog/history.html

Order lighthouse posters, calendars, Christmas cards, books, and videos at this site. The lighthouse store is now two floors of lighthouse collectibles from around the world.

Alien Antiques

http://home.earthlink.net/~asimov/

Books, ephemera, furniture, and pottery are some of what is available at the Alien Antiques site. Items are listed by category in alphabetical order. Find what you're interested in and e-mail your request.

Auntie Q's Antiques & Collectibles

http://www.teleport.com/~auntyq/

Claimed to be the world's first Internet antique shop, this site provides a catalog of collectibles, depression glass information and buying opportunities, and reference books. This site is updated weekly.

BJS Enterprises Collectibles and Crafts Mini Mall

http://www.cato.com/bjs/

Offers sports collectibles, trading cards, and comics, and also lists addresses for interesting sites, such as the White House, *PC Magazine*, and the 1996 Olympic games.

Bob's Rock Shop

http://www.rtd.com/~bkeller/rockshop/rockshop.html

Bob's Rock Shop is a non-commercial site containing an extensive mineral collection, a gallery of specimen images, classified ads, and articles and essays about minerals.

Campus Collectibles

http://www.umich.edu/~webspin/cc-ind.html

Carries all sorts of unique gift ideas from autographs to comics to fantasy role-playing games. Primarily advertises, but does provide some information and a catalog.

The Canadian Online Bottle Collecting Network

http://www.netaccess.on.ca/~mhall

Provides information for anyone interested in painted pop bottles from Canada and elsewhere. Presents links to other bottle collecting sites.

Cape Cod Teddy Bear

http://virtumall.com/cgi-bin/shop?/CCTeddyBear/main.html

Presents an online collection of teddy bears and lets you order one. Also contains a catalog of bears (including pictures).

Casecrafters

http://www.iminet.com/casecrafters/

Makes and sells display cases for collectibles, such as dolls, trains, and sports memorabilia. Offers premade and custom cases. Lets you order by phone or mail. Makes all cases from fine hardwoods and lets you choose the finish style.

Cellophane Square

http://www.cellophane.com/~music/

Online music store. Features new and used collectible editions of albums, autographs, and other memorabilia. Also offers links to Billboard, American Recordings, and more cool music sites.

CG Publishing, Inc. Home Page

http://www.icom.ca/cgpinc/

Offers collectibles from Star Wars and various musicians, including Elvis Presley. Accompanies each product with a picture to give you a better feel for the product.

Classifieds–Collectibles–Selling

http://www.wwcd.com/classified/collect_sell/collect_sell.html

Provides a collection of ads for collectibles (including toys, sports-related merchandise, and stamps) for sale. Lets you read or post ads.

Collectibles by R&T

http://www.rt66.com/olworld/mall/mall_us/c_gifts/m_colrt/

Features gift items, such as jewelry boxes, music boxes, and rocking horses. Also offers an extensive collection of miniatures for the doll house enthusiast. Lets you view and order products.

Collectibles by R&T Musical Merry-Go-Rounds

`http://www.olworld.com/olworld/mall/mall_us/c_gifts/`
`m_colrt/40musme1/index.html`

Presents catalog of musical merry-go-rounds and carousels. Includes pictures of each item and an online order form.

Collector Online

`http://together.net/~collect/`

Focuses on antiques and collectibles. Offers classifieds, collector e-mail listings, and file-exchange libraries.

Collectors COIN UNIVERSE

`http://www.coin-universe.com/index.html`

Comprehensive site for anyone interested in coin collecting. Presents coin dealers, clubs, classifieds, coin directory, chat opportunities, and more.

The Collectors' Index

`http://www.bdt.com:80/home/k55k`

Provides collectors of everything a way to locate and network with each other. Lets you register yourself as a collector of a variety of items or just browse to find others with similar interests in your area. Also includes a calendar of upcoming events.

Cottage Catalogs

`http://www.olworld.com/olworld/mall/mall_us/c_toys/`
`m_cotcat/index.html`

Features collectible porcelain dolls, each of which are accompanied by a picture and complete description. Includes an enlargement feature that lets you look at the pictures in greater detail.

Cybercinema Links

`http://www.indirect.com/www/jonbrown/cinema/`

If collecting movie posters is your hobby, this site's for you. Most are in the $20 range, and they're categorized by Top 25, Classics, '96 Winter Catalog, and Top Movies of All Time, among others.

Dolls By Christine

`http://www.imsweb.net/cweb/dollsbc/`

Offers porcelain dolls created to order by artist Christine Sanders. Each doll is unique and comes with a Certificate of Authenticity.

Dr. Wax

`http://www.metamor.com/drwax/`

Offers new and used CDs, cassettes, and LPs, as well as collectibles pertaining to music albums (unreleased versions and more).

Dream-Land Dollies!!!

`http://www.mind.net/chrystal/dolls.html`

Serves as an online shop for antique porcelain dolls. Creator Sally Salazar will make a replica of a doll if you have the picture and she has the mold. Dolls are made to order.

East Coast Cards and Collectibles

`http://www.wwcd.com/eccc/eccc.html`

Specializes in NFL, NBA, NHL, and other sports-related trading cards, but also offers collectible card games such as Star Trek and Magic: The Gathering.

Funtiques Antiques Home Page

`http://rivendell.com/funtiques/`

Offers collectibles to fit your budget. Provides a collection of books, magazines, cookbooks, pottery, and more that can be found by category or by using a keyword search. Layaway plan is also available.

Glass Insulators

`http://www.insulators.com`

Contains photographs, history, and reference materials about collecting glass insulators, one of the newer hobbies. The opportunity is also there for joining an insulator club, hearing about upcoming shows, and reading personal pages from other glass insulator collectors.

Global Art Marketing

`http://vvv.com/IslandArt/`

Provides information and services to art collectors, as well as artists and people who want to buy repro-ductions of fine art. Offers open market listings, reproductions for sale, and original art.

Haynet on the Web

`http://nehalem.rain.com/haynet`

Includes FAQs, chats, resources, and personal pages for model horse collectors.

Henry Gitner Philatelists, Inc.

http://www.hgitner.com/ll.html

Contains published price lists, rarities, year sets pages, and special offers for the avid stamp collector. Discounted postage (for both U.S. and international) is available. Special requests and want lists are welcomed.

Hershey's Collectibles

http://www.padutch.com/html/hersheys/collectibles/collectibles.html

Order the Christmas KISSES light set, trading cards, pewter spoons, and other novelties from the Hershey Chocolate Company. You can also tour Hershey to find out who M. S. Hershey was, the history of chocolate, and nutrition facts. (Hey, who said chocolate was bad for you anyway?)

Ilene & WAYNE Productions: Collectibles

http://www.aloha.com/~shakacat/

Offers some Hawaii collectibles and provides information on collectible POGs (milk caps). Includes a Collectibles Wanted page.

Incredible Collectibles Home Page

http://rivendell.com/antiques/stores/IC/

Includes a catalog of antiques (contains many pictures) as well as an antique museum online. Includes a form-based survey.

The Internet Auction List

http://ssi.syspac.com/~usaweb/auction.html

Enables the serious collector to keeps tabs on auctions that occur around the country. Lists the times and locations (including maps) for these auctions, and includes at least a partial list of items to be auctioned off.

Internet Classifieds: 1500–1599 Collectibles Index

http://ad.wwmedia.com/classified/indexed/1500.1599.html

Lets you view or place advertisements. Lists ads under subjects such as antiques, stamps, and rare art. Also includes a miscellaneous subject for subjects not listed specifically.

Island Imports, Ltd.

http://www.rt66.com/olworld/mall/mall_us/c_gifts/m_islan2/index.html

Features handcrafted Jamaican walking canes. Also showcases Caribbean Hook Bracelets.

Jan-Ken-Po—The Trading Card Game for Kids of All Ages

http://www.aloha.com/~hollis

A collectible trading card game that is based on the Rock, Paper, Scissors game that everyone played as a kid. Features Manga style artwork with socially responsible storyline.

Just Matchbox!!

http://members.aol.com/jstmtchbx/

This site is for lovers of matchbox cars. It presents the opportunity to join collectors' clubs; tells of upcoming shows and events; provides buying, selling, and trading options; and lists books related to matchbox cars.

Kaila's Country Collectibles

http://www.isystems.com/kaila/laurie.html

Offers tie ons, dolls, baskets, and barrettes for the country collector. Pictures are included. Orders can be customized for a certain color combination or personalized for someone special.

KBC Antiques and Collectibles Sites List

http://kbc.com:80/html/antiques.htm

If you're interested in finding out where the used book stores are in your state, downloading a nature picture, or collecting antiques, old postcards, jewelry, coins, and more, the Kaiser Books & Computers site is for you.

Kringle Kottage Collectibles

http://www.prairieweb.com/kringle/

Features Christmas items and collectibles from Christmas past. Includes pictures and descriptions for each item, and offers to send you more information via e-mail.

Medals of America

http://www.usmedals.com/

Medals of America provides a catalog of U.S. and Allied military medals, ribbons, badges, patches, insignia, and display cases. Offers custom mounting and personal service from the veterans themselves.

Moments On-Line

http://www.exp-online.com/moments/index.htm

For those collectors of Precious Moments figurines, this site should appeal to you. Found here is collector information, an online catalog, history, and new and retired pieces.

MOODY'S Sports Autographs and Memorabilia

http://www.wwcd.com/moodys/moodys.html

Provides autographed sports memorabilia, programs, tickets, and other collectibles.

Numismatists Online

http://www.numismatists.com:8000/q/index.html

Offers interactive coin auctioning and fixed price sales. Also provides a want list service and a dealer directory.

Perfect Image Sportscards and Memorabilia

http://www.wwcd.com/pimage/image.html

A collectibles stop. Offers trading cards, game cards, comic cards, and collectibles supplies, in addition to non-sports collectibles such as Power Rangers, *X-Files*, and Coca-Cola.

Portal Disney FANtasEARS-Mouse-Sell-aneous Forum

http://www.portal.com/~rkoster/sell.html

Provides information about Disney, Disney collectibles, souvenirs and merchandise, news about WDCC new releases, and Disneyana discussions. Also offers a link to a Disney discussion room to chat with other Disney fans.

Railroad Scripophily

http://www.dnai.com/~tcarson/pages/scrip.html

Scripophily is the hobby of collecting old stock and bond certificates. Shares the history of scripophily, introduces interested individuals to the stocks and bonds of old railroad companies, and provides a listing of links to other railroad resources on the Net.

Rick's GAMEROOM Collectibles

http://www-odp.tamu.edu/~schulte/

Visit Rick's GAMEROOM Collectibles site if you're interested in collecting or restoring jukeboxes, arcade machines, advertising signs, classic cars, radios, carousel animals, soda fountains, and other nostalgia. Also lists links to other nostalgia sites.

Roger's Collector's Marketplace

http://iquest.com/~cws/rogers/

Presents information about receiving the Collectors' Marketplace, a 20-page monthly newsletter that serves as a marketplace for such popular collectibles as Precious Moments, Cherished Teddies, Hummel, Harbor Lights, and Armani.

Rusty Zipper—Vintage Clothing on the Web

http://www.rustyzipper.com/

Shop for vintage clothing from the '40s through the '70s at the site whose motto is "The Brady's would be proud." Also offered here are home accessories such as light switch plates, address numbers, and Beach Glass hooks, drawer pulls, and knobs.

Santa Fe Southwest Artists Marketspace

http://www.ARTSANTAFE.com/sfm/sfmhome.html

Provides a collection of works from fine southwestern artists, musicians, photographers, and weavers. Includes a wide variety of products to browse.

Santa Fe Traditions, Inc.

http://www.rt66.com/olworld/mall/mall_us/c_gifts/m_sftrad/index.html

Features Native American jewelry and crafts from the Southwest. Includes pictures and an online ordering form.

Sea Creations

http://cyberactive-1.com/sea-creations/

Features gifts from the sea, such as jewelry, collectible lighthouses, and Atocha collectible reproductions. Opportunity to adopt a whale or sponsor a dolphin.

Sports, Collectibles, and Money

http://www.primenet.com/~collect

Offers a sports collectible program. Combines making money with sports cards and building a collection, and creating valuable contacts.

SportsCards, Etc.

http://www.nauticom.net/users/sce/

Deals in all kinds of cards. Offers sports cards and nonsports cards in factory-sealed wax boxes. Also offers Magic: The Gathering cards and other collectible card games, as well as complete sets of cards.

Sun Tile

http://www.rt66.com/olworld/mall/mall_us/c_gifts/m_suntil/index.html

Features hand-painted ceramic art tile. Offers online ordering and a complete catalog.

Web Mill Business District—Bears By The Sea

http://webmill.com/web/mill/bears

The online store sells everyday bears, theme bears (for special holidays, sports, professions, and so on), featured collectibles (such as teddy bear stamps, books, and jewelry), and Barbie. Also includes pointers to other bear-related sites.

Web Mill Business District—Teddy Bear Directory

http://webmill.com/web/mill/bears/dir

Offers a collection of teddy bear manufacturers and retailers, organized by region and by state so that teddy bear enthusiasts can find a source close to home. Includes listing of people who repair teddy bears and dolls, and also includes links to other teddy bear sites.

Whispers in Time

http://www.pev.com/whispers.htm

Old prints, music boxes, toys and trains, furniture, and antiques can be found here. Call for ordering information. Several Currier and Ives prints are available, which can be viewed online.

World Wide Collectors Digest—Your Collectibles Outlet

http://www.wwcd.com/hp/collectibles.html

Provides collectibles, but also serves anyone interested in any of the following: baseball, football, basketball, hockey, nonsports, comic cards, trading cards, memorabilia, comic books, autographs, stadiums, sports arenas, seating charts, events, figurines, classifieds, chat, toys, Star Trek, milk caps, pogs, standings, schedules, trade shows, trains, baseball cards, price guides, shopping malls, conventions, games, odds, racing tickets, and more.

World Wide Mall:™ Arts, Crafts, & Antiques

http://www.olworld.com/olworld/mall/mall_us/c_arts/m_tyler/index.html

Some of what's available at this site include the following: Southwestern and Native American arts and crafts, Chinese antiques, decorative wooden calendars and kitchen accessories, handcrafted boxes, and fine art.

World Wide Mall:™ Collectibles, Dolls, & More

http://www.rt66.com/olworld/mall/mall_us/c_gifts/m_abover/index.html

This site used to carry only sports collectibles, but now offers everything from dolls to Beatles' memorabilia, Southwestern art to His and Her puzzle rings. There's something here for everyone.

Astronomy

Astronomy and Astrophysics

http://www.w3.org/hypertext/DataSources/bySubject/astro/educational.html

Includes over 50 educational resources for astronomy and links to the WWW Virtual Library. Some of the educational resources include the Algonquin Space Campus, the Arizona Mars K–12

Education Program, NSCORT on Controlled Ecological Life Support Systems (CELSS) from Purdue University, and the Research Institute for Space Education (RISE).

The Galaxy Page

http://www.seds.org/galaxy/

Provides links to four areas—Planets: the Solar System, Astronomy and Space Sciences, Aerospace and Astronautics, and Visions of the Future. From here, there are links to various astronomy sites on the Internet including amateur astronomy, educational resources in astronomy and astrophysics, astronomical data sources, astronomy news, astronomy publications and periodicals, astronomy software, celestial events, observatories, space sciences, cosmology, and SETI: the Search for Extra-Terrestrial Intelligence.

NASA

http://www.nasa.gov/NASA_homepage.html

The NASA home page enables you to link to their Aeronautics, Space and Science, Mission to Planet Earth, Technology Development, Human Space Flight, Gallery for searchable photos and movies, Q&A, and other areas. This site is updated daily to bring you the most up-to-date information on what our space telescopes and probes are finding.

National Space Science Data Center (NSSDC)

http://nssdc.gsfc.nasa.gov/

Provides access to a wide variety of astrophysics, space physics, solar physics, and lunar and planetary data from NASA space flight missions. Includes the latest version of the NSSDC newsletter, extensive photo gallery, ftp sites, link to the World Data Center, and a listing of frequently asked questions.

Novagraphics Space Art Gallery

http://www.novaspace.com/

Includes the world's first and largest gallery devoted to space art. Information from *Sky & Telescope* and *Astronomy* magazines, and links to various comets is also available.

Raben Software & Graphics

http://www.raben.com/planet/index.html

Home of the PlanetWatch v2.1 software, a multimedia guide to our solar system including breathtaking photos and up-to-date information from various space probes. You can view the PlanetWatcher online newsletter or link to other astronomy sites such as the Jet Propulsion Laboratory.

Radio-Sky Publishing

http://www.win.net/~radiosky/

Focuses on amateur radio astronomers who make radio observations of cosmic phenomena. Information, such as digital converter resources, Jupiter noise storm predictions, the history of radio astronomy, and projects for radio telescopes, is also available.

Skywatcher's Diary

http://www.pa.msu.edu/abrams/SWD/SWD_9506.html

Abrams Planetarium and the Michigan State University's Department of Physics and Astronomy prepare a diary/calendar of each day's most striking sights in the sky. Morning events are mentioned in the diary one day prior to the event, but you can sometimes see next month's diary in advance. Sites can include the moon passing near planets or bright stars.

The Society of Amateur Radio Astronomers (SARA)

http://irsociety.com/0c:/sara.htm¦/

Provides information about SARA, an international nonprofit society to learn, trade technical information, and observe the radio sky. Includes information about observation programs, how to join the group, an index of SARA's journal articles since 1983, and sources of components, software, and general radio astronomy information.

Students for the Exploration and Development of Space (SEDS)

http://seds.lpl.arizona.edu/

SEDS from the University of Arizona provide galaxy images, information about the Ascending Node, links to a multimedia solar system tour of the nine planets, the Messier Deep-Sky catalog, the Web Nebulae, the astro ftp list, space images archives, the Xprize foundation, and the space chat room.

Birding

The Academy of Natural Sciences

http://www.acnatsci.org/

Provides a vast biological collection of life forms and their evolution, survival, and extinction. The Birds of North America series is a comprehensive, authoritative summary of currently known habits of the breeding bird species of North America. It has been acclaimed the standard reference on North American birds.

The Backyard Birdfeeder

http://www.sienna.com/

Provides information about bird feeders, bird-watching for kids, bird feeding products, bird feeding tips, bird houses, bird seed, binocular tips, contests, and other Web birding links. Includes an ever changing collection of facts, fun, and trivia about birds as well.

The Bird Guide, Inc.

http://www.teleport.com/~guide/

The only magazine that teaches you how to watch birds in the Pacific Northwest, the history of the area, and where to find some of the area's birds. Each issue includes the habitat, range, plumage, and individuality of a particular bird in the Pacific Northwest. Includes links to various sites on the Internet for birding in other areas of the world, such as Birding in British Columbia, The Oregon Weekly Wildlife Viewing Report, BirdWest Digest, and The Geographical Birdline Guide.

Birding in Southeast Arizona

http://soliton.physics.arizona.edu/~elbryan/birds.html

Provides trip reports from various states, images of birds of the Southeast, birding hot spots, a listing of Arizona parks, field trips, local birding organizations, and links to other great birding sites.

Birding on the Web

http://compstat.wharton.upenn.edu:8001/~siler/birding.html

Provides a bird's classification, hot lists, bird chat, popular links, FAQs, references, and announcements of exhibitions.

Birding on the Web

http://www.birder.com/

Provides upcoming exhibit information, a place to direct your questions about birding, a listing of books, videos, and CD-ROMs on birding, and an extensive list of birding sites such as EuroBirding, the Nova Scotia Bird Society, and the African Bird Club.

Fugleskue Birdwatch Birdbase

http://home.sol.no/tibjonn/

Provides 17 birding resources, other birding Web sites, real-world birding sites, birder mailing groups, information about recent observations and bird feeding, a bird photo gallery, and registration projects to participate in, such as the NTT World Bird Count and the YouthEurope BarnSwallow.

Hotspot for Birds

http://www.lainet.com/hotspot/birdhome.htm

Sells exotic birds anywhere that government and weather permits, includes information and sells brooders and incubators, bird heaters, bird houses and placement, bird food, bird seed savers, and bird cages. Includes information about bird nutrition and how to build your own bird seed cleaner.

NPFauna and NPFlora

http://ice.ucdavis.edu/US_National_Park_Service/NPS_birds.html

Preliminary PC-based databases of birds at over 175 selected parks including Assateague Island National Seashore, Big Bend National Park, Everglades National Park, Guadalupe Mountains National Park, Ozark National Seashore Riverways, and Yosemite National Park.

Ontario Birdwatching Home Page

http://www.interlog.com/~gallantg/ontario.html

Provides field checklists, Ontario hotspots, recent birding reports, graphic birding guide to North America, rare bird alerts, bird-finding guides, weather and climate, raptor watch, links to other birding Web sites, and upcoming birding events.

Wild Bird Marketplace

http://www.wildbird.com/

Provides a listing of all of their stores nationwide and backyard birding tips. Their newsletter has information about the placement of feeders, food, feeder care, and different kinds of birds and their habitat.

Ceramics & Pottery

Archie Bray Foundation for the Ceramic Arts

http://www.imageplaza.com/archiebray/

The Bray Foundation is an educational institution for enriching ceramic arts, offering residencies and specialized workshops to ceramic artists. Provides a complete history of the Bray Foundation, their on-site gallery, and a listing of all the ceramic supplies, materials, and equipment they sell.

Carl Baker Stoneware and Raku Pottery

http://reality.sgi.com/employees/raster/cb/index.html

Includes photos and information about Raku pottery and crackle glazed Raku pottery, where to order Raku pottery, answers to frequently asked questions, and how to be put on their mailing list.

CDI Ceramic Devices, Inc.

http://www.compdist.com/ceramic/products.html

Provides information about the world's smallest screw-in filters, eyelet style filters, filter pins, bolt style filters, broad band filters, custom filter assemblies, and discoidal ceramic capacitors and custom caparrays.

CEEN, The Crafts Equipment Exchange Newsletter

http://www.sonic.net/ceen/

Provides a listing of used craft equipment, over-stocked supplies, going-out-of-business sales, and recycled materials from all over the United States. Items include accessories, ceramics, jewelry, weaving, and wood.

Centre for Technical Ceramics, CTK

http://www.chem.tue.nl/ctk/

Provides information about ceramics, research areas for Eindhoven University of Technology, their facilities, and curriculum. They carry out research and development on advanced ceramics. Research areas include powder processing, ceramic coatings, continuous fibre composites, and sintering and metalceramic joining.

Ceramic Industry

http://www.bnp.com/ceramic_industry/

Provides an online ceramic manufacturing magazine. It includes information about ceramics, glass, whiteware, structural clay, refractories, and porcelain enamel products. Includes subscription, advertising, editorial, list rental, Web sponsorship, and lists related publications.

Ceramic Solutions

http://www.aros.net/~lonepeak/ceramics/

Provides the most recent and innovative products for today's problems, such as fine ceramic kitchen knives and golf putters. Includes information about ceramics and a catalog displaying various types of products already created.

Ceramics and Artifacts Restoration

http://astral.magic.ca/%7Emarwill/Restoration/Restorationpage.html

Provides a ceramic restoration question and answer area, information on the Hans van de Berg restoration of ancient Egyptian artifacts, art from the Warda Stevens Stout collection of the 18th century, information about arita porcelain and traditional pottery, and how to attend a ceramics restoration course.

Dynamic Ceramic

http://www.smart.co.uk/dynamic/dynamic.htm

Provides information about an advanced ceramic manufacturing, trading, and consultancy company. Includes information about new developments in the industry, such as new coatings, ceramic injection moulding, agents, and alumina tubes. Provides up-to-date information regarding material sourcing and finishing.

The Forum On-Line Antiques Mall for Potter, Porcelain and Ceramics

http://www.the-forum.com/pottery/index.htm

Includes information and color photos on American art pottery tiles, American pottery, European pottery, and collectible pottery and porcelain.

Keith Ceramic Materials LTD

http://www.ceramics.com/~ceramics/keith/

Manufactures synthetic mullite, bonds, plasticizers, stuccos, and fillers for casting industries. Their customers can produce glass and steel refractories, filn furniture, and ceramic molds. Provides a detailed list of what products they carry.

Mesa Verde Pottery

http://www.hwi.com/mvp/home.html

Provides handmade Native American pottery crafted by Navajo and Ute artisans, and a gallery featuring original and limited editions of pottery pieces.

Orton's Firing Tips

http://www.zoom.com/personal/jimberry/ortontips.html

Provides tips on firing lead-free glazes, solving glaze defects, firing handbuilt ware, correctly loading a kiln, using the three-cone system, cracking and warping caused by drying and casting, firing red glaze, and having success with decals, china paints, and lusters.

The Potter's Page

http://www.aztec.co.za/users/theo/

Provides information about the ancient art of making clay pots. Includes Internet resources to various sites, pottery software, current exhibitions, magazines and newsletters, and a list of potters around the United States and in Africa.

Pottery

http://www.ftech.net/~regia/pottery.htm

Provides a complete explanation of what pottery is and has been used for, the step-by-step process of how early Ango-Saxons made pottery, and describes 13 different types of pottery, including St. Neots, Lincoln, York, and Fine Whitby.

Scientific Report, Chapter 2: Ceramics and Ceramic Composites

http://www.mtm.kuleuven.ac.be/Reports/
ScientificReport92-94/Chap2Toc.html

Provides information on chemical preparation methods, powder injection moulding, electrophoretic forming, microwave processing, liquid phase processing, and processing and properties of monolithic and particle toughened ceramics.

Virtual Ceramics Exhibit

http://www.uky.edu/Artsource/vce/VCEhome.html

Provides over 45 color photos of ceramic pieces from various artists, who are listed. Includes information about clay art, and links to Ceramics Gopher, which includes clay art archives, technical data, and articles on ceramics.

WWW Virtual Library: Technical Ceramics

http://www.ikts.fhg.de/ceramics.html

Provides a listing of new commercial and non-commercial ceramics sites and information about silicate ceramics, nitride ceramics, ferroelectric ceramics, superconducting ceramics, journals, upcoming conferences, and ceramics arts.

Coins

American Gold Coins

http://www.opennet.com/townesquare/coins/coins.htm

Provides a listing of some of the most sought after gold coins minted in the United States from 1840–1933. Shows full color photos of the Double Eagle $20, Eagle $10, Half Eagle $5, Quarter Eagle $2.50, and One Dollar $1 coins. Includes information about the different kinds of coin terminology, such as RAW, Very Fine, Xtra Fine, About Uncirculated, Commercial, Brilliant, SLAB, and MS.

The American Numismatic Association

http://www.money.org/

Provides information about the nonprofit, educational organization chartered by Congress, which studies coins, paper money, tokens, and medals. Includes information about conferences, clubs, the Money Museum, the Money Market Catalog, and links to other Numismatic sites.

Ancient and Medieval Coins

http://www_wwrc.uwyo.edu/coinnet/coinnet.html

Provides information about ancient Roman coins, Medieval Italian and English coins, and how to submit coins for identification.

Buying Gold Silver Jewelry Coins

http://www1.minn.net/~richcook/gold.html

Provides information about how to buy and sell gold jewelry, gold watches, class rings, dental gold, and silver or gold coins. Includes current market prices and investment tips.

Coin Universe

http://www.coin-universe.com/index.html

Provides information about the CoinMarket for coin shows and auctions, CoinChat, coin terms, silver coin tables, the United States coin directory, dealers, the CoinClub, and classified ads for coin collectors. Includes information about paper money collecting and what you should know before buying rare coins for investment.

Coins

http://zow00.desy.de:8000/~chlebana/coins/coins.html

Provides a bibliography/library of coin books, tips on taking photos of coins, information on grading coins, frequently asked questions, various articles, and historical information regarding currency.

The Department of the Treasury of the United States

http://www.ustreas.gov/treasury/bureaus/mint/mint.html

Provides information about the background of the United States Mint, currently available commemorative coins, and information about the American Eagle and Silver Bullion coins.

E Pluribus Unum

http://atheist.tamu.edu/~ratboy/Coins/coins.html

Provides descriptions of United States coin types, a trader section for exchanging coins, grading guides and other numismatic writings, and reviews of coin software, which can also be downloaded.

History of Money from Ancient Times to the Present Day

http://www.ex.ac.uk/~RDavies/arian/llyfr.html

Provides a pendulum metatheory of money, origins of money and banking, warfare and financial history, information about Celtic coinage, the Vikings and money in England, money in North American history, Britain and European Monetary Union, the democracy and government control of the money supply, and Third World money and debt in the Twentieth Century.

Superior Stamp and Coin

http://www.PrimeNet.Com:80/amark/

Provides information about ordering coin and stamp auction catalogs, schedules of upcoming coin auctions, and consignment information.

Furniture Refinishing & Repair

BUILD.COM: The Building and Home Improvement Products Network

http://www.build.com/

Includes a listing of manufacturers for building materials from construction equipment to wall coverings, merchants, over 40 associations, resources from books to masonry, services, and other Internet sites dealing with furniture repair and restoration.

Furniture and Refinishing

http://www.antiques-on-line.com/Books/Book17.html

Provides a listing of over ten books relating to furniture refinishing. Book subjects include oak furniture, Victorian furniture, Hoosier cabinets, furniture of the Depression Era, antique wicker, and reupholstering.

Furniture Medic®

http://members.aol.com/furnmedic/index.html

Provides information on furniture restoration, refurbishing and repair for restaurants, motels, hotels, and offices. This site also includes a list of furniture services and examples of work before and after restoration.

The Furniture Repair and Refinishing Wizard

http://www.netoasis.com/info/wizard/

Provides a Q&A area for furniture refinishers, refinishing techniques, care and maintenance information, and archives of past furniture technique documents. These technique documents include antique restoration tips and furniture repair strategies.

Book

http://www.picturephone.com/survey.htm

Get a free copy of "Videoconferencing and Money, Money, Money" when you complete a questionnaire.

Hartmann House Antiques

http://www.island.net/~hartmann/antiques/antiques.html

Provides information about buying and selling antiques, furniture restoration and refinishing, rebuilding and part replacement, woodworking and furniture design, upholstery and interior design, and manufacturing living room suites and furniture.

LIBERON/Star Finishing Supplies

http://www.mcn.org/MenComNet/Business/Retail/Lib/liberon.html

Lists LIBERON finishing materials and supplies as well as information about wood finishing and supply sources. This site also includes the LIBERON Supply Catalog, which even includes books and videos for furniture refinishing.

North American Refinisher's Association

http://www.tclsystems.com/nara/

This site has been awarded the Seal of Approval from Cyberspace WebNut. It provides a listing of refinishers, homeowners, suppliers, franchisors, dealers, distributors, and training facilities.

Technical Guidelines, Finishing Schedules & Product Information

http://www.mcn.org/MenComNet/Business/Retail/Lib/StarTechSchedules.html

Discusses various finishing techniques and what materials you will need to create each technique. Steps are included for refinishing cabinets and applying lacquer. There are also technical bulletins and articles dealing with finishing issues.

Gardening

AgriGator

http://www.ifas.ufl.edu/WWW/AGATOR_HOME.HTM

The home page for the Institute of Food and Agricultural Sciences, which is part of the University of Florida. Includes lists of related Web sites, upcoming conferences, and various programs such as the Acid Rain Program and PANNA (Pesticide Action Network North America).

The Garden Gate

http://www.prairienet.org/ag/garden/homepage.htm

Provides gardeners and nature lovers links to various gardening sites from around the world, tips for gardeners, and access to the Garden Exchange, where gardeners can post requests for seeds and plants, as well as offer items for sale or trade.

Gardening

http://www.rt66.com/~telp/garden.htm

Provides information on irises, hostas, hardy succulents, and gardening catalogs. Includes information about what makes a garden, and about organic gardening. This site include several beautiful photos of irises, hostas, daylilies, and sedums.

The Gardening Archive

http://www.lysator.liu.se/garden/index.html

Provides an emphasis on plants suitable for a temperate or cold temperature climate. Lists specific plants and their uses, including edible plants, herbs, and ornamentals. Has a frequently asked questions area for dealing with fertilizers, soil, and wildflowers.

The Gardens at Thunder Ridge

http://www.msn.fullfeed.com/~thunder/garden/

Provides growing information on organic methods of growing gardens, including organic controls that prove successful. Includes information about how to landscape for birds and wildlife, related Web sites, and how to obtain their garden supply/seed catalogs.

The Germinator

http://pages.prodigy.com/germinator/

Provides information sharing for growers and consumers of vegetables, fruits, herbs, and flowers. Includes a journal about the day-to-day happenings on a farm, documents dealing with tomatos and how to build an affordable greenhouse, horticultural Web links, and farming jokes and quotes.

Howard Garrett's Basic Organic Program

http://www.msn.fullfeed.com/~thunder/garden/

Provides a biannual newsletter with a basic program for organic gardeners, information for beginners, and tips for specific gardening problems. Includes principles of organic gardening, information on controlling insects, organic recipes, flea control, how to save sick Photinias, a listing of Howard Garett's books, recommended nonprofit organizations, and how to submit questions.

Joe and Mindy's WebGarden

http://www.nhn.uoknor.edu/~howard/garden2.html

Provides a of helpful books and magazines on gardening and a wealth of links to such Web sites as GardenNet, The Ardent Gardener, Mirror's Garden Patch, Gardens+Gardening, Garden Spider's Web, Ohio State WebGarden, and The Armchair Gardener.

The Virtual Garden

http://www.pathfinder.com/@@KQHKcoOzHgAAQE@9/vg/

Provides an online resource for the home gardener. Includes gardening content from several well-known magazines such as *Southern Living* and *Homeground*, an interactive plant encyclopedia, a house plant directory, garden project documents, excerpts from the best books on the market, an online bookstore for ordering books, garden literature discussion sessions, some of the world's finest botanical gardens, and inside information from plant authorities.

Jewelry Making & Metalworking

Ancient Circles

http://www.pacific.net/~ancient/

Provides a listing of various symbolic jewelry, jewelry with images of gods and goddesses, Celtic reproductions, and why this jewelry is protective and magical. Includes a listing of over 30 circles from ancient times and their meanings.

Associate Jeweler's Tradeshop

http://www.teleport.com/~raylc/

Provides a wholesale jewelry union tradeshop and service facility, centered in Portland, Oregon. Includes a shop tour, a listing of their current work, references, information about diamond cuts, colors, clarity, how a diamond is measured, and a complete online catalog of everything they carry.

Design in Metal

http://www.kcom.com:80/art/company/001/price.htm

Provides photos and descriptions of various products by Walt Mendenhall, including three heavy firs 30" high, a stainless steel sea whirl and water wall, and three small wheat stalks.

Hansen Designs—Fine Art Jewelry and Gems

http://www.homecom.com/global/index/
HansenDesigns-FineArtJewelryandGems.html

Provides a directory of jewelry gifts and distinctive, contemporary, and fine art jewelry that sometimes uses exotic materials.

Keith Farley/Metalsmith

http://wuarchive.wustl.edu/edu/arts/metal/Gallery/
Farley_K.html

Provides color photos of various types of jewelry Keith Farley has made, information about the latest ArtMetal project, and ArtMetal gallery with displays of work using forged metal, sand matrix metalwork, forged steel, and metal sculptors.

Main Lobby for Jewelry Making

http://www.teleport.com/~raylc/master/lobby.html

Shows how ideas turn into fine jewelry and lists various types of diamond cuts, qualities, and sizes. Includes information about gold mountings, grading diamonds, price tables of stones, colored stones, and prices of current inventory at Accurate Gem Labs, Inc.

The Making of JEEP COLLINS Jewelry

http://www.ktc.com/Jeepcollins/mknjwlry.html

Provides a sales catalog of Jeep Collins pieces and information about how to make handmade jewelry and cast pieces.

Metalwork Using the Sand-Matrix Design Process

http://www.uark.edu/ALADDIN/artexp/hank/kaminsky.html

Provides information on Sand-Matrix designs, where molten metal is poured into holes in the sand. Includes a gallery of Sand-Matrix designed objects such as the bronze belt buckle, 14-gold and amethyst ring, and a pewter, bronze, and padouk chalice.

Models

Aero-Pac

http://www.aeropac.org/aeropac/

Provides information about the Tripoli Rocketry Association, upcoming Aero-Pac launches and meetings, the dangers of igniters being triggered by radio transmitters, rocketry related manufacturers and distributors, and rocketry research.

Books/Videos

http://www.cybergate.net/~jpowell/mrrref.html

Provides an extensive list of multiple scale books, magazines, online magazines, videos, and photographs. Some of the sites include Bookmine, a searchable index of old, rare, and used books; *German Railways Magazine*, for all scales of German railroads; and model railroad how-to videos.

C & M Train Depot

http://www.xmission.com/~gastown/trains/train.htm

Provides a mail order site for ordering all kinds of trains from over 35 manufacturers, include American Model Builders, Grandt Line Products, K-Line, Micro-Trains, Pola, and Tichy Train Group.

DP Industries Home Page

http://www.modelrailroad.com/dpi/dpwelm.html

DP Industries manufactures revolutionary scenery and detail products for model railroaders. You can order a Bag O' Junk or a Tire Pile for little or no money. Their products include advertising signs, as well as plaster and plastering products.

Florida's Largest Train Store

http://www.hrtrains.com/

Provides innovative solutions for model railroading in all scales. Includes information about gauges and sizes, children's trains and toys, collectibles, engine and car shop, and the class and conference schedule.

Logic Rail Technologies

http://ourworld.compuserve.com/homepages/LogicRailTech/

Includes model railroad electronics. This site has some products unique to the marketplace, such as their signaling circuits, BlockMaster™, SignalMaster™, and HO and N scale resistance wheelsets. Includes a complete price list, ordering information, and links to railroad-related Internet resources such as the Cyberspace World Railroad.

Mini Automania

http://www.masternet.it/market/automini/home.htm

Provides information about Quartzo's 1/43ʳᵈ scale models with die-cast body models, the Studio 1050 Schuco model, 11 models by Victoria, the Traxxas Rustler, the Traxxas Stampede, Tamiya's Fiatabarth Berlina Corsa, Revival models, the Pego Maserati, and Brumm's Porsche and Ferrari models.

Model Railroad.Com

http://www.cybergate.net/~jpowell/

Provides information and related model railroad links. The more popular your scale, the more information and links available.

Monroe Astronomical Rocket Society

http://nysernet.org/staff/billowens/mars/mars.html

Provides information about contests, sport flying, high impulse rocketry, a photo archive, and how to subscribe to the *Upstate Rocketeer* magazine. Includes links to various resources such as clubs and associations, rocketry humor, rocket Web servers for historical archives, and rocketry companies.

Nautical Research and Shipmodeling Links

http://www.seaways.com/nautres.html

Provides information about scale model boats, frequently asked questions for beginning and intermediate shipmodelers about finding tools, books, plans, and paint for shipmodeling. Includes information about the Big Gun R/C Warship Combat, nautical documents, pictures of U.S. ships from 1775–1941, and various model ship museums.

Palatine Hobby's Railroad Page

http://members.aol.com/phlhobby/railroad/railroad.html

Provides a listing of one of the biggest selections of model trains in the Chicago area. Includes links to other popular railroad sites and 12 of the most well-known manufacturers. There is also a list of products from the Historical Society.

Pmcg's Vicious Model Boat Page

http://www.tiac.net/users/pmcg/boat.html

Features model boats, exhibit photos, descriptions and avi videos of some exotic radio controlled model boats, manufacturers of model powerboat hulls, marine motors, and accessories. Includes information about the F-41 Stryker Cat and the 56" Aeromarine Apache model.

Polyterrain Water Soluble Scenery Materials

http://www.tttrains.com/polyt/

Provides a wide selection of water soluble materials, an alternative to plaster and hard shell scenery. Includes information about the polyterrain materials, supplies, and techniques, and videos that you can order through this site.

Rocket Works

http://www.tyrell.net/~smcatee/

Provides launch reports, upcoming launches in the central U.S., links to weather information sources, photos of model and high powered rockets, and links to other related sites.

Roecks Railroad Concepts

http://www.largescale.com/rrc/

Provides electronic modules that can turn train sets into railroads by performing realistic operations without the use of complex wiring or the use of computers. Includes documentation for track hookups and a price list for a Train Decelerator System, a Switching Interface Module, and a SwitchMaster.

The RR Depot

http://www.virtual-village.com/rrdepot/index.html

Offers a selection of the world's best values in scale models, track, and accessories. You can read reviews and articles about models and prototypes, and instruction books and tapes, HO starter kits, and the list of products they carry by manufacturer.

Rutger Friberg's World of Model Railroad Electronics

http://www.hobby.se/Rutger/Rutger.html

Provides a list of books Rutger has written, updates to the books, and railroad projects from each. Projects include blinking lights, flashing railroad crossings, flashing lights, engine code tester, and sound control decoder.

S. Shiota's Model Rocket Page

http://www.st.rim.or.jp/~shushi/rocket.html

Includes model rocket components, the launch and recovery system, NAR/HIA model rocketry safety codes, model rocket collections, and the launch schedule for Japan.

A Scale Model Collection

http://ourworld.compuserve.com/homepages/k_oltean/

Provides a precision scale models gallery of planes, trains, and automobiles. Includes the scale model aircraft of the Jet Age and WW II and a variety of profiles of model scale cars.

Scale Modeling

http://vms.www.uwplatt.edu/~boelterj/scalemodeling.html

Includes construction tips and techniques for civilian and military models for land, sea, and air. Some models include the Model T, land-based military vehicles, old sailing ships, aircraft carriers, destroyers, cargo ships, stunt planes, the Cessna, glider planes, barnstormer planes, and planes from World War I and II.

South Bay Model Shipwrights

http://home.earthlink.net/free/gswiercz1/webdocs/sbms.html

Provides a club for builders and admirers of wooden models of old sailing ships. Includes meeting schedules, membership information, kits, plans, fittings, magazines, a listing of hobby shops, tools, and Internet resources for ship modelers.

TraiNutz

http://members.aol.com/rome154/trainutz.html

Provides puzzles, pictures, and information about real trains as well as model trains. Some of the pictures include Aerotrain, Oriana Bay model railroad, Santa Fe Erie-Built Diesel, Rock Island Bicentennial E8, and New York City's Lightning Stripes.

Movie Memorabilia

Big Reel

http://www.csmonline.com/bigrpage.html

Provides thousands of advertisements for movies, videos, movie memorabilia, autographs, and posters for sale or wanted. Includes stories and interviews with stars and information on upcoming conventions and shows.

CinaMedia

http://www.gu.edu.au/gwis/cinemedia/CineMedia.home.html

Is the largest film and media directory available on the Internet. Includes over 4,000 links to actors, animation, radio, cinema, festivals, images, journals, films, sounds, new media, television, and much more.

Collecting

http://www.inreach.com/odyssey/coll396.htm

Collecting is a publication for collectibles, autographs, movies, television, rock and roll, props, costumes, movie posters and memorabilia, sports, space collectibles, animation, and art. Includes authentic original historical autographs, letters, documents, and signed photographs of personalities.

CyberCinema

http://www.indirect.com/www/jonbrown/cinema/

Provides a World Wide Web movie poster store specializing in the sale of current releases and upcoming movies, as well as classic movies. Includes a listing of all the box office hits of 1995, the top 25 posters, and the classic movie poster catalog, as well as the top 10 current movies in the United States.

Hollywood Toy and Poster Company

http://www.mbnet.mb.ca/hollywdposter/

Provides scripts, photos, posters, presskits, back issues of *Marquee* and *Tribute* magazines, and a large selection of collector toys. Includes a poster photo gallery, The Star Wars Store, The Bargain Department, and information on how to consign items.

Movie Collector's World

http://www.arenapub.com/mcw/

Is the world's leading publication for collectors of movie memorabilia, such as old, new, common and rare movie posters, autographs, stills and cels, videos, and celebrity memorabilia. Includes an extensive fan club directory and up-to-date events center.

Movie Poster Warehouse

http://www.io.org/~mpw/

Provides the latest announcements, frequently asked questions about movie posters, and a poster list arranged chronologically by year. Includes various 4×6 and 8×10 photos of music and movie personalities, and cast photos of popular movies and TV series.

Sources for Still Photographs, Posters and Other Film Memorabilia

http://www.amctv.com/memorabilia/index.html

Provides a resource from the American Movie Classics. Includes a list of contacts from Peter Jones of persons interviewed by him for a broadcast on American Movie Classics.

World Collectible Center

http://home.earthlink.net/free/wcc/webdocs/

Is the world's largest collectible store for memorabilia, nostalgia, and vintage toys. Includes sports, movies, TV, rock and roll, science fiction, political, and advertising collectibles.

Origami

The Electric Origami Shop

http://www.ibm.com/Stretch/EOS/

Includes several origami products: The Fridge Gallery, high-tech art, some products from IBM, various puzzles, fractals, kaleidoscope images, Deep Blue, Mood Ringo, Site Traveler, and Alien Snow.

An Introduction to Origami and The Peace of Paper

http://www.jumpmedia.com/peace/intro.html

Includes the history and tradition of origami, the Chinese, Japanese, Western, and Zen Buddhist traditions.

Jasper's Origami Menagerie

http://www.mit.edu:8001/people/jasper/origami/menagerie/origami.html

Provides examples, galleries of related models, and related Web links. The galleries include mammals, birds, bugs and spiders, animals from the jungle, reptiles, symbols, objects, and the Dark Side. Includes a step-by-step display on how to make some basic folds.

Joseph Wu's Origami Page

http://www.cs.ubc.ca/spider/jwu/origami.html

Provides origami photo galleries from artists such as J.C. Nolan and other famous people, information on origami, various files and diagrams, and other origami home pages in Australia, Europe, Japan, and the United States.

Marbleized Paper

http://www.southwind.net/~rjones/marble.html

Discusses the history behind marbleized paper since the 12th Century, detailed information on how to marbleize paper, several marble images, and a listing of paper marbler resources.

Origami Books in Local Libraries

http://www.contrib.andrew.cmu.edu/org/origami/library.html

Lists over 90 books on origami from the CMU Hunt Library, the Pitt Hillman Library, and the Carnegie Library of Pittsburgh. The list includes books written from 1961–present. Some of the more recently written titles are *Brilliant Origami* by David Brill, and *Spirals II* by Tomoko Fuse.

Origami Tips

http://www2.gsu.edu/~gs01yyj/origami/oritip.html

Provides the types of papers you can use for origami, how to correctly combine two or more types of paper, and preserving origami models by spraying, painting, or dipping them.

Origami USA Main Menu

http://www2.gsu.edu/~gs01yyj/ousa/ousa.html

Includes information about Origami USA and Origami USA membership a complete listing of Origami USA suppliers, and information about the annual origami convention that takes place in New York City.

The Pavilion of Polyhedreality

http://www.li.net/~george/pavilion.html

Provides an assortment of images, such as the Paper Ball, the Puzzle, If You Build It, He Will Come, and apples and oranges. Includes several links to other sites, such as David Eppstein's Geometry Junkyard, Jim Plank's Origami Page, and Kirby Urner's Plyhedra Gallery.

Schoolhouse Videos and CDs

http://www.nando.net/ads/gift/videos/v2200.htm

Provides a unique video revealing the secrets of origami, the ancient paper-folding art form. The video teaches you how to make a sailboat, a cup, a flying bird, a butterfly, a snake, and a whale using their step-by-step process.

The Word Chains

http://www.mandrak.com/ablau/oring.htm

Includes an interactive display of an origamic creation. Enables you to open cards on the screen and watch as the paper comes apart and takes form. Explores the transformation from the two dimensional plane to three dimensional.

Photography

@rtweb Art Gallery

http://www.bitech.com/gallery

Eugene, Oregon's first online gallery, specializes in digital photography, but features new work in all two-dimensional media. Current exhibit changes each month.

1002situations

http://fgidec1.tuwien.ac.at/1002situations/

Place the text, photos, and sounds that define your *heimat* (homeland) into this virtual museum. Not only do you visit, you can participate and interact.

ABC of Bird Photography

http://www.netshop.net/~cloughs/abcbird.html

Includes a discussion about everything you will ever need to know about bird photography—essential equipment, habitat of the birds, hiding places, how to get close shots, overseas travel, whether to get prints or slides, shutter speed, and even how to use a tripod outdoors.

Alan Dorow Gallery

http://www.picture.com/Alan-Dorow.html

This site includes photographs of people and their surroundings. Many of Dorow's photographs are humorous, but tasteful.

Alder Yarrow's Photography

http://www-leland.stanford.edu/~alder/photography.html

Contains five portfolios of Alder Yarrow's latest photographic work, as well as links to photography related resources on the Web. He works in the 4×5-inch format, primarily in black and white. The majority of his work would be considered landscape photography, although he would not classify the majority of his photographs as pure landscapes.

Allen Rose

http://www.metronet.com/~arose

Photos from the news and a portfolio are included at this site. Rose puts his daily work here.

Anderson Galleries

http://www.spectra.net/mall/anderson/

Exhibits the professional work of Richard Anderson, a professional photographer who specializes in portraits.

Ansel Adams—*Fiat Lux*

http://bookweb.cwis.uci.edu:8042/AdamsHome.html

Exhibits *Fiat Lux*, the book of photographs Ansel Adams produced to commemorate the University of California's centennial celebration. Here, there are essays, a chronology, and some other links, as well as an exhibition of the photographs. You can place electronic orders here for these and other works by Adams and others.

Atlanta Photography Group

http://www.mindspring.com/~baird/apg/index.html

A group of photographers from Atlanta presents their photographs at this site. It is intended for students of photography, as well as others who might enjoy the visit.

Atlanta Photojournalism Seminar

http://www.mindspring.com/~frankn/atlanta

This seminar has become an internationally known contest for photography. This site presents some of the winning photographs from recent exhibitions.

Australian Outback Gallery Photography

http://matahari.tamu.edu/People/Ewen/Outback.html

Offers a collection of images from the heart of Australia's arid zone, the Outback.

Barry Anderson Photography

http://www.eden.com/~alyosha

Presents a selection of photographs from Barry Anderson Photography.

California Museum of Photography

http://cmp1.ucr.edu/

Some photos, but mostly essays, are present at this site. Although a bit disorganized, this site is the home to a huge collection of photographs and photography materials.

Chiossone Studio, NYC

http://www.photostudio.com/

Beauty/fashion photo studio in New York dedicated to editorial and advertising photography. Includes advertising photos.

The Discovery Catalogue

http://prostar-int.com/gogg

Contains a pictorial essay on the journey of Captain George Vancouver to the Pacific Northwest Coast of North America in 1792.

Figure 1: The Visual Sector

http://www.interport.net/~edb

Dedicated to the anonymous pleasure of found photos. Accepts submissions of photos from people on the Net and posts them (see the Web site for more information). Also maintains a biased listing of photographic sites of passing interest for the Web community.

Hans de Kort Photography

http://www.xs4all.nl/~hdekort/

Presents fashion and advertising photography.

Home Page of Photographer, Sculptor David C. Franson

http://www.eciad.bc.ca/~dfranson/dfranson.htm

Offers images of David Franson's photographs and sculptures for viewing and for sale.

Hot Pictures: Russian Photography

http://www.kiae.su/www/wtr/hotpictures/gallery.html

Russian photographers and artists are present at this site. There are several exhibitions by different photographers that students of photography from the West may never have seen.

Impact Studio

http://www.netaxs.com/~impact/index.html

This site may be of interest to both students of photography and people in advertising and design. Some very skilled photographers flex their digital muscles with fine camera and computer work.

Jay Stoegbauer Photography

http://www.stoegbauer.com/Pages/Prtflo.html

Provides a color portfolio Jay Stoegbauer, a commercial photographer who specializes in digital photography. This page includes information about why high-end digital photography surpasses scanned transparencies in quality, information about the tonal limitations of film, the dynamic tonal control of high-end digital photography, a discussion on the various types of digital cameras, and a discussion about color-bit versus number of pixels.

The Jazz Photography of Ray Avery

http://bookweb.cwis.uci.edu:8042/Jazz/jazz.html

Traces jazz beginnings through records and photography. Also includes Ray Avery's online jazz exhibition, which is grouped into four major areas: The Lighthouse All Stars—Hermosa Beach and Laguna Beach; Nightclubs, Festivals and Concerts; Recording Sessions—Los Angeles; and Stars of Jazz—TV Series.

Kodak

http://www.kodak.com/

The granddaddy of the photography industry maintains this site where employees from Kodak show their photographic skills.

Michigan Press Photographers

http://www.cris.com/~Mppa/

News and feature photographers from the Michigan Press have this gallery. This site is well-maintained and well-designed.

Mythago

http://www.umich.edu/~cjericks/gallery/gallery.html

Figure studies and landscapes are featured at this site. Largely a study in the human figure, this site does feature some nudes (albeit tasteful).

Northwest College Photographic Communications

http://photo.nwc.whecn.edu/

Provides information about Northwest College's Photographic Communications. Northwest offers sample student portfolios, faculty and alumni portfolios, what courses they offer, and information about scholarships. They focus on commercial portraiture, studio illustration, photojournalism, digital imaging, medical photography, color lab management, public relations, aerial photography, and freelance.

Online PhotoWeb

http://www.web-search.com/photo.html

Provides links to several image enhancement software, such as Paint Shop Pro, Kai's Power Tools, and Fractal Design. There are links to photojournalist commercial graphics and design, commercial photography and imaging, personal photography, scenic photography galleries, sports, digital images collections, miscellaneous photography collections, clubs, photography instruction and schools, photo finishers, and camera and film supplies.

The Photography Spot

http://www.cris.com/~Bubaluba/photo_spot.html

Dedicated to photography and photographers. Links you to the work of photographers around the world. You can add the Web site that shows your work or the work of another. Also visit Photo Stuff to look at or add companies and services that deal with photography.

The Photography Yellow Pages

http://theyellowpages.com/photography.htm

Provides links to the Cloud Gallery, InfoVid Outlet for photography, film and video, Panoramic Photography, various stock photography, wedding photography, and Wenger International Photography.

The Photojournalist's Coffee House

http://www.intac.com/~jdeck/index2.html

This site (as its name implies) features photojournalists' documentaries and photo-essays. Maintained by John Decker, this site includes his famous Covington's Homeless display.

PhotoServe

http://www.photoserve.com/

Publishes the latest work of professional photographers, their home pages, an industry resource center, a bulletin board, and a new talent section.

Professional Photography Portfolios

http://www.best.com/~casner/personal/photo_index.shtml

Provides extensive portfolios of photography from over 35 artists, a listing of photojournalists, several photographic home pages, photographic essays, digital photography, digital photorealistic imaging, stereoscopic photography, photography schools, some history of photography, and an online photo gallery.

Ron Lowry's Home Page

http://goofy.iafrica.com:80/~gabriela/

Provides links for digital photographers to Adobe, Kodak, the Photoshop newsgroup, the Digital Imaging newsgroup, and the NPPA-L and Photoforum mailing lists.

Sacred Faces, Sacred Spaces

http://www.artsantafe.com/sfm/jyoung/youngphoto.html

Exhibits Polaroid transfer, color, and black and white images of the American Southwest, Australia, Mexico, Greece, and more.

Scott Freeman's Underwater Photography Page

http://weber.u.washington.edu/~scotfree

Focuses on underwater photography in the Northwest, namely Puget Sound.

Specializing in Natural Light and Nature Images

http://www.halcyon.com/pacimage/outland/

Provides several photos from Outland Images that can be used for personal use upon request. The library of images includes plantlife, national parks, water, buildings, mountains, skies, and sunsets.

Travels with Samantha

http://martigny.ai.mit.edu/samantha/travels-with-samantha.html

Depicts writer Philip Greenspun's experiences as he traveled throughout North America. Offers

photographs of United States and Canadian landscapes, wildlife cultures, and youthful women.

Virtual Gallery (Korea)

http://203.248.135.66/gallery/

Many of Korea's best photographers are featured here. You will have no trouble finding great photography, even though some of the menus are written in a misleading fashion.

Virtual Portfolio (London)

http://www.dircon.co.uk/maushaus/folio.html

This site featuring some of London's most talented artists offers the opportunity to both view and purchase some of their stunning photographs (and some illustrations).

The Web Nebulae

http://seds.lpl.arizona.edu/billa/twn/

Introduces a few of the spectacular objects that unfold in the night sky when you have a camera and a telescope.

Rocks, Gems, & Minerals

Arris International Corporation

http://www.metroguide.com/arris/

Provides an extensive selection of rare earth materials and other metals for sale. A complete chemical analysis of each material can be provided, and samples for independent analysis can be obtained. Some of the rare earth metals include erbium, gadolinium, holmium, terbium, and yttrium.

Crystals and Minerals

http://www.pb.net/usrwww/w_celestyte/crystals.htm

Displays color photos and information about the gems found in the Smithsonian Gem and Mineral Collection, the history of amber, flourescent minerals, and rock collecting.

Gems

http://www.treasurenet.com/treasure/calgold/books/subject/gems.html

Provides an extensive listing of rock and gem books available on the market.

Hunterian Museum of Rocks and Minerals

http://www.dcs.gla.ac.uk/~sagemp/Museum/HuntMus/rocks/

The Hunterian Museum contains a collection of rocks and minerals originating elsewhere in the solar system. The museum pieces, which include over three-quarters of a million specimens, are those that have fallen to the earth as meteorites. Includes a virtual or guided tour of the museum. Some individual exhibitions include The Romans in Scotland, Ancient Greeks, and the Vikings.

Mineralogical Meanderings

http://www.rtd.com/~bkeller/rockshop/meander.html

Provides information on collecting Micrometeorites and Crystal Lattice Models. Model kits are available for building display models of mineral crystal lattices. Provides mineral postage stamps and information about the mysterious powers of crystals and gemstones.

Rockhounds Information Page

http://www.rahul.net/infodyn/rockhounds/rockhounds.html

Provides rock shops and galleries, images and pictures from the Museum of Minerology, articles about minerals, general earth science info, paleontology-related sites, collecting sites and trips, clubs and societies, and software.

Web Dexter

http://www.3wnet.com/webdex/recreati/hobbies/rocks__1.html

Provides information about birthstones, the Columbus Rock and Mineral Society, French Association of Microminerology, Irving family rock collecting, and tips on topaz mountain rockhounding.

Stamps

Bjorn Much's Stamps Page

http://www.idt.unit.no/~bjornmu/stamp.html

Provides frequently asked questions, information about the Internet Stamp Database project, and how to obtain CTO's (Cancelled to Order), which are unusable canceled stamps.

ELA Auctions, Inc.

http://www.virtualcities.com/~virtual/col/ela/stamp/0elarst.htm

Shows color photos, size, and price of various stamp plate blocks, U.S. airmail, hunting permit stamps for sale, and how to obtain a catalog for an upcoming auction.

The Icelandic Stamp's Page

http://xanadu.centrum.is/~vip/english.htm

Provides color photos of stamps from 1873–present. Includes stamps depicting animals, birds, communications, cars, fish, the Olympic games, the Boy Scouts movement, the Vikings, volcanic eruptions, and mountains.

Joseph Luft's Philatelic Resources on the Web

http://www.execpc.com/~joeluft/resource.html

Provides a complete philatelic resource. Includes a listing of what stamps are for sale from around the world and information about the Rossica Society of Russian Philately, the Austrian postal authority, the Philatelic Dealer's Group, the Philatelic Trading Post, the National Stamp Dealer's Association, how to obtain a stamp catalog, and stamp dealers.

New Zealand First Day Covers

http://www.efn.org/%7Ecne/

Provides information about stamps first day covers and information about the New Zealand Stamp Dealer's Association, which provides a means for stamp collectors to buy, sell, or trade stamps. Includes a member list of the New Zealand Philatelic Society.

The Philatelic Trading Post

http://www.clark.net/pub/stamps/

Provides stamp auction information, Cuban price lists, books, pamphlets, stamp magazines, supplies, and how to attend stamp societies and clubs.

Software

http://www.grasp.com/lycos/dbeta.htm

Download a free 30-day demo of *Know*It All, designed to simplify information collection. Register to receive discounts on future upgrades as well.

Revenue and Telegraph Stamps

http://www.pbbooks.com/revenue.htm

Provides a historical reference of the revenue stamps of the U.S., such as the Private Die Proprietary stamps, Beer stamps, Wine Revenue stamps, and Internal Revenue stamps. Includes Telegraph stamps such as Indian Telegraphs from 1851–1914 and Foreign Revenue stamps.

Stamp Collecting Basics

http://www.best.com/~linns/Collecting_Basics.html

Provides an introduction to stamp collecting, information about postage stamps, stamp condition, postmarks, stamp care and handling, stamp albums, postal stationery, essays and proofs, and souvenir cards.

Stamps, Covers, and Anything Philatelic

http://www.supernet.net/~spitzerp/

Provides information about philately, how to have a stamp scanned, cartophilately, rules for reserving stamps or covers for purchase, how to find out what a stamp is worth, how to receive free stamps and supplies for schools, and a glossary of stamp acronyms.

U.S. 1995 Stamp Program

http://www.realtime.net/~efdietz/stamps/95stamps.htm

Lists more than 60 stamps and postal stationery assembled from U.S. Postal Service Stamp News releases. Includes information on how to get first day covers and about the Philatelic fulfillment Service Center.

Ukrainian Stamps

http://wvnvaxa.wvnet.edu/~roman/Ukstamps.html

Provides information about Ukrainian stamps, a complete chronological listing of Ukrainian stamps, and photos of stamps from 1991–1995 including Soviet-era stamps overstamped as Ukrainian postage stamps and 1993 definitive stamps.

Textiles

Amish Quilts

http://www.folkart.com/~latitude/amish/amish.htm

Explains what quilts mean to the Amish. This site explains appliques, bar, center diamond and center square, contemporary, log cabin, ninepatch, star, sunshine and shadow, traditional, and tumbling block designs. You can custom order Amish quilts or wall hangings.

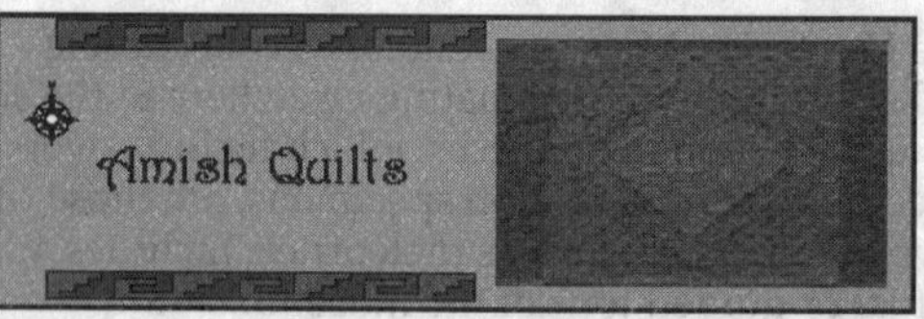

A Brief History of Quilting

http://204.249.244.10/QuiltHistoryPage.html

Discusses the history of quilting, such as origins of quilting styles, quilt blocks and techniques, and quilting in different countries. There are links to pictures of quilts found in the Smithsonian and links to various quilt study groups.

Computers and Quilting

http://204.249.244.10/ComputerQuiltingPage.html

The Computers and Quilting home page lists various computer quilting software. It reviews some computer quilting software and includes software demos for download directly from this site.

Counted Cross Stitch, Needlework, and Stitchery Page

http://www.crl.com/~kdyer/xstitch.html

Counted Cross Stitch, Needlework, and Stitchery Page provides links to various cross stitch and other forms of needlework. There is an area for FAQs (frequently asked questions), limericks, poems, songs, jokes, and puzzles relating to quilting and sewing. There are online resource links to supplies, media (such as books, magazines, television, and videotapes), stores, stitching information, activities, and historical and cultural references.

Creative Quilting

http://www.iplaza.com/quilting/

The Creative Quilting page is an online quilting catalog that includes quilting items from batting to irons at discount prices. This site includes a classified ad area enabling you to buy, sell, or trade your quilting supplies, as well as a questions and tips corner that is updated daily.

International Web Exchange: Quilting Exchange

http://www.iwe.com/quilting.html

Includes everything you need for sewing, even gift baskets. You can sign up for beginner and advanced quilting classes at The Quilting Bee through this site as well.

Misc Quilting Information

http://ttsw.com/MiscQuiltingPage.html

Lists interesting facts, stories, and ideas about quilting. Information includes quilter's commandments, gift wrapping quilts, pressing quilt tops, quilting for a good cause, computer-generated templates and foundations, and 71 reasons to buy fabric.

The Quilting Page

http://www.peinet.pe.ca:80/PEIhomepage/fyi/quilt/ quilt.html

Includes the World Wide Quilting Page, Carnegie Threads Quilting Club, John Hopkins University quilt photographs, and Michiana Free-Net's Quilting Book Reviews. The World Wide Quilting area displays color photos of contest winners for the WORST Quilt In The World Contest.

The True PA Dutch Country Souvenir

http://padutch.welcome.com/quilts.html

The True Pennsylvania Dutch Country Souvenir page discusses Amish quilts and their meaning. From this page you can link to the Pennsylvania Dutch Convention and Service Bureau, which explains more about the Amish and where to purchase these beautiful works of art.

World Wide Quilting Page

http://ttsw.com/mainquiltingpage.html

This quilting page includes an archive for quilting enthusiasts and crafters. Quilting information, special techniques, diagrams, and foundations for making quilts are discussed. There is also a calendar of upcoming quilting events.

Arbortech

http://www.iinet.net.au/~arbortec/

Provides freehand power shaping tools for developing innovative new products. Includes various products and distributors, free plans for a bowl and coat stand, and a gallery of Bishwa Oaks and Arthur Clark.

Carleton Woodworking

http://members.gnn.com/carleton/carleton.htm

Provides information about custom furniture, wood turning, making architectural and furniture parts for other woodworkers, how to turn wooden bowls, and a listing a good resources for woodworking.

Chris Melhorn's Woodworking Gallery

http://www.electrotek.com/staff/powersys/chris/wood/ frames/WoodMain.htm

Provides photographs and details on how to make a valance or cornice board, cradle for a newborn baby, mirror/coat hanger, toy box, baby bottle holder, stool, wooden spaghetti utensils, picture frame, and tree house.

The Oak Factory Bulletin Board

http://theoak.com/wwwboard.html

Provides information about mini-lathes, footbridge plans, cleaning saw blades, upholstery springs, what routers to buy, what radius of circle to use, woodburning stoves, oak flooring, painting oily concrete floors, tool grinder, finishing problems with pine, and more.

Prairie Woodworking

http://ourworld.compuserve.com/homepages/ prairie_woodwork/

Provides photos showing examples of Japanese lattice, Frank Lloyd Wright look, fillets and bevels, square slats, and the use of brass. Includes information on measuring for enclosures.

Quality Woodwork and Supply, Inc.

http://www.metrolink.net/quality/qwsmain.htm

Provides an online hardwood lumber store including domestic wood price quotes, a listing of what laminates are available and a listing of what hardware lines they carry.

W5: Woodworking on the World Wide Web

http://www.iucf.indiana.edu/~brown/hyplan/wood.html

Provides useful information about handtools, machines, finishings, patent information, The Woodworking Catalog, woodworking books from BookServe (the world's largest bookseller on the Web), color theory and mixing stains, saw sharpening instructions, woodturning and woodcarving techniques, and woodworking shareware and software.

WoodLink

http://www.vicnet.net.au/~woodlink/woodlink.htm

Provides information on Victorian Woodworker's Association, Australian woodwork and woodworkers, and timber.

Woods of the World

http://www.woodweb.com/~treetalk/price_discount.html

Provides a multimedia database for woodworkers, wood researchers, and wood users. Includes information to help you search for woods, examine a species' data, compare woods, and view movies or photo libraries of wood.

WoodWeb

http://www.woodweb.com/

An information resource for the woodworking industry. Includes links to the Woodworking Machinery Distributors Association, Wood Machinery Manufacturers of America, and the Wood Machinery Importers Association.

Woodworking in Western Montana

http://www.ronan.net/~woodwork/

Services provided include antique refinishing, antique repair, cabinets, construction consultation, custom furniture, and general carpentry work.

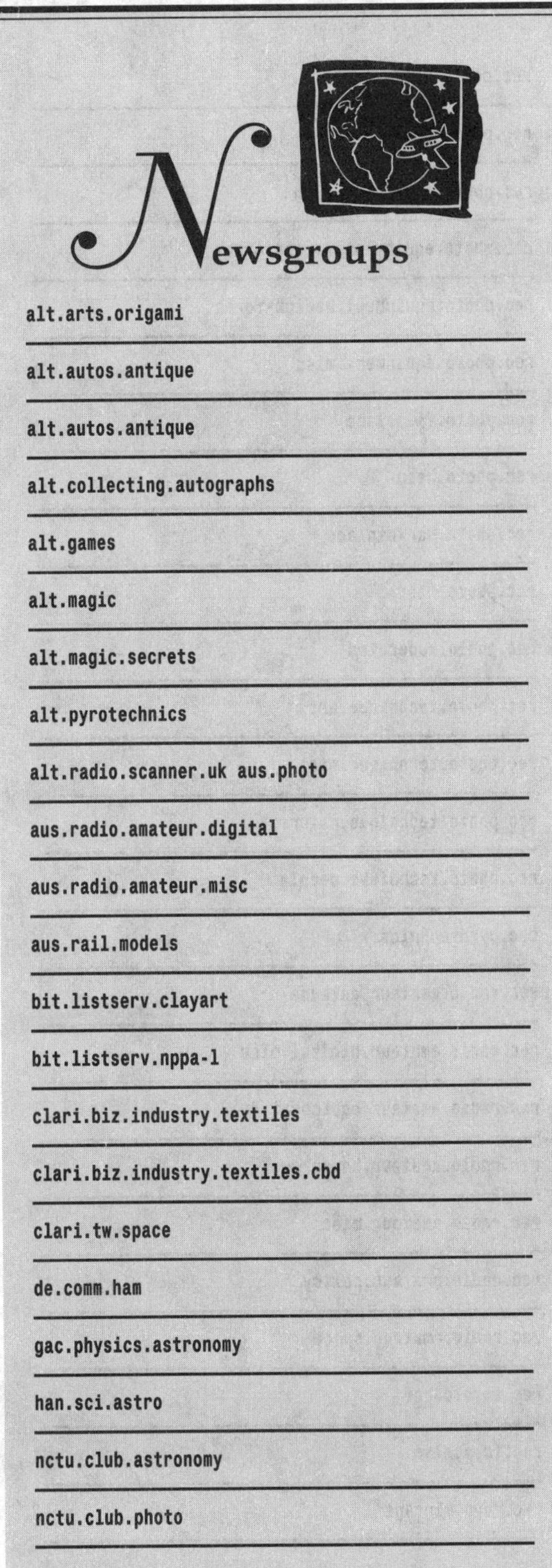

Newsgroups

alt.arts.origami

alt.autos.antique

alt.autos.antique

alt.collecting.autographs

alt.games

alt.magic

alt.magic.secrets

alt.pyrotechnics

alt.radio.scanner.uk aus.photo

aus.radio.amateur.digital

aus.radio.amateur.misc

aus.rail.models

bit.listserv.clayart

bit.listserv.nppa-1

clari.biz.industry.textiles

clari.biz.industry.textiles.cbd

clari.tw.space

de.comm.ham

gac.physics.astronomy

han.sci.astro

nctu.club.astronomy

nctu.club.photo

pdaxs.ads.antiques

pnet.rec.antiques

pnet.rec.radio.amateur.announce

pnet.rec.radio.amateur.talk

rec.antiques

rec.antiques.marketplace

rec.antiques.radio+phono

rec.arts.anime.models

rec.arts.bonsai

rec.arts.puppetry

rec.autos.antique

rec.birds

rec.crafts.polymer-clay

rec.collecting

rec.collecting.cards

rec.collecting.cards.discuss

rec.collecting.cards.non-sports

rec.collecting.coins

rec.collecting.phonecards

rec.collecting.sport.baseball

rec.collecting.sport.basketball

rec.collecting.sport.football

rec.collecting.sport.hockey

rec.collecting.sport.misc

rec.collecting.stamps

rec.crafts.beads

```
rec.crafts.jewelry

rec.crafts.metalworking

rec.crafts.pottery

rec.crafts.textiles.misc

rec.crafts.textiles.needlework

rec.crafts.textiles.quilting

rec.crafts.textiles.sewing

rec.crafts.textiles.yarn

rec.games.design

rec.games.miniatures

rec.games.miniatures.historical

rec.games.miniatures.misc

rec.games.miniatures.warhammer

rec.games.misc

rec.games.video.arcade.collecting

rec.juggling

rec.kites

rec.models.railroad

rec.models.rc.air

rec.models.rc.land

rec.models.rc.misc

rec.models.rc.water

rec.models.rockets

rec.models.scale

rec.pets.birds

rec.photo
```

```
rec.photo.advanced

rec.photo.darkroom

rec.photo.equipment.35mm

rec.photo.equipment.large-format

rec.photo.equipment.medium-format

rec.photo.equipment.misc

rec.photo.film+labs

rec.photo.help

rec.photo.marketplace

rec.photo.misc

rec.photo.moderated

rec.photo.technique.art

rec.photo.technique.misc

rec.photo.technique.nature

rec.photo.technique.people

rec.pyrotechnics

rec.radio.amateur.antenna

rec.radio.amateur.digital.misc

rec.radio.amateur.equipment

rec.radio.amateur.homebrew

rec.radio.amateur.misc

rec.radio.amateur.policy

rec.radio.amateur.space

rec.toys.cars@

rec.toys.misc

rec.toys.vintage
```

rec.woodworking

relcom.fido.ru.photo

relcom.fido.su.astronomy

relcom.radio.ham

sbay.hams

sci.astro

sci.astro.amateur

sci.astro.research

sci.materials.ceramics

swnet.sci.astro

tnn.radio.amateur

tw.bbs.sci.astronomy

uiuc.org.synton

uiuc.pubs.messenger

uk.org.starlink.misc

uk.radio.amateur

uwarwick.societies.amateur-radio

Listservs

AANDC—Arts and Crafts Era Collectors list

You can join this group by sending the message "sub AANDC your name" to
listserv@home.ease.lsoft.com

ASTRONOMY—This is a Discussion List for Amateur and Professional Astronomy

You can join this group by sending the message "sub ASTRONOMY your name" to
listserv@lime.ease.lsoft.com

ATCA—Antique Telephone Collectors

St. John's University, Jamaica, NY

You can join this group by sending the message "sub ATCA your name" to
listserv@sjuvm.stjohns.edu

BIRDCHAT—National Birding Hotline Cooperative (Chat Line)

University of Arizona, Tucson, AZ

You can join this group by sending the message "sub BIRDCHAT your name" to
listserv@listserv.arizona.edu

BIRDCNTR—National Birding Hotline Cooperative (Central)

University of Arizona, Tucson, AZ

You can join this group by sending the message "sub BIRDCNTR your name" to
listserv@listserv.arizona.edu

BIRDEAST—National Birding Hotline Cooperative (East)

University of Arizona, Tucson, AZ

You can join this group by sending the message "sub BIRDEAST your name" to
listserv@listserv.arizona.edu

BIRD_RBA—National Birding Hotline Cooperative Business List

University of Arizona, Tucson, AZ

You can join this group by sending the message "sub BIRD_RBA your name" to
listserv@listserv.arizona.edu

BIRDTECH-L—The Companion Bird Forum

You can join this group by sending the message "sub BIRDTECH-L your name" to
listserv@home.ease.lsoft.com

BIRDWEST—National Birding Hotline Cooperative (West)

University of Arizona, Tucson, AZ

You can join this group by sending the message "sub BIRDWEST your name" to `listserv@listserv.arizona.edu`

CLAYART—Ceramic Arts Discussion List

You can join this group by sending the message "sub CLAYART your name" to `listserv@lsv.uky.edu`

CLOTEX-L—Extension Textile and Clothing List

University of Nebraska Computing Services Network, Lincoln, NE

You can join this group by sending the message "sub CLOTEX-L your name" to `listserv@unlvm.unl.edu`

FUNASTR-—Interesting New Discoveries in Astronomy

NE Regional Data Center, Univ. of Florida campus, Gainesville, FL

You can join this group by sending the message "sub FUNASTR- your name" to `listserv@nervm.nerdc.ufl.edu`

GARDENS—Gardens & Gardening

You can join this group by sending the message "sub GARDENS your name" to `listserv@lsv.uky.edu`

OGL—Organic Gardening Discussion List

You can join this group by sending the message "sub OGL your name" to `listserv@lsv.uky.edu`

PHOTOASSIST—The Photographer's Assistant Mail List

You can join this group by sending the message "sub PHOTOASSIST your name" to `listserv@internet.com`

PHOTOPRO—The Professional Photographers Mail List

You can join this group by sending the message "sub PHOTOPRO your name" to `listserv@internet.com`

PHOTOTECH—The Photographers Technical Mail List

You can join this group by sending the message "sub PHOTOTECH your name" to `listserv@internet.com`

SEW-OLD—Sew-Old Antique Sewing Machine Collectors List

You can join this group by sending the message "sub SEW-OLD your name" to `listserv@kbs.net`

SQFT—Square Foot Gardening

University of Missouri-St. Louis

You can join this group by sending the message "sub SQFT your name" to `listserv@umslvma.umsl.edu`

SSUG-L—ShopSmith Woodworking Users Group List

State University of New York at Buffalo

You can join this group by sending the message "sub SSUG-L your name" to `listserv@ubvm.cc.buffalo.edu`

STAMPS—The Stamps List

Pennsylvania State University

You can join this group by sending the message "sub STAMPS your name" to `listserv@psuvm.psu.edu`

WOODWORK—Woodworking Discussions

You can join this group by sending the message "sub WOODWORK your name" to `listserv%ipfwvmb.bitnet@listserv.net`

HOME IMPROVEMENT

Architecture

Architecture & Design

http://www.vnr.com/vnr/adhome.html

Publisher of books on architecture, interior design, graphic design, landscape architecture, and urban design.

Art for Architecture

http://www.artarch.com/

A service company for architects and designers. AFA works closely with clients on projects that require artwork in various mediums.

HBA Architecture and Interior Design

http://www.infi.net/~hbaarch/

Site describes HBA Architecture and Interior Design's current projects, lists key personnel, and shows examples of their work.

International Architecture and Design Home Page

http://www.escape.ca/~jmorgan/timothy

Provides information on types of architecture, information on famous architects, links to other sites, a picture gallery, and design picks of the week and year.

MBT Architecture

http://www.dnai.com:80/~mbt/

Advertises the firm that offers services in project management. Provides an online gallery and brochure. Learn about the latest projects they have been involved with, visit the Galleries of Architecture, Interiors, Laboratories, and Renderings. Employment opportunities are also available.

Open Building Architecture For Residential Construction

http://www.access.digex.net/~david/OB.html

Open Building (OB) is a set of principles for making an architecture of variety and coherence. It is a new approach to housing construction and marketing. These principles are useful for constructing and renovating buildings when decisions are organized on several levels among a number of parties who prefer to act independently while expecting a coherent architecture to result.

V.C.net

http://www.webfac.com/VCnet/

V.C.net is an educational tool for architecture students and a place to visit to learn more about architecture.

Automation

CBI Systems, Inc.

http://www.hyperf.com/cbi/

A Kentucky-based company that designs and installs control systems for homes and businesses. A listing is provided for several different packages for residential and business needs.

DHSL: Data Home Systems Limited

http://Fox.nstn.ca/~datahome/

A Hantsport, Nova Scotia company, employing the latest in electrical system technologies and offering an alternative to conventional wiring systems. The benefits that are explained are cost savings, security, entertainment, increased value, and ecology.

Home Automation Association

http://www.hometeam.com/haa/

You are invited to join others who manufacture, distribute, install, and service home automation products. Provides objectives of the association and the benefits of becoming a member.

Home Automation Association (HAA)

http://www.smarthome.com/smarthome/hajump.htm

A supplier of home automation, control, and security equipment. Provides an online catalog of over 500 products. A few of the categories are visual surveillance, phones, wiring, audio/visual, security, and computer control.

Home Automator

http://www.hometeam.com/automator

The Home Automator Newsletter includes do-it-yourself home automation ideas. Each issue contains projects, unbiased product reviews, schematics, feature homes, and interviews with industry experts.

The Home Team

http://www.hometeam.com/

Contains information on intelligent home design, lighting controls, standards, security systems, communication systems, and more. Involves many industries and numerous members who represent a wide range, from manufacturing to service providers. Members are dedicated to spreading the word about the latest technologies for homes and are primarily directed by trade associations. Does not sell any of the products described, other than a few educational products. Provides information and remains neutral and unbiased to the industry.

HomeTheater Com

http://www.virtualmarketing.com/ht/home_theater.html

Offers recommendations and advice related to home theaters. Provides various hyperlinks.

Intelligent Home Technologies, Inc.

http://www.builder.net/hometech/

IHT provides D.C.-area builders and homeowners with the latest in home technology, including home automation, home theater, electrical architecture, audio/video systems, telephone systems, and more.

JDS Technologies

http://www.hometeam.com/jds/

Manufacturer of telephone and computer control products for intelligent homes. Products are described in detail. A free home control software demo can be downloaded.

Media Dimensions

http://www.floridaguide.com/media/

Media Dimensions creates and installs custom home entertainment systems. Additional information is provided for worldwide services, home theater automation, and yacht and aircraft entertainment areas.

ProSpec

http://ilab.com/prosphme.htm

Interactive Labs ProSpec Home Electronics Database is a free resource for consumers to view products from many manufacturers. Full-color pictures and text for thousands of products covering the spectrum of home electronics. The site is geared toward the custom installation industry and has many useful features for consumers. The service is free to users. Manufacturers can submit their products for free.

The Spectacular Powerhouse Page

http://csbh.mhv.net/~powerhouse/mainmenu.html

A necessary page for electricians, engineers, and home owners. Provides information regarding the electrical industry by featuring subjects such as Q & A, help wanted page, and various links to other related Web sites for information on a particular topic of interest.

Vantage

http://www.transera.com/vantage

Vantage provides advanced automation systems for lighting, HVAC, audio/visual, and home theater control systems. With a combination of superior technology and fabulous design, they produce a very sophisticated home automation system.

Construction & Woodworking

The Construction Zone

http://www.constructionzone.com/~homezone

Provides a resource for your home improvement needs. Their growing service offers listings of contractors and related businesses specializing in home repair, home improvement, remodeling, and other related services covering the U.S. Visit their free handy hints forum or join their monthly online newsletter for ideas and tips. Contractors can also find out how to list their companies with this national registry.

Cyberwood Express

http://www.woodexpress.com/

Dedicated to the "small shop" woodworker. Provides information about hand-crafted products, wooden toys, and more. Welcomes suppliers of quality wood products.

The Dulux Paint Assistant

http://www.dulux.com

Describes the Dulux paint range of decorative paint products for buildings. The site has a paint selection program, a paint calculator, and painting tips to help solve your paint problems. A valuable resource for the home improvement enthusiast and the professional decorator.

THE HOME IMPROVEMENT and CONSTRUCTION CONNECTION

http://www.geopages.com/RodeoDrive/1618

Includes topics related to new house construction, remodeling, and woodworking.

Home Improvement Home Page

http://www.homeless.com/homepages/
jsrader@intergate.com.html

A & M Roofing Home Improvement Home page. Offers tips, home improvement videos, and links to other sites.

Home Improvement Net

http://www.homeimprove.com/~plans

A "how to" informational resource for home improvement activities. Advertisers welcome!

HomeSource

http://www.earthlink.net/~donvander/

Columnist and author Don Vandervort provides free home-improvement information and ideas for remodelers and do-it-yourselfers.

Jonathan Press Woodworking and Home Improvement Books and Plans

http://members.aol.com/jonpress/index.html

A source for home improvement and woodworking books and plans, such as projects for gazebos, arbors, decks, outdoor furniture, and storage units.

New Home Builders

http://www.NewHomeBuilders.com

The Ultimate national resource for new home construction. Use the database to select a state, city, neighborhood, or subdivision. Then set your price limit, the number of bedrooms and bathrooms you want, and you're well on your way to finding the home of your dreams. There are also lists of builders and industry-related articles.

New Home Interactive Cyber Home Building Site

http://www.emi.net/newhome

New Home Interactive allows you to create your own dream home. Visit the site to download a short demo program.

Pete's Dry Dock

http://www.pacificharbor.com/whpier/pdd/

Home maintenance and remodeling advice from handyman Pete Prlain. Help for do-it-yourselfers from deck repair and tool suggestions to drippy faucets and leaky roofs.

Professional Woodgraining Kits

http://members.aol.com/ffreeze

Details about products and services available to produce professional woodgraining results at home.

Quality Woodwork & Supply, Inc.

http://www.tach.net/public/quality.html

Carries a wide variety of woods, from the common to the exotic, as well as an array of other woodworking supplies. Offers an online price lookup system that enables you to enter the type and amount of wood you need and gives a price for the wood.

Remodeler Online

http://www.remodelers.com

A homeowners guide to finding home improvement remodelers across the country.

The Sound Home Resource Web Home Page

http://www.soundhome.com

A comprehensive site of home improvement and construction information for homeowners and prospective homeowners.

The Woodworking Catalog

http://www.woodworking.com/

Contains useful information on lumber, hardware, power tools, finishing supplies, books and plans, woodworking schools, workshops, stores, accessories, hand tools, wooden products, and machinery. Also contains a collection of links to other woodworking-related sites. Offers a downloadable DOS program called Woodpro (a lumber database and wood selection expert system).

Education

DO IT YOURSELF HQ

http://pwp.usa.pipeline.com/~sivprob

Money-saving information and links for the home handyman and do-it-yourself practitioner.

Home Improvement

http://www.learninglane.com/Learning/hmimprov.html

Visit any one of their classrooms with this site's Learning Lane. Provides instructional videos on the following subjects: home improvement and interior decorating, carpentry and woodworking, construction, home buying/selling, repair/remodeling, and home security.

Home Improvement How-to Videos

http://www.intellinet.com/~jdutton/homeimprov.html

Offers dozens of step-by-step instructional videos to guide you through any home repair. Paint your house, build a deck, fix the plumbing, install a security system, and more. Visit the Video Vault for a complete catalog.

Hometime

http://www.hometime.com/

Home page of the popular PBS television series. Offers text and still frame highlights from the show and step-by-step instruction on several home improvement projects.

Lamb Home Videos U-DO IT YOURSELF

http://www.fixitvideos.com/homefix

Award-winning do-it-yourself instructional videos. Learn to do-it-yourself from professional, certified instructors. Step-by-step instruction on the proper tools and techniques you'll need to get the job done. Subjects include tile setting for floors, walls, or counters; installation of marble or Mexican tile; faux finishing (decorative painting techniques); installation of glass block; and basic plumbing.

Materials Engineering and Research Laboratory

http://donews.do.usbr.gov/merl/reprhome.html

Provides information on the research of new materials and methods for concrete maintenance, repair, and preservation. Also presents publications on the results of technical studies about conventional and new repair methods and materials.

Flooring

Advanced Flooring, Inc.

http://www.icanect.net/advance

Provides information about Dupont Stainmaster carpet, as well as ceramic tile, marble, porcelain, vinyl, and more.

Anderson Hardwood Floors

http://www.andersonfloors.com

Provides information on one of America's leading manufacturers of prefinished, laminated hardwood floors.

Carpets.com

http://www.carpets.com/

Provides a large number of colors, textures, fibers, and styles of carpet that can be shipped to you. Also gives a cost and information guide on buying hardwood and vinyl flooring. Also provides links to other carpet manufacturers.

Carpet One

http://www.carpet1.com/index.html

Learn more about Carpet One and how to buy the right carpet for your home. Also visit the Bigelow Carpet Collection and learn the history of Bigelow carpet.

Country Oak Flooring

http://www.hway.com/oakfloor

Quality T&G Oak Flooring at discount prices. Delivered factory direct anywhere in the U.S.A.

Dalton Carpet Outlets

http://www.hickory.nc.us:80/ncnetworks/carpets.html

Provides a listing of carpet dealers in Dalton, GA, home of more than 100 carpet outlets and dealers.

Floor Coverings International

http://kaos.deepcove.com/carpet/

Advertises products offered by Floor Coverings International. Obtain information on carpet terminology, types of carpet styles and fibers, carpet cleaning, and answers to frequently asked questions related to carpets. Visit their showroom and check out the Hit Lists.

Sculptured Carpet Selections

http://scsi-inc.com/carpet/

Specializes in affordable decorator rugs using inlay and sculpting techniques. Almost any design can be incorporated in these high quality carpet creations, including company logos. These rugs can be ordered in any size or color(s). Some design samples are shown at this site.

TrustMark

http://www.shawinds.com/trustmark/

Play the TrustMark Wheel of Fortune Sweepstakes for cash rebates and prizes while you learn about carpet construction, performance, and durability factors. Receive decorating tips and find your nearest TrustMark carpet retailer among more than 1,750 participants.

Furniture

Amboan & Badinia Furniture of Spain

http://www.servtech.com/public/amboan/

Offers online catalog of classic, hand-finished furniture. Also provides a directory of sales representatives worldwide.

Bayviewer Chair Company

http://www.xmission.com:80/~gastown/balaam/bayview.htm

Provides advertising and ordering information for the Bayviewer Chair Company.

Blue Canyon Woodworks

http://www.rt66.com/blue/

Advertises Blue Canyon Woodworks, makers of New Mexican furniture. Offers several images of products and provides ordering information.

Crazy Creek Products

http://www.sccsi.com/CrazyCreek/home.html

Advertises products offered by Crazy Creek, including the original Crazy Creek chair and the ThermaLounger. Also provides various accessories and ordering information.

The Family Room Store

http://www.shopperusa.com/Furniture/Familyroom

Features exclusively designed computer and entertainment cabinets, and furniture in various laminate and wood finishes. Offers a complete line of additional services, including space planning for commercial and residential interiors, design consultation, and complete furniture ordering service.

Furniture First Aid

http://www.homefurnish.com/firstaid.htm

Offers tips on furniture care and repair, stain removal, fabric protection, and carpet cleaning.

Furniture, Furniture, Furniture

http://www.hickory.nc.us:80/ncnetworks/furnitur.html

Offers a collection of links to various furniture manufacturers near Hickory and High Point, North Carolina, as well as an online color catalog, a factory tour, and many needlework designs.

Furniture On Line

http://www.furnitureonline.com

Allows you to browse any of the following categories for furniture: living room, entertainment, home office, bedroom, children, accessories, dining, rugs, and outdoor. Click any category and be linked to pages of furniture plus advice and design tips. Includes dealer locators for leading furniture manufacturers.

Leisure Home Center

http://www.hearth.com/directfire

Advertises their products through showrooms. Casual furniture for the home, including wicker, rattan, wrought iron, cast aluminum, and outdoor furniture. Special orders can be shipped to your home anywhere.

The Online Furniture Refinisher

http://www.win.net/~amwood

Offers a comprehensive manual on furniture refinishing and an e-mail consultation service ensuring that the do-it-yourselfer achieves perfect results.

THE ON LINE FURNITURE REFINISHER

The Sturdy Artistics Catalogue Pages

http://www.matlcon.com/Sturdy/Cover.html

Available furniture includes a complete hickory bedroom. Also metal and wicker furniture, including a step basket, TV/VCR/printer table, plant stand, baker's rack, wine rack, sling chair, and grills.

Welcome to the Furniture Fair!

http://www.bemarnet.es/moble/welcome.e.html

Offers clients the opportunity to explore different exhibits. Learn what a virtual fair actually is and how you can offer your products.

General Home Improvement

Builders Graphics

http://www.homeplan.com/homeplan/

Provides three main categories that present a wide range of interesting information. Home Plans includes topics such as custom home planning, contact information, sample WWW projects, online reviews, affordable stock plans, sample stock plans, and willows subdivision. Home Info includes repair tips, construction terms, roof types, and home business. Home Links includes software, designers, builders, landscaping, automation, virtual tours, home projects, Realtors, and buyer information. Also join in various chat rooms.

Home Ideas

http://www.homeideas.com

Offers articles to help you plan home projects, a guide to Internet sites, and a request section to get free catalogs and brochures sent to you by mail. A joint project between *Home Mechanix* magazine and Build.com.

Home Line Talk Radio

http://rampages.onramp.net/~homeline

Home improvement, house building, construction, and remodeling questions are answered on-the-air and on the Internet with Home Line Talk Radio, Houston, TX.

Home Repair Hotline

http://www.deltanet.com/allstar/homerepr.htm

Provides information about a 1-900 number that gives instructions related to the following topics: plumbing improvements, electricity, small and large appliances, heating and cooling units, and home improvement projects ($2.49 a minute).

Lowe's Home Improvement Warehouse

http://www.lowes.com/

Lowe's Companies, Inc. is one of America's top 30 retailers serving home improvement, home decor, home electronics, and home construction markets. Lowe's Web site offers step-by-step guides for home improvement projects, featured products, and tips from Lowe's Home Safety Council. There's also a store locator, recent corporate financial data, and a list of employment opportunities.

National Consumer Alert Hotline

http://www.deltanet.com/allstar/conalert.htm

Provides information on recalls and product warnings. Provides information on many types of appliances, as well as service providers, such as motels, dentists, and carpet cleaners.

On The House with The Carey Brothers

http://www.onthehouse.com/

On The House is a weekly syndicated radio talk show offering advice, hints, and solutions relating to all aspects of home maintenance, repair, and improvement.

This Old House

http://www.pathfinder.com/TOH/

An interactive doorway into This Old House, featuring articles and columns from the magazine, as well as topics related to building, renovation, and restoration. Current news, information on personal appearances by the TV series crew, and project house updates are posted regularly.

United Consumers Club

http://www.boomernet.com/boom/products.htm

A national buying service that enables members to save money buying furniture, carpet, and other home improvement, furnishing, and decorating items at manufacturers' cost prices.

Voyager Plus Home Improvement Specialists

http://msn.fullfeed.com/~kim/vplus/

Provides information on kitchen remodeling, decks, recreation rooms, garage additions, and window replacements. Estimates and financial assistance available.

Inspection

Accu-Spect Home Inspection Institute

http://www.tiac.net/users/mmc1/accu

You can learn the tools of the home inspection business through Accu-Spect Home Inspector Institute. Certification available upon completion. These comprehensive videos are based on over a decade of residential home inspections. The videos also explain details and guide you through the home inspection business.

Advanced Home Inspection

http://www.hmw.com/advanced_home/

Answers frequently asked questions regarding the home inspection process. Provides information to buyers such as knowing what the contract should include, what are some causes for alarm, and how

to deal with problems that arise. Sellers learn about issues, such as how an inspection can help set a realistic price for the house and how the "Buyer Beware" catch phrase can become "Seller Beware."

American Society of Home Inspection

http://www1.mhv.net/~dfriedman/ashihome.htm

Provides information on the Association as a whole. Contains sections that give information on what new things homeowners, buyers, and inspectors should be aware of. Assists in finding a certified home inspector. Provides information on specific topics relating to electrical wiring, plumbing, the environment, structural foundations, heating systems, and chimneys and flues.

AmeriSpec Home Inspection Service

http://www.io.org/~amrspec/Overview.html

AmeriSpec is a franchised company that provides information on how to pursue a franchise opportunity. Frequently asked questions from buyers are answered.

Home Inspection Resources

http://pages.prodigy.com/LHKF55D/main.htm

Provides information in the following categories: homebuyers assistance, market messages, home inspection forum, and Web site information.

Home Spec Inspection Services, Inc.

http://www.mindspring.com/~homespec/homespec.html

This Atlanta, GA, company is code-certified in both residential and commercial inspections. Answers commonly asked questions regarding home inspection. Also describes problems that can be discovered during a normal home inspection.

HomeSpec 101

http://www.homespec101.com/

Describes a pamplet that is purchased by first-time homebuyers, retired people, or people interested in learning what to look for when purchasing a house. Site also features future pamplets that will be available.

Professional Home Inspections, Inc.

http://www.acxes.com/hm/phi/hmpg.html

Provides sample home inspection reports that describe the exact services the company performs. Many color radon graphs are available to learn more about radon.

Wedgwood Service Group, Inc.

http://www.wwsg.com/index.htm

Provides information and answers to the following topics: real estate inspection; seminars, audio tapes, marketing services, and a monthly industry newsletter for real estate inspectors; and a professional discussion forum.

Interior Decorating

Cascade Blinds

http://www.youdo.com

Order factory direct blinds at wholesale prices.

Colton, Inc.

http://www.cc.utah.edu/~jc3908/colton.htm

Advertises the products of Colton, Inc., a drapery manufacturing company in Salt Lake City, Utah.

Cuvs Factory Outlet Store

http://www.cuvs.com

Offers information about slipcovers for casual furniture cushions, picnic tables, accent pillows, window treatments, lamp shade covers, dust ruffles, and pillow shams.

Decorating Dimensions, Inc.

http://www.decdim.com/homepage.htm

Carries decorating products for the home. Wallcovering (wallpaper), windowcoverings, floorcoverings (carpet, vinyl, woodflooring), and paint.

Decorating Online

http://www.netrix.net/saverud

Professionals at Saverud Paint Shop provide customers with decorating products and advice. Saverud's is a full-service decorating center that offers paint, wallpaper, window blinds, and related items.

Dion's Secrets of Home Decorating guide

http://www.doubleclickd.com/dion.html

Reveals projects anyone can do to change the look of their home. This guide shows you how to recover chairs, redo your walls, dye your carpeting, and much more. Also allows you to subscribe to Dion's special newsletter.

Home Decorator

http://www.homefurnish.com/hmdeco_m.htm

Offers home decorating and interior design information, tips, and ideas. Subjects include furniture placement and room arrangement, accessorizing your home, color themes, combining patterns, and monthly design topics.

Mainely Shades

http://www.maineguide.com/maineshade

Add to your home decoration with lampshades (cut and pierced, traditional, victorian) that you create. Complete kits available through mail order.

National Decorating Products Association

http://www.hygexpo.com/ndpa

Provides consumer information on decorating products and industry information for decorating product retailers and manufacturers.

Roc On Drywall Paint & Wallpaper

http://www.mv.igs.net/~rocon

Designed to help the average urban dweller by providing tips on painting, decorating, and drywalling.

Southwest Decor

http://swdecor.cpeq.com

Includes over 40 pages (including pictures) of information. Specializes in Southwestern, western, and contemporary furnishings, decorating accessories, and gifts.

Sudberry House new Location!

http://connix.com/~sudberry/

Displays fine wood accessories used for mounting needlework and crafts, as well as an online color catalog, a factory tour, and many needlework designs.

Suzanne Seely's "Make it Beautiful" Decorating Newsletter

http://www.aiminc.com/seely

Suzanne Seely brings her knowledge of styles, design, color, resources, and years of interior decorating experience to Internet subscribers in her newsletter.

Symbol-Talk

http://www.teleport.com:80/~symbol/index.html

Advertises meditation pillows made by Symbol-Talk. Provides information on the various types and styles of pillows, cloth color, and how to order.

Landscaping

Centre for Landscape Research

http://www.clr.toronto.edu:1080/

Provides a collaborative environment for the exploration of ideas related to the design, planning, and policies of the environment. Focuses primarily on developing and utilizing electronic media to foster more informed decision-making.

Jeff Chorba Landscape Design

http://home.ptd.net/~jchorba/

Provides design and horticultural documents, links to their related landscaping sites, future site for a BBS Connection, and a photo gallery of various landscape designs.

LandNET—American Society of Landscape Architects

http://www.asla.org/asla/

Learn what ASLA is and how to become a member. Obtain access to the bookstore, marketplace, file library, spotlight (a bi-monthly discussion group that has an online interview with a professional landscape architect), and join in discussion groups. Provides educational links, job links, and landscape architecture links.

Landscape Architecture Virtual Library

http://www.clr.toronto.edu:1080/VIRTUALLIB/LARCH/comp.html

Provides valuable links to Internet-based electronic information on a wide range of subjects that pertain to the landscape architecture field.

Pennsylvania Horticultural Society

http://www.libertynet.org:80/~phs/service.html

Provides a library with over 14,000 types of reference materials. Receive information about garden tours in Pennsylvania, Delaware, New Jersey, New York, and New England. PHS also has their own exhibits and gardens to visit. Learn how to become a member and read various publications.

University of Delaware Botanic Gardens

http://bluehen.ags.udel.edu/udgarden.html

Tour the gardens of the University of Delaware. The tour includes eight different gardens. Descriptions of plants that are contained in the gardens are available.

Plumbing

Best Mfg. Co.

http://pages.prodigy.com/best/

Offers wholesale plumbing supplies. Some of the products in their line include faucets, water heaters, fixtures, pipes, valves, and fittings.

Faucet Outlet Online

http://www.faucet.com/

Contains selections of faucets. Provides information about installing and selecting a faucet.

GROHE

`http://www.grohe.com/`

This company is known for its faucet brands used in custom homes and upscale remodeling projects. Lists the latest products, as well as how to contact GROHE. Also, look at a showroom and learn about their various promotional programs for dealers.

Pipe Trades Association

`http://www.PipeTA.org/`

The Pipe Trades Association's purpose is to bring together members of the Bay Area Local Unions. This site describes the Association and provides information regarding Local Unions 342, 343, and 467. Also lists topics such as craftsmanship, training and education, quality, contractors, labor management cooperation, hot links, and a discussion forum.

theplumber.com

`http://www.theplumber.com/`

Hills Plumbing page provides answers to frequently asked questions. Offers a selection of plumbing links and newsgroups. Also learn about the history of plumbing.

Baking Papers

`http://www.wholesalepaper.com/samples.html`

Send for baking paper samples in all shapes and sizes. Available to professionals and Betty Crocker wanna-bes.

Newsgroups

alt.architecture

alt.architecture.alternative

alt.architecture.int-design

alt.binaries.pictures.furniture

alt.building.architecture

alt.building.construction

alt.building.consulting-specialty

alt.building.engineering

alt.building.environment

alt.building.finance

alt.building.health-safety

alt.building.jobs

alt.building.manufacturing

alt.building.realestate

alt.building.survey-mapping

alt.landscape.architecture

clari.biz.industry.construction.cbd.misc

clari.biz.industry.household

clari.biz.industry.household.cbd

comp.home.automation

intalt.building.interior-design

landalt.building.landscape

pdaxs.ads.furniture

pdaxs.services.plumbing

relcom.commerce.household

tieee.ces.home-automation

umn.cs.bldg

Listservs

ARCITRON—Architronic: The Electronic Journal of Architecture

You can join this group by sending the message "sub ARCITRON your name" to listserv@listserv.kent.edu

DESIGN-L—Basic and Applied Design (Art and Architecture)

Pennsylvania State University

You can join this group by sending the message "sub DESIGN-L your name" to listserv@psuvm.psu.edu

LARCH-L—Landscape Architecture Electronic Forum

Syracuse University

You can join this group by sending the message "sub LARCH-L your name" to listserv@listserv.syr.edu

PLUMBERS-L—Plumbers Discussion List

America Online, Inc. (1-800-827-6364 in USA/ Canada)

You can join this group by sending the message "sub PLUMBERS-L your name" to listserv@listserv.aol.com

TREETM-L—Sustainable Landscapes, Woody etc. Plants

University of Nebraska Computing Services Network, Lincoln, NE

You can join this group by sending the message "sub TREETM-L your name" to listserv@unlvm.unl.edu

Anthropology

ANTHAP—The Applied Anthropology Computer Network

http://www.acs.oakland.edu/~dow/anthap.html

ANTHAP offers information to practicing anthropologists and to the public interested in applied anthropology. Applied anthropology is a growing branch of the anthropological sciences devoted to applying anthropological knowledge to the solution of human problems. Applied anthropologists solve problems in the areas of business, education, law, medicine, historical preservation, and others. ANTHAP has been providing e-mail conferencing services to professional anthropologists since 1991.

Anthropoetics: The Electronic Journal of Generative Anthropology

http://www.humnet.ucla.edu/humnet/anthropoetics/home.html

Here you will find a description of generative anthropology, as well as an online version of Anthropoetics, including full articles and subscription information. This site also runs a mailing list for those interested in this field.

Anthropology of East Europe Review (AEER)

http://condor.depaul.edu/~rrotenbe/aeer/aeer.html

This journal is a publication of the East European Anthropology Group (EEAG), an international network of anthropologists working in Central and Eastern Europe and in the Post-Soviet Regions of Europe and Asia. Online you will find information about the EEAG, full-text articles and abstracts, and submission information.

Anthropology Resources on the Internet

http://www.nitehawk.com/alleycat/anth-faq.html

This page offers a comprehensive set of links to anthropology sites worldwide, sorted by resource type (for example, WWW servers, Gopher indexes, and FTP sites). Of particular interest is the lengthy list of mailing lists and newsgroups to which those interested in various aspects of anthropology can subscribe.

The Ascent of Mind: Ice Age Climates and the Evolution of Intelligence

http://weber.u.washington.edu/wcalvin/bk5.html

Here is the full text of a book by William H. Calvin, with illustrations. The site is organized to give an abstract of each chapter, which you can then read if interested. Other books by Mr. Calvin are available at this same site.

The Castles of Wales

http://www.wp.com/castlewales/home.html

This site offers photographs and descriptions of castles in Wales. Not only includes the full history of castle building, but is an online study of the whys of castles. So you will find here history, archaeology, anthropology, and a bit of psychology—just about everything you could ever want to know about castles and their builders.

Center for Anthropology Communications Home Page

http://pegasus.acs.ttu.edu/~wurlr/anthro.html

The Center for Anthropology Communications serves to promote communication between journalists, the media, and anthropologists. The Center promotes the communication of anthropology through the media in a responsible and accurate way. This WWW home page serves to reach this goal by utilizing advanced technology in order to reach an extremely wide audience in an efficient manner.

Center for Visual Anthropology (CVA)

http://www.usc.edu/dept/elab/anth/cvadesc.html

The CVA provides training in ethnographic filmmaking and a home to documentary filmmakers who are exploring ways in which films can express ideas generated in ethnography. The CVA and its Web site are run out of the University of Southern California Department of Anthropology.

Centre for Social Anthropology and Computing (CSAC) Ethnographics Gallery

http://lucy.ukc.ac.uk/

The aim of the Centre is to advance anthropology by developing new methods and means for investigating anthropological problems, to promote the use of computers in "ordinary" anthropology, and to provide advice and information resources for the anthropology community worldwide. This site provides information on CSAC-sponsored research projects, general resources for anthropologists, bibliographies and abstracts, publications, software, and links to other sites.

Exploring Ancient World Cultures

http://cedar.evansville.edu/~wcweb/wc101/

Exploring Ancient World Cultures provides an introduction to Web research on the eight cultures represented here: the Near East, India, Egypt, China, Greece, the Roman Empire, the Islamic World, and Medieval Europe.

Fourth World Documentation Project

http://www.halcyon.com/FWDP/fwdp.html

At this site dedicated to the study of unrecognized nations (such as tribal groups), you will find project descriptions, related government documents, background information, and more. Includes a searchable index to find just what you're looking for.

Gnostic Institute of Anthropology—London U.K.

http://www.lookup.com/homepages/70749/

Gnosis is a Greek word of Indo-European origin, meaning intuitive knowledge, related to the English "know" and the Sanskrit "jnana." Anthropology originates etymologically from the Greek words "anthropo," meaning man, and "logia," meaning study. We can say that Gnostic Anthropology is the study and understanding of man through a knowledge of oneself. This site of an interesting blend of anthropology, philosophy, and psychology—see for yourself.

The Gorilla Home Page

http://larch.ukc.ac.uk:2001/gorillas/index.html

If you are interested in primate anthropology, here's a lot of good information on the background, social behavior, and habitat of mountain gorillas. This Web author is also attempting to set up a computer simulation of gorilla life.

Grottos of the American Midwest

http://www.lafayette.edu/niless/awsthome.htm

Throughout the American Midwest are examples of a distinctive folk building tradition. Known locally as grottos, these structures are built of concrete studded with glass, stone, ceramics, and sometimes whole objects. At this Web site, you will find photographs of some of these structures, along with the corresponding research report.

Hopi Basketry Presentation

http://hanksville.phast.umass.edu/defs/independent/
baskets/baskets.html

At this graphics-intensive site, you will find a self-guided "tour" of the study of Hopi (Native American) baskets, including ceremonial uses, symbolism, and craftsmanship.

Journal of World Anthropology

gopher://wings.buffalo.edu/11/academic/department/
anthropology/jwa

The Journal of World Anthropology is an electronic journal dedicated to scholarship in all fields of anthropology, and publishes articles on academic research, matters of theory and methodology, and the education of the public, as well as book, software and film reviews. This Gopher site contains current and back issues as well as subscription and submission information.

Maxwell Museum of Anthropology

http://www.unm.edu/~maxwell/Maxwell/MMhp.html

The Maxwell Museum of Anthropology, University of New Mexico, holds over 10 million individual items in its archaeological, ethnological, archival, photographic, and skeletal collections. Online you will find graphics files depicting a portion of the museum's collection.

Maya Adventure

http://www.sci.mus.mn.us/sln/ma/

This is a Web site that highlights science activities and information related to ancient and modern Maya culture. Includes many multimedia activities developed at the Science Museum of Minnesota. Includes images from the Science Museum's anthropological collections.

MayaQuest '96 Home Page

http://www.mecc.com/mayaquest.html

Aimed particularly at grades 4–8 (with high school and family applications), this online interactive experience will, among other things, let followers lead the team, chat with other kids and educators, view images from the journey, and learn about the ancient Maya and contemporary Central America.

Museum of Anthropology—University of Michigan

http://www.umma.lsa.umich.edu/

The Museum of Anthropology is one of the major archaeological research and teaching facilities in the United States. The Museum does not maintain exhibit space and its collections are usually not available for public viewing. This Web site is designed to make available images and information about selected collections from the Museum holdings. As a result, this is a graphics-intensive site. A high-speed connection is recommended.

Native American Net Server

gopher://alpha1.csd.uwm.edu:70/11/UWM%20Information/
Native%20American%20Net%20Server

This Gopher site provides information relevant to current studies of the Native American population. Also includes a bulletin board service to post your own information.

NativeWeb

http://www.maxwell.syr.edu/nativeweb/

The goal of this site is "to provide a cyber-place for Earth's indigenous peoples." The creators have accomplished this goal by putting together a comprehensive collection of articles and links to hundreds of different sites, such as organizations, newsletters, languages, mailing lists, and much more.

Nicole's AnthroPage

http://www.wsu.edu:8000/~i9248809/anthrop.html

This "personal" anthropology page provides many links to related sites. The catch here is that the links are organized by the sub-field of anthropology to which the corresponding site belongs. Look here for a link to anything you could possibly want to know about the online world of anthropology.

Origins Of Mankind Home Page

http://www.pro-am.com/origins/origins.htm

This site provides a service for discussion on the origins of humanity. Includes a bulletin board, chat room, text covering various theories, and more.

Primate Info Net (PIN)

http://uakari.primate.wisc.edu:80/pin/

This HTML front for a Gopher server leads you into a network for people with an interest in the field of primatology. Among the resources accessible in PIN

are a taxonomy of the primates, audiovisual resources, a list of specialized bibliographies, information about Primate-Talk (an e-mail–based listserver), the latest issue of the Laboratory Primate Newsletter, and other resources pertinent to the field.

Seeker1's CyberAnthropology Home Page

http://www.clas.ufl.edu/anthro/cyberanthro/newhome.html

CyberAnthropology is the study of humans in virtual communities and networked environments, and this home page provides a rather sidelong look at this newer field of anthropology. Contains original essays, other resources, related links, and much more.

Sisseton Wahpeton Sioux Tribe

http://swcc.cc.sd.us/homepage.htm

Anthropology is not just a study of "fringe" societies, but also a study of portions of our own society. In that respect, learn about the history, culture, and current status of the Dakota Sioux with a visit to this site maintained by a tribe in South Dakota. Includes an online course to learn the Dakota language.

The Society for the Anthropology of Europe (SAE) Web Site

http://h-net.msu.edu/~sae/

Other than just provide information about their organization, the Webmasters at SAE also sponsor the H-SAE discussion list for anyone interested in the anthropology of Europe. This discussion list is also used to post academic announcements such as conferences and calls for papers and to provide online course materials. A searchable archive is available.

Society for Economic Anthropology

http://www.lawrence.edu/~peregrip/seahome.html

The Society for Economic Anthropology is an association of anthropologists, archaeologists, and economists interested in understanding diversity and change in the economic systems of the world. This site includes information on membership, conferences, student papers, and books for sale.

Chemical Light Sticks

http://nwlink.com/epicenter/free.html

Chemical light sticks are perfect for your next party—request your free sample from this site.

UCSB Anthropology Web Site

http://www.sscf.ucsb.edu/anth/index.html

Instead of just giving information about the courses offered by the Anthropology Department at the University of California at Santa Barbara, this well-done Web site contains student projects, including a complete 3D computer reconstruction of the Chetro Ketl Great Kiva, a prehistoric ceremonial structure found in Chaco Canyon of northern New Mexico, and various multimedia computer software packages devoted to the teaching of anthropology.

University of Chicago Press Anthropology and Archaeology Catalog

http://press-gopher.uchicago.edu:70/1s/Subjects/Anthropology

This page is the entry-point into U of Chicago's Gopher-based online catalog and ordering system for anthropology texts. Search by author and subject or read the whole catalog, including book summaries.

University of Manitoba Anthropology Department

http://www.umanitoba.ca/anthropology/index.html

In addition to providing course information from Canada's University of Manitoba, this set of pages includes a couple of projects of particular interest. The first is an interactive tutorial about Kinship and Social Organization, and the second is a full archaeological study of the history of Manitoba, Canada, from BC 10,000 to the present.

The UVa AnthroNet

http://darwin.clas.virginia.edu/~dew7e/anthronet/

The UVa AnthroNet maintains links to anthropology-related Internet sites, including a series of forms to use in subscribing to anthropology-related e-mail discussion lists and clickable links to many Usenet newsgroups. The AnthroNet also features a description of the Anthropology Graduate Program at the University of Virginia, as well as pages describing the work and interests of UVa Anthropology faculty and graduate students.

World Scripture: A comparative anthology of sacred texts

http://rain.org/~origin/ws.html

This collection contains over 4,000 scriptural passages from 268 sacred texts and 55 oral traditions, and is organized in terms of 164 different themes. The text is the result of a five-year project involving the collaboration of an international team of 40 recognized scholars representing all the major religious traditions of the world. This archive contains the complete text of the original hardbound version.

Archaeology

The Aerial Archaeology Newsletter

http://www.nmia.com/~jaybird/AANewsletter/

This site provides information on an "off-beat" branch of archaeology. Here you will find aerial photographs of archaeological sites (mainly in the southwestern USA). In addition, a complete history of aerial archaeology and detailed text descriptions of the photographs are offered.

The Ancient City of Athens

http://www.indiana.edu/~kglowack/Athens/Athens.html

The Ancient City of Athens is a photographic archive of the archaeological and architectural remains of ancient Athens (Greece). It is intended primarily as a resource for students of classical languages, civilization, art, archaeology, and history who may wish to take a "virtual tour" of the chief excavated regions and extant monuments.

Anasazi Archaeology

http://www.swcolo.org/Tourism/ArchaeologyHome.html

This site maintained by the tourism industry of Montezuma County, Colorado, USA, provides good introductory information on the many Native American archaeological sites in southwestern Colorado. So in addition to learning a little archaeology, you can make detailed plans to visit the sites to possibly participate in the digs by following the appropriate tourism links from these pages.

Annual Egyptological Bibliography (AEB)

http://www.leidenuniv.nl/nino/aeb.html

The AEB is a listing with summaries of all articles and books published within a given year on the various fields of Egyptology. The most recent full text given is for 1992, but a selection is given for each of the years 1993–1995; however, this comprehensive bibliography does not provide a search interface.

Archaeological Fieldwork Opportunities

http://durendal.cit.cornell.edu/

This service is designed to allow those seeking archaeological fieldwork opportunities to browse postings submitted by those who have them to offer. Included here are positions for volunteers, paid workers, field schools, contract jobs—whatever is submitted or found on various lists and news groups. This server does not contain position announcements for professional academic or staff archaeologists.

Archaeological Resource Guide for Europe

http://www.bham.ac.uk/BUFAU/Projects/EAW/index.html

This Web page points to current archaeology Web resources in or about Europe. Currently thematic and geographic access is provided to these resources, and an improved system, which will include an index and keyword search, should be available soon.

Archaeology at Mt. Vernon Plantation

http://www.mountvernon.org/image/archaeology.html

Ever wanted to know more about the first president of the United States? This site gives information on the excavations underway at his home at Mt. Vernon. Volunteers are encouraged to help with the archaeological dig.

Archaeology Magazine

http://www.he.net/~archaeol/index.html

In addition to providing subscription information, this site provides abstracts and tables of contents for current and past issues of *Archaeology* magazine, an official publication of the Archaeological Institute of America. Also offered is a full list of links to other archaeology sites on the Web.

ArchNet: WWW Virtual Library— Archaeology

http://www.lib.uconn.edu/ArchNet/ArchNet.html

Provides links to and information regarding archaeology on the Internet. Includes the following subject areas: archeometry, ceramics, educational materials, ethnohistory, ethnoarchaeology, geo-archaeology, and more. This information is categorized by both geographic region and subject.

Biblical Archaeologist

http://scholar.cc.emory.edu/scripts/ASOR/BA/BAHP.html

Contains abstracts of articles from current issues of the magazine *Biblical Archaeologist*. Also includes a full index to articles published from 1983–1987.

British Archaeology

http://britac3.britac.ac.uk:80/cba/ba/ba.html

This is the online version of this journal from the Council on British Archaeology. Includes full articles, reviews, an archive of past issues, and a searchable index. Subscription information for the print version is also given.

Classics and Mediterranean Archaeology Home Page

http://rome.classics.lsa.umich.edu/welcome.html

Focuses on Mediterranean and classical archaeology, but also provides access to all sorts of archaeological links, including articles, journals, projects, exhibits, images, related academics, museums, geographic information, other Internet resources, and more.

COMBINED CAESAREA EXPEDITIONS— Underwater Excavations of Sebastos: King Herod's Harbor

http://www.carleton.ca/~ereinhar/CaesareaHome.html

This site provides information on this research project of marine archaeology. Includes volunteer requests, research summaries, and links to other sites about this excavation.

The Council for Independent Archaeology

http://www.compulink.co.uk/~archaeology/cia/

This is a "professional" society for non-professional archaeologists. If you just enjoy archaeology, but can't study it seriously, this group will hook you up with the resources you need, including advice from experts and a placement service.

Dino Russ's Lair

http://128.174.172.76/isgsroot/dinos/dinos_home.html

Maintained as part of the Illinois State Geological Survey Web site, this page provides information on and links to sites about dinosaurs and paleontology across the U.S. Includes information on archaeological digs you can join.

Dinosaur Provincial Park

http://www.worldweb.com/AEP/parks/Dinosaur/

This Web site for Dinosaur Provincial Park in Alberta, Canada, gives detailed information on the archaeological finds within the park, tour information, contact information (to plan your vacation), and much more.

Duke Papyrus Archive

http://scriptorium.lib.duke.edu/papyrus/

This site is a full online study of the ancient Egyptian papyrus archives at Duke University. Includes graphics, the history of the archives, research papers, and more.

Encyclopedia Smithsonian: Archaeology

http://www.si.edu/welcome/faq/arclogy.htm

This portion of the Smithsonian Institution's immense Web presence is devoted to information about archaeology careers within the Smithsonian and in general. Includes contact addresses and a suggested reading list.

FAQ—Career in Archaeology in the U.S.

http://www.museum.state.il.us/ismdepts/anthro/dlcfaq.html

At this site David L. Carlson, an Associate Professor of Anthropology at Texas A & M University, answers frequently asked questions concerning how to go about starting and continuing a career as an archaeologist.

Field Museum Online

http://www.bvis.uic.edu/museum/Dna_To_Dinosaurs.html

Chicago's Field Museum has prepared an excellent online multimedia dinosaur exhibit entitled "From DNA to Dinosaurs." Bring your kids, high-speed modem, and have fun.

GIS and Remote Sensing for Archaeology: Burgundy, France

http://deathstar.rutgers.edu/projects/france/france.html

This site sums up most of the major technological techniques for use at archaeological digs by following the analysis of the Arroux River Valley region of Burgundy (France) for nearly two decades. The techniques discussed include satellite remote sensing, archival aerial photographs, predictive modeling, and many, many more.

The Indiana Jones WWW Page

http://www.softaid.net/msjohnso/

Okay, humor us… This fictional archaeologist did a lot to bring attention to the discipline. Here's a Web site filled with information on the movies, books, and television series. Includes many still images, video clips, and sound files. For those interested,

there are also links to real-world sites concerning the same adventures Indiana Jones went on.

Institute of Nautical Archaeology (INA)

http://nautarch.tamu.edu/napina.htm

Based at Texas A&M University, this Institute owns its own research vessel and coordinates studies with museums worldwide. This Web page contains information on the INA's research, publications, and membership.

Internet Archaeology

http://intarch.york.ac.uk/

Internet Archaeology aims to become one of the world's archaeological journals of record, having set itself the task of publishing papers of high academic standing which also utilize the full potential of electronic publication. Although not starting publication until August, 1996, this site already contains some advance articles.

National Park Service: Links to the Past—Archaeology

http://www.cr.nps.gov/archeo.html

Here you will find information on archaeological digs sponsored by the U.S. government at national parks across the United States. In addition, there is information on how to participate in these projects, no matter what your level of knowledge. Finally, this site provides a primary link to the NPS-sponsored National Archeological Database, which provides a Web-searchable index to archaeological research nationwide.

Native American History and Archaeology Resources on the Internet

http://hanksville.phast.umass.edu/misc/NAhistory.html

This index page provides links to many other sites concerning the Native American oral and written traditions, as well as archaeology and anthropology sites dealing with the study of Native American culture past and present.

The Oriental Institute—University of Chicago

http://www-oi.uchicago.edu/OI/default.html

The Oriental Institute is a museum and research organization devoted to the study of the ancient Near East. Included on this Web site are descriptions of archaeological projects underway by the Institute and images from their museum collection.

Pan-American Institute of Maritime Archaeology (PIMA)

http://www.wbm.ca/users/nfisher/

This site provides a view of archaeology other than "just digging in the dirt." Here you will find information on the history of ships and seafaring as demonstrated by underwater finds. You can also volunteer to join the non-profit PIMA on its excavation of a 17th-century shipwreck near the Dominican Republic. Now there's adventure!

Papers from the Institute of Archaeology (UCL)

http://www.ucl.ac.uk/archaeology/pia/

This journal's primary aim is to provide an outlet for research at the graduate level, much of which would not otherwise be published. Find online abstracts and full articles, as well as contribution guidelines and subscription information.

Prehistory Press

http://www.fullfeed.com/prehistory/

A site for the professional archaeologist, Prehistory Press specializes in the publication and distribution of data-oriented archaeological monographs worldwide. Prehistory Press is now publishing a peer-reviewed series in Old and New World archaeology, and is actively seeking manuscript submissions.

RADIOCARBON WWW Server

http://packrat.aml.arizona.edu/

Aimed at professional archaeologists, this site provides information for *Radiocarbon*, the main international journal of record for research articles and datelists related to C-14 and other radioisotopes and techniques used in archaeological, geophysical, oceanographic, and related dating. This page also contains a list of links to other sites providing online radiocarbon labs, related databases, computer programs, and much more.

Reeder's Egypt Page

http://www.sirius.com/~reeder/egypt.html

This comprehensive site will tell you just about anything you want to know about the history, art, and archaeological study of Egypt. Besides a list of links to many Egypt-related sites, the main focuses of Reeder's Egypt Page are a detailed tour of the tomb of Niankhkhnum and Khnumhotep from the 5th dynasty and information on "KMT: A Modern Journal of Ancient Egypt," including online articles.

ROMARCH—Roman Art and Archaeology

http://www-personal.umich.edu/~pfoss/ROMARCH.html

ROMARCH is a crossroads for resources on the art and archaeology of ancient Italy and the Roman Empire, ca. BC 100–AD 600; it is the original Roman index, and has links to more than 175 sites of interest, organized by province, geographically with a clickable map. ROMARCH is also an Internet discussion group with over 450 professionals and laypersons worldwide who discuss the economy, history, art, architecture and archaeology of the ancient Roman Empire. The archives for the messages posted to the listserv are also available at the Web site.

Royal Commission on the Ancient and Historical Monuments of Scotland (RCAHMS)

http://www.open.gov.uk/scotoff/heritage.htm

Provides information on archaeological projects within Scotland as they pertain to a further understanding of mankind's history in that country. Three areas in particular that concern archaeology are the National Archaeological Survey (NAS), Afforestable Land Survey (ALS), and Aerial Photographic Survey (APS).

Royal Tyrrell Museum Web Site

http://tyrrell.magtech.ab.ca/

Fun for the whole family, this Web site contains a virtual tour of the museum, information on educational programs, volunteer programs, and much more. The Royal Tyrrell Museum bills itself as a destination vacation spot for families with children interested in dinosaurs (or anyone else for that matter).

SAAweb—Society for American Archaeology

http://www.saa.org/textmenu.html

The Society for American Archaeology (SAA) is an international organization dedicated to the research, interpretation, and protection of the archaeological heritage of the Americas. The SAA Web site contains information on various archaeological projects sponsored by the SAA, online versions of the group's publications, and membership details.

The Skull Page

http://www.cet.com/~mwalters/hominid/skulls.htm

In an effort to further the understanding of human evolution, the Washington State University Anthropology Department is now offering for sale reproductions of fossil hominid skulls. If you're in need of skulls or parts of skulls, here's the place to buy them. It's also rather fun just to look, in an odd sort of way.

South Dakota Archaeology

http://www.usd.edu/anth/SDarch.html

Based at the University of South Dakota in Vermillion, this Web page provides site reports and organization information concerning digs within the state of South Dakota (primarily Native American).

SouthWestern Archaeology

http://seamonkey.ed.asu.edu/swa/

This site provides detailed information on the practice of archaeology in the American Southwest. Includes not only the standard research summaries, but also information on how to prepare yourself (supplies, contact addresses, and so on).

Stone Pages

http://joshua.micronet.it/utenti/dmeozzi/HomEng.html

These graphics-intensive pages provide photographs and information on the many stone megaliths (such as Stonehenge) in Europe, primarily England, Scotland, and Ireland.

T.W. Rutledge

http://www.skypoint.com/members/magic/captn/terry.html

This is a site portraying the works of T.W. Rutledge, a modern artist who is a well-known illustrator of archaeological sites. His work has appeared in *National Geographic* magazine. Includes both thumbnails and full-screen images.

U.C. Berkeley Museum of Paleontology

http://ucmp1.berkeley.edu:80/welcome.html

Tour the online exhibits (dinosaurs, mammals, and so on), browse the online catalog of type specimens, and more at this thorough Web depiction of the U.C. Museum of Paleontology. Very graphics-intensive, so a high-speed connection is recommended.

UK Archaeology on the Internet

http://www.ccc.nottingham.ac.uk/~aczkdc/links.html

This site provides information about the current state of archaeology in the United Kingdom and Europe. Contains many links to related sites, including academics, museums, businesses, and more.

General Humanities

Center for Electronic Texts in the Humanities

http://www.ceth.rutgers.edu/

The Center for Electronic Texts in the Humanities is working mostly with primary source material for research and teaching in the humanities. This includes, but is not limited to, works of literature (prose, verse, drama), documentary and archival material, inscriptions, papyri, charters, and historical dictionaries in any natural language.

Center for the Humanities

http://www.nypl.org/research/chss/chss.html

This is an online catalog of the humanities resources available at the New York Public Library. But you don't have to go to New York to find what you're looking for, as many texts are available at this Web site.

Computing in the Humanities Users Group (CHUG)

http://www.stg.brown.edu/resources/chug/
chug_overview.html

CHUG provides a forum for discussing the use of computers in the humanities and for sharing ideas and information about computing techniques and applications. Primarily for people at Brown University, the online discussion summaries give very interesting views on CHUG-related subjects.

H-Net—Humanities OnLine

http://h-net.msu.edu/

H-Net is an international initiative to assist humanities scholars and teachers to go online, using their personal computers. Currently, H-Net sponsors over 70 electronic newsletters. Subscription, posting, and membership information is all available at this site.

Humanities and Social Sciences— University of Chicago LibInfo

http://www.lib.uchicago.edu:80/LibInfo/SourcesBySubject/HumSocSci/

Besides providing information about the humanities collection at the University of Chicago Library, this site also gives a broad range of links to other humanities-related sites (organized by subject).

Humanities HUB

http://132.234.1.8/gwis/hub/hub.index.html

This site provides a very comprehensive set of links to humanities sources worldwide. Organized by subjects such as Anthropology, Gender Studies, Film & Media, Political Economy, and many more.

Humanities National Database Search

http://susan.chin.gc.ca:8003/BASIS/NATH/USER/WWWE/SF

The Humanities National Database is provided by the Canadian Heritage Information Network. This search form allows you to delve into various aspects of humanities studies from Canada, although the current focus is on Canadian artists, including many graphics.

The Humanities Report

http://www.nps.gov/history/index.html

This site provides the background and full text of a report written by the Humanities Review Committee of the U.S. National Park Service Advisory Board. The report studies how the national park system can join with education institutions to further the study of the humanities.

Institute for Human Sciences—Vienna

http://www.ping.at/iwm/iwmhome.htm

An independent, interdisciplinary Institute for Advanced Study which offers in-residence fellowships for scholars in the humanities primarily from Eastern and Western Europe and the United States, and further operates a number of long-term policy projects in the nations of the former Eastern bloc.

National Endowment for the Humanities (NEH)

http://www.neh.fed.us/

The NEH is an independent agency of the United States Government that makes grants for projects in history, languages, philosophy, and other areas of the humanities. The NEH Web site contains links to NEH-sponsored projects, overviews of those programs, and information on writing NEH grant requests.

National Humanities Institute Home Page

http://www.access.digex.net/~nhi/

Promotes research and publishing. Emphasizes ethical preconditions of culture and society, the centrality of personal freedom and creativity, and the historical nature of human existence. Web site includes articles, book reviews, and poetry.

Literature

http://villagenet.com/imta

Learn all about the international trunked radio industry from the International Mobile Telecommunications Association (a sister of the American Mobile Telecommunications Association).

The Stanford Electronic Humanities Review

http://shr.stanford.edu:80/shreview/

Here you will find online articles on topics from all branches of the humanities. Includes information on how to subscribe to the printed *Stanford Humanities Review*.

Research Institute for the Humanities (RIH)

http://www.arts.cuhk.hk/

This site provides information on the RIH's publications, conferences, and research programs. Includes a searchable index of articles and Internet links on a wide variety of subjects available via Gopher, FTP, or the Web.

Voice of the Shuttle: Web Page for Humanities Research

http://humanitas.ucsb.edu/

VoS is a large, multi-disciplinary page of well-organized links to online resources for research in the humanities. Currently comprising some 70 sub-pages, VoS is designed specifically with the academic or research professional in mind (as opposed to the general user).

WWW Virtual Library—Humanities

http://www.hum.gu.se/w3vl/VL.html

This is the main subject index at the World-Wide Web Virtual Library for Humanities-related topics. One of the best starting points around for humanities research on the Internet.

Geography

AGI GIS Dictionary

http://www.geo.ed.ac.uk/root/agidict/html/welcome.html

The University of Edinburgh and the Association of Geographic Information have teamed up to bring you this online dictionary of Geographic Information Systems (GIS) terminology. It might be useful to visit this site before looking at the rest of this geography section!

Area Accurate Map / The Peters Projection

http://www.webcom.com/~bright/petermap.html

This site provides information on the Peters Projection map. This new type of mapmaking is technically more accurate than current standards. An example given is Greenland versus Africa; Greenland appears larger on conventional maps, but in reality Africa is almost 14 times bigger. At this site, you can also order your own copy of the Peters Projection map.

The Association of American Geographers

http://www.aag.org/

The Association of American Geographers (AAG) is a scientific and educational society with members who share interests in the theory, methods, and practice of geography, which they cultivate through the AAG. This site contains basic information about the group, including contact addresses (e-mail and U.S. postal).

The Association of Chinese Professionals in Geographic Information Systems

http://gegsun.merrick.miami.edu/~cpgis/home.htm

This site provides general information about the Association, including online publications, conferences, and a FAQ list.

Canadian WWW Central Index/Liste centrale des serveurs WWW canadiens

http://www.csr.ists.ca/w3can/Welcome.html

This index is a listing of WWW servers in Canada that can be searched by province, city, or subject matter. Text available in English and French.

Cartography—Indiana State University

http://www.indstate.edu/gga/gga_cart/index.html

In addition to the standard course descriptions, this academic site also provides a basic introduction to the study of cartography (map making), links to map-related sites worldwide, and, of course, online maps of just about everywhere. A high-speed connection is recommended for the large map graphics files.

ChartWrite's Data-on-the-Map

http://chartwrite.josnet.se/index.html

Data-on-the-Map is a desktop software package for GIS mapping. This site includes a free demo version of the software, sample maps, a free run-time DM-MapServer SDK, and, of course, ordering information for the full package.

E-scapes: Electronic Resources for the Study of Ancient Landscapes

http://perseus.holycross.edu:80/e-scapes/

This site uses the Geographic Information System (GIS) to reconstruct the landscapes of the ancient Mediterranean area in order to facilitate the study of history, archaeology, biology, geography, and other disciplines. Includes an online lexicon of ancient place-names and geographic terms.

Federal Geographic Data Committee (FGDC)

http://fgdc.er.usgs.gov/fgdc.html

The FGDC was established through the Office of Management and Budget (OMB) and charged with the responsibility to coordinate various surveying, mapping, and spatial data activities of federal agencies to meet the needs of the United States. Online you will find the results of the FGDC's work.

Geographic Institutes around the World

http://ftp.geog.ucl.ac.be/GEOG/Einstgg.html

This site provides links to geographic organizations around the world, whether they are affiliated with governments, universities, or independent. Available in French and English.

Geographic Nameserver

http://www.mit.edu:8001/geo

Find information such as latitude and longitude, population, and elevation of just about any place on Earth, just enter the place-name and let the Nameserver do the rest.

GEOGRAPHY USA: A Virtual Textbook

http://www.for.nau.edu/~alew/ustxtwlc.html

This site by Alan Lew of Northern Arizona University contains a full online geography textbook that teaches U.S. geography at an introductory college level. A good continuing education area for adults.

The Global Positioning System (GPS)

http://wwwhost.cc.utexas.edu/ftp/pub/grg/gcraft/notes/gps/gps.html

This site maintained by the University of Texas at Austin gives detailed information on the Global Positioning System—its history, current projects, data summaries, and much more. Also provided are many links to other GPS-related sites.

Heritage Map Museum

http://www.carto.com/

Displays hundreds of original 15th- and 19th-century antique maps. Focuses on displaying and selling original works of the masters of cartography. Offers the works of Schedel, Munster, Ortelius, Mercator, Blaeu, Hondus, and many others.

The History of Cartography Project

http://feature.geography.wisc.edu/histcart/

The History of Cartography Project is a research, editorial, and publishing endeavor drawing international attention to the history of maps and mapping. The Project brings together scholars in the arts, sciences, and humanities under the direction of the University of Wisconsin Department of Geography. By considering previously ignored aspects of map history, such as ideological patronage and religious symbolism, the Project encourages a broader view of maps.

How far is it?

http://www.indo.com/distance/

Just for fun, enter the names, ZIP codes, or coordinates of any two places in the world. The search engine at this site will check the University of Michigan Geographic Name Server and related servers to tell you the distance between the two points, plus additional information about each.

Institute of Arctic and Alpine Research

http://instaar.colorado.edu/

The Institute of Arctic and Alpine Research (INSTAAR) is an interdisciplinary research institute of the Graduate School at the University of Colorado that emphasizes the environmental sciences (geology, geography, and biology), especially as they pertain to high altitudes, high latitudes, and former cold environments of the Quaternary period.

Interactive Geographical Index

http://www.hcc.hawaii.edu/htbin/plotd

A different kind of Web-searching service. Click on part of the world map (or enter a search string) to see a listing of sites registered for that area—then enter your own.

International Map Trade Association (IMTA)

http://www.maine.com/maptrade/Welcome.html

Have you ever wanted to know where to get a map? Well, this home page of the IMTA is a linked-list of publishers, manufacturers, retailers, and distributors of maps and related products from around the world. If you need a map, this is the place to check first, not the corner drugstore.

The Laboratory for Remote Sensing and Geographic Information Systems (LRSGIS)

http://lrsgis.memphis.edu/

LRSGIS is an academic and research facility which undertakes interdisciplinary research projects requiring the development and processing of digital data and images for applications in the cultural, physical, biological, and mapping sciences. This site contains research project summaries, workshop information, and much more.

Making Maps Easy to Read

http://acorn.educ.nottingham.ac.uk/ShellCent/maps/

Do you have trouble reading maps? Well then, this site could help you out by giving details of a study conducted at the University College London, at the Royal College of Art and at the University of Nottingham, concerning what makes maps easy to read and use. Areas covered include symbols, typography, relief styles, and more.

Mapmaker, Mapmaker, Make Me a Map

http://loki.ur.utk.edu/ut2Kids/maps/map.html

This site gives a history of cartography (mapmaking), as well as a full description of how maps are made using various processes. The text and recommended reading list at this site are aimed at younger children, but are informative for us all.

MAPublisher

http://www.avenza.com/

MAPublisher is a set of plug-ins for Adobe Illustrator that can translate rough GIS data into graphical maps within Illustrator. A piece of software definitely meant for the geographic professional, this site contains product details, samples, and ordering information from Avenza Software.

NAISMap WWW-GIS Home Page

http://ellesmere.ccm.emr.ca/naismap/naismap.html

With NAISMap, you can view and manipulate National Atlas spatial data layers and construct your own map of Canada. This is a very graphics-intensive site, and requires a forms-enabled browser.

National Center for Geographic Information and Analysis (NCGIA)

http://ncgia.geog.buffalo.edu//ncgia/NCGIA.html

The NCGIA provides information about research with computer technologies that enable scientists and policy makers to visualize geographic problems through maps, images, and data. Located at the State University of New York at Buffalo, this site details the research, policies, and educational programs of the NCGIA.

The Natural Area Coding System

http://www.io.org/~nac/

This site provides details on the Natural Area Coding System developed by NAC Geographic Products Inc. The NAC System was developed to give a global standard for site location for applications such as navigation, postal addressing, telecommunications, and much more.

Oregon Geographic Alliance (OGA)

http://geog.pdx.edu/oga.html

This page provides information about the OGA, based at Portland State University, which works with various publications and government services to try to increase public awareness of the importance of geographic education, especially at the K–12 level.

Project GeoSim

http://geosim.cs.vt.edu/index.html

Project GeoSim is a joint research project of the Departments of Computer Science and Geography at Virginia Tech. The project is creating education modules for introductory geography courses. These software modules are available for several different computer platforms.

RETKI GPS Land Navigation Software

http://www.intex.net/safensnd/retki.html

RETKI is a Windows-based software package that works with the NAVSTAR Global Positioning System from your laptop computer. Software designed for the traveling professional, the RETKI site contains full product information, system requirements, and a free downloadable demo.

The RYHINER-Project at the University Library of Berne

http://ubeclu.unibe.ch/STUB/RYHINER/RYHINER.HTML

The Ryhiner map collection is one of the most valuable and considerable collections of the world. It consists of more than 15,000 maps, charts, plans and views from the 16th to the 18th century, covering the whole globe. This Web site not only contains online versions of some of this rare maps, but general information on map/geographic conservation projects.

Spatial Odyssey: GIS Literature Database

http://www.odyssey.maine.edu/gisweb/

The Univeristy of Maine had collaborated with worldwide professional geographic organizations to provide this online, searchable database of the proceedings and papers of those organizations. The database includes images and the full text of the papers, not just summaries—a lot of technical information recommended for the professional geographer.

TIGER Mapping Service

http://tiger.census.gov/

This service provided by the United States Bureau of the Census enables you to create detailed maps of anywhere in the U.S. You control how much detail is given, such as highways, national parks, rivers and lakes, congressional districts, and everything else. However, a high-speed connection is recommended for this intensive site.

TOPO!™ Interactive Maps

http://www.topo.com/index.shtml

The company Wildflower Productions has developed this CD-ROM product that provides browsable topographic maps for several regions within the U.S. This site contains sample maps and ordering information.

U.S. Geological Survey (USGS) National Mapping Information World Wide Web Server

http://www-nmd.usgs.gov/

The USGS National Mapping Program provides accurate and up-to-date cartographic data and information for the United States. This site gives background information on the program, tips on using the USGS maps for educational purposes, and maps for sale (samples are viewable online).

Xerox PARC Map Viewer

http://mapweb.parc.xerox.com/map/

This mapping server provided by the Xerox Palo Alto Research Center lets you click anywhere on the world map to zoom in on details such as rivers, roads, and borders (state and country). Zoom in up to 6000x normal to download a map of your part of the world, although about 1500x normal is just as useful.

Languages/Linguistics

The American Dialect Society (ADS)

http://www.msstate.edu/Archives/ADS/

This is the home page of the ADS, the only scholarly association dedicated to the study of the English language in North America—and of other languages, or dialects of other languages, influencing it or influenced by it. Includes membership information, conference schedules, and calls for papers.

American Sign Language Linguistic Research Project

http://web.bu.edu/ASLLRP/

This is a collaborative research project, involving researchers at Boston University, Dartmouth College, Rutgers University, and Gallaudet University. Information is provided at this site on the two main parts of this project: investigation of the syntactic structure of American Sign Language (ASL) and development of multimedia tools for sign language research.

The Association for Computational Linguistics

http://www.cs.columbia.edu/~acl/home.html

Includes background information on the Association, conference schedules, abstracts from the *Computational Linguistics* journal, plus links to related sites.

Ink

http://www.cyserv.com:80/opco/index.html

Craving the latest in ink samples? Check out the Organic Products Web site. Don't forget to request samples of the Wornow Epoxy ink.

Australian National Dictionary Centre

http://online.anu.edu.au/ANDC/

This center provides information on research into the usage of Australian English. Includes details on various Australian dictionaries published by Oxford Univesity Press, with plans for an online dictionary.

CELEX Dutch Centre for Lexical Information

http://www.kun.nl/celex/index.html

CELEX has compiled three large electronic databases which can provide online and offline users with detailed English, German, and Dutch lexical data. Aimed at the professional linguist, this database contains representations of the phonological, morphological, syntactic, and frequency properties of lemmata for each of the three languages included.

Center for Applied Linguistics (CAL)

http://www.cal.org/cal/calhome.html-ssi

CAL is a private nonprofit organization that has been applying research and information about language and culture to educational, cultural, and social concerns for 37 years. This site provides information about CAL's history, current projects, and future mission.

Center for Machine Translation

http://www.mt.cs.cmu.edu/cmt/CMT-home.html

The Center for Machine Translation (CMT) at the School of Computer Science at Carnegie Mellon University conducts advanced research and development in a suite of technologies for natural language processing. At this site you will find project details, personnel profiles, technical reports, and more.

Center for Spoken Language Understanding

http://www.cse.ogi.edu/CSLU/

This group from the Oregon Graduate Institute of Science and Technology has a mission to perform basic research leading to advances in the state of the art of spoken language systems. Their Web site follows that mission by providing research summaries, publications, including the full text and illustrations of the Human Lanquage Technology Survey, and more.

The Chomskybot

http://www.ling.lsa.umich.edu/cgi-bin/chomsky.pl

The focal point of this site is a Web robot that assembles random phrases from the works of Noam Chomsky into nearly coherent paragraphs. Also provided is a detailed discussion of the programming behind this robot and the linguistic principles it uses.

Colibri Home Page

http://colibri.let.ruu.nl/

Colibri is an electronic newsletter and WWW service for people interested in the fields of language, speech, logic, or information. A searchable index of current and past issues is available, along with subscription directions and many links to related topics.

English as a Second Language Home Page

http://www.lang.uiuc.edu/r-li5/esl/

This home page is a starting point for ESL learners who want to learn English through the World Wide Web. Many people have created ESL learning materials for the Web. This home page links you to those ESL sites and other interesting places. The variety of materials will allow you to choose something appropriate for yourself.

ETHNOLOGUE: Languages of the World

http://www.sil.org/ethnologue/ethnologue.html

If you've ever wanted to know what people are saying all over the world, this is the place to come. This site includes a detailed study of the names, number of speakers, location, dialects, linguistic affiliation, multilingualism of speakers, and much more information on over 360 languages currently spoken on this planet. A searchable database and clickable maps are provided to help you find just the language you are looking for.

EUROLANG *Optimizer*

http://www.eurolang.fr/

Provides information on the EUROLANG *Optimizer* software package. This program is designed to work with the most popular word processors and RDBMS to provide language translation. Download the demo version from this site. Pages available in French or English.

FoLLI, the European Association for Logic, Language and Information

http://www.fwi.uva.nl/research/folli/

This site contains information FoLLI's background, current and future projects, and publications. Also find out how to join FoLLI and receive their journal.

Haskins Laboratories

http://www.haskins.yale.edu/

Haskins Laboratories, New Haven, Connecticut, is a private, nonprofit research laboratory. Currently, most of the Laboratories' research projects are focused on problems in human communication and related topics, including speech perception, speech production, reading, linguistics, motor behavior, cognitive science, nonlinear dynamics, medical imaging, functional MRI, and so on.

The Human-Languages Page

http://www.willamette.edu/~tjones/Language-Page.html

This page is devoted to bringing together information about the languages of the world. The language resources listed here come from all around the world, and range from dictionaries to language tutorials to spoken samples of languages. Offers the page in several languages. Provides Quick-Jump links for easy navigation.

Journal of Child Language

http://www.cup.cam.ac.uk/Journals/JNLSCAT95/jcl/jcl.html

Journal of Child Language publishes articles on all aspects of the scientific study of language behaviour in children, the principles which underlie it, and the theories which may account for it. At this site you will find submission requirements, tables of contents for past issues, and subscription information.

Journal of Pidgin and Creole Languages

http://www.siu.edu/departments/cola/ling/

JPCL presents the results of current research in theory and description of pidgin and creole languages in the wider sense. Includes glossary of linguistic terminology.

The Klingon Language Institute

http://www.kli.org/

Just for fun or for the serious linguist, this site details the development of the "artificial" Klingon language from the *Star Trek* series and movies. At this site, you can also teach yourself Klingon to speak with your friends.

Kualono: 'Olelo Hawai'i

http://www.olelo.hawaii.edu/OP/help/

This Web site is dedicated to providing information on the native Hawaiian language, both for preservation and teaching. Among its many resources are Hawaiian fonts (Mac and IBM), an online dictionary, and instructional materials for purchase.

Lexeme-Morpheme Base Morphology (LMBM)

http://www.bucknell.edu/~rbeard/

The LMBM lexicon is exclusively the domain of lexemes which are defined specifically as noun, verb, and adjective stems and the lexical categories that define them (number, gender, transitivity, and so on). LMBM distinguishes itself from other lexeme-based theories in that it maintains a pristine distinction between lexemes and grammatical morphemes and consequently predicts this distinction at every level of language and speech.

The Lingua Project

http://www.loria.fr/exterieur/equipe/dialogue/lingua/

This page is devoted to the Lingua Parallel Concordancing Project which aims at managing a multilingual corpus to ease students' and teachers' work in second language learning. More specifically some implementation issues of the Text Encoding Initiative guidelines are shown, along with the corresponding tools which have been developed. Currently, this project has translated various texts into English, French, German, Dutch, Greek, or Italian, and cross-referenced each work in a searchable index of the languages.

The LINGUIST Network

http://engserve.tamu.edu/files/linguistics/linguist/

LINGUIST is an electronic network maintained at Texas A&M and Eastern Michigan Universities. LINGUIST serves as a research and discussion facility for the linguistic academic community through an electronic mailing list and its World Wide Web sites. Join a discussion or read archived discussion threads from this site.

Linguistic Fun

http://www.bucknell.edu/departments/linguistics/fun.html

A Bucknell professor has put together this fun and interesting introduction to the study of linguistics. It all begins with the question, "What do a hippo and a feather have in common?"

Loglan

`http://www.halcyon.com/loglan/welcome.html`

Loglan is an artificial human language originally designed/invented by James Cooke Brown in the late 1950s. This site details the construction and usage of this language. An HTML primer to learn Loglan is scheduled to be available soon, but some translations are already online.

The Mayan Epigraphic Database Project

`http://jefferson.village.virginia.edu/med/home.html`

The Mayan Epigraphic Database Project (MED) is an experiment in networked scholarship with the purpose of enhancing Classic Mayan epigraphic research. MED is an Internet-accessible database of primary and secondary sources of epigraphic, iconographic, and linguistic data in a multimedia format.

Mayan Hieroglyphic Syllabary

`http://www.he.net/~nmcnelly/`

Intended for primarily for researchers already familiar with Mayan language and history, this site contains GIFs of Mayan hieroglyphics, associated sound files, and much more information on the Mayan culture. However, this site is also fun to browse, not only to see the hieroglyphics, but also because of the VRML walkthrough of the 900 AD Palace of the Governor in Uxmal, Yucatan, Mexico.

Model Languages

`http://ourworld.compuserve.com/homepages/jeffrey_henning/`

The electronic newletter contains discussions and articles on made-up languages. Includes subscrip-

tion information and a software package (Windows) for making your own language.

Multilingual PC Directory

`http://www.knowledge.co.uk/xxx/mpcdir/book.htm`

The Multilingual PC Directory is designed to help you find products which support non-English languages on PCs and compatibles. A search option by language is available. Includes software reviews, company profiles, and links to Web resources.

Natural Language Computing Home Page

`http://www.nyu.edu/pages/linguistics/ling.html`

This page is part of a larger Web site that discusses the design and implementation of a computer programming language that works using real English syntax, not the cryptic commands of languages such as C++. This page relates the linguistic theories of Noam Chomsky to the larger project.

Old English Pages

`http://www.georgetown.edu/cball/oe/old_english.html`

This site contains nearly everything you could want to know about Old English. Includes links to online texts and translations, discussion groups, fonts, audio recordings, course materials, instructional software, and much more.

Russian Manual Alphabet

`http://weber.u.washington.edu/~jkautz/russian.sign.html`

This small page provides graphics that demonstrate the use of sign language to speak Russian.

Semiotics for Beginners

`http://www.aber.ac.uk/~dgc/semiotic.html`

As the title suggests, this site provides an online course in the study of signs/communication in society (semiotics). Here you get the history of this discipline, current applications and research, and lists of suggested reading material.

TsaLaGi (English/Cherokee Dictionary)

`http://www.idsonline.com/ssb/tsalagi.htm`

This is a downloadable software program for Windows that provides translation and fonts from English to Cherokee. Site includes system requirements, registration, and ordering information.

UCREL—University Centre for Computer Corpus Research on Language

http://www.comp.lancs.ac.uk/computing/research/ucrel/

The University Centre for Computer Corpus Research on Language is a Lancaster University research center shared between the Department of Linguistics and Modern English Language and the Department of Computing. Its objective is to carry out computer-based research on the analysis and processing of natural language data. This site provides details on the Centre's research, including data summaries, online papers, and conference schedules.

University of Chicago Press Cognitive Science and Linguistics Catalog

http://press-gopher.uchicago.edu:70/1s/Subjects/Linguistics

This page is the entry-point into U of Chicago's Gopher-based online catalog and ordering system for linguistics texts. Search by author and subject or read the whole catalog, including book summaries.

The Web Journal of Modern Language Linguistics

http://www.ncl.ac.uk/~njw5/

This recently created online journal includes articles, book reviews, and subscription and submission information. (A print version will also be available.) Submissions are encouraged from any branch of modern lanquages.

Word Manager

http://www.idsia.ch/wordmanager.html

Word Manager is a system for the acquisition and management of reusable morphological and phrasal dictionaries. Learn about this system developed in Europe; a demo version is downloadable for Macintosh.

WordSmith Tools

http://www1.oup.co.uk/cite/oup/elt/software/wsmith/

Wordsmith Tools is an integrated suite of programs for looking at how words behave in texts. It is intended for linguists, language teachers, and anyone who needs to examine language as part of their work. Download a full demo version from this site at the Oxford University Press.

The Yuen Ren Society

http://weber.u.washington.edu/~yuenren/index.html

Founded for the Promotion of Chinese Dialect Fieldwork, the Yuen Ren Society is a loose group of descriptive linguists working in Hann Chinese. The central focus of this Web site is a guide to Gwoyeu Romatzyh Tonal Spelling of Chinese for the romanization of the Chinese language.

Psychology

Ages & Stages

gopher://tinman.mes.umn.edu:4242/11/ChildCare/ChildDevel

This Gopher menu contains fact sheets from the National Network for Child Care detailing the physical and mental development of children ages newborn to 11 years. Available in English and Spanish.

Altered States of Consciousness

http://www.utu.fi/~jounsmed/asc/asc.html

This site provides online papers and related links on varoius psychological topics, including dreams, parapsychology, hypnosis, out-of-body experiences, and more.

The American Academy of Child & Adolescent Psychiatry Homepage (AACAP)

http://www.psych.med.umich.edu/web/aacap/

Here you will find information about the AACAP, including membership, conferences, publications, and research plans. Of general interest are the Facts for Families sheets that provide information about child psychiatry. Available in English, Spanish, or French.

American Psychoanalytic Association

http://apsa.org/

This home page for the American Psychoanalytic Association includes a history of psyhchoanalysis, a searchable database of related papers, a list of members, information on upcoming conferences, and online summaries of the organization's journals.

American Psychological Association— PsychNET

http://www.apa.org/

This organization's Web page covers psychological and cognitive science resources, the practice of psychology, APA's large publishing operation, and information for the public on the field and the association. Of interest to the general public is the APA's Help section, which provides text and resource listings for those looking for psychological assistance.

American Psychological Society (APS)

`http://psych.hanover.edu/APS/`

Contains full information on this organization's membership and research, including a Gopher database of the APS *Observer* articles. Also provides online classified ads for job postings in the field of psychology.

The Arc, a national organization on mental retardation

`http://TheArc.org/welcome.html`

This home page for The Arc provides information on mental retardation, The Arc activities and local chapters, and a discussion board. Includes a searchable index of topics discussed.

Attention Deficit Disorder WWW Archive

`http://www.seas.upenn.edu/~mengwong/add/`

This site provides an archive of ariticles on Attention Deficit Disorder, from introductory materials to professional evaluations to medication reviews. Many of the articles are local to this server, but several are just links.

C.G. Jung, Analytical Psychology, and Culture

`http://www.cgjung.com/cgjung`

What would a section on pyschology be like without pages devoted to one of the most well-known figures in the discipline's history? This site provides resources for Jungians, such as conference schedules, online papers, and links to associated sites.

The C.G. Jung Institute of Los Angeles

`http://home.earthlink.net/users/junginla/./webdocs/./`

The Jung Institute of Los Angeles is a nonprofit center based on the concepts and discoveries of C.G. Jung, the founder of Analytical Psychology. Also available from this site is an online bookstore from which you can order texts by Jung and Jungian psychologists.

Canadian Psychological Association

`http://www.cycor.ca/Psych/home.html`

This site provides membership information for Canadian psychologists, career advertisements, publication abstracts, conference schedules, and a listing of psychological resources in Canada. Available in both French- and English-language versions.

Cyber-Psych

`http://www.charm.net/~pandora/psych/index.html`

Cyber-Psych is committed to bringing high-quality, professional psychological care and information to the online community. This site does this through a well-organized and comprehensive set of psychology-related links.

Depression FAQ

`http://avocado.pc.helsinki.fi/~janne/asdfaq/index.html`

This site provides answers to all types of questions concerning this common but undiagnosed illness. Topics covered include definitions, concepts, causes, treatment, how to find a doctor, various resources, and more.

DreamLink

`http://www.iag.net/~hutchib/.dream/`

This site is an open forum for those interested in dreams and dreaming. It is dedicated to an open exchange of thoughts, feelings, and ideas from people at all levels of knowledge. In DreamLink you can read the dreams of others, offer interpretations of another's dream, and submit your own dream for translation, all anonymously. This site also offers different techniques on how to remember dreams, as well as the latest theories concerning dream interpretation.

The ERIC Digests

`gopher://INET.ed.gov:12002/7waissrc%3A/Eric`

The Gopher site opens with a one-line search interface. Enter the psychological subject of your choice, and the server will search an incredible list of articles for related information. Most of the articles contained here appear to deal with school-age psychological disorders.

Evolution's Voyage

http://www.Evoyage.com/

Is world peace possible? This man thinks so. See how the new science of evolutionary psychology has affected him and how he sees the world around him.

The Institute of Psychology, Russian Academy of Sciences (IP RAS)

http://www.glasnet.ru/~vega/ipras/index.html

Discover how psychology is studied in the Russian Federation. This site contains information on the educational programs, publishing activities, international relations, and research projects of the IP RAS. Yes, the text is in English.

International Association for Cross-Cultural Psychology (IACCP)

http://www.fit.edu/ft-orgs/iaccp/

The IACCP was founded in 1972 and aims to facilitate communication among persons interested in cross-cultural psychology and to pursue the universal validity of psychological theories in all branches of psychology and related disciplines. Included on this site is information on membership, papers, conferences, and publications.

Internet Mental Health

http://www.mentalhealth.com/

This is an online encyclopedia of mental health information put together by a Canadian psychiatrist. Lots of good general information, plus more detailed information on the Canadian mental health system.

Institute for the Psychological Study of the Arts (IPSA)

http://www.clas.ufl.edu/ipsa/

The discipline of literature-and-psychology explores literary questions using psychology, often psycho-analytic psychology, but other psychologies as well. Here you will find electronic publications, conference schedules, and more relating to this mix of literature and psychology.

The Journal of Mind and Behavior (JMB)

http://kramer.ume.maine.edu/~jmb/welcome.html

JMB is an educational and professional journal dedicated to the interdisciplinary approach within psychology and related fields and is interested in: the psychology, philosophy, and sociology of experimentation and the scientific method; the relationship between methodology, operationism, and theory construction; the mind/body problem in the social sciences, psychiatry and the medical sciences, and the physical sciences; and much, much more.

The Keirsey Temperament Sorter

http://sunsite.unc.edu/personality/keirsey.html

Find out more than you ever wanted to know about yourself. Take this personality test based on the professional Meyers-Briggs test. The results include a general description of your personality type (out of 16 possible). The Web author reminds you several times that this is just for fun.

KidsPeace®, The National Center for Kids in Crisis

http://www.kidspeace.org/

KidsPeace is an organization devoted to promoting the mental well-being of children. At this Web site you will find research summaries and parenting tips that lead to this goal.

The Mental Edge—Sport Psychology

http://www.iii.net/users/dupcak/mntledge.html

Sport psychology involves preparing the mind of an athlete, just as thoroughly as one prepares the body. Sport psychology is an emerging field in the worlds of psychology and athletics. This site contains detailed information on the field of sport psychology, including a full list of recommended reading.

Mental Relativity

http://www.well.com/user/melanie/relative.html

Mental relativity is a model of psychology based on chaos theory, fractals, and a new concept called frictals (from friction and fraction). Because of its frictal description of the mind's processes of problem solving and justification, Mental relativity not only explains the underlying foundations of self-awareness, but can equally be applied to other human and scientific issues as well.

Mind Tools

http://www.gasou.edu/psychweb/mtsite/index.html

Mind Tools is a resource of high-quality, problem-solving software, thought techniques, practical psychology and links to related topics, designed to help you optimise the performance of your mind and achieve your dreams and ambitions.

National Institute of Mental Health (NIMH)

`gopher://gopher.nimh.nih.gov:70/1`

NIMH is the U.S. government agency that conducts and supports research on mental illness and mental health, including studies of the brain, behavior, and mental health services. This Gopher site provides very detailed information on NIMH-sponsored projects, publications, grants, membership, and much more, including a searchable bibliography.

Online Psychological Services

`http://www.onlinepsych.com/`

Online Psychological Services is a comprehensive information service serving the needs of psychological professionals and consumers. On this public page you will find interesting and useful connections to many different areas of psychological concern.

Personality Test

`http://www.users.interport.net/~zang/personality.html`

Mainly for fun, this site provides you with nine pictures of which you choose one to be "rewarded" with a general description of your personality type

PREP—Psychology Preprint Server

`http://www.ccsnet.com:80/prep/`

As an academic preprint archive and distribution system, PREP is designed to augment current practice in academic psychology research, by circulating—by mail or e-mail—copies of your paper prior to acceptance or actual publication in the journal literature. PREP does not require copyright transfer; the author retains full copyright ownership. Both text and illustrations may be posted.

The Primal Psychotherapy Page

`http://www.net-connect.net/~jspeyrer/`

The object of primal psychotherapy is to enhance one's life by first lowering the tension levels of the material stored in the unconscious. This site provides a history of this discipline, as well as an online newsletter and links to psychotherapists who practice the techniques of primal psychotherapy.

Professional Psychology

`http://www.psy.it/propsy1.html`

Professional Psychology is an international non-profit association that provides psychologists with continuous education and professional services, in the specific areas of legal and forensic psychology,

medical psychology, clinical psychology and psychotherapy, and organizational psychology. Only the introductory page is available in English, the remainder of the site is in Italian.

Psychology of Religion Page

`http://www.gasou.edu/psychweb/psyrelig/psyrelig.htm`

This site describes the way that psychologists use scientific research methods to study religion. The author has included a list of psychologists around the world who study the psychology of religion, as well as links to related resources, a recommended reading list, and a brief commentary on the future of this field.

Psychguide

`http://www.designers-int.com/Psychguide/`

Indexes psychology-related sites on the Net. Includes universities, journals, and conferences across the Web.

Psychiatry & Psychotherapy

`http://www-leland.stanford.edu/~corelli/`

Offers links to mental health information and resources. Provides information on psychiatric diagnosis and on personality disorders and other areas of pssychological interest. Offers links to information on psychotherapy and psychopharmacology. Includes an extensive reading list in areas of psychiatry, psychotherapy, and Jungian psychology.

Psychiatry On-Line

`http://www.cityscape.co.uk/users/ad88/psych.htm`

This Web-based, peer-reviewed electronic journal contains articles, book reviews, an online bookstore (in the works), and more. Includes subscription (it's free) and submission information.

Psychological Type Profiles

`http://sacam.oren.ortn.edu/~jabutt/profiles/profiles.html`

This site provides full summaries of the 16 psychological profile types as defined by the Myers-Briggs Type Indicator, as well as a link to an online version of the Keirsey Temperment Sorter (a test that will tell you which profile type you are).

Psychology of Invention

`http://hawaii.cogsci.uiuc.edu/invent/invention.html`

This page is a gateway to three collections relevant to the theme of the psychology of invention.

Specifically, it is concerned with the thought processes that inventors employ to create new artifacts and pro-cesses. Includes studies on the invention of the airplane and the invention of the telephone.

Psychology Self-Help Resources on the Internet

http://www.gasou.edu/psychweb/resource/selfhelp.htm

This page contains links to non-commercial sites providing information and help about specific disorders related to psychology. Links are organized both alphabetically by site title and by subject.

Psychology Software Tools, Inc.

http://www.pstnet.com/

Psychology Software Tools, Inc., is dedicated to serving the field of psychology by producing commercial-software products to facilitate the implementation of computerized experiments and enhance the teaching of psychology. Site includes product descriptions, ordering information, and job postings.

Rorschach Inkblot Test

http://www-students.biola.edu/~markm/rorsch.html

This site provides a history of the Rorschach tests, online "Cyber-blots," and an IRC chat room for discussion of Rorschach-related issues.

School Psychology Resourses Online

http://www.bcpl.lib.md.us/~sandyste/school_psych.html

Provides links to information of interest to school psychologists. Sorted by subjects such as Attention Deficit Disorder, Autism, Tourette's Disorder, Substance Abuse, and much more.

Sigmund Freud

http://austria-info.at/personen/freud/index.html

An online biography of Freud's life and work, this site is part of the Austrian National Tourism Office Web site.

The Society for Computers in Psychology

http://www.lafayette.edu/allanr/scip.html

The Society for Computers in Psychology is a nonprofit organization of researchers interested in the application of computers in psychology. Its primary purpose is to "increase and diffuse knowledge of the use of computers in psychological research." Membership is open to any person who has an academic degree and who is active in scientific applications of computers to psychological research. Site includes calls for papers and conference information.

Subintellect's Personality Test

http://anonym.com/aboutest.html

A twisted approach to personality evaluation by the Subintellect's Anonym Research Institute. All that can be said is "See for yourself!" Personality types are called "cults." The only real drawback to this site (besides the questions) is that test results are not instantaneous. Also includes an index of Web pages sorted by personality cult.

Teaching Clinical Psychology

http://www1.rider.edu/~suler/tcp.html

This site is devoted to sharing ideas and resources for the teaching of clinical psychology, especially undergraduate courses on abnormal psychology, psychotherapy, group dynamics, psychological testing, and clinical components of introductory psychology.

Tools for Practical Self Development

http://www.azstarnet.com/~lehrman/

Information and articles on mindfulness, Quantum Psychology, Hakomi Psychotherapy, Buddhist Psychology, Morita, Naikan, Constructive Living, programs in personal self development, and related links.

The Whole Brain Atlas

http://www.med.harvard.edu/AANLIB/home.html

This site maintained by the Harvard Medical School provides a full tour of the structure of the human brain with associated reports on brain diseases and infections. An interactive portion of the tour is available for Java-enabled browsers.

Sociology

American Civilization Homepage

http://www.infi.net/amcivilization/

The American Civilization Web site is designed as the point in cyberspace to discuss, define, and articulate a vision for the future of American civilization. You can upload your own views on topics discussed, which will be updated daily and summarized in a monthly journal.

American Sociological Association (ASA)

http://www.asanet.org/

The ASA is a nonprofit membership association dedicated to advancing sociology as a scientific discipline and profession serving the public good. On their Web site you will find membership information, several online bulletins, employment listings, and much more of interest to professional sociologists.

Association for Humanist Sociology

http://www.kutztown.edu/~ehrensal/ahshome.html

Humanist sociologists strive as professionals, as scholars and as activists to uncover and address social issues, working with others to lessen the pain of social problems. This site includes a mission statement, conference schedule, and membership information.

The Canadian Journal of Sociology (CJS)

http://gpu.srv.ualberta.ca/~cjscopy/cjs.html

The CJS is a rigorously peer-reviewed, quarterly journal published at the University of Alberta. Online you will find abstracts of past and forthcoming issues, selected articles and reviews, and subscription and submission information.

Center for Rural Studies (CRS)

http://www.uvm.edu/~cdae/crs/

The Center for Rural Studies (CRS) is a nonprofit, fee-for-service research organization that addresses social, economic, and resource-based problems of rural people and communities. This combined Web and Gopher site provides information on CRS's five main research areas: agriculture, human services, economic development, energy, and environment/natural resources.

Center for the Study of Online Communities

http://www.sscnet.ucla.edu/soc/csoc/

The Center for the Study of Online Community seeks to present and foster studies that focus on how computers and networks alter people's capacity to form groups, organizations, institutions, and how those social formations are able to serve the collective interests of their members. Includes papers on related topics.

Centre for Media Sociology (CeMeSo)

http://www.vub.ac.be/SCOM/cemeso/index.html

The Centre for Media Sociology, a research center attached to the Free University Brussels, primarily investigates the role of the media in the transformation of the public sphere. Specific fields of scientific interest include: intercultural communication, racism and minorities, media, and the fourth estate.

Centre for Social Theory and Technology (CSTT)

http://www.keele.ac.uk/depts/stt/home.htm

The CSTT is a new leading research center for social, information, and organization theory sponsored by the departments of management and sociology/social anthropology at Keele University in Staffordshire, UK. Find details here on research projects and publications.

Consortium for International Earth Science Information Network (CIESIN)

http://www.ciesin.org/

The CIESIN is developing ways to help you access and use data and information that will help you understand the impacts of global environmental change and support sustainable development. At this Web site you will find information on current projects, information resources, and much more.

Book

http://www.nestle.com

Dazzle your friends and family with a lovely new addition to your coffee table. Just correctly answer three questions about Nestle and receive an illustrated copy of *Nestle: 125 years*.

CTHEORY

http://www.ctheory.com/

CTHEORY is an international, electronic review of books on theory, technology, and culture. Sponsored by the Canadian Journal of Political and Social Theory, reviews are posted periodically of key books in contemporary discourse as well as theorisations of major "event-scenes" in the mediascape. It is possible to search for online articles by date submitted, but not by subject.

The Economic and Social Research Council Data Archive

http://dawww.essex.ac.uk/

The Economic and Social Research Council Data Archive at the University of Essex houses the largest collection of accessible computer-readable data in the social sciences and humanities in the United Kingdom. Several different search engines are available at this site to access the collected data, as well as information on internship programs.

Electronic Journal of Sociology©

http://gpu1.srv.ualberta.ca:8010/

In this electronic journal, you will find abstracts and full-text versions of hundreds of sociology articles, including reviews of the same. All text is published in both HTML and ASCII versions. Submission requirements are also detailed.

European Research Centre on Migration and Ethnic Relations (ERCOMER)

http://www.ruu.nl/ercomer/index.html

ERCOMER studies issues of growing cultural complexity and problems of social integration and social exclusion, primarily from the European perspective. This site details the Centre's research efforts, publications, and conferences. Includes a full annual report from the 1994–1995 academic year.

European Sociological Association (ESA)

http://www.qub.ac.uk/socsci/miller/esaintro.html

This home page for the ESA offers membership information, conference schedules, and an online newsletters. Also includes a full history of the organization. ESA is not only for European members, but for anyone interested in European issues.

Filmakers Library

http://www.filmakers.com/

Filmakers Library distributes award-winning documentaries on social issues, global concerns and academic subjects, such as psychology and anthropology, to educational institutions and libraries.

The Future of Children

http://www.futureofchildren.org/

The primary purpose of The Future of Children is to disseminate timely information on major issues related to children's well-being, with special emphasis on providing objective analysis and evaluation, translating existing knowledge into effective programs and polices, and promoting constructive institutional change. Online articles and subscription information are given at this Web site.

GALLERY OF SOCIAL STRUCTURES: Network Visualization

http://www.mpi-fg-koeln.mpg.de/~lk/netvis.html

The Network gallery documents work in progress in our efforts to visualize social structures. The aim is to develop experience about how automatic procedures can be combined with aesthetics to ease insight into usually complex phenomena. This site provides research summaries and demonstrations, a bulletin board service, and more.

The Human Rights Web Home Page

http://www.traveller.com/~hrweb/hrweb.html

This informative site provides a history of the human rights movement, links to organizations involved in the fight to promote human rights, and information on what you can do to be involved. Also includes legal and political documents from organizations such as the United Nations.

The Institute for Propaganda Analysis

http://carmen.artsci.washington.edu/propaganda/ipa.htm

The Institute for Propaganda Analysis was created in 1937 to educate the American public about the widespread nature of political propaganda. This site details the Institute's publications and research.

International Network for Social Network Analysis (INSNA)

http://thecore.socy.scarolina.edu/insna.html

This page contains information about the International Network for Social Network Analysis (INSNA) and related subjects. Here you will find Social Networks information, reference sources and links to related home pages. They hope that future additions to these pages will include areas for automated data collection.

International Sociological Association (ISA)

http://www.ucm.es/OTROS/isa/

The goal of the Association, as stated in these pages, is to represent sociologists everywhere, regardless of their school of thought, scientific approaches or ideological opinion, and to advance sociological knowledge throughout the world. Online you will find research summaries, conference information, abstracts, links to national sociligical groups, and more. Pages available in English, French, and Spanish.

Journal of Criminal Justice and Popular Culture

http://www.scj.albany.edu:90/jcjpc/

This online journal serves the criminal justice/criminological community by publishing reviews of all types of popular culture artifacts and original essays pertaining to the intersection of popular culture and criminal justice. Here you will find the full text online, along with an index searchable by author. Of course, submission information is also given.

The Journal of Latin American Perspectives

http://wizard.ucr.edu/~asampaio/lap.html

Latin American Perspectives is a theoretical and scholarly journal for debate and discussion on the political economy of capitalism, imperialism, and socialism in the Americas. The journal offers a multidisciplinary view of the most powerful forces shaping the Americas, such as economics, political science, international relations, history, sociology, and culture.

Journal of World-Systems Research

http://csf.colorado.edu/wsystems/jwsr.html

The *Journal of World-Systems Research* is an electronic journal dedicated to scholarly research on the modern world-system and earlier, smaller intersocietal

networks. At this Web site you will find subscription information and archived copies of past issues.

National Criminal Justice Reference Service (NCJRS)

http://www.ncjrs.org/

This site provides detailed information on the U.S. criminal justice system, encompassing several differenct government organizations. Includes a searchable index of topics and research information.

Population Index

http://opr.princeton.edu/popindex/

This quarterly bibliography publication from Princeton University is now available online. The entire published database for 1986–1995 is available and can be searched by author, subject matter, geographical region, and year of publication. Also find out how to subscribe to the printed version of the *Population Index*.

Population Reference Bureau (PRB)

http://www.prb.org/prb/

PRB is dedicated to providing timely, objective information on U.S. and international population trends. This site includes publications, membership information, and the chance to query the *1995 World Population Data Sheet* as prepared by PRB.

Population Studies Center— University of Michigan

http://www.psc.lsa.umich.edu/index.html

PSC is one of the outstanding demographic research and training institutions in the world, located at the intersection of social science and demography across the nation and world. Included at this Web site are a searchable data archive, research papers, a publications listing, and many related links.

Society for Applied Sociology

http://www.indiana.edu/~appsoc/

The Society for Applied Sociology, founded in 1978, is an international organization for professionals involved in applying sociological knowledge in a wide variety of settings. Here you will information on conferences, membership, and publications.

Sociological Research Online

http://www.soc.surrey.ac.uk/socresonline/

This is the Web site for a new online sociological journal (first issue March, 1996). Contains full articles, reviews, calls for papers, and more. This project is partially funded by the British Sociological Association.

Sociology Gopher Resources

`gopher://marvel.loc.gov:70/11/global/socsci/soc`

This Gopher server at the Library of Congress provides links to dozens of other sociology-related Gopher servers and institutes worldwide. A good starting point for sociology research.

The SocioWeb

`http://www.socioweb.com/~markbl/socioweb/`

This site provides resources for sociologists, such as conference schedules, calls for papers, university job listings, research topics, and much more. One additional area included here not included in more "professional" sites is a forum for undergraduate research.

SOCNET

`http://www.mcmaster.ca/socscidocs/socnet.htm`

SOCNET provides a sorted index of sociology courses and curricula resources on the Internet. Here you will find links to online courses covering nearly any topic that relates to sociology.

United Nations Scholars' Workstation at Yale University

`http://www.library.yale.edu/un/unhome.htm`

The United Nations Scholars' Workstation, developed by the Yale University Library and the Social Science Statistical Laboratory, is a collection of texts, finding aids, data sets, maps, and pointers to print and electronic information. Subject coverage includes disarmament, economic and social development, environment, human rights, international relations, international trade, peacekeeping, and population and demography.

United Nations Population Information Network (POPIN)

`gopher://gopher.undp.org:70/11/ungophers/popin/`

This Gopher server is funded by the United Nations to improve the flow of population information worldwide, and to encourage, initiate and facilitate exchange of population information and experience among population and information experts. Includes research information and links on many demographics-related subjects.

University of Chicago Press Sociology Catalog

`http://press-gopher.uchicago.edu:70/1s/Subjects/Sociology`

This page is the entry-point into U of Chicago's Gopher-based online catalog and ordering system for sociology texts. Search by author and subject or read the whole catalog, including book summaries.

U.S. Agency for International Development

`http://www.info.usaid.gov/`

This site provides information about the U.S. government's aid programs worldwide: who is being helped and how, the reciprocal benefits of foreign aid, and general information on developing countries. Includes many summary graphs of the information presented.

U.S. Civil Rights Code

`http://www.law.cornell.edu/uscode/42/ch21.html`

This site at Cornell Univerisity provides the full text of the U.S. Civil Rights Code browsable by part in HTML format, not just a text listing. Includes a WAIS searchable index.

World Neighbors

`http://www.halcyon.com/fkroger/wn.html`

World Neighbors is a U.S.-based nonprofit organization working at the forefront of worldwide efforts to eliminate hunger, disease and poverty in Asia, Latin America and Africa. This Web site contains information on how you can join their efforts, as well as description of World Neighbors projects searchable by country.

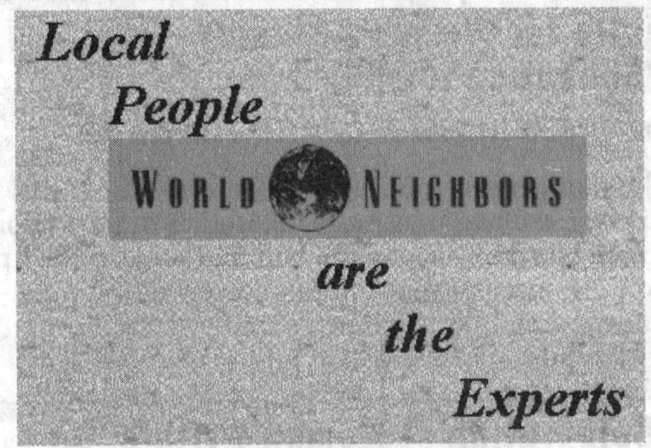

Worldwide Demography Resources

`http://www.esrc.bris.ac.uk/Subjects/demog.html`

Provides links to demographic resources based on the Internet, including data archives, mailing lists, discussion groups, research centers, and more.

Women's Studies

American Association of University Women (AAUW)

http://www.aauw.org/index.html

The American Association of University Women is a national organization that promotes education and equity for all women and girls. This Web site describes AAUW issues, research programs, grants and fellowships, membership information, and much more.

The Center for the American Woman and Politics (CAWP)

http://www.rci.rutgers.edu/~cawp/

The CAWP is a university-based research, education and public service center. Its mission is to promote greater understanding and knowledge about women's relationship to politics and government and to enhance women's influence and leadership in public life. CAWP is a unit of the Eagleton Institute of Politics at Rutgers, The State University of New Jersey.

Center for Women's Global Leadership (CWGL)

gopher://gopher.igc.apc.org:70/00/orgs/cwgl/cwglgo

The Gopher server provided by this Center in New Jersey provides information on group publications, women's forums, and more in an effort to work toward the recognition of women's human rights at all levels.

Centre for Women's Studies in Education (CWSE)

gopher://porpoise.oise.on.ca:70/11/resources/CWSE

This Gopher server in Toronto, Ontario, Canada is run by the Ontario Institute for Studies in Education. Among its many pages you will find project descriptions, research papers, information on CWSE publications, and links to women's studies sites worldwide.

A Celebration of Women Writers

http://www.cs.cmu.edu/afs/cs.cmu.edu/user/mmbt/www/women/celebration.html

This site provides links to complete online editions of books by women writers. Currently an index by author is provided, with expansion plans in the works. Volunteers to help with this project are requested; submissions must be either public domain titles (i.e., the classics) or be authorized by the copyright holder.

Colleen's Feminism Home Page

http://pages.prodigy.com/HYEW27A/feminism.htm

This personal home page summarizes many women's issues, including nonsexist language, quotations, women's right to vote, and much more.

CRLP: Women of the World

http://www.echonyc.com/~jmkm/wotw/

This site provided by The Center for Reproductive Law & Policy, Inc., provides a review of women's reproductive freedom in six countries around the world—Brazil, China, Germany, India, Nigeria, and the United States. Each country's pertinent laws and policies are discussed on a wide range of topics.

Cybergrrl Webstation

http://www.cybergrrl.com/cg.html

This site bills itself as the "First Stop on the Web" for women's resources. Includes articles, movie and book reviews, family information, and more. The server for this site also houses many other feminism-related sites.

Diotima: Women & Gender in the Ancient World

http://www.uky.edu/ArtsSciences/Classics/gender.html

This Web site is intended to serve as a resource for anyone interested in patterns of gender around the ancient Mediterranean and as a forum for collaboration among instructors who teach courses about women and gender in the ancient world. Includes research articles, course materials, a comprehensive bibliography, and more.

Encyclopedia of Women's History

http://www.teleport.com/~megaines/women.html

Part of a "K12-opedia," this site presents essays, stories, poetry, and so on about women in history researched and written by K–12 students worldwide. Instructions are given for adding your own (or your child's) work to the site. (Sorry, it is requested that submissions be in English.)

Electronic Access to Research on Women: A Short Guide, 2nd Edition

gopher://cscgoph2.ALBANY.EDU/00/.DEPTS/.WS/
WS%20Network%20Resources/%20%2a%20%2a%20Guide%20-
%20By%20Hudson%20and%20Turek%20%2a%20%2a

This Gopher document provides the full text of a guide to how to conduct research on women's issues on the Internet. A study from the University of Albany, the guide is also available in a printed edition.

Expect the Best from a Girl

http://www.academic.org/

This site prepared by the Women's College Coalition contains information about what parents and others can do to encourage girls in academic areas, particularly math and the sciences. Includes a listing of programs and institutes that can be contacted.

Feminism and Women's Resources

http://www.ibd.nrc.ca/~mansfield/feminism.html

A large collection of feminist and women's resources on the Internet.

Feminist Bookstores

http://www.igc.apc.org/women/bookstores/booknets.html

This page provides a comprehensive listing of women's bookstores in the U.S. and Canada arranged by state and province. Includes postal addresses and Internet links (if applicable).

Feminist Majority Online

http://www.feminist.org/

This site, subtitled Women's WebWorld, contains information on government actions for and against women, an online discussion group, publication information, and much more.

Feminist Science Fiction, Fantasy, & Utopia

http://www.uic.edu/~lauramd/sf/femsf.html

This site provides very detailed information on the page's title topic. An indexed bibliography, book reviews, and author biographies, as well as non-fiction information literary criticism, conferences, and much more. Also included is like information on related literary genres and links to related sites.

Feminist Studies in Aotearoa Electronic Journal (FMST)

http://www.massey.ac.nz/~wwwms/FMST/Info.html

FMST is produced by and for those interested in feminist theory, feminist perspectives in philosophy, and contemporary feminist debates, publications and research, and is operated out of Dunebin, New Zealand. Besides an index of issues and online articles, FMST also provides a service called FMST-TALK for service subscribers.

FEMINIST.COM

http://feminist.com/

Feminist.com is a site aimed at helping women network more effectively on the Internet. Includes the abridged text of articles and speeches, women's health resources, women-owned businesses, and more.

Gender Equity in Sports

http://www.arcade.uiowa.edu/proj/ge/

Gender Equity in Sports is designed to serve as a resource for any individual investigating the state of affairs in interscholastic or intercollegiate sport. This site provides detailed information on this research project conducted at the University of Iowa.

Global Fund for Women

http://www.igc.apc.org/gfw/

The Global Fund for Women is an international organization which focuses on female human rights. Includes information on supported programs, news articles, a FAQ sheet, and describes what you can do to help.

Guerrilla Girls

http://www.voyagerco.com/gg/gg.html

The Guerrilla Girls is a group of women artists and arts professionals who make posters about discrimination. They dub themselves as the "feminist counterparts to the mostly male tradition of anonymous do-gooders like Robin Hood, Batman, and the Lone Ranger." Available online is information on their cause, reactions to their work, and, of course, posters for sale.

Her Own Words®

http://netopia.com/herwords/

This Web site for Her Own Words® Women's History, Literature, & Art Videotapes gives company history, video reviews, an online newletter, and ordering information. The videos produced by this company all present primary-source, first-person accounts of women's history which are recommended for educational use.

InforM Women's Studies Database

http://inform.umd.edu:86/Educational_Resources/
AcademicResourcesByTopic/WomensStudies/

The women's studies database serves those people interested in the women's studies profession and in general women's issues. The searchable database contains collections of conference announcements, calls for papers, and employment opportunities, as well as a picture gallery, a significant number of government documents, and much more.

Internet Resources for Women's Legal and Public Policy Information

http://asa.ugl.lib.umich.edu/chdocs/womenpolicy/
womenlawpolicy.html

This guide at the University of Michigan is intended to assist individuals seeking information related to women's and feminist legal, public policy, and political issues. Included are Gopher, WWW, and ftp sites; as well as listservs and Usenet newsgroups. An ACSII version of the index is available for download, if you want a hardcopy of the URLs provided.

Isis

http://www.netdiva.com/isisplus.html

Isis is a World Wide Web page that features the art and culture of women of the African diaspora. Included on this Web site is information about movies, music, books, businesses, and the many other accompishments of black women.

Library Resources for Women's Studies

http://sunsite.unc.edu/cheryb/women/librcws.html

At the site title indicates, this page provides links to university and research center libraries across the U.S. that contain "useful or unique collections" related to women's studies. Includes Telnet, Gopher, FTP, and Web addresses.

Lifetime Online

http://www.lifetimetv.com/

This is the World Wide Web extension of Lifetime Television, the women's network. Provides not only information about Lifetime's television schedule and programs, but articles on health and fitness, parenting, sports, and more. Includes a searchable index of topics covered.

Linkages FOURTH WORLD CONFERENCE ON WOMEN site

http://www.iisd.ca/linkages/4wcw/

This site provides summary information about the Fourth World Conference on Women that was held in Beijing, China, during September of 1995; the first such conference in 10 years. Includes news articles, photographs, sound files, and more.

The Legal Rights of Women

http://www.electriciti.com/womenrts/

Legal Rights of Women is a legal reference text. This is the abridged version of the printed book; ordering information is provided if you like what you see. The purpose of this text is to bring to one source the legal principles most affecting the personal, business, family, and civil rights of women.

The National Organization for Women (NOW)

http://now.org:80/now/home.html

This home page for NOW offers press releases and articles, issues NOW is currently involved in, information on joining (with e-mail or Web addresses for many local chapters), and the history of NOW. Also provided is a search form if you're looking for a specific topic at NOW's site.

Resources for Feminist Research/ Documentation sur la recherche féministe (RFR/DRF)

http://www.oise.on.ca/rfr/

RFR/DRF is a bilingual (English/French) Canadian scholarly journal at the Ontario Institute for Studies in Education which addresses Canadian and international feminist research issues and debates. At this Web site you will find abstracts of current and back issues, calls for papers, and subscription information.

Spinsters Ink

http://www.lesbian.org:80/spinsters-ink/

Spinsters Ink publishes novels and non-fiction works that deal with significant issues in women's lives from a feminist perspective. Included on their Web site are book reviews, ordering information, and submission information.

The United Nations and the Status of Women

http://www.un.org/Conferences/Women/PubInfo/Status/Home.htm

This site from the United Nations provides information about what the UN has done during its 52-year history to further the status of women. Included are conference findings, general articles, and commission reports.

VOWworld: Voices of Women

http://www.voiceofwomen.com/VOWworld.html

This online women's group offers articles, an electronic newsletter, snail-mail magazine subscriptions, lists of women's conferences, links to women-owned businesses, and much more. As the site introduction states, "In these pages, real women are telling their stories, discussing issues, sharing hard-won wisdom."

WIDNET (Women In Development NETwork)

http://www.synapse.net/~focusint/

The WIDNET site presents information pertaining to women's resources throughout the Internet. Also includes the WIDNET magazine, a searchable resource database, business contacts, and much more. Available in English and French.

The Women & Politics Home Page

http://www.westga.edu/~wandp/w+p.html

Women & Politics is an academic journal published at West Georgia College in Carrollton, GA. The goal of the journal is to foster research and the development of theory on women's political participation, the role of women in society, and the impact of public policy upon women's lives. Included online are article abstracts, calls for papers, and subscription information.

Women Leaders Online (WLO)

http://worcester.lm.com/women/women.html

WLO is an organization dedicated to stopping the Radical Right/Contract With America agenda. This Web site contains information about Women Leaders Online and a variety of other women-related issues.

Women's Books Online

http://www.cybergrrl.com/review/

This site calls itself a cooperative book review, which means that it provides a place for women to post reviews of women's books available at women's bookstores. The only drawback is that submission instructions are not posted.

Women's History Month

http://socialstudies.com/mar/women.html

This Web site, part of the Social Studies School Service, provides teachers with several lessons, student exercises, and reviews of special materials that present exciting ways to bring women's history into their classrooms. Topics include Women in Wartime, American Women at Work, Ameila Earhart, and others.

The Women's Studies Reference Roadmap

http://women-www.uia.ac.be/women/roadmap/women/w0000000.html

This resource listing from the Universty of Antwerp, Belgium, contains links to women's studies Internet sites around Europe. Also contains a relatively complete directory of mailing lists and Usenet newsgroups talking about women's studies and feminism.

Women's Wire

http://www.women.com/

This online magazine includes sections on news and entertainment, career information, a question and answer area, links to women's businesses, and much more. There is an archive area for perusing back issues, and a guide to find just the subject you're looking for.

Toys

http://www.macromedia.com/Toys/index.html

Get free toys and software from Macromedia.

WomensNet@igc

`http://www.igc.apc.org/womensnet/`

WomensNet is a nonprofit computer network for women, activists, and organizations using computer networks for information sharing and increasing women's rights. WomensNet provides e-mail accounts, Internet access, WWW publishing, consulting, and training. Site contains WomensNet's online newsletter and descriptions of projects in which the group is currently involved.

WomenSpace

`http://www.womenspace.com/spring/index.html`

This is a quarterly online 'zine that discusses various women's issues. Includes a discussion area, a market square with promo items, relevant articles, an archive of past issues, and more.

The World's Women On-Line!

`http://wwol.inre.asu.edu/toc.html`

The World's Women On-Line! is an electronic art networking project that was begun in conjunction with the Fourth World Conference on Women in September, 1995. Here you will find online artwork from female artists around the world, along with the chance to upload your own image file.

Yale Journal of Law and Feminism

`http://www.yale.edu/lawnfem/law&fem.html`

The *Yale Journal of Law and Feminism* is committed to publishing pieces about women's experiences, especially as they have been structured, affected, controlled, discussed, or ignored by the law. This Web site contains subscription information, Telnet access to past issues, the chance to submit your own article, and even order a T-shirt.

Newsgroups

alt.archaeology

alt.fan.noam-chomsky

alt.feminism

alt.feminism.individualism

alt.psychology

alt.psychology.help

alt.psychology.jung

alt.psychology.nlp

alt.psychology.personality

alt.psychology.synchronicity

alt.psychology.transpersonal

alt.sci.sociology

bit.listserv.ioob-l

bit.listserv.geograph

bit.listserv.sportpsy

clari.news.women

fj.sci.psychology

humanities.answers

humanities.design.misc

humanities.language.sanskrit

humanities.misc

school.subjects.humanities

sci.anthropology

sci.anthropology.paleo

sci.archaeology

sci.archaeology.mesoamerican

sci.classics

sci.lang

sci.lang.translation

sci.psychology.announce

sci.psychology.consciousness

sci.psychology.journals.psyche

sci.psychology.journals.psycoloquy

sci.psychology.misc

sci.psychology.personality

sci.psychology.psychotherapy

sci.psychology.research

sci.psychology.theory

soc.culture

soc.culture.african

soc.culture.african.american

soc.culture.asian.american

soc.culture.esperanto

soc.women

thelinq.geography

Listservs

ABSLST-L—Association of Black Sociologists

Central Michigan University, Mt. Pleasant, MI

You can join this group by sending the message "sub ABSLST-L your name" to `listserv@cmuvm.csv.cmich.edu`

AGGRESS—Aggression-Psychology

St. John's University, Jamaica, New York

You can join this group by sending the message "sub AGGRESS your name" to `listserv@sjuvm.stjohns.edu`

ALT—The Association for Linguistic Typology

Texas A&M University Computing Services Center

You can join this group by sending the message "sub ALT your name" to `listserv@tamvm1.tamu.edu`

ANIMUS—Philosophy in the Third Millenium

Memorial University of Newfoundland, St. John's, Newfoundland, Canada

You can join this group by sending the message "sub ANIMUS your name" to `listserv@morgan.ucs.mun.ca`

ANTHRO-L—General Anthropology Bulletin Board

State University of New York at Buffalo

You can join this group by sending the message "sub ANTHRO-L your name" to `listserv@ubvm.cc.buffalo.edu`

APASD-L—APA Research Psychology Network

Virginia Tech

You can join this group by sending the message "sub APASD-L your name" to `listserv@vtvm1.cc.vt.edu`

ARCH-L—Archaeology List

Texas A&M University Computing Services Center

You can join this group by sending the message "sub ARCH-L your name" to `listserv@tamvm1.tamu.edu`

ARCHCOMP-L—Computational Archaeology

State University of New York at Buffalo

You can join this group by sending the message "sub ARCHCOMP-L your name" to `listserv@listserv.acsu.buffalo.edu`

ARCO—Arco/Art & Literature, Psychology and Communication

St. John's University, Jamaica, NY

You can join this group by sending the message "sub ARCO your name" to `listserv@sjuvm.stjohns.edu`

ASAONET—Oceanic Anthropology Discussion Group

University of Illinois at Chicago, Chicago, IL

You can join this group by sending the message "sub ASAONET your name" to `listserv@listserv.uic.edu`

ASASCAN—Computers and Sociology

Temple University, Philadelphia, PA

You can join this group by sending the message "sub ASASCAN your name" to `listserv@vm.temple.edu`

ASPSYCH—Applied Social Psychology Discussion Group

The George Washington University Computer Center, Washington, DC

You can join this group by sending the message "sub ASPSYCH your name" to `listserv@gwuvm.gwu.edu`

ASSESS-P—Psychological Assessment-Psychometrics Discussion

St. John's University, Jamaica, NY

You can join this group by sending the message "sub ASSESS-P your name" to `listserv@sjuvm.stjohns.edu`

C-PSYCH—Cross-Cultural Psychology Discussion List

St. John's University, Jamaica, NY

You can join this group by sending the message "sub C-PSYCH your name" to `listserv@sjuvm.stjohns.edu`

CAPSYCH—CAPsych Child-Psych

St. John's University, Jamaica, NY

You can join this group by sending the message "sub CAPSYCH your name" to `listserv@sjuvm.stjohns.edu`

CLINICAL-PSYCHOLOGISTS—Clinical Psychologists

You can join this group by sending the message "sub CLINICAL-PSYCHOLOGISTS your name" to `listserv@listserv.nodak.edu`

COMPSYCH—Community Psychology Listserv

Michigan State University, East Lansing, MI

You can join this group by sending the message "sub COMPSYCH your name" to `listserv@msu.edu`

COUNPSY—Counseling Psychology Practice and Science

The University of Georgia, Athens, GA

You can join this group by sending the message "sub COUNPSY your name" to `listserv@uga.cc.uga.edu`

E-SAE—Society for Anthropology of Europe Editorial Board List

University of Illinois at Chicago, Chicago, IL

You can join this group by sending the message "sub E-SAE your name" to `listserv@uicvm.uic.edu`

FORENPSY—Forenpsy Forensic Psychology

St. John's University, Jamaica, NY

You can join this group by sending the message "sub FORENPSY your name" to `listserv@sjuvm.stjohns.edu`

FUNKNET—Discussion of Issues in Functional Linguistics

Rice University Information Systems, Houston, TX

You can join this group by sending the message "sub FUNKNET your name" to `listserv@ricevm1.rice.edu`

GEOGED—Geography Education List

You can join this group by sending the message "sub GEOGED your name" to `listserv@lsv.uky.edu`

H-SAE—An H-Net List for the Society for Anthropology of Europe

Michigan State University, East Lansing, MI

You can join this group by sending the message "sub H-SAE your name" to `listserv@msu.edu`

IAPSY-L—Interamerican Psychologists List (SIPNET)

You can join this group by sending the message "sub IAPSY-L your name" to `listserv%albnyvm1.bitnet@listserv.net`

IFPE—Psychoanalysis and Education

You can join this group by sending the message "sub IFPE your name" to `listserv@listserv.kent.edu`

IOOB-L—Industrial Psychology

The University of Georgia, Athens, GA

You can join this group by sending the message "sub IOOB-L your name" to `listserv@uga.cc.uga.edu`

IOPSYCH—Industrial/Organizational Psychology Discussion Group

The George Washington University Computer Center, Washington, DC

You can join this group by sending the message "sub IOPSYCH your name" to `listserv@gwuvm.gwu.edu`

JWA—The Journal of World Anthropology

State University of New York at Buffalo

You can join this group by sending the message "sub JWA your name" to `listserv@ubvm.cc.buffalo.edu`

LEFTGEOG—Socialist/Radical Geography

You can join this group by sending the message "sub LEFTGEOG your name" to `listserv@lsv.uky.edu`

LINGUIST—The LINGUIST Discussion List

Texas A&M University Computing Services Center

You can join this group by sending the message "sub LINGUIST your name" to `listserv@tamvm1.tamu.edu`

LITHICS-L—The Archaeological Lithic Analysis Discussion List

State University of New York at Buffalo

You can join this group by sending the message "sub LITHICS-L your name" to `listserv@listserv.acsu.buffalo.edu`

MATHSOC—Mathematical Sociology Discussion Group

Dartmouth College, Hanover, NH

You can join this group by sending the message "sub MATHSOC your name" to `listserv@listserv.dartmouth.edu`

PAN-L—Physical Anthropology News List

Portland State University, Portland, OR

You can join this group by sending the message "sub PAN-L your name" to `listserv@freya.cc.pdx.edu`

PHILOS-L—Paleoanthropological & Biological Basis of Ethics & Aesthetics

West Virginia Network for Educational Telecomputing

You can join this group by sending the message "sub PHILOS-L your name" to `listserv@wvnvm.wvnet.edu`

PSA-ED—Psychoanalysis and Education Discussion Network

You can join this group by sending the message "sub PSA-ED your name" to `listserv@listserv.kent.edu`

PSI-L—Parapsychology Discussion Forum

Rensselaer Polytechnic Institute, Troy, NY

You can join this group by sending the message "sub PSI-L your name" to `listserv@vm.its.rpi.edu`

PSY-LANG—Language and Psychopathology Discussion

St. John's University, Jamaica, NY

You can join this group by sending the message "sub PSY-LANG your name" to `listserv@sjuvm.stjohns.edu`

PSYART—Institute for Psychological Study of the Arts

NE Regional Data Center, Univ. of Florida campus, Gainesville, FL

You can join this group by sending the message "sub PSYART your name" to `listserv@nervm.nerdc.ufl.edu`

PSYADMIN—Psych-Admin Psychiatry Administration

St. John's University, Jamaica, NY

You can join this group by sending the message "sub PSYADMIN your name" to
listserv@sjuvm.stjohns.edu

PSYCH-CI—List Name PSYCH-CI - Current Issues in Psychology and Psychiatry

St. John's University, Jamaica, NY

You can join this group by sending the message "sub PSYCH-CI your name" to
listserv@sjuvm.stjohns.edu

PSYCH-DD—Developmental Disabilities

You can join this group by sending the message "sub PSYCH-DD your name" to
listserv@listserv.nodak.edu

PSYCHL—PSYCHL Psychiatry

Country: USA

St. John's University, Jamaica, NY

You can join this group by sending the message "sub PSYCHL your name" to
listserv@sjuvm.stjohns.edu

PSYCHAT—PsyUSA Network - Collegial Chat

St. John's University, Jamaica, NY

You can join this group by sending the message "sub PSYCHAT your name" to
listserv@sjuvm.stjohns.edu

PSYCHNEWS—PsychNews International

You can join this group by sending the message "sub PSYCHNEWS your name" to
listserv@listserv.nodak.edu

PSYCHOAN—Psychoanalysis

St. John's University, Jamaica, NY

You can join this group by sending the message "sub PSYCHOAN your name" to
listserv@sjuvm.stjohns.edu

PSYCHOLOGICAL-TYPE—Psychological-Type Discussion List

Virginia Tech

You can join this group by sending the message "sub PSYCHOLOGICAL-TYPE your name" to
listserv@listserv.vt.edu

PSYMEA-L—Developmental Psychology

State University of New York at Buffalo

You can join this group by sending the message "sub PSYMEA-L your name" to
listserv@listserv.acsu.buffalo.edu

PSYSTS-L—Psychology Statistics Discussion

University of Missouri-Columbia, Columbia, MO

You can join this group by sending the message "sub PSYSTS-L your name" to
listserv@mizzou1.missouri.edu

RADANTH-L—Radical Anthropologists List

The American University, Washington, DC

You can join this group by sending the message "sub RADANTH-L your name" to
listserv@american.edu

RES-GARD—Research & Educational Gardens—Urban & Socio-Horticulture

Texas A&M University Computing Services Center

You can join this group by sending the message "sub RES-GARD your name" to
listserv@tamvm1.tamu.edu

RURSOC-L—Rural Sociology Discussion List

You can join this group by sending the message "sub RURSOC-L your name" to
listserv@lsv.uky.edu

SANALST—Study of North American Anthropology Discussion

Temple University, Philadelphia, PA

You can join this group by sending the message "sub SANALST your name" to
`listserv@vm.temple.edu`

SLLING-L—Sign Language Linguistics List

Yale University Computer Center; New Haven, CT

You can join this group by sending the message "sub SLLING-L your name" to
`listserv@yalevm.cis.yale.edu`

SOCTALK—Sociology Discussion List

University of Missouri-St. Louis

You can join this group by sending the message "sub SOCTALK your name" to
`listserv@umslvma.umsl.edu`

SPIRAMED—Spiramed Spiritual Implications for Medicine and Psychology

St. John's University, Jamaica, NY

You can join this group by sending the message "sub SPIRAMED your name" to
`listserv@sjuvm.stjohns.edu`

SPORTPSY—Exercise and Sports Psychology

Temple University, Philadelphia, PA

You can join this group by sending the message "sub SPORTPSY your name" to
`listserv@vm.temple.edu`

SPORTSOC—Sociological Aspects of Sports Discussion

Temple University, Philadelphia, PA

You can join this group by sending the message "sub SPORTSOC your name" to
`listserv@vm.temple.edu`

SUB-ARCH—Underwater Archaeology Discussion List

Arizona State University, Tempe, AZ

You can join this group by sending the message "sub SUB-ARCH your name" to
`listserv@asuvm.inre.asu.edu`

SWIP-L—Society for Women in Philosophy Information and Discussion List

University of South Florida, Tampa, FL

You can join this group by sending the message "sub SWIP-L your name" to
`listserv@cfrvm.cfr.usf.edu`

TRANSCULTURAL-PSYCHOLOGY

You can join this group by sending the message "sub TRANSCULTURAL-PSYCHOLOGY your name" to `listserv@listserv.nodak.edu`

WMST-L—Women's Studies List

University of Maryland CSC, College Park, MD

You can join this group by sending the message "sub WMST-L your name" to
`listserv%umdd.bitnet@listserv.net`

WISE-L—European Women's Studies

FUNET (CSC/Finnish University and research NETwork), Espoo, Finland

You can join this group by sending the message "sub WISE-L your name" to
`listserv@fiport.funet.fi`

WSCC-L—Women's Studies Curriculum Committee

You can join this group by sending the message "sub WSCC-L your name" to
`listserv@listserv.kent.edu`

WSCD—Women's Studies Collection Development List

Massachusetts Institute of Technology, Cambridge, MA

You can join this group by sending the message "sub WSCD your name" to `listserv@mitvma.mit.edu`

URBGEOG—Urban Geography

University of Arizona, Tucson, AZ

You can join this group by sending the message "sub URBGEOG your name" to
`listserv@listserv.arizona.edu`

Access Providers

Charm Net Personal IP Page

http://www.charm.net/pip.html

Provides information on how to connect your computer directly to the Internet. It leans toward PPP and MS-Windows, but includes information for users of Macs, Windows, Windows NT, and OS/2.

CyberSight

http://cybersight.com/cgi-bin/cs/s?main.gmml

The information hotline for online hipsters. It also just happens to be a service provider and consultant to some of the largest corporations in the world, including Visa, Pepsi, and K2 Sports.

EFF's (Extended) Guide to the Internet

http://www.eff.org/papers/bdgtti/eegtti.html

Features a list of Internet providers, organized by state, and describes e-mail, Usenet groups, ftp, Telnet, and BBS.

Enterprise Internet Services

http://www.enterprise.net

Acts as a major provider of Internet Services, based on the Isle of Man, British Isles. It also specializes in providing Web-based applications that utilize a secure Netscape Commerce Server. Offers a diverse and extensive Web server for all applications.

Fountainhead Internet Systems

http://www.fountainhead.com/

A full-service Internet presence provider based in Los Angeles. Provides Internet hookups, consulting, Web page design, and training. Also publishes the Los Angeles Superstation.

Fusion Advertising and Communications

http://usa.net/fusion/

A link from the www.usa.net page, an internet service provider based in Colorado Springs. Provides links to transfer rate information on the usa.net page. Not of interest to the average Internet surfer.

GeoCities

http://www.geocities.com/

Award-winning Internet presence provider based in Beverly Hills, California. Contains hundreds of free home pages, organized into neighborhoods reflecting various sites, such as Wall Street or Hollywood. Presents a thriving community, including live video feeds from all over, as well as the freshest hot lists.

GHG Corp

http://www.ghgcorp.com/ghg/InternetServices/

A Houston company offering computer training and consulting services such as Web page development for businesses. Provides links to business home pages and newsgroups of interest.

GTLug ISP Index

http://www.gtlug.org/isp/

Lists Internet Service Providers. Helps you you find ISPs by entering an area code or by clicking on a map of the United States. A new feature critiques providers.

How To Select an Internet Service Provider

http://web.cnam.fr/Network/Internet-access/how_to_select.html

Describes what you should look for when you set out to purchase an Internet connection. Includes information on network topology, network link speeds, technical staff, and more.

I-2000

http://i-2000.com/

An access provider for the east coast. Includes links for connection information, services, server residents, and tech support.

Icanect

http://www.icanect.net/~sunny/

Provides Internet consulting to get you connected with a service provider and up and running on the Internet. Provides downloads of Web and Internet software, along with contests, giveaways, and much more.

ICNet: The Original Internet Provider for the Eastern Shore

http://www.intercom.net/

This provider for the eastern U. S. provides links to Internet and computer classes, computer resellers, search engines, local weather, news, and entertainment.

Imagine.com

`http://www.imagine.com/`

A service provider in Hartford, Connecticut, connecting individuals, businesses, government, and educational institutions to the Web. Offers Web site development, links to Imagine.com offerings (Web servers and firewalls), user's pages, and other creative services.

Industrial Peer-to-Peer

`http://www.callamer.com/~pfahey/`

Based in California, a network integration product and service provider for your organization. Includes links to products and services, management profiles, clients, and contact info.

InReach

`http://www.inreach.com/`

An internet access provider for the Northern California area. Provides connection and service information as well as local job openings, news, and related sites.

Inspiration Software

`http://www.rdrop.com/`

Dial-up access for those in the Portland, Oregon area. Includes links to search engines, software to download, html info, movies, and other interesting Web sites.

InstaNet (Instant Internet Corp.)

`http://www.instanet.com/`

Dial-up access for the Los Angeles area. Provides links to local business, traffic info, other users' pages, how to write in HTML, and more.

Infonet

`http://www.infonet.net/`

A service provider that also presents information on navigation aids and search utilities, help files and FAQs, and other Internet services.

Internet Access Phoenix Arizona

`http://neta.com/`

An access provider of Phoenix, Arizona, with links to information and renting Web space, business and personal home pages, Internet shopping, search engines, interesting sites, and more. Features new sites often.

Internet Application Services, Inc.

`http://www.mindspring.com/~netserve/`

Internet Service provider for the Atlanta, Georgia area.

Internet Channel

`http://www.inch.com/`

New York City-based Internet service provider. Links to services, accounts, clients, and the home page creator.

Internet Delaware

`http://www.delnet.com/`

Internet access and Web publishing for individuals and businesses. A cool site with many, many links to search tools, software, Web sites, government info, products, and more.

Internet Direct

`http://idirect.com/welcome.html`

Internet access for the novice Internet user. Includes links to lots of free stuff online. Other links to membership options, products and prices, and more.

Internet Express, Inc.

`http://www.inxpress.net/`

An access provider based in Madison, Wisconsin, with many links to services, subscriptions and rates, news access, global and local links, search engines, business and personal pages, and new user info.

Internet Front

`http://www.internetfront.com/`

An Internet service provider for businesses. Includes links to images, movies, software, other products, and more.

Intergate

`http://www.intergate.net/`

A full-service network provider for everything from e-mail to dedicated lines for corporations. A complete listing of products, services, and pricing is available.

Internet Interface Systems

`http://www.webnet.com.au/`

An Internet access provider for businesses and individuals in Australia. A really cool interactive site with links to search engines, clients, games, newsgroups, and much more.

Internet Light and Power

http://www.ilap.com/

A Canadian-based Internet access provider for individuals and businesses in North America. Includes links to client services, search tools, cool sites, and more.

Internet MainStreet

http://www.mainstreet.net/

A full-service internet provider for your business. Based in California, it provides links to other Web pages on its server.

Internet North

http://www.internorth.com/

An Internet service provider for Northern Canada. Includes links to Northern Canada's Net Index, local weather info, user's home pages, and more.

Internet On-Ramp, Inc.

http://www.ior.com/

A full-service Internet service provider based in Spokane, Washington. Includes links to support, Web info, businesses, members, Alta Vista search engine, and more.

Internet Services Montana

http://www.ism.net/index.html

A full-service Internet provider based in Montana. Provides links to user pages, cool sites, businesses, Web searches, support, and more.

InterServe Communications

http://www.interserve.com/

Low cost, high baud rate Internet access for individuals or businesses. Includes links to clients' pages, services and prices, and company info.

IntrepidNet

http://www.intrepid.net/

Internet access for individuals or businesses in eastern West Virginia and Washington County, Maryland. Provides access to businesses on the Internet, services, support, local sites, and more.

ISDN Internet Access

http://www.nettechsys.com/

A full-service Internet provider in the San Francisco Bay area with links to and information on Internet connectivity, the Web, support, products and services, and more.

LavaNet, Inc.

http://www.lava.net/

Honolulu's Internet connection. Includes links to tech support, service and rates, clients' Web pages, the Hawaii home page, and more.

LI.Net

http://www.li.net/

The Internet service provider for the Long Island area. Includes links to resources, news, service, local living, and more.

Linkage Online

http://www.hk.linkage.net/

An Internet service provider for all your business needs and the largest service provider in Asia. Find out about what it offers, businesses online, free classifieds, and more.

Magnetic Page

http://www.magpage.com/

An Internet service provider for areas of Delaware and Pennsylvania. Provides links to its corporate user pages, other user pages, subscriber services, Web searchers, and more cool stuff.

MapleNet Technologies, Inc.

http://www.maple.net/maple.html

Interhop Network Services, Inc., is now the owner of MapleNet's system. Interhop is an Internet service provider offering residential, Webmaster, and business packages for moderate prices.

Medius Communications, Inc.

http://www.medius.com

Medius Communications, Inc., provides corporate Internet access and presence services, enabling organizations to plan, build, implement, and promote complete online information and application services.

Michigan Internet Cooperative Association

http://www.mica.net/

A full-service Internet service provider for businesses, offering high-bandwidth/low-cost connectivity. Check out its product announcements, its press releases, the Business Solutions Group, and more.

Micron Internet Services

http://www.micron.net/

A full-service Internet provider with links to subscriber information and access, tech support, Micron products and services, and Web search tools.

MJC Inc. Computer Services

http://www.holonet.net/mjc/

A full-service Internet provider with on-site service or remote service call capability. Call and answer a few simple questions to get a 30-day trial membership.

Minnesota MicroNet

http://www.mm.com/

An Internet service provider for the Minneapolis/ St. Paul, Minnesota area. Includes links to business directories, community pages, customer support, and services.

Minnesota Regional Network (MRNet)

http://www.mr.net/MRNet.html

The most experienced Internet service provider located in Minnesota. Includes links to services, members, and resources.

MonadNet

http://www.monad.net/

An Internet service provider for individuals or organizations in the Monadnock area of New Hampshire. Includes links to how to get started, services and tech support, and frequently asked questions.

Mojoski Net Tools

http://www.mojoski.com/nettools.html

A group of experienced Internet professionals who provide Internet access to the world. Offers Finger and Archie, with more tools on the way.

Moran Communications Group

http://www.moran.com/

An Internet access provider offering myriad services, including Web services and connections, training, programming, networking, hardware and software. Also, two cool links to a movie database and to an Internet card creator. Send a virtual greeting card to anyone with an e-mail address.

Mountain Internet

http://www.mountain-inter.net/

An Internet service provider for areas in British Columbia, Canada. In addition to links to member services, it includes links to summer camps for kids, flight instruction classes, logger sports, auto racing, real estate, magazines, and other sites of local interest.

Nantucket.Net

http://www.nantucket.net/NN/

The Internet service provider for Nantucket Island. All the information you need to get started, including access info and pricing.

National Knowledge Networks, Inc.

http://www.nkn.edu/

The Internet service provider for North Texas, with links to Web info, services, news, and ideas.

NetAccess Worldwide List

http://www.best.be/iap.html

Offers a list of Internet access providers from every continent in the world.

NetAxis

http://www.netaxis.qc.ca/

An Internet access provider based in Montreal, with links including local sites and businesses, search engines, local and community events and culture, and health sites, as well as links to sister sites.

NETCOM Online Communications Services, Inc.

http://www.netcom.com

Contains information about Netcom, the nation's largest Internet provider. Offers local access numbers online for subscribers on the go. Subscription information is also available online.

NetDepot

`http://www.netdepot.com/`

Internet access and services for individuals. Provides information about using and navigating the Internet, skills, and fun places to go.

NETHEAD

`http://www.nethead.co.uk/`

An Internet service provider for most of the United Kingdom. Offers Web publishing and consulting services to clients.

NetPoint Communications, Inc.

`http://www.netpoint.net/`

An international Internet service provider based in Miami, Florida, for individuals and corporations. Internet consulting provided in both English and Spanish. Provides access to a long list of interesting sites.

NetPress Communications

`http://www.netpress.com/`

NetPress Communications provides links to the following home pages: Collabra Software, Institute for Management Studies, Lithocraft, Inc., the Law Office of Kirsten Keith, and Bay Rep, Inc.

NetReach

`http://www.reach.net/`

An Internet service provider for the Quinte region located in Canada. Includes links to products and services, community and school information, Web sites, and resources.

Netropolis

`http://www.dash.com/`

A local Internet service provider for the Denver, Colorado area. Includes many links to art, business, education, government, entertainment, shopping, news, weather, and other sites.

Netside Network

`http://www.netside.com/index.html`

Internet access, computer sales, and networking for the Southeast U.S., with links to search engines, software sites, news and weather, user pages, advertising, and subscribing information.

NETWave Internet Access Provider

`http://maui.netwave.net/info.html`

The Internet service provider for the Chicagoland area. Includes many links to art, business, education, entertainment, government, kids, local news, and weather sites; info; members' home pages; *Chicago Tribune*; search engines and subscription information; and much more.

Northwest Link

`http://nwlink.com/`

An Internet service provider for the Seattle, Washington area, with links to local news and weather, personal pages, new sites, rates, and service information.

Novagate

`http://www.novagate.com`

West Michigan's Internet service provider, with gateway information, services and pricing, yellow pages, local city information, and more.

Valiquet Lamothe, Inc.

`http://www.vli.ca`

Offers access to the Internet and provides information on links to French and English sites. Also provides information on tourism and levels of government.

Browsers & Interfaces

About Web/Genera

`http://gdbdoc.gdb.org/letovsky/genera/genera.html`

Offers Web/Genera, a software package that uses Mosaic 2.4 to integrate Sybase databases into the Web. Offers downloadable alpha-mode (pretest) software.

Cyberspace Connection

`http://www.main.com/~kirton/index.html`

Offers a variety of resources, from search engines to personal and commercial Web links. Provides "your jumppoint to Cyberspace."

Easy Mosaic and Introductory Web Surfing

http://www.lm.com/~lmann/docs/easymosaic.html

Serves as a basic primer on using the Mosaic Web browser. Provides a history of how information was disseminated before the Web.

Global Network Navigator Home Page

http://gnn.com/gnn/index.html

Presents GNN, the creators of the Web browser Mosaic. Provides information on Mosaic and GNN's Internet access service. Includes its Whole Internet Catalog and offers perusable online publications on virtually every topic.

Hill Holliday Advertising

http://www.hhcc.com/

A site that provides links to download Shockwave, Java, and Netscape. Other than that, all links return the user to this page.

Internet Group/Internet Business Center

http://home.tig.com/cgi-bin/genobject/index

A Web and Internet resource and home page provider. Offers Manage! IT, a browsing tool.

Chats, Messaging, & Conferences

Internet Conference Calendar

http://www.automatrix.com/conferences/

Lists upcoming conferences, symposia, and workshops related to the Internet. Lets you use the submission form to add your own events to the calendar. Also lets you list upcoming events geographically. Provides links to separate pages for each event listed, if available.

Internet Relay Chat Games

http://calypso.cs.uregina.ca/Games/

Offers information and history on the most popular games played on the IRC network. Offers information on Risky Business, Chaos, Boggle, and Acrophobia.

IRC Galley

http://www.powertech.no/IRCGallery/

A place where people using IRC can put up images of themselves. Allows you to search by country or name.

IRC Poker Channels Home Page

http://maelstrom.cc.mcgill.ca/poker/poker.html

Offers everything you need to know to play IRC poker. Lets you play poker with people anywhere in the world in real time.

MeGALiTH's Sensational Visual IRC Beta Home Page

http://apollo3.com/~acable/virc.html

Visual IRC is the first of a "new generation" of IRC clients for Windows, incorporating state-of-the-art file transfer, audio, and advanced IRC features. Features channel surf and other great features. Grab the latest beta from this page.

Quarterdeck Global Chat

http://www.qdeck.com/chat/

Formerly owned by Prospero. Focuses on adding live interaction to the Web. Allows you to download the software for free, and also offers discussion areas.

TeamWARE AB

http://www.pro.icl.se

A Swedish company that provides the Internet e-mail and Web product EMBLA.

World Wide Web Consortium

http://www.w3.org/pub/WWW

Offers information about the upcoming WWW International Conference. Also contains a wealth of information on various Web issues, such as security, HTTP, and graphics standards.

Worlds Chat

http://www.worlds.net/wc/

Provides a 3D multiuser chatting system. Allows you to use images and sound while you chat with others, interacting *through* your computer instead of with it.

Cyberspace Issues

BBN on the World Wide Web

http://www.bbn.com/home.html

An online version of *BBN* magazine. Offers an Internet tutorial, an Internet timeline, the BBN Planet, press releases, and job postings.

Blacklist of Internet Advertisers

http://math-www.uni-paderborn.de/~axel/BL/blacklist.html

One of several blacklists targeting Internet advertisers who violate "netiquette" when hawking their wares. Provides more information on the issue and advice on what to do to avoid getting blacklisted when you advertise on the Internet.

c|net: the computer network

http://www.cnet.com/

c|net: the computer network, creators of c|net online and the television series c|net central, is an on-air and online interactive showcase for computers, multimedia, and digital technologies.

Censorship and the Internet

http://dis.strath.ac.uk/people/paul/Control.html

Offers a growing collection of links about censorship and associated issues on the Internet. Provides resources on the legal and ethical issues of running a Web service.

Cybertown

http://www.cybertown.com/cybertown

Presents an off-world 21st-century town with spectacular graphics that load quickly. Offers many areas to explore, including the Spaceport, the Time Machine, and the mysterious Cyberhood.

EFFweb—The Electronic Frontier Foundation

http://www.eff.org/

A nonprofit civil liberties organization working in the public interest to protect privacy, free expression, and access to online resources and information. Includes many online resources and references. Contains its publication *EFFector Online*.

Executive Guide to Marketing on the New Internet

http://www.industry.net/guide.html

An online paper that focuses on the effects of the Internet on business. Talks about the changing role between the Internet and the marketing executive and speculates on the future on the Internet.

Hermes Project

http://www.umich.edu/~sgupta/hermes

Presents an ongoing research project that is trying to determine the commercial uses of the Web. Offers an online consumer survey for people on the Web.

Information Economy

http://www.sims.berkeley.edu/resources/infoecon/

Formerly called Economics and the Internet, this site provides a collection of documents related to information goods, intellectual property, and related issues. Includes high-resolution slides.

Internet Companion

http://www.obs-us.com/obs/english/books/editinc/obsxxx.htm

An online version of *Internet Companion: A Beginner's Guide to Global Networking, 2nd Edition*. Provides book reviews and answers such questions as "Who runs the Internet?"

Internet Society

http://www.isoc.org/

The closest thing to a governing organization to be found on the Net. Offers information services, ISOC chapter data, conferences and papers, and Internet standards.

Mapping the Internet

http://www.uvc.com/gbell/promo.html

Presents Gordon Bell, one of the pioneers of the Internet, discussing his views on the direction in which the Internet should now proceed. Discusses his proposal for ending the problems with limited bandwith and the increased traffic on the Internet. Includes a slide show and sound bites with the presentation.

Netscape: J.P. Morgan's Equities Research

http://www.jpmorgan.com/MarketDataInd/Research/
WebReport/TOC.html

A rather large report by J.P. Morgan & Associates on the impact the World Wide Web has and will continue to have on business. Includes useful tables and appendices.

NetWatchers Legal Cyberzine

http://www.ionet.net/~mdyer/netwatch.shtml

A monthly e-zine that reports on legal developments in cyberspace and the online world.

SurfWatch Home Page

http://www.surfwatch.com/

Presents SurfWatch, a program for reducing the risk of children uncovering sexually explicit material on the Internet.

What's New in Japan

http://www.ntt.jp/WHATSNEW/index.html

Provides information on recent happenings or recent changes on the Web in Japan. Offers a Japanese language version of the site.

Educational & Tutorial Listings

Beginner's Guide to Effective E-mail

http://www.webfoot.com/advice/email.top.html?Yahoo

Talks about the ways to express intonation and gestures thru e-mail. Gives information on page layouts and the format of e-mail as well.

Center for the Application of Information Technology

http://www.cait.wustl.edu/cait/

A consortium whose mission is "to be a center of learning in the field of information management and to provide our member companies with world-class educational and leadership programs."

FutureNet

http://www.futurenet.co.uk/netmag/Issue1/Easy/index.html

Europe's leading electronic magazine. Serves as a complete in-depth Internet beginner's guide. Provides information on how to hook up your machine, how to use information to your advantage, and more. Also provides a history of the Internet.

Gestalt Systems, Inc.

http://www.gestalt-sys.com/

Provides links to computer training classes, courseware, educational support, and information for downloading its training software.

Global Institute for Interactive Multimedia

http://www.thegiim.org/

Provides information and guides for teaching people how to create a home page. Divides the information according to the audience; for example, provides a different tutorial for teachers than for business owners.

Glossary of Internet Terms

http://www.matisse.net/files/glossary.html

Lists and defines Internet and computer-related terms and acronyms.

Hideki's Home Page: How To Use Japanese on Internet

http://www.jweb.com/~hirayama/

Offers many links to Japanese resources, including information on Netscape's Japanese Capable WWW Browser. Also provides many links on Japan.

How To Search a WAIS Database

http://town.hall.org/util/wais_help.html

Provides information on how to begin and structure a Wide Area Internet Server search. Describes how to use Boolean operators, wild cards, relevance ranking, and so on. Offers a tutorial on using a WAIS search engine.

ICC Seminar Series

http://www.icons.com/seminar.html

Provides for businesses information concerning security, firewalls, and server design and implementation.

INFO Online

http://www.pona.com

Focuses on "Information Networking For Oncologists," and specifically provides information for physicians dealing with networks, integration, and pharmaceutical companies. Also offers information for people involved with oncology, including patients.

INFOMINE

`http://lib-www.ucr.edu/`

An online library at the University of California-Riverside. Aims to make resources available to UCR students and staff, but is open to the public. Offers many online card catalogs and articles.

Information Management Group

`http://www.imginfo.com/`

A Windows development and Internet educational and consulting firm offering university courses, consulting, and tips and tricks for developers. Provides links to services and classes offered.

Information Resources

`http://www.si.umich.edu/hp/Websites.html`

Although focusing primarily on the University of Michigan School of Information, also offers links to a variety of Internet resources.

Inter-Links

`http://www.nova.edu/Inter-Links/start.html`

A site for browsing the Internet and locating specific resources. Features Internet resources, guides and tutorials, news and weather, library resources, fun and games, a reference shelf, and a miscellaneous section. Includes several original search engines as well. Millions of visitors can't be wrong.

Internet Learning Center

`http://oeonline.com/~emoryd`

Offers tutorial columns and "where to go" columns. Also includes links to the Unix Reference Center, the Hyptertext Guide, Rinaldi's Netiquette, Odd de Presno's Online World book, and other Internet resources. Past columns are archived.

Internet Web Text

`http://www.december.com/web/text/index.html`

A hypertext guide to the Internet, written by Net guru John December. Begins with Internet orientation and clicks through all the major Internet tools. Highly recommended.

Introduction to the Internet II

`http://uu-gna.mit.edu:8001/uu-gna/text/internet/index.html`

One of several prototype classes and texts sponsored through the Globewide Network Academy. Introduces the user to various resources available via the Internet, with particular emphasis on allowing a neophyte to access GNA services as quickly as possible.

Kids on Campus (Cornell Theory Center)

`http://www.tc.cornell.edu/Kids.on.Campus`

The Cornell Theory Center sponsors Kids On Campus as part of its celebration of National Science and Technology Week. The purpose of this event is to increase computer awareness and scientific interest among Ithaca, New York-area third, fourth, and fifth grade students. Hands-on computer activities, innovative videos, and exciting demonstrations help the children develop interest and excitement in computers and science.

Learning Edge Corp.

`http://www.io.org/~tle/`

Offers products and services to the private and public sectors, including courseware and training, animation, videos, interfaces, and more. Contains links to clients, services, portfolio, and more.

Library Solutions Institute and Press

`http://www.internet-is.com/library/`

Internet training information and seminars for both students and trainers. Self-paced tutorials including HTML tutorial, K-12 resources, publications, and more.

Magnett Internet Gateway

`http://www.magnet.ca/`

Links to various Internet browsers and gateways such as software archives, helper applications, Netscape questions and answers, and customer service for subscribers of Magnett Internet Gateway.

Management Concepts, Inc.

`http://www.MgmtConcepts.com/`

A corporation providing training in personal property management, property leasing, grants management, and computer and financial applications. Provides access to new courses and special events, publications, and links to other sites of related interest.

MicroMedium, Inc.

`http://www.micromedium.com/`

Check out MicroMedium's Digital Trainer Professional® multimedia computer-based training software for your organization. Already in use by AT&T, MCI, Long John Silver's, and others. Includes links to product reviews, demos, tech support, the MicroMedium training library, and ordering information.

Multimedia Help Page

`http://www.sdcs.k12.ca.us/people/schumsky/greg.html`

Provides quick access to sources of multimedia tools and tips on the Web. Also provides links and tips for video production, search engines, and production tools for the Apple Newton.

Net Guru Technologies, Inc.

`http://www.ngt.com/`

On-site training and consulting by certified Webmasters. Some courses include these topics: Webmaster specialists, security and firewalls, Unix, networking, TCP/IP, and more. If you register online, you will receive a rebate!

Net: User Guidelines and Netiquette, by Arlene Rinaldi

`http://www.fau.edu/rinaldi/net/index.html`

Offers a collection of Internet user guidelines and netiquette. Discusses legal and ethical issues involved.

Netscape Tutorial

`http://w3.ag.uiuc.edu/AIM/Discovery/Net/www/netscape/index.html`

Gives a step-by-step tutorial on using Netscape—it can be very in-depth. Allows for different levels of expertise.

Online World Resources Handbook

`http://login.eunet.no/~presno/`

Provides practical advice on using the Internet to get information or programs. Breaks topics down into various topics, such as how to get free expert assistance, how to read your electronic daily news, and more.

Patrick Crispen's Internet Roadmap

`http://www.brandonu.ca/~ennsnr/Resources/Roadmap/Welcome.html`

This is the Internet Roadmap online training course, available in HTML. This is a well-written tutorial and is very user-friendly. A must for any Internet coordinator's bookmark list!

Setting Up Shop on the Internet

`http://www.netrex.com/business.html`

Provides information regarding commercial-use strategies, including dos and don'ts of online marketing.

Surfin' the Net

`http://www.shore.net/~adfx/video`

Introduces the Internet via a video made "with two real people." Ideal for beginners, skeptics, or the perpetual questioner.

Teach Yourself the Internet Support Page

`http://randall.uwaterloo.ca/tyi.htm`

Provides a structured tutorial to teaching yourself how to use the Internet and all of its tools in 21 days. Targets beginners, but serves as a good tutorial for all. Spends one week teaching the basic Internet tools, then focuses on personal and professional uses of the Internet.

UK Index Beginner's Guide: the Net

`http://www.ukindex.co.uk/begin0.html`

Serves as a beginners guide to using the Internet, and includes pointers to more resources.

Web Weavers: Tools for Aspiring Web Authors

Provides a comprehensive listing of Web tools and techniques, including a sample page and search engine.

Winsock Connections

`http://omni.cc.purdue.edu/~xniu/winsock.htm`

Explains both the hardware and software issues concerning setting up your Windows PC to access the Internet. Explains where to get the software you need and how to configure it. Also provides information on creating HTML documents.

Writing the Information Superhighway

`http://www.umich.edu/~wbutler/UC153Syl.html`

Offers information regarding how to write literature for the Internet (originally an online class at University of Michigan). Lets you direct questions to the professors who originally taught the class. Also includes a linked bibliography of other sites.

Youth Quake

`http://emall.com/yq/home.html`

Serves as a destination for computer-literate youth. Plans to cater to education all around the world.

Zen and the Art of the Internet

`http://www.cs.indiana.edu/docproject/zen/zen-1.0_toc.html`

A beginner's guide to the Internet. Offers information on the search engines available and even a section on how to create a newsgroup.

Guides, Tours, & Cool Site Resources

Best of the Net

`http://gnn.com/gnn/wic/botn/index.html`

A listing of favorite resources, picked by the editors of GNN.

George Coates Performance Works

`http://www.georgecoates.org/`

Just a diversional site where you fill out a questionnaire (it's short) and are then matched with a character who most fits your personality type. Your character is described, and you can change characters often. You are encouraged to visit your multiple personalities often!

GO! Online Communications

`http://www.jumppoint.com`

An exclusive Internet club of advertisers. Includes links to businesses, professionals, employment opportunities, Kids Corner, and more.

Greene Communications Design, Inc.

`http://www.greene.com/`

A graphics design firm expanded to Web publishing. Greene will design anything for the business, educational, advertising or marketing executive (including letterheads, logos, promotional or educational materials, press releases, and so on). Provides links to projects, clients, and the Internet development group.

Hajjar/Kaufman New Media Lab

`http://www.hkweb.com/`

A small marketing and development company that gives you all the benefits and expertise of a large company. Hajjar/Kaufman will develop your business Web site. Provides links to clients and to contact information.

Cool Site of the Day

`http://www.infi.net/cool.html`

Connects you to the cool site of the day on the Internet, determined by the moderator. This works better than a random-site connector because the sites are more likely to be pretty cool.

Exploring the Internet

`http://www.cen.uiuc.edu/exploring.html#BlindSpin`

Introduces you to blindspinning—spinning around and then going in a random direction. Thus, it provides all sorts of random links. Also includes a link to What's New lists, searching tools, subject directories, server and other directories, tutorials, multimedia exhibits and demonstrations, computer information, weather, and more.

Latex Gloves

`http://www.howardmedical.com/gan2.htm`

Howard Medical Company offers free samples of a variety of Gantex gloves including surgeon gloves, procedure gloves, and extra thick paramedic gloves.

Glass Wings

`http://www.aus.xanadu.com/GlassWings/`

A site whose stated purpose is "to have fun, help improve the state of the world, inform, provide an interesting and useful commercial site, and have fun (yes, I intentionally mentioned fun twice)." Provides a collection of links and a search site only for fun and nonbusiness-oriented stuff. Includes an online mall where you can buy things, links to humorous sites, and more.

GNN Select Top 50

`http://gnn.com/wic/wics/top.new.html`

Offers the 50 most-accessed links in GNN Select over the past week.

GNN Tour

`http://gnn.com/gnn/join/tour/tourmain.html`

Provides a graphical interface that shows the locations of all the GNN sites around the world.

Guided Web Tours

`http://www.netgen.com/tour.html`

Through the use of "server-push," presents guided tours of the Web. Best when used with Netscape and audio support.

Handy Guide

`http://www.ahandyguide.com/`

Serves as a complete guide to thousands of sites on the Internet and Web. Lets you search by category or company name, and teaches American Sign Language (ASL) as you go.

High-Tech Investor

`http://www.interlog.com/~mathewi/invest.htm`

Written by an investment and markets reporter at the *Toronto Globe and Mail*, this site discusses investment-related resources on the Web and offers a collection of links to some of those resources.

Hit The Beach!

`http://www.hitthebeach.com/`

If you like the beach, you'll love this site. Provides links to a chat café, the swimsuit shot of the week, a virtual trip to the beach, a beach shop, and food. Register to win a trip to Cancun or to Jamaica, mon. Also a beach-related search engine.

Hybrid Communications

`http://gs1.com/homepages/dir.html`

A virtual metropolis of culture, government, art and antiques, restaurants, public service, business, retail, travel, and entertainment sites. Click on whatever interests you.

InfoMedia

`http://www.cgenterprises.com/infomedia/`

This page solicits information on the Olympic Park bombing and provides information on terrorism, contacting your government, and other interesting links.

Internet ProLink SA/AG

`http://www.iprolink.ch/`

Provides links to businesses on the Web, Web tools and services, and the "culture café." Also available in other languages.

Internet Resources

`http://www.brandonu.ca/~ennsnr/Resources/`

Contains pointers to more than 100 guides, lists, and indices of documents that help you learn how to use the Internet. Includes pointers to The December and Yanoff Lists, Patrick Crispen's Internet Roadmap (in HTML), The Awesome List, and many others.

Internet Tour

`http://www.globalcenter.net/gcweb/tour.html`

An overview of the Internet. Incorporates many graphics and a laid-back attitude. This site shows you how, for example, to check the stock market, find a government document, or send birthday flowers.

Meta-list of What's New Pages

`http://homepage.seas.upenn.edu/~mengwong/whatsnew.list.html`

Offers a collection of links to all the different Internet What's New sites for the Web. By the author's own admission, "the Web is growing so fast that this document can be considered, at best, a historical artifact."

Mirsky's Worst of the Web

`http://mirsky.com/wow/Worst.html`

Provides an alternative to the many sites that serve up a "cool" site of the day or point you to "great" places. Offers links to sites that exemplify why some people shouldn't be allowed to make their own Web sites.

Net Trek Cafe

`http://www.nettrek.com.au/`

The first Internet café in Australia, offering a variety of links and services, including Internet training, a business directory, links to Internet search engines and catalogs, Australian links, outer space and *Star Trek* links, links for kids and music lovers, sports, news media, and much much more.

nicejob Media

`http://www.earthlink.net/~mrnicejob/`

An odd assortment of home pages, including Two Moms Named Alma, An Illusion Dog, Unexplained Art, and more. If you're looking for an interesting site, look no further.

NickNet

`http://www.pinc.com/nburger/home.html`

More than 3,200 links to dazzle and amaze you! If Web surfing were any more fun, they would have to ban it! Everything you could ever want is here and categorized so it is all easy to find. Web addicts beware!

Overall Knowledge Company, Inc.

`http://www.okc.com`

Overall Knowledge Company, Inc. is a general Web presence provider with an emphasis on the film and television trades as well and the arts and entertainment industries. Also publishes several industry-specific directories on the World Wide Web.

Point Survey and Escort

`http://www.pointcom.com/`

Provides a large collection of reviews of Web sites. Rates sites for content, presentation, and experience. Includes more than 1,000 reviews across many categories. Helps you get started on the Web with answers to common questions and guided tours of browsing software and sites.

Thousand Points of Sites

`http://inls.ucsd.edu/y/OhBoy/randomjump1.html`

Sends you to a Web site randomly selected from its listings.

ThreadTreader's WWW Contests Guide

`http://www.4cyte.com/ThreadTreader/`

Presents ThreadTreader's WWW Contests Guide, a complete, current compilation of contests on the Web. Provides easy ways to browse through an extensive index of online contests, drawings, raffles, sweepstakes, and other prize-oriented promotions. Even lets you add your own contest to the ThreadTreader's Guide.

Today Page

`http://www.vossnet.co.uk/local/today/index.html`

Offers a collection of links to sites that change daily; for example, includes links to news, your horoscope, and weather photos.

UnderWorld Links

`http://www.nd.edu/StudentLinks/jkeating/links.html`

Offers some of the more offbeat links. Provides *Star Wars* information, audio and video clips from movies, weather maps, and more.

Unusual or Deep Site of the Day

`http://adsint.bc.ca/deepsite/`

Offers links to sites that provide some sort of intellectually stimulating purpose.

The Unusual or Deep Site of the Day

Virtual Town City Limits

`http://wwwcsif.cs.ucdavis.edu/virt-town/welcome.html`

Contains many links to stores, public offices, and other things you might find in a real town. Allows you to manuever around it the way you do around a real town.

WEBula

`http://www.eg.bucknell.edu/cgi-bin/webula/index.html`

Allows you to search the site to find links to all sorts of random things. Also lets you add your page to the existing categories.

HTML & Other Languages

Bare Bones Guide to HTML

`http://werbach.com/barebones/`

Lists every HTML 2.0 tag and most of the 3.0 tags, with a special section on Netscape extensions.

Beginner's Guide to HTML

`http://www.ncsa.uiuc.edu/General/Internet/WWW/`
`HTMLPrimer.html`

Talks about linking to other documents, trouble-shooting, and creating forms. Focuses on Mosaic, but includes other browsers.

Cerebral Systems Development—Home of Webber™

`http://www.csdcorp.com/Welcome.html`

Offers Webber™, a fast, friendly, and flexible HTML editor for Windows. Provides full-featured help, including HTML tag descriptions and an easy-to-use validation system to help you create valid HTML documents. Allows you to download Webber as shareware; also offers a registered version.

ColorEditor for Windows

`http://www.bbsinc.com/colorEditor_FAQ.html`

Provides standalone MS Windows shareware to assist the Web page author develop a HTML page color scheme using extensions to the HTML 3.0 specification. Also provides a Style Box that enables users to edit, save, and retrieve color schemes. Runs on Windows 3.1, Windows 3.1 for Workgroups, Windows 95, and Windows NT 3.5.

David B. Martin's VRML Page

`http://www.kfu.com/~dbmartin/vrml.html`

Provides a decent page of Virtual Reality Modelling Language (VRML) links, describes what VRML is, and offers a little bit about its inventors.

HTML Info Page

`http://www.ohiou.edu/~jvannest/info/`

Lists HTML-related information. Encourages you to add links to other informational pages. Also includes links to CGI, forms, imagemaps, tables, and lists, and information on the latest developments in these areas.

Introduction to HTML: Table of Contents

`http://www.cwru.edu/help/introHTML/toc.html`

Presents a guide to authoring Web pages. Divides sections by different images, lists, and anchors, and offers information on how to take advantage of Netscape functions.

Personal Home Page of Bob Hunter

`http://www.awinc.com/users/bhunter/`

Focuses on testing HTML coding examples and pushing the limits of HyperText Markup Language and all of its extensions.

Primer for Creating Web Resources

`http://www-slis.lib.indiana.edu/Internet/`
`programmer-page.html`

Offers a list of links to HTML resources. Also offers links to Perl and CGI languages for creating top-of-the-line Web pages.

tkHTML Editor Information

`http://www.ssc.com/~roland/tkHTML/tkHTML.html`

Presents tkHTML, a simple HTML editor based on the Tcl script language and the Tk toolkit for X11 that enables you to quickly compose and edit HTML-formatted documents as well as rapidly convert text documents to the HTML format.

Web Letter, a Guide to HTML/Web Publishing

`http://www.writething.com/`

Serves as an HTML resource. Includes a newsletter, a video, and training books, as well as numerous links to help you build your own Web.

Web Resources

`http://www.wwwa.com/resource.html`

Serves as a complete Web resource site with HTML commands, software for publishing, searches, libraries, and high-speed Web host connections for your company or home page.

Resources

Aether Madness

`http://www.aether.com/Aether/`

Provides an online version of the book *Aether Madness: An Offbeat Guide to the On-line World*. The site contains the full original text, with hypertext links to most of the places recommended in it.

All-Internet Shopping Directory

`http://www.webcom.com/~tbrown/`

Serves as an easy-to-use, fast-loading central hot link to products, services, malls, and stores on the Web. Selected as one of *PC Magazine's* top 100 Web sites (2/13/96).

Ansible's Web Page Design Services

http://www.cyberenet.net/center/

Helpful to anyone from newbies to expert Internauts, this site offers links to online Internet resources, software, search tools, and a list of favorite Internet sites.

Argus/Univeristy of Michigan Clearinghouse

http://www.lib.umich.edu/chhome.html

"The Premier Internet Research Library," this site serves as a clearinghouse for subject-oriented Internet resources guides. Allows you to submit your own guides or obtain guides written on various Internet-related topics.

Aspen Systems Corp.

http://www.aspensys.com

Provides complete Internet services. Also discusses requirements and needs analysis, Internet publishing services, systems support, and customer support. Specializes in identifying, gathering, and analyzing online information.

Association of Internet Users

http://beach.com/welcome/aiu.html

An organization for individuals and companies seeking to effectively promote their products or services on the Internet. Benefits of membership include the INTERNET REPORT newsletter, free DNS registration, e-mail forwarding service, and Internet insurance.

Association of University Technology Managers

http://autm.rice.edu/autm/

Features resources for the technology transfer field, once called the "unknown profession." Offers links to other resources and includes information about AUTM (publications, membership, events), job postings, and a way to search lists of technologies you can license from more than 20 different university, government, and organizational sites in one query (via a harvest gatherer).

Autopilot

http://www.mit.edu:8001/people/mkgray/autopilot.html

Uses Netscape and connects you to a different Web site every 12 seconds. Helps you find totally random sites with little effort. Also allows you to change the amount of time between connections.

Autorama

http://www.hooked.net/users/1auto

Provides information, software, and links related to Web authoring and automated cybernetic delivery. Offers a download site for Web hot spots, an image map editor, and the Cyberspace Shuttle Loading Kit (a toolkit for creating single-step Web smart Zip files).

Babbs's Bookmarks

http://www.aquila.com/babbs.bookmarks/

A monthly column featured in *Boardwatch Magazine*. Focuses on Web sites that help you make the most of the amazing resources available on the Web.

Banana Report Easy Visual Basic Tips

http://www.infohaus.com/access/by-seller/
BananaReport_Visual_Basic_Tips/i.free.html

Provides a way for programmers to get quick tips and techniques that solve common Visual Basic programming problems.

Canada Net Pages

http://www.visions.com/netpages

This page's stated goal is to "be recognized as the most comprehensive resource of Canadian business and finance data." Also provides links for various pages, such as Canada Net Financial Pages and Canada Net Business Directory.

Canadian Internet Handbook/Advantage Home Page

http://www.csi.nb.ca/handbook/

Presents guides to Internet access in Canada. Lets you add your Canadian Internet address to the handbook, find out more about its publications, send the authors e-mail, and more.

Categorical Catapult

http://www.clark.net/pub/cargui/links.html

Offers a database of more than 3,250 links in 160 categories, organized hierarchically.

Cnet—Canada

http://cnet.unb.ca/cnet/

Provides information specific to Canada. Allows you to search the database by clicking on the geographical regions on a map or by using standard keywords.

Commercial Services on the Net

http://www.directory.net/

Provides a collection of links to commercial Web sites on the Internet. Lets you search by a word or name of a company.

Common Internet File Formats

http://www.matisse.net/files/formats.html

Provides information on the different file types and formats on the Internet. Each blurb about a specific file type also gives links to obtaining readers for that type.

Connect, Inc.—Audio Innovations

http://www.tc.net/connect

Harnesses the power of audio on the Internet. Provides applications that enable you to instantly update your Web page or e-mail applications by simply picking up your telephone and calling a fully automated system. Also qualifies as an authorized AT&T 900 service bureau, so you can set up and run any 900 or 800 voice or data application.

CRAYON—CReAte Your Own Newspaper

http://www.eg.bucknell.edu/~boulter/crayon/

Serves as an interactive news agent. Lets you choose from sections such as News, Sports, Entertainment, and others to find the best periodical information on the Internet. Enables you to organize it into your own personal newspaper—you may never read a print publication again.

CSUSM Windows World

http://coyote.csusm.edu/cwis/winworld/winworld.html

Provides virtually any Windows shareware. Allows you to search the entries by keyword. A GNN "Best of the Net" nominee for 1995.

E-Minder Free Reminder-By-E-mail Service

http://www.netmind.com/e-minder/

Offers to send you automatically generated reminder messages for any event or occasion for which you register. Requires an e-mail address, but otherwise is completely anonymous. Lets you specify the number of days in advance you want a reminder. It also provides a simple e-mail interface that you can use to list or delete reminders.

Economics of Networks Internet Site

http://edgar.stern.nyu.edu/networks/

Provides information and links to the economics behind all networks. Includes downloadable papers on topics ranging from network compatibility to financial networks.

EINet Galaxy

http://www.einet.net

A search site provided free of charge by Trade-Wave Corp. Includes general topics and sublists under each of these. Also offers a list of job opportunities.

FLFSoft, Inc. Home Page

http://www.execpc.com/~flfsoft/

Develops Windows-based utilities and Internet software and services. Features Web Spinner, a Windows-based HTML editor.

FutureMedia Services

http://www.futuremedia.com/

Provides Internet access to small businesses interested in taking their services to the Internet. Provides Web site development and consulting services, ftp and Gopher service space, and links to current projects.

FutureTel, Inc.

http://www.ftelinc.com

Possesses leading technology in both compression and telecommunications, so it is uniquely positioned to serve the needs of the digital video publishing and distribution markets. Provides the most complete solution to the challenges of distributing and publishing digital video on CDs and wired and wireless networks. The company's digital video publishing product line includes PrimeView, a family of real-time PC-based MPEG encoders; and MPEGWORKS, a comprehensive encoding control software package for human-assisted or pass-through compression.

Glistening Trail Records

http://membrane.com/

For those in Pennsylvania (primarily the Philadelphia area), this site lists places for adventure, music, food, shopping, real estate opportunities, computer and business services, churches, credit card services, medical services, and more. Click on individual listings for more descriptions and some pictures.

Global Village Stock Footage

http://www.nbn.com:80/footage/

For multimedia and video professionals. Search the huge database of stock video footage to download or order the disk. Includes links to sample images and demos. Global Village will find the clip you're looking for.

G.T.A. Business Solutions

http://www.elknet.com/gta/hpgta.html

Provides businesses and organizations presence on the Internet with Web page design, training and classes. Includes access to price lists and sample client pages.

Harter Image Archives

http://www.tddc.net/geo/harter/

Better than any clip-art gallery, here you will find general images, images of men, and images of women. Provides samples to download and ordering information.

Hippermedia

http://www.io.org/~farellc/hipper.html

An independent consulting company based in Toronto that specializes in getting businesses and organizations on the Web as simply and as inexpensively as possible.

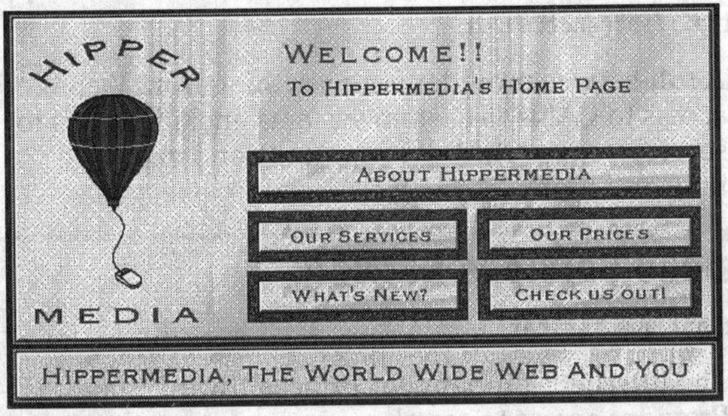

HFSI

http://www.hfsi.com/

Workflow and imaging technologies, providing products and services for the federal government and government contractors. Provides links to products, services, resource centers, and education and training opportunities. Offers workload management seminars to help your office run more efficiently and on less paper.

Hirt & Carter Owlnet

http://www.owlnet.co.za/

A link from the Disc Imaging Photo Page, based in South Africa. Provides links to Owlnet and its images of birds that show you what they can do. Owlnet will take your images and load them into your Web site.

Home Run Pictures

http://www.zdepth.com/homerun/

This company creates online animation and special effects for ad agencies, corporations, TV stations, and interactive producers. Includes links to samples, contacts, and pricing information.

Information Age, Inc.

http://www.informationage.com/

A software- and data-intensive Web site development company with links to applications, articles, services, the Information Age team, and general information.

InfoScan

http://www.machinasapiens.qc.ca/machina/infoscanang.html

A filtering tool that reads and evaluates your e-mail, news, or databases according to key words you provide, and alerts you to the most interesting ones. Includes links to several frequently asked questions, including how to get your own copy.

Innovative Computer Associates, Inc.

http://www.icai.com/icai/

A software engineering firm for database and Web page development, located near Denver, Colorado. Provides information about Internet classes offered and services such as online application development, multimedia marketing campaigns, corporate training, cross-platform application development, and much more.

Instruction Set, Inc.

http://www.inset.com/

Broad curriculum of courses for the software development technology of today. Links to courses and seminars, consulting, courseware development services, employment opportunities, and more.

InteliSys Technologica, Inc.

http://www.intelinet.net/

Networking and programming solutions for businesses around the world. Will also provide Web development services. Links to Web services. Watch up-to-date company info scroll across the bottom of your screen.

Interactive Data Systems, Inc.

http://www.idsinc.com/

A software engineering service provider, especially for object-oriented tools. Includes links to services, database and development environment info and software, freeware, and other interesting links.

Interactive Voice Applications

http://www.tc.net/voice/

Streaming audiofile technology to enable you to send voice messages around the world for a fraction of the regular cost. Expedite your business transactions while also reducing expenditures. Includes access to demos, contact info, and many other services.

International Industrial Intelligence

http://international.com/

Internet connections and WWW space for the business to advertise on the Web. Increase your company's exposure without increasing costs. Includes links to advertising, online info and connections, multimedia demos, and more.

Internet Business Solutions

http://inbs.coop.net/

A Colorado company that will develop database systems to help your company promote services and products on the Internet. Provides links to current customers.

Internet Info Store Directory

http://www.openmarket.com/stores/walsh@internetinfo.com/store/StoreFront.html

Tracks commercial activity on the Internet and offers special reports online about financial service firms, public software companies, and venture capital firms on the Internet.

Internet Resources Newsletter

http://www.hw.ac.uk/libWWW/irn/irn.html

A free monthly Web newsletter. Focuses on higher education and the Internet. Features lists of new Internet resources and other items of interest.

Internet Servers for the Mac OS

http://www.freedonia.com/ism/

Contains many links to Macintosh-specific software packages for running a Mac-based server. Topics include mail servers, mail gateways, ftp servers, Telnet servers, and more.

Internet World

http://pubs.iworld.com/iw-online/

An online version of this popular magazine devoted to the Internet. Allows you to search back issues by cover or by keyword.

Internet Systems, Inc.

http://www.isi.net/

Business, educational, and government institution Internet services. Provides site architecture, access, service, and maintenance for your high-volume site. Also provides access to clients' pages.

iWORLD

http://www.mecklerweb.com/

Touting itself as "all Net, all the time," this site offers Internet news, features, resources, and tools. Supported by Mecklermedia, publisher of *Internet World* magazine.

INTRANET Technologies, Inc.

http://intranet.on.ca/

A full-service provider for everything from Web access to LANs to custom systems. Includes links to services, support, Web community and exposure info, and more.

Island Services Network

http://www.isn.net/

The Internet Company for Prince Edward Island. Provides access to search engines, user services, news and entertainment, local weather, and other Internet services.

Knighted Computers

http://www.knighted.com/

An Internet service provider based in Fulton, New York, with links to local newspapers, games, software, hardware, services, and more.

Knossopolis

`http://www.knosso.com/`

A Web site design and architecture, training, teaching, and consulting firm with links to its resources and information, clients, projects, and more.

Life on the Internet

`http://www.screen.com/understand/welcome.html`

Provides a large collection of links to many resources on the Internet. Gives sources for browsers, software, page development, and more.

List of WWW Archie Services

`http://pubweb.nexor.co.uk/public/archie/`

Offers a list of hypertext links to Archie (archive) servers. Helps you find files anywhere on the Internet and lists Archie servers that use forms and others that don't.

Logical Operations

`http://www.logicalops.com`

Training products and services for professional trainers.

LookUp!

`http://www.lookup.com/`

Offers a directory service that provides easy-to-use names to e-mail address mapping.

Lopez Communications

`http://www.interport.net/peoplelink/`

Lopez Communications offers a variety of on- and offline services, including integrated marketing to progressive organizations, online publishing, Web design, and other Web projects for socially responsible companies.

Marketing Masters

`http://surveysaid.ostech.com:8080/`

An Internet host with links to hosted sites, including Ham Radio Forums, Marketing Masters, and JF Computer Leasing.

MindSphere Design for Communication

`http://www.mindsphere.com/`

For businesses and individuals looking to develop an identity on the Internet. Services include business multimedia, interface, advertising, and packaging. Includes links to MindSphere's creativity, clients, and more.

Miramar Productions

`http://useattle.uspan.com/miramar/`

Browse Miramar's catalog of latest releases, or go to its Top Five section for interactive previews, video and audio clips, computer animation, performance samplers, and much much more.

Media Connection of New York—Links Page

`http://www.mcny.com/linkspage/`

Offers a collection of links to Web resources in or about New York City.

Monster FTP Sites List

`http://hoohoo.ncsa.uiuc.edu/ftp/`

A comprehensive listing of anonymous ftp sites.

Network Hardware Suppliers List

`http://www.ua.com/hardware/hardware.html`

Look here to find a list of recommended telecommunications and hardware dealers. These dealers have been recommended by various people all over the Internet. As the author states, "Caveat Emptor."

Newton Online

`http://www.newtonline.com`

Newton Online provides business consulting (and a quirky sense of humor) for companies who want to compliment marketing and communications strategies by using the Internet.

Norcov Research

`http://www.norcov.com/`

Offers scientific research, programming, Internet services, and Unix administration. Check out the complete list of products and services as well as the Norcov customer pages.

Novia Internetworking

`http://www.novia.net/`

A personal and business connection to the Internet. Check out its partial list of hosted business pages, LAN integration capability, and its services and search engines.

Omega West

`http://cascade.cs.ubc.ca:12000/omega/omega.html`

A site with something for everyone. Well-organized into a hierarchical structure, it includes everything from business resources and financial tips to a broad spectrum of entertainment and Web developer resources. Omega West, an international distribution and services company, will soon have an "intelligent interface" that is capable of adapting to users' actions. This, of course, will mean that return visits and continued interaction will provide users with a personalized interface.

Presence—An Information Design Studio

`http://www.presence.com/`

Focuses on providing innovative and effective marketing solutions through the Internet. Also includes many interesting Internet-related links.

Q-D Software Development

`http://www.q-d.com`

Presents the creators of WebForms, the Web forms generator; and WinBrowse, the multiple-PC database utility. Also includes a variety of shareware programs available for download.

RealAudio Home Page

`http://www.realaudio.com/`

Provides RealAudio, software you can use to both record and play your own sound. Many Web sites on the Internet use RealAudio to provide sounds.

Sibylla: The WWW Software Development Kit

`http://www.cib.unibo.it/guests/ariadne/sibylla/sibyllaeng.html`

Provides information on Sibylla, a development kit geared toward creating Web software, whose purpose is to provide access to information sources (such as company databases) through the Web. Also provides pricing information on the software.

SpectraFAX Corp. Home Page

`http://naples.com/spectrafax/`

Describes fax broadcast and fax-on-demand technology. Also compares costs for reaching U.S. markets via fax and via postal service from locations outside the United States. Introduces the SpectraFAX Service Bureau and enables you use an online form to arrange for fax services.

Strategis

`http://strategis.ic.gc.ca/engdoc/site.html`

A business information site sponsored by the Canadian federal government's economic flagship department, dedicated "to the success of all Canadian businesses at home and abroad."

SWITCH—Swiss Academic and Research Network

`http://www.switch.ch/`

Presents SWITCH, an Internet Service Provider that interconnects all Swiss universities, many libraries, and research labs, as well as other Swiss and international organizations. Also presents the WWW Rent-A-Page service.

Timothy W. Amey Resource Links

`http://www.netins.net/showcase/amey/twa`

Offers a collection of resource links and information regarding OS/2 resources, OS/2 advocacy, Lotus resources, Intel alternatives, religion, Ford advocacy, and IT/IS resources.

Virtual Tourist

`http://www.vtourist.com/webmap/europe.htm`

Provides a graphical map interface that you can click on to find and then jump to Web servers operating in many countries around the world.

Washington Web

`http://www.washweb.net:8000/`

Presents an online guide of Internet resources for the greater Washington, D.C. area.

Web Week

`http://pubs.iworld.com/ww-online/`

An electronic publication that serves as a repository of Web-related topics. Categories include News, Commericial, Intranet, Products, Under Construction, Industry, and Opinion.

Welcome to Netscape

`http://home.mcom.com/`

Offers information about the new security measures being built into HTML; also offers a downloadable version of Netscape for Windows 95 and technical support.

Windows95 InterNetworking Headquarters

`http://www.windows95.com`

Offers Windows 95 shareware, Internet setup information, networking across the Internet, and more.

WorldTel Global Marketing Network

`http://www.worldtel.com/home.html`

Lists businesses and individuals offering products, services, or opportunities to the world market.

Searchers & Databases

Business Directions International

`http://www.business.com.au/`

An Internet search directory using numerous search engines to find business sites on the Internet.

InterNIC Directory of Directories

`http://ds.internic.net/ds/dsdirofdirs.html`

Contains an index of links to various resources, products, and services on the Net, including agriculture, the arts, business, dictionaries, education, health and medicine, religion, sports and hobbies, and weather. Allows you to add your site.

Four11 White Page Directory

`http://www.Four11.com/`

Enables you to search for people and their e-mail addresses and Web pages. Contains more than 5.5 million listings. Allows you to register and put your name on the directory.

Business Researcher's Interests

`http://www.pitt.edu/~malhotra/interest.html`

Provides more than 2,800 sites relevant to contemporary organizational issues concerning information processes, information systems, and information technology. Categories include electronic markets, organizational learning, emerging organizations, WWW design, and journals and magazines.

College and University Home Pages

`http://www.mit.edu:8001/people/cdemello/univ.html`

Provides links to the Web pages of more than 750 colleges and universities around the world. Allows you to search alphabetically or just browse.

COMMA Hotlist Database

`http://arachnid.cm.cf.ac.uk/htbin/AndrewW/Hotlist/hot_list_search.csh`

Provides a graphical, searchable Web database. Choose your search criteria from their list, and then it searches and gives you an output list. Also enables you to add your own hot list to the database.

Database Demos

`http://bristol.onramp.net/`

Shows you how to set up your Oracle-based database management system (DBMS) for access via the Web. Good for creating your own search engine or providing Web access to large bodies of information.

Explorer

`http://www.rtis.com/explorer/`

Serves as a search site for finding resources on the Internet. Arranges areas by subject.

High Performance Cartridges

`http://www.netpoint.net/hpcart/hpcart.html`

A re-manufacturer of laser toner cartridges for large institutional settings. Also provides a search engine, a database of shareware on the Internet, and other cool links with software to download.

Index

`http://www.library.vanderbilt.edu/law/acqs/pubr.html`

If you're looking for a publisher or vender on the Internet, this is the database to search. Search by name, subject, e-mail address, or geographic location.

Index of Australian Indexes

`http://www.moreinfo.com.au/ausindex/`

A meta-index of Australian Web site indexes. Over a dozen are described, with links to each.

T'rific! Skin Care

`http://www.trific.com/sample.html`

T'rific! will send you a color brochure with product information, one Splasher Handi-pack, and one Clear Z'it Up Handi-pack at your request.

InfoCafé

http://www.infocafe.com/

A complete bookstore on the Web. Members may order any book currently in print, or even books out of print, and InfoCafé will do the search. Books are indexed by department: for example, computers, business, fiction.

International Business Resources on the WWW

http://ciber.bus.msu.edu/busres.htm

Serves as an index of business, economics, trade, marketing, and government sites with an international focus.

Internet Pearls Index

http://www.execpc.com/~wmhogg

Features collections of the best of the Internet. Includes sections for beginners as well as comprehensive coverage of topics such as business, medicine, jobs, cinema, shareware, astronomy, futuristic technologies, fun, cartoons, comics, virtual reality, and more.

Internet Sleuth

http://www.charm.net/~ibc/sleuth/

Offers a collection of more than 500 searchable databases on a wide variety of subjects. includes links to a search form or a page that lists a number of related searchable databases. Also allows you search by keyword or browse alphabetically or by category.

Joel's Hierarchical Subject Index

http://www.cen.uiuc.edu/~jj9544/index.html

A lesser-known but fairly thorough search site.

Lycos Home Page: Hunting WWW Information

http://lycos.cs.cmu.edu/

Provides a Web search engine. Contains more than 5.5 million Web pages in its database. Provides context for evaluating whether a document or page is relevant to your search.

Media Logic's Index of Economic and Financial Resources

http://www.mlinet.com/mle/

This index of resources is provided by Media Logic as a service for the Internet community. It provides a searchable index of data, news, and services that are of interest to investors, researchers, and other members of the financial community. Unlike many other Internet indexes, all entries here are subject to editorial review to ensure that they are useful, relevant, and current.

MediaTel's Newsline

http://www.mediatel.co.uk/

Based in the United Kingdom, an online information database used most often by ad agencies and media owners. Includes databases for subscribers and nonsubscribers, as well as links to "free daily media news."

Micro Service & Training

http://www.ici.net/cust_pages/jsouza/jsouza.html

This is a resource database for computer hardware, software, and training. If you are searching for hardware or software, or if you need training or consulting for your business or organization, you can search for it here.

Montana Communications Network (MCN)

http://www.mcn.net/index.html

A resource page for Montana events, businesses, and information. Includes access to businesses, real estate, and other Montana links, local newspapers on line, news and weather, classified ads, and more.

Mother-of-all BBS

http://wwwmbb.cs.colorado.edu/~mcbryan/bb/summary.html

Seeks to collect all Web addresses of all companies, universities, research centers, government agencies, research projects, and hardware and software annoucements into one searchable database.

NET Compass

http://home.cc.umanitoba.ca/~umwittma

Serves as a meta-index for searching the Web by subject or by keyword, and for searching ftp software by file name or by file description.

New Riders' Official World Wide Web Yellow Pages

http://www.mcp.com/nrp/wwwyp/

The online version of this book (with thousands of additional sites). Searchable by keyword. Obviously the most complete and useful search site available. (Talk about your shameless plug!)

New User's Directory

http://hcs.harvard.edu/~calvarez/newuser.html

Presents a large collection of links to information. Offers tips for specific kinds of computers (MAC, IBM, Unix, and so forth), links to search engines, and more. Also provides information on how to create Web pages and download software.

NlightN: Finding What You Want To Know Now

http://www.nlightn.com

Claims to be "the Web's largest library of meaningful information." With a single query, the NlightN Universal Index searches the Web, World News, Online Databases, and traditional reference sources.

Nothin' But Net

http://www.xmission.com/~vothcom/ltompkins/index.html

Nothin' But Net (NBN) is a complete Internet Encyclopedia covering more than 200 categories packed with 2,500-plus non-commercial, resourceful Internet sites. Provides a sample excerpt from the A-B categories, as well as full ordering information.

Planet Earth Home Page

http://www.nosc.mil/planet_earth/info.html

A search site on the Internet, organized like a library. Offers a library floorplan that you can use to browse the sites in its database. Also lets you search the database by keyword.

Publicize Your Home Page

http://www.ntg-campus.com/ntg/public.htm

Provides a collection of links to various search engines. Focuses on connecting you to the part of these search engines that allows you to register and add your own home page.

Recondite Reference Desk

http://www.unt.edu/~ns0003/

Serves as a starting place for Web searches. Features an online form that is linked to the search forms of major data sites, including nine different (and popular) search engines.

Search, Find—Internet Resource Locators

http://ananse.irv.uit.no/law/nav/find.html

Provides a graphically oriented set of links to search engines on the Internet, such as Open Text Web Index, InfoSeek Search, and others.

Searching the Web

http://union.ncsa.uiuc.edu/HyperNews/get/www/searching.html

Provides information, strategies, and links to searching for information on the Web. Offers links to searching services, searching software, and searching references.

shareware.com

http://www.shareware.com/

Formerly the Virtual Software Library, offers a tool for searching for shareware and freeware on the Internet.

Starting Point

http://www.stpt.com/

Offers "everything you need to work the Web every day." Provides a starting site for finding information on the Web. Offers many links.

Starting Points for Internet

http://www.ncsa.uiuc.edu/SDG/Software/Mosaic/StartingPoints/NetworkStartingPoints.html

NCSA's comprehensive links to Internet resources. Includes Gopher, Veronica, Finger, Usenet, WAIS, and many others. Also presents representative Web home pages. Highly recommended (nay, essential).

URL-Minder: Your Own Personal Web Robot

http://www.netmind.com/URL-minder/URL-minder.html

Presents the URL-minder, your own personal Web robot, which retrieves your registered URLs regularly and reports back to you by e-mail when they change. The URL-minder also runs searches on Web databases regularly and lets you know when anything new that matches your search shows up. It also keeps track of the places you've been, so you can spend your time (and money) doing new things on the Web.

Virtual Libraries

http://www.w3.org/hypertext/DataSources/bySubject/Virtual_libraries/Overview.html

Offers links to collections of information, based on the subject matter of those sites.

VSL Front Desk at the OAK Repository

http://www.acs.oakland.edu/cgi-bin/vsl-front

Enter a keyword, and the engine searches the major Internet shareware archives for the program you want.

WAIS Access Through the Web

http://www.ai.mit.edu/the-net/wais.html

Provides information about WAIS, a system that enables you to retrieve documents from databases via full-text searches. Allows you to search by name or by topic.

WebAnts Home Page

http://thule.mt.cs.cmu.edu:8001/webants/

Provides information about project WebAnts, to develop an information retrieval system for the Web using cooperative agents. Offers information about its approach and current progress reports.

Yahoo!

http://www.yahoo.com

Possibly the most popular search site on the Web. Considered to be the place to go for anything, as long as it isn't too technically oriented. Offers links only to sources, which is different from something such as Lycos, which also searches directories and files themselves.

Statistics & History

Economic FAQs about the Internet

http://gopher.econ.lsa.umich.edu/FAQs/FAQs.html

Presents a collection of FAQs about the economics behind the Internet. Discusses the technology behind the Internet, the NSF backbone.

Internet Business Center

http://www.tig.com/IBC/index.html

Provides information about conducting business on the Internet. Includes Internet statistics, maps, and charts. Also lists hot sites and services.

Rampages

http://rampages.onramp.net/new/index.html

A service provider that offers automated usage statistics, bookmarks, counters, and online tutorials. High-powered clients are also candidates for the Rampage of the Month. Web directories are organized by user name.

World Wide Web: Origins and Beyond

http://homepage.seas.upenn.edu/~lzeltser/WWW/

Gives the origins of the Web and also talks about some of the other uses of hypertext, such as the Xanadu project. Also discusses some disadvantages of the Web.

Web Publishing

5 Top Internet Marketing Successes of 1994

http://arganet.tenagra.com/Tenagra/awards95.html

Showcases Tenagra Corp.'s picks for the top Internet marketing success stories of the year. The 1995 winners are Federal Express, Ragu Spaghetti Sauce, Yahoo!, NetPOST™, Software.Net, and Virtual Vineyards.

Artzilla Surf Constructions

http://www.earthlink.net/~Artzilla

A group of designers and illustrators who left the corporations and now do what they love—provide the Web with high-quality graphics.

Building Web Servers

http:// www.cybergroup.com/

Provides a collection of and links to information on how to create a Web, ftp, or Gopher server. Covers most operating systems, including Windows, Macintosh, and Unix. Includes a tutorial.

Business of the Internet

http://www.rtd.com/people/rawn/business.html

Introduces the Internet for commercial organizations. Offers information about the structure and history of the Internet, how the Internet can help business, and how to connect your business to the Internet.

Carter & Associates WEB Studios

http://www.biddeford.com/~axs.

Specializes in Web page construction for individuals and companies who want to advertise on a personal or corporate scale on the Internet. Offers to create and maintain an established business presence on the Internet, customized to the personal tastes of clients.

Copyright Website

http://www.benedict.com/

Provides copyright information for the general public and interested parties. Includes categories of fundamentals on copyrights and issues related to copyright over the Net. Also contains a section for relevant sources and links.

Dunn & Edwards Services

http://www.iwc.com/des/index.html

Provides a variety of services and resources related to career and employment, hypertext résumés, and home page services and development.

Dynamic Diagrams Home Page

http://dynamicDiagrams.com/

Focuses on the organization and presentation of information in print and electronic forms, interactive publication and prototype design, SGML applications, Web servers, and computer kiosks for museums.

Four Lakes Colorgraphics, Inc.

http://www.fourlakes.com/

This company provides prepress and publishing services to publishers, advertisers, and educational service providers. Four Lakes will design and publish CD-ROMs and home pages. Provides links to its target sights.

Free Range Media, Inc.

http://www.freerange.com

A full-scale Web production and Internet services company with expertise in creative design, new technology, and account management. Specializes in keeping track of the newest tools. Produces a wide variety of Web-related products. Also shares many tips and techniques.

FRS Associates Training and Education Division

http://www.frsa.com/

A Web presence provider that specializes in graphics, interactive programming, Java, Javascript, and animation. Also provides Web training for the novice to the professional developer and links to designed sights and the FRS business directory.

Garry's Web Services

http://tusconbiz.com/

Internet presence provider in Tuscon, Arizona. Garry's will design Web pages for businesses. Describe what you want, and an estimate will be provided. Proficient in animation, graphics, and can provide security for credit card orders on your Web site. Provides links to other services and example sites.

Gates, Jeff

http://www.tmn.com/Community/jgates/home.html

Jeff Gates's personal home page is a sample of what he can do for your personal or business use. Provides links to contact Jeff to set up a site of your own.

Headquarters.Com Internet

http://www.headquarters.com/

Internet/Intranet Web sites for individuals and businesses. Provides links to current and upcoming projects and their client base. Offers complete multimedia design, including Java, graphics, and CGI scripting, among others.

Hijinx

http://www.hijinx.com.au/

Communications software to give your Web pages memorable pictures and sounds. Provides links to a sample page, product info, and downloading info. Be sure to check out the "latest screen shot."

Home Space Builder

http://www.paragraph.com/whatsnew/homespce.htm

A 3D Web authoring tool that enables you to create a 3D home space using a standard Windows personal computer. Offers shareware and commercial versions.

Hourglass Internet Services

http://www.halcyon.com/hourglass/

Hourglass will publish and design your résumé, home page, or business information on the Web. Provides links to company information, services, and pricing information.

HudsoNet

http://www.hudsonet.com/

A New York-based service and Web page designer that will get your business on the Internet. Provides links to client pages and services offered.

Hyper Design Technologies

http://www.redshift.com/~montpres/hdt.html

A multimedia graphic design firm for corporations, offering Web pages, 3D illustrations, and video. Provides links to services, prices, art, and other interesting links.

Iconomics

`http://linden.fortnet.org/FORTNET/business/Iconomics/`
`Iconomics.html`

Your global illustration resource for graphics design via modem, mail, ftp, or floppy disk. Provides links to custom art, images, ordering, prices, and policy information.

Image Alchemy Digital Imaging

`http://imalchemy.com`

Presents a gallery of digital and traditional art and photography. Offers services such as photo retouching and manipulation. Also designs Web sites.

Image Compression for Publishing Online

`http://www.jgc.com`

Provides information about Johnson-Grace company, a multimedia software development that developed an image compression format called ART. Suggests that using ART enables image compression three times more efficient than when you use JPEG or GIF.

Image House Digital Photography Studio

`http://www.concom.com/~whitcomb/ih_home.html`

A digital photo studio for your business publishing needs. Provides training and camera installation information, Web site design, and messages from clients.

imedia

`http://www.imedia-sf.com`

A corporate multimedia development service the the company that wants to develop a 3D Internet presence. Includes access to company profiles and tours and current projects.

Infowerks Creative Web Services

`http://www.infowerks.com/`

College students who will set up your Web server and write your Web page with the help of art students. Cheap rates! Includes links to rates and services, and other links to art students of San Francisco.

Integra Software Corp.

`http://www.xmission.com/~americom/integra-credit.html`

Internet applications such as Web development for your business. Also includes access to contact

information if your company would like to develop an Internet presence.

Inter//Web Development

`http://www.iwd.com/`

A company specializing in Web page design and development for your business. Choose from many custom services to develop a unique Internet presence. Includes links to sample pages, services, pricing info, and more.

INTERCAT

`http://www.intercat.com/`

If you have a catalog or other information you want to get on the Web, Intercat will develop a complete multimedia Web presence for you. Includes links to sample sights, catalogs, and contact information.

Interglobal Mutltimedia

`http://www.interglobal.com/`

Web solutions for your corporate multimedia Web presence, including Web hosting, design, and security. Provides access to customer profiles, catalog, video, and much more.

International Business Center

`http://www.niagara.com/blmc`

A graphic design and ad agency based in Ontario, Canada. A company exploring the relationship among art, design, and technology for individuals or organizations.

Internet Advertising Solutions

`http://iaswww.com/`

These people will develop your company's Web site and get your information on the Internet. Winner of many awards for innovative site development. Includes links to services, clients, and more.

Internet Business Connection

`http://www.intbc.com/`

A virtual mall specializing in home page development and marketing services to any business seeking an Internet presence.

Internet Pilots

`http://www.xmission.com/~ip/ip.html`

A consulting firm based in Vancouver, British Columbia, specializing in Web publishing and

Internet training for individuals, businesses, organizations, and church groups. Includes access to more information and sample sites.

Making Money on Internet

http://cism.bus.utexas.edu/ravi/making_money.html

Offers information on electronic publishing, Internet economics, education, and other areas.

Manhattan MultiMedia, Inc.

http://www.m-m-m.com/

Manhattan will help your company plan, develop, and maintain a unique Internet presence by using the most advanced tools possible, including Java, C++, Perl, Oracle, Unix, Shockwave, and others.

MediaBox Communications

http://www.mediabox.com/

Web publishing, specializing in creative marketing strategies, graphic design and production, multimedia, and advertising for the Web. Click on the MediaBox electronic portfolio to get a sample of its work.

Metrotel Multi-Media Ltd

http://mmm.wwa.com/mmm/why.html

Web design and Internet consulting for your company. Develop a Web presence and find out how to surf the Internet to your advantage.

MFD Consult

http://login.dknet.dk/~mortenf/

A consulting company in Copenhagen, Denmark, specializing in Web publishing for small companies as well as individuals.

MGL Systems

http://www.mgl.ca/

A computer technologies firm based in Cambridge, Ontario, offering Web publishing as well as several other cool links to its customer base, shareware sites, search engines, and more.

Moshofsky/Plant Creative Services

http://moshplant.com

Using Shockwave and Director, its creative services can do anything for you or your company, including logos, image manipulation, illustration, presentations, and design. Check out what these folks have already done.

MultiMedia Dimensions—New Horizons in Sight and Sound

http://www.mmdimensions.com

MultiMedia Dimensions is a full-service interactive multimedia and Web page design and consulting company helping people find the right business solutions for their needs and budget.

NetCasters, Inc.

http://www.netcasters.com/

Your site for customized Web services, including Intranet and database system development, Web publishing, graphic design, site hosting, consulting, and more. Check out NetCaster's electronic portfolio.

NetWorXs of California

http://www.garlic.com/~dennisa/

Offers a full range of Web home page authoring and design services. Also offers full turn-key systems, including training in-house personnel so that you can enhance your Web server as your services or products change.

new3, Inc.

http://www.new3.com/

A leading-edge Web site architectural and development firm. With high-level technical knowledge of programming and a creative focus, new3, Inc. has played a role in bringing some of the best sites to the Web. Its speciality is areas of development considered too complex for many developers.

Program One Online Service

http://www.prgone.com/

Helps businesses and individuals learn and exploit the new Internet culture. Provides information about Internet marketing, and explains how companies can survive their ride on the Information Superhighway.

RAMWORKS

http://www.ramworks.com/ramworks/

Provides cutting-edge technology blended with award-winning traditional design to offer interactive multimedia services, Internet presence, Web pages, CD-ROM and CD-I authoring, interactive touch-screen kiosks, and corporate communications.

Stannet WWW Designing and Publishing Company

`http://www.webcom.com/~stannet`

Focuses on authoring, designing, and publishing Web pages for businesses and individuals. Performs custom graphics work and maintains and upgrades customers' sites as needed. Offers to meet customers in their offices in the greater New York City area.

Vannevar New Media

`http://www.vannevar.com`

An Internet publishing and applications company that puts businesses on the Web. Located in Houston, it boasts a strong NASA influence.

Web Developer

`http://pubs.iworld.com/wd-online/`

An online publication for programmers, Webmasters, network administrators, and other technically oriented personnel, responsible for developing and maintaining software, hardware, and security on the Web.

Web Publishing Australia

`http://AusWeb.com.au/`

Introduces you to a professional Web publishing and promotion company based in Queensland, Australia.

WebDesigns

`http://www.execpc.com/~jeffo/webdes/`

A Web page creation service. Focuses on posting and maintenance, logo and graphic design, photography (including improvement of existing photographs), image maps, online newsletters, and getting your page listed in directories like this one, among others.

Winfield Design Group

`http://www.gate.net/~winfield/index.html`

Internet site developers and Internet providers. Winfield will design an Internet site from the primary concept to its completion and to the final indexing of the site or home page. Offers CGI scripting, C++, Perl, and programs.

WorldWide Information and Netcasting Services

`http://www.corcom.com/wins/wins.html`

A full-service Internet marketing and communication company specializing in Web page design, product/service marketing, form CGI programming, and graphic design.

World Wide exPRess

`http://www.wwe.com/WWE/`

An Internet marketing and presence provider for all your home or office needs. Provides links to benefits, cost, and project samples.

Newsgroups

alt.best.of.internet

alt.bbs.internet

alt.culture.internet

alt.culture.www

alt.cybercafes

alt.folklore.internet

alt.internet.access.wanted

alt.internet

alt.internet.commerce

alt.internet.guru

alt.internet.media-coverage

alt.internet.services

alt.life.internet

alt.online-service

alt.online-service.*

alt.www.hotjava

aus.net.access

aus.org.waia

austin.internet

az.internet

ba.internet

chi.internet

comp.infosystems.announce

comp.infosystems.interpedia

comp.infosystems.www

comp.infosystems.www.advocacy

comp.infosystems.www.authoring.cgi

comp.infosystems.www.authoring.html

comp.infosystems.www.authoring.images

comp.infosystems.www.browsers.mac

comp.infosystems.www.browsers.misc

comp.infosystems.www.browsers.ms-windows

comp.infosystems.www.browsers.x

comp.infosystems.www.misc

comp.infosystems.www.providers

comp.infosystems.www.Servers.mac

comp.infosystems.www.Servers.misc

comp.infosystems.www.Servers.ms-windows

comp.infosystems.www.Servers.unix

comp.infosystems.www.users

comp.lang.java

comp.lang.javascript

comp.mail.list-admin.policy

comp.mail.list-admin.software

comp.mail.mime

comp.org.isoc.interest

comp.protocols.*

comp.protocols.ppp

```
dfw.internet.providers

misc.news.internet.announce

misc.news.internet.discuss

news.admin.net-abuse.announce

news.admin.net-abuse.misc

news.announce.newusers

nz.org.isocnz

phl.internet

tnn.internauts

tnn.internet

tnn.internet.address

tnn.internet.broadcast

tnn.internet.firewall

tnn.internet.isode

tnn.internet.library

tnn.internet.life

tnn.internet.mobile

tnn.internet.routing

tnn.internet.www

tnn.marketing

tw.bbs.rec.mud
```

Listservs

AOL-MONITOR—AOL Internet Systems Root-Mail List

You can join this group by sending the message "sub AOL-MONITOR your name" to `listserv@services.web.aol.com`

BEYON—User Services Internet in the Colleges Working List

Rice University Information Systems, Houston, TX

You can join this group by sending the message "sub BEYON your name" to `listserv@ricevm1.rice.edu`

BONSAI—Internet Bonsai Club

You can join this group by sending the message "sub BONSAI your name" to `listserv@home.ease.lsoft.com`

CLICK4HP—Health Promotion on the Internet (Discussion)

You can join this group by sending the message "sub CLICK4HP your name" to `listserv@yorku.ca`

EDRES-DB—Educational Resources on the Internet - Database

University of New Brunswick, Fredericton, N.B., Canada

You can join this group by sending the message "sub EDRES-DB your name" to `listserv@listserv.unb.ca`

GNN-MONITOR—GNN Internet Systems Root-Mail List

You can join this group by sending the message "sub GNN-MONITOR your name" to `listserv@services.web.aol.com`

IAP—Small Internet Access Providers

University of Notre Dame, Notre Dame, IN

You can join this group by sending the message "sub IAP your name" to `listserv@vma.cc.nd.edu`

IBASICS—Internet Basics: An Online Tutorial

Syracuse University

You can join this group by sending the message "sub IBASICS your name" to `listserv@listserv.syr.edu`

IDA—Internet Developers Association Announcement Mailing List

You can join this group by sending the message "sub IDA your name" to `listserv@internet.com`

IE-HTML—Internet Explorer—HTML

You can join this group by sending the message "sub IE-HTML your name" to `listserv@listserv.msn.com`

IMARCOM—The Internet Marketing Communications Mailing List

You can join this group by sending the message "sub IMARCOM your name" to `listserv@internet.com`

INBUSINESS—Internet In Business Discussion List

America Online, Inc. (1-800-827-6364 in USA/Canada)

You can join this group by sending the message "sub INBUSINESS your name" to `listserv@listserv.aol.com`

INET-L—OCC Internet Committee

Oakland Community College, West Bloomfield, MI

You can join this group by sending the message "sub INET-L your name" to `listserv@vm.occ.cc.mi.us`

INETUSE—Internet Use Discussion List

You can join this group by sending the message "sub INETUSE your name" to `listserv%emuvm1.bitnet@listserv.net`

INTERCAT—OCLC Internet Cataloging project

OCLC, Inc., Dublin, Ohio USA

You can join this group by sending the message "sub INTERCAT your name" to `listserv@oclc.org`

IO-MUG—Internet ONLY Macintosh User's Group

You can join this group by sending the message "sub IO-MUG your name" to `listserv%utarlvm1.bitnet@listserv.net`

ISP-ADMIN-LIST—Internet Service Provider Admin Resource Mailing List

America Online, Inc. (1-800-827-6364 in USA/Canada)

You can join this group by sending the message "sub ISP-ADMIN-LIST your name" to `listserv@listserv.aol.com`

IUFOG-L—Administrative Discussions of the Internet UFO Group Project

America Online, Inc. (1-800-827-6364 in USA/Canada)

You can join this group by sending the message "sub IUFOG-L your name" to `listserv@listserv.aol.com`

IUS-L—Internet Ultra Society

The American University, Washington, DC

You can join this group by sending the message "sub IUS-L your name" to `listserv@american.edu`

MMATRIX—Internet Medical Resource Development

St. John's University, Jamaica, NY

You can join this group by sending the message "sub MMATRIX your name" to `listserv@sjuvm.stjohns.edu`

NANOSNET—Neuro-Ophthalmology Internet Mail Group

The George Washington University Computer Center, Washington DC

You can join this group by sending the message "sub NANOSNET your name" to
listserv@gwuvm.gwu.edu

NETEX—The Internet Experience

America Online, Inc. (1-800-827-6364 in USA/Canada)

You can join this group by sending the message "sub NETEX your name" to
listserv@listserv.aol.com

NETHELP—TJL Internet User Help

University of Missouri-St. Louis

You can join this group by sending the message "sub NETHELP your name" to
listserv@umslvma.umsl.edu

PACESIG—Special Internet Group

Pace University, Pleasantville, NY

You can join this group by sending the message "sub PACESIG your name" to
listserv@pacevm.dac.pace.edu

PRIE-L—Packet Radio Internet Extension List

University of California, San Francisco, CA

You can join this group by sending the message "sub PRIE-L your name" to
listserv@itssrv1.ucsf.edu

SHAMANS—Shamans Impact of the Internet on Religion

University of Arkansas Main Campus - Fayetteville

You can join this group by sending the message "sub SHAMANS your name" to
listserv@uafsysb.uark.edu

STCMD-L—Internet Star Trek Command Council

University of Arkansas Main Campus - Fayetteville

You can join this group by sending the message "sub STCMD-L your name" to
listserv@uafsysb.uark.edu

TOURBUS—The Internet TourBus - A Virtual Tour of Cyberspace

America Online, Inc. (1-800-827-6364 in USA/Canada)

You can join this group by sending the message "sub TOURBUS your name" to
listserv@listserv.aol.com

WEB-INT—Internet Integration Team

You can join this group by sending the message "sub WEB-INT your name" to
listserv@services.web.aol.com

WEBLIST—Internet Workshop Discussion Group

You can join this group by sending the message "sub WEBLIST your name" to
listserv@listserv.kent.edu

WWWIIG-L—UA World Wide Web Internet Interest Group Discussion

University of Arkansas Main Campus - Fayetteville

You can join this group by sending the message "sub WWWIIG-L your name" to
listserv@uafsysb.uark.edu

Criminal Law

Cecil Greek's Criminal Justice Page

`http://www.stpt.usf.edu/~greek/cj.html`

Links to criminal justice and the media—including high-profile cases such as the O.J. Simpson trial and the Susan Smith case—also, online criminal justice discussion groups and e-journals, criminal justice education, prisons and the death penalty, crime-related Web sites, agencies providing criminal justice information, international criminal justice resources, and federal criminal justice agencies (just to name a few). Over 300 links!

COPNet & Police Resource List

`http://police.sas.ab.ca/`

The law enforcement officer's home in cyberspace. An international collection of works by and for other law enforcement officers. While many of the items found here are useful for their job and professional development, others are here solely for their entertainment.

Criminal Law Links

`http://dpa.state.ky.us:80/~rwheeler/`

Top 5% Web site by the Point system. Well-designed and laid out. Has a focus that concentrates on aspects of crime and criminal law. Also includes a focus index and links to other sites about criminal law. Has news abstracts and links to full articles on current events related to criminal law.

Guide to Internet Resources in Criminal Law and Criminal Justice

`http://www.law.ubc.ca/international/guide.html`

Defines and links to networking resources such as mailing lists and USENET groups that deal with criminal law. Also includes information resources such as Gopher, WWW, FTP, and Telnet sites. Sites are listed in alphabetical order. An exhaustive listing.

Justice Information Center (NCJRS)

`http://www.ncjrs.org/`

Besides access to thousands of links on courts, crime prevention, criminal justice statistics, drugs and crime, juvenile justice, law enforcement, and victims, site has pertinent articles and abstracts that deal with crimes and criminal justice. Links also included to various bureaus and organizations that deal with crimes and criminal law.

Partnerships Against Violence Network (PAVNET)

`gopher://cyfer.esusda.gov:70/11/violence`

Gopher site. Library of information about violence and youth with data from seven different United States federal agencies. Deals with issues of: community violence, criminal and juvenile justice, family violence, substance abuse, youth violence, and victims. Variety of papers and studies available on these issues.

Scott Carpenter's TOP Page

`http://www.usit.net/public/rscarp/law.htm`

Various links to pages specifically on criminal law and on law in general. Includes link to resources in forensic science and the National Archive of Criminal Justice Data. Also links to searchable law sites.

U.S. Criminal Law

`http://www.law.cornell.edu/topics/criminal.html`

The Legal Information Institute from Cornell Law School maintains this page. Mostly text, provides primary source material from the U.S. Constitution and U.S. Code and recent legislation. Also includes federal agencies that are related to or deal with crimes, criminal law, and criminal justice.

Cyber Law

CyberLaw™ World Wide

`http://www.cyberlaw.com/cylw_home.html`

Site houses CyberLaw, an educational service focusing on legal issues concerning computer technology, and CyberLex, which reports legal developments touching the computer industry. Links to articles from both are found here.

CyberSpace Law Center

`http://www.cybersquirrel.com/clc/clcindex.html`

For those interested in legal issues related to or concerning cyberspace. Link to information about commerce, privacy, cybercrimes, freedom of expression, intellectual property, and other resources that cover cyberspace law. Also includes links to general legal information and general Internet information.

E-Law 3.0

`http://www.leepfrog.com/E-Law/E-Law/Contents.html`

Table of contents for a paper by David Loundy about computer information systems law and system operator liability. Paper covers what computer information systems are, legal issues involved, computer crime, copyright issues, trademark issues, and suggestions for regulation.

ICLU—Your Rights in Cyberspace

http://www.law.indiana.edu/law/iclu.html

Site provides resources and information regarding cyberspace and law. Links to information on how the Internet works, ownership of public materials, who pays for the Internet, the Clipper Chip, criminal law issues, pornography, free speech, and much more.

Information Highway Advisory Counsel (IHAC) of Canada

http://info.ic.gc.ca/info-highway/ih.html

Site provides information about the establishment of this Counsel and its intent and purpose. Read the final report of the Counsel, *Connection, Community, Content: The Challenge of the Information Highway*, or review the reports and studies used by the Counsel. Site also includes links to other documents of related topics, and contains summaries of all the Counsel meetings.

The Information Law Web

http://seamless.com/rcl/infolaw.html

Visit this site to access people, places, and things that help you understand your rights in the information age. People has links to lawyers and specialists who work in this field. Places links you to sites containing information on copyright, patent, trademarks, and intellectual property.

Internet, the Law, and Related Topics

gopher://ming.law.vill.edu:70/11/.efl/

A Gopher menu containing various papers on subjects related to the Internet and the law. Some topics include an electronic town meeting, the commercialization of electronic networks, metaphors and network law, and strategies for protecting intellectual property on networks.

OwlLex Law Links—The CyberSpace Law Links

http://www.dcez.com/~alewine/CyberLawLinks.html

Find links from the Federal Communications Bar Association to the Cyberspace Law Library, and everything in between. Also gain access to Cyberspace Law News Links such as the Entertainment Law Resource Center and HotWired Index of Privacy Resources. Dozens of links to all aspects of cyberspace and cyberlaw: commissions, committees, journals, resource sites, and more.

Netwatchers Cyberzine

http://www.ionet.net/~mdyer/front.shtml

Home to the e-zine that covers legal developments in cyberspace and the online community. Link to current issue's contents, letters to the editor, past issues, find out if you can be a NetWatcher, or subscribe to the cyberzine. Or connect to other legal links through the Hot Links button—home to the NetWatchers Legal Hotlink of the week. Site also has bookmarks to various legal sites on the Internet.

Environmental Law

CCE - CCA - CEC (Commission for Enviromental Cooperation)

http://cec.org/english/index.html

Home page of the Commission for Environmental Cooperation, this site has links to the North American Agreement on Environmental Cooperation, what's new at the CEC, what the CEC is about, CEC publications, and the CEC resource center. Also included are links to an enviornmental law info-base, the North American Environment Fund, the EcoRegion newsletter, and contracts and job vacancies. The site is available in French and Spanish as well as English, and has a searchable database. Other environmental links are included.

Environmental Law Alliance Worldwide

http://open.igc.org/elaw/

Site is virtual home to the E-LAW. Contains the newsletter issued by the U.S. office. Each issue is a hot link: click and read. You can also access the Telnet session and join a electronic discussion conference. If you would rather, you can browse the index of topic discussed in this electronic conference. See who participated in the E-LAW annual meeting, or meet some of its members. Site's basic purpose is to promote understanding of E-LAW.

Environmental Law Around the World

`http://www.igc.apc.org/envlaw/`

Click on the area of the world whose environmental law interests you, and you are whisked away to a page containing links to treaties, papers, and organizations for individual countries in that part of the world. Areas include Middle East, Europe, Asia, Americas, and Africa. Site also has connection to treaties and other links involving environment and the law.

Environmental Law Resources

`http://http1.brunel.ac.uk:8080/depts/chem/advanced/resource/law.htm`

Site contains sources of environmental law and regulations from the Internet along with some discussion from the environmental newsgroups. Links include Standards, Law, Environmental Conventions, and Ecotaxes. Covers international environmental laws and regulations.

Environmental Law World Wide Web Site

`http://www.webcom.com/~staber/welcome.html`

Site is a plethora of information about environment and the law. Divided into sections: What's new, United States Environmental Law at a Glance, Recent Information Regarding Environmental Law, Articles, Speeches, Press Releases and Announcements Concerning Environmental Law, and Environmental Forum. Each section contains links to various types of information including laws, statutes, articles, and press releases.

U.S. Environmental Protection Agency

`http://www.epa.gov/`

The home page of the U.S. Environmental Protection Agency boasts access to mountains of information. Links include standard about the EPA, what's new, and what's hot. Also, offices, programs, EPA news and events, contracts, grants, environmental financing, jobs, rules, regulations, and legislation. Not all links that are provided are listed here. Page has access to other Internet resources and has a searchable database and index.

United Nations Environment Programme

`http://unep.unep.no/`

Find out what the UN is doing to promote the environment. Link to a discussion of what the UNEP is, access the UNEP Internet Information Exchange, read about Environmental Current Events, or search documents at UNEP. Page also can link you to other UN organizations, and the UNEP staff.

The WWW Virtual Library: Law: International & Environmental Law

`http://www.law.indiana.edu/law/intenvlaw.html`

Part of the WWW Virtual Library, this site has links and links and links to conferences, papers, collections, services, laws, and on and on about international and environmental law. Materials are organized alphabetically by source.

Family Law

Divorce Helpline Home Page

`http://www.divorcehelp.com/`

Keep the law out of your divorce! This site provides resources to the consumer who is looking to stay out of court for his or her divorce. Divided into sections: Helpline Center, Short Cource, Directory, Book Shop, Work Room, and Reading Room. Also includes link to Divorce Helpline's California Center and a Directory of Self-help Services. Obligatory links to other sites included.

Divorce Law Home Page

`http://www.agate.net/~corbeau/lyons.html#toc`

Henry Lyons is his name, family law is his game. Site has nicely set up table of contents for easy searching in the following categories: state-by-state family law, case law, bankruptcy and divorce, health insurance, child custody and support, women's resources, men's resources, newsgroups and mailing lists, and articles on divorce and family law. Site also has access to Find People Fast, a national information service dedicated to locating missing persons. Do a Yahoo search from here, access other legal links, or find a lawyer.

The Divorce Page

`http://www.primenet.com/~dean/legal.html`

Site has incredible range of links that access information from the 'lectric Law Library to an overview of marriage contracts in 15th-century Normandy. Basically a starting point for persons who are in need of legal advice. This page pinpoints certain areas of the U.S. including New Jersey, Arizona, and California, but its information is not limited to these areas.

Family Law

http://www.njlawnet.com/famlaw.htm

Concise page with links that identify laws that affect families, government agencies for families, family law news, family law articles, and family law sites. Short and to the point.

Family Law Advisor Home Page

http://www.divorcenet.com/law/

Site provides support and legal information for persons going through or having gone through a divorce. Divided into sections: frequently asked questions, Online Newsletter and Index, State-by-State Resource Center, Interactive Bulletin Board, Paternity Establishment, Lawyer to Lawyer, and International Parental Abduction. Link to information through each of these sections. Page also includes a search engine that covers the entire site. Other legal and law links are available through this site, too.

Fathers' Rights and Equality Exchange

http://www.vix.com/free/index.html

Site contains much information about the legal rights of fathers. You can find out about the first annual F.R.E.E. conference, join F.R.E.E., discover the benefits of F.R.E.E., read the F.R.E.E. case file, and read a message from the founder of F.R.E.E. Other links include the F.R.E.E. case file and testimonies from F.R.E.E. members.

Legal dot Net—Family Law, and Overview

http://www.legal.net/family.htm

An overview of family law and what is involved in the leaglities of divorce. Covers the legal talk about negotiated settlements, discovery, disclosure statements, temporary orders, petitions, and responses. Site also links to other legal sites, and attorney and non-attorney topics.

Same-Sex Marriage Home Page

http://www.nether.net/~rod/html/sub/marriage.html

Site contains much legal information about same-sex marriages, including which states have banned them, which states have failed to ban them, and which states are currently trying to ban them. Also access same-sex lobby groups, the marriage mailing list, and articles on same-sex relationships and marriage. General information about how solid gay unions are is also included.

International Law

American Journal of International Law

http://www.enews.com/magazines/ajil/

Complete summary of goals and mission of the Americal Journal of International Law. Also, links to current issue, the archive, subscription information, and even a virtual comment card.

Foreign and International Law Page

http://lawlib.wuacc.edu/forint/forint3m.html

Provides searchable links to foreign legal materials (searchable by subject and geographic location), International law related materials, and other international law resources. Also contains access to embassies around the world. Law firms, and legal-related Web pages around the world.

The International Law Page

http://www.noord.bart.nl/~bethlehem/law.html

Access to hundreds of international law links, including links to international organizations, international treaties, European treaties, international law journals, and universities involved in international law. Also, links to environmental law, and other Web law resources.

International Trade Law—ITL

http://itl.irv.uit.no/trade_law/

Site enables you to type in a keyword or concept for a search of information related to the legal field. Site also includes various links that contain information about International trade treaties, International organizations related to trade, country profiles, links to other law-related sites, the Trade Law Library, and various Internet search engines.

The Internet Immigration Law Center

http://catalog.com/immlaw/

Home page contains links to resources on immigration law topics and information, immigration news bulletins, links to other Internet immigration law resources, and attorney/client immigration law. Linked sites are set up in easy-to-follow formats for the quickest searches.

JurWeb

http://www.uni-bayreuth.de/students/elsa/jura/geo/jurweb-geo-home.html

In both German and English, this site has access to hundreds of countries (broken down by continent), the United Nations and its organizations, international organizations, international treaties. Each link leads to a Gopher menu containing general information about that country or organization, and the constitution of the nation, where appropriate.

United Nations Crime and Justice Information Network

http://www.ifs.univie.ac.at/uncjin/mosaic/

"The International exchange and dissemination of information on crime prevention and criminal justice issues." Much information available here regarding International law, criminal, and legal issues. Links include United Nations documents, information on various countries, international statistics and research sources, constitutions, treaties, laws, and court decisions, and other organizations that have similar goals as the United Nations.

Law Schools

FindLaw: Law Schools of Canada

http://www.findlaw.com/02lawschools/canada.html

Part of the FindLaw database. Links to the law schools in Canada. Information given for each school includes a link to the university home page and contact information (snail mail address and telephone number).

FindLaw: US News Top 25 Law Schools

http://www.findlaw.com/02lawschools/USNEWSlist.html

Part of the FindLaw database. Search through the top 25 law schools in the nation based on the *US News and World Report* survey. Each school's listing provides home page links, library links, and snail mail contact information.

ILRG: Brennan's Law School Rankings

http://www.uts.cc.utexas.edu/~juris/rankings/rankings.html

Chief Justice Thomas E. Brennan's *Judging the Law Schools*. Table of contents provided. Includes author biography, methodology used to judge the schools, top 20 law schools based on the following: composite index, quality index, instutional index, faculty index, library index, diversity index, and value index.

Law School Admission Council Online

Http://www.lsac.org/

Features "Reggie" the online LSAT registration service. Link to their Web site and get information on law school forums, LSAT preparation materials, and law school financial aid. Page also includes link to WWW sites at LSAC-member law schools.

Law School and the LSAT

http://www.kaplan.com/lsat

From Kaplan, everything you need to know about the LSAT and law school, including scoring, sections, and dates and registration. Page also includes links to help you through law school admission and financial aid. Access to law schools and law student resources also found on page.

Law School Dot Com

http://www.lawschool.com/

The lighter side of law school. Access games and diversions, law school information, and bar exam information. Also search the career center database for a job. Speak your mind in the newsgroup. Many valuable and entertaining links.

Law School Quotes

http://www.shore.net/~djn/law.html

Lighten up with this page of law school quotes compiled by a student. Witty, funny, and you can contribute, too. Also includes a link to Boston College Law School. Send your funny, quirky, or just plain off-the-wall quote to this page.

The Law Student Web

http://darkwing.uoregon.edu/~ddunn/l_schl.htm

The main Web site for law students. A comprehensive index of law student pages, law schools, sites of importance to law students, and strange case law and statutes.

The Princeton Review: Law School and the LSAT

http://www.review.com/law/LAW_HOMEPAGE.html

Provides links and information regarding the law school entrance exam—the LSAT. Access to information on financial aid, tips for getting into law school, the LSAT test, and the MBE. Also includes links to law school databases and to other law-related sites on the Internet.

Yale Law School Homepage

http://www.yale.edu/lawweb/lawschool/ylshp.htm

Number one ranked law school in the nation based on the *US News and World Report* survey. Link to admissions information, the 1995-96 Bulletin, faculty biographies, and occasional papers. Also access Dean Kronman's welcoming address to the class of 1998.

Legal Organizations

ACLU Freedom Network

http://www.aclu.org/

The home page for the American Civil Liberties Union takes you to the latest happenings from congress, current events, and what's happening in the nation's courts. You can also join the ACLU, browse their cyberstore, and read about current events. Other links take you to highlights of cases that the ACLU has involvement in.

American Bar Association

http://www.abanet.org/

The ABA Network connects you to any information you need pertaining to this world's largest voluntary professional association. Links to information about the various entities of the ABA (each entity has its own link), a calendar of events, and public information are just a few starting points on this top 5% Web site.

American Immigration Lawyers Association

http://www.aila.org/

Links to information about the AILA, how to join, and AILA conferences can be found here. Also, writings about immigration as it pertains to America, the role of immigration lawyers, and recent legislative affairs that affect immigration law. Provided, too, is a searchable index of AILA members, and immigration lawyers on the Web.

The Better Business Bureau

http://www.igc.apc.org/cbbb

Links to information about the Better Business Bureau, local BBBs, and programs and services provided by the BBB. Also access to members of the BBB, frequently asked questions, and publications of the BBB.

International Association of Constitutional Law

http://www.eur.nl/iacl/index.html

Provides access to general information about the IACL, an invitation for the adherence to the IACL, a link to more information about the Fourth World Congress, and access to the constitutions of countries of the world, in both the native language and English.

NYSDA Public Defense Backup Center Home Page

http://www.nysda.org/

This is the front page of an extensive collection of links related to the New York State Defenders Association. This not-for-profit organization seeks to improve the quality of defense services in New York State. The site indexes the various departments of NYSDA through various links, including those on membership, the Board of Directors, and the Defender News Archives.

The Sovereign Patriot Group

http://www.ecst.csuchico.edu/~spg/index.html

Provides access to information regarding constitutional issues and laws. Link to two electronic journals that report local and national news in sovereign events. Also has link to the White House, and to other sovereign Web pages.

Legal Publications

The American Indian Law Review

`http://www.law.uoknor.edu/departments/ailr.html`

This Review is published by the University of Oklahoma College of Law. This site gives background information about the Review, and contact information for getting a copy of the current, or back, issues.

American Journal of Criminal Law

`http://tarlton.law.utexas.edu/journals/ajcl/ajcl.html`

Maintained by the University of Texas School of Law. From here gain information about subscriptions, how to submit a manuscript to the Journal, and send mail to the journal members.

European Law Journal

`http://www.iue.it/LAW/ELJ/Welcome.html`

Find out about the Journal by clicking on the aims and scope link. Get the table of contents, issues covered in the Journal, the editorial board, the advisory board, and information about contributing to the Journal through links from this site.

Federal Communications Law Journal

`http://www.law.indiana.edu/fclj/fclj.html`

The official journal of the Federal Communications Bar Association. Site includes links to electronic versions of currently available issues. Access also available to information about the Federal Communications Bar Association and Indiana University School of Law. Journal is maintained by student editorial board at Indiana Univeristy School of Law.

Global Legal Studies Journal

`http://www.law.indiana.edu/glsj/glsj.html`

Published by the Indiana University School of Law, this site contins all back issues of the Journal, information on how and why it was started, subscription information, and editorial board information. A search engine is available to help you locate the information you need.

Human Rights Brief

`http://www.wcl.american.edu/pub/journals/hmnrghts.htm`

Maintained by the Washington College of Law Center of Human Rights and Humanitarian Law,

this site has links that access the available issues of this journal. Link to the issue and receive a full table of contents, as well as a calendar of events and information about the copyrights and credits for that issue.

Journal of Information, Law, and Technology

`http://ltc.law.warwick.ac.uk/elj/jilt/`

This site, home to the e-journal JILT, enables you to access past and present issues, link to what is new, regular features, special features, and information about the people who put JILT together. Also link to information about JILT, how it got started, what its purpose is, and why it is maintained the way it is.

Journal of International Law and Practice

`http://ic.net/~jilp/`

This site is the home of the Journal of International Law and Practice. Topics covered range from international human rights to recent developments in private and public international law. Links include subscription information, submission information, back issues, forthcoming issues, and general information about the Journal.

The Journal of Online Law

`http://www.law.cornell.edu/jol/jol.table.html`

E-journal with essays pertaining law and online communications—law and cyberspace. Read the articles, subscribe, get information about the Journal of Online Law, or meet the editorial staff from this Web site.

Bean Bag Color Samples

`http://www.beanbag.com/ordersam.htm`

Can't decide which bean bag would look best in your living room? Bean Bag City can send you free color samples including quick silver, milk chocolate, and glacier blue.

Law Journal Extra!

`http://www.ljx.com/`

Updated daily! Journal highlights current events that affect the legal and political professions. Articles on high-profile cases and suits, court-room updates, and new rulings are just some of the interesting and resourceful links on this page. Also included is access to national legal journals online, the market-place, employment center, and law firms online.

Law Library Journal

`gopher://ukoln.bath.ac.uk:7070/11/BUBL_Main_Menu/E/E2/E2EL22`

A Gopher menu that enables you to access the most recent volumes of the Library Law Journal. Volume contains article title, author, and abstract of the article.

legal.online

`http://www.legalonline.com/`

Home to the monthly newsletter for legal profession-als using the Internet. Link to information about legal.online, view a sample issue, check out the index of back issues, fill out the ordering informa-tion, read the guide to courts on the Net, and look over the statutes and bill on the Net.

Legal Resources

ALSO! Main Page

`http://www.lawsource.com/also/alsohome.htm`

Provides a comprehensive, uniform, and useful compilation of links to all online sources of Ameri-can law that are available without charge. Source documents are stored in various file formats in many separately maintained databases located in several countries.

AMERICAN LAW SOURCES ON-LINE

Counsel Connect Web

`http://www.counsel.com/`

Updated daily, this site provides links to the hottest legal topics and discussions of the day, current updates on high-profile cases, and breaking legal news. Or click on Law Links and get access to links to legal topics, government, world law, libraries, non-legal sites, or use the search engine. Go inside Counsel Connect to find out what's online,

upcoming seminars, and read the newsletter. You can also search the Lawyers database for legal help, classi-fieds, a lawyer search, and the Quick Request for Proposals.

CourtTV Home Page

`http://www.courttv.com/index.html#Top`

Something for people of all ages. Includes links to legal help, the law library, and case files. Provides access to updates on high-profile cases. Read about what are currently the "hot topics" in the legal world. But don't overlook the fun side of law—click to CourtTV games and pages for kids. Finally, stop in the CourtTV store for a look around.

Hieros Gamos

`http://www.hg.org/`

Comprehensive resource for legal professionals, law students, and persons seeking law-related informa-tion. Links include bar associations, legal associa-tions, law schools, publishers, law firms, law sites, governments sites, vendors, and online services. Site available in English, Spanish, German, French, and Italian. More resources than can be listed.

Law.Net

`http://law.net/`

A resourceful page that links to a directory of lawyers and law firms separated into specialization. Page also includes how to join information, the newsletter, access to the library, articles of interest.

LawMall

`http://www.lawmall.com/`

A virtual mall for the legal profession with a pot-pourri of links, including classified ads, editorials, articles, expert witness wanted ads, LawMall information, and others. Page also includes links to other law-related resources, and lawyers and firms by state and city.

LawMarks...The Legal Resource Database

`http://www.iwc.com/entropy/marks/bkmrkjsm.html`

A comprehensive digest of all available legal and law-related resources on the Internet. After reading about LawMarks, choose from the General Directory of Resources menu, or the General Directory of Other Internet Search Engines menu. The General Directory includes links to rules of court, law schools, law journals, legal news, legal directories, federal documents, and law libraries, to name a few.

The 'Lectric Law Library

http://www.lectlaw.com/

Grab your library card and search the not-so-dusty shelves of the 'Lectric Law Library. The Rotunda leads to various rooms housing information on business law, legal and business forms, legal research guides, and more. Also has a room for the weird laws, cases, and court filings. Includes jokes, bloopers, and anecdotes. Comprehensive legal resource.

Legal Information Institute

http://www.law.cornell.edu/index.html#main_menus

If you can't find it here, it isn't on the Web. This is thoroughly comprehensive in its presentation of legal information. Search by keyword or through an alphabetical index. Locate information on all topics of law and the legal profession. If the LII can't locate the information you need, there are links to other legal and general search engines that can help.

P-LAW Legal Resources Locator

http://www.dorsai.org/p-law/

For anyone who is looking for legal resources on the Internet. Link to legislative and other government information sites, multicategory reference sites such as universities and the United Nations, specialized topic sites such as advertising law, criminal law, statistical information sites, and miscellaneous sites such as The ACLU Reading Room and The National Criminal Justice Reference Service.

Web Journal of Current Legal Issues

http://www.ncl.ac.uk/~nlawwww/

Click and you're connected to past and present issues of the Web JCLI. Covers current legal issues. Site includes other legal links, a welcome message, and information on becoming an author of the Web Journal of Current Legal Issues. A top 5% Web Site by Point.

Miscellaneous Law Sites

The Constitution of the United States of America

http://www.law.cornell.edu:80/constitution/
constitution.overview.html

Site gives you access to the U.S. Constitution in a series of links: Credits and Condition, Context, The

Preamble, Articles I through VII (separate links), Signers, and Amendments. Articles are broken down into Sections, one link per section.

LAW EMPLOYMENT CENTER

http://www.lawjobs.com/

The law classifieds. Find legal job listings, legal recruiting, and the law employment library here. Access the NLJ top 250 index of the nation's largest law firms. Link to the National Law Journal salary survey. Also link to the market update, telling you which fields are hot and which are not.

LawTalk

http://www.law.indiana.edu/law/lawtalk.html

RealAudio files dealing with some aspect of law or legal studies. Segments are authored by a faculty member at IU School of Law in Bloomington or Indianapolis. Titles include: Amendments to the U.S. Constitution, Business and Personal Finance Law, Criminal Law, and Civil Law.

Lawyer Jokes

http://nearnet.gnn.com/gnn/bus/nolo/jokes.html

Lawyer bashing, the new American past time. This site has hundreds of jokes poking fun at lawyers. Some jokes are question and answer, such as what's the difference between baseball and law? In baseball, if you are caught stealing, you're out. Other jokes are humorous anecdotes. You can hot link to you favorite type of lawyer joke, or just browse through the page, laughing along the way.

Legalitees T-Shirts Home Page

http://attorneysatlaw.com/

On the lighter side... Site has humorous T-shirts for sale with law-related themes. Gifts for lawyers, law students, law enforcement officers, legal scholars, and law professors. Links take you to preview of T-shirt. Order through site.

Murphy's Law

http://dmawww.epfl.ch/~muller/murphy.html

"Anything that can go wrong, will." Ah, Murphy's Law. Even the non-technical, non-legal person knows about Murphy and his laws. This site has a great collection of the most popular Murphy's Laws,

laws that deal with the military, with science and technology, with love, and with sex. It also includes an abridged collection of interdisciplinary laws.

THE SEAMLESS WEBsite...lawyer law firm expert

http://www.seamless.com/

First commercial legal Web site. Four main categories: The Chambers contains news and information about this site; the Commons contains original writings on topics related to law; The Shingle features the home pages of lawyers and legal service providers; and the Crossroads contains roads to over 1,000 other law sites. Site also offers free job listing service, listing of expert witnesses, and an interactive bulleting board. Also has a live chat line.

Newsgroups

alt.law-enforcement

alt.lawyers.sue.sue.sue

alt.privacy

alt.society.resistance

alt.visa.us

aus.legal

aw.school.legal-prof

bit.listserv.lawsch-l

bit.listserv.lawsch.internships

can.legal

clari.nb.law

clari.news.law_enforce

clari.news.usa.law

clari.usa.law

clari.usa.law.misc

clari.usa.law.supreme

clari.world.law

fido7.civil-law

fido7.law

law.court.federal

law.listserv.election-law

law.listserv.net-lawyers

law.school.anti-trust

law.school.clinic.info-law

law.school.copyright

law.school.corps

law.school.legal-prof

law.school.tax.basic

law.school.tax.busiplan

law.school.tax.business

misc.immigration.usa

misc.int-property

misc.legal

misc.legal.computing

misc.legal.moderated

misc.taxes

pdaxs.services.legal

pnet.talk.legal

relcom.comp.law

tuk.legal

Listservs

ADA-LAW—Americans with Disabilities Act Law

You can join this group by sending the message "sub ADA-LAW your name" to listserv@listserv.nodak.edu

ALSBFEM—Academy of Legal Studies in Business (ALSB) Feminist

Miami University, Oxford, OH

You can join this group by sending the message "sub ALSBFEM your name" to `listserv@miamiu.muohio.edu`

ALSBNEWS—Academy of Legal Studies in Business (ALSB) News

Miami University, Oxford, OH

You can join this group by sending the message "sub ALSBNEWS your name" to `listserv@miamiu.muohio.edu`

ALSBTALK—Academy of Legal Studies in Business (ALSB) Talk

Miami University, Oxford, OH

You can join this group by sending the message "sub ALSBTALK your name" to `listserv@miamiu.muohio.edu`

BUSLAW-L—Business Law List

Humber College, Toronto, Ontario, Canada

You can join this group by sending the message "sub BUSLAW-L your name" to `listserv@admin.humberc.on.ca`

CALL-L—Canadian Association of Law Libraries List

University of New Brunswick, Fredericton, N.B., Canada

You can join this group by sending the message "sub CALL-L your name" to `listserv@listserv.unb.ca`

CYBERIA-L—Law & Policy of Computer Communications

America Online, Inc. (1-800-827-6364 in USA/Canada)

You can join this group by sending the message "sub CYBERIA-L your name" to `listserv@listserv.aol.com`

EDLAW—Law and Education

You can join this group by sending the message "sub EDLAW your name" to `listserv@lsv.uky.edu`

FEMJUR—Discussions and Information About Feminist Legal Issues

Syracuse University

You can join this group by sending the message "sub FEMJUR your name" to `listserv@listserv.syr.edu`

INTLAW-L—Internet and Computer Law Association

NE Regional Data Center, Univ. of Florida campus, Gainesville, FL

You can join this group by sending the message "sub INTLAW-L your name" to `listserv@nervm.nerdc.ufl.edu`

LAT-LAW—Latin American Legal Discussion Group

University of Arizona, Tucson, AZ

You can join this group by sending the message "sub LAT-LAW your name" to `listserv@listserv.arizona.edu`

LAWCOM-L—Commission on Communication and Law Discussion List

University of Arkansas Main Campus - Fayetteville

You can join this group by sending the message "sub LAWCOM-L your name" to `listserv@uafsysb.uark.edu`

LAWSCH-L—Law School Discussion List

The American University, Washington, DC

You can join this group by sending the message "sub LAWSCH-L your name" to `listserv@american.edu`

LEGALTEN—Topical Evaluation Network Legal List

St. John's University, Jamaica, NY

You can join this group by sending the message "sub LEGALTEN your name" to `listserv@sjuvm.stjohns.edu`

LGUILD-L—The National Lawyers Guild Electronic Mailing List

State University of New York at Buffalo

You can join this group by sending the message "sub LGUILD-L your name" to `listserv@listserv.acsu.buffalo.edu`

LRW—Legal Research and Writing Adjuncts' Discussion Group

The George Washington University Computer Center, Washington DC

You can join this group by sending the message "sub LRW your name" to `listserv@gwuvm.gwu.edu`

LSE—Legal Studies Education

Wayne State University, Detroit, MI

You can join this group by sending the message "sub LSE your name" to `listserv@cms.cc.wayne.edu`

MAALL—Mid-America Association of Law Libraries

Washington University, St. Louis, MO

You can join this group by sending the message "sub MAALL your name" to `listserv@wuvmd.wustl.edu`

MALSLC—Mid-America Law School Library Consortium Resource Sharing

Washington University, St. Louis, MO

You can join this group by sending the message "sub MALSLC your name" to `listserv@wuvmd.wustl.edu`

MINLAW-L—Law School Experiences of Minorities

University of Arkansas Main Campus - Fayetteville

You can join this group by sending the message "sub MINLAW-L your name" to `listserv@uafsysb.uark.edu`

MPLA—Minority Pre-Law Association

University of Arizona, Tucson, AZ

You can join this group by sending the message "sub MPLA your name" to `listserv@listserv.arizona.edu`

NCLSMTG—National Conference of Lawyers and Scientists

The George Washington University Computer Center, Washington, DC

You can join this group by sending the message "sub NCLSMTG your name" to `listserv@gwuvm.gwu.edu`

PSYCOP—PsyUSA Network - Psychologists in Law Enforcement

St. John's University, Jamaica, NY

You can join this group by sending the message "sub PSYCOP your name" to `listserv@sjuvm.stjohns.edu`

PSYLAW-L—Psychology and Law, International Discussion

You can join this group by sending the message "sub PSYLAW-L your name" to `listserv%utepa.bitnet@listserv.net`

SPORTLAW

Central Missouri State University

You can join this group by sending the message "sub SPORTLAW your name" to `listserv%cmsuvmb.bitnet@listserv.net`

TECHLAW—"Journal of Technology Law & Policy"

NE Regional Data Center, Univ. of Florida campus, Gainesville, FL

You can join this group by sending the message "sub TECHLAW- your name" to `listserv@nervm.nerdc.ufl.edu`

WRIFELL—Legal Research and Writing Fellows Discussion Group

The George Washington University Computer Center, Washington, DC

You can join this group by sending the message "sub WRIFELL your name" to listserv@gwuvm.gwu.edu

YLOPEARL—Asian Pacific American Law Professors Discussion Group

Syracuse University

You can join this group by sending the message "sub YLOPEARL your name" to listserv@listserv.syr.edu

MEDIA

Access ET

http://www.telegraph.co.uk/

Online version of the *Electronic Telegraphy*, a United Kingdom newspaper. Presents European and international stories. Offers information that has a different slant. Registration is required.

Acoustic Musician Magazine

http://www.netshop.net/acoustic/

Online edition of the *Acoustic Musician* magazine. Covers all aspects of acoustic music for the folk musician. Features articles, a music festival guide, the table of contents for the forthcoming issue, and a place to submit letters to the editor. Also presents covers of back issues.

Adventure Online Gaming

http://www.gameworld.com

Monthly fantasy fiction Web magazine featuring original art and fiction. Includes exciting interactive graphical hypertext adventures. Describes a human and computer refereed true role-playing game. Features intelligent talking monsters, multiple players, 3D graphics, and advanced chat.

Adventurous Traveler Bookstore

http://www.gorp.com/atbook.htm

Provides helpful books and maps to assist in planning fun and safe trips around the world. Allows for searching by location, geographically, and particular activities. Carries both books and videos that may be ordered via phone or fax.

Advertising Age

http://www.adage.com/

Presents images for viewing. Contains archives, ad market information, and a daily top story. Lets you join the Ad Age mailing list.

AE Magazine

http://www.onscreen.com/

AE Magazine's site of new movie reviews, programming information, and actor biographies.

American Country Collectibles

http://rivendell.com/antiques/pubs/gcr/country/

Provides jumps to descriptions and subscription information for GCR Publishing Group, Inc.'s magazines: *American Country Collectibles, Collectibles Flea Market Finds*, and *Victorian Decorating and Lifestyle*. Contains an editorial profile and a guide to where to buy each magazine, as well as the table of contents for the current month's issues.

American Wine

http://www.2way.com:80/food/wine/

American Wine magazine online. Focuses on American vineyards and their products. Features in-depth listings of wine and wine-related links. Also includes the complete text of the magazine, a wine glossary, and a beginner's guide to wine.

Aquanaut

http://bighorn.terra.net/aquanaut/

Online magazine that focuses on scuba diving. Includes classified ads, maps, destination, reviews of products, and lists of training agencies. Allows subscription to an e-mail version.

Architronic Home Page

http://arcrs4.saed.kent.edu/Architronic/

Architectural magazine online. Includes archives of past issues and subscription information.

Asia, Inc. Online

http://www.asia-inc.com/

Business magazine from Asia online. Includes financial news, the Asia Report, and other information for Asian business people.

Astronomer Magazine

http://www.demon.co.uk/astronomer/

A British publication online. Targets the advanced amateur but does contain items for the beginner. Also contains information on comets, asteroids, supernovae, and a variety of other topics that pertain to astronomy.

basilisk

http://swerve.basilisk.com/

Online quarterly journal of film, architecture, philosophy, literature, music, and perception.

Fish Food

http://www.tir.com/~dmccord/fishfood.html

Get free samples of fish food.

Boardwatch Magazine

http://www.boardwatch.com/

Boardwatch magazine online. Focuses on BBSs and the Internet. Provides subscription information (offers the entire publication free online), and enables you to contact the specific departments or editors of the magazine.

Car Collector Home Page

http://www.carcollector.com/

Car Collector magazine online. Features back issues, advertising information, subscription information, and automotive news.

Chicago Moving Image Scene

http://www.rtvf.nwu.edu/chicago/

Serves as a resource for media people in Chicago and around the world. Includes links, phone numbers, and information about media production.

Column that Nobody Reads

http://www.londonmall.co.uk/thecol

The new column in the London Mall Magazine. Mixes contemporary politics and the quirks of life in an attempt to entertain you, whatever your mood.

Condé Nast Traveler

http://www.cntraveler.com/

Condé Nast Traveler online. Previews the current issue on the newsstands and provides articles for travelers who want to save money.

Cyber Cyclist

http://cyberbike.com:80/E0020/
SUI.HpilcNcwU-729cwdFyw9jjMcFjki/index.htm

Web magazine for bicyclists. Includes information about bikes, product reviews, current bicycle events, and other news.

cyberSPOKESMAN

http://tecnet2.jcte.jcs.mil:8000/cybrspke/cybrspke.html

The Air Force online in the form of a magazine. Interesting for military personnel and buffs. Provides information about news and events in the Air Force.

Cyberwest Magazine

http://www.netway.net:80/cyberwest/

The magazine of the American West online. Features articles and offers links about the West. Entertaining, informative magazine that also gives vacation ideas.

Dirty Linen

http://kiwi.futuris.net/linen/

Abridged edition of top American magazine for folk, electric folk, Celtic, and world music. Features a selection of articles, reviews, interviews, and letters to the editor from the current issue. Also includes a guide to concerts and festivals.

Discover Magazine

http://www.enews.com:80/magazines/discover/

Discover magazine online. Science magazine including text of issues, photos, links related to articles, and a subscription service.

Editor & Publisher

http://www.mediainfo.com/edpub/ep/index.htm

Editor & Publisher magazine online. Offers selected articles from the printed version of the magazine, as well as Web-only content. Offers comprehensive coverage of new media news and trends affecting the newspaper industry.

Electronic Green Journal

http://drseuss.lib.uidaho.edu:70/docs/egj.html

Environmental journal online. Contains information about environmental issues. Also lists the contents of the recent issues of the journal.

Electronic Newsstand

http://internet.com/

Offers sample articles and subscription information for more than 300 magazines.

Esquireb2b

http://www.esquireb2b.com

An interactive service provided by the publishing operations of *Esquire Magazine*.

Family World Home Page

http://family.com/homepage.html

Offers selections from more than 40 monthly publications on parenting. Offers links to Internet resources for parents, children and schools.

Felix Culpa Home Page

http://cq-pan.cqu.edu.au/felix-culpa/felix-culpa.html

Australian student magazine. Provides information geared towards Australian students. Features news, community events, and other school-related issues.

FH: Canada Travel Home Page

http://www.fleethouse.com/fhcanada/fhc_expl.htm

Canada Travel magazine online. Provides information about travel to Canada. Offers information the traveler will want while planing a trip to Canada.

Fix—Funkier Than Blown Vinyl

http://www.easynet.co.uk/fix/fix.htm

Exemplifies twentysomethings on the net. Resembles a coffee shop—somewhat pretentious and smoke-filled, frequently raunchy, but interesting nonetheless.

Folk Roots Home Page

http://www.cityscape.co.uk/froots/

Condensed, electronic version of *Folk Roots*. Features their guide to folk and world music events in Britain and Europe, CD reviews, charts and lists of best selling music, a playlist from *Folk Route*s radio program on the BBC World Service, a complete table of contents from the current issue, and much more.

Fortran Journal

http://www.fortran.com/fortran/fug_fj.html

Fortran Journal online. Includes simple form to order the magazine and an in-depth description of the magazine.

FutureNet:.net—Index

http://www.futurenet.co.uk/netmag/net.html

.net magazine online. Covers Internet-related topics. Features their news page. Provides an Internet tutorial, job listings, and back issues. Also provides articles online that don't appear in the published magazine.

Galaxy Entertainment

http://www..starz.com/index.html

Provides information, entertainment and business opportunities in the field of show business. Contains

hot links to show business tips, talent, and an entrepreneur's manual.

Gigaplex

http://www.gigaplex.com/wow

Presents an arts and entertainment Web magazine with departments for film, TV, music, books, theater, photography, food and restaurants, and more. Includes celebrity interviews with actors, musicians, authors, playwrights, directors, and photographers.

Glass Wings: Sensual Celebrations

http://www.aus.xanadu.com/GlassWings/sexual/celebrations.html

Online magazine. Focuses on the sensual side of humanity.

Good Medicine Magazine

http://none.coolware.com/health/good_med/ThisIssue.html

Good Medicine Magazine online. Provides stories and information, such as guided imagery, holistic skin and body care, Reiki (energy healing), and network chiropractic. Proposes that holistic and traditional Western medicine should be combined and considered together as "medicine."

Grass Roots Magazine

http://www.bendtech.com/library/grassroots/

Grass Roots magazine online. Includes feature articles, text of speeches, and links to other environmental sites.

Great Lakes Skier Magazine

http://www.iquest.com/michweb/glskier/

Skiing magazine online. Includes articles and contact information for a subscription. Includes a few skiing links.

High Country News Home Page

http://www.infosphere.com:80/clients/HCNArchive/

High Country News online. Reports biweekly on the West's natural resources, public lands, and changing communities.

Interactive Age Home Page

http://techweb.cmp.com:80/techweb/ia/current

Interactive Age Magazine online. Focuses on tracking electronic Commerce. Enables you to contact the magazine staff, find out the 100 best business Web sites, use their hot link section, or look at their traffic analysis of the most visited Internet sites. Also features daily articles online for registered users.

Internet Writer Resource Guide

http://www.math.uio.no/faq/writing/resources.html

Provides a guide to writing on the Internet. Includes e-mail submissions, a FAQ, and tips on how to improve your writing.

InterText: The Online Fiction Magazine

http://ftp.etext.org/Zines/InterText/intertext.html

Monthy online fiction magazine. Contains short stories. Features five authors whose work has been published in this magazine and have won awards.

JEST Home Page

http://www.uoregon.edu/~roc/jest/index.html

JEST (Journal of Extraneous Scientific Topics) online. Includes very humorous looks at science.

KLON'S JazzAvenue Jazz Information Service

http://www.klon.org/~jazzave/

Features include a biography of featured artist (updated daily), a weekly top 20, CD covers and track listings, and weekly playlists. Also provides local concert information, and a list of Los Angeles area jazz venues.

Knowledge Industry Publications, Inc.

http://www.KIPInet.com/

Offers links to Knowledge Industry's magazines: *AV Video, Multimedia Producer*, and *Tape/Disc Business*. Also contains sports links to companies in the audio visual and multimedia fields.

LIFE Photo Home Page

http://www.pathfinder.com/@@egQ6VwAAAAAAAIMR/Life/lifehome.html

The magazine that pioneered photojournalism has reimagined itself for cyberspace. A visually stunning site that includes many images.

Living Poets, EJournal Home Page

http://dougal.derby.ac.uk/lpoets/

Online magazine. Presents new poetry on the Web.

Logical Alternative—Front Door

http://shell.conknet.com/fusion/

Online magazine that targets multimedia authors. Contains reviews, tips, and other information.

MacNet Journal

http://www.dgr.com/web_mnj/

Contains *MacNet Journal*. Lets you suggest ideas on improving the Macintosh operating system, peruse a free help wanted page, obtain guidelines for submitting articles, and search past issues. Also lets you browse the current issue or subscribe (it's free).

Macworld Online Web Server

http://www.macworld.com/

Macworld online. Lets you search past issues and read articles. Also provides Internet tips.

Mercury Center Home Page

http://www.sjmercury.com/

The *San Jose Mercury* online. Offers in-depth coverage of news events and utilizes hypertext links within stories.

Millennium Whole Earth Catalog

http://www.well.net/mwec/home.html

A limited edition of Howard Rheingold's *Whole Earth Catalog* online. Provides many online excerpts from the catalog book.

MMWIRE WEB

http://www.mmwire.com/

Electronic magazine. Focuses on multimedia and design. Provides much information about current and future multimedia trends.

Mobilia Magazine

http://www.mobilia.com/

Mobilia magazine online. Focuses on the worlds of motoring and collecting. Lets you read it online and offers subscription information. Includes a classified ad section.

MoJo Wire

http://www.mojones.com/

Mother Jones online. Provides insightful information with a Mother Jones slant.

Motorcycle Online

http://www.motorcycle.com/motorcycle.html

Online magazine. Covers all aspects of motorcycles. Includes new model reviews, daily news, technical help, pictures, and tours.

Muse Magazine

http://www.val.net/VillageSounds/Muse/index.html

Online magazine. Focuses on women in music. Features CD reviews, book reviews, and the full text of the magazine.

NCS Career Magazine

http://www.careermag.com/careermag/index.html

Career online. Offers listings of available jobs and employer contact information. Features employment news, college recruiting activity, company profiles, and a résumé bank. Includes a search engine.

Net Traveler

http://www.primenet.com/~ntravel/

Contains *Net Traveler* magazine. Provides information about their list of sites and tools. Offers links to brand new things to hit the Internet. Includes a collection of links to sites of importance, as well as a files archive.

Oceanography—The Magazine

http://www.tos.org/tos/tos_magazine_menu.html

Does not contain full text versions of the articles, but does list the table of contents and biography information about editors of the magazine.

Online Access Web Edition

http://www.oamag.com/online/access.html

Contains *Online Access* magazine. Serves as a guide to online services, bulletin boards, and the Internet. Offers an online events catalog of events happening in cyberspace, a list of the magazines links, and a monthly column devoted to ground breaking shareware software. Also offers subscription information.

Online Educator

http://ole.net/ole/

Offers lesson plans, sample articles from the *Online Educator* magazine, and many other resources. Offers the magazine itself for subscription in both print and electronic forms.

Outside Online

http://web2.starwave.com:80/outside/online/

Offers sections on news, going places, activities, and gear for the outdoor enthusiast.

Pan Asian Publications Home Page

http://www.panap.com/

The source for Asian Publications online. Provides searching and online ordering.

Penthouse on the Internet

http://www.penthousemag.com/

Penthouse online. Features an Internet edition of the magazine and contains many images. Also includes an erotic toy store.

Perspective

http://hcs.harvard.edu/~perspy/

Monthly liberal magazine from Harvard University. Recent issues have focused on the Web.

Playboy Home Page

http://www.playboy.com/

Playboy magazine online. Includes interviews, reviews, and a Playboy forum.

PM Zone

http://popularmechanics.com/

Popular Mechanics online. Provides movies, pictures, and information about new and useful products and technology.

Popular Science Magazine

http://bwn.popsci.com/

Electronic version of *Popular Science* magazine. Aims to be the most timely and authoritative source of enlightened and practical information about what's new in science and technology.

Positive Planet

`http://www.ppmedia.com/planet`

Presents *Positive Planet* magazine and dateline. Features many personal ads from around the world. Also includes a technosexual dating magazine.

PowerPC News

`http://power.globalnews.com/ppchome.htm`

Online biweekly magazine. Features current news about major companies that produce PowerPC microprocessors, software that runs on the PowerPC chip, and products that incorporate the chip. Lets you sign up for an e-mail version of the magazine.

Redundantly, Online

`http://www.unt.edu/~price/red/`

Presents online version of the printed literary magazine. Concentrates on multimedia and using cyberspace creatively. The print version focuses on the humanities.

Rippin' Good Yarn

`http://www.3rdplanet.com/rippin.html`

Online magazine of science fiction and fantasy.

Scripps Howard Home Page

`http://www.scripps.com/`

Presents the media giant on the Web. Scripps Howard owns 18 daily newspapers, 9 TV stations, and a host of other stuff you might want to check out.

Sea Frontiers

`http://www.rsmas.miami.edu/sea-frontiers/sea-frontiers.html`

Oceanography journal online. Contains full-text versions of articles from recent editions.

Serif: The Magazine of Type & Typography

`http://www.quixote.com/serif/`

Online magazine that targets the desktop publisher. Features sample articles, subscription information, and desktop publishing links on the Internet.

South Carolina Point

`http://www.mindspring.com/~scpoint/point/`

Provides online site for *South Carolina Point* news monthly. Includes current and back issues along with contact information.

Tharunka Home

`http://www.real.com.au/magazines/tharunka/`

Australian university student magazine. Offers a different angle on the news (often quite funny).

Travel Weekly

`http://www.novalink.com/travel/`

Travel Weekly online. Serves the travel agency community in the U.S. and internationally. Includes feature travel-related articles and news. Also offers hundreds of links to sites associated with hotels, airlines, cruises, car rentals, railroads, and tour operators.

TravelASSIST Magazine

`http://travelassist.com/mag/mag_home.html`

Online magazine. Contains articles on travel and travel spots around the United States and the world. Includes back issues for online reading.

Typofile Magazine—Home

`http://www.will-harris.com/type.htm`

Online magazine. Focuses on type and its uses. Includes articles and links to other type and desktop publishing sites.

Unix News

`http://apt.usa.globalnews.com/UNI/`

Contains the current issue of *Unix News International*, a monthly publication about Unix systems.

UT Science Bytes

`http://loki.ur.utk.edu/ut2kids/science.html`

Online hypertext magazine. Focuses on UT scientists' research projects. Describes the projects at a level appropriate for elementary school students and links any unfamiliar words or concepts to a definition or explanation.

FREE STUFF

ArchiGopher

`gopher://libra.arch.umich.edu/`

Download images of ancient architecture and study architectural history.

Videomaker's Camcorder & Desktop Video Site

http://www.videomaker.com/

Videomaker magazine online. Includes a product search engine, back issues, and other information about camcorders and video.

Virtual Pathways

http://edge.edge.net/~jhbryan/pathways/toc.html

Backpacking magazine online. Includes reviews of trails and locations around the United States.

Walls & Ceilings Magazine

http://www.wco.org/wac.html

Contains the official publication of the walls and ceilings industry—*Walls & Ceilings Magazine*. Serves contractors, suppliers, and distributors. Contains a virtual library of features on specialty subjects and offers links to an online bookstore and virtual library.

Wave~Length Paddling Network

http://interchange.idc.uvic.ca/~wavenet/magazine.html

Kayaking and Paddling magazine online. Includes archives of past articles and current issues with pictures.

Web Week Home Page

http://www.mecklerweb.com/mags/ww/

Contains *WebWeek Magazine*. Targets Web developers. Offers an online-only column every Monday. Also previews the printed issues and lets you read some of the articles.

Welcome to Carbon 14

http://www.rsabbs.com/carbon14/

Online magazine. Focuses on underground music in all its forms. Features interactive graphics and samples from currently featured albums.

Welcome to Computer Shopper

http://www.zdnet.com/~cshopper/

Provides an online edition of the current *Computer Shopper* magazine. Lets you search through the advertisers for the lowest prices on computer components, or browse through current and past articles.

Welcome To HotWired!

http://www.hotwired.com/

Wired! online. Includes information not found in the paper version of the magazine. Offers many links.

Welcome to Infobahn Magazine

http://www.postmodern.com/

Contains *Infobahn* magazine, a publication devoted to covering the Internet from a cultural point of view. Lets you sign up for a free trial issue, contact the editors, get advertising information and prices, and find out how to submit articles.

Welcome to Pathfinder

http://www.pathfinder.com/@@5NGfxQAAAAAAwIIQ/pathfinder/welcome.html

Time Warner's site. Offers links to *Time* online, *Sports Illustrated* online, *Money Magazine* online, and more.

Welcome to ZD Net

http://www.ziff.com/

Ziff-Davis publishes many computer magazines. Provides articles and information about computers, as well as links to other Ziff-Davis publications, including *PC Magazine*, *PC Week*, *Mac Week*, *Mac User*, *Computer Life*, and more.

Where the Buffalo Roam

http://internet-plaza.net/wtbr

Presents a cartoon published weekly on the Web. Provides cartoons published in the last five weeks. Tells fans about ordering books and T-shirts.

News

American Reporter

http://www.newshare.com/Reporter/today.html

A six day a week electronic "newshare" that is free on a trial basis. Set up by the writers whose work it features, it covers most general topics covered by a daily newspaper with wide coverage of foreign news.

Associated Press

http://www1.trib.com/NEWS/APwire.html

The Associated Press online. Requires free login, but then offers full access to the AP news wires.

FCC Welcome Page

http://www.fcc.gov/

Federal Communications Commission online. Serves as a forum for public discussion concerning FCC issues (including broadcasting). Contains current legislation, full text of relevant speeches, agenda, and the FCC daily digest. Also lists e-mail addresses to which to send comments and concerns about television.

infoMCI

http://www.fyionline.com/infoMCI/

Provides news summaries about business, sports, and headlines. Features industry spotlights for the business surfer.

International Pages

http://www.omroep.nl/international.html

The Dutch public broadcasting system's Web site. Includes program information and other information about the Netherlands.

Internet Disaster Information Center

http://www.disaster.net/

Offers information about ongoing disasters, historical information about disasters, and links to other disaster sites on the Web.

libraries.americas

ftp://ftp.ping.at/pub/info/internet/libraries/libraries.americas

Provides information on information retrieval from online libraries.

NewsLink Menu

http://www.newslink.org/menu.html

Offers a free service that provides access to many online newspapers, periodicals, and so on, around the world every day.

NJ Online Weather

http://www.nj.com/weather/

The Old Farmers Almanac online. Includes weather forecasts for the United States, helpful tips, and other information—just like the hard copy.

NOS TeleTekst

http://www.nos.nl/cgi-bin/tt/nos/page

Dutch Broadcasting Service. Provides an interface to news and other information off the Dutch wire services. Includes English menus but provides the articles in Dutch.

Omnivore

http://way.net/omnivore/

Provides a free daily news service designed to quickly and concisely deliver coverage of events around the world as they happen (uncensored news, straight from the source and original point of view). Provides many links to other news services.

RadioSpace Home Page

http://www.radiospace.com/welcome.html

Serves as a resource for radio station programming and news staffs. Provides ready-for-broadcast sound bites, news, and programming.

RealAudio: ABC News

http://www.realaudio.com/contentp/abc.html

Offers ABC Radio news, available with the RealAudio player. Lets you download audio files of daily and hourly news broadcasts.

South African Broadcasting Corporation Welcome Page

http://www.sabc.co.za/

South African Broadcasting online. Provides many phone numbers and other information. Includes sports scores and news services.

Time Daily News Summary

http://www.pathfinder.com/time/daily/

Provides one paragraph summaries of current stories and provides a searching engine you can use for a more in-depth look.

USIA International Broadcasting

http://www.usia.gov/usiahome/bbureau.html

The United States Information Agency. Provides information about *Voice of America* and other programs.

Newspapers

Campus Newspapers on the Internet

http://beacon-www.asa.utk.edu/resources/papers.html

Lists student newspapers available on the Internet. Includes listings for dailies, weeklies, and less frequent publications.

The Capital

http://www.infi.net/capital/

Online site for the daily newspaper for the Anapolis, Maryland area. Provides a supplemental net version of the paper update five to six times a week. Includes links and area background of the area.

City Paper

http://www.cpcn.com/

Provides online interactive newspaper for Philadelphia, Pennsylvania. Includes local news and events for the Philadelphia metropolitan area. A good place to check if you are looking for entertainment and art in Philly.

Financial Times Group

http://www.nsa.ft.com/

Offers highlights from *Financial Times*, news, and stock indices, updated daily.

Gazeta Wyborcza

http://info.fuw.edu.pl/gw/0/gazeta.html

Presents Gazette Online, an electronic version of Poland's largest daily newspaper, *Gazeta Wyborcza*.

Hastings Tribune Internet Edition

http://www.cnweb.com/tribune/index.html

Nebraska's first online newspaper. Links to news, sports, major stories, subscriber info, comics, want ads, and other info and back issues. Includes color graphics.

Indianapolis Star and News

http://www.starnews.com/

The current editions of the *Indianapolis Star* and the *Indianapolis News*. Access to sports, weather, local and state news, political coverage, and a visitor's guide to Indianapolis.

Jerusalem Post

http://www.jpost.co.il/

The Internet edition of the *Jerusalem Post*. Access to news, business, features, sports, tourism sections and more. Includes graphics.

Kamloops Daily News—Online

http://www.netshop.net/dailynews/daily_news.html

A Canadian-based online newspaper with features such as local news, sports, weather, business, opinion page, and more.

Knoxville News Sentinel

http://www.knoxnews.com/

Knoxville, Tennessee newspaper with links to headlines and features stories, sports, news, weather, classifieds, and more. Includes graphics.

Maui News

http://www.maui.net/~mauinews/news.html

The *Maui News* is a local newspaper featuring news, entertainment, classifieds, features, weather, and other sections of the newspaper. The site also features a link to "Maui County at a Glance."

Money & Investing Update—Welcome

http://update.wsj.com/

The Wall Street Journal online. A free subscription lets business surfers access the daily *Wall Street Journal*.

Newspaper / Diario LA NACION—San Jose, Costa Rica

http://www.nacion.co.cr/

Presents news in Spanish. *La Nacion*, the largest newspaper in Costa Rica, provides news and information of Central America and the world.

Newsshare Corporation

http://www.crocker.com/~densmore/

Supplies interactive media products to newspapers, broadcasters, and the public.

Personal Technology Home Page

http://ptech.wsj.com/

Features the personal technology section from *The Wall Street Journal*. Provides information related to technology and contains archival data.

Private Eye

http://www.intervid.co.uk/intervid/eye/gateway.html

Provides online site for the *Private Eye* newspaper based in London, England. Includes samples of the papers articles and artwork. Also includes subscription information. This paper is similar to the *National Enquirer*; hence, it is good fun.

Providence Business News

http://www.pbn.com/

Provides online site for the *Providence Business News*. Includes resources, circulation, past issues, and a search index. Also incudes subscription information.

Southam, Inc.

http://www.southam.com/

Provides home site and information about *Southam, Inc.*, which publishes 17 daily newspapers, 33 weekly newspapers, along with magazines and new media in Canada. Includes corporate profile, trade show appearance dates, new media services offered, and links to Southam's various newspapers and magazines.

The St. Petersburg Times

http://www.spb.su/sppress/

English language weekly newspaper from St. Petersburg, Russia. Covers news, business news, commentary, culture, and classifieds.

Stanford Daily Home Page

http://daily.stanford.org/

Provides a good example of daily newspapers available on the Internet. Contains news and information.

Sydney Morning Herald

http://www.smh.com.au/

Provides home site and online version of the *Syndey Morning Herald*. Includes stories, advertising information, and various features for this Syndey, Austrailia paper.

Tech

http://the-tech.mit.edu/

MIT bi-weekly student newspaper. Provides articles, including national news wires.

Telluride Times-Journal

http://www.adone.com/telluride/

Provides online site for the *Telluride Times-Journal* from Telluride, Colorado. Includes online version of the paper and subscription information.

Times Higher Education Supplement

http://www.timeshigher.newsint.co.uk/

Provides home site and online supplement for the *Times Higher Education* newspaper from the United Kingdom. Includes stories and features dealing with higher education and career opportunities.

Vocal Point

http://bvsd.k12.co.us/cent/Newspaper/Newspaper.html

High school newspaper online. Offers monthly news from a teen's perspective.

Wall Street Journal Link

http://journal.link.wsj.com/

Provides an online advertising directory of *The Wall Street Journal*. Contains links to advertiser Web sites and e-mail addresses.

Welcome to USA TODAY

http://www.usatoday.com/web1.htm

USA Today online. Features headlines, subscription information, and daily news reports.

Publishing

Academic Press

http://www.apnet.com/

Offers information about their new publications and insight into future releases. Also has a book catalog and textbook shop. Features direct contact to their customer service.

Addison Wesley Longman

http://www.aw.com/

Provides information about the publishing company and the published titles. Also offers information about other publishing houses affiliated with Addison Wesley.

Albion Books

http://www.bookport.com/source/albion9501.html

Provides information and background about the San Francisco-based computer book and online servcice publisher. Includes calendar of events, author chats, novel discussions, and a handy channel programming guide to all services and related sites.

Alldata

http://www.alldata.tsb.com/

Home site for electronic automotive repair publisher. Provides locations of Alldata repair shops, automotive chat room, recall notices, and technical service bulletin titles for vehicles. Also includes corporation background, employment opportunies with Alldata, and an extensive link sheet to various automotive sites.

Association of American University Presses

http://aaup.pupress.princeton.edu/

Features an index of university presses and includes a searchable index of books.

Astrology et al Bookstore

http://www.wolfe.net/~astroetl/index.html

Largest U.S. astrology and metaphysical bookstore. Search the online catalog and place orders online.

Atomic Books "Literary Finds for Mutated Minds"

http://www.atomicbooks.com/

Alternative bookstore online. Features comics, alternative fiction, magazines, and more. Includes online ordering.

Audiobook Source

http://www.webcom.com/absource/

Audiobooks online. Lets you search the catalog and place orders for more than 7,000 titles. Holds monthly specials and has sale items.

Baltzer Science Publishers

http://www.NL.net/~baltzer/

Publishes scientific journals and related books. Provides catalog of journals, ordering information, and author submission guidelines.

BDD: Home Page

http://www.bdd.com/

Bantam Doubleday Dell online. Features intimate visits with authors, information about new books, and a daily horoscope.

Beach Holme Publishing

http://www.swifty.com/Beach/

Provides company background, author biographies, bookseller information, and submission guidelines for this Canadian publisher. Beach Holme publishes

books in many areas from fiction to children's books. Includes *Swiftsure* online magazine and Wiccan spiritual titles.

Bioenergetics Press

http://www.msn.fullfeed.com/rschenk/bioecat.html

Publishes books about men's and gender issues. Provides samples of their books, a catalog of tapes and books available, and ordering information. Includes links to sites and newsgroups that deal with men's issues.

Blackwell Science

http://www.blacksci.co.uk/

Publishes medical and scientific journals and books. Provides company news, catalog, upcoming publications information, and service listings of their products. Includes links to all of Blackwell Science's sites worldwide.

Blue Heron Publishing

http://www.teleport.com/~bhp/

Provides company profile, catalog, author background, and submissions guidelines for Blue Heron Publishing. Publishes fiction and nonfiction books for adults, and children. Catalog also includes information titles for writers, librarians, and teachers.

Book Stacks—Home Page

http://www.books.com/

Online bookstore. Includes the Book Cafe and a virtual coffee shop in where literary discussion occurs.

Bookish

http://www.bic.org.uk/bic/

U.K.-based Book Industry Communications home page that provides links to over 100 publishers and numerous links with booksellers, library suppliers, and service suppliers. A very valuable site for anyone doing business or research on United Kingdom publishers and book industry.

BookWire—The First Place To Look for Book Information

http://www.bookwire.com/

Includes indices of book and publishing-related sites, a reading room, the comic of the day, bestseller lists, and book reviews.

BookZone

http://ttx.com/bookzone

BookZone, "the Internet source for extraordinary books," enables you to learn more about and order books directly from publishers. Includes works from small, medium-size, and alternative publishers whose works you don't always find in the typical bookstore.

Borders Books and Music

http://www.borders.com/

Enables you to search for books and then order them from Borders' large selection of books and magazines. Also provides a list of store locations and lets you browse their titles.

BradyGAMES Home Page

http://www.mcp.com/brady/

Includes a combination of strategies, how-to information, game background, editorial content, valuable "inside" information, interviews with game creators, and more.

BRP Publications, Inc.

http://brpinc.com/

Provides access to selected articles from more than 20 newsletters that cover the fields of telecommunications, multimedia, data networking, technology, and human resources.

Cambridge University Press

http://www.cup.cam.ac.uk/

Features information about the publisher and its different publications. Offers ordering and contact information and other online services.

Carswell Publishing

http://www.carswell.com/carswell.home

Publishes professional books, pamplets, electronic media, catalogs, and other documents for the legal, medical, banking and corporate fields. Provides company history, services offered, listings of published items, clients served, and additional product information.

Catalogue Index

http://www.firmware.com.au/cgi-bin/mediacat.cgi

Offers multimedia developer books and resources for purchasing them.

CatchWord Ltd

http://www.catchword.co.uk/

Publishes and republishes scholarly journals from the United States, Australia, Canada, and the United Kingdom on the Internet. Provides full books with the ability to search through text by subscription or payment-per-page basis. Includes links to CatchWord sites across the globe.

ChemTech Publishing

http://www.io.org/~chemtec/

Publishes journals, books and software that deal with the chemical polymers industry. Provides full catalog of products offered and links to related sites. Includes submission guidelines and ordering information.

Christian Warehouse

http://christwh.com/cw/index.html

Online bookstore that offers best-selling books. Allows online ordering.

Cocoon

http://www.leonardo.net/cocoon

Online book and publisher. Focuses on dissolving depression.

Cold Spring Harbor Laboratory Press

http://www.cshl.org/about_cshl_press.html

Publishes scholarly journals, books, manuals, and videotapes. Topics covered include biology, genetics, neurobiology, and closly related sciences. Includes information for publishing proposals.

Colorado Independent Publisher's Association

http://usa.net/cipa/

Provides Web site to members' sites by book title, subject, or by publishers. Includes contact and membership information. Also includes small publishing links.

Imprinted Pen

http://www.pens.com/cgi-win/cluegen.exe

Win a free imprinted pen by reading the online catalog from National Pen and finding three hidden clues.

Commercial Publications

http://www.spub.ksu.edu/other/journlist/commercial.html

Lists of commercial magazines that are on the Internet.

Conari Press

http://www.organic.com/Books/Conari/index.html

Provides home site for Conari Press. Includes company catalog with cover art and book descriptions. Produces self-spirituality and emotional exploration books. Includes mailing list and ordering information.

Coteau Books

http://coteau.unibase.com/welcome.html

Provides home site for Coteau Books, a small literary house based out of Saskatchewan, Canada that produces fiction and nonfiction. Includes new upcoming titles, company catalog, and information about Coteau's Men by Men and Women's Work lines. Also includes recommended links and ordering information.

Creative Virtue Press

http://www.eskimo.com/~telical/

Provides home site for Creative Virtue Press, which features technology-based philosophical writings. Catalog includes both nonfiction and fiction that is specifically aimed at the study of the future and next directions. Alsp provides book and author backgrounds with ordering information.

Doody Publishing, Inc.

http://www.doody.com/

Produces "Doodie's Health Sciences Book Review" and home page that covers the health science industry. Also produces other titles that cover the health industry. Includes submissions guidelines, reviews, company profile, and purchasing information. Also includes directories of publishers, and other health science Web pages.

Drama Book Publishers

http://www.interport.net/~dramapub/

Publishes plays, musicals and other theatre projects. Includes new electronic publishing and CD-ROMs. Provides company catalog and related theatre links.

Dream Garden Press

http://www.dreamgarden.com/

Provides home site for Dream Garden Press based in Salt Lake City, Utah. Specializes in regional-themed books about Utah and the American West. Includes company catalog, upcoming titles, and ordering information.

East View Publications, Inc. Home Page

http://www.eastview.com/

Offers books, magazines, CDs, maps, microforms and newspapers published in Central Europe, the CIS, and former Soviet Union. Offers online delivery of newspapers.

Editorial Experts, Inc. (EEI)

http://www.eei-alex.com/

Provides design, editorial, and production services along with publishing style and usage texts. Includes sevices listings, technologies utilized, work examples, and a catalog of texts created. Also includes contact information and company profile.

Elsevier Science—Home Page

http://www.elsevier.nl/

Contains extensive information about publishing. Includes books about writing and publishing.

HarperCollins Publishers Home Page

http://www.harpercollins.com

HarperCollins online. Includes information about best sellers, new releases, and an online bookstore.

Harvard Advocate Home Page

http://hcs.harvard.edu/~advocate/

Venerable literary site on the net from Harvard. Offers many links to other online literary resources.

Hayden Books

http://www.mcp.com/adobe/

Hayden Books online. Publishes Adobe Press Books as well as books that focus on Macintosh computers and Macintosh programs. Features a Macintosh tip of the day.

HMSO

http://www.hmso.gov.uk/

An England-based publishing house devoted to being a forerunner in the industry through Internet service, publications, and commitment to the community.

Hodder & Stoughton

http://www.u-net.com/hodder/

A book publishing company advertising for the first time on the net. Their latest publication is *BEING DIGITAL*, a book about the net. The company publishes books in the UK, everything from children's literature to adult fiction and nonfiction.

Houghton Mifflin Company

http://www.hmco.com/

Houghton Mifflin Company online. Publishes educational books and materials for elementary through college levels. Includes links to subsidiaries.

IDG Books

http://www.idg.com/

Computer book publisher featuring information about their current titles and previews of future ones.

index.html

http://iww.org/~monkeywrench/index.html

Monkeywrench Press online. Caters to the anarchist in all of us. Features information about authors and current books.

Information SuperLibrary

http://www.mcp.com/

Macmillan Publishing presents this site as a resource to the many computer books it publishes. Provides information on books published by Que, SAMS, New Riders, Brady, The Waite Group, and Hayden, and lets you review sample chapters of the latest computer books and order online. Enables you to subscribe to The SuperLibrary Newsletter, a monthly that offers a wide variety of articles and features. Contains hundreds of Macmillan programs and software packages.

INFOSEARCH—PrintNet

http://www.xmission.com/~insearch/printnet.html

Lists publishing sites on the net.

Internet Book Fair: Publishers Index

http://www.bookfair.com/Publishers/PublishersIndex.html

Features several different guides to publishers on the Internet. Allows for searching through different categories and indexes or conducting a search by name or keyword. Makes for easy access to many publishing houses.

Internet Road Map to Books

http://www.bookport.com/b_welcomehome.html

A great site for anyone interested in books. Provides links to many major publishers, booksellers, and online editions of books. Also provides links to bibliographies, bestsellers lists, and news about books and the publishing industry. This is a site to bookmark for anyone who loves to read or works in the publishing industry.

IPL Books

http://ipl.sils.umich.edu/ref/RR/ENT/Books-rr.html

An Internet library, complete with information about books and authors in specific genres. Concentrates on children's literature, comics, horror, nonfiction, and romance.

iWORLD Home Page

http://www.mecklerweb.com/

Meckler Media online. Includes Internet news, features, resources and tools. Offers many links and provides information. Includes a newsstand.

Jacobs Publishing, Ltd.

http://www.awa.com/jacobs/jacobs.html

An electronic book publisher featuring authors Katharine Kerr and Kevin J. Anderson. Author information is provided.

Karoma Publishers

http://www.infop.com/karoma/

Technical publishers and developers for your business needs. Get your Guide to EDI and International Electronic Trading, links to what's new, learn how to showcase your company.

Keski-Uusimaa

http://www.cardinal.fi/keski-uusimaa/ekeskari.htm

A publisher of newspapers and trade journals in the Keski-Uusimaa county.

Kluwer Academic Publishers

gopher://gopher.wkap.nl/

Offers information about the publisher, a full catalog and journal information, and links to other related sites. Also allows for author submission.

Koinonia House

http://www.khouse.org/

Christian book publisher online. Includes information about books and magazines and offers links to other Christian sites on the Internet.

Kraken Press, Titles

http://webster.skypoint.net/members/mfinley/booklist.htm

Considered a "last resort" publisher by some, admittedly by the publisher and primary author himself. Publisher of novels, poetry, children's books and more.

Little, Brown & Company

http://www.pathfinder.com/@@9B66QQAAAAAAIcR/twep/Little_Brown/Little_Brown.html

Little, Brown & Company publishing company online. Features reviews and summaries of current books.

Manic D Press

http://www.well.com/user/manicd/

Smaller publishing house dealing with books and comics. Features online ordering and a listing of bookstores carrying their works.

McGraw Hill

http://www.cityscape.co.uk/bookshop/mccat.html

Online bookstore. Enables you to browse through McGraw Hill titles.

M.E. Sharpe

http://usa.net/mesharpe/mesh.html

A book and journal publisher specializing in the areas of Asian and Russian studies, economics, history and political science. Browse their book listing, which include the following categories: anthropology, business, education, health journalism, legal studies, literature, philosophy, religion, and much more. Ordering information and manuscript submission guidelines included.

MIT Press

http://www-mitpress.mit.edu/

Offers an online bookstore, search information, journals and textbook information. Also features sale items and links to other sites of interest. Gives previews to new and future releases.

Monterey Press

http://www.redshift.com/~montpres/

A small press publishing eight to ten works of fiction or nonfiction per year. Links to books and authors, reviews, and press releases.

Multimedia Newsstand home

http://mmnewsstand.com/index.html

Offers a collection of subscription information and forms for more than 500 magazines, books, and videos. Also contains a number of different contests sponsored by the various magazines.

Natural History Book Service— Home Page

http://www.nhbs.co.uk/

British online bookstore. Focuses on natural history, books on environmental issues, and science books. Provides information in English, Spanish, Italian, and German.

New Riders Publishing

http://mcp.com/newriders/

New Riders concentrates on staying current and delivering the necessary depth and breadth of computer-related information—all in a timely fashion. Stay ahead of the game, and check out this Web site for the latest information on the hottest computer topics—from networking and AutoCAD to communications/Internet and multimedia/graphics.

Nomad Press

http://www.awa.com/nomad/

If you're interested in going to "paperless publishing," then check out the e-book Sampler. Links to publishing and writing resources, and electronic publishing services.

Norwegian Bookshop Home Page

http://www.oslonett.no/home/paul/nw.html

Norwegian bookshop online. Provides Norwegian books or books about Norway. Also includes information about Norwegian language and education. Includes a currency converter for international orders.

O'Reilly Home Page

http://www.ora.com:80/staff/

Acts as a source for computer books about topics such as Unix, TCP/IP, and the Internet.

Online Islamic Bookstore— Home Page

http://www.sharaaz.com/

Online bookstore. Features Islamic books, music, and CD-ROMs. Offers online ordering.

Oxford University Press

http://www.oup.co.uk/

Features information about Oxford University Press and its publications. Also includes previews of future titles and links to other Oxford University Press Web sites.

Para Publishing

http://www.zpub.com/para/

Provides home site for Para Publishing, which specializes in skydiving and parachute texts. Includes Para catalog, ordering information, and links to other skydiving sites. Also includes information and links about small press publishing.

Peachpit Press

http://www.peachpit.com/

Provides home page and online ordering for Peachpit Press. Specializes in computer books from personal PC use to online communication service books. Includes indexed catalog, author background, upcoming titles and discussion forums.

Penguin USA

http://www.penguin.com/usa/

Features sections devoted to new titles, a complete reading room, academic books, electronic publishing, and information about Penguin Books.

PennWell Publishing Company

http://www.pennwell.com/

Produces a wide array of magazines, books, newsletters, and trade journals that cover many industries inlcluding petroleum, electric utlities, computers, communications, and information technologies. Includes complete company catalog indexed by industry, ordering, and contact information.

pgrmli.txt

http://www.library.nwu.edu:80/media/resources/pgrmli.txt

Burrelle's Transcripts, a leading transcription company for more than 20 years, provides transcripts and, where indicated, videotapes, of more than 75 news, public affairs, health, and talk shows.

Prentice Hall Home Page

http://www.prenhall.com/

Publishes college textbooks and technical books. Offers Prentice Hall's online catalog of books and information, as well as links to their Gopher site and to fun Internet sites, including other Viacom sites. Contains a searchable database by title, author, ISBN number and subject.

Press Association

http://www.cais.com/djackson/tpa.html

Provides home site for Press Association publishing which specializes in nonfiction travel, computing, and how-to books. Includes company catalog, book discriptions, and contact information.

Publisher's Catalogues Home Page

http://northern.lights.com:80/publisher/

Provides a listing of publishers from all over the world and their home pages, indexed by country.

Putnam Berkley Online

http://www.mca.com/putnam/

Provides home site for Putnam Berkley and their related imprints. Includes featured books and a search index of all titles published. Also includes author profiles, book samples, and ordering information.

QUE Publishing Home Page

http://www.mcp.com/que/

QUE publishes books on every major category of personal computer technology, from end-user applications to programming languages, from the Internet to new hardware and software technologies. The home page provides information about the technology you've come to depend on, and explains how you can gain access to QUE computer books.

Random House

http://www.randomhouse.com/

Features a smattering of information, but includes the Del Rey Books (science fiction and fantasy) home page and the Knopf Publishing Group's home page.

Reed Interactive

http://www.reedbooks.com.au/index.html

Provides home site for Reed Educational Publishing and imprints.

Resolution Business Press

http://www.respress.com/

Publishes books dealing with the Internet. Includes company catalog, book discriptions, cover art, and ordering information. Also provides links to many family oriented sites on the WWW.

Saint Mary's Press

http://wwwsmp.smumn.edu/

Publishes Christian religious texts and related books for English and Spanish markets. Includes indexed catalog and links to other religious sites. Provides resources and contact information.

Sams Publishing

http://www.mcp.com/sams/

Sams Publishing online. Produces professional references on computer topics. Specializes in programming books. Also features recent titles on emerging technologies. Contains advertising information, a searchable database and software library.

Sapphire Press UNCAT

http://www.digimark.net/UNCAT/

UNCAT is a catalog of uncatalog titles like trade papers, pamphelts, government agency reports, self-published titles, video and audio cassettes. Includes company and UNCAT background. Provides search index and contact information.

Shogakukan Home Page

http://www.toppan.co.jp/bookshop/

Shogakukan publishes magazines for children, comic magazines, weeklies, dictionaries, encyclopedia, and art books. Features Japanese links, books, and magazines. Provides English and Japanese language versions.

Small Media and Large

http://smallmedia.com/

Independent publisher of gay and lesbian books. Also features feminist books. Offers online ordering.

Software Net Product Menu

http://software.net/automenu.htm/1521/
SK:kfbfkoafbmahjacj

Lets you order desktop publishing and graphics software online.

Springer-Verlag

http://www.springer.de/

Publishing house devoted to scientific, medical, and technical writings. Features press releases, catalogs, and samples of different works. Also contains links to its national Web sites.

Straight Line Medium, Inc.

http://www.infi.net/~slm/slm.html

Produces destination CD-ROMs. Includes titles about Caribbean travel and destinations. Provides title background and ordering information.

Strangelove Internet Enterprises

http://www.phoenix.ca/sie/

Internet business publishing, consulting, and training organization. Includes information on their book, *How to Advertise on the Internet*, and on their publication, *The Internet Business Journal*.

Thomsom Publishing

http://www.thomsom.com/

International publisher devoted to science, technology, business, medicine, defense, and the humanities social science. Offers customer support, information about new releases, and a catalog.

Time-Life Explorer

http://www.timelife.com/

Contains a visual database of all the Time-Life products. Lets you browse and order products.

Times Mirror Higher Education Group

http://www.tmhe.com

Publishes printed and multimedia educational products for businesses and schools. Includes an online catalog broken down into various imprints and background information. Also provides site search index and complementary copy request forms.

TOR SF and Fantasy

`http://www.tor.com/`

TOR online. Publishes science fiction and fantasy books. Includes links to other science fiction and fantasy sites on the Web, offers a browsable database of books, and allows online ordering.

W. W. Norton & Company, Inc.

`http://www.wwnorton.com/`

Provides home site, online catalog, and ordering information for W.W. Norton & Company publishing. Includes a complete catalog indexed and broken down by publishing imprints. Also includes featured books, author profiles, company history, and signing appearance dates.

Warner Aspect

`http://pathfinder.com/twep/Aspect/Aspect.html`

Publishes science fiction, fantasy, and horror titles under the Warner Books label. Includes author profiles, upcoming release information, search index, bulletin boards, and ordering information.

Web Art Publishing

`http://www.webart.com/`

Web site publishers devoted to high-quality page production and publishing. Offers information about their services and price structure.

Wellsweep Press

`http://www.poptel.org.uk/password/wellswee.html`

Publishes literature translated from Chinese. Includes company catalog, book discriptions, sample poems, and ordering information.

West Publishing

`http://www.westpub.com/`

West Publishing online, a legal and educational publisher. Includes information on their products. Lets you use West's Legal Directory to find a lawyer, law firm, or corporate or governmental lawyer located in the United States or Canada.

Wiley

`http://www.wiley.com/`

Publishing house that develops, publishes, and sells both printed and electronic media for educational, professional, scientific, technical, and consumer uses. Features information about the company, press releases, worldwide links, and online products and services.

WWW VL Electronic Journals List: Publishers

`http://www.edoc.com/ejournal/publishers.html`

Complete listing to publishing companies. Contains listing by: academic, computer, science and technology, electronic, and other commercial publishing companies. Also allows for searching.

Radio

Amateur Radio Books and Open Repeater Database

`http://www.earthlink.net/~artsci`

Produces amateur radio books, including Radio Modifications, Repeater Mapbook, cartoon license manuals, frequency guides, and reference manuals.

Brent Albert's Radioland

`http://hightech.iadfw.net/brent.htm`

Examines the life and radio adventures of Brent Alberts. Includes pictures and audio airchecks from radio stations dating back to the late 60s.

Chris Smolinski's Radio Page

`http://www.access.digex.net/~cps/radio.html`

Provides information (and links to other pages with similar information) about short-wave and amateur radio.

Deutche Welle Radio & TV—English Home Page

`http://www.dwelle.de/english/`

Provides online program schedules and news and other reports.

Condom

`http://www.linkmag.com/trojan/GIFT.html`

Get a free condom from Trojan just for giving them your name and address. They also send a letter to your parents telling them what a good investment your computer and monthly Internet service charge is. (Just kidding.)

Javiation

http://www.demon.co.uk/javiation

Scanner and associated equipment distributor in the United Kingdom. Producer and publisher of the "Airband Guide." Links to products and purchase information and other related sites.

Monitor Radio

http://town.hall.org/radio/Monitor/

The *Christian Science Monitor* radio program online. Includes program information and a behind-the-scenes look at Monitor Radio.

NPR Online

http://www.npr.org/

National Public Radio online. Provides information about NPR and other topics. Includes audio version of daily noon news casts, transcripts of other programs, and in-depth looks at current events.

Old Time Radio (OTR) WWW Page

http://www.old-time.com/

Focuses on radio programs from "radio's golden age." Contains pointers to many entertaining and educational areas for fans of nostalgic radio shows.

Radio Centro

http://www.internet.com.mx/empresas/radiocen/index.html

Contains listings and information about Spanish language radio stations.

Radio HK

http://hkweb.com/radio/

Hong Kong Radio. Broadcasts exclusively into the Internet, real-time and nonstop. Provides information in addition to the real-time radio broadcasts.

Radio JAPAN

http://www.ntt.jp/japan/NHK/

Provides information about Japanese radio. Includes transmission maps and program schedules.

Radio Prague

http://town.hall.org/Archives/radio/Mirrors/Prague/

Radio Prague provides information about radio programming and offers audio broadcasts of radio programs.

RadioWorld Europe

http://www.vhc.se/radio.html

Includes a listing of radio stations in Europe that are online. Also includes a listing of radio networks in Europe.

RealTime

http://realtime.cbcstereo.com

Radio show heard across Canada. Includes music and guests. Features a great deal of RealAudio.

Rob Mayfield

http://wattle.itd.adelaide.edu.au/~mayfield

Includes a collection of amateur radio links and more.

RTHK on the Internet Home Page

http://www.cuhk/rthk/

Radio Television Hong Kong provides program schedule information and content information.

Thistle and Shamrock Stations List at the Ceolas Archive

http://celtic.stanford.edu/pmurphy/thistle.html

Provides a list of stations arranged alphabetically by state and city. Broadcasts a popular Celtic music radio program on National Public Radio. Includes broadcast times.

Welcome to BBC Radio

http://www.bbcnc.org.uk/radio/index.html

BBC Radio online. Contains information about program schedules and information about specific programs carried on the BBC radio network.

Newsgroups

alt.binaries.fashion.magazines

alt.binaries.zines Images

alt.ezines

alt.fan.cfny

alt.fan.don-imus

alt.fan.don-n-mike

alt.fan.fi.glover

alt.fan.howard-stern

alt.fan.kroq

alt.fan.mark-brian

alt.good.news

alt.internet.talk-radio

alt.journalism

alt.journalism.criticism

alt.journalism.freelance

alt.journalism.gay-press

alt.journalism.gonzo

alt.journalism.moderated

alt.journalism.music

alt.journalism.newspapers

alt.journalism.photo

alt.journalism.print

alt.journalism.students

alt.mag.playboy

alt.magazine.the.new.republic

alt.news-media

alt.publish.newspaper

alt.pulp

alt.radio.college

alt.radio.digital

alt.radio.networks.cbc

alt.radio.networks.npr

alt.radio.online-tonight

alt.radio.paul-harvey

alt.radio.pirate

alt.radio.scanner

alt.radio.scanner.uk

alt.radio.talk

alt.radio.uk

alt.radio.uk.talk-radio

alt.radio.whadya-know

alt.radio.wpkn

alt.rush-limbaugh

alt.sex.magazines

alt.sports.radio

alt.sports.radio.ferrall

alt.testing.testing

alt.zines

```
aus.radio.broadcast
ba.broadcast
bit.listserv.radio-l
chi.media
chinese.rec.magazines.multiworld
clari.biz.industry.media
clari.biz.industry.media.entertainment
clari.biz.industry.media.releases
clari.news.*@
clari.sports.*@
clari.world.*
clari.world.africa
clari.world.africa.south_africa
clari.world.americas.canada
clari.world.americas.canada.business
clari.world.americas.canada.review
clari.world.americas.caribbean
clari.world.americas.central
clari.world.americas.mexico
clari.world.americas.south
clari.world.asia.central
clari.world.asia.china
clari.world.asia.hong_kong
clari.world.asia.india
clari.world.asia.japan
clari.world.asia.koreas
clari.world.asia.south
clari.world.asia.southeast
clari.world.asia.taiwan
clari.world.briefs
clari.world.europe.alpine
clari.world.europe.balkans
clari.world.europe.benelux
clari.world.europe.central
clari.world.europe.eastern
clari.world.europe.france
clari.world.europe.germany
clari.world.europe.greece
clari.world.europe.iberia
clari.world.europe.ireland
clari.world.europe.italy
clari.world.europe.northern
clari.world.europe.russia
clari.world.europe.uk
clari.world.europe.union
clari.world.mideast
clari.world.mideast.arabia
clari.world.mideast.iran
clari.world.mideast.iraq
clari.world.mideast.israel
clari.world.mideast.turkey
clari.world.oceania
```

clari.world.oceania.new_zealand

clari.world.organizations

clari.world.top

comp.publish.cdrom.multimedia

comp.publish.electronic.misc

dc.media

ieee.pub.announce

ieee.pub.general

misc.news.bosnia

misc.news.east-europe.rferl

misc.news.southasia

no.alt.radio-tv.irma-1000

no.radio-tv

pdaxs.ads.printing

pdaxs.arts.print

pdaxs.arts.radio

phl.media

pnet.rec.radio.amateur.announce

pnet.rec.radio.amateur.talk

rec.antiques.radio+phono

rec.arts.wobegon

rec.models.rc.air

rec.models.rc.land

rec.models.rc.misc

rec.models.rc.water

relcom.commerce.publishing

relcom.radio

tnn.books.magazine

tnn.internet.itr

triangle.radio

tw.bbs.rec.radio

uiuc.org.synton

uk.media.radio.archers

uk.media.radio.bbc-r4

Listservs

ADEC-STC—ADEC Satellite Telecommunications Coordinators

University of Nebraska Computing Services Network, Lincoln, NE

You can join this group by sending the message "sub ADEC-STC your name" to listserv@unlvm.unl.edu

AHECTA-L—Assoc. of Higher Education Cable Television Administrators

The University of Georgia, Athens, GA, 30602

You can join this group by sending the message "sub AHECTA-L your name" to listserv@uga.cc.uga.edu

ALAORPC—ALAO Research and Publication Committee

You can join this group by sending the message "sub ALAORPC your name" to listserv@listserv.kent.edu

CAN-MEDIA—Canadian Student Media Mailing List

Memorial University of Newfoundland, St. John's, Newfoundland, Canada

You can join this group by sending the message "sub CAN-MEDIA your name" to
listserv@morgan.ucs.mun.ca

CURRENT—Campus Newspaper Discussion List

University of Missouri-St. Louis

You can join this group by sending the message "sub CURRENT your name" to
listserv@umslvma.umsl.edu

DUBNET—A Forum for Public Radio Folks to Swap Dubs

Texas A&M University Computing Services Center

You can join this group by sending the message "sub DUBNET your name" to
listserv@tamvm1.tamu.edu

FANZINE—Discussion of Fanzines, Small Press and Self Publishing

Pennsylvania State University

You can join this group by sending the message "sub FANZINE your name" to
listserv@psuvm.psu.edu

IBSRAD-L—College/Community Radio Association

The University of Connecticut, Storrs, CT

You can join this group by sending the message "sub IBSRAD-L your name" to
listserv@uconnvm.uconn.edu

L-MEDIA—Media Discussion Group

State University of New York at Buffalo

You can join this group by sending the message "sub L-MEDIA your name" to
listserv@listserv.acsu.buffalo.edu

MAGAZINE

Rensselaer Polytechnic Institute, Troy, New York

You can join this group by sending the message "sub MAGAZINE your name" to
listserv@vm.its.rpi.edu

MEDIA-L—Media in Education

State University of New York at Binghamton

You can join this group by sending the message "sub MEDIA-L your name" to
listserv@bingvmb.cc.binghamton.edu

NETV-L—IBM's NETView Discussion List

Marist College

You can join this group by sending the message "sub NETV-L your name" to listserv@vm.marist.edu

NV-L—Discussion of IBM NetView and POLYCENTER Manager on NetView

University of California at Santa Barbara

You can join this group by sending the message "sub NV-L your name" to listserv@ucsbvm.ucsb.edu

P-ONS—Traffic Departments of Public Television Stations

You can join this group by sending the message "sub P-ONS your name" to listserv@listserv.uh.edu

PRFORUM—Public Radio Discussion Group

Boise State University, Boise, ID

You can join this group by sending the message "sub PRFORUM your name" to
listserv@idbsu.idbsu.edu

PTV-DCOM—Public Television Station Development & Communications Departments

You can join this group by sending the message "sub PTV-DCOM your name" to
listserv@listserv.uh.edu

PUBRADIO—Public Radio Discussion Group

Boise State University, Boise, ID

You can join this group by sending the message "sub PUBRADIO your name" to
`listserv@idbsu.idbsu.edu`

SCREEN-L—Film and TV Studies Discussion List

The University of Alabama, Tuscaloosa, AL

You can join this group by sending the message "sub SCREEN-L your name" to
`listserv@ua1vm.ua.edu`

SNPA—Southern Newspaper Publishers Association

The University of Georgia, Athens, GA

You can join this group by sending the message "sub SNPA your name" to `listserv@uga.cc.uga.edu`

TELECOM—Telecommunications List

You can join this group by sending the message "sub TELECOM your name" to `listserv@yorku.ca`

WISP-L—Women in Scholarly Publishing Discussion List

University Computing Services, Indiana University

You can join this group by sending the message "sub WISP-L your name" to
`listserv@iubvm.ucs.indiana.edu`

Movies

Action/Adventure

Alien

http://ng.netgate.net/~alvaro/alien/alien.htm

Find behind-the-scenes info, stills, lines, scripts, and lots of other goodies from all three films in the series at this site.

Apollo 13

http://www.digiplanet.com/universal_pictures/apollo13/

Get up close and personal with Ron Howard, find out what goes into making a movie that'll make you stand up and cheer for your country, and link to other space-related sites.

Braveheart

http://www.aloha.net/~brvhrt/index.html

Maybe you don't share this page creator's opinion that *Braveheart* is easily the best movie ever made, but it's worth it to let him try to convince you he's right.

Congo the Movie

http://www.paramount.com/Congo.html

Find out what this movie is all about, take a look at what went on behind the scenes, and take a closer look at some pivotal parts of the movie.

Crimson Tide: Danger Runs Deep

http://pantheon.cis.yale.edu/~sting/crimson/

Whether you've seen the movie yet or not, the links here to information about the cast, including Gene Hackman and Denzel Washington, submarines, or the behind the scenes show you something you'll be interested in.

Dr. NO

http://www.dur.ac.uk/~dcs3pjb/jb/drno.html

This 007 classic from the period when Sean Connery was still playing Bond can be found here with raw data, trivia, pictures, and plot summary.

The Hunt for Red October

http://www.susx.ac.uk/Users/ccfk0/index.htm

Listen to a wide array of sound bites from the Sean Connery film.

In the Name of the Father

http://www.fsu.umd.edu/students/dhiggins/movies.htm

Look here for sound bites from the film starring Daniel Day Lewis, conveying the tale of the Conlon family. The site publisher promises to have pictures up soon, and it's worth checking back occasionally just to use some of the links at the bottom.

The Indiana Jones WWW Page

http://www.softaid.net/msjohnso/

From Indy's childhood to what's in store for the fourth installment, this page contains all of the theories and artifacts that went into making Indiana Jones an American icon.

James Bond 007

http://www.mcs.net/~klast/www/bond.html

If you like the Bond genre, you'll enjoy information on the actors, the Bond girls link, previews of the next Bond film, and information on Bond-esque films. Check out the Mondo Bondo section for a look at funny Bond knockoffs from the Sixties.

The Killer

http://www.hooked.net/~clayton/movies/the_killer/

If you haven't familiarized yourself yet with John Woo, here's your opportunity. Read about the plot and actors in this film, as well as checking out some pictures from this action-thriller.

Killing Zoe

`http://w3.nationalnet.com/~berube/kill_zoe.htm`

You've never seen a movie like this. Check out images and sounds from what fans consider a masterpiece of filmmaking.

Last of the Mohicans

`http://ac.acusd.edu/History/filmnotes/mohicansnotes.html`

This site is a great reference source to learn more about the book that the movie is based on. Makes sense because it is the Web site for a class discussion of it—complete with overhead.

Nathan's Apocalypse Now Page

`http://www.luhsd.k12.ca.us/~nc670597/apocnow.html`

Loosely based on Joseph Conrad's *Heart of Darkness*, this movie is well covered on this page that interviews the assistant director and has a "why you liked the movie" survey included, among other things.

The Professional

`http://pages.prodigy.com/stansfield/profess.html`

It's important to know that this film is called *Leon* everywhere else in the world. If you've seen the movie, you know why, and will enjoy visiting this page. The uninitiated will enjoy the page as an introduction to a great movie.

Terminator/Terminator 2: Judgment Day FAQ List

`http://www.cis.ohio-state.edu/hypertext/faq/usenet/movies/terminator-faq/faq.html`

Truly a FAQ list, with no graphics, but plenty of links to other fans, this page is for those wishing to expand their Terminator knowledge.

Tombstone

`http://www-scf.usc.edu/~garnold/tombston.htm`

Not only are there links to the actors from *Tombstone*, links to the characters that they played are available. See how good a job Kurt Russell did as Wyatt Earp when you compare him to the real thing. Lots of great downloadable quotes, too.

Actors & Actresses

Looking for information about your favorite movie star? Here's just a sampling of what's available on the Web:

Kevin Bacon	`http://www.primenet.com/~fnargle/erisson/bacon/`
Antonio Banderas	`http://www.missouri.edu/~c617756/Antonio.html`
Humphrey Bogart	`http://www.macconsult.com/mikerose/bogart/bogart.html`
Kenneth Branagh	`http://users.aol.com/luvvy/kbfaq.htm`
Pierce Brosnan	`http://www.goldeneye.com/brosnan.htm`
Sandra Bullock	`http://www.develop.american.edu/~tlawson/sandyfaq.html`
Nicolas Cage	`http://us.imdb.com/M/person-exact?Cage,+Nicolas`
Jackie Chan	`http://pages.nyu.edu/~gqn1193/jackie.html`
Sean Connery	`http://www.wsu.edu:8080/~dock/`
Tom Cruise	`http://www.cyberhighway.net/~phlacin/cruise.html`
James Dean	`http://www.americanlegends.com/jamesdean/`
Richard Dreyfuss	`http://us.imdb.com/M/person-exact?Dreyfuss,+Richard`
Harrison Ford	`http://www.mit.edu:8001/people/lpchao/harrison.ford.html`
Jodie Foster	`http://weber.u.washington.edu/~jnorton/jodie/jodie.html`
Judy Garland	`http://members.aol.com/judygumm/homepage.htm`
Mel Gibson	`http://s9000.furman.edu/~riley/mel_gibson.html`
Steve Martin	`http://www.dundee.ac.uk/~dcyork/steve.htm`
Bette Midler	`http://www.interactive8.com/bette/`
Demi Moore	`http://showbiz.starwave.com/showbiz/memorybank/starbios/demimoore/a.html`
Sean Penn	`http://showbiz.starwave.com/showbiz/memorybank/starbios/seanpenn/index.html`
Keanu Reeves	`http://www.empirenet.com/~jahvah/skc/skc.html`
Molly Ringwald	`http://www.iag.net/~alladin/ring.html`
Jimmy Stewart	`http://www.jimmy.org/`
Meryl Streep	`http://pathfinder.com/@@TanbUPPMBwAAQBu6/twep/bridges/meryl.streep.html`
John Travolta	`http://www.execpc.com/~aemog/travolta.html`
Bruce Willis	`http://www.accsyst.com/writers/bruno.htm`

Clint Eastwood The World Wide Web Page

http://www.pyramid.net/eastwood/

Before he was the mayor of a beautiful resort town, Clint Eastwood made a movie or two. In a great Old West style, this page presents everything you could want to know about this king of the screen.

KeanuNet

http://www.aok.com/keanunet/

Bet you didn't know Keanu Reeves was so well-rounded. Come to this page to see all of his contributions to the arts and catch a glimpse of this dreamy star.

The Marilyn Pages

http://www.ionet.net:80/~jellenc/marilyn.html

Marilyn fans will appreciate the lengthy biography, images, and filmography included on this page. Check out the great images by her photographer and friend, Richard Avedon. Also includes memoribilia information.

Welcome to Brandoland

http://www.best.com/~wcleere

Presents Brandoland, an amusement park devoted entirely to Marlon Brando. Enter through the gates to find out more about Brando in every movie he's ever done. This site also includes exerpts of his controversial interviews on *Larry King Live*, and a Brando for President poster.

Children's

The Adventures of Pinocchio

http://www.pinocchio.com/

Read about Jonathan Taylor Thomas in this movie of the classic children's tale. Pepe will be your guide on your Internet tour of the film.

All Dogs Go To Heaven 2

http://www.mgmua.com/alldogs2/

If someone you know enjoyed this movie, show them the Web page so that they can continue the adventure.

Ariel Forever

http://www.nashville.com/~Merdoug/index.html

For some reason, every *Little Mermaid* page is all about Ariel, understandably—she's the main character—but people really love her, including the author of this site. Find links to plenty of other pages if this one doesn't have quite what you're looking for.

Babe

http://www.geocities.com/Hollywood/3713/babe.htm

Something makes this film extraordinarily popular. It's a talking pig, how could it not be? Visit this site to find many other swine related pages, and maybe get a hint why the movie is such a family favorite.

Beauty and the Beast Trivia

Looking for an excuse to watch this Disney classic for the 32nd time? If you miss any of the following questions, you may just want to. (Check out the following Web site for more on this classic pair.)

1. What is the name of the horse in Beauty and the Beast?

   Philippe

2. What four types of animals do Belle and Maurice have on their farm?

   Pigs, chickens, goats, and a horse

3. What four weapons does Gaston use?

   Gun (Blunderbuss), bow and arrow, knife, and makeshift club

4. What is the name of Gaston's sidekick?

   Lefou

5. What is the color of Belle's eyes?

   Brown

6. What is the color of the suit that Gaston wore to propose to Belle in?
   Burgundy with gold trim

7. What was the Beast's first line?
   "There's a stranger in here."

8. What are the color of Gaston's socks?
   Red with white (heel and toe) patches

9. How many times is the magic mirror used?
   Three

10. What two foods is Cogsworth submerged in?
   Jello and pudding (en flambe)

Beauty and the Beast

http://falcon.jmu.edu/~pollarpe/batb.html

This animated version of the classic fairy tale has a link to the Beast's Page and trivia questions (and answers), as well as pages about the story and music.

Casper Audio/Video Library

http://www.mca.com/universal_pictures/casper/casper_inv/audio.html

The site includes bits of audio and video footage of the movie made from the classic TV cartoon.

The Dark Crystal

http://www.fairfield.net/wyvern/darkcrys/

The movie that brought us the line, "Of course I have wings, I'm a girl, all girl's have wings," has its own unofficial page. The movie's been around for 15 years, plenty of time for people to figure out all of the symbolism behind it.

The Dove Foundation's Home Page

http://www.dove.org

Nonprofit foundation that lists "family-friendly" movies and reviews these films. Click on the Movie and Video List or the Top 10 List to see which movies are family-friendly. Includes links to other family sites on the Web, a Who's Who directory of Dove members and staff, and information on the Dove seal for video retailers.

Hunchback of Notre Dame

http://www.disney.com/DisneyPictures/Hunchback_of_Notre_Dame/

There are regular features about the characters, animation, and the film itself, as well as a page du jour on this very entertaining Disney page.

It Takes Two

http://www.rysher.com/film/ittakes2/index.html

Read about the adventures of the Olsen twins in this tale of finding your exact twin.

James and the Giant Peach

http://www.hotwired.com/renfeatures/96/15/index4a.html

It's hard to believe that somebody could do justice to this great Roald Dahl book, but Hotwired has done it. See how the magic was made and join a discussion about whether the movie lives up to your memories of the book.

Lion King

http://falcon.jmu.edu/~pollarpe/lionking.html

If you know anyone under the age of 10, you've probably seen this movie at least once. You don't really need the excuse of a niece or nephew to enjoy this movie, though. If nothing else, visit this site to find the hidden Mickey.

Mighty Morphin Power Rangers Megadventure

http://www.tcfhe.com/mmpr/

With the White Ranger as your guide, visit this site to see just what being a Power Ranger is all about.

Miracle on 34th Street

http://www.tcfhe.com/miracle/

Visit the site of the remake of this Christmas classic to be reminded of what made it so great, and to remind you of why it's important to be good the whole year. Santa is always watching.

Muppet Movie Links

http://www.ncsa.uiuc.edu/VR/BS/Muppets/net_movies.html

Start here to find your way, or someone you love's, to any of the great muppet movies, *The Muppet Movie*, *The Great Muppet Caper*, *The Muppets Take Manhattan*, *Muppetvision 3-D*, *The Muppet Christmas*, *Muppet Treasure Island*, *The Dark Crystal*, and *Labyrinth*.

Pocahontas

http://www.disney.com/DisneyPictures/Pocahontas/
?referer=^DisneyPictures^index.html&GL=H

Disney's official page lets you explore Pocahantas' own home page, offers information about the movie, and lets you sample some multimedia treats from the film.

Toy Story

http://www.disney.com/ToyStory/?GL=H

This quiet site talks about the story, the characters in the film, and the movie release dates in different countries. Join the Internet fan club. Be sure to check out the Woody versus Buzz section. Download Buzz/Woody WAVs from the film.

Willy Wonka and the Chocolate Factory

http://www.fred.net/gregg/html/willy/willy.html#index

Sample sounds and characters from this classic with Gene Wilder as the candy master.

Classics

Casablanca

http://users.aol.com/VRV1/index.html

Granted, everyone will know you're looking at this site when you can't resist the urge to play "As Time Goes By" while you're looking at it, but this site is well worth any embarrassment you might experience.

Citizen Kane

http://www.voyagerco.com/CC/gh/welles/p.makingkane.html

This site covers the making of, problems with, and controversy over this American classic. Only use this page as a refresher or an introduction, nothing can substitute for the real thing.

Gone With the Wind

http://www.angelfire.com/pages1/slbGWTW/index.html

Find out what the Scarlet Hoax is, refresh yourself on some of the best lines, pick up on some little known facts and bloopers, or link to two pages worth of pictures and many other sites pertaining to Rhett, Scarlet, and Tara.

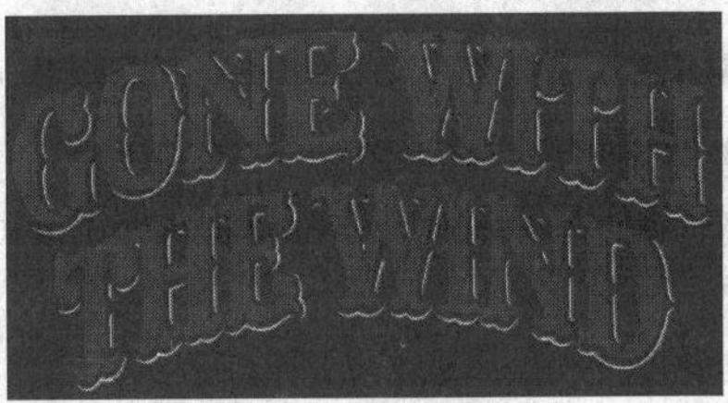

The Jazz Singer (1927)

http://www.cwrl.utexas.edu/~nick/e309k/texts/jazzsinger/
jazzsinger.html

Very little information is available on the film, but check out the images that are around, and link to other pages on topics related to one of the first movies to use synchronous sound.

Metropolis

http://www.loop.com/~ecb/loser.html

If you aren't already familiar with this Fritz Lang film, once you navigate around the page you're sure to recognize many of the images. Lots of information is out there on the Web about *Metropolis*, and you can find the links here.

The Wizard of Oz

http://www.shore.net/~kdonovan/oz.html

What movie list would be complete without this all-time classic? The creator of this page spent a lot of time finding all of the sources on the WWW and put all of his links here. And, of course, you click on the ruby slippers to get back home.

Comedies

Airplane!—The Movie

http://www.d.umn.edu/~elindsko/Airplane/airplane.html

Just when you thought you wouldn't hear "Ever seen a grown man naked?" again for a long time, here it is. There are also stills and mini-movies, along with pages on all of the players.

Brazil

http://poppy.kaist.ac.kr/cinema/brazil/

This site is primarily a FAQ site, but because of an unexplained correlation between people who use the Web and Brazil fans, you'll find plenty of discussion. (Best used when trying to not sound confused about the message of the movie.)

Caddyshack Movie Sound Archive

http://www.ee.duke.edu/~ceh/caddy/caddy.html

So many great quotes, so little time. Some smaller links are off this page to information on the movie, but it's the lines that really make this movie—you can find most of the great ones here.

Cher Horowitz's Home Page

http://www.paramount.com/Clueless.html

Yes *Clueless* fans, you have a place on the Web, too. Visit with the star and brush up on your Beverly Hills vocabulary and ideas.

A Christmas Story

http://www.fishingworld.com/pdlg/c-story/

Maybe it's the defining difference between generations—now the family gathers around to watch this every Christmas as well as *Miracle on 34th Street*. You can get a taste here with some of the best quotes, but be sure to catch it this year.

Clerks

http://www.us.itd.umich.edu/~mingchen/clerks/

Haven't heard of Silent Bob? Here's your chance to get acquainted with the crew of this movie that's surely destined for cult classic stature.

Ferris Bueller's Day Off

http://www.dartmouth.edu/~bueller/

Ferris was a slacker when slacking wasn't cool. Visit the master of getting away with it and link to related movies and the TV series inspired by the movie.

Four Rooms

http://www.miramax.com/dlpages/fourrodl.html#video

Catch lots of pictures and clips from this crazy movie at this site. Tim Roth is the Bell Boy holding together four seemingly unrelated tales.

Ghostbusters

http://www.miramax.com/dlpages/fourrodl.html#video

See if you would qualify to be a Ghostbuster. Look at the actual script for the film and read about the history of the *Ghostbusters* or even Tobin's Spirit Guide. It's all here at the most comprehensive *Ghostbusters* site around.

The Goon Docks

http://www.rpi.edu/~thompe2/goonies/welcome.html

You'll have to do the truffle shuffle to get into the Goonies page, but it'll be worth it. Get the scoop on the kids who only wanted to save their homes.

Groundhog Day

http://powered.cs.yale.edu:8000/~miller/hog/groundhog.html

Not just a site about the making of the Bill Murray/Harold Ramis film, you can also find out a lot about the festivities that surround the town of Punxsutawney, where the story took place during an actual Groundhog Day.

The Jerk

http://www.hirons.com/~lburgess/jerk.html

The page is definitely for fans, otherwise you'll miss most of the great references to this classic Steve Martin film.

Joe Versus the Volcano

http://sashimi.wwa.com/~shopnet/jvv/

The film that gives you Meg Ryan in many different lights has its own Web page. Check out screen shots, the script, and music.

Kids in the Hall Brain Candy

http://web.syr.edu/~rahammer/brain.html

Read reviews of the Kids in the Hall's first movie or visit Scott Thompson's personal home page, Scottland!

Loser

http://www.loop.com/~ecb/loser.html

A low budget film that's been shown at film festivals around the world. Read its reviews and see if you think it's worth a trip out to the video store.

National Lampoon's Animal House

http://www.calspan.com/users/lundvall/animal_house-page/animal_house-page.html

Relive the cherished images of the movie that set the standard for college partying. A link to the only other *Animal House* page is also offered up. Why Pinto? Why not?

October Films Presents, Nadja

http://www.inch.com/user/october/nadja/index.html

Presents Michael Almereyda's *Nadja*, a spellbinding brew of droll comedy, hallucinatory fantasy, and lush eroticism. Click on one of the other Web pages here to find out more about this film.

The Princess Bride

http://faraday.clas.virginia.edu/~dan8s/pbride.html

If you can't recite it line for line, you haven't seen it enough times. Link to different parts of the movie by choosing a picture, and then check out how other people have paid homage to Buttercup.

Reality Bites

http://www.geocities.com/Athens/1894/reality.html

Link to pages about Ethan Hawke, Winona Ryder, and Ben Stiller and to movies that you'll like if you enjoyed this one. Also be sure to run through the quote page.

Rosencrantz and Guildenstern Are Dead

http://www.susqu.edu/ac_depts/arts_sci/english/lharris/class/stoppard/rose.htm

Find out more about the movie that follows around Hamlet's friends from college on their misadventures while things are afoot at the castle.

The Saxonian Blues Brothers Page

http://www.inf.tu-dresden.de/~mb21/eblues.htm

People around the world love the Blues Brothers, and this page is proof. Find links to other BB pages, as well as information on the cast and making of the film.

Shaft

http://www.rapidcity.com/~wforster/index.html

With the stated goal of being as cheesy as possible achieved, this site will remind you why most people are glad it's the Nineties and not the Seventies anymore.

Shallow Grave

http://www.hollywood.com/movies/shallow/text/tsshallow.html

So what's a movie with a title like that doing in the comedy section? Blackest of the black comedies, find out more about its players and story line at this site.

Smoke

http://www.miramax.com/movies/smoke_.html

This technical page will link you to downloadable stills from the film as well as to the impromptu movie made during the filming of *Smoke—Blue in the Face*.

Super Fly

http://student-www.uchicago.edu/users/bra9/fly.html

If you aren't familiar with *Super Fly*, it's high time you become so. Read a plot summary and link to production notes, related sites, and some images from the film.

Salsa

http://www.redfoxsalsa.com/freestuf.htm

Receive a surprise gift and enter to win a free jar of Red Fox Salsa when you fill out the guest book. Hot-cha-cha.

Tank Girl

`http://www.cs.ucl.ac.uk/staff/b.rosenberg/tg/index.html`

You know this site has to be good because the studio that made the film has a link to it. Visit the *Tank Girl* gallery and see what other people have had to say about this futuristic spoof.

Three O'Clock High

`http://ccwf.cc.utexas.edu/~ifde474/three.html`

This 80s favorite's site has links to all of the main characters, the story, and stills from the film.

To Wong Foo, Thanks for Everything! Julie Newmar

`http://www.mca.com/universal_pictures/to_wong_foo/index.html`

It's hard to think of a time when cross-dressing isn't entertaining. That's especially true when you put Wesley Snipes and Patrick Swayze in dresses. Visit this site for introductions to the characters and behind the scenes peaks.

The Unofficial Addams Family Movie Home Page

`http://users.deltanet.com/~beaker/movie.html`

The one stop for both of the *Addams Family* movies. You can check out Raul Julia's last film, and then pay homage by linking to all of the different *Addams Family* sites, including the TV show and the cartoon.

Companies

Buena Vista MoviePlex

`http://www.wdp.com/MoviePlex/MooVPlex.html?LO=D&GL=V`

Includes information on Buena Vista and Touchstone Picture's movies currently in theaters. Click on a movie of interest to read about the film, download the soundtrack and production stills, and more. Click on the box office to go inside the movieplex for more choices.

Elstree—remember me?

`http://www.moose.co.uk/userfiles/elstree/index.html`

Don't feel uninformed if you don't remember this studio that's responsible for such classics as *2001*, *The Shining*, and *Star Wars*—they've been on hiatus for a few years. You can still find out about their old productions and what's waiting for them in the near future at this site, though.

Fine Line

`http://www.flf.com/`

This is the studio that brought you the likes of Robert Altman and *Hoop Dreams*. Visit and see what they have in store for the coming months, how Cannes went for them, and look up some of their past films.

Fox Film

`http://www.fox.com/film.htm`

Of course, the primary attraction of this page is its current releases, but there are also links to previews and other "insider" information.

The Lion's Den

`http://www.mgmua.com/`

Check out new movies from Metro Goldwyn Mayer and United Artists.

MCA/Universal

`http://www.mca.com/`

Find out the latest on this mega entertainment company, which includes Universal Pictures, Universal Theme Parks, Spencer Gifts, Winterland Productions, and MCA Records. Download stills from current and soon-to-be released movies, learn about Universal's production studios, Universal Theme Parks' latest rides and events, and upcoming shows and pay-per-view movies on the Universal Channel.

Media House Films

`http://www.ultranet.com/~msavino/MHFHome.html`

Into campy horror films? Good. These guys are too. Link to some of their recent productions and enjoy.

Miramar Productions

`http://useattle.uspan.com/miramar/`

Miramar is a multimedia company, but they are leaders in cutting edge movies like *The Gate to the Mind's Eye*. They're very happy to have you, and you're encouraged to see what else they have to offer.

Miramax Cafe

http://www.miramax.com/

This studio may be smaller than the other guys, but it more than holds its own when it comes to great movies. Look here for films that are a bit off-beat, and that is meant in the best way possible.

Movies.Com

http://www.movies.com/

So maybe you were looking for information on movies and already found this site, and to your chagrin, it was a movie studio. Hollywood Pictures puts out plenty of titles you'll recognize if you decide to stay, and it's worth the visit.

New Line Cinema

http://www.newline.com/

As of this printing, New Line is still finalizing their page, but keep checking back to find out what they have to offer.

October Films

http://www.octoberfilms.com/

For the movies that might not be in your local theater too long, or even make it there, be sure to check out this studio's site. These movies are the ones that a good friend tells you about, and it helps you understand your friends a little bit better after you've seen the movie.

Paramount Pictures Online Studio

http://www.paramount.com/

See what Paramount movies are playing in theaters and are out on video and read about Paramount's upcoming film and digital products.

Polygram Filmed Entertainment

http://www.reellife.com/PFE/

If you're familiar with or looking for Gramercy Films, this site is the one you'll want to come to. Get updates on what's currently showing and what will be showing soon. Or, find out what videos are available and what some reviewers have to say about this studio's productions.

Sony Pictures Entertainment Page

http://www.spe.sony.com/Pictures/index.html

Find out about Sony's latest movies, theaters, TV shows, and home videos. This site also describes their CyberPassage and pay-per-view information. It may take a while to see everything this site has to offer. If you're looking for pictures by Columbia or Tri-Star, look here as well.

Walt Disney

http://www.disney.com/News/docs/movies.html

Not only can you read about Disney's current theatrical releases, you can link to a host of other pages that deal with their products and productions.

Warner Bros. Online

http://www.movies.warnerbros.com/

Warner Brothers doesn't just do animation (although you can get to their site for that from here), they also make big name movies. Check here to see what they currently have playing in a theater near you.

Cult

Bloodlust

http://www.ozemail.com.au/~jswjon/

The only Australian film banned in Britain has a site to show you exactly why that's the case. Well done page; creepy movie.

The Buckaroo Banzai Jump-Station

http://ourworld.compuserve.com/homepages/ecline/banzai.htm

Find every link and commentary you'll ever need for the *Adventures of Buckaroo Banzai Across the 8th Dimension*. It is just a jump-station, with a few images, but very complete.

A Clockwork Orange

`http://www.lehigh.edu/~pjl2/films/clockwork.html`

Every major player is covered in this classic movie's page, from Anthony Burgess to Stanley Kubrick. Full of sound bites and images, as well as links to papers on the film, a chapter from the book that's missing, and other *Clockwork Orange* pages.

The Cult Shop

`http://lasarto.cnde.iastate.edu/Movies/CultShop/`

If you don't have a favorite cult movie, but are pretty sure that they would appeal to you, this site is a good place to start. Links to current releases are here as well as what's on video, as well as directories of traditionally cult actors and directors.

Dr. Strangelove Or: How I Learned to Stop Worrying and Love the Bomb

`http://www.voyagerco.com/CC/sfh/strangelove.html`

This film is from the same man who brought us *A Clockwork Orange*. Come to the sight to get an overview of the movie and see just what makes it so popular.

Heathers

`http://www.inf.tu-dresden.de/~mb21/eblues.htm`

"A lurid glimpse into the dark shadowed underbelly of the American psyche." With a description like that, how could it not be a cult classic? Check out Winona Ryder in one of her first roles.

Mystery Science Theater 3000: The Movie

`http://www.reellife.com/PFE/mystery/mystery-home.html`

If you're already a fan of the TV show, check out what happens to Mike on this adventure. If not, give it a chance and see what people are talking about when they mention *MST3K*.

Ray Wolfe's Online Guide to Eraserhead

`http://users.aol.com/RayWolf1/eraser.htm`

On this page dedicated to David Lynch, you can find a synopsis of one of his first and darkest movies, as well as a glossary of symbolism.

Rocky Horror Picture Show

`http://www.rockyhorror.com/`

This is the official site for the midnight showing classic, so there aren't any worries about licensing rights that other sites might encounter. You can find background info and memorabilia, as well as ground rules for participation.

Spinal Tap

`http://www.spinaltap.com/`

As they say, "This page goes to 11." If that means nothing to you, then you need to get in touch with *Spinal Tap*. Devotees will appreciate just how far *Spinal Tap* can carry out a joke.

The Unofficial Monty Python Home Page

`http://www2.cybernex.net/~mikes2/python.html`

Even though the page is dedicated to true Monty Python fans, everyone can enjoy it. Link to the *Holy Grail*, *Life of Brian*, *Meaning of Life*, *The Crimson Permanent Assurance*, and other films with some of the Python players.

Drama

Barton Fink

`http://poppy.kaist.ac.kr/cinema/barton_fink/esch1.html`

This is a good site if you've already seen the movie and are wondering if you missed out on some of its symbolism, or just visit to have your curiosity piqued.

Basketball Diaries

`http://underground.net/BDiaries/`

If you think this compelling drama about Jim Carroll may be a little too much for you, visit the Web site and see what it's about for yourself. The fact that Leonardo DiCaprio is in it certainly couldn't hurt.

The Crow

http://www4.ncsu.edu/unity/users/b/bsspiche/www/crow/crowpage2.html

If the movie intrigued you, be sure to link to sites about the book from this page. Or you can introduce yourself to the sites and sounds of the film where the tragic death of Brandon Lee took place.

Dead Man Walking

http://www.reellife.com/PFE/dead/dead-homepage.html

Find out more about the stars, Susan Sarandon and Sean Penn, the real-life events that inspired the movie, or what went on behind the scenes at this site for the film nominated for four Academy Awards.

Forrest Gump

http://rhf.bradley.edu/~willy/gump.html

When you get there, and you should make a point of it, be sure to check out the Celebrity Gumpisms and the link to Gary Sinise.

The Godfather Trilogy

http://www.exit109.com/~jgeoff/godfathr.html

Focuses on *The Godfather* trilogy. Find out everything imaginable about this famous trilogy. This award-winning site includes pointers to each film, a trivia challenge, soundtrack and dialogue WAVs, stills from the films, and contest information.

Goodfellas

http://www-personal.umich.edu/~geordyg/goodfell.html

This site is still heavily under construction, but you can at least download sound bites and pictures of another great Scorsese film.

Hackers

http://www.mgmua.com/hackers/index.html

Even if you're not a hacker, the site promises that you will still enjoy this movie (real hackers will enjoy the message it claims). Play the hacking game at the site, read letters from hackers, and link to related sites.

Heat

http://www.hooked.net/~clayton/movies/heat/

How can a film that stars Al Pacino and Robert DeNiro be anything but powerful? This site is currently under construction, but check back frequently and read the character bios for the two mentioned above as well as Val Kilmer and writer/director Michael Mann.

Il Postino (The Postman)

http://www.cecchigori.com/cinema/postino/home.htm

Visit the site for this Academy Award nominated picture, and get a glimpse of what's in store for you when you get a chance to see this great film.

Jane Eyre

http://www.alliance.ca/theatre/movies/eyre.html

With a stellar cast and Charlotte Bronte's classic work holding it up, this movie holds great promise. Read about the actors and the story itself at this page.

Leaving Las Vegas

http://www.mgmua.com/vegas/index.html

This is the film that Nicholas Cage won best actor honors for. Be sure to explore Cage, Elizabeth Shue, and others involved in the making of this deeply disturbing movie at their Web site.

Martin Scorsese

`http://www.hooked.net/~clayton/directors/`
`martin_scorsese/`

Look up pictures, related links, the complete works, or a biography of one of the greatest directors of our time. Or look at clips from some of his movies.

Mean Streets

`http://www.hooked.net/~clayton/movies/mean_streets/`

The site for this Scorsese film set in Little Italy gives you a synopsis of the film, a sound bite teaser, and an image of the laser disc cover.

Othello

`http://othello.guide.com/`

Read up on interviews with the filmmakers; preview the CD-ROM; and get the chance to learn more about Shakespeare, his other plays, and festivals around the country.

Photographic Gallery of the Film Trilogy of Krzysztof Kieslowski, Three Colors

`http://www.mty.itesm.mx/~dch/centros/cinema16/`
`tres_colores/texto/tres_colores.html`

If you're looking for stills from *Blue*, *White*, or *Red*, be sure to check out this page. The images alone may be haunting enough to convince you that these three films are worth seeing.

Powder

`http://www.angelfire.com/pages0/powder/index.html`

This page manages to avoid a lot of the controversy that surrounded this film's making. Presents a fan's page with links to pages on all of the main actors.

Pulp Fiction Apothecarys Page

`http://www.pla-net.net/~apoth/pulp/`

Links to every *Pulp Fiction* page currently out there, plus a coupon off the purchase of the movie!

Quiz Show

`http://cybermart.com/sundance/movies.html`

Because this film is so intricately tied to the Sundance Film Festival, you can view clips from the film and from the Sundance Institute at the site.

Reservoir Dogs

`http://www.miramax.com/dlpages/reservdl.html`

Here's the place to come to download stills and clips from the film that put Tarantino on the map.

Scarface

`http://www.exit109.com/~jgeoff/scarface/`

It would be silly to say anything disparaging about this site wouldn't it? There's no need to, though. Lots of links for buffs and people who wouldn't know Tony Montana from a hole in the ground—their mistake.

Showgirls

`http://Showgirls.directnet.com/Showgirls/`
`ShowGirlsMainPage.html`

One rumor is that *Showgirls* could become the next *Rocky Horror Picture Show*, with back talk and audience members dressing (or undressing as the case may be) like characters in the film.

A Taxi Driver Page

`http://pilot.msu.edu/user/svoboda1/taxi_driver/`

Even if this movie didn't have Robert DeNiro or Jodie Foster in one of her first roles, it would still be great, hard to imagine, but great. Be sure to check out the counter at the bottom of the first page.

True Romance

`http://www.hooked.net/~clayton/movies/true_romance/`

Let's see, between Quentin Tarantino, Christian Slater, Patricia Arquette, Dennis Hopper, Gary Oldman, and Val Kilmer, someone should be of interest to you. If not, check out the site for its multimedia showcase and links to related sites.

(Unofficial) Hoop Dreams

`http://www.well.com/user/srhodes/hoopdreams.html`

While not a very graphical page, it is full of links to seemingly every article written about this great documentary.

Festivals

Cannes Film Festival Official Web Site

http://www.festival-cannes.fr/

Be sure to click on the English "Welcome" when you get there, it'd be a shame to miss anything this page has to offer. You can count on this site to give you the latest results and goings on at the festival and in the town where it's held year after year.

Chicago Underground Film Festival

http://www.deafear.com/cuff/

The pages for this annual event allow the visitor to download special software to view clips of some of the experimental pieces that will be shown in the upcoming year. You may also read about special events at the festival and find links to other major film festivals.

Cinema Festivals

http://www.coproductions.com/cnfestad.htm

This search engine allows you to find specific film festivals by month, home page, topic, name, type of festival (competition or exhibition), city, state, or country, in both French and English.

The Film Festivals Server

http://filmfestivals.com/

What a great site. Whether you have the money and time to make it to these festivals or not, so much information is to be had on these pages that you might feel like you've been there. All the major festivals can be found, plus city guides to go along with them.

Low Res film and video festival

http://www.lowres.com/

This film festival is meant to showcase and encourage young film makers by showing just how much can be accomplished on a small budget.

Sundance Film Festival

http://sundancefilm.com/festival/

Take a tour through the independent filmmaker's festival created by Robert Redford. You can look at this year's entries or review past winners.

Film & Production Resources

The Character Shop

http://www.character-shop.com/

This special effects shop produces some of the most famous animals on the big screen. Read how the Budweiser frogs and anteater were created using puppets and animatronics. Check out the story about the largest animatronic robots ever created for Disney's *Operation Dumbo Drop*. Includes a resume of every film, TV show, and commercial shot with Character Shop animals, FAQs about their work, a tour of the facility, and semi-regular updates on their work. A fascinating visit!

CinemaSpace

http://cinemaspace.berkeley.edu/

Home page for the film studies program at Berkeley. Choose a department related to science fiction, art direction, Web pages by Berkeley students, and more.

Dolby Laboratories

http://www.dolby.com/

Find out just what Dolby Surround sound is after all these years. If you're in production, bookmark this page right away, you'll come back to it frequently for information and resources. You'll also learn how to set up your home stereo for optimal performance.

DTS Theatrical

http://www.dtstech.com/theatrical/

Visit the Web page of the leaders in movie theater sound, whether you're going to open a theater, or in the more likely event that you're just curious.

Newsletters

http://www.tpbrain.com/freesample.html

Did you know that certain kinds of music contribute to intelligence and problem solving? Or that you should eat leafy green vegetables, apples, and eggs for optimal learning? Visit The Brain Store to receive free research-based newsletters.

Movies

Film Resources

http://www.magicnet.net/enzian-bin/resource

A searchable Web site of every link known related to film. Includes film festivals, film schools, critiques of films, and resources for filmmakers. An excellent bookmark for the budding screenwriter and director.

The Independent Film and Video Makers Internet Resource Guide

http://www.echonyc.com/~mvidal/Indi-Film+Video.html

A valuable resource guide for filmmakers on a professional and political level, there's something here that you need.

Knight Productions, Inc.

http://www.msen.com/~knight/

Link to other sites and "tangents," as well as gaining access to informative databases when you visit this site.

LucasArts

http://www.lucasarts.com/

Never one to be behind the times in technology, George Lucas' production company has its own site. Come find technical support and sneak glimpses of what they're working on.

Makin' Waves Studio

http://cyberzine.org/html/Waves/wavepage.html

Sample some of their special "Aussie" WAV files, or order your own custom .WAV. You can even order a broadcast-quality commercial voice over.

Mass F/X

http://www.ultranet.com/~msavino/fx/fx.html

A favorite of Media House Films, this group produces special effects for your film or simply your pleasure.

New York Film and Animation Co. Ltd.

http://www.okc.com/nyfac

Home page for NY-based computer animators. Read about NYFAC, check out their gallery of cool graphics, and see what's cooking with current projects.

Production Magic

http://www.ProductionMagic.com/

Read about their shot logger, a special tool for nonlinear editing. Specifications for the tool, instructions for use, questions and answers, and some examples of it in use are included in the site.

Rhythm & Hues Studios

http://www.rhythm.com/

This visual effects production company has created a number of entertaining rides, exhibits, commercials, and movie effects. Read about their work on the award winning *Babe* (1995), the Coca-Cola polar bears, and effects for EuroDisneyland. Click on Sights and Sounds to see how these special effects are created.

Shades of Light Studios

http://www.ernestallen.com/shadesoflight/

A new studio that would like to offer its facilities to those who need a place to film. Read about their specific studios and vision for production and see if they offer what you need, or just get an inside look at what goes on at a studio.

THX

http://www.thx.com/thx/

For home and theater sound, visit this site to see what one of the leaders in effects, LucasArts, is doing for your listening pleasure.

Virtual Studio Ltd, London

http://www.vrworlds.com/

This computer graphics, audio, and custom software studio provides information on virtual reality and links to the biggest VR companies on the Web. Check out the Graphics Studio link to see samples of their work.

WAVE—Wognum Art's Virtual Exchange

http://www.pi.se/wognum-art

Home page for this Stockholm-based art studio. Read about their recent work with clients incorporating interface design, CD-ROM programming, corporate profiling, typography, graphics, 3D modeling, and animation.

Welcome to EPSONE.COM

http://www.amug.org/~eps/

Home of Entertainment Production Service, a multimedia and corporate event production company.

Horror

The Cabinet of Dr. Casey

http://www.cat.pdx.edu/~caseyh/horror/index.html

A great site for horror movie buffs. Check out the extensive Horror Movie Posters Archive, the Horror audio and graphics sections, and Horror in Literature and the Movies.

David Cronenberg Home Page

http://www.netlink.co.uk/users/zappa/cronen.html

Read interviews and reviews, see what's around the corner, and generally be grossed out by this master of horror and creator of many classics of our time.

Halloween

http://ourworld.compuserve.com/homepages/
Garrick_Bernard/

Find out about the beginning of Michael Myers' legacy at this page that pays tribute to all of the *Halloween* movies. You can read up on John Carpenter and others who deserve credit for this slumber party mainstay.

The Hannibal Lecter Home Page

http://cyberstation.net/~mariah/lecter.html

Of course you can link to *The Silence of the Lambs* page from this site, but anyone who has seen the movie knows that the real lure is the deranged psychiatrist. Read all about him and his wacky exploits here, and link to pages related to some of his more obscure references.

Jaws

http://www.winternet.com/~tandj04/jaws.html

Did you remember that *Jaws* was rated PG? Visit and refresh yourself on one of the most truly frightening movies of our time.

Lord of Illusions

http://www.dimensionx.com/archive/reeltalk/promo/
lordofillusions.html

Check out some clips and stills from one of Clive Barker's masterpieces, and brush up on who's who in the horror business.

A Nightmare on the Web

http://www-personal.umich.edu/~rexerm/nightmare/
index.html

Link off of Freddy Kreuger's fingernails to links pertaining to all of the installments of the horror classic, *Nightmare on Elm Street*.

The Return of the Texas Chainsaw Massacre

http://chainsaw.crimson.com/rtcm/

Because just once isn't enough. Spy on Leatherface, but don't think that he's not looking for you too. As they say on the page, check out some of their "tasty cuts."

The Shining

http://pubweb.acns.nwu.edu/~mdk899/overlook.html

The maker of this page believes *The Shining* is destined to live on forever in the pages of the movie greats. Visit the Overlook Hotel and let him show you why. He'll take you through all the rooms you remember and the symbolism that you didn't know was there.

Miscellaneous

And the Winner Is

Having trouble deciding what movie to rent tonight? Why not check out one of the classics. Here's a list of the academy Award winning films for Best Picture. For more information about Oscar, check out the Academy of Motion Picture Arts and Sciences Web site.

Year	Film
1927-28	Wings
1928-29	Broadway Melody
1929-30	All Quiet on the Western Front
1930-31	Cimarron
1931-32	Grand Hotel
1932-33	Cavalcade

Movies

Year	Film
1934	It Happened One Night
1935	Mutiny on the Bounty
1936	The Great Zigfield
1937	The Life of Emile Zola
1938	You Can't Take It With You
1939	Gone with the Wind
1940	Rebecca
1941	How Green Was My Valley
1942	Mrs. Miniver
1943	Casablanca
1944	Going My Way
1945	The Lost Weekend
1946	The Best Years of Our Lives
1947	Gentleman's Agreement
1948	Hamlet
1949	All the King's Men
1950	All About Eve
1951	An American in Paris
1952	The Greatest Show on Earth
1953	From Here to Eternity
1954	On the Waterfront
1955	Marty
1956	Around the World in Eighty Days
1957	The Bridge on the River Kwai
1958	Gigi
1959	Ben-Hur
1960	The Apartment
1961	West Side Story
1962	Lawrence of Arabia
1963	Tom Jones
1964	My Fair Lady
1965	The Sound of Music
1966	A Man for All Seasons
1967	In the Heat of the Night
1968	Oliver!
1969	Midnight Cowboy
1970	Patton
1971	The French Connection
1972	The Godfather
1973	The Sting
1974	The Godfather, Part II
1975	One Flew Over the Cuckoo's Nest
1976	Rocky
1977	Annie Hall
1978	The Deer Hunter
1979	Kramer vs. Kramer
1980	Ordinary People
1981	Chariots of Fire
1982	Gandhi
1983	Terms of Endearment
1984	Amadeus
1985	Out of Africa
1986	Platoon
1987	The Last Emperor
1988	Rain Man
1989	Driving Miss Daisy
1990	Dances with Wolves
1991	The Silence of the Lambs
1992	Unforgiven
1993	Schindler's List
1994	Forrest Gump
1995	Braveheart

The Academy of Motion Picture Arts and Sciences

http://www.ampas.org/ampas/

Check out the latest press releases and new Web features by the Academy. This site also includes the Interactive Guide to the Academy Awards, the winners of the latest Academy Awards, and information on the Academy itself.

American Cinema Page

http://www.netcenter.com/netcentr/entertain/cinema.html

This page includes links to the major motion picture Web sites (Buena Vista, MGM, Disney, and so forth) and fan pages devoted to special movies. Part of the NetCenter, a directory of topics and links.

Best Video

http://www.tagsys.com:80/Ads/BestVideo/index.html

This site isn't a must-see movie, it's an online video store that helps you find and buy movies. You have the option of buying previously viewed movies, reading about films in the monthly reviews, or linking to other Web sites. Good when you know what you want but not where to get it.

Bright Lights Film Journal

http://www.slip.net/~gmm/bright.html

This quarterly journal explores the issue of movies as propaganda. They'll take you through all the angles of movie interpretation and impact, and encourage you to give them a piece of your mind.

Cinema Sites

http://www.vir.com/VideoFilm/davidaug/Movie_Sites.html

One of the most complete sites around for movie buffs. Find links to awards, databases that allow you to find a movie by a quote and other obscure facts, reviews, specific films and actors, the history of film, and many other useful tools.

Cinemania Online

http://www.msn.com/Cinemania/

This site, maintained by Microsoft, will keep you abreast of the newest theatrical releases, allow you to participate in on-going debates about great actors, or read biographies and regularly updated special features.

Critics Roost

http://useattle.uspan.com/maven/

Includes the Women's Lip, Movie Avenger, Movie Assassin, and J-Man critics circles. These critics not only review movies, but explain their take on the big studios' perversion of the movie art. Includes valuable reviews of a number of films. Visit this site before you crack the entertainment section of the newspaper.

Early Motion Pictures 1897–1916

http://lcweb2.loc.gov/papr/mpixhome.html

Download AVI files of early motion pictures of New York, San Francisco before and after the earthquake (1906), and different presidents. This fascinating site also includes essays on film at the turn of the century, the actuality film genre, and early motion picture information.

Films in the Works

http://www.boxoff.com/cgi/
filmwork.pl?filename=filmwork.txt

This kind of site is what the Web is all about, getting information before your friends. You can search for key words, if you're looking for a sequel, or just browse through the titles and link to information about the movie.

The Internet Movie Database

http://www.msstate.edu/Movies/

The Internet movie resource provides information on over 65,000 movies and TV shows. Search for a film of interest to learn about the cast, production company, and staff on the film. This site also includes stills from films, sound clips, and synopses of the films. Check out the Goofs and Location sections for some hilarious info on screwups and hellish conditions.

Movie Reviews.com

http://moviereviews.com/

Don't let the name fool you, this site is much more than your ordinary review site. Joining in is more than welcome. You may join experts, or pick a topic like sex in films or chick flicks to talk about, but, best of all, there's a place to rate the worst movie of all time.

The Movies Cliché List

http://www.well.com/user/vertigo/cliches.html

Contains a hilarious list of movie clichés and logic flaws from hundreds of films. Choose a cliché of interest (Clothing, Monsters, Women, Wood, and so forth) to see lengthy descriptions (complaints?) of clichés. Give your e-mail address and updates will be sent your way.

The Movie Sounds Page

http://www.netaxs.com/people/dgresh/snddir.html

Sounds from many popular movies can be downloaded for customizing your computer. Check out the Now Playing and Mystery Sounds sections for great WAVs of current movies and older films.

Movie Target

http://www.hooked.net/~clayton/movies/

This group of devoted movie fans are constantly expanding the number of movie pages you can link to. Their tastes cover the likes of Stanley Kubrick, Michael Mann, Martin Scorsese, Quentin Tarantino, and John Woo.

MovieLink 777-FILM Online

http://www.movielink.com

If you live in one of America's larger cities, enter your ZIP code to see current show times. Local theater locations and up-to-the-minute show times for movies in 25 cities are part of this site. The Café includes previews, reviews of films, a parents guide, and a list of relevant newsgroups.

Movienet

http://www.movienet.com/

Find listings by city or movie of what's showing at Landmark Theaters, read about upcoming films, or just see what's new in the movie business.

MovieWEB

http://movieweb.com/

The definitive site for movie information. Lists films by production company, and has places for you to rate films you've seen, and read what other people have said.

MPEG Movie Archive

http://www.eeb.ele.tue.nl/mpeg/index.html

Download MPEG movies of different topics, such as nature, racing, space, movies, supermodels, and animation. Make sure you have an MPEG viewer—you can download one from this site.

Mr. Showbiz

http://web3.starwave.com/showbiz/

A great site for Hollywood gossip queens. Read crazy interviews about the latest films, participate in pure fluff about serious American events, and enjoy it! Not only does this site look good, but it has "substance!"

San Francisco Chronicle Film Review

http://www.sfgate.com/chronicle/pink-section/film.html

The movie reviewer for this page certainly takes his work seriously, if the extensive list of reviewed movies is any indication. The site does not include links to the movies, but it's good to read about movies from someone other than the person who made it.

Showtimes Home Page

http://www.showtimes.com/

A great place to find links to the pages of movies currently in the theater.

Star Seeker Movie Page

http://www.starseeker.com/Movie.htm

Information on this page includes past, present, and future movies, directors, sound bites, the past week's ticket sales and the top 50 ever in the box office, current movie listings, the Oscars since 1927, a daily bit of movie trivia, and upcoming festivals.

United Film Distributors

http://www.unitedleisure.com/ufd/

A distributing house with some movie names you may not recognize, but actors you probably will. An interesting look at smaller films.

Widescreen Links

http://www.abdn.ac.uk/~u15cs/wslinks.htm

Touting itself as "THE one-stop site for movie fans," this site does a thorough job of allowing you to look by country, studio, or star for a movie, and also has links to articles that are of interest to the movie-going public.

Mystery

Clue

http://www.fortnet.org/~meltdown/clue.htm

Get pictures from the movie that had three endings and links to other fans' pages.

Fargo

http://www.reellife.com/PFE/fargo/fargo-home.html

If you're already a fan of the Coen brothers, you probably already know that *Fargo* continues a tradition of great films from these two. If you haven't heard of them, think *Raising Arizona*, *Blood Simple*, and *Miller's Crossing*, and if that doesn't help, check out the page anyway.

The Hitchcock Page

http://www.primenet.com/~mwc/

Tribute page to one of the greatest film directors. Read a biography, check out the Filmography and Hitchcock on TV sections, and read about his awards and honors. The Pure Cinema section includes an animation of Hitchcock's shower sequence.

Seven

http://corail.plg.u-nancy.fr/~bellili/seven.html

Just so that you don't have to go all the way to the page if you don't want to, here they are: gluttony, greed, sloth, envy, wrath, pride, and lust. Lots of other things can be found at the site though—definitely worth the trip.

Usual Suspects

http://www.servtech.com/public/funkman/usual/

Even if you haven't seen this movie, the ending won't be ruined for you by visiting this site. In fact, the writer makes a point of it. So feel free to explore the cast, crew, and story here, and pass on the consideration of not ruining this great movie.

Vertigo

http://www.soton.ac.uk/~ajm194/vertigo.html

Read a big fan's interpretation of this American classic, and tell him how you agree and disagree. There are links to other critical essays on Hitchcock's work from this page too.

Products

CyberCinema

http://www.indirect.com/www/jonbrown/cinema

Want a movie poster for that bare wall? This online movie poster store lets you order posters of the latest hits. Be sure to check out the Classic Movie Catalog and the Our Catalog of Favorite Posters. You can order online or send away for their catalog.

The Entertainment Connection

http://econnection.com/bin/evan.dll/tec/users/htxreg/&/tec/user/home.htx#banner

The long URL is worth it. Come here and get a virtual shopping cart that you can fill with all sorts of movie paraphernalia, and then store them until you're ready to buy them. You'll have a personal page and your own guide.

HSS Wholesale Home Page

http://www.direct.ca:80/hss

Offers a collection of more than 200 life-size stand-up cardboard posters of famous movie stars, singers, *Star Trek* characters, and more. Check their index, or click on What's New to see the latest full-size cutouts.

Movie Madness Merchandise

http://www.MovieMadness.com/

If you didn't realize that you liked the movie that much until it was already out on video, here's your chance to still get products that show your devotion.

The Movie Poster Page

http://musicman.com/mp/posters.html

Learn about the new movie poster collecting frenzy hitting the auction houses. This site includes poster images of leading movies and thumbnails of many other movie posters. You can read about movie poster preservation, poster investing, and the reprint business. This site also includes a movie poster catalog and information on Disney, Elvis, and James Bond movie posters. A busy site!

The Ultimate Resource for Vintage Posters

`http://www.panix.com/~jerry/chisholm/`

Visit the only movie poster search service on the Web. This site also provides examples of extremely rare movie posters and a gallery index for New York.

Science Fiction/Fantasy

2001: A Space Odyssey

`http://www.hooked.net/~clayton/movies/2001/`

Visit this site to remind yourself what a great movie this is, or to convince yourself to go out and rent it today. There are links to information on the movie, as well as more generally related sites.

2019: Off-World (Blade Runner Page)

`http://kzsu.stanford.edu/uwi/br/`

From links to small sites with a few pictures and essays to a huge site with nothing but *Blade Runner* info, as well as a warehouse of information on the page itself, you won't have any questions left after visiting.

Back to the Future

`http://www.pi.net/~eeersel/`

The author of this page would like to have an individual page for each installment in this trilogy starring Michael J. Fox, but for now, he has synopses of each on the front page.

Bob's Godzilla Shrine

`http://ccwf.cc.utexas.edu/~rloftin/gpage.html`

Read about Bob's personal collection of *Godzilla* artifacts, or link to the pages of others who worship at the *Godzilla* shrine.

Dune

`http://www.eerie.fr/~tassin/Dune/dune.html`

Frank Herbert's science fiction classic can be found here with links to the main characters, the book, and more information about Herbert's legacy.

Flash Gordon

`http://www.geocities.com/Hollywood/4262/`

Read other people's comments and contribute your own after you look through the credits, pictures, plot, music, and quotes. You also have the opportunity to buy the movie right from this page.

Harp on Batman Forever

`http://www.lungfish.com/alteregos/velcro/soforth/batman.html`

A very critical look at the most recent Batman film, the author gets the ball rolling and encourages others to contribute inconsistencies they noticed in the film. Not a site for someone who hasn't seen the film and plans to.

Mithral Web

`http://mithral.iit.edu:8080/highlander/`

The unofficial *Highlander* site will link you to many other pages run by people who share a passion for this film, as well as to the pages that fans like to visit.

Nuke Home Page

`http://www.nuke.com`

Web site for computer and video game fanatics and sci-fi movie buffs. Check out *Cinescape* magazine's site or visit *Electronic Gaming Monthly*. Try out their Chat feature, which lets you talk to others in real-time, or visit the James Bond site.

Phantasm

`http://www.phantasm.com/`

When a movie's been around this long, and still has a unique URL, you know it's here to stay. Take a tour of the Tall Man's Mausoleum, or check out what he has to say to you. It is a site definitely worth checking out, even if it's only for job openings.

Star Trek: WWW

http://www.vol.it/luca/startrek/index.html

Not surprisingly, *Star Trek* pages abound on the Web. Use this one as a starting point, and then link away to many other pages and see what pieces of Trek lore you can pick up along the way.

The Star Wars Collectors Home Page

http://www.cs.washington.edu/homes/lopez/collectors.html

This site has tons of information on *Star Wars* toys, posters, movie props, food, new collectibles, bootlegs, and many more types of *Star Wars* collectibles. This page also has links to *Toy Shop*, *Action Figure Digest*, and *The Star Wars Collector Magazine*.

Star Wars Home Page at UPENN

http://stwing.resnet.upenn.edu:8001/~jruspini/starwars.html

A great site that includes *Star Wars* FAQs, art, the Dark Forces Demo, and dozens of articles on different *Star Wars* characters and equipment used in the trilogy. If you can't access this site, it's because the page has been shut down by LucasArts. Their new policy is to not allow fans to have Web pages of *Star Wars* related material. Is this the beginning of the end of the Internet as a virtual community for everyone, not just companies?

The Tron Home Page

http://www.aquila.com/guy.gordon/tron/tron.htm

Was Disney's 1984 movie *Tron* ahead of its time? Find out here. Download images and sounds and use the read time chat feature to discuss *Tron* with others. Neat!

Until the End of the World

http://www.panix.com/~archii/uteotw/

If you've seen the movie, you'll recognize the wallpaper throughout the sight, which is a great effect. Hopefully it'll intrigue you if you haven't seen it. Check out the themes link, as well as those that take you to the people involved.

War Games Fan Page

http://www.students.uiuc.edu/~lneumann/wargames/

Only at the *War Games* site can Dabney Coleman give you quotes for everyday life. You can take the trivia quiz, or explore alternate endings to one of the first movies to introduce us to what a boy and his computer can do.

Waterworld

http://www.mca.com/unicity/waterworld/

Somebody out there had to like *Waterworld*. If that was you, here's the site you need to visit. You can be part of this interactive adventure, and make fun of all your friends for not giving it a chance.

Safety and Regulatory Guides

http://www.jjkeller.com/samples.htm

Features monthly freebies and a variety of catalogs about transportation safety, training materials, software, and more. J.J. Keller and Associates, Inc., provides safety and regulatory publications, products, and services.

Newsgroups

alt.ascii-art.animation

alt.asian-movies

alt.binaries.sounds.movies

alt.binaries.starwars

alt.cult-movies

alt.cult-movies.alien

alt.cult-movies.evil-deads

alt.cult-movies.rocky-horror

alt.fan.actors

alt.fan.alicia-slvrstone

alt.fan.blade-runner

alt.fan.blues-brothers

alt.fan.brad-pitt

alt.fan.bruce-campbell

alt.fan.drew-barrymore

alt.fan.dune

alt.fan.harrison-ford

alt.fan.james-bond

alt.fan.keanu-reeves

alt.fan.mandy-patinkin

alt.fan.michael.biehn

alt.fan.ricci.christina

alt.fan.sam-raimi

alt.fan.sandra-bullock

alt.fan.woody-allen

alt.horror

alt.movies.branagh-thmpsn

alt.movies.chaplin

alt.movies.christian-bale

alt.movies.cinematography

alt.movies.hitchcock

alt.movies.independent

alt.movies.indian

alt.movies.joe-vs-volcano

alt.movies.kubrick

alt.movies.monster

alt.movies.scorsese

alt.movies.silent

alt.movies.spielberg

alt.movies.terry-gilliam

alt.movies.tim-burton

alt.movies.visual-effects

alt.sex.movies

aus.films

clari.living.movies

fido.ger.movie

fj.rec.animation

fj.rec.movies

kw.movies

pdaxs.ads.movies

pdaxs.arts.auditions

pdx.movies

rec.arts.movies.announce

rec.arts.movies.current-films

rec.arts.movies.lists+surveys

rec.arts.movies.local.indian

rec.arts.movies.misc

rec.arts.movies.movie-going

rec.arts.movies.past-films

rec.arts.movies.people

rec.arts.movies.production

rec.arts.movies.reviews

rec.arts.movies.tech

rec.arts.sf.movies

rec.arts.sf.reviews

rec.arts.sf.starwars.games

rec.arts.startrek.current

rec.music.movies

sdnet.movies

triangle.movies.

tw.bbs.rec.movie

umn.general.movies

Listservs

CINEMA-L—Discussions on All Forms of Cinema

The American University, Washington, DC

You can join this group by sending the message "sub CINEMA-L your name" to listserv@american.edu

Film Music Discussion List

University Computing Services, Indiana University

You can join this group by sending the message "sub FILMUS-L your name" to listserv@iubvm.ucs.indiana.edu

FRAMEWORKS—Experimental Film Discussion List

America Online, Inc. (1-800-827-6364 in USA/ Canada)

You can join this group by sending the message "sub FRAMEWORKS your name" to listserv@listserv.aol.com

H-FILM—H-NET List for Scholarly Studies and Uses of Media

You can join this group by sending the message "sub H-FILM your name" to listserv@h-net.msu.edu

Movie Poster Discussion

The American University, Washington, DC

You can join this group by sending the message "sub MOPO-L your name" to listserv@american.edu

SCREEN-L—Film and TV Studies Discussion List

The University of Alabama, Tuscaloosa, Alabama

You can join this group by sending the message "sub SCREEN-L your name" to listserv@ua1vm.ua.edu

Alternative

Be Happy or Die!

http://www.emba.uvm.edu/~jross/aonhome.html

Focuses on the techno-pop group Art of Noise. Includes a complete discography with covers of each album above the track titles. Also includes a summary of all information from the liner notes in each album.

The Cure

http://miso.wwa.com/~anaconda/cure2.html

Focuses on The Cure. Includes fan club information, lyrics, images, and more. Also includes a few sound bites and tablatures.

D'CuCKOO

http://www.well.com/user/tcircus/Dcuckoo/index.html

The techno-tribal band made up of six women from Oakland who build and play their own percussion instruments, including 6-foot bamboo "trigger sticks." Features the band's interactive "showtoys" MidiBall and RiGBy.

Depeche Mode Home Page

http://www.commline.com

Focuses on the eclectic alternative band. Includes lyrics, song parodies, dozens of pictures, and several links to other Depeche Mode resources. Also provides information on how to subscribe to the BONG mailing list.

Ectophiles' Guide to Good Music

http://weber.u.washington.edu/~neile/EctoGuide/ectophiles.guide.html

Based on Ecto, the singer/songwriter Happy Rhodes' mailing list. Provides a searchable index of similar music and explains the ectophile phenomenon.

fourtuoh

http://www.seanet.com/Users/dphil420/fourtuoh.html

Offers links to Seattle-area bands page, including Phat Sidy Smokehouse, Kilgore Trout, and Ganja Farmers. Also includes show times and audio samples.

The High Lonesome

http://www.io.com/~thl/high_lonesome

Focuses on the band The High Lonesome. Features bios, history, lyrics, photos, sound, ordering information, upcoming gigs, and more.

Hyperreal

http://hyperreal.com/

An alternative culture site for anyone interested in raves, music, or recreational drugs. Links to music info, sound and graphics tools, and more, including links to other cool sites.

Index

http://www.cs.ucl.ac.uk/external/T.Wicks/ill/index.html

If you like independent-label music, this "way-cool" site is for you. Search for general info, music lists, label info, or follow the links to the featured label of the day.

Kraftwerk infobahn

http://wwwtdb.cs.umu.se/~dvlawm/kraftwerk.html

Includes pictures, sounds, videos, and a collection of Kraftwerk MIDI sequences. Lets you add your name to the list of Kraftwerk fans.

MEGO

http://www.icf.de/mego/

If you're looking for something out of the ordinary, this is it. Listen to their refrigerator tracks (yes, they put a microphone in a refrigerator and recorded), ambient treatments of the moon landing, and many more experimental tracks.

Lou Reed's Web Home

http://www.rocknroll.net/loureed/

Provides information about Lou Reed and more. Includes a bootleg gallery, a couple of guitar tabs, and plenty more.

Linux

http://emile.math.ucsb.edu:8000/giveaway.html

A complete list of all the sites where you can download your free copy of the Linux operating system.

Pet Shop Boys Virtually

http://www.dsv.su.se/~mats-bjo/psb/psbhome.html

The European site that provides a huge picture library, fan club information, monthly updates, and sound files. Also includes a FAQ list, news hotlines, biographies, articles, and a pricing guide.

R.E.M. Home Page

http://www.halcyon.com/rem/index.html

Includes notes on the R.E.M. tour, all about Mike Mills, and a Frequently Asked Questions sheet. Offers a discography, lyrics, and guitar chord sheets. Also includes a photo archive.

Talking Heads

http://129.237.17.3/Heads/Talking_Heads.html

Provides Talking Heads information. Spares nothing—includes digitized songs, images, and more. Also includes information on signing up for the Talking Heads mailing list and "The Members: Life After Heads."

They Might Be Giants: Home-away-from-Home Page

http://www-personal.engin.umich.edu/~athaler/TMBG/TMBG.html

Focuses on TMBG. Now lets you dial-a-song online and get previously unreleased material. Includes lyrics, graphics, and FAQs.

Tom Waits Digest

http://www.nwu.edu/waits/index.htm

All the latest Tom Waits news, plus an encyclopedic collection of references. Includes album cover art for all Waits' records, song lists, band member lists, interviews, reviews, links to song lyrics and guitar tablature, and much more.

Turmoil's Seattle Music Web

http://www.blarg.com/~turmoil

Focuses on alternative and underground music in Seattle. Contains many WAV clips and whole songs. Also furnishes a Seattle music calendar and related art.

Wood and Wire

http://www.seekoc.com./woodwire/interface/home.html

Provides links to alternative, independent music sites. Includes record labels, band sites, and online zines. This site offers many cool links for fans of all types of music under the tag "alternative."

Awards

Academy Awards® for Music, 1960s and 1970s

http://www.msstate.edu/Movies/Oscars/1960_Music.html

Lists music awards and nominees for both song, score, and adaptation. Includes release information about the film and other works of the composer or artist.

Grammy Awards on the Internet

http://grammy.apple.com/

Focuses on the 1996 Grammy Awards. Lists all nominees and winners. Includes previews of video and audio files, Grammy trivia, and a hearsay column. Also provides QuickTime files.

Bluegrass

Bluegrass Unlimited Reviews

http://www.clark.net/pub/warnock/WWW/review_toc.html

Offers reviews of bluegrass-related recordings by Archie Warnock III, originally published in *Bluegrass Unlimited Magazine*.

Central Texas Bluegrass Association

http://www.zilker.net/~ctbg/

Offers information about the Central Texas Bluegrass Association, a nonprofit corporation. Includes a calendar of events, as well as workshop and membership information.

Doc Hamilton's Bluegrass Home Page

http://ccwf.cc.utexas.edu/~docham/

Presents a photo gallery of bluegrass greats.

Doc Watson

http://sunsite.unc.edu/doug/DocWat/DocWat.html

Contains a brief biography, a discography, a concert schedule, and a performance by Doc Watson accompanied by his son Merle. Includes links to pages on other bluegrass greats, such as Bill Monroe.

Old Time Music Bulletin Board

http://140.190.128.190/oldtime/oldtime.html

Enables readers to exchange and sell instruments and discuss banjo playing, fiddling, songs and lyrics, reviews, and anything else regarding American old-time music. Lets you post messages to the Anything Else? page.

Welcome to Planet Bluegrass!

http://www.csn.net:80/planet/

Blue Planet Music, organizers of the legendary Telluride Bluegrass Festival, is now online. Contains festival schedule and information, as well as information about Blue Planet recordings and their mail order operation.

Charts

Air Top 20 Chart

http://www-personal.umich.edu/~fishrfun/chart.html

Lawrence Birks picks for the top 20 in music. Most of the songs on the chart are alternative, and he has a good ear for them. Most bands listed have hyperlinks to the band's home page, while songs listed might contain links to the song's lyrics.

Alternative World

http://webser.lcs.k12.me.us/mssm/student/ethan/pages/main

See what's hot in the world of alternative music. View the top 20 of the week, or visit "The Summit" where you can find the best alternative music of all time. Also at the site are quizzes and a chance to vote for the 1996 music awards.

Black Music Department Top R&B Album and Singles Chart

http://www.cluster.com/frontier/chart/chart.html

As the title implies, the top 25 singles and albums in the R&B genre. Statistics for the page are provided by Frontier Entertainment group and reflect what is being bought and listened to in the community. This page is updated biweekly.

Casey's Top 40

http://www.ncf.carleton.ca/~aj627/HomePage.kclatest.html

The details from the latest broadcast of "Casey's Top 40." Includes the top 40 pop songs and their position in the chart last week, as well as the top songs in the other categories such as rock, R&B, and adult contemporary. This site is text only, but contains a link to a graphical version.

CD Album Top 100 of All Time

http://www.club.innet.be/~erikdl/

Cast your vote for your favorite album of all time and see what the results are. Votes are taken from all over the world and the results are presented in the form of the top 100 list, available in table or plain text form. There is also an archive of the previous lists.

DJ Dom A's Top Twenty Club Charts

http://www.djdoma.com/mychart.html

The top 20 dance club hits, updated biweekly. Many of the songs on the charts have WAV samples available, and DJ Dom A even provides a link to download a WAV player if you don't already have one.

DJ Special Blend's Top 10

http://www.uic.edu/~robertf/top10.html

A weekly top 10 list of urban contemporary music. This site is easy on the eyes with album covers or video stills for each and every song on the chart. DJ Special Blend's comments are insightful and give a feel for how the public accepts both artist and song.

HitsWorld

http://www.hitsworld.com/

The site to find out about music charts—Internet Top 30, Casey's Top 40, Personal Top 20, Rick Dee's Weekly Top 40, Billboard, MTV Top 20 Music Videos, and many, many more. Features reviews and links to other music sites.

Hype! One Hit Wonder Compilation

http://www.hype.com/nostalgia/onehit/onehitin.htm

A lengthy list of groups and artists that had one tremendously popular hit and then faded away into obscurity. When it is known, the current fate of the artist is also listed.

Rick Dee's Weekly Top 40

http://rick.com/Top-40/Chart.html

The online version of the top 40 list that is currently aired on over 500 radio stations across the United States. Links are provided to the artists' home pages, and you can participate in Rick Dee's Weekly Top 40 Challenge online.

Christian

"Almost" Definitive Contemporary Christian Music Hot

http://www.afn.org/~mrblue/ccm/ccm.html#what

Defines contemporary Christian music and serves as a guide to Web-related Christian music sources for all styles of music. Provides links to Christian artists and labels, related publications, and more.

Christian Music Online

http://www.cmo.com/cmo/index.html

Provides information about different types of Christian music, including contemporary, alternative, praise/worship, and rap. Includes concert dates, artists' biographies, and sound files.

Michael W. Smith

http://www.cs.rose-hulman.edu/~schaefsm/mws/

Focuses on contemporary Christian/pop artist Michael W. Smith. Includes information on contacting the fan club and the Michael's Best Friend newsletter.

Susan Ashton

http://rendall.notis.com/ashton/ashton.html

Serves as a resource page for contemporary Christian singer Susan Ashton. Includes the expected Net resources, as well as many metalinks that point to other Christian music resources.

Classical

Allegro

http://www.teleport.com/~allegro/

Allegro bills itself "the largest independent distributor of Classical Music in America." Features sound bytes from recent releases, as well as instructions on how to subscribe to Allegro's catalogs and automatic mailing list. This site also provides a link to the Magellan search engine.

American Music Center

http://www.ingress.com/amc/

Nonprofit contemporary music information and resource center. Provides lists of scores, opportunities for composers and performers, and information on grants, as well as links to Web music indices and Internet newsgroups.

Aspen Music Festival

http://www.infosphere.com:80/aspenonline/directory/ae/sponsors/artscouncil/sponsors/amf/index.amf.html

This site provides information about the Festival, its concert schedule, tickets, performing groups, master classes. There is also an audition schedule for the Aspen Music School that is a part of the Festival.

BalletWeb

http://users.aol.com/balletweb/balletweb.html

Devoted to classical ballet and occasionally to modern dance, this site offers a photo of the week, a gallery of photos, articles from online magazines, reviews, commentaries, analyses, and links to other ballet sites.

Boston Chamber Ensemble

http://www.mit.edu:8001/people/jcb/BCE/bce.html

This instrumental group's concerts are devoted to the music from the Renaissance Era to the present day. The BCE is particularly committed to supporting contemporary composers, and therefore holds an annual nationwide composition competition in an effort to expand its interaction with American composers. Learn more about this competition and the BCE's upcoming concert schedule at this site.

Building a Library: A Collector's Guide

http://www.ncsa.uiuc.edu/SDG/People/marca/barker-beethoven.html

Having trouble deciding what recording of Beethoven's Fifth to buy? This page offers you some tips on classical record collecting. It also reviews certain selected well-known classical works. There's a lot of reading involved here, so be prepared.

Cecilia Bartoli FanWeb (Unofficial)

http://www.nwu.edu/music/bartoli/

Cecilia's admirers are many and vocal (not surprisingly) in singing her praises! Lots of information about this talented mezzo-soprano's recordings and career. You can converse with other fans and view their Web pages. Contains sound and image files, as well as links to other Bartoli pages.

Chamber Music Conferences

http://www.ultranet.com/~cwholl/cmc/cmc.html

Provides a guide to chamber music conferences for amateur musicians and students. Contains information, schedules, fees, and application forms for more than 30 conferences.

Chicago Concert Search

http://student-www.uchicago.edu/users/achatche/music/concerts.html

Features a searchable database that contains classical music concert schedules, including festivals, for the Chicago area. Lets you search by calendar, performer, composer, or work.

Classical MIDI Archives

http://www.prs.net/midi.html

This multiple award-winning site provides archives of classical music audio files in MIDI format. Listen to your favorite works by Handel, Brahms, Scarlatti, and Albinoni. If you want to copy some of the sequences for your Web site, you must get the permission of the compiler.

Classical Music Home Page

http://www.webcom.com/~music/

Provides information on classical and early music. Includes a guide to building a basic CD collection, a buying guide for the serious collector, lists of more than 1,850 recommended CDs, and informative composer profiles. Searchable.

Classical Music on the Web

http://www.einet.net/galaxy/Leisure-and-Recreation/Music/douglas-bell/Index.html

According to Dr. Douglas Bell, mastermind behind this site, navigating the Internet without a guide is like finding yourself in New York City without a map. With the help of this site, you'll at least be able to find the Internet landmarks of classical music that are equivalent to the Big Apple's Metropolitan Opera! While you're at it, enjoy Dr. Bell's "Ask the Musical Doctor" column.

Cleveland Concert Search

http://student-www.uchicago.edu/users/achatche/music/Cleveland/concerts.html

Provides a searchable database that contains comprehensive classical music concert schedules, including festivals, for the Cleveland area. Lets you search by time period, performer, composer, or work.

Current Opera Website

http://www.webcom.com/~redwards/

Focuses on live opera. Features Current Opera Digest, a "daily gleaning of highlights from opera discussions on the Net," an article about a "conspiracy" to prevent a little-known composer from receiving his due, and links to other opera resources on the Net.

CyberDance: Ballet on the Web

http://www.thepoint.net/~raw/dance.htm

Contains an extensive alphabetical list of U.S. and Canadian professional, regional, and school-affiliated ballet and dance companies, with links to their home pages. There are also many links to schools and international ballet companies.

DCI: Drum Corps International

http://www.dci.org/

Keep up with your favorite drum and bugle corps' competition schedule and scores as it participates in the Summer Music Games. Includes profiles of the Top 12, the Open Class, and the Division II and III corps. Contains links to various member corps' home pages.

Electronic Early Music

http://www.hike.te.chiba-u.ac.jp/eem/

Features several dozen audio files, primarily of Renaissance dance music played on various MIDI instruments.

FAQ: rec.music.classical

http://www.cis.ohio-state.edu/hypertext/faq/usenet/music/classical-faq/faq.html

Contains useful information for the novice classical music lover. Answers questions on how to select recordings, which books to read to learn more, how to identify a classical piece heard on the radio, TV, or in a movie, what distinguishes different genres of music, how to pronounce names of composers, performers, and conductors, and more.

FutureNet: Classic CD

http://www.futurenet.co.uk/music/classiccd.html

Contains articles and reviews, a CD finder, and subscription information. Provides a beginner's guide that includes features on classical music in the media, and a history of classical music, plus a classical CD top 100 and an at-a-glance guide to the composers, A–Z.

Galliard String Quartet

http://planet-hawaii.com/wanui/svend.cgi/
pg15?alKWMV8j;;12

This ensemble performs string quartet music written in the tradition of the 19th century. It has recently released a CD of music written by Queen Liliuo- kalani of Hawaii. You can order CDs from this site.

Gilbert and Sullivan Archive

http://math.idbsu.edu/gas/GaS.html

Wandering Minstrels and Modern Major Generals alike will be enchanted by this multiple-award- winning site devoted to the famous William S. Gilbert/Arthur S. Sullivan collection of light operas. Here you can find out where and when your favorite Gilbert and Sullivan works will be staged. You can also search the complete libretti of all 14 Gilbert and Sullivan operas, and link to Web pages by local Gilbert and Sullivan performing ensembles in the United States, Great Britain, Canada, and Australia.

Gregorian Chant Home Page

http://www.music.princeton.edu:80/chant_html/

For the serious scholar, this award-winning site sponsored by Princeton University contains exten- sive information pertaining to the study of Gregorian liturgical music. There are links to related pages that include sound files of early music compositions. Also included are links to sites of ecclesiastical and musicological interest, as well as downloadable texts and tutorials.

Indiana University School of Music

http://www.music.indiana.edu/

Presents information about IU's renowned music school online, including its programs, schedules, and concerts. Offers a resource page that can help you find nearly anything related to classical music. Also includes an index of music resources on the Internet.

Indianapolis Symphony Orchestra

http://www.in.net/iso/

Contains a history of the Indianapolis Symphony Orchestra (ISO) and its present home, the historic Circle Theater. Also features biographical informa- tion about conductor/composer/musicologist Raymond Leppard, and the ISO's monthly concert schedule, as well as the schedule of Instrument Petting Zoo—a program sponsored by the ISO that teaches children about musical instrument families by allowing them to handle and play a collection of donated instruments.

Katia and Marielle Labeque Home Page

http://shrine.cyber.ad.jp/~hartline/labequehome.html

Meet the French sisters who have taken the music world by storm with their interpretations of classical two-piano literature. There's a CD list that also includes their jazz/fusion recordings. A fans and links page connects you with other Labeque lovers.

La Ma de Guido

http://ww1.grn.es/guido/

Title means "Guido's Hand." Guido was a medieval theorist, who supposedly used a diagram of the hand to teach students how to read music. You can see the diagram at this site, maintained by a publish- ing house that specializes in classical music and CDs by Spanish and Catalan artists. Biographies of the artists are included.

Le Nozze di Figaro

http://server.music.vt.edu/lenozze/lenozzehome.html

Contains information on Mozart's opera *The Marriage of Figaro*. Offers sections about Figaro's composition, its music, and its dramatis personae.

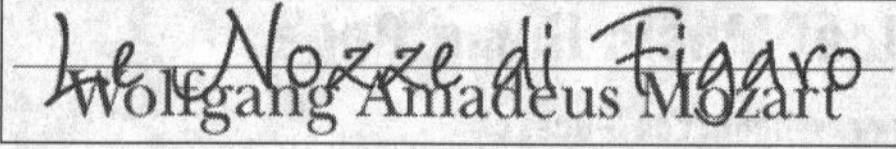

Maestronet

http://www.maestronet.com/

Players and collectors of classical stringed instru- ments will find Maestronet's site useful for finding and pricing the Stradivari of their dreams. The Instrument Showroom databases provide listings of instruments from around the world, as well as price information. The Conservatory section includes sheet music in Adobe Acrobat format, which you can download and print. MIDI files of this music are also available so that your computer can accompany you as you play!

Music Hall

http://www.ncsa.uiuc.edu/SDG/Experimental/
vatican.exhibit/exhibit/e-music/Music.html

Presents the music area of the Vatican Exhibit at the Library of Congress online. Contains four "rooms" of art treasures, primarily pages from Medieval and Renaissance illuminated music manuscripts. Provides notes with all the art works.

Music under Soviet Rule

http://www.webcom.com/~beatlebk/musov/musov.html

If you would like to explore the relationship between music and politics, or simply enjoy the music of Prokofiev, Shostokovitch, or any other classical composer active in the Soviet Union between 1917 and 1991, this site's collection of documents will be of interest to you. There are also links to other Soviet music-related pages.

New York Philharmonic

http://www.nyphilharmon.org/

The home page of one of the most highly respected symphony orchestras in the United States. Provides schedule and ticket information, profiles members of the orchestra, and supplies historical and archival facts about the orchestra and about its home at Avery Fisher Hall.

Opera Schedule Server

http://www.fsz.bme.hu/opera/main.html

Offers a searchable database that contains the schedules of opera companies around the world. Also contains basic information on major opera houses worldwide.

opera-l_home_page

http://www.physics.su.oz.au/~neilb/operah.html

Includes a guide to recorded opera, an A–Z guide to composers, an A–Z guide to operas, synopses of operas (you are invited to contribute a synopsis if your favorite opera is not already listed), photos of opera stars, and links to other opera sites.

Opera Stories and Background

http://www.classicalmus.com/bmgclassics/opera/index.html

Provided by BMG Music, this site offers a thorough synopsis, complete with sound clips, of such opera favorites as *Aida*, *Carmen*, and *Madama Butterfly*. Also includes historical information about featured operas and their respective composers. Opera afficionados will find the recommended recordings of great interest. There is also a Classics World search engine of classical music composers, conductors, and ensembles.

Performing Arts Sites

http://artsnet.heinz.cmu.edu/Artsites/
PerformingArts.html

Sponsored by Carnegie Mellon University, this site includes links—carefully chosen for their quality—to opera, theater, Broadway musical, music, and dance pages. If you are looking for a place to stage your performance art, this site also provides links to possible locations.

Renaissance Consort

http://www.hike.te.chiba-u.ac.jp/cons1/

Lets you see and hear the instruments that make up a typical Renaissance consort. Provides photographs (accompanied by audio clips) of recorders, crumhorns, flutes, viols, and more.

SCA Music and Dance Home Page

http://fermi.clas.virginia.edu/~gl8f/
music_and_dance.html

Society for Creative Anachronism, online. Focuses on Renaissance dance and dance music. Includes dance "cheat sheets," a discography of Renaissance dance music, a collection of articles taken from the society's newsletter on Renaissance dance, articles on troubadours and bardic songs, and many links to other early music and dance sites.

T. M. McComb: Music Home Page

http://www.best.com:80/~mccomb/music/

Provides one music writer's recommendations of classical, early music, and world music CDs. Contains informative notes on the different styles of music.

Unknown Composers Page

http://homepage.seas.upenn.edu/~jimmosk/TOC.html

Here's where underrated, obscure, and anonymous composers the likes of Nikolai Miaskovski and Robert Fuchs hang out. Most of the biographical sketches say "his music reminds me of so-and-so's" —alas, the fate of those who somehow missed the mark. Appropriately, there's a Special Mystery Moment/Guess the Composer test, and some of the composers have accompanying sound clips. Your contributions are welcome.

Worldwide Internet Music Resources

http://www.music.indiana.edu/music_resources/

If you are planning on doing any sort of music research online, this is the place to start. Sponsored by Indiana University's Music Library, this site provides an extensive list of music types, performers, and popular/classical musical ensembles. Other lists include schools and departments of music around the world, music industry leaders, and music-related journals and magazines.

Music

Commercial Music Resources

Ace Ticket Service—Concert Tickets

http://www.mindspring.com/~acetix/concerts.html

Buys and sells tickets to concerts and other events. Search for concert information by artist, city, or venue. Also features an artist of the week, tour gossip, and information on new and top 10 tours.

Akers Mic

http://www.oslonett.no/akersmic/musikk/ztv.html

Online CD store. Presents a catalog and other offerings within multimedia, surroundsound, and high-end HIFI. Contains more than 62,000 titles.

Andrak Music

http://www.andrak.com/

Formerly Planet Music. Specializes in thousands of hard-to-find domestic and import CDs. Also sells video tapes and music T-shirts.

HMV Toronto Superstore

http://www.hmv.ca/

Contains new releases, charts, and reviews of CDs and videos. Also contains a Canadian Indie Music Archive.

Hot Platters

http://home.earthlink.net/~oversight/HotPlatters.html

Serves as an auction for record lovers. Offers thousands of hard-to-find LPs, 45s, and 78s. Also offers posters, buttons, and other music memorabilia. Includes instructions on how to bid, and lets you submit bids by e-mail, fax, or the postal system. Also invites you to send an order or a want-list to Hot Platters.

Jazz Music Stores around the World

http://www.acns.nwu.edu/jazz/lists/stores.html

Serves as a guide to jazz record stores worldwide, arranged alphabetically by location. Includes useful information on shops' strengths in terms of formats and new/used, bargains, and more.

Rounder Records

http://harp.rounder.com:70/1/

Presents a catalog for a variety of independent labels including bluegrass, pop, alternative, Celtic, Latin sounds, and more. Features sound samples from recordings of several of their most popular artists. Also features artist profiles and discographies.

Transatlantic Management

http://euphoria.org/home/transmgt/index.html

Provides management and marketing services to unsigned musicians and bands. Includes company background, artist roster, and contact information.

Virtual Radio

http://www.microserve.net/vradio/

Do you want to hear new music? Here is an online service that does not offer sound byte clips, it offers entire songs. Virtual Radio provides a listener programmable station. Includes index by band with musician biographies and songs. This is a cool site.

WholeARTS Directory of Musical Entertainment

http://www.wholarts.com/mdir/

Provides directory of musical entertainment artists for hire. Includes artist profiles, site background, and contact information.

Country

Basket Full of Country

http://www.hcc.cc.fl.us/services/staff/dawn/basketc.htm

Offers a personal collection of country-related sites for country western music fans and cowboys. Also provides fan club information and a pen pal list.

History of Country Music

http://www.roughstock.com/roughstock/history/home.htm

Focuses on influential country artists as far back as the beginning of country music itself. Features history on artists such as Roy Acuff, Hank Williams, Gene Autry, Patsy Cline, Charley Pride, and more. Includes country styles such as western swing, urban cowboy, honky tonk, the Nashville sound, and others.

Obvious Gossip Home Page

http://www.infohouse.com/obviousgossip/home.html

Welcomes you to the official k.d. lang fan club. Lets you investigate the purchase of various k.d. lang paraphernalia and provides the latest album and concert information.

planet garth

`http://www.inlink.com/~brandon/`

Provides the latest on country sensation Garth Brooks. Includes world tour information, reviews, chart positions, pictures, and downloadable songs in RealAudio format.

Reba McENTIRE

`http://ruby.ph.utexas.edu/RebaWWW/Reba.html`

Provides a wealth of Reba resources. Tells you how to join Reba's International Fan Club. Offers the latest Reba news, a schedule of appearances, Reba's Special Events, and more. Also lets you add your favorite Reba pictures.

Databases

AMG Online Music

`http://allmusic.com/amg/om/omroot.html`

Access All-Music Guide's mega music database. Includes articles and reviews of hundreds of titles and artists from more than 200 freelance writers. Includes information on recent and upcoming releases and reissues, the latest in music news and discographies. Many feature similar and related artist suggestions as well as artists' biographies, their influences, and the time period in which they were popular or active.

Digital Tradition Folk Song Database

`http://web2.xerox.com/digitrad`

Here you can search the Xerox Palo Alto Research Center's Folk Song Database. Search by keywords, titles, or full text.

Discographies (and More)

`http://www.swcp.com/~lazlo/Discographies.html`

Indexes many varied discographies of many bands, including Erasure, Falco, Devo, Men Without Hats, and many more. Be sure to check out the Discography Search Engine.

Friedman/Fairfax Publishers

`http://www.webcom.com/~friedman/`

Freidman Publishing publishes a variety of nonfiction titles and this page provides an overview of their Life, Times, and Music Series. Provides links to

jazz, rock, classical, Broadway, weddings, kids, music polls, etc.

GEMM: Global Electronic Music Marketplace

`http://gemm.com`

Enables you to search for information about artists, albums, and companies. Lets you register to be notified when a particular item you want is mentioned elsewhere in the marketplace.

Hype! Music

`http://www.hype.com/music/home.htm`

Provides a searchable database of music reviews for all genres. Enables you to submit your own review of a CD for inclusion in the database. Includes a list of one-hit wonders.

Mammoth Music Meta-List @ VIBE

`http://www.pathfinder.com/@@DSzPaQAAAAAAANkP/vibe/mmm/`

Contains a directory of music-oriented Web sites. Includes folk, bluegrass, blues, jazz, world, classical, rock, and other styles of music.

Monsterbit Media

`http://monsterbit.com/`

A firm that develops Web sites for the entertainment industry. Use this to search for your favorite artist, band, label, merchandise, tours, music software, and other cool music sites.

Random '80s Lyrics

`http://itg-pc1.acns.nwu.edu/cgi-bin/lyric`

Generates random '80s lyrics. Once you start, it's almost impossible to stop!

Random Band Name

`http://www.terranet.ab.ca/~aaron/band_names.html`

Helps you find a name for that band you're starting. Serves entertainment purposes and generates names that actually come close to some current actual bands. Examples include Bellybutton Fuzz, No Tears of Happiness, and Barking Seagulls.

Rockmine Archives

`http://www.rockmine.music.co.uk/`

Provides a collection (based on 750,000 text clippings, 7,000 hours of rock video, 25,000 hours of audio material, and various memorabilia) of information about British rock and roll. Includes—among other things—rock film posters and artist information.

Similarities Engine

http://www.ari.net/se/

Enter the names of your favorite artists to receive a list of other bands or artists in which you might also be interested.

Ultimate Band List

http://american.recordings.com/wwwofmusic/ubl/ubl.shtml

Offers links to information about any genre or style of music. Includes information not only on Web pages, but on newsgroups, mailing lists, and more.

Worldwide Internet Music Resources

http://www.music.indiana.edu/music_resources/

Hosted by the William and Gayle Cook Music Library at Indiana University. Contains links to almost every imaginable music-related sites—artists/ensembles, composers, genres, publications, the music industry, general and miscellaneous resources, Usenet groups, research, and more.

Education

Brent Hugh's Music Instruction Software Page

http://205.138.183.1/~bhugh/musici.cgi#intro

Focuses on freeware that introduces ear training, music theory and history, and note reading. Also includes lists of instructional materials, online sheet music, and a Music Instruction Video of the Week. Features a brief introduction to Braille music.

MIDI Home Page

http://www.eeb.ele.tue.nl/midi/index.html

Introduces novice and advanced users about how to work with MIDI (Musical Instrument Digital Interface). Includes MIDI archives, explanation of GM and GS formats, downloadable MIDI sequences, as well as links to other MIDI sites and newsgroups.

Neil Hume DJ Page

http://www.magna.com.au/~neilham/how1.html

Provides information on what DJs do and how to go about becoming one. Lessons include an overview of the equipment you'll need and how to use it, as well as how music works.

Ethnic Music

Abayudaya Jews in Uganda: Music

http://www.intac.com/PubService/uganda/music.html

Documents the songs of the Abayudaya people of Uganda, who converted to Judaism in the 1920s. Contains several audio files of songs, most of which are versions of American-Jewish songs. Also offers photos and information on the history and culture of the Abayudaya people.

Afro-Caribbean Music

http://www.ina.fr/Music/index.en.html

Yes, there's reggae music here, but there's also everything from Afro Funk to Ziglibithy to suit your musical tastes. Explore Africa and the Caribbean by artist, geographical location, and style. If you get tired exploring this site in English, you can exercise your French capabilities by clicking on the French flag. You'll also find a list of African/Caribbean nightclubs and restaurants in Paris.

Afropop Worldwide

http://majorca.npr.org/programs/afropop/

Presents National Public Radio's popular African/world music program online. Features a station guide and program listings, as well as concert schedules, suggested disc lists, artist photos, and even recipes.

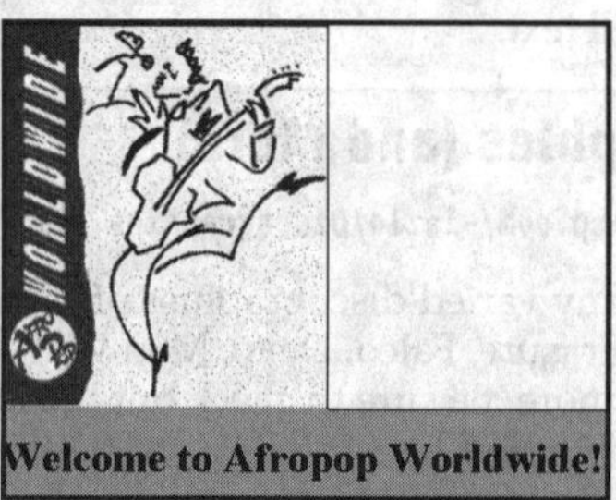

Ain't Whistlin' Dixie

http://mothra.nts.uci.edu/~dhwalker/dixie/

Offers a collection of Irish, Scottish, and English traditional tunes played on the pennywhistle and ocarina. Each tune is presented in AU and AIFF formats. *Note:* AIFF takes two to three times longer to download.

Ari Davidow's Klezmer Page

`http://www.well.com/user/ari/klez/`

Focuses on Klezmer music—a blend of traditional Jewish folk music and jazz. Contains articles, artist profiles, CD reviews, concert and festival information, a guide to radio programs, and contact information for Klezmer musicians. There are also links to sites where you can purchase Klezmer CDs.

Australian Music World Wide Web Site

`http://www.slnsw.gov.au/ausmusic/index.html`

The goal of this site is to provide information about as many Australian musicians and musical organizations as possible. Currently the site lists more than 1,160 Australian musicians in all areas of music, with links to more than 309 pages. One particularly useful link—Australian Arts and Cultural Sites—contains a wealth of music- and other media-related links.

Bali & Beyond Home Page

`http://www.kaiwan.com/~gamelan/balihome.html`

Contains information on gamelan music in general (a form of Indonesian orchestral music characterized by gongs, chimes, and percussion), and Balinese and Javanese gamelan in particular. Also offers some technical information on musical scales and structure and a glossary of Indonesian music terms.

Batish Institute of Indian Music and Fine Arts

`http://hypatia.ucsc.edu:70/1/RELATED/Batish`

This award-winning site provides information about the Batish Institute, located in Santa Cruz, California, as well as information about Hindustani (North Indian) and Carnatic (South Indian) music. An online journal—RagaNet—includes lessons in sitar and tabla performance.

Celtic Music Index Page

`http://www.execpc.com/~danb/celtic.html`

Focuses on Irish music. Contains sheet music for traditional tines, reviews of recent CDs, audio excerpts, and more. If you happen to be in the Milwaukee area and are a Celtic music enthusiast, there's an open invitation to join Dan (this site's creator) in a music session or two at Nash's Irish Castle or the Nomad World Pub.

Ceolas Celtic Music Archive

`http://celtic.stanford.edu/ceolas.html`

Claims to contain the largest collection of Celtic music information that is available online. Receives about 1,000 visits a day. The concentration is on Irish and Scottish music, though the music of Wales and Brittany is also represented. Provides a guide to Celtic music resources, artist profiles, discographies, reviews, sound samples, concert and festival schedules. Also featured are tune indexes, music software, a guide to musical isntruments, and links to countless other sites.

Chinese Music Page

`http://vizlab.rutgers.edu/~jaray/sounds/chinese_music/chinese_music.html`

Presents an archive of Chinese and Taiwanese music from the pre- and post-liberation eras. Contains many audio samples of traditional instrumental and vocal forms, and music from the folk, ceremonial, and military music genres.

Clannad WWW Home Page

`http://www.empire.net/~whatmoug/clanhome.htm`

Features a discography, lyrics, images, interviews, sound bytes, and information about the Irish band, Clannad.

Classical Music Home Page: N.S. Sundar

`http://www.cis.ohio-state.edu/~sundar/`

Provides information on North and South Indian classical music, Indian classical dance forms, an FAQ for rec.music.indian.classical, and an eclectic gallery of photos ranging from musicians to Hindu deities to Mahatma Gandhi. Also includes databases of song lyrics and great personalities of Carnatic (South Indian) music.

Cuban Music

`http://itre.uncecs.edu/music/cuban-music.html`

Provides music samples, Spanish lyrics, and English translations of a wide variety of Cuban songs. Most of the audio files are pickups of Cuban radio transmissions collected in the Florida Keys.

Scholarships

`http://users.aol.com/scholarshp/cc3.html`

You can get financial help for college from the Web. Hit this site to see what scholarships are available to undergraduates, graduates, and those attending vocational schools.

Flamenco Home Page

http://solea.quim.ucm.es/flamenco.html

Focuses on the flamenco scene in Madrid. Contains useful information for the would-be tourist and flamenco aficionado about where to see live flamenco performances. There are links to other flamenco sites on the Web. Some information is in Spanish.

Hindi Movie Songs

http://www.cs.wisc.edu/~navin/india/songs/index.html

Focuses on Indian movie songs in the Hindi language. Contains song information and full lyrics. Includes categorized indexes of singers, music directors, lyricists, films, actors/actresses, as well as a searchable song title index.

Home Page of MT&C Music Club

http://www.pacificsurf.com

Contains information about Mandarin, Taiwanese, and Cantonese music and recent CD releases. Also presents an opportunity to browse and shop online. Contains full-track listings and pictures of all CDs.

Indian Classical Music

http://www.vt.edu:10021/org/malhaar/music.html

Features an introduction to Indian classical music, excellent biographies of master musicians, and some detailed information about the different ragas and styles of music. Also offers links to online catalogs of Indian CDs and to other Indian music sites.

Indian Music: Recordings and Instruments

http://www.winternet.com/~khazana/cd1.html

Serves as an online source for CDs of Indian music. Claims to be able to get anything in print and carries over 1,000 titles. Also offers a gallery of Indian musicians featuring photos, biographies, and audio selections. There is also a gallery of music instruments that offers illustrations, descriptive material, and sound samples.

Indonesian Music

http://www.umanitoba.ca/indonesian/music.html

Features information on various types of Balinese, Javanese, and Sundanese music and instruments, including the gamelan (Indonesian percussion orchestra) and angklung (a bamboo instrument). Also offers Indonesian song lyrics and links to North American gamelan orchestra pages.

Irish Folk Songs

http://www.cs.hut.fi/%7Ezaphod/search/

Provides a searchable database containing the lyrics to more than 300 Irish folk songs. Also provides an alphabetic index for easy browsing.

Larry Aronson Home Page

http://www.interport.net/~laronson/WorldBeat.html

Contains a variety of information on Afro-pop music, particularly Soukous, a variety of pan-African dance music that originated in Zaire and the Congo. Features recommendations on bands, CDs, and other useful information.

MIZIK

http://www.unik.no/~robert/mizik/mizik.html

Presents an eclectic collection of world music information and extensive links to other ethnomusicology-related sites. Includes discographies, sound samples, reviews, and more.

Music from Africa and the African Diaspora

http://matisse.net/~jplanet/afmx/ahome.htm

Contains information on African and African-influenced music and musicians from all over the world, including South America and the Caribbean. Includes articles, artist profiles, and sound samples. Also offers links to the home pages of the various countries. Provides text in English and Spanish.

Northern Journey: Canadian Folk Music Website

http://www.io.org/~njo/

This site claims to be the definitive guide to Canadian folk music. Covers excerpts from the book *Northern Journey: A Guide to Canadian Folk Music*, contains information about Canadian folk artists and folk festivals, and reviews some new and recent Canadian folk CDs. There is also a *Northern Journey* online journal.

Rashid Sales Co.

http://virtumall.com/Rashid/home.html

Provides home site and online sale for Rashid Sales Co., which distributes and sells Arabic music. Includes online catalog, artist background, and ordering information.

Richard Robinson's Tunebook

http://www.leeds.ac.uk/music/Info/RRTuneBk/tunebook.html

Offers a collection of sheet music of traditional tunes, primarily from the Celtic lands and Scandinavia. Lets you you access them by title, country, or type (jig, reel, waltz, and so on).

Roots/World Music FAQ

http://www.acns.nwu.edu/WNUR/drift/faq/

Offers definitions for the terms world music and roots music. Provides basic information on musical styles, notable artists, and musical instruments from a wide geographical area.

RootsWorld: Music on the Net

http://www.rootsworld.com/rw/rw1.html

Offers news, CD reviews, articles, and special features, such as ethnomusicologist Philip Blackburn's "Voices of Vietnam" essay. There is also a great guide to the music and musicians of Finland.

Russian Music

http://mars.uthscsa.edu/Russia/Music/

Contains an archive of Russian singers and their songs. Includes photos, discographies, song lyrics, and audio and video clips. Also offers recommended recordings and where to buy them. Includes folk and pop music.

Samba in Sweden

http://www.algonet.se/~johanw/

Focuses on the thriving Brazilian music scene in Sweden. Provides information about current Samba groups and sample some of their music. Offers links to Samba pages, including Finnish and Scottish sites!

Sami's Urdu/Hindi Film Music Page

http://www.lehigh.edu/sm0e/public/www-data/sami.html

Serves fans of Urdu and Hindi film music. Offers articles on various singers, musical directors, and lyricists, lists of songs indexed by singer, music director, and so forth. Also provides notes and chords of songs and presents many photos.

Shona Music

http://www.teleport.com/~dbullock/shona_music.shtml

Provides information about Shona Music from Zimbabwe, and its typical mix of mbira, marimba, and other indigenous instruments. Contains a directory of Shona musicians and a Shona music

bulletin board, and offers many links to other sites with information on Zimbabwe and on African music in general.

Some Peruvian Music

http://www.rcp.net.pe/snd/snd_ingles.html

A page from the World Wide Web Server of Peru— Red Cientifica Peruana—this site contains sound files of Andean flute music as well as links to related Peruvian music topics.

Tara: The World of Jewish Music

http://www.jewishmusic.com/

Offers a wide variety of Jewish music selections. Provides an online catalog, sound clips, and jumps to other Jewish music links.

Temple Records

http://www.rootsworld.com/temple/

Provides home site and online ordering for Temple Records, which specializes in Scottish traditional music. Includes online catalog, artist descriptions, and ordering information.

TuneWeb

http://www.ece.ucdavis.edu/~darsie/tunebook.html

Provides an archive of traditional tunes of mostly Celtic (Irish, Scottish, Breton), American, and English origin. Provides complete sheet music for all the tunes, with audio excerpts for many. Categorizes by tune type (jig, reel, hornpipe, and so on).

Turkish Music Home Page

http://vizlab.rutgers.edu/~jaray/sounds/turkish/turkish.html

Hosgeldiniz! This site presents a Turkish music archive and index to other Turkish music sites. Includes articles on Turkish music genres, audio files, discographies, and links to classical, folk, religious, and other music styles from Turkey and Cyprus.

WOMEX '96

http://www.eunet.fi/gmc/womex/womex.html

This year's "Summit Worldwide of World, Roots, Folk, Ethnic and Traditional Music" will be held in Copenhagen, Denmark. WOMEX is a combination of conference, trade fair, and musical showcase. Provides the complete history of WOMEX, a conference schedule, and registration information.

World Music/Boston

http://www.arts-online.com/worldmusic.html

Provides schedules and ticket information for world music concerts and festivals happening in Boston. Also supplies short but informative biographies of the performers.

Events

29th Montreux Jazz Festival Official Site

http://www.mhm.fr/festival/montreux/

Covers an international jazz festival held annually in Montreux, Switzerland. Contains general festival information, programs, artists' photos and bios, band lineups, a catalog of festival merchandise, and more.

ABSOLUTELY WORTHLESS Calendar of New England Folk Concerts

http://theory.lcs.mit.edu/~wald/calendar.html

Offers a calendar of concerts, festivals, and events, organized by month, for folk fans in the New England area. Also contains a guide to other print and electronic folk calendars.

Creation 96

http://www.creationfest.com/

Provides information on Creation, the nation's largest Christian festival, held annually in Mt. Union, Pennsylvania. Includes what visitors can expect, festival history, schedules, performers, speakers, directions, children's events, and volunteer and merchandise information.

Lollapalooza Information (Unofficial)

http://nimitz.mcs.kent.edu/~cstone/lolla.html

Focuses on what Lollapalooza was and is. Includes details about the multiband festival for every year since 1991. Includes links to the individual home pages of featured bands.

MBNA College Quartet Contest

http://webpages.marshall.edu/~bennett7/cqc.html

Includes information on dates, rules, and previous winners of the MBNA Collegiate Quartet Contest. Provides contacts for general information and ways to get involved.

Musi-Cal Performer Index

http://www.automatrix.com/cgi-bin/list-performers

Provides an international concert calendar for folk, bluegrass, blues, and world music performers, organized alphabetically by artist. Also, add your own concerts.

National Folk Festival

http://www.adfa.oz.au/NFF/NFF.html

Presents the Australian folk festival. Provides information on the festival, including schedules, performers, tickets, and food and lodging.

Rob Kenney Presents: Kerrville Folk Festival

http://www.fmp.com/~kerrfest/

Provides information about the Kerrville Folk Festival (held in Texas), a major United States folk festival that continues for 25 days starting every May. Contains performance schedules, ticket information, upcoming events, and their limited edition 10-CD set.

Ron Smith Oldies Calendar

http://homepage.interaccess.com/~ronsmith/cal.htm

A "this week" of events in rock 'n' roll history. Includes charts for the number one songs of the '50s, '60s, and '70s, as well as links to featured artists.

Strawberry Music Festivals

http://www.newart.com:80/strawberry/

Contains an eclectic variety of music and presents the "Strawberry Way" to produce "the finest festival of its type, anywhere."

UFOJOE Presents: Information about Canadian Folk Festivals

http://www.interlog.com/~ufojoe/

Provides information and schedules for dozens of Canadian folk music festivals. Also features a festival discussion group and links to other festival information.

Folk

Fasola Home Page

http://medinfo.labmed.umn.edu/Docs/.www/fasola_homepage.html

Provides information resources for Sacred Harp (a form of early American three- and four-part a cappella folk music that traces its roots back to Reformation and Renaissance England) and other American Shape Note traditions of singing.

Folk Music Home Page

`http://www.eit.com/web/folk/folkhome.html`

Covers every aspect of folk music: artists, albums, commercial resources, concerts, and folk music on the radio. Also contains information on ftp sites, mailing lists, and Usenet newsgroups, as well as links to many other folk music sites.

Folk on the Radio

`http://www.hidwater.com/folkdj/folkdj.html`

Provides information on folk and bluegrass music on the radio, submitted by the programs' disc jockeys. Contains station lists, show profiles, and playlists.

Folk Stuff

`http://www.lm.com/~dshu/folkstuff.html`

Presents a directory of information for folk musicians and people designing and building folk and experimental musical instruments. Covers catalogs, books, and periodicals for a wide variety of instruments, including hammered dulcimers, folk flutes, and many others.

FolkBook

`http://www.cgrg.ohio-state.edu/folkbook/`

Contains all sorts of information about folk music and folk musicians. Provides information on venues, festivals and concerts, artist profiles, discographies, record labels and distributors, song lyrics, tablatures, and more. Also contains links to Usenet newsgroups of interest.

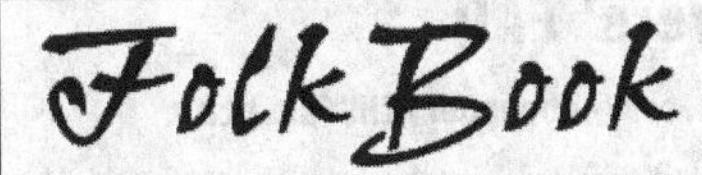

Mary Chapin Carpenter

`http://www.sony.com/Music/ArtistInfo/MaryChapinCarpenter.html`

Provides all the latest and most accurate information about what's coming up. Includes a biography, discography, and tour information.

Southern Folklife Collection

`http://ils.unc.edu/barba/sfc.html`

Contains archives of Southeastern American tradition-derived music that includes numerous photographs, interviews, oral histories, video and film documentaries, books, and periodicals. Contains pages on music and musicians in the following categories: early country music, old-time string bands, gospel and spiritual song, and southeastern blues traditions, all illustrated with photos.

Unofficial John Prine Page

`http://www.atw.fullfeed.com/~bix/prine.htm`

Up close and personal with John Prine, this site provides an interview with the popular musician. Also contains "The Prine Times," a question and answers session, lyrics, tour dates, and a digitized version of an autographed photo.

Karaoke

Karaoke

`http://www.karaokeusa.com/`

Features the history of karaoke, FAQs, and a glossary of terms. Also includes order information for karaoke tunes of all genres from PRO SING and information on karaoke equipment.

Karaoke Home Page

`http://ourworld.compuserve.com/homepages/karaoke/`

Dedicated to karaoke education. Send for your karaoke catalog and information on ordering karaoke DJ shows. Includes links to cyberspace karaoke sites.

Instruments

Accumulated Accordian Annotations

`http://www.cs.cmu.edu/afs/cs/user/phoebe/mosaic/accordion.html`

Provides information on accordians, concertinas, and all free-reed instruments. Includes where to purchase instruments, where to study, and where to get accordion music. Also includes a bibliography of books about accordions.

Autoharp Page

`http://www.autoharp.org/harppage`

Brought to you by the Cyberpluckers, this site tells you everything you want to know about the autoharp, including publications, recordings, concert and festival schedules, and how to buy and get started playing an autoharp.

Banjo Tablature Archive

http://www.vuw.ac.nz/~gnat/banjo/tab/

Contains five-string banjo tablature archives in a variety of musical styles, including classical, bluegrass, and jazz.

Bodhran Page

http://www.panix.com/~mittle/bodhran.html

Focuses on an Irish musical instrument, the bodhran, a goat-skin drum. Includes everything from making, buying, and caring for a bodhran to learning how to play. Provides information on bodhran players, recordings, and concerts.

Bottom Line Archive

http://syy.oulu.fi/tbl.html

Electronic version of this magazine for electric bassists. Features articles for the practicing electric bass player. Contains all back issues. Also offers photos of musicians and links to various bassists' home pages.

CONCERTINA!

http://funnelweb.utcc.utk.edu/~tkoosman/boxlinks.html

The concertina is a free-reed, bellows-operated instrument related to the accordian. This site contains links to Web sites for concertina or would-be concertina players. Includes information on associated music forms, such as Irish and Morris Dance music, as well as links to tune books.

Digeridoo Page

http://www.well.com/user/nhunter/didj/index.html

Provides information about modern musicians who use the digeridoo—an Australian aboriginal instrument—in their music. Contains artist biographies, discographies, and record labels.

DREAMTIME, The Didjeridu W3 Server

http://www.nd.edu/~sborman/didjeridu/

Focuses on didjeridu players around the world. Contains myths, legends, and literature related to this Australian aboriginal instrument, audio samples, CD reviews, cover photos, information on building and repairing didjeridus, lessons and tips on playing, and a didjeridu player's resource guide.

Drums and Percussion Page

http://www.cse.ogi.edu/Drum/

Targets the active drummer or percussionist in all genres of music. Offers transcriptions of drum and percussion pieces, a searchable list of percussionists on the Net, a directory of drum and percussion-related organizations, assorted articles and bibliographies, FAQs, jokes, and links to other drum sites.

GUITAR.NET

http://www.netcentral.net/guitar/index.html

Offers instruction via the guitar chord of the week (including sound clip) for those learning guitar. Lets you ask Abe Wechter questions. Also provides access to many files from the Online Guitar Archives.

Harmonica World

http://www.bekkoame.or.jp/~mshige/

A harmonica page located in Japan. Provides harmonica photos and sounds, as well as information on harmonica players, CDs, concerts, even a harmonica festival. Represents all styles of music, although blues and classical predominate.

Harp Page

http://www.tns.lcs.mit.edu/harp/harp.html

Targets the harp or folk harp enthusiast. Includes information on harp societies, publications, and events, as well as links to various harpists' home pages and shops where you can obtain harps.

Historical Harp Society Page

http://www.tns.lcs.mit.edu/harp/HHS/

Promotes the appreciation and use of historical harps (i.e. non-modern, folk and art music harps). Contains details about the Society's history, purpose, membership, and—of special interest to historical harp enthusiasts—information about the Annual Historical Harp Conference and Workshop.

Horn Players' FAQ

http://www.io.com/~rboerger/IHSfaq.html

Provides answers to commonly asked questions about the French horn. Here, you can find lists of horn music, manufacturers, and dealers, as well as tips on performance techniques and information about horn summer camps and other horn-related Web sites.

IDRS WWW

http://idrs.colorado.edu/

International Double Reed Society online. Provides information for double reed players (oboists, bassoonists). Contains information on the society, its conference, and membership. Also offers online editions of their two publications, the *Double Reed* and the *Journal of the International Double Reed Society*, which contain many articles of interest to practicing musicians, from current and back issues.

Lark in the Morning

http://www.mhs.mendocino.k12.ca.us/MenComNet/Business/
Retail/Larknet/larkhp.html

Provides information on music instruments for the performance of all types of acoustic music. Provides a wide selection of instruments, books, recordings, and videos for purchase. Also contains various informative articles.

Mandolin Pages

http://www.execpc.com/~danb/mandolin.html

Focuses on mandolins and related instruments (citterns, octave mandolins, bouzoukis, and more). Features instrument guides, historical information, and images of mandolins. There is also a list of the creator's favorite mandolin recordings.

Musicmaker's Kits, Inc.

http://www.primenet.com/~musikit/

Displays online catalog of instruments, providing descriptions and sound samples with each image.

Official Hammered Dulcimer Page

http://tfnet.ils.unc.edu/~gotwals/hd/dulcimer.html

Provides information on hammered dulcimers, including workshops, festivals, publications, photos, sound samples, musicians, and information on building or buying an instrument.

Phillip Mann's Banjo Tab Collection and Bluegrass Information Site

http://www.wsnet.com/~phil/banjo.html

Contains a collection of banjo tablatures and a variety of other banjo and bluegrass-related information. Also includes Tab Transcriber, a program that transcribes MIDI files for you.

Piano Page

http://www.prairienet.org/arts/ptg/homepage.htm

Advice and suggestions on everything from buying a piano to its maintenance and service needs. Includes information on humidity control, voicing, and more. Also features the Piano Technicians Guild.

Violette Instruments

http://www.lightlink.com/violette/

Marti Violette is a builder of custom electric basses. You can view and order his products from this site. There are also many other bass-related links here.

Wayne's Lute Page

http://www.cs.dartmouth.edu/~wbc/lute.html

Offers a collection of lute information. Includes a gallery of old lute artworks and photos of new lutes, as well as additional photos of various harps and bagpipes.

Will Clifton, Double Basses and Some Other Things

http://www.gonix.com/wgcabp

Will is principal bass player with the Omaha Symphony. This page offers some of his favorite music links—such as to the International Society of Bassists—and miscellaneous information about playing classical or jazz styles on the double bass.

Jazz

Alabama Jazz Hall of Fame

http://www.the-matrix.com/jazz/aljazz.html

Contains information about the organization whose stated mission is "to foster, encourage, educate, and cultivate a general appreciation of the medium of jazz music." Includes information on jazz events, their museum, instrument recycling, and the Jazz In Schools Program.

Arizona Jazz, Rhythm and Blues Festival

http://www.infomagic.com/~azjazz/index.html

Offers complete schedules and ticket information for this fairly new jazz and blues event held in Flagstaff and brought to you by the organizers of the famous Telluride Jazz Festival. Also provides information on travel and accommodations.

Electric Gallery

http://www.egallery.com/egallery/jazz.html

Features paintings and sound samples of blues and jazz greats.

Hard Bop Cafe™

http://www.mbnet.mb.ca/~mcgonig/hardbop.html

Serves as a complete guide to jazz in Canada. Includes concert and festival information, jazz on the radio, jazz publications, CD reviews, and more.

Jazz Central Station

http://www.jazzcentralstation.com

Features worldwide club, concert, and festival information, interactive reviews from *JazzTimes* magazine, recent and upcoming releases, artist reviews, the Jazz Cafe, and the Jazz Market. Also includes official site for the International Association of Jazz Educators.

Jazz Improvisation

http://gopher.adp.wisc.edu/jazz/

Presents a series of articles for a course on jazz improvisation, taught at the University of Wisconsin. Serves as an introduction to the subject. Includes many images of musical notation and photos of jazz musicians.

Jazz in France

http://www.erb.com/cdeus/jazzfr/

Surveys the entire French jazz scene, including festivals, magazines, musicians, jazz on radio and TV, and jazz awards. Provides texts in English and French.

Jazz Net

http://www.dnai.com/~lmcohen/index.html

Your guide to jazz on the Internet. Offers weekly updates and reviews of new jazz sites, as well as links to jazz-related sites.

Jazz Roots

http://redlt.com/tom/next/JazzRoots/Introduction.html

Provides information on the early jazz masters, such as Fats Waller and Benny Goodman. Includes photos, bios, band members, discographies, and other information on the artists' careers.

Pacific Blues & Jazz

http://www.speakeasy.org/nwjazz/

Contains a potpourri of jazz information, pertaining to the northwestern United States (mostly Washington). Includes area artists and their recordings, concert and festival schedules, jazz publications, and visual art.

Tom Morgan's Web Site for Jazz and Blues

http://redlt.com/tom/

Presents Tom Morgan, alternative radio station director, freelance writer, and author of *From Cakewalks to Concert Halls: An Illustrated History of African-American Popular Music 1895–1930*. Features several articles and columns on blues and jazz. One of the best collections of record companies on the Web with links to more than 100 recording labels.

Traditional Jazz (Dixieland)

http://www.best.com/~kquick/dixie.html

Focuses on Dixieland music. Provides information on the bands, festivals, publications, societies, and places to hear Dixieland on the radio all over North America. Offers many links to newsgroups, mailing lists, and other jazz Web sites.

Virtual Jazz Fest!

http://yatcom.com/neworl/jfest/jfesttop.html

The New Orleans Jazz and Heritage Festival. Provides complete performance schedules, notes on the different musical styles, accommodation information, a survival guide, and a decade of festival posters.

William Ransom Hogan Archive of New Orleans Jazz

http://www.tulane.edu/~lmiller/JazzHome.html

Contains oral history interviews, recorded music, photographic collections and film, sheet music and orchestrations, and numerous files containing manuscript materials, clippings, and bibliographic references. Contains information about the archive, photos, sound clips, and a complete index to the oral history interviews.

WNUR-FM JazzWeb

http://www.acns.nwu.edu/jazz/

Contains information on jazz. Includes essays on the different styles of jazz (accessible from a unique hypermap that reveals their interrelationships), artist bios, discographies, and reviews. Also offers information on festivals, venues, regional concerts, instruments, jazz in the media (radio, television, press), jazz art, and various jazz resources. Continually updated.

Lyrics

Jessica Ross and Her Amazing Mondegreen Circus

http://www.mcs.net/~bingo/lyrics.html

A site devoted to misunderstood lyrics from all genres. The line, "Sing us a song yellow pian man," is a misunderstood line from Billy Joel's "Piano Man" that goes "Sing us a song, you're the piano man." Contains hundreds of lyrics as well as information on how to submit your own.

Lyrics Page

http://archive.uwp.edu/pub/music/lyrics/

Search for lyrics by selected text, artist, or song title. Results return full text of songs, including titles and artists.

Twisted Tunes

http://www.twistedtunes.com/

Bob Rivers as Weird Al Yankovich. Features downloadable hits such as "Strawberry Rehabs Forever" and "I Shot the White House."

Magazines

Addicted To Noise

http://www.addict.com/ATN/

Includes interviews with artists like Lou Reed, Iggy Pop, and Neil Young. Provides columns by rock critics, including Dave Marsh and Greil Marcus. Offers daily rock news reports. Serves as a guide to rock spots on the Web. Also offers album reviews with sound bytes, movie reviews, rock book reviews, and music and technology columns. Use RealAudio to listen in on Radio ATN, one of the Internet's only real-time audio radio stations.

Cybergrass—The Internet Bluegrass Magazine

http://www.banjo.com/BG/

Features everything you'd expect in a magazine, including articles, artist profiles, and an events calendar. Includes reader comments and bluegrass want ads. Also includes a guide to magazines and newsletters and offers links to other bluegrass sites.

Electric Magic—The Led Zeppelin Chronicle

http://www.pathcom.com/~rapallof/emagic.html

Online edition of the fan magazine and rated "the best" Zeppelin site on the Net. Features photo and article archives, a video vault, information about the band's appearance on the MuchMusic special and the Montreux concerts, plus much more.

ICE On-Line

http://www.webcom.com/~ice/

Based on the printed publication and offers free trial subscription. ICE provides information and exclusive articles on upcoming album releases. Also includes release dates that are updated weekly.

Northern Journey: Canadian Folk Music Website

http://www.io.org/~njo/

Northern Journey: A Guide to Canadian FolkMusic, the online edition. Claims to be "the definitive guide" to Canadian folk music. Overviews excerpts from the book, contains information about Canadian folk artists and folk festivals, and music, book and video reviews. Also features the electronic version of *Maple Roots*, a publication of the Canadian Caucus of the North American Folk Alliance.

OffBeat Magazine

http://www.NeoSoft.com/~offbeat/

Online edition of the monthly print magazine of the same name, "New Orleans' and Louisiana's only music and entertainment magazine." Features interviews, articles, reviews, polls, and more on the New Orleans jazz scene, as well as club, concert, and festival information, and classified ads.

Stirrings Folk Mag

http://www.cityscape.co.uk/users/ah98/

Online edition of British folk music magazine. Features CD, book, and concert reviews, interviews, concert and festival schedules, news, and more.

Synthesis: Electronic Dance Music Page

`http://www.isisnet.com/spacelab/synthesis/index.html`

A bimonthly, online magazine format that emphasizes alternative and dance-oriented sounds, including the rave/techno scene, electropop, house, new beat/hardbeat, industrial, and experimental music. Also features the Force One Music service where you can purchase import CDs.

Musicals

Les Miserables Home Page

`http://www.ot.com/lesmis/`

A summary of the musical's storyline, a complete libretto, a variety of sounds and images from the musical, a list of tour dates and the list of the musical's credits. This site also provides information about the Victor Hugo novel that inspired the musical.

On Broadway WWW Information Page

`http://artsnet.heinz.cmu.edu:80/OnBroadway/`

Here you can find a list of plays and musicals that are currently performing on Broadway, off Broadway, and even off-off Broadway. The site also maintains a year-by-year listing of Tony award winners dating back to the 1940s.

The Really Useful Company Presents Sir Andrew Lloyd Webber

`http://www.reallyuseful.com/`

A bevy of information about Webber and his musicals which include *Cats*, *Jesus Christ Superstar*, *Evita*, and *Sunset Boulevard*. Find out when the shows are touring, read background information on the shows, purchase show-related merchandise, or enter a trivia contest to possibly win tickets.

Rec.Arts.Theatre.Musicals

`news:rec.arts.theatre.musicals`

A Usenet newsgroup devoted to the discussion of musicals. Here you can find stimulating conversation about famous musicals like *Cats* or *Les Miserables*, the New York cabaret scene, or anything else related to musicals and those who are involved with them.

New Age

Björk's—Web Sense

`http://www.centrum.is/bjork/`

Presents the Web site "of the six senses… where sight, hearing, smell, taste, touch, and intuition" serve as the focus.

Enya—Unofficial World Wide Web Home Page

`http://www.bath.ac.uk/~ccsdra/enya/homepage.html`

Provides pictures, sounds, translations of the Irish lyrics, the popular Enya Pages, transcripts of interviews with Enya, QuickTime movies and sound files.

Malahat Mountain Music

`http://www.islandnet.com/~dobro/`

A Canadian booking agency and record label for acoustic musicians. Download your free sample of RealAudio to listen to the music samples provided. Also order music after browsing their database.

Vangelis—The Man and The Music

`http://bau2.uibk.ac.at/perki/Vangelis.html`

Provides information about the man and his music and movies (*Bladerunner* being the most popular so far). Contains an array of pictures, sounds, and digitized film sequences, as well as a page with links to all of the Vangelis fans in the world.

Organizations & Clubs

American Music Center

`http://www.ingress.com/amc/`

Nonprofit contemporary music information and resource center. Provides lists of scores, opportunities for composers and performers, information on grants, and links to music indices and AMC publications.

BMG

`http://www.bmg.de/`

Lets you explore the universe of music and download sound samples, pictures, and videos of various artists. Provides much of the information in German.

Club ZigZag

http://www.interverse.com/clubzigzag/

Club ZigZag is an "online night club presenting an eclectic mix of performance and presentation from around Cyberspace and beyond."

Muscle Music, Inc.

http://www.hiwaay.net/mm

Serves the entertainment industry "through a number of services designed to increase the quality and efficiency of music and audio producers, publishers, and record companies." Contains information about music, video and Web services, and previews of artists and bios of Alabama music achievers.

National Music Foundation

http://www.nmc.org/

The nonprofit organization "dedicated to American music and the people who bring it to us." Features a newsletter, press releases, the American Music Calendar, and links to music sites of all types. Also offers gift shop that includes a cookbook with recipes provided by your favorite country musicians.

Wolverine Antique Music Society

http://www.teleport.com/~rfrederi/

Presents the Wolverine Antique Music Society. Focuses on the preservation of music originally recorded for 78 rpm records. Offers much to the 78 collector and early jazz aficionado. Contains many articles on the music, collecting, and all sorts of technical and resource information pertaining to antique audio. Also contains information on the early record labels, 78 album cover art, and sound clips.

ABBAnatic

http://www.dlc.com/funnyguy/abba.html

Serves as a source for all the ABBA lyrics. Also includes pictures and links to other ABBA pages on the Web. Contains information on bootlegs and post-ABBA projects.

Amy Grant Site in College Park, MD

http://www.wam.umd.edu/~xiaoqin/ag.html

Provides information on Amy Grant, including lyrics, the Friends of Amy Newsletter, an articles index, video clips, and the CDLink Voyager page, which lets you play your CDs in a whole new way.

and through the wire

http://www.cs.clemson.edu/~junderw/pg.html

Offers a collection of goodies about Peter Gabriel. Includes lyrics, pictures, and sound bytes. Also includes excepts from his authorized biography, recent news, B-side titles, updates on his "Real World" theme park, and Mojo.

Beastie Boys

http://www.nando.net/BeastieBoys/

Contains all conceivable data regarding the '80s hard rock band, along with more that you probably haven't conceived of.

Financial Aid

http://www.ed.gov/prog_info/SFA/StudentGuide/

Price of college got you down? Send for a free guide to financial aid supplied by the U.S. Department of Education. Who says the government doesn't care about the little people?

Music

The Boy George Home Page

http://www.umich.edu/~geena/boygeorge.html

Presents information about Boy George in the form of a fan magazine. Includes a discography with all lyrics, pop chart information, photo gallery, sound bytes, and articles and interviews.

Bryan Adams Home Page

http://www.glue.umd.edu/~xiaoqin/music/adams.html

Offers lyrics, reviews, pictures, and more. Also provides charts and statistics from around the world.

Clash

http://www.idiscover.co.uk/paul/rob/clash.html

Features a complete discography of all Clash albums and the lyrics to every track. Also offers a chart history of all the hits that made it big.

Caribbean Soul: The Jimmy Buffett Parrot(t)head Page

http://www.homecom.com/buffett/

Includes resources for finding Jimmy Buffett on the Net. Offers tour dates, pictures, sound bytes, and the National Parrothead Raffle to benefit the Alzheimer's Association.

Chicago O(+> Nation

http://www.mcs.net/~nation/home/cpn.htm

Serves as a resource for Chicago-area O(+> fans and collectors about the Artist Fomerly Known As Prince and his new wife, Mayte. Also shows the entire Former Prince community what Chicago has to offer.

Counting Crows

http://hammers.wwa.com/hammers/crows/crows.html

Provides Counting Crows information. Offers a complete discography, pictures, and an extensive FAQs file. Tells you who "Mr. Jones" really is.

Disgraceland

http://www.wmin.ac.uk/%7Etjdec/welcome2.html

Provides information about Belinda Carlisle and the Go-Gos. Includes a large image bank.

ELP—Emerson, Lake & Palmer

http://bliss.berkeley.edu/elp/

Provides Emerson, Lake & Palmer (ELP) information. Includes online back issues of the ELP digest and links to other ELP sites.

Elvis Costello Home Page

http://www.east.isx.com/~schnitzi/elvis.html

Focuses on Elvis Costello. Includes mailing lists, concert reviews, lyrics, interviews, photos, guitar tablatures, and a complete discography. Also features a page of closely related artists.

Enigma

http://www.stud.his.no/~joarg/Enigma.html

Provides information on Enigma. Provides a discography of the band and its founding father, Michael Cretu. Also provides mailing list information, a picture gallery, and reviews of Enigma.

EXCESS OF INXS, AN

http://www.columbia.edu/~nak6/inxs.html

Includes INXS biographies, discographies, lyrics, pictures, guitar tabs, digital songs, and more.

Finally Found a Page: A Web Site Dedicated to Huey Lewis and the News

http://www.prism.gatech.edu/~jw157/hl/

Provides biographies, pictures, and information on the band's obscure releases. Features a Questions and Answers Page as well as a Merchandise Mart, and more.

Frankie Goes to Hollywood Fan Pages

http://www.cs.rulimburg.nl/~antal/fgth/fgth-home.html

Presents Frankie Goes to Hollywood, the band, online. Provides numerous FGTH resources.

Future Love Paradise: The Seal WWW Site

http://pantheon.cis.yale.edu/~ariedels/seal.html

Includes an image oasis, the Seal FAQ file, a lyric library, and more. Includes transcriptions of online conferences with Seal.

Gaia: Olivia Newton-John Home Page

http://www-leland.stanford.edu/~clem/

Provides information about Olivia. Offers links to SoulKiss, the ONJ Internet Mailing list, movie information, videos, and a photo collection. Also offers information on how to join the fan clubs.

Gloria Estefan/MSM

http://www.almetco.com/estefan/gloria-1.html

Features Gloria and the Miami Sound Machine. Features background information, photo galleries, album lists, and where to read articles about the artist. Also contains video information, recent news, and fan club and mailing list info.

Lloyd Robbins' Moody Blues Page

http://www.ids.net/~lrobbins/moodys.html

Serves as a site for people who believe that all the best music was written 25 years ago. Offers links to information about the Moody Blues, including pictures and a discography. Also contains links to Alan Parsons Project information.

Madonna Home Page

http://www.mit.edu:8001/people/jwb/Madonna.html

Serves as a means to finding any of myriad pages about Madonna on the Web. Includes a link to the Madonna Lyrics Archive, a complete discography, and Madonna's Top 10 List from the infamous Letterman episode. Also includes many pictures.

Men Without Hats: The (Unofficial) Home Page

http://www.mit.edu:8001/people/tobye/mwh/mwh.html

Offers all the latest discoveries about this '80s band. Includes a complete discography and a few pictures.

Mike Markowski's Beatles Page

http://www.eecis.udel.edu/~markowsk/beatles/

Includes a metaindex of other Beatles resources. Provides all the information you need about the Fab Four, including sounds, pictures, lyrics, merchandise, backwards messages, MIDI files, bios, bootleg records, and close encounters stories. Even non-fans will enjoy this site.

Nicks Fix

http://web2.iadfw.net/jkinney/

Features Stevie Nicks, former singer of Fleetwood Mac. Contains Stevie news, album and video

information, song lyrics, photos, and more. Also includes several links to other Stevie-related pages.

Original Mariah Carey Home Page

http://biogopher.wustl.edu/audio/mariah.html

Targets the Mariah Carey fan. Includes many pictures, links to other Mariah pages, and audio and video files. Also provides fan club information.

Original Unofficial Elvis Home Page

http://sunsite.unc.edu/elvis/elvishom.html

Everything you ever wanted to know about Elvis. Reports recent sightings and lets you download some pictures and sounds. Brings Graceland to the Net. Includes lyrics, a collectors' page, a copy of Elvis' will, and links to other Elvis sites. Also lets you make an Elvis connection and find an Elvis pen pal on the Net.

Pete Lambie's Bruce Springsteen Page

http://www.gla.ac.uk/~gkrx11/Bruce/

Provides many pictures, lyrics, and more. Links to people who are willing to help you create your own bootleg collection and suggests a way to bring your bootlegs to life by making your own covers.

Planet Janet

http://web.mit.edu/afs/athena/user/a/g/agoyo1/www/janet2.html

Focuses on Janet Jackson. Includes the latest news, tour information, sounds, image gallery, lyrics, and more.

ROSS

http://www.knoware.nl/music/diana/ross1.htm

Focuses on singer Diana Ross and includes plenty of reminiscence about the Supremes. Also provides information on how to subscribe to *ROSS*, the official Diana Ross fan club magazine, as well as how to join the fan club.

Roxette: Home Page

http://babylon.caltech.edu/roxette/roxette.html

Offers information about some tour information, an interactive discography, and many pictures. Also includes information on soloists Marie Fredriksson, Per Gessle, and Gyllene Tider.

Sarah McLachlan Homepage

http://www.iupui.edu/~jrshepar/sarah1.html

Focuses on the music and activities of Sarah McLachlan. Includes a biography of Sarah, concert descriptions, FAQs, and links to other must-visit McLachlan sites.

Simon and Garfunkel Home Page

http://www.dur.ac.uk/~d213ga/

Offers Simon and Garfunkel and some Paul Simon solo stuff containing many guitar tabs and some information on the duo. Contains a picture gallery and lyrics.

Simple Minds—Good News From the Web

http://matahari.cv.com/people/Simon.Cornwell/simple_minds/

Contains information about the '80s band Simple Minds. Includes a full discography, lyrics, FAQs files, rumors and facts, an auction, biographies, and bootlegs. Also includes many links to other Simple Minds resources on the Net.

Sinead O'Connor Home Page

http://www.engr.ukans.edu/~jrussell/music/sinead/sinead.html

Contains an official discography, a biography of Sinead, pictures (including two photos of Sinead with hair), quotations, and additional Sinead information. Serves as a master index to all sorts of goodies.

Sting—The Soul Pages

http://www.ot.com/sting/

Focuses on Sting. Provides the usual information such as lyrics, images, and sounds. Also provides information on Sting's nonmusical projects, his work with charity organizations, and his artwork. Includes a personal letter to Sting from the Web page's author.

22nd Row

http://itchy.faa.uiuc.edu/elton.html

The site for Elton John fans. Features the Elton John AIDS Foundation, bibliography of books about Elton and Bernie Taupin, and information on third-party publications. Links to "A Most Excellent Discography."

Tori Amos

http://www.mit.edu:8001/people/nocturne/tori.html

Includes a special link to Really Deep Thoughts, a mailing list digest about the music of Tori Amos. Also includes many pictures and sounds, and a few QuickTime videos.

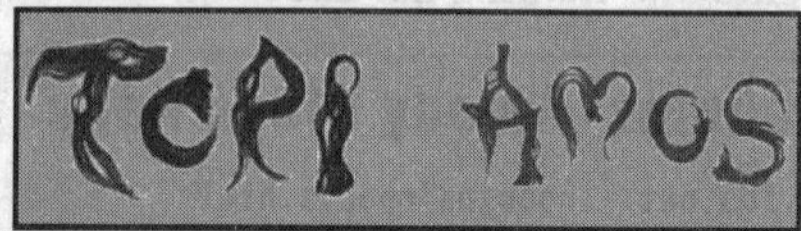

VH1 Music First

http://vh1.com/

VH1 online. Features the latest information on various artists, from biographies and videographies to news updates and special features such as downloadable files. Also spotlights the videos and specials playing on VH1. Provides special coverage of events in music culture, a sounding board, and a multimedia library.

Welcome to HIStory!

http://www.music.sony.com/Music/ArtistInfo/MichaelJackson.html

Serves as the official Sony page for Michael Jackson. Includes graphics and considerable information and depth of thought.

Zar's Paula Abdul

http://www2.csn.net/~danzirin/paula.html

Lionizes Paula Abdul, complete with sound bytes, QuickTime videos, and plenty of pictures. Also includes personal information about Paula.

R&B

Biscuit Time on Blues Web

http://www.island.net/~blues/

Possibly everything you ever wanted to know about the blues. Offers news, CD reviews, a great selection of audio files, photos, extensive biographies of musicians, articles, links to other blues sites, and more.

Blue Highway

http://www.umn.edu/nlhome/m161/schn0170/index.html

Offers a tour through delta blues country, introducing the blues immortals along the way. Includes photos and biographies accompanied by a road map of the route you take. Also lets you enter comments and read those of others who have traveled the blues highway.

Bluenote

http://www.cis.ohio-state.edu/hypertext/faq/usenet/music/bluenote/top.html

Contains the FAQs from the Usenet newsgroup rec.music.bluenote. Contains basic information on blues and jazz.

BluesNet

http://dragon.acadiau.ca/~rob/blues/blues.html

Contains biographies of musicians, an archive of photos (many previously unpublished), a feature on teachers, and many informative articles. Lets you leave your comments in the guest book. Offers links to other major blues sites.

DC Blues Home Page

http://www.intelus.com/dcblues/

Provides information on concerts, events, and venues in the Washington, D.C. area. Lets musicians submit information regarding their own concerts to include in the schedule. Features sounds, pictures, and reviews of D.C. area musicians. Also provides information on the DC Blues Society.

House of Blues

http://hob.com/hob.html

Offers QuickTime virtual reality scenes. Includes concert schedules, music and video samples, blues bios, and more.

Live Blues and Blues Radio, Steamin' Stan Ruffo

http://www.primenet.com/~steamin

Introduces Steamin' Stan Ruffo to the Internet community as a singer, songwriter, blusician, world-reknowned harmonicator, as well as producer and host of the blues radio show, Blues On Tap, on Visalia's K100 99.7FM. Also offers links to other music- and nonmusic-related sites.

Record Labels

About Time Music Company

http://www.numenet.com/sc/about_time/

Provides direct information and sales of the acoustic instrumental-based About Time Music Catalog. Also provides background about the artists and sound byte samples of music on the label.

Acorn Music

http://www.sirius.com/~acorn/

Provides a catalog of traditional and nontraditional folk and world music. Includes background of the label and its artists, including tour dates.

Alternet Sonic Realities

http://www.iuma.com/ASR/

Provides label background, artist history, sound clips, and ordering information for this small, independent "cyber-label." Musicians on Alternet Sonic vary from Australian techno to east coast United States alternative rock.

American Gramaphone Records

http://www.amgram.com/

Provides background and history of the label and their artists. Includes detailed essay about Chip Davis the leader of Manneheim Steamroller, Fresh Aire, and American Gramaphone Records. Also provides tour and lecture dates.

American Recordings Home Page

http://american.recordings.com/

The label that publishes acts such as Frank Black, Julian Cope, Pete Droge, Slayer, Lords of Acid, and more. Includes discographies, audio and video clips, tour schedules, online chat with the artists and more.

Angel Thorne Music

http://www.e-MediaWeb.com/ATM.html

Provides news, reviews, and ordering information for this music production company and record label based out of Danbury, Connecticut. Includes audio samples, performance dates, group backgrounds, and photography. Record label concentrates on progressive rock.

Asphodel Records

`http://www.w2.com/docs2/a3/asphodel.html`

Eclectic is the self-described philosophy of San Francisco, California's Asphodel Records. Provides record reviews and artist descriptions. If strange music is your tune, this might be your site.

Atlantic Records Home Page

`http://www.atlantic-records.com/`

Biographies on most of the label's recording artists, online chat with famous artists, tour dates, and "Stereo-Type," Atlantic's new newsletter for gays and lesbians.

Axiom/Laswell Web Site

`http://hyperreal.com/music/labels/axiom/`

Home site for Bill Laswell and Axiom records. Includes label catalog, upcoming releases, Bill Laswell discography, and links to related musical sites. Also provides extensive history of Laswell's career in music that covers all grounds in rock, funk, experimental, and beyond. Fans of eclectic music and those looking for something different would do very well to visit this site.

Badcat Records

`http://www.opendoor.com/badcat/BCR_Home.html`

Provides home site for Badcat Records. Includes label catalog, artist photos, and downloadable music samples of their records. Provides many choices of information players.

Bedazzled

`http://www.iuma.com/Bedazzled/`

A label that publishes eclectic bands such as Mistle Thrush, Siddal, Viola Peacock, and more. You can request a copy of the entire catalog to be e-mailed to you or download samples recorded in MPEG format, some of them complete songs.

Black Rock Coalition

`http://users.aol.com./brcny/home.html`

To fight the notion that all black artists must play either R&B or hip-hop, the BRC have put out compilation albums containing all rock and roll songs recorded entirely by black groups and artists. Check out an overview of the coalition, reviews of their albums, and interviews with progressive black artists, writers, and industry leaders.

Bogus Records

`http://www.w2.com/bogus.html`

Founded in 1979 by a local guitar shop owner, this label puts out a variety of albums. Check out the records, download some audio clips, and then purchase them online.

Boy's Life Records

`http://www.iuma.com/Boy's_Life/`

Provides sound samples, cover art, and catalog for Los Angeles-based label. Includes ordering information. Boy's Life Records artists' music is described as psychedelic rock.

Caroline Records

`http://www.caroline.com/`

A very animated Web page containing band biographies, audio and QuickTime video clips from bands such as Engine 88 and Ben Folds Five, and e-mail access to the bands and various departments of Caroline Records.

Castle von Buhler Records

`http://world.std.com/~amb/`

Provides home site for this Illinois-based independent, alternative label. Includes band promos and reviews for such acts as Turkish Delight, Splashdown, and sirensong. Also includes sound bytes, album artwork, and ordering information.

Catasonic Records

`http://underground.net/Weba/catasonic.html`

Yet another indie label that publishes such bands as Weba World, Mechanical Sound Orchestra, and Gynomite. Read press clippings about the bands and download sound clips of some of their works.

Caulfield Records

`http://www.acton.com/bernie/`

Provides home site for Caulfield Records and their bands. Includes sound bytes, album cover artwork, tour dates, and upcoming releases information. Also includes the Caulfield Web Board for use as newsgroup.

Changing Tones Records

`http://www.inch.com/~macmusic/chngtone.html`

Provides recording and music books catalog along with ordering information for Changing Tones Records. Also provides event calendar and links to music lists and newsgroups. Changing Tones Records and books concentrate on jazz, blues, and traditional rock and roll.

China Records

http://www.china.co.uk/china/

Provides home site for British label China Records. Includes label catalog, current news, band background, and ordering information. Also provides tour dates, reviews, and sound bytes for such artists as The Levellers and Blameless among others.

Curb Records

http://www.curb.com/

Provides home site for Curb Records that specializes in, but is not limited to, country and traditional American song forms such as blues and zydeco. Artists on the Curb catalog site include Tim McGraw, Wynonna, Junior Brown, Hank Williams, Jr., Lyle Lovett, and Kool and the Gang to name a few. Includes artist background, tour dates, record catalog, lyrics, sound bytes, and ample information on Curb artists. Also includes ordering information. This is a nice music site and is highly recommended for fans of the above artists.

East Side Digital Records

http://www.w2.com/esd.html

An independent label that provides a large number of sound clips from their bands which include Go To Blazes, Blood Oranges, and Bottle Rockets. CDs can be purchased online.

Geffen Records

http://www.geffen.com/

A very well-put-together page from the giant recording label. Features a variety of information about its various artists including QuickTime video clips, AU sound files, biographies, rare photos, and more.

Go Kart Records

http://www.w2.com/gokart.html

A Record Company and link from the World Square home page. Links to recording artists and CD ordering information. Click on the CD or song title and download for your viewing and listening pleasure.

Grand Royal

http://www.southern.net/grandroyal/

The recording label of the Beastie Boys, "where you're sure to find plenty of beats, rhymes, threads and snaps." Check out information on the various bands published by the label including Luscious Jackson, Noise Addict, and Ween.

Hi-Bias Records Inc.

http://www.interlog.com/~hibias/

A Canadian-based record label, originally developed by DJs and music enthusiasts, producing CDs and music videos. Provides links to their catalog, artists, new releases, features, club hibias, etc.

ID&T Records

http://www.dance.nl/id&t/

Originally a rave organizer based in Holland and in Germany, now provides CD releases, album info, DJ info, and fashion and party info to the alternative music enthusiast.

Indochina

http://www.china.co.uk/china/indochina/

A listing of new releases on the Indochina record label, a sort of ambient, house, hip-hop kind of sound. Descriptions of and links to new releases.

Landphil Records' Online Information Dump

http://www.novia.net/~landphil/

A growing independent label whose Web site provides audio samples in WAV format, products such as T-shirts and stickers, a guide to Omaha's indie music scene and a listing of indie record stores throughout the U.S. and Canada.

Lunch Records

http://www.lunch.com:2500/

Formerly Breakfast Records, this is an independent label that publishes such alternative acts as Orbit, Kent 25, Damn You Peter Pan, and more. Depending on which act you want to check out, you can access bios, sound clips, reviews, home pages, and more.

Carpet Samples

http://www.dalton.net/access

Fill out the demographic information and walk away with carpet samples from Access carpets in Dalton, Georgia.

Magic Island

http://www.magicisland.com/

If you like the music of Bob James, Jazz Stuff, the Island Dwellers, or any other jazz-like sound, check out this site. Links to the home pages of many jazz musicians.

Manifest Records

http://www.pacifier.com/~coldwave/

Christ Analogue's official Web site, an industrial band from Seattle, Washington. Find out about their upcoming releases and touring information.

Marathon Records

http://www.netads.com/netads/arts/music/marathon/

A group of indie bands who decided to put their pages together on the Internet. Links to alternative bands' pages such as Able Cain, Animator, Fairwell to Juliet, Sunny Day Roses, Soulstice, and others.

Metal Blade Records

http://www.iuma.com/Metal_Blade/

If you like Metallica, check out this Web site of heavy metal, gothic, and doom bands. You can also browse and order from their mail order catalog.

Monkeyland Records

http://www.primenet.com/~tripmon/

Another page for all you indie music lovers. Includes artwork, CD reviews, soundbytes, ordering info, tour dates, and related music links.

Moonshine Music

http://www.moonshine.com/

Musical compilations not often found on top 40 labels. Includes ambient, techno, house, and many more. Links to bands and releases.

Mute Liberation Technologies

http://www.mutelibtech.com/mute/

The Web site of Mute Records, with links to an artist database including Depeche Mode and Erasure, music news, and a full color catalog.

Nettwerk

http://www.nettwerk.com/artists/index.html

A label based in British Columbia that is home to Sarah McLachlan, Skinny Puppy, Barenaked Ladies

and other lesser-known artists. The site features discographies and biographies, although there were no sound clips to be found.

Oh Boy Records

http://www.nashville.net/ohboy/

Record label formed by John Prine. Contains pages devoted to John and Heather Eatman. Includes discographies, lyrics, pictures, mail order catalogs, and more. Also covers Red Pajamas Records and Blue Plate Music.

PolyGram Records, Inc.

http://www.polygram.com/polygram/Music.html

Provides home site for PolyGram Records and artists. Includes links to artist sites including Blues Traveler, P.J. Harvey, Rusted Root, Brian Adams, and many, many more. Also includes worldwide tour dates, upcoming releases, and online ordering information.

Pop Gun Records

http://www.camtech.com.au/popgun/

Provides home site and online sales for Pop Gun Records, a small independent record company based in Adelaide, Australia. Specializes in 7-inch vinyl singles and groove-based rock music. Includes catalog and online ordering information.

Propulsion Records

http://www.w2.com/docs2/b/propulsion.html

Provides home site for Propulsion Records. Includes online catalog, sound bytes, album artwork, and artist background. Also includes ordering information.

Rage Records

http://www.w2.com/rage.html

Provides home site and online ordering for Rage Records, a New York City-based hip-hop label. Includes company catalog, artist profiles, and sound bytes.

RCA Victor

http://www.rcavictor.com/

Provides home site for RCA Victor, home of many great artists from jazz to classical and rock. Site features new releases information, links to artist sites, and sound bytes.

Red Phraug Modern Medium

http://www.teleport.com/~noise/

Provides home site for Red Phraug Modern Medium label collective. Specializes in ambient and house dance music. Includes company catalog, sound bytes, and ordering information.

Reservoir Records

http://monsterbit.com/reservoir/reservoir.html

Provides home site for Reservoir Records. Includes catalog, artist profiles, and ordering information.

Restless Records

http://www.restless.com/

Provides online site for Restless Records. Includes artist profiles, video clips, sound bytes, upcoming release information, and company catalog. Catalog includes artists such as the Sex Pistols, Jack Logan, Wire, and many more.

Rhino Records Home Page

http://pathfinder.com/Rhino/

Search for your favorite artist or song in their 2000-plus title catalog, check out the upcoming releases, chat with an artist, order Rhino merchandise, read the online version of the Retroactive newsletter, and enter the monthly contests for free stuff.

Rockadillo Records

http://www.sjoki.uta.fi/~latvis/levyyht/rockad.html

Provides home site for Rockadillo Records based in Finland. Includes company catalog, artist profiles (not all are Finnish), and contact information. Rockadillo focuses upon rock with jazz, ethnic, and country overtones.

Sesha Press Records

http://www.sesha.com/index.html

Provides home site and online ordering for Sesha Press Records. Includes artist profiles and album artwork for groups such as Luxo Crush and Granite Path. Also includes sound bytes, tour dates, and ordering information.

Silver Girl Records

http://www.tumyeto.com/tydu/music/labels/silver/silver.htm

Provides home site and ordering information for Silver Girl Records based in San Diego, California. Includes company catalog, record artwork, and descriptions for such bands as Everready, Fluf, and Ruby Falls.

Sin-Drome Records

http://www.kspace.com/KM/music.sys/SinDrome/pages/home.html

Provides home site for Sin-Drome records. Includes artist background, sound bytes, cover art, and ordering information. Also includes record reviews and a mailbox for Sin-Drome artists.

Slumberland Records

http://www.denizen.com/trout/slumberland/

Provides home site and online ordering for Slumberland Records. Includes label catalog, artist profiles, upcoming releases, and contact information.

Squealer Music

http://www.mal.com/~squealer/

Provides home site for Squealer Music. Includes online catalog, artist profiles, tour dates, label news, and links to other independent labels and zines.

Supernova Records

http://www.intr.net/supernova/

Provides home site for Supernova Records based in Arlington, Virginia. Includes background and ordering information for Supernova's two artist compilations. Also includes links to many band, zine, and tour dates.

Surfdog Records

http://www.professionals.com/~surfdog/records.html

Provides home site for Surfdog Records. Includes artist profiles, label catalog, and contact information. Surfdog artists concentrate on the surfer music styles including reggae and instrumental guitar rock.

TeenBeat Records

http://www.iuma.com/TeenBeat/

Provides home site for TeenBeat Records. Includes online catalog with artist and sound descriptions. Also includes label news and contact information.

Verb Audio

http://www.mindspring.com/~brydaguy/verb.html

Home site for the Verb Audio label that specializes in electronic dance music. Includes label profile, philosophy, catalog, DJ booking information, and information about the Atlanta dance scene. This site has some unbelievable graphics. Very cool.

Village Pulse

`http://www.rootsworld.com/rw/villagepulse/outpost.html`

Provides home site for Village Pulse, a record label that specializes in Mandinka drum music and other West African drum artists. Includes label catalog, artist background, photos, and contact information.

Wa Nui Records

`http://planet-hawaii.com/wanui/`

Provides home site and label information for Wa Nui Records based in Honolulu, Hawaii. Includes artist profiles, label catalog, sound bytes, and contact information. Also includes links to other Hawaiian sites.

Warner Bros. Records

`http://www.wbr.com/`

Provides home site for Warner Brothers Records and artists. Includes information about groups such as Van Halen, k.d. lang, Ministry, Lou Reed, the Artist Formally Known As Prince, and many, many more. Also includes discussion groups and links to related sites. There are quite a few famous musicians on Warner Brothers.

Windham Hill Records

`http://www.windham.com/`

Provides home site for Windham Hill Records. Includes artist profiles, sound bytes, tour dates, label catalog, and ordering information. Windham Hill artists include George Winston, Michael Hedges, Tuck & Patti, Timbuk 3, and much more.

Recording

Marketing Music on the Web

`http://www.magicnet.net/rz/web_music/markmus.html`

Provides marketing information for independent labels and alternative groups. Includes catalog services with price lists and sound bytes, online ordering information, and links to promotional sites.

Moneymaking Music Resources

`http://www.mcs.net/~fishercg/`

Everything you need to know about how to turn a profit from your musical talents. Features marketing and sales secrets, and tips on improving composition and songwriting. Also includes the S.U.R.V.I.V.A.L resource guide and a one-year free subscription to Musician's Business Building Bookshelf.

Patrick's Musicians' Page

`http://www.crl.com/~patrickk/music.html`

Contains information about Patrick's musician's referral service and Web page service. Also provides information about Patrick's band and offers links to other regional/unsigned bands of all types.

Planet StarChild

`http://streams.com/starchild`

Serves as a music resource for artists and new music fans around the world. Offers home pages and Internet marketing help for indpendent artists and labels.

Rock

Aerosmith

`http://coos.dartmouth.edu/~joeh/`

Focuses on Aerosmith. Includes pictures of the band and downloadable sound bytes. Provides tour dates, concert tickets, quotes from lead singer Stephen Tyler, and other recent Aerosmith news. Also offers tabs and chord charts.

The David Bowie File

`http://liber.stanford.edu/~torrie/Bowie/BowieFile.html`

Chronicles the life of David Bowie. Provides information about his albums, movies, and videos.

The Death of Rock 'n' Roll

`http://weber.u.washington.edu/~jlks/pike/DeathRR.html`

Contains samples from Jeff Pike's book of the same name. Features "Untimely Demises, Morbid Preoccupations, and Premature Forecasts of Doom in Pop Music." Sections include heroin deaths, famous death dates, and "Beatles Bugouts."

The Grateful Dead

`http://www.cs.cmu.edu/afs/cs.cmu.edu/user/mleone/web/dead.html`

Helps you keep your Eyes on the Dead. Includes everything from lyrics, pictures, and sounds to song chords, rumors, and Dead icons. Offers links to Garcia memorial pages, set lists, and tape trading networks. No need to keep surfing down the Web feelin' bad.

Green Day

http://www.greenday.com

Focuses on the band Green Day. Also offers links to plenty of other Green Day Net resources and links to other bands that sport a similar sound.

Hanspeter Niederstrasser's Def Leppard Page

http://www.princeton.edu/~nieder/defleppard/def.html

Focuses on this '80s band that defined modern metal. Provides all you might need to complete your collection. Includes complete lyrics, band history, images, and sounds. Also presents a guest book and survey to fill out so you can express your opinion about the band.

Hyper Idol II

http://pantheon.cis.yale.edu/~markl/idol/index.html

Represents every album as a separate page with images and lyrics to every song. Contains a growing collection of images besides those found on the albums.

Iron Maiden Page

http://www.cs.tufts.edu/~stratton/maiden/maiden.html

Offers a collection of album covers and a running commentary on the meaning and value of each album. Includes many pictures.

Jane's Addiction and Porno for Pyros

http://www.links.net/vita/muzik/janes/

Contains the latest facts on the bands. Provides detailed discographies, pictures, and sound samples from both Jane's Addiction and Porno for Pyros. Also contains links to many other Web pages (like Woodstock '94) and ftp sites.

Jethro Tull Music Archive

http://remus.rutgers.edu/JethroTull/

Focuses on the band Jethro Tull. Provides information about the band and its whereabouts. Includes lyrics to all the band's songs, tour dates, a comprehensive FAQ list, and more.

Kinks Web Sites

http://hobbes.it.rit.edu/kinks/kinks.html

Includes everything from pictures, sounds, and videos to a complete discography and lyric database.

KISS OTAKU

http://www.otaku.net/kissotaku.html

Details on KISS conventions, the reunion tour and tribute bands, and fanzines. Features a fan finder, sound files, trade pages, and photos (including candid shots and Beavis and Butthead as Gene and Paul).

L.A. Rock & Roll Road Map

http://www.net101.com/rocknroll/page2.html

Contains L.A.-area maps, addresses, and pictures of hangouts where you can run into or reminisce about your favorite musicians and bands. Visit Chateau Marmont, former "home" of the Doors' Jim Morrison, or The Rainbow, the hangout of the likes of Led Zeppelin, Keith Moon, and John Lennon.

Led Zeppelin Home Page

http://www.cs.virginia.edu/~jsw2y/zeppelin/zeppelin.html

Focuses on Led Zeppelin. Includes links to the Digital Graffiti mailing list, plenty of pictures, a discography, lyrics, and guitar tabs. Also offers a link to a Zeppelin page written in French.

Mazzy Star Home Page

http://www.unc.edu/~hondo/mazzy.html

Focuses on Mazzy Star. Includes an "unofficial" discography and an ever-growing picture page. Also includes a video clip from the Jesus & Mary Chain.

Meat Puppets Home Page

http://www.nando.net/music/gm/puppets/index.html

Offers information on the band Meat Puppets, including photos, sound files, interviews, band art, discography, and guitar tabs.

Merger

http://www.wp.com/Merger/home.htm

Presents Merger, an original rock-and-roll band in the Los Angeles, California area.

Metallica

http://www.algonet.se/~medex/

Features photos, tablatures, links to other Metallica sites, and information about the band—including the members' favorite beers.

MÖTLEY CRÜE

`http://pathfinder.com/@@H33bgYNwygEAQJC8/elektra/artists/motley/motley.html`

Contains general information about the band Mötley Crüe, as well as sound and video clips and a discography. Links to other Mötley sites.

nine inch nails: the unofficial home page

`http://nothing.nin.net/op.html`

Targets the intense fan. Provides photos, lyrics, and frequently asked questions. Also offers chords, interviews, and reviews.

Phish.Net

`http://www.phish.net`

Leave thoughts of Wilson behind as you enter this world of FAQs, photos, graphics, and show reviews, then run like an antelope through links to phan pages, the Helping Phriendly Book, and more. Stay up-to-date on tour info and band rumors. Unite, Lizards, and free Gamehendge!

Pink Floyd Home Page

`http://humper.student.princeton.edu/floyd/`

Includes many pictures, lyrics, a discography, and more. Also offers transcribed interviews with band members. Also offers a downloadable Pink Floyd screen saver.

Queen

`http://queen-fip.com/`

Includes an art gallery, lyrics and discography, video samples, audio samples of classic tracks, and reviews. Discussions on Queen's last album, "Made in Heaven," information on the upcoming Queen game, and frequently updated news.

RADISH—Hot Original Rock!

`http://www.rockhouse.com/radish/`

Presents RADISH, an original rock band from Greenville, Texas (just east of Dallas), that plays original rock music as well as other classic rock. Introduces RADISH band members, Ben Kweller, Lauren Hamilton, and John David Kent.

Rock and Roll Hall of Shame

`http://pathfinder.com/@@VwQROsNXPgIAQJ@8/people/hall/`

Features "performers who deserve a very special place on the mantelpiece—right up there with, say, your mood ring collection." Categories includes the Kings Of Shame (Milli Vanilli), Lyrical Letdowns, Haute Rocks, and Flops on Film.

Rolling Stones Web Site

`http://www.stones.com/`

Contains a vast collection of sounds, pictures, and interviews. Includes a few pages especially for the new HotJava browser by Sun Systems.

Room Full of Mirrors: The Official Jimi Hendrix Web Site

`http://www.wavenet.com/~jhendrix/index.html`

Provides many Jimi goodies. Sponsored by the Jimi Hendrix Foundation. Includes information about the "On the Road Again," traveling exhibition, astrological charts, the "Searching for Jimi Hendrix" documentary, a personal memoir and the Virtual Museum.

Stranglehold—The Ted Nugent Page

`http://thunder.indstate.edu/h5/jngonzo/.nuge.html`

Provides information about the Nuge. Includes a complete discography, pictures, articles, reviews, tour dates, FAQs, lyrics, and information on the fan club. Also features his "Spirit of the Wild" television show.

Welcome to the Jungle

`http://www.teleport.com/~boerio/gnr-home.html`

Features information about the band Guns 'n' Roses. Includes a complete discography, lyrics, image gallery, and tour information. Also includes guitar tabs and interviews with the band.

Software

`http://www.pcmag.com/download/dl-home.htm`

Get free copies of software and utilities from PC Magazine's download area.

Newsgroups

alt.emusic

alt.fan.depeche-mode

alt.fan.elvis-costello

alt.fan.henry-rollins

alt.fan.kinks

alt.fan.rickie-lee-jones

alt.fan.weird-al

alt.fan.yanni

alt.music.+live+

alt.music.4-track

alt.music.abba

alt.music.alanis

alt.music.alternative

alt.music.alternative.female

alt.music.america

alt.music.barenaked-ladies

alt.music.bee-gees

alt.music.beethoven

alt.music.black-sabbath

alt.music.blamed

alt.music.brian-eno

alt.music.bruce-springsteen

alt.music.cheap-trick

alt.music.clash

alt.music.counting-crows

alt.music.cranberries

alt.music.ct-dummies

alt.music.dave-matthews

alt.music.def-leppard

alt.music.depeche-mode

alt.music.faith-no-more

alt.music.filk

alt.music.fleetwood-mac

alt.music.foo-fighters

alt.music.guthrie

alt.music.iggy-pop

alt.music.j-s-bach

alt.music.journey

alt.music.karaoke

alt.music.lou-reed

alt.music.lyrics

alt.music.modern-rock

alt.music.pearl-jam

alt.music.polkas

alt.music.pop-eat-itself

alt.music.ramones

alt.music.rockabilly

alt.music.savoy-brown

alt.music.saxophone

alt.music.soul

alt.music.squeeze

alt.music.swedish-pop

alt.music.synthpop

alt.music.tape-culture

alt.music.the-band

alt.music.thecure

alt.music.tragically-hip

alt.music.world

alt.niteclub.alternative

alt.punk

alt.punk.europe

alt.punk.straight-edge

alt.rock-n-roll

alt.rock-n-roll.acdc

alt.rock-n-roll.aerosmith

alt.rock-n-roll.classic

alt.rock-n-roll.hard

alt.rock-n-roll.metal

alt.rock-n-roll.metal.death

alt.rock-n-roll.metal.gnr

alt.rock-n-roll.metal.groove

alt.rock-n-roll.metal.heavy

alt.rock-n-roll.metal.ironmaiden

alt.rock-n-roll.metal.megadeth

alt.rock-n-roll.metal.metallica

alt.rock-n-roll.metal.motley-crue

alt.rock-n-roll.metal.progressive

alt.rock-n-roll.oldies

alt.rock-n-roll.psychedelic

alt.rock-n-roll.stones

bit.listserv.bgrass-l

fido7.music.lyrics

han.rec.artrock

it.arti.musica

rec.music.artists.amy-grant

rec.music.artists.beach-boys

rec.music.artists.bruce-hornsby

rec.music.artists.kiss

rec.music.artists.mariah-carey

rec.music.artists.neil-young

rec.music.artists.rage-machine

rec.music.artists.trich-yearwood

rec.music.beatles

rec.music.bluenote

rec.music.bluenote.blues

rec.music.christian

rec.music.classical

rec.music.classical.guitar

rec.music.classical.performing

rec.music.classical.recordings

rec.music.country.old-time

rec.music.country.western

rec.music.dylan

rec.music.early

rec.music.folk

rec.music.funky

rec.music.gaffa

rec.music.gdead

rec.music.hip-hop

rec.music.indian.classical

rec.music.makers.builders

rec.music.makers.guitar.jazz

rec.music.makers.percussion

rec.music.makers.piano

rec.music.makers.trumpet

rec.music.newage

rec.music.opera

rec.music.phish

rec.music.reggae

rec.music.rem

rec.music.tori-amos

tnn.music.jazz-fusion

tw.bbs.music.classical

tw.bbs.music.pop

tw.bbs.music.rocknroll

tw.bbs.rec.guitar

tw.bbs.rec.instrument

uk.music.folk

uk.music.guitar

uk.music.rhythm-n-blues

Listservs

ACTMUS-L—Asian Contemporary Music Discussion Group

State University of New York at Buffalo

You can join this group by sending the message "sub ACTMUS-L your name" to listserv@ubvm.cc.buffalo.edu

ALLMUSIC—Discussions on All Forms of Music

The American University, Washington, DC

You can join this group by sending the message "sub ALLMUSIC your name" to listserv@american.edu

BGRASS-L—Bluegrass Music Discussion

You can join this group by sending the message "sub BGRASS-L your name" to listserv@lsv.uky.edu

BLUE-EYED-POP—Bjork/Sugarcubes/ Icelandic Music Mailing List

Memorial University of Newfoundland, St. John's, Newfoundland, Canada

You can join this group by sending the message "sub BLUE-EYED-POP your name" to listserv@morgan.ucs.mun.ca

BLUES-L—Blues Music List

Brown University, Providence, RI

You can join this group by sending the message "sub BLUES-L your name" to
`listserv@brownvm.brown.edu`

BOSTON-M—Boston Music Scene

NetSpace Project, Brown University, Providence, RI

You can join this group by sending the message "sub BOSTON-M your name" to
`listserv@netspace.org`

C-OPERA—Contemporary Opera and Music Theatre

University of New Brunswick, Fredericton, N.B., Canada

You can join this group by sending the message "sub C-OPERA your name" to
`listserv@listserv.unb.ca`

CLASSICAL—Moderated Classical Music List

You can join this group by sending the message "sub CLASSICAL your name" to
`listserv@home.ease.lsoft.com`

CLASSM-L—Classical Music List

Brown University, Providence, RI

You can join this group by sending the message "sub CLASSM-L your name" to
`listserv@brownvm.brown.edu`

COLLAB-L—Theatre and Musical Artists, Composers, etc.

Pennsylvania State University

You can join this group by sending the message "sub COLLAB-L your name" to
`listserv@psuvm.psu.edu`

EMUSIC-L—Electronic Music Discussion List

The American University, Washington, DC

You can join this group by sending the message "sub EMUSIC-L your name" to
`listserv@american.edu`

FILMUS-L—Film Music Discussion List

University Computing Services, Indiana University

You can join this group by sending the message "sub FILMUS-L your name" to
`listserv@iubvm.ucs.indiana.edu`

FOLKBIZ—Folk Musician Issues

Pennsylvania State University

You can join this group by sending the message "sub FOLKBIZ your name" to
`listserv@psuvm.psu.edu`

IRTRAD-L—Irish Traditional Music List

You can join this group by sending the message "sub IRTRAD-L your name" to
`listserv@listserv.hea.ie`

LAMC-L—Academic Discussion of Latin American Music

University Computing Services, Indiana University

You can join this group by sending the message "sub LAMC-L your name" to
`listserv@iubvm.ucs.indiana.edu`

ROCKLIST—Academic Discussion of Popular Music

You can join this group by sending the message "sub ROCKLIST your name" to
`listserv@listserv.kent.edu`

STABWEST-L—The College Rock Music Interest Group

University of Illinois, Urbana, IL

You can join this group by sending the message "sub STABWEST-L your name" to
`listserv@postoffice.cso.uiuc.edu`

SYNTH-L—Electronic Music "Gearhead" List

The American University, Washington, DC

You can join this group by sending the message "sub SYNTH-L your name" to listserv@american.edu

WMUSIC-L—Center for the Study of World Musics

You can join this group by sending the message "sub WMUSIC-L your name" to listserv@listserv.kent.edu

Music

Alchemy

Alchemy, Taoism, God & all that Stuff

http://www.fablor.com/open/alchemy1.htm

For those who aspire in alchemy, stop here for a review of the rules and advice from a self-proclaimed alchemist. Be sure to make a note of the 10 Golden Threads.

The Alchemy Virtual Library

http://www.levity.com/alchemy/home.html

This site is the original and best alchemy site of the WWW. It contains information ranging from general historic data to alchemical journals and even an image of a reconstructed alchemical laboratory. Chemists and laymen alike will be fascinated by the online translated texts from the journals of alchemists.

Philosophers of Nature

http://www.mcs.net/~alchemy/

Home page for the "leading school for the study of practical alchemy." Site contains information about courses and study in Qabala and Esotericism. Site also contains *The Stone*, an alchemy newsletter.

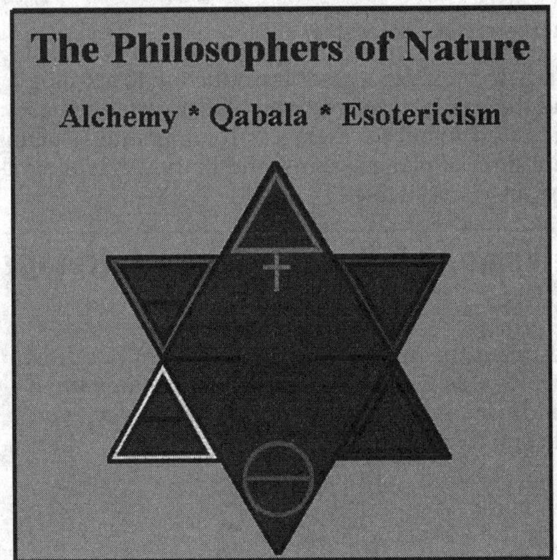

Philosopher's Stone/Elixir of Life

http://www.teleport.com/~boydroid/gold.html

Site details the research of Dean Stonier, director of the Global Sciences Group. The page details the chemistry involved in the purification and transmutation of transition row metals and their societal applications.

Astrology

Asian Astrology

http://users.deltanet.com/~wcassidy/astro/astroindex.html

This site features aspects of Asian divination. Specialized links to Chinese, Tibetan, and Vietnamese astrology are available. Also provides current news in Asian astrology and a mailing list.

The Astrological Association of Great Britain

http://www.astrologer.com/aanet/index.html

Site gives information about the founding of the AA and promotes its three publications. Site also gives information about annual seminars on all aspects of astrology.

Astrology Alive!

http://www.lightworks.com/Astrology/Alive/

A professional astrologer for over 20 years, Barbara Schermer offers astrological reports via e-mail, horoscopes by mail, book lists, and guest astrologers, all at a "great price," of course. Also features information about Schermer's Book, *Astrology Alive!*

Astrology Online Magazine

http://www.dimensional.com/%7Esolheart/so00002.htm

This is the home page for the *Magazine of Astrology*. Site contains professional astrological forecasting, editorials, and information about astrology as a profession. Site also contains articles about ethics in astrology and the current trends in commercial astrological forecasting.

Astrology: A Theological Science

http://zeta.cs.adfa.oz.au/Spirit/Astro/western-astro-theology-01.html

This site takes a serious look at astrology and its biblical roots. Site lays out the limitations of modern commercial astrology and attempts to define its true meaning and place in daily life.

Astrology—The Ultimate Original Science

http://www.the-ultimate.com/s[ace/astro.htm

Provides a speculative historical description of astrology. Also contains a mathematical description of planetary movements and the movements of the zodiac. Site contains an alphabetical listing of other links as well.

The Cosmic Palette

http://nen.sedona.net/haizen/

This light and fluffy site features information about current lunar phases and signs, as well as reasons why people believe and disbelieve astrology. Site describes the astrologer Haizen Paige as a "renaissance man" and describes his interests and qualifications.

The Harmony of Heaven

http://ruls41.fsw.leidenuniv.nl/ProZodiac/

Contains a musical interpretation of the movements of the planets. Billed as relaxing when used in a state of meditation.

How and Why Astrology Works

http://premium.caribe.net/~ezekiel/file0008.html

This site attempts to rationalize astrology through spiritual laws traditionally accepted by science and religion. Site provides a somewhat logical argument for astrology. Regardless of your view, the page provides a slew of information on astrology rather than just an advertisement.

Kramer—Fishing guide to the Stars

http://www.io.com/~fgs/

One of the wittiest astrology pages on the WWW, Kramer gives entertaining horoscopes rather than the usual predigested planetessimal garbage. A refreshing look at astrology.

The Metalog Yellow Pages

http://www.astrologer.com/metalog/

Probably the definitive source in astrological online searching. Site maintains links to professional astrologers, student astrologers, national associations, and schools in 48 countries. Site also contains information about how to register with this directory for the astrologically inclined.

The Nine Planets

http://seds.lpl.arizona.edu/nineplanets/nineplanets/nineplanets.html

This astounding multimedia tour of the planets contains a wealth of information about mythological significance, scientific understanding, as well as some very neat facts, not to mention the good images. Site is a very good educational tool for the astronomical and astrological novice.

Oracle's Astrology Chart

http://www.idirect.com/astrology/

Site offers a free astrological chart based on information entered by the user. Page also gives information about the author of the site, as well as links to other astrological chart servers.

The Skeptics Dictionary—Astrology

http://wheel.ucdavis.edu/%7Ebtcarrol/skeptic/astrology.html

Site offers a thorough historical and critical investigation of astrology. Although at times highly opinionated, this site presents a very detailed and somewhat logical argument.

The Underground Astrologer

http://www.links.net/astro/

This site provides a great introduction to astrology and the basics of astrological planetary movements and interpretations. Breaks astronomy into an acting paradigm of planets, signs, and houses. A bibliography also is available.

Welcome to Daka's Buddhist Astrology

http://www.mala.bc.ca/~shanemanj/asto.htm

Describes the fundamental principles of Buddhist astrology, as well as the history of astrology in Buddhism. Also offers a free-of-charge system of Tibetan divination.

Zodiacal Zephyr

http://metro.turnpike.net/S/SRozhon/index.html

Organized as one of the Web's jumping off points for astrology. Contains many links to different areas of astrology including articles by Sandra Hozhon, links to a WWW index, conference information, and even an O.J. Simpson case commentary.

Ghost Stories

Arcadia

http://www2ios.com/%7Etidwell/ghost/ghost.html

Site describes the fictional and well-illustrated story of Elisa Cameron, who loses her life in the metropolis of Arcadia. Site contains nine issues of this saga.

Are Ghosts For Real?

http://mason.gmu.edu/~jmartinj/docs/buu.html

This site contains an in-depth essay on the psychology of believing in ghosts. Essay also probes the history of believing, as well as other cultures' beliefs and disbeliefs in spirits.

Asylum

http://www.hallucinet.com/asylum2/as_paramount.html

Site describes spirits that reside in one of Los Angeles' oldest movie studios. Speculation as to the identity of the ghosts ranges from Lucille Ball to Redd Foxx. Regardless of the identity, the page is an entertaining read.

A Directory of Haunted Dining and Lodging in the U.S.

http://web2.airmail.et/spectre1/source/page0.html

Yes, it really is a list of haunted dining and lodging in the United States. Browsers are able to select haunted establishments based on geographical location. Also contains a short explanation of the previous identity of the ghost.

The Earthlight Productions Haunted Page

http://www.primenet.com/~sgoodman/Halloween/spookhouse.html

Site contains a wealth of ghost stories and supernatural spook tales. Page contains Halloween stories and vampire tales as well. This Web page was assembled very nicely—try it.

Ghost Hunters Gallery

http://www.aone.com/~starwest/index.html

Ghost photos and spooky tales are found in this Web site sponsored by two paranormal investigators. Also contains links to the "UFO Realm."

Ghost Lore

http://virtual.park.uga.edu/~clandrum/category_html/ghost.html

Site explains how a personal-experience narrative can evolve into a ghost story. Also contains links to other types of lore.

The Ghost Watcher

http://www.flyvision.org/sitelite/houston/ghostwatcher/basement/index.html

This site brings forth the question "What is happening in June's basement?" Site contains pictures and images, and the browser is asked interpret what is wrong.

Ghosts

http://users.aol.com/shadoland2/ghost.html

Site tells of the author's experiences with hauntings. Contains a long list of ghost stories and spooky tales.

Ghosts—The Charles J. Adams Home Page

http://www.iconservices.com/propages/cadams/

Site author describes his work in the field and provides a catalog of books on ghost stories, shipwrecks, and train wrecks. Site also invites believers and observers to share their stories.

Ghosts of New Mexico

http://hoggan1.atiin.com/redrabbit/

Site is the home page for the *Adobe Angels Ghost* book series. Stories relate to the experiences of Native Americans, Hispanics, and Anglos. Site contains ordering information and forms.

Haunted Toys R Us

http://www.lido.com/ghosts/toysrus.html

Uncovers the story of a haunted Toys R Us store and a seance held to communicate with the ghost employee. Site also describes the increased business due to the activities.

Hauntings Today

http://www.hauntings.com/today.htm

An organization of over 22 years wants to hear your ghost stories. Submission by e-mail from this site is possible. You also can order a T-shirt, if you want.

The Legend of Sleepy Hollow

http://auden.fac.utexas.edu/%7Edaniel/amlit/sleepy/sleepy.htm

Page provides an interactive version of the classic Washington Irving tale. User is able to read and make comments on characters, symbolism, and other aspects of the work.

The Ooga Booga Page

http://www.star06.atklab.yorku.ca/~peterpan/

If you are looking for vampires, werewolves, ghosts, and witchcraft links, go no further. Site also contains short voice messages and video-clips.

Paranormal Belief Survey

http://galileo.metatech.com/surveys/paranorm/paranorm.htm

Site invites the browser to offer his or her opinion for or against paranormal phenomena. Site attempts to evaluate the level of belief in modern myths, such as UFOs and a living Elvis.

A Philippine Ghost Story

http://www.emerald-empire.com/zines/travel/philgh%7E1.htm

Site contains the haunting story of a little boy from the Philippines and his religious experience at Easter. Site also contains travel information for those interested.

Schloss Reichenstein

http://www.caltim.com/reichenstein/

Beautiful site depicting the haunted castle Reichenstein along the Rhine River of Germany. Not only does this site contain stories of a man without a head, it provides an informative tour of the stronghold.

The Virtual Library—Angel Encounters

http://www.crown.net/X/AngelStories.html

Site contains stories told by the page author and anonymous spectators pertaining to angel visitations. Site also contains links to other paranormal phenomena.

The WWW Virtual Library—Ghost Stories and Folklore

http://www.crown.net/X/GhostStories.html

Site is a conglomeration of information gathered from various electronic resources. Contains extensive list of ghost stories and links to similar sites.

Numerology

Animals and Karma

http://www.hyperlink.com/E0020/4NXJP+e2CbgNy+Jx6R9+7G8ZZP6xlugd/weaver/95/25_8/dev/numerical/animals.htm

Site explains the connection between the number seven and the animal kingdom, through the upper and lower astral planes. Site also contains links to *The Weaver*, a spiritual publication.

Astro-numerology

http://www.reu.com/kier/

Site provides information and acts as an advertisement for numerologist Yaakov Kier. User can input personal information and questions and e-mail them to Kier.

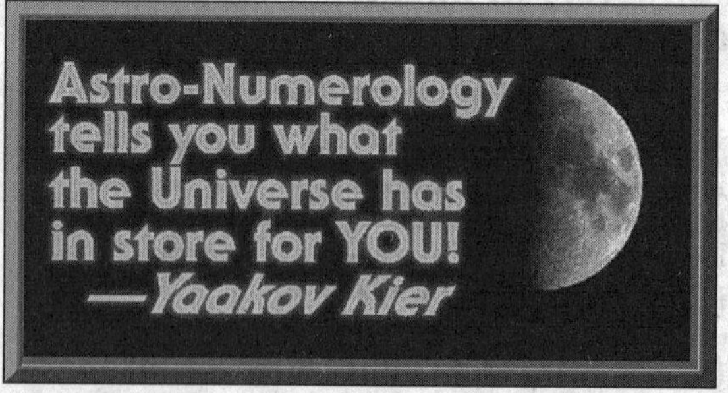

Entropic Fine Art Inc.

http://www.entropic-art.com/

Site gives an unusual approach to art based on arcane law, geometry, and numerology. Home page provides an online quest to decipher and interpret the meaning of five works by Peter Robson.

How Does the Kalabalarian Philosophy Differ from Numerology?

http://www.kabalarians.com/articles/differ.htm

Site compares and contrasts the different dogmas of both philosophical endeavors. Site offers a unique analysis of the browser's name, try it!

Numerology

http://www.luna.co.uk/~npharris/number.htm

If you need help discovering your life purpose, you might try here. Nigel Harris provides numerology readings using your name and date of birth. Also contains information about computer programs for numerologists.

Numerology

http:///www.numerology.com/

Site gives a synopsis of numerology and metaphysical descriptions of numbers 1 through 9. Site also features numerological charts and how the user can obtain his or her own.

Numerology by Cheryl Lee Terry

http://www.ellemag.com/cgi-unprot/pn

This site provides a refreshing change to those bogged down in daily horoscopes. This site also provides a free reading by simply entering your birth date.

Numerology—I've Got Your Number

http://www.kaiwan.com%7Emcivr/numbers.html

This site features a vast array of information about numerology relating to astrological signs; love, sex, and marriage; numerology and religion; and information about how to receive your own reading. Also contains links to incense and oils.

Numerology, The Science of Vibration

http://ww.cosmic-web.com/num.html

This page gives a descriptive introduction to numerology and a broad history. Site also contains three brief lessons to practicing numerology and interpreting your results.

Numerology—What do the Numbers Mean?

http://www.diro.com/clara/nmean.htm

Site provides information about basic meanings of the letters of the alphabet and their numerological meanings. Also contains a life lessons section and tells how to order your chart.

Prime—Advanced Numerology Profiler

http://www.inforamp.net%7Ehfeist/

Prime is a software package that predicts dates, gives individual profiles, matchmakes, and interprets numerology profiles. This software can be downloaded from their Web site.

Six Hundred and Sixty Six But not 666

http://www.math.gatech.edu/~jkatz/Religions/Numerics.six.html

This site provides a detailed and opinionated discussion of the number 666 and its biblical meanings. Author attempts to dispel the current connotations and misrepresentation of the infamous number.

The Skeptics Dictionary—Numerology

http://wheel.dcn.davis.ca.us/~btcarrol/skeptic/numerology.html

Site provides intriguing information about numerology and public response to numerology. Also provides a cynical, skeptical, and highly opinionated look at the pseudo-science.

Sun Angel

http://www.sun-angel.com/interact/numquest/numquest.html

One of the only free online numerology services of the WWW. It provides a lengthy reading that will surprise you at times and bore you at others. Regardless, it's still free, so investigate!

The Wonderful World of Numerology

http://www.valdosta.peachnet.edu/~abernste/numer.html

This fascinating page gives numerological interpretations into the JFK assassination, Shakespeare, the Bible, and presidential deaths.

Occult

The Alternative Spiritualities Club Home Page

http://yoyo.cc.monash.edu.au/%7Edarmou/occult/Occult_home.html

Site features the exploration of alternative spiritualities. Contains links to commercial organizations, pagan links, rituals, and other spiritual home pages. Also available is a membership in the ASC.

Angelnet

`http://alive.mcn.org:80/angelnet.html/`

Site contains links to sights and sounds created by dolphins and angels to inspire the believer. Also contains a downloadable dolphin movie.

Aunt Agatha's Occult Emporium

`http://web.idirect.com/~agatha/`

Site serves as a pagan/metaphysical gathering place and seeks to promote the occult through links to events, artists, magazines, and of course, merchandise sales. Also contains a spell book link and a registry.

The Land of Oz

`http://members.gnn.com/schickman/index.htm`

An amazing site containing information ranging from wisdom of the earth to Mayan astronomical techniques. Also contains poetry, magical lands links, and much more.

Necronomi.com—The Familiar Spirit BBS

`http://www.necronomi.com/`

Site is fundamentally dedicated to expanding human horizons and promotes alternate religion across the Web. Also contains links to business, discussion forums, sex, and magic.

The Nine Houses of Gaia

`http://edgewood.portland.or.us:80/9houses/`

Site describes the NHOG as a nonprofit organization promoting Earth-based religions. Features their newsletter, *Open Ways*, plus links to the Northwest Fall Equinox Festival and occult resources.

Occult Gateway

`http://www.think.com/users/cward/WWW/occult.html`

Site provides a large number of links to occult sites on the WWW. Site also contains links to search engine listings of certain topics.

Occult Page

`http://www.uib.no/zoo/wolf/bjorn/occult.html`

Site contains a great index to occult sites on the Net. Some include links to newsgroups, neopagans, and magic.

Occultism—The Shawn Knight Page

`http://www.contrib.andrew.cmu.edu/~shawn/occult/`

This is another occult site containing a massive number of links. Links are organized into categories, which are in alphabetical order.

Paganlink

`http://www.brad.ac.uk/~kmhether/paganlink/plhome.html`

This site contains information and links for those who celebrate the spirit of the Earth. Also contains links to pagan art, pagan news, and other pagan events.

Pentagram—the Internet's Pagan and Occult Superstore

`http://www.psinet.co.uk/pentagram/index.html`

If you need a deluxe ceremonial dagger or a wall pentagram finished in gold, this is your site. Also contains links to events, groups, and psychics.

Servants of the Light—School of Occult Science

`http://www.algonet.se/~sol_swe/`

Site describes mystery school correspondence teachings. Site offers a history of the school, course descriptions, information about lectures and workshops, contact addresses, and recommended occult literature.

The Shroud of Turin

`http://www.cais.com/npacheco/shroud/turin.html`

You've seen it on the Discovery Channel, now check it out online—the Shroud of Turin. Site gives information about the research endeavors on the shroud, as well as shroud literature and a frequently asked questions section.

Urdco's Mystic Visions

`http://www.olworld.com/olworld/m_urdco/`

Site serves as a guide to the occult, mystic books, and other material. Site offers a $3, 90-page catalog.

Norse lore, mythology, and mysticism material are available as well.

You lack Slack, Jack—The Church of the Subgenius

http://www-usa.iona.com/www/slack

This site contains excerpts from *The Book of the Subgenius* by J.R. "Bob" Dobbs. Site boasts intellectual salvation from the doldrums and evils of society and promises "physical attractiveness—overnight." A very strange site, but check it out.

Reincarnation

22 Topics on Past Lives

http://pastlives.com/topics.html

Site serves as the contact site for Bud Hollowell, reincarnationist. Mr. Hollowell claims to help people remember past lives. Also mentions past lives seminars.

Electronic Newsletter—Reincarnation

http://www.pix.za/mbs/spirit/nacvc95b.htm

Site explores the concept of the biblical Moses' reincarnation as Dr. Martin Luther King. Site is strewn with biblical quotes and conclusions drawn from them. The skeptic might view this site with several pounds of salt and a doubting eye.

Human Understood Reincarnation

http://www.canuck.com/~akwu/

Site features the bizarre Addison Brown and his efforts at reincarnation. Brown outlines his theories about how reincarnation is possible due to rotations of celestial bodies. Site also contains New Age links.

Joe's Reincarnation Link

http://www.intercall.com/~joe/reinc.htm

This page explores Joe's unified spirituality theory and his attempts to understand the meaning of life. Also contains links to other paranormal phenomena.

Karma and Reincarnation—Yoga

http://www.sivanda.org/krma&rei.htm

Part of the Sivanda Yoga Vendanta Center, this Web site explains the subject of reincarnation through quotes from the Bhagavad Gita and the laws of Karma. Also contains a poem about reincarnation.

Past Lives and Reincarnation

http://www.execpc.com/~mholmes/passt.html

Site is part of the "Phenomena of the Psyche and Other Inexplicable Anomalies." Site contains links to ftp sites, search engines, Gopher sites, and Web sites on reincarnation.

Reincarnation

http://www.spiritweb.org/Spirit/reincarnation.htm

Site attempts to explain the concept of soul evolution and application of the Karma principle. Page provides personal reincarnation examples, definitions of reincarnation, and past-life therapy links.

Reincarnation 101

http://xis.com/~bhs/24Reincarnation101-t.html

Ben H. Swett gives an interesting look at reincarnation through a Christian perspective. Site contains an essay by Mr. Swett, a few tidbits on the Wheel of Karma, and many interesting stories.

Reincarnation & Karma

http://www.spiritweb.org/Spirit/reincarnation-karma-omni.html

Site discusses reincarnation based on the laws of Karma. Page attempts to correct misconceptions about Karma and elucidates this as an anecdote.

Reincarnation Case History

http://www.best.com/~dna/don/CaseHistory.html

Site provides a case history of a reincarnation event taped in 1976, provided by Don Showen. Home page is set up in a question/answer therapy session, which at times is very eerie.

Reincarnation—Have We Lived Before?

http://www.ip.net/are/reincarnation.html

The writings of Edgar Cayce, a deceased psychic, are displayed to give his view of reincarnation. The page, however, is the platform of the Association for Research and Enlightenment, Inc., which seeks to build its membership, as well as promote its publications on reincarnation, ESP, and health and healing.

Reincarnation—Is Reincarnation a Christian Concept?

http://the700club.org/cbn/teach/rcn2.html

Site looks into the biblical meaning of reincarnation from a very Christian investigator. A good site for a brief overview of reincarnation and biblical reincarnation.

Reincarnation and the Theory of Tri-chart

http://www.canuck.com/~akwu/trichart.html

One of the strangest pages yet encountered in the reincarnation corner of the Web. An eclectic page combining the tri-chart theory of reincarnation based on conception and birth dates, and an author's obsession with Einstein.

Synthetic Reincarnation

http://www3ios.com/~osiris/qru/syntcarn.htm

A nuts and bolts approach to reincarnation based on the simplistic view of carbon-based life forms. Also contains some neat graphics and poetry.

The True Reincarnation of Panchen Rinpoche

http://www.hyperlink.com/E0030/
bb8f3dbob82936c50e8440e0721of396be52c392f3f32c8d/weaver/
96/25_1/east/buddhism/reincpr.htm

Site profiles the Dali Lama's recognition of a six-year-old boy, Gehun Choekyi Nyima, as the authentic reincarnation of the 10th Panchen Lama. Contains links to letters to the Chinese government and press releases.

What is Reincarnation?

http://www.elstore.com/Unity/dtpsb.htm

Brad Jensen gives a Christian perspective of reincarnation based on self-examination and exploration. Site also contains links to other essays pertaining to discovering the power within you.

Tarot

Innerspace Station

http://web.idirect.com/%7Einnerspa/

Page offers tarot readings and psychic guidance. Page contains a well-thought-out graphic scheme, as well as interesting links to the spiritual realm.

Introduction To Tarot Magic

http://magitech.tcastle.is.net:80/tarot/
tarot_spells.html

Not an introductory page, but a site that claims to be a manual for use of tarot cards in spells. Site contains numerous tarot combinations to remedy troubles or create them.

Learning the Tarot—An Online Course

http://www2.dgsys.com/~bunning/top.html

Joan Bunning provides an excellent in-depth online tarot tutorial. The entire package can also be downloaded from this site. This is an excellent place to start for those interested in entering the tarot realm.

Lord of Illusions—Clive Barker's Tarot Cards

http://www.mgmua.com/lord/wom/tarot_wom.html

Site gives a explanatory tarot reading for Clive Barker. Also contains links to Clive's home page and other occult sites.

Michael's Tarot Pages

http://www.tcd.net/~mwalden/taort/tarot.html

Page contains information based on a "Hermetic Order of the Golden Dawn" approach to tarot reading. Site contains links to meanings and origins of tarot, as well as a brief book list on tarot.

Michele's Tarot Page

http://www.infi.net/~jacksn/

Site yields information for tarot enthusiasts in the form of links to tarot decks, publications, reviews, and software. Page also contains a useful online beginner course taught by Michele Jackson, for free! Site provides a very useful tarot source.

The Original WWW Tarot Site

http://www.facade.com/attraction/tarot/

Site has been providing free tarot readings since 1993. Contains several different deck readings and schools of tarot thought. Site also contains links to tarot-related topics and other occult interests.

The Tarot Cards

http://www.ipcc.com/market/newage/tarot.html

Provides background information on tarot plus a brief lesson in reading tarot cards. Also contains explanations of deck types, the Rider deck, and the Crowley deck.

Tarot Cards—Maelstrom

http://www.fsu.umd.edu/students/dhiggins/tarot.htm

Site gives a brief and informative overview of tarot cards. Site is the home page for Daniel Higgins, amateur tarot card reader.

Tarot Inspiration

http://www.geocities.com/Paris/2110/index.html

Site gives information on tarot relating to the Book of Troth (Crowley Deck). Site contains a discussion forum and an entire visualized deck.

Tarot—Tools and Rites of Transformation

http://www.nccn.net%7Etarot/

If talking to tarot people like yourself is what you want, stop here first. This is the site to order the T.A.R.O.T. newsletter from and check out links to other tarot stuff. Site features the work of Mary K. Greer and Ed Buryn.

Tarot Web

http://www2dgsys.com%7Ebunning/osites.html

A very useful tarot site that contains an extensive alphabetical list of tarot decks and brief history of tarot. Also contains a nifty list of U.S. stores that sell tarot decks.

Tarot Weekly

http://wwwlabs.com/tarot/notes.html

This site describes and promotes the use of tarot to explore one's self, in essence, tarot solitaire. Page also contains a nice "Tree of Life" link that leads to further explanations.

Vibrations—The Layman's Answer to Tarot Cards!

http://www.tntonline.com/card/card.htm

Site is designed to equip the non-professional with the means to read their own cards. But, it isn't free.

UFOs

8-Tracks and UFOs

http://virtumall.com/zines/8track/ufo.html

This excellent UFO page not only contains UFO stories, but it links William Lear, inventor of the 8-track tape, to some very strange happenings. Site also hints—or screams—of government cover-ups and covert intelligence.

Alien Bob's Command Post

http://www.pnn.com/~boba/alien1.htm

Another site not for the paranoid. Alien Bob provides an entertaining and thought-provoking site. Site provides a unique perspective on UFO and alien invasion that must be seen and not explained.

Alien Information

http://www.iinet.net.au/~bertino/alien.html

Another phenomenal site boasting alien information, photos, and sightings. Site also provides access to the Alien Archive—its search engine.

Digital Postcards

http://www.kodak.com:80/daiHome/postcard/picturePostcard.shtml

Download Picture Postcard software for free. Enables you to choose a picture, create a card, and send it to a friend.

Area 51

http://www.ufomind.com/area51/

Home page, not government-sponsored, for the secret military installation that has sparked curiosity in UFO enthusiasts for years. Site contains links to newsletters, testimonials, photos, cartoons, and newspaper articles.

Aufora—The Alberta UFO Research Association

http://ume.med.ucalgary.ca/aufor/news/index.html

You'll find the latest UFO news and sighting information at this site. Site contains links to scientific and not-so-scientific information, but browsers can still subscribe to a free newsletter here.

BUFORA—British UFO Research Association

http://www.citadel.co.uk/citadel/eclipse/futura/bufora/aboutbuf.htm

Home page for the organization provides historical UFO information and research goals of the organization. Discusses BUFORA's publication, *UFO Times*, and annual meetings.

The Conspiracy Pages

http://w3one.net/~conspira

Clandestine operations in the Reagan-Bush years covering up military affairs and UFO contacts are discussed here. Various conspiracy links also can be found, as well as some other tripped-out theories, including a take on the Kennedy assassination.

Flying Saucer Review

http://www.cee.hw.ac.uk/~ceewb/fsr/fsrhome.htm

FSR is an international journal established in 1955, and this is its home page. Site contains a fine picture library of UFO sittings.

Internet UFO Group—Government

http://www.shmitzware.com/IUFOG/iufog-gov.html

A home page for governmental cover-up utilizing

the Freedom of Information Act. Site contains government-released documents about UFO encounters and other bits of fascinating information attempting to prove a cover-up.

Jody's "ET Phone-Home!" Page

http://nic2.hawaii.net%7Eboyne/#Time

This page claims its purpose is "...to foster this awareness and communication between all beings on this planet and elsewhere." Page includes author's own "awakening story" and her work as psychiatric counselor. A strange page for the firmly grounded unbeliever.

PBS' Nova Solves UFO and Alien Abduction Phenomena!

http://lovecraft.cc.utexas.edu/clarity/Nova-Abduction/index.html

Page describes the plight of Budd Hopkins' work with PBS and PBS's molestation of the material. Hopkins accuses the show of a message that "...all people who claim to be abductees are delusional, victims of repeat hallucinations..." Sight contains the links to Nova and the program.

Roswell UFO Crash Page

http://www.execpc.com/vjentpr/jroswell.html#images

An astounding page providing alien autopsy images, crash photos, sketches of the most famous UFO crash ever, and information about the cover-up. Page also contains Air Force reports on the incident.

Smitty's UFO Page

http://www.schmitzware.com/Ufo.html

Site gives a somewhat scientific view of extraterrestrial alien civilization with the "drake equation," first proposed by Carl Sagan. Also contains information about the secret air base known as Groom Lake.

Stan Friedman's UFO Page

http://medianet.nbnet.nb.ca/ufo/index.htm

Nuclear physicist, Stan Friedman, provides his Web page for discussion and presentation of new information in "Ufology." Site contains some fascinating images of UFO wreckage and astronomical data. Page also contains UFO sighting report forms and UFO publication information.

UFO Books—The Serious Literature

http://www.cs.bgsu.edu/~jzawodn/ufo/ufo-books.html

This site contains a book list of semiserious literature from UFO researchers. Although the preface to the book list is over-dramatic, the list is a good source of information for those who want to believe and participate in the debate.

UFO Sightings by Astronauts

http://www.cs.bgsu.edu/~jzawodn/ufo/astro-sightings.html#Cooper

Either a great information source or a governmental cover-up, you decide. Site contains unconfirmed stories of 10 astronauts and their encounters with UFOs and aliens.

Unidentified Flying Objects

http://www.ee.fit.edu/users/lpinto/sec-ufo.html

A wealth of information on the cover-up, the conspiracy, sightings, and even a *Newsweek* poll. Page contains enough information to satisfy and convince the browser with images and stories.

The X-Files

http://www.rutgers.edu/x-files.html

You've waited for it, here it is. The home page for the popular TV show. Site contains all sorts of *X-Files* information, from fan club news to episode surveys and frequently asked questions.

Voodoo

African Religion Syncretism

http://www.ncf.carleton.ca/freenet/rootdir/menus/sigs/religion/pagan/faqs/voodoo

Informative text-only page provides a lengthy discussion about the origins of voodoo and attempts to clear up some misconceptions about the religion. Article also addresses differences in Haitian, Creole, and African voodoo.

The Electric Gallery-Voodoo Flags

http://www.egallery.com/flags.html

Site provides an online gallery of Voodoo flags, which can be viewed and purchased from this site.

Features several flags depicting the hybridization of traditional religions.

A New Look at Juju

http://www.ulcoa.com/~mcivr/juju.html

Site contains an article by N. Adu Kwabena-Essem discussing the Catholic Church's recent recognition of the religions of Africa and its apology for years of scorn. Site also details the inner workings of the voodoo religion and relations to daily life.

A Primer on Voodoo

http://falcon.cc.ukans.edu/~beleiver/setites/vocab.html

Site provides a quick introduction to voodoo vocabulary and figures associated with voodoo. Also contains several voodoo links.

The Role of the Patient's Religion in Healthcare Setting

http://www-hbp.usc.edu:8376/%7Egellerma/health1.html

Frances A. Bono writes an in-depth and well-referenced article about the influences of religion in healing, especially voodoo and hybrids of voodoo. The article attempts to dispel myths and to speculate about medical causes for illnesses other than voodoo. A very interesting read nonetheless.

Voodoo

http://www.oberlein.edu/~kcross/Afrikan1.html

Site provides a brief overview of voodoo and explains the birth of modern voodoo in Haiti. Site also contains links to creation myths and voodoo ceremonies.

Voodoo-Angelique Kidjo

http://www.imaginet.fr/~kidjo/cult1.html

Home page of Angelique Kidjo gives a modern-day look at the role of voodoo practices in daily life of the residents of Benin. Site also has a few photos of West African voodoo ceremonies.

National Computer Security Association

http://www.ncsa.com/

Download "The Catalog"—a free guide to published material on firewalls and other aspects of Internet security.

Voodoo and Cemeteries

`http://www.neworleans.com/voodoo.html`

This site gives a handy overview of voodoo and a nice history. Also contains a useful voodoo term glossary and information about a haunted history tour of New Orleans.

Voodoo Culture in the US Bibliography

`http://www.afrinet.net/&7Egriot/voodoo.html`

Site contains a lengthy bibliographic list of books and authors pertaining to voodoo. Also contains references to newspaper articles and a map of Africa.

Voodoo: From Medicine to Zombies

`http://www.nando.net/prof/caribe/voodoo.html`

This page contains links to African voodoo information. Links include: the origins of voodoo, gods and goddesses, Afro-Caribbean deities, and other Africa links.

Voodoo Information Pages

`http://www.vmedia.com/shannon/voodoo/voodoo.html`

Page is one of the most comprehensive voodoo pages on the WWW, although there are few, if any, pictures. Start here if you are a neophyte to the religion of voodoo or just want a lot of information.

Voodoo Museum

`http://www.neosoft.com/%7Enodust/mus.html`

Site is the home page for the New Orleans Voodoo Museum. Site provides a brief description of the exhibits and the people involved in making them happen.

Voodoo Products and Information

`http://www.tiac.net/users/bpantry/voodoo`

This site provides voodoo products to the online shopper. Site contains price lists and images of the products. Also present are other interesting religious African links.

The Voodoo Queen

`http://mardi.gras.com/voodoo.html`

Superb graphics make this voodoo page worth visiting. Contains several voodoo cards and meanings. Links also can be found to Mardi Gras pages.

VoodooTour—A Cultural Trip to Benin

`http://www.fotoarchiv.com/`

Site promotes a tour of Benin on the West Coast of Africa. Discover the ancient roots of voodoo from your air-conditioned hotel on the beach, if you've got the money.

Witchcraft

About Witchcraft

`http://www.cog.org/cog/general/about.html`

The Covenant of the Goddess, a nonprofit religious corporation, provides information about the religion of witchcraft and attempts to clear up "thousands of years of bad press." Site contains links to philosophy, holidays, and general practices.

Bewitched

`http://www.erols.com/bewitchd/index.html`

If you are obsessed with Elizabeth Montgomery and *Bewitched*, you have probably already found this page. Site contains a great record of the 60s TV show *Bewitched* and a great deal more information about Samantha. Also features downloadable images of Elizabeth and a silly slide show.

The Hazelnut

`http://www.duc.auburn.edu/~kerrlin/index.html`

The Hazelnut is an online/print Wiccan magazine whose philosophy is based on the Celtic tree calendar/alphabet. The messages deal with aspects of herbal uses, folklore, mythology, lunar happenings, and more.

The Killing of Witches-A Chronicle of the Burning Times

http://www.priment.com/~ioseph/burnwitc.htm

Page serves as a body count for those who lost their lives due to witch persecution. The site contains a long alphabetical list of the persecuted dating back to medieval times.

Rosegate—The Council of Elders

http://users.ids.net/rosegate/

Home page for a organization founded in 1985 for practicing the beliefs of the ancient Celts and Witches from Tuscany. This organization publishes a semiannual magazine with news and information about their following. Information on instruction in their tradition also can be found here.

Satanism and the History of Wicca

http://ourworld.compuserve.com/homepages/hpaulis/swc.htm

Ever wondered what the ties between Satanism and Wicca are? You'll find the answer here. Page contains a lengthy text article containing information about the birth of Wicca from 19th-century literary Satanism and the direction of present day Wiccan philosophy.

Strand by Strand

http://www.3rdplanet.com/~ravnglas/

A collective based in Portland, SbS practices feminist witchcraft and encourages modern living through conservation, ecology, and education. Browser can also find other witchcraft and activism links here.

What about Witches

http://saturn.star.net/salem/witches.htm

One of the best sites dealing with the Salem witch trials. Site contains great images and information in the form of an online tour of Salem.

Witchcraft

http://www.acts17-11.com/witchcraft.html

While most WWW sites inform and support witchcraft, this site looks to condemn it through biblical verse and interpretation. Site also contains a list of biblical passages on aspects of the occult. The phrase "spiritual adultery" also is coined here and used to explain a highly one-sided view.

Witchcraft

http://newreach.net/people/taliesin/witch.html

Site is the home page for Taliesin Athor Govannon, a self-proclaimed witch. Page contains a who's who of Gardnerian Wicca, starting with the founder, Geral B. Gardner. Also contains a historical timeline starting with events in 1749.

Witchcraft

http://www.ucmb.ulb.ac.be/~joan/witches/

Site uses the *Malleus Malificarum*, a 15th century witch hunting manual, to learn about witches. Site also contains witchcraft and pagan links.

Witchcraft in Salem

http://www1.usa1.com/~arachne/hist.html

Site gives a brief overview of the infamous history surrounding the Salem witch trials. Site also blends the art of witchcraft with tarot cards and offers psychic services.

Witchcraft: Some Answers for the Curious

http://www.databahn.net/esp/pgcurous.html

An extensive list of questions and answers regarding witchcraft and aspects of witchcraft you might never think of nor want to think about is located here. Answers to questions like "Do witches believe in Jesus?" are found within. Also contains a handful of links to occult sites.

Witchcraft (Wicca)

http://www.iag.net/~dakins/wicca.html

Page discusses the origins and dark history of Wicca, the religion of the ancient Celtic people. Site also explains the role of Wicca and pagan sources in the formation of Christianity.

Witches League for Public Awareness

http://www.celticcrow.com/

Another page based in Salem, Massachusetts, this informative witching page provides a unique resource for witches and pagans to congregate on the Web. Site contains current events links and many more relevant links of interest to occult types. Great page to start searching the WWW for witchcraft.

Witch's Brew—For All of Mother's Children

http://www.witchs-brew.com/

Witch's Brew is a nicely done page providing information on witchcraft and the occult, as well as great graphics. Site also contains several interesting witchcraft, pagan, Wicca, occult, and commercial links.

Newsgroups

alt.alien.research

alt.alien.visitors

alt.alien.wanderers

alt.aliens.imprisoned

alt.astrology

alt.consciousness

alt.magick

alt.magick.chaos

alt.magick.ethics

alt.magick.order

alt.magick.sex

alt.magick.tyagi

alt.out-of-body

alt.paranormal

alt.paranet.abduct

alt.paranet.metaphysics

alt.paranet.paranormal

alt.paranet.psi

alt.paranet.science

alt.paranet.skeptic

alt.paranet.ufo

alt.paranormal

alt.paranormal.channeling

alt.paranormal.crop-circles

alt.paranormal.pyramid

alt.paranormal.spells.hexes.magic

alt.tarot

alt.ufo.reports

Listservs

IUFOG-L—Administrative Discussions of the Internet UFO Group Project

America Online, Inc. (1-800-827-6364 in USA/Canada)

You can join this group by sending the message "sub IUFOG-L your name" to listserv@listserv.aol.com

UFO-L—FORUM FOR UFOLOGY

You can join this group by sending the message "sub UFO-L your name" to listserv%brufpb.bitnet@listserv.net

Calendars

The Calendar

http://www.ast.cam.ac.uk/RGO/leaflets/calendar/calendar.html

An information leaflet from the Royal Greenwich Observatory, this page details the history of the calendar as a method for keeping track of the passage of time.

CalendarLand

http://www.juneau.com/home/janice/calendarland/

Offering a list of links to other calendar pages, CalendarLand is a comprehensive resource of general, event, celestial, interactive, and cultural and religious calendars. The site also offers links to calendar indexes and directories, calendar information and resources, and calendar software.

Calendars and Their History

http://astro.nmsu.edu/~lhuber/leaphist.html

This site reprints an essay by L. E. Doggett about the history of various calendars, including the Gregorian, the Julian, the Hebrew, the Islamic, the Indian, and the Chinese. Additionally, the essay explains the astronomical bases of calendars, calendar reform movements, and historical eras and chronologies. This site is an important first step for anyone trying to understand where calendars originate and how they are created.

Chinese Astrology Calendar

http://found.cs.nyu.edu/liaos/calendar.html

By using this simple interface, you can click any year in the Twentieth Century and be given a chart that tells you, for example, that 1996 is the Year of the Rat and that 1997 will be the Year of the Ox. The backgrounds at this site are beautiful, but might be slow to download.

Compact Calendar

http://icarus.uic.edu/~rfelic2/calendar.html

This site will generate a calendar, in the year of your choosing, which you can then print onto a single piece of paper.

Conversion Between Chinese and Gregorian Calendar

http://ifcss.org:8001/www/lunar.html

Enter either a Gregorian or a Chinese date and this forms-based site will convert your date into the other.

Ecclesiastical Calendar

http://cssa.stanford.edu/~marcos/ec-cal.html

The Ecclesiastical Calendar site offers Christian calendars for any year you specify. The calendar calculates when Easter and its attendant Christian holidays (Ash Wednesday, Good Friday, and others) will fall in a particular year and also when other feast days in the Roman Catholic tradition will occur. The Web author explains the various algorithms used to calculate Easter's date, discusses when certain cultures adopted the Western method for determining the Easter date, and even posits that current formulas for determining the Easter date might not be valid in the far future.

Gregorian-Hijri Dates Converter

http://bert.cs.pitt.edu/~tawfig/convert/

Converts Gregorian dates into the Islamic calendar.

The Hebrew Date for Today

http://www.doe.carleton.ca/doebin/dfs_dispatch?hebdate

This site translates today's Gregorian date into the Hebrew calendar (for example, 20 April 1996 is 1 Ayar 5756) and offers a list of upcoming holidays.

Heichal Shlomo Interactive Calendar

http://www.jer1.co.il/calendar/calfrm.htm

This frames-based calendar from Virtual Jerusalem offers the Hebrew calendar. Clicking a hyperlinked date brings up information about events and religious observations on that date and even "translates" the Hebrew date into the Gregorian (or Western) calendar.

Home Page for Calendar Reform

http://ecuvax.cis.ecu.edu/~pymccart/calendar-reform.html

This site details several attempts that have been made to reform the Gregorian calendar. Included here are the World Calendar, the 13-month calendar, and the Positivist Calendar, in addition to a history of calendar reform.

J World

http://globall.com/j/

Billing itself as a "comprehensive calendar of birthdays, holidays, historical events, and fun dates," J World's interface allows you to look up a date, either within the current week or one of your choosing, and find a list of celebrities and historical figures born on that day plus holidays and historical events that occur on that date.

Leap Years

http://www.ast.cam.ac.uk/RGO/leaflets/leapyear/leapyear.html

This page, from the Royal Greenwich Observatory in Great Britain, reprints an Information Leaflet the Observatory published explaining the astronomical reasons that leap years exist.

Literary Hyper Calendar

http://www.yasuda-u.ac.jp/LitCalendar.html

Offering a "this day in literary history" service, the Literary Hyper Calendar has an interface consisting of the calendar for the current month. The calendar is a clickable imagemap and you simply click the date in which you are interested. In addition, you can choose from a list of other months and days.

Olivian Calendar

http://boondox.org/vague/olivian.htm

Another 13-month calendar proposal, this one lightly humorous. Common to all 13-month calendar propositions are 13 months of four weeks and 28 days. In this way, January 1 falls on the same weekday, year after year, unlike the current calendar, in which January 1 falls on a different day from one year to the next.

One-World Global Calendar

http://www.zapcom.net/phoenix.arabeth/1world.html

Offering festivals, celebrations, and holidays from ancient and modern cultures around the world, this is an excellent multicultural resource. The calendar is updated weekly.

Ron Smith Oldies Calendar

http://homepage.interaccess.com/~ronsmith/cal.htm

This calendar offers a this-week-in-rock-and-roll-history service, which details the anniversaries of births, deaths, and famous events occurring in that week.

Steffen Thorsen's Calendar Page

http://www.stud.unit.no/USERBIN/steffent/kalender.pl

This page displays a calendar for the current year and offers, in addition, calendars for any year that you specify. You can look up the day of the week on which you were born or find out which weekday will begin the new millenium (Monday, January 1, 2001).

Census

1990 U.S. Census Lookup

http://cedr.lbl.gov/cdrom/doc/lookup_doc.html

Contains links to WWW servers for accessing 1990 census data from tapes.

TIGER Mapping Service

http://tiger.census.gov/

This site, a service of the United States Census, generates detailed maps of anywhere in the United States. Images are large and, because the service actually *creates* the maps while you wait, download times can be slow.

U.S. Gazetteer

http://www.census.gov/cgi-bin/gazetteer

Search engine for retrieving state and local census information from the 1990 census.

Dictionaries & Thesauri

ARTFL Project: ROGET'S Thesaurus Search Form

http://humanities.uchicago.edu/forms_unrest/ROGET.html

The ARTFL (American and French Research on the Treasury of the French Language) Project, located at the University of Chicago, have provided this online version of Roget's Thesaurus. The interface is simple—type in the word you want, and the form will return synonyms and antonyms. This site is among PC Magazine's Top 100 Web Sites.

The Climbing Dictionary

http://www.fm.bs.dlr.de:/dlr/abt_12/climbing/climbing_dict.html

Browse the only dictionary of rock/mountain climbing terms in English, along with translations in German, French, Dutch, Italian, Spanish, Swedish, and Polish.

Dictionary of Cell Biology

http://www.mblab.gla.ac.uk/~julian/Dict.html

Searchable cell biology index. Is the online counterpart to *The Dictionary of Cell Biology, 2nd Ed.*, plus some additions.

The Free On-Line Dictionary of Computing

http://wombat.doc.ic.ac.uk/

Searchable dictionary of computer terms. Along with the definition of the term, the site also provide hypertext links to the terms in the dictionary alphabetically immediately before and immediately after the requested term. Also includes a list of links to other reference sites — some general Internet reference sites, some specifically computer reference sites.

Hacker's Jargon

http://www.tu-graz.ac.at/
C0x811be681_0x0000001f;sk=B41155D9

Dictionary of computer terms, especially those used by hackers. Both browsable and searchable by keyword.

Hypertext Webster Interface

http://c.gp.cs.cmu.edu:5103/prog/webster/

A simple way to look up word definitions on the Web. You type in the word you want, click Look up definition, and, within seconds, the Interface returns the definition of the word. For example, a search on "frontier" brought back the word, broke the word down into its components (fron-tier), and provided the definition.

LC Thesaurus for Graphic Material: Topical Terms for Subject Access

http://palimpsest.stanford.edu/lex/lctgm/lctgm.html

This site is for catalogers, indexers, and researchers looking for subject terms to use when indexing or researching pictures and photographs. It can be both browsed and searched by keyword.

STING software engineering glossary

http://dxsting.cern.ch/sting/glossary-intro.html

Searchable by keyword. In addition to definitions of terms, also provides links to sites with more information about selected term.

The WorldWideWeb Acronym and Abbreviation Server

http://www.ucc.ie/info/net/acronyms/acro.html

As simple as it sounds, this site offers a dictionary of acronyms and abbreviations. You can even offer new acronyms to add to their list or request an acronym definition via e-mail if you cannot access the Web.

English Language

Oxymorons

An *oxymoron* is a pairing of contradictory or incongruous words. For more information about the English language, check out the sites in this section.

bittersweet

idiot savant

good grief

home office

jumbo shrimp

linear curve

liquid gas

nonalcoholic beer

nondairy creamer

old news

same difference

sweet sorrow

war games

working vacation

The 11 Rules of Grammar

http://ucsu.colorado.edu/~giaquint/grammar.htm

Another grammar reference, this site explains the eleven rules (according to the author, these are the most common errors he's seen while grading papers) and offers both correct and incorrect examples of the rules in action.

The American Dialect Society

http://www.msstate.edu/Archives/ADS/

This site, dedicated to the study of North American English, offers information about ADS publications, meetings, and membership. The site also contains an online version of the Society's newsletter, a link to a Gopher site containing an index of American speech, and information about the ADS mailing list.

BritSpeak: English as a Second Language for Americans

http://pages.prodigy.com/NY/NYC/britspk/main.html

Have you ever heard anyone say, "I'll knock you up tomorrow morning"? This statement would be shocking only if you didn't realize that, to the British, the term *knock up* means to awaken someone by knocking on that person's door. This site attempts to clear up many such opportunities for misunderstanding, and provides a dictionary that converts British words and phrases to American and vice versa.

The Collective Nouns

http://www.1rcs.com/collectives/

If a group of fish is called a school, and a group of lions equals a pride, then what is the name of a group of whales? Would you believe a *pod*? This fun site catalogs well over fifty collective nouns, many of them humorous. For example, you might see a colony of penguins, a siege of herons, a bunch of things, or a giggle of girls.

Cool Word of the Day

http://www.dsu.edu/projects/word_of_day/word.html

As you might imagine, this site provides an exercise in vocabulary-building. The page's best feature is that, when the page first appears on your screen, all you see is the word itself. If you don't already know the word's meaning, click the Definition link below the word. The interface also allows you to view past words or even submit a cool word of your own.

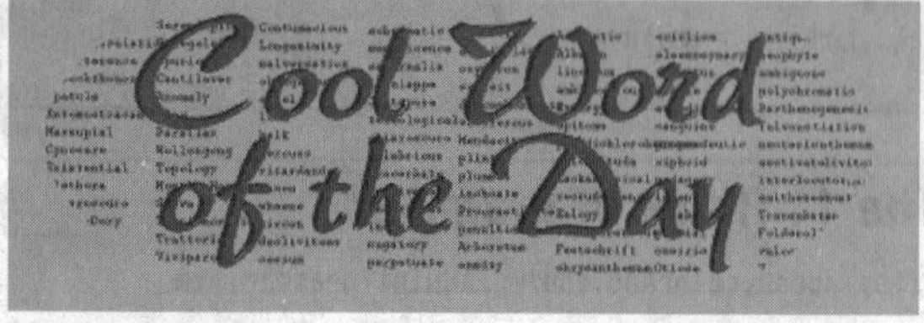

The Electronic *Beowulf*

http://www.uky.edu/ArtsSciences/English/Beowulf/

A project of the British Library and the University of Kentucky, the goal of The Electronic *Beowulf* is to make available, on the Web, access to digitized photographs of an early manuscript of *Beowulf*, one of the earliest surviving works of English literature. This project, in addition to making the manuscript much more widely available for study, would also allow the manuscript to be studied through electronic and computerized methods which would otherwise be impossible.

The Electronic Text Center at the University of Virginia

http://www.lib.virginia.edu/etext/ETC.html

This site contains thousands of texts, in Modern, Early Modern, and Middle English, plus French, German, Japanese, and Latin. Here you will find fiction, science fiction, poetry, theology, essays, histories, and many other types of materials. This site is excellent and thorough. Although a huge number of these texts are freely available, some texts are available only to users at the University of Virginia—the licensors of these texts have not permitted the University to make them widely available.

ENGL 310: History of the English Language

http://engserve.tamu.edu/files/linguistics/ling410/

This page is the Web-based supplement to a course taught at Texas A&M University by Dr. Anthony Aristar, a Professor of English. You will not earn course credit on the Web, but you won't be expected to sit for the mid-term or the final, either. You will, however, learn about the Indo-European and Germanic roots of English and trace the development of English from its Anglo-Saxon beginnings up through its emergence as a world language.

The Etymology of First Names

http://www.engr.uvic.ca/~mcampbel/etym.html

Aaron, Zoe, and all their friends will be interested to learn the origins and meanings of their names at this site, which will also provide plenty of ideas for parents to be.

Grammar and Style Notes

http://www.english.upenn.edu/~jlynch/grammar.html

Quick! What's the difference between affect and effect? Jack Lynch has the answer and he's offered it up on this site, an online guide to the complexities of English grammar. Lynch clearly explains the difference between commonly confused words, defines terms such as dangling participle, and offers his own opinions on a variety of style issues.

The Logical World of Etymology

http://www.phoenix.net/~melanie/thelogic.htm

Melanie (no last name please), the creator of this site, offers an abundance of information about word origins in this site. In addition to explaining how words are created and providing information about Greek and Latin roots and affixes, she answers etymology-related questions that have been e-mailed to her. Recent words included jazz, mafia, Cheyenne, and passion.

Old English Pages

http://www.georgetown.edu/cball/oe/old_english.html

Catherine N. Ball, a linguist at Georgetown University, has developed these pages devoted to the study of Old English. The page contains links to electronic texts, manuscript images, and the historical context of the language. Professor Ball has even included downloadable font packages to display Old English characters that no longer exist in our language.

The On-line Books Page

http://www.cs.cmu.edu/Web/books.html

Over 1,500 English-language books are offered on this site, which you can search or browse by author or by title. In addition, you can browse new book listings or browse by subject. Philosophy, religion, science, computer science, literature, law, and medicine are among the subjects you can browse.

A.Word.A.Day

http://lrdc5.lrdc.pitt.edu/awad/home.html

This is the home page for the A.Word.A.Day mailing list, which sends a new word and its definition to your e-mail box each day.

Word for Word

http://www.peg.apc.org/~toconnor/welcome.html

Another site detailing the origins of words and phrases, Word for Word reprints installments from Terry O'Connor's column of the same name appearing in the Queensland (Australia) *Courier-Mail*.

The Word Page

http://users.aol.com/jomnet/words.html

Build your vocabulary! (Or, to express it another way, augment your lexicon!) This page offers ten new words and their definitions a week. This week's offerings included transcendental, soliloquy, aesthete, and multifarious.

WordNet

http://www.cogsci.princeton.edu/~wn/

A lexical reference work, WordNet is designed to map out the relationships and connections between words and their synonyms. Created by the Cognitive Science Laboratory at Princeton University, this site is being developed as an educational tool for improving vocabulary and reading comprehension.

The WWW Anagram Generator

http://csugrad.cs.vt.edu/~eburke/anagrams.html

This cool site will form an anagram from any word, name, or phrase you type in. For example, the phrase "New Riders," when anagrammed forms the phrases, "Sir, we rend" and "sewn drier," among others.

Etiquette

Dance Floor Etiquette

http://www.apci.net/%7Edrdeyne/flooretq.htm

Provides a diagram of a dance floor with the dance areas outlined (i.e. line dances, flow dances, swing dances, etc.).

Toilet Training: An Online Guide to Urinal Etiquette

http://gpu.srv.ualberta.ca/~msykes/thome.html

The title speaks for itself.

USENET Etiquette

http://unix1.sncc.lsu.edu/internet/usenet/
usenet-etiquette.html

Provides information about politely posting messages to Usenet newsgroups.

Flags

Betsy Ross Homepage

http://libertynet.org/iha/betsy/

Provides information about Betsy Ross, history of the U.S. Flag, pictures of U.S. flags, and links to other flag-related sites. Also has instructions for cutting a five-pointed star in one snip.

The Flag of the United States of America

http://www.icss.com/usflag/

Provides flag etiquette, history of the U.S. flag, text of the Declaration of Independence, National Anthem, and Pledge of Allegiance to the flag. The Pledge is in English, German, and Spanish. Information about obtaining a flag that was flown over the U.S. Capitol. Links to other flag-related sites. Poetry, songs, etc. about the flag.

The Flag-Burning Page

http://www.indirect.com/user/warren/flag.html

Yes, this is the page where you can burn a virtual flag. This site provides information about the proposed Constitutional amendment on flag burning, information on the history of flag-burning, a legal definition of "flag," and information on contacting members of Congress.

Flags of the 19th and 20th Century

http://www.pi.net/~marksens/

Provides pictures of flags, primarily from the Netherlands and surrounding countries, plus a few African countries.

National Flag Foundation

http://www.icss.com/usflag/nff.html

Information about how to become a member of the National Flag Foundation.

Save Old Glory From Flames Home Page

http://www.pic.net/flameout/oldglory/

This site is in response to the Flag-Burning Page. One can add one's name to a list of people that support the Constitutional amendment to outlaw flag-burning. Also has links to other politics-related sites.

Genealogy

Cool Site of the Month for Genealogists

http://www.cogensoc.org/cgs/cgs-cool.htm

The Colorado Genealogy Society sponsors this site, which provides links to sites that meet the following criteria: they are not widely known to genealogists working on the Web, they provide an example of good genealogical work, or they contain valuable information for genealogists.

The Genealogy Home Page

http://ftp.cac.psu.edu/~saw/genealogy.html

This extensive set of pages offers information about maps and geography, communication with other genealogists, a compendium or genealogy databases, a list of other genealogy home pages, and other genealogy resources, both in North America and around the world.

The Genealogy Page

http://ocf.berkeley.edu/~andyneal/g-home.html

This poignant site specializes in genealogy advice for those who lost relatives in the Holocaust, but offers links to other genealogy sites as well.

Genealogy Resources on the Internet

http://www-personal.umich.edu/~cgaunt/gen_int1.html

Chris Gaunt and John Fuller, creators of this site, offer a comprehensive list of genealogy information accessible through mailing lists, newsgroups, Telnet, e-mail, and ftp, Gopher, and World Wide Web sites.

Genealogy Resources on the Internet

http://pmgmac.micro.umn.edu/genealogy.html

Paula M. Goblirsch offers another comprehensive list of Internet resources devoted to genealogical research, plus a collection of German surnames that she is researching.

Roots Surname List Name Finder

http://www.rand.org/cgi-bin/Genea/rsl

This forms-based site contains over 92,000 surnames contributed by over 6,000 genealogists. It enables you to type in any surname and, if a match is found, it will display the surname along with a list of people researching that name.

Treasure Maps: The "How-To" Genealogy Site

http://www.firstct.com/fv/tmaps.html

Offering a wealth of information about researching family history, this site offers tips for newcomers to genealogy and what to do if you "hit a wall" in your research.

Holidays

National Holidays

The following is a list of the United States' national holidays. Visit the sites in this section to learn more about them and other holidays around the world.

New Year's Day	January 1
Martin Luther King Day	Monday closest to January 15
Lincoln's Birthday	February 12
Washington's Birthday	Third Monday in February
Memorial Day	Last Monday in May
Independence Day	July 4
Labor Day	First Monday in September
Columbus Day	Monday closest to October 12
Veteran's Day	November 11
Thanksgiving	Fourth Thursday in November
Christmas Day	December 25

Happy Birthday, America!

`http://banzai.neosoft.com/citylink/usa/`

Offering audio files of Vice President Al Gore and the Star Spangled Banner, this page celebrates the Fourth of July with multimedia, in addition to providing links to important governmental and historical sites.

Christmas around the World

`http://www.christmas.com/christmas.html`

Asia, Europe, Latin America, the Middle East, and the Netherlands are among the regions with Christmas traditions explained on this site. Here you will also learn how to say "Merry Christmas" in over 30 languages and you will find a list of other holidays that fall around the Christmas season.

Chinese New Year

`http://bronze.ucs.indiana.edu/~hyuan/newyear.html`

Because the Chinese New Year is celebrated at a different time each year, this site explains how to determine when the New Year falls, offers a history of the Chinese New Year, and explains its traditions.

Easter in Cyberspace: A Christian Perspective

`http://members.aol.com/REMinistry/devotionals/easter.html`

This page reminds Easter celebrators of the "true meaning" of the holiday. You might not find jelly beans or bunnies, but you will find a collection of links about the death and resurrection of Jesus Christ.

Kwanzaa Information Center

`http://www.melanet.com/melanet/kwanzaa/kwanzaa.html`

Here you'll find reams of information about the background and purpose, symbols, and principles of Kwanzaa, as well as a schedule for Kwanzaa Celebration.

KWANZAA YENU IWE NA HERI (HAPPY KWANZAA)!!!

Passover on the Net

`http://www.melizo.com/holidays/passover/`

This beautifully illustrated page offers the story of Passover, information about the Seder meal (plus recipes), and a collection of downloadable Passover songs in MIDI format. Be aware though that the lavish backgrounds won't show up in all browsers and the graphics might be a memory drain.

Fonts

`http://www.linotype.com/freefont.htm`

Fill out a registration card to receive three cool fonts, product and industry information, and special offers from Linotype-Hell.

World Wide Holidays and Events

http://www.classnet.com/holidays/

This cool, searchable calendar lists the holidays and events celebrated on any given day. You can look up the holidays that fall on the day you access the calendar (April 13 is Songkran Day in Thailand, for example) or you can search the full calendar for a day of your choosing.

The Yom Tov Page

http://www.torah.org/learning/yomtov/index.html

On this page is a collection of links and information about the Jewish holidays.

Libraries

AcqWeb

http://www.library.vanderbilt.edu/law/acqs/acqs.html

This site contains a list of links to information that is especially useful for acquisitions librarians. Some of the links include Telnet links to searchable databases such as OCLC, RLIN, WLN, Dialog, Lexis/Nexis, LOCIS, and HYTELNET; links to Web sites for publishers, vendors, and library associations; links for newsletters and journals; and links to general reference resources.

American Society of Indexers home page

http://www.well.com/user/asi/

Provides links to online resources for indexers, information about conferences and workshops, local chapter meeting and contact information. List of links to various online reference resources such as dictionaries, encyclopedias, thesauri, etc.

Building Digital Libraries on the Web

http://www.texshare.edu/TexShareServices/Professional/digital.html

Provides links to various digital libraries, hardware/software needed to establish digital libraries, and copyright information. This page is helpful for someone wanting to establish a digital library or wanting to keep abreast of the new technologies for digital libraries and other Web searching. Also includes Web searching capabilities.

Celebrate Libraries

http://www.gale.com/gale/cl.html

This site was established for National Library Week and contains information about Log On Day at Gardiner Public Library in Maine, the library of the year in Charlotte, NC, a quiz about libraries and their history, trivia about libraries, a link to "Who Reads What?" which details the reading interests of various celebrities, and information about joining FOLUSA (Friends of Libraries USA).

Christian Classics Ethereal Library

http://ccel.wheaton.edu/

With hundreds of fiction and non-fiction titles, hymns and choral music, and even a study bible, this site offers an extensive collection of excellent spiritual titles, all in the public domain.

Internet Public Library

http://www.ipl.org/

Includes resources for children, teenagers, and adults. The reference center allows one to ask questions of a live librarian (not a computer). The youth services and teen divisions have links to both books and other resources, such as writing contests, college information, science projects, and author question-and-answer sessions. A section is also devoted to information for libraries and other information professionals. Other features include tutorials, an exhibit hall, reading room with browsable full-text resources, links to Web search engines, and a MOO (Multi-User Object Oriented) environment for browsing the library.

Internet Resources for Cataloging

http://asa.ugl.lib.umich.edu/chdocs/libcat/libcat.htm

Contains list of links and detailed information about accessing various Web, Gopher, and Telnet sites especially useful when cataloging library materials.

Librarians' professional resources

http://www.cfcsc.dnd.ca/links/lib/index.html

Provides list of links to other library-related sites, arranged into categories of "indexes," "topics in library science," "types of libraries and collections," and "computers and libraries."

Library Job Hunting

http://tigger.cc.uic.edu/~aerobin/libjob.html

Provides information for library professionals who are searching for a job. Contains links to Web sites for library-related associations, Web and Gopher sites for career information, and addresses for library-related mailing lists.

The Library of Congress

http://www.loc.gov/

Provides access to the Library of Congress online catalog through Telnet searches of LOCIS, Gopher searches of LC MARVEL, the Library of Congress FTP site, and the Library of Congress Z39.50 Gateway. Other databases available for searching include Vietnam Era Prisoner of War/Missing in Action database, Task Force Russia database, Global Legal Information Network (GLIN), THOMAS (full-text legislative information), and the National Digital Library. This site is a must for librarians because it includes valuable information about Library of Congress standards for cataloging, acquisitions, and book preservation; frequently asked reference questions; links to international, federal, state, and local government information; links to Internet search engines and meta-indexes; a link to the U.S. Copyright Office home page; and information about Library of Congress special events and exhibits.

Library Resource List

http://www.state.wi.us/agencies/dpi/www/lib_res.html

This site contains lists of links to other sites, arranged into the categories of Reference Resources, New Sites and Search Engines, Government Resources, Library Sites, Professional Information, and Libraries, the Net and the NII (National Information Infrastructure). Although the site is geared toward libraries and government information, there is still information here that is valuable for anyone doing research on the Internet or just surfing the Net for fun.

National Archives and Records Administration

http://www.nara.gov/

Includes both searchable and browsable services for locating government information via the Government Information Locator Service (GILS). Has links to the Federal Register, the National Archives and Records Administration Library, and the presidential libraries. The presidential libraries' page also includes the addresses, phone numbers, fax numbers, e-mail addresses, and links to the home pages for the presidential libraries. Also has links for geneological research.

OCLC Online Computer Library Center, Inc.

http://www.oclc.org/

Contains information especially useful for librarians and other information professionals. Has links to OCLC documents and forms, a search engine for searching OCLC information, and demonstrations of OCLC services. Actual logon to some OCLC services is available by subscription only.

A Plethora of Web Sites: The Librarian's Meta-List

http://ainet.com/scfl/plethora.htm

Table of contents consists of a couple dozen very broad categories which then provide links to relevant sites. Extremely useful as a starting place for Web browsing or research. Some of the categories include libraries, law, health and medicine, music, travel, government, education, and religion.

School Libraries on the Web: A Directory

http://www.libertynet.org/~bertland/libs.html

Contains a browsable list of school library Web pages, arranged alphabetically by state. Also contains links to school libraries in Australia, Canada, Japan, and Sweden.

Smithsonian Institution Libraries

http://www.sil.si.edu/

Includes links to the various Smithsonian Museums, a search engine for locating information within the Smithsonian, information about visiting Washington, DC, information about how to become a member of the Smithsonian, a map showing the locations of most of the Smithsonian Museums, and a browsable shopping area.

Smithsonian Institution Libraries

"...for the increase and diffusion of knowledge..."

Understanding Call Numbers

http://www.hcc.hawaii.edu/education/hcc/library/
callno.html

This site explains how to read Library of Congress classification call numbers to locate materials on the shelves. The location prefixes information is specific to the Honolulu Community College Library, but the call number descriptions and Library of Congress classification tables are useful for locating materials in any library that uses LC call numbers (as opposed to Dewey Decimal system).

WWW Library Directory

http://www.albany.net/~ms0669/cra/libs/libs.html

Click on a country name to be presented with a list of links to libraries in that country. Most of the countries currently represented are European (both East and West) and North American, although there are a few Asian, Middle Eastern, and South American countries also. Also has links to other library-related resources.

Maps

Color Landform Atlas of the United States

http://fermi.jhuapl.edu/states/states.html

This service, offered by the John Hopkins University Applied Physics Laboratory, provides topographical and county maps for every state in the U. S. plus links to map lists at Yahoo, City Net, and Virtual Tourist.

Country Maps from W3 Servers in Europe

http://www.tue.nl/europe/

This clearinghouse site offers a clickable image-map that lists the countries of Europe. Clicking a country's flag takes you to a map of that country. Maps vary in quality (the United Kingdom's map mainly listed universities, not cities or regions, while the link to the European Union didn't even offer a map), but all of Europe is represented. The pages offer English descriptions in addition to commentary in the country's native tongue.

International Map Trade Association

http://www.maine.com/maptrade/Welcome.html

Offers links to member stores' Web sites and a geographical directory of map and travel book retailers.

Mapmaker, Mapmaker, Make Me a Map

http://loki.ur.utk.edu/ut2Kids/maps/map.html

Although this site is ostensibly aimed at children, adults and kids alike will enjoy this site's presentation of how cartographers create maps.

MapQuest

http://www.mapquest.com/

This remarkable but graphics-intensive site offers a number of map-related services. First, MapQuest has an interactive atlas that enables you to find virtually any street address or business in the continental United States. TripQuest will plot out a route from any city in the U.S. to any other. MapQuest offers Java applets and an interactive "walk" through their site.

National Atlas Information Service (of Canada)

http://ccm-10.ccm.emr.ca/

The NAIS offers for sale at this site both conventional and digital maps of Canada.

The Perry-Castañeda Library Map Collection

http://www.lib.utexas.edu/Libs/PCL/Map_collection/
Map_collection.html

This collection, based at the University of Texas at Austin, contains over 230,000 maps from all over the world. Be aware that the electronic version of the maps can be quite large—many of them are 300 KB or larger. Download times can be slow and the maps might tax your browser. The Frequently Asked Questions page offers tips for viewing these maps.

Rare Map Collection at the Hargrett Library

http://scarlett.libs.uga.edu/darchive/hargrett/maps/
maps.html

The Hargrett Library, at the University of Georgia Library, offers over 800 rare maps from the16th through the early 20th century. Early maps depict the New World, while others chart Colonial and Revolutionary America, the Civil War, and Georgia's Revolutionary period, cities, and coastal areas. File sizes are large and downloads are slow.

National Atlas of Canada on SchoolNet

http://www-nais.ccm.emr.ca/schoolnet/

This site, offered in both English and French, offers demographic maps based on Canada's languages and aging population, maps of wetlands and natural hazards, an atlas of Canadian communities, and an interactive geography quiz.

VIBE's World Map

http://pathfinder.com/vibe/vibeworld/worldmap.html

VIBE, an online magazine on Time-Warner's Pathfinder site, offers this world map page. Clicking on the time zone colors brings up the local time for that area plus a list of Web sites of cities in the region.

Measurements

Conversion Factor Table

http://www.uwosh.edu/students/wallip27/convert.html

The interface is a bit clumsy, but the information is thorough. Here's how it works: You want to know how many centimeters are in 10 meters. You find meters in the table, see that the conversion factor (or c.f.) is 100 (100 centimeters equal 1 meter), and multiply that number by 10. Ten meters equal 1000 centimeters.

Engineering, Scientific Unit Converter

http://www.webcom.com/~legacysy/convert2/convert2.html

This forms-based tool will convert values in a number of categories: acceleration, angle, area, current, force, inductance, mass, power, time, torque, velocity, volume, and many others.

Measurements Converter

http://www.mplik.ru/~sg/transl/

Select from a list of measurement types that includes weight, volume, length, area, speed, pressure, temperature, circular measure, and time; the script will convert miles to kilometers, ounces to metric tons, and centuries to seconds.

Miscellaneous Reference

The Better Business Bureau

http://www.cbbb.org/cbbb/

Consumers and businesses alike will find reams of valuable information on this site, which provides membership information, offers tips on how and when to file a complaint, explains what a reliability report is and how to obtain one, lists online publications for consumers and businesses, and links to local Bureaus.

Bow Brummell: Where Cyberians Learn the Manly Art of Tying a Bow Tie

http://www.tcf.ua.edu/bowtie/

This humorous page offers diagrams and instructions on how to tie a bow tie. Arguably the most noteworthy thing about the diagrams is that the man in the picture is clearly *not* tying his own tie.

Central Notice

http://www.notice.com/

Billing itself as the place to find information that you aren't aware of not knowing about (as opposed to information that you don't know, but you realize that you don't know it—make sense?), Central Notice posts listings of product recalls, class action lawsuits, and missing children while also assisting with consumer problems and providing lists of holidays, both important and trivial.

Clocks and Time

http://glen-ellyn.iit.edu/~clocks/clocks/clocks.html

More than you ever wanted to know about how time is measured and clocks and watches are made. This site offers articles about clockmaking and watchmaking; links to books, journals, and museums dedicated to clocks and watches; bulletin boards that discuss timepieces; and national and international agencies for time.

The Consumer Information Center

http://www.pueblo.gsa.gov/

With a browsable catalog, consumer news on topics like car- and home-buying and children's health, lists of publications, and links to other consumer sites, the CIC's site is another valuable consumer resource.

The DataStar Information Retrieval Service

http://www.rs.ch/www/rs/datastar.html

This service of Knight-Ridder Information provides a searchable index to over 400 databases culled widely from sources such as automotive industry data; import/export trade statistics; pharmaceutical, biomedical, and healthcare information; and European news organizations.

Disaster Information Network

http://www.disaster.net/

Offering information about current and historical disasters, this site covers natural disasters, fires (both natural and manmade), and acts of terrorism.

Find-A-Grave

http://www.orci.com/personal/jim/index.html

Listing the final resting places for hundreds of celebrities and VIPs, this macabre site offers notable graves geographically or alphabetically, pictures of famous graves, and links to other tomb-related sites.

Gray Ghost: The Links You Use Everyday

http://www.whytel.com/ftp/users/pwirth/index.htm

A cornucopia of references is what this site offers. Standard, office, scientific, World Wide Web, computer industry, and government and military references, plus links to maps and geographical sites, and museums are all located here.

Internet Nonprofit Center

http://www.human.com/inc/

This excellent and extensive grouping of links to non-profit sites offers a search engine that will locate almost any U.S. charity, provides links to home pages for non-profit groups, and even offers a library of rankings of charities and a "Donor Defense Kit" to help separate the wheat from the chaff when charities contact you for donations.

Jumble & Crossword Solver

http://odin.chemistry.uakron.edu/cbower/jumble.html

Stumped by a scrambled word game or a crossword puzzle? This simple interface allows you to either enter the jumbled letters (for example, "tbona") or the word you need with question marks in the spaces you can't fill (for instance, "ba?o?") and this page will return a word or list of words that answers your query. In the first example, this page unjumbled "tbona" into "baton" and, in the second, provided "bacon," "baron," "baton," and "bayou" for "ba?o?."

Morse Code and the Phonetic Alphabets

http://www.soton.ac.uk/~scp93ch/refer/alphabet.html

Contains the phonetic alphabets in British English, American English, international English, international aviation English, Italian, and German and the Morse code equivalent for all letters plus some punctuation marks.

Morse Code Translator

http://www.soton.ac.uk/~scp93ch/refer/morseform.html

Translates typewritten Morse code (i.e. dots and dashes) into text and text into Morse code.

MRX - Morse Receive and Transmit Training

http://www.ozemail.com.au/~jwsamin/

Download a copy of MRX from this Web site. MRX is a software program designed to provide training in Morse code. Software system requirements are DOS 4.0, 286 PC, sound card or PC Speaker, VGA monitor, and a joystick port.

My Virtual Reference Desk

http://www.refdesk.com/

This site bills itself as a "one-stop reference for all things Internet." Although it is mainly a collection of links, it maintains a thorough and comprehensive database of references on a vast array of subjects

The Nobel Foundation

http://www.nobel.se/

In addition to offering a list of present winners, this official site presents a searchable database for past winners. Unfortunately, however, you cannot browse the list of winners or see biographical information about each winner. This site does, however, offer a bio of Alfred Nobel and discusses his motivations for founding the Prizes, in addition to explaining how Nobel Laureates are nominated and selected.

The Nobel Prize Internet Archive

http://mgm.mit.edu:8080/pevzner/Nobel.html

Listing both the 1995 Nobel Prize winners (announced in October) and all previous winners in every category, this site also links to biographical information about many of the winners. The interface is much easier to navigate than the Noble Foundation's official site.

The Obituary Page

http://catless.ncl.ac.uk/Obituary/README.html

This morbidly fascinating page offers death hoaxes, in addition to the lifespans of famous figures from literature, movies, music, politics, sciences, sports, radio and TV, and visual arts.

The Official Wicked Hair-Dyeing Page

http://www-leland.stanford.edu/~mizraith/dyeing.html

The authors, a brother and sister at Stanford University, provide a great deal of information here about the equipment needed to dye hair; some dos and don'ts for those who wish to dye; variables such as natural hair color, shampoos, conditioners, heat, and moisture; permanent versus semipermanent dyes; and products that they have tried.

On-Line Reference Works

http://www.cs.cmu.edu/Web/references.html

Carnegie Mellon University provides this list of links to dictionaries, Internet resources, geographical references, bibliographies, and legal and government resources.

The Reporter's Internet Survival Guide

http://www.qns.com/~casey/

Patrick Casey, an Associated Press reporter in Oklahoma, created this online catalog of reference materials for reporters on a deadline. Despite that, this is a valuable reference for anyone needing access to a wide variety of information.

Research-It!

http://www.iTools.com/research-it/research-it.html

By using forms you can search through dictionaries and thesauri; find acronyms or quotations; translate words between English and French and English and Japanese; find maps, area codes, and 800 numbers; look up currency exchange rates and stock quotes; and even track packages through the United States Postal Service, UPS, and FedEx.

The Scout Report

http://rs.internic.net/scout/report/

Net Scout Services publishes this weekly report (via e-mail and the Web) cataloging new and newly discovered resources and tools available on the Internet. Aimed at researchers and educators, The Scout Report offers its archives on the Web for both browsing and searching.

Standard Industrial Classifications (SIC) Index

http://www.wave.net/upg/immigration/sic_index.html

Browsable list of the 1987 edition of the SIC index (latest available). List is arranged alphabetically by subject.

"Ten Codes"

http://www.jaxnet.com/~habedd/10codes.html

Lists the official meanings of the 10 codes used by police departments.

THOR+: The Virtual Reference Desk

http://thorplus.lib.purdue.edu/reference/index.html

This information-rich site at the Purdue University Library provides references to many Web resources including the following: government documents, information technology, dictionaries and language reference, phone books and area codes, maps and travel information, science data, time and date information, and ZIP and postal codes.

Tipping

http://www.cpmc.columbia.edu/homepages/gonzalu/tipping.html

This page offers general guidelines for how much to tip in certain situations: restaurants, hotels, valet parking, train stations and airports, cruise ships, and the like.

Today's Fun Fact

http://www.actwin.com/csn/WardoWorld/410.html

Compiled from different sources, this site offers one new bit of trivia every day.

The WWW Virtual Library

http://www.w3.org/hypertext/DataSources/bySubject/Overview.html

This Web-based library offers hundreds of subjects in science, mathematics, art, literature, music, culture, museums, religion, spirituality, sport, finance, and transportation. Truly eclectic, some of its more unusual categories include beer and brewing, paranormal phenomena, roadkill (!), whale watching Web, and yeasts.

UTLink: Resources by Subject

http://library.utoronto.ca/www/subjects.html

The University of Toronto Library maintains this site, which offers lists of resources, at U of T and beyond, in academic fields ranging from African and Black Studies to Women's Studies.

The World Fact Book 1995

http://www.odci.gov/cia/publications/95fact/index.html

Browsable list is arranged alphabetically by country. Contains the text of the CIA World Fact Book for 1995, including the appendices and reference maps. The information provided for each individual country includes a map of the country with major cities marked and other information broken down into the categories of geography, people, government, economy, transportation, communications, and defense forces.

World Population

http://sunsite.unc.edu/lunarbin/worldpop

This site offers an estimate of the current world population at the time you access it.

World Population Figures

http://www1.tip.nl/users/t865190/index.html

This excellent and extensive site clearly presents population data for every region of the world. You can find here as well lists of the 25 countries with the largest surface area, the 25 countries with the largest population, and the 25 largest cities in the world. The data are presented in tables, which means that not all browsers can display the information.

Patents

European Patent Office

http://www.epo.co.at/epo/

Contains information about the European Patent Office, information about obtaining a European patent, and links to other patent information sites.

National Association of Patent Practitioners

http://www.napp.org/

Provides links to Web sites for international patent offices, U.S. patent laws and court rulings, intellectual property organizations and newsletters, patent search engines, and specific patent firms. Also has membership information for joining the National Association of Patent Practitioners.

Source Translation & Optimization (STO) Internet Patent Search System

http://sunsite.unc.edu/patents/intropat.html

Searchable by either class/subclass code or patent number. Provides a browsable list of the U.S. Patent and Trademark Office (PTO) classification system to determine the class/subclass code. Search returns patent number, title, and year of issue for all patents that meet the search criteria.

U.S. Patent and Trademark Office

http://www.uspto.gov/

Provides both search and browse capabilities for the U.S. Patent Bibliographic database and the AIDS Patent database, information on ordering copies of patents, links to legal information relating to patents, and links to other related Web sites.

Wacky Patent of the Month

http://colitz.com/site/wacky.htm

Clicking on the patent number of the winning patent will give you a complete description of the patented device along with all the figures that accompanied the patent when it was applied for. Also available are the prior winners of the "Wacky Patent of the Month," from September 1995 to the present.

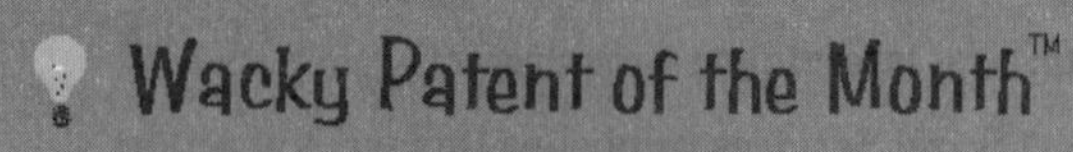

Phone Numbers

555-1212.com Area Code Look-Up

http://www.555-1212.com/aclookup.html

Searchable by city and/or state name for U.S. or Canadian area codes, or browsable by area code or state name. Returns area code and corresponding city/state. Area code links lead to a business look-up directory that is browsable by category or searchable by business name.

Airline Toll-Free Numbers and Websites

http://www.princeton.edu/Main/air800.html

Browsable list of both domestic and international airlines with corresponding 800 numbers and links to Web sites if available.

American Computer Resources, Inc.

`http://www.the-acr.com/cntrycd.html`

Provides browsable list of international country and city telephone codes, plus instructions for dialing overseas (outside of the United States) phone numbers. Also includes a link to "Telephone Directories on the Web."

The AmeriCom Long Distance AREA DECODER

`http://www.xmission.com/~americom/aclookup.html`

Input city, state, and/or country to receive the area or country code and AmeriCom rates. Input the area code, country code, AmeriCom per minute rate, and/or AmeriCom in state rate to receive the city, state, or country and the AmeriCom rates. Also has information about AmeriCom international business opportunities.

AT&T Internet Toll Free 800 Directory

`http://www.tollfree.att.net/dir800/`

Browsable by category, or searchable by company name, city, state, and/or category. Also includes information about AT&T.

BigBook

`http://www.bigbook.com/`

Searchable by business name, category, city, and/or state for a quick search. Search can also be narrowed by using the ZIP code, area code, street name, or map location. Search returns name, address, and telephone number of businesses matching search criteria. Option is available for seeing business location on a map.

BigYellow

`http://s10.bigyellow.com/`

Search for businesses by city, state, business name, category, address, and/or ZIP code. Returns full address including ZIP+4 and telephone number for all businesses matching the search criteria. Also includes links to other world-wide telephone directories and Web search engines, business infor-mation for setting up Web sites, and advertising information for advertising at this BigYellow site.

Central Source Yellow Pages

`http://www.telephonebook.com/`

Searchable by category, company name, phone number, and/or business opportunity. Includes links for international yellow pages, dictionaries, newspapers, and other online resources. Contains browsable list of Internet service providers throughout the United States, although this list is not complete. List is browsable by state name only.

The Internet 800 Directory

`http://inter800.com/`

Searchable by keyword and state. Returns businesses matching the search criteria and their corresponding 1-800 telephone numbers, up to a maximum of 100 businesses.

Mutual Fund Company Directory

`http://www.cs.cmu.edu/~jdg/funds.html`

Lists mutual fund companies from the United States, Bahamas, Canada, Germany, Great Britain, Hong Kong, Hungary, and Luxembourg. Browsable list of companies is arranged alphabetically by country and includes the telephone number (usually a 1-800 number) of the mutual fund company and a link to their Web site, if available.

National Telephone & Communications (NTC) Tele-Locator

`http://www.natltele.com/form.html`

Searchable by state name, area code, city code, telephone number prefix, telephone number, or country code (for countries outside the United States). Returns city, state, area code, and/or telephone number prefix as applicable.

Glue Sticks

`http://www.craftnet.org/adtech/atsurvey.htm`

Are you a glue guru? Do you want to be? Test you glue knowledge with a quiz (lots of hints provided) to win a packet of glue sticks.

PC Phone List

http://foundation.mit.edu/cgi-bin/search-phone-list

Provides technical support phone numbers for computer hardware and software. Enter the name of the company or the software, and the program returns all technical support telephone numbers (and bulletin board services if available) that match the search terms.

Period.Com Airlines!

http://www.period.com/airlines/airlines.shtml

Browsable list of domestic, foreign, and shipping airlines with their 800 numbers. Provides links to airline Web sites where available.

PhoNETic

http://www.soc.qc.edu/phonetic/

Enter a phone number to receive all possible letter combinations for that phone number, or enter letters to receive the phone number corresponding to those letters. Also includes information about obtaining phonetic telephone numbers and an explanation for why calculator and telephone keypads are different.

Switchboard

http://www.switchboard.com/

Search for either businesses or people. For people searches, enter last name, first name, city, and/or state to return name, address, and phone number of all people matching the search criteria. For business searches, enter the company name, city, and/or state to return the name, address, and phone number of all businesses matching the search criteria. Registered users may also personalize and update their own listings.

Telephone Directories on the Web

http://www.c2.org/~buttle/tel/

List of links to telephone directories all over the world, plus one or two lines about each directory detailing what it covers, what language it is in, and whether it is very good or not. Also includes a few other phone-related links, plus a link to an art gallery and a link for international television schedules.

What does your phone number spell?

http://www.best.com/~jgro/phoneSearch.shtml

Enter a 3-digit prefix, a 7-digit phone number, or some letters. Returns real words (not just letter combinations) that match the given numbers; returns the phone number that matches the letters if letters are given as the search criteria.

World Telecom Directories

http://infolab.ms.wwa.com/wtx/

Select country name from list, then type in company name. Returns list of companies and corresponding fax numbers. This address is for locating fax numbers for Asian and Pacific region countries.

World Yellow Pages Network (wyp.net)

http://wyp.net/

U.S. and Canadian businesses are searchable by company name and state, phone number, or ZIP code. The white pages are searchable by name, phone number, or keyword. Searches return all entries matching the search criteria, up to a maximum of 100 returns. The white pages also contain search capabilities for locating e-mail addresses of individuals. In addition to providing yellow and white pages searches, this site also allows businesses and individuals to create their own home page for this site and to update it at their convenience.

Yellow Pages Online, Inc.

http://www.ypo.com/

Searchable by heading keyword, company name, or brand name. Returns company name and phone number for all entries that match the search criteria.

YellowNet

http://www.yellownet.com/

Searchable by geographic area (city, state, county), company name, and/or heading keyword. Returns name, address, and phone number for all entries that match the search criteria.

Postal Information

Geographic Nameserver

http://www.mit.edu:8001/geo

Index is searchable by ZIP code or city name. Results returned include city, county, state, country, and ZIP code. Latitude, longitude, population, and elevation are returned if available. If more than one city matches the search criteria, then information on all matching cities is returned.

National Address and ZIP+4 Browser

http://www.semaphorecorp.com/

Searchable by company name, street address, city, state, and ZIP code. Returns closest matches along with ZIP+4 code. After information is returned, option is given to browse addresses in the same geographical location. Also includes list of state code abbreviations.

United States Postal Service

http://www.usps.gov/

Includes information about stamp releases, pictures of stamps available, searchable index for ZIP+4 codes, state and address abbreviations, preferred addressing methods, size standards for mail, postage rates for both domestic and international mail delivery, history of the USPS, news releases, calendar of events, and other postal-related information. The business section of this Web site includes information both for the mailing needs of businesses and for the business needs of the USPS. Businesses wishing to sell products to the USPS will find a purchasing manual and information about selling products to the USPS at this Web site.

The Zipper

http://www.stardot.com/zipper/

Input a five-digit ZIP code to obtain the name, address, and phone number of either the Congressional representative or Senators for that ZIP code. Search returns name, Washington office address, phone number, fax number, and e-mail address (if available) of representative or Senator. A link to the representative's or Senator's home page is provided if available. Also includes a couple of links to other sites for Congressional information.

Quotations

Advertising Quotes

http://www.utexas.edu/coc/adv/research/quotes/

Jef Richards, an Adverising Professor at the University of Texas at Austin, has collected here a set of quotations about the world of advertising. The Index includes over 60 subcategories, ranging from Advertising Is... to Wearout. Highlights along the way include Billboards, Critics, Evil, Fantasy & Dreams, Honesty, Manipulation, Morality & Ethics, Puffery, Sex, and Value.

Ash's Choice Quotations

http://www.he.net/~morgoth/quotes/index.html

A list of dozens of quotations sorted by last name.

Bartlett's Familiar Quotations

http://www.columbia.edu/acis/bartleby/bartlett/

The Ninth Edition of John Bartlett's famous book, published in 1901, has been converted to HTML format and posted to the Web by Project Bartleby, an

extensive Web-based literature library established by Columbia University.

The "Best of" Edward Gibbon's *Decline and Fall of the Roman Empire*

http://www.alumni.caltech.edu/~zimm/gibbon.html

This set of quotes, some quite lengthy, have been posted to the Web by Mark Zimmerman, who finds Gibbon's work to be quite relevant to current events.

Bon Mots from the Supermodels

http://www.sils.umich.edu/~sooty/thoughts.html

This witty site of quotations from the glamorous proves once again that you don't need to be an intellectual to be internationally famous.

Conventional Wisdom: Selected Quotations Illustrating the Illusions of Popular History

http://nickel.ucs.indiana.edu/~mtmurphy/cw.html

This set of quotations debunks popular notions about history and society. Among the subjects are The Fall of the Roman Empire, Columbus and the Spanish Conquest, Pocahontas, Our Founding Fathers, A Day That Will Live in Infamy, Lucky Lindy, and The March of Science. For example, the page's author uses Abraham Lincoln's own quotations to prove that he once supported slavery.

The Curmudgeon Quotelist

http://www.lm.com/~rww/

If a curmudgeon is a cantankerous person, as the dictionary says, then this site will be a curmudgeon's dream. Be sure to check out the reasons the Web author found these quotes worth including.

Dave's Searchable Quote Database

http://cornelius.cc.vanderbilt.edu/users/lilly/cgi-bin/search.cgi

This forms-based database contains over 6,500 quotes. You can search them by subject—say, *death* or *taxes*—or you can select to have the form randomly draw a quote from the database.

Don's Doctor Who Interesting Quote Archive

http://www.mit.edu:8001/people/dasmith/Who/Quotes.html

This frames-based archive is accessible only on Netscape Navigator 2.0. The quotes originated on the British low-tech science fiction show *Doctor Who*. Topics include art, history, the human race, love, politics, and other pithy topics.

Frank Lloyd Wright Quotes

http://marin.org/parks/flw.quotes.html

Read on as the master architect expounds on architecture, government, nature, and life. This site is part of a larger Frank Lloyd Wright page offered by the Marin County (California) Convention and Visitors Bureau.

Labor Quotes Page

http://www.igc.apc.org/laborquotes/

LaborNet, a community of labor unions and activists using the Internet to communicate, gathered together this compendium of quotes about labor-related issues. Subjects include solidarity, strikes and other acts of civil disobedience, working conditions, negotiations, hope, attitudes of the rich and famous, oppression, politics and politicians, women in the labor movement, and class and inequality.

The Official Internet Quayle Quote List

http://www.xmission.com/~mwalker/DQ/quayle/qq/
quayle.quotes.html

Okay, maybe we should finally be leaving our former Vice-President alone, but when the material he's provided is so funny, how can you refuse to enjoy it? This collection is divided into a number of subcategories, making Quayle's comments on issues such as International Affairs easy to locate. Ironically, though, the Webmaster here has inadvertantly included some "Quayle-isms" of his own: In lamenting Quayle's departure from public life, for example, the Webmaster consoles himself with, "We do have his book to look forward to as well as his bid for the presidency in 1994."

Outriders of Reality Reference Manual & Travel Guide

http://www.sols.on.ca/stuff/outriders.html

According to David Harvie, the "Chief Scout" of Outriders of Reality, this oddball listing of quotes

"…is a collection of errant pieces of knowledge, quips of non-conventional wisdom found in graffiti, e-mail taglines, bumperstickers, buttons, and snatches of conversions heard while standing in fast-food checkout lines." Subjects are covered with irreverent humor.

Quotations

http://www.lexmark.com/data/quote.html

This collection of over 5,000 quotations is grouped into recent quotes, advice, great leaders, proverbial wisdom, sarcasm, annoying proverbs, malapropisms, random visions, poetry, aphorisms, definitions, miscellaneous or anonymous quotes, and selections from William Shakespeare and comedian Steven Wright. This site also maintains an extensive collection of links to other quotation pages.

Quotations About Libraries and Librarians

http://www.nlc-bnc.ca/ifla/I/humour/author.htm

The International Federation of Libraries Associations and Institutions has put together this selection of quotes from authors, statesmen, and celebrities regarding the importance of libraries.

Quotations of William Blake

http://www.mcs.net/~jorn/html/blake.html

This page offers, in somewhat of a hodgepodge, a list of quotations by the radical poet.

Quotes, Quotes, and More Quotes

http://www.sccs.swarthmore.edu/~dansac/quotes.html

Offering quotes from movies and song lyrics, this site also includes quotes about sex, music, love, and God.

Welcome to the Introspect Library

http://www.lasertone.com/~rc/il1.html

Here are gathered quotes written to inspire and motivate. The page is billed as "a place for quiet inspiration and meditation."

Zappa Quote of the Day

http://www.fwi.uva.nl/~heederik/zappa/quote/

Offers a new random quote each day from one of the geniuses of rock music.

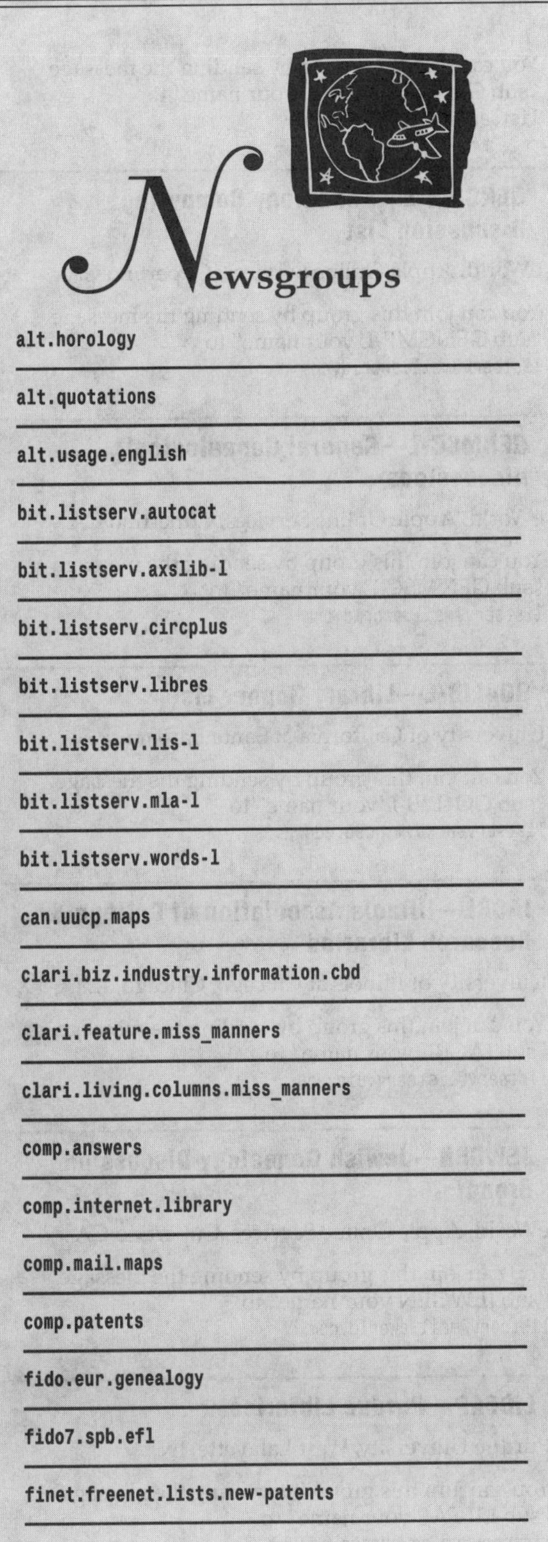

Newsgroups

alt.horology

alt.quotations

alt.usage.english

bit.listserv.autocat

bit.listserv.axslib-l

bit.listserv.circplus

bit.listserv.libres

bit.listserv.lis-l

bit.listserv.mla-l

bit.listserv.words-l

can.uucp.maps

clari.biz.industry.information.cbd

clari.feature.miss_manners

clari.living.columns.miss_manners

comp.answers

comp.internet.library

comp.mail.maps

comp.patents

fido.eur.genealogy

fido7.spb.efl

finet.freenet.lists.new-patents

ie.news.map

mi.map

misc.answers

misc.education.language.english

news.answers

pnet.community.library

pnet.rec.genealogy.announce

pnet.rec.genealogy.talk

sci.answers

slac.library.hepths

slac.library.ppf

slac.library.ppf.string

sci.answers

soc.genealogy.african

soc.genealogy.australia+nz

soc.genealogy.benelux

soc.genealogy.computing

soc.genealogy.french

soc.genealogy.german

soc.genealogy.hispanic

soc.genealogy.jewish

soc.genealogy.marketplace

soc.genealogy.medieval

soc.genealogy.methods

soc.genealogy.misc

soc.genealogy.nordic

```
soc.genealogy.slavic
```

```
soc.genealogy.surnames
```

```
soc.genealogy.uk+ireland
```

```
soc.libraries.talk
```

```
stgt.maps
```

```
talk.answers
```

```
tamu.electronic.library.resources
```

```
tnn.internet.librar
```

```
tw.bbs.lang.english
```

```
uk.net.maps
```

```
za.net.maps
```

Listservs

3MPLUS-LIST—3 Million Library Volumes

State University of New York at Buffalo

You can join this group by sending the message "sub 3MPLUS-LIST your name" to `listserv@listserv.acsu.buffalo.edu`

GEDCOM-L—Genealogical Data Communications Specs

You can join this group by sending the message "sub GEDCOM-L your name" to `listserv@listserv.nodak.edu`

GEN-MEDIEVAL—Medieval Genealogy Discussion List

eWorld, Apple Online Services, Cupertino CA

You can join this group by sending the message "sub GEN-MEDIEVAL your name" to `listserv@mail.eworld.com`

GENCMP-L—Genealogy Computing Discussion List

eWorld, Apple Online Services, Cupertino CA

You can join this group by sending the message "sub GENCMP-L your name" to `listserv@mail.eworld.com`

GENMSC-L—General Genealogical Discussions

eWorld, Apple Online Services, Cupertino CA

You can join this group by sending the message "sub GENMSC-L your name" to `listserv@mail.eworld.com`

GO4LIB-L—Library Gopher List

University of California at Santa Barbara

You can join this group by sending the message "sub GO4LIB-L your name" to `listserv@ucsbvm.ucsb.edu`

IACRL—Illinois Association of College & Research Libraries

University of Illinois at Chicago, Chicago, IL

You can join this group by sending the message "sub IACRL your name" to `listserv@listserv.uic.edu`

JEWGEN—Jewish Genealogy Discussion Group

eWorld, Apple Online Services, Cupertino CA

You can join this group by sending the message "sub JEWGEN your name" to `listserv@mail.eworld.com`

LIBFAP—Purdue Libraries

Purdue University, West Lafayette, IN

You can join this group by sending the message "sub LIBFAP your name" to `listserv@vm.cc.purdue.edu`

LIBREF-L—Discussion of Library Reference Issues

You can join this group by sending the message "sub LIBREF-L your name" to `listserv@listserv.kent.edu`

LINES-L—LifeLines Genealogical System

You can join this group by sending the message "sub LINES-L your name" to `listserv@listserv.nodak.edu`

ROOTS-L—ROOTS-L Genealogy List

You can join this group by sending the message "sub ROOTS-L your name" to `listserv@mail.eworld.com`

TFTD-L—Thought for the Day

You can join this group by sending the message "subscribe TFTD-L" to `LISTSERV@tamvm1.tamu.edu`

TJLDESK—TJL Reference Desk

University of Missouri-St. Louis

You can join this group by sending the message "sub TJLDESK your name" to `listserv@umslvma.umsl.edu`

TJLREF-L—Thomas Jefferson Library Reference List

University of Missouri-St. Louis

You can join this group by sending the message "sub TJLREF-L your name" to `listserv@umslvma.umsl.edu`

RELIGION & PHILOSOPHY

Atheism

Atheist Manifesto

http://206.126.103.21/dan/atheist-manifesto.html

Jeffrey Clark's popular twenty-three point argument against placing one's faith in the Almighty. Has link to alt.atheism.

International Atheistic Secular Humanist Conspiracy [Canada Division]

http://infoweb.magi.com/~godfree/index.html

Provides links to areas of interest to humanists, atheists, agnostics, and freethinkers. Encourages the investigation of a diversity of viewpoints. Features cartoons and On Line Baptism Removal.

The Secular Web

http://freethought.tamu.edu/

A page of interest to atheists, agnostics, humanists, and freethinkers. Links to a variety of Internet resources, including Usenet newsgroups, IRC channels, and other Web pages. The library contains several documents, historical and otherwise.

Bible Study & Christian Research

Bible Gateway

http://www.calvin.edu/cgi-bin/bible

This award-winning site provides a search form for the Bible and handles many common translations. Lets you conduct searches and output verses in French, German, Swedish, Tagalog, Latin, or English.

ECOLE Institute

http://www.evansville.edu/~ecoleweb/

This scholarly site seeks to create a hypertext encyclopedia of the works of early Christian church authors. Covers such "isms" as docetism, mithraism, and stoicism, and their impact on early Christianity, as well as other topics of theological interest. There is also a glossary and links to other sites related to early Church history.

Holy Bible—King James Version

http://www.iadfw.net/webchap/kjvb/

A complete text of the King James Version of the Bible in HTML 3 format. Each chapter is a separate HTML file that provides quick access to any verse. Verses can be referenced by the URL of the file followed by a # and the verse number. There is also a 13,857-word concordance that is hyperlinked to the Bible.

Logos Research Systems

http://www.logos.com/

An electronic publishing firm that offers CD-ROMs of biblical translations, ranging from the King James to Revised Standard Version. Also includes many other titles.

New Media Communications

http://www.iac.net/~dlature

Seeks to gather resources to enable seminaries and theological organizations to bring theological education to all who desire it. Provides links to schools of theology, as well as sociological and hypertext studies.

Our Daily Bread

http://www.gospelcom.net/rbc/odb/

Presents a short, daily devotional guide for Christians. Includes an archive page for access to previous months' devotions.

RTS's Totally Righteous Home Page for Paul the Apostle

http://www.magicnet.net/rts/paul.html

If you think research plus religion equals "Dullsville," you need to visit this site and get to know the Apostle Paul—as you never knew him before! Written, compiled, and designed by graduate students of Dr. Reggie Kidd at Reformed Theological Seminary in Orlando, Florida, these pages explore Paul's cultural background, ministry, letters (from a Perfectly Practical Perspectival Approach), theology, and impact on world culture.

Scrolls from the Dead Sea

http://sunsite.unc.edu/expo/deadsea.scrolls.exhibit/intro.html

This exhibit from the Library of Congress is a great scholastic site. The published text of the Quamran scrolls, commonly known as the Dead Sea Scrolls.

These works have been extensively studied by Bible scholars. The site offers a link to the Expo Bookstore where a printed copy of the exhibition catalog can be purchased.

University of St. Michael's College, Faculty of Theology

`http://www.utoronto.ca/stmikes/index.html`

Contains the APS Research Guide to Resources for Theological and Religious Sites—an award-winning guide created by St. Michael's graduate students.

Buddhism

Buddha's Four Noble Truths

1. Suffering is always present in life.

2. Desire causes suffering.

3. Suffering ends when desire is overcome.

4. Freedom from life is achieved by nirvana (release from the cycle of birth, death, rebirth). Eightfold Path leads to nirvana.

Eightfold Path

1. Right understanding

2. Right thought

3. Right speech

4. Right action

5. Right livelihood

6. Right effort

7. Right awareness

8. Right concentration

Access to Insight

`http://world.std.com/~metta/`

Focuses on supporting and deepening Buddhist meditation practice. Emphasizes teachings from the Theravada Buddhist tradition, but represents other Buddhist traditions as well.

Buddhist Scripture Information Retrieval

`http://www.mahidol.ac.th/budsir/budsir-main.html`

Promotes the BUDSIR database and search engine for researching the Pali cannon of the sayings of Buddha.

DEFA Home Page

`http://sunsite.unc.edu/dharma/defa.html`

DharmaNet Electronic Files Archive. Contains the online Buddhist libraries maintained by DharmaNet International. Offers links to the Dharma Newsstand, Buddhist Info Web, BBS listings, and more.

International Meditation Centres (in the Tradition of Sayagyi U Ba Khin)

`http://www.webcom.com/~imcuk/welcome.html`

Offers information on 10-day Vipassana meditation courses as well as a newsletter, Theravada Buddhist publications, and images of pagodas.

International Research Institute for Zen Buddhism

`http://www.iijnet.or.jp/iriz/irizhtml/irizhome.htm`

This site contains, among other things, the largest searchable collection of Zen Buddhist primary text materials on the Internet. Also has a searchable database of Zen centers around the world.

Journal of Buddhist Ethics

`http://www.cac.psu.edu/jbe/jbe.html`

The *Journal of Buddhist Ethics* is a free online publication that promotes academic research in Buddhist ethics. Offers current and back issues. Includes a number of articles in Adobe Acrobat format.

New Kadampa Tradition

`http://www.webcom.com/~nkt/`

A Mahayana Buddhist organization. Aims to preserve and promote the essence of Buddha's teachings in a form suited to the Western mind and way of life. Offers information on books, meditation programs, and a directory of NKT centers.

Nichiren Shoshu Buddhism

`http://www.primenet.com/~martman/ns.html`

Offers a look into this Japanese school of Buddhism that emphasizes the Lotus Sutra. Includes a list of temples and articles from the The Nichiren Shoshu Monthly.

Shin Buddhism Network

http://www.aloha.net/~rtbloom/shinran

Award-winning scholarly site. Contains English and Japanese articles on Shin Buddhism, as well as a list of links to Buddhist resources. Includes a self-study course.

Shin Buddhist Resource Center

http://www.well.com/user/shinshu/SBRC/

Includes an online library of text and a bookstore, in cooperation with the Buddhist Bookstore in San Francisco.

Tiger Team Buddhist Information Network

http://www.newciv.org/TigerTeam/

The Tiger Team Buddhist Information Network is a not-for-profit online service dedicated to serving the worldwide Buddhist community. Offers online files, conferencing, and shopping. Includes links to Buddhist resources and to the table of contents for the CyberSangha Journal.

Zen Garden

http://www.nomius.com/~zenyard/zenyard.htm

A fun, multimedia introduction to the Zen mind. Features Koans such as, "If you want to realize such a thing, you must be such a person. Once you are such a person, why worry about such a thing?" Updated weekly.

Zen Mountain Monastery

http://www1.mhv.net/~dharmacom/

Features Questions for Cybermonk, Buddhist resources, a list of worldwide affiliates, Zen art, a Zen environmental studies center, meditation, and a journal.

Zen@SunSITE

http://sunsite.unc.edu/zen

Created as an online home for the Gateless Gate, a collection of koans. New koans presented daily. Features other Zen sites, including links to the Zen Hospice Project and to Zen and Taoist texts.

Christian Denominations

American Baptist Churches Mission Center Online

http://www.abc-usa.org/

Contains information about local American Baptist churches, and American Baptist Green Lakes Conferences, as well as national, international, and educational ministries.

Anglicans Online

http://infomatch.com/~haibeck/anglican.html

Provides information about the Anglican church (Church of England). Includes Anglican news, as well as links to related North American and world sites. Offers other links that cover resources, Synod news, schools, newsgroups, and mailing lists.

Association of Vineyard Churches

http://groke.beckman.uiuc.edu/AVC/avc-home.html

This site supplies information about the Vineyard churches around the world, such as its statement of faith, values, and priorities. There's a directory of Vineyard churches for you to explore, as well as a directory of e-mail addresses of those who attend Vineyard churches.

Baptist Faith and Message

http://www.utm.edu/martinarea/fbc/bfm.html

Contains statement of faith adopted by the Southern Baptist convention.

Canada Toronto East Mission

http://www.goodnet.com/~rob

Sponsored by the Church of Jesus Christ of Latter Day Saints. Provides former missionary e-mail addresses, information about upcoming reunions, mission history and experiences, and access to Toronto resources. Lots of information about Canada too!

Catholic Online

http://www.catholic.org/index.html

Bills itself as the "world's largest and most comprehensive Roman Catholic information service." Provides message centers, forums, and research materials related to Roman Catholicism. There is also information about Catholic organizations, dioceses and archdioceses, publications, software, and doctrines.

East 7th Street Baptist Ministry— Graffiti

http://soho.ios.com/~dwna/grafhome.html

Aims to foster faith, hope, and love in the Lower East Side of Manhattan, New York, through ministries to help meet the spiritual, social, educational, and economic development needs of the community.

Evangelical Lutheran Church in America Home Page

http://www.elca.org/

Contains news and pointers to areas of interest to the Evangelical Lutheran denomination. You can browse through the home pages of local Evangelical Lutheran-affiliated churches.

Famous Unitarian Universalists

http://www.execpc.com/~biblogic/cvuufamo.html

Provides a list of well-known contemporary and historical figures who have been involved with the Unitarian Universalist movement and offers links to sites that provide information about these people.

Harvest Online

http://www.harvest.org/

Provides the history of the Harvest Christian Fellowship. Includes dates for upcoming Harvest Crusades, along with information about the "A New Beginning with Greg Laurie" broadcasts.

Lutheran Church-Missouri Synod Home Page

http://tcm.nbs.net/~cc/lcms/

The unofficial home page for the Missouri Synod of the Lutheran Church. Provides membership information and other statistics. Contains many useful FAQs, including "What is a Lutheran?" and "What do Lutherans believe?" Also online is a variety of reference material useful to Christians and links to other Christian sites.

Orthodox Christian Page

http://www.ocf.org/OrthodoxPage/

What is Greek Orthodox Christianity all about? This site tells you and provides links to European and American Orthodox sites. There are pages covering scriptures and liturgy, icons, prayers, readings, and links to other resources.

Orthodox Ministry ACCESS

http://goa.goarch.org/access/

Provides information about Orthodox Christianity; the Greek Orthodox Archdiocese; the Orthodox Ministry ACCESS Bulletin Board System (accessible via the Internet); Orthodox Christian resources; Orthodox Christian organizations; and more.

Presbyterian Church USA

http://www.pcusa.org/

Contains news from the Presbyterian News Service, reports and proceedings of the General Assembly, mission news, religious humor, and the PresbyNet conferencing system. There also are links to other Presbyterian-related sites, such as the Web pages of local churches.

Religious Society of Friends WWW site

http://www.quaker.org/

Offers a list of links about Quakers on the Web. Includes links to sites focusing on Quaker schools, journals, The American Friends Service Committee, geneaology sites, Quaker history, newsgroups, and more.

SBC "Maverick" Home Page

http://www.io.com/~tarrytwn/SBC/sbcmain.htm

This unofficial site of the Southern Baptist Convention contains information about this denomination, links to Yahoo and GOSHEN lists of local church home pages, as well as links to an SBC bulletin board and SBC-related sites.

SDANet

http://www.sdanet.org/

This is the site for the Seventh Day Adventist (SDA) WWW server. Links to Gopher sites, SDA institutions and Bible Study forums can be found here.

United Church of Christ

http://www.apk.net/ucc

Provides information and demographics concerning The United Church of Christ. Topics include news, ministries, missions, educational outreach, hymns, as well as ecumenical concerns.

United Pentecostal Church International

http://www.prairienet.org/community/religion/fire/upc.html

Serves as an unofficial page for this denomination. Contains information about Pentecostalism and the Pentecostal Church on both regional and general levels.

Christian Media

Baker Book House

http://www.bakerbooks.com/

Baker Book House publishes approximately 200 Christian books a year in the categories of fiction, non-fiction, children's books, academic textbooks, and references. It also sells BakerBytes reference software. Published authors include Ruth Bell Graham and Robert Schuller, among others.

Christian Articles Archive

http://www.garlic.com/rfwilson/archive/

Contains articles for Christian newsletters, religious periodicals, brochures, and sermon illustrations. Also provides information about using Internet e-mail conferencing for Christian teaching and discipleship.

Christian Book Connection

http://www.xmission.com/~seer/Christian-Book/index.html

Online bookstore that features nearly 30,000 items. Offers a selection of books, Bibles, software, and research, all of which can be ordered at 20% to 50% off the retail price.

Christian Classics Ethereal Library

http://ccel.wheaton.edu/

Presents classic Christian literature in electronic format. Contains works from St. Augustine to Wesley. There are also links to a catalog of church music and to the World Wide Study Bible.

Christian Computing Magazine

http://www.website.net/~ccmag/

Online edition of *Christian Computing Magazine.* Contains current as well as back issues of the printed magazine. Provides subscription information and links to Christian resources and literature as well.

Christian Cyberspace Companion

http://www.bakerbooks.com/ccc/

This site promotes the *Christian Cyberspace Companion*—a hard-cover "handbook for Christians using the Internet" that is available at many Christian bookstores. Also included is a Christian Internet directory and links to various Christian information sources and denominational sites.

Christian Poetry

http://www.pennet.net/resident/hoffman/crossway.html

Publishes works of Christians who want to share the gospel of Jesus Christ through the medium of poetry. Presently building a biographical index of Christian poets and welcome contributions.

Electronic Book of Common Prayer

http://listserv.american.edu/anglican/bcp

Contains the sacraments, prayers, liturgies, and other rites used in the Anglican and Episcopal Churches. Also contains the Psalms.

Gospel Films, Inc.

http://www.gospelcom.net/gf/

Distributes Christian videos in a range of subjects, from children's tapes to historical/biblical and true life stories. Also features a monthly Bible crossword, Christian games, articles, and news.

GROKNet—Comedyatre and Resources

http://www.ozemail.com.au/~grok/

Presents an Australian Christian two-man comedy theatrical team. Includes information on GROK's performance history, reviews, and schedules.

ICMC Home Page

http://www.xc.org/icmc/

The International Christian Media Commission's vision is to proclaim the Good News through all the types of existing media. This site provides an electronic magazine members can use to browse directories. Maintains a list of links to resources for Christians.

Jesus Film Project

http://www.mdalink.com/JESUSproject/index.html

Presents the Campus Crusade for Christ's Jesus Film project. Includes well-designed graphics pages. Offers links to other Campus Crusade for Christ sites in the United States and abroad.

Minister's Reference Center

http://www.rr-mrc.com/

Serves as a subscription site from which you can download other ministers' sermons for a fee each month. Offers a free trial period as well as a discount for lay members and students.

National Religious Broadcasters

http://www.mnsinc.com/nrb/

The NRB strives to promote ethical standards in all aspects of broadcasting and exists to safeguard free access to religious broadcasting. You can get information about NRB conventions and publications here, as well as issues of concern to the NRB.

Saint Mary's Press

http://wwwsmp.smumn.edu/

This award-winning site features St. Mary's Press' online catalog of Catholic-related materials for young people. Their Prophets of Hope series is aimed at Hispanic youths. You can order materials from this site, as well as access links to other Christian publishers.

Serious Developments—Christian Software Catalog

http://www.viper.net/clients/serious/

A good source for Christian software, featuring hundreds of products, including Bible Study software, clipart, games, and religious studies. You can select from a choice of free software, just for visiting this Web page. There are also links to other Christian sites from this page.

This Week in Bible Prophecy

http://www.niagara.com:80/~twibp/

This Web site supplements a television program on Bible prophecy that is aired over the Trinity Broadcasting Network in the United States and over Vision TV in Canada. You can receive transcripts of recently aired programs through this site, as well as read magazine articles and select videos and books.

Tien Dao Christian Media

http://www.webcom.com/~tiendao/tiendao.html

Focuses on Chinese Christianity. Offers software and an online bookstore (includes text in both Chinese and English). Interesting fact: Because of the Chinese government's strict laws about Bible distribution/importation, 60 million Christian homes in China do not have Bibles.

Wire

http://www.roehampton.ac.uk/link/wire/

Presents an ecumenical Christian communications periodical, published electronically using the Acrobat PDF format. Includes issues of interest to Christian computer users.

Christian Ministries & Organizations

Christian Recovery Connection

http://www.fileshop.com/personal/iugm/

Enables you to participate in a 12-step recovery program for abuse, addiction, or grief. Offers links to other recovery programs on the Web that offer support from a Christian point of view.
Christian Singles Online
http://www.miami.net/Two4Christ/

A Christian dating service online. Offers a six-month membership that entitles you to at least 10 matches with a compatible Christian single (for a fee).

Computerized AIDS Ministries

http://hwmin.gbgm-umc.org/CAM/index.html

"There's more to living with AIDS than AIDS" is the motto of this site for people and the friends/families of people who have AIDS or are HIV-positive. Here, an emphasis is placed on love and caring for AIDS patients and their families. You will find inspiring stories, memorials, a bulletin board service, and many links to other AIDS-related sites.

Family Research Council

http://www.townhall.com/townhall/FRC/

This organization seeks to reaffirm and promote the traditional family unit and the Judeo-Christian value system. Many online publications through which you can search, on such topics as child abuse, parental rights, home schooling, to name but a few.

Greater Grace World Outreach

http://www.ggwo.org/

An international ministry with links to associated ministries including: The Grace Hour International Radio Show, missionary outreaches, and the Maryland Bible College and Seminary. This site also contains daily faith thoughts as well as information about upcoming conferences.

InterVarsity Christian Fellowship

http://www.gospelcom.net/iv/

The aim of this site is to promote collegiate fellowships and "develop students who employ Biblical values." There are links to affiliated chapters on various campus. Also offers online ordering for books published by InterVarsity Press.

Jesus Army

http://www.tecc.co.uk/jesusa/

What is the Jesus Revolution? Find out on this award-winning British-based site. Contains an electronic magazine and many pictures.

Jesus Fellowship Home Page

http://jf.org/

A family church, a Christian teaching center, a covenant community, a worldwide outreach center, a campus ministry, a neighborhood Bible fellowship, and much more. Links to Miami Christian University, where you can earn theological degrees online.

Life and Faith Network

http://www.telos.ca/lf/index.html

Membership in this network enables you to access a group of conferences for people interested in discussing their faith and how it affects their lives.

Lutheran Marriage Encounter

http://www.pic.net/~speed/lme.html

Focuses on providing married couples the opportunity to examine their lives together. Contains links to marriage encounters sponsored by other denominations and organizations.

Monastery of Christ in the Desert

http://www.christdesert.org/pax.html

Truly one of the most beautiful Web sites out there! The Benedictine monks of this monastery will help you design and illuminate your home page, and if theirs is any indication, they do an inspired job!

National Association of Evangelicals

http://nae.goshen.net/

The NAE is composed of 42,500 congregations across the United States that subscribe to the NAE's statement of faith. The intent of the NAE is to provide cooperation in subsidiary ministries such as the World Relief Corporation. Site contains resolutions, press releases, and the NAE statement of conscience.

Promise Keepers Unofficial Home Page

http://www.whitedove.com/pk/

Promise Keepers is a nationwide ministry "calling men to reconciliation, discipleship, and godliness." This site provides information about the ministry's aims, beliefs, and history. Included are the seven Promises or commitments that a Promise Keeper makes. There are links to regional PK Web pages and schedules of upcoming PK meetings.

Renewal Ministries: De Colores and Ultreya

http://www.seas.smu.edu/~jackson/communities/

Provides information on various faith-renewal weekends, such as Chrysalis and Teens Encounter Christ, led by lay people and clergy. Also provides information on Kairos weekends—a program for prison inmates.

St. Louis Life News

`http://www.afn.org/~slli/`

Presents pro-life news and information, including opinion pieces and links to pro-life and pro-abortion sites.

Tough Guys

`http://basix.com/~ps91/`

Testimonies of drug addicts, convicted criminals, and former gang members who radically turned their lives around after giving themselves to Christ.

Web Chapel—Prayer Request

`http://web2.airmail.net/webchap/`

Web Chapel is a mission to cyberspace, providing Web access to Christian writings and sermons, an online Bible study and devotional material, information on how to become a Christian, and prayer requests.

Christian Philosophy

Answers in Action Home Page

`http://www.power.net/users/aia/`

Seeks to train Christians to "adopt and promote a Christian world view in every area of their lives." Features book reviews, information on contemporary issues, the Bible, Christian apologetics, and cults.

APOLOGIA—To Offer a Reason

`http://diakonos.hum.utah.edu/philosophy/religion/apologia/`

Focuses on a reasoned defense of the Christian faith and ethics. Presents a positive Christian world view.

In the Footsteps of the Lord

`http://www.xensei.com/users/Angel/Home/CR.html`

Created by a Christian from India who is studying at the University of Houston, this site offers testimonials, articles, and many Christian resource links.

Project Wittenberg

`http://www.iclnet.org/pub/resources/text/wittenberg/wittenberg-home.html`

This award-winning site provides the thought of Martin Luther online. Plans to accumulate all of Luther's work, along with that of other theologians.

Christian Resources

Brother Mark's Christian Material

`http://www.tit.fi/~mark/Christian/`

Provides a collection of links to Christian sites and resources. Offers a diversity of links that include humor, magazines, history, Christian organizations, Christian home pages, and theology. Provides some material in Finnish, but most in English.

Christian Connections

`http://tcm.nbs.net/~cc/cchome.html`

Aims to inspire and educate the Christian community in online resourcing and communication. Offers reference materials, Web page storage/development training, and direct dial-in for the northwest part of the state of Washington. Offers many indexed Christian reference lists, such as a job bank, as well as an index of Web sites relating to Lutheranism.

Christian Resource Network

`http://www.cresnet.org`

This award-winning site contains hundreds of documents, including Christianity, cults, missions, evangelism, and pastors' sermon notes. Also features a wide selection of Christian shareware including electronic Bibles, church management software, an online Bible, Christian educational software, and games.

GOSHEN Internet Christian Resource Directory

`http://www.goshen.net/`

GOSHEN stands for Global Online Service Helping to Evangelize Nations. Its goal is to provide free access to Christian resources on the Web. It provides a site for Christian organizations and church-related businesses to add their home pages to the Web with no storage fees. Supplies access to the GoSearch search engine for Christian resources.

Not Just Bibles

`http://www.iclnet.org/pub/resources/christian-resources.html`

An incredibly vast collection of Christian resource materials provided for Christians in search of material on "Classical Christianity." Among the myriad of links are mail-based services, Gopher servers, Christian College Web sites, electronic journals, bulletin boards, Usenet newsgroups, and much, much more.

Creation/Evolution

Answers About Evolution

http://www.rt66.com/diamond/cre_answ.html

An in-depth response to the questions posed at another page devoted to Creation Science. The questions are answered in a polite, fair manner, making the page a pleasure to read for anyone interested in the creation/evolution debate.

Center for Scientific Creation

http://www.indirect.com/www/wbrown/

Here you can read the full text of Dr. Brown's book *In the Beginning: Compelling Evidence for Creation and the Flood* and place an order for the print edition. This a very well put together book that has been generously provided for online use.

Creation Science Home Page

http://emporium.turnpike.net/C/cs/

A site that provides arguments for creationism and against evolutionism. Poses questions to evolutionists. Contains a list of recommended books on the subject of creation and a list of creationist bulletin boards.

Creationism Connection

http://members.gnn.com/DWReynolds/Creation.html

A wealth of information for creationists. This page provides synopses of creationist books, lists other creationist sites and newsgroups, and maintains a list of creationist organizations sorted by state.

Evolution vs. Creation Science

http://web.canlink.com/ocrt/evolutio.htm

Explains the differences between the various theories of creationism and evolution. Examines what the Bible has to say about creation, how creation scientists believe the Earth was formed, and how evolutionists might interpret the Bible.

Talk.Origins Archive

http://earth.ics.uci.edu:8080/origins/faqs.html

A large collection of FAQs generated by the Usenet newsgroup talk.origins. The site maintains FAQs on creationism, evolution, flood geology, catastrophism, and more. The collection is basically an argument for evolutionism.

Cults

A-Z of Cults

http://www.guardian.co.uk/observer/cults/a-z-cults/index.html

A list of cults, each with a corresponding entry. Entries include a brief synopsis of the cult, reasons to join, reasons not to join, and the bottom line.

AFF Cultic Studies

http://www.csj.org/

Studies psychological manipulation and cultic groups, and aims to assist those who have been victims of such. Books and periodicals such as *Cultic Studies Journal*, *Cult Observer*, and *Young People & Cults* are available for order online.

Cults

http://www.the700club.org/cbn/teach/cults.html

A teaching sheet for Christians on the subjects of cults and cultism. Provides scriptural references and information on how to recognize a cult.

Cults 'R Us

http://www.mayhem.net/Crime/cults1.html

This "hit list" from the pages of the Internet Crime Archives gives general information about a number of cult figures whose cultish practices included murder, human sacrifice, and suicide.

Destructive Cults

http://www.algonet.se/~teodor/Cults/welcome.html

Good general information about cults, without going into the various differences between cults. Contains lists of cult characteristics, signs a person might be involved in a cult, recruitment tactics, and the consequences of becoming a cult member.

.ex-cult Archive

http://www.ex-cult.org/

Contains general information about cults, archives of cult-related Usenet groups, information about specific cults, and a list of addresses for ex-cult support groups. Also includes a list of books that are suggested reading. This is a very informative page.

Jehovah's Christian Witnesses

http://www.eskimo.com/~jcw/index.html

An analytical view of the beliefs of Jehovah's Witnesses. Contains many informative articles, including "A Short History of the Watchtower Organization," "Tips on Dealing with the Witnesses," and "Jehovah's Witnesses a Cult?" The articles are intelligently written and will provide timely information for current, past, or potential members of the group.

Jehovah's Witnesses

http://www.magna.com.au/~tony/j_w/

Contains information about the Witnesses from an eight-year member of the church. Read a basic overview of what Jehovah's Witnesses believe and their feelings about the cross.

Loki Cult Web Page

http://www.memoria.com/loki/

A page for those who profess to worship Loki, the "boogeyman of Norse mythology." Features a variety of articles on Loki worship from "Lokasenna: The Flighting of Loki from the Poetic Edda" to "Loki the Fool."

Ms. Guidance on Strange Cults

http://www.t0.or.at/msguide/devilgd1.htm

A plethora of links to all sorts of cult subjects. Several cult categories are addressed, including generic magick, paganism, freemasons, Gnostics, and many more.

Sacrespace

http://www.sound.net/lordvrtigo/

The home of Tribe Eros, an extremist sport freestyle religion, on the Net. This cult strives to attain apotheosis, Godhood, and immortality. Read their lengthy manifesto and find out what their views are on psychedelic drugs, self-realization, and other religions.

Waco Never Again

http://www.mainelink.net/~mswett/

A comprehensive site about David Koresh and the Branch Davidians. Contains many pictures of Koresh, quotes from Koresh, tracts and letters written by Koresh, and a list of strange coincidences between David Koresh and Jesus Christ.

Hinduism

Bhagavad Gita

http://www.cc.gatech.edu/gvu/people/Phd/Rakesh.Mullick/gita/gita.html

For students of Hinduism's most revered scripture, this site offers the Bhagavad Gita in the original Sanskrit (requires a PostScript viewer, such as Ghostscript). Also offers Arnold's complete English translation.

Global Hindu Electronic Network

http://rbhatnagar.csm.uc.edu:8080/hindu_universe.html

Rich site including complete texts of major Hindu scriptures. Contains the alt.hindu newsgroup, information on publications, Hindu festivals, and links to Jain, Buddhist, and Sikh dharmas. Also has pictures of famous saints.

Hinduism

http://www.geocities.com/RodeoDrive/1415/indexd.html

An award-winning one-stop overview of the diverse world of Hinduism. Has links to detailed descriptions of the Veda and Vedic literature, Hinduism's secular source. Also discusses Sanskrit, the language of nature, and the main Hindu gods.

Hinduism Today Home Page

http://www.HinduismToday.kauai.hi.us/ashram/htoday.html

A Hindu family newspaper online. Provides an index of issues, along with subscription information. Explains vegetarianism, Vedas, and non-violence.

Kundalini Research Foundation, Ltd.

http://www.renature.com/krf/

Concerned with the Kundalini Paradigm, an offshoot of Tantra Yoga and Shaivism. Center for scholarly study of the "serpent energy" and its relationship to higher consciousness. Founded by Gopi Krishna.

Spirituality, Yoga, and Hinduism

http://www.geocities.com/RodeoDrive/1415/index1.html

A gentle introduction to Hinduism, Yoga, Kundalini, and eastern spirituality. Preaches renunciation and meditation.

Islam

CyberMuslim Information Collective

http://www.uoknor.edu:80/cybermuslim/

Provides information and resources regarding Islam worldwide. Offers links to the HyperQur'an project. Includes information on Islamic culture, schools, computing services, bookstores, and digital activism.

Ibrahim Shafi's Page in Islam

http://www.wam.umd.edu/~ibrahim/

Rich in links focusing on the cornerstones of Islamic religious life. Connects to Muslim organizations, texts, ftp, Gopher sites, newsgroups, and other resources. Also offers links to Muslim countries. Great starting point for study of Islam.

Islam

http://www-leland.stanford.edu/~yusufali/islam/index.html

Many introductory essays. Includes the Shi'ite encyclopedia and information about the Ahlul Bayt. Features a daily verse from the Qur'an and a daily saying that represents Islamic principles.

Islam's Home Page

http://www.utexas.edu/students/amso/

A valuable Islamic resource containing articles about various Islamic issues including the Renaissance of Islam, women in Islam, and Jesus in Islam. An English translation of the Holy Qur'an and several Islamic prayers can be found at this site, as well as a collection of Islamic images.

Islamic Society of Wichita

http://www.southwind.net/~masjid

For the serious researcher. Multiple databases for the Qur'an, mosques, prayer timings, and numerous other topics of interest to Muslims. International in flavor.

Online Islamic Bookstore

http://www.sharaaz.com

Provides information about the books, tapes, and software. Offers links to Islamic sites and book reviews of important books. "To encourage the Muslim community to read again. To assert the importance of spiritual knowledge especially in this modern age."

Salaam Ailaikum

http://www.wco.com/~altaf/altaf.html

Contains Islamic and social justice poetry, articles, links, and stories. Also contains several articles by the Islamic author, the late Dr. Ali Shariati.

WAMY IslamNet (World Assembly of Muslim Youth)

http://www.cais.com/islamic/index.html

Presents links of interest to students and practitioners of Islam. Includes sounds, magazines, and the Fiqeh database online, among other resources.

Jainism

Jain Studies

http://www.dmu.ac.uk/~pka/guides/jain.html

Web site of De Montfort University. Provides a starting point for people looking for resources on the Internet for Jainism, a religion of non-violence and avoidance of greed. Offers many links to resources.

Jain World Wide Web Page

http://www.wavefront.com/~raphael/jain/jain.html

Overviews Jain resources on the Web. Describes its Jain mailing list and presents its archives. Offers links to Gopher sites, ftp sites, Web sites, organizations, books and periodicals.

Financial Column

http://www.stretcher.com/dollar/index.htm

The Dollar Stretcher is a weekly online column that can be sent to you free of charge. Learn how to maximize your family finances without sacrificing your quality of living.

Judaism & Messianic Judaism

A–Z of Jewish & Israel-Related Resources

http://www.ort.org/anjy/a-z/

Links to a wide variety of Jewish topics, organizations, and resources can be found at this site. The links are organized alphabetically for easy access.

Aish Ha Torah Discovery

http://j51.com:80/~jrsflw

Presents a Jewish adult-education seminar called "Discovery." Provides information ranging from the basics of Judaism to the latest research by mathematicians and computer specialists on the existence of hidden codes in the Bible.

Chabad Lubavitch in Cyberspace

http://www.chabad.org

Offers information pertaining to Chabad philosophy and Chassidic Judaism. Includes Kosher recipe and children's links, multimedia, listserv, and Gopher resources.

Jerusalem One WWW Network

http://www.jer1.co.il/

Calls itself "the most popular Jewish and Israel information source on the Internet." Contains Aliya information, Torah and Judaic studies, a Jewish calendar of events, current news and views from Israel and the world's largest Jewish software, and a clip art library.

Jewish Federation/Jewish Exponent

http://www.libertynet.org/~exponent/index.html

The Jewish Federation of Greater Philadelpha has existed since 1901 to serve Philadelphia's Jewish citizens. The Jewish Exponent is the online version of this Philadelphia newspaper that features articles of interest to Jews. This site contains lists of Jewish organizations and referrals in the Philadelphia area.

Jewish on the WELL

http://www.well.com/user/ari/jewish/jewish.html

Contains local religious and cultural information for Jews in the San Francisco area. There are links to the San Francisco Jewish Film Festival home page, and klezmer music pages here.

Jewish Theological Seminary

http://www.jtsa.edu/

Represents this conservative seminary online. Provides a wealth of resources and links to conservative Jewish synagogues and institutions.

Jewishnet

http://jewishnet.net/

Offers a list of Jewish-related sites. Offers links to Gopher sites, home pages, libraries, ftp sites, and provides information on Jewish newsgroups and mailing lists.

Jews for Jesus Home Page

http://www.jews-for-jesus.org/index.html

Serves as a means to finding Jewish Christians. Contains documents on Messianic Judaism, along with a music and concert schedule and a fun quiz.

Judaism and Jewish Resources

http://shamash.org/trb/judaism.html

Quite possibly the most complete source of Jewish information and Jewish-related links on the Web. Lists of links include media, singles groups, communities, newsgroups, reading lists, and museums, as well as commerce sites.

Menorah Ministries

http://rainbow.rmii.com/~menorah

Menorah Ministries is a Messianic Jewish resource and referral site. Offers information and articles regarding the Messiah, the Biblical Jewish roots of Christianity, and Israel. There is an "Ask Pastor Reuben" section that answers pertinent questions about Messianic Judaism, such as "Does a Jew stop being Jewish when he/she believes in Jesus?"

Messianic Jewish Alliance of America

http://www.mjaa.org/

Established in 1915 for Jews who believe Yeshua (Jesus) is the Messiah, the MJAA is the largest association of its kind in the world. This site contains information on the MJAA's mission, purpose, and ministries. There are also links to other Messianic Jewish sites.

National Jewish Committee on Scouting

http://shamash.nysernet.org/scouts/

Offers boy scouting opportunities for Jewish youth. Also offers information on scouting and links to other Jewish youth resources.

Shamash

http://shamash.org/

This award-winning site run by the Jewish Internet Consortium offers links to various Jewish religious organizations ranging from Hillel to the World Zionist Organization. Includes FAQs pertaining to various facets of Judaism.

Shtetl, Yiddish Language and Culture Home Page

http://sunsite.unc.edu/yiddish/shtetl.html

"Shtetl" means "small town" in Yiddish. This site aims to be a virtual small town on the Web. Provides information on Yiddish culture, as well as resources that point towards a wide range of links—ranging from recommended books to kosher recipes.

Society Hill Synagogue of Philadelphia

http://www-leland.stanford.edu/~nadav/shs.html

An independent, conservative egalitarian synagogue that offers numerous programs in all aspects of Jewish religious and cultural life. Includes detailed descriptions, a brochure, a monthly newsletter, and some nice graphics.

World ORT Union

http://www.ort.org/

Serves as a host site to ANJY (A Network for Jewish Youth), The Jewish Quarterly, and other Jewish resources. Exhibits on this server are of special interest to young people.

Yaohushua, the Genuine Messiah

http://metro.turnpike.net/Y/yaohush/index.html

This site, from Jerusalem, contains information about the original, archaic Hebrew names of the Creator and the Messiah, Yaohushua. Also includes files on various doctrinal beliefs. Topics covered include: salvation, health, wealth, love, family, marriage, success, and deliverance.

Miscellaneous Religion

Baha'i Resources on the Internet

http://www.bcca.org/srb/resources.html

A rich trove of links and information for those new to the eclectic and young religion Baha'i. Complete coverage of foundational and institutional texts. Covers IRC fellowship.

The Bastard Son of the Lord

http://www.trog.com/jesus/

The home page of Jesus Christ, as maintained by Steve. Jesus visits daily and leaves messages in his "Messiah Log." Site features lists of people that are going to heaven and hell, a 3D stereogram of a nude Jesus, and a downloadable version of Jesus' birthday song, "Spank Me, Jesus." Warning—this page is a bit on the blasphemous side.

The Church of the SubGenius BRAIN TOOLKIT AND SURREALITY REBOOT

http://sunsite.unc.edu/subgenius/

An official home page for a bona fide bogus religion. Founded by the fictional J.R. "Bob" Dobbs, this church believes in the promotion of "slack" at all costs, and the appeasement of the Subgenius god of wrath. Eternal salvation guaranteed or triple your money back.

CyberINDIA: India at your Fingertips

http://www.cyberindia.net/cyberindia/links/i1religi.htm

A component of CyberINDIA focusing on the varied religions of the land of spiritual receptivity. Features links to all the main eastern religions.

Free Daism

http://www.he.tdl.com/~fdac/

Presents Free Daism, the "ancient, eternal, and always new religion of self-transcending God-Realization," based on the teaching of Adi Da (Da Free John). Information on books and other publications.

Friends of Osho

http://earth.path.net/osho/

Introduction to the work of Osho (Bhagwan Shri Rajneesh), popular and controversial teacher of Tantra Yoga.

Haqqani Foundation Home Page

http://www.best.com/~informe/mateen/haqqani.html

Offers a look into the teachings and precepts of Sufism. Offers many pages of information, pictures, and links intended to spread Sufi teachings of the brotherhood of man. Focuses on Sufi leader Shaykh Muhammad Nazim al-Haqqani.

Hare Krishna Home Page

http://www.webcom.com/~ara/

Official ISKCON site, detailing the religion of Krishna Consciousness founded by A.C. Bhaktivedanta Swami Prabhupada. Identifies spirit as primary and matter as secondary.

Israelite Handbook

http://www.interport.net/~barzel

Serves as the base of operations on the Internet for blacks and Latinos who want to forge a new cultural and religious identity as Hebrew Israelites. Discusses such topics as Islam, Christianity, atheism, Afrocentricity, drugs, and slavery.

Logictarian Christian Home Page

http://www.geopages.com/CapitolHill/1205

Focuses on the quest for the meaning of life. Offers a blend of Christianity, Shintoism, martial arts, and science. Also serves as a division of the UFG/ECD, Inc., a Canada-based non-profit research body. Oversized text makes for difficult reading.

McChurch

http://mcchurch.org/

Over 29,713 saved! The place to go when you need a "Happy Meal" for your eternal soul. Join the Rev. Dr. O.L. Jaggers, D.D. Litt.D. Phd., Miss Velma, and the Holy McDonna as they make McWorship.

Pagan Pages

http://www.eor.com/pages

Provides free advertising, announcements, and networking for Pagan (witchcraft and nature worship) and Pagan-friendly people and their businesses in hopes of strengthening community ties. The Pagan Pages is arranged as a village setting with sub-conferences.

Pathways to Metaphysics

http://digital.net/~egodust/

For those involved in the new physics, metaphysics, or the exploration of that which lies beneath the appearance of things. Introduction to Vedanta which explores the manifestation of diversity from underlying unity. Links for novices, veterans, and sadhus.

Stanford University Zoroastrian Group

http://www-leland.stanford.edu/group/zoroastrians/

Presents a student group interested in exploring the Zoroastrian religion (one of the world's first monotheisms), history, and culture. Presents a short overview of Zoroastrianism, daily prayers, and links to other Zoroastrian groups.

Taoism Philosophy

Taoism was founded by tradition in the 6th century BC by Lao Zi. The following are central to its philosophy. To learn more about Taoism, visit the Taoism Information Page Web site or the Taoist Resource Center site.

1. All is in flux except Tao.

2. Yin balances Yang.

3. Belief in meditation and simplicity.

4. Te (virtue) and Ch'i (energy) the power of effortless action.

5. Quest for immortality.

6. Heaven rules earth, earth rules man, Tao rules heaven.

7. Tao produces and sustains all things.

8. All move in harmony.

Taoism Information Page

http://www.cnu.edu/~patrick/taoism.html

Offers a look into the Taoist tradition. Provides alternate, complete translations of the Tao Te Ching, Sun Tzu's The Art of War, and the I Ching, including all hexagrams.

Taoist Resource Center

http://members.aol.com/gr8tao/index.html

A great source of information about Taoism, especially for those just beginning to learn about it. Great explanations of what Tao is, the differences between philosophical and religious Taoism, snippets of wisdom from the "I Ching," and more.

Theosophical Society

http://users.aol.com/tstec/hmpage/tsintro.htm

The society was founded in 1875 in an effort to promote the expressed awareness of the Oneness of Life. This site links to descriptions of foundational, esoteric texts by Blavatsky and others. Acts as a guide for personal exploration of truth.

Universal Life Church

http://ulc.org/ulc/about.html

The church that feels that everyone is already a member, they just don't know it yet. This church will ordain anyone that asks, just choose the "Become Ordained" option on their page. There is no fee, and you are taken to a page with a certificate of ordination that you can save and/or print out.

Urantia Book

http://zeta.cs.adfa.oz.au/Urantia/

A simple but huge site, containing the entire text of The Urantia Book. Claimed to be a channeled description of the entire universe and of hyperuniverses.

Yoga Paths, An Overview Of Different Schools and Traditions

http://zeta.cs.adfa.oz.au/Spirit/Yoga/Overview.html

Covers dozens of paths of Yoga, the science of self-realization. Includes IRC, Web-Chat, and newsgroup links.

Mysticism

Al Azif: The Manuscript Liber Logaeth

http://www.primenet.com/~ottinge/n.html

Also known as "The Book of the Arab, Abdul Alhazred" and the "Necronomicon," this site provides an electronic version of the manuscript that inspired H.P. Lovecraft to write about the Cthulhu mythos.

Aleister Crowley

http://www.crl.com/~thelema/crowley.html

Learn about the life of the famous mystic. This one-time member of the Golden Dawn is famous for his "Book of the Law," which was dictated to him from behind by the Egyptian god Horus.

The Egyptian Book of the Dead

http://www.lysator.liu.se/~drokk/BoD/

Learn all about the ancient Egyptian's view on death and the afterlife. The Book of the Dead is here in its full-translated glory, everything from "Hymn to Osiris" to "Making the Transformation to the Crocodile God."

The Golden Dawn FAQ

http://www.bartol.udel.edu/~cranmer/cranmer_gdfaq.html

Anything and everything you ever wanted to know about the Hermetic Order of the Golden Dawn, a "society devoted to spiritual, philosophical, and magical development."

The Kabballah Connection

http://www.netvoyage.net/~dalfin/

What's more important, a dira or a lichtiker dira? Find out in this page devoted to Kabbalah, the hidden secrets of Judaism. This site includes "Kabballah & Self Improvement," "Kabbalistic Resources," "Kabballah & the Rebbe," and other Kabballah resources.

Mysticism in World Religions

http://www.bga.com/~rlp/dwp/mystic/index.html

Systematic comparison of Jewish, Christian, Muslim, Buddhist, Hindu, and Taoist scriptures with respect to twenty-one mystical concepts.

Shawn's Rituals Collection

http://www.andrew.cmu.edu/user/shawn/occult/rites/

A collection of rituals from various authors, for a variety of intents and purposes. The rituals included range from "The Lesser Pentagram Banishing Ritual" to "Getting Pop Cans Out of Machines."

Tarot Reading

http://www.Facade.com/Occult/tarot/

Here you can have your fortune told through the magic of an Internet tarot reading. Choose from five beautifully rendered decks.

Wayfarer's Rest

http://www.compulink.co.uk/~wayfarer/

Articles on mysticism, water healing, and problem solving. Links to various other mystical sites.

Philosophy

American Philosophical Association

http://www.oxy.edu/apa/apa.html

Provides information on how to join APA and offers links to APA's Proceedings and Electronic Bulletin Board. Also offers links to other Web resources for philosophers. Includes information on upcoming events sponsored by APA and/or of interest to philosophers.

ANALYSIS Home Page

http://www.shef.ac.uk/uni/academic/N-Q/phil/analysis/homepage.html

Provides information about the philosophy journal ANALYSIS and its monthly e-mail supplement ANALYST. Provides information on how to subscribe to both ANALYSIS and ANALYST. Includes recent and current contents of ANALYSIS, as well as links to the ANALYST ftp archive.

Arisbe: A Home for Charles S. Peirce Studies

http://204.119.173.21/peirce/

Contains hypertext versions of Charles Peirce's papers and information on various subjects relating to Peirce.

Augustine

http://ccat.sas.upenn.edu/jod/augustine.html

Contains translations and texts of Augustine. Also includes other research materials and reference aids. Also contains papers from an online seminar and images.

Australasian Philosophy Network: Home Page

http://www.arts.su.edu.au/Arts/departs/philos/APS/APS.home.html

Focuses on philosophy in Australian and New Zealand. Contains information on AP net, Australasian philosophers, departments, conferences, and job postings.

BEARS in Moral and Political Philosophy

http://www.netspace.org/bears/

Brown Electronic Article Review Service on Moral and Political Philosophy. Contains short reviews of articles that have appeared in the last six months. Provides information on contributors and a list of reviews.

Cybernetics and Systems Theory

http://pespmc1.vub.ac.be/CYBSYSTH.html

Contains information gathered through the Principia Cybernetica Project. Contains general information and background material on cybernetics and systems theory.

Electronic Journal of Analytic Philosophy

http://www.phil.indiana.edu/ejap/ejap.html

Includes three issues in hypertext, simple text, or PostScript; provides analytical philosophy articles. Provides information on how to subscribe to the journal via a listserv. Includes topics for upcoming issues, and invites submissions. Also contains links to other philosophy sites.

Environmental Ethics

http://www.cep.unt.edu/

Provides information on environmental ethics. Focuses on environmental ethics resources. Provides book reviews and site summaries and links of interest to environmental philosophy.

International Philosophical Preprint Exchange

http://phil-preprints.l.chiba-u.ac.jp/IPPE.html

Part of an international working group coordinating access to philosophy preprints. Provides information in a visual index, as well as a textual one. Includes subject access, submissions, and directory links.

Mechanosphere

http://www.scsn.net/~efolley/

Provides an index of links to resources relating to the French philosophers, Gilles Deleuze and Felix Guattari.

Nietzsche Page at USC

http://www.usc.edu/dept/annenberg/thomas/nietzsche.html

Provides information on all aspects of study. Contains the complete text of Nietzsche's Thus Spoke

Zarathustra; information on the available e-mail lists for Nietzsche studies; assorted mixed opinions and maxims from Nietzsche; and many other documents and links.

Philosophy and Religion

gopher://marvel.loc.gov/11/global/phil

Presents the Library of Congress' Gopher guide to philosophy and religion. Contains links and documents relating to philosophy from all over the world.

Philosophy in Cyberspace—Home Page

http://www.monash.edu.au/cc/staff/phi/dey/WWW/phil.html

Provides an annotated guide to philosophy resources and tools available over the Internet. Includes information a novice needs and offer links even the most experienced user can use.

Philosophy Resources

gopher://gopher.liv.ac.uk/11/phil

Contains a list of all the philosophy departments in the United Kingdom, their addresses, contact information, and their head. Also provides information on conferences, workshops, and calls for papers.

PSYCHE: an interdisciplinary journal of research and consciousness

http://psyche.cs.monash.edu.au/

Provides direct access to PSYCHE's archives. Also contains a FAQ associated with the journal that covers the following topics: general introduction; notes for authors; book reviews; subscriptions to the electronic version of PSYCHE; subscriptions to the MIT Press version of PSYCHE; the discussion list Psyche-D; archival information; the executive editor, associate editors, and editorial board.

Tech Classics Archive

http://the-tech.mit.edu/Classics

Contains full text documents by many philosophers spanning the ages. Includes a full text copy of Candide (English).

University of Chicago Philosophy Project

http://csmaclab-www.uchicago.edu/philosophyProject philos.html

Serves as a forum for electronically mediated scholarly discussion of philosophical works. Contains several moderated philosophical discussions between small groups of participants.

White Mountain Education— A Source for the Ageless Wisdom

http://www.primenet.com/~wtmtn

Provides articles, lectures, the online publication Meditation Monthly International, esoteric astrology, and psychology.

Sikhism

Fort: Panth Khalsa

http://www.community.net/~khalsa/

Provides a glimpse into the culture of the Sikh Nation. Posts Hukam-Namah (daily verses from the Sikh Scriptures) in native Gurmukhi format. Contains information about Sikh history and current events relevant to the Sikh people.

Sikhism: Religion of the Sikh People

http://www.io.org/~sandeep/sikhism.htm

Provides information about Sikhism, which preaches a message of love of one God, truthful living, and the equality of mankind, through the teachings of its Gurus enshrined in the Sri Guru Granth Sahib, the Sikh Holy Book, and Eternal Guru.

Scientology

Alt.religion.scientology

news:alt.religion.scientology

A Usenet forum for the discussion of the Church of Scientology, Dianetics, L. Ron Hubbard, and anything else associated with the Church.

The Church of Scientology vs. The Net

http://www.cybercom.net/~rnewman/scientology/home.html

A Web page put up by a non-Scientologist, who sees the Church as "a religious cult which has unwisely decided to declare war against the Usenet and Internet communities." The page includes information about lawsuits, raids, spams, and more.

Dianetics Home Page

http://www.dianetics.org/

Dianetics is a book written by the founder of Scientology, L. Ron Hubbard in 1950. It is used as a basis for the Church of Scientology. More information about the book and its contents can be found at this page.

Johnny Get Your Modem—Scientology's War with the Internet

http://www.primenet.com/~stevem/scieno_java.html

An article by Stephen E. Marinick, an individual who is none too happy with the practices of the Church of Scientology. This page also links to Steve's home page, which contains a response from the Church to this article.

L. Ron Hubbard Home Page

http://www.lronhubbard.org/

Read an overview of the life of L. Ron Hubbard, the founder of Scientology. See him portrayed as humanitarian, music maker, poet/lyricist, yachtsman, and philosopher. Also home to an online bookstore, where Mr. Hubbard's work can be purchased.

Scientology Home Page

http://www.scientology.org/

The official Web site for Dianetics/the Church of Scientology. Available in English, French, Spanish, Italian, and German, this site is a wealth of information. Features 3D tours of actual Scientology churches, RealAudio lectures from founder L. Ron Hubbard, and complete explanations of the Scientology faith.

Newsgroups

alt.atheism

alt.atheism.moderated

alt.atheism.satire

alt.bible.prophecy

alt.binaries.scientology

alt.birthright

alt.christnet

alt.christnet.bible

alt.christnet.christianlife

alt.christnet.ethics

alt.christnet.evangelical

alt.christnet.hypocrisy

alt.christnet.nudism

alt.christnet.philosophy

alt.christnet.prayer

alt.christnet.second-coming.real-soon-now

alt.christnet.sex

alt.christnet.theology

alt.education.home-school.christian

alt.fan.jesus-christ

alt.hindu

alt.islam.sufism

alt.messianic

alt.meditation

alt.meditation.quanyin

alt.music.jewish

alt.org.promisekeepers

alt.pagan

alt.pagan.conacts

alt.pagan.contacts

alt.pagan.magick

alt.paranet.metaphysics

alt.personals.jewish

alt.philosophy.debate

alt.philosophy.jarf

alt.philosophy.objectivism

alt.philosophy.taoism

alt.philosophy.zen

alt.religion.buddhism.nichiren

alt.religion.buddhism.tibetan

alt.religion.christian

alt.religion.christian.20-something

alt.religion.christian.anabaptist.brethren

alt.religion.christian.calvary-chapel

alt.religion.christian.last-days

alt.religion.druid

alt.religion.islam

alt.religion.islam.arabic

alt.religion.mormon

alt.religion.scientology

alt.religion.scientology.squick.squick.squick

alt.religion.shamanism

alt.religion.subgenius

alt.religion.urantia-book

alt.religion.vaishnava

alt.religion.wicca

alt.religion.zoroastrianism

alt.society.neutopia

alt.zen

alt.zen+budo

aus.religion.christian

bit.listserv.christia

bit.listserv.muslims

christnet.admin

christnet.bible

christnet.christianlife

christnet.christnews

christnet.ethics

christnet.evangelical

christnet.general

christnet.healing.herbs

christnet.ladies

christnet.philosophy

christnet.poetry

christnet.prayer

christnet.religion

christnet.theology

christnet.writers

clari.news.jews

clari.news.religion

fido7.christianity

misc.education.home-school.christian

nctu.club.buddhism

own.buddhism

pdaxs.religion.christian

pdaxs.religion.jewish

pnet.religion.pagan

rec.music.christian

relcom.sci.philosophy

sci.logic

sci.philosophy.meta

sci.philosophy.tech

shamash.israelisusa

shamash.j-scouts

shamash.jewish-psy

shamash.jewishdigest

shamash.jewishhikers

shamash.jewishweek

shamash.mail-jewish

shamash.torch-d

```
shamash.travel

soc.atheism

soc.culture.jewish

soc.culture.jewish.holocaust

soc.culture.jewish.parenting

soc.genealogy.jewish

soc.religion.bahai

soc.religion.christian

soc.religion.christian.bible-study

soc.religion.christian.youth-work

soc.religion.eastern

soc.religion.gnosis

soc.religion.hindu

soc.religion.islam

soc.religion.quaker

soc.religion.sikhism

soc.religion.unitarian-univ

talk.atheism

talk.origins

talk.philosophy.humanism

talk.philosophy.misc

talk.religion.buddhism

tnn.religion.buddhism.shinshu

talk.religion.misc

talk.religion.newage

tw.bbs.sci.philosophy

uk.religion.buddhist
```

```
uk.religion.christian

uk.religion.hindu

uk.religion.islam

uk.religion.jewish
```

Listservs

ACE-NET-L—Association of Christian Economists

University of Illinois, Urbana, IL

You can join this group by sending the message "sub ACE-NET-L your name" to `listserv@postoffice.cso.uiuc.edu`

ALPHA-CHURCH—A Place for Christians Who Share 1st Century Church Beliefs

You can join this group by sending the message "sub ALPHA-CHURCH your name" to `listserv@home.ease.lsoft.com`

AMERCATH—AMERCATH - A Discussion List on the History of American Catholicism

You can join this group by sending the message "sub AMERCATH your name" to `listserv@lsv.uky.edu`

ANIMUS—Philosophy in the Third Millenium

Memorial University of Newfoundland, St. John's, Newfoundland, Canada

You can join this group by sending the message "sub ANIMUS your name" to `listserv@morgan.ucs.mun.ca`

APACIC-L—American Philosophical Association

You can join this group by sending the message "sub APACIC-L your name" to
`listserv%ucbcmsa.bitnet@listserv.net`

ARCANA—ARCANA Discussion List for the Study of the Occult

You can join this group by sending the message "sub ARCANA your name" to
`listserv%unccvm.bitnet@listserv.net`

ARIL-L—"Association for Religion and Intellectual Life"

University of California at Santa Barbara

You can join this group by sending the message "sub ARIL-L your name" to `listserv@ucsbvm.ucsb.edu`

AYN-RAND—Moderated Discussion of Objectivist Philosophy

University Computing Services, Indiana University

You can join this group by sending the message "sub AYN-RAND your name" to
`listserv@iubvm.ucs.indiana.edu`

AYN-REVU—Moderated Discussion of Objectivist Philosophy

University Computing Services, Indiana University

You can join this group by sending the message "sub AYN-REVU your name" to
`listserv@iubvm.ucs.indiana.edu`

AYN-TECH—Moderated Discussion of Objectivist Philosophy — Technical

University Computing Services, Indiana University

You can join this group by sending the message "sub AYN-TECH your name" to
`listserv@iubvm.ucs.indiana.edu`

BETMIDRASH—Information from the Seminary of Judaic Studies, Jerusalem

Jewish Theological Seminary of America, New York, NY

You can join this group by sending the message "sub BETMIDRASH your name" to
`listserv@jtsa.edu`

BUDDHA-L—Buddhist Academic Discussion Forum

You can join this group by sending the message "sub BUDDHA-L your name" to
`listserv@ulkyvm.louisville.edu`

BUSSOC—Business and Society Course, Philosophy Dept.

Villanova University, Villanova, PA

You can join this group by sending the message "sub BUSSOC your name" to
`listserv%villvm.bitnet@listserv.net`

CAGS-L—Christian Anthropology Grad Students

The American University, Washington, DC

You can join this group by sending the message "sub CAGS-L your name" to `listserv@american.edu`

CCC_VT—Campus Crusade for Christ Mailing List

Virginia Tech

You can join this group by sending the message "sub CCC_VT your name" to
`listserv@listserv.vt.edu`

CHPSSTU—Committee On The History And Philosophy Of Science At UMCP

University of Maryland CSC, College Park, MD

You can join this group by sending the message "sub CHPSSTU your name" to
`listserv%umdd.bitnet@listserv.net`

CHRISTIANITY-ONLINE—Christianity Online Connection Newsletter

America Online, Inc. (1-800-827-6364 in USA/Canada)

You can join this group by sending the message "sub CHRISTIANITY-ONLINE your name" to `listserv@listserv.aol.com`

CJ-L—Discussion of Beliefs and Practices of Conservative Judaism

You can join this group by sending the message "sub CJ-L your name" to `listserv%albnyvm1.bitnet@listserv.net`

COMETHIC—Ethical Issues and Computer Science Course Philosophy Dept.

Villanova University, Villanova, PA

You can join this group by sending the message "sub COMETHIC your name" to `listserv%villvm.bitnet@listserv.net`

CONCHR-L—Conservative Christian Discussion List

Temple University, Philadelphia, PA

You can join this group by sending the message "sub CONCHR-L your name" to `listserv@vm.temple.edu`

COVR—Colloquium on Violence and Religion

East Carolina University, Computing and Info systems, Greenville, NC

You can join this group by sending the message "sub COVR your name" to `listserv@ecuvm.cis.ecu.edu`

CYBERMIND—Philosophy and Psychology of Cyberspace

America Online, Inc. (1-800-827-6364 in USA/Canada)

You can join this group by sending the message "sub CYBERMIND your name" to `listserv@listserv.aol.com`

DIG-NEWS—LesBiGay Catholic News

The American University, Washington, DC

You can join this group by sending the message "sub DIG-NEWS your name" to `listserv@american.edu`

DIGNITY—LesBiGay Catholic List

The American University, Washington, DC

You can join this group by sending the message "sub DIGNITY your name" to `listserv@american.edu`

EDPHIL2-L—Philosophy of Education, Open Access

University of Illinois, Urbana, IL

You can join this group by sending the message "sub EDPHIL2-L your name" to `listserv@postoffice.cso.uiuc.edu`

EJAP—The Electronic Journal of Analytic Philosophy

University Computing Services, Indiana University

You can join this group by sending the message "sub EJAP your name" to `listserv@iubvm.ucs.indiana.edu`

FEMREL-L—Open Discussion of Women, Religion, and Feminist Theology

America Online, Inc. (1-800-827-6364 in USA/Canada)

You can join this group by sending the message "sub FEMREL-L your name" to `listserv@listserv.aol.com`

HINDU-D—Hindu Digest

You can join this group by sending the message "sub HINDU-D your name" to `listserv@listserv.nodak.edu`

HOPOS-L—A Forum for Discussion of the History of the Philosophy of Science

You can join this group by sending the message "sub HOPOS-L your name" to `listserv@lsv.uky.edu`

IMBAS—The IMBAS List for Celtic Pagans

America Online, Inc. (1-800-827-6364 in USA/Canada)

You can join this group by sending the message "sub IMBAS your name" to
`listserv@listserv.aol.com`

ISL-SCI—Issues on Islam and Science

Virginia Tech

You can join this group by sending the message "sub ISL-SCI your name" to
`listserv@vtvm1.cc.vt.edu`

ISLAM—Islam Discussion List

Virginia Tech

You can join this group by sending the message "sub ISLAM your name" to `listserv@listserv.vt.edu`

ISLAM-L—History of Islam

You can join this group by sending the message "sub ISLAM-L your name" to
`listserv@ulkyvm.louisville.edu`

IVCF-L—InterVarsity Christian Fellowship List

State University of New York at Buffalo

You can join this group by sending the message "sub IVCF-L your name" to
`listserv@ubvm.cc.buffalo.edu`

JEWGEN—Jewish Genealogy Discussion Group

eWorld, Apple Online Services, Cupertino, CA

You can join this group by sending the message "sub JEWGEN your name" to
`listserv@mail.eworld.com`

LDS-PHIL—LDS Philosophy List

University of Notre Dame, Notre Dame, IN

You can join this group by sending the message "sub LDS-PHIL your name" to
`listserv@vma.cc.nd.edu`

MSA-L—Muslim Student Association List

Pennsylvania State University

You can join this group by sending the message "sub MSA-L your name" to `listserv@psuvm.psu.edu`

MUSLIMS—The Islamic Information & News Network

Arizona State University, Tempe, AZ

You can join this group by sending the message "sub MUSLIMS your name" to
`listserv@asuvm.inre.asu.edu`

NEWLIFE—Helping the New Christian on Their Walk with God

America Online, Inc. (1-800-827-6364 in USA/Canada)

You can join this group by sending the message "sub NEWLIFE your name" to
`listserv@listserv.aol.com`

PHILCOMM—Philosophy of Communication

Rensselaer Polytechnic Institute, Troy, NY

You can join this group by sending the message "sub PHILCOMM your name" to
`listserv@vm.its.rpi.edu`

PHILOS-L—Paleoanthropological & Biological Basis of Ethics & Aesthetics

West Virginia Network for Educational Telecomputing

You can join this group by sending the message "sub PHILOS-L your name" to
`listserv@wvnvm.wvnet.edu`

PHTECH-L—Philosophy and Technology

Pennsylvania State University

You can join this group by sending the message "sub PHTECH-L your name" to
`listserv@psuvm.psu.edu`

POMO—Discussions in Post-Modern Jewish Philosophy and Theology

Jewish Theological Seminary of America, New York, NY, USA

You can join this group by sending the message "sub POMO your name" to listserv@jtsa.edu

RELNET—Religious Internet

You can join this group by sending the message "sub RELNET your name" to listserv%emuvm1.bitnet@listserv.net

RENEW-L—Catholic Reform and Renewal

The American University, Washington, DC

You can join this group by sending the message "sub RENEW-L your name" to listserv@american.edu

SHAMANS—Shamans Impact of the Internet on Religion

University of Arkansas Main Campus - Fayetteville

You can join this group by sending the message "sub SHAMANS your name" to listserv@uafsysb.uark.edu

SSREL-L—Scientific Study of Religion

The University of Tennessee, Knoxville

You can join this group by sending the message "sub SSREL-L your name" to listserv@utkvm1.utk.edu

SWIP-L—Society for Women in Philosophy Information and Discussion List

University of South Florida, Tampa, FL

You can join this group by sending the message "sub SWIP-L your name" to listserv@cfrvm.cfr.usf.edu

VINCENT—Vincent Vincentian Philosophy and Practice

St. John's University, Jamaica, NY

You can join this group by sending the message "sub VINCENT your name" to listserv@sjuvm.stjohns.edu

VISIONS—Christian Visions Discussion List

State University of New York at Buffalo

You can join this group by sending the message "sub VISIONS your name" to listserv@listserv.acsu.buffalo.edu

WMSPRT-L—Women's Spirituality and Feminist-Oriented Religions

State University of New York at Buffalo

You can join this group by sending the message "sub WMSPRT-L your name" to listserv@ubvm.cc.buffalo.edu

SCIENCE & ENGINEERING

Agriculture

Ag-Links

http://www.gennis.com/aglinks.html

Features news, weather, professional and non-professional associations, research, and newsletters related to the agriculture industry. Also contains links to other agricultural sites.

Agriculture Online

http://www.agriculture.com/

Contains current news of interest to the agricultural community. Also offers links to sites on the Internet related to agriculture issues.

AgriGator Commercial Agriculture Sites

http://www.ifas.ufl.edu/WWW/AGATOR/HTM/AGCOMMERCIAL.HTM

Contains links to businesses on the Internet related to agriculture, including subjects on gardening, farming, fishing, birds, insects, and food research.

Agrinet

http://www.spectramedia.com/agrinet/

General agricultural resource site offering links to farm, ranch, family, and commercial sites. Site provides great starting place for agricultural sites.

Center for Soybean Tissue and Genetic Engineering

http://mars.cropsoil.uga.edu/homesoybean/index.htm

Describes efforts to develop and refine a complete soybean genetic engineering system.

Economic Research Service

http://www.econ.ag.gov/

Provides economic and social science information and analysis for public and private decisions on agriculture, food, natural resources, and rural America. Features reports, catalogs, publications and USDA data statistics. Also offers other agriculture-related links.

Farmland Information Library

http://farm.fic.niu.edu/fic/home.html

Site devoted to individuals interested in agriculture. Contains information about upcoming events, legislation, literature, Internet resources, and an agricultural library.

GrainsGenes

http://wheat.pw.usda.gov/graingenes.html

Database sponsored by the USDA that provides molecular and phenotypic information on wheat, barley, rye, oats, and sugarcane.

High Plains Journal—The Farmer-Rancher Paper

http://www.hpi.com/

Site summarizes the weekly publication. Site includes information on farm shows, livestock sales, new product news, harvest reports, a classified section, and subscription information.

John Deere—Agricultural Equipment

http://www.deere.com/ag/index.htm

Offers product information on entire farm machinery line, as well as other Deere products. Includes lists of dealers in the U.S. and Canada.

NewCrop

http://newcrop.hort.purdue.edu/

Provides detailed descriptions about many different kinds of crops, as well as access to reference material. Also contains links to experts on specific crops.

Pest & Crop Management Production Newsletter

http://www.entm.purdue.edu/entomology/Pest&Crop/index.html

Site offers the latest information on pests and their impact on crops. Several back issues of the periodical are accessible from this site (Adobe Acrobat Reader required).

Rationale

http://www.bae.uga/dept/research/cropsim/rationale.html

Site gives information about the uses of computer simulations in crop development taught through fee-based workshops. Also gives links to universities, as well as workshop dates and reservation information.

USDA

http://www.usda.gov/

Contains information about USDA programs, news releases, and legislation dealing with the agricultural industry. Also contains employment lists and opportunities links.

The Voice of Agriculture

http://www.fb.com/home.shtml

Provides links to agricultural and farm-related sites as well as state and county farm bureaus. Also offers links to national and rural news and educational materials.

Astronomy

Air Force Maui Optical Station (AMOS)

http://ulua.mhpcc.edu/amos.html

Provides information about the Air Force Maui Optical Station (AMOS), located in Hawaii, and operated by the Phillips Laboratory. Describes telescopes and sensors at AMOS, as well as how visiting experimenters can request use of the facilities.

American Astronomical Society

http://www.aas.org/

Provides general astronomy information of interest to professionals and amateur enthusiasts. Maintains links to other astronomy resources on the Net.

Art of Renaissance Science: Galileo and Perspective

http://bang.lanl.gov/video/stv/arshtml/lanlarstitle.html

Features the life of Galileo, including many images from the period; based on a videotape entitled "The Art of Renaissance Science: Galileo and Perspective."

Astro!Info

http://ezinfo.ethz.ch/ezinfo/astro/astro.html

Aims to provide general information about a variety of astronomical events (large portion written in German, but some parts written in English).

Astronomical Data Center

http://nssdc.gsfc.nasa.gov/adc/adc.html

Element of the National Space Science Data Center (NSSDC) / A World Data Center for Rockets and Satellites (WDC-A-R&S). Part of an international federation of astronomical data centers. Acquires, verifies, formats, documents, and distributes files that contain astronomical data in computer-readable form. Also develops and maintains software tools to access these data.

Astronomical Museum in Bologna

http://boas3.bo.astro.it/dip/Museum/MuseumHome.html

Provides background on the history of astronomy and the instruments at this museum.

Houston, We Have A Problem

Well, not really. Here are just a few stats about this incredible universe we call home. To learn more, check out the sites in this Astronomy section.

Planet	Diameter	Distance from Sun	Orbits Sun	Rotates on Axis
Mercury	3,100 miles	36 million miles	Every 88 days	In 59 days
Venus	7,700 miles	67 million miles	Every 225 days	In 244 days
Earth	7,920 miles	93 million miles	Every 365 days	In 24 hours
Mars	4,200 miles	141 million miles	Every 687 days	In 24 hours 24 minutes
Jupiter	88,640 miles	483 million miles	Every 11.9 years	In 9 hours 50 minutes
Saturn	74,500 miles	886 million miles	Every 29.5 years	In 10 hours 39 minutes
Uranus	32,000 miles	1,782 million miles	Every 84 years	In 23 hours
Neptune	31,000 miles	2,793 million miles	Every 165 years	In 15 hours 48 minutes
Pluto	1,500 miles	3,670 million miles	Every 248 years	In 6 days 7 hours

Astronomical Resources on the Internet

http://stsci.edu/net-resources.html

Contains lists of sites broken down into Gopher, Telnet, ftp, and WWW resources. Offers many links as well.

Astronomy HyperText Book

http://zebu.uoregon.edu/text.html

A hypertextual astronomy textbook written at the college level. Contains interactive information about astronomy. Also offers links to sites that offer astronomy assistance.

Astronomy-Related Web Sites

http://www.skypub.com/links/astroweb.html

Offers listing of astronomy-related Web sites and includes brief descriptions.

AstroWeb Astronomy/Astrophysics on the Internet

http://msowww.anu.edu.au/~anton/astroweb/

Provides a searchable index of information about astronomy and astrophysics that you can find on the Internet. Contains a keyword or string search option.

Aztec Books

http://world.std.com/~aztec/

Features books on UFOs, ghosts and the spirit world, unexplained phenomena, freemasonry, ancient and lost civilizations, science, ESP and psychic phenomena, holy grail, apocrypha, Kabbalah, Gnostic texts, astral projection, occult sciences, knights templar, theosophy, Nikola Tesla, Wilhelm Reich, and more.

Brief Tour of Our Universe!

http://149.159.15.26/~space/index.html

Presents an image-enhanced interactive virtual tour of the universe.

Caltech Space Society

http://www.seds.org/seds/chapters/css/CSS.html

Provides information about space-related projects, such as conferences and educational programs, that are open to the public.

CCD Images of Galaxies

http://zebu.uoregon.edu/galaxy.html

Presents a collection of images that specializes in photographs of galaxies. Also offers educational resources.

Center for Advanced Space Studies (CASS) Home Page

http://cass.jsc.nasa.gov/CASS_home.html

Provides information about this national research center, as well as general information about space science.

Compton Observatory Science Support Center

http://cossc.gsfc.nasa.gov/cossc/cossc.html

Contains links to various instrument home pages, bulletin board access, announcements, and public data archives.

CyberSky

http://www.astro.ucla.edu/staff/stephen/cybersky.html

CyberSky is an educational shareware program that allows you to turn your computer into an animated traditional planetarium.

Discovery Program Home Page

http://mercury.hq.nasa.gov/office/discovery/

Discover information about the different missions that NASA hopes to undertake.

HEASARC Video Archive

http://heasarc.gsfc.nasa.gov/docs/heasarc/videos/videos.html

Contains a directory of video clips that highlight high-energy astrophysics missions (in various formats).

Henrietta Leavitt Flat Screen Space Theater

http://ucsu.colorado.edu/~peterscc/Home.html

Explores astronomy topics in a planetarium-show style, designed to present astronomy to a wide variety of readers.

High Energy Astrophysics Science Archive Research Center

http://heasarc.gsfc.nasa.gov/docs/HEASARC_HOME_PAGE.html

Contains general information on supernovae, x-ray binaries, and black holes.

Humans in Space

http://medlib.jsc.nasa.gov/intro/humans.html

Provides information on physiological needs, spacecraft systems, and general information about humans living in space.

Information Leaflets

http://www.ast.cam.ac.uk/RGO/leaflets/

Lists online explanations of a variety of astronomy-related topics.

Institute for Space Astrophysics C.N.R.

http://titan.ias.fra.cnr.it/ias-home/ias-home.html

Offer some links in Italian but the majority in English. Includes the "Electronic Atlas of Dynamical Evolutions of Short-Period Comets."

International Astronomical Union

http://www.lsw.uni-heidelberg.de/iau.html

Contains access to current and past bulletins, as well as reports posted by association members.

International Occultation Timing Association (I.O.T.A.) Home Page

http://www.sky.net/~robinson/iota.htm

Specializes in organizing reliable ways to view occultations and eclipses. Provides information on how nonmembers can become involved. Offers a list of members' addresses to help you locate a member near you who would be willing to help you properly view occultations and eclipses.

The Long Duration Exposure Facility

http://setas-www.larc.nasa.gov/setas/ldef.html

Describes the LDEF satellite, which contained 57 experiments and spent 69 months in space. Provides the baseline on space environments and their effects.

Mount Wilson Observatory

http://www.mtwilson.edu/

Overviews several ongoing astronomy projects using innovative techniques and modern detectors.

Provides information for professionals, amateurs, tourists, and educators.

NASA Astrophysics Data System Home Page—Classic System

http://adswww.colorado.edu/adswww/adshomepg.html

Offers free software, developed and operated on behalf of NASA, aimed at the astrophysics community. Provides access to a variety of astronomical data for the scientific user community. Presents a tutorial that allows users to get a taste of the software.

NASA-JSC Digital Image Collection

http://images.jsc.nasa.gov/html/home.htm

Features more than 9,000 images since the Mercury space program.

NASA World Wide Web Information Services

http://www.gsfc.nasa.gov/NASA_homepage.html

Contains news and resources of value to a variety of people. Provides scientific information for professionals as well as educational information for teachers and students.

NCSA Relativity Group

http://jean-luc.ncsa.uiuc.edu/

Provides software tools, original documents (on black holes, cosmology, hydrodynamics, and so on), scientific movies, multimedia exhibits, and visualization projects.

Planetary Society Home Page

http://wea.mankato.mn.us:80/tps/

Encourages the exploration of the solar system and the search for extraterrestrial life. Provides information about organization projects, important space news, activities for the classroom, and links to information on the Internet.

Purdue SEDS (Students for the Exploration and Development of Space)

http://expert.cc.purdue.edu/~puseds/

Provides information about the Purdue SEDS group and serves as a place to discuss space exploration and development.

SEDS Internet Space Warehouse

http://seds.lpl.arizona.edu/

Contains many links to space resources on the Internet, a few multimedia documents, and information about the organization.

Sensors and Instrument Technology Planetary Tour Guide

http://ranier.oact.hq.nasa.gov/Sensors_page/Planets.html

Contains links to Web sites that have tours of the planets.

Sky Online Home Page

http://www.skypub.com/

Contains astronomy-related information and a large number of resources. Also contains a regularly updated listing of astronomical events.

Solar System Live

http://www.fourmilab.ch/solar/solar.html

Allows you to view a model of the solar system. Offers adjustable settings so you can see how the solar system would be at any given time or on any given date.

Southern Cross Astronomical Society

http://www.mangonet.com/scas/

Lets you check out the Southern Cross Astronomical Society.

Space Explorer's Guide

http://nyquist.ee.ualberta.ca/~wanigar/spacelink/space_explorer.html

Contains links to space resources all over the globe by country. Provides information on space news and jobs.

Space Settlement

http://www.nas.nasa.gov/NAS/SpaceSettlement/

Provides information on developing orbital space settlements, including who, what, where, when, and how much.

StarBits—Acronyms, Abbreviations, and More

http://cdsweb.u-strasbg.fr/~heck/sfbits.htm

Furnishes a searchable dictionary/glossary of astronomy acronyms, abbreviations, and terms.

StarWorlds—Astronomy and Related Organizations

http://cdsweb.u-strasbg.fr/~heck/sfworlds.htm

Furnishes a searchable listing of the addresses of organizations, institutions, associations, companies, and other groups involved in astronomy and related space sciences.

STELAR Project Demos

http://ssdoo.gsfc.nasa.gov/stelar/stelar_demos.html

Study of Electronic Literature for Astronomical Research. Explores the use of electronic means for improving access to scientific literature, and using astronomical publications to evaluate distribution, search, and retrieval techniques for full text and graphics display. Contains a listing of hypertext journal articles on astronomy.

Usenet FAQs Space

http://www.cis.ohio-state.edu/hypertext/faq/usenet/space/top.html

Presents FAQ list of general questions about planetary probes or information about solar system bodies.

Views of the Solar System

http://bang.lanl.gov/solarsys/

Offers an educational view of the solar system. Contains images and information about the sun, planets, moons, asteroids, comets, and meteoroids.

Web Nebulae

http://seds.lpl.arizona.edu/billa/twn/top.html

Contains a collection of images of various objects in our galaxy. Includes images and explains how to classify nebulae.

WebStars Astrophysics in Cyberspace

http://www.stars.com/WebStars/

Provides information about astronomy. Contains online journals as well as searchable indexes and listings of other sites.

Welcome to Loch Ness Productions

http://www.lochness.com/

Specializes in producing planetarium program materials. Includes access to samples of planetarium music and art, as well as a listing of planetariums around the world.

Welcome to Project CLEA

http://www.gettysburg.edu/project/physics/clea/CLEAhome.html

Contemporary Laboratory Experiences in Astronomy. Contains educational resources that can be used to incorporate astronomy into a science curriculum.

Welcome to SkyView

http://skview.gsfc.nasa.gov/skyview.html

Serves as a virtual observatory on the Net that enables visitors to view a generated image of any part of the sky in a variety of wavelengths.

Welcome to the Planets

http://stardust.jpl.nasa.gov/planets/

Presents collection of photos from NASA, organized by planet and the space craft that took the picture. Also includes textual explanations of the photos.

World Wide Web Home Page of the Canadian Astronomy Data Centre (CADC)

http://cadcwww.dao.nrc.ca/CADC-homepage.html

Contains general information on astronomy. Enables users to access programs and full-text copies of articles from several CD-ROMs.

Wormhole Interactive

http://www.intr.net/bertwillco/

Serves both educational and entertaining purposes. Focuses on wormholes.

Aviation

Air Affair

http://www.airaffair.com/

Focuses on different types of flying machines. Includes a calendar of flying shows, a listing of aviation fuel prices, and an aviation library.

Airship: The Home Page for Lighter-Than-Air Craft

http://spot.colorado.edu/~dziadeck/airship.html

Offers links for finding information about lighter-than-air craft. Includes information on these craft in fiction, models, and pictures; a bibliography; and links to Internet resources and discussion groups.

Aviation Enthusiast Corner

http://omni.brooklyn.cuny.edu/rec/air/air.html

Provides many resources, including picture libraries, airshow information, and aircraft locators.

Aviation Image Archives

http://www.landings.com/aviation.html

Contains links to many aviation images and movies, including aircraft, aerobatics, combat, hang gliding, and logos from around the world.

Basics of Space Flight Learners' Workbook

http://www.jpl.nasa.gov/basics/

Provides orientation to space flight and related topics, including the solar system, gravity and mechanics, interplanetary trajectories, orbits, electromagnetic phenomena, space craft types, telecommunications, onboard subsystems, navigation, and phases of flight.

Canard's Aviator's Page

http://www.intercom.net/local/aviation/

Provides information for the aviation enthusiast. Offers links to Canard aircraft that provide information on each aircraft and other related information.

Federal Aviation Regulations

http://www.landings.com/aviation.html

Furnishes searchable database of FAA regulations.

First General Aviation WWW Server

http://aviation.jsc.nasa.gov/

Offers a resource on aviation. Provides information about learning to fly, piloting tips, model airplanes, simulator information, FAA information, and other aviation-related items.

NASA Dryden Flight Research Center

http://www.dfrf.nasa.gov/dryden.html

Provides information about the activities of this research center. Includes a photo archive of research aircraft, research documents, and program information.

NASA Information Services via World Wide Web

http://www.nasa.gov/

Acts as the starting point for all of NASA's Web-based information. Offers links to resources, including space shuttle information, home pages for the NASA centers around the country, space images, and educational resources.

NASA Television on CU-SeeMe

http://btree.lerc.nasa.gov/NASA_TV/NASA_TV.html

Helps visitors learn how to access live images and audio from NASA using CU-SeeMe software. Provides a link for obtaining the CU-SeeMe software.

On Board STS-70

http://shuttle.nasa.gov/

Provides data about the current space shuttle mission. Includes images, schedules, mission information, video clips, technical information. Lets you access status reports for every day for the last two years, including things to be done, concerns, and activities undertaken that day.

Biology

Anatomy Images

ftp://grind.isca.uiowa.edu/image/gif/anatomy/

Contains a directory of anatomy images.

Anderson's Timesaving Comparative Guide

http://www.atcg.com/atcg/

Serves as reference for molecular biologists, providing the world's most comprehensive listing of restriction enzymes, modifying enzymes, commercial DNA libraries, and more.

Auditory Perception

http://www.music.mcgill.ca/~welch/auditory/Auditory.html

Offers a multimedia document about auditory perception, including demonstrations, discussions, and experiments.

BiochemWeb

http://biochemweb.slu.edu/

Provides a service for people involved in biochemistry and molecular biology: those considering applying to the St Louis University graduate program, those involved in the graduate program, and professors.

Biodiversity and Biological Collections Web Server

http://muse.bio.cornell.edu/

Provides information about specimens in biological collections, taxonomic authority files, directories of biologists, reports by various standards bodies (IOPI, ASC, SA2000, and so on), an archive of the Taxacom (MUSE-L and CICHLID-L listservs), access to online journals (including Flora On-line), and MUSE and Delta.

BioForce Labs

http://mac10201.zool.iastate.edu

Focuses on expanding the use of scanning probe microscopy and molecular force detection in basic and applied research and molecular diagnostics. Focuses in particular on manufacturing and selling BioTipsä, biologically modified force transducers for molecular detection. Includes the following services and activities: on-site SPM setup and training, collaborations, providing services, and supply sales.

BIOS Scientific Publishers

http://www.bookshop.co.uk/bios/default.htm

Publisher and bookseller offering a wide variety of scientific books. Site provides detailed descriptions of books and an online ordering option.

BioSupplyNet

http://www.biosupplynet.com/bsn/

Serves as an online product directory for the biomedical/lifescience research community. Offers searchable database that contains more than 15,000 products from 1,400 vendors. Provides information on new products and special offers, an opportunity for users to share expertise through product user groups, and immediate access to suppliers via e-mail for technical support and ordering information.

CSU BIOWEB

`http://130.17.2.215/index.html`

Consolidates existing WWW biological science teaching and research resources and creates and distributes original multimedia resources for teaching biology. Offers general biology links and short descriptions of the sites as well as the separate category for multimedia sites related to biology, which consist mostly of image databases on the Internet.

The Gene Expression Information Resource Project

`http://linus.informatics.jax.org/doc/gxdgen.html`

Site gives an introduction and general background information, as well as query-based searching, about the mouse genome project for gene expression. Site provides other relevant links to the gene expression database. Genetic researchers will find the genotypic, phenotypic, and physical mappings useful.

The Genome Database

`http://gdbwww.gdb.org/`

Site serves as the outlet to the Human Genome Project through the genome database. Database can be searched by keyword, gene name, or symbol. Offers current news and relevant links, as well as the ability to add to the database.

Horizon Scientific Press: Molecular Biology Books

`http://www.apollo.co.uk/a/horizon`

A resource for books in molecular biology and microbiology. Contains useful links to other sites of interest to molecular biologists.

Journals, Conferences, and Current Awareness Services (Biosciences)

`http://golgi.harvard.edu/journals.html`

Site provides links to biomedical WWW sites, online journals, addresses of biologists, and bio-orientated gophers. Also offers access to The Pasteur Institute's search service. Anyone interested in searching specific biological topics will find this site useful.

LLNL Biology and Biotechnology Research Program

`http://www-bio.llnl.gov/bbrp/bbrp.homepage.html`

Introduces you to the Lawrence Livermore National Laboratory's Biology and Biotechnology Research Program (BBRP). Provides information related to their research projects in the areas of the human genome project, DNA repair, x-ray crystallography, and more.

Mendelweb

`http://www.netspace.org/mendelweb/`

Provides an educational resource based on the work of Mendel. Mendel's original 1865 paper on plant hybridization can be downloaded. The site is intended to benefit students by giving interesting information about Mendel's work, as well as links to interactive "MOO" games.

Microworlds Exploring the Structure of Materials

`http://www.lbl.gov/MicroWorlds/`

Explores scientific issues being investigated at the Lawrence Berkeley Laboratory in an understandable and fun way. Provides information on research dealing with issues such as light, conductivity, and wetlands.

National Center for Biotechnology Information

`http://www.ncbi.nlm.nih.gov/`

Responsible for building, maintaining, and distributing GenBank, the NIH genetic sequence database that collects all known DNA sequences from scientists worldwide. Also provides searchable database for DNA sequences.

NRC Biotechnology Research Institute

`http://www.bri.nrc.ca/irbgenen.html`

Provides information about the Biotechnology Research Institute (BRI) of the National Research Council of Canada. BRI has more than 400 specialists and state-of-the-art facilities and equipment to perform cutting-edge R&D in biopharmaceuticals, environmental biotechnology, and bioprocess.

Tools for Molecular Biology, Genetics, and Microbiology

`http://www.genetics.utah.edu%7Erafael/tool.html`

Site contains extensive links to many biological sites involving molecular biology, genetics, microbiology, and virology. Also includes links to databases and professional and commercial organizations. Offers unique links to protocols for laboratory techniques.

Tree of Life

http://phylogeny.arizona.edu/tree/phylogeny.html

Serves as "a map to biological information," a cooperative group of WWW sites on the Internet. Provides information on biology arranged like a phylogenetic tree; the further along you go, the more specific the information becomes.

Virus Databases Online

http://life.anu.edu.au/viruses/welcome.html

Provides links to Internet resources on biological viruses. Includes links to plant and animal viruses, tutorials, genome sequences, and virus news.

Welcome to Virtual FlyLab

http://vflylab.calstatela.edu/edesktop/VirtApps/Vfly/
IntroVflylab.html

Site provides a teaching tool for the genetics of inheritance based on the common fruit fly. The program offers the ability to selectively breed flies with certain mutations, and it requires the user to interpret the results. Virtual FlyLab has been used successfully at the collegiate level as a supplementary tool to laboratory work.

The World Wide Web Virtual Library, Evolution (Biosciences)

http://golgi.harvard.edu/biopages/evolution.html

Provides lists of books and journals. Also gives extensive links to evolution servers, collections, phylogenetics, systematics, taxonomy, and museums. Excellent place to begin searching about biological evolution.

Botany

Balogh Scientific Books

http://www.balogh.com/~balogh/

Publisher and bookseller specializing in botany. Features information on books, an online ordering desk, new book releases, and news about botany. Also offers a mailing list and book trading list.

Botanical Gardens

http://www.btw.com/urls/garden/botanic.htm

Provides links to several online botanical gardens. Links feature a variety of botanical ecosystems from the desert environment to an alpine meadow.

Botany

http://www.ncsa.uiuc.edu/SDG/experimental/
vatican.exhibit/exhibit/g-nature/Botany.html

Site yields information on the history and tradition of botany using the Vatican Library. Contains GIF images of botany texts from the late eighth or early ninth and tenth centuries.

Brief Overview of the National Herbarium

http://nmnhwww.si.edu/botany/collover.html

Includes information about the National Herbarium, a government organization. Includes searchable databases of plants and historical documents.

Connecticut Botanical Society

http://www.vfr.com/cbs/

Site describes the activities of the botanical society: field trips, programs, ecology, and conservation. Also gives information about membership.

Geobotanical Institue

http://www.geobot.umnw.ethx.ch/

Features an overview of the institute and contact information. Also includes research topics, plant ecology, systematics, mycology, archeobotany, libraries, and a herbarium.

Internet Directory for Botany

http://www.helsinki.fi/kmus/botmenu.html

Site provides many botanical sites in science, economy, universities, and applicable software. Also provides mirror sites in nine countries.

National Institute of Agricultural Botany

http://www.open.gov.uk/niab/niabhome.htm

Includes comprehensive index to the science and study of botany. Features articles on training, lab tests, and chemical and plant diseases.

Nature Described: Learning to Look at the World

http://www.ncsa.uiuc.edu/SDG/Experimental/
vatican.exhibit/exhibit/g-nature/Nature.html

Provides historical data about nature and botany.

University of Wisconsin-Madison Botanical Garden

http://www.wisc.edu/edu/botany/garden/

Provides an informative pictorial tour of the University of Wisconsin Botanical Garden. Site contains many colorful floral photographs.

Chemistry

The American Chemical Society

http://www.acs.org/

Site provides access to the American Chemical Society products and news, all ACS journals, as well as limited access to Chemical Literature Abstracts. Also provides access to U.S. chemical patents from 1971 to the present. Excellent site for anyone in an academic or professional chemical field.

The Armchair Scientist

http://www.areacom.it/html/ita/loris/armchair/html#Index

Site describes the contents of a quasiperiodic publication, which features recent hot areas of scientific research. Users can download back issues of the magazine from the site. Also gives access to a mailing list.

Atmospheric Chemistry

http://asd-www.larc.nasa.gov/atmchem/ASDatchem.html

Provides general information about goals and reasons for atmospheric chemical research. Also provides links to major experiments of the Atmospheric Sciences Division, such as tropospheric ozone and biomass emission.

Brain Page

http://maui.net/~jms/brainuse.html

Presents study of how brain chemicals affect emotion, personality, and sexuality. Also offers links to related sites.

ChemCAI: Instructional Software for Chemistry

http://www.sfu.ca:80/chemed/

Contains links to software sources, demonstration materials, and other information for chemists.

Chemical Demonstrations—Table of Contents

http://chemwww.byu.edu/chamed/toc_demo.htm

Site gives a table of contents of a wide variety of chemical demonstrations. Science teachers will find the page extremely useful in finding an appropriate demonstration. Each experiment gives a literature reference where the full description can be found.

Chemistry Hypermedia Project

http://www.chem.vt.edu/chem-ed/vt-chem-ed.html

Provides a library of hypermedia tutorials related to chemistry.

Chemistry Teacher Resources

http://rampages.onramp.net/~jaldr/chemtchr.html

Provides resources for teachers and high school students of chemistry and original documents created by a science teacher.

Composite Materials Research Group—University of Mississippi

http://cypress.mcsr.olemiss.edu/~melackey

Features research conducted by the Composite Materials Research Group at the University of Mississippi. Focuses on the optimization of the pultrusion process for the manufacture of composite materials and mechanical and physical property characterization of composite materials. Features faculty research, facilities and equipment, and graduate school opportunites.

CTI Centre for Chemistry Software Catalogue

http://www.liv.ac.uk/ctichem/catmain.html

Lists software you can use in many areas of science, including general science, crystallography, and all areas of chemistry. Covers a wide variety of software types and platforms.

Dalton Chemical Laboratories, Inc.

http://www.dalton.com/dalton/

Specializes in the synthesis of phosporamidites, oligonucleotides, custom synthesis, and research contracts.

George Goble (GHG) Extended Home Page

http://ghg.ecn.purdue.edu/

View JPEG images of an outdoor barbecue with liquid oxygen. Also contains audio tracks and an MPEG movie of the grill lighting and subsequent disintegration of the grill.

Introduction to Alchemy

http://www.levity.com/alchemy/index.html

Site describes the past of chemistry in alchemy (as well as the future), current applications, and uses of alchemy. Site gives links to mysticism, metaphysical, and allegorical journeys in alchemy. Also provides links to alchemical literature and alchemical societies.

Los Alamos National Laboratory of Energetic Materials

http://sonhp.lanl.gov/dx16.html

Site features fantastic images of exploding objects, as well as information on new explosives, unique applications of explosives, explosives safety, and remediation. Site also stresses the availability of internships and employment at the National Laboratories.

Mendeleev Communications

http://mc.ioc.ac.ru/mc.htm

International journal of short communications in chemistry, published jointly by The Royal Society of Chemistry and The Russian Academy of Sciences since 1991. Presents preliminary accounts of original and significant work from Russia, other states of the former Soviet Union, and elsewhere.

Periodic Table of the Elements

http://www-c8.lanl.gov/infosys/html/periodic/periodic-main.html

Contains a periodic table from which you can select an element and get more information, including atomic number, weight, electrons, and a history of its discovery.

SoftShell Online

http://www.softshell.com/

Offers discussions and information on chemistry topics, including electronic publishing, the free ChemWeb GIF structure editor, and other chemistry

software (such as ChemWindow and ChemIntosh). Focuses on worldwide access to chemical information. Presents a magazine in which anything can be published. Serves as a resource, a classroom, a library, a bulletin board, and a hangout.

Software Reviews from the CTI Centre for Chemistry

http://www.liv.ac.uk/ctichem/swrev.html

Reprints software reviews from the Centre's journal Software Reviews. Helps educators and researchers locate appropriate chemistry-related software.

STM Image Gallery

http://www.almaden.ibm.com/vis/stm/gallery.html

Site features a virtual tour of Scanning Tunneling Microscopy Image gallery. Also features many nanoscale images of quantum intereference, as well as images of the famous Quantum Corrals.

Understanding Our Planet Through Chemistry

http://helios.cr.usgs.gov/gips/aii-home.htm

Explains the history of the earth and the chemistry concepts involved in its formation.

WWW Chemistry Sites at Academic Institutions

http://www.chem.ucla.edu/chempointers.html#Academic

Site provides links to chemistry departments at academic institutions in over 40 countries worldwide.

Intel Software

http://www.intel.com/iaweb/bizapps.htm

Download an application that creates hyperlinks between applications for Windows 95, an application that provides access to Usenet newsgroups using intelligent agent technology, or Windows 95 and Windows NT experimental software.

Cognitive Science

Esoteric Psychology

http://users.aol.com/psychosoph/intropsych.html

Provides an alternative look at psychology and relationships based on spiritual ideas and values. Also contains links to interesting charts on soul evolution, auras, and energies.

Frequently Asked Questions about Parapsychology

http://eeyore.lv-hrc.nevada.edu/~cogno/para1.html

Attempts to explain the current thinking about parapsychology from a scientific point of view. Includes discussions of ESP, ghosts, channeling, and a review of the criticisms.

Internet Resources for Cognitive Science

http://gort.ucsd.edu/ds/sophia/cogsci.html

Site provides links to major cognitive science academic departments. Also contains links to the library of the University of California at San Diego.

Interpsych

http://www.shef.ac.uk/%7Epsysc/InterPsych/inter.html

Site provides an Internet forum discussion of mental health issues and contains links to electronic conferences on topics such as addiction, group-psychotherapy, hypnosis, neuropsych, and many more.

MIT Artificial Intelligence Laboratory

http://www.ai.mit.edu/

Provides information and publications about MIT's latest work on artificial intelligence, including information on computer vision, humanoid robotics, and artificial muscles.

Neurosciences on the Internet

http://www.lm.com/~nab

Lists sites suggested as starting points for exploring neuroscience. Also lists some essential biological and medical resource sites and some World Wide Web sites invaluable for any type of information retrieval.

North West Artificial Intelligence Applications Group

http://www.airtime.co.uk/NWAIAG/Welcome.html

Promotes the application of artificial intelligence.

Psych Central—Dr. John Grohol's Mental Health Page

http://www.coil.com/~grohol/web.htm

Site provides comprehensive links to psychological and mental health topics. Links are broken into two categories—general and professional resources. Site provides a good place to begin searching for information about psychological disorders.

Scholarly Psychology Resources on the Web

http://www.gasou.edu/psychweb/resource/bytopic/htm

The PsychWeb home page contains links to subtopics within the field of psychology. Site contains the traditional subdisciplines of psychology, as well as links in animal neuroscience, ethology, and evolutionary psychology. Page also features a job listing section.

The Social Worker Networker

http://www.spring-board.com/two/SocialWorkerNet/

Site gives access to social work resources on the Internet, as well as chat channels, job opportunities, public policy, legal information, and journals. A mailing list link also is available.

Computer Science

Brussels Free University (ULB) Computer Science Department: Bookmarks

http://www.ulb.ac.be/di/bookmarks/book.html

Collects bookmarks about computer science, mathematics, computer firms, technical reports in these fields, bibliographies, and more.

Computer Vision and Image Processing Group

http://poseidon.csd.auth.gr:80/

Covers digital image processing and related areas. Includes the areas of multichannel and color image processing, parallel image processing, medical signal processing, ultrasonic image processing and storage, fast algorithms and architectures for digital filtering and image processing, morphological image analysis.

Computing Center, Academy of Sciences, Russia

http://sunny.ccas.ru/

Provides computing services to the institutes of the Academy and other users.

Cornell Theory Center

http://www.tc.cornell.edu/

Contains information about high-end computing theory. Offers a visualization link that includes animations, graphics, and tools.

Electronic Desktop Project Home Page

http://vflylab.calstatela.edu/Welcome.html

Focuses on improving the way science is taught and learned by bringing the power of advanced workstation technology to introductory science students in both major and general education classes. Details some of EDP's projects and offers links to interactive demonstrations.

Electronic Visualization Lab

http://www.ncsa.uiuc.edu/EVL/docs/html/homePage.html

Merges art, computers, and science in electronic visualization. Contains visualization projects, as well as student home pages that display visualizations.

European Software Institute (ESI)

http://www.esi.es/

Provides information about Europe's movement toward improving the competitiveness of the European software industry. Includes training information, a list of upcoming events, and new improvements to their server.

Los Alamos Group XTM Home Page

http://www-xdiv.lanl.gov/XTM/

Supports X-Division's mission by developing state-of-the-art computational tools to investigate and solve complex problems in radiation hydrodynamics and transport. Applies these tools to problems that are important to the nation's security and well-being.

Projects in Scientific Computing

http://www.sdsc.edu/MetaScience/welcome.html

National Science Foundation Research Center. Online version of the Pittsburgh Supercomputing Center (PSC)'s annual publication. Features current research in various fields, written at a nonspecialist level.

San Diego Supercomputer Center

http://www.sdsc.edu

National laboratory for computational science and engineering established in 1985. Advances research and promotes United States economic competitiveness with state-of-the-art computational tools. Features a variety of collaborative research and educational programs, high-performance computational and visualization tools, and a nationally recognized staff.

UCSD Optoelectronic Computing Group

http://soliton.ucsd.edu/

Researches and develops massively parallel optoelectronic computer systems using the optimal utilization of microelectronic and photonic technologies. Pursues a plan of research that spans the areas of optoelectronic materials and devices, diffractive and micro-optics, nonlinear optics, optical storage technologies, parallel computing algorithms and architectures, including database and neural systems, computer modeling, and optoelectronic packaging.

Earth Science

Earth Sciences and Resources Institute

http://www.esri.utah.edu

Focuses on university-based research applied to fossil fuel, mineral, geothermal, and environmental assessment. Presents an electronic brochure about the Institute. Also offers links to energy/environmental/mineral/geothermal-relevant reference sites. Includes a photo and quote of the week.

EOS Buchantiquariat Benz

http://www.iprolink.ch/eos/

Catalog of antiquarian books concerning botany, earth science, geology, natural history, paleontology, and zoology. Also contains a search tool, some illustrations, terms and ordering information, and links to other earth science related sites.

Hanford Site

http://www.hanford.gov/

Department of Energy Web site supporting programs in waste management, environmental science restoration, and energy. Contains information on news and events, projects and activities, business opportunities, and the history of Hanford. Also features searchable database and links to other related Web sites.

Idaho National Engineering Laboratory

http://www.inel.gov/

Site dedicated to the research in basic and applied sciences to solve problems related to the environment, energy production and use, economic competitiveness, and national security. Features educational resources, news releases, calendar events, environmental articles, and links to other environmental related sites.

National Center for Atmospheric Research

http://www.ucar.edu/oceanmodel.html

Presents a high-resolution simulation of the North Atlantic Ocean that represents circulation, designed to show the utility of some current scientific visualization tools to interpret highly complex data—making these data both meaningful and instructive to the viewer.

Online Earth Science Journals

http://www.glg.ed.ac.uk/~ajsw/doc/journals_FAQ.html

Lists online resources for earth science.

Rain Forest Action Network Home Page

http://www.ran.org/ran/

Discusses environmental issues of the rain forest. Includes numerous reports, statistics, information on other groups, and lists of companies to boycott. Also presents a children's corner and information about what you can do.

Science and Public Policy Program

http://www.uoknor.edu/spp/

Contains general information about the program, new trends, activities, and publications concerning policy research on environmental, energy, and sustainable development.

Science and Technology Corporation (STC)

http://www.stcnet.com/

Specializes in the atmospheric and environmental sciences.

Science Applications International Corp. (SAIC)

http://www.saic.com/

Firm devoted to high-tech products and services in the fields of national security, environment, health, energy, transportation, and systems integration. Features separate categories on energy, environment, government, information technology, health care technology, the Internet, telecommunication, transportation, a search tool, and career opportunities.

Supplements to Atmospheric & Oceanic Publications

http://www-cmpo.mit.edu/met_links/index.html

Provides data sets, source codes, and other supplements to published papers on the Web. Includes the means for visitors to the listing to add their own supplemental material if appropriate.

Technadyne Engineering Consultants

http://www.indirect.com/www/technady/

Consulting firm specializing in energy applications, earth sciences, environmental and defense-related issues. Site features information about the firm and their clients and reports on some of their projects.

VolcanoWorld

http://volcano.und.nodak.edu/

Provides information on volcanoes. Includes current news, images and articles about eruptions, background information, and an online expert who answers questions.

Ecology

Abbey's Web

http://www.abalon.se/beach/aw/abbey.html

Site honors the militant environmentalist Edward Abbey and provides information about his writings and current ecological causes he promoted. Site also contains interesting links to outdoor photos.

The Access Fund

`http://www.sportsite.com/accessfund/`

Seeks to preserve America's diverse rock climbing areas through education, instruction in conservation, and promoting environmentally sound climbing practices. Site also contains board of directors information, as well as information regarding participation and protection of areas.

Earth Viewer

`http://www.fourmilab.ch/earthview/vplanet.html`

Enables you to use the Earth Viewer online mapping tool to see Earth from above by setting specifications such as longitude and latitude, look at satellite imagery, composite the image with cloud cover, and much more. Presents the Solar System Live, which shows the locations of the planets at any time. Also presents Terranova, a series of images of hypothetical planets created each day.

EcoLink

`http://www.envirolink.org/EcoLink/`

Online eco-Web journal. Delves into one ecological topic each week, including real-life stories, photos, and scientific information. Offers links to related Net resources.

Ecology and Human Rights Information

`http://paul.spu.edu/~koberst/green/green.html`

Site contains various links to general ecological resources on the WWW, domestic and foreign. Site contains lists of major environmental and human rights special interest groups.

The Ecology Channel

`http://www.ecology.com/`

Web site features news and information about current ecological problems and solutions. Offers excellent links to business, current ecological publications, and various activism groups.

Ecovote Online

`http://www.ecovote.org/ecovote/`

Site features the platform of the California League of Conservation Voters. Contains links to environmental issues, press releases, an environmental scorecard, 1996 bill tracking, and links to other WWW environmental resources.

Greenpeace

`http://www.greenpeace.org/`

Promoter of biodiversity and enemy of ecological and environmental pollution, Greenpeace and its links are accessible through this site. Links include the biodiversity campaign, the North Sea oil rig tour, a hotpage, and more.

Natural Resources Conservation Service—U.S. Dept. of Agriculture

`http://www.ncg.nrcs.usda.gov/`

Site describes the goals and services of the Natural Resources Conservation Service (NRCS). Formerly the Soil Conservation Service, the NRCS provides assistance to preserve the natural resources. Site also contains workforce organizations and state directories.

Rainforest Workshop Home Page

`http://mh.osd.wednet.edu/`

Provides information about the rainforest. Contains many links to Internet resources, including lesson plans, plant and animal information, ecology, and more.

Ralph Maughan's Wolf Report

`http://ww.greywolf.com/rm/maughan.html`

Dr. Ralph Maughan, a political scientist specializing in natural resource policies, reports on the status of the grey wolf's reintroduction to Yellowstone. Site contains daily to weekly updates on the status of the wolf packs.

Sierra Club

`http://www.sierraclub.org/`

Home page for the nonprofit public interest conservation organization. Site focuses on activist news, current critical "ecoregions," Sierra Club National Outings Program, as well as an internal Sierra Club search engine.

U.I.A. Freshwater Ecology (The Chironomid Home Page)

http://alt-www.uia.ac.be/u/intpanis/

Focuses on chironomidae (non-biting midges). Provides several bibliographies with scientific papers, lists of colleagues around the world, and more. Also provides the opportunity to ask questions or share general messages.

U.S. Fish and Wildlife Service

http://www.nwi.fws.gov/

Site provides a list of the national wetlands and news related to them. Nineteen files are available for downloading, including a list of plant species that are found in wetlands. Also contains links to product information, ecology, and educator information.

Welcome to Coastal America's Home Page

http://kingfish.ssp.nmfs.gov/coastamer/coastamer.html

The Coastal America program is a collaborative effort between organizations to protect the ecological systems and wildlife of America's coastal regions. Provides general information on the program itself and placeholders for more specific information yet to come.

World Forum for Acoustic Ecology

http://interact.uoregon.edu/MediaLit/WFAEHomePage

Seeks to investigate natural and human-made soundscapes. Offers links to sound resources and links to the online discussion forum.

Energy

Alternative Energy Engineering

http://www.asia.com/aee/

Site devoted to helping individuals make electricity from solar, wind, or water power. Features a Web catalog including a 120-page design information packet.

The American Nuclear Society

http://www.ans.neep.wisc.edu/

Provides information on membership, upcoming conferences, links to student chapters, and links to other WWW resources.

Bioenergy

http://calvin.biotech.wisc.edu/jeffries/

Resource page for bioenergy, bioconversion, and bioprocess technology. Contains an archive of related papers, information on liquid fuels from feedstocks and enzymatic methods. Personnel offer to assist in bioprocess development.

Brookhaven National Laboratory

http://www.bnl.gov/PUBAF/pubaf_home.html

Department of Energy research laboratory is dedicated to basic and applied investigation in several scientific disciplines. Contains an educational section geared for all ages, calendar of events, bulletin board, weekly newspaper, and departmental information.

Clustron Science Corporation

http://www.gslink.com/~ncmcn/Clustron/

Features information about the Nucleon Clustron Model of the atomic nucleus. Also contains company information and an atomic and nuclear periodic table of elements and isotopes.

CREST'S Guide to Alternative Energy

http://solstice.crest.org/online/aeguide/index.html

Contains features and articles related to alternative energy. Also includes links to other related sites and a searchable database.

Ed's News Page

http://www.hubcom.com/edsnews/index.html

Daily newspaper devoted to the oil and gas industry. Contains images, news summaries, and links to other news sources.

Energy Science and Technology Software Center

http://www.doe.gov/html/osti/estsc/estsc.html

Features software for sale funded by the Department of Energy or the Nuclear Regulatory Commission. Contains a searchable database, title information, ordering specifications, and other general information about the center.

Home Power Magazine

http://www.homepower.com/hp/

Magazine designed to assist home or business owners in lowering electric costs through solar, hydroelectric, or wind energy. Contains articles and stories, subscription information, and links to other alternative energy-related sites.

Investigating Wind Energy

http://sln.fi.edu/tfi/units/energy/windguide.html

Set up in an educational format by The Franklin Institute Science Museum, this site contains discussions and articles relating to wind energy, information on building windmills, and different ideas and exhibits.

Nova Structure

http://www.bergen.gov/ATC/nova_structure2.html

Academy for the Advancement of Science and Technology Web site. Features information about, pictures of, and the general process for their project to design an energy-efficient house.

Engineering

All Electrical Engineering Academic Programs (Almost)

http://www.ee.umr.edu/schools/ee_programs.html

Contains a complete listing of electrical engineering academic programs, organized by country.

American Institute of Chemical Engineers

http://www.che.ufl.edu/WWW-CHE/aiche/

Provides information on the group's mission, the upcoming world conference, and its programs. Also offers membership information.

Chemical Engineering URLs Directory

http://www.ciw.uni-karlsruhe.de/chem-eng.html

Offers a collection of links to information about chemical engineering resources outside the United States. Also offers a collection of links to chemical engineering sites all over the world. Provides information on upcoming conferences and includes many search links.

Crazy about Constraints!

http://www.lm.com/~dshu/toc/cac.html

Provides information regarding mechanical engineering manufacturing issues, such as the theory of constraints, the thinking processes, and other Goldratt techniques.

D Banks—Microengineering/MEMS

http://www.ee.surrey.ac.uk/Personal/D.Banks/ueng.html

Provides information on microengineering. Offers a small collection of tutorials and documents. Focuses on micromachining and the fabrication of structures the size of microns.

Fraunhofer Institute for Materials Physics and Surface Engineering

http://www.iws.fhg.de/ext/iwseng.htm

Focuses on basic and applied research for surface processing of materials and components by means of laser and other high-power energy sources.

Institution of Electrical Engineers Home Page

http://www.iee.org.uk/

Provides information about membership in the Institution of Electrical Engineers, upcoming events, information services (including searchable databases), and a collection of links to other Internet resources.

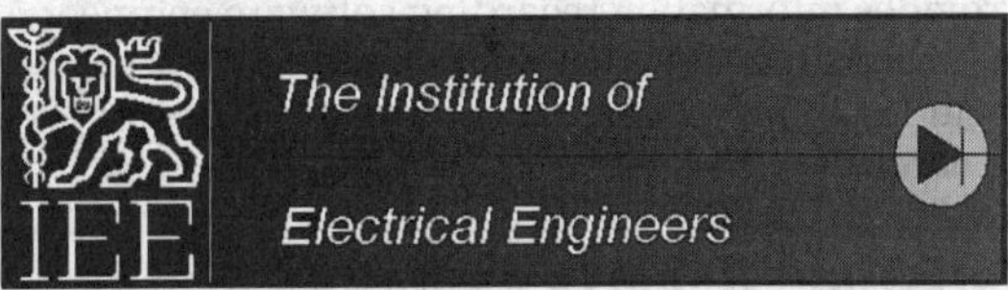

Meetings Information

http://www.tms.org

Provides information about materials-related resources and publications. Also offers a list of national or international conferences and seminars on materials engineering.

Micromath's Home Page

http://www.MicroMath.com/

Develops software for scientists and engineers, primarily for solving equation systems and fitting experimental data. Offers Mac and IBM software. Also offers MMCalc, a downloadable Macintosh desktop utility program (free).

National Society Of Black Engineers at SDSU

http://rohan.sdsu.edu/home/nsbe/index.html

Provides information about the organization, links to other chapter home pages, and an assortment of links to other Web sites. Also includes membership information.

NU Student Chapter ASCE

http://www.civil.nwu.edu/asce/

Provides information regarding the American Society of Civil Engineers. Includes information concerning membership, and offers a calendar and information about other chapters.

Reliability Analysis Center (RAC) Home Page

http://www.iitri.com/RAC/

Provides many links to information about reliability engineering. Also provides information on RAC products and offers a large collection of learning resources.

Software Engineering Archives

http://www.qucis.queensu.ca/Software-Engineering/

Provides information regarding software engineering. Offers links to other related information. Includes archives searchable by vendor, category, or name.

Statistical Reports on United States Science and Engineering

http://www.nsf.gov/sbe/srs/stats.htm

Includes the education of scientists and engineers, the science and engineering work force, research and development expenditures and performance, science and technology outputs and impacts, and public attitudes on science.

UAB Thermal and Fluids Engineering Group

http://mmewww.eng.uab.edu/me/tfrl/

Focuses on computational/experimental research related to modeling problems, primarily those involving fluids and heat transfer interactions.

UCF ASET

http://pegasus.cc.ucf.edu/~aset/

Provides information about the Electric Car project and offers a collection of links to student engineering groups and organizations, along with research-related links.

Unofficial Chemical Engineering Home Page

http://raffles0005.pc.nus.sg/~rekcah/ChE/

Describes chemical engineering and offers a collection of links to information about or for chemical engineers.

Virginia Geotechnical Services

http://www.infi.net/~vageo/

Specializes in geotechnical engineering, geoenvironmental services, and construction monitoring. Provides useful information concerning professional consulting, the environment, and business practice.

Welcome to Internet Directory of Biotechnology Resources

http://biotech.chem.indiana.edu/

Provides information on biotechnology engineering on the Internet.

World Wide Web Virtual Library: Aerospace

http://macwww.db.erau.edu/www_virtual_lib/Aerospace.html

Offers collection of links on aerospace engineering.

WWW Archive for Electric Power Engineering Education

http://www.uow.edu.au/pwrsysed/homepage.html

Provides resources for electric power educators. Focuses on the Asia-Pacific region. Also provides information about books and software packages.

Environmental Science

BCRI On-Line

http://www.bcr.bc.ca

Centre for Alternative Transportation Fuels. Focuses on forest biotechnology, environment, advanced transportation systems, ocean engineering, and ergonomics.

Earth and Environmental Science

http://info.er.usgs.gov/network/science/earth/earth.html

Site is a registry of Earth and environmental science internet resources, maintained by the U.S. Geological Survey. Mainly provides links to university departments of Earth and environmental science.

EMF-Link

http://infoventures.com

Serves as a resource on biological effects of electric and magnetic fields for the general public and professionals. Contains key documents, resources, and literature for those interested in possible health effects from power lines, computer monitors, magnetic resonance imaging equipment, radio communications, cellular telephones, radar, microwave transmissions, and other sources.

Environmental Chemical Corporation

http://w3.one.net/~webcon/clients/environ/html/index.html

Deals with safety solvents, industrial cleaning, biological products, maintenance supplies, equipment cleaning, truck wash, sewage treatment, degreasers, disinfectant, food processing chemicals, food service, drain maintenance, HVAC, heating ventilation and air conditioning, vehicle maintenance, vehicle cleaning, printing industry, de-icers, and odor control, among other things, as partners for a cleaner, safer environment.

Florida Center for Environmental Studies' Home Page

http://www.ces.fau.edu/

Provides environmental resources concerning the management of Florida ecosystems and other tropical and subtropical water-dominated freshwater and estuarine ecosystems worldwide.

Giovanni Guglielmo's Research Page on Salt Tectonics

http://www.utexas.edu/research/beg/giovanni/

Contains free computer animations, 3D visualization, and interpretations of physical and finite element models of salt tectonics.

Greenspan Technology

http://peg.pegasus.oz.au/~greenspan/

Specializes in leading-edge water quality monitoring technology for the water resources, environmental, and pollution markets. Offers services ranging from the deployment of single water quality sensors, installation of sophisticated multiparameter monitors, to project management of major hydrological studies worldwide.

IFIAS

http://www.ifias.ca

A global network of scientific research institutions that collaborate on projects relating to science, technology and innovation policy, ecosystem management, gender science and development, the implications of the human genome project for developing countries, and the international system of science.

Infrastructure Technology Institute (ITI)

http://iti.acns.nwu.edu/

Provides information about current research, technology transfer, and education regarding America's infrastructure.

National Soil Erosion Research Laboratory

http://soils.ecn.purdue.edu:200-2/%7Ewepp/nserl.html

Focuses on water erosion of soil and seeks to preserve the soil for future generations. Site also contains downloadable Water Prediction Project software and the Crop Parameter Intelligent Database System.

United Nations Environment Programme (UNEP), Geneva

http://www.unep.ch/

Contains many treaties and programs on preserving the environment. Includes information on topics including the "Convention on Biodiversity," climate change, endangered species, and toxic chemicals.

Rocky Mountain High

Sorry, John Denver, but as the following indicates, the tallest of the world's mountains are in the Himalayas. For more geographical information, check out the sites in the Geography section.

Mountain	Range	Feet
Everest	Himalayas	29,022
K2 (Godwin Austen)	Karakoram	28,251
Kanchenjunga	Himalayas	28,208
Lhotse	Himalayas	27,923
Yalung	Himalayas	27,893
Makalu	Himalayas	27,824
Dhaulagiri	Himalayas	26,811
Manaslu	Himalayas	26,758
Cho Oyu	Himalayas	26,748
Nanga Parbat	Himalayas	26,660

WWW Virtual Library—Environment

http://ecosys.drdr.virginia.edu/all.shtml

Site provides hundreds of links to environmental causes, environmentally friendly living, and recycling. Also contains many photos and images.

Geography

Althausen's WWW Wonderland

http://www.stpt.usf.edu/~johnalt/index.html

Provides information and links to the wonderful world of geography, concentrating on the fields of remote sensing and geographic information systems. Also provides links to pages that deal with the topic. Althausen tosses in pages for his favorite professional teams and musicians as well. Offers links to numerous government agencies.

Chesapeake Bay Program

http://www.epa.gov/r3chespk

Page contains information on the health and history of the waterway. Features trends in pollution and restoration projects of Chesapeake Bay that are underway. Also contains links to scientific data and research about the bay and other bay resources.

Clinch River Restoration Program

http://www.esd.orni.gov/programs/crerp/index.htm

An astounding page that describes geographical measurements on the Clinch River in Tennessee. Color geographical images and animated sequences provide excellent entertainment and also make this page educational.

Color Landform Atlas of the United States

http://fermi.jhuapl.edu/states/states.html

Site provides beautiful colorform maps of the United States. Topographic maps and a "virtual tour" of each state can be found, as well as an elevation key.

Geographic Nameserver

http://www.mit.edu:8001/geo

Provides geographic information about a specific location, including county, state, country, population, area code, latitude, longitude, and elevation.

Geography—A Diverse Discipline

http://www.umanitoba.ca/faculties/arts/geography/
geoginfo.html

Site is part of the geography department of the University of Manitoba. This page gives a broad overview of the disciplines of geography, as well as an explanation of the different disciplines. A good place to start for the novice interested in geography and its subfields.

Internet Resources for Geographers

http://www.utexas.edu/depts/grg/virtdept/resources/contents.html

Provides WWW resources and information for geographers and laymen alike. Also contains great satellite imagery, mapping information, and other geographically relevant links.

Michael Braun's Home Page

http://www.cla.sc.edu/geog/geogdocs/departdocs/stddocs/mbraun.html

Provides information about geographical techniques such as remote sensing and fractal dimensions in geography. Other interesting geographical links are present too.

TIGER Mapping Service

http://tiger.census.gov/

Allows you to generate a high-quality, detailed map of anywhere in the United States, using public geographic data.

United States Gazetteer

http://tiger.census.gov/cgi-bin/gazetteer/

Identifies places you can use the Tiger Map Server and the 1990 Census Lookup to view. Lets you search for a place by entering the name and state abbreviation.

Xerox PARC Map Viewer

http://www.xerox.com/map

Enables you to click on a region and zoom in to see areas in more detail.

Geology

Centre for Earth and Ocean Research—University of Victoria

http://wikyonos.seaoar.uvic.ca/ceor.home.html

Focuses on earth and ocean research.

Civil Engineer's Calendar

http://audrey.fagg.uni-lj.si/ICARIS/dates.ce/

Provides information about upcoming events of interest to civil engineers, in a searchable index or obtainable by e-mail.

CNC Relief Maps

http://www.nerosworld.com/www/MassProduction/reliefmap.html

Provides models of any size, scale, or vertical exaggeration. Serves the National Forest Service for interpretive centers, fire/watershed analysis, and maintenance.

Data Catalog

http://rainbow.ldgo.columbia.edu/datacatalog.html

Presents a catalog of climate-related datasets, with an interface that enables you to make plots, tables, and files from any dataset, its subsets, or processed versions thereof.

Data Zoo

http://www-ccs.ucsd.edu/ccs/about_datazoo.html

Contains data collected by various California coastal data collection programs and studies.

Earthquake Info from the U.S.G.S.

http://quake.wr.usgs.gov/

Provides earthquake information. Includes plots, news, regional studies, maps, and references.

Nevada Bureau of Mines and Geology

http://www.nbmg.unr.edu

Conducts research and publishes results of the studies for the general public, as well as geologic and minerals specialists.

New Mexico Bureau of Mines and Mineral Resources

http://www.nmt.edu/~nmbmmr/homepage.html

Provides a database of mineral images from New Mexico as well as a geologic map.

Lotus Notes Applications

http://www.lotus.com/edgefree/default.htm

More downloadable fun stuff. Hit this site to download trial or freeware versions of Notes tools.

Niel's Timelines and Scales of Measurement List

http://xalph.ast.cam.ac.uk/public/niel/scales.html

Provides information in the areas of evolutionary time, geological time, scales of measurement, and so forth.

Smithsonian Gem and Mineral Collection

http://galaxy.einet.net/images/gems/gems-icons.html

Contains nearly 100 images and short descriptions of gems and minerals.

United States Department of the Interior/Geological Survey/ Pacific Marine Geology

http://walrus.wr.usgs.gov/

Strives to address key marine and coastal issues, increase understanding of geological processes affecting these realms, and ultimately improve predictive capabilities to help guide the preservation and sustainable development of the nation's marine and coastal regions. Offers links to information on seismic activity, information on the Monterey bay area, and sea floor images. Also features a link to a more graphic-intensive version of the site. Contains many resources.

United States Geological Survey: Earth and Environmental Science

http://info.er.usgs.gov/network/science/earth/
earthquake.html

Offers links to pages about earthquakes, federal emergency management, oceanography, earth science, geology, and more.

Mathematics

AMATH, Inc.

http://www.smartpages.com/amath/

A pre-algebra course for students who have trouble learning math. Provides both a preview and ordering information.

Beauty of Chaos

http://i30www.ira.uka.de/~ukrueger/fractals/

Provides interactive journey through fractal images. Takes you through most of the database, which consists of hundreds of images.

Ben Cheng's Home Page

http://198.68.160.16/~benny/benny.htm

Offers a weekly math teaser (which also appears in the journal *Matematika*) to entertain and stretch your advanced math knowledge. Also presents an art gallery that contains chaos images.

Calculus & Mathematica Home Page

http://www-cm.math.uiuc.edu/

Calculus & Mathematica is a calculus-reform project started at the University of Illinois and Ohio State University. Uses Mathematica, a software package from Wolfram Research, to teach calculus to high school and college students.

Chaos at Maryland

http://www-chaos.umd.edu/chaos.html

Provides information on the various applications of chaos theory. Includes dimensions, fractal basin boundaries, chaotic scattering, and controlling chaos. Includes online papers, a searchable database, and general references. Also offers the Chaos Gallery.

Chaos Network Sign-In

http://www.prairienet.org/business/ptech/

Offers many links to topics relating to chaos theory, such as fractal mathematics. Recommends books to peruse.

Chartwell-Bratt

http://www.studli.se/brattint/welcUSE.html

Provides an online catalog for Swedish book publisher, Chartwell-Bratt. Offers English or Swedish databases you can search by title, author, or subject. Includes books on mathematics, computer science, and engineering.

Common Weights and Measures

http://www.cchem.berkeley.edu/ChemResources/
Weights-n-Measures/index.html

Contains information on converting to and from metric and United States measurements.

Computational Logic, Inc.

http://www.cli.com/

Performs advanced research and development in math modeling of digital hardware and software systems. Includes software and technical reports. Also provides education and consulting services.

Offers jumps to university sites that contain information on the mathematical modeling of digital systems.

CPLEX Optimization, Inc. Home Page

http://www.cplex.com/

Develops large-scale mathematical programming software and services. Provides lists of products and services and offers linear and mixed-integer programming software.

CSC Mathematical Topics

http://www.csc.fi/math_topics/

Provides information about mathematical software and guidebooks available at the Center for Scientific Computing (CSC, Finland). Also points to application specialists at CSC for help on specific topics. Provides several kinds of search mechanisms to help find documents. Displays examples of mathematical animations and visualizations made at CSC. Also contains some guidebooks and newsletters published by CSC.

CSC Mathematical Topics: Visualizations

http://www.csc.fi/math_topics/Movies/

Displays animations (MPG format) of various mathematical theories and areas. Includes Klein bottle, genetic algorithms, Fourier series, and so on.

Data Modeling Web Site

http://www.fred.net/mandalay/

Offers links to many other sites. Builds custom nonlinear curve-fitting software based on your problem.

Dave's Math Links

http://www.azstarnet.com/~maxinfo/index.htm

Provides a Mathcad files library, links to math resources on the Web, and image-processing applications.

Design-By-Example

http://www.uta.fi/~hs/dbe.html

Develops tools for database design and reverse engineering.

Dynamical Systems and Technology Project

http://math.bu.edu/DYSYS/dysys.html

Provides information on contemporary mathematics, such as fractals and chaos. Includes computer demos, as well as movies on some famous fractal sets.

e-Math Home Page

http://www.ams.org/

Home of the American Mathematical Society. Offers professional memberships. Publishes electronic journals, books on math, and the fee-based MathSci database, which features comprehensive coverage of research in mathematics, computer science, and statistics.

Eisenhower National Clearinghouse DCL

http://www.enc.org/

Supports improving teaching and learning in math and science in secondary schools. Offers links to other Internet resources. Presents online catalog and databases, as well as a collection of Internet software and information.

Electronic Textbook: Integrated Course in Chemistry, Mathematics, and Physics

http://dept.physics.upenn.edu/courses/gladney/mathphys/Contents.html

Contains information in the areas of trigonomics, velocity, acceleration, Newton's Laws, chaotic systems, and more.

Fractal Gallery

http://eulero.cineca.it/~strumia/FractalGallery.htm

Presents downloadable color fractal images that show different mathematics problems. Includes the Curve of Von Koch, the Mandelbot Set, and trees, ferns, and mountains.

Fractal Image Compression

http://inls3.ucsd.edu/y/Fractals

Contains links and information regarding fractal image compression. Offers an online bibliography, book reviews, conference announcements, and papers.

Fractal Microscope

http://www.ncsa.uiuc.edu/Edu/Fractal/Fractal_Home.html

Provides information on basic fractals, why they should be discussed, their purposes in the real world, and why supercomputers are necessary for fractals.

Fractals Calendar Home Page

http://fas.sfu.ca/0/cs/research/projects/FractalCal/cal.html

Provides information on obtaining the Fractal Calendar, a calendar specifically designed to show off some of the newer discoveries in fractal mathematics. Also offers previous editions of the calendar.

Fractals Frequently Asked Questions and Answers

http://www.marshall.edu/~stepp/fractal-faq/faq.html

Contains all the frequently asked questions about fractals.

Future Graph, Inc. Home Page

http://www.futuregraph.com/

Offers many links to math-related sites.

GAMS: Guide to Available Mathematical Software

http://gams.nist.gov/

Gateway to NIST guide to available mathematical software. Allows searching by package name or, more interestingly, by what problem it solves.

Guide to Math Resources

http://www.ama.caltech.edu/resources.html

Offers resource jump list to various math resources, including the Latex, Tex, and Maple packages. Also contains jumps to math-related Gopher sites, newsgroups, math institutes, and a math software index.

History of Mathematics

http://www-groups.dcs.st-and.ac.uk:80/~history/

Contains biographies of mathematicians, searchable by alphabetical or chronological index (and some include pictures).

IMA WWW Server

http://www.ima.umn.edu/

Institute for Mathematics and its Applications. Provides the newsletter and back issues of the newsletters of this professional organization.

IMSA Home Page

http://www.imsa.edu/

Provides information about the Illinois Mathematics and Science Academy, a residential public high school for students talented in the fields of math and science.

Intercall

http://www.maths.monash.edu.au/people/tdr/welcome.html

Lets you import code into Mathematica. Gives users a way to organize and use Mathematica Notebooks. Also displays graphics rendered in Mathematica.

Internet Center for Mathematics Problems

http://www.mathpro.com/math/mathCenter.html

Attempts to identify and list all sources of math puzzles on the Internet. Lists problems from back issues of the *Missouri Journal of Mathematical Sciences* and the *Fibonacci Quarterly* and contains information about other sources of math puzzlers such as newsgroups and books.

Logal Software Home Page

http://www.logal.com/

Develops and markets math software for middle school through college.

Math Teaching Assistant

http://www.csun.edu/~vcact00g/math.html

Contains a math tutoring program developed for classroom computer labs aimed at secondary school students.

Mathematica World

`http://www.vut.edu.au/MW/`

Electronic distribution center and support center for various math-related newsletters, most of which are based on Mathematica software.

Mathematics Archives WWW Server

`http://archives.math.utk.edu/`

Provides ftp access to shareware and public domain software for teaching math on the college level. Also provides information and software for people interested in math, as well as links to secondary school software. Includes considerable information on software.

Mathlab

`http://www.scar.utoronto.ca/homes/mathlab/mathlab.html`

A mathematics computer lab. Features downloadable undergraduate level courseware (designed to run under Unix and Mathematica) on geometry, graph theory, and complex analysis.

MathSearch—Search a Collection of Mathematical Web Material

`http://www.maths.usyd.edu.au:8000/MathSearch.html`

Allows you to search a collection of over 19,000 documents on mathematics and statistics servers.

MathSoft Home Page

`http://www.mathsoft.com/`

Offers technical support, news, and product catalog.

MathSolutions, Inc. Home Page

`http://smc.vnet.net/Christensen.html`

Distributes MathTensor, an add-on for Mathematica that performs tensor analysis. Also provides links to resources and offers papers.

MathSource Home Page

`http://www.wri.com/WWWDocs/mathsource/`

Provides a collection of downloadable Mathematica packages, notebooks, examples, and programs. Offers list of related Web sites.

MathType Home Page

`http://www.mathtype.com/mathtype/`

Houses an equation editor for Mac and Windows machines. Offers technical support, registration, and product information.

MathWorks Home Page

`http://www.mathworks.com/`

Offers MATLAB, a high-end mathematics software package, as well as links to jobs, news, and books. Provides information on the Pentium chip flaw. Also presents products and services and an online copy of the MATLAB newsletter.

More Fractal Pictures

`http://www.lerc.nasa.gov/Other_Groups/K-12/fracpage.html`

Serves as a resource for fractal images that show the concepts of chaos theory (geared to grades K through 12).

Netlib Repository at UTK/ORNL

`http://www.netlib.org/`

Contains a large number of downloadable math-related programs (most of the software is shareware). Contains papers about different research on mathematical topics, many of which involve computers. Also offers links to other math-related databases.

Numerical Algorithms Group Ltd.

`http://www.nag.co.uk:70/`

Produces numerical, symbolic, statistical, and visualization software for science, engineering, financial analysis, and research.

Online Image Archiver

`http://www.maths.tcd.ie/pub/images/images.html`

Presents math-related images, such as Mobius strips and Kleinband.

Precision Large-Scale Dimensional Metrology/Measurement

`http://worldmall.com/et/ethome.htm`

Offers precision large-scale measurement, typically dimensional measurements with .001-inch accuracy.

Principia Consulting Home Page

http://www.csn.net/princon/

Offers training on Mathematica, gives Mathematica support, and does custom programming. Lists fees and availability of training. Provides information on fine-tuning performance with Mathematica.

Quantum Books Home Page

http://www.quantumbooks.com/

Online technical bookstore. Specializes in computer topics such as the Internet, programming, and graphics, as well as in books pertaining to mathematics and physics.

Steven M. Christensen and Associates, Inc.

http://smc.vnet.net/Christensen.html

Offers scientific computing software. Provides information on MathTensor, Schur, and Mathematica. Also offers consulting, which includes porting software to Sun systems. Offers links to Mathgroup, a Mathematica support group.

TMP at Imperial College London

http://othello.ma.ic.ac.uk/

Uses Mathematica to make learning modules for first-year university science and engineering students. Provides learning modules for calculus, algebra, matrices, and so on.

Transmath—A CBL Mathematics Tutor

http://caliban.leeds.ac.uk/

Offers mathematics courseware using Toolbook (hypertext) documents with Microsoft Windows. Provides instruction on algebra, matrices, vectors, and sequences.

Union Mathematica Argentina

http://www.famaf.uncor.edu/uma/

Organizes workshops, talks, meetings, and conferences, and edits several magazines in mathematics and education.

Video Vita

http://evlweb.eecs.uic.edu/spiff/videovita/index.html

Produces "edutainment" products in mathematics, science, and technology. Offers an online video sample.

Waterloo Fractal Compression Page

http://links.uwaterloo.ca/

Provides information on fractal compression software and papers on fractal compression.

World-Wide Web Virtual Library: Mathematics

http://euclid.math.fsu.edu/Science/math.html

Provides links to all things mathematical. Includes jumps to math software, Gophers, newsgroups, electronic journals, preprints, bibliographies, TeX Archives, and high school and university math sites.

Meteorology

AgriWeather

http://www.agriweather.com/

Presents an online catalog of weather instruments and related products. Also offers a customized weather forecast service that provides separate weather forecasts for agricultural, business, and corporate needs.

Alden Electronics

http://www.alden.com/

Provides weather data systems, marine electronics, and specialized imaging products and papers. Offers software, hardware, and customized data products.

Atlantic Tropical Weather Center

http://www.neosoft.com/citylink/blake/tropical.html

Provides the latest hurricane information and other weather information dealing with tropical cyclones.

Automated Weather Source— Nationwide School Weather Network

http://www.aws.com/index.html

Provides national weather information from images to textual data. Also presents a photo gallery of severe weather by storm chasers throughout the country.

Current Weather Maps/Movies

http://clunix.cl.msu.edu/weather/

Offers timely JPEG weather maps and MPEG movies of radar motion (also offers a text version).

Defense Meteorological Satellite Program

http://web.ngdc.noaa.gov/dmsp/dmsp.html

Two satellite constellations of near-polar orbiting, sun-synchronous satellites that monitor meteorological, oceanographic, and solar-terrestrial physics environments. Features currently occurring meteorological phenomena.

Earth Watch Communications, Inc.

http://www.earthwatch.com/

Contains many images of 3D satellite views from space. Also plugs its 3D software package that integrates 3D weather visualization with a global database to create a virtual world.

Intellicast

http://www.intellicast.com/

Serves as a guide to weather, ski reports, and ocean conditions. Provides information for weather novices and professionals.

Interactive Marine Observations

http://thunder.met.fsu.edu/~nws/buoy/

Gives access to meteorological and oceanographic data being reported by buoys and CMAN stations in the Atlantic, United States, and Pacific. Reloads automatically every two minutes if you have Netscape.

Interactive Weather Browser

http://rs560.cl.msu.edu/weather/interactive.html

Provides the capability to type any city's station ID and receive up-to-the-minute conditions. Also enables you to build a weather map, checking off only the options you want to include on the surface map.

International Weather Watchers Official Home Page

http://groundhog.sprl.umich.edu/IWW/

Nonprofit group of weather enthusiasts. Includes information about the group, links to weather-related information, and an offer to receive a free bulletin the group puts out.

NASA Weather Archive

ftp://explorer.arc.nasa.gov/pub/Weather/

Provides archive of weather images taken by the space shuttle and NASA satellite systems.

National Center for Atmospheric Research

http://www.ucar.edu/

Consists of several scientific divisions and programs working together with member universities on research activities to better understand Earth's climate systems. Includes information on resources, facilities, and services; the research data archives; and weather-related information.

National Hurricane Center Tropical Prediction Center

http://www.nhc.noaa.gov/

Contains resources for the researcher, advanced student, and hobbyist interested in the latest information on tropical weather conditions, as well as archival information on weather data and maps. Provides links to other NOAA information and satellite data.

National Severe Storms Laboratory

http://www.nssl.uoknor.edu/

Provides information about the laboratory, including current research and programs. Does not offer specific information on severe weather but does provide links to sites that do. Also includes an extensive list of links to "Web literacy" sites.

National Weather Service

http://www.nws.noaa.gov/

Provides all information output by the NWS, including national and international weather in graphical and textual formats, and information about regional offices. Also offers links to NOAA and other NWS programs.

Seismological Laboratory

http://www.gps.caltech.edu/seismo/seismo.page.html

Provides many seismology-related resources, including the record of the day, recent earthquake activity, and publications.

Space Science and Engineering Center (SSEC) Real-Time Data

http://www.ssec.wisc.edu/data/index.html

Includes weather information and ocean temperatures.

Storm Chaser Home Page

http://taiga.geog.niu.edu/chaser.html

Includes information about storm chasers, a photo gallery of storms, and the latest news about the Storm Chasers group. Also provides information about storm chasing at home, including how to contact the NWS.

Warren Faidley's Storm Chasing Home Page

http://www.indirect.com/www/storm5/

Presents photos of severe weather taken by Warren Faidley, full-time storm chaser.

Weather and Climate Images

http://grads.iges.org/pix/head.html

Offers short- and medium-range forecasts for North America and current weather maps and climate anomaly models for the rest of the world. Provides a key to the weather maps and a table of weather symbols.

Weather and Global Monitoring

http://life.anu.edu.au/weather.html

Provides pointers to various weather services worldwide.

Weather Channel

http://www.weather.com/

Includes information about the Weather Channel and also provides novice weather enthusiasts with simple weather maps.

Weather Net

http://cirrus.sprl.umich.edu/wxnet/

Tries to list every weather-related link on the Internet. Includes not only WWW sites, but ftp sites, Gophers, and Telnet sites. Includes commercial sites as well as educational and governmental sites.

Weather Page

http://www.landings.com/aviation.html

Lists weather links out of Harvard University. Includes brief descriptions of each link. Also provides links to aviation information.

Miscellaneous Science Sites

American Electronics Association

http://www.aeanet.org/

Provides information on AEA and its activities and services, including an events calendar, a directory of services, and a membership roster. Provides instant links to more than 100 high-tech firms.

The Aphrodisiac Home Page

http://www.bart.nl/~sante/aphrodis/aphrhome.htm

Site gives an overview of seven main categories of aphrodisiacs, as well as some special collections. The main aphrodisiacs include food and drink, spices, pharmaceuticals, and others.

California Academy of Sciences

http://www.calacademy.org/

"From the exhibits we build, to the research we conduct, lectures we sponsor, courses we teach, magazines and books we publish, symposia we host, the Academy's aim is to shed light on the wonders and value of the natural world." The academy's site contains links to exhibits, research departments, educational classes at Cal Academy, a newsletter, and other museum-related information.

CMU Artificial Intelligence Repository

http://www.cs.cmu.edu/afs/cs.cmu.edu/project/
ai-repository/ai/html/air.html

Contains public domain and freely distributable software, publications, and other materials of interest to AI researchers, educators, students, and practitioners.

Consciousness Research Laboratory

http://eeyore.lv-hrc.nevada.edu/~cogno/cogno.html

Contains a bibliography of alternative research, parapsychology, cognitive science, human factors, and science fiction. Includes an online experiment in which visitors can participate.

Exploratorium

http://www.exploratorium.edu

Provides this interactive science museum's exhibits, workshops, projects, programs, events, and schedules. Includes a quarterly magazine, gifts, learning publication tools and resources, and images and sounds.

Explorer Home Page

http://unite.ukans.edu/

Provides access to thousands of science and math documents, lesson plans, and software for use in educational settings. Provides information about each item before you download, as well as how they fit into curriculum goals.

Fun with Grapes—A Case Study

http://www.sci.tamucc.edu/~pmichaud/grape/

Site yields an interesting experiment in culinary entertainment. Describes the easy, at-home process of exploding grapes in any microwave-equipped kitchen.

Great Canadian Scientists

http://fas.sfu.ca/css/gcs/main.html

Presents a collection of material on Canadian scientists and science. Includes biographies of several scientists, descriptions of their greatest claims to fame, and activities. Presents an interactive quiz that tests knowledge and guides users around the site looking for answers. Also includes images and text.

ISB Working Group on Footwear Biomechanics

http://www.teleport.com/~biomech/sneakers.html

Organization of biomechanics experts who study footwear for sports and other functional applications. Includes information on the organization and abstracts of papers.

National Chipcard Forum

http://www.dds.nl/~ncp/indexe.html

Provides information about smartcards and chipcards on the Net, as well as on the outcome of the forum's studies and projects. Also presents brochures and more.

National Museum of Natural History

http://nmnhwww.si.edu/nmnhweb.html

Provides information about the museum, exhibits, and what a visitor might expect. Contains useful information about various programs and several searchable databases.

National Science Foundation

http://www.nsf.gov/

Provides information on government-funded efforts to improve science in this country. Also provides information on past and present grant information and presents NSF publications.

Nondestructive Testing Information Analysis Center Home Page

http://www.dtic.dla.mil/iac/ntiac/ntiachome.html

Contains current and past issues of the NTIAC Newsletter, calendars of events, calls for papers, NDE book reviews, cross links to other NDE sites, and other information.

Nye Labs

http://nyelabs.kcts.org/

Houses PBS's Bill Nye the Science Guy. Serves as a place for students to learn science and have fun at the same time. Includes a set of links to science on the Web, show listings, and activities to do at home.

Olivetti Research Laboratory

http://www.cam-orl.co.uk/index.html

Contains research reports on various activities of the Lab in the area of computer multimedia architecture, gestural input, face recognition, and so on. Also of interest is the link to "The World Right Now," which shows live outdoor images from different parts of the world. Also available in Italian.

On Being a Scientist: Responsible Conduct in Research

http://xerxes.nas.edu:70/1/nap/online/obas

Presents a publication that addresses issues relevant to being a responsible scientist and researcher. Covers issues such as values, experimental technique, authorship practices, and the scientist in society.

Point Source Ltd.

http://www.hpsource.com/psource.html

Designs and manufactures customized fiber-optic and laser diode systems for the photonics industry. Provides flexible fiber-optic solutions to equipment manufacturers and research establishments throughout the world.

Sargent Welch Scientific Company

http://www.sargentwelch.com

Lists catalog items and links them to science education references on the Web. Includes MSDS, safety checklist, and other references.

Science Television

http://www.service.com/stv/

Specializes in producing programs for the professional and educational use of the scientific community. Provides MPEG clips that help visualize complex sets of scientific data.

Society for Scientific Exploration

http://www.jse.com/

Explores issues ignored or not studied adequately in the mainstream scientific community. Contains abstracts to some articles published in their journal.

SRI's Optical Technology Group

http://aeol-www.sri.com/optics.html

Performs research in optics and related disciplines and applies optical and infrared technologies to practical problems. Includes research in optical oceanography and laser eye and sensor protection.

Superplasticity

http://www.mm.mtu.edu/~drjohn/superplasticity.html

Provides information relating to the topic of superplasticity. Offers literature databases, experimental results, and software relating to superplasticity.

Systems Realization Laboratory

http://www.srl.gatech.edu/

Develops mechanical design techniques, higher learning, and environmentally friendly designs.

Technology Review Magazine

http://web.mit.edu/techreview/www/

Covers technology and its implications. Addresses the practical applications of science, as opposed to laboratory breakthroughs and theoretical abstractions. Emphasizes policy issues rather than nuts and bolts.

Vibrant Technology, Inc.

http://www.mlode.com/~vibrant/

Offers a downloadable application demo for a modal analysis system for viewing and analyzing noise and vibration in structures.

Virtually Hawaii

http://www.satlab.hawaii.edu/space/hawaii/

Provides easy access to earth and space science data. Focuses on Hawaii. Offers a database of satellite, space shuttle, and aircraft remote sensing images of Hawaii. Enables you to view image navigators for Landsat, Spaceborne Radar, or aerial photographic images. Also includes a collection of images in oceanography, meteorology, and volcanology.

Web Station—New Media Science

http://www.mediascience.no/

Serves Nordic companies and institutions that want to strengthen their position in their markets by using multimedia as one of several business tools.

Westinghouse Science and Technology Center

http://www.stc.westinghouse.com/

Information center for the Westinghouse Science & Technology Center.

X-Ray and Gamma-Ray Coefficients

http://www1.usa1.com/~aic/2121.html

Displays graphic presentation of all X-ray and gamma-ray coefficients. Includes links to other nuclear data and a program for calculating shielding and dose deposition.

Yale NMR Research Group

http://mri.med.yale.edu/

Concentrates on biomedical magnetic resonance imaging and spectroscopy.

Oceanography

ASLO Home Page

http://www.ngdc.noaa.gov/paleo/aslo/aslo.html

"The purposes of ASLO are to promote the interests of limnology, oceanography and related sciences, to foster the exchange of information across the range of aquatic science, and to further investigations dealing with these subjects." Contains general information about the organization, as well as information on careers and job listings.

Coral Health and Monitoring Home Page

http://coral.aoml.erl.gov/

Provides services to help improve and sustain coral reef health throughout the world. Contains general information about coral, as well as a listing of links to other sites about coral.

CSIRO Division of Oceanography

http://www-ocean.ml.csiro.au/

Offers two links: The Climate and Ocean Processes link provides information on research in this area, and the Marine Environment and Resources link contains additional information on current research.

El Nino Theme Page

http://www.pmel.noaa.gov/toga-tao/el-nino/home.html

Explains El Nino (frequently referred to on oceanography pages), a disruption of the ocean-atmosphere system in the tropical Pacific that affects weather around the globe.

GLOBEC Information

http://www.ccpo.odu.edu/globec_menu.html

Designed to be a collaborative effort between physicists, biologists, and chemists. Attempts to more rapidly further research on oceanography through collaboration (made possible by Internet technology, including this Web site).

List of Oceanography Resources

http://www.esdim.noaa.gov/ocean_page.html

Lists oceanography Web sites. Contains a listing of the major NOAA Web sites and links to some of the better Web sites of educational institutions.

National Marine Fisheries Service

http://kingfish.ssp.nmfs.gov/

Provides services and products to support domestic and international fisheries management operations, fisheries development, trade and industry assistance activities, enforcement, protected species and habitat conservation operations, and the scientific and technical aspects of NOAA's marine fisheries program. Offers links to oceanographic information, particularly data concerning fish life.

NEMO—Oceanographic Data Server

http://nemo.ucsd.edu/

Provides a collection of data sets for physical oceanographers. Offers many holdings only to local users. Offers information on shore temperature and winds to all users.

NOAA Coastal & Estuarine Oceanography Branch

http://www-ceob.nos.noaa.gov/

Contains information on the physics of coastal waterways and the movement of the waters and the causes of those movements.

Yogi's Cassette

http://members.gnn.com/Threadmail/yogi/yogi.html

Yogi—smarter than your average site. No, not the cartoon character. This musician will send you a free cassette if you ask for it. Check out the cool animated graphics, too.

NOAA Home Page

http://www.noaa.gov/

Provides information about National Oceanic and Atmospheric Administration (NOAA) research, current weather information, and links to all other NOAA projects. Also includes latest news involving NOAA and the NOAA mission statement. Includes information about seasonal forecasts, fisheries, protected species, coastal ecosystems, and navigation.

NOAA Paleoclimatology Program

http://www.ngdc.noaa.gov/paleo/paleo.html

Includes searchable databases on climate modeling, ice cores, paleoceanographic, paleovegetation, tree-ring, and other data. Provides alternate search engines for users who cannot use tables.

Ocean Planet Home Page

http://seawifs.gsfc.nasa.gov/ocean_planet.html

Presents an online version of an exhibition at the Smithsonian Institution's National Museum of Natural History. Also contains many resources.

Oceanography Links: Oceanography on the World Wide Web

http://www.ocgy.ubc.ca/links/

Lists Web sites dealing with the field of oceanography. There are sublistings of educational and government institutions as well as listings of other online resources such as images, project descriptions, and research articles.

Oceanography Society

http://www.tos.org/

Offers general membership information. Maintains a news posting system. Covers a wide variety of topics ranging from highly scientific issues to elementary level oceanography education under the "News System" heading.

Parallel Ocean Program (POP) Simulation

http://dubhe.cc.nps.navy.mil/~braccio/

Simulates the global ocean circulation. Covers research being conducted by scientists at Los Alamos National Laboratory and the Naval Postgraduate School. Contains an array of images as well as MPEG movies.

Pathfinder Cafe

http://satori.gso.uri.edu/archive/images.html

Contains more than 28,000 images. Serves as resource for finding oceanography images. Provides an interface for acquiring and viewing Pathfinder images.

Safari Splash

http://oberon.educ.sfu.ca/splash.htm

Links people around the world and in classrooms to students and experts diving in an ocean environment. Features the Safari Touch Tank, in which you click on an image of plants and animals to call up a description, large image, 3D animation, and Webster definition of the item you choose.

Satellite Oceanography Laboratory

http://satftp.soest.hawaii.edu/

Contains real-time data for meteorology and oceanography, as well as images and archives of publications. Includes video footage and offers the capability to make comments on the site and its contents.

Scripps Institution of Oceanography Library

http://orpheus.ucsd.edu/sio/inst/index.html

Caters to the information needs of the research and educational activities of Scripps Institution.

Sea Surface Temperature Satellite Images

http://dcz.gso.uri.edu/avhrr-archive/archive.html

Provides access to the University of Rhode Island, Graduate School of Oceanography's archive of sea surface temperature satellite images. Also includes an online lesson plan for teachers who want to incorporate the images into a lesson.

SeaWiFS Project Home Page

http://seawifs.gsfc.nasa.gov/scripts/SEAWIFS.html

Provides access into the background, status, and documentation for NASA's upcoming global ocean color monitoring mission. Offers online documentation on this project, including educational resources.

SelectSite Ocean Technology

http://www.selectsite.com/oceantech/

Provides pointers to businesses that specialize in ocean technology. Also lists conferences and reference sites, some of which might have something to offer someone doing non-business related research.

TAMU Oceanography Welcome Page

http://www-ocean.tamu.edu/welcome.html

Contains a variety of information. Includes a section on questions about careers in oceanography. Also offers links to online journals and research articles and resources related to oceanography.

Topex/Poseidon—The Ocean Topography Experiment

http://topex-www.jpl.nasa.gov/

Cooperative project between the United States and France to develop and operate an advanced satellite system dedicated to observing the Earth's oceans. Contains archives and updates for the project.

United States JGOFS Home Page

http://www1.whoi.edu/

Contains information on current professional programs and studies. Includes current images of the world's major oceans as viewed with satellite technology. Also contains recent oceanography references on the Web.

United States WOCE Home Page

http://www-ocean.tamu.edu/WOCE/uswoce.html

Provides information about the present United States WOCE plans and details the status of current work.

Welcome to OCEANIC

http://diu.cms.udel.edu/

Maintains information on World Ocean Circulation Experiment (WOCE), TOGA Coupled Ocean-Atmosphere Response Experiment (TOGA COARE), research ship information and cruise schedules, and other oceanographic information sources.

Woods Hole Oceanographic Institution (WHOI)

http://www.whoi.edu/index.html

Contains general oceanographic information. Includes a listing of oceanography Web sites.

Word about the International Oceanographic Foundation

http://www.rsmas.miami.edu/iof/

Explains the mission of the International Oceanographic and contains an excellent definition/explanation of the field of oceanography.

World Wide Web Virtual Library: Oceanography

http://www.mth.uea.ac.uk/ocean/oceanography.html

Provides links to a variety of Internet resources on oceanography. Offers links to Web resources by geographic area. Links to the "What's New" link, which contains a listing of sites that have recently announced or renovated their Web sites.

Paleontology

Columbus Rock and Mineral Society

http://ourworld.compuserve.com/homepages/JHAYES/CRMS.HTM

This site is dedicated to information on rocks, minerals, and fossils. Lists schedules of meetings and field trips and links to other sites devoted to the collection and study of fossils and minerals.

Dino Russ's Laur

http://128.174.172.76/isgsroot/dinos/dinos_home.html

Web site devoted to information about varius dinosaurs. Features links to dinosaur and vertebrate paleontology, and earth and geoscience sites. Also contains information concerning contacts for those interested in participating in actual dinosaur digs.

Dinosauria On-Line

http://www.dinosauria.com/

Features dinosaur articles, discussions and essays, reference materials and dinosaur products for sale. Also contains the names and dates of all the geological time periods and links to other dinosaur related Web sites.

Palaeolithic Painted Cave at Vallon-Pont-d'Arc

`http://www.culture.fr/culture/gvpda-en.htm`

Presents recently discovered ancient cave paintings from the south of France, created during the last ice-age, which makes them between 17,000 and 20,000 years old.

Exposure Excursions

`http://dns.magtech.ab.ca/digdino/dinotour.htm`

Vacation planners that arrange paleontological excursions into the "badlands" of Alberta Canada.

Gulf Of St. Lawrence Microfossil Catalogue

`http://www.cs.uwindsor.ca/meta-index/mcat/html-docs/woop.html`

Contains searchable database of microfossil images.

Museum of Paleontology

`http://ucmp1.berkeley.edu/exhibittext/entrance.html`

Devoted to the explanation and understanding of paleontology. Also contains sections on phylogeny, geological time, and evolutionary thought.

Raymond M. Alf Museum

`http://www.webb.pvt.k12.ca.us/webb/Alf/AlfHome.html`

Features a paleontologic museum tour. Also contains information about various collections the museum carries.

UC Berkeley's Museum of Paleontology

`http://ucmp1.berkeley.edu/welcome.html`

Online museum covering the different aspects of paleontology. Features educational catalogs and exhibits.

University of California Museum of Paleontology: Bringing Life's Past and People Together

`http://ucmp1.berkeley.edu/`

Presents dinosaurs and fossils. Simulates a visit to a real museum of paleontology. Enables you to visit different exhibits to discover fossil images, background data, and geological information.

Physics

Like a Rolling Stone

The study of how objects move is called *mechanics*. Isaac Newton (1643-1727) discovered the laws that govern this. The following are his three laws of motion. For more information about other aspects of physics, check out the sites in this section. (For more information about the Rolling Stones, check out their Web site in the Music chapter.)

1. An object remains at rest or moves in a straight line until a force acts upon it.

2. When a force acts on a moving object its rate of acceleration is proportional to the force and in the direction of the force.

3. Action and reaction are equal and opposite. This means that the action of a force always produces a reaction in the object.

Accelerator Physics at SLAC

`http://beam.slac.stanford.edu/`

Describes accelerator physics at the Stanford Linear Accelerator Center. Includes links to most accelerator physics and resources on the Web, including almost all accelerator labs in the world, lab-specific and general news and job-listing sites, physics societies and organizations, texts, and more.

American Institute of Physics

`http://aip.org/`

Provides general information on physics. Contains lists of other Web sites, as well as services such as online journals and software archives. Offers information varying from news about what is happening in the field of physics, presented at a newspaper reading level, to listings of job openings in the field of physics.

American Physical Society

`http://aps.org/`

American Physical Society is an organization of more than 41,000 physicists. The group publishes research journals, including the *Physical Review*, *Physical Review Letters*, and *Review of Modern Physics*. Their site contains links to information on the organization's meetings, membership information, and career/employment opportunities, as well as links to their numerous publications publications.

The American Physical Society

ASM International Home Page

http://www.asm-intl.org/

Provides information about ASM, the Materials Information Society. Provides a searchable collection of Web sites, a calendar of events, and a collection of materials producers of interest to materials engineers.

CERN European Laboratory for Particle Physics

http://www.cern.ch/

Birthplace of the World Wide Web. Provides general information on the Web and maintains archives of information on particle physics and listings of links to other sites pertaining to the field of physics.

CMB Astrophysics Research Program

http://spectrum.lbl.gov

Surveys ongoing research and lists current personnel in the George Smoot Astrophysics Research Group.

Fermilab—Discovering the Nature of Nature

http://fnnews.fnal.gov/

Site describes the activities of the Department of Energy National Accelerator Laboratory. Features information about the Top Quark discovery, high energy physics, and Fermilab activities.

HyperSpace at UBC

http://axion.physics.ubc.ca/hyperspace/

Contains articles related to gravity and relativity, current news on relativity, job listings, and conference information, among other information.

Interactive Physics Problem Set

http://info.itp.berkeley.edu/Vol1/Contents.html

Contains almost 100 practice problems accompanied by detailed solutions and interactive computer experiments.

Jean-Marie Vaneskahian's Physics Home Page

http://www.fiu.edu/~jvanes01

Offers physics-related links and software, including Net software.

Lawrence Livermore National Laboratory

http://www.llnl.gov/

Provides information about the laboratory and its research projects, as well as links to other sites of general interest. Specializes in the study of nuclear, ecological, and bioscience topics.

Laws List

http://www.alcyone.com/max/

Online dictionary of physics terms and ideas. Covers laws, rules, principles, effects, paradoxes, limits, constants, experiments, and thought experiments in physics.

Listing of Physics Resources on the World Wide Web

http://aip.org/aip/physres.html

Lists various types of physics resources currently available on the Web.

Livermore Labs Atmospheric Research

http://www-ep.es.llnl.gov/www-ep/atm.html

Provides technical information with research on global and regional climate change, atmospheric physics and chemistry, biogeochemical cycles of anthropogenic gases and aerosols, cloud physics, and real-time modeling of the transport of contaminants in the atmosphere.

Nanotechnology

http://nano.xerox.com/nano

Nanotechnology is an expected future manufacturing technology that should enable us to inexpensively build almost any structure consistent with the laws of chemistry and physics with molecular precision.

Nanoworld Home Page

http://www.uq.oz.au/nanoworld/nanohome.html

Research and service facility dedicated to understanding the structure and composition of all materials. Provides links to several resources. Offers database of microscopic images.

NIH Guide to Molecular Modeling

http://www.nih.gov/molecular_modeling/gateway.html

Features information on modeling, software, and images.

Nuclear Physics

http://www.riken.go.jp/rarf/np/nplab.html

Contains a catalog of sites pertaining to the field of physics. Contains a variety of links to sites and an alphabetical listing that consists predominately of links to research centers around the world but that also includes links to a variety of associations.

Physics and Space Technology Directorate

http://www-phys.llnl.gov/

Provides information on physics—particularly physics pertaining to space technology.

Physics around the World

http://www.physics.mcgill.ca/physics-services/

Provides a catalog of physics and related resources on the Web. Includes all major fields in physics, science education, history of science, physical constants, laws, data and tables, journals, software, and more. Also includes bulletin boards for summer schools and workshops and for buying and selling used instruments and equipment.

Physics Demonstrations at UC Berkeley

http://www.mip.berkeley.edu/physics/physics.html

Demonstrations for the subjects of mechanics, waves, heat and matter, electricity, magnetism, and optics.

Physics News

http://www.het.brown.edu/news/index.html

Contains up-to-date information on current events in the world of physics. Offers a listing of various online publications and resource sites.

Physics Problems

http://zebu.uoregon.edu/~dmason/probs/probm.html

Contains more than 30 problems in basic concepts, mechanics, and thermal physics.

Physics Servers and Services around the World

http://www.physics.mcgill.ca/deptdocs/physics_services.html

Serves as a starting place to find physics resources on the Internet. Includes links to academic institutions, organizations, documents, and mailing lists.

Physics Unbound

http://uptown.turnpike.net/L/lindeman/physics_ub.html

Contains a collection of texts about issues and topics in physics. Encourages readers to add to the wealth of knowledge already present.

Physics World Electronic News

http://www.ioppublishing.com/

An online newsletter. Allows subscribers to receive e-mail that provides up-to-date accounts of news in the field of physics.

Quantum Magazine Home Page

http://www.nsta.org:80/quantum/

Provides information about Quantum magazine. Contains primarily physics-related contents, but does include a "toy store" of "mathematical amusements." Includes back issues and a sample.

Virtual Science Class

http://visualsystems.com/main.html

Site featuring educational software for science related topics. Includes energy flow, physics lab simulator, and producing energy. Also gives highlights on new or future products.

WARP Home

http://www.hia.com/hia/pcr/home.html

Offers a collection of multimedia documents pertaining to various aspects of "alternative" science, including warp technology, fantasy stories of time travel, quantum mechanics, and so on.

Welcome to the Institute of Physics

http://www.ioppublishing.com/iopwelcome.html

Provides information in the field of physics. Restricts use of some items and aspects to registered members only. Users who choose to register can browse text abstracts or download full text versions of any article. To register, you must be a member of a subscribing institution.

Welcome to the Laboratory for Terrestrial Physics

`http://ltpwww.gsfc.nasa.gov/`

Provides information, documents and simulations related to terrestrial physics. Features links to images of various terrestrial phenomena, such as magnetic models of the crust.

World Wide Web Virtual Library: Physics

`http://www.w3.org/hypertext/DataSources/bySubject/Physics/Overview.html`

Offers a general listing of physics sites. Also contains links to listings of more specific sites on geophysics, astrophysics, nuclear physics, and energy science.

Zoology

Absearch

`http://www.commquest.com/business/absearch/`

A professional literature database containing abstracts about wildlife, ecology, fisheries, ornithology, biology, and zoology.

AlpacaNet

`http://www.alpacanet.com/`

Serves as a resource for Alpaca ranchers, breeders, weavers, spinners, investors, and anyone who wants more information about alpacas.

Cornell Ornithology Collection

`http://muse.bio.cornell.edu/museums/cubird.html`

Provides information about the history of the ornithology program at Cornell. Offers a useful link to a Gopher search tool for scientific information on bird species.

Electronic Zoo

`http://netvet.wustl.edu/e-zoo.htm`

Contains information about animals and animal-related resources. Offers many links to information on nearly any animal.

Insect Behavior Group

`http://www.zoo.utoronto.ca/ibg.html`

Site run by zoology professors and students at the University of Toronto. Contains several articles about insect behavior and communication.

NetVet Veterinary Resources

`http://netvet.wustl.edu/`

Provides information related to veterinary medicine. Offers the Electronic Zoo, a large collection of animal-related computer resources.

NetVet Veterinary Resources and the Electronic Zoo

`http://netvet.wustl.edu/`

Provides lists for animal resources. Includes links organized by animal (cats, dogs, insects, and so forth), electronic publications, legislation, organizations, biology, and medicine.

Virtual Emu

`http://www.vicnet.net.au/~raou/raou.html`

A biodiversity and bird conservation group in Australia. Features a library of bird images and listings of threatened birds.

Zoology Department

`http://www.utas.edu.au/docs/zoology/HomePage.html`

Zoology department at The University of Tasmania Web site. Contains information about the department and its programs. Also has information for contacting the department.

Zoological Record

`http://www.york.biosis.org/index.htm`

Contains links to various zoological resources. Provides an online glossary.

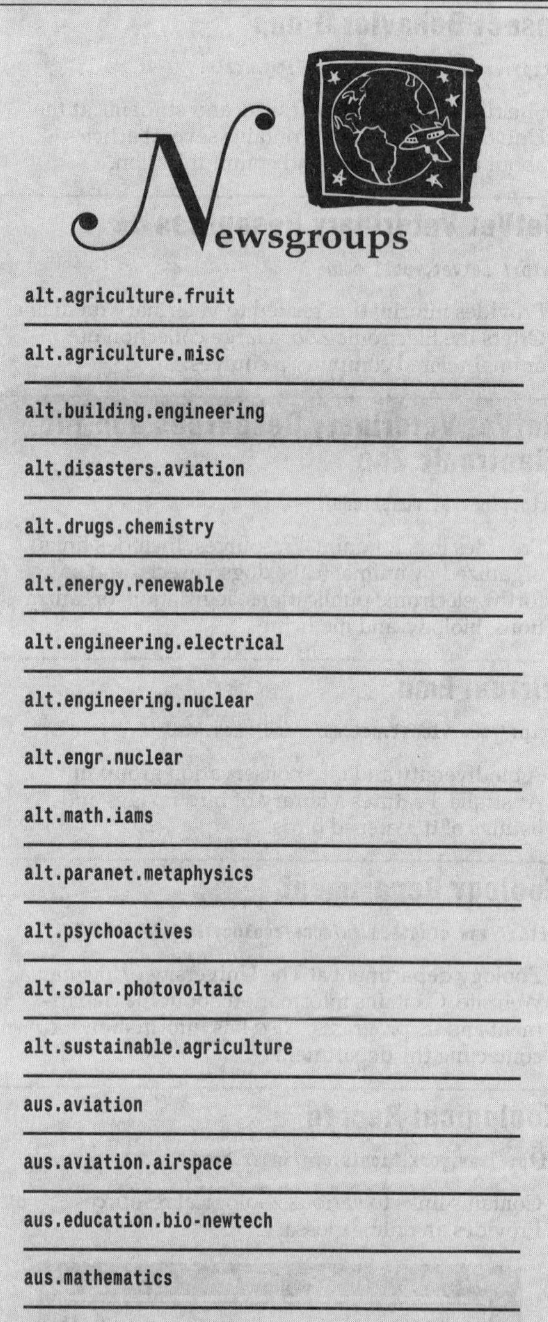

Newsgroups

alt.agriculture.fruit

alt.agriculture.misc

alt.building.engineering

alt.disasters.aviation

alt.drugs.chemistry

alt.energy.renewable

alt.engineering.electrical

alt.engineering.nuclear

alt.engr.nuclear

alt.math.iams

alt.paranet.metaphysics

alt.psychoactives

alt.solar.photovoltaic

alt.sustainable.agriculture

aus.aviation

aus.aviation.airspace

aus.education.bio-newtech

aus.mathematics

aus.mbio

bionet.biology.cardiovascular

bionet.biology.computational

bionet.biology.deepsea

bionet.biology.grasses

bionet.biology.n2-fixation

bionet.biology.symbiosis

bionet.biology.tropical

bionet.biology.vectors

bionet.cellbiol

bionet.cellbiol.insulin

bionet.drosophila

bionet.ecology.physiology

bionet.journals

bionet.journals.note

bionet.microbiology

bionet.molbio.hiv

bionet.molbio.yeast

bionet.plants

bionet.plants.education

bionet.population-bio

bionet.prof-society.ascb

bionet.prof-society.faseb

bionet.prof-society.navbo

bionet.software

bionet.software.sources

bionet.users.addresses

bionet.women-in-bio

can.aviation.rgs

can.schoolnet.biomed.jr

can.schoolnet.biomed.sr

can.schoolnet.chem.jr

can.schoolnet.chem.sr

can.schoolnet.comp.jr

can.schoolnet.comp.sr

can.schoolnet.earth.jr

can.schoolnet.earth.sr

can.schoolnet.eng.jr.

can.schoolnet.eng.sr.

can.schoolnet.math.jr

can.schoolnet.math.sr

can.schoolnet.phys.jr

can.schoolnet.phys.sr

clari.biz.industry.agriculture

clari.biz.industry.agriculture.releases

clari.biz.industry.aviation

clari.biz.industry.aviation.releases

clari.biz.industry.energy

clari.biz.industry.energy.releases

clari.tw.space

eunet.aviation

fido.ger.aviation

fido7.aviation

fj.education.math

fj.engr.control

fj.engr.elec

fj.engr.materials

fj.engr.mech

fj.engr.misc

fj.rec.aerospace

fj.sci.bio

fj.sci.chem

fj.sci.geo

fj.sci.physics

francom.aviation

gac.physics.astronomy

han.sci.astro

han.sci.earth

hepnet.conferences

hepnet.freehep

hepnet.general

hepnet.hepix

hepnet.heplib

hepnet.jobs

hepnet.lang.c++

hepnet.videoconf

misc.jobs.fields.chemistry

mit.eecs.discuss

nctu.applied.math

nctu.ce.general

ncsc.chemistry

nctu.club.astronomy

nctu.cm.general

nctu.com.ecology

nctu.ee.general

nctu.mat-sci-eng

nctu.me.general

oh.chem

rec.aviation.announce

rec.aviation.answers

rec.aviation.hang-gliding

rec.aviation.homebuilt

rec.aviation.ifr

rec.aviation.marketplace

rec.aviation.military

rec.aviation.misc

rec.aviation.owning

rec.aviation.piloting for aviators

rec.aviation.products

rec.aviation.questions

rec.aviation.rotorcraft

rec.aviation.simulators

rec.aviation.soaring

rec.aviation.stories

rec.aviation.student

rec.aviation.ultralight

relcom.commerce.energy

relcom.ecology

relcom.fido.su.astronomy

sci.agriculture

sci.agriculture.beekeeping

sci.astro

sci.astro.amateur

sci.astro.research

sci.bio.botany

sci.bio.conservation

sci.bio.ecology

sci.bio.ethology

sci.bio.evolution

sci.bio.fisheries

sci.bio.herp

sci.bio.microbiology

sci.bio.misc

sci.chem

sci.chem.analytical

sci.chem.electrochem

sci.chem.organomet

sci.energy

sci.energy.hydrogen

sci.engr

sci.engr.biomed

sci.engr.chem

sci.engr.civil

sci.engr.control

sci.engr.mech

sci.engr.metallurgy

sci.engr.semiconductors

sci.environment

sci.geo.geology

sci.materials

sci.med.aids

sci.med.physics

sci.med.psychobiology

sci.physics

sci.physics.accelerators

sci.physics.computational.fluid-dynamics

sci.physics.cond-matter

sci.physics.electromag

sci.physics.fusion

sci.physics.particle

sci.physics.plasma

sci.research

sci.research.careers

sci.skeptics

soc.culture.scientists

swnet.sci.astro

tnn.bio

tnn.math

tw.bbs.sci.astronomy

tw.bbs.sci.biology

tw.bbs.sci.math

tw.bbs.sci.physics

ucb.erg

ucb.geology

ucd.geology

uiuc.pubs.messenger

uk.org.starlink.misc

ukr.commerce.energy

umn.general.energy

wyo.energy

AAASEST—Perspectives on Ethical Issues in Science and Technology

The George Washington University Computer Center, Wash DC

You can join this group by sending the message "sub AAASEST your name" to listserv@gwuvm.gwu.edu

ANSCI-L—Animal Science Students

You can join this group by sending the message "sub ANSCI-L your name" to listserv@listserv.okstate.edu

ASEE-L—American Society of Engineering Education Students

Virginia Tech

You can join this group by sending the message "sub ASEE-L your name" to listserv@vtvm1.cc.vt.edu

ASUSCI—ASU Science and Research Press Release Distribution List

Arizona State University, Tempe, AZ

You can join this group by sending the message "sub ASUSCI your name" to
listserv@asuvm.inre.asu.edu

AWISNEOC—Association of Women In Science — N. E. Ohio Chapter

You can join this group by sending the message "sub AWISNEOC your name" to
listserv@listserv.kent.edu

BIOM-SCI—Events Concerning the Biomedical Sciences Graduate Program

University of California, San Francisco, CA

You can join this group by sending the message "sub BIOM-SCI your name" to
listserv@itssrv1.ucsf.edu

CECS-L—MU Computer Engineering and Computer Science

University of Missouri-Columbia, Columbia, MO

You can join this group by sending the message "sub CECS-L your name" to
listserv@mizzou1.missouri.edu

CHEME-L—Chemical Engineering List

You can join this group by sending the message "sub CHEME-L your name" to
listserv@ulkyvm.louisville.edu

COUNPSY—Counseling Psychology Practice and Science

The University of Georgia, Athens, GA

You can join this group by sending the message "sub COUNPSY your name" to
listserv@uga.cc.uga.edu

DISTLABS—Teaching Science Labs Via Distance

You can join this group by sending the message "sub DISTLABS your name" to
listserv@listserv.iupui.edu

EARLYSCIENCE-L—History of Science Society - Early Science Interest Group

Virginia Tech

You can join this group by sending the message "sub EARLYSCIENCE-L your name" to
listserv@listserv.vt.edu

EMFLDS-L—Electromagnetics in Medicine, Science & Comunications

State University of New York at Buffalo

You can join this group by sending the message "sub EMFLDS-L your name" to
listserv@ubvm.cc.buffalo.edu

ENG263-L—Popular Literature of Contemporary Science

State University of New York at Buffalo

You can join this group by sending the message "sub ENG263-L your name" to
listserv@listserv.acsu.buffalo.edu

ESIPLIST—Elementary Science Integration Project

University of Maryland CSC, College Park, MD

You can join this group by sending the message "sub ESIPLIST your name" to
listserv%umdd.bitnet@listserv.net

FAMLYSCI—Family Science Network

You can join this group by sending the message "sub FAMLYSCI your name" to listserv@lsv.uky.edu

GEOED-L—Geology and Earth Science Education Discussion Forum

University of West Florida, Pensacola, Florida

You can join this group by sending the message "sub GEOED-L your name" to
listserv@uwf.cc.uwf.edu

GEONET-L—GEONET-L Geoscience Librarians & Information Specialists

University Computing Services, Indiana University

You can join this group by sending the message "sub GEONET-L your name" to `listserv@iubvm.ucs.indiana.edu`

H-NEXA—H-NEXA: the Science-Humanities Convergence Forum

You can join this group by sending the message "sub H-NEXA your name" to `listserv@h-net.msu.edu`

HEC-L—Higher Education Consortium for Mathematics and Science

University of West Florida, Pensacola, Florida

You can join this group by sending the message "sub HEC-L your name" to `listserv@uwf.cc.uwf.edu`

HUMSCI—Human Sciences Program

The George Washington University Computer Center, Washington DC

You can join this group by sending the message "sub HUMSCI your name" to `listserv@gwuvm.gwu.edu`

IMSE-L—Institute for Math and Science Education

University of Illinois at Chicago, Chicago, IL

You can join this group by sending the message "sub IMSE-L your name" to `listserv@listserv.uic.edu`

ISL-SCI—Issues on Islam and Science

Virginia Tech

You can join this group by sending the message "sub ISL-SCI your name" to `listserv@vtvm1.cc.vt.edu`

KSUSCI-L—KSU Science News

Kansas State University, Manhattan, KS

You can join this group by sending the message "sub KSUSCI-L your name" to `listserv@ksuvm.ksu.edu`

KYCCS—Center for Computational Sciences

You can join this group by sending the message "sub KYCCS your name" to `listserv@lsv.uky.edu`

MAES-L—Society of Mexican American Engineers and Scientists

Texas A&M University Computing Services Center

You can join this group by sending the message "sub MAES-L your name" to `listserv@tamvm1.tamu.edu`

MEDDCHEM—Macromolecular Engineering, Drug Design and Chemistry

Wayne State University, Detroit, MI

You can join this group by sending the message "sub MEDDCHEM your name" to `listserv@cms.cc.wayne.edu`

MEDSCI-L—Medieval Science Discussion List

Brown University, Providence, RI

You can join this group by sending the message "sub MEDSCI-L your name" to `listserv@brownvm.brown.edu`

MSIRE-L—RI Math & Science Resource Discussion List

You can join this group by sending the message "sub MSIRE-L your name" to `listserv@uriacc.uri.edu`

MST—Math, Science and Technology Mentors

OCM BOCES, Syracuse, NY

You can join this group by sending the message "sub MST your name" to `listserv@ocmvm.cnyric.org`

NCLSMTG—National Conference of Lawyers and Scientists

The George Washington University Computer Center, Washington DC

You can join this group by sending the message "sub NCLSMTG your name" to
`listserv@gwuvm.gwu.edu`

NCPRSE-L—Reform Discussion List for Science Education

East Carolina University, Computing and Info systems, Greenville, North Carolina

You can join this group by sending the message "sub NCPRSE-L your name" to
`listserv@ecuvm.cis.ecu.edu`

NEURL—Neuroscience Strategic Planning

University of Illinois at Chicago, Chicago, IL

You can join this group by sending the message "sub NEURL your name" to
`listserv@listserv.uic.edu`

NSBELINE—NSBE National Society of Black Engineers

Syracuse University

You can join this group by sending the message "sub NSBELINE your name" to
`listserv@listserv.syr.edu`

NYSESM-L—Earth Science Mentors List

State University of New York at Buffalo

You can join this group by sending the message "sub NYSESM-L your name" to
`listserv@ubvm.cc.buffalo.edu`

ORNITH-L—The Scientific Discussion of Ornithology

University of Arkansas Main Campus - Fayetteville

You can join this group by sending the message "sub ORNITH-L your name" to
`listserv@uafsysb.uark.edu`

QMSTE-L—Mathematics, Science, and Technology Education Group

Queen's University Computing Services

You can join this group by sending the message "sub QMSTE-L your name" to
`listserv@qucdn.queensu.ca`

SCI-CULT—Science-as-Culture

St.John's University, Jamaica, NY

You can join this group by sending the message "sub SCI-CULT your name" to
`listserv@sjuvm.stjohns.edu`

SCIALL-L—NIH Science Alliance

You can join this group by sending the message "sub SCIALL-L your name" to `listserv@list.nih.gov`

SCIFRAUD—Discussion of Fraud in Science

You can join this group by sending the message "sub SCIFRAUD your name" to
`listserv%albnyvm1.bitnet@listserv.net`

SCINEWS—News Service Science News releases

Purdue University, W. Lafayette, IN

You can join this group by sending the message "sub SCINEWS your name" to
`listserv@vm.cc.purdue.edu`

SMART—Science/Math Teacher Training List

You can join this group by sending the message "sub SMART your name" to `listserv@uriacc.uri.edu`

SSREL-L—Scientific Study of Religion

The University of Tennessee, Knoxville

You can join this group by sending the message "sub SSREL-L your name" to
`listserv@utkvm1.utk.edu`

STPPNEWS—Science, Technology, and Public Policy News Group

The George Washington University Computer Center, Wash DC

You can join this group by sending the message "sub STPPNEWS your name" to `listserv@gwuvm.gwu.edu`

SUSIG—Teaching in the Mathematical Sciences with Spreadsheets

Miami University, Oxford, OH

You can join this group by sending the message "sub SUSIG your name" to `listserv@miamiu.muohio.edu`

SWE-L—Society of Women Engineers

Rensselaer Polytechnic Institute, Troy, NY

You can join this group by sending the message "sub SWE-L your name" to `listserv@vm.its.rpi.edu`

TSS-LIST—Transportation Science Section List

Massachusetts Institute of Technology, Cambridge, MA

You can join this group by sending the message "sub TSS-LIST your name" to `listserv@mitvma.mit.edu`

WISENET—Women In Science and Engineering NETwork

University of Illinois at Chicago, Chicago, IL

You can join this group by sending the message "sub WISENET your name" to `listserv@listserv.uic.edu`

WVUSTW-L—Scientific and Technical Writing Group

West Virginia Network for Educational Telecomputing

You can join this group by sending the message "sub WVUSTW-L your name" to `listserv@wvnvm.wvnet.edu`

SEXUALITY

Abuse

Breaking the Cycle

http://www.stolaf.edu/people/bierlein/noxxx/noxxx.html

A site to help men addicted to pornography. Provides a nonjudgmental, accepting, and supportive place for people struggling with pornography in all its various forms. Pornography is dealt with at the point it becomes an addictive, unhealthy force.

Child Sexual Abuse

http://www.commnet.edu/QVCTC/student/LindaCain/sexabuse.html#horror

One woman's labor of love—her compiled index of sites helpful to the families of victims.

Images of Children, Crime, and Violence

http://www.iglou.com/first-principles/abstract.html

The online version of a study conducted from 1954-1984 concerning the view of children in mainstream adult magazines.

National Coalition Against Sexual Assault

http://www.cs.utk.edu/~bartley/ncasa/ncasa.html

Offers a huge index of informational pages ranging from acquaintance rape to women's resources. Provides forms for becoming a member or making a donation.

No More Victims

http://www.casti.com/NMV/html/nmv.html

Provides links and back issues of the mailing list. Serializes Peter B's book, *Breaking the Cycle*, archived at the site.

Stop It Now

http://www.inetcon.com/stopit.html

Discusses sexual abuse as the epidemic that it is. Offers an e-mail link to the Stop It Now organization.

Survivors Network of Those Abused by Priests

http://www.ece.orst.edu/~barreta/snap/

Focuses on self help and education. Gives links to related sites.

Dating Services

Christian Singles

http://www.kiss.com/cs/

This site for the intimacy-deprived focuses on helping people achieve spiritual maturity and emotional stability through seminars, classes, newsletters, books, and so forth. Helps individuals achieve harmony and unity in their lives by stressing a proper relationship with God and Christ, themselves, and then with other people.

Christian Single Online

http://www.miami.net/Two4Christ/

Dedicated to connecting you with potential mates who closely match your beliefs, interests, and specifications. Identify your tastes and profile the person you are seeking, and they'll find compatible matches based on your top 5 preferences.

Jewish Singles Connection

http://www.zdepth.com/jsc/index.html

An attempt to help reconnect young, single Jews across the U.S. and the world to each other and re-create some of the community of yesteryear. Utilizes the Internet to help create a new community paradigm.

Match.Com—"We met on the net"

http://www.match.com

Join this Web matchmaking service or enter as a guest. Try a free ten-day membership and enter your personal profile. This site also includes the Matchbook online e-zine, with interviews of famous authors, member events, and a dating counselor. Thousands sign up every month to be included on match.com's roster.

Ulti-Mate Dating Service

http://www.primenet.com/~jekagan/dating/

Internet-only singles dating service that provides complete anonymity and no registration or startup fees. View their database free, answer the latest survey, or sign up.

Webpersonals.com

http://www.webpersonals.com:80/date/subdex.html

Offers a variety of free services to the Internet community. Maintains a database of thousands of people from all over the world and enables you to contact them. Provides a nightly scouting report, called *Love Hound*, that automatically mails you the new ads posted that meet the criteria you select. Offers anonymous mailings for those people who are a little shy. Just pick the service you wish to use, and come back often—it's free!

Erotic E-Zines, Publications, and Other Resources

The Aphrodisiac Home Page

http://www.bart.nl/~sante/aphrodis/aphrhome.htm

Advice on mixing and finding true love potion number nines. Broken into categories, including food & drink and plant preparations. Visitors in a hurry (which they likely will be) are directed to the pine nut recipes.

The Bio Keeper Archives

http://www.cris.com/~abend/AdultStars.html

Biographies and rumors of adult film stars and makers. Provides film critiques (what can *really* be said? One never ends a description of a XXX movie with, "The dialogue in *Backalley Babes* rivals that of O'Neill and Wilder—that soliloquy by Peter North was amazing...so deep!").

Body Politic

http://the.arc.co.uk/body/home.html

Charts men's reaction to the challenge of feminism and documents changes in the social construction of masculinity. Describes women's explorations of sexual desire and gratification through the eroticizing of men's bodies. Analyses the sexual/political changes as they take place in the world at large. Review books, exhibitions, films, television, and other media events. Celebrate sexual and social diversity and creative collisions of political cultures.

The Church of Tantra

http://www.AAArt.com/tantra/

Learn why the word Tantra is generally misused in the West. Your basic how-to guide. Thank you, Vatasyayana.

Dark Nites

http://falcon.cc.ukans.edu/~lafemme/darknite.htm

The Dark Nite Trilogy online, as well as other erotic serial stories.

eaRoS

http://www.calweb.com/~ilk/earotic.html

Downloadable sound bites (pun fully intended). Unrehearsed, real-audio recordings of couples and (so far) females in flagrante delicto. The webmaster even provides extraordinary messages left on his answering machine.

EroticaTender

http://www.etzine.com/

Provides information for Judeo-Christian marrieds who are interested in improving or re-sparking their love lives by introducing them gently into the (forced) underground world of kink. Even provides children links to encourage the peering eyes of youth to jump to more appropriate sites.

The Erotic Pen

http://www.cris.com/~markth/epen/epen1.shtml

A list of stories penned by the webmaster and others, as well as links to other erotica sites.

Libido Magazine

http://www.indra.com/libido/cover3.html

Online Libido with online stories, as well as information for those who would like to try their hand at penning stories or submitting photos.

Penthouse Online

http://www.penthousemag.com/home.html

See this month's table of contents, cropped figures (due to the CDA), subscription information, toy store connections, and a link to the sister publication, *Omni*.

Red Hot Amsterdam

http://www.demon.co.uk/redhot/hotsex3.html

Join the online zine and gain access to downloadable pictorials, movies, and gay material. FAQs include the question, Why pay for online erotica when it can be obtained for free on the Net. Answer: You get what you pay for.

The Stories of Mary Anne Mohanraj

`http://mud.bsd.uchicago.edu/~mohanraj/stories.html`

Although she's gone professional, Ms. Mohanraj has provided many of her stories on the Web. Included are links to other writers' works that she admires.

The Loving Center: Your Source for Information on Tantric Loving

`http://heartfire.com/tantric/loving.html`

Helps stressed couples relearn how to be intimate—mentally, emotionally, and physically. Considers the needs of corporate lovers with little time or changing schedules. Offers Tantric Loving weekend getaways for practicing Power of Love techniques. As one graduate put it, "It's like making love before you make love."

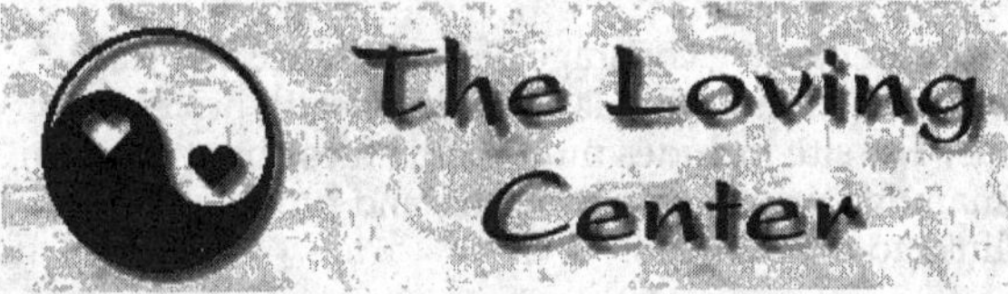

Yellow Silk

`http://www.dc.enews.com/magazines/yellow_silk/`

The Yellow Silk online magazine. Download online stories, or view lists of recommended videos, books, and poetry.

Erotiproducts

Classic Lady

`http://www.telepath.com/~roblow/`

Dedicated to classic nylons from the 50s, 60s, and 70s. Tastefully designed online lingerie shop.

Cyber-Sex-Toys

`http://www.sextoy.com/`

Another form of safe sex is the avoidance of sexual intercourse altogether. Over 400 sexy products for driving yourself or lover(s) crazy. 'Nuff said. ;-) ;-)

EVN Mail Order Factory Outlet

`http://www.evn.com/index2.html`

Like adult movies but hate the dark, smoky places where you get them? Now, in these days of AIDS and safe sex, you can order these movies from the privacy of your own home. Order your copy of John Wayne Bobbit's own cinematic masterpiece.

Exxxtasy Adult Television

`http://www.xtc-com.com/chandis.htm`

For the connoisseur. Provides info about all of the Exxxtasy International satellite and cable adult channels, which show uncut, uncensored, unadulterated movies. Features Specialty Nights, so be sure to set the VCR! Gives a whole new meaning to the phrase "boob tube."

Plainwrapped Chocolates

`http://www.eden.com/~plainwrp/choco/`

Great gift ideas for those wanting to taunt their in-laws on Easter. Double your pleasure with anthropomorphic bunnies, x-rated suckers, and busty lollipops, which all come together to make one of the most interesting and tasty sites on the Web. MMMmmmmmm. Choooocolate.

Playware Limited

`http://www.playware.com/`

Select tasteful playware for men or women, broken down by type, such as teddies, garters, panties, boxers, and briefs. Choose to view them in either .JPEG or .GIF. The models, male and female, are worth the trip alone.

Sensuous You

`http://www.dynamo.com/sensuous/index.html`

More toys than you can shake a...er...you get the idea. Assumes pleasure needs for both men and women (not that these toys have an F or M on them to tell you whom they're to be used on).

Sin

`http://www.sin-inc.com/`

Shoes for foot fetishers. A small step for man; a giant leap for man's kind of shopping.

TriRSex

`http://www.trirsex.com/index.html`

Online adult film and CD-ROM store. Order from the privacy of your home and choose from a score of "preference" catalogs. Gives new meaning to "Satisfaction guaranteed."

Rocky Road Resources

The Chamber of Goddess Dianna Vesta

http://www.geocities.com/SunsetStrip/1185/

Insights of a modern-day dominatrix. Check out her biography.

The Different Loving Page

http://gloria-brame.com/diflove.htm

Covers topics ranging from your basic D&S and foot fetishes to infantilism, body piercing, water sports, and more, extending as far as the human imagination. Features interviews from the book, *Different Loving: The World of Sexual Dominance & Submission*. More links to related sites than can be counted.

Sex and Food

http://www.directnet.com/Crash/Purgatory/SexAndFood/

Brought to you by vegetarian sex lovers, this site defines many words you didn't know existed, such as meatology and ophidicism, and offers alternative recipes, such as Jackasserole and Ketchuppasta. Scrumptious, and all in good fun, though it was expected the two topics would be mixed. Oh, well.

Stasya's Main Zoo Page

http://www.av.qnet.com/~stasya/text.htm

Interesting site for a topic most people know very little about. Gives a whole new twist to the command, "Come, Spot, come."

Safer Sex Resources

Condoms Express/Condom Club International

http://www.webcom.com/~condom/

You'll never have to experience the knowing smirks of clerks again! Besides links to related sites, use the Internet to buy contraceptives to be delivered to your door. Easy way to sample all the erotic varieties without the fuss of not knowing where to start.

Contraceptive Research and Development Program

http://www.conrad.org/

Help the CONRAD program come up with improved contraceptive devices and methods.

Information about Contraception and Reproductive Health

http://opr.princeton.edu/ec/contrac.html

Learn more about contraceptives and methods with links to pages about emergency contraception, device failure rates, Planned Parenthood, and more. Also links to general reproductive information pages.

The Safer Sex Page

http://www.cmpharm.ucsf.edu/~troyer/safesex.html

Comprehensive coverage of many aspects of safer sex. Serves individuals as well as health professionals. The site includes multimedia files about condom manufacturing and sex myths, and provides many links to related sites.

Same Sex Resources

Blair

http://www.youth.org/zines/blair/

Billed as the online "superzine for kooks and retards such as yrself!" An interesting array of articles for the most alternative of alternative people, ranging from academic discussions about the "ugliest shoes on the planet" (Clark Wallabees) to Pippi Longstocking movies.

Dyke TV

http://www.dyketv.org/index.html

A weekly show produced by lesbians for lesbians, the show mixes news, commentary, and the arts. Lesbian filmmakers all around the country are encouraged to help create the public access show's segments.

The Gay & Lesbian Bar Guide

http://www.webpost.com/barguide/

Pick a state and learn where to go to have an alternative time. A form is even provided to submit bars not yet in the guide.

The Gay & Lesbian National Hotline

http://www.escape.com/~irany/index.html

A new nonprofit organization that provides a vital service to the gay community by providing nationwide toll-free peer counseling, information, and referrals. Offers links, a business referral database, and the opportunity to join the hotline.

Grassroots Queers

http://critpath.org/~tracy/gq/queers.html

Dedicated to fighting hatred and bigotry and promoting equal rights for self-proclaimed "queers" through networking, organizing, and direct action.

The Isle of Lesbos

http://www.sappho.com/

Well-designed pages of poetry, art, and links to other lesbian-related sites. Coverage of sapphic poetry is extensive.

The Lesbian Herstory Project

http://www-lib.usc.edu/~retter/main.html

Site dedicated to record, archive, and publicize work on lesbian history in any geographic area or time period, with an emphasis on lesbians of color in general and Southern California in particular.

OutNOW Live

http://www.outnow.com/

"The Internet's gay newspaper" offers sections for news, opinions, arts, classified ads, and more.

The Pines Guesthouse

http://www.travelbase.com/destinations/keywest/pines-keywest/

The home page of a Key West resort devoted to providing a friendly, relaxed, affordable atmosphere. Clothing optional.

Sexual Health Resources

American Social Health Association

http://sunsite.unc.edu/ASHA/

Covers topics relevant to helping people and families affected by sexually transmitted diseases.

Camp Heartland

http://www.digital.com/cust/camp/

A charitable, non-profit organization dedicated to helping children infected with or affected by HIV/AIDS by providing recreational opportunities, support, and AIDS education. Children are helped to make friends, have fun, and gain the acceptance to overcome the isolation and misunderstanding they often face. Peer education and AIDS awareness seminars encourage America's youth to do their part to eliminate the tragedy of AIDS.

Herpes Zone

http://www.worldpassage.net/herpeszone/

Contains information for sufferers and non-sufferers alike. Knowledge about herpes viruses has really only begun in the last 25 years, and this site very professionally discusses living and coping with the virus, which also causes shingles and chicken pox, among other diseases.

International Planned Parenthood Federation

http://www.oneworld.org/ippf/

Provides news, statistics for the need for planning, publications, and links to other organizations interested in population control.

Coupons

http://www.kooponz.com

Print coupons to use nationally or locally, based upon your locale.

SHAPE: Sexual Health Advocate Peer Education

http://www.missouri.edu/~shape/

This college peer education program is founded on the belief that students can be effective in influencing the health knowledge, attitudes, and behaviors of other students, concerning all types of sexually transmitted diseases. SHAPE members discuss the importance of communication, decision making, and safer behaviors in the expression of sexuality.

Sexual Purity Tests

The 100-Point Purity Test for Non-Virgins

http://www.circus.com/~omni/purity.html

The place to go to see how you compare to other World's Great Lovers. Answer 100 blue questions to see how you "rate."

The 100-Point Bondage/Dominance Sadism/Masochism Purity Test

http://www.lungfish.com/friday/bdsm_purity.html

Learn your kinkiness level with this questionnaire. Take it with friends. Compare and contrast your scores.

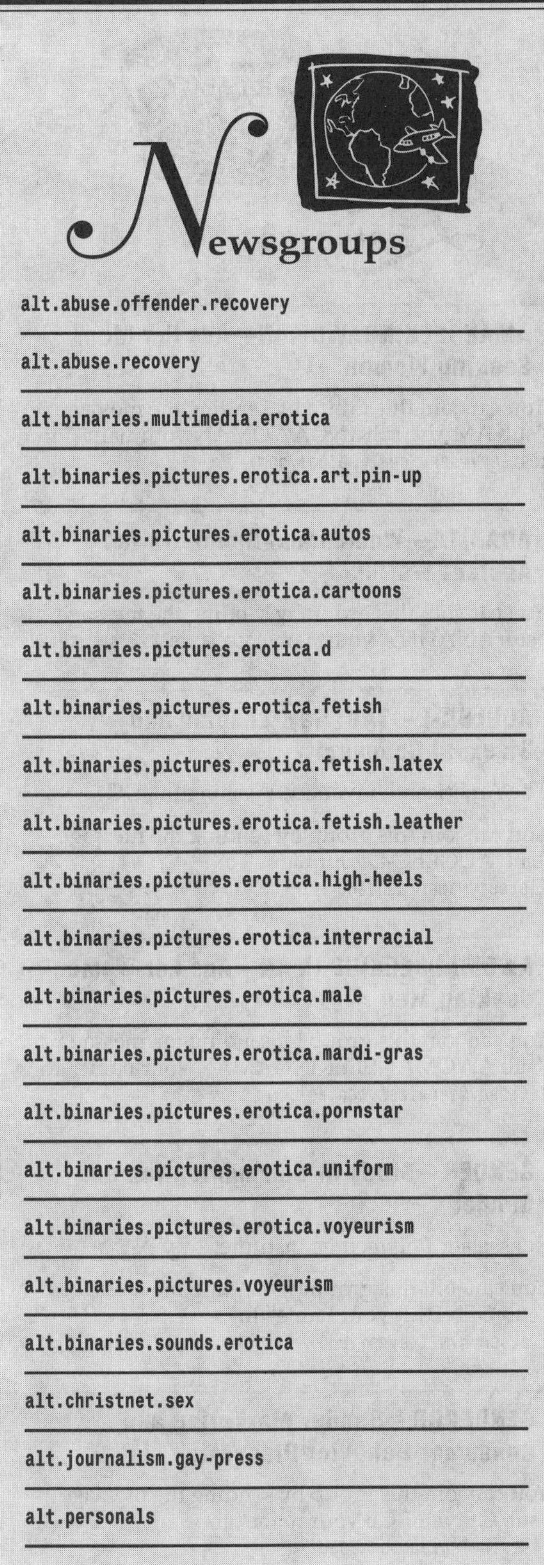

Newsgroups

alt.abuse.offender.recovery

alt.abuse.recovery

alt.binaries.multimedia.erotica

alt.binaries.pictures.erotica.art.pin-up

alt.binaries.pictures.erotica.autos

alt.binaries.pictures.erotica.cartoons

alt.binaries.pictures.erotica.d

alt.binaries.pictures.erotica.fetish

alt.binaries.pictures.erotica.fetish.latex

alt.binaries.pictures.erotica.fetish.leather

alt.binaries.pictures.erotica.high-heels

alt.binaries.pictures.erotica.interracial

alt.binaries.pictures.erotica.male

alt.binaries.pictures.erotica.mardi-gras

alt.binaries.pictures.erotica.pornstar

alt.binaries.pictures.erotica.uniform

alt.binaries.pictures.erotica.voyeurism

alt.binaries.pictures.voyeurism

alt.binaries.sounds.erotica

alt.christnet.sex

alt.journalism.gay-press

alt.personals

alt.personals.ads

alt.personals.bi

alt.personals.big-folks

alt.personals.bondage

alt.personals.fat

alt.personals.fetish

alt.personals.herpes

alt.personals.intercultural

alt.personals.intergen

alt.personals.jewish

alt.personals.misc

alt.personals.motss

alt.personals.poly

alt.personals.psychedelic

alt.personals.spanking

alt.personals.tall

alt.personals.teen

alt.personals.transgendered

alt.romance

alt.romance.chat

alt.romance.online

alt.romance.teen

alt.sex.erotica.marketplace

alt.sex.movies

alt.sex.safe

alt.sex.stories.gay

alt.sex.wanted

alt.sexual.abuse.recovery

alt.startrek.creative.erotica

alt.support.abuse-partners

alt.transgendered

bit.listserv.gaynet

can.motss

clari.news.crime.abuse

clari.news.crime.sex

clari.news.gays

clari.news.minorities

rec.arts.erotica

seattle.gay.news

soc.couples.intercultural

soc.singles

soc.support.transgendered

soc.support.youth.gay-lesbian-bi

talk.rape

ucb.erotica.sensual

ucd.q-news

uk.gay-lesbian-bi

Listservs

AMANSEEKINGAWOMAN—Ads For Men Seeking Women

You can join this group by sending the message "sub AMANSEEKINGAWOMAN your name" to listserv@services.web.aol.com

ANAHITA—Women and Gender in the Ancient World

You can join this group by sending the message "sub ANAHITA your name" to listserv@lsv.uky.edu

AUGLBC-L—TAU: Gay, Lesbian and Bisexual Community

The American University, Washington, DC

You can join this group by sending the message "sub AUGLBC-L your name" to listserv@american.edu

AWOMANSEEKINGAMAN—Ads For Women Seeking Men

You can join this group by sending the message "sub AWOMANSEEKINGAMAN your name" to listserv@services.web.aol.com

GENDER—Study of Communication and Gender

Rensselaer Polytechnic Institute, Troy, NY

You can join this group by sending the message "sub GENDER your name" to listserv@vm.its.rpi.edu

GENDERCB—Gender Marketing and Consumer Behavior Discussion List

You can join this group by sending the message "sub GENDERCB your name" to listserv@uriacc.uri.edu

GENDEREQ—RI Gender Equity Discussion & Information List

You can join this group by sending the message "sub GENDEREQ your name" to `listserv@uriacc.uri.edu`

GLMGLBCN—Great Lakes/Midwest Gay, Lesbian, Bisexual College Network

University of Illinois at Chicago, Chicago, IL

You can join this group by sending the message "sub GLMGLBCN your name" to `listserv@listserv.uic.edu`

LEADER—Gender and Leadership Case Studies Discussion Group

St. John's University, Collegeville, MN

You can join this group by sending the message "sub LEADER your name" to `listserv@moe.computing.csbsju.edu`

MINERVA—Discussion of Women and the Military and Women in War

Site: The George Washington University Computer Center, Washington, DC

You can join this group by sending the message "sub MINERVA your name" to `listserv@gwuvm.gwu.edu`

NGLB-L—List for NASPA Network on Gay, Lesbian, and Bisexual Concerns

East Carolina University, Computing and Info systems, Greenville, NC

You can join this group by sending the message "sub NGLB-L your name" to `listserv@ecuvm.cis.ecu.edu`

NGO-CONF—Global Women's Issues Discussed in World Women's Conferences

You can join this group by sending the message "sub NGO-CONF your name" to `listserv%albnyvm1.bitnet@listserv.net`

RSVPP—RSVPP List for Research in Sex, Violence, and Pregnancy Prevention

The University of Alabama, Tuscaloosa, AL

You can join this group by sending the message "sub RSVPP your name" to `listserv@ua1vm.ua.edu`

SEX-L—For General Discussion of Sexual Issues

Texas A&M University Computing Services Center

You can join this group by sending the message "sub SEX-L your name" to `listserv@tamvm1.tamu.edu`

SEXTALK—For Intellectual Discussion on Issues Related to Sexuality

Texas A&M University Computing Services Center

You can join this group by sending the message "sub SEXTALK your name" to `listserv@tamvm1.tamu.edu`

STOPRAPE—Sexual Assault Activist List

Brown University, Providence, RI

You can join this group by sending the message "sub STOPRAPE your name" to `listserv@brownvm.brown.edu`

STWTTF-L—Gender Issues in Science Fiction

University of Notre Dame, Notre Dame, IN

You can join this group by sending the message "sub STWTTF-L your name" to `listserv@vma.cc.nd.edu`

WITCHHNT—Is There a Child Sex Abuse Witchhunt?

Massachusetts Institute of Technology, Cambridge, MA

You can join this group by sending the message "sub WITCHHNT your name" to `listserv@mitvma.mit.edu`

WOMEN-IN-MINISTRY—Women in Ministry

You can join this group by sending the message "sub WOMEN-IN-MINISTRY your name" to `listserv@home.ease.lsoft.com`

SHOPPING

2(x)ist Underwear

`http://www.digex.net/2xist.html`

Provides a virtual catalog of men's underwear. Includes a closer view of boxers, briefs, tanks, and tees, as well as a size chart and guarantee.

America's Tall Catalog

`http://www.a1.com/shirt/bigtall.html`

Offers 100% cotton and button-down pinpoint oxfords for the big and tall. Web-direct, same day shipping. Prices and sizes available are listed.

Bonté Casuals

`http://www.catalog.com/corner/bonte`

Offers children's casualwear made with environmentally friendly fabrics. For every garment sold, the company purchases 25 square feet of rainforest or wetlands acreage or helps sponsor a whale. If you send in your hangtag, they give you the deed to the property.

Camalgori: A Representative Collection of Fashion Made in Italy

`http://www.nettuno.it/btw/cmlgr`

Offers the Camalgori collection of women's clothing.

Discreet Boutique

`http://www.mbnet.mb.ca:80/flatland/mall/discreet/`

Offers an online lingerie catalog and an 800 number for convenient ordering. Site includes plus sizes. Sign up for the new arrival mailing list.

Express Online

`http://express.style.com/`

Provides news about fashions, trends, and upcoming merchandise. Ask the Express fashion director for fashion tips and tricks. Members are eligible for exclusive offers from Express.

Genius T-Shirts

`http://www.a1.com/shirt/t-shirt.html`

Carries a collection of 50 artistic, scholarly T-shirts and sweatshirts, including Einstein, Socrates, Mozart, Geronimo, Dickinson, and more. Will ship internationally.

Graphiti

`http://libertynet.org/~graphiti`

Lets you design your own T-shirts, sweatshirts, jackets, caps, and more. Lets you order as many or as few items as you want.

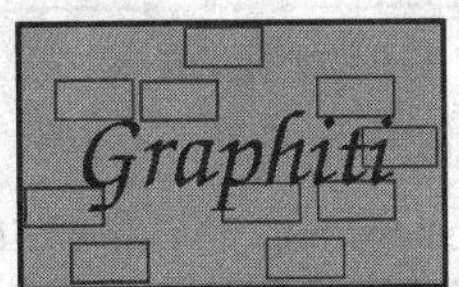

Hot Couture Clothing Company

`http://www.hotcouture.com`

Designs and manufactures clothing for women. Designs and sews every garment individually to produce distinctive garments that represent the wearer's individual sense of style.

Lebow Bros. Clothing for Men and Boys

`http://www.tiac.net/users/lebow/`

Offers fine clothing for men and boys, including sizes for the hard-to-fit individual. (In English and Chinese.)

Main Sequence Astronomical Apparel

`http://www.treknet.net/astronomytees`

Offers a full line of wholesale astronomy T-shirts, sweats, and caps for purchase by planetariums, science centers, and museums. Select designs are also available for individual purchase.

Menswear Unlimited

`http://www.clark.net/pub/menswear/suits.html`

Presents a catalog of men's tailored clothing.

Planet Greek

`http://www.nemonet.com/planet/plntgrek.htm`

Offers a selection of custom screen-printed and embroidered Greek apparel, including event T-shirts and elaborately embroidered fraternity or sorority crests.

Rainbow Rags

`http://www.promotion.com/rainbow/`

Offers high-quality, durable children's clothing featuring embroidered and appliquéd trim for a unique look.

Salonwear

http://visi.com/~ibonk/

Offers factory-direct fashionable career attire for stylists, including a complete line of uniforms, aprons, capes, gowns, lab coats, and sundries.

Soft Wear by ColorTech

http://www.holli.com/colortech

Offers T-shirt designs and a wide variety of shirts, jackets, hats, and coffee mugs. Also puts your own full-color images on products.

Automobiles

AutoPages of Internet

http://www.clark.net/pub/networx/autopage/autopage.html

Features full-color photographs and detailed descriptions of automobiles and motorcycles for sale across the United States. Also includes information about manufacturers, restorers, trade shows, and auctions.

CAR-LINK

http://www.car-link.com/

Provides opportunity to view cars for sale. Lets you submit an ad, including a color picture of the car for $5. Offers listings by the month.

Hot Rods World Wide

http://www.america.net/com/hotrods/hrhome.html

Departments include hot rods for sale, car shows and coming events, and advertising rates. Submit your own ad or add a link.

The Ultimate New Auto Club in Canada

http://www.barint.on.ca/cybermal/autoclub.html

Offers economic service for the whole family. Works on a reimbursement program. Also available in the U.S.

Flowers

1-800-FLOWERS

http://www.800flowers.com/

Advertises the services and products of 1-800-FLOWERS. Offers home decorating ideas, card message suggestions, and the latest in floral trends. Shop by occasion, product category, or price range. Special contests and promotions available.

1-800-Roses

http://www.1stresource.com/r/roses/default.htm

Specializes in long stem roses. Other floral arrangements available. Open 24 hours. Free delivery. Order flowers over the Internet or by calling the toll-free number.

Absolutely Fresh Flowers

http://www.cts.com/~flowers/

Specializes in nearly 150 different kinds of miniature carnations. Sells and ships flowers directly all over the U.S. via next day service. Offers satisfaction guarantee.

Buning the Florist

http://www.paradise.net/flowers

Serves the needs of the flower-buying public as one of the largest retail florists in the United States. Includes an online catalog of flower arrangements sorted by occasion.

Fleurs d'Eté

http://www.webguide.com/fleurs.html

Advertises the flowers offered by Fleurs d'Eté of Miami, Florida. Contains product list with color photos and a price list.

Flora Designs

http://www.nav.com/FDI/flora.html

Advertises the services of Flora Designs, a worldwide floral and fruit, gourmet, and champagne basket delivery service.

Flower Stop

http://www.flowerstop.com/fstop/

Advertises floral arrangements provided by Flower Stop. Flowers come directly from the grower and are shipped overnight. Price lists for different bouquets are available. Order flowers by using online order form, calling their toll free number, or sending e-mail.

3D Glasses

http://www.insight.com/web/form3d.html

Complete a questionnaire and get a free pair of 3D glasses and a free subscription to Insight catalog.

FTD Internet

`http://www.ftd.com/`

Offers FTD's official flower catalog. Provides domestic and international delivery. Contains images of the products available and a free personal reminder service.

Royer's Flowers

`http://go.flowerlink.com/html/dship/dship.html`

Catalog of the various types of floral arrangements available for shipment, including bouquets, foliage, flowering plants, gift baskets, and specialty items.

Teleflora—at the Spectra.Net Mall

`http://www.spectra.net/mall/teleflora/`

Teleflora is the world's largest privately owned floral wire service. Provides bouquet suggestions and special offers.

Total Flower Exports

`http://www.iinet.net.au/~total/`

Provides information about this exporter of fresh and dried flowers located in Australia. Lets you view some unusual flowers and order a sampler of dried flowers.

Gifts

à la Gift Basket Headquarters

`http://www.gifthq.com/gifthq/`

Offers 30 different food, wine, and all-occasion gift baskets. Secured credit card ordering nationwide. A detailed catalog provides prices and shipping and handling information for each basket.

Christmas Shop

`http://www.ChristmasNet.com`

Offers gifts for children year round. Specializes in Steinbach Nutcrackers, Department 56 villages, and ornaments of all types, sizes, and shapes. Lets you visit Santa in Long Grove, Illinois, where we all know he keeps a summer home.

Crafter's Showcase

`http://www.northcoast.com/unlimited/product_directory/cs/cs.html`

Provides color photographs and information about a wide array of items including dolls and plaques. Also provides pricing and ordering information.

Erre Esse Gifts

`http://www.erresse.com/erresse/index.html`

Advertises fine silverware and sterling silver gifts. Includes tea and coffee sets, jewel cases, candelabras, and children's gifts. Contains prices and images of various pieces, as well as ordering information.

Giftnet

`http://www.demon.co.uk/giftnet/`

Lets you order a variety of novelty gifts, such as coffee blends, flowers, and gardening kits. Detailed descriptions and prices of items are provided.

Parkleigh World-Wide

`http://www.parkleigh.com`

Offers a selection of coffees, chocolates, writing instruments, stationery, and other fine gifts.

The Private Source

`http://metroux.metrobbs.com/PrivateSource/index.htm`

Advertises Private Source's collection of personal gifts through an online catalog.

Health & Beauty

American Supply International

`http://www.amsupply.com/`

ASI already has a good reputation with overseas Americans who've used it for years to order everything from special and dietetic foods, automotive parts, hardware, small appliances, and much more. Offers link to other commercial- and consumer-related sites.

The Beauty Department at CyberShop

`http://www.nfic.com/Cybershop/Online/pe_dept.htm`

Order cosmetics, perfume, and personal goods online. Advertisers include Drakkar Noir, Moschino, and Terme di Saturnia.

Body Doubles Skin Care

`http://www.primenet.com/~doubles`

Offers a line of facial cremes, gentle body lotions, and aromatic bathing essentials created to nourish, protect, and care for your skin.

Certified European Image Consultant

http://www.islandnet.com/~cvcprod/bartz.htm

Provides head-to-toe image makeovers, skin care and cosmetics, wardrobe, fashion and shopping assistance, color analysis, business presentations, and European costume jewelry.

Health-Max Your Maximum Health Connection

http://www.ieway.com/business/max/welcome.html

Offers a product line developed using the latest scientific discoveries combined with natural ingredients to help achieve healthy bodies. Products are designed to help cleanse, nourish, and balance the body, helping it to resist disease. Includes an online catalog.

J. Crow Company—Herbs, Spices, Oils, Incense

http://www.ronin.com/jcrow

Offers culinary herbs, spices, essential oil fragrances, and insights into other traditions and techniques for health and well-being. Includes links to other related sites.

Le Parfum

http://www.netview.com/leparfum/

Carries more perfume labels than any other store in California and lets you order many of them online. Offers fragrances for men and women. Includes catalog of their most popular and hard to find fragrances.

Maui Amenities

http://planet-hawaii.com/~amen

Offers Maui Island Formula skin and hair care products with all-natural Hawaiian ingredients. Lets you order via a secured line.

Nature's Wealth

http://branch.com/nature/wealth.htm

Dedicated to providing the highest quality health and fitness products that cannot be found in stores. Focus on vitamin supplements, moisturizers and lotions, water and air filters, and more.

Home & Office

Atlas Pen and Pencil Corporation

http://pwr.com/ATLAS/

Produces promotional advertising products for your business or organization by imprinting your logo on their products. Presents highlights of their catalog of products. You can request a complete copy of the catalog. A sponsor of the Creative Times Newsletter.

Cyberian Outpost

http://www.cybout.com/

Serves as a virtual computer store. Offers software, accessories, and peripherals at unbeatable prices with overnight delivery. Features a Product of the Day, detailed information on the hundreds of featured products—including reviews, screen shots, and product demos (as available).

The Electronics Department at CyberShop

http://www.nfic.com/Cybershop/Online/el_dept.htm

Provides a variety of products to fill all your electronics needs. Purchase televisions, stereos, laser printers, cordless phones, word processors, and more. Guided graphics tours available.

Haworth Furniture for What's Next

http://www.haworth-furn.com

Offers office furniture and office design and reconfiguration services. Includes a catalog and a listing of showroom locations.

In Home Shopping

http://users.mwci.net/~intp

Purchase environmentally friendly products, such as detergents, cosmetics, soaps, hair styling products, and vitamins. Provides catalog of products, toll-free ordering, and 100 percent satisfaction guarantee.

Leonardo Collection Co.

http://www.crl.com/~bidlccca

Features a fine selection of high quality corporate and personal wooden gift items, including organizers, pen sets, desk accessories, and custom-designed gifts.

Marshall on the Internet

http://www.marshall.com

Contains product information and data sheets from more than 140 electronic parts and components manufacturers. Lets you order all products directly through the Internet.

Shopping Planet

http://www.shopplanet.com

Advertises the best online prices for computer hardware and software. Also provides airline information and the top 10 games on CD-ROM.

Southern Reprographics

http://www.mindspring.com/~srepro/southern.html

Supplies drafting, computer drafting, blueprinting, plotter, electrostatic, and xerographic products. Serves the architectural engineering, construction, surveying, home-building, and manufacturing design industries.

STI Internet Toner Depot

http://www.itsnet.com/commercial/sti

Offers a complete line of supplies for copiers, fax machines, and laser, line, dot-matrix, and inkjet printers.

Valentine & Company

http://ireland.iol.ie/~nova/nova1/pages/valentns.htm

Serves as an Internet department store from Ireland. Specializes in linen by Thomas Ferguson. The Ferguson Gift Collection includes double damask tablecloths, damask linen bathrobes, and Irish linen sheets.

WoodWrite Wood Pens

http://www.ip.net/shops/WoodWrite__Wood_Pens/

Offers a variety of wooden pens and pencils hand-turned and ergonomically designed for proper balance and comfort made in a variety of hardwoods selected for beauty of color and grain pattern.

Internet & Multimedia Services

After Hours Media Duplication Service

http://www.afterhours.com/

Provides CD mastering and duplication, floppy disk duplication, audio cassette and video cassette duplication, international video standards conversion, and film to video transfer.

Allegro New Media

http://www.allegronm.com/

Publishes interactive multimedia CD-ROMs. Includes Allegro Home PC Library, the growing "Learn To Do" series, business references, cooking, travel in Europe, and educational titles.

AzTech Interactive

http://www.bga.com/aztech

Multimedia and WWW production studio based in Austin, TX. Produces CD-ROM, enhanced CD, and electronic brochures, and designs WWW sites for clients.

Connect Homepage

http://www.audiowav.com/connect/

Offers cutting edge communications solutions for businesses, including 900 number services, Internet services, and interactive voice applications.

Punch & Brodie Productions

http://www.rockisland.com/~leo/punch/

Provides live animation for video, film, and live productions. Specializes in corporate events, training videos, commercials, and entertainment.

Jewelry

Abundant Discoveries

http://amsquare.com/abundant/index.html

Provides sales of traditional hand-crafted jewelry made in Native American styles. Products only utilize natural and original materials. Includes high-definition photographs of all pieces of Abundant Discoveries line.

The Amber Lady

http://goldray.com/amberlady/

Features genuine 40 million-year-old insects in polished honey-colored amber, as seen in *Jurassic Park* and featured in *Smithsonian Magazine*. Also offers more traditional amber jewelry.

Gem Search International

http://www.pixi.com/gem_international/

Advertises the products of Gem Search International and contains diamond buying and selling information guides.

J & M Coin, Stamp, and Jewellery Ltd.

http://www.jandm.com

J & M buys, sells, and trades coins, stamps, bullion, and jewelry. Offers a current list of products.

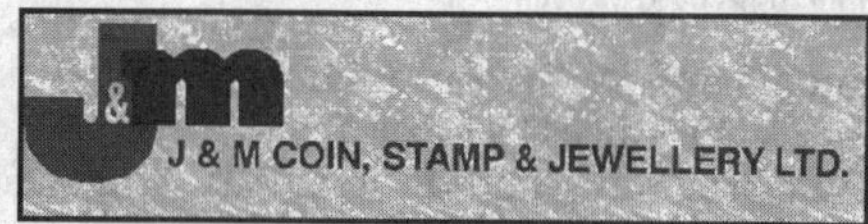

The Jewelers of Las Vegas

http://www.manifest.com/Jewelers

Manufacturers, wholesalers, importers, and distributors of fine jewelry. Offers an online catalog of their products, as well as information on custom-made jewelry and advice on how to shop for jewelry.

Milne Jewelry Company

http://www.xmission.com/~turq

Presents an online catalog of Southwestern jewelry, including traditional Navajo, Zuni, and Hopi designs. Provides sections on "Guide to Southwest Indian Jewelry" and "Care of Silver and Turquoise Jewelry." (In English and Japanese.)

NetDiamonds, Inc.

http://www.bnt.com/netdiamonds/

Advertises products offered by NetDiamonds, Inc. of New York, New York. Provides a catalog, images of specific products, and prices and ordering information.

Rhinestone Jewelry Word Pins

http://www.rhinestone.com/rhinestone

Provides online sales of Austrian Crystal rhinestone jewelry. Includes catalog with pictures and ordering information.

Silver Jewellery

http://www.he.net/~lensam/ak/

Displays samples of work done at Sir John Cass Faculty of Arts, Jewellery, and Silversmithing.

Miscellaneous Shopping Sites

A&H Internet Shopping Service

http://www.beicomm.com/ah/

Offers one-stop shopping for jewelry and computers. Can help you customize your teleconferencing needs. Descriptions and prices of all products available. Warranty and return information also provided.

Ada's Store

http://adaweb.com/adaweb/items/store.html

An eclectic collection of artists wares makes up Ada's Store. This on-line shopping site features hats, T-shirts, Ada soaps, magazines, videos, and books.

AmericaNet.Com—Free Classified Advertising

http://www.AmericaNet.Com/classified.html

Provides free national classified advertising, including help wanted, cars, trucks, RVs, commercial real estate, and residential real estate. Lets you submit your ad.

The Americas

http://www.integctr.com/americas/

Specializes in folk art and artifacts by Indian and Indigenous peoples of the American Southwest, Mexico, and South America. Includes a catalog and photo gallery of artwork. E-mail questions are encouraged.

AMOC (A Matter of Clay)

http://www.systemv.com/infonet/gtg/

Searching for unusual gifts for the eclectically minded? A Matter of Clay specializes in ceramic Gargoyles, Cherubs, and new age articles. Features catalog with photos and online ordering. Also features other artwork, such as Smooth Creek Leather and ceramic figures from Mexico.

Ancient World

http://www.mindspring.com/~ancient/ancient.html

Manufacturers of museum-quality reproductions of historical and archaeological artifacts from the ancient and contemporary world. Offers a catalog of more than 400 items. Also manufactures molds of almost any type of artistic or architectural element to your custom specifications.

Another Victim of Santa Fe Style

http://www.neosoft.com/~victim

Serves as online curio shop. Offers the art of the late Tommie Macaione, as well as T-shirts, notecards, and posters from some of the Southwest's most singular talents.

Antiques World

http://www.webcom.com/~antiques

Features online antique shops, classified ads of antiques and collectibles for sale and wanted, and other resources for collectors and antiquers.

Aquarium World Market

http://www.io.com/~kslandry/Aquarium_World_Market.html

Provides current availability and price lists for over 20 mail-order companies offering aquarium fish and supplies.

Art of the States

http://www.pol.com/states/

Offers limited-edition prints and collector series Christmas ornaments. Features a collection of native birds and wildflowers, along with the capital building of its respective state. (All paintings by W.D. Gaither MSB.)

Blue Green Algae Enzymes

http://www.roughguys.com/bluegreen

Presents information about the health benefits of Super Blue Green Algae and how to become an independent distributor of the product.

Builders Graphics

http://www.primenet.com/~mrclark/builders.html

Designs customized dream homes from your sketches. Offers downloadable GIF files from a home project by Builders Graphics. Also offers home plans for Southwest style homes.

Business and Safety Cartoons by Goff

http://www.fileshop.com/personal/tgoff/

Presents samples of cartoons by professional cartoonist Ted Goff. Geared to people who are responsible for an in-house newsletter, training manual, presentation, brochure, or other publication. Available cartoons have safety, teamwork, quality, management, sales, technology, and computer themes. Also provides links to other related sites.

California Crafts Marketplace

http://www.catalog.com/giftshop/index.htm

Serves as a guide to crafts and gifts, including clothing, furniture, and jewelry.

Cartoon Heaven

http://www.aardvark.ie/cartoon-heaven/

Presents an animation art gallery in Melbourne, Australia, including artwork from all the major studios. Includes an online catalog and links to related sites.

Castle Attic

http://emporium.turnpike.net/~castle.home/index.html

Offers a selection of swords, daggers, and armor for medieval and renaissance fans, SCA members, or anyone who just likes a good blade. And there's no waiting period!

Catalog Live

http://cataloglive.com

Top shopping site winner! Shop for great upscale items, including Williams Sonoma, Preserves by Viki's, Hoop Backboards, and Golf Gifts. Other shopping categories include wine, flowers, gourmet foods, cookies, sporting goods, and much more.

Charleston: A Magical History Tour

http://sc.net/organizations/farrow/magic-tour.html

Provides background and ordering information for "Charleston: A Magical History Tour," a 70-minute video introduction to Charleston, South Carolina. Includes author background and video contents.

Coherent Communications Systems Corporation

http://www.coherent.com

Offers voice enhancement technology, including echo cancellation platforms and associated network software. Also provides teleconferencing products for audio, video, and desktop conferencing applications.

Area Code Finder

http://www.555-1212.com/aclookup.html

Find the area code for any area.

CouponNet

`http://coupon.com/coupon.html`

Do you want to save money? Here is the ultimate online coupon and rebate connection. Includes reference library, recipes, and a coupon trading center. A site for anyone looking to save money while shopping to their heart's content.

CraftBase

`http://www.cerf.net/vistek`

Offers craft kits, patterns, and information, including a craft catalog for kids. Includes photos of completed projects. The Kangaroo Korner includes craft tips, links to other craft-related sites, and craft news.

Dakota Engraving, Etc.

`http://www.getnet.com/engrave/`

Specializes in key tags personalized with your name, URL, e-mail address, and N-Number. Also offers bicycle plates and license plate frames.

Delblau Company

`http://www.travelaccessories.com`

Who is watering your plants while you're basking in the hot Caribbean sun? And who is watching your traveler's checks while you're snorkeling? What you need is the Plant Oasis Self-Watering System and the SurfSafe Waterproof Wallet. They're available here, along with many other handy gadgets for travelers.

Discovering Success with Gary Viterise, Ph.D.

`http://www.infoanalytic.com/viterise/`

Offers a wide collection of presentations that cover motivation, self-esteem, and leadership. Includes programs for stress management, the psychology of selling, positive morale development, and leadership models. Also offers audio tapes. First advise? Turn off the computer and go play outside!

Distant Caravans

`http://www.greatbasin.com/~caravan/`

Serves people interested in the Middle Ages, renaissance, belly dancing, ethnic jewelry, amber, and more. Imports goods from Afghanistan, India, Pakistan, and Poland.

dotSpiegel

`http://www.spiegel.com/spiegel/`

Spiegel's new online catalog and magazine, including features, merchandise, stories, tips, and contests. Experts also answer questions about interior design, travel, gardening, and more.

eShop Inc.

`http://www.eshop.com`

Tower Records, 1-800-Flowers, Spiegel, and more advertise at this site. Job listings also provided. Merchants can create promotions tailored to each shopper.

Essex Wood Products

`http://www.snswwide.com/essex.html`

A wood fabrication shop. Combines computerized routing equipment with skilled hand-finishing to provide quality woodworking. Products offered include precision-engineered storage cases, plaques, craft kits, and game boards.

Eureka! The Web Junction

`http://www.wilder.com/eureka.html`

Provides access to an array of unique products. Appellation Spring's Winery T-shirts, Sweet Enhancement candy, solar panel power products, and software can be purchased from this site.

Facet Collector's Showcase

`http://www.inetbiz.com/facet/`

Provides a catalog of various collectibles from many famous manufacturers and designers, such as Armani, Royal Copenhagen, Versace, and many more. Includes product pictures and ordering information.

Fanco International Corp.

`http://www.webcom.com/~stannet/fanco/fanco.html`

Imports PVC laundry, storage, and shopping bags. Also imports slippers and luggage carts from China. Includes an online catalog.

Feathered Friends

`http://www.halcyon.com/featherd/welcome.htm`

Produces down sleeping bags, outerwear, and accessories. Really, the friends aren't feathered anymore.

For Sale By Owner Magazine

http://www.human.com/mkt/fsbo/

Lets you place ads for selling homes. You can view property listings, refer to area maps, and see property advertising rates.

Fox Color and Light Home Page

http://www.microweb.com/jimfox/index.html

Creates CyberFashions and CyberToys, including electronic, interactive, programmable clothing, jewelry, gifts, toys, and accessories.

The Front Page

http://www.thefrontpage.com/welcome.html

Offers an extensive mix of shops and services, such as recreational activities, art, computer consulting, and more. American Indian collectibles, telecommunication services, health and weight management products, Havana Cigar Club memberships, and psychic cards included.

Gilltro-Electronics, Inc.

http://www.giltronix.com

Offers remote access systems, local connectivity products, and peripheral sharing devices. Includes product overviews, service and support, and order forms.

Global Innovations

http://www.icw.com/global/global.html

Online novelty products shop. Carries an Internet watch, Star Trek T-shirts, Aura's virtual reality vest, cooling products for those hot summer days, and stereogram posters and software.

Good Stuff Cheap

http://www.onramp.net/goodstuf

Get new, brand-name products below wholesale. Provides an enormous selection of products. Categories include automotive, clothing, baby needs, luggage, tools, and fitness.

The Hahn Company

http://hahncompany.com

The Hahn Company owns and manages more than 40 shopping malls throughout North America. Shop for toys, jewelry, home entertainment, clothing, and more. Also presents retail leasing space information and retail tenant lists. News and games categories offered as well.

Handcrafts Unlimited

http://www.awod.com/gallery/crafts/hu/

Offers a variety of quality hand-crafted items, including clothing, costumes, calligraphy and art, lamp shades, ornaments, miniatures, tole painting, and many other items by request.

Hawaiian Express Unlimited

http://planet-hawaii.com/~hawnexp/

Take a virtual shopping trip to Hawaii. Purchase clothing, coffee, flowers and baskets, hand-crafted jewelry, Hawaiian art, and photos.

Ideal Engraving Co., Inc.

http://www.cybercom.com/~rbeir

Manufactures a complete line of marking products, including steel hand stamps and dies, interchangeable type and holders, numbering heads, and bench presses.

InfoWell

http://www.infowell.com/~infowell

Offers exciting products from around the world, delivered to your door. Includes art, gifts, electronic marketing programs, and kits to check your home for asbestos insulation and lead paint. You can finally measure whether it's time to add more asbestos and lead paint!

Internet Auction List

http://www.usaweb.com/usaweb/auction

Serves as a source for auctions on the Internet. Provides auction listings for automobile, real estate, antiques, collectibles, wines, and much more. No Jackie O stuff, though.

Internet Green Marketplace

http://envirolink.org/products/

Features services and products of environmentally and socially responsible companies. Also provides links to related sites.

J.R. Antiques and China Registry

http://www.islandnet.com/~cvcprod/jrantiq.html

Specializes in a matching service for current and discontinued china patterns. Serves as a registry for people interested in selling china or trying to find missing pieces.

John Charles Antiques

http://www.londonmall.co.uk/antiques

Deals mainly in furniture originating from the 17th century to the beginning of the 20th century. Buys and sells fine oil and watercolor paintings, old and new prints, clocks, chandeliers, china, glass, mirrors, pewter, copper, brass, bronze, silver, and gold.

Jordan Manufacturing Company, Inc.

http://www.empgal.com/~jordan

Sells cedar birdhouses and feeders, squirrel feeders, replacement cushions, umbrellas, wooden picnic tables, sawhorses, workbenches, and umbrella frames.

Keller's Appaloosas

http://www.babcom.com/keller/

Offers breeding quality Appaloosa horses for sport, halter, and performance. Provides online sales and pedigree information, as well as photos and pricing. Also has links to related sites.

KRAMER Handgun Leather

http://shop-utopia.com/kramer_leather/kramer.html

Sells horsehide concealment holsters and accessories for the armed professional. Offers specialized designs for government covert operations, military special warfare, undercover police, and dignitary protection details.

Laid Back Designs

http://www.travelsource.com/travelstore/lbd/lbd.html

Offers a catalog of sammocks—high quality, comfortable, versatile, portable hammocks. Great for the office.

LifeTime Filters

http://www.sccsi.com/LifeTime/lifetime_welcome.html

Advertises electrostatic air filters sold by LifeTime Filters. Provides information about these air-cleaning products, including how they work, their benefits, and how to clean them.

Lucia's Little Houses

http://media1.hypernet.com/knight.html

Offers Grand Ideas for Small Houses, a portfolio of 12 designs for small homes by an architectural firm in Maine.

Made in America

http://amsquare.com/america/made.html

Offers American hand-made goods and services. Offers a separate section on career and résumé management. Also has links to related sites.

Magazine Warehouse

http://cdnow.com/mags

Offers subscriptions to more than 300 magazines in more than 80 categories, including computing, music, science, sports, fitness, and fashion. What, no million dollar winners?

Maude Asbury

http://www.deltanet.com/intersphere/ma

Offers distinctive photo albums and desk accessories hand-crafted in the United States.

Maverick Communications

http://www.maverickcomm.com

Offers online shopping for radio and communications equipment, as well as repair and customer services for such equipment.

Musicmaker's Kits, Inc.

http://www.primenet.com/~musikit/index.html

Makers of unusual stringed instruments, kits, plans, supplies, and completed instruments, including dulcimers, mandolins, zithers, banjos, and harps. Provides pictures, prices, and an audio sample of each instrument. Also provides information about the company and links to related sites.

Neuromedical Supplies, Inc.

http://www.neuro.com/

Ordering catalog for neuromedical supplies such as caps, gowns, lab supplied, needs, and more. Check out their catalog for a full list of items available.

Next to Nothing

http://www.winternet.com/~julie/ntn.html

Provides information on getting free stuff both on and off the Internet. Includes free offers from magazines, Internet sites, newsletters, TV, and more.

Newbury Comics, Interactive

http://www.newbury.com

"Shop here and die happy," they say. Newbury Comics is an online retailer, selling thousands of compact discs as well as funky rock and pop culture merchandise such as T-shirts, posters, boots, hats, videos, lava lamps, and so forth. There's also the Guide to Boston's Underground and Boston's Music Scene.

Northwest Neon

http://www.peak.org/~omarab/nwneon.html

Designs and manufactures custom neon signs for shipment all over the U.S. They specialize in interior wall and window signs displaying logos, products, and services.

Paramount Custom Cabinetry

http://www.bizlink.com/paramount

Specializes in custom cabinetry, kitchens, computer furniture, and wall units. Offers the latest computerized designs and layouts.

Perspective Visuals, Inc.

http://haven.ios.com/~dinosaur/

Provides information and sales for the Smithsonian Dinosaur Museum CD-ROM. Includes background, sample graphics, and contact information.

Pet Supplies On-line

http://www.awa.com/pets

No matter whether your furry, feathery, or scaly companion is carnivorous or vegetarian, this site enables you to obtain all the food and treats it needs, as well as such pet essentials as brushes, shampoos, treats, toys, and training aids.

PolyEster Records and Books

http://www.glasswings.com.au/PolyEster/index.html

Provides online sales of records, CDs, and books for PolyEster Records and Books, based in Melbourne, Australia. Includes online catalog of hard to find records, books, and magazines.

Posters from Your Photos and Computer Files

http://www.pacificrim.net/~bydesign/poster.html

Makes posters, T-shirts, and mouse pads from your photos and computer files.

The Quiltery

http://mmink.com/mmink/dossiers/quilt/quilt.html

Provides online sales of hand-made quilts. Includes photos, pricing, and ordering information.

Rip-Tie

http://www.riptie.com/riptie/

Sells velcro cable organizers. Designs Rip-Tie products for maximum speed, flexibility, and safety, letting you easily insert, remove, or rearrange cables as you need without damage.

Roctronics Lighting

http://www.roctronics.com/

Provides lighting, laser graphics, and special effects for nightclubs, theaters, stage performances, exhibits, trade shows, museums, concerts, amusement centers, and special events.

Rubber Stamp Queen

http://www.dol.com/queen/

Provides sales of uniquely designed rubber stamps. Includes catalog information, examples of stamps, links to related pages, and contact addresses.

SCHWA Online

http://kzsu.stanford.edu/uwi/schwa/schwa.html

Provides online sales of the SCHWA line of products. What exactly are the SCHWA line of products? Well, let's say they are not of this world—assorted T-shirts, stickers, and other alien defense products. Weird? Yes. Interesting? Yes. Check this site out, it's unlike any other out there.

Scintilla Alternative Lighting, Gifts, and Accessories

http://www.mindspring.com/~bart/scintilla.html

Presents a collection of functional art in forms of lighting fixtures, jewelry, frames, and other choice accessories.

SeaVision USA

http://www.seavisionusa.com

Offers the finest in underwater vision technology, from color-correcting filters to prescription lenses for your diving mask.

Shopping2000

`http://www.shopping2000.com/shopping2000/ross_simon/`

Offers over 50 catalogs and thousands of products for sale.

Stealth Technologies

`http://www.peak.org/~omarab/index.html`

Provides wholesale stereo equipment, custom computer programming, hardware sales, computer setup assistance, and local limousine service. You can see the connection, of course.

Sumeria Product List

`http://www.service.com/D3/sumeria/sumeria.html`

Produces and provides sales of CD-ROMs on various subjects. Includes QuickTime movie examples of catalog. Also includes CD-ROM background and ordering information.

Surplus United States Government Sales

`http://www.drms.dla.mil/index.html`

The Defense Reutilization and Marketing Service sells surplus Department of Defense properties to the general public, including computers, vehicles, aircraft parts, scrap metal, clothing, and furniture.

Tampa Machinery Auction, Inc.

`http://www.usaweb.com/usaweb/tma`

Holds a government surplus auction every month. Includes surplus and seized vehicles and equipment from cities, counties, sheriffs' departments, utilities, and many others. Offers lists of inventory for the next auction. Here's your chance to buy your neighbor's car you've always wanted.

Tickets and Travel, Inc.

`http://www.inetdirect.net/tnt`

Provides online sales for tickets to events including sports, concerts, and more. Also provides travel reservation services and includes company and contact information.

Tough Traveler Gear

`http://www.travelsource.com/travelstore/toughtraveler/toughtraveler.html`

Presents Tough Traveler Gear online. Features soft luggage, backpacks, camera bags, duffel bags, and child carriers. Guarantee information available.

Traders' Connection

`http://www.trader.com`

Presents more than 500,000 classified ads online. Lets you browse or search ad papers from all over the United States and Canada. Offers more than 40 publications online. Also offers full BBS services and nationwide Internet access for as little as $3.95 per month.

Uncommon Connections

`http://www.mps.org/uncommon/`

Offers online marketplace. Includes some unique products and unusual gift items such as coffee, off-the-wall checks, sportswear, and art. Provides secure credit card transactions for all online merchants.

Winona

`http://www.mps.org/~winona.inc/`

Offers a selection of gifts organized by theme: kids, outdoors, loons, wolves, golf, sweaters, and care products.

Woman Made Catalog Showroom

`http://www.megamed.com/womanmade`

Features art and crafts made by women-owned businesses. Includes jewelry, pottery, clothing, stained and etched glass, and more.

The World Shopping & Information Network

`http://www.wsin.com`

Shopping, travel, real estate, news, entertainment and more. Comprehensive listings, exciting colorful graphics, easy-to-navigate directories and search engines on site to locate anything, anytime!

Amish Recipe

`http://www.kraftmaid.com/`

Get a free Amish recipe from KraftMaid—the folks who know cabinets and cabinetry.

Security & Surveillance Equipment

Alarm Systems

http://www.mindspring.com/~ko4ta/alarm.html

Offers alarm equipment at installer-direct prices, including fire alarms, closed-circuit TVs, and gate systems.

The Codex

http://www.thecodex.com/

Provides electronic eavesdropping detection services and equipment, anti-bugging and anti-wiretapping equipment, privacy, protection, and security products, forensic audio restoration, and secure communications equipment. Also includes links to other security, investigative, and related sites.

Electronic Countermeasures, Inc.

http://www.t8000.com/eci/eci.htm

Provides security management, consulting, and investigative services. Focuses on corporate security services and information loss in the oil, brokerage, and legal communities. Also offers analysis, surveillance, monitoring systems, and vehicle tracking systems.

Special Electronic Security Products Ltd.

http://sesp.co.il/~tunik

Specializes in the design and manufacturing of surveillance and counter-surveillance equipment and systems. Offers direct purchase worldwide.

Spy Supply Online

http://wbrt.wb.psu.edu/~galt/spy.html

Offers a wide array of items dealing with surveillance and privacy assurance, including audio recorders, bug detectors, phone tapping devices, and locksmithing tools. Paranoia heaven.

STANCOM, Inc.

http://www.mindspring.com/~stancom

Specializes in all types of security systems and equipment. Performs in-house service on cameras on monitors, video tape recorders, amplifiers, intercoms, and other equipment.

Software

Confluent, Inc.

http://www.confluent.com

Offers Visual Thought, a multipurpose Unix diagramming and flowcharting tool. Provides product information and lets you place orders.

Diskovery Educational Systems

http://www.diskovery.com/Diskovery/

Furnishes an electronic pricing guide for computer software, hardware, CD-ROMs, books, videos, and laser discs. Also offers a printed catalog. Categorizes products by title, category, and publisher.

KeyStone Learning Systems Corporation

http://www.keylearnsys.com

Provides video training for Windows applications. Describes their video training library and provides order forms.

Layer Eight Systems, Inc.

http://www.eight.com/

Provides financial engineering and software systems for the financial derivatives market. Describes their interest rate derivatives real-time pricing software system.

Lighten, Inc.

http://www.lighten.com/

Provides Advance 1.0 for Windows, a tool used for business modeling and analysis. Offers an evaluation guide and an animated demo.

Lumina Decision Systems, Inc.

http://www.lumina.com/

A computer software and services company that develops and markets software for modeling and decision support. Contains a product description and links to information about decision risk analysis.

MECC

http://www.mecc.com/

Contains information about its innovative and fun software programs for kids of all ages. Offers technical support and links to various other Internet sites of interest to kids, parents, and teachers. Includes titles such as The Oregon Trail, MathKeys, Storybook Weaver, MayaQuest, and Science Sleuths.

NeuroSolutions: The Neural Network Simulation Environment

http://www.nd.com/

Provides information on NeuroSolutions, a neural network design and simulation software product for Unix and Windows. Includes a demo and ordering information.

ObjectSpace, Inc.

http://www.objectspace.com

Offers object-oriented software products, consulting, and training. Provides information on training classes and schedules, product descriptions, and support information.

Ovation Software Testing, Inc.

http://world.std.com/~ovation/ovation.html

Specializes in software test automation technology. Provides technical information and information on training programs and implementation guidelines and modules.

Second Chair Corporation

http://www.secondchair.com/

Manufactures legal-specific Windows software for the legal research and litigation community. Offers trial downloads of legal software products.

Sunquest Information Systems, Inc.

http://www.sunquest.com/

Provides laboratory information systems and computer solutions to hospitals in the U.S., Canada, and Europe.

Virtual AdVentures

http://www.virtualadventures.com

Produces multimedia travel and adventure experiences, including "Fly Fishing: Great Rivers of the West," and "Virtual AdVentures, Grand Canyon." Includes reviews and ordering information.

Sporting Goods

The Amazing Baseball Card Auction

http://www.execpc.com/~mosey/auction.html

This silent auction is a great place to buy cards or sell them on consignment. You can view the cards, place a bid, and see after two weeks whether your bid is the highest.

New England Ski and Scuba

http://awebs.com/06066/NewEnglandSkiScuba/

Serves as a full service ski and scuba center. Carries all major brands of ski and scuba equipment and offers instruction and service on all their equipment.

Online Sports

http://www.onlinesports.com/

Online catalog for the secure purchase of any type of sports-related product for every sport known in the universe. You can also sign up for the newsletter, search through a sports career database, and more.

S & S Enterprises

http://www.usaweb.com/usaweb/ss

Provides a wholesale sports supplement catalog. Supplies sports nutrition products for professional and amateur bodybuilders.

Score It

http://www.scoreit.com/

Tired of drawing a score card as you watch the Big Game (and all the little games that precede it)? This software provides everything you need to track at bats, player summaries, automatically calculate stats, and a lot more!

Steve's Multi-Sport Catalog

http://www.source.net/steves/

Dedicated to providing the finest in bicycling, swimming, nutritional, and other related products. Where else on the Web can you buy a wet suit and a helmet?

SunFun Collection

http://www.sunfun.com

Offers innovative items for your sun protection, travel comfort, great reading, and sports and outdoor fun.

Sunglasses.Com

http://www.sunglasses.com/def2.htm

Pictorial catalog from which you can order every kind of sunglasses known to sea and sand. Calvin Klein, Bolle, Ray Ban, Vuarnet, and more.

The Sunglasses, Shavers, and More Home Page

`http://www.shades.com/sunglass/shop`

Offers sunglasses, shavers, and more. Offers a large selection of sunglasses, including Ray-Ban, Serengeti, Revo, Reebok, Guess, and Marilyn Monroe.

Toys

Baby Joy Toys

`http://www.pacific.net/~joy/bjt/`

Offers toys and accessories for babies and young children.

MotoMini—Quality Motorcycle Collectibles

`http://www.homepage.com/motomini/`

Presents an online catalog of MotoMini's collectible motorcycle models.

PGT Toys

`http://www.tias.com/stores/pgt`

Offers a variety of unusual toys for sale. TV and movie toys, superheroes, and novelty items are included. Prices and purchasing information provided.

Stratton's Collector Toy Network

`http://www.umsi.com/stratton/ctn.htm`

Offers collectible scale replica toys at discount prices. Includes NASCAR die-cast cars, John Deere farm toys, licensed Coca-Cola toys and banks, and software for tracking and cataloging a collection of scale replicas.

The Virtual Toy Store

`http://www.halcyon.com/uncomyn/home.html`

Targeted toward science fiction and fantasy enthusiasts. Offers a fully interactive toy store, complete with sound and video clips. Specializes in hard-to-find gifts, toys, T-shirts, and jewelry.

The World of Breyer Model Horses

`http://www.aa.net/~cascade`

A model horse mail-order service that offers all current Breyer model horses and accessories. Also carries a wide variety of discontinued and used models. Includes links to other model horse sites.

Virtual Malls

American Shopping Mall

`http://www.greenearth.com`

Provides a wide array of products and services. Computer software, coupons, professional video editing, classifieds, and personal ads included. Free products daily.

BizCafe Mall

`http://www.bizcafe.com`

Serves as a WWW mall. Includes categories such as travel, books, getting ahead, printing, office, home, consulting, business, financial, legal, sports, fitness, gifts, manufacturing, and autos.

Branch Mall

`http://www.branchmall.com`

An online shopping mall containing listings for dozens of retail stores and business centers.

CityMart Shopping Mall

`http://usasights.inter.net/usasights/citymart/welcome.html`

usaSights offers a unique shopping experience in categories such as health and nutrition, jewelry, sports, and pet supplies. Purchase products like American Indian jewelry, billiard supplies, and pet supplies for your dogs, cats, and reptiles.

The Cyber-Shopping Network

`http://www.cybershopping.net`

Offers a variety of shopping categories, including art and photography, books, pet supplies, real estate, restaurants, formal wear, and sporting goods. Opportunity for free products. Businesses can sign up to advertise on their site.

Flea Market @FUW

`http://info.fuw.edu.pl/market/market.html`

Serves as an online flea market for products. Lets you place ads, as well as search ads in the long and short form, or search for a specific item.

IndustryNET Industry's Online Mall

`http://www.industry.net`

Presents up-to-date information about engineering design, automation, and manufacturing news from IndustryNET. Includes application assistance, new products, demo software, online trade shows, tested shareware programs, employment opportunities, and used industrial equipment.

Internet Shopping Galleria

`http://www.intergal.com/intergal.htm`

Shop in different categories like art, audio books, auto gallery, bikes, computers, jewelry, magazines, and sports. Also offers corporate service and travel information.

Internet Shopping Network

`http://www.Internet.net:80/`

Lets you join online shopping club for deals on everything from software to flowers. Provides an alphabetical listing of more than 600 companies.

Leonardo Park

`http://www.hobbies.com`

Internet shopping mall for hobbies, crafts, and collectibles. Includes products and services information. Lists categories in stamp collecting, photography, gardening, comics, military memorabilia, and much more.

Meetings Industry Mall

`http://www.mim.com`

Serves as a virtual mall specifically for industry professionals. Lets suppliers open shop to meeting planners and buyers throughout the world.

Microplay Video Game Stores

`http://www.canadamalls.com/provider/microp.html`

Have fun in Canada's largest virtual mall. Search the mall by keyword or by store name, browse the new additions, check out the featured store of the month.

Roblyn's Shopping Mall

`http://www.roblyn.com/mallhome.htm`

Offers products and services from Canada's top businesses, including 18th century inspired funiture, hydroponic gardening supplies, virtual bookstore, fishing tips, and more.

Shopper's Utopia

`http://shop-utopia.com`

Contains a variety of custom shops, ranging from leather products, fashion jewelry, and salsa, to a full-fledged graphics design shop.

Spectra.Net Mall

`http://www.spectra.net/`

Brings the convenience of home shopping to you with electronic classified ads in an array of topics, such as health and beauty and home furnishings. Adds new storefronts, new products, and new services daily.

Star-Byte Shopping Mall

`http://www.starbyte.com/mall.html`

Provides online shopping in numerous virtual stores for many different items. Includes mass media, business, computers, and other products.

The UK Shopping City

`http://www.ukshops.co.uk:8000`

Provides predominantly British products and services. Offers 180,000 books, 56,000 videos, and 14,000 CDs, plus computer software, watches, jewelry, art, and more. Enables businesses to reach their market quickly and economically through Internet and interactive advertising, as well as joint venture management and referral services.

WebMart Virtual Mall And Web Development Services

`http://www.webmart.com/icc/webmart.html`

Provides online shopping and services from the comfort of your own home. Includes links to many different stores based in the eastern United States.

The Web Plaza—Online Marketplace

`http://www.webplaza.com/`

Serves as an online marketplace. Provides categorizes in employment services, electronics, and real estate. Also provides solutions for effectively marketing products and services on the Web.

Xplore Shopping

`http://www.xplore.com/xplore500/medium/shopping.html`

At Xplore Shopping, you can get almost anything—even your own personal shopper to help you out with those tough shopping decisions. Provides links to FAO Schwartz, L.L. Bean, Land's End, Spencer Gifts, Spiegel, Ticketmaster Online, and more.

Newsgroups

comp.os.os2.marketplace

comp.sys.amiga.marketplace

comp.sys.ibm.pc.games.marketplace

comp.sys.mac.games.marketplace

comp.sys.next.marketplace

misc.computers.forsale

misc.forsale

misc.forsale.computer

misc.forsale.computers

misc.forsale.computers.d

misc.forsale.computers.discussion

misc.forsale.computers.mac

misc.forsale.computers.mac-specific.cards.misc

misc.forsale.computers.mac-specific.cards.video

misc.forsale.computers.mac-specific.misc

misc.forsale.computers.mac-specific.portables

misc.forsale.computers.mac-specific.software

misc.forsale.computers.mac-specific.systems

misc.forsale.computers.memory

misc.forsale.computers.modems

misc.forsale.computers.monitors

misc.forsale.computers.net-hardware

misc.forsale.computers.other

misc.forsale.computers.other.misc

misc.forsale.computers.other.software

misc.forsale.computers.other.systems

misc.forsale.computers.pc-specific.audio

misc.forsale.computers.pc-specific.cards.misc

misc.forsale.computers.pc-specific.cards.video

misc.forsale.computers.pc-specific.misc

misc.forsale.computers.pc-specific.motherboards

misc.forsale.computers.pc-specific.portables

misc.forsale.computers.pc-specific.software

misc.forsale.computers.pc-specific.systems

misc.forsale.computers.printers

misc.forsale.computers.storage

misc.forsale.computers.workstation

misc.forsale.misc

misc.forsale.non-computer

misc.forsale.other

rec.arts.anime.marketplace

rec.arts.books.marketplace

rec.arts.comics.marketplace

rec.arts.sf.marketplace

rec.audio.marketplace

rec.autos.marketplace

rec.aviation.marketplace

rec.bicycles.marketplace

rec.boats.marketplace

rec.crafts.marketplace

rec.games.board.marketplace

rec.games.frp.marketplace

rec.games.trading-cards.marketplace

rec.games.trading-cards.marketplace.magic.auctions

rec.games.trading-cards.marketplace.magic.sales

rec.games.trading-cards.marketplace.magic.trades

rec.games.video.marketplace

rec.music.makers.marketplace

rec.music.marketplace

rec.photo.marketplace

rec.skiing.marketplace

rec.travel.marketplace

soc.genealogy.marketplace

Listservs

ACCIBD—American Council on Consumer Interests

You can join this group by sending the message "sub ACCIBD your name" to listserv@lsv.uky.edu

BIG-E-DEALS—Discounts, Deals, and Bargains for Consumers by E-mail

L-Soft International, Inc.

You can join this group by sending the message "sub BIG-E-DEALS your name" to listserv@indian.dc.lsoft.com

GENDERCB—Gender Marketing and Consumer Behavior Discussion List

You can join this group by sending the message "sub GENDERCB your name" to listserv@uriacc.uir.edu

SOCIETY & CULTURE

Alternative Living

AERO—The Alternative Education Resource Organization

http://www.speakeasy.org/~aero/home.html

Covering both home schooling and other alternative schools, these pages help you familiarize yourself with what works and what doesn't in education. All levels of education are covered, and there are tools to help your child learn no matter what the situation.

Alternative Living

http://www.bestcom.com/health/

If you're not looking to make a radical change to your lifestyle, but would still like to live by some of the ideals of intentional living, this page is your guide to ensuring that you support companies whose policies you agree with.

Cohousing Network

http://www.cohousing.org/

This group developed in response to the impersonal living experienced in many suburbs in America. It provides links to a state-by-state list of communities throughout the country that have adopted this manner of living, and it explains the benefits of the lifestyle.

Eco-Village Information Service

http://www.gaia.org/

Eco-villages are primarily concerned with integrating comfortable living spaces with their surroundings. This site provides background and links to successful communities.

Fellowship for Intentional Community

http://www.well.com/user/cmty/fic/

Promoting the ideals of cooperative living, this page is a springboard to help you find communities throughout the country, as well as links to places that will assist you if you're already living in a cooperative.

The Intentional Family Connection

http://www.dimensional.com/~family/index.html

This site is what personal ads should be. Tales of successful and failed matches within intentional communities can be found. You also can enter yourself into the pool of prospective members and read about others who would like to live in a cooperative environment.

Vision of Sanctuary

http://www.newciv.org/millennium_matters/vision.html

Full of deeply nested links and going off the fundamental belief that we need to simplify our lives, these pages explore the background of cooperative living and expand on some of the shared ideas within particular communities.

Censorship

24 Hours of Democracy

http://www.hotwired.com/staff/userland/24/

Hotwired's page is full of links to essays about freedom of expression and the Internet's role in it. Other links expose the novice or experienced Web surfer to the power that the Web holds.

Bonfire of Liberties: Censorship of the Humanities

http://www.humanities-interactive.org/

If the opportunity does not present itself to see this traveling showcase on the history and roots of censorship, this site is the next best thing. Click on the burning books to enter the exhibit.

Citizens Internet Empowerment Coalition

http://www.cdt.org/ciec/index.html

Rulings and reactions from officials involved, as well as concerned observers, regarding the Communications Decency Act. Regularly updated with new developments in the case, as well as links to the background of the case and those involved in it.

The Indecency Page

http://cctr.umkc.edu/userx/bhugh/indecent.html

Dedicated to making as much fun of the Communications Decency Act as possible, though this page could in no way be called indecent. Links to many related sites.

Index on Censorship

http://www.oneworld.org/index_oc/index.html

The most recent and back issues of this magazine are available in their entirety online. Look here for well-written articles on the repercussions of freedom of speech in our everyday lives.

Know Your Enemies

http://www.eff.org/pub/Groups/BCFE/bcfenatl.html

Where to go to find brief summaries on many of the more notorious enemies of free speech. Within each description are links to other articles dealing with their histories and cohorts.

Project Censored

http://zippy.sonoma.edu/ProjectCensored/

Devoted to listing online news stories that impact all of us, but that weren't well publicized. Not the place to go if you want to remain in a good mood. This site might cause the hairs on your neck to rise and fists to form.

Project 2000: The Cyberporn Debate

http://www2000.ogsm.vanderbilt.edu/
cyberporn.debate.cgi#background

Here is a clearinghouse of links on the Rimm case and its far-reaching implications regarding censorship on the Web. Be sure to check out Project 2000's other research projects after becoming familiar with this landmark study.

Sex, Censorship, and the Internet

http://www.eff.org/CAF/cafuiuc.html#Outline

A comprehensive list of occurrences of censorship in academia around the world. Links to pages describing past incidents where the viewer can decide what should have been done, then compare reactions to "Library Policy."

Civil Rights

American Civil Liberties Union

http://www.aclu.org/

Provides info on every front at which the ACLU is battling, including Net censorship, separation of church and state, abortion rights, the death penalty, and immigrant rights. Closely follows the ACLU v Reno anti-CDA trial and rightfully argues against

anti-terrorism legislation resulting from the Oklahoma bombing.

Amnesty International Online

http://www.amnesty.org/

The human rights defenders go online to provide information about rights violations and what you can do to help. Topics include China and women.

Center for Democracy and Technology

http://www.cdt.org/

Links to a host of issues concerning civil liberties. Includes updated headlines of articles regarding the Internet, with further links to the events that caused issues to come to the forefront of the public's attention.

Cornucopia of Disability Information Gopher Server

gopher://val-dor.cc.buffalo.edu/1

With links to sites pertaining to disability issues from a local to an international level, this site is not just for the disabled, but also for people who provide services to those who are.

Euthanasia World Directory

http://www.efn.org/~ergo/

This very delicate subject is handled well and extensively by the Euthanasia Research & Guidance Organization's page. It contains comprehensive lists of links to right to die organizations, as well as information on their stands and legislation they would like to see passed.

Fear—Forfeiture Endangers American Rights

http://www.fear.org/

Dedicated to reforming the country's recent, unconstitutional forfeiture laws that impose double jeopardy on undeserving defendants by taking property without a hearing, while convicting the person to jail and heavy fines.

Global Vision—The Other Network...Rights & Wrongs

`http://www.igc.apc.org/globalvision/`

Gopher links to areas throughout the world keep you updated on current events in human rights. Lists shows pertaining to the issues covered in the page and where they can be viewed, as well as the transcripts from previous shows.

Human Rights Web

`http://www.traveller.com/~hrweb/hrweb.html`

A globally comprehensive list of links for information about human rights, who's trying to violate them, and what you can do to protect them.

The Martin Luther King Jr. Directory

`http://www-leland.stanford.edu/group/King/index.html`

Maintained by the MLK Center in Atlanta, this site is the storehouse for all of the Reverend's papers, speeches, and history.

Votelink...the Voice of the Net

`http://www.votelink.com/`

A highly interactive site that encourages you to voice your opinion about pertinent civil rights issues of the day. You can vote or just read about the pro and con sides to an issue, as well as participate in a forum discussion on the topic.

Crime

Crime-Free America

`http://announce.com/cfa/cfa.htm`

Dedicated to providing info about prevention, the criminal justice system, and articles about how crime affects American society.

Crime Prevention Initiatives

`http://www.crime-prevention.org.uk/`

Find online guides to teach you how to better protect yourself and your belongings. Not intended to replace the need for police officers, but to help them help you.

Emergency Net

`http://www.emergency.com/`

This page is not limited to accounts of crimes. However, there is so much to look at about real occurrences police, firemen, military personnel, and others have encountered, that surely you'll find something of interest.

Fugitive Watch

`http://www.fugitive.com/`

This site not only gives names, pictures, and information about fugitives from the law, it also provides links to information about how to better protect yourself and past solved crimes.

Justice Net

`http://www.igc.org/justice/`

While some links are still under construction as of this printing, this site currently contains a wide array of articles pertaining to our prison system, from the inside and out.

National Victim Center

`http://www.nvc.org/`

Stop here if you are a recent victim of crime. Site offers info about what you and supporters can do to fight for victims' rights. Discusses legislation and statistics, offers an index of books, links, and other helpful publications.

Software

`http://www.iminet.com/software/shack/`

Get free software from the Shareware Shack.

Parents of Murdered Children

http://www.metroguide.com/pomc/

Organization offers info to parents and friends of youth killed by violence.

Prison Legal News

http://www.synapse.net/~arrakis/pln/pln.html

Written by prisoners for other prisoners, their friends, and loved ones, this online journal has current and back issues available. The articles pertain to prisoners' rights in America and throughout the world.

Rape Victim Advocates

http://www.lib.uchicago.edu/~loakleaf/RVA.html

Read survivors' stories and find out how to help someone who has been raped. Very straightforward and very informative, this page replaces myths about rape with facts.

Rate Your Risk

http://www.Nashville.Net/~police/risk/

Answer simple questions to see your risk of being assaulted, robbed, raped, stabbed, or murdered. Offers a virtual police academy so you can learn what being an officer is like. Provides pages about specific self-defense techniques.

Serial Killers

http://www.mayhem.net/Crime/serial.html

An informational, albeit disturbing, page about what's different in a serial killer's mind than in other people's.

Shattered Love Broken Lives

http://www.s-t.com/projects/DomVio/

Includes investigative articles about domestic violence, links to everything you should know about it, as well as links to other guides on the Internet and other articles.

United Nations Crime and Justice Information Network

gopher://uacsc2.albany.edu:70/11/newman

This site is purely for links to articles pertaining to crime statistics and occurrences throughout the world, bills and resolutions pertaining to crime, and home pages of justice agencies.

United States Department of Justice

http://www.usdoj.gov/

The Department of Justice is here to serve you, so find out what they're doing and what's on their minds. You can link to other justice servers, other government sites, or explore the different branches of the Justice Department from this page.

Cross-Cultural Resources

Diversity and Pluralism

http://www.msue.msu.edu/msue/imp/moddp/masterdp.html

This database of articles allows you to search by keyword or letter, and is cross-referenced by subject and author. The links are varied and the directions clear, making it a good starting point for information.

The ERaM Programme

http://www.brad.ac.uk/bradinfo/research/eram/eram.html

To find out about current trends in the area of ethnicity and racism studies, take a look at this page. Then, if you'd like to read more, link to the ERaM WWW pages to look at the sources that went into the research you've just read about.

Interracial Voice

http://www.webcom.com/intvoice/

Published every other month to serve the mixed-race/interracial community. Advocates universal recognition of mixed-race individuals as constituting a separate "racial" entity and supports the initiative to establish a multiracial category on the 2000 Census.

ITI's Multi-Cultural Network

http://www.fcg.com/iti/iti_cultnet.html

Intended as a tool for businesses, this site serves a purpose for people who are interested in learning about the different cultures that make up the United States, including African, Irish, Jewish, Puerto-Rican, and Native American.

Minority Affairs Forum

`ftp://heather.cs.ucdavis.edu/pub/README.html`

Dedicated to in-depth discussions of race relations, immigration, affirmative action, and bilingual education.

Museum of Tolerance

`http://www.wiesenthal.com/mot/`

A high-tech, hands-on experiential museum that focuses on two themes through unique interactive exhibits: the dynamics of racism and prejudice in America, and the history of the Holocaust. Includes info about visiting the museum's 3D site in LA.

National Civil Rights Museum

`http://www.mecca.org/~crights/ncrm.html`

Take a tour of this Memphis-based museum, which starts from the beginning—Brown v Board of Education—and provides links to related sites.

The National Multicultural Institute

`http://www.nmci.org/nmci/history.html`

Provides a forum for the discussion of the critical issues of multiculturalism through conferences in February, June, and November, and through training and consulting programs.

The Web of Culture

`http://www.worldculture.com/`

Designed to educate and entertain on the topic of cross-cultural communications. Offers useful info to the student and the educator on global language (and a body language page is under construction), religion, embassies, business and currency, and more.

Senior Citizens

AARP

`http://www.aarp.org/`

This very user-friendly site contributes to AARP's goal of allowing senior citizens to lead the rich and

fulfilling lives that they are accustomed to. Not only by staying well-informed, but also by staying active.

The Adopt a Grandparent Program

`http://hanksville.phast.umass.edu/misc/Grandparents.html`

The program's online resource for people interested in volunteering or learning about regional activities.

Caregiver Network, Inc.

`http://www.caregiver.on.ca/`

The Canadian woman who maintains this site became a caregiver herself overnight. She is very aware of what resources you need to take care of someone you care about. Most links are in the United States, and many will refer you to services in your own area.

Elderhostel

`http://www.elderhostel.org/`

With the fundamental belief that no one should ever stop learning, this site provides access to resources around the world to continue your education. Currently, you must register through postal mail, but all of the registration information is at the site.

Grand Times

`http://www.grandtimes.com/`

An e-zine dedicated to the needs of active retirees. Example topics include travel, useful products, beating the casino, high-tech bird feeders, and relief from arthritis, back pain, and migraines.

Seniors-Site

`http://seniors-site.com/`

If you're already acquainted with Yahoo, this site will look very familiar to you. The wide array of links here all keep senior citizens in mind, though, from travel information to fraud, scams, and abuses.

SWT Age Page

http://elo.mediasrv.swt.edu/Departments/Honors_Program/
AGE_NET/agenetf/AGENET

Designed for use by long-term care administrators and anyone seeking information about the social, emotional, and physical concerns of the elderly and their caregivers.

Social Issues

American Firearms Association

http://www.firearms.org/afa/

Visit this page if you feel that the NRA is too extremist, but you still believe in a gun owner's rights. Here you can read about the group's position on many issues dealing with the right to bear arms.

Drug Use is Life Abuse/Project: No Gangs

http://www.duila.org/

Looking to empower families to help young people resist the temptations of drugs and gangs, this site provides three primary links to groups that help accomplish these goals.

EZ Connect

http://ezconnect.web.aol.com/socia.htm

A very well-managed site that doesn't just link to its own articles and journals. It has gone out and found the best of the Web at other sites and links you to social issues from homelessness and abuse to guns, disasters, and so on.

Gunfree

http://www.gunfree.inter.net/

Concerned primarily with eliminating handgun violence, this group has put together pages of information and links to data on crimes and accidents that involved guns, as well as what you can do to help (besides just joining their organization).

Institute for Global Communications

gopher://gopher.igc.apc.org/1

With the ability to link to five major social action groups, PeaceNet, EcoNet, ConflictNet, LaborNet, and WomensNet, as well as to general information on current social issues, this Gopher page is a good place to begin your search.

just

http://libertynet.org/~zelson/publish/just.html

This collection of personal experiences and encounters with real social issues is invaluable. The goal here is to put a human face to issues that are too often decided on by people who will never feel the ramifications of their actions.

The Knowledge Source

http://www.sirs.com/tree/social.htm

This page is set up by a larger group called SIRS. Their intention is to provide an easier means of access to information for schools and libraries. What they have a complied here are meta-links to most of the relevant social issues of the day.

NARAL

http://www.naral.org/publications/facts/fact.html

A very political wing of the pro-choice movement, this site is an effort to keep Americans informed of current trends in the battle to defend reproductive rights.

National Right to Life

http://www.nrlc.org/

Visit this page for an informed introduction to the Right to Life's stands and beliefs. Links to politicians' voting records and articles to keep you up-to-date on the newest developments in the movement.

Planned Parenthood Federation of America

http://www.ppfa.org/ppfa/index.html

Access links to a varied list of resources, find out how to contact them to either utilize their services or volunteer time, or read about PP's past and where it's going.

Soapbox Issues

http://www.pangalactic.com/soapbox/

Pick a topic, any topic. This site picks an issue a month, features an article about it, and gives you a forum to voice your opinion on how to fix what's wrong with society. Each topic then has links to experts in the field.

Soundprint Historical and Social Issues

http://soundprint.brandywine.american.edu/~soundprt/historical_and_social.html

Partially funded by the National Endowment for the Arts, this page introduces many topics of historical and social importance, along with where to find out more. Some of the topics included also have reading and resource lists.

Urban Legends Archive

http://www.urbanlegends.com/

Our urban legends say a lot about us as a society, what we're afraid of and what we hope for. This site is aiming to be the most comprehensive one out there, and the stories that it doesn't have links to can be found through links to other urban legends pages.

U.S. Pro-Life Directory

http://user.mc.net/dougp/prolist1.html

There are several extensive lists to be found at this site. Many nondenominational groups, as well as some that are affiliated with organized religions can be found. Information on the pro-life movement also is available.

Today in Perspective

http://www.iquest.net/~gtemp/

This online journal covers the right and the left, not trying to placate, just deliver from both sides of the spectrum. There are links to issues such as family violence and poverty, as well as other, more political matters.

Vote Smart Web

http://www.vote-smart.org/

This page not only helps voters make informed choices in their voting, it also introduces those who might not be familiar with the electoral college to some of the nuances of how our government works.

American Red Cross

http://www.crossnet.org/

Yes, one of the most recognized symbols of help also has a Web page. On their home page, you can find out where the nearest Red Cross is, as well as what projects they are currently working on.

The Carter Center

http://www.emory.edu/CARTER_CENTER/homepage.htm

Atlanta, Georgia is where the former U.S. President and his wife have based their public policy institute. Visit the site to get information about their current and past work, as well as to find out what you can do to help.

Contact Center Network

http://www.contact.org/

This group's stated purpose is to provide links to and between nonprofit organizations so that they might better help themselves and each other. You can find groups by country or keyword, or explore how Contact can help your organization.

HandsNet

http://www.igc.apc.org/handsnet/

Intended as a site for sharing information, links can be made to basic information or specific issues, where further links take you to the sites of those who know the topic best. A valuable resource for community service groups.

National Civic League

http://www.ncl.org/ncl/

When Theodore Roosevelt founded this group with the goal of improving communities, he surely didn't realize how helpful and accessible it would become. This site will link you to mission statements, recent progress in the area, and how you can assist your own community.

The National Coalition for the Homeless

http://www2.ari.net/home/nch/

With the primary goal of abolishing homelessness in mind, this group relates tales of people's struggles with homelessness and provides links to information on recent developments and legislation that pertain to homelessness.

River of Hope

http://www.riverhope.org/

River of Hope is not itself a service organization; instead, it provides links to groups that it believes in. As of this printing, there are links to groups that deal with drug abuse, eating disorders, and emotionally troubled children.

An Unofficial Guide to Rotary

http://www.tecc.co.uk/public/PaulHarris/

Provides information about the entire history of the Rotary Club, current service projects, and how you can join.

VISTA Web

http://libertynet.org/~zelson/vweb.html

Volunteers in Service to America has been around since 1964, and it is now part of the larger AmeriCorps program. Find out about both groups' successes in the past, what they're planning to do in the future, as well as how to find someone that you might have worked with in either group.

Who Cares

http://www.whocares.org/

This site dedicated to community service not only includes complete coverage of current issues that need attention, but listings of social activism events nationwide. You also can read about what others are doing to help out various causes.

Veterans' Affairs

The American Legion

http://www.legion.org/

Offers info about the Legion's stance on patriotic programs (such as for education, the Boy Scouts, and scholarships), veteran health issues, flag protection, news releases, Bosnia topics, and more.

Baudo's Vet Links

http://www.teleport.com/~baudo/

A crossroads for veterans and their supporters, this site directs surfers to relevant sites organized as news, chat, support, politics, surveys, and miscellaneous.

Department of Veterans Affairs

http://www.va.gov/

An up-to-the-minute report about where veterans can go to find out about benefits, facilities, and special programs available to them.

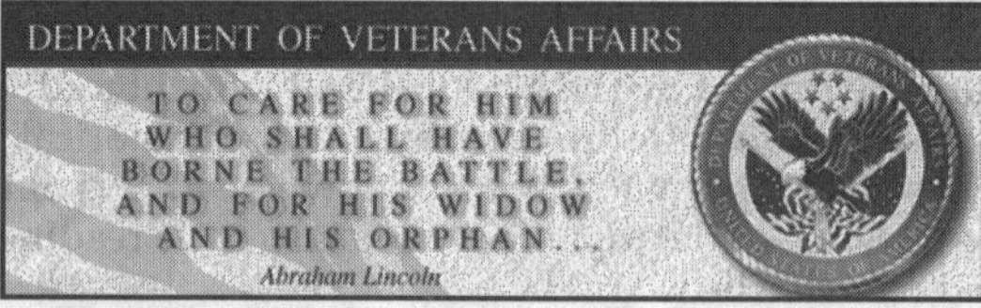

Military Family Institute

http://mfi.marywood.edu/

This Department of Defense sponsored research deals with how the entire family is affected by military service. There are also links for "military brats," and be sure to check out the guest book to see if anyone is looking for you.

Veterans Archive

http://home.earthlink.net/~beerborn/index.html

A database of veterans looking for old friends.

Vietnam Veterans Home Page

http://grunt.space.swri.edu/

An index of events pertaining to Vietnam vets, as well as links to works by vets themselves. This page will let you in on current goings on in the veteran community, as well as what's being done to assist veterans.

FREE STUFF

Unix Versions

http://axp745.gsfc.nasa.gov/niles/info/software_sites.html

Obtain a list of sites where you can get free versions of the Unix operating system (or is it UNIX?—depends on how old your book is).

Newsgroups

alt.abortion

alt.abortion.inequity

alt.activism

alt.activism.children

alt.activism.death-penalty

alt.angst

alt.censorship

alt.consciousness.near-death-exp

alt.crime

alt.culture.alaska!

alt.culture.arab-league!

alt.culture.argentina!

alt.culture.austrian!

alt.culture.beaches!

alt.culture.bullfight!

alt.culture.cajun!

alt.culture.egyptian!

alt.culture.french-polynesia!

alt.culture.hawaii!

alt.culture.hawaii.irc!

alt.culture.indonesia!

alt.culture.internet!

alt.culture.jamming!

alt.culture.knights!

alt.culture.kuwait!

alt.culture.military-brats!

alt.culture.ny-upstate!

alt.culture.oregon!

alt.culture.saudi!

alt.culture.somalia!

alt.culture.southasianet!

alt.culture.tamil!

alt.culture.us.1970s!

alt.culture.us.1980s!

alt.culture.us.asian-indian!

alt.culture.us.southwest!

alt.culture.usenet!

alt.culture.www!

alt.culture.zippies!

alt.current-events.antigua!

alt.current-events.bosnia!

alt.current-events.clinton.whitewater!

alt.current-events.cuny-crisis!

alt.current-events.epidemics!

alt.current-events.haiti!

alt.current-events.net-abuse!

alt.current-events.russia!

alt.current-events.somalia!

alt.current-events.ukraine!

alt.current-events.usa!

alt.dads-rights

alt.dads-rights.unmoderated

alt.disasters.aviation!

alt.disasters.earthquake!

alt.disasters.misc!

alt.drugs!

alt.drugs.caffeine!

alt.drugs.chemistry!

alt.drugs.culture!

alt.drugs.hard!

alt.drugs.pot!

alt.drugs.pot.cultivation!

alt.drugs.psychedelics!

alt.drugs.usenet!

alt.gathering.rainbow

alt.gothic

alt.gothic.fashion

alt.individualism

alt.lefthanders

alt.mens-rights

alt.peace-corps!

alt.prisions

alt.smokers

alt.smokers.cigars

alt.smokers.pipes

alt.skinheads

alt.skinheads.moderated

alt.society.anarchy!

alt.society.civil-disob!

alt.society.civil-liberties!

alt.society.civil-liberty!

alt.society.cnd.global!

alt.society.conservatism!

alt.society.futures!

alt.society.generation-x!

alt.society.high-school!

alt.society.kindness!

alt.society.labor-unions!

alt.society.mental-health!

alt.society.neutopia!

alt.society.paradigms!

alt.society.resistance!

alt.society.revolution!

alt.society.sovereign!

alt.support.abortion

alt.support.househusbands

alt.true-crime

asu.general.crime_stop

clari.news.aging

clari.news.civil_rights

clari.news.censorship

clari.news.conflict

clari.news.crime

clari.news.crime.abductions

clari.news.crime.assaults

clari.news.crime.fraud+embezzle

clari.news.crime.general

clari.news.crime.hate

clari.news.crime.juvenile

clari.news.crime.misc

clari.news.crime.murders

clari.news.crime.murders.misc

clari.news.crime.murders.political

clari.news.crime.organized

clari.news.crime.sex

clari.news.crime.theft

clari.news.crime.top

clari.news.gays

clari.news.issues.human_rights

clari.news.poverty

soc.culture.afghanistan!

soc.culture.african!

soc.culture.african.american!

soc.culture.albanian!

soc.culture.algeria!

soc.culture.arabic!

soc.culture.argentina!

soc.culture.asean!

soc.culture.asian.american!

soc.culture.assyrian!

soc.culture.australia!

soc.culture.australian!

soc.culture.austria!

soc.culture.azeri!

soc.culture.baltics!

soc.culture.bangladesh!

soc.culture.basque!

soc.culture.bavarian!

soc.culture.belarus!

soc.culture.belgium!

soc.culture.bengali!

soc.culture.berber!

soc.culture.bolivia!

soc.culture.bosna-herzgvna!

soc.culture.brazil!

soc.culture.british!

soc.culture.bulgaria!

soc.culture.burma!

soc.culture.cambodia!

soc.culture.canada!

soc.culture.caribbean!

soc.culture.celtic!

soc.culture.chile!

soc.culture.china!

soc.culture.colombia!

soc.culture.costa-rica!

soc.culture.croatia!

soc.culture.cuba!

soc.culture.czech!

soc.culture.czecho-slovak!

soc.culture.dominican-rep!

soc.culture.ecuador!

soc.culture.egyptian!

soc.culture.esperanto!

soc.culture.estonia!

soc.culture.ethiopia!

soc.culture.europe!

soc.culture.filipino!

soc.culture.french!

soc.culture.galician!

soc.culture.german!

soc.culture.greek!

soc.culture.haiti!

soc.culture.hongkong!

soc.culture.hongkong.entertainment!

soc.culture.jamaican!

soc.culture.indian!

soc.culture.indian.delhi!

soc.culture.indian.info!

soc.culture.indian.kerala!

soc.culture.indian.marathi!

soc.culture.indian.telugu!

soc.culture.indonesia!

soc.culture.iranian!

soc.culture.iraq!

soc.culture.irish!

soc.culture.israel!

soc.culture.italian!

soc.culture.japan!

soc.culture.jewish!

soc.culture.jewish.holocaust!

soc.culture.jewish.parenting!

soc.culture.jordan!

soc.culture.korean!

soc.culture.kurdish!

soc.culture.kuwait!

soc.culture.laos!

soc.culture.latin-america!

soc.culture.lebanon!

soc.culture.maghreb!

soc.culture.magyar!

soc.culture.malagasy!

soc.culture.malaysia!

soc.culture.mexican!

soc.culture.mexican.american!

soc.culture.misc!

soc.culture.mongolian!

soc.culture.native!

soc.culture.nepal!

soc.culture.netherlands!

soc.culture.new-zealand!

soc.culture.nigeria!

soc.culture.nordic!

soc.culture.pacific-island!

soc.culture.pakistan!

soc.culture.palestine!

soc.culture.peru!

soc.culture.polish!

soc.culture.portuguese!

soc.culture.prussian!

soc.culture.puerto-rico!

soc.culture.punjab!

soc.culture.quebec!

soc.culture.rep-of-georgia!

soc.culture.romanian!

soc.culture.russia!

soc.culture.russian!

soc.culture.scientists!

soc.culture.scottish!

soc.culture.siberia!

soc.culture.sicilian!

soc.culture.sierra-leone!

soc.culture.singapore!

soc.culture.slovak!

soc.culture.slovenia!

soc.culture.somali!

soc.culture.somalia!

soc.culture.south-africa!

soc.culture.south-africa.afrikaans!

soc.culture.soviet!

soc.culture.spain!

soc.culture.sri-lanka!

soc.culture.swiss!

soc.culture.syria!

soc.culture.taiwan!

soc.culture.tamil!

soc.culture.thai!

soc.culture.tibet!

soc.culture.turkish!

soc.culture.ukrainian!

soc.culture.uruguay!

soc.culture.usa!

soc.culture.venezuela!

soc.culture.vietnamese!

soc.culture.welsh!

soc.culture.yugoslavia!

soc.culture.zimbabwe!

soc.men

soc.penpals

soc.retirement

soc.rights.human

soc.veterans

soc.women

talk.abortion

Listservs

AAASHRAN—AAAS Human Rights Action Network

The George Washington University Computer Center, Washington, DC

You can join this group by sending the message "sub AAASHRAN your name" to listserv@gwuvm.gwu.edu

AASNET-L—African American Student Network

You can join this group by sending the message "sub AASNET-L your name" to listserv@listserv.uh.edu

AFAM-L—African-American Research

University of Missouri-Columbia, Columbia, MO

You can join this group by sending the message "sub AFAM-L your name" to listserv@mizzou1.missouri.edu

AFAMHED—African-Americans in Higher Education

Wayne State University, Detroit, MI

You can join this group by sending the message "sub AFAMHED your name" to listserv@cms.cc.wayne.edu

AFAMLIT—African American Literature Discussion Forum

You can join this group by sending the message "sub AFAMLIT your name" to listserv@listserv.kent.edu

AFRICA-L—Pan-Africa Discussion List

Virginia Tech

You can join this group by sending the message "sub AFRICA-L your name" to listserv@vtvm1.cc.vt.edu

BIRG—Black Issues Research Group

You can join this group by sending the message "sub BIRG your name" to listserv@uriacc.uri.edu

BLKCRIM—Black Criminologists Discussion List

University of Maryland CSC, College Park, MD

You can join this group by sending the message "sub BLKCRIM your name" to listserv%umdd.bitnet@listserv.net

CJMOVIES—Journal of Criminal Justice and Popular Culture

You can join this group by sending the message "sub CJMOVIES your name" to listserv%albnyvm1.bitnet@listserv.net

CJUST-L—CJUST-L: Criminal Justice Discussion List

City University of New York/University Computing Center

You can join this group by sending the message "sub CJUST-L your name" to listserv@cunyvm.cuny.edu

FREE-L—Fathers' Rights and Equality Exchange

You can join this group by sending the message "sub FREE-L your name" to
`listserv@listserv.iupui.edu`

H-AFRLITCINE—H-NET List for African Literature and Cinema

You can join this group by sending the message "sub H-AFRLITCINE your name" to
`listserv@h-net.msu.edu`

HRS-L—Systematic Studies of Human Rights

State University of New York at Binghamton

You can join this group by sending the message "sub HRS-L your name" to
`listserv@bingvmb.cc.binghamton.edu`

NCS-L—National Crime Survey Discussion

University of Maryland CSC, College Park, MD

You can join this group by sending the message "sub NCS-L your name" to
`listserv%umdd.bitnet@listserv.net`

NSBELINE—NSBE National Society of Black Engineers

Syracuse University

You can join this group by sending the message "sub NSBELINE your name" to
listserv@listserv.syr.edu

SA_TALK—South African Social and Political Issues Forum

Temple University, Philadelphia, PA

You can join this group by sending the message "sub SA_TALK your name" to
`listserv@vm.temple.edu`

VPAD-L—Veterans Program Administrators Discussion List/VPAD-L

Arizona State University, Tempe, AZ

You can join this group by sending the message "sub VPAD-L your name" to
`listserv@asuvm.inre.asu.edu`

Y-RIGHTS—Y-Rights: Kid/Teen Rights Discussion Group

St. John's University, Jamaica, NY

You can join this group by sending the message "sub Y-RIGHTS your name" to
`listserv@sjuvm.stjohns.edu`

SPORTS

Auto Racing

candelaMotorsport

`http://www.ozemail.com.au/~candela`

Provides all the latest news, press releases, pictures, and generally, anything involving motorsport in Australia and the rest of the world.

GALE FORCE F1

`http://www.monaco.mc/f1/`

Provides Formula One motor racing results and track information. Also offers subscription to mailing list that provides up-to-date race results via e-mail.

The IndyCar Enthusiast

`http://ucsu.colorado.edu/~sauerb/Home.html`

Provides information on upcoming IndyCar races. Also offers links to other sites.

Matt's Solar Car Page

`http://www-lips.ece.utexas.edu/~delayman/solar.html`

Provides race information, team listings (United States and Canada), and official results of previous races. Also offers images of solar cars, as well as a race route map across Australia.

Motorsports Media Service International Home Page

`http://www.west.net/~webpages`

Provides information about auto racing—drivers, teams, sponsors, art and photography, merchandise, and more.

The Racer Archive

`http://student-www.eng.hawaii.edu/carina/ra.home.page.html`

Provides information about Formula One, IndyCar, and NASCAR racing. Also includes race results, point standings, schedules, history, links to other sites, ancecdotes, and more.

Specialty Car Page

`http://www.infiniteweb.com/cars.html`

Includes free classified ads with photos of hundreds of cars, as well as vendor, car club, and car show pages.

Baseball

The following are Web sites for Major League Baseball teams:

Team	URL
Atlanta Braves	`http://www.atlantabraves.com/`
Baltimore Orioles	`http://www2.pcy.mci.net/mlb/al/bal/index.html`
Boston Red Sox	`http://www.nesn.com/sox.cgi`
California Angels	`http://www.sportsnetwork.com/mlb/teams/angels.html`
Chicago Cubs	`http://www.students.uiuc.edu/~k-jerbi/cubs/home.html`
Cincinnati Reds	`http://www.sportsnetwork.com/mlb/teams/reds.html`
Cleveland Indians	`http://www.indians.com/`
Colorado Rockies	`http://www.sportsnetwork.com/mlb/teams/rockies.html`
Detroit Tigers	`http://www.sportsnetwork.com/mlb/teams/tigers.html`
Florida Marlins	`http://www.sportsnetwork.com/mlb/teams/marlins.html`
Houston Astros	`http://www.astros.com/`
Kansas City Royals	`http://www.sportsnetwork.com/mlb/teams/royals.html`
Los Angeles Dodgers	`http://www.sportsnetwork.com/mlb/teams/dodgers.html`
Milwaukee Brewers	`http://www.sportsnetwork.com/mlb/teams/brewers.html`
Minnesota Twins	`http://www.wcco.com/sports/twins/`
Montreal Expos	`http://www.sportsnetwork.com/mlb/teams/expos.html`
New York Mets	`http://www.sportsnetwork.com/mlb/teams/mets.html`
New York Yankees	`http://www.yankees.com/`
Oakland A's	`http://www.oaklandathletics.com/`
Philadelphia Phillies	`http://www.sportsnetwork.com/mlb/teams/phillies.html`
Pittsburgh Pirates	`http://www.pirateball.com/`
San Diego Padres	`http://www.sportsnetwork.com/mlb/teams/padres.html`
San Fransisco Giants	`http://www.sfgiants.com/`
Seattle Mariners	`http://www.mariners.org/`
St. Louis Cardinals	`http://www.stlcardinals.com/`
Texas Rangers	`http://www.sportsnetwork.com/mlb/teams/rangers.html`
Toronto Blue Jays	`http://www.bluejays.ca/bluejays`

Baseball Hall of Fame

http://www.enews.com/bas_hall_fame/overview.html

The Hall of Fame site provides admission prices and hours of operation. You can link to directions on how to get to Cooperstown, access the Hall of Fame newsletter, *Around the Horn*, and view online special exhibits like the current one on the history of the World Series.

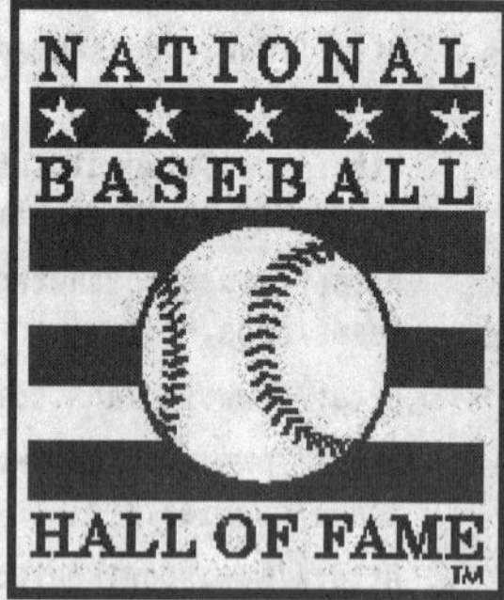

ESPNet SportsZone: Major League Baseball

http://espnet.sportszone.com/mlb/

A site with everything you've come to expect from ESPN, just concentrated on baseball. Here you'll find links to the top stories of the day, but you'll also find 1996 attendance figures, team payroll lists and the latest injury reports. Subscription information available; ideal for both the casual observer and baseball enthusiast.

Fastball

http://www.fastball.com/

With scores and stats updated every three minutes, this is a great resource for followers of the game. There is hometown coverage of the Braves, Rockies, Reds, Astros, Marlins, and Rangers that is just a click away. Dugout Chatter is a unique link to chat rooms and baseball topics.

Instant Baseball

http://www.InstantSports.com/baseball.html

Truly instant in the sense that game updates are done about every two minutes so you can follow the game without your television or radio. They are currently running beta tests that will bring animated games live to the Web. Now available are up-to-the-minute standings, statistics and schedules for all MBL teams.

Japanese Professional Baseball

http://www.inter.co.jp/Baseball/

Provides final statistics in this league from 1936–present. Team rosters, schedules, and statistics are provided as well.

John Skilton's Baseball Links

http://www.pc-professor.com/baseball/

Popular and informative site that contains over 1,000 links to different areas of baseball. You can find out about the majors, the minors, youth and international leagues as well as fantasy and rotisserie leagues. Of course, links to collectible and online merchandise are provided as well.

Little League Baseball

http://www.littleleague.org/

Provides lists of past state champions and a thorough FAQ page. The World Series link details the happenings of that event. Information on summer camps is provided along with gift and equipment supply purchasing information.

Major League Baseball

http://www.majorleaguebaseball.com/

Official site of Major League Baseball contains an up-to-date scoreboard, photo of the day and a section for kids. Also included are links to each team that provide individual team member stats and career highlights, as well as links to each team's home page. The MLB Library and Digest are useful for learning facts about the game.

Nando Baseball Server

http://www.nando.net/SportServer/baseball/

The baseball link of the Nando SportServer breaks down the MLB by leagues and divisions. Each league section has a listing of that day's starting pitchers. Also included are current statistics, team transactions, and a preview of that day's games.

NASA CD

http://southport.jpl.nasa.gov/education/cdrom/
OrderCD.html

Grab a free CD-ROM from the folks at NASA (who brought us that wonderful breakfast drink—TANG—that you can only find at fine restaurants).

New York Yankees Home Plate

`http://www.yankees.com/`

Yankee fans can order season tickets, subscribe to *Yankee Magazine,* and order merchandise from this site. Team rosters and statistics for both the Yankees and their minor league affiliates are also available.

World Youth Baseball

`http://www.brandonu.ca/~ennsnr/WYB/`

Unofficial server of World Youth Baseball. Provides links to league standings and schedules. Teams from all over the world play in this league. The site provides words to the official song of the WYB and a link to find out about former WYB players now in the major leagues.

Basketball

The following are the home pages for teams of the National Basketball Association:

Team	URL
Atlanta Hawks	`http://www.nba.com/hawks/`
Boston Celtics	`http://www.nba.com/celtics/`
Charlotte Hornets	`http://www.nba.com/hornets/`
Chicago Bulls	`http://www.nba.com/bulls/`
Cleveland Cavaliers	`http://www.nba.com/cavs/`
Dallas Mavericks	`http://www.nba.com/mavericks/`
Denver Nuggets	`http://www.nba.com/nuggets/`
Detroit Pistons	`http://www.nba.com/pistons/`
Golden State Warriors	`http://www.nba.com/warriors/`
Houston Rockets	`http://www.nba.com/rockets/`
Indiana Pacers	`http://www.nba.com/pacers/`
Los Angeles Clippers	`http://www.nba.com/clippers/`
Los Angeles Lakers	`http://www.nba.com/lakers/`
Miami Heat	`http://www.nba.com/heat/`
Milwaukee Bucks	`http://www.nba.com/bucks/`
Minnesota Timberwolves	`http://www.nba.com/timberwolves/`
New Jersey Nets	`http://www.nba.com/nets/`
New York Knicks	`http://www.nba.com/knicks/`
Orlando Magic	`http://www.nba.com/magic/`
Philadelphia 76ers	`http://www.nba.com/sixers/`

Team	URL
Phoenix Suns	`http://www.nba.com/suns/`
Portland Trail Blazers	`http://www.nba.com/blazers/`
Sacramento Kings	`http://www.nba.com/kings/`
San Antonio Spurs	`http://www.nba.com/spurs/`
Seattle Supersonics	`http://www.nba.com/sonics/`
Toronto Raptors	`http://www.nba.com/raptors/`
Utah Jazz	`http://www.nba.com/jazz/`
Vancouver Grizzlies	`http://www.nba.com/grizzlies/`
Washington Bullets	`http://www.nba.com/bullets/`

College Basketball Page

`http://www.cs.cmu.edu/afs/cs.cmu.edu/user/wsr/Web/bball/`

Has all the usual: schedules, rosters, conference breakdowns, and team nicknames. But, this site also includes All-American lists, recruiting information, academic standards, and rule changes for the next season. Includes information for both men and women, Division IA and below.

Michael Jordan's Home Page

`http://gagme.wwa.com/~boba/mj1.html`

As much a home page for the Bulls as for Jordan. Here you'll find information on Jordan's career, stats, links to other Jordan pages, those of his teammates as well those about the Bulls. Included are team rosters and schedules, as well as stories about their 70+ win season.

Nando Basketball Server

`http://www.nando.net/SportServer/basketball/`

The basketball link of the Nando SportServer. Provides links to national and collegiate level teams, scores and statistics. Also includes links to important sports stories like tournament results and happenings like Jordan's return to basketball.

On Hoops

`http://www.onhoops.com/`

A forum for those who love to discuss and critique basketball, its players, coaches, and referees as much as they love to watch the games. You won't find just lists of stats and team rosters here. You will find links to the Police Blotter, which chronicles the latest NBA player brushes with the law, as well as a place to vote for your favorite chump player. A nice change of pace for basketball enthusiasts.

Scottie Pippen's Home Court

http://www.clark.net/pub/cardman/pippen/

The complete guide to Pippen's career including links to both his college and professional stats. There are over 20 photos to download and video files highlighting memorable plays and games from the past season.

Ultimate Basketball Home Page

http://www.odyssey.com.au/sports/bball.html

This site is very graphics-oriented. You can download logos from NBA teams as well as photos of several current NBA players. This site also provides links to popular sports pages by ESPN and featuring Michael Jordan.

Unofficial Australian National Basketball League (NBL) Page

http://natsem.canberra.edu.au/nbl/nbl.html

Provides the latest Australian NBL results and news. Includes complete team, player, and game statistics, and links to teams' home pages.

Boating & Sailing

Adventure Schools, Inc.

http://jstart.com/kayak/kayak.html

Offers kayaking lessons for people of every ability level as well as kayaking vacations all over the world.

Boatnet

http://www.boatnet.com/boatnet/

Initally focused on the Northwest, Boatnet is expanding to include information for the entire country. You can find out about new and used boats for sale, chartered trips as well as links to online publications.

Common Sense Design's Home Page

http://www.hevanet.com/berniew/index.htm

Offers boat plans designed by the world famous designer Phil Bolger specially for first time boat builders who want a quick, easy, and inexpensive boat.

The Flying Scot Page

http://www.ansoft.com/palmer/sail/fs.html

Provides information about Flying Scot sailboats, news about regattas and results, new and used boats

and equipment for sale, tips on boatspeed, tactics, and more.

Internet Sea Kayaking

http://intelenet.com/clubs/ckf/other.html

This site provides a list of links to national paddling resources, magazines, associations, and clubs. Also included are links to several mailing lists to get in touch with other kayakers in your area.

Offshore Powerboat Racing

http://www.offshorepage.com

Provides race results, recaps, schedules. Contains current news, rules, and team information.

Perception, Inc.'s Kayaking Home Page—20 Years of Fun

http://www.kayaker.com/perception/

Kayak manufacturer's site that celebrates 20 years of fun and invites you to visit. Contains FAQs about the sport, a listing of their products, updates on upcoming events, the Olympics, and links to clubs/organizations.

RC—Sailing Infocenter

http://honeybee.helsinki.fi/surcp/rcsail.htm

Offers descriptions and pictures of radio-control sailing, the Finnish competition schedule, and online results. Provides the results of all Finnish competitions and some international competitions. Includes information on how to build a boat and some links to other organizations.

SailWeb

http://www.bga.com/~dkern/sail.html

Dedicated to sailboat racing of all types and provides links to weather and yacht club information. A link to boat designs leads you to each design's home page or association.

United States Power Squadrons Web Page

http://www.ronin.com/USPS/

Presents USPS, a private boating organization. Focuses on USPS's Basic Boating Course and the purpose of the club. Provides FAQs, link, and how to locate a squadron near you.

White Water Rafting

http://whirl.speech.cs.cmu.edu/WhiteWaterRafting.html

While this site is still under construction, you will already find river classifications, links to equipment and trip outfitters, as well as classification descriptions and permit requirements.

WWW Sailing Index

http://www.ualberta.ca/~sjones/urls.html

A list of links to other sailing/yachting pages as well as to online publications, clubs, and sailing series results.

Cycling

Cyber Cylcery

http://cyclery.com/index.html

Provides links to cycling manufacturers, publications, tour organizations and associations for both bicycle racing and mountain biking. Shown in both graphic and quick link formats.

CycLinks

http://www.velonews.com/VeloNews/cyclinks/cyclinks.html

This site has links to manufacturers and organizations associated with cycling. An unique feature is the online classifieds where you can buy, sell, and trade cycling equipment, post and peruse cycling-related job opportunities, and learn about touring and clinic opportunities.

Emory Bicycle Manufacturing Company

http://www.tdg.com/emory/emory.html

Factory direct bicycles. Forty years in the bicycle business. Offers products ranging from beach cruisers to collectables to mountain bikes, all for sale.

Fat Tire Wire

http://www.Fat-Tire-Wire.com/ftw/

The Fat Tire Wire is a meeting place for those who want to learn what's new, buy/sell/trade bikes and equipment, learn about upcoming races, and contact mountain biking manufacturers.

MuDsLuTs

http://www.mudsluts.com/pigseye/index2.html

Home page of the Northwest Mountain Biking Free Zone. Provides links to maps of the top trails in the Northwest United States as well as updates on product recalls, and direct links to biking suppliers and manufacturers all over the country.

Spring City Cycles

http://iquest.com/~topcycle/

Provides fun and useful information on bikes and info on how to order. Includes stats and photos on your favorite bike.

VeloNet

http://www.cycling.org/

Information center for the Global Cycling Network. Provides links to mailing lists of cycling clubs throughout the U.S. and the world. This is a sister site to Cyber Cyclery, listed previously, but includes links for things like BMX racing and Tandem riding as well as links to relevant publications.

The Velonews

http://www.velonews.com/VeloNews/

A journal of competitive cycling. Offers news, Tour de France info, and links to other pages. You can also browse the classified section, which lists bikes for sale, clinics, and a calendar of events.

VeloZine

http://www.wsmith.com/velolinq

Serves as a source for current cycling news, cutting-edge racing results, product information, online cycling publications, and links to other sites.

WOMBATS on the Web

http://www.wombats.org/

Home page of the Women's Mountain Bike and Tea Society. Geared toward women and their growing involvement in the sport, this site has links for upcoming clinics and group events as well as links to clubs and zines from across the country.

The WWW Bicycle Lane

http://www.cs.purdue.edu/homes/dole/bikelane.html

Similar to other cycling sites in content by providing links to manufacturers and publications. But the section on Bicycle Commuting and Advocacy is worth checking out; Bikelane offers links to other popular cycling sites as well.

Extreme Sports

Edge Magazine

http://www.fanzine.se/edgemag/

Covers snowboard, skateboard, surf, sound, and daredevil sports. Lets you download movie clips, some really radical photos, a preview of the latest issue of *Edge Magazine*, and more. Also offers many links to Internet sites on the edge.

Hang Gliding Page

http://www.mainelink.net/SKYADVENTURES/

Provides info about hang gliding festivals and tour dates. Includes mountain images and a directory of pilot home pages. Also has many links to tour operators and other related pages.

Hang Gliding WWW Server

http://cougar.stanford.edu:7878/HGMPShomePage.html

Contains information for both hang gliding and paragliding. Photo links and galleries make up the bulk of this site, but there are links to Hang Gliding digests. There is also a great link to comics related to the sport.

ISF World Snowboarding Rankings

http://deepcove.com/isf/

Presents International Snowboard Federation World & National Ranking lists, compiled from snowboarding competition results received from all over. Covers primarily Parallel Slalom, GS, Halfpipe, and Boarder Cross.

The Maui Windsurfing Report

http://maui.net/~mauiwind/MWR/mwr.html

The MWR is the center of windsurfing on the WWW. Offers action photos, news and views, contest to win a sail, and weather reports.

New England Windsurfing Journal

http://www.rscomm.com/adsports/newj/index.html

Offers past issues of the *New England Windsurfing Journal*—online.

Parachute Industry Association

http://www.pia.com/

The objectives of the Parachute Industry Association are to advance and promote the growth, development, and safety of parachuting and to engage and serve participants in the parachute industry. The PIA consists of companies and individuals united by a common desire to improve business opportunities in this segment of aviation. Site contains PIA publications, parachuting "Yellow Pages," a product listing, meeting schedule, and more.

Sailboard Vacations

http://www.sailboardvac.com/

Serves as a travel agency for windsurfers. Offers detailed travel information on the finest windsurfing spots. Features the latest in quality windsurfing equipment from Mistral. Provides information on how to windsurf.

SkyDance SkyDiving

http://www.webcom.com/~skydance/skydance.html

Here you can find out where to learn to dive, but also find out how much any level of dive will cost. The site provides an online newsletter, a list of related skydiving sites, and memorable images to download.

Skydive Archive

http://www.afn.org/skydive/

A resource for those who want to learn to skydive, and learn about safety and training techniques. You can link to the different disciplines of skydiving, find out where to dive, and what organizations are available for you to join.

Windsight Windsurfing Wind Reports

http://www.gorge.net/windsight

Provides text, graphics, and video coverage of windsurfing sites in the Columbia River Gorge, Oregon Coast, San Francisco Bay, Baja, and Maui. Also covers meteorological concepts as they apply to windsurfing. Explains how to use Windsight's 800 number voice phone service and the Windsight software.

Fantasy Leagues

Conway's Sports Research

http://www.wwcd.com/sportsa/sports/odds.html

Offers all the daily and future gaming odds. Includes an in-depth explanation of sports gambling terms and strategies.

Cosmic Baseball Association

http://www.clark.net/pub/cosmic/cba1.html

In a league all its own. This site pits teams like the Washington Presidents with third base coach Pat Buchanan against the Vestal Virgins with catcher Uma Thurman. Games are generated by CBA computers and new members are always welcome. The home page invites those who see baseball as a metaphor for the life of the mind to continue. An interesting change of pace.

CyberSoccer

http://www.cybersports.co.uk/soccer/index.html

Presents fantasy football (soccer) based on English FA Premiership.

Fantasy Baseball

http://arachnid.cm.cf.ac.uk/User/Gwyn.Price/fantasy_baseball/

Offers a collection of information links useful to fantasy league players. Includes rosters, up-to-date transactions, and statistics from past seasons.

Fantasy Baseball Home Page

http://www.usatoday.com/sports/baseball/sbfant.htm

Includes links to get free FanTrack software to track your players. The site tells you to "check here daily for everything you need to manage your fantasy baseball team." Complete listings of players from both leagues, broken down by position, as well as predicted player values and comparisons.

Fantasy Insights

http://www.best.com/~football/football.html

The complete resource for the fantasy football fanatic. This site boosts sleeper picks, trade activity, free agent movement, and other important aspects of Fantasy Football. They also have an "Ask the Master" area where you can get your questions about fantasy football answered. Some services require subscription.

Football Stats Analyzer Shareware

http://www.webcom.com/~liberty

Offers shareware you can use to predict future football game outcomes by analyzing historical statistics. Also offers links to other sports sites.

The Grandstand

http://www.gstand.com

Offers fantasy leagues, simulation leagues, and contests. Serves as a forum where sports fans can watch, talk, and play sports. Also offers links to other sports sites.

Highlight Fantasy—The Draft Kit

http://gmg.gmgnet.com/fantasy/

Presents The Draft Kit for fantasy and rotisserie sports, such as football, baseball, hockey, and basketball. Includes jumbo size 10-foot draft boards. Also offers a line of fantasy sports T-shirts.

Midwest Express Fantasy Game Co.

http://www.iquest.net/~mwexp

Headquarters for Online Fantasy Sports. Hosts the World Wide Weekly Challenge. Enables you to pick, trade, or waive your players online. Also the home of Weebe Technologies (Statmaster Football and Baseball).

NFL POOL

http://webcom.net/~dunny/nfl.htm

Offers information on the National Football League and a shareware program that runs a recreational football pool on the NFL.

Onondaga/Oswego Fantasy Football Page

http://www.servtech.com/public/newt

Devoted to a fantasy football league, contains its standings, rules, recaps of games, and links to sports sites.

Sports

Small World

http://baseball.smallworld.com/

Presents Small World Baseball and Hockey, online sports strategy games that allows fans to draft and trade a team of real players on an active, national market. Lets you organize a league with your friends and compete with thousands of opponents from across the globe.

WinAmerica! Fantasy Football

http://www.cdmnet.com/winAmerica/winam.html

Lets you engage in fantasy football on the Internet. Licensed by The NFL Players Association and sponsored by Dodge. Provides weekly results via Internet and on Prime Sports cable Thursday nights.

Fishing

Anglers Online

http://www.inetmkt.com/fishpage/index.html

Links to weather centers and fish report pages throughout the world to help you plan your next trip. Also included are current product reviews, links to manufacturers, related publications, and buy/sell/trade lists.

Flyfishing Antventures

http://www.teleport.com/~anthonyn/

Subtitled flyfishing and the full-time job. You will find links to pictures, stories, trip reports and future trip "dream seeds" here.

J.P.'s Fishing Page

http://www.geo.mtu.edu/~jsuchosk/fish/fishpage

Links to fishing newsgroups and other fishing home pages around the country make up this site. There is also a place to vote for the home page logos and plenty of graphics relating to fishing to download.

King of the Hill Fly Fishing Co.

http://www.kinghill.com

Full service fly fishing outfitter and supplier carries complete line of fly tying and fly fishing products. Provides product and books reviews, and links. Also represents worldwide fishing destinations, with a listing of charter boats.

Nautical Net

http://www.nauticalnet.com

A recreational watersports site that contains a tackle shop, marine electronics, boat brokers and manufacturers, clubs, fishing reports, and links to charter boats.

Nor'east Saltwater Magazine

http://www.noreast.com

A weekly sportfishing magazine for New York's saltwater anglers. Includes weeky fishing reports, sportfishing news, new product information, boats for charter, partyboat schedules, weekly saltwater fly fishing column, editorials, reader feedback, classifieds, and more. Updated weekly from April to November, monthly from December to March.

Sportfishing Industry Newsletter

http://www.kinghill.com/sportfishing

Offers a comprehensive closeup of the business of sportfishing: what's new, what's hot, who's who, and why. Targets fishing tackle manufacturers, ad agencies, marketers, and informed consumers.

Virtual Flyshop

http://www.flyshop.com/

Comprehensive page that has reports of fishing conditions on Canadian rivers. Offers an online magazine, a forum that includes an interactive discussion, and an "Ask the Experts" section.

DNA Purification System Sample Kit

http://www.promega.com/uk/
newpro.htm#Wizard_Plus_Samples

Have you been searching for that perfect DNA purification system? The Wizard™ Plus Miniprep DNA Purification System might be your answer. Visit this site to learn more about the system and other special offers.

World of Fishing

`http://www.fishingworld.com`

Offers all types of fishing information, services, products, tournament information, magazines, and servers as a place to visit other fishermen.

Football

The following are home pages for National Football League teams:

Team	URL
Arizona Cardinals	`http://nfl.com/teams/cardinals/cardinals.html`
Atlanta Falcons	`http://nfl.com/teams/falcons/falcons.html`
Baltimore Ravens	`http://nfl.com/teams/ravens/ravens.html`
Buffalo Bills	`http://nfl.com/teams/bills/bills.html`
Carolina Panthers	`http://nfl.com/teams/panthers/panthers.html`
Chicago Bears	`http://nfl.com/teams/bears/bears.html`
Cincinnati Bengals	`http://nfl.com/teams/bengals/bengals.html`
Dallas Cowboys	`http://nfl.com/teams/cowboys/cowboys.html`
Denver Broncos	`http://nfl.com/teams/broncos/broncos.html`
Detroit Lions	`http://nfl.com/teams/lions/lions.html`
Green Bay Packers	`http://nfl.com/teams/packers/packers.html`
Houston Oilers	`http://nfl.com/teams/oilers/oilers.html`
Indianapolis Colts	`http://nfl.com/teams/colts/colts.html`
Jacksonville Jaguars	`http://nfl.com/teams/jaguars/jaguars.html`
Kansas City Chiefs	`http://nfl.com/teams/chiefs/chiefs.html`
Miami Dolphins	`http://nfl.com/teams/dolphins/dolphins.html`
Minnesota Vikings	`http://nfl.com/teams/vikings/vikings.html`
New England Patriots	`http://nfl.com/teams/patriots/patriots.html`
New Orleans Saints	`http://nfl.com/teams/saints/saints.html`
New York Giants	`http://nfl.com/teams/giants/giants.html`

Team	URL
New York Jets	`http://nfl.com/teams/jets/jets.html`
Oakland Raiders	`http://nfl.com/teams/raiders/raiders.html`
Philadelphia Eagles	`http://nfl.com/teams/eagles/eagles.html`
Pittsburgh Steelers	`http://nfl.com/teams/steelers/steelers.html`
San Diego Chargers	`http://nfl.com/teams/chargers/chargers.html`
San Fransisco 49ers	`http://nfl.com/teams/49ers/49ers.html`
Seattle Seahawks	`http://nfl.com/teams/seahawks/seahawks.html`
St. Louis Rams	`http://nfl.com/teams/rams/rams.html`
Tampa Bay Buccaneers	`http://nfl.com/teams/buccaneers/bucs.html`
Washington Redskins	`http://nfl.com/teams/redskins/redskins.html`

AllSports.Com Football Hotlist

`http://allsports.questtech.com/nfl/football.html`

In addition to links to all the NFL team home pages, there is a NFL trivia game worth checking out, and an online weekly betting pool. Sorry guys, no money exchanged.

College Football WWW Site

`http://www.engr.wisc.edu/~dwilson/rsfc/`

Along with the usual schedules, preseason magazines and notes on each conference, this site links you to all the team logos, as well as information about stadiums, fight songs, and rules of the game.

College Sports Internet Channel

`http://www.xcscx.com/colsport/`

Provides access to Division 1A football teams by conference as well as by choosing from a map of the states. Links to other Sports Channel supported sites are also listed.

Nando Football Server

`http://www.nando.net/SportServer/football/`

The football arm of the Nando SportServer, this site gives access to professional and collegiate levels, a Cyber Road to the Superbowl and a look back at season's past.

NFL Executive Accessories

http://www.executive-accessories.com

Offers NFL executive accessories, including: NFL golf accessories, NFL desk accessories, NFL personal accessories, NFL travel luggage, NFL business luggage, and how to order.

Team NFL

http://nflhome.com/

Provides top-notch reports of football happenings like the draft and playoffs. Links to NFL headlines, and free agent questions and answers keep the football fan well-informed. There are also links for kids and places to find out more about your favorite NFL broadcaster.

Traveller Information Service

http://www.traveller.com/sports/ncaa_fb/

You can vote for the best Division I team, check out this week's picks, preview upcoming games, see who won last week, and access information for NCAA football teams.

Two-Minute Warning

http://www.dtd.com/tmw/

This site is for those who want to test their football knowledge. Two-Minute Warning is an NFL trivia game that allows participants to win prizes for correct answers. On the site you can check out the rules, play the trivia game, and see what prizes are available for winners.

USA Football Center Online

http://cybergsi.com/foot2.htm

Provides scores and updates to college and pro football games, standings, player stats, betting lines, and weekly stats. Also features a pregame show that talks about the games to be played that day, and provides the picks of the day.

Golf

The 19th Hole

http://www.sport.net

Serves as a place where fans and participants of the sport can gather, share a few stories, and settle a bet or two. Provides Daily Golf News and Almanac sections that let you keep up with the game on a daily basis and an Art section that brings a little laughter and color to your day. Also includes the Classified Ads area.

Alberta

http://www.cuug.ab.ca:8001/~mcleods/golf/golf.html

Provides in-depth descriptions of the many golf courses located in and around Alberta.

Fore Play Golf Home Page

http://www.4play.com/frame1.htm

Offers pro-line and custom golf equipment for sale. Features newsletters, tips from pros, quiz about the rules of golf, and links to other sites.

The Golf Circuit

http://www.sdgolf.com/

Thorough site that offers golf products for sale and provides the PGA schedule. Features many golf related topics and provides tips on everything from putting to the psychology of golf. Also contains an Internet golf directory which lists schools, golf product manufacturers and other related sites.

Golf Courses of British Columbia

http://www.sunnugolf.com/golfbc.html

Offers much to golfers of all skill levels. A point-and click map of British Columbia provides links to more than 100 golf courses. Also provides links to other golf-related Web servers.

The Golf Depot

http://www.golfdepot.com

Offers a line of Australian-made DINT putters, including info on how to order.

Golf Magazine

http://www.golfonline.com/

An online version of the current issue of *Golf Magazine,* you can also link to updates about past and future tournaments. A unique feature provided is a link to the current day in golf history. Information about *Golf Magazine* subscriptions is also available.

Golf Web

http://www.golfweb.com/

Here you can access the regualr golf stuff: tournament results, online pro shops, etc. But you can also link to the Lesson Tee for golfing tips, go to a link for Women in Golf as well as write a personal message to the winner of a current tournament.

NBC Golf Tour

http://www.gdol.com/

Offers a bundle of links related to golf, including travel packages, golf publications, course information, tournament and association information. Provides additional links to other golf servers.

Official PGA Championship Web Site

http://www.championship.pga.org/

Features live results from the Riviera Country Club. Provides results and features information about every hole, all the players, news and daily photographs/artwork, past and future PGA Championship events, other events run by the PGA of America, and more.

Princeton Golf Archives

http://dunkin.princeton.edu/.golf

Offers an education in designing a golf club and calculating slope and handicaps. Provides information about GolfData Online—a bulletin board that offers a database of 14,000 golf courses, tips from Jeff Maggert (PGA professional), discount coupons, and more (including .GIF and .BMP images).

Ryder Cup Home Page

http://www.RochesterDandC.com/sports/ryder/rydhome.html

Offers complete coverage of the Ryder Cup golf tournament in Rochester, New York. Includes history of the event, links to other golf sites, and a detailed map of the course.

Hiking

Above the Clouds

http://www.gorp.com/abvclds.htm

Highlights destinations that focus on the Himalayas, Europe, the Americas, and Africa. The group provides leaders for treks throughout these countries and this site discusses those, as well as the trip ethic they endorse.

Backcountry Home Page

http://io.datasys.swri.edu/Overview.html

Geared toward the rugged hiker, you will find links to backcountry maps, recipe links, and weather reports, all to make your trip more successful. There are also links to backcountry hiking publications.

Orienteering and Rogaining Home Page

http://www2.aos.Princeton.EDU:80/rdslater/orienteering/

Offers a general description of the two sports (which are types of cross-county hiking) and provides announcements, a schedule of events, and club activities. Also offers links to other orienteering and rogaining servers.

Volksmarch and Walking Index

http://www.telport.com/~walking/hiking.html

Volksmarching is a *different* kind of walk. This site tells you how to get involved or start a volksmarching club. You can also link to their publications, get a list of the 1,100 most unique trails to walk, and read about interesting things, like which walking shoe is the best.

Hockey

The following are Web sites for the teams of the National Hockey League:

Team	URL
Anaheim Mighty Ducks	http://www.nhl.com/teams/ana/index.htm
Boston Bruins	http://www.nhl.com/teams/bos/index.htm
Buffalo Sabres	http://www.nhl.com/teams/buf/index.htm
Calgary Flames	http://www.nhl.com/teams/cal/index.htm
Chicago Blackhawks	http://www.nhl.com/teams/chi/index.htm

Team	URL
Colorado Avalanche	`http://www.nhl.com/teams/col/index.htm`
Dallas Stars	`http://www.nhl.com/teams/dal/index.htm`
Detroit Red Wings	`http://www.nhl.com/teams/det/index.htm`
Edmonton Oilers	`http://www.nhl.com/teams/edm/index.htm`
Florida Panthers	`http://www.nhl.com/teams/flo/index.htm`
Hartford Whalers	`http://www.nhl.com/teams/har/index.htm`
Los Angeles Kings	`http://www.nhl.com/teams/la/index.htm`
Montreal Canadiens	`http://www.nhl.com/teams/mon/index.htm`
New Jersey Devils	`http://www.nhl.com/teams/nj/index.htm`
New York Islanders	`http://www.nhl.com/teams/nyi/index.htm`
New York Rangers	`http://www.nhl.com/teams/nyr/index.htm`
Ottawa Senators	`http://www.nhl.com/teams/ott/index.htm`
Philadelphia Flyers	`http://www.nhl.com/teams/phi/index.htm`
Pittsburgh Penguins	`http://www.nhl.com/teams/pit/index.htm`
San Jose Sharks	`http://www.nhl.com/teams/sjo/index.htm`
St. Louis Blues	`http://www.nhl.com/teams/stl/index.htm`
Tampa Bay Lightning	`http://www.nhl.com/teams/tam/index.htm`
Toronto Maple Leafs	`http://www.nhl.com/teams/tor/index.htm`
Vancouver Canucks	`http://www.nhl.com/teams/van/index.htm`
Washington Capitals	`http://www.nhl.com/teams/was/index.htm`
Winnipeg Jets	`http://www.nhl.com/teams/win/index.htm`

Hockey Hall of Fame

`http://www.hype.com/hhof/`

An information page about the Hockey Hall of
Fame, including admission prices and hours of
operation.

National Hockey League Players' Association

`http://www.nhlpa.com/`

With great links like Be a Player (a trivia link), Hot
Shots, Player of the Day, and player stats, this site is
for the person who knows about hockey and those
who want to find out more.

NHL OPEN NET

`http://www.nhl.com/nhl/Page2.html`

The complete hockey reference and Web site. This site
will link you to season standings as well as tell you all
about the current Stanley Cup champion. The link to
the Celebrity All-Star hockey team offers information
about the fund raising aspect of the sport.

NHL Schedule

`http://www.cs.ubc.ca/nhl`

Provides the schedules for each of the 26 NHL
hockey teams. Has an interactive interface that
enables you to see schedules in a list or calendar
format and when a specific team plays another.

NHL Wreckroom

`http://amadeus.ccs.queensu.ca/Hockey/Hockey.html`

This site contains primarily NHL player images.
You can also access The Hockey News—online.

Horse Sports

Horse Country

`http://www.pathology.washington.edu/Horse/index.html`

Here you'll find out about horse stories, history,
sounds and images, as well as barn smells. There are
links to horse training tips and links for kids to
Junior Riders Digest.

Thoroughbred Horse Racing and Breeding

`http://www.swcp.com/~hyperion/horse.html`

Links to pedigree and bloodline information as well
as to track and individual race results. You can help
a horse farm name its foals and check out the latest
equestrian publications.

Three Chimneys Farm Home Page

`http://www.threechimney.com/farm/`

Provides photos and statistics of some of the world's leading thoroughbred stallions, as well as information and photographs of Three Chimneys Farm, one of the world's leading thoroughbred breeding farms.

The Washington Handicapper

http://www.webcom.com/~sris/wh/wahandicapper.html

Serves thoroughbred horse racing fans in the state of Washington by providing pre-race analyses and post-race summaries about stakes races run at Washington race tracks. Provides occasional stats-based features about racing in the state and offers links to related sites.

Martial Arts

Aikido Information

http://www.cse.ucsd.edu/users/paloma/Aikido/

For the student of Aikido. This site provides links to the Aikido archives at UCSD, a dojo directory by continent, and lists of suppliers and equipment. Also useful are links to phone directories in the U.S. and Europe to find Aikido centers.

CyberDojo

http://www.ryu.com/CyberDojo/

Karate lovers offer lots of karate-related information. A wide range of resources include a karate lexicon, mailing lists, FAQs, events calendar, and a bibliography.

The Danzan-Ryu Jujutsu Homepage

http://www.radix.net/~danzan

Contains authoritative information on Danzan-Ryu Jujutsu, the martial art of Henry Seishiro Okazaki. Offers history, photos, and a list of dojos—schools that teach this sport.

Judo Information Site

http://www.rain.org/~ssa/judo.htm

A learning tool about Judo, you will find links to Japanese terms used in Judo, to the origins and principles used in Judo, and to the techniques of Judo in words and pictures. But the site is not all serious; there is also a link to a little Judo humor.

The Martial Arts As I've Learned Them

http://student-www.uchicago.edu/users/fun5/martial.html

If you want to broaden your horizons beyond Judo and Karate, this is the site. The author outlines different techniques and tells of their origins. The section on Bruce Lee and his contributions to the Martial Arts is interesting and the author provides several links to allow you to learn more.

Piedmont Budokan (Judo and JuJitsu)

http://www.cpcc.cc.nc.us/clubs/judo.htm

Emphasizes developing the individual and provides information on Judo throws and the proper way to work out. Also has history of the sport and how to join the club.

The T'ai Chi Connection

http:// www.islandnet.com/~gmuir/homepage.html

Links to finding a teacher, improving your posture, training tips, and chat areas. When the page is completed they will have links to bookstores and herb stores.

Miscellaneous Sports Sites

American Poolplayers Association

http://www.bimagic.com/pages/apa/apa_home.htm

This home page has links that outline league/team structure, step-by-step game rules, and playing instructions. There is also online association registration and links to billard club home pages, technique sites, and equipment manufacturers.

The Art of Fencing

http://www.ii.uib.no/~arild/fencing.html

Here you will find a link to the main fencing newsgroup, articles about fencing as well as books, photos, tournament results, and links to other fencing organizations and their home pages.

AWESOME Sports Site of the Week

http://www.awesomesports.com/

Scans the Web looking for the best, the coolest, the most awesome sports site of the week.

Ballistic Batteries

http://cybermart.com/web/ballistic/

Provides reliable high-quality batteries for use in your remote controlled cars, trucks, planes, helicopters, or boats. Also contains a company overview, FAQs, and links.

British Society of Sports History

http://info.mcc.ac.uk/UMIST_Sport/bssh.html

Promotes research and publications about British sports history and physical education. Also provides information about past and upcoming sports conferences. Includes important dates in British sports history and profiles of sports legends.

Canada's Sports Hall of Fame

http://www.inforamp.net/~cshof

A guide to Canada's best and most honored athletes and to Canada's Sports Hall of Fame, located in Toronto, Canada.

College Athletics WWW Pages

http://www.intellinet.com/~bryan/colleges.html

This site lists the Division I college teams by conference and provides a link that connects you, in most cases, with the home page of each school's athletic program. Also available here are a list of team nicknames, Top 25 statistics, and a chronicle of Notre Dame football.

College Lacrosse USA

http://www.centennial.fandm.edu/lacrosse/mainmenu

Provides links for men's and women's lacrosse at all collegiate levels, including club teams. Polls, stats, and tournament results are also available.

David B. Martin's Water Polo Page

http://www.kfu.com/~dbmartin/polo.html

Focuses on water polo and offers many water polo links—university and independent club teams. Also contains photos of water polo action.

ESPNET Sports Zone

http://espnet.sportszone.com

Provides up-to-date information for the following sports: football, basketball, hockey, and baseball (for professional and college teams/players). Also offers scores, previews, statistics, and highlight photos for some of the big games.

Frisbee Freestyle

http://www.users.interport.net/~rmeier/disc/disc.html

Links to photos you can download, tournament rankings and schedules, as well as links to other frisbee pages that contain more frisbee information. These links include lots of good frisbee trivia.

The Gym Forum

http://rainbow.rmii.com/~rachele/gymhome.html

A good resource for followers of gymnastics to keep up-to-date on the happenings in the sport. There are extensive meet results for American, Canadian, and International meets. Several photos to view and download as well.

Internet Athlete

http://www.athlete.com

Provides an extensive calendar of events for running, swimming, cycling, and triathlon/duathlon. Offers results, team and training directories, and features.

Irish Sports Report

http://irishsports.com/

Focuses on Notre Dame sports. Offers Irish news, trivia, photographs, and chances to win a book about Lou Holtz's first eight years as head coach. Provides a feature article, game summary, photo of the week, plus insider information you won't find anywhere else.

La Tauromaquia: The Art of Bullfighting

http://www.clark.net/pub/jgbustam/toros/toros.html

Provides links to learn more about the history of bullfighting, especially in Spain. Text links are coupled extensively with photo links. Knowing Spanish is helpful when visiting this site since some links are in Spanish only.

Mart's In-Line Stating Page

http://ourworld.compuserve.com/Homepages/Martin_Rivers

Do you want to learn how to become adept at Stair Riding? Or do the Backwards Powerslide? This site gives you all the instructions you need to master these and other techniques, plus tips on the best places in London to blade.

Nando.Net Sports Server

http://www.nando.net/SportServer/

Provides links to the NCAA and NIT post-season tournament results, as well as the latest sports news-clips and photos. SportsServer is broken down into separate baseball, basketball, hockey, and football servers, and provides access to general and specialized chat rooms.

PBA Tour

`http://www.pba.org/`

The Professional Bowlers Association links you to their history, gives you the dates and locations of their current tours as well as links to bowling association home pages around the country.

Physique Techniques Fitness Consultants

`http://rampages.onramp.net/~pthomas/`

Offers complete fitness programs, nutritional analysis, personal training, supplementation, steroid information, bodybuilding, training advice, fitness columns, and so on. Specializes in *metabolic manipulation* (making your body work for you—not being trapped by your body). Also offers a list of gyms and personal trainers, a bodybuilding contest schedule, and links to other sites.

Planet Reebok

`http://planetreebok.com/`

Offers information about Reebok's corporate history and news about fitness, human rights, activism, and research. Also offers the stats of athletes who endorse Reebok.

Quick Stats Service

`http://www.quickstats.com`

This site requires a subscription to access the information for baseball, football, basketball, and hockey. They do provide subscription information and will be offering online subscription soon. A perfect site for the fantasy leaguer.

Rowing

`http://www.comlab.ox.ac.uk/archive/other/rowing.html`

Provides definitions, rules, statistics, and photographs for the sport of rowing. Also provides Regatta results, a link to the River and Rowing Museum, list of Newsgroups, organizations, and companies on the Internet.

The Sporting Life

`http://www.sfgate.com/sports/`

Primary focus is on California-based sports teams of all types, but links to general NFL information also provided. Interesting feature is the chat room link where discussion is moderated and guests appear to discuss sports-related topics.

Sports Illustrated

`http://www.pathfinder.com/si/`

An online version of the current *Sports Illustrated* issue with photo links to top stories. Also includes links to the popular Swimsuit edition and a breakdown of individual sport highlights. You will also find a link to the current edition of *SI for Kids*.

Sports Network

`http://www.sportsnetwork.com/`

An up-to-the-minute resource for scores and news. Sports Network provides links to sports at the collegiate and professional level as well as auto racing, horse racing and boxing. Their headline news coverage is very thorough and the Java link and forum are added bonuses.

Sports Source

`http://s2.com/`

This site relates to the emerging sports of inline skating and snowboarding as well as extreme sports like skydiving and windsurfing. The focus is on outdoor sports and links to related catalogs, organization home pages, and magazines are provided.

Sports Souvenirs & Memorabilia

`http://nashville.net/~mold`

Presents Team Fan, which carries a wide variety of sports memorabilia and souvenirs. Carries items from the NHL, MLB, and NFL. Includes a list of hard-to-find items, including many for the Dallas Cowboys.

Sports Videos

`http://www.intellinet.com/~jdutton/sports.html`

Offers basketball, football, baseball, hockey, golf, tennis, track and field, fishing, camping, hunting, skiing, and more. Features dozens of selections of sports videos and includes plenty of tips and instructions from Dave Stockton, Billy Casper, Andre Aggasi, and many other well-known sports heroes.

FREE STUFF

Personal Lubricant

`http://www.davryan.com/probe-sample.html`

The body needs additional lubrication every now and then, so grab a free sample of Probe—it's Ph balanced and preserved by a unique citrus extract.

SportsArena

`http://www.awa.com/arena`

A site with links to virtually all sports. SportsArena includes the usual football, soccer, and hockey links, but also provides curling, kayaking, korfball, and ultimate frisbee links. This site also includes links to well-known sporting events like the Tour de France and the 1994 Goodwill Games.

Sportsworld

`http://sportsworld.com/`

The Sports Information Resource. Provides worldwide sports information, merchandise, facts, trivia, and results (both professional and amateur). Includes results for running, triathlons, duathlons, and cycling (with a unique individual results page for each athlete).

Sprague Mat Club

`http://www.teleport.com/~mitchell`

A kids wrestling club. Lists upcoming events, results, and how to join the club. Also includes general information about wrestling—how to watch a match and links to other sites.

Stadiums and Arenas

`http://www.wwcd.com/stadiums.html`

Offers seating charts and information of hundreds of stadiums and arenas throughout the world. Includes all NBA, NHL, MLB, and NFL arenas, and many college sites. Also includes phone numbers for ticket ordering and links to sports teams' home pages.

Sumo Infomation Page

`http://akebono.stanford.edu/users/jerry/sumo/`

This sumo wrestling home page provides a link to sumo facts and terms, tournament results for the past two years, and sumo-related news links.

Tenpin World

`http://www.shef.ac.uk/~sutbc/`

Contains information about the American Bowling Congress and the World International Bowling Congress. Links to tenpin organizations in Europe are abundant as are links to bowling articles and a complete bowler's dictionary.

The Ultimate Internet Sports Guide

`http://www.sportinfo.com/sportinfo/`

Serves as an Internet guide to professional and college sporting events. Offers schedules, accommodations, ticket information, and links.

The Ultimate Sports Page

`http://sportsone.radix.net`

Provides sports information: includes the pros, college sports, and the Olympics. Sponsors free fantasy basketball, baseball, and hockey teams. Also offers top sports headlines and editorial columns.

United States Air-Table-Hockey Association (USAA)

`http://www.compassnet.com/tweissm/`

This site provides links to upcoming tournament schedules, a complete list of rules of the sport, player biographies, and an ordering service for supplies. Also included is a database of players listed geographically to help those interested find each other and a dictionary of terms relevant to the game.

US Fencing Association Online

`http://www.usfa.org/`

Events, standings, and tournament results make up the bulk of the information on this home page. You can also stay up-to-date on association meetings and decisions through online press releases and meeting minutes. The online rule book is currently in the works.

USA Today Sports

`http://./www.usatoday.com/sports/sfront.htm`

As complete a reference as the newspaper itself. Photo links to top stories, as well as quick links to seasonal sports information. For baseball enthusiasts a link to *Baseball Weekly* is provided. This site also gives complete coverage of all the day's sporting events, available by clicking a key topic. *USA Today* updates the site often, so reloading for updates is advised.

the virtual greensward

`http://www.comzone.com/croquet/`

This page is run by a true lover of croquet. The links you find here to croquet organizations, teams, and clubs are the result of his efforts to locate croquet-related site on the Web. You'll even find a link to the croquet game mentioned in *Alice In Wonderland*.

Wide Web of Sports

http://tns-www.lcs.mit.edu/cgi-bin/sports

Offers a collection of sports statistics, schedules, rosters, facts, figures, and information. Covers the NBA, NFL, NHL, soccer, golf, frisbee, rowing, fencing, rugby, and other popular and little-known sports.

World Squash Federation

http://ptoon.ccit.arizona.edu/NMSRA/Rules.html

A complete list of rules of the game including techniques and scoring. Provides a glossary of terms as well.

Motorcycle Racing

AFMWeb

http://www.afmracing.org

Focuses on motorcycle roadracing. Offers New Racer School, practices, and schedule of races. Also includes a FAQ list, rulebook, links, membership information, race results, and a classified section.

Speedway Home Page

http://www.amg.gda.pl./speedway/speedway.html

Provides links to motorcycle racing forums in Britain, Australia, Canada and the United States. An all event calendar link is provided as well as information involving ice, land, and asphalt track motorcycle racing around the world.

Olympics

Guide to the 1996 Olympic Games

http://www.atlanta.olympic.org/

The commemorative site has information about the '96 games. There is also a link to the Olympic torch relay page with photos and relay maps.

The XVIII Olympic Winter Games

http://www.linc.or.jp/Nagano/index.html

You can access the page in Japanese and English. You will find links to the mission statement of the games, event and venue information as well as travel information to Nagano, Japan, the site of the 1998 Winter Games.

Outdoors

Arkatents USA—High Quality Camping Accessories

http://www.homepage.com/arkatent/

Offers a catalog of camping accessories and tents. Includes ordering information and photos of products.

Great Outdoor Recreation Pages (GORP)

http:///www.gorp.com/

Sort of an online newsletter, complete with feature story links, attraction listings and ratings, and a well-organized travel assistance page.

Outside Online

http://outside.starwave.com/outside/online/

The online version of the outdoor magazine. Topics address environmental issues and awareness as well as equipment reviews and destination planning.

Roller Warehouse News

http://albert.bu.edu/~spectre/rw-news.html

Provides information about rollerblading and skating. Includes an archive for the *Roller Warehouse News* newsletter, distributed via mailing list. Also contains deals from Roller Warehouse and articles from the newsletter editor.

Sk8er's Home Page

http://www.eden.com/~sk8er/

Offers instructions on inline skating techniques. Reviews equipment and places to skate. Provides a messages bulletin board, newsgroup, links to other pages and manufacturers. Also provides information on figureblade skating school programs.

The Upper Midwest Traveler and Adventure Guide

http://www.execpc.com/~midwest

Provides information about this splendid region known as the Upper Midwest. Covers recreation activities ranging from participation sports to pure travel and adventure. Tells you where to hike, bike, golf, ride, and canoe in the summer and fall and where to downhill and cross-country ski in the winter. Also leads you to unique attractions, festivals, and events the Upper Midwest has to offer.

Rugby

International Rugby League Home Page

`http://www.brad.ac.uk/~cgrussel/`

With an Austrailan twist, this site has a glossary of rugby league terms that is under construction. You can also access the home pages of various rugby leagues and clubs as well as get information about fantasy rugby league competitions.

WWW Rugby Information Service

`http://rugby.phys.edu/rugby.html`

Rules and basics of rugby catered to the beginner and sophisticate. This is an international site with country-specific contact information about clubs and contacts, as well as tournament schedules and results.

Running

Running Page

`http://sunsite.unc.edu/drears/running/running.html`

Provides information on notable trails, clubs, races, marathons, race results, and "the running scene" worldwide.

Sportsworld

`http://sportsworld.com/`

Link to in-depth update of the latest races and triathalons and shop in the Sportsworld mall using a secured browser. You can also link to SportSite and investigate other sports.

Scuba Diving

Aquanaut

`http://bighorn.terra.net/aquanaut`

Among other things, this scuba site tells you where to train, where to dive, rates the gear you use, and tells you the weather and temperature at the site where you are diving.

Diving Server

`http://www.cru.uea.ac.uk/ukdiving/`

Provides information about underwater diving, specifically in the United Kingdom. Some of the available links are to tide and weather information, underwater wildlife, and inland dive sites throughout England and Europe.

Mad Dog Expeditions

`http://www.mad-dog.net/`

Seeks to expand the experience of sport diving into realms traditionally reserved for scientists and heavily sponsored exploration teams. Offers challenging expeditions and training for serious divers of all ability levels.

Maui Scuba Page—Ed Robinson's Diving Adventures

`http://www.maui.net/robinson/erda.html`

Provides information on dive sites, weather and sea conditions, and other dive-related aspects of island life, including articles on underwater photography.

NAUI (National Association of Underwater Instructors)

`http://www.naui.org/`

Serves as the official site for the National Association of Underwater Instructors (NAUI) for use by scuba divers of all associations to promote diving safety and education.

Scuba Central

`http://www.scubacentral.com/`

Not only provides online magazines, links to reviews of programs and equipment, but Scuba Humor, Scuba Chat and The Wall, where you can post bulletin board messages.

Scuba Net

`http://www.scuba.net/`

Focuses on California Monterey Bay area, but links to other diving areas across the country are provided. A combination trivia/FAQ page provides a standard diving table for you to use.

Skiing

CRN—Colorado Resort Net

http://www.toski.com

Serves as a guide to Colorado resort communities, including hotel, restaurant, arts, event, real estate, and shopping information.

The FALL LINE Home Page

http://www.uvm.edu/~smiller/skihome.html

Devoted to the sport of skiing. Offers weather reports, trail ratings, links to resorts, and equipment manufacturers.

Jump

http://www.cdnsport.ca/jump/

Here you can find out how to ski jump and how your jump will be scored. You can link to major competitions and find out about the National Ski Jumping team as well.

Northern Vermont X-Country, Backcountry, and Telemark Skiing

http://salus.uvm.edu/VTXCSki.html

Provides information about free heel skiing in Northern Vermont. Includes trail maps, trail discriptions, and links to clubs, organizations, and resorts related to back-country or telemark skiing.

Pedersen's Ski and Sport

http://www.pedersens.com

Sells mountain bikes, inline skates, skis, snowboards, accessories, clothing, and more. Provides free shipping within the continental United States. Includes contests and links to other resources.

Powder Hound Ski Report

http://www.icw.com/skireport.html

Provides information about ski conditions and weather reports throughout the world. Also offers specific resort forecasts for Utah.

The SnowPage

http://rmd-www.mr.ic.ac.uk/snow/snowpage.html

Provides information about winter sports, including skiing and snow boarding, as well as information on resorts, weather reports, and trail maps. Also offers a picture gallery, e-zines, and Usenet newsgroups.

Wasatch Powderbird Guides

http://www.xmission.com/~act/wpb.htm

Offers helicopter powder skiing in Snowbird, Utah, just 35 minutes from Salt Lake City International Airport. Offers a price of trips available.

World Skiing

http://www.cs.colorado.edu/~mcbryan/bb/ski/ski.html

Provides bulletin boards for reporting world skiing conditions, both alpine and backcountry. The lists are extensive, but there is the chance to link a report for your ski area.

Soccer

ESPNet SportZone Soccer

http://espnet.sportszone.com/soccer

Provides links to soccer's hot zone, Europe, but also to World Cup qualification coverage worldwide. As Major League Soccer grows in the U.S., expect ESPN's current coverage to grow with it.

International Soccer

http://www2.webbernet.net/~bob/international.html

With links to soccer information the world over, both conferenced teams and clubs, this page is a good place to get soccer facts. Also available is a link to the World Cup history.

Soccer Cybertour

http://www.sybergoal.com/soccer/

This site focuses on the people who play the game, and seems youth-oriented. There are links to find penpals, a soccer parents meeting room, and a coaches/referees meeting place.

SoccerNet

`http://soccernet.com`

For followers of English and Scottish soccer leagues. You can link to pages for each premiere league team and follow the latest in FA Cup coverage.

SoccerNews Online

`http://www.csn.net/~eid/soccer/sccrindx.html`

Gives you access to soccer information all over the world by linking to the confederation name you want. This site has information about men and women's soccer, their tournaments, players, and national competitions.

TSI Soccer

`http://www.webpress.net/tsi/`

Provides catalogs of soccer products for teams and individuals. Includes information about TSI services. Provides Major League Soccer's schedule, photo gallery, information on "The Instep"— a program to help players get into college. Links to other soccer pages.

U.S. Soccer Web Pages

`http://www.cs.cmu.edu/afs/cs/usr/mdwheel/www/soccer/us~soccer.html`

The Web page for U.S. soccer updates. Provides complete coverage of Major League Soccer and links to the Major Fantasy Soccer League. Also available is information on the U.S. National team, U.S. Pro Leagues, and all U.S. soccer news.

Surfing & Waterskiing

Bodysurfing

`http://www.oceangroup.com/bodysurf.html`

Home page for the Santa Cruz Body Surfing Association. You'll find tide reports, bodysurfing articles, contest postings, and bodysurfing images to download.

Drop In

`http://www.ohana.com/hisurfad/links/links.html`

Disccover the best places to surf, as well as join Surfrider Foundation USA, an environmental group committed to protecting the beaches and waves.

FreeSurf

`http://www.iaaccess.com.au/freesurf/home.html#contents`

Relevant information especially for Australian surfers. Those interested in the surfing culture and familiar with surfing terms will enjoy links to competition results and top pro surfer home pages.

Surf Lingo

`http://www.sd.monash.edu.au/~jasonl/Dropin/lingo.html`

Dedicated to providing a page of surfing/body boarding lingo and slang.

Water Skier's Web

`http://waterski.net/`

Links to barefoot, air chair, and wake boarding techniques. Also provides links to talk about water skiing and visit the mall for products and vendor links.

Welcome to the Lip

`http:// www.lighthouse.com/~kieffer/TheLip/index.html`

Avoids being a list of links but instead wants to provide innovative resources of its own. Provides an interesting *Surfari Trip Database* to help you plan your next surfing adventure.

Windsurfer.com

`http://www.windsurfer.com/`

A thorough windsurfing database divided into organized categories. A link to maps and technical info is helpful in using the page and links to member sites and online publications give other areas to explore.

Swimming

Home Page for United States Swimming, Inc.

`http://www.usswim.org/usswim`

Presents United States Swimming, Inc., the national governing body for amateur competitive swimming in the United States. Provides history of organization, meet results, and Olympic trial info.

Web Swim

`http://alf2.tcd.ie/~smftzger/swim/header.html`

This site grew from the FAQ Swimming page. The authors are compiling a list of sport participants that you can become part of. Links to find training sites while on the road, nutrional information and swimming information for all ability levels are available.

Tennis

ATP Tour Home Page

`http://www.atptour.com/`

Get rankings, results, and tennis news from this site. Also a tournament calendar and profiles of top ATP players.

Tennis Country

`http://www.tenniscountry.com/`

Follow the latest tennis news, talk with other fans and players, take a free tennis lesson, win free trips, or check out your next tennis destination.

United States Tennis Association/ Mid-Atlantic Section

`http://www.clark.net/pub/mrosen/usta/`

Provides information about the USTA/Mid-Atlantic section, USTA programs, results, tournament schedules, and more.

World Wide Web Tennis Server

`http://www.tennisserver.com/`

Offers tournament updates, camp information, photos, daily tennis news, and hyperlinks to the Tennis Rules and Tennis Code. Also offers extensive list of other links.

Volleyball

USA Volleyball Home Page

`http://Volleyball.ORG:80/usav/`

Links to youth and junior programs as well as rosters for top men and women's teams.

Volleyball WorldWide

`http://www.volleyball.org/`

Fact page and links for both indoor and beach volleyball, men and women's. Provides information for all levels of volleyball: amateur, collegiate, and professional. Links to related associations like the U.S. Disabled Volleyball Team home pages also provided.

Winter Sports

Figure Skater's Web Page

`http://www.webcom.com/~dnkorte/sk8_0000.html`

Of most interest to those actually involved in amateur figure skating. Here you can find out where to learn to skate, if a person in your area needs a partner, as well as how much difficulty that new jump you just learned really has. Also included are links to clubs, skating organizations, and list of upcoming competitions.

Snow Page

`http://rmd-www.mr.ic.ac.uk/snow/snowpage.html`

Stuff on skiing and snowboarding. Links to zines, trail maps, travel services and snow resorts.

Speed Skating

`http://www.twi.tudelft.nl/~penninx/skate/`

This page gives you all you want to know about speed skating in the past and the future. Overviews of Olympic venues are available along with lists of national and world records and competition results.

The Winter Sports Page

`http://www.wintersports.org/`

This page is still under construction. The current links relate to the promotion of winter sports alternatives and introducing sports to children in general.

Promotional Items

`http://www.voyager.net/allstar/talkback.html`

Looking to promote your company, Web site, or yourself? Get free samples of promotional items such as notepads, pens, or towels.

Newsgroups

alt.arts.bujinkan

alt.autos.karting

alt.autos.sport.nhra

alt.fishing

alt.flame.football.notre-dame

alt.motorcycle.sportbike alt.sailing.asa

alt.olympics

alt.sport.basketball.pro.fantasy

alt.sport.foosball

alt.sport.horse-racing

alt.sport.horse-racing.systems

alt.sport.street-hockey

alt.sports.baseball.atlanta-braves

alt.sports.baseball.az-diamondbacks

alt.sports.baseball.balt-orioles

alt.sports.baseball.bos-redsox

alt.sports.baseball.calif-angels

alt.sports.baseball.chi-whitesox

alt.sports.baseball.chicago-cubs

alt.sports.baseball.cinci-reds

alt.sports.baseball.cleve-indians

alt.sports.baseball.col-rockies

alt.sports.baseball.detroit-tigers

alt.sports.baseball.fla-marlins

alt.sports.baseball.houston-astros

alt.sports.baseball.kc-royals

alt.sports.baseball.la-dodgers

alt.sports.baseball.minor-leagues

alt.sports.baseball.mke-brewers

alt.sports.baseball.mn-twins

alt.sports.baseball.montreal-expos.

alt.sports.baseball.ny-mets

alt.sports.baseball.ny-yankees

alt.sports.baseball.oakland-as

alt.sports.baseball.phila-phillies

alt.sports.baseball.pitt-pirates

alt.sports.baseball.sd-padres

alt.sports.baseball.sea-mariners

alt.sports.baseball.sf-giants

alt.sports.baseball.stl-cardinals

alt.sports.baseball.texas-rangers

alt.sports.baseball.tor-bluejays

alt.sports.basketball.big8.kansas

alt.sports.basketball.college.big-5

alt.sports.basketball.ivy.penn

alt.sports.basketball.nba.atlanta-hawks

alt.sports.basketball.nba.boston-celtics

alt.sports.basketball.nba.char-hornets

alt.sports.basketball.nba.chicago-bulls

alt.sports.basketball.nba.dallas-mavs

alt.sports.basketball.nba.denver-nuggets

alt.sports.basketball.nba.det-pistons

alt.sports.basketball.nba.gs-warriors

alt.sports.basketball.nba.hou-rockets

alt.sports.basketball.nba.ind-pacers

alt.sports.basketball.nba.la-lakers

alt.sports.basketball.nba.miami-heat

alt.sports.basketball.nba.mil-bucks

alt.sports.basketball.nba.mn-wolves

alt.sports.basketball.nba.nj-nets

alt.sports.basketball.nba.orlando-magic

alt.sports.basketball.nba.phila-76ers

alt.sports.basketball.nba.phx-suns

alt.sports.basketball.nba.port-blazers

alt.sports.basketball.nba.sa-spurs San

alt.sports.basketball.nba.sac-kings

alt.sports.basketball.nba.seattle-sonics

alt.sports.basketball.nba.tor-raptors

alt.sports.basketball.nba.utah-jazz

alt.sports.basketball.nba.vanc-grizzlies

alt.sports.basketball.nba.wash-bullets

alt.sports.basketball.pro.ny-knicks

alt.sports.football.arena

alt.sports.football.college.fsu-seminoles

alt.sports.football.mn-vikings

alt.sports.football.oak-raiders

alt.sports.football.pro.ariz-cardinals

alt.sports.football.pro.atl-falcons

alt.sports.football.pro.baltimore

alt.sports.football.pro.buffalo-bills

alt.sports.football.pro.car-panthers

alt.sports.football.pro.chicago-bears

alt.sports.football.pro.cinci-bengals

alt.sports.football.pro.cleve-browns

alt.sports.football.pro.dallas-cowboys

alt.sports.football.pro.denver-broncos

alt.sports.football.pro.detroit-lions

alt.sports.football.pro.gb-packers

alt.sports.football.pro.houston-oilers

alt.sports.football.pro.indy-colts

alt.sports.football.pro.jville-jaguars

alt.sports.football.pro.kc-chiefs

alt.sports.football.pro.la-raiders

alt.sports.football.pro.la-rams

alt.sports.football.pro.miami-dolphins

alt.sports.football.pro.ne-patriots

alt.sports.football.pro.no-saints

alt.sports.football.pro.ny-giants

alt.sports.football.pro.ny-jets

alt.sports.football.pro.oak-raiders

alt.sports.football.pro.phila-eagles

alt.sports.football.pro.phoe-cardinals.

alt.sports.football.pro.pitt-steelers

alt.sports.football.pro.sd-chargers San

alt.sports.football.pro.sea-seahawks

alt.sports.football.pro.sf-49ers

alt.sports.football.pro.stl-rams

alt.sports.football.pro.tampabay-bucs

alt.sports.football.pro.wash-redskins

alt.sports.hockey.ahl

alt.sports.hockey.cohl

alt.sports.hockey.echl

alt.sports.hockey.fantasy

alt.sports.hockey.ihl

alt.sports.hockey.nhl.Que-Nordiques

alt.sports.hockey.nhl.ana-mighty-ducks

alt.sports.hockey.nhl.boston-bruins

alt.sports.hockey.nhl.buffalo-sabres

alt.sports.hockey.nhl.chat

alt.sports.hockey.nhl.chi-blackhawks

alt.sports.hockey.nhl.clgry-flames

alt.sports.hockey.nhl.col-avalanche

alt.sports.hockey.nhl.dallas-stars

alt.sports.hockey.nhl.det-redwings

alt.sports.hockey.nhl.edm-oilers

alt.sports.hockey.nhl.fla-panthers

alt.sports.hockey.nhl.hford-whalers

alt.sports.hockey.nhl.la-kings

alt.sports.hockey.nhl.mtl-canadiens

alt.sports.hockey.nhl.nj-devils

alt.sports.hockey.nhl.ny-islanders

alt.sports.hockey.nhl.ny-rangers

alt.sports.hockey.nhl.ott-senators

alt.sports.hockey.nhl.phila-flyers

alt.sports.hockey.nhl.pit-penguins

alt.sports.hockey.nhl.pitt-penguins

alt.sports.hockey.nhl.que-nordiques

alt.sports.hockey.nhl.sj-sharks

alt.sports.hockey.nhl.stl-blues

alt.sports.hockey.nhl.tor-mapleleafs

alt.sports.hockey.nhl.vanc-canucks

alt.sports.hockey.nhl.wash-capitals

alt.sports.hockey.nhl.winnipeg-jets

alt.sports.hockey.rhi

alt.sports.hockey.uhf

alt.sports.hockey.vhf

alt.sports.hockey.whl

alt.sports.soccer.european

alt.sports.soccer.european.uk

alt.surfing

alt.surfing.bodyboard

alt.tennis

alt.zen+budo

aus.sport.rugby-league

aus.sport.scuba

clari.sports.baseball

clari.sports.baseball.major

clari.sports.baseball.major.al.games

clari.sports.baseball.major.al.stats

clari.sports.baseball.major.nl.games

clari.sports.baseball.major.nl.stats

clari.sports.baseball.minor

clari.sports.basketball

clari.sports.basketball.college

clari.sports.basketball.college.men

clari.sports.basketball.college.men.games

clari.sports.basketball.college.men.stats

clari.sports.basketball.college.women

clari.sports.basketball.minor

clari.sports.basketball.nba

clari.sports.basketball.nba.games

clari.sports.basketball.nba.stats

clari.sports.football

clari.sports.football.cfl

clari.sports.football.college

clari.sports.football.college.games

clari.sports.football.college.stats

clari.sports.football.nfl

clari.sports.football.nfl.games

clari.sports.football.nfl.stats

clari.sports.golf

clari.sports.hockey

clari.sports.hockey.ahl

clari.sports.hockey.ihl

clari.sports.hockey.nhl

clari.sports.hockey.nhl.games

clari.sports.hockey.nhl.stats

clari.sports.horse_racing

clari.sports.soccer

clari.sports.tennis

dc.redskins

fido7.martial_arts

fido7.sport.football

finet.freenet.harrastus.judo

fj.rec.fishing

fj.rec.sports.american.football

fj.rec.sports.baseball

fj.rec.sports.basketball

fj.rec.sports.football

fj.rec.sports.golf

fj.rec.sports.keiba

fj.rec.sports.rugby

fj.rec.sports.ski

fj.rec.sports.soccer

fj.rec.sports.volleyball

git.club.sailing

git.club.swim

git.olympics.official

git.olympics.volunteer

nctu.club.baseball

pdaxs.schools.martial

pdaxs.schools.sports

pdaxs.sports.baseball

pdaxs.sports.basketball

pdaxs.sports.football

pdaxs.sports.golf

pdx.golf

pdx.running

phl.outdoors

pnet.rec.fishing

pnet.rec.windsurfing

rec.autos.sport.f1

rec.autos.sport.indy

rec.autos.sport.info

rec.autos.sport.nascar

rec.autos.sport.tech

rec.bicycles.marketplace

rec.bicycles.misc

rec.bicycles.off-road

rec.bicycles.soc

rec.bicycles.tech

rec.boats

rec.boats.marketplace

rec.collecting.sport.baseball

rec.collecting.sport.basketball

rec.collecting.sport.football

rec.collecting.sport.hockey

rec.equestrian

rec.martial-arts

rec.motorcycles.racing

rec.outdoors.camping

rec.outdoors.fishing

rec.outdoors.fishing.bass

rec.outdoors.fishing.fly

rec.outdoors.fishing.saltwater

rec.outdoors.marketplace

rec.outdoors.national-parks

rec.outdoors.rv-travel

rec.scuba

rec.skiing.alpine

rec.skiing.announce

rec.skiing.backcountry

rec.skiing.marketplace

rec.skiing.nordic

rec.skiing.resorts.europe

rec.skiing.resorts.misc

rec.skiing.resorts.north-america

rec.skiing.snowboard

rec.sport.baseball

rec.sport.baseball.analysis

rec.sport.baseball.college

rec.sport.baseball.data

rec.sport.baseball.fantasy

rec.sport.basketball.college

rec.sport.basketball.europe

rec.sport.basketball.misc

rec.sport.basketball.pro

rec.sport.basketball.women

rec.sport.football.australian

rec.sport.football.canadian

rec.sport.football.college

rec.sport.football.fantasy

rec.sport.football.misc

rec.sport.football.pro

rec.sport.golf

rec.sport.hockey

rec.sport.hockey.field

rec.sport.olympics

rec.sport.rugby.league rec.sport.rugby.union

rec.sport.skating

rec.sport.skating.ice.figure

rec.sport.skating.ice.recreational

rec.sport.skating.misc

rec.sport.skating.racing

rec.sport.soccer

rec.sport.swimming

rec.sport.table-soccer

rec.sport.table-tennis

rec.sport.tennis

rec.sport.unicycling

rec.sport.volleyball

rec.sport.waterski

rec.running

rec.windsurfing

relcom.rec.tourism

tw.bbs.sports.baseball

tw.bbs.sports.basketball

tw.bbs.sports.fishing

tw.bbs.sports.tennis

ucd.sports.volleyball.mens

uiuc.sport.basketball

uiuc.sport.football

uk.rec.walking

uk.sport.horseracing

uwarwick.societies.shotokan-karat

Listservs

AUTORACE—A Discussion of Auto Racing

Virginia Tech

You can join this group by sending the message "sub AUTORACE your name" to listserv@vtvm1.cc.vt.edu

B10WB-L—Big 10 Women's Basketball

Pennsylvania State University

You can join this group by sending the message "sub B10WB-L your name" to listserv@psuvm.psu.edu

CBR—Honda CBR motorcycles

You can join this group by sending the message "sub CBR your name" to listserv@gu.uwa.edu.au

HRACING—Horse Racing Discussion

You can join this group by sending the message "sub HRACING your name" to listserv@ulkyvm.louisville.edu

MUFC—Manchester United Football Club (Soccer)

University Computing Services, Indiana University

You can join this group by sending the message "sub MUFC your name" to listserv@iubvm.ucs.indiana.edu

NYMETS-L—New York Mets Baseball Talk

You can join this group by sending the message "sub NYMETS-L your name" to listserv@listserv.aol.com

PHILS—Phillies Discussion List

You can join this group by sending the message "sub PHILS your name" to listserv@listserv.uoguelph.ca

RANGERS—Discussion of Texas Rangers Major League Baseball Team

Texas A&M University Computing Services Center

You can join this group by sending the message "sub RANGERS your name" to listserv@tamvm1.tamu.edu

SOCCER-L—Soccer Boosters List

You can join this group by sending the message "sub SOCCER-L your name" to listserv@lsv.uky.edu

SOCREF-L—Discussion of Topics for Soccer Referees

You can join this group by sending the message "sub SOCREF-L your name" to listserv@uriacc.uri.edu

SPORTS-CARDS—Buy/Sell/Trade and Discussion of Sports Cards

You can join this group by sending the message "sub SPORTS-CARDS your name" to listserv@listserv.aol.com

STATLG-L—Baseball (and Lesser Sports) Discussion List

Brown University, Providence, RI

You can join this group by sending the message "sub STATLG-L your name" to listserv@brownvm.brown.edu

UTAHJAZZFANS—Discussion of Utah Jazz Basketball

America Online, Inc. (1-800-827-6364 in USA/Canada)

You can join this group by sending the message "sub UTAHJAZZFANS your name" to listserv@listserv.aol.com

VB-CLUB—Club Volleyball Discussion List

You can join this group by sending the message "sub VB-CLUB your name" to listserv@ulkyvm.louisville.edu

The Internet is full of Web sites about television personalities. Here is just a sampling of what's available:

Personality	URL
Pamela Anderson	`http://www.infolink.net/~hokh/pamela/pamela.html`
Jennifer Aniston	`http://www.escape.ca/~hazlitt/jaclub.htm`
George Burns	`http://www.premrad.com/celeb/burns.html`
George Clooney	`http://www.hooked.net/users/cpatubo/clooney.html`
Kelsey Grammer	`http://www.nbc.com/entertainment/shows/frasier/biogrammer.html`
Helen Hunt	`http://www.ltm.com/dinan/hhunt/html/hhunt.html`
Lisa Kudrow	`http://www.rpi.edu/~dohnm/1107.html`
Heather Locklear	`http://www.geocities.com/Hollywood/2155/`
David Schwimmer	`http://users.aol.com/loraj/dspage.html`
Jerry Seinfeld	`http://www.nbc.com/entertainment/shows/seinfeld/bioseinfeld.html`
Will Smith	`http://www.nbc.com/entertainment/shows/prince/biosmith.html`
Patrick Stewart	`http://ourworld.compuserve.com/homepages/psas/`

Children

2 Stupid Dogs

`http://www.sn.no/~tbk/2stupid.html`

Produced by Hanna Barbara, *2 Stupid Dogs* is about, well, two dogs that aren't that smart. There are plenty of pictures, sounds, and links available at this site. (And, if you can get here, then you are probably smarter than our heroes.)

The Adventures of Pete and Pete

`http://www.cs.indiana.edu/entertainment/pete-and-pete/`

Nickelodeon's television program *The Adventures of Pete and Pete* chronicles the adventures of two brothers who experience very strange happenings. There is always someone interesting on the show, ranging from Iggy Pop to Hunter S. Thompson to Adam West.

The alt.tv.tiny-toon FAQ

`http://kumo.swcp.com/synth/tta-faq.html`

A comprehensive site for fans of Fox's *Tiny Toons*. Includes every conceivable question possible about this cartoon.

Animaniacs

`http://www.wbanimation.com/bin/wb.cgi?MIval=an_100.htm`

Yakko, Wacko, and Dot (the cute one) have their home page here on the Warner Brothers studio lot. There is information, downloads, credits, and a bunch of other stuff that you can't get anywhere else on the Web.

Bananas in Pajamas

`http://www.prairienet.org/~dbrown/bananas.html`

A page dedicated to B1 and B2 and their adventures. It has images and storylines that you can check out.

Batfink

`http://www.cybercomm.net/~dmackey/animation/batfink.html`

Batfink is a parody of the *Batman* series from the sixties. This site has its history, some pictures, and some other information about this Hal Seeger animated gem.

Batman: The Animated Series

`http://www.math.ufl.edu/~wdn/comics/batman/BTAS/`

Although some would argue that this is not merely a children's TV show, who knows a kid who doesn't like Batman? This site is for that kid—it has cast and credits lists, an episode guide, and some nice pictures from this animated series.

Beakman's World Home Page

`http://www.spe.sony.com/Pictures/tv/beakman/beakman.html`

The MTV generation's version of Mr. Wizard, *Beakman's World* started as a syndicated info-comic strip and has become a Saturday morning show. There's much to learn about science, so look here for a head start.

Captain Caveman

http://www.hype.com/nostalgia/tv/capcav/capcavin.htm

"What can't he pull out of his fur?" is the question of the hour with this superhero. Look here for some Captain Caveman quotes, pictures, and other stuff about this popular kid's cartoon.

Captain Planet

http://www.turner.com/planet/

Shown on the Turner Broadcasting System, *The Adventures of Captain Planet* provides a superhero for the nineties. Smart. Ecological. Blue. This is his official Web page and has lots of stuff to look at and download.

Cartoon World

http://www.cet.com/~rascal/

Cartoons through the ages reside at this site. There are pictures and information here that you thought you'd never see again. A cartoon lover's paradise!

Cartoons of the '80s Home Page

http://hertz.njit.edu/~sxs7502/80sCartoons/

A tribute page to cartoons that were shown on over-the-air television in the 1980s. They are separated in a well-ordered outline for your convenience.

Children's Television Workshop

http://www.ctw.org/

From the people who brought you *Sesame Street*, this page gives parenting information and stuff for kids to do. It includes some nice pictures of Muppets (and the like) and coloring pages for printing out.

Clarissa Explains It All

http://www.ee.surrey.ac.uk/Contrib/Entertainment/Clarissa/

Episode guides, interviews, and other information about Nickelodeon's young adult comedy *Clarissa Explains It All*.

Count Duckula Page

http://www.ghgcorp.com/vision/Lupine/Duckula/index.html

Count Duckula was one of the original wacky ducks presented for kids' amusement (after Daffy, but before Darkwing). This page is his unoffical site.

Craig's Comic & Cartoon Page

http://137.52.232.11/~nadlerc/craig.html

Looney Toons, Animaniacs, Wile E. Coyote, and others are here at the Cartoon Links site. You can also find other comic strip links including Peanuts, Calvin and Hobbes, and Dilbert here.

Danger Mouse

http://www.charm.net/~altera/dm/

Download images and sounds of this popular Nickelodeon cartoon. Includes info on the show's characters, a lengthy video list, and links to fan pages.

Davey and Goliath

http://www.itserve.com/~tfitz/DG1.html

Davey and Goliath is a show from the famous maker of *Gumby*, Art Clokey. This show is different than *Gumby* in that it has a religious (Christian) message to give.

Deron's Muppet Page

www-leland.stanford.edu/~dsedy/muppets.html

Pictures, sounds, links, and information about the popular kids' program from the late '70s to the early '80s. Even Statler and Waldorf are here!

Dinosaucers

http://www.public.iastate.edu/~bovy/Dinosaucers.html

Complete with an episode guide, graphics, and sound, the Dinosaucers home page is dedicated to the sci-fi/fantasy cartoon of the same name.

Dungeons and Dragons

http://ada.hofstra.edu/~bferri1/accaaa/great_cartoons/
dung_and_drag/

With downloadable movies, pictures, and sound, the Dungeons and Dragons cartoon's Web site is a wonderful piece of nostalgia.

Earthworm Jim

http://www.wbanimation.com/bin/wb.cgi?MIval=ej_500.htm

Based on a popular game for the Nintendo Entertainment System, Earthworm Jim is based in a very strange world where goldfish are evil and, well, an earthworm is a superhero. You can download sounds, movies, and other stuff from this, the official Web site.

The Flintstones Unofficial Home Page

http://www.chickasaw.com/~cchamber/flint.html

This is a great page with a Desktop Theme for Windows 95, pictures, broadcast schedule, and an updated Sites for Kids feature. These pages have also been translated into Ukrainian and Russian (just in case you were wondering).

Fraggle Rock

http://www.clark.net/pub/cvaughn/html/frindex.htm

This page is dedicated to the Muppet-like Fraggles. It has a complete *Fraggle Rock* Guide and other information of interest.

Freakazoid!

http://www.wbanimation.com/bin/wb.cgi?MIval=f_600.htm

Presented by Steven Spielberg, *Freakazoid!* is a popular Warner Brothers cartoon with a teenage superhero. Actually, Freakazoid was once mild-mannered Dexter Douglas, but was transformed by a "crash on the information superhighway." See where the Internet will get you?

Frostbite Falls

http://www.pomona.claremont.edu//frostbite/
frostbite.html

Not a pretty site, but definitely valuable for fans of the crazy cartoon show, *Rocky and Bullwinkle*. Includes FAQs about the show, voice actor lists, sound clips, and publications about and interviews with the show's creator, Jay Ward.

G.I. Joe—A Real American Hero

http://ada.hofstra.edu/~bferri1/accaaa/great_cartoons/
gijoe/

The famous soldier has a home here with pictures, sounds, videos, and an episode guide.

Goosebumps

http://scholastic.com/Goosebumps/index.html

Based on the popular children's books, *Goosebumps* has become the most popular kid's TV show in the United States. This is its official Web presence and features links to a fan club, a photo gallery, information concerning R.L. Stine (writer of the popular books), and items for purchase.

Gumby on the Web

http://www.emsphone.com/gumby/

Complete with the Gumby theme song, pictures, and other wonderful Gumby memorabilia, Gumby on the Web can satisfy any person's appetite for green clay. There's even a link to an essay on Gumby's Eastern mystic philosophy.

The Jetsons

http://www.turner.com/tbs/disaster/jetsons.htm

The Jetsons was one of Hanna Barbara's attempts at making a family cartoon for kids and adults. Not as successful as the Flintstones, the Jetsons has won over many fans, and now has a home on TBS. This site has pictures and trivia from the futuristic family of the past.

Keeper's Cartoon Files

`http://www2.cruzio.com/~keeper/toons.html`

This isn't a pretty site, but it does include a ton of information on Warner Brothers' cartoons, such as *Animaniacs* and *Pinky and the Brain*. Download a complete episode list of Warner cartoons and lyric files, screenplays of particular shows, and learn more about the Warner Internet Fan Association.

Kids.Cool

`http://www.kmsp.com/kidscool.html`

Kids.Cool is a program produced by UPN-9 for kids. It uses the latest technology—such as computers—to relay this message. This site has many interactive Kids.Cool links and includes a newsletter and a page dedicated to the host, Brian Z.

Mighty Morphin Power Documents

`http://mason.gmu.edu/~tguingab/power/`

Includes up-to-date FAQs on the show and movies, episode guides for each season, and a quotes file (strange). Check out links to other sites for more MMPR info.

Mister Rogers' Neighborhood

`http://www.pbs.org:80/rogers/mrr_home.html`

Of course Mister Rogers has a home page. One of the nicest parts of his page, though, is its use of RealAudio in conjunction with his information. There are lyrics to songs and a book list for suggested reading.

Muppets Home Page

`http://www.ncsa.uiuc.edu/VR/BS/Muppets/muppets.html`

Although this site is thin on sounds and images, valuble info for Muppets fans abounds. A must see are the Episode Guides for all of Jim Henson's productions, including *The Muppet Show*, *Fraggle Rock*, and *Dinosaurs*. Travel to Official and fan-related Muppets sites on the Web and read online articles on the Muppets. Die-hard Muppets fans should check out the Muppography, a list of everything known on the Muppets.

Phil's Faboo Animaniacs Web Page

`http://www.novia.net/~wakko/warner.html`

This fan page for the *Animaniacs* cartoon show includes images, funny sound clips, and links to other fan pages. You can also join the Animaniacs with a Life fan club if you love the show and also have time for a real life—difficult!

Pigs in CyberSpaaaaaaaaaaace...

`http://www-leland.stanford.edu/~rosesage/Muppet.html`

A fun site from the creator of the Fabulous Miss Piggy Page. Includes info on the new Muppets show and movie, the MuppetZine, Muppet CD-ROMs and interactive products, mailing lists, and the Muppet museum exhibit.

Pinky and the Brain

`http://www.wbanimation.com/bin/wb.cgi?MIval=pb_300.htm`

Pinky and the Brain are the Odd Couple of lab rats. Apparently they've moved their scheming to take over the world to the World Wide Web.

The ReBoot Home Page

`http://uts.cc.utexas.edu/~ifex534/main.html`

Includes information on the characters of the Saturday morning cartoon show, *ReBoot*. You can also read the episode guide and general info. Check out the episode guide and the "Did you notice" section for funny info on the show's more subtle additions.

The School House Rock Page

`http://hera.life.uiuc.edu/rock.html`

Any Generation Xer will remember these songs. Check out "Grammar Rock," "America Rock," "Science Rock," and "Multiplication Rock." Which song is your favorite "Interjections?"

The Secret World of Alex Mack Unofficial Home Page

`http://hot.hotcc.com/users/bennettd/alexmack/`

With trivia, cast lists, and other entertaining information, this site is dedicated to the popular Nickelodeon series.

Some of the 100 or Some Odd Smurfs

`http://www.umich.edu/~starchld/hannabarbera/smurfs/`

Forgot who all those blue male Smurfs were living with the lonely Smurfette? Find out here! This site provides names of and images of dozens of these little blue devils from the early '80s Saturday morning cartoon. A riot!

The Superfriends Archive

`http://fantasia.ncsa.uiuc.edu/Doug/superhtml/`

With the Flash, Batman and Robin, Superman, Aquaman, and Wonder Woman, the Superfriends are here! Of course, there are pictures, sounds, and other stuff you can download from the site. There also is a complete listing of the Superfriends, just in case you've forgotten some of their names.

The Sylvester and Tweety Mysteries

http://www.wbanimation.com/bin/wb.cgi?MIval=st_400.htm

Based on characters from the same series that produced television legend Bugs Bunny, the *Sylvester and Tweety Mysteries* Web site has bios, credits, and sounds and movies to download. There is also a schedule of times the show is aired.

Taz-Mania Page

http://www.itouch.net/~jeff/taz-mania/index.html

Fan page for the craziest cartoon character ever. Read the Taz-Mania FAQ, download TAZ images, or check out the Taz Episode List. This site also connects to the Tazmanian Devil Usenet group.

Teen Court TV

http://www.courttv.com/teens/

Games, previews, forums, and a miniature digital law library are showcased at this site. You can also fill out quizzes, register to be on TV, go shopping, or read about this new show just for teens shown on Saturday mornings.

That's Warner Bros.!

http://www.wbanimation.com/bin/wb.cgi?MIval=wb_200.htm

Bugs Bunny, Sylvester, Yosemite Sam, and Pepe LePew (you remember these guys, right?) call this their official Web page. It is based at the Warner Brothers studio's server and has plenty of stuff to look at, download, and read about.

Thomas the Tank Engine

http://www.webcom.com/reeduk/thomas/

The engine from *Shining Time Station* has his home on the Web here. There are histories, stories, and coloring sheets available for downloading.

Thunderbirds

http://www.ludd.luth.se/~kavli/Tbirds.html

The Gerry Anderson TV series produced in the 1960s has been popular for years. Made in claymation, the famous cold-war jet-plane show now has information on the Web. There are pictures, info, and a Gerry Anderson FAQ available here.

The Tick Page

http://www.cipsinc.com:80/TICK/tickpage.html

Home of the alternative superhero Tick. Learn about Tick do-gooders and evil-doers, recurring Tick characters, Tick toys, and the latest Tick news. View images by Tick fans in ArticTICK, read funny quotes in TICKisms, and check out Diversions. Someone went a little crazy with frames.

The Unofficial Sid and Marty Krofft Home Page

http://www.west.net/~popomatic/Krofft.html

This page is dedicated to the brothers Krofft, creators of shows such as *H.R. Pufnstuf* and *Bugaloos*. This is a beautifully designed page and has many links, including theme songs, "Krofftware," and a Family Photo Album.

Welcome to Casper's Whipstaff Manor

http://www.atlas.co.uk/casper/welcome.htm

Order merchandise from the movie or visit Casper at this official Web site for the film. This site includes info on the cast, the story, and a description of the Casper character.

You Can't Do That On Television

http://www.PERnet.net/~rbarrow1/ycdtotv.htm

Read why Nickelodeon's *You Can't Do That On Television* was such a hit in the eighties. Includes interviews, scripts from the show, the Sausage Factory (a virtual mess!), and the Locker Room, where you can leave messages.

Comedies & Sitcoms

Absolutely Fabulous

http://www.comcentral.com/abfab/abfab.htm

Download images of the hit Comedy Central TV show, *Absolutely Fabulous*. This page also includes an episode guide, air schedule, and merchandise info.

The ALF Page by Kyle

http://www.webcom.com/pleasant/kyle/alf/alf.html

The alien life form (ALF) that landed in Willy Tanner's backyard calls this place home. You will find a biography of ALF and his characters, a trivia archive, and even Melmac holidays of the month here.

The Alice TV-Show Home Page

http://yakko.cs.wmich.edu/~ochs/guides/alice.html

Remember Mel's Diner, Vera, Flo, and the gang? Want to read the subtle differences in the theme song season to season? Well, you can. It's here—the *Alice* TV-show home page.

All in the Family

http://pmwww.cs.vu.nl/service/sitcoms/AllInTheFamily/

The show that shook up a nation in the 1970s, starring Carrol O'Connor. There is an episode guide and some pictures here. "Gee, our old LaSalle ran great…"

alt.tv.brisco-county

news://alt.tv.brisco-county

Have the need to talk about the combination of Bruce Campbell and cowboys? Look here.

America's Favorite Radio Station

http://www.tir.com/~rtw/krp.htm

Baby, if you've ever wondered, this site concentrates on *WKRP in Cincinnati*. It calls itself a fan guide and has articles, photos, stories, and other remembrances from the late '70s–early '80s sitcom.

"Nip It in the Bud"

Missed your local TV station's 24-hour *Andy Griffith Show* marathon? Don't despair—here are a few tidbits to hold you over. Be sure to check out the The Andy Griffith Show Home Page.

- Number of times Barney wore a dress: 3.

- Number of times Barney accidentally fired his pistol: 8. 3 into courthouse floor, 1 into courthouse ceiling, 2 into the air, 1 into Andy's front porch, and 1 into a tire on a squad car.

- Number of panes of glass and/or windows broken by someone: 23.

- Percentage of that glass broken by Ernest T. Bass: 78%.

- Things wrong with the car Barney bought from "Hubcaps" Lesh for $297.50: plugs, points, bearings, valves, rings, fuel pump, starter switch, ignition wires, water pump, oil pump, clutch, clutch bearings, clutchplate, brake lining, brake shoes, radiator hose cover, sawdust in the transmission. And it could stand a good wash.

- Number of stoplights in Mayberry: 1.

- Number of miles on Aunt Bee's car: 145,000.

- Number of steps up to the Taylors' front porch: 2.

- Number of steps up to the church (which isn't air-conditioned): 6.

- Number of jars of Miracle Salve delivered to Andy's house: 946.

The Andy Griffith Show Home Page

http://www.winternet.com/~muff/andy-griffith.html

The show that made stars out of several people including Ron Howard and Don Knotts. This site has an episode guide, Mayberry Trivia, links, and other strange, fun, and seemingly worthless stuff for the Mayberry fanatic.

Beavis and Butthead

http://mtv.com/animation/beavbutt/

The official Beavis and Butthead site—this is offered by MTV in order to control our minds. There is megabyte after megabyte of movies, sound clips, and pictures.

Better Dead Than SMEG

http://www.dwarflander.com/reddwarf.htm

The Red Dwarf unofficial Web page is bandwidth-heavy and extremely Netscape formatted, but deserves a look if you are a fan of the almost-famous British comedy.

Bewitched Home Page

http://www.sappho.com/bewitchd/index.shtml

Elizabeth Montgomery and her TV show have many fans, but none seem as Web-savvy as the creator of this site. It has the look and feel of the television program and much information about people related to the show.

Blossom

http://pmwww.cs.vu.nl/service/sitcoms/Blossom/

Unofficial Web page for this television comedy. Provides interviews with Mayim Bialik, Jenna Von Oy, episode guides to *Blossom*, and more.

The Bob Newhart Unofficial Homepage

http://www.mindspring.com/~i20west/bob.htm

This page is dedicated to all of Bob Newhart's shows from 1972–present, but concentrates mainly on *The Bob Newhart Show*, which lasted from 1972-1978. There are links to episode guides, broadcast listings, trivia, and other pieces of Newhart interest.

Bosom Buddies Home Page

http://www.ozemail.com.au/~peterv/bb/index.html

Remember Kip and Henry? They lived in an all-women's apartment complex and worked in an advertising agency. Well, anyway, this is their Web site, and it's very complete—there's an episode guide, reviews, sounds, and loads of other information about this show that helped start Tom Hanks's career. (No offense to Peter Scolari, of course.)

Boston Common

http://www.nbc.com/entertainment/shows/boston/

Boyd Pritchett is a Virginia handyman who ends up getting a job in the student union of his sister's college. Read more about the show, the characters, and the actors at this official NBC Web site.

Boy Meets World

http://www.tvplex.com/TVplex/Touchstone/BoyMeetsWorld/
BoyMeetsWorldG.html?GL=H

On for three seasons, this popular Friday night sitcom airs on ABC and stars Ben Savage as Cory

Matthews. This would be the thing to watch if you were in high school and didn't have the car. Oh, and if you weren't on the Web.

Café Nervosa

http://www-personal.umich.edu/~geena/frasier.html

This site is dedicated to the NBC comedy *Frasier*, starring Kelsey Grammer and Moose the dog (as Eddie). With the theme song, photos, and much more to come, this page is well worth seeing. It has some nice animated GIFs and other stuff that is, well, Frasier-riffic!

California Dreams

http://www.nbc.com/entertainment/shows/california/
index.html

California Dreams is to NBC's Saturday morning line-up what *Saved By The Bell* once was to, well, NBC's Saturday morning line-up. You can read about its stars and characters at this official site.

The Carol Burnett Show Episode Guide

http://www-personal.umich.edu/~mcgee/cbsguide.txt

Just what it says it is: a no-nonsense text file filled with information about the *Carol Burnett Show*, which aired from 1968–1979.

Caroline in the City

http://www.av.qnet.com/~melodyc/rcpage.htm

Perhaps destined for the same fate as the once popular show *Angie*, *Caroline in the City* now has a large following. This page chronicles her life and times, as well as her relationship (or lack thereof) with Richard. There are also some links to the Caroline mailing list.

Cheers Home Page

http://s9000.furman.edu/~treu/cheers.html

Online fan site of the TV show *Cheers*. Includes an archive of pictures, audio of famous Cheers quotes, information about every cast member, and the lyrics to Woody's classic "Kelly's Song."

Clueless

http://www.abctelevision.com/clueless.html

Based on the 1995 film, *Clueless* continues the adventures of Cher and her friends. At this page you can see a slide show from the program and download movies of the show.

C'mon, Get Happy!

http://www.geocities.com/Hollywood/5255/

This is the unofficial home page of the Partridge family. It has pictures, links, and other stuff relating to the show *The Partridge Family* and its original cast.

The Comedy Store Fan Club Home Page

http://www.macom.co.il/Channel2/ComedyStore/index.html

Next time you are in Israel, check out this popular Hebrew program. But if you can't make it there and are curious what happens on Israeli TV, you can access it from this fan club home page.

Common Law

http://www.abctelevision.com/comlaw.html

Part of ABC's new fall lineup for 1996–1997, *Common Law* stars Greg Giraldo as a Harvard-trained attorney. From what is present at the site, you can obtain a brief summary of the premise of the show and some scenes from the program.

The Critic

http://www.geocities.com/Hollywood/3894/index.html

Jay Sherman is a movie critic, but he always bashes what the general public loves. This site is truly complete with links to sound clips, a newsgroup, other links, an art gallery, an episode guide, and video clips.

Dinosaurs

http://www.sci.kun.nl/thalia/funpage/dinosaurs/
dinos_en.html

You can read this page in both English and Dutch, but what you'll get is basically the same content. It has pictures, cast member bios, a sound library, and more dino-oriented stuff.

Dr. Katz

http://home.dwave.net/~jscott/katz.html

Almost as neurotic as his patients, Dr. Katz sees a couple of stand-up comedians an episode. Oh yeah, he's a therapist. And a cartoon.

Dream On

http://www.mca.com/tv/dreamon/

The popular HBO adult sitcom has come to Comedy Central on cable TV. There are bios, credits, a forum, and more available for your perusal at this site.

Duckman!

http://bluejay.creighton.edu/~jduche/duckman.html

Tons of information about this crazy animated show. Check out random *Duckman!* quotes, synopses of each season, and graphics from the show. Great wallpaper!

Eerie, Indiana

http://www.imc.sfu.ca/eerie/

This strange, short-lived program has many fans, and this Web site was written by one of the most fanatic. It is very complete with links, credits, pictures, sounds, an episode guide, and a mailing list.

Encyclopedia Brady

http://www.primenet.com/~dbrady/

The Encyclopedia Brady is comprehensive in nature, filled with a FAQ, an episodes guide, links to other Brady sites, and a glossary. If you are addicted to Mike and Carol and Sam and Alice, you'll love this site.

The Facts of Life Unofficial Home Page

http://fly.hiwaay.net/~djberry/fol/fol.shtml

You take the good, you take the bad, you take some Netscape extensions… Anyway, this page is very complete with everything you probably forgot about this *Diff'rent Strokes* spin-off. Be warned, though, this page is graphics-heavy and formatted to the nines.

Family Ties

http://pmwww.cs.vu.nl/service/sitcoms/FamilyTies/

With pictures, the theme song, and other broadcast information, the *Family Ties* home page is where you'll find all the Keatons, except maybe Buster.

Fawlty Towers Episode Guide

http://www.cm.cf.ac.uk/Fun/FawltyTowers.html

Perfect for those PBS British comedy extravaganzas, the *Fawlty Towers* episode guide will give you a description of each episode, including what the sign outside says.

The Fresh Prince of Bel-Air

http://www.nbc.com/entertainment/shows/prince/index.html

This is the official site of the popular Will Smith program. It has a schedule, bios, and synopses of the show.

Friends

http://www.nbc.com/entertainment/shows/friends/index.html

The official *Friends* home page. Click on your favorite character to see a bio of the actor.

Full House

http://home.sn.no/home/edinb/fh/fhpage.htm

This is THE *Full House* site. Here you'll find everything you wanted to know about this ABC comedy, but were afraid to ask, including pictures, sound clips, links, articles, bios, and a complete episode guide.

Get a Life Program Guide

http://math-www.uio.no/faq/tv/program-guides/get-a-life.html

This site simply hosts the *Get a Life* Program Guide. Did you know that .0017 people each year die from tonsillectomies?

The Get Smart Home Page

http://www.bcpl.lib.md.us/~cbirkmey/getsmart.html

This site is devoted to Maxwell Smart and all his buddies at Control. This site disseminates all sorts of information, including cast lists, episode guides, and other Smart-related info.

Gilligan's Island

http://www.lookup.com/homepages/58181/homea.html

This site has daily quizzes, a free *Gilligan's Island* information package, and a three hour tour. There is also information about every character present on the show. Did you know that Mrs. Howell's name was actually Eunice?

The Golden Girls

http://www.innotts.co.uk/~kburton/gg/

The show with Bea Arthur, Rue McClanahan, Betty White, and Estelle Getty finds its home at this site. There are character bios, the title song, and a book of scripts located here.

Grace Under Fire

http://pmwww.cs.vu.nl/service/sitcoms/GraceUnderFire/

Information about Brett Butler's popular ABC sitcom can be found here. There are movies, sounds, an episode guide, and links to other *Grace Under Fire* resources here.

Growing Pains

http://pmwww.cs.vu.nl/service/sitcoms/GrowingPains/

Remember the Seavers? They're here in all of their Kirk Cameron and Alan Thicke glory. You'll find broadcast schedules around the world, the theme song, and other information concerning this '80s TV show at this site.

The Hangin' with Mr. Cooper Home Page

http://www.geocities.com/Hollywood/2984/cooper.html

The unofficial home of Mark Curry and Raven-Symoné's popular program is here. This site is truly complete with pictures, sounds, and anything else you wanted concerning *Hangin' with Mr. Cooper*.

Herman's Head

http://pmwww.cs.vu.nl/service/sitcoms/HermansHead/

Now in international syndication, *Herman's Head* is a Freudian dream. There is plenty of information here concerning the show that gave insight into a man, his life, and (most importantly) his head.

Hogan's Heroes

http://kirk.microsys.net/personal/franklin/hogan.htm

As if World War II was any fun at all, this program gave a "wacky" view of being a POW in wartime Germany. What you'll find here is a storehouse of Hogan information, like program guides, sounds, pictures, and the like about this '60s program that has recently found popularity in, of all places, Germany.

Home of Home Improvement Cyberfans

http://www.morepower.com/homeimpr.html

More information than you probably ever wanted about Tim Allen, Tool Time, or that hunky Jonathan Taylor Thomas. This page has won all kinds of awards and is worth seeing even if just out of respect for the sheer amount of time taken to create it.

The Honeymooners Picture Depot

http://www.intercall.com/~python/honymoon/honymoon.htm

This page has information about Jackie Gleason, Art Carney, and Joyce Randolph, as well as the popular '50s TV show, *The Honeymooners*.

Hudson Street Home Page

http://www.spe.sony.com/Pictures/tv/hudson/hudson.html

Tony Danza has yet another TV show on which he is called Tony. This time, it's called *Hudson Street*. This site has video clips, audio clips, and even shots from the set.

The Indispensable I Dream of Jeannie Page

http://www.pi.net/~ahijdra/home.html

This page is written by a computer programmer and big Jeannie fan. This site has tons of information, as well as pictures, sounds, and nicely animated GIFs. The author is also currently working on a "Jeannie Adventure" game, which promises to have a virtual representation of Major Nelson's house. You can't tell this guy to get a hobby.

The John Larroquette Show

http://www.nbc.com/entertainment/shows/larroquette/index.html

The John Laroquette Show is about a recovering alcoholic in St. Louis. His adventures are usually quite strange—everything is just a little bit absurd. That may explain his character's love of Samuel Beckett.

Kids In the Hall by Jeff

http://siksik.learnnet.nt.ca/yk1/sjf/JeffK/Kids.html

This site features pictures of the cast and other strangeness. It has everything you would want from a *Kids in the Hall* page, including links to other *Kids in the Hall* pages.

The Larry Sanders Show

http://pmwww.cs.vu.nl/service/sitcoms/LarrySanders/

Originally aired on HBO, *The Larry Sanders Show* stars Garry Shandling as a talk show host (in the Johnny Carson vein) named, appropriately enough, Larry Sanders. This site gives episode guides, links, and other information about the show.

Mad About You

http://hubcap.clemson.edu/~rwsloan/may.html

This is the site for the complete *Mad About You* fan. It has links to a photo gallery, an episode guide, the *Mad About You* newsgroup, merchandise, and other sites related to the program.

The Mad TV Home Page

http://gilmour.pvt.k12.oh.us/~zobera/madhome.htm

This is the home page for the skit comedy show that brought us skits like "The Triple X Files" and "Apollo the 13th: Jason Takes NASA." Of course, there are pictures and other information available here.

Mama's Family

http://ourworld.compuserve.com/homepages/MFREIER/mamas.htm

The official unofficial *Mama's Family* site, complete with an episode guide, quotes, cast information, and other links.

Maniac Mansion

http://alcor.concordia.ca/~vipond/maniac.htm

From the show starring Joe Flaherty as Fred Edison, this home page is dedicated to what many believe to be the "funniest television program in history." Of course, those people are probably Canadian.

Married...With Children Home Page

http://inet.uni-c.dk/~pegasus1/index.html

If you were looking for information or links for *Married…With Children*, this is the place to go. It has episode guides, pictures, and the coveted Bundybase.

MASH Archives

http://www.best.com/~dijon/tv/mash/index.html

This *MASH* TV show site includes cast photos, the opening theme, a FAQ, and more.

Mel Loves I Love Lucy

http://www-bcf.usc.edu/~msoriano/ill/

This page has tons of *I Love Lucy* info and pictures, as well as links to other Lucy sites.

Mook's the Simpsons Page

http://alpha1.curtin.edu.au/~emerrick/Simpsons.html

This fun site includes sound clips and a multimedia section with images and videos. Check out the links to other Simpsons pages.

Moon Over Parma

http://www.geocities.com/Hollywood/6663/parma.htm

A tribute to *The Drew Carrey Show*, Moon Over Parma is very complete. It has an episode guide, pictures, bios, and links to other Drew Carey-oriented Net sites.

Moonlighting, on the Web

http://www.ici.net/cust_pages/ddemelo/moonlighting.html

The show that launched Bruce Willis's career and revived Cybill Shepherd's finds a great fan page here. There are links to background information, an episode guide, related pages, and even an IRC chat channel.

Murphy Brown

http://pmwww.cs.vu.nl/service/sitcoms/MurphyBrown/

This site boasts broadcast schedules, episode guides, and pictures from the program.

My So-Called Life

http://www.umn.edu/nlhome/g564/lask0008/mscl.html

Official site for the TV show about teenagers and high school. Includes cast info, images, scripts, video and audio downloads, and pleas to keep the show on the air.

The Nanny Unofficial Home Page

http://www.perfect.com/nanny.html

This site has FAQs, an episode guide, links, pictures, and cast references about the popular CBS show *The Nanny*. It also has sound bites, but who would want Fran Drescher's voice on their SoundBlaster card?

The Ned and Stacey Home Page

http://www.spe.sony.com/Pictures/tv/ned/ned.html

Ned and Stacey is a strange show starring Thomas Hayden Church (who played Lowell on *Wings*). Visit this site to find out more background information or to download sound clips, pictures, and other tidbits about this Fox comedy.

The New Web Site of Love Mystery Science Theatre 3000

http://www.usgcc.odu.edu/~ty/mst3k/MST3K.html

Find out the latest on *MST3K's* move from Comedy

CD-ROMs

http://www.west.net/~cdromug/freecds.shtml

If you're a CD-ROM user, this site will put a smile on your face. Provides a giant list of free promotional CD-ROM offers (for PCs only).

Central and their film. This site also includes episode guides, FAQs, and ratings of each show.

The NewsRadio Station

http://shaflik.com/shaflik/newsradio/

NewsRadio stars David Foley from *Kids in the Hall* and Phil Hartman from *Saturday Night Live*. This site has an episode guide, cast info, sounds, and other links, including the infamous "Jimmy's List."

The Official Unofficial Seinfeld Page

http://wagga.tpgi.com.au/~summer96/grahamm.htm

Includes tons of pix, FAQs, episode guides, sounds, and bio info on the Seinfeld show and its characters. A licensing attorney's nightmare!

Parker Lewis Can't Lose

http://www.geo.mtu.edu/flamingo/

Digests, archives, and the whos, whats, whens, and wheres of the short-lived cult-followed Fox television program.

The Red Green Show

http://www.redgreen.com/

This is the official site of the new *Red Green Show*. There are bios, an episode guide, a comment board, and merchandise information located here. Visit the Possom Lodge if you dare.

The R.M.P.S.S.

http://ugWeb.cs.ualberta.ca/~stuart/monty.cgi/

Every time you access this site, a different Monty Python sketch appears. You can also choose to see any of dozens of Monty Python TV and movie skits.

Roseanne

http://pmwww.cs.vu.nl/service/sitcoms/Roseanne/

Strangely, the only Rosanne fan pages that we could find were either this one, located in the Netherlands, and one in Germany. Wonder if that says anything about her popularity in the States? Anyway, you can find broadcast schedules, pictures, sounds, and episode guides at this site.

Saturday Night Archives

http://www.best.com:80/~dijon/tv/snl/

A number of FAQs on characters, parodies, song lyrics, Wayne's World, band information, and more are provided at this site. This site also includes a monthly schedule of SNL, links to Web sites of

former cast members, and of course the Deep Thought of the Day.

Saved By The Bell

http://pages.prodigy.com/90210/sbtb.htm

If you like Zach, Screech, and the rest of the rowdy bunch on *Saved By The Bell* or *Saved By The Bell: The College Years*, you'll love this site.

The Simpsons Source

http://bird.taponline.com/~simpsons/

Pictures, sounds, movies, articles, whatever you can think of concerning the Simpsons, you'll find it here. The only thing that leaves one wondering is how did the author of this site find a place to put the megs and megs of files used to create this page?

The Single Guy ("How about something simple, like...")

http://camel.conncoll.edu/ccother/sf.folder/single/index.html

Here is where you can hang out in "The Bachelor Pad" to download pictures, news, and information about the NBC sitcom starring Jonathan Silverman.

Sledge Hammer! Arsenal

http://www.phrank.com/sh/

Remember David Rasche? Remember when comedy was wacky? Alright, maybe that's a bit too cheesy, but if you remember this show, you'll be glad to know that there is now a place to get sounds, pictures, and information about this short-lived ABC sitcom.

Spin City

http://www.abctelevision.com/spin.html

A new comedy starring Michael J. Fox, *Spin City* is about the deputy mayor of New York. This site gives you information, a slide show, and a RealAudio clip about this new comedy.

The State's Virtual Whatever...

http://www.thstate.com/

The State comedy troupe has now set up a Web site with e-mail links to each of the members and information about what they are all now doing. Originally brought to TV by MTV, The State has a new show on Comedy Central.

Sup's Blackadder Page

http://www.people.memphis.edu/~jgwright/bladder.htm

The British comedy starring Rowan Atkinson as Blackadder has a very well-done fan page here. This site hosts many sounds, an interview, and other links related to Rowan Atkinson, *Blackadder*, and British comedy.

Third Page from the Official

http://www.nexusprime.org/personal/algermissen/3rdRock/index.html

Although this site is very bandwidth-heavy, it is worth checking out. There are sounds, character bios and quotes, and other information about this popular new show.

Townies

http://www.abctelevision.com/townies.html

This is a new show on ABC starring Molly Ringwald. This Web site has information about the program, QuickTime movies, and RealAudio clips from the show.

TV Nation

http://www.spe.sony.com/Pictures/tv/tvnation/tvnation.html

Michael Moore's brilliant TV show mixing serious issues with comical reporting is now off the air, but his home page remains. Check this home page out if you miss it.

Welcome Back, Kotter

http://village.ios.com/~horshack/kotter.html

Pictures and information about Vinny Barbarino, Freddie "Boom-Boom" Washington, Mr. Kotter, and the rest of the Sweathogs can be found at this site written by a guy who calls himself Horshack.

Whose Line Is It Anyway?

http://www.geocities.com/WestHollywood/1770/wliia.html

Read about this improvisational game show, which has aired since 1988 in England. You can find the show on Comedy Central and read more about the rules and stars. Be sure to read about the Drinking Game!

Wings

http://expert.cc.purdue.edu/~c88dink/Frames.htm

A beautifully formatted page, this site gives information about characters, actors, scenes, and sounds from this NBC comedy.

The Wonder Years

http://www.sfc.keio.ac.jp/~t93272at/wonder.html

A site for the complete *Wonder Years* fan. This page contains loads of information about Kevin Arnold and his entourage. Join the mailing list, read the articles, but most of all, enjoy the site.

Dramas

Chicago Hope Home Page

http://www-cs-students.stanford.edu/~clee/chicagohope.html

The *Chicago Hope* Home Page is based on the CBS drama that centers around a hospital and its doctors. This site is filled with pictures, FAQs, and episode guides, as well as other information about this popular show.

Dangerous Minds

http://www.abctelevision.com/dangerous.html

Based on the movie from the autumn of 1995, this show is about an ex-marine who goes to bat for her students. You can view it on ABC, and you can get information about the program at this site.

Dead At 21

http://www.uaep.co.uk/pages/deadep1.html

A strange MTV drama about a man who discovers that he was part of a government bioengineering experiment and is set to die at age 21. This page hosts the episode guide and some stills from the film.

The Dr. Quinn, Medicine Woman Official Web Site

http://www.DrQuinn.com/

Chat rooms at the Saloon, documents at the Library, merchandise at the Mercantile shop, and Dr. Quinn's office are available to check out at this site.

ER

http://www.nbc.com/entertainment/shows/er/index.html

This show is wildly popular on Thursday nights. It stars Anthony Edwards, George Clooney, Eriq La Salle, and Sherry Stringfield as doctors at County General Memorial Hospital. Written by Michael Crichton, this show takes place in Chicago. And, of course, you can read all about it at this site on the Web.

The Little House on the Prairie Unofficial Home Page

http://www.angelfire.com/pages1/LittlHouse/index.html

A well-formatted site that utilizes Netscape extensions to make itself look like it is supposed to. There is information about the popular program here, including mailing lists, schedules, and character information.

A Random Quote from Northern Exposure

Here's a classic dialog among Shelly, Holling, and Chris that you can find at The Moose's Guide to Northern Exposure site:

Do you take me for your lawfully wedded squeeze?

Yes I do, certainly, most assuredly.

Me too. Chris, put a knot on it.

By the power vested in me, I now pronounce you legal.

Can I kiss the bride?

Yep.

Oh! We'll suck face later, babe. Right now, I've got to check something out.

The Moose's Guide to Northern Exposure

http://www.netspace.org/~moose/moose.html

Online guide to *Northern Exposure*. Includes graphics, sound bites, FAQs, episode guides, rerun schedules, and a lengthy bibliography.

My So-Called Life

http://www.tc.umn.edu/nlhome/g564/lask0008/mscl.html

Information, multimedia, feedback, images, scripts, and links are present at this page. This show that had a strange air-life can sometimes be caught now on MTV, but there is no real rhyme or reason to when they show it—just like being a teenager.

NYPD Blue Home Page

http://src.doc.ic.ac.uk/public/media/tv/collections/tardis/us/drama/NYPDBlue/index.html

Includes detailed info for each episode and text files on the cast, characters, the NYPD drinking game, and several FAQs.

Party of Five

http://www.csua.berkeley.edu/~byron/PartyOf5/

Fan page for the Fox TV show, *Party of Five*, including an episode guide, a FAQ about the show, recent publicity, and links to other fan sites.

The Perry Mason Pages

http://www.ozemail.com.au/~jsimko/

This unofficial Perry Mason home page features links and suggested readings to all things Perry Mason. Don't forget to check out the episode guides to find out which case Perry lost.

The Real World

http://www.grrl.com/real.html

The *Real World*'s unofficial Web site is for "all the folks out there who enjoy watching a group of young people whine, cry, bitch, laugh, talk, and share their constant confessions." There is a FAQ, episode guide, and other stuff for the *Real World* fanatic.

The thirtysomething Episode Guide

http://duplox.wz-berlin.de/people/oswald/30/guide.ascii

This is the printable episode guide for the *thirtysomething* fan. Perhaps you forgot what exactly happened in an episode, or you were wanting a reference by which to write a drinking game. Here, you've found it.

The Twin Peaks Lodge

http://www.sci.fi/~mike*/tp/tplodge.html

A fan page for the bizarre television show from David Lynch—*Twin Peaks*. Includes links to the David Lynch filmography, information on each major *Twin Peaks* actor, a *Twin Peaks* FAQ, and actor list. Click on the Black Lodge for bizarre, interesting info on the *Twin Peaks* time line and random quote generator.

The Unofficial Picket Fences Home Page

`http://www.lewis.edu/fences/fences.html`

At this site you'll find information about the show starring Tom Skerritt as the sheriff of a small town. There is a FAQ, cast photos and info, links, and sounds from this popular CBS drama.

Educational

Bill Nye the Science Guy's Nye Labs Online

`http://nyelabs.kcts.org/`

One of the hippest geeks on television, Bill Nye is from Seattle and sometimes has the guests to prove it. Entertaining as well as educational, *Bill Nye the Science Guy*'s Web site has listings, a search mechanism, and other goodies.

Biography

`http://www.biography.com/`

A Web site based on the A&E program of the same name, Biography has a 15,000 person search engine, quizzes and games, and chapters from written biographies of important people. You can also get VDO clips and a calendar of upcoming programs.

Building America—Eye On Business

`http://www.batv.com/ba.html`

A program that looks at how local companies are driving America's regional economies. You can download a video clip or read about companies, regions, or opinions of the program.

Collecting Across America

`http://www.collectin.com/`

A program airing on Public Television, *Collecting Across America* spotlights what you'd think it would—collectors and the things they hoarde. If you'd like to be on the show or have a suggestion, there is a reply form where you can voice your opinions.

CTN

`http://www.phoenix.net/USERS/ace/ctn.html`

Producers of the TV show *Computer Workshop*, a show about business and personal computing. Includes general info, a contact list, and program information.

The Doctor Is In

`http://www.dartmouth.edu/~drisin/`

Shown on PBS, the *Doctor Is In* has links to letters, awards, reviews, and dossiers of the production team. Also, every show from the program is featured with a link to a quick description and videotape purchase information.

Great Canadian Parks

`http://www.interlog.com/~parks/`

Great Canadian Parks is shown Tuesdays on the Discovery Channel. It "explores the diverse natural and human histories within one of the most comprehensive parks systems in the world." A different park is showcased every week.

The Joy of Painting with Bob Ross

`http://bobross.com/`

Bob Ross's legacy of painting for the common person lives on at this, the official *Joy of Painting* Web site. If you like happy trees, you'll love this site!

Newton's Apple

`http://ericir.syr.edu/Projects/Newton/`

Newton's Apple is a program shown on PBS affiliates around the nation. Each show has a particular theme and has guests who explain certain scientific concepts.

No Dogs or Philosophers Allowed

`http://www.access.digex.net/~kknisely/philosophy.tv.html`

Although it has a tricky title, this program is a philosophy program and is available only in a limited area. Check the site out even if you haven't seen it, though—you might like it enough to beg your cable company to get it.

Where in the World Is Carmen Sandiego?

http://www.boston.com/wgbh/pages/carmensandiego/
carmenhome.html

The popular geography computer game has gone from the computer to the television screen and back to the computer via the World Wide Web. Based at Boston's public television station, WGBH, this site has many links for students, teachers, and others who enjoy the game and the program.

News

The C-Span Networks

http://www.c-span.org/

See what's playing today on C-Span. Includes info on Congress Today, daily live video of congress, C-SPAN in the Classroom, and Campaign '96. Check out the RealAudio section with sound clips from the President and others.

CNN Newsroom

http://www.nmis.org/NewsInteractive/CNN/Newsroom/
contents.html

CNN goes online with up-to-the-minute news. Click on the day you're interested in to see videos on current stories. Take the pop quiz to see how current you are on the news.

Science Fiction & Fantasy

Babylon 5 file Area

http://www.hyperion.com/b5/

Includes FAQs, Usenet groups, pictures, quotes, episode synopses, actors' lists, show history, and interviews with the show's creator.

Battlestar Galactica

http://mcmfh.acns.carleton.edu/BG//

Includes archives with FAQs, reviews of the show, and program guides. The Gallery and Sound Bytes areas include great images and sound clips from the show. Check out the Software area for fonts used on the show; the Future pointer includes information on reviving this successful TV series.

Broadsword

http://modjadji.anu.edu.au/steve/broadsword

The Web page for *Doctor Who, the New and Missing Adventures*. This e-zine Web site includes interviews with actors, a writer's guide, articles on the missing adventures, and a list of books published about *Doctor Who*. Don't click on New Adventures if you don't want to know what happens in these stories.

Dark Shadows

http://members.aol.com/darkkshad/super/natural.htm

Premiering in 1966 on ABC television, this show was a soap opera based on ghouls, goblins, vampires, and the like. There are storylines, photo galleries, fan fictions, and other points of interest for Dark Shadows' fans at this Web site.

The Dominion Sci-fi Channe

http://www.scifi.com/

Click on Table of Contents to see the wealth of info at this site. The Free Zone includes audio clips, images, and video clips. Be sure to check out Sci-fi Live, a CU-SeeMe area that contains live video on the Internet. Nicely designed site.

The Extraterrestrial Biological Entity (EBE) Page

http://sloop.ee.fit.edu/users/lpinto/index.html

Haven't kept up on the latest abduction stories and Area 51 sightings? Catch up by reading about Crop Circles, UFO Sightings, Area 51, and the latest Roswell news. A search engine is provided for finding exactly the info you need.

Forever Knight

http://www.spe.sony.com/Pictures/tv/forever/forever.html

This program chronicles the life of Nick Knight. He is a vampire from the 13th century living in a modern metropolis. He wishes to once again enter the mortal world and end the pain of bloodlust, while keeping his enemies at bay. At this site, you'll find screen savers and other goodies available for download.

Hyperlight Enterprises

http://www.iceonline.com/home/roxanneb/www/
hyperlight.html

Retailer of *X-Files*, *Star Trek*, and *Star Wars* collectibles and clothing. Click on an item of interest in their product line to see what is in stock. Offers many science fiction and fantasy products, including card games and autographs.

Lurker's Guide to Babylon 5

`http://www.hyperion.com/lurk/lurker.html`

Nice site provides information on the show. Watch out for spoilers if you haven't watched a show yet. Includes info on the making of the show, its cast and characters, images of the amazing special effects, and episode information.

Planet X

`http://www.microserve.net/PlanetX/`

A virtual community for science fiction fanatics. If you join (it's free), you will be a member of their mailing lists, which are devoted to everything science fiction. This site also includes a note board, Planet X events info, a survey, and a photo album.

Sliders

`http://www.xtc.net/~lucast/sliders/sliders.html`

Up-to-date information on the Fox television show, *Sliders*. Description of the latest episodes, a *Sliders* photo gallery, and WAVs of the intro to episodes are included. Includes links to other *Sliders* sites.

Songs of the Blue Bird

`http://www.iquest.net/~jeneric/songs.html`

A virtual zine and news source for fans of the CBS television drama *Beauty and the Beast*. Includes unaired scripts, images and paintings by fans, back issue catalogs, and information about conventions for this cult TV show.

Starship Portfolio

`http://www.mag-net.co.uk/Starship/`

Examine, then order one of five prints of the Star Trek Enterprise (old and new). These paintings were commissioned by English artist G. W. Hutchins.

Starship Store

`http://www.halcyon.com/uncomyn/startrek.html`

Includes collectors items, memorabilia, and clothing of every *Star Trek* series. Order T-shirts of your favorite characters, key chains, toys, and other items.

Tales from the Crypt

`http://www.cryptnet.com/`

A huge site from the dungeons that are *Tales from the Crypt*. You can check out the Laboratory, the Vault, the Episode Graveyard, the Screaming Room, and the Cryptique.

Terminal X

`http://www.neosoft.com/sbanks/xfiles/xfiles.html`

Click on multimedia to download the theme song (WAV or RealAudio), images and video clips, and audio clips. This section also includes links to the IRS, CIA, and of course the FBI. Be sure to check the Episode Guide for news on each show. A must see are the bloopers.

Trader 800 Trekker

`http://www.scifi.com/trader/trekker/trekker.html`

Part of the Sci-Fi Channel Web site. The Trader includes collectibles you can purchase about the *X-Files*, *Star Wars*, *Star Trek*, *Doctor Who*, and *Babylon 5*. Click on the show you're interested in to see what merchandise is available.

CD-ROM and Screen Saver

`http://pentium.intel.com/comm-net/sns/offers/tflcd.htm`

Find out what's going on in LANtropolis with Intel's free CD-ROM and screen saver.

Trek Reviews Archive

http://www.mcs.net/~forbes/trek-reviews/

This nicely designed Web site for the rec.arts.startrek.reviews Usenet group includes an archive of reviews of every *Star Trek* show and episode by season, movie and book reviews, and links to other *Star Trek* Web pages.

Soap Operas

All My Children

http://purplenet.com/soaps/AllMyChildren.html

Read about the show, its characters, and the story-line of this successful soap opera. Includes a current cast list and family tree, FAQs about the show, and humor in the press.

The Another World Fan Club Official Home Page

http://members.aol.com/jensfan/awfc.html

There is loads of information about the popular NBC daytime soap opera here. Cast photos, luncheon schedules, and gossip are plentiful for the perusing.

As the World Turns

http://www.cbs.com/daytime/atwt/

The official site boasts set shots, links, family trees, star bios, and polls. And, if you wish to write to *As the World Turns*, there is a place to write your message.

The Bold and the Beautiful

http://www.cbs.com/daytime/bb/

The *Bold and the Beautiful*'s official home page on the Web. You can take a *Bold and the Beautiful* poll, send e-mail, check out fan club info, and get a sneak preview of what's coming up on the show.

Days of Our Lives Page

http://Weber.u.washington.edu/~pfloyd/days/index.html

Complete online information site for the soap opera *Days of Our Lives*. Includes a list and photos of the cast, a chat area, and a place to exchange videos.

General Hospital

http://www.cts.com/~jeffmj/

Provides daily updates for fans of the daytime drama *General Hospital*. Check out the Message Exchange, Cast News, Top Ten lists, and Calendar of Events for the latest on the show. This site also includes fan club, cast birthday, and filmography info. You can even read about shows that haven't aired yet. Everything imaginable!

Guiding Light

http://server.berkeley.edu/soaps/gl/update.html

If you missed today's show, you can check out this *Guiding Light* home page to get the low-down on what happened. You can also peruse the archives for a past program.

One Life To Live: The History Page

http://www.bowdoin.edu/~sbodurt2/oltl/

Filled with story lines, histories, family trees, and whatever else you might like to know about this long-running ABC soap opera, this site will make you feel at home.

Soap Opera Pen Pal Page

http://www.angelfire.com/pages2/OLTL/index.html

Looking for someone to write to who might have the same interests? Want to talk about your favorite soaps with someone who will understand? You can find someone here! Whether you want to use e-mail or conventional mail, it's as simple as filling out a form.

The Young and the Restless

http://www.weicomp.com/php.cgi/yr/index.htm

This site is a veritable warehouse of information on the popular and long-lasting soap opera. You can read recaps, spoilers, and just about anything else you want to know about this show.

Talk Shows

alt.fan.howard-stern

news://alt.fan.howard-stern

The newsgroup for fans of the ultra-abrasive television and radio man, Howard Stern. If you have something to say about this self-proclaimed "King of All Media," here's where you can.

alt.tv.talkshows.daytime

news://alt.tv.talkshows.daytime

Check out this Usenet newsgroup for all the gossip and information that was on any of the daytime talk shows.

alt.tv.talkshows.late

news://alt.tv.talkshows.late

If you want to talk about Dave's hair, Jay's chin, or Conan's baby-face, you'll want to do it here. This is where you can make your mark on late night TV.

Andy Richter: King of the Couch

http://www.well.com/user/xkot/andy.htm

Fans of Andy Richter know he's not just another sidekick gathering moss. Includes pictures and biographical information.

Canned Hams Anyone?

Remember this classic line from the most powerful man in television? Check out other monologue moments at the David Letterman home page.

"Congratulations to American Astronaut Shannon Lucid, she now holds the record for most time in space, more than any other American. Of course, the old record was held by Jerry Garcia. You know it's really quite an accomplishment when you think about it. The only other woman who has spent that much time in a state of weightlessness was Kate Moss."

David Letterman

http://www.cbs.com/lateshow/lateshow.html

Find out who will be on the show each day and check out the latest Top Ten list at this official site for *Late Show with David Letterman*.

The Ed Sullivan Show

http://www.edsullivan.com/

Ed Sullivan is the man that they all learned it from; Johnny Carson, David Letterman, Jay Leno, and Conan O'Brien would all have to bow their heads to this man. Now he has a home on the Web. You can order tapes, read bios, and visit the Ed Sullivan store, if you'd like.

FAQ—alt.tv.talkshows.late

http://www.cis.ohio-state.edu/hypertext/faq/usenet-faqs/ bygroup/alt/tv/talkshows/late/top.html

Read this FAQ if you want to get really involved in the discussions happening on alt.tv.talkshows.late.

The George and Alana Show Home Page

http://www.rysher.com/tv/george/index.html

This morning talk show starring divorcées (from each other) George Hamilton and Alana Stewart is one of the hottest new daily talk shows. You can read all about it here.

Hereeeeeeeeeeee's Conan

http://styx.ios.com/~damone/gconan.html

Late Night With Conan O'Brien is a strange beast. As this page says: "Born in pathetic confusion, treated like an illegitimate, idiot son, and ignored by millions, [this show] is the best thing going on late night talk shows." Well, whether or not that is true, it was Dave's time slot once. Check out this page for loads of information and pictures from this red-headed step-child of a talk show.

The Late Late Show with Tom Snyder

http://www.cbs.com/snyder/

This is the official World Wide Web home of Tom Snyder's *Late Late Show*. You can write him via e-mail from here, read about upcoming guests, and find out other information about this veteran talk show host.

Later with Greg Kinnear

http://www.nbc.com/entertainment/shows/later/

This well-designed Web site has quotes, a photo gallery, biography, and plenty of other information about Greg and his program.

Lauren Hutton

http://www.turner.com/laurenhutton/

This is the home page for the show called *Lauren Hutton and…* You will find show overviews, a library, and links to find where the show is playing in your hometown.

The Oprah Winfrey Show

http://www.finearts.yorku.ca/jstockman/museum/Oprah.html

This is the home of one of the most widely syndicated programs in television. Available in Afghanistan, Bhutan, Chad, and other out-of-the-way places, this show has a history of presenting people's lives to the world every day. Pictures, an Oprah exhibit, and information about this long-time #1 show are available at this Web site.

The Politically Incorrect Unofficial Home Page

http://www.nbtw.com/pi/

Bill Maher is the host of this popular Comedy Central panel discussion show. This page is filled with information about him, this show, and other bits of Politically Incorrect Trivia.

The Richard Bey Show

http://www.richardbey.com/

Richard Bey's "less talk and more action" talk show goes hand-in-hand with this, the official Web site. Take a few minutes to browse around these pages, you'll find out everything you wanted to know about Richard Bey and his talk show.

The Ricki Lake Show Home Page

http://www.spe.sony.com/Pictures/tv/rickilake/ricki.html

This is the official Ricki Lake home page with audio clips, video and still pictures, and a behind-the-scenes set opportunity.

Rolonda

http://www.kingworld.com/rolonda/index.html

Rolanda Watts' talk show has been on for several seasons, and seems like it will stay around. You can visit this Web site to read about its history, Rolanda's biography, or submit show topic ideas.

The Rosie O'Donnell Show

http://www.rosieo.com/

Updated daily, this site has scheduled guests for today and tomorrow, show descriptions, and a list of where you can catch the show.

Sony Pictures Before They Were Stars

http://www.spe.sony.com/Pictures/tv/before/before.html

Includes information on the television show hosted by Scott Baio. You can also access other Sony TV shows from this page, or return to the Sony TV home page. Includes pictures of television and movie stars before they were famous.

Tempestt

http://www.spe.sony.com/Pictures/tv/tempestt/tempestt.html

You might remember Tempestt Bledsoe from the *Cosby Show*. Well, now she's grown up, has her own talk show, and people are talking about her on the Web. This is her official home page, and you can download sounds, pictures, and other Tempestt goodies.

The Tonight Show with Jay Leno

http://www.nbc.com/entertainment/shows/tonight/index.html

This show and time slot has been the traditional late night talk show place to be. Jay Leno is the host, and you can find sounds, pictures, and other information about the cornerstone of the NBC late night lineup.

The Unofficial Talk Soup Web Page

http://home.ptd.net/~mstill/talksoup/index.htm

Mostly filled with sound clips, there are also pictures available at this site dedicated to E! Entertainment Television's *Talk Soup*.

Television Resources

All TVs Center

http://www.netcenter.com/netcentr/entertain/tv.html

Includes links to every cable channel, popular TV show, and TV network on the Web. Click on a channel or show and go directly to the site.

Columbia Music Video Resources

`http://www.sony.com/Music/VideoStuff/vidfaq.htm`

Find out if an alternative to MTV and VH-1 exists in your town. This page includes a list of hundreds of public access and cable shows for music videos.

Comedy Central

`http://www.comcentral.com/`

The home to many popular comedy shows, there is a download area with QuickTime movies available to fill up that annoying extra space you may have on your hard drive.

NBC

`http://www.nbc.com/`

NBC's home page. Daily updates let you access ground breaking news stories and weather. This site also includes CNBC and sports information. If you like late night TV, be sure to check out Conan O'Brien's Web page.

PBS Online

`http://www.pbs.org/Welcome.html`

This home page for the Public Broadcasting System includes the latest shows on PBS, classroom resources, an inside look at the corporation, and the PBS store.

Tooncers Web Page Fantasmic

`http://www.mind.net/worksj`

A crazy site that's the home of the Internet Cola Page, the "Unofficial" WWIV Web server (a collection of software for Telnetting to BBSs from the Web), and the Toon Town BBS, a collection of animation from cartoons. This site also provides real time animation and cartoons. Fun!

TV5

`http://www.tv5.ca/eng_tv5.html`

This worldwide French language channel Web site includes a global satellite map, technical data on the station, a Life in America special, and information on learning French on TV5.

The Ultimate TV List

`http://www.tvnet.com/UTVL/utvl.html`

Describes over 745 TV shows in every genre imaginable. You can find what you're looking for a number of ways: search using the search engine, click on a letter to find an alphabetical list, or choose a genre such as Science Fiction or Comedy. This site also includes pointers to TV-related newsgroups and Web sites.

Vanderbilt Television News Archive

`http://tvnews.vanderbilt.edu/`

This site may not be pretty, but it includes abstracts of every nightly news broadcast on the big three networks since 1968! See what happened on a particular date over the past 25 years. Be sure to visit the Special Reports and Specialized News Collections areas for news on major events, such as the Persian Gulf War.

Welcome to the BBC

`http://www.bbc.co.uk/`

The British Broadcasting Corporation on the Web includes pointers to BBC Radio, BBC TV, BBC Internet, BBC Education, and more.

Newsgroups

alt.binaries.sounds.tv.

alt.cable-tv.re-regulate

alt.fan.actors!

alt.fan.actors.dead!

alt.fan.addams.family!

alt.fan.alicia-slvrstone!

alt.fan.another.world!

alt.fan.bill-nye!

alt.fan.bill.nye.the.science.guy!

alt.fan.chris-elliott!

alt.fan.conan-obrien!

alt.fan.dennis-miller!

alt.fan.disney.afternoon!

alt.fan.greg-kinnear!

alt.fan.hawaii-five-o!

alt.fan.heather-locklear!

alt.fan.jay-leno!

alt.fan.jon-stewart!

alt.fan.letterman!

alt.fan.letterman.guests.female!

alt.fan.letterman.top-ten!

alt.fan.mandy-patinkin!

alt.fan.marcia-clark!

alt.fan.monty-python!

alt.fan.pam-anderson!

alt.fan.penn-n-teller!

alt.fan.ren-and-stimpy!

alt.fan.rush-limbaugh.tv-show

alt.fan.wings!

alt.radio.networks.cbc

alt.radio.networks.npr

alt.radio.online-tonight

alt.satellite.tv.australasia

alt.satellite.tv.europe

alt.tv.90210!

alt.tv.absolutely_fabulous!

alt.tv.air-farce!

alt.tv.amer-gothic!

alt.tv.animaniacs!

alt.tv.babylon-5!

alt.tv.barney!

alt.tv.beakmans-world!

alt.tv.beavis-n-butthead!

alt.tv.bill.nye!

alt.tv.brady-bunch!

alt.tv.brisco-county!

alt.tv.casper!

alt.tv.chicago-hope!

```
alt.tv.christy!
alt.tv.comedy-central!
alt.tv.commercials!
alt.tv.dark_shadows!
alt.tv.discovery!
alt.tv.duckman!
alt.tv.due-south!
alt.tv.dweebs!
alt.tv.earth2!
alt.tv.eek-the-cat!
alt.tv.er!
alt.tv.fifteen!
alt.tv.forever-knight!
alt.tv.frasier!
alt.tv.friends!
alt.tv.game-shows!
alt.tv.hermans-head!
alt.tv.highlander!
alt.tv.home-imprvment!
alt.tv.homicide!
alt.tv.infomercials!
alt.tv.kids-in-hall!
alt.tv.knight-rider!
alt.tv.kungfu!
alt.tv.la-law!
alt.tv.liquid-tv!

alt.tv.lois-n-clark!
alt.tv.mad-about-you!
alt.tv.magnum-pi!
alt.tv.man-from-uncle!
alt.tv.mantis.mockery!
alt.tv.mash!
alt.tv.max-headroom!
alt.tv.melrose-place!
alt.tv.models-inc!
alt.tv.mst3k!
alt.tv.mtv!
alt.tv.muppets!
alt.tv.murder-one!
alt.tv.mwc!
alt.tv.my-s-c-life!
alt.tv.networks.cbc!
alt.tv.news-shows!
alt.tv.newsradio!
alt.tv.nickelodeon!
alt.tv.northern-exp!
alt.tv.nowhere-man!
alt.tv.nypd-blue!
alt.tv.party-of-five!
alt.tv.picket-fences!
alt.tv.prisoner!
alt.tv.public-access!
```

```
alt.tv.quantum-leap.creative!

alt.tv.real-world!

alt.tv.reboot!

alt.tv.red-dwarf!

alt.tv.ren-n-stimpy!

alt.tv.road-rules!

alt.tv.robotech!

alt.tv.rockford-files!

alt.tv.roseanne!

alt.tv.saved-bell!

alt.tv.sctv!

alt.tv.seaquest!

alt.tv.seinfeld!

alt.tv.sentai!

alt.tv.sesame-street!

alt.tv.simpsons!

alt.tv.simpsons.itchy-scratchy!

alt.tv.sliders!

alt.tv.sliders.creative!

alt.tv.snl!

alt.tv.space-a-n-b!

alt.tv.star-trek.ds9!

alt.tv.star-trek.tos!

alt.tv.star-trek.voyager!

alt.tv.talkshows.daytime!

alt.tv.talkshows.late!

alt.tv.taz-mania!

alt.tv.tekwar!

alt.tv.the-critic!

alt.tv.the-jihad!

alt.tv.time-traxx!

alt.tv.tiny-toon!

alt.tv.tv-nation!

alt.tv.twin-peaks!

alt.tv.vr5!

alt.tv.weird-science!

alt.tv.wild-palms!

alt.tv.wings!

alt.tv.wiseguy!

alt.tv.x-files!

alt.tv.x-files.creative!

americast.usa-today.telcom

bit.listserv.screen-l

chi.media

clari.living.tv

clari.nb.broadcast

clari.nb.telecom

fj.rec.tv

rec.arts.sf.tv

rec.arts.startrek.creative

rec.arts.startrek.current

rec.arts.startrek.fandom
```

rec.arts.startrek.info

rec.arts.startrek.reviews

rec.arts.startrek.tech

rec.arts.tv!

rec.arts.tv-frasier!

rec.arts.tv.interactive!

rec.arts.tv.mst3k!

rec.arts.tv.mst3k.announce!

rec.arts.tv.mst3k.misc!

rec.arts.tv.soaps!

rec.arts.tv.soaps.abc!

rec.arts.tv.soaps.cbs!

rec.arts.tv.soaps.misc!

rec.arts.tv.uk!

rec.arts.tv.uk.comedy!

rec.video

rec.video.cable-tv

rec.video.cable-tv

rec.video.production

rec.video.professional

rec.video.satellite.dbs

rec.video.satellite.europe

rec.video.satellite.misc

rec.video.satellite.tvro

sci.engr.television.advanced

sci.engr.television.advanced

sci.engr.television.broadcast

sci.engr.television.broadcast

DQMW-L—Dr. Quinn Medicine Woman TV Show

You can join this group by sending the message "sub DQMW-L your name" to listserv%emuvm1.bitnet@listserv.net

FORKNI-L—Forever Knight TV show

Pennsylvania State University

You can join this group by sending the message "sub FORKNI-L your name" to listserv@psuvm.psu.edu

HIGHLA-L—Highlander movies and TV series

Pennsylvania State University

You can join this group by sending the message "sub HIGHLA-L your name" to listserv@psuvm.psu.edu

LAW-AND-ORDER—Discussion of the TV Series

America Online, Inc. (1-800-827-6364 in USA/Canada)

You can join this group by sending the message "sub LAW-AND-ORDER your name" to listserv@listserv.aol.com

MASTVF-L—Martial Arts in Television and films

You can join this group by sending the message "sub MASTVF-L your name" to listserv@psuvm.psu.edu

PTV-SERV—Public Television Station Service

You can join this group by sending the message "sub PTV-SERV your name" to listserv@listserv.uh.edu

SCREEN-L—Film and TV Studies Discussion List

The University of Alabama, Tuscaloosa, Alabama

You can join this group by sending the message "sub SCREEN-L your name" to listserv@ua1vm.ua.edu

SO-CALLED—Discussion of the TV series "My So-Called Life"

You can join this group by sending the message "sub so-called email-address" to listserv@netcom.com

Alternative Fuel Vehicles

Citicar: My Electric Vehicle

http://tile.net/john/citicar.html

A page put up by an owner of the first production electric automobile. The site contains many pictures of the car, information about the cost of electricity, and contact information in case you'd like to acquire your own.

Electric Vehicle Association of the Americas

http://www.evaa.org/

Your one-stop clearinghouse for information concerning electric vehicles. Here you will find news releases from the association and its member companies and details from various conferences and symposiums on the subject of electric automobiles.

Formula Lightning

http://www.ece.wvu.edu/~formula/

Information about the high-performance electric race cars used in the Formula Lightning competition. Several colleges have elected to compete in the events, having fun while improving the technology of electric vehicles. The site includes pictures, specifications, a race schedule, and more.

Buyer's Guides

AutoPlus

http://www.autoplus.com/

A car buyer's guide aimed mainly at the Boston area, but applicable elsewhere as well. You'll find a listing of used cars for sale and can add yours if you like. There also is information about new cars, including a searchable database of over 16 years of car reviews done by the Boston Globe.

Car and Driver Buyer's Guide 1996

http://www.caranddriver.com/hfm/cgi-unprot/bg

The official buyer's guide of the famous automotive magazine. Pick a manufacturer, price range, and vehicle type, and browse the results complete with photos. Or take the shortcuts and browse by all of any one category. Vehicle specifications are also provided.

Car Tips

http://www.tex-net.net/tex-net/cartips.html

When buying a car from a dealership, do you feel like you're walking into a spider's web? These tips are provided to make you feel less like a victim and more in control of your automobile purchase. Tips include—what time of the month you can get the best price, what to do before going to the dealership, and what cars really cost the dealer.

CARveat Emptor

http://www.well.com/user/kr2/

An enlightening set of tips for dealing with dealers when buying a car. The site shows you common tricks of the trade to look out for and methods you can use to get a better deal. Read all of this lengthy advice, and you'll be more than ready for your next purchase.

Edmund's Automobiles Buying Guides

http://www.edmunds.com/

The place to go when thinking of buying a new or used car. A multitude of information is available, including price guides, dealer cost information, buyer advice and recommendations, recall information, and much, much more. Best of all, it's absolutely free.

The Internet CarGuide

http://www.carguide.com/

Select a car by looking through makes, models, and classes. When you narrow your search down to a single vehicle, you are presented with a photo and the option of viewing all of its specifications. A glossary is also provided, which is very useful for giving meaning to sometimes cryptic automobile terms.

New Car Comparison Guide

http://www.iac.net/~jasongg/newcarrankings.html

If you're thinking of buying a new compact car, check out this Web site first. It contains ranking information from a variety of sources, such as AAA, Consumer Guides, The Car Book, and more, to help you find out which compact is best for you.

Tallweb—Cars

http://www.bluplanet.com/tallweb/cars.html

Without giving any consideration whatsoever to the performance of the vehicles, a bunch of tall people sat in a bunch of cars and decided which were the best (and worst) based solely on interior room and comfort. Trucks, sport-utilities, minivans, and even subcompacts are compared.

Used Car Buying Guide

http://lyre.mit.edu/~powell/sherman/files/used_car.html

A very lengthy set of questions designed to completely evaluate the condition of a used car before purchasing it. Included are questions you should ask of the seller and of yourself, and checklists for inside, outside, and under the car. A plain text version of this document is available and would be very handy to print out and take when looking at a car.

Clubs

CHVA

http://www.classicar.com/clubs/chva/chva.htm

The Contemporary Historical Vehicles Association is a club dedicated to the preservation of vehicles from the Action Era, which is defined as any car 25 years old or older, back to 1928. Members receive free classified ads, access to an extensive club library, and CHVAID, a volunteer-based roadside assistance program.

Hudson-Essex-Terraplane Club, Inc.

http://www.classicar.com/clubs/hudson/Hethome.htm

A worldwide organization founded in 1959 that is dedicated to the preservation of the automobiles produced by the Hudson corporation, and later by American Motors. Members enjoy parts locators, annual meetings, and "The White Triangle," a 60-page bimonthly magazine.

Rolls-Royce Owners' Club

http://www.virtualforum.com/rroc/

For those lucky enough to own a Rolls-Royce or Bentley automobile, this club provides a variety of services. There is a parts exchange service and national events. The Web site also includes a FAQ and maintenance tips.

Driving

Art of Driving

http://sunsite.unc.edu/rdu/p-drv.html

Sensible driving tips everyone can benefit from. Tips include real-world driving tips, how to set your mirrors, two-lane driving, the trucker's perspective, and the actual physics of racing.

Natural Born Drivers

http://www.cts.com/browse/jccasey/nbd/

A hangout for those among us who might appear to be lunatics, but who in reality are merely confident of their driving ability, do not obstruct traffic, know the capabilities of their vehicle, and have a passion for driving. If you fit the bill, hang out and chat with the rest of the NBD gang.

Teen New Drivers' Home Page

http://www.ai.net/~ryanb/

Now there's no need to abandon the roads once your little sister gets her license—as long as she's seen this page! This is a wonderful collection of possibly life-saving advice that inexperienced drivers can greatly benefit from. There are tips for driving to/from school, in rural areas, in bad weather, dealing with fatigue, and much more.

Very Usable Film and Cinema Directory

http://www.movies.net

Contains the best of the best and all the usual—as well as some unique—features, such as production information and a list of local theater show times called "Now Playing."

Four Wheel Drives

4WD: Four Wheel Drive and All Wheel Drive

http://www.sofcom.com.au/4WD/4WD.html

An Internet magazine devoted to off-roading. FAQs and pictures can be found about all sorts of vehicles including military, amphibious, and vehicles with as many as eight wheels. There is also an events page, with off-road events posted from all over the world, although the majority are Australian.

America's 4×4 4U Video Magazine

http://www.4x44u.com/pub/k2/am4x44u/4x4.html

Get the lowdown on trails, technical truck information, clubs and events, and 4×4 products. Then zoom on into the 4×4 chat room and talk shop with fellow off-roaders.

Dakar Official Site

http://www.dakar.com/

All the information on the famous Dakar road rally. Browse route information, information on the Dakar organization, photos from the race, and view the sponsors.

My Jeep Adventures

http://www.halcyon.com/csutton/myjeepadventures

An ongoing story by Chris Sutton about his adventures with his 1952 flatfender jeep. Details are provided about everything from buying the jeep and fixing it up with various parts to coping with particular off-road situations.

Off-Road.com

http://www.off-road.com/

A well-put-together site of interest to off-road aficionados. Features include various articles on anything from a specific vehicle to land use. Also available are photo galleries, links to manufacturers'

home pages, and a classified service where you can advertise your vehicle or parts.

Warn Adventure Morocco '96

http://www.vision210.es/warn/uk/

Details from the Moroccan Warn Adventure off-road race. The six-day event required precise navigation, teamwork, and endurance. Interesting reading to anyone involved in off-road racing.

Makes & Models

AC Cobra Page

http://www.xs4all.nl/~luukb/

The AC Cobra isn't just a car, it's a way of life; this Web page is dedicated to it. Here you will find listings of Cobra owners on the Web, the history of Carrol Shelby, pictures, stories, and much more. Of interest to anyone who's ever dreamed of owning one of these roadsters.

Alfa Romeo GTA

http://www.xmission.com/~gtaj/

A page dedicated to this light racing car that the Italian automaker put out in the 1960s. Includes information about all the various flavors of the car, and an image gallery of every GTA the author has ever seen.

Aston Martin

http://www.ultranet.com/~dwc/am/

The car often driven by the world's most famous spy, James Bond. This page contains images, technical information, links to other Aston Martin pages, and an assortment of Aston Martin trivia.

DeLorean Home Page

http://www.delorean.org/

This page is sure to take you back to a time when the DeLorean was the coolest gullwing car in production. You'll find images, lists of known DeLorean owners on the Internet, a history of DMC, a DeLorean newsletter, and more.

Javelin AMX Home Page

http://www.intercall.com/~javelin/

A page dedicated to the Javelin, a sports car produced by American Motors in the early 1970s. Here you will find a bevy of information and links including images, original artwork, humor, cars owned by the site's visitors, and much more.

Paul Murtagh's Lamborghini Web Site

http://sparky.elec.uq.edu.au/lambo/index.html

A site containing a brief history of the Italian automaker known as Automobili Lamborghini and a collection of almost every model of car they ever produced, sorted by year, which includes photos and statistics.

Waletail's Porsche and 959 Home Page

http://www.olemiss.edu/~waletail/ben.htm

True Porsche lovers live by the motto "Porsche: There Is No Substitute." At this site you can find information and photos from every major Porsche produced, from a humble 11 horsepower Porsche tractor to the sleek new 986 convertible.

Motorcycles

Longriders Internet Bikers' Club House

http://www.longriders.com/wwwboard/wwwboard.html

A Web-based chat board of particular interest to bikers. Whether you're looking to buy/sell that rare Harley-Davidson, find a travel partner, or ask fix-it questions, this is the place to go.

Motorcycle Tips and Techniques

http://home.earthlink.net/~jamesdavis/TIPS.html

A collection of tips to keep the potentially dangerous hobby of motorcycling as safe as possible. Read through the collection of tips, peruse a case study on women motorcyclists, and link to a variety of other motorcycle pages.

WetLeather Home Page

http://mom.isc-br.com/wetleather/

What is WetLeather? It's what you're wearing if you do much motorcycle riding in America's Pacific Northwest! This motorcycle enthusiast group's Web site features a mailing list, several photos of mem-

bers at rallies, a registry of members and their bikes, and much more.

Museums

Auto Museum at Wells

http://www.classicar.com/museums/wells/wells.htm

Home to a number of historic cars from the "brass era" of automobiles. Features over 70 gas, electric, and steam automobiles from over 45 different makes. The museum is located in New England and admission is charged.

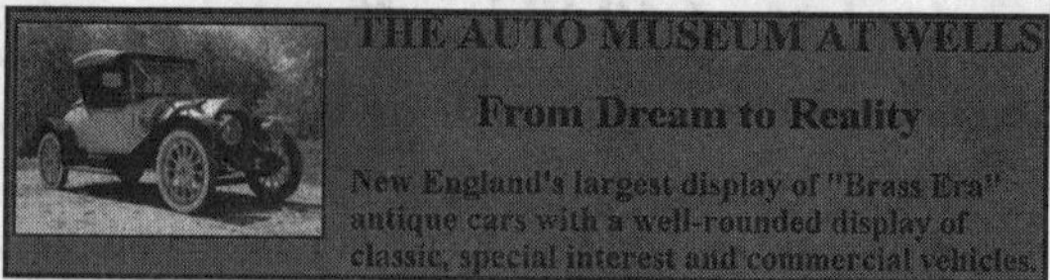

Cole Land Transportation Museum

http://www.classicar.com/museums/coleland/cole.htm

Information about and directions to the Cole Land Transportation Museum in Bangor, Maine. The museum is home to over 200 Maine land transportation vehicles; a full-size locomotive, freight car, and caboose; and various other items of interest.

Henry Ford Museum & Greenfield Village On-Line

http://hfm.umd.umich.edu/

Founded by Henry Ford in 1929, the nation's largest indoor/outdoor museum complex draws over one million visitors per year. Online, you can browse the highlights of the museum, get tips on planning your visit, and even browse the gift shop.

Vette Americana On-Line

http://www.corvette-americana.com/

The official Web site of the Corvette Hall of Fame and Americana Museum, located in Cooperstown, New York. At the museum, the Corvette is recognized as being a cultural icon, and as such, is used as a timeline to record the story of America in the 20th century.

Organizations

American Truck Historical Society

http://www.the-matrix.com/aths/truck.html

An organization dedicated to the assimilation of information regarding the history of the American trucking industry. The society publishes "Wheels of Time," a magazine distributed to members worldwide. They maintain a reference library and archives and hold a truck show every year.

Mid-America Old Time Auto Association

http://www.classicar.com/clubs/motaa/motaa.htm

MOTAA was devised in 1958 to be a collection of small antique car clubs, since most of the larger clubs were too far away to be of any use. The organization publishes a bimonthly newsletter, "The Antique Car Times." Membership in member auto clubs is not required for MOTAA membership, but it is recommended.

Trains

Amtrak

http://www.amtrak.com/

Information about Amtrak, the popular passenger railway system. Read background information about Amtrak, what they have planned for the future, learn about their routes, and get practical travel tips.

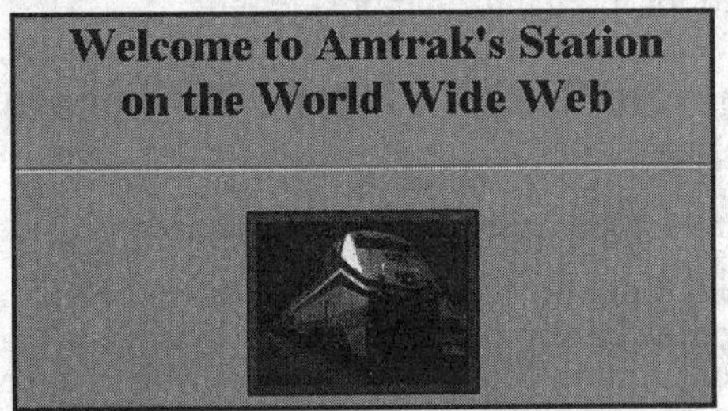

Burlington Northern Santa Fe Corporation

http://www.bnsf.com/

Official home page of the largest rail network in the United States. BNSF provides transportation for a variety of goods including coal, grains, automobiles, and forest products.

Grand Canyon Railway

http://www.thetrain.com/

Information about the Grand Canyon Railway, a train that runs from Williams, Arizona through forests, plains, and small canyons to deliver you to the Grand Canyon. The page shows schedules, fares, and timetables, as well as a map of the railroad and information on the fleet.

Trucks

European Trucks

http://www.indigo.ie/poreilly/european-trucks.html

A source of information for those interested in European truck makers. Links to a variety of company home pages, including Scania, Volvo, and Mercedes-Benz. There is also an image gallery with photos of the more popular of the European trucks.

Sport Trucks

http://home.sprynet.com/sprynet/steinwan/

A page of interest to those who prefer a sportier truck to the traditional rugged look. Information is provided for sport trucks straight from the factory and those that have been custom modified. There is a lengthy image gallery that might take a while to load at slower connection speeds.

Truck Safety Page

http://www.e-z.net/~ts/ts/ts.html

Professional trucking is a very dangerous occupation, and this page is designed to give truckers some vital information that might save their lives. The page gives some information on fires, but its main focus is rollovers and how to avoid dying in them.

Trucking Times

http://www.ttol.com

The online version of the bimonthly print magazine. Here you will find comprehensive listings of accessories for light trucks and the manufacturers who make them, news stories, and links to other sites of interest to people who own trucks.

Vintage Automobiles

Boulder Bob's Roadster Page

http://members.aol.com/boulderbob/roadster.htm

Boulder Bob is a guy from Colorado who took a classic 1929 roadster and turned it into a piece of art. Check out his "rod" and read all the details that went into getting it into the shape it's in today.

Car Junkie

http://members.aol.com/carjunke/carjunke.htm

A couple of pages that are "dedicated to the love and preservation of antique, classic, and just plain old cars (and trucks)." Browse the classifieds, or check out the winners of the photo contest.

Classic Car Gallery

http://www.aclassic-car.com/

View the current inventory in their image gallery. If they don't have what you want, they also provide a locator service to find the car of your dreams. They also maintain a classified listing in which you can advertise your car free for 30 days. They will even appraise your car for a fee.

Classic Car Pictures Archive

http://dutoc74.io.tudelft.nl/voitures/

A collection of over 600 images of classic automobiles, a large number of which are from Bugatti. Take a look at the car of the week, and then browse the subcategories for your favorites. There are over 46 megabytes of pictures available.

Classic Showcase

http://www.classicshowcase.com/

Provides fine vintage cars, automobiles, and motorcycles, as well as a locator service for the machines they don't happen to have in stock. Photos are available for much of their inventory, and an inventory list is available and can be e-mailed to you on a regular basis.

Coys of Kensington

http://www.coys.co.uk/

A dealership in England that specializes in historic automobiles. Browse their online showroom for photos of automobiles currently available for sale, or peruse their auction catalogs. They also offer various pieces of automobilia, such as old race posters.

Hillsborough Concours d'Elegance

http://users.aimnet.com/~jfox/hcd/

Features cars shown at the 40th annual showing of vintage automobiles. Cars shown were from the mid 50s and included the Corvette and the Thunderbird. There are a number of cars pictured that you are challenged to identify.

Schiemer's Page

http://members.aol.com/pschiemer/index.html

An interesting collection of automobiles for sale. Cars are available from Porsche, Ferrari, and Hudson, with Grand Prix cars also for sale. In addition, there are even some aircraft for sale. Pictures are provided, and the owner can be contacted for more information.

Tangerine Dream Vintage Car Locator Service

http://www.tangerinedream.inter.net/welnt.htm

Having trouble finding that '69 Boss 409? Perhaps Tangerine Dream can help. They specialize in finding vintage Mustangs, Porsches, Volkswagens, big steel, and muscle cars. Browse their FAQ, and then it's as simple as submitting a form telling them what you're looking for.

Wambo!

http://www.kent.net/wambo/

The 10th annual Wallaceburgh Antique Motor and Boat Outing features antique automobiles, motorcycles, fire engines, boats, and tractors. In addition to the antiques, there is entertainment provided for all ages.

XK's Unlimited

http://www.xks.com/

Specializes in Jaguars from 1948 to present, but also deals with other European sports cars of the same era. They have a facility dedicated to restoration, and they maintain a large supply of Jaguar parts. Also, check out some information on the racing of vintage automobiles.

Newsgroups

alt.hotrod

alt.motorcycles.harley

alt.motorcycle.sportbike

alt.scooter

alt.scooter.classic

clari.biz.industry.automotive

rec.autos.4x4

rec.autos.antique

rec.autos.driving

rec.autos.makers.chrysler

rec.autos.makers.ford.mustang

rec.autos.makers.honda

rec.autos.makers.mazda.miata

rec.autos.makers.mg

rec.autos.makers.saturn

rec.autos.makers.vw.aircooled

rec.autos.makers.vw.watercooled

rec.autos.marketplace

rec.autos.misc

rec.autos.sport

rec.autos.sport.f1

rec.autos.sport.indy

rec.autos.sport.info

rec.autos.sport.misc

rec.autos.sport.nascar

rec.autos.sport.rally

rec.autos.subaru

rec.autos.rod-n-custom

rec.autos.tech

rec.autos.vw

rec.motorcycles

rec.motorcycles.dirt

rec.motorcycles.harley

rec.motorcycles.racing

Listservs

AEROSP-L—Aeronautics & Aerospace History

Smithsonian Institution, Washington, DC

You can join this group by sending the message "sub AEROSP-L your name" to listserv@sivm.si.edu

AIRCRAFT—The Aircraft Discussion List

You can join this group by sending the message "sub AIRCRAFT your name" to LISTSERV@iubvn.ucs.indiana.edu

AUTORECY—Automobile Recycling

You can join this group by sending the message "sub AUTORECY your name" to listserv@pdomain.uwindsor.ca

CCEVS—Carolinas Consortium for Electrical Vehicles

You can join this group by sending the message "sub CCEVS your name" to `listserv%unccvm.bitnet@listserv.net`

CETM-L—Canadian Executive Transportation Management

You can join this group by sending the message "sub CETM-L your name" to `listserv@vm1.mcgill.ca`

CYCLNG-L—UGA Cycling Club Discussion List

You can join this group by sending the message "sub CYCLNG-L your name" to `listserv@uga.cc.uga.edu`

EV—Electric Vehicle Discussion List

San Jose State University, San Jose, CA

You can join this group by sending the message "sub EV your name" to `listserv@sjsuvm1.sjsu.edu`

EM_TRANS—Emerging Methods in Transportation

You can join this group by sending the message "sub EM_TRANS your name" to `listserv@listserv.uic.edu`

HYDROGEN—Hydrogen as an Alternative Fuel

You can join this group by sending the message "sub HYDROGEN your name" to `listserv@uriacc.uri.edu`

NTEAA-L—North Texas Electric Auto Association

Texas Christian University, Fort Worth, TX

You can join this group by sending the message "sub NTEAA-L your name" to `listserv@tcubvm.is.tcu.edu`

NUMAP—Nuclear Utility Materials and Procurement

L-Soft International, Inc.

You can join this group by sending the message "sub NUMAP your name" to `listserv@peach.ease.lsoft.com`

RBIKE—Road Bicycling

You can join this group by sending the message "sub rbike your name" to `listserv@bucknell.edu`

Adventure Travel

Adventure Travel

http://www.rscomm.com/adsports/at.html

This interesting site provides links to resources for sporting travel companies like Windsurfing World and Above the Clouds. Vacations vary from hiking in the Himalayas, to windsurfing in the Caribbean. Also provides links to many related gear and wear companies.

Adventure Travel for Women

http://www.gorge.net/business/adventure/women

Tired of all the machismo of high adventure trips? Try a "woman only" trip. Provides information about hiking and backpacking in some very scenic places with a little less testosterone.

Alaska—Mt. McKinley

http://www.inch.com/%7Edipper/ak.html

Denali, as the locals call it, is Alaska's beacon to the world. This is adventure travel at its best, not to mention at its most dangerous. But armchair travel is fun, too.

Alpine Guides Alaska

http://www.alaska.net/%7Epaoletti/AGA/AlpineGuides.html

Need some life-risking excitement in your life? Try some alpine adventures. You'll need a guide if you're inexperienced—that way you'll stay alive. Who knows, you might even have fun. Check here for glacial adventures in beautiful Alaska.

Arctic Adventours, Inc.

http://www.oslonett.no/html/adv/AA/AA.html

Advertises Arctic Adventours, a Norwegian company that specializes in creating exciting expeditions and explorations in the Arctic area, including Northern Norway, Jan Mayen, Spitzbergen (Svalbard), Franz Josef's Land, and Northern Russia/Siberia.

Big Island Air

http://www.ilhawaii.net:80/pt/bigair.html

Offers twin engine air tours of Hawaii and some of its most inaccessible areas, including volcano tours. Experience some breathtaking views that even some of the residents don't get to see. Also offers a reservation service.

Eagle Canyon Airlines

http://cybermart.com/eagle/

The airline to tour the Grand Canyon. Also offers ground tours. Tour information available in German, French, Spanish, Italian, Chinese, Korean, and Japanese.

EarthWise Journeys

http://www.teleport.com/~earthwyz/

Provides information about adventure travel packages with an ecological and socially responsible philosophy. Provides information about socially responsible travel, packages available, and a lengthy company background.

Helinet Helicopter Tours

http://travelassist.com/tcd/helinet.html

Presents an unusual tour of Los Angeles—by helicopter! Provides information on beach tours and a dinner tour in which you land atop a skyscraper. Preview images of what you might see on a helicopter tour.

Mayuc—Ecological Tourism

http://www.ascinsa.com/MAYUC/#intro

Trekking in Peru might be the highlight of your South American experience this year. This page features float trips and treks in the Amazon and the Andes.

New Brunswick, Canada Outdoor Adventures

http://www.csi.nb.ca/tourism/

Advertises Outdoor Adventures vacation packages, which include whale watching, scuba-diving, sailing, kayaking, canoeing, hiking, bird-watching, and cycling in various national parks and other locations.

Resort Sports Network

http://www.rsn.com/

Provides information on packages, rates, and opportunities for the avid athlete and vacationer. Includes wind, surf, and snow conditions for the extremist on vacation.

Safari Helicopters

http://hoohana.aloha.net/safari/

Offers helicopter tours of Kauai and the Big Island. Includes a "Virtual Helicopter Tour" with QuickTime movies and a photo gallery of locations toured. Book your reservations online in advance and receive a free T-shirt upon your arrival.

Sierra Mountain Guides

http://www.climbnet.com/smg/

Quit climbing your office walls and get outside in the fresh air of California and Nevada. Certified guides are found at this page to help you, whether you prefer ice climbing, rock climbing, mountaineering, or trekking.

Touring Exchange

http://www.bajatravel.com/tourex/index.htm

Sea kayaking and bike trips can be found, purchased, and enjoyed from this nicely done site. Learn to Eskimo roll with the best of them or change a flat in some vicious conditions.

TravelBase

http://www.travelbase.com/

Focuses primarily on sport-oriented vacation spots. Claims to have a list of all the ski resorts available on the Web. Also offers extensive information on Florida cities and most western states. Conduct a search from image maps or a search form.

Wildwest Travel, Inc.

http://www.webcom.com/~wildwest/

Provides information about western adventure travel packages, such as snowmobile tours, cowboy vacations, Alaskan cruises, and wilderness travels. Provides package background and pricing and includes contact information.

Airlines

Above It All

http://hoohana.aloha.net/~above/index.htm

Serves as a charter service for Hawaii and the islands. Includes flight reservation, charter information, and flight lessons.

Aer Lingus

http://www.hursley.ibm.com/aer/

Includes departures, news, special business programs, and a photo gallery that shows Aer Lingus history.

Aeroflot

http://www.seanet.com/Bazar/Aeroflot/Aeroflot.html

Includes pictures of aircraft, departure schedules, and a map of Moscow's Sheremetyevo-2 Airport.

Air Canada

http://www.aircanada.ca/

The official Web site for Air Canada. Includes a news desk, schedules, a program, and a special section called Netguide, which provides information on Internet and HTML basics. Also provides a French version.

Air Charter Guide

http://www.shore.net/acg/

The online edition of *The Air Charter Guide*, a limited version of the book. Serves as a guide for locating charter operators, arranged by state, name. Also includes tips on planning and pricing a charter.

Air Travel Card Control Tower

http://air-travel-card.com/atc/home.htm

Provides news and trends in the business travel industry and information about Air Travel Card.

Air UK

http://www.neptune.com/scotland/airuk.html

Provides information about the airline for travel to Scotland, but no schedule or service information. Offers links to a site that provides information on Scotland.

Airlines of the Web

http://haas.berkeley.edu/~seidel/airline.html

Provides information about airlines, organized by geographic region. Also provides information about cargo airlines, newsgroups, and airports.

American Airlines

http://www.amrcorp.com/aa_home/aa_home.htm

Includes schedules, travel awards program information, special products, and a helpful alphabetical index to access information quickly. Also includes an employment opportunity section.

Ansett Australia

http://www.ansett.com.au/

Provides information, timetables, rates, and special offers on flights. Site has information and links about Australia's currency, history, major cities, and general facts.

Canadian Airlines Intl.

http://www.cdnair.ca/

An airline that obviously cares about its Web presence. Find out flight schedules from a complete searchable index by destination and departure. Find out about business travel fares and accommodation arrangements made in conjunction with Canadian Airlines.

Cathay Pacific

http://www.cathaypacific-air.com/../index2_1.html

The home page of this airline offers information about service to locations in Asia, such as Hong Kong, Bangkok, and Singapore. Includes rates and special deals. Also includes a link to traveling in Hong Kong.

Comair

http://fly-comair.com/

Provides flight schedules, frequent flyer program information, and special weekend fare information for patrons of Comair—a Delta Connection.

Eagle Canyon Airlines

http://cybermart.com/eagle/

Provides air tours of the Grand Canyon, including an extensive air/ground south rim tour. Provides contact information and translations of the site into many other languages.

Emirates Airline Page

http://www.innotravel.com/emirate/home.htm

Emphasizes the variety of services this airline offers. Provides an overview of the several vacation packages available in addition to the core purpose of this site—route, class, and plane information.

Finnair

http://www.interactive.line.com/finland/.tic.index.html

Provides background information on Finland and the other locations Finnair services. Includes a section on available tours.

Frontier Airlines

http://www.cuug.ab.ca:8001/~busew/frontier.html

Provides links regarding the history, development, flight information, and reservation information of Frontier Airlines.

International Airport Codes

http://www-iwi.unisg.ch/~mmarchon/airline/

Sports an inclusive list of the codes for all United States and world airports, in addition to international airline codes arranged alphabetically by airport code. Learn to decipher airport departure/arrival monitors.

Japan Airlines

http://mmm.wwa.com/travlog/jal.html

Accommodates travelers to Taiwan, Korea, and Japan. Offers frequent flyer information, as well as virtual tours of Asian countries. Also provides a Japanese language version.

Lauda Air

http://www.laudaair.com/engl/indexe.htm

Promotes an Austrian airline that services Milan, Munich, London, Brussels, and Paris. Includes basic schedule and airline information, as well as a historical and financial analysis of the company.

Way of Tea

http://www.wayoftea.com/

If you love tea and want a free sample, this is the site for you. Just sign the guest book and send your "happy thoughts."

Lufthansa Timetable Info

`http://www.tkz.fh-rpl.de/tii/lh/lhflug-e.html`

Focuses on departure information on Lufthansa flights to and from Europe. Furnishes a German version of the page.

Mexicana Airlines

`http://www.catalog.com/cgibin/var/mx/index.html`

Provides a graphics-intensive airline Web site for Mexico. Includes maps, vacation specials, and online reservations. Also provides links to other travel-related sites.

Mount Cook Airlines

`http://www.clearfield.co.nz/mount_cook/`

Offers graphics-rich information helpful to those planning to visit New Zealand. Also offers flight schedules, booking arrangements, and exchange rates.

New England Airlines

`http://www.ids.net/flybi/nea/`

Offers flights to Block Island, Nantucket, Martha's Vineyard, and Cape Cod. Emphasizes Block Island and provides information on the island itself.

Quantas Airlines

`http://www.anzac.com/qantas/qantas.htm`

Includes a history of the airline, schedules, rates, and links to related sites on Australia and other airlines. Offers pictures of koalas, too.

Scenic Airlines

`http://www.scenic.com/scenic.htm`

Specializes in airplane tours of the Grand Canyon, Monument Valley, Bryce, and more. Includes current prices. Lets you make reservations online through their domestic and international travel offices. Support for most North American and European languages.

Virgin Atlantic Airlines

`http://www.fly.virgin.com/atlantic/`

Provides information about special offers, frequent flyer miles, and more. Lets you plan your flight online from a detailed form. Offers City Guides—travel tips for major North American, Asian, British, Irish, and Greek cities. Also furnishes articles from their magazine, *Hot Air*.

Automobile Travel

ASIRT-Association for International Road Travel

`http://www.horizon-web.com/asirt/`

Want to know which countries are the most dangerous to drive in? You'll find this fact here, as well as other road information and safety data.

Bumper Stickers

`http://www.csc.calpoly.edu/~sstaffor/humor/bmprstkr.html`

Look here for dozens and dozens of bumper stickers ranging from gut-wrenching hilarity to worrisome, as well as other forms of travel humor.

National Auto League

`http://www.nal-path.com/auto.html`

Insurance discounts and travel insurance packages provide the primary focus of this site. Other forms of insurance are also available from this site for what-ever your needs might be.

Rental Agencies

`http://www.yahoo.com/Business/Corporations/Automotive/Rentals/`

Yahoo's lengthy list of rental agencies is located here, which include over 50 rental agency home page links. Also recreational vehicle links are situated here.

Route 66

`http://route66.netvision.be/`

Get your kicks on the famous roadway Route 66. This site is packed with photos, stories, and a wealth of helpful information. Also features a locator map.

Scenic Byways and Other Recreational Drives

`http://www.gorp.com/gorp/activity/byway/byway.htm`

Organized into categories such as Far West, Desert Southwest, Great Plains, and Great Lakes, this site helps you locate the scenic route to your destination. Contains links to a majority of the 50 states.

Traveling in the USA

`http://www.travelingusa.com/a1/assistance/youhere.html`

These pages will help the U.S. traveler find information on parks, campgrounds, resorts, and recreation.

From relief maps to kiddie activities, you'll probably satisfy your travel needs here.

Books & Publications

Adventurous Traveler Bookstore

http://www.gorp.com/atbook.htm

The claim "The world's most complete source of outdoor adventure books and maps" pretty much says it all. You can search this bookstore's entire database from this site.

Travel Publications

http://www.yahoo.com/business_and_Economy/companies/Travel/publications/Books/

Yahoo's list of companies and agencies specializing in travel publications. This list contains sites that deal with a wide spectrum of travel.

Traveler's Book Club

http://members.aol.com/travbkclub/index.html

Home page for a discount service that offers "substantial discounts on guidebooks and travel titles." You have to be a member, though.

Travels with Samantha

http://www-swiss.ai.mit.edu/samantha/travels-with-samantha.html

Philip Greenspun, a graduate student at MIT, provides this summer travel log entirely online. Download chapters or browse the spectacular images; it is worth your time.

World of Maps

http://www.worldofmaps.com/

So you'll never feel lost, a professional cartographer, Brad Green, operates this plentiful online travel site. Mostly Canadian travel information is featured here.

Cruise Ships

Accent's Cruise Connection

http://www.premier.net/~accent/

Provides information about cruises of all kinds including riverboat, masted sailing ship, European river, and literally worldwide cruising areas' ports of call. This site, while still under construction, has ample information about taking cruises in China,

Canada's Maritime Provinces, and more familiar destinations in the Caribbean and Mediterranean. Also provided are links to order forms for all said destinations.

Adventure Cruising in the North Atlantic

http://www.centrum.is/com/vinland.html

Provides information on the pleasure cruiser, Liefur Eriksson, which sails in the North Atlantic.

Cruise Review Library

http://www.solutions.net/rec-travel/cruises/rtc.html

Serves as a Usenet newsgroup archive for discussing travel by cruise ships. Offers candid reviews of many of the major cruise ship lines. Don't plan a cruise without hearing what other people have to say. Also offers links to other cruise-related sites.

Cruise Shoppes America, Ltd.

http://www.cruiseshoppes.com/

Provides full-service cruise travel services. Includes destinations, monthly specials, and contact information. Includes an association directory with links to agencies by region.

Cruises, Inc.

http://www2.csn.net/cruises/

Provides information and profiles about many different cruises and destinations. Includes company backgrounds, photo albums, cruise reviews, and ordering information. Includes links to cruise lines on the Web.

Freighter World Cruises

http://www.gus.com/travel/fwc/fwc.html

Advertises Freighter World Cruises, Inc., a travel agency that focuses on freighter travel. Provides information on various freighter lines and their destinations. Cruise in economy style.

Norwegian Cruise Line

http://www.cruisematch.com/norweg.htm

Provides information on Norwegian Cruise Line's various cruise ships, their destinations, itineraries, and travel fees.

Royal Caribbean Cruise Line

http://mmink.com/mmink/kiosks/costa/rccl.html

A stripped-down overview of cruise destinations, itineraries, and prices offered by Royal Caribbean Cruise Line cruise ships.

Travel Discounts Cruise Index

http://www.traveldiscounts.com/cruises/

Provides discount cruise information, arranged by region and cruise line. Includes up-to-date information and the option to make online reservations.

International Travel

Once Upon a Time, In a Land Far Far Away

Tired of the *Meatballs II* reruns on those international flights? Next time, why not read one of the following author's classic travel books—maybe learn a thing or two about your destination that you can't get in a Frommers or Fodors.

- **Marco Polo** (1254-1324), Venetian traveler: *Divisament dou Monde*, the major source of information on Asia during the Renaissance.

- **James Boswell** (1740-1795), Scottish writer: *Journal of a Tour of the Hebrides,* accompanying Samuel Johnson.

- **Alexis de Tocqueville** (1805-1859), French historian: *Journeys to England and Ireland.*

- **Henry James** (1843-1916), American writer: *Portrait of Places.*

- **Robert Louis Stevenson** (1850-1894), Scottish novelist: *Travels with a Donkey in the Cevennes.*

- **Paul Theroux** (1941-present), American writer: *The Great Railway Bazaar.*

Air Brokers International World Travel Specialist

http://www.aimnet.com/~airbrokr/

Provides information about international travel, specifically air flight, lodgings, and sightseeing tours. Also provides a list of favorite sites that deal with travel worldwide.

Alchemy of Africa

http://www.aztec.co.za/biz/africa

Provides information all about Africa. Lets you download African Music while you stroll through the Art Gallery, browse the Market for shops and business listings, chat online in the chat rooms, armchair travel to African destinations via the Mystical Launch pad, and more.

Ansett Australia

http://www.ansett.com.au/homepage.html

Features an airline that flies to exotic places such as Norfolk Island, Bali, and Christmas Island, in addition to places in Australia.

Antigua & Barbuda

http://www.candw.ag/

Provides a guide to Antigua and Bermuda with links to related sites. Home page does not offer detailed information or pictures, but the links to local tourist sites are worthwhile for anyone considering traveling to the area.

Australia Travel Directory

http://www.anzac.com/aust/aust.htm

Offers links to information on tourism, VISA, individual states, and transportation.

Automated Travel Center

http://www.ananda.com/plg/travel/

Provides full online service travel arrangements and reservations. Includes international and domestic United States destination packages for both business and leisure.

Brochure Flow

http://www.broflo.com.au/broflo.html

Provides a home for The Australia Travel Arcade and Brochure Flow Travel agency. Offers full-service travel services, including airline reservations, hotel accommodations, and tourist packages. Includes links by area to any business one might need when planning a trip to Australia. A very handy site for anyone planning to go Down Under.

The Civilized Explorer

http://www.crl.com/~philip/home.html

Contains information on the French West Indies and Guadeloupe, including information about beaches, restaurants, activities, and places to stay. Also includes photographs and links to maps, satellite pictures, and other Web resources.

Costa Travel Online

http://www.ciee.org:80/cts/ctshome.htm

Offers worldwide tour packages. Includes links to Alamo Rent A Car, Carnival Cruises, Cunard, and Royal Caribbean. Special discounts given to the academic community.

Council Travel

http://www.elderhostel.org/

Specializes in student and youth budget travelers. Provides information on youth hostels, international student ID cards, and rail passes. Index to study abroad programs.

Country Maps of Europe

http://www.tue.nl/europe/

Provides links to sites that detail regional and city maps of Great Britain, European, and Slavic countries.

Cyprus

http://www.wam.umd.edu/~cyprus/tourist.html

Serves as a comprehensive guide to Cyprus—its history, its beauty, and why it's definitely worth planning a trip to. Includes sections on cities and advice on where to stay. Provides information on where to shop, what to buy, the cuisine of Cyprus, music sites, and where to have fun.

Czech Info Center

http://www.muselik.com/

An incredibly well-organized guide to the Czech Republic. Includes general information, bulletin boards (such as finding an ancestor), helpful travel information, and a section on the city of Prague.

Dublin Pub Review

http://www.dsg.cs.tcd.ie:/dsg_people/czimmerm/pubs.html

Provides a self-admittedly biased opinion of pubs and nightclubs in Dublin. Takes you on a virtual pub crawl and provides a price and visitability rating for each one.

Endeavour Travel

http://www.anzac.com/endvr/endvr.htm

Specializes in travel services to Australia, New Zealand, and the South Pacific for both business and leisure. Includes package vacations to exotic locals such as Fiji and the Antarctic. Includes links to Australian and New Zealand sites for travel information.

European and British Rail Passes

http://www.eurail.com/eurail/passes/passlist.htm

Provides information on the Eurorail pass and rail passes for other countries such as Germany, Austria, Italy, Czech Republic, and Scandinavia. This site is a must for those considering traveling Europe by Eurorail.

Eurostar Internet

http://www.eurostar.com/eurostar/

Presents Eurostar, a direct passenger train service that connects Paris, Brussels, and London using the Chunnel (English Channel Tunnel). Includes timetables, prices, booking information, special fares, and general information about trains that travel this civil engineering masterpiece.

Far & Away Travel Services

http://www.faraway.com/default.htm

Provides full travel services to vacation sites worldwide. Includes many package deals and current specials. The site provides ordering and contact information.

FranceEscape

http://www.cerf.net/cei/1/South_Am/index.htm

Informative site on planning and vacationing in France. Includes studies in France, festivals, transportation, and classifieds.

Freesun News

http://www.freesun.be/

This Belgium site provides links to international travel all over the world. Links to airline information, restaurants, accommodations, bookstores, fairs, and real estate indexed by country.

Going to Belgium

http://www.france.com/francescape/top.html

Provides links to Belgium cities and travel interests, passport and customs information, and information for establishing residency.

Great Australian Travel Co.

http://www.magna.com.au/~hideaway/snow_ind.html

If you like to go skiing, how about skiing in Australia or New Zealand? Check out airfares, ski travel packages, and prices.

Hong Kong Online Guide

http://www.hk.super.net/~webzone/hongkong.html

A Java-enhanced site providing information about Hong Kong, including shopping, dining, culture, hotel information, and places of interest. Offers links to sites related to Chinese and Hong Kong culture.

Indonesia

http://www.sino.net/asean/indonesa.html

Serves as a guide to Indonesia—its customs, traveling within the country, entertainment, useful phrases, currency, and other traveler tips. Includes a recording of the National Anthem of Indonesia and a soon-to-be-available video clip.

InteleTravel International

http://inteletravel.com/inteletravel/

This is the Web site for one of InteleTravel's Independent Agents. You can book any international travel through this agent. Links to the company, employment travel information, and specials.

International Travel Agency (ITA)

http://www.comprez.com/ita/

A full-service travel agency based in Canada to handle all your corporate international travel needs. Links to services, specials, travel management, contact information, and more.

The Internet Guide to Hostels

http://www.hostels.com/hostels/

Includes a Worldwide Hostel Guide for locations throughout the world; "Talk Backpacking," a forum for asking questions; and a guide to Budget guidebooks.

Intra Travel

http://qb.island.net/~intra/

Your full-service travel agency based in Vancouver, Canada. Will take care of your travel and accommodation needs, from a cruise to an around-the-world trip.

Jerusalem Mosaic

http://www1.huji.ac.il/jeru/jerusalem.html

Provides a virtual welcome to the city of Jerusalem. Offers many interesting historical and religious facts and pictures pertaining to Jerusalem. Includes a view of Jerusalem from the sky and an option to hear the song of Jerusalem.

Jordan

http://www.mit.edu:8001/activities/jordanians/jordan/

A graphics-rich guide to the Hashemite Kingdom of Jordan, its culture, people, and tourism. Also provides accommodation listings and traveler tips, as well as links to Jordanian sites of interest.

Lanka Internet Services

http://www.lanka.net

The Sri Lanka Web Server page with links to travel and business guides, maps, gems, news, and Internet access information.

Lonely Planet Travel Centre

http://www.lonelyplanet.com.au/

Concentrates on travel in the various regions of India and the attractions of each. These snippets are obviously extracts from the Lonely Planet guides that provide travelers information somewhat off the beaten path (fax an order for your copy today).

Middle World

http://www.centrum.is/english/index.html

Provides home page for Icelandic Internet server service. Interesting site for its links, in English, about Iceland's business, culture, and links to Internet Servers. This site is excellent for anyone interested in Iceland for business or pleasure.

The Monaco Home Page

http://www.monaco.mc/

Presents the Principality of Monaco and its tourism, business, and motor racing. Includes English and French versions.

Salzburg, Austria

http://www.tcs.co.at/fvp.html

Provides seasonal tourist information about Salzburg, Austria and its surrounding regions. Offers alternatives to traditional holiday plans when abroad (in German and English).

Sinbad Travel

http://www.spb.su/ryh/sindbad.html

Provides online travel agency services for Sinbad Travel based in St.Petersberg, Russia. Includes information about student travel packages and hostel information in Russia.

TGV French High Speed Train

http://mercurio.iet.unipi.it/tgv/tgvindex.html

Features TGV, the French high-speed train. Includes background, graphics, and schedules (in French) and links to other high-speed train sites around the world.

Tour Canada without Leaving Your Desk

http://www.cs.cmu.edu/Web/Unofficial/Canadiana/
Travelogue.html

Take a virtual vacation in Canada and each of its provinces via the Web site links provided. This site is a good resource for anything you'd like to find out about Canada and what it has to offer for tourists.

Tourist Office of Spain Homepage

http://www.cais.com/usa/visitors/visitors.html

General information on travel in Spain provided by the Spanish Tourism Office. Includes sites for National Parks, special events, and social customs.

Travel Home

http://www.kern.com/travelhome.html

Provides travel agency services, including plane reservations and lodgings. Specializes in travel to the Far East, India, and Pakistan. Includes contact information.

Travel to Finland

http://www.travel.fi/Welcome.html

Provides information about Finland, including the usual fare of information a tourist might want, such as hotels, sights, culture, shopping, and maps (clickable). Offers the language preferences in English or Suomi.

United Kingdom Pages

http://www.neosoft.com/~dlgates/uk/ukindex.html

Provides information about the United Kingdom in many categories: higher education, cities, country-side, culture, government, travel, employment, and other miscellaneous information. Provides more than a thousand links to other sites, primarily within the United Kingdom. Also lists bed-and-breakfast accommodations, picturesque pubs, and so forth. Offers several photo albums of downloadable images, including a page of photographs of the Royals.

Vancouver, British Columbia

http://freenet.vancouver.bc.ca

Provides FreeNet's information and links about Vancouver. Also offers links to the British Columbia home page and other Canadian home pages.

Victoria, British Columbia

http://freenet.victoria.bc.ca/vifa.html

A community-based network available at no cost to residents and visitors of Victoria. Provides easy access to businesses, individuals, government, and more.

Welcome to Future Net—Queensland, Australia

http://peg.apc.org/~futurecom

Future Net's Sunzine presents a collection of graphics concerning life online, from Queensland, Australia. Offers links to many facets of Web lifestyle, including education, vacationing, and travel. Take a cybertour of Queensland and experience a taste of Australia you might never get to.

Travel

http://www.developnet.com/travel/index.html

Learn how to travel for no or little money with the tips obtained at this site.

Island Travel

America's Caribbean Paradise

`http://noc.usvi.net:80/`

Provides information about the Virgin Islands, including wedding and vacation information, holidays, carnivals and other events, and weather forecasts. Also offers a section on real estate, vacation rentals, recipes, and Caribbean products.

Bahamas Online

`http://TheBahamas.com/`

Provides Bahamian facts, available accommodations, restaurants, banks, and bars. A good resource for those looking to visit the islands and sample some Goombay punch.

CaribWeb

`http://www.caribweb.com/caribweb/`

Serves as a resource for travelers and Caribophiles alike. Provides online travel publications and a conversation area. Also provides information from all the Caribbean tourist-board home pages and other relevant links to the Caribbean. Includes a searchable database, called CaribSearch, which contains information on hundreds of hotels, yacht charter companies, and restaurants.

Charlotte's Caribbean Connection

`http://www.coe.uncc.edu/~demccoy/ccc.html`

Serves as a starting point for the traveler who wants to become familiar with the Caribbean. Jump to island Web pages from a clickable image map of the isles. A good springboard site for those searching for information on the Caribbean.

Holman Travel

`http://www.wwwa.com/holman/`

A travel service with links to travel specials and exotic travel, including Hawaii, Tahiti, Fiji, and other islands. Airline, accommodations, and pricing information included.

Maui Interactive

`http://maui.net/~kelii/MIA/MI.html`

A full-blown interactive guide to Maui. Contains information on travel, entertainment, maps, photography, magazines, and art.

NetWeb Bermuda Home Page

`http://www.bermuda.com/`

Offers links to Bermuda travel and cultural information. Also serves as an advertising site for Bermuda businesses.

Lodging

American Youth Hostels

`http://www.taponline.com/tap/travel/hostels/pages/hosthp.htm`

Start here to plan your inexpensive getaway or rock-bottom budget spring break. Over 5,000 youth hostels are located in the U.S and can be found within this site. You can also learn about Richard Shirrmann, the founder of the youth hostel movement.

Bed & Breakfast Inns Online

`http://www.bbonline.com/`

Do large hotels have you down? Try this site to find that quaint little hideaway. Pictures and sketches help describe over 600 of these travel gems in the U.S.

California Travel and Parks Association

`http://www.campgrounds.com/ctpa/`

This site will help you find camping sites in California, Nevada, and Oregon. Get information on over 400 campgrounds here.

Campground Directory

`http://www.holipub.com/camping/director.htm`

Look here for a place in the 50 states, Great Britain, or Canada to pitch a tent. Site is still expanding so links are limited.

Choice Hotels

`http://www.senior.com/choice/choice.html`

Over 3,500 of the Choice Hotels International are available from this site, which includes branches of Econolodge, Clarion, Comfort Inn, and more. Reservations are available from this site.

Homeless Shelters in the United States

`http://www.nmc.edu/~lanninl/us.htm`

Homeless shelters provide a roof over thousands of people's heads every night. Look here for a national directory of homeless shelters.

Hostelling International

http://ww.fuaj.fr/index.htm

Try hostels if you're tired of being overcharged and hate being alone. This page features information about hostels located mainly in France. Site also features a Frequently Asked Questions site.

International Bed And Breakfast Guide

http://www.inntraveler.com/innbook.html

National and international B&Bs dot this site. Countries featured other than the U.S. include Canada, Great Britain, New Zealand, and Argentina.

Nude 2000

http://www.nude2000.com/

You'll satisfy all your needs for a campground here, if you subscribe to the philosophy. Other nudist information available here includes newsletters, updates, and government affairs.

Professional Association of Innkeepers International

http://www.paii.org/

You'll find more than just the *Innkeeping Weekly* at this site, but do look at that, too. The book *So You Want to be an Innkeeper* is available from this site, as are stimulating topics such as "Cutting Deals with Unlikely Allies" and B&B management tips.

Travel Web

http://www.travelweb.com/

This huge travel monster will provide more information than just lodging. This site features a unique section of independent hotels to help you stay away from the lodging machine of franchised establishments, if that is what you're looking for; however, you can find chain hotels here, too.

United Hostels of Europe

http://www.hostelwatch.com/hostels.eurgreen.html

You can find information about the five most famous hostels in Europe, plus 20 more, at this European hostel page. Site focuses on hostels in Germany, Great Britain, Sweden, Norway, Denmark, and Finland. Links to other parts of Europe can be accessed here.

World Wide Lodging Guide

http://www.lgww.com/

It's not called the World Wide Lodging guide for nothing. Reservations in most major cities around the world can be made here.

Train Travel

Burlington Northern—Sante Fe

http://www.bnsf.com/webdocs/210e.html

For the Woody Guthrie types, here is a basic freight train route map for those who wish to travel by questionable means. But remember, you didn't see it here.

Canadian National

http://www.cn.ca/english/maps/sysmap01.htm

Again, another travel agency whose office you can't visit. If you need some Beatnik experiences in Canada, plan your route here.

European Rail System

http://www.starnetic.com/eurorail/railindx.htm

Get the Eurorail pass information you've been desperately looking for here. You will also find tips about how to travel by train, including the "Plan it, Do it" scheme.

Liberty's Amtrak Page

http://www.aho.com/amtrak.html

Site provides a more personal look at Amtrak services and train travel in general. Also includes rail-fan information, travelogues, and photos and drawings.

Union Pacific Railroad Excursion Information

http://www.uprr.com/upr/ffh/excurs/

Are you craving a steam locomotive billowing down the rail with a monstrous cow-catcher? Try here for a few nostalgic trips on the original monster of all locomotives.

VI Rail-Canada's Passenger Train Network

http://www.virail.ca/

This is the home page for the railway lining the Great White North. Get travel times, destinations, fares, and more from this iron horse site.

Welcome to Amtrak's Station on the WWW

http://www.amtrak.com/

The country's foremost train authority, Amtrak, is accessed through this page. Find everything from the latest high-speed train info to travel tips and reservations on this useful home page.

Travel Databases

America's Best

http://www.americasbest.com/abest/welcome.html

Provides links to the best travel sites of the 50 states. Visit the launch pad to be directed to a random site within the U.S.—a different launch every time. A great resource for travel and historical information about America.

City Net

http://www.city.net/

The first Web site stop any cybertraveler should make. Contains a well organized index of most features of over 2,090 cities and 780 other locations worldwide. Lets you take a virtual tour of Marseille, check the subway schedule for Philadelphia, or find out what types of entertainment are available in Victoria.

GNN Travel Center

http://gnn.com/gnn/meta/travel/

GNN furnishes a Web site for feature stories on special travel sites and links to other travel-related Web sites. A wealth of information for the cybertraveler.

The Inn Traveler—International Bed & Breakfast and Country Inn Guide

http://www.inntraveler.com/

A grant-funded site providing information about bed and breakfast inns. Currently covers the United States (arranged alphabetically) and Canada. Includes room descriptions, reservations (forms), newsletters, and audio clips recorded by the innkeepers. Also offers links to other travel-related sites.

The North American Virtual Tourist

http://www.vtourist.com/webmap/na.htm

An incredible resource for North American travel! One click on the image map of North America will lead you to every WWW resource available for the selected state or region. This site is heaven for those looking for an all-encompassing site on the United States, Canada, and Mexico. Make a bookmark and visit frequently!

rec.travel.library

http://www.solutions.net/rec-travel/

A true library of Internet travel resources. Features a searchable database to find the exact topic you're looking for. Also includes hotel, tour operators, and worldwide rail information.

Round-The-World Travel Guide

http://www.solutions.net/rec-travel/rtw/html/faq.html

Offers links to sites that help you make travel decisions and choose transportation and accommodations, and provides information on money matters and communications. Covers travel-related newsgroups.

TII—Tourism Info Internet

http://www.tii.de/

Award-winning site providing an index to information on flights, rails, hotels, tourist news, newsgroups, and countries around the world. Includes English and German versions.

Travel & Entertainment Network (TEN-IO) Home Page

http://www.ten-io.com/index.html

Fulfill your personal and business travel needs with a searchable database of travel-related information, including a seperate Frequent Flyer information database. Also offers a downloadable demo copy of their Trip Finder for Travelers software.

Travel Information

http://galaxy.einet.net/GJ/travel.html

A searchable index of links to Web sites on domestic and international travel.

Travel Online

http://TravelOnLine.com/

Provides information about travel locations, tour packages, accommodations, travel bargains, and many more travel topics. Also lets you make reservations and purchases online.

The Travel Page

`http://www.travelpage.com/`

A thorough travel planning site for visitors. Make hotel, airline, and cruise reservations online. Provides vacation recommendations ranging from the more popular to the truly unique.

Travel Web Search Page

`http://www.travelweb.com/thisco/global/travel.html`

Lists hotels by city and country. Lets you search for the right type of hotel by location, property type, and lodging chain. Also offers links to the required hotels.

TravelSearch

`http://205.179.48.54/`

Provides extensive information from visitors bureaus, offers a searchable database to arrange travel accommodations, and offers a map delivery service to alleviate the hassles of getting your geographical plans together.

TravelSource

`http://www.travelsource.com/`

Includes information about different vacation packages and locations. Also provides links to travel agents and other travel resources to fine tune your vacation plans. Whether you're looking to scuba dive, white water raft, take a cruise, or simply kick back, this site is your one-stop vacation planner.

Virtual Tourist II

`http://www.vtourist.com/vt/`

Provides information on various countries, including city information, culture and language, education, maps, news, and so forth. Select the country you're interested in from the globe image map or jump to City.Net for a more precise search. Provides a text-based version for faster access of the information.

The Webfoot's Travel Guides

`http://www.webfoot.com/travel/guides/`

Serves as a "thinking person's guide" to traveling in Austria, British Virgin Islands, France, Germany, Italy, Spain, Vatican City, and the state of Hawaii. Provides links to good overall information about each location, such as general information, city/site information, public transportation, language, museums, historic sites, literature and culture, and tips for tourists.

WL The World Library From Scescape

`http://www.scescape.com/wl/business/companies/traveagent.html`

Provides a broad listing of travel sites with an emphasis on business travel.

The Yankee Traveler

`http://www.tiac.net/users/macgyver/ne.html`

Provides a compilation of travel-related sources of New England. Includes state Web pages, information on Cape Cod and the Islands, bed and breakfast inns, and map links. Also provides information about real estate, local businesses, and more.

Travel Tips

Air Traveler's Handbook

`http://www.cs.cmu.edu/afs/cs/user/mkant/Public/Travel/airfare.html`

Offers links to information on courier travel, consolidators and bucket shops, charters, newsgroups, mailing lists, general travel information, background notes, tourist information, destination information, embassies, car rental agencies, hotels, bed and breakfasts, hosteling, home exchanges, health, money and currency, weather, foreign languages, packing, insurance, maps, travel publishers, publications, periodicals, travel bookstores, travel software, student/budget travel, round-the-world, travelogues, aviation, miscellaneous usage statistics, and entry submissions.

Currency Exchange Rates

`http://www.dna.lth.se/cgi-bin/kurt/rates`

Presents the exchange rate for 23 currencies. Don't be taken for an ignorant tourist and robbed blind when touring another country. If you need to know what Indian rupees are worth in Dutch Guilders, this site will not let you down. Exchange rates are updated daily.

The Electronic Embassy

`http://www.embassy.org/`

Serves as a source for information that is useful to the staff of embassies in Washington, D.C., as well as for those interested in embassy affairs. Offers links to embassy Web sites, an index of all D.C. embassies, and jumps to federal executive agencies and a list of Washington events.

ELVIS+, Co.

http://www.elvis.msk.su/

Provides information about USD exchange rates in Russia, a Russian-English dictionary, advertisements, and more. Offers a keyword search engine. Provides English and Russian versions.

Foreign Language for Travelers

http://insti.physics.sunysb.edu/~mmartin/languages/languages.html

Discusses common words and phrases of just about any language you might be interested in, including German, French, Italian, Russian, Czech, Turkish, Finnish, Danish Esperanto, English, Spanish, Portuguese, Dutch, Polish, Romanian, Swedish, Norwegian, and Icelandic. Furnishes sound files for each language. Offers links to other sites that feature translation dictionaries and general information. Won a GNN Best of the Net award.

GNN/Koblas Money Converter

http://bin.gnn.com/cgi-bin/gnn/currency/

Presents a currency converter that is updated weekly for accuracy. Put your calculator to the side and let this site do all the math for you.

Information about Duty Free/Tax Free Shopping

http://www.stelcom.com/duty_free/homepage.html

Provides information on duty-free shopping—allowances, origins, and future developments in this popular method of shopping when traveling.

Interactive Travel Guide

http://www.developnet.com/travel/

Provides information for people traveling on a budget. Includes tips about money, documents, protection against theft, travel organizations, making accommodation arrangements, and lists the essentials for any traveler. Also contains links to other travel-related sites.

International Traveler's Clinic

http://www.intmed.mcw.edu/ITC/Health.html

Provides information about diseases, environmental concerns, and immunizations for travelers. Includes tips on what to pack in your travel medicine kit and concerns for pregnant women who are traveling.

Railroad Timetables

http://www-cse.ucsd.edu/users/bowdidge/railroad/rail-gopher.html

Offers links to railroad timetables for United (Amtrak) and commuter lines, Canada, Europe, Asia, and Oceania. Also provides links to sightseeing tours by rail.

Travel Discounts

http://www.traveldiscounts.com/

A business travel-oriented site providing information about discounts on car rentals, railroads, tours, cruises, airlines, and specific tour packages arranged by region.

Travel Web Sites

http://www.cybershow.com/travel.html

Contains U.S. and international travel tips submitted by college students, travelogues, links to travel agency Web sites, U.S. travel Web sites, and international travel Web sites. A good springboard resource for finding travel information on the Web.

United States State Department Travel Warnings and Consular Info Sheets

http://www.stolaf.edu/network/travel-advisories.html

Provides up-to-date information for international travelers, including warnings, entry requirements, medical requirements, political status, and crime information for travel sites abroad. Also includes the location of the U.S. embassy in each country. Countries are easy to find in an alphabetical index.

Web Travel Review

http://swissnet.ai.mit.edu/webtravel/

Award-winning site, including more than 600 pages of text and more than 2,000 photographs from the travelogues of travel writer, Philip Greenspun. Showcases many pictures. Offers more of a personal overview than you'll get with traditional travel Web sites.

U.S. Travel

Access New Hampshire

http://www.nh.com/

A comprehensive guide to the state of New Hampshire, including information about tourism, historical legacy, local happenings, and everything else under the sun.

ACUMUG—Arkansas Index of Internet Resources

http://acumug.ualr.edu/ar-map.html

A clickable image map of the state of Arkansas that allows you to search for information by region whether it's corporate or travel information you're looking for. A valuable reference tool for visitors and residents.

Alabama

http://www.eng.auburn.edu/alabama/map.html

A detailed clickable image map of Alabama by city or region. Provides information of interest to the cybertraveler in the different regions of Alabama. Offers links to other Alabama-related sites. Awarded an America's Best! site award.

Alaska Information Cache

http://www.neptune.com/alaska/alaska.html

Overviews things to see and do in Alaska. Includes tour information.

Allons! Acadiana

http://www.allons.com/

A multimedia-enhanced online magazine devoted to the sights, sounds, and smells of Cajun country—southern Louisiana. Provides the What to Do, Where to Go, and How to Get There of traveling through Acadian country. This site is a virtual tour in itself.

America's Land of Enchantment

http://www.nets.com/newmextourism/

A traveler's guide to New Mexico. Provides information about culture, outdoor activities, area ruins, regional events, and skiing. Also includes maps and historical tidbits for travelers.

AMI News—Recreation and Travel

http://www.omix.com/ami/

A travel site catering to the outdoors enthusiast. Provides ski and weather reports. Offers transportation and accommodation reservations and discounts for sports-oriented vacations.

The Arizona Guide

http://www.arizonaguide.com/

The official site for the Arizona Office of Tourism organized by region in text format and image map format. Provides up-to-date weather information, maps, and state information. Features golf resorts and, of course, the Grand Canyon and the many touring packages for exploring it. Well worth visiting even if you're not planning a trip to Arizona any time soon.

Atlanta Web Guide

http://www.webguide.com/

Take a virtual tour of Atlanta, Georgia, which was home to the 1996 Summer Olympics. Features businesses, restaurants, historic sites, art galleries, nightlife spots, and other areas worth visiting.

Boston Area Map of WWW Resources

http://donald.phast.umass.edu/misc/boston.html

A complete and easily navigable site listing all (or most) sites pertinent to the Boston area. Find what you need from the clickable image map or browse the alphabetized text listing. Everything you want to find out about Boston is right here.

California Do Your Own Thing

http://gocalif.ca.gov:8000/

A comprehensive guide to the West Coast's tourism mecca. Provides a clickable image map organized by region that delivers the goods on where to stay, eat, shop, and visit, and what to do in the various parts of the state. Also offers traveler tips, a calendar of events, and high-resolution downloadable maps of specific areas.

Cambridge, Massachusetts

http://www.ci.cambridge.ma.us/

Features Cambridge city resources and more. Offers information on the city's art, entertainment, museums, and tourism, and more general information for those looking to relocate.

Vitamins

http://www.up-time.com/form.html

Check out the free offer from Up-time Vitamins.

Chicago Information System

http://reagan.eecs.uic.edu

Provides visitor and resident information about Chicago including a calendar of events, tourism, how to get around, government, education, and updated weather forecasts.

CLEVE.NET A Guided Tour of the North Coast

http://www.en.com/cleve.net/

Invites you to take a tour of the North Coast. Presents Cleveland, a city once full of urban decay, as a beautiful mecca you can visit and enjoy. Focuses on entertainment, the arts, government, commerce, and other general information for travelers and those considering making Cleveland their permanent residence.

Clickable Connecticut Area Map

http://www.scsu-cs.ctstateu.edu/lib/map.html

Just what it says it is. Organized by region, this site offers tourist and general information on the state of Conneticut and its surrounding areas.

Front Desk

http://www.vegas.com/vegascom/front_desk/front.html

This link from the Vegas.com page provides other links to restaurants, business services, sports, accommodations, sight seeing, special events, weddings, etc., for the Las Vegas traveler.

Gold Canyon Multimedia

http://www.goldcanyon.com

If you're planning a trip to Gold Canyon, Arizona, this site lists business information, history and images of the canyon, desert survival tips, trails and waterways to explore, and other regional Web sites of interest.

Grand Rapids, Michigan

http://www.grfn.org/

A user-intensive searchable index to Grand Rapids, Michigan and what it has to offer to the traveler.

Greensboro Online

http://www.greensboro.nc.us/gol/

A comprehensive and visually stimulating site devoted to Greensboro, North Carolina and what it

offers to visitors. Contains detailed image maps of the area and its attractions.

HobokenX

http://www.stevens-tech.edu/hobokenx/hobokenx.html

Provides information about Hoboken, New Jersey and what makes it a viable place to explore for travelers and residents alike. Offers restaurants, bars, nightlife, transit information, and a map to find all of these places.

Idaho Home Page

http://www.state.id.us/

Provides information on regional attractions, state parks, national forests, a calendar of events, and more general information on the state of Idaho.

Index

http://www.vegas.com/

If you're planning a trip to Las Vegas, check out this page for travel and tourist info, shows, casinos, entertainment, real estate, sports, and much more.

Index

http://199.201.186.116/info/casinos.htm

If you would like casino information for the Mississippi Gulf coast, look no further. Provides hotels and contact information, including phone numbers, recreational info, maps, and employment opportunities.

Indiana Virtual Tourist

http://www.cica.indiana.edu/news/servers/tourist/index.html

Take a virtual tour of Indiana's diverse offerings via a clickable image map of the state. This site also acts as a directory for all Web servers found in Indiana.

Information Access Websites

http://www.info-access.com/iAW/Contact.htm

Services Web sites featuring most areas of Florida, including Boca Raton, Coral Springs, Ft. Lauderdale, Miami, the Florida Keys, South Florida, and Tampa. Each site features a hotel finder/reservation maker, lists of attractions of the region, corporate information, weather conditions, a map of the area, and links to other Web sites devoted to the region.

Iowa Virtual Tourist

http://www.jeonet.com/tourist/

A detailed clickable image map separated by region linking you to any information resources available on Iowa. Take a cybertour before you go for real or just enjoy the wealth of information.

Kentucky Network Services

http://www.uky.edu/kentucky-network-services.html

A huge clickable image map of recreational and corporate Web sites in the state of Kentucky. Valuable as a reference source as well as a springboard for the cybertraveler.

Las Vegas

http://www.vegas.com

Includes a wide range of vacation-planning information concerning Las Vegas, ranging from hotel information and reservations, to show schedules, sports, conventions, betting tips, employment opportunities, and business services.

Los Angeles Traffic Report

http://www.scubed.com/caltrans/la/la_transnet.html

Features real-time traffic data for Los Angeles, updated once a minute. Contains current areas of congestion, five-minute and real-time maps, and tables of current speeds on freeways.

Maine WWW Resources

http://www.destek.net/Maps/ME.html

An invaluable site containing every Web and Gopher site located in or dedicated to the state of Maine, from the Bangor public library to L.L. Bean.

Minneapolis

http://www.minneapolis.org

The official site of the city of Minneapolis, the city of lakes. Contains a searchable database for narrowing the scope of your search for travel information whether you're in town for a convention or on vacation with the family. From accommodations to dining and entertainment, it's all right here.

Missouri WWW Resources

http://micromedia.com/WWW/StLouis/Missouri.html

A complete alphabetical listing of all corporate Web sites, city home pages, and other recreational sites located in the state of Missouri.

Nashville Scene

http://www.nashscene.com/

An award-winning online newspaper providing the traveler a guide to dining and events in Nashville, Tennessee in addition to offering some insight into the Tennessean mindset.

Nebraska Travel and Tourism

http://www.ded.state.ne.us/tourism.html

A well-presented documentation of the attractions, campgrounds, hotels, and tourist sites of Nebraska presented in a colorful interface organized by locale and topic.

The Oklahoma Image Map

http://www.mstm.okstate.edu/students/jjohnson2/oklahoma.htm

An attractively laid out site featuring information on Native American culture; regional events and festivals; and an impressive collection of travel and recreation sites highlighting state parks, museums, zoos, and other tourist attractions throughout the state.

Oregon Online

http://www.state.or.us/

Provides information on the government, education, and commerce of Oregon. Of particular interest to the tourist is the section on communities, which provides links to the various regions of the state that may be more pertinent to your travel plans.

Palo Alto, California

http://www.city.palo-alto.ca.us/home.html

Why is Palo Alto on the Internet? This site attempts to explain with information about medical facilities, schools, parks, recreation, entertainment, and government in Palo Alto, California.

Peaks—An Online Magazine About Montana

http://www.cyberport.net/peaks/v01i03/peaks.html

A colorful and clever online magazine focusing on the recreational activities, culture, and art and literature of Montana. Find out about white water rafting and fly-fishing in Montana. Take a virtual tour of Flathead Valley or sample the writing of some local authors.

RING. Online Michigan's Electronic Magazine

http://www.ring.com/michigan.html

Offers comprehensive information on what Michigan has to offer, such as local news and events, sightseeing, travel, entertainment, and more. Make sure to visit this site before you find yourself in Michigan.

Santa Barbara County

http://www.internet-cafe.com/sb/sb.html

Provides information about businesses, community service, events, leisure activities, and visitor information in the sunny county of Santa Barbara.

South Carolina Supernet—LocalNet

http://www.scsn.net/local/

A portion of South Carolina's Supernet online services devoted to regional interests including arts and entertainment, people, organizations, and other regional information.

South Dakota World Wide Web Site

http://www.state.sd.us/

The official state page of South Dakota, replete with travel information including area attractions, available accommodations, events, state parks, outdoor recreation, and travel tips available from an accurate clickable image map. Also provides general information about South Dakota in addition to links to other South Dakota sites.

Staunton, Virginia

http://www.elpress.com:80/staunton/

Invites you on a virtual tour of historical Staunton, Virginia, founded in the 1740s. Offers historical tours, maps, and access to many visitor attractions.

St. Louis, Missouri

http://www.st-louis.mo.us/

Invites you to visit the "Gateway to the West." Provides information about tourist sites, restaurants, museums, and more.

Texas, Austin

http://www.quadralay.com/Austin/austin.html

Provides information about Austin's government and the local area, including attractions, culture, restaurants, accommodations, universities, and more.

U/Seattle

http://useattle.uspan.com

Serves as a guide to events, restaurants, accommodations, shopping, sports, and nightlife in the greater Seattle area. Also includes a weather link and news information.

USA CityLink

http://banzai.neosoft.com/citylink/

A fantastic guide to touring the 50 U.S. states. This site is organized alphabetically by state and further broken down by city. Offers links to pertinent travel information for each city. A thoroughly indexed site for the virtual or planning tourist.

Utah! Travel and Adventure Online

http://www.utah.com/

Visit the Rocky mountains, Sand dunes, and Salt Lake of Utah via a virtual tour. This site also provides general tourist information including maps and travel tips. Find out about a selection of vacation packages ranging from guided adventures to traditional family adventures. A visually breathtaking site not to be missed.

The Vail Valley Home Page

http://vail.net/internetworks/home.html?0

An easily navigable Web site that provides information on what makes Vail famous—skiing. Also offers information about other outdoor activities and what Vail valley has to offer during the summer. Gives a listing of area ski shops in addition to essential travel information such as where to shop, dine, and sleep. Provides a graphic clickable menu in addition to a searchable database.

Vermont/New Hampshire WWW Resources

http://www.destek.net/Maps/VT-NH.html

A full listing of every Web and Gopher site based in or devoted to the small New England communities located in these adjoining states. Among the links included are ski areas, area universities, museums, and Ben & Jerry's Ice Cream.

VISIT Virginia

http://www2.virginia.org/cgi-shl/VISITVA/Tourism/Welcome

An eye-pleasing site containing general tourism in addition to recreational activities, where to stay, restaurants, local events, theme attractions, and other points of interest in the state for lovers.

The Washington DC City Pages

http://dcpages.ari.net/

Contains information on what the nation's capitol has to offer to visitors and residents alike. Provides content on entertainment, the arts, culture, tourism, travel, dining, and other general information about the city.

Washington State Online Travel Information

http://www.tourism.wa.gov/

Provides things to see and do in the state of Washington, including white water rafting/kayaking, museums, winery tours, whale watches, golf courses, and children-oriented activities. Also provides a regional database of available accommodations in addition to general and historical information about this northwestern state.

Web Texas

http://www.utexas.edu/texas/

A comprehensive searchable index of every Web site connected with the Lone Star state. From commercial to recreational sites, Web Texas' interface makes it easy for the inquisitive visitor to locate what they want.

Weekend Getaways

http://www.wknd.com/wknd/index.htm

A good site to consider when you need to escape the responsibilities of the real world. Provides an index of inns and resorts in most eastern states and California.

Welcome to the Ohio Web

http://www.zygaena.com/ohio/

Take a virtual tour of the various regions of Ohio via alphabetical listings and search engines of Ohio interest sites. Anything that can be found online in Ohio is here.

The West Virginia Web

http://wvweb.com

Serves as West Virginia's main entry ramp to the worldwide information superhighway and the Internet. Pertains to the West Virginia travel industry, economic development, government, and virtually any other area of interest within West Virginia.

Poster

http://www.execpc.com/~cpi/form.html

Get a free poster from CPI—the National Crisis Prevention Institute. CPI offers training in the safe management of disruptive and assualtive behavior.

Travel

Newsgroups

alt.airline.schedules

alt.flame.airlines

alt.rv

alt.travel.canada

alt.travel.new-orleans

alt.travel.road-trip

bit.listserv.travel-l

clari.biz.industry.aviation

clari.biz.industry.aviation.releases

clari.biz.industry.travel+leisure

clari.biz.industry.travel+leisure.cbd CBD:

clari.biz.industry.travel+leisure.releases

dc.driving Highway

misc.transport.air-industry

rec.gambling.misc

rec.outdoors.rv-travel

rec.photo.technique.nature

rec.scuba.locations

rec.travel

rec.travel.africa

rec.travel.air

rec.travel.asia

rec.travel.australia+nz

rec.travel.caribbean

rec.travel.cruises

rec.travel.europe

rec.travel.latin-america

rec.travel.marketplace

rec.travel.misc

rec.travel.usa-canada

tnn.travel

tnn.travel.globe

tnn.travel.report

tw.bbs.rec.trave

Listservs

AGING-L—University of Connecticut's Traveler's Center on Aging

You can join this group by sending the message "sub AGING-L your name" to listserv@uconnvm.uconn.edu

SCUBA-SE—SouthEast US Scuba Diving Travel list

University of Tennessee at Chattanooga

You can join this group by sending the message "sub SCUBA-SE your name" to listserv@utcvm.utc.edu

TRAVABLE—Travel for the Disabled

St.John's University, Jamaica, NY

You can join this group by sending the message "sub TRAVABLE your name" to
`listserv@sjuvm.stjohns.edu`

TRAVEL-L—Travel-L Discussion of Travel Experiences

Ege University Bornova, Izmir, Turkey

You can join this group by sending the message "sub TRAVEL-L your name" to
`listserv@vm3090.ege.edu.tr`

TRAVELUK-L—Travel in the United Kingdom

You can join this group by sending the message "sub TRAVELUK-L your name" to
`listserv@listserv.aol.com`

WEDDINGS

Announcements, Invitations, & Registries

Bridal Gallery

http://www.shewey.com/wedding/

Contains online registration with a complete list of registered couples. Also contains planning services, a list of bridal fairs, and a resource for purchasing gifts for the wedding party.

Bridal Net: Online Bridal Registry

http://www.bridalnet.com

Offers information on everything from wedding registries to honeymoon destinations to wedding services and tips. Contains a geographical image map with nationwide listings of services. Provides an online shopping and bridal registry with images of china and silverware patterns. Also offers links to other online bridal services and honeymoon destinations.

Club Wed Press

http://www.interlog.com/~amy/phpl.cgi?ClubWed.html

Advertises a service that provides a personal *Club Wed Press Newsletter/Invitation* that introduces you to guests and helps them plan for the ceremony, reception, and other special events. Also offers some tips on how to use the newsletter. Links to other wedding-related pages.

Historical Wedding Invitations

http://members.aol.com/qwerx/

Custom designed wedding invitations are available to order in three period styles: Celtic, Renaissance, and Victorian.

Personal Wedding Pages on the Net

http://www.wam.umd.edu/~sek/readwed/readwed.html

Helps you announce your wedding over the Web. Offers to link to your wedding page or create a page for you. Lists couples by the year of wedding and includes many photos.

The Wedding Center

http://peachtreedata.com/bricol/weddings.htm

A site designed mainly for advertisers and wedding announcements. Also contains a page for visitors to exchange hints and ideas.

Gifts

Groom's Gift Collection

http://www.bridalnet.com/states/nt/jds/jds.htm

Advertises select gifts for the groomsmen and other men in the wedding party. Choose from items such as glassware, brassware, and other cool stuff.

Peachtree Circle Inc.

http://www.mindspring.com/~pcircle/pcircle.html

Advertises distinctive gifts for wedding attendants. Includes personalized, sterling silver, and pearl items. Also provides links to other sites.

Sophisticated Chocolates

http://branch.com/sophisticated/

Advertises services by Sophisticated Chocolates Mfg., Inc. Specializes in supplying gift box chocolate assortments, chocolate corporate logos, chocolate-filled gift baskets, personalized wedding favors, and many other chocolate products.

Wedding Decorations and Gifts

http://www.olworld.com/olworld/mall/mall_us/c_gifts/m_colrt/41weding/

Handmade and painted figures and musicals are available to order from Collectibles by R&T.

Wedding Marketplace

http://www.weddingmarketplace.com/

An online shopping mall dedicated to wedding-related products. Information on reception sites, gifts for the wedding party, guest favors, wedding cameras, and accessories.

The Wedding Registries Directory

http://www.bridess.com/index.htm

Couples can place their gift registry online for wedding guests to access. Also contains a directory of vendors that provide a wedding registry service. Unique wedding gift ideas.

Miscellaneous Wedding Sites

The Alt.Wedding Home Page

http://www.pacificnet.net/~jkdyson/aw/altwedding.html

The Web page for the newsgroup alt.wedding contains information on almost every subject imaginable. It has been organized under the categories engagement, wedding, and honeymoon, which make it easy to find the desired topic. This site also contains an area to annouce weddings and anniversaries as well as add personal experince to the store of information. Offers an area for vendors to submit information about their services.

The American Humanist Association

http://freethought.tamu.edu/org/aha/#weddings

Contains a collection of articles, essays, commentaries, lists, and so on. Contains information in the Special Occasions section on how to conduct various types of humanist wedding ceremonies.

Automatic Wedding Speech Writer

http://iconz.co.nz/commercial/speech_writer/auto.htm

A clever site by David Slack that allows you to fill in a form with drop down boxes to create a general outline for a speech. Also offers some tips on making a speech and an e-mail address for speech editing and advice.

The Bride and Groom's World Wedding Fair

http://www.opendoor.com/bridefair/main_dir.html

This site combines advertisement with informative articles. Vendors can advertise their wedding services and there are articles on how to choose and hire the best service provider for a wedding. There is also a bulletin board for visitors to post messages to each other.

The Bride's Page

http://www.omnigroup.com/People/hollie/bride_page.html

A site put together by a bride without any commerical vendor influence. It contains information on every stage of planning a wedding and provides an opportunity for the visitor to leave their own advice and anecdotes.

Celebration Vineyards

http://www.deltanet.com/intersphere/cv/

Advertises Vineyard Celebrations, which provides personalized wedding favors, such as customized labels for champagne and sparkling cider table favors. Shows examples of each.

Collected Domestic Partners Information

http://www.cs.cmu.edu/afs/cs.cmu.edu/user/scotts/domestic-partners/mainpage.html

Contains information and links to information on topics related to domestic partnerships and same-sex marriages. Offers excellent resources on policies in various companies and universities, family leave and adoption policies, and legal opinions.

Elegant Bride

http://www.webpress.net/leading-edge/ebride/

The home page for *Elegant Bride* magazine is currently being expanded to contain more information. It currently has a questionnaire for visitors to answer and a list of other links to visit.

I Do

http://www.i-do.com/

A site that changes its information every month much like a bridal magazine. Topics can range from fashion and planning tips to instructions on how to create your own wedding home page.

Rialto Archive: Period and SCA Weddings

http://www.pbm.com/~lindahl/rialto/idxweddings.html

Provides a collection of articles about various types of weddings, including medieval, early Christian, middle Eastern, and SCA (Society for Creative Anachronism).

Same-Sex Marriage Home Page

http://www.nether.net/~rod/html/sub/marriage.html

Contains links to Internet resources, state news, lobby groups, articles, and general information related to same-sex marriages.

soc.couples.wedding WWW Page

http://www.wam.umd.edu/~sek/wedding.html

Web page for the newsgroup soc.couples.wedding, a forum for discussing all aspects of wedding planning, from engagement through honeymoon. Includes, but isn't limited to, information about purchasing engagement/wedding jewelry and gifts, announcing the engagement, setting a wedding date, hiring professionals such as caterers and photographers, renting facilities such as churches and halls, planning the ceremony, wedding-related etiquette, registering for gifts, selecting wedding attire, and dealing with relationship/family problems associated with wedding planning.

A Way Cool Wedding Every Week

http://tribeca.ios.com/~whitey/waycool/

A site dedicated to picking the best personal wedding page every week. Also provides a list of past winners and a list of vendors and other wedding-related sites.

Wedding Bell Blueprint

http://www.videomaker.com/edit/mag/weddin~1.htm

An article that tells the professional secrets of how to videotape a wedding with a single camera. Gives advice on story visualization, rehearsals, and how to best capture the ceremony.

Wedding Bells

http://www.weddingbells.com/

A well-designed site by *Wedding Bells* magazine based in Canada. Information is broken down into interesting categories such as trends and traditions, inside scoop, ideas and inspirations, romance central, and stores and services. A good source for making a wedding more creative.

Wedding Circle Home Page

http://www.cipsinc.com/wedding/

Contains information on products and services, customs and traditions, honeymoons, speeches and toasts, general questions and links to other sites. Offers free announcement space for couples.

The Wedding Source

http://www.pep.com/pep/tws/tws.html

Provides information on wedding vendors and serves as a place to find and exchange ideas. Contains links to other sites relating to weddings or wedding-related products.

The Wedding Spot

http://www.weddingspot.com/

Information is broken down by geographical region that allows specific searches for vendors. There is also general topics as well as bridal show announcements, wedding software, and links to other sites.

Weddings Online, The Internet's Wedding Information Resource

http://weddings-online.com/wol.html

A comprehensive site with listings in every category from attire to videography. Contains a search engine which enables users to search for specific key words. Also offers explicit directions on entering Internet chat rooms dedicated to discussing weddings.

Wedding & Honeymoon Locations

Caribmoon

http://www.caribweb.com/caribweb/caribmoon/

Provides information for couples wanting to get married or honeymoon in the Caribbean Islands. Offers specific wedding instructions and requirements pertaining to each island.

Island Weddings, SuperClubs

http://www.webcom.com/~travel/island.html

Advertises the services of SuperClubs Resorts. Offers honeymoon escapes, and free wedding services at Jamaica-Jamaica, Sans Souci Lido, and Grand Lido.

Wedding Gardens

http://www.olympus.net/gardens/gwedd.htm

Serves as a complete guide to gardens in the United States that allow weddings on the grounds. Offers a detailed description of each garden along with contact information.

A Wedding Made in Paradise

http://www.maui.net/~wedmaui/

Advertises wedding locations and custom planning services for couples getting married in Maui, Hawaii.

Weddings, with Makana

http://204.182.49.10/wed.html

Advertises a private estate that offers wedding locations and a full range of onsite wedding services, including videographers, musicians, vocalists, dancers and drummers, photographers, florals, champagnes, and wedding cakes.

Wedding Gowns & Accessories

Ans Bolk Personal Design Bridal Couture

http://www.xs4all.nl/~gijs/ansbolk.htm

Advertises custom-made bridal and evening gowns. Designs gowns that suit the personality of the client in style and cut. Also offers links to other wedding Web sites.

The Bridal Veil Home Page

http://www.hooked.net/users/sraney/

Provides information about bridal veils. Offers a short history of bridal attire and information on matching your veil and hair.

The Dessy Creations Home Page

http://www.Dessy.com/

Advertises bridesmaid, flower girl, and special occasion dresses designed by Dessy Creations. Provides thumbnail pictures of dresses and the opportunity to locate a retailer near you.

Hora Bridal Accessories

http://www.netmart.com/hora/

Advertises discounted bridal accessories offered by Hora. Includes items such as bouquets, combs, pillows, and garters.

Imagi-Nations

http://www.netmart.com/imagi-nations/

Advertises discounted bridal gowns offered by Imagi-Nations, styles by Watters and Watters. Contains photographs of gowns.

NetDiamonds, Inc.

http://www.bnt.com/netdiamonds/

A direct source of diamonds and other fine jewelry. Includes a catalogue of various types of jewelry including engagement rings, and orders can be placed while online.

Sposabella Bridal—La Sposa Veil

http://www.hydra.com/sposa/sposa.html

Shows veils and head attire offered by Sposabella Bridal of New York. Also offers information on other accessories. Offers images of their products.

Watters and Watters

http://wwi.computek.net/

Advertises a dress designer well-known for gowns that can be worn for many special occasions. The site includes a search engine to find a retailer near the shopper and a photographic catalogue of dresses.

The Wedding Band Center

http://www.r8w.com/

A Philadelphia-based company that offers advice and information on selecting wedding bands. Includes information on designs, common mistakes, how to propose, and a catalogue of pictures.

Wedding Planning

Bridal Expo Online

http://www.wsol.com/expo/

A resource for planning weddings in the Chicago area. This site contains a list of local vendors, planning information, an area to announce a wedding and a direct e-mail to a professional wedding consultant.

Coconut Coast Weddings and Honeymoons

http://hoohana.aloha.net/cocowed/

Advertises the services of Coconut Coast Weddings and Honeymoons, which specializes in planning and coordinating weddings, vow renewals, and honeymoons. Also offers a list of various packages and the marriage licence requirements for Hawaii.

Poster

http://www.execpc.com/~cpi/form.html

Get a free poster from CPI—the National Crisis Prevention Institute. CPI offers training in the safe management of disruptive and assaultive behavior.

Emily Post's Complete Guide to Weddings

http://www.harpercollins.com/hci/edu/wedh.htm

Advertises a CD-ROM program designed to help plan and coordinate a wedding. Contains video of Emily Post as well as tracking programs for expenses, gifts, and invitations.

Leslie's Guide to Wedding Planning

http://acm.vt.edu/~lfowler/wed/wedding.html

Contains information on ceremony and reception music, readings, flowers and their meanings, links to other wedding Web sites, a bride's emergency kit, shower games, a photo checklist, a list of places to register, honeymoons in Hawaii, ceremonies, cookware, invitations, and miscellaneous other things.

Melanet Online African Wedding Guide

http://www.melanet.com/wedding/

Focuses on giving you ideas and guiding you to resources. Represents a hodgepodge of African traditions, as well as adaptations to the ways of African Americans. Includes examples of how others have had African-centered weddings. Also provides consumer and retail information.

My Wedding Companion

http://jax.jaxnet.com/~fivestar/

Advertises wedding planning software. Contains planning and tracking guides as well as the opportunity to create invitations, maps, and wedding programs.

Ninga Software Corporation: "The Wedding Planner"

http://www.freenet.calgary.ab.ca/trade/ninga.html#wedding

Advertises Ninga Software Corporation's "The Wedding Planner," a program that helps the organizer (usually the bride) with the invitations, RSVPs, gifts, and thank-you cards.

Northwest Wedding Network

http://www.teleport.com/~ecanning/wedding-pages/

A guide to planning weddings in the pacific northwest. Provides online registry and an opportunity for vendors to advertise their services.

A Pagan Wedding

http://inner-sanctum.com/magus/Hecate/a2.html

A wedding service written by Rel Davis, a ceremony for the bride and groom in the pagan tradition.

Simply Software: "Bridesmaids for Windows"

http://infolane.com/infolane/simply/bride.html

Advertises "Bridesmaids for Windows," a Windows application that helps the wedding planner organize invitations, gifts, RSVPs, thank-you notes, expenses, and important dates.

The TouchSoft: "I Do Ultimate Wedding Planner"

http://www.worldport.com:80/touchsoft/

Advertises a Windows-based software application that helps you organize, plan, and budget your wedding. Provides information on its features, how it works, and how to order it.

Wedding Web Home Page

http://www.weddingweb.com/

A complete guide to planning a wedding with a wide variety of information ranging from vendor listings to general hints and tips and information on how to get a marriage license and change your name. Also contains planning guides that can be downloaded and implemented for free.

Wedding Wise

http://www.bridal-guide.com/

A weekly Internet magazine dedicated to how to plan a wedding. Topics include a wedding etiquette guide, budget planning, tips, resources, checklists, and an opportunity to ask personal questions.

Weddings by IPS

http://www.usvi.net/wedding/wedbyips/index.htm

Advertises a service to help plan your island wedding in the Virgin Islands. Choose from a la carte options or select a pre-packaged wedding. Plenty of advice and tips on how to plan an island wedding.

WedNet —The Wedding Network

http://www.wednet.com/

Contains many informative articles concerning all aspects of planning a wedding. Announce a wedding, browse shows and events or ask a wedding-related question. Contains a wedding service database covering the country.

Newsgroups

alt.marriage-minded.women

alt.wedding

soc.couples.wedding

Listservs

1YEAR2GO—Planning and Information for Upcoming Weddings

Dartmouth College, Hanover, NH

You can join this group by sending the message "sub 1YEAR2GO your name" to
listserv@listserv.dartmouth.edu

COUPLES-L—Aspects of Concern in Heterosexual Relationships

You can join this group by sending the message "sub COUPLES-L your name" to
listserv@cornell.edu

FAMCOMM—Marital/Family & Relational Communication

Rensselaer Polytechnic Institute, Troy, NY

You can join this group by sending the message "sub FAMCOMM your name" to
listserv@vm.its.rpi.edu

FAMLYSCI—To Enhance Communication among Family Scientists

You can join this group by sending the message "sub FAMLYSCI your name" to
listserv@ukcc.uky.edu

MFTC-L—Marriage and Family Therapy Counseling Discussion

St.John's University, Jamaica, NY

You can join this group by sending the message "sub MFTC-L your name" to
listserv@sjuvm.stjohns.edu

PHOTOWED—The Wedding Photographers Mailing List

You can join this group by sending the message "sub PHOTOWED your name" to
listserv@internet.com

WME-L—Worldwide Marriage Encounter Discussion

The American University, Washington, DC

You can join this group by sending the message "sub WME-L your name" to listserv@american.edu

APPENDIX A
COLLEGES & UNIVERSITIES

The following list contains the names and Uniform Resource Locators (URLs) of more than 1,500 World Wide Web sites maintained by colleges and universities. These sites provide information on degree programs, curricula, research, student life, and other areas of interest associated with institutions of higher learning.

Aachen University of Technology
http://www.informatik.rwth-aachen.de/RWTH/

Aalborg Business College
http://www.aalborges.dk/

Aalborg University
http://www.auc.dk/

Abilene Christian University
http://www.acu.edu/

Academy Canada
http://www.compusult.nf.ca/~micronet/academycanada/

Acadia University
http://www.acadiau.ca/

Agder College
http://www.aid.no/

Agnes Scott College
http://www.scottlan.edu/

Agricultural University of Norway
http://www.nlh.no/Studie_kontor/info_eng/info_eng.html

Akita University
http://quartet.bb.akita-u.ac.jp/index-e.html

Albert Szentgyorgyi Medical University
http://www.szote.u-szeged.hu/

Albertson College of Idaho
http://www.acofi.edu/

Albion College
http://www.albion.edu/

Allentown College
http://www.allencol.edu/

Altai State University
http://dcn-asu.altai.su/ENTRY.en.html

American University
http://www.american.edu/

American University in Bulgaria
http://www.aubg.bg/

Amherst College
http://www.amherst.edu/

Andrews University School of Business
http://www.cs.andrews.edu/index.html

Anglia Polytechnic University
http://www.anglia.ac.uk/

Anna University
http://www.engr.uky.edu/~arunp/anna.html

Annamalai University
http://wwwvms.utexas.edu/~thaths/auhome.html

Antioch University
http://college.antioch.edu/

Aoyama Gakuin
http://www.bb.aoyama.ac.jp/index-e.html

Appalachian State University
http://www.acs.appstate.edu/

Aristotle University of Thessaloniki
http://www.lance.colostate.edu/auth/

Arizona State University
http://www.asu.edu/

Arizona Western College
http://www.awc.cc.az.us/

Armstrong State College
http://www.armstrong.edu/

Ashland University
http://www.ashland.edu/

Asian Institute of Technology
http://emailhost.ait.ac.th/

Askeri Elektronik Sanayi
http://www.aselsan.com.tr/

Assumption College
http://www.assumption.edu:80/

Assumption University
http://www.au.ac.th/

Aston University
http://www.aston.ac.uk/

Ateneo de Manila University
http://kilaw.admu.edu.ph/

Athena University
http://symnet.net/~VOU/au.html

Atlantic Community College
http://www.atlantic.edu/

Attila Jozsef University
http://www.jate.u-szeged.hu/

Auburn University
http://mallard.duc.auburn.edu/

Augsburg College
http://www.augsburg.edu/

Augustana College, Rock Island, Illinois
http://www.augustana.edu/

Austin College
http://www.austinc.edu/

Australian International Hotel School
http://hotelschool.cornell.edu/aihs/

Azusa Pacific University
http://apu.edu/

Baker University
http://www.bakeru.edu/

Ball State University
http://virgo.bsu.edu:8080/

Bangkok University
http://www.bu.ac.th/

Barnard College
http://www.barnard.columbia.edu/

Bates College
http://abacus.bates.edu/

Baylor College of Dentistry
http://www.ont.com/baylords/

Baylor College of Medicine
http://www.bcm.tmc.edu/

Baylor University
http://www.baylor.edu/

Beaver College
http://www.beaver.edu/

Beijing Agricultural University
http://www.ihep.ac.cn:3000/uni/BAU/agri.html

Beijing University of Chemical Technology
http://www.buct.edu.cn/

Belmont University
http://acklen.belmont.edu/

Beloit College
http://stu.beloit.edu/

Bemidji State University
http://bsuweb.bemidji.msus.edu/

Benedictine College
http://www.benedictine.edu/

Berea College
http://www.berea.edu/

Bergen College
http://www.hib.no/

Bergen University
http://www.uib.no/index-eng.html

Bermuda College
http://www.bercol.bm/

Berufsakademie Ravensburg
http://www.ba-ravensburg.de/home.htm

Bessenyei Gyorgy Teachers Training College
http://www.bgytf.hu/

Bethel College and Seminary, St. Paul Minnesota
http://www.bethel.edu/

Bethel College, Newton, Kansas
http://www.bethelks.edu/

Bilkent University
http://www.bilkent.edu.tr/bilkent.html

Binghamton University
http://www.binghamton.edu/

Biola University
http://www.biola.edu/

Birkbeck College
http://www.bbk.ac.uk/

Birmingham-Southern College
http://www.bsc.edu/

Bishop's University
http://venus.ubishops.ca/

Black Hills State University
http://www.bhsu.edu/

Blackburn College
http://www.mcs.net/~kwplace/bc.htm

Bloomsburg University
http://www.bloomu.edu/

Bluffton College
http://www.bluffton.edu/

Bogazici University
http://www.boun.edu.tr/

Boise State University
http://www.idbsu.edu/

Bond University
http://bond.edu.au/

Boston College
http://infoeagle.bc.edu/

Boston University
http://web.bu.edu

Bowdoin College
http://www.bowdoin.edu/

Bowling Green State University
http://www.bgsu.edu/

Bradley University
http://www.bradley.edu/

Brandeis University
http://www.cs.brandeis.edu/

Bridgewater College
http://www.bridgewater.edu/

Brigham Young University
http://www.byu.edu/

Brigham Young University, Hawaii
http://www.byuh.edu/

Bristol University
http://www.bris.ac.uk/

Brock University
http://spartan.ac.brocku.ca/

Brookdale Community College
http://soho.ios.com/~andrewjr/

Brooklyn College
http://146.245.2.151/

Brown University
http://www.brown.edu/

Brunel University
http://http1.brunel.ac.uk:8080/

Brussels University
http://sun4.iihe.ac.be/

Bryant College
http://www.bryant.edu/

Bryn Mawr College
http://www.brynmawr.edu/

Bucknell University
http://www.bucknell.edu/

Buena Vista College, Storm Lake IA
http://othmar.bvc.edu/

Butler University
http://www.butler.edu/

Butte Community College
http://www.cin.butte.cc.ca.us/

Cabot College of Applied Arts, Technology and Continuing Education
http://www.cabot.nf.ca/

California Coast University
http://www.calcoastuniv.edu/ccu/

California Institute of Technology
http://www.caltech.edu/

California Institute of the Arts
http://www.calarts.edu/

California Lutheran University
http://callutheran.edu/

California Polytechnic State University, San Luis Obispo
http://www.calpoly.edu/

California State Polytechnic University, Pomona
http://www.csupomona.edu/

California State University
http://www.calstate.edu/

California State University, Bakersfield
http://www.csubak.edu/

California State University, Chico
http://www.csuchico.edu/

California State University, Fresno
http://athena.lib.csufresno.edu/csuf.htm

California State University, Hayward
http://www.mcs.csuhayward.edu/

California State University, Long Beach
http://www.csulb.edu/

California State University, Los Angeles
http://www.calstatela.edu/

California State University, Northridge
http://www.csun.edu/

California State University, Sacramento
http://www.csus.edu/

California State University, San Bernardino
http://www.csusb.edu/

California State University, San Marcos
http://coyote.csusm.edu/

California State University, Stanislaus
http://lead.csustan.edu/

Calvin College
http://www.calvin.edu/

Cambridge University
http://www.cam.ac.uk/

Camosun College
http://www.camosun.bc.ca/camosun.html

Canadore College
http://www.canadorec.on.ca/

Capital Community-Technical College
http://neo-oreo.commnet.edu/

Cardinal Stritch College
http://acs.stritch.edu/

Carleton College
http://www.carleton.edu/

Carleton University
http://www.carleton.ca/

Carnegie Mellon University
http://www.cmu.edu/

Carroll College
http://carroll1.cc.edu/

Case Western Reserve University
http://litwww.cwru.edu/

Catholic University of America
http://www.cua.edu/

Catholic University of Louvain
http://www.sc.ucl.ac.be/UCL/gb/intro.html

Cedarville College
http://www.cedarville.edu/

Centenary College of Louisiana
http://alpha.centenary.edu/busy

Central Connecticut State University
http://neal.ctstateu.edu/Home.html

Central Florida Community College
http://205.129.12.3/

Central Institute of Technology
http://www.cit.ac.nz/

Central Michigan University
http://www.cmich.edu/

Central Missouri State University
http://cmsuvmb.cmsu.edu/

Central Oregon Community College
http://www.cocc.edu/

Central Queensland University
http://www.cqu.edu.au/

Central Washington University
http://www.cwu.edu/

Centre College
http://www.centre.edu/

Cerritos College
http://www.cerritos.edu

Chalmers University of Technology
http://www.chalmers.se/Home-E.html

Chandler-Gilbert Community College
http://140.198.129.30/

Chapman University
http://www.chapman.edu/

Charles University, Prague
http://www.cuni.cz/

Chemeketa Community College
http://web.chemek.cc.or.us/

Chiba University
http://www.hike.te.chiba-u.ac.jp/chiba-u/

Chicago-Kent College of law
http://www.kentlaw.edu/

Chinese University of Hong Kong
http://www.cuhk.hk/

Christchurch Polytechnic
http://vesta.chch.planet.co.nz/polytech/polytech.html

Christian Brothers University
http://www.cbu.edu/

Christopher Newport University
http://www.pcs.cnu.edu/

Chukyo University
http://www.sccs.chukyo-u.ac.jp/

Chulalongkorn University
http://www.netserv.chula.ac.th/

Chung Ang University
http://www.cau.ac.kr/

Chung Hua Polytechnic Institute
http://www.chpi.edu.tw/

Chung-Ang University
http://bbs.cba.cau.ac.kr/

Chungbuk National University
http://cbubbs.chungbuk.ac.kr/~jeongjh/cbnu/
welcome.html

ChungNam National University
http://infocomm2.chungnam.ac.kr/busy

Citadel
http://macs01.mathcs.citadel.edu/

City University
http://web.city.ac.uk/

City University of Hong Kong
http://www.cityu.edu.hk/

City University of New York
http://www.cuny.edu/

City University, Seattle WA
http://www.cityu.edu/

Claremont College
http://www.clare.tased.edu.au/

Clark University
http://www.clarku.edu/

Clarkson University
http://fire.clarkson.edu/

Clemson University
http://www.clemson.edu/home.html

Cleveland State University
http://www.csuohio.edu/

Coe College
http://www.coe.edu

Colby College
http://www.colby.edu/

Colgate University
http://arachnid.colgate.edu/

**Collaborative Information Technology
Research Institute**
http://www.citri.edu.au/

College of Aeronautics
http://www.mordor.com/coa/coa.html

College of Charleston
http://www.cofc.edu/

College of Eastern Utah
http://www.ceu.edu/

College of St. Catherine
http://www.stkate.edu/

College of Staten Island
http://www.csi.cuny.edu/

College of William and Mary
http://www.wm.edu/

College of Wooster
http://www.wooster.edu/

Colorado Christian University
http://www.ccu.edu/

Colorado College
http://www.cc.colorado.edu/

Colorado School of Mines
http://gn.mines.colorado.edu:80/

Colorado State University
http://www.colostate.edu/

Columbia College
http://www.colum.edu/

Columbia University
http://www.columbia.edu/

Concordia College
http://www.cord.edu/

Concordia University
http://www.concordia.ca/

Concordia University, River Forest
http://www.cuis.edu/www/curf/home.html

Connecticut College
http://camel.conncoll.edu/

Cooper Union
http://www.cooper.edu/

Copenhagen Business School
http://www.cbs.dk/

Cornell College
http://www.cornell-iowa.edu/

Cornell University
http://www.cornell.edu/

Cornerstone College
http://www.grfn.org/~cstone/

Cranfield University
http://www.cranfield.ac.uk/

Creighton University
http://bluejay.creighton.edu/

Curtin University, Western Australia
http://www.curtin.edu.au/

Czech Technical University, Prague
http://www.cvut.cz/

Da-Yeh Institute of Technology
http://www.dyit.edu.tw/

Dakota State University
http://www.dsu.edu/

Dalhousie University
http://www.dal.ca/

Dalian University of Technology
http://www-personal.engin.umich.edu/~leijiang/DUT/
index.html

Dallas County Community College District
http://www.dcccd.edu/

Dana College
http://www.dana.edu/

Daniel Webster College
http://www.dwc.edu/

Dartmouth College
http://www.dartmouth.edu/

Davidson College
http://www.davidson.edu/

De La Salle University
http://www.dlsu.edu.ph/

De Montfort University
http://www.dmu.ac.uk/

Deakin University
http://www.deakin.edu.au/

Delaware Technical & Community College
http://www.dtcc.edu/

Delft University of Technology
http://www.tudelft.nl/

Democritus University
http://www.cc.duth.gr/

Denison University
http://www.denison.edu/

DePaul University
http://www.depaul.edu/

Devry Institute of Technology
http://www.devrycols.edu/

Diablo Valley College
http://www.dvc.edu/

Dixie College
http://sci.dixie.edu/

Dokkyo University School of Medicine
http://www.dokkyomed.ac.jp/

Dongguk University
http://www.dongguk.ac.kr/DGU/

DongSeo University
http://www.dongseo.ac.kr/

Dortmund University
http://www.uni-dortmund.de/

Downing College
http://www.dow.cam.ac.uk/

Drake University
http://www.drake.edu/default.html

Drew University
http://tarzan.drew.edu/athome.html

Drexel University
http://www.drexel.edu/

Dublin City University
http://www.dcu.ie/

Dublin Institute of Technology
http://147.252.133.152/

Duke University
http://www.duke.edu/

Dundee University
http://alpha.mic.dundee.ac.uk/dusa/dusa.html

Duquesne University
http://www.duq.edu/

Earlham College
http://www.earlham.edu/

East Carolina University
http://ecuvax.cis.ecu.edu/

East Central University, Ada OK
http://student.ecok.edu/

East Stroudsburg University
http://www.esu.edu/

East Tennessee State University
http://etsu.east-tenn-st.edu

East Texas State University
http://www.etsu.edu/

Eastern Illinois University
http://www.eiu.edu/

Eastern Mediteranean University
http://salamis.emu.edu.tr/

Eastern Mennonite University
http://www.emu.edu/

Eastern Michigan University
http://www.emich.edu/

Eastern New Mexico State University
http://www.enmu.edu/

Eastern Washington University
http://www.ewu.edu/

Ecole Centrale Paris
http://www.ecp.fr/

Ecole Nationale Superieure des Télécomunnications de Paris
http://www.enst.fr/

Ecole Polytechnique de Montreal
http://www.polymtl.ca/

Edinboro University
http://www.edinboro.edu/

Edith Cowan University
http://www.cowan.edu.au/

Edmonds Community College
http://www.edmonds.ctc.edu/

Ege University
http://www.ege.edu.tr/

Ehime University
http://ccs42.dpc.ehime-u.ac.jp:8000/

Eindhoven University of Technology
http://www.tue.nl/

Embry Riddle Aeronautical University
http://macwww.db.erau.edu/

Emerson College
http://www.emerson.edu/

Emmanuel College
http://www.emmanuel.edu/

Emory University
http://www.cc.emory.edu/welcome.html

Engineering School of St. Gallen
http://www.bodan.net/isg/index.html

Eotvos Lorand University of Sciences
http://dtalk.elte.hu/www/welcome.html

Erasmus University of Rotterdam
http://www.eur.nl/

Erie Community College
http://davey.sunyerie.edu/

Ernst-Moritz-Arndt-University Greifswald
http://www.uni-greifswald.de/

Escuela de Administracion de Negocios para Graduados
http://www.esan.edu.pe/

Estrella Mountain Community College
http://www.emc.maricopa.edu/

Europa-University Viadrina Frankfurt
http://www.euv-frankfurt-o.de/

European Institute of Business Administration
http://www.insead.fr/

Ewha Women's University
http://arch.ewha.ac.kr/

Fayetteville State University
http://www.fsufay.edu/

Feng Chia University
http://www.fcu.edu.tw/

Ferris State University
http://about.ferris.edu/

Findhorn College
http://www.tiac.net/biz/fcie/

Fisk University
http://www.fisk.edu/

Flinders University
http://www.flinders.edu.au/

Florida A&M University
http://www-wane-leon.scri.fsu.edu:80/~jippolit/
FAMU_html/html_s/FAMU_top.html

Florida Atlantic University
http://www.fau.edu/

Florida Institute of Technology
http://www.fit.edu/

Florida International University
http://www.fiu.edu/

Florida State University
http://www.fsu.edu

Foothill College
http://www.fhda.edu/foothill/

Fort Hays State University
http://www.fhsu.edu/fhsu.html

Franklin and Marshall College
http://www.fandm.edu/

Franklin Pierce College
http://www.fpc.edu/

Franklin Pierce Law Center
http://www.fplc.edu/

Fredonia State University
http://www.cs.fredonia.edu/

Freie University Berlin
http://www.chemie.fu-berlin.de/fub/index.html

Friends University
http://www.friends.edu/

Fudan University
http://www.cs.wisc.edu/~mshen/fudan.html

Fujita Health University
http://pathy.fujita-hu.ac.jp/

Fukuoka Institute of Technology
http://www.fit.ac.jp/

Fukuoka Junior College of Technology
http://www.fjct.fit.ac.jp/

Fukushima Medical College
http://www.fmu.ac.jp/index.html

Fukushima University
http://www.fukushima-u.ac.jp/

Fullerton College
http://www.fullcoll.edu/

Furman University
http://www.furman.edu/

Gainesville College
http://www.gc.peachnet.edu/

Gallaudet University
http://www.gallaudet.edu/

Gannon University
http://www.gannon.edu/

Gazi University
http://cc.gazi.edu.tr/

Gdansk Medical Academy
http://www.amg.gda.pl/

Gdansk Technical University
http://www.pg.gda.pl/pg.html

George Mason University
http://www.gmu.edu/

George Washington University
http://gwis.circ.gwu.edu/

Georgetown University
http://www.georgetown.edu/

Georgia Institute of Technology
http://www.gatech.edu/TechHome.html

Georgia State University
http://www.gsu.edu/

Gettysburg College
http://www.gettysburg.edu/

Glasgow University
http://www.gla.ac.uk/

GMI Engineering & Management Institute
http://www.gmi.edu/

Golden West College
http://www.gwc.cccd.edu/

Goldsmiths College, University of London
http://www.gold.ac.uk/

Gonzaga University
http://www.gonzaga.edu/

Goshen College
http://www.goshen.edu/

Goucher College
http://www.goucher.edu/

Grace College
http://www.grace.edu/

Graduate Institute of International Studies
http://heiwww.unige.ch/

Grant MacEwan Community College
http://www.gmcc.ab.ca/

Graz University of Technology
http://www.tu-graz.ac.at/

Griffith University
http://www.gu.edu.au/

Grinnell College
http://www.math.grin.edu/

Grossmont-Cuyamaca Community College District
http://www.gcccd.cc.ca.us/

Guilford College
http://www.guilford.edu/

Gunma University
http://www.la.gunma-u.ac.jp/

Gustavus Adolphus College
http://www.gac.edu/

Gvdvllu University of Agricultural Sciences
http://www.ktg.gau.hu/

Haagse Hogeschool
http://www.hhs.nl/Welcome.html

Hacettepe University
http://www.ee.hun.edu.tr/

Hachinohe Institute of Technology
http://www.hi-tech.ac.jp/

Hahnemann University
http://www.hahnemann.edu/

Hallym University
http://myrinae.hallym.ac.kr/welcome.html

Halmstad University
http://www.hh.se:7777/

Hamilton College
http://www.hamilton.edu/

Hamline University
http://www.hamline.edu/

Hampden-Sydney College
http://www.hsc.edu/

Hampshire College
http://www.hampshire.edu/

Hampton University
http://cs.hamptonu.edu/

Hangzhou University
http://bronze.ucs.indiana.edu/~zerping/hangda.htm

Hanover College
http://www.hanover.edu/

Hanyang University
http://166.104.36.75/

Harbin Engineering University
http://www.tuns.ca/~hey/hsei.html

Harding University
http://www.harding.edu/

Harvard University
http://www.harvard.edu/

Harvey Mudd College
http://www.hmc.edu/

Hastings College of Law
http://www.uchastings.edu

Hawaii Pacific University
http://www.hpu.edu/

Heald Institute Of Technology
http://www.heald.edu/

Hebrew University of Jerusalem
http://www1.huji.ac.il

Heidelberg College
http://www.heidelberg.edu/

Heinrich-Heine-University Duesseldorf
http://www.rz.uni-duesseldorf.de/

Helsinki Business Polytechnic
http://www.helbp.fi/

Helsinki School of Economics
http://www.hkkk.fi/

Helsinki University
http://www.helsinki.fi/

Helsinki University of Technology
http://www.hut.fi/index.html

Hendrix College
http://192.131.98.11/

Heriot-Watt University
http://www.cee.hw.ac.uk/

Hillsdale College
http://www.hillsdale.edu/

Hiram College
http://www.hiram.edu/

Hirosaki University
http://www.hirosaki-u.ac.jp/

Hiroshima City University
http://www.hiroshima-cu.ac.jp/

Hiroshima Institute of Technology
http://www.cc.it-hiroshima.ac.jp/

Hiroshima Shudo University
http://www.shudo-u.ac.jp/

Hiroshima University
http://www.hiroshima-u.ac.jp/

Hiroshima-Denki Institute of Technology
http://www.c.hiroshima-dit.ac.jp/

Hitotsubashi University
http://www.higashi.hit-u.ac.jp/info-ind.html

Hobart and William Smith Colleges
http://hws3.hws.edu:9000/

Hofstra University
http://www.hofstra.edu/

Hogeschool Eindhoven
http://www.hi.ft.hse.nl/

Hogeschool van Amsterdam
http://www.hva.nl

Hogeschool van Utrecht
http://www.hvu.nl/index_english.html

Hokkaido University
http://www.hokudai.ac.jp/welcome-e.html

Hokkaido University of Education
http://www.iwa.hokkyodai.ac.jp/

Hong Kong Baptist University
http://www.hkbu.edu.hk/

Hong Kong University of Science and Technology
http://sunsite.ust.hk/

Honolulu Community College
http://www.hcc.hawaii.edu/

Hope College
http://www.hope.edu/

Howard Community College
http://www.howardcc.edu/

Howard University
http://www.howard.edu/

Hudson Valley Community College
http://www.hvcc.edu/

Humber College of Applied Arts and Technology
http://www.humberC.on.ca/

Humboldt State University,
http://rocky.humboldt.edu/

Humboldt-University, Berlin
http://www.hu-berlin.de/

Huntingdon College
http://www.huntingdon.edu/

Huntington College
http://www.huntcol.edu/

ICI University
http://www.ici.edu/

Idaho State University
http://www.isu.edu/

Illinois Benedictine College
http://www.ibc.edu/

Illinois Institute of Technology
http://www.iit.edu/

Illinois State University
http://www.ilstu.edu/

Imperial College of Science and Technology
http://www.doc.ic.ac.uk/

Incarnate Word College
http://www.iwctx.edu/

Indian Institute of Science, Bangalore
http://ece.iisc.ernet.in/iisc.html

Indian Institute of Technology, Bombay
http://sarang.ee.iitb.ernet.in/

Indian Institute of Technology, Delhi
http://kriti.iitd.ernet.in/menu/iitd-home.html

Indian Institute of Technology, Kanpur
http://www.cs.wisc.edu/~shubu/iitk/iitk.html

Indian Institute of Technology, Kharagpur
http://www.rahul.net/kgpnet/iit/iit.html

Indian Institute of Technology, Madras
http://sol.rutgers.edu/~sabesan/iit.html

Indiana Institute of Technology
http://www.indtech.edu/

Indiana State University
http://www-isu.indstate.edu/

Indiana University
http://www.indiana.edu/

Indiana University of Pennsylvania
http://www.lib.iup.edu/

Indiana University Purdue University, Indianapolis
http://indyunix.iupui.edu/

Indiana University, Bloomington
http://www-iub.indiana.edu/

Indiana University, South Bend
http://www.iusb.edu/

Inha University
http://nms.inha.ac.kr/

Institut d'Informatique d'Entreprise
http://iie.cnam.fr/

Institut des Mathematiques Appliquees de Grenoble
http://imag.fr/

Institut f. Semantische Informationsverarbeitung
http://hal.cl-ki.uni-osnabrueck.de/

Institut fur Lasertechnik
http://www.ilt.fhg.de/WELCOME.HTML

Institut Jozef Stefan
http://www.ijs.si/

Institut National de Physique Nucleaire et de Physique des Particules
http://info.in2p3.fr/

Institut National des Sciences Appliquees de Toulouse
http://www.insa-tlse.fr/

Institut National des Télécommunications
http://arctique.int-evry.fr/eng/menu_eng.html

Institut Universitari de l'Audiovisual
http://www.iua.upf.es/

Institute for Mathematical Sciences
http://www.imsc.ernet.in/

Institute of Paper Science and Technology
http://www.ipst.edu/

Institute of Telecommunications and Information Technology
http://ittm.com.my/

Instituto Politecnico Nacional
http://www.ipn.mx/

Instituto Tecnologico y de Estudios Superiores de Monterrey
http://www.mty.itesm.mx/

Instituto Tecnologico y de Estudios Superiores de Occidente
http://www.gdl.iteso.mx/

International College Penang
http://mimos.my/icp/start.html

International Islamic University, Malaysia
http://scc.mimos.my/uia/uia.html

International School for Advanced Studies
http://www.sissa.it/

Iowa State University
http://www.iastate.edu/

Istanbul Technical University
http://www.itu.edu.tr/

Ithaca College
http://www.ithaca.edu/

Jackson State University
http://tiger.jsums.edu/html/homepage.html

Jacksonville State University
http://jsucc.jsu.edu/welcome.html

Jacksonville University
http://junix.ju.edu/

Jagiellonian Univeristy
http://www.if.uj.edu.pl/

James Cook University
http://www.jcu.edu.au/

James Madison University
http://www.jmu.edu/

Janus Pannonius University of Sciences
http://ipisun.jpte.hu/

Japan Advanced Institute of Science and Technology
http://www.jaist.ac.jp/

Japan Women's University
http://www.jwu.ac.jp/

Johannes Kepler University of Linz
http://www.ifs.uni-linz.ac.at/home.html

John Brown University
http://www.jbu.edu/

John Marshall Law School
http://www.jmls.edu/

Johns Hopkins University
http://www.jhu.edu/

Juhasz Gyula Teacher Training College
http://berreh.cab.jgytf.u-szeged.hu/jgytfeng.html

Kagoshima University
http://www.kagoshima-u.ac.jp/

Kalamazoo College
http://kzoo.edu/

Kanazawa University
http://kipcwww.ipc.kanazawa-u.ac.jp:8080/

Kansas State University
http://www.ksu.edu/

Karl Franzens University
http://www.kfunigraz.ac.at/

Karolinska Institute
http://www.ki.se/

Katholieke Universiteit Leuven
http://www.kuleuven.ac.be/

Kazan University
http://www.ksu.ras.ru/

Keele University
http://www.keele.ac.uk/

Keene State College
http://kilburn.keene.edu/

Keimyung University
http://kmucc.keimyung.ac.kr/

Keio University
http://www.sfc.keio.ac.jp/index.en.html

Keio University of Science and Technology
http://www.st.keio.ac.jp/

Kent State University
http://www.kent.edu/homepage.html

Kenyon College
http://www.kenyon.edu/

King's College London
http://www.kcl.ac.uk/

Kingston University
http://www.kingston.ac.uk/

Kinjo Gakuin University
http://www.kinjo-u.ac.jp/Welcome.html

Kitasato University
http://www.kitasato-u.ac.jp/

Kobe University
http://www.kobe-u.ac.jp/

Koc University
http://u6065.ku.edu.tr:70/0h/ku/ku.guide.html/

Kochi National College of Technology
http://www.kochi-ct.ac.jp/

Kochi University
http://www.is.kochi-u.ac.jp/

Koga Kuin University
http://www.kogakuin.ac.jp/

Konan University
http://www.ipc.konan-u.ac.jp/

Korea Advanced Institute of Science & Technology
http://camis.kaist.ac.kr:8080/

Korea University
http://www.cs.columbia.edu/~dongwon/KU/

Kossuth Lajos University of Sciences
http://www.lib.klte.hu/index.english.html

Kumamoto National College of Technology
http://www.cs.knct.ac.jp/

Kumamoto Prefecture College
http://www.pu-kumamoto.ac.jp/

Kumamoto University
http://www.eecs.kumamoto-u.ac.jp/

Kurume institute of Technology
http://www.kurume-it.ac.jp/

Kutztown University of Pennsylvania
http://www.kutztown.edu/

Kuwait University
http://kuc01.kuniv.edu.kw/

Kwangwoon University
http://128.134.70.44/main-eng.html

Kyoto Institute of Technology
http://www.kit.ac.jp/

Kyoto University
http://www.kyoto-u.ac.jp/English/

KyungSung University
http://sarang.kyungsung.ac.kr/

Kyushu Institute of Design
http://www.kyushu-id.ac.jp/

Kyushu Institute of Technology
http://www.kyutech.ac.jp/

Kyushu Sangyo University
http://www.ip.kyusan-u.ac.jp/

Kyushu University
http://www.kyushu-u.ac.jp/

La Salle University
http://www.lasalle.edu/home.html

La Sierra University
http://www.lasierra.edu/

La Trobe University
http://www.latrobe.edu.au/

Lafayette College
http://www.lafayette.edu/

LaGrange College
http://www.lgc.peachnet.edu/

Lahti Polytechnic
http://web.lahti-poly.fi/

Lake Forest College
http://www.lfc.edu/

Lake Superior State University
http://www.lssu.edu/

Lakehead University
http://www.lakeheadu.ca/menu.html

Lamar University
http://www.lamar.edu/

Lambton College
http://www.lambton.on.ca/

Lancaster University
http://www.lancs.ac.uk/

Langston University
http://www.lunet.edu/

Lappeenranta University of Technology
http://www.lut.fi/english.html

Lawrence University
http://www.lawrence.edu/

Lehigh University
http://www.lehigh.edu/

Lewis & Clark College
http://www.lclark.edu/

Lewisham College
http://www.lewisham.ac.uk/college/index.html

Liberec University of Technology
http://www.vslib.cz/

Libero Istituto Universitario Carlo Cattaneo
http://www.liuc.it/

Liberty University
http://www.liberty.edu/

Lillehammer College
http://www.hil.no/

Limburgs Universitair Centrum
http://www.luc.ac.be/

Lincoln University
http://www.lincoln.ac.nz/

Linkoping University
http://www.liu.se/

Liverpool John Moores University
http://www.livjm.ac.uk/

Lock Haven University of Pennsylvania
http://www.lhup.edu/

Lodz Technical University
http://zsku.p.lodz.pl/

London Business School
http://www.lbs.lon.ac.uk/

London School of Economics
http://www.blpes.lse.ac.uk/

Loughborough University of Technology
http://info.lut.ac.uk/

Lousiana College
http://www.lacollege.edu/

Louisiana State University
http://unix1.sncc.lsu.edu/

Louisiana Tech University
http://aurora.latech.edu/

Loyola College
http://www.loyola.edu/

Loyola Marymount University
http://www.lmu.edu/

Loyola University, Chicago
http://www.luc.edu/

Lulea University
http://www.luth.se/

Lund Institute of Technology
http://www.lth.se/

Lund University
http://www.lu.se/

Lycoming College
http://www.lycoming.edu/

Macalester College
http://www.macalstr.edu/

Macquarie University
http://www.mq.edu.au/

Madison Area Technical College
http://www.madison.tec.wi.us/

Mahidol University
http://www.mahidol.ac.th/mahidol.html

Malaspina University-College
http://www.mala.bc.ca/

Manchester Metropolitan University
http://www.mmu.ac.uk/

Manhattan College
http://www.cc.mancol.edu/

Mankato State University
http://www.mankato.msus.edu/

Mansfield University
http://157.62.12.80/

Maria Curie-Sklodowska University
http://www.umcs.lublin.pl/

Maricopa Community Colleges
http://www.maricopa.edu/

Marine Institute St. John's
http://inseine.ifmt.nf.ca/mi.html

Marist College
http://148.100.176.70/mcollege.htm

Marlboro College
http://www.marlboro.edu/

Marquette University
http://vinny.csd.mu.edu/marquette.html

Marshall University
http://www.marshall.edu/

Martin Luther University Halle-Wittenberg
http://www.uni-halle.de/

Mary Washington College
http://www.mwc.edu/

Maryland Institute, College of Art
http://www.mica.edu/

Marymount College
http://www.marymt.edu/

Marywood College
http://www.marywood.edu/

Masaryk University
http://www.fi.muni.cz/

Massachusetts Institute of Technology
http://web.mit.edu/

Massachusetts Maritime Academy
http://www.mma.mass.edu/mma.html

Massey University
http://www.massey.ac.nz/

Masters College
http://www.masters.edu/

Matej Bel University
http://nic.uakom.sk/hypertext/home.html

Mathematical Institute of the Hungarian Academy of Sciences
http://www.math-inst.hu/

Matsuyama University
http://iyokan.cc.matsuyama-u.ac.jp/

McGill University
http://www.mcgill.ca/

McMaster University
http://www.mcmaster.ca/

Medical College of Georgia
http://www.mcg.edu/

Medical College of Ohio
http://www.mco.edu/

Medical College of Wisconsin
http://www.mcw.edu/

Medical University of South Carolina
http://www.radonc.musc.edu/

Meharry Medical College
http://ccmac.mmc.edu/

Meiji University
http://www.meiji.ac.jp/

Meisei University
http://www.meisei-u.ac.jp/

Memorial University of Newfoundland
http://www.ucs.mun.ca/

Mercer University
http://www.mercer.peachnet.edu/

Mercyhurst College
http://utopia.mercy.edu/

Meredith College
http://www.meredith.edu/meredith/

Merton College, Oxford
http://info.ox.ac.uk/~mertinfo/

Mesa Community College
http://www.mc.maricopa.edu/

Messiah College
http://www.messiah.edu/

Metropolitan State College of Denver
http://www.mscd.edu/

Miami Bible Institute
http://www.fiu.edu/~wgreen01/mbi.html

Miami University, Ohio
http://www.muohio.edu/

Miami-Dade Community College
http://www.mdcc.edu/

Michigan State University
http://www.msu.edu/

Michigan Technological University
http://www.mtu.edu/

Mid Sweden University
http://www.forv.mh.se/estart.html

Middle East Technical University
http://www.metu.edu.tr/

Middle Tennessee State University
http://www.mtsu.edu/

Middlebury College
http://www.middlebury.edu/

Middlesex University
http://www.mdx.ac.uk/

Midwestern State University
http://www.mwsu.edu/

Mie University
http://www.mie-u.ac.jp/english.html

Millersville University
http://cs.millersv.edu/

Millsaps College
http://www.millsaps.edu/

Milwaukee School of Engineering
http://www.msoe.edu/

Mindanao State University—Iligan Institute of Technology
http://www.msuiit.edu.ph/

Minneapolis College of Art and Design
http://www.mcad.edu/

Minot State University
http://warp6.cs.misu.nodak.edu/

Mississippi College
http://www.mc.edu/

Mississippi State University
http://www.msstate.edu/

Missouri Western State College
http://www.mwsc.edu/

Miyazaki International College
http://www.miyazaki-mic.ac.jp/

Miyazaki Medical College
http://www.miyazaki-med.ac.jp/

Miyazaki University
http://www.miyazaki-u.ac.jp/

Monash University
http://www.monash.edu.au/

Monmouth College
http://pippin.monm.edu/

Monmouth University
http://www.monmouth.edu/

Montana State University-Bozeman
http://www.montana.edu/

Montana State University-Northern Havre
http://www.nmclites.edu

MontanUniversity Leoben
http://www.unileoben.ac.at/oehwww/

Montclair State University
http://www.montclair.edu/

Monterey Institute of International Studies
http://www.miis.edu/

Moscow Institute of Physics and Technology
http://www.crec.mipt.ru/MIPT

Moscow State University
http://www.rector.msu.su/

Mount Allison University
http://www.mta.ca/

Mount Holyoke College
http://www.mtholyoke.edu/

Mount Saint Mary College
http://www.msmc.edu/

Mount Saint Mary's College
http://www.msmary.edu/

Mount Saint Vincent University
http://www.msvu.ca/

Mount Union College
http://www.muc.edu/

Munich University of Technology
http://www.informatik.tu-muenchen.de/HOME-PAGE_e.html

Murdoch University
http://www.murdoch.edu.au/

Muroran Institute of Technology
http://www.muroran-it.ac.jp/

Musashi Institute of Technology
http://www.musashi-tech.ac.jp/

Musashi University
http://www.cc.musashi.ac.jp/

Muskingum College
http://www.muskingum.edu/

Nagano University
http://www.nagano.ac.jp/

Nagasaki University
http://www.cc.nagasaki-u.ac.jp/

Nagoya Institute of Technology
http://www.nitech.ac.jp/

Nagoya University
http://www.nagoya-u.ac.jp/

Nanyang Polytechnic
http://WWW.nyp.ac.sg/

Nanyang Technological University, Singapore
http://www.ntu.ac.sg/

Nanzan University
http://www.nanzan-u.ac.jp/

Napier University
http://www.napier.ac.uk/

Nara Institute of Science and Technology
http://www.aist-nara.ac.jp/

Naruto University of Education
http://www.naruto-u.ac.jp/

National Central University
http://www.mgt.ncu.edu.tw/

National Cheng Kung University
http://www.ncku.edu.tw/

National Chiao Tung University
http://www.nctu.edu.tw/

National Chung Cheng University
http://www.ccu.edu.tw/

National College of Art & Design, Norway
http://samson.shks.no/

National Defense University
http://www.ndu.edu/

National Taichung Institute of Commerce
http://alpha.ntcic.edu.tw/

National Taiwan Normal University
http://www.ntnu.edu.tw/

National Taiwan University
http://www.ntu.edu.tw/

National Technological University
http://www.ntu.edu/

National Tsing-Hua University
http://www.nthu.edu.tw/

National University
http://nunic.nu.edu/

National University of Mexico
http://www.noc.unam.mx/UNAM/hpunam.html

National University of Singapore
http://www.nus.sg/

Naval Postgraduate School
http://www.nps.navy.mil/

Nesna College
http://oter.hinesna.no/

New Jersey Institute of Technology
http://www.njit.edu/

New Mexico Institute of Mining and Technology
http://www.nmt.edu/

New Mexico State University
http://www.nmsu.edu/

New School for Social Research
http://dialnsa.edu/home.html

New York Institute of Technology
http://ftp.nyit.edu/

New York University
http://www.nyu.edu/

Nicholls State University
http://server.nich.edu/

Nicolaus Copernicus University
http://www.cc.uni.torun.pl/

Nihon University
http://ftp.nc.nihon-u.ac.jp/

Niigata University
http://www.cc.niigata-u.ac.jp/

Nijenrode University
http://www.nijenrode.nl/

Nippon Bunri University
http://www.mc.nbu.ac.jp/NBU/e/nbu-e.html

Nippon Medical School
http://www.nms.ac.jp/

Noordelijke Hogeschool Leeuwarden
http://www.tem.nhl.nl/

North Carolina Agricultural and Technical State University
http://www.ncat.edu/

North Carolina State University
http://www.ncsu.edu/

North Central Bible College
http://www.ncbc.edu/

North Dakota State University
http://toons.cc.ndsu.nodak.edu/ndsu/Home.html

North Dakota University System
http://www.nodak.edu/

North East Wales Institute of Higher Education
http://www.newi.ac.uk/

North Park College and Theological Seminary
http://www.npcts.edu/

Northeast Louisiana University
http://www.nlu.edu/

Northeast Missouri State University
http://www.nemostate.edu/

Northeastern University
http://www.dac.neu.edu/

Northern Arizona University
http://www.nau.edu/

Northern Michigan University
http://www.nmu.edu/

Northern Statue University
http://www.northern.edu/

Northern Territory University
http://www.ntu.edu.au/

Northern University of Malaysia
http://161.142.40.1/0c:\versi.htm|/

Northwest Nazarene College
http://www.nnc.edu/Homepage.html

Northwestern Michigan College
http://leo.nmc.edu/

Northwestern State University
http://server.nsula.edu/

Northwestern University
http://www.nwu.edu/

Notre Dame Women's College
http://www.notredame.ac.jp/

Nova Southeastern University
http://www.nova.edu/Inter-Links/

Novgorod State University
http://www.novsu.ac.ru/

Novosibirsk State University
http://www.nsu.nsk.su/

Oakland University
http://www.acs.oakland.edu/

Oberlin College
http://www.oberlin.edu/

Occidental College
http://www.oxy.edu/

Ohio Northern University
http://www.onu.edu/

Ohio State University
http://www.acs.ohio-state.edu/

Ohio University
http://www.ohiou.edu/

Ohio Wesleyan University
http://192.68.223.4:8000/

Oita University
http://www.oita-u.ac.jp/

Okanagan University College
http://oksw01.okanagan.bc.ca/home.html

Okayama Prefectural University
http://www.oka-pu.ac.jp/

Oklahoma City University
http://frodo.okcu.edu/

Oklahoma State University
http://www.okstate.edu/

Old Dominion University
http://www.odu.edu/

Olivet Nazarene University
http://www.olivet.edu/

Open University of the Netherlands
http://www.ouh.nl/

Oppland College
http://www.odh.no/

Oral Roberts University
http://www.oru.edu/

Orange Coast College
http://www.lib.occ.cccd.edu/OCC/OCCHomePage.html

Oregon Graduate Institute of Science and Technology
http://www.ogi.edu/welcome.html

Oregon Health Sciences University
http://www.ohsu.edu/

Oregon State University
http://www.orst.edu/

Osaka Kyoiku University
http://okumedia.cc.osaka-kyoiku.ac.jp/

Osaka Medical College
http://www.osaka-med.ac.jp/

Osaka University
http://www.osaka-u.ac.jp/Osaka-u.html

Oulu Institute of Tecnology
http://www.otol.fi/index.uk.html

Oxford Brookes University
http://www.brookes.ac.uk/

Oxford University
http://www.ox.ac.uk/

Pace University
http://pacevm.dac.pace.edu/

Pacific Lutheran University
http://plu.edu/

Palomar College
http://www.palomar.edu/

Peking University
http://www.pku.edu.cn/

Pennsylvania State System of Higher Education
http://sshe2.sshechan.edu/sshe.html

Pennsylvania State University
http://www.psu.edu/

Pepperdine University
http://moon.pepperdine.edu/HomeSBM.html

Perugia University
http://www.unipg.it/welcomeEn.html

Phoenix College
http://www.pc.maricopa.edu/

Pima Community College
http://www.pima.edu/

Pittsburgh State University
http://www.pittstate.edu/

Pitzer College
http://www.pitzer.edu/

Plymouth State College
http://www.plymouth.edu/

Pohang University of Science and Technology
http://firefox.postech.ac.kr/

Point Loma Nazarene College
http://192.147.249.89/

Point Park College
http://www.lm.com/~markv20/ppc.html

Politecnico di Milano
http://www.polimi.it/

Politecnico di Torino
http://www.polito.it/

Polytechnic University of New York
http://www.poly.edu/

Polytechnical University of Bucharest
http://www.cs.pub.ro/

Pomona College
http://www.pomona.claremont.edu/

Pontifica University Catolica de Chile
http://www.puc.cl/

Portland Community College
http://www.pcc.edu/

Portland State University
http://www.pdx.edu/

Princeton University
http://www.princeton.edu/

PUC-Rio
http://www.puc-rio.br/

Purdue University
http://www.purdue.edu/

Pusan National University
http://164.125.64.41/pnu/pnu.html

Pusan Women's University
http://lotus.pwu.ac.kr/

Queen's University, Belfast
http://www.qub.ac.uk/

Queen's University, Kingston, Ontario
http://info.queensu.ca/index.html

Queensland University of Technology
http://www.qut.edu.au/

Quincy University
http://www.quincy.edu/

Radford University
http://www.runet.edu/

Rand Afrikaans University
http://www.rau.ac.za/

Randolph-Macon College
http://www.rmc.edu/

Randolph-Macon Woman's College
http://www.rmwc.edu/

Reading University
http://www.reading.ac.uk/

Reed College
http://www.reed.edu/

Regent University
http://www.regent.edu/

Regional Engineering College
http://www.cis.ufl.edu/~sk0/recw.html

Regional Engineering College, Tiruchirappalli, India
http://tam2k.tamu.edu/~ssk8291/rect.html

Reitaku University
http://www.reitaku-u.ac.jp/

Rensselaer Polytechnic Institute
http://www.rpi.edu/

Rhodes College
http://www.rhodes.edu/

Rhodes University
http://www.ru.ac.za/rhodes.html

Rice University
http://www.rice.edu/

Richard Stockton University
http://odin.stockton.edu/

Richland College
http://www.rlc.dcccd.edu/

Rider University
http://www.rider.edu/

Riga Technical University
http://www.eef.rtu.lv/

Ritsumeikan University
http://www.ritsumei.ac.jp/

Roanoke College
http://www.roanoke.edu/

Rochester Institute of Technology
http://www.rit.edu/

Rockefeller University
http://www.rockefeller.edu/

Rockhurst College
http://vax1.rockhurst.edu/

Rollins College
http://www.rollins.edu/

Rose-Hulman Institute of Technology
http://www.rose-hulman.edu/

Roskilde University
http://frederik.ruc.dk/

Rowan College of New Jersey
http://www.rowan.edu/

Royal Danish School of Pharmacy
http://info.dfh.dk/

Royal Holloway College
http://www.rhbnc.ac.uk/

Royal Institute of Technology, Stockholm
http://www.kth.se/

Royal Melbourne Institute of Technology
http://www.rmit.edu.au/

Royal Military Academy
http://www.rma.ac.be/

Royal Military College of Canada
http://www.rmc.ca/

Royal Postgraduate Medical School
http://www.rpms.ac.uk/index.html

Ruhr-University Bochum
http://www.ruhr-uni-bochum.de/

Russian Academy of Sciences
http://www.ras.ru/

Rutgers University
http://www.rutgers.edu/index.html

Rutgers University, Camden
http://camden-www.rutgers.edu/

Ryerson Polytechnic University
http://www.acs.ryerson.ca/

Sacramento City College
http://wheel.ucdavis.edu/~btcarrol/sac_city/Sac_City.html

Saga University
http://www.cc.saga-u.ac.jp/

Sage Colleges
http://www.sage.edu/

Saint Joseph College
http://www.sjc.edu/

Saint Joseph's College
http://www.saintjoe.edu/

Saint Joseph's University
http://www.sju.edu/

Saint Mary's University
http://www.stmarys.ca:70/

Saint Xavier University
http://www.sxu.edu/

Saitama University
http://www.ke.ics.saitama-u.ac.jp/index_english.html

Sam Houston State University
http://www.shsu.edu/

Samford University
http://www.samford.edu/

San Diego State University
http://www.sdsu.edu/

San Francisco State University
http://www.sfsu.edu/

San Joaquin Delta College
http://www.sjdccd.cc.ca.us/

San Jose State University
http://www.sjsu.edu/

Sangamon State University
http://www.sangamon.edu/

Santa Clara University
http://www.scu.edu/

Santa Fe Community College
http://www.santafe.cc.fl.us/

Santa Rosa Junior College
http://www.santarosa.edu/

Sapporo Medical University
http://www.sapmed.ac.jp/

Saskatchewan Institute of Applied Science and Technology
http://www.siast.sk.ca/

Scarborough College, University of Toronto
http://www.scar.toronto.edu/

School of Engineering of Bern HTL
http://www.isbe.ch/index_e.html

School of Engineering of Burgdorf HTL
http://www.isburg.ch/hpageeng.html

School of Oriental and African Studies
http://www.soas.ac.uk/

School of the Art Institute of Chicago
http://www.artic.edu/saic/saichome.html

School of the Visual Arts
http://www.sva.edu/

Science University of Tokyo
http://www.sut.ac.jp/

Scuola Superiore di Studi Universitari e di Perfezionamento Sant'Anna
http://www.sssup.it/

Seattle Central Community College
http://scc.cc.wa.us/

Seattle Pacific University
http://www.spu.edu/

Seattle University
http://www.seattleu.edu/

Semmelweis University of Medical Sciences
http://www.sote.hu/

Sendai National College of Technology
http://www.sendai-ct.ac.jp/welcome-e.html

Seoul National University
http://www.snu.ac.kr/

Seton Hall University
http://www.shu.edu/

Shandong University
http://www.inf-wiss.uni-konstanz.de/~zhang/SDUni/sduni.html

Shanghai Medical University
http://www.ucc.uconn.edu/~xuchen/smu.html

Sheffield Hallam University
http://pine.shu.ac.uk/

Sheffield University
http://www.shef.ac.uk/

Shiga Polytechnic College
http://www.shiga-pc.ac.jp:8080/

Shimane Medical University
http://www.shimane-med.ac.jp/

Shippensburg University
http://www.ship.edu/

Silesian Technical University
http://www.gliwice.edu.pl/

Simon Fraser University
http://www.sfu.ca/

Simon's Rock College
http://www.simons-rock.edu/

Simpson College
http://www.simpson.edu/

Skidmore College
http://www.skidmore.edu/

Slippery Rock University
http://www.sru.edu/

Slovak Technical University
http://sun.sanet.sk/info/efstu-sl.html

Smith Chapel Bible College
http://144.174.145.13/

Smith College
http://www.smith.edu/

Sogang University
http://www.sogang.ac.kr/

Soka University
http://www.t.soka.ac.jp/

Sonoma State University
http://www.sonoma.edu/

Sophia University
http://www.sophia.ac.jp/

South Bank University
http://www.sbu.ac.uk/

South Dakota School of Mines and Technology
http://www.sdsmt.edu/

South Dakota State University
http://www.sdstate.edu/

Southeast Missouri State University
http://www.semo.edu/

Southern College of Seventh-day Adventists
http://www.southern.edu/

Southern College of Technology
http://www.sct.edu/

Southern Connecticut State University
http://scwww.ctstateu.edu/

Southern Cross University
http://www.scu.edu.au/

Southern Denmark Business School
http://www.hhs.dk/

Southern Illinois University
http://www.siu.edu/

Southern Illinois University at Edwardsville
http://www.siue.edu/

Southern Methodist University
http://www.smu.edu/

Southern University
http://www.subr.edu/

Southern Utah University
http://www.suu.edu/suuhome.html

Southwest Missouri State University
http://www.smsu.edu/

Southwest Texas State University
http://www.swt.edu/

Southwestern Adventist College
http://www.swac.edu/

St. Andrews University
http://www.st-and.ac.uk/~www_/index.html

St. Cloud State University
http://www.stcloud.msus.edu/

St. Edward's University
http://www.cs.stedwards.edu/

St. Francis Xavier University
http://www.stfx.ca/

St. John's College, Annapolis
http://www.sjca.edu/

St. John's University
http://www.stjohns.edu/

St. John's University, College of St. Benedict
http://www.csbsju.edu/

St. Louis College of Pharmacy
http://www.stlcop.edu/

St. Louis University, Baguio
http://www.slu.edu.ph/

St. Mary's College of California
http://www.stmarys-ca.edu/

St. Mary's College of Minnesota
http://140.190.128.190/SMC/HomePage.html

St. Olaf College
http://www.stolaf.edu/

St. Petersburg University
http://www.pu.ru/

St. Thomas University
http://www.stthomasu.ca/

Stanford University
http://www.stanford.edu/

Stanislaw Staszic University of Mining And Metallurgy
http://www.uci.agh.edu.pl/

State Engineering University of Armenia
http://www.darmstadt.gmd.de/~dressler/seua.html

State University of New York at Geneseo
http://mosaic.cc.geneseo.edu/geneseo.html

State University of New York at Oswego
http://www.oswego.edu/

State University of New York at Potsdam
http://www.potsdam.edu/

State University of New York College at Cortland
http://www.cortland.edu/

State University of New York Institute of Technology
http://woody.c2tc.rl.af.mil/

State University of New York, Albany
http://cscmosaic.albany.edu/

State University of New York, Brockport
http://www.acs.brockport.edu/

State University of New York, Buffalo
http://wings.buffalo.edu/

State University of New York, New Platz
http://npeeserv.eelab.newpaltz.edu/

State University of New York, Oneonta
http://137.141.153.38/

State University of New York, Plattsburgh
http://bio420.hawk.plattsburgh.edu/SUNYHomePage.html

State University of New York, Stony Brook
http://www.sunysb.edu/

Stavanger College
http://www.hsr.no/

Stephen F. Austin State University
http://www.sfasu.edu/

Stetson University
http://www.stetson.edu/

Stevens Institute of Technology
http://www.stevens-tech.edu/

Stockholm School of Economics
http://www.hhs.se/

Stockholm University
http://www.su.se/

Stord/Haugesund College
http://www.ssh.no/

Strasbourg University
http://www.u-strasbg.fr/

Susquehanna University
http://www.susqu.edu/

Suzhou University
http://kantaro.sk.tsukuba.ac.jp/Shi/public_html/Suzhou_U.html

Swansea University
http://www.swan.ac.uk/

Swarthmore College
http://www.swarthmore.edu

Swedish School of Economics and Business Administration, Finland
http://www.shh.fi/

Swedish University of Agricultural Sciences
http://www.radek.slu.se/

Sweet Briar College
http://www.sbc.edu/

Swinburne University of Technology
http://www.swin.edu.au/

Swiss Federal Institute of Technology, Zurich
http://www.ethz.ch/

Syracuse University
http://cwis.syr.edu/

Szeged University
http://www.u-szeged.hu/

Taegu University
http://www.taegu.ac.kr/

Takuma National College of Technology
http://www.takuma-ct.ac.jp/

Tallinn Technical University
http://zaphod.cc.ttu.ee/

Tama Institute of Management and Information Sciences
http://www.timis.ac.jp/Timishome.html

Tamkang University
http://www.tku.edu.tw/

Tampere Institute of Technology
http://www.tit.fi/

Tampere University of Technology
http://www.cc.tut.fi/

Tartu University
http://www.ut.ee/

Tatung Institute of Technology
http://www.cse.ttit.edu.tw/

Technical University Kosice
http://hron.ef.tuke.sk/tu/tuke-a.html

Technical University of Budapest, Hungary
http://www.bme.hu/

Technical University of Denmark
http://www.dtu.dk/cwis/welcome.html

Technical University of Nova Scotia
http://www.tuns.ca/

Technical University of Timisoara
http://www.utt.ro/

Technikum Vorarlberg
http://www.tvlbg.ac.at/

Technion, Israel Institute of Technology
http://www.technion.ac.il/

Technische University Berlin
http://www.tu-berlin.de/

Technische University Braunschweig
http://www.tu-bs.de/

Technische University Chemnitz-Zwickau
http://www.tu-chemnitz.de/index-e.html

Technische University Clausthal
http://www.tu-clausthal.de/

Technische University Darmstadt
http://www.th-darmstadt.de/

Technische University Dresden
http://www.tu-dresden.de/

Technische University Hamburg-Harburg
http://www.tu-harburg.de/indexus.html

Technische University Ilmenau
http://www.tu-ilmenau.de/

Teikyo University
http://www.teikyo-u.ac.jp/

Tel Aviv University
http://www.tau.ac.il/

Telemark College
http://www.tdh.no/

Temple University
http://astro.ocis.temple.edu/

Tennessee Technological University
http://www.tntech.edu/

Texas A&M University
http://www.tamu.edu

Texas Christian University
http://www.tcu.edu/

Texas State Technical College
http://www.tstc.edu/

Texas Tech University
http://www.ttu.edu/

Texas Woman's University
http://192.135.186.50/twu/1.html

Thamasat University
http://ipied.tu.ac.th/

Thomas College
http://www.thomas.edu

Thomas Jefferson University
http://www.tju.edu/

Thomas More College
http://www.thomasmore.edu/welcome.html

Tianjin University
http://www.tju.edu.cn/

Tilburg University
http://www.kub.nl:2080/

Tohoku University
http://www.tohoku.ac.jp/

Tokai University
http://www.cc.u-tokai.ac.jp/

Tokyo Institute of Technology
http://www.titech.ac.jp/

Tokyo International University
http://www.tiu.ac.jp/

Tokyo Kaseigakuin Tsukuba Junior College
http://www.kasei.ac.jp/

Tokyo Kogei Tanki University
http://www.win.or.jp/~takahara/

Tokyo Medical and Dental University
http://www.i-mde.tmd.ac.jp/I-MDE.html

Tokyo Metropolitan College of Aeronautical Engineering
http://www.kouku-k.ac.jp/

Tokyo University of Agriculture & Technology
http://www.tuat.ac.jp/

Tokyo Woman's Christian University
http://www.twcu.ac.jp/

Tokyo Women's Medical College
http://www.twmc.ac.jp/

Tomsk State University
http://www.tsu.tomsk.su/

Towson State University
http://www.towson.edu/

Toyama Medical and Pharmaceutical University
http://www.toyama-mpu.ac.jp/

Toyama University
http://www.toyama-u.ac.jp/

Transylvania University
http://www.transy.edu/

Trenton State College
http://www.trenton.edu/

Trinity College
http://www.trincoll.edu/homepage.html

Trinity University
http://www.trinity.edu/

Tsinghua University
http://www.net.edu.cn/

Tufts University
http://www.tufts.edu/

Tulane University
http://www.tulane.edu/

Ube College
http://www.ube-c.ac.jp

Ulsan University
http://munsu.ulsan.ac.kr:8080/

Uludag
http://www.uludag.edu.tr/

Umea University
http://macavity.umdc.umu.se/~roland/

Uniformed Services University of the Health Sciences
http://www.usuhs.mil/

UNIK - Center for Technology at Kjeller, University of Oslo
http://www.unik.no/ENGELSK/presentengelsk.html

Union College
http://www.union.edu/

United Medical and Dental Schools of Guy's and St Thomas's Hospitals
http://www.umds.ac.uk/

United States Air Force Academy
http://www.usafa.af.mil/

United States Military Academy
http://euler.math.usma.edu/Introduction.html

United States Naval Academy
http://xtreme2.acc.iit.edu/~trygray/USNA.html

United States Sports Academy
http://www.sport.ussa.edu/

Université du Québec
http://www.uquebec.ca/

University degli studi di Brescia
http://www.unibs.it/

University of Connecticut
http://www.uconn.edu/

University of Dallas
http://www.udallas.edu/

University Anahuac
http://www.dcc.anahuac.mx/

University Anahuac del Sur
http://www.uas.mx/

University Autonoma de Barcelona
http://www.uab.es/

University Autonoma de Nayarit
http://www.uan.mx/

University Autonoma de Nuevo Leon
http://www.dsi.uanl.mx/

University Autonoma Metropolitana
http://tonatiuh.uam.mx/

University Bamberg
http://www.uni-bamberg.de/

University Basel
http://www.unibas.ch/

University Bayreuth
http://www.uni-bayreuth.de/homes/bayreuth.html

University Bielefeld
http://www.techfak.uni-bielefeld.de/indexengl.html

University Bonn
http://www.informatik.uni-bonn.de/unibo.html

University Bremen
http://www.uni-bremen.de/

University Central de Venezuela
http://www.sagi.ucv.edu.ve/

University College London
http://www.ucl.ac.uk/home.html

University College of Kalmar
http://www.hik.se/

University College Salford
http://www.ucsalf.ac.uk/

University College, Cork
http://www.ucc.ie/webentry.html

University College, Dublin
http://www.ucd.ie/

University College, Galway
http://www.ucg.ie/

University Complutense de Madrid
http://www.ucm.es/UCMD.html

University de Barcelona
http://www.ub.es/

University de Chile
http://www.uchile.cl/

University de Colima
http://www.ucol.mx/

University de Cordoba
http://www.uco.es/UCOhome.english.html

University de Costa Rica
http://www.ucr.ac.cr/

University de Granada
http://www.ugr.es/

University de Guadalajara
http://www.udg.mx/Ingles/udg.html

University de Guanajuato
http://www.ugto.mx/

University de La Frontera
http://www.enlaces.ufro.cl/

University de la Republica Oriental del Uruguay
http://fisica.edu.uy/

University de las Palmas de Gran Canaria
http://www.ulpgc.es/

University de Lausanne
http://www.unil.ch/

University de Los Andes
http://mozart.ing.ula.ve/ula.html

University de Marne la Vallée
http://indy.univ-mlv.fr/

University de Oviedo
http://www.uniovi.es/

University de Savoie
http://www.univ-savoie.fr/

University de Technologie Compiegne
http://delta.si.univ-compiegne.fr/

University del Valle
http://www.univalle.edu.co/

University del Zulia
http://www.luz.ve/

University des Saarlandes
http://www.rz.uni-sb.de/

University des Sciences et Technologies de Lille
http://www.univ-lille1.fr/

University di Cagliari
http://www.unica.it/welcome.html

University do Estado do Rio de Janeiro
http://www.uerj.br/

University du Quebec a Hull
http://www.uqah.uquebec.ca/welcome.htm

University EAFIT
http://www.eafit.edu.co/home.html

University Erlangen-Nuremberg
http://www.uni-erlangen.de/docs/index_e.html

University Federal de Minas Gerais
http://www.cpdee.ufmg.br/

University Federal de Pernambuco
http://www.di.ufpe.br/

University Federal de Santa Catarina
http://www.inf.ufsc.br/

University Federal de Santa Maria
http://www.ufsm.br/

University Federal do Rio de Janeiro
http://www.ufrj.br/

University Federal do Rio Grande do Sul
http://www.cesup.ufrgs.br/

University Freiburg
http://www.uni-freiburg.de/

University G.d'Annunzio
http://mars.unich.it/

University Gesamthochschule Essen
http://www.uni-essen.de/

University Hamburg
http://www.uni-hamburg.de/welcome_english.html

University Hannover
http://www.tnt.uni-hannover.de/data/info/www/tnt/welcome.html

University Heidelberg
http://www.urz.uni-heidelberg.de/index.html

University Hildesheim
http://www.uni-hildesheim.de/EWelcome.html

University Institute of Architecture
http://www.iuav.unive.it/

University Javeriana
http://javercol.javeriana.edu.co/

University Kaiserslautern
http://www.uni-kl.de/

University Karlsruhe
http://www.rz.uni-karlsruhe.de/Uni/

University Konstanz
http://www.uni-konstanz.de/index.html

University Laval
http://www.rsvs.ulaval.ca/

University Leipzig
http://www.uni-leipzig.de/

University Libre de Bruxelles
http://www.ulb.ac.be/

University Lumiere Lyon
http://web.univ-lyon2.fr/Universite.html

University Malaysia Sarawak
http://www.fit.unimas.my:8080/

University Mannheim
http://www.uni-mannheim.de/

University Medical School off Debrecen
http://www.dote.hu/

University Michoacana
http://www.ccu.umich.mx/

University Nacional Autonoma de Mexico
http://www.noc.unam.mx/unam/historia.html

University Nacional de La Plata
http://www.unlp.edu.ar/

University Nueva Esparta
http://www.une.edu.ve/

University of Aarhus
http://www.aau.dk/

University of Aberdeen
http://www.abdn.ac.uk/

University of Abertay Dundee
http://www.dct.ac.uk/

University of Adelaide
http://www.adelaide.edu.au/

University of Aizu
http://www.u-aizu.ac.jp/

University of Akron
http://www.uakron.edu/

University of Alabama
http://www.ua.edu/

University of Alabama, Birmingham
http://www.lhl.uab.edu/

University of Alabama, Huntsville
http://info.uah.edu/

University of Alaska
http://www.alaska.edu/

University of Alaska, Anchorage
http://orion.alaska.edu/www/cwis.html

University of Alaska, Fairbanks
http://zorba.uafadm.alaska.edu/

University of Alberta
http://web.cs.ualberta.ca/UAlberta.html

University of Amsterdam
http://www.uva.nl/00/english.html

University of Antwerp
http://www.ua.ac.be/

University of Arizona
http://www.arizona.edu/

University of Arkansas, Fayetteville
http://www.uark.edu/

University of Arkansas, Little Rock
http://www.ualr.edu/

University of Arkansas, Monticello
http://cotton.uamont.edu/

University of Art and Design Helsinki
http://www.uiah.fi/default.html

University of Auckland
http://www.auckland.ac.nz/

University of Baltimore
http://www.ubalt.edu/

University of Bath
http://www.bath.ac.uk/home.html

University of Bergen
http://www.uib.no/

University of Berne
http://arwen.unibe.ch/

University of Birmingham
http://www.bham.ac.uk/

University of Bologna Department of Computer Science
http://www.cs.unibo.it/

University of Boras
http://www.hb.se/

University of Bradford
http://www.brad.ac.uk/bradinfo/bradinfo.html

University of British Columbia
http://view.ubc.ca/

University of Calgary
http://www.ucalgary.ca/

University of California at Santa Barbara
http://id-www.ucsb.edu/

University of California, Berkeley
http://www.berkeley.edu/

University of California, Davis
http://www.ucdavis.edu/

University of California, Irvine
http://www.uci.edu/

University of California, Los Angeles
http://www.ucla.edu/

University of California, Riverside
http://www.ucr.edu/

University of California, San Diego
http://www.ucsd.edu/

University of California, San Francisco
http://www.ucsf.edu/

University of California, Santa Cruz
http://www.ucsc.edu/

University of Campinas
http://www.unicamp.br/

University of Canberra
http://services.canberra.edu.au/home.html

University of Cantabria
http://www.gae.unican.es/

University of Canterbury
http://www.canterbury.ac.nz/

University of Capetown
http://www.uct.ac.za/

University of Central Arkansas
http://aix1.uca.edu/

University of Central Florida
http://www.ucf.edu/home.html

University of Chicago
http://www.uchicago.edu/

University of Cincinnati
http://www.uc.edu/

University of Colorado at Denver
http://www.cudenver.edu/

University of Colorado, Boulder
http://www.colorado.edu/

University of Colorado, Colorado Springs
http://www.uccs.edu/

University of Copenhagen
http://www.ku.dk/welcome-e.html

University of Dallas
http://acad.udallas.edu/

University of Dayton
http://www.udayton.edu

University of Delaware
http://www.udel.edu/

University of Denver
http://www.du.edu/

University of Dublin - Trinity College
http://www.tcd.ie/

University of Duisburg
http://www.uni-duisburg.de/

University of Durham
http://www.dur.ac.uk/

University of East Anglia
http://cpca3.uea.ac.uk/welcome.html

University of East London
http://www.uel.ac.uk/

University of Economics, Vienna
http://www.wu-wien.ac.at/

University of Edinburgh
http://www.ed.ac.uk/

University of Electro-Communications
http://www.uec.ac.jp/

University of Essex
http://www.essex.ac.uk/

University of Evansville
http://www.evansville.edu/

University of Exeter
http://info.ex.ac.uk/

University of Florida
http://www.ufl.edu/

University of Fribourg
http://www.unifr.ch/

University of Gazi Antep
http://www.gantep.edu.tr/

University of Geneva
http://www.unige.ch/

University of Georgia
http://www.uga.edu/

University of Ghent
http://www.rug.ac.be/

University of Glamorgan
http://www.glam.ac.uk/home.html

University of Greenwich
http://www.gre.ac.uk/

University of Groningen
http://www.rug.nl/rug/startuk.html

University of Guelph
http://www.uoguelph.ca/

University of Haifa
http://www.haifa.ac.il/

University of Hartford
http://www.hartford.edu/UofHWelcome.html

University of Hawaii
http://www.hawaii.edu/uhinfo.html

University of Hawaii, West Oahu
http://www.uhwo.hawaii.edu/

University of Hertfordshire
http://www.herts.ac.uk/

University of Hong Kong
http://www.hku.hk/

University of Houston
http://www.uh.edu/

University of Houston, Clear Lake
http://129.7.160.115/

University of Hull
http://www.hull.ac.uk/

University of Iceland
http://www.rhi.hi.is/

University of Idaho
http://www.uidaho.edu/

University of Illinois, Chicago
http://www.uic.edu/

University of Illinois, Urbana-Champaign
http://www.uiuc.edu/

University of Indianapolis
http://www.uindy.edu/

University of Indonesia
http://www.ui.ac.id/

University of Innsbruck
http://info.uibk.ac.at/

University of Iowa
http://www.uiowa.edu/

University of Joensuu
http://cc.joensuu.fi/

University of Kansas
http://kuhttp.cc.ukans.edu/cwis/UDK/KUhome/KUHome.html

University of Kansas Medical Center
http://www.kumc.edu/

University of Karlskrona/Ronneby
http://www.hk-r.se/

University of Karlstad
http://www.hks.se/

University of Kent at Canterbury
http://www.ukc.ac.uk/

University of Kentucky
http://www.uky.edu/

University of King's College
http://www.ukings.ns.ca/Docs/

University of Klagenfurt
http://info.uni-klu.ac.at/

University of Kuopio
http://www.uku.fi/

University of L'Aquila
http://www.univaq.it/EnglishIndex.html

University of Latvia
http://www.latnet.lv/

University of Leeds
http://www.leeds.ac.uk/

University of Leicester
http://www.le.ac.uk/

University of Lethbridge
http://www.uleth.ca/

University of Library and Information Science
http://ulispsn.ulis.ac.jp:8001/html/ENG_homepage.html

University of Liège
http://www.ulg.ac.be/

University of Limburg
http://www.cs.rulimburg.nl/

University of Limerick
http://www.ul.ie/

University of Liverpool
http://www.liv.ac.uk/

University of Ljubljana
http://www.uni-lj.si/

University of London
http://www.ulcc.ac.uk/

University of Los Andes
http://www.uniandes.edu.co/

University of Louisville
http://www.louisville.edu/

University of Macau
http://sftw.umac.mo:8000/

University of Maine
http://www.maine.edu/

University of Maine at Farmington
http://www.umf.maine.edu/

University of Maine at Fort Kent
http://www.umfk.maine.edu/

University of Manchester
http://info.mcc.ac.uk/UofM.html

University of Manitoba
http://www.umanitoba.ca/UofM_homepage.html

University of Maribor
http://www.uni-mb.si/

University of Maryland
http://www.umd.edu/

University of Maryland University College
http://www.umuc.edu/

University of Maryland, Baltimore County
http://www.umbc.edu/

University of Maryland, College Park
http://inform.umd.edu/

University of Massachusetts
http://www.umassp.edu/

University of Massachusetts, Amherst
http://www.umass.edu/

University of Massachusetts, Boston
http://www.umb.edu/

University of Massachusetts, Dartmouth
http://www.umassd.edu/welcome.html

University of Massachusetts, Lowell
http://www.uml.edu/

University of Medicine and Dentistry of New Jersey
http://njmsa.umdnj.edu/umdnj.html

University of Melbourne
http://www.unimelb.edu.au/

University of Memphis
http://www.memphis.edu

University of Miami
http://www.ir.miami.edu/

University of Michigan, Ann Arbor
http://www.umich.edu/

University of Michigan, Dearborn
http://www.umd.umich.edu/

University of Milano
http://www.dsi.unimi.it/home.html

University of Minho
http://www.uminho.pt/

University of Minnesota
http://www.umn.edu/

University of Minnesota, Duluth
http://www.d.umn.edu/

University of Minnesota, Morris
http://www.mrs.umn.edu/

University of Miskolc
http://silver.uni-miskolc.hu:8080/

University of Miskolc, Hungary
http://gold.uni-miskolc.hu/

University of Mississippi
http://www.olemiss.edu/

University of Missouri St. Louis
http://www.umsl.edu/

University of Missouri, Columbia
http://www.missouri.edu/

University of Missouri, Kansas City
http://www.umkc.edu/

University of Missouri, Rolla
http://www.umr.edu/

University of Modena
http://www.casa.unimo.it/

University of Montana
http://www.umt.edu

University of Montreal
http://www.iro.umontreal.ca/

University of Namur
http://www.fundp.ac.be/

University of Natal
http://www.und.ac.za/

University of Natal, Pietermaritzburg
http://www.unp.ac.za/

University of Nebraska at Kearney
http://betty-boop.unk.edu/

University of Nebraska, Lincoln
http://www.unl.edu/index.html

University of Nebraska, Omaha
http://www.unomaha.edu/

University of Neuchatel
http://www.unine.ch/www/welcome-e.html

University of Nevada System
http://www.nevada.edu/

University of Nevada, Las Vegas
http://www.nscee.edu/

University of Nevada, Reno
http://www.scs.unr.edu/

University of New Brunswick
http://www.unb.ca/

University of New England
http://www.une.edu.au/

University of New Hampshire, Durham
http://samizdat.unh.edu:70/1/unh

University of New Haven
http://www.newhaven.edu/

University of New Mexico
http://www.unm.edu/

University of New Orleans
http://www.uno.edu/

University of New South Wales
http://www.unsw.edu.au/

University of Newcastle
http://www.newcastle.edu.au/

University of Newcastle upon Tyne
http://www.ncl.ac.uk/

University of Nijmegen
http://www.kun.nl/

University of North Carolina at Wilmington
http://www.uncwil.edu/

University of North Carolina, Asheville
http://www.unca.edu/

University of North Carolina, Chapel Hill
http://www.unc.edu/

University of North Carolina, Charlotte
http://unccvm.uncc.edu/

University of North Carolina, Greensboro
http://www2.uncg.edu/

University of North Dakota, Grand Forks
http://www.und.nodak.edu/

University of North Florida
http://www.unf.edu/

University of North London
http://www.unl.ac.uk:80/welcome.html

University of North Texas
http://www.unt.edu/

University of Northern Colorado
http://www.univnorthco.edu/

University of Northern Iowa
http://www.uni.edu/

University of Notre Dame
http://www.nd.edu/NDHomePage/NDHomePage.html

University of Nottingham
http://www.nott.ac.uk/

University of Oklahoma
http://www.uoknor.edu/

University of Oldenburg
http://www.informatik.uni-oldenburg.de/homepage.e.html

University of Oregon
http://www.uoregon.edu/

University of Oslo
http://www.uio.no/

University of Otago
http://www.otago.ac.nz/

University of Ottawa
http://www.uottawa.ca/

University of Oulu
http://www.oulu.fi/homepage.html

University of Padua
http://www.unipd.it/

University of Palermo
http://cucaix.cuc.unipa.it/Public/welcome.html

University of Parma
http://www.unipr.it/

University of Pavol Jozef Safarik
http://kosice.upjs.sk/upjs.html

University of Pennsylvania
http://www.upenn.edu/

University of Pereslavl
http://u-pereslavl.botik.ru/UP/

University of Phoenix
http://www.uophx.edu/

University of Picardie
http://www.u-picardie.fr/

University of Pisa
http://www.unipi.it/welcome.html

University of Pittsburgh
http://www.pitt.edu/

University of Port Elizabeth
http://www.upe.ac.za/

University of Portland
http://www.up.edu/

University of Portsmouth
http://www.port.ac.uk/

University of Pretoria
http://www.up.ac.za/

University of Prince Edward Island
http://www.upei.ca/

University of Puerto Rico
http://www.upr.clu.edu/english/home.html

University of Puget Sound
http://www.ups.edu/

University of Quebec, Montreal
http://www.uqam.ca/

University of Queensland
http://www.uq.edu.au/

University of Reading
http://www.rdg.ac.uk/

University of Redlands
http://www.uor.edu/

University of Regina
http://www.uregina.ca/

University of Rennes 1
http://www.univ-rennes1.fr/welcome.html

University of Rhode Island
http://www.uri.edu/

University of Richmond
http://www.urich.edu/

University of Rochester
http://www.rochester.edu/

University of Salford
http://www.salford.ac.uk/

University of Salzburg
http://www.edvz.sbg.ac.at/home.html

University of San Carlos
http://www.usc.edu.ph/

University of San Diego
http://www.acusd.edu/

University of San Francisco
http://www.usfca.edu/

University of Saskatchewan
http://www.usask.ca/

University of Science and Technology of China
http://math.wisc.edu/~cliu/ustc/

University of South Africa
http://www.unisa.ac.za/

University of South Australia
http://cutl.city.unisa.edu.au/

University of South Carolina
http://www.csd.scarolina.edu/

University of South Carolina at Aiken
http://www.usca.scarolina.edu/

University of South Dakota
http://www.usd.edu/

University of South Florida
http://www.usf.edu/

University of Southampton
http://ilc.ecs.soton.ac.uk/welcome.html

University of Southern California
http://cwis.usc.edu/

University of Southern Indiana
http://www.usi.edu/

University of Southern Maine
http://www.usm.maine.edu/

University of Southern Mississippi
http://www.usm.edu/

University of Southern Queensland
http://www.usq.edu.au/

University of Southwestern Louisiana
http://www.usl.edu/

University of St. Andrews
http://www.st-andrews.ac.uk/

University of St. Gallen
http://www-iwi.unisg.ch/

University of St. Thomas
http://www.stthomas.edu/

University of Stellenbosch
http://lib.sun.ac.za/

University of Stirling
http://www.stir.ac.uk/

University of Strathclyde
http://www.strath.ac.uk/

University of Sunderland
http://www.sunderland.ac.uk/

University of Surrey
http://www.surrey.ac.uk/

University of Sussex
http://www.susx.ac.uk/

University of Sydney
http://www.usyd.edu.au/

University of Tampere
http://www.uta.fi/

University of Tasmania
http://info.utas.edu.au/

University of Technology, Sydney
http://www.uts.edu.au/

University of Teesside
http://www.tees.ac.uk/

University of Tennessee, Chattanooga
http://www.utc.edu/

University of Tennessee, Knoxville
http://www.utk.edu/

University of Tennessee, Martin
http://www.utm.edu/

University of Texas at Arlington
http://www.uta.edu/

University of Texas at Austin
http://www.utexas.edu/

University of Texas at Dallas
http://www.utdallas.edu/

University of Texas at El Paso
http://cs.utep.edu/utep/utep.html

University of Texas at Houston
http://www.uth.tmc.edu/

University of Texas at San Antonio
http://rabbit.cs.utsa.edu/Welcome.html

University of Texas Health Center at Tyler
http://pegasus.uthct.edu/UTHCT-Home/Welcome.html

University of Texas Health Science Center, San Antonio
http://www.uthscsa.edu/

University of Texas Medical Branch
http://www.utmb.edu/

University of Texas Southwestern Medical Center
http://www.swmed.edu/

University of Texas-Pan American
http://www.panam.edu/

University of the Americas
http://info.pue.udlap.mx/

University of the Basque Country
http://www.sc.ehu.es/

University of the Pacific
http://www.uop.edu/

University of the Philippines, Diliman
http://www.upd.edu.ph/

University of the Ryukyus
http://www.ie.u-ryukyu.ac.jp/

University of the Virgin Islands
http://www.uvi.edu/

University of the West Indies
http://www.uwimona.edu.jm/

University of the West of England
http://gate.uwe.ac.uk:8000/uwe/uwe.html

University of Tokushima
http://www.tokushima-u.ac.jp/

University of Tokyo
http://web.yl.is.s.u-tokyo.ac.jp/ut/ut.html

University of Tokyo, Institute of Industrial Science
http://www.iis.u-tokyo.ac.jp/

University of Toledo
http://www.utoledo.edu/

University of Toronto
http://www.utoronto.ca/uoft.html

University of Trieste
http://www.univ.trieste.it/e_utshom.html

University of Trondheim
http://www.unit.no/

University of Tsukuba
http://www.tsukuba.ac.jp/

University of Tulsa
http://www.utulsa.edu/

University of Turku
http://www.utu.fi/

University of Twente
http://www.nic.utwente.nl/

University of Udine
http://www.uniud.it/www/welcome.html

University of Ulster
http://www.ulst.ac.uk/

University of Utah
http://www.utah.edu/

University of Vaasa
http://www.uwasa.fi/samjay/index.html

University of Valladolid
http://www.uva.es/

University of Venice
http://www.unive.it/HomePage.html

University of Vermont
http://www.uvm.edu/

University of Veterinary Medicine Vienna
http://www.vu-wien.ac.at/

University of Victoria
http://www.uvic.ca/

University of Vienna
http://www.univie.ac.at/

University of Virginia
http://www.virginia.edu/

University of Waikato
http://www.waikato.ac.nz/default.html

University of Wales
http://WWW.Lamp.Ac.UK/

University of Wales College of Medicine
http://www.uwcm.ac.uk/

University of Wales, Bangor
http://www.bangor.ac.uk/

University of Wales, Cardiff
http://www.cf.ac.uk/index.html

University of Warwick
http://www.csv.warwick.ac.uk/default.html

University of Washington
http://www.washington.edu/

University of Waterloo
http://www.uwaterloo.ca/

University of Western Australia
http://www.uwa.edu.au/

University of Western Ontario
http://www.uwo.ca/

University of Western Sydney, Hawkesbury
http://www.hawkesbury.uws.edu.au/

University of Western Sydney, Macarthur
http://www.macarthur.uws.edu.au/

University of Western Sydney, Nepean
http://www.nepean.uws.edu.au/

University of Westminster
http://www.wmin.ac.uk/

University of Windsor
http://www.uwindsor.ca/

University of Wisconsin, Eau Claire
http://www.uwec.edu/

University of Wisconsin, Madison
http://www.wiscinfo.wisc.edu/

University of Wisconsin, Milwaukee
http://www.uwm.edu/

University of Wisconsin, Oshkosh
http://www.uwosh.edu/

University of Wisconsin, Parkside
http://www.uwp.edu/

University of Wisconsin, River Falls
http://www.uwrf.edu/

University of Wisconsin, Steven's Point
http://www.uwsp.edu/

University of Wisconsin, Stout
http://www.uwstout.edu/

University of Wisconsin-Platteville
http://www.uwplatt.edu/

University of Wisconsin-Whitewater
http://www.uww.edu/

University of Witwatersrand
http://www.wits.ac.za/

University of Wollongong
http://www.uow.edu.au/

University of Wolverhampton
http://www.wlv.ac.uk/

University of Wyoming
http://www.uwyo.edu/

University of York
http://www.york.ac.uk/

University of Zambia
http://www.zamnet.zm/unza/unza.html

University of Zurich
http://www.unizh.ch/

University Paris IX Dauphine
http://www.bu.dauphine.fr/

University Passau
http://www.uni-passau.de/welcome.html

University Pertanian Malaysia
http://w3.cs.upm.my/

University Potsdam
http://www.uni-potsdam.de/

University Regensburg
http://www.wiwi.uni-regensburg.de/

University Regiomontana
http://www.ur.mx/

University Rostock
http://www.informatik.uni-rostock.de/Uni/

University Rovira i Virgili
http://www.urv.es/

University Sains Malaysia
http://www.cs.usm.my/

University San Francisco de Quito
http://mail.usfq.edu.ec/

University Santa Maria La Antigua
http://www.usma.pa/

University Stuttgart
http://www.uni-stuttgart.de/

University Tecnica Federico Santa Maria
http://www.inf.utfsm.cl/

University Teknologi Malaysia
http://www.utm.my/

University Trier
http://www.uni-trier.de/

University Ulm
http://www.informatik.uni-ulm.de/index.eng.html

University Zagreb
http://www.zvne.etf.hr/uniinfo.html

University-GH Paderborn
http://www.uni-paderborn.de/

Uppsala University
http://www.uu.se/

Ursinus College
http://www.ursinus.edu

Utah State University
http://www.usu.edu/

Utah Valley State College
http://www.uvsc.edu/

Utrecht University
http://www.ruu.nl/

Utsunomiya University
http://www.utsunomiya-u.ac.jp/

Valdosta State University
http://www.valdosta.peachnet.edu/home.html

Valparaiso University
http://www.valpo.edu/

Vanderbilt University
http://www.vanderbilt.edu/

Vassar College
http://vasweb.vassar.edu/

Vaxjo University
http://www.hv.se/eng/eng_home.html

Vermont Technical College
http://www.vtc.vsu.edu/

Vesalius College
http://www.vub.ac.be/VECO/VECO-intro.html

Victoria Jubilee Technical Institute
http://www.ece.iit.edu/~hchhaya/vjti/vjti.html

Victoria University of Technology
http://www.vut.edu.au/

Victoria University of Wellington
http://www.vuw.ac.nz/

Vienna University of Technology
http://info.tuwien.ac.at/ROOT

Villanova University
http://www.vill.edu/

Virginia Commonwealth University
http://www.vcu.edu/

Virginia Tech
http://www.vt.edu/

Volda College
http://www.hivolda.no/

Vrije University
http://www.cca.vu.nl/

Wabash College
http://ruby.wabash.edu/

Wageningen Agricultural University
http://www.wau.nl/welcome.html

Wakayama University
http://www.wakayama-u.ac.jp/

Wake Forest University
http://www.wfu.edu/start.html

Walden University
http://www.waldenu.edu/

Walla Walla College
http://www.wwc.edu/

Warren Wilson College
http://www.warren-wilson.edu/

Warsaw Technical University
http://www.ia.pw.edu.pl/

Warsaw University
http://info.fuw.edu.pl/

Washburn University
http://www.wuacc.edu/

Washington & Lee University
http://liberty.uc.wlu.edu/

Washington College
http://www.washcoll.edu/

Washington State University
http://www.wsu.edu/

Washington University in St. Louis
http://www.wustl.edu/

Washtenaw Community College
http://northernspy.washtenaw.cc.mi.us/

Wayne State University
http://www.wayne.edu/

Waynesburg College
http://waynesburg.edu/

Weber State University
http://www.weber.edu/

Weizmann Institute of Science
http://wissgi.weizmann.ac.il/

Wellesley College
http://www.wellesley.edu/

Wesleyan University
http://www.wesleyan.edu/

West Chester University of Pennsylvania
http://albie.wcupa.edu/

West Coast University
http://katz.wcula.edu/

West Georgia College
http://www.westga.edu/

West Texas A&M University
http://www.wtamu.edu/

West Virginia University
http://www.wvu.edu/

Western Baptist College
http://www.wbc.edu/

Western Carolina University
http://www.wcu.edu/

Western Iowa Community College
http://www.witcc.ia.us/

Western Kentucky University
http://www.wku.edu/

Western Maryland College
http://ns1.wmc.car.md.us/

Western Michigan University
http://www.wmich.edu/

Western State College of Colorado
http://www.wester.edu/Welcome.html

Western Washington University
http://www.wwu.edu/

Westmont College
http://www.westmont.edu/

Wharton School
http://www.wharton.upenn.edu/

Wheaton College
http://www.wheatonma.edu/

Whitman College
http://www.whitman.edu/

Whittier College
http://www.whittier.edu/

WHU Koblenz School of Corporate Management
http://www.whu-koblenz.de/

Wichita State University
http://www.twsu.edu/

Wilkes University
http://www.wilkes.edu/

Willamette University
http://www.willamette.edu/

William Penn College
http://www.wmpenn.edu/

William Rainey Harper College
http://www.harper.cc.il.us/

William Woods University
http://www.wmwoods.edu/

Williams College
http://www.williams.edu/

Wilmington College
http://www.wilmington.edu/

Winona State University, Minnesota
http://gopher.winona.msus.edu/

Winthrop University
http://lurch.winthrop.edu/WinthropHomePage.html

Wolfson College, Oxford
http://www.wolfson.ox.ac.uk/

Worcester Polytechnic Institute
http://www.wpi.edu/

Wright State University
http://pogo.wright.edu/

Wroclaw Technical University
http://www.ict.pwr.wroc.pl/

Xavier University
http://www.xu.edu.ph/

Xi'an Jiao Tong University
http://www.cs.bham.ac.uk/~yxh/xjtu.html

Yale University
http://www.yale.edu/

Yamanashi University
http://www.yamanashi.ac.jp/

Yasuda Women's University
http://www.yasuda-u.ac.jp/

Yerevan Physics Institute
http://www.yerphi.am/

Yeshiva University, Albert Einstein College of Medicine
http://www.aecom.yu.edu/

Yeungnam University
http://165.229.11.3/

Yildiz Technical University
http://www.ce.yildiz.edu.tr/

York College
http://www.yorkcol.edu/

York University
http://www.yorku.ca/

Youngstown State University
http://gateway.cis.ysu.edu/

Yuan-Ze Institute of Technology
http://www.yzit.edu.tw/

Zhongshan University
http://www.sci.ccny.cuny.edu:80/~jdong/zhongda/index.html

FTP Sites

ftp://161.105.2.22

Centre Commune d'Etude de Telecommunication et de Telediffusion (joint France Telecom and TDF research center, CCETT), Rennes

Files: MPEG: audio (decod, parser, sound) video (ccett)

ftp://acavax.lynchburg.edu

Lynchburg College, Lynchburg, Virginia

Files: bourne; Mac; Nicely: program to test Pentium FPU bug; roussos

ftp://acfcluster.nyu.edu

New York University, New York, New York

Files: VMS UUCP; news; DECUS library catalog; vsmnet.sources; Info-VAX code segments

ftp://afutub.extern.tu-berlin.de

Technische Universitaet Berlin (Berlin University of Technology), Berlin

Files: Amateurfunk-Software; Geraetemodifikationen; Tips & Tricks

ftp://aix.rpi.edu

Rensselaer Polytechnical Institute, Troy, New York

Files: TCP/IP benchmarks

ftp://ajpo.sei.cmu.edu

Carnegie-Mellon University, Pittsburgh, Pennsylvania, ADA Joint Program Office (AJPO)

Files: All the ADA you could ask for

ftp://alb.uib.no

University of Bergen, Bergen

Files: Editors; comp.editors FAQ and related material

ftp://allspice.lcs.mit.edu

Massachusetts Institute of Technology (MIT), Cambridge, Massachusetts

Files: CMU-PCIP; dartnet; disktab; ecma-desd; mcode; netsim; PCMAIL; SNMP; SNPP; white-pages; WP

ftp://anna.stanford.edu

Stanford University, Menlo Park, California

Files: Anna (annotated Ada) software and docs

ftp://aql.gatech.edu

Georgia Tech, Atlanta, Georgia

Files: 40Hex magazine archives; Computer Underground Digest (CuD); crypto (mirror of the cypherpunks archive and more); EFF (small parts of ftp.eff.org); Netinfo (NetInfo mailing list archive); OTIS Project (from 141.214.4.135 and sunsite.unc.edu); seasame; security; utils; virii; Virtual Culture; Xfiles; Zines (incl. Voices from the Net)

ftp://archie.au

Australian Academic and Research Network (AARNet), Canberra

Files: AARNet; alex; archie; mirrors: 4.4BSD, ACS, Amiga, CIAC, FreeBSD, GNU, gopher, graphics, Kermit, Linux, Mac, micros, MicroSoft, NCSA, packet-drivers, RFCs, security, Simtel Software Repository mirror (/micros/pc/oak), garbo.uwasa.fi (/micros/pc/garbo), talk-radio, Unix, Usenet, WAIS, wu-ftpd; NetWorkShop; projects; Weather; X11

ftp://archive.orst.edu

Oregon State University, Corvallis, Oregon

Files: astro-data; comm; doc; Doom; gaming; lang; mailing-lists; mirrors:

Linux (sunsite.unc.edu), ucs.orst.edu, Simtel Software Repository, CICA Windows archive: ftp.cica.indiana.edu; network; news; noc; OSU-gopher; packages; publishers; security; skunk-works; SNMP; Sun; systems; Usenet; WAIS

ftp://arp.anu.edu.au

Australian National University

Files: abelson; akcl; blackhole; bridge; CISR; compress; exedit; Finder; haskell; HPFF; kripke; lam228; license-forms; lisp; MaGIC; mizar; ml; mpi; multicast; otter; papers; PAWS; Solaris 2.3; tech-reports; tptp

ftp://asylum.sf.ca.us

Apocalypse, San Francisco, California

Files: apocalypse; asylum; bingbong; bps; Cerebus (read the rec.arts.comics FAQ for details); circlet; clover; dsp; filter; flash; fsb; GOLD; gub; internet-drafts; itc; leadheads; leather; multitone; mystery-hill; norn; omnium; ranchers; RFCs; sappho; Slackware; tcp-encryption; Usenet; User public directories; void; wintalk (see ftp.elf.com)

ftp://audrey.levels.unisa.edu.au

University of Southern Australia, Signal Processing Institute, Digital Communications Group

Files: lemacs; space flight info (manifests, launch times, etc.); satellite modems; speech

ftp://biomol.univ-lyon1.fr

Universite de Lyon (University of Lyon), Lyon

Files: ACNUC nucleic acid sequences database

ftp://brawl.mindlink.net/pub

MIND LINK! Communications Corp., Vancouver, British Columbia

Files: audio and textual information related to arcade one-on-one fighting video games (Street Fighter II, etc.); pictures

ftp://butler226a.dorm.tulane.edu

Tulane University, New Orleans, Louisiana

Files: Files are related to the new country in development, Oceania.

ftp://byrd.mu.wwnet.edu

Marshall University, West Virginia

Files: aircraft-related files; ejvc; ejvdeds; estepp; history; merton; NATO documents; Novell; vleadr; yeager

ftp://c.scs.uiuc.edu

University of Illinois - Urbana/Champaign, Urbana, Illinois

Files: ROSAT; some astronomy GIFs; StarChart

ftp://cambridge.apple.com

Apple Computer, Cambridge, Massachusetts

Files: clim; comp.lang.lisp; dropbox; dylan; gsb; MacL; mail-archive; MCL2; shlib; X3J13

ftp://cao-vlsi.ibp.fr

University Pierre et Marie Curie - MASI Lab., Paris

Files: Alliance (CAD system for teaching VLSI digital CMOS design); GNU; Mach; Mirrors: Simtel20, Cica, Linux (sunsite.unc.edu); pub directory of ftp.ibp.fr; TeX; Unix

ftp://cdcnac.aspensys.com (page 2)

Aspen Systems Corporation, Rockville, Maryland

Files: CDCNAC (CDC National AIDS Clearinghouse); housing (US Dept. of Housing HUD User); Internet; NCJRS (National Criminal Justice Reference Service); software (DOS (archie, gopher, kermit, telnet,trumpet, utils), Mac (archie, communications, compress, email, ftp, gopher, kermit, mosaic, netscape, news, tcp, telnet, utils, viewers, wais), MPEG, OS/2, QT, SCO (archie, editors, email, gopher, kermit, lynx, mosaic, news, utils, viewers), SlipKnot, SunSoft (archie, editors, email, ftp server, gnu, gopherclient, gopherserver, kermit, listserver, mosaic, news, security, utils, viewers, wais, webserver), Unixware (archie, editors, email, gopher, kermit, mosaic, news, utils, viewers), Windows (archie, cello, email, extensions, ftp, gopher, htmleditors, kermit, mosaic, netscape, news, sockets, telnet, trumpet, utils, viewers, winqvt, winsock), WindowsNT, Windows for WorkGroups)

ftp://celtic.stanford.edu

Stanford University, Menlo Park, California

Files: Anything related to celtic music. Currently has artist bios, discographies, tour schedules, lists of radio shows, music sessions, festivals, publications.

ftp://cert.org

Carnegie-Mellon University, Pittsburgh, Pennsylvania, Software Engineering Institute (SEI), Computer Emergency Response Team (CERT)

Files: CERT information and files; COPS; FIRST; network tools; NIST; ssphgw; Virus-L/comp.virus archives

ftp://chopin.forest.dnj.ynu.ac.jp/

Yokohama National University, Yokohama, Electrical and Computer Engineering dept., Mori Laboratory

Files: doc; doc-tools; fonts; games; GNU; ifs; images [empty?]; IPAL; lang; Linux; mirror of kites.its.hawaii.edu; MS-DOS; MS-Windows; ncd; net; NLP; NetBSD; PostScript; Prolog; security; Sun-info; TeX; X; X11R6; XFree86; YNU

ftp://cirrus.com/

Cirrus Logic Inc.

Files: Drivers and utilities for video cards using Cirrus chipsets

ftp://clementine.s1.gov/

Department of Defense

Files: Clementine Spacecraft currently orbiting the moon images + viewers

ftp://climate.gsfc.nasa.gov/

NASA - Goddard Space Flight Center, Greenbelt, Maryland

Files: IRIS and HPUX; IRIS apps; Mac software; NeXTfax; wu

ftp://clr.nmsu.edu

New Mexico State University, , New Mexico, Consortium for Lexical Research (CLR)/Computer Research Lab (CRL)

Files: CLR archives (natural language oriented materials including fonts, dictionaries and such)

ftp://coast.cs.purdue.edu/

Purdue University, West-Lafayette, Indiana, CS dept., Computer Operations, Audit and Security Technology (COAST) archive

Files: alert (CERT, CIAC, DEC, HP, Mac, NIST, NeXT, SERT, SGI, Solbourne, Sun); COAST info; dict (several dictionaries mirrored from ftp.funet.fi and ftp.netsys.com); doc (documents relating to computer security and security tools); mirrors (numerous sites with security info are mirrored here); news+lists (several mirrored magazines and mailing list archives); patches; Purdue info; response teams; tools

ftp://coombs.anu.edu.au/

Australian National University, Canberra, Research Schools of Social Sciences and Pacific and Asian Studies (RSSS/RSPAS), Coombs (ANU Social Sciences Research Data Bank)

Files: Coombspapers (Asian/Pacific studies, humanities, Social Sciences): Aboriginal history journal, Anthropology, Asian Pacific economic literature, Australia/Japan research centre, Australian dict of biography, cartography unit, contemporary China centre, coombs computing, demography, economic history, economic policy research, economics rspacs, economics rsss, federalism research centre, history, history of ideas, immigration multicult studies, indonesia-project, international relations, land management project, linguistics, national centre for development studies, national social sciences survey, Pacific/Asian history, Pacific Islands group, Pacific manuscripts bureau, peace research centre, philosophy, political and social change, political science, prehistory, rspacs annual report 91, rspacs publications, rsss annual report 91, social science data archives, sociology, southeast Asia economic history, strategic and defence studies, Thai Yunnan project, urban research project; Other archives - research documents and materials originating from elsewhere: Aboriginal studies archives, archaeology prehistory archives, Asian religions archives, asian-studies-archives [Bhutan archives, Burma archives, Cambodia archives, Central Asia archives, China archives, Indonesia archives, Papua New Guinea archives, Philippines archives, South East Asia archives, Thailand archives, Tibetan archives, Vietnam archives, Australian National University archives, Australian science archives, caut archives, cipsh unesco archives, electronic buddhist archives, human communication archives, Pacific studies archives, raia archives, reach journal archives, social science directories, social science software, sociology research archives, uk nra archives

ftp://corsa.ucr.edu/

University of California - Riverside, Riverside, California

Files: anti-virus tools; Linux; papers; Virus-L (mirror of ftp.cert.org)

ftp://crab.rutgers.edu/

Rutgers University, Piscataway, New Jersey

Files: Mac (audio, graphics, hypercard, kermit, pspice); MS-DOS (kermit, Linux, PC-Xremote, popmail, pspice, slip, zip); Unix (graphics, icons)

ftp://cutl.city.unisa.edu.au/

University of Southern Australia

Files: Mac; MS-DOS; multimedia; Windows

ftp://darwin.cc.nd.edu/

Notre Dame University

Files: comics (X-Men, see the rec.arts.comics FAQ for details); gopher; NAFTA; NeXT; PC; Soviet archive; Unix

ftp://datacom.ee.ubc.ca/

University of Britsh Columbia

Files: audio (NCD audio extensions, rplay); doc;

Linux (local stuff only); PC (IDE (EIDE drivers), network (mostly TCP/IP, software for PC's), NFS (for DOS and WFW), programmer (C source), TeX/ LaTeX (installation based on EmTeX with PS fonts enhancements), Windows add-ons, winsock apps); SPW; TeX (alternate format file, PSTricks); Unix; WWW (PS and text docs); X11 (some clients)

ftp://debra.dbgt.doc.ca/

Files: Canadian Broadcasting Corporation (CBC) radio programs stored as 8-bit, 8KHz .AU files; chat; IRC; dvi; freenet; ISC; opengov; sox sound conversion tool for .AU to .VOC, .WAV conversion for PC use; usenet-survey

ftp://elbereth.rutgers.edu/

Rutgers University, Piscataway, New Jersey

Files: SF-lovers archive; lots of text files about tv series; program guides; text files on a number of subjects; FAQs related to SF (Bladerunner); info on SF awards and writers (Hugo Awards, Adams, Asimov, and more)

ftp://explorer.arc.nasa.gov/

NASA - Ames Research Center, Moffett Field, California

Files: Images and data mostly of Jet Propulsion Laboratory space probes Viking, Voyager, Magellan etc.; partial sci.space.news archive

ftp://flinux.tu-graz.ac.at/

Technischer Universitaet Graz (Graz Institute of Technology), Graz

Files: Doom; graphics (33, 3D, boris, BSD, fantasy, hajime, icons, mpg, ted-kimer); Linux (Debian, handbuch, Linus, lst, network, slacksrc, slackware, source, sunsite.unc.edu); MS-DOS (archiver, ATI, djgpp, info, network, Novell, romulus, turbo_C, turbo_pascal, TurboVision, Ultrasound, virus, XWindows, zip); MUD; Qdeck; Wine

ftp://freeware.dit.co.jp/

Files: MacTCP Exchanger; NCSA Telnet

ftp://ftp.adelaide.edu.au/

University of Adelaide, Adelaide

Files: 4.3BSD; Apple; Apple2; aus.comms; AUUG; av; CERT; compression; cyberterm; funnelweb; KA9Q; lynx; mailers; Minix; minplot; Modula-3; Mosaic; netinfo; news; NTP; PC; Perl Quickref; Rocksoft; S; security; sendmail; servers; Sun (icons,

sounds, source, spots); tcsh; training; URT; Usenet; vt100art; whitepages; whois; WWW

ftp://ftp.adobe.com/

Adobe Systems Inc., Mountain View, California

Files: Adobe info, patches, programs, textfiles, updates; AFM files; Developer support

ftp://ftp.ae.keio.ac.jp/

Files: 386BSD; database; dic; doc; emacs-lips; FreeBSD; GNU; jndoc; KEIO; LaiTeX; languages; lingual; Mac; MS-DOS (386, 486, archivers, docs, GNU, GNUish, lang, TeX, tools, tsr-devd, utils); Nethack; OS/2; statistics; Sun-dist; superpipe; text; YaTeX

ftp://ftp.aimnet.com/

AIMNet

Files: Mac; MIME; Netscape; network; PC (AIMNet config); ranger; sysutils (security, sendmail); UUCP; user directories: adam, advancednet, aes, airbrokr, akvitka, alanlee, alotz, alvin, amavisca, anne7777, ark, aron, arrow, arthurw, arun, asmo, asr10, ausiguy, aviv, aztech (accessories, cdrom, mmkits, NT, OS/2, patches, soundcards, videocards, win95), bai, bambam, banzai, barth, bazaar, bbb, belmont, brentw, bretts, briareos, bsch, bschec, buggysft, burney, bwatson, cadboys, cadint, calves4, calvinl, capp, carroll, cbm, cdserv, cgate, cgi, cheese, chinabus, chlyman, chops, cindyk, ckim, cliu, cmd, cmyers, concep, cordero, craig, csa, ctsze, darrenw, dav3d, dcarroll, dcrocker, dgv, dieter, digit, djlang, dmolony, documagx, dragnet, dsallen, dseitel, dslayer, dtpu, dukester, dwainej, dwalker, dwaters, dyuhas, ebeck, ebigas, eclectic, ecrutch, ed, edmyers, edwardk, egad, egadient, egan, egis, eman, escort, esis, falcon2, forecast, fpeter, fred, frerking, friedman, fse-power, fsoul, futuret, fwb, gaird, gaius, gameman, gamvcm, gander, gizmo, global, gmgraves, gointeract, grafica, grail, grob, gwachob, hacman, hal, happycat, hassan, heising, herring, hia, hudsons, hyperion, ianj, iceman, icsinc, immerse, impact, infobaan, ipd, jackb, james, jaques, jar, jasonb, jaye, jbv, jcarver, jdanner, jen, jennings, jensen, jerryc, jester, jfox, jharris, jhw1, jianto, jjoaquin, jnavas, jnewton, joes, john, johnbwrs, johnc, jon, jpc, jswitzer, jwilley, kathy, kcheung, kclsf, kdyer, keng, kmp, kwh, kzim, larry, lazar, lemon, lenz, letgo, limon, livermor, lkreuzer, llin, loco, lordsoth, lynnb, lynng, madden, maluku, manabu, marcos, markg, mbarone, mbl, mdwelter, mdwlter, michelle, mickeyt, mijo, mikeeth, miken, minh, mitchell, modtiger, molinari, mozart, mtnmath, mwall, myu, napann, neil, nicoli, nnpann, nutec, oaktree, omd, onlinefocus, orlando, oxymoron, paulwang, pbell, pbennett, penguins, pete, peters, pfarrah, philmr, phummel, pkahn, plss, procket, profile, qsite, qssnet, racine, radicade, raleigh, ralph, rat, raynault, remax, reoneill, reproguy, res, rhardwic, rickg, rickl, rjg, rjone, rluening, rob, rodelq, samhahn, schwett, scj, scot, scottja, shaw, sleek, sooho, steve-o, synergy, tgirard, thixot, thom, thomaslw, tim, tim1, todd, tonydd, topsoft, toucan, tourism, triton, ttaylor, turbo, twain, unibio, unknown, uspot, vance, vasudev, vki, vsp, vyau, webster, wei, wes, wirth, writers, ycc, yuki, zarzycki

ftp://ftp.aol.com/

America Online, Vienna, Virginia

Files: Access software for AOL for Macintosh and MS-Windows

ftp://ftp.best.com/

Best Internet Communications

Files: abcnet; acceptance; acix; analytic; babylon; best; compusa1; ecafe; english; entcafe; excel; fanclub; flatline; hal9000; ii; indigo; infoasia; infoent; informe; infowerk; integra; intentrs; kilsdonk; newmedia; quantum; quarium; siggraph; software [?]; spectrex; starnet; support [?]

ftp://ftp.borland.com/

Borland International

Files: Borland related file: Borland C++, Turbo C, Turbo Pascal, etc.

ftp://ftp.ccmail.com/

Lotus Development Corporation, Mountain View, California

Files: 3rd party, admin tools, cc:Mail utils, DOS updates, general info, Link products, Mac updates, modem info, OS/2 updates, PD utils, remote (Mobile), router, TCP/IP, technotes, Unix, Lotus VIM, Windows updates, Windows Mobile

ftp://ftp.ccu.edu.tw/

National Chung Cheng Uuniversity (CCU), Chiayi, CC

Files: AARnet; anime; CCU; cdrom; Chinese; database; document; FAQs; gopher; Internet; language; Mac; MS-DOS; NCSA; netlib; NeXT; Novell; OS/2; package2; packet drivers; TeX; Unix

ftp://ftp.cd.chalmers.se/

Chalmers University of Technology, Gothenburg

Files: anim; InterTeX; MUD (LPMUD) related files; NetBSD; Netrek; OS; PC; words; xibc; ZyXel

ftp://ftp.cdconnection.com/

Files: Billboard Top 10; CDcatalog: classical, country, jazz, rock, shows, soundtracks; Golden Ears; IBM PC off-line search prog.

ftp://ftp.cdrom.com/

Walnut Creek CDROM, Concord/Walnut Creek, California

Files: ADA (ftp.wustl.edu /languages/ada); Aminet; ASCII text files; BSD-sources; CD-ROM related stuff; Delphi; Descent; Doom; Doom2; dresden; FreeBSD; games (ftp.uml.edu); garbo.uwasa.fi mirror; GNU (prep.ai.mit.edu); Gutenberg (mirror of etext.archive.umich.edu); Hamradio (qrz.com, oak.oakland.edu /pub/ hamradio); handicap; Heretic; Hornet demos; ID games; Internet (ftp.uu.net, is.internic.net, rtfm.mit.edu); Japanese (ftp.cs.titech.ac.jp, kuso.shef.ac.uk, mindseye.berkeley.edu, ftp.monash.edu.au, theta.iis.u-tokyo.ac.jp, uesama.tjp.washington.edu, utsun.is.s.u-tokyo.ac.jp); languages; Linux (Slackware home & more: Bogus: phys-pc61.med.unc.edu, sunsite.unc.edu, tsx-11.mit.edu); Mac (ra.nrl.navy.mil, funet_mac, ftp.wustl.edu (mac.archive.umich.edu implicity)); math; MS-Windows (mirror of ftp.cica.indiana.edu); MS-Windows NT; Newt NT; OBI (On-line Book Initiative, ftp.std.com/obi); OS/2 Hobbes; Perl; Point Of View-ray (povray.cdrom.com); security archive (coast.cs.purdue.edu); SimTel; stereograms; Supreme Court (ftp.cwru.edu); Tcl; TeX; Unix-C; Visual Engineering; Walnut Creek Avalon 3D objects; Win32s; Windows 95; XFree86; X11R6 (ftp.x.org)

ftp://ftp.cnit.nsk.su/

Novosibirsk State University, Novosibirsk

Files: archiver; ccphys.nsu.nsk.su (AD&D; adventure games; D&D; DDL; games; MUD; RPG; SSG; strategic/economic/role-playing engines and description languages to develop several types of software; wargames); CD; dataproc; ftpsites (partial mirrors of elvis.msk.su,ftp.cert.org, ftp.csn.net, ftp.demos.su, ftp.funet.fi, ftp.kiae.su,ftp.ncsa.uiuc.edu, ftp.novell.de, ftp.ripe.net, ftp.uga.edu,garbo.uwasa.fi); games (Doom levels); GNU; GUI; HTML; Internet; IRC collection; mirrors of ftp.funet.fi Pascal archive, Pegasus software, teeri.oulu.fi; MS-DOS; MS-Windows; OS/2; Perl; PGP; pictures; RunNet; SCO (SLS and TLS); security; Sound; Textdoc; Unixware (updates and parts); WWW; X11

ftp://ftp.coe.montana.edu/

Files: fractals; MUD related files; WWW

ftp://ftp.coe.ufrj.br/

Universidade Federal do Rio de Janeiro (Rio Janeiro State University), Rio de Janeiro

Files: Acmg; docs; jonny (KillDoom, Pentium test (p5test)); Linux; MBONE; meteosat; MS-DOS; network; Novell; pictures; Sun; teleinfo; urantia; vendor; Windows

ftp://ftp.coli.uni-sb.de/

Universitaet des Saarlandes (University of the Saarland), Saarbruecken

Files: Amiga; Atari; Toy files

ftp://ftp.comlab.ox.ac.uk/

Oxford University, Oxford, Computing Laboratory (OUCL)

Files: CSP; documents; microprocessor cards; music research; OBJ forum; Occam; packages; programs; Transputer; Z forum

ftp://ftp.compaq.com/

Compaq Computer Corp.

Files: 386BSD; SCO; softpaq

ftp://ftp.cray.com/

Cray Research, Eagan, Minnesota

Files: craysoft, cray: announcements, applications, articles, artwork, product info; FAQs: linear and non-linear programming; comp.lang.verilog; misc.fitness; nqe; nqs

ftp://ftp.creaf.com/

Creative Labs, Santa Clara, California

Files: SoundBlaster related files (patches, press releases, utils for all platforms)

ftp://ftp.cs.bilkent.edu.tr/

Bilkent University, Ankara

Files: graphics programs (Motif, Ray, Render, VolumeRendering); Machine_Learning; tech-reports; Turklang

ftp://ftp.cs.brown.edu/

Brown University, Providence, Rhode Island

Files: alt.quotations; Brown CS Field and Thread

packages; ccel; comp.lang.postscript; comp.robotics; comp.sources.postscript; eim; fnord; graphics; graphtext; hyperbole; iclp94; optbook; postscript; ppcp93; splitup; tech-reports; XMX

ftp://ftp.cs.colorado.edu/

University of Colorado - Boulder, Boulder, Colorado

Files: cs; docs; energy shootout; Esperanto; faces; Ghostscript; HPSC; Netfind sources; standards; tech-reports; time-series; Texas92; Vis

ftp://ftp.cs.few.eur.nl/

Erasmus Universiteit Rotterdam (Erasmus University Rotterdam), Rotterdam

Files: cs; docs; GNU; network (samba); OS (Net2 BSD); PC (Cirrus, PC NFS, Perl, protect); pk; Sun; tech-reports; Unix; WWW

ftp://ftp.cs.indiana.edu/

Indiana University, Bloomington, Indiana

Files: CIC; conacyt; elisp (w3, tcp, mime-rtm, pop, netrek); eopl (Essentials_of_Programming_Languages supplements); faces & picons archives (sources & icons); goo; le (Logic Engine); lics & logic (Logic in CS); mosis; phonedir (Russian long distance); scheme-repository; stiquito; techreports; ucstri (world CS techreport index); oracle (Usenet Oracle); vsh (Visual Shell)

ftp://ftp.cs.keio.ac.jp/

Keio University, Keio

Files: 4.4BSD-Lite; arch; dbms; doc; GNU; inet; jtex; KEIO-CS; lang; Mac; mh; net; NeXT; OS; security; soft-eng; Solaris2; TeX; X11; X11R6

ftp://ftp.cs.kun.nl/

Katholieke Universiteit Nijmegen (University of Nijmegen), Nijmegen

Files: ArMaTuReS (TeX); clean; cip-s; compmath.{alcom,found,numanal}; csi; eag; GLASS; LDB; rail; softweng.{functlang,infsyst,progrmeth}; school; technapp.{exp,theor}; ToalTeX; TeX-bnf; Z80-dis

ftp://ftp.cs.mcgill.ca/

McGill University, Montreal, Quebec

Files: AIX; Aarchie; docs; images; labs; Linux (kernel, Slackware); mail-list; MS-DOS; Netrek (COW and COW-lite); news; NeXT; PC Unix; SGI; Unix; X

ftp://ftp.cs.pdx.edu/

Portland State University, Portland, Oregon

Files: aber (MUD); blackadder; csqr; Dylan; Elvis; frp; games; gks; GNU; Ileaf; League for programming freedom; Keanu-L archive; LPMUD; mexpress; music; NeXT sounds; Parker Lewis archive; Perl; politics; Pratchett; utek; yama; zmodem

ftp://ftp.cs.rochester.edu/

University of Rochester, Rochester, New York

Files: comp.std.lisp archive; ftp.faq [!]; knowledge tools; Lisp standards; Mint; Papers and tech reports; rao; rcs; rec.woodworking; simulator; xarchie

ftp://ftp.cs.ruu.nl/

Rijks Universiteit Utrecht (Utrecht University), Utrecht

Files: Aircraft images; archivers; Atari ST; docs; Elm; GNU; HP-UX; LPF; Linux; MIDI; MIDI ftp sitelist; news.answers archive; NN-6.4; Perl; PINE; RUU; security; SGI; STOP; TeX; Unix; X11

ftp://ftp.cs.tcd.ie/

Trinity College, Dublin

Files: alpha; BSD; cosine-p8; crash; docs; fonts; GNU; graphics; languages; Mac; mail; mcast; multimedia; network; OSF; PC; security; Sun; TCD; text; Unix; utils; windows; X

ftp://ftp.cs.titech.ac.jp/

Tokyo Institute of Technology, Tokyo

Files: docs; games; GNU; GNU-rel; IEICE; Japanese; lang; Mac; mail; net; news; NeXT; OS; security; shell; Sun; TeX; text; tool; wnn; wwfs; X11

ftp://ftp.cs.toronto.edu/

Orgnization: University of Toronto, Toronto

Files: CA domain reg. csri-tech-reports; C-News; cogrob; combin; coopis; CS; darwin; dgp; dkbs; dt; dvix; emv; ftpd; Jove; mirror of nic.ddn.mil; molbio; NeXT; onet; pathalias; PC; reports; scheme; SGI; sigview; SunOS SLIP; Sun-spots; Sun-WP; S/SL; TeX; tff; tron; UofT BIND; usenet; VIS; X11R4; X11R5; xerion; zen; zmailer

ftp://ftp.cs.tulane.edu/

Tulane University, New Orleans, Louisiana

Files: bb; ck; cpen240; fs; lang; mb; prabhu; rpg;

SCSI (files from the SCSI BBS: ESDI, Fiber Channel, IPI, SCSI docs); TAI; tech; wbt; wmr

ftp://ftp.cs.ubc.ca/

University of British Columbia, British Columbia

Files: archive (mirrors): Apollo, doc (RFCs), GNU, Mac, Sun, Unix; ca-domain; cdnnet; cicsr; example images and data files; graphics bibliography in BiBTeX format; images; mirrors: Linux (tsx-11.mit.edu, nighty), NeXT, djgpp (ftp.clarkson.edu, nightly), GNU (prep.ai.mit.edu, nightly), Mach (mach.cs.cmu.edu, weekly), ftp.x.org (X-contrib, nightly), 386BSD (mirrored agate.berkeley.edu, weekly), EFF (ftp.eff.org, nightly), BSD-sources (ftp.uu.net, weekly), canarie (unbmvs1.csd.unb.ca, daily), EmTeX (ftp.cs.ruu.nl, weekly), IETF (ftp.wustl.edu, daily), internet drafts (ftp.wustl.edu, daily), MS-DOS (ftp.wustl.edu, daily), ndtl (hsdndev.harvard.edu, daily), RFCs (ftp.isi.edu, daily), SNMP-MIBs (ftp.3com.com and venera.isi.edu, daily); PCpickup; raster; Raven; security; snacc; Sun-fixes; Tourism in British Columbia (Hypercard Stack); UBC crest bitmaps; UBC CS tech-reports; UBC Unix Users Group; vista (software for computer vision research); X11R6

ftp://ftp.cs.uit.no/

Universitetet i Tromsoe (Tromsoe University), Tromsoe

Files: Amiga; Amiga BSD; Linux; local stuff; OS/2; XPilot

ftp://ftp.cs.umd.edu/

University of Maryland, Maryland

Files: amanda; BSD; classes; coltbib; complex; cyrillic; declarative languages bib; dept.; faculty; hcil; hpsl; MaRS; misc nonlin; omega; papers; prism; realtime; security; skiplists; style-guide; Sun-patches

ftp://ftp.cs.umn.edu/

University of Minnesota, Minnesota

Files: docs; elisp-archive; epoch; GNU; Internet Talk Radio (ITR); LaTeX; Linux; maccabe; networking; security; sparse; systems [?]; Usenet; X

ftp://ftp.cs.unlv.edu/

University of Nevada - Las Vegas, Las Vegas, Nevada

Files: Chimera; Mac (comm, oztex, privacy, utils, virus); MS-DOS (asme, bcf77, emtex, ghostscript, GNU, kermit, oemacs); Unix (Linux distribution and installation HOWTO)

ftp://ftp.cs.uwm.edu/

University of Wisconsin - Milwaukee, Milwaukee, Wisconsin

Files: comp-literacy; comp.privacy (CPD archives Vol 1-4, Privacy Library); crypto94; FreeBSD; NetBSD; OS/2; PC-DOS; shuttle-GIFs (Columbia); soft-eng (Software Engineering class software); tech-reports; uwm-tools (locally developed software tools)

ftp://ftp.cs.vu.nl/

Vrije Universiteit (Free University), Amsterdam

Files: acm; amoeba; ast; Atari (archivers, games); bal; bonsangue; ceriel; ctv (C++, CPL++, draft, Prolog); DejaVU; dick (biddulph, cvs, deskjet & laserjet fonts, magtape handling, MS-DOS, PLE, PTAPG, similarity tester, tartan: loads of GIFs of Scottish design it seems); dictionaries; ecai94; eliens (book, GIFs of Dutch ships, , papers); eptreur; golding; gvw; harpoon; idraw; IOA; ipoorten (Atari 8bit (images, docs, pinouts), Prince (images, PMLs, reviews), Unix); Minix-386vm (ANSI compilers, demo, pascal, simulator); nlroei (successor of rulglj.leidenuniv.nl); papers (AI, amoeba, math, orca, theory); public (RadioAmsterdamNews); Sater (bridge, software); SGML; xemp

ftp://ftp.cs.widener.edu/

Widener University

Files: Simpsons archive, nixpub listing, Archie clients (home of Kehoe's C client); Zen and the Art of the Internet

ftp://ftp.cs.wisc.edu/

University of Wisconsin, Madison, Wisconsin

Files: 007; afs-tools; AIX; Approximation Theory; bolo; CDIFF; computer-vision; condor; connectivity table; coral; Exodus; galileo; ghost; goodman; HP; list-archives; machine learning; markhill; math prog; mcplib; Novell; par-distr-sys; paradise; shore; sohi; spim; spimsal; swartz; tech-reports; Ultimate Frisbee files; UW; warts; wisc; wwt; X; xunet

ftp://ftp.csc.ncsu.edu/

North Carolina State University, Raleigh, North Carolina

Files: anime; bitmaps; classes; communications; compilers; CSC tech-reports; docs; fts; GNU; graduate and undergraduate info; graphics; locked; mail; markov; multimedia; ncsu_motif; network; paracomp; rn; rtcomm; SGI; tdcada; tech; Ultrasound; Unix; utils; wg25; X11; Xinu

ftp://ftp.csce.kyushu-u.ac.jp/

University of Kyushu, Kyushu

Files: 386BSD; 4.4BSDLite; FreeBSD; GNU; internet-drafts; kyushu-u; lang; Linux; Mac; MS-DOS; misc; net; netdocs; Quake info; RFCs; security; system; TeX; utils; X; X11R5

ftp://ftp.cse.psu.edu/

Pennsylvania State University, Pennsylvania

Files: BSDI; cdrom; DNS.Talk; docs; Ethics; ICPP94; ioccc; laser-set; laser-status; mirror of ftp.eff.org; moon; plan9-fans; PSU domain; resource guide; RFCs; Sun-dist; Unix-admin; Vision; VLSI-CAD; winsboro; worm; ZED

ftp://ftp.cse.ucsc.edu/

University of California - Santa Cruz, Santa Cruz, California

Files: amoeba; bibliographies; carafe; colt; comp.os.research; csl; hpdc3; images; item; karplus; mcmc; morph; plan9; protein; qnx; refdbms; rna; tcos; tr; UCSC; xnf-xs

ftp://ftp.csie.nctu.edu.tw/

National Chiao Tung University, Hsin Chu

Files: BBS; BIOS; books; Chinese; cna-news; CSIE; docs; FAQ; GNU; graphics formats; IRIS; liny; Mach docs; MS-DOS; MS-Windows 3.x (mirror of papa.indstate.edu); music; news; news-archive; NeXT; NSC; Phoenix BBS; RFCs; RFC-C; RS6000; security; Sun; Unix; X11; ZyXEL

ftp://ftp.csn.net

Colorado Supernet Inc./Metacard Corporation, Colorado

Files: aap_support; AATA; AATA_China-Link; Advance; Aescon; aimhigh-info; aimhigh; alt.book.reviews; Altia; apptech; aquaengr; ASTI; bbell-assoc; BHPLAW; blackhawk; boulder; CCDC; CGM; ClassicSoft; CloudNine; CMS; COGS; Cogwheel; Columbia; Compatible; Computech; ConferTech; crlhq; CSN; CSNews; Cygnus; cytomation; databases; dea; densoft; disability; DMK; docdev; dos dovetail; dsi; Edgenet; ForteNet; fruug; gat; GEOSYN; gifted; GLP; GMG; golden; gopher; gvnet; HDI; HDL; health; hms; hydrosphere; icc; ices; ILE; Infozone; internet-talk-radio; interpex; interprise; ISAaC; isdn; IST; JournalG; k12; Laserdisc; Libnet; library; LucasRadio; mac; mail-list-archives; mail; mantic; mapinfo; maps; Mathcom; McCallum; Menu; MetaCard (multimedia authoring for Unix/X11); mhhc; MINC;

Minimus; Minitel; misc; modem; net; news; novalink; OldColoCity; OmniRes; other; Pipeline; Platte; povsb; PowerPlay; PPB; prime; ProBook; psi-japan; psi-usa; PTI; QED; qtrack; quarkxt; quipinfo; R2; ramtron; RMDP; RN+; rpgtools; Schreiber; security; seltzer; slip; SOS; Spatial; sudo; Sycon; tiag; tin; Tunguska; Unidata; Unimac; uucp; vprof; wais; Whitestar; XVT

ftp://ftp.cso.uiuc.edu/

University of Illinois - Urbana/Champaign, Urbana, Illinois

Files: Amiga; BBS; Compression programs/formats chart; docs; Mac; mail; math; mods; MS-DOS: ADF, Exec-PC, PC-SIG files; mrc; net-nav; Tandy; UIUC; Unix-PC tools

ftp://ftp.csua.berkeley.edu/

University of California - Berkeley, Berkeley, California

Files: archie; ars-magica; btech; campus-maps; cd-rom; cerebus; chaosium;classes; corewar; crossfire; culture; ctulhu; Cypherpunks archive; dikued; eap; enscriptor; evers; frua; frudge; go-bears archive; help-sessions; hiking-club; ikiru; Linux; lpf; Mach; mcb130; net-growth; Netrek; NNTPscan; novel; palladium; quayletool; rec.gambling; rpg-index; runequest; scheme_class; Sequent; sfraves; sockets; storyteller; strangeness; sugar; the4thnation; typing injury FAQ; vt100.animation; war_cry; wordoftheday; wortzumtag; X11R5; xbattlefront

ftp://ftp.csuohio.edu/

Cleveland State University, Cleveland, Ohio

Files: CSU (Mac, MS-DOS, Windows: misc SLIP software configured for CSU); news: alt.sources, alt.sources.{amiga,d,index,mac,mac.d, patches,wanted}, bit.listserv.{notis-l,novell}, comp.infosystems.gopher, comp.os.vms, comp.protocols.tcp-ip, comp.protocols.tcp-ip.{domains,ibmpc}, comp.soft-sys.nextstep, comp.sources.{misc,unix,x}, comp.sys.dec, comp.sys.dec.micro, comp.sys.next, comp.sys.next.{advocacy,announce,bugs,hardware, marketplace,misc,programmer,software,sysadmin}, comp.sys.novell, comp.sys.sun.{admin,announce, apps,hardware,misc,wanted}, comp.unix.osf.{misc,osf1}, comp.unix.solaris, comp.unix.ultrix

ftp://ftp.cup.hp.com/

Hewlett-Packard, Cupertino, California
Files: dist: courtney, networking, pcapi, socks, tftpexts, tools

ftp://ftp.cuslm.ca/

Centre Universitaire Saint-Louis-Maillet/Universite de Moncton (University of Moncton), Edmonton, New Brunswick

Files: canarie; games; Internet; MIDI; MS-DOS; NB; network; powerpoint; virus; WfW; Win3

ftp://ftp.cwi.nl/

Centrum voor Wiskunde en Informatica (Centre for Mathematics and Computer Science), Amsterdam

Files: ABC; ADPCM lossy algorithm; audio; bootstrap; compare; concur2; cweb; CWI: conferences, courses, drafts, location maps, Quarterly; data; dcab; dinesh; dynload; gipe; gollum; Made; manifold; mcvl; md5; mm papers; moorkop II; morphology; outerjoins; ozsl; parallels project; pascal; pictures; premo; python; qvolume; RIDDLE; SGI trace; stdwin; views

ftp://ftp.cwru.edu/

Case Western Reserve University, Cleveland, Ohio
Files: adf; alt.beer; Art of Prolog; biology; FreeNet; games; hermes; Japanese; math; Mathematica; mercury (OH Appeals 8th dist); NeXT; picture; physics; prolog1000; security; sendmail CWRU; US Supreme Court rulings

ftp://ftp.cyberspace.com/

Files: archive (aviation, bolo, botham, defcon, fastjack, girls, jchaase, mica, mtway, rodman, tierra, timoney, towe, wsantee, zone); DOS (games, qmodem, qwk, upgrade, utils); Mac (appl, comm, compression, extensions, games, ppp); MUD (LambdaMOO); OS/2 (IBM, network, PPP, SLIP); PPP (Mac, Unix, Windows); Unix (FreeBSD (1.1.5.1, 2.0), games, Linux (sunsite.unc.edu: epoch, fgrabber, lilo, slackware, SLS, snap, sound, WordPerfect for Linux, X11), packages: layers, qpopper, telnet); Video (CUSeeMe: extras, Mac, PC)

ftp://ftp.cyberstore.ca/

Files: Atari; bookreviews (antivirus book-reviews by Robert Slade; CIXCan; docs; IETF; Mac; merit (meritrr, pride, ripe, transition); MS-DOS (archivers, termprogs); Net (netmgmt, pcip96, pdtar, qcnw96); OLA; OS/2; realtime; rtfm (alt.answers, comp.mail.sendmail, comp.mail.uucp, comp.os.msdos.mail-news, news.admin.misc, news.admin.technical); Solaris 2.x; Sun; talk; webmaint; windows (apps, cyber-ppp, htmlasst, lwp, mosaic, netscape, win32s)

ftp://ftp.cyf-kr.edu.pl/

CYFRONET, Cracow, Academic Computer Center

Files: agh (mounted, including GIFs in /agh/reserve/gifs); Cyfronet (local info); ecuc94 (European Convex Users Conference); ifuj (mounted); lfs (mounted); mirrors: AMI info (ftp.megatrends.com), Comm programs (boombox.micro.umn.edu:/pub/pc), GNU, JPG viewers (ftp.portal.com), MS-DOS (ftp.coast.net via ftp.switch.ch), MS-Windows (ftp.cica.indiana.edu:/pub/win3 via ftp.switch.ch), NCSA Telnet (ftp.ncsa.uiuc.edu:/PC/Telnet), RFCs, Unix-arcers (garbo.uwasa.fi:/unix/arcers), X11R5, X contrib (ftp.x.org:/contrib); netinfo (mostly outdated); TeXmex; Unix

ftp://ftp.dante.de/

Comprehensive TeX Archive Network (CTAN Germany), Heidelberg

Files: TeX (CTAN)

ftp://ftp.dartmouth.edu/

Dartmouth College

Files: ATT6300+; csmp-digest; Dante; Dartmouth stuff (rn; mail; etc.); Exceptions; GNUplot; Hyperbooks; ICMA library; LLTI-IALL; Mac; Prologue users; protein; PTSD; Renal-function; security; SOP; VWPROJ

ftp://ftp.datasrv.co.il/

DataServ, Jeruzalem

Files: Datasrv customer support: Linux, PC, Unix utis; Hebrew and Jewish software; InVirCible /pub/usr/netz; networking; security

ftp://ftp.dcc.uchile.cl/

Universidad de Chile (University of Chile), DCC

Files: chile; dccinfo; edo; GNU; gopher; graphics; Internet; Lang; lib; Linux (docs, Slackware, TinyX); Mac; MUD; network; news; PC (4dos, antivirus, binaries, comm, games, graph, lang, latex, mac, network, os2, pov, sound, uucp, vga, win); pictures [empty]; redinfo; security [only some zip stuff]; Sinclair (almost all there is on ftp.ijs.si); Sparc; Sun; TeX; Unix; VLDB; X11

ftp://ftp.dcs.ed.ac.uk/

University of Edinburgh, Edinburgh, Scotland

Files: Acorn; BBC; bind; cao; cap; fonts; graphics; ident; ifip; ladm; lego; Mac; netutils; pic; POP; Postscript utils; rasmol; RFCs; TeX; Tk; TolkLang; utils; VLSI-CAD; X11R5

ftp://ftp.dcs.gla.ac.uk/

University of Glasgow, Glasgow, Scotland

Files: actress; Ansible; Avalanche; BCS; fide; flare; gist; glasgow-fp; haskell; hug94; iii; imis; Linux; Mac; merill; mail; NASA; news; pj-lester book; recipes; src; SF archives; theory; triangle; types

ftp://ftp.demon.co.uk/

Demon Internet, London

Files: 4.3BSD; ACCU (/pub/cug); Amiga; Antivirus (comprehensive across all platforms); Archimedes; Atari; books; commercial demos; CP/M; CUG; Dialup IP, PGP and Usenet software; doc; games; GNU; ham-radio; KA9Q; images; Mac; mail; MS-DOS (SimTel); news; NetBSD (mirror of sun-lamp.cs.berkeley.edu); NeXt; NT; OS/2; perl; PGP; pick; PPP; roundhill; SCO; SLIP; Sun; trumphurst; Unix; Xenix; XWindows; XFree86 (mirror of ftp.xfree86.org)

ftp://ftp.demos.su/

Files: arcers; astrology; books; databases; demo; Demos; esperanto; graph; hosts (fantom); languages; Mac; maps; math; MS-DOS; music; net; news; RFCs; servers [old ftp-list]; Unix

ftp://ftp.dfv.rwth-aachen.de/

RWTH Aachen, Aachen

Files: Linux (sunsite.unc.edu)

ftp://ftp.di.fc.ul.pt/

Lisbon University, Lisbon

Files: antivirus; cadeiras; doc; FAQ; games; net; papers; programming; systems

ftp://ftp.difi.unipi.it/

University of Pisa, Pisa

Files: 386ix; gated; graphics; Khoros; kinet; Linux; Mac; Mosaic; mpeg; NetEC; preprints; Rexx; RS6000; TeX

ftp://ftp.digex.net/

Digital Express Group Inc.

Files: access; avernus; bibliobytes; binaries; cbooks; crest; davei; deckmaster; diversity; GNU; mail; mms; networking; news; newsreaders; OS; RFCs; scibooks; shells; TeX; text-processing; TFactors; vendor-specific; wash; X11

ftp://ftp.digibd.com/

DigiBoard

Files: Digiboard (digifax, digiline: drivers, isdn); pub: HP4laser (lp model for autohandling of PCL/PostScript jobs), SCO-ports, uiarchive (archive of the defunct Unix International effort), unixware, WWW

ftp://ftp.digifix.com/

Digifix

Files: binaries; documents; drivers; mailinglist-archives; newsletters;NeXT: NeXT-In-Line, comp.sys.next.announce archives; source; submissions; vendors

ftp://ftp.dkfz-heidelberg.de/

DKFZ, Heidelberg

Files: Atlas; cica; docs; embnet; gdb; igd; Linux; MS-DOS; PostScript; UTS; Windows3

ftp://ftp.dmu.ac.uk/

DeMontfort University, Leicester

Files: clb_comp; cms (cph, imaging, moo, tattoo, VR); netcomm (docs, Linux, Mac, MS-DOS, Solaris 1.x, Solaris 2.x, src); pharmacy (addresses, drug-info, mednews, meetings, net-info, pme, posts, pse, schools, software, usenet-smp, www); sun (dmu)

ftp://ftp.doc.ic.ac.uk/

Imperial College of Science, Technology and Medicine, London

Files: Aminet; biology; faces; geology; GNU; IAFA-SITEINFO; info; literary; media; mirrors: SimTel Software Repository (/pub/packages/simtel20), games from ftp.uml.edu (/computing/systems/ibmpc/msdos-games/Games), MS-Windows from ftp.cica.indiana.edu; politics; RFCs; Sun; Tcl/Tk (packages/tcl from ftp.cs.berkeley.edu); TeX from ftp.tex.ac.uk; UKUUG; Unix; Usenet; weather

ftp://ftp.dungeon.com/

Files: Amiga (AmiTCP, networking); cartoons [empty]; cd1 (cdrom, OS/2, windows); dungeon (Amiga, docs, Mac, MS-DOS, news, Windows, WWW); homeo; Linux (MOO, sunsite.unc.edu); MS-DOS (antivirus, BBS, comms, diskutils, dtp, games, genutils, graphics, IDgames, programming, ray-tracing, sound, StarTrek, vendor [?], win); music (BTL, cathyden, MODs); nap

ftp://ftp.ea.com/

Electronic Arts, San Mateo, California

Files: demos (bioforge, crusader, cybermage, f2b, fifa, little big adventure (Twinsen's adventure: Europe), magic carpet, need 4 speed, relentless (Twinsen's adventure: USA), system shock, theme park, usnf (US Navy Fighters), wing4, wings of glory); eaweb (graphics, patches, pictures); gifs (screen captures of crusader, cybermage, space hulk 3do, super wing, system shock, wing3 3do, wing commander III, wings of glory); movies; patches; press releases

ftp://ftp.earn.net/

European Academic Research Network (EARN)

Files: cnre; docs; earnest; general EARN info; gophermail; listserv archives; nethelp; networking info; networking services; nsc; tools

ftp://ftp.earthlink.net

Earthlink Network, Los Angeles, California

Files: Earthlink info; Software: Amiga, ISDN (Windrider), Mac (net related utils, PC (AWE32, CTHUGHA, DOS_SLIP, games, ghostview, mstcpip, mosaic, netscape, offlinereaders, tiskwin (mirror of ftp.halcyon.com), , PGP, SGI (ESPModeller); Constitution (legal and gov files)

ftp://ftp.ece.concordia.ca/

Concordia University, Montreal, Quebec

Files: eng; HP calc; info; ISODE-8; math; OS (Amiga, Linux, Mac, MS-DOS, MS-Windows 3.1, OS/2, Sun, Ultrix, Unix); simulator; soft-dev; sysadm (Sendmail)

ftp://ftp.ecn.bgu.edu/

Western Illinois University, Macomb, Illinois

Files: archive; cs-research; ecn; eiu; fine-art (alt.binaries.pictures. fine-art.{d,digitized,graphics} archive; gopher; gsu; micro; perl; ph; Sun-admin; Sun-fixes; wiu

ftp://ftp.ecs.soton.ac.uk/

Orgnization: University of Southampton, Southampton

Files: admin; benchmarks; digits; docs; eefl; elm; etet; Mac; misc; MS-DOS (demos (overlord), patches (ufo1-2)); netweek; news; occam; papers; pastpapers; PC; SGI; transputer; UC; Unix; X11

ftp://ftp.ed.ac.uk/

University of Edinburgh, Edinburgh, Scotland

Files: a2ps; courses; EdLAN; emwac [mirror of emwac.ed.ac.uk?]; GNU; IUSC; JIPS; lrtt; mail; mmaccess; maps; MFT; Motif FAQ; netdocs; PC-NFS; pdps; smrsh; Solaris; spooling; Sun: ecl, fixes, papers; UCSG; uniras; Unixhelp; whiteosi; X.400; X11 FAQ

ftp://ftp.ed.gov/

US Dept. of Education, Washington, D.C.

Files: ED_wide (Dept. of Education Initiatives and Legislation); OERI gopher; National Center for Education Statistics (NCES) gopher; WWW

ftp://ftp.edv.agrar.tu-muenchen.de/

Technische Universitaet Muenchen (Munich Institute of Technology), Munich

Files: IDOLON imagemanipulationsystem; OS/2; Unix; Windows; X11

ftp://ftp.edu.tw/

National Chiao Tung University, Campus Computer Communication Association, Taipei

Files: Aminet; BSD; Chinese Apps (ifcss.org); Computing Languages; E-Text; ftp-list (documents/networking/guides/ftp-list); Images; GNU; Linux; MaasInfo files (documents/Internet/Maasinfo); Mac; mirrors: coombs.anu.edu.au, garbo.uwasa.fi (/PC/garbo), ftp.uml.edu (/Ulowell/msdos or /PC/uwp), ftp.cica.indiana.edu, Simtel Software Repository (/pub/mirrors/msdos); MS-DOS; MS-Windows; NCSA Apps; NCTU; Netlib; Next; OS/2; Packages; Sound; Statlib; Unix; Usenet; Vendors; VLSI; X-Windows; XFree86 (mirror of ftp.xfree86.org)

ftp://ftp.ee.auth.gr/

Aristotle University of Thessaloniki, Thessaloniki

Files: animations; games; images (Bablyon5, fantasy, formula1, misc, music, Startrek, Starwars); MS-DOS; MS-Windows; music (many songs in S3M/MTM/XM formats); NeXTStep; OS/2; Unix

ftp://ftp.ee.und.ac.za/

University of Natal - Durban, Durban, Natal.

Files: Alternet ZA (alt.za domain info); archiving; bible; crypto; docs; Internet info (drafts, netinfo, RFCs); ioccc (International Obfuscated C Code Competition); mail; MS-DOS (including network-ing); Novell; optics; Perl; security; superconductiv-ity; TeX; time; UniNet ZA; Unix; Usenet news; WAIS

ftp://www.eff.org/

Electronic Frontier Foundation (EFF), Washington, District of Columbia

Files: EFF-related materials (newsletters, press releases, legislative analyses, etc.); legal and govt. information (crypto/privacy, case law, bill and govt. report texts, action alerts, censorship & free speech, NII/GII/III); network information (Internet guidebooks, FAQs, resource lists, net.culture articles, networking utilities, PGP); online non-profit organizations (SEA, EFF-Austin, etc.); electronic publications (e-journals, CuD, Phrack, Cyberwire Dispatch - many zines on networking issues and home site of the Computer underground Digest archives); Computers and Academic Freedom project archive (AUPs, university censorship issues, intellectual freedom, legal texts).

ftp://ftp.ege.edu.tr/

Files: Amiga; docs; GIF (EGE, Movies, Tourism); MEDCAMP; MS-DOS (4DOS, demos, docs, filedocs, games, graphics, gscript, info, memman, networks, sound, virus, win3, xwindows, zip); OS/2 (bbs, perfbeta, servpack, tcputils); RFCs; Unix

ftp://ftp.einet.net/

EINet

Files: cyberspace; EINet info; EINet MacWeb/WinWeb/WinWAIS (mirrored on www.jsc.nasa.gov); gopherhunt; gopherjewels; handbook on population; hardin; iceimt; Perl5; POP; Samba; WWWorder

ftp://ftp.elf.stuba.sk/

STU Bratislava, Bratislava

Files: audio; images; lyrics; mod; PC (gxf, sac); pomoc (docs, C++, faq, X); Unix (cs, scripts, Sun); vtipy; zakony; zx

ftp://ftp.elka.pw.edu.pl/

Technical University of Warsaw, Warsaw

Files: docs; DOS (clipper, doc, dos_unix, dpmi, gnu, gopher, graph, gs, html, ka91, novell, pcbridge, pcroute, pegasus, perl, pkt, tcp, telnet.win, TeX, waterloo, windows, wintcp, xapeal); ELKA; FAQs; IAPW; ISO; RFCs; Unix (database, DTP, GNU, gopher, graphics, Ks, Linux, mail, network, news, programming, publishing, shells, TeX, WWW, X11R5

ftp://ftp.eng.auburn.edu/

Files: 3D; Ada; bt; doug (security stuff including klaxon, netwho, satan); ecos; emap; engext; gauss; isa; lists; modem; MOSCAP; mutools; Perl5; Prolog; ROADMAP; SEGA; SMCC; Solaris; tech-reports; Usenix; wu; xdm

ftp://ftp.eni.co.jp/

ENI

Files: mirrors: ALL (asustek.asus.com.tw, ftp.3com.com, ftp.adaptec.com, ftp.ascend.com, ftp.atitech.ca, ftp.buslogic.com, ftp.cirrus.com, ftp.cnds.canon.co.jp, ftp.creaf.com, ftp.diamondmm.com, ftp.dpt.com, ftp.farallon.com, ftp.fore.com, ftp.freebsd.org, ftp.funet.fi, ftp.intel.com, ftp.maxtor.com, ftp.ncr.com, ftp.netbsd.org, ftp.newton.uiowa.edu, ftp.next.com, ftp.nine.com, ftp.pc.digital.com, ftp.rtpro.yamaha.co.jp, ftp.seagate.com, ftp.service.digital.com, ftp.shiva.com, ftp.smc.com, ftp.symbios.com, ftp.tenon.com, ftp.tut.ac.jp, ftp.wdc.com, ftp.wiretap.spies.com, ftp.wpine.com, ftp.xircom.com, papa.indstate.edu, wcarchive.cdrom.com), ftp.adobe.com, OS (ftp.cnds.canon.co.jp, ftp.freebsd.org, ftp.netbsd.org, ftp.next.com, ftp.tenon.com, ftp.tut.ac.jp); nnr; Winsock (papa.indstate.edu)

ftp://ftp.ens.fr/

Ecole Normale Superieure, Service de Prestations Informatique

Files: Bitnet; ens; FAQs; Internet (economics, libraries, services); listserv; Mac; math; meteo; mod2mag; Mosaic; NeXT; PC (arc-lbr, comm, dos, lang, Linux, net, tex, virus); pomp; pompc; primes; reports; security; sun-managers; TeX; Unix

ftp://ftp.enst.fr/

Ecole National Superieure des Telecoms (ENST), Paris

Files: afa; archivers; bench; docs; ENST; FAQs; games; GNU; infosystems; Internet; Mac; mail; network; PC; prog; reports; RFCs; security; sesame; sounds; SSBA (mirrored on ftp.univ-lyon1.fr); TeX; tools; tribunix; Unix; VMS; X-paleolitic; X11

ftp://ftp.enterprise.net/

Enterprise

Files: mirrors: Linux (sunsite.unc.edu complete), Mac (mac.umich.umich.edu), MS-Windows (ftp.winsite.com: borland, menu, starter, win3, win95, winnt), Winsock (papa.indstate.edu complete); netdial

ftp://ftp.eos.hokudai.ac.jp/

Hokkaido University, Hokkaido

Files: archiver; Canna; doc; emacs; Geo; GNU; Info-Mac; lang; Mac; mail; MPEG; MS-DOS; MS-Windows; mule; netnews; network; Postscript; RFCs; security; skk; Sun; TeX; tools; umich; Unix; VMS; Wnn; WU-ftpd; WWW; X

ftp://ftp.epcc.ed.ac.uk/

University of Edinburg, Edinburgh, Scotland, Edinburgh Center for Parallel Computing (EPCC)

Files: chimp; cs9; cupid; DCS; explorer; ftpmail.help [?]; ifip; paramics; parintro; pul; RCS; rpl2; ss; t3d-docs; th; tn; tr; ug; vispad; visualization

ftp://ftp.es.ele.tue.nl/

Technische Universiteit Eindhoven

Files: esprit; graph3d; Linux (edatools (spice, twolf), games, kernel, telnetd patched, xemacs, ZyXEL); LP_solve; neat (asd-expander, dfg, emacs-info, neat, nwgen, papers); poster; primes examples; tiggr

ftp://ftp.estec.esa.nl/

European Space Agency (ESA), Noordwijk

Files: CODE; csds; ers; esbtc; ESIS (European Science Information System) data files including current ESA science program project files (CLUSTER, ISO, POEM etc); gp; network files and ESA administrative documents; ntp; opex; piers; poem; public relations documents + PC/MAC files; soho; TOPSIM; TST; WDP; wm; xe; ypa

ftp://ftp.etext.org/

Private site

Files: CERT Advisories; CPSR; Gutenberg; Legal; Libellus; Mailing lists; Objectivism; Poetry; Politics; Quartz; Religious texts; Sports; Text files and electronic journals: Computer Underground Digest (CuD) archives, other zines (electronic magazines); Well; X11; Zines

ftp://ftp.evitech.fi/

Espoo/Vanta Institute of Technology, Espoo

Files: doc (Netdocs, RFCs); Linux (Slackware); Mac (Mosaic); MS-DOS (math, multimedia, util); Novell; Taik; Unix (HP-UX 9); WWW (doc, html, httpd, Lynx, Mosaic, Perl, rootitus)

ftp://ftp.eunet.be/

EUnet Belgium

Files: bootstrap; BUUG; comp; customers (interackt, sail4u); docs; EUnet; Eunet BE; GNU; mail; network; news; OS (Linux); people; RIPE; security (CERT reports); utils

ftp://ftp.eunet.ch/

CHUUG/EUnet Switzerland (CH), Zurich

Files: Amiga BSD; Aminet; CHUUG; docs; FSP; Gopher; Mirrors: GNU, X11 contrib, RFCs; NetBSD Amiga; network; news-archive; NeXT (mirror from ftp.informatik.uni-muenchen.de); Unix; vendor; WAIS

ftp://ftp.eunet.cz/

EUnet Czechoslavakia

Files: Big Dummy's Guide to the Internet; cdrom; CERT; GNU; Guidebooks; Kermit; MERIT; network; NIC; Novell; RIPE; security; SURANet info; Telnet; Web/WWW; Winsock; X11

ftp://ftp.eunet.es/

EUnet Spain (ES), Madrid

Files: Anuncios (announcements of Spanish events on networking); Documents/CE (Spanish related information about the European Commission); EUnet/Spain (Spanish service provider information); FAQs; Interstand (information from Spanish sites and institutions); mirrors: sites relating to communication, mostly Internet software docs (gopher, MIME, RFCs, Wais, winsock, WWW)

ftp://ftp.eunet.no/

EUnet Norge AS, Oslo

Files: docs (CERT advisories, ORA, RFC, RIPE); GNU; languages (Perl, Tcl); Mac (Internet); MS-DOS (archivers, demodisk, ggdata, win3); networking (security, services, snmp); NT; text; Unix (4BSD, FreeBSD, mail, networking, news, shell, utilities); vendors (bnti, cascade, livingston, morningstar, sgi); X11R6

ftp://ftp.eunet.sk/

EUnet Slovakia (SK), Bratislava

Files: CD-ROM (NLUUG CD-ROM: best public SW); EUNet SK; Internet Talk Radio; Slackware; X11R6

ftp://ftp.euronet.nl/

EuroNet Internet, Amsterdam

Files: Aminet; EuroNet; Mac (comms, info-mac, system, util); MS-DOS; MS-Windows (cica, comms, support); Unix (Netscape)

ftp://europa.com/

Europa Communications Inc., Portland, Oregon

Files: Amiga; database; Mac; MS-DOS (docs, SLIP-PPP, terminal, utils); MS-Windows (docs, SLIP-PPP, trumpet, utils, WinIPKit); OS/2 (docs, fixpak, SLIP-PPP, terminal, utils); outgoing (user public directories: Bax, DOORS, FDMGR, NU, RAR, sasidata, sf, telemate, tossftp); pierian

ftp://ftp.expa.fnt.hvu.nl/

Hogeschool van Utrecht (Utrecht Polytechnical Institute), Utrecht

Files: ameraal; cdrom; graphics; hunt; inun; jobs; Linux (some FAQs, Oberon); MS-DOS (dsfree, minuarc, misc utils, sio); network; pba (fuzzy, interet); projects; sdt; unpo

ftp://ftp.farallon.com/

Farallon Computing Inc., Alameda, California

Files: Farallon product info, updates, drivers

ftp://ftp.fdn.fr/

Oragnization: French Data Network, Paris

Files: Mac; NeXT (mirror of ftp.informatik.uni-muenchen.de)

ftp://ftp.fedworld.gov/

FedWorld

Files: a-dr-cmt; cals; cim; comments; commerce; ctn; d-rule; healthact; healthrpt; jobs; media; nafta; nii; npr; ntis; ota-pres; p-dr-cmt; patent; results; ruleinfo; s-cmts; s-draft; sat-images; sca; teltrend; whitehouse

ftp://ftp.fee.vutbr.cz/

Technical University of Brno, Brno

Files: bible; books; docs; GNU; Hyper-G; languages; MS-DOS (Borland, Buttonware, games, Garbo, McAfee, Novell, Pmail, Qdeck, Share, Simtel, TCP/IP); networking (mirror of ftp.uu.net/networking: AppleTalk, applic, archival, athena, cisco, fax, gopher, ident, info-service, IP, isis, Lynx, mail, news, OSI, RPC, serial, terms, UUCP, uumap, wais, WWW, x25); sources; systems (FreeBSD, Linux, mach, NetBSD, SCO, Unixware); usenet (comp.sources.(d,games,misc, postscript,unix,x)); X; X11; X11R5; X11R6; XFree86 (mirror of ftp.xfree86.org)

ftp://ftp.fenk.wau.nl/

Landbouw Universiteit Wageningen (Wageningen Agricultural University), Wageningen

Files: International Association of Colloid and Interface (IACI) scientists info; mirrors: info-mac.stanford.edu, jagubox.gsfc.nasa.gov (Mac); Linux (Slackware); Molecular Modelling progs bases on the Scheutjens-Fleer theory; pceudora; popper; Simula/simed; Sun-fixes; verman

ftp://ftp.fh-wolfenbuettel.de/

Fachhochschule Wolfenbuettel (Wolfenbuettel Polytechnical Institute), Wolfenbuettel

Files: alliance; archiver; Atari; audio; doc (Filter, Lyrics, O'Reilly, Posix, SCSI); games; gametool; ghostscript; graphics; Khoros; infosys; languages; Linux (Linus, Slackware, SLS, sunsite.unc.edu, tsx-11.mit.edu); LPMUD; lyrics; magazine; MS-DOS; nethack; Netrek; network; Oberon; parallel; shells; Simulation; Sun; TeX; Terminal; TinyMUD; tools; Unix (games, PVM); WWW-FHWF; X11 (contrib, misc and more misc)

ftp://ftp.fht-mannheim.de/

Fachhochschule der Technik Mannheim (Mannheim Polytechnical Institute), Mannheim

Files: 386BSD (from ftp.uni-stuttgart.de); AIX PC; BSD 4.3 src; Emtex PC; Linux; MS-DOS (Simtel-20); MS-DOS games (from ftp.urz.uni-heidelberg.de); OS/2 (comp.binaries.os2); PasTeX (Amiga, from ftp.uni-passau.de); RS6000; Trumpet

ftp://ftp.fi.upm.es/

Technical University of Madrid (UPM)

Files: aix; amiga; archie; docs; faculty; gopher; MS-DOS; news; OS/2; suit; Unix; VMS; X11

ftp://ftp.fibronics.de/

Fibronics GmbH, Dietzenbach

Files: FreeBSD; Linux; MS-DOS; MS-Windows; Software for Fibronics products

ftp://ftp.fnal.gov/

Fermi National Accelerator Laboratories, Chicago, Illinois

Files: admin; AIX; cps; declared; FermiTools; frc; histoscope; html; generic Unix; HP-UX; IRIX; juke; murmur_kit; nedit; OSF/1; plot_widgets; spuds; SunOS; VxWorks; Unix KITS (registered users only)

ftp://ftp.fonorola.net/

Fonorola

Files: ca-domain; Fonorola; Internet Business Journal; Internet information; Mac Gopher servers; networking; training; Usenet; Veronica; WAIS-sources

ftp://ftp.forthnet.gr/

Foundation for Research and Technology, Heraklion, Crete

Files: Archie; Cisco; docs; Ebone; GNU; Gopher; Greek (FAQ, fonts, Mosaic, PC-drivers, soc.culture.greek); Isode; Mac; Mail; News; networking (dns, ftpd, mail, monster, osi, ppp, ripe, routing, slip, tip, tools, ttcp, uucp-x25, uupc); pub (GNU, guitar (mirror),

infosystems, Linux, Mac, NetBSD, X); RFCs; RIPE; Sun; WAIS; WWW; X11

ftp://ftp.fourmilab.ch/

Fourmi Lab

Files: kelvin: secure voice conversation over the Internet through Netfone (Sun and SGI), Speak Freely (MS-Windows)

ftp://ftp.francenet.fr/

FranceNet BBS

Files: cdrom; gopher; htdocs; mirrors (DOS: reseau, windows3 (demo, drivers, programr), GNU); systems (Mac (TCP/IP), Unix (networking)); wincode

ftp://ftp.fujixerox.co.jp/

Fuji Xerox Co. Ltd., Kawasaki, Kanagawa

Files: DeleGate (etlport.etl.go.jp); FlexFax; FujiXerox; GNU (utsun.s.u-tokyo.ac.jp); images; Internet drafts (ds.internic.net) InterViews (sragw.sra.co.jp); MIME (etlport.etl.go.jp); mirrors not mentioned in the rest of this entry (bash.keio.ac.jp, cs.ucl.ac.uk, cs.uiuc.edu, ftp.aist-nara.ac.jp, ftp.ascii.co.jp, ftp.center.osaka-u.ac.jp ftp.cs.titech.ac.jp, ftp.cs.wisc.edu, ftp.foretune.co.jp, ftp.ics.uci.edu, ftp.lysator.liu.se, ftp.sra.co.jp, ftp.tis.com, info.cern.ch, lab4imgw.kuis.kyoto-u.ac, opcom.sun.ca, riksun.riken.go.jp, self.stanford.edu, sgi.com, sprite.berkeley.edu, xtel.co.uk; MS-DOS; Mosaic-l10n+ (ftp.fujitsu.co.jp); mule (etlport.etl.go.jp); NetBSD; OSI; product; RFCs (ftp.dit.co.jp); security; sendmail (ftp.cs.berkeley.edu); Tcl (sragw.sra.co.jp); TeX; Unix; Windows; X (ftp.iij.ad.jp); X11-i18n; Zaurus

ftp://ftp.funet.fi/

Finland University & Research Network (FUNET) NIC, Espoo

Files: Amiga; Astro; Atari; cae; CBM; cryptography; Computer Underground nDigest (CuD) archives; csc; culture; docs; dx; FUNET; GNU; graphics; ham-radio; IRC clients, GIFs of IRC and Relay people: pub/pics/gif/pics/people/misc; kermit; languages; lyhty; Mac; Mach; microprocs; Minix; MS-DOS; netinfo; networking; NeXT; org; OS/2; pictures; sci; security docs and apps; Simtel20 mirror (/pub/msdos/SimTel-mirror); Sony NeWS OS software; sounds; sports; standards; Tao; Unix; VM; VMS; Windows, Windows NT (ftp.cica.indiana.edu); X11; XFree86 (mirror of ftp.xfree86.org under consideration)

ftp://ftp.geod.emr.ca/

Natural Resources Canada (Energy, Mines and Resources Canada and Forestry Canada), Ottawa, Ontario

Files: docs; GSD; Linux (mail); Mac; MS-DOS (4DOS, archive, communications, editors, games, GNU, infosystems, internettools, McAfee, Perl, pictures, security, sysutils, Tcl, Textutils, Unixlike, USNO, viewers); OS/2; recipes; Unix; vegetarian; ziptools

ftp://ftp.germany.eu.net/

German EUnet backbone, Dortmund

Files: 386BSD; Amiga; archiver; Atari; benchmark; books; CT-Magazin; docs; EUnet; GNU; GUUG; infosystems; IX-Magazin; Linux (sunsite.unc.edu); mail; Motif; MS-DOS; Network docs; news; newsarchive; OS/2 programming; RFCs; RIPE; sources and binaries for various systems; X11 (official server)

ftp://ftp.gmu.edu/

George Mason University, Fairfax, Virginia

Files: aic; ascime; bcox; cff; library; support (TIA, winsock); system (docs)

ftp://ftp.grolier.fr/

Grolier, Neuilly

Files: Aminet; images; IRC; Linux; Mac; mods; PC; SimTel; traque; Unix

ftp://ftp.gu.edu.au/

Griffith University, Security Emergency Response Team (SERT)

Files: qps; rex; security; sendmail; smrsh; The Hessling Editor (THE) macro package

ftp://ftp.gui.uva.es/

Universidad de Valladolid (Valladolid University), Castilla y Leo'n, Facultad de Ciencias, Grupo Universitario de Informatica (GUI)

Files: Amiga (pub/aminet, almost finished constructing); Bridge (/pub/bridge): Public Domain PC Bridge & Router; GNU (pub/gnu): daily mirror of GNU licensed soft; HP48 calculators (pub/hp48): soft & utils; IRC (pub/Irc): progs & utils; Linux (pub/linux.new): Official Spanish Mirror of Slackware distribution, plus kernels & lots of soft & utils, & mirror of the Linux Documentation Project (also available in our Web); Electronic Magazines (pub/magazine), including our own magazine "Login:"; MSDOS (pub/pc): 2M & other Ciriaco Garci'a de Celis' programs home site (Ciriaco is a member of our association), 4DOS (mirror of ftp.std.com), astronomy, BBS, chemistry, chess (lots of info), clipper, communications-Telix, Terminate, etc.-, compression, file, disk, screen, system & test utils, editors, emulators, FreeDOS project mirror (very recent), games & cheats, graphic utils, info (hard disks, mirror of the Interrupt List, OnLine Book, this ftp-list :-), microsoft upgrades & info, Movies (MS Video & Quicktime), NCSA, NFS, Postscript, POV-Ray, printer drivers, rip, sound,TeX, virus (includes FProt & Scan mirror); Music area (pub/music) for several machines; OS/2 (pub/os2); sinclair (pub/sinclair, all such machines covered & mirrors); tsx-lite (pub/tsx-lite), unix (pub/unix, misc progs); info about international contests (Assembly, Obfuscated C); The Internet Adapter (pub/TIA) and MS-Windows area (recently moved to pub/windows from pub/pc, with Win3.x and Win95 areas)

ftp://ftp.hab-weimar.de/

HAB-Weimar, Weimar, CC

Files: GIF; graphics; MS-DOS; sound; Windows

ftp://ftp.hacktic.nl/

Hack-Tic, Amsterdam

Files: crypto; etext (Cypher-Rebels Electronic Book); PGP (pgp-add-on, pgpfone); remailer; security

ftp://ftp.halcyon.com/

Northwest NEXUS Inc., Bellevue, Washington

Files: activism; alt.missing-kids.gifs; artcrit; Computer Underground Digest (CuD) archives; esdl; Eudora; faf; fluke; FWDP; FX (UUCICO/ UUCP); go; handicap; HUG; II (Infinite Ink); ITR; jargon; Linux; nag-hammadi; North West Nexus; Pink Floyd; recipes; RKBA; seabird; SLIP; Supra; Tidbits (TIA); tiskwin; Waffle; wuarchive

ftp://ftp.health.org/

Files: DOS, MAC, UNIX and WP text files relating to all kinds of health issues (alcoholism, child abuse, drugs, etc.)

ftp://ftp.hiof.no/

Ostfold College

Files: adate; adm; Atari (Jaguar); comics (rec.arts.comics archive, read the FAQ for that group on material available: Annotations, Batman, Beanworld, Cerebus, Comics-L, Database, Disney, FAQ, Fanfiction, Fanzines, Film_and_TV, Guide-lines, Misc, Pictures, Previews, Reference, Releases, Reviews, Sandman, Software, Statistics, Strips, Superman, Toys, Trading_Cards, Watchmen, X-Men)); cyber; dimensions; FR-MUD; fuzzy; GIF; inet-maps; levant; lyd; Mac; mid-east; miniboard; ml; multimedia; NeXT; Novell; pan and tilt; PC; PGP; sarpinger; teleconferencing; weather

ftp://ftp.hitachi-sk.co.jp/

Hitachi Software Engineering Co.

Files: 386BSD (Compaq, PC98); 4.3BSD-Reno; CAP; CERT; database; demacs; doc (IEN, RFCs); emacs-lisp; font; FreeBSD; gambit; GNU; haskell (MacGopher); Info-Mac; IntelligentPad; MIME; MS-DOS; MS-Windows; mule (multi-lingual enhance-ment to GNU Emacs); NetBSD; news; Novell; OSI; PCTE (portable common tool environment); penpoint; SunRPC; X11R5/R6 (core, contrib)

ftp://ftp.hk.super.net/

Hong Kong SuperNet, HKUST, Sai Kung

Files: mirrors of AutoDesk, CICA, Creative, FAQs,

FreeBSD, Games (ftp.uml.edu), Info-MAC, GNU, Linux, Mcafee Antivirus, Newton, Omega (ftp.wiwi.uni-frankfurt.de), OS2 (ftp-os2.nmsu.edu), RFCs, Simtel (MSDOS), Slackware (ftp.cdrom.com)

ftp://ftp.hobby.nl/

HobbyNet (HCC), Utrecht

Files: 68000; 6805; 6809; C++; docs; HobbyNet; mirror (Cica); MS-DOS; Newton; start pakketten (Amiga, Linux, MS-Windows, OS/2); Unix

ftp://ftp.hq.eso.org/

European Southern Observatory (ESO), Garching

Files: Astronomical images; ESO Preprints (some); FITS documents/testfiles; MIDAS (astronomical image processing) files; NTT; SAO; Star Catalogs; StyleGuide; TeX DVI drivers

ftp://ftp.hsrc.ac.za/

Human Sciences Research Council

Files: census; comet (Shoemaker-Levy 9 (SL9) pictures); FAQs; GNU; mirrors: 3COM (ftp.3com.com/pub/adapters/drivers), Borland (ftp.borland.com/pub), CD-ROM (ftp.cdrom.com), CICA (ftp.cica.indiana.edu), ftp.sun.ac.za/pub, Intel (ftp.intel.com), Microsoft (ftp.microsoft.com), Novell (ftp.novell.com), OS/2 (software.watson.ibm.com), TeX (sunsite.unc.edu/ TeX), WU-archive (ftp.wustl.edu); RFCs

ftp://ftp.htwm.de/

HTW Mittweida, Mittweide, CC

Files: HP-UX; HP external; misc

ftp://ftp.iaehv.nl/

Internet Access Eindhoven, Eindhoven

Files: NLnet material (FAQ and ftp list); Rnf; several public user directories in /pub/users: perry (Integral Dutch Course and some modem AT code docs)

ftp://ftp.iastate.edu/

Iowa State University, Iowa

Files: 386BSD; abc; afs-kerb; condor; console; crash; IRC; ITR (Interney Talk Radio); Linux; lyrics; Mac; NetBSD; Netinfo; news; NT; PC; Utah-raster; Vax; Wylber; mirrors galore and ftp.uwp.edu (lyrics); XFree86 (mirror of ftp.xfree86.org under consideration)

ftp://ftp.ibp.fr/

University Pierre et Marie Curie - MASI Lab., Paris, CentreNational de la Recherche Scientifique (National Center forScientific Research, CNRS), Institut Blaise Pascal (Blaise Pascal Institute, IBP)/Centre de Calcul Recherche (CCR) Jussieu

Files: Annex; AppleTalk; CERT; distributed_systems; docs; emacs; faces; FreeBSD; ghost; gnat; GNU; IBP info; IFIP; iman; Linux; Mac; Mach; meteo; MS-DOS; NetBSD; parallel; RFCs; sfca95; Sun; Tcl/Tk (ftp.cs.berkeley.edu); TeX; Unix; vsta; Windows3; WWW

ftp://ftp.icce.rug.nl/

Rijks Universiteit Groningen (RUG, University of Groningen), Groningen, ICCE

Files: 4tex (TeX for 4dos); Adobe (Fonts); AI stuff (/pub/peter); Atari; dictionaries; fonts (PostScript); Ghostscript; MIDI2TeX;

ftp://ftp.iclnet.org/

ICL

Files: astronomy; bench; calculators; cccoalition; cdrom; cisco; clm; cygnus; database; docs; facdialogue; games; GNU; graphics; InterVarsity; mail; math; multimedia; music; network; news; NeWS; postscript; programming; rainet; resources; RFCs; security; shells; simulation; Solaris; Sun; SunOS-patches; sysadmin; text; UCB; X11; XView

ftp://ftp.ics.forth.gr/

Foundation of Research and Technology (FORTH), Heraklion, Crete, Institute of Computer Science (ICS)

Files: CERN-HTTPD; ercim; greek (FAQ, fonts, PC-drivers, soc.culture.greek); httpd; lydia; PC; pub (audio, conferencing, EDI, HOMER, IPNG, lang, MBONE, pager, ROOMS, Sun-dist, WWW); tech-reports

ftp://ftp.ics.uci.edu/

University of California - Irvine, Irvine, California

Files: arcadia; GNU; honig; Internet (e-mail, ifip); ISODE; pub (adaptive, anime, answer-garden, antenor, atm, cadlab-releases, cadlab-trs, classweb-code, CSP-repository, dbox, dos-virus, et, hls-book, ibl, Mac, machine learning (databases, papers, programs), mentoring workshop, mh, ml-list, mrose, origins); Sun; TeX; Unix; Usenet

ftp://ftp.icsi.berkeley.edu/

University of California - Berkeley, Berkeley, California

Files: Emacs lisp code; FTP client program; FTP mail help; ICSI: AI group

ftp://ftp.idsoftware.com/

ID Software

Files: FSP; IDStuff (Doom, Doom2, Heretic, IDSIRS, Strife); MikeAB (Michael Abrash little going on's); Tonsmore (3rd party stuff: deathmatch, docs, graphics, idstuff, levels, lmps, utils)

ftp://ftp.ilt.columbia.edu/

Columbia University, New York, New York

Files: copyright; FAQs; gallery; ilt (docs, ILTinfo, misc, projects); Internet (net docs); livetext; Mac (Bobs_HTML_Editor, communication, CUSeeMe, FirstClass, HTML, icons, MacWeb, maven, Mosaic, netscape, rapmaster, QuickTime, Toolkits, tr-www, utilities, Webstat; PC (browsers, CUSeeMe, FirstClass, htmlassist, pkzip, SLIPKnot, TCP apps, viewers, wordhtml); projects; texts (McClintock, Dewey)

ftp://ftp.ime.usp.br/

Universidade de Sao Paulo (University of Sao Paulo), Sao Paulo

Files: am; articles; CEC; exel; gold; info; Khoros 2.0; Latin95; Linux (docs, faqs, Slackware, soda); Mac; music; PC; PS; reports; security-docs; semi-groups; toolbox; Unix; words

ftp://ftp.ims.uni-stuttgart.de/

Universitaet Stuttgart (University of Stuttgart), Stuttgart

Files: charon; communication; corpora; cuf; DOS; dyana2; et10-52; games; GNU; homophones; ICL; ilr; info; languages; lexicase; lfg; Mac; NeXT; papers; TeX; TFS; tools; Unix; vmob; Wordnet; X11

ftp://ftp.inbe.net/

INnet Belgium, Geel

Files: docs: atm, cdma, dsis, esdi, faq, iana, ieee802, ien, internet, ipx-spx, iso, mobility, netbios, performance, protocols, rfc, x.25, x3t9.2, x3t9.5; networking: alex, appletalk, archie, bbs, cmot, cso-nameserver, dnet, essence, fsp, gopher, hytelnet, icmp, ipx-spx, irc, isode, osi, prospero, routing, snmp, veronica, wais, whois++, www, x.25, x.500, xns; Unix: BSDI, FreeBSD, GNU, Linux, mail, shells, XFree86; vendors: 3COM, ATI, Adaptec, Borland, cdrom.com, Crynwr, FTPSoftware, IBM, Intel, Intercon, Microsoft, Netmanage, OReilly, prenhall, Quest, Telebit

ftp://ftp.indirect.com/

Internet Direct, Phoenix, Arizona

Files: aci; admin; cr; drc; ics; information about the 'Greencard' posting; mm; software (depot, hamradio, Linux, Mac, MS-DOS, MUD, Netscape, offline, OS/2, OS/2 Warp, pics, Role Playing Game material: (Cyberpunk 2020, cyberpunk genre, engines, general RPG material, miniature and strategic gaming, FUDGE, SORD, NUELOW, Circa7000, Call of Cthulhu related files, clients, servers etc.), slip, telix, Windows 3.1, Windows 95, Windows NT

ftp://ftp.info.apple.com/

Apple Computer, Austin, Texas

Files: Apple Support; DRC; dts (pr, utils); standards

ftp://ftp.informatik.tu-muenchen.de/

Technische Universitaet Muenchen (Munich University of Technology), Munich

Files: comp (database, devices, doc (ORA (ftp.ora.com), iX magazine (ftp.uni-paderborn.de), RFCs (nic.ddn.mil), GNU (prep.ai.mit.edu), graphics, infosys, networking (mail: zmailer MTA (ftp.funet.fi) newsreaders: ftp.eu.net, updates and info for ZyXEL modems: ftp.zyxel.com), OS (FreeBSD: ref.tfs.com, ftp.cdrom.com, ftp.freebsd.org), BSDI: ftp.bsdi.com, CT software listings ftp.uni-paderborn.de), DES for *BSD (braae.ru.ac.za), IRC (cs-ftp.bu.edu), Linux (LST: ftp.uni-erlangen.de, sunsite.unc.edu, tsx-11.mit.edu), NetBSD (ftp.iastate.edu), NetBSD for Mac (cray-ymp.acm.stuorg.vt.edu)), platforms (Amiga Aminet: (ftp.uni-paderborn.de; drivers for Deskjet, LaserJet, plotter and scanner (ftp-boi.external.hp.com)), programming, security, typesetting (TeX: ftp.dante.de), usenet, X11); rec (cooking (fatfree recipes (ftp.rahul.net)), fun, games, images, magic (magic, tarot, wizardry (ftp.lysator.liu.se)), medicine, movies, music (ftp.uwp.edu), sounds, travel); science (cs, math, neural-nets, physics)

ftp://ftp.informatik.uni-oldenburg.de/

Universitaet Oldenburg (Oldenburg University), Oldenburg

Files: Amiga; dkbtrace; IRC; netpbm; PoV raytracer; Star Trek

ftp://ftp.informatik.uni-rostock.de/

Universitaet Rostock (Rostock University), Rostock

Files: antivirus; doc; graphics; Linux; magazine; Unix

ftp://ftp.informatik.uni-stuttgart.de/

Universitaet Stuttgart (University of Stuttgart), Stuttgart

Files: AERO; apricots; ArabTeX; Atari ST; cinema; cio; dfg; diplomarbeiten; dkfz; ei3; Eiffel; fractal compression; GNU; graphics; GRIDS; inet; ipvrpub; jb93; lgrammar; library; Linux; load_balancing; ludewig; Melody; Minix; modula_p; movie; MS-DOS; net; parallaxis; performance; petri-nets; PoliFlow; polygloss; postgres; postleitzahlen; RandomDots; RS6000; security; SNNS; statinfo; Sun; swift; tech-reports; TeX; TI; Tiempo; traces; visAvis; vistra; VS; Windows; X11R4; X11R5; X11R6; xit; Xlocal

ftp://ftp.inria.fr/

INRIA

Files: associations; banner; games; GNU; graphics; inet; INRIA; lang; network; postscript; prog; research; RFCs; TeX; X; X11R5; Yabba

ftp://ftp.intel.com/

Intel Corp.

Files: benchmarks; dmtf; EtherExpress; i960; Intel Archictecture Labs (IAL); ipg; isv; landesk; mcs51; mcs96; neural; papers; pld_fpga; rmx; support; tis; x86

ftp://ftp.intergraph.com/

Intergraph Corporate Information Services, Huntsville, Alabama

Files: CLIX; Intergraph BBS files, Product information, Customer Services, Evaluation Software; Net Software compiled for Intergraph hardware; Win32s

ftp://ftp.internic.net/

Internet NIC - Directory and Database Services by AT&T and the NSF

Files: EDI; IETF; IESG; Internet-drafts; RFC; InterNIC info; resource databases (plus files from ftp.nisc.sri.com)

ftp://ftp.interport.net/

InterPort

Files: Mac (several useful Mac utils); NetBack (pub/fmkatz); SLIPKnot (pub/pbrooks); Windows (some Internet related Windows programs and other utils)

ftp://ftp.invircible.com/

Invircible - Vine Computer Industry, Cicero, Illinois
Files: antivirus software

ftp://ftp.io.com/

Illuminati On-Line, Austin, Texas

Files: convergence (e-zine); fasa; fwi (FringeWare Inc. catalogs etc.); hartgr; IO; netinfo; netfobs; oenabler; sjgames (Steve Jackson games); SoB (e-zine); tekumel (Empire of the Petal Throne src); user dirs: 12vman (7FP, Buffet (alt.fan.jimmy-buffet: faqs, Guitar, images, lyrics, MargRecords), IHL); aicinfo; averyc (gameboy, nintendo, snes); btorres (NewtNews); cedavis (multimedia: mods, samples: brass, percussion, strings, voice, woodwind); dmg (dmg-humor, fnord); draco (AA, pb, pw images); dwomack (Dragon (FAQ and support materials for alt.dragons-inn and alt.books.sf.melanie-rawn); ebartley (StoryTeller: amusing, archive, camarilla, campaigns, character sheets, fiction, general, mage, vampire, werewolf); games (GURPS); gibbonsb (futures, misc.invest, standards); gomer (picts: males (brewer twins, gif, jpeg)); infinite (chops, diplomacy, eps, gif, gifcatalog, in, info, software); jam237 (The Bears Project: basic, bears, dos, unix, windows); kerry (BSE, misc, ogre); mimir (asatru: mythology); pmonti (ICARO, avp, virus info); qor (MUD); torin (mage, nexus [!], sarah); zboray (4-newbies, coding, shareware: DOSQue scheduler and more, W3); zebulon (fonts, images, programs, shadows edge); zxcvb (mostly WWW material and for sale stuff)

ftp://ftp.ior.com/

Internet On-Ramp

Files: Lamplight; Linux (kernel, redhat, Slackware); Mac (MacTCP); PC (comm, games, MS-Windows, MS Windows NT, OS/2, utils, uucp (FX-UUCICO))

ftp://ftp.irisa.fr/

Institute de Recherche en Informatique et Systemes Aleatoires (IRISA, INRIA/CNRS, Universite de Rennes I/Insa de Rennes), Rennes, Brittany
Files: AFUU-BPL; bench; C++; com; compress; docs; FrameMaker; games; GNUplot; graphics;

m-emac; micro-spell; mirrors; mp; mtools; Post-script; Sather; siames; tcsh; tech-reports; VT100; X11

ftp://ftp.is.co.za/

The Internet Solution

Files: African IETF document mirror; applications; comp.sources.{games,,misc, reviewed, unix}; GNU; Internet (Internet drafts, RFCs); Linux (big chunk of sunsite.unc.edu); NetBSD; networking (dns, info-service (incl. Netscape), ip, Mac, mail); security; The Internet Solution (TIS) info; Usenet; utilities; vendor; windows; X

ftp://ftp.isi.edu/

University of Southern California, California
Files: GNU Chess; RFCs, FYIs, IEN from ftp.nisc.sri.com (internet tour etc.); statspy (NNstat)

ftp://ftp.iunet.it/

IUNet, Genova, NOC

Files: astro; benchmark; comp.sources; compilers; Cosine; docs; games; GNU; graphics; HP; Internet Talk Radio; IUNet; ix386; Mac; Mach; mail; math; mirror; MS-DOS; multimedia; network; news; NeXT; OS; papers; performance; programming; security; SFS; simulators; Sun-dist; TeX; Unix; vendor; X11

ftp://ftp.ix.de/

iX Multiuser Multitasking Magazine, Hannover
Files: benchmarks; CERT; CT; doc; FAQs; iX (benches, Linux (docs, iX-terminal, misc, nfsd), iX listings, MS-DOS); RFCs

ftp://ftp.mimos.my/

Jaring Network

Files: archives; BSDI; budget95; C; cancare; cert; cica (mirror of winftp.cica.indiana.edu); conf; GNU; info; Internet; Internet drafts; IRC; Jalinan; Jaring; Linux; Mac; Mosaic; MS-DOS (SimTel Software Repository mirror); NCSA (mirror of ftp.ncsa.uiuc.edu, WWW software); Novell (dosup, ipx-tcp, winup); OS; PC-DOS (bbs, cdrom, data-base, dcom, demo, games, gopher, graphics, jaring, misc, modem, news, slip, slipdisk, snews, snuupm, trumpet, utility, uucp, uupc, vb); radio; RFCs; src; Usenet; WWW

ftp://ftp.jpl.nasa.gov/

NASA - Jet Propulsion Laboratory, Pasadena, California, Public Information Office

Files: educator (for teachers); fsheets (fact sheets about missions); images (anim, hi-res, sl9); news; releases; sircxsar (Spaceborne Imaging Rader-C/X-band Synethetic Aperture Radar); software (misc. software); status; topex (TOPEX/Poseidon oceanographic mission); universe (local magazine archive)

ftp://ftp.jvnc.net/

John von Neumann Super Computer Centre NIC, Princeton, New Jersey

Files: beta; dialin-tiger; docs; JvNC Net info; k12; Mac; mail-list; Meaddata; Meckler; megabytes; MS-DOS; network info; NOCOL (NOC On Line); packages; RFCs; site-reps; traffic-reports; Unix

ftp://ftp.kaist.ac.kr/

Korea Advanced Institute of Science and Technology, Center for Artificial Intelligence Research

Files: CAIR; Hangul; NLPRS-95; Winsock (papa.indstate.edu); Usenet

ftp://ftp.kcl.ac.uk/

King's College, London, CC

Files: alarm; archie; bison; boss; bulletin; cmu-tcpip; cproto; datebook; deliver; dism32; dumper32; dx; elvis; emacs; etek; ethermon; fdvd; fidogate; fileutils; finger; flex; flist; fts; games; gas; gawk; gifsixel; GNU; GNUchess; GNUplot; gopher; hassle; hpgl2ps; hytelnet; irc; iupop; jed; juicer; kermit; laser; ldb; lex; lynx; lzw; madgoat; make; mftu; micro-support; mosaic; mpeg; mx; name-router; nanny; news; nsquery; patch_diff; pbmplus; pcx; perf_meter; perl; pgp; psutils; que_mon; rcs; rz/sz; scanuaf; sed; setpql; sixel_print; spell; sunclock; swim; swing; tcl; tcsh; tex-lsedit; tscon; twm; vaxtrek; vds; vi; vitpu; vmstpc; vms_share; vnews; watcher; X11; XDVI; XFIG; XFORECAST; XSCOPE; XSHARE; XTERM; XV; XVIEWGL; XWINDOWS; YACC; zenternet; zip/unzip; zmodem; zoo

ftp://ftp.kfki.hu/

Central Research Institute for Physics, Budapest

Files: GNU; infosystems; Linux; ll; local; packages; PC Soft; RFCs; Sun; WWW; X11

ftp://ftp.khoros.unm.edu/

University of New Mexico, Albuquerque, New Mexico

Files: crypt breakers workbench (cbw); dist (aegis, amd, c-to-ansic,,contool, DEC, duel, elm, epoch,

f2c, GB, Gems, GNU, GNUplot, hp2pbm, IETF, ioccc, ispell, jpeg, lapack, map, MAEstro, mh, moira, mush, netlib, netman, ntalk, pbmplus, pmake, psroff, resource-guide, rkive, rn, sc, security, sendmail, SunOS patches, sysinfo, tcsh, tiff, TeX, Utah toolkit, vis5d, vogle, wais, X, X11R5, xntp, zephyr, zsh); ftp-list [old!]; Internet info; istec; Khoros; League for Programming Freedom (LPF); Mac; misc network related utils; network maps (AARnet, Alternet, ANS, BARRnet, bitnet, canet, cerfnet, cicnet, concert, csunet, esnet, ilan, jvncnet, mae-east, michnet, midnet, mixnet, mrnet, nearnet, nordunet, nsfnet, nwnet, oarnet, onet, pipex, prepnet, psi, ripe, sesquinet, suranet, switch, thenet, twbnet, ucb, uhnet, vernet, westnet; pa-risc; papers; PC; perl; procmail; rec.games.abstract; RFCs; Sun patches (4.1.1, 4.1.2); Usenet info; wu-ftpd

ftp://ftp.kiae.su/

KIAE

Files: 386BSD; Apple; FreeBSD; GNU; Internet (archives, docs, FAQs, maps, Mosaic-papers, multimedia, RFCs); Linux; MS-DOS (arcers, arcutil, astronomy, bat, bbs, biology, cad, calculator, cdrom, comm, compress, convert, crypto, database, deskpub, doc, dos, dskutil, education, emulator, execomp, fido, filutil, finance, games, genealogy, gnu, graphics, hardware, lan, language, magick, multitask, news-mail, plot, printer, programming, qtrdeck, relcom, schedule, shell, sound, spread-sheet, sys, tape, tcpip, text, unixlike, virus, x11); NetBSD; OS/2 (arcers, arcutil, bugfixes, comm, convert, cyr, doc, drivers, dskutil, fido, games, gnu, graphics, ibm, lan, misc, pmtool, programming, rexx, shell, sound, systools, tcpip, user); Relcom net info and support files; Unix (arcers, astronomy, bbs, benchmarks, books, cad, comm, compress, convert, cprog, crypto, database, emulator, fido, fileutl, games, graphics, lang, magick, mail, math, misc, msdos, news, os, relcom, shell, sound, sysadm, sysutl, tcpip,text, viewer); tar313 source and binaries; VMS; Windows (arcers, astronomy, bbs, cad, cdrom, comm, crypto, cyrillic, database, demo, desktop, doc, drivers, education, faq, finance, fonts, games, genealogy, graphics, icons, lan, language, magick, mail, medicine, microsoft, misc, multimedia, nt, oo, patches, printer, programmer, sdl, sound, tcpip, text, toolbook, util, viewer, virus, winword, wp, wp4win, wrk, x11); X11

ftp://ftp.kiam1.rssi.ru/

Russian Academy of Sciences (RSSI), Moscow

Files: antivirus (adinf, aidstest, v-hunter); books; drweb; MS-DOS; texts;

ftp://ftp.knoware.nl/

Stichting Knoware (Knoware Foundation), Utrecht

Files: delta; emulator (Mac on PC); Internet tools: IRCclient, KA9Q, NUPOP, SLIP, Trumpet, Winsock, Wintrumpet

ftp://ftp.kodak.com/

Kodak

Files: digital camera (DCS, sample images, software updates, technical tips [under construction]; gem; images; ips; nitfs; photo CD (color, general, iamges, international, news, portfolio, prepress, printers, processors, software, writable); security (tiger); www; ycc

ftp://ftp.konbib.nl/

Koninklijke Bibliotheek (Royal Library), The Hague

Files: Gopher Editor

ftp://ftp.krl.caltech.edu/

California Institute of Technology, Pasadena, California, Kellogg Radiation Lab

Files: avida; NetHack (reed spoilers, weapons guide); sf2

ftp://ftp.ksc.nasa.gov/

NASA - Kennedy Space Center, Florida

Files: Amiga; ddcu; images; info (DOS, other, Posix, RFCs); lisp; MS-DOS (misc. network utils); MS-Windows; VMS; Win32; WinVN (docs, NT, source, Win3); WWW

ftp://ftp.kyoto.wide.ad.jp/

WIDE, Kyoto

Files: docs; GNU; IRC (chat, ircII, pirc, server, zircon); mail (bind, CF, sendmail); multicast; net; Perl; Tcl

ftp://ftp.laas.fr/

LAAS, Toulouse

Files: antibes-93; Atari; bafleur; cesame; designtest; docs; Emacs; esorics; estim; ia; kheops; lcs; logiciels; NetBSD; NEXUS; nic; pcl; reports; RFCs; Sorel; TeX; theses-rapports; tsf2lri

ftp://ftp.lanl.gov/

Los Alamos National Laboratory, Los Alamos, New Mexico

Files: AlphaVMS; ASCI; doc; hippi; HP; IBM; Mac; MS-DOS; MS-Windows; NeXT; SGI; Sun3; Sun4; Ultrix; Unix; VMS

ftp://ftp.lantronix.com/

Lantronix

Files: software for Lantronix products: EPS1/2, EPS4/12, ETS8/16, MPS1, bridge (LB and LSB code), rtel (src and binaries), configd (VMS), maccon (Macintosh config util), Novell tools, docs, tech Q&A

ftp://ftp.lasermoon.co.uk/

Lasermoon, Fareham

Files: crisp (THE editor); dBMAN (Database Management); flagship (database); FreeBSD; games; Lasermoon catalogue; Linux; mirror of ftp.ora.com; Perl; RedHat (Linux distribution); Slackware; SWiM (Motif for Linux); Systek; Tcl; vendors (ACC Corp.); Xad (Motif applications builder)

ftp://ftp.law.cornell.edu/

Cornell University, Ithaca, New York

Files: Cello (WWW client for MS-Windows, mirrored on many sites); CILP; Folio Views version of Legal Academia; humor; Internet; Jim Milles Internet Training files; listservs; TRI

ftp://ftp.lcs.mit.edu/

Massachusetts Institute of Technology, Cambridge, Massachusetts

Files: inquir; Internet drafts; LCS; mailinglists; Map; MIT e-club; MIT-LPF; nets; nmsgs; PCLU; RFCs; student-workshop; Supertech; telecom-archives; terminus; thor; ulana

ftp://ftp.leo.chubu.ac.jp/

Chubu University, LEO

Files: animation; au; canna (ftp.astec.co.jp); CU-SeeME-jp; DeleGate (etlport.etl.go.jp); FreeBSD; FreeBSD packages (ftp.hitachi-sk.co.jp); fvwm (ftp.eos.hokudai.ac.jp); GNU; GUI; hips; HP; InterViews; ipm94; Japanese; Java; jvim; kinput2; lang; Linux-towns (ftp.meiji.ac.jp); Mac (ftp.phys.keio.ac.jp); Mach; midia; minmin-patch; mnews; mpeg play; MS-DOS (ftp.phys.keio.ac.jp); mule; ncftp (ftp.eos.hokudai.ac.jp); NCSA-telnet (freeware.dit.co.jp); network; news; NeXT; PNG code; security; sendmail (ftp.kyoto.wide.ad.jp); Solaris; Sun (faq, fixes, patches); telnetx (gladys.cs.uec.ac.jp); TeX; TeX-macros (ftp.center.osaka-u.ac.jp); this; top (eecs.nwu.edu); tua; vt-animation; Windows (etlport.etl.go.jp); Winsock-L (papa.indstate.edu from ftp.riken.go.jp); Wnn; WWW; X (contrib, R5, R6); XFree86 (chopin.forest.dnj.ynu.ac.jp)

ftp://ftp.lightside.com/

Lightside

Files: Bolo; FTP Primer; Internet User's Manual; Mac Internet software; MS-Windows Internet software; other Mac utilities; other MS-Windows utilities

ftp://ftp.linux.org/

Linux

Files: Linux (distributions, kernel, mirrors, network)

ftp://ftp.livingston.com/

Livingston

Files: Livingston software releases incl. FireWall, IRX, PM2, RADIUS (Remote Authentication Dial In User Service)

ftp://ftp.lm.com/

Telerama/LM, Pittsburg, Pennsylvania

Files: Computer Privacy Digest; Interpedia; pdial

ftp://ftp.loc.gov/

Library of Congress, Washington, DC

Files: american.memory; client software; collections services; copyright; crs; exhibit images; Federal Library and Information Center Committee (flicc); folklife (Folkline); general info; iug (Internet Users Group); Library of Congress: access (LOC Information System (LOCIS) client software, internet, online (on-line search of LOCIS, USMARC classification records; listproc; nls (National Library Service); proceedings; reference guides; z3950 (Z39.50 standard)

ftp://ftp.loria.fr/

Centre de Recherche en Informatique de Nancy (CRIN-CNRS) / INRIA Lorraine, Nancy

Files: Loria: info, Equipe-Projet; mirrors: Linux, Simtel20, Macintosh, Multicast, Tex (CTAN mirror); some text document (obi, dico, kahaner, ...)

ftp://ftp.lrz-muenchen.de/

Leibniz RechenZentrum der Bayerischen Akademie der Wissenschaften (Leibniz Research and Super Computing Center of the Bavarian Academy of Sciences), Munich

Files: comp (docs, math, networking, parallel, platforms, programing, sysadmin, typesetting, usenet, X11); culture (commsci, east-asia); science (geodesy, geology, metereology)

ftp://ftp.luna.nl/

Luna Internet Access/Lunatech Research, Rotterdam, Dutch Luna archive

Files: Mac (Internet software, utils); Windows (Internet software)

ftp://ftp.lunatech.com/

Luna Internet Access/Lunatech Research

Files: Luna Internet Access info; Lunatech Research info; STAClassArchive; Software: Mac (connectivity, games, graphics, internet, sounds), Newton (apps, books, dev, games, system, utils), OS/2 (networking), Windows (networking, winnfs)

ftp://ftp.luth.se/

University of Lulee, Lulee

Files: 386bsd; infosystems; Amiga (Aminet); demos (from ftp.uwp.edu); FAQs; Linux; mods; OS/2; songs (from ftp.sdsu.edu); Tcl/Tk (languages/tcl from ftp.cs.berkeley.edu); X11; X11-contrib

ftp://ftp.lysator.liu.se/

Linnkoping University, Linnkoping, Lysator ACS

Files: abc1600; Amiga; Apollo; archivers; asl; aviation; Blake 7; comics (Disney, see the rec.arts.comics FAQ for details); comm; daemons; doc; dynix; emacs; emulators; europa; faces; games; gardening; geography; GNU; gopher; HP28; HP48; ident; IRC; ispell; kiwi; languages; libraries; Linux; LPF; LPMUD; Lysator; LysKOM; Mac; Mach; magick; mail; marine mammals; mgr; mods; MS-DOS; net; news; NYS; PC Eudora; PDP10; Postgres; Prime/PRIMOS; religion; rmt; rom; runeberg; science fiction; sgml; shell; solutions; standards; Sun; Sunview; SvenskMUD; texts; Windows NT; WWW; X11

ftp://ftp.math.uni-hamburg.de/

Universitaet Hamburg (University of Hamburg), Hamburg

Files: C; CD; chess (daily mirror of

chess.uoknor.edu); ct; emx; fortran; ix; lam; lapack; library; linpack; Linux; Mac; magazine; mail; math; mcafee; minpack; mirrors: ftp.informatik.uni-hamburg.de, ftp.uni-hamburg.de; MS-DOS game solutions; mod2; netlib; news; os2; pack; parallel; pas; pc; pic; plz; postscript; programming; pvm3; RS6000; sesc; SimTel; sites; tarzan; tex; Tolkien JPG graphics files, FAQs etc.; Unix stuff (magazines, network)

ftp://ftp.math.utah.edu/

University of Utah, Salt Lake City, Utah

Files: awk; benchmarks; DEC Alpha; doc; elefunt; IAFA-{description, list archive, maillists, services, siteinfo}; IBM PC; Mac; Math; mf; mg; RFCs; SGI; Solaris; Stardent; TeX; Ultrix; uuthesis; VAX; Xdvi

ftp://ftp.mbfys.kun.nl/

Katholieke Universiteit Nijmegen (Nijmegen University), Nijmegen

Files: snn (Neural Networks Foundation archive: neuro-intro, neuro-software, reports, tex)

ftp://ftp.mcc.ac.uk/

University of Manchester/University of Manchester Institute of Science and Technology

Files: 386BSD (mirrored agate.berkeley.edu); Andrew; CGU; Cubase archive; DECUS; DJGPP; DOS; EMagic; EmTeX; GNU (mirror of prep.ai.mit.edu); Linux (mirror of ftp.funet.fi); Mach; Mantec; Matclass; NCSA telnet; ndr; ON-U; SG; TeX

ftp://ftp.mcom.com/

Netscape Communications Corp.

Files: Netscape (WWW browser) Home site (Mac, Unix, Windows); unsupported: mozilize (conv. Mosaic INI files to Mozilla bookmark), mozock (dll file to use Netscape without a network for files on local disks)

ftp://ftp.mcs.com/

MCSnet, Chicago, Illinois

Files: acmesoft; AKCS; Books & Bytes; copyright; Dell software; Mac: Packet, Packrat utils; MCSnet info; MS-Windows Winsock archive; NeXT; user sponsored ftp-directories in /mcsnet.users: damir: Croatia and Bosnia related material, falcon/add (Att'n Deficit Disorder mirror for the CompuServe ADD forum libraries, falcon/addult.news (ADDult News Online magazine archive site), jorn/ascii-art (mirror of ASCII art archives)

ftp://ftp.mechnet.liv.ac.uk/

University of Liverpool, Liverpool, Mechanical Engineering Dept.

Files: crusher; mods; Novell utils (setuname); Pascal; patches; PC demos; Phrack; viewers; Wing

ftp://ftp.med.nyu.edu/

New York University, New York, New York, Medical Center

Files: AFP resource; AWB; binhex; GCG docs; gopher; IMR; MDPP; Mosaic2; MS-DOS; tidbits; VAX info; WWW

ftp://ftp.med.rug.nl/

Rijks Universiteit Groningen (RUG, University of Groningen), Groningen, Medical Dept.

Files: 4DOS; antivirus; clinical genetics [empty]; DOS (6.22, communication: Telix 3.22); Windows (AVI, desktop, icons, jpg, Mosaic, mpg, postscript, screensaver, utils, winsock)

ftp://cumulus.met.ed.ac.uk/

University of Edinburgh, Edinburgh

Files: animations; calmet: Computer Aided Learning in Metereology software; Meteosat3 and Meteosat4 images

ftp://ftp.metrics.com/

Software Metrics

Files: archive (newsgroup archives: comp.unix.bsd.bsdi.announce); auto (Audi, Audi Quattro, Formula One, Indy Car, Racetrak, VW); MS-Windows FAQs; pub: client, comt, Mad About You, pkzip 2.04g, ripb61nt, wincd

ftp://ftp.mfi.com/

Miller Freeman

Files: cadence (magazine, code for AutoCAD users); gamedev; keyboard; PC; source; Unix-review

ftp://ftp.michnet.net/

Michigan Education & Research Infrastructure Triad/National Science Foundation, Michigan

Files: Acceptable Use Policies; cise; conference proceedings; docs; IETF; Internet Info; Internet-drafts; internet-monthly report; Introducing the Internet; maps; Merit's Internet Cruise; Michnet info; newsletters; NFSNET Link Letter, statistics, maps; NREN info; OMB; resources; RFCs; statistics; working groups; X11R6

ftp://ftp.micromuse.co.uk/

Micromuse PLC, London

Files: mirrors the following packages daily: GNU
(ftp.doc.ic.ac.uk); HTML conversion utilities/filters
(ftp.doc.ic.ac.uk); Linux (Slackware,
ftp.cdrom.com); PC utils (server.berkeley.edu);
sendmail (ftp.cs.berkeley.edu); X86Solaris
(server.berkeley.edu)

ftp://ftp.microsoft.com/

Microsoft Corp.

Files: Microsoft utilities and updates: Developer
Relations Group, Lan

ftp://ftp.mid.net/

MIDnet, Oklahoma/South Dakota

Files: announce; archive; FAQs; Info-Mac; Mac;
mindvision; MS-DOS; net; newsletter; noc; NSFnet;
PC-DOS; PC-Windows; regulus; RFCs; templates;
vitalimages; Unix

ftp://ftp.midisoft.com/

Midisoft Corp., Issaquah, Washington

Files: Midisoft product demo; multimedia (MIDI,
wave, images); utils (video, sound).

ftp://ftp.morningstar.com/

Morning Star Technologies

Files: C++; Express (Link, Plus); Interop93Spring;
netinfo; nslookup; papers; PPP (staging, wg-drafts);
press-releases; PSI; RFCs; SIP (wg-drafts); SCO
Unix tools; snaplink; SNMP; X.25; ZIP

ftp://ftp.mpd.co.za/

M+PD, Johannesburg

Files: Borland (mirror of ftp.borland.com); Chase
Research Supplements; Epson Printer Drivers;
Fujitsu Printer Drivers; garbo.uwasa.fi mirror (of /
pub/pc); GIFs; HugSoft demo; Intel Networking
Produtcs (mirror of ftp.intel.com); Linux
(Slackware); M+PD patches; Novell (mirror of
ftp.novell.com); Racal Interlan Network Adapters;
RSA (Republic of South Africa) files; SCO specific
files; text files; Unix BBS programs; Xircom (Xircom
adapters drivers and utils)

ftp://ftp.mpgn.com/

Multi-Player Games Network

Files: gaming (ADND, fantasy, Hero, HomeBrew,
Traveller, utilities, Warhammer); MPG-Net

(DrakVision, EmpireBuilder, MarketGarden,
StarCruiser)

ftp://ftp.mpi-sb.mpg.de/

Max Planck Gesellschaft, Saarbruecken, Max Planck
CS Institute - Saarbruecken

Files: ACID; ALCOM; ALF; benchmarks; c't index;
DOS-networking; GNU; iX-index; LEDA; Linux;
MOTEL; MS-DOS; Novell; OS/2; papers; SATU-
RATE; SPECTRAL; Tcl; TeX

ftp://ftp.ms.uky.edu/

University of Kentucky, Kentucky

Files: 7300; Amiga; Apple II; Atari; BSD; calculus;
cs505; GNU; games; graphics; images; IRC; Linux;
lpnmr; Mac (incl. MacBSD); mailinglists; MS-DOS;
music; NetBSD; NeXT; NSF; primos; RFCs;
robinson; sounds; statistics; tech-reports; Unix;
UUCP; X11R5; zipcodes

ftp://ftp.msu.edu/

Michigan State University, Lansing, Michigan

Files: CMS (POP3-EMC2); docs (MSUnet, others);
education (Internet & ED); MacOS; MS-DOS
(gopher, kermit, LWP4DOS, newsreaders, NUPOP,
PCPrint, Pegasus, Packet Drivers, PPP, utils); MS-
Windows (gopher, Mosaic, Netscape, PC Eudora,
utils, winvn); Unix (apE, editors, gopher, news,
NeXTOS, sendmail, SunOS, utils, XWindows)

Site; ftp://dcs.muni.cz/

Masaryk University, Brno

Files: Amiga; archives; bibliography;
informatics.muni.cz; Internet drafts; math.muni.cz;
MS-DOS CZ; music (guitar, lyrics, scripts, vax);
NFS-client; ORA; RFCs; scb; software (BSDI, Linux,
NetBSD, share, Sol2 Sparc); TeX

ftp://ftp.nc.nihon-u.ac.jp/

Nihon University

Files: 386BSD; astro; CERT; cvdb; docs; emulator;
fj.sources; games; GNU; languages; Linux; Mac;
Mathematica; MS-DOS; multimedia; network;
NeXT; news; OS; reference list on image processing;
scitech; SGI; TeX; Wnn; X11 (R5, R6); X68000

ftp://ftp.ncl.ac.uk/

University of Newcastle, Newcastle, England

Files: cba; CDBOOT; dialup; DNS; ethernet; info;
internet; itti; Mac; MS-DOS; network-training; ngg;
nrs; ntp; parallel; sendmail Sundumps; Sunstuff

ftp://ftp.ncr.com/

AT&T Global Information Solutions (Formerly NCR Corp)

Files: comp.sys.ncr; drube; NCR chips; NCR products (3600sys, comten, federal, france, msgsc, pc, stargroup, teradb, vistium, wavelan; parallel (conf.announcements); standards (io, nmf, performance)

ftp://ftp.ncsa.uiuc.edu/

University of Illinois - Urbana/Champaign, Urbana, Illinois

Files: aff; BIMA; brochure; DEC_ALPHA; DTM; Docs; education; Global Models; HDF (Hierarchical Data File system); LCA; Mac; misc (scientific and file) formats; Mosaic (homesite); NCSA (Telnet/ FTP/WWW programs); PC; SGI; samples; sc22wg5; survey; Unix; Visualization; VR; Web (WWW, mirrored on www.jsc.nasa.gov and numerous other sites); x3j3

ftp://ftp.near.net/

New England Academic Regional Network NIC

Files: CERFnet; Commerce Business Daily (in / cbd); docs; forms; Gopher; image; Internet Talk Radio (ITR, in /talk-radio); internet-drafts; internet-information; K12; mail-archives; maps; NEARNet info; NeTraMet; nosupport directory; RFCs; seminars; ucp

ftp://ftp.nec.com/

NEC System Labs Inc., Irving/Dallas, Texas

Files: ecpa; GNU; Japan; Linux; mail; misc; modems; multimedia; news; PC misc; PC net; products; RFCs; security; sendmail; slip; Sun-fixes; TCL-TK; Unix; WWW; Weath; X11; X-misc

ftp://ftp.nectec.or.th/

National Electronic and Computer Technology Center (NECTEC), Ministry of Science, Technology and Environment, Nonthaburi/Bangkok

Files: Dharma Electronic File Archive (mirror of sunsite.unc.edu, buddhism); Electronic Frontier Foundation (mirror of ftp.eff.org); GNU (mirror of prep.ai.mit.edu); Intel Corp (mirror of ftp.intel.com); Internet drafts; Lao information (mirror of mono1.cc.monach.edu.au); Linux (mirror of sunsite.unc.edu); Leaque of Programming Freedom (mirror of prep.ait.mit.edu); Macintosh software; Microsoft docs (mirror of ftp.microsoft.com); MS-DOS games (mirror of ftp.uml.edu and ftp.uwp.edu); MS-Windows 3

(mirror of ftp.cica.indiana.edu); NetBSD (mirror of ftp.iastate.edu); OS/2 (mirror of hobbes.nmsu.edu); rec.travel archive (mirror of ftp.cc.umanitoba.ca); RFCs; SimTel Software Repository (mirror both msdos and win3); Software for Motorola MPUs; Thai/Lao MS-DOS software (/pub/pc); Thailand info (/pub/info); Thai daily news (/pub/news); soc.culture.thai FAQ (/soc.culture.thai); Unix PD software (/pub/unix); USENET archives for soc.culture.{burma,cambodia,laos,thai} and comp.sources.{unix, misc} (/pub/archives); USENET Frequently Asked Questions (mirror of rtfm.mit.edu); X11R6 and X contribution (mirror of ftp.x.org); XFree86 (mirror of ftp.xfree86.org)

ftp://ftp.netcom.com/

Netcom On-Line Communications Services Inc., Santa Clara, California

Files: computer game development stuff; several informational files in /pub directory: every user has his/her own /pub directory; Netcom info; aamram; AB1264; Acme; activis; alumlist; ASCUS; billa (Space/Astro related GIFs, e.g. Shoemaker-Levey 9 (SL9), HST GIFs) and SL9 sitelist; boutell (FAQ); bradleym (40Hex, IRC, KOH, NuKE); gamedir; geoi310 (Japanese A6 CD-ROM products); GNO; GTU; Guides; imagecft; Infes-station BBS (infes-station); info-deli; Iris; Isis; kaminski; KBBS (tcsmith); lotus-cars; ltubbs (Enigma archive: DiskExpress (DXP), Finfo, PMatno, VX-REXX runtime (VROBJ)); metal; micromed; microspc; Militia; mnemonic; mushroom; Nascent (Linux CD); net app; Netcom; netmail; newmedia; notgnu; Nutec; OPN; pearl-jam; PineSoft; PPS-info; Seti; Silk; Simpsons (calliope); skylines; softhelp; surfgear; Tetra-Soft; thinknet; Trek; tweek (FAQ); urimud; US Network; UUCP; VE3SUN; veritools; vidgames; WD6CMU; Weitek; X3H6; Yggdrasil (Linux CD); Zytek

ftp://ftp.netlib.org/

University of Tennessee, Knoxville, Tennessee

Files: aicm; alliant; amos; ampl; anl-reports; Apollo; att.com; benchmark; bibnet; bihar; blas; bmp; C; C++; cephes; chammp; cheney-kincaid; clapack; confdb; conformal; contin; crc; crpc; ddsv; domino; eispack; elefunt; errata; f2c; fdlibm; fftpack; fishpack; fitpack; floppy; fmm; fn; Fortran; Fortran-M; fp; gcv; genome; gmat; go; graphics; harwell; hence; hompack; hpf; hypercube; IEEEcss; ijsa; image; imsl; itpack; keyword; kincaid-cheney; la-net; lanczos; lanz; lapack; laso; libs; linalg; linpack; list; listL; lp; machines; magic; maspar; master; microscope; minpack; misc; mpi; na-digest; na-net; nac.no; nag; napack; national software exchange (nse); netlib; new2admin; news; newtoms; numeralgo; ode; odepack; odrpack; opt;

p4; papers; paragraph; parallel; paranoia; parkbench; parmacs; pascal; patents; pbwg; pchip; pdes; performance; picl; pltmg; poly2; polyhedra; polyhedron; popi; port; Posix; pppack; presto; problem-set; pu; pvm; pvm3; quadpack; random; reqlog; research; rkpack; scalapack; sched; scilib; seispack; Sequent; sfmm; shpcc94; slap; slatec; sminpack; sort-pascal; sparse; sparse-blas; sparspak; specfun; spin; sscpack; statistics; stoeplitz; stringsearch; svdpack; templates; tennessee; toeplitz; toms; treegr; typesetting; uncon; UTK; vanhuffel; vfftpack; vfftpk; vfnlib; voronoi; whois; xmagic; xnetlib; xnl4; xnlindex; y12m

---

ftp://ftp.netmanage.com/

Netmanage

Files: demos; Product info (Chameleon); SDK tools; Unix tools; WinStandards

---

ftp://ftp.netsys.com/

Netsys Inc.

Files: 40Hex magazine archives; aleph1; freedom; getsat; irc; lanwan; mtrek; NetSys info; Novell; patches; Phrack magazine archives; pictures; quake; satellite; smc; smh; Sun; tklgifs; trinity; worldlists

---

ftp://ftp.nevada.edu/

University of Nevada - Las Vegas, Las Vegas, Nevada

Files: bass; bitnet; guitar; IBM PC; heathers; Las Vegas BBS list; liaison; Linux; Mac; Minix; network; photo; RFCs; shadow3; Unix; VMS

---

ftp://ftp.next.com/

NeXT Computer

Files: NeXT files (some sources still on next.com)

---

ftp://ftp.ngs.noaa.gov/

NOAA - National Geodetic Survey, Silver Sring, Maryland

Files: Geodetic applications (PC, Unix); mirrors: CERT (ftp.cert.org /pub/tools), gated (gated.cornell.edu /pub/gated), GNU (prep.ai.mit.edu /pub/gnu), mail (ftp.cs.berkeley.edu /ucb/sendmail, thumper.bellcore.com /pub/nsb), NCFTP (ftp.cs.unl.edu /pub/ncftp), NTP (ftp.udel.edu / pub/ntp), WU-ftpd (ftp.wustl.edu /packages/ wuarchive-ftpd), WWW (ftp.ncsa.uiuc.edu /pub/ Web), X11R6 (ftp.x.org /pub/R6, /contrib)

---

ftp://ftp.nic.surfnet.nl/

INFOSERVICES: Royal (National) Library and Stichting Universitaire Reken Faciliteiten (SURFnet), Utrecht

Files: CERT-NL info; EARN info; FAQs; IETF; Internet Resource Guide; mirrors: gopher, SimTel Software Repository: MS-DOS, MS-Windows, windows (ftp.cica.indiana.edu), winsock; RARE; security; SURFnet Info/Gids; University of Leiden

---

ftp://ftp.nig.ac.jp/

National Institute of Genetics

Files: data; db; DDBJ; DNA; graphic; JOHO; lang; Mac; mirror [?]; MS-DOS; NCBI toolbox; nentrez; news; PPP; protein; security; Unix

---

ftp://ftp.nikhef.nl/

Nationaal Instituut voor Kernfysica en Hoge-Energie Fysica (Dutch National Institute for Nuclear and High-Energy Physics, NIKHEF), Amsterdam

Files: AIO school; Atari; atlas; drift tube sim; enigma; eps; ff; form; gajet; hepmix; lhcb tracking; network; nucphys; preprints; rd11; RFCs; rtd94; siteinfo; teleconferencing; vmdlep; vme2tp

---

ftp://ftp.nine.com/

Number Nine Visual Technology

Files: GX; GXE; GXE64; GXE64Pro; GXI; Imagine; Motion 531; Motion 771; Pepper; Pro 1280; Revolution; Tiga; Trio; Vision 330

---

ftp://ftp.njit.edu/

Organization; New Jersey Institute of Technology, New Jersey

Files: 4BSD; bieber; db; DNS; hamradio; images; jazz-primer; LaTeX; MS-DOS; NJIT; ntp; parallel; passwd; patch; PC-Unix; Perl; Plan9; recdb; rmb-lists; rt; security; sendmail; snmp-tools; sounds; sunlibs; sunspots; Ultrix; Unix-wizards; vt100-text

---

ftp://ftp.nl.net/

NLUUG (Netherlands Unix User Group)/NLNet, Amsterdam

Files: ABC; some comp.sources groups; ITR; some mirrors (GNU, C-News, Linux (Slackware, SLS, from ftp.funet.fi), archive.eu.net); FAQs; RFCs; graphics and docs; networksoftware; X; newsarchive; CERT warnings; mirror of the RIPE databases; Sun; TeX; 386BSD; UC (archiver)

ftp://ftp.novell.com/

Novell, Provo, Utah

Files: Novell utilities, patches, fixes, information etc.: Netwire, Unixware; WWW

ftp://ftp.novell.de/

Novell Germany, Duesseldorf

Files: doc; Linux; Mosaic; netwire; Novell utilities, patches, fixes, information, on-line technical support database etc.; OS/2; sjf-lwp; Unix; Unixware; Windows3

ftp://ftp.nus.sg/

National University of Singapore

Files: bio; docs; du.info; infoserver; infosystems; Mac; misc; multimedia; NT; NUS; OOT; Opensys; PC; Unix (Linux, sunsite.unc.edu); Windows; Winsock (Sunsite)

ftp://ftp.nvg.unit.no/

University of Trondheim, Trondheim

Files: CUD archives; IRC; Linux (Bogus release: mirror of phys-pc61.med.unc.edu); Sam-Coupe files; Sinclair ZX-Spectrum; Sounds; Usenet News including sources, binaries and FAQ's

ftp://ftp.nysernet.org/

NYSERNET, New York, New York

Files: gain; guides; npt; nyserlink; nysernet; nysertech; provision; resources; rfp; software

ftp://ftp.paradise.com/

Paradise Software

Files: Erlangen; images; movies; multicast; parallax; Simplicity (video teleconferencing package PSVC and white board); tomp; Uniflix (software toolkit for decompression and display of digital video); videopix

ftp://ftp.parc.xerox.com/

Xerox - Palo Alto Research Center (PARC), Palo Alto, California

Files: MOO (MUD) clients

ftp://ftp.pasteur.fr/

Internet World

Files: 4.3BSD; Empire; FAQ; games; gensoft; GNU; Go; gopher; Logo; Mac; MycDB; network; news;

PC; Perl; PolyDoc; resig; RFCs; security; sendmail; SimpleTimes; systems; TeX; X11R5

ftp://ftp.pcnet.com/

PCNet, Connecticut

Files: IBM-PC; Mac; SLIP-PPP; user directories: actnet, beeline, brianw, cambridge, circellar, dodge, dpg, edrauh, eischen, fapinc, gbs, gdelius, gerrat, ibexgraphics, infinity, john, lexipub, mbsii, midi-classics, ndma, nds, netcraft-sw, objex, protech, quilt, ras,

recol, rkw, sdn, sis, sscnet, tob, wconley, winzip, wshu ;winsock

ftp://ftp.pku.edu.cn/

Peking University, Beijing

Files: cica (ftp.cica.indiana.edu); docs; emTeX; FAQs; GNU; Linux; Netscape; SCO; SimTel; Slackware; Solaris 2.4; Sun-info; Unix; X11R6

ftp://ftp.pkware.com/

Internet Connect Inc.

Files: Appalachian Trail; AWE32 (AWE-L, drivers, editors, info, midi, samples, sbk, utils); Internet Connect (dns, mail, netbsd, news, nic-templates); Merge Technologies (dicom, toolkits (mc3_adv, mc3_basic, mergecom)); PK-Ware (PKWare Products, such as PKZip, PKZMenu, PKZFind, PKZoom, PKLite, StupenDOS, QDPMI, REName ZIP, VLMUP, ZZAP); security (Phrack, wordlists (lots))

ftp://ftp.pi.net/

Planet Internet

Files: PIShell; Planet: beeld & geluid (picture and sound: win32, windows), docs (Daily Planet, handleiding, Internet, Planet Internet info), games (Mac, MS-DOS (action, adventure, platform, platform), MS-Windows), Internet software (Ms-Windows, Unix, win32), multimedia (pictures, sound, video), utils (Mac, MS-DOS, MS-Windows, OS/2, Unix, win32)

ftp://ftp.pica.army.mil/

U.S. Army PICA

Files: Computer Privacy Digest; images; Info-Labview; Mosaic; paladin; Picatinny race results; prism; security; training; usenet; WWW; Xclass

ftp://ftp.pop.psu.edu/

Pennsylvania State University, Pennsylvania

Files: computer-papers; Internet Talk Radio (PSU only); maps; papers: working papers for population and rural centers; PSU; src (Unix source - networking, utilities, X11); Sun-patches (4.1.3 and OpenWindows3)

ftp://ftp.primenet.com/

PrimeNet

Files: files (Amiga, Linux, Mac, Netscape, OS/2, PC, PrimePPP, Windows3); games (Mac, MS-DOS); lippard; RFCs; rincon; skeptic; swr (misc. images)

ftp://ftp.proxima.alt.za/

Proxima

Files: MS-DOS; Oberon; PiX: South Afican BBS info; Unix

ftp://ftp.prz.tu-berlin.de/

Technische Universitaet Berlin (Berlin University of Technology), Berlin

Files: aladdin; atm; audio-video; DEC and Sun related papers; HP; HTML; hypertubkom; MBone; mmc; motemes; multimedia; Music; MusicAnalysis; networking papers; NeXT; PC; Pink Floyd and Sonic Youth related stuff; PRZ info; recipes (~12000 English and German); security; Sun; Solaris X86 binaries (gcc, emac, TeX); whoami; wisstrans; X11R5 (interactive Unix); xtp

ftp://ftp.psc.edu/

Pittsburgh Supercomputing Center, Pittsburgh, Pennsylvania

Files: award; biomed; cgm; cmrad; depot; dqs; gall; gplot; grants; guide; Kecks; lvr; Mac gplot; malloc_dbg; matmul; net_tools; P3D; PC gplot; PC scub; psr; spr

ftp://ftp.psg.com/

RAINet/PSG, Oregon/Washington

Files: bbslists; CIX; docs; Eiffel; Elvis; FIDONet; GNU; Intel; Internet; IP-for-PC; K12; lists; Mac; Modula-2; MS-DOS; nets; Oberon; Pascal; Python; RAINet; SCSI (Adaptec); unced; Unix; UUCP-for-PC

ftp://ftp.psi.com/

Performance Systems International

Files: archive; dns; doc; gopsi; ien; ietf; info; Internet Talk Radio (ITR); irg; isode; maps; netinfo; newsletter; pilot; press releases; psilink; psisnmp; radio; RFCs; sendmail; snmp; snmpstats; src; srmftp; Sun; Usenet; uuftp; waan; WP

ftp://ftp.psychol.utas.edu.au/

University of Tasmania, Hobart, Tasmania

Files: Mac network news-reader; Winsock; Trumpet DOS/Windows; some games; antivirus utilities (most of this stuff is mirrored from sites much closer to users from Europe or North-America)

ftp://ftp.psychologie.uni-freiburg.de/

Universitaet Freiburg (University of Freiburg), Freiburg

Files: Research related information - documents and software (psychology, cognitive psychology, cognitive science, artificial intelligence); Sun related software, patches, and documents

ftp://ftp.pu-toyama.ac.jp/

Toyama Prefectural University (TPU)

Files: 386BSD; Archiver; bible; doc; DosV; FreeBSD; ftpmail; games; GNU; HP100LX; info; infosystems; JPNIC; JUNET-DB; Linux; Mac; MS-DOS; net; net-2; NeXT; NetBSD; news archives; RFCs; security; SL9; Sun-dist; Tahoe; TeX; Toyama prefecture; Triton; Wine; X11; X11R5; XFree86; zaurus

ftp://ftp.rau.ac.za/

Rand Afrikaans University

Files: drivers (3COM, Trident); Internet (pmail, some docs); Linux; listings; MS-DOS (arcers, bios, comm, cutcp, dbase, demos, emulators, games, graphics, graphics_workshop, int, menus, mod_players, network, pascal, pc-bench, programming, screen, upgrade, ZA); multimedia; networks; Novell (dosup_winup, ipx, mercury, mhs, nlm, odi, pmail, tcpip, trumpet, util); NT (patches); Unix; Windows (bench, drivers, ghostscript, graphics_workshop, infosystems, network, util, visual_basic, win32s)

ftp://ftp.rc.tudelft.nl/

Technische Universiteit Delft (Delft University of Technology), Delft, CC

Files: PC (gopher, MS-DOS, OS/2, Windows, Winsock); Unix (PC NFSD, POP)

ftp://ftp.rdt.monash.edu.au/

Monash University - Clayton Campus, Melbourne

Files: images; Monash info; netinfo; Shoemaker-Levy 9 (SL9) images in /pub/jupiter-sl9; RDT; tech-reports; weathermap; wp60mini.zip

ftp://ftp.riken.go.jp/

Institute of Physical and Chemical Research (RIKEN), Saitama, Ring Cyclotron

Files: astro (SL9 from ftp.seds.arizona.edu); cica (ftp.cica.indiana.edu); GNU; GPS; Mac (KT, mac.archive.umich.edu, sumex-aim.stanford.edu, TeX); net; OpenVMS/AXP; Quake info; RFCs; security (CERT, CIAC); SimTel; Sun-dist; TeX (CTAN); UCB; VAX/VMS; Winsock (papa.indstate.edu); Wnn; WWW

ftp://ftp.rpi.edu/

Rensselaer Polytechnical Institute, Troy, New York

Files: antivirus; communications; consulting; doc; dses; elc; faculty; Internet-Tools; its (papers, releases); languages (chinese, ethiopia, mule); laser disks; mail; math; misc; networking; org; pctcp; printing; programming; resources; Sun-fixes; sysadmin; thesis; usenet; workshop92; WWW

ftp://ftp.rug.nl/

Rijks Universiteit Groningen (University of Groningen), Groningen

Files: 386BSD; GopherE; graphics; listserv archive; MS-DOS; NetBSD; networks; Novell; Origami; pacxnet; RC_msdos; RUGnet; Surfnet; Unix

ftp://info.rutgers.edu/

Rutgers University, Piscataway, New Jersey

Files: caipworks; forms (bicycle, camden1, citadel, corporate, Eisenhower, eisenreg); gopher; Info; International Connectivity; Internet; maps; Mosaic; MS-DOS (mirror of wuarchive:/mirror/msdos); Performance; RFCs; Rutgers Press; soc.religion.christian; sounds; WWII; X-files

ftp://ftp.sausage.com/

Sausage Software

Files: HotDog and Hotdog Pro HTML Editors; mIRC; mozock; vbrun300

ftp://ftp.sccsi.com/

South Coast Computing Services Inc., Houston, Texas

Files: comet; communications; doc (history, howto, internet-resource guide, internet worm, InterNIC RFCs, jokes, NIC); dos; internet; local; macintosh; newtnet; os2; sas; sass; serial; tnic; unix; uupcb; win-nt; windows; winsock

ftp://ftp.schnet.edu.au/

SchoolsNet

Files: Electronic Frontiers Australia; lukeh (cert, Linux, NeXT, Netware, syslog, w3, win95, windows); xedoc (fabrik, netinfo)

ftp://ftp.scn.de/

Siemens Corporate Network (SCN)

Files: archivers; databases (db, msql, onyx, ssql); docs (RFCs); editors; GNU; graphics (tools); infosystems (archie, gopher, wais); mail (clients, dns, filters, servers, tools); MS-DOS (misc. tools/ utils); net (tools); networking (samba, tcpdump, traceroute); news (inn, tin newsreader home, winvn, xrn); OS (Amiga, FreeBSD, HP-UX, Linux, Mac, Sun); security; src (cforms, databases, fwf, patch, pgp, postscript, programming, psroff, TeX, tools, X11); TeX; tools (cflow, perl, Tcl/Tk); weather; WWW (browsers, cgi-bin, editors, Hyper-G, indexers, servers, tools)

ftp://ftp.scri.fsu.edu/

Florida State University, Florida

Files: Amiga; BUB; CLASsoft; cluster-workshop; comp.graphics.research; DQS; DSM; GAO; genetics; genome92; hep-lat; Mac; MC93; MS-DOS; netinfo; Norton; NSPCG; parallel-workshop; Sage; SciAn; super93; TFN; uci; Unix; Usenet

ftp://ftp.sdd.com/

Siltek Distribution Dynamics, Johannesburg

Files: Adaptec; AST; Borland; Chase; CICA (ftp.cica.indiana.edu); Compaq; Corel; Creative; demos; DFI; Epson; FreeBSD; Fujitsu; GIF; hotfiles; HP; HP2; HPCalc; HugSoft; Intel; JSB; market; Microsoft; Novell; PD; Proteon; Quarterdeck; Racal; RFCs; RSA; SCO; Seagate; SMC; Symantec; txt; WWW; Xircom

ftp://ftp.sdsc.edu/

San Diego Supercomputer Centre, San Diego, California

Files: ccms; CERFnet; Khoros; Multics; security; supercomputer center info; SuperComputing 95; X; ZyXel

ftp://ftp.seds.lpl.arizona.edu/

University of Arizona, Tucson, Arizona

Files: anim; astro; clementine; dosdirs; FAQs; images (Apollo, asteroid, ccd, charts, clementine, comets, dcx, deepspace, earth, eclipse, HST, Hubble, jpeg, Jupiter, launcher, logos, Mars, Mercury, misc, Moon, Neptune, observatories, Pluto, rme, Saturn, scans, shuttle, space, spacestation, spacecolony, spacecraft, stsci, Sun, supercomputing, supernova, Uranus, Venus, WFPC2); info; sat; SEDS; Shoemaker-Levy 9 (SL9) images; software (Amiga, Atari, CP/M, general, HP48, instruments, Mac, NeWS, NeXT, obsdbase, obsprog, OS/2, PC, Space, Spacelink, text, Unix, VMS); spacecraft

ftp://ftp.servtech.com/

ServiceTech Inc.

Files: Mac (MacTCP apps for MacOS 7.x); OS/2 (TCP/IP apps from IBM); Unix (TCP/IP src); Windows (winsock apps for Windows 3.x/95/NT: antivirus, archie, browsers, compression, essential apps, finger, ftp clients, gopher, html apps, IRC, mailers, newsreaders, ping, telnet, viewers, z-attic); misc. user public directories: acdsys, ami4000, baracuda, excalibur, pscnet, roadrun, tech5

ftp://ftp.seti-inst.edu/

Search for Extra-Terrestrial Intelligence (SETI) Institute

Files: GNU (prep.ai.mit.edu); perl; security (ftp.win.tue.nl, xinetd); skey; util (misc. network utils)

ftp://ftp.shsu.edu/

Sam Houston State University, Huntsville, Texas

Files: cdrom; Comprehensive TeX Archive Network (CTAN) in /tex-archive;

docs; economics; ftp-list; lib; MaasInfo; mirror of garbo.uwasa.fi /pc/doc-net highlights; utils; VMS

ftp://ftp.sls.wau.nl/

Landbouw Universiteit Wageningen (Wageningen Agricultural University), Wageningen

Files: Linux (document project and Pascal for Linux); mirror of ftp.wau.nl; MS-DOS (Borland, Banyan, Doom, languages (BorlandPascal/C/ C++/ Clipper/TurboPascal/VisualBasic), games (mirror of offical game archive: Apogee, Epic, ID), Quarterdeck, utils (virus, winsock, zip), www)

ftp://smartdocs.com/

Smart Docs

Files: Mac; misc; MS-DOS; Unix (Perl, pmaster, samba); Windows (mirror of papa.indstate.edu)

ftp://ftp.smc.com/

Standard Microsystems Corporation

Files: Network Interface Cards drivers; Hubs and LAN switch products

ftp://ftp.snu.ac.kr/

Seoul National University, Seoul

Files: FAQs; GNU (prep.ai.mit.edu); Hangul (garam.kreonet.re.kr [user anonymous unknown]); Internet; Linux (ftp.cdrom.com); KRNIC; MS-DOS; networking (ftp.uu.net); news; published; SNUNet; security; Unix; Xwindows

ftp://ftp.sra.co.jp/

SRA Inc., Tokyo

Files: cmd; doc; GNU; lang; Mach; MS-DOS; net; news archive (mokuroku.jis, newsgroups: alt.sources, comp.archives, comp.binaries.ibm.pc, comp.binaries.mac, comp.binaries.ms-windows, comp.bugs.4bsd, comp.bugs.4bsd.ucb-fixes, comp.sources.misc, comp.sources.postscript, comp.sources.reviewed, comp.sources.sun, comp.sources.unix, comp.sources.x, fj.archives, fj.binaries.mac, fj.binaries.msdos, fj.sources, gnu.emacs.sources, news.answers); OS (386BSD, 4.4BSD-Lite, BSD, FreeBSD, Linux, Mac, Mach, Minix, MS-DOS (driver, editor, network, program-ming, text, utility), MS-Windows, MS-Windows NT, MS-Windows95, NetBSD, Xinu); Smalltalk; TeX; Wnn; X11

ftp://ftp.sri.ucl.ac.be/

Universite Catholique de Louvain (Catholic Univer-sity of Louvain), Louvain-la-Neuve

Files: Anarchie; Eudora/Macintosh; Eudora/ Windows; FTPd; Fetch; Finger; Gopher; ISO.3166; ISO.8859-1; InternetConfig; Mac.lpr.lpd; MacPPP; MacTCP-F; MacTCP-Switcher; MacTCP-Watcher; MailShare; Minuet; NCSA_Telnet; News/ NewsWatcher; News/YANewsWatcher; ph; poppassd; RFCs; Talk; tn3270; WWW/MacWeb; WWW/NCSA_Mosaic

ftp://ftp.srv.ualberta.ca/

University of Alberta, Edmonton, Alberta, Computing and Network Services

Files: docs; DOS; ECS (beta) for MS-Windows; faculty; Mac; Novell; OS/2; pictures; Unix; Windows; WWW

ftp://ftp.st.nepean.uws.edu.au/

UWS - Nepean

Files: Amiga; doc; images; Mac; movies; PC (analysis, anti-virus, archive, cdrom, chemistry, clipper, cobol, comms, demos, disk, editor, emtex, emulate, games, graphics, modula2, os/2, palmtop, pascal, pentium, prolog, rhubarb, sb_awe32, spim, UltraSound, unix-utils, web, win3, win95, winsock); sounds; Unix

ftp://ftp.std.com/

Software Tool and Die - The World Public Access Unix, Boston, Massachusetts

Files: activist forum; alt.religion.kibology; amo; Apropos; arj; arj2; AW; astronomy; Atari; b100demo; bball; bbedit; bcs; bitnet addresses; bmug; boston rsi; catnip; cenvi; clipart; cmellow; consultants; dance; dj500; DSPdev; epimbe; fbpro; fix; fontutil; freelance; fullview; funne-archive; genesoft; GNU; graph; ham-radio; idg2; IMA; info-futures; ipv7; IsetlSymdiff; Kluwer; lawyer; Lexicor; liant; lingua; majordomo; MenuDropper; MetaCard; mmodel; NE; obi; OBS; onset; QLS; Quantum; patents; periodicals; python; ra; radio; RAT-archive; renascence; Rgirls; sable; sabre; ScreenSaverKit; SShare; Softpro; sold; talk.bizarre; TECO; Termcomp; Tierra; toolbox; tv-networks; ultracom; vendors (JP Software: 4DOS, 4NT, 4OS2, TC); winmag; World info; WWW; Xtty

ftp://ftp.sterling.com/

Sterling Software

Files: comp.sources.misc, comp.sources.x, comp.sources.reviewed, TSIG archives, USENET Moderators archive and US Mirror && mailing list site for ZSH; extensive EDI archive and unofficial mirrors for many other net.packages; dodiis; gatekeeper; isode; mail; ncsa; news RFCs; rkive; security; std; style; sun-dist; talk-radio; Tcl (programming/languages/tcl from ftp.aud.alcatel.com); usenet (archive for: alt.sources, alt.sources.mac, comp.archives, comp.archives.admin, comp.sources.3b1, comp.sources.acorn, comp.sources, amiga, comp. sources.apple2, comp.sources.atari.st, comp.sources.bugs, comp.sources.games, comp.sources.hp48, comp.sources.mac, comp.sources.misc, comp.sources.postscript, comp.sources.reviewed, comp.sources.sun, comp.sources.unix, comp.sources.x, gnu.emacs.sources, net.sources, news.answers, u3b.sources, unix-pc, vmsnet.sources; uumap; whitehouse; WWW; zsh

ftp://ftp.stolaf.edu/

St. Olaf College

Files: acts; Amiga; anylchem experiments; Apple2; Budapest; diffEQ; IECC (Intercultural Email Classroom Connections); Indian Music; Kierkegaard; 1acnet; Linux-doc; Macpsych mailinglist and software archive; mn-math; mnpsych; MuTeX and MusicTeX mailinglist and software archive; newlist; NeXT managers mailinglist and software archive; oscar (Omni Cultural Academic Resource); origami; OZ; perseus; PEW; Plan9; sca; sci; smlcoll; snap; stat-ed; steen; Tamil;, tchechon; teach; trainset; travel-advisories (U.S. State dept.); xcp (Cross Cultural Psychology)

ftp://ftp.stsci.edu/

Space Telescope Science Institute Electronic Information Service

Files: ExInEd; cdbs; docs; godfrey; Hubble space telescope archive; instrument_news/ sci.astro.hubble; listserver archives; net-resources; observer; pasp; policy; proposer; searchtools; stsci

ftp://ftp.su.oz.au/

University of Sydney, Sydney, Information Services

Files: AARNet; ads; anaed; av; casmac; cygnus; docs; Eudora; GNU; IETF; INET93; itpc; Mosaic; NCSA; Netware (Novell); nsw-minutes; ohs-manuals; RFCs; soviet archive; talk-radio; Telebit; UB; Zsh

ftp://ftp.sun.ac.za/

University of Stellenbosch, Cape Town

Files: 386BSD; daily weather image; doom; FreeBSD; Games hacks; GNU; Linux (from tsx-11.mit.edu and sunsite.unc.edu); MS-DOS; mirrors: Simtel Software Repository, ftp.uml.edu (/pub/msdos/uml); NETBSD; Oberon, OS/2 (ftp.cdrom.com); packages (archie, describe, elm, emtex, fsp, ftpmail, irc, listproc, mirror, musictex, ntp, procmail, smail, tex, texshell, tin, wu-ftpd, xarchie); RFCs; South Africa; Stellenbosch; Tcl; Tex (incl. emTeX); Ultrasound; Unix (ispell, ncftp, octave, remind, tcsh, zsh); Usenet (FAQs); X11 (ftp.x.org)

ftp://ftp.sun.ca/

Sun Canada, OpCom

Files: bin.x86; demos; docs (cookbook, internet-drafts, networking, papers, RFCs, SCSI, security, smk, Solaris, Sun-info, tnftools, volmgt); drivers; freeware; hw; ITR; migration (survey, tools); newsletter; packages; R5; reseller; scripts; specials; staging; Sun-info; tars; threads; X11R5

ftp://ftp.sunet.se/

Swedish University Network (SUNET), Stockholm, NIC

Files: anim; benchmark; comics; conferencing; docs; etext; games; global-net; GNU; Gopher; graphics; Internet documents; Internet drafts; lang; library; Mac; MIME; molbio; movies; multimedia; music (mirror of ftp.uwp.edu /pub/music/lyrics, /pub/music/pictures); network; Network User Guides; news; NIDR tools; NT; PC; pictures (advertisments, animals, anime-manga, architecture, art, ascii, astro-images, chem, collections, comics, computer, fantasy, fractals, history, maps, misc, money, music, people, plants, raytrace, satellite-views, sports, stereograms, tv.film, uploads, vehicles, views); radio; security; text-processing; tv+movies; Unix; Usenet; vendor; Wais; Windows (mirror of papa.indstate.edu); WWW; X500

ftp://ftp.supra.com/

Supra Corp.

Files: Amiga; Atari; BBS config; generic info [interesting stuff]; Mac; MS-DOS; Supra; Windows

ftp://ftp.sura.net/

South-eastern Universities Research Association network, Maryland

Files: archie; articles from the SURAnet newsletter; books; databases; DNS (bind); FDIC (Federal Deposit Insurance Corporation); forms (templates for DNS requests); loads; maps; MBONE; meetings; network info/maps; news; NIC; RIPE; security; sendmail; SURAnet information

ftp://ftp.switch.ch/

Swiss Academic & Research Network (SWITCH), Zurich

Files: docs : CERT, ftp-list, FYI, IESG, IETF, Internet-Draft, Internet-Monthly-Report, Internet-Resources-Guide, OIW, RFC, Unicode, UNT-library-guide; mirrors: CU-SeeMe (mirror/ CU-SeeMe from gated.cornell.edu), Eudora (mirror/eudora from ftp.qualcomm.com), GNU (mirror/gnu from prep.ai.mit.edu), Info-Mac (mirror/info-mac from sumex-aim.stanford.edu), Kermit (mirror/kermit from watsun.cc.columbia.edu), Khoros (mirror/khoros from ftp.khoros.unm.edu), Linux (mirror/linux from sunsite.unc.edu), MachTen (mirror/MachTen from ftp.tenon.com), MH (mirror/mh from ics.uci.edu), MSDOS (/mirror/simtel/msdos from SimTel), Novell (mirror/novell from netlab1.usu.edu), Oberon (mirror/MachTen from ftp.inf.ethz.ch), OS/2 (mirror/os2 from ftp-os2.cdrom.com), OSF1 (mirror/osf1 from various sites), OzTeX (mirror/oztex from midway. uchicago.edu), UCSD-hamradio (mirror/ucsd from ftp.ucsd.edu), UoMichigan-Mac (mirror/umich-mac from mac.archive.umich.edu), Tcl (mirror/tcl from ftp.aud.alcatel.com), TeX (mirror/tex from ftp.tex.ac.uk), VMS (mirror/vms from various sites), WAIS (mirror/wais from sunsite.unc.edu), Windows 3 (mirror/win3 from ftp.cica.indiana. edu, mirror/simtel/win3 from SimTel), WWW (mirror/www from various sites), X11 (mirror/X11 from ftp.x.org), XFree86 (mirror/XFree86 from ftp.xfree86.org);news archive (only a few groups); Swiss resource network info

ftp://ftp.symantec.com/

Symantec

Files: Antivirus (CPAV, NAV); apps; devtools; utils

ftp://ftp.symbios.com/

Symbios Logic (formerly NCR Microelectronics Products Division)

Files: benchmarking (Netware, NT, Unix); NCR chips (graphics, SCSI:drivers for DOS, ISA, NeXTStep, Netware3, Netware4, OS/2, PCI, PCI Win95, PCMCIA, SCO, Unixware1, Unixware2, utils, Windows NT 3.1, Windows NT 3.5), sample code, SCSI docs); standards (I/O: ATA, ATA2, ATA3, CAM, FC, PNPSCSI, rflt list, SCSI1, SCSI2, SCSI3, SSA, X3T10, X3T10.1)

ftp://ftp.synapse.net/

Synapse Internet

Files: contrib (FreeBSD, Mac (networking), MS-DOS (demos, games, multimedia, networking), Netscape (networking), OS/2 (demos, multimedia, networking, updates, utilities), Unix (networking), Windows (games, misc, multimedia, networking, updates)); info (ad&d, apipr, cad (CADalog, AutoCAD shareware catalog, AutoLISP and other AutoCAD utils), cohousing, dsce, infozone, nashinfo, optotek, slrclnt, vysor, wishlist); packages (winnet); shareware (bbsee, icom, kentrol, orpheus, recipes, vbreader); Synapse (active, newsgroups, scripts, templates)

ftp://ftp.syr.edu/

Syracuse University, Syracuse, New York

Files: AFA-Objects; archives (bit.listserv.big-lan); isr; math; networks: hosts, info; news; novell; Sun-fixes; Unix; virus

ftp://ftp.tardis.ed.ac.uk/

University of Edinburgh, Edinburgh, Scotland

Files: bcs; computing; etext; images; internet; media; mpeg; net; papers; Queer Resources Directory (QRD); stormcock; tardis; underground;

ftp://ftp.tcp.com/

The Commnet Project Archives, Seattle, Washington

Files: 90210; anime; anime-manga; ben-pics; clarissa; crow; ftp; image; introspective; jl-pics; jpeg; jpop; lullaby; maiko; melrose-place; MUD clients; neph; Queer Resource Directory (QRD); sundoom; SVR4; tapestries; text; vincent-clarke

ftp://ftp.tenon.com/

Tenon

Files: MachTen (apps, bug fixes, docs, mailing list archive, ports, software, tech notes, tools, updates, upgrades)

ftp://ftp.terena.nl/

Terena, Amsterdam

Files: COA; collaborations; executive committee; general assembly; JENC6 (6th Joint European Networking Conference); liaisons; projects; publications; rare council; ripe ncc; rtc; telematics (info on how to submit a proposal under the EU 4th Framework program)

ftp://ftp.th-darmstadt.de/

Technische Hochschule Darmstadt (Darmstadt Polytechnical Institute), Darmstadt

Files: Amiga; Archie; archivers; databases; dicts; doc; editors; fixes; GNU; graphics; hhlrinfo; lang; Linux; machines; mods; MS-DOS; networking; OS; OS/2; programming; RFCs; starter; sysadmin; TeX; thd; usenet; X11

ftp://ftp.truevision.com/

Truevision/RasterOps, Santa Clara, California

Files: docs; faqs_Q&A; images; Mac; PC; press_releases; Sun; Telefinder

ftp://ftp.trumpet.com.au/

Trumpet

Files: IRC; SLIPper; TCP-ABI; Trumpet newsreader home: dostrump, LWP, view, winsock, wintrump; WinIRC

ftp://ftp.u.washington.edu/

University of Washington, Seattle, Washington

Files: DEC OSF; docs; IBM PC; RS6000; user-supported (airplanes, alt.drugs, alt.fan.fabio, alt.locksmithing, amnesty, animaniacs, anime, Anne Frank, Applets, arthistory, BOE, CALI, CARTAH, CHMC audiology, Chimaera, Chinese Fieldwork, Christmas, cinema, classics, climbing, cmedicine, cogsci, cypherpunks, depeche mode, design-l, Doom, Duran Duran, ECSEL, fugate, GNU, go, hades, health reform, hockey, Holocaust, homecare, hpoadocs, hsis94, ICSC, logistic data, LOTRmush, MRwww, MS-DOS, music gifs, netstudy, new media, NGS, NetBSD-Amiga, obsidian, peru, phantom, PIX, positron, psycho, pyrite, rainman, realestate, RR, Red Dwarf, script-tex, seasonic, seattle-maps, SimTel20, slovene, TMBG, tobit, UKC, USTC, UW_IRC, V-Man, venice, Virtual Reality, virtual worlds (sci.virtual-worlds archive), vislab, webber, webinfo, WeNa, xor, XXXX, yellow submarine, zarathustra

ftp://ftp.ua.pt/

Universidade de Aveiro (University of Aveiro), Aveiro, Centro de Informatica (CS dept.)

Files: Amiga; cisco; docs (mirror of ns.dns.pt, PT, RCCN); GNU; ham-radio; HP48; local: dicts, hypermedia, music (basement, docs, guitar, software), news, PC (sound, tcp, win3, win32s), pictures+sounds; Mac (comm, compression, developer, diskfile, graphicsutil, hypercardutil, multifinder, network, print, screensaver, security, text, unix, virus); misc (AI, ASCII-art, Khoros, matlab, minuet, mpack, NCSA-telnet, Novell-patches, nupop, pegasus, pop, ps_graphics, smile, stereo, TeX); netnews; PC (SimTel Software Repository mirror, papa.indstate.edu); programming; Unix (adm, debug, editors, games, graphics, Mac, mail, misc, net, news, pack, security, sounds, TIA, X)

ftp://ftp.uakom.sk/

Matej Bel University, Banska Bystrica, UAKOM UMB

Files: 602; Enviro+Med; finex; GNU; hypertext; infoserv; Inzercia; mailinglists; MS-DOS (compression, freeware, McAfee, MS-Windows); MSV-SR; multimedia; MZP-SR; network (cutcp, dial-up-ip, gopher, ISODE, lynx, mail, mbone, Mosaic, netfind, Netscape, news, PC-Mosaic, Pmail, security, SNMP, time, tools, wn, WWW, X.500, Xtools); OS (Linux); quelle; radio; reports; SAIA; SANET; SAZP; SimTel; STB; teletext; UAKOM; Unix; weather; WWW

ftp://ftp.ucdavis.edu/

University of California - Davis, Davis, California

Files: bitsites; cpumeter; dialppp; domain-info; Eclipse; econet; Hitchhikers Guide to the Internet; INET93; inet-drafts; Internet Resource Guide; JIS; Kanji; lacnet; listoflists; Mac; MS-DOS (old archivers); PC lisp; peacenet; popmail; RFCs; sendmail; slnet; UCD info; Unix; USGS; VMS

ftp://ftp.uct.ac.za/

University of Cape Town, Cape Town

Files: archives (List of South African ftp sites); data (geminivirus, potyvirus); depts (library); FreeBSD; Geo; mirrors (EC); PC (archive, biblio, delphi, encode, internet, misc, scan); Unix

ftp://ftp.ugcs.caltech.edu/

California Institute of Technology, Pasadena, California

Files: caltech.house.dabney; cilibrar; cms (bonsia, bosnia, cms, hadith, islamic timer, quran, shakir-suras); cyberboarder; diplomacy; disney; dragonslair; elef; gifs (Pakistan: bit.listserv.{pakistan, pns-l}); plan; showppm; stale-urine; zee

ftp://ftp.uidaho.edu/

University of Idaho, Moscow, Idaho

Files: Electronic Green Journal (EGJ)

ftp://ftp.iupui.edu/

Indiana University - Purdue University at Indianapolis, Indianapolis

Files: doc (Internet, RFC); indycert (Mac, PC, Unix); library; logos; Mac (eudora, gopher, hypercard, mackermit, pegasus, utilities, web); PC; psychiatry; Unix (ntp, sendmail, web, web-tools)

ftp://ftp.umd.umich.edu/

University of Michigan, Ann Arbor, Michigan

Files: Doom; FRP; graphics; Mac; MS-DOS; MUD; Red Dwarf material (gifs/lyrics/scripts etc.); Sandman/Death Gallery; sound; text; Unix; Windows

ftp://ftp.uml.edu/

University of Massachusetts - Lowell, Lowell, Massachusetts

Files: Babylon-5; comp.binaries.ibm.pc archive & submissions; FreeBSD; GNU; Linux; MS-DOS games and demo's: (3D, 3DRealms, adventures, Apogee, arcade, BBSdoors, cards, cheet sheets, copysoft, demos, editors, education, Epic, Flightsimulators, FPS football, Game Dev, Game Bytes, ID, kids, Links386, MVP, MahJongg, Moraff, patches,

puzzle, RPG, sports, Tetris, TextAd, Top100, Trivia, utils, VGAPlanets, Windows; Netscape; Sonic; TV

ftp://ftp.une.edu.au/

University of New England - Armidale, Armidale, New South Wales

Files: Adobe (AFM, Acrobat, Applications, PPD); Amateur Radio Topics (Ham-radio: aus.radio, buffalo, f6bb-utils, funet, icom, kiss, Mac-files, Pacsat, Rose, UCSD); DEC (DEC-Info); FreeBSD; GNU; Gopher (Unix); NCSA (Mac, PC, Telnet, Web); Novell (Netwire); Otherrealms

ftp://ftp.uni-duisburg.de/

Universitaet Duisburg (University of Duisburg), Duisburg

Files: 386BSD; CAD; compiler; ghost; GNU; graphics; HP48; lang; Linux; MS-DOS; OS/2; source files; TeX; Unix; Windows 3; X11

ftp://ftp.uni-erlangen.de/

Friedrich Alexander Universitaet Erlangen (University of Erlangen), Erlangen

Files: Adobe; Amiga; Aminet; Atari; audio; Auth; Aviator; beam; BSD; C++; docs; doc.epix; du-s; duu; ebs; faces; flexfax; Fun; games; GNU; graphics; HP28; HP48; IERS; IMMD2; IMMD4; inventories; IP; IRC; ISO; iwi4; Khoros; Lemacs; Linux (sunsite.unc.edu); Lisp; Mac; media; Modula3; Motorola; Multimedia; net; news; Newton; papers; PC; pc-freeware; pictures; psion3; snm; snmp; sounds; Sun; TeX; utilities; wafe; WAIS; X11; X11R6; X25; X400; XBtx; XCept; ZyXEL

ftp://ftp.uni-kl.de/

Universitaet Kaiserslautern (University of Kaiserslautern), Kaiserslautern

Files: Acorn; Amiga; Aminet; amoeba; Apple II; Astro; Atari; Athena; bio; BSD-sources; docs; EMBL; FUN; game-solutions; GNU; gopher; graphics; ham-radio; helios; HP48; humor (incl. real programmers don't use Pascal); Info-Mac (sumex-aim.stanford.edu); info KL; informatik; Internet; IRC; ISIS; languages; Linux; lists; Mac; Mach3; Minix; MS-DOS; netinfas; netlib; NeXT; Novell; panda; Pegasus; RFCs; sat.met; security; Sun; TCP/IP; tech-reports; TeX; Transputer; Unix; vektorproz; vendor; X11R5

ftp://ftp.uni-mainz.de/

Universitaet Mainz (University of Mainz), Mainz

Files: amd; Amiga; Atari; Athena; batch; chaos; GNU; images (gif, jpg, NASA); internet (alex, archie, dos, gopher, hyper-g, isode, kermit, kurs, news, security, sendmail, wais, www); JOGUbits; Linux; Mac; misc (autostereogramme, ebooks, ZyXel); MS-DOS (antivirus, catalog, CIP, DOS, Novell, Windows); muwiinf; NetBSD; news-archive (alt.comp.periphs.mainboard.asus, comp.benchmarks, comp.lang.perl, comp.lang.tcl, comp.os.386bsd.announce, comp.os.386bsd.apps, comp.os.386bsd.bugs, comp.os.386bsd.development, comp.os.386bsd.misc, comp.os.386bsd.questions, comp.os.linux, comp.os.linux.admin, comp.os.linux.announce, comp.os.linux.development, comp.os.linux.help, comp.os.linux.misc, comp.os.research, comp.os.vms, comp.parallel, comp.parallel.pvm, comp.sources.misc, comp.sources.postscript, comp.sources.reviewed, comp.sources.unix, comp.sources.x, comp.sys.dec, comp.sys.hp, comp.sys.hp.apps, comp.sys.hp.hardware, comp.sys.hp.hpux, comp.sys.hp.misc, comp.sys.hp.mpe, comp.sys.sgi.admin, comp.sys.sgi.announce, comp.sys.sgi.apps, comp.sys.sgi.bugs, comp.sys.sgi.graphics, comp.sys.sgi.hardware, comp.sys.sgi.misc, comp.sys.sun.admin, comp.sys.sun.hardware, comp.unix.aix, comp.unix.bsd, comp.unix.osf.misc, comp.unix.osf.osf1, comp.unix.solaris, comp.unix.ultrix, de.comp.os.linux, gnu.emacs.sources, jogu.announce, jogu.bull, jogu.linux, jogu.net, jogu.talk, jogu.vms, stgt.general, stgt.net, stgt.uni-s.general, stgt.uni-s.rus, vmsnet.sources, vmsnet.sources.d, vmsnet.sysmgt); OS/2; SCO; security; Tcl/Tk; TeX; X11

ftp://ftp.unicamp.br/

Universidad de Campinas (University of Campinas), Sao Paulo

Files: ahand; AIX; backup; ccuec; cdrom; communications; condor; cso; databases; djgpp; docs; e-books; education; fapesp; ftpd; FreeBSD; GNU (mirror of prep.ai.mit.edu); gopher; gzip; humor; iicm; images; internet; irpf95; kerberos; kerberos-

mit; khoros; languages; Linux; listproc; lpf; Mac; mail; mathtools; medicine; multimedia; music; news.software; Novell; OS/2; PC; postmodern; prlaser; ProTeM; RFCs; security; shells; SimTel; simulation; Sun; systems (DOS, Windows, OS/2, Macintosh, Unix software);; TCP/IP; TeX; Unix; UUNET; WAIS; WWW browsers (lynx, mosaic, netscape); X11

ftp://ftp.univie.ac.at/

Universitaet Wien (University of Vienna), Vienna, EDV

Files: Austria; docs; GNU; Mac; netinfo (aconet, docs, EARN, Europanet, FYI, IEN, IETF, infos, internet-drafts, ISO, networking, RFCs, zone-info); Novell; OS/2 (hobbes, servicepack-gr); packages (compression, GNU, grass, khoros, lapack, mathematica, network, oberon, octave, TeX, X11); PC; security; systems (HP-UX, Linux, Mac, MS-DOS, Novell, OS/2, Solaris, Unix, Windows3); TeX; UniVie

ftp://ftp.uqam.ca/

University of Quebec at Montreal, Montreal, Quebec

Files: Linux (AVIS, SLS); Mac (docs, Eudora, MacTCP, MacWeb, Netscape, Nuntius, Pegasus, Telnet, TurboGopher, tn3270, utils); PC (drivers, internet, kermit, ncsa, news, pmail, sapi, tn3270, util, win31);

ftp://ftp.urz.uni-heidelberg.de/

Universitaet Heidelberg (University of Heidelberg), Heidelberg

Files: AIX RS/6000; Amiga; BSD-sources; div-sources; fonts; games (mirrored on ftp.fht-mannheim.de); games solutions; GNU; gopher; graphics; Heidelberg info; Linux; MS-DOS (archivers, astronomy, comm, demos, educ, educgames, graphics, libs, music, Novell, physics, SCSI, sounds, utilities, virus, windows3, X11); NCSA; net; OS/2; SAS; Simtel Software Repository (mirror of ftp.coast.net); Sun-dist; Unix; X11; xed

ftp://ftp.usask.ca/

University of Saskatchewan, Saskatchewan

Files: Amiga; cwi; dcs-docs; dec-fixes; email; Gutenberg project; Hytelnet (Hypertext list of Telnet sites); incometax; Library of Congress rule interpretations; Literature works of many kinds; Mac; MS-DOS; MS-Windows; MS-Windows NT; netinfo; ntp; OS/2; selected Sun-fixes; Sun-gcc Solaris binaries; Unix; U of S logo; vendor; weather

ftp://ftp.usitc.gov/

US International Trade Commission

Files: general info about the USITC; jobs; lawbib (bibliography of trade-related law journal articles); news releases; notices (Federal Register notices covering USITC investigations, Commission meetings and votes, rules); reports (general factfinding reports, Commission opinions, for selected countervailing-duty and anti-dumping investigations, industry trade and technology reviews); stamps; telephone (analysts' names and numbers

ftp://ftp.uu.net/

UUNET Technologies, Falls Church, Virginia

Files: AI; Athena; BSD-sources; C-utils; cake; calc; CLIM; comp.sources: 3b1, amiga, games, misc, reviewed, unix, x; comp.std.unix; database; economics; editors; faces (Usenix); franzinc; FTPNUZ (/support/pubdom); games; GNU; government; graphics; Internet docs; ioccc; languages; library; linguistics; Mach; mail; math; mirror of coombs.anu.edu.au; mtools; music; news; networking galore; nutshell; opinions; packages [?]; physics; printers; prob-tracking; prog-libs; published; SCO; security; shells; Simtel Software Repository mirror (/systems/ibmpc/msdos/simtel20); Sun-fixes; sysadm; Unix Today; Unix World; UUmap; UUnet info; vendor [?]; window-sys; X

ftp://ftp.uwp.edu/

University of Wisconsin - Parkside, Kenosha, Wisconsin

Files: Music related **Files:** lyrics (also on ftp.sunet.se /pub/music/lyrics, ftp.informatik.tu-muenchen.de /pub/rec/music/vocal/lyrics, http://www.informatik.tu-muenchen.de /isar/archive/music), pictures (ftp.sunet.se /pub/music/pictures), discographies, many music mailing lists and press kits; Official ID software games distribution; several site mirrors; ftp-list; Tin; programs for SB, ProAudio etc.; mirror of ftp.uml.edu (/pub/msdos/games/ulowell): MS-DOS games and ftp.luth.se (/pub/msdos/demos), ftp.eng.ufl.edu (/pub/msdos/demos), ftp.edu.tw /PC/uwp/demos: MS-DOS demos, mirror of ftp.edu.tw /PC/uwp/romulus (hints and cheats for MS-DOS)

ftp://ftp.vector.co.za/

The Vector Group, Durban

Files: docs (info, RFCs, Solaris Q&A); FAQ; GNU; MS-DOS; Solaris (binaries, patches); Sun (expansion options, hardware, OS, performance, software, SPARC5, SPARC20, SPARCcenter1000, SPARCcenter2000, SPARCcluster); utils; TeX; X11

ftp://ftp.wang.com/

Wang Labs

Files: fitz (aix-bind, expect, used-music); lar3ry (Creative (poem, song, story, top10), dnd (wirenews, archives), FAQs (rec.arts.disney, wdw), Lyrics (aladdin, aristocats, batb, cinderella, dumbo, dw, junglebook, oliver, peterpan, rescuers, robinhood, sb, snowwhite, tfath, tgmd, tlm, tlmsfts, tlmtv, tsits, wtp); SCO (bind, cpio, emacs, gcc, gzip, ispell)

ftp://ftp.wariat.org/

WARIAT/APK

Files: alt.beer; APK; cdroms; Clipper; command (AVP, encode, HS, virus info, tests; cupid; dougmenu; news; NT; OS/2; sports; tiny; uniboard; user public directories; winsock

ftp://ftp.warwick.ac.uk/

Warwick University, Coventry

Files: C64; Computer Underground Digest (CuD) archives; fiction; games; GNU; HTML; MS-DOS; MUD related; Novell; SNMP; Solaris2; Statlib; TeX; usenet; X11

ftp://ftp.wgs.com/

WorkGroup Solutions, Inc, hosted by Rocky Mountain Internet Inc RMII), Colorado Springs, Colorado

Files: FlagShip & CA-Clipper programming, and product information. Fox, Dbase, and "C" also supported. FlagShip is a 4GL, with no Royalties on code you create. It is a great prototyping language, yet strong enough to create industrial strength applications. Integrates well with "C"; Linux; Mac; MS-DOS; OS/2; RFCs; SCO; Sun; Unix; user public directories

ftp://ftp.wordperfect.com/

WordPerfect Corp., Orem, Utah

Files: CIS; corpinfo; demos; netwareIP; Unixware; WP Corp (drivers, Internet Publisher, patches, utils)

ftp://ftp.world.net/

Internetworks Inc. Worldnet, Oregon

Files: Crossfire (Roguelike game); Nethack; mirrors: ftp.ifi.uio.no, ftp.ruf.uni-freiburg.de; news; soc.religion.eastern; tools; World info; zcat

ftp://ftp.xensei.com/

Xensei Corporation, Quincy, Massachusetts

Files: GIFs; HTML; Linux (TCP/IP); Mac (TCP/IP); MS-Windows(TCP/IP: archie, chat, ftp, finger, irc, mail, mosaic, news, ping, telnet, wincode, winsock, xensei navigator, xentime); news (Usenet newsgroup listings); RFCs; Spypond; TechTips; user pub directories

ftp://ftp.xircom.com/

Xircom

Files: drivers (ce, ce2, cem, cem2, cnw, ee, epp, iib, iip, mpm, p3270, pa, pa2, pe, pe2, pe3, pem, peps, ppx, pt, pt2, pt3, ptps)

ftp://ftp.yars.free.net/

Yaroslavl State University, Yaroslavl

Files: Russian, programming (Russian), Systems, Hardware (more in Russian), Software: Orac software (MS-DOS: games, network, language (asm, C, Fortran, Perl5); Windows: games, network (winsock, pathway, pcnfs50, chameleon), desktop; unix: Linux (slackware), network, X11, Perl5; Novell; WWW (tools: hypermail, converters, editors(htmlasst, htmledit, htmlwrit, hotmetal, phoenix), imagemap; HTTPD: Cyrillic version of NCSA daemon, Win-HTTPD; clients: Netscape, Lynx, Mosaic, WinWeb, Cello, HotJava, Sesam)

ftp://ftp.zam.kfa-juelich.de/

Forschungszentrum Juelich GmbH (KFA), Juelich, ZAM

Files: antivirus utilities; ftp-info; graphics; HP UX; MS-DOS; Tex

ftp://ftpboi.external.hp.com/

Hewlett-Packard

Files: International drivers for HP products; Printerdrivers; Scanjet; SNMPmib

ftp://gatekeeper.dec.com/

Digital Equipment Corp - Palo Alto, Palo Alto, California

Files: Alpha; Athena; BSD (386BSd and NetBSD, used to mirror agate.berkeley.edu); case; Cica (ftp.cica.indiana.edu) mirror; comm; conferences; database; DEC; Digital; docs; editors; forums; games; GNU; graphics; Larry Wall stuff; Mach; mail; maps; micro; misc;

multimedia; net; NetScape; news; NIST; plan; published; recipes; sf; Standards; sysadm; text; UCB; Usenet; Usenix; VMS; X11; X11-contrib

ftp://geom.umn.edu/

University of Minnesota, Minnesota, Geometry Center

Files: Differential Geometry Stuff: Geomview (pub/software/geomview), Surface Evolver (pub/software/evolver), SnapPea (pub/software/snappea); docs; images

ftp://grind.isca.uiowa.edu/

University of Iowa, Iowa, Iowa Student Computer Association

Files: MS-DOS; Windows 3.x (mirrors ftp.cica.indiana.edu)

ftp://hcrl.open.ac.uk/

Open University, Human Cognition Research Laboratory

Files: bugtales; dm863; docs; misc; Psion3; psyche; software (Mac (Logomedia, Transparent Prolog Machine, Timelines application), PC (Micro Interpreter for Knowledge Engineering (MIKE)), Qtc)

ftp://hplvopen.lvld.hp.com/

Hewlett-Packard Co., Loveland, Colorado

Files: HP product bug lists, docs, drivers, example files, price lists, revision history, tutorials, utilities

ftp://images.jsc.nasa.gov/

NASA - Johnson Space Center

Files: Earth observations from STS-59; Public Affairs images

ftp://infant2.sphs.indiana.edu/

University of Indiana, Bloomington, Indiana

Files: Doom; Netrek

ftp://jagubox.gsfc.nasa.gov/

NASA - Goddard Space Flight Center, Greenbelt, Maryland

Files: A/UX (Apple, daemons, GNU, info, patches, security, sys, technotes, UUCP, utilities, web); Mac; misc (Monty Python, rem.lyrics)

ftp://lesvos.med.auth.gr

Aristotle University of Thessaloniki, Thessaloniki

Files: antivirus; archivers; ARJ; authoring systems; benchmarks; clipart; communication; demos;

desktop publishing; drivers (printer, various, video); editors; emulators; fax; games (APOGEE, EPIC, mind);,graphics viewers; greek (images, info, programs, songs); images: car, nature, space, various); INERTIA player; Internet info files; LONGWORD; medical programs; medical images; medical info; modem; MPEG (mpeg files, players); OS/2; programs (drawing, education, recreation); security; sound (editors, mod files, players, wav files); Unix (docs, programs, sources); utilities (copy, disk, file, system); various information files; Windows (applications, games, network programs); word processors

ftp://lifshitz.ph.utexas.edu/

University of Texas - Austin, Austin, Texas

Files: Atari; aviation; fortran; ghostscript for the atari; graphics; hg; images (PS, sunicons); multidimensional fast fourier transform (fft); mwc; Myer's ICTP lectures and related programs (/pub/graphics); plain TeX goodies (/pub/tex); publicly available sources (/pub/src); qsp; rcsin front end to rcs ci command; sounds; TeXsis macros for TeX (/texsis); utseal

ftp://mail.ncku.edu.tw/

National Cheng Kung University, Taiwan

Files: et-word; gopher; graphics; guitar; Internet tools; LaTeX; Mac; MBONE; Mosaic; MS-DOS; multimedia; NCKU-net-docs; news; OS; RFCs; seminars; tools; Unix; X

ftp://media-lab.media.mit.edu/

Massachusetts Institute of Technology, Cambridge, Massachusetts

Files: access; audio; books; DEC; EDS; elwin; Foner; framer; galatea; holography; interface-agents; jill; k-arith-code; mc; MediaMOO; medimage; monkeyBrains; mrconsole; music; ne-raves; NeXT; noname; nuno; physics; point_icon; Pro Audio Spectrum (PAS); saus; sci.vw.a; SGI; sparce-dyn; stoneRave; sysadmin; thinking-about-thinking; VietNet; WavesWorld

ftp://mirrors.aol.com/

America Online, Vienna, Virginia

Files: AOL Mac and Windows client software (from ftp.aol.com as /aol_mac and /aol-win); FAQs and other info (from rtfm.mit.edu:/pub as /pub/rtfm); guitar (from ftp.nevada.edu:/pub/guitar as pub/guitar); ID games (from ftp.cdrom.com:/pub/idgames); Mac (sumex-aim.stanford.edu:/info-mac as /pub/info-mac and mac.archive.umich.edu:/ as /pub/mac); MS-Windows (from ftp.winsite.com as

pub/cica); music (ftp.uwp.edu:/pub/music as /pub/music); PC games (from ftp.uwp.edu and ftp.uml.edu as /pub/pc_games); PC games development (x2ftp.oulu.fi:/pub as /pub/x2ftp); Peter Lewis Shareware as /pub/peterlewis (from ftp.pht.com:/pub/gamehead)

ftp://mirror.apple.com/

Apple Computer, Inc.

Files: Mirrors of: The Info-Mac Archive, The Macintosh sofware archive from mac.archive.umich.edu, The AppleScript archive from gaea.scriptweb.com, The software archive from jagubox.gsfc.nasa.gov (A/UX, Mac), The Apple_SW_Updates archive from Apple's support servers

ftp://mscmga.ms.ic.ac.uk/

Imperial College of Science, Technology and Medicine, London

Files: OR library, you have to know what you're looking for here or read the info.txt file

ftp://mthvax.cs.miami.edu/

University of Miami, Miami, Florida

Files: homebrew; US Constitution; worm papers; Elm; nn

ftp://naic.nasa.gov/

NASA - Ames Research Center, Moffet Field, California

Files: april drafts; DECnet; DMS; FBI; images; Internet Resource Guide; maps; NASA Resource Guide; NASA Science Internet Russia Mgt Plan; OSS tables; packet video; RFCs; software (max500 v2.0, motif-dua, turbogopher, utilities, windows-dua); UNABOM info (/files/fbi); WWW framework

ftp://newton.uiowa.edu/

University of Iowa, Iowa

Files: Newton technology site (tools for Mac and MS-DOS: FAQ, helpline, WWW)

ftp://next.com/

NeXT Computer

Files: NeXT files

ftp://nic.ddn.mil/

U.S. Department of Defense Defense Data Network - Internet NIC

Files: DDN news; domain; FYIs; gosip; IEN; IETF; internet drafts; netinfo; protocols;RFCs; scc (DDN security bulletins); STDs; TCP/IP

ftp://niord.shsu.edu/

Sam Houston State University, Huntsville, Texas

Files: ACADlist; accountability; additions; archie; asaetr; astrosym; autoindent; babel; bbfig; bbm; bibclean; bibdb; bibextract; bibliobuilder; bm2font; boxedeps; brief_t; bsn; bst; c2latex; checksum; chemtex; chess; cjethics-l; cjintro-l; clip; cmbb; cmrps; cmttss; cnoweb; commutative; comp.text.tex; cope-author-instructions; cope; cpp2latex; crossword; cso-stuff; ctan (see pip.shsu.edu); ctt; cweb-Mac; d-VMSlsv; deu-l; deu-listings; devanagari; diagramf; doc; domain codes; dosnoweb; drivers; drutpu; dtk-l; dvgt; dvi2pcl; dvi2tty; dvidvi; dviln03; dvips547; dvips5490; dvips5495; dvips5516; econbib; econdata; economics; eepic; efe; ega2me; egopher; ejournl; emtex-texshell; epic; explain; epmtex; essential; etpu; eveplus; exercise; faq; fedtax-l; fig2mf; fileserv tools; fillform; finale; flist; floatfig; fontname; fonts; fontsel; footnpag; french; ftnright; funnelweb; fweb-faq; fweb; gawk; gentle; GhostScript (MS-DOS); gopher plus; GreekTeX; harvard; headache; hp2pbm; hp2pk; hp2xx; IAFA; impatient; include; Info-TeX; Info-TPU; inrstex; Internet; ir-comm; IRC; itrans; jed; kermit; knuth; kr-cweb; labor; LACheck (MS-DOS); LameTeX; LaTeX3; LaTeXInfo; lexitex; ling-tex; litprog-bib; lollipop; LP-Intro; LTX3pub; ludica; lzw; lzw_sources; MaasInfo files; mailgopher; makeindex; maltby-intro; mamath; mfpic; mftu; midnight; modes; MSWin LaTeX; MultiNet FTP mode LZ; mweb; mx; nassflow; newsletter; nfss; novfc; noweb; nuweb; ozgis; PC-Web; PC-Dviware; Perl; pgframe; PH; pictex; pkzip; plain; pmtex; pol-econ; PP; PPHLP; PS2PK; PSBOX; PSFIGTeX; PSNFSS; PS tricks; PS utils; RevTeX; RTF; RTF2LaTeX; S2LaTeX; sals; sauter; scriptTeX; seminar; sfware; smcro; special; spfontware; spiderweb; squiggle; St. Mary; sty; tbefiles; TeX-XeT; TeX-CD; TeX-LSEdit; TeX-News; Texas; TeXHax; TeXinfo; TeXxMag; TeXserver; TeXshell-CMS; TeXtools; TeXtugn; TeXtures-FIGS; TeXexample; TeX-primer; theorem; tgrind; TPU; TPUHDR; TR2LaTeX; TRIES-L; tries; troff to TeX; trombone; tspell; ttn; tug-lug; tug-suggest; tugabs; tugboat; tugproc; twg-tds; twg; UCtheses; UCX support; UK TeX; Unix-TeX; unmacro; unsplit; unzip (Amiga, Atari, BCC, Mac, MS-DOS, NT, OS2, VMS); uucode (Unix); vaxbook; vertex; VMS LaTeX; VMS mail; VMS Tar; VMS WAIS; vol-task; vvcode; WAIS; WEB2C; Windows3; wizunzip; wkbf; wordweb; WP2LaTeX; XDvi; Xetal; XPPT; ZCrypt; ZIP (Atari, Mac, MS-DOS, NT, OS/2, VMS); ZOO

ftp://nlmpubs.nlm.nih.gov/

U.S. National Institute of Health, National Library of Medicine

Files: aids; alerts; bibs; grants; grateful; hstat (Health Services Technology Assessment Text); nlminfo; online; umls

ftp://novell.nrc.ca/

National Research Council

Files: mirror of netlab2.usu.edu (Novell Netwire); STAMP (Parallax microcontroller)

ftp://oak.oakland.edu/

Oakland University, Rochester, Michigan

Files: BBS lists; ham radio; ka9q TCP/IP; Mac; modem protocol info; MS-DOS; MS-Windows; PC Blue; PostScript; SimTel; Unix

ftp://ocf.berkeley.edu/

Organization; University of California - Berkeley, Berkeley, California

Files: Amiga; Apollo; Cal Band; Cal Band History; Cal graphics; Calsol; comics (Kid Dynamo, read the rec.arts.comics FAQ for details); crossfire; FTP sites; games; gobears; Hello World archive; Help Sessions; Library; Network Info; netrek; NFL draft; OCF;

purity; RFCs; Space; Traveller; Usenet Olympics

ftp://pacific.mps.ohio-state.edu/

Ohio State University, Columbus, Ohio

Files: dcmp (teX macros for preparing DCMP invited talks); dvi3ps (merging of many dvi2ps versions); gentle-tex (intro to TeX crossref. with TeXbook); facilities-guide (configurable user guide for Unix, VMS, TOPS-20, Mac, PC); dvidj (dvi to HP Deskjet); LabanWriter (tool for doing Laban (dance) notation)

ftp://pc.usl.edu/

University of Southwestern Louisiana, Lafayette, Louisiana

Files: alt.os.multics archives; Jnos ham tcp/ip package

ftp://polyslo.calpoly.edu/

California Polytechnical Institute, California

Files: anime (Japanese animation); crow (From the Crow's nest Newsletter); GA scheduler; hgi (Hitch Hiker's Guide to the Internet); magic (Magic The Gathering price list); mdurkin (PC Shareware); NeXT (Graphics Workshop for a NeXT); ocr (PD Optical Character Recognition software); ood_and_i; RFCs; tech-reports; xglib

ftp://princeton.edu/

Princeton University

Files: aabd; amr; Apogee; ASD; Atlas1; BBS; benchmarks; Bicycles; Bioethics; Bitnet; bpw; BT; cwisp; diku; diver; draine; EDV; fort; fusion; Graphics; hk; hosts (info on Internet and Princeton Hosts); iams; IRC; katak; lcc; libmast; Maastricht Treaty; ml; morph; Mosaic; mp-render; MS-DOS; MUMBLE; music; netchat; Networking Tools; ntalk; Oberon; PC anti-virus; PC ann; PC gopher; pnn; rec.music.a-cappella; sendmail; sendmail.satellite; SGI fixes; srk; standard ML; Sun; Sun-fixes; t2demo; trees; USGS; uw; vfs; Video; virus; Web; Whitney-Graustein; wolf; xtank; xtetris; yoga; yugo; zsh; zxx

ftp://publications.ai.mit.edu/

Massachusetts Institute of Technology, Cambridge, Massachusetts

Files: Artificial Intelligence Laboratory publications

ftp://qiclab.scn.rain.com/

Research And Info Network

Files: astronomy; bench; calculators; cdrom; cisco; cygnus; database; docs; games; GNU; graphics; mail; math; misc (huge); multimedia; music network; NeWS; pas-lovers; pinecone; PostScript; programming; rea; RFC; security; shells; simulation; Solaris; Sun; SunOS-patches; sysadmin; text; ucb; vlsi; wordlists; X11; xview

ftp://robotics.eecs.berkeley.edu/

University of California - Berkeley, Berkeley, California

Files: ACRobot; computational geometry and algebra: software, docs and publications; ConvexHull; Fingerlike; MixedVolume; multimedia; Robot assembly, control, grasping, motion; RobotPrimitives; SparseResultant; vision

ftp://s2k-ftp.cs.berkeley.edu/

University of California - Berkeley, Berkeley, California

Files: Ingres (University Ingres DataBaseManagementSystem); multimedia (MPEG software and lots of MPEG movies); Picasso (GUI development system); Postgres (Postgres DBMS); RCS; scan (incoming scanned tech-reports); Sequoia 2000 (Global Change Project); teaching (CS lecture notes); tech-reports (outgoing CS tech-reports); WWW

ftp://seabass.st.usm.edu/

University of Southern Mississippi, Hattiesburg, Mississippi

Files: BBS; css; diag (diagramming language); Eagle's BBS; ELAS (remote sensing software); FAQs; Glenda (environment for parallel programming using PVM); Linux; tars

ftp://sepftp.stanford.edu/

Stanford University, Menlo Park, California, Stanford Exploration Project

Files: astronomy; CLOP; Cerveny-92; Dmo3D; ERUUG; Earth_Images; Earth_Topography; geology; lowercrust; SCCM240; SEGTeX; sep-dist; SPP; Worldmap; X; Xtpanel

ftp://server.berkeley.edu/

University of California - Berkeley, Berkeley, California

Files: AIcons (Athony's Icon Collection); anime (Anime & Manga archive: KOR-chive); brie (Binary files for BRIE working papers); CAA (Cal-Animage, Alpha Chapter); dsql (Distributed SQL); htlj (High-Tech Law Journal); Mac (Macintosh software); map; marvel (Marvel Comics: Generation X); mblga (Queer Resource Center); media-cov (Media Coverage class); misc (misc programs for wrangling QuickTime files, etc.); MPEG-2 audio recordings; mpeg_utils (utilities for playing/converting mpeg audio files); music; netscape (Netscape WWW browser); PC (PC Software); quiz-bowl; src (source for newsgroup archiving program); ucb-www (archive of ucb-www mailing list); Unix (Unix software); www (WWW statistics programs); www-docs (Postscript docs about creating HTML files); x86solaris

ftp://service.boulder.ibm.com/

IBM, Boulder, Colorado

Files: OS/2 fixes

ftp://sgi.com/

Silicon Graphics

Files: comp.sys.mips; comp.sys.sgi/info-iris mailinglist; FAQ; ftp2job; Flexfax software + sources; IRIS; OpenGL graphics programs, source from Paul Haeberli; sage; various sources including ttcp, whois and fax; xtp

ftp://sgigate.sgi.com/

Silicon Graphics

Files: archie-aux; aub; audio; devprogram; dwarf; expo; Inventor; intercolor; IRIS stuff; Mosaic; net-services; OpenGL; Performer; releases; SciTeX; security; support; Surf; Usergroups

ftp://sunsite.sut.ac.jp/

Science University of Tokyo, Tokyo, SunSITE Japan

Files: academic (agriculture, art, astronomy, athletics, biology, business, chemistry, communications, computer-science, data_analysis, economics, education, engineering, environment, geography, geology, history, languages, literature, mathematics, medicine, music, pharmacy, physics, political-science, psychology, religious_studies, russian-studies, water); archives (clipart, documents, games, GNU (prep.ai.mit.edu), intro, Linux, math, networking, packages, qt, Unix-utils, X (ftp.x.org)); asia-info; multimedia (3D, animation, Chinese music, emusic, MAEstro, mods, Sun-sounds, Taiwanese music, utils); sun-info (Sun JP, Sun US)

ftp://sunsite.unc.edu/

University of North Carolina, Chapel Hill, North Carolina, Office for Information Technology (OIT), SunSITE USA

Files: academic; docs; electronic-publications; GNU; humor; IAFA; Internet Talk Radio (ITR); languages; Linux archive; micro; mirror of byrd.mu.wvnet.edu; multimedia; packages; Politics; SAS; sci.econ.research archive; Sun related Usenet newsgroups & announcements; UNC; Unix; WAIS client (nov-cli-visual.zip); X11; XFree86 (mirror of ftp.xfree86.org); Z39.50

ftp://the-tech.mit.edu/

Massachusetts Institute of Technology, Cambridge, Massachusetts, The Tech (MIT's oldest and largest newspaper)

Files: Emacs (Emacs FAQ and scripts); Egal-Minyan; FAQ-Quark; KPT (Kai's Power Tools tips, imaging tool for the Mac); MacPerl; WWW: CGI programs (incl. formmail)

ftp://theory.lcs.mit.edu/

Massachusetts Institute of Technology, Cambridge, Massachusetts

Files: aflent; algorithms; BOAZ; docs; comics: Books of Magic, Sandman, Suicide Squid, Watch-men, see the rec.arts.comics FAQ for details; Emacs; hilbert; IAFA; papers; Pratchett; SPAA94; TeX; theory seminars; timekeeper

ftp://tsx-11.mit.edu/

Massachusetts Institute of Technology, Cambridge, Massachusetts

Files: Linux (one of the primary sites); XFree86 (Linux binaries only)

ftp://uiarchive.cso.uiuc.edu/

University of Illinois - Urbana/Champaign, Urbana, Illinois

Files: doc (RFCs, rtfm); etext (Project Gutenberg); games; GNU; infosystems (gopher, www); lang (eLisp, Perl, Python, Smalltalk, Tcl); math; packages (mail, news); security (CERT, COAST, wordlists); systems (Linux, Mac, Novell, OS/2, PC: SimTel); X11

ftp://urvax.urich.edu/

University of Richmond, Richmond, Virginia

Files: MS-DOS: anti-virus utilities; archivers; comm; generic utilities; Rainbow; VMS

ftp://utelscin.el.utwente.nl/

Universiteit Twente (University of Twente), Enschede

Files: amiga; dislite; hardware; iphone; irc; graphics; mime64; mirror (erlangen: adapter, erlangen, imagepro, pay-tv, vc-info, vc-refer); network; novell (TCP/IP utils); pic prog; schijven (nuffic, ptt, stufi); util; virus; vcrypt (mirror of helvetica-gw.chnet.ch); Windows (IPhone)

ftp://wuarchive.wustl.edu/

Washington University St. Louis, St. Louis, Missouri

Files: decus; doc (bible, coombspapers (coombs.anu.edu.au), EFF, graphic-formats, ietf, internet-drafts, internet-info, mailings-lists, minsky, misc, network-reading-list, noctools, nsfnet, nsfnet-stats, org, publications, RFCS, STD, tech-reports); edu; graphics (comp.sources.x, GIFs, GIF-news, graphics, lpr-art, magellan, radiology trains, x3l3); info; languages; multimedia (audio, images);

packages (architec, benchmarks, caben,
clips2sybase, cmip, compression, dialslip, dist,
ferret, first-virtual, fpsmath, gopher, ingres, ISODE,
kinsim, la, lcs.mit.edu, mail, mail-servers, NCSA
(ftp.ncsa.uiuc.edu), news, Oak (oak.oakland.edu),
pccts, pcr, ph, postgres, ppp, prospero, security,
shells, snmp, TeX, uSystem, wuarchive-ftpd, www,
X11R6, XFree86); pub (Aminet, baseball, culture,
emkt-book, MSDOS_UPLOADS, science, SiteView);
systems (AIX, Amiga, Amoeba, Apple2, Atari, aux,
CP/M, CP/MUG, GNU, HP, hz100, IBMPC, Linux,
Mac, Mach3, Minix, MS-DOS, Newton, NeXT,
Novell, OS/2, OS9, sigm, sinclair, svr5-PC, Unix,
zsys); usenet (alt.sources, bionet.molbio,
comp.archives, comp.benchmarks,
comp.binaries.amiga, comp.binaries.apple2,
comp.binaries.atari.st, comp.binaries.ibm.pc,
comp.binaries.ms-windows, comp.binaries.newton,
comp.graphics.algorithms, comp.internet.library,
comp.lang.eiffel, comp.sources.amiga,
comp.sources.apple2, comp.sources.atari.st,
comp.sources.games, comp.sources.hp48,
comp.sources.mac, comp.sources.misc,
comp.sources.postscript, comp.sources.reviewed,
comp.sources.sun, comp.sources.unix,
comp.sources.x, comp.std.announce,
comp.sys.hp48, comp.unix.aix, comp.virus,
gnu.emacs.sources, rec.food.recipes,
sci.med.telemedicine); vendor (datastorm)

INDEX

Symbols

3D action games
3D Gaming Scene, 159
All-Time Best Doom Levels, 159
CyberMage, 159
Dark Forces Editors and Utilities, 159
Djinni's Hexen-Editing Page, 159
Doom and Doom II Secrets, 159
Duke Nukem 3D Resource Page, 159
GameNet, 159
ID Archives—Doom, 338
id software, 159
Mech Warrior 2 and Clan of the Ghost Bear Page, 159
Quake, 159
Tenth Planet, 160
Terminator, 160
Welcome to the Web Wumpus, 342

3D strategy games
Crusader, 160
Diablo, 160
Ishi Press, 160
Justin's Command and Conquer Web Page, 160
Player's Lists, 160
Raptor's Warcraft and Warcraft II Page, 160
Welcome to Dave's Warcraft 2 Page, 160

4×4 trucking, *see* **off-road vehicles**

A

Aaron-Taylor, Susan, 88
abortion, St. Louis Life News, 730
access providers
Charm Net Personal IP Page, 553
CyberSight, 553
EFF's (Extended) Guide to the Internet, 553
Fountainhead Internet Systems, 553
Fusion Advertising and Communications, 553
GeoCities, 553
GHG Corp, 553
GTLug ISP Index, 553
How To Select an Internet Service Provider, 553
I-2000, 553
Icanect, 553
ICNet: The Original Internet Provider for the East, 553
Imagine.com, 554
Industrial Peer-to-Peer, 554
Infonet, 554
InReach, 554

Inspiration Software, 554
InstaNet (Instant Internet Corp.), 554
Intergate, 554
Internet Access Phoenix Arizona, 554
Internet Application Services, Inc., 554
Internet Channel, 554
Internet Delaware, 554
Internet Direct, 554
Internet Express, Inc., 554
Internet Front, 554
Internet Interface Systems, 554
Internet Light and Power, 555
Internet MainStreet, 555
Internet North, 555
Internet On-Ramp, Inc., 555
Internet Services Montana, 555
InterServe Communications, 555
IntrepidNet, 555
ISDN Internet Access, 555
Knighted Computers, 570
LavaNet, Inc., 555
LI.Net, 555
Linkage Online, 555
Magnetic Page, 555
MapleNet Technologies, Inc., 555
Medius Communications, Inc., 555
Michigan Internet Cooperative Association, 556
Micron Internet Services, 556
Minnesota MicroNet, 556
Minnesota Regional Network (MRNet), 556
MJC Inc. Computer Services, 556
Mojoski Net Tools, 556
MonadNet, 556
Moran Communications Group, 556
Mountain Internet, 556
Nantucket.Net, 556
National Knowledge Networks, Inc., 556
NetAccess Worldwide List, 556
NetAxis, 556
NETCOM Online Communications Services, Inc., 556
NetDepot, 557
NETHEAD, 557
NetPoint Communications, Inc., 557
NetPress Communications, 557
NetReach, 557
Netropolis, 557
Netside Network, 557
NETWave Internet Access Provider, 557
Northwest Link, 557
Novagate, 557
Valiquet Lamothe Inc., 557

accessing Web sites, 16-18
accordians, Accumulated Accordian Annotations, 661
accounting, Farg's Cost Accounting Home Page, 130
action movies
Alien, 623
Apollo 13, 623
Braveheart, 623
Crimson Tide Danger Runs Deep, 623
Dr. NO, 623
Hunt for Red October, 623
In the Name of the Father, 623
James Bond 007, 623
Killer, 623
Killing Zoe, 624
Nathan's Apocalypse Now Page, 624
Professional, 624
Terminator/Terminator 2: Judgment Day FAQ List, 624
actors, 624-625
Casting on the Web, 335
CastingOnline, 335
Hollywood Actors Network, 335
KeanuNet, 625
Marilyn Pages, 625
Mr. Showbiz, 348
television, 867
VCV Stunts-Stuntmen on the Net, 335
Virtual Headbook, 335
Welcome to Brandoland, 625
see also movies
acupuncture, 428, 449
addresses
e-mail, 22-23
Geographic Nameserver, 716
LookUp!, 571
National Address and ZIP+4 Browser, 716
searchers, 573-574
United States Postal Service, 717
Zipper, 717
adoptions
Adoptee & Genealogy Page from Carrie's Crazy Quilt, 381
Adoptees and Birthparents, 381
Adoption Advocates: Adoption Policy Resource Center, 379
Adoption Benefits: Employers as Partners in Family Building, 379
Adoption on the Usenet, 381
Adoption Resources on the Internet, 379
Adoption-Where Do I Start?, 379
AdoptioNetwork, 379

Index

Adoptions, 379

Adoptions Connections Project:
  Women's Journeys, 379

AIS Exchange List 1996-Community
  Resources, 379

Alliance for Children, 380

BirthQuest, 381

Christian World Adoption, 380

Domestic Infant Adoption Advice,
  380

Faces of Adoptin-America's Waiting
  Children, 380

Family Law Center-Adoption, 380

Growing Families Inc., 380

Having Your Adopted, 380

Help the Children, 380

Holt International Children's
  Services, 380

Independent Adoption Center Home
  Page, 380

Jeff Hartung's Adoptees Resources
  Home Page, 381

National Adoption Organizations,
  380

Precious in HIS Sight-Adoption
  Information on the Internet, 380

Roots and Wings Adoption
  Magazine, 381

Tapestry Books— Adoption/
  Infertility Book Catalog, 429

Texas Adoption Resource Exchange,
  381

Treasure Maps, 381

Voices of Adoption, 381

**Advanced Research Projects Agency
  (ARPA), 9**

adventure movies

Congo, 623

Indiana Jones WWW Page, 623

Last of the Mohicans, 624

Tombstone, 624

see also movies

adventure travel

Adventure Travel, 901

Adventure Travel for Women, 901

Alaska—Mt. McKinley, 901

Alpine Guides Alaska, 901

Arctic Adventours, Inc., 901

Big Island Air, 901

Eagle Canyon Airlines, 901

EarthWise Journeys, 901

Helinet Helicopter Tours, 901

Mayuc—Ecological Tourism, 901

New Brunswick, Canada Outdoor
  Adventures, 901

Resort Sports Network, 901

Safari Helicopters, 902

Sierra Mountain Guides, 902

Touring Exchange, 902

TravelBase, 902

Wildwest Travel, Inc., 902

see also travel

advertising, 7

Advertising Age, 599

Advertising, Boelter & Lincoln, 138

Advertising Quotes, 717

AfterHours Communications Corp.,
  138

Allen & Associates, Ltd., 138

Another Color Inc., 139

Association of Internet Users, 567

Austin Knight's KnightNet, 139

B.A.A.S. Boating Advertising,
  Advice, and Service, 139

Biggs Gilmore Communications, 139

Black list of Internet Advertisers, 559

BMP DDB Needham, 139

Carter & Associates WEB Studios,
  576

Carter Waxman, 139

CEO Access: Across the Street, 139

Chiat/Day Inc., 139

Chiossone Studio, NYC, 494

Cohn & Wells, 139

Cortex Marketing Resources, 139

curious pictures, 139

Dynamic Diagrams Home Page, 577

Electronic Product Catalog Systems,
  140

Executive Guide to Marketing on the
  New Internet, 559

Farago Advertising, 140

Forest Green Media, 140

Galaxy Communications Inc., 140

GBH Handsfree Communication, 140

Goswick Advertising, 140

Hans de Kort Photography, 494

HERMES, Consumer and Corporate
  Surveys, 140

Impact Studio, 495

Ingalls, Quinn & Johnson, 140

Institute for the Study of Business
  Markets, 140

Internet Business Connection, 578

Kern Media Associates, 140

Liggett Stashower, 142

Marcus Advertising, 140

Market Place Media, 141

Marketing to Consumers: A Guide,
  141

McMonigle & Spooner, 141

Michael J. Motto Advertising, 141

Mintz & Hoke Advertising and
  Public Relations, 141

Mousetracks-NSNS Marketing
  Resources, 141

Newton Online, 571

O'KEEFE WORLD, 141

Online Source Register (Services), 78

Presence—An Information Design
  Studio, 572

Program One Online Service, 579

Reckless Design Limited, 141

Richards Group, 141

Sales Plus, 141

Setting Up Shop on the Internet, 562

Sidea, 142

TAL Marketing Services, Inc. 142

Time Machine, 134

Tom Davis+Company, 142

Usenet newsgroups, 19

Wahlstrom & Company, 142

Wall Street Journal, 142

Web Digest for Marketers, 142

WebReach: Internet Advertising and,
  142

Weightman Group, 142

Winkler McManus, 142

WorldTel Global Marketing Network,
  573

WorldWide Information and
  Netcasting Services, 580

Young & Roehr, Inc., 143

aeronautics, 304

**aerospace engineering, World Wide
  Web Virtual Library: Aerospace, 766**

Africa

African Sky Video, 123

Edoardo Villa, 85

hiking, 849

Isis, 544

Melanet Online African Wedding
  Guide, 927

music

  Afro-Caribbean Music, 656

  Afropop Worldwide, 656

  Larry Aronson Home Page, 658

  *Music from Africa and the African
    Diaspora, 658*

  Shona Music, 659

South African Futures Exchange, 126

African-Americans

art, 71

dance, 89

design, OBD-Organization of Black
  Designers, 78

history
   African American History, 455
   Amistad Research, 291
   Isis: Our Story, 455
   Kwanzaa Information Center, 707
aging
   Aging Research Centre, 439
   Creative Learning Stroke Support
      Web Site, 439
   Geropsychology, 439
   Institute for Brain Aging and
      Dementia, 440
   Portals Aging, 440
   see also senior citizens
agriculture, 414
   Ag-Links, 749
   Agriculture Online, 749
   AgriGator, 488, 749
   Agrinet, 749
   Center for Rural Studies (CRS), 538
   Center for Soybean Tissue and
      Genetic Engineering, 749
   Economic Research Service, 749
   Farmland Information Library, 749
   GrainsGenes, 749
   High Plains Journal-The Farmer-
      Rancher Paper, 749
   John Deere-Agricultural Equipment,
      749
   NewCrop, 749
   Oregon—World War II Farming, 456
   Pest & Crop Management Production
      Newsletter, 749
   Rationale, 749
   USDA, 749
   Voice of Agriculture, 750
AIDS
   Camp Heartland, 799
   Roxane Pain Institute, 435
air filters, LifeTime Filters, 814
Air Force, cyberSPOKESMAN, 600
airlines
   Above It All, 902
   Aer Lingus, 902
   Aeroflot, 902
   Air Canada, 902
   Air Charter Guide, 902
   Air Travel Card Control Tower, 902
   Air Traveler's Handbook, 913
   Air UK, 902
   Airline Toll-Free Numbers and
      Websites, 714
   Airlines of the Web, 902
   American Airlines, 902
   Ansett Australia, 903
   Canadian Airlines Intl., 903
   Cathay Pacific, 903

Comair, 903
   Eagle Canyon Airlines, 903
   Emirates Airline Page, 903
   Finnair, 903
   Frontier Airlines, 903
   Healthy Flying, 448
   International Airport Codes, 903
   Japan Airlines, 903
   Lauda Air, 903
   Lufthansa Timetable Info, 904
   Mexicana Airlines, 904
   Mount Cook Airlines, 904
   New England Airlines, 904
   Period.Com Airlines!, 716
   Quantas Airlines, 904
   Scenic Airlines, 904
   Virgin Atlantic Airlines, 904
airplanes
   Scale Model Collection, 491
   Schiemer's Page, 898
   see also aviation
Akar, Monique, 85
Alabama
   Alabama, 915
   Alabama Supercomputer Authority,
      305
Alaska
   Alaska Information Cache, 915
   Alaskan Dance Theater, 89
alchemy
   Alchemy, Taoism, God & all that
      Stuff, 685
   The Alchemy Virtual Library, 685
   Philosophers of Nature, 685
   Philosopher's Stone/Elixir of Life,
      685
alcoholic beverages
   Acats Internet Bar Pages, 393
   Beamish & Crawford Brewery, 393
   Brew Hawaii Magazine, 393
   Bud On-Line, 393
   Cat's Meow 3: Internet Beer Recipe
      Database, 393
   Celebration Vineyards, 393
   Chris' Collection of Drinking Misc.,
      337
   Cocktail.Com, 393
   Cyber Grape and Grain, 393
   Edinburgh Malt Whisky Tour, 394
   Eric's Simple Fermented Beverages,
      394
   Glenfiddich—Weird and Wonderful
      Websites, 347
   Grapevine, 394
   Heineken, 394
   Jack Daniel's, 394
   Napa Valley Virtual Visit, 394

Newcastle Brown Home Page, 394
   Redhook Brewery, 395
   Rosswog Farm Distillery, 395
   S.P.S. Beer Stuff, 395
   SmartWine Online, 395
   Stoli Central, 395
   Virtual Pub, 395
   Virtual Vineyards, 396
   Wines on the Internet, 396
   World Wide Web Winemaking Home
      Page, 396
   zima.com, 396
alcoholism
   Drinkwise, 427
   Recovery Home Page, 427
aliases, 27
**alphabets, Morse Code and the
   Phonetic Alphabets, 712**
alternative energy
   Alternative Energy Engineering, 764
   BCRI On-Line, 766
   CREST'S Guide to Alternative
      Energy, 764
   Home Power Magazine, 764
**alternative housing, Intentional
   Communities, 463**
alternative living
   AERO-The Alternative Education
      Resource Organization, 823
   Alternative Living, 823
   Cohousing Network, 823
   Eco-Village Information Service, 823
   Fellowship for Intentional
      Community, 823
   Intentional Family Connection, 823
   Vision of Sanctuary, 823
alternative medicine
   Actual Natural Source, 427
   Acupuncture Home Page, 427
   Alexandra Health Center, 427
   Alternative Medicine Home Page
      from Falk Library of the Health
      Science-University of Pittsburgh,
      427
   Cell Tech Super Blue Green Algae,
      428
   Code Four Medical, 428
   Conscious Choice, 427
   D&M Sales, 428
   Designs for Health, 428
   Doody Publishing Health Science
      Book Reviews, 429
   Dragon Herbarium, 429
   HANS—The Health Action Network
      Society, 428
   Health and Longevity, 428
   Herbal Hall, 428

Marijuana as a Medicine, 441

Natural Health and Nutrition Shop, 428

Nature's Medicine, 428

People's Place, 428

SPA in Italy, 441

Welcome to Acupuncture, 428

WorldWide Wellness, 428

alternative music

94.7 NRK: The New Rock Revolution, 348

Air Top 20 Chart, 649

Alternative World, 649

Be Happy or Die!, 647

Beastie Boys, 667

Cure, 647

Depeche Mode Home Page, 647

fourtuoh, 647

High Lonesome, 647

Hyperreal, 647

Jane's Addiction and Porno for Pyros, 677

Lollapalooza Information (Unofficial), 660

Lou Reed's Web Home, 647

Mazzy Star Home Page, 677

Meat Puppets Home Page, 677

MEGO, 647

nine inch nails: the unofficial home page, 678

R.E.M. Home Page, 648

Talking Heads, 648

They Might Be Giants, 648

Tom Waits Digest, 648

Turmoil's Seattle Music Web, 648

Welcome to Carbon 14, 605

Wood and Wire, 648

Alzheimer's disease, Alzheimer Disease Web Site, 433

amateur radio

100 Years of Radio, 477

Amateur Radio Elmers Resource Directory, 477

Amateur Radio Resources, 477

American Radio Relay League's World Wide Web Service, 477

Ham Radio Outlet, 477

List of Mail Order Electronics Companies, 477

Packet Radio Home Page, 477

Personal Database Applications, 477

WWW Ham Radio Servers List, 477

America Online, 26, 41

American art

911 Gallery Home Page, 82

National Museum of American Art, 77

American history, *see* **United States history**

American Midwest, Grottos of the American Midwest, 518

American Southwest

Aerial Archaeology Newsletter, 520

Anasazi Archaeology, 520

Sacred Faces, Sacred Spaces, 496

SouthWestern Archaeology, 524

Amish

Amish Recipe, 816

quilts

Amish Quilts, 498

True PA Dutch Country Souvenir, 499

anagrams, 705

analog design, 306

analytical psychology

C.G. Jung, Analytical Psychology, and Culture, 534

C.G. Jung Institute of Los Angeles, 534

anatomy, *see* **biology**

ancient history

ABZU, 456

Akkadian Language (Babylonian and Assyrian Cuneiform Texts), 456

Alexandria, Egypt, 456

Ancient and Medieval Coins, 486

Ancient City of Athens, 456

Archaeological Survey in the Eastern Desert of Egypy, 456

Assyria On-line, 456

Didaskalia: Home Page, 457

Diotima: Women & Gender in the Ancient World, 457, 542

E-scapes: Electronic Resources for the Study of Ancient Landscapes, 527

Exploring Ancient World Cultures, 457, 518

Kelsey Museum Educational and Outreach Program, 457

Oriental Institute, 457

Perseus Project Home Page, 457

Peter Konin's Ancient Rome Page, 457

Pompeii, 457

Pompeii Forum, 457

angels

Angelnet, 690

Virtual Library—Angel Encounters, 688

Anglican church, Anglicans Online, 725

animals

Adam's Fox Box, 64

Amphibian and Reptile Collection, 62

Animal Rights Resource Site, 62

Animals, 62

birds, 57-58

Bunny Thymes, 62

cats

Cat Fanciers' Home Page, 58

Cat House (EFBC/FCC) Home Page, 58

Cats on the Internet, 58

Happy Household Pet Cat Club, 58

Index of /multimed/pics/feline, 58

JESSICATS Home Page, 59

LAL Cat Archive, 59

Savage Studios Homepage, 59

Traditional Cat Association Home Page, The, 59

Zoe Foundation, 59

dogs

Akbash Dog Home Page, 59

Bernese Mountain Dog Home Page, 59

Border Collies, 59

Borzoi Info Online, 59

Canine Activity Calendar, 59

Canine Vaccination Schedule, 59

Caucasian Ovcharka Info, 59

Choosing a Dog Breed, 60

Dog Breeding, 60

Dog Play, 60

Dog Term Glossary, 60

Greyhound Starting Gate, 60

ImageMaker Gifts for Dog Lovers, 85

Pomeranian Dog Home Page, 60

Portuguese Water Dog Index, 60

Pug Dog Home Page, 60

Rhodesian Ridgebacks, 60

Rottweiler Home Page, 60

Schipperke Page, 60

Tibetan Mastiff Home Page, 61

Visual Rhodesian Ridgeback, 61

Westies Home Page, 61

dolphins, 61

Donald Firsching's Chicken Page, 62

endangered

American Association of Zoo Keepers, 361

Atlantic Salmon Federation, 362

Australian Environment Online, 368

The Butterfly Website: Conservation and Ecology, 362

Conservation Breeding Specialist Group, 362

Endangered Species, 62, 362

Fragile Legacy, 369

GreenLife Society—North America, 362

The Video Project, 372

Whale and Dolphin Conservation Society, 369

Whale Museum's Orca Adoption Program, 370

Exotic Pets, 62

ferrets, 61

Getting a Pet, 62

horses, 63-64

House Rabbit Society Home Page, The, 63

How to Put Your Pet on the Web, 63

Index of /animal_gifs/, 63

Inter–species Telepathic Communication, 63

listservs, 68-70

Nature Subject Page, 63

newsgroups, 67

Pet Care Corner, 63

Pet Grief Support, 63

PetBunny Home Page, 63

Remembrance Page, 63

Viva La Tortuga!, 374

wildlife

Adam's Fox Box, 64-66

Antarctica and Its Environment, 64

art, 72

Bear Den, 65

Cochrane Wildlife Reserve, 65

Deer Net, 65

Eastern Slop Grizzly, 65

Frontier Technologies's Lion Gallery, 65

GORP–Nature & Wildlife, 65

Hyenas, 65

Introduced Wild Animals in Australia, 65

Kaehler's Mill Farm, 65

Kids's Action: Rainforest Animals, 66

Lion Pictures of the Month, 66

LlamaWeb, 66

Manatees, 66

OSU's Breeds of Livestock, 66

Polar Regions, 66

Turtle Trax–A Marine Turtle Page, 66

Wolf Resource Page, 66

Wolf Studies Project, 66

Wolf's Den: Home Page of Wolf McSherry, 66

Wombats, Marsupials, and Other Animals, 66

Wonderful Skunk and Opposum Page, 66

World Wide Raccoon Web, 66

zoos, 57

animation

Austin Anime-Niacs Association, 335

Calvin and Hobbes on the World Wide Web, 335

Gen13: Animation's Next GEN, 336

Lysator Computer Society, 77

Museum of Fine Arts, 3D Animation, 336

Sirius Entertainment, 336

VI&P Animation Art Resources, 79

answering services, Inland Answering Service, 131

Antarctica, Live from Antarctica, 299

anthropology

ANTHAP—The Applied Anthropology Computer Network, 517

Anthropoetics: The Electronic Journal of Generative Anthropology, 517

Anthropology of East Europe Review (AEER), 517

Anthropology Resources on the Internet, 517

Ascent of Mind: Ice Age Climates and the Evolution of Intelligence, 517

Castles of Wales, 517

Center for Anthropology Communications Home Page, 517

Center for Visual Anthropology (CVA), 517

Centre for Social Anthropology and Computing (CSAC): Ethnographics Gallery, 517

Exploring Ancient World Cultures, 518

Fourth World Documentation Project, 518

Gnostic Institute of Anthropology—London U.K., 518

Gorilla Home Page, 518

Grottos of the American Midwest, 518

Hopi Basketry Presentation, 518

Journal of World Anthropology, 518

Maxwell Museum of Anthropology, 518

Maya Adventure, 518

MayaQuest '96 Home Page, 518

Museum of Anthropology— University of Michigan, 518

Native American Net Server, 519

NativeWeb, 519

Nicole's AnthroPage, 519

Origins Of Mankind Homepage, 519

Primate Info Net (PIN), 519

Seeker1's CyberAnthropology Home Page, 519

Sisseton Wahpeton Sioux Tribe, 519

Society for Economic Anthropology, 519

Society for the Anthropology of Europe (SAE) Web Site, 519

UCSB Anthropology Web Site, 520

University of Chicago Press Anthropology and Archeaology Catalog, 520

University of Manitoba Anthropology Department, 520

UVa AnthroNet, 520

World Scripture: A comparative anthology of sacred texts, 520

antique automobiles

Boulder Bob's Roadster Page, 898

CHVA, 894

Classic Car Pictures Archive, 898

Classic Showcase, 898

Coys of Kensington, 898

Hillsborough Concours d'Elegance, 898

Hudson-Essex-Terraplane Club, Inc., 894

Mid-America Old Time Auto Association, 897

Wambo!, 898

XK's Unlimited, 898

see also automobiles

antiques

A–Z Antique & Collectible Directory, 477

Alien Antiques, 478

Antiques World, 811

Auntie Q's Antiques & Collectibles, 478

Collector Online, 479

Funtiques Antiques Home Page, 479

Furniture and Refinishing, 487

Hartmann House Antiques, 488

Incredible Collectibles Home Page, 480

Internet Classifieds: 1500–1599 Collectibles Index, 480

J.R. Antiques and China Registry, 813

John Charles Antiques, 814

KBC Antiques and Collectibles Sites List, 480

Railroad Scripophily, 481

Rick's GAMEROOM Collectibles, 481

Whispers in Time, 482

Woodworking in Western Montana, 500

World Wide Mall:™ Arts, Crafts, & Antiques, 482

aphrodisiacs, Aphrodisiac Home Page, 776

API (application programming interface), 15

Apple

Apple Higher Education: The Apple Virtual Campus, 291

apple.com, 235

World of Newton, 211

aquariums, Aquarium World Market, 811

arcade games

Alexander Jean-Claude Bottema's Home Page, 336

The Destruction Derby Games, 337

archaeology

Aerial Archaeology Newsletter, 520

Anasazi Archaeology, 520

Ancient City of Athens, 520

Annual Egyptological Bibliography (AEB), 520

Archaeological Fieldwork Opportunities, 520

Archaeological Resource Guide for Europe, 521

Archaeology at Mt. Vernon Plantation, 521

Archaeology Magazine, 521

ArchNet: Main Menu, 457

ArchNet: WWW Virtual Library—Archaeology, 521

Biblical Archaeologist, 521

British Archaeology, 521

Classics and Mediterranean Archaeology Home Page, 457, 521

COMBINED CAESAREA EXPEDI-TIONS—Underwater Excavations of Sebastos: King Herod's Harbor, 521

Council for Independent Archaeology, 521

Dino Russ's Lair, 521

Dinosaur Provincial Park, 521

Duke Papyrus Archive, 522

Encyclopedia Smithsonian: Archaeology, 522

FAQ—Career in Archaeology in the U.S., 522

Field Museum Online, 522

Fossil Hominids, 457

GIS and Remote Sensing for Archaeology: Burgundy, France, 458, 522

Gopher and WWW Servers, 458

Indiana Jones WWW Page, 522

Institute of Egyptian Art and Archaeology, 458

Institute of Nautical Archaeology (INA), 522

Internet Archaeology, 522

Leptiminus Archaeological Project, 458

National Park Service: Links to the Past—Archaeology, 522

Native American History and Archaeology Resources on the Internet, 522

NEH Archaeology Projects Online, 458

Newstead Project, 458

Ohio State University Excavations at Isthmia, 458

Online Archaeology-An Electronic Journal of Archaeological Theory, 458

Oriental Institute Archaeology, 458

Oriental Institute—University of Chicago, 523

OWAN, 458

Pan-American Institute of Maritime Archaeology (PIMA), 523

Papers from the Institute of Archaeology (UCL), 523

Prehistory Press, 523

RADIOCARBON WWW Server, 523

Reeder's Egypt Page, 523

ROMARCH—Roman Art and Archaeology, 523

Royal Commission on the Ancient and Historical Monuments of Scotland (RCAHMS), 523

Royal Tyrrell Museum Web Site, 523

SAAweb—Society for American Archaeology, 524

Skull Page, 524

South Dakota Archaeology, 524

SouthWestern Archaeology, 524

Stone Pages, 524

T.W. Rutledge, 524

U.C. Berkeley Museum of Paleontology, 524

UK Archaeology on the Internet, 524

University of Chicago Press Anthropology and Archaeology Catalog, 520

archie servers, 571

architecture

ArchiGopher, 604

Architecture & Design, 505

Architronic Home Page, 599

Art for Architecture, 505

basilisk, 599

Builders Graphics, 811

Frank Lloyd Wright Quotes, 718

HBA Architecture and Interior Design, 505

International Architecture and Design Home Page, 505

Lucia's Little Houses, 814

MBT Architecture, 505

new3, Inc., 579

Open Building Architecture For Residential Construction, 505

Southern Reprographics, 809

V.C.net, 505

archives

humor

Oracle Service Humor Archive, 345

Planet Wallywood One Liner Comedy Diner, 345

Spam Haiku Archive, 346

TEI's Random Joke Server, 346

music

AMG Online Music, 655

Classical MIDI Archives, 651

Digital Tradition Folk Song Database, 655

Discographies (and More), 655

Ectophiles' Guide to Good Music, 647

GEMM: Global Electronic Music Marketplace, 655

HitsWorld, 649

Hype! Music, 655

Index, 647

Mammoth Music Meta-List @ VIBE, 655

Monsterbit Media, 655

Rockmine Archives, 655

Similarities Engine, 656

Ultimate Band List, 656

WholeARTS Directory of Musical Entertainment, 654

Worldwide Internet Music Resources, 653, 656

Arctic studies, Institute of Arctic and Alpine Research, 527

area codes, Area Code Finder, 811

Arizona

Arizona Guide, 915

Arizona Museum for Youth, 72

Birding in Southeast Arizona, 484

Gold Canyon Multimedia, 916

Arkansas, ACUMUG-Arkansas Index, 915

Armenia, Armenian Research Center Home Page, 458

ARPA (Advanced Research Projects Agency), 9

art

Ancient World, 810

Anti-Art Productions, 83

Art by Belinda Di Leo, 83

Art by Tim Pascoe, 83

Art Cellar Exchange service, 83

Art Crimes Index, 72

Art for Architecture, 505

Art Online, 72

ArtScene, 73

ArtScape, 72

Art?, 72

Asian, Asian Arts, 83

Australian

AusArts, 84

West Australian Virtual Arts Community, 79

Brookhouse Studio, 73

BYU Performing Arts Management, 73

Canadian

Front Home, 75

Vancouver Arts Index, 79

Capacity Index, 73

ceramics

Archie Bray Foundation for the Ceramic Arts, 485

Carl Baker Stoneware and Raku Pottery, 485

CDI Ceramic Devices, Inc., 485

CEEN, The Crafts Equipment Exchange Newsletter, 485

Centre for Technical Ceramics, CTK, 485

Ceramic Industry, 485

Ceramic Solutions, 485

Ceramics and Artifacts Restoration, 485

Dynamic Ceramic, 485

Forum On-Line Antiques Mall for Potter, Porcelain and Ceramics, 485

Keith Ceramic Materials LTD, 485

Mesa Verde Pottery, 486

Orton's Firing Tips, 486

Potter's Page, 486

Pottery, 486

Scientific Report, Chapter 2: Ceramics a Ceramic Composites, 486

Sun Tile, 482

Virtual Ceramics Exhibit, 486

WWW Virtual Library: Technical Ceramics, 486

dance, 74, 89

Daum On-line, 74

decorative

Hal's Virtual Furniture Gallery, 75

iGallery, 76

Stained Glass by Steve, 88

Virtual Design Center, 135

design, 71

education

ArtsEdge Network, 299

Ballinakill Studios, 73

Rittners School of Floral Design, 78

electronic

@art gallery, 80

Alternative Virtual Biennial, 80

Atelier Nord, 80

Auricular Homepage, 80

Center for Research in Computing and the Arts (CRCA), 73

Crosswire Images, 84

Cyberbabe, 80

Digital Cathedral, 84

Digital Giraffe, 85

Donajski's Digital Gallery, 85

Duncan Hopkins web site, 80

Electronic Chronicles, 85

FineArt Forum Gallery, 85

Graficas Art and Design, 80

Hillustration, 81

Hiway Technologies Graphics Portfolio, 81

HypArt, 81

Lectro-Art, 81

Martin Action Art, 81

Media West Editions, 81

NCSA Digital Gallery CD-ROM, 81

Netwash, 81

place, The, 82

Rainbow of Chaos, 82

Sample the Dog Design, 82

Spanky Welcome (The Spanky Fractal Database), 82

Vancouver Cyberspace Association, 82

WebWeavers, 82

Enterzone, 74

galleries

Citizen Kane Gallery, 91

Edgerton Center's Online Photo Gallery, 91

FocalPoint f/8, 91

GallerySight, 92

Heirloom Art, 85

Mythago, 92

Nature Gallery, 92

New Mexico, 92

New York Public Library Photography Collection, 92

Novagraphics Space Art Gallery, 483

PPSA Photo Gallery, 93

Rogers Virtual Gallery (Beauty #2), 94

Ruby's Gallery, 94

Russian Reminiscence, 94

Zone I Gallery, 94

graffiti, Art Crimes Index, 72

graphical

Artzilla Surf Constructions, 576

DigiPen Applied Computer Graphics School, 74

Dynamic Diagrams Home Page, 577

Free Range Media, Inc., 577

IBM—the Electric Origami Shop, 338

Optical Illusions—A Collection, 340

Stannet WWW Designing and Publishing Company, 580

Syracuse University Computer Graphics for the VA, 78

WebDesigns, 580

Her Own Words®, 544

history

Age of Enlightenment, 71

ArchiGopher, 604

ArtServe, 71

restoration, 71

Risk Map of Cultural Heritage in Italy, 71

INM Home Page, 76

Internet Classifieds: 1500–1599 Collectibles, 480

Ireland

Exhibition of Paintings by Stanley Pettigrew, 85

Patrick Gallagher, Celtic Art, 78

Isis, 544

Italian, WebArtWed, 79

jewelry

Ancient Circles, 489

Associate Jeweler's Tradeshop, 489

Hansen Designs—Fine Art Jewelry and Gems, 489

Main Lobby for Jewelry Making, 489

Making of JEEP COLLINS Jewelry, 489

Santa Fe Southwest Artists Marketspace, 481

Santa Fe Traditions, Inc., 481

Kaleidospace Home Page, 76

listservs, 95–96

Luxembourg, Musée National D'Histoire Et D'Art, 87

metalworking

ArtMetal Project, 83

Design in Metal, 489

Keith Farley/Metalsmith, 489
Metalwork Using the Sand-Matrix Design Process, 489
Mexico, Galeria MexPlaza, 85
multimedia
Metaverse, 77
Multimedia Cultural Information Service, 77
museums
Akron Art Museum, 82
Allen Memorial Art Museum, 82
Andy Warhol Museum, 83
Arizona Museum for Youth, 72
Ashmolean Museum of Art and Archaeology, 71
Bruce Museum, 84
Butler Institute of American Art, 73
Center on Contemporary Art, 84
Centre for Contemporary Art in Warsaw, 84
Chrysler Museum, 74
DaliWeb: The Official Salvador Dali, 84
Dallas Museum of Art Online, 84
Dia Center for the Arts, 74
Getty Art History Information Program, 75
Heard Museum, 76
International Museum of Art, 86
Israel Museum-Jerusalem, 71
Krannert Art Museum, 76
La Trobe University Art Museum, 86
Le Ministère de la Culture, 77
Los Angeles County Museum of Art, 86
Meridian Gallery: Contemporary Art, 86
Michael C. Carlos Museum, Emory University, 77
Minneapolis Institute of Arts, 86
MIT Center for Educational Computing Initiatives Virtual Museum, 86
Musée National D'Histoire Et D'Art, 87
Musée des Arts et Métiers's World Wide Web (Museum of Art and Craft), 77
Museum Web from Art-ROM, 77
Museums in the Netherlands, 77
National Museum of American Art, 77
RACE: Research into Artifacts, 87
REIFF II Museum, 82
Tel Aviv Museum of Art, 88
Tokugawa Art Museum, 78

Treasure of the Louvre, 88
Tucson Museum of Art and Historic Block, 88
University Art Museum: Art Exhibitions, 79
University of Wyoming Art Museum, 88
WebMuseum, 89
Whitney Museum Information, 89
Wonders of the World, 80
National Museum of American Art, 77
National Museum of the American Indian, 77
Native American, 72
natural
Earth Folk Catalog, 370
National Audubon Society, 363
nautical, 72
neon, Krypton Neon—The Internet's Neon Shop, 76
newsgroups, 95
nonprofit organizations, Business Volunteers for the Arts-Houston, 73
Okanagan University College, Department of Fine Arts, 87
Optical Illusions, 78
origami
Electric Origami Shop, 492
Introduction to Origami and The Peace of Paper, 492
Jasper's Origami Menagerie, 492
Joseph Wu's Origami Page, 492
Marbleized Paper, 493
Origami Books in Local Libraries, 493
Origami Tips, 493
Origami USA Main Menu, 493
Pavilion of Polyhedreality, 493
Schoolhouse Videos and CDs, 493
Word Chains, 493
performance, Performing Arts Sites, 653
photography
@rtweb Art Gallery, 493
(Art)ⁿ Galleries, 90
(Microscapes), 92
3-D Stuff, 90
50th Bristol International Salon of Photography, 90
Alan Dorow Gallery, 493
Alder Yarrow's Photography, 493
Allen Rose, 494
Anderson Galleries, 494
Ansel Adams—Fiat Lux, 494
Atlanta Photography Group, 494

Atlanta Photojournalism Seminar, 494
Attic Window (by Diane Fenster), 90
Australian Outback Gallery Photography, 494
Barry Anderson Photography, 494
Black and White Gallery, 90
California Museum of Photography, 494
Cemetery, 90
Cincinnati Parks' Butterfly Show, 91
Citizen Kane Gallery, 91
Crayon Design & Communications, 91
Cypress College Photography Department (First Stop), 91
Detroit Publishing Company Photographic Collection, 91
Digital Photography Exhibit, 91
digital wave photography gallery, 91
Discovery Catalogue, 494
Edgerton Center's Online Photo Gallery, 91
Eye Produce CD ROM Home Page, 74
Florida Wildflower Showcase, 91
FocalPoint f/8, 91
Fotogruppe der Studiobühne und Filmwerkstatt, 91
Frolic, 91
GallerySight, 92
Hans de Kort Photography, 494
Hiroshima and Nagasaki Gallery Exhibition, 92
Home Page of Photographer, Sculptor David C. Franson, 194
Hot Pictures: Russian Photography, 494
Image Alchemy Digital Imaging, 578
imago, 92
Impact Studio, 495
Jay Stoegbauer Photography, 495
Jazz Photography of Ray Avery, 495
Kodak, 495
Michael's Photo Gallery, 92
Michigan Photo Contest, 92
Michigan Press Photographers, 495
Misa, 92
Mythago, 92, 495
Nature Gallery, 92
New Mexico, 92
New York Public Library Photography Collection, 92
Non Facturé, 92
Northwest College Photographic Communications, 495
Online PhotoWeb, 495

Oxford Photographs, 92

Photo Archive, 92

Photo Perspectives, 93

Photographers Gallery, 93

Photography Spot, 495

Photography Yellow Pages, 495

Photojournalist's Coffee House, 495

PhotoLink Gallery, 93

PhotoServe, 495

Picture Projects, 93

Portfolio of Architectural Photographs, 93

Postcards from Bahia, 93

PPSA Photo Gallery, 93

Prairie Dog Artworks, 93

Probus Photos, 93

Professional Photography Portfolios, 496

Remembering Nagasaki, 93

Rogers Virtual Gallery (Beauty #2), 94

Russian Reminiscence, 94

Ron Lowry's Home Page, 496

Ruby's Gallery, 94

Sacred Faces, Sacred Spaces, 496

Sam's Shoebox, 94

Scott Freeman's Underwater Photography Page, 496

Shot in the Dark, 94

SITO, 94

Solar Color Photography by Michael Fastoso, 94

Specializing in Natural Light andNature Images, 496

Stereoscopic Imaging by Ray 3D, 94

Travels with Samantha, 496

United in Anger, 94

Unofficial Cincinnati Butterfly Show, 94

Vintage Postcards, 94

Virtual Gallery (Korea), 496

Virtual Portfolio (London), 496

Zone I Gallery, 94

prints, 72

    Art to Live with Original Prints, 72

    Framers Corner, 75

    Global Art Marketing, 479

Scintilla: Alternative Lighting, Gifts, and Access, 815

sculpture

    Crucible Chicago, 84

    Daddazio-The Bronze Necktie, 84

    International Sculpture Center's On-line Resource, 76

    Koh-Varilla Guild, 86

    Sculptor/Stone Carver, 87

    Sculpture Tour, 88

Southwestern: Another Victim of Santa Fe Style, 811

Visa Olympics of the Imagination, 154

World Wide Mall:™ Arts, Crafts, & Antiques, 482

World's Women On-Line!, 546

arthritis, Pediatric Rheumatology home page, 435

artificial intelligence,

    Brunel University Artificial: Intelligence Area, 305

    CMU Artificial Intelligence Repository, 777

    MIT Artificial Intelligence Laboratory, 760

    North West Artificial Intelligence Applications Group, 760

artists

    Allen Toney's Home Page, 71

    Art by Belinda Di Leo, 83

    Art by Tim Pascoe, 83

    Art of Barbara Weigel, 83

    Art on the Net, 83

    Arthole, 83

    Artworld (ArtMap) Online, 73

    Attic Window (by Diane Fenster), 90

    Booth Milton: Sculptor, 89

    Buron Levitsky, 84

    Christine Thea Partridge* Gallery, 80

    Connie Tunick's Paintings in Watermedia, 84

    DaliWeb: The Official Salvador, 84

    Daniel Vogel, 74

    Eagle Aerie Gallery (Roy Henry Vickers), 85

    Edoardo Villa, 85

    Eric Boutilier-Brown, 74

    Exhibition of Paintings by Stanley Pettigrew, 85

    Framers Corner, 75

    Free Art Website (Laurie McCanna's Home Page), 75

    freelance, Graphix Exchange, 75

    Gen Art, 75

    Guerrilla Girls, 543

    Herbert R. Mears, Contemporary American Artist, 85

    Identity Box Collective, The (Sam Jennings), 85

    ImageMaker Gifts for Dog Lovers (Monique Akar's), 85

    J.C. Mareschal, 71

    jewel (Julieann M. Brown-Micklo), 74

    Joe Walker's Page, 81

    Jordan, Robert, 102

    Kaufman, Karin, 86

    Kjell Ringi Art Exhibition, 86

    Lectro-Art (Dave Parmley), 81

    Michael Rubin, 86

    Nico Roos, 87

    Noel Ford Cartoonist/Illustrator/Author, 77

    Patrick Gallagher, Celtic Art, 78

    rEX's wORLd, 78

    Robert Derr's Virtual Gallery, 82

    Robert Jordan, 76

    Roger Whitney Gallery of Artists, 87

    SolarColor Photography by Michael Fastoso, 94

    Sonoma State University: Alumni Art Exhibition, 88

    Stained Glass by Steve, 88

    Susan Aaron-Taylor: Profile of an Artist, 88

    T.W. Rutledge, 524

    The Art Kelderie (Theo Kelderman), 83

    Tom Reed/Photographer, 82

    Watercolors of Sherry Zuker, 88

    Welcome to the aRt_sLab @ UCSD, 89

    Will James Art Company, 89

    Windshadow (Michael Duncan), 89

    women, Cyberbabe, 80

Asia

    Anthropology of East Europe Review (AEER), 517

    Asia, Inc. Online, 599

    Asian Arts, 83

    Asian Business Daily, 124

    Bali & Beyond Home Page, 657

    Cathay Pacific, 903

    Econsult Group WWW Page, 125

    Faculty of Asian Studies, Australian National University, 304

    Indonesian Music, 658

    Oriental Institute, 457

    Oriental Institute Archaeology, 458

    Oriental Institute—University of Chicago, 523

    Pan Asian Publications Home Page, 603

    War from a Parlor: Stereoscopic Images of American War and Soldiers's Letters Home, 462

    World Telecom Directories, 716

    WWW Archive for Electric Power Engineering Education, 766

Index

astrology
Asian Astrology, 685
The Astrological Association of Great Britain, 685
Astrology Alive!, 685
Astrology et al Bookstore, 609
Astrology Online Magazine, 685
Astrology—The Ultimate Original Science, 685
Astrology: A Theological Science, 685
Chinese Astrology Calendar, 701
The Cosmic Palette, 686
The Harmony of Heaven, 686
How and Why Astrology Works, 686
Kramer—Fishing Guide to the Stars, 686
The Metalog Yellow Pages, 686
The Nine Planets, 686
Oracle's Astrology Chart, 686
The Skeptics Dictionary—Astrology, 686
The Underground Astrologer, 686
Welcome to Daka's Buddhist Astrology, 686
Zodiacal Zephyr, 687

astronomy
Air Force Maui Optical Station (AMOS), 750
American Astronomical Society, 750
Art of Renaissance Science Galileo and Perspective, 750
Astro!Info, 750
Astronomical Data Center, 750
Astronomical Museum in Bologna, 750
Astronomical Resources on the Internet, 751
Astronomy and Astrophysics, 482
Astronomy HyperText Book, 751
Astronomy-Related Web Sites, 751
AstroWeb: Astronomy/Astrophysics on the Internet, 751
Brief Tour of Our Universe!, 751
Caltech Space Society, 751
CCD Images of Galaxies, 751
Center for Advanced Space Studies (CASS) Home Page, 751
Compton Observatory Science Support Center, 751
CyberSky, 751
Discovery Program Home Page, 751
Galaxy Page, 483
HEARSARC Video Archive, 751
Henrietta Leavitt Flat Screen Space Theater, 751
High Energy Astrophysics Science Archive Research, 752

History of Astronomy, 465
Humans in Space, 752
Information Leaflets, 752
Institute for Space Astrophysics C.N.R., 752
International Astronomical Union, 752
International Occultation Timing Association (I.O.T.A.) Home Page, 752
Lesson Plans and Activities, 310
Long Duration Exposure Facility, 752
Mount Wilson Observatory, 752
NASA, 483
NASA Astrophysics Data System Home Page–Classic System, 752
NASA World Wide Web Information Services, 752
NASA-JSC Digital Image Collection, 752
National Space Science Data Center (NSSDC), 483
NCSA Relativity Group, 752
Novagraphics Space Art Gallery, 483
Planetary Society Home Page, 752
Posters, 363, 400
Purdue SEDS (Students for the Exploration and Development of Space), 752
Raben Software & Graphics, 483
Radio-Sky Publishing, 483
SEDS Internet Space Warehouse, 753
Sensors and Instrument Technology Planetary Tour Guide, 753
Sky Online Home Page, 753
Skywatcher's Diary, 483
Society of Amateur Radio Astronomers (SARA), 483
Solar System Live, 753
Southern Cross Astronomical Society, 753
Space Explorer's Guide, 753
Space Settlement, 753
StarBits-Acronyms, Abbreviations, and More, 753
StarWorlds-Astronomy and Related Organizations, 753
STELAR Project Demos, 753
Students for the Exploration and Development of Space (SEDS), 483
Usenet FAQs: Space, 753
Views of the Solar System, 753
Web Nebulae, 496, 753
WebStars Astrophysics in Cyberspace, 753
Welcome to Loch Ness Productions, 754

Welcome to Project CLEA, 754
Welcome to SkyView, 754
Welcome to the Planets, 754
World-Wide Web Home Page of the Canadian Astronomy Data Centre (CADC), 754
Wormhole Interactive, 754

atheism
Atheist Manifesto, 723
International Atheistic Secular Humanist Conspiracy (Canada Division), 723
Secular Web, 723

audio, Internet Connect, Inc.—Audio Innovations, 568

audio hardware, 34

Australia
arts, 71
AusArts, 84
West Australian Virtual Arts Community, 79
Australian National Dictionary Centre, 530
Australian Outback Gallery of Photography, 494
Australian Stock Market Web Pages, 124
basketball, 842
Felix Culpa Home Page, 601
Index of Australian Indexes, 573
motorcycle racing, 855
music
Australian Music World Wide Web Site, 657
Digeridoo Page, 662
DREAMTIME, The Didjeridu W3 Server, 662
National Folk Festival, 660
Quantas Airlines, 904
Sacred Faces, Sacred Spaces, 496
Tharunka Home, 604
Web Publishing Australia, 580
WoodLink, 500

Austria
Austrian Worldport, 124
Lauda Air, 903

authors
Albert Camus, 99
Alice Walker, 105
Amy Tan, 105
Anaïs Nin, 103
Anne McCaffrey, 103
Anne Rice, 104
Aphra Behn Page, 98
Ayn Rand, 104
Barbara Kingsolver, 102

Brontë Sisters, 98
C.S. Lewis (Into the Wardrobe), 103
C.S. Lewis and the Inklings, 102
Charles Bukowski, 98
Charlotte Brontë, 98
Clive Barker, 97
Cormac McCarthy, 103
David Brin, 98
Dean Koontz, 102
Donald Barthelme, 97
Douglas Adams, 97
Douglas Coupland-Snapshots, 100
Edgar Allen Poe, 104
Edgar Rice Burroughs, 98
Edward Bellamy, 98
Ernest Hemingway (The Papa Page), 101
Eudora Welty, 105
F. Scott Fitzgerald, 101
Fyodor Dostoevsky, 100
George Sand, 104
Gertrude Stein, 105
Gore Vidal, 105
H. P. Lovecraft, 103
Henry Miller (18, villa seurat), 103
Herman Melville, 103
Ian Fleming, 101
Isaac Asimov, 97
J.D. Salinger (The Bananafish Home Page), 104
Jack Kerouac, 102
Jim Carroll, 99
Johann Wolfgang von Goethe, 101
John Grisham, 101
John Steinbeck, 105
Jonathan Kellerman, 102
Jorge Luis Borges-The Garden of Forking Paths, 98
Joyce Carol Oates (Celestial Timepiece), 104
Jules Verne, 105
Kate Chopin Project, 99
L. Ron Hubbard, 101
Le Marquis de Sade, 100
Lewis Carroll: An Overview, 99
listservs, 117-119
Louis L'Amour, 102
Louisa May Alcott: Flower Fables, 97
Marcel Proust (Proust Said That), 104
Margaret Atwood Information Site, 97
Marguerite Duras, 100
Mark Twain (Ever the Twain Shall Meet), 105
Mary Shelley, 105

Michael Crichton, 100
Miguel de Cervantes, 99
N. Scott Momaday, 103
Nathaniel Hawthorne, 101
newsgroups, 116-117
Nicholson Baker, 97
Oscar Wilde (The Wild Wilde Web), 105
Philip Roth, 104
Piers Anthony, 97
Raymond Carver, 99
Richard Bausch, 97
Richard Brautigan, 98
Ring Lardner (Lardnermania), 102
Rita Brown, 98
Roald Dahl, 100
Robert Jordan, 102
Roger Zelazny, 106
Stephen Crane, 100
Stephen King, 102
Thomas Hardy, 101
Thomas Wolfe, 106
Tom Clancy, 99
Tom Robbins (The AFTRLife), 104
Truman Capote, 99
Umberto Eco, 100
Ursula K. Le Guin, 102
V.C. Andrews, 97
Virginia Woolf, 106
Vladmir Nabokov (Zembla), 103
Willa Cather, 99
William Faulkner, 101
William S. Burroughs, 99
William T. Vollmann, 105
Yukio Mishima Archive, 103
Zora Neale Hurston, 101
autoharps, Autoharp Page, 661
automation, home
CBI Systems, Inc., 505
DHSL: Data Home Systems Limited, 505
Home Automation Association, 505
Home Automator, 506
Home Team, 506
HomeTheater Com, 506
Intelligent Home Technologies, Inc., 506
Media Dimensions, 506
ProSpec, 506
Spectacular Powerhouse Page, 506
Vantage, 506
automobile travel
ASIRT-Association for International Road Travel, 904-905
Bumper Stickers, 904

National Auto League, 904
Rental Agencies, 904
Route 66, 904
Scenic Byways and Other Recreational Drives, 904
Traveling in the USA, 904
automobiles
antiques
Boulder Bob's Roadster Page, 898
Car Collector Home Page, 600
CHVA, 894
Classic Car Pictures Archive, 898
Classic Showcase, 898
Coys of Kensington, 898
Hillsborough Concours d'Elegance, 898
Hudson-Essex-Terraplane Club, Inc., 894
Mid-America Old Time Auto Association, 897
Wambo!, 898
XK's Unlimited, 898
AutoPages of Internet, 806
buyer's guides
AutoPlus, 893
Car and Driver Buyer's Guide 1996, 893
Car Tips, 893
CARveat Emptor, 893
Edmund's Automobile Buying Guides, 893
Internet CarGuide, 893
New Car Comparison Guide, 893
Tallweb—Cars, 894
Used Car Buying Guide, 894
Car Junkie, 898
CAR-LINK, 806
classifieds
AmericaNet.Com-Free Classified Advertising, 810
Classic Car Gallery, 898
Good Stuff Cheap, 813
Schiemer's Page, 898
Tangerine Dream Vintage Car Locator Service, 898
driver's tips
Art of Driving, 894
Natural Born Drivers, 894
Teen New Drivers' Home Page, 894
electric, 371
Citicar: My Electric Vehicle, 893
Eco-Motion, 370
Electric Vehicle Association of the Americas, 893
Formula Lightning, 893
ZAP Power Systems, 372

luxury, Rolls-Royce Owners' Club, 894

Mobilia Magazine, 602

off-road

   4WD: Four Wheel Drive and All Wheel Drive, 895

   America's 4×4 4U Video Magazine, 895

   My Jeep Adventures, 895

   Off-Road.com, 895

PM Zone, 603

sports cars

   AC Cobra Page, 895

   Alfa Romeo GTA, 895

   Aston Martin, 895

   DeLorean Home Page, 895

   Hot Rods World Wide, 806

   Javelin AMX Home Page, 895

   Paul Murtagh's Lamborghini Web Site, 896

   Vette Americana On-Line, 896

   Waletail's Porsche and 959 Home Page, 896

Ultimate New Auto Club in Canada, 806

autoracing

candelaMotorsport, 839

GALE FORCE F1, 839

IndyCar Enthusiast, 839

Matt's Solar Car Page, 839

Motorsports Media Service International Home Page, 839

Racer Archive, 839

Specialty Car Page, 839

aviation

Air Affair, 754

Airship: The Home Page for Lighter-Than-Air Craft, 754

Aviation Enthusiast Corner, 754

Aviation Image Archives, 754

Basics of Space Flight Learners' Workbook, 754

BIOS Scientific Publishers, 755

Canard's Aviator's Page, 754

Federal Aviation Regulations, 754

First General Aviation WWW Server, 754

Florida Institute of Technology— School of Aeronautics, 304

NASA Dryden Flight Research Center, 755

NASA Information Services via World Wide Web, 755

NASA Television on CU-SeeMe, 755

On Board STS-70, 755

Weather Page, 776

awards

Academy Awards for Music, 1960s and 1970s, 648

Academy of Motion Picture Arts and Sciences, 637

GrammyAwards on the Internet, 648

Nobel Foundation, 712

Nobel Prize Internet Archive, 712

B

ballet

BalletWeb, 650

CyberDance: Ballet on the Web, 651

see also dance

ballroom dancing, *see* **dance**

banjos

Banjo Tablature Archive, 662

Phillip Mann's Banjo Tab Collection, 663

bankruptcy, Internet Bankruptcy Library, 131

Baptists

American Baptist Churches Mission Center Online, 725

Baptist Faith and Message, 725

East 7th Street Baptist Ministry- Graffiti, 726

SBC "Maverick" Home Page, 726

baseball

Amazing Baseball Card Auction, 818

Baseball Hall of Fame, 840

Cosmic Baseball Association, 845

ESPNet SportsZone: Major League Baseball, 840

Fantasy Baseball, 845

Fantasy Baseball Home Page, 845

Fastball, 840

Instant Baseball, 840

Japanese Professional Baseball, 840

John Skilton's Baseball Links, 840

Little League Baseball, 840

Major League Baseball, 840

Nando Baseball Server, 840

New York Yankees Home Plate, 841

Score It, 818

teams, 839

World Youth Baseball, 841

baseball cards, SportsCards, Etc., 482

basketball

College Basketball Page, 841

Michael Jordan's Home Page, 841

Nando Basketball Server, 841

On Hoops, 841

Scottie Pippen's Home Court, 842

teams, 841

Ultimate Basketball Home Page, 842

Unofficial Australian National Basketball League (NBL) Page, 842

bass

Bottom Line Archive, 662

Will Clifton, Double Basses and Some Other Things, 663

bauds, 32

bee pollen, 427

beer

Beamish & Crawford Brewery, 393

Brew Hawaii Magazine, 393

Bud On-Line, 393

Cat's Meow 3: Internet Beer Recipe Database, 393

Heineken, 394

Newcastle Brown Home Page, 394

Real Beer Page, 395

Redhook Brewery, 395

S.P.S. Beer Stuff, 395

Virtual Pub, 395

Bermuda: Ask Us For, 124

Berners-Lee, Tim, 4

beta programs, 42

beverages

Cafe MAM, 393

Capulin Coffee, 393

Celebration Vineyards, 393

Coca-Cola, 393

Cyber Grape and Grain, 393

Food Works by Swiss Connection, 399

Jolt Cola, 394

Lloyd's Coke Machine, 339

Moxie Collector's Page, 394

Perrier, 395

Snapple, 395

Way of Tea, 903

see also alcoholic beverages

Bible studies, Biblical Archaeologist, 521

big band music, Jazz Roots, 664

billiards, 851

binary files, 26, 29

biology

Anatomy Images, 755

Anderson's Timesaving Comparative Guide, 755

Auditory Perception, 755

BiochemWeb, 755

Biodiversity and Biological Collections Web Server, 755

BioForce Labs, 755

BioSupplyNet, 755

CSU BIOWEB, 756

Dictionary of Cell Biology, 703

educational projects, Net Frog, 348

Gene Expression Information Resource Project, 756

Genome Database, 756

Horizon Scientific Press: Molecular Biology Books, 756

Journals, Conferences, and Current Awareness Services (Biosciences), 756

LLNL Biology and Biotechnology Research Program, 756

Mendelweb, 756

National Center for Biotechnology Information, 756

NRC Biotechnology Research Institue, 756

Tools for Molecular Biology, Genetics, and Microbiology, 756

Tree of Life, 757

Virus Databases Online, 757

Welcome to Virtual FlyLab, 757

World Wide Web Virtual Library, Evolution, 757

biotechnology, Chastain Research Group, Inc., 130

bird watching

Academy of Natural Sciences, 484

Backyard Birdfeeder, 484

Bird Guide, Inc., 484

Birding in Southeast Arizona, 484

Birding on the Web, 484

Fugleskue Birdwatch Birdbase, 484

Hotspot for Birds, 484

NPFauna and NPFlora, 484

Ontario Birdwatching Home Page, 484

Wild Bird Marketplace, 484

birds

Audubon, 57

Birds, United States National Park Service (NPS) (Information Center for the Environment), 57

Caring for Your New Bird, 57

Eagle Page from Rocky Mountain High, 58

Fabulous Kakapo (Strigops Habroptilus), 58

Hirt & Carter Owlnet, 569

Jordan Manufacturing Company, Inc., 814

Michael's Photo Gallery, 58

Pet Bird Page, The, 58

UAS Home Page, 58

United States Fish and Wildlife Service Home Page, 58

Virtual Birding in Tokyo, 58

birthparents, *see* **adoption**

blindspinning, 563

bluegrass music

Bluegrass Unlimited Reviews, 648

Central Texas Bluegrass Association, 648

Cybergrass—The Internet Bluegrass Magazine, 665

Doc Watson, 648

Doc Hamilton's Bluegrass Home Page, 648

Musi-Cal Performer Index, 660

Old Time Music Bulletin Board, 648

Phillip Mann's Banjo Tab Collection and Bluegrass Information Site, 663

Welcome to Planet Bluegrass!, 649

blues music

Biscuit Time on Blues Web, 670

Blue Highway, 670

Bluenote, 671

BluesNet, 671

DC Blues Home Page, 671

Electric Gallery, 663

House of Blues, 671

Live Blues and Blues Radio, Steamin' Stan Ruffo, 671

Musi-Cal Performer Index, 660

Pacific Blues & Jazz, 664

see also jazz

boating/sailing

Adventure Schools, Inc., 842

Boatnet, 842

Common Sense Design's Home Page, 842

Flying Scot Page, 842

Internet Sea Kayaking, 842

Offshore Powerboat Racing, 842

Perception, Inc.'s Kayaking Home Page-20 Years of, 842

RC-Sailing Infocenter, 842

SailWeb, 842

Wambo!, 898

White Water Rafting, 843

WWW Sailing Index, 843

boats, models

Nautical Research and Shipmodeling Links, 490

Pmcg's Vicious Model Boat Page, 490

South Bay Model Shipwright, 491

books

Adventures of Tom Sawyer, 106

Adventurous Traveler Bookstore, 599

Aether Madness, 566

Agatha Christie, 99

Alice's Adventures in Wonderland, 106

alt.books.reviews, 110

alt.books.technical, 110

Amazon.com, 110

American Literary Classics, 106

Anne McCaffrey, 103

Antiquarian Booksellers' Association of America, 112

Architecture & Design, 505

Arthur C. Clarke Chapter of The Silicon Jungle, 100

Association of American University Presses (AAUP), 112

Aztec Books, 751

Baker Street Connection, 106

Balogh Scientific Books, 757

Banned Books On-line, 110

Bantam Doubleday Dell-BDD Online, 112

Bonder Bookstore Inc., 112

Book Banning, Burning, and Censorship, 110

Book Hunter, 112

Book Nook, 299

Bookbinding, a tutorial, 110

BookLink, 112

Books/Videos, 490

BookSite, 112

Bookstore at Houghton Mifflin, 112

BookWorld, 110

C.S. Lewis and the Inklings, 102

Christian Book Connection, 113

Citadell of Riva, 106

Clean Well-Lighted Place For Books, 113

Cody's Books, 113

Comics at Bendigo Books, 113

Commonplace Book, 106

Conservation OnLine, 110

Cyber-Seuss, 100

David Morrison Books, 113

Deep Politics Bookstore, 113

Domanski-Irvine Book Company, 224

Doody Publishing Health Science Book Reviews, 429

Electronic Library, 106

Fast Books, 113

Feminist Bookstores, 543

Funtiques Antiques Home Page, 479

Gareth Stevens Publishing, 113

Garfield Co. Public Library System, 302

Gary Holmes Books, 113

Great Books of Western Civilization, 107

Greg Bear, 97

Gutter Press, 107

Horizon Scientific Press: Molecular Biology Books, 756

Hundred Highlights from the Koninklijke Bibliotheek, 110

Hungry Mind Review Discussion, 111

Hunting of the Snark: An Agony in Eight Fits, 107

Indiana Jones WWW Page, 522

Isaac Asimov, 97

It's a Mystery, 113

Jonathan Press Woodworking and Home Improvement Books and Plans, 507

Joseph-Beth Booksellers, 113

JourneyWare Media, 113

Katherine Kurtz, 102

KBC Antiques and Collectibles Sites List, 480

L'Art Medical Antiquarian Books, 111

listservs, 117-119

Little Women-DataText, 107

Loganberry Books, 114

Login Brothers Book Company, 114

Lost World (Randomhouse), 107

Macmillan Publishing USA (The Information SuperLibrary), 111

Mage Publishing, 114

Mare's Nest Publishing, 114

Mark Twain; Huckleberry Finn, 107

Martian Chronicles Study Guide, 107

Midnight Special Bookstore, 114

Moe's Books, 114

Navrang, Inc., 114

New World Books, 114

newsgroups, 116-117

Norwegian Bookshop, 114

Notable Children's Books, 111

Old Bookroom, 114

On-line Books, 78

On-line Books Page, 705

Online Books FAQ, 107

Origami Books in Local Libraries, 493

Pacific Book Auction Galleries, 114

Pantera Publishing, 114

Pas de chance, 114

Piers Anthony, 97

Polonia Bookstore, 115

Preservation Educators' Exchange, 111

Primary Colors, 418

Quantum Books Home Page, 774

Ray Bradbury, 98

ReadersNdex, 111

rec.arts.books, 111

Revolution Books, 115

Roger Zelazny, 106

Romance Pages, 111

Science Express, Inc., 115

Secret Staircase Bookshop, 115

Shen's Books and Supplies, 115

Sherlockian Holmepage, 111

SPITE! Books, 115

Stephen King, 102

Stone Bridge Press, 115

Svoboda's Books Online, 115

Svoboda's Books Online-State College, PA, 115

TeleRead, 107, 109

Time-Life Explorer, 115

Tree Fiction on the World Wide Web, 108

Ultimate Romance Novel Website, 111

UNARIUS Academy of Science, 115

Ursula K. Le Guin, 102

V.C. Andrews, 97

Vintage Books Reading Group Guides, 112

Willy Wonka Lyrics, 112

Women's Books Online, 545

Wonderful Wizard of Oz, 108

Zanadu Comics, 115

Zuzu's Petals Literary Resource, 108

see also authors

Boston

Boston Restaurant Guide, 406

Larry Stark's Theater Mirror, 351

World Music/Boston, 660

botany

The Tele-Garden, 341

Balogh Scientific Books, 757

Botanical Gardens, 757

Botany, 757

Brief Overview of the National Herbarium, 757

Connecticut Botanical Society, 757

Conservation Breeding Specialist Group, 362

Endangered Plants: Images, 362

Geobotanical Institute, 757

GreenLife Society—North America, 362

Internet Directory for Botany, 757

Missouri Botanical Garden, 365

National Institue of Agricultural Botany, 757

Nature Described Learning to Look at the World, 757

Okefenokee Joe's Natural Education Center, 366

bottles, Canadian Online Bottle Collecting Network, 478

Boutilier-Brown, Eric, 74

bowling, 853-854

brainteasers

Crejaculabryrinth, 337

The Fruit Game, 338

Mindgames, 340

Riddle du Jour, 340

The Vain Game, 341

Webcube, 342

Brazil

CRLP: Women of the World, 542

Samba in Sweden, 659

breast cancer, 449

bridal registries

Bridal Gallery, 923

Bridal Net: Online Bridal Registry, 923

Club Wed Press, 923

Historical Wedding Invitations, 923

Wedding Center, 923

Wedding Registries Directory, 923

bridal wear

Ans Bolk Personal Design: Bridal Couture, 926

Bridal Veil Home Page, 926

Dessy Creations Home Page, 926

Elegant Bride, 924

Hora Bridal Accessories, 926

Imagi-Nations, 926

Sposabella Bridal-La Sposa Veil, 926

Watters and Watters, 926

Britain, *see* **England; United Kingdom**

browsers, 4, 11, 17, 41-42

About Web/Genera, 557

ActiveX, 45

AIR Mosaic, 53

Cello, 53

customizing, 46

Cyberspace Connection, 557

Easy Mosaic and Introductory Web Surfing, 558

Global Network Navigator Home Page, 558

Hill Holliday Advertising, 558

installing, 46

Internet Explorer 3.0, 52

Internet Group/Internet Business Center, 558

Lynx, 54

Microsoft Internet Explorer, 51

Mosaic, 5-6

Navigator, 5

NCSA Mosaic 2.1.1, 51

NetCruiser, 54
Netscape Extensions, 43
Netscape Navigator 2.0, 50
Netscape Navigator Gold 2.0, 51
Netscape Plug-Ins, 44
SlipKnot, 54
Spyglass Enhanced Mosaic, 52
support tools, 49
viewing capabilities, 47
VRML, 44
Buddhism, 724
Access to Insight, 724
Buddhist Scripture Information
Retrieval, 724
DEFA Home Page, 724
Hell's Buddhas, 347
International Meditation Centres, 724
International Research Institute for
Zen Buddhism, 724
Journal of Buddhist Ethics, 724
New Kadampa Tradition, 724
Nichiren Shoshu Buddhism, 724
Shin Buddhism Network, 725
Shin Buddhist Resource Center, 725
Tiger Team Buddhist Information
Network, 725
Welcome to Daka's Buddhist
Astrology, 686
Zen Garden, 725
Zen Mountain Monastery, 725
Zen@SunSITE, 725
bullfighting, 852
business, 414
Acer America Career Opportunities,
129
AdMorInk, 129
Adnet, 123
advertising
Advertising Age, 599
Advertising, Boelter & Lincoln, 138
Advertising Quotes, 717
*AfterHours Communications Corp.,
138*
Allen & Associates, Ltd., 138
Another Color Inc., 139
Association of Internet Users, 567
Austin Knight's KnightNet, 139
*B.A.A.S. Boating Advertising,
Advice, and Service, 139*
Biggs Gilmore Communications, 139
Black list of Internet Advertisers, 559
BMP DDB Needham, 139
*Carter & Associates WEB Studios,
576*
Carter Waxman, 139

CEO Access: Across the Street, 139
Chiat/Day Inc., 139
Chiossone Studio, NYC, 494
Cohn & Wells, 139
Cortex Marketing Resources, 139
curious pictures, 139
Dynamic Diagrams Home Page, 577
*Electronic Product Catalog Systems,
140*
*Executive Guide to Marketing on the
New Internet, 559*
Farago Advertising, 140
Forest Green Media, 140
Galaxy Communications Inc., 140
*GBH Handsfree Communication,
140*
Goswick Advertising, 140
Hans de Kort Photography, 494
*HERMES, Consumer and Corporate
Surveys, 140*
Impact Studio, 495
Ingalls, Quinn & Johnson, 140
*Institute for the Study of Business
Markets, 140*
Internet Business Connection, 578
Kern Media Associates, 140
Liggett Stashower, 142
Marcus Advertising, 140
Market Place Media, 141
*Marketing to Consumers: A Guide,
141*
McMonigle & Spooner, 141
Michael J. Motto Advertising, 141
*Mintz & Hoke Advertising and
Public Relations, 141*
*Mousetracks-NSNS Marketing
Resources, 141*
Newton Online, 571
O'KEEFE WORLD, 141
Online Source Register (Services), 78
*Presence—An Information Design
Studio, 572*
Program One Online Service, 579
Reckless Design Limited, 141
Richards Group, 141
Sales Plus, 141
Setting Up Shop on the Internet, 562
Sidea, 142
TAL Marketing Services, Inc. 142
Time Machine, 134
Tom Davis+Company, 142
Usenet newsgroups, 20
Wahlstrom & Company, 142
Wall Street Journal, 142
Web Digest for Marketers, 142
*WebReach: Internet Advertising and,
142*

Weightman Group, 142
Winkler McManus, 142
*WorldTel Global Marketing Network,
573*
*WorldWide Information and
Netcasting Services, 580*
Young & Roehr, Inc., 143
American Computer Resources, Inc.,
129
AT&T Internet Toll Free 800
Directory, 715
Australasian World Publishing
Systems, 124
Australian Pacific Advertising, 124
Automation Specialists, 129
Batey Ads Singapore, 124
BigBook, 715
BigYellow, 715
Bubble Technology Industries Inc.,
130
Business Incorporating Guide, 130
Bytewise Consulting, Inc., 130
Canada
Canada Net Pages, 567
Strategis, 572
Central Source Yellow Pages, 715
Copyright Clearance Center Online,
130
Duoforce Enterprises, Inc., 130
Economics of Networks Internet Site,
568
Global Business Network, 130
Global Trade Center, 131
Hippermedia, 569
ICC Communications Centre, 125
ICC Seminar Series, 560
Interactive Age Home Page, 601
Internet 800 Directory, 715
Internet Business Center, 576
Internet Business Connection, 578
Internet Info Store Directory, 570
Junior Achievement Purpose/Facts,
304
listservs, 146-148
management
Benchmarking Exchange, 121
*Leverage Technologists Home Page,
121*
*Navatar-Organizational Renewal
and Business Reengineering, 121*
Phoenix Business Renewal Site, 121
MicroBiz, 132
Minority Business Development
Agency, 414
Money & Investing Update—
Welcome, 607

Mutual Fund Company Directory, 715

Netscape: J.P. Morgan's Equities Research, 560

newsgroups, 144-146

Omega West, 572

Period.Com Airlines!, 716

Porter Novelli, 133

Pristine Communications, 126

Providence Business News, 608

Regional Economic Models, Inc., 133

Research Dynamics, 133

searchers

   Business Directions International, 573

   MediaLogic's Index of Economic and Financial Resources, 574

Service Bureau, LLC, 134

small

   Bucknell University Small Business Development Center, 143

   Cobweb, 143

   Creative Edge, 143

   Entrepreneur Network, 143

   FranNet, 143

   GROW-Opportunity Wales, 304

   Inc. Business Resources Library, 143

   On-Line Marketing, 143

   SBA, 143

   Simple Solutions, 143

   Small and Home-Based Business Links, 143

   Xerox Small Office, 144

Society for Economic Anthropology, 519

Standard Industrial Classifications (SIC) Index, 713

Switchboard, 716

tradeshows, EXPOguide Home Page, 130

Wall Street Journal, 142

Wall Street Journal Link, 608

Welcome to MLMBBS, 135

World Bank Home Page, 121

World of Commercial Ballooning, 135

World Telecom Directories, 716

World Yellow Pages Network (wyp.net), 716

Yellow Pages Online, Inc., 716

YellowNet, 716

C

cable

Habia Cable AB, 131

Rip-Tie, 815

Submarine Cables of the World, 134

calendars

CalendarLand, 701

Calendars and Their History, 701

Chinese Astrology Calendar, 701

Chinese New Year, 707

Compact Calendar, 701

Conversion Between Chinese and Gregorian Calendar, 701

Ecclesiastical Calendar, 701

Gregorian-Hijri Dates Converter, 701

Hebrew Date for Today, 701

Heichal Shlomo Interactive Calendar, 701

Home Page for Calendar Reform, 701

J World, 701

Leap Years, 702

Literary Hyper Calendar, 702

Olivian Calendar, 702

One-World Global Calendar, 702

Ron Smith Oldies Calendar, 702

Steffen Thorsen's Calendar Page, 702

The Calendar, 701

World Wide Holidays and Events, 708

California

art galleries, 73

California Academy of Sciences, 776

California Do Your Own Thing, 915

L.A. Rock & Roll Road Map, 677

Legal dot Net, 384

Los Angeles Traffic Report, 917

Palo Alto, California, 917

Placer County Office of Education, 295

Santa Barbara County, 918

Scuba Net, 856

Southern California Real Time Traffic Report, 348

Weekend Getaways, 919

Camalgori, A Representative Collection of Fashion Made in Italy, 805

campaigns, *see* **politics**

camping

Arkatents USA-High Quality: Camping Accessories, 855

Great Outdoor Recreation Pages (GORP), 855

Outside Online, 855

Upper Midwest Traveler and Adventure Guide, 855

Canada

Advanced Cultural Technologies, 71

Air Canada, 902

arts, 73

   Front Home, 75

   Vancouver Arts Index, 79

   Vancouver Cyberspace Association, 82

Bird Guide, Inc., 484

broadcasting, 73

Canada Net Pages, 124, 567

Canada Toronto East Mission, 725

Canada's Sports Hall of Fame, 852

Canadian Airlines Intl., 903

Canadian Business InfoWorld, 124

Canadian Institute of Applied Learning, Inc., 300

Canadian Internet Handbook/ Advantage Home Page, 567

Canadian Journal of Sociology (CJS), 538

Canadian Kids' Page, 301

Canadian Online Bottle Collecting Network, 478

Canadian Psychological Association, 534

Canadian WWW Central Index/Liste centrale des serveurs WWW canadiens, 526

Child CyberSEARCH: English Home Page, 385

Cnet—Canada, 567

CTHEORY, 539

Dinosaur Provincial Park, 521

Exposure Excursions, 782

FH: Canada Travel Home Page, 601

FindLaw: Law Schools of Canada, 589

fishing (Virtual Flyshop), 846

Golf Courses of British Columbia, 848

Great Canadian Scientists, 777

Hard Bop Cafe, 664

Heritage Post Interactive, 463

Humanities National Database Search, 525

Internet Mental Health, 535

Malahat Mountain Music, 666

Mega-Directory of US/Canada International Exports-U.S. Trade Center Directory, 125

motorcycle racing, 855

National Atlas Information Service (of Canada), 710

National Atlas of Canada on SchoolNet, 710

Northern Journey: Canadian Folk, 658

Northern Journey: Canadian Folk Music Website, 665

Ontario Birdwatching Home Page, 484

RealTime, 617

Southam, Inc., 608

Strategis, 572

TN-1 NAFTA Home Page, 126

Travels with Samantha, 496

UFOJOE Presents, 660

Ultimate New Auto Club in Canada, 806

University of Manitoba Anthropology Department, 520

Welcome to Molson Canadian, 127

women, Resources for Feminist Research/Documentation sur la recherche féministe (RFR/DRF), 544

World-Wide Web Home Page of the Canadian Astronomy Data Centre (CADC), 754

cancer

breast, 449

International Cancer Alliance, 442

Prostate Cancer InfoLink, 435

Roxane Pain Institute, 435

Testicular Cancer: Survival High, 445

candy

Ann Hemyng Candy, Inc.'s Chocolate FACTORY, 399

Candy, 399

ChocolateTown U.S.A., 399

Godiva Online, 399

I Need My Chocolate!, 399

Sophisticated Chocolates, 923

canes, Island Imports, Ltd., 480

card games, Wizards of the Coast, Inc., 342

cardiovascular diseases

Cardiovascular Institute of the South, 433

Heart Mind Body Institute, 434

careers

Acer America Career Opportunities, 129

Airbase, 321

Airline Employment Assistance Corps, 321

Attorney Jobs, 321

BackStreet Studios, 321

Bolack Total Travel Academy, 321

Career Atlas for the Road, 321

Career Crafting, 321

Career Management International, 321

Career Resource Homepage, 321

CareerWEB, 321

Cybermania!, 321

employment services, 322-325

Federal Law Enforcement Careers Employment Guide, 321

Getting Past Go, 322

High Technology Careers, 322

Hot Jobs, 322

How To Find a Creative Job in The Real World, 322

human resources, 325-326

job fairs, 326

Library Job Hunting, 322

MECA (MBA Employment Connection Association), 322

NetConnections, 322

Occupational Resources, 322

résumé services, 326-327

Ronaldi's MBA Job Finder, 322

training services, 327-329

Westech Career Expo, 322

see also employment

Caribbean Islands

Canboulay, The Caribbean Literature Quarterly, 108

Island Imports, Ltd., 480

carousels

Collectibles by R&T Musical Merry-Go-Rounds, 479

Rick's GAMEROOM Collectibles, 481

carpentry

Arbortech, 499

Carleton Woodworking, 499

Chris Melhorn's Woodworking Gallery, 499

Oak Factory Bulletin Board, 499

Prairie Woodworking, 499

Quality Woodwork and Supply, Inc., 499

W5: Woodworking on the World Wide Web, 500

WoodLink, 500

Woods of the World, 500

WoodWeb, 500

Woodworking in Western Montana, 500

carpeting

Advanced Flooring, Inc., 508

Carpet One, 508

Carpet Samples, 673

Carpets.com, 508

Dalton Carpet Outlets, 509

Floor Coverings International, 509

Sculptured Carpet Selections, 509

TrustMark, 509

cars, *see* automobiles

cartography

Area Accurate Map/The Peters Projection, 526

Association of American Geographers, 526

Association of Chinese Professionals in Geographic Information Systems, 526

Canadian WWW Central Index/Liste centrale des serveurs WWW canadiens, 526

Cartography—Indiana State University, 526

ChartWrite's Data-on-the-Map, 526

Color Landform Atlas of the United States, 710

Country Maps from W3 Servers in Europe, 710

E-scapes: Electronic Resources for the Study of Ancient Landscapes, 527

Federal Geographic Data Committee (FGDC), 527

Geographic Institutes around the World, 527

Global Positioning System (GPS), 527

Heritage Map Museum, 292, 527

History of Cartography Project, 527

International Map Trade Association (IMTA), 527, 710

Laboratory for Remote Sensing and Geographic Information Systems (LRSGIS), 528

Mapmaker, Mapmaker, Make Me a Map, 528, 710

MapQuest, 710

MAPublisher, 528

NAISMap WWW-GIS Home Page, 528

National Atlas Information Service (of Canada), 710

National Atlas of Canada on SchoolNet, 710

Oregon Geographic Alliance (OGA), 528

Perry-Castañeda Library Map Collection, 710

Rare Map Collection at the Hargrett Library, 710

Research-It!, 713

RYHINER-Project at the University Library of Berne, 528

Spatial Odyssey: GIS Literature Database, 529

TIGER Mapping Service, 529

TOPO!™ Interactive Maps, 529

U.S. Geological Survey (USGS) National Mapping Information World Wide Web Server, 529

VIBE's World Map, 711

Xerox PARC Map Viewer, 529

Index

cartoons
  Business and Safety Cartoons by Goff, 811
  Cartoon Heaven, 811
  Cartoon Laws of Physics, 291
  election.html, 301
  Kids's WB, 152
  Looney Tunes Karaoke, 339
  Marvin the Martian, 347
  The Tick's Dart Games, 341
  Where the Buffalo Roam, 605

castles
  Castles on the Web, 462
  Schloss Reichenstein, 688

Catholicism, Catholic Online, 726

cats
  Cat Fanciers' Home Page, 58
  Cat House (EFBC/FCC) Home Page, 58
  Cats on the Internet, 58
  Happy Household Pet Cat Club, 58
  Index of /multimed/pics/feline, 58
  JESSICATS Home Page, 59
  LAL Cat Archive, 59
  Savage Studios Homepage, 59
  Traditional Cat Association Home Page, 59
  Zoe Foundation, 59

CCITT (Consultative Committee for International Telephone and Telegraphy), 32

CD-ROMs
  After Hours Media Duplication Service, 809
  Allegro New Media, 809
  AzTech Interactive, 809
  Sumeria Product List, 816

CDs (compact discs), Dr. Wax, 479

Cello (Web browser), 53

Celtic art, Patrick Gallagher, Celtic Art, 78

cemeteries, Find-A-Grave, 712

censorship
  24 Hours of Democracy, 823
  American Civil Liberties Union, 824
  Banned Books Online, 303
  Bonfire of Liberties: Censorship of the Humanities, 823
  Censorship and the Internet, 559
  Citizens Internet Empowerment Coalition, 823
  Indecency Page, 823
  Index on Censorship, 823
  Know Your Enemies, 824
  Media Watchdog, 349
  Project 2000: The Cyberporn Debate, 824
  Project Censored, 824
  Sex, Censorship, and the Internet, 824

census
  1990 U.S. Census Lookup, 702
  Population Index, 540
  Population Reference Bureau (PRB), 540
  Population Studies Center—University of Michigan, 540
  TIGER Mapping Service, 702
  U.S. Gazetteer, 702
  United Nations Population Information Network (POPIN), 541
  United Nations Scholars' Workstation at Yale University, 541
  World Population, 714
  World Population Figures, 714
  Worldwide Demography Resources, 541

Central America
  Mayan Hieroglyphic Syllabary, 532
  Newspaper/Diario LA NACION—San Jose, Costa Rica, 607

central processing units, 33

ceramics
  Archie Bray Foundation for the Ceramic Arts, 485
  Carl Baker Stoneware and Raku Pottery, 485
  CDI Ceramic Devices, Inc., 485
  CEEN, The Crafts Equipment Exchange Newsletter, 485
  Centre for Technical Ceramics, CTK, 485
  Ceramic Industry, 485
  Ceramic Solutions, 485
  Ceramics and Artifacts Restoration, 485
  Dynamic Ceramic, 485
  Forum On-Line Antiques Mall for Potter, Porcelain and Ceramics, 485
  Funtiques Antiques Home Page, 479
  Keith Ceramic Materials LTD, 485
  Mesa Verde Pottery, 486
  Orton's Firing Tips, 486
  Potter's Page, 486
  Pottery, 486
  Scientific Report, Chapter 2: Ceramics and Ceramic Composites, 486
  Sun Tile, 482
  Virtual Ceramics Exhibit, 486
  WWW Virtual Library: Technical Ceramics, 486

CerfNet, Inc., 36

CERN (European Particle Physics Laboratory), 4

chamber music
  Boston Chamber Ensemble, 650
  Chamber Music Conferences, 651

chats, *see* **Internet; IRC**

chemical waste, Khem Products, Inc., 132

chemistry
  American Chemical Society, 758
  Armchair Scientist, 758
  Atmospheric Chemistry, 758
  Brain Page, 758
  ChemCAI: Instructional Software for Chemistry, 758
  Chemical Demonstrations—Table of Contents, 758
  Chemistry Hypermedia Project, 758
  Chemistry Teacher Resources, 758
  Composite Materials Research Group—University of, 758
  CTI Centre for Chemistry Software Catalogue, 758
  Dalton Chemical Laboratories, Inc., 758
  George Goble (GHG) Extended Home Page, 759
  Introduction to Alchemy, 759
  Los Alamos National Laboratory of Energetic Materials, 759
  Mendeleev Communications, 759
  Periodic Table of the Elements, 759
  SoftShell Online, 759
  Software Reviews from the CTI Centre for Chemistry, 759
  STM Image Gallery, 759
  Understanding Our Planet Through Chemistry, 759
  Waters Corporation, 135
  WWW Chemistry Sites at Academic Institutions, 759

Chicago
  Chicago Moving Image Scene, 600
  Field Museum Online, 522
  Humanities and Social Sciences—University of Chicago LibInfo, 525

children
  4Kids Treehouse, 149
  Academy One, 291
  AHA! Kids Network, 149
  Arkansas Children's Hospital, 442
  Awesome Site for All Ages, 149
  BigKid Network, 149
  Blind Childrens Center, Inc., Home Page, 432

Build Your Own Critter, 336
Canadian Kids' Page, 301
Center for Talented Youth (CTY) of
the Johns Hopkins University, 291
CHATBACK Trust, 432
child abuse
  *Amber Hagerman's Missing
    Children Home Page, 384*
  Blain Nelson's Abuse Pages, 384
  *Child Abuse Prevention Network,
    384*
  *Child Abuse: Statistics, Research,
    and Resources, 385*
  Child Sexual Abuse, 385, 795
  *Child Sexual Abuse or Exploitation:
    What to Do, 385*
  *Family Law Center—Child Abuse
    and Neglect, 386*
  How to Identify Child Abuse, 386
  *Institute for the Prevention of Child
    Abuse, 386*
  *Mental Health Net: Responding to
    Sexual Child Abuse, 386*
  *National Center for Missing and
    Exploited Children, 387*
  *National Center on Child Abuse and
    Neglect, 387*
  *SAVE: Survivors and Victims
    Empowered, 387*
  Stop It Now, 795
  *Survivor Organizations and
    Agencies, 387*
  *Survivors Network of those Abused
    by Priests, 795*
child care, Children's House Home
  Page, 385
Child Prodigies, 149
Childaware, 291
Children Page, 149
Children's Pages at WombatNet, 149
Children's Stories, Poems and
  Pictures, 149
Childrens Internet Site, Upstate SC,
  149
Classroom Connect, 301
Colgate Kid's World, 149
Cool Lego Site of the Week, 337
CraftBase, 812
custody, 382-384
Cyber-Seuss, 100
Cyberhaunts for Kids, 149
CyberKids Home, 307
Cynthia and Winston's Kids' Page,
  149
  Dr. Seuss, 100

election.html, 301
Encyclopedia of Women's History,
  542
Expect the Best from a Girl, 543
Exploratorium Homepage, 301
Flitter Adventure Land, 150
Free Kids Page, 150
FreeZone, 150
Girl Talk, 150
Global Show-n-Tell Museum Wings,
  150
health care
  Camp Heartland, 799
  *Children's Safety Network Home
    Page, 385*
  KidsHealth.org, 388
  Our Kids, 388
  Parent's Place.Com, 389
Hemp Baby, 371
Hillside Elementary School, 293
Horse Country, 150
I Spy, 150
Info Guide-For Kids Only, 150
Inkspot, 308
Interesting Places for Kids, 150
Internet for Kids, 150
ISN KidNews, 293
Jackson's Page for Five Year Olds,
  151
Jan-Ken-Po—The Trading Card
  Game for Kids of All Ages, 480
Katie's Workshop, 151
Kay's Kid's Collection, 151
KID List, 151
Kidland, 151
kidlinks, 151
Kids Club, 151
Kids Hits, 151
Kids on Campus, 151
Kids on Campus (Cornell Theory
  Center), 561
Kids on the Web, 151
Kids' Space, 308
Kids' Web, 152
Kid's Web, 151
Kids Web A World Wide Web Digital
  Library for Schoolkids, 308
Kid's Window, 151
Kids World 2000, 152
Kid's Zone, 151
KidsCom Home Page, 152
KidsHealth.org, 152
KidsNet, 152
Kids's Place, 152
Kids's WB, 152

KidStuff, 152
KidWeb, 152
Knowledge Adventure, 152
Knox Junior High Homepage, 293
LEGO Group, 152
Link-4-Kids, 152
listservs, 156-158
Lite Board, 339
literature
  Book Nook, 299
  *Children's Literature Web Guide,
    307*
  Cyber-Seuss, 100
  Dr. Seuss, 100
  Moe's Books, 114
  thekids.com, 154
Little Toy Store on the Net, 293
Maddy Mayhem's Kid's Stuff, 152
MATHMOL-K-12 Mathematics and
  Molecules, 293
MayaQuest '96 Home Page, 518
MBG Network, 153
MCA Home Entertainment
  Playroom, 153
movies
  Adventures of Pinocchio, 625
  All Dogs Go To Heaven 2, 625
  Ariel Forever, 625
  Babe, 625
  Beauty and the Beasty Trivia, 625
  Casper Audio/Video Library, 626
  Dark Crystal, 626
  Dove Foundation's Home Page, 626
  Hunchback of Notre Dame, 626
  It Takes Two, 626
  James and the Giant Peach, 626
  Lion King, 626
  *Mighty Morphin Power Rangers
    Megadventure, 626*
  Miracle on 34th Street, 627
  Muppet Movie Links, 627
  Pocahontas, 627
  Toy Story, 627
  *Willy Wonka and the Chocolate
    Factory, 627*
Munchkin Lady, 153
newsgroups, 155
NFL Kids, 153
Nicky's Kid Links, 153
Notable Children's Books, 111
Nucleus Kids' Page, 153
Oasis, Here and There, Kids Corner,
  153
Palos Verdes Kid's Corner, 153
Pasadena Kid's Pages, 153
Patricia's Kids' Links, 153

Index

Pediatric Rheumatology home page, 435

Persimmon Software for Children, 295

Planet Blortland, 153

Platypus Family Playroom, 153

Playroom, 154

psychology
> *Ages & Stages*, 533
> *American Academy of Child & Adolescent Psychology Homepage (AACAP)*, 533
> *ERIC Digests*, 534
> *KidsPeace®, The National Center for Kids in Crisis*, 535

Rachel's Kids Page, 154

Ranger Rick, 374

REACH Summer Science Camp, 154

Reference links, 154

Rock, Paper, Scissors, 340

Route 6-16, 154

Royal Tyrrell Museum Web Site, 523

safety
> *KEYEYE Making Kids Safe Page*, 386
> *KidsPeace: The National Center for Kids in Crisis*, 386
> *OUDPS: Kids Safety on the Internet*, 387

Shogakukan Home Page, 615

Sprague Mat Club, 854

Street Cents Online, 296

Sudden Infant Death Syndrome (SIDS) Information Page, 435

Sugar Bush, 154

SurfWatch Home Page, 560

Terrific Web Sites, 154

Tessa's Cool Links for Kids, 154

thekids.com, 154

Theodore Tugboat, 296

Tic-Tac-Toe, 341

Tirstan and Tiffany's Daily Cool Stuff for Kids, 154

Uncle Bob's Kid's Page, 154

Virtual Mr. Spud Head, 342

Visa Olympics of the Imagination, 154

Web-a-Sketch, 342

WebBattleship, 342

Webcube, 342

Web Kids, 155

Web66: K-12 Schools Registry, 297

Welcome to MegaMath, 297

Welcome to the Adventures of Spacedog, 348

Welcome To the Connect Four Homepage, 342

Whales: A Thematic Web Unit, 297

Willy Wonka Lyrics, 112

World Kids Press Home, 299

World Surfari, 155

World Wide Kids, 'Welcome Aboard!', 155

Xplore Kids, 155

Yahooligans, 155

Youth Central Community, 155

Youth Connection, 155

Youth Quake, 563

children's television

2 Stupid Dogs, 867

Adventures of Pete and Pete, 867

alt.tv.tiny-toon FAQ, 867

Animaniacs, 867

Bananas in Pajamas, 867

Batfink, 867

Batman: The Animated Series, 867

Beakman's World Home Page, 867

Captain Caveman, 868

Captain Planet, 868

Cartoon World, 868

Cartoons of the 80s Home Page, 868

Children's Television Workshop, 868

Clarissa Explains It All, 868

Count Duckula Page, 868

Craig's Comic & Cartoon Page, 868

Danger Mouse, 868

Davey and Goliath, 868

Deron's Muppet Page, 868

Dinosaucers, 868

Dungeons and Dragons, 869

Earthworm Jim, 869

Flintstones Unofficial Home Page, 869

Fraggle Rock, 869

Freakazoid!, 869

Frostbite Falls, 869

G.I. Joe—A Real American Hero, 869

Goosebumps, 869

Gumby on the Web, 869

Jetsons, 869

Keeper's Cartoon Files, 870

Kids.Cool, 870

Mighty Morphin Power Documents, 870

Mister Rogers' Neighborhood, 870

Muppets Home Page, 870

Phil's Faboo Animaniacs Web Page, 870

Pigs in CyberSpaaaaaaaaaace..., 870

Pinky and the Brain, 870

ReBoot Home Page, 870

School House Rock Page, 870

Secret World of Alex Mack Unofficial Home Page, 870

Some of the 100 or Some Odd Smurfs, 870

Superfriends Archive, 870

Sylvester and Tweety Mysteries, 871

Taz-Mania Page, 871

Teen Court TV, 871

That's Warner Bros.!, 871

Thomas the Tank Engine, 871

Thunderbirds, 871

Tick Page, 871

Unofficial Sid and Marty Krofft Home Page, 871

Welcome to Casper's Whipstaff Manor, 871

You Can't Do That On Television, 871

China

Chinese Music Page, 657

Chinese New Year, 707

CRLP: Women of the World, 542

Empires Beyond the Great Wall: The Heritage of Genghis Khan, 460

Home Page of MT&C Music Club, 658

Precious in HIS Sight-Adoption Information on the Internet, 380

Radio HK, 617

RTHK on the Internet Home Page, 617

World Wide Mall:™ Arts, Crafts, & Antiques, 482

china dishware, J.R. Antiques and China Registry, 813

chocolates

Ann Hemyng Candy, Inc.'s Chocolate FACTORY, 399

Candy, 399

ChocolateTown U.S.A., 399

Food Works by Swiss Connection, 399

Godiva Online, 399

Hershey's Collectibles, 480

I Need My Chocolate!, 399

Christianity

Anglican church, Anglicans Online, 725

APOLOGIA—To Offer a Reason, 730

Association of Vineyard Churches, 725

Baker Book House, 727

Baptists
> *American Baptist Churches Mission Center Online*, 725
> *Baptist Faith and Message*, 725

East 7th Street Baptist Ministry-Graffiti, 726

SBC "Maverick" Home Page, 726

Brother Mark's Christian Material, 730

Canada Toronto East Mission, 725

Catholicism, Catholic Online, 726

Christian Articles Archive, 727

Christian Book Connection, 727

Christian Classics Ethereal Library, 708, 727

Christian Computing Magazine, 727

Christian Connections, 730

Christian Cyberspace Companion, 727

Christian Philosophy, 730

Christian Poetry, 727

Christian Recovery Connection, 728

Christian Resource Network, 730

Christian Singles Online, 728

Christian Warehouse, 610

Christian World Adoption, 380

Church of Jesus Christ of Latter Day Saints Canada Toronto East Mission, 725

Computerized AIDS Ministries, 728

Easter in Cyberspace: A Christian Perspective, 707

Ecclesiastical Calendar, 701

Electronic Book of Common Prayer, 727

Family Research Council, 729

GOSHEN Internet Christian Resource Directory, 730

Gospel Films, Inc., 727

Greater Grace World Outreach, 729

Greek Orthodox
   Orthodox Christian Page, 726
   Orthodox Ministry ACCESS, 726

GROKNet-Comedyatre and Resources, 727

Harvest Online, 726

ICMC Home Page, 728

In the Footsteps of the Lord, 730

InterVarsity Christian Fellowship, 729

Jesus Army, 729

Jesus Fellowship Home Page, 729

Jesus Film Project, 728

Koinonia House, 613

Life and Faith Network, 729

Lutheran
   Evangelical Lutheran Church in America Home Page, 726
   Lutheran Church-Missouri Synod Home Page, 726
   Lutheran Marriage Encounter, 729

Minister's Reference Center, 728

Mithraism, 464

Monastery of Christ in the Desert, 729

Musei, 464

music
   "Almost", 650
   Christian Music Online, 650
   Creation 96, 660
   Michael W. Smith, 650
   Susan Ashton, 650

National Association of Evangelicals, 729

National Religious Broadcasters, 728

Not Just Bibles, 730

Pentecostal Church, United Pentecostal Church International, 727

Presbyterian, Presbyterian Church USA, 726

Project Wittenberg, 730

Promise Keepers Unofficial Home Page, 729

Quaker, Religious Society of Friends WWW site, 726

Renewal Ministries: De Colores and Ultreya, 729

research
   Bible Gateway, 723
   ECOLE Institute, 723
   Holy Bible-King James Version, 723
   Logos Research Systems, 723
   New Media Communications, 723
   Our Daily Bread, 723
   RTS's Totally Righteous Home Page for Paul the Apostle, 723
   Scrolls from the Dead Sea, 723
   University of St. Michael's College, Faculty of Theology, 724

Saint Mary's Press, 728

Serious Developments-Christian Software Catalog, 728

Seventh Day Adventist, SDANet, 727

St. Louis Life News, 730

This Week in Bible Prophecy, 728

Tien Dao Christian Media, 728

Tough Guys, 730

Unitarian, Famous Unitarian Universalists, 726

United Church of Christ, United Church of Christ, 727

Web Chapel—Prayer Request, 730

Wire, 728

Christmas

Christmas around the World, 707

Kringle Kottage Collectibles, 480

chromatography, Waters Corporation, 135

cinema, *see* film; movies

civil liberties, Center for Democracy and Technology, 824

civil rights, U.S. Civil Rights Code, 541

Civil War, American Civil War Home Page, 455

CIX (Commercial Internet Exchange), 7

classic movies
   Casablanca, 627
   Citizen Kane, 627
   Gone With the Wind, 627
   Jazz Singer (1927), 627
   Metropolis, 627
   Wizard of Oz, 628

classical archaeology, Classics and Mediterranean Archaeology Home Page, 521

classical music
   Allegro, 650
   American Music Center, 650
   Aspen Music Festival, 650
   BalletWeb, 650
   Boston Chamber Ensemble, 650
   Building a Library: A Collector's Guide, 650
   Cecilia Bartoli FanWeb (Unofficial), 650
   Chamber Music Conferences, 651
   Chicago Concert Search, 651
   Classical MIDI Archives, 651
   Classical Music Home Page, 651
   Classical Music on the Web, 651
   Cleveland Concert Search, 651
   Current Opera Website, 651
   CyberDance: Ballet on the Web, 651
   DCI: Drum Corps International, 651
   Electronic Early Music, 651
   FAQs, rec.music.classical, 651
   FutureNet: Classic CD, 651
   Galliard String Quartet, 652
   Indiana University School of Music, 652
   Indianapolis Symphony Orchestra, 652
   Katia and Marielle Labeque Home Page, 652
   La Ma de Guido, 652
   Le Nozze di Figaro, 652
   Maestronet, 652
   Music Hall, 652
   Music under Soviet Rule, 653
   New York Philharmonic, 653
   Performing Arts Sites, 653

Renaissance Consort, 653

SCA Music and Dance Home Page, 653

T. M. McComb: Music Home Page, 653

Unknown Composers Page, 653

Worldwide Internet Music Resources, 653

clients, 11

clinical psychology, Teaching Clinical Psychology, 537

clockmaking, Clocks and Time, 711

clothing

2(x)ist Underwear, 805

America's Tall Catalog, 805

Bont, Casuals, 805

Bow Brummell: Where Cyberians Learn the Manly Art of Tying a Bow Tie, 711

California Crafts Marketplace, 811

Camalgori, A Representative Collection of Italian Fashion, 805

children, Hemp Baby, 371

Earth Shirts, 370

Eco-Heads, 370

Express Online, 805

Fanco International Corp., 812

Fox Color and Light Home Page, 813

Genius T-Shirts, 805

Good Stuff Cheap, 813

Graphiti, 805

Hot Couture Clothing Company, 805

Lebow Bros. Clothing for Men and Boys, 805

Legalitees T-Shirts Home Page, 593

Main Sequence Astronomical Apparel, 805

Menswear Unlimited, 805

Planet Greek, 805

Rainbow Rags, 805

Rusty Zipper—Vintage Clothing on the Web, 481

Salonwear, 806

SCHWA Online, 815

Soft Wear by ColorTech, 806

Sunglasses, Shavers, and More Homepage, 818

Sunglasses.Com, 818

Tough Traveler Gear, 816

coffee

Cafe MAM, 393

Capulin Coffee, 393

Food Works by Swiss Connection, 399

Mother City Espresso, 394

Neu Coffee, 398

Over the Coffee, 394

Parkleigh World-Wide, 807

The Tin Cup Coffee House, 352

cognitive science

American Psychological Association—PsychNET, 533

Consciousness Research Laboratory, 777

Esoteric Psychology, 760

Frequently Asked Questions about Parapsychology, 760

Haskins Laboratories, 531

Internet Resources for Cognitive Science, 760

Interpsych, 760

MIT Artificial Intelligence Laboratory, 760

Neurosciences on the Internet, 760

North West Artificial Intelligence Applications Group, 760

Psych Central-Dr. John Grohol's Mental Health Page, 760

Scholarly Psychology Resources on the Web, 760

Social Worker Networker, 760

University of Chicago Press Cognitive Science and Linguistics Catalog, 533

cohousing communities, Cohousing Network, 823

coin collecting

American Gold Coins, 486

American Numismatic Association, 486

Ancient and Medieval Coins, 486

Buying Gold Silver Jewelry Coins, 486

Coin Universe, 487

Coins, 487

Collectors COIN UNIVERSE, 479

Department of the Treasury of the United States, 487

E Pluribus Unum, 487

History of Money from Ancient Times to the Present Day, 487

Numismatists Online, 481

Superior Stamp and Coin, 487

collectibles

A–Z Antique & Collectible Directory, 477

About the Lighthouse Depot, 477

American Country Collectibles, 599

Art of the States, 811

Auntie Q's Antiques & Collectibles, 478

BJS Enterprises Collectibles and Crafts Mini Mall, 478

Cape Cod Teddy Bear, 478

Casecrafters, 478

CG Publishing Inc. Home Page, 478

Classifieds–Collectibles–Selling, 478

Collectibles by R&T, 478

Collectibles by R&T Musical Merry-Go-Rounds, 479

Collector Online, 479

Collectors' Index, 479

Cottage Catalogs, 479

East Coast Cards and Collectibles, 479

Facet Collector's Showcase, 812

Global Art Marketing, 479

Hershey's Collectibles, 480

Ilene & Wayne Productions: Collectibles, 480

Incredible Collectibles Home Page, 480

Internet Auction List, 480

Internet Classifieds: 1500–1599 Collectibles Index, 480

Island Imports, Ltd., 480

Jan-Ken-Po—The Trading Card Game for Kids of All Ages, 480

Kaila's Country Collectibles, 480

KBC Antiques and Collectibles Sites List, 480

Kringle Kottage Collectibles, 480

Medals of America, 481

Moments On-Line, 481

Perfect Image Sportscards and Memorabilia, 481

porcelain dolls

Dolls By Christine, 479

Dream-Land Dollies!!!, 479

Portal Disney FANtasEARS- Mouse-Sell-aneous Forum, 481

Railroad Scripophily, 481

Rick's GAMEROOM Collectibles, 481

Roger's Collector's Marketplace, 481

Spider Man Figure Archive, 336

Sports, Collectibles, and Money, 482

teddy bears

Web Mill Business District—Bears By The Sea, 482

Web Mill Business District—Teddy Bear Directory, 482

World Wide Collectors Digest—Your Collectibles Outlet, 482

colleges, *see* **universities**
Colorado
Anasazi Archaeology, 520
CRN-Colorado Resort Net, 857
Vail Valley Home Page, 918
comedians
Planet Wallywood One Liner
Comedy Diner, 345
Rodney Dangerfield Home Page, 346
comedies (movies)
Airplane!, 628
Brazil, 628
Caddyshack Movie Sound Archive,
628
Cher Horowitz's Home Page, 628
Christmas Story, 628
Clerks, 628
Ferris Bueller's Day Off, 628
Four Rooms, 628
Ghostbusters, 628
Goon Docks, 628
Groundhog Day, 628
Jerk, 628
Joe Versus the Volcano, 628
Kids in the Hall Brain Candy, 629
Loser, 629
National Lampoon's Animal House,
629
October Films Presents, Nadja, 629
Princess Bride, 629
Reality Bites, 629
Rosencrantz and Guildenstern Are
Dead, 629
Saxonian Blues Brothers Page, 629
Shaft, 629
Shallow Grave, 629
Smoke, 629
Super Fly, 629
Tank Girl, 630
Three O'Clock High, 630
To Wong Foo, Thanks for Everything!
Julie Newmar, 630
Unofficial Addams Family Movie
Home Page, 630
Whose Line Is It Anyway?, 879
comedies (television)
Beavis and Butthead, 872
Carol Burnett Show Episode Guide,
873
Comedy Store Fan Club Home Page,
874
New Web Site of Love Mystery
Science Theatre 3000, 877
R.M.P.S.S., 878
Saturday Night Archives, 878
TV Nation, 879

comedy
Lawyer Jokes, 593
Legalitees T-Shirts Home Page, 593
Murphy's Law, 593
PDX TheatreSports, 90
see also humor
comic books
3-D Zone, 335
Alternative Comics: A WWW Guide,
335
Atomic Books Literary Finds for
Mutated Minds, 609
BJS Enterprises Collectibles and
Crafts Mini Mall, 478
Comics at Bendigo Books, 113
Comics 'n Stuff, 335
Jonah Weiland's Comic Book
Resources, 336
Marvel Comics, 336
Newbury Comics, Interactive, 815
Planet Millenium, 336
Sirius Entertainment, 336
Spider Man Figure Archive, 336
SPITE! Books, 115
Zanadu Comics, 115
commerce, *see* **business**
Commercial Internet Exchange (CIX), 7
compact discs
Dr. Wax, 479
PolyEster Records and Books, 815
companies
Alps Electric USA, 177
Altera, 177
Amdahl Open Enterprise Systems,
177
American Digital Network, 177
Apache Digital Corporation, 177
Apple Computer Home Page, 177
AST Support Information, 177
AT&T Global Information Solutions
WWW Homepage!, 177
Belhaven Group, 177
Bell Microproducts, Inc., 177
Beyond 2000 Systems, 177
CGI Systems, Inc., 178
Citac Corporation, 178
Client Systems, Inc., 178
Comdisco Inc., 178
CommTech Systems, Inc., 178
Compaq Online, 178
Computer House/ISMAX, 178
CTE Computer Training Center, 178
Cunningham & Cunningham, Inc.,
178
Darwin Micro Systems, 178
Data Exchange Corporation, 178

Data-Doc Electronics, Inc., 178
Database Excelleration Systems, 179
Dataserv Middle East & Africa Ltd,
179
DataWave Technologies, 179
DayStar Digital, 179
DDB Needham Interactive
Communications, 179
Dell Computer, 179
Digital PC, 179
Distinct Corporation, 179
Downtown Digital, 179
DPI, 179
DVC Company, 179
Eltec International, 180
EMD, 180
eSoft, Inc., 180
Explorer Communication, 180
Fujitsu Systems Business of America,
180
Global Computing, Inc., 180
Great Computer, 180
Hewlett Packard, 180
IBM Client/Server Computing, 180
IBM Person to Person Conferencing,
180
Meiko Computers, 180
Micropolis Corporation, 181
Nightware Energy Saving Switch for
Laser Printers, 181
Parsytec Computer GmbH, 181
Perfection Services, Inc., 181
Performance Engineering
Corporation, 181
Persoft Inc., 181
Planet Xerox Products, 181
Point & Click Software, Inc., 181
PRC Inc., 181
Quality HiTec Services, 181
Quantum Research Corporation, 181
Schofield Computer Organization,
181
Sea Change Corporation, 182
SEIKO EPSON, 182
SITE Computer Services, Inc., 182
Speech Systems, Inc., 182
Sprague Magnetics, 182
SRA International, Inc., 182
Storage Computer Corp. Presents,
182
Storage Systems Solutions, 182
Sun Microsystems, 182
Sybex, 182
Sylvest Management Systems, 182
Synapse Communications, Inc., 183

Synergetic Resource Corporation, 183

Systems Solutions, 183

TechWorks, 183

Tecnation Digital World, 183

Texas Micro Home Page, 183

TradeNet International, Inc., 183

Turbosales, 183

Twenty Twenty, 183

Unicomp, Inc., 183

UniPress Worldwide, 183

VA Research, Inc., 184

Validity Corporation, 184

Vive Synergies, Inc., 184

Voice Recognition Systems, 184

Willow Peripherals, 184

Wordlink, Inc., 184

XPRO Systems, 184

compression, 568, 578

CompuServe, Inc, 26, 36

computer games

3D action, 159

3D strategy, 160

adventure, 161

companies, 161

developer sites, 164

flight simulator, 163

hardware, 165

horror, 166

humorous, 167

life simulators, 167

listservs, 173-175

magazines, 167

MUDs (Multiple User Dungeons), 168

newsgroups, 172-173

shareware/freeware, 169

sports-related, 170

war simulations, 170

computer science

Argonne National Laboratory: Mathematics, 184

Brussels Free University (ULB) Computer Science Department, 760

Center for Machine Translation, 530

Computer Oriented Abbreviations and Acronyms, 184

Computer Vision and Image Processing Group, 760

Computing Center, Academy of Sciences, Russia, 761

Cornell Theory Center, 184, 761

Cray Research, 184

CS-100: The History of Computing, 185

Electronic Desktop Project Home Page, 761

Electronic Visualization Lab, 761

European Software Institute (ESI), 761

Historic Computer Images, 185

IEEE Communications Society Technical Committee on Gigabit Networking, 185

Innovation Network, 185

Intelligent Systems Integration Program, 185

Los Alamos Group XTM Home Page, 761

MetaCenter Computational Science Highlights, 185

MIT Artificial Intelligence Laboratory, 185

NASA High Performance Computing and Communications, 185

North Carolina Supercomputing Center Home Page, 185

PARC: Xerox Palo Alto Research Center, 185

Projects in Scientific Computing, 761

San Diego Supercomputer Center, 761

Smithsonian Computer History, 186

Software Tools for Logistics Problem Solving, 186

Spectral Research Technologies, 186

UCSD Optoelectronic Computing Group, 761

Welcome to The Computer Museum, 186

computers

A&H Internet Shopping Service, 810

Alabama Supercomputer Authority, 305

Alps Electric USA, 177

Altera, 177

Amdahl Open Enterprise Systems, 177

American Computer Resources, Inc., 129

American Digital Network, 177

Apache Digital Corporation, 177

Apple Computer Home Page, 177

Apple Higher Education: The Apple Virtual Campus, 291

AST Support Information, 177

AT&T Global Information Solutions WWW Homepage!, 177

Banana Report Easy Visual Basic Tips, 567

Belhaven Group, 177

Bell Microproducts, Inc., 177

Beyond 2000 Systems, 177

Bytewise Consulting, Inc., 130

c|net, the computer network, 559

Canadian Institute of Applied Learning, Inc., 300

Center for the Study of Online Communities, 538

Centre for Social Anthropology and Computing (CSAC) Ethnographics Gallery, 517

CGI Systems, Inc., 178

Citac Corporation, 178

Client Systems, Inc., 178

Comdisco, Inc., 178

CommTech Systems, Inc., 178

Compaq Online, 178

Computer as Learning Partner, 292

Computer House/ISMAX, 178

Computer Related Repetitive Strain Injury, 450

consultants

123 Consulting, 186

Action Call Help Desk Service, 186

AHK & Associates, 186

AIT, 186

Amadeus Consulting, 186

Apple Support, 186

Bennet Products-Computer Sales/Networking/Consulting/Internet, 186

Cambridge Technology Partners, 187

Cascade Consulting, 187

CCI Consulting, 187

Clara Vista Corporation, 187

Commonwealth Data Systems, Inc., 187

Communicopia Environmental Research, 187

CompAdept Corporation, 187

Comport Consulting Corporation, 187

Compusult Limited, 187

Computer Power Group, 187

Computerized Data Management, 188

ComputerPeople/Dci, 188

CooperSoft, 188

CoreLAN Communications, Inc, 188

CP Systems, 188

CSI.NET, Inc., 188

Daedalus Design Group, 188

Dokken Consulting, Inc., 188

Dowdell Business Services, 188

Durango Computer Classroom, 188

Eccosys, Ltd., 188

EPMOD Consultants, Inc., 188

ESDX, 189
FIEN Group, 189
Fly-By-Day Consulting, 189
Folio Corporation, 189
For-to-Win, 189
Full Spectrum Communications, 189
Galaxy Systems Inc., 189
Garbee and Garbee, 189
Genoa Technology, 189
Georg Heeg, 189
GlobalNET, 189
Godin London Incorporated, 190
GroupWise Information, 190
GulfNet Technologies, 190
Guru Technologies, Inc., 190
Halo Network Management, 190
Hartford Computer Group, 190
HD Industries, 190
Hieroglyphics, 190
hot-n-GUI, 190
HTA Link, 190
Ian Freed Consulting, Inc., 190
IC Group, Inc., 190
Inacom Corp., 191
Index, 191
Information Builders, Inc., 191
Ingres Consultant, 191
Integrated Systems Solutions
  Corporation, 191
InterComp Internet, Unix, and
  World Wide Web Services, 191
IPC Technologies, Inc. on the World
  Wide Web, 191
J P Mclaughlin & Associates Inc.,
  191
Jackson-Reed, Inc., 191
Jewell, Chris, 191
JimWare, Inc., 191
JM Consulting and Cheap Advice,
  191
Keystone Technology, 191
Kitchen Wisdom Publishing, 192
Kratzer Computer Consultants, 192
Lavallée & Associates, 192
Lodestone Research, L.L.C., 192
MacMedic, 192
MBS Industries, Inc., 192
MC2 Cyberspace Research, 192
MediaGlobe, 192
MetaCase Consulting, 192
Mike Salitter Consultant Services,
  192
Millennium Solution, 192
Minerva Technology, 192

MultiMedia Enterprises, 192
MVS Training, Inc., 193
Mystech Enterprises, 193
Netplan ApS. Consultants in
  Telecommunications, 193
Pangea Visions, 193
Phoenix Systems Internet
  Publishing, 193
PLATINUM Solutions, 193
PRC Inc. Home Page, 193
ProSoft Consulting, 193
Relational Information Systems, Inc.,
  193
SAIC Los Altos Home Page, 193
Software Dynamics Consulting, 193
Specs™ Manufacturing Instruc-
  tions, 194
Spire Technologies, 194
Sterling Information Group, 194
STS, 194
Technology Futures, Inc., 194
TeKnowlogy Education Centers, 194
Telecommunications Technology
  Corp., 194
Whole Shebang, 194
Winsor Computing, 194
Word Master, Inc., 194
Xephon, 194
CTE Computer Training Center, 178
CTN, 881
Cunningham & Cunningham, Inc.,
  178
Cyberian Outpost, 808
CyberLaw™ World Wide, 585
Darwin Micro Systems, 178
Data Exchange Corporation, 178
Data-Doc Electronics, Inc., 178
Database Excelleration Systems, 179
Dataserv Middle East & Africa Ltd.,
  179
DataWave Technologies, 179
DayStar Digital, 179
DDB Needham Interactive
  Communications, 179
Dell Computer, 179
desktop publishing, 194
Digital PC, 179
Distinct Corporation, 179
Downtown Digital, 179
DPI, 179
DVC Company, 179
E-Law 3.0, 585
EDUCOM-Homepage, 292
Eltec International, 180
EMD, 180

eSoft, Inc., 180
Explorer Communication, 180
Free On-Line Dictionary of
  Computing, 703
Fujitsu Systems Business of America
  Home Page, 180
Global Computing, Inc., 180
Great Computer, 180
Hacker's Jargon, 703
hardware, see hardware
Hayden Books, 611
Health and Computers, 450
Hewlett Packard, 180
IBM Client/Server Computing, 180
IBM Person to Person Conferencing,
  180
ICDL, 293
IDG Books, 612
Information SuperLibrary, 612
JDS Technologies, 506
Kids on Campus (Cornell Theory
  Center), 561
Kids' Space, 308
KidsNet, 152
Kids' Web, 152
languages
  Amzi! Prolog + Logic Server, 207
  Benaroya, 207
  C Programming v.2.6, 207
  C++ Virtual Library, 208
  CONSULTIX, the UNIX Training
    Experts, 207
  Free Compilers and Interpreters, 207
  hav.Software, 207
  Hyperparallel Technologies, 207
  Index of /1/perlinfo/scripts/, 207
  LEARN C/C ++ TODAY (A list of
    resources/tutorials), 207
  Management Information Technolo-
    gies, Inc., 208
  OC Systems AdaMania Page, 208
  Rigal language home page, 208
  Software Translation Tools, 208
  Tutorials, 208
  Unofficial FutureBASIC Web Page,
    208
  Welcome to the WWW Home of
    COBOL, 208
Linux, 647
listservs, 281-290
MacNet Journal, 602
Macworld Online Web Server, 602
magazines
  BYTE Magazine, 208
  Communications Week Interactive,
    208

Computer Shopper Online, 208
Computer Sun Times, 208
HotWired, 209
Ice-9 Publications, 209
List of Free Computer-related
    Publications, 209
MacUser/MacWeek Special on
    Apple's Future, 209
PC-TRANS, 209
PurePower, 209
Scientific Computing and
    Automation Magazine, 209
Virtual Computer Library Journals,
    209
ZDNet, 209
McDonnell Information Systems, 132
Meiko Computers, 180
Micropolis Corporation, 181
Mining the Internet Columns, 310
mobile
    Adaptec AIRport Family, 209
    Apex PCMCIA Modems, 209
    BarCode1-A Web of Information
        about Bar Code, 209
    Cellular Works, 209
    Columbia University Mobile
        Computing Laboratory, 210
    DataLink by Timex, 210
    Introduction to ARDIS, 210
    It's a Wireless World, 210
    Mobile and Wireless Computing, 210
    Mobile Office Magazine, 210
    Mobile Planet, 210
    MobileWare Corporation, 210
    NDS Distributing, 210
    Psion Incorporated, 210
    Road Warrior Outpost, 210
    Special Topics in Engineering, 210
    World of Newton, 211
multimedia
    Atomic Vision Inc., 211
    Auricle Control Systems, 211
    Avalanche Systems, Inc., 211
    AVM Summit, 211
    CA Natalie Associates, 211
    CD Warehouse, 211
    CD Works, 211
    CD-ROM Online, 211
    Chick Enterprises Ltd., 212
    Cinax Designs Inc., 212
    Constant Synthesis Project, 212
    Crystal River Engineering, 212
    Darim Vision Co., 212
    DayStar Digital, Inc., 212
    Demo and Tutorial Builders, 212

Digital Creators, 212
Digital Movie News, 212
Due North, 213
EDGE Interactive Media, Inc., 213
Edit & Copy Communications, 213
EMA Multimedia, Inc., 213
Entertainment Through Technology
    Consortium, 213
HJF Digital Media, 213
IBM 3D Interaction Accelerator, 213
IDM, 213
Incite, 213
Jack, 213
Loviel Computer Corporation, 213
Magnum Resources, 214
Media Solutions International, 214
Metatec Corporation, 214
MidiMan's Official Web Site, 214
Mimesis Technology, 214
Multimedia Archives, 214
Murray MultiMedia, 214
Music Screeners, 214
Net-One System's Personalized CDs,
    214
North Communications, 214
NuReality, 214
Pangea Creative Media, 214
Photodex Corporation, 215
Pinnacle Post, 215
QuickMedia, 215
QuickMedia-Living Album, 215
Ramworks, 215
Scala Computer Television AS
    (Norway), 215
Sealworks, Inc., 215
SimPhonics, Inc., 215
Software Tools for Artists, 215
Sound & Vision Media, 215
Sprite Interactive, 215
StarMan Group, Multimedia
    Productions, 216
Station Graphics, Inc., 216
ThreeToad Multimedia, 216
Two Guys Named Hank, 216
Virtual Artists, 216
Visionary Designs, 216
vivid studios, 216
Welcome to macromedia.com, 216
Worlds Inc., 216
X Communications Multimedia, 216
Xpand, Inc., 217
XSI MeDIA, 217
Zfx, Inc., 217
National Computer Security
Association, 395, 695

Natural Language Computing Home
    Page, 532
Network Nuggets, 294
networking, see networking
New Riders, 613
News-Planet Xerox Products, 181
newsgroups, 270-281
Nightware Energy Saving Switch
    for Laser Printers, 181
online services, 228
operating systems, 235
O'Reilly Home Page, 613
Parsytec Computer GmbH, 181
PCs, 236
Perfection Services, Inc., 181
Performance Engineering
    Corporation, 181
Persoft, 181
Point & Click Software, Inc., 181
PowerPC News, 604
PRC, 181
Quality HiTec Services, 181
Quantum Research Corporation, 181
Que's Home Page, 614
sales
    BreakThrough Technologies, 222
    Campus Network Solutions, 222
    CJC Graphic Design, Inc., 222
    Computer Direct, 222
    Computer Express, 222
    Computer Literacy Bookshops, Inc.,
        222
    Computer Marketplace, Inc., 223
    Computer Price Cruncher, 223
    Computer Recycler, 223
    Computer Warehouse, 223
    Comstar, 223
    Continental Resources, 223
    Cyberian Outpost, 223
    CyberStar, 223
    DAKCO PC Products Division, Inc.,
        223
    Datalink Direct, 223
    Datamini Systems, 223
    Digital Dimensions, 223
    Direct Connections, 223
    Egghead Software, 224
    EMJ Data Systems Limited, 224
    Essential Data, Inc., 224
    EZ Systems, 224
    F. F. Tronixs, 224
    Global Union Square Internet
        Shopping Mall, 224
    Grey-Tech Computer, Inc., 224
    Hamilton Rentals Place, 224

HNR Computers, 224
Icon Technologies, Inc., 225
IPC Technologies, Inc., 225
L & H Computers, 225
Laser Express, 225
Laser Products and Services Group, 225
Laser Renewal, 225
LinkStor, 225
LMB Microcomputers, 225
Logic Approach, 225
Lotus Selects Catalog, 225
Mac Talk, Inc's WWW Page, 225
MacZone Internet Superstore, 225
Mantissa Computer Systems, 225
Micro-Rent Corporation, 226
Micro/Station at UIC, 226
Microtrader, 226
MicroWarehouse, Inc., 226
National Parts Depot, 226
NCA Computer Products, 226
Networks Plus Computers, 226
New England Computer Supply, 226
New Technology Computers, 226
New Wave Computers, 226
Newman Group Computer Services, 226
North American Digital, 227
PC Heidens, 227
Phoenix Software Solutions, Inc., 227
Powercom and One Com, 227
Printer Works, 227
Q Group, 227
S.P.C. Microcomputer, 227
SBI Computer Distribution, 227
SNC International, 227
Spectrum Trading, 227
Sunshine Computers, 228
Team America, 228
TENET Computer Group, Inc., 228
Total Systems, Inc. (TSI) Home Page, 228
United Computer Exchange Corp. (UCE), 228
Used Computers, Etc, 228
Welcome to the Computer Shop, 228
Z-Law Software, Inc., 228
SAMS Home Page, 615
Schofield Computer Organization, 181
Sea Change Corporation, 182
security, 238
SEIKO EPSON, 182
Seven Technologies, 134

Shopping Planet, 809
Simple Solutions, 143
SITE Computer Services Inc., 182
Society for Computers in Psychology, 537
Software, 678, 825
software, *see* software
Speech Systems, Inc., 182
Sprague Magnetics, 182
SRA International, Inc., 182
STING software engineering glossary, 703
Storage Computer Corp. Presents, 182
Storage Systems Solutions, 182
Sun Microsystems, 182
Sybex, 182
Sylvest Management Systems, 182
Synapse Communications, Inc., 183
Synergetic Resource Corporation, 183
Systems Solutions, 183
TechWorks, 183
Tecnation Digital World, 183
telecommunications, 265-268
Texas Micro Home Page, 183
Timothy W. Amey Resource Links, 572
TradeNet International, Inc., 183
Turbosales, 183
Twenty Twenty, 183
UCREL—University Centre for Computer Corpus Research on Language, 533
Unicomp, Inc., 183
UniPress Worldwide, 183
UNIX News International, 604
Unix Versions, 830
USENET Etiquette, 705
user groups
Autodesk North American User Groups, 268
Computing in the Humanities Users Group (CHUG), 524
GUIDE International-An IBM User Group, 268
Hull Community Artworks, 268
IEEE Computer Society-Purdue Student Chapter, 268
InfoWest Windows 95 Software Archive, 268
International Computer Association Home Page, 268
Newsletters on the Web, 268
Ottawa Microsoft Users Group (TOMUG), 269
Portland PC Users Group, 269

SGI User Groups, 269
Sun User Group Java SIG, 269
Tampa Bay Linux GNU Technical Society, 269
Victoria Macintosh Users Group, 269
VA Research, Inc., 184
Validity Corporation, 184
Vive Synergies, Inc., 184
Voice Recognition Systems, 184
Welcome to Computer Shopper, 605
Welcome to ZD Net, 605
Willow Peripherals, 184
Wordlink, Inc., 184
XPRO Systems, 184
concert tickets, Ace Ticket Service—Concert Tickets, 654
concertinas
Accumulated Accordian Annotations, 661
CONCERTINA!, 662
concerts, *see* festivals
conditions
Arthritis-Doctor's Guide to the Internet, 433
Bad Breath Research, 433
Eye Diseases and Conditions, 433
Gastroenterology Consultants, 434
HYPHECAN Fingertip Cap, 434
Condoms Express/Condom Club International, 798
conferences
Internet Conference Calendar, 558
World Wide Web Consortium, 558
configuration, Windows 95, Internet, 38-40
Connecticut, Clickable Connecticut Area Map, 916
connecting to the Internet, 10-11
conservation
Alaska Safari Club Home Page, 361
Arbor Day, 361
Arctic National Wildlife Refuge, 368
Australian Environment Online, 368
The Butterfly Website: Conservation and Ecology, 362
Chrysler Corporation—Recycling & Conservation, 361
Conservation International, 362
Conservation OnLine, 110
The Coral Reef Alliance, 362
Department of the Navy Environmental Programs, 361
The Dying Sea, 372
GREENGUIDE—How to Trim Your Office Waste, 366

Index

Headwaters Forest, 369

International Center for Tropical Ecology, 365

International Palm Society, 362

Jade Mountain, 371

John Muir Exhibit, 363

League of Conservation Voters, 363

Maine Solar House, 363

Marine Fish Conservation Network, 363

Mr. Solar Home Page, 363

National Audobon Society, 363

Real Goods, 371

Sempervirens Fund, 363

Surfrider Foundation USA, 363

USDA—Natural Resources Conservation Service, 363

The Video Project, 372

Welcome to Sherwood, 369

see also ecology; environment

conspiracies, Conspiracy Pages, 694

construction

BUILD.COM: The Building and Home Improvement Products Network, 487

Builders Graphics, 510

Construction Zone, 506

Cyberwood Express, 506

DO IT YOURSELF HQ, 508

Dulux Paint Assistant, 507

Home Ideas, 510

Home Improvement, 508

HOME IMPROVEMENT and CONSTRUCTION CONNECTION, 507

Home Improvement How-to Videos, 508

Home Improvement Net, 507

Home Line Talk Radio, 510

Home Repair Hotline, 510

HomeSource, 507

Hometime, 508

Jonathan Press Woodworking and Home Improvement Books and Plans, 507

Lamb Home Videos U-DO IT YOURSELF, 508

Levien-Rich Associates, Inc., 137

Lowe's Home Improvement Warehouse, 510

Materials Engineering and Research Laboratory, 508

National Consumer Alert Hotline, 510

New Home Interactive Cyber Home Building Site, 507

On The House with The Carey Brothers, 510

Open Building Architecture For Residential Construction, 505

Pete's Dry Dock, 507

Quality Woodwork and Supply, Inc., 499

Remodeler Online, 507

Sound Home Resource Web Home Page, 507

This Old House, 511

United Consumers Club, 511

Voyager Plus Home Improvement Specialists, 511

Walls and Ceilings Magazine, 605

consultants (computers)

123 Consulting, 186

ActionCall Help Desk Service, 186

AHK & Associates, 186

AIT, 186

Amadeus Consulting, 186

Apple Support, 186

Bennett Products, 186

Cambridge Technology Partners, 187

Cascade Consulting, 187

CCI Consulting, 187

Clara Vista Corporation, 187

Commonwealth Data Systems, Inc., 187

Communicopia Environmental Research, 187

CompAdept Corporation, 187

Comport Consulting Corporation, 187

Compusult Limited, 187

Computer Power Group, 187

Computerized Data Management, 188

ComputerPeople/Dci, 188

CooperSoft, 188

CoreLAN Communications, Inc, 188

CP Systems, 188

CSI.NET, Inc., 188

Daedalus Design Group, 188

Dokken Consulting Inc., 188

Dowdell Business Services, 188

Durango Computer Classroom, 188

Eccosys, Ltd., 188

EPMOD Consultants, Inc., 188

ESDX, 189

FIEN Group, 189

Fly-By-Day Consulting, 189

Folio Corporation, 189

For-to-Win, 189

Full Spectrum Communications, 189

Galaxy Systems Inc., 189

Garbee and Garbee, 189

Genoa Technology, 189

Georg Heeg, 189

GlobalNET, 189

Godin London Incorporated, 190

GroupWise Information, 190

GulfNet Technologies, 190

Guru Technologies, Inc., 190

Halo Network Management, 190

Hartford Computer Group, 190

HD Industries, 190

Hieroglyphics, 190

hot-n-GUI, 190

HTA Link, 190

Ian Freed Consulting, Inc., 190

IC Group, Inc., 190

Inacom Corp., 191

Index, 191

Information Builders, Inc, 191

Ingres Consultant, 191

Integrated Systems Solutions Corporation, 191

InterComp Internet, Unix, and World Wide Web Services, 191

IPC Technologies, Inc., 191

J P Mclaughlin & Associates Inc., 191

Jackson-Reed, Inc., 191

Jewell, Chris, 191

JimWare Inc., 191

JM Consulting and Cheap Advice, 191

KAB Konsult AB, 132

Keystone Technology, 191

Kitchen Wisdom Publishing, 192

Kratzer Computer Consultants, 192

Lavallée & Associates, 192

Lodestone Research, L.L.C., 192

MacMedic, 192

MBS Industries, Inc., 192

MC2 Cyberspace Research, 192

MediaGlobe, 192

MetaCase Consulting, 192

Mike Salitter Consultant Services, 192

Millennium Solution, 192

Minerva Technology, 192

MultiMedia Enterprises, 192

MVS Training, Inc., 193

Mystech Enterprises, 193

Netplan ApS. Consultants, 193

Pangea Visions, 193

Phoenix Systems Internet Publishing, 193

PLATINUM Solutions, 193

PRC Inc. Home Page, 193

ProSoft Consulting, 193

Relational Information Systems, Inc., 193

SAIC Los Altos Home Page, 193

Software Dynamics Consulting, 193

Specs™ Manufacturing Instructions, 194

Spire Technologies, 194

Sterling Information Group, 194

STS, 194

Technology Futures, Inc., 194

TeKnowlgy Education Centers, 194

Telecommunications Technology Corp., 194

Whole Shebang, 194

Winsor Computing, 194

Word Master, Inc., 194

Xephon, 194

Consultative Committee for International Telephony and Telegraphy (CCITT), 32

consumer information

AutoPlus, 893

Better Business Bureau, 590, 711

Car and Driver Buyer's Guide 1996, 893

Car Tips, 893

CARveat Emptor, 893

Central Notice, 711

ClearStar Security Network, 122

Consumer Fraud Alert Network, 122

Consumer Information Center, 711

Consumer Law Page, 122

Criminal Enforcement Bulletin, 122

DataStar Information Retrieval Service, 711

Diamond Resources, 122

Edmund's Automobiles Buying Guides, 893

Get Organized, 122

Gray Ghost: The Links You Use Everyday, 712

Internet CarGuide, 893

National Consumer Alert Hotline, 510

New Car Comparison Guide, 893

Street Cents Online, 296

Tallweb—Cars, 894

Used Car Buying Guide, 894

contests

MBNA College Quartet Contest, 660

Thread Treader's WWW Contests Guide, 565

cooking, *see* **food; recipes**

cooperative living

Fellowship for Intentional Community, 823

Intentional Family Connection, 823

Vision of Sanctuary, 823

copyrights, 576

coronary heart diseases, *see* **cardiovascular diseases**

corporations

3M Innovation Network, 122

AT&T Home Page, 122

Commercial Services on the Net, 568

computer games, 161

FedEx Home Page, 122

GE Home Page, 123

Goodyear Tire and Rubber Company, 123

JCPenney Home Page, 123

McDonnell Douglas Aerospace, 123

MCI Home Page, 123

Planet Reebok, 853

Shell Oil Company, 123

SONY Online, 123

Tandy Corporation, 123

UPS Home Page, 123

Walgreen Co., 123

cosmetology

Certified European Image Consultant, 808

Maui Amenities, 808

Nature's Wealth, 808

Official Wicked Hair-Dyeing Page, 712

Salonwear, 806

costume design, History of Costume by Braun, 463

country music

Basket Full of Country, 654

History of Country Music, 654

Mary Chapin Carpenter, 661

Obvious Gossip Home Page, 654

planet garth, 655

Reba McENTIRE, 655

coupons, CouponNet, 812

CPU (central processing units), 33

crackers, 22

crafts

listservs, 503-504

newsgroups, 501-503

creationism

Center for Scientific Creation, 731

Creation Science Home Page, 731

Creationism Connection, 731

Evolution vs. Creation Science, 731

Talk.Origins Archive, 731

credit card transactions, 15

credit reporting services, Service Bureau, LLC, 134

crime

Crime Prevention Initiatives, 825

Crime-Free America, 825

Drug Use is Life Abuse/Project: No Gangs, 828

Emergency Net, 825

Fugitive Watch, 825

Images of Children, Crime, and Violence, 795

just, 828

Justice Net, 825

National Victim Center, 825

Parents of Murdered Children, 826

Poster, 919, 926

Prison Legal News, 826

Rape Victim Advocates, 826

Rate Your Risk, 826

Serial Killers, 826

Shattered Love Broken Lives, 826

United Nations Crime and Justice Information Network, 826

United States Department of Justice, 826

criminal law

Cecil Greek's Criminal Justice Page, 585

COPNet & Police Resource List, 585

Criminal Law Links, 585

Guide to Internet Resources in Criminal Law and Criminal Justice, 585

Justice Information Center (NCJRS), 585

Partnerships Against Violence Network (PAVNET), 585

Scott Carpenter's TOP Page, 585

U.S. Criminal Law, 585

croquet, 854

cross stitch, Counted Cross Stitch, Needlework, and Stitchery Page, 498

cross-cultural psychology, International Association for Cross-Cultural Psychology (IACCP), 535

cross-platform support, 44

cruises

Accent's Cruise Connection, 905

Adventure Cruising in the North Atlantic, 905

Cruise Review Library, 905

Cruise Shoppes America, Ltd., 905

Cruises, Inc., 905

Freighter World Cruises, 905
Norwegian Cruise Line, 905
Royal Caribbean Cruise Line, 906
Travel Discounts Cruise Index, 906
crystals, Crystals and Minerals, 497
Cuba, Cuban Music, 657
cult movies
Bloodlust, 631
Buckaroo Banzai Jump-Station, 631
Clockwork Orange, 632
Cult Shop, 632
Dr. Strangelove Or: How I Learned to Stop Worrying, 632
Heathers, 632
Mystery Science Theater 3000 The Movie, 632
Ray Wolfe's Online Guide to Eraserhead, 632
Rocky Horror Picture Show, 632
Spinal Tap, 632
Unofficial Monty Python Home Page, 632
cults
.ex-cult Archive, 731
A-Z of Cults, 731
AFF Cultic Studies, 731
Cults, 731
Cults 'R Us, 731
Destructive Cults, 731
Jehovah's Christian Witnesses, 732
Jehovah's Witnesses, 732
Loki Cult Web Page, 732
Ms. Guidance on Strange Cults, 732
Sacrespace, 732
Waco Never Again, 732
culture
listservs, 836-837
newsgroups, 831-836
seventies, Oeno Phile's Mood Detector, 340
Web culture
Cruel Site of the Day, 343
The Daily Double Awards, 343
Internet Advertising Hall of Shame, 344
Mirky's Worst of the Web, 345
Top Ten Ways to Tell if You Have a Sucky Home Page, 346
currency, History of Money from Ancient Times to the Present Day, 487
customizing browsers, 46
cyber law
CyberLaw™ World Wide, 585
CyberSpace Law Center, 585
E-Law 3.0, 585
ICLU—Your Rights in Cyberspace, 586
Information Highway Advisory Counsel (IHAC) of Canada, 586
Information Law Web, 586
Internet, the Law, and Related Topics, 586
Netwatchers Cyberzine, 586
OwlLex Law Links—The CyberSpace Law Links, 586
cycling
Cyber Cyclist, 600
Cyber Cyclery, 843
CycLinks, 843
Emory Bicycle Manufacturing Company, 843
Fat Tire Wire, 843
MuDsLuTs, 843
Spring City Cycles, 843
VeloNet, 843
Velonews, 843
VeloZine, 843
WOMBATS on the Web, 843
WWW Bicycle Lane, 843
Czech Republic
Radio Prague, 617
Virtual Business Plaza, 126

D

daemons, 17
Dali, Salvador, 84
dance
Alaskan Dance Theater, 89
Arthur Hall and Black Dance in America, 89
As-Sayf Oriental Dance Home Page, 89
AXIS Dance Troupe, 89
BalletWeb, 650
CyberDance, 651
Dancescape, 89
Danclink, 74
Henry's Dance Hotlist, 90
International Folk Dancers of Ottawa Home Page, 90
Internet Dance Resources, 90
Marjan, 90
Ohio State University, Department of Dance Home Page, 90
PDX TheatreSports, 90
Performing Arts Sites, 653
Renaissance: SCA Music and Dance Home Page, 653
Talk about Dance, 90
Tango Dance Notation Argentina Artentine, 90
database management system (DBMS), 573
databases, *see* **archives; searchers**
dating services
Christian Single Online, 795
Christian Singles, 795
Jewish Singles Connection, 795
Match.Com-"We met on the net," 795
Ulti-Mate Dating Service, 795
Webpersonals.com, 795
death
Internet Cremation Society, 429
Natural Death Centre, 430
Sociology of Death and Dying, 430
Summum Mummification, 430
Delphi (online service), 26
demographic research
Geographic Nameserver, 527
Population Index, 540
Population Reference Bureau (PRB), 540
Population Studies Center—University of Michigan, 540
United Nations Population Information Network (POPIN), 541
United Nations Scholars' Workstation at Yale University, 541
World Population, 714
World Population Figures, 714
Worldwide Demography Resources, 541
dentistry
Dental Ethics, 430
Dental Information Home Page, 430
Dental Implant Home Page, 430
Dental Related Internet Resources, 430
DENTal TRAUMA Server, 430
Frequently Asked Questions, 430
Mercury Page, 430
Oral Health Country Profiles, 430
Scholarly Opportunities in Dentistry, 430
So, You Want to be a Dentist?, 430
depression, Depression FAQ, 534
Derr, Robert, 82
design
African-American, OBD-Organization of Black Designers, 78
graphic, Architecture & Design, 505
interior
Architecture & Design, 505

Art for Architecture, 505

HBA Architecture and Interior Design, 505

International Architecture and Design Home Page, 505

MBT Architecture, 505

V.C.net, 505

desktop publishing

Adobe PageMaker, 194

DTP Internet Jumplist, 195

ECS: Custom Personalized, 195

First Guide to Postscript, 195

Free Software from Adobe, 195

Freedom System Integrators, Inc., 195

i am Iomega, 195

Imagine Adobe, 195

INFOSEARCH PrintNet, 195

MacroMedia Fontgrapher, 195

New World Graphics and Publishing, 195

Newspaper Production Using PageMaker 5, 195

Quark, Inc., 196

Serif, Inc., 196

Simple Solutions, 143

So Cal Graphics, 196

Software Net Product Menu, 615

Tomato Foundry Technical Writing and Design, 196

Typofile Magazine—Home, 604

What's New at Quark, Inc.'s Web Site, 196

Xpresso Bar, 196

Di Leo, Belinda, 83

dictionaries

A.Word.A.Day, 705

AGI GIS Dictionary, 526

Climbing Dictionary, 702

Dictionary of Cell Biology, 703

Free On-Line Dictionary of Computing, 703

Glossary of Internet Terms, 560

Hacker's Jargon, 703

Hypertext Webster Interface, 703

Jumble & Crossword Solver, 712

Morse Code and the Phonetic Alphabets, 712

Morse Code Translator, 712

MRX - Morse Receive and Transmit Training, 712

On-Line Reference Works, 713

Research-It!, 713

STING software engineering glossary, 703

THOR+: The Virtual Reference Desk, 713

Word Manager, 533

Word Page, 705

WordNet, 705

World Wide Web Acronym and Abbreviation Server, 703

dieting

AromaTrim Weight Loss System, 430

Body/Mind Restoration Retreats 1996, 430

CyberDiet, 431

Fat Person's Home Page, 431

FITE-Fat is the Enemy, 431

Hacker's Diet, 431

Health Vision, 431

International No Diet Day, 431

Magic of Believing, 431

Medical Sciences Bulletin, 431

Michael D. Myers MD, Inc./Myers Information Service, 431

Modern Methods-Fat Burning Specialists, 431

Nutri/System Online, 431

NutriGenie, 438

TOPS-Take Off Pounds Sensibly, 431

Weight Watchers, 431

digeridoo

Digeridoo Page, 662

DREAMTIME, The Didjeridu W3 Server, 662

digital libraries, *see* **libraries**

dinosaurs

Columbus Rock and Mineral Society, 781

Dino Russ's Lair, 521

Dino Russ's Laur, 781

Dinosaur Provincial Park, 521

Dinosauria On-Line, 781

Exposure Excursions, 782

Field Museum Online, 522

Gulf of St. Lawrence Microfossil Catalogue, 782

Museum of Paleontology, 782

Perspective Visuals, Inc., 815

Raymond M. Alf Museum, 782

Royal Tyrrell Museum Web Site, 523

U.C. Berkeley Museum of Paleontology, 524, 782

University of California Museum of Paleontology, 782

directories, The Bottom 95% of the WWW, 343

disabilities

Ability OnLine Support Network, 432

Access Ability Travel, 432

Archimedes Project, 432

Blind Childrens Center, Inc. Home Page, 432

Cornucopia of Disability Information Gopher Server, 824

Deaf World Web, 432

Disability Net, 432

Mankato State University Department of Communication Disorders, 432

National Sports Center for the Disabled, 432

Rusty Chambers Insurance Agent— Life, DI, Disability, Health, 442

Sibling Support Project, 432

diseases

AIDS Bytes, 432

AIDS Information for Young People, 432

American Diabetes Association, 433

American Heart Association National Center, 433

American Lyme Disease Foundation, 433

Breast Cancer Information, 433

Caring for People With Huntington's Disease, 433

CDC National AIDS Clearinghouse, 433

Down Syndrome WWW Page, 434

Endometriosis, 433

Eye Diseases and Conditions, 433

Herpes: The Hidden Disease, 434

Introduction to Skin Cancer, 434

Kaiser Family Foundation, 434

Malaria Weekly, 434

Merck Manual, 434

Muscular Dystrophy Association, 434

National Osteoporosis Foundation, 435

Scoliosis, 435

Skin (Diseases) Page, 435

Sudden Infant Death Syndrome (SIDS) Information Page, 435

World of Multiple Sclerosis, 435

Disney, collectibles, Portal Disney FANtasEARS- Mouse-Sell-aneous Forum, 481

display cases, *see* **collectibles**

divorce

10 Questions About Child Custody, 382

C.H.I.L.D.: Children Hurt in Legal Decisions, 382

CCADE Web, 382

Child Custody in the USA, 382

Index

Child Custody: Building Agreements that Work, 382

Child Support Home Page, 382

Children's Rights Counsel Home Page, 382

CourtTV Divorce, 382

Custody and Access, 382

Divorce, 382

Divorce Care Home Page, 382

Divorce Helpline Home Page, 383, 587

Divorce Helpline: The legal divorce vs. the real divorce, 383

Divorce Law Home Page, 383, 587

Divorce Online, 383

Divorce Page, 587

Divorce Page: Child Support and Custody, 383

Divorce Page: Parenting and Children, 383

Divorce Roadmap: Help Around the Legal System, 383

Family Law Advisor Home Page, 383, 588

Family Law Advisor Message Board, 383

Family Law Links, 383

Fathers' Rights and Equality Exchange, 588

Kids' Turn, 383

Law Offices of Keith M. Carter: Child Custody and Visitation, 384

Legal dot Net, 384

Legal dot Net—Family Law, and Overview, 588

Nolo's Fast Facts: Custody and Visitation, 384

DNA, *see* **biology**

DNS (Domain Name System), 10

Document Type Definition (DTD), 14

dogs

Akbash Dog Home Page, 59

Bernese Mountain Dog Home Page, 59

Border Collies, 59

Borzoi Info Online, 59

Canine Activity Calendar, 59

Canine Vaccination Schedule, 59

Caucasian Ovcharka Info, 59

Choosing a Dog Breed, 60

Dog Breeding, 60

Dog Play, 60

Dog Term Glossary, 60

Greyhound Starting Gate, 60

ImageMaker Gifts for Dog Lovers, 85

Pomeranian Dog Home Page, 60

Portuguese Water Dog Index, 60

Pug Dog Home Page, 60

Rhodesian Ridgebacks, 60

Rottweiler Home Page, 60

Schipperke Page, 60

Tibetan Mastiff Home Page, 61

Visual Rhodesian Ridgeback, 61

Westies Home Page, 61

dolls

Cottage Catalogs, 479

Dolls By Christine, 479

Dream-Land Dollies!!!, 479

Kaila's Country Collectibles, 480

Salon Betty's Interactive Paper Doll, 341

World Wide Mall ™ Collectibles, Dolls, & More, 482

dolphins

Dolphin Alliance, 61

Dolphin Information Server–Home Page, 61

Dolphin Page, 61

Sea Creations, 482

Wild Dolphin Project, 61

domain addresses, 23

Domain Name System (DNS), 10

domain names, 10

domestic violence

Domestic Violence Page, 386

Kathy's Resources on Parenting, Domestic Violence, Abuse, Trauma, and Disassociation, 386

Minnesota Higher Education Center Against Violence & Abuse, 386

Shattered Love Broken Lives, 826

U.S. Recovery, Addiction, and Abuse Resources, 427

double reed instruments, IDRS WWW, 662

downloading Web sites, 50

dramas (television)

Chicago Hope Home Page, 879

Dangerous Minds, 879

Dead At 21, 879

Dr. Quinn, Medicine Woman Official Web Site, 879

ER, 880

Little House on the Prairie Unofficial Home Page, 880

Moose's Guide to Northern Exposure, 880

My So-Called Life, 880

NYPD Blue Home Page, 880

Party of Five, 880

Perry Mason Pages, 880

Real World, 880

thirtysomething Episode Guide, 880

Twin Peaks Lodge, 880

Unofficial Picket Fences Home Page, 881

dramatic movies

Barton Fink, 632

Basketball Diaries, 632

Crow, 633

Dead Man Walking, 633

Forrest Gump, 633

Godfather Trilogy, 633

Goodfellas, 633

Hackers, 633

Heat, 633

Hoop Dreams, 634

Il Postino (The Postman), 633

Jane Eyre, 633

Leaving Las Vegas, 633

Martin Scorsese, 634

Mean Streets, 634

Othello, 634

Photographic Gallery of the Film Trilogy, 634

Powder, 634

Pulp Fiction Apothecarys Page, 634

Quiz Show, 634

Reservoir Dogs, 634

Scarface, 634

Showgirls, 634

Taxi Driver Page, 634

True Romance, 634

draperies, *see* **interior decorating**

dreams

Altered States of Consciousness, 533

DreamLink, 305, 534

drinking games, Chris' Collection of Drinking Misc., 337

drinks

listservs, 411-412

newsgroups, 409-410

drug abuse

Cenikor Foundation, Inc., 427

Drinkwise, 427

Habit Smart, 427

Prevline: Prevention Online, 427

drug-testing services, Windy Hills Professional Laboratories, 135

drums

Bodhran Page, 662

Drums and Percussion Page, 662

DTD (Document Type Definition), 14

Duncan, Michael, 89

E

e-mail, 21
addresses, 22-23
aliases, 27
binary files, 26-27
creating messages, 25
domain addresses, 23
filtering, 27
folders, 27
handles, 23
interface, 27
mailing lists, 24
Netscape manager, 24
security, 22
Send an Electronic Postcard, 341
sending, 25
sorting, 27
subdomains, 23
TeamWARE AB, 558
tooltips, 25
uuencode, 26
Virtual Flowers, 348

e-zines
@Ezine, 108
Alternative-X, 108
American Planet Galactic News, 108
Plaintext, 109
Renditions, 109
Wespennest, 110

earth sciences
Earth and Environmental Science, 767
Earth Sciences and Resources Institute, 761
EOS Buchantiquariat Benz, 761
Hanford Site, 762
Idaho National Engineering Laboratory, 762
National Center for Atmospheric Research, 762
National Soil Erosion Research Laboratory, 767
Online Earth Science Journals, 762
Rain Forest Action Network Home Page, 762
Science and Public Policy Program, 762
Science and Technology Corporation (STC), 762
Science Applications International Corp. (SAIC), 762
Supplements to Atmospheric & Oceanic Publications, 762
Technadyne Engineering Consultants, 762

VolcanoWorld, 762
WWW Virtual Library-Environment, 768

earthquakes, 770, 776
eating disorders, 431
Medical Sciences Bulletin, 431
Michael D. Myers MD, Inc./Myers Information Service, 431
Tell-Me-Y, Inc., 432

eclipses, 752
ecology
Abbey's Web, 762
Access Fund, 763
BASF Ecology, 361
The Butterfly Website: Conservation and Ecology, 362
Cliff Ecology Research Group, 364
Connecting With Nature, 365
Department of the Navy Environmental Programs, 361
The Dying Sea, 372
Earth Viewer, 763
Earth Watch, 364
EcoLink, 763
Ecologia, 364
Ecological Monitoring and Assessment Network, 364
Ecology Action Centre, 364
Ecology and Human Rights Information, 763
Ecology Channel, 763
Ecovote Online, 763
FICUS, 366
Global Ecology Study Abroad/IHP, 304
Greenpeace, 763
International Center for Tropical Ecology, 365
Natural Resources Conservation Service—U.S. Dept., 763
Okefenokee Joe's Natural Education Center, 366
PlanetKeepers, 365
Questions About Biodiversity, 365
Rainforest Workshop Home Page, 763
Ralph Maughan's Wolf Report, 763
Sierra Club, 763
Suncoast Wildlife/Ecology, 374
U.I.A. Freshwater Ecology (The Chironomid Home Page), 764
U.S. Fish and Wildlife Service, 764
The Video Project, 372
Welcome to Coastal America's Home Page, 764

World Forum for Acoustic Ecology, 764
see also conservation; environment
economics
Economic Research Service, 749
Society for Economic Anthropology, 519
education
A.Word.A.Day Home Page, 291
About the NDLC, 299
Academy One, 291
Adult Education, 291
AERO-The Alternative Education Resource Organization, 823
AIMS Education Foundation, 291
Ainsworth Keyboard Training Systems, 308
Alpine Valley School-Homepage, 299
Ameritech Education Resources, 309
Apple Higher Education: The Apple Virtual Campus, 291
arts, 73, 78
ArtsEdge Network, 299
AskERIC Virtual Library, 291
astronomy
Caltech Space Society, 751
CCD Images of Galaxies, 751
CyberSky, 751
NCSA Relativity Group, 752
STELAR Project Demos, 753
Beginner's Guide to Effective E-mail, 560
biology,
Biology(Science), 291
CSU BIOWEB, 756
Brooke High WWW Server, 299
CALI: The Center for Computer-Assisted Legal Instruction, 291
Canadian Kids' Page, 301
Carrie's Sites for Educators, 309
CASAA Student Leadership Resource Center, 307
Center for Talented Youth (CTY) of the Johns Hopkins University, 291
Center for the Application of Information Technology, 560
chemistry
ChemCAI, 758
Chemistry Hypermedia Project, 758
Chemistry Teacher Resources, 758
Software Reviews from the CTI Centre for Chemistry, 759
children
Childaware, 291
Children's Literature Web Guide, 307

Index

Welcome to MegaMath, 297
Whales: A Thematic Web Unit, 297
CIC, Center for Library Initiatives, 292
Cisco Educational Archives and Resources Catalog, 309
Classroom at the Internet Schoolhouse, 307
Classroom Connect, 301
Cold Spring Harbor Fish Hatchery and Aquarium, 299
College Prep Page, 307
Columbia Public Schools Homepage, 300
Comer School Development Program, 292
Community Learning Network, 301
Computer as Learning Partner, 292
Cornell Computer Science Graphics Course, 301
Cornell Theory Center Math and Science Gateway, 292
Council of the Great City Schools Online, 300
CyberKids Home, 307
Cyberspace Middle School, 300
Digital Frog, 292
Distance Ed, 301
Distance Education Clearinghouse, 301
Distance Education Resources, 301
Distance Learning Directory, 301
Distance Learning Resources, 301
Dole 5-A-Day Homepage, 309
Ed Web Homepage, 309
Education Sites, 309
Education Virtual Library-Primary School, 292
Educational Online Sources, 301
EDUCOM-Homepage, 292
eduMail, 309
ELTI Charlotte's English Aids, 309
employment, DPI InfoWeb, 309
Encyclopedia of Women's History, 542
English as a Second Language, 307
environmental
Arizona EarthVision, 365
Ask An Earth Scientist, 365
Earth System Science Community Home Page, 366
EE Link, 366
Environmental Information Center, 366

Environmental Training Group Inc.'s ENVIROPAGE, 306
GLOBE Program, 366
Handbook for a Better Future, 366
Institute for Earth Education, 366
Plastic Bag Information Clearinghouse, 366
Second Nature, 295
Exchange-Learning English Language Culture, 307
Exploratorium Homepage, 301
Explorer Homepage, 309
Federal and State-Run Servers, 292
films, VFS Multimedia, 79
financial aid
Financial Aid Information Page, 298
Money for College, 298
FredNet MOO, 307
Garfield Co. Public Library System, 302
GENII Homepage, 309
geography
GEOGRAPHY USA: A Virtual Textbook, 527
Oregon Geographic Alliance (OGA), 528
Project GeoSim, 528
Geometry Forum, 292
Gestalt Systems, Inc., 560
Getting Past Go, 322
Gifted and Talented (TAG) Resources Homepage, 310
Grolier Interactive, 304
Guidelines for Educational Uses of Networks, 306
health care, New York Open Center, 294
Heinemann World, 310
Hillside Elementary School, 293
history, World of Benjamin Franklin, 297
Home Schooling Resources, 298
Homework Page, 308
HotList of K-12 Internet School Sites, 300
humanities
Center for Electronic Texts in the Humanities, 524
Center for the Humanities, 524
Computing in the Humanities Users Group (CHUG), 524
H-Net—Humanities OnLine, 525
Humanities and Social Sciences—University of Chicago LibInfo, 525
Humanities HUB, 525
Humanities National Database Search, 525

Humanities Report, 525
Institute for Human Sciences—Vienna, 525
National Endowment for the Humanities (NEH), 525
National Humanities Institute Home Page, 525
Research Institute for the Humanities (RIH), 526
Stanford Electronic Humanites Review, 526
Voice of the Shuttle: Web Page for Humanities Research, 526
WWW Virtual Library—Humanities, 526
HyperLiterature/HyperTheory, 107
ICDL, 293
Ideal Point Home Page, 131
ILTweb: LiveText: Index, 306
InfoList Homepage, 310
InforMNs, 310
inQuiry Almanack, March 1995, 310
Institute of Psychiatry, 445
Integrating Technology Schools Homepage at University of New Mexico, 310
Interactive Multimedia Education Resources, 293
Intercultural E-Mail Classroom Connections, 302
international
Friends and Partners, 298
Global Ecology Study Abroad/IHP, 304
GROW-Opportunity Wales, 304
Hello India!, 298
Human-Languages Page, 298
*I*EARN*, 298
IMD International Institute for Management Development, 299
JASON Project, 302
Landegg Academy Online, 302
Le Coin des Francophones et Autres Grenouilles, 299
Live from Antarctica, 299
Reed Interactive's Global Classroom, 303
Study in the USA Online Directory, 303
World Kids Press Homepage, 299
International Federation of Library Associations and Institutions (IFLA), 304
Internet Educational Resources Guide, 293
Internet Learning Center, 561

Internet Web Text, 561
Introduction to the Internet II, 561
IPL Building Directory, 293
ISN KidNews, 293
Jefferson-Scranton Community
  Schools, 308
Jon's Home-School Resource Page,
  298
Judi Harris' Network-Based
  Educational Activity Collection, 310
Junior Achievement Purpose/Facts,
  304
K-12 Education, 300
K-12 Technology, 300
Kidding Around, 310
Kids on Campus (Cornell Theory
  Center), 561
Kids Web A World Wide Web Digital
  Library for Schoolkids, 308
Knowledge Source, 828
Knox Junior High Homepage, 293
Lesson Plans and Activities, 310
listservs, 313-319
Little Toy Store on the Net, 293
Magic Learning Systems, 293
Mark Twain Library, 293
mathematics
    *Calculus & Mathematica Home
      Page, 770*
    IMSA Home Page, 772
    Math Teaching Assistant, 772
    Math Education Resources, 302
    *Math and Science Gateway (Cornell
      Theory Center), 293*
    MathMagic Internet, 302
    *MATHMOL-K-12 Mathematics and
      Molecules, 293*
Media History, Studies, and
  Education, 463
Media Literacy Online Project
  Homepage, 294
MediaPro, 294
Medical/Clinical/Occupational
  Toxicology Resource Homepage, 294
MEOL, 294
Middlebrook's Structured Analog
  Design, 306
Mining the Internet Columns, 310
Monterey Academy of Oceano-
  graphic Science, 306
Mount St. Helens, 294
MU CoE LInks to Education
  Resources, 294
music
    *Brent Hugh's Music Instruction
      Software Page, 656*

    MIDI Home Page, 656
    Neil Hume DJ Page, 656
NASA Education Sites, 294
NASA Spacelink-An Electronic
  Information System For Educators,
  310
National Science Foundation World
  Wide Web Server, 310
National Teachers Enhancement
  Network, 310
Natural Resources Defense Council
  (NRDC), 304
NCSA Education Program, 300
Network Nuggets, 294
newsgroups, 312-313
Newton's Apple Educational
  Materials, 311
Nine Planets, 294
Norm's Homepage, 306
North American Historical Re-
  Enactor Web Site (West Site), 308
North Central Regional Educational
  Laboratory, 307
North Dakota ICICLE Project, 311
Northwest Service Academy Page,
  304
NYSERNet, 300
Old School House Studio, 311
Online Educator, 603
Online Reference Works, 302
Open University, 302
OSPI Math, Science, and Technology
  Server, 294
parents, Parenting Skills on Video,
  295
Patrick Crispen's Internet Roadmap,
  562
Peterson's Education Center, 295
Placer County Office of Education,
  295
Private School Resource, 295
Private Schools Online, 308
Project LEAP (Learn Earn and
  Prosper), 295
psychology, Teaching Clinical
  Psychology, 537
public policy, Harry Singer
  Foundation, 304
Research at BYU Integrated
  Microelectronics Lab, 306
Scholarly Electronic Forums Web
  Page, 295
School and Community Networking
  Resources, 311
Schoolhouse Videos and CDs
  (CD-ROMs), 295

SciEd: Science and Mathematics
  Education Resources, 295
science
    Expect the Best from a Girl, 543
    Science Television, 778
    Small is Beautiful, 295
    Welcome to Project CLEA, 754
SERESC, 295
Smithsonian Institution Homepage,
  305
Social Sciences, 309
sociology, SOCNET, 541
Sylvan Learning Centers, 308
Teach Yourself the Internet Support
  Page, 562
Tech Classes Archive, 311
Technology and Distance Education
  Branch, 303
Technology for All Americans
  Project, 307
Tecla Homepage form Birkbeck
  College London, 296
TENET, 296
TERC, 305
TESL-EJ Master Page, 296
Theodore Tugboat, 296
TIESnet, 296
Times Higher Education
  Supplement, 608
Total Recall, 303
Turner Adventure Learning, 300
UEWeb, 296
United States Education
  Department/OERI, 296
Virtual English Language Center, 311
Virtual Frog Dissection Kit, 303
Voices of Youth Homepage, 308
VOTEC Homepage, 296
Washington Center for Internships &
  Academic Seminars, 296
Waterford Institute, 306
Web66: K-12 Schools Registry, 297
Welcome K-12, 300
Welcome to TEAMSnet, 303
Welcome to the Council of the Great
  City Schools Online, 305
Welcome to the DeweyWeb, 308
Welcome to Virtual FlyLab, 308
Winston Churchill High School Web
  Server, 297
WisDPI-The Wisconsin Department
  of Public Instruction, 297
women's studies
    *Centre for Women's Studies in
      Education (CWSE), 542*
    Women in Higher Education, 297

World Lecture, 297
Writing at MU, 308
Youth Quake, 563
Zen and the Art of the Internet, 563

educational games
Bluedog Can Count, 336
Husband Lover Spy, 338
Lemonade Stand, 339

educational television programs
Bill Nye the Science Guy's Nye Labs Online, 881
Biography, 881
Building America—Eye On Business, 881
Collecting Across America, 881
CTN, 881
Doctor Is In, 881
Great Canadian Parks, 881
Joy of Painting with Bob Ross, 881
Newton's Apple, 881
No Dogs or Philosophers Allowed, 881
Where in the World Is Carmen Sandiego?, 882

Egypt
ABZU, 456
Alexandria, Egypt, 456
Annual Egyptological Bibliography (AEB), 520
Archaeological Survey in the Eastern Desert of Egypt, 456
Duke Papyrus Archive, 522
Egyptian Gallery, 292
HealthNet, 448
Institute of Egyptian Art and Archaeology, 458
Reeder's Egypt Page, 523

EIDE (extended IDE), 34

electric automobiles, 371
Citicar: My Electric Vehicle, 893
Eco-Motion, 370
Electric Vehicle Association of the Americas, 893
ZAP Power Systems, 372

electric fields, 450, 767

electrical systems
CBI Systems, Inc., 505
DHSL: Data Home Systems Limited, 505
Home Automation Association (HAA), 505
Home Automator, 506
Home Team, 506
HomeTheater Com, 506

Intelligent Home Technologies, Inc., 506
Media Dimensions, 506
ProSpec, 506
Spectacular Powerhouse Page, 506
Vantage, 506

electronic art
@art gallery, 80
Alternative Virtual Biennial, 80
Atelier Nord, 80
Auricular Homepage, 80
Center for Research in Computing and the Arts (CRCA), 73
Crosswire Images, 84
Cyberbabe, 80
DigiPen Applied Computer Graphics School, 74
Digital Cathedral, 84
Digital Giraffe, 85
Donajski's Digital Gallery, 85
Duncan Hopkins Web site, 80
Electronic Chronicles, 85
FineArt Forum Gallery, 85
Hillustration, 81
Hiway Technologies Graphics Portfolio, 81
HypArt, 81
Lectro-Art, 81
Martin Action Art, 81
Media West Editions, 81
NCSA Digital Gallery CD-ROM, 81
Netwash, 81
place, The, 82
Rainbow of Chaos, 82
Sample the Dog Design, 82
Spanky Welcome (The Spanky Fractal Database), 82
Syracuse University Computer Graphics for the Visual Arts, 78
Vancouver Cyberspace Association, 82
WebWeavers, 82

electronic mail, *see* **e-mail**

electronics
American Electronics Association, 776
CES News, 350
Electronics Department at CyberShop, 808
FutureNet, 560
Gilltro-Electronics, Inc., 813
HADCO Corporation, 131
HSiN Semiconductor Pte Ltd, 131
List of Mail Order Electronics Companies, 477

Maverick Communications, 814
Peters-de Laet, Inc., 133
Roctronics Lighting, 815
Scope Systems-Worldwide Industrial Electronics Repair and Services, 134

Elvis, Original Unoffical Elvis Home Page, 669

embassies
Electronic Embassy, 417
Embassy Page, 418

employment
4Work, 322
Access Careers & Jobs Resources, 323
America's Employers, 323
American Sociological Association (ASA), 538
Amerisoft, 323
Archaeological Fieldwork Opportunities, 520
Atlantic Management Resources, 323
BBN on the World Wide Web, 559
Best Jobs in the USA Today, 323
Butterfass, Pepe & MacCallan, Inc., 323
CACEE WorkWeb, 323
Caldwell Partners On-line Directory, 323
CareerMart, 323
CareerSite, 323
Center for Talented Youth (CTY) of the Johns Hopkins University, 291
College Prep Page, 307
Cromwell Partners Interactive, 323
D.L. Weaver Difference, 324
DPI InfoWeb, 309
Dunn & Edwards Services, 577
E-Span, 324
EINet Galaxy, 568
EMBBS: Emergency Medicine and Primary Care Home, 436
Employment Search International, Inc., 324
Employment Search Productions, 324
Encyclopedia Smithsonian: Archaeology, 522
eShop Inc., 812
FAQ—Career in Archaeology in the U.S., 522
Freelance Online, 324
Groupweb, 324
InforM Women's Studies Database, 544
InPursuit's Employment Network, 324
JobExchange, 324
LAW EMPLOYMENT CENTER, 593

Library Job Hunting, 709
listservs, 332-334
MBT Architecture, 505
MedLink International, 444
MedSearch America, 441
MEOL, 294
Michael Latas & Associates, Inc., 324
Michigan Association of Personnel Services, 324
Monster Board, 324
NASA Spacelink-An Electronic Information System For Educators, 310
National Association of Colleges and Employers, 324
National Consulting Network, 325
National Internship Directory, 325
NCS Career Magazine, 603
newsgroups, 330-332
OSHA (Occupational Safety and Health Administration), 443
Patti Peeples' Guide to Health Economics, Medical, and Pharmacy Resources on the Net, 441
Pharmacokinetics, Pharmacodynamics, Biopharmaceutics Home Page, 447
Project LEAP (Learn Earn and Prosper), 295
ProMatch '96, 325
Recruiters OnLine Network, 325
SEAMLESS WEBsite...lawyer law firm expert, 594
SocioWeb, 541
VOTEC Homepage, 296
whatNOW?, 325
encyclopedias, Nothin' But Net, 575
endangered animals
American Association of Zoo Keepers, 361
Atlantic Salmon Federation, 362
Australian Environment Online, 368
The Butterfly Website: Conservation and Ecology, 362
Conservation Breeding Specialist Group, 362
Endangered Species, 362
Fragile Legacy, 369
GreenLife Society—North America, 362
The Video Project, 372
Whale and Dolphin Conservation Society, 369
Whale Museum's Orca Adoption Program, 370

energy
Alternative Energy Engineering, 764
American Nuclear Society, 764
Bioenergy, 764
Brookhaven National Laboratory, 764
Center for Rural Studies (CRS), 538
Clustron Science Corporation, 764
conservation
Maine Solar House, 363
Mr. Solar Home Page, 363
Real Goods, 371
CREST'S Guide to Alternative Energy, 764
Ed's News Page, 764
Energy Science and Technology Software Center, 764
Home Power Magazine, 764
Investigating Wind Energy, 765
North American Power Brokers, 132
Nova Structure, 765
engineering
All Electrical Engineering Academic Programs (Almost), 765
American Institute of Chemical Engineers, 765
architectural, Southern Reprographics, 809
Chemical Engineering URLs Directory, 765
Crazy about Constraints!, 765
D Banks—Microengineering/MEMS, 765
Fraunhofer Institute for Materials Physics and Surface Engineering, 765
genetics
Center for Soybean Tissue and Genetic Engineering, 749
Genetic Engineering Taught Through Telecommunication, 302
Ingvar's Home Page, 125
Institution of Electrical Engineers Home Page, 765
listservs, 789-793
Meetings Information, 765
Micromath's Home Page, 765
National Society Of Black Engineers at SDSU, 766
newsgroups, 786-789
NU Student Chapter ASCE, 766
Reliability Analysis Center (RAC) Home Page, 766
San Diego Supercomputer Center, 761
Software Engineering Archives, 766

Statistical Reports on United States Science and Engineering, 766
TechExpo on WWW, 134
UAB Thermal and Fluids Engineering Group, 766
UCF ASET, 766
Unofficial Chemical Engineering Home Page, 766
Virginia Geotechnical Services, 766
Welcome to Internet Directory of Biotechnology Resources, 766
World-Wide Web Virtual Library Aerospace, 766
WWW Archive for Electric Power Engineering Education, 766
England
Ain't Whistlin' Dixie, 656
American and British History Resources, 455
British Archaeology, 521
London Mall: Magazine and HQ, 125
Mobile Phones for UK Users, 125
SoccerNet, 858
Welcome to BBC Radio, 617
English
11 Rules of Grammar, 703
A.Word.A.Day, 705
American Dialect Society, 529, 704
Australian National Dictionary Centre, 530
BritSpeak: English as a Second Language for Americans, 704
CELEX Dutch Centre for Lexical Information, 530
Collective Nouns, 704
Cool Word of the Day, 704
ELTI Charlotte's English Aids, 309
ENGL 310: History of the English Language, 704
English as a Second Language, 307, 530
Etymology of First Names, 704
Exchange-Learning English Language Culture, 307
Grammar and Style Notes, 704
Impact! Online Homepage, 302
Lexeme-Morpheme Base Morphology (LMBM), 531
Logical World of Etymology, 705
Morse Code and the Phonetic Alphabets, 712
Old English Pages, 532, 705
Research-It!, 713
TESL-EJ Master Page, 296
TsaLaGi (English/Cherokee Dictionary), 532

UCREL—University Centre for Computer Corpus Research on Language, 533

University of Chicago Press Cognitive Science and Linguistics Catalog, 533

Virtual English Language Center, 311

Word for Word, 705

Word Page, 705

WWW Anagram Generator, 705

engraving

Dakota Engraving, Etc., 812

Ideal Engraving Co., Inc., 813

entertainment

listservs, 357-359

newsgroups, 353-356

entomology, The Butterfly Website: Conservation and Ecology, 362

environment

listservs, 376-378

newsgroups, 376

environmental sciences

activisim

Community Environmental Action Web, 365

Environmental Defense Fund, 369

Friends of the Earth Local Groups, 367

Greenpeace USA, 369

Air & Waste Management Association, 368

American Association of Zoo Keepers, 361

Arbor Day, 361

Arctic National Wildlife Refuge, 368

Atlantic Salmon Federation, 362

Australian Environment Online, 368

awards, Goldman Prize Winners, 361

BCRI On-Line, 766

Center for Rural Studies (CRS), 538

companies

Amway, 361

Anatomy, 370

BASF Ecology, 361

Black-Gold Oil Conditioning Systems, 370

Buy Green, 370

Chrysler Corporation—Recycling & Conservation, 361

Department of the Navy Environmental Programs, 361

Disaster's Edge Environmental Education Center, 361

DuPont: Safety, Health, and the Environment, 361

Earth Shirts, 370

Eco Store, 370

Eco-Heads, 370

Eco-Motion, 370

Environmental Software Resources, 370

Environmentally Sound Products, 371

Ford Environmental Report, 361

Geotechnical & Geo-environmental Software Director, 371

Green Bean, 371

Greenway, 371

Hemp Baby, 371

Hugg-A-Planet, 371

Jade Mountain, 371

Mother Nature's General Store, 371

Real Goods, 371

Smokeless Cooking Products, 372

ZAP Power Systems, 372

Connecting With Nature, 365

Consortium for International Earth Science Information Network (CIESIN), 538

The Coral Reef Alliance, 362

disaster recovery

Most Contaminated Spot on the Planet, 364

Oil Spill Public Information Center, 364

Sea Empress Oil Spill, 364

Earth Watch, 364

Ecologia, 364

Ecology Action Centre, 364

education

Arizona EarthVision, 365

Ask An Earth Scientist, 365

Earth System Science Community Home Page, 366

EE Link, 366

Environmental Education Network, 306

Environmental Information Center, 366

GLOBE Program, 366

Handbook for a Better Future, 366

Institute for Earth Education, 366

Plastic Bag Information Clearing-house, 366

Second Nature, 295

Electronic Green Journal, 600

EMF-Link, 767

Endangered Plants: Images, 362

Envirolink, 364

Envirolink Freenet, 365

Environmental Chemical Corporation, 767

Environmental Training Group, Inc.'s ENVIROPAGE, 306

FICUS, 366

Florida Center for Environmental Studies' Home Page, 767

Giovanni Guglielmo's Research Page on Salt Tectonics, 767

Grass Roots Magazine, 601

Green Cross International, 369

GREENGUIDE—How to Trim Your Office Waste, 366

GreenLife Society—North America, 362

Greenspan Technology, 767

IFIAS, 767

In Home Shopping, 808

Infrastructure Technology Institute (ITI), 767

Internet Green Marketplace, 813

John Muir Exhibit, 363

Natural Resources Defence Council (NRDC), 304

Northwest Service Academy Page, 304

Okefenokee Joe's Natural Education Center, 366

PlanetKeepers, 365

political affiliates

Electronic Lobbyist for Renewable Energy, 370

International Greens, 369

League of Conservation Voters, 363

US Environmental Protection Agency, 369

pollution issues

Air That Kills Us, 367

Black-Gold Oil Conditioning Systems, 370

Breath Taking, 367

Burning Issues/Clean Air Revival, 367

Ecocide in the U.S.S.R., 367

Economics of Industrial Pollution Home Page, 367

EPIC Home Page, 367

Georgia Pollution Prevention Assistance Division, 367

Geothermal Energy, 368

How To Survive Without a Car, 368

Impact of Lead-Contaminated Soil on Public Health, 368

National Pollution Prevention Center for Higher Education, 368

Pollution, 368

publications

Atlantic Monthly Election Connection, 372

CNN—Environment News Main Page, 372

Conscious Choice, 372

Duke Environment Magazine, 372

The Dying Sea, 372

E Online, 372

Earth First! Journal, 372

The Earth Times Home Page, 372

EcoLink, 373

Electronic Green Journal, 373

Environmental Ethics Journal, 373

Environmental News Network, 373

Forty Tips to Go Green, 373

Grassroots Youth Magazine, 373

GreenBeat!, 373

GreenDesign, 371

GREENLines, 373

Greenpeace Magazines & Newsletters, 373

Natural Areas Journal, 373

Natural History Book Service, 368

The Online Better World Magazine, 374

Our Environment—Online, 374

People and the Planet, 374

Rachel's Environment & Health Weekly, 374

Ranger Rick, 374

Science & The Environment, 374

SCOPE Newsletter, 374

Senior Network News, 374

Suncoast Wildlife/Ecology, 374

Viva La Tortuga!, 374

The WWW Virtual Library— Environment, 374

Questions About Biodiversity, 365

Sci.environment, 365

Sempervirens Fund, 363

Surfrider Foundation USA, 363

Talk.environment, 365

Texas Environmental Center, 367

United Nations Environment Programme (UNEP), Geneva, 767

USDA—Natural Resources Conservation Service, 363

The Video Project, 372

Welcome to Sherwood, 369

World Transformation, 367

see also conservation; ecology

environmental law

CCE - CCA - CEC (Commission for Enviromental Cooperation), 586

Environmental Law Alliance Worldwide, 586

Environmental Law Around the World, 587

Environmental Law Resources, 587

Environmental Law World Wide Web Site, 587

U.S. Environmental Protection Agency, 587

United Nations Environment Programme, 587

WWW Virtual Library: Law: International & Environmental Law, 587

enzymes, 755

erotica

Cyber-Sex-Toys, 797

Dark Nites, 796

Erotic Pen, 796

ErtocaTender, 796

Libido Magazine, 796

Loving Center: Your Source for Information on Tant, 797

Plainwrapped Chocolates, 797

Red Hot Amsterdam, 796

Sensuous You, 797

Sin, 797

Stories of Mary Anne Mohanraj, 797

Yellow Silk, 797

essays, Electronic Labyrinth, 106

ethics, Ethical, Legal, and Social Issues in Science, 303

ethnic food

Cape Breton Pictorial Cookbook, 403

Creole and Cajun Recipe Page, 403

Culinary World Tour, 403

Filipino Cuisine, 404

Friends and Partners Kitchen, 404

FYNet's Collection of Malaysian Recipes, 404

Hawaiian Electric Kitchen, 404

Hawaii's Favorite Recipes, 404

Kosher Express, 404

La Comeda Mexicana, 404

La Pagina dela Salsa Mole, 404

Mama's Cookbook, 404

Native American Foods, 407

Nomius Eye—Sasa Recipes, 405

Pedro's Kitchen, 405

Prapapun's Hobby Kitchen, 405

Recipe Archive Index, 405

Recipes for Traditional Food in Slovenia, 405

Restaurant Le Cordon Bleu, 405

Rolling Your Own Sushi, 402

Stuart's Chinese Recipes, 405

Turkish Cuisine, 405

VNO: Food—Cooking and Recipes, 406

World-Wide Sushi Restaurant Reference, 407

YACB (Yet Another CookBook), 406

see also food; recipes

etiquette

Dance Floor Etiquette, 705

Toilet Training: An Online Guide to Urinal Etiquette, 705

etymology, Logical World of Etymology, 705

Europe

Anthropology of East Europe Review (AEER), 517

Archaeological Resource Guide for Europe, 521

Catalogue Production Management Services, 124

Country Maps from W3 Servers in Europe, 710

East View Publications, Inc. Home Page, 611

European Law Journal, 591

European Patent Office, 714

European Research Centre on Migration and Ethnic Relations (ERCOMER), 539

European Sociological Association (ESA), 539

FoLLI, the European Association for Logic, Language and Information, 530

hiking, 849

history

Europe/Russia/Eastern Europe, 458

European History, 458

Historical Text Archive, 459

History Pages, 459

REESWeb: Russian and East European Studies, 459

Institute for Human Sciences— Vienna, 525

RadioWorld Europe, 617

Society for the Anthropology of Europe (SAE) Web Site, 519

Stone Pages, 524

UK Archaeology on the Internet, 524

Welcome to the European Market, 126

euthanasia, 429, 824

Evangelical Lutheran, Evangelical Lutheran Church in America Home Page, 726

evolution

Answers About Evolution, 731

Evolution vs. Creation Science, 731

Evolution's Voyage, 535

Talk.Origins Archive, 731

see also anthropology

excavations, *see* archaeology

extended IDE (EIDE), 34

extraterrestrials

Aztec Books, 751

Planetary Society Home Page, 752

eyeglasses, *see* **visually impaired**

F

family issues

listservs, 390-392

newsgroups, 390

family law

Divorce Helpline Home Page, 587

Divorce Law Home Page, 587

Divorce Page, 587

Family Law, 588

Family Law Advisor Home Page, 588

Fathers' Rights and Equality Exchange, 588

Legal dot Net—Family Law, and Overview, 588

Same-Sex Marriage Home Page, 588

FAQs, 19

farming, *see* **agriculture**

fashion

Bon Mots from the Supermodels, 717

Chiossone Studio, NYC, 494

Department of Clothing, Design, and Technology, MMU, 292

Hans de Kort Photography, 494

faucets, *see* **plumbing**

fax machines, Spectra FAX Corp. Home Page, 572

fax numbers, 716

feminism

American Association of University Women (AAUW), 542

Body Politic, 796

Celebration of Women Writers, 542

Center for the American Woman and Politics (CAWP), 542

Center for Women's Global Leadership (CWGL), 542

Centre for Women's Studies in Education (CWSE), 542

Colleen's Feminism Home Page, 542

CRLP: Women of the World, 542

Cybergrrl Webstation, 542

Diotima: Women & Gender in the Ancient World, 542

Electronic Access to Research on Women: A short Guide, 2nd Edition, 543

Encyclopedia of Women's History, 542

Expect the Best from a Girl, 543

Feminism and Women's Resources, 543

Feminist Bookstores, 543

Feminist Majority Online, 543

Feminist Science Fiction, Fantasy, & Utopia, 543

Feminist Studies in Aotearoa Electronic Journal (FMST), 543

FEMINIST.COM, 543

Gender Equity in Sports, 543

Global Fund for Women, 543

Guerrilla Girls, 543

Her Own Words®, 544

InforM Women's Studies Database, 544

Internet Resources for Women's Legal and Public Policy Informatio, 544

Isis, 544

Largesse: The Network for Size Esteem, 431

Legal Rights of Women, 544

Library Resources for Women's Studies, 544

Lifetime Online, 544

Linkages FOURTH WORLD CONFERENCE ON WOMEN site, 544

National Organization for Women (NOW), 544

Resources for Feminist Research/ Documentation sur la recherche féministe (RFR/DRF), 544

Spinsters Ink, 545

United Nations and the Status of Women, 545

VOWworld: Voices of Women, 545

WIDNET (Women In Development NETwork), 545

Women & Politics Home Page, 545

Women Leaders Online (WLO), 545

Women's Books Online, 545

Women's History Month, 545

Women's Studies Reference Roadmap, 545

Women's Wire, 545

WomensNet @igc, 546

WomenSpace, 546

World's Women On-Line!, 546

Yale Journal of Law and Feminism, 546

fencing, 851, 854

ferrets

Electronic Zoo/NetVet–Ferret Page, 61

Ferret Central, 61

Ferret World, 61

festivals, music

29th Montreux Jazz Festival Official Site, 660

ABSOLUTELY WORTHLESS Calendar, 660

Creation 96, 660

Lollapalooza Information (Unofficial), 660

MBNA College Quartet Contest, 660

Musi-Cal Performer Index, 660

National Folk Festival, 660

Rob Kenney Presents: Kerrville Folk Festival, 660

Strawberry Music Festivals, 660

UFOJOE Presents, 660

WOMEX '96, 659

World Music/Boston, 660

fiction

Agatha Christie, 99

Atomic Books Literary Finds for Mutated Minds, 609

Baker Street Connection, 106

David Brin, 98

Dean Koontz, 102

Douglas Adams, 97

Dr. Seuss, 100

eSCENE 1995, 74

Flaming Jewels, 74

Flapping, 75

H.P. Lovecraft, 103

InterText: The Online Fiction Magazine, 602

IPL Books, 612

Jayhawk, 76

Jonathan Kellerman, 102

Katherine Kurtz, 102

Lewis Carroll Home Page, 77

Little Women-DataText, 107

Lost World (Randomhouse), 107

On-line Books, 78

Project Gutenberg, 87

Romance Pages, 111

Science Fiction Weekly, 109

Sherlockian Holmepage, 111

Stephen King, 102

Tolkien Society, 111

Tree Fiction on the World Wide Web, 108

Ultimate Romance Novel Website, 111

Ursula K. Le Guin, 102

V.C. Andrews, 97

Wonderful Wizard of Oz, 108

see also authors; books

file formats, Common Internet File Formats, 568

file transfer protocol, *see* **FTP**

films

A Very Usable Film and Cinema Directory, 79

basilisk, 599

Daum On-line, 74

festivals

Cannes Film Festival Official Web Site, 635

Chicago Underground Film Festival, 635

Cinema Festivals, 635

Film Festivals Server, 635

Low Res film and video festival, 635

Mill Valley Film Festival, 77

Sundance Film Festival, 635

Filmakers Library, 539

Fox Film, 630

Hollywood Archaeology, 76

Lion's Den, 630

Screenwriters Online, 134

University Art Museum and Pacific Film Archive, 79

Very Usable Film and Cinema Directory, 894

VFS Multimedia, 79

see also movies

filtering e-mail, 27

financial aid, Money for College, 298

financial sites

A.S.K. Financial Digest, 127

Accel Partners, 127

Adnet, 123

Allegiance Financial Advisors, 127

American Stock Exchange, The, 127

American Stock Report, Inc., 127

Chicago Mercantile Exchange, 127

Credit Union Home Page, 121

CyberFund, 127

Evolving Technologies Corporation, 130

FFP Securities, 127

Fin-Atlantic Securities, Inc., 127

High-Tech Investor, 564

How to Become a Real-Time commodity, Futures Trader—From Home, 127

Infogroup S.p.A., 121

InterQuote, 127

Mutual Fund Home Page, 128

Nesbitt Burns Inc., 128

Olsen & Associates, 128

Pawws Financial Network, 128

Perception Global Market Predictions, 128

Philadelphia Stock Exchange, 128

Precision Investment Services, Inc., 128

Quote.Com, 128

Security APL Quote Server, 128

SGA Goldstar Research, 128

Siegel Group, Inc., 128

Silicon Investor, 129

STAT-USA, 134

Stockdeck Online, 129

StockMaster at MIT, 129

Trader's Financial Resource Guide, 129

Wall Street Net, 129

Wall Street Online, 129

Woodbridge and Associates, 129

World Bank Home Page, 121

World Currency Converter, 121

fingerprinting, Seals on Wheels, 134

Finland

Finnair, 903

RootsWorld: Music on the Net, 659

VR Cargo International Home Page, 126

firearms

American Firearms Association, 828

Gunfree, 828

fish

Atlantic Salmon Federation, 362

Cold Spring Harbor Fish Hatchery and Aquarium, 299

Fish Food, 599

Marine Fish Conservation Network, 363

fisheries

Aquatic Network, 129

National Marine Fisheries Service, 779

fishing

Anglers Online, 846

ArtStudio, 83

Flyfishing Antventures, 846

J.P.'s Fishing Page, 846

King of the Hill Fly Fishing Co., 846

Nautical Net, 846

Nor'east Saltwater Magazine, 846

Sportfishing Industry Newsletter, 846

Virtual Flyshop, 846

World of Fishing, 847

fitness

Alexander Technique, 436

Healthtouch, 438

listservs, 453-454

newsgroups, 451-453

see also health

flags

Betsy Ross Homepage, 705

Flag of the United States of America, 706

Flag-Burning Page, 706

Flags of the 19th and 20th Century, 706

National Flag Foundation, 706

Save Old Glory From Flames Home Page, 706

flaming, 18, 28

floating point units (FPU), 33

flooring

Advanced Flooring, Inc, 508

Anderson Hardwood Floors, 508

Carpet One, 508

Carpet Samples, 673

Carpets.com, 508

Country Oak Flooring, 509

Dalton Carpet Outlets, 509

Floor Coverings International, 509

Sculptured Carpet Selections, 509

TrustMark, 509

Florida

Florida Institute of Technology-School of Aeronautics, 304

Florida Wildflower Showcase, 91

Information Access Websites, 916

florists

1-800-FLOWERS, 806

1-800-Roses, 806

Absolutely Fresh Flowers, 806

Buning the Florist, 806

Fleurs d'Eté, 806

Flora Designs, 806

Flower Stop, 806

FTD Internet, 807

Rittners School of Floral Design, 78

Royer's Flowers, 807

Teleflora-at the Sprectra.Net Mall, 807

Total Flower Exports, 807

Virtual Flowers, 348

flying saucers, *see* **UFOs**

folk art, Americas, 810

folk music

ABSOLUTELY WORTHLESS Calendar, 660

Digital Tradition Folk Song Database, 655

Dirty Linen, 600
Fasola Home Page, 660
Folk Music Home Page, 661
Folk on the Radio, 661
Folk Roots Home Page, 601
Folk Stuff, 661
Folkbook, 661
Irish Folk Songs, 658
Mary Chapin Carpenter, 661
National Folk Festival, 660
Northern Journey: Canadian Folk, 658
Northern Journey: Canadian Folk Music Website, 665
Rob Kenney Presents: Kerrville Folk Festival, 660
Southern Folklife Collection, 661
Stirrings Folk Mag, 665
UFOJOE Presents, 660
folklore
Khazana, 86
Urdco's Mystic Visions, 690
WWW Virtual Library—Ghost Stories and Folklore, 688
fonts, ECS, Custom Personalized, 195
food
American Supply International, 807
Amish Recipe, 816
Anytime Snacks, 396
Aunt Ida's Southern Kitchen, 396
Bagel Page, 400
BBQ-A Southern Cultural Icon, 400
Ben & Jerry's, 396
Blonz Guide to Nutrition, Food Science, and Health, 436
Bovril Shrine, 400
Bread, 400
Breakfast Cereal Hall of Fame, 400
Broccoli Central, 400
B's Cucumber Page, 400
Buckeye Beans & Herbs, Inc., 396
Buffalo Chicken Wing Home Page, 400
Burrito Page, 400
CalWine Gourmet Food Shop, 396
Campbell Soup Company, 396
Caroline Gold Cheese, 396
Caviar & Caviar, Ltd., 400
Cheeseburger in Paradise, 400
CheeseNet 95, 401
ChefsOnline, 396
Chicken Wing Central, 401
Chile Today Hot Tamale, 397
Constant Creation, 397
Cranberry Home Page, 401

Crunch, 343
Dan's Doner Kebab Registry, 401
Dean & Deluca, 397
Dinner Co-op, 401
Fax Foods, 397
Food & Nutrition Information Center, 436
Food Pyramid, 437
Food Resource, 401
FoodPlex, 401
Frito-Lay Main Menu, 397
Garlic Page, 401
Hacienda Flores Salsa, 397
Highland Trail Company, 397
Hot Hot Hot, 397
Hot Roast Beef Sandwiches, 401
Idaho Potato Expo, 401
Ipizza, 339
It's the French Fries, 344
Italian Food Market, 401
J.R. Wood, Inc., 397
Kitchens of Gordon Bleu, 404
Krema Nut Company, 397
Linsey Foods, 397
listservs, 411-412
Lotsa Hotsa Salsas, Hot Sauces and More, 397
Mmmm... Toast, 401
Myer's Gourmet Popcorn, 398
National Pork Producer's Council, 402
newsgroups, 409-410
North Fork Exchange, 398
Official French Fries Page, 401
Oils of Aloha, 399
Olympia Bakery and Catering, 398
Ore-Ida Foods, Inc., 398
Oregon Cupboard, 398
Pasta Home Page, 402
Pickle Preservation Society, 402
PizzaHut, 398
Pop 'n Stuff, Inc., 398
Potato Miscellany, 402
Professor Geoff Skurray's Food & Nutrition Information, 437
Queen's Kitchen & Pantry, 398
Ranch Worship Page, 402
Raspberry Web Page, 402
Rhubarb Compendium, 402
Rolling Your Own Sushi, 402
Saguaro Food Products, 398
Scubber's, 398
Snax.Com, 402
Spam Page, 402
Strawberry Facts Page, 402

Taste of Texas, 398
Taste of Texas Market, 398
Thai Fruits, 402
Truly Special Gourmet Foods, 399
Virtual Gourmet, 399
Watkins Recipes, 399
Wild Mushrooms, 402
see also ethnic food; health food; recipes
food manufacturing, 749
football, 847-848
Fantasy Insights, 845
Football Stats Analyzer Shareware, 845
NFL POOL, 845
Onondaga/Oswego Fantasy Football Page, 845
WinAmerica! Fantasy Football, 846
foreign languages
Classical: Project Libellus, 295
Climbing Dictionary, 702
Cursing in Swedish, 343
Education Virtual Library—Primary School, 292
French, TV-5, 887
German, CELEX Dutch Centre for Lexical Information, 530
Handy Spanish Phrase, 338
Human-Languages Page, 298
Japanese
Hideki's Home Page, 560
Traveler's Japanese with Voice, 303
What's New in Japan, 560
Morse Code and the Phonetic Alphabets, 712
Online Reference Works, 302
Spanish
Radio Centro, 617
Tecla Homepage from Birkbeck College London, 296
World Kids Press Home, 299
forms, 21
Fortes Free Agent, 29
fortune telling
Introduction To Tarot Magic, 692
Learning the Tarot—An Online Course, 692
Lord of Illusions—Clive Barker's Tarot Cards, 692
Michael's Tarot Pages, 692
Michele's Tarot Page, 692
Original WWW Tarot Site, 693
Tarot, 692
Tarot Cards, 693
Tarot Cards—Maelstrom, 693

Index

Tarot Inspiration, 693
Tarot Web, 693
Tarot Weekly, 693
Tarot—Tools and Rites of Transformation, 693
Vibrations—The Layman's Answer to Tarot Cards!, 693
FPUs (floating point units), 33
fractals, 771-772, 774
France
GIS and Remote Sensing for Archaeology: Burgundy, France, 522
Le Coin des Francophones et Autres Grenouilles, 299
music, Jazz in France, 664
Paris Museums, 464
fraternities, Planet Greek, 805
freeware, 15, 169, 575
French horns, Horn Players' FAQ, 662
Frequently Asked Questions (FAQs), 19
Freud, Sigmund, 537
FTP (file transfer protocol), 9
Monster FTP Sites List, 571
fuels, Centre for Alternative Transportation Fuels, 305
full-duplex modes, 33
funerals
Internet Cremation Society, 429
Natural Death Centre, 430
funk, Afro-Caribbean Music, 656
furniture
Alien Antiques, 478
Amboan & Badinia Furniture of Spain, 509
Bayviewer Chair Company, 509
Blue Canyon Woodworks, 509
BUILD.COM: The Building and Home Improvement Products Network, 487
California Crafts Marketplace, 811
Carleton Woodworking, 499
Chris Melhorn's Woodworking Gallery, 499
Construction Zone, 506
Crazy Creek Products, 509
Cyberwood Express, 506
Family Room Store, 509
Furniture and Refinishing, 487
Furniture First Aid, 509
Furniture Medic, 487
Furniture On Line, 509
Furniture Repair and Refinishing Wizard, 487
Hal's Virtual Furniture Gallery, 75
Hartmann House Antiques, 488

Haworth: Furniture for What's Next, 808
HOME IMPROVEMENT and CONSTRUCTION CONNECTION, 507
iGallery, The, 76
John Charles Antiques, 814
Jonathan Press Woodworking and Home Improvement Books and Plans, 507
Laid Back Designs, 814
Leisure Home Center, 509
LIBERON/Star Finishing Supplies, 488
North American Refinisher's Association, 488
Oak Factory Bulletin Board, 499
Online Furniture Refinisher, 510
Paramount Custom Cabinetry, 815
Prairie Woodworking, 499
Sturdy Artistics Catalogue Pages, 510
Technical Guidelines, Finishing Schedules & Product Information, 488
Virtual Design Center, 135
Welcome to the Furniture Fair!, 510
Whispers in Time, 482
Woodworking in Western Montana, 500

G

galleries
(Art)n Galleries, 90
@rtweb Art Gallery, 493
Abulafia Gallery, 82
Advanced Cultural Technologies, 71
Art Links on the World Wide Web, 72
Arthur Ross Gallery Homepage, The, 83
Artix, 72
ArtMap, 72
ArtScene, 73
ArtSource, 73
AS220, 73
Asian Arts, 83
Black and White Gallery, 90
California, 73
Center on Contemporary Art, 84
Christine Thea Partridge* Gallery, 80
Citizen Kane Gallery, 91
Cloud Gallery, 74
digital wave photography gallery, 91
Douglas Albert Gallery—State College, PA, 85

Duane Hilton High Sierra Fine Art, 85
Eagle Aerie Gallery (Roy Henry Vickers), 85
Edgerton Center's Online Photo Gallery, 91
Electric Gallery, 85
Electronic Art, 80
FineArt Forum Gallery, 85
Florida Wildflower Showcase, 91
FocalPoint f/8, 91
gallery.html (Edison Gallery), 75
GallerySight, 92
Hal's Virtual Furniture Gallery, 75
Heirloom Art, 85
International Masters Group, 86
Khazana, 86
Lightside Art Gallery, 81
Liros Gallery, 86
Motorcycle Collectable Art Gallery, 77
Museum Web, 81
Museum Web from Art-ROM, 77
Mythago, 92
Na-Te-So Workshop, 87
Nature Gallery, 92
New Mexico, 92
New York Public Library Photography Collection, 92
Novagraphics Space Art Gallery, 483
Ohio State University at Newark, 87
Parallax, 87
Pavilion of Polyhedreality, 87
Pearl St. Online Gallery, 87
Pix Gallery, 81
PPSA Photo Gallery, 93
Rare Treasures, 78
Rhode Island, 73
Robert Derr's Virtual Gallery, 82
Roger Whitney Gallery of Artists, The, 87
Rogers Virtual Gallery (Beauty #2), 94
Ruby's Gallery, 94
Russian Reminiscence, 94
Santa Fe Fine Art, 87
Sierra Wave Art Gallery, 88
U'Mista Cultural Centre, 79
Zone I Gallery, 94
gambling, Virtual Vegas, 352
games
3D action
3D Gaming Scene, 159
All-Time Best Doom Levels, 159
CyberMage, 159
Dark Forces Editors and Utilities, 159

Index

Djinni's Hexen-Editing Page, 159
Doom and Doom II Secrets, 159
Duke Nukem 3D Resource Page, 159
GameNet, 159
ID Archives—Doom, 338
id software, 159
Mech Warrior 2 and Clan of the Ghost Bear Page, 159
Quake, 159
Tenth Planet, 160
Terminator, 160
Welcome to the Web Wumpus, 342

3D strategy
Crusader, 160
Diablo, 160
Ishi Press, 160
Justin's Command and Conquer Web Page, 160
Player's Lists, 160
Raptor's Warcraft and Warcraft II Page, 160
Welcome to Dave's Warcraft 2 Page, 160

adventure
Activision Zork Nemesis, 161
Daggerfall, 161
Dungeon Keeper, 161
Myst Hint Guide, 161
Prepare to Get Maxxed, 161
Return to Krondor, 161
Review of Phantasmagoria, 161
Welcome to the Shrine of Zork, 161

Adventure Online Gaming, 599

arcade
Alexander Jean-Claude Bottema's Home Page, 336
The Destruction Derby Games, 337

BradyGAMES Home Page, 610

brainteasers
Crejaculabryrinth, 337
The Fruit Game, 338
Mindgames, 340
Riddle du Jour, 340
The Vain Game, 341

cards
IRC Poker Channels Home Page, 558
Wizards of the Coast, Inc., 342

Carlo's Coloring Book, 337

childhood
Build Your Own Critter, 336
Cool Lego Site of the Week, 337
Lite Board, 339
Rock, Paper, Scissors, 340
Tic-Tac-Toe, 341
Virtual Mr. Spud Head, 342

Web-a-Sketch, 342
WebBattleship, 342
Webcube, 342
Welcome To the Connect Four Homepage, 342

companies
7th Level, 161
Aristoplay, Ltd., 161
Bethesda Software, 161
Capstone Software, 162
Cosmic JamStain, 162
Epic Megagames, 162
InterPlay Productions, 162
LucasArts Entertainment Company Presents, 162
Microprose Software, 162
Pop Rocket, Inc., 162
Shadow Island Games, 162
Sierra On-Line, 162
Sony Electronic Publishing, 162
Virgin Zesty Bytes, 163
Virtual Entertainment, 163

developer sites
3D Engine List, 164
Commercial 3D Graphic Game Engines, 164
Digital Dialect, 164
EVPA, 165
G.A.C. Computer Services, 165
Gray Design Associates, 165
IBM OS/2 Games Home Page, 165
Jeff Lander's Home Page, 165
Pie in the Sky Software, 165

drinking, Chris' Collection of Drinking Misc., 337

educational
Bluedog Can Count, 336
Husband Lover Spy, 338
Lemonade Stand, 339

flight simulators
Air Havoc Controller for Windows, 163
Battlecruiser 3000AD Unofficial FAQ and Homepage, 163
Embry-Riddle Flight Simulation Links, 163
First Eurofighter Air Wing, 163
Flight Unlimited, 163
Military Simulations Back to Baghdad, 163
Military Simulations, Inc., 163
TekMate, 163
Terran Confederate Underground, 164
Thrustmaster Home Page, 164

U.S. Navy Fighters, 164
USENET Guide to Falcon 3, 164
Warbirds, 164
Welcome to CRC and the Air Warrior Community, 164
Werewolf vs. Commanche, 164

hardware
CH Products, 165
Creative Zone, 165
Diamond Multimedia, 165
Forte Vfxl, 165
head on by Eiger Labs, 165
Mag zine, 166
Virtual I/O, 166
Welcome to the SpaceTec IMC WebKeep, 166

horror
Computer Games Rating Guide, 166
Fade to Black, 166
Gabriel Knight, 166
Into the Void, 166
Psychic Detective, 166
Shivers, 166
Trilobyte Software, 166

humorous
Cannon Fodder II, 167
Earthworm Jim II, 167
Ferret Frenzy, 337
Gearheads, 167
Home Appliance Shooting, 338
How Bored Are You, 338
Information about Lemming 3D-the Demo, 167
Orion Burger, 167
Salon Betty's Interactive Paper Doll, 341
The Tick's Dart Games, 341
Welcome to Faces, 342
Welcome to Find-the-Spam, 342
You Don't Know Jack, 167

life simulators
Civilization Page, 167
Cybertown, 559
Jerry Moore's Sim Stuff Web Page, 167
Maxis, Inc. Home Page, 167

magazines
Coming Soon! Magazine, 167
Computer Gaming World, 168
Electronic Gaming Monthly, 168
Game Guide, 168
Game Informer, 168
hyper@ctive, 168
NEXT Generation Magazine, 168
Nuke InterNETWORK, 168
PC Gamer Online, 168

MUDs, Multiple User Dungeons, 168-169
puzzles
   Duck Hunt—Find the Fowl, 337
   Manic Maze, 340
   WWW Interactive Crossword, 342
role playing, Lee's Useless Superhero Generator, 339
scavenger hunts, Funny Bunny Trail, 338
screen savers, Dogz, 337
shareware/freeware
   Gamer's Inn, 169
   Games Domain, 169
   Happy Puppy's PC Hit 100 Game Downloads, 169
   Intel Software Showcase, 169
   Moonlite Software, 170
   shareware.com, 170
   Welcome to the New Guru Online, 170
sports-related
   Computer Baseball and Basketball Games, 170
   Trophy Bass, 170
   Unofficial Need for Speed Page, 170
   VR Soccer, 170
   Welcome to My NBA Live 96 Page, 170
   Whiplash, 170
   X-Car, 170
strategic, Play Chess on the Net, 340
trivia
   The Daily 100, 337
   Makin Bacon, 339
   Rock Mall's Trivia Challenge, 340
war simulators
   Avalon Hill, 170
   E-Hawk Cadre, 171
   Enemy Lock On!, 171
   Goat Locker, 171
   Great War Series, 171
   HPS Simulations, 171
   Multiplayer Games and Simulations, 171
   Silent Service Wargaming Club, 171
   Tanker's Homepage, 171
   War Page, 171
word games, Boggle, 336
gardening
AgriGator, 488
Garden Gate, 488
Gardening, 488
Gardening Archive, 488
Gardens at Thunder Ridge, 488

Germinator, 488
Howard Garrett's Basic Organic Program, 488
Joe and Mindy's WebGarden, 489
Magazine, 153
Organic Gardening, 447
Tele-Garden, 78
Virtual Garden, 489
gems
Crystals and Minerals, 497
Gems, 497
genealogy
Adoptee & Genealogy Page from Carrie's Crazy Quilt, 381
Cool Site of the Month for Genealogists, 707
Genealogy Home Page, 706
Genealogy Page, 706
Genealogy Resources on the Internet, 706
Roots Surname List Name Finder, 706
Treasure Maps, 381
Treasure Maps: The "How-To" Genealogy Site, 706
genetic engineering
Center for Soybean Tissue and Genetic Engineering, 749
Genetic Engineering Taught Through Telecommunications, 302
geography
AGI GIS Dictionary, 526
Althausen's WWW Wonderland, 768
Area Accurate Map/The Peters Projection, 526
Association of American Geographers, 526
Association of Chinese Professionals in Geographic Information Systems, 526
Canadian WWW Central Index/Liste centrale des serveurs WWW canadiens, 526
Cartography—Indiana State University, 526
ChartWrite's Data-on-the-Map, 526
Chesapeake Bay Program, 768
Clinch River Restoration Program, 768
Color Landform Atlas of the United States, 768
E-scapes: Electronic Resources for the Study of Ancient Landscapes, 527
Federal Geographic Data Committee (FGDC), 527
Geographic Institutes around the World, 527

Geographic Nameserver, 527
GEOGRAPHY USA: A Virtual Textbook, 527
Global Positioning System (GPS), 527
Heritage Map Museum, 527
History of Cartography Project, 527
How far is it?, 527
Institute of Arctic and Alpine Research, 527
Interactive Geographical Index, 527
International Map Trade Association (IMTA), 527
Internet Resources for Geographers, 769
Laboratory for Remote Sensing and Geographic Information Systems (LRSGIS), 528
Making Maps Easy to Read, 528
Mapmaker, Mapmaker, Make Me a Map, 528
MAPublisher, 528
Michael Braun's Home Page, 769
NAISMap WWW-GIS Home Page, 528
National Center for Geographic Information and Analysis (NCGIA), 528
Natural Area Coding System, 528
Oregon Geographic Alliance (OGA), 528
Project GeoSim, 528
RETKI GPS Land Navigation Software, 528
RYHINER-Project at the University Library of Berne, 528
Spatial Odyssey: GIS Literature Database, 529
TIGER Mapping Service, 529, 769
TOPO!™ Interactive Maps, 529
U.S. Geological Survey (USGS) National Mapping Information World Wide Web Server, 529
United States Gazetteer, 769
Xerox PARC Map Viewer, 529, 769
geology
Centre for Earth and Ocean Research—University of Victoria, 769
Civil Engineer's Calendar, 769
CNC Relief Maps, 769
Data Catalog, 769
Data Zoo, 769
Earthquake Info from the U.S.G.S., 769
Geographic Nameserver, 768
Nevada Bureau of Mines and Geology, 768

New Mexico Bureau of Mines and Mineral Resources, 769

Niel's Timelines and Scales of Measurement List, 770

Smithsonian Gem and Mineral Collection, 770

United States Department of the Interior/Geological Survey/Pacific Marine Geology, 770

United States Geological Survey, 770

Georgia

Atlanta Photography Group, 494

Atlanta Photojournalism Seminar, 494

Atlanta Web Guide, 915

geriatrics

AARP, 827

Adopt a Grandparent Program, 827

Aging Research Centre, 439

Caregiver Network Inc., 827

Elderhostel, 827

Grand Times, 827

Seniors-Site, 827

SWT Age Page, 828

Germany

Berlin Wall Falls Project, 458

CRLP: Women of the World, 542

Germany—Database of German Nobility, 459

Lufthansa Timetable Info, 904

ghosts

Arcadia, 687

Are Ghosts For Real?, 687

Asylum, 687

A Directory of Haunted Dining and Lodging in the U.S., 687

The Earthlight Productions Haunted Page, 687

Ghost Hunters Gallery, 687

Ghost Lore, 687

The Ghost Watcher, 687

Ghosts, 687

Ghosts of New Mexico, 687

Ghosts—The Charles J. Adams Home Page, 687

Haunted Toys R Us, 688

Hauntings Today, 688

Legend of Sleepy Hollow, 688

Ooga Booga Page, 688

Paranormal Belief Survey, 688

Philippine Ghost Story, 688

Schloss Reichenstein, 688

Virtual Library—Angel Encounters, 688

WWW Virtual Library—Ghost Stories and Folklore, 688

GIF (Graphics Interchange Format) files, 12

gifts

… la Gift Basket Headquarters, 807

Catalog Live!, 811

Christmas Shop, 807

Collectibles by R&T, 478

Collectibles by R&T Musical Merry-Go-Rounds, 479

Crafter's Showcase, 807

Eureka! The Web Junction, 812

Front Page, 813

Giftnet, 807

Global Innovations, 813

Moments On-Line, 481

Parkleigh World-Wide, 807

Private Source, 807

Roger's Collector's Marketplace, 481

Sea Creations, 482

Uncommon Connections, 816

Valentine & Company, 809

Winona, 816

WoodWrite Wood Pens, 809

glass

Glass Insulators, 479

Process Technologies Incorporated, 133

GNN, Global Network Navigator Home Page, 558

golf, 848-849

gorillas, 518

government

BosniaLINK, 413

C-Span Networks, 882

Census Bureau, 413

CIAWEB: Central Intelligence Agency Website, 413

DefenseLINK, 413

Federal and State-Run Servers, 292

Federal Election Commission, 413

Federal Information Exchange, 413

Federal Justice Center, 413

Federal Web Locator, 413

FedWorld Information Network, 413

House of Representatives WWW Service, 413

Japan Technology Program, 413

Know Your Enemies, 824

Library of Congress Home Page, 414

listservs, 423-426

Minority Business Development Agency, 414

National Archives and Records Administration, 709

National Criminal Justice Reference Service (NCJRS), 540

National Endowment for the Arts, 414

National Endowment for the Humanities (NEH), 525

National Humanities Institute Home Page, 525

National Institute of Mental Health (NIMH), 536

newsgroups, 420-422

Office of Management and Budget, 414

SERESC, 295

Social Security On Line, 414

surplus sales, 816

Thomas: The U. S. Congress, 414

U.S. Agency for International Development, 541

U.S. Department of Agriculture, 414

U.S. Department of Commerce: Stat-USA, 414

U.S. Department of Education, 414

U.S. Department of Energy, 414

U.S. Department of Health and Human Services, 415

U.S. Department of Housing and Urban Development, 415

U.S. Department of Justice, 415

U.S. Department of Labor, 415

U.S. Department of the Interior, 415

U.S. Department of Transportation, 415

U.S. Patent and Trademark Office, 415

U.S. Postal Service, 415

U.S. Travel and Tourism Administration, 415

United States Senate WWW Server, 415

Votelink...the Voice of the Net, 825

Zipper, 717

White House Home Page, 415

graffiti art, 72

grammar

11 Rules of Grammar, 703

Collective Nouns, 704

Grammar and Style Notes, 704

Lexeme-Morpheme Base Morphology (LMBM), 531

Word for Word, 705

Word Page, 705

WordNet, 705

graphic design

Architecture & Design, 505

Artzilla Surf Constructions, 576

Dynamic Diagrams Home Page, 577

Free Range Media, Inc., 577

IBM—the Electric Origami Shop, 338

MMWIRE WEB, 602

NetWorXs of California, 579

Optical Illusions—A Collection, 340

Stannet WWW Designing and Publishing Company, 580

Surrey Institute of Art and Design's World Wide Web Server, 88

WebDesigns, 580

graphical user interfaces (GUIs), 8

graphics

Adobe Illustrator What's New, 196

AnimaTek, Inc., 196

Anton's Freehand Page, 196

Artifice, Inc., 196

Astrobyte, 197

Autodesk Home Page, 197

BackStreet Studios, 321

Blue Sky Research, 197

Cadkey Corp., 197

CadSoft Computer GmbH, 197

Caema Ltd., 197

CGD.Graphix, 197

CHRIS DICKMAN'S CorelNet, 197

Cimio CADCAM Conversion Software, 197

Click 3x, 197

ComCom Systems, Inc., 197

Computer Chrome Presentation Graphics, 198

Computer Graphics Systems Development Corporation, 198

Creative Eye, 198

Creative Services, 198

CyberTec Commercial Art, Inc., 198

Cytopia Software Incorporated, 198

DAIR Computer Systems Logo Design, 198

Data Image Systems, 198

DesignSphere Online, 198

Digio Media, 199

displaying on Web sites, 49

Edifika, 199

EDS Unigraphics Division, 199

Electronic Design Automation Companies, 199

Evans & Sutherland Computer Corporation, 199

Fractal Design Corporation, 199

Graphics Gallery, 199

Hamrick Software, 199

hardware, 34

ICE, 199

IDEAL Scanners & Systems, 199

InfoImaging Technologies Home Page, 199

Intergraph Corp., 200

Kai's Power Tips and Tricks for Adobe Photoshop, 200

Lightscape Technologies, Inc., 200

Limit X, 200

Live Picture, Inc., 200

Lockheed Martin REAL3D, 200

MacroMedia Freehand Page, 200

Management Graphics, Inc. USA, 200

Marine Graphics, Inc., 200

MaxVision Online, 200

Mentor Graphics Corporation, 200

Number Nine Visual Technologies, 201

Optix: The Internet Document, 201

Pacific Animated Imaging, 201

Parallel Performance Group, 201

Parametric Technology Corporation, 201

Pathtrace Systems, 201

Pattern Corporation, 201

Paul Mace Software, 201

Performing Graphics Company, 201

PhotoModeler, 201

Photoshop Folder FTP Site, 201

Play Incorporated, 201

Precision Graphics of Texas, 202

Quadrat Communications, 202

Renaissance Technologies, 202

Render-Cam Images, 202

Scientific Visualization Sites, 202

Silicon Surf, 202

Software Publishing Corporation Home Page, 202

Stephens Design, 202

Subia, 202

team smartyPANTS!, 202

tela computer consulting + design, 202

Triffet Design Group, 203

Ventana's Photoshop f/x Online Companion, 203

Virtus Corporation, 203

Visual CADD Home Page, 203

WebFlow Communications Group, 203

Zycad Corporation, 203

Graphics Interchange Format (GIF), 12

graphs, Web sites, 49

Great Britain

Castles of Wales, 517

UK Archaeology on the Internet, 524

Greece

Ancient City of Athens, 456, 520

Ohio State University Excavations at Isthmia, 458

Perseus Project Home Page, 457

Project Libellus, 295

Greek Orthodox

Orthodox Christian Page, 726

Orthodox Ministry ACCESS, 726

GUIs (graphical user interfaces), 8

guitars, GUITAR.NET, 662

gymnastics, 852

H

hackers, 22

hair care products, Maui Amenities, 808

hair loss, Hair Loss Handbook and Support Group Network, 442

half-duplex modes, 33

ham radio, *see* **amateur radio**

handguns, KRAMER Handgun Leather, 814

handles, 23

hardware

ACCESS Computer Hardware, 203

American Power Conversion, 203

ATI Technologies Online, 203

audio, 34

Autotime Corp., 203

Bandwidth Brokers International (BBI), 203, 204

BizWeb Category Computer Hardware, 204

Black Box Corporation, 204

Boca Research, 204

BusLogic, Inc., 204

BVM, 204

Canadian Institute of Applied Learning, Inc., 300

Central Data, 204

Colorgraphic Communications Corporation, 204

Commax Technologies, Inc., 204

Computer Companies and Vendor WWW Home Pages, 204

computer games, 165

Computer Hardware Page, 204

DTK Computers Inc., 204

graphics, 34

Hauppauge Computer, 205

Hewlett Packard Products, 205

ICS, 205

Image, 205

Image Manipulation Systems, 205

IMT Systems, 205

Information Data Products Corp., 205

Intel Information for Developers, 205

Intergraph Corporation, 205

Maxtor Current Product Information, 205

Memory USA, 205

Micro House International, 205

MIPS Product Information, 205

Network Hardware Suppliers List, 571

Power Computing Corporation, 206

Praegitzer Industries Web Server, 206

PSI Ltd., 206

Rockwell Collins Printed Circuits, 206

Samsung Group, 206

SCEPTRE, 206

Tadpole Technology, 206

TechnoGraphy & Storage Computer in Japan, 206

Thinking Machines Corporation, 206

TouchWindow, 206

TTi Technologies, Inc., 206

ViewSonic Corporation, 207

Web requirements, 31

hardwood floors

Anderson Hardwood Floors, 508

Carpets.com, 508

see also flooring

harmonicas, Harmonica World, 662

harps

Harp Page, 662

Historical Harp Society Page, 662

Hawaii

Above It All, 902

Air Force Maui Optical Station (AMOS), 750

Hawaiian Express Unlimited, 813

Ilene & Wayne Productions: Collectibles, 480

Kualono: 'Olelo Hawai'i, 531

Oils of Aloha, 407

Virtually Hawaii, 778

headers in newsgroups, 29

health

Blonz Guide to Nutrition, Food Science, and Health, 436

Kaiser Family Foundation, 434

listservs, 453-454

newsgroups, 451-453

health care, 415

American College of Healthcare Executives, 440

American Social Health Association, 799

Aspen Publishers, Inc., 440

BONES (Biomedically Oriented Navigator), 440

Camp Heartland, 799

Catholic Health Association of Wisconsin, 442

Center for Rural Health and Social Service Developers, 440

Charities USA, 442

Chiropractic Page, 441

Colgate Kid's World, 149

Colorado HealthNet, 441

employment, MedSearch America, 441

Healthcare Financial Management Association, 440

Healthcare Information and Management Systems Society, 440

HealthCom, Inc., 438

Herpes Zone, 799

holistic, New York Open Center, 294

HomeCareNurse Web Page, 446

Indigent Patient Services, 441

Innervation Technology Corp., 440

Interactive Patient, 443

Internal Capsule, 441

International Planned Parenthood Federation, 799

KidsHealth.org, 152

Linda Sy Skin Care, 439

Marquette University Program in Physical Therapy, 441

MDB Information Network, 441

Medical Education Page, 443

Medical/Clinical/Occupational Toxicology Resource Homepage, 294

men

Chronic Prostatitis, 444

Circumcision Issues, 444

Male Factor Infertility, 444

Male Fertility, 444

Men's Health, 444

Men's Health Issues, 445

Successfully Treating Impotence, 445

Survival High, 445

Urologic and Male Genital Diseases, 445

mental

Acclaim Professional Counseling, 445

Cyber-Psych, 445

Institute of Psychiatry, 445

National Alliance for the Mentally Ill Home Page, 445

National Coalition of Arts Therapies Associations, 445

Noodles's Panic-Anxiety Page, 445

Psychiatry and Psychotherapy, 445

Psyrix Help-Net and High Performance Consultants, 446

Recreational Therapy Home Page, 446

Missouri Institute of Mental Health, 442

Narhex, 439

National Association of Health Authorities and Trusts, 440

Natracare, LLC, 439

nursing

ADN/RN Concepts, 446

Idea Nurse, 446

International Network for Interfaith Heal Practices, 446

MacNursing, 446

Nursing Lists, 446

Telephone Triage and Nurse Consultation, 446

WholeNurse, 446

occupational

American Industrial Hygiene Association, 450

Computer Related Repetitive Strain Injury, 450

CTD News Online, 450

Eastern Analytical Services, 450

EMF-Link, 450

Health and Computers, 450

Howger Services, Inc., 450

NewsPage, 450

OSHA-DATA, 450

Rocky Mountain Center for Occupation Environmental Health, 450

Typing Injury FAQ, 450

Pain Reliever, 414, 686

Patti Peeples' Guide to Health Economics, Medical, and Pharmacy Resources on the Net, 441

Personal Lubricant, 853

Physical Therapy WWW Page, 441

SHAPE: Sexual Health Advocate Peer Education, 800

Society for Medical Decision Making, 440

travel

AEE Wilderness Safety and Emergency Care, 448

Comprehensive Healthcare for International Wilderness Travelers, 448

Executive Registry, 448

HealthNet, 448

Healthy Flying, 448

International Traveler's Clinic, 448

Moon Publications, 448

Outdoor Action Guide to High Altitude Acclimatization and Illness, 448

Travel First Aid Kit, 448
Traveler's Diarrhea, 448
Traveler's Medical and
   Immunization Service, 448
World Wide Drugs, 449
Vitamins, 915
women
   Atlanta Reproductive Health Centre,
      449
   Avon's Breast Cancer Awareness
      Crusade, 449
   Breast Cancer Information, 449
   Bright Innovations, 449
   Emergency Contraception, 449
   Endometriosis, 449
   Health and Science, 449
   Health Articles by Patricia Older,
      449
   Labor of Love, 449
   OB/GYN Toolbox, 449
   S.P.O.T., 449
   Women of the World, 449
   WomenCare, 449
   WomenSpace, 449
health care products
   Health-Max: Your Maximum Health
      Connection, 808
   J. Crow Company-Herbs, Spices,
      Oils, Incense, 808
health food
   Algy's Herb Page, 407
   Alliance Health Products, 428
   BabyfishNet's Vegan Recipes, 407
   Blue Green Algae Enzymes, 811
   Earthrise Spirulina home page, 407
   Gardenburger, 407
   Herbs & Spices, 407
   Index to Gluten-Free and Wheat-free
      Diets pages, 407
   Mycelium, 407
   Natural Food Samples, 368, 418
   Noah's Ark, 407
   U.S. Soyfoods Directory, 408
   Vegetarian Pages, 408
   Veggies Unite!, 408
   Whole Foods Market, 408
   World Guide To Vegetarianism, 408
health insurance
   AFLAC, 441
   Employers Health Insurance, 441
   FHP Health Care, 442
   Inscon: Insurance Consultants, Inc.,
      442
   Insurance for Students, Inc., 442

Insurance Research Network, 442
Managed Health Care, 442
Rusty Chambers Insurance Agent—
   Life, DI, Disabliity, Health, 442
Value-Care, 442
Worldwide Med, 442
**health regulations, Environmental
Training Group Inc.'s ENVIROPAGE,
306**
heart diseases, *see* **cardiovascular
disease**
herbariums, *see* **botany**
herbology, 428-429
high latency, 32
hiking, 849
Hinduism
   Bhagavad Gita, 732
   Global Hindu Electronic Network,
      732
   Hinduism, 732
   Hinduism Today Home Page, 732
   Kundalini Research Foundation, Ltd.,
      732
   Spirituality, Yoga, and Hinduism, 732
history
   ADFA History: History on the
      Internet, 462
   African-American
      African American History, 455
      Amistad Research, 291
      Isis: Our Story, 455
   agriculture, Oregon—World War II
      Farming, 456
   American and British History
      Resources, 455
   ancient
      ABZU, 456
      Akkadian Language (Babylonian and
         Assyrian Cuneiform Texts), 456
      Alexandria, Egypt, 456
      Ancient and Medieval Coins, 486
      Ancient City of Athens, 456
      Archaeological Survey in the Eastern
         Desert of Egy, 456
      Assyria On-line, 456
      Didaskalia: Home Page, 457
      Diotima: Women & Gender in the
         Ancient World, 457, 542
      E-scapes: Electronic Resources for the
         St Ancient Landscapes, 527
      Exploring Ancient World Cultures,
         457, 518
      Kelsey Museum Educational and
         Outreach Program, 457
      Oriental Institute, 457

Perseus Project Home Page, 457
Peter Konin's Ancient Rome Page,
   457
Pompeii, 457
Pompeii Forum, 457
Ari's Today Page, 462
Armenia, Armenian Research Center
   Home Page, 458
Best of Edward Gibbon's Decline and
   Fall of the Roman Empire, 717
BUBL Information Service Web
   Server, 462
Castles on the Web, 462
China, Empires Beyond the Great
   Wall: The Heritage of Genghis Khan,
   460
Civil War: American Civil War Home
   Page, 455
Conventional Wisdom: Selected
   Quotations Illustrating the Illusions
   of Popular History, 717
Europe
   Europe/Russia/Eastern Europe, 458
   European History, 458
   Historical Text Archive, 459
   History Pages, 459
   REESWeb: Russian and East
      European Studies, 459
Gangsters!, 462
Germany
   Berlin Wall Falls Project, 458
   Germany—Database of German
      Nobility, 459
Heritage Post Interactive, 463
Historical Text Archive, 463
History Computerization Project, 463
History of Costume by Braun, 463
History of Money from Ancient
   Times to the Present Day, 487
History of Space Exploration, 465
Hungary, Hungarian Images and
   Historical Background, 459
Index of /expo/, 463
Institute for Human Sciences—
   Vienna, 465
Internet
   Economic FAQs about the Internet,
      576
   Internet Business Center, 576
   Rampages, 576
   World Wide Web, 576
Ireland
   Irish History on the Web, 459
   Irish Potato Famine, 459
Italy, Romarch List Home Page, 464
James B. Ross' Home Page, 463

Leonardo da Vinci Museum, 460
listservs, 467-475
Lords of the Earth: Maya/Aztec/Inca Exchange, 463
Maritime History Virtual Archives, 463
Martin Luther King Jr. Directory, 825
Mary Rose Virtual Maritime Museum, 463
Maya, 463
Maya Astronomy Page, 463
Mayan Hieroglyphic Syllabary, 532
Media History, Studies, and Education, 463
medieval studies
 Ancient and Medieval Coins, 486
 Articles on Medieval/Renaissance Subjects, 460
 Avalon: Arthurian Heaven, 460
 Byzantium: The Byzantine Studies Page, 460
 Labyrinth WWW Home Page, 460
 Vikings Home Page, 461
 WWW Medieval Resources, 461
military
 Cold War Hot Links, 461
 Cybrary of the Holocaust, 461
 D-Day, 461
 George Rarey's Journals of the 379th Fighter Squadron, 461
 Gulf War Photo Gallery, 461
 Korean War Project, 461
 Medals of America, 481
 Military History, 461
 Operation Desert Storm Debriefing Book, 461
 Remembering Nagasaki, 461
 Salvation of Bulgarian Jews during WW II, 461
 Salzburg 1945–1955: Introduction, 461
 Vietnam Veterans Home Page, 462
 War from a Parlot: Stereoscopic Images of American War and Soldiers's Letters Home, 462
 World War I (1914-1918), 462
 World War II on the Web, 462
 Worlds of Late Antiquity, 462
Native American Cultural Resources on the Internet, 464
nautical
 Mutiny on the HMS Bounty, 464
 Pan-American Institute of Maritime Archaeology (PIMA), 523
 Pirates, 464
newsgroups, 466

North American Historical Re-Enactor Web Site (West Site), 308
Papyrology Home Page, 464
Rare Map Collection at the Hargrett Library, 710
Russia
 Russian Information, 459
 Soviet Archives: Entrance Room, 459
science and technology, Art of Renaissance Science, 465
Shikhin, 464
Shore Line Trolley Museum, 465
Spectrum Biography Library, 460
Twisted Freaks of History, 460
UNESCO World Heritage List, 465
United States
 Abraham Lincoln Online, 459
 American Civilization Internet Resources, 455
 American History, 455
 American Memory, 455
 American Revolution and the Struggle for Independence, 455
 American Studies Web, 455
 Anti-Imperialism in the United States, 1898–1935, 455
 Educational Sources for George Washington, 459
 Fair Play, 460
 Indiana Historical Society, 455
 JFK Resources Online, 460
 Life Histories—American Memory Project, 456
 Thomas Jefferson, 460
 Thomas Paine, 460
 United States Presidents: Welcome Page, 460
 United States—History, 456
 Welcome to the United States Civil War Center, 297
Voice of the Shuttle Home Page, 465
Web, 4-5
women
 Encyclopedia of Women's History, 542
 Her Own Words®, 544
 Women's History Month, 545
World of Benjamin Franklin, 297
hobbies
listservs, 503-504
newsgroups, 501-503
hockey, 849-850
holistic medicine
Actual Natural Source, 427
Acupuncture Home Page, 427
Alexandra Health Center, 427

Alternative Medicine Home Page from Falk Library of the Health Science-University of Pittsburgh, 427
Cell Tech Super Blue Green Algae, 428
Code Four Medical, 428
Conscious Choice, 427
Doody Publishing Health Science Book Reviews, 429
Dragon Herbarium, 429
Good Medicine Magazine, 601
HANS—The Health Action Network Society, 428
Health and Longevity, 428
Herbal Hall, 428
My Life International, 429
Nature's Medicine, 428
Natural Health and Nutrition Shop, 428
New York Open Center, 294
Pain Reliever, 414, 686
People's Place, 428
SPA in Italy, 441
Springboard Health and Nutrition Products, 429
Welcome to Acupuncture, 428
WorldWide Wellness, 428
Holocaust
Cybrary of the Holocaust, 461
Genealogy Page, 706
home entertainment systems, Media Dimensions, 506
home improvement
Advanced Flooring, Inc, 508
automation
 CBI Systems, Inc., 505
 DHSL: Data Home Systems Limited, 505
 Home Automation Association, 505
 Home Automation Association (HAA), 505
 Home Automator, 506
 Home Team, 506
 HomeTheater Com, 506
 Intelligent Home Technologies, Inc., 506
 Media Dimensions, 506
 ProSpec, 506
 Vantage, 506
Builders Graphics, 510
Carpet One, 508
Carpet Samples, 673
Carpets.com, 508
construction
 Advant Home, 135

Construction Zone, 506
dotSpiegel, 812
Home Line Talk Radio, 510
Country Oak Flooring, 509
Cyberwood Express, 506
DO IT YOURSELF HQ, 508
Dulux Paint Assistant, 507
Floor Coverings International, 509
Home Ideas, 510
Home Improvement, 508
HOME IMPROVEMENT and CONSTRUCTION CONNECTION, 507
Home Improvement Home Page, 507
Home Improvement How-to Videos, 508
Home Improvement Net, 507
Home Line Talk Radio, 510
Home Repair Hotline, 510
HomeSource, 507
Hometime, 508
Jonathan Press Woodworking and Home Improvement Books and Plans, 507
Lamb Home Videos U-DO IT YOURSELF, 508
listservs, 515-516
loans
Fidelity Union Mortgage, 136
Home Improvement Loans, 136
Lowe's Home Improvement Warehouse, 510
Materials Engineering and Research Laboratory, 508
National Consumer Alert Hotline, 510
New Home Interactive Cyber Home Building Site, 507
newsgroups, 515
On The House with The Carey Brothers, 510
Remodeler Online, 507
Sculptured Carpet Selections, 509
Sound Home Resource Web Home Page, 507
This Old House, 511
TrustMark, 509
United Consumers Club, 511
Voyager Plus Home Improvement Specialists, 511
home inspection
Accu-Spect Home Inspection Institute, 511
Advanced Home Inspection, 511
American Society of Home Inspection, 511

AmeriSpec Home Inspection Service, 511
Home Inspection Resources, 511
Home Spec Inspection Services, Inc., 511
HomeSpec 101, 511
Professional Home Inspections, Inc., 511
Wedgwood Service Group, Inc., 512
home schooling, AERO-The Alternative Education Resource Organization, 823
home security
DHSL: Data Home Systems Limited, 505
Home Automation Association (HAA), 505
Home Team, 506
homeopathy, 427-428
homosexuality
Gay & Lesbian Bar Guide, 798
Gay & Lesbian National Hotline, 799
Grassroots Queers, 799
OutNOW Live, 799
Pines Guesthouse, 799
Same-Sex Marriage Home Page, 588
Small Media and Large, 615
honeymoons
Caribmoon, 925
Coconut Coast Weddings and Honeymoons, 926
Island Weddings, SuperClubs, 925
Wedding Gardens, 925
Wedding Made in Paradise, 925
horoscopes, Today Page, 565
horror games, 166
horror movies
Cabinet of Dr. Casey, 637
David Cronenberg Home Page, 637
Halloween, 637
Hannibal Lecter Home Page, 637
Jaws, 637
Lord of Illusions, 637
Nightmare on the Web, 637
Return of the Texas Chainsaw Massacre, 637
The Shining, 637
horses
EquiLinQ, 63
Horse Country, 150, 850
Horse Zone, 63-64
Horseman's Advisor, The, 64
Keller's Appaloosas, 814
models, Haynet on the Web, 479
Thoroughbred Horse Racing and Breeding, 850

Three Chimneys Farm Home Page, 850
Washington Handicapper, 851
WWW Library–Livestock Section, 64
horticulture
The Tele-Garden, 341
Conservation Breeding Specialist Group, 362
International Palm Society, 362
John Muir Exhibit, 363
Okefenokee Joe's Natural Education Center, 366
see also gardening; landscaping
hospitals
Arkansas Children's Hospital, 442
Cyberspace Hospital, 443
Department of Neurosurgery at New York University, 443
Department of Otorhinolaryngology at Baylor College of Medicine, 443
New England Medical Center, 443
hotels and motels
American Youth Hostels, 910
Bed & Breakfast Inns Online, 910
California Travel and Parks Association, 910
Campground Directory, 910
Choice Hotels, 910
Homeless Shelters in the United States, 910
Hostelling International, 911
International Bed And Breakfast Guide, 911
Nude 2000, 911
Professional Association of Innkeepers International, 911
Travel Web, 911
United Hostels of Europe, 911
World Wide Lodging Guide, 911
house music, DJ Dom A's Top Twenty Club Charts, 649
housewares
Dean & Deluca, 397
North Fork Exchange, 398
HTML (HyperText Markup Language), 4, 11, 43
Bare Bones Guide to HTML, 565
Beginner's Guide to HTML, 566
Cerebral Systems Development— Home of Webber™, 566
Color Editor for Windows, 566
HTML Editor Information, 566
HTML Info Page, 566
Introduction to HTML: Table of Contents, 566
Personal Home Page of Bob Hunter, 566

Primer for Creating Web Resources, 566

tags, 43

Web Letter, a Guide to HTML/Web Publishing, 566

Web Resources, 566

HTTP (HyperText Transfer Protocol), 15

human evolution, *see* **anthropology; evolution**

human resources

Achievement Corporation, 325

Analysis Group, 325

Benefit Associates, 325

CareerLab, 325

Edwards and Associates, 325

Fortune Personnel Consultants, 326

Human Resource News and Issues, 326

Pemberton and Associates, 326

Total Human Resources, 326

human rights

Human Rights Brief, 591

Human Rights Web Home Page, 539

humanist sociology, Association for Humanist Sociology, 538

humanities

Bonfire of Liberties: Censorship of the Humanities, 823

Center for Electronic Texts in the Humanities, 524

Center for the Humanities, 524

Computing in the Humanities Users Group (CHUG), 524

H-Net—Humanities OnLine, 525

Humanities and Social Sciences— University of Chicago LibInfo, 525

Humanities HUB, 525

Humanities National Database Search, 525

Humanities Report, 525

Institute for Human Sciences— Vienna, 525

listservs, 548-552

National Endowment for the Humanities (NEH), 525

National Humanities Institute Home Page, 525

newsgroups, 547

Research Institute for the Humanities (RIH), 526

Stanford Electronic Humanites Review, 526

Voice of the Shuttle: Web Page for Humanities Research, 526

WWW Virtual Library—Humanities, 526

humor

Air Guitar, 343

The Amazing Pecking Chicken, 343

Big Green Button, 343

Center for the Easily Amused, 343

comedians, Rodney Dangerfield Home Page, 346

Cruel Site of the Day, 343

Crunch, 343

Cursing in Swedish, 343

The Daily Muse, 343

David Hasselhoff is the AntiChrist, 343

A Duck's Memoirs, 344

Evil Little Brother's Excuse Generator, 344

Exploding Heads, 344

Fun with Grapes, 338

Georgetown Gonzo, 344

The Great Barbie Naming Contest, 344

Heather Has Two Mommies, 344

It's the French Fries, 344

Jadie's Warped Mind, 344

Jim's All New, Fresher Smelling Home Page, 344

Kurt Cobain's Talking Eight Ball, 339

LaughWeb, 344

Lawyer Jokes, 593

Legalitees T-Shirts Home Page, 593

Lip Balm Anonymous, 345

The Lunacy Catapult, 345

The Magic 8 Bra, 347

Make James Earl Jones Speak, 345

The Miraculous Winking Jesus, 345

Murphy's Law, 593

Oracle Service Humor Archive, 345

Pelvis, 345

Piercing Mildred, 340

Punch Rush Limbaugh Page, 345

Random Elizabethan Curse Generator, 345

Random Jokes about Yo Mama, 346

Rock and Roll Hall of Shame, 678

The Scamizdat Memorial, 346

Solid Space, 346

Spam Haiku Archive, 346

Spatula City, 346

Supermarket Tabloid Headlines, 348

TEI's Random Joke Server, 346

The Textual Abuse Page, 346

Thinking Bob's Image of the Day, 346

Twisted Tunes Home Page, 346

Webcrawler—Deep Thought of the Day, 347

White Trash Homepage—Phrantic's Trailerpark, 347

World Headquarters for Burrito and Burrito-Related Information, 347

WWW Fights, 347

humorous games

Ferret Frenzy, 337

Home Appliance Shooting, 338

How Bored Are You, 338

Salon Betty's Interactive Paper Doll, 341

The Tick's Dart Games, 341

Welcome to Faces, 342

Welcome to Find-the-Spam, 342

Hungary, Hungarian Images and Historical Background, 459

Hunt, Alan, 75

hurricanes, *see* **meteorology**

hydrology, Macroscale Land Surface Hydrology Modeling at the UW, 304

hypermedia, 3-4, 14

hypertext, 3, 576

HyperText Markup Language, *see* **HTML**

HyperText Transfer Protocol (HTTP), 15

I

Iceland, Invgar's Home Page, 125

Idaho, Idaho Home Page, 916

IDE (integrated drive electronics), 34

Illinois, Chicago Information System, 916

image compression, 568

FutureTel, Inc., 568

Image Compression for Publishing Online, 578

image processing, 760

immigration

American Civil Liberties Union, 824

American Immigration Lawyers Association, 590

Internet Immigration Law Center, 588

Minority Affairs Forum, 827

impotence

Geddings Osbon, Sr. Foundation Impotence Resource Center, 444

Successfully Treating Impotence, 445

improvement, home, *see* **home improvements**

independent label music

Alternet Sonic Realities, 671

Asphodel Records, 672

Axiom/Laswell Web Site, 672

Badcat Records, 672

Bedazzled, 672

Bogus Records, 672

Boy's Life Records, 672

Caroline Records, 672

Castle von Buhler Records, 672

Catasonic Records, 672

Caulfield Records, 672

East Side Digital Records, 673

Hi-Bias Records Inc., 673

Index, 647

Landphil Records' Online Information Dump, 673

Lunch Records, 673

Manifest Records, 674

Marathon Records, 674

Monkeyland Records, 674

Moonshine Music, 674

Planet StarChild, 676

Pop Gun Records, 674

Propulsion Records, 674

Rage Records, 674

Red Phraug Modern Medium, 674

Rounder Records, 654

Sesha Press Records, 675

Silver Girl Records, 675

Sin-Drome Records, 675

Slumberland Records, 675

Squealer Music, 675

Supernova Records, 675

Surfdog Records, 675

Verb Audio, 675

Wa Nui Records, 676

Wood and Wire, 648

indexing

American Society of Indexers home page, 708

LC Thesaurus for Graphic Material: Topical Terms for Subject Access, 703

India

Batish Institute of Indian Music and Fine Arts, 657

Classical Music Home Page N.S. Sundar, 657

CRLP: Women of the World, 542

Hello India!, 298

Hindi Movie Songs, 658

Indian Classical Music, 658

Indian Music: Recordings and Instruments, 658

Sami's Urdu/Hindi Film Music Page, 659

Indiana, Indiana Virtual Tourist, 916

indigenous peoples, NativeWeb, 519

Indonesia, Indoesian Music, 658

infertility

Atlanta Reproductive Health Centre, 449

Male Factor Infertility, 444

Male Fertility, 444

Tapestry Books— Adoption/ Infertility Book Catalog, 429

inline skating, 855

insects, *see* **entomology**

insolvency, Internet Bankruptcy Library, 131

installing browsers, 46

instruments, *see* **musical instruments**

insurance

AFLAC, 441

Employers Health Insurance, 441

FHP Health Care, 442

Inscon, 442

Insurance for Students, Inc., 442

Insurance Research Network, 442

Managed Health Care, 442

Rusty Chambers Insurance Agent— Life, DI, Disability, Health, 442

Value-Care, 442

Worldwide Med, 442

integrated drive electronics (IDE), 34

Integrated Services Digital Networks (ISDN) connection, 8, 33

interfaces, AboutWeb/Genera, 557

interior decorating

BUILD.COM: The Building and Home Improvement Products Network, 487

Carpet Samples, 673

Cascade Blinds, 512

Colton Inc., 512

Cuvs Factory Outlet Store, 512

Decorating Dimensions, Inc., 512

Decorating Online, 512

Dion's Secrets of Home Decorating guide, 512

Home Decorator, 512

Mainely Shades, 513

National Decorating Products Association, 513

Roc On Drywall Paint & Wallpaper, 512

Southwest Decor, 512

Sudberry House new Location!, 513

Suzanne Seely's "Make it Beautiful" Decorating Newsletter, 513

Symbol-Talk, 513

interior design

Architecture & Design, 505

Art for Architecture, 505

HBA Architecture and Interior Design, 505

International Architecture and Design Home Page, 505

MBT Architecture, 505

V.C.net, 505

international business

Adnet, 123

African Sky Video, 123

Agora Language Marketplace, 124

Asian Business Daily, 124

Ask Us For, 124

Australasian World Publishing Systems, 124

Australian Pacific Advertising, 124

Australian Stock Market Web Page, 124

Austrian Worldport, 124

Batey Ads Singapore, 124

Canada Net Pages, 124

Canadian Business InfoWorld, 124

Catalogue Production Management Services, 124

Cyber Planet Korea, 125

Econsult Group WWW Page, 125

Extra Trade, Inc., 125

How to Do Business in Mexico, 125

ICC Communications Centre, 125

INFOCENTRO, 125

Ingvar's Home Page, 125

London Mall Magazine and HQ, 125

Mega-Directory of US/Canada International Exports-U.S. Trade Center Directory, 125

Microswiss-Centre North-South, 125

Mobile Phones for UK Users, 125

Moscow Libertarium, 125

NAFTA Watch, 125

OCEANOR-Oceanographic Company of Norway, 126

Octagon Technology Group, Inc., 126

Pristine Communications, 126

Rainforest Health Project, 126

searchers, International Business Resources on the WWW, 574

Selling Your Products Abroad, 126

South African Futures Exchange, 126

TN-1 NAFTA Home Page, 126

U.S. Council for International Business, 126

Valore International, 126

Virtual Business Plaza, 126

VR Cargo International Home Page, 126

Index

Welcome to Molson Canadian, 127

Welcome to the European Market, 126

international education

Friends and Partners, 298

Global Ecology Study Abroad/IHP, 304

GROW-Opportunity Wales, 304

Hello India!, 298

Human-Languages Page, 298

I*EARN, 298

IMD International Institute for Management Development, 299

Intercultural E-Mail Classroom Connection, 302

JASON Project, 302

Landegg Academy Online, 302

Le Coin des Francophones et Autres Grenouilles, 299

Live from Antarctica, 299

Reed Interactive's Global Classroom, 303

Study in the USA Online Directory, 303

World Kids Press Homepage, 299

international law

American Journal of International Law, 588

Foreign and International Law Page, 588

International Law Page, 588

International Trade Law—ITL, 588

Internet Immigration Law Center, 588

Journal of International Law and Practice, 591

JurWeb, 588

United Nations Crime and Justice Information Network, 589

WWW Virtual Library: Law: International & Environmental Law, 587

international radio, Blue Planet, 348

international relations, Web of Culture, 827

international travel

Air Brokers International World Travel Specialist, 906

Alchemy of Africa, 906

Ansett Australia, 906

Antigua & Barbuda, 906

Australia Travel Directory, 906

Automated Travel Center, 906

Brochure Flow, 906

Civilized Explorer, 907

Costa Travel Online, 907

Council Travel, 907

Country Maps of Europe, 907

Cyprus, 907

Czech Info Center, 907

Dublin Pub Review, 907

Endeavour Travel, 907

European and British Rail Passes, 907

Eurostar Internet, 907

Far & Away Travel Services, 907

FranceEscape, 907

Freesun News, 908

Going to Belgium, 908

Great Australian Travel Co., 908

Hong Kong Online Guide, 908

Indonesia, 908

InteleTravel International, 908

International Travel Agency (ITA), 908

Internet Guide to Hostels, 908

Intra Travel, 908

Jerusalem Mosaic, 908

Jordan, 908

Lanka Internet Services, 908

Lonely Planet Travel Centre, 908

Middle World, 908

Monaco Home Page, 909

Salzburg, Austria, 909

Sinbad Travel, 909

TGV French High Speed Train, 909

Tour Canada without Leaving Your Desk, 909

Tourist Office of Spain Homepage, 909

Travel Home, 909

Travel to Finland, 909

United Kingdom Pages, 909

Vancouver, British Columbia, 909

Victoria, British Columbia, 909

Welcome to Future Net— Queensland, Australia, 909

Internet

access providers

Charm Net Personal IP Page, 553

CyberSight, 553

EFF's (Extended) Guide to the Internet, 553

Fountainhead Internet Systems, 553

Fusion Advertising and Communications, 553

GeoCities, 553

GHG Corp, 553

GTLug ISP Index, 553

How To Select an Internet Service Provider, 553

I-2000, 553

Icanect, 553

ICNet: The Original Internet Provider for the East, 553

Imagine.com, 554

Industrial Peer-to-Peer, 554

Infonet, 554

InReach, 554

Inspiration Software, 554

InstaNet (Instant Internet Corp.), 554

Intergate, 554

Internet Access Phoenix Arizona, 554

Internet Application Services, Inc., 554

Internet Channel, 554

Internet Delaware, 554

Internet Direct, 554

Internet Express, Inc., 554

Internet Front, 554

Internet Interface Systems, 554

Internet Light and Power, 555

Internet MainStreet, 555

Internet North, 555

Internet On-Ramp, Inc., 555

Internet Services Montana, 555

InterServe Communications, 555

IntrepidNet, 555

ISDN Internet Access, 555

Knighted Computers, 570

LavaNet, Inc., 555

LI.Net, 555

Linkage Online, 555

Magnetic Page, 555

MapleNet Technologies, Inc., 555

Medius Communications, Inc., 555

Michigan Internet Cooperative Association, 556

Micron Internet Services, 556

Minnesota MicroNet, 556

Minnesota Regional Network (MRNet), 556

MJC Inc. Computer Services, 556

Mojoski Net Tools, 556

MonadNet, 556

Moran Communications Group, 556

Mountain Internet, 556

Nantucket.Net, 556

National Knowledge Networks, Inc., 556

NetAccess Worldwide List, 556

NetAxis, 556

NETCOM Online Communications Services, Inc., 556

NetDepot, 557

NETHEAD, 557

NetPoint Communications, Inc., 557

NetPress Communications, 557

NetReach, 557

Netropolis, 557

Netside Network, 557

NETWave Internet Access Provider, 557

Northwest Link, 557

Novagate, 557

Valiquet Lamothe Inc., 557

advertising

Blacklist of Internet Advertisers, 559

Carter & Associates WEB Studios, 576

Executive Guide to Marketing on the New Internet, 559

Internet Business Connection, 578

Newton Online, 571

Presence-An Information Design Studio, 572

Program One Online Service, 579

Setting Up Shop on the Internet, 562

WorldTel Global Marketing Network, 573

WorldWide Information and Netcasting Services, 580

Ansible's Web Page Design Services, 567

Argus/Univeristy of Michigan Clearinghouse, 567

Artzilla Surf Constructions, 576

Aspen Systems Corporation, 567

Association of Internet Users, 567

Association of University Technology Managers, 567

audio, Connect, Inc.—Audio Innovations, 568

Autopilot, 567

Autorama, 567

Babbs's Bookmarks, 567

Banana Report Easy Visual Basic Tips, 567

Best of the Net, 563

Boardwatch Magazine, 600

browsers, Internet Explorer 3.0, 52

business, Information Economy, 559

Canada, Cnet—Canada, 567

censorship, Censorship and the Internet, 559

Center for the Study of Online Communities, 538

Classroom at the Internet Schoolhouse, 307

Classroom Connect, 301

Common Internet File Formats, 568

conferences

Internet Conference Calendar, 558

World Wide Web Consortium, 558

connecting, 10

consumer information, Hermes Project, 559

Cool Site of the Day, 563

copyrights, 576

corporations, Commercial Services on the Net, 568

CRAYON—CReAte Your Own Newspaper, 568

credit card transactions, 15

CSUSM Windows World, 568

domain names, 10

Economics of Networks Internet Site, 568

education, Gestalt Systems, Inc., 560

EINetGalaxy, 568

Environmental Education Network, 306

Exploring the Internet, 563

FAQs (Frequently Asked Questions), 19

Federal and State-Run Servers, 292

FLFSoft, Inc. Home Page, 568

FutureNet, 560, 601

FutureTel, Inc., 568

George Coates Performance Works, 563

Glass Wings, 564

Glossary of Internet Terms, 560

GNN Select Top 50, 564

GO! Online Communications, 563

Greene Communications Design, Inc., 563

Hajjar/Kaufman New Media Lab, 563

Handy Guide, 564

Hippermedia, 569

history, 9

Economic FAQs about the Internet, 576

Internet Business Center, 576

Rampages, 576

World Wide Web, 576

Hit The Beach!, 564

How To Search a WAIS Database, 560

HTML language

Cerebral Systems Development- Home of Webber, 566

Color Editor for Windows, 566

HTML Editor Information, 566

HTML Info Page, 566

Introduction to HTML, 566

Web Letter, a Guide to HTML/Web Publishing, 566

Web Resources, 566

Hybrid Communications, 564

InfoList Homepage, 310

InfoMedia, 564

Inter-Links, 561

Internet Companion, 559

Internet Educational Resources Guide, 293

Internet Info Store Directory, 570

Internet ProLink SA/AG, 564

Internet Resources, 564

Internet resources

Home Run Pictures, 569

Information Age, Inc., 569

InfoScan, 569

Innovative Computer Associates, Inc., 569

Instruction Set, Inc., 569

InteliSys Technologica, Inc., 569-570

Interactive Data Systems, Inc., 570

Interactive Voice Applications, 570

International Industrial Intelligence, 570

Internet Business Solutions, 570

Internet Systems, Inc., 570

Marketing Masters, 571

Miramar Productions, 571

Internet Resources Newsletter, 570

Internet Servers for the Mac OS, 570

Internet Society, 559

Internet, the Law, and Related Topics, 586

Internet Tour, 564

Internet Web Text, 561

Internet World, 570

Internet Writer Resource Guide, 602

Introduction to the Internet II, 561

IP addresses, 10

IP connections, 11

IRC network

Internet Relay Chat Games, 558

IRC Poker Channels Home Page, 558

MeGALiTH's Sensational Visual IRC Beta Home Page, 558

ISO Easy, 131

iWORLD, 570

Japanese, Hideki's Home Page, 560

Jefferson-Scranton Community Schools, 308

John and Janice's Research Page, 306

Journal of Online Law, 591

Knox Junior High Homepage, 293

Learning Edge Corp., 561

legal.online, 592
Library Solutions Institute and Press, 561
Life on the Internet, 571
List of WWW Archie Services, 571
listservs, 582-584
LookUp!, 571
Magnett Internet Gateway, 561
Management Concepts Inc., 561
Meta-list of What's New Pages, 564
MicroMedium, Inc., 561
Mining the Internet Columns, 310
Monster FTP Sites List, 571
National Computer Security Association, 395, 695
Net Guru Technologies, Inc., 562
Net Trek Cafe, 565
Net Watchers Legal Cyberzine, 560
Netscape Tutorial, 562
Netscape: J.P. Morgan's Equities Research, 560
Netwatchers Cyberzine, 586
Network Hardware Suppliers List, 571
Network Nuggets, 294
New York City, Media Connection of New York—LinksPage, 571
newsgroups, 581-582
nicejob Media, 565
Nick Net, 565
OmegaWest, 572
Online Access Web Edition, 603
Online World Resources Handbook, 562
packet-switching, 9
Patrick Crispen's Internet Roadmap, 562
Quarter deck Global Chat, 558
routers, 10
searchers
Business Directions International, 573
Business Researcher's Interests, 573
Categorical Catapult, 567
College and University Home Pages, 573
COMMA Hotlist Database, 573
Database Demos, 573
Explorer, 573
Four11 White Page Directory, 573
FutureMedia Services, 568
G.T.A. Business Solutions, 569
Glistening Trail Records, 568
Global Village Stock Footage, 569
Harter Image Archives, 569
HFSI, 569

Index of Australian Indexes, 573
International Business Resources on the WWW, 574
Internet Sleuth, 574
InterNIC Directory of Directories, 573
Joel's Hierarchical Subject Index, 574
Lycos Home Page, 574
MediaTel's Newsline, 574
Micro Service & Training, 574
Montana Communications Network (MCN), 574
Mother-of-all BBS, 574
NET Compass, 574
New Rider's Official World Wide Web Yellow Pages, 574
New User's Directory, 575
NlightN, 575
Nothin' But Net, 575
Planet Earth Home Page, 575
Publicize Your Home Page, 575
Q-D Software Development, 572
Recondite Reference Desk, 575
Search, Find—Internet Resource Locators, 575
Searching the Web, 575
shareware.com, 575
Starting Point, 575
Starting Points for Internet, 575
URL-Minder, 575
Virtual Libraries, 575
VSL Front Desk at the OAK Repository, 575
WAIS Access Through the Web, 576
WebAnts_ Home Page, 576
Yahoo, 576
shareware, Windows95 InterNetworking Headquarters, 573
software
Real Audio Home Page, 572
Sibylla, 572
Spectra FAX Corp. Home Page, 572
Surfin' the Net, 562
Switzerland, SWITCH-Swiss Academic and Research Network, 572
Teach Yourself the Internet Support Page, 562
TeamWARE AB, 558
Timothy W. Amey Resource Links, 572
UK Index Beginner's Guide the Net, 562
Unusual or Deep Site of the Day, 565
Virtual Town City Limits, 565

VRML language, David B. Martin's VRML Page, 566
Washington D.C., Washington Web, 572
Web publishing
5 Top Internet Marketing Successes of 1994, 576
Building Web Servers, 576
Business of the Internet, 576
Copyright Website, 576
CRAYON-CReAte Your Own Newspaper, 568
Dunn & Edwards Services, 577
Free Range Media, Inc., 577
Home Space Builder, 577
Image Alchemy Digital Imaging, 578
Image Compression for Publishing Online, 578
Knossopolis, 571
Making Money on Internet, 579
new 3, Inc., 579
RAMWORKS, 579
Sight and Sound, 579
Stannet WWW Designing and Publishing Company, 580
Vannevar New Media, 580
Web Designs, 580
Web Developer, 580
Winfield Design Group, 580
Web Weavers, Tools for Aspiring Web Authors, 562
Web Week, 572
Welcome to Infobahn Magazine, 605
Welcome to Netscape, 572
Windows 95, configuring, 38-40
Winsock Connections, 562
Worlds Chat, 558
Writing the Information Superhighway, 563
Zen and the Art of the Internet, 563
Internet Explorer, 6, 52
inventions, National Inventors Hall of Fame, 464
inventors, Entrepreneur Network, 143
IOMA Information Services for Professionals, 122
Iowa Virtual Tourist, 917
IP addresses, 10
IP connections, 11
IPL Building Directory, 293
IRC (Internet Relay Chat), 11
Internet Relay Chat Games, 558
IRC Galley, 558
MeGALiTH's Sensational Visual IRC Beta Home Page, 558

Ireland

Aer Lingus, 902

art, 73

Exhibition of Paintings by Stanley Pettigrew, 85

Patrick Gallagher, Celtic Art, 78

Clannad WWW Home Page, 657

history

Irish History on the Web, 459

Irish Potato Famine, 459

Irish Sports Report, 852

music

Ain't Whistlin' Dixie, 656

Celtic Music Index Page, 657

Ceolas Celtic Music Archive, 657

Irish Folk Songs, 658

TuneWeb, 659

Thistle and Shamrock Stations List at the Ceolas Archive, 617

Valentine & Company, 809

Isaac Asimov, 97

ISDN (Integrated Services Digital Network), 8, 33

ISF World Snowboard Rankings, 844

Islam

CyberMuslim Information Collective, 733

Ibrahim Shafi's Page in Islam, 733

Islam, 733

Islamic Society of Wichita, 733

Islam's Home Page, 733

Online Islamic Bookstore, 733

Online Islamic Bookstore—Home Page, 614

Salaam Ailaikum, 733

WAMY IslamNet (World Assembly of Muslim Youth), 733

ISO (International Standards Organization), 4

ISPs (Internet Service Providers), 35

assignments, 37

Charm Net Personal IP Page, 553

CyberSight, 553

EFF's (Extended) Guide to the Internet, 553

Fountainhead Internet Systems, 553

Fusion Advertising and Communications, 553

GeoCities, 553

GHG Corp, 553

GTLug ISP Index, 553

How To Select an Internet Service Provider, 553

I-2000, 553

Icanect, 553

ICNet: The Original Internet Provider for the East, 553

Imagine.com, 554

Industrial Peer-to-Peer, 554

Infonet, 554

InReach, 554

Inspiration Software, 554

InstaNet (Instant Internet Corp.), 554

Intergate, 554

Internet Access Phoenix Arizona, 554

Internet Application Services, Inc., 554

Internet Channel, 554

Internet Delaware, 554

Internet Direct, 554

Internet Express, Inc., 554

Internet Front, 554

Internet Interface Systems, 554

Internet Light and Power, 555

Internet MainStreet, 555

Internet North, 555

Internet On-Ramp, Inc., 555

Internet Services Montana, 555

InterServe Communications, 555

IntrepidNet, 555

ISDN Internet Access, 555

Knighted Computers, 570

LavaNet, Inc., 555

LI.Net, 555

Linkage Online, 555

Magnetic Page, 555

MapleNet Technologies, Inc., 555

Medius Communications, Inc., 555

Michigan Internet Cooperative Association, 556

Micron Internet Services, 556

Minnesota MicroNet, 556

Minnesota Regional Network (MRNet), 556

MJC Inc. Computer Services, 556

Mojoski Net Tools, 556

MonadNet, 556

Moran Communications Group, 556

Mountain Internet, 556

Nantucket.Net, 556

National Knowledge Networks, Inc., 556

NetAccess Worldwide List, 556

NetAxis, 556

NETCOM Online Communications Services, Inc., 556

NetDepot, 557

NETHEAD, 557

NetPoint Communications, Inc., 557

NetPress Communications, 557

NetReach, 557

Netropolis, 557

Netside Network, 557

NETWave Internet Access Provider, 557

Northwest Link, 557

Novagate, 557

Valiquet Lamothe Inc., 557

Israel

art history, 71

Shikhin, 464

Italy

Camalgori, A Representative Collection of, 805

history

Peter Konin's Ancient Rome Page, 457

Pompeii, 457

Pompeii Forum, 457

Romarch List Home Page, 464

Newstead Project, 458

ROMARCH—Roman Art and Archaeology, 523

WebArtWed, 79

J

Jainism

Jain Studies, 733

Jain World Wide Web Page, 733

Jamaica, Island Imports, Ltd., 480

James, Will, 89

Japan

1998 Winter Olympics, 855

animation

Austin Anime-Niacs Association, 335

Lysator Computer Society, 77

art. Tokugawa Art Museum, 78

Hideki's Home Page: How To Use Japanese on Interne, 560

Japan Airlines, 903

Japanese Professional Baseball, 840

Kid's Window, 151

Radio JAPAN, 617

Remembering Nagasaki, 93

Shogakukan Home Page, 615

Traveler's Japanese with Voice, 303

What's New in Japan, 560

Java programming language, 6, 33, 44

JavaScript, 44

jazz

29th Montreux Jazz Festival Official Site, 660

Alabama Jazz Hall of Fame, 663
Arizona Jazz, Rhythm and Blues Festival, 663
Bluenote, 671
Electric Gallery, 663
Hard Bop Cafe, 664
Jazz Central Station, 664
Jazz Improvisation, 664
Jazz in France, 664
Jazz Music Stores around the World, 654
Jazz Net, 664
Jazz Photography of Ray Avery, 495
Jazz Roots, 664
Katia and Marielle Labeque Home Page, 652
KLON'S JazzAvenue Jazz Information Service, 602
Magic Island, 674
Pacific Blues & Jazz, 664
Tom Morgan's Web Site for Jazz, 664
Traditional Jazz (Dixieland), 664
Virtual Jazz Fest!, 664
William Ransom Hogan Archive, 664
WNUR-FM JazzWeb, 664
see also blues music; rhythm and blues
Jefferson, Thomas, 460
Jennings, Sam, 85
jewelry
A&H Internet Shopping Service, 810
Amber Lady, 809
Ancient Circles, 489
Associate Jeweler's Tradeshop, 489
Buying Gold Silver Jewelry Coins, 486
California Crafts Marketplace, 811
Colorburst Studio Online, 74
Design in Metal, 489
Diamond Resources, 122
Gem Search International, 810
Hansen Designs—Fine Art Jewelry and Gems, 489
iGallery, The, 76
J & M Coin, Stamp, and Jewellery Ltd., 810
Jewelers of Las Vegas, 810
Keith Farley/Metalsmith, 489
Main Lobby for Jewelry Making, 489
Making of JEEP COLLINS Jewelry, 489
Metalwork Using the Sand-Matrix Design Process, 489
Milne Jewelry Company, 810
Net Diamonds, Inc., 810
NetDiamonds, Inc., 926

Rhinestone Jewelry Word Pins, 810
Santa Fe Southwest Artists Marketspace, 481
Santa Fe Traditions, Inc., 481
Sea Creations, 482
Silver Jewellery, 810
job fairs
Career Expo, 326
CyberFair, 326
Job Fair Home Page, 326
SENET Career Expo Home Page, 326
Virtual Job Fair, 326
Which Job Fair Is Right for You?, 326
jobs
Business Job Finder, 121
Chancellor and Chancellor, Inc., 121
Dick Williams and Associates, 121
DXI Corporation, 122
employment services, 322-325
FutureScan, 150
GE Home Page, 123
IOMA Information Services for Professionals, 122
Opportunity Network, 133
Walgreen Co., 123
see also employment; employment services
Joint Photographics Experts Group (JPEG) files, 12
jokes, *see* **humor**
Jordan, Robert, 76, 102
journalism
Center for Anthropology Communications Home Page, 517
CRAYON—CReAte Your Own Newspaper, 568
ISN KidNews, 293
Reporter's Internet Survival Guide, 713
journals
@Ezine, 108
American Indian Law Review, 591
American Journal of Criminal Law, 591
American Journal of International Law, 588
Anagram, 108
Canboulay, The Caribbean Literature Quarterly, 108
Cream City Review, 108
CrossConnect, 108
De Proverbio, 108
Dimension2, 108
Early Modern Literary Studies, 109
Electronic Journal of Sociology©, 539
European Law Journal, 591
Exemplaria, 109

Federal Communications Law Journal, 591
Global Legal Studies Journal, 591
Harvard Gay and Lesbian Review, 109
Human Rights Brief, 591
Internet Archaeology, 522
Journal of Child Language, 531
Journal of Criminal Justice and Popular Culture, 540
Journal of Information, Law, and Technology, 591
Journal of International Law and Practice, 591
Journal of Latin American Perspectives, 540
Journal of Online Law, 591
Journal of World Anthropology, 518
Law Journal Extra!, 592
Law Library Journal, 592
Milton Quarterly, 109
NorthWords, 109
Papers from the Institute of Archaeology (UCL), 523
Qui Parle, 109
Romanticism On the Net, 109
Sapphic Ink, 109
Stanford Electronic Humanites Review, 526
Transculture, 110
Web Journal of Current Legal Issues, 593
Women & Politics Home Page, 545
Yale Journal of Law and Feminism, 546
JPEG (Joint Photographics Experts Group) file, 12
Judaism
A–Z of Jewish & Israel-Related Resources, 734
Aish Ha Torah Discovery, 734
Chabad Lubavitch in Cyberspace, 734
Cybrary of the Holocaust, 461
Genealogy Page, 706
Hebrew Date for Today, 701
Heichal Shlomo Interactive Calendar, 701
Jerusalem One WWW Network, 734
Jewish Federation/Jewish Exponent, 734
Jewish on the WELL, 734
Jewish Singles Connection, 795
Jewish Theological Seminary, 734
Jewishnet, 734
Jews for Jesus Home Page, 734
Judaism and Jewish Resources, 734

Menorah Ministries, 734

Messianic Jewish Alliance of America, 734

Museum of Tolerance, 827

National Jewish Committee on Scouting, 735

Passover on the Net, 707

Salvation of Bulgarian Jews during WW II, 461

Shamash, 735

Shtetl, Yiddish Language and Culture Home Page, 735

Society Hill Synagogue of Philadelphia, 735

Tara: The World of Jewish Music, 659

Tel Aviv Museum of Art, 88

World ORT Union, 735

Yaohushua, the Genuine Messiah, 735

Yom Tov Page, 708

Jung, Carl, 534

K

Kahlo, Frida, 75

karaoke

Internet Karoake Store, 349

Karaoke, 661

Karaoke Home Page, 661

Looney Tunes Karaoke, 339

Kaufman, Karin, 86

kayaking, *see* **boating/sailing**

Kelderman, Theo, 83

Kennedy, John Fitzgerald, 460

Kentucky, Kentucky Network Services, 917

kiosks, marketing, N-Vision Systems, 132

Korea

Cyber Planet Korea, 125

Virtual Gallery (Korea), 496

L

labor unions, Labor Quotes Page, 718

lacrosse, 852

lampshades, *see* **interior decorating**

landscaping

Architecture & Design, 505

Centre for Landscape Research, 513

Jeff Chorba Landscape Design, 513

LandNET—American Society of Landscape Architects, 513

Landscape Architecture Virtual Library, 513

Magazine, 153

Pennsylvania Horticultural Society, 513

University of Delaware Botanic Gardens, 513

languages

ARTFL Project: ROGET'S Thesaurus Search Form, 702

Center for Applied Linguistics (CAL), 530

Center for Machine Translation, 530

Center for Spoken Language Understanding, 530

Chinese, Yuen Ren Society, 533

Dutch, CELEX Dutch Centre for Lexical Information, 530

English

American Dialect Society (ADS), 529

Australian National Dictionary Centre, 530

CELEX Dutch Centre for Lexical Information, 530

English as a Second Language Home Page, 530

Old English Pages, 532

ETHNOLOGUE: Languages of the World, 530

EUROLANG Optimizer, 530

FoLLI, the European Association for Logic, Language and Information, 530

German, CELEX Dutch Centre for Lexical Information, 530

Haskins Laboratories, 531

Hawaiian, Kualono: 'Olelo Hawai'i, 531

Human-Languages Page, 531

Journal of Child Language, 531

Klingon Language Institute, 531

Lexeme-Morpheme Base Morphology (LMBM), 531

Lingua Project, 531

LINGUIST Network, 531

Linguistic Fun, 531

Loglan, 532

Mayan Epigraphic Database Project, 532

Mayan Hieroglyphic Syllabary, 532

Model Languages, 532

Multilingual PC Directory, 532

Native American, TsaLaGi (English/Cherokee Dictionary), 532

Natural Language Computing Home Page, 532

Pidgin/Creole: Journal of Pidgin and Creole Languages, 531

Russian, Russian Manual Alphabet, 532

Semiotics for Beginners, 532

sign, American Sign Language Linguistic Research Project, 529

UCREL—University Centre for Computer Corpus Research on Language, 533

University of Chicago Press Cognitive Science and Linguistics Catalog, 533

Web Journal of Modern Language Linguistics, 533

Word Manager, 533

WordSmith Tools, 533

LANs (Local Area Networks), INTRANET Technologies, Inc., 570

Las Vegas

Front Desk, 916

Virtual Vegas, 352

Latin America, Journal of Latin American Perspectives, 540

Latin language, Project Libellus, 295

law

ACLU Freedom Network, 590

adoption, 380, 381

ALSO! Main Page, 592

American Bar Association, 590

American Civil Liberties Union, 824

American Immigration Lawyers Association, 590

Better Business Bureau, 590

CALI: The Center for Computer-Assisted Legal Instruction, 291

Censorship and the Internet, 559

Central Notice, 711

Constitution of the United States of America, 593

Consumer Law Page, 122

Counsel Connect Web, 592

CourtTV Home Page, 592

Crime Prevention Initiatives, 825

Crime-Free America, 825

criminal

Cecil Greek's Criminal Justice Page, 585

COPNet & Police Resource List, 585

Criminal Enforcement Bulletin, 122

Criminal Law Links, 585

Guide to Internet Resources in Criminal Law and Criminal Justice, 585

Justice Information Center (NCJRS), 585

Partnerships Against Violence Network (PAVNET), 585

Scott Carpenter's TOP Page, 585
U.S. Criminal Law, 585
CRLP: Women of the World, 542
cyber
CyberLaw™ World Wide, 585
CyberSpace Law Center, 585
E-Law 3.0, 585
ICLU—Your Rights in Cyberspace, 586
Information Law Web, 586
Information Highway Advisory Counsel (IHAC) Canada, 586
Internet, the Law, and Related Topics, 586
Netwatchers Cyberzine, 586
OwlLex Law Links—The CyberSpace Law Links, 586
DeathNET, 429
divorce, 382-384
EFFweb-The Electronic Frontier Foundation, 559
Emergency Net, 825
environmental
CCE - CCA - CEC (Commission for Env. Cooperation), 586
Environmental Law Alliance Worldwide, 586
Environmental Law Around the World, 587
Environmental Law Resources, 587
Environmental Law World Wide Web Site, 587
U.S. Environmental Protection Agency, 587
United Nations Environment Programme, 587
WWW Virtual Library: Law: International & Environmental Law, 587
Ethical, Legal, and Social Issues in Science, 303
family
Divorce Helpline Home Page, 587
Divorce Law Home Page, 587
Divorce Page, 587
Family Law, 588
Family Law Advisor Home Page, 588
Fathers' Rights and Equality Exchange, 588
Legal dot Net—Family Law, and Overview, 588
Same-Sex Marriage Home Page, 588
Fear-Forfeiture Endangers American Rights, 824
Hieros Gamos, 592
Human Rights Web Home Page, 539

international
American Journal of International Law, 588
Foreign and International Law Page, 588
International Law Page, 588
International Trade Law—ITL, 588
Internet Immigration Law Center, 588
JurWeb, 588
United Nations Crime and Justice Information Network, 589
International Association of Constitutional Law, 590
Internet Resources for Women's Legal and Public Policy Informatio, 544
Jones, Hall, Hill, and White, 131
Justice Net, 825
LAW EMPLOYMENT CENTER, 593
Law.Net, 592
LawMall, 592
LawMarks...The Legal Resource Database, 592
LawTalk, 593
Lawyer Jokes, 593
Legal Information Institute, 593
Legal Rights of Women, 544
LEXIS-NEXIS Communication Center, 132
listservs, 595-598
National Criminal Justice Reference Service (NCJRS, 540
National Organization for Women (NOW), 544
NetWatchers Legal Cyberzine, 560
newsgroups, 595
NYSDA Public Defense Backup Center Home Page, 590
On-Line Reference Works, 713
P-LAW Legal Resources Locator, 593
publications
American Indian Law Review, 591
American Journal of Criminal Law, 591
European Law Journal, 591
Federal Communications Law Journal, 591
Global Legal Studies Journal, 591
Human Rights Brief, 591
Journal of Criminal Justice and Popular Culture, 540
Journal of Information, Law, and Technology, 591

Journal of International Law and Practice, 591
Journal of Online Law, 591
Law Journal Extra!, 592
Law Library Journal, 592
legal.online, 592
Yale Journal of Law and Feminism, 546
schools
FindLaw: Law Schools of Canada, 589
FindLaw: US News Top 25 Law Schools, 589
ILRG: Brennan's Law School Rankings, 589
Law School Admission Council Online, 589
Law School and the LSAT, 589
Law School Dot Com, 589
Law School Quotes, 589
Law Student Web, 589
Princeton Review: Law School and the LSAT, 589
Yale Law School Homepage, 589
Seals on Wheels, 134
SEAMLESS WEBsite...lawyer law firm expert, 594
Second Chair Corporation, 818
Social Security Online, 440
Sovereign Patriot Group, 590
Web Journal of Current Legal Issues, 593
Welcome to the Council of the Great City Schools Online, 305
West Publishing, 616
Women of the World, 449
law enforcement, "Ten Codes", 713
Lee, Bruce, 851
lesbian interests
Dyke TV, 798
Gay & Lesbian Bar Guide, 798
Gay & Lesbian National Hotline, 799
Isle of Lesbos, 799
Lesbian Herstory Project, 799
OutNOW Live, 799
Same-Sex Marriage Home Page, 588
Small Media and Large, 615
lexemes, 531
libraries
AcqWeb, 708
American Society of Indexers home page, 708
AskERIC Virtual Library, 291
Building Digital Libraries on the Web, 708

Celebrate Libraries, 708

Christian Classics Ethereal Library, 708

CIC, Center for Library Initiatives, 292

Education Virtual Library-Primary School, 292

Electronic Text Center at the University of Virginia, 704

Filmakers Library, 539

Garfield Co. Public Library System, 302

Humanities and Social Sciences—University of Chicago LibInfo, 525

INFOMINE, 561

Information Resources, 561

International Federation of Library Associations and Institutions (IFLA), 304

Internet Resources for Cataloging, 708

IPL Building Directory, 293

IUB Libraries: Research Collections and Services Department, 306

Knowledge Source, 828

Librarians' professional resources, 709

Library Job Hunting, 709

Library of Congress, 709

Library Resource List, 709

Library Resources for Women's Studies, 544

National Archives and Records Administration, 709

New York Public Library Center for the Humanities, 524

OCLC Online Computer Library Center, Inc., 709

Plethora of Web Sites: The Librarian's Meta-List, 709

Quotations About Libraries and Librarians, 718

RYHINER-Project at the University Library of Berne, 528

School Libraries on the Web: A Directory, 709

Smithsonian Institution Libraries, 709

Understanding Call Numbers, 710

Welcome to the Introspect Library, 718

WisDPI-The Wisconsin Department of Public Instruction, 297

World-Wide Web Virtual Library, 303

WWW Library Directory, 710

WWW Virtual Library, 713

WWW Virtual Library—Humanities, 526

licensing services, International Typeface Corporation, 131

life simulator games, 167, 559

lighthouses

About the Lighthouse Depot, 477

Sea Creations, 482

Lincoln, Abraham, 459

lingerie

Classic Lady, 797

Discreet Boutique, 805

Playware Limited, 797

linguistics

American Dialect Society (ADS), 529

Association for Computational Linguistics, 529

Australian National Dictionary Centre, 530

CELEX Dutch Centre for Lexical Information, 530

Center for Applied Linguistics (CAL), 530

Center for Spoken Language Understanding, 530

Chomskybot, 530

Colibri Home Page, 530

ENGL 310: History of the English Language, 704

FoLLI, the European Association for Logic, Language and Information, 530

Haskins Laboratories, 531

Human-Languages Page, 531

Journal of Child Language, 531

Journal of Pidgin and Creole Languages, 531

Klingon Language Institute, 531

Kualono: 'Olelo Hawai'i, 531

Lexeme-Morpheme Base Morphology (LMBM), 531

Lingua Project, 531

LINGUIST Network, 531

Linguistic Fun, 531

Logical World of Etymology, 705

Loglan, 532

Mayan Epigraphic Database Project, 532

Mayan Hieroglyphic Syllabary, 532

Model Languages, 532

Multilingual PC Directory, 532

Old English Pages, 532, 705

Russian Manual Alphabet, 532

Semiotics for Beginners, 532

TsaLaGi (English/Cherokee Dictionary), 532

UCREL—University Centre for Computer Corpus Research on Language, 533

University of Chicago Press Cognitive Science and Linguistics Catalog, 533

Web Journal of Modern Language Linguistics, 533

Word Manager, 533

WordSmith Tools, 533

Yuen Ren Society, 533

Linux, Slackware Professional Linux, 236

listservs

animals, 68-70

art, 95-96

books & authors, 117-119

business, 146-148

children, 156-158

computer games, 173-175

computers, 281-290

education, 313-319

employment, 332-334

entertainment, 357-359

environment, 376-378

family Issues, 390-392

food & drink, 411-412

government & politics, 423-426

health & fitness, 453-454

history, 467-475

hobbies & crafts, 503-504

home improvement, 515-516

humanities, 548-552

Internet resources, 582-584

law, 595-598

media, 620-622

movies, 645-646

music, 681-683

paranormal phenomena, 699

reference, 720-721

religion & philosophy, 743-747

science & engineering, 789-793

sexuality, 802-803

shopping, 822

society & culture, 836-837

sports, 866

television, 891-892

transportation, 899-900

travel, 920-921

weddings, 929

literacy

Arrow Publishing, 303

Banned Books On-line, 303

Parents and Children Together Online, 389

Project LEAP (Learn Earn and Prosper), 295
SITCOM Home Page, 351
VOTEC Homepage, 296

literary psychology, Institute for the Psychological Study of the Arts (IPSA), 535

literature
Adventures of Tom Sawyer, 106
Albert Camus, 99
Alice Walker, 105
Alice's Adventures in Wonderland, 106
alt.books.reviews, 110
alt.books.technical, 110
Amazon.com, 110
American Literary Classics, 106
Amy Tan, 105
Anagram, 108
Anaïs Nin, 103
Anne McCaffrey, 103
Anne Rice, 104
Antoine de Saint-Exupery, 104
Aphra Behn Page, 98
Arthur C. Clarke Chapter of The Silicon Jungle, 100
Ayn Rand, 104
Banned Books On-line, 110
Barbara Kingsolver, 102
Bartlett's Familiar Quotations, 717
Book Banning, Burning, and Censorship, 110
Book Nook, 299
Bookbinding, a tutorial, 110
BookWorld, 110
Brontë Sisters, 98
C.S. Lewis (Into the Wardrobe), 103
C.S. Lewis and the Inklings, 102
Canboulay, The Caribbean Literature Quarterly, 108
Celebration of Women Writers, 542
Center for Electronic Texts in the Humanities, 524
Charles Bukowski, 98
Charlotte Brontë, 98
Children's Literature Web Guide, 307
Clive Barker, 97
Commonplace Book, 106
Complete Works of William Shakespeare, 350
Conservation OnLine, 110
Cormac McCarthy, 103
Cream City Review, 108
David Brin, 98
De Proverbio, 108

Dimension2, 108
Donald Barthelme, 97
Douglas Coupland-Snapshots, 100
Early Modern Literary Studies, 109
Edgar Allen Poe, 104
Edgar Rice Burroughs, 98
Edward Bellamy, 98
Electronic Beowulf, 704
Electronic Labyrinth, 106
Electronic Library, 106
Electronic Text Center at the University of Virginia, 704
Ernest Hemingway (The Papa Page), 101
eSCENE 1995, 74
Eudora Welty, 105
Exemplaria, 109
F. Scott Fitzgerald, 101
Flaming Jewels, 74
Fyodor Dostoevsky, 100
George Sand, 104
Gertrude Stein, 105
Gore Vidal, 105
Great Books of Western Civilization, The, 75, 107
Gutter Press, 107
Henry Miller (18, villa seurat), 103
Her Own Words®, 544
Herman Melville, 103
Hundred Highlights from the Koninklijke Bibliotheek, 110
Hungry Mind Review Discussion, 111
HyperLiterature/HyperTheory, 107
Ian Fleming, 101
J.D. Salinger (The Bananafish Home Page), 104
Jack Kerouac, 102
Jim Carroll, 99
Johann Wolfgang von Goethe, 101
John Grisham, 101
John Steinbeck, 105
Jorge Luis Borges-The Garden of Forking Paths, 98
Joyce Carol Oates (Celestial Timepiece), 104
Jules Verne, 105
Kate Chopin Project, 99
L. Ron Hubbard, 101
L'Art Medical Antiquarian Books, 111
Le Marquis de Sade, 100
Lewis Carroll: An Overview, 99
Libyrinth, 103
Literary Hyper Calendar, 702
Literary Works: Mark Twain, 107

Louis L'Amour, 102
Louisa May Alcott: Flower Fables, 97
Marcel Proust (Proust Said That), 104
Margaret Atwood Information Site, 97
Marguerite Duras, 100
Mark Twain (Ever the Twain Shall Meet), 105
Mark Twain Library, 293
Mark Twain; Huckleberry Finn, 107
Mary Shelley, 105
Michael Crichton, 100
Miguel de Cervantes, 99
Milton Quarterly, 109
N. Scott Momaday, 103
Nathaniel Hawthorne, 101
Nicholson Baker, 97
NorthWords, 109
Online Books FAQ, 107
Oscar Wilde (The Wild Wilde Web), 105
Persimmon Software for Children, 295
Philip Roth, 104
Plaintext, 109
Preservation Educators' Exchange, 111
Project Gutenberg, 87
Qui Parle, 109
Raymond Carver, 99
ReadersNdex, 111
rec.arts.books, 111
Renditions, 109
Richard Bausch, 97
Richard Brautigan, 98
Ring Lardner (Lardnermania), 102
Rita Brown, 98
Roald Dahl, 100
Romanticism On the Net, 109
Shakespeare, 78
Stephen Crane, 100
Stephen King, 102
TeleRead, 107, 109
Thomas Hardy, 101
Thomas Wolfe, 106
Tolkien Society, 111
Tom Clancy, 99
Tom Robbins (The AFTRLife), 104
Transculture, 110
Tree Fiction on the World Wide Web, 108
Truman Capote, 99
Umberto Eco, 100
Ursula K. Le Guin, 102
Vintage Books Reading Group Guides, 112

Virginia Woolf, 106
Vladmir Nabokov (Zembla), 103
Wespennest, 110
Willa Cather, 99
William Faulkner, 101
William S. Burroughs, 99
William T. Vollmann, 105
Writing the Information
  Superhighway, 563
Yukio Mishima Archive, 103
Zora Neale Hurston, 101
Zuzu's Petals Literary Resource, 108
**liturgical music, Gregorian Chant
  Home Page, 652**
lodging
  American Youth Hostels, 910
  Bed & Breakfast Inns Online, 910
  California Travel and Parks
    Association, 910
  Campground Directory, 910
  Choice Hotels, 910
  Homeless Shelters in the United
    States, 910
  Hostelling International, 911
  International Bed And Breakfast
    Guide, 911
  Nude 2000, 911
  Professional Association of
    Innkeepers Internation, 911
  Travel Web, 911
  United Hostels of Europe, 911
  World Wide Lodging Guide, 911
London
  Gnostic Institute of Anthropology—
    London U.K., 518
  London Theatre Guide-Online, 351
  Virtual Portfolio (London), 496
**long distance services, FiberNet
  Communications, 130**
Los Angeles
  L.A. Rock & Roll Road Map, 677
  Los Angeles County Museum of Art,
    86
Lotus, Lotus Selects Catalog, 225
Louisiana, Allons! Acadiana, 915
LSAT (Law School Admissions Test)
  Law School Admission Council
    Online, 589
  Law School and the LSAT, 589
  Princeton Review: Law School and
    the LSAT, 589
  Yale Law School Homepage, 589
lumber
  Professional Woodgraining Kits, 507

Quality Woodwork & Supply, Inc.,
  507
Quality Woodwork and Supply, Inc.,
  499
Woods of the World, 500
WoodWeb, 500
Woodworking Catalog, 507, 508
lutes, Wayne's Lute Page, 663
Lutheran
  Evangelical Lutheran Church in
    America Home Page, 726
  Lutheran Church-Missouri Synod
    Home Page, 726
**Luxembourg, Musée National
  D'Histoire Et D'Art, 87**
**luxury automobiles, Rolls-Royce
  Owners' Club, 894**
Lynx, 54

M

Macintosh
  Cult of Macintosh, 236
  DayStar Digital, 179
  Hayden Books, 611
  Internet Servers for the Mac OS, 570
  Mac Talk, Inc's WWW
    Page.i.computers sales, 225
  MacNet Journal, 602
  MacUser/MacWeek Special on
    Apple's Future.i.computers, 209
  Macworld Online Web Server, 602
  MacZone Internet Superstore, 225
  New User's Directory, 575
  Well Connected Mac, 235
magazines
  Access ET, 599
  Acoustic Musician Magazine, 599
  Adventure Online Gaming, 599
  Adventurous Traveler Bookstore, 599
  Advertising Age, 599
  AE Magazine, 599
  American Country Collectibles, 599
  American Wine, 599
  Aquanaut, 599
  Archaeology Magazine, 521
  Architronic Home Page, 599
  Asia, Inc. Online, 599
  Astronomer Magazine, 599
  ave~Length Paddling Network, 605
  basilisk, 599
  BBN on the World Wide Web, 559
  Boardwatch Magazine, 600
  Car Collector Home Page, 600
  Chicago Moving Image Scene, 600

Christian Computing Magazine, 727
Column that Nobody Reads, 600
Condé Nast Traveler, 600
Cyber Cyclist, 600
cyberSPOKESMAN, 600
Cyberwest Magazine, 600
Dirty Linen, 600
Discover Magazine, 600
Editor & Publisher, 600
Electronic Green Journal, 600
Electronic Newsstand, 600
Esquireb2b, 600
Family World Home Page, 600
Felix Culpa Home Page, 601
FH, Canada Travel Home Page, 601
Fix—Funkier Than Blown Vinyl, 601
Folk Roots Home Page, 601
For Sale By Owner Magazine, 813
Fortran Journal, 601
Funtiques Antiques Home Page, 479
FutureNet, 560, 601
Galaxy Entertainment, 601
Gigaplex, 601
Glass Wings: Sensual Celebrations,
  601
Golf Magazine, 848
Good Medicine Magazine, 601
Grass Roots Magazine, 601
Great Lakes Skier Magazine, 601
High Country News Home Page, 601
Interactive Age Home Page, 601
Internet Writer Resource Guide, 602
InternetWorld, 570
InterText: The Online Fiction
  Magazine, 602
JEST Home Page, 602
KLON'S JazzAvenue Jazz Informa-
  tion ServiceKLON'S Ja, 602
Knowledge Industry Publications,
  Inc., 602
Libido Magazine, 796
LIFE Photo Home Page, 602
Living Poets, EJournal Home Page,
  602
Logical Alternative—Front Door, 602
MacNet Journal, 602
Macworld Online Web Server, 602
Magazine, 153
Magazine Warehouse, 814
Mercury Center Home Page, 602
Millennium Whole Earth Catalog,
  602
MMWIRE WEB, 602
Mobilia Magazine, 602
MoJo Wire, 603

Motorcycle Online, 603
Muse Magazine, 603
music
  Addicted To Noise, 665
  Cybergrass—The Internet Bluegrass
    Magazine, 665
  Electric Magic—The Led Zeppelin
    Chronicle, 665
  ICE On-Line, 665
  OffBeat Magazine, 665
  Stirrings Folk Mag, 665
  Synthesis: Electronic Dance Music
    Page, 666
NCS Career Magazine, 603
Net Traveler, 603
Nor'east Saltwater Magazine, 846
Oceanography—The Magazine, 603
Online Access Web Edition, 603
Online Educator, 603
Outside Online, 603
Pan Asian Publications Home Page,
  603
Penthouse on the Internet, 603
Penthouse Online, 796
Perspective, 603
Playboy Home Page, 603
Popular Science Magazine, 603
Positive Planet, 604
PowerPC News, 604
Quantum Magazine Home Page, 784
Redundantly, Online, 604
Rippin' Good Yarn, 604
Scripps Howard Home Page, 604
Sea Frontiers, 604
Serif: The Magazine of Type &
  Typography, 604
South Carolina Point, 604
Sports Illustrated, 853
Tharunka Home, 604
Travel Weekly, 604
TravelASSIST Magazine, 604
Typofile Magazine—Home, 604
UNIX News International, 604
UT Science Bytes, 604
Videomaker's Camcorder & Desktop
  Video Site, 605
Virtual Pathways, 605
Walls and Ceilings Magazine, 605
Web Week Home Page, 605
Welcome to Carbon 14, 605
Welcome to Computer Shopper, 605
Welcome To HotWired!, 605
Welcome to Infobahn Magazine, 605

Welcome to Pathfinder, 605
Welcome to ZD Net, 605
Where the Buffalo Roam, 605
magnetic fields, 450, 767
Maine, Maine WWW Resources, 917
mandolins, Mandolin Pages, 663
manufacturing
  Manufacturing Resources, 132
  Rodex: Technologies for the, 133
maps
  Antiquarian Booksellers's
    Association of America, 112
  Area Accurate Map/The Peters
    Projection, 526
  Association of American Geogra-
    phers, 526
  Association of Chinese Professionals
    in Geographic Information Systems,
    526
  Canadian WWW Central Index/Liste
    centrale des serveurs WWW
    canadiens, 526
  Cartography—Indiana State
    University, 526
  ChartWrite's Data-on-the-Map, 526
  Color Landform Atlas of the United
    States, 710
  Country Maps from W3 Servers in
    Europe, 710
  E-scapes: Electronic Resources for the
    Study of Ancient Landscapes, 527
  Federal Geographic Data Committee
    (FGDC), 527
  Geographic Institutes around the
    World, 527
  Global Positioning System (GPS), 527
  Heritage Map Museum, 292, 527
  History of Cartography Project, 527
  International Map Trade Association,
    710
  International Map Trade Association
    (IMTA), 527
  Laboratory for Remote Sensing and
    Geographic Information Systems
    (LRSGIS), 528
  Mapmaker, Mapmaker, Make Me a
    Map, 528, 710
  MapQuest, 710
  MAPublisher, 528
  NAISMap WWW-GIS Home Page,
    528
  National Atlas Information Service
    (of Canada), 710
  National Atlas of Canada on
    SchoolNet, 710

  Old Bookroom, 114
  Oregon Geographic Alliance (OGA),
    528
  Perry-Castañeda Library Map
    Collection, 710
  Rare Map Collection at the Hargrett
    Library, 710
  Research-It!, 713
  RYHINER-Project at the University
    Library of Berne, 528
  Spatial Odyssey: GIS Literature
    Database, 529
  TIGER Mapping Service, 529
  TOPO!™ Interactive Maps, 529
  U.S. Geological Survey (USGS)
    National Mapping Information
    World Wide Web Server, 529
  VIBE's World Map, 711
  Xerox PARC Map Viewer, 529
**marines, OCEANOR-Oceanographic
Company, 126**
marine geology, 770
marine science, Aquatic Network, 129
marketing
  Advertising, Boelter & Lincoln, 138
  AfterHours Communications Corp.,
    138
  Allen & Associates, Ltd., 138
  American Demographics/Marketing
    Tools, 138
  Another Color Inc., 139
  Austin Knight's KnightNet, 139
  B.A.A.S. Boating Advertising,
    Advice, and Service, 139
  Biggs Gilmore Communications, 139
  BMP DDB Needham, 139
  Business-to-Business Marketing
    Exchange, 139
  Carter Waxman, 139
  CEO Access Across the Street or
    Around the World, 139
  Chiat/Day Inc., 139
  Cohn & Wells, 139
  Cortex Marketing Resources, 139
  curious pictures, 139
  Electronic Product Catalog Systems,
    140
  Farago Advertising, 140
  Forest Green Media, 140
  furnishing, Virtual Design Center,
    135
  Galaxy Communications Inc., 140
  GBH Handsfree Communication, 140
  Goswick Advertising, 140
  HERMES, Consumer and Corporate
    Surveys, 140

Ingalls, Quinn & Johnson, 140
Institute for the Study of Business
  Markets, 140
Kern Media Associates, 140
Liggett Stashower, 142
Marcus Advertising, 140
Market Place Media, 141
Marketing to Consumers: A Guide,
  141
McMonigle & Spooner, 141
Michael J. Motto Advertising, 141
Mintz & Hoke Advertising and
  Public Relations, 141
Mousetracks-NSNS Marketing
  Resources, 141
music
  Marketing Music on the Web, 676
  Moneymaking Music Resources, 676
  Patrick's Musicians' Page, 676
  Planet StarChild, 676
N-Vision Systems, 132
O'KEEFE WORLD, 141
On-Line Marketing, 143
Reckless Design Limited, 141
Richards Group, 141
Sales Plus, 141
Selling Your Products Abroad, 126
Setting Up Shop on the Internet, 562
Sharrow Advertising and Marketing
  and Marketing Information
  Resource Center, 141
Sidea, 142
Small and Home-Based Business
  Links, 143
TAL Marketing Services, Inc., 142
TEAMS Marketing and Sales
  Assessment Software, 142
Tech Image, Ltd., 142
Tom Davis+Company, 142
Wahlstrom & Company, 142
Web Digest for Marketers, 142
WebReach, Internet Advertising and,
  142
Weightman Group, 142
Western Direct's Home Page, 142
Winkler McManus, 142
World of Commercial Ballooning, 135
Young & Roehr, Inc., 143
martial arts, 851
Massachusetts
  Boston Area Map of WWW
    Resources, 915
  Cambridge, Massachusetts, 915
  education, MEOL, 294

matchbox cars, Just Matchbox!!, 480
math
  AIMS Education Foundation, 291
  AMATH, Inc., 770
  Beauty of Chaos, 770
  Ben Cheng's Home Page, 770
  Calculus & Mathematica Home Page,
    770
  Chaos at Maryland, 770
  Chaos Network Sign-In, 770
  Chartwell-Bratt, 770
  children, Welcome to MegaMath, 297
  Common Weights and Measures, 770
  Computational Logic, Inc., 770
  Conversion Factor Table, 711
  Cornell Theory Center Math and
    Science Gateway, 292
  CPLEX Optimization, Inc. Home
    Page, 771
  CSC Mathematical Topics, 771
  Data Modeling Web Site, 771
  Dave's Math Links, 771
  Design-By-Example, 771
  Dynamical Systems and Technology
    Project, 771
  e-Math Home Page, 771
  Eisenhower National Clearinghouse
    DCL, 771
  Electronic Textbook Integrated
    Course in, 771
  Engineering, Scientific Unit
    Converter, 711
  Fractal Gallery, 771
  Fractal Image Compression, 772
  Fractal Microscope, 772
  Fractals Calendar Home Page, 772
  Fractals Frequently Asked Questions
    and Answers, 772
  Future Graph, Inc. Home Page, 772
  GAMS-Guide to Available Math-
    ematical Software, 772
  Geometry Forum, 292
  Guide to Math Resources, 772
  History of Mathematics, 772
  IMA WWW Server, 772
  IMSA Home Page, 772
  Intercall, 772
  Internet Center for Mathematics
    Problems, 772
  Logal Software Home Page, 772
  Math and Science Gateway (Cornell
    Theory Center), 293
  Math Education Resources, 302
  Math Teaching Assistant, 772
  Mathematica World, 773

  Mathematics Archives WWW Server,
    773
  Mathlab, 773
  MathMagic Internet, 302
  MATHMOL-K-12 Mathematics and
    Molecules, 293
  MathSearch—Search a Collection of
    Mathematical Web Material, 773
  MathSoft Home Page, 773
  MathSolutions, Inc. Home Page, 773
  MathSource Home Page, 773
  MathType Home Page, 773
  MathWorks Home Page, 773
  Measurements Converter, 711
  More Fractal Pictures, 773
  MU CoE LInks to Education
    Resources, 294
  Netlib Repository at UTK/ORNL,
    773
  Numerical Algorithms Group Ltd.,
    773
  Online Image Archiver, 773
  NASA Education Sites, 294
  OSPI Math, Science, and Technology
    Server, 294
  Precision Large-Scale Dimensional
    Metrology/Measurement, 773
  Principia Consulting Home Page, 774
  Quantum Books Home Page, 774
  SciEd: Science and Mathematics
    Education Resources, 295
  Steven M. Christensen and Associ-
    ates, Inc., 774
  TERC, 305
  TMP at Imperial College London, 774
  Transmath—A CBL Mathematics
    Tutor, 774
  Union Mathematica Argentina, 774
  Video Vita, 774
  Videodiscovery, 296
  Waterloo Fractal Compression Page,
    774
  World-Wide Web Virtual Library
    Mathematics, 774
math co-processors, 33
Matrix, 9
McCanna, Laurie, 75
Mears, Herbert R., 85
measurements
  Conversion Factor Table, 711
  Engineering, Scientific Unit
    Converter, 711
  Measurements Converter, 711
media
  listservs, 620-622
  newsgroups, 618-620

media arts, 72
Centre for MediaSociology (CeMeSo), 538
Institute for Propaganda Analysis, 539

medical ethics, Ethical, Legal, and Social Issues in Science, 303

medical research, Radiation Effects Research Foundation, 443

medical simulations
Interactive Media Lab, 442
Three-Dimensional Medical Reconstruction, 444
Virtual Environments and Real-time Deformations for Surgery Simulation, 444

medicine
AIDS Walk Los Angeles, 432
alternative
Actual Natural Source, 427
Acupuncture Home Page, 427
Alexandra Health Center, 427
Alternative Medicine Home Page from Faulk Library of the Health Sciences, University of Pittsburgh, 427
Cell Tech Super Blue Green Algae, 428
Code Four Medical, 428
Conscious Choice, 427
Doody Publishing Health Science Book Reviews, 429
Dragon Herbarium, 429
HANS—The Health Action Network Society, 428
Health and Longevity, 428
Herbal Hall, 428
Nature's Medicine, 428
Welcome to Acupuncture, 428
WorldWide Wellness, 428
Alzheimer Disease Web Site, 433
Cardiovascular Institute of the South, 433
DeathNET, 429
Emergency, 436
employment
EMBBS, 436
MedLink International, 444
Euthanasia World Directory, 429
Experimental Organ Preservation, 443
Harvard Biological Labratories' Biosciences-Medicine, 443
Heart Mind Body Institute, 434
History of Science, Technology and Medicine, 465

Internet Medical Products Guide, 441
Introduction to Vision Correcting Procedures by Med-Source, Inc., 434
Jeffrey Modell Foundation, 434
Marijuana as a Medicine, 441
Medicine On Line, 434
MEDMarket Virtual Industrial Park, 439
Medscrip Windows Prescription Writer for Physician, 444
Michigan Digital Historical Initiative in the Health Sciences, 443
Minority Health Network, 439
Northwestern University Department of Radiology, 444
Osteopathic Source, 444
Parkinson's Web, 435
Pediatric Rheumatology home page, 435
PLink—The Plastic Surgery Link, 444
Prostate Cancer InfoLink, 435
Rehabilitation Learning Center, 435
Roxane Pain Institute, 435
Scientific and Medicinal Antiques, 443
search and rescue missions
Avalanche Dogs!, 435
Mountain Rescue Association, 436
SkinCare Program, 439
Sudden Infant Death Syndrome (SIDS) Information Page, 435
Telemedicine Information Exchange—TIE, 444
trauma
Emergency Preparedness Information eXchange, 436
Global Emergency Medicine Archives, 436
National Collegiate EMS Foundation Home Page, 436
Team Dispatch, 436
UBC (University of British Columbia) Multi-Research Network, 436
UTHSCSA Trauma Home Page, 436
Vision Impairments, A Guide for the Perplexed, 435

medieval collectibles
Castle Attic, 811
Distant Caravans, 812

medieval studies
Ancient and Medieval Coins, 486
Articles on Medieval/Renaissance Subjects, 460
Avalon: Arthurian Heaven, 460
Byzantium: The Byzantine Studies Page, 460

Electronic Beowulf, 704
Labyrinth WWW Home Page, 460
Old English Pages, 532, 705
Vikings Home Page, 461
WWW Medieval Resources, 461

memory, Total Recall, 303

men, Fathers' Rights and Equality Exchange, 588

menopause, *see* **women, healthcare**

mental health
Center for Anxiety and Stress Treatment, 445
Cybernetic Stress Control, 445
Internet Mental Health, 535
Mental Health Net: Responding to Sexual Child Abuse, 386
Mental Relativity, 535
National Institute of Mental Health (NIHM), 536

mental retardation, Arc, a national organization on mental retardation, 534

merry-go-rounds
Collectibles by R&T Musical Merry-Go-Rounds, 479
Rick's GAMEROOM Collectibles, 481

messages, reminders, E-Minder Free Reminder-By-E-mail Service, 568

metalworking
Ancient Circles, 489
Arris International Corporation, 497
ArtMetal Project, The, 83
Associate Jeweler's Tradeshop, 489
Design in Metal, 489
Hansen Designs—Fine Art Jewelry and Gems, 489
Keith Farley/Metalsmith, 489
Main Lobby for Jewelry Making, 489
Making of JEEP COLLINS Jewelry, 489
Metalwork Using the Sand Matrix Design Process, 489

meteorology
AgriWeather, 774
Alden Electronics, 774
Atlantic Tropical Weather Center, 775
Automated Weather Source— Nationwide School Weather Network, 775
Current Weather Maps/Movies, 775
Defense Meteorological Satellite Program, 775
Earth Watch Communications, Inc., 775
Intellicast, 775

Interactive Marine Observations, 775
Interactive Weather Browser, 775
International Weather Watchers Official Home Page, 775
NASA Weather Archive, 775
National Center for Atmospheric Research, 775
National Hurricane Center Tropical Prediction Center, 775
National Severe Storms Laboratory, 775
National Weather Service, 776
NJ Online Weather, 606
Seismological Laboratory, 776
Space Science and Engineering Center (SSEC) Real-Time Data, 776
Storm Chaser Home Page, 776
Today Page, 565
Warren Faidley's Storm Chasing Home Page, 776
Weather and Climate Images, 776
Weather and Global Monitoring, 776
Weather Channel, 776
Weather Net, 776
Weather Page, 776
Mexico
Galeria MexPlaza, 85
How to Do Business in Mexico, 125
INFOCENTRO, 125
Mayan Hieroglyphic Syllabary, 532
Mexicana Airlines, 904
NAFTA Watch, 125
Sacred Faces, Sacred Spaces, 496
Michigan
Grand Rapids, 916
Michigan Digital Historical Initiative, 443
Michigan Photo Contest, 92
RING. Online Michigan's Electronic Magazine, 918
microbreweries, *see* **alcoholic beverages**
Microsoft, shortcuts, 47
Microsoft Internet Explorer, 41, 51
Microsoft Network, 26
military history
Cold War Hot Links, 461
Cybrary of the Holocaust, 461
D-Day, 461
George Rarey's Journals of the 379th Fighter Squadron, 461
Gulf War Photo Gallery, 461
Korean War Project, 461
Medals of America, 481
Military History, 461

Operation Desert Storm Debriefing Book, 461
Remembering Nagasaki, 461
Salvation of Bulgarian Jews during WW II, 461
Salzburg 1945–1955: Introduction, 461
Vietnam Veterans Home Page, 462
War from a Parlor: Stereoscopic Images of American War and Soldiers' Letters Home, 462
World War I (1914-1918), 462
World War II on the Web, 462
Worlds of Late Antiquity, 462
Milton, Booth, 89
MIME (Multipurpose Internet Mail Extensions), 12-13
minerals, 769-770, 781
Arris International Corporation, 496
Bob's Rock Shop, 478
Crystals and Minerals, 497
Hunterian Museum of Rocks and Minerals, 497
Mineralogical Meanderings, 497
mini blinds, *see* **interior decorating**
Minnesota
Minneapolis, 917
Minneapolis Institute of Arts, 86
Minnesota Higher Education Center Against Violence & Abuse, 386
TIESnet, 296
mirror sites, 18
missing children
America's Lost Children Television Network, 384
Child CyberSEARCH: English Home Page, 385
Child Quest International, 385
Child Search: National Missing Children's Center, 385
CyberPages International Inc: Missing Children, 385
Kevin Collins Foundation for Missing Children, 386
National Center for Missing and Exploited Children, 387
PeaceDove, 387
Safe-T-Child Online, 387
Mississippi, Index, 916
Missouri
Missouri WWW Resources, 917
St. Louis, Missouri, 918
modeling
airplanes, Scale Model Collection, 491

boats
Nautical Research and Shipmodeling Links, 490
Pmcg's Vicious Model Boat Page, 490
South Bay Model Shipwright, 491
cars, Mini Automania, 490
Casting on the Web, 335
horses, Haynet on the Web, 479
planes, Scale Model Collection, 491
polyterrain, Polyterrain Water Soluble Scenery Materials, 491
rockets
Aero-Pac, 489
Monroe Astronomical Rocket Society, 490
Rocket Works, 491
S.Shiota's Model Rocket Page, 491
Scale Modeling, 491
trains
C & M Train Depot, 490
DP Industries Home Page, 490
Florida's Largest Train Store, 490
Interactive Model Railroad, 339
Logic Rail Technologies, 490
Model Railroad.Com, 490
Palatine Hobby's Railroad Page, 490
RR Depot, 491
Rutger Friberg's World of ModelRailroad Electronic, 491
TraiNutz, 491
modems, 32
modes
full-duplex, 33
half-duplex, 33
molecular modeling, Concepts in Science through Molecular Modeling, 305
Montana, Peaks-An Online Magazine About Montana, 917
Monterey Academy of Oceanographic Science, 306
Moore, Daniel, 75
morphology, 531
Word Manager, 533
mortgages
Eastern Mortgage Services, Inc., 136
Fidelity Union Mortgage, 136
First Pacific Financial, 136
FractalNet Real Estate Server, 136
Home Builder's Utopia, 136
Home Improvement Loans, 136
HomeOwners Finance Center, 136
J.C. Mortgage, 137
LOAN STORE, 137

Index

Mortgage Calculator, 137
Mortgage Manager, 137
Mortgages Manager Version 5.00, 137
National Homes Online, 137
National InterAd Real Estate Page, 137
Real Estate Junction, 137
Real Estate Pages, 137
Security First Funding, 138
Mosaic, 5
About Web/Genera, 557
Easy Mosaic and Introductory Web Surfing, 558
Global Network Navigator Home Page, 558
newsreaders, 29
motels and hotels
American Youth Hostels, 910
Bed & Breakfast Inns Online, 910
California Travel and Parks Association, 910
Campground Directory, 910
Choice Hotels, 910
Homeless Shelters in the United States, 910
Hostelling International, 911
International Bed And Breakfast Guide, 911
Nude 2000, 911
Professional Association of Innkeepers Internation, 911
Travel Web, 911
United Hostels of Europe, 911
World Wide Lodging Guide, 911
motorcycle racing, 855
motorcycles
Classic Showcase, 898
Harley-Davidson: Motorcycle Collectible Art Gallery, 77
Hell's Buddha's, 347
Longriders Internet Bikers' Club House, 896
Motorcycle Online, 603
Motorcycle Tips and Techniques, 896
Motorsports Media Service International Home Page, 839
Wambo!, 898
WetLeather Home Page, 896
movies
101 Hollywood Blvd., 347
Academy of Motion Picture Arts and Sciences, 638
action
Alien, 623
Crimson Tide Danger Runs Deep, 623

Dr. NO, 623
Hunt for Red October, 623
In the Name of the Father, 623
James Bond 007, 623
Killer, 623
Killing Zoe, 624
Nathan's Apocalypse Now Page, 624
Professional, 624
Terminator/Terminator 2: Judgment Day FAQ List, 624
action movies
Apollo 13, 623
Braveheart, 623
actors, 624-625
actresses, 624-625
adventure
Congo, 623
Indiana Jones WWW Page, 623
Last of the Mohicans, 624
Tombstone, 624
AE Magazine, 599
American Cinema Pages, 639
Best Video, 639
Big Reel, 491
Bright Lights Film Journal, 639
Buena Vista MoviePlex, 630
CG Publishing Inc. Home Page, 478
children's
Adventures of Pinocchio, 625
All Dogs Go To Heaven 2, 625
Ariel Forever, 625
Babe, 625
Beauty and the Beasty Trivia, 625
Casper Audio/Video Library, 626
Dark Crystal, 626
Dove Foundation's Home Page, 626
Hunchback of Notre Dame, 626
It Takes Two, 626
James and the Giant Peach, 626
Lion King, 626
Mighty Morphin Power Rangers Megadventure, 626
Miracle on 34th Street, 627
Muppet Movie Links, 627
Pocahontas, 627
Toy Story, 627
Willy Wonka and the Chocolate Factory, 627
CinaMedia, 491
Cinema Sites, 639
Cinemania Online, 639
classics
Casablanca, 627
Citizen Kane, 627

Gone With the Wind, 627
Jazz Singer (1927), 627
Metropolis, 627
Wizard of Oz, 628
Collecting, 492
comedies
Airplane!, 628
Brazil, 628
Caddyshack Movie Sound Archive, 628
Cher Horowitz's Home Page, 628
Christmas Story, 628
Clerks, 628
Ferris Bueller's Day Off, 628
Four Rooms, 628
Ghostbusters, 628
Goon Docks, 628
Groundhog Day, 628
Jerk, 628
Joe Versus the Volcano, 628
Kids in the Hall Brain Candy, 629
Loser, 629
National Lampoon's Animal House, 629
October Films Presents, Nadja, 629
Princess Bride, 629
Reality Bites, 629
Rosencrantz and Guildenstern Are Dead, 629
Saxonian Blues Brothers Page, 629
Shaft, 629
Shallow Grave, 629
Smoke, 629
Super Fly, 629
Tank Girl, 630
Three O'Clock High, 630
To Wong Foo, Thanks for Everything! Julie Newmar, 630
Unofficial Addams Family Movie Home Page, 630
Critics Roost, 639
cult movies
Bloodlust, 631
Buckaroo Banzai Jump-Station, 631
Clockwork Orange, 632
Cult Shop, 632
Dr. Strangelove Or: How I Learned to Stop Worrying, 632
Heathers, 632
Mystery Science Theater 3000 The Movie, 632
Ray Wolfe's Online Guide to Eraserhead, 632
Rocky Horror Picture Show, 632

Spinal Tap, 632
Unofficial Monty Python Home Page, 632
CyberCinema, 492, 641
Cybercinema Links, 479
Digital Movie News, 212
dramas
 Barton Fink, 632
 Basketball Diaries, 632
 Crow, 633
 Dead Man Walking, 633
 Forrest Gump, 633
 Godfather Trilogy, 633
 Goodfellas, 633
 Hackers, 633
 Heat, 633
 Hoop Dreams, 634
 Il Postino (The Postman), 633
 Jane Eyre, 633
 Leaving Las Vegas, 633
 Martin Scorsese, 634
 Mean Streets, 634
 Othello, 634
 Photographic Gallery of the Film Trilogy, 634
 Powder, 634
 Pulp Fiction Apothecarys Page, 634
 Quiz Show, 634
 Reservoir Dogs, 634
 Scarface, 634
 Showgirls, 634
 Taxi Driver Page, 634
 True Romance, 634
Early Motion Pictures 1897–1916, 639
Elstree-remember me?, 630
Entertainment Connection, 641
EVN Mail Order Factory Outlet, 797
film festivals
 Cannes Film Festival Official Web Site, 635
 Chicago Underground Film Festival, 635
 Cinema Festivals, 635
 Film Festivals Server, 635
 Low Res film and video festival, 635
 Sundance Film Festival, 635
Films in the Works, 639
Fine Line, 630
games, Makin Bacon, 339
Hollywood Toy and Poster Company, 492
HomeTheater Com, 506
horror
 Cabinet of Dr. Casey, 637
 David Cronenberg Home Page, 637
 Halloween, 637

Hannibal Lecter Home Page, 637
Jaws, 637
Lord of Illusions, 637
Nightmare on the Web, 637
Return of the Texas Chainsaw Massacre, 637
Shining, 637
HSS Wholesale Home Page, 641
Indiana Jones WWW Page, 522
Internet Movie Database, 639
listservs, 645-646
Lucasfilm's THX Home Page, 350
MCA/Universal, 630
Media House Films, 630
Miramar Productions, 630
Miramax Cafe, 631
Movie Collector's World, 492
Movie Madness Merchandise, 641
Movie Poster Page, 641
Movie Poster Warehouse, 492
Movie Reviews.com, 639
Movie Sounds Page, 640
Movie Target, 640
MovieLink 777-FILM Online, 640
Movienet, 640
Movies Cliché List, 639
Movies.Com, 631
MovieWEB, 640
MPEG Movie Archive, 640
Mr. Showbiz, 640
music
 Hindi Movie Songs, 658
 Sami's Urdu/Hindi Film Music Page, 659
 Vangelis—The Man and The Music, 666
mystery
 Clue, 641
 Fargo, 641
 Hitchcock Page, 641
 Seven, 641
 Usual Suspects, 641
 Vertigo, 641
New Line Cinema, 631
newsgroups, 644-645
October Films, 631
Overall Knowledge Company, Inc., 565
Paramount Pictures Online Studio, 631
Polygram Filmed Entertainment, 631
production resources
 Character Shop, 635
 CinemaSpace, 635
 Dolby Laboratories, 635

DTS Theatrical, 635
Film Resources, 636
Independent Film and Video Makers Internet Resourc, 636
Knight Productions, Inc., 636
LucasArts, 636
Makin' Waves Studio, 636
Mass F/X, 636
New York Film and Animation Co. Ltd., 636
Production Magic, 636
Rhythm & Hues Studios, 636
Shades of Light Studios, 636
THX, 636
Virtual Studio Ltd, London, 636
WAVE—Wognum Art's Virtual Exchange, 636
Welcome to EPSONE.COM, 637
San Francisco Chronicle Film Review, 640
science fiction
 2001: A Space Odyssey, 642
 2019: Off-World (Blade Runner Page), 642
 Back to the Future, 642
 Bob's Godzilla Shrine, 642
 Dune, 642
 Flash Gordon, 642
 Harp on Batman Forever, 642
 Mithral Web, 642
 Nuke Home Page, 642
 Phantasm, 642
 Star Trek: WWW, 643
 Star Wars Collectors Home Page, 643
 Star Wars Home Page at UPENN, 643
 Tron Home Page, 643
 Until the End of the World, 643
 War Games Fan Page, 643
 Waterworld, 643
Showtimes Home Page, 640
Sony Pictures Entertainment Page, 631
Sources for Still Photographs, Posters and Other Film Memorabilia, 492
Star Seeker Movie Page, 640
trivia
 The Daily 100, 337
 The Oracle of Bacon at Virginia, 345
Ultimate Resource for Vintage Posters, 642
United Film Distributors, 640
VCV Stunts—Stuntmen on the Net, 335

Index

Walt Disney, 631
Warner Bros. Online, 631
Widescreen Links, 640
World Collectible Center, 492
see also film
MUDs, Lee's Useless Superhero Generator, 339
multimedia
art
Metaverse, 77
Multimedia Cultural Information Service, The; 77
Atomic Vision Inc., 211
Auricle Control Systems, 211
Avalanche Systems Inc., 211
AVM Summit, 211
CA Natalie Associates, 211
CD Learn: Personalized Training for Your, 211
CD Warehouse, 211
CD Works, 211
Chick Enterprises Ltd., 212
Cinax Designs Inc., 212
Constant Synthesis Project, 212
Crystal River Engineering, 212
Darim Vision Co., 212
DayStar Digital, Inc., 212
Demo and Tutorial Builders from MIKSoft, Inc., 212
Digital Creators, 212
Digital Movie News, 212
Due North, 213
EDGE Interactive Media, Inc., 213
Edit & Copy Communications, 213
EMA Multimedia, Inc., 213
Entertainment Through Technology Consortium, 213
HJF Digital Media, 213
IBM 3D Interaction Accelerator, 213
IDM, 213
Incite, 213
Jack, 213
Knowledge Industry Publications, Inc., 602
Loviel Computer Corporation, 213
Magnum Resources, 214
MakeMPEG-the Home Page, 214
Media Solutions International, 214
Metatec Corporation, 214
MidiMan's Official Web Site, 214
Mimesis Technology, 214
MMWIRE WEB, 602
Multimedia Archives, 214
Murray MultiMedia, 214

Music Screeners, 214
Net-One System's Personalized CDs, 214
North Communications, 214
NuReality, 214
Pangea Creative Media, 214
Photodex Corporation, 215
Pinnacle Post, 215
QuickMedia, 215
QuickMedia-Living Album, 215
Ramworks, 215
Redundantly, Online, 604
Scala Computer Television AS (Norway), 215
Sealworks, Inc., 215
SimPhonics, Inc., 215
Software Tools for Artists, 215
Sound & Vision Media, 215
Sprite Interactive, 215
StarMan Group, Multimedia Productions, 216
Station Graphics, Inc., 216
ThreeToad Multimedia, 216
Two Guys Named Hank, 216
Virtual Artists, 216
Visionary Designs, 216
vivid studios, 216
Welcome to Macromedia.com, 216
Welcome to macromedia.com, 216
Worlds Inc., 216
X Communications Multimedia, 216
Xpand Inc., 217
XSI MeDIA, 217
Zfx, Inc., 217
Multipurpose Internet Mail Extensions (MIME), 12-13
mummification, 430
museums
Advanced Cultural Technologies, 71
Artix, 72
California, 73
California Museum of Photography, 494
Field Museum Online, 522
Heritage Map Museum, 292, 527
Leonardo da Vinci Museum, 460
Mary Rose Virtual Maritime Museum, 463
Maxwell Museum of Anthropology, 518
Museum of Anthropology— University of Michigan, 518
Museum of Fine Arts, 3D Animation, 336

Museums in the Netherlands, 77
Museum of Paleontology, 782
Museum of Television and Radio, 349
Museum of Tolerance, 827
Museum Professional, 464
National Civil Rights Museum, 827
Paris Museums, 464
Raymond M. Alf Museum, 782
Royal Tyrrell Museum Web Site, 523
Shore Line Trolley Museum, 465
transportation
Auto Museum at Wells, 896
Cole Land Transportation Museum, 896
Henry Ford Museum & Greenfield Village, 896
U'Mista Cultural Centre, 79
University of California Museum of Palentology, 782
music
94.7 NRK: The New Rock Revolution, 348
Acoustic Musician Magazine, 599
agents: Transatlantic Management, 654
alternative
Air Top 20 Chart, 649
Alternative World, 649
Be Happy or Die!, 647
Beastie Boys, 667
Cure, 647
Depeche Mode Home Page, 647
fourtuoh, 647
High Lonesome, 647
Hyperreal, 647
Jane's Addiction and Porno for Pyros, 677
Lou Reed's Web Home, 647
Mazzy Star Home Page, 677
Meat Puppets Home Page, 677
MEGO, 647
nine inch nails: the unofficial home page, 678
R.E.M. Home Page, 648
Talking Heads, 648
They Might Be Giants, 648
Tom Waits Digest, 648
Turmoil's Seattle Music Web, 648
Welcome to Carbon 14, 605
Wood and Wire, 648
archives
AMG Online Music, 655
Classical MIDI Archives, 651
Ectophiles' Guide to Good Music, 647

HitsWorld, 649
Hype! Music, 655
Mammoth Music Meta-List @ VIBE, 655
Monsterbit Media, 655
Rockmine Archives, 655, 656
Similarities Engine, 656
Ultimate Band List, 656
WholeARTS Directory of Musical Entertainment, 654
Worldwide Internet Music Resources, 653, 656
awards
    Academy Awards for Music, 1960s and 1970s, 648
    Grammy Awards on the Internet, 648
Blue Planet, 348
bluegrass
    Bluegrass Unlimited Reviews, 648
    Central Texas Bluegrass Association, 648
    Doc Hamilton's Bluegrass Home Page, 648
    Doc Watson, 648
    Old Time Music Bulletin Board, 648
    Phillip Mann's Banjo Tab Collection, 663
    Welcome to Planet Bluegrass!, 649
blues
    Biscuit Time on Blues Web, 670
    Blue Highway, 670
    Bluenote, 671
    BluesNet, 671
    DC Blues Home Page, 671
    House of Blues, 671
    Live Blues and Blues Radio, Steamin' Stan Ruffo, 671
Cellophane Square, 478
CERN MusiClub, 73
CG Publishing Inc. Home Page, 478
Christian
    "Almost," 650
    Christian Music Online, 650
    Creation 96, 660
    Michael W. Smith, 650
    Susan Ashton, 650
classical
    Allegro, 650
    American Music Center, 650
    Aspen Music Festival, 650
    Ballet Web, 650
    Boston Chamber Ensemble, 650
    Building a Library, 650
    Chamber Music Conferences, 651

Chicago Concert Search, 651
Classical MIDI Archives, 651
Classical Music Home Page, 651
Classical Music on the Web, 651
C level and Concert Search, 651
CyberDance, 651
DCI, 651
Electronic Early Music, 651
FAQ, 651
FutureNet, 651
Galliard String Quartet, 652
Indianapolis Symphony Orchestra, 652
Indiana University School of Music, 652
Katia and Marielle Labeque Home Page, 652
La Ma de Guido, 652
Maestronet, 652
Music Hall, 652
Music under Soviet Rule, 653
New York Philharmonic, 653
Performing Arts Sites, 653
Renaissance Consort, 653
SCA Music and Dance Home Page, 653
T.M.Mc Comb, 653
Unknown Composers Page, 653
Worldwide Internet Music Resources, 653
concert tickets
    Ace Ticket Service—Concert Tickets, 654
country
    Basket Full of Country, 654
    History of Country Music, 654
    Obvious Gossip Home Page, 654
    planetgarth, 655
    Reba McENTIRE, 655
databases, Similarities Engine II, 341
Dr. Wax, 479
education
    Brent Hugh's Music Instruction Software Page, 656
    MIDI Home Page, 656
    Neil Hume DJ Page, 656
festivals
    29th Montreux Jazz Festival Official Site, 660
    ABSOLUTELY WORTHLESS Calendar, 660
    Lollapalooza Information (Unofficial), 660
    MBNA College Quartet Contest, 660

Musi-Cal Performer Index, 660
National Folk Festival, 660
Rob Kenney Presents: Kerrville Folk Festival, 660
Strawberry Music Festivals, 660
UFOJOE Presents, 660
WOMEX '96, 659
World Music/Boston, 660
folk
    Digital Tradition Folk Song Database, 655
    Dirty Linen, 600
    Fasola Home Page, 660
    Folk Book, 661
    Folk Music Home Page, 661
    Folk on the Radio, 661
    Folk Stuff, 661
    Mary Chapin Carpenter, 661
    Northern Journey: Canadian Folk Music Website, 665
    Southern Folklife Collection, 661
Harmony Music List, 75
house, DJ Dom A's Top Twenty Club Charts, 649
humor, Twisted Tunes Home Page, 346
independent label
    Alternet Sonic Realities, 671
    Asphodel Records, 672
    Axiom/Laswell Web Site, 672
    Badcat Records, 672
    Bedazzled, 672
    Bogus Records, 672
    Boy's Life Records, 672
    Caroline Records, 672
    Castle von Buhler Records, 672
    Catasonic Records, 672
    Caulfield Records, 672
    East Side Digital Records, 673
    Hi-Bias Records Inc., 673
    Index, 647
    Landphil Records' Online Information Dump, 673
    Lunch Records, 673
    Manifest Records, 674
    Marathon Records, 674
    Monkeyland Records, 674
    Moonshine Music, 674
    Pop Gun Records, 674
    Propulsion Records, 674
    Rage Records, 674
    Red Phraug Modern Medium, 674
    Sesha Press Records, 675

Index

Index

Silver Girl Records, 675
Sin-Drome Records, 675
Slumberland Records, 675
Squealer Music, 675
Supernova Records, 675
Surfdog Records, 675
Verb Audio, 675
Wa Nui Records, 676
Wood and Wire, 648
jazz
    Alabama Jazz Hall of Fame, 663
    Arizona Jazz, Rhythm and Blues
        Festival, 663
    Electric Gallery, 663
    Hard Bop Cafe, 664
    Jazz Central Station, 664
    Jazz Improvisation, 664
    Jazz in France, 664
    Jazz Net, 664
    Jazz Photography of Ray Avery, 495
    Jazz Roots, 664
    KLON'S JazzAvenue Jazz
        Information Service, 602
    Magic Island, 674
    Pacific Blues & Jazz, 664
    Tom Morgan's Web Site for Jazz, 664
    Traditional Jazz (Dixieland), 664
    Virtual Jazz Fest!, 664
    William Ransom Hogan Archive,
        664
    WNUR-FM JazzWeb, 664
karaoke
    Karaoke, 661
    Karaoke Home Page, 661
    Looney Tunes Karaoke, 339
listservs, 681-683
liturgical, Gregorian Chant Home
    Page, 652
lyrics
    Jessica Ross and Her Amazing
        Mondegreen Circus, 665
    Lyrics Page, 665
    Twisted Tunes, 665
magazines
    Addicted To Noise, 665
    Cybergrass—The Internet Bluegrass
        Magazine, 665
    Electric Magic—The Led Zeppelin
        Chronicle, 665
    ICE On-Line, 665
    OffBeat Magazine, 665
    Stirrings Folk Mag, 665
    Synthesis: Electronic Dance Music
        Page, 666
marketing
    Marketing Music on the Web, 676
    Moneymaking Music Resources, 676

Patrick's Musicians' Page, 676
Planet StarChild, 676
new age
    Björk's—Web Sense, 666
    Enigma, 668
    Enya—Unofficial World Wide Web
        Home Page, 666
    Malahat Mountain Music, 666
    Vangelis—The Man and The Music,
        666
newsgroups, 679-681
online stores
    Akers Mic, 654
    Andrak Music, 654
    GEMM: Global Electronic Music
        Marketplace, 655
    HMV Toronto Superstore, 654
    Hot Platters, 654
    Jazz Music Stores around the World,
        654
    Rounder Records, 654
opera
    Cecilia Bartoli FanWeb (Unofficial),
        650
    Current Opera Web site, 651
    Gilbert and Sullivan Archive, 652
    Le Nozze di Figaro, 652
    Opera Schedule Server, 653
    opera-l_home_page, 653
    Opera Stories and Background, 653
organizations
    American Music Center, 666
    Black Rock Coalition, 672
    Club ZigZag, 667
    Muscle Music, Inc., 667
    National Music Foundation, 667
    Wolverine Antique Music Society,
        667
percussive
    D'CuCKOO, 647
    Official Hammered Dulcimer Page,
        663
    Village Pulse, 675, 676
pop
    22nd Row, 670
    ABBAnatic, 667
    Amy Grant Site in College Park,
        MD, 667
    and through the wire, 667
    The Boy George Home Page, 668
    Bryan Adams Home Page, 668
    Caribbean Soul: Jimmy Buffett
        Parrotheads, 668
    Casey's Top 40, 649

Chicago O(+> Nation, 668
Counting Crows, 668
Discographies (and More), 655
Disgraceland, 668
DJ Special Blend's Top 10, 649
ELP—Emerson, Lake & Palmer, 668
Elvis Costello Home Page, 668
EXCESS OF INXS, AN, 668
Frankie Goes to Hollywood Fan
    Pages, 668
Future Love Paradise: The Seal
    WWW Site, 668
Gaia: Olivia Newton-John Home
    Page, 668
Gloria Estefan/MSM, 669
Huey Lewis and the News, 668
Hype! One Hit Wonder Compilation,
    649
Madonna Home Page, 669
Men Without Hats: The (Unofficial)
    Home Page, 669
Nicks Fix, 669
Original Mariah Carey Home Page,
    669
Pet Shop Boys Virtually, 648
Planet Janet, 669
Random '80s Lyrics, 655
Rick Dee's Weekly Top 40, 649
ROSS, 669
Roxette: Home Page, 669
Sarah McLachlan Homepage, 670
Simon and Garfunkel Home Page,
    669
Simple Minds—Good News From
    the Web, 670
Sinead O'Connor Home Page, 670
Sting—The Soul Pages, 670
Tori Amos, 670
VH1 Music First, 670
Welcome to HIStory!, 670
Zar's Paula Abdul, 670
punk
    Clash, 668
    Green Day, 677
record clubs, BMG, 666
record labels
    About Time Music Company, 671
    Acorn Music, 671
    American Gramaphone Records, 671
    American Recordings Home Page,
        671
    Angel Thorne Music, 671
    Atlantic Records Home Page, 672
    Changing Tones Records, 672

China Records, 673

Curb Records, 673

Geffen Records, 673

Go Kart Records, 673

Grand Royal, 673

ID&T Records, 673

Indochina, 673

Metal Blade Records, 674

Mute Liberation Technologies, 674

Nettwerk, 674

Oh Boy Records, 674

PolyGram Records, Inc., 674

RCA Victor, 674

Reservoir Records, 675

Restless Records, 675

Rhino Records Home Page, 675

Rockadillo Records, 675

TeenBeat Records, 675

Warner Bros. Records, 676

Windham Hill Records, 676

rhythm and blues, Black Music
Department Top R&B, 649

rock

Aerosmith, 676

The David Bowie File, 676

The Death of Rock 'n' Roll, 676

The Grateful Dead, 676

Hanspeter Niederstrasser's Def
Leppard Page, 677

Hyper Idol II, 677

Iron Maiden Page, 677

Jethro Tull Music Archive, 677

Kinks Web Sites, 677

KISS OTAKU, 677

L.A. Rock & Roll Road Map, 677

Led Zeppelin Home Page, 677

Lloyd Robbins' Moody Blues Page,
669

Merger, 677

Metallica, 677

Mike Markowski's Beatles Page, 669

MÖTLEY CRÜE, 678

Original Unoffical Elvis Home Page,
669

Pete Lambie's Bruce Springsteen
Page, 669

Phish.Net, 678

Pink Floyd Home Page, 678

Queen, 678

RADISH—Hot Original Rock!, 678

Rock and Roll Hall of Shame, 678

Rolling Stones Web Site, 678

Ron Smith Oldies Calendar, 660

Room Full of Mirrors: The Official
Jimi Hendrix We, 678

Stranglehold—The Ted Nugent Page,
678

Welcome to the Jungle, 678

Ron Smith Oldies Calendar, 702

See Hollywood and Vine, 350

sound bytes, Virtual Radio, 654

surveys, CD Album Top 100 of All
Time, 649

Synergy Music and Art Workshop, 78

techno, Kraftwerk infobahn, 647

trivia, The Rock and Roll Hall of
Shame, 346

The Virtual Keyboard, 348

weddings, Wedding Band Center, 926

women, Muse Magazine, 603

world

Abayudaya Jews in Uganda: Music,
656

Afro-Caribbean Music, 656

Afropop Worldwide, 656

Ain't Whistlin' Dixie, 656

Ari Davidow's Klezmer Page, 657

Australian Music
World Wide Web Site, 657

Bali & Beyond Home Page, 657

Batish Institute of Indian Music and
Fine Arts, 657

Celtic Music Index Page, 657

Ceolas Celtic Music Archive, 657

Chinese Music Page, 657

Clannad WWW Home Page, 657

Classical Music Home Page, 657

Cuban Music, 657

Flamenco Home Page, 658

Hindi Movie Songs, 658

Home Page of MT&C Music Club,
658

Indian Music: Recordings and
Instrumentals, 658

Indian Classical Music, 658

Indonesian Music, 658

Irish Folk Songs, 658

Larry Aronson Home Page, 658

MIZIK, 658

Music from Africa and the African
Diaspora, 658

Northern Journey: Canadian Folk,
658

Rashid Sales Co., 658

Richard Robinson's Tunebook, 659

Roots/World Music FAQ, 659

RootsWorld: Music on the Net, 659

Russian Music, 659

Samba in Sweden, 659

Sami's Urdu/Hindi Film Music
Page, 659

Shona Music, 659

Some Peruvian Music, 659

T. M. McComb: Music Home Page,
653

Tara: The World of Jewish Music,
659

Temple Records, 659

TuneWeb, 659

Turkish Music Home Page, 659

World Music/Boston, 660

Zappa Quote of the Day, 718

music videos, Columbia Music Video
Resources, 887

musical instruments

Accumulated Accordian
Annotations, 661

autoharps, Autoharp Page, 661

banjo

Banjo Tablature Archive, 662

Phillip Mann's Banjo Tab Collection,
663

bass

Bottom Line Archive, 662

Will Clifton, Double Basses and
Some Other Thin, 663

concertina, CONCERTINA!, 662

digeridoo

Digeridoo Page, 662

DREAMTIME, The Didjeridu W3
Server, 662

drums, Drums and Percussion Page,
662

French horns, Horn Players' FAQ,
662

guitars, GUITAR.NET, 662

harmonicas, Harmonica World, 662

harps

Harp Page, 662

Historical Harp Society Page, 662

Lark in the Morning, 663

lutes, Wayne's Lute Page, 663

mandolins, Mandolin Pages, 663

Musicmaker's Kits, Inc., 663, 814

Official Hammered Dulcimer Page,
663

percussion, Bodhran Page, 662

reeds, IDRS WWW, 662

sitars, Batish Institute of Indian
Music and Fine Arts, 657

musicals

Les Miserables Home Page, 666

On Broadway WWW Information
Page, 666

Really Useful Company Presents Sir Andrew Lloyd Webber, 666
Rec.Arts.Theatre.Musicals, 666
mutual funds, 715
mysteries
Agatha Christie, 99
Baker Street Connection, 106
mystery movies
Clue, 641
Fargo, 641
Hitchcock Page, 641
Seven, 641
Usual Suspects, 641
Vertigo, 641
Mysticism
Al Azif: The Manuscript Liber Logaeth, 737
Aleister Crowley, 737
Egyptian Book of the Dead, 737
Golden Dawn FAQ, 737
Kabballah Connection, 737
Mysticism in World Religions, 737
Shawn's Rituals Collection, 737
Tarot Reading, 737
Wayfarer's Rest, 738

N

NASA
Discovery Program Home Page, 751
MTAC Home Page, 132
NASA, 483
NASA Astronautics History, 465
NASA Astrophysics Data System Home Page-Classic Sy, 752
NASA CD, 840
NASA Dryden Flight Research Center, 755
NASA Education Sites, 294
NASA Information Services via World Wide Web, 755
NASA Spacelink-An Electronic Information System For Educators, 310
NASA Television on CU-SeeMe, 755
NASA Weather Archive, 775
NASA World Wide Web Information Services, 752
NASA-JSC Digital Image Collection, 752
Nicky's Kid Links, 153
Nine Planets, 294
SeaWiFS Project Home Page, 781
Welcome to the Planets, 754
national parks
Humanities Report, 525

National Park Service: Links to the Past—Archaeology, 522
Native Americans
Anasazi Archaeology, 520
art, 72
Heard Museum, 76
National Museum of the American Indian, 77
Hopi Basketry Presentation, 518
Mesa Verde Pottery, 486
Milne Jewelry Company, 810
Native American Cultural Resources on the Internet, 464
Native American History and Archaeology Resources on the Internet, 522
Native American Net Server, 519
Santa Fe Traditions, Inc., 481
Sisseton Wahpeton Sioux Tribe, 519
South Dakota Archaeology, 524
World Wide Mall:™ Arts, Crafts, & Antiques, 482
natural art
Earth Folk Catalog, 370
National Audubon Society, 363
natural disasters
Disaster Information Network, 711
Internet Disaster Information Center, 606
natural history, Natural History Book Service—Home Page, 613
naturopathy, 428
nautical history
Maritime History Virtual Archives, 463
Mutiny on the HMS Bounty, 464
Nautical Net, 846
Pan-American Institute of Maritime Archaeology, 523
Pirates, 464
Navigator, 5
Navigator Gold 2.0, 41, 51
Navy, United States Naval Sea Cadet Corps, 305
NCSA Mosaic 2.1.1, 51
near-death experiences, 429
Nebraska, Nebraska Travel and Tourism, 917
nebulae, 753
needlepoint, Counted Cross Stitch, Needlework, and Stitchery Page, 498
neon
Krypton Neon—The Internet's Neon Shop, 76
Northwest Neon, 815
NetCruiser, 54

NetGuide, 36
Netherlands
Flags of the 19th and 20th Century, 706
Museums in the Netherlands, 77
Nijenrode Business Webserver, 132
Netiquette, 18
flames, 18, 28
signatures, 18
spamming, 28
Netscape, 5-6, 12, 41, 50
beta programs, 42
binary files, 29
e-mail manager, 24
Extensions, 43
graphics, 50
newsreaders, 29
Plug-Ins, 44
Netscape Navigator Gold 2.0, 41, 51
networking
Alcatel Data Networks, 217
AppWare Developers Association, 217
Banyan Systems Inc., 217
Capella Networking, 217
CD-ROM Online, 211
CrossComm Corporation, 217
CygnaCom Solutions, Inc., 217
Designed Information Systems Corporation, 218
DIgital Network Product Business, 218
Economics of Networks Internet Site, 568
Emulex Network Systems, 218
Engage Communication, 218
Enterprise Network Solutions, 218
Florida Atlantic University, 218
HDS Network Systems, 218
HELIOS Software, 218
Integrated Communications, 218
Intel Smart Network Devices, 218
Internet Database Consultants, 218
Interphase, 219
InterWorking Labs, 219
INTRANET Technologies, Inc., 570
Island Services Network, 570
John Mayes & Associates, 219
K-Net Ltd, 219
KarlBridge, 219
Kinesix, 219
Klever Computers, 219
LAN Solutions, 219
Lancom Technologies, 219
Maxperts, Inc., 219

MSI Communications, 219
Myricom, Inc., 219
Net Guru Technologies, 219
NETiS Technology, Inc., 219
NetMagic, Inc., 220
Network Communication Computers and Arrays, 220
Networks Incorporated, 220
NeuroDimension, Inc., 220
Newbridge Networks Corporation, 220
Nortel Northern Telecom, 220
Novell, Inc., 220
Novia Internetworking, 571
NTG International, 220
NTT Data Communications Systems, 220
Onion Peel Software Home, 220
Ornetix Network Computing, 221
PC DOCS, Inc., 221
Plaintree Systems, 221
Retix Web, 221
Rnet, 221
routers, 10
Sietec Document Management and Archives, 221
SoftLinx, Inc. Web Page, 221
StonyBrook Software, 221
Strategic Networks Consulting, Inc., 221
Structured Network Systems, 221
System Resources Corporation, 221
TENET Computer Group, Inc., 222
VISIT Computer Telephony Integration, 222
Word Master, Inc., 222
XLNT Designs, Inc, 222
Yost Serial Device Wiring Standard, 222
neurosurgery, Department of Neurosurgery at New York University, 443
Nevada
Front Desk, 916
Index, 916
Las Vegas, 917
Nevada Bureau of Mines and Geology, 768
Virtual Vegas, 352
new age music
Björk's—Web Sense, 666
Clannad WWW Home Page, 657
Enigma, 668
Enya—Unofficial World Wide Web Home Page, 666
Malahat Mountain Music, 666

Vangelis—The Man and The Music, 666
Windham Hill Records, 676
World Transformation, 367
New England
New England Windsurfing Journal, 844
surfing, 844
New Hampshire
Access New Hampshire, 914
Vermont/New Hampshire WWW Resources, 918
New Jersey, HobokenX, 916
New Mexico, 92, 389
America's Land of Enchantment, 915
New York
Albany, theater, 351
fishing, Nor'east Saltwater Magazine, 846
New York City
Media Connection of New York— Links Page, 571
New York Public Library: Center for the Humanities, 524
New York City Theater, 351
New York Open Center, 294
TenEyck Design Studio, 351
NYSDA Public Defense Backup Center Home Page, 590
New Zealand
Mount Cook Airlines, 904
New Zealand First Day Covers, 497
news
American Reporter, 605
Associated Press, 605
C-Span Networks, 882
C-SPAN Networks Site, 416
CBS News: Campaign '96, 416
CNN Newsroom, 882
CNN/Time: All Politics, 416
DataStar Information Retrieval Service, 711
Decision '96, 416
Deutche Welle Radio & TV—English Home Page, 616
ElectionLine, 416
FCC Welcome Page, 606
infoMCI, 606
International Pages, 606
Internet Disaster Information Center, 606
iWORLD, 570
Japan, What's New in Japan, 560
libraries.americas, 606
Mercury Center Home Page, 602

Monitor Radio, 617
NewsLink Menu, 606
NJ Online Weather, 606
NOS TeleTekst, 606
NPR Online, 617
Omnivore, 606
RadioSpace Home Page, 606
RealAudio: ABC News, 606
Tharunka Home, 604
Time Daily News Summary, 606
USIA International Broadcasting, 606
Vanderbilt Television News Archive, 887
newsgroups, 9, 21, 28
advertising, 19
animals, 67
art, 95
books & authors, 116-117
business, 144-146
children, 155
computer games, 172-173
computers, 270-281
education, 312-313
employment, 330-332
entertainment, 353-356
environment, 376
family issues, 390
flaming, 28
food & drink, 409-410
government & politics, 420-422
headers, 29
health & fitness, 451-453
history, 466
hobbies & crafts, 501-503
home improvement, 515
humanities, 547
Internet resouces, 581-582
law, 595
media, 618-620
movies, 644-645
music, 679-681
paranormal phenomena, 699
posting, 18
reference, 719-720
religion & philosophy, 741-743
replying, 29
science & engineering, 786-789
sci.environment, 365
sexuality, 801-802
shopping, 821-822
society & culture, 831-836
spamming, 28
sports, 860-865
Talk.environment, 365

television, 888-891
threading, 29
transportation, 899
travel, 920
weddings, 929
newsletters
Aerial Archaeology Newsletter, 520
Colibri Home Page, 530
Home Automator, 506
Internet Resources Newsletter, 570
legal.online, 592
Physics World Electronic News, 784
Sportfishing Industry Newsletter, 846
Suzanne Seely's "Make it Beautiful"
Decorating Newsletter, 513
newspapers
Access ET, 599
Campus Newspapers on the Internet,
606
Capital, 607
City Paper, 607
CRAYON—CReAte Your Own
Newspaper, 568
Editor & Publisher, 600
Financial Times Group, 607
Gazeta Wyborcza, 607
Hastings Tribune Internet Edition,
607
Indianapolis Star and News, 607
Jerusalem Post, 607
Kamloops Daily News, 607
Knoxville News Sentinel, 607
Maui News, 607
Money & Investing Update—
Welcome, 607
Newspaper / Diario LA NACION—
San Jose, Costa Rica, 607
Newsshare Corporation, 607
Personal Technology Home Page, 607
Private Eye, 607
Providence Business News, 608
Scripps Howard Home Page, 604
Southam, Inc., 608
Stanford Daily Home Page, 608
Sydney Morning Herald, 608
Tech, 608
Telluride Times-Journal, 608
Times Higher Education Supple-
ment, 608
USA Today Sports, 854
Vocal Point, 608
Welcome to USA TODAY, 608
newsreaders, 29
Fortes Free Agent, 29
in Netscape 2.0, 29

NFL (National Football League), 853
NFL Executive Accessories, 848
NFL Kids, 153
NFL POOL, 845
**Nigeria, CRLP: Women of the World,
542**
nonprofit organizations
arts, 73
Cenikor Foundation, Inc., 427
Internet Nonprofit Center, 712
North Carolina
Greensboro Online, 916
North Central Regional Educational
Laboratory, 307
**North Dakota, North Dakota ICICLE
Project, 311**
**Norway, Norwegian Bookshop Home
Page, 114, 613**
nostalgia radio, 617
notary publics, Seals on Wheels, 134
novelty gifts, Global Innovations, 813
**nuclear war, Radiation Effects Research
Foundation, 443**
numerology
Animals and Karma, 688
Astro-numerology, 688
Entropic Fine Art Inc., 688
How Does the Kalabalarian
Philosophy Differ from Numerol-
ogy, 689
Numerology, 689
Numerology by Cheryl Lee Terry, 689
Numerology, The Science of
Vibration, 689
Numerology—I've Got Your
Number, 689
Numerology—What do the Numbers
Mean?, 689
Prime—Advanced Numerology
Profiler, 689
Six Hundred and Sixty Six
But not 666, 689
Skeptics Dictionary—Numerology,
689
Sun Angel, 689
Wonderful World of Numerology,
689
numismatics, *see* **coin collecting**
nursing
ADN/RN Concepts, 446
HomeCareNurse Web Page, 446
International Network for Interfaith
Healing Practices, 446
MacNursing, 446
Neuromedical Supplies, Inc., 814
Nursing Lists, 446

Telephone Triage and Nurse
Consultation, 446
nutrition
Alliance Health Products, 428
Arizona Health Sciences Library, 446
Austin Reference Guide for Vitamins,
446
balance, Fitness on the Net, 436
Blonz Guide to Nutrition, Food
Science, and Health, 436
Center for Food Safety and Applied
Nutrition, 446
CyberNutrition Online Dole 5 A Day,
437
D&M Sales, 428
Department of Food Science &
Nutrition, 399
Designs for Health, 428
Dietetics Online, 447
Dole 5 A Day, 437
Dole 5 a Day, 399
Dole 5-A-Day Homepage, 309
Electronic Gourmet Guide (eGG), 399
Fast Food Finder, 447
Food & Nutrition Information
Center, 436
Food Pyramid, 437
General Complementary Medicine,
438
Good Health Web, 438
Green Page-Natural Health/
Nutrition, 429
Health and Longevity, 428
Health Resource, 438
Healthtouch, 438
Herbal Hall, 428
IFIC Foundation, 437
International Health News, 439
Krispin Komments, 437
Macrobiotics Online, 447
Magnesium Deficiency, Heart Attack,
and Drinking Water, 447
Mirkin Report, 437
MN-NET Home Page, 447
Natural Food Samples, 368, 418
Natural Health and Nutrition Shop,
428
Navigator's Health and Nutrition
Page, 439
Netlife Health Products, 437
NutriGenie, 438
Nutrition Expert, 438
Nutrition Pages, 438, 447
Nutritive Value of Foods, 438
Organic Gardening, 447

Pharmavite Corporation, 429
Professor Geoff Skurray's Food & Nutrition Informa, 437
Professor Geoff Skurray's Food, Nutrition, and Health Information Page, 400
Sci.Med.Nutrition, 438
Springboard Health and Nutrition Products, 429
Virtual Health, 406
Vitamins, 915
Word on Health, 439
World Health Network, 439
NYSERNet, 300

O

obesity, *see* **weight loss**
obituaries, Obituary Page, 712
occult
Alternative Spiritualities Club Home Page, 689
Aunt Agatha's Occult Emporium, 690
Land of Oz, 690
Lord of Illusions—Clive Barker's Tarot Cards, 692
Necronomi.com—The Familiar Spirit BBS, 690
Nine Houses of Gaia, 690
Occult Gateway, 690
Occult Page, 690
Occultism—The Shawn Knight Page, 690
Original WWW Tarot Site, 693
Pentagram—the Internet's Pagan and Occult Superstore, 690
Servants of the Light—School of Occult Science, 690
Shroud of Turin, 690
Urdco's Mystic Visions, 690
Witchcraft, 697
Witchcraft: Some Answers for the Curious, 697
Witch's Brew—For All of Mother's Children, 698
You lack Slack, Jack—The Church of the Subgenius, 691
see also paganism; witchcraft
occultations, 752
occupational safety, Environmental Training Group Inc.'s ENVIROPAGE, 306
oceanography, 770
Aquatic Network, 129
ASLO Home Page, 779

Coral Health and Monitoring Home Page, 779
CSIRO Division of Oceanography, 779
El Nino Theme Page, 779
GLOBEC Information, 779
List of Oceanography Resources, 779
Monterey Academy of Oceanographic Science, 306
National Marine Fisheries Service, 779
NEMO—Oceanographic Data Server, 779
NOAA Coastal & Estuarine Oceanography Branch, 779
NOAA Home Page, 780
NOAA Paleoclimatology Program, 780
Ocean Planet Home Page, 780
Oceanography Links: Oceanography on the World Wide, 780
Oceanography Society, 780
Oceanography—The Magazine, 603
OCEANOR-Oceanographic Company, 126
Parallel Ocean Program (POP) Simulation, 780
Pathfinder Cafe, 780
Safari Splash, 780
Satellite Oceanography Laboratory, 780
Scripps Institution of Oceanography Library, 780
Sea Frontiers, 604
Sea Surface Temperature Satellite Images, 780
SeaWiFS Project Home Page, 781
SelectSite Ocean Technology, 781
TAMU Oceanography Welcome Page, 781
Topex/Poseidon—The Ocean Topography Experiment, 781
United States JGOFS Home Page, 781
United States WOCE Home Page, 781
Welcome to OCEANIC, 781
Woods Hole Oceanographic Institution (WHOI), 781
Word about the International Oceanographic Foundat, 781
World-Wide Web Virtual Library Oceanography, 781
off-road vehicles
4WD: Four Wheel Drive and All Wheel Drive, 895

America's 4×4 4U Video Magazine, 895
My Jeep Adventures, 895
Off-Road.com, 895
office supplies
Atlas Pen and Pencil Corporation, 808
Cyberian Outpost, 808
Haworth: Furniture for What's Next, 808
Imprinted Pen, 610
Ink, 529
Leonardo Collection Co., 808
Marshall on the Internet, 809
Southern Reprographics, 809
STI Internet Toner Depot, 809
WoodWrite Wood Pens, 809
Ohio
CLEVE.NET A Guided Tour of the North Coast, 916
Ohio State University at Newark, 87
Welcome to the Ohio Web, 919
oil industry
ODIN Oil Network, 133
Shell Oil Company, 123
Oklahoma, Oklahoma Image Map, 917
Olympics
1996 Olympic Games Site, 149
Guide to teh 1996 Olympic Games, 855
XVIII Olympic Winter Games, 855
oncology, INFOOnline, 560
online publishing, *see* **Web publishing**
online services
Allegro Group, 228
Alta Vista digital.com, 228
Amris, Ltd., 228
APCiNet, 229
AT&T Business Network, 229
Axess Communications, 229
BrainLINK International, 229
Brazilnet BBS, 229
CDM Distributors, 229
CNI Communications Network International GmbH, 229
Cogent Software, Inc., 229
CommNet Data Systems, 229
Community ConneXion, 229
CompuHelp Online, 230
ConnectUSA, 230
CrossLink Internet Access, 230
Cyber Technologies International, 230
CyberDiner Internet Cafe Systems, 230

Damar Group, 230
Dataworld, 230
DirectNet, 230
Dream Machine, 230
E-Doc, 230
e.m.a.N.a.t.e., 230
Emporium, 231
ENVISIONET, Inc., 231
Epublish, 231
Excite, 231
Flamingo Communications Inc., 231
Florida Online, 231
Global One, 231
Green Bay Online!, 231
GroMedia, 231
Hot City Networking, 231
I. Net Solutions, Inc., 231
Icanet, 232
Indiana University's UCS Knowledge Base, 232
Intercom, 232
Internet Home Users Group (IHUG), 232
Interstate FiberNet, 232
Intertex, 232
JUMBO! Shareware Archive, 232
Lopez Communications, 571
Merisel's Sun Division, 232
OAK Software Repository, 232
pixel Generation, inc., 232
Planet Communications, 232
PObox EMail Service, 233
QPage.Com, 233
Quay Information, 233
Quick.Net, 233
r.u.there?, 233
SenseMedia Online, 233
SoftInfo Software Information Center, 233
Sojourn Systems, 233
Southwest Web, 233
SPAN Information Technology Inc., 233
Stat Tech, 233
SuperLink.NET, 233
System Optimization Information, 234
ThoughtPort Authority, Inc., 235
Tiger Mountain Productions, 234
Total Connectivity Providers, 234
TRG, Inc., 234
U-NET, 234
Vector Internet Services, 234
Virtual Communications, 234
Web Professionals, Inc., 234

Web Weavers Publishing, 234
WebPub Communications, 234
WebSpace, 234
Whitey's Web Works & Internet Services, 235
WonderNet Digital Communications, Inc., 235
World Information Network, 235
XXL, 235

opera
Cecilia Bartoli FanWeb (Unofficial), 650
Current Opera Website, 651
Gilbert and Sullivan Archive, 652
Le Nozze di Figaro, 652
Opera Stories and Background, 653
opera-l_home_page, 653
Opera Schedule Server, 653

operating systems
Apple Software Updates (ftp.info.apple.com), 235
ARDI Executor, 235
Current Operating Systems Projects and OS-related research, 235
Linux, 647
OS/2 Warp Product Family Home Page, 236
PC-DOS, 236
Que's Complete List of Windows 95 Products, 236
Randy's Windows 95 Resource Center, 236
Slackware Professional Linux, 236
Web browsers, 42
Week's Popular Unix Downloads, 236
Windows: Information Management Group, 561
Xiaomu Niu's Internet Application Collection for Windows, 236

optoelectronic computer systems, 761

Oregon
Bird Guide, Inc., 484
Oregon Online, 917

organ transplants, 443

organic gardening
Gardening, 488
Gardens at Thunder Ridge, 488
Howard Garrett's Basic OrganicProgram, 488
Noah's Ark, 407

organized crime, Gangsters!, 462

origami
Electric Origami Shop, 492
Introduction to Origami and The Peace of Paper, 492

Jasper's Origami Menagerie, 492
Joseph Wu's Origami Page, 492
Marbleized Paper, 493
Origami Books in Local Libraries, 493
Origami Tips, 493
Origami USA Main Menu, 493
Pavilion of Polyhedreality, 493
Schoolhouse Videos and CDs, 493
Word Chains, 493

ornithology, 785
ABC of Bird Photography, 493

Orthodox
Orthodox Christian Page, 726
Orthodox Ministry ACCESS, 726

Oswald, Lee Harvey, 460

outdoor sports, 855
Feathered Friends, 812
Hiking and Walking Home Page, 437
Outside Online, 603
Virtual Pathways, 605
Wave~Length Paddling Network, 605

P

packet-switching, 9

paganism
Alternative Spiritualities Club Home Page, 689
Aunt Agatha's Occult Emporium, 690
Necronomi.com—The Familiar Spirit BBS, 690
Nine Houses of Gaia, 690
Occult Page, 690
Paganlink, 690
Pentagram—the Internet's Pagan and Occult Superstore, 690
Witchcraft (Wicca), 697
Witches League for Public Awareness, 697
Witch's Brew—For All of Mother's Children, 698
see also occult

Paine, Thomas, 460

paleontology, 781
Columbus Rock and Mineral Society, 781
Dino Russ's Lair, 521
Dino Russ's Laur, 781
Dinosaur Provincial Park, 521
Dinosauria On-Line, 781
Electronic Prehistoric Shark Museum, 301
Exposure Excursions, 782

Gulf Of St. Lawrence Microfossil Catalogue, 782

Museum of Paleontology, 782

Palaeolithic Painted Cave at Vallon-Pont-d'Arc, 782

Raymond M. Alf Museum, 782

Royal Tyrrell Museum Web Site, 523

U.C. Berkeley Museum of Paleontology, 524

UC Berkeley's Museum of Paleontology, 782

University of California Museum of Paleontology, 782

papyrology, Duke Papyrus Archive, 522

paranormal phenomena

listservs, 699

newsgroups, 699

parapsychology, 760, 777

Altered States of Consciousness, 533

Arcadia, 687

Are Ghosts For Real?, 687

Asylum, 687

A Directory of Haunted Dining and Lodging in the U, 687

The Earthlight Productions Haunted Page, 687

Ghost Hunters Gallery, 687

Ghost Lore, 687

The Ghost Watcher, 687

Ghosts, 687

Ghosts of New Mexico, 687

Ghosts—The Charles J. Adams Home Page, 687

Haunted Toys R Us, 688

Hauntings Today, 688

Legend of Sleepy Hollow, 688

Ooga Booga Page, 688

Paranormal Belief Survey, 688

Philippine Ghost Story, 688

Schloss Reichenstein, 688

Virtual Library—Angel Encounters, 688

WWW Virtual Library—Ghost Stories and Folklore, 688

parenting

365 TV-Free Activities, 387

All About Kids Online, 387

D.O.S.A. Parenting Home Page, 387

Empowering People Home Page, 387

Expect the Best from a Girl, 543

Family Planet Home Page, 388

Family Resiliency, 388

Family World Home Page, 600

family.com, 388

International Planned Parenthood Federation, 799

KidsHealth.org, 388

Mommy Times, 388

Moms-at-Home Page, 388

Nashville Parent, 388

National Child Care Information Center Home Page, 388

Our Kids, 388

Parent Soup, 388

Parenting New Mexico, 389

Parenting Skills on Video, 295

ParentingMatters, 389

Parents and Children Together Online, 389

Parents of Murdered Children, 826

Parent's Place.Com, 389

Positive Parenting Home Page, 389

Toilet Training: An Online Guide to Urinal Etiquet, 705

Twins Magazine Home Page, 389

Wonderwise Parent Home Page, 389

see also adoption

Parkinson's disease, Parkinson's Web, 435

Parmley, Dave, 81

parodies, *see* **satire**

Partridge, Christine Thea, 80

Pascoe, Tim, 83

patents, 415

European Patent Office, 714

Information Law Web, 586

National Association of Patent Practitioners, 714

Patent Portal: Internet Patent Resources, 135

SBH: Patent Marketing Group, 135

Shadow Patent Office, 135

Source Translation & Optimization (STO) Internet Patent Search System, 714

U.S. Patent and Trademark Office, 135, 714

Wacky Patent of the Month, 714

PCs

Acer Computer, 236

Acorn Computer Group, 236

Dell Computer Home Page, 237

Elek-Tek, 237

GW2K.COM, 237

IBM Personal Computers Home Page, 237

IBM Personal Computers in the U.S. Aptiva, 237

Micron, 237

NEC Home Page, 237

New Wave Computers, 226

Northstar, 237

Packard Bell, 237

Swan Technologies, 237

PDF (Portable Document Format), 14, 46

Pentecostal Church, United Pentecostal Church International, 727

percussive music

D'CuCKOO, 647

Drums and Percussion Page, 662

Official Hammered Dulcimer Page, 663

Village Pulse, 675

performance arts

Alaskan Dance Theater, 89

Arthur Hall and Black Dance in America, 89

As-Sayf Oriental Dance Home Page, 89

AXIS Dance Troupe, 89

B.A.W.P. Spoken Word Audio, 89

Dancescape, 89

Danclink, 74

Drama Book Publishers, 611

Galaxy Entertainment, 601

Gigaplex, 601

Henry's Dance Hotlist, 90

International Folk Dancers of Ottawa Home Page, 90

Internet Dance Resources, 90

Marjan, 90

Millennium Productions, 77

Ohio State University, Department of Dance Home Page, 90

PDX TheatreSports, 90

Performing Arts Sites, 653

Tango Dance Notation Argentina, 90

perfumes

Beauty Department at CyberShop, 807

Le Parfum, 808

personal computers, *see* **PCs**

Peru

Rainforest Health Project, 126

Some Peruvian Music, 659

pets

Exotic Pets, 62

Fish Food, 599

Getting a Pet, 62

How to Put Your Pet on the Web, 63

Pet Care Corner, 63

Pet Grief Support, 63

Pet Supplies On-line, 815

PetBunny Home Page, 63
Remembrance Page, 63
Summum Mummification, 430
see also animals

Pettigrew, Stanley, 85

PGP (Pretty Good Privacy), 22

pharmacology
Chastain Research Group, Inc., 130
Controlled Substances: Uses and
Effects, 447
Evolving Technologies Corporation,
130
Fischer Pharmaceuticals
Laboratories, 447
Hedonistic Imperative, 447
Patti Peeples' Guide to Health
Economics, Medical, and Pharmacy
Resources on the Net, 441
Pharmaceutical Information
Network, 447
PhRMA Home Page, 447
PPS OnLine, 448
RxList: The Internet Drug Index, 448
WomenSpace, 449

philately, *see* **stamp collecting**

philosophy
American Philosophical Association,
738
ANALYSIS Home Page, 738
Arisbe: A Home for Charles S. Peirce
Studies, 738
Augustine, 738
Australasian Philosophy Network:
Home Page, 738
BEARS in Moral and Political
Philosophy, 738
creationism
Center for Scientific Creation, 731
Creation Science Home Page, 731
Creationism Connection, 731
Evolution vs. Creation Science, 731
Talk.Origins Archive, 731
Cybernetics and Systems Theory, 738
Electronic Journal of Analytic
Philosophy, 738
Environmental Ethics, 738
evolution
Answers About Evolution, 731
Evolution vs. Creation Science, 731
Talk.Origins Archive, 731
Feminist Studies in Aotearoa
Electronic Journal (FMST), 543
International Philosophical Preprint
Exchange, 738
listservs, 743-747
Mechanosphere, 738

Mysticism
Al Azif: The Manuscript Liber
Logaeth, 737
Aleister Crowley, 737
Egyptian Book of the Dead, 737
Golden Dawn FAQ, 737
Kabballah Connection, 737
Mysticism in World Religions, 737
Shawn's Rituals Collection, 737
Tarot Reading, 737
Wayfarer's Rest, 738
newsgroups, 741-743
Nietzsche Page at USC, 738
Philosophy and Religion, 739
Philosophy in Cyberspace—Home
Page, 739
Philosophy Resources, 739
PSYCHE: an interdisciplinary journal
of research, 739
Taoism, 736
Taoism Information Page, 736
Taoist Resource Center, 737
Theosophical Society, 737
Universal Life Church, 737
Urantia Book, 737
Tech Classics Archive, 739
University of Chicago Philosophy
Project, 739
White Mountain Education—A
Source for the Ageless, 739

photography
(Art)ⁿ Galleries, 90
(Microscapes), 92
@rtweb Art Gallery, 493
1002situations, 493
3-D Stuff, 90
50th Bristol International Salon of
Photography, 90
ABC of Bird Photography, 493
Alan Dorow Gallery, 493
Alder Yarrow's Photography, 493
Allen Rose, 494
Anderson Galleries, 494
Ansel Adams—Fiat Lux, 494
Arthole, 83
artists, Eric Boutilier-Brown, 74
Atlanta Photography Group, 494
Atlanta Photojournalism Seminar,
494
Attic Window (by Diane Fenster), 90
Australian Outback Gallery
Photography, 494
Barry Anderson Photography, 494
Black and White Gallery, 90
California Museum of Photography,
494

Cemetery, 90
Chiossone Studio, NYC, 494
Cincinnati Parks' Butterfly Show, 91
Citizen Kane Gallery, 91
Crayon Design & Communications,
91
Cypress College Photography
Department (First Stop, 91
Daum On-line, 74
Detroit Publishing Company
Photographic Collection, 91
Digital Photography Exhibit, 91
digital wave photography gallery, 91
Discovery Catalogue, 494
Edgerton Center's Online Photo
Gallery, 91
Eye Produce CD ROM Home Page,
The, 74
Figure 1: The Visual Sector, 494
Florida Wildflower Showcase, 91
FocalPoint f/8, 91
Fotogruppe der Studiobühne und
Filmwerkstatt, 91
Frolic, 91
GallerySight, 92
Hans de Kort Photography, 494
Hiroshima and Nagasaki Gallery
Exhibition, 92
Home Page of Photographer,
Sculptor David C. Franson, 494
Hot Pictures: Russian Photography,
494
Image Alchemy Digital Imaging, 578
imago, 92
Impact Studio, 495
Jay Stoegbauer Photography, 495
Jazz Photography of Ray Avery, 495
Kodak, 495
Maude Asbury, 814
Michael's Photo Gallery, 92
Michigan Photo Contest, 92
Michigan Press Photographers, 495
Misa, 92
MIT Center for Educational
Computing Initiatives Virtual
Museum, 86
Mythago, 92, 495
Nature Gallery, 92
New Mexico, 92
New York Public Library
Photography Collection, 92
Non Facturé, 92
Northwest College Photographic
Communications, 495
Online PhotoWeb, 495

Oxford Photographs, 92
Photo Archive, 92
Photo Perspectives, 93
Photographers Gallery, 93
Photography Spot, 495
Photography Yellow Pages, 495
Photojournalist's Coffee House, 495
PhotoLink Gallery, 93
PhotoServe, 495
Picture Projects, 93
Portfolio of Architectural
  Photographs, 93
Postcards from Bahia, 93
PPSA Photo Gallery, 93
Prarie Dog Artworks, 93
Probus Photos, 93
Professional Photography Portfolios,
  496
Remembering Nagasaki, 93
Rogers Virtual Gallery (Beauty #2),
  94
Ron Lowry's Home Page, 496
Ruby's Gallery, 94
Russian Reminisence, 94
Sacred Faces, Sacred Spaces, 496
Sam's Shoebox, 94
Scott Freeman's Underwater
  Photography Page, 496
Shot in the Dark, 94
SITO, 94
SolarColor Photography by Michael
  Fastoso, 94
Specializing in Natural Light and
  Nature Images, 496
Stereoscopic Imaging by Ray 3D, 94
Tom Reed/Photographer, 82
Travels with Samantha, 496
underwater, Mau Scuba Page-Ed
  Robinson's Diving Adventures, 856
United in Anger, 94
Unofficial Cincinnati Butterfly Show,
  94
Vintage Postcards, 94
Virtual Gallery (Korea), 496
Virtual Portfolio (London), 496
Wedding Bell Blueprint, 925
Zone I Gallery, 94

photojournalism
Atlanta Photojournalism Seminar,
  494
Michigan Press Photographers, 495
Photojournalist's Coffee House, 495

physical fitness
Aerobics!, 436
balance, Fitness on the Net, 436
Health Resource, 438

Hiking and Walking Home Page, 437
International Health News, 439
International Yoga School, 437
Mirkin Report, 437
MSU Athletic Training, 437
Navigator's Health and Nutrition
  Page, 439
Online Digital Fitness Solutions, 438
Peak Performance, 438
Physique Techniques Fitness
  Consultants, 853
World Health Network, 439
Yoga Paths: An Overview of
  Different Schools, 438

physical therapy
Marquette University Program in
  Physical Therapy, 441
Physical Therapy WWW Page, 441

physics
Accelerator Physics at SLAC, 782
American Institute of Physics, 782
American Physical Society, 782
ASM International Home Page, 783
CERN European Laboratory for
  Particle Physics, 783
CMB Astrophysics Research
  Program, 783
Fermilab-Discovering the Nature of
  Nature, 783
HyperSpace at UBC, 783
Interactive Physics Problem Set, 783
Jean-Marie Vaneskahian's Physics
  Home Page, 783
Lawrence Livermore National
  Laboratory, 783
Laws List, 783
Listing of Physics Resources on the
  World Wide Web, 783
Livermore Labs Atmospheric
  Research, 783
Nanotechnology, 783
Nanoworld Home Page, 783
NIH Guide to Molecular Modeling,
  784
Nuclear Physics, 784
Physics, 785
Physics and Space Technology
  Directorate, 784
Physics around the World, 784
Physics Demonstrations at UC
  Berkeley, 784
Physics News, 784
Physics Problems, 784
Physics Servers and Services around
  the World, 784
Physics Unbound, 784

Physics World Electronic News, 784
Quantum Magazine Home Page, 784
Virtual Science Class, 784
WARP Home, 784
Welcome to the Institute of Physics,
  784
Welcome to the Laboratory for
  Terrestrial Physics, 785
World-Wide Web Virtual Library
  Physics, 785

planets, *see* **astronomy**
plants, Delblau Company, 812
plastic surgery, 444
plug-ins, 12
plumbing
Best Mfg. Co., 513
Faucet Outlet Online, 513
GROHE, 514
Pipe Trades Association, 514
theplumber.com, 514

poetry
Flaming Jewels, 74
Hunting of the Snark: An Agony in
  Eight Fits, 107
Living Poets, EJournal Home Page,
  602
Purgatory of Semiotics, A, 78
Quotations of William Blake, 718
Ursula K. Le Guin, 102

Point-to-Point Protocol (PPP), 11
Points of Presence (POP), 10
Poland, Gazeta Wyborcza, 607
political humor
The Daily Muse, 343
Punch Rush Limbaugh Page, 345

political interest groups
American Civil Liberties Union, 824
American Firearms Association, 828
Amnesty International Online, 824
Center for Democracy and
  Technology, 824
Citizens Internet Empowerment
  Coalition, 823
Cornucopia of Disability Information
  Gopher Server, 824
Fear-Forfeiture Endangers American
  Rights, 824
Global Vision The Other
  Network...Rights & Wrongs, 825
Human Rights Web, 825
NARAL, 828
National Right to Life, 828

political parties
College Democrats of America, 419
College Republican National
  Committee Homepage, 419
Democratic Caucus, 419

Democratic National Committee, 419
Independence/Reform Party, 419
Libertarian Party Headquarters, 419
Republican National Committee, 419
Republicans Abroad International, 419
Young Republican National Federation Homepage, 419

politics
All Things Political, 416
Almanac of American Politics, 416
American Political Network, 416
American Voter '96, 416
BEARS in Moral and Political Philosophy, 738
C-SPAN Networks Site, 416
Campaign and Elections Online, 416
CBS News: Campaign '96, 416
Center for the American Woman and Politics (CAWP), 542
CNN/Time: All Politics, 416
Decision '96, 416
ElectionLine, 416
ElectNet, 416
Gallup Organization: 1996 Presidential Elections, 416
GoverNet, 417
Greer, Margolis, Mitchell, Burns & Associates, 418
Grossfeld/Severin, Inc., 418
Hardball '96, 418
Institute for Propaganda Analysis, 539
KidsNet: Election '96, 417
League of Women Voters' Election '96, 417
listservs, 423-426
Majority '96, 417
Mother Jones Magazine's On the Campaign Trail, 417
NetVote '96, 417
newsgroups, 420-422
Official Internet Quayle Quote List, 718
Political Americana Online, 418
Political Participation Project, 417
PoliticsUSA, 417
Praxis Online Campaigns, 418
President '96, 418
Primary Colors, 418
Project Vote Smart, 417
Right Company, 418
Silicon Media, Inc., 418
Women & Politics Home Page, 545
Women Leaders Online (WLO), 545

pollution
Air That Kills Us, 367
Black-Gold Oil Conditioning Systems, 370
Breath Taking, 367
Burning Issues/Clean Air Revival, 367
Ecocide in the U.S.S.R., 367
Economics of Industrial Pollution Home Page, 367
EPIC Home Page, 367
Georgia Pollution Prevention Assistance Division, 367
Geothermal Energy, 368
How To Survive Without a Car, 368
Impact of Lead-Contaminated Soil on Public Health, 368
National Pollution Prevention Center for Higher Education, 368
Pollution, 368

polyterrain, models, Polyterrain Water Soluble Scenery Materials, 491

POP (Points of Presence), 10

pop music
22nd Row, 670
ABBAnatic, 667
Amy Grant Site in College Park, MD, 667
and through the wire, 667
The Boy George Home Page, 668
Bryan Adams Home Page, 668
Caribbean Soul: Jimmy Buffett Parrot(t)heads, 668
Casey's Top 40, 649
Chicago O(+> Nation, 668
Counting Crows, 668
Discographies (and More), 655
Disgraceland, 668
DJ Special Blend's Top 10, 649
ELP—Emerson, Lake & Palmer, 668
Elvis Costello Home Page, 668
Enigma, 668
EXCESS OF INXS, AN, 668
Frankie Goes to Hollywood Fan Pages, 668
Future Love Paradise: The Seal WWW Site, 668
Gaia: Olivia Newton-John Home Page, 668
Gloria Estefan/MSM, 669
Huey Lewis and the News, 668
Hype! One Hit Wonder Compilation, 649
Madonna Home Page, 669
Men Without Hats: The (Unofficial) Home Page, 669

Mike Markowski's Beatles Page, 669
Nicks Fix, 669
Original Mariah Carey Home Page, 669
Pet Shop Boys Virtually, 648
Planet Janet, 669
Random '80s Lyrics, 655
Rick Dee's Weekly Top 40, 649
ROSS, 669
Roxette: Home Page, 669
Sarah McLachlan Homepage, 670
Simon and Garfunkel Home Page, 669
Simple Minds—Good News From the Web, 670
Sinead O'Connor Home Page, 670
Sting—The Soul Pages, 670
Tori Amos, 670
VH1 Music First, 670
Welcome to HIStory!, 670
Zar's Paula Abdul, 670

population studies
Population Index, 540
Population Reference Bureau (PRB), 540
Population Studies Center—University of Michigan, 540

porcelain dolls
Cottage Catalogs, 479
Dolls By Christine, 479
Dream-Land Dollies!!!, 479

pornography
Bio Keeper Archives, 796
Breaking the Cycle, 795
Playboy Home Page, 603

Portable Document Format (PDF), 14, 46

postal information
Geographic Nameserver, 716
National Address and ZIP+4 Browser, 716
United States Postal Service, 717
Zipper, 717

posting to newsgroups, 18, 29

pottery
AMOC (A Matter of Clay), 810
Archie Bray Foundation for the Ceramic Arts, 485
Carl Baker Stoneware and Raku Pottery, 485
CDI Ceramic Devices, Inc., 485
CEEN, The Crafts Equipment Exchange Newsletter, 485
Centre for Technical Ceramics, CTK, 485
Ceramic Industry, 485

Ceramic Solutions, 485

Ceramics and Artifacts Restoration, 485

Dynamic Ceramic, 485

Forum On-Line Antiques Mall for Potter, Porcelain and Ceramics, 485

Funtiques Antiques Home Page, 479

Keith Ceramic Materials LTD, 485

Mesa Verde Pottery, 486

Orton's Firing Tips, 486

Potter's Page, 486

Pottery, 486

Scientific Report, Chapter 2: Ceramics and Ceramic Composites, 486

Sun Tile, 482

Virtual Ceramics Exhibit, 486

WWW Virtual Library: TechnicalCeramics, 486

Powder Hound Ski Report, 857

PPP (Point-to-Point Protocol), 11

premenstrual syndrome, 449

Pretty Good Privacy (PGP), 22

primatology, *see* **anthropology**

prints, limited edition, Framers Corner, 75

Prodigy, 26, 41

production resources (movies)

Character Shop, 635

CinemaSpace, 635

Dolby Laboratories, 635

DTS Theatrical, 635

Film Resources, 636

Independent Film and Video Makers Internet Resourc, 636

Knight Productions, Inc., 636

LucasArts, 636

Makin' Waves Studio, 636

Mass F/X, 636

New York Film and Animation Co. Ltd., 636

Production Magic, 636

Rhythm & Hues Studios, 636

Shades of Light Studios, 636

THX, 636

Virtual Studio Ltd, London, 636

WAVE—Wognum Art's Virtual Exchange, 636

Welcome to EPSONE.COM, 637

products (movies)

CyberCinema, 641

Entertainment Connection, 641

HSS Wholesale Home Page, 641

Movie Madness Merchandise, 641

Movie Poster Page, 641

Ultimate Resource for Vintage Posters, 642

psychiatry

American Academy of Child & Adolescent Psychiatry Homepage (AACAP), 533

Psychiatry & Psychotherapy, 536

Psychiatry On-Line, 536

psychics

Introduction To Tarot Magic, 692

Learning the Tarot—An Online Course, 692

Lord of Illusions—Clive Barker's Tarot Cards, 692

Michael's Tarot Pages, 692

Michele's Tarot Page, 692

Original WWW Tarot Site, 693

Tarot, 692

Tarot Cards, 693

Tarot Cards—Maelstrom, 693

Tarot Inspiration, 693

Tarot Web, 693

Tarot Weekly, 693

Tarot—Tools and Rites of Transformation, 693

Vibrations—The Layman's Answer to Tarot Cards!, 693

psychology

American Psychological Association—PsychNET, 533

American Psychological Society (APS), 534

analytical

C.G. Jung, Analytical Psychology, and Culture, 534

C.G. Jung Institute of Los Angeles, 534

Attention Deficit Disorder WWW Archive, 534

Canada

Canadian Psychological Association, 534

Internet Mental Health, 535

child

Ages & Stages, 533

American Academy of Child & Adolescent Psychology Homepage (AACAP), 533

ERIC Digests, 534

KidsPeace®, The National Center for Kids in Crisis, 535

clinical, Teaching Clinical Psychology, 537

computers, Society for Computers in Psychology, 537

cross-cultural, International Association for Cross-Cultural Psychology (IACCP), 535

Cyber-Psych, 534

Depression FAQ, 534

dreams

Altered States of Consciousness, 533

DreamLink, 534

evolutionary, Evolution's Voyage, 535

interdisciplinary, Journal of Mind and Behavior (JMB), 535

International Association for Cross-Cultural Psychology (IACCP), 535

Keirsey Temperament Sorter, 535

literary, Institute for the Psychological Study of the Arts (IPSA), 535

mental health

Internet Mental Health, 535

Mental Relativity, 535

National Institute of Mental Health (NIHM), 536

mental retardation, Arc, a national organization on mental retardation, 534

Online Psychological Services, 536

parapsychology, Altered States of Consciousness, 533

Personality Test, 536

PREP—Psychology Preprint Server, 536

Primal Psychotherapy Page, 536

Professional Psychology, 536

Psychguide, 536

Psychiatry On-Line, 536

Psychiatry & Psychotherapy, 536

psychoanalysts, American Psychoanalytic Association, 533

Psychological Type Profiles, 536

Psychology of Invention, 536

Psychology Self-Help Resources on the Internet, 537

Psychology Software Tools, Inc., 537

religion, Psychology of Religion Page, 536

Rorschach Inkblot Test, 537

Russia, Institute of Psychology, Russian Academy of Sciences (IP RAS), 535

School Psychology Resourses Online, 537

self help, Mind Tools, 535

Sigmund Freud, 537

sports, Mental Edge—Sport Psychology, 535

Subintellect's Personality Test, 537

Tools for Practical Self Development, 537

Whole Brain Atlas, 537

Index

psychotherapy
   Primal Psychotherapy Page, 536
   Psychiatry & Psychotherapy, 536
pubishing, Web, Internet Business Connection, 578
public policy, Harry Singer Foundation, 304
public relations
   Porter Novelli, 133
   Tech Image, Ltd., 142
publications, law
   American Indian Law Review, 591
   American Journal of Criminal Law, 591
   European Law Journal, 591
   Federal Communications Law Journal, 591
   Global Legal Studies Journal, 591
   Human Rights Brief, 591
   Journal of Information, Law, and Technology, 591
   Journal of International Law and Practice, 591
   Journal of Online Law, 591
   Law Journal Extra!, 592
   Law Library Journal, 592
   legal.online, 592
publishers
   Academic Press, 608
   Addison Wesley, 608
   Albion Books, 608
   Alldata, 608
   Arrow Publishing, 303
   Aspen Publishers, Inc., 440
   Astrology et al Bookstore, 609
   Atomic Books Literary Finds for Mutated Minds, 609
   Audiobook Source, 609
   Aztec Books, 751
   Baltzer Science Publishers, 609
   Bantam Doubleday Dell-BDD Online, 112
   BDD Home Page, 609
   Beach Holme Publishing, 609
   Bioenergetics Press, 609
   Blackwell Science, 609
   Blue Heron Publishing, 609
   Book Stacks—Home Page, 609
   Bookish, 609
   BookWire—The First Place To Look for Book Information, 609
   BookZone, 610
   Borders Books and Music, 610
   BradyGAMES Home Page, 610
   BRP Publications, Inc., 610

   Cambridge University Press, 610
   Carswell Publishing, 610
   Catalogue Index, 610
   CatchWord Ltd, 610
   ChemTech Publishing, 610
   Cold Spring Harbor Laboratory Press, 610
   Colorado Independent Publisher's Association, 610
   Conari Press, 611
   Coteau Books, 611
   Creative Virtue Press, 611
   Christian Warehouse, 610
   Cocoon, 610
   Commercial Publications, 611
   Domanski-Irvine Book Company, 224
   Doody Publishing, Inc., 611
   Drama Book Publishers, 611
   Dream Garden Press, 611
   East View Publications, Inc. Home Page, 611
   Editorial Experts, Inc. (EEI), 611
   Elsevier Science—Home Page, 611
   Grolier Interactive, 304
   HarperCollins Publishers Home Page, 611-612
   Harvard Advocate Home Page, 611
   Hayden Books, 611
   HMSO, 611
   Hodder & Stoughton, 611
   Houghton Mifflin Company, 612
   IDG Books, 612
   index.html, 612
   Information Superlibrary, 612
   INFOSEARCH—PrintNet, 612
   Internet Book Fair, Publishers Index, 612
   Internet Road Map to Books, 612
   IPL Books, 612
   iWORLD Home Page, 612
   Jacobs Publishing, Ltd., 612
   Javiation, 617
   KAB Konsult AB, 132
   Karoma Publishers, 612
   Keski-Uusimaa, 612
   Kraken Press, Titles, 613
   Kluwer Academic Publishers, 612
   Koinonia House, 613
   Little, Brown & Company, 613
   M.E. Sharpe, 613
   Manic D Press, 613
   McGraw Hill, 613
   Mendeleev Communications, 759
   MIT Press, 613

   Monterey Press, 613
   Multimedia Newsstand home, 613
   Natural History Book Service— Home Page, 613
   New Riders, 613
   Nomad Press, 613
   Norwegian Bookshop Home Page, 613
   O'Reilly Home Page, 613
   Oxford University Press, 614
   Para Publishing, 614
   Peachpit Press, 614
   Penguin USA, 614
   PennWell Publishing Company, 614
   pgrmli.txt, 614
   Prehistory Press, 523
   Prentice Hall Home Page, 614
   Press Association, 614
   Publishers' Catalogues Home Page, 614
   Putnam Berkley Online, 614
   Que's Home Page, 614
   Random House, 614
   Reed Interactive, 615
   Resolution Business Press, 615
   Saint Mary's Press, 615
   SAMS Home Page, 615
   Sapphire Press UNCAT, 615
   Shogakukan Home Page, 615
   Small Media and Large, 615
   Software Net Product Menu, 615
   Springer-Verlag, 615
   Straight Line Medium, Inc., 615
   Strangelove Internet Enterprises, 615
   Thomsom Publishing, 615
   Time Life Explorer, 615
   Times Mirror Higher Education Group, 615
   Tor SF and Fantasy, 616
   University of Chicago Press Anthropology and Archaeology Catalog, 520
   Video Publishing House, 135
   W. W. Norton & Company, Inc., 616
   Warner Aspect, 616
   Web Art Publishing, 616
   Wellsweep Press, 616
   West Publishing, 616
   Wiley, 616
   WWW VL Electronic Journals List Publishers, 616
publishing, Web
   5 Top Internet Marketing Successes of 1994, 576

Artzilla Surf Constructions, 576

Aspen Systems Corporation, 567

Building Web Servers, 576

Carter & Associates WEB Studios, 576

Copyright Website, 576

CRAYON—CReAte Your Own Newspaper, 568

Dunn & Edwards Services, 577

Dynamic Diagrams Home Page, 577

Free Range Media, Inc., 577

Home Space Builder, 577

Image Alchemy Digital Imaging, 578

Image Compression for Publishing Online, 578

Making Money on Internet, 579

new3, Inc., 579

Program One Online Service, 579

RAMWORKS, 579

Stannet WWW Designing and Publishing Company, 580

Vannevar New Media, 580

WebDesigns, 580

Web Developer, 580

Winfield Design Group, 580

World Wide Information and Netcasting Services, 580

punk music

Clash, 668

Green Day, 677

puzzle games

Duck Hunt—Find the Fowl, 337

Jumble & Crossword Solver, 712

Manic Maze, 340

Riddle du Jour, 340

The Vain Game, 341

Webcube, 342

WWW Interactive Crossword, 342

Q

Quaker, Religious Society of Friends WWW site, 726

quilts

Amish Quilts, 498

Brief History of Quilting, 498

Computers and Quilting, 498

Counted Cross Stitch, Needlework, and Stitchery Page, 498

Creative Quilting, 498

International Web Exchange: Quilting Exchange, 499

Misc Quilting Information, 499

Quiltery, 815

Quilting Page, 499

True PA Dutch Country Souvenir, 499

World Wide Quilting Page, 499

quotations

Advertising Quotes, 717

Ash's Choice Quotations, 717

Bartlett's Familiar Quotations, 717

Best of" Edward Gibbon's Decline and Fall of the Roman Empire, 717

Bon Mots from the Supermodels, 717

Conventional Wisdom: Selected Quotations Illustrating the Illusions of Popular History, 717

Curmudgeon Quotelist, 717

Dave's Searchable Quote Database, 717

Don's Doctor Who Interesting Quote Archive, 718

Frank Lloyd Wright Quotes, 718

Labor Quotes Page, 718

Official Internet Quayle Quote List, 718

Outriders of Reality Reference Manual & Travel Guide, 718

Quotations, 718

Quotations About Libraries and Librarians, 718

Quotations of William Blake, 718

Quotes, Quotes, and More Quotes, 718

Welcome to the Introspect Library, 718

Zappa Quote of the Day, 718

R

race relations

Diversity and Pluralism, 826

ERaM Programme, 826

Interracial Voice, 826

ITI's Multi-Cultural Network, 826

Minority Affairs Forum, 827

Museum of Tolerance, 827

National Civil Rights Museum, 827

National Multicultural Institute, 827

radiation, Radiation Effects Research Foundation, 443

radiation hydrodynamics, 761

radio

440 Satisfaction, 348

amateur

100 Years of Radio, 477

Amateur Radio Elmers Resource Directory, 477

Amateur Radio Resources, 477

American Radio Relay League's World Wide Web Service, 477

Ham Radio Outlet, 477

List of Mail Order Electronics Companies, 477

Packet Radio Home Page, 477

Personal Database Applications, 477

WWW Ham Radio Servers List, 477

Amateur Radio Books and Open Repeater Database, 616

AudioNet: The Broadcast Network on the Internet, 348

Blue Planet, 348

Brent Alberts' Radioland, 616

CBC Radio Trial, 73

Chris Smolinski's Radio Page, 616

Cinemedia Radio, 349

Deutche Welle Radio & TV—English Home Page, 616

FCC, 349

Howard Stern Show Sounds Page, 349

international, Blue Planet, 348

Internet Karoake Store, 349

Literature, 525

Media Watchdog, 349

Monitor Radio, 617

Museum of Television and Radio, 349

NPR Online, 617

Old Time Radio (OTR) WWW Page, 617

Radio Centro, 617

Radio HK, 617

Radio JAPAN, 617

Radio on the Internet, 349

Radio Online: Radio's Starting Point on the Net, 349

Radio Prague, 617

RadioWorld Europe, 617

RealTime, 617

Rob Mayfield, 617

RTHK on the Internet Home Page, 617

Sounds of Silence, 349

Thistle and Shamrock Stations List at the Ceolas A, 617

Welcome to BBC Radio, 617

radiology, 444

railroad modeling, Interactive Model Railroad, 339

railroads

Amtrak, 897

Burlington Northern Santa Fe Corporation, 897

Grand Canyon Railway, 897

models
  C & M Train Depot, 490
  DP Industries Home Page, 490
  Florida's Largest Train Store, 490
  Logic Rail Technologies, 490
  Model Railroad.Com, 490
  Palatine Hobby's Railroad Page, 490
  Roecks Railroad Concepts, 491
  RR Depot, 491
  Rutger Friberg's World of ModelRailroad Electronic, 491
  TraiNutz, 491
Railroad Timetables, 914

rape
National Coalition Against Sexual Assault, 795
U.S. Recovery, Addiction, and Abuse Resources, 427

real estate
ADLIST Real Estate Database, 135
Advant Home, 136
ALWAYS OPEN!-HouseLink US. Real Estate Guide, 136
bestagents.com, 136
Eastern Mortgage Services, Inc., 136
Electronic Resource Services Property Finder, 136
Exquisite Homes and Properties, 136
Fidelity Union Mortgage, 136
First Pacific Financial, 136
For Sale By Owner Magazine, 813
FractalNet Real Estate Server, 136
Home Builder's Utopia, 136
Home Improvement Loans, 136
HomeOwners Finance Center, 136
How I Made 1 Million Dollars in Real Estate with No Money Down, 136
Insiders Track Capital Funding Aid, 137
Internet Real Estate Listings, 137
Internet Real Estate Network, 137
J.C. Mortgage, 137
Levien-Rich Associates, Inc., 137
LOAN STORE, 137
Mortgage Calculator, 137
Mortgage Manager, 137
Mortgages Manager Version 5.00, 137
National Homes Online, 137
National InterAd Real Estate Page, 137
Real Estate Junction, 137
Real Estate Pages, 137
Real Estate Recruiting/Careers/ Education, 138
Real Estate Registry, 138

Real Estate Shop, 138
Real Estate Web, 138
Security First Funding, 138
Timbergreen Custom Homes, 138
Who's Who in Luxury Real Estate?, 138
WRENet-World Real Estate Network, 138

rebates, CouponNet, 812

recipes
Amish Recipe, 816
Callahan's Cookbook, 403
Cape Breton Pictorial Cookbook, 403
Chicken Wing Central, 403
Chil E-Heads, 403
Chili!, 403
Cooking Recipes of the Institute of Nuclear Chemistry, 403
Culinary World Tour, 403
Directory of /pub/rec.food.recipes, 403
Directory of /pub/Vegetarian/ Recipes/FatFree, 403
Epicurious, 403
FATFREE Vegetarian Mailing List Archive, 403
Filipino Cuisine, 404
Friends and Partners Kitchen, 404
FYNet's Collection of Malaysian Recipes, 404
Hawaiian Electric Kitchen, 404
Hawaii's Favorite Recipes, 404
Janet Starosta's Recipes, 404
Ketchum Kitchen, 404
Kitchens of Gordon Bleu, 404
Kosher Express, 404
Krispin Komments, 437
La Comeda Mexicana, 404
La Pagina dela Salsa Mole, 404
Linsey Foods, 397
Mama's Cookbook, 404
Medieval/Renaissance Food Home Page, 404
My Favorite Recipes, 405
New England Lobster, 405
Nomius Eye -Sasa Recipes, 405
Notte's Cookbook, 405
Pedro's Kitchen, 405
Prapapun's Hobby Kitchen, 405
Recipe Archive Index, 405
RecipeNet, 405
Recipes for Traditional Food in Slovenia, 405
Recipes from Kathy, 405
Restaurant Le Cordon Bleu, 405

Ridiculously Easy Recipes, 405
Spam Page, 402
Stuart's Chinese Recipes, 405
Turkish Cuisine, 405
USENET Cookbook, 405
Virtual Health, 406
Virtual Kitchen, 405-406
VNO: Food—Cooking and Recipes, 406
YACB: Yet Another CookBook, 406

recording, 8-Track Heaven, 349

records and tapes, PolyEster Records and Books, 815

recycling
Chrysler Corporation—Recycling & Conservation, 361
Cleaning Up C.E. Cole, 374
Commonly Recycled Materials, 375
The Consumer Recycling Guide: Index to Local Recycling Centers, 375
Ford Environmental Report, 361
GreenDisk, 375
GREENGUIDE—How to Trim Your Office Waste, 366
GREENGUIDE—Reduce/Reuse/ Recycle, 375
National Oil Recycler's Association, 375
Plastic Bag Information Clearinghouse, 366
The Recycle Link, 375
Recycle Locally, 375
Recycler's World, 375

Redlin, Terry, 75

reed instruments, IDRS WWW, 662

Reed, Tom, 82

reference
ARTFL Project: ROGET'S Thesaurus Search Form, 702
Climbing Dictionary, 702
foreign language, Handy Spanish Phrase, 338
LC Thesaurus for Graphic Material: Topical Terms for Subject Access, 703
listservs, 720-721
My Virtual Reference Desk, 712
newsgroups, 719-720
Online Reference Works, 302
Simple Rhyming Dictionary, 336
THOR+: The Virtual Reference Desk, 713
UTLink: Resources by Subject, 714
World Fact Book 1995, 714
WWW Virtual Library, 713

refinishing, *see* furniture; woodworking

reggae music, Afro-Caribbean Music,
656

reincarnation

22 Topics on Past Lives, 691

Electronic Newsletter—Reincarnation, 691

Human Understood Reincarnation, 691

Joe's Reincarnation Link, 691

Karma and Reincarnation—Yoga, 691

Past Lives and Reincarnation, 691

Reincarnation & Karma, 691

Reincarnation 101, 691

Reincarnation and the Theory of Tri-chart, 692

Reincarnation Case History, 691

Reincarnation—Have We Lived Before?, 692

Reincarnation—Is Reincarnation a Christian Concept?, 692

Synthetic Reincarnation, 692

True Reincarnation of Panchen Rinpoche, 692

What is Reincarnation?, 692

religion

atheism

Atheist Manifesto, 723

International Atheistic Secular Humanist Conspirac, 723

Secular Web, 723

Bahai Resources on the Internet, 735

Bastard Son of the Lord, 735

Buddhism, 724

Access to Insight, 724

Buddhist Scripture Information Retrieval, 724

DEFA Home Page, 724

Hell's Buddha's, 347

International Meditation Centres, 724

International Research Institute for Zen Buddhism, 724

Journal of Buddhist Ethics, 724

New Kadampa Tradition, 724

Nichiren Shoshu Buddhism, 724

Shin Buddhism Network, 725

Shin Buddhist Resource Center, 725

Tiger Team Buddhist Information Network, 725

Welcome to Daka's Buddhist Astrology, 686

Zen Garden, 725

Zen Mountain Monastery, 725

Zen@SunSITE, 725

Christian Singles, 795

Christianity

American Baptist Churches Mission Center Online, 725

Anglicans Online, 725

APOLOGIA—To Offer a Reason, 730

Association of Vineyard Churches, 725

Baker Book House, 727

Baptist Faith and Message, 725

Bible Gateway, 723

Brother Mark's Christian Material, 730

Canada Toronto East Mission, 725

Catholic Online, 726

Christian Articles Archive, 727

Christian Book Connection, 113, 727

Christian Classics Ethereal Library, 708, 727

Christian Computing Magazine, 727

Christian Connections, 730

Christian Cyberspace Companion, 727

Christian Philosophy, 730

Christian Poetry, 727

Christian Recovery Connection, 728

Christian Resource Network, 730

Christian Singles Online, 728, 795

Christian Warehouse, 610

Computerized AIDS Ministries, 728

East 7th Street Baptist Ministry-Graffiti, 726

Easter in Cyberspace: A Christian Perspective, 707

Ecclesiastical Calendar, 701

ECOLE Institute, 723

Electronic Book of Common Prayer, 727

Evangelical Lutheran Church in America Home Page, 726

Family Research Council, 729

Famous Unitarian Universalists, 726

GOSHEN Internet Christian Resource Directory, 730

Gospel Films, Inc., 727

Greater Grace World Outreach, 729

GROKNet-Comedyatre and Resources, 727

Holy Bible-King James Version, 723

ICMC Home Page, 728

In the Footsteps of the Lord, 730

InterVarsity Christian Fellowship, 729

Jesus Army, 729

Jesus Fellowship Home Page, 729

Jesus Film Project, 728

Koinonia House, 613

Life and Faith Network, 729

Logos Research Systems, 723

Lutheran Church-Missouri Synod Home Page, 726

Lutheran Marriage Encounter, 729

Minister's Reference Center, 728

Mithraism, 464

Monastery of Christ in the Desert, 729

Musei, 464

National Association of Evangelicals, 729

National Religious Broadcasters, 728

New Media Communications, 723

Not Just Bibles, 730

Orthodox Christian Page, 726

Orthodox Ministry ACCESS, 726

Our Daily Bread, 723

Presbyterian Church USA, 726

Project Wittenberg, 730

Promise Keepers Unofficial Home Page, 729

Religious Society of Friends WWW site, 726

Renewal Ministries: De Colores and Ultreya, 729

RTS's Totally Righteous HomePage for Paul the Apos, 723

Saint Mary)s Press, 728

SBC "Maverick" Home Page, 726

Scrolls from the Dead Sea, 723

SDANet, 727

Serious Developments-Christian Software Catalog, 728

Shroud of Turin, 690

St. Louis Life News, 730

This Week in Bible Prophecy, 728

Tien Dao Christian Media, 728

Tough Guys, 730

United Church of Christ, 727

United Pentecostal Church International, 727

University of St. Michael's College, Faculty of Theology, 724

Web Chapel—Prayer Request, 730

Wire, 728

Church of the SubGenius BRAIN TOOLKIT AND SURREALISM, 735

cults

.ex-cult Archive, 731

A-Z of Cults, 731

AFF Cultic Studies, 731

Cults, 731

Cults 'R Us, 731

Destructive Cults, 731
Jehovah's Christian Witnesses, 732
Jehovah's Witnesses, 732
Loki Cult Web Page, 732
Ms. Guidance on Strange Cults, 732
Sacrespace, 732
Waco Never Again, 732
CyberINDIA: India at your Fingertips, 735
Free Daism, 735
Friends of Osho, 736
Haqqani Foundation Home Page, 736
Hare Krishna Home Page, 736
Hinduism
  Bhagavad Gita, 732
  Global Hindu Electronic Network, 732
  Hinduism, 732
  Hinduism Today Home Page, 732
  Kundalini Research Foundation, Ltd., 732
  Spirituality, Yoga, and Hinduism, 732
Islam
  CyberMuslim Information Collective, 733
  Ibrahim Shafi's Page in Islam, 733
  Islam, 733
  Islamic Society of Wichita, 733
  Islam's Home Page, 733
  Online Islamic Bookstore, 733
  Online Islamic Bookstore—Home Page, 614
  Salaam Ailaikum, 733
  WAMY IslamNet (World Assembly of Muslim Youth), 733
Israelite Handbook, 736
Jainism
  Jain Studies, 733
  Jain World Wide Web Page, 733
Judaism
  A-Z of Jewish & Israel-Related Resources, 734
  Aish Ha Torah Discovery, 734
  Chabad Lubavitch in Cyberspace, 734
  Hebrew Date for Today, 701
  Heichal Shlomo Interactive Calendar, 701
  Jerusalem One WWW Network, 734
  Jewish Federation/Jewish Exponent, 734
  Jewish on the WELL, 734
  Jewish Singles Connection, 795
  Jewish Theological Seminary, 734

Jewishnet, 734
Jews for Jesus Home Page, 734
Judaism and Jewish Resources, 734
Menorah Ministries, 734
Messianic Jewish Alliance of America, 734
National Jewish Committee on Scouting, 735
Passover on the Net, 707
Shamash, 735
Shtetl, Yiddish Language and Culture Home Page, 735
Society Hill Synagogue of Philadelphia, 735
World ORT Union, 735
Yaohushua, the Genuine Messiah, 735
Yom Tov Page, 708
listservs, 743-747
Logictarian Christian Home Page, 736
McChurch, 736
new age, World Transformation, 367
newsgroups, 741-743
Pagan Pages, 736
Pathways to Metaphysics, 736
Philosophy and Religion, 739
psychology, Psychology of Religion Page, 536
Scientology
  Alt.religion.scientology, 739-740
  Church of Scientology vs. The Net, 739
  Dianetics Home Page, 739
  Johnny Get Your Modem-Scientology's War with the Internet, 740
  L. Ron Hubbard Home Page, 740
  The Scamizdat Memorial, 346
  Scientology Home Page, 740
  Yoga Paths, An Overview Of Different Schools and Traditions, 737
Stanford University Zoroastrian Group, 736
voodoo
  African Religion Syncretism, 695
  Electric Gallery-Voodoo Flags, 695
  New Look at Juju, 695
  Primer on Voodoo, 695
  Voodoo, 695
  Voodoo and Cemeteries, 696
  Voodoo Culture in the US Bibliography, 696
  Voodoo Information Pages, 696
  Voodoo Museum, 696

Voodoo Products and Information, 696
Voodoo Queen, 696
Voodoo-Angelique Kidjo, 695
Voodoo: From Medicine to Zombies, 696
VoodooTour—A Cultural Trip to Benin, 696
World Scripture: A comparative anthology of sacred texts, 520
reminder messages, E-Minder Free Reminder-By-E-mail Service, 568
remodeling, see construction; home improvement
Renaissance
  dance, SCA Music and Dance Home Page, 653
  music
    Electronic Early Music, 651
    Music Hall, 652
    Renaissance Consort, 653
    SCA Music and Dance Home Page, 653
renovation, Open Building Architecture For Residential Construction, 505
replying to newsgroups, 29
reproductive rights, 542
research
  Ideal Point Home Page, 131
  Research-It!, 713
  Scout Report, 713
restaurants
  Boston Restaurant Guide, 406
  Chrone's Virtual Diner, 406
  Diner's Grapevine, 406
  Dining Out on the Web, 406
  MenuNet FoodFinder, 406
  Paolo's, 406
  Sally's Place, 406
  Tipping, 713
  Virginia Diner, 407
restoration, art, 71
résumé services
  Career Résumés, 326
  Employnet, Inc., 326
  Extreme Résumé Drop, 327
  Graphiti Printing & Graphics' Online Résumé Services, 327
  Job-Link, 327
  unisoft.net, 327
  see also employment; employment services
retirement, Guide to Retirement Living Online, 439
reupholstering, see furniture
Rhode Island, art galleries, 73

rhythm and blues
  Arizona Jazz, Rhythm and Blues Festival, 663
  Black Music Department Top R&B Album and Singles Chart, 649
rock collecting
  Arris International Corporation, 496
  Bob's Rock Shop, 478
  Hunterian Museum of Rocks and Minerals, 497
  Mineralogical Meanderings, 497
  Rockhounds Information Page, 497
  Web Dexter, 497
rock music
  Addicted To Noise, 665
  Aerosmith, 676
  The David Bowie File, 676
  The Death of Rock 'n' Roll, 676
  Electric Magic—The Led Zeppelin Chronicle, 665
  The Grateful Dead, 676
  Hanspeter Niederstrasser's Def Leppard Page, 677
  Hyper Idol II, 677
  Iron Maiden Page, 677
  Jethro Tull Music Archive, 677
  Kinks Web Sites, 677
  KISS OTAKU, 677
  Led Zeppelin Home Page, 677
  Lloyd Robbins' Moody Blues Page, 669
  Merger, 677
  Metallica, 677
  Mike Markowski's Beatles Page, 669
  MÖTLEY CRÜE, 678
  Original Unoffical Elvis Home Page, 669
  Pete Lambie's Bruce Springsteen Page, 669
  Phish.Net, 678
  Pink Floyd Home Page, 678
  Queen, 678
  RADISH—Hot Original Rock!, 678
  Rock and Roll Hall of Shame, 678
  Rockmine Archives, 655, 656
  Rolling Stones Web Site, 678
  Ron Smith Oldies Calendar, 660
  Room Full of Mirrors: The Official Jimi Hendrix We, 678
  Stranglehold—The Ted Nugent Page, 678
  Welcome to the Jungle, 678
rockets, models
  Aero-Pac, 489
  Monroe Astronomical Rocket Society, 490
  Rocket Works, 491
  S. Shiota's Model Rocket Page, 491
role playing games, Lee's Useless Superhero Generator, 339
rollerblading, 855
Roman Catholicism, Catholic Online, 726
romance fiction
  Romance Pages, 111
  Romanticism On the Net, 109
  Ultimate Romance Novel Website, 111
Roos, Nico, 87
routers, 10
rubber stamps, Rubber Stamp Queen, 815
Rubin, Michael, 86
rugby, 856
running, 856
rural studies, Center for Rural Studies (CRS), 538
Russia
  Aeroflot, 902
  art, Liros Gallery, 86
  ELVIS+, Co., 914
  Friends and Partners, 298
  history
    Russian Information, 459
    Soviet Archives: Entrance Room, 459
  Hot Pictures: Russian Photography, 494
  Moscow Libertarium, 125
  music, Russian Music, 659
  Music under Soviet Rule, 653
  Precious in HIS Sight-Adoption Information on the Internet, 380
  psychology, Institute of Psychology, Russian Acade Sciences (IP RAS), 535
  Russian Manual Alphabet, 532
  Russian Reminisence, 94
  St. Petersburg Press Home Page, 608
  Window-To-Russia Homepage, 297

S

sailing, *see* **boating**
sales, *see* **marketing**
Satanism, Satanism and the History of Wicca, 697
satire
  Georgetown Gonzo, 344
  Heather Has Two Mommies, 344
  PElvis, 345
  The Scamizdat Memorial, 346
  Solid Space, 346
  Twisted Tunes Home Page, 346
  White Trash Homepage—Phrantic's Trailerpark, 347
Scandanavia, World of the Vikings Homepage, 298
scavenger hunts, Funny Bunny Trail, 338
science
  agriculture
    Ag-Links, 749
    Agriculture Online, 749
    AgriGator, 749
    Agrinet, 749
    Economic Research Service, 749
    Farmland Information Library, 749
    GrainsGenes, 749
    High Plains Journal-The Farmer-Rancher Paper, 749
    John Deere-Agricultural Equipment, 749
    NewCrop, 749
    Pest & Crop Management Production Newsletter, 749
    Rationale, 749
    USDA, 749
    Voice of Agriculture, 750
  AIMS Education Foundation, 291
  anatomy, Skull Page, 524
  Aphrodisiac Home Page, 776
  astronomy, 750
    History of Astronomy, 465
    Posters, 363, 400
    WebStars Astrophysics in Cyberspace, 753
  aviation, 754
    Air Affair, 754
    Airship, 754
    Aviation Enthusiast Corner, 754
    Aviation Image Archives, 754
    Basics of Space Flight Learners' Workbook, 754
    Canard's Aviator's Page, 754
    Federal Aviation Regulations, 754
    First General Aviation WWW Server, 754
    NASA Dryden Flight Research Center, 755
    NASA Information Services via World Wide Web, 755
    NASA Television on CU-SeeMe, 755
    On Board STS-70, 755
  biology, 291, 755
    Dictionary of Cell Biology, 703
    Net Frog, 348
  Blackwell Science, 609
  botany, 757

California Academy of Sciences, 776

chemistry, 758

cognitive science, 760

American Psychological Association—PsychNET, 533

Consciousness Research Laboratory, 777

Esoteric Psychology, 760

Haskins Laboratories, 531

Internet Resources for Cognitive Science, 760

Psych Central-Dr. John Grohol's Mental Health Pag, 760

Scholarly Psychology Resources on the Web, 760

Social Worker Networker, 760

University of Chicago Press Cognitive and Linguistics Catalogue, 533

computer science, 760

Concepts in Science through Molecular Modeling, 305

Cornell Computer Science Graphics Course, 301

Cornell Theory Center Math and Science Gateway, 292

Cyberspace Middle School, 300

Cynthia and Winston's Kids's Page, 149

Discover Magazine, 600

earth science, 761

ecology, 763

education, Expect the Best from a Girl, 543

electronics, American Electronics Association, 776

energy, 764

engineering, *see* engineering

environmental, *see* environmental sciences

Air & Waste Management Association, 368

Ethical, Legal, and Social Issues in Science, 303

evolution, Answers About Evolution, 731

Exploratorium, 777

Exploratorium Homepage, 301

Explorer Home Page, 777

Fun with Grapes-A Case Study, 777

Galileo, 300

GCRIO Online Student Activities, 302

geography, *see* geography

geology, *see* geology

Great Canadian Scientists, 777

history, Art of Renaissance Science, 465

History of Science, Technology and Medicine, 465

HotList: Virtual Exhibits, 302

humor, Fun with Grapes, 338

Interactive Frog Dissection: An Online Tutorial, 302

Interactive Multimedia Education Resources, 293

ISB Working Group on Footwear Biomechanics, 777

JASON Project, 302

JEST Home Page, 602

Kids on Campus, 151

Kids on Campus (Cornell Theory Center), 561

listservs, 789-793

Math and Science Gateway (Cornell Theory Center), 293

mathematics, 770

MATHMOL-K-12 Mathematics and Molecules, 293

meterology, 774

MU CoE LInks to Education Resources, 294

NASA Education Sites, 294

National Chipcard Forum, 777

National Museum of Natural History, 777

National Science Foundation, 777

National Science Foundation World Wide Web Server, 310

NCSA Education Program, 300

newsgroups, 786-789

Nondestructive Testing Information Analysis Center Home Page, 777

Norcov Research, 571

Nye Labs, 777

Olivetti Research Laboratory, 777, 778

On Being a Scientist Responsible Conduct in, 778

OSPI Math, Science, and Technology Server, 294

paleontology, 781

Dino Russ's Lair, 521

Dinosaur Provincial Park, 521

U.C. Berkeley Museum of Paleontology, 524

physics, 782

Point Source Ltd., 778

Popular Science Magazine, 603

REACH Summer Science Camp, 154

Sargent Welch Scientific Company, 778

SciEd: Science and Mathematics Education Resources, 295

Science Television, 778

Small is Beautiful, 295

Society for Scientific Exploration, 778

Springer-Verlag, 615

SRI's Optical Technology Group, 778

Superplasticity, 778

Systems Realization Laboratory, 778

Technology Review Magazine, 778

TERC, 305

UT Science Bytes, 604

Vibrant Technology, Inc., 778

Videodiscovery, 296

Virtual Frog Dissection Kit, 303

Virtually Hawaii, 778

Web Station—New Media Science, 778

Welcome to Virtual FlyLab, 308

Westinghouse Science and Technology Center, 778

X-Ray and Gamma-Ray Coefficients, 778

Yale NMR Research Group, 779

zoology, 785

science fiction

East Coast Cards and Collectibles, 479

Feminist Science Fiction, Fantasy, & Utopia, 543

Flapping, 75

Isaac Asimov, 97

Jayhawk, 76

Martian Chronicles Study Guide, 107

Ray Bradbury, 98

Rippin' Good Yarn.i.magazines Rippin' Good Yarn, 604

Virtual Toy Store, 819

Web Kids, 155

What I Believe by J.G. Ballard, 79

Wizards of the Coast, Inc., 342

science fiction (movies)

2001: A Space Odyssey, 642

2019: Off-World (Blade Runner Page), 642

Back to the Future, 642

Bob's Godzilla Shrine, 642

Dune, 642

Flash Gordon, 642

Harp on Batman Forever, 642

Mithral Web, 642

Nuke Home Page, 642

Phantasm, 642

Star Trek: WWW, 643

Star Wars Collectors Home Page, 643

Star Wars Home Page at UPENN, 643

Tron Home Page, 643

Until the End of the World, 643

War Games Fan Page, 643
Waterworld, 643

science fiction (television)
Babylon 5 file Area, 882
Battlestar Galactica, 882
Broadsword, 882
Dark Shadows, 882
Dominion Sci-fi Channel, 882
Extraterrestrial Biological Entity (EBE) Page, 882
Forever Knight, 882
Hyperlight Enterprises, 882
Lurker's Guide to Babylon 5, 883
Planet X, 883
Sliders, 883
Songs of the Blue Bird, 883
Star Trek: The Next Generation—The Daily Test, 341
Starship Portfolio, 883
Starship Store, 883
Tales from the Crypt, 883
Terminal X, 883
Trader 800 Trekker, 883
Trek Reviews Archive, 884
The X-Files, 695

scientology
Alt.religion.scientology, 739-740
Church of Scientology vs. The Net, 739
Dianetics Home Page, 739
Johnny Get Your Modem-Scientology's War with the Internet, 740
L. Ron Hubbard Home Page, 740
Scientology Home Page, 740
The Scamizdat Memorial, 346
Yoga Paths, An Overview Of Different Schools and Traditions, 737

Scotland
music
Ain't Whistlin' Dixie, 656
Ceolas Celtic Music Archive, 657
Temple Records, 659
TuneWeb, 659
Royal Commission on the Ancient and Historical Monuments of Scotland (RCAHMS), 523
SoccerNet, 858

screen savers, Dogz, 337
screenwriting, Hollywood Actors Network, 335
SCSI (small computer system interface), 34
scuba diving, 815, 856
Aquanaut, 599
Scuba Central, 856
Scuba Net, 856

sculpture
Booth Milton: Sculptor, 89
Crucible Chicago, 84
Daddazio-The Bronze Necktie, 84
International Sculpture Center's On-line Resource, 76
Koh-Varilla Guild, 86
Sculptor/Stone Carver, 87
Sculpture Tour, 88

search and rescue missions
Avalanche Dogs!, 435
Mountain Rescue Association, 436

searchers
addresses, Four11 White Page Directory, 573
business
Business Directions International, 573
Media Logic's Index of Economic and Financial Resources, 574
Categorical Catapult, 567
colleges, College and University Home Pages, 573
FutureMedia Services, 568
G.T.A. Business Solutions, 569
Glistening Trail Records, 568
Global Village Stock Footage, 569
Handy Guide, 564
Harter Image Archives, 569
HFSI, 569
Index of Australian Indexes, 573
International Business Resources on the WWW, 574
MediaTel's Newsline, 574
Micro Service & Training, 574
Montana Communications Network (MCN), 574
Nothin' But Net, 575
Planet Earth Home Page, 575
universities, College and University Home Pages, 573
Yahoo!, 576

security
Alarm Systems, 817
American Power Conversion, 238
Anonymity and Privacy on the Internet, 239
Atlantic Systems Group, 238
ByteBox Computer Enclosures, 238
ClearStar Security Network, 122
Codex, 817
Community Connextion, 238
Computer Security Day, 238
crackers, 22
Cryptography and PGP Page, 238

DHSL: Data Home Systems Limited, 505
e-mail, 22
Electronic Countermeasures, Inc., 817
Exide Electronics, 238
hackers, 22
Home Automation Association (HAA), 505
Home Team, 506
Index of Privacy Resources, 238
Internet Firewalls FAQs, 238
McAfee VirusScan for Windows, 238
National Computer Security Association, 239, 395, 695
Network Systems Corporation, 239
NH&A, 239
NIST Computer Security Resource Clearinghouse, 239
Raptor Systems, Inc, 239
S&S International PLC-Dr. Solomon's Online, 239
Secure Computing Corporation, 239
Security Engineering Services, Inc., 239
Special Electronic Security Products Ltd., 817
Spy Supply Online, 817
STANCOM, Inc., 817
UN*X Net for Computer Security, 239, 242
VeriSign, Inc., 239
ViaCrypt, 240
World Wide Web Security FAQ, 240
ZD Net Trailblazer Security, 240

Seery-Lester, John, 75
seismology, 776
self help
A Place to Honor Grief, 429
Acclaim Professional Counseling, 445
Bereavement Research Network, 429
Breaking the Cycle, 795
Cocoon, 610
Discovering Success with Gary Viterise, Ph.D, 812
Habit Smart, 427
Hair Loss Handbook and Support Group Network, 442
Lenair Technique, Inc., 427
Mind Tools, 535
Planet Millenium, 336
Psychology Self-Help Resources on the Internet, 537
Sex and Love Addiction Recovery Home Page, 427
Shyness Home Page, 446
Tools for Practical Self Development, 537

U.S. Recovery, Addiction, and Abuse Resources, 427

sending e-mail messages, 25

senior citizens

AARP, 827

Adopt a Grandparent Program, 827

Caregiver Network Inc., 827

Elderhostel, 827

Grand Times, 827

Home Modification: A NARIC Resource Guide, 439

Seniors-Site, 827

SeniorSites, 440

Social Security Online, 440

SWT Age Page, 828

servers, 11, 15

Seventh Day Adventist, SDANet, 727

seventies culture, Oeno Phile's Mood Detector, 340

sexual assault, *see* **rape**

sexuality

100-Point Purity Test for Non-Virgins, 800

Aphrodisiac Home Page, 796

Church of Tantra, 796

Condom, 616

Condoms Express/Condom Club International, 798

Contraceptive Research and Development Program, 798

eaRoS, 796

ErtocaTender, 796

Glass Wings: Sensual Celebrations, 601

Information about Contraception and Reproductive Health, 798

listservs, 802-803

Mirkin Report, 437

newsgroups, 801-802

Planned Parenthood Federation of America, 828

Safer Sex Page, 798

SHAPE: Sexual Health Advocate Peer Education, 800

Sex and Food, 798

SGML (Standard General Makeup Language), 4, 14

Shakespeare, William, 78, 350

shareware, 575

CSUSM Windows World, 568

CyberSky, 751

SlipKnot, 54

Software, 825

shareware games, 169

sharks, Electronic Prehistoric Shark Museum, 301

shopping

Antiquarian Booksellers' Association of America, 112

Association of American University Presses (AAUP), 112

Astrology et al Bookstore, 112

Bantam Doubleday Dell-BDD Online, 112

Bonder Bookstore Inc., 112

Book Hunter, 112

BookLink, 112

BookSite, 112

Bookstore at Houghton Mifflin, 112

Clean Well-Lighted Place For Books, 113

Cody's Books, 113

Comics at Bendigo Books, 113

Coupons, 799

Crafter's Showcase, 807

David Morrison Books, 113

Deep Politics Bookstore, 113

Fast Books, 113

FrameMakers, 75

Gareth Stevens Publishing, 113

Gary Holmes Books, 113

Glass Wings, 564

Hahn Company, 813

Handcrafts Unlimited, 813

InfoWell, 813

Internet Auction List, 813

It's a Mystery, 113

Joseph-Beth Booksellers, 113

JourneyWare Media, 113

listservs, 822

Loganberry Books, 114

Login Brothers Book Company, 114

Made in America, 814

Mage Publishing, 114

malls

American Shopping, 819

BizCafe Mall, 819

Branch Mall, 819

CityMart Shopping Mall, 819

Cyber-Shopping Network, 819

Flea Market @FUW, 819

IndustryNET Industry's Online Mall, 820

Internet Shopping Galleria, 820

Internet Shopping Network, 820

Leonardo Park, 820

Meetings Industry Mall, 820

Microplay Video Game Stores, 820

Roblyn's Shopping Mall, 820

Shopper's Utopia, 820

Spectra.Net Mall, 820

Star-Byte Shopping Mall, 820

UK Shopping City, 820

Web Plaza-Online Marketplace, 820

WebMart Virtual Mall And Web Development Services, 820

Xplore Shopping, 820

Mare's Nest Publishing, 114

Midnight Special Bookstore, 114

Moe's Books, 114

Navrang Inc., 114

New World Books, 114

newsgroups, 821-822

Next to Nothing, 814

Norwegian Bookshop, 114

Old Bookroom, 114

Pacific Book Auction Galleries, 114

Pantera Publishing, 114

Pas de chance, 114

Polonia Bookstore, 115

Posters from Your Photos and Computer Files, 815

Potomac Mills, 459

Revolution Books, 115

Science Express, Inc., 115

Secret Staircase Bookshop, 115

Shen's Books and Supplies, 115

Shopping2000, 816

SPITE! Books, 115

Stone Bridge Press, 115

Surplus United States Government Sales, 816

Svoboda's Books Online, 115

Tampa Machinery Auction, Inc., 816

Time-Life Explorer, 115

Traders' Connection, 816

UNARIUS Academy of Science, 115

Woman Made Catalog Showroom, 816

World Shopping & Information Network, 816

Zanadu Comics, 115

shortcuts, 47

sign language, American Sign Language Linguistic Research Projects, 529

signatures, e-mail, 18

Sikhism

Fort: Panth Khalsa, 739

Sikhism: Religion of the Sikh People, 739

silverware, Erre Esse Gifts, 807

Simple Mail Transport Protocol (SMTP), 12

simplex devices, 33

singles

Christian Single Online, 795

Christian Singles, 795

Jewish Singles Connection, 795
Match.Com-"We met on the net", 795
Positive Planet, 604
Ulti-Mate Dating Service, 795
Webpersonals.com, 795
sitars, Batish Institute of Indian Music and Fine Arts, 657
sitcoms
  Absolutely Fabulous, 871
  ALF Page by Kyle, 872
  Alice TV-Show Home Page, 872
  All in the Family, 872
  alt.tv.brisco-county, 872
  America's Favorite Radio Station, 872
  Andy Griffith Show, 872
  Better Dead Than SMEG, 872
  Bewitched, 696
  Bewitched Home Page, 872
  Blossom, 873
  Bob Newhart Unofficial Homepage, 873
  Bosom Buddies Home Page, 873
  Boston Common, 873
  Café Nervosa, 873
  California Dreams, 873
  Caroline in the City, 873
  Cheers Home Page, 873
  Clueless, 874
  C'mon, Get Happy!, 874
  Common Law, 874
  Critic, 874
  Dinosaurs, 874
  Dr. Katz, 874
  Dream On, 874
  Duckman!, 874
  Eerie, Indiana, 874
  Encyclopedia Brady, 874
  Facts of Life Unofficial Home Page, 874
  Family Ties, 874
  Fawlty Towers Episode Guide, 875
  The First Simpson Dating Game on the Web, 337
  Fresh Prince of Bel-Air, 875
  Friends, 875
  Full House, 875
  Get a Life Program Guide, 875
  Get Smart Home Page, 875
  Gilligan's Island, 875
  Golden Girls, 875
  Grace Under Fire, 875
  Growing Pains, 875
  Hangin' with Mr. Cooper Home Page, 875
  Herman's Head, 875

Hogan's Heroes, 876
Home of Home Improvement Cyberfans, 876
Honeymooners Picture Depot, 876
Hudson Street Home Page, 876
Indispensable I Dream of Jeannie Page, 876
John Larroquette Show, 876
Kids In the Hall by Jeff, 876
Kramer—Fishing Guide to the Stars, 686
Larry Sanders Show, 876
Mad About You, 876
Mad TV Home Page, 876
Mama's Family, 876
Maniac Mansion, 877
Married…With Children Home Page, 877
MASH Archives, 877
Mel Loves I Love Lucy, 877
Mook's the Simpsons Page, 877
Moon Over Parma, 877
Moonlighting, on the Web, 877
Murphy Brown, 877
My So-Called Life, 877
Nanny Unofficial Home Page, 877
Ned and Stacey Home Page, 877
NewsRadio Station, 878
Official Unofficial Seinfeld Page, 878
Parker Lewis Can't Lose, 878
Planet Wallywood One Liner Comedy Diner, 345
Red Green Show, 878
Roseanne, 878
Saved By The Bell, 878
Simpsons Source, 878
Single Guy ("How about something simple, like…"), 878
SITCOM Home Page, 351
Sledge Hammer! Arsenal, 878
Spin City, 878
State's Virtual Whatever…, 878
Sup's Blackadder Page, 878
Third Page from the Official, 879
Townies, 879
Welcome Back, Kotter, 879
Wings, 879
Wonder Years, 879
site links, Gray Ghost: The Links You Use Everyday, 712
sites, 16
  accessing, 17
  Best of the Net, 563
  Cool Site of the Day, 563
  mirror, 18

skating
  Figure Skater's Web Page, 859
  Speed Skating, 859
skiing, 857
  AMI News-Recreation and Travel, 915
  Great Lakes Skier Magazine, 601
  Snow Page, 859
skin care products
  Body Doubles Skin Care, 807
  Certified European Image Consultant, 808
  Maui Amenities, 808
  Nature's Wealth, 808
skydiving
  SkyDance SkyDiving, 844
  Skydive Archive, 844
SlipKnot browser, 41, 54
small businesses, Get Organized, 122
small computer system interface (SCSI), 34
SMTP (Simple Mail Transport Protocol), 12
snowboarding, 844
soap operas
  All My Children, 884
  Another World Fan Club Official Home Page, 884
  As the World Turns, 884
  Bold and the Beautiful, 884
  Days of Our Lives Page, 884
  General Hospital, 884
  Guiding Light, 884
  One Life To Live: The History Page, 884
  Soap Opera Pen Pal Page, 884
  Young and the Restless, 884
soccer
  CyberSoccer, 845
  Soccer Cybertour, 857
  SoccerNet, 858
  SoccerNews Online, 858
social action groups, Institute for Global Communications, 828
social issues
  American Firearms Association, 828
  Drug Use is Life Abuse/Project: No Gangs, 828
  EZ Connect, 828
  Gunfree, 828
  Institute for Global Communications, 828
  just, 828
  Knowledge Source, 828
  Landegg Academy Online, 302

Index

Index

listservs, 836-837
NARAL, 828
National Right to Life, 828
newsgroups, 831-836
Planned Parenthood Federation of America, 828
Soapbox Issues, 828
Soundprint Historical and Social Issues, 829
Today in Perspective, 829
U.S. Pro-Life Directory, 829
Urban Legends Archive, 829
Vote Smart Web, 829

social services
American Red Cross, 829
Carter Center, 829
Contact Center Network, 829
HandsNet, 829
National Civic League, 829
National Coalition for the Homeless, 830
River of Hope, 830
Unofficial Guide to Rotary, 830
VISTA web, 830
Who Cares, 830

sociology
American Civilization Homepage, 537
American Sociological Association (ASA), 538
Association for Humanist Sociology, 538
Canada: CTHEORY, 539
Canadian Journal of Sociology (CJS), 538
Center for Rural Studies (CRS), 538
Center for the Study of Online Communities, 538
Centre for MediaSociology (CeMeSo), 538
Centre for Social Theory and Technology (CSTT), 538
Consortium for International Earth Science Information Network (CIESIN), 538
Economic and Social Research Council Data Archive, 539
Electronic Journal of Sociology©, 539
European Research Centre on Migration and Ethnic Relations (ERCOMER), 539
European Sociological Association (ESA), 539
Future of Children, 539
GALLERY OF SOCIAL STRUCTURES: Network Visualization, 539

Human Rights Web Home Page, 539
Institute for Propaganda Analysis, 539
International Network for Social Network Analysis (INSNA), 540
International Sociological Association (ISA), 540
Journal of Criminal Justice and Popular Culture, 540
Journal of Latin American Perspectives, 540
Journal of World-Systems Research, 540
National Criminal Justice Reference Service (NCJRS, 540
Population Index, 540
Population Reference Bureau (PRB), 540
Population Studies Center— University of Michigan, 540
Society for Applied Sociology, 540
Sociological Research Online, 540
Sociology Gopher Resources, 541
SocioWeb, 541
SOCNET, 541
U.S. Agency for International Development, 541
U.S. Civil Rights Code, 541
United Nations Population Information Network (POPIN), 541
United Nations Scholars' Workstation at Yale University, 541
University of Chicago Press Sociology Catalog, 541
World Neighbors, 541
Worldwide Demography Resources, 541

soft drinks, *see* **beverages**
software
20/20 Software, 240
4GL Computing Ltd, 240
Ablaze Business Systems, Inc., 240
Absoft Corporation, 240
Abstract Technologies, 240
ACC Corp., Inc., 240
Accsys Corporation, 240
Achieve Technology, 240
ACI Company, 240
Advanced Computing Systems Company, 241
Advanced Quick Circuits, L.P., 241
Agorics, Inc., 241
Aladdin Knowledge Systems Ltd., 241
Aliah, Inc., 241

Alpha Microsystems Services Operation, 241
Analytical Software Packages, Inc., 241
ANGOSS Software ntl., 241
Applix, Inc., 242
AquaNet, 242
Arcada Software, 242
Archive Comparison Test (A.C.T.), 242
ARGUS, 242
Aslan Computing Inc, 242
ATI Technologies, 242
Atlantic Information Systems, Inc., 243
Attachmate Internet Products Group, 243
Austin Software Foundry, 243
Automata Design, Inc. (ADI), 243
Axis Communications AB, 243
B & E Technology Group, 243
Bentley Systems, 243
Bernstein & Associates, Inc., 243
BGS Systems, 243
Bismarck Group, 243
Bluestone, Inc., 243
Blyth Software, 243
BMC Software, 243
Brent Hugh's Music Instruction Software Page, 656
Brickell Research, Inc., 244
Brightware Corporation, 244
Broadcast Management Plus, 244
Bryant Software, 244
Business Systems of America Inc., 244
Caldera Inc., 244
Cambridge Computer Corp., 244
Camellia Software Corporation, 244
Canadian Institute of Applied Learning, Inc., 300
Candle Corporation, 244
Caravelle Networks Corporation, 244
CastCAE, 245
Catron Custom Software, 245
CE Software, 245
CEO Software, 245
CharterHouse Software Corporation, 245
ChartWrite's Data-on-the-Map, 526
Chemical Safety, 245
Chicago-Soft, Ltd, 245
CIAO Software Solutions, Inc., 245
Clarion for Windows Icetips, 245

Classic Variety AIPS, 245

Clayton Wallis, 246

clySmic Software, 246

Coconut Info, 246

Cogent Computing Software, 246

Collabra Software, Inc., 246

Columbia Data Products, Inc., 246

Computers and Learning A/S, 246

Computers and Quilting, 498

Computervision Corp., 246

Compuware Corporation, 246

Confluent, Inc., 817

Connectivity Custom Controls, 246

Core Systems, 246

Cornelius Concepts, 247

Cort Directions, Inc., 247

CPI Electronic Publishing, 247

CPLEX Optimization, Inc. Home Page, 771

CPsoft Consulting, 247

Crescent Division, 247

CrossWind Technologies, Inc., 247

Custom Innovative Solutions (CIS), 247

CVS Bubbles, 247

CyberMedia, 247

CyberMedia, Inc. WWW Home Page, 247

Cyclic Software, 248

Cygnus Support Information Gallery, 248

Data Logic, 248

Databyte, 248

DataViz, 248

David Whitt & Associates, Inc., 248

Delphi Information Systems, 248

Delphic Medical Systems, 248

DGA, 248

Diamond International Systems Ltd., 248

Diskovery Educational Systems, 817

Dragon's Eye Software, 248

DS Diagonal Systems, 249

Dubl-Click Software, 249

Dun & Bradstreet Software, 249

Egghead Software, 224

Eisenhower National Clearinghouse DCL, 771

Élan Computer Group, 249

Electric Gypsy Software & Consulting, 249

Electronic Book Technologies, 249

Electronic Learning Systems, Inc., 249

emotion, Inc., 249

Engineering Graphical Solutions, 249

EnviroAccount Software, 249

Environmental Software Resources, 370

Environmental Systems Research Institute, 249

Eòlas Technologies Incorporated, 250

ERDAS, 250

European Software Institute (ESI), 761

ExperTelligence, 250

FCR Software, 250

Fineware Systems, 250

Focus GbR Software, 250

Fundamental Software, 250

Futuristic Software & Computing Group, 250

Gamma Productions, Inc., 250

GAMS: Guide to Available Mathematical Software, 772

Gemini Systems Software, Inc., 250

GeneCraft, 250

Generator, 251

Geotechnical & Geo-environmental Software Director, 371

Global Computing, Inc., 224

Golden Diamonds, 251

GrafTek Inc., 251

Gryphon Software Corporation, 251

Guide to Math Resources, 772

Harlequin, 251

Hearne Scientific Software, 251

Helios Software, 251

HMS Software, 251

Honeysuckle Computing, 251

Hummingbird Software, 251

I-Kinetics, Inc., 251

iambic Software, 252

Illustra Information Technologies, Inc., 252

ImageFX, 252

Imageware, 252

Imagix, 252

Imaja Home Page, 252

IMB: Managing for Profit, 252

Immortal Software Productions, 252

InContext Systems, 252

Inference, 252

Infogroup S.p.A., 121

INFORIUM, The Information Atrium Inc., 252

Information Builders, Inc., 253

Information Systems Manager, Inc., 253

Insight Designs, Inc., 253

Insignia Solutions, 253

Integrated Research, 253

Interactive Data Systems, Inc., 570

Interactive Software Engineering, 253

InterMind, 253

International Knowledge Systems, 253

International Software Systems Inc., 253

Interpretive Software, 253

ISPW, 253, 254

J-MAC System Inc., 254

Jandel Scientific Software, 254

Jean-Marie Vaneskahian's Physics Home Page, 783

JOBSCOPE Manufacturing Management System, 254

KeyStone Learning Systems Corporation, 817

Kinfonetics Technology, 254

Knowledge Engineering Pty Ltd., 254

LandWare, 254

Law Enforcement/Police Software, 254

Layer Eight Systems, Inc., 817

Legal Computer Solutions, 254

Leverage Technologists Home Page, 121

Lex Systems, 254

Lexitech, Inc., 254

LifeGuide, 254

Lighten, Inc., 817

Lighthouse Software, Inc., 254

Lilly Software Associates, Inc., 255

LMSoft, 255

Look Software Systems Inc., 255

Lumina Decision Systems, Inc., 817

MacNeal-Schwendler Corporation, 255

Macola Software from Osiris, 255

MAcZone Internet Superstore, 225

Magna Computer Corp., 255

MathWorks Home Page, 773

Maui Software, 255

Mayflower Software, 255

MCAE Inc., 255

McDonnell Information Systems, 132

MECC, 817

Medlin Accounting Shareware, 255

MentorPlus Software, Inc., 255

Merlin Software, 255

Message Board System, 256

MetaWare Incorporated, 256

Micro-Frame Technologies, Inc., 256

MicroExcel Software, 256

Micromath's Home Page, 765

Microstar Software Ltd., 256

Microsystems Software, Inc., 256

Milestone Technologies, Inc. (MTI), 256

MKS Source Integrity Product, 256

MLL Software and Computers, 256

Modular Software Corporation, 256

Molloy Group, Inc., 257

MRX - Morse Receive and Transmit Training, 712

NeoLogic Systems, 257

NeuroSolutions: The Neural Network Simulation Envi, 818

new stuff inc., 257

Notes Solution Software, 257

Numerical Algorithms Group Ltd., 257

ObjectSpace Inc., 818

Online PhotoWeb, 495

Ovation Software Testing, Inc., 818

Pacific Numerix Corporation, 257

PaperFree Systems, 257

Peninsula Advisors, Inc., 257

Personal Library Software, Inc., 257

Pierian Spring Educational Software, 257

Pinnacle Software, 258

Plant Software, Inc., 258

Praxis International, 258

Prime Time Freeware, 258

Process Analysts, Inc., 258

Prode, 258

ProSoft International, Inc., 258

Psychology Software Tools, Inc., 537

Q-D Software Development, 572

Qbik Software, 258

Quadrillion: Data Analysis Software, 258

Quality America Incorporated, 258

Quality Software Management, 258

Quarterdeck Global Chat, 558

Quest Software Inc., 259

RABA Technologies, Inc., 259

Raben Software & Graphics, 483

Rachel's Kids Page, 154

RealAudio Home Page, 572

Robert McNeel & Associates, 259

S.S.I.T.E. Windows 3.x Utilities, 259

Safetynet, Inc. AntiVirus and Security, 259

Sage Solutions, Inc., 259

Sanctuary Woods Multimedia, 259

Scandinavian Softline Technology, 259

Second Chair Corporation, 818

Second Nature Software, Inc., 259

Sequent Computer Systems, Inc., 259

Shana Corporation, 259

Shock Software, 260

Sibylla: The WWW Software Development Kit, 572

SiliconSoft, 260

Simply Software: "Bridesmaids for Windows", 927

Simucad, 260

Sirius Software, 260

Skylonda Group, 260

Smithmicro, 260

SoftPlan Systems, 260

SoftSell Business Systems Inc., 260

Software, 678, 825

Software Consulting Services, 260

Software Net Product Menu, 615

Software Tailors, 260

Solid Oak Software, Inc., 260

SouthWare Innovations, Inc., 261

SPARTA, Inc., 261

Specialized Business Solutions, 261

SpeedSim, Inc., 261

SST Inc., 261

Steven M. Christensen and Associates, Inc., 774

Stonehand Inc., 261

StrandWare Home Page, 261

Strawberry Tree, Inc., 261

Subtle Software, 261

Sunbelt Software, 261

Sunvalley Software, 261

Superlative Software Solutions, 261

SurfWatch Software, 261

SW International Systems Pte Ltd, 262

SymCon Software, 262

Synapse Communications, Inc., 262

Syntax, 262

Systemcorp, 262

Systems Alliance, Inc., 262

TEC Solutions, 262

TECHCO, 262

Technetix Unix/Internet Tools, 262

Thermal Solutions, 262

Thinque Systems Corporation, 262

Thomson Software Products, 262

Thunderstone Software, 262

Tibco, 263

Time Crafter (shareware), 263

TimeLess Technologies Schedule Wizard Software, 263

Tosoft Children's Education and Quit Smoking Page, 263

Total Point of Sale Solution, 263

Tower Concepts, Inc., 263

Toys, 545

Traffic Software, 263

Trax Softworks, Inc., 263

Tumbleweed Software Corp., 263

Ubi Soft, 263

UCSB Anthropology Web Site, 520

UNIBOL, 263

Uniplex, 263

Uptime Computer Solutions, Inc., 263-264

Van Dyke Technologies, 264

Vantageware, 264

Veritas Software, 264

VersaFax, 264

Viewpoint Software Solutions, 264

Virtual AdVentures, 818

Visigenic, 264

Vision XXI, 264

VYSOR Integration Inc., 264

Wall Street Software, 264

Web requirements, 34

Welcome to Computer Associates, 264

Welcome to HPI on the World Wide Web, 265

Welcome to Microsoft, 265

Wind River Systems, 265

Wingra Technologies, 265

Z-Law Software, Inc., 228

Zinc Software Inc., 265

solar energy

Maine Solar House, 363

Mr. Solar Home Page, 363

solar system

Earth Viewer, 763

Nine Planets, 294

Planetary Society Home Page, 752

Sensors and Instrument Technology Planetary Tour G, 753

Solar System Live, 753

Usenet FAQs Space, 753

Views of the Solar System, 753

Web Nebulae, 496

see also astronomy

sororities, Planet Greek, 805

sorting e-mail, 27

sound

8-Track Heaven, 349

CES News, 350

Lucasfilm's THX Home Page, 350

Make James Earl Jones Speak, 345

RealAudio: Audio on Demand for the Internet, 350

Secrets of Home Theater and High
Fidelity, 350
See Hollywood and Vine, 350
The Sneeze Page, 348
Sound Site, 350
The Virtual Keyboard, 348
Virtual Media, 342
Welcome to Dolby Laboratories, 350
Xing Technology's StreamWorks, 350
**South Carolina, South Carolina
Supernet—LocalNet, 918**
South Dakota
Sisseton Wahpeton Sioux Tribe, 519
South Dakota Archaeology, 524
South Dakota World Wide Web Site,
918
Southwest, *see* **American Southwest**
Southwestern art
Another Victim of Santa Fe Style, 811
Na-Te-So Workshop, 87
space shuttles
NASA Spacelink-An Electronic
Information System For Educators,
310
On Board STS-70, 755
Spain, Flamenco Home Page, 658
spamming, 28
Spanish
Radio Centro, 617
Tecla Homepage form Birkbeck
College London, 296
spectroscopy, 779
**speech pathology, Mankato State
University Department of Communi-
cation Disorders, 432**
**spoken word performances, B.A.W.P.
Spoken Word Audio, 89**
**sport psychology, Mental Edge—Sport
Psychology, 535**
**sporting goods, Sunglasses, Shavers,
and More Home Page, 819**
sporting trips
Adventure Travel, 901
Adventure Travel for Women, 901
Alaska—Mt. McKinley, 901
Alpine Guides Alaska, 901
Arctic Adventours, Inc., 901
Big Island Air, 901
Eagle Canyon Airlines, 901
EarthWise Journeys, 901
Helinet Helicopter Tours, 901
Mayuc—Ecological Tourism, 901
New Brunswick, Canada Outdoor
Adventures, 901
Resort Sports Network, 901

Safari Helicopters, 902
Sierra Mountain Guides, 902
Touring Exchange, 902
TravelBase, 902
Wildwest Travel, Inc., 902
sports
autoracing
candelaMotorsport, 839
Dakar Official Site, 895
Formula Lightning, 893
GALE FORCE F1, 839
IndyCar Enthusiast, 839
Matt's Solar Car Page, 839
*Motorsports Media Service
International Home Page, 839*
Racer Archive, 839
Specialty Car Page, 839
Warn Adventure Morocco '96, 895
AWESOME Sports Site of the Week,
851
baseball
Baseball Hall of Fame, 840
Cosmic Baseball Associationn, 845
*ESPNet SportsZone: Major League
Baseball, 840*
Fantasy Baseball, 845
Fantasy Baseball Home Page, 845
Fastball, 840
Instant Baseball, 840
Japanese Professional Baseball, 840
John Skilton's Baseball Links, 840
Little League Baseball, 840
Major League Baseball, 840
Nando Baseball Server, 840
New York Yankees Home Plate, 841
teams, 839
World Youth Baseball, 841
basketball
College Basketball Page, 841
Michael Jordan's Home Page, 841
Nando Basketball Server, 841
Nando Net Sports Server, 852
On Hoops, 841
Scottie Pippen's Home Court, 842
teams, 841
*Unofficial Australian National
Basketball League (NBL) Page, 842*
Ultimate Basketball Home Page, 842
billiards, American Poolplayers
Association, 851
boating/sailing
Adventure Schools, Inc., 842
Boatnet, 842
*Common Sense Design's Home Page,
842*

Flying Scot Page, 842
Internet Sea Kayaking, 842
Offshore Powerboat Racing, 842
*Perception, Inc.'s Kayaking Home
Page-20 Years of, 842*
RC-Sailing Infocenter, 842
SailWeb, 842
White Water Rafting, 843
WWW Sailing Index, 843
bowling
PBA Tour, 853
Tenpin World, 854
bullfighting, La Tauromaquia: The
Art of Bullfighting, 852
Canada's Sports Hall of Fame, 852
collegiate, College Atheletics WWW
Pages, 852
Conway's Sports Research, 845
croquet, virtual greensward, 854
cycling
Cyber Cyclist, 600
Cyber Cyclery, 843
CycLinks, 843
*Emory Bicycle Manufacturing
Company, 843*
Fat Tire Wire, 843
MuDsLuTs, 843
Spring City Cycles, 843
VeloNet, 843
Velonews, 843
VeloZine, 843
WOMBATS on the Web, 843
WWW Bicycle Lane, 843
equestrian
Horse Country, 850
*Thoroughbred Horse Racing and
Breeding, 850*
*Three Chimneys Farm Home Page,
850*
Washington Handicapper, 851
ESPNET Sport Zone, 852
fencing
Art of Fencing, 851
US Fencing Association Online, 854
fishing
Anglers Online, 846
Flyfishing Antventures, 846
J.P.'s Fishing Page, 846
King of the Hill Fly Fishing Co., 846
Nautical Net, 846
Nor'east Saltwater Magazine, 846
*Sportfishing Industry Newsletter,
846*
Virtual Flyshop, 846
World of Fishing, 847

fitness, Physique Techniques Fitness Consultants, 853
football
  AllSports.Com Football Hotlist, 847
  College Football WWW Site, 847
  College Sports Internet Channel, 847
  Fantasy Insights, 845
  Football Stats Analyzer Shareware, 845
  Nando Football Server, 847
  NFL Executive Accessories, 848
  NFL POOL, 845
  Onondaga/Oswego Fantasy Football Page, 845
  Team NFL, 848
  teams, 847
  Traveller Information Service, 848
  Two-Minute Warning, 848
  USA Football Center Online, 848
  WinAmerica! Fantasy Football, 846
Frisbee Freestyle, 852
Gender Equity in Sports, 543
golf
  19th Hole, 848
  Alberta, 848
  Fore Play Golf Home Page, 848
  Golf Circuit, 848
  Golf Courses of British Columbia, 848
  Golf Depot, 848
  Golf Magazine, 848
  Golf Web, 849
  NBC Golf Tour, 849
  Official PGA Championsh Web Site, 849
  Princeton Golf Archives, 849
  Ryder Cup Home Page, 849
Grandstand, 845
gymnastics, Gym Forum, 852
hang gliding
  Hang Gliding Page, 844
  Hang Gliding WWW Server, 844
Highlight Fantasy-The Draft Kit, 845
hiking
  Above the Clouds, 849
  Backcountry Home Page, 849
  Orienteering and Rogaining Home Page, 849
  Volksmarch and Walking Index, 849
history, British Society of Sports History, 852
hockey
  Hockey Hall of Fame, 850
  National Hockey League Players' Association, 850
  NHL OPEN NET, 850

NHL Schedule, 850
NHL Wreckroom, 850
teams, 849-850
inline skating
  Roller Warehouse News, 855
  Sk8er's Home Page, 855
Internet Athlete, 852
Irish Sports Report, 852
lacrosse, College Lacrosse USA, 852
listservs, 866
magazines, Sports Illustrated, 853
marketing, Planet Reebok, 853
martial arts
  Aikido Information, 851
  CyberDojo, 851
  Danzan-Ryu Jujutsu Homepage, 851
  Judo Information Site, 851
  Martial Arts As I've Learned Them, 851
  Piedmont Budokan (Judo and JuJitsu), 851
  T'ai Chi Connection, 851
memorabilia, Sports Souvenirs & Memorabilia, 853
Midwest Express Fantasy Game Co., 845
motorcycle racing
  AFMWeb, 855
  Speedway Home Page, 855
news, Sports Network, 853
newsgroups, 860-865
Olympics
  Guide to the 1996 Olympic Games, 855
  XVIII Olympic Winter Games, 855
outdoor
  Arkatents USA-High Quality Camping Accessories, 855
  Feathered Friends, 812
  Great Outdoor Recreation Pages (GORP), 855
  Hiking and Walking Home Page, 437
  Outside Online, 855
  Upper Midwest Traveler and Adventure Guide, 855
  Virtual Pathways, 605
  Wave~Length Paddling Network, 605
remote controlled, Ballistic Batteries, 851
rowing, 853
rugby
  International Rugby League Home Page, 856
  WWW Rugby Information Service, 856

running
  Running Page, 856
  Sportsworld, 856
scuba diving
  Aquanaut, 856
  Diving Server, 856
  Mad Dog Expeditions, 856
  Maui Scuba Page-Ed Robinson's Diving Adventures, 856
  NAUI (National Association of Underwater Instructors, 856
  New England Ski and Scuba, 818
  Scuba Central, 856
  Scuba Net, 856
  SeaVision USA, 815
skiing
  CRN-Colorado Resort Net, 857
  FALL LINE Home Page, 857
  Great Lakes Skier Magazine, 601
  Jump, 857
  Northern Vermont X-Country, Backcountry, and Telem, 857
  Pedersen's Ski and Sport, 857
  Powder Hound Ski Report, 857
  SnowPage, 857
  Wasatch Powderbird Guides, 857
  World Skiing, 857
skydiving
  SkyDance SkyDiving, 844
  Skydive Archive, 844
Small World, 846
snowboarding, ISF World Snowboard Rankings, 844
soccer
  CyberSoccer, 845
  ESPNet SportZone Soccer, 857
  International Soccer, 857
  Soccer Cybertour, 857
  SoccerNet, 858
  SoccerNews Online, 858
  TSI Soccer, 858
  U.S. Soccer Web Pages, 858
Sports Source, 853
Sports Videos, 853
SportsArena, 854
squash, World Squash Federation, 855
Stadiums and Arenas, 854
statistics, Quick Stats Service, 853
sumo wrestling, Sumo Information Page, 854
surfing
  Bodysurfing, 858
  Drop In, 858

Edge Magazine, 844

FreeSurf, 858

Maui Windsurfing Report, 844

New England Windsurfing Journal, 844

Parachute Industry Association, 844

Sailboard Vacations, 844

Surf Lingo, 858

Welcome to the Lip, 858

Windsight Windsurfing Wind Report, 844

Windsurfer.com, 858

swimming

Home Page for United States Swimming, Inc., 858

Web Swim, 859

tennis

ATP Tour Home Page, 859

Tennis Country, 859

United States Tennis Association/ Mid-Atlantic Sect, 859

World Wide Web Tennis Server, 859

trivia

Sportsworld, 854

Wide Web of Sports, 855

Ultimate Internet Sports Guide, 854

Ultimate Sports Page, 854

United States Air-Table Hockey Association (USAA), 854

USA Today Sports, 854

volleyball

USA Volleyball Home Page, 859

Volleyball WorldWide, 859

water polo, David B. Martin's Water Polo Page, 852

waterskiing, Water Skier's Web, 858

winter

Figure Skater's Web Page, 859

Snow Page, 859

Speed Skating, 859

Winter Sports Page, 859

wrestling, Sprague Mat Club, 854

sports cars

AC Cobra Page, 895

Alfa Romeo GTA, 895

Aston Martin, 895

DeLorean Home Page, 895

Javelin AMX Home Page, 895

Paul Murtagh's Lamborghini Web Site, 896

Vette Americana On-Line, 896

Waletail's Porsche and 959 Home Page, 896

sports equipment

ISB Working Group on Footwear Biomechanics, 777

Online Sports, 818

S & S Enterprises, 818

Steve's Multi-Sport Catalog, 818

SunFun Collection, 818

Sunglasses, Shavers, and More Homepage, 818

Sunglasses.Com, 818

Sports Illustrated, 853

sports memorabilia

BJS Enterprises Collectibles and Crafts Mini Mall, 478

East Coast Cards and Collectibles, 479

MOODY'S Sports Autographs and Memorabilia, 481

Perfect Image Sportscards and Memorabilia, 481

Sports, Collectibles, and Money, 482

SportsCards, Etc., 482

World Wide Collectors Digest—Your Collectibles Outlet, 482

World Wide Mall ™ Collectibles, Dolls, & More, 482

sports-related games, 170

Sprint, 37

Spry/CompuServe Internet, 37

Spyglass Enhanced Mosaic, 52

squash, 855

stamp collecting

Bjorn Much's Stamps Page, 497

ELA Auctions, Inc., 497

Henry Gitner Philatelists, Inc., 480

Icelandic Stamp's Page, 497

Joseph Luft's Philatelic Resources on the Web, 497

New Zealand First Day Covers, 497

Philatelic Trading Post, 497

Revenue and Telegraph Stamps, 498

Stamp Collecting Basics, 498

Stamps, Covers, and AnythingPhilatelic, 498

Superior Stamp and Coin, 487

U.S. 1995 Stamp Program, 498

Ukrainian Stamps, 498

United States Postal Service, 717

stamps, rubber, Rubber Stamp Queen, 815

Standard General Makeup Language (SGML), 4, 14

stocks & bonds

A.S.K. Financial Digest, 127

Accel Partners, 127

American Stock Exchange, 127

American Stock Report, Inc., 127

Australian Stock Market Web Page, 124

Chicago Mercantile Exchange, 127

CyberFund, 127

Fin-Atlantic Securities, Inc., 127

Financial Times Group, 607

How to Become a Real-Time Commodity Futures Trader-From Home, 127

InterQuote, 127

Mutual Fund Company Directory, 715

Nesbitt Burns Inc., 128

Pawws Financial Network, 128

Perception Global Market Predictions, 128

Philadelphia Stock Exchange, 128

Precision Investment Services, Inc., 128

Quote.Com, 128

Railroad Scripophily, 481

Research-It!, 713

Security APL Quote Server, 128

SGA Goldstar Research, 128

Siegel Group, Inc., 128

Silicon Investor, 129

Stockdeck Online, 129

StockMaster at MIT, 129

Trader's Financial Resource Guide, 129

Wall Street Net, 129

Wall Street Online, 129

Woodbridge and Associates, 129

stone megaliths, 524

storm chasers, 775-776

storytelling, Campfire Tales, 347

strategy games

Play Chess on the Net, 340

Welcome To the Connect Four Homepage, 342

strokes, Creative Learning Stroke Support Web Site, 439

students

CASAA Student Leadership Resource Center, 307

College Prep Page, 307

CyberKids Home, 307

Felix Culpa Home Page, 601

Homework Page, 308

mathematics, Calculus & Mathematica Home Page, 770

Private Schools Online, 308

Sylvan Learning Centers, 308

Welcome to the DeweyWeb, 308

Welcome to Virtual FlyLab, 308

Writing at MU, 308

subdomains, 23
sumo wrestling, 854
supernatural, *see* **parapsychology**
support tools, browsers, 49
surfing, 858
    Edge Magazine, 844
    Maui Windsurfing Report, 844
    New England Windsurfing Journal, 844
    Parachute Industry Association, 844
    Sailboard Vacations, 844
    Windsight Windsurfing Wind Report, 844
surgical equipment
    Scientific and Medicinal Antiques, 443
    Swan Medical, Inc., 429
surveys, music, CD Album Top 100 of All Time, 649
Switzerland
    Microswiss-Centre North-South, 125
    SWITCH—Swiss Academic and Research Network, 572
synonyms, 705

T

tabloids, Private Eye, 607
Taiwan
    Chinese Music Page, 657
    Home Page of MT&C Music Club, 658
talk shows
    alt.fan.howard-stern, 884
    alt.tv.talkshows.daytime, 884
    alt.tv.talkshows.late, 885
    Andy Richter: King of the Couch, 885
    David Letterman, 885
    Ed Sullivan Show, 885
    FAQ-alt.tv.talkshows.late, 885
    George and Alana Show Home Page, 885
    Hereeeeeeeeee's Conan, 885
    Late Late Show with Tom Snyder, 885
    Later with Greg Kinnear, 885
    Lauren Hutton, 885
    Oprah Winfrey Show, 885
    Politically Incorrect Unofficial Home Page, 886
    Richard Bey Show, 886
    Ricki Lake Show Home Page, 886
    Rolonda, 886
    Rosie O'Donnell Show, 886
    Sony Pictures Before They Were Stars, 886
    Tempestt, 886
    Tonight Show with Jay Leno, 886
    Unofficial Talk Soup Web Page, 886
tampons, 449
Taoism, 736
    Taoism Information Page, 736
    Taoist Resource Center, 737
    Theosophical Society, 737
    Universal Life Church, 737
    Urantia Book, 737
tapes and records, PolyEster Records and Books, 815
tarot
    Introduction To Tarot Magic, 692
    Learning the Tarot—An Online Course, 692
    Michael's Tarot Pages, 692
    Michele's Tarot Page, 692
    Original WWW Tarot Site, 693
    Tarot, 692
    Tarot Cards, 693
    Tarot Cards—Maelstrom, 693
    Tarot Inspiration, 693
    Tarot Web, 693
    Tarot Weekly, 693
    Tarot—Tools and Rites of Transformation, 693
    Vibrations—The Layman's Answer to Tarot Cards!, 693
tasteless humor
    Cruel Site of the Day, 343
    Exploding Heads, 344
    Heather Has Two Mommies, 344
    Kurt Cobain's Talking Eight Ball, 339
    The Magic 8 Bra, 347
    The Miraculous Winking Jesus, 345
    Piercing Mildred, 340
    Random Jokes about Yo Mama, 346
taxes
    Citizens for an Alternative Tax System, 144
    L.A. Professionals Online, 144
    TaxSites-INcome Tax Information in Internet, 144
    United States Tax Code Online, 144
TCP/IP (Transmission Control Protocol/ Internet Protocol), 6-10
tea, Way of Tea, 903
teachers
    Ainsworth Keyboard Training Systems, 308
    Ameritech Education Resources, 309
    Busy Teachers WebSite K-12, 299
    Carrie's Sites for Educators, 309
    chemistry
        Chemistry Teacher Resources, 758
        Software Reviews from the CTI Centre for Chemistry, 759
    Children's Literature Web Guide, 307
    Cisco Educational Archives and Resources Catalog, 309
    Dole 5-A-Day Homepage, 309
    DPI InfoWeb, 309
    Ed Web Homepage, 309
    Education, 309
    Education (Social Sciences), 309
    Education Sites, 309
    eduMail, 309
    ELTI Charlotte's English Aids, 309
    Expect the Best from a Girl, 543
    Explorer Homepage, 309
    Galileo, 300
    GENII Homepage, 309
    Gifted and Talented (TAG) Resources Homepage, 310
    Heinemann World, 310
    InfoList Homepage, 310
    InforMNs, 310
    inQuiry Almanack, March 1995, 310
    Integrating Technology Schools Homepage at University of New Mexico, 310
    Judi Harris' Network-Based Educational Activity Collection, 310
    Kidding Around, 310
    Lesson Plans and Activities, 310
    mathematics
        Calculus & Mathematica Home Page, 770
        Math Teaching Assistant, 772
    Mining the Internet Columns, 310
    National Science Foundation World Wide Web Server, 310
    National Teachers Enhancement Network, 310
    Newton's Apple Educational Materials, 311
    North Dakota ICICLE Project, 311
    Old School House Studio, 311
    School and Community Networking Resources, 311
    Tech Classes Archive, 311
    Virtual English Language Center, 311
techno music
    Kraftwerk infobahn, 647
    nine inch nails: the unofficial home page, 678

technology
3M Innovation Network, 122
8-Track Heaven, 349
BRP Publications, Inc., 610
Coherent Communications Systems Corporation, 811
Connect Homepage, 809
GE Home Pages, 123
history, Art of Renaissance Science, 465
Intelligent Home Technologies, Inc., 506
JDS Technologies, 506
Lucasfilm's THX Home Page, 350
McDonnell Douglas Aerospace, 123
MTAC Home Page, 132
MU CoE LInks to Education Resources, 294
Paracel, Inc., 133
Perceptics Corporation, 133
Personal Technology Home Page, 607
Process Technologies Incorporated, 133
ProSpec, 506
Resource Group, 133
Rodex: Technologies for the, 133
Scope Systems-Worldwide Industrial Electronics Repair and Services, 134
Seven Technologies, 134
Shape Memory Applications, Inc., 134
Silicon Investor, 129
SONY Online, 123
Stealth Technologies, 816
Tandy Corporation, 123
TechExpo on WWW, 134
TERC, 305
Thomsom Publishing, 615
Welcome To HotWired!, 605
teddy bears
Cape Cod Teddy Bear, 478
Web Mill Business District—Bears By The Sea, 482
Web Mill Business District—Teddy Bear Directory, 482
teens
Academy One, 291
BigKid Network, 149
Classroom Connect, 301
Encyclopedia of Women's History, 542
Expect the Best from a Girl, 543
FreeZone, 150
FutureScan, 150

Girl Talk, 150
Internet Public Library, 708
ISN KidNews, 293
Jefferson-Scranton Community Schools, 308
Junior Achievement Purpose/Facts, 304
Kidding Around, 310
KidsCom Home Page, 152
Knox Junior High Homepage, 293
MATHMOL-K-12 Mathematics and Molecules, 293
Route 6-16, 154
Tessa's Cool Links for Kids, 154
Vocal Point, 608
Voices of Youth Homepage, 308
Web66: K-12 Schools Registry, 297
Winston Churchill High School Web Server, 297
TEI (Text Encoding Initiative), 48
telecommunications
Applied Signal Technology, 265
Archtek Telecom Corp., 265
AT&T Home Page, 122
Commercial Speech Recognition, 265
Cromack Industries, Inc., 265
EMJ Data Systems, 265
FAQ: How can I use the Internet, 266
Genesys LLC Home Page-Premier Telephony Products for Windows, 266
Internet Phone: Download a Free Copy, 266
ISDN Infocentre, 266
Kingston Telecommunication Laboratories, 132
M&S Hourdakis SA, 266
MCI Home Page, 123
MedConnect, 266
MediaLogic, ADL Inc., 266
MediaSoft Telecom, 266
Metricon Welcome, 266
MindSphere Design for Communication, 571
Motorola Information Systems Group, 266
Multi-Tech Systems, Inc., 266
National Telecommunications and Information Administration, 267
Network Hardware Suppliers List, 571
Nokia, 267
Online Source Register (Services), 78
Practinet Practical Peripherals, 267

Research Program on Communications Policy, 267
Rogers Communications Inc., 133
Siegel Group, Inc., 128
Source Inc., 267
Stylus Innovation, Inc., 267
Symplex Communications, 267
Tascomm Engineering, 267
Tele-Communications, Inc. (TCI), 134
Telecommunications News and Journals, 267
TeleService Resources, Inc., 134
Terminate Home Page, the Final Terminal, 267
Universal Group Of Companies, 268
Vaughn Communications Inc., 134
Videoconferencing Systems, Inc., 268
Welcome to Sprint Stop, 268
Welcome to the Fibersphere, 268
World Wide Web Virtual Library: Communications and Telecommunications, 268
telemarketing, Western Direct's Home Page, 142
telephone directories
555-1212.com Area Code Look-Up, 714
American Computer Resources, Inc., 715
AmeriCom Long Distance AREA DECODER, 715
AT&T Internet Toll Free 800 Directory, 715
BigBook, 715
BigYellow, 715
Central Source Yellow Pages, 715
Internet 800 Directory, 715
Mutual Fund Company Directory, 715
National Telephone & Communications (NTC), Tele-Locator, 715
Period.Com Airlines!, 716
PhoNETic, 716
Switchboard, 716
Telephone Directories on the Web, 716
What does your phone number spell?, 716
World Telecom Directories, 716
World Yellow Pages Network (wyp.net), 716
Yellow Pages Online, Inc., 716
YellowNet, 716
telephone services
FiberNet Communications, 130

Harris Digital Telephone Systems, 131

Inland Answering Service, 131

television

All TVs Center, 886

children

2 Stupid Dogs, 867

Adventures of Pete and Pete, 867

alt.tv.tiny-toon FAQ, 867

Animaniacs, 867

Bananas in Pajamas, 867

Batfink, 867

Batman: The Animated Series, 867

Beakman's World Home Page, 867

Captain Caveman, 868

Captain Planet, 868

Cartoon World, 868

Cartoons of the 80's Home Page, 868

Children's Television Workshop, 868

Clarissa Explains It All, 868

Count Duckula Page, 868

Craig's Comic & Cartoon Page, 868

Danger Mouse, 868

Davey and Goliath, 868

Deron's Muppet Page, 868

Dinosaucers, 868

Dungeons and Dragons, 869

Earthworm Jim, 869

Flintstones Unofficial Home Page, 869

Fraggle Rock, 869

Freakazoid!, 869

Frostbite Falls, 869

G.I. Joe—A Real American Hero, 869

Goosebumps, 869

Gumby on the Web, 869

Jetsons, 869

Keeper's Cartoon Files, 870

Kids.Cool, 870

Mighty Morphin Power Documents, 870

Mister Rogers' Neighborhood, 870

Muppets Home Page, 870

Phil's Faboo Animaniacs Web Page, 870

Pigs in CyberSpaaaaaaaaaace..., 870

Pinky and the Brain, 870

ReBoot Home Page, 870

School House Rock Page, 870

Secret World of Alex Mack Unofficial Home Page, 870

Some of the 100 or Some Odd Smurfs, 870

Superfriends Archive, 870

Sylvester and Tweety Mysteries, 871

Taz-Mania Page, 871

Teen Court TV, 871

That's Warner Bros.!, 871

Thomas the Tank Engine, 871

Thunderbirds, 871

Tick Page, 871

Unofficial Sid and Marty Krofft Home Page, 871

Welcome to Casper's Whipstaff Manor, 871

You Can't Do That On Television, 871

Columbia Music Video Resources, 887

comedies

Beavis and Butthead, 872

Carol Burnett Show Episode Guide, 873

Comedy Store Fan Club Home Page, 874

New Web Site of Love Mystery Science Theatre 3000, 877

R.M.P.S.S., 878

Saturday Night Archives, 878

TV Nation, 879

Whose Line Is It Anyway?, 879

Comedy Central, 887

CourtTV Home Page, 592

dramas

Chicago Hope Home Page, 879

Dangerous Minds, 879

Dead At 21, 879

Dr. Quinn, Medicine Woman Official Web Site, 879

ER, 880

Little House on the Prairie Unofficial Home Page, 880

Moose's Guide to Northern Exposure, 880

My So-Called Life, 880

NYPD Blue Home Page, 880

Party of Five, 880

Perry Mason Pages, 880

Real World, 880

thirtysomething Episode Guide, 880

Twin Peaks Lodge, 880

Unofficial Picket Fences Home Page, 881

educational

Bill Nye the Science Guy's Nye Labs Online, 881

Biography, 881

Building America—Eye On Business, 881

Collecting Across America, 881

CTN, 881

Doctor Is In, 881

Great Canadian Parks, 881

Joy of Painting with Bob Ross, 881

Newton's Apple, 881

No Dogs or Philosophers Allowed, 881

Where in the World Is Carmen Sandiego?, 882

Exxxtasy Adult Television, 797

games, Guess the Dictator and/or Television Sit-com Chara, 338

Indiana Jones WWW Page, 522

Lifetime Online, 544

listservs, 891-892

Museum of Television and Radio, 349

NBC's home page, 887

news

C-Span Networks, 882

CNN Newsroom, 882

newsgroups, 888-891

PBS Online, 887

personalities, 867

science fiction

Babylon 5 file Area, 882

Battlestar Galactica, 882

Broadsword, 882

Dark Shadows, 882

Dominion Sci-fi Channel, 882

Extraterrestrial Biological Entity (EBE) Page, 882

Forever Knight, 882

Hyperlight Enterprises, 882

Lurker's Guide to Babylon 5, 883

Planet X, 883

Sliders, 883

Songs of the Blue Bird, 883

Starship Portfolio, 883

Starship Store, 883

Tales from the Crypt, 883

Terminal X, 883

Trader 800 Trekker, 883

Trek Reviews Archive, 884

Siegel Group, Inc., 128

SITCOM Home Page, 351

sitcoms

Absolutely Fabulous, 871

ALF Page by Kyle, 872

Alice TV-Show Home Page, 872

All in the Family, 872

alt.tv.brisco-county, 872

America's Favorite Radio Station, 872

Andy Griffith Show, 872

Better Dead Than SMEG, 872

Bewitched, 696

Bewitched Home Page, 872

Blossom, 873

Bob Newhart Unofficial Homepage, 873

Bosom Buddies Home Page, 873

Boston Common, 873

Boy Meets World, 873

Café Nervosa, 873

California Dreams, 873

Caroline in the City, 873

Cheers Home Page, 873

Clueless, 874

C'mon, Get Happy!, 874

Common Law, 874

Critic, 874

Dinosaurs, 874

Dr. Katz, 874

Dream On, 874

Duckman!, 874

Eerie, Indiana, 874

Encyclopedia Brady, 874

Facts of Life Unofficial Home Page, 874

Family Ties, 874

Fawlty Towers Episode Guide, 875

The First Simpson Dating Game on the Web, 337

Fresh Prince of Bel-Air, 875

Friends, 875

Full House, 875

Get a Life Program Guide, 875

Get Smart Home Page, 875

Gilligan's Island, 875

Golden Girls, 875

Grace Under Fire, 875

Growing Pains, 875

Hangin' with Mr. Cooper Home Page, 875

Herman's Head, 875

Hogan's Heroes, 876

Home of Home Improvement Cyberfans, 876

Honeymooners Picture Depot, 876

Hudson Street Home Page, 876

Indispensable I Dream of Jeannie Page, 876

John Larroquette Show, 876

Kids In the Hall by Jeff, 876

Kramer—Fishing guide to the Stars, 686

Larry Sanders Show, 876

Mad About You, 876

Mad TV Home Page, 876

Mama's Family, 876

Maniac Mansion, 877

Married…With Children Home Page, 877

MASH Archives, 877

Mel Loves I Love Lucy, 877

Mook's the Simpsons Page, 877

Moon Over Parma, 877

Moonlighting, on the Web, 877

Murphy Brown, 877

My So-Called Life, 877

Nanny Unofficial Home Page, 877

Ned and Stacey Home Page, 877

NewsRadio Station, 878

Official Unofficial Seinfeld Page, 878

Parker Lewis Can't Lose, 878

Planet Wallywood One Liner Comedy Diner, 345

Red Green Show, 878

Roseanne, 878

Saved By The Bell, 878

Simpsons Source, 878

Single Guy ("How about something simple, like…"), 878

Sledge Hammer! Arsenal, 878

Spin City, 878

State's Virtual Whatever…, 878

Sup's Blackadder Page, 878

Third Page from the Official, 879

Townies, 879

Welcome Back, Kotter, 879

Wings, 879

Wonder Years, 879

soap operas

All My Children, 884

Another World Fan Club Official Home Page, 884

As the World Turns, 884

Bold and the Beautiful, 884

Days of Our Lives Page, 884

General Hospital, 884

Guiding Light, 884

One Life To Live: The History Page, 884

Soap Opera Pen Pal Page, 884

Young and the Restless, 884

talk shows

alt.fan.howard-stern, 884

alt.tv.talkshows.daytime, 884

alt.tv.talkshows.late, 885

Andy Richter: King of the Couch, 885

David Letterman, 885

Ed Sullivan Show, 885

FAQ-alt.tv.talkshows.late, 885

George and Alana Show Home Page, 885

Hereeeeeeeeee's Conan, 885

Late Late Show with Tom Snyder, 885

Later with Greg Kinnear, 885

Lauren Hutton, 885

Oprah Winfrey Show, 885

Politically Incorrect Unofficial Home Page, 886

Richard Bey Show, 886

Ricki Lake Show Home Page, 886

Rolonda, 886

Rosie O'Donnell Show, 886

Sony Pictures Before They Were Stars, 886

Tempestt, 886

Tonight Show with Jay Leno, 886

Unofficial Talk Soup Web Page, 886

Tooncers Web Page Fantasmic, 887

TV-5, 887

Ultimate TV List, 887

Vanderbilt Television News Archive, 887

Welcome to the BBC, 887

The X-Files, 695

Tennessee, Nashville Scene, 917

tennis

ATP Tour Home Page, 859

Tennis Country, 859

United States Tennis Association/ Mid-Atlantic Sect, 859

World Wide Web Tennis Server, 859

Texas

art, WORD-guide to the arts, The, 80

Texas Adoption Resource Exchange, 381

Texas, Austin, 918

Web Texas, 919

text, Web sites, 47

Text Encoding Initiative (TEI), 48

textiles

Amish Quilts, 498

Brief History of Quilting, 498

Computers and Quilting, 498

Counted Cross Stitch, Needlework, and Stitchery Page, 498

Creative Quilting, 498

International Web Exchange: Quilting Exchange, 499

Misc Quilting Information, 499

Quilting Page, 499

True PA Dutch Country Souvenir, 499

World Wide Quilting Page, 499

theater

Complete Works of William Shakespear, 350

Larry Stark's Theater Mirror, 351

London Theatre Guide-Online, 351

Index

musicals
    Les Miserables Home Page, 666
    On Broadway WWW Information Page, 666
    Rec.Arts.Theatre.Musicals, 666
    Sir Andrew Lloyd Webber, 666
New York City Theater, 351
New York's Capital District Theater Page, 351
Performing Arts Sites, 653
Raymond Interactive Theatre, Ltd., 335
Red Herring Productions, 351
SITCOM Home Page, 351
TenEyck Design Studio, 351
Triad Productions Presents, 351

thesauri
ARTFL Project: ROGET'S Thesaurus Search Form, 702
LC Thesaurus for Graphic Material: Topical Terms for Subject Access, 703

threading, newsgroups, 29
tickets, Tickets and Travel, Inc., 816
time wasters
Air Guitar, 343
Big Green Button, 343
Center for the Easily Amused, 343
Internet Squeegee Guy, 344
The Sneeze Page, 348
Spatula City, 346
Thinking Bob's Image of the Day, 346
Virtual Bubble Wrap, 341
Welcome to Find-the-Spam, 342

Toney, Allen, 71
tooltips, 25
tourism, *see* **travel**
toys
3-D Glasses, 806
Baby Joy Toys, 819
Cape Cod Teddy Bear, 478
Chemical Light Sticks, 519
Classifieds–Collectibles–Selling, 478
Dolls By Christine, 479
Fox Color and Light Home Page, 813
Haynet on the Web, 479
Just Matchbox!!, 480
Little Toy Store on the Net, 293
Moto-Mini Motorcycle Collectibles, 819
PGT Toys, 819
porcelain dolls
    Cottage Catalogs, 479
    Dream-Land Dollies!!!, 479

Stratton's Collector Toy Network, 819
teddy bears
    Web Mill Business District—Bears By The Sea, 482
    Web Mill Business District—Teddy Bear Directory, 482
Toys, 545
Virtual Toy Store, 819
Whispers in Time, 482
World Collectible Center, 492
World of Breyer Model Horses, 819

trademarks, 415
trading cards
East Coast Cards and Collectibles, 479
Jan-Ken-Po—The Trading Card Game for Kids of All Ages, 480
MOODY'S Sports Autographs and Memorabilia, 481
Perfect Image Sportscards and Memorabilia, 481
Sports, Collectibles, and Money, 482
SportsCards, Etc., 482
World Wide Collectors Digest—Your Collectibles Outlet, 482

train travel
Burlington Northern-Sante Fe, 911
Canadian National, 911
European Rail System, 911
Liberty's Amtrak Page, 911
Union Pacific Railroad Excursion Information, 911
VI Rail-Canada's Passenger Train Network, 911
Welcome to Amtrak's Station on the WWW, 912

training services
ACME Training, Inc., 327
Advanced Training Professionals, 327
American Management Association, 327
Ankarlo Training Group Home Page, 327
CaBiT Development, 327
Career Connection, 327
ClearWord Communications and Training, 327
Conceptual Systems, Inc., 328
Damar Group, 328
Image Maker, 328
InfoDesign Group, 328
Jacks Institute, 328
Logical Operations, 571
McKinley Group, Inc., 328
National Center for Tooling &

Precision Components, 328
Peritas Online, 328
Practical Management, Inc., 328
RootLearning, Inc., 328
Scaffold Training Institute, 328
Stressmaster, 329
Success Express Journal, 329
TLC Seminars, 329
Training Express, 329
Vital Learning Corporation, 329

trains
Amtrak, 897
Burlington Northern Santa Fe Corporation, 897
Grand Canyon Railway, 897
models
    C & M Train Depot, 490
    DP Industries Home Page, 490
    Florida's Largest Train Store, 490
    Interactive Model Railroad, 339
    Logic Rail Technologies, 490
    Model Railroad.Com, 490
    Palatine Hobby's Railroad Page, 490
    Roecks Railroad Concepts, 491
    RR Depot, 491
    Rutger Friberg's World of ModelRailroad Electronic, 491
    TraiNutz, 491

Transmission Control Protocol/Internet Protocol (TCP/IP), 6-10
transportation
listservs, 899-900
newsgroups, 899
transportation museums
Auto Museum at Wells, 896
Cole Land Transportation Museum, 896
Henry Ford Museum & Greenfield Village, 896
trauma
Emergency Preparedness Information eXchange, 436
Global Emergency Medicine Archives, 436
National Collegiate EMS Foundation Home Page, 436
Team Dispatch, 436
UTHSCSA Trauma Home Page, 436
travel
accommodations
    Inn Traveler-International Bed & Breakfast, 912
    Travel Web Search Page, 913
    TravelSearch, 913

adventure
  Adventure Travel, 901
  Adventure Travel for Women, 901
  Adventurous Traveler Bookstore, 599
  Alaska—Mt. McKinley, 901
  Alpine Guides Alaska, 901
  Arctic Adventours, Inc., 901
  Big Island Air, 901
  Eagle Canyon Airlines, 901
  EarthWise Journeys, 901
  Helinet Helicopter Tours, 901
  Mayuc—Ecological Tourism, 901
  New Brunswick, Canada Outdoor
    Adventures, 901
  Resort Sports Network, 901
  Safari Helicopters, 902
  Sierra Mountain Guides, 902
  Touring Exchange, 902
  TravelBase, 902
  Wildwest Travel, Inc., 902
AEE Wilderness Safety and Emer-
  gency Care, 448
airlines
  Above It All, 902
  Aer Lingus, 902
  Aeroflot, 902
  Air Canada, 902
  Air Charter Guide, 902
  Air Travel Card Control Tower, 902
  Air Traveler's Handbook, 913
  Air UK, 902
  Airlines of the Web, 902
  American Airlines, 902
  Ansett Australia, 903
  Canadian Airlines Intl., 903
  Cathay Pacific, 903
  Comair, 903
  Eagle Canyon Airlines, 903
  Emirates Airline Page, 903
  Finnair, 903
  Frontier Airlines, 903
  International Airport Codes, 903
  Lauda Air, 903
  Lufthansa Timetable Info, 904
  Mexicana Airlines, 904
  Mount Cook Airlines, 904
  New England Airlines, 904
  Quantas Airlines, 904
  Scenic Airlines, 904
  Virgin Atlantic Airlines, 904
America's Best, 912
automobile travel
  ASIRT-Association for International
    Road Travel, 904-905
  Bumper Stickers, 904

  National Auto League, 904
  Rental Agencies, 904
  Route 66, 904
  Scenic Byways and Other Recre-
    ational Drives, 904
  Traveling in the USA, 904
Bolack Total Travel Academy, 321
Canada, Exposure Excursions, 782
City Net, 912
Comprehensive Healthcare for
  International and Wilderness
  Travelers, 448
cruises
  Accent's Cruise Connection, 905
  Adventure Cruising in the North
    Atlantic, 905
  Cruise Review Library, 905
  Cruise Shoppes America, Ltd., 905
  Cruises Inc., 905
  Freighter World Cruises, 905
  Norwegian Cruise Line, 905
  Royal Caribbean Cruise Line, 906
  Travel Discounts Cruise Index, 906
domestic, Southern California Real
  Time Traffic Report, 348
DOSFAN: Department of State
  Foreign Affairs Networ, 417
Earthwise Travels, 369
Electronic Embassy, 913
exchange rates
  Currency Exchange Rates, 913
  ELVIS+, Co., 914
  GNN/Koblas Money Converter, 914
FH, Canada Travel Home Page, 601
GNN Travel Center, 912
HealthNet, 448
Healthy Flying, 448
hiking, 849
Information about Duty Free/Tax
  Free Shopping, 914
international
  Air Brokers International World
    Travel Specialist, 906
  Alchemy of Africa, 906
  Ansett Australia, 906
  Antigua & Barbuda, 906
  Australia Travel Directory, 906
  Automated Travel Center, 906
  Brochure Flow, 906
  Civilized Explorer, 907
  Costa Travel Online, 907
  Council Travel, 907
  Country Maps of Europe, 907
  Cyprus, 907
  Czech Info Center, 907

  Dublin Pub Review, 907
  Endeavour Travel, 907
  European and British Rail Passes,
    907
  Eurostar Internet, 907
  Far & Away Travel Services, 907
  FranceEscape, 907
  Freesun News, 908
  Going to Belgium, 908
  Great Australian Travel Co., 908
  Hong Kong Online Guide, 908
  Indonesia, 908
  InteleTravel International, 908
  Interactive Travel Guide, 914
  International Travel Agency (ITA),
    908
  International Traveler's Clinic, 914
  Internet Guide to Hostels, 908
  Intra Travel, 908
  Jerusalem Mosaic, 908
  Jordan, 908
  Lanka Internet Services, 908
  Lonely Planet Travel Centre, 908
  Middle World, 908
  Monaco Home Page, 909
  Round-The-World Travel Guide, 912
  Salzburg, Austria, 909
  Sinbad Travel, 909
  TGV French High Speed Train, 909
  Tour Canada without Leaving Your
    Desk, 909
  Tourist Office of Spain Homepage,
    909
  Travel Home, 909
  Travel to Finland, 909
  United Kingdom Pages, 909
  Vancouver, British Columbia, 909
  Victoria, British Columbia, 909
  Welcome to Future Net—
    Queensland, Australia, 909
islands
  American's Caribbean Paradise, 910
  Bahamas Online, 910
  CaribWeb, 910
  Charlotte's Caribbean Connection,
    910
  Maui Interactive, 910
  NetWeb Bermuda Home Page, 910
language, Foreign Language for
  Travelers, 914
listservs, 920-921
lodging
  American Youth Hostels, 910
  Bed & Breakfast Inns Online, 910

California Travel and Parks Association, 910
Campground Directory, 910
Choice Hotels, 910
Homeless Shelters in the United States, 910
Hostelling International, 911
International Bed And Breakfast Guide, 911
Nude 2000, 911
Professional Association of Innkeepers Internation, 911
Travel Web, 911
United Hostels of Europe, 911
World Wide Lodging Guide, 911
Net Traveler, 603
newsgroups, 920
North American Virtual Tourist, 912
Outdoor Action Guide to High Altitude Acclimatization and Illness, 448
publications
Adventurous Traveler Bookstore, 905
Condé Nast Traveler, 600
Moon Publications, 448
Travel Publications, 905
TravelASSIST Magazine, 604
Traveler's Book Club, 905
Travels with Samantha, 905
World of Maps, 905
railroads, Railroad Timetables, 914
rec.travel.library, 912
SABRE Decision Technologies, 133
Sunglasses, Shavers, and More Home Page, 819
TII-Tourism Info Internet, 912
Tough Traveler Gear, 816
train travel
Burlington Northern-Sante Fe, 911
Canadian National, 911
European Rail System, 911
Liberty's Amtrak Page, 911
Union Pacific Railroad Excursion Information, 911
VI Rail-Canada's Passenger Train Network, 911
Welcome to Amtrak's Station on the WWW, 912
Travel, 909
Travel & Entertainment Networ (TEN-10) Home Page, 912
Travel Discounts, 914
Travel First Aid Kit, 448
Travel Information, 912
Travel Online, 912
Travel Page, 913

Travel Web Sites, 914
Travel Weekly, 604
Traveler's Diarrhea, 448
Traveler's Japanese with Voice, 303
Traveler's Medical and Immunization Service, 448
TravelSource, 913
U.S. Travel and Tourism Administration, 415
United States
Access New Hampshire, 914
ACUMUG-Arkansas index of Internet Resources, 915
Alabama, 915
Alaska Information Cache, 915
Allons! Acadiana, 915
America's Land of Enchantment, 915
AMI News-Recreation and Travel, 915
Arizona Guide, 915
Atlanta Web Guide, 915
Boston Area Map of WWW Resources, 915
California, 915
Cambridge, Massachusetts, 915
Chicago Information Sytem, 916
CLEVE.NET, 916
Clickable Connecticut Area Map, 916
Grand Rapids, Michigan, 916
Greensboro Online, 916
HobokenX, 916
Idaho Home Page, 916
Indiana Virtual Tourist, 916
Information Access Websites, 916
Iowa Virtual Tourist, 917
Kentucky Network Services, 917
Las Vegas, 917
Los Angeles Traffic Report, 917
Maine WWW Resources, 917
Minneapolis, 917
Missouri WWW Resources, 917
Nashville Scene, 917
Nebraska Travel and Tourism, 917
Oklahoma Image Map, 917
Oregon Online, 917
Palo Alto, California, 917
Peaks-An Online Magazine About Montana, 917
RING.Online, 918
Santa Barbara County, 918
South Carolina Supernet-LocalNet, 918
South Dakota World Wide Web Site, 918

St. Louis, Missouri, 918
Staunton, Virginia, 918
Texas, Austin, 918
U/Seattle, 918
United States State Department Travelers Warnings and Consular Info Sheets, 914
USA CityLink, 918
Utah! Travel and Adventure Online, 918
Vail Valley Home Page, 918
Vermont/New Hampshire WWW Resources, 918
VISIT Virginia, 919
Washington DC City Pages, 919
Washington State Online Travel Information, 919
Web Texas, 919
Weekend Getaways, 919
Welcome to the Ohio Web, 919
West Virginia Web, 919
Yankee Traveler, 913
Virtual Tourist II, 913
Web Travel Review, 914
Webfoot's Travel Guides, 913
WL: The World Library From Scescape, 913
World Wide Drugs, 449
trivia
Kooks Museum, 339
The Oracle of Bacon at Virginia, 345
The Rock and Roll Hall of Shame, 346
Rock Mall's Trivia Challenge, 340
sports, Quick Stats Service, 853
Star Trek: The Next Generation—The Daily Test, 341
Today's Fun Fact, 713
trivia games
The Daily 100, 337
Makin Bacon, 339
trucks
European Trucks, 897
off-road
4WD: Four Wheel Drive and All Wheel Drive, 895
America's 4×4 4U Video Magazine, 895
My Jeep Adventures, 895
Off-Road.com, 895
organizations, American Truck Historical Society, 896
Sport Trucks, 897
Truck Safety Page, 897
Trucking Times, 897

Tunick, Connie, 84

Turkey, Turkish Music Home Page, 659

turtles, Viva La Tortuga!, 374

tutorials, Gestalt Systems, Inc., 560

typography, Serif, The Magazine of Type & Typography, 604

U

U.S. Air Force, Airbase, 321

U.S. Patent and Trademark Office, 135

U.S. Soccer Web Pages, 858

UEWeb, 296

UFOs

    8-Tracks and UFOs, 693

    Alien Bob's Command Post, 693

    Alien Information, 693

    Area 51, 694

    Aufora—The Alberta UFO Research Association, 694

    BUFORA—British UFO Research, 694

    Conspiracy Pages, 694

    Flying Saucer Review, 694

    Internet UFO Group—Government, 694

    Jody's "ET Phone-Home!" Page, 694

    PBS' Nova Solves UFO and Alien Abduction Phenomena, 694

    Roswell UFO Crash Page, 694

    Smitty's UFO Page, 694

    Stan Friedman's UFO Page, 694

    UFO Books—The Serious Literature, 694

    UFO Sightings by Astronauts, 695

    Unidentified Flying Objects, 695

Ukraine, Ukrainian Stamps, 498

Uniform Resource Locators (URLs), 15

United Kingdom

    Air UK, 902

    Ain't Whistlin' Dixie, 656

    Blue Planet, 348

    BritSpeak: English as a Second Language for Americans, 704

    Diving Server, 856

    GROW-Opportunity Wales, 304

    London Theatre Guide-Online, 351

    motorcycle racing, 855

    Noel Ford Cartoonist/Illustrator/Author, 77

    Open University, 302

    Welcome to the BBC, 887

United Nations, 418

United States

    Almanac of American Politics, 416

    American Airlines, 903

    American Civilization Homepage, 537

    American Political Network, 416

    American Voter '96, 416

    Archaeology at Mt. Vernon Plantation, 521

    Betsy Ross Homepage, 705

    census

        1990 U.S. Census Lookup, 702

        TIGER Mapping Service, 702

        U.S. Gazetteer, 702

    Color Landform Atlas of the United States, 710

    Community Learning Network, 301

    Constitution of the United States of America, 593

    CRLP: Women of the World, 542

    Department of the Treasury of the United States, 487

    E Pluribus Unum, 487

    embassies

        Electronic Embassy, 417

        Embassy Page, 418

    Federal Geographic Data Committee (FGDC), 527

    Flag of the United States of America, 706

    Flag-Burning Page, 706

    foreign policy

        DOSFAN: Department of State Foreign Affairs Network, 417

    GEOGRAPHY USA: A Virtual Textbook, 527

    government agencies

        National Criminal Justice Reference Service (NCJRS), 540

        National Endowment for the Humanities (NEH), 525

        U.S. Agency for International Development, 541

    Happy Birthday, America!, 707

    history

        Abraham Lincoln Online, 459

        American and British History Resources, 455

        American Civilization Internet Resources, 455

        American Memory, 455

        American Revolution and the Struggle for Independence, 455

        American Studies Web, 455

        Anti-Imperialism in the United States, 1898–1935, 455

        Educational Sources for George Washington, 459

        Fair Play, 460

        Indiana Historical Society, 455

        JFK Resources Online, 460

        Life Histories—American Memory Project, 456

        Medals of America, 481

        Thomas Jefferson, 460

        Thomas Paine, 460

        United States Presidents: Welcome Page, 460

        United States—History, 456

    HotList of K-12 Internet School Sites, 300

    International Association of Constitutional Law, 590

    Minority Business Development Agency, 414

    National Archives and Records Administration, 709

    National Association of Patent Practitioners, 714

    National Endowment for the Arts, 414

    National Flag Foundation, 706

    National Humanities Institute Home Page, 525

    national parks

        Humanities Report, 525

        NPFauna and NPFlora, 484

        National Park Service: Links to the Past—Archaeology, 522

    NATO: The North Atlantic Treaty Organization, 418

    political parties

        College Democrats of America, 419

        College Republican National Committee Homepage, 419

        Democratic Caucus, 419

        Democratic National Committee, 419

        Independence/Reform Party, 419

        Libertarian Party Headquarters, 419

        Republican National Committee, 419

        Republicans Abroad International, 419

        Young Democrats of America, 419

        Young Republican National Federation Homepage, 419

    politics

        Institute for Propaganda Analysis, 539

    Save Old Glory From Flames Home Page, 706

    Social Security On Line, 414

    Sovereign Patriot Group, 590

    Study in the USA Online Directory, 303

    Thomas: The U. S. Congress, 414

TIGER Mapping Service, 529

Travels with Samantha, 496

U.S. 1995 Stamp Program, 498

U.S. Civil Rights Code, 541

U.S. Department of Agriculture, 414

U.S. Department of Commerce: Stat-USA, 414

U.S. Department of Education, 414

U.S. Department of Energy, 414

U.S. Department of Health and Human Services, 415

U.S. Department of Housing and Urban Development, 415

U.S. Department of Justice, 415

U.S. Department of Labor, 415

U.S. Department of the Interior, 415

U.S. Department of Transportation, 415

U.S. Patent and Trademark Office, 415, 714

U.S. Postal Service, 415

U.S. Travel and Tourism Administration, 415

United States Senate WWW Server, 415

veterans affairs

   American Legion, 830

   Baudo's Vet Links, 830

   Department of Veterans Affairs, 830

   Military Family Institute, 830

   Veterans Archive, 830

   Vietnam Veterans Home Page, 830

Web sites, accessing, 16

Welcome to the Council of the Great City Schools Online, 305

West

   Cyberwest Magazine, 600

   High Country News Home Page, 601

White House Home Page, 415

universities

College and University Home Page, 573

College Athletics WWW Pages, 852

College Football WWW Site, 847

College Prep Page, 307

College Sports Internet Channel, 847

Faculty of Asian Studies, Australian National University, 304

FindLaw: Law Schools of Canada, 589

FindLaw: US News Top 25 Law Schools, 589

ILRG: Brennan's Law School Rankings, 589

Indiana University School of Music, 652

Irish Sports Report, 852

IUB Libraries: Research Collections and Services Department, 306

La Trobe University Art Museum, 86

Law Student Web, 589

Ohio State University at Newark, 87

Okanagan University College, Department of Fine Arts, 87

Open University, 302

Princeton Review: Law School and the LSAT, 589

Sonoma State University Alumni Art Exhibition, 88

South Dakota Archaeology, 524

SWITCH—Swiss Academic and Research Network, 572

Syracuse University Computer Graphics for the Visual Arts, 78

UCSB Anthropology Web Site, 520

University of California, Berkeley, University Art Museum, 79

University of Chicago Press Anthropology and Archaeology Catalog, 520

University of Manitoba Anthropology Department, 520

University of Oregon , Farg's Cost Accounting Home Page, 130

University of Pennsylvania Arthur Ross Gallery Home Page, 83

University of Tennessee Sculpture Tour, 88

University of Wyoming Art Museum, 88

UTLink: Resources by Subject, 714

UVa AnthroNet, 520

Vanderbilt Television News Archive, 887

Virginia Commonwealth University (VCU) Arts Home Page, 79

Yale Law School Homepage, 589

university presses, *see* **publishers**

UNIX

Florida Tech HELP DESK, 235

This Week's Popular UNIX Downloads, 236

upholstering, *see* **furniture**

URLs (Uniform Resource Locators), 15

Usenet newsgroups, 9, 21, 28

advertising, 19

etiquette, 705

user groups, 268

Utah

BYU Performing Arts Management, 73

Powder Hound Ski Report, 857

Utah! Travel and Adventure Online, 918

Wasatch Powderbird Guides, 857

utilities, North American Power Brokers, 132

uuencode, 26

V

vegetarian food

BabyfishNet's Vegan Recipes, 407

FATFREE Vegetarian Mailing List Archive, 403

Gardenburger, 407

Kitchens of Gordon Bleu, 404

People's Place, 428

Tamilian Cuisine, 407

U.S. Soyfoods Directory, 408

Vegetarian Pages, 408

Veggies Unite!, 408

Whole Foods Market, 408

World Guide To Vegetarianism, 408

Vermont

Northern Vermont X-Country, Backcountry, and Telemark Skiing, 857

Vermont/New Hampshire WWW Resources, 918

veterans affairs

American Legion, 830

Baudo's Vet Links, 830

Department of Veterans Affairs, 830

Military Family Institute, 830

Veterans Archive, 830

Vietnam Veterans Home Page, 830

veterinary medicine, 785

victim support

National Victim Center, 825

Rape Victim Advocates, 826

Videodiscovery, 296

videography

After Hours Media Duplication Service, 809

Charleston: A Magical History Tour, 811

Punch & Brodie Productions, 809

Sports Videos, 853

Videomaker's Camcorder & Desktop Video Site.i.magaz, 605

Virtual Media, 342

Wedding Bell Blueprint, 925

viewing capabilities, browsers, 47

vintage clothing
Rusty Zipper—Vintage Clothing on the Web, 481

Virginia
Staunton, Virginia, 918
VISIT Virginia, 919

virtual environments
Cyber City '96, 347
Desiderata—The Reststop, 352
Electric Saloon, 352
Enterprise City Home Page, 352
Mariam's Cyberspace Park, 352
Social Cafe, 352
Tin Cup Coffee House, 352
Virtual Vegas, 352
World of Paths Headquarters, 352

virtual reality
Brief Tour of Our Universe!, 751
Virtual AdVentures, 818

Virtual Reality Modeling Language (VRML), 6, 12

Visual Basic
Banana Report Easy Visual Basic Tips, 567

visually impaired
E-Zee Vision™ Prescription Eyeglasses, 429
Introduction to Vision Correcting Procedures by Med-Source, Inc., 434
Vision Impairments, A Guide for the Perplexed, 435

vitamins, *see* **nutrition**

volleyball, 859

voodoo
African Religion Syncretism, 695
Electric Gallery-Voodoo Flags, 695
New Look at Juju, 695
Primer on Voodoo, 695
Role of the Patient's Religion in Healthcare Setting, 695
Voodoo, 695
Voodoo and Cemeteries, 696
Voodoo Culture in the US Bibliography, 696
Voodoo Information Pages, 696
Voodoo Museum, 696
Voodoo Products and Information, 696
Voodoo Queen, 696
Voodoo-Angelique Kidjo, 695
Voodoo: From Medicine to Zombies, 696
VoodooTour—A Cultural Trip to Benin, 696

voting, *see* **politics**

VRML (Virtual Reality Modeling Language), 6, 12, 44
David B. Martin's VRML Page, 566

W

Wales, Ceolas Celtic Music Archive, 657

walking canes, Island Imports, Ltd., 480

wallcoverings, *see* **interior decorating**

war simulation games, 171

Washington
Bird Guide, Inc., 484
U/Seattle, 918
Washington State Online Travel Information, 919

Washington D.C.
Washington DC City Pages, 919

Washington, George, 459

Washington state
Mount St. Helens, 294
Scott Freeman's Underwater Photography Page, 496

watches, Akteo Watch Boutique, 71

water polo, 852

waterskiing, 858

weather forecasts, *see* **meteorology**

Web
advertising, 7
Berners-Lee, Tim, 4
browsers, 11, 41
   AIR Mosaic, 53
   Cello, 53
   HTML 3.2 support, 43
   Lynx, 54
   Microsoft Internet Explorer, 51-52
   NCSA Mosaic 2.1.1, 51
   NetCruiser, 54
   Netscape Navigator 2.0, 50
   Netscape Navigator Gold 2.0, 51
   operating systems, 42
   SlipKnot, 54
   Spyglass Enhanced Mosaic, 52
   TCP/IP connections, 41
CERN (European Particle Physics Laboratory), 4
FAQs (Frequently Asked Questions), 19
growth, 7
hardware requirements, 31
history, 4-5
hypermedia documents, 11
HyperText Transfer Protocol (HTTP), 11
modems, 32
navigators, 46

publishing
5 Top Internet Marketing Successes of 1994, 576
Artzilla Surf Constructions, 576
Building Web Servers, 576
Carter & Associates WEB Studios, 576
Copyright Website, 576
CRAYON—CReAte Your Own Newspaper, 568
Dunn & Edwards Services, 577
Dynamic Diagrams Home Page, 577
Four Lakes Colorgraphics, Inc., 577
Free Range Media, Inc., 577
FRS Associates Training and Education Division, 577
Garry's Web Services, 577
Gates, Jeff, 577
Headquarters.Com Internet, 577
Hijinx, 577
Home Space Builder, 577
Hourglass Internet Services, 577
HudsoNet, 577
Hyper Design Technologies, 577
Iconomics, 578
Image Alchemy Digital Imaging, 578
Image Compression for Publishing Online, 578
Image House Digital Photography Studio, 578
imedia, 578
Infowerks Creative Web Services, 578
Integra Software Corp., 578
Inter//Web Development, 578
INTERCAT, 578
Interglobal Mutltimedia, 578
International Business Center, 578
Internet Advertising Solutions, 578
Internet Business Connection, 578
Internet Pilots, 578
Knossopolis, 571
Making Money on Internet, 579
Manhattan MultiMedia, Inc., 579
MediaBox Communications, 579
Metrotel Multi-Media Ltd, 579
MFD Consult, 579
MGL Systems, 579
Moshofsky/Plant Creative Services, 579
MultiMedia Dimensions—New Horizons in Sight and Sound, 579
NetCasters, Inc., 579
new3, Inc., 579

Program One Online Service, 579
RAMWORKS, 579
Stannet WWW Designing and Publishing Company, 580
Vannevar New Media, 580
Web Developer, 580
WebDesigns, 580
Winfield Design Group, 580
World Wide exPRess, 580
WorldWide Information and Netcasting Services, 580
servers, 7, 15
sites, 7
accessing, 17
downloading, 50
forms, 21
graphics, 49
mirror, 18
non-U.S., 16
text, 47
United States, 16
software requirements, 34
Uniform Research Locator (URL), 11
Web culture
Cruel Site of the Day, 343
The Daily Double Awards, 343
Internet Advertising Hall of Shame, 344
Mirky's Worst of the Web, 345
Top Ten Ways to Tell if You Have a Sucky Home Page, 346
weddings
African
Melanet Online African Wedding, 927
attire
Ans Bolk Personal Design Bridal Couture, 926
Bridal Veil Home Page, 926
Dessy Creations Home Page, 926
Elegant Bride, 924
Hora Bridal Accessories, 926
Imagi-Nations, 926
Sposabella Bridal-La Sposa Veil, 926
Watters and Watters, 926
gifts
Bridal Gallery, 923
Bridal Net: Online Bridal Registry, 923
Club Wed Press, 923
Groom's Gift Collection, 923
Historical Wedding Invitations, 923
Peachtree Circle Inc., 923
Personal Wedding Pages on the Net, 923

Sophisticated Chocolates, 923
Wedding Center, 923
Wedding Decorations and Gifts, 923
Wedding Marketplace, 923
Wedding Registries Directory, 923
honeymoons
Caribmoon, 925
Coconut Coast Weddings and Honeymoons, 926
Island Weddings, SuperClubs, 925
Wedding Gardens, 925
Wedding Made in Paradise, 925
listservs, 929
newsgroups, 929
photography, Wedding Bell Blueprint, 925
planning
Alt.Wedding Home Page, 924
American Humanist Association, 924
Automatic Wedding Speech Writer, 924
Bridal Expo Online, 926
Bride and Groom's World Wedding Fair, 924
Bride's Page, 924
Celebration Vineyards, 924
Collected Domestic Partners Information, 924
Emily Post's Complete Guide to Weddings, 927
I Do, 924
Leslie's Guide to Wedding Planning, 927
My Wedding Companion, 927
Ninga Software Corporation: "The Wedding Planner," 927
Northwest Wedding Network, 927
Pagan Wedding, 927
Rialto Archive: Period and SCA Weddings, 924
Same-Sex Marriage Home Page, 924
Simply Software: "Bridesmaids for Windows," 927
soc.couples. wedding WWW Page, 924
TouchSoft: "I Do Ultimate Wedding Planner," 927
Way Cool Wedding Every Week, 925
Wedding Bells, 925
Wedding Circle Home Page, 925
Wedding Source, 925
Wedding Spot, 925
Wedding Web Home Page, 927
Wedding Wise, 927
Weddings by IPS, 928

Weddings Online, The Internet's Wedding Information, 925
Weddings with Makana, 926
WedNet-The Wedding Network, 928
rings, NetDiamonds, Inc., 926
weight loss
AromaTrim Weight Loss System, 430
Body/Mind Restoration Retreats 1996, 430
CyberDiet, 431
Fat Person's Home Page, 431
FITE-Fat is the Enemy, 431
Health Vision, 431
International No Diet Day, 431
Magic of Believing, 431
Medical Sciences Bulletin, 431
Michael D. Myers MD Inc./Myers Information Service, 431
Modern Methods—Fat Burning Specialists, 431
Nutri/System Online, 431
NutriGenie, 438
TOPS—Take Off Pounds Sensibly, 431
Weight Watchers, 431
West Virginia
Brooke High WWW Server, 299
West Virginia Web, 919
whales
Canada Whale Watching, 64
Sea Creations, 482
Welcome to the Tirpitz Whaling Web Page, 64
Whale Adoption Project Home Page, 64
Whale and Dolphin Conservation Society, 309
Whale Information Network, 64
Whale Songs, 64
Whale Watching Web, 64
wicca
The Hazelnut, 696
Satanism and the History of Wicca, 697
Witchcraft (Wicca), 697
Witch's Brew—For All of Mother's Children, 698
wildlife
Adam's Fox Box, 64-66
Antarctica and Its Environment, 64
art, 72
Bear Den, The, 65
Cochrane Wildlife Reserve, 65
Deer Net, 65
Eastern Slop Grizzly, 65

Frontier Technologies's Lion Gallery, 65
GORP–Nature & Wildlife, 65
Hyenas, 65
Introduced Wild Animals in Australia, 65
Kaehler's Mill Farm, 65
Kids's Action: Rainforest Animals, 66
Lion Pictures of the Month, 66
LlamaWeb, 66
Manatees, 66
OSU's Breeds of Livestock, 66
Polar Regions, 66
Turtle Trax–A Marine Turtle Page, 66
Wolf Resource Page, 66
Wolf Studies Project, 66
Wolf's Den: Home Page of Wolf McSherry, 66
Wombats, Marsupials, and Other Animals, 66
Wonderful Skunk and Opposum Page, 66
World Wide Raccoon Web, 66

wind energy, *see* **energy**

windmills, 765

window blinds, *see* **interior decorating**

Windows
ColorEditor for Windows, 566
CSUSM Windows World, 568
FLFSoft, Inc. Home Page, 568
Information Management Group, 561
Openstep for Windows, 235
Winsock Connections, 562

Windows 95
configuring Internet, 38-40
OS/2 versus Windows 95-Battle for Operating System Domination, 236
Randy's Windows 95 Resource CenterDescribes in deta, 236
Windows95 InterNetworking Headquarters, 573
WWW.WIN.COM, 235

windsurfing, *see* **surfing**

wine
American Wine, 599
Celebration Vineyards, 393
Cyber Grape and Grain, 393
Grapevine, 394
Internet Wine Rack, 394
Napa Valley Virtual Visit, 394
SmartWine Online, 395
Virtual Vineyards, 395, 396
Wines on the Internet, 396
World Wide Web Winemaking Home Page, 396

winter sports, 859

witchcraft
About Witchcraft, 696
Aunt Agatha's Occult Emporium, 690
Bewitched, 696
The Hazelnut, 696
Killing of Witches-A Chronicle of the Burning Time, 697
Necronomi.com—The Familiar Spirit BBS, 690
Occult Page, 690
Ooga Booga Page, 688
Rosegate—The Council of Elders, 697
Satanism and the History of Wicca, 697
Strand by Strand, 697
What about Witches, 697
Witchcraft, 697
Witchcraft (Wicca), 697
Witchcraft in Salem, 697
Witchcraft: Some Answers for the Curious, 697
Witches League for Public Awareness, 697
Witch's Brew—For All of Mother's Children, 698
see also occult; wicca

women, 796
Adoptions Connections Project: Women's Journeys, 379
Adventure Travel for Women, 901
artists, Cyberbabe, 80
Body Politic, 796
cycling, WOMBATS on the Web, 843
health care
Atlanta Reproductive Health Centre, 449
Avon's Breast Cancer Awareness Crusade, 449
Breast Cancer Information, 449
Bright Innovations, 449
Emergency Contraception, 449
Endometriosis, 449
Health and Science, 449
Health Articles by Patricia Older, 449
Labor of Love, 449
OB/GYN Toolbox, 449
S.P.O.T., 449
Women of the World, 449
WomenCare, 449
WomenSpace, 449
history, Diotima: Women & Gender in the Ancient World, 457

Largesse, The Network for Size Esteem, 431
Muse Magazine, 603
SoccerNews Online, 858
Social Cafe, 352
Women in Higher Education, 297

women's studies
American Association of University Women (AAUW), 542
Celebration of Women Writers, 542
Center for the American Woman and Politics (CAWP), 542
Center for Women's Global Leadership (CWGL), 542
Centre for Women's Studies in Education (CWSE), 542
Colleen's Feminism Home Page, 542
CRLP: Women of the World, 542
Cybergrrl Webstation, 542
Diotima: Women & Gender in the Ancient World, 542
Electronic Access to Research on Women: A short Guide, 2nd Edition, 543
Encyclopedia of Women's History, 542
Expect the Best from a Girl, 543
Feminism and Women's Resources, 543
Feminist Bookstores, 543
Feminist Majority Online, 543
Feminist Science Fiction, Fantasy, & Utopia, 543
Feminist Studies in Aotearoa Electronic Journal (FMST), 543
FEMINIST.COM, 543
Gender Equity in Sports, 543
Global Fund for Women, 543
Guerrilla Girls, 543
Her Own Words®, 544
InforM Women's Studies Database, 544
Internet Resources for Women's Legal and Public Policy Information, 544
Isis, 544
Legal Rights of Women, 544
Library Resources for Women's Studies, 544
Lifetime Online, 544
Linkages FOURTH WORLD CONFERENCE ON WOMEN site, 544
National Organization for Women (NOW), 544

Resources for Feminist Research/ Documentation sur la recherche féministe (RFR/DRF), 544

Spinsters Ink, 545

United Nations and the Status of Women, 545

VOWworld: Voices of Women, 545

WIDNET (Women In Development NETwork), 545

Women & Politics Home Page, 545

Women Leaders Online (WLO), 545

Women's Books Online, 545

Women's History Month, 545

Women's Studies Reference Roadmap, 545

Women's Wire, 545

WomensNet @igc, 546

WomenSpace, 546

World's Women On-Line!, 546

Yale Journal of Law and Feminism, 546

woodworking

Arbortech, 499

Carleton Woodworking, 499

Chris Melhorn's Woodworking Gallery, 499

Construction Zone, 506

Essex Wood Products, 812

Furniture Repair and Refinishing Wizard, 487

Hartmann House Antiques, 488

LIBERON/Star Finishing Supplies, 488

North American Refinisher'sAssociation, 488

Oak Factory Bulletin Board, 499

Prairie Woodworking, 499

Professional Woodgraining Kits, 507

Quality Woodwork & Supply, Inc., 507

Quality Woodwork and Supply, Inc., 499

Technical Guidelines, Finishing Schedules & Product Information, 488

W5: Woodworking on the World Wide Web, 500

WoodLink, 500

Woods of the World, 500

WoodWeb, 500

Woodworking Catalog, 507

Woodworking in Western Montana, 500

word games, Boggle, 336

word generators

Complaint Letter Generator, 337

The Crystal Ball, 337

The Cyrano Server, 337

Dave's Web of Lies, 343

Evil Little Brother's Excuse Generator, 344

The First Simpson Dating Game on the Web, 337

Guess the Dictator and/or Television Sit-com Character, 338

Handy Spanish Phrase, 338

Heretical Rhyme Generator, 338

The Insult Page, 338

Joe's Amazing Relationship Problem Solver, 339

Mark's Apology Note Generator, 340

Penny's Skulls of Fate, 345

Personalized Shakespearean Insult Service, 345

PhoNETic, 340

Pig Latin Converter, 340

Random '80s Lyrics, 655

Random Band Name, 655

Random Elizabethan Curse Generator, 345

Random Topic Generator, 340

Supermarket Tabloid Headlines, 348

Test Borkifier, 341

The Textual Abuse Page, 346

The Dog Ate my Homework—1,001 excuses for Home, Work, and Play, 343

The Ultimate Oracle—Pray Before the Head of Bob, 341

WWW Anagram Generator, 342

The WWW Fortune Cookie Machine, 342

world hunger, World Neighbors, 541

world music

Abayudaya Jews in Uganda: Music, 656

Afro-Caribbean Music, 656

Afropop Worldwide, 656

Ain't Whistlin' Dixie, 656

Ari Davidow's Klezmer Page, 657

Australian Music World Wide Web Site, 657

Bali & Beyond Home Page, 657

Batish Institute of Indian Music and Fine Arts, 657

Celtic Music Index Page, 657

Ceolas Celtic Music Archive, 657

Chinese Music Page, 657

Clannad WWW Home Page, 657

Classical Music Home Page N.S.Sundar, 657

Cuban Music, 657

Enya—Unofficial World Wide Web Home Page, 666

Flamenco Home Page, 658

Hindi Movie Songs, 658

Home Page of MT&C Music Club, 658

Indian Classical Music, 658

Indian Music Recordings and Instruments, 658

Indonesian Music, 658

Irish Folk Songs, 658

Larry Aronson Home Page, 658

MIZIK, 658

Musi-Cal Performer Index, 660

Music from Africa and the African Diaspora, 658

Northern Journey: Canadian Folk, 658

Rashid Sales Co., 658

Richard Robinson's Tunebook, 659

Roots/World Music FAQ, 659

RootsWorld: Music on the Net, 659

Russian Music, 659

Samba in Sweden, 659

Sami's Urdu/Hindi Film Music Page, 659

Shona Music, 659

Some Peruvian Music, 659

T. M. McComb: Music Home Page, 653

Tara: The World of Jewish Music, 659

Temple Records, 659

TuneWeb, 659

Turkish Music Home Page, 659

WOMEX '96, 659

World Music/Boston, 660

World Wide Web (WWW), *see* **Web**

wormholes, 754

wrestling, 854

writers, *see* **authors; books**

writing

Inkspot, 308

Internet Writer Resource Guide, 602

Writing at MU, 308

Writing the Information Superhighway, 563

WWW (World Wide Web), *see* **Web**

Y-Z

yoga, Karma and Reincarnation—Yoga, 691

Zimbabwe, Shona Music, 659

ZIP codes

Geographic Nameserver, 716

National Address and ZIP+4 Browser, 716

United States Postal Service, 717

Zipper, 717

zoology

Absearch, 785

AlpacaNet, 785

American Association of Zoo Keepers, 361

Cornell Ornithology Collection, 785

Electronic Zoo, 785

Insect Behavior Group, 785

NetVet Veterinary Resources, 785

NetVet Veterinary Resources and the Electronic Zoo, 785

Virtual Emu, 785

Zoological Record, 785

Zoology Department, 785

zoos

National Zoological Park Home Page, 57

Neopolis Zoo, 57

San Diego Wild Animal Park, 57

Sea World/Busch Gardens, 57

Singapore Zoological Gardens, 57

Terry Polk's Zoological E-mail Directory, 57

Zoo, 57

ZooNet, 57

Index

Check Us Out Online!

New Riders has emerged as a premier publisher of computer books for the professional computer user. Focusing on CAD/graphics/multimedia, communications/internetworking, and networking/operating systems, New Riders continues to provide expert advice on high-end topics and software.

Check out the online version of *New Riders' Official World Wide Yellow Pages, 1996 Edition* for the most engaging, entertaining, and informative sites on the Web! You can even add your own site!

Brave our site for the finest collection of CAD and 3D imagery produced today. Professionals from all over the world contribute to our gallery, which features new designs every month.

From Novell to Microsoft, New Riders publishes the training guides you need to attain your certification. Visit our site and try your hand at the CNE Endeavor, a test engine created by VFX Technologies, Inc. that enables you to measure what you know—and what you don't!

http://www.mcp.com/newriders

WHAT'S ON THE CD-ROM?

The *New Riders' Official World Wide Web Yellow Pages CD-ROM* is designed to make World Wide Web browsing easier than ever with hyperlinks! With the *New Riders' Official World Wide Web Yellow Pages CD-ROM*, you can link to the Web without having to remember the URLs of the sites you want to go to.

You can:

- Use this CD with a Windows, Macintosh, or Unix browser

- Edit the files to include newly discovered links

All of the Web sites in the book have been converted to HTML files (the same kind used on the Web). You simply load the Welcome.htm file into your favorite Web browser (Netscape, Explorer, or Mosaic, for example) and point and click your way onto the World Wide Web.

You need Web browser software loaded on your computer to use this CD.

Although you can load the entire contents of this CD-ROM onto your computer's hard drive, it is recommended that you instead run this CD-ROM each time you need to use its data.

The files on the CD-ROM have been organized into the following categories:

Animals	Humanities
Art	Internet Resources
Books & Authors	Law
Business	Media
Children	Movies
Colleges & Universities	Music
Computer Games	Paramornal Phenomena
Computers	Reference
Education	Religion & Philosophy
Employment	Science & Engineering
Entertainment	Sexuality
Environment	Shopping
Family Issues	Society & Culture
Food & Drink	Sports
Government & Politics	Television
Health & Fitness	Transportation
History	Travel
Hobbies & Crafts	Weddings
Home Improvement	